Webster's
Spanish-English DICTIONARY

NEW EDITION

Webster's
Diccionario Español-Inglés

Webster's
Spanish-English DICTIONARY

❖❖❖❖❖ NEW EDITION ❖❖❖❖❖

Webster's
Diccionario Español-Inglés

Created in Cooperation with the Editors of
MERRIAM-WEBSTER

Federal Street Press is a trademark of Federal Street Press, a division of Merriam-Webster, Incorporated.

This 2013 edition published by arrangement with
Federal Street Press,
a division of Merriam-Webster, Incorporated

The Popular Group LLC
1700 Broadway
New York, NY 10019

ISBN 978-1-59695-158-7

Printed in the United States of America

1st printing RR Donnelley Harrisonburg, VA 9/2013

Contents

Índice

Contents	Page	Índice
Preface	6a	
	7a	Prefacio
60 New Spanish Words	8a	60 palabras nuevas en español
60 New English Words	9a	60 palabras nuevas en inglés
Explanatory Notes	10a	
	17a	Notas explicativas
Spanish Grammar	25a	
	34a	Gramática inglesa
Conjugation of Spanish Verbs	42a	
	50a	Verbos irregulares en inglés
	54a	Contracciones en inglés
	55a	Prefijos y sufijos en inglés
Abbreviations in this Work	57a	Abreviaturas empleadas en este libro
Pronunciation Symbols	58a	Símbolos de pronunciación
Spanish–English Dictionary	**1**	**Diccionario Español–Inglés**
English–Spanish Dictionary	**287**	**Diccionario Inglés–Español**
100 Common English Idioms	722	100 Frases idiomáticas importantes en inglés
Numbers	729	Números
Common Spanish Abbreviations	731	Abreviaturas comunes en español
Common English Abbreviations	733	Abreviaturas comunes en inglés
Nations of the World	737	Naciones del mundo
Metric System: Conversions	741	Sistema métrica: conversiones

Preface

This Spanish-English Dictionary is designed to meet the needs of English and Spanish speakers in a time of ever-expanding communication among the countries of the Western Hemisphere. It is intended for language learners, teachers, office workers, tourists, business travelers—anyone who needs to communicate effectively in the Spanish and English languages as they are spoken and written in the Americas.

This new dictionary provides accurate and up-to-date coverage of current vocabulary in both languages, as well as abundant examples of words used in context to illustrate idiomatic usage. The selection of Spanish words and idioms was based on evidence drawn from a wide variety of modern Latin-American sources and interpreted by trained Merriam-Webster bilingual lexicographers. The English entries were chosen by Merriam-Webster editors from the most recent Merriam-Webster dictionaries, and they represent the current basic vocabulary of American English.

All of this material is presented in a format which is based firmly upon and, in many important ways, is similar to the traditional styling found in the Merriam-Webster monolingual dictionaries. The reader who is familiar with Merriam-Webster dictionaries will immediately recognize this style, with its emphasis on convenience and ease of use, clarity and conciseness of the information presented, precise discrimination of senses, and frequent inclusion of example phrases showing words in actual use. Also included are pronunciations (in the International Phonetic Alphabet) for all English words, full coverage of irregular verbs in both languages, a section on basic Spanish grammar, written in English for the English speaker, and one on English grammar written in Spanish, a section of the most common Spanish and English abbreviations, and a detailed Explanatory Notes section, written in English and Spanish, which answers any questions the reader might have concerning the use of this book.

This edition has been brought up-to-date with 60 new Spanish terms and 60 new English terms immediately following this Preface. And readers will appreciate the section of 100 common English idioms in the back, along with a restructured chart of numbers showing English and Spanish names side by side, as well as sections covering the nations of the world and the metric system. We believe the user will find this an extremely helpful resource.

Prefacio

Este diccionario está diseñado con el fin de satisfacer las necesidades de lenguaje de angloparlantes e hispanoparlantes en una era de continuo crecimiento en la comunicación entre los países del hemisferio occidental. El diccionario está destinado a los estudiantes de estos idiomas, así como a los maestros, oficinistas, turistas, viajeros de negocios, o a cualquier persona que necesite expresarse claramente y eficazmente en inglés o español tal como se hablan y se escriben en las Américas.

Este diccionario provee una cobertura exacta y actualizada del vocabulario corriente en ambos idiomas, así como abundantes ejemplos de palabras empleadas en contexto para ilustrar su uso idiomático. La selección de vocablos y modismos en español se efectuó a base de una vasta gama de fuentes latinoamericanas modernas y fue interpretada por especialistas en lexicografía bilingüe de Merriam-Webster. Las voces inglesas fueron extraídas de los más recientes diccionarios Merriam-Webster por editores de Merriam-Webster, y representan el vocabulario básico actual del inglés americano.

El material se ha organizado en un formato basado en el estilo tradicional característico de los diccionarios monolingües Merriam-Webster. El lector ya familiarizado con los diccionarios Merriam-Webster reconocerá de inmediato este estilo, con su énfasis en la conveniencia y la facilidad de uso, en la claridad y la concisión de la información presentada, en el preciso discernimiento de los sentidos de cada vocablo, y en la frecuente inclusión de frases ejemplares que ilustran el uso de una palabra. Aparecen también pronunciaciones (compuestas en el Alfabeto Fonético Internacional) para todas las voces inglesas, así como una cobertura plena de verbos irregulares en ambos idiomas, una sección de gramática inglesa básica, tablas de abreviaturas comunes, y una sección de Notas explicativas que contesta en detalle cualquier pregunta que pueda tener el lector tocante al uso de este libro.

Esta edición ha sido actualizada con 60 términos nuevos en español y 60 términos nuevos en inglés, los cuales se relacionan a continuación. Los lectores también apreciarán la sección de 100 modismos ingleses comunes que aparece al final, la tabla de números rediseñada para mostrar los nombres en inglés y en español uno al lado del otro, y las secciones sobre las naciones del mundo y el sistema métrico. Creemos que éstas proporcionarán al lector un recurso sumamente útil.

60 New Spanish Words
60 palabras nuevas en español

aerodeslizador *nm* : hovercraft

aerogenerador *nm* : wind-powered generator

amenaza de bomba *nf* : bomb threat

amenaza de muerte *nf* : death threat

ancho de banda *nm* : bandwidth

aprontar *vt Chile, Uru* : to prepare, to ready — **aprontarse** *vr*

arroba *nf* (*used for the symbol* @) : at sign ⟨arroba merriam-webster punto com : at merriam-webster dot com⟩

auriculares *nmpl* : headphones, earphones

avatar *nm* **1** : avatar **2 avatares** *nmpl* : vagaries, vicissitudes

banda ancha *nf* : broadband

barra de herramientas *nf* : toolbar

berma *nf Chile, Col, Ecua, Peru* : shoulder (of a road)

bisexualidad *nf* : bisexuality

blog [ˈblox] *nm, pl* **blogs** BITÁCORA : blog

buscador *nm* : search engine

buzón de voz *nm* : voicemail

caficultor, -tora *n* : coffee grower

calentamiento global *nm* : global warming

camarín *nm, pl* **-rines** **1** *Chile, Peru, Uru* : locker room **2** *Arg, Uru* : dressing room

cantautor, -tora *n* : singer-songwriter

cargada *nf Arg, Uru* : joke

casquete polar *nm* : polar ice cap

chat *nm or* **sala de chat** : chat room

cifrar *vt* : to encrypt (a file, etc.)

clic *nm, pl* **clics** : click ⟨haz clic aquí : click here⟩ ⟨doble clic : double click⟩

ciudad deportiva *nf* : sports complex

código de barras *nm* : bar code

consumismo *nm* : consumerism

conversatorio *nm CA, Carib, Mex* : talk, discussion

cuantificar *vt* : to quantify

cuarto oscuro *nm* : darkroom

descargable *adj* : downloadable

digitalizar *vt* : to digitalize

dióxido de carbono *nm* : carbon dioxide

e–book [ˈibuk] *nm, pl* **e–books** : electronic book, e-book

email *nm, pl* **emails** : e-mail ⟨enviar algo por email : to e-mail something⟩

euro *nm* : euro

fluorescente *nm* : fluorescent light

guay *adj Spain fam* : cool, neat

garzón, -zona *n, mpl* **-zones** *Chile* : waiter *m*, waitress *f*

habiloso, -sa *adj Chile fam* : bright, smart, clever

hiperenlace *nm* : hyperlink

hipermercado *nm* : large supermarket, hypermarket

interfón *nm, pl* **-fones** *Mex* : intercom

internauta *nmf* : Internet user

infografía *nf* : computer graphics *pl*

monovolumen *nm, pl* **-lúmenes** *Spain* : minivan

motoneta *nf Mex* : scooter

MP3 [emepeˈtres] *nm, pl* **MP3** : MP3

panela *nf Col, Ecua* : unrefined sugar

pipí *nm fam* : pee *fam* ⟨hacer pipí : to take a pee⟩

podcast [podˈkast] *nm, pl* **podcasts** : podcast

portátil *nmf* : laptop computer

regalón, -lona *adj, mpl* **-lones** *Chile fam* : spoiled (of a person)

SMS [ˈeseˈemeˈese, ˈesˈemˈes] *nm, pl* **SMS** : text message

todoterreno *nm* : all-terrain vehicle

transgénico, -ca *n* : genetically modified plant or animal

ultrasónico, -ca *adj* : ultrasonic

videojuego *nm* : video game

zapping [ˈsapin, ˈθapin] *nm* : channel surfing

60 New English Words
60 palabras nuevas en inglés

acid rain *n* : lluvia *f* ácida

all–terrain vehicle [ˈɔltəˈreɪn-] *n* : todoterreno *m*, vehículo *m* todoterreno

antiviral [ˌæntiˈvaɪrəl, ˌæntaɪ-] *adj* : antiviral

at sign *n* (*usado para el símbolo @*) : arroba *f*

bed and breakfast *n* : pensión *f* con desayuno

ATV [ˌeɪˌtiːˈviː] → **all-terrain vehicle**

avatar [ˈævəˌtɑr] *n* : avatar *m*

bar code *n* : código *m* de barras

bike lane *or* **bicycle lane** *n* : carril *m* para bicicletas

biological weapon *n* : arma *f* biológica

biotechnological [ˌbaɪoˌtɛknəˈlɑdʒɪkəl] *adj* : biotecnológico, -ca

birth control *n* : control *m* de natalidad

bisexuality [ˌbaɪˌsekʃʊˈæləti] *n* : bisexualidad *f*

blog [ˈblɔg, ˈblɑg] *n* : blog *m*, bitácora *f*

bookmark[1] [ˈbʊkˌmɑrk] *n* : marcador *m* (de Internet)

bookmark[2] *vt* : marcar (una página web)

bootleg[1] [ˈbuːtˌlɛg] *adj* : pirata ⟨bootleg software : software pirata⟩

bootleg[2] *vt* : piratear (un video, etc.)

broadband [ˈbrɔdˌbænd] *n* : banda *f* ancha — **broadband** *adj*

browser [ˈbraʊzər] *n* : navegador *m* (para la Internet)

call center *n* : centro de atención *f* (telefónica)

carbon dioxide [-daɪˈɑkˌsaɪd] *n* : dióxido *m* de carbono

carbon footprint *n* : huella *f* de carbono

channel surfing *n* : zapping *m*

chat room *n* : chat *m*, sala *f* de chat

digitalize [ˈdɪdʒətəˌlaɪz] *vt* **-ized; -izing** : digitalizar

downloadable [ˈdaʊnˌloːdəbəl] *adj* : descargable

e–book [ˈiːˌbʊk] *n* : libro *m* electrónico, e-book *m*

emoticon [iˈmotɪˌkɑn] *n* : emoticono *m*, emoticón *m*

enchilada [ˌɛntʃəˈlɑdə] *n* : enchilada *f*

euro [ˈjʊrˌoː] *n, pl* **-ros** *or* **-ro** : euro *m*

FAQ [ˈfæk, ˌɛfˌeɪˈkjuː] *n, pl* **FAQs** : FAQ *m* (lista)

flamenco [fləˈmɛŋko] *n* : flamenco *m* (música o baile) — **flamenco** *adj*

globalization [ˌgloːbələˈzeɪʃən] *n* : globalización *f*

global warming *n* : calentamiento *m* global

hovercraft [ˈhʌvərˌkræft] *n* : aerodeslizador *m*

hyperlink [ˈhaɪpərˌlɪŋk] *n* : hiperenlace *m*

hypermarket [ˈhaɪpərˌmɑrkət] *n* : hipermercado *m*

information technology *n* : informática *f*

intercom [ˈɪntərˌkɑm] *n* : interfono *m*, interfón *m Mex*

keypad [ˈkiːˌpæd] *n* : teclado *m* numérico

lip–read [ˈlɪpˌriːd] *vi* : leer los labios

maraca [məˈrɑkə] *n* : maraca *f*

maté [ˈmɑˌteɪ] *n* : yerba *f*, mate *m*

MP3 [ˌɛmˌpiːˈθriː] *n* : MP3 *m*

nuke *vt* **1** : atacar con armas nucleares **2** *fam* : cocinar en el microondas

paella [pɑˈɛlə, -ˈeɪljə, -ˈeɪə] *n* : paella *f*

pee [ˈpiː] *vi fam* URINATE : hacer pipí

podcast [ˈpɑdˌkæst] *n* : podcast *m*

rainforest [ˈreɪnˌfɔrəst] *n* : bosque *m* tropical

reggae [ˈrɛˌgeɪ, ˈreɪ-] *n* : reggae *m*

search engine *n* : buscador *m*

soap opera *n* : telenovela *f*, culebrón *m*

special effects *n* : efectos *mpl* especiales

surfer [ˈsərfər] *n* **1** : surfista *mf* **2** : internauta *mf*

text message *n* : mensaje *m* de texto, SMS *m*

ultrasonic [ˌʌltrəˈsɑnɪk] *adj* : ultrasónico

webcam [ˈwɛbˌkæm] *n* : webcam *f*

Web page *n* : página *f* web

zit [ˈzɪt] *n* : grano *m*

Explanatory Notes

Entries

A boldface letter, word, or phrase appearing flush with the left-hand margin of each column of type is a **main entry** or entry word.

cafetalero[1], **-ra** *adj* . . .
eye-opener . . . *n* . . .
walk out *vi* . . .

The main entry, together with the material that follows it on the same line and succeeding indented lines, constitutes a **dictionary entry**.

Alphabetical order throughout the book follows the order of the English alphabet, without regard to intervening spaces or hyphens, with one exception: words beginning with the Spanish letter *ñ* follow all entries for the letter *n*.

Homographs (words with the same spelling) having different parts of speech are usually given separate dictionary entries and are distinguished by superscript numerals.

hail[1] . . . *vt* . . .
hail[2] *n* . . .
hail[3] *interj* . . .
madrileño[1], **-ña** *adj* . . .
madrileño[2], **-ña** *n* . . .

Homographs having the same part of speech are normally included at the same dictionary entry, without regard to their different semantic origins. On the English-to-Spanish side, however, separate entries are made if the homographs have distinct inflected forms or if they have distinct pronunciations.

A pair of **guide words** is printed at the top of each page, indicating the first and last main entries that appear on that page.

When a main entry is followed by the word *or* and another spelling, the two spellings are **variants** and both are standard.

jailer *or* **jailor** . . . *n* . . .
quizá *or* **quizás** *adv* . . .

Occasionally, a variant spelling is used only for a particular sense of a word. In these cases, the variant spelling is listed after the sense number of the sense to which it pertains:

electric . . . *adj* **1** *or* **electrical** . . .

Sometimes the entry word is used interchangeably with a longer phrase containing the entry word. For the purposes of this dictionary, such phrases are considered variants of the headword:

bunk[2] *n* **1** *or* **bunk bed** . . .
angina *nf* **1** *or* **angina de pecho** : angina . . .

Variant wordings of boldface phrases may also be shown:

madera *nf* . . . **3 madera dura** *or* **madera noble** . . .
atención[1] *nf* . . . **2 poner atención** *or* **prestar atención** . . .

A main entry may be followed by one or more derivatives or by a homograph with a different functional label. These are **run-on entries**. Each is introduced by a boldface dash and each has a functional label. They are not defined, however, since their equivalents can be readily derived by adding the corresponding foreign-language suffix to the terms used to define the entry word or, in the case of homographs, simply substituting the appropriate part of speech:

> **illegal** . . . *adj* : ilegal — **illegally** *adv* (the Spanish adverb is *ilegalmente*)
> **transferir** . . . *vt* TRASLADAR : to transfer — **transferible** *adj* (the English adjective is *transferable*)
> **Bosnian** *n* : bosnio *m,* -nia *f* — **Bosnian** *adj* (the Spanish adjective is *bosnio, -nia*)

On the Spanish side of the book, reflexive verbs are sometimes run on undefined:

> **enrollar** *vt* : to roll up, to coil — **enrollarse** *vr*

The absence of a definition means that *enrollarse* has the simple reflexive meaning "to become rolled up or coiled," "to roll itself up."

A main entry may be followed by one or more phrases containing the entry word or an inflected form of the entry word. These are **bold notes**. Each bold note is defined at its own numbered sense:

> **álamo** *nm* **1** : poplar **2 álamo temblón** : aspen
> **hold**[1] . . . *vi* . . . **4 to hold to** : . . . **5 to hold with** : . . .

If the bold note consists only of the entry word and a single preposition, the entry word is represented by a boldface swung dash **~**.

> **pegar** . . . *vi* . . . **3 ~ con** : to match, to go with . . .

The same bold note phrase may appear at two or more senses if it has more than one distinct meaning:

> **wear**[1] . . . *vt* . . . **3 to wear out** : gastar <he wore out his shoes . . . > **4 to wear out** EXHAUST : agotar, fatigar <to wear oneself out . . . > . . .
> **estar** . . . *vi* . . . **15 ~ por** : to be in favor of **16 ~ por** : to be about to <está por cerrar . . . > . . .

If the use of the entry word is commonly restricted to one particular phrase, then a bold note may be given as the entry word's only sense:

> **ward**[1] . . . *vt* **to ward off** : . . .

Pronunciation of English Entry Words

The matter between a pair of brackets [ ] following the entry word of an English-to-Spanish entry indicates the **pronunciation**. The symbols used are explained in the chart of Pronunciation Symbols.

The presence of variant pronunciations indicates that not all educated speakers pronounce words the same way. A second-place variant is not to be regarded as less acceptable than the pronunciation that is given first. It may, in fact, be used by as many educated speakers as the first variant, but the requirements of the printed page are such that one must precede the other:

> **tomato** [tə'meɪt̬o, -'mɑ-] . . .

When a compound word has less than a full pronunciation, the missing part is to be supplied from the pronunciation at the entry for the unpronounced element of the compound:

gamma ray [ˈgæmə] . . .
ray [ˈreɪ] . . .
smoke[1] [ˈsmoːk] . . .
smoke detector [dɪˈtɛktər] . . .

In general, no pronunciation is given for open compounds consisting of two or more English words that are main entries at their own alphabetical place:

water lily *n* : nenúfar *m*

Only the first entry in a series of numbered homographs is given a pronunciation if their pronunciations are the same:

dab[1] [ˈdæb] *vt* . . .
dab[2] *n* . . .

No pronunciation is shown for principal parts of verbs that are formed by regular suffixation, nor for other derivative words formed by common suffixes.

Pronunciation of Spanish Entry Words

Spanish pronunciation is highly regular, so no pronunciations are given for most Spanish-to-English entries. Exceptions have been made for certain words (such as foreign borrowings) whose Spanish pronunciations are not evident from their spellings:

pizza [ˈpitsa, ˈpisa] . . .
footing [ˈfuˌtɪŋ] . . .

Functional Labels

A **functional label** is an italic label indicating a part of speech or some other functional classification of the main entry. It follows the pronunciation if one is given. The eight traditional parts of speech, adjective, adverb, conjunction, interjection, noun, preposition, pronoun, and verb, are indicated as follows:

daily[2] *adj* . . .
vagamente *adv* . . .
and . . . *conj* . . .
huy *interj* . . .
jackal . . . *n* . . .
para *prep* . . .
neither[3] *pron* . . .
leer . . . *v* . . .

Verbs that are intransitive are labeled *vi,* and verbs that are transitive are labeled *vt.* Entries for verbs that are both transitive and intransitive are labeled *v;* if such an entry includes irregular verb inflections, it is labeled *v* immediately after the main entry, with the labels *vt* and *vi* serving to introduce transitive and intransitive subdivisions when both are present:

deliberar *vi* : to deliberate
necessitate . . . *vt* **-tated; -tating** : necesitar, requerir
satisfy . . . *v* **-fied; -fying** *vt* . . . — *vi* . . .

Two other labels are used to indicate functional classifications of verbs: *v aux* (auxiliary verb) and *v impers* (impersonal verb).

may . . . *v aux, past* **might** . . .
haber[1] . . . *v aux* **1** : have . . . — *v impers* **1 hay** : there is, there are . . .

In Spanish-to-English noun entries, italic **gender labels** indicate masculine (*m*), feminine (*f*), or masculine or feminine (*mf*) genders of nouns.

magnesio *nm* . . .
galaxia *nf* . . .
turista *nmf* . . .

If both the masculine and feminine forms are shown for a noun referring to a person, the label is simply *n:*

director, -tora *n* . . .

Spanish noun equivalents of English entry words are also labeled for gender:

amnesia . . . *n* **:** amnesia *f*
earache . . . *n* **:** dolor *m* de oído
gamekeeper . . . *n* **:** guardabosque *mf*

The **plurals** of nouns (inflected forms) are shown in this dictionary when they are irregular, when plural suffixation brings about a change in accentuation or in the spelling of the root word, when an English noun ends in a consonant plus *-o* or in *-ey,* when an English noun ends in *-oo,* when an English noun is a compound that pluralizes any element but the last, when a noun has variant plurals, or whenever the dictionary user might have reasonable doubts regarding the spelling of a plural:

tooth . . . *n, pl* **teeth** . . .
garrafón *nm, pl* **-fones** . . .
potato . . . *n, pl* **-toes** . . .
abbey . . . *n, pl* **-beys** . . .
cuckoo[2] *n, pl* **-oos** . . .
brother-in-law . . . *n, pl* **brothers-in-law** . . .
quail[2] *n, pl* **quail** *or* **quails** . . .
hábitat *nm, pl* **-tats** . . .
tahúr *nm, pl* **tahúres** . . .

Cutback inflected forms are used for most nouns on the English-to-Spanish side, regardless of the number of syllables. On the Spanish-to-English side, cutback inflections are given for nouns that have three or more syllables; plurals for shorter words are written out in full:

shampoo[2] *n, pl* **-poos** . . .
calamity . . . *n, pl* **-ties** . . .
mouse . . . *n, pl* **mice** . . .
sartén *nmf, pl* **sartenes** . . .
hámster *nm, pl* **hámsters** . . .
federación *nf, pl* **-ciones** . . .

If only one gender form has a plural which is irregular, that plural form will be given with the appropriate label:

campeón, -ona *n, mpl* **-ones :** champion

The plurals of nouns are usually not shown when the base word is unchanged by the addition of the regular plural suffix or when the noun is unlikely to occur in the plural:

apple . . . *n* **:** manzana *f*
inglés[3] *nm* **:** English (language)

Nouns that are plural in form and that regularly occur in plural constructions are labeled as *npl* (for English nouns), *nmpl* (for Spanish masculine nouns), or *nfpl* (for Spanish feminine nouns):

knickers . . . *npl* . . .

enseres *nmpl* . . .
mancuernas *nfpl* . . .

Entry words that are unchanged in the plural are labeled *ns & pl* (for English nouns), *nms & pl* (for Spanish masculine nouns), *nfs & pl* (for Spanish feminine nouns), and *nmfs & pl* (for Spanish gender-variable nouns):

deer . . . *ns & pl* . . .
lavaplatos *nms & pl* . . .
tesis *nfs & pl* . . .
rompehuelgas *nmfs & pl* . . .

The **principal parts of English verbs** are shown when they are irregular, when suffixation brings about a change in spelling of the root word, when the verb ends in *-ey,* when there are variant inflected forms, or whenever it is believed that the dictionary user might have reasonable doubts about the spelling of an inflected form:

break[1] . . . *v* **broke** . . .; **broken** . . .; **breaking** . . .
drag[1] . . . *v* **dragged; dragging** . . .
monkey[1] . . . *vi* **-keyed; -keying** . . .
label[1] . . . *vt* **-beled** *or* **-belled; -beling** *or* **-belling** . . .
imagine . . . *vt* **-ined; -ining** . . .

Cutback inflected forms are usually used when the verb has two or more syllables:

multiply . . . *v* **-plied; -plying** . . .
bevel[1] . . . *v* **-eled** *or* **-elled; -eling** *or* **-elling** . . .
forgo *or* **forego** . . . *vt* **-went; -gone; -going** . . .
commit . . . *vt* **-mitted; -mitting** . . .

The principal parts of an English verb are not shown when the base word is unchanged by suffixation:

delay[1] . . . *vt*
pitch[1] . . . *vt*

Entries for **irregular Spanish verbs** are cross-referenced by number to the model conjugations appearing in the Conjugation of Spanish Verbs section:

abnegarse {49} *vr* . . .
volver {89} *vi* . . .

Entries for Spanish verbs with regular conjugations are not cross-referenced; however, model conjugations for regular Spanish verbs are included in the Conjugation of Spanish Verbs section.

The **comparative and superlative forms** of English adjective and adverb main entries are shown when suffixation brings about a change in spelling of the root word, when the inflection is irregular, and when there are variant inflected forms:

wet[2] *adj* **wetter; wettest** . . .
good[2] *adj* **better** . . .; **best** . . .
evil[1] . . . *adj* **eviler** *or* **eviller; evilest** *or* **evillest** . . .

The superlative forms of adjectives and adverbs of two or more syllables are usually cut back; the superlative is shown in full, however, when it is desirable to indicate the pronunciation of the inflected form:

early[1] . . . *adv* **earlier; -est** . . .
gaudy . . . *adj* **gaudier; -est** . . .
secure[2] *adj* **-curer; -est** . . .

but

young[1] . . . *adj* **younger** [ˈjʌŋgər];
youngest [-gəst] . . .

At a few entries only the superlative form is shown:

mere *adj, superlative* **merest** . . .

The absence of the comparative form indicates that there is no evidence of its use.
The comparative and superlative forms of adjectives and adverbs are usually not shown when the base word is unchanged by suffixation:

quiet[3] *adj* **1** . . .

Usage

Two types of **usage labels** are used in this dictionary—regional and stylistic. Spanish words that are limited in use to a specific area or areas of Latin America, or to Spain, are given labels indicating the countries in which they are most commonly used:

guarachear *vi Cuba, PRi fam* . . .
bucket . . . *n* : . . . cubeta *f Mex*

The following regional labels are used in this book: *Arg* (Argentina), *Bol* (Bolivia), *CA* (Central America), *Car* (Caribbean), *Chile* (Chile), *Col* (Colombia), *CoRi* (Costa Rica), *Cuba* (Cuba), *DomRep* (Dominican Republic), *Ecua* (Ecuador), *Sal* (El Salvador), *Guat* (Guatemala), *Hond* (Honduras), *Mex* (Mexico), *Nic* (Nicaragua), *Pan* (Panama), *Par* (Paraguay), *Peru* (Peru), *PRi* (Puerto Rico), *Spain* (Spain), *Uru* (Uruguay), *Ven* (Venezuela).

Since this book focuses on the Spanish spoken in Latin America, only the most common regionalisms from Spain have been included in order to allow for more thorough coverage of Latin-American forms.

A number of Spanish words are given a *fam* (familiar) label as well, indicating that these words are suitable for informal contexts but would not normally be used in formal writing or speaking. The stylistic label *usu considered vulgar* is added for a word which is usually considered vulgar or offensive but whose widespread use justifies its inclusion in this book. The label is intended to warn the reader that the word in question may be inappropriate in polite conversation.

Definitions are sometimes preceded by parenthetical **usage notes** that give supplementary semantic information:

not . . . *adv* **1** (*used to form a negative*) : no . . .
within[2] *prep* . . . **2** (*in expressions of distance*) : . . . **3** (*in expressions of time*) : . . .
e[2] *conj* (*used instead of* **y** *before words beginning with i or hi*) : . . .
poder[1] . . . *v aux* . . . **2** (*expressing possibility*) : . . . **3** (*expressing permission*) : . . .

Additional semantic orientation is also sometimes given in the form of parenthetical notes appearing within the definition:

calibrate . . . *vt* . . . : calibrar (armas), graduar (termómetros)
palco *nm* : box (in a theater or stadium)

Occasionally a usage note is used in place of a definition. This is usually done when the entry word has no single foreign-language equivalent. This type of usage note will be accompanied by examples of common use:

> **shall** . . . *v aux* . . . **1** (*used to express a command*) <you shall do as I say : harás lo que te digo> . . .

Definitions are sometimes followed by **verbal illustrations** that show a typical use of the word in context or a common idiomatic usage. These verbal illustrations include a translation and are enclosed in angle brackets:

> **lejos** *adv* **1 :** far away, distant <a lo lejos : in the distance, far off> . . .
> **make**[1] . . . **9** . . . **:** ganar <to make a living : ganarse la vida> . . .

Senses

A boldface colon is used to introduce a definition and boldface numerals separate the senses of a word:

> **fable** . . . *n* **:** fábula *f*
> **laguna** *nf* **1 :** lagoon **2 :** lacuna, gap

Whenever some information (such as a synonym, a boldface word or phrase, a usage note, a cross-reference, or a label) follows a sense number, it applies only to that specific numbered sense:

> **abanico** *nm* . . . **2** GAMA **:** . . .
> **tonic**[2] *n* . . . **2** *or* **tonic water :** . . .
> **grillo** *nm* . . . **2 grillos** *nmpl* **:** . . .
> **fairy** . . . *n, pl* **fairies** . . . **2 fairy tale :** . . .
> **myself** . . . *pron* **1** (*used reflexively*) **:** . . .
> **pike** . . . *n* . . . **3 → turnpike**
> **atado**[2] *nm* . . . **2** *Arg* **:** . . .

Cross-references

Three different kinds of **cross-references** are used in this dictionary: synonymous, cognate, and inflectional. In each instance the cross-reference is readily recognized by the boldface arrow following the entry word.

Synonymous and cognate cross-references indicate that a definition at the entry cross-referred to can be substituted for the entry word:

> **scapula** . . . **→ shoulder blade**
> **amuck** . . . **→ amok**

An inflectional cross-reference is used to identify the entry word as an inflected form of another word (as a noun or verb):

> **fue, etc. → ir, ser**
> **mice → mouse**

Synonyms

At many entries or senses in this book, a **synonym** in small capital letters is provided before the boldface colon and the following defining text. These synonyms are all main entries or bold notes elsewhere in the book. They serve as a helpful guide to the meaning of the entry or sense and also give the reader an additional term that might be substituted in a similar context. On the English-to-Spanish side synonyms are particularly abundant, since special care has been taken to guide the English speaker—by means of synonyms, verbal illustrations, or usage notes—to the meaning of the Spanish terms at each sense of a multisense entry.

Notas explicativas

Entradas

Toda letra, palabra o frase en negrita que aparece al extremo del margen izquierdo de la columna de texto de la que forma parte es una **entrada principal**, o lema.

> **cafetalero**[1], **-ra** *adj* . . .
> **eye-opener** . . . *n* . . .
> **walk out** *vi* . . .

La entrada principal, junto con el texto que la sigue tanto en la misma línea como en las líneas sangradas subsiguientes, constituyen una **entrada del diccionario**.

El orden alfabético del diccionario concuerda con el orden del alfabeto inglés, con la excepción de las entradas españolas que comienzan con la letra *ñ-*. Éstas aparecen después de las entradas que comienzan con *n-*. Las entradas principales aparecen alfabéticamente, letra por letra, sin tener en cuenta guiones o espacios intermediarios.

Los homógrafos (palabras que se escriben igual) que pertenecen a distintas categorías gramaticales por lo general aparecen en entradas individuales. A estas entradas se les identifica con un número superíndice:

> **hail**[1] . . . *vt* . . .
> **hail**[2] *n* . . .
> **hail**[3] *interj* . . .
> **madrileño**[1], **-ña** *adj* . . .
> **madrileño**[2], **-ña** *n* . . .

Los homógrafos que se clasifican bajo una misma categoría gramatical aparecen incluidos bajo la misma entrada del diccionario, sin tener en cuenta diferencias de origen semántico. Sin embargo, en la sección Inglés-Español se les asigna a cada uno de estos homógrafos una entrada individual si existe entre ellos alguna diferencia ya sea en la inflexión o en la pronunciación.

En el margen superior de cada página aparecen dos **palabras guía** que indican la primera y última entrada de la página correspondiente.

Cuando una entrada principal aparece seguida de la palabra *or* y otra ortografía, las dos ortografías se consideran **variantes**. Ambas ortografías son estándar, y cualquiera de las dos puede usarse según se prefiera:

> **jailer** *or* **jailor** . . . *n* . . .
> **quizá** *or* **quizás** *adv* . . .

Hay ocasiones en las que una variante ortográfica se emplea únicamente para una de las acepciones de una palabra. En tales casos, la variante ortográfica aparece después del número de la acepción a la cual corresponde:

> **electric** . . . *adj* **1** *or* **electrical** . . .

En otros casos, el lema puede intercambiarse con una frase de la que forma parte. Para los fines de este diccionario, tales frases se consideran como variantes del lema:

> **bunk**[2] *n* **1** *or* **bunk bed** . . .
> **angina** *nf* **1** *or* **angina de pecho** : angina . . .

Las frases en negrita también pueden, a su vez, presentar variantes:

> **madera** *nf* . . . **3 madera dura** *or* **madera noble** . . .
> **atención**[1] *nf* . . . **2 poner atención** *or* **prestar atención** . . .

Una entrada principal puede ser seguida por uno o más derivados del lema, o de un homógrafo de distinta categoría gramatical. Éstas son **entradas secundarias.** Cada una de estas entradas aparece después de un guión en negrita, y cada una posee su propio calificativo. Tales entradas aparecen sin definición, ya que sus equivalentes en el idioma extranjero pueden derivarse fácilmente al combinar la definición del lema con el sufijo correspondiente, o como sucede con los homógrafos, al sustituir la categoría gramatical por otra. Véase por ejemplo:

> **illegal** . . . *adj* : ilegal — **illegally** *adv* (el adverbio español es *ilegalmente*)
> **transferir** . . . *vt* TRASLADAR : to transfer — **transferible** *adj* (el adjetivo inglés es *transferable*)
> **Bosnian** *n* : bosnio*m,* -nia *f* — **Bosnian** *adj* (el adjetivo español es *bosnio, -nia*)

En la sección Español-Inglés, los verbos pronominales aparecen en ocasiones como entradas secundarias, sin definición:

> **enrollar** *vt* : to roll up, to coil — **enrollarse** *vr*

La ausencia de la definición en este caso comunica al lector de habla inglesa que el verbo *enrollarse* tiene una función expresamente reflexiva. Esto elimina la necesidad de agregar una definición que resultaría superflua como "to become rolled up or coiled," o "to roll itself up."

Una entrada principal puede aparecer acompañada de una o varias **frases en negrita** (generalmente locuciones o términos compuestos) que contienen ya sea el lema, o una inflexión de éste. Cada una de estas frases se presenta como una de las acepciones numeradas del lema:

> **álamo** *nm* **1** : poplar **2 álamo temblón** : aspen
> **hold**[1] . . . *vi* . . . **4 to hold to** : . . . **5 to hold with** : . . .

Cuando la frase en negrita consta únicamente de una combinación del lema con una preposición, el lema se representa entonces por medio de una tilde en negrita **~**.

> **pegar** . . . *vi* . . . **3 ~ con** : to match, to go with . . .

Si la frase en cuestión tiene más de un sentido, entonces puede aparecer en dos o más acepciones de la misma entrada principal:

> **wear**[1] . . . *vt* . . . **3 to wear out** : gastar <he wore out his shoes . . . > **4 to wear out** EXHAUST : agotar, fatigar <to wear oneself out . . . > . . .
> **estar** . . . *vi* . . . **15 ~ por** : to be in favor of **16 ~ por** : to be about to <está por cerrar . . . > . . .

Si el uso común de una palabra está generalmente limitado a una frase determinada, la frase es presentada como la única acepción del lema:

> **ward**[1] . . . *vt* **to ward off** : . . .

Pronunciación de los lemas ingleses

El texto que aparece entre corchetes [ ] inmediatamente después de un lema en la sección Inglés-Español indica la **pronunciación** del lema. Para una explicación de los símbolos empleados, véase la tabla titulada Símbolos de pronunciación.

La presencia de variantes de pronunciación indica que no todos los hablantes educados del idioma pronuncian una palabra determinada de igual forma. El hecho de que una variante aparezca después de otra no significa que sea menos apropiada que la que aparece primero. De hecho, la segunda variante puede ser tan común como la primera, pero las restricciones de la página impresa exigen que una preceda a la otra.

tomato [təˈmeɪt̬o, -ˈmɑ-] . . .

Cuando un término compuesto aparece con sólo una pronunciación parcial, la pronunciación del resto del término puede obtenerse bajo la entrada correspondiente a la palabra cuya pronunciación se ha omitido:

gamma ray [ˈgæmə] . . .
ray [ˈreɪ] . . .
smoke[1] [ˈsmoːk] . . .
smoke detector [dɪˈtɛktər] . . .

En general, no se indica la pronunciación de términos compuestos cuando éstos están formados de dos o más palabras inglesas que aparecen en el diccionario como entradas principales:

water lily *n* : nenúfar *m*

Solamente la primera entrada en una serie de homógrafos numerados incluye la pronunciación si ésta es la misma para todos los otros homógrafos:

dab[1] [ˈdæb] *vt* . . .
dab[2] *n* . . .

No se indica la pronunciación de las partes principales de los verbos formados por sufijación regular, ni por otros derivados formados por sufijos comunes.

Pronunciación de los lemas españoles

Dada la alta regularidad de la pronunciación del español, no se indica la pronunciación de la mayor parte de las entradas que aparecen en la sección Español-Inglés. Sin embargo, se han hecho excepciones para ciertas palabras (tales como aquéllas que se han adaptado de otras lenguas) cuya pronunciación en español no puede derivarse naturalmente de su ortografía:

pizza [ˈpitsɑ, ˈpisɑ] *nf* : pizza
footing [ˈfuˌtɪŋ] . . .

Calificativos funcionales

Un **calificativo** en itálicas que indica la **categoría gramatical** u otra clasificación funcional del lema aparece inmediatamente después de la pronunciación, o si la pronunciación se ha omitido, después del lema. Las ocho categorías gramaticales tradicionales, el adjetivo, el adverbio, la conjunción, la interjección, el sustantivo, la preposición, el pronombre, y el verbo, se indican como sigue:

daily[2] *adj* . . .
vagamente *adv* . . .
and . . . *conj* . . .

huy *interj* . . .
jackal . . . *n* . . .
para *prep* . . .
neither[3] *pron* . . .
leer . . . *v* . . .

Los verbos intransitivos se identifican con el calificativo *vi*, y los transitivos, *vt*. Las entradas para aquellos verbos que son a la vez transitivos e intransitivos llevan el calificativo *v*. Si una de estas entradas incluye inflexiones irregulares, el calificativo *v* aparece inmediatamente después del lema, y las acepciones transitivas e intransitivas son introducidas con los calificativos *vt* y *vi* respectivamente.

deliberar *vi* : to deliberate
necessitate . . . *vt* **-tated; -tating** : necesitar, requerir
satisfy . . . *v* **-fied; -fying** *vt* . . . — *vi* . . .

Por último, dos otros calificativos se emplean para indicar la clasificación funcional de los verbos: *v aux* (verbo auxiliar) y *v impers* (verbo impersonal).

may . . . *v aux, past* **might** . . .
haber[1] . . . *v aux* **1** : have . . . — *v impers*
1 hay : there is, there are . . .

En toda entrada cuyo lema es un sustantivo español, el **género** de éste se indica con los calificativos *m* (masculino), *f* (femenino), o *mf* (masculino o femenino), que aparecen inmediatamente después del calificativo funcional:

magnesio *nm* . . .
galaxia *nf* . . .
turista *nmf* . . .

Si se dan las formas tanto masculina como femenina de un sustantivo que denota a una persona, se aplica el calificativo *n*.

director, -tora *n* . . .

Todo sustantivo español que aparece como definición de un lema inglés es acompañado de un calificativo de género:

amnesia . . . *n* : amnesia *f*
earache . . . *n* : dolor *m* de oído
gamekeeper . . . *n* : guardabosque *mf*

En este diccionario se indica el **plural** de un sustantivo en los siguientes casos: cuando el plural es irregular, cuando la sufijación del plural produce un cambio en la acentuación o la ortografía del vocablo raíz, cuando un sustantivo inglés termina en una consonante seguida de *-o* o de *-ey*, cuando un sustantivo inglés termina en *-oo*, cuando un sustantivo inglés es un término compuesto del cual el elemento a pluralizar no es el último, cuando un sustantivo tiene variantes en el plural, o cuando podría suscitarse una duda razonable en cuanto a la ortografía del plural:

tooth . . . *n, pl* **teeth** . . .
garrafón *nm, pl* **-fones** . . .
potato . . . *n, pl* **-toes** . . .
abbey . . . *n, pl* **-beys** . . .
cuckoo[2] *n, pl* **-oos** . . .
brother-in-law . . . *n, pl* **brothers-in-law** . . .
quail[2] *n, pl* **quail** *or* **quails** . . .
hábitat *nm, pl* **-tats** . . .
tahúr *nm, pl* **tahúres** . . .

En la sección Inglés-Español, la forma plural de la mayor parte de los sustantivos se indica por medio de una inflexión reducida, sin tener en cuenta el número de sílabas que el lema contenga. En la sección Español-Inglés, se dan inflexiones reducidas sólo para aquellos sustantivos que contengan tres o más sílabas, mientras que las formas plurales de sustantivos más breves se presentan enteras:

shampoo[2] *n, pl* **-poos** . . .
calamity . . . *n, pl* **-ties** . . .
mouse . . . *n, pl* **mice** . . .
sartén *nmf, pl* **sartenes** . . .
hámster *nm, pl* **hámsters** . . .
federación *nf, pl* **-ciones** . . .

Si se produce un plural irregular en sólo uno de los géneros, la forma plural se da con el calificativo correspondiente:

campeón, -ona *n, mpl* **-ones** : champion

La forma plural de un sustantivo generalmente no aparece si el vocablo raíz permanece inalterado por la adición del sufijo plural regular, o cuando no es probable que el sustantivo se use en el plural:

apple . . . *n* : manzana *f*
inglés[3] *nm* : English (language)

Aquellos sustantivos que son plurales en forma y que ocurren regularmente en construcciones plurales son clasificados *npl* (si son sustantivos ingleses), *nmpl* (si son sustantivos masculinos españoles), o *nfpl* (si son sustantivos femeninos españoles):

knickers . . . *npl* . . .
enseres *nmpl* . . .
mancuernas *nfpl* . . .

Toda entrada que permanece inalterada en el plural es clasificada *ns & pl* (sustantivos ingleses), *nms & pl* (sustantivos masculinos españoles), *nfs & pl* (sustantivos femeninos españoles), y *nmfs & pl* (sustantivos españoles de género variable):

deer . . . *ns & pl* . . .
lavaplatos *nms & pl* . . .
tesis *nfs & pl* . . .
rompehuelgas *nmfs & pl* . . .

En la sección Inglés-Español, las **partes principales de los verbos** se indican en los siguientes casos: cuando el verbo es irregular, cuando la sufijación produce un cambio en la ortografía del vocablo raíz, cuando el verbo termina en *-ey*, cuando una inflexión tiene variantes, o cuando puede suscitarse una duda razonable en cuanto a la ortografía de una inflexión:

break[1] . . . *v* **broke** . . . ; **broken** . . . ; **breaking** . . .
drag[1] . . . *v* **dragged; dragging** . . .
monkey[1] . . . *vi* **-keyed; -keying** . . .
label[1] . . . *vt* **-beled** *or* **-belled; -beling** *or* **-belling** . . .
imagine . . . *vt* **-ined; -ining** . . .

Si el verbo consta de dos o más sílabas, se da generalmente una forma reducida de la inflexión:

multiply . . . *v* **-plied; -plying** . . .
bevel[1] . . . *v* **-eled** *or* **-elled; -eling** *or* **-elling** . . .
forgo *or* **forego** . . . *vt* **-went; -gone; -going** . . .
commit . . . *vt* **-mitted; -mitting** . . .

Las partes principales de un verbo inglés no aparecen cuando el vocablo raíz permanece inalterado por la sufijación.

delay[1] . . . *vt*
pitch[1] . . . *vt*

En cada entrada correspondiente a un **verbo irregular español** aparece un número entre llaves que remite al lector a los modelos de conjugación que aparecen en la sección titulada Conjugación de verbos españoles:

abnegarse {49} *vr* . . .
volver {89} *vi* . . .

Aunque estas remisiones no aparecen en las entradas que corresponden a los verbos regulares españoles, los modelos de conjugación de estas formas pueden consultarse en la susodicha sección.

Las entradas principales de adjetivos y adverbios ingleses incluyen las **formas comparativas y superlativas** cuando la sufijación produce un cambio en la ortografía del vocablo raíz, cuando la inflexión es de forma irregular, o cuando existen variantes de la inflexión:

wet[2] *adj* **wetter; wettest** . . .
good[2] *adj* **better** . . . ; **best** . . .
evil[1] . . . *adj* **eviler** *or* **eviller; evilest** *or* **evillest** . . .

Las formas superlativas de adjetivos y adverbios de dos o más sílabas son presentadas generalmente en forma reducida:

early[1] . . . *adv* **earlier; -est** . . .
gaudy . . . *adj* **gaudier; -est** . . .
secure[2] *adj* **-curer; -est** . . .
pero
young[1] . . . *adj* **younger** [ˈjʌŋgər]; **youngest** [-gəst] . . .

En algunas entradas aparece únicamente la forma superlativa:

mere *adj, superlative* **merest** . . .

La ausencia de la forma comparativa indica que no existe evidencia suficiente de su uso.

Las formas comparativas y superlativas de los adjetivos y adverbios generalmente no se muestran si la sufijación no altera el vocablo raíz:

quiet[3] *adj* **1** . . .

Uso

En este diccionario se emplean dos tipos de **calificativo de uso**: regional y estilístico. Las palabras españolas cuyo uso se limita a ciertas regiones de Latinoamérica o a España, reciben calificativos que indican los países en que suelen usarse con más frecuencia:

guarachear *vi Cuba, PRi fam* . . .
bucket . . . *n* : . . . cubeta *f Mex*

Los siguientes calificativos regionales se han empleado en la redacción de este libro: *Arg* (Argentina), *Bol* (Bolivia), *CA* (Centroamérica), *Car* (el Caribe), *Chile* (Chile), *Col* (Colombia), *CoRi* (Costa Rica), *Cuba* (Cuba), *DomRep* (República Dominicana), *Ecua* (Ecuador), *Sal* (El Salvador), *Guat* (Guatemala), *Hond* (Honduras), *Mex* (México), *Nic* (Nicaragua), *Pan* (Panamá), *Par*

(Paraguay), *Peru* (Perú), *PRi* (Puerto Rico), *Spain* (España), *Uru* (Uruguay), *Ven* (Venezuela).

Dado el foco primordialmente latinoamericano de este diccionario, la mayoría de los regionalismos que contiene provienen de América Latina. Sin embargo, se han incluido también algunos regionalismos comunes de España.

Varios vocablos en español reciben un calificativo de *fam* (familiar), lo cual indica que el uso de tales palabras es apropiado solamente en contextos informales. El calificativo estilístico *usu considered vulgar* se emplea para indicar que el uso de la palabra indicada puede considerarse como vulgar u ofensivo. Se han omitido la mayoría de este tipo de voces, pero hay algunas cuyo uso es tan común que el omitirlas resultaría negligente. El propósito de este calificativo es, pues, de servir de advertencia al lector.

En algunos casos, una acepción puede venir precedida de una **nota parentética** que proporciona al lector información semántica suplementaria:

> **not** . . . *adv* **1** (*used to form a negative*) : no . . .
> **within**[2] *prep* . . . **2** (*in expressions of distance*) : . . . **3** (*in expressions of time*) : . . .
> **e**[2] *conj* (*used instead of* **y** *before words beginning with i or hi*) : . . .
> **poder**[1] . . . *v aux* . . . **2** (*expressing possibility*) : . . . **3** (*expressing permission*) : . . .

Este tipo de orientación semántica puede aparecer también entre paréntesis como parte de la definición:

> **calibrate** . . .*vt* . . . : calibrar (armas), graduar (termómetros)
> **palco** *nm* : box (in a theater or stadium)

En algunas ocasiones, una **nota de uso** aparece en lugar de una definición. Esto ocurre sólo cuando el lema carece de equivalente en el idioma extranjero. Estas notas de uso aparecen acompañadas de ejemplos que ilustran el uso común del lema:

> **shall** . . . *v aux* . . . **1** (*used to express a command*) <you shall do as I say : harás lo que te digo> . . .

Varias definiciones vienen acompañadas de **ejemplos de uso**. Estos ejemplos sirven para ilustrar un empleo típico del lema en un contexto dado, o un uso idiomático común de la palabra. Los ejemplos de uso incluyen una traducción, y aparecen entre paréntesis angulares:

> **lejos** *adv* **1** : far away, distant <a lo lejos : in the distance, far off> . . .
> **make**[1] . . . **9** . . . : ganar <to make a living : ganarse la vida> . . .

División de las acepciones

Se presenta una **acepción o definición** por medio de dos puntos en negrita:

> **fable** . . . *n* : fábula *f*

Cuando una entrada principal tiene varias acepciones, éstas se indican con un número arábigo, compuesto también en negrita:

> **laguna** *nf* **1** : lagoon **2** : lacuna, gap

Cuando alguna información (como un sinónimo, una palabra o frase en negrita, una nota de uso, una remisión, o un calificativo) aparece después de un número de acepción, ésta se aplica única y específicamente a dicha acepción, y no a otras que puedan aparecer bajo la misma entrada principal:

abanico *nm* . . . **2** GAMA : . . .
tonic[2] *n* . . . **2** *or* **tonic water** : . . .
grillo *nm* . . . **2 grillos** *nmpl* : . . .
fairy . . . *n, pl* **fairies** . . . **2 fairy tale** : . . .
myself . . . *pron* **1** (*used reflexively*) : . . .
pike . . . *n* . . . **3** → **turnpike**
atado[2] *nm* . . . **2** *Arg* : . . .

Remisiones

Las **remisiones** empleadas en este diccionario se clasifican en tres categorías: sinónima, cognada, e inflexional. Toda remisión puede identificarse inmediatamente por la flecha en negrita que aparece a continuación del lema.

Las remisiones de tipo sinónimo y cognado indican que la definición correspondiente al lema que precede a la flecha puede encontrarse en la entrada a la cual se remite:

scapula . . . → **shoulder blade**
amuck → **amok**

Las remisiones de tipo inflexional se utilizan para indicar que el lema que precede a la flecha es meramente una inflexión de la entrada a la cual se remite (generalmente un verbo o un sustantivo):

fue, etc. → **ir, ser**
mice → **mouse**

Sinónimos

En varias entradas y acepciones del diccionario se encuentra, entre los dos puntos en negrita y el texto de la definición, un **sinónimo** compuesto en mayúsculas pequeñas. Toda palabra empleada como sinónimo tiene su propia entrada en el diccionario, ya sea como entrada principal o como frase en negrita. El propósito de estos sinónimos es de orientar al lector y ayudarlo a elegir la acepción correcta, así como de proveer un término que podría usarse alternativamente en el mismo contexto.

Spanish Grammar

Accentuation

Spanish word stress is generally determined according to the following rules:

- Words ending in a vowel, or in *-n* or *-s,* are stressed on the next to last syllable (*zapato, llaman*).
- Words ending in a consonant other than *-n* or *-s* are stressed on the last syllable (*perdiz, curiosidad*).

Exceptions to these rules have a written accent mark over the stressed vowel (*fácil, hablará, último*). There are also a few words which take accent marks in order to distinguish them from homonyms (*si, sí; que, qué; el, él;* etc.).

Adverbs ending in *-mente* have two stressed syllables since they retain both the stress of the root word and of the *-mente* suffix (***lentamente***, ***dificilmente***). Many compounds also have two stressed syllables (*limpiaparabrisas*).

Punctuation and Capitalization

Questions and exclamations in Spanish are preceded by an inverted question mark ¿ and an inverted exclamation mark ¡, respectively:

¿Cuándo llamó Ana?
Y tú, ¿qué piensas?
¡No hagas eso!
Pero, ¡qué lástima!

In Spanish, unlike English, the following words are not capitalized:

- Names of days, months, and languages (*jueves, octubre, español*).
- Spanish adjectives or nouns derived from proper nouns (*los nicaragüenses, una teoría marxista*).

Articles

1. Definite Article

Spanish has five forms of the definite article: *el* (masculine singular), *la* (feminine singular), *los* (masculine plural), *las* (feminine plural), and *lo* (neuter). The first four agree in gender and number with the nouns they limit (*el carro,* the car; *las tijeras,* the scissors), although the form *el* is used with feminine singular nouns beginning with a stressed *a-* or *ha-* (*el águila, el hambre*).

The neuter article *lo* is used with the masculine singular form of an adjective to express an abstract concept (*lo mejor de este método,* the best thing about this method; *lo meticuloso de su trabajo,* the meticulousness of her work; *lo mismo para mí,* the same for me).

Whenever the masculine article *el* immediately follows the words *de* or *a,* it combines with them to form the contractions *del* and *al,* respectively (*viene del campo, vi al hermano de Roberto*).

The use of *el, la, los,* and *las* in Spanish corresponds largely to the use of *the* in English; some exceptions are noted below.

The definite article is used:

- When referring to something as a class (*los gatos son ágiles,* cats are agile; *me gusta el café,* I like coffee).
- In references to meals and in most expressions of time (*¿comiste el almuerzo?,* did you eat lunch?; *vino el año pasado,* he came last year; *son las dos,* it's two o'clock; *prefiero el verano,* I prefer summer; *la reunión es el lunes,* the meeting is on Monday; but: *hoy es lunes,* today is Monday).

- Before titles (except *don, doña, san, santo, santa, fray,* and *sor*) in third-person references to people (*la señora Rivera llamó,* Mrs. Rivera called; but: *hola, señora Rivera,* hello, Mrs. Rivera).
- In references to body parts and personal possessions (*me duele la cabeza,* my head hurts; *dejó el sombrero,* he left his hat).
- To mean "the one " or "the ones " when the subject is already understood (*la de madera,* the wooden one; *los que vi ayer,* the ones I saw yesterday).

The definite article is omitted:

- Before a noun in apposition, if the noun is not modified (*Caracas, capital de Venezuela;* but: *Pico Bolívar, la montaña más alta de Venezuela*).
- Before a number in a royal title (*Carlos Quinto,* Charles the Fifth).

2. Indefinite Article

The forms of the indefinite article in Spanish are *un* (masculine singular), *una* (feminine singular), *unos* (masculine plural), and *unas* (feminine plural). They agree in number and gender with the nouns they limit (*una mesa,* a table; *unos platos,* some plates), although the form *un* is used with feminine singular nouns beginning with a stressed *a-* or *ha-* (*un ala, un hacha*).

The use of *un, una, unos,* and *unas* in Spanish corresponds largely to the use of *a, an,* and *some* in English, with some exceptions:

- Indefinite articles are generally omitted before nouns identifying someone or something as a member of a class or category (*Paco es profesor/católico,* Paco is a professor/Catholic; *se llama páncreas,* it's called a pancreas).
- They are also often omitted in instances where quantity is understood from context (*vine sin chaqueta,* I came without a jacket; *no tengo carro,* I don't have a car).

Nouns

1. Gender

Nouns in Spanish are either masculine or feminine. A noun's gender can often be determined according to the following guidelines:

- Nouns ending in *-aje, -o,* or *-or* are usually masculine (*el traje, el libro, el sabor*), with some exceptions (*la mano, la foto, la labor,* etc.).
- Nouns ending in *-a, -dad, -ión, -tud,* or *-umbre* are usually feminine (*la alfombra, la capacidad, la excepción, la juventud, la certidumbre*). Exceptions include: *el día, el mapa,* and many learned borrowings ending in *-ma* (*el idioma, el tema*).

Most nouns referring to people or animals agree in gender with the subject (*el hombre, la mujer; el hermano, la hermana; el perro, la perra*). However, some nouns referring to people, including those ending in *-ista,* use the same form for both sexes (*el artista, la artista; el modelo, la modelo;* etc.).

A few names of animals exist in only one gender form (*la jirafa, el sapo,* etc.). In these instances, the adjectives *macho* and *hembra* are sometimes used to distinguish males and females (*una jirafa macho,* a male giraffe).

2. Pluralization

Plurals of Spanish nouns are formed as follows:

- Nouns ending in an unstressed vowel or an accented *-é* are pluralized by adding *-s* (*la vaca, las vacas; el café, los cafés*).
- Nouns ending in a consonant other than *-s,* or in a stressed vowel other than *-é,* are generally pluralized by adding *-es* (*el papel, los papeles; el rubí, los rubíes*). Exceptions include *papá* (*papás*) and *mamá* (*mamás*).

- Nouns with an unstressed final syllable ending in *-s* usually have a zero plural (*la crisis, las crisis; el jueves, los jueves*). Other nouns ending in *-s* add *-es* to form the plural (*el mes, los meses; el país, los países*).
- Nouns ending in *-z* are pluralized by changing the *-z* to *-c* and adding *-es* (*el lápiz, los lápices; la vez, las veces*).
- Many compound nouns have a zero plural (*el paraguas, los paraguas; el aguafiestas, los aguafiestas*).
- The plurals of *cualquiera* and *quienquiera* are *cualesquiera* and *quienesquiera*, respectively.

Adjectives

1. Gender and Number

Most adjectives agree in gender and number with the nouns they modify (un chico *alto,* una chica *alta,* unos chicos *altos,* unas chicas *altas*). Some adjectives, including those ending in *-e* and *-ista* (*fuerte, altruista*) and comparative adjectives ending in *-or* (*mayor, mejor*), vary only for number.

Adjectives whose masculine singular forms end in *-o* generally change the *-o* to *-a* to form the feminine (*pequeño → pequeña*). Masculine adjectives ending in *-án, -ón,* or *-dor,* and masculine adjectives of nationality which end in a consonant, usually add *-a* to form the feminine (*holgazán → holgazana*; *llorón → llorona*; *trabajador → trabajadora*; *irlandés → irlandesa*).

Adjectives are pluralized in much the same manner as nouns:

- The plurals of adjectives ending in an unstressed vowel or an accented *-é* are formed by adding an *-s* (un postre *rico,* unos postres *ricos;* una camisa *café,* unas camisas *cafés*).
- Adjectives ending in a consonant, or in a stressed vowel other than *-é,* are generally pluralized by adding *-es* (un niño *cortés,* unos niños *corteses;* una persona *iraní,* unas personas *iraníes*).
- Adjectives ending in *-z* are pluralized by changing the *-z* to *-c* and adding *-es* (una respuesta *sagaz*, unas respuestas *sagaces*).

2. Shortening

- The following masculine singular adjectives drop their final *-o* when they occur before a masculine singular noun: *bueno* (*buen*), *malo* (*mal*), *uno* (*un*), *alguno* (*algún*), *ninguno* (*ningún*), *primero* (*primer*), *tercero* (*tercer*).
- *Grande* shortens to *gran* before any singular noun.
- *Ciento* shortens to *cien* before any noun.
- The title *Santo* shortens to *San* before all masculine names except those beginning with *To-* or *Do-* (*San Juan, Santo Tomás*).

3. Position

Descriptive adjectives generally follow the nouns they modify (*una cosa útil, un actor famoso*). However, adjectives that express an inherent quality often precede the noun (*la blanca nieve*).

Some adjectives change meaning depending on whether they occur before or after the noun: *un pobre niño,* a poor (pitiable) child; *un niño pobre,* a poor (not rich) child; *un gran hombre,* a great man; *un hombre grande,* a big man; *el único libro,* the only book; *el libro único,* the unique book, etc.

4. Comparative and Superlative Forms

The comparative of Spanish adjectives is generally rendered as *más . . . que* (more . . . than) or *menos . . . que* (less . . . than): *soy más alta que él,* I'm taller than he; *son menos inteligentes que tú,* they're less intelligent than you.

The superlative of Spanish adjectives usually follows the formula *definite arti-*

cle + (*noun* +) *más/menos* + *adjective: ella es la estudiante más trabajadora,* she is the hardest-working student; *él es el menos conocido,* he's the least known.

A few Spanish adjectives have irregular comparative and superlative forms:

Adjective	Comparative/Superlative
bueno (good)	**mejor** (better, best)
malo (bad)	**peor** (worse, worst)
grande[1] (big, great), **viejo** (old)	**mayor** (greater, older; greatest, oldest)
pequeño[1] (little), **joven** (young)	**menor** (lesser, younger; least, youngest)
mucho (much), **muchos** (many)	**más** (more, most)
poco (little), **pocos** (few)	**menos** (less, least)

[1]These words have regular comparative and superlative forms when used in reference to physical size: *él es más grande que yo; nuestra casa es la más pequeña.*

ABSOLUTE SUPERLATIVE

The absolute superlative is formed by placing *muy* before the adjective, or by adding the suffix *-ísimo* (*ella es muy simpática* or *ella es simpatiquísima,* she is very nice). The absolute superlative using *-ísimo* is formed according to the following rules:

- Adjectives ending in a consonant other than *-z* simply add the *-ísimo* ending (*fácil → facilísimo*).
- Adjectives ending in *-z* change this consonant to *-c* and add *-ísimo* (*feliz → felicísimo*).
- Adjectives ending in a vowel or diphthong drop the vowel or diphthong and add *-ísimo* (*claro → clarísimo; amplio → amplísimo*).
- Adjectives ending in *-co* or *-go* change these endings to *qu* and *gu,* respectively, and add *-ísimo* (*rico → riquísimo; largo → larguísimo*).
- Adjectives ending in *-ble* change this ending to *-bil* and add *-ísimo* (*notable → notabilísimo*).
- Adjectives containing the stressed diphthong *ie* or *ue* will sometimes change these to *e* and *o,* respectively (*ferviente → fervientísimo* or *ferventísimo; bueno → buenísimo* or *bonísimo*).

Adverbs

Adverbs can be formed by adding the adverbial suffix *-mente* to virtually any adjective (*fácil → fácilmente*). If the adjective varies for gender, the feminine form is used as the basis for forming the adverb (*rápido → rápidamente*).

Pronouns

1. Personal Pronouns

The personal pronouns in Spanish are:

Person	Singular		Plural	
FIRST	**yo**	I	**nosotros, nosotras**	we
SECOND	**tú**	you (familiar)	**vosotros**[2], **vosotras**[2]	you, all of you
	vos[1]	you		
	usted	you (formal)	**ustedes**[3]	you, all of you
THIRD	**él**	he	**ellos, ellas**	they
	ella	she		
	ello	it (neuter)		

[1]Familiar form used in addition to tú in South and Central America.
[2]Familiar form used in Spain.
[3]Formal form used in Spain; familiar and formal form used in Latin America.

FAMILIAR VS. FORMAL

The second person personal pronouns exist in both familiar and formal forms. The familiar forms are generally used when addressing relatives, friends, and children, although usage varies considerably from region to region; the formal forms are used in other contexts to show courtesy, respect, or emotional distance.

In Spain and in the Caribbean, *tú* is used exclusively as the familiar singular "you." In South and Central America, however, *vos* either competes with *tú* to varying degrees or replaces it entirely. (For a more detailed explanation of *vos* and its corresponding verb forms, refer to the Conjugation of Spanish Verbs section.)

The plural familiar form *vosotros, -as* is used only in Spain, where *ustedes* is reserved for formal contexts. In Latin America, *vosotros, -as* is not used, and *ustedes* serves as the all-purpose plural "you."

It should be noted that while *usted* and *ustedes* are regarded as second person pronouns, they take the third person form of the verb.

USAGE

In Spanish, personal pronouns are generally omitted (*voy al cine,* I'm going to the movies; *¿llamaron?,* did they call?), although they are sometimes used for purposes of emphasis or clarity (*se lo diré yo,* I will tell them; *vino ella, pero él se quedó,* she came, but he stayed behind). The forms *usted* and *ustedes* are usually included out of courtesy (*¿cómo está usted?,* how are you?).

Personal pronouns are not generally used in reference to inanimate objects or living creatures other than humans; in these instances, the pronoun is most often omitted (*¿es nuevo? no, es viejo,* is it new? no, it's old).

The neuter third person pronoun *ello* is reserved for indefinite subjects (as abstract concepts): *todo ello implica . . . ,* all of this implies . . . ; *por si ello fuera poco . . . ,* as if that weren't enough. . . . It most commonly appears in formal writing and speech. In less formal contexts, *ello* is often either omitted or replaced with *esto, eso,* or *aquello.*

2. Prepositional Pronouns

Prepositional pronouns are used as the objects of prepositions (*¿es para mí?,* is it for me?; *se lo dio a ellos,* he gave it to them).

The prepositional pronouns in Spanish are:

Singular		Plural	
mí	me	**nosotros, nosotras**	us
ti	you	**vosotros[1], vosotras[1]**	you
usted	you (formal)	**ustedes**	you
él	him	**ellos, ellas**	them
ella	her		
ello	it (neuter)		
sí	yourself, himself, herself, itself, oneself	**sí**	yourselves, themselves

[1]Used primarily in Spain.

When the preposition *con* is followed by *mí, ti,* or *sí,* both words are replaced by *conmigo, contigo,* and *consigo,* respectively (*¿vienes conmigo?,* are you coming with me?; *habló contigo,* he spoke with you; *no lo trajo consigo,* she didn't bring it with her).

3. Object Pronouns

DIRECT OBJECT PRONOUNS

Direct object pronouns represent the primary goal or result of the action of a verb. The direct object pronouns in Spanish are:

Singular		Plural	
me	me	**nos**	us
te	you	**os**[1]	you
le[2]	you, him	**les**[2]	you, them
lo	you, him, it	**los**	you, them
la	you, her, it	**las**	you, them

[1]Used only in Spain.
[2]Used mainly in Spain.

Agreement

The third person forms agree in both gender and number with the nouns they replace or the people they refer to (*pintó las paredes,* she painted the walls → *las pintó,* she painted them; *visitaron al señor Juárez*, they visited Mr. Juárez → *lo visitaron*, they visited him). The remaining forms vary only for number.

Position

Direct object pronouns are normally affixed to the end of an affirmative command, a simple infinitive, or a present participle (*¡hazlo!,* do it!; *es difícil hacerlo,* it's difficult to do it; *haciéndolo, aprenderás,* you'll learn by doing it). With constructions involving an auxiliary verb and an infinitive or present participle, the pronoun may occur either immediately before the construction or suffixed to it (*lo voy a hacer* or *voy a hacerlo,* I'm going to do it; *estoy haciéndolo* or *lo estoy haciendo,* I'm doing it). In all other cases, the pronoun immediately precedes the conjugated verb (*no lo haré,* I won't do it).

Regional Variation

In Spain and in a few areas of Latin America, *le* and *les* are used in place of *lo* and *los* when referring to or addressing people (*le vieron,* they saw him; *les vistió,* she dressed them). In most parts of Latin America, however, *los* and *las* are used for the second person plural in both formal and familiar contexts.

The second person plural familiar form *os* is restricted to Spain.

INDIRECT OBJECT PRONOUNS

Indirect object pronouns represent the secondary goal of the action of a verb (*me dio el regalo,* he gave me the gift; *les dije que no,* I told them no). The indirect object pronouns in Spanish are:

Singular		Plural	
me	(to, for, from) me	**nos**	(to, for, from) us
te	(to, for, from) you	**os**[1]	(to, for, from) you
le	(to, for, from) you, him, her, it	**les**	(to, for, from) you, them
se[2]		**se**[2]	

[1]Used only in Spain.
[2]See explanation below.

Position

Indirect object pronouns follow the same rules as direct object pronouns with regard to their position in relation to verbs. When they occur with direct object pronouns, the indirect object pronoun always precedes (*nos lo dio,* she gave it to us; *estoy trayéndotela,* I'm bringing it to you).

Use of *Se*

When the indirect object pronouns *le* or *les* occur before any direct object pronoun beginning with an *l-*, the indirect object pronouns *le* and *les* convert to *se* (*les mandé la carta,* I sent them the letter → *se la mandé,* I sent it to them; *vamos a comprarle los aretes,* let's buy her the earrings → *vamos a comprárselos,* let's buy them for her).

4. Reflexive Pronouns

Reflexive pronouns are used to refer back to the subject of the verb (*me hice daño,* I hurt myself; *se vistieron,* they got dressed, they dressed themselves; *nos lo compramos,* we bought it for ourselves).

The reflexive pronouns in Spanish are:

Singular		Plural	
me	myself	**nos**	ourselves
te	yourself	**os**[1]	yourselves
se	yourself, himself, herself, itself	**se**	yourselves, themselves

[1]Used only in Spain.

Reflexive pronouns are also used:

- When the verb describes an action performed to one's own body, clothing, etc. (*me quité los zapatos,* I took off my shoes; *se arregló el pelo,* he fixed his hair).
- In the plural, to indicate reciprocal action (*se hablan con frecuencia,* they speak with each other frequently).
- In the third person singular and plural, as an indefinite subject reference (*se dice que es verdad,* they say it's true; *nunca se sabe,* one never knows; *se escribieron miles de páginas,* thousands of pages were written).

It should be noted that many verbs which take reflexive pronouns in Spanish have intransitive equivalents in English (*ducharse,* to shower; *quejarse,* to complain; etc.).

5. Relative Pronouns

Relative pronouns introduce subordinate clauses acting as nouns or modifiers (*el libro que escribió . . . ,* the book that he wrote . . . ; *las chicas a quienes conociste . . . ,* the girls whom you met . . .). In Spanish, the relative pronouns are:

que (that, which, who, whom)
quien, quienes (who, whom, that, whoever, whomever)
el cual, la cual, los cuales, las cuales (which, who)
el que, la que, los que, las que (which, who, whoever)
lo cual (which)
lo que (what, which, whatever)
cuanto, cuanta, cuantos, cuantas (all those that, all that, whatever, whoever, as much as, as many as)

Relative pronouns are not omitted in Spanish as they often are in English: *el carro que vi ayer,* the car (that) I saw yesterday. When relative pronouns are used with prepositions, the preposition precedes the clause (*la película sobre la cual le hablé,* the film I spoke to you about).

The relative pronoun *que* can be used in reference to both people and things. Unlike other relative pronouns, *que* does not take the personal *a* when used as a direct object referring to a person (*el hombre que llamé,* the man that I called; but: *el hombre a quien llamé,* the man whom I called).

Quien is used only in reference to people. It varies in number with the explicit or implied antecedent (*las mujeres con quienes charlamos . . . ,* the women we chatted with; *quien lo hizo pagará,* whoever did it will pay).

El cual and *el que* vary for both number and gender, and are therefore often used in situations where *que* or *quien(es)* might create ambiguity: *nos contó algunas cosas sobre los libros, las cuales eran interesantes,* he told us some things about the books which (the things) were interesting.

Lo cual and *lo que* are used to refer back to a whole clause, or to something indefinite (*dijo que iría, lo cual me alegró,* he said he would go, which made me happy; *pide lo que quieras,* ask for whatever you want).

Cuanto varies for both number and gender with the implied antecedent: *conté a cuantas (personas) pude,* I counted as many (people) as I could. If an indefinite mass quantity is referred to, the masculine singular form is used (*anoté cuanto decía,* I jotted down whatever he said).

Possessives

1. Possessive Adjectives

UNSTRESSED FORMS

Singular		Plural	
mi(s)	my	**nuestro(s), nuestra(s)**	our
tu(s)	your	**vuestro(s)[1], vuestra(s)[1]**	your
su(s)	your, his, her, its	**su(s)**	your, their

[1]Used only in Spain.

STRESSED FORMS

Singular		Plural	
mío(s), mía(s)	my, mine, of mine	**nuestro(s), nuestra(s)**	our, ours, of ours
tuyo(s), tuya(s)	your, yours, of yours	**vuestro(s)[1], vuestra(s)[1]**	your, yours, of yours
suyo(s), suya(s)	your, yours, of yours; his, of his; her, hers, of hers; its, of its	**suyo(s), suya(s)**	your, yours, of yours; their, theirs, of theirs

[1]Used only in Spain.

The unstressed forms of possessive adjectives precede the nouns they modify (*mis zapatos,* my shoes; *nuestra escuela,* our school).

The stressed forms occur after the noun and are often used for purposes of emphasis (*el carro tuyo,* your car; *la pluma es mía,* the pen is mine; *unos amigos nuestros,* some friends of ours).

All possessive adjectives agree with the noun in number. The stressed forms, as well as the unstressed forms *nuestro* and *vuestro,* also vary for gender.

2. Possessive Pronouns

The possessive pronouns have the same forms as the stressed possessive adjectives (see table above). They are always preceded by the definite article, and they agree in number and gender with the nouns they replace (*las llaves mías,* my keys → *las mías,* mine; *los guantes nuestros,* our gloves → *los nuestros,* ours).

Demonstratives

1. Demonstrative Adjectives

The demonstrative adjectives in Spanish are:

Singular		Plural	
este, esta	this	**estos, estas**	these
ese, esa	that	**esos, esas**	those
aquel, aquella	that	**aquellos, aquellas**	those

Demonstrative adjectives agree with the nouns they modify in gender and number (*esta chica, aquellos árboles*). They normally precede the noun, but may occasionally occur after for purposes of emphasis or to express contempt: *en la época aquella de cambio,* in that era of change; *el perro ese ha ladrado toda la noche,* that (awful, annoying, etc.) dog barked all night long.

The forms *aquel, aquella, aquellos,* and *aquellas* are generally used in reference to people and things that are relatively distant from the speaker in space or time: *ese libro,* that book (a few feet away); *aquel libro,* that book (way over there).

2. Demonstrative Pronouns

The demonstrative pronouns in Spanish are orthographically identical to the demonstrative adjectives except that they take an accent mark over the stressed vowel (*éste, ése, aquél,* etc.). In addition, there are three neuter forms— *esto, eso,* and *aquello*—which are used when referring to abstract ideas or unidentified things (*¿te dijo eso?,* he said that to you?; *¿qué es esto?,* what is this?; *tráeme todo aquello,* bring me all that stuff).

Except for the neuter forms, demonstrative pronouns agree in gender and number with the nouns they replace (*esta silla,* this chair → *ésta,* this one; *aquellos vasos,* those glasses → *aquéllos,* those ones).

Gramática inglesa

El adjetivo

El adjetivo inglés es invariable en cuanto a número o género, y suele preceder al sustantivo que modifica:

the tall woman	the tall women
a happy child	happy children

Las **formas comparativas y superlativas del adjetivo** inglés se pueden construir de tres maneras. Cuando el adjetivo positivo consta de una sola sílaba, la construcción más común es de añadir los sufijos *-er* o *-est* al vocablo raíz; si el adjetivo positivo consta de más de dos sílabas, suele entonces combinarse con los adverbios *more*, *most*, *less* o *least;* al adjetivo positivo de dos sílabas puede aplicarse cualquiera de las dos fórmulas; y por último, existen los adjetivos irregulares cuyas formas comparativas y superlativas son únicas.

Positivo	Comparativo	Superlativo
clean	cleaner	cleanest
narrow	narrower	narrowest
meaningful	more/less meaningful	most/least meaningful
good	better	best
bad	worse	worst

El **adjetivo demostrativo** *this* o *that* corresponde al adjetivo español *este* o *ese*. Debe notarse que este tipo de adjetivo es el único que tiene forma plural:

Singular	Plural
this	these
that	those

Un **adjetivo descriptivo** describe o indica una cualidad, clase o condición (a fascinating conversation; a positive attitude; a fast computer).

Un **adjetivo indefinido** se usa para designar personas o cosas no identificadas (some children; other hotels).

El **adjetivo interrogativo** se usa para formular preguntas:

Whose office is this? *Which* book do you want?

Un **sustantivo** puede usarse para **modificar otro sustantivo**. De esta manera el sustantivo funciona igual que un adjetivo (the Vietnam War; word processing).

Llámase **adjetivo posesivo** a la forma posesiva del pronombre personal:

Singular	Plural
my	our
your	your
his/her/its	their

Where's *my* watch?	Where are *our* coats?
Your cab's here.	*Your* tables are ready.
It was *her* idea.	We paid for *their* tickets.
They read *his* book.	the box and *its* contents

Un **adjetivo predicativo** modifica el sujeto de un verbo copulativo (como *be, become, feel, taste, smell,* o *seem*):

She is *happy* with the outcome. The milk tastes *sour*.
The student seems *puzzled*.

Un **adjetivo propio** es derivado de un nombre propio y suele escribirse con mayúscula:

Victorian furniture a *Puerto Rican* product

Un **adjetivo relativo** (tal como *which, that, who, whom, whose, where*) se emplea para introducir una cláusula adjetival o sustantiva:

toward late April, by ***which*** time the report should be finished
not knowing ***whose*** advice she should follow

El adverbio

La mayor parte de los adverbios ingleses se forman a partir de un adjetivo al que se le agrega el sufijo *-ly*:

mad***ly*** wonderful***ly***

Para formar un adverbio de un adjetivo que termina en *-y*, suele cambiarse primero esta terminación a una *-i*, y luego se añade el sufijo *-ly*:

happ***ily*** daint***ily***

La forma adverbial que corresponde a varios adjetivos que terminan en *-ic* recibe el sufijo *-ally*:

basic***ally*** numeric***ally***

Si un adjetivo termina en *-ly*, el adverbio que le corresponde suele escribirse de la misma manera:

she called her mother ***daily*** the show started ***early***

Por último, hay adverbios que no terminan en *-ly* (por ejemplo, *again, now,* y *too*).

Al igual que el adjetivo, la mayoría de los adverbios ingleses poseen tres grados de comparación: **positivo, comparativo,** y **superlativo.** Como regla general, a un adverbio monosilábico se le añade el sufijo *-er* cuando es comparativo, y *-est* cuando es superlativo. Si el adverbio consta de tres o más sílabas, las formas comparativas y superlativas se forman al combinarlo con los adverbios *more/most* o *less/least*. Las formas comparativas y superlativas de un adverbio de dos sílabas pueden obtenerse empleando uno u otro de los dos métodos:

Positivo	**Comparativo**	**Superlativo**
fast	faster	fastest
easy	easier	easiest
madly	more madly	most madly
happily	more happily	most happily

Finalmente, hay algunos adverbios, tales como *quite* y *very*, que no poseen comparativo.

Adverbios tales como *just* y *only* suelen usarse para poner el énfasis en otras palabras. El énfasis producido puede cambiar según la posición del adverbio en la oración:

He ***just*** nodded to me as he passed.
Sólo me saludó con la cabeza al pasar.
He nodded to me ***just*** as he passed.
Me saludó con la cabeza ***justamente*** cuando me pasó.

Los **adverbios relativos** (tales como *when*, *where*, y *why*) se utilizan principalmente para introducir preguntas:

When will he return? ***Where*** have the children gone?
Why did you do it?

El artículo

En inglés existe solamente una forma del **artículo definido**, *the*. Este artículo es invariable en cuanto a género o número.

The boys were expelled. *The* First Lady dined with *the* ambassador.

El **artículo indefinido** *a* se usa con cualquier sustantivo o abreviatura que comience ya sea con una consonante, o con un *sonido* consonántico:

a door	a hat
a B.A. degree	a one-way street
a union	a U.S. Senator

El artículo *a* se emplea también antes de un sustantivo cuya primera sílaba comienza con *h-*, y esta sílaba no es acentuada o tiene solamente una acentuación moderada (a historian, a heroic attempt, a hilarious performance). Sin embargo, en el inglés hablado, suele más usarse el artículo *an* en estos casos (an historian, an heroic attempt, an hilarious performance). Ambas formas son perfectamente aceptables.

El artículo indefinido *an* se usa con cualquier sustantivo o abreviatura que comience con un sonido vocal, sin tener en cuenta si la primera letra del sustantivo es vocal o consonante (an icicle, an nth degree, an honor, an FBI investigation).

La conjunción

Existen tres tipos principales de conjunciones: la conjunción coordinante, la correlativa, y la subordinante.

Las **conjunciones coordinantes**, tales como *and, because, but, for, or, nor, since, so,* y *yet,* se emplean para unir elementos gramaticales de igual valor. Estos elementos pueden ser palabras, frases, cláusulas subordinadas, cláusulas principales, u oraciones completas. Las conjunciones coordinantes se emplean para unir elementos similares (she ordered pencils, pens, and erasers), para excluir o contrastar (he is a brilliant *but* arrogant man), para indicar una alternativa (she can wait here *or* go on ahead), para indicar una razón (the report is useless, *for* its information is no longer current), o para precisar un resultado (his diction is excellent, *so* every word is clear).

Las **conjunciones correlativas** se usan en pares, y sirven para unir alternativas y elementos de igual valor gramatical.

Either you go ***or*** you stay. He had ***neither*** looks ***nor*** wit.

Las **conjunciones subordinantes** se usan para unir una cláusula subordinada a una cláusula principal. Estas conjunciones pueden emplearse para expresar la causa (*because* she learns quickly, she is doing well in her new job), la condición o concesión (don't call *unless* you are coming), el modo (we'll do it *however* you tell us to), el propósito o resultado (he distributes the mail early *so* that they can read it), el tiempo (she kept meetings to a minimum *when* she was president), el lugar o la circunstancia (*wherever* he goes, he is welcomed with open arms), así como las condiciones o posibilidades alternativas (they were undecided *whether* to go or stay).

El sustantivo

A diferencia del sustantivo español, el sustantivo inglés generalmente carece de género. En algunos sustantivos, el género femenino se identifica por la presencia del sufijo - *ess* (empress, hostess); existen también aquellos sustantivos que sólo se aplican a miembros de uno u otro sexo, por ejemplo: *husband, wife, father, mother, brother, sister,* así como nombres de ciertos animales: *bull, cow, deer, doe,* etc. Sin embargo, la mayoría de los sustantivos ingleses son neutros. Cuando es preciso atribuirle un género a un sustantivo neutro, suele combinarse éste con palabras como *male, female, man, woman,* etc., por ejemplo:

a *male* parrot *women* writers

Los sustantivos ingleses suelen usarse como **sujetos** (the *office* was quiet), **objetos directos** (he locked the *office*), **objetos de una preposición** (the file is in the *office*), **objetos indirectos** (he gave his *client* the papers), **objetos retenidos** (his client was given the *papers*), **nominativos predicativos** (Mrs. Adams is the managing *partner*), **complementos objetivos** (they made Mrs. Adams managing *partner*), **construcciones apositivas** (Mrs. Adams, the managing *partner,* wrote that memo), y **en trato directo** (*Mrs.* Adams, may I present Mr. Bonkowski).

Los sustantivos desempeñan una función adjetival cuando preceden a otros sustantivos:

olive oil business management
emergency room

La mayoría de los sustantivos ingleses se pluralizan añadiendo *-s* al final del singular (book, books; cat, cats; dog, dogs; tree, trees).

Cuando el sustantivo singular termina en *-s, -x, -z, -ch,* o *-sh,* su forma plural se obtiene añadiendo *-es* al final (cross, crosses; fox, foxes; fez, fezes; witch, witches; wish, wishes).

Si el sustantivo singular termina en *-y* precedida de una consonante, la *-y* es convertida en *-i* y se le añade la terminación *-es* (fairy, fairies; pony, ponies; guppy, guppies).

No todos los sustantivos ingleses obedecen estas normas. Hay algunos sustantivos (generalmente nombres de animales) que no siempre cambian en el plural (fish, fish o fishes; caribou, caribou o caribous). Por último, hay algunos sustantivos que poseen una forma plural única (foot, feet; mouse, mice; knife, knives).

La forma posesiva del sustantivo singular generalmente se obtiene al añadir un apóstrofe seguido de una *-s* al final:

Jackie's passport this hat is *Billy's*

Cuando el sustantivo termina en *-s,* suele añadirse únicamente el apóstrofe, como sigue:

the *neighbors's* dog Mr. *Ross's* briefcase

La preposición

La preposición inglesa se combina generalmente con un sustantivo, un pronombre, o el equivalente de un sustantivo (como una frase o cláusula) para formar una frase con función adjetival, adverbial, o sustantiva. Suele distinguirse dos tipos de preposiciones: la preposición simple, es decir, aquélla que consta de una sola palabra (por ejemplo, *against, from, near, of, on, out,* o *without*), y la compuesta, que consta de más de un elemento (como *according to, by means of,* o *in spite of*).

La preposición se emplea generalmente para unir un sustantivo, un pronombre, o el equivalente de un sustantivo al resto de la oración. Una frase preposicional suele emplearse como adverbio o adjetivo.

She expected resistance *on* his part. He sat down *beside* her.

Las palabras inglesas *after, before, but, for,* y *since* pueden funcionar como preposiciones así como conjunciones. El papel que desempeñan estas palabras suele determinarse según su posición dentro de la oración. Las conjunciones generalmente sirven para unir dos elementos de igual valor gramatical, mientras que las preposiciones suelen preceder a un sustantivo, un pronombre, o una frase sustantiva.

conjunción: I was a bit concerned *but* not panicky.
[*but* vincula dos adjetivos]
preposición: I was left with nothing *but* hope.
[*but* precede a un sustantivo]

conjunción: The device conserves fuel, *for* it is battery-powered. [*for* vincula dos cláusulas]
preposición: The device conserves fuel *for* residual heating. [*for* precede a una frase sustantiva]

Una preposición puede aparecer antes de un sustantivo o un pronombre (*below* the desk, *beside* them), después de un adjetivo (antagonistic *to,* insufficient *in,* symbolic *of*), o después de un elemento verbal con el cual combina para formar una frase con función verbal (take *for,* take *over,* come *across*).

A diferencia de la preposición española, la preposición inglesa puede aparecer al final de una oración, lo cual sucede frecuentemente en el uso común, especialmente si la preposición forma parte de una frase con función verbal.

After Rourke left, Joyce took *over.* What does this all add up *to*?

El pronombre

Los pronombres pueden poseer las características siguientes: caso (nominativo, posesivo, u objetivo); número (singular o plural); persona (primera, segunda, o tercera), y género (masculino, femenino, o neutro). Los pronombres ingleses se clasifican en siete categorías principales, de las cuales cada una juega un papel específico.

Las palabras *this, that, these* y *those* se consideran como pronombres cuando funcionan como sustantivos. (Se les clasifica como adjetivos demostrativos cuando modifican un sustantivo.) El **pronombre demostrativo** indica a una persona o cosa para distinguirla de otras.

These are the best designs we've seen to date. *Those* are strong words.

El pronombre demostrativo también se usa para distinguir a una persona o cosa cercana de otra que se encuentre a mayor distancia (*this* is my desk; *that* is yours).

El **pronombre indefinido** se emplea para designar a una persona o cosa cuya identidad se desconoce o no se puede establecer de inmediato. Estos pronombres se usan generalmente como referencias en la tercera persona, y no se distinguen en cuanto a género. A continuación se listan ejemplos de pronombres indefinidos.

all	either	none
another	everybody	no one
any	everyone	one
anybody	everything	other
anyone	few	several
anything	many	some
both	much	somebody
each	neither	someone
each one	nobody	something

Los pronombres indefinidos deben concordar en cuanto a número con los verbos que les corresponden. Los siguientes pronombres son singulares y deben usarse con un verbo conjugado en singular: *another, anything, each one, everything, much, nobody, no one, one, other, someone, something.*

Much is being done. *No one wants* to go.

Los pronombres indefinidos *both, few, many, several* entre otros son plurales, y por lo tanto deben emplearse con verbos conjugados en plural:

Many were called; *few were* chosen.

Algunos pronombres, tales como *all, any, none,* y *some,* pueden presentar un problema ya que pueden usarse tanto con verbos singulares como plurales. Como regla general, los pronombres que se usan con sustantivos no numerables emplean verbos singulares, mientras que aquéllos que se usan con sustantivos numerables suelen tomar un verbo plural.

con sustantivo no numerable: ***All*** of the *property* is affected.
None of the *soup* was spilled.
Some of the *money* was spent.

con sustantivo numerable: ***All*** of my *shoes* are black.
None of the *clerks* were available.
Some of your *friends* were there.

Los **pronombres interrogativos** *what, which, who, whom,* y *whose,* así como las combinaciones de estos con el sufijo *-ever* (*whatever, whichever,* etc.) se usan para introducir una pregunta:

Who is she? He asked me ***who*** she was.
Whoever can that be? We wondered ***whoever*** that could be.

El **pronombre personal** refleja la persona, el número, y el género del ser u objeto que representa. La mayoría de los pronombres personales toman una forma distinta para cada uno de estos tres casos.

Persona	Nominativo	Posesivo	Objetivo
PRIMERA			
SINGULAR:	I	my, mine	me
PLURAL:	we	our, ours	us
SEGUNDA			
SINGULAR:	you	your, yours	you
PLURAL:	you	your, yours	you
TERCERA			
SINGULAR:	he	his, his	him
	she	her, hers	her
	it	its, its	it
PLURAL:	they	their, theirs	them

Nótese que los pronombres personales en el caso posesivo no llevan apóstrofe, y no deben confundirse con los homófonos *you're, they're, there's, it's.*

Los **pronombres recíprocos** *each other* y *one another* se emplean para indicar una acción o relación mutua:

They do not quarrel with ***one another***.
Lou and Andy saw ***each other*** at the party.

Un pronombre recíproco puede usarse también en el caso posesivo:

They always borrowed ***one another*'s** money.
The two companies depend on ***each other*'s** success.

Los **pronombres reflexivos** se forman al combinar los pronombres personales *him, her, it, my, our, them* y *your* con *-self* o *-selves.* El pronombre reflexivo se usa generalmente para expresar una acción reflexiva, o bien para recalcar el sujeto de una oración, cláusula, o frase.

She dressed ***herself.*** He asked ***himself*** if it was worth it.
I ***myself*** am not concerned. They wanted to do it ***themselves.***

Los **pronombres relativos** son *that, what, which, who, whom,* y *whose,* así como las combinaciones de éstos con la terminación *-ever.* Estos pronombres se emplean para introducir oraciones subordinadas con función sustantiva o adjetival. El pronombre relativo *who* se usa para referirse a personas y, en ciertas ocasiones, algunos animales. *Which* suele usarse para referirse a animales o cosas, y *that* puede usarse para personas, animales, o cosas.

a man ***who*** sought success a woman ***whom*** we trust
Kentucky Firebolt, ***who*** won yesterday's horse race
an author ***whose*** novels are well-known
a movie ***which*** was a big hit a dog ***which*** kept barking
a boy ***that*** behaves well a movie ***that*** was a big hit

a dog *that* kept barking give it to *whomever* you wish
whoever thought of it pick *whichever* you want

En ciertas ocasiones el pronombre relativo puede omitirse:

The man [*whom*] I was talking to is the senator.

El verbo

El verbo inglés posee típicamente las siguientes características: inflexión (por ejemplo, *help, helps, helping, helped*), persona (primera, segunda, o tercera), número (singular o plural), tiempo (presente, pasado, futuro), aspecto (categorías temporales distintas a los tiempos simples de presente, pasado y futuro), voz (activa o pasiva), y modo (indicativo, subjuntivo e imperativo).

Los verbos regulares ingleses tienen cuatro **inflexiones** diferentes, las cuales se producen al añadir los sufijos *-s* o *-es, -ed,* e *-ing.* La mayoría de los verbos irregulares poseen cuatro o cinco inflexiones (por ejemplo, *see, sees, seeing, saw, seen*); y el verbo *be* tiene ocho (*be, is, am, are, being, was, were, been*).

Los verbos que terminan en una *-e* muda conservan por lo general la *-e* al añadírsele un sufijo que comienza con una consonante (como *-s*), pero esta *-e* desaparece si el sufijo comienza con una vocal (como sucede con *-ed* o *-ing*).

arrange; arranges; arranged; arranging hope; hopes; hoped; hoping

Sin embargo, algunos de estos verbos conservan la *-e* final para no ser confundidos con otras palabras de ortografía igual, por ejemplo:

dye; dyes; dyed; dyeing [vs. *dying,* del verbo *die*]
singe; singes; singed; singeing [vs. *singing,* del verbo *sing*]

Si un verbo consta de una sílaba y termina en una sola consonante a la cual precede una sola vocal, la consonante final se repite en algunas inflexiones:

brag; bragged; bragging grip; gripped; gripping

Cuando un verbo posee esta misma terminación, pero consta de dos o más sílabas, y la última de éstas es acentuada, se repite también la consonante final:

commit; committed; committing occur; occurred; occurring

Los verbos que terminan en *-y*, precedida de una consonante, suelen cambiar esta *-y* en *-i* en toda inflexión excepto cuando el sufijo correspondiente es *-ing.*

carry; carried; carrying study; studied; studying

Cuando un verbo termina en *-c,* se le añade una *-k* en inflexiones cuyos sufijos comienzan con *-e* o *-i*.

mimic; mimics; mimicked; mimicking
traffic; traffics; trafficked; trafficking

Los verbos ingleses exhiben generalmente su **presente simple** o **pasado simple** en una sola palabra, por ejemplo:

I do, I did we write, we wrote

El **tiempo futuro** suele expresarse al combinar el verbo auxiliar *shall* o *will* con la forma presente simple o presente progresiva del verbo:

I *shall* do it. We *will* come tomorrow.

Llámase aspecto de un verbo a aquellos tiempos que difieren del presente simple, pasado simple, o futuro simple. A continuación se presentan cuatro de estos tiempos o aspectos: el progresivo, el presente perfecto, el pasado perfecto, y el futuro perfecto.

El **tiempo progresivo** expresa una acción que está teniendo lugar en el presente o en el futuro.

He *is* reading the paper.

El **presente perfecto** se emplea para expresar una acción que ha comenzado en el pasado y que continúa en el presente, o también para expresar una acción que haya tenido lugar en un momento indefinido del pasado.

She *has* written a book.

El **pasado perfecto** expresa una acción que fue llevada a cabo antes de otra acción o evento en el pasado.

She *had* written many books previously.

El futuro perfecto indica una acción que será llevada a cabo antes de una acción o evento en el futuro.

We *will* have finished the project by then.

La **voz (activa o pasiva)** indica si el sujeto de la oración es el que desempeña la acción del verbo o si es el objeto de esta acción:

Voz activa: His colleagues *respected* him.
Voz pasiva: He *was* respected by his colleagues.

En inglés existen tres modos: indicativo, imperativo, y subjuntivo.

El **modo indicativo** se emplea ya sea para indicar un hecho, o para hacer una pregunta:

He *is* here. *Is* he here?

El **modo imperativo** se usa para expresar una orden o una petición:

Come here. Please *come* here.

El modo subjuntivo expresa una condición contraria a los hechos. El modo subjuntivo en inglés ha caído en desuso, pero suele aparecer en cláusulas introducidas por *if*, y después del verbo *wish*.

I wish he *were* here. If she *were* there, she could answer that.

Como en español, el verbo inglés puede ser transitivo o intransitivo. El **verbo transitivo** es el que puede llevar un complemento directo:

She *sold* her car. *Vendió* su coche.

El **verbo intransitivo** no lleva un complemento directo:

He *talked* all day. *Habló* todo el día.

Conjugation of Spanish Verbs

Simple Tenses

Tense	Regular Verbs Ending in -AR hablar	
PRESENT INDICATIVE	hablo hablas habla	hablamos habláis hablan
PRESENT SUBJUNCTIVE	hable hables hable	hablemos habléis hablen
PRETERIT INDICATIVE	hablé hablaste habló	hablamos hablasteis hablaron
IMPERFECT INDICATIVE	hablaba hablabas hablaba	hablábamos hablabais hablaban
IMPERFECT SUBJUNCTIVE	hablara hablaras hablara *or* hablase hablases hablase	habláramos hablarais hablaran hablásemos hablaseis hablasen
FUTURE INDICATIVE	hablaré hablarás hablará	hablaremos hablaréis hablarán
FUTURE SUBJUNCTIVE	hablare hablares hablare	habláremos hablareis hablaren
CONDITIONAL	hablaría hablarías hablaría	hablaríamos hablaríais hablarían
IMPERATIVE	— habla hable	hablemos hablad hablen
PRESENT PARTICIPLE (GERUND)	hablando	
PAST PARTICIPLE	hablado	

Regular Verbs Ending in -ER comer		Regular Verbs Ending in -IR vivir	
como	comemos	vivo	vivimos
comes	coméis	vives	vivís
come	comen	vive	viven
coma	comamos	viva	vivamos
comas	comáis	vivas	viváis
coma	coman	viva	vivan
comí	comimos	viví	vivimos
comiste	comisteis	viviste	vivisteis
comió	comieron	vivió	vivieron
comía	comíamos	vivía	vivíamos
comías	comíais	vivías	vivíais
comía	comían	vivía	vivían
comiera	comiéramos	viviera	viviéramos
comieras	comierais	vivieras	vivierais
comiera	comieran	viviera	vivieran
or		*or*	
comiese	comiésemos	viviese	viviésemos
comieses	comieseis	vivieses	vivieseis
comiese	comiesen	viviese	viviesen
comeré	comeremos	viviré	viviremos
comerás	comeréis	vivirás	viviréis
comerá	comerán	vivirá	vivirán
comiere	comiéremos	viviere	viviéremos
comieres	comiereis	vivieres	viviereis
comiere	comieren	viviere	vivieren
comería	comeríamos	viviría	viviríamos
comerías	comeríais	vivirías	viviríais
comería	comerían	viviría	vivirían
—	comamos	—	vivamos
come	comed	vive	vivid
coma	coman	viva	vivan
comiendo		viviendo	
comido		vivido	

Compound Tenses

1. Perfect Tenses

The perfect tenses are formed with *haber* and the past participle:

PRESENT PERFECT
he hablado, etc. (*indicative*);
haya hablado, etc. (*subjunctive*)

PAST PERFECT
había hablado, etc. (*indicative*);
hubiera hablado, etc. (*subjuntive*)
or
hubiese hablado, etc. (*subjunctive*)

PRETERIT PERFECT
hube hablado, etc. (*indicative*)

FUTURE PERFECT
habré hablado, etc. (*indicative*)

CONDITIONAL PERFECT
habría hablado, etc. (*indicative*)

2. Progressive Tenses

The progressive tenses are formed with *estar* and the present participle:

PRESENT PROGRESSIVE
estoy llamando, etc. (*indicative*);
esté llamando, etc. (*subjunctive*)

IMPERFECT PROGRESSIVE
estaba llamando, etc. (*indicative*);
estuviera llamando, etc. (*subjunctive*)
or
estuviese llamando, etc. (*subjunctive*)

PRETERIT PROGRESSIVE
estuve llamando, etc. (*indicative*)

FUTURE PROGRESSIVE
estaré llamando, etc. (*indicative*)

CONDITIONAL PROGRESSIVE
estaría llamando, etc. (*indicative*)

PRESENT PERFECT PROGRESSIVE
he estado llamando, etc. (*indicative*);
haya estado llamando, etc. (*subjunctive*)

PAST PERFECT PROGRESSIVE
había estado llamando, etc. (*indicative*);
hubiera estado llamando, etc. (*subjunctive*)
or
hubiese estado llamando, etc. (*subjunctive*)

Use of *Vos*

In parts of South and Central America, *vos* often replaces or competes with *tú* as the second person familiar personal pronoun. It is particularly well established in the Río de la Plata region and much of Central America.

The pronoun *vos* often takes a distinct set of verb forms, usually in the present tense and the imperative. These vary widely from region to region; examples of the most common forms are shown below.

INFINITIVE FORM	hablar	comer	vivir
PRESENT INDICATIVE	vos hablás	vos comés	vos vivís
PRESENT SUBJUNCTIVE	vos hablés	vos comás	vos vivás
IMPERATIVE	hablá	comé	viví

In some areas, *vos* may take the *tú* or *vosotros* forms of the verb, while in others (as Uruguay), *tú* is combined with the *vos* verb forms.

Irregular Verbs

The *imperfect subjunctive,* the *future subjunctive,* the *conditional*, and the remaining forms of the *imperative* are not included in the model conjugations list, but can be derived as follows:

The *imperfect subjunctive* and the *future subjunctive* are formed from the third person plural form of the preterit tense by removing the last syllable (*-ron*) and adding the appropriate suffix:

PRETERIT INDICATIVE, THIRD PERSON PLURAL (querer)	quisieron
IMPERFECT SUBJUNCTIVE (querer)	quisiera, quisieras, etc. *or* quisiese, quisieses, etc.
FUTURE SUBJUNCTIVE (querer)	quisiere, quisieres, etc.

The conditional uses the same stem as the future indicative:

FUTURE INDICATIVE (poner)	pondré, pondrás, etc.
CONDITIONAL (poner)	pondría, pondrías, etc.

The third person singular, first person plural, and third person plural forms of the *imperative* are the same as the corresponding forms of the present subjunctive.

The second person plural *(vosotros)* form of the *imperative* is formed by removing the final *-r* of the infinitive form and adding a *-d* (ex.: *oír* → *oíd*).

Model Conjugations of Irregular Verbs

The model conjugations below include the following simple tenses: the *present indicative* (*IND*), the *present subjunctive* (*SUBJ*), the *preterit indicative* (*PRET*), the *imperfect indicative* (*IMPF*), the *future indicative* (*FUT*), the second person singular form of the *imperative* (*IMPER*), the *present participle* or *gerund* (*PRP*), and the *past participle* (*PP*). Each set of conjugations is preceded by the corresponding infinitive form of the verb, shown in bold type. Only tenses containing irregularities are listed, and the irregular verb forms within each tense are displayed in bold type.

Each irregular verb entry in the Spanish-English section of this dictionary is cross-referred by number to one of the following model conjugations. These cross-reference numbers are shown in curly braces { } immediately following the entry's functional label.

1 **abolir** *(defective verb)* : *IND* abolimos, abolís *(other forms not used); SUBJ (not used); IMPER (only second person plural is used)*
2 **abrir** : *PP* abierto
3 **actuar** : *IND* **actúo, actúas, actúa**, actuamos, actuáis, **actúan;** *SUBJ* **actúe, actúes, actúe**, actuemos, actuéis, **actúen;** *IMPER* **actúa**
4 **adquirir** : *IND* **adquiero, adquieres, adquiere**, adquirimos, adquirís, **adquieren;** *SUBJ* **adquiera, adquieras, adquiera**, adquiramos, adquiráis, **adquieran;** *IMPER* **adquiere**
5 **airar** : *IND* **aíro, aíras, aíra**, airamos, airáis, **aíran;** *SUBJ* **aíre, aíres, aíre**, airemos, airéis, **aíren;** *IMPER* **aíra**
6 **andar** : *PRET* **anduve, anduviste, anduvo, anduvimos, anduvisteis, anduvieron**
7 **asir** : *IND* **asgo**, ases, ase, asimos, asís, asen; *SUBJ* **asga, asgas, asga, asgamos, asgáis, asgan**
8 **aunar** : *IND* **aúno, aúnas, aúna**, aunamos, aunáis, **aúnan;** *SUBJ* **aúne, aúnes, aúne**, aunemos, aunéis, **aúnen;** *IMPER* **aúna**
9 **avergonzar** : *IND* **avergüenzo, avergüenzas, avergüenza**, avergonzamos, avergonzáis, **avergüenzan;** *SUBJ* **avergüence, avergüences, avergüence, avergoncemos, avergoncéis, avergüencen;** *PRET* **avergoncé;** *IMPER* **avergüenza**
10 **averiguar** : *SUBJ* **averigüe, averigües, averigüe, averigüemos, averigüéis, averigüen;** *PRET* **averigüé**, averiguaste, averiguó, averiguamos, averiguasteis, averiguaron
11 **bendecir** : *IND* **bendigo, bendices, bendice**, bendecimos, bendecís, **bendicen;** *SUBJ* **bendiga, bendigas, bendiga, bendigamos, bendigáis, bendigan;** *PRET* **bendije, bendijiste, bendijo, bendijimos, bendijisteis, bendijeron;** *IMPER* **bendice**
12 **caber** : *IND* **quepo**, cabes, cabe, cabemos, cabéis, caben; *SUBJ* **quepa, quepas, quepa, quepamos, quepáis, quepan;** *PRET* **cupe, cupiste, cupo, cupimos, cupisteis, cupieron;** *FUT* **cabré, cabrás, cabrá, cabremos, cabréis, cabrán**
13 **caer** : *IND* **caigo**, caes, cae, caemos, caéis, caen; *SUBJ* **caiga, caigas, caiga, caigamos, caigáis, caigan;** *PRET* caí, **caíste, cayó, caímos, caísteis, cayeron;** *PRP* **cayendo;** *PP* **caído**
14 **cocer** : *IND* **cuezo, cueces, cuece**, cocemos, cocéis, **cuecen;** *SUBJ* **cueza, cuezas, cueza, cozamos, cozáis, cuezan;** *IMPER* **cuece**
15 **coger** : *IND* **cojo**, coges, coge, cogemos, cogéis, cogen; *SUBJ* **coja, cojas, coja, cojamos, cojáis, cojan**
16 **colgar** : *IND* **cuelgo, cuelgas, cuelga**, colgamos, colgáis, **cuelgan;** *SUBJ* **cuelgue, cuelgues, cuelgue, colguemos, colguéis, cuelguen;** *PRET* **colgué**, colgaste, colgó, colgamos, colgasteis, colgaron; *IMPER* **cuelga**
17 **concernir** *(defective verb; used only in the third person singular and plural of the present indicative, present subjunctive, and imperfect subjunctive) see* 25 **discernir**
18 **conocer** : *IND* **conozco**, conoces, conoce, conocemos, conocéis, conocen; *SUBJ* **conozca, conozcas, conozca, conozcamos, conozcáis, conozcan**
19 **contar** : *IND* **cuento, cuentas, cuenta**, contamos, contáis, **cuentan;** *SUBJ* **cuente, cuentes, cuente**, contemos, contéis, **cuenten;** *IMPER* **cuenta**
20 **creer** : *PRET* creí, **creíste, creyó, creímos, creísteis, creyeron;** *PRP* **creyendo;** *PP* **creído**
21 **cruzar** : *SUBJ* **cruce, cruces, cruce, crucemos, crucéis, crucen;** *PRET* **crucé**, cruzaste, cruzó, cruzamos, cruzasteis, cruzaron
22 **dar** : *IND* **doy**, das, da, damos, **dais**, dan; *SUBJ* **dé**, des, **dé**, demos, **deis**, den; *PRET* **di, diste, dio, dimos, disteis, dieron**
23 **decir** : *IND* **digo, dices, dice**, decimos, decís, **dicen;** *SUBJ* **diga, digas, diga, digamos, digáis, digan;** *PRET* **dije, dijiste, dijo, dijimos, dijisteis, dijeron;** *FUT* **diré, dirás, dirá, diremos, diréis, dirán;** *IMPER* **di;** *PRP* **diciendo;** *PP* **dicho**
24 **delinquir** : *IND* **delinco**, delinques, delinque, delinquimos, delinquís, delinquen; *SUBJ* **delinca, delincas, delinca, delincamos, delincáis, delincan**
25 **discernir** : *IND* **discierno, disciernes, discierne**, discernimos, discernís, **disciernen;** *SUBJ* **discierna, disciernas, discierna**, discernamos, discernáis, **disciernan;** *IMPER* **discierne**
26 **distinguir** : *IND* **distingo**, distingues, distingue, distinguimos, distinguís, distinguen; *SUBJ* **distinga, distingas, distinga, distingamos, distingáis, distingan**
27 **dormir** : *IND* **duermo, duermes, duerme**, dormimos, dormís, **duermen;** *SUBJ* **duerma, duermas, duerma, durmamos, durmáis, duerman;** *PRET* dormí, dormiste, **durmió**, dormimos, dormisteis, **durmieron;** *IMPER* **duerme;** *PRP* **durmiendo**

28 **elegir** : *IND* **elijo, eliges, elige,** elegimos, elegís, **eligen;** *SUBJ* **elija, elijas, elija, elijamos, elijáis, elijan;** *PRET* elegí, elegiste, **eligió,** elegimos, elegisteis, **eligieron;** *IMPER* **elige;** *PRP* **eligiendo**
29 **empezar** : *IND* **empiezo, empiezas, empieza,** empezamos, empezáis, **empiezan;** *SUBJ* **empiece, empieces, empiece, empecemos, empecéis, empiecen;** *PRET* **empecé,** empezaste, empezó, empezamos, empezasteis, empezaron; *IMPER* **empieza**
30 **enraizar** : *IND* **enraízo, enraízas, enraíza,** enraizamos, enraizáis, **enraízan;** *SUBJ* **enraíce, enraíces, enraíce, enraicemos, enraicéis, enraícen;** *PRET* **enraicé,** enraizaste, enraizó, enraizamos, enraizasteis, enraizaron; *IMPER* **enraíza**
31 **erguir** : *IND* **irgo** *or* **yergo, irgues** *or* **yergues, irgue** *or* **yergue,** erguimos, erguís, **irguen** *or* **yerguen;** *SUBJ* **irga** *or* **yerga, irgas** *or* **yergas, irga** *or* **yerga, irgamos, irgáis, irgan** *or* **yergan;** *PRET* erguí, erguiste, **irguió,** erguimos, erguisteis, **irguieron;** *IMPER* **irgue** *or* **yergue;** *PRP* **irguiendo**
32 **errar** : *IND* **yerro, yerras, yerra,** erramos, erráis, **yerran;** *SUBJ* **yerre, yerres, yerre,** erremos, erréis, **yerren;** *IMPER* **yerra**
33 **escribir** : *PP* **escrito**
34 **estar** : *IND* **estoy, estás, está,** estamos, estáis, **están;** *SUBJ* **esté, estés, esté,** estemos, estéis, **estén;** *PRET* **estuve, estuviste, estuvo, estuvimos, estuvisteis, estuvieron;** *IMPER* **está**
35 **exigir** : *IND* **exijo,** exiges, exige, exigimos, exigís, exigen; *SUBJ* **exija, exijas, exija, exijamos, exijáis, exijan**
36 **forzar** : *IND* **fuerzo, fuerzas, fuerza,** forzamos, forzáis, **fuerzan;** *SUBJ* **fuerce, fuerces, fuerce, forcemos, forcéis, fuercen;** *PRET* **forcé,** forzaste, forzó, forzamos, forzasteis, forzaron; *IMPER* **fuerza**
37 **freír** : *IND* **frío, fríes, fríe, freímos,** freís, **fríen;** *SUBJ* **fría, frías, fría, friamos, friáis, frían;** *PRET* freí, **freíste, frió, freímos, freísteis, frieron;** *IMPER* **fríe;** *PRP* **friendo;** *PP* **frito**
38 **gruñir** : *PRET* gruñí, gruñiste, **gruñó,** gruñimos, gruñisteis, **gruñeron;** *PRP* **gruñendo**
39 **haber** : *IND* **he, has, ha, hemos,** habéis, **han;** *SUBJ* **haya, hayas, haya, hayamos, hayáis, hayan;** *PRET* **hube, hubiste, hubo, hubimos, hubisteis, hubieron;** *FUT* **habré, habrás, habrá, habremos, habréis, habrán;** *IMPER* **he**
40 **hacer** : *IND* **hago,** haces, hace, hacemos, hacéis, hacen; *SUBJ* **haga, hagas, haga, hagamos, hagáis, hagan;** *PRET* **hice, hiciste, hizo, hicimos, hicisteis, hicieron;** *FUT* **haré, harás, hará, haremos, haréis, harán;** *IMPER* **haz;** *PP* **hecho**
41 **huir** : *IND* **huyo, huyes, huye,** huimos, huís, **huyen;** *SUBJ* **huya, huyas, huya, huyamos, huyáis, huyan;** *PRET* huí, huiste, **huyó,** huimos, huisteis, **huyeron;** *IMPER* **huye;** *PRP* **huyendo**
42 **imprimir** : *PP* **impreso**
43 **ir** : *IND* **voy, vas, va, vamos, vais, van;** *SUBJ* **vaya, vayas, vaya, vayamos, vayáis, vayan;** *PRET* **fui, fuiste, fue, fuimos, fuisteis, fueron;** *IMPF* **iba, ibas, iba, íbamos, ibais, iban;** *IMPER* **ve;** *PRP* **yendo;** *PP* **ido**
44 **jugar** : *IND* **juego, juegas, juega,** jugamos, jugáis, **juegan;** *SUBJ* **juegue, juegues, juegue, juguemos, juguéis, jueguen;** *PRET* **jugué,** jugaste, jugó, jugamos, jugasteis, jugaron; *IMPER* **juega**
45 **lucir** : *IND* **luzco,** luces, luce, lucimos, lucís, lucen; *SUBJ* **luzca, luzcas, luzca, luzcamos, luzcáis, luzcan**
46 **morir** : *IND* **muero, mueres, muere,** morimos, morís, **mueren;** *SUBJ* **muera, mueras, muera, muramos, muráis, mueran;** *PRET* morí, moriste, **murió,** morimos, moristeis, **murieron;** *IMPER* **muere;** *PRP* **muriendo;** *PP* **muerto**
47 **mover** : *IND* **muevo, mueves, mueve,** movemos, movéis, **mueven;** *SUBJ* **mueva, muevas, mueva,** movamos, mováis, **muevan;** *IMPER* **mueve**
48 **nacer** : *IND* **nazco,** naces, nace, nacemos, nacéis, nacen; *SUBJ* **nazca, nazcas, nazca, nazcamos, nazcáis, nazcan**
49 **negar** : *IND* **niego, niegas, niega,** negamos, negáis, **niegan;** *SUBJ* **niegue, niegues, niegue, neguemos, neguéis, nieguen;** *PRET* **negué,** negaste, negó, negamos, negasteis, negaron; *IMPER* **niega**
50 **oír** : *IND* **oigo, oyes, oye, oímos,** oís, **oyen;** *SUBJ* **oiga, oigas, oiga, oigamos, oigáis, oigan;** *PRET* oí, **oíste, oyó, oímos, oísteis, oyeron;** *IMPER* **oye;** *PRP* **oyendo;** *PP* **oído**
51 **oler** : *IND* **huelo, hueles, huele,** olemos, oléis, **huelen;** *SUBJ* **huela, huelas, huela,** olamos, oláis, **huelan;** *IMPER* **huele**
52 **pagar** : *SUBJ* **pague, pagues, pague, paguemos, paguéis, paguen;** *PRET* **pagué,** pagaste, pagó, pagamos, pagasteis, pagaron

53 **parecer** : *IND* **parezco,** pareces, parece, parecemos, parecéis, parecen; *SUBJ* **parezca, parezcas, parezca, parezcamos, parezcáis, parezcan**

54 **pedir** : *IND* **pido, pides, pide,** pedimos, pedís, **piden;** *SUBJ* **pida, pidas, pida, pidamos, pidáis, pidan;** *PRET* pedí, pediste, **pidió,** pedimos, pedisteis, **pidieron;** *IMPER* **pide;** *PRP* **pidiendo**

55 **pensar** : *IND* **pienso, piensas, piensa,** pensamos, pensáis, **piensan;** *SUBJ* **piense, pienses, piense,** pensemos, penséis, **piensen;** *IMPER* **piensa**

56 **perder** : *IND* **pierdo, pierdes, pierde,** perdemos, perdéis, **pierden;** *SUBJ* **pierda, pierdas, pierda,** perdamos, perdáis, **pierdan;** *IMPER* **pierde**

57 **placer** : *IND* **plazco,** places, place, placemos, placéis, placen; *SUBJ* **plazca, plazcas, plazca, plazcamos, plazcáis, plazcan;** *PRET* plací, placiste, plació *or* **plugo,** placimos, placisteis, placieron *or* **pluguieron**

58 **poder** : *IND* **puedo, puedes, puede,** podemos, podéis, **pueden;** *SUBJ* **pueda, puedas, pueda,** podamos, podáis, **puedan;** *PRET* **pude, pudiste, pudo, pudimos, pudisteis, pudieron;** *FUT* **podré, podrás, podrá, podremos, podréis, podrán;** *IMPER* **puede;** *PRP* **pudiendo**

59 **podrir** *or* **pudrir** : *PP* **podrido** *(all other forms based on* pudrir*)*

60 **poner** : *IND* **pongo,** pones, pone, ponemos, ponéis, ponen; *SUBJ* **ponga, pongas, ponga, pongamos, pongáis, pongan;** *PRET* **puse, pusiste, puso, pusimos, pusisteis, pusieron;** *FUT* **pondré, pondrás, pondrá, pondremos, pondréis, pondrán;** *IMPER* **pon;** *PP* **puesto**

61 **producir** : *IND* **produzco,** produces, produce, producimos, producís, producen; *SUBJ* **produzca, produzcas, produzca, produzcamos, produzcáis, produzcan;** *PRET* **produje, produjiste, produjo, produjimos, produjisteis, produjeron**

62 **prohibir** : *IND* **prohíbo, prohíbes, prohíbe,** prohibimos, prohibís, **prohíben;** *SUBJ* **prohíba, prohíbas, prohíba,** prohibamos, prohibáis, **prohíban;** *IMPER* **prohíbe**

63 **proveer** : *PRET* proveí, **proveíste, proveyó, proveímos, proveísteis, proveyeron;** *PRP* **proveyendo;** *PP* **provisto**

64 **querer** : *IND* **quiero, quieres, quiere,** queremos, queréis, **quieren;** *SUBJ* **quiera, quieras, quiera,** queramos, queráis, **quieran;** *PRET* **quise, quisiste, quiso, quisimos, quisisteis, quisieron;** *FUT* **querré, querrás, querrá, querremos, querréis, querrán;** *IMPER* **quiere**

65 **raer** : *IND* rao *or* **raigo** *or* **rayo,** raes, rae, raemos, raéis, raen; *SUBJ* **raiga** *or* **raya, raigas** *or* **rayas, raiga** *or* **raya, raigamos** *or* **rayamos, raigáis** *or* **rayáis, raigan** *or* **rayan;** *PRET* **raí, raíste, rayó, raímos, raísteis, rayeron;** *PRP* **rayendo;** *PP* **raído**

66 **reír** : *IND* **río, ríes, ríe, reímos,** reís, **ríen;** *SUBJ* **ría, rías, ría, riamos, riáis, rían;** *PRET* reí, **reíste, rió, reímos, reísteis, rieron;** *IMPER* **ríe;** *PRP* **riendo;** *PP* **reído**

67 **reñir** : *IND* **riño, riñes, riñe,** reñimos, reñís, **riñen;** *SUBJ* **riña, riñas, riña, riñamos, riñáis, riñan;** *PRET* reñí, reñiste, **riñó,** reñimos, reñisteis, **riñeron;** *IMPER* **riñe;** *PRP* **riñendo**

68 **reunir** : *IND* **reúno, reúnes, reúne,** reunimos, reunís, **reúnen;** *SUBJ* **reúna, reúnas, reúna,** reunamos, reunáis, **reúnan;** *IMPER* **reúne**

69 **roer** : *IND* roo *or* **roigo** *or* **royo,** roes, roe, roemos, roéis, roen; *SUBJ* roa *or* **roiga** *or* **roya,** roas *or* **roigas** *or* **royas,** roa *or* **roiga** *or* **roya,** roamos *or* **roigamos** *or* **royamos,** roáis *or* **roigáis** *or* **royáis,** roan *or* **roigan** *or* **royan;** *PRET* roí, **roíste, royó, roímos, roísteis, royeron;** *PRP* **royendo;** *PP* **roído**

70 **romper** : *PP* **roto**

71 **saber** : *IND* **sé,** sabes, sabe, sabemos, sabéis, saben; *SUBJ* **sepa, sepas, sepa, sepamos, sepáis, sepan;** *PRET* **supe, supiste, supo, supimos, supisteis, supieron;** *FUT* **sabré, sabrás, sabrá, sabremos, sabréis, sabrán**

72 **sacar** : *SUBJ* **saque, saques, saque, saquemos, saquéis, saquen;** *PRET* **saqué,** sacaste, sacó, sacamos, sacasteis, sacaron

73 **salir** : *IND* **salgo,** sales, sale, salimos, salís, salen; *SUBJ* **salga, salgas, salga, salgamos, salgáis, salgan;** *FUT* **saldré, saldrás, saldrá, saldremos, saldréis, saldrán;** *IMPER* **sal**

74 **satisfacer** : *IND* **satisfago,** satisfaces, satisface, satisfacemos, satisfacéis, satisfacen; *SUBJ* **satisfaga, satisfagas, satisfaga, satisfagamos, satisfagáis, satisfagan;** *PRET* **satisfice, satisficiste, satisfizo, satisficimos, satificisteis, satisficieron;** *FUT* **satisfaré, satisfarás, satisfará, satisfaremos, satisfaréis, satisfarán;** *IMPER* **satisfaz** *or* satisface; *PP* **satisfecho**

75 **seguir** : *IND* **sigo, sigues, sigue,** seguimos, seguís, **siguen;** *SUBJ* **siga, sigas, siga, sigamos, sigáis, sigan;** *PRET* seguí, seguiste, **siguió,** seguimos, seguisteis, **siguieron;** *IMPER* **sigue;** *PRP* **siguiendo**

76 **sentir** : *IND* **siento, sientes, siente,** sentimos, sentís, **sienten;** *SUBJ* **sienta, sientas, sienta, sintamos, sintáis, sientan;** *PRET* sentí, sentiste, **sintió,** sentimos, sentisteis, **sintieron;** *IMPER* **siente;** *PRP* **sintiendo**

77 **ser** : *IND* **soy, eres, es, somos, sois, son;** *SUBJ* **sea, seas, sea, seamos, seáis, sean;** *PRET* **fui, fuiste, fue, fuimos, fuisteis, fueron;** *IMPF* **era, eras, era, éramos, erais, eran;** *IMPER* **sé;** *PRP* **siendo;** *PP* **sido**

78 **soler** *(defective verb; used only in the present, preterit, and imperfect indicative, and the present and imperfect subjunctive) see* 47 **mover**

79 **tañer** : *PRET* tañí, tañiste, **tañó,** tañimos, tañisteis, **tañeron;** *PRP* **tañendo**

80 **tener** : *IND* **tengo, tienes, tiene,** tenemos, tenéis, **tienen;** *SUBJ* **tenga, tengas, tenga, tengamos, tengáis, tengan;** *PRET* **tuve, tuviste, tuvo, tuvimos, tuvisteis, tuvieron;** *FUT* **tendré, tendrás, tendrá, tendremos, tendréis, tendrán;** *IMPER* **ten**

81 **traer** : *IND* **traigo,** traes, trae, traemos, traéis, traen; *SUBJ* **traiga, traigas, traiga, traigamos, traigáis, traigan;** *PRET* **traje, trajiste, trajo, trajimos, trajisteis, trajeron;** *PRP* **trayendo;** *PP* **traído**

82 **trocar** : *IND* **trueco, truecas, trueca,** trocamos, trocáis, **truecan;** *SUBJ* **trueque, trueques, trueque, troquemos, troquéis, truequen;** *PRET* **troqué,** trocaste, trocó, trocamos, trocasteis, trocaron; *IMPER* **trueca**

83 **uncir** : *IND* **unzo,** unces, unce, uncimos, uncís, uncen; *SUBJ* **unza, unzas, unza, unzamos, unzáis, unzan**

84 **valer** : *IND* **valgo,** vales, vale, valemos, valéis, valen; *SUBJ* **valga, valgas, valga, valgamos, valgáis, valgan;** *FUT* **valdré, valdrás, valdrá, valdremos, valdréis, valdrán**

85 **variar** : *IND* **varío, varías, varía,** variamos, variáis, **varían;** *SUBJ* **varíe, varíes, varíe,** variemos, variéis, **varíen;** *IMPER* **varía**

86 **vencer** : *IND* **venzo,** vences, vence, vencemos, vencéis, vencen; *SUBJ* **venza, venzas, venza, venzamos, venzáis, venzan**

87 **venir** : *IND* **vengo, vienes, viene,** venimos, venís, **vienen;** *SUBJ* **venga, vengas, venga, vengamos, vengáis, vengan;** *PRET* **vine, viniste, vino, vinimos, vinisteis, vinieron;** *FUT* **vendré, vendrás, vendrá, vendremos, vendréis, vendrán;** *IMPER* **ven;** *PRP* **viniendo**

88 **ver** : *IND* veo, **ves, ve, vemos, veis, ven;** *PRET* **vi, viste, vio, vimos, visteis, vieron;** *IMPER* **ve;** *PRP* **viendo;** *PP* **visto**

89 **volver** : *IND* **vuelvo, vuelves, vuelve,** volvemos, volvéis, **vuelven;** *SUBJ* **vuelva, vuelvas, vuelva,** volvamos, volváis, **vuelvan;** *IMPER* **vuelve;** *PP* **vuelto**

90 **yacer** : *IND* **yazco** *or* **yazgo** *or* **yago,** yaces, yace, yacemos, yacéis, yacen; *SUBJ* **yazca** *or* **yazga** *or* **yaga, yazcas** *or* **yazgas** *or* **yagas, yazca** *or* **yazga** *or* **yaga, yazcamos** *or* **yazgamos** *or* **yagamos, yazcáis** *or* **yazgáis** *or* **yagáis, yazcan** *or* **yazgan** *or* **yagan;** *IMPER* yace *or* **yaz**

Los verbos irregulares en inglés

Los verbos regulares en inglés, como *call* o *trust*, siguen un patrón previsible en las formas del pasado y el participio pasado (las cuales se llaman las "partes principales"). Éstas se forman agregando *-ed* al infinitivo. A veces, la adición de esta terminación (o *desinencia*) resulta en una sílaba más (*trusted* [ˈtrʌstəd]) y otras veces no (*called* [ˈkɔld]).

Un verbo se considera regular incluso cuando al añadir *-ed* hace que la consonante final se dobla (*abet, abetted, abetted*) o la *-e* final se elimina (*die, died, died*).

Un verbo se considera irregular si la forma del pasado o del participio pasado no sigue el patrón normal de agregar *-ed* (*swim, swam, swum*) o si una o ambas de éstas tienen otra grafía además de la que termina en *-ed* (*saw, sawed, sawed* o *sawn*). Muchas veces, esta variante ortográfica se forma sustituyendo la *-ed* por *-t* (*burn, burned* o *burnt*), la cual representa una pronunciación típica.

A continuación se ofrece una lista de algunos verbos irregulares en inglés que muestra las formas del pasado y el participio pasado junto con cualquier variante ortográfica que corresponda.

INFINITIVO	**PASADO**	**PARTICIPIO PASADO**
arise	arose	arisen
awake	awoke	awoken
	también awaked	*o* awaked
		también awoke
be	was, were	been
bear	bore	borne
		también born
beat	beat	beaten
		o beat
become	became	become
befall	befell	befallen
begin	began	begun
behold	beheld	beheld
bend	bent	bent
beseech	besought	besought
	o beseeched	*o* beseeched
beset	beset	beset
bet	bet	bet
	también betted	*también* betted
bid	bade	bidden
	o bid	*o* bid
		también bade
bind	bound	bound
bite	bit	bitten
		también bit
bleed	bled	bled
blow	blew	blown
break	broke	broken
breed	bred	bred
bring	brought	brought
build	built	built
burn	burned	burned
	o burnt	*o* burnt
burst	burst	burst
	también bursted	*también* bursted
buy	bought	bought
can (auxiliary verb)	could	—
cast	cast	cast
catch	caught	caught
choose	chose	chosen
cling	clung	clung
come	came	come
cost	cost	cost
creep	crept	crept

cut	cut	cut
deal	dealt	dealt
dig	dug	dug
do	did	done
draw	drew	drawn
dream	dreamed *o* dreamt	dreamed *o* dreamt
drink	drank	drunk *o* drank
drive	drove	driven
dwell	dwelt *o* dwelled	dwelt *o* dwelled
eat	ate	eaten
fall	fell	fallen
feed	fed	fed
feel	felt	felt
fight	fought	fought
find	found	found
flee	fled	fled
fling	flung	flung
fly	flew	flown
forbid	forbade *también* forbad	forbidden
forecast	forecast *también* forecasted	forecast *también* forecasted
forego	forewent	foregone
foresee	foresaw	foreseen
foretell	foretold	foretold
forget	forgot	forgotten *o* forgot
forgive	forgave	forgiven
forsake	forsook	forsaken
freeze	froze	frozen
get	got	got *o* gotten
give	gave	given
go	went	gone
grind	ground	ground
grow	grew	grown
hang	hung *también* hanged	hung *también* hanged
have	had	had
hear	heard	heard
hide	hid	hidden *o* hid
hit	hit	hit
hold	held	held
hurt	hurt	hurt
keep	kept	kept
kneel	knelt *o* kneeled	knelt *o* kneeled
know	knew	known
lay	laid	laid
lead	led	led
lean	leaned *también* leant	leaned
leap	leapt *o* leaped	leapt *o* leaped
leave	left	left
lend	lent	lent
let	let	let
lie (to recline)	lay	lain
light	lit *o* lighted	lit *o* lighted
lose	lost	lost

make	made	made
may	might	—
mean	meant	meant
meet	met	met
mow	mowed	mowed
		o mown
pay	paid	paid
put	put	put
quit	quit	quit
	también quitted	*también* quitted
read	read	read
rend	rent	rent
rid	rid	rid
	también ridded	*también* ridded
ride	rode	ridden
ring (to sound)	rang	rung
rise	rose	risen
run	ran	run
saw	sawed	sawed
		o sawn
say	said	said
see	saw	seen
seek	sought	sought
sell	sold	sold
send	sent	sent
set	set	set
shake	shook	shaken
shall (auxiliary verb)	should	—
shear	sheared	sheared
		o shorn
shed	shed	shed
shine	shone	shone
	o shined	*o* shined
shoot	shot	shot
show	showed	shown
		o showed
shrink	shrank	shrunk
	o shrunk	*o* shrunken
shut	shut	shut
sing	sang	sung
	o sung	
sink	sank	sunk
	o sunk	
sit	sat	sat
slay	slew	slain
sleep	slept	slept
slide	slid	slid
sling	slung	slung
smell	smelled	smelled
	o smelt	*o* smelt
sow	sowed	sown
		o sowed
speak	spoke	spoken
speed	sped	sped
	o speeded	*o* speeded
spell	spelled	spelled
spend	spent	spent
spill	spilled	spilled
	también spilt	*también* spilt
spin	spun	spun
spit (to eject saliva)	spit	spit
	o spat	*o* spat
split	split	split
spoil	spoiled	spoiled
	o spoilt	*o* spoilt

spread	spread	spread
spring	sprang *o* sprung	sprung
stand	stood	stood
steal	stole	stolen
stick	stuck	stuck
sting	stung	stung
stink	stank *o* stunk	stunk
stride	strode	stridden
strike	struck	struck *también* stricken
swear	swore	sworn
sweep	swept	swept
swell	swelled	swelled *o* swollen
swim	swam	swum
swing	swung	swung
take	took	taken
teach	taught	taught
tear (to rip)	tore	torn
tell	told	told
think	thought	thought
throw	threw	thrown
thrust	thrust	thrust
tread	trod	trodden *o* trod
wake	woke *también* waked	woken *también* waked *o* woke
waylay	waylaid	waylaid
wear	wore	worn
weave	wove *o* weaved	woven *o* weaved
wed	wedded *también* wed	wedded *también* wed
weep	wept	wept
will (auxiliary verb)	would	—
win	won	won
wind (to encircle)	wound *también* winded	wound *también* winded
withdraw	withdrew	withdrawn
withhold	withheld	withheld
withstand	withstood	withstood
wring	wrung	wrung
write	wrote	written *también* writ

Contracciones en inglés

Los hablantes nativos de inglés frecuentemente acortan (o contraen) nueve palabras comunes en el habla coloquial. Ocho de éstas son verbos: *have, has, had, is, am, are, will*, y *would*. Una es un adverbio: *not*. Estas palabras también se acortan con frecuencia en la escritura informal. La forma acortada de la palabra está unida con la palabra que la precede; cuando la contracción es por escrito, un apóstrofo (') sustituye las letras omitidas.

La tabla siguiente demuestra cómo los ocho verbos son contraídos cuando siguen un pronombre personal.

I have → **I've**	you have → **you've**	she has → **she's**	they have → **they've**
I had → **I'd**	you had → **you'd**	he had → **he'd**	we had → **we'd**
I am → **I'm**	you are → **you're**	it is → **it's**	we are → **we're**
I will → **I'll**	you will → **you'll**	he will → **he'll**	they will → **they'll**
I would → **I'd**	you would → **you'd**	she would → **she'd**	we would → **we'd**

I would have → **I'd have; I would've**
you would have → **you'd have; you would've**
it would have → **it would've; it'd have**
they would have → **they'd have; they would've**

Observe como *-'s* puede sustituir *is* o *has*. (También puede formar el genitivo, como en el ejemplo "Sarah's dog.") La forma contraída *-'d* puede sustituir las palabras *had* o *would*. En preguntas, *-'d* algunas veces sustituye la palabra *did* ("Where'd he go?" "Why'd you do it?").

Las contracciones se forman comúnmente con otros pronombres también: "Who's that?" "What's happening?" "Someone's coming." "Who'd have guessed it?" "That'll be all." "This'll work. " Frecuentemente se forman con sustantivos: "Michael's here." "The coffee's hot." "Time's passing." etc. Y comúnmente se usan con *here* y *there*: "Here's the book." "There'd be plenty of food. "

Las contracciones comúnmente se forman al añadir *-'ve* (*have*) a los verbos modales *would, could, should*, y *might*: "Argentina could've won." "Those should've been better." "I might've known."

Puede contraer el adverbio *not* a *-n't* y combinarlo con los verbos en esta lista:

are → **aren't**	has → **hasn't**	ought → **oughtn't**
can → **can't**	have → **haven't**	should → **shouldn't**
could → **couldn't**	is → **isn't**	was → **wasn't**
did → **didn't**	might → **mightn't**	were → **weren't**
do → **don't**	must → **mustn't**	will → **won't**
does → **doesn't**	need → **needn't**	would → **wouldn't**
had → **hadn't**		

Observe que *will/won't* es el único ejemplo irregular.

La contracción *let's* (*let us*) se utiliza comúnmente incluso en la escritura formal. *Ain't* (*am not, are not, is not, have not, has not*) es común en el habla informal pero nunca se utiliza en la escritura formal. *Y'all* (*you all*) es común en el habla del sur de los Estados Unidos.

Prefijos y sufijos en inglés

El aprendizaje de los prefijos y sufijos comunes en inglés le ayudará a comprender y recordar el significado de muchas palabras inglesas.

PREFIJOS

PREFIJO	SIGNIFICADO	EJEMPLOS
a-, an-	*not, without*	asexual
ante-	*before*	antedate, anteroom
anti-	*against, opposite*	antidote, anticlimax
arch-	*chief, extreme*	archbishop, archenemy
bi-	*two, every other, twice a*	bicycle, bipartisan, biweekly, biannual
co-	*with, together*	coexist, coauthor
counter-	*opposite, against*	counterclockwise, counteract
dis-	*exclude, not*	disbar, disagreeable
ex-	*former*	ex-husband, ex-president
extra-	*outside, beyond*	extracurricular, extraterrestrial
hyper-	*very, too much*	hypercritical, hyperactive, hypertension
hypo-	*under, down, below normal*	hypothermia, hypoallergenic
in-	*not*	incapable, inconsistent
inter-	*between, among*	intermarry, international
mis-	*bad, wrongly*	mistake, mislead
non-	*not*	nonalcoholic, nontoxic
out-	*more than*	outgrow, outnumber
over-	*go beyond, too much, very*	overachieve, overambitious
pre-	*before*	prehistoric, premature
pro-	*favoring, supporting*	pro-American
re-	*again, back*	retell, recall
semi-	*twice a, half, partly, partial*	semiannual, semicircle, semiconsciousness
sub-	*under, division*	subsoil, substandard, subtopic
super-	*more than*	superhighway, superhuman
tri-	*three*	triangle, tricycle
un-	*not, contrary to, reverse, remove*	unable, unethical, unfold, untie
under-	*below, too low or little*	underlying, underpaid

SUFIJOS

SUFIJO	SIGNIFICADO	EJEMPLOS
-able, -ible	*tending to, fit for*	agreeable, collectible
-al	*relating to, action*	fictional, rehearsal
-ant	*one that does, doing or acting*	assistant, coolant, hesitant
-ee	*one who does or receives*	escapee, trainee
-eer	*one who does or makes*	auctioneer, profiteer
-er	*one that has, is, does, or is connected with*	double-decker, foreigner, reporter, prisoner
-ful	*characterized by, amount that fills*	peaceful, helpful, cupful
-fy	*cause to become*	simplify, purify
-ion	*act or process, state or condition*	ignition, perfection
-ish	*almost, approximately*	greenish
-istic, -istical	*relating to, characterized by*	altruistic, egotistical
-itis	*disease, inflammation*	arthritis, bronchitis
-ize	*treat like, become like*	idolize, crystallize
-less	*not having, doing, or becoming*	witless, childless, tireless
-like	*resembling*	apelike, childlike
-ment	*action or process, result, condition*	development, entertainment, excitement
-ness	*condition, quality*	alertness, goodness
-ous	*full of, having or containing*	glamorous, poisonous
-ship	*condition, skill, position, status*	friendship, penmanship, professorship
-ward	*toward*	westward, upward
-y	*characterized by*	dirty, icy, sleepy

Abreviaturas empleadas en este libro/Abbreviations used in this work

	EXPAÑOL/SPANISH	INGLÉS/ENGLISH
adj	adjetivo	adjective
adv	adverbio	adverb
Arg	Argentina	Argentina
Bol	Bolivia	Bolivia
CA	Centroamérica	Central America
Car	Región del Caribe	Caribbean region
Col	Colombia	Colombia
conj	conjunción	conjunction
CoRi	Costa Rica	Costa Rica
DomRep	República Dominicana	Dominican Republic
Ecua	Ecuador	Ecuador
f	femenino	feminine
fam	familiar o coloquial	familiar or colloquial
fpl	femenino plural	feminine plural
Guat	Guatemala	Guatemala
Hond	Honduras	Honduras
interj	interjección	interjection
m	masculino	masculine
Mex	México	Mexico
mf	masculino o femenino	masculine or feminine
mpl	masculino plural	masculine plural
n	sustantivo	noun
nf	sustantivo femenino	feminine noun
nfpl	sustantivo plural femenino	feminine plural noun
nfs & pl	sustantivo plural femenino, invariable en cuanto a número	invariable singular or plural feminine noun
Nic	Nicaragua	Nicaragua
nm	sustantivo masculino	masculine noun
nmf	sustantivo masculino o femenino	masculine or feminine noun
nmfpl	sustantivo plural, invariable en cuanto a género	plural noun invariable for gender
nmfs & pl	sustantivo invariable en cuanto a género y número	noun invariable for both gender and number
nmpl	sustantivo plural masculino	masculine plural noun
nms & pl	sustantivo masculino, invariable en cuanto a número	invariable singular or plural masculine noun
npl	sustantivo plural	plural noun
ns & pl	sustantivo invariable en cuanto a número	noun invariable for plural
Pan	Panamá	Panama
Par	Paraguay	Paraguay
pl	plural	plural
prep	preposición	preposition
PRi	Puerto Rico	Puerto Rico
pron	pronombre	pronoun
Sal	El Salvador	El Salvador
Uru	Uruguay	Uruguay
usu	generalmente	usually
v	verbo	verb
v aux	verbo auxiliar	auxiliary verb
Ven	Venezuela	Venezuela
vi	verbo intransitivo	intransitive verb
v impers	verbo impersonal	impersonal verb
vr	verbo pronominal	reflexive verb
vt	verbo transitivo	transitive verb

Pronunciation Symbols

VOWELS

æ	ask, bat, glad
ɑ	cot, bomb
a	*New England* aunt, *British* ask, glass, *Spanish* casa
e	*Spanish* peso, jefe
ɛ	egg, bet, fed
ə	about, javelin, Alabama
ə	when italicized as in *ə*l, *ə*m, *ə*n, indicates a syllabic pronunciation of the consonant as in bottle, prism, button
i	very, any, thirty, *Spanish* piña
iː	eat, bead, bee
ɪ	id, bid, pit
o	Ohio, yellower, potato, *Spanish* óvalo
oː	oats, own, zone, blow
ɔ	awl, maul, caught, paw
ʊ	sure, should, could
u	*Spanish* uva, culpa
uː	boot, few, coo
ʌ	under, putt, bud
eɪ	eight, wade, bay
aɪ	ice, bite, tie
aʊ	out, gown, plow
ɔɪ	oyster, coil, boy
ər	further, stir
ɒ	*British* bond, god
ː	indicates that the preceding vowel is long. Long vowels are almost always diphthongs in English, but not in Spanish.

STRESS MARKS

ˈ	high stress	**pen**manship
ˌ	low stress	penman**ship**

CONSONANTS

b	baby, labor, cab
β	*Spanish* cabo, óvalo
d	day, ready, kid
ʤ	just, badger, fudge
ð	then, either, bathe
f	foe, tough, buff
g	go, bigger, bag
ɣ	*Spanish* tragar, daga
h	hot, aha
j	yes, vineyard
k	cat, keep, lacquer, flock
l	law, hollow, boil
m	mat, hemp, hammer, rim
n	new, tent, tenor, run
ŋ	rung, hang, swinger
ɲ	*Spanish* cabaña, piña
p	pay, lapse, top
r	rope, burn, tar
s	sad, mist, kiss
ʃ	shoe, mission, slush
t	toe, button, mat
t̬	indicates that some speakers of English pronounce this as a voiced alveolar flap [ɾ], as in later, catty, battle
ʧ	choose, batch
θ	thin, ether, bath
v	vat, never, cave
w	wet, software
x	*German* Bach, *Scots* loch, *Spanish* gente, jefe
z	zoo, easy, buzz
ʒ	jaborandi, azure, beige
h, k, p, t	when italicized indicate sounds which are present in the pronunciation of some speakers of English but absent in that of others, so that *whence* [ˈ*h*wɛn*t*s] can be pronounced as [ˈwɛns], [ˈhwɛns], [ˈwɛnts], or [ˈhwɛnts]

Spanish–English Dictionary

a[1] *nf* : first letter of the Spanish alphabet

a[2] *prep* **1** : to ⟨nos vamos a México : we're going to Mexico⟩ **2** (*used before direct or indirect objects referring to persons*) ⟨¿llamaste a tu papá? : did you call your dad?⟩ ⟨como a usted le guste : as you wish⟩ **3** : in the manner of ⟨papas a la francesa : french fries⟩ **4** : on, by means of ⟨a pie : on foot⟩ **5** : per, each ⟨tres pastillas al día : three pills per day⟩ **6** : at ⟨a las dos : at two o'clock⟩ ⟨al principio : at first⟩ **7** (*with infinitive*) ⟨enséñales a leer : teach them to read⟩ ⟨problemas a resolver : problems to be solved⟩

ábaco *nm* : abacus

abad *nm* : abbot

abadesa *nf* : abbess

abadía *nf* : abbey

abajo *adv* **1** : down ⟨póngalo más abajo : put it further down⟩ ⟨arriba y abajo : up and down⟩ **2** : downstairs **3** : under, beneath ⟨el abajo firmante : the undersigned⟩ **4** : down with ⟨¡abajo la inflación! : down with inflation!⟩ **5 ~ de** : under, beneath **6 de ~** : bottom ⟨el cajón de abajo : the bottom drawer⟩ **7 hacia ~** *or* **para ~** : downwards **8 cuesta abajo** : downhill **9 río abajo** : downstream

abalanzarse {21} *vr* : to hurl oneself, to rush

abanderado, -da *n* : standard-bearer

abandonado, -da *adj* **1** : abandoned, deserted **2** : neglected **3** : slovenly, unkempt

abandonar *vt* **1** DEJAR : to abandon, to leave **2** : to give up, to quit ⟨abandonaron la búsqueda : they gave up the search⟩ — **abandonarse** *vr* **1** : to neglect oneself **2 ~ a** : to succumb to, to give oneself over to

abandono *nm* **1** : abandonment **2** : neglect **3** : withdrawal ⟨ganar por abandono : to win by default⟩

abanicar {72} *vt* : to fan — **abanicarse** *vr*

abanico *nm* **1** : fan **2** GAMA : range, gamut

abaratamiento *nm* : price reduction

abaratar *vt* : to lower the price of — **abaratarse** *vr* : to go down in price

abarcar {72} *vt* **1** : to cover, to include, to embrace **2** : to undertake **3** : to monopolize

abaritonado, -da *adj* : baritone

abarrotado, -da *adj* : packed, crammed

abarrotar *vt* : to fill up, to pack

abarrotería *nf CA, Mex* : grocery store

abarrotero, -ra *n Col, Mex* : grocer

abarrotes *nmpl* **1** : groceries, supplies **2 tienda de abarrotes** : general store, grocery store

abastecedor, -dora *n* : supplier

abastecer {53} *vt* : to supply, to stock — **abastecerse** *vr* : to stock up

abastecimiento → **abasto**

abasto *nm* : supply, supplying ⟨no da abasto : there isn't enough for all⟩

abatido, -da *adj* : dejected, depressed

abatimiento *nm* **1** : drop, reduction **2** : dejection, depression

abatir *vt* **1** DERRIBAR : to demolish, to knock down **2** : to shoot down **3** DEPRIMIR : to depress, to bring low — **abatirse** *vr* **1** DEPRIMIRSE : to get depressed **2 ~ sobre** : to swoop down on

abdicación *nf, pl* **-ciones** : abdication

abdicar {72} *vt* : to relinquish, to abdicate

abdomen *nm, pl* **-dómenes** : abdomen

abdominal *adj* : abdominal

abecé *nm* : ABC's *pl*

abecedario *nm* ALFABETO : alphabet

abedul *nm* : birch (tree)

abeja *nf* : bee

abejorro *nm* : bumblebee

aberración *nf, pl* **-ciones** : aberration

aberrante *adj* : aberrant, perverse

abertura *nf* **1** : aperture, opening **2** AGUJERO : hole **3** : slit (in a skirt, etc.) **4** GRIETA : crack

abeto *nm* : fir (tree)

abierto[1] *pp* → **abrir**

abierto[2], **-ta** *adj* **1** : open **2** : candid, frank **3** : generous — **abiertamente** *adv*

abigarrado, -da *adj* : multicolored, variegated

abigeato *nm* : rustling (of livestock)

abismal *adj* : abysmal, vast

abismo *nm* : abyss, chasm ⟨al borde del abismo : on the brink of ruin⟩

abjurar *vi* **~ de** : to abjure — **abjuración** *nf*

ablandamiento *nm* : softening, moderation

ablandar *vt* **1** SUAVIZAR : to soften **2** CALMAR : to soothe, to appease — *vi* : to moderate, to get milder — **ablandarse** *vr* **1** : to become soft, to soften **2** CEDER : to yield, to relent

ablución *nf, pl* **-ciones** : ablution

abnegación *nf, pl* **-ciones** : abnegation, self-denial

abnegado, -da *adj* : self-sacrificing, selfless

abnegarse {49} *vr* : to deny oneself

abobado, -da *adj* **1** : silly, stupid **2** : bewildered

abocarse {72} *vr* **1** DIRIGIRSE : to head, to direct oneself **2** DEDICARSE : to dedicate oneself

abochornar *vt* AVERGONZAR : to embarrass, to shame — **abochornarse** *vr*

abofetear *vt* : to slap

abogacía *nf* : law, legal profession

abogado, -da *n* : lawyer, attorney

abogar {52} *vi* **~ por** : to plead for, to defend, to advocate

abolengo *nm* LINAJE : lineage, ancestry

abolición *nf, pl* **-ciones** : abolition

abolir {1} *vt* DEROGAR : to abolish, to repeal

abolladura *nf* : dent

abollar *vt* : to dent

abombar *vt* : to warp, to cause to bulge — **abombarse** *vr* : to decompose, to go bad

abominable *adj* ABORRECIBLE : abominable

abominación *nf, pl* **-ciones** : abomination

abominar *vt* ABORRECER : to abominate, to abhor

abonado, -da *n* : subscriber

abonar *vt* **1** : to pay **2** FERTILIZAR : to fertilize — **abonarse** *vr* : to subscribe

abono *nm* **1** : payment, installment **2** FERTILIZANTE : fertilizer **3** : season ticket

abordaje *nm* : boarding

abordar *vt* **1** : to address, to broach **2** : to accost, to waylay **3** : to come on board

aborigen[1] *adj, pl* **-rígenes** : aboriginal, native

aborigen[2] *nmf, pl* **-rígenes** : aborigine, indigenous inhabitant

aborrecer {53} *vt* ABOMINAR, ODIAR : to abhor, to detest, to hate

aborrecible *adj* ABOMINABLE, ODIOSO : abominable, detestable

aborrecimiento *nm* : abhorrence, loathing

abortar *vi* : to have an abortion — *vt* **1** : to abort **2** : to quash, to suppress

abortista *nmf* : abortionist

abortivo, -va *adj* : abortive

aborto *nm* **1** : abortion **2** : miscarriage

abotonar *vt* : to button — **abotonarse** *vr* : to button up

abovedado, -da *adj* : vaulted

abrasador, -dora *adj* : burning, scorching

abrasar *vt* QUEMAR : to burn, to sear, to scorch

abrasivo[1], **-va** *adj* : abrasive

abrasivo[2] *nm* : abrasive

abrazadera *nf* : clamp, brace

abrazar {21} *vt* : to hug, to embrace — **abrazarse** *vr*

abrazo *nm* : hug, embrace

abrebotellas *nms & pl* : bottle opener

abrelatas *nms & pl* : can opener

abrevadero *nm* BEBEDERO : watering trough

abreviación *nf, pl* **-ciones** : abbreviation

abreviar *vt* **1** : to abbreviate **2** : to shorten, to cut short

abreviatura → **abreviación**

abridor *nm* : bottle opener, can opener

abrigadero *nm* : shelter, windbreak

abrigado, -da *adj* **1** : sheltered **2** : warm, wrapped up (with clothing)

abrigar {52} *vt* **1** : to shelter, to protect **2** : to keep warm, to dress warmly **3** : to cherish, to harbor ⟨abrigar esperanzas : to cherish hopes⟩ — **abrigarse** *vr* : to dress warmly

abrigo *nm* **1** : coat, overcoat **2** : shelter, refuge

abril *nm* : April

abrillantador *nm* : polish

abrillantar *vt* : to polish, to shine

abrir {2} *vt* **1** : to open **2** : to unlock, to undo **3** : to turn on (a tap or faucet) — *vi* : to open, to open up — **abrirse** *vr* **1** : to open up **2** : to clear (of the skies)

abrochar *vt* : to button, to fasten — **abrocharse** *vr* : to fasten, to hook up

abrogación *nf, pl* **-ciones** : abrogation, annulment, repeal

abrogar {52} *vt* : to abrogate, to annul, to repeal

abrojo *nm* : bur (of a plant)

abrumador, -dora *adj* : crushing, overwhelming

abrumar *vt* **1** AGOBIAR : to overwhelm **2** OPRIMIR : to oppress, to burden

abrupto, -ta *adj* **1** : abrupt **2** ESCARPADO : steep — **abruptamente** *adv*

absceso *nm* : abscess

absolución *nf, pl* **-ciones** **1** : absolution **2** : acquittal

absolutismo *nm* : absolutism

absoluto, -ta *adj* **1** : absolute, unconditional **2 en ~** : not at all ⟨no me gustó en absoluto : I did not like it at all⟩ — **absolutamente** *adv*

absolver {89} *vt* **1** : to absolve **2** : to acquit

absorbente *adj* **1** : absorbent **2** : absorbing, engrossing

absorber *vt* **1** : to absorb, to soak up **2** : to occupy, to take up, to engross

absorción *nf, pl* **-ciones** : absorption

absorto, -ta *adj* : absorbed, engrossed

abstemio[1], **-mia** *adj* : abstemious, teetotal

abstemio[2], **-mia** *n* : teetotaler

abstención *nf, pl* **-ciones** : abstention

abstenerse {80} *vr* : to abstain, to refrain

abstinencia *nf* : abstinence

abstracción *nf, pl* **-ciones** : abstraction

abstracto, -ta *adj* : abstract

abstraer {81} *vt* : to abstract — **abstraerse** *vr* : to lose oneself in thought

abstraído, -da *adj* : preoccupied, withdrawn

abstruso, -sa *adj* : abstruse

abstuvo, etc. → **abstenerse**

absuelto *pp* → **absolver**

absurdo[1], **-da** *adj* DISPARATADO, RIDÍCULO : absurd, ridiculous — **absurdamente** *adv*

absurdo[2] *nm* : absurdity

abuchear *vt* : to boo, to jeer

abucheo *nm* : booing, jeering

abuela *nf* **1** : grandmother **2** : old woman **3 ¡tu abuela!** *fam* : no way!, forget about it!

abuelo *nm* **1** : grandfather **2** : old man **3 abuelos** *nmpl* : grandparents, ancestors

abulia *nf* : apathy, lethargy

abúlico, -ca *adj* : lethargic, apathetic

abultado, -da *adj* : bulging, bulky

abultar *vi* : to bulge — *vt* : to enlarge, to expand

abundancia *nf* : abundance

abundante *adj* : abundant, plentiful — **abundantemente** *adv*

abundar *vi* **1** : to abound, to be plentiful **2 ~ en** : to be in agreement with

aburrido, -da *adj* **1** : bored, tired, fed up **2** TEDIOSO : boring, tedious

aburrimiento *nm* : boredom, weariness

aburrir *vt* : to bore, to tire — **aburrirse** *vr* : to get bored

abusado, -da *adj Mex fam* : sharp, on the ball

abusador, -dora *n* : abuser

abusar *vi* **1** : to go too far, to do something to excess **2 ~ de** : to abuse (as drugs) **3 ~ de** : to take unfair advantage of

abusivo, -va *adj* **1** : abusive **2** : outrageous, excessive

abuso *nm* **1** : abuse **2** : injustice, outrage

abyecto, -ta *adj* : despicable, contemptible

acá *adv* AQUÍ : here, over here ⟨¡ven acá! : come here!⟩

acabado[1], -da *adj* **1** : finished, done, completed **2** : old, worn-out

acabado[2] *nm* : finish ⟨un acabado brillante : a glossy finish⟩

acabar *vi* **1** TERMINAR : to finish, to end **2 ~ de** : to have just (done something) ⟨acabo de ver a tu hermano : I just saw your brother⟩ **3 ~ con** : to put an end to, to stamp out — *vt* TERMINAR : to finish — **acabarse** *vr* TERMINARSE : to come to an end, to run out ⟨se me acabó el dinero : I ran out of money⟩

acacia *nf* : acacia

academia *nf* : academy

académico[1], -ca *adj* : academic, scholastic — **académicamente** *adv*

académico[2], -ca *n* : academic, academician

acaecer {53} *vt* (*3rd person only*) : to happen, to take place

acalambrarse *vr* : to cramp up, to get a cramp

acallar *vt* : to quiet, to silence

acalorado, -da *adj* : emotional, heated

acaloramiento *nm* **1** : heat **2** : ardor, passion

acalorar *vt* : to heat up, to inflame — **acalorarse** *vr* : to get upset, to get worked up

acampada *nf* : camp, camping ⟨ir de acampada : to go camping⟩

acampar *vi* : to camp

acanalar *vt* **1** : to groove, to furrow **2** : to corrugate

acantilado *nm* : cliff

acanto *nm* : acanthus

acantonar *vt* : to station, to quarter

acaparador, -dora *adj* : greedy, selfish

acaparar *vt* **1** : to stockpile, to hoard **2** : to monopolize

acápite *nm* : paragraph

acariciar *vt* : to caress, to stroke, to pet

ácaro *nm* : mite

acarrear *vt* **1** : to haul, to carry **2** : to bring, to give rise to ⟨los problemas que acarrea : the problems that come along with it⟩

acarreo *nm* : transport, haulage

acartonarse *vr* **1** : to stiffen **2** : to become wizened

acaso *adv* **1** : perhaps, by any chance **2 por si acaso** : just in case

acatamiento *nm* : compliance, observance

acatar *vt* : to comply with, to respect

acaudalado, -da *adj* RICO : wealthy, rich

acaudillar *vt* : to lead, to command

acceder *vi* **~ a 1** : to accede to, to agree to **2** : to assume (a position) **3** : to gain access to

accesar *vt* : to access (on a computer)

accesibilidad *nf* : accessibility

accesible *adj* ASEQUIBLE : accessible, attainable

acceso *nm* **1** : access **2** : admittance, entrance

accesorio[1], -ria *adj* **1** : accessory **2** : incidental

accesorio[2] *nm* **1** : accessory **2** : prop (in the theater)

accidentado[1], -da *adj* **1** : eventful, turbulent **2** : rough, uneven **3** : injured

accidentado[2], -da *n* : accident victim

accidental *adj* : accidental, unintentional — **accidentalmente** *adv*

accidentarse *vr* : to have an accident

accidente *nm* **1** : accident **2** : unevenness **3 accidente geográfico** : geographical feature

acción *nf, pl* **acciones 1** : action **2** ACTO : act, deed **3** : share, stock

accionamiento *nm* : activation

accionar *vt* : to put into motion, to activate — *vi* : to gesticulate

accionario, -ria *adj* : stock ⟨mercado accionario : stock market⟩

accionista *nmf* : stockholder, shareholder

acebo *nm* : holly

acechar *vt* **1** : to watch, to spy on **2** : to stalk, to lie in wait for

acecho *nm* **al acecho** : lying in wait

acedera *nf* : sorrel (herb)

acéfalo, -la *adj* : leaderless

aceitar *vt* : to oil

aceite *nm* **1** : oil **2 aceite de ricino** : castor oil **3 aceite de oliva** : olive oil

aceitera *nf* **1** : cruet (for oil) **2** : oilcan **3** *Mex* : oil refinery

aceitoso, -sa *adj* : oily

aceituna *nf* OLIVA : olive

aceituno *nm* OLIVO : olive tree

aceleración *nf, pl* **-ciones** : acceleration, speeding up

acelerado, -da *adj* : accelerated, speedy

acelerador *nm* : accelerator

aceleramiento *nm* → **aceleración**

acelerar *vt* **1** : to accelerate, to speed up **2** AGILIZAR : to expedite — *vi* : to accelerate (of an automobile) — **acelerarse** *vr* : to hasten, to hurry up

acelga *nf* : chard, Swiss chard

acendrado, -da *adj* : pure, unblemished

acendrar *vt* : to purify, to refine

acento *nm* **1** : accent **2** : stress, emphasis

acentuación *nf, pl* **-ciones** : accentuation

acentuado, -da *adj* : marked, pronounced

acentuar {3} *vt* **1** : to accent **2** : to emphasize, to stress — **acentuarse** *vr* : to become more pronounced

acepción *nf, pl* **-ciones** SIGNIFICADO : sense, meaning

aceptabilidad *nf* : acceptability

aceptable *adj* : acceptable

aceptación *nf, pl* **-ciones** **1** : acceptance **2** APROBACIÓN : approval

aceptar *vt* **1** : to accept **2** : to approve

acequia *nf* **1** : irrigation ditch **2** *Mex* : sewer

acera *nf* : sidewalk

acerado, -da *adj* **1** : made of steel **2** : steely, tough

acerbo, -ba *adj* **1** : harsh, cutting ⟨comentarios acerbos : cutting remarks⟩ **2** : bitter — **acerbamente** *adv*

acerca *prep* **~ de** : about, concerning

acercamiento *nm* : rapprochement, reconciliation

acercar {72} *vt* APROXIMAR, ARRIMAR : to bring near, to bring closer — **acercarse** *vr* APROXIMARSE, ARRIMARSE : to approach, to draw near

acería *nf* : steel mill

acerico *nm* : pincushion

acero *nm* : steel ⟨acero inoxidable : stainless steel⟩

acérrimo, -ma *adj* **1** : staunch, steadfast **2** : bitter ⟨un acérrimo enemigo : a bitter enemy⟩

acertado, -da *adj* CORRECTO : accurate, correct, on target — **acertadamente** *adv*

acertante[1] *adj* : winning

acertante[2] *nmf* : winner

acertar {55} *vt* : to guess correctly — *vi* **1** ATINAR : to be correct, to be on target **2** **~ a** : to manage to

acertijo *nm* ADIVINANZA : riddle

acervo *nm* **1** : pile, heap **2** : wealth, heritage ⟨el acervo artístico del instituto : the artistic treasures of the institute⟩

acetato *nm* : acetate

acético, -ca *adj* : acetic ⟨ácido acético : acetic acid⟩

acetileno *nm* : acetylene

acetona *nf* **1** : acetone **2** : nail-polish remover

achacar {72} *vt* : to attribute, to impute ⟨te achaca todos sus problemas : he blames all his problems on you⟩

achacoso, -sa *adj* : frail, sickly

achaparrado, -da *adj* : stunted, scrubby ⟨árboles achaparrados : scrubby trees⟩

achaques *nmpl* : aches and pains

achatar *vt* : to flatten

achicar {72} *vt* **1** REDUCIR : to make smaller, to reduce **2** : to intimidate **3** : to bail out (water) — **achicarse** *vr* : to become intimidated

achicharrar *vt* : to scorch, to burn to a crisp

achicoria *nf* : chicory

achispado, -da *adj fam* : tipsy

achote *or* **achiote** *nm* : annatto seed

achuchón *nm, pl* **-chones** **1** : push, shove **2** *fam* : squeeze, hug **3** *fam* : mild illness

aciago, -ga *adj* : fateful, unlucky

acicalar *vt* **1** PULIR : to polish **2** : to dress up, to adorn — **acicalarse** *vr* : to get dressed up

acicate *nm* **1** : spur **2** INCENTIVO : incentive, stimulus

acidez *nf, pl* **-deces** **1** : acidity **2** : sourness **3** **acidez estomacal** : heartburn

acidificar {72} *vt* : to acidify

ácido[1], **-da** *adj* AGRIO : acid, sour

ácido[2] *nm* : acid

acierto *nm* **1** : correct answer, right choice **2** : accuracy, skill, deftness

acimut *nm* : azimuth

acitronar *vt Mex* : to fry until crisp

aclamación *nf, pl* **-ciones** : acclaim, acclamation

aclamar *vt* : to acclaim, to cheer, to applaud

aclaración *nf, pl* **-ciones** CLARIFICACIÓN : clarification, explanation

aclarar *vt* **1** CLARIFICAR : to clarify, to explain, to resolve **2** : to lighten **3** **aclarar la voz** : to clear one's throat — *vi* **1** : to get light, to dawn **2** : to clear up — **aclararse** *vr* : to become clear

aclaratorio, -ria *adj* : explanatory

aclimatar *vt* : to acclimatize — **aclimatarse** *vr* **~ a** : to get used to — **aclimatación** *nf*

acné *nm* : acne

acobardar *vt* INTIMIDAR : to frighten, to intimidate — **acobardarse** *vr* : to be frightened, to cower

acodarse *vr* **~ en** : to lean (one's elbows) on

acogedor, -dora *adj* : cozy, warm, friendly

acoger {15} *vt* **1** REFUGIAR : to take in, to shelter **2** : to receive, to welcome — **acogerse** *vr* **1** REFUGIARSE : to take refuge **2** **~ a** : to resort to, to avail oneself of

acogida *nf* **1** AMPARO, REFUGIO : refuge, protection **2** RECIBIMIENTO : reception, welcome

acolchar *vt* **1** : to pad (a wall, etc.) **2** : to quilt

acólito *nm* **1** MONAGUILLO : altar boy **2** : follower, helper, acolyte

acomedido, -da *adj* : helpful, obliging

acometer *vt* **1** ATACAR : to attack, to assail **2** EMPRENDER : to undertake, to begin — *vi* **~ contra** : to rush against
acometida *nf* ATAQUE : attack, assault
acomodado, -da *adj* **1** : suitable, appropriate **2** : well-to-do, prosperous
acomodador, -dora *n* : usher, usherette *f*
acomodar *vt* **1** : to accommodate, to make room for **2** : to adjust, to adapt — **acomodarse** *vr* **1** : to settle in **2 ~ a** : to adapt to
acomodaticio, -cia *adj* : accommodating, obliging
acomodo *nm* **1** : job, position **2** : arrangement, placement **3** : accommodation, lodging
acompañamiento *nm* : accompaniment
acompañante *nmf* **1** COMPAÑERO : companion **2** : accompanist
acompañar *vt* : to accompany, to go with
acompasado, -da *adj* : rhythmic, regular, measured
acomplejado, -da *adj* : full of complexes, neurotic
acondicionado, -da *adj* **1** : equipped, fitted-out **2 bien acondicionado** : in good shape, in a fit state
acondicionador *nm* **1** : conditioner **2 acondicionador de aire** : air conditioner
acondicionar *vt* **1** : to condition **2** : to fit out, to furnish
acongojado, -da *adj* : distressed, upset
acongojarse *vr* : to grieve, to become distressed
aconsejable *adj* : advisable
aconsejar *vt* : to advise, to counsel
acontecer {53} *vt* (*3rd person only*) : to occur, to happen
acontecimiento *nm* SUCESO : event
acopiar *vt* : to gather, to collect, to stockpile
acopio *nm* : collection, stock
acoplamiento *nm* : connection, coupling
acoplar *vt* : to couple, to connect — **acoplarse** *vr* : to fit together
acoquinar *vt* : to intimidate
acorazado[1], -da *adj* BLINDADO : armored
acorazado[2] *nm* : battleship
acordado, -da *adj* : agreed upon
acordar {19} *vt* **1** : to agree on **2** OTORGAR : to award, to bestow — **acordarse** *vr* RECORDAR : to remember, to recall
acorde[1] *adj* **1** : in agreement, in accordance **2 ~ con** : in keeping with
acorde[2] *nm* : chord
acordeón *nm, pl* **-deones** : accordion — **acordeonista** *nmf*
acordonar *vt* **1** : to cordon off **2** : to lace up **3** : to mill (coins)
acorralar *vt* ARRINCONAR : to corner, to hem in, to corral
acortar *vt* : to shorten, to cut short — **acortarse** *vr* **1** : to become shorter **2** : to end early
acosar *vt* PERSEGUIR : to pursue, to hound, to harass
acoso *nm* ASEDIO : harassment ⟨acoso sexual : sexual harassment⟩
acostar {19} *vt* **1** : to lay (something) down **2** : to put to bed — **acostarse** *vr* **1** : to lie down **2** : to go to bed
acostumbrado, -da *adj* **1** HABITUADO : accustomed **2** HABITUAL : usual, customary
acostumbrar *vt* : to accustom — *vi* : to be accustomed, to be in the habit — **acostumbrarse** *vr*
acotación *nf, pl* **-ciones** **1** : marginal note **2** : stage direction
acotado, -da *adj* : enclosed
acotamiento *nm Mex* : shoulder (of a road)
acotar *vt* **1** ANOTAR : to note, to annotate **2** DELIMITAR : to mark off (land), to demarcate
acre[1] *adj* **1** : acrid, pungent **2** MORDAZ : caustic, biting
acre[2] *nm* : acre
acrecentamiento *nm* : growth, increase
acrecentar {55} *vt* AUMENTAR : to increase, to augment
acreditación *nf, pl* **-ciones** : accreditation
acreditado, -da *adj* **1** : accredited, authorized **2** : reputable
acreditar *vt* **1** : to accredit, to authorize **2** : to credit **3** : to prove, to verify — **acreditarse** *vr* : to gain a reputation
acreedor[1], -dora *adj* : deserving, worthy
acreedor[2], -dora *n* : creditor
acribillar *vt* **1** : to riddle, to pepper (with bullets, etc.) **2** : to hound, to harass
acrílico *nm* : acrylic
acrimonia *nf* **1** : pungency **2** : acrimony
acrimonioso, -sa *adj* : acrimonious
acriollarse *vr* : to adopt local customs, to go native
acritud *nf* **1** : pungency, bitterness **2** : intensity, sharpness **3** : harshness, asperity
acrobacia *nf* : acrobatics
acróbata *nmf* : acrobat
acrobático, -ca *adj* : acrobatic
acrónimo *nm* : acronym
acta *nf* **1** : document, certificate ⟨acta de nacimiento : birth certificate⟩ **2 actas** *nfpl* : minutes (of a meeting)
actitud *nf* **1** : attitude **2** : posture, position
activación *nf, pl* **-ciones** **1** : activation, stimulation **2** ACELERACIÓN : acceleration, speeding up
activar *vt* **1** : to activate **2** : to stimulate, to energize **3** : to speed up
actividad *nf* : activity
activista *nmf* : activist
activo[1], -va *adj* : active — **activamente** *adv*
activo[2] *nm* : assets *pl* ⟨activo y pasivo : assets and liabilities⟩

acto *nm* **1** ACCIÓN : act, deed **2** : act (in a play) **3 el acto sexual** : sexual intercourse **4 en el acto** : right away, on the spot **5 acto seguido** : immediately after

actor *nm* ARTISTA : actor

actriz *nf, pl* **actrices** ARTISTA : actress

actuación *nf, pl* **-ciones** **1** : performance **2 actuaciones** *nfpl* DILIGENCIAS : proceedings

actual *adj* PRESENTE : present, current

actualidad *nf* **1** : present time ⟨en la actualidad : at present⟩ **2 actualidades** *nfpl* : current affairs

actualización *nf, pl* **-ciones** : updating, modernization

actualizar {21} *vt* : to modernize, to bring up to date

actualmente *adv* : at present, nowadays

actuar {3} *vi* : to act, to perform

actuarial *adj* : actuarial

actuario, -ria *n* : actuary

acuarela *nf* : watercolor

acuario *nm* : aquarium

Acuario *nmf* : Aquarius, Aquarian

acuartelar *vt* : to quarter (troops)

acuático, -ca *adj* : aquatic, water

acuchillar *vt* APUÑALAR : to knife, to stab

acuciante *adj* : pressing, urgent

acucioso, -sa → **acuciante**

acudir *vi* **1** : to go, to come (someplace for a specific purpose) ⟨acudió a la puerta : he went to the door⟩ ⟨acudimos en su ayuda : we came to her aid⟩ **2** : to be present, to show up ⟨acudí a la cita : I showed up for the appointment⟩ **3 ~ a** : to turn to, to have recourse to ⟨hay que acudir al médico : you must consult the doctor⟩

acueducto *nm* : aqueduct

acuerdo *nm* **1** : agreement **2 estar de acuerdo** : to agree **3 de acuerdo con** : in accordance with **4 de ~** : OK, all right

acuicultura *nf* : aquaculture

acullá *adv* : yonder, over there

acumulación *nf, pl* **-ciones** : accumulation

acumulador *nm* : storage battery

acumular *vt* : to accumulate, to amass — **acumularse** *vr* : to build up, to pile up

acumulativo, -va *adj* : cumulative — **acumulativamente** *adv*

acunar *vt* : to rock, to cradle

acuñar *vt* : to coin, to mint

acuoso, -sa *adj* : aqueous, watery

acupuntura *nf* : acupuncture

acurrucarse {72} *vr* : to cuddle, to nestle, to curl up

acusación *nf, pl* **-ciones** **1** : accusation, charge **2 la acusación** : the prosecution

acusado[1], -da *adj* : prominent, marked

acusado[2], -da *n* : defendant

acusador, -dora *n* **1** : accuser **2** FISCAL : prosecutor

acusar *vt* **1** : to accuse, to charge **2** : to reveal, to betray ⟨sus ojos acusaban la desconfianza : his eyes revealed distrust⟩ — **acusarse** *vr* : to confess

acusativo *nm* : objective (in grammar)

acusatorio, -ria *adj* : accusatory

acuse *nm* **acuse de recibo** : acknowledgment of receipt

acústica *nf* : acoustics

acústico, -ca *adj* : acoustic

adagio *nm* **1** REFRÁN : adage, proverb **2** : adagio

adalid *nm* : leader, champion

adaptable *adj* : adaptable — **adaptabilidad** *nf*

adaptación *nf, pl* **-ciones** : adaptation, adjustment

adaptado, -da *adj* : suited, adapted

adaptador *nm* : adapter (in electricity)

adaptar *vt* **1** MODIFICAR : to adapt **2** : to adjust, to fit — **adaptarse** *vr* : to adapt oneself, to conform

adecentar *vt* : to tidy up

adecuación *nf, pl* **-ciones** ADAPTACIÓN : adaptation

adecuadamente *adv* : adequately

adecuado, -da *adj* **1** IDÓNEO : suitable, appropriate **2** : adequate

adecuar {8} *vt* : to adapt, to make suitable — **adecuarse** *vr* **~ a** : to be appropriate for, to fit in with

adefesio *nm* : eyesore, monstrosity

adelantado, -da *adj* **1** : advanced, ahead **2** : fast (of a clock or watch) **3 por ~** : in advance

adelantamiento *nm* **1** : advancement **2** : speeding up

adelantar *vt* **1** : to advance, to move forward **2** : to overtake, to pass **3** : to reveal (information) in advance **4** : to advance, to lend (money) — **adelantarse** *vr* **1** : to advance, to get in front **2 ~ a** : to forestall, to preempt

adelante *adv* **1** : ahead, in front, forward **2 más adelante** : further on, later on **3 ¡adelante!** : come in!

adelanto *nm* **1** : advance, progress **2** : advance payment **3** : earliness ⟨llevamos una hora de adelanto : we're running an hour ahead of time⟩

adelfa *nf* : oleander

adelgazar {21} *vt* : to thin, to reduce — *vi* : to lose weight

ademán *nm, pl* **-manes** **1** GESTO : gesture **2 ademanes** *nmpl* : manners

además *adv* **1** : besides, furthermore **2 ~ de** : in addition to, as well as

adenoides *nfpl* : adenoids

adentrarse *vr* **~ en** : to go into, to penetrate

adentro *adv* : inside, within

adentros *nmpl* **decirse para sus adentros** : to say to oneself ⟨me dije para mis adentros que nunca regresaría : I told myself that I'd never go back⟩

adepto[1], -ta *adj* : supportive ⟨ser adepto a : to be a follower of⟩

adepto[2], -ta *n* PARTIDARIO : follower, supporter

aderezar {21} *vt* **1** SAZONAR : to season, to dress (salad) **2** : to embellish, to adorn
aderezo *nm* **1** : dressing, seasoning **2** : adornment, embellishment
adeudar *vt* **1** : to debit **2** DEBER : to owe
adeudo *nm* **1** DÉBITO : debit **2** *Mex* : debt, indebtedness
adherencia *nf* **1** : adherence, adhesiveness **2** : appendage, accretion
adherente *adj* : adhesive, sticky
adherirse {76} *vr* : to adhere, to stick
adhesión *nf, pl* **-siones** **1** : adhesion **2** : attachment, commitment (to a cause, etc.)
adhesivo[1], **-va** *adj* : adhesive
adhesivo[2] *nm* : adhesive
adicción *nf, pl* **-ciones** : addiction
adición *nf, pl* **-ciones** : addition
adicional *adj* : additional — **adicionalmente** *adv*
adicionar *vt* : to add
adictivo, -va *adj* : addictive
adicto[1], **-ta** *adj* **1** : addicted **2** : devoted, dedicated
adicto[2], **-ta** *n* **1** : addict **2** PARTIDARIO : supporter, advocate
adiestrador, -dora *n* : trainer
adiestramiento *nm* : training
adiestrar *vt* : to train
adinerado, -da *adj* : moneyed, wealthy
adiós *nm, pl* **adioses** **1** DESPEDIDA : farewell, good-bye **2 ¡adiós!** : good-bye!
aditamento *nm* : attachment, accessory
aditivo *nm* : additive
adivinación *nf, pl* **-ciones** **1** : guess **2** : divination, prediction
adivinanza *nf* ACERTIJO : riddle
adivinar *vt* **1** : to guess **2** : to foretell, to predict
adivino, -na *n* : fortune-teller
adjetivo[1], **-va** *adj* : adjectival
adjetivo[2] *nm* : adjective
adjudicación *nf, pl* **-ciones** **1** : adjudication **2** : allocation, awarding, granting
adjudicar {72} *vt* **1** : to adjudge, to adjudicate **2** : to assign, to allocate ⟨adjudicar la culpa : to assign the blame⟩ **3** : to award, to grant
adjuntar *vt* : to enclose, to attach
adjunto[1], **-ta** *adj* : enclosed, attached
adjunto[2], **-ta** *n* : deputy, assistant
adjunto[3] *nm* : adjunct
administración *nf, pl* **-ciones** **1** : administration, management **2 administración de empresas** : business administration
administrador, -dora *n* : administrator, manager
administrar *vt* : to administer, to manage, to run
administrativo, -va *adj* : administrative
admirable *adj* : admirable, impressive — **admirablemente** *adv*
admiración *nf, pl* **-ciones** : admiration
admirador, -dora *n* : admirer
admirar *vt* **1** : to admire **2** : to amaze, to astonish — **admirarse** *vr* : to be amazed
admirativo, -va *adj* : admiring
admisibilidad *nf* : admissibility
admisible *adj* : admissible, allowable
admisión *nf, pl* **-siones** : admission, admittance
admitir *vt* **1** : to admit, to let in **2** : to acknowledge, to concede **3** : to allow, to make room for ⟨la ley no admite cambios : the law doesn't allow for changes⟩
admonición *nf, pl* **-ciones** : admonition, warning
admonitorio, -ria *adj* : admonitory
ADN *nm* (*á*cido *d*esoxirribo*n*ucleico) : DNA
adobar *vt* : to marinate
adobe *nm* : adobe
adobo *nm* **1** : marinade, seasoning **2** *Mex* : spicy marinade used for cooking pork
adoctrinamiento *nm* : indoctrination
adoctrinar *vt* : to indoctrinate
adolecer {53} *vi* PADECER : to suffer ⟨adolece de timidez : he suffers from shyness⟩
adolescencia *nf* : adolescence
adolescente[1] *adj* : adolescent, teenage
adolescente[2] *nmf* : adolescent, teenager
adonde *conj* : where ⟨el lugar adonde vamos es bello : the place where we're going is beautiful⟩
adónde *adv* : where ⟨¿adónde vamos? : where are we going?⟩
adondequiera *adv* : wherever, anywhere ⟨adondequiera que vayas : anywhere you go⟩
adopción *nf, pl* **-ciones** : adoption
adoptar *vt* **1** : to adopt (a measure), to take (a decision) **2** : to adopt (children)
adoptivo, -va *adj* **1** : adopted (children, country) **2** : adoptive (parents)
adoquín *nm, pl* **-quines** : paving stone, cobblestone
adorable *adj* : adorable, lovable
adoración *nf, pl* **-ciones** : adoration, worship
adorador[1], **-dora** *adj* : adoring, worshipping
adorador[2], **-dora** *n* : worshipper
adorar *vt* : to adore, to worship
adormecer {53} *vt* **1** : to make sleepy, to lull to sleep **2** : to numb — **adormecerse** *vr* **1** : to doze off **2** : to go numb
adormecimiento *nm* **1** SUEÑO : drowsiness, sleepiness **2** INSENSIBILIDAD : numbness
adormilarse *vr* : to doze, to drowse
adornar *vt* DECORAR : to decorate, to adorn
adorno *nm* : ornament, decoration
adquirido, -da *adj* **1** : acquired **2 mal adquirido** : ill-gotten
adquirir {4} *vt* **1** : to acquire, to gain **2** COMPRAR : to purchase

adquisición *nf, pl* **-ciones** **1** : acquisition **2** COMPRA : purchase
adquisitivo, -va *adj* **poder adquisitivo** : purchasing power
adrede *adv* : intentionally, on purpose
adrenalina *nf* : adrenaline
adscribir {33} *vt* : to assign, to appoint — **adscribirse** *vr* **~ a** : to become a member of
adscripción *nf, pl* **-ciones** : assignment, appointment
adscrito *pp* → **adscribir**
aduana *nf* : customs, customs office
aduanero[1], **-ra** *adj* : customs
aduanero[2], **-ra** *n* : customs officer
aducir {61} *vt* : to adduce, to offer as proof
adueñarse *vr* **~ de** : to take possession of, to take over
adulación *nf, pl* **-ciones** : adulation, flattery
adulador[1], **-dora** *adj* : flattering
adulador[2], **-dora** *n* : flatterer, toady
adular *vt* LISONJEAR : to flatter
adulteración *nf, pl* **-ciones** : adulteration
adulterar *vt* : to adulterate
adulterio *nm* : adultery
adúltero[1], **-ra** *adj* : adulterous
adúltero[2], **-ra** *n* : adulterer
adultez *nf* : adulthood
adulto, -ta *adj & n* : adult
adusto, -ta *adj* : harsh, severe
advenedizo, -za *n* **1** : upstart, parvenu **2** : newcomer
advenimiento *nm* : advent
adverbio *nm* : adverb — **adverbial** *adj*
adversario[1], **-ria** *adj* : opposing, contrary
adversario[2], **-ria** *n* OPOSITOR : adversary, opponent
adversidad *nf* : adversity
adverso, -sa *adj* DESFAVORABLE : adverse, unfavorable — **adversamente** *adv*
advertencia *nf* AVISO : warning
advertir {76} *vt* **1** AVISAR : to warn **2** : to notice, to tell ⟨no advertí que estuviera enojada : I couldn't tell she was angry⟩
Adviento *nm* : Advent
adyacente *adj* : adjacent
aéreo, -rea *adj* **1** : aerial, air **2 correo aéreo** : airmail
aeróbic *nm* : aerobics
aeróbico, -ca *adj* : aerobic
aerobio, -bia *adj* : aerobic
aerodinámica *nf* : aerodynamics
aerodinámico, -ca *adj* : aerodynamic, streamlined
aeródromo *nm* : airfield
aeroespacial *adj* : aerospace
aerolínea *nf* : airline
aeromozo, -za *n* : flight attendant, steward *m,* stewardess *f*
aeronáutica *nf* : aeronautics
aeronáutico, -ca *adj* : aeronautical
aeronave *nf* : aircraft
aeropostal *adj* : airmail
aeropuerto *nm* : airport
aerosol *nm* : aerosol, aerosol spray
aeróstata *nmf* : balloonist
aerotransportado, -da *adj* : airborne
aerotransportar *vt* : to airlift
afabilidad *nf* : affability
afable *adj* : affable — **afablemente** *adv*
afamado, -da *adj* : well-known, famous
afán *nm, pl* **afanes** **1** ANHELO : eagerness, desire **2** EMPEÑO : effort, determination
afanador, -dora *n Mex* : cleaning person, cleaner
afanarse *vr* : to toil, to strive
afanosamente *adv* : zealously, industriously, busily
afanoso, -sa *adj* **1** : eager, industrious **2** : arduous, hard
afear *vt* : to make ugly, to disfigure
afección *nf, pl* **-ciones** **1** : fondness, affection **2** : illness, complaint
afectación *nf, pl* **-ciones** : affectation
afectado, -da *adj* **1** : affected, mannered **2** : influenced **3** : afflicted **4** : feigned
afectar *vt* **1** : to affect **2** : to upset **3** : to feign, to pretend
afectísimo, -ma *adj* **suyo afectísimo** : yours truly
afectivo, -va *adj* : emotional
afecto[1], **-ta** *adj* **1** : affected, afflicted **2** : fond, affectionate
afecto[2] *nm* CARIÑO : affection
afectuoso, -sa *adj* CARIÑOSO : affectionate, caring
afeitadora *nf* : shaver, electric razor
afeitar *vt* RASURAR : to shave — **afeitarse** *vr*
afelpado, -da *adj* : plush
afeminado, -da *adj* : effeminate
aferrado, -da *adj* : obstinate, stubborn
aferrarse {55} *vr* : to cling, to hold on
affidávit *nm, pl* **-dávits** : affidavit
afgano, -na *adj & n* : Afghan
AFI *nm* (*A*lfabeto *F*onético *I*nternacional) : IPA
afianzar {21} *vt* **1** : to secure, to strengthen **2** : to guarantee, to vouch for — **afianzarse** *vr* ESTABLECERSE : to establish oneself
afiche *nm* : poster
afición *nf, pl* **-ciones** **1** : enthusiasm, penchant, fondness ⟨afición al deporte : love of sports⟩ **2** PASATIEMPO : hobby
aficionado[1], **-da** *adj* ENTUSIASTA : enthusiastic, keen
aficionado[2], **-da** *n* **1** ENTUSIASTA : enthusiast, fan **2** : amateur
áfido *nm* : aphid
afiebrado, -da *adj* : feverish
afilado, -da *adj* **1** : sharp **2** : long, pointed ⟨una nariz afilada : a sharp nose⟩
afilador *nm* : sharpener
afilalápices *nms & pl* : pencil sharpener
afilar *vt* : to sharpen
afiliación *nf, pl* **-ciones** : affiliation

afiliado[1], **-da** *adj* : affiliated

afiliado[2], **-da** *n* : member

afiliarse *vr* : to become a member, to join, to affiliate

afín *adj, pl* **afines 1** PARECIDO : related, similar ⟨la biología y disciplinas afines : biology and related disciplines⟩ **2** PRÓXIMO : adjacent, nearby

afinación *nf, pl* **-ciones 1** : tune-up **2** : tuning (of an instrument)

afinador, -dora *n* : tuner (of musical instruments)

afinar *vt* **1** : to perfect, to refine **2** : to tune (an instrument) — *vi* : to sing or play in tune

afincarse {72} *vr* : to establish oneself, to settle in

afinidad *nf* : affinity, similarity

afirmación *nf, pl* **-ciones 1** : statement **2** : affirmation

afirmar *vt* **1** : to state, to affirm **2** REFORZAR : to make firm, to strengthen

afirmativo, -va *adj* : affirmative — **afirmativamente** *adj*

aflicción *nf, pl* **-ciones** DESCONSUELO, PESAR : grief, sorrow

afligido, -da *adj* : grief-stricken, sorrowful

afligir {35} *vt* **1** : to distress, to upset **2** : to afflict — **afligirse** *vr* : to grieve

aflojar *vt* **1** : to loosen, to slacken **2** *fam* : to pay up, to fork over — *vi* : to slacken, to ease up — **aflojarse** *vr* : to become loose, to slacken

afloramiento *nm* : outcropping, emergence

aflorar *vi* : to come to the surface, to emerge

afluencia *nf* **1** : flow, influx **2** : abundance, plenty

afluente *nm* : tributary

afluir {41} *vi* **1** : to flock ⟨la gente afluía a la frontera : people were flocking to the border⟩ **2** : to flow

aforismo *nm* : aphorism

aforo *nm* **1** : appraisal, assessment **2** : maximum capacity (of a theater, highway, etc.)

afortunado, -da *adj* : fortunate, lucky — **afortunadamente** *adv*

afrecho *nm* : bran, mash

afrenta *nf* : affront, insult

afrentar *vt* : to affront, to dishonor, to insult

africano, -na *adj & n* : African

afroamericano, -na *adj & n* : Afro-American

afrodisiaco *or* **afrodisíaco** *nm* : aphrodisiac

afrontamiento *nm* : confrontation

afrontar *vt* : to confront, to face up to

afrutado, -da *adj* : fruity

afuera *adv* **1** : out ⟨¡afuera! : get out!⟩ **2** : outside, outdoors

afueras *nfpl* ALEDAÑOS : outskirts

agachadiza *nf* : snipe (bird)

agachar *vt* : to lower (a part of the body) ⟨agachar la cabeza : to bow one's head⟩ — **agacharse** *vr* : to crouch, to stoop, to bend down

agalla *nf* **1** BRANQUIA : gill **2** **tener agallas** *fam* : to have guts, to have courage

agarradera *nf* ASA, ASIDERO : handle, grip

agarrado, -da *adj fam* : cheap, stingy

agarrar *vt* **1** : to grab, to grasp **2** : to catch, to take — *vi* **agarrar y** *fam* : to do (something) abruptly ⟨el día siguiente agarró y se fue : the next day he up and left⟩ — **agarrarse** *vr* **1** : to hold on, to cling **2** *fam* : to get into a fight ⟨se agarraron a golpes : they came to blows⟩

agarre *nm* : grip, grasp

agarrotarse *vr* **1** : to stiffen up **2** : to seize up

agasajar *vt* : to fête, to wine and dine

agasajo *nm* : lavish attention

ágata *nf* : agate

agave *nm* : agave

agazaparse *vr* **1** AGACHARSE : to crouch **2** : to hide

agencia *nf* : agency, office

agenciar *vt* : to obtain, to procure — **agenciarse** *vr* : to manage, to get by

agenda *nf* **1** : agenda **2** : appointment book

agente *nmf* **1** : agent **2** **agente de viajes** : travel agent **3** **agente de bolsa** : stockbroker **4** **agente de tráfico** : traffic officer

agigantado, -da *adj* GIGANTESCO : gigantic

agigantar *vt* **1** : to increase greatly, to enlarge **2** : to exaggerate

ágil *adj* **1** : agile, nimble **2** : sharp, lively (of a response, etc.) — **ágilmente** *adv*

agilidad *nf* : agility, nimbleness

agilizar {21} *vt* ACELERAR : to expedite, to speed up

agitación *nf, pl* **-ciones 1** : agitation **2** NERVIOSISMO : nervousness

agitado, -da *adj* **1** : agitated, excited **2** : choppy, rough, turbulent

agitador, -dora *n* PROVOCADOR : agitator

agitar *vt* **1** : to agitate, to shake **2** : to wave, to flap **3** : to stir up — **agitarse** *vr* **1** : to toss about, to flap around **2** : to get upset

aglomeración *nf, pl* **-ciones 1** : conglomeration, mass **2** GENTÍO : crowd

aglomerar *vt* : to cluster, to amass — **aglomerarse** *vr* : to crowd together

aglutinar *vt* : to bring together, to bind

agnóstico, -ca *adj & n* : agnostic

agobiado, -da *adj* : weary, worn-out, weighted-down

agobiante *adj* **1** : exhausting, overwhelming **2** : stifling, oppressive

agobiar *vt* **1** OPRIMIR : to oppress, to burden **2** ABRUMAR : to overwhelm **3** : to wear out, to exhaust

agonía *nf* : agony, death throes

agonizante *adj* : dying

agonizar {21} *vi* **1** : to be dying **2** : to be in agony **3** : to dim, to fade

agorero, -ra *adj* : ominous

agostar *vt* **1** : to parch **2** : to wither — **agostarse** *vr*

agosto *nm* **1** : August **2 hacer uno su agosto** : to make a fortune, to make a killing

agotado, -da *adj* **1** : exhausted, used up **2** : sold out **3** FATIGADO : worn-out, tired

agotador, -dora *adj* : exhausting

agotamiento *nm* FATIGA : exhaustion

agotar *vt* **1** : to exhaust, to use up **2** : to weary, to wear out — **agotarse** *vr*

agraciado[1], **-da** *adj* **1** : attractive **2** : fortunate

agraciado[2], **-da** *n* : winner

agradable *adj* GRATO, PLACENTERO : pleasant, agreeable — **agradablemente** *adv*

agradar *vi* : to be pleasing ⟨nos agradó mucho el resultado : we were very pleased with the result⟩

agradecer {53} *vt* **1** : to be grateful for **2** : to thank

agradecido, -da *adj* : grateful, thankful

agradecimiento *nm* : gratitude, thankfulness

agrado *nm* **1** GUSTO : taste, liking ⟨no es de su agrado : it's not to his liking⟩ **2** : graciousness, agreeableness **3 con ~** : with pleasure, willingly ⟨lo haré con agrado : I will be happy to do it⟩

agrandar *vt* **1** : to exaggerate **2** : to enlarge — **agrandarse** *vr*

agrario, -ria *adj* : agrarian, agricultural

agravación *nf, pl* **-ciones** : aggravation, worsening

agravante *adj* : aggravating

agravar *vt* **1** : to increase (weight), to make heavier **2** EMPEORAR : to aggravate, to worsen — **agravarse** *vr*

agraviar *vt* INJURIAR, OFENDER : to offend, to insult

agravio *nm* INJURIA : affront, offense, insult

agredir {1} *vt* : to assail, to attack

agregado[1], **-da** *n* **1** : attaché **2** : assistant professor

agregado[2] *nm* **1** : aggregate **2** AÑADIDURA : addition, something added

agregar {52} *vt* **1** AÑADIR : to add, to attach **2** : to appoint — **agregarse** *vr* : to join

agresión *nf, pl* **-siones 1** : aggression **2** ATAQUE : attack

agresividad *nf* : aggressiveness, aggression

agresivo, -va *adj* : aggressive — **agresivamente** *adv*

agresor[1], **-sora** *adj* : hostile, attacking

agresor[2], **-sora** *n* **1** : aggressor **2** : assailant, attacker

agreste *adj* **1** CAMPESTRE : rural **2** : wild, untamed

agriar *vt* **1** : to sour, to make sour **2** : to embitter — **agriarse** *vr* : to turn sour

agrícola *adj* : agricultural

agricultor, -tora *n* : farmer, grower

agricultura *nf* : agriculture, farming

agridulce *adj* **1** : bittersweet **2** : sweet-and-sour

agrietar *vt* : to crack — **agrietarse** *vr* **1** : to crack **2** : to chap

agrimensor, -sora *n* : surveyor

agrimensura *nf* : surveying

agrio, agria *adj* **1** ÁCIDO : sour **2** : caustic, acrimonious

agriparse *vr* : to catch the flu

agroindustria *nf* : agribusiness

agronomía *nf* : agronomy

agropecuario, -ria *adj* : pertaining to livestock and agriculture

agrupación *nf, pl* **-ciones** GRUPO : group, association

agrupamiento *nm* : grouping, concentration

agrupar *vt* : to group together

agua *nf* **1** : water **2 agua oxigenada** : hydrogen peroxide **3 aguas negras** *or* **aguas residuales** : sewage **4 como agua para chocolate** *Mex fam* : furious **5 echar aguas** *Mex fam* : to keep an eye out, to be on the lookout

aguacate *nm* : avocado

aguacero *nm* : shower, downpour

aguado, -da *adj* **1** DILUIDO : watered-down, diluted **2** *CA, Col, Mex fam* : soft, flabby **3** *Mex, Peru fam* : dull, boring

aguafiestas *nmfs & pl* : killjoy, stick-in-the-mud, spoilsport

aguafuerte *nm* : etching

aguamanil *nm* : ewer, pitcher

aguanieve *nf* : sleet ⟨caer aguanieve : to be sleeting⟩

aguantar *vt* **1** SOPORTAR : to bear, to tolerate, to withstand **2** : to hold **3 aguantar las ganas** : to resist an urge ⟨no pude aguantar las ganas de reír : I couldn't keep myself from laughing⟩ — *vi* : to hold out, to last — **aguantarse** *vr* **1** : to resign oneself **2** : to restrain oneself

aguante *nm* **1** TOLERANCIA : tolerance, patience **2** RESISTENCIA : endurance, strength

aguar {10} *vt* **1** : to water down, to dilute **2 aguar la fiesta** *fam* : to spoil the party

aguardar *vt* ESPERAR : to wait for, to await — *vi* : to be in store

aguardiente *nm* : clear brandy

aguarrás *nm* : turpentine

agudeza *nf* **1** : keenness, sharpness **2** : shrillness **3** : witticism

agudizar {21} *vt* : to intensify, to heighten

agudo, -da *adj* **1** : acute, sharp **2** : shrill, high-pitched **3** PERSPICAZ : clever, shrewd

agüero *nm* AUGURIO, PRESAGIO : augury, omen

aguijón *nm, pl* **-jones 1** : stinger (of a bee, etc.) **2** : goad

aguijonear *vt* : to goad
águila *nf* **1** : eagle **2 águila o sol** *Mex* : heads or tails
aguileño, -ña *adj* : aquiline
aguilera *nf* : aerie, eagle's nest
aguilón *nm, pl* **-lones** : gable
aguinaldo *nm* **1** : Christmas bonus, year-end bonus **2** *PRi, Ven* : Christmas carol
agüitarse *vr Mex fam* : to have the blues, to feel discouraged
aguja *nf* **1** : needle **2** : steeple, spire
agujerear *vt* : to make a hole in, to pierce
agujero *nm* **1** : hole **2 agujero negro** : black hole (in astronomy)
agujeta *nf* **1** *Mex* : shoelace **2 agujetas** *nfpl* : muscular soreness or stiffness
agusanado, -da *adj* : worm-eaten
aguzar {21} *vt* **1** : to sharpen ⟨aguzar el ingenio : to sharpen one's wits⟩ **2 aguzar el oído** : to prick up one's ears
ah *interj* : oh!
ahí *adv* **1** : there ⟨ahí está : there it is⟩ **2 por ~** : somewhere, thereabouts **3 de ahí que** : with the result that, so that
ahijado, -da *n* : godchild, godson *m*, goddaughter *f*
ahijar {5} *vt* : to adopt (a child)
ahínco *nm* : eagerness, zeal
ahogar {52} *vt* **1** : to drown **2** : to smother **3** : to choke back, to stifle — **ahogarse** *vr*
ahogo *nm* : breathlessness, suffocation
ahondar *vt* : to deepen — *vi* : to elaborate, to go into detail
ahora *adv* **1** : now **2 ahora mismo** : right now **3 hasta ~** : so far **4 por ~** : for the time being
ahorcar {72} *vt* : to hang, to kill by hanging — **ahorcarse** *vr*
ahorita *adv fam* : right now, right away
ahorquillado, -da *adj* : forked
ahorrador, -dora *adj* : thrifty
ahorrar *vt* **1** : to save (money) **2** : to spare, to conserve — *vi* : to save up — **ahorrarse** *vr* : to spare oneself
ahorrativo, -va *adj* : thrifty, frugal
ahorro *nm* : saving ⟨cuenta de ahorros : savings account⟩
ahuecar {72} *vt* **1** : to hollow out **2** : to cup (one's hands) **3** : to plump up, to fluff up
ahuizote *nm Mex fam* : annoying person, pain in the neck
ahumar {8} *vt* : to smoke, to cure
ahuyentar *vt* **1** : to scare away, to chase away **2** : to banish, to dispel ⟨ahuyentar las dudas : to dispel doubts⟩
airado, -da *adj* FURIOSO : angry, irate
airar {5} *vt* : to make angry, to anger
aire *nm* **1** : air **2 aire acondicionado** : air-conditioning **3 darse aires** : to give oneself airs
airear *vt* : to air, to air out — **airearse** *vr* : to get some fresh air
airoso, -sa *adj* **1** : elegant, graceful **2 salir airoso** : to come out winning
aislacionismo *nm* : isolationism
aislacionista *adj & nmf* : isolationist
aislado, -da *adj* : isolated, alone
aislador *nm* : insulator (part)
aislamiento *nm* **1** : isolation **2** : insulation
aislante *nm* : insulator, nonconductor
aislar {5} *vt* **1** : to isolate **2** : to insulate
ajado, -da *adj* **1** : worn, shabby **2** : wrinkled, crumpled
ajar *vt* : to wear out, to spoil
ajardinado, -da *adj* : landscaped
ajedrecista *nmf* : chess player
ajedrez *nm, pl* **-dreces** **1** : chess **2** : chess set
ajeno, -na *adj* **1** : alien **2** : of another, of others ⟨propiedad ajena : somebody else's property⟩ **3 ~ a** : foreign to **4 ~ de** : devoid of, free from
ajetreado, -da *adj* : hectic, busy
ajetrearse *vr* : to bustle about, to rush around
ajetreo *nm* : hustle and bustle, fuss
ají *nm, pl* **ajíes** : chili pepper
ajo *nm* : garlic
ajonjolí *nm, pl* **-líes** : sesame
ajuar *nm* : trousseau
ajustable *adj* : adjustable
ajustado, -da *adj* **1** CEÑIDO : tight, tight-fitting **2** : close, tight ⟨una ajustada victoria : a close victory⟩
ajustar *vt* **1** : to adjust, to adapt **2** : to take in (clothing) **3** : to settle, to resolve — **ajustarse** *vr* : to fit, to conform
ajuste *nm* **1** : adjustment **2** : tightening
ajusticiar *vt* EJECUTAR : to execute, to put to death
al *prep* (contraction of a and el) → **a**[2]
ala *nf* **1** : wing **2** : brim (of a hat)
Alá *nm* : Allah
alabanza *nf* ELOGIO : praise
alabar *vt* : to praise — **alabarse** *vr* : to boast
alabastro *nm* : alabaster
alabear *vt* : to warp — **alabearse** *vr*
alabeo *nm* : warp, warping
alacena *nf* : cupboard, larder
alacrán *nm, pl* **-cranes** ESCORPIÓN : scorpion
alado, -da *adj* : winged
alambique *nm* : still (to distill alcohol)
alambre *nm* **1** : wire **2 alambre de púas** : barbed wire
alameda *nf* **1** : poplar grove **2** : tree-lined avenue
álamo *nm* **1** : poplar **2 álamo temblón** : aspen
alar *nm* : eaves *pl*
alarde *nm* **1** : show, display **2 hacer alarde de** : to make show of, to boast about
alardear *vi* PRESUMIR : to boast, to brag
alargado, -da *adj* : elongated, slender
alargamiento *nm* : lengthening, extension, elongation
alargar {52} *vt* **1** : to extend, to lengthen **2** PROLONGAR : to prolong — **alargarse** *vr*

alarido *nm* : howl, shriek
alarma *nf* : alarm
alarmante *adj* : alarming — **alarmantemente** *adv*
alarmar *vt* : to alarm
alazán *nm, pl* **-zanes** : sorrel (color or animal)
alba *nf* AMANECER : dawn, daybreak
albacea *nmf* TESTAMENTARIO : executor, executrix *f*
albahaca *nf* : basil
albanés, -nesa *adj & n, mpl* **-neses** : Albanian
albañil *nmf* : bricklayer, mason
albañilería *nf* : bricklaying, masonry
albaricoque *nm* : apricot
albatros *nm* : albatross
albedrío *nm* : will ⟨libre albedrío : free will⟩
alberca *nf* **1** : reservoir, tank **2** *Mex* : swimming pool
albergar {52} *vt* ALOJAR : to house, to lodge, to shelter
albergue *nm* **1** : shelter, refuge **2** : hostel
albino, -na *adj & n* : albino — **albinismo** *nm*
albóndiga *nf* : meatball
albor *nm* **1** : dawning, beginning **2** BLANCURA : whiteness
alborada *nf* : dawn
alborear *v impers* : to dawn
alborotado, -da *adj* **1** : excited, agitated **2** : rowdy, unruly
alborotador[1]**, -dora** *adj* **1** : noisy, boisterous **2** : rowdy, unruly
alborotador[2]**, -dora** *n* : agitator, troublemaker, rioter
alborotar *vt* **1** : to excite, to agitate **2** : to incite, to stir up — **alborotarse** *vr* **1** : to get excited **2** : to riot
alboroto *nm* **1** : disturbance, ruckus **2** MOTÍN : riot
alborozado, -da *adj* : jubilant
alborozar {21} *vt* : to gladden, to cheer
alborozo *nm* : joy, elation
álbum *nm* : album ⟨álbum de recortes : scrapbook⟩
albúmina *nf* : albumin
albur *nm* **1** : chance, risk **2** *Mex* : pun
alca *nf* : auk
alcachofa *nf* : artichoke
alcahuete, -ta *n* CHISMOSO : gossip
alcaide *nm* : warden (in a prison)
alcalde, -desa *n* : mayor
alcaldía *nf* **1** : mayoralty **2** AYUNTAMIENTO : city hall
álcali *nm* : alkali
alcalino, -na *adj* : alkaline — **alcalinidad** *nf*
alcance *nm* **1** : reach **2** : range, scope
alcancía *nf* **1** : piggy bank, money box **2** : collection box (for alms, etc.)
alcanfor *nm* : camphor
alcantarilla *nf* CLOACA : sewer, drain
alcanzar {21} *vt* **1** : to reach **2** : to catch up with **3** LOGRAR : to achieve, to attain — *vi* **1** DAR : to suffice, to be enough **2 ~ a** : to manage to
alcaparra *nf* : caper
alcapurria *nf PRi* : stuffed fritter made with taro and green banana
alcaravea *nf* : caraway
alcatraz *nm, pl* **-traces** : gannet
alcázar *nm* : fortress, castle
alce[1]**, etc.** → **alzar**
alce[2] *nm* : moose, European elk
alcoba *nf* : bedroom
alcohol *nm* : alcohol
alcohólico, -ca *adj & n* : alcoholic
alcoholismo *nm* : alcoholism
alcoholizarse {21} *vr* : to become an alcoholic
alcornoque *nm* **1** : cork oak **2** *fam* : idiot, fool
alcurnia *nf* : ancestry, lineage
aldaba *nf* : door knocker
aldea *nf* : village
aldeano[1]**, -na** *adj* : village, rustic
aldeano[2]**, -na** *n* : villager
aleación *nf, pl* **-ciones** : alloy
alear *vt* : to alloy
aleatorio, -ria *adj* : random, fortuitous — **aleatoriamente** *adv*
alebrestar *vt* : to excite, to make nervous — **alebrestarse** *vr*
aledaño, -ña *adj* : bordering, neighboring
aledaños *nmpl* AFUERAS : outskirts, surrounding area
alegar {52} *vt* : to assert, to allege — *vi* DISCUTIR : to argue
alegato *nm* **1** : allegation, claim **2** *Mex* : argument, summation (in law) **3** : argument, dispute
alegoría *nf* : allegory
alegórico, -ca *adj* : allegorical
alegrar *vt* : to make happy, to cheer up — **alegrarse** *vr* : to be glad, to rejoice
alegre *adj* **1** : glad, cheerful **2** : colorful, bright **3** *fam* : tipsy
alegremente *adv* : happily, cheerfully
alegría *nf* : joy, cheer, happiness
alejado, -da *adj* : remote
alejamiento *nm* **1** : removal, separation **2** : estrangement
alejar *vt* **1** : to remove, to move away **2** : to estrange, to alienate — **alejarse** *vr* **1** : to move away, to stray **2** : to drift apart
alelado, -da *adj* **1** : bewildered, stupefied **2** : foolish, stupid
aleluya *interj* : hallelujah!, alleluia!
alemán[1]**, -mana** *adj & n, mpl* **-manes** : German
alemán[2] *nm* : German (language)
alentador, -dora *adj* : encouraging
alentar {55} *vt* : to encourage, to inspire — *vi* : to breathe
alerce *nm* : larch
alérgeno *nm* : allergen
alergia *nf* : allergy
alérgico, -ca *adj* : allergic
alero *nm* **1** : eaves *pl* **2** : forward (in basketball)

alerón *nm, pl* **-rones** : aileron

alerta[1] *adv* : on the alert

alerta[2] *adj & nf* : alert

alertar *vt* : to alert

aleta *nf* **1** : fin **2** : flipper **3** : small wing

aletargado, -da *adj* : lethargic, sluggish, torpid

aletargarse {52} *vr* : to feel drowsy, to become lethargic

aletear *vi* : to flutter, to flap one's wings

aleteo *nm* : flapping, flutter

alevín *nm, pl* **-vines** **1** : fry, young fish **2** PRINCIPIANTE : beginner

alevosía *nf* **1** : treachery **2** : premeditation

alevoso, -sa *adj* : treacherous

alfabético, -ca *adj* : alphabetical — **alfabéticamente** *adv*

alfabetismo *nm* : literacy

alfabetizado, -da *adj* : literate

alfabetizar {21} *vt* : to alphabetize

alfabeto *nm* : alphabet

alfalfa *nf* : alfalfa

alfanje *nm* : cutlass, scimitar

alfarería *nf* : pottery

alfarero, -ra *n* : potter

alféizar *nm* : sill, windowsill

alfeñique *nm fam* : wimp, weakling

alférez *nmf, pl* **-reces** **1** : second lieutenant **2** : ensign

alfil *nm* : bishop (in chess)

alfiler *nm* **1** : pin **2** BROCHE : brooch

alfiletero *nm* : pincushion

alfombra *nf* : carpet, rug

alfombrado *nm* : carpeting

alfombrar *vt* : to carpet

alfombrilla *nf* : small rug, mat

alforfón *nm, pl* **-fones** : buckwheat

alforja *nf* : saddlebag

alforza *nf* : pleat, tuck

alga *nf* **1** : aquatic plant, alga **2** : seaweed

algarabía *nf* **1** : gibberish, babble **2** : hubbub, uproar

álgebra *nf* : algebra

algebraico, -ca *adj* : algebraic

álgido, -da *adj* **1** : critical, decisive **2** : icy cold

algo[1] *adv* : somewhat, rather <es simpático, pero algo tacaño : he's nice but rather stingy>

algo[2] *pron* **1** : something **2 ~ de** : some, a little <tengo algo de dinero : I've got some money>

algodón *nm, pl* **-dones** : cotton

algoritmo *nm* : algorithm

alguacil *nm* : constable

alguien *pron* : somebody, someone

alguno[1], **-na** *adj* (**algún** *before masculine singular nouns*) **1** : some, any <algún día : someday, one day> **2** (*in negative constructions*) : not any, not at all <no tengo noticia alguna : I have no news at all> **3 algunas veces** : sometimes

alguno[2], **-na** *pron* **1** : one, someone, somebody <alguno de ellos : one of them> **2 algunos, -nas** *pron pl* : some, a few <algunos quieren trabajar : some want to work>

alhaja *nf* : jewel, gem

alhajar *vt* : to adorn with jewels

alharaca *nf* : fuss

alhelí *nm* : wallflower

aliado[1], **-da** *adj* : allied

aliado[2], **-da** *n* : ally

alianza *nf* : alliance

aliarse {85} *vr* : to form an alliance, to ally oneself

alias *adv & nm* : alias

alicaído, -da *adj* : depressed, discouraged

alicates *nmpl* PINZAS : pliers

aliciente *nm* **1** INCENTIVO : incentive **2** ATRACCIÓN : attraction

alienación *nf, pl* **-ciones** : alienation, derangement

alienar *vt* ENAJENAR : to alienate

aliento *nm* **1** : breath **2** : courage, strength **3 dar aliento a** : to encourage

aligerar *vt* **1** : to lighten **2** ACELERAR : to hasten, to quicken

alijo *nm* : cache, consignment (of contraband)

alimaña *nf* : pest, vermin

alimentación *nf, pl* **-ciones** NUTRICIÓN : nutrition, nourishment

alimentar *vt* **1** NUTRIR : to feed, to nourish **2** MANTENER : to support (a family) **3** FOMENTAR : to nurture, to foster — **alimentarse** *vr* **~ con** : to live on

alimentario, -ria → **alimenticio**

alimenticio, -cia *adj* **1** : nutritional, food, dietary **2** : nutritious, nourishing

alimento *nm* : food, nourishment

aliñar *vt* **1** : to dress (salad) **2** CONDIMENTAR : to season

alineación *nf, pl* **-ciones** **1** : alignment **2** : lineup (in sports)

alineamiento *nm* : alignment

alinear *vt* **1** : to align **2** : to line up — **alinearse** *vr* **1** : to fall in, to line up **2 ~ con** : to align oneself with

aliño *nm* : seasoning, dressing

alipús *nm, pl* **-puses** *Mex fam* : booze, drink

alisar *vt* : to smooth

aliso *nm* : alder

alistamiento *nm* : enlistment, recruitment

alistar *vt* **1** : to recruit **2** : to make ready — **alistarse** *vr* : to join up, to enlist

aliteración *nf, pl* **-ciones** : alliteration

aliviar *vt* MITIGAR : to relieve, to alleviate, to soothe — **aliviarse** *vr* : to recover, to get better

alivio *nm* : relief

aljaba *nf* : quiver (for arrows)

aljibe *nm* : cistern, well

allá *adv* **1** : there, over there **2 más allá** : farther away **3 más allá de** : beyond **4 allá tú** : that's up to you

allanamiento *nm* **1 :** (police) raid **2 allanamiento de morada :** breaking and entering

allanar *vt* **1 :** to raid, to search **2 :** to resolve, to solve **3 :** to smooth, to level out

allegado[1], **-da** *adj* : close, intimate

allegado[2], **-da** *n* : close friend, relation ⟨parientes y allegados : friends and relations⟩

allegar {52} *vt* : to gather, to collect

allende[1] *adv* : beyond, on the other side

allende[2] *prep* : beyond ⟨allende las montañas : beyond the mountains⟩

allí *adv* : there, over there ⟨allí mismo : right there⟩ ⟨hasta allí : up to that point⟩

alma *nf* **1 :** soul **2 :** person, human being **3 no tener alma :** to be pitiless **4 tener el alma en un hilo :** to have one's heart in one's mouth

almacén *nm, pl* **-cenes 1** BODEGA : warehouse, storehouse **2** TIENDA : shop, store **3 gran almacén** *Spain* : department store

almacenaje → **almacenamiento**

almacenamiento *nm* : storage ⟨almacenamiento de datos : data storage⟩

almacenar *vt* : to store, to put in storage

almacenero, -ra *n* : shopkeeper

almacenista *nm* MAYORISTA : wholesaler

almádena *nf* : sledgehammer

almanaque *nm* : almanac

almeja *nf* : clam

almendra *nf* **1 :** almond **2 :** kernel

almendro *nm* : almond tree

almiar *nm* : haystack

almíbar *nm* : syrup

almidón *nm, pl* **-dones** : starch

almidonar *vt* : to starch

alminar *nm* MINARETE : minaret

almirante *nm* : admiral

almizcle *nm* : musk

almohada *nf* : pillow

almohadilla *nf* **1 :** small pillow, cushion **2 :** bag, base (in baseball)

almohadón *nm, pl* **-dones** : bolster, cushion

almohazar {21} *vt* : to curry (a horse)

almoneda *nf* SUBASTA : auction

almorranas *nfpl* HEMORROIDES : hemorrhoids, piles

almorzar {36} *vi* : to have lunch — *vt* : to have for lunch

almuerzo *nm* : lunch

alocado, -da *adj* **1 :** crazy **2 :** wild, reckless **3 :** silly, scatterbrained

alocución *nf, pl* **-ciones** : speech, address

áloe *or* **aloe** *nm* : aloe

alojamiento *nm* : lodging, accommodations *pl*

alojar *vt* ALBERGAR : to house, to lodge — **alojarse** *vr* : to lodge, to room

alondra *nf* : lark, skylark

alpaca *nf* : alpaca

alpinismo *nm* : mountain climbing, mountaineering

alpinista *nmf* : mountain climber

alpino, -na *adj* : Alpine, alpine

alpiste *nm* : birdseed

alquilar *vt* ARRENDAR : to rent, to lease

alquiler *nm* ARRENDAMIENTO : rent, rental

alquimia *nf* : alchemy

alquimista *nmf* : alchemist

alquitrán *nm, pl* **-tranes** BREA : tar

alquitranar *vt* : to tar, to cover with tar

alrededor[1] *adv* **1 :** around, about ⟨todo temblaba alrededor : all around things were shaking⟩ **2 ~ de :** around, approximately ⟨alrededor de quince personas : around fifteen people⟩

alrededor[2] *prep* **~ de** : around, about ⟨corrió alrededor de la casa : she ran around the house⟩ ⟨llegaré alrededor de diciembre : I will get there around December⟩

alrededores *nmpl* ALEDAÑOS : surroundings, outskirts

alta *nf* **1 :** admission, entry, enrollment **2 dar de alta :** to release, to discharge (a patient)

altanería *nf* ALTIVEZ, ARROGANCIA : arrogance, haughtiness

altanero, -ra *adj* ALTIVO, ARROGANTE : arrogant, haughty — **altaneramente** *adv*

altar *nm* : altar

altavoz *nm, pl* **-voces** ALTOPARLANTE : loudspeaker

alteración *nf, pl* **-ciones 1** MODIFICACIÓN : alteration, modification **2** PERTURBACIÓN : disturbance, disruption

alterado, -da *adj* : upset

alterar *vt* **1** MODIFICAR : to alter, to modify **2** PERTURBAR : to disturb, to disrupt — **alterarse** *vr* : to get upset, to get worked up

altercado *nm* DISCUSIÓN, DISPUTA : altercation, argument, dispute

alternador *nm* : alternator

alternancia *nf* : alternation, rotation

alternar *vi* **1 :** to alternate **2 :** to mix, to socialize — *vt* : to alternate — **alternarse** *vr* : to take turns

alternativa *nf* OPCIÓN : alternative, option

alternativo, -va *adj* **1 :** alternating **2 :** alternative — **alternativamente** *adv*

alterno, -na *adj* : alternate ⟨corriente alterna : alternating current⟩

alteza *nf* **1 :** loftiness, lofty height **2 Alteza :** Highness

altibajos *nmpl* **1 :** unevenness (of terrain) **2 :** ups and downs

altímetro *nm* : altimeter

altiplanicie *nf* → **altiplano**

altiplano *nm* : high plateau, upland

altisonante *adj* **1 :** pompous, affected (of language) **2** *Mex* : rude, obscene (of language)

altitud *nf* : altitude

altivez *nf, pl* **-veces** ALTANERÍA, ARROGANCIA : arrogance, haughtiness
altivo, -va *adj* ALTANERO, ARROGANTE : arrogant, haughty
alto[1] *adv* **1** : high **2** : loud, loudly
alto[2], **-ta** *adj* **1** : tall, high **2** : loud <en voz alta : aloud, out loud>
alto[3] *nm* **1** ALTURA : height, elevation **2** : stop, halt **3 altos** *nmpl* : upper floors
alto[4] *interj* : halt!, stop!
altoparlante *nm* ALTAVOZ : loudspeaker
altozano *nm* : hillock
altruismo *nm* : altruism
altruista[1] *adj* : altruistic
altruista[2] *nmf* : altruist
altura *nf* **1** : height **2** : altitude **3** : loftiness, nobleness **4 a la altura de** : near, up by <en la avenida San Antonio a la altura de la Calle Tres : on San Antonio Avenue up near Third Street> **5 a estas alturas** : at this point, at this stage of the game
alubia *nf* : kidney bean
alucinación *nf, pl* **-ciones** : hallucination
alucinante *adj* : hallucinatory
alucinar *vi* : to hallucinate
alucinógeno[1], **-na** *adj* : hallucinogenic
alucinógeno[2] *nm* : hallucinogen
alud *nm* AVALANCHA : avalanche, landslide
aludido, -da *n* **1** : person in question <el aludido : the aforesaid> **2 darse por aludido** : to take it personally
aludir *vi* : to allude, to refer
alumbrado *nm* ILUMINACIÓN : lighting
alumbramiento *nm* **1** : lighting **2** : childbirth
alumbrar *vt* **1** ILUMINAR : to light, to illuminate **2** : to give birth to
alumbre *nm* : alum
aluminio *nm* : aluminum
alumnado *nm* : student body
alumno, -na *n* **1** : pupil, student **2 ex-alumno, -na** : alumnus, alumna *f* **3 ex-alumnos, -nas** *npl* : alumni, alumnae *f*
alusión *nf, pl* **-siones** : allusion, reference
alusivo, -va *adj* **1** : allusive **2 ~ a** : in reference to, regarding
aluvión *nm, pl* **-viones** : flood, barrage
alza *nf* SUBIDA : rise <precios en alza : rising prices>
alzamiento *nm* LEVANTAMIENTO : uprising, insurrection
alzar {21} *vt* **1** ELEVAR, LEVANTAR : to lift, to raise **2** : to erect — **alzarse** *vr* LEVANTARSE : to rise up
ama *nf* → **amo**
amabilidad *nf* : kindness
amable *adj* : kind, nice — **amablemente** *adv*
amado[1], **-da** *adj* : beloved, darling
amado[2], **-da** *n* : sweetheart, loved one
amaestrar *vt* : to train (animals)
amafiarse *vr Mex fam* : to conspire, to be in cahoots
amagar {52} *vt* **1** : to show signs of (an illness, etc.) **2** : to threaten — *vi* **1** : to be imminent, to threaten **2** : to feint, to dissemble
amago *nm* **1** AMENAZA : threat **2** : sign, hint
amainar *vi* : to abate, to ease up, to die down
amalgama *nf* : amalgam
amalgamar *vt* : to amalgamate, to unite
amamantar *v* : to breast-feed, to nurse, to suckle
amanecer[1] {53} *v impers* **1** : to dawn **2** : to begin to show, to appear **3** : to wake up (in the morning)
amanecer[2] *nm* ALBA : dawn, daybreak
amanerado, -da *adj* : affected, mannered
amansar *vt* **1** : to tame **2** : to soothe, to calm down — **amansarse** *vr*
amante[1] *adj* : loving, fond
amante[2] *nmf* : lover
amañar *vt* : to rig, to fix, to tamper with — **amañarse** *vr* **amañárselas** : to manage
amaño *nm* **1** : skill, dexterity **2** : trick, ruse
amapola *nf* : poppy
amar *vt* : to love — **amarse** *vr*
amargado, -da *adj* : embittered, bitter
amargar {52} *vt* : to make bitter, to embitter — *vi* : to taste bitter
amargo[1], **-ga** *adj* : bitter — **amargamente** *adv*
amargo[2] *nm* : bitterness, tartness
amargura *nf* **1** : bitterness **2** : grief, sorrow
amarilis *nf* : amaryllis
amarillear *vi* : to yellow, to turn yellow
amarillento, -ta *adj* : yellowish
amarillismo *nm* : yellow journalism, sensationalism
amarillo[1], **-lla** *adj* : yellow
amarillo[2] *nm* : yellow
amarra *nf* **1** : mooring, mooring line **2 soltar las amarras de** : to loosen one's grip on
amarrar *vt* **1** : to moor (a boat) **2** ATAR : to fasten, to tie up, to tie down
amartillar *vt* : to cock (a gun)
amasar *vt* **1** : to amass **2** : to knead **3** : to mix, to prepare
amasijo *nm* : jumble, hodgepodge
amasio, -sia *n* : lover, paramour
amateur *adj & nmf* : amateur — **amateurismo** *nm*
amatista *nf* : amethyst
amatorio, -ria *adj* : amatory, sexual <poesía amatoria : love poems>
amazona *nf* **1** : Amazon (in mythology) **2** : horsewoman
amazónico, -ca *adj* : amazonian
ambages *nmpl* **sin ~** : without hesitation, straight to the point
ámbar *nm* **1** : amber **2 ámbar gris** : ambergris
ambición *nf, pl* **-ciones** : ambition
ambicionar *vt* : to aspire to, to seek

ambicioso, -sa *adj* : ambitious — **ambiciosamente** *adv*
ambidextro, -tra *adj* : ambidextrous
ambientación *nf, pl* **-ciones** : setting, atmosphere
ambiental *adj* : environmental — **ambientalmente** *adv*
ambientalista *nmf* : environmentalist
ambientar *vt* : to give atmosphere to, to set (in literature and drama) — **ambientarse** *vr* : to adjust, to get one's bearings
ambiente *nm* **1** : atmosphere **2** : environment **3** : surroundings *pl*
ambigüedad *nf* : ambiguity
ambiguo, -gua *adj* : ambiguous
ámbito *nm* : domain, field, area
ambivalencia *nf* : ambivalence
ambivalente *adj* : ambivalent
ambos, -bas *adj & pron* : both
ambulancia *nf* : ambulance
ambulante *adj* **1** : traveling, itinerant **2 vendedor ambulante** : street vendor
ameba *nf* : amoeba
amedrentar *vt* : to frighten, to intimidate — **amedrentarse** *vr*
amén *nm* **1** : amen **2 ~ de** : in addition to, besides **3 en un decir amén** : in an instant
amenaza *nf* : threat, menace
amenazador, -dora *adj* : threatening, menacing
amenazante → **amenazador**
amenazar {21} *v* : to threaten
amenguar {10} *vt* **1** : to diminish **2** : to belittle, to dishonor
amenidad *nf* : pleasantness, amenity
amenizar {21} *vt* **1** : to make pleasant **2** : to brighten up, to add life to
ameno, -na *adj* : agreeable, pleasant
amento *nm* : catkin
americano, -na *adj & n* : American
amerindio, -dia *adj & n* : Amerindian
ameritar *vt* MERECER : to deserve
ametralladora *nf* : machine gun
amianto *nm* : asbestos
amiba → **ameba**
amigable *adj* : friendly, amicable — **amigablemente** *adv*
amígdala *nf* : tonsil
amigdalitis *nf* : tonsilitis
amigo[1], **-ga** *adj* : friendly, close
amigo[2], **-ga** *n* : friend
amigote *nm* : crony, pal
amilanar *vt* **1** : to frighten **2** : to daunt, to discourage — **amilanarse** *vr* : to lose heart
aminoácido *nm* : amino acid
aminorar *vt* : to reduce, to lessen — *vi* : to diminish
amistad *nf* : friendship
amistoso, -sa *adj* : friendly — **amistosamente** *adv*
amnesia *nf* : amnesia
amnésico, -ca *adj & n* : amnesiac, amnesic
amnistía *nf* : amnesty
amnistiar {85} *vt* : to grant amnesty to
amo, ama *n* **1** : master *m,* mistress *f* **2** : owner, keeper (of an animal) **3 ama de casa** : housewife **4 ama de llaves** : housekeeper
amodorrado, -da *adj* : drowsy
amolar {19} *vt* **1** : to grind, to sharpen **2** : to pester, to annoy
amoldable *adj* : adaptable
amoldar *vt* **1** : to mold **2** : to adapt, to adjust — **amoldarse** *vr*
amonestación *nf, pl* **-ciones 1** APERCIBIMIENTO : admonition, warning **2 amonestaciones** *nfpl* : banns
amonestar *vt* APERCIBIR : to admonish, to warn
amoníaco *or* **amoniaco** *nm* : ammonia
amontonamiento *nm* : accumulation, piling up
amontonar *vt* **1** APILAR : to pile up, to heap up **2** : to collect, to gather **3** : to hoard — **amontonarse** *vr*
amor *nm* **1** : love **2** : loved one, beloved **3 amor propio** : self-esteem **4 hacer el amor** : to make love
amoral *adj* : amoral
amoratado, -da *adj* : black-and-blue, bruised, livid
amordazar {21} *vt* **1** : to gag, to muzzle **2** : to silence
amorfo, -fa *adj* : shapeless, amorphous
amorío *nm* : love affair, fling
amoroso, -sa *adj* **1** : loving, affectionate **2** : amorous <una mirada amorosa : an amorous glance> **3** : charming, cute — **amorosamente** *adv*
amortiguación *nf* : cushioning, absorption
amortiguador *nm* : shock absorber
amortiguar {10} *vt* : to soften (an impact)
amortizar {21} *vt* : to amortize, to pay off — **amortización** *nf*
amotinado[1], **-da** *adj* : rebellious, insurgent, mutinous
amotinado[2], **-da** *n* : rebel, insurgent, mutineer
amotinamiento *nm* : uprising, rebellion
amotinar *vt* : to incite (to riot), to agitate — **amotinarse** *vr* **1** : to riot, to rebel **2** : to mutiny
amparar *vt* : to safeguard, to protect — **ampararse** *vr* **1 ~ de** : to take shelter from **2 ~ en** : to have recourse to
amparo *nm* ACOGIDA, REFUGIO : protection, refuge
amperímetro *nm* : ammeter
amperio *nm* : ampere
ampliable *adj* : expandable, enlargeable, extendible
ampliación *nf, pl* **-ciones** : expansion, extension
ampliar {85} *vt* **1** : to expand, to extend **2** : to widen **3** : to enlarge (photographs) **4** : to elaborate on, to develop (ideas)
amplificador *nm* : amplifier
amplificar {72} *vt* : to amplify — **amplificación** *nf*

amplio, -plia *adj* : broad, wide, ample — **ampliamente** *adj*
amplitud *nf* **1** : breadth, extent **2** : spaciousness
ampolla *nf* **1** : blister **2** : vial, ampoule
ampollar *vt* : to blister — **ampollarse** *vr*
ampolleta *nf* **1** : small vial **2** : hourglass **3** *Chile* : light bulb
ampulosidad *nf* : pompousness, bombast
ampuloso, -sa *adj* GRANDILOCUENTE : pompous, bombastic — **ampulosamente** *adv*
amputar *vt* : to amputate — **amputación** *nf*
amueblar *vt* : to furnish
amuleto *nm* TALISMÁN : amulet, charm
amurallar *vt* : to wall in, to fortify
anacardo *nm* : cashew nut
anaconda *nf* : anaconda
anacrónico, -ca *adj* : anachronistic
anacronismo *nm* : anachronism
ánade *nmf* **1** : duck **2 ánade real** : mallard
anagrama *nm* : anagram
anal *adj* : anal
anales *nmpl* : annals
analfabetismo *nm* : illiteracy
analfabeto, -ta *adj & n* : illiterate
analgésico[1], -ca *adj* : analgesic, painkilling
analgésico[2] *nm* : painkiller, analgesic
análisis *nm* : analysis
analista *nmf* **1** : analyst **2** : annalist
analítico, -ca *adj* : analytical, analytic — **analíticamente** *adv*
analizar {21} *vt* : to analyze
analogía *nf* : analogy
analógico, -ca *adj* **1** : analogical **2** : analog ⟨computadora analógica : analog computer⟩
análogo, -ga *adj* : analogous, similar
ananá *or* **ananás** *nm, pl* **-nás** : pineapple
anaquel *nm* REPISA : shelf
anaranjado[1], -da *adj* NARANJA : orange-colored
anaranjado[2] *nm* NARANJA : orange (color)
anarquía *nf* : anarchy
anárquico, -ca *adj* : anarchic
anarquismo *nm* : anarchism
anarquista *adj & nmf* : anarchist
anatema *nm* : anathema
anatomía *nf* : anatomy — **anatomista** *nmf*
anatómico, -ca *adj* : anatomical — **anatómicamente** *adv*
anca *nf* **1** : haunch, hindquarter **2 ancas de rana** : frogs' legs
ancestral *adj* **1** : ancient, traditional **2** : ancestral
ancestro *nm* ASCENDIENTE : ancestor, forefather *m*
ancho[1], -cha *adj* **1** : wide, broad **2** : ample, loose-fitting
ancho[2] *nm* : width, breadth
anchoa *nf* : anchovy
anchura *nf* : width, breadth
ancianidad *nf* SENECTUD : old age
anciano[1], -na *adj* : aged, old, elderly
anciano[2], -na *n* : elderly person
ancla *nf* : anchor
ancladero → **anclaje**
anclaje *nm* : anchorage
anclar *v* FONDEAR : to anchor
andadas *nfpl* **1** : tracks **2 volver a las andadas** : to go back to one's old ways, to backslide
andador[1] *nm* **1** : walker, baby walker **2** *Mex* : walkway
andador[2], -dora *n* : walker, one who walks
andadura *nf* : course, journey ⟨su agotadora andadura al campeonato : his exhausting journey to the championship⟩
andaluz, -luza *adj & n, mpl* **-luces** : Andalusian
andamiaje *nm* **1** : scaffolding **2** ESTRUCTURA : structure, framework
andamio *nm* : scaffold
andanada *nf* **1** : volley, broadside **2 soltar una andanada a** : to reprimand
andanzas *nfpl* : adventures
andar[1] {6} *vi* **1** CAMINAR : to walk **2** IR : to go, to travel **3** FUNCIONAR : to run, to function ⟨el auto anda bien : the car runs well⟩ **4** : to ride ⟨andar a caballo : to ride on horseback⟩ **5** : to be ⟨anda sin dinero : he's broke⟩ — *vt* : to walk, to travel
andar[2] *nm* : walk, gait
andas *nfpl* : stand (for a coffin), bier
andén *nm, pl* **andenes 1** : (train) platform **2** *CA, Col* : sidewalk
andino, -na *adj* : Andean
andorrano, -na *adj & n* : Andorran
andrajos *nmpl* : rags, tatters
andrajoso, -sa *adj* : ragged, tattered
andrógino, -na *adj* : androgynous
andurriales *nmpl* : remote place
anea *nf* : cattail
anduvo, etc. → **andar**
anécdota *nf* : anecdote
anecdótico, -ca *adj* : anecdotal
anegar {52} *vt* **1** INUNDAR : to flood **2** AHOGAR : to drown **3** : to overwhelm — **anegarse** *vr* : to be flooded
anejo *nm* → **anexo[2]**
anemia *nf* : anemia
anémico, -ca *adj* : anemic
anémona *nf* : anemone
anestesia *nf* : anesthesia
anestesiar *vt* : to anesthetize
anestésico[1], -ca *adj* : anesthetic
anestésico[2] *nm* : anesthetic
anestesista *nmf* : anesthetist
aneurisma *nmf* : aneurysm
anexar *vt* : to annex, to attach
anexión *nf, pl* **-xiones** : annexation
anexo[1], -xa *adj* : attached, joined, annexed
anexo[2] *nm* **1** : annex **2** : supplement (to a book), appendix
anfetamina *nf* : amphetamine

anfibio[1], **-bia** *adj* : amphibious

anfibio[2] *nm* : amphibian

anfiteatro *nm* **1** : amphitheater **2** : lecture hall

anfitrión, -triona *n, mpl* **-triones** : host, hostess *f*

ánfora *nf* **1** : amphora **2** *Mex, Peru* : ballot box

ángel *nm* : angel

angelical *adj* : angelic, angelical

angélico, -ca *adj* → **angelical**

angina *nf* **1** *or* **angina de pecho** : angina **2** *Mex* : tonsil

anglicano, -na *adj & n* : Anglican

angloparlante[1] *adj* : English-speaking

angloparlante[2] *nmf* : English speaker

anglosajón, -jona *adj & n, mpl* **-jones** : Anglo-Saxon

angoleño, -ña *adj & n* : Angolan

angora *nf* : angora

angostar *vt* : to narrow — **angostarse** *vr*

angosto, -ta *adj* : narrow

angostura *nf* : narrowness

anguila *nf* : eel

angular *adj* : angular — **angularidad** *nf*

ángulo *nm* **1** : angle **2** : corner **3 ángulo muerto** : blind spot

anguloso, -sa *adj* : angular, sharp ⟨una cara angulosa : an angular face⟩ — **angulosidad** *nf*

angustia *nf* **1** CONGOJA : anguish, distress **2** : anxiety, worry

angustiar *vt* **1** : to anguish, to distress **2** : to worry — **angustiarse** *vr*

angustioso, -sa *adj* **1** : anguished, distressed **2** : distressing, worrisome

anhelante *adj* : yearning, longing

anhelar *vt* : to yearn for, to crave

anhelo *nm* : longing, yearning

anidar *vi* **1** : to nest **2** : to make one's home, to dwell — *vt* : to shelter

anillo *nm* SORTIJA : ring

ánima *n* ALMA : soul

animación *nf, pl* **-ciones 1** : animation **2** VIVEZA : liveliness

animado, -da *adj* **1** : animated, lively **2** : cheerful — **animadamente** *adv*

animador, -dora *n* **1** : (television) host **2** : cheerleader

animadversión *nf, pl* **-siones** ANIMOSIDAD : animosity, antagonism

animal[1] *adj* **1** : animal **2** ESTÚPIDO : stupid, idiotic **3** : rough, brutish

animal[2] *nm* : animal

animal[3] *nmf* **1** IDIOTA : idiot, fool **2** : brute, beastly person

animar *vt* **1** ALENTAR : to encourage, to inspire **2** : to animate, to enliven **3** : to brighten up, to cheer up — **animarse** *vr*

anímico, -ca *adj* : mental ⟨estado anímico : state of mind⟩

ánimo *nm* **1** ALMA : spirit, soul **2** : mood, spirits *pl* **3** : encouragement **4** PROPÓSITO : intention, purpose ⟨sociedad sin ánimo de lucro : nonprofit organization⟩ **5** : energy, vitality

animosidad *nf* ANIMADVERSIÓN : animosity, ill will

animoso, -sa *adj* : brave, spirited

aniñado, -da *adj* : childlike

aniquilación *nf* → **aniquilamiento**

aniquilamiento *nm* : annihilation, extermination

aniquilar *vt* **1** : to annihilate, to wipe out **2** : to overwhelm, to bring to one's knees — **aniquilarse** *vr*

anís *nm* **1** : anise **2 semilla de anís** : aniseed

aniversario *nm* : anniversary

ano *nm* : anus

anoche *adv* : last night

anochecer[1] {53} *v impers* : to get dark

anochecer[2] *nm* : dusk, nightfall

anodino, -na *adj* : insipid, dull

ánodo *nm* : anode

anomalía *nf* : anomaly

anómalo, -la *adj* : anomalous

anonadado, -da *adj* : dumbfounded, speechless

anonadar *vt* : to dumbfound, to stun

anonimato *nm* : anonymity

anónimo, -ma *adj* : anonymous — **anónimamente** *adv*

anorexia *nf* : anorexia

anoréxico, -ca *adj* : anorexic

anormal *adj* : abnormal — **anormalmente** *adv*

anormalidad *nf* : abnormality

anotación *nf, pl* **-ciones 1** : annotation, note **2** : scoring (in sports) ⟨lograron una anotación : they managed to score a goal⟩

anotar *vt* **1** : to annotate **2** APUNTAR, ESCRIBIR : to write down, to jot down **3** : to score (in sports) — *vi* : to score

anquilosado, -da *adj* **1** : stiff-jointed **2** : stagnated, stale

anquilosamiento *nm* **1** : stiffness (of joints) **2** : stagnation, paralysis

anquilosarse *vr* **1** : to stagnate **2** : to become stiff or paralyzed

anquilostoma *nm* : hookworm

ánsar *nm* : goose

ansarino *nm* : gosling

ansia *nf* **1** INQUIETUD : apprehensiveness, uneasiness **2** ANGUSTIA : anguish, distress **3** ANHELO : longing, yearning

ansiar {85} *vt* : to long for, to yearn for

ansiedad *nf* : anxiety

ansioso, -sa *adj* **1** : anxious, worried **2** : eager — **ansiosamente** *adv*

antagónico, -ca *adj* : conflicting, opposing

antagonismo *nm* : antagonism

antagonista[1] *adj* : antagonistic

antagonista[2] *nmf* : antagonist, opponent

antagonizar {21} *vt* : to antagonize

antaño *adv* : yesteryear, long ago

antártico, -ca *adj* **1** : antarctic **2 círculo antártico** : antarctic circle

ante[1] *nm* **1** : elk, moose **2** : suede

ante[2] *prep* **1** : before, in front of **2** : considering, in view of **3 ante todo** : first and foremost, above all

anteanoche *adv* : the night before last

anteayer *adv* : the day before yesterday

antebrazo *nm* : forearm

antecedente[1] *adj* : previous, prior

antecedente[2] *nm* **1** : precedent **2 antecedentes** *nmpl* : record, background

anteceder *v* : to precede

antecesor, -sora *n* **1** ANTEPASADO : ancestor **2** PREDECESOR : predecessor

antedicho, -cha *adj* : aforesaid, above

antelación *nf, pl* **-ciones 1** : advance notice **2 con ~** : in advance, beforehand

antemano *adv* **de ~** : in advance ⟨se lo agradezco de antemano : I thank you in advance⟩

antena *nf* : antenna

antenoche → **anteanoche**

anteojera *nf* **1** : eyeglass case **2 anteojeras** *nfpl* : blinders

anteojos *nmpl* GAFAS : glasses, eyeglasses

antepasado[1], **-da** *adj* : before last ⟨el domingo antepasado : the Sunday before last⟩

antepasado[2], **-da** *n* ANTECESOR : ancestor

antepecho *nm* **1** : guardrail **2** : ledge, sill

antepenúltimo, -ma *adj* : third from last

anteponer {60} *vt* **1** : to place before ⟨anteponer al interés de la nación el interés de la comunidad : to place the interests of the community before national interest⟩ **2** : to prefer

anteproyecto *nm* **1** : draft, proposal **2 anteproyecto de ley** : bill

antera *nf* : anther

anterior *adj* **1** : previous **2** : earlier ⟨tiempos anteriores : earlier times⟩ **3** : anterior, forward, front

anterioridad *nf* **1** : priority **2 con ~** : beforehand, in advance

anteriormente *adv* : previously, beforehand

antes *adv* **1** : before, earlier **2** : formerly, previously **3** : rather, sooner ⟨antes prefiero morir : I'd rather die⟩ **4 ~ de** : before, previous to ⟨antes de hoy : before today⟩ **5 antes que** : before ⟨antes que llegue Luis : before Luis arrives⟩ **6 cuanto antes** : as soon as possible **7 antes bien** : on the contrary

antesala *nf* **1** : anteroom, waiting room, lobby **2** : prelude, prologue

antiaborto, -ta *adj* : antiabortion

antiácido *nm* : antacid

antiadherente *adj* : nonstick

antiaéreo, -rea *adj* : antiaircraft

antiamericano, -na *adj* : anti-American

antibalas *adj* : bulletproof

antibiótico[1], **-ca** *adj* : antibiotic

antibiótico[2] *nm* : antibiotic

antichoque *adj* : shockproof

anticipación *nf, pl* **-ciones 1** : expectation, anticipation **2 con ~** : in advance

anticipado, -da *adj* **1** : advance, early **2 por ~** : in advance

anticipar *vt* **1** : to anticipate, to forestall, to deal with in advance **2** : to pay in advance — **anticiparse** *vr* **1** : to be early **2** ADELANTARSE : to get ahead

anticipo *nm* **1** : advance (payment) **2** : foretaste, preview

anticlerical *adj* : anticlerical

anticlimático, -ca : anticlimactic

anticlímax *nm* : anticlimax

anticomunismo *nm* : anticommunism

anticomunista *adj & nmf* : anticommunist

anticoncepción *nf, pl* **-ciones** : birth control, contraception

anticonceptivo *nm* : contraceptive

anticongelante *nm* : antifreeze

anticuado, -da *adj* : antiquated, outdated

anticuario[1], **-ria** *adj* : antique, antiquarian

anticuario[2], **-ria** *n* : antiquarian, antiquary

anticuario[3] *nm* : antique shop

anticuerpo *nm* : antibody

antidemocrático, -ca *adj* : antidemocratic

antideportivo, -va *adj* : unsportsmanlike

antidepresivo *nm* : antidepressant

antídoto *nm* : antidote

antidrogas *adj* : antidrug

antier → **anteayer**

antiestético, -ca *adj* : unsightly, unattractive

antifascista *adj & nmf* : antifascist

antifaz *nm, pl* **-faces** : mask

antifeminista *adj & nmf* : antifeminist

antífona *nf* : anthem

antígeno *nm* : antigen

antigualla *nf* **1** : antique **2** : relic, old thing

antiguamente *adv* **1** : formerly, once **2** : long ago

antigüedad *nf* **1** : antiquity **2** : seniority **3** : age ⟨con siglos de antigüedad : centuries-old⟩ **4 antigüedades** *nfpl* : antiques

antiguo, -gua *adj* **1** : ancient, old **2** : former **3** : old-fashioned ⟨a la antigua : in the old-fashioned way⟩ **4 Antiguo Testamento** : Old Testament

antihigiénico, -ca *adj* INSALUBRE : unhygienic, unsanitary

antihistamínico *nm* : antihistamine

antiimperialismo *nm* : anti-imperialism

antiimperialista *adj & nmf* : anti-imperialist

antiinflacionario, -ria *adj* : anti-inflationary

antiinflamatorio, -ria *adj* : anti-inflammatory

antillano[1], **-na** *adj* CARIBEÑO : Caribbean, West Indian

antillano[2], **-na** *n* : West Indian

antílope *nm* : antelope

antimilitarismo *nm* : antimilitarism

antimilitarista *adj & nmf* : antimilitarist

antimonio *nm* : antimony

antimonopolista *adj* : antimonopoly, antitrust

antinatural *adj* : unnatural, perverse

antipatía *nf* : aversion, dislike

antipático, -ca *adj* : obnoxious, unpleasant

antipatriótico, -ca *adj* : unpatriotic

antirrábico, -ca *adj* : antirabies ⟨vacuna antirrábica : rabies vaccine⟩

antirreglamentario, -ria *adj* **1** : unlawful, illegal **2** : foul (in sports)

antirrevolucionario, -ria *adj & n* : antirevolutionary

antirrobo, -ba *adj* : antitheft

antisemita *adj* : anti-Semitic

antisemitismo *nm* : anti-Semitism

antiséptico[1], -ca *adj* : antiseptic

antiséptico[2] *nm* : antiseptic

antisocial *adj* : antisocial

antitabaco *adj* : antismoking

antiterrorista *adj* : antiterrorist

antítesis *nf* : antithesis

antitoxina *nf* : antitoxin

antitranspirante *nm* : antiperspirant

antojadizo, -za *adj* CAPRICHOSO : capricious

antojarse *vr* **1** APETECER : to be appealing, to be desirable ⟨se me antoja un helado : I feel like having ice cream⟩ **2** : to seem, to appear ⟨los árboles se antojaban fantasmas : the trees seemed like ghosts⟩

antojitos *nmpl Mex* : traditional Mexican snack foods

antojo *nm* **1** CAPRICHO : whim **2** : craving

antología *nf* **1** : anthology **2 de ~** *fam* : fantastic, incredible

antónimo *nm* : antonym

antonomasia *nf* **por ~** : par excellence

antorcha *nf* : torch

antracita *nf* : anthracite

antro *nm* **1** : cave, den **2** : dive, seedy nightclub

antropofagia *nf* CANIBALISMO : cannibalism

antropófago[1], -ga *adj* : cannibalistic

antropófago[2], -ga *n* CANÍBAL : cannibal

antropoide *adj & nmf* : anthropoid

antropología *nf* : anthropology

antropológico, -ca *adj* : anthropological

antropólogo, -ga *n* : anthropologist

anual *adj* : annual, yearly — **anualmente** *adv*

anualidad *nf* : annuity

anuario *nm* : yearbook, annual

anudar *vt* : to knot, to tie in a knot — **anudarse** *vr*

anuencia *nf* : consent

anulación *nf, pl* **-ciones** : annulment, nullification

anular *vt* : to annul, to cancel

anunciador, -dora *n* → **anunciante**

anunciante *nmf* : advertiser

anunciar *vt* **1** : to announce **2** : to advertise

anuncio *nm* **1** : announcement **2** : advertisement, commercial

anzuelo *nm* **1** : fishhook **2 morder el anzuelo** : to take the bait

añadido *nm* : addition

añadidura *nf* **1** : additive, addition **2 por ~** : in addition, furthermore

añadir *vt* **1** AGREGAR : to add **2** AUMENTAR : to increase

añejar *vt* : to age, to ripen

añejo, -ja *adj* **1** : aged, vintage **2** : age-old, musty, stale

añicos *nmpl* : smithereens, bits ⟨hacer(se) añicos : to shatter⟩

añil *nm* **1** : indigo **2** : bluing

año *nm* **1** : year ⟨en el año 1990 : in (the year) 1990⟩ ⟨tiene diez años : she is ten years old⟩ **2** : grade ⟨cuarto año : fourth grade⟩ **3 año bisiesto** : leap year **4 año luz** : light-year **5 Año Nuevo** : New Year

añoranza *nf* : longing, yearning

añorar *vt* **1** DESEAR : to long for **2** : to grieve for, to miss — *vi* : to mourn, to grieve

añoso, -sa *adj* : aged, old

aorta *nf* : aorta

apabullante *adj* : overwhelming, crushing

apabullar *vt* : to overwhelm

apacentar {55} *vt* : to pasture, to put to pasture

apache *adj & nmf* : Apache

apachurrado, -da *adj fam* : depressed, down

apachurrar *vt* : to crush, to squash

apacible *adj* : gentle, mild, calm — **apaciblemente** *adv*

apaciguador, -dora *adj* : calming

apaciguamiento *nm* : appeasement

apaciguar {10} *vt* APLACAR : to appease, to pacify — **apaciguarse** *vr* : to calm down

apadrinar *vt* **1** : to be a godparent to **2** : to sponsor, to support

apagado, -da *adj* **1** : off, out ⟨la luz está apagada : the light is off⟩ **2** : dull, subdued

apagador *nm Mex* : switch

apagar {52} *vt* **1** : to turn off, to shut off **2** : to extinguish, to put out — **apagarse** *vr* **1** : to go out, to fade **2** : to wane, to die down

apagón *nm, pl* **-gones** : blackout (of power)

apalancamiento *nm* : leverage

apalancar {72} *vt* **1** : to jack up **2** : to pry open

apalear *vt* : to beat up, to thrash

apantallar *vt Mex* : to dazzle, to impress

apañar *vt* **1** : to seize, to grasp **2** : to repair, to mend — **apañarse** *vr* : to manage, to get along

apaño *nm fam* **1** : patch **2** HABILIDAD : skill, knack

apapachar *vt Mex fam* : to cuddle, to caress — **apapacharse** *vr*

aparador *nm* **1** : sideboard, cupboard **2** ESCAPARATE, VITRINA : shop window
aparato *nm* **1** : machine, appliance, apparatus ⟨aparato auditivo : hearing aid⟩ ⟨aparato de televisión : television set⟩ **2** : system ⟨aparato digestivo : digestive system⟩ **3** : display, ostentation ⟨sin aparato : without ceremony⟩ **4 aparatos** *nmpl* : braces (for the teeth)
aparatoso, -sa *adj* **1** : ostentatious **2** : spectacular
aparcamiento *nm Spain* **1** : parking **2** : parking lot
aparcar {72} *v Spain* : to park
aparcero, -ra *n* : sharecropper
aparear *vt* **1** : to mate (animals) **2** : to match up — **aparearse** *vr* : to mate
aparecer {53} *vi* **1** : to appear **2** PRESENTARSE : to show up **3** : to turn up, to be found — **aparecerse** *vr* : to appear
aparejado, -da *adj* **1 ir aparejado con** : to go hand in hand with **2 llevar aparejado** : to entail
aparejar *vt* **1** PREPARAR : to prepare, to make ready **2** : to harness (a horse) **3** : to fit out (a ship)
aparejo *nm* **1** : equipment, gear **2** : harness, saddle **3** : rig, rigging (of a ship)
aparentar *vt* **1** : to seem, to appear ⟨no aparentas tu edad : you don't look your age⟩ **2** FINGIR : to feign, to pretend
aparente *adj* **1** : apparent **2** : showy, striking — **aparentemente** *adv*
aparición *nf, pl* **-ciones** **1** : appearance **2** PUBLICACIÓN : publication, release **3** FANTASMA : apparition, vision
apariencia *nf* **1** ASPECTO : appearance, look **2 en ~** : seemingly, apparently
apartado *nm* **1** : section, paragraph **2 apartado postal** : post office box
apartamento *nm* DEPARTAMENTO : apartment
apartar *vt* **1** ALEJAR : to move away, to put at a distance **2** : to put aside, to set aside, to separate — **apartarse** *vr* **1** : to step aside, to move away **2** DESVIARSE : to stray
aparte[1] *adv* **1** : apart, aside ⟨modestia aparte : if I say so myself⟩ **2** : separately **3 ~ de** : apart from, besides
aparte[2] *adj* : separate, special
aparte[3] *nm* : aside (in theater)
apartheid *nm* : apartheid
apasionado, -da *adj* : passionate, enthusiastic — **apasionadamente** *adv*
apasionante *adj* : fascinating, exciting
apasionar *vt* : to enthuse, to excite — **apasionarse** *vr*
apatía *nf* : apathy
apático, -ca *adj* : apathetic
apearse *vr* **1** DESMONTAR : to dismount **2** : to get out of or off (a vehicle)
apedrear *vt* : to stone, to throw stones at
apegado, -da *adj* : attached, close, devoted ⟨es muy apegado a su familia : he is very devoted to his family⟩
apegarse {52} *vr* **~ a** : to become attached to, to grow fond of
apego *nm* AFICIÓN : attachment, fondness, inclination
apelación *nf, pl* **-ciones** : appeal (in court)
apelar *vi* **1** : to appeal **2 ~ a** : to resort to
apelativo *nm* APELLIDO : last name, surname
apellidarse *vr* : to have for a last name ⟨¿cómo se apellida? : what is your last name?⟩
apellido *nm* : last name, surname
apelotonar *vt* : to roll into a ball, to bundle up
apenar *vt* : to aggrieve, to sadden — **apenarse** *vr* **1** : to be saddened **2** : to become embarrassed
apenas[1] *adv* : hardly, scarcely
apenas[2] *conj* : as soon as
apéndice *nm* **1** : appendix **2** : appendage
apendicectomía *nf* : appendectomy
apendicitis *nf* : appendicitis
apercibimiento *nm* **1** : preparation **2** AMONESTACIÓN : warning
apercibir *vt* **1** DISPONER : to prepare, to make ready **2** AMONESTAR : to warn **3** OBSERVAR : to observe, to perceive — **apercibirse** *vr* **1** : to get ready **2 ~ de** : to notice
aperitivo *nm* **1** : appetizer **2** : aperitif
apero *nm* : tool, implement
apertura *nf* **1** : opening, aperture **2** : commencement, beginning **3** : openness
apesadumbrar *vt* : to distress, to sadden — **apesadumbrarse** *vr* : to be weighed down
apestar *vt* **1** : to infect with the plague **2** : to corrupt — *vi* : to stink
apestoso, -sa *adj* : stinking, foul
apetecer {53} *vt* **1** : to crave, to long for ⟨apeteció la fama : he longed for fame⟩ **2** : to appeal to ⟨me apetece un bistec : I feel like having a steak⟩ ⟨¿cuándo te apetece ir? : when do you want to go?⟩ — *vi* : to be appealing
apetecible *adj* : appetizing, appealing
apetito *nm* : appetite
apetitoso, -sa *adj* : appetizing
apiario *nm* : apiary
ápice *nm* **1** : apex, summit **2** PIZCA : bit, smidgen
apicultor, -tora *n* : beekeeper
apicultura *nf* : beekeeping
apilar *vt* AMONTONAR : to heap up, to pile up — **apilarse** *vr*
apiñado, -da *adj* : jammed, crowded
apiñar *vt* : to pack, to cram — **apiñarse** *vr* : to crowd together, to huddle
apio *nm* : celery
apisonadora *nf* : steamroller
apisonar *vt* : to pack down, to tamp
aplacamiento *nm* : appeasement
aplacar {72} *vt* APACIGUAR : to appease, to placate — **aplacarse** *vr* : to calm down

aplanadora *nf* : steamroller
aplanar *vt* : to flatten, to level
aplastante *adj* : crushing, overwhelming
aplastar *vt* : to crush, to squash
aplaudir *v* : to applaud
aplauso *nm* **1** : applause, clapping **2** : praise, acclaim
aplazamiento *nm* : postponement
aplazar {21} *vt* : to postpone, to defer
aplicable *adj* : applicable — **aplicabilidad** *nf*
aplicación *nf, pl* **-ciones 1** : application **2** : diligence, dedication
aplicado, -da *adj* : diligent, industrious
aplicador *nm* : applicator
aplicar {72} *vt* : to apply — **aplicarse** *vr* : to apply oneself
aplique *or* **apliqué** *nm* : appliqué
aplomar *vt* : to plumb, to make vertical
aplomo *nm* : aplomb, composure
apocado, -da *adj* : timid
apocalipsis *nms & pl* : apocalypse ⟨el Libro del Apocalipsis : the Book of Revelation⟩
apocalíptico, -ca *adj* : apocalyptic
apocamiento *nm* : timidity
apocarse {72} *vr* **1** : to shy away, to be intimidated **2** : to humble oneself, to sell oneself short
apócrifo, -fa *adj* : apocryphal
apodar *vt* : to nickname, to call — **apodarse** *vr*
apoderado, -da *n* : proxy, agent
apoderar *vt* : to authorize, to empower — **apoderarse** *vr* **~ de** : to seize, to take over
apodo *nm* SOBRENOMBRE : nickname
apogeo *nm* : acme, peak, zenith
apología *nf* : defense, apology
apoplejía *nf* : apoplexy, stroke
apoplético, -ca *adj* : apoplectic
aporrear *vt* : to bang on, to beat, to bludgeon
aportación *nf, pl* **-ciones** : contribution
aportar *vt* CONTRIBUIR : to contribute, to provide
aporte *nm* → **aportación**
apostador, -dora *n* : bettor, better
apostar {19} *v* : to bet, to wager ⟨apuesto que no viene : I bet he's not coming⟩
apostasía *nf* : apostasy
apóstata *nmf* : apostate
apostilla *nf* : note
apostillar *vt* : to annotate
apóstol *nm* : apostle
apostólico, -ca *adj* : apostolic
apóstrofe *nmf* : apostrophe
apostura *nf* : elegance, gracefulness
apoyacabezas *nms & pl* : headrest
apoyapiés *nms & pl* : footrest
apoyar *vt* **1** : to support, to back **2** : to lean, to rest — **apoyarse** *vr* **1 ~ en** : to lean on **2 ~ en** : to be based on, to rest on
apoyo *nm* : support, backing
apreciable *adj* : appreciable, substantial, considerable
apreciación *nf, pl* **-ciones 1** : appreciation **2** : appraisal, evaluation
apreciar *vt* **1** ESTIMAR : to appreciate, to value **2** EVALUAR : to appraise, to assess — **apreciarse** *vr* : to appreciate, to increase in value
aprecio *nm* **1** ESTIMO : esteem, appreciation **2** EVALUACIÓN : appraisal, assessment
aprehender *vt* **1** : to apprehend, to capture **2** : to conceive of, to grasp
aprehensión *nf, pl* **-siones** : apprehension, capture, arrest
apremiante *adj* : pressing, urgent
apremiar *vt* INSTAR : to pressure, to urge — *vi* URGIR : to be urgent ⟨el tiempo apremia : time is of the essence⟩
apremio *nm* : pressure, urgency
aprender *v* : to learn — **aprenderse** *vr*
aprendiz, -diza *n, mpl* **-dices** : apprentice, trainee
aprendizaje *nm* : apprenticeship
aprensión *nf, pl* **-siones** : apprehension, dread
aprensivo, -va *adj* : apprehensive, worried
apresamiento *nm* : seizure, capture
apresar *vt* : to capture, to seize
aprestar *vt* : to make ready, to prepare — **aprestarse** *vr* : to get ready
apresuradamente *adv* **1** : hurriedly **2** : hastily, too fast
apresurado, -da *adj* : hurried, in a rush
apresuramiento *nm* : hurry, haste
apresurar *vt* : to quicken, to speed up — **apresurarse** *vr* : to hurry up, to make haste
apretado, -da *adj* **1** : tight **2** *fam* : cheap, tightfisted — **apretadamente** *adv*
apretar {55} *vt* **1** : to press, to push (a button) **2** : to tighten **3** : to squeeze — *vi* **1** : to press, to push **2** : to fit tightly, to be too tight ⟨los zapatos me aprietan : my shoes are tight⟩
apretón *nm, pl* **-tones 1** : squeeze **2 apretón de manos** : handshake
apretujar *vt* : to squash, to squeeze — **apretujarse** *vr*
aprieto *nm* APURO : predicament, difficulty ⟨estar en un aprieto : to be in a fix⟩
aprisa *adv* : quickly, hurriedly
aprisionar *vt* **1** : to imprison **2** : to trap, to box in
aprobación *nf, pl* **-ciones** : approval, endorsement
aprobar {19} *vt* **1** : to approve of **2** : to pass (a law, an exam) — *vi* : to pass (in school)
aprobatorio, -ria *adj* : approving
apropiación *nf, pl* **-ciones** : appropriation
apropiado, -da *adj* : appropriate, proper, suitable — **apropiadamente** *adv*
apropiarse *vr* **~ de** : to take possession of, to appropriate
aprovechable *adj* : usable

aprovechado[1], -da *adj* **1** : diligent, hardworking **2** : pushy, opportunistic

aprovechado[2], -da *n* : pushy person, opportunist

aprovechamiento *nm* : use, exploitation

aprovechar *vt* : to take advantage of, to make good use of — *vi* **1** : to be of use **2** : to progress, to improve — **aprovecharse** *vr* **~ de** : to take advantage of, to exploit

aprovisionamiento *nm* : provisions *pl*, supplies *pl*

aprovisionar *vt* : to provide, to supply (with provisions)

aproximación *nf, pl* **-ciones** **1** : approximation, estimate **2** : rapprochement

aproximado, -da *adj* : approximate, estimated — **aproximadamente** *adv*

aproximar *vt* ACERCAR, ARRIMAR : to approximate, to bring closer — **aproximarse** *vr* ACERCARSE, ARRIMARSE : to approach, to move closer

aptitud *nf* : aptitude, capability

apto, -ta *adj* **1** : suitable, suited, fit **2** HÁBIL : capable, competent

apuesta *nf* : bet, wager

apuesto, -ta *adj* : elegant, good-looking

apuntador, -dora *n* : prompter

apuntalar *vt* : to prop up, to shore up

apuntar *vt* **1** : to aim, to point **2** ANOTAR : to write down, to jot down **3** INDICAR, SEÑALAR : to point to, to point out **4** : to prompt (in the theater) — *vi* **1** : to take aim **2** : to become evident — **apuntarse** *vr* **1** : to sign up, to enroll **2** : to score

apunte *nm* : note

apuñalar *vt* : to stab

apuradamente *adv* **1** : with difficulty **2** : hurriedly, hastily

apurado, -da *adj* **1** APRESURADO : rushed, pressured **2** : poor, needy **3** : difficult, awkward **4** : embarrassed

apurar *vt* **1** APRESURAR : to hurry, to rush **2** : to use up, to exhaust **3** : to trouble — **apurarse** *vr* **1** APRESURARSE : to hurry up **2** PREOCUPARSE : to worry

apuro *nm* **1** APRIETO : predicament, jam **2** : rush, hurry **3** : embarrassment

aquejar *vt* : to afflict

aquel, aquella *adj, mpl* **aquellos** : that, those

aquél, aquélla *pron, mpl* **aquéllos** **1** : that (one), those (ones) **2** : the former

aquello *pron* (*neuter*) : that, that matter, that business ⟨aquello fue algo serio : that was something serious⟩

aquí *adv* **1** : here **2** : now ⟨de aquí en adelante : from now on⟩ **3 por ~** : around here, hereabouts

aquiescencia *nf* : acquiescence, approval

aquietar *vt* : to allay, to calm — **aquietarse** *vr* : to calm down

aquilatar *vt* **1** : to assay **2** : to assess, to size up

ara *nf* **1** : altar **2 en aras de** : in the interests of, for the sake of

árabe[1] *adj & nmf* : Arab, Arabian

árabe[2] *nm* : Arabic (language)

arabesco *nm* : arabesque — **arabesco, -ca** *adj*

arábigo, -ga *adj* **1** : Arabic, Arabian **2 número arábigo** : Arabic numeral

arable *adj* : arable

arado *nm* : plow

aragonés, -nesa *adj & n, mpl* **-neses** : Aragonese

arancel *nm* : tariff, duty

arándano *nm* : blueberry

arandela *nf* : washer (for a faucet, etc.)

araña *nf* **1** : spider **2** : chandelier

arañar *v* : to scratch, to claw

arañazo *nm* : scratch

arar *v* : to plow

arbitraje *nm* **1** : arbitration **2** : refereeing (in sports)

arbitrar *v* **1** : to arbitrate **2** : to referee, to umpire

arbitrariedad *nf* **1** : arbitrariness **2** INJUSTICIA : injustice, wrong

arbitrario, -ria *adj* **1** : arbitrary **2** : unfair, unjust — **arbitrariamente** *adv*

arbitrio *nm* **1** ALBEDRÍO : will **2** JUICIO : judgment

árbitro, -tra *n* **1** : arbitrator, arbiter **2** : referee, umpire

árbol *nm* **1** : tree **2 árbol genealógico** : family tree

arbolado[1], -da *adj* : wooded

arbolado[2] *nm* : woodland

arboleda *nf* : grove, wood

arbóreo, -rea *adj* : arboreal

arbusto *nm* : shrub, bush, hedge

arca *nf* **1** : ark **2** : coffer, chest

arcada *nf* **1** : arcade, series of arches **2 arcadas** *nfpl* : retching ⟨hacer arcadas : to retch⟩

arcaico, -ca *adj* : archaic

arcángel *nm* : archangel

arcano, -na *adj* : arcane

arce *nm* : maple tree

arcén *nm, pl* **arcenes** : hard shoulder, berm

archidiócesis *nfs & pl* : archdiocese

archipiélago *nm* : archipelago

archivador *nm* : filing cabinet

archivar *vt* **1** : to file **2** : to archive

archivero, -ra *n* : archivist

archivista *nmf* : archivist

archivo *nm* **1** : file **2** : archive, archives *pl*

arcilla *nf* : clay

arco *nm* **1** : arch, archway **2** : bow (in archery) **3** : arc **4** : wicket (in croquet) **5** PORTERÍA : goal, goalposts *pl* **6 arco iris** : rainbow

arder *vi* **1** : to burn ⟨el bosque está ardiendo : the forest is in flames⟩ ⟨arder de ira : to burn with anger, to be seething⟩ **2** : to smart, to sting, to burn ⟨le ardía el estómago : he had heartburn⟩

ardid *nm* : scheme, ruse

ardiente *adj* **1** : burning **2** : ardent, passionate — **ardientemente** *adv*
ardilla *nf* **1** : squirrel **2** *or* **ardilla listada** : chipmunk
ardor *nm* **1** : heat **2** : passion, ardor
ardoroso, -sa *adj* : heated, impassioned
arduo, -dua *adj* : arduous, grueling — **arduamente** *adv*
área *nf* : area
arena *nf* **1** : sand ⟨arena movediza : quicksand⟩ **2** : arena
arenga *nf* : harangue, lecture
arengar {52} *vt* : to harangue, to lecture
arenilla *nf* **1** : fine sand **2 arenillas** *nfpl* : kidney stones
arenisca *nf* : sandstone
arenoso, -sa *adj* : sandy, gritty
arenque *nm* : herring
arepa *nf* : cornmeal bread
arete *nm* : earring
argamasa *nf* : mortar (cement)
argelino, -na *adj & n* : Algerian
argentino, -na *adj & n* : Argentinian, Argentine
argolla *nf* : hoop, ring
argón *nm* : argon
argot *nm* : slang
argucia *nf* : sophistry, subtlety
argüir {41} *vi* : to argue — *vt* **1** ARGUMENTAR : to contend, to argue **2** INFERIR : to deduce **3** PROBAR : to prove
argumentación *nf, pl* **-ciones** : line of reasoning, argument
argumentar *vt* : to argue, to contend
argumento *nm* **1** : argument, reasoning **2** : plot, story line
aria *nf* : aria
aridez *nf, pl* **-deces** : aridity, dryness
árido, -da *adj* : arid, dry
Aries *nmf* : Aries
ariete *nm* : battering ram
arisco, -ca *adj* : surly, sullen, unsociable
arista *nf* **1** : ridge, edge **2** : beard (of a plant) **3 aristas** *nfpl* : rough edges, complications, problems
aristocracia *nf* : aristocracy
aristócrata *nmf* : aristocrat
aristocrático, -ca *adj* : aristocratic
aritmética *nf* : arithmetic
aritmético, -ca *adj* : arithmetic, arithmetical — **aritméticamente** *adv*
arlequín *nm, pl* **-quines** : harlequin
arma *nf* **1** : weapon **2 armas** *nfpl* : armed forces **3 arma de fuego** : firearm
armada *nf* : navy, fleet
armadillo *nm* : armadillo
armado, -da *adj* **1** : armed **2** : assembled, put together **3** *PRi* : obstinate, stubborn
armador, -dora *n* : shipowner
armadura *nf* **1** : armor **2** ARMAZÓN : skeleton, framework
armamento *nm* : armament, arms *pl*, weaponry
armar *vt* **1** : to assemble, to put together **2** : to create, to cause ⟨armar un escándalo : to cause a scene⟩ **3** : to arm — **armarse** *vr* **armarse de valor** : to steel oneself
armario *nm* **1** CLÓSET, ROPERO : closet **2** ALACENA : cupboard
armatoste *nm fam* : monstrosity, contraption
armazón *nmf, pl* **-zones 1** ESQUELETO : framework, skeleton ⟨armazón de acero : steel framework⟩ **2** : frames *pl* (of eyeglasses)
armenio, -nia *adj & n* : Armenian
armería *nf* **1** : armory **2** : arms museum **3** : gunsmith's shop **4** : gunsmith's craft
armiño *nm* : ermine
armisticio *nm* : armistice
armonía *nf* : harmony
armónica *nf* : harmonica
armónico, -ca *adj* **1** : harmonic **2** : harmonious — **armónicamente** *adv*
armonioso, -sa *adj* : harmonious — **armoniosamente** *adv*
armonizar {21} *vt* **1** : to harmonize **2** : to reconcile — *vi* : to harmonize, to blend together
arnés *nm, pl* **arneses** : harness
aro *nm* **1** : hoop **2** : napkin ring **3** *Arg, Chile, Uru* : earring
aroma *nm* : aroma, scent
aromático, -ca *adj* : aromatic
arpa *nf* : harp
arpegio *nm* : arpeggio
arpía *nf* : shrew, harpy
arpillera *nf* : burlap
arpista *nmf* : harpist
arpón *nm, pl* **arpones** : harpoon — **arponear** *vt*
arquear *vt* : to arch, to bend — **arquearse** *vr* : to bend, to bow
arqueología *nf* : archaeology
arqueológico, -ca *adj* : archaeological
arqueólogo, -ga *n* : archaeologist
arquero, -ra *n* **1** : archer **2** PORTERO : goalkeeper, goalie
arquetípico, -ca *adj* : archetypal
arquetipo *nm* : archetype
arquitecto, -ta *n* : architect
arquitectónico, -ca *adj* : architectural — **aquitectónicamente** *adv*
arquitectura *nf* : architecture
arrabal *nm* **1** : slum **2 arrabales** *nmpl* : outskirts, outlying area
arracada *nf* : hoop earring
arracimarse *vr* : to cluster together
arraigado, -da *adj* : deep-seated, ingrained
arraigar {52} *vi* : to take root, to become established — **arraigarse** *vr*
arraigo *nm* : roots *pl* ⟨con mucho arraigo : deep-rooted⟩
arrancar {72} *vt* **1** : to pull out, to tear out **2** : to pick, to pluck (a flower) **3** : to start (an engine) **4** : to boot (a computer) — *vi* **1** : to start an engine **2** : to get going — **arrancarse** *vr* : to pull out, to pull off

arrancón *nm, pl* **-cones** *Mex* **1** : sudden loud start (of a car) **2 carrera de arrancones** : drag race

arranque *nm* **1** : starter (of a car) **2** ARREBATO : outburst, fit **3 punto de arranque** : beginning, starting point

arrasar *vt* **1** : to level, to smooth **2** : to devastate, to destroy **3** : to fill to the brim

arrastrar *vt* **1** : to drag, to tow **2** : to draw, to attract — *vi* : to hang down, to trail — **arrastrarse** *vr* **1** : to crawl **2** : to grovel

arrastre *nm* **1** : dragging **2** : pull, attraction **3 red de arrastre** : dragnet, trawling net

arrayán *nm, pl* **-yanes 1** MIRTO : myrtle **2 arrayán brabántico** : bayberry, wax myrtle

arrear *vt* : to urge on, to drive — *vi* : to hurry along

arrebatado, -da *adj* **1** PRECIPITADO : impetuous, hotheaded, rash **2** : flushed, blushing

arrebatar *vt* **1** : to snatch, to seize **2** CAUTIVAR : to captivate — **arrebatarse** *vr* : to get carried away (with anger, etc.)

arrebato *nm* ARRANQUE : fit, outburst

arreciar *vi* : to intensify, to worsen

arrecife *nm* : reef

arreglado, -da *adj* **1** : fixed, repaired **2** : settled, sorted out **3** : neat, tidy **4** : smart, dressed-up

arreglar *vt* **1** COMPONER : to repair, to fix **2** : to tidy up ⟨arregla tu cuarto : pick up your room⟩ **3** : to solve, to work out ⟨quiero arreglar este asunto : I want to settle this matter⟩ — **arreglarse** *vr* **1** : to get dressed (up) ⟨arreglarse el pelo : to get one's hair done⟩ **2 arreglárselas** *fam* : to get by, to manage

arreglo *nm* **1** : repair **2** : arrangement **3** : agreement, understanding

arrellanarse *vr* : to settle (in a chair)

arremangarse {52} *vr* : to roll up one's sleeves

arremeter *vi* EMBESTIR : to attack, to charge

arremetida *nf* EMBESTIDA : attack, onslaught

arremolinarse *vr* **1** : to crowd around, to mill about **2** : to swirl (about)

arrendador, -dora *n* **1** : landlord, landlady *f* **2** : tenant, lessee

arrendajo *nm* : jay

arrendamiento *nm* **1** ALQUILER : rental, leasing **2 contrato de arrendamiento** : lease

arrendar {55} *vt* ALQUILAR : to rent, to lease

arrendatario, -ria *n* : tenant, lessee, renter

arreos *nmpl* GUARNICIONES : tack, harness, trappings

arrepentido, -da *adj* : repentant, remorseful

arrepentimiento *nm* : regret, remorse, repentance

arrepentirse {76} *vr* **1** : to regret, to be sorry **2** : to repent

arrestar *vt* DETENER : to arrest, to detain

arresto *nm* **1** DETENCIÓN : arrest **2 arrestos** *nmpl* : boldness, daring

arriar {85} *vt* **1** : to lower (a flag, etc.) **2** : to slacken (a rope, etc.)

arriate *nm Mex, Spain* : bed (for plants), border

arriba *adv* **1** : up, upwards **2** : above, overhead **3** : upstairs **4 ~ de** : more than **5 de arriba abajo** : from top to bottom, from head to foot

arribar *vi* **1** : to arrive **2** : to dock, to put into port

arribista *nmf* : parvenu, upstart

arribo *nm* : arrival

arriendo *nm* ARRENDAMIENTO : rent, rental

arriero, -ra *n* : mule driver, muleteer

arriesgado, -da *adj* **1** : risky **2** : bold, daring

arriesgar {52} *vt* : to risk, to venture — **arriesgarse** *vr* : to take a chance

arrimado, -da *n Mex fam* : sponger, freeloader

arrimar *vt* ACERCAR, APROXIMAR : to bring closer, to draw near — **arrimarse** *vr* ACERCARSE, APROXIMARSE : to approach, to get close

arrinconar *vt* **1** ACORRALAR : to corner, to box in **2** : to push aside, to abandon

arroba *nf* : arroba (Spanish unit of measurement)

arrobamiento *nm* : rapture, ecstasy

arrobar *vt* : to enrapture, to enchant — **arrobarse** *vr*

arrocero[1], -ra *adj* : rice

arrocero[2], -ra *n* : rice grower

arrodillarse *vr* : to kneel (down)

arrogancia *nf* ALTANERÍA, ALTIVEZ : arrogance, haughtiness

arrogante *adj* ALTANERO, ALTIVO : arrogant, haughty

arrogarse {52} *vr* : to usurp, to arrogate

arrojado, -da *adj* : daring, fearless

arrojar *vt* **1** : to hurl, to cast, to throw **2** : to give off, to spew out **3** : to yield, to produce **4** *fam* : to vomit — **arrojarse** *vr* PRECIPITARSE : to throw oneself, to leap

arrojo *nm* : boldness, fearlessness

arrollador, -dora *adj* : sweeping, overwhelming

arrollar *vt* **1** : to sweep away, to carry away **2** : to crush, to overwhelm **3** : to run over (with a vehicle)

arropar *vt* : to clothe, to cover (up) — **arroparse** *vr*

arrostrar *vt* : to confront, to face (up to)

arroyo *nm* **1** RIACHUELO : brook, creek, stream **2** : gutter

arroz *nm, pl* **arroces** : rice

arrozal *nm* : rice field, rice paddy

arruga *nf* : wrinkle, fold, crease

arrugado, -da *adj* : wrinkled, creased, lined

arrugar {52} *vt* : to wrinkle, to crease, to pucker — **arrugarse** *vr*

arruinar *vt* : to ruin, to wreck — **arruinarse** *vr* **1** : to be ruined **2** : to fall into ruin, to go bankrupt

arrullar *vt* : to lull to sleep — *vi* : to coo

arrullo *nm* **1** : lullaby **2** : coo (of a dove)

arrumaco *nm fam* : kissing, cuddling

arrumbar *vt* **1** : to lay aside, to put away **2** : to floor, to leave speechless

arsenal *nm* : arsenal

arsénico *nm* : arsenic

arte *nmf* (*usually m in singular, f in plural*) **1** : art ⟨artes y oficios : arts and crafts⟩ ⟨bellas artes : fine arts⟩ **2** HABILIDAD : skill **3** : cunning, cleverness

artefacto *nm* **1** : artifact **2** DISPOSITIVO : device

artemisa *nf* : sagebrush

arteria *nf* : artery — **arterial** *adj*

arteriosclerosis *nf* : arteriosclerosis, hardening of the arteries

artero, -ra *adj* : wily, crafty

artesanal *adj* : pertaining to crafts or craftsmanship, handmade

artesanía *nf* **1** : craftsmanship **2** : handicrafts *pl*

artesano, -na *n* : artisan, craftsman *m*, craftsperson

artesiano, -na *adj* : artesian ⟨pozo artesiano : artesian well⟩

ártico, -ca *adj* : arctic

articulación *nf, pl* **-ciones** **1** : articulation, pronunciation **2** COYUNTURA : joint

articular *vt* **1** : to articulate, to utter **2** : to connect with a joint **3** : to coordinate, to orchestrate

articulista *nmf* : columnist

artículo *nm* **1** : article, thing **2** : item, feature, report **3 artículo de comercio** : commodity **4 artículos de primera necesidad** : essentials **5 artículos de tocador** : toiletries

artífice *nmf* **1** ARTESANO : artisan **2** : mastermind, architect

artificial *adj* **1** : artificial, man-made **2** : feigned, false — **artificialmente** *adv*

artificio *nm* **1** HABILIDAD : skill **2** APARATO : device, appliance **3** ARDID : artifice, ruse

artificioso, -sa *adj* **1** : skillful **2** : cunning, deceptive

artillería *nf* : artillery

artillero, -ra *n* : artilleryman *m*, gunner

artilugio *nm* : gadget, contraption

artimaña *nf* : ruse, trick

artista *nmf* **1** : artist **2** ACTOR, ACTRIZ : actor, actress *f*

artístico, -ca *adj* : artistic — **artísticamente** *adv*

artrítico, -ca *adj* : arthritic

artritis *nfs & pl* : arthritis

artrópodo *nm* : arthropod

arveja *nf* GUISANTE : pea

arzobispado *nm* : archbishopric

arzobispo *nm* : archbishop

as *nm* : ace

asa *nf* AGARRADERA, ASIDERO : handle, grip

asado[1], -da *adj* : roasted, grilled, broiled

asado[2] *nm* **1** : roast **2** : barbecued meat **3** : barbecue, cookout

asador *nm* : spit, rotisserie

asaduras *nfpl* : entrails, offal

asalariado[1], -da *adj* : wage-earning, salaried

asalariado[2], -da *n* : wage earner

asaltante *nmf* **1** : mugger, robber **2** : assailant

asaltar *vt* **1** : to assault **2** : to mug, to rob **3 asaltar al poder** : to seize power

asalto *nm* **1** : assault **2** : mugging, robbery **3** : round (in boxing) **4 asalto al poder** : coup d'etat

asamblea *nf* : assembly, meeting

asambleísta *nmf* : assemblyman *m*, assemblywoman *f*

asar *vt* : to roast, to grill — **asarse** *vr fam* : to roast, to be dying from heat

asbesto *nm* : asbestos

ascendencia *nf* **1** : ancestry, descent **2 ~ sobre** : influence over

ascendente *adj* : ascending, upward ⟨un curso ascendente : an upward trend⟩

ascender {56} *vt* **1** : to ascend, to rise up **2** : to be promoted ⟨ascendió a gerente : she was promoted to manager⟩ **3 ~ a** : to amount to, to reach ⟨las deudas ascienden a 20 millones de pesos : the debt amounts to 20 million pesos⟩ — *vt* : to promote

ascendiente[1] *nmf* ANCESTRO : ancestor

ascendiente[2] *nm* INFLUENCIA : influence, ascendancy

ascensión *nf, pl* **-siones** **1** : ascent, rise **2 Fiesta de la Ascensión** : Ascension Day

ascenso *nm* **1** : ascent, rise **2** : promotion

ascensor *nm* ELEVADOR : elevator

asceta *nmf* : ascetic

ascético, -ca *adj* : ascetic

ascetismo *nm* : asceticism

asco *nm* **1** : disgust ⟨¡qué asco! : that's disgusting!, how revolting!⟩ **2 darle asco (a alguien)** : to sicken, to revolt **3 estar hecho un asco** : to be filthy **4 hacerle ascos a** : to turn up one's nose at

ascua *nf* **1** BRASA : ember **2 estar en ascuas** *fam* : to be on edge

asear *vt* **1** : to wash, to clean **2** : to tidy up — **asearse** *vr*

asechanza *nf* : snare, trap

asechar *vt* : to set a trap for

asediar *vt* **1** SITIAR : to besiege **2** ACOSAR : to harass

asedio *nm* **1** : siege **2** ACOSO : harassment

asegurador[1], -dora *adj* **1** : insuring, assuring **2** : pertaining to insurance

asegurador[2], -dora *n* : insurer, underwriter

aseguradora *nf* : insurance company

asegurar *vt* **1** : to assure **2** : to secure **3** : to insure — **asegurarse** *vr* **1** CERCIORARSE : to make sure **2** : to take out insurance, to insure oneself

asemejar *vt* **1** : to make similar ⟨ese bigote te asemeja a tu abuelo : that mustache makes you look like your grandfather⟩ **2** *Mex* : to be similar to, to resemble — **asemejarse** *vr* **~ a** : to look like, to resemble

asentaderas *nfpl fam* : bottom, buttocks *pl*

asentado, -da *adj* : settled, established

asentamiento *nm* : settlement

asentar {55} *vt* **1** : to lay down, to set down, to place **2** : to settle, to establish **3** *Mex* : to state, to affirm — **asentarse** *vr* **1** : to settle **2** ESTABLECERSE : to settle down, to establish oneself

asentimiento *nm* : assent, consent

asentir {76} *vt* : to consent, to agree

aseo *nm* : cleanliness

aséptico, -ca *adj* : aseptic, germ-free

asequible *adj* ACCESIBLE : accessible, attainable

aserción *nf* → **aserto**

aserradero *nm* : sawmill

aserrar {55} *vt* : to saw

aserrín *nm, pl* **-rrines** : sawdust

aserto *nm* : assertion, affirmation

asesinar *vt* **1** : to murder **2** : to assassinate

asesinato *nm* **1** : murder **2** : assassination

asesino[1], -na *adj* : murderous, homicidal

asesino[2], -na *n* **1** : murderer, killer **2** : assassin

asesor, -sora *n* : advisor, consultant

asesoramiento *nm* : advice, counsel

asesorar *vt* : to advise, to counsel — **asesorarse** *vr* **~ de** : to consult

asesoría *nf* **1** : consulting, advising **2** : consultant's office

asestar {55} *vt* **1** : to aim, to point (a weapon) **2** : to deliver, to deal (a blow)

aseveración *nf, pl* **-ciones** : assertion, statement

aseverar *vt* : to assert, to state

asexual *adj* : asexual — **asexualmente** *adv*

asfaltado[1], -da *adj* : asphalted, paved

asfaltado[2] *nm* PAVIMENTO : pavement, asphalt

asfaltar *vt* : to pave, to blacktop

asfalto *nm* : asphalt

asfixia *nf* : asphyxia, asphyxiation, suffocation

asfixiar *vt* : to asphyxiate, to suffocate, to smother — **asfixiarse** *vr*

asga, etc. → **asir**

así[1] *adv* **1** : like this, like that **2** : so, thus ⟨así sea : so be it⟩ **3 ~ de** : so, about so ⟨una caja así de grande : a box about so big⟩ **4 así que** : so, therefore **5 ~ como** : as well as **6 así así** : so-so, fair

así[2] *adj* : such, such a ⟨un talento así es inestimable : a talent like that is priceless⟩

así[3] *conj* AUNQUE : even if, even though ⟨no irá, así le paguen : he won't go, even if they pay him⟩

asiático[1], -ca *adj* : Asian, Asiatic

asiático[2], -ca *n* : Asian

asidero *nm* **1** AGARRADERA, ASA : grip, handle **2** AGARRE : grip, hold

asiduamente *adv* : regularly, frequently

asiduidad *nf* **1** : assiduousness **2** : regularity, frequency

asiduo, -dua *adj* **1** : assiduous **2** : frequent, regular

asiento *nm* **1** : seat, chair ⟨asiento trasero : back seat⟩ **2** : location, site

asignación *nf, pl* **-ciones** **1** : allocation **2** : appointment, designation **3** : allowance, pay **4** *PRi* : homework, assignment

asignar *vt* **1** : to assign, to allocate **2** : to appoint

asignatura *nf* MATERIA : subject, course

asilado, -da *n* : exile, refugee

asilo *nm* : asylum, refuge, shelter

asimetría *nf* : asymmetry

asimétrico, -ca *adj* : asymmetrical, asymmetric

asimilación *nf, pl* **-ciones** : assimilation

asimilar *vt* : to assimilate — **asimilarse** *vr* **~ a** : to be similar to, to resemble

asimismo *adv* **1** IGUALMENTE : similarly, likewise **2** TAMBIÉN : as well, also

asir {7} *vt* : to seize, to grasp — **asirse** *vr* **~ a** : to cling to

asistencia *nf* **1** : attendance **2** : assistance **3** : assist (in sports)

asistente[1] *adj* : attending, in attendance

asistente[2] *nmf* **1** : assistant **2 los asistentes** : those present, those in attendance

asistir *vi* : to attend, to be present ⟨asistir a clase : to attend class⟩ — *vt* : to aid, to assist

asma *nf* : asthma

asmático, -ca *adj* : asthmatic

asno *nm* BURRO : ass, donkey

asociación *nf, pl* **-ciones** **1** : association, relationship **2** : society, group, association

asociado[1], -da *adj* : associate, associated

asociado[2], -da *n* : associate, partner

asociar *vt* **1** : to associate, to connect **2** : to pool (resources) **3** : to take into partnership — **asociarse** *vr* **1** : to become partners **2 ~ a** : to join, to become a member of

asolar {19} *vt* : to devastate, to destroy

asoleado, -da *adj* : sunny

asolear *vt* : to put in the sun — **asolearse** *vr* : to sunbathe

asomar *vt* : to show, to stick out — *vi* : to appear, to become visible — **aso-**

marse *vr* 1 : to show, to appear 2 : to lean out, to look out ⟨se asomó por la ventana : he leaned out the window⟩

asombrar *vt* MARAVILLAR : to amaze, to astonish — **asombrarse** *vr* : to marvel, to be amazed

asombro *nm* : amazement, astonishment

asombroso, -sa *adj* : amazing, astonishing — **asombrosamente** *adv*

asomo *nm* 1 : hint, trace 2 **ni por asomo** : by no means

aspa *nf* : blade (of a fan or propeller)

aspaviento *nm* : exaggerated movement, fuss, flounce

aspecto *nm* 1 : aspect 2 APARIENCIA : appearance, look

aspereza *nf* RUDEZA : roughness, coarseness

áspero, -ra *adj* : rough, coarse, abrasive — **ásperamente** *adv*

aspersión *nf, pl* **-siones** : sprinkling

aspersor *nm* : sprinkler

aspiración *nf, pl* **-ciones** 1 : inhalation, breathing in 2 ANHELO : aspiration, desire

aspiradora *nf* : vacuum cleaner

aspirante *nmf* : applicant, candidate

aspirar *vi* ~ **a** : to aspire to — *vt* : to inhale, to breathe in

aspirina *nf* : aspirin

asquear *vt* : to sicken, to disgust

asquerosidad *nf* : filth, foulness

asqueroso, -sa *adj* : disgusting, sickening, repulsive — **asquerosamente** *adv*

asta *nf* 1 : flagpole ⟨a media asta : at half-mast⟩ 2 : horn, antler 3 : shaft (of a weapon)

ástaco *nm* : crayfish

astado, -da *adj* : horned

aster *nm* : aster

asterisco *nm* : asterisk

asteroide *nm* : asteroid

astigmatismo *nm* : astigmatism

astil *nm* : shaft (of an arrow or feather)

astilla *nf* 1 : splinter, chip 2 **de tal palo, tal astilla** : like father, like son

astillar *vt* : to splinter — **astillarse** *vr*

astillero *nm* : dry dock, shipyard

astral *adj* : astral

astringente *adj & nm* : astringent — **astringencia** *nf*

astro *nm* 1 : heavenly body 2 : star

astrología *nf* : astrology

astrológico, -ca *adj* : astrological

astrólogo, -ga *n* : astrologer

astronauta *nmf* : astronaut

astronáutica *nf* : astronautics

astronáutico, -ca *adj* : astronautic, astronautical

astronave *nf* : spaceship

astronomía *nf* : astronomy

astronómico, -ca *adj* : astronomical — **astronómicamente** *adv*

astrónomo, -ma *n* : astronomer

astroso, -sa *adj* DESALIÑADO : slovenly, untidy

astucia *nf* 1 : astuteness, shrewdness 2 : cunning, guile

astuto, -ta *adj* 1 : astute, shrewd 2 : crafty, tricky — **astutamente** *adv*

asueto *nm* : time off, break

asumir *vt* 1 : to assume, to take on ⟨asumir el cargo : to take office⟩ 2 SUPONER : to assume, to suppose

asunción *nf, pl* **-ciones** : assumption

asunto *nm* 1 CUESTIÓN, TEMA : affair, matter, subject 2 **asuntos** *nmpl* : affairs, business

asustadizo, -za *adj* : nervous, jumpy, skittish

asustado, -da *adj* : frightened, afraid

asustar *vt* ESPANTAR : to scare, to frighten — **asustarse** *vr*

atacante *nmf* : assailant, attacker

atacar {72} *v* : to attack

atado[1], **-da** *adj* : shy, inhibited

atado[2] *nm* 1 : bundle, bunch 2 *Arg* : pack (of cigarettes)

atadura *nf* LIGADURA : tie, bond

atajar *vt* 1 IMPEDIR : to block, to stop 2 INTERRUMPIR : to interrupt, to cut off 3 CONTENER : to hold back, to restrain — *vi* ~ **por** : to take a shortcut through

atajo *nm* : shortcut

atalaya *nf* 1 : watchtower 2 : vantage point

atañer {79} *vt* ~ **a** (*3rd person only*) : to concern, to have to do with ⟨eso no me atañe : that does not concern me⟩

ataque *nm* 1 : attack, assault 2 : fit ⟨ataque de risa : fit of laughter⟩ 3 **ataque de nervios** : nervous breakdown 4 **ataque cardíaco** *or* **ataque al corazón** : heart attack

atar *vt* AMARRAR : to tie, to tie up, to tie down — **atarse** *vr*

atarantado, -da *adj fam* 1 : restless 2 : dazed, stunned

atarantar *vt fam* : to daze, to stun

atarazana *nf* : shipyard

atardecer[1] {53} *v impers* : to get dark

atardecer[2] *nm* : late afternoon, dusk

atareado, -da *adj* : busy, overworked

atascar {72} *vt* 1 ATORAR : to block, to clog, to stop up 2 : to hinder — **atascarse** *vr* 1 : to become obstructed 2 : to get bogged down 3 PARARSE : to stall

atasco *nm* 1 : blockage 2 EMBOTELLAMIENTO : traffic jam

ataúd *nm* : coffin, casket

ataviar {85} *vt* : to dress, to clothe — **ataviarse** *vr* : to dress up

atavío *nm* ATUENDO : dress, attire

ateísmo *nm* : atheism

atemorizar {21} *vt* : to frighten, to intimidate — **atemorizarse** *vr*

atemperar *vt* : to temper, to moderate

atención[1] *nf, pl* **-ciones** 1 : attention 2 **poner atención** *or* **prestar atención** : to pay attention 3 **llamar la atención** : to attract attention 4 **en atención a** : in view of

atención[2] *interj* 1 : attention! 2 : watch out!

atender {56} *vt* **1** : to help, to wait on **2** : to look after, to take care of **3** : to heed, to listen to — *vi* : to pay attention
atenerse {80} *vr* : to abide ⟨tendrás que atenerte a las reglas : you will have to abide by the rules⟩
atentado *nm* : attack, assault
atentamente *adv* **1** : attentively, carefully **2** (*used in correspondence*) : sincerely, sincerely yours
atentar {55} *vi* **∼ contra** : to make an attempt on, to threaten ⟨atentaron contra su vida : they made an attempt on his life⟩
atento, -ta *adj* **1** : attentive, mindful **2** CORTÉS : courteous
atenuación *nf, pl* **-ciones** **1** : lessening **2** : understatement
atenuante[1] *adj* : extenuating, mitigating
atenuante[2] *nmf* : extenuating circumstance, excuse
atenuar {3} *vt* **1** MITIGAR : to extenuate, to mitigate **2** : to dim (light), to tone down (colors) **3** : to minimize, to lessen
ateo[1], **atea** *adj* : atheistic
ateo[2], **atea** *n* : atheist
aterciopelado, -da *adj* : velvety, downy
aterido, -da *adj* : freezing, frozen
aterrador, -dora *adj* : terrifying
aterrar {55} *vt* : to terrify, to frighten
aterrizaje *nm* : landing (of a plane)
aterrizar {21} *vt* : to land, to touch down
aterrorizar {21} *vt* **1** : to terrify **2** : to terrorize — **aterrorizarse** *vr* : to be terrified
atesorar *vt* : to hoard, to amass
atestado, -da *adj* : crowded, packed
atestar {55} *vt* **1** ATIBORRAR : to crowd, to pack **2** : to witness, to testify to — *vi* : to testify
atestiguar {10} *vt* : to testify to, to bear witness to — *vi* DECLARAR : to testify
atiborrar *vt* : to pack, to crowd — **atiborrarse** *vr* : to stuff oneself
ático *nm* **1** : penthouse **2** BUHARDILLA, DESVÁN : attic
atigrado, -da *adj* : tabby (of cats), striped (of fur)
atildado, -da *adj* : smart, neat, dapper
atildar *vt* **1** : to put a tilde over **2** : to clean up, to smarten up — **atildarse** *vr* : to get spruced up
atinar *vi* ACERTAR : to be accurate, to be on target
atingencia *nf* : bearing, relevance
atípico, -ca *adj* : atypical
atiplado, -da *adj* : shrill, high-pitched
atirantar *vt* : to make taut, to tighten
atisbar *vt* **1** : to spy on, to watch **2** : to catch a glimpse of, to make out
atisbo *nm* : glimpse, sign, hint
atizador *nm* : poker (for a fire)
atizar {21} *vt* **1** : to poke, to stir, to stoke (a fire) **2** : to stir up, to rouse **3** *fam* : to give, to land (a blow)
atlántico, -ca *adj* : Atlantic
atlas *nm* : atlas
atleta *nmf* : athlete
atlético, -ca *adj* : athletic
atletismo *nm* : athletics
atmósfera *nf* : atmosphere
atmosférico, -ca *adj* : atmospheric
atole *nm Mex* **1** : thick hot beverage prepared with corn flour **2 darle atole con el dedo (a alguien)** : to string (someone) along
atollarse *vr* : to get stuck, to get bogged down
atolón *nm, pl* **-lones** : atoll
atolondrado, -da *adj* **1** ATURDIDO : bewildered, dazed **2** DESPISTADO : scatterbrained, absentminded
atómico, -ca *adj* : atomic
atomizador *nm* : atomizer
atomizar {21} *vt* FRAGMENTAR : to fragment, to break into bits
átomo *nm* : atom
atónito, -ta *adj* : astonished, amazed
atontar *vt* **1** : to stupefy **2** : to bewilder, to confuse
atorar *vt* ATASCAR : to block, to clog — **atorarse** *vr* **1** ATASCARSE : to get stuck **2** ATRAGANTARSE : to choke
atormentador, -dora *n* : tormenter
atormentar *vt* : to torment, to torture — **atormentarse** *vr* : to torment oneself, to agonize
atornillar *vt* : to screw (in, on, down)
atorrante *nmf Arg* : bum, loafer
atosigar {52} *vt* : to harass, to annoy
atracadero *nm* : dock, pier
atracador, -dora *n* : robber, mugger
atracar {72} *vt* : to dock, to land — *vt* : to hold up, to rob, to mug — **atracarse** *vr fam* **∼ de** : to gorge oneself with
atracción *nf, pl* **-ciones** : attraction
atraco *nm* : holdup, robbery
atractivo[1], **-va** *adj* : attractive
atractivo[2] *nm* : attraction, appeal, charm
atraer {81} *vt* : to attract — **atraerse** *vr* **1** : to attract (each other) **2** GANARSE : to gain, to win
atragantarse *vr* : to choke (on food)
atrancar {72} *vt* : to block, to bar — **atrancarse** *vr*
atrapada *nf* : catch
atrapar *vt* : to trap, to capture
atrás *adv* **1** DETRÁS : back, behind ⟨se quedó atrás : he stayed behind⟩ **2** ANTES : ago ⟨mucho tiempo atrás : long ago⟩ **3 para ∼** *or* **hacia ∼** : backwards, toward the rear **4 ∼ de** : in back of, behind
atrasado, -da *adj* **1** : late, overdue **2** : backward **3** : old-fashioned **4** : slow (of a clock or watch)
atrasar *vt* : to delay, to put off — *vi* : to lose time — **atrasarse** *vr* : to fall behind
atraso *nm* **1** RETRASO : lateness, delay ⟨llegó con 20 minutos de atraso : he was 20 minutes late⟩ **2** : backwardness **3 atrasos** *nmpl* : arrears

atravesar {55} *vt* **1** CRUZAR : to cross, to go across **2** : to pierce **3** : to lay across **4** : to go through (a situation or crisis) — **atravesarse** *vr* **1** : to be in the way ⟨se me atravesó : it blocked my path⟩ **2** : to interfere, to meddle
atrayente *adj* : attractive
atreverse *vr* **1** : to dare **2** : to be insolent
atrevido, -da *adj* **1** : bold, daring **2** : insolent
atrevimiento *nm* **1** : daring, boldness **2** : insolence
atribución *nf, pl* **-ciones** : attribution
atribuible *adj* IMPUTABLE : attributable, ascribable
atribuir {41} *vt* **1** : to attribute, to ascribe **2** : to grant, to confer — **atribuirse** *vr* : to take credit for
atribular *vt* : to afflict, to trouble — **atribularse** *vr*
atributo *nm* : attribute
atril *nm* : lectern, stand
atrincherar *vt* : to entrench — **atrincherarse** *vr* **1** : to dig in, to entrench oneself **2 ~ en** : to hide behind
atrio *nm* **1** : atrium **2** : portico
atrocidad *nf* : atrocity
atrofia *nf* : atrophy
atrofiar *v* : to atrophy
atronador, -dora *adj* : thunderous, deafening
atropellado, -da *adj* **1** : rash, hasty **2** : brusque, abrupt
atropellamiento → **atropello**
atropellar *vt* **1** : to knock down, to run over **2** : to violate, to abuse — **atropellarse** *vr* : to rush through (a task), to trip over one's words
atropello *nm* : abuse, violation, outrage
atroz *adj, pl* **atroces** : atrocious, appalling — **atrozmente** *adv*
atuendo *nm* ATAVÍO : attire, costume
atufar *vt* : to vex, to irritate — **atufarse** *vr* **1** : to get angry **2** : to smell bad, to stink
atún *nm, pl* **atunes** : tuna fish, tuna
aturdimiento *nm* : bewilderment, confusion
aturdir *vt* **1** : to stun, to shock **2** : to bewilder, to confuse, to stupefy
atuvo, etc. → **atenerse**
audacia *nf* OSADÍA : boldness, audacity
audaz *adj, pl* **audaces** : bold, audacious, daring — **audazmente** *adv*
audible *adj* : audible
audición *nf, pl* **-ciones** **1** : hearing **2** : audition
audiencia *nf* : audience
audífono *nm* **1** : hearing aid **2 audífonos** *nmpl* : headphones, earphones
audio *nm* : audio
audiovisual *adj* : audiovisual
auditar *vt* : to audit
auditivo, -va *adj* : auditory, hearing, aural ⟨aparato auditivo : hearing aid⟩
auditor, -tora *n* : auditor
auditoría *nf* : audit
auditorio *nm* **1** : auditorium **2** : audience
auge *nm* **1** : peak, height **2** : boom, upturn
augur *nm* : augur
augurar *vt* : to predict, to foretell
augurio *nm* AGÜERO, PRESAGIO : augury, omen
augusto, -ta *adj* : august
aula *nf* : classroom
aullar {8} *vt* : to howl, to wail
aullido *nm* : howl, wail
aumentar *vt* ACRECENTAR : to increase, to raise — *vi* : to rise, to increase, to grow
aumento *nm* INCREMENTO : increase, rise
aun *adv* **1** : even ⟨ni aun en coche llegaría a tiempo : I wouldn't arrive on time even if I drove⟩ **2 aun así** : even so **3 aun más** : even more
aún *adv* **1** TODAVÍA : still, yet ⟨¿aún no ha llegado el correo? : the mail still hasn't come?⟩ **2 más aún** : furthermore
aunar {8} *vt* : to join, to combine — **aunarse** *vr* : to unite
aunque *conj* **1** : though, although, even if, even though **2 aunque sea** : at least
aura *nf* **1** : aura **2** : turkey buzzard
áureo, -rea *adj* : golden
aureola *nf* **1** : halo **2** : aura (of power, fame, etc.)
aurícula *nf* : auricle
auricular *nm* : telephone receiver
aurora *nf* **1** : dawn **2 aurora boreal** : aurora borealis
ausencia *nf* : absence
ausentarse *vr* **1** : to leave, to go away **2 ~ de** : to stay away from
ausente[1] *adj* : absent, missing
ausente[2] *nmf* **1** : absentee **2** : missing person
auspiciar *vt* **1** PATROCINAR : to sponsor **2** FOMENTAR : to foster, to promote
auspicios *nmpl* : sponsorship, auspices
austeridad *nf* : austerity
austero, -ra *adj* : austere
austral[1] *adj* : southern
austral[2] *nm* : former monetary unit of Argentina
australiano, -na *adj & n* : Australian
austriaco *or* **austríaco, -ca** *adj & n* : Austrian
autenticar {72} *vt* : to authenticate — **autenticación** *nf*
autenticidad *nf* : authenticity
auténtico, -ca *adj* : authentic — **auténticamente** *adv*
autentificar {72} *vt* : to authenticate — **autentificación** *nf*
autismo *nm* : autism
autista *adj* : autistic
auto *nm* : auto, car
autoayuda *nf* : self-help
autobiografía *nf* : autobiography
autobiográfico, -ca *adj* : autobiographical
autobús *nm, pl* **-buses** : bus

autocompasión *nf* : self-pity
autocontrol *nm* : self-control
autocracia *nf* : autocracy
autócrata *nmf* : autocrat
autocrático, -ca *adj* : autocratic
autóctono, -na *adj* : indigenous, native ‹arte autóctono : indigenous art›
autodefensa *nf* : self-defense
autodestrucción *nf* : self-destruction — **autodestructivo, -va** *adj*
autodeterminación *nf* : self-determination
autodidacta[1] *adj* : self-taught
autodidacta[2] *nmf* : self-taught person, autodidact
autodidacto[1], **-ta** *adj* → **autodidacta**[1]
autodidacto[2], **-ta** *n* → **autodidacta**[2]
autodisciplina *nf* : self-discipline
autoestima *nf* : self-esteem
autogobierno *nm* : self-government
autografiar *vt* : to autograph
autógrafo *nm* : autograph
autoinfligido, -da *adj* : self-inflicted
automación → **automatización**
autómata *nm* : automaton
automático, -ca *adj* : automatic — **automáticamente** *adv*
automatización *nf* : automation
automatizar {21} *vt* : to automate
automotor, -tora *adj* **1** : self-propelled **2** : automotive, car
automotriz[1] *adj, pl* **-trices** : automotive, car
automotriz[2] *nf, pl* **-trices** : automaker
automóvil *nm* : automobile
automovilista *nmf* : motorist
automovilístico, -ca *adj* : automobile, car ‹accidente automovilístico : automobile accident›
autonombrado, -da *adj* : self-appointed
autonomía *nf* : autonomy
autónomo, -ma *adj* : autonomous — **autónomamente** *adv*
autopista *nf* : expressway, highway
autoproclamado, -da *adj* : self-proclaimed, self-appointed
autopropulsado, -da *adj* : self-propelled
autopsia *nf* : autopsy
autor, -tora *n* **1** : author **2** : perpetrator
autoría *nf* : authorship
autoridad *nf* : authority
autoritario, -ria *adj* : authoritarian
autorización *nf, pl* **-ciones** : authorization
autorizado, -da *adj* **1** : authorized **2** : authoritative
autorizar {21} *vt* : to authorize, to approve
autorretrato *nm* : self-portrait
autoservicio *nm* **1** : self-service restaurant **2** SUPERMERCADO : supermarket
autostop *nm* **1** : hitchhiking **2 hacer autostop** : to hitchhike
autostopista *nmf* : hitchhiker
autosuficiencia *nf* : self-sufficiency — **autosuficiente** *adj*
auxiliar[1] *vt* : to aid, to assist
auxiliar[2] *adj* : assistant, auxiliary
auxiliar[3] *nmf* **1** : assistant, helper **2 auxiliar de vuelo** : flight attendant
auxilio *nm* **1** : aid, assistance **2 primeros auxilios** : first aid
aval *nm* : guarantee, endorsement
avalancha *nf* ALUD : avalanche
avalar *vt* : to guarantee, to endorse
avaluar {3} *vt* : to evaluate, to appraise
avalúo *nm* : appraisal, evaluation
avance *nm* ADELANTO : advance
avanzado, -da *adj* **1** : advanced **2** : progressive
avanzar {21} *v* : to advance, to move forward
avaricia *nf* CODICIA : greed, avarice
avaricioso, -sa *adj* : avaricious, greedy
avaro[1], **-ra** *adj* : miserly, greedy
avaro[2], **-ra** *n* : miser
avasallador, -dora *adj* : overwhelming
avasallamiento *nm* : subjugation, domination
avasallar *vt* : to overpower, to subjugate
ave *nf* **1** : bird **2 aves de corral** : poultry **3 ave rapaz** *or* **ave de presa** : bird of prey
avecinarse *vr* : to approach, to come near
avecindarse *vr* : to settle, to take up residence
avellana *nf* : hazelnut, filbert
avellano *nm* : hazel
avena *nf* **1** : oat, oats *pl* **2** : oatmeal
avenencia *nf* : agreement, pact
avenida *nf* : avenue
avenir {87} *vt* : to reconcile, to harmonize — **avenirse** *vr* **1** : to agree, to come to terms **2** : to get along
aventajado, -da *adj* : outstanding
aventajar *vt* **1** : to be ahead of, to lead **2** : to surpass, to outdo
aventar {55} *vt* **1** : to fan **2** : to winnow **3** *Col, Mex* : to throw, to toss — **aventarse** *vr* **1** *Col, Mex* : to hurl oneself **2** *Mex fam* : to dare, to take a chance
aventón *nm, pl* **-tones** *Col, Mex fam* : ride, lift
aventura *nf* **1** : adventure **2** RIESGO : venture, risk **3** : love affair
aventurado, -da *adj* : hazardous, risky
aventurar *vt* : to venture, to risk — **aventurarse** *vr* : to take a risk
aventurero[1], **-ra** *adj* : adventurous
aventurero[2], **-ra** *n* : adventurer
avergonzado, -da *adj* **1** : ashamed **2** : embarrassed
avergonzar {9} *vt* APENAR : to shame, to embarrass — **avergonzarse** *vr* APENARSE : to be ashamed, to be embarrassed
avería *nf* **1** : damage **2** : breakdown, malfunction
averiado, -da *adj* **1** : damaged, faulty **2** : broken down
averiar {85} *vt* : to damage — **averiarse** *vr* : to break down
averiguación *nf, pl* **-ciones** : investigation, inquiry

averiguar {10} *vt* **1** : to find out, to ascertain **2** : to investigate
aversión *nf, pl* **-siones** : aversion, dislike
avestruz *nm, pl* **-truces** : ostrich
avezado, -da *adj* : seasoned, experienced
aviación *nf, pl* **-ciones** : aviation
aviador, -dora *n* : aviator, flyer
aviar {85} *vt* **1** : to prepare, to make ready **2** : to tidy up **3** : to equip, to supply
avicultor, -tora *n* : poultry farmer
avicultura *nf* : poultry farming
avidez *nf, pl* **-deces** : eagerness
ávido, -da *adj* : eager, avid — **ávidamente** *adv*
avieso, -sa *adj* **1** : twisted, distorted **2** : wicked, depraved
avinagrado, -da *adj* : vinegary, sour
avío *nm* **1** : preparation, provision **2** : loan (for agriculture or mining) **3 avíos** *nmpl* : gear, equipment
avión *nm, pl* **aviones** : airplane
avioneta *nf* : light airplane
avisar *vt* **1** : to notify, to inform **2** : to advise, to warn
aviso *nm* **1** : notice **2** : advertisement, ad **3** ADVERTENCIA : warning **4 estar sobre aviso** : to be on the alert
avispa *nf* : wasp
avispado, -da *adj fam* : clever, sharp
avispero *nm* : wasps' nest
avispón *nm, pl* **-pones** : hornet
avistar *vt* : to sight, to catch sight of
avituallar *vt* : to suppy with food, to provision
avivar *vt* **1** : to enliven, to brighten **2** : to strengthen, to intensify
avizorar *vt* **1** ACECHAR : to spy on, to watch **2** : to observe, to perceive ⟨se avizoran dificultades : difficulties are expected⟩
axila *nf* : underarm, armpit
axioma *nm* : axiom
axiomático, -ca *adj* : axiomatic
ay *interj* **1** : oh! **2** : ouch!, ow!
ayer[1] *adv* : yesterday
ayer[2] *nm* ANTAÑO : yesteryear, days gone by
ayote *nm CA, Mex* : squash, pumpkin
ayuda *nf* **1** : help, assistance **2 ayuda de cámara** : valet
ayudante *nmf* : helper, assistant
ayudar *vt* : to help, to assist — **ayudarse** *vr* **~ de** : to make use of
ayunar *vi* : to fast
ayunas *nfpl* **en ~** : fasting ⟨este medicamento ha de tomarse en ayunas : this medication should be taken on an empty stomach⟩
ayuno *nm* : fast
ayuntamiento *nm* **1** : town hall, city hall **2** : town or city council
azabache *nm* : jet ⟨negro azabache : jet black⟩
azada *nf* : hoe
azafata *nf* **1** : stewardess *f* **2** : hostess *f* (on a TV show)
azafrán *nm, pl* **-franes 1** : saffron **2** : crocus
azahar *nm* : orange blossom
azalea *nf* : azalea
azar *nm* **1** : chance ⟨juegos de azar : games of chance⟩ **2** : accident, misfortune **3 al azar** : at random, randomly
azaroso, -sa *adj* **1** : perilous, hazardous **2** : turbulent, eventful
azimut *nm* : azimuth
azogue *nm* : mercury, quicksilver
azorar *vt* **1** : to alarm, to startle **2** : to fluster, to embarrass — **azorarse** *vr* : to get embarrassed
azotar *vt* **1** : to whip, to flog **2** : to lash, to batter **3** : to devastate, to afflict
azote *nm* **1** LÁTIGO : whip, lash **2** *fam* : spanking, licking **3** : calamity, scourge
azotea *nf* : flat roof, terraced roof
azteca *adj & nmf* : Aztec
azúcar *nmf* : sugar — **azucarar** *vt*
azucarado, -da *adj* : sweetened, sugary
azucarera *nf* : sugar bowl
azucarero, -ra *adj* : sugar ⟨industria azucarera : sugar industry⟩
azucena *nf* : white lily
azuela *nf* : adze
azufre *nm* : sulphur — **azufroso, -sa** *adj*
azul *adj & nm* : blue
azulado, -da *adj* : bluish
azulejo *nm* : ceramic tile, floor tile
azuloso, -sa *adj* : bluish
azulete *nm* : bluing
azur[1] *adj* CELESTE : azure
azur[2] *n* CELESTE : azure, sky blue
azuzar {21} *vt* : to incite, to egg on

B

b *nf* : second letter of the Spanish alphabet
baba *nf* **1** : spittle, saliva **2** : dribble, drool (of a baby) **3** : slime, ooze
babear *vi* **1** : to drool, to slobber **2** : to ooze
babel *nmf* : babel, chaos, bedlam
babero *nm* : bib
babor *nm* : port, port side
babosa *nf* : slug (mollusk)
babosada *nf CA, Mex* : silly act or remark
baboso, -sa *adj* **1** : drooling, slobbering **2** : slimy **3** *CA, Mex fam* : silly, dumb
babucha *nf* : slipper
babuino *nm* : baboon
bacalao *nm* : cod (fish)

bache *nm* **1** : pothole **2** *PRi* : deep puddle **3** : bad period, rough time ⟨bache económico : economic slump⟩

bachiller *nmf* : high school graduate

bachillerato *nm* : high school diploma

bacilo *nm* : bacillus

bacon *nm Spain* : bacon

bacteria *nf* : bacterium

bacteriano, -na *adj* : bacterial

bacteriología *nf* : bacteriology

bacteriológico, -ca *adj* : bacteriologic, bacteriological

bacteriólogo, -ga *n* : bacteriologist

báculo *nm* **1** : staff, stick **2** : comfort, support

badajo *nm* : clapper (of a bell)

badén *nm, pl* **badenes** **1** : (paved) ford, channel **2** : dip, ditch (in a road) **3** : speed bump

bádminton *nm* : badminton

bafle *or* **baffle** *nm* **1** : baffle **2** : speaker, loudspeaker

bagaje *nm* **1** EQUIPAJE : baggage, luggage **2** : background ⟨bagaje cultural : cultural baggage⟩

bagatela *nf* : trifle, trinket

bagre *nm* : catfish

bahía *nf* : bay

bailar *vt* : to dance — *vi* **1** : to dance **2** : to spin **3** : to be loose, to be too big

bailarín[1], -rina *adj, mpl* **-rines** **1** : dancing **2** : fond of dancing

bailarín[2], -rina *n, mpl* **-rines** **1** : dancer **2** : ballet dancer, ballerina *f*

baile *nm* **1** : dance **2** : dance party, ball **3 llevarse al baile a** *Mex fam* : to take for a ride, to take advantage of

baja *nf* **1** DESCENSO : fall, drop **2** : slump, recession **3** : loss, casualty **4 dar de baja** : to discharge, to dismiss **5 darse de baja** : to withdraw, to drop out

bajada *nf* **1** : descent **2** : dip, slope **3** : decrease, drop

bajar *vt* **1** DESCENDER : to lower, to let down, to take down **2** REDUCIR : to reduce (prices) **3** INCLINAR : to lower, to bow (the head) **4** : to go down, to descend **5 bajar de categoría** : to downgrade — *vi* **1** : to drop, to fall **2** : to come down, to go down **3** : to ebb (of tides) — **bajarse** *vr* **~ de** : to get off, to get out of (a vehicle)

bajeza *nf* **1** : low or despicable act **2** : baseness

bajío *nm* **1** : lowland **2** : shoal, sandbank, shallows

bajista *nmf* : bass player, bassist

bajo[1] *adv* **1** : down, low **2** : softly, quietly ⟨habla más bajo : speak more softly⟩

bajo[2], -ja *adj* **1** : low **2** : short (of stature) **3** : soft, faint, deep (of sounds) **4** : lower ⟨el bajo Amazonas : the lower Amazon⟩ **5** : lowered ⟨con la mirada baja : with lowered eyes⟩ **6** : base, vile **7 los bajos fondos** : the underworld

bajo[3] *nm* **1** : bass (musical instrument) **2** : first floor, ground floor **3** : hemline

bajo[4] *prep* : under, beneath, below

bajón *nm, pl* **bajones** : sharp drop, slump

bajorrelieve *nm* : bas-relief

bala *nf* **1** : bullet **2** : bale

balacera *nf* TIROTEO : shoot-out, gunfight

balada *nf* : ballad

balance *nm* **1** : balance **2** : balance sheet

balancear *vt* **1** : to balance **2** : to swing (one's arms, etc.) **3** : to rock (a boat) — **balancearse** *vr* **1** OSCILAR : to swing, to sway, to rock **2** VACILAR : to hesitate, to vacillate

balanceo *nm* **1** : swaying, rocking **2** : vacillation

balancín *nm, pl* **-cines** **1** : rocking chair **2** SUBIBAJA : seesaw

balandra *nf* : sloop

balanza *nf* BÁSCULA : scales *pl,* balance

balar *vi* : to bleat

balaustrada *nf* : balustrade

balaustre *nm* : baluster

balazo *nm* **1** TIRO : shot, gunshot **2** : bullet wound

balboa *nf* : balboa (monetary unit of Panama)

balbucear *vi* **1** : to mutter, to stammer **2** : to prattle, to babble ⟨los niños están balbuceando : the children are prattling away⟩

balbuceo *nm* : mumbling, stammering

balbucir → **balbucear**

balcánico, -ca *adj* : Balkan

balcón *nm, pl* **balcones** : balcony

balde *nm* **1** CUBO : bucket, pail **2 en ~** : in vain, to no avail

baldío[1], -día *adj* **1** : fallow, uncultivated **2** : useless, vain

baldío[2] *nm* **1** : wasteland **2** *Mex* : vacant lot

baldosa *nf* LOSETA : floor tile

balear *vt* : to shoot, to shoot at

balero *nm* **1** *Mex* : ball bearing **2** *Mex, PRi* : cup-and-ball toy

balido *nm* : bleat

balín *nm, pl* **balines** : pellet

balística *nf* : ballistics

balístico, -ca *adj* : ballistic

baliza *nf* **1** : buoy **2** : beacon (for aircraft)

ballena *nf* : whale

ballenero[1], -ra *adj* : whaling

ballenero[2], -ra *n* : whaler

ballenero[3] *nm* : whaleboat, whaler

ballesta *nf* **1** : crossbow **2** : spring (of an automobile)

ballet *nm* : ballet

balneario *nm* : spa, bathing resort

balompié *nm* FUTBOL : soccer

balón *nm, pl* **balones** : ball

baloncesto *nm* BASQUETBOL : basketball

balsa *nf* **1** : raft **2** : balsa **3** : pond, pool

balsámico, -ca *adj* : soothing

bálsamo *nm* : balsam, balm

báltico, -ca *adj* : Baltic

baluarte *nm* BASTIÓN : bulwark, bastion

bambolear *vi* **1** : to sway, to swing **2** : to wobble — **bambolearse** *vr*

bamboleo *nm* **1** : swaying, swinging **2** : wobbling

bambú *nm, pl* **bambúes** *or* **bambús** : bamboo

banal *adj* : banal, trivial

banalidad *nf* : banality

banana *nf* : banana

bananero[1], **-ra** *adj* : banana

bananero[2] *nm* : banana tree

banano *nm* **1** : banana tree **2** *CA, Col* : banana

banca *nf* **1** : banking **2** BANCO : bench

bancada *nf* **1** : group, faction **2** : workbench

bancal *nm* **1** : terrace (in agriculture) **2** : plot (of land)

bancario, -ria *adj* : bank, banking

bancarrota *nf* QUIEBRA : bankruptcy

banco *nm* **1** : bank ⟨banco central : central bank⟩ ⟨banco de datos : data bank⟩ ⟨banco de arena : sandbank⟩ ⟨banco de sangre : blood bank⟩ **2** BANCA : stool, bench **3** : pew **4** : school (of fish)

banda *nf* **1** : band, strip **2** *Mex* : belt ⟨banda transportadora : conveyor belt⟩ **3** : band (of musicians) **4** : gang (of persons), flock (of birds) **5 banda de rodadura** : tread (of a tire, etc.) **6 banda sonora** *or* **banda de sonido** : sound track

bandada *nf* : flock (of birds), school (of fish)

bandazo *nm* : swerving, lurch

bandearse *vr* : to look after oneself, to cope

bandeja *nf* : tray, platter

bandera *nf* : flag, banner

banderazo *nm* : starting signal (in sports)

banderilla *nf* : banderilla, dart (in bullfighting)

banderín *nm, pl* **-rines** : pennant, small flag

bandidaje *nm* : banditry

bandido, -da *n* BANDOLERO : bandit, outlaw

bando *nm* **1** FACCIÓN : faction, side **2** EDICTO : proclamation

bandolerismo *nm* : banditry

bandolero, -ra *n* BANDIDO : bandit, outlaw

bangladesí *adj & nmf* : Bangladeshi

banjo *nm* : banjo

banquero, -ra *n* : banker

banqueta *nf* **1** : footstool, stool, bench **2** *Mex* : sidewalk

banquete *nm* : banquet

banquetear *v* : to feast

banquillo *nm* **1** : bench (in sports) **2** : dock, defendant's seat

bañadera *nf* → **bañera**

bañar *vt* **1** : to bathe, to wash **2** : to immerse, to dip **3** : to coat, to cover ⟨bañado en lágrimas : bathed in tears⟩ — **bañarse** *vr* **1** : to take a bath, to bathe **2** : to go for a swim

bañera *nf* TINA : bathtub

bañista *nmf* : bather

baño *nm* **1** : bath **2** : swim, dip **3** : bathroom **4 baño María** : double boiler

baqueta *nf* **1** : ramrod **2 baquetas** *nfpl* : drumsticks

bar *nm* : bar, tavern

baraja *nf* : deck of cards

barajar *vt* **1** : to shuffle (cards) **2** : to consider, to toy with

baranda *nf* : rail, railing

barandal *nm* **1** : rail, railing **2** : bannister, handrail

barandilla *nf Spain* : bannister, handrail, railing

barata *nf* **1** *Mex* : sale, bargain **2** *Chile* : cockroach

baratija *nf* : bauble, trinket

baratillo *nm* : rummage sale, flea market

barato[1] *adv* : cheap, cheaply ⟨te lo vendo barato : I'll sell it to you cheap⟩

barato[2], **-ta** *adj* : cheap, inexpensive

baratura *nf* **1** : cheapness **2** : cheap thing

barba *nf* **1** : beard, stubble **2** : chin

barbacoa *nf* : barbecue

bárbaramente *adv* : barbarously

barbaridad *nf* **1** : barbarity, atrocity **2 ¡qué barbaridad!** : that's outrageous!

barbarie *nf* : barbarism, savagery

bárbaro[1] *adv fam* : wildly ⟨anoche lo pasamos bárbaro : we had a wild time last night⟩

bárbaro[2], **-ra** *adj* **1** : barbarous, wild, uncivilized **2** *fam* : great, fantastic

bárbaro[3], **-ra** *n* : barbarian

barbecho *nm* : fallow land ⟨dejar en barbecho : to leave fallow⟩

barbero, -ra *n* : barber

barbilla *nf* MENTÓN : chin

barbitúrico *nm* : barbiturate

barbudo[1], **-da** *adj* : bearded

barbudo[2] *nm* : bearded man

barca *nf* **1** : boat **2 barca de pasaje** : ferryboat

barcaza *nf* : barge

barcia *nf* : chaff

barco *nm* **1** BARCA : boat **2** BUQUE, NAVE : ship

bardo *nm* : bard

bario *nm* : barium

barítono *nm* : baritone

barlovento *nm* : windward

barman *nm* : bartender

barniz *nm, pl* **barnices** **1** LACA : varnish, lacquer **2** : glaze (on ceramics, etc.)

barnizar {21} *vt* **1** : to varnish **2** : to glaze

barométrico, -ca *adj* : barometric

barómetro *nm* : barometer

barón *nm, pl* **barones** : baron

baronesa *nf* : baroness

baronet *nm* : baronet

barquero, -ra : boatman *m,* boatwoman *f*

barquillo *nm* : wafer, thin cookie or cracker

barra *nf* : bar

barraca *nf* **1** CABAÑA, CHOZA : hut, cabin **2** : booth, stall

barracuda *nf* : barracuda

barranca *nf* **1** : hillside, slope **2** → **barranco**

barranco *nm* : ravine, gorge

barredora *nf* : street sweeper (machine)

barrena *nf* **1** TALADRO : drill, auger, gimlet **2** : tailspin

barrenar *vt* **1** : to drill **2** : to undermine

barrendero, -ra *n* : sweeper, street cleaner

barrer *v* : to sweep — **barrerse** *vr* : to slide (in sports)

barrera *nf* OBSTÁCULO : barrier, obstacle ⟨barrera de sonido : sound barrier⟩

barreta *nf* : crowbar

barriada *nf* **1** : district, quarter **2** : slums *pl*

barrica *nf* BARRIL, TONEL : barrel, cask, keg

barricada *nf* : barricade

barrida *nf* **1** : sweep **2** : slide (in sports)

barrido *nm* : sweeping

barriga *nf* PANZA : belly, paunch

barrigón, -gona *adj, mpl* **-gones** *fam* : potbellied, paunchy

barril *nm* **1** BARRICA : barrel, keg **2** **cerveza de barril** : draft beer

barrio *nm* **1** : neighborhood, district **2** **barrios bajos** : slums *pl*

barro *nm* **1** LODO : mud **2** ARCILLA : clay **3** ESPINILLA, GRANO : pimple, blackhead

barroco, -ca *adj* : baroque

barroso, -sa *adj* ENLODADO : muddy

barrote *nm* : bar (on a window)

barrunto *nm* **1** SOSPECHA : suspicion **2** INDICIO : sign, indication, hint

bártulos *nmpl* : things, belongings ⟨liar los bártulos : to pack one's things⟩

barullo *nm* BULLA : racket, ruckus

basa *nf* : base, pedestal

basalto *nm* : basalt

basar *vt* FUNDAR : to base — **basarse** *vr* FUNDARSE **~ en** : to be based on

báscula *nf* BALANZA : balance, scales *pl*

base *nf* **1** : base, bottom **2** : base (in baseball) **3** FUNDAMENTO : basis, foundation **4** **base de datos** : database **5** **a base de** : based on, by means of **6** **en base a** : based on, on the basis of

básico, -ca *adj* FUNDAMENTAL : basic — **básicamente** *adv*

basílica *nf* : basilica

basquetbol *or* **básquetbol** *nm* BALONCESTO : basketball

basset *nm* : basset hound

bastante[1] *adv* **1** : enough, sufficiently ⟨he trabajado bastante : I have worked enough⟩ **2** : fairly, rather, quite ⟨llegaron bastante temprano : they arrived quite early⟩

bastante[2] *adj* : enough, sufficient

bastante[3] *pron* : enough ⟨hemos visto bastante : we have seen enough⟩

bastar *vi* : to be enough, to suffice

bastardilla *nf* CURSIVA : italic type, italics *pl*

bastardo, -da *adj & n* : bastard

bastidor *nm* **1** : framework, frame **2** : wing (in theater) ⟨entre bastidores : backstage, behind the scenes⟩

bastilla *nf* : hem

bastión *nf, pl* **bastiones** BALUARTE : bastion, bulwark

basto, -ta *adj* : coarse, rough

bastón *nm, pl* **bastones** **1** : cane, walking stick **2** : baton **3** **bastón de mando** : staff (of authority)

basura *nf* DESECHOS : garbage, waste, refuse

basurero[1], **-ra** *n* : garbage collector

basurero[2] *nm Mex* : garbage can

bata *nf* **1** : bathrobe, housecoat **2** : smock, coverall, lab coat

batalla *nf* **1** : battle **2** : fight, struggle **3** **de ~** : ordinary, everyday ⟨mis zapatos de batalla : my everyday shoes⟩

batallar *vi* LIDIAR, LUCHAR : to battle, to fight

batallón *nm, pl* **-llones** : battalion

batata *nf* : yam, sweet potato

batazo *nm* HIT : hit (in baseball)

bate *nm* : baseball bat

batea *nf* **1** : tray, pan **2** : flat-bottomed boat, punt

bateador, -dora *n* : batter, hitter

batear *vi* : to bat — *vt* : to hit

bateo *nm* : batting (in baseball)

batería *nf* **1** PILA : battery **2** : drum kit, drums *pl* **3** **batería de cocina** : kitchen utensils *pl*

baterista *nmf* : drummer

batido *nm* LICUADO : milk shake

batidor *nm* : eggbeater, whisk, mixer

batidora *nf* : (electric) mixer

batir *vt* **1** GOLPEAR : to beat, to hit **2** VENCER : to defeat **3** REVOLVER : to mix, to beat **4** : to break (a record) — **batirse** *vr* : to fight

batista *nf* : batiste, cambric

batuta *nf* **1** : baton **2** **llevar la batuta** : to be the leader, to call the tune

baúl *nm* : trunk, chest

bautismal *adj* : baptismal

bautismo *nm* : baptism, christening

bautista *adj & nmf* : Baptist

bautizar {21} *vt* : to baptize, to christen

bautizo → **bautismo**

bávaro, -ra *adj & n* : Bavarian

baya *nf* **1** : berry **2** **baya de saúco** : elderberry

bayeta *nf* : cleaning cloth

bayoneta *nf* : bayonet

baza *nf* **1** : trick (in card games) **2** **meter baza en** : to butt in on

bazar *nm* : bazaar

bazo *nm* : spleen

bazofia *nf* **1** : table scraps *pl* **2** : slop, swill **3** : hogwash, rubbish

bazuca *nf* : bazooka

beagle *nm* : beagle

beatificar {72} *vt* : to beatify — **beatificación** *nf*

beatífico, -ca *adj* : beatific

beatitud *nf* : beatitude

beato, -ta *adj* **1** : blessed **2** : pious, devout **3** : sanctimonious, overly devout

bebé *nm* : baby

bebedero *nm* **1** ABREVADERO : watering trough **2** *Mex* : drinking fountain

bebedor, -dora *n* : drinker

beber *v* TOMAR : to drink

bebida *nf* : drink, beverage

beca *nf* : grant, scholarship

becado, -da *n* : scholar, scholarship holder

becerro, -rra *n* : calf

begonia *nf* : begonia

beige *adj & nm* : beige

beisbol *or* **béisbol** *nm* : baseball

beisbolista *nmf* : baseball player

beldad *nf* BELLEZA, HERMOSURA : beauty

belén *nf, pl* **belenes** NACIMIENTO : Nativity scene

belga *adj & nmf* : Belgian

beliceño, -ña *adj & n* : Belizean

belicista[1] *adj* : militaristic

belicista[2] *nmf* : warmonger

bélico, -ca *adj* GUERRERO : war, fighting ⟨esfuerzos bélicos : war efforts⟩

belicosidad *nf* : bellicosity

belicoso, -sa *adj* **1** : warlike, martial **2** : aggressive, belligerent

beligerancia *nf* : belligerence

beligerante *adj & nmf* : belligerent

bellaco[1]**, -ca** *adj* : sly, cunning

bellaco[2]**, -ca** *n* : rogue, scoundrel

belleza *nf* BELDAD, HERMOSURA : beauty

bello, -lla *adj* **1** HERMOSO : beautiful **2** **bellas artes** : fine arts

bellota *nf* : acorn

bemol *nm* : flat (in music) — **bemol** *adj*

benceno *nm* : benzene

bendecir {11} *vt* **1** CONSAGRAR : to bless, to consecrate **2** ALABAR : to praise, to extol **3** **bendecir la mesa** : to say grace

bendición *nf, pl* **-ciones** : benediction, blessing

bendiga, bendijo etc. → **bendecir**

bendito, -ta *adj* **1** : blessed, holy **2** : fortunate **3** : silly, simple-minded

benedictino, -na *adj & n* : Benedictine

benefactor[1]**, -tora** *adj* : beneficent

benefactor[2]**, -tora** *n* : benefactor, benefactress *f*

beneficencia *nf* : beneficence, charity

beneficiar *vt* : to benefit, to be of assistance to — **beneficiarse** *vr* : to benefit, to profit

beneficiario, -ria *n* : beneficiary

beneficio *nm* **1** GANANCIA, PROVECHO : gain, profit **2** : benefit

beneficioso, -sa *adj* PROVECHOSO : beneficial

benéfico, -ca *adj* : charitable, beneficent

benemérito, -ta *adj* : meritorious, worthy

beneplácito *nm* : approval, consent

benevolencia *nf* BONDAD : benevolence, kindness

benévolo, -la *adj* BONDADOSO : benevolent, kind, good

bengala *nf* **luz de bengala 1** : flare (signal) **2** : sparkler

bengalí[1] *adj & nmf* : Bengali

bengalí[2] *nm* : Bengali (language)

benignidad *nf* : mildness, kindness

benigno, -na *adj* : benign, mild

beninés, -nesa *adj & n* : Beninese

benjamín, -mina *n, mpl* **-mines** : youngest child

beodo[1]**, -da** *adj* : drunk, inebriated

beodo[2]**, -da** *n* : drunkard

berberecho *nm* : cockle

berbiquí *nm* : brace (in carpentry)

berenjena *nf* : eggplant

bergantín *nm, pl* **-tines** : brig (ship)

berilo *nm* : beryl

bermudas *nfpl* : Bermuda shorts

berrear *vi* **1** : to bellow, to low **2** : to bawl, to howl

berrido *nm* **1** : bellowing **2** : howl, scream

berrinche *nm fam* : tantrum, conniption

berro *nm* : watercress

berza *nf* : cabbage

besar *vt* : to kiss

beso *nm* : kiss

bestia[1] *adj* **1** : ignorant, stupid **2** : boorish, rude

bestia[2] *nf* : beast, animal

bestia[3] *nmf* **1** IGNORANTE : ignoramus **2** : brute

bestial *adj* **1** : bestial, beastly **2** *fam* : huge, enormous ⟨hace un frío bestial : it's terribly cold⟩ **3** *fam* : great, fantastic

besuquear *vt fam* : to cover with kisses — **besuquearse** *vr fam* : to neck, to smooch

betabel *nm Mex* : beet

betún *nm, pl* **betunes 1** : shoe polish **2** *Mex* : icing

bianual *adj* : biannual

biatlón *nm, pl* **-lones** : biathlon

biberón *nm, pl* **-rones** : baby's bottle

biblia *nf* **1** : bible **2** **la Biblia** : the Bible

bíblico, -ca *adj* : biblical

bibliografía *nf* : bibliography

bibliográfico, -ca *adj* : bibliographic, bibliographical

bibliógrafo, -fa *n* : bibliographer

biblioteca *nf* : library

bibliotecario, -ria *n* : librarian

bicameral *adj* : bicameral

bicarbonato *nm* **1** : bicarbonate **2** **bicarbonato de soda** : sodium bicarbonate, baking soda

bicentenario *nm* : bicentennial

bíceps *nms & pl* : biceps
bicho *nm* : small animal, bug, insect
bici *nf fam* : bike
bicicleta *nf* : bicycle
bicolor *adj* : two-tone
bicúspide *adj* : bicuspid
bidón *nm, pl* **bidones** : large can, (oil) drum
bien[1] *adv* **1** : well ⟨¿dormiste bien? : did you sleep well?⟩ **2** CORRECTAMENTE : correctly, properly, right ⟨hay que hacerlo bien : it must be done correctly⟩ **3** : very, quite ⟨el libro era bien divertido : the book was very amusing⟩ **4** : easily ⟨bien puede acabarlo en un día : he can easily finish it in a day⟩ **5** : willingly, readily ⟨bien lo aceptaré : I'll gladly accept it⟩ **6 bien que** : although **7 más bien** : rather
bien[2] *adj* **1** : well, OK, all right ⟨¿te sientes bien? : are you feeling all right?⟩ **2** : pleasant, agreeable ⟨las flores huelen bien : the flowers smell very nice⟩ **3** : satisfactory **4** : correct, right
bien[3] *nm* **1** : good ⟨el bien y el mal : good and evil⟩ **2 bienes** *nmpl* : property, goods, possessions
bienal *adj & nf* : biennial — **bienalmente** *adv*
bienaventurado, -da *adj* **1** : blessed **2** : fortunate, happy
bienaventuranzas *nfpl* : Beatitudes
bienestar *nm* **1** : welfare, well-being **2** CONFORT : comfort
bienhechor[1], **-chora** *adj* : beneficent, benevolent
bienhechor[2], **-chora** *n* : benefactor, benefactress *f*
bienintencionado, -da *adj* : well-meaning
bienvenida *nf* **1** : welcome **2 dar la bienvenida a** : to welcome
bienvenido, -da *adj* : welcome
bies *nm* : bias (in sewing)
bife *nm Arg, Chile, Uru* : steak
bífido, -da *adj* : forked
bifocal *adj* : bifocal
bifocales *nmpl* : bifocals
bifurcación *nf, pl* **-ciones** : fork (in a river or road)
bifurcarse {72} *vr* : to fork
bigamia *nf* : bigamy
bígamo, -ma *n* : bigamist
bigote *nm* **1** : mustache **2** : whisker (of an animal)
bigotudo, -da *adj* : mustached, having a big mustache
bikini *nm* : bikini
bilateral *adj* : bilateral — **bilateralmente** *adv*
bilingüe *adj* : bilingual
bilioso, -sa *adj* **1** : bilious **2** : irritable
bilis *nf* : bile
billar *nm* : pool, billiards
billete *nm* **1** : bill ⟨un billete de cinco dólares : a five-dollar bill⟩ **2** BOLETO : ticket ⟨billete de ida y vuelta : round-trip ticket⟩
billetera *nf* : billfold, wallet
billón *nm, pl* **billones** **1** : billion (Great Britain) **2** : trillion (U.S.A.)
bimestral *adj* : bimonthly — **bimestralmente** *adv*
bimotor *adj* : twin-engined
binacional *adj* : binational
binario, -ria *adj* : binary
bingo *nm* : bingo
binocular *adj* : binocular
binoculares *nmpl* : binoculars
binomio *nm* **1** : binomial **2** PAREJA : pair, duo
biodegradable *adj* : biodegradable
biodegradarse *vr* : to biodegrade
biodiversidad *nf* : biodiversity
biofísica *nf* : biophysics
biofísico[1], **-ca** *adj* : biophysical
biofísico[2], **-ca** *n* : biophysicist
biografía *nf* : biography
biográfico, -ca *adj* : biographical
biógrafo, -fa *n* : biographer
biología *nf* : biology
biológico, -ca *adj* : biological, biologic — **biológicamente** *adv*
biólogo, -ga *n* : biologist
biombo *nm* MAMPARA : folding screen, room divider
biomecánica *nf* : biomechanics
biopsia *nf* : biopsy
bioquímica *nf* : biochemistry
bioquímico[1], **-ca** *adj* : biochemical
bioquímico[2], **-ca** *n* : biochemist
biosfera *or* **biósfera** *nf* : biosphere
biotecnología *nf* : biotechnology
biótico, -ca *adj* : biotic
bipartidismo *nm* : two-party system
bipartidista *adj* : bipartisan
bípedo *nm* : biped
birlar *vt fam* : to swipe, to pinch
birmano, -na *adj & n* : Burmese
bis[1] *adv* **1** : twice, again (in music) **2** : a, A ⟨artículo 47 bis : Article 47A⟩ ⟨calle Bolívar, número 70 bis : Bolívar Street, number 70A⟩
bis[2] *nm* : encore
bisabuelo, -la *n* : great-grandfather *m*, great-grandmother *f*, great-grandparent
bisagra *nf* : hinge
bisecar {72} *vt* : bisect — **bisección** *nf*
bisel *nm* : bevel
biselar *vt* : to bevel
bisexual *adj* : bisexual
bisiesto *adj* **año bisiesto** : leap year
bismuto *nm* : bismuth
bisnieto, -ta *n* : great-grandson *m*, great-granddaughter *f*, great-grandchild
bisonte *nm* : bison, buffalo
bisoñé *nm* : hairpiece, toupee
bisoño[1], **-ña** *adj* : inexperienced, green
bisoño[2], **-ña** *n* : rookie, greenhorn
bistec *nm* : steak, beefsteak
bisturí *nm* ESCALPELO : scalpel
bisutería *nf* : costume jewelry
bit *nm* : bit (unit of information)
bivalvo *nm* : bivalve
bizarría *nf* **1** : courage, gallantry **2** : generosity

bizarro, -rra *adj* **1** VALIENTE : courageous, valiant **2** GENEROSO : generous

bizco, -ca *adj* : cross-eyed

bizcocho *nm* **1** : sponge cake **2** : biscuit **3** *Mex* : breadstick

bizquera *nf* : crossed eyes, squint

blanco[1], **-ca** *adj* : white

blanco[2], **-ca** *n* : white person

blanco[3] *nm* **1** : white **2** : target, bull's-eye ⟨dar en el blanco : to hit the target, to hit the nail on the head⟩ **3** : blank space, blank ⟨un cheque en blanco : a blank check⟩

blancura *nf* : whiteness

blancuzco, -ca *adj* **1** : whitish, off-white **2** PÁLIDO : pale

blandir {1} *vt* : to wave, to brandish

blando, -da *adj* **1** SUAVE : soft, tender **2** : weak (in character) **3** : lenient

blandura *nf* **1** : softness, tenderness **2** : leniency

blanqueador *nm* : bleach, whitener

blanquear *vt* **1** : to whiten, to bleach **2** : to shut out (in sports) **3** : to launder (money) — *vi* : to turn white

blanquillo *nm CA, Mex* : egg

blasfemar *vi* : to blaspheme

blasfemia *nf* : blasphemy

blasfemo, -ma *adj* : blasphemous

blazer *nm* : blazer

bledo *nm* **no me importa un bledo** *fam* : I couldn't care less, I don't give a damn

blindado, -da *adj* ACORAZADO : armored

blindaje *nm* **1** : armor, armor plating **2** : shield (for cables, machinery, etc.)

bloc *nm, pl* **blocs** : writing pad, pad of paper

blof *nm Col, Mex* : bluff

blofear *vi Col, Mex* : to bluff

blondo, -da *adj* : blond, flaxen

bloque *nm* **1** : block **2** GRUPO : bloc ⟨el bloque comunista : the Communist bloc⟩

bloquear *vt* **1** OBSTRUIR : to block, to obstruct **2** : to blockade

bloqueo *nm* **1** OBSTRUCCIÓN : blockage, obstruction **2** : blockade

blusa *nf* : blouse

blusón *nm, pl* **blusones** : loose shirt, smock

boa *nf* : boa

boato *nm* : ostentation, show

bobada *nf* **1** : stupid remark or action **2 decir bobadas** : to talk nonsense

bobalicón, -cona *adj, mpl* **-cones** *fam* : silly, stupid

bobina *nf* CARRETE : bobbin, reel

bobo[1], **-ba** *adj* : silly, stupid

bobo[2], **-ba** *n* : fool, simpleton

boca *nf* **1** : mouth **2 boca arriba** : face up, on one's back **3 boca abajo** : face down, prone **4 boca de riego** : hydrant **5 en boca de** : according to

bocacalle *nf* : entrance to a street ⟨gire a la última bocacalle : take the last turning⟩

bocadillo *nm Spain* : sandwich

bocado *nm* **1** : bite, mouthful **2** FRENO : bit (of a bridle)

bocajarro *nm* **a ~** : point-blank, directly

bocallave *nf* : keyhole

bocanada *nf* **1** : swig, swallow **2** : puff, mouthful (of smoke) **3** : gust (of air) **4** : stream (of people)

boceto *nm* : sketch, outline

bochinche *nm fam* : ruckus, uproar

bochorno *nm* **1** VERGÜENZA : embarrassment **2** : hot and humid weather **3** : hot flash

bochornoso, -sa *adj* **1** EMBARAZOSO : embarrassing **2** : hot and muggy

bocina *nf* **1** : horn, trumpet **2** : automobile horn **3** : mouthpiece (of a telephone) **4** *Mex* : loudspeaker

bocinazo *nm* : honk (of a horn)

bocio *nm* : goiter

bocón, -cona *n, mpl* **bocones** *fam* : blabbermouth, loudmouth

boda *nf* : wedding

bodega *nf* **1** : wine cellar **2** *Chile, Col, Mex* : storeroom, warehouse **3** (*in various countries*) : grocery store

bofetada *nf* CACHETADA : slap on the face

bofetear *vt* CACHETEAR : to slap

bofetón *nm* → **bofetada**

bofo, -fa *adj* : flabby

boga *nf* : fashion, vogue ⟨estar en boga : to be in style⟩

bogotano[1], **-na** *adj* : of or from Bogotá

bogotano[2], **-na** *n* : person from Bogotá

bohemio, -mia *adj & n* : bohemian, Bohemian

boicot *nm, pl* **boicots** : boycott

boicotear *vt* : to boycott

boina *nf* : beret

boiserie *nf* : wood paneling, wainscoting

boj *nm, pl* **bojes** : box (plant), boxwood

bola *nf* **1** : ball ⟨bola de nieve : snowball⟩ **2** *fam* : lie, fib **3** *Mex fam* : bunch, group ⟨una bola de rateros : a bunch of thieves⟩ **4** *Mex* : uproar, tumult

bolear *vt Mex* : to polish (shoes)

bolera *nf* : bowling alley

bolero *nm* : bolero

boleta *nf* **1** : ballot **2** : ticket **3** : receipt

boletería *nf* TAQUILLA : box office, ticket office

boletín *nm, pl* **-tines** **1** : bulletin **2** : journal, review **3 boletín de prensa** : press release

boleto *nm* BILLETE : ticket

boliche *nm* **1** BOLOS : bowling **2** *Arg* : bar, tavern

bólido *nm* **1** : race car **2** METEORO : meteor

bolígrafo *nm* : ballpoint pen

bolillo *nm* **1** : bobbin **2** *Mex* : roll, bun

bolívar *nm* : bolivar (monetary unit of Venezuela)

boliviano[1], **-na** *adj & n* : Bolivian

boliviano[2] *nm* : boliviano (monetary unit of Bolivia)

bollo *nm* : bun, sweet roll
bolo *nm* : bowling pin, tenpin
bolos *nmpl* BOLICHE : bowling
bolsa *nf* **1** : bag, sack **2** *Mex* : pocketbook, purse **3** *Mex* : pocket **4 la Bolsa** : the stock market, the stock exchange **5 bolsa de trabajo** : employment agency
bolsear *vi Mex* : to pick pockets
bolsillo *nm* **1** : pocket **2 dinero de bolsillo** : pocket change, loose change
bolso *nm* : pocketbook, handbag
bomba *nf* **1** : bomb **2** : bubble **3** : pump ⟨bomba de gasolina : gas pump⟩
bombachos *nmpl* : baggy pants, bloomers
bombardear *vt* **1** : to bomb **2** : to bombard
bombardeo *nm* **1** : bombing, shelling **2** : bombardment
bombardero *nm* : bomber (airplane)
bombástico, -ca *adj* : bombastic
bombear *vt* : to pump
bombero, -ra *n* : firefighter, fireman *m*
bombilla *nf* : lightbulb
bombillo *nm CA, Col, Ven* : lightbulb
bombo *nm* **1** : bass drum **2** *fam* : exaggerated praise, hype ⟨con bombos y platillos : with great fanfare⟩
bombón *nm, pl* **bombones 1** : bonbon, chocolate **2** *Mex* : marshmallow
bonachón[1], -chona *adj, mpl* **-chones** *fam* : good-natured, kindhearted
bonachón[2], -chona *n, mpl* **-chones** *fam* BUENAZO : kindhearted person
bonaerense[1] *adj* : of or from Buenos Aires
bonaerense[2] *nmf* : person from Buenos Aires
bonanza *nf* **1** PROSPERIDAD : prosperity ⟨bonanza económica : economic boom⟩ **2** : calm weather **3** : rich ore deposit, bonanza
bondad *nf* BENEVOLENCIA : goodness, kindness ⟨tener la bondad de hacer algo : to be kind enough to do something⟩
bondadoso, -sa *adj* BENÉVOLO : kind, kindly, good — **bondadosamente** *adv*
bonete *nm* : cap, mortarboard
boniato *nm* : sweet potato
bonificación *nf, pl* **-ciones 1** : discount **2** : bonus, extra
bonito[1] *adv* : nicely, well ⟨¡qué bonito canta tu hermana! : your sister sings wonderfully!⟩
bonito[2], -ta *adj* LINDO : pretty, lovely ⟨tiene un apartamento bonito : she has a nice apartment⟩
bonito[3] *nm* : bonito (tuna)
bono *nm* **1** : bond ⟨bono bancario : bank bond⟩ **2** : voucher
boqueada *nf* : gasp ⟨dar la última boqueada : to give one's last gasp⟩
boquear *vi* **1** : to gasp **2** : to be dying
boquete *nm* : gap, opening, breach
boquiabierto, -ta *adj* : open-mouthed, speechless, agape
boquilla *nf* : mouthpiece (of a musical instrument)
borbollar *vi* : to bubble
borbotar *or* **borbotear** *vi* : to boil, to bubble, to gurgle
borboteo *nm* : bubbling, gurgling
borda *nf* : gunwale
bordado *nm* : embroidery, needlework
bordar *v* : to embroider
borde *nm* **1** : border, edge **2 al borde de** : on the verge of ⟨estoy al borde de la locura : I'm about to go crazy⟩
bordear *vt* **1** : to border, to skirt ⟨el Río Este bordea Manhattan : the East River borders Manhattan⟩ **2** : to border on ⟨bordea la irrealidad : it borders on unreality⟩ **3** : to line ⟨una calle bordeada de árboles : a street lined with trees⟩
bordillo *nm* : curb
bordo *nm* **a ~** : aboard, on board
boreal *adj* : northern
borgoña *nf* : burgundy
bórico, -ca *adj* : boric ⟨ácido bórico : boric acid⟩
boricua *adj & nmf fam* : Puerto Rican
borinqueño, -ña → **boricua**
borla *nf* **1** : pom-pom, tassel **2** : powder puff
boro *nm* : boron
borrachera *nf* : drunkenness ⟨agarró una borrachera : he got drunk⟩
borrachín, -china *n, mpl* **-chines** *fam* : lush, drunk
borracho[1], -cha *adj* EBRIO : drunk, intoxicated
borracho[2], -cha *n* : drunk, drunkard
borrador *nm* **1** : rough copy, first draft ⟨en borrador : in the rough⟩ **2** : eraser
borrar *vt* : to erase, to blot out — **borrarse** *vr* **1** : to fade, to fade away **2** : to resign, to drop out **3** *Mex fam* : to split, to leave ⟨me borro : I'm out of here⟩
borrascoso, -sa *adj* : gusty, blustery
borrego, -ga *n* **1** : lamb, sheep **2** : simpleton, fool
borrico → **burro**
borrón *nm, pl* **borrones** : smudge, blot ⟨borrón y cuenta nueva : let's start on a clean slate, let's start over again⟩
borronear *vt* : to smudge, to blot
borroso, -sa *adj* **1** : blurry, smudgy **2** CONFUSO : unclear, confused
boscoso, -sa *adj* : wooded
bosnio, -nia *adj & n* : Bosnian
bosque *nm* : woods, forest
bosquecillo *nm* : grove, copse, thicket
bosquejar *vt* ESBOZAR : to outline, to sketch
bosquejo *nm* **1** TRAZADO : outline, sketch **2** : draft
bostezar {21} *vi* : to yawn
bostezo *nm* : yawn
bota *nf* **1** : boot **2** : wineskin
botana *nf Mex* : snack, appetizer
botanear *vi Mex* : to have a snack
botánica *nf* : botany

botánico[1], **-ca** *adj* : botanical
botánico[2], **-ca** *n* : botanist
botar *vt* **1** ARROJAR : to throw, to fling, to hurl **2** TIRAR : to throw out, to throw away **3** : to launch (a ship)
bote *nm* **1** : small boat ⟨bote de remos : rowboat⟩ **2** : can, jar **3** : jump, bounce **4** *Mex fam* : jail
botella *nf* : bottle
botica *nf* FARMACIA : drugstore, pharmacy
boticario, -ria *n* FARMACÉUTICO : pharmacist, druggist
botín *nm, pl* **botines 1** : baby's bootee **2** : ankle boot **3** : booty, plunder
botiquín *nm, pl* **-quines 1** : medicine cabinet **2** : first-aid kit
botón *nm, pl* **botones 1** : button **2** : bud **3** INSIGNIA : badge
botones *nmfs & pl* : bellhop
botulismo *nm* : botulism
boulevard [ˌbule'var] → **bulevar**
bouquet *nm* **1** : fragrance, bouquet (of wine) **2** RAMILLETE : bouquet (of flowers)
boutique *nf* : boutique
bóveda *nf* **1** : vault, dome **2** CRIPTA : crypt
bovino, -na *adj* : bovine
box *nm, pl* **boxes 1** : pit (in auto racing) **2** *Mex* : boxing
boxeador, -dora *n* : boxer
boxear *vi* : to box
boxeo *nm* : boxing
boya *nf* : buoy
boyante *adj* **1** : buoyant **2** : prosperous, thriving
bozal *nm* **1** : muzzle **2** : halter (for a horse)
bracear *vi* **1** : to wave one's arms **2** : to make strokes (in swimming)
bracero, -ra *n* : migrant worker, day laborer
braguero *nm* : truss (in medicine)
bragueta *nf* : fly, pants zipper
braille *adj & nm* : braille
bramante *nm* : twine, string
bramar *vi* **1** RUGIR : to roar, to bellow **2** : to howl (of the wind)
bramido *nm* : bellowing, roar
brandy *nm* : brandy
branquia *nf* AGALLA : gill
brasa *nf* ASCUA : ember, live coal
brasero *nm* : brazier
brasier *nm Col, Mex* : brassiere, bra
brasileño, -ña *adj & n* : Brazilian
bravata *nf* **1** JACTANCIA : boast, bravado **2** AMENAZA : threat
bravo, -va *adj* **1** FEROZ : ferocious, fierce ⟨un perro bravo : a ferocious dog⟩ **2** EXCELENTE : excellent, great ⟨¡bravo! : bravo!, well done!⟩ **3** : rough, rugged, wild **4** : annoyed, angry
bravucón, -cona *n, mpl* **-cones** : bully
bravuconadas *nfpl* : bravado
bravura *nf* **1** FEROCIDAD : fierceness, ferocity **2** VALENTÍA : bravery
braza *nf* **1** : breaststroke **2** : fathom (unit of length)
brazada *nf* : stroke (in swimming)
brazalete *nm* PULSERA : bracelet, bangle
brazo *nm* **1** : arm **2 brazo derecho** : right-hand man **3 brazos** *nmpl* : hands, laborers
brea *nf* ALQUITRÁN : tar, pitch
brebaje *nm* : potion, brew
brecha *nf* **1** : gap, breach ⟨estar siempre en la brecha : to be always there when needed, to stay in the thick of things⟩ **2** : gash
brécol *nm* : broccoli
brega *nf* **1** LUCHA : struggle, fight **2** : hard work
bregar {52} *vi* **1** LUCHAR : to struggle **2** : to toil, to work hard **3 ~ con** : to deal with
brete *nm* : jam, tight spot
breve *adj* **1** CORTO : brief, short **2 en ~** : shortly, in short — **brevemente** *adv*
brevedad *nf* : brevity, shortness
breviario *nm* : breviary
brezal *nm* : heath, moor
brezo *nm* : heather
bribón, -bona *n, mpl* **bribones** : rascal, scamp
bricolaje *or* **bricolage** *nm* : do-it-yourself
brida *nf* : bridle
brigada *nf* **1** : brigade **2** : gang, team, squad
brigadier *nm* : brigadier
brillante[1] *adj* : brilliant, bright — **brillantemente** *adv*
brillante[2] *nm* DIAMANTE : diamond
brillantez *nf* : brilliance, brightness
brillar *vi* : to shine, to sparkle
brillo *nm* **1** LUSTRE : luster, shine **2** : brilliance
brilloso, -sa *adj* LUSTROSO : lustrous, shiny
brincar {72} *vi* **1** SALTAR : to jump around, to leap about **2** : to frolic, to gambol
brinco *nm* **1** SALTO : jump, leap, skip **2 pegar un brinco** : to give a start, to jump
brindar *vi* : to drink a toast ⟨brindó por los vencedores : he toasted the victors⟩ — *vt* OFRECER, PROPORCIONAR : to offer, to provide — **brindarse** *vr* : to offer one's assistance, to volunteer
brindis *nm* : toast, drink ⟨hacer un brindis : to drink a toast⟩
brinque, etc. → **brincar**
brío *nm* **1** : force, determination **2** : spirit, verve
brioso, -sa *adj* : spirited, lively
briqueta *nf* : briquette
brisa *nf* : breeze
británico[1], **-ca** *adj* : British
británico[2], **-ca** *n* **1** : British person **2 los británicos** : the British
brizna *nf* **1** : strand, thread **2** : blade (of grass)

broca *nf* : drill bit

brocado *nm* : brocade

brocha *nf* : paintbrush

broche *nm* **1** ALFILER : brooch **2** : fastener, clasp **3 broche de oro** : finishing touch

brocheta *nf* : skewer

brócoli *nm* : broccoli

broma *nf* **1** CHISTE : joke, prank **2** : fun, merriment **3 en ~** : in jest, jokingly

bromear *vi* : to joke, to fool around ⟨sólo estaba bromeando : I was only kidding⟩

bromista[1] *adj* : fun-loving, joking

bromista[2] *nmf* : joker, prankster

bromo *nm* : bromine

bronca *nf fam* : fight, quarrel, fuss

bronce *nm* : bronze

bronceado[1], **-da** *adj* **1** : tanned, suntanned **2** : bronze

bronceado[2] *nm* **1** : suntan, tan **2** : bronzing

broncearse *vr* : to get a suntan

bronco, -ca *adj* **1** : harsh, rough **2** : untamed, wild

bronquial *adj* : bronchial

bronquio *nm* : bronchial tube, bronchus

bronquitis *nf* : bronchitis

broqueta *nf* : skewer

brotar *vi* **1** : to bud, to sprout **2** : to spring up, to stream, to gush forth **3** : to break out, to appear

brote *nm* **1** : outbreak **2** : sprout, bud, shoot

broza *nf* **1** : brushwood **2** MALEZA : scrub, undergrowth

brujería *nf* HECHICERÍA : witchcraft, sorcery

brujo[1], **-ja** *adj* : bewitching

brujo[2], **-ja** *n* : warlock *m*, witch *f*, sorcerer

brújula *nf* : compass

bruma *nf* : haze, mist

brumoso, -sa *adj* : hazy, misty

bruñir {38} *vt* : to burnish, to polish (metals)

brusco, -ca *adj* **1** SÚBITO : sudden, abrupt **2** : curt, brusque — **bruscamente** *adv*

brusquedad *nf* **1** : abruptness, suddenness **2** : brusqueness

brutal *adj* **1** : brutal **2** *fam* : incredible, terrific — **brutalmente** *adv*

brutalidad *nf* CRUELDAD : brutality

brutalizar {21} *vt* : to brutalize, to maltreat

bruto[1], **-ta** *adj* **1** : gross ⟨peso bruto : gross weight⟩ ⟨ingresos brutos : gross income⟩ **2** : unrefined ⟨petróleo bruto : crude oil⟩ **3** : brutish, stupid

bruto[2], **-ta** *n* **1** : brute **2** : dunce, blockhead

bubónico, -ca *adj* : bubonic

bucal *adj* : oral

bucanero *nm* : buccaneer, pirate

buccino *nm* : whelk

buceador, -dora *n* : diver, scuba diver

bucear *vi* **1** : to dive, to swim underwater **2** : to explore, to delve

buceo *nm* **1** : diving, scuba diving **2** : exploration, searching

buche *nm* **1** : crop (of a bird) **2** *fam* : belly, gut **3** : mouthful ⟨hacer buches : to rinse one's mouth⟩

bucle *nm* **1** : curl, ringlet **2** : loop

bucólico, -ca *adj* : bucolic

budín *nm, pl* **budines** : pudding

budismo *nm* : Buddhism

budista *adj & nmf* : Buddhist

buen *adj* → **bueno**[1]

buenamente *adv* **1** : easily **2** : willingly

buenaventura *nf* **1** : good luck **2** : fortune, future ⟨le dijo la buenaventura : she told his fortune⟩

buenazo, -za *n fam* BONACHÓN : kindhearted person

bueno[1], **-na** *adj* (**buen** *before masculine singular nouns*) **1** : good ⟨una buena idea : a good idea⟩ **2** BONDADOSO : nice, kind **3** APROPIADO : proper, appropriate **4** SANO : well, healthy **5** : considerable, goodly ⟨una buena cantidad : a lot⟩ **6 buenos días** : hello, good day **7 buenas tardes** : good afternoon **8 buenas noches** : good evening, good night

bueno[2] *interj* **1** : OK!, all right! **2** *Mex* : hello! (on the telephone)

buey *nm* : ox, steer

búfalo *nm* **1** : buffalo **2 búfalo de agua** : water buffalo

bufanda *nf* : scarf, muffler

bufar *vi* : to snort

bufet *or* **bufé** *nm* : buffet-style meal

bufete *nm* **1** : law firm, law office **2** : writing desk

bufido *nm* : snort

bufo, -fa *adj* : comic

bufón, -fona *n, mpl* **bufones** : clown, buffoon, jester

bufonada *nf* **1** : jest, buffoonery **2** : sarcasm

buhardilla *nf* **1** ÁTICO, DESVÁN : attic **2** : dormer window

búho *nm* **1** : owl **2** *fam* : hermit, recluse

buhonero, -ra *n* MERCACHIFLE : peddler

buitre *nm* : vulture

bujía *nf* : spark plug

bula *nf* : papal bull

bulbo *nm* : bulb

bulboso, -sa *adj* : bulbous

bulevar *nm* : boulevard

búlgaro, -ra *adj & n* : Bulgarian

bulla *nf* BARULLO : racket, rowdiness

bullicio *nm* **1** : ruckus, uproar **2** : hustle and bustle

bullicioso, -sa *adj* : noisy, busy, turbulent

bullir {38} *vi* **1** HERVIR : to boil **2** MOVERSE : to stir, to bustle about

bulto *nm* **1** : package, bundle **2** : piece of luggage, bag **3** : size, bulk, volume **4** : form, shape **5** : lump (on the body), swelling, bulge

bumerán *nm, pl* **-ranes** : boomerang
búnker *nm, pl* **búnkers** : bunker
búnquer → **búnker**
buñuelo *nm* : fried pastry
buque *nm* BARCO : ship, vessel
burbuja *nf* : bubble, blister (on a surface)
burbujear *vi* **1** : to bubble **2** : to fizz
burbujeo *nm* : bubbling
burdel *nm* : brothel, whorehouse
burdo, -da *adj* **1** : coarse, rough **2** : crude, clumsy ⟨una burda mentira : a clumsy lie⟩ — **burdamente** *adj*
burgués, -guesa *adj & n, mpl* **burgueses** : bourgeois
burguesía *nf* : bourgeoisie, middle class
burla *nf* **1** : mockery, ridicule **2** : joke, trick **3 hacer burla de** : to make fun of, to mock
burlar *vt* ENGAÑAR : to trick, to deceive — **burlarse** *vr* **~ de** : to make fun of, to ridicule
burlesco, -ca *adj* : burlesque, comic
burlón[1], -lona *adj, mpl* **burlones** : joking, mocking
burlón[2], -lona *n, mpl* **burlones** : joker
burocracia *nf* : bureaucracy
burócrata *nmf* : bureaucrat
burocrático, -ca *adj* : bureaucratic
burrada *nf fam* : stupid act, nonsense
burrito *nm* : burrito
burro[1], -rra *adj fam* : dumb, stupid
burro[2], -rra *n* **1** ASNO : donkey, ass **2** *fam* : dunce, poor student
burro[3] *nm* **1** : sawhorse **2** *Mex* : ironing board **3** *Mex* : stepladder
bursátil *adj* : stock-market
bursitis *nf* : bursitis
burundés, -desa *adj & n* : Burundian
bus *nm* : bus
busca *nf* : search
buscador, -dora *n* : hunter (for treasure, etc.), prospector
buscapersonas *nms & pl* : beeper, pager
buscapleitos *nmfs & pl* : troublemaker
buscar {72} *vt* **1** : to look for, to seek **2** : to pick up, to collect **3** : to provoke — *vi* : to look, to search ⟨buscó en los bolsillos : he searched through his pockets⟩
buscavidas *nmf & pl* **1** : busybody **2** : go-getter
busque, etc. → **buscar**
búsqueda *nf* : search
busto *nm* : bust
butaca *nf* **1** SILLÓN : armchair **2** : seat (in a theatre) **3** *Mex* : pupil's desk
butano *nm* : butane
buzo[1], -za *adj Mex fam* : smart, astute ⟨¡ponte buzo! : get with it!, get on the ball!⟩
buzo[2] *nm* : diver, scuba diver
buzón *nm, pl* **buzones** : mailbox
byte *nm* : byte

C

c *nf* : third letter of the Spanish alphabet
cabal *adj* **1** : exact, correct **2** : complete **3** : upright, honest
cabales *nmpl* **no estar en sus cabales** : not to be in one's right mind
cabalgar {52} *vi* : to ride (on horseback)
cabalgata *nf* : cavalcade, procession
cabalidad *nf* **a ~** : thoroughly, conscientiously
caballa *nf* : mackerel
caballada *nf* **1** : herd of horses **2** *fam* : nonsense, stupidity, outrageousness
caballar *adj* EQUINO : horse, equine
caballeresco, -ca *adj* : gallant, chivalrous
caballería *nf* **1** : cavalry **2** : horse, mount **3** : knighthood, chivalry
caballeriza *nf* : stable
caballero[1] → **caballeroso**
caballero[2] *nm* **1** : gentleman **2** : knight
caballerosidad *nf* : chivalry, gallantry
caballeroso, -sa *adj* : gentlemanly, chivalrous
caballete *nm* **1** : ridge **2** : easel **3** : trestle (for a table, etc.) **4** : bridge (of the nose) **5** : sawhorse
caballista *nmf* : horseman *m*, horsewoman *f*
caballito *nm* **1** : rocking horse **2 caballito de mar** : seahorse **3 caballitos** *nmpl* : merry-go-round
caballo *nm* **1** : horse **2** : knight (in chess) **3 caballo de fuerza** *or* **caballo de vapor** : horsepower
cabalmente *adv* : fully, exactly
cabaña *nf* CHOZA : cabin, hut
cabaret *nm, pl* **-rets** : nightclub, cabaret
cabecear *vt* : to head (in soccer) — *vi* **1** : to nod one's head **2** : to lurch, to pitch
cabecera *nf* **1** : headboard **2** : head ⟨cabecera de la mesa : head of the table⟩ **3** : heading, headline **4** : headwaters *pl* **5 médico de cabecera** : family doctor **6 cabecera municipal** *CA, Mex* : downtown area
cabecilla *nmf* : ringleader, kingpin
cabellera *nf* : head of hair, mane
cabello *nm* : hair
cabelludo, -da *adj* **1** : hairy **2 cuero cabelludo** : scalp
caber {12} *vi* **1** : to fit, to go ⟨no sé si cabremos todos en el coche : I don't know if we'll all fit in the car⟩ **2** : to be possible ⟨no cabe duda alguna : there's no doubt about it⟩ ⟨cabe que llegue mañana : he may come tomorrow⟩
cabestrillo *nm* : sling ⟨llevo el brazo en cabestrillo : my arm is in a sling⟩
cabestro *nm* : halter (for an animal)
cabeza *nf* **1** : head **2 cabeza hueca** : scatterbrain **3 de ~** : head first **4 dolor de cabeza** : headache

cabezada *nf* **1** : butt, blow with the head **2** : nod ⟨echar una cabezada : to take a nap, to doze off⟩
cabezal *nm* : bolster
cabezazo *nm* : butt, blow with the head
cabezón, -zona *adj, mpl* **-zones** *fam* **1** : having a big head **2** : pigheaded, stubborn
cabida *nf* **1** : room, space, capacity **2 dar cabida a** : to accommodate, to hold
cabildear *vi* : to lobby
cabildeo *nm* : lobbying
cabildero, -ra *n* : lobbyist
cabildo *nm* AYUNTAMIENTO **1** : town or city hall **2** : town or city council
cabina *nf* **1** : cabin **2** : booth **3** : cab (of a truck), cockpit (of an airplane)
cabizbajo, -ja *adj* : dejected, downcast
cable *nm* : cable
cableado *nm* : wiring
cabo *nm* **1** : end ⟨al cabo de dos semanas : at the end of two weeks⟩ **2** : stub, end piece **3** : corporal **4** : cape, headland ⟨el Cabo Cañaveral : Cape Canaveral⟩ **5 al fin y al cabo** : after all, in the end **6 llevar a cabo** : to carry out, to do
caboverdiano, -na *adj & n* : Cape Verdean
cabrá, etc. → **caber**
cabra *nf* : goat
cabrestante *nm* : windlass
cabrío, -ría *adj* : goat, caprine
cabriola *nf* **1** : skip, jump **2 hacer cabriolas** : to prance
cabriolar *vi* : to prance
cabrito *nm* : kid, baby goat
cabús *nm, pl* **cabuses** *Mex* : caboose
cacahuate *or* **cacahuete** *nm* : peanut
cacalote *nm Mex* : crow
cacao *nm* : cacao, cocoa bean
cacarear *vi* : to crow, to cackle, to cluck — *vt fam* : to boast about, to crow about ⟨cacarear un huevo : to brag about an accomplishment⟩
cacareo *nm* **1** : clucking (of a hen), crowing (of a rooster) **2** : boasting
cacatúa *nf* : cockatoo
cace, etc. → **cazar**
cacería *nf* **1** CAZA : hunt, hunting **2** : hunting party
cacerola *nf* : pan, saucepan
cacha *nf* : butt (of a gun)
cachar *vt fam* : to catch
cacharro *nm* **1** *fam* : thing, piece of junk **2** *fam* : jalopy **3 cacharros** *nmpl* : pots and pans
cache *nm* : cache, cache memory
caché *nm* : cachet
cachear *vt* : to search, to frisk
cachemir *nm* : cashmere
cachetada *nf* BOFETADA : slap on the face
cachete *nm* : cheek
cachetear *vt* BOFETEAR : to slap
cachiporra *nf* : bludgeon, club, blackjack
cachirul *nm Mex fam* : cheating ⟨hacer cachirul : to cheat⟩
cachivache *nm fam* : thing ⟨mete tus cachivaches en el maletero : put your stuff in the trunk⟩
cacho *nm fam* : piece, bit
cachorro, -rra *n* **1** : cub **2** PERRITO : puppy
cachucha *nf Mex* : cap, baseball cap
cacique *nm* **1** : chief (of a tribe) **2** : boss (in politics)
cacofonía *nf* : cacophony
cacofónico, -ca *adj* : cacophonous
cacto *nm* : cactus
cactus → **cacto**
cada *adj* **1** : each ⟨cuestan diez pesos cada una : they cost ten pesos each⟩ **2** : every ⟨cada vez : every time⟩ **3** : such, some ⟨sales con cada historia : you come up with such crazy stories⟩ **4 cada vez más** : more and more, increasingly **5 cada vez menos** : less and less
cadalso *nm* : scaffold, gallows
cadáver *nm* : corpse, cadaver
cadavérico, -ca *adj* **1** : cadaverous **2** PÁLIDO : deathly pale
caddie *or* **caddy** *nmf, pl* **caddies** : caddy
cadena *nf* **1** : chain **2** : network, channel **3 cadena de montaje** : assembly line **4 cadena perpetua** : life sentence
cadencia *nf* : cadence, rhythm
cadencioso, -sa *adj* : rhythmic, rhythmical
cadera *nf* : hip
cadete *nmf* : cadet
cadmio *nm* : cadmium
caducar {72} *vi* : to expire
caducidad *nf* : expiration
caduco, -ca *adj* **1** : outdated, obsolete **2** : deciduous
caer {13} *vi* **1** : to fall, to drop **2** : to collapse **3** : to hang (down) **4 caer bien** *fam* : to be pleasant, to be likeable ⟨me caes bien : I like you⟩ **5 caer mal** *or* **caer gordo** *fam* : to be unpleasant, to be unlikeable — **caerse** *vr* : to fall down
café[1] *adj* : brown ⟨ojos cafés : brown eyes⟩
café[2] *nm* **1** : coffee **2** : café
cafeína *nf* : caffeine
cafetal *nm* : coffee plantation
cafetalero[1], **-ra** *adj* : coffee ⟨cosecha cafetalera : coffee harvest⟩
cafetalero[2], **-ra** *n* : coffee grower
cafetera *nf* : coffeepot, coffeemaker
cafetería *nf* **1** : coffee shop, café **2** : lunchroom, cafeteria
cafetero[1], **-ra** *adj* : coffee-producing
cafetero[2], **-ra** *n* : coffee grower
cafeticultura *nf Mex* : coffee industry
caguama *nf* **1** : large Caribbean turtle **2** *Mex* : large bottle of beer
caída *nf* **1** BAJA, DESCENSO : fall, drop **2** : collapse, downfall
caiga, etc. → **caer**
caimán *nm, pl* **caimanes** : alligator, caiman

caimito *nm* : star apple

caja *nf* **1** : box, case **2** : cash register, checkout counter **3** : bed (of a truck) **4** *fam* : coffin **5 caja fuerte** *or* **caja de caudales** : safe **6 caja de seguridad** : safe-deposit box **7 caja torácica** : rib cage

cajero, -ra *n* **1** : cashier **2** : teller **3 cajero automático** : automated teller machine, ATM

cajeta *nf Mex* : a sweet caramel-flavored spread

cajetilla *nf* : pack (of cigarettes)

cajón *nm, pl* **cajones 1** : drawer, till **2** : crate, case **3 cajón de estacionamiento** *Mex* : parking space

cajuela *nf Mex* : trunk (of a car)

cal *nf* : lime, quicklime

cala *nf* : cove, inlet

calabacín *nm, pl* **-cines** : zucchini

calabacita *nf Mex* : zucchini

calabaza *nf* **1** : pumpkin, squash **2** : gourd **3 dar calabazas a** : to give the brush-off to, to jilt

calabozo *nm* **1** : prison **2** : jail cell

calado[1], **-da** *adj* **1** : drenched **2** : openworked

calado[2] *nm* **1** : draft (of a ship) **2** : openwork

calafatear *vt* : to caulk

calamar *nm* **1** : squid **2 calamares** *nmpl* : calamari

calambre *nm* **1** ESPASMO : cramp **2** : electric shock, jolt

calamidad *nf* DESASTRE : calamity, disaster

calamina *nf* : calamine

calamitoso, -sa *adj* : calamitous, disastrous

calaña *nf* : ilk, kind, sort ⟨una persona de mala calaña : a bad sort⟩

calar *vt* **1** : to soak through **2** : to pierce, to penetrate — *vi* : to catch on — **calarse** *vr* : to get drenched

calavera[1] *nf* **1** : skull **2** *Mex* : taillight

calavera[2] *nm* : rake, rogue

calcar {72} *vt* **1** : to trace **2** : to copy, to imitate

calce, etc. → **calzar**

calceta *nf* : knee-high stocking

calcetería *nf* : hosiery

calcetín *nm, pl* **-tines** : sock

calcificar {72} *v* : to calcify — **calcificarse** *vr*

calcinar *vt* : to char, to burn

calcio *nm* : calcium

calco *nm* **1** : transfer, tracing **2** : copy, image

calcomanía *nf* : decal, transfer

calculador, -dora *adj* : calculating

calculadora *nf* : calculator

calcular *vt* **1** : to calculate, to estimate **2** : to plan, to scheme

cálculo *nm* **1** : calculation, estimation **2** : calculus **3** : plan, scheme **4 cálculo biliar** : gallstone **5 hoja de cálculo** : spreadsheet

caldas *nfpl* : hot springs

caldear *vt* : to heat, to warm — **caldearse** *vr* **1** : to heat up **2** : to become heated, to get tense

caldera *nf* **1** : cauldron **2** : boiler

caldo *nm* **1** CONSOMÉ : broth, stock **2 caldo de cultivo** : culture medium, breeding ground

caldoso, -sa *adj* : watery

calefacción *nf, pl* **-ciones** : heating, heat

calefactor *nm* : heater

caleidoscopio → **calidoscopio**

calendario *nm* **1** : calendar **2** : timetable, schedule

caléndula *nf* : marigold

calentador *nm* : heater

calentamiento *nm* **1** : heating, warming **2** : warm-up (in sports)

calentar {55} *vt* **1** : to heat, to warm **2** *fam* : to annoy, to anger **3** *fam* : to excite, to turn on — **calentarse** *vr* **1** : to get warm, to heat up **2** : to warm up (in sports) **3** *fam* : to become sexually aroused **4** *fam* : to get mad

calentura *nf* **1** FIEBRE : temperature, fever **2** : cold sore

calibrador *nm* : gauge, calipers *pl*

calibrar *vt* : to calibrate — **calibración** *nf*

calibre *nm* **1** : caliber, gauge **2** : importance, excellence **3** : kind, sort ⟨un problema de grueso calibre : a serious problem⟩

calidad *nf* **1** : quality, grade **2** : position, status **3 en calidad de** : as, in the capacity of

cálido, -da *adj* **1** : hot ⟨un clima cálido : a hot climate⟩ **2** : warm ⟨una cálida bienvenida : a warm welcome⟩

calidoscopio *nm* : kaleidoscope

caliente *adj* **1** : hot, warm ⟨mantenerse caliente : to stay warm⟩ **2** : heated, fiery ⟨una disputa caliente : a heated argument⟩ **3** *fam* : sexually excited, horny

califa *nm* : caliph

calificación *nf, pl* **-ciones 1** NOTA : grade (for a course) **2** : rating, score **3** CLASIFICACIÓN : qualification, qualifying ⟨ronda de calificación : qualifying round⟩

calificar {72} *vt* **1** : to grade **2** : to describe, to rate ⟨la calificaron de buena alumna : they described her as a good student⟩ **3** : to qualify, to modify (in grammar)

calificativo[1], **-va** *adj* : qualifying

calificativo[2] *nm* : qualifier, epithet

caligrafía *nf* **1** ESCRITURA : handwriting **2** : calligraphy

calipso *nm* : calypso

calistenia *nf* : calisthenics

cáliz *nm, pl* **cálices 1** : chalice, goblet **2** : calyx

caliza *nf* : limestone

callado, -da *adj* : quiet, silent — **calladamente** *adv*

callar *vi* : to keep quiet, to be silent — *vt* **1** : to silence, to hush ⟨¡calla a los niños! : keep the children quiet!⟩ **2** : to keep secret — **callarse** *vr* : to remain silent ⟨¡cállate! : be quiet!, shut up!⟩

calle *nf* : street, road

callejear *vi* : to wander about the streets, to hang out

callejero, -ra *adj* : street ⟨perro callejero : stray dog⟩

callejón *nm, pl* **-jones** **1** : alley **2 callejón sin salida** : dead-end street

callo *nm* **1** : callus, corn **2 callos** *nmpl* : tripe

calloso, -sa *adj* : callous

calma *nf* : calm, quiet

calmante[1] *adj* : calming, soothing

calmante[2] *nm* : tranquilizer, sedative

calmar *vt* TRANQUILIZAR : to calm, to soothe — **calmarse** *vr* : to calm down

calmo, -ma *adj* TRANQUILO : calm, tranquil

calmoso, -sa *adj* **1** TRANQUILO : calm, quiet **2** LENTO : slow, sluggish

calor *nm* **1** : heat ⟨hace calor : it's hot outside⟩ ⟨tener calor : to feel hot⟩ **2** : warmth, affection **3** : ardor, passion

caloría *nf* : calorie

calórico, -ca *adj* : caloric

calorífico, -ca *adj* : caloric

calque, etc. → **calcar**

calumnia *nf* : slander, libel — **calumnioso, -sa** *adj*

calumniar *vt* : to slander, to libel

caluroso, -sa *adj* **1** : hot **2** : warm, enthusiastic

calva *nf* : bald spot, bald head

calvario *nm* **1** : Calvary **2** : Stations of the Cross *pl* **3 vivir un calvario** : to suffer great adversity

calvicie *nf* : baldness

calvo[1], **-va** *adj* : bald

calvo[2], **-va** *n* : bald person

calza *nf* : block, wedge

calzada *nf* : roadway, avenue

calzado *nm* : footwear

calzador *nm* : shoehorn

calzar {21} *vt* **1** : to wear (shoes) ⟨¿de cuál calza? : what is your shoe size?⟩ ⟨siempre calzaban tenis : they always wore sneakers⟩ **2** : to provide with shoes

calzo *nm* : chock, wedge

calzoncillos *nmpl* : underpants, briefs

calzones *nmpl* : underpants, panties

cama *nf* **1** : bed **2 cama elástica** : trampoline

camada *nf* : litter, brood

camafeo *nm* : cameo

camaleón *nm, pl* **-leones** : chameleon

cámara *nf* **1** : camera **2** : chamber, room **3** : house (in government) **4** : inner tube

camarada *nmf* **1** : comrade, companion **2** : colleague

camaradería *nf* : camaraderie

camarero, -ra *n* **1** MESERO : waiter, waitress *f* **2** : bellhop *m,* chambermaid *f* (in a hotel) **3** : steward *m,* stewardess *f* (on a ship, etc.)

camarilla *nf* : political clique

camarógrafo, -fa *n* : cameraman *m,* camerawoman *f*

camarón *nm, pl* **-rones** **1** : shrimp **2** : prawn

camarote *nm* : cabin, stateroom

camastro *nm* : small hard bed, pallet

cambalache *nm fam* : swap

cambiante *adj* **1** : changing **2** VARIABLE : changeable, variable

cambiar *vt* **1** ALTERAR, MODIFICAR : to change **2** : to exchange, to trade — *vi* **1** : to change **2 cambiar de velocidad** : to shift gears — **cambiarse** *vr* **1** : to change (clothing) **2** MUDARSE : to move (to a new address)

cambio *nm* **1** : change, alteration **2** : exchange **3** : change (money) **4 en cambio** : instead **5 en cambio** : however, on the other hand

cambista *nmf* : exchange broker

camboyano, -na *adj & n* : Cambodian

cambur *nm Ven* : banana

camelia *nf* : camellia

camello *nm* : camel

camellón *nm, pl* **-llones** *Mex* : traffic island

camerino *nm* : dressing room

camerunés, -nesa *adj, mpl* **-neses** : Cameroonian

camilla *nf* : stretcher

camillero, -ra *n* : orderly (in a hospital)

caminante *nmf* : wayfarer, walker

caminar *vi* ANDAR : to walk, to move — *vt* : to walk, to cover (a distance)

caminata *nf* : hike, long walk

camino *nm* **1** : path, road **2** : journey ⟨ponerse en camino : to set off⟩ **3** : way ⟨a medio camino : halfway there⟩

camión *nm, pl* **camiones** **1** : truck **2** *Mex* : bus

camionero, -ra *n* **1** : truck driver **2** *Mex* : bus driver

camioneta *nf* : light truck, van

camisa *nf* **1** : shirt **2 camisa de fuerza** : straitjacket

camiseta *nf* **1** : T-shirt **2** : undershirt

camisón *nm, pl* **-sones** : nightshirt, nightgown

camorra *nf fam* : fight, trouble ⟨buscar camorra : to pick a fight⟩

camote *nm* **1** : root vegetable similar to the sweet potato **2 hacerse camote** *Mex fam* : to get mixed up

campal *adj* : pitched, fierce ⟨batalla campal : pitched battle⟩

campamento *nm* : camp

campana *nf* : bell

campanada *nf* TAÑIDO : stroke (of a bell), peal

campanario *nm* : bell tower, belfry

campanilla *nf* **1** : small bell, handbell **2** : uvula

campante *adj* : nonchalant, smug ⟨seguir tan campante : to go on as if nothing had happened⟩

campaña *nf* **1** CAMPO : countryside, country **2** : campaign **3 tienda de campaña** : tent
campañol *nm* : vole
campechana *nf Mex* : puff pastry
campechanía *nf* : geniality
campechano, -na *adj* : open, cordial, friendly
campeón, -peona *n, mpl* **-peones** : champion
campeonato *nm* : championship
cámper *nm* : camper (vehicle)
campero, -ra *adj* : country, rural
campesino, -na *n* : peasant, farm laborer
campestre *adj* : rural, rustic
camping *nm* **1** : camping **2** : campsite
campiña *nf* CAMPO : countryside, country
campista *nmf* : camper
campo *nm* **1** CAMPAÑA : countryside, country **2** : field ⟨campo de aviación : airfield⟩ ⟨su campo de responsabilidad : her field of responsibility⟩
camposanto *nm* : graveyard, cemetery
campus *nms & pl* : campus
camuflaje *nm* : camouflage
camuflajear *vt* : to camouflage
camuflar → **camuflajear**
can *nm* : hound, dog
cana *nf* **1** : gray hair **2 salirle canas** : to go gray, to get gray hair **3 echar una cana al aire** : to let one's hair down
canadiense *adj & nmf* : Canadian
canal[1] *nm* **1** : canal **2** : channel
canal[2] *nmf* : gutter, groove
canalé *nm* : rib, ribbing (in fabric)
canaleta *nf* : gutter
canalete *nm* : paddle
canalizar {21} *vt* : to channel
canalla[1] *adj fam* : low, rotten
canalla[2] *nmf fam* : bastard, swine
canapé *nm* **1** : hors d'oeuvre, canapé **2** SOFÁ : couch, sofa
canario[1], **-ria** *adj* : of or from the Canary Islands
canario[2], **-ria** *n* : Canarian, Canary Islander
canario[3] *nm* : canary
canasta *nf* **1** : basket **2** : canasta (card game)
cancel *nm* **1** : sliding door **2** : partition
cancelación *nf, pl* **-ciones** **1** : cancellation **2** : payment in full
cancelar *vt* **1** : to cancel **2** : to pay off, to settle
cáncer *nm* : cancer
Cáncer *nmf* : Cancer
cancerígeno[1], **-na** *adj* : carcinogenic
cancerígeno[2] *nm* : carcinogen
canceroso, -sa *adj* : cancerous
cancha *nf* : court, field (for sports)
canciller *nm* : chancellor
cancillería *nf* : chancellery, ministry
canción *nf, pl* **canciones** **1** : song **2 canción de cuna** : lullaby
cancionero[1] *nm* : songbook
cancionero[2], **-ra** *n Mex* : songster, songstress *f*
candado *nm* : padlock
candela *nf* **1** : flame, fire **2** : candle
candelabro *nm* : candelabra
candelero *nm* **1** : candlestick **2 estar en el candelero** : to be the center of attention
candente *adj* : red-hot
candidato, -ta *n* : candidate, applicant
candidatura *nf* : candidacy
candidez *nf* **1** : simplicity **2** INGENUIDAD : naïveté, ingenuousness
cándido, -da *adj* **1** : simple, unassuming **2** INGENUO : naive, ingenuous
candil *nm* : oil lamp
candilejas *nfpl* : footlights
candor *nm* : naïveté, innocence
candoroso, -sa *adj* : naive, innocent
canela *nf* : cinnamon
canesú *nm* : yoke (of clothing)
cangrejo *nm* JAIBA : crab
canguro *nm* **1** : kangaroo **2 hacer de canguro** *Spain* : to baby-sit
caníbal[1] *adj* : cannibalistic
caníbal[2] *nmf* ANTROPÓFAGO : cannibal
canibalismo *nm* ANTROPOFAGIA : cannibalism
canibalizar {21} *vt* : to cannibalize
canica *nf* : marble ⟨jugar a las canicas : to play marbles⟩
caniche *nm* : poodle
canijo, -ja *adj* **1** *fam* : puny, weak **2** *Mex fam* : tough, hard ⟨un examen muy canijo : a very tough exam⟩
canilla *nf* **1** : shin, shinbone **2** *Arg, Uru* : faucet
canino[1], **-na** *adj* : canine
canino[2] *nm* **1** COLMILLO : canine (tooth) **2** : dog, canine
canje *nm* INTERCAMBIO : exchange, trade
canjear *vt* INTERCAMBIAR : to exchange, to trade
cannabis *nm* : cannabis
cano, -na *adj* : gray ⟨un hombre de pelo cano : a gray-haired man⟩
canoa *nf* : canoe
canon *nm, pl* **cánones** : canon
canónico, -ca *adj* **1** : canonical **2 derecho canónico** : canon law
canónigo *nm* : canon (of a church)
canonizar {21} *vt* : to canonize — **canonización** *nf*
canoso, -sa → **cano**
cansado, -da *adj* **1** : tired ⟨estar cansado : to be tired⟩ **2** : tiresome, wearying ⟨ser cansado : to be tiring⟩
cansancio *nm* FATIGA : fatigue, weariness
cansar *vt* FATIGAR : to wear out, to tire — *vi* : to be tiresome — **cansarse** *vr* **1** : to wear oneself out **2** : to get bored
cansino, -na *adj* : slow, weary, lethargic
cantaleta *nf fam* : nagging ⟨la misma cantaleta : the same old story⟩
cantalupo *nm* : cantaloupe
cantante *nmf* : singer
cantar[1] *v* : to sing

cantar[2] *nm* : song, ballad
cántaro *nm* **1** : pitcher, jug **2 llover a cántaros** *fam* : to rain cats and dogs
cantata *nf* : cantata
cantera *nf* : quarry ⟨cantera de piedra : stone quarry⟩
cántico *nm* : canticle, chant
cantidad[1] *adv fam* : really ⟨ese carro me costó cantidad : that car cost me plenty⟩
cantidad[2] *nf* **1** : quantity **2** : sum, amount (of money) **3** *fam* : a lot, a great many ⟨había cantidad de niños en el parque : there were tons of kids in the park⟩
cantimplora *nf* : canteen, water bottle
cantina *nf* **1** : tavern, bar **2** : canteen, mess, dining quarters *pl*
cantinero, -ra *n* : bartender
canto *nm* **1** : singing **2** : chant ⟨canto gregoriano : Gregorian chant⟩ **3** : song (of a bird) **4** : edge, end ⟨de canto : on end, sideways⟩ **5 canto rodado** : boulder
cantón *nm, pl* **cantones 1** : canton **2** *Mex fam* : place, home
cantonés[1], **-nesa** *adj & n, mpl* **-neses** : Cantonese
cantonés[2] *nm, pl* **-neses** : Cantonese (language)
cantor[1], **-tora** *adj* **1** : singing **2 pájaro cantor** : songbird
cantor[2], **-tora** *n* **1** : singer **2** : cantor
caña *nf* **1** : cane ⟨caña de azúcar : sugarcane⟩ **2** : reed **3 caña de pescar** : fishing rod **4 caña del timón** : tiller (of a boat)
cañada *nf* : ravine, gully
cáñamo *nm* : hemp
cañaveral *nm* : sugarcane field
cañería *nf* TUBERÍA : pipes *pl*, piping
caño *nm* **1** : pipe **2** : spout **3** : channel (for navigation)
cañón *nm, pl* **cañones 1** : cannon **2** : barrel (of a gun) **3** : canyon
cañonear *vt* : to shell, to bombard
cañoneo *nm* : shelling, bombardment
cañonero *nm* : gunboat
caoba *nf* : mahogany
caolín *nm* : kaolin
caos *nm* : chaos
caótico, -ca *adj* : chaotic
capa *nf* **1** : cape, cloak **2** : coating **3** : layer, stratum **4** : (social) class, stratum
capacidad *nf* **1** : capacity **2** : capability, ability
capacitación *nf, pl* **-ciones** : training
capacitar *vt* : to train, to qualify
caparazón *nm, pl* **-zones** : shell, carapace
capataz *nmf, pl* **-taces** : foreman *m*, forewoman *f*
capaz *adj, pl* **capaces 1** APTO : capable, able **2** COMPETENTE : competent **3** : spacious ⟨capaz para : with room for⟩
capcioso, -sa *adj* : cunning, deceptive ⟨pregunta capciosa : trick question⟩
capea *nf* : amateur bullfight
capear *vt* **1** : to make a pass with the cape (in bullfighting) **2** : to dodge, to weather ⟨capear el temporal : to ride out the storm⟩
capellán *nm, pl* **-llanes** : chaplain
capilar *nm* : capillary — **capilar** *adj*
capilla *nf* : chapel
capirotada *nf Mex* : traditional bread pudding
capirotazo *nm* : flip, flick
capital[1] *adj* **1** : capital **2** : chief, principal
capital[2] *nm* : capital ⟨capital de riesgo : venture capital⟩
capital[3] *nf* : capital, capital city
capitalino[1], **-na** *adj* : of or from a capital city
capitalino[2], **-na** *n* : inhabitant of a capital city
capitalismo *nm* : capitalism
capitalista *adj & nmf* : capitalist
capitalizar {21} *vt* : to capitalize — **capitalización** *nf*
capitán, -tana *n, mpl* **-tanes** : captain
capitanear *vt* : to captain, to command
capitanía *nf* : captaincy
capitel *nm* : capital (of a column)
capitolio *nm* : capitol
capitulación *nf, pl* **-ciones** : capitulation
capitular *vi* : to capitulate, to surrender
capítulo *nm* **1** : chapter, section **2** : matter, subject
capó *nm* : hood (of a car)
capón *nm, pl* **capones** : capon
caporal *nm* **1** : chief, leader **2** : foreman (on a ranch)
capota *nf* : top (of a convertible)
capote *nm* **1** : cloak, overcoat **2** : bullfighter's cape **3** *Mex* COFRE : hood (of a car)
capricho *nm* ANTOJO : whim, caprice
caprichoso, -sa *adj* ANTOJADIZO : capricious, fickle
Capricornio *nmf* : Capricorn
cápsula *nf* : capsule
captar *vt* **1** : to catch, to grasp **2** : to gain, to attract **3** : to harness, to collect (waters)
captor, -tora *n* : captor
captura *nf* : capture, seizure
capturar *vt* : to capture, to seize
capucha *nf* : hood, cowl
capuchina *nf* : nasturtium
capuchino *nm* **1** : Capuchin (monk) **2** : capuchin (monkey) **3** : cappuccino
capullo *nm* **1** : cocoon **2** : bud (of a flower)
caqui *adj & nm* : khaki
cara *nf* **1** : face **2** ASPECTO : look, appearance ⟨¡qué buena cara tiene ese pastel! : that cake looks delicious!⟩ **3** *fam* : nerve, gall **4 ~ a** *or* **de cara a** : facing **5 de cara a** : in view of, in the light of
carabina *nf* : carbine
caracol *nm* **1** : snail **2** CONCHA : conch, seashell **3** : cochlea **4** : ringlet

caracola *nf* : conch
carácter *nm, pl* **caracteres 1** ÍNDOLE : character, kind, nature **2** TEMPERAMENTO : disposition, temperament **3** : letter, symbol ⟨caracteres chinos : Chinese characters⟩
característica *nf* RASGO : trait, feature, characteristic
característico, -ca *adj* : characteristic — **característicamente** *adv*
caracterizar {21} *vt* : to characterize — **caracterización** *nf*
caramba *interj* **1** (*expressing annoyance*) : darn!, heck! **2** (*expressing disgust or surprise*) : jeez!
carámbano *nm* : icicle
carambola *nf* **1** : carom **2** : ruse, trick ⟨por carambola : by a lucky chance⟩
caramelo *nm* **1** : caramel **2** DULCE : candy
caramillo *nm* **1** : pipe, small flute **2** : heap, pile
caraqueño[1], -ña *adj* : of or from Caracas
caraqueño[2], -ña *n* : person from Caracas
carátula *nf* **1** : title page **2** : cover, dust jacket **3** CARETA : mask **4** *Mex* : face, dial (of a clock or watch)
caravana *nf* **1** : caravan **2** : convoy, motorcade **3** REMOLQUE : trailer
caray → **caramba**
carbohidrato *nm* : carbohydrate
carbón *nm, pl* **carbones 1** : coal **2** : charcoal
carbonatado, -da *adj* : carbonated
carbonato *nm* : carbonate
carboncillo *nm* : charcoal
carbonera *nf* : coal cellar, coal bunker (on a ship)
carbonero, -ra *adj* : coal
carbonizar {21} *vt* : to carbonize, to char
carbono *nm* : carbon
carbunco *or* **carbunclo** *nm* : carbuncle
carburador *nm* : carburetor
carburante *nm* : fuel
carca *nmf fam* : old fogy
carcacha *nf fam* : jalopy, wreck
carcaj *nm* : quiver (for arrows)
carcajada *nf* : loud laugh, guffaw ⟨reírse a carcajadas : to roar with laughter⟩
carcajearse *vr* : to roar with laughter, to be in stitches
cárcel *nf* PRISIÓN : jail, prison
carcelero, -ra *n* : jailer
carcinogénico, -ca *adj* : carcinogenic
carcinógeno *nm* CANCERÍGENO : carcinogen
carcinoma *nm* : carcinoma
carcomer *vt* : to eat away at, to consume
carcomido, -da *adj* **1** : worm-eaten **2** : decayed, rotten
cardán *nm, pl* **cardanes** : universal joint
cardar *vt* : to card, to comb
cardenal *nm* **1** : cardinal (in religion) **2** : bruise
cardíaco *or* **cardiaco, -ca** *adj* : cardiac, heart
cárdigan *nm, pl* **-gans** : cardigan
cardinal *adj* : cardinal
cardiología *nf* : cardiology
cardiólogo, -ga *n* : cardiologist
cardiovascular *adj* : cardiovascular
cardo *nm* : thistle
cardumen *nm* : school of fish
carear *vt* : to bring face-to-face
carecer {53} *vi* **~ de** : to lack ⟨el cheque carecía de fondos : the check lacked funds⟩
carencia *nf* **1** FALTA : lack **2** ESCASEZ : shortage **3** DEFICIENCIA : deficiency
carente *adj* **~ de** : lacking (in)
carero, -ra *adj fam* : pricey
carestía *nf* **1** : rise in cost ⟨la carestía de la vida : the high cost of living⟩ **2** : dearth, scarcity
careta *nf* MÁSCARA : mask
carey *nm* **1** : hawksbill turtle, sea turtle **2** : tortoiseshell
carga *nf* **1** : loading **2** : freight, load, cargo **3** : burden, responsibility **4** : charge ⟨carga eléctrica : electrical charge⟩ **5** : attack, charge
cargado, -da *adj* **1** : loaded **2** : bogged down, weighted down **3** : close, stuffy **4** : charged ⟨cargado de tensión : charged with tension⟩ **5** FUERTE : strong ⟨café cargado : strong coffee⟩ **6 cargado de hombros** : stoop-shouldered
cargador[1], -dora *n* : longshoreman *m*, longshorewoman *f*
cargador[2] *nm* **1** : magazine (for a firearm) **2** : charger (for batteries)
cargamento *nm* : cargo, load
cargar {52} *vt* **1** : to carry **2** : to load, to fill **3** : to charge — *vi* **1** : to load **2** : to rest (in architecture) **3 ~ sobre** : to fall upon
cargo *nm* **1** : burden, load **2** : charge ⟨a cargo de : in charge of⟩ **3** : position, office
cargue, etc. → **cargar**
carguero[1], -ra *adj* : freight, cargo ⟨tren carguero : freight train⟩
carguero[2] *nm* : freighter, cargo ship
cariarse *vr* : to decay (of teeth)
caribe *adj* : Caribbean ⟨el mar Caribe : the Caribbean Sea⟩
caribeño, -ña *adj* : Caribbean
caribú *nm* : caribou
caricatura *nf* **1** : caricature **2** : cartoon
caricaturista *nmf* : caricaturist, cartoonist
caricaturizar {21} *vt* : to caricature
caricia *nf* **1** : caress **2 hacer caricias** : to pet, to stroke
caridad *nf* **1** : charity **2** LIMOSNA : alms *pl*
caries *nfs & pl* : cavity (in a tooth)
carillón *nm, pl* **-llones 1** : carillon **2** : glockenspiel
cariño *nm* AFECTO : affection, love
cariñoso, -sa *adj* AFECTUOSO : affectionate, loving — **cariñosamente** *adv*
carioca[1] *adj* : of or from Rio de Janeiro

carioca[2] *nmf* : person from Rio de Janeiro
carisma *nf* : charisma
carismático, -ca *adj* : charismatic
carita *adj Mex fam* : cute (said of a man) ⟨tu primo se cree muy carita : your cousin thinks he's gorgeous⟩
caritativo, -va *adj* : charitable
cariz *nm, pl* **carices** : appearance, aspect
carmesí *adj & nm* : crimson
carmín *nm, pl* **carmines 1** : carmine **2 carmín de labios** : lipstick
carnada *nf* CEBO : bait
carnal *adj* **1** : carnal **2 primo carnal** : first cousin
carnaval *nm* : carnival
carnaza *nf* : bait
carne *nf* **1** : meat ⟨carne molida : ground beef⟩ **2** : flesh ⟨carne de gallina : goose bumps⟩
carné → carnet
carnero *nm* **1** : ram, sheep **2** : mutton
carnet *nm* **1** : identification card, ID **2** : membership card **3 carnet de conducir** *Spain* : driver's license
carnicería *nf* **1** : butcher shop **2** MATANZA : slaughter, carnage
carnicero, -ra *n* : butcher
carnívoro[1], **-ra** *adj* : carnivorous
carnívoro[2] *nm* : carnivore
carnoso, -sa *adj* : fleshy, meaty
caro[1] *adv* : dearly, a lot ⟨pagué caro : I paid a high price⟩
caro[2], **-ra** *adj* **1** : expensive, dear **2** QUERIDO : dear, beloved
carpa *nf* **1** : carp **2** : big top (of a circus) **3** : tent
carpelo *nm* : carpel
carpeta *nf* : folder, binder, portfolio (of drawings, etc.)
carpetazo *nm* **dar carpetazo a** : to shelve, to defer
carpintería *nf* **1** : carpentry **2** : carpenter's workshop
carpintero, -ra *n* : carpenter
carraspear *vi* : to clear one's throat
carraspera *nf* : hoarseness ⟨tener carraspera : to have a frog in one's throat⟩
carrera *nf* **1** : run, running ⟨a la carrera : at full speed⟩ ⟨de carrera : hastily⟩ **2** : race **3** : course of study **4** : career, profession **5** : run (in baseball)
carreta *nf* : cart, wagon
carrete *nm* **1** BOBINA : reel, spool **2** : roll of film
carretel → carrete
carretera *nf* : highway, road ⟨carretera de peaje : turnpike⟩
carretero, -ra *adj* : highway ⟨el sistema carretero nacional : the national highway system⟩
carretilla *nf* **1** : wheelbarrow **2 carretilla elevadora** : forklift
carril *nm* **1** : lane ⟨carretera de doble carril : two-lane highway⟩ **2** : rail (on a railroad track)
carrillo *nm* : cheek, jowl
carrito *nm* : cart ⟨carrito de compras : shopping cart⟩
carrizo *nm* JUNCO : reed
carro *nm* **1** COCHE : car **2** : cart **3** *Chile, Mex* : coach (of a train) **4 carro alegórico** : float (in a parade)
carrocería *nf* : bodywork, body (of a vehicle)
carroña *nf* : carrion
carroñero, -ra *n* : scavenger (animal)
carroza *nf* **1** : carriage **2** : float (in a parade)
carruaje *nm* : carriage
carrusel *nm* **1** : merry-go-round **2** : carousel ⟨carrusel de equipaje : luggage carousel⟩
carta *nf* **1** : letter **2** NAIPE : playing card **3** : charter, constitution **4** MENÚ : menu **5** : map, chart **6 tomar cartas en** : to intervene in
cártamo *nm* : safflower
cartearse *vr* ESCRIBIRSE : to write to one another, to correspond
cartel *nm* : sign, poster
cártel *or* **cartel** *nm* : cartel
cartelera *nf* **1** : billboard **2** : marquee
cartera *nf* **1** BILLETERA : wallet, billfold **2** BOLSO : pocketbook, purse **3** : portfolio ⟨cartera de acciones : stock portfolio⟩
carterista *nmf* : pickpocket
cartero, -ra *n* : letter carrier, mailman *m*
cartilaginoso, -sa *adj* : cartilaginous, gristly
cartílago *nm* : cartilage
cartilla *nf* **1** : primer, reader **2** : booklet ⟨cartilla de ahorros : bankbook⟩
cartografía *nf* : cartography
cartógrafo, -fa *n* : cartographer
cartón *nm, pl* **cartones 1** : cardboard ⟨cartón madera : fiberboard⟩ **2** : carton
cartucho *nm* : cartridge
cartulina *nf* : poster board, cardboard
carúncula *nf* : wattle (of a bird)
casa *nf* **1** : house, building **2** HOGAR : home **3** : household, family **4** : company, firm **5 echar la casa por la ventana** : to spare no expense
casaca *nf* : jacket
casado[1], **-da** *adj* : married
casado[2], **-da** *n* : married person
casamentero, -ra *n* : matchmaker
casamiento *nm* **1** : marriage **2** BODA : wedding
casar *vt* : to marry — *vi* : to go together, to match up — **casarse** *vr* **1** : to get married **2 ~ con** : to marry
casateniente *nmf Mex* : landlord, landlady *f*
cascabel[1] *nm* : small bell
cascabel[2] *nf* : rattlesnake
cascada *nf* CATARATA, SALTO : waterfall, cascade
cascajo *nm* **1** : pebble, rock fragment **2** *fam* : piece of junk
cascanueces *nms & pl* : nutcracker

cascar {72} *vt* : to crack (a shell) — **cascarse** *vr* : to crack, to chip
cáscara *nf* **1** : skin, peel, rind, husk **2** : shell (of a nut or egg)
cascarón *nm, pl* **-rones** **1** : eggshell **2** *Mex* : shell filled with confetti
cascarrabias *nmfs & pl fam* : grouch, crab
casco *nm* **1** : helmet **2** : hull **3** : hoof **4** : fragment, shard **5** : center (of a town) **6** *Mex* : empty bottle **7 cascos** *nmpl* : headphones
caserío *nm* **1** : country house **2** : hamlet
casero[1], **-ra** *adj* **1** : domestic, household **2** : homemade
casero[2], **-ra** *n* DUEÑO : landlord *m*, landlady *f*
caseta *nf* : booth, stand, stall ⟨caseta telefónica : telephone booth⟩
casete → **cassette**
casi *adv* **1** : almost, nearly, virtually **2** (*in negative phrases*) : hardly ⟨casi nunca : hardly ever⟩
casilla *nf* **1** : booth **2** : pigeonhole **3** : box (on a form)
casino *nm* **1** : casino **2** : (social) club
caso *nm* **1** : case **2 en caso de** : in case of, in the event of **3 hacer caso de** : to pay attention to, to notice **4 hacer caso omiso de** : to ignore, to take no notice of **5 no venir al caso** : to be beside the point
caspa *nf* : dandruff
casque, etc. → **cascar**
casquete *nm* **1** : skullcap **2 casquete glaciar** : ice cap **3 casquete corto** *Mex* : crew cut
casquillo *nm* : case, casing (of a bullet)
cassette *nmf* : cassette
casta *nf* **1** : caste **2** : lineage, stock ⟨de casta : thoroughbred, purebred⟩ **3 sacar la casta** *Mex* : to come out ahead
castaña *nf* : chestnut
castañetear *vi* : to chatter (of teeth)
castaño[1], **-ña** *adj* : chestnut, brown
castaño[2] *nm* **1** : chestnut tree **2** : chestnut, brown
castañuela *nf* : castanet
castellano[1], **-na** *adj & n* : Castilian
castellano[2] *nm* ESPAÑOL : Spanish, Castilian (language)
castidad *nf* : chastity
castigar {52} *vt* : to punish
castigo *nm* : punishment
castillo *nm* **1** : castle **2 castillo de proa** : forecastle
casto, -ta *adj* : chaste, pure — **castamente** *adv*
castor *nm* : beaver
castración *nf, pl* **-ciones** : castration
castrar *vt* **1** : to castrate, to spay, to neuter, to geld **2** DEBILITAR : to weaken, to debilitate
castrense *adj* : military
casual *adj* **1** FORTUITO : fortuitous, accidental **2** *Mex* : casual (of clothing)
casualidad *nf* **1** : chance **2 por ~** *or* **de ~** : by chance, by any chance
casualmente *adv* : accidentally, by chance
casucha *or* **casuca** *nf* : shanty, hovel
cataclismo *nm* : cataclysm
catacumbas *nfpl* : catacombs
catador, -dora *n* : wine taster
catalán[1], **-lana** *adj & n, mpl* **-lanes** : Catalan
catalán[2] *nm* : Catalan (language)
catálisis *nf* : catalysis
catalítico, -ca *adj* : catalytic
catalizador *nm* **1** : catalyst **2** : catalytic converter
catalogar {52} *vt* : to catalog, to classify
catálogo *nm* : catalog
catamarán *nm, pl* **-ranes** : catamaran
cataplasma *nf* : poultice
catapulta *nf* : catapult
catapultar *vt* : to catapult
catar *vt* **1** : to taste, to sample **2** : to look at, to examine
catarata *nf* **1** CASCADA, SALTO : waterfall **2** : cataract
catarro *nm* RESFRIADO : cold, catarrh
catarsis *nf* : catharsis
catártico, -ca *adj* : cathartic
catástrofe *nf* DESASTRE : catastrophe, disaster
catastrófico, -ca *adj* DESASTROSO : catastrophic, disastrous
catcher *nmf* : catcher (in baseball)
catecismo *nm* : catechism
cátedra *nf* **1** : chair, professorship **2** : subject, class **3 libertad de cátedra** : academic freedom
catedral *nf* : cathedral
catedrático, -ca *n* PROFESOR : professor
categoría *nf* **1** CLASE : category **2** RANGO : rank, standing **3 categoría gramatical** : part of speech **4 de ~** : first-rate, outstanding
categórico, -ca *adj* : categorical, unequivocal — **categóricamente** *adv*
catéter *nm* : catheter
cátodo *nm* : cathode
catolicismo *nm* : Catholicism
católico, -ca *adj & n* : Catholic
catorce *adj & nm* : fourteen
catorceavo *nm* : fourteenth
catre *nm* : cot
catsup *nm* : ketchup
caucásico, -ca *adj & n* : Caucasian
cauce *nm* **1** LECHO : riverbed **2** : means *pl*, channel
caucho *nm* **1** GOMA : rubber **2** : rubber tree **3** *Ven* : tire
caución *nf, pl* **cauciones** FIANZA : bail, security
caudal *nm* **1** : volume of water **2** RIQUEZA : capital, wealth **3** ABUNDANCIA : abundance
caudillaje *nm* : leadership
caudillo *nm* : leader, commander

causa *nf* **1** MOTIVO : cause, reason, motive ⟨a causa de : because of⟩ **2** IDEAL : cause ⟨morir por una causa : to die for a cause⟩ **3** : lawsuit

causal[1] *adj* : causal

causal[2] *nm* : cause, grounds *pl*

causalidad *nf* : causality

causante[1] *adj* **~ de** : causing, responsible for

causante[2] *nmf Mex* : taxpayer

causar *vt* **1** : to cause **2** : to provoke, to arouse ⟨eso me causa gracia : that strikes me as being funny⟩

cáustico, -ca *adj* : caustic

cautela *nf* : caution, prudence

cautelar *adj* : precautionary, preventive

cauteloso, -sa *adj* : cautious, prudent — **cautelosamente** *adv*

cauterizar {21} *vt* : to cauterize

cautivador, -dora *adj* : captivating

cautivar *vt* HECHIZAR : to captivate, to charm

cautiverio *nm* : captivity

cautivo, -va *adj & n* : captive

cauto, -ta *adj* : cautious, careful

cavar *vt* : to dig — *vi* **~ en** : to delve into, to probe

caverna *nf* : cavern, cave

cavernoso, -sa *adj* **1** : cavernous **2** : deep, resounding

caviar *nm* : caviar

cavidad *nf* : cavity

cavilar *vi* : to ponder, to deliberate

cayado *nm* : crook, staff, crosier

cayena *nf* : cayenne pepper

cayó, etc. → **caer**

caza[1] *nf* **1** CACERÍA : hunt, hunting **2** : game

caza[2] *nm* : fighter plane

cazador, -dora *n* **1** : hunter **2 cazador furtivo** : poacher

cazar {21} *vt* **1** : to hunt **2** : to catch, to bag **3** *fam* : to land (a job, a spouse) — *vi* : to go hunting

cazatalentos *nmfs & pl* : talent scout

cazo *nm* **1** : saucepan, pot **2** CUCHARÓN : ladle

cazuela *nf* **1** : pan, saucepan **2** : casserole

cazurro, -ra *adj* : sullen, surly

CD *nm* : CD, compact disk

cebada *nf* : barley

cebar *vt* **1** : to bait **2** : to feed, to fatten **3** : to prime (a pump, etc.) — **cebarse** *vr* **~ en** : to take it out on

cebo *nm* **1** CARNADA : bait **2** : feed **3** : primer (for firearms)

cebolla *nf* : onion

cebolleta *nf* : scallion, green onion

cebollino *nm* **1** : chive **2** : scallion

cebra *nf* : zebra

cebú *nm, pl* **cebús** *or* **cebúes** : zebu (cattle)

cecear *vi* : to lisp

ceceo *nm* : lisp

cecina *nf* : dried beef, beef jerky

cedazo *nm* : sieve

ceder *vi* **1** : to yield, to give way **2** : to diminish, to abate **3** : to give in, to relent — *vt* : to cede, to hand over

cedro *nm* : cedar

cédula *nf* : document, certificate

céfiro *nm* : zephyr

cegador, -dora *adj* : blinding

cegar {49} *vt* **1** : to blind **2** : to block, to stop up — *vi* : to be blinded, to go blind

cegatón, -tona *adj, mpl* **-tones** *fam* : blind as a bat

ceguera *nf* : blindness

ceiba *nf* : ceiba, silk-cotton tree

ceja *nf* **1** : eyebrow ⟨fruncir las cejas : to knit one's brows⟩ **2** : flange, rim

cejar *vi* : to give in, to back down

celada *nf* : trap, ambush

celador, -dora *n* GUARDIA : guard, warden

celda *nf* : cell (of a jail)

celebración *nf, pl* **-ciones** : celebration

celebrado, -da *adj* CÉLEBRE, FAMOSO : famous, celebrated

celebrante *nmf* OFICIANTE : celebrant

celebrar *vt* **1** FESTEJAR : to celebrate **2** : to hold (a meeting) **3** : to say (Mass) **4** : to welcome, to be happy about — *vi* : to be glad — **celebrarse** *vr* **1** : to be celebrated, to fall **2** : to be held, to take place

célebre *adj* CELEBRADO, FAMOSO : celebrated, famous

celebridad *nf* **1** : celebrity **2** FAMA : fame, renown

celeridad *nf* : celerity, swiftness

celeste[1] *adj* **1** : celestial **2** : sky blue, azure

celeste[2] *nm* : sky blue

celestial *adj* : heavenly, celestial

celibato *nm* : celibacy

célibe *adj & nmf* : celibate

cello *nm* : cello

celo *nm* **1** : zeal, fervor **2** : heat (of females), rut (of males) **3 celos** *nmpl* : jealousy ⟨tenerle celos a alguien : to be jealous of someone⟩

celofán *nm, pl* **-fanes** : cellophane

celosía *nf* **1** : lattice window **2** : latticework, trellis

celoso, -sa *adj* **1** : jealous **2** : zealous — **celosamente** *adv*

celta[1] *adj* : Celtic

celta[2] *nmf* : Celt

célula *nf* : cell

celular *adj* : cellular

celuloide *nm* **1** : celluloid **2** : film, cinema

celulosa *nf* : cellulose

cementar *vt* : to cement

cementerio *nm* : cemetery

cemento *nm* : cement

cena *nf* : supper, dinner

cenador *nm* : arbor

cenagal *nm* : bog, quagmire

cenagoso, -sa *adj* : swampy

cenar *vi* : to have dinner, to have supper — *vt* : to have for dinner or supper

⟨anoche cenamos tamales : we had tamales for supper last night⟩
cencerro *nm* : cowbell
cenicero *nm* : ashtray
ceniciento, -ta *adj* : ashen
cenit *nm* : zenith, peak
ceniza *nf* **1** : ash **2 cenizas** *nfpl* : ashes (of a deceased person)
cenizo, -za *n* : jinx
cenote *nm Mex* : natural deposit of spring water
censar *vt* : to take a census of
censo *nm* : census
censor, -sora *n* : censor, critic
censura *nf* **1** : censorship **2** : censure, criticism
censurable *adj* : reprehensible, blameworthy
censurar *vt* **1** : to censor **2** : to censure, to criticize
centauro *nm* : centaur
centavo *nm* **1** : cent (in English-speaking countries) **2** : unit of currency in various Latin-American countries
centella *nf* **1** : lightning flash **2** : spark
centellear *vi* **1** : to twinkle **2** : to gleam, to sparkle
centelleo *nm* : twinkling, sparkle
centenar *nm* **1** : hundred **2 a centenares** : by the hundreds
centenario[1], **-ria** *adj & n* : centenarian
centenario[2] *nm* : centennial
centeno *nm* : rye
centésimo[1], **-ma** *adj* : hundredth
centésimo[2] *nm* : hundredth
centígrado *adj* : centigrade, Celsius
centigramo *nm* : centigram
centímetro *nm* : centimeter
centinela *nmf* : sentinel, sentry
central[1] *adj* **1** : central **2** PRINCIPAL : main, principal
central[2] *nf* **1** : main office, headquarters **2 central camionera** *Mex* : bus terminal
centralita *nf* : switchboard
centralizar {21} *vt* : to centralize — **centralización** *nf*
centrar *vt* **1** : to center **2** : to focus — **centrarse** *vr* **~ en** : to focus on, to concentrate on
céntrico, -ca *adj* : central
centrífugo, -ga *adj* : centrifugal
centrípeto, -ta *adj* : centripetal
centro[1] *nmf* : center (in sports)
centro[2] *nm* **1** MEDIO : center ⟨centro de atención : center of attention⟩ ⟨centro de gravedad : center of gravity⟩ **2** : downtown **3 centro de mesa** : centerpiece
centroamericano, -na *adj & n* : Central American
ceñido, -da *adj* AJUSTADO : tight, tight-fitting
ceñir {67} *vt* **1** : to encircle, to surround **2** : to hug, to cling to ⟨me ciñe demasiado : it's too tight on me⟩ — **ceñirse** *vr* **~ a** : to restrict oneself to, to stick to
ceño *nm* **1** : frown, scowl **2 fruncir el ceño** : to frown, to knit one's brows
cepa *nf* **1** : stump (of a tree) **2** : stock (of a vine) **3** LINAJE : ancestry, stock
cepillar *vt* **1** : to brush **2** : to plane (wood) — **cepillarse** *vr*
cepillo *nm* **1** : brush ⟨cepillo de dientes : toothbrush⟩ **2** : plane (for woodworking)
cepo *nm* : trap (for animals)
cera *nf* **1** : wax ⟨cera de abejas : beeswax⟩ **2** : polish
cerámica *nf* **1** : ceramics *pl* **2** : pottery
cerámico, -ca *adj* : ceramic
ceramista *nmf* ALFARERO : potter
cerca[1] *adv* **1** : close, near, nearby **2 ~ de** : nearly, almost
cerca[2] *nf* **1** : fence **2** : (stone) wall
cercado *nm* : enclosure
cercanía *nf* **1** PROXIMIDAD : proximity, closeness **2 cercanías** *nfpl* : outskirts, suburbs
cercano, -na *adj* : near, close
cercar {72} *vt* **1** : to fence in, to enclose **2** : to surround
cercenar *vt* **1** : to cut off, to amputate **2** : to diminish, to curtail
cerceta *nf* : teal (duck)
cerciorarse *vr* ASEGURARSE **~ de** : to make sure of, to verify
cerco *nm* **1** : siege **2** : cordon, circle **3** : fence
cerda *nf* **1** : bristle **2** : sow
cerdo *nm* **1** : pig, hog **2 carne de cerdo** : pork
cereal *nm* : cereal — **cereal** *adj*
cerebelo *nm* : cerebellum
cerebral *adj* : cerebral
cerebro *nm* : brain
ceremonia *nf* : ceremony — **ceremonial** *adj*
ceremonioso, -sa *adj* : ceremonious
cereza *nf* : cherry
cerezo *nm* : cherry tree
cerilla *nf* **1** : match **2** : earwax
cerillo *nm* (*in various countries*) : match
cerner {56} *vt* : to sift — **cernerse** *vr* **1** : to hover **2 ~ sobre** : to loom over, to threaten
cernidor *nm* : sieve
cernir → **cerner**
cero *nm* : zero
ceroso, -sa *adj* : waxy
cerque, etc. → **cercar**
cerquita *adv fam* : very close, very near
cerrado, -da *adj* **1** : closed, shut **2** : thick, broad ⟨tiene un acento cerrado : she has a thick accent⟩ **3** : cloudy, overcast **4** : quiet, reserved **5** : dense, stupid
cerradura *nf* : lock
cerrajería *nf* : locksmith's shop
cerrajero, -ra *n* : locksmith
cerrar {55} *vt* **1** : to close, to shut **2** : to turn off **3** : to bring to an end — *vi* **1** : to close up, to lock up **2** : to close down — **cerrarse** *vr* **1** : to close **2** : to fasten, to button up **3** : to conclude, to end

cerrazón *nf, pl* **-zones** : obstinacy, stubbornness
cerro *nm* COLINA, LOMA : hill
cerrojo *nm* PESTILLO : bolt, latch
certamen *nm, pl* **-támenes** : competition, contest
certero, -ra *adj* : accurate, precise — **certeramente** *adv*
certeza *nf* : certainty
certidumbre *nf* : certainty
certificable *adj* : certifiable
certificación *nf, pl* **-ciones** : certification
certificado[1], **-da** *adj* **1** : certified **2** : registered (of mail)
certificado[2] *nm* **1** : certificate **2** : registered letter
certificar {72} *vt* **1** : to certify **2** : to register (mail)
cervato *nm* : fawn
cervecera *nf* : brewery
cervecería *nf* **1** : brewery **2** : beer hall, bar
cerveza *nf* : beer ⟨cerveza de barril : draft beer⟩
cervical *adj* : cervical
cerviz *nf, pl* **cervices** : nape of the neck, cervix
cesación *nf, pl* **-ciones** : cessation, suspension
cesante *adj* : laid off, unemployed
cesantía *nf* : unemployment
cesar *vi* : to cease, to stop — *vt* : to dismiss, to lay off
cesárea *nf* : cesarean, C-section
cese *nm* **1** : cessation, stop ⟨cese del fuego : cease-fire⟩ **2** : dismissal
cesio *nm* : cesium
cesión *nf, pl* **cesiones** : transfer, assignment ⟨cesión de bienes : transfer of property⟩
césped *nm* : lawn, grass
cesta *nf* **1** : basket **2** : jai alai racket
cesto *nm* **1** : hamper **2** : basket (in basketball) **3 cesto de (la) basura** : wastebasket
cetrería *nf* : falconry
cetrino, -na *adj* : sallow
cetro *nm* : scepter
chabacano[1], **-na** *adj* : tacky, tasteless
chabacano[2] *nm Mex* : apricot
chacal *nm* : jackal
cháchara *nf fam* **1** : small talk, chatter **2 cháchara**s *nfpl* : trinkets, junk
chacharear *vi fam* : to chatter, to gab
chacra *nf Arg, Chile, Peru* : small farm
chadiano, -na *adj & n* : Chadian
chal *nm* MANTÓN : shawl
chalado[1], **-da** *adj fam* : crazy, nuts
chalado[2], **-da** *n* : nut, crazy person
chalán *nm, pl* **chalanes** *Mex* : barge
chalé → **chalet**
chaleco *nm* : vest
chalet *nm Spain* : house
chalupa *nf* **1** : small boat **2** *Mex* : small stuffed tortilla
chamaco, -ca *n Mex fam* : kid, boy *m*, girl *f*
chamarra *nf* **1** : sheepskin jacket **2** : poncho, blanket
chamba *nf Mex, Peru fam* : job, work
chambear *vi Mex, Peru fam* : to work
chamo, -ma *n Ven fam* **1** : kid, boy *m*, girl *f* **2** : buddy, pal
champaña *or* **champán** *nm* : champagne
champiñón *nm, pl* **-ñones** : mushroom
champú *nm, pl* **-pus** *or* **-púes** : shampoo
champurrado *nm Mex* : hot chocolate thickened with cornstarch
chamuco *nm Mex fam* : devil
chamuscar {72} *vt* : to singe, to scorch — **chamuscarse** *vr*
chamusquina *nf* : scorch
chance *nm* OPORTUNIDAD : chance, opportunity
chancho[1], **-cha** *adj fam* : dirty, filthy, gross
chancho[2], **-cha** *n* **1** : pig, hog **2** *fam* : slob
chanchullero, -ra *adj fam* : shady, crooked
chanchullo *nm fam* : shady deal, scam
chancla *nf* **1** : thong sandal, slipper **2** : old shoe
chancleta → **chancla**
chanclo *nm* **1** : clog **2 chanclos** *nmpl* : overshoes, galoshes, rubbers
chancro *nm* : chancre
changarro *nm Mex* : small shop, stall
chango, -ga *n Mex* : monkey
chantaje *nm* : blackmail
chantajear *vt* : to blackmail
chantajista *nmf* : blackmailer
chanza *nf* **1** : joke, jest **2** *Mex fam* : chance, opportunity
chapa *nf* **1** : sheet, panel, veneer **2** : lock **3** : badge
chapado, -da *adj* **1** : plated **2 chapado a la antigua** : old-fashioned
chapar *vt* **1** : to veneer **2** : to plate (metals)
chaparrón *nm, pl* **-rrones** **1** : downpour **2** : great quantity, torrent
chapeado, -da *adj Col, Mex* : flushed
chapopote *nm Mex* : tar, blacktop
chapotear *vi* : to splash about
chapucero[1], **-ra** *adj* **1** : crude, shoddy **2** *Mex fam* : dishonest
chapucero[2], **-ra** *n* **1** : sloppy worker, bungler **2** *Mex fam* : cheat, swindler
chapulín *nm, pl* **-lines** *CA, Mex* : grasshopper, locust
chapuza *nf* **1** : botched job **2** *Mex fam* : fraud, trick ⟨hacer chapuzas : to cheat⟩
chapuzón *nm, pl* **-zones** : dip, swim ⟨darse un chapuzón : to go for a quick dip⟩
chaqueta *nf* : jacket
charada *nf* : charades (game)
charango *nm* : traditional Andean stringed instrument
charca *nf* : pond, pool
charco *nm* : puddle, pool

charcutería *nf* : delicatessen
charla *nf* : chat, talk
charlar *vi* : to chat, to talk
charlatán[1], **-tana** *adj* : talkative, chatty
charlatán[2], **-tana** *n, mpl* **-tanes** **1** : chatterbox **2** FARSANTE : charlatan, phony
charlatanear *vi* : to chatter away
charol *nm* **1** : lacquer, varnish **2** : patent leather **3** : tray
charola *nf Bol, Mex, Peru* : tray
charreada *nf Mex* : charro show, rodeo
charretera *nf* : epaulet
charro[1], **-rra** *adj* **1** : gaudy, tacky **2** *Mex* : pertaining to charros
charro[2], **-rra** *n Mex* : charro (Mexican cowboy or cowgirl)
chascarrillo *nm fam* : joke, funny story
chasco *nm* **1** BROMA : trick, joke **2** DECEPCIÓN, DESILUSIÓN : disillusionment, disappointment
chasis *or* **chasís** *nm* : chassis
chasquear *vt* **1** : to click (the tongue, fingers, etc.) **2** : to snap (a whip)
chasquido *nm* **1** : click (of the tongue or fingers) **2** : snap, crack
chatarra *nf* : scrap metal
chato, -ta *adj* **1** : pug-nosed **2** : flat
chauvinismo *nm* : chauvinism
chauvinista[1] *adj* : chauvinistic
chauvinista[2] *nmf* : chauvinist
chaval, **-vala** *n fam* : kid, boy *m,* girl *f*
chavo[1], **-va** *adj Mex fam* : young
chavo[2], **-va** *n Mex fam* : kid, boy *m,* girl *f*
chavo[3] *nm fam* : cent, buck ⟨no tengo un chavo : I'm broke⟩
chayote *nm* : chayote (plant, fruit)
checar {72} *vt Mex* : to check, to verify
checo[1], **-ca** *adj & n* : Czech
checo[2] *nm* : Czech (language)
checoslovaco, -ca *adj & n* : Czechoslovakian
chef *nm* : chef
chelín *nm, pl* **chelines** : shilling
cheque[1], **etc.** → **checar**
cheque[2] *nm* **1** : check **2 cheque de viajero** : traveler's check
chequear *vt* **1** : to check, to verify **2** : to check in (baggage)
chequeo *nm* **1** INSPECCIÓN : check, inspection **2** : checkup, examination
chequera *nf* : checkbook
chévere *adj fam* : great, fantastic
chic *adj & nm* : chic
chica → **chico**
chicano, -na *adj & n* : Chicano *m,* Chicana *f*
chicha *nf* : fermented alcoholic beverage made from corn
chícharo *nm* : pea
chicharra *nf* **1** CIGARRA : cicada **2** : buzzer
chicharrón *nm, pl* **-rrones** **1** : pork rind **2 darle chicharrón a** *Mex fam* : to get rid of
chichón *nm, pl* **chichones** : bump, swelling
chicle *nm* : chewing gum
chicloso *nm Mex* : taffy
chico[1], **-ca** *adj* **1** : little, small **2** : young
chico[2], **-ca** *n* **1** : child, boy *m,* girl *f* **2** : young man *m,* young woman *f*
chicote *nm* LÁTIGO : whip, lash
chiffon → **chifón**
chiflado[1], **-da** *adj fam* : nuts, crazy
chiflado[2], **-da** *n fam* : crazy person, lunatic
chiflar *vi* : to whistle — *vt* : to whistle at, to boo — **chiflarse** *vr fam* **~ por** : to be crazy about
chiflido *nm* : whistle, whistling
chiflón *nm, pl* **chiflones** : draft (of air)
chifón *nm, pl* **chifones** : chiffon
chilango[1], **-ga** *adj Mex fam* : of or from Mexico City
chilango[2], **-ga** *n Mex fam* : person from Mexico City
chilaquiles *nmpl Mex* : shredded tortillas in sauce
chile *nm* : chili pepper
chileno, -na *adj & n* : Chilean
chillar *vi* **1** : to squeal, to screech **2** : to scream, to yell **3** : to be gaudy, to clash
chillido *nm* **1** : scream, shout **2** : squeal, screech, cry (of an animal)
chillo *nm PRi* : red snapper
chillón, -llona *adj, mpl* **chillones** **1** : piercing, shrill **2** : loud, gaudy
chilpayate *nmf Mex fam* : child, little kid
chimenea *nf* **1** : chimney **2** : fireplace
chimichurri *nm Arg* : traditional hot sauce
chimpancé *nm* : chimpanzee
china *nf* **1** : pebble, small stone **2** *PRi* : orange
chinchar *vt fam* : to annoy, to pester — **chincharse** *vr fam* : to put up with something, to grin and bear it
chinchayote *nm Mex* : chayote root
chinche[1] *nf* **1** : bedbug **2** *Ven* : ladybug **3** : thumbtack
chinche[2] *nmf fam* : nuisance, pain in the neck
chinchilla *nf* : chinchilla
chino[1], **-na** *adj* **1** : Chinese **2** *Mex* : curly, kinky
chino[2], **-na** *n* : Chinese person
chino[3] *nm* : Chinese (language)
chip *nm, pl* **chips** : chip ⟨chip de memoria : memory chip⟩
chipote *nm Mex fam* : bump (on the head)
chipotle *nm Mex* : type of chili pepper
chipriota *adj & nmf* : Cypriot
chiquear *vt Mex* : to spoil, to indulge
chiquero *nm* POCILGA : pigpen, pigsty
chiquillada *nf* : childish prank
chiquillo[1], **-lla** *adj* : very young, little
chiquillo[2], **-lla** *n* : kid, youngster
chiquito[1], **-ta** *adj* : tiny
chiquito[2], **-ta** *n* : little one, baby
chiribita *nf* **1** : spark **2 chiribitas** *nfpl* : spots before the eyes
chiribitil *nm* **1** DESVÁN : attic, garret **2** : cubbyhole

chirigota *nf fam* : joke
chirimía *nf* : traditional reed pipe
chirimoya *nf* : cherimoya, custard apple
chiripa *nf* **1** : fluke **2 de ~** : by sheer luck
chirivía *nf* : parsnip
chirona *nf fam* : slammer, jail
chirriar {85} *vi* **1** : to squeak, to creak **2** : to screech — **chirriante** *adj*
chirrido *nm* **1** : squeak, squeaking **2** : screech, screeching
chirrión *nm, pl* **chirriones** *Mex* : whip, lash
chisme *nm* **1** : gossip, tale **2** *Spain fam* : gadget, thingamajig
chismear *vi* : to gossip
chismoso¹, **-sa** *adj* : gossipy, gossiping
chismoso², **-sa** *n* **1** : gossiper, gossip **2** *Mex fam* : tattletale
chispa¹ *adj* **1** *Mex fam* : lively, vivacious ⟨un perrito chispa : a frisky puppy⟩ **2** *Spain fam* : tipsy
chispa² *nf* **1** : spark **2 echar chispas** : to be furious
chispeante *adj* : sparkling, scintillating
chispear *vi* **1** : to give off sparks **2** : to sparkle
chisporrotear *vi* : to crackle, to sizzle
chiste *nm* **1** : joke, funny story **2 tener chiste** : to be funny **3 tener su chiste** *Mex* : to be tricky
chistoso¹, **-sa** *adj* **1** : funny, humorous **2** : witty
chistoso², **-sa** *n* : wit, joker
chivas *nfpl Mex fam* : stuff, odds and ends
chivo¹, **-va** *n* **1** : kid, young goat **2 chivo expiatorio** : scapegoat
chivo² *nm* **1** : billy goat **2** : fit of anger
chocante *adj* **1** : shocking **2** : unpleasant, rude
chocar {72} *vi* **1** : to crash, to collide **2** : to clash, to conflict **3** : to be shocking ⟨le chocó : he was shocked⟩ **4** *Mex, Ven fam* : to be unpleasant or obnoxious ⟨me choca tu jefe : I can't stand your boss⟩ — *vt* **1** : to shake (hands) **2** : to clink glasses
chochear *vi* **1** : to be senile **2 ~ por** : to dote on, to be soft on
chochín *nm, pl* **-chines** : wren
chocho, **-cha** *adj* **1** : senile **2** : doting
choclo *nm* **1** : ear of corn, corncob **2** : corn **3 meter el choclo** *Mex fam* : to make a mistake
chocolate *nm* **1** : chocolate **2** : hot chocolate, cocoa
chofer *or* **chófer** *nm* **1** : chauffeur **2** : driver
choke *nm* : choke (of an automobile)
chole *interj Mex fam* **¡ya chole!** : enough!, cut it out!
cholo, **-la** *adj & n* : mestizo
cholla *nf fam* : head
chollo *nm Spain fam* : bargain
chongo *nm* **1** *Mex* : bun (chignon) **2 chongos** *nmpl Mex* : dessert made with fried bread
choque¹, **etc.** → **chocar**
choque² *nm* **1** : crash, collision **2** : clash, conflict **3** : shock
chorizo *nm* : chorizo, sausage
chorrear *vi* **1** : to drip **2** : to pour out, to gush out
chorrito *nm* : squirt, splash
chorro *nm* **1** : flow, stream, jet **2** *Mex fam* : heap, ton
choteado, **-da** *adj Mex fam* : worn-out, stale ⟨esa canción está bien choteada : that song's been played to death⟩
chotear *vt* : to make fun of
choteo *nm* : joking around, kidding
chovinismo, **chovinista** → **chauvinismo**, **chauvinista**
choza *nf* BARRACA, CABAÑA : hut, shack
chubasco *nm* : downpour, storm
chuchería *nf* : knickknack, trinket
chueco, **-ca** *adj* **1** : crooked, bent **2** *Chile, Mex fam* : dishonest, shady
chulada *nf Mex, Spain fam* : cute or pretty thing ⟨¡qué chulada de vestido! : what a lovely dress!⟩
chulear *vt Mex fam* : to compliment
chuleta *nf* : cutlet, chop
chulo¹, **-la** *adj* **1** *fam* : cute, pretty **2** *Spain fam* : cocky, arrogant
chulo² *nm Spain* : pimp
chupada *nf* **1** : suck, sucking **2** : puff, drag (on a cigarette)
chupado, **-da** *adj fam* **1** : gaunt, skinny **2** : plastered, drunk
chupaflor *nm* COLIBRÍ : hummingbird
chupamirto *nm Mex* : hummingbird
chupar *vt* **1** : to suck **2** : to absorb **3** : to puff on **4** *fam* : to drink, to guzzle — *vi* : to suckle — **chuparse** *vr* **1** : to waste away **2** *fam* : to put up with **3 ¡chúpate esa!** *fam* : take that!
chupete *nm* **1** : pacifier **2** *Chile, Peru* : lollipop
chupetear *vt* : to suck (at)
chupón *nm, pl* **chupones** **1** : sucker (of a plant) **2** : baby bottle, pacifier
churrasco *nm* **1** : steak **2** : barbecued meat
churro *nm* **1** : fried dough **2** *fam* : botch, mess **3** *fam* : attractive person, looker
chusco, **-ca** *adj* : funny, amusing
chusma *nf* GENTUZA : riffraff, rabble
chutar *vi* : to shoot (in soccer)
chute *nm* : shot (in soccer)
cianuro *nm* : cyanide
cibernética *nf* : cybernetics
cicatriz *nf, pl* **-trices** : scar
cicatrizarse {21} *vr* : to form a scar, to heal
cíclico, **-ca** *adj* : cyclical
ciclismo *nm* : bicycling
ciclista *nmf* : bicyclist
ciclo *nm* : cycle
ciclomotor *nm* : moped
ciclón *nm, pl* **ciclones** : cyclone
cicuta *nf* : hemlock
cidra *nf* : citron (fruit)
ciega, **ciegue etc.** → **cegar**

ciego[1], **-ga** *adj* **1** INVIDENTE : blind **2 a ciegas** : blindly **3 quedarse ciego** : to go blind — **ciegamente** *adv*
ciego[2], **-ga** *n* INVIDENTE : blind person
cielo *nm* **1** : sky **2** : heaven **3** : ceiling
ciempiés *nms & pl* : centipede
cien[1] *adj* **1** : a hundred, hundred ⟨las primeras cien páginas : the first hundred pages⟩ **2 cien por cien** *or* **cien por ciento** : a hundred percent, through and through, wholeheartedly
cien[2] *nm* : one hundred
ciénaga *nf* : swamp, bog
ciencia *nf* **1** : science **2** : learning, knowledge **3 a ciencia cierta** : for a fact, for certain
cieno *nm* : mire, mud, silt
científico[1], **-ca** *adj* : scientific — **científicamente** *adv*
científico[2], **-ca** *n* : scientist
ciento[1] *adj* (*used in compound numbers*) : one hundred ⟨ciento uno : one hundred and one⟩
ciento[2] *nm* **1** : hundred, group of a hundred **2 por ～** : percent
cierne, etc. → **cerner**
cierra, etc. → **cerrar**
cierre *nm* **1** : closing, closure **2** : fastener, clasp, zipper
cierto, -ta *adj* **1** : true, certain, definite ⟨lo cierto es que . . . : the fact is that . . . ⟩ **2** : certain, one ⟨cierto día de verano : one summer day⟩ ⟨bajo ciertas circunstancias : under certain circumstances⟩ **3 por ～** : in fact, as a matter of fact — **ciertamente** *adv*
ciervo, -va *n* : deer, stag *m*, hind *f*
cifra *nf* **1** : figure, number **2** : quantity, amount **3** CLAVE : code, cipher
cifrar *vt* **1** : to write in code **2** : to place, to pin ⟨cifró su esperanza en la lotería : he pinned his hopes on the lottery⟩ — **cifrarse** *vr* : to amount ⟨la multa se cifra en millares : the fine amounts to thousands⟩
cigarra *nf* CHICHARRA : cicada
cigarrera *nf* : cigarette case
cigarrillo *nm* : cigarette
cigarro *nm* **1** : cigarette **2** PURO : cigar
cigoto *nm* : zygote
cigüeña *nf* : stork
cilantro *nm* : cilantro, coriander
cilíndrico, -ca *adj* : cylindrical
cilindro *nm* : cylinder
cima *nf* CUMBRE : peak, summit, top
cimarrón, -rrona *adj, mpl* **-rrones** : untamed, wild
címbalo *nm* : cymbal
cimbel *nm* : decoy
cimbrar *vt* : to shake, to rock — **cimbrarse** *vr* : to sway, to swing
cimentar {55} *vt* **1** : to lay the foundation of, to establish **2** : to strengthen, to cement
cimientos *nmpl* : base, foundation(s)
cinc *nm* : zinc
cincel *nm* : chisel
cincelar *vt* **1** : to chisel **2** : to engrave
cincha *nf* : cinch, girth
cinchar *vt* : to cinch (a horse)
cinco *adj & nm* : five
cincuenta *adj & nm* : fifty
cincuentavo[1], **-va** *adj* : fiftieth
cincuentavo[2] *nm* : fiftieth (fraction)
cine *nm* **1** : cinema, movies *pl* **2** : movie theater
cineasta *nmf* : filmmaker
cinematográfico, -ca *adj* : movie, film, cinematic ⟨la industria cinematográfica : the film industry⟩
cingalés[1], **-lesa** *adj & n* : Sinhalese
cingalés[2] *nm* : Sinhalese (language)
cínico[1], **-ca** *adj* **1** : cynical **2** : shameless, brazen — **cínicamente** *adv*
cínico[2], **-ca** *n* : cynic
cinismo *nm* : cynicism
cinta *nf* **1** : ribbon **2** : tape ⟨cinta métrica : tape measure⟩ **3** : strap, belt ⟨cinta transportadora : conveyor belt⟩
cinto *nm* : strap, belt
cintura *nf* **1** : waist, waistline **2 meter en cintura** *fam* : to bring into line, to discipline
cinturón *nm, pl* **-rones** **1** : belt **2 cinturón de seguridad** : seat belt
ciñe, etc. → **ceñir**
ciprés *nm, pl* **cipreses** : cypress
circo *nm* : circus
circón *nm, pl* **circones** : zircon
circonio *nm* : zirconium
circuitería *nf* : circuitry
circuito *nm* : circuit
circulación *nf, pl* **-ciones** **1** : circulation **2** : movement **3** : traffic
circular[1] *vi* **1** : to circulate **2** : to move along **3** : to drive
circular[2] *adj* : circular
circular[3] *nf* : circular, flier
circulatorio, -ria *adj* : circulatory
círculo *nm* **1** : circle **2** : club, group
circuncidar *vt* : to circumcise
circuncisión *nf, pl* **-siones** : circumcision
circundar *vt* : to surround — **circundante** *adj*
circunferencia *nf* : circumference
circunflejo, -ja *adj* **acento circunflejo** : circumflex
circunlocución *nf, pl* **-ciones** : circumlocution
circunloquio *nm* → **circunlocución**
circunnavegar {52} *vt* : to circumnavigate — **circunnavegación** *nf*
circunscribir {33} *vt* : to circumscribe, to constrict, to limit — **circunscribirse** *vr*
circunscripción *nf, pl* **-ciones** **1** : limitation, restriction **2** : constituency
circunscrito *pp* → **circunscribir**
circunspección *nf, pl* **-ciones** : circumspection, prudence
circunspecto, -ta *adj* : circumspect, prudent
circunstancia *nf* : circumstance
circunstancial *adj* : circumstantial, incidental

circunstante *nmf* **1** : onlooker, bystander **2 los circunstantes** : those present
circunvalación *nf, pl* **-ciones** : surrounding, encircling ⟨carretera de circunvalación : bypass, beltway⟩
circunvecino, -na *adj* : surrounding, neighboring
cirio *nm* : large candle
cirro *nm* : cirrus (cloud)
cirrosis *nf* : cirrhosis
ciruela *nf* **1** : plum **2 ciruela pasa** : prune
cirugía *nf* : surgery
cirujano, -na *n* : surgeon
cisma *nm* : schism, rift
cisne *nm* : swan
cisterna *nf* : cistern, tank
cita *nf* **1** : quote, quotation **2** : appointment, date
citable *adj* : quotable
citación *nf, pl* **-ciones** EMPLAZAMIENTO : summons, subpoena
citadino[1]**, -na** *adj* : of the city, urban
citadino[2]**, -na** *n* : city dweller
citado, -da *adj* : said, aforementioned
citar *vt* **1** : to quote, to cite **2** : to make an appointment with **3** : to summon (to court), to subpoena — **citarse** *vr* **~ con** : to arrange to meet (someone)
cítara *nf* : zither
citatorio *nm* : subpoena
citoplasma *nm* : cytoplasm
cítrico[1]**, -ca** *adj* : citric
cítrico[2] *nm* : citrus fruit
ciudad *nf* **1** : city, town **2 ciudad universitaria** : college or university campus **3 ciudad perdida** *Mex* : shantytown
ciudadanía *nf* **1** : citizenship **2** : citizenry, citizens *pl*
ciudadano[1]**, -na** *adj* : civic, city
ciudadano[2]**, -na** *n* **1** NACIONAL : citizen **2** HABITANTE : resident, city dweller
ciudadela *nf* : citadel, fortress
cívico, -ca *adj* **1** : civic **2** : public-spirited
civil[1] *adj* **1** : civil **2** : civilian
civil[2] *nmf* : civilian
civilidad *nf* : civility, courtesy
civilización *nf, pl* **-ciones** : civilization
civilizar {21} *vt* : to civilize
civismo *nm* : community spirit, civic-mindedness, civics
cizaña *nf* : discord, rift
clamar *vi* : to clamor, to raise a protest — *vt* : to cry out for
clamor *nm* : clamor, outcry
clamoroso, -sa *adj* : clamorous, resounding, thunderous
clan *nm* : clan
clandestinidad *nf* : secrecy ⟨en la clandestinidad : underground⟩
clandestino, -na *adj* : clandestine, secret
clara *nf* : egg white
claraboya *nf* : skylight
claramente *adv* : clearly
clarear *v impers* **1** : to clear, to clear up **2** : to get light, to dawn — *vi* : to go gray, to turn white
claridad *nf* **1** NITIDEZ : clarity, clearness **2** : brightness, light
clarificación *nf, pl* **-ciones** ACLARACIÓN : clarification, explanation
clarificar {72} *vt* ACLARAR : to clarify, to explain
clarín *nm, pl* **clarines** : bugle
clarinete *nm* : clarinet
clarividencia *nf* **1** : clairvoyance **2** : perspicacity, discernment
clarividente[1] *adj* **1** : clairvoyant **2** : perspicacious, discerning
clarividente[2] *nmf* : clairvoyant
claro[1] *adv* **1** : clearly ⟨habla más claro : speak more clearly⟩ **2** : of course, surely ⟨¡claro!, ¡claro que sí! : absolutely!, of course!⟩ ⟨claro que entendió : of course she understood⟩
claro[2]**, -ra** *adj* **1** : bright, clear **2** : pale, fair, light **3** : clear, evident
claro[3] *nm* **1** : clearing **2 claro de luna** : moonlight
clase *nf* **1** : class **2** ÍNDOLE, TIPO : sort, kind, type
clasicismo *nm* : classicism
clásico[1]**, -ca** *adj* **1** : classic **2** : classical
clásico[2] *nm* : classic
clasificación *nf, pl* **-ciones** **1** : classification, sorting out **2** : rating **3** CALIFICACIÓN : qualification (in competitions)
clasificado, -da *adj* : classified ⟨aviso clasificado : classified ad⟩
clasificar {72} *vt* **1** : to classify, to sort out **2** : to rate, to rank — *vi* CALIFICAR : to qualify (in competitions) — **clasificarse** *vr*
claudicación *nf, pl* **-ciones** : surrender, abandonment of one's principles
claudicar {72} *vi* : to back down, to abandon one's principles
claustro *nm* : cloister
claustrofobia *nf* : claustrophobia
claustrofóbico, -ca *adj* : claustrophobic
cláusula *nf* : clause
clausura *nf* **1** : closure, closing **2** : closing ceremony **3** : cloister
clausurar *vt* **1** : to close, to bring to a close **2** : to close down
clavadista *nmf* : diver
clavado[1]**, -da** *adj* **1** : nailed, fixed, stuck **2** *fam* : punctual, on the dot **3** *fam* : identical ⟨es clavado a su padre : he's the image of his father⟩
clavado[2] *nm* : dive
clavar *vt* **1** : to nail, to hammer **2** HINCAR : to plunge, to stick **3** : to fix (one's eyes) on — **clavarse** *vr* : to stick oneself (with a sharp object)
clave[1] *adj* : key, essential
clave[2] *nf* **1** CIFRA : code **2** : key ⟨la clave del misterio : the key to the mystery⟩ **3** : clef **4** : keystone
clavel *nm* : carnation
clavelito *nm* : pink (flower)

clavicémbalo *nm* : harpsichord
clavícula *nf* : collarbone
clavija *nf* **1** : plug **2** : peg, pin
clavo *nm* **1** : nail ‹clavo grande : spike› **2** : clove **3 dar en el clavo** : to hit the nail on the head
claxon *nm, pl* **cláxones** : horn (of an automobile)
clemencia *nf* : clemency, mercy
clemente *adj* : merciful
cleptomanía *nf* : kleptomania
cleptómano, -na *n* : kleptomaniac
clerecía *nf* : ministry, ministers *pl*
clerical *adj* : clerical
clérigo, -ga *n* : cleric, member of the clergy
clero *nm* : clergy
cliché *nm* **1** : cliché **2** : stencil **3** : negative (of a photograph)
cliente, -ta *n* : customer, client
clientela *nf* : clientele, customers *pl*
clima *nm* **1** : climate **2** AMBIENTE : atmosphere, ambience
climático, -ca *adj* : climatic
climatización *nf, pl* **-ciones** : air-conditioning
climatizar {21} *vt* : to air-condition — **climatizado, -da** *adj*
clímax *nm* : climax
clínica *nf* : clinic
clínico, -ca *adj* : clinical — **clínicamente** *adv*
clip *nm, pl* **clips 1** : clip **2** : paper clip
clítoris *nms & pl* : clitoris
cloaca *nf* ALCANTARILLA : sewer
clocar {82} *vi* : to cluck
cloche *nm CA, Car, Col, Ven* : clutch (of an automobile)
clon *nm* : clone
cloqué, etc. → **clocar**
cloquear *vi* : to cluck
clorar *vt* : to chlorinate — **cloración** *nf*
cloro *nm* : chlorine
clorofila *nf* : chlorophyll
cloroformo *nm* : chloroform
cloruro *nm* : chloride
clóset *nm, pl* **clósets 1** : closet **2** : cupboard
club *nm* : club
clueca, clueque etc. → **clocar**
coa *nf Mex* : hoe
coacción *nf, pl* **-ciones** : coercion, duress
coaccionar *vt* : to coerce
coactivo, -va *adj* : coercive
coagular *v* : to clot, to coagulate — **coagulación** *nf*
coágulo *nm* : clot
coalición *nf, pl* **-ciones** : coalition
coartada *nf* : alibi
coartar *vt* : to restrict, to limit
cobalto *nm* : cobalt
cobarde[1] *adj* : cowardly
cobarde[2] *nmf* : coward
cobardía *nf* : cowardice
cobaya *nf* : guinea pig
cobertizo *nm* : shed, shelter
cobertor *nm* COLCHA : bedspread, quilt
cobertura *nf* **1** : coverage **2** : cover, collateral
cobija *nf* FRAZADA, MANTA : blanket
cobijar *vt* : to shelter — **cobijarse** *vr* : to take shelter
cobra *nf* : cobra
cobrador, -dora *n* **1** : collector **2** : conductor (of a bus or train)
cobrar *vt* **1** : to charge **2** : to collect, to draw, to earn **3** : to acquire, to gain **4** : to recover, to retrieve **5** : to cash (a check) **6** : to claim, to take (a life) **7** : to shoot (game), to bag — *vi* **1** : to be paid **2 llamar por cobrar** *Mex* : to call collect
cobre *nm* : copper
cobrizo, -za *adj* : coppery
cobro *nm* : collection (of money), cashing (of a check)
coca *nf* **1** : coca **2** *fam* : coke, cocaine
cocaína *nf* : cocaine
cocal *nm* : coca plantation
cocción *nf, pl* **cocciones** : cooking
cocear *vi* : to kick (of an animal)
cocer {14} *vt* **1** COCINAR : to cook **2** HERVIR : to boil
cochambre *nmf fam* : filth, grime
cochambroso, -sa *adj* : filthy, grimy
coche *nm* **1** : car, automobile **2** : coach, carriage **3 coche cama** : sleeping car **4 coche fúnebre** : hearse
cochecito *nm* : baby carriage, stroller
cochera *nf* : garage, carport
cochinada *nf fam* **1** : filthy language **2** : disgusting behavior **3** : dirty trick
cochinillo *nm* : suckling pig, piglet
cochino[1]**, -na** *adj* **1** : dirty, filthy, disgusting **2** *fam* : rotten, lousy
cochino[2]**, -na** *n* : pig, hog
cocido[1]**, -da** *adj* **1** : boiled, cooked **2 bien cocido** : well-done
cocido[2] *nm* ESTOFADO, GUISADO : stew
cociente *nm* : quotient
cocimiento *nm* : cooking, baking
cocina *nf* **1** : kitchen **2** : stove **3** : cuisine, cooking
cocinar *v* : to cook
cocinero, -ra *n* : cook, chef
cocineta *nf Mex* : kitchenette
coco *nm* **1** : coconut **2** *fam* : head **3** *fam* : bogeyman
cocoa *nf* : cocoa, hot chocolate
cocodrilo *nm* : crocodile
cocotero *nm* : coconut palm
coctel *or* **cóctel** *nm* **1** : cocktail **2** : cocktail party
coctelera *nf* : cocktail shaker
codazo *nm* **1 darle un codazo a** : to elbow, to nudge **2 abrirse paso a codazos** : to elbow one's way through
codearse *vr* : to rub elbows, to hobnob
códice *nm* : codex, manuscript
codicia *nf* AVARICIA : avarice, covetousness
codiciar *vt* : to covet
codicilo *nm* : codicil
codicioso, -sa *adj* : avaricious, covetous

codificación *nf, pl* **-ciones 1** : codification **2** : coding, encoding

codificar {72} *vt* **1** : to codify **2** : to code, to encode

código *nm* **1** : code **2 código postal** : zip code **3 código morse** : Morse code

codo[1], -da *adj Mex* : cheap, stingy

codo[2], -da *n Mex* : tightwad, cheapskate

codo[3] *nm* : elbow

codorniz *nf, pl* **-nices** : quail

coeficiente *nm* **1** : coefficient **2 coeficiente intelectual** : IQ, intelligence quotient

coexistir *vi* : to coexist — **coexistencia** *nf*

cofa *nf* : crow's nest

cofre *nm* **1** BAÚL : trunk, chest **2** *Mex* CAPOTE : hood (of a car)

coger {15} *vt* **1** : to seize, to take hold of **2** : to catch **3** : to pick up **4** : to gather, to pick **5** : to gore — **cogerse** *vr* AGARRARSE : to hold on

cogida *nf* **1** : gathering, harvest **2** : goring

cognición *nf, pl* **-ciones** : cognition

cognitivo, -va *adj* : cognitive

cogollo *nm* **1** : heart (of a vegetable) **2** : bud, bulb **3** : core, crux ⟨el cogollo de la cuestión : the heart of the matter⟩

cogote *nm* : scruff, nape

cohabitar *vi* : to cohabit — **cohabitación** *nf*

cohechar *vt* SOBORNAR : to bribe

cohecho *nm* SOBORNO : bribe, bribery

coherencia *nf* : coherence — **coherente** *adj*

cohesión *nf, pl* **-siones** : cohesion

cohesivo, -va *adj* : cohesive

cohete *nm* : rocket

cohibición *nf, pl* **-ciones 1** : (legal) restraint **2** INHIBICIÓN : inhibition

cohibido, -da *adj* : inhibited, shy

cohibir {62} *vt* : to inhibit, to make self-conscious — **cohibirse** *vr* : to feel shy or embarrassed

cohorte *nf* : cohort

coima *nf Arg, Chile, Peru* : bribe

coimear *vt Arg, Chile, Peru* : to bribe

coincidencia *nf* : coincidence

coincidente *adj* **1** : coincident **2** ACORDE : coinciding

coincidir *vi* **1** : to coincide **2** : to agree

coito *nm* : sexual intercourse, coitus

coja, etc. → **coger**

cojear *vi* **1** : to limp **2** : to wobble, to rock **3 cojear del mismo pie** : to be two of a kind

cojera *nf* : limp

cojín *nm, pl* **cojines** : cushion, throw pillow

cojinete *nm* **1** : bearing, bushing **2 cojinete de bola** : ball bearing

cojo[1], -ja *adj* **1** : limping, lame **2** : wobbly **3** : weak, ineffectual

cojo[2], -ja *n* : lame person

cojones *nmpl usu considered vulgar* **1** : testicles *pl* **2** : guts *pl,* courage

col *nf* **1** REPOLLO : cabbage **2 col de Bruselas** : Brussels sprout **3 col rizada** : kale

cola *nf* **1** RABO : tail ⟨cola de caballo : ponytail⟩ **2** FILA : line (of people) ⟨hacer cola : to wait in line⟩ **3** : cola, drink **4** : train (of a dress) **5** : tails *pl* (of a tuxedo) **6** PEGAMENTO : glue **7** *fam* : buttocks *pl,* rear end

colaboracionista *nmf* : collaborator, traitor

colaborador, -dora *n* **1** : contributor (to a periodical) **2** : collaborator

colaborar *vi* : to collaborate — **colaboración** *nf*

colación *nf, pl* **-ciones 1** : light meal **2** : comparison, collation ⟨sacar a colación : to bring up, to broach⟩ **3** : conferral (of a degree)

colador *nm* **1** : colander, strainer **2** *PRi* : small coffeepot

colapso *nm* **1** : collapse **2** : standstill

colar {19} *vt* : to strain, to filter — **colarse** *vr* **1** : to sneak in, to cut in line, to gate-crash **2** : to slip up, to make a mistake

colateral[1] *adj* : collateral — **colateralmente** *adv*

colateral[2] *nm* : collateral

colcha *nf* COBERTOR : bedspread, quilt

colchón *nm, pl* **colchones 1** : mattress **2** : cushion, padding, buffer

colchoneta *nf* : mat (for gymnastic sports)

colear *vi* **1** : to wag its tail **2 vivito y coleando** *fam* : alive and kicking

colección *nf, pl* **-ciones** : collection

coleccionar *vt* : to collect, to keep a collection of

coleccionista *nmf* : collector

colecta *nf* : collection (of donations)

colectar *vt* : to collect

colectividad *nf* : community, group

colectivo[1], -va *adj* : collective — **colectivamente** *adv*

colectivo[2] *nm* **1** : collective **2** *Arg, Bol, Peru* : city bus

colector[1], -tora *n* : collector ⟨colector de impuestos : tax collector⟩

colector[2] *nm* **1** : sewer **2** : manifold (of an engine)

colega *nmf* **1** : colleague **2** HOMÓLOGO : counterpart **3** *fam* : buddy

colegiado[1], -da *adj* : collegiate

colegiado[2], -da *n* **1** ÁRBITRO : referee **2** : member (of a professional association)

colegial[1], -giala *adj* **1** : school, collegiate **2** *Mex fam* : green, inexperienced

colegial[2], -giala *n* : schoolboy *m,* schoolgirl *f*

colegiatura *nf Mex* : tuition

colegio *nm* **1** : school **2** : college ⟨colegio electoral : electoral college⟩ **3** : professional association

colegir {28} *vt* **1** JUNTAR : to collect, to gather **2** INFERIR : to infer, to deduce
cólera[1] *nm* : cholera
cólera[2] *nf* FURIA, IRA : anger, rage
colérico, -ca *adj* **1** FURIOSO : angry **2** IRRITABLE : irritable
colesterol *nm* : cholesterol
coleta *nf* **1** : ponytail **2** : pigtail
coletazo *nm* : lash, flick (of a tail)
colgado, -da *adj* **1** : hanging, hanged **2** : pending **3 dejar colgado a** : to disappoint, to let down
colgante[1] *adj* : hanging, dangling
colgante[2] *nm* : pendant, charm (on a bracelet)
colgar {16} *vt* **1** : to hang (up), to put up **2** AHORCAR : to hang (someone) **3** : to hang up (a telephone) **4** *fam* : to fail (an exam) — **colgarse** *vr* **1** : to hang, to be suspended **2** AHORCARSE : to hang oneself **3** : to hang up a telephone
colibrí *nm* CHUPAFLOR : hummingbird
cólico *nm* : colic
coliflor *nf* : cauliflower
colilla *nf* : butt (of a cigarette)
colina *nf* CERRO, LOMA : hill
colindante *adj* CONTIGUO : adjacent, neighboring
colindar *vi* : to adjoin, to be adjacent
coliseo *nm* : coliseum
colisión *nf, pl* **-siones** : collision
colisionar *vi* : to collide
collage *nm* : collage
collar *nm* **1** : collar (for an animal) **2** : necklace ⟨collar de perlas : string of pearls⟩
colmado, -da *adj* : heaping
colmar *vt* **1** : to fill to the brim **2** : to fulfill, to satisfy **3** : to heap, to shower ⟨me colmaron de regalos : they showered me with gifts⟩
colmena *nf* : beehive
colmenar *nm* APIARIO : apiary
colmillo *nm* **1** CANINO : canine (tooth), fang **2** : tusk
colmilludo, -da *adj Mex, PRi* : astute, shrewd, crafty
colmo *nm* : height, extreme, limit ⟨el colmo de la locura : the height of folly⟩ ⟨¡eso es el colmo! : that's the last straw!⟩
colocación *nf, pl* **-ciones** **1** : placement, placing **2** : position, job **3** : investment
colocar {72} *vt* **1** PONER : to place, to put **2** : to find a job for **3** : to invest — **colocarse** *vr* **1** SITUARSE : to position oneself **2** : to get a job
colofón *nm, pl* **-fones** **1** : ending, finale **2** : colophon
colofonia *nf* : rosin
colombiano, -na *adj & n* : Colombian
colon *nm* : (intestinal) colon
colón *nm, pl* **colones** : Costa Rican and Salvadoran unit of currency
colonia *nf* **1** : colony **2** : cologne **3** *Mex* : residential area, neighborhood
colonial *adj* : colonial
colonización *nf, pl* **-ciones** : colonization
colonizador[1], **-dora** *adj* : colonizing
colonizador[2], **-dora** *n* : colonizer, colonist
colonizar {21} *vt* : to colonize, to settle
colono, -na *n* **1** : settler, colonist **2** : tenant farmer
coloquial *adj* : colloquial
coloquio *nm* **1** : discussion, talk **2** : conference, symposium
color *nm* **1** : color **2** : paint, dye **3 colores** *nmpl* : colored pencils
coloración *nf, pl* **-ciones** : coloring, coloration
colorado[1], **-da** *adj* **1** ROJO : red **2 ponerse colorado** : to blush **3 chiste colorado** *Mex* : off-color joke
colorado[2] *nm* ROJO : red
colorante *nm* : coloring ⟨colorante de alimentos : food coloring⟩
colorear *vt* : to color — *vi* **1** : to redden **2** : to ripen
colorete *nm* : rouge, blusher
colorido *nm* : color, coloring
colorín *nm, pl* **-rines** **1** : bright color **2** : goldfinch
colosal *adj* : colossal
coloso *nm* : colossus
coludir *vi* : to be in collusion, to conspire
columna *nf* **1** : column **2 columna vertebral** : spine, backbone
columnata *nf* : colonnade
columnista *nmf* : columnist
columpiar *vt* : to push (on a swing) — **columpiarse** *vr* : to swing
columpio *nm* : swing
colusión *nf, pl* **-siones** : collusion
colza *nf* : rape (plant)
coma[1] *nm* : coma
coma[2] *nf* : comma
comadre *nf* **1** : godmother of one's child **2** : mother of one's godchild **3** *fam* : neighbor, female friend **4** *fam* : gossip
comadrear *vi fam* : to gossip
comadreja *nf* : weasel
comadrona *nf* : midwife
comanche *nmf* : Comanche
comandancia *nf* **1** : command headquarters **2** : command
comandante *nmf* **1** : commander, commanding officer **2** : major
comandar *vt* : to command, to lead
comando *nm* **1** : commando **2** : command (for computers)
comarca *nf* REGIÓN : region
comarcal *adj* REGIONAL : regional, local
comatoso, -sa *adj* : comatose
combar *vt* : to bend, to curve — **combarse** *vr* **1** : to bend, to buckle **2** : to warp, to bulge, to sag
combate *nm* **1** : combat **2** : fight, boxing match
combatiente *nmf* : combatant, fighter
combatir *vt* : to combat, to fight against — *vi* : to fight

combatividad *nf* : fighting spirit
combativo, -va *adj* : combative, spirited
combinación *nf, pl* **-ciones** **1** : combination **2** : connection (in travel)
combinar *vt* **1** UNIR : to combine, to mix together **2** : to match, to put together — **combinarse** *vr* : to get together, to conspire
combo *nm* **1** : (musical) band **2** *Chile, Peru* : sledgehammer **3** *Chile, Peru* : punch
combustible[1] *adj* : combustible
combustible[2] *nm* : fuel
combustión *nf, pl* **-tiones** : combustion
comedero *nm* : trough, feeder
comedia *nf* : comedy
comediante *nmf* : actor, actress *f*
comedido, -da *adj* MESURADO : moderate, restrained
comediógrafo, -fa *n* : playwright
comedor *nm* : dining room
comején *nm, pl* **-jenes** : termite
comelón[1], **-lona** *adj, mpl* **-lones** *fam* : gluttonous
comelón[2], **-lona** *n, pl* **-lones** *fam* : big eater, glutton
comensal *nmf* : dinner guest
comentador, -dora *n* → **comentarista**
comentar *vt* **1** : to comment on, to discuss **2** : to mention, to remark
comentario *nm* **1** : comment, remark ⟨sin comentarios : no comment⟩ **2** : commentary
comentarista *nmf* : commentator
comenzar {29} *v* EMPEZAR : to begin, to start
comer[1] *vt* **1** : to eat **2** : to consume, to eat up, to eat into — *vi* **1** : to eat **2** CENAR : to have a meal **3 dar de comer** : to feed — **comerse** *vr* : to eat up
comer[2] *nm* : eating, dining
comercial *adj & nm* : commercial — **comercialmente** *adv*
comercializar {21} *vt* **1** : to commercialize **2** : to market
comerciante *nmf* : merchant, dealer
comerciar *vi* : to do business, to trade
comercio *nm* **1** : commerce, trade **2** NEGOCIO : business, place of business
comestible *adj* : edible
comestibles *nmpl* VÍVERES : groceries, food
cometa[1] *nm* : comet
cometa[2] *nf* : kite
cometer *vt* **1** : to commit **2 cometer un error** : to make a mistake
cometido *nm* : assignment, task
comezón *nf, pl* **-zones** PICAZÓN : itchiness, itching
comible *adj fam* : eatable, edible
comic *or* **cómic** *nm* : comic strip, comic book
comicastro, -tra *n* : second-rate actor, ham
comicidad *nf* HUMOR : humor, wit
comicios *nmpl* : elections, voting
cómico[1], **-ca** *adj* : comic, comical
cómico[2], **-ca** *n* HUMORISTA : comic, comedian, comedienne *f*
comida *nf* **1** : food **2** : meal **3** : dinner **4 comida basura** : junk food **5 comida rápida** : fast food
comidilla *nf* : talk, gossip
comienzo *nm* **1** : start, beginning **2 al comienzo** : at first **3 dar comienzo** : to begin
comillas *nfpl* : quotation marks ⟨entre comillas : in quotes⟩
comilón, -lona → **comelón, -lona**
comilona *nf fam* : feast
comino *nm* **1** : cumin **2 me vale un comino** *fam* : not to matter to someone ⟨no me importa un comino : I couldn't care less⟩
comisaría *nf* : police station
comisario, -ria *n* : commissioner
comisión *nf, pl* **-siones** **1** : commission, committing **2** : committee **3** : percentage, commission ⟨comisión sobre las ventas : sales commission⟩
comisionado[1], **-da** *adj* : commissioned, entrusted
comisionado[2], **-da** *n* → **comisario**
comisionar *vt* : to commission
comité *nm* : committee
comitiva *nf* : retinue, entourage
como[1] *adv* **1** : around, about ⟨cuesta como 500 pesos : it costs around 500 pesos⟩ **2** : kind of, like ⟨tengo como mareos : I'm kind of dizzy⟩
como[2] *conj* **1** : how, as ⟨hazlo como dijiste que lo harías : do it the way you said you would⟩ **2** : since, given that ⟨como estaba lloviendo, no salí : since it was raining, I didn't go out⟩ **3** : if ⟨como lo vuelva a hacer lo arrestarán : if he does that again he'll be arrested⟩ **4 como quiera** : in any way
como[3] *prep* **1** : like, as ⟨ligero como una pluma : light as a feather⟩ **2 así como** : as well as
cómo *adv* : how ⟨¿cómo estás? : how are you?⟩ ⟨¿a cómo están las manzanas? : how much are the apples?⟩ ⟨¿cómo? : excuse me?, what was that?⟩ ⟨¿se puede? ¡cómo no! : may I? please do!⟩
cómoda *nf* : bureau, chest of drawers
comodidad *nf* **1** : comfort **2** : convenience
comodín *nm, pl* **-dines** **1** : joker, wild card **2** : all-purpose word or thing **3** : pretext, excuse
cómodo, -da *adj* **1** CONFORTABLE : comfortable **2** : convenient — **cómodamente** *adv*
comodoro *nm* : commodore
comoquiera *adv* **1** : in any way **2 comoquiera que** : in whatever way, however ⟨comoquiera que sea eso : however that may be⟩
compa *nm fam* : buddy, pal
compactar *vt* : to compact, to compress
compacto, -ta *adj* : compact

compadecer {53} *vt* : to sympathize with, to feel sorry for — **compadecerse** *vr* **1** ~ **de** : to take pity on, to commiserate with **2** ~ **con** : to fit, to accord (with)
compadre *nm* **1** : godfather of one's child **2** : father of one's godchild **3** *fam* : buddy, pal
compaginar *vt* **1** COORDINAR : to combine, to coordinate **2** : to collate
compañerismo *nm* : comradeship, camaraderie
compañero, -ra *n* : companion, mate, partner
compañía *nf* **1** : company ⟨llegó en compañía de su madre : he arrived with his mother⟩ **2** EMPRESA, FIRMA : firm, company
comparable *adj* : comparable
comparación *nf, pl* **-ciones** : comparison
comparado, -da *adj* : comparative ⟨literatura comparada : comparative literature⟩
comparar *vt* : to compare
comparativo¹, -va *adj* : comparative, relative — **comparativamente** *adv*
comparativo² *nm* : comparative degree or form
comparecencia *nf* **1** : appearance (in court) **2 orden de comparecencia** : subpoena, summons
comparecer {53} *vi* : to appear (in court)
compartimiento *or* **compartimento** *nm* : compartment
compartir *vt* : to share
compás *nm, pl* **-pases 1** : beat, rhythm, time **2** : compass
compasión *nf, pl* **-siones** : compassion, pity
compasivo, -va *adj* : compassionate, sympathetic
compatibilidad *nf* : compatibility
compatible *adj* : compatible
compatriota *nmf* PAISANO : compatriot, fellow countryman
compeler *vt* : to compel
compendiar *vt* : to summarize, to condense
compendio *nm* : summary
compenetración *nf, pl* **-ciones** : rapport, mutual understanding
compenetrarse *vr* **1** : to understand each other **2** ~ **con** : to identify oneself with
compensación *nf, pl* **-ciones** : compensation
compensar *vt* : to compensate for, to make up for — *vi* : to be worth one's while
compensatorio, -ria *adj* : compensatory
competencia *nf* **1** : competition, rivalry **2** : competence
competente *adj* : competent, able — **competentemente** *adv*
competición *nf, pl* **-ciones** : competition
competidor¹, -dora *adj* RIVAL : competing, rival
competidor², -dora *n* RIVAL : competitor, rival
competir {54} *vi* : to compete
competitividad *nf* : competitiveness
competitivo, -va *adj* : competitive — **competitivamente** *adv*
compilar *vt* : to compile — **compilación** *nf*
compinche *nmf fam* **1** : buddy, pal **2** : partner in crime, accomplice
complacencia *nf* : pleasure, satisfaction
complacer {57} *vt* : to please — **complacerse** *vr* ~ **en** : to take pleasure in
complaciente *adj* : obliging, eager to please
complejidad *nf* : complexity
complejo¹, -ja *adj* : complex
complejo² *nm* : complex
complementar *vt* : to complement, to supplement — **complementarse** *vr*
complementario, -ria *adj* : complementary
complemento *nm* **1** : complement, supplement **2** : supplementary pay, allowance
completamente *adv* : completely, totally
completar *vt* TERMINAR : to complete, to finish
completo, -ta *adj* **1** : complete **2** : perfect, absolute **3** : full, detailed
complexión *nf, pl* **-xiones** : (physical) constitution
complicación *nf, pl* **-ciones** : complication
complicado, -da *adj* : complicated
complicar {72} *vt* **1** : to complicate **2** : to involve — **complicarse** *vr*
cómplice *nmf* : accomplice
complicidad *nf* : complicity
complot *nm, pl* **complots** CONFABULACIÓN, CONSPIRACIÓN : conspiracy, plot
componenda *nf* : shady deal, scam
componente *adj & nm* : component, constituent
componer {60} *vt* **1** ARREGLAR : to fix, to repair **2** CONSTITUIR : to make up, to compose **3** : to compose, to write **4** : to set (a bone) — **componerse** *vr* **1** : to improve, to get better **2** ~ **de** : to consist of
comportamiento *nm* CONDUCTA : behavior, conduct
comportarse *vr* : to behave, to conduct oneself
composición *nf, pl* **-ciones 1** OBRA : composition, work **2** : makeup, arrangement
compositor, -tora *n* : composer, songwriter
compostura *nf* **1** : composure **2** : mending, repair
compra *nf* **1** : purchase **2 ir de compras** : to go shopping **3 orden de compra** : purchase order

comprador, -dora *n* : buyer, shopper
comprar *vt* : to buy, to purchase
compraventa *nf* : buying and selling
comprender *vt* **1** ENTENDER : to comprehend, to understand **2** ABARCAR : to cover, to include — *vi* : to understand ⟨¡ya comprendo! : now I understand!⟩
comprensible *adj* : understandable — **comprensiblemente** *adv*
comprensión *nf, pl* **-siones 1** : comprehension, understanding, grasp **2** : understanding, sympathy
comprensivo, -va *adj* : understanding
compresa *nf* **1** : compress **2** *or* **compresa higiénica** : sanitary napkin
compresión *nf, pl* **-siones** : compression
compresor *nm* : compressor
comprimido *nm* PÍLDORA, TABLETA : pill, tablet
comprimir *vt* : to compress
comprobable *adj* : verifiable, provable
comprobación *nf, pl* **-ciones** : verification, confirmation
comprobante *nm* **1** : proof ⟨comprobante de identidad : proof of identity⟩ **2** : voucher, receipt ⟨comprobante de ventas : sales slip⟩
comprobar {19} *vt* **1** : to verify, to check **2** : to prove
comprometedor, -dora *adj* : compromising
comprometer *vt* **1** : to compromise **2** : to jeopardize **3** : to commit, to put under obligation — **comprometerse** *vr* **1** : to commit oneself **2 ~ con** : to get engaged to
comprometido, -da *adj* **1** : compromising, awkward **2** : committed, obliged **3** : engaged (to be married)
compromiso *nm* **1** : obligation, commitment **2** : engagement ⟨anillo de compromiso : engagement ring⟩ **3** : agreement **4** : awkward situation, fix
compuerta *nf* : floodgate
compuesto[1] *pp* → **componer**
compuesto[2], **-ta** *adj* **1** : fixed, repaired **2** : compound, composite **3** : decked out, spruced up **4 ~ de** : made up of, consisting of
compuesto[3] *nm* : compound
compulsión *nf, pl* **-siones** : compulsion
compulsivo, -va *adj* **1** : compelling, urgent **2** : compulsive — **compulsivamente** *adv*
compungido, -da *adj* : contrite, remorseful
compungirse {35} *vr* : to feel remorse
compuso, etc. → **componer**
computable *adj* : countable ⟨años computables : years accrued⟩ ⟨ingresos computables : qualifying income⟩
computación *nf, pl* **-ciones** : computing, computers *pl*
computador *nm* → **computadora**
computadora *nf* **1** : computer **2 computadora portátil** : laptop computer
computar *vt* : to compute, to calculate
computarizar {21} *vt* : to computerize
cómputo *nm* : computation, calculation
comulgar {52} *vi* : to receive Communion
común *adj, pl* **comunes 1** : common **2 común y corriente** : ordinary, regular **3 por lo común** : generally, as a rule
comuna *nf* : commune
comunal *adj* : communal
comunicación *nf, pl* **-ciones 1** : communication **2** : access, link **3** : message, report
comunicado *nm* **1** : communiqué **2 comunicado de prensa** : press release
comunicar {72} *vt* **1** : to communicate, to convey **2** : to notify — **comunicarse** *vr* **~ con 1** : to contact, to get in touch with **2** : to be connected to
comunicativo, -va *adj* : communicative, talkative
comunidad *nf* : community
comunión *nf, pl* **-niones 1** : communion, sharing **2** : Communion
comunismo *nm* : communism, Communism
comunista *adj & nmf* : communist
comúnmente *adv* : commonly
con *prep* **1** : with ⟨vengo con mi padre : I'm going with my father⟩ ⟨¿con quién hablas? : who are you speaking to?⟩ **2** : in spite of ⟨con todo : in spite of it all⟩ **3** : to, towards ⟨ella es amable con los niños : she is kind to the children⟩ **4** : by ⟨con llegar temprano : by arriving early⟩ **5 con (tal) que** : as long as, so long as
conato *nm* : attempt, effort ⟨conato de robo : attempted robbery⟩
cóncavo, -va *adj* : concave
concebible *adj* : conceivable
concebir {54} *vt* **1** : to conceive **2** : to conceive of, to imagine — *vi* : to conceive, to become pregnant
conceder *vt* **1** : to grant, to bestow **2** : to concede, to admit
concejal, -jala *n* : councilman *m,* councilwoman *f,* alderman *m,* alderwoman *f*
concejo *nm* : council ⟨concejo municipal : town council⟩
concentración *nf, pl* **-ciones** : concentration
concentrado *nm* : concentrate
concentrar *vt* : to concentrate — **concentrarse** *vr*
concéntrico, -ca *adj* : concentric
concepción *nf, pl* **-ciones** : conception
concepto *nm* NOCIÓN : concept, idea, opinion
conceptuar {3} *vt* : to regard, to judge
concernir {17} *vi* : to be of concern
concertar {55} *vt* **1** : to arrange, to set up **2** : to agree on, to settle **3** : to harmonize — *vi* : to be in harmony
concesión *nf, pl* **-siones 1** : concession **2** : awarding, granting
concha *nf* : conch, seashell

conciencia *nf* **1** : conscience **2** : consciousness, awareness
concientizar {21} *vt* : to make aware — **concientizarse** *vr* **~ de** : to realize, to become aware of
concienzudo, -da *adj* : conscientious
concierto *nm* **1** : concert **2** : agreement **3** : concerto
conciliador[1], **-dora** *adj* : conciliatory
conciliador[2], **-dora** *n* : arbitrator, peacemaker
conciliar *vt* : to conciliate, to reconcile — **conciliación** *nf*
conciliatorio, -ria *adj* → **conciliador**[1]
concilio *nm* : (church) council
conciso, -sa *adj* : concise — **concisión** *nf*
conciudadano, -na *n* : fellow citizen
cónclave *nm* : conclave, private meeting
concluir {41} *vt* **1** TERMINAR : to conclude, to finish **2** DEDUCIR : to deduce, to infer — *vi* : to end, to conclude
conclusión *nf, pl* **-siones** : conclusion
concluyente *adj* : conclusive
concomitante *adj* : concomitant
concordancia *nf* : agreement, accordance
concordar {19} *vi* : to agree, to coincide — *vt* : to reconcile
concordia *nf* : concord, harmony
concretar *vt* **1** : to pinpoint, to specify **2** : to fulfill, to realize — **concretarse** *vr* : to become real, to take shape
concretizar → **concretar**
concreto[1], **-ta** *adj* **1** : concrete, actual **2** : definite, specific ⟨en concreto : specifically⟩ — **concretamente** *adv*
concreto[2] *nm* HORMIGÓN : concrete
concubina *nf* : concubine
concurrencia *nf* **1** : audience, turnout **2** : concurrence
concurrente *adj* : concurrent — **concurrentemente** *adv*
concurrido, -da *adj* : busy, crowded
concurrir *vi* **1** : to converge, to come together **2** : to concur, to agree **3** : to take part, to participate **4** : to attend, to be present ⟨concurrir a una reunión : to attend a meeting⟩ **5 ~ a** : to contribute to
concursante *nmf* : contestant, competitor
concursar *vt* : to compete in — *vi* : to compete, to participate
concurso *nm* **1** : contest, competition **2** : concurrence, coincidence **3** : crowd, gathering **4** : cooperation, assistance
condado *nm* **1** : county **2** : earldom
conde, -desa *n* : count *m,* earl *m,* countess *f*
condecoración *nf, pl* **-ciones** : decoration, medal
condecorar *vt* : to decorate, to award (a medal)
condena *nf* **1** REPROBACIÓN : disapproval, condemnation **2** SENTENCIA : sentence, conviction
condenable *adj* : reprehensible
condenación *nf, pl* **-ciones** **1** : condemnation **2** : damnation
condenado[1], **-da** *adj* **1** : fated, doomed **2** : convicted, sentenced **3** *fam* : darn, damned
condenado[2], **-da** *n* : convict
condenar *vt* **1** : to condemn **2** : to sentence **3** : to board up, to wall up — **condenarse** *vr* : to be damned
condensación *nf, pl* **-ciones** : condensation
condensar *vt* : to condense
condesa *nf* → **conde**
condescendencia *nf* : condescension
condescender {56} *vi* **1** : to condescend **2** : to agree, to acquiesce
condición *nf, pl* **-ciones** **1** : condition, state **2** : capacity, position **3 condiciones** *nfpl* : conditions, circumstances ⟨condiciones de vida : living conditions⟩
condicional *adj* : conditional — **condicionalmente** *adv*
condicionamiento *nm* : conditioning
condicionar *vt* **1** : to condition, to determine **2 ~ a** : to be contingent on, to depend on
condimentar *vt* SAZONAR : to season, to spice
condimento *nm* : condiment, seasoning, spice
condiscípulo, -la *n* : classmate
condolencia *nf* : condolence, sympathy
condolerse {47} *vr* : to sympathize
condominio *nm* : condominium, condo
condón *nm, pl* **condones** : condom
cóndor *nm* : condor
conducción *nf, pl* **-ciones** **1** : conduction (of electricity, etc.) **2** DIRECCIÓN : management, direction
conducir {61} *vt* **1** DIRIGIR, GUIAR : to direct, to lead **2** MANEJAR : to drive (a vehicle) — *vi* **1** : to drive a vehicle **2 ~ a** : to lead to — **conducirse** *vr* PORTARSE : to behave, to conduct oneself
conducta *nf* COMPORTAMIENTO : conduct, behavior
conducto *nm* : conduit, channel, duct
conductor[1], **-tora** *adj* : conducting, leading
conductor[2], **-tora** *n* : driver
conductor[3] *nm* : conductor (of electricity, etc.)
conectar *vt* : to connect — *vi* **~ con** : to link up with, to communicate with
conector *nm* : connector
conejera *nf* : rabbit hutch
conejillo *nm* **conejillo de Indias** : guinea pig
conejo, -ja *n* : rabbit
conexión *nf, pl* **-xiones** : connection
confabulación *nf, pl* **-ciones** COMPLOT, CONSPIRACIÓN : plot, conspiracy
confabularse *vr* : to plot, to conspire
confección *nf, pl* **-ciones** **1** : preparation **2** : tailoring, dressmaking
confeccionar *vt* : to make, to produce, to prepare

confederación *nf, pl* **-ciones** : confederation
confederarse *vr* : to confederate, to form a confederation
conferencia *nf* **1** REUNIÓN : conference, meeting **2** : lecture
conferenciante *nmf* : lecturer
conferencista → **conferenciante**
conferir {76} *vt* : to confer, to bestow
confesar {55} *v* : to confess — **confesarse** *vr* : to go to confession
confesión *nf, pl* **-siones 1** : confession **2** : creed, denomination
confesionario *nm* : confessional
confesor *nm* : confessor
confeti *nm* : confetti
confiable *adj* : trustworthy, reliable
confiado, -da *adj* **1** : confident, self-confident **2** : trusting — **confiadamente** *adv*
confianza *nf* **1** : trust ⟨de poca confiaza : untrustworthy⟩ **2** : confidence, self-confidence
confianzudo, -da *adj* : forward, presumptuous
confiar {85} *vi* : to have trust, to be trusting — *vt* **1** : to confide **2** : to entrust — **confiarse** *vr* **1** : to be overconfident **2** ∼ **a** : to confide in
confidencia *nf* : confidence, secret
confidencial *adj* : confidential — **confidencialmente** *adv*
confidencialidad *nf* : confidentiality
confidente *nmf* **1** : confidant, confidante *f* **2** : informer
configuración *nf, pl* **-ciones** : configuration, shape
configurar *vt* : to shape, to form
confín *nm, pl* **confines** : boundary, limit
confinamiento *nm* : confinement
confinar *vt* **1** : to confine, to limit **2** : to exile — *vi* ∼ **con** : to border on
confirmación *nf, pl* **-ciones** : confirmation
confirmar *vt* : to confirm, to substantiate
confiscación *nf, pl* **-ciones** : confiscation
confiscar {72} *vt* DECOMISAR : to confiscate, to seize
confitado, -da *adj* : candied
confite *nm* : comfit, candy
confitería *nf* **1** DULCERÍA : candy store, confectionery **2** : tearoom, café
confitero, -ra *n* : confectioner
confitura *nf* : preserves, jam
conflagración *nf, pl* **-ciones 1** : conflagration, fire **2** : war
conflictivo, -va *adj* **1** : troubled **2** : controversial
conflicto *nm* : conflict
confluencia *nf* : junction, confluence
confluir {41} *vi* **1** : to converge, to join **2** : to gather, to assemble
conformar *vt* **1** : to form, to create **2** : to constitute, to make up — **conformarse** *vr* **1** RESIGNARSE : to resign oneself **2** : to comply, to conform **3** ∼ **con** : to content oneself with, to be satisfied with
conforme[1] *adj* **1** : content, satisfied **2** ∼ **a** : in accordance with
conforme[2] *conj* : as ⟨entreguen sus tareas conforme vayan saliendo : hand in your homework as you leave⟩
conformidad *nf* **1** : agreement, consent **2** : resignation
confort *nm* : comfort
confortable *adj* CÓMODO : comfortable
confortar *vt* CONSOLAR : to comfort, to console
confraternidad *nf* : brotherhood, fraternity
confraternización *nf, pl* **-ciones** : fraternization
confraternizar *vi* : to fraternize
confrontación *nf, pl* **-ciones** : confrontation
confrontar *vt* **1** ENCARAR : to confront **2** : to compare **3** : to bring face-to-face — *vi* : to border — **confrontarse** *vr* ∼ **con** : to face up to
confundir *vt* : to confuse, to mix up — **confundirse** *vr* : to make a mistake, to be confused ⟨confundirse de número : to get the wrong number⟩
confusión *nf, pl* **-siones** : confusion
confuso, -sa *adj* **1** : confused, mixed-up **2** : obscure, indistinct
congelación *nf, pl* **-ciones 1** : freezing **2** : frostbite
congelado, -da *adj* HELADO : frozen
congelador *nm* HELADORA : freezer
congelamiento *nm* → **congelación**
congelar *vt* : to freeze — **congelarse** *vr*
congeniar *vi* : to get along (with someone)
congénito, -ta *adj* : congenital
congestión *nf, pl* **-tiones** : congestion
congestionado, -da *adj* : congested
congestionamiento *nm* → **congestión**
congestionarse *vr* **1** : to become flushed **2** : to become congested
conglomerado[1]**, -da** *adj* : conglomerate, mixed
conglomerado[2] *nm* : conglomerate, conglomeration
congoja *nf* ANGUSTIA : anguish, grief
congoleño, -ña *adj & n* : Congolese
congraciarse *vr* : to ingratiate oneself
congratular *vt* FELICITAR : to congratulate
congregación *nf, pl* **-ciones** : congregation, gathering
congregar {52} *vt* : to bring together — **congregarse** *vr* : to congregate, to assemble
congresista *nmf* : congressman *m,* congresswoman *f*
congreso *nm* : congress, conference
congruencia *nf* **1** : congruence **2** COHERENCIA : coherence — **congruente** *adj*
cónico, -ca *adj* : conical, conic
conífera *nf* : conifer

conífero, -ra *adj* : coniferous
conjetura *nf* : conjecture, guess
conjeturar *vt* : to guess, to conjecture
conjugación *nf, pl* **-ciones** : conjugation
conjugar {52} *vt* **1** : to conjugate **2** : to combine
conjunción *nf, pl* **-ciones** : conjunction
conjuntivo, -va *adj* : connective ⟨tejido conjuntivo : connective tissue⟩
conjunto[1], **-ta** *adj* : joint
conjunto[2] *nm* **1** : collection, group **2** : ensemble, outfit ⟨conjunto musical : musical ensemble⟩ **3** : whole, entirety ⟨en conjunto : as a whole, altogether⟩
conjurar *vt* **1** : to exorcise **2** : to avert, to ward off — *vi* CONSPIRAR : to conspire, to plot
conjuro *nm* **1** : exorcism **2** : spell
conllevar *vt* **1** : to bear, to suffer **2** IMPLICAR : to entail, to involve
conmemorar *vt* : to commemorate — **conmemoración** *nf*
conmemorativo, -va *adj* : commemorative, memorial
conmigo *pron* : with me ⟨habló conmigo : he talked with me⟩
conminar *vt* AMENAZAR : to threaten, to warn
conmiseración *nf, pl* **-ciones** : pity, commiseration
conmoción *nf, pl* **-ciones 1** : shock, upheaval **2** *or* **conmoción cerebral** : concussion
conmocionar *vt* : to shake, to shock
conmovedor, -dora *adj* EMOCIONANTE : moving, touching
conmover {47} *vt* **1** EMOCIONAR : to move, to touch **2** : to shake up — **conmoverse** *vr*
conmutador *nm* **1** : switch **2** : switchboard
conmutar *vt* **1** : to commute (a sentence) **2** : to switch, to exchange
connivencia *nf* : connivance
connotación *nf, pl* **-ciones** : connotation
connotar *vt* : to connote, to imply
cono *nm* : cone
conocedor[1], **-dora** *adj* : knowledgeable
conocedor[2], **-dora** *n* : connoisseur, expert
conocer {18} *vt* **1** : to know, to be acquainted with ⟨ya lo conocí : I've already met him⟩ **2** : to meet **3** RECONOCER : to recognize — **conocerse** *vr* **1** : to know each other **2** : to meet **3** : to know oneself
conocido[1], **-da** *adj* **1** : familiar **2** : well-known, famous
conocido[2], **-da** *n* : acquaintance
conocimiento *nm* **1** : knowledge **2** SENTIDO : consciousness
conque *conj* : so, so then, and so ⟨¡ah, conque esas tenemos! : oh, so that's what's going on!⟩
conquista *nf* : conquest
conquistador[1], **-dora** *adj* : conquering
conquistador[2], **-dora** *n* : conqueror
conquistar *vt* : to conquer
consabido, -da *adj* : usual, typical
consagración *nf, pl* **-ciones** : consecration
consagrar *vt* **1** : to consecrate **2** DEDICAR : to dedicate, to devote
consciencia → **conciencia**
consciente *adj* : conscious, aware — **conscientemente** *adv*
conscripción *nf, pl* **-ciones** : conscription, draft
conscripto, -ta *n* : conscript, inductee
consecución *nf, pl* **-ciones** : attainment
consecuencia *nf* **1** : consequence, result ⟨a consecuencia de : as a result of⟩ **2 en ~** : accordingly
consecuente *adj* : consistent — **consecuentemente** *adv*
consecutivo, -va *adj* : consecutive, successive — **consecutivamente** *adv*
conseguir {75} *vt* **1** : to get, to obtain **2** : to achieve, to attain **3** : to manage to ⟨consiguió acabar el trabajo : she managed to finish the job⟩
consejero, -ra *n* : adviser, counselor
consejo *nm* **1** : advice, counsel **2** : council ⟨consejo de guerra : court-martial⟩
consenso *nm* : consensus
consentido, -da *adj* : spoiled, pampered
consentimiento *nm* : consent, permission
consentir {76} *vt* **1** PERMITIR : to consent to, to allow **2** MIMAR : to pamper, to spoil — *vi* **~ en** : to agree to, to approve of
conserje *nmf* : custodian, janitor, caretaker
conserva *nf* **1** : preserve(s), jam **2 conservas** *nfpl* : canned goods
conservación *nf, pl* **-ciones** : conservation, preservation
conservacionista *nmf* : conservationist
conservador[1], **-dora** *adj & n* : conservative
conservador[2] *nm* : preservative
conservadurismo *nf* : conservatism
conservante *nm* : preservative
conservar *vt* **1** : to preserve **2** GUARDAR : to keep, to conserve
conservatorio *nm* : conservatory
considerable *adj* : considerable — **considerablemente** *adv*
consideración *nf, pl* **-ciones 1** : consideration **2** : respect **3 de ~** : considerable, important
considerado, -da *adj* **1** : considerate, thoughtful **2** : respected
considerar *vt* **1** : to consider, to think over **2** : to judge, to deem **3** : to treat with respect
consigna *nf* **1** ESLOGAN : slogan **2** : assignment, orders *pl* **3** : checkroom
consignación *nf, pl* **-ciones 1** : consignment **2** ASIGNACIÓN : allocation
consignar *vt* **1** : to consign **2** : to record, to write down **3** : to assign, to allocate

consigo *pron* : with her, with him, with you, with oneself ⟨se llevó las llaves consigo : she took the keys with her⟩
consiguiente *adj* **1** : resulting, consequent **2 por ~** : consequently, as a result
consistencia *nf* : consistency
consistente *adj* **1** : firm, strong, sound **2** : consistent — **consistentemente** *adv*
consistir *vi* **1 ~ en** : to consist of **2 ~ en** : to lie in, to consist in
consola *nf* : console
consolación *nf, pl* **-ciones** : consolation ⟨premio de consolación : consolation prize⟩
consolar {19} *vt* CONFORTAR : to console, to comfort
consolidar *vt* : to consolidate — **consolidación** *nf*
consomé *nm* CALDO : consommé, clear soup
consonancia *nf* **1** : consonance, harmony **2 en consonancia con** : in accordance with
consonante[1] *adj* : consonant, harmonious
consonante[2] *nf* : consonant
consorcio *nm* : consortium
consorte *nmf* : consort, spouse
conspicuo, -cua *adj* : eminent, famous
conspiración *nf, pl* **-ciones** COMPLOT, CONFABULACIÓN : conspiracy, plot
conspirador, -dora *n* : conspirator
conspirar *vi* CONJURAR : to conspire, to plot
constancia *nf* **1** PRUEBA : proof, certainty **2** : record, evidence ⟨que quede constancia : for the record⟩ **3** : perseverance, constancy
constante[1] *adj* : constant — **constantemente** *adv*
constante[2] *nf* : constant
constar *vi* **1** : to be evident, to be on record ⟨que conste : believe me, have no doubt⟩ **2 ~ de** : to consist of
constatación *nf, pl* **-ciones** : confirmation, proof
constatar *vt* **1** : to verify **2** : to state
constelación *nf, pl* **-ciones** : constellation
consternación *nf, pl* **-ciones** : consternation, dismay
consternar *vt* : to dismay, to appall
constipación *nf, pl* **-ciones** : constipation
constipado[1], **-da** *adj* **estar constipado** : to have a cold
constipado[2] *nm* RESFRIADO : cold
constiparse *vr* : to catch a cold
constitución *nf, pl* **-ciones** : constitution — **constitucional** *adj* — **constitucionalmente** *adv*
constitucionalidad *nf* : constitutionality
constituir {41} *vt* **1** FORMAR : to constitute, to make up, to form **2** FUNDAR : to establish, to set up — **constituirse** *vr* **~ en** : to set oneself up as, to become
constitutivo, -va *adj* : constituent, component
constituyente *adj & nmf* : constituent
constreñir {67} *vt* **1** FORZAR, OBLIGAR : to constrain, to oblige **2** LIMITAR : to restrict, to limit
construcción *nf, pl* **-ciones** : construction, building
constructivo, -va *adj* : constructive — **constructivamente** *adv*
constructor, -tora *n* : builder
constructora *nf* : construction company
construir {41} *vt* : to build, to construct
consuelo *nm* : consolation, comfort
consuetudinario, -ria *adj* **1** : customary, habitual **2 derecho consuetudinario** : common law
cónsul *nmf* : consul — **consular** *adj*
consulado *nm* : consulate
consulta *nf* **1** : consultation **2** : inquiry
consultar *vt* : to consult
consultor[1], **-tora** *adj* : consulting ⟨firma consultora : consulting firm⟩
consultor[2], **-tora** *n* : consultant
consultorio *nm* : office (of a doctor or dentist)
consumación *nf, pl* **-ciones** : consummation
consumado, -da *adj* : consummate, perfect
consumar *vt* **1** : to consummate, to complete **2** : to commit, to carry out
consumible *adj* : consumable
consumición *nf, pl* **-ciones** **1** : consumption **2** : drink (in a restaurant)
consumido, -da *adj* : thin, emaciated
consumidor, -dora *n* : consumer
consumir *vt* : to consume — **consumirse** *vr* : to waste away
consumo *nm* : consumption
contabilidad *nf* **1** : accounting, bookkeeping **2** : accountancy
contabilizar {21} *vt* : to enter, to record (in accounting)
contable[1] *adj* : countable
contable[2] *nmf Spain* : accountant, bookkeeper
contactar *vt* : to contact — *vi* **~ con** : to get in touch with, to contact
contacto *nm* : contact
contado[1], **-da** *adj* **1** : counted ⟨tenía los días contados : his days were numbered⟩ **2** : rare, scarce ⟨en contadas ocasiones : on rare occasions⟩
contado[2] *nm* **al contado** : cash ⟨pagar al contado : to pay in cash⟩
contador[1], **-dora** *n* : accountant
contador[2] *nm* : meter ⟨contador de agua : water meter⟩
contaduría *nf* **1** : accounting office **2** CONTABILIDAD : accountancy
contagiar *vt* **1** : to infect **2** : to transmit (a disease) — **contagiarse** *vr* **1** : to be contagious **2** : to become infected
contagio *nm* : contagion, infection

contagioso, -sa *adj* : contagious, catching
contaminación *nf, pl* **-ciones** : contamination, pollution
contaminante *nm* : pollutant, contaminant
contaminar *vt* : to contaminate, to pollute
contar {19} *vt* **1** : to count **2** : to tell **3** : to include — *vi* **1** : to count (up) **2** : to matter, to be of concern ⟨eso no cuenta : that doesn't matter⟩ **3 ~ con** : to rely on, to count on — **contarse** *vr* **~ entre** : to be numbered among
contemplación *nf, pl* **-ciones** : contemplation — **contemplativo, -va** *adj*
contemplar *vt* **1** : to contemplate, to ponder **2** : to gaze at, to look at
contemporáneo, -nea *adj & n* : contemporary
contención *nf, pl* **-ciones** : containment, holding
contencioso, -sa *adj* : contentious
contender {56} *vi* **1** : to contend, to compete **2** : to fight
contendiente *nmf* : contender
contenedor *nm* **1** : container, receptacle **2** : Dumpster™
contener {80} *vt* **1** : to contain, to hold **2** ATAJAR : to restrain, to hold back — **contenerse** *vr* : to restrain oneself
contenido[1], **-da** *adj* : restrained, reserved
contenido[2] *nm* : contents *pl,* content
contentar *vt* : to please, to make happy — **contentarse** *vr* : to be satisfied, to be pleased
contento[1], **-ta** *adj* : contented, glad, happy
contento[2] *nm* : joy, happiness
contestación *nf, pl* **-ciones** **1** : answer, reply **2** : protest
contestar *vt* RESPONDER : to answer — *vi* **1** RESPONDER : to answer, to reply **2** REPLICAR : to answer back
contexto *nm* : context
contienda *nf* **1** : dispute, conflict **2** : contest, competition
contigo *pron* : with you ⟨voy contigo : I'm going with you⟩
contiguo, -gua *adj* COLINDANTE : contiguous, adjacent
continencia *nf* : continence
continente *nm* : continent — **continental** *adj*
contingencia *nf* : contingency, eventuality
contingente *adj & nm* : contingent
continuación *nf, pl* **-ciones** **1** : continuation **2 a ~** : next ⟨lo demás sigue a continuación : the rest follows⟩ **3 a continuación de** : after, following
continuar {3} *v* : to continue
continuidad *nf* : continuity
continuo, -nua *adj* : continuous, steady, constant — **continuamente** *adv*
contonearse *vr* : to sway one's hips
contoneo *nm* : swaying, wiggling (of the hips)
contorno *nm* **1** : outline **2 contornos** *nmpl* : outskirts
contorsión *nf, pl* **-siones** : contortion
contra[1] *nf* **1** *fam* : difficulty, snag **2 llevar la contra a** : to oppose, to contradict
contra[2] *nm* : con ⟨los pros y los contras : the pros and cons⟩
contra[3] *prep* : against
contraalmirante *nm* : rear admiral
contraatacar {72} *v* : to counterattack — **contraataque** *nm*
contrabajo *nm* : double bass
contrabalancear *vt* : to counterbalance — **contrabalanza** *nf*
contrabandear *v* : to smuggle
contrabandista *nmf* : smuggler, black marketeer
contrabando *nm* **1** : smuggling **2** : contraband
contracción *nf, pl* **-ciones** : contraction
contracepción *nf, pl* **-ciones** : contraception
contraceptivo *nm* ANTICONCEPTIVO : contraceptive
contrachapado *nm* : plywood
contracorriente *nf* **1** : crosscurrent **2 ir a contracorriente** : to go against the tide
contractual *adj* : contractual
contradecir {11} *vt* DESMENTIR : to contradict — **contradecirse** *vr* DESDECIRSE : to contradict oneself
contradicción *nf, pl* **-ciones** : contradiction
contradictorio, -ria *adj* : contradictory
contraer {81} *vt* **1** : to contract (a disease) **2** : to establish by contract ⟨contraer matrimonio : to get married⟩ **3** : to tighten, to contract — **contraerse** *vr* : to contract, to tighten up
contrafuerte *nm* : buttress
contragolpe *nm* **1** : counterblow **2** : backlash
contrahecho, -cha *adj* : deformed, hunchbacked
contraindicado, -da *adj* : contraindicated — **contraindicación** *nf*
contralor, -lora *n* : comptroller
contralto *nmf* : contralto
contramaestre *nm* **1** : boatswain **2** : foreman
contramandar *vt* : to countermand
contramano *nm* **a ~** : the wrong way (on a street)
contramedida *nf* : countermeasure
contraorden *nf* : countermand
contraparte *nf* **1** : counterpart **2 en ~** : on the other hand
contrapartida *nf* : compensation
contrapelo *nm* **a ~** : in the wrong direction, against the grain
contrapeso *nm* : counterbalance
contraponer {60} *vt* **1** : to counter, to oppose **2** : to contrast, to compare
contraposición *nf, pl* **-ciones** : comparison
contraproducente *adj* : counterproductive

contrapunto *nm* : counterpoint
contrariar {85} *vt* **1** : to contradict, to oppose **2** : to vex, to annoy
contrariedad *nf* **1** : setback, obstacle **2** : vexation, annoyance
contrario, -ria *adj* **1** : contrary, opposite ⟨al contrario : on the contrary⟩ **2** : conflicting, opposed
contrarrestar *vt* : to counteract
contrarrevolución *nf, pl* **-ciones** : counterrevolution — **contrarrevolucionario, -ria** *adj & n*
contrasentido *nm* : contradiction
contraseña *nf* : password
contrastante *adj* : contrasting
contrastar *vt* **1** : to resist **2** : to check, to confirm — *vi* : to contrast
contraste *nm* : contrast
contratar *vt* **1** : to contract for **2** : to hire, to engage
contratiempo *nm* **1** PERCANCE : mishap, accident **2** DIFICULTAD : setback, difficulty
contratista *nmf* : contractor
contrato *nm* : contract
contravenir {87} *vt* : to contravene, to infringe
contraventana *nf* : shutter
contribución *nf, pl* **-ciones** : contribution
contribuidor, -dora *n* : contributor
contribuir {41} *vt* **1** APORTAR : to contribute **2** : to pay (in taxes) — *vi* **1** : contribute, to help out **2** : to pay taxes
contribuyente[1] *adj* : contributing
contribuyente[2] *nmf* : taxpayer
contrición *nf, pl* **-ciones** : contrition
contrincante *nmf* : rival, opponent
contrito, -ta *adj* : contrite, repentant
control *nm* **1** : control **2** : inspection, check **3** : checkpoint, roadblock
controlador, -dora *n* : controller ⟨controlador aéreo : air traffic controller⟩
controlar *vt* **1** : to control **2** : to monitor, to check
controversia *nf* : controversy
controversial → **controvertido**
controvertido, -da *adj* : controversial
controvertir {76} *vt* : to dispute, to argue about — *vi* : to argue, to debate
contubernio *nm* : conspiracy
contumacia *nf* : obstinacy, stubbornness
contumaz *adj, pl* **-maces** : obstinate, stubbornly disobedient
contundencia *nf* **1** : forcefulness, weight **2** : severity
contundente *adj* **1** : blunt ⟨un objeto contundente : a blunt instrument⟩ **2** : forceful, convincing — **contundentemente** *adv*
contusión *nf, pl* **-siones** : bruise, contusion
contuvo, etc. → **contener**
convalecencia *nf* : convalescence
convalecer {53} *vi* : to convalesce, to recover
convaleciente *adj & nmf* : convalescent
convección *nf, pl* **-ciones** : convection
convencer {86} *vt* : to convince, to persuade — **convencerse** *vr*
convencimiento *nm* : belief, conviction
convención *nf, pl* **-ciones** **1** : convention, conference **2** : pact, agreement **3** : convention, custom
convencional *adj* : conventional — **convencionalmente** *adv*
convencionalismo *nm* : conventionality
conveniencia *nf* **1** : convenience **2** : fitness, suitability, advisability
conveniente *adj* **1** : convenient **2** : suitable, advisable
convenio *nm* PACTO : agreement, pact
convenir {87} *vi* **1** : to be suitable, to be advisable **2** : to agree
convento *nm* **1** : convent **2** : monastery
convergencia *nf* : convergence
convergente *adj* : convergent, converging
converger {15} *vi* **1** : to converge **2** ~ **en** : to concur on
conversación *nf, pl* **-ciones** : conversation
conversador, -dora *n* : conversationalist, talker
conversar *vi* : to converse, to talk
conversión *nf, pl* **-siones** : conversion
converso, -sa *n* : convert
convertible *adj & nm* : convertible
convertidor *nm* : converter
convertir {76} *vt* **1** : to convert **2** : to transform, to change **3** : to exchange (money) — **convertirse** *vr* ~ **en** : to turn into
convexo, -xa *adj* : convex
convicción *nf, pl* **-ciones** : conviction
convicto[1], **-ta** *adj* : convicted
convicto[2], **-ta** *n* : convict, prisoner
convidado, -da *n* : guest
convidar *vt* **1** INVITAR : to invite **2** : to offer
convincente *adj* : convincing — **convincentemente** *adv*
convivencia *nf* **1** : coexistence **2** : cohabitation
convivir *vi* **1** : to coexist **2** : to live together
convocación *nf, pl* **-ciones** : convocation
convocar {72} *vt* : to convoke, to call together
convocatoria *nf* : summons, call
convoy *nm* : convoy
convulsión *nf, pl* **-siones** **1** : convulsion **2** : agitation, upheaval
convulsionar *vt* : to shake, to convulse — **convulsionarse** *vr*
convulsivo, -va *adj* : convulsive
conyugal *adj* : conjugal
cónyuge *nmf* : spouse, partner
coñac *nm* : cognac, brandy
cooperación *nf, pl* **-ciones** : cooperation
cooperador, -dora *adj* : cooperative

cooperar *vi* : to cooperate

cooperativa *nf* : cooperative, co-op

cooperativo, -va *adj* : cooperative

cooptar *vt* : to co-opt

coordenada *nf* : coordinate

coordinación *nf, pl* **-ciones** : coordination

coordinador, -dora *n* : coordinator

coordinar *vt* COMPAGINAR : to coordinate, to combine

copa *nf* **1** : wineglass, goblet **2** : drink ⟨irse de copas : to go out drinking⟩ **3** : cup, trophy

copar *vt* **1** : to take ⟨ya está copado el puesto : the job is already taken⟩ **2** : to fill, to crowd

copartícipe *nmf* : joint partner

copete *nm* **1** : tuft (of hair) **2 estar hasta el copete** : to be completely fed up

copia *nf* **1** : copy **2** : imitation, replica

copiadora *nf* : photocopier

copiar *vt* : to copy

copiloto *nmf* : copilot

copioso, -sa *adj* : copious, abundant

copla *nf* **1** : popular song or ballad **2** : couplet, stanza

copo *nm* **1** : snowflake **2 copos de avena** : rolled oats **3 copos de maíz** : cornflakes

copra *nf* : copra

cópula *nf* : copulation

copular *vi* : to copulate

coque *nm* : coke (fuel)

coqueta *nf* : dressing table

coquetear *vi* : to flirt

coqueteo *nm* : flirting, coquetry

coqueto[1], -ta *adj* : flirtatious, coquettish

coqueto[2], -ta *n* : flirt

coraje *nm* **1** VALOR : valor, courage **2** IRA : anger ⟨darle coraje a alguien : to make someone angry⟩

corajudo, -da *adj* : brave

coral[1] *nm* **1** : coral **2** : chorale

coral[2] *nf* : choir

Corán *nm* **el Corán** : the Koran

coraza *nf* **1** : armor, armor plating **2** : shell (of an animal)

corazón *nm, pl* **-zones 1** : heart ⟨de todo corazón : wholeheartedly⟩ ⟨de buen corazón : kindhearted⟩ **2** : core **3** : darling, sweetheart

corazonada *nf* : hunch, impulse

corbata *nf* : tie, necktie

corcel *nm* : steed, charger

corchete *nm* **1** : hook and eye, clasp **2** : square bracket

corcho *nm* : cork

corcholata *nf Mex* : cap, bottle top

corcovear *vi* : to buck

cordel *nm* : cord, string

cordero *nm* : lamb

cordial[1] *adj* : cordial, affable — **cordialmente** *adv*

cordial[2] *nm* : cordial (liqueur)

cordialidad *nf* : cordiality, warmth

cordillera *nf* : mountain range

córdoba *nf* : Nicaraguan unit of currency

cordón *nm, pl* **cordones 1** : cord ⟨cordón umbilical : umbilical cord⟩ **2** : cordon

cordura *nf* **1** : sanity **2** : prudence, good judgment

coreano[1], -na *adj & n* : Korean

coreano[2] *nm* : Korean (language)

corear *vt* : to chant, to chorus

coreografía *nf* : choreography

coreografiar {85} *vt* : to choreograph

coreográfico, -ca *adj* : choreographic

coreógrafo, -fa *n* : choreographer

corista *nmf* **1** : chorister **2** : chorus girl *f*

cormorán *nm, pl* **-ranes** : cormorant

cornada *nf* : goring, butt (with thehorns)

córnea *nf* : cornea

cornear *vt* : to gore

cornejo *nm* : dogwood (tree)

corneta *nf* : bugle, horn, cornet

cornisa *nf* : cornice

cornudo, -da *adj* : horned

coro *nm* **1** : choir **2** : chorus

corola *nf* : corolla

corolario *nm* : corollary

corona *nf* **1** : crown **2** : wreath, garland **3** : corona (in astronomy)

coronación *nf, pl* **-ciones** : coronation

coronar *vt* **1** : to crown **2** : to reach the top of, to culminate

coronario, -ria *adj* : coronary

coronel, -nela *n* : colonel

coronilla *nf* **1** : crown (of the head) **2 estar hasta la coronilla** : to be completely fed up

corpiño *nm* **1** : bodice **2** *Arg* : brassiere, bra

corporación *nf, pl* **-ciones** : corporation

corporal *adj* : corporal, bodily

corporativo, -va *adj* : corporate

corpóreo, -rea *adj* : corporeal, physical

corpulencia *nf* : corpulence, stoutness, sturdiness

corpulento, -ta *adj* ROBUSTO : robust, stout, sturdy

corpúsculo *nm* : corpuscle

corral *nm* **1** : farmyard **2** : corral, pen, stockyard **3** *or* **corralito** : playpen

correa *nf* : strap, belt

correcaminos *nms & pl* : roadrunner

corrección *nf, pl* **-ciones 1** : correction **2** : correctness, propriety **3** : rebuke, reprimand **4 corrección de pruebas** : proofreading

correccional *nm* REFORMATORIO : reformatory

correctivo, -va *adj* : corrective ⟨lentes correctivos : corrective lenses⟩

correcto, -ta *adj* **1** : correct, right **2** : courteous, polite — **correctamente** *adv*

corrector, -tora *n* : proofreader

corredizo, -za *adj* : sliding ⟨puerta corrediza : sliding door⟩

corredor[1], -dora *n* **1** : runner, racer **2** : agent, broker ⟨corredor de bolsa : stockbroker⟩

corredor[2] *nm* PASILLO : corridor, hallway

correduría *nf* → **corretaje**
corregir {28} *vt* **1** ENMENDAR : to correct, to emend **2** : to reprimand **3 corregir pruebas** : to proofread — **corregirse** *vr* : to reform, to mend one's ways
correlación *nf, pl* **-ciones** : correlation
correo *nm* **1** : mail ⟨correo aéreo : airmail⟩ **2** : post office
correoso, -sa *adj* : leathery, rough
correr *vi* **1** : to run, to race **2** : to rush **3** : to flow — *vt* **1** : to travel over, to cover **2** : to move, to slide, to roll, to draw (curtains) **3 correr un riesgo** : to run a risk — **correrse** *vr* **1** : to move along **2** : to run, to spill over
correspondencia *nf* **1** : correspondence, mail **2** : equivalence **3** : connection, interchange
corresponder *vi* **1** : to correspond **2** : to pertain, to belong **3** : to be appropriate, to fit **4** : to reciprocate — **corresponderse** *vr* : to write to each other
correspondiente *adj* : corresponding, respective
corresponsal *nmf* : correspondent
corretaje *nm* : brokerage
corretear *vi* **1** VAGAR : to loiter, to wander about **2** : to run around, to scamper about — *vt* : to pursue, to chase
corrida *nf* **1** : run, dash **2** : bullfight
corrido[1], **-da** *adj* **1** : straight, continuous **2** : worldly, experienced
corrido[2] *nm* : Mexican narrative folk song
corriente[1] *adj* **1** : common, everyday **2** : current, present **3** *Mex* : cheap, trashy **4 perro corriente** *Mex* : mutt
corriente[2] *nf* **1** : current ⟨corriente alterna : alternating current⟩ ⟨direct current : corriente continua⟩ **2** : draft **3** TENDENCIA : tendency, trend
corrillo *nm* : small group, clique
corro *nm* : ring, circle (of people)
corroboración *nf, pl* **-ciones** : corroboration
corroborar *vt* : to corroborate
corroer {69} *vt* **1** : to corrode **2** : to erode, to wear away
corromper *vt* **1** : to corrupt **2** : to rot — **corromperse** *vr*
corrompido, -da *adj* CORRUPTO : corrupt, rotten
corrosión *nf, pl* **-siones** : corrosion
corrosivo, -va *adj* : corrosive
corrugar {52} *vt* : to corrugate — **corrugación** *nf*
corrupción *nf, pl* **-ciones** **1** : decay **2** : corruption
corruptela *nf* : corruption, abuse of power
corrupto, -ta *adj* CORROMPIDO : corrupt
corsario *nm* : privateer
corsé *nm* : corset
cortada *nf* : cut, gash
cortador, -dora *n* : cutter
cortadora *nf* : cutter, slicer
cortadura *nf* : cut, slash
cortafuegos *nms & pl* **1** : firebreak **2** : firewall (program)
cortante *adj* : cutting, sharp
cortar *vt* **1** : to cut, to slice, to trim **2** : to cut out, to omit **3** : to cut off, to interrupt **4** : to block, to close off **5** : to curdle (milk) — *vi* **1** : to cut **2** : to break up **3** : to hang up (the telephone) — **cortarse** *vr* **1** : to cut oneself ⟨cortarse el pelo : to cut one's hair⟩ **2** : to be cut off **3** : to sour (of milk)
cortauñas *nms & pl* : nail clippers
corte[1] *nm* **1** : cut, cutting ⟨corte de pelo : haircut⟩ **2** : style, fit
corte[2] *nf* **1** : court ⟨corte suprema : supreme court⟩ **2 hacer la corte a** : to court, to woo
cortejar *vt* GALANTEAR : to court, to woo
cortejo *nm* **1** GALANTEO : courtship **2** : retinue, entourage
cortés *adj* : courteous, polite — **cortésmente** *adv*
cortesano[1], **-na** *adj* : courtly
cortesano[2], **-na** *n* : courtier
cortesía *nf* **1** : courtesy, politeness **2 de ~** : complimentary, free
corteza *nf* **1** : bark **2** : crust **3** : peel, rind **4** : cortex ⟨corteza cerebral : cerebral cortex⟩
cortijo *nm* : farmhouse
cortina *nf* : curtain
cortisona *nf* : cortisone
corto, -ta *adj* **1** : short (in length or duration) **2** : scarce **3** : timid, shy **4 corto de vista** : nearsighted
cortocircuito *nm* : short circuit
corvejón *nm, pl* **-jones** JARRETTE : hock
corvo, -va *adj* : curved, bent
cosa *nf* **1** : thing, object **2** : matter, affair **3 otra cosa** : anything else, something else
cosecha *nf* : harvest, crop
cosechador, -dora *n* : harvester, reaper
cosechadora *nf* : harvester (machine)
cosechar *vt* **1** : to harvest, to reap **2** : to win, to earn, to garner — *vi* : to harvest
coser *vt* **1** : to sew **2** : to stitch up — *vi* : to sew
cosmético[1], **-ca** *adj* : cosmetic
cosmético[2] *nm* : cosmetic
cósmico, -ca *adj* : cosmic
cosmonauta *nmf* : cosmonaut
cosmopolita *adj & nmf* : cosmopolitan
cosmos *nm* : cosmos
cosquillas *nfpl* **1** : tickling **2 hacer cosquillas** : to tickle
cosquilleo *nm* : tickling sensation, tingle
cosquilloso, -sa *adj* : ticklish
costa *nf* **1** : coast, shore **2** : cost ⟨a toda costa : at all costs⟩
costado *nm* **1** : side **2 al costado** : alongside
costar {19} *v* : to cost ⟨¿cuánto cuesta? : how much does it cost?⟩
costarricense *adj & nmf* : Costa Rican
costarriqueño, -ña → **costarricense**
coste → **costo**
costear *vt* : to pay for, to finance

costero, -ra *adj* : coastal, coast
costilla *nf* **1** : rib **2** : chop, cutlet **3** *fam* : better half, wife
costo *nm* **1** : cost, price **2 costo de vida** : cost of living
costoso, -sa *adj* : costly, expensive
costra *nf* **1** : crust **2** POSTILLA : scab
costumbre *nf* **1** : custom **2** HÁBITO : habit
costura *nf* **1** : seam **2** : sewing, dressmaking **3 alta costura** : haute couture
costurera *nf* : seamstress *f*
cotejar *vt* : to compare, to collate
cotejo *nm* : comparison, collation
cotidiano, -na *adj* : daily, everyday ⟨la vida cotidiana : daily life⟩
cotización *nf, pl* **-ciones 1** : market price **2** : quote, estimate
cotizado, -da *adj* : in demand, sought after
cotizar {21} *vt* : to quote, to value — **cotizarse** *vr* : to be worth
coto *nm* **1** : enclosure, reserve **2 poner coto a** : to put a stop to
cotorra *nf* **1** : small parrot **2** *fam* : chatterbox, windbag
cotorrear *vi fam* : to chatter, to gab, to blab
cotorreo *nm fam* : chatter, prattle
coyote *nm* **1** : coyote **2** *Mex fam* : smuggler (of illegal immigrants)
coyuntura *nf* **1** ARTICULACIÓN : joint **2** : occasion, moment
coz *nf, pl* **coces** : kick (of an animal)
crac *nm, pl* **cracs** : crash (of the stock market)
cozamos, etc. → **cocer**
craneal *adj* : cranial
cráneo *nf* : cranium, skull — **craneano, -na** *adj*
cráter *nm* : crater
crayón *nm, pl* **-yones** : crayon
creación *nf, pl* **-ciones** : creation
creador[1], -dora *adj* : creative, creating
creador[2], -dora *n* : creator
crear *vt* **1** : to create, to cause **2** : to originate
creatividad *nf* : creativity
creativo, -va *adj* : creative
crecer {53} *vi* **1** : to grow **2** : to increase
crecida *nf* : flooding, floodwater
crecido, -da *adj* **1** : grown, grown-up **2** : large (of numbers)
creciente *adj* **1** : growing, increasing **2 luna creciente** : waxing moon
crecientemente *adv* : increasingly
crecimiento *nm* **1** : growth **2** : increase
credencial *adj* **cartas credenciales** : credentials
credenciales *nfpl* : documents, documentation, credentials
credibilidad *nf* : credibility
crédito *nm* : credit
credo *nm* : creed, credo
credulidad *nf* : credulity
crédulo, -la *adj* : credulous, gullible
creencia *nf* : belief
creer {20} *v* **1** : to believe **2** : to suppose, to think ⟨creo que sí : I think so⟩ — **creerse** *vr* **1** : to believe, to think **2** : to regard oneself as ⟨se cree guapísimo : he thinks he's so handsome⟩
creíble *adj* : believable, credible
creído, -da *adj* **1** *fam* : conceited **2** : confident, sure
crema *nf* **1** : cream **2 la crema y nata** : the pick of the crop
cremación *nf, pl* **-ciones** : cremation
cremallera *nf* : zipper
cremar *vt* : to cremate
cremoso, -sa *adj* : creamy
crepa *nf Mex* : crepe (pancake)
crepe *or* **crep** *nmf* : crepe (pancake)
crepé *nm* **1** → **crespón 2 papel crepé** : crepe paper
crepitar *vi* : to crackle
crepúsculo *nm* : twilight
crescendo *nm* : crescendo
crespo, -pa *adj* : curly, frizzy
crespón *nm, pl* **crespones** : crepe (fabric)
cresta *nf* **1** : crest **2** : comb (of a rooster)
creta *nf* : chalk (mineral)
cretino, -na *n* : cretin
creyente *nmf* : believer
creyó, etc. → **creer**
crezca, etc. → **crecer**
cría *nf* **1** : breeding, rearing **2** : young **3** : litter
criadero *nm* : hatchery
criado[1], -da *adj* **1** : raised, brought up **2 bien criado** : well-bred
criado[2], -da *n* : servant, maid *f*
criador, -dora *n* : breeder
crianza *nf* : upbringing, rearing
criar {85} *vt* **1** : to breed **2** : to bring up, to raise
criatura *nf* **1** : baby, child **2** : creature
criba *nf* : sieve, screen
cribar *vt* : to sift
cric *nm, pl* **crics** : jack
crimen *nm, pl* **crímenes** : crime
criminal *adj & nmf* : criminal
crin *nf* **1** : mane **2** : horsehair
criollo[1], -lla *adj* **1** : Creole **2** : native, national ⟨comida criolla : native cuisine⟩
criollo[2], -lla *n* : Creole
criollo[3] *nm* : Creole (language)
cripta *nf* : crypt
críptico, -ca *adj* **1** : cryptic, coded **2** : enigmatic, cryptic
criptón *nm* : krypton
críquet *nm* : cricket (game)
crisálida *nf* : chrysalis, pupa
crisantemo *nm* : chrysanthemum
crisis *nf* **1** : crisis **2 crisis nerviosa** : nervous breakdown
crisma *nf fam* : head ⟨romperle la crisma a alguien : to knock someone's block off⟩
crisol *nm* **1** : crucible **2** : melting pot
crispar *vt* **1** : to cause to contract **2** : to irritate, to set on edge ⟨eso me crispa : that gets on my nerves⟩ — **crisparse** *vr* : to tense up

cristal *nm* **1** VIDRIO : glass, piece of glass **2** : crystal
cristalería *nf* **1** : glassware shop ⟨como chivo en cristalería : like a bull in a china shop⟩ **2** : glassware, crystal
cristalino[1], **-na** *adj* : crystalline, clear
cristalino[2] *nm* : lens (of the eye)
cristalizar {21} *vi* : to crystallize — **cristalización** *nf*
cristiandad *nf* : Christendom
cristianismo *nm* : Christianity
cristiano, -na *adj & n* : Christian
Cristo *nm* : Christ
criterio *nm* **1** : criterion **2** : judgment, sense
crítica *nf* **1** : criticism **2** : review, critique
criticar {72} *vt* : to criticize
crítico[1], **-ca** *adj* : critical — **críticamente** *adv*
crítico[2], **-ca** *n* : critic
criticón[1], **-cona** *adj, mpl* **-cones** *fam* : hypercritical, captious
criticón[2], **-cona** *n, mpl* **-cones** *fam* : faultfinder, critic
croar *vi* : to croak
croata *adj & nmf* : Croatian
crocante *adj* : crunchy
croché *or* **crochet** *nm* : crochet
cromático, -ca *adj* : chromatic
cromo *nm* **1** : chromium, chrome **2** : picture card, sports card
cromosoma *nm* : chromosome
crónica *nf* **1** : news report **2** : chronicle, history
crónico, -ca *adj* : chronic
cronista *nmf* **1** : reporter, newscaster **2** HISTORIADOR : chronicler, historian
cronología *nf* : chronology
cronológico, -ca *adj* : chronological — **cronológicamente** *adv*
cronometrador, -dora *n* : timekeeper
cronometrar *vt* : to time, to clock
cronómetro *nm* : chronometer
croquet *nm* : croquet
croqueta *nf* : croquette
croquis *nm* : rough sketch
cruce[1], **etc.** → **cruzar**
cruce[2] *nm* **1** : crossing, cross **2** : crossroads, intersection ⟨cruce peatonal : crosswalk⟩
crucero *nm* **1** : cruise **2** : cruiser, warship **3** *Mex* : intersection
crucial *adj* : crucial — **crucialmente** *adv*
crucificar {72} *vt* : to crucify
crucifijo *nm* : crucifix
crucifixión *nf, pl* **-fixiones** : crucifixion
crucigrama *nm* : crossword puzzle
crudo[1], **-da** *adj* **1** : raw **2** : crude, harsh
crudo[2] *nm* : crude oil
cruel *adj* : cruel — **cruelmente** *adv*
crueldad *nf* : cruelty
cruento, -ta *adj* : bloody
crujido *nm* **1** : rustling **2** : creaking **3** : crackling (of a fire) **4** : crunching
crujiente *adj* : crunchy, crisp
crujir *vi* **1** : to rustle **2** : to creak, to crack **3** : to crunch
crup *nm* : croup
crustáceo *nm* : crustacean
crutón *nm, pl* **crutones** : crouton
cruz *nf, pl* **cruces** : cross
cruza *nf* : cross (hybrid)
cruzada *nf* : crusade
cruzado[1], **-da** *adj* : crossed ⟨espadas cruzadas : crossed swords⟩
cruzado[2] *nm* **1** : crusader **2** : Brazilian unit of currency
cruzar {21} *vt* **1** : to cross **2** : to exchange (words, greetings) **3** : to cross, to interbreed — **cruzarse** *vr* **1** : to intersect **2** : to meet, to pass each other
cuaderno *nm* LIBRETA : notebook
cuadra *nf* **1** : city block **2** : stable
cuadrado[1], **-da** *adj* : square
cuadrado[2] *nm* : square ⟨elevar al cuadrado : to square (a number)⟩
cuadragésimo[1] *adj* : fortieth, forty-
cuadragésimo[2], **-ma** *n* : fortieth, forty- (in a series)
cuadrante *nm* **1** : quadrant **2** : dial
cuadrar *vi* : to conform, to agree — *vt* : to square — **cuadrarse** *vr* : to stand at attention
cuadriculado *nm* : grid (on a map, etc.)
cuadrilátero *nm* **1** : quadrilateral **2** : ring (in sports)
cuadrilla *nf* : gang, team, group
cuadro *nm* **1** : square ⟨una blusa a cuadros : a checkered blouse⟩ **2** : painting, picture **3** : baseball diamond, infield **4** : panel, board, cadre
cuadrúpedo *nm* : quadruped
cuadruple *adj* : quadruple
cuadruplicar {72} *vt* : to quadruple — **cuadruplicarse** *vr*
cuajada *nf* : curd
cuajar *vi* **1** : to curdle **2** COAGULAR : to clot, to coagulate **3** : to set, to jell **4** : to be accepted ⟨su idea no cuajó : his idea didn't catch on⟩ — *vt* **1** : to curdle **2** ~ **de** : to fill with
cual[1] *prep* : like, as
cual[2] *pron* **1 el cual, la cual, los cuales, las cuales** : who, whom, which ⟨la razón por la cual lo dije : the reason I said it⟩ **2 lo cual** : which ⟨se rió, lo cual me dio rabia : he laughed, which made me mad⟩ **3 cada cual** : everyone, everybody
cuál[1] *adj* : which, what ⟨¿cuáles libros? : which books?⟩
cuál[2] *pron* **1** (*in questions*) : which (one), what (one) ⟨¿cuál es el mejor? : which one is the best?⟩ ⟨¿cuál es tu apellido? : what is your last name?⟩ **2 cuál más, cuál menos** : some more, some less
cualidad *nf* : quality, trait
cualitativo, -va *adj* : qualitative — **cualitativamente** *adv*
cualquier *adj* → **cualquiera**[1]
cualquiera[1] (**cualquier** *before nouns*) *adj, pl* **cualesquiera** **1** : any, whichever ⟨cualquier persona : any person⟩ **2** : everyday, ordinary ⟨un hombre cualquiera : an ordinary man⟩

cualquiera[2] *pron, pl* **cualesquiera** **1** : anyone, anybody, whoever **2** : whatever, whichever

cuán *adv* : how ⟨¡cuán risible fue todo eso! : how funny it all was!⟩

cuando[1] *conj* **1** : when ⟨cuando llegó : when he arrived⟩ **2** : since, if ⟨cuando lo dices : if you say so⟩ **3 cuando más** : at the most **4 de vez en cuando** : from time to time

cuando[2] *prep* : during, at the time of ⟨cuando la guerra : during the war⟩

cuándo *adv & conj* **1** : when ⟨¿cuándo llegará? : when will she arrive?⟩ ⟨no sabemos cuándo será : we don't know when it will be⟩ **2 ¿de cuándo acá?** : since when?, how come?

cuantía *nf* **1** : quantity, extent **2** : significance, import

cuántico, -ca *adj* : quantum ⟨teoría cuántica : quantum theory⟩

cuantioso, -sa *adj* **1** : abundant, considerable **2** : heavy, grave ⟨cuantiosos daños : heavy damage⟩

cuantitativo, -va *adj* : quantitative — **cuantitativamente** *adv*

cuanto[1] *adv* **1** : as much as ⟨come cuanto puedas : eat as much as you can⟩ **2 cuanto antes** : as soon as possible **3 en ~** : as soon as **4 en cuanto a** : as for, as regards

cuanto[2], **-ta** *adj* : as many, whatever ⟨llévate cuantas flores quieras : take as many flowers as you wish⟩

cuanto[3], **-ta** *pron* **1** : as much as, all that, everything ⟨tengo cuanto deseo : I have all that I want⟩ **2 unos cuantos, unas cuantas** : a few

cuánto[1] *adv* : how much, how many ⟨¿a cuánto están las manzanas? : how much are the apples?⟩ ⟨no sé cuánto desean : I don't know how much they want⟩

cuánto[2], **-ta** *adj* : how much, how many ⟨¿cuántos niños tiene? : how many children do you have?⟩

cuánto[3] *pron* : how much, how many ⟨¿cuántos quieren participar? : how many want to take part?⟩ ⟨¿cuánto cuesta? : how much does it cost?⟩

cuarenta *adj & nm* : forty

cuarentavo[1], **-va** *adj* : fortieth

cuarentavo[2] *nm* : fortieth (fraction)

cuarentena *nf* **1** : group of forty **2** : quarantine

Cuaresma *nf* : Lent

cuartear *vt* **1** : to quarter **2** : to divide up — **cuartearse** *vr* AGRIETARSE : to crack, to split

cuartel *nm* **1** : barracks, headquarters **2** : mercy ⟨una guerra sin cuartel : a merciless war⟩

cuartelazo *nm* : coup d'état

cuarteto *nm* : quartet

cuartilla *nf* : sheet (of paper)

cuarto[1], **-ta** *adj* : fourth

cuarto[2], **-ta** *n* : fourth (in a series)

cuarto[3] *nm* **1** : quarter, fourth ⟨cuarto de galón : quart⟩ **2** HABITACIÓN : room

cuarzo *nm* : quartz

cuate, -ta *n Mex* **1** : twin **2** *fam* : buddy, pal

cuatrero, -ra *n* : rustler

cuatrillizo, -za *n* : quadruplet

cuatro *adj & nm* : four

cuatrocientos[1], **-tas** *adj* : four hundred

cuatrocientos[2] *nms & pl* : four hundred

cuba *nf* BARRIL : cask, barrel

cubano, -na *adj & n* : Cuban

cubertería *nf* : flatware, silverware

cubeta *nf* **1** : keg, cask **2** : bulb (of a thermometer) **3** *Mex* : bucket, pail

cúbico, -ca *adj* : cubic, cubed

cubículo *nm* : cubicle

cubierta *nf* **1** : covering **2** FORRO : cover, jacket (of a book) **3** : deck

cubierto[1] *pp* → **cubrir**

cubierto[2] *nm* **1** : cover, shelter ⟨bajo cubierto : under cover⟩ **2** : table setting **3** : utensil, piece of silverware

cubil *nm* : den, lair

cúbito *nm* : ulna

cubo *nm* **1** : cube **2** BALDE : pail, bucket, can ⟨cubo de basura : garbage can⟩ **3** : hub (of a wheel)

cubrecama *nm* COLCHA : bedspread

cubrir {2} *vt* : to cover — **cubrirse** *vr*

cucaracha *nf* : cockroach, roach

cuchara *nf* : spoon

cucharada *nf* : spoonful

cucharilla *or* **cucharita** *nf* : teaspoon

cucharón *nm, pl* **-rones** : ladle

cuchichear *vi* : to whisper

cuchicheo *nm* : whisper

cuchilla *nf* **1** : kitchen knife, cleaver **2** : blade ⟨cuchilla de afeitar : razor blade⟩ **3** : crest, ridge

cuchillada *nf* : stab, knife wound

cuchillo *nm* : knife

cuclillas *nfpl* **en ~** : squatting, crouching

cuco[1], **-ca** *adj fam* : pretty, cute

cuco[2] *nm* : cuckoo

cucurucho *nm* : ice-cream cone

cuece, cueza etc. → **cocer**

cuela, etc. → **colar**

cuelga, cuelgue etc. → **colgar**

cuello *nm* **1** : neck **2** : collar (of a shirt) **3 cuello del útero** : cervix

cuenca *nf* **1** : river basin **2** : eye socket

cuenco *nm* : bowl, basin

cuenta[1], **etc.** → **contar**

cuenta[2] *nf* **1** : calculation, count **2** : account **3** : check, bill **4 darse cuenta** : to realize **5 tener en cuenta** : to bear in mind

cuentagotas *nfs & pl* **1** : dropper **2 con ~** : little by little

cuentista *nmf* **1** : short story writer **2** *fam* : liar, fibber

cuento *nm* **1** : story, tale **2 cuento de hadas** : fairy tale **3 sin ~** : countless

cuerda *nf* **1** : cord, rope, string **2 cuerdas vocales** : vocal cords **3 darle cuerda a** : to wind up (a clock, a toy, etc.)

cuerdo, -da *adj* : sane, sensible

cuerno *nm* **1** : horn, antler **2** : cusp (of the moon) **3** : horn (musical instrument)

cuero *nm* **1** : leather, hide **2 cuero cabelludo** : scalp

cuerpo *nm* **1** : body **2** : corps

cuervo *nm* : crow, raven

cuesta[1], **etc.** → **costar**

cuesta[2] *nf* **1** : slope <cuesta arriba : uphill> **2 a cuestas** : on one's back

cuestión *nf, pl* **-tiones** ASUNTO, TEMA : matter, affair

cuestionable *adj* : questionable, dubious

cuestionar *vt* : to question

cuestionario *nm* **1** : questionnaire **2** : quiz

cueva *nf* : cave

cuidado *nm* **1** : care **2** : worry, concern **3 tener cuidado** : to be careful **4 ¡cuidado!** : watch out!, be careful!

cuidador, -dora *n* : caretaker

cuidadoso, -sa *adj* : careful, attentive — **cuidadosamente** *adv*

cuidar *vt* **1** : to take care of, to look after **2** : to pay attention to — *vi* **1 ~ de** : to look after **2 cuidar de que** : to make sure that — **cuidarse** *vr* : to take care of oneself

culata *nf* : butt (of a gun)

culatazo *nf* : kick, recoil

culebra *nf* SERPIENTE : snake

culi *nmf* : coolie

culinario, -ria *adj* : culinary

culminante *adj* **punto culminante** : peak, high point, climax

culminar *vi* : to culminate — **culminación** *nf*

culo *nm* **1** *fam* : backside, behind **2** : bottom (of a glass)

culpa *nf* **1** : fault, blame <echarle la culpa a alguien : to blame someone> **2** : sin

culpabilidad *nf* : guilt

culpable[1] *adj* : guilty

culpable[2] *nmf* : culprit, guilty party

culpar *vt* : to blame

cultivado, -da *adj* **1** : cultivated, farmed **2** : cultured

cultivador, -dora *n* : cultivator

cultivar *vt* **1** : to cultivate **2** : to foster

cultivo *nm* **1** : cultivation, farming **2** : crop

culto[1], **-ta** *adj* : cultured, educated

culto[2] *nm* **1** : worship **2** : cult

cultura *nf* : culture

cultural *adj* : cultural — **culturalmente** *adv*

cumbre *nf* CIMA : top, peak, summit

cumpleaños *nms & pl* : birthday

cumplido[1], **-da** *adj* **1** : complete, full **2** : courteous, correct

cumplido[2] *nm* : compliment, courtesy <por cumplido : out of courtesy> <andarse con cumplidos : to stand on ceremony, to be formal>

cumplimentar *vt* **1** : to congratulate **2** : to carry out, to perform

cumplimiento *nm* **1** : completion, fulfillment **2** : performance

cumplir *vt* **1** : to accomplish, to carry out **2** : to comply with, to fulfill **3** : to attain, to reach <su hermana cumple los 21 el viernes : her sister will be 21 on Friday> — *vi* **1** : to expire, to fall due **2** : to fulfill one's obligations <cumplir con el deber : to do one's duty> <cumplir con la palabra : to keep one's word> — **cumplirse** *vr* **1** : to come true, to be fulfilled <se cumplieron sus sueños : her dreams came true> **2** : to run out, to expire

cúmulo *nm* **1** MONTÓN : heap, pile **2** : cumulus

cuna *nf* **1** : cradle **2** : birthplace <Puerto Rico es la cuna de la música salsa : Puerto Rico is the birthplace of salsa music>

cundir *vi* **1** : to propagate, to spread <cundió el pánico en el vecindario : panic spread throughout the neighborhood> **2** : to progress, to make headway

cuneta *nf* : ditch (in a road), gutter

cuña *nf* : wedge

cuñado, -da *n* : brother-in-law *m*, sister-in-law *f*

cuño *nm* : die (for stamping)

cuota *nf* **1** : fee, dues **2** : quota, share **3** : installment, payment

cupé *nm* : coupe

cupo[1], **etc.** → **caber**

cupo[2] *nm* **1** : quota, share **2** : capacity, room

cupón *nm, pl* **cupones 1** : coupon, voucher **2 cupón federal** : food stamp

cúpula *nf* : dome, cupola

cura[1] *nm* : priest

cura[2] *nf* **1** CURACIÓN, TRATAMIENTO : cure, treatment **2** : dressing, bandage

curación *nf, pl* **-ciones** CURA, TRATAMIENTO : cure, treatment

curandero, -ra *nm* **1** : witch doctor **2** : quack, charlatan

curar *vt* **1** : to cure, to heal **2** : to treat, to dress **3** CURTIR : to tan **4** : to cure (meat) — *vi* : to get well, to recover — **curarse** *vr*

curativo, -va *adj* : curative, healing

curiosear *vi* **1** : to snoop, to pry **2** : to browse — *vt* : to look over, to check

curiosidad *nf* **1** : curiosity **2** : curio

curioso, -sa *adj* **1** : curious, inquisitive **2** : strange, unusual, odd — **curiosamente** *adv*

currículo → **currículum**

currículum *nm, pl* **-lums 1** : résumé, curriculum vitae **2** : curriculum, course of study

curry [ˈkurri] *nm, pl* **-rries 1** : curry powder **2** : curry (dish)

cursar *vt* **1** : to attend (school), to take (a course) **2** : to dispatch, to pass on

cursi *adj fam* : affected, pretentious

cursilería *nf* **1** : vulgarity, poor taste **2** : pretentiousness

cursiva *nf* BASTARDILLA : italic type, italics *pl*
curso *nm* **1** : course, direction **2** : school year **3** : course, subject (in school)
cursor *nm* : cursor
curtido, -da *adj* : weather-beaten, leathery (of skin)
curtidor, -dora *n* : tanner
curtiduría *nf* : tannery
curtir *vt* **1** : to tan **2** : to harden, to weather — **curtirse** *vr*
curva *nf* : curve, bend
curvar *vt* : to bend
curvatura *nf* : curvature
curvilíneo, -nea *adj* : curvaceous, shapely
curvo, -va *adj* : curved, bent
cúspide *nf* : zenith, apex, peak
custodia *nf* : custody
custodiar *vt* : to guard, to look after
custodio, -dia *n* : keeper, guardian
cúter *nm* : cutter (boat)
cutícula *nf* : cuticle
cutis *nms & pl* : skin, complexion
cuyo, -ya *adj* **1** : whose, of whom, of which **2 en cuyo caso** : in which case

D

d *nf* : fourth letter of the Spanish alphabet
dable *adj* : feasible, possible
dactilar *adj* **huellas dactilares** : fingerprints
dádiva *nf* : gift, handout
dadivoso, -sa *adj* : generous
dado, -da *adj* **1** : given **2 dado que** : given that, since
dador, -dora *n* : giver, donor
dados *nmpl* : dice
daga *nf* : dagger
dalia *nf* : dahlia
dálmata *nm* : dalmatian
daltónico, -ca *adj* : color-blind
daltonismo *nm* : color blindness
dama *nf* **1** : lady **2 damas** *nfpl* : checkers
damasco *nm* : damask
damisela *nf* : damsel
damnificado, -da *n* : victim (of a disaster)
damnificar {72} *vt* : to damage, to injure
dance, etc. → **danzar**
dandi *nm* : dandy, fop
danés[1], **-nesa** *adj* : Danish
danés[2], **-nesa** *n, mpl* **daneses** : Dane, Danish person
danza *nf* : dance, dancing ⟨danza folklórica : folk dance⟩
danzante, -ta *n* BAILARÍN : dancer
danzar {21} *v* BAILAR : to dance
dañar *vt* **1** : to damage, to spoil **2** : to harm, to hurt — **dañarse** *vr*
dañino, -na *adj* : harmful
daño *nm* **1** : damage **2** : harm, injury **3 hacer daño a** : to harm, to damage **4 daños y perjuicios** : damages
dar {22} *vt* **1** : to give **2** ENTREGAR : to deliver, to hand over **3** : to hit, to strike **4** : to yield, to produce **5** : to perform **6** : to give off, to emit **7 ~ como** *or* **~ por** : to regard as, to consider — *vi* **1** ALCANZAR : to suffice, to be enough ⟨no me da para dos pasajes : I don't have enough for two fares⟩ **2 ~ a** *or* **~ sobre** : to overlook, to look out on **3 ~ con** : to run into **4 ~ con** : to hit upon (an idea) **5 dar de sí** : to give, to stretch — **darse** *vr* **1** : to give in, to surrender **2** : to occur, to arise **3** : to grow, to come up **4 ~ con** *or* **~ contra** : to hit oneself against **5 dárselas de** : to boast about ⟨se las da de muy listo : he thinks he's very smart⟩
dardo *nm* : dart
datar *vt* : to date — *vi* **~ de** : to date from, to date back to
dátil *nm* : date (fruit)
dato *nm* **1** : fact, piece of information **2 datos** *nmpl* : data, information
dé → **dar**
de *prep* **1** : of ⟨la casa de Pepe : Pepe's house⟩ ⟨un niño de tres años : a three-year-old boy⟩ **2** : from ⟨es de Managua : she's from Managua⟩ ⟨salió del edificio : he left the building⟩ **3** : in, at ⟨a las tres de la mañana : at three in the morning⟩ ⟨salen de noche : they go out at night⟩ **4** : than ⟨más de tres : more than three⟩
deambular *vi* : to wander, to roam
debacle *nf* : debacle
debajo *adv* **1** : underneath, below, on the bottom **2 ~ de** : under, underneath **3 por ~** : below, beneath
debate *nm* : debate
debatir *vt* : to debate, to discuss — **debatirse** *vr* : to struggle
debe *nm* : debit column, debit
deber[1] *vt* : to owe — *v aux* **1** : must, have to ⟨debo ir a la oficina : I must go to the office⟩ **2** : should, ought to ⟨deberías buscar trabajo : you ought to look for work⟩ **3** (*expressing probability*) : must ⟨debe ser mexicano : he must be Mexican⟩ — **deberse** *vr* **~ a** : to be due to
deber[2] *nm* **1** OBLIGACIÓN : duty, obligation **2 deberes** *nmpl, Spain* : homework
debidamente *adv* : properly, duly
debido, -da *adj* **1** : right, proper, due **2 ~ a** : due to, owing to
débil *adj* : weak, feeble — **débilmente** *adv*
debilidad *nf* : weakness, debility, feebleness
debilitamiento *nm* : debilitation, weakening

debilitar *vt* : to debilitate, to weaken — **debilitarse** *vr*
debilucho[1], **-cha** *adj* : weak, frail
debilucho[2], **-cha** *n* : weakling
debitar *vt* : to debit
débito *nm* **1** DEUDA : debt **2** : debit
debut [deˈbut] *nm, pl* **debuts** : debut
debutante[1] *nmf* : beginner, newcomer
debutante[2] *nf* : debutante *f*
debutar *vi* : to debut, to make a debut
década *nf* DECENIO : decade
decadencia *nf* **1** : decadence **2** : decline
decadente *adj* **1** : decadent **2** : declining
decaer {13} *vi* **1** : to decline, to decay, to deteriorate **2** FLAQUEAR : to weaken, to flag
decaiga, etc. → **decaer**
decano, -na *n* **1** : dean **2** : senior member
decantar *vt* : to decant
decapitar *vt* : to decapitate, to behead
decayó, etc. → **decaer**
decena *nf* : group of ten
decencia *nf* : decency
decenio *nm* DÉCADA : decade
decente *adj* : decent — **decentemente** *adv*
decepción *nf, pl* **-ciones** : disappointment, letdown
decepcionante *adj* : disappointing
decepcionar *vt* : to disappoint, to let down — **decepcionarse** *vr*
deceso *nm* DEFUNCIÓN : death, passing
dechado *nm* **1** : sampler (of embroidery) **2** : model, paragon
decibelio *or* **decibel** *nm* : decibel
decidido, -da *adj* : decisive, determined, resolute — **decididamente** *adv*
decidir *vt* **1** : to decide, to determine <no he decidido nada : I haven't made a decision> **2** : to persuade, to decide <su padre lo decidió a estudiar : his father persuaded him to study> — *vi* : to decide — **decidirse** *vr* : to make up one's mind
decimal *adj* : decimal
décimo, -ma *adj* : tenth — **décimo, -ma** *n*
decimoctavo[1], **-va** *adj* : eighteenth
decimoctavo[2], **-va** *n* : eighteenth (in a series)
decimocuarto[1], **-ta** *adj* : fourteenth
decimocuarto[2], **-ta** *n* : fourteenth (in a series)
decimonoveno[1], **-na** *or* **decimonono, -na** *adj* : nineteenth
decimonoveno[2], **-na** *or* **decimonono, -na** *n* : nineteenth (in a series)
decimoquinto[1], **-ta** *adj* : fifteenth
decimoquinto[2], **-ta** *n* : fifteenth (in a series)
decimoséptimo[1], **-ma** *adj* : seventeenth
decimoséptimo[2], **-ma** *n* : seventeenth (in a series)
decimosexto[1], **-ta** *adj* : sixteenth
decimosexto[2], **-ta** *n* : sixteenth (in a series)
decimotercero[1], **-ra** *adj* : thirteenth
decimotercero[2], **-ra** *n* : thirteenth (in a series)
decir[1] {23} *vt* **1** : to say <dice que no quiere ir : she says she doesn't want to go> **2** : to tell <dime lo que estás pensando : tell me what you're thinking> **3** : to speak, to talk <no digas tonterías : don't talk nonsense> **4** : to call <me dicen Rosy : they call me Rosy> **5 es decir** : that is to say **6 querer decir** : to mean — **decirse** *vr* **1** : to say to oneself **2** : to be said <¿cómo se dice "lápiz" en francés? : how do you say "pencil" in French?>
decir[2] *nm* DICHO : saying, expression
decisión *nf, pl* **-siones** : decision, choice
decisivo, -va *adj* : decisive, conclusive — **decisivamente** *adv*
declamar *vi* : to declaim — *vt* : to recite
declaración *nf, pl* **-ciones** **1** : declaration, statement **2** TESTIMONIO : deposition, testimony **3 declaración de derechos** : bill of rights **4 declaración jurada** : affidavit
declarado, -da *adj* : professed, open — **declaradamente** *adv*
declarar *vt* : to declare, to state — *vi* ATESTIGUAR : to testify — **declararse** *vr* **1** : to declare oneself, to make a statement **2** : to confess one's love **3** : to plead (in court) <declararse inocente : to plead not guilty>
declinación *nf, pl* **-ciones** **1** : drop, downward trend **2** : declination **3** : declension (in grammar)
declinar *vt* : to decline, to turn down — *vi* **1** : to draw to a close **2** : to diminish, to decline
declive *nm* **1** DECADENCIA : decline **2** : slope, incline
decodificador *nm* : decoder
decolar *vi Chile, Col, Ecua* : to take off (of an airplane)
decolorar *vt* : to bleach — **decolorarse** *vr* : to fade
decomisar *vt* CONFISCAR : to seize, to confiscate
decomiso *nm* : seizure, confiscation
decoración *nf, pl* **-ciones** **1** : decoration **2** : decor **3** : stage set, scenery
decorado *nm* : stage set, scenery
decorador, -dora *n* : decorator
decorar *vt* ADORNAR : to decorate, to adorn
decorativo, -va *adj* : decorative, ornamental
decoro *nm* : decorum, propriety
decoroso, -sa *adj* : decent, proper, respectable
decrecer {53} *vi* : to decrease, to wane, to diminish — **decreciente** *adj*
decrecimiento *nm* : decrease, decline
decrépito, -ta *adj* : decrepit
decretar *vt* : to decree, to order
decreto *nm* : decree
decúbito *nm* : horizontal position <en decúbito prono : prone> <en decúbito supino : supine>

dedal *nm* : thimble
dedalera *nf* DIGITAL : foxglove
dedicación *nf, pl* **-ciones** : dedication, devotion
dedicar {72} *vt* CONSAGRAR : to dedicate, to devote — **dedicarse** *vr* **~ a** : to devote oneself to, to engage in
dedicatoria *nf* : dedication (of a book, song, etc.)
dedo *nm* **1** : finger ⟨dedo meñique : little finger⟩ **2 dedo del pie** : toe
deducción *nf, pl* **-ciones** : deduction
deducible *adj* **1** : deducible, inferable **2** : deductible
deducir {61} *vt* **1** INFERIR : to deduce **2** DESCONTAR : to deduct
defecar {72} *vi* : to defecate — **defecación** *nf*
defecto *nm* **1** : defect, flaw, shortcoming **2 en su defecto** : lacking that, in the absence of that
defectuoso, -sa *adj* : defective, faulty
defender {56} *vt* : to defend, to protect — **defenderse** *vr* **1** : to defend oneself **2** : to get by, to know the basics ⟨su inglés no es perfecto pero se defiende : his English isn't perfect but he gets by⟩
defendible *adj* : defensible, tenable
defensa[1] *nf* : defense
defensa[2] *nmf* : defender, back (in sports)
defensiva *nf* : defensive, defense
defensivo, -va *adj* : defensive — **defensivamente** *adv*
defensor[1], **-sora** *adj* : defending, defense
defensor[2], **-sora** *n* **1** : defender, advocate **2** : defense counsel
defeño, -ña *n* : person from the Federal District (Mexico City)
deferencia *nf* : deference
deficiencia *nf* : deficiency, flaw
deficiente *adj* : deficient
déficit *nm, pl* **-cits** **1** : deficit **2** : shortage, lack
definición *nf, pl* **-ciones** : definition
definido, -da *adj* : definite, well-defined
definir *vt* **1** : to define **2** : to determine
definitivamente *adv* **1** : finally **2** : permanently, for good **3** : definitely, absolutely
definitivo, -va *adj* **1** : definitive, conclusive **2 en definitiva** : all in all, on the whole **3 en definitiva** *Mex* : permanently, for good
deflación *nf, pl* **-ciones** : deflation
deforestación *nf, pl* **-ciones** : deforestation
deformación *nf, pl* **-ciones** **1** : deformation **2** : distortion
deformar *vt* **1** : to deform, to disfigure **2** : to distort — **deformarse** *vr*
deforme *adj* : deformed, misshapen
deformidad *nf* : deformity
defraudación *nf, pl* **-ciones** : fraud
defraudar *vt* **1** ESTAFAR : to defraud, to cheat **2** : to disappoint
defunción *nf, pl* **-ciones** DECESO : death, passing
degeneración *nf, pl* **-ciones** **1** : degeneration **2** : degeneracy, depravity
degenerado, -da *adj* DEPRAVADO : degenerate
degenerar *vi* : to degenerate
degenerativo, -va *adj* : degenerative
degollar {19} *vt* **1** : to slit the throat of, to slaughter **2** DECAPITAR : to behead **3** : to ruin, to destroy
degradación *nf, pl* **-ciones** **1** : degradation **2** : demotion
degradar *vt* **1** : to degrade, to debase **2** : to demote
degustación *nf, pl* **-ciones** : tasting, sampling
degustar *vt* : to taste
deidad *nf* : deity
deificar {72} *vt* : to idolize, to deify
dejado, -da *adj* **1** : slovenly **2** : careless, lazy
dejar *vt* **1** : to leave **2** ABANDONAR : to abandon, to forsake **3** : to let be, to let go **4** PERMITIR : to allow, to permit — *vi* **~ de** : to stop, to quit ⟨dejar de fumar : to quit smoking⟩ — **dejarse** *vr* **1** : to let oneself be ⟨se deja insultar : he lets himself be insulted⟩ **2** : to forget, to leave ⟨me dejé las llaves en el carro : I left the keys in the car⟩ **3** : to neglect oneself, to let oneself go **4** : to grow ⟨nos estamos dejando el pelo largo : we're growing our hair long⟩
dejo *nm* **1** : aftertaste **2** : touch, hint **3** : (regional) accent
del (*contraction of* **de** *and* **el**) → **de**
delación *nf, pl* **-ciones** : denunciation, betrayal
delantal *nm* **1** : apron **2** : pinafore
delante *adv* **1** ENFRENTE : ahead, in front **2 ~ de** : before, in front of
delantera *nf* **1** : front, front part, front row ⟨tomar la delantera : to take the lead⟩ **2** : forward line (in sports)
delantero[1], **-ra** *adj* **1** : front, forward **2 tracción delantera** : front-wheel drive
delantero[2], **-ra** *n* : forward (in sports)
delatar *vt* **1** : to betray, to reveal **2** : to denounce, to inform against
delegación *nf, pl* **-ciones** : delegation
delegado, -da *n* : delegate, representative
delegar {52} *vt* : to delegate
deleitar *vt* : to delight, to please — **deleitarse** *vr*
deleite *nm* : delight, pleasure
deletrear *vi* : to spell ⟨¿como se deletrea? : how do you spell it?⟩
deleznable *adj* **1** : brittle, crumbly **2** : slippery **3** : weak, fragile ⟨una excusa deleznable : a weak excuse⟩
delfín *nm, pl* **delfines** **1** : dolphin **2** : dauphin, heir apparent
delgadez *nf* : thinness, skinniness
delgado, -da *adj* **1** FLACO : thin, skinny **2** ESBELTO : slender, slim **3** DELICADO : delicate, fine **4** AGUDO : sharp, clever
deliberación *nf, pl* **-ciones** : deliberation

deliberado, -da *adj* : deliberate, intentional — **deliberadamente** *adv*

deliberar *vi* : to deliberate

deliberativo, -va *adj* : deliberative

delicadeza *nf* **1** : delicacy, fineness **2** : gentleness, softness **3** : tact, discretion, consideration

delicado, -da *adj* **1** : delicate, fine **2** : sensitive, frail **3** : difficult, tricky **4** : fussy, hard to please **5** : tactful, considerate

delicia *nf* : delight

delicioso, -sa *adj* **1** RICO : delicious **2** : delightful

delictivo, -va *adj* : criminal

delictuoso, -sa → **delictivo**

delimitación *nf, pl* **-ciones** **1** : demarcation **2** : defining, specifying

delimitar *vt* **1** : to demarcate **2** : to define, to specify

delincuencia *nf* : delinquency, crime

delincuente[1] *adj* : delinquent

delincuente[2] *nmf* CRIMINAL : delinquent, criminal

delinear *vt* **1** : to delineate, to outline **2** : to draft, to draw up

delinquir {24} *vi* : to break the law

delirante *adj* : delirious

delirar *vi* **1** DESVARIAR : to be delirious **2** : to rave, to talk nonsense

delirio *nm* **1** DESVARÍO : delirium **2** DISPARATE : nonsense, ravings *pl* ⟨delirios de grandeza : delusions of grandeur⟩ **3** FRENESÍ : mania, frenzy ⟨¡fue el delirio! : it was wild!⟩

delito *nm* : crime, offense

delta *nm* : delta

demacrado, -da *adj* : emaciated, gaunt

demagogia *nf* : demagogy

demagógico, -ca *adj* : demagogic, demagogical

demagogo, -ga *n* : demagogue

demanda *nf* **1** : demand ⟨la oferta y la demanda : supply and demand⟩ **2** : petition, request **3** : lawsuit

demandado, -da *n* : defendant

demandante *nmf* : plaintiff

demandar *vt* **1** : to demand **2** REQUERIR : to call for, to require **3** : to sue, to file a lawsuit against

demarcar {72} *vt* : to demarcate — **demarcación** *nf*

demás[1] *adj* : remaining ⟨acabó las demás tareas : she finished the rest of the chores⟩

demás[2] *pron* **1 lo (la, los, las) demás** : the rest, everyone else, everything else ⟨Pepe, Rosa, y los demás : Pepe, Rosa, and everybody else⟩ **2 estar por demás** : to be of no use, to be pointless ⟨no estaría por demás : it couldn't hurt, it's worth a try⟩ **3 por demás** : extremely **4 por lo demás** : otherwise **5 y demás** : and so on, et cetera

demasía *nf* **en ~** : excessively, in excess

demasiado[1] *adv* **1** : too ⟨vas demasiado aprisa : you're going too fast⟩ **2** : too much ⟨estoy comiendo demasiado : I'm eating too much⟩

demasiado[2], **-da** *adj* : too much, too many, excessive

demencia *nf* **1** : dementia **2** LOCURA : madness, insanity

demente[1] *adj* : insane, mad

demente[2] *nmf* : insane person

demeritar *vt* **1** : to detract from **2** : to discredit

demérito *nm* **1** : fault **2** : discredit, disrepute

democracia *nf* : democracy

demócrata[1] *adj* : democratic

demócrata[2] *nmf* : democrat

democrático, -ca *adj* : democratic — **democráticamente** *adv*

democratizar {21} *vt* : to democratize, to make democratic

demografía *nf* : demography

demográfico, -ca *adj* : demographic

demoledor, -dora *adj* : devastating

demoler {47} *vt* DERRIBAR, DERRUMBAR : to demolish, to destroy

demolición *nf, pl* **-ciones** : demolition

demonio *nm* DIABLO : devil, demon

demora *nf* : delay

demorar *vt* **1** RETRASAR : to delay **2** TARDAR : to take, to last ⟨la reparación demorará varios días : the repair will take several days⟩ — *vi* : to delay, to linger — **demorarse** *vr* **1** : to be slow, to take a long time **2** : to take too long

demostración *nf, pl* **-ciones** : demonstration

demostrar {19} *vt* : to demonstrate, to show

demostrativo, -va *adj* : demonstrative

demudar *vt* : to change, to alter — **demudarse** *vr* : to change one's expression

denegación *nf, pl* **-ciones** : denial, refusal

denegar {49} *vt* : to deny, to turn down

denigrante *adj* : degrading, humiliating

denigrar *vt* **1** DIFAMAR : to denigrate, to disparage **2** : to degrade, to humiliate

denodado, -da *adj* : bold, dauntless

denominación *nf, pl* **-ciones** **1** : name, designation **2** : denomination (of money)

denominador *nm* : denominator

denominar *vt* : to designate, to name

denostar {19} *vt* : to revile

denotar *vt* : to denote, to show

densidad *nf* : density, thickness

denso, -sa *adj* : dense, thick — **densamente** *adv*

dentado, -da *adj* SERRADO : serrated, jagged

dentadura *nf* **1** : teeth *pl* **2 dentadura postiza** : dentures *pl*

dental *adj* : dental

dentellada *nf* **1** : bite **2** : tooth mark

dentera *nf* **1** : envy, jealousy **2 dar dentera** : to set one's teeth on edge

dentición *nf, pl* **-ciones** **1** : teething **2** : dentition, set of teeth

dentífrico *nm* : toothpaste

dentista *nmf* : dentist

dentro *adv* **1** : in, inside **2** : indoors **3** **~ de** : within, inside, in **4 dentro de poco** : soon, shortly **5 dentro de todo** : all in all, all things considered **6 por ~** : inwardly, inside

denuedo *nm* : valor, courage

denuesto *nm* : insult

denuncia *nf* **1** : denunciation, condemnation **2** : police report

denunciante *nmf* : accuser (of a crime)

denunciar *vt* **1** : to denounce, to condemn **2** : to report (to the authorities)

deparar *vt* : to have in store for, to provide with ⟨no sabemos lo que nos depara el destino : we don't know what fate has in store for us⟩

departamental *adj* **1** : departmental **2 tienda departamental** *Mex* : department store

departamento *nm* **1** : department **2** APARTAMENTO : apartment

departir *vi* : to converse

dependencia *nf* **1** : dependence, dependency ⟨dependencia emocional : emotional dependence⟩ ⟨dependencia del alcohol : dependence on alcohol⟩ **2** : agency, branch office

depender *vi* **1** : to depend **2** **~ de** : to depend on **3** **~ de** : to be subordinate to

dependiente[1] *adj* : dependent

dependiente[2], **-ta** *n* : clerk, salesperson

deplorable *adj* : deplorable

deplorar *vt* **1** : to deplore **2** LAMENTAR : to regret

deponer {60} *vt* **1** : to depose, to overthrow **2** : to abandon (an attitude or stance) **3 deponer las armas** : to lay down one's arms — *vi* **1** TESTIFICAR : to testify, to make a statement **2** EVACUAR : to defecate

deportación *nf, pl* **-ciones** : deportation

deportar *vt* : to deport

deporte *nm* : sport, sports *pl* ⟨hacer deporte : to engage in sports⟩

deportista[1] *adj* **1** : fond of sports **2** : sporty

deportista[2] *nmf* **1** : sports fan **2** : athlete, sportsman *m,* sportswoman *f*

deportividad *nf Spain* : sportsmanship

deportivo, **-va** *adj* **1** : sports, sporting ⟨artículos deportivos : sporting goods⟩ **2** : sporty

deposición *nf, pl* **-ciones** **1** : statement, testimony **2** : removal from office

depositante *nmf* : depositor

depositar *vt* **1** : to deposit, to place **2** : to store — **depositarse** *vr* : to settle

depósito *nm* **1** : deposit **2** : warehouse, storehouse

depravación *nf, pl* **-ciones** : depravity

depravado, **-da** *adj* DEGENERADO : depraved, degenerate

depravar *vt* : to deprave, to corrupt

depreciación *nf, pl* **-ciones** : depreciation

depreciar *vt* : to depreciate, to reduce the value of — **depreciarse** *vr* : to lose value

depredación *nf* SAQUEO : depredation, plunder

depredador[1], **-dora** *adj* : predatory

depredador[2] *nm* **1** : predator **2** SAQUEADOR : plunderer

depresión *nf, pl* **-siones** **1** : depression **2** : hollow, recess **3** : drop, fall **4** : slump, recession

depresivo[1], **-va** *adj* **1** : depressive **2** : depressant

depresivo[2] *nm* : depressant

deprimente *adj* : depressing

deprimir *vt* **1** : to depress **2** : to lower — **deprimirse** *vr* ABATIRSE : to get depressed

depuesto *pp* → **deponer**

depuración *nf, pl* **-ciones** **1** PURIFICACIÓN : purification **2** PURGA : purge **3** : refinement, polish

depurar *vt* **1** PURIFICAR : to purify **2** PURGAR : to purge

depuso, etc. → **deponer**

derecha *nf* **1** : right **2** : right hand, right side **3** : right wing, right (in politics)

derechazo *nm* **1** : pass with the cape on the right hand (in bullfighting) **2** : right (in boxing) **3** : forehand (in tennis)

derechista[1] *adj* : rightist, right-wing

derechista[2] *nmf* : right-winger

derecho[1] *adv* **1** : straight **2** : upright **3** : directly

derecho[2], **-cha** *adj* **1** : right **2** : right-hand **3** RECTO : straight, upright, erect

derecho[3] *nm* **1** : right ⟨derechos humanos : human rights⟩ **2** : law ⟨derecho civil : civil law⟩ **3** : right side (of cloth or clothing)

deriva *nf* **1** : drift **2 a la deriva** : adrift

derivación *nf, pl* **-ciones** **1** : derivation **2** RAMIFICACIÓN : ramification, consequence

derivar *vi* **1** : to drift **2** **~ de** : to come from, to derive from **3** **~ en** : to result in — *vt* : to steer, to direct ⟨derivó la discusión hacia la política : he steered the discussion over to politics⟩ — **derivarse** *vr* : to be derived from, to arise from

dermatología *nf* : dermatology

dermatológico, **-ca** *adj* : dermatological

dermatólogo, **-ga** *n* : dermatologist

derogación *nf, pl* **-ciones** : abolition, repeal

derogar {52} *vt* ABOLIR : to abolish, to repeal

derramamiento *nm* **1** : spilling, overflowing **2 derramamiento de sangre** : bloodshed

derramar *vt* **1** : to spill **2** : to shed (tears, blood) — **derramarse** *vr* **1** : to spill over **2** : to scatter

derrame *nm* **1** : spilling, shedding **2** : leakage, overflow **3** : discharge, hemorrhage

derrapar *vi* : to skid

derrape *nm* : skid

derredor *nm* **al derredor** *or* **en derredor** : around, round about

derrengado, -da *adj* **1** : bent, twisted **2** : exhausted

derretir {54} *vt* : to melt, to thaw — **derretirse** *vr* **1** : to melt, to thaw **2** ~ **por** *fam* : to be crazy about

derribar *vt* **1** DEMOLER, DERRUMBAR : to demolish, to knock down **2** : to shoot down, to bring down (an airplane) **3** DERROCAR : to overthrow

derribo *nm* **1** : demolition, razing **2** : shooting down **3** : overthrow

derrocamiento *nm* : overthrow

derrocar {72} *vt* DERRIBAR : to overthrow, to topple

derrochador[1], **-dora** *adj* : extravagant, wasteful

derrochador[2], **-dora** *n* : spendthrift

derrochar *vt* : to waste, to squander

derroche *nm* : extravagance, waste

derrota *nf* **1** : defeat, rout **2** : course (at sea)

derrotar *vt* : to defeat

derrotero *nm* RUTA : course

derrotista *adj & nmf* : defeatist

derruir {41} *vt* : to demolish, to tear down

derrumbamiento *nm* : collapse

derrumbar *vt* **1** DEMOLER, DERRIBAR : to demolish, to knock down **2** DESPEÑAR : to cast down, to topple — **derrumbarse** *vr* DESPLOMARSE : to collapse, to break down

derrumbe *nm* **1** DESPLOME : collapse, fall ⟨el derrumbe del comunismo : the fall of Communism⟩ **2** : landslide

desabastecimiento *nm* : shortage, scarcity

desabasto *nm Mex* : shortage, scarcity

desabrido, -da *adj* : tasteless, bland

desabrigar {52} *vt* **1** : to undress **2** : to uncover **3** : to deprive of shelter

desabrochar *vt* : to unbutton, to undo — **desabrocharse** *vr* : to come undone

desacatar *vt* **1** DESAFIAR : to defy **2** DESOBEDECER : to disobey

desacato *nm* **1** : disrespect **2** : contempt (of court)

desacelerar *vi* : to decelerate, to slow down

desacertado, -da *adj* **1** : mistaken **2** : unwise

desacertar {55} *vi* ERRAR : to err, to be mistaken

desacierto *nm* ERROR : error, mistake

desaconsejable *adj* : inadvisable

desaconsejado, -da *adj* : ill-advised, unwise

desacorde *adj* **1** : conflicting **2** : discordant

desacostumbrado, -da *adj* : unaccustomed, unusual

desacreditar *vt* DESPRESTIGIAR : to discredit, to disgrace

desactivar *vt* : to deactivate, to defuse

desacuerdo *nm* : disagreement

desafiante *adj* : defiant

desafiar {85} *vt* RETAR : to defy, to challenge

desafilado, -da *adj* : blunt

desafinado, -da *adj* : out-of-tune, off-key

desafinarse *vr* : to go out of tune

desafío *nm* **1** RETO : challenge **2** RESISTENCIA : defiance

desafortunado, -da *adj* : unfortunate, unlucky — **desafortunadamente** *adv*

desafuero *nm* ABUSO : injustice, outrage

desagradable *adj* : unpleasant, disagreeable — **desagradablemente** *adv*

desagradar *vi* : to be unpleasant, to be disagreeable

desagradecido, -da *adj* : ungrateful

desagrado *nm* **1** : displeasure **2 con** ~ : reluctantly

desagravio *nm* **1** : apology **2** : amends, reparation

desagregarse {52} *vr* : to break up, to disintegrate

desaguar {10} *vi* : to drain, to empty

desagüe *nm* **1** : drain **2** : drainage

desahogado, -da *adj* **1** : well-off, comfortable **2** : spacious, roomy

desahogar {52} *vt* **1** : to relieve, to ease **2** : to give vent to — **desahogarse** *vr* **1** : to recover, to feel better **2** : to unburden oneself, to let off steam

desahogo *nm* **1** : relief, outlet **2 con** ~ : comfortably

desahuciar *vt* **1** : to deprive of hope **2** : to evict — **desahuciarse** *vr* : to lose all hope

desahucio *nm* : eviction

desairar {5} *vt* : to snub, to rebuff

desaire *nm* : rebuff, snub, slight

desajustar *vt* **1** : to disarrange, to put out of order **2** : to upset (plans)

desajuste *nm* **1** : maladjustment **2** : imbalance **3** : upset, disruption

desalentador, -dora *adj* : discouraging, disheartening

desalentar {55} *vt* DESANIMAR : to discourage, to dishearten — **desalentarse** *vr*

desaliento *nm* : discouragement

desaliñado, -da *adj* : slovenly, untidy

desalmado, -da *adj* : heartless, callous

desalojar *vt* **1** : to remove, to clear **2** EVACUAR : to evacuate, to vacate **3** : to evict

desalojo *nm* **1** : removal, expulsion **2** : evacuation **3** : eviction

desamor *nm* **1** FRIALDAD : indifference **2** ENEMISTAD : dislike, enmity

desamparado, -da *adj* DESVALIDO : helpless, destitute

desamparar *vt* : to abandon, to forsake

desamparo *nm* **1** : abandonment, neglect **2** : helplessness

desamueblado, -da *adj* : unfurnished

desandar {6} *vt* : to go back, to return to the starting point

desangelado, -da *adj* : dull, lifeless

desangrar *vt* : to bleed, to bleed dry — **desangrarse** *vr* **1** : to be bleeding **2** : to bleed to death

desanimar *vt* DESALENTAR : to discourage, to dishearten — **desanimarse** *vr*
desánimo *nm* DESALIENTO : discouragement, dejection
desanudar *vt* : to untie, to disentangle
desapacible *adj* : unpleasant, disagreeable
desaparecer {53} *vt* : to cause to disappear — *vi* : to disappear, to vanish
desaparecido[1], **-da** *adj* **1** : late, deceased **2** : missing
desaparecido[2], **-da** *n* : missing person
desaparición *nf, pl* **-ciones** : disappearance
desapasionado, -da *adj* : dispassionate, impartial — **desapasionadamente** *adv*
desapego *nm* : coolness, indifference
desapercibido, -da *adj* **1** : unnoticed **2** DESPREVENIDO : unprepared, off guard
desaprobación *nf, pl* **-ciones** : disapproval
desaprobar {19} *vt* REPROBAR : to disapprove of
desaprovechar *vt* MALGASTAR : to waste, to misuse — *vi* : to lose ground, to slip back
desarmador *nm Mex* : screwdriver
desarmar *vt* **1** : to disarm **2** DESMONTAR : to disassemble, to take apart
desarme *nm* : disarmament
desarraigado, -da *adj* : rootless
desarraigar {52} *vt* : to uproot, to root out
desarreglado, -da *adj* : untidy, disorganized
desarreglar *vt* **1** : to mess up **2** : to upset, to disrupt
desarreglo *nm* **1** : untidiness **2** : disorder, confusion
desarrollar *vt* : to develop — **desarrollarse** *vr* : to take place
desarrollo *nm* : development
desarticulación *nf, pl* **-ciones** **1** : dislocation **2** : breaking up, dismantling
desarticular *vt* **1** DISLOCAR : to dislocate **2** : to break up, to dismantle
desaseado, -da *adj* **1** : dirty **2** : messy, untidy
desastre *nm* CATÁSTROFE : disaster
desastroso, -sa *adj* : disastrous, catastrophic
desatar *vt* **1** : to undo, to untie **2** : to unleash **3** : to trigger, to precipitate — **desatarse** *vr* : to break out, to erupt
desatascar {72} *vt* : to unblock, to clear
desatención *nf, pl* **-ciones** **1** : absentmindedness, distraction **2** : discourtesy
desatender {56} *vt* **1** : to disregard **2** : to neglect
desatento, -ta *adj* **1** DISTRAÍDO : absentminded **2** GROSERO : discourteous, rude
desatinado, -da *adj* : foolish, silly
desatino *nm* : folly, mistake
desautorizar {21} *vt* : to deprive of authority, to discredit
desavenencia *nf* DISCORDANCIA : disagreement, dispute
desayunar *vi* : to have breakfast — *vt* : to have for breakfast
desayuno *nm* : breakfast
desazón *nf, pl* **-zones** INQUIETUD : uneasiness, anxiety
desbalance *nm* : imbalance
desbancar {72} *vt* : to displace, to oust
desbandada *nf* : scattering, dispersal
desbarajuste *nm* DESORDEN : disarray, disorder, mess
desbaratar *vt* **1** ARRUINAR : to destroy, to ruin **2** DESCOMPONER : to break, to break down — **desbaratarse** *vr* : to fall apart
desbloquear *vt* **1** : to open up, to clear, to break through **2** : to free, to release
desbocado, -da *adj* : unbridled, rampant
desbocarse {72} *vr* : to run away, to bolt
desbordamiento *nm* : overflowing
desbordante *adj* : overflowing, bursting ⟨desbordante de energía : bursting with energy⟩
desbordar *vt* **1** : to overflow, to spill over **2** : to surpass, to exceed — **desbordarse** *vr*
descabellado, -da *adj* : outlandish, ridiculous
descafeinado, -da *adj* : decaffeinated
descalabrar *vt* : to hit on the head — **descalabrarse** *vr*
descalabro *nm* : setback, misfortune, loss
descalificación *nf, pl* **-ciones** **1** : disqualification **2** : disparaging remark
descalificar {72} *vt* **1** : to disqualify **2** DESACREDITAR : to discredit — **descalificarse** *vr*
descalzarse {21} *vr* : take off one's shoes
descalzo, -za *adj* : barefoot
descansado, -da *adj* **1** : rested, refreshed **2** : restful, peaceful
descansar *vi* : to rest, to relax — *vt* : to rest ⟨descansar la vista : to rest one's eyes⟩
descansillo *nm* : landing (of a staircase)
descanso *nm* **1** : rest, relaxation **2** : break **3** : landing (of a staircase) **4** : intermission
descapotable *adj & nm* : convertible
descarado, -da *adj* : brazen, impudent — **descaradamente** *adv*
descarga *nf* **1** : discharge **2** : unloading
descargar {52} *vt* **1** : to discharge **2** : to unload **3** : to release, to free **4** : to take out, to vent (anger, etc.) — **descargarse** *vr* **1** : to unburden oneself **2** : to quit **3** : to lose power
descargo *nm* **1** : unloading **2** : defense ⟨testigo de descargo : witness for the defense⟩
descarnado, -da *adj* : scrawny, gaunt
descaro *nm* : audacity, nerve

descarriado, **-da** *adj* : lost, gone astray
descarrilar *vi* : to derail — **descarrilarse** *vr*
descartar *vt* : to rule out, to reject — **descartarse** *vr* : to discard
descascarar *vt* : to peel, to shell, to husk — **descascararse** *vr* : to peel off, to chip
descendencia *nf* **1** : descendants *pl* **2** LINAJE : descent, lineage
descendente *adj* : downward, descending
descender {56} *vt* **1** : to descend, to go down **2** BAJAR : to lower, to take down, to let down — *vi* **1** : to descend, to come down **2** : to drop, to fall **3** ~ **de** : to be a descendant of
descendiente *adj & nm* : descendant
descenso *nm* **1** : descent **2** BAJA, CAÍDA : drop, fall
descentralizar {21} *vt* : to decentralize — **descentralizarse** *vr* — **descentralización** *nf*
descifrable *adj* : decipherable
descifrar *vt* : to decipher, to decode
descodificar {72} *vt* : to decode
descolgar {16} *vt* **1** : to take down, to let down **2** : to pick up, to answer (the telephone)
descollar {19} *vi* SOBRESALIR : to stand out, to be outstanding, to excel
descolorarse *vr* : to fade
descolorido, **-da** *adj* : discolored, faded
descomponer {60} *vt* **1** : to rot, to decompose **2** DESBARATAR : to break, to break down — **descomponerse** *vr* **1** : to break down **2** : to decompose
descomposición *nf, pl* **-ciones** **1** : breakdown, decomposition **2** : decay
descompresión *nf* : decompression
descompuesto[1] *pp* → **descomponer**
descompuesto[2], **-ta** *adj* **1** : broken down, out of order **2** : rotten, decomposed
descomunal *adj* **1** ENORME : enormous, huge **2** EXTRAORDINARIO : extraordinary
desconcertante *adj* : disconcerting
desconcertar {55} *vt* : to disconcert — **desconcertarse** *vr*
desconchar *vt* : to chip — **desconcharse** *vr* : to chip off, to peel
desconcierto *nm* : uncertainty, confusion
desconectar *vt* **1** : to disconnect, to switch off **2** : to unplug
desconfiado, **-da** *adj* : distrustful, suspicious
desconfianza *nf* RECELO : distrust, suspicion
desconfiar {85} *vi* ~ **de** : to distrust, to be suspicious of
descongelar *vt* **1** : to thaw **2** : to defrost **3** : to unfreeze (assets — **descongelarse** *vr*
descongestionante *adj & nm* : decongestant
desconocer {18} *vt* **1** IGNORAR : to be unaware of **2** : to fail to recognize
desconocido[1], **-da** *adj* : unknown, unfamiliar
desconocido[2], **-da** *n* EXTRAÑO : stranger
desconocimiento *nm* : ignorance
desconsiderado, **-da** *adj* : inconsiderate, thoughtless — **desconsideradamente** *adj*
desconsolado, **-da** *adj* : disconsolate, heartbroken
desconsuelo *nm* AFLICCIÓN : grief, distress, despair
descontaminar *vt* : to decontaminate — **descontaminación** *nf*
descontar {19} *vt* **1** : to discount, to deduct **2** EXCEPTUAR : to except, to exclude
descontento[1], **-ta** *adj* : discontented, dissatisfied
descontento[2] *nm* : discontent, dissatisfaction
descontrol *nm* : lack of control, disorder, chaos
descontrolarse *vr* : to get out of control, to be out of hand
descorazonado, **-da** *adj* : disheartened, discouraged
descorazonador, **-dora** *adj* : disheartening, discouraging
descorrer *vt* : to draw back
descortés *adj, pl* **-teses** : discourteous, rude
descortesía *nf* : discourtesy, rudeness
descrédito *nm* DESPRESTIGIO : discredit
descremado, **-da** *adj* : nonfat, skim
describir {33} *vt* : to describe
descripción *nf, pl* **-ciones** : description
descriptivo, **-va** *adj* : descriptive
descrito *pp* → **describir**
descuartizar {21} *vt* **1** : to cut up, to quarter **2** : to tear to pieces
descubierto[1] *pp* → **descubrir**
descubierto[2], **-ta** *adj* **1** : exposed, revealed **2** **al descubierto** : out in the open
descubridor, **-dora** *n* : discoverer, explorer
descubrimiento *nm* : discovery
descubrir {2} *vt* **1** HALLAR : to discover, to find out **2** REVELAR : to uncover, to reveal — **descubrirse** *vr*
descuento *nm* REBAJA : discount
descuidado, **-da** *adj* **1** : neglectful, careless **2** : neglected, unkempt
descuidar *vt* : to neglect, to overlook — *vi* : to be careless — **descuidarse** *vr* **1** : to be careless, to drop one's guard **2** : to let oneself go
descuido *nm* **1** : carelessness, negligence **2** : slip, oversight
desde *prep* **1** : from **2** : since **3** **desde ahora** : from now on **4** **desde entonces** : since then **5** **desde hace** : for, since (a time) ‹ha estado nevando desde hace dos días : it's been snowing for

two days⟩ **6 desde luego** : of course **7 desde que** : since, ever since **8 desde ya** : right now, immediately
desdecir {11} *vi* **1 ~ de** : to be unworthy of **2 ~ de** : to clash with — **desdecirse** *vr* **1** CONTRADECIRSE : to contradict oneself **2** RETRACTARSE : to go back on one's word
desdén *nm, pl* **desdenes** DESPRECIO : disdain, scorn
desdentado, -da *adj* : toothless
desdeñar *vt* DESPRECIAR : to disdain, to scorn, to despise
desdeñoso, -sa *adj* : disdainful, scornful — **desdeñosamente** *adv*
desdibujar *vt* : to blur — **desdibujarse** *vr*
desdicha *nf* **1** : misery **2** : misfortune
desdichado[1], **-da** *adj* **1** : unfortunate **2** : miserable, unhappy
desdichado[2], **-da** *n* : wretch
desdicho *pp* → **desdecir**
desdiga, desdijo etc. → **desdecir**
desdoblar *vt* DESPLEGAR : to unfold
deseable *adj* : desirable
desear *vt* **1** : to wish ⟨te deseo buena suerte : I wish you good luck⟩ **2** QUERER : to want, to desire
desecar {72} *vt* : to dry (flowers, etc.)
desechable *adj* : disposable
desechar *vt* **1** : to discard, to throw away **2** RECHAZAR : to reject
desecho *nm* **1** : reject **2 desechos** *nmpl* RESIDUOS : rubbish, waste
desembarazarse {21} *vr* **~ de** : to get rid of
desembarcadero *nm* : jetty, landing pier
desembarcar {72} *vi* : to disembark — *vt* : to unload
desembarco *nm* **1** : landing, arrival **2** : unloading
desembarque → **desembarco**
desembocadura *nf* **1** : mouth (of a river) **2** : opening, end (of a street)
desembocar {72} *vi* **~ en** *or* **~ a 1** : to flow into, to join **2** : to lead to, to result in
desembolsar *vt* PAGAR : to disburse, to pay out
desembolso *nm* PAGO : disbursement, payment
desempacar {72} *v* : to unpack
desempate *nm* : tiebreaker, play-off
desempeñar *vt* **1** : to play (a role) **2** : to fulfill, to carry out **3** : to redeem (from a pawnshop) — **desempeñarse** *vr* : to function, to act
desempeño *nm* **1** : fulfillment, carrying out **2** : performance
desempleado[1], **-da** *adj* : unemployed
desempleado[2], **-da** *n* : unemployed person
desempleo *nm* : unemployment
desempolvar *vt* **1** : to dust off **2** : to resurrect, to revive
desencadenar *vt* **1** : to unchain **2** : to trigger, to unleash — **desencadenarse** *vr*
desencajar *vt* **1** : to dislocate **2** : to disconnect, to disengage
desencantar *vt* : to disenchant, to disillusion — **desencantarse** *vr*
desencanto *nm* : disenchantment, disillusionment
desenchufar *vt* : to disconnect, to unplug
desenfadado, -da *adj* **1** : uninhibited, carefree **2** : confident, self-assured
desenfado *nm* **1** DESENVOLTURA : self-assurance, confidence **2** : naturalness, ease
desenfrenadamente *adv* : wildly, with abandon
desenfrenado, -da *adj* : unbridled, unrestrained
desenfreno *nm* : abandon, unrestraint
desenganchar *vt* : to unhitch, to uncouple
desengañar *vt* : to disillusion, to disenchant — **desengañarse** *vr*
desengaño *nm* : disenchantment, disillusionment
desenlace *nm* : ending, outcome
desenlazar {21} *vt* **1** : to untie **2** : to clear up, to resolve
desenmarañar *vt* : to disentangle, to unravel
desenmascarar *vt* : to unmask, to expose
desenredar *vt* : to untangle, to disentangle
desenrollar *vt* : to unroll, to unwind
desentenderse {56} *vr* **1 ~ de** : to want nothing to do with, to be uninterested in **2 ~ de** : to pretend ignorance of
desenterrar {55} *vt* **1** EXHUMAR : to exhume **2** : to unearth, to dig up
desentonar *vi* **1** : to clash, to conflict **2** : to be out of tune, to sing off-key
desentrañar *vt* : to get to the bottom of, to unravel
desenvainar *vt* : to draw, to unsheathe (a sword)
desenvoltura *nf* **1** DESENFADO : confidence, self-assurance **2** ELOCUENCIA : eloquence, fluency
desenvolver {89} *vt* : to unwrap, to open — **desenvolverse** *vr* **1** : to unfold, to develop **2** : to manage, to cope
desenvuelto[1] *pp* → **desenvolver**
desenvuelto[2], **-ta** *adj* : confident, relaxed, self-assured
deseo *nm* : wish, desire
deseoso, -sa *adj* : eager, anxious
desequilibrar *vt* : to unbalance, to throw off balance — **desequilibrarse** *vr*
desequilibrio *nm* : imbalance
deserción *nf, pl* **-ciones** : desertion, defection
desertar *vi* **1** : to desert, to defect **2 ~ de** : to abandon, to neglect
desertor, -tora *n* : deserter, defector
desesperación *nf, pl* **-ciones** : desperation, despair

desesperado, -da *adj* : desperate, despairing, hopeless — **desesperadamente** *adv*
desesperanza *nf* : despair, hopelessness
desesperar *vt* : to exasperate — *vi* : to despair, to lose hope — **desesperarse** *vr* : to become exasperated
desestimar *vt* **1** : to reject, to disallow **2** : to have a low opinion of
desfachatez *nf, pl* **-teces** : audacity, nerve, cheek
desfalcador, -dora *n* : embezzler
desfalcar {72} *vt* : to embezzle
desfalco *nm* : embezzlement
desfallecer {53} *vi* **1** : to weaken **2** : to faint
desfallecimiento *nm* **1** : weakness **2** : fainting
desfasado, -da *adj* **1** : out of sync **2** : out of step, behind the times
desfase *nm* : gap, lag <desfase horario : jet lag>
desfavorable *adj* : unfavorable, adverse — **desfavorablemente** *adv*
desfavorecido, -da *adj* : underprivileged
desfigurar *vt* **1** : to disfigure, to mar **2** : to distort, to misrepresent
desfiladero *nm* : narrow gorge, defile
desfilar *vi* : to parade, to march
desfile *nm* : parade, procession
desfogar {52} *vt* **1** : to vent **2** *Mex* : to unclog, to unblock — **desfogarse** *vr* : to vent one's feelings, to let off steam
desforestación *nf, pl* **-ciones** : deforestation
desgajar *vt* **1** : to tear off **2** : to break apart — **desgajarse** *vr* : to come apart
desgana *nf* **1** INAPETENCIA : lack of appetite **2** APATÍA : apathy, unwillingness, reluctance
desgano *nm* → **desgana**
desgarbado, -da *adj* : ungainly
desgarrador, -dora *adj* : heartrending, heartbreaking
desgarradura *nf* : tear, rip
desgarrar *vt* **1** : to tear, to rip **2** : to break (one's heart) — **desgarrarse** *vr*
desgarre → **desgarro**
desgarro *nm* : tear
desgarrón *nm, pl* **-rrones** : rip, tear
desgastar *vt* **1** : to use up **2** : to wear away, to wear down
desgaste *nm* : deterioration, wear and tear
desglosar *vt* : to break down, to itemize
desglose *nm* : breakdown, itemization
desgobierno *nm* : anarchy, disorder
desgracia *nf* **1** : misfortune **2** : disgrace **3 por ~** : unfortunately
desgraciadamente *adv* : unfortunately
desgraciado[1], -da *adj* **1** : unfortunate, unlucky **2** : vile, wretched
desgraciado[2], -da *n* : unfortunate person, wretch
desgranar *vt* : to shuck, to shell
deshabitado, -da *adj* : unoccupied, uninhabited
deshacer {40} *vt* **1** : to destroy, to ruin **2** DESATAR : to undo, to untie **3** : to break apart, to crumble **4** : to dissolve, to melt **5** : to break, to cancel — **deshacerse** *vr* **1** : to fall apart, to come undone **2 ~ de** : to get rid of
deshecho[1] *pp* → **deshacer**
deshecho[2], -cha *adj* **1** : destroyed, ruined **2** : devastated, shattered **3** : undone, untied
desheredado, -da *adj* MARGINADO : dispossessed, destitute
desheredar *vt* : to disinherit
deshicieron, etc. → **deshacer**
deshidratar *vt* : to dehydrate — **deshidratación** *nf*
deshielo *nm* : thaw, thawing
deshilachar *vt* : to fray — **deshilacharse** *vr*
deshizo → **deshacer**
deshonestidad *nf* : dishonesty
deshonesto, -ta *adj* : dishonest
deshonra *nf* : dishonor, disgrace
deshonrar *vt* : to dishonor, to disgrace
deshonroso, -sa *adj* : dishonorable, disgraceful
deshuesar *vt* **1** : to pit (a fruit, etc.) **2** : to bone, to debone
deshumanizar {21} *vt* : to dehumanize — **deshumanización** *nf*
desidia *nf* **1** APATÍA : apathy, indolence **2** NEGLIGENCIA : negligence, sloppiness
desierto[1], -ta *adj* : deserted, uninhabited
desierto[2] *nm* : desert
designación *nf, pl* **-ciones** NOMBRAMIENTO : appointment, naming (to an office, etc.)
designar *vt* NOMBRAR : to designate, to appoint, to name
designio *nm* : plan
desigual *adj* **1** : unequal **2** DISPAREJO : uneven
desigualdad *nf* **1** : inequality **2** : unevenness
desilusión *nf, pl* **-siones** DESENCANTO, DESENGAÑO : disillusionment, disenchantment
desilusionar *vt* DESENCANTAR, DESENGAÑAR : to disillusion, to disenchant — **desilusionarse** *vr*
desinfectante *adj & nm* : disinfectant
desinfectar *vt* : to disinfect — **desinfección** *nf*
desinflar *vt* : to deflate — **desinflarse** *vr*
desinhibido, -da *adj* : uninhibited, unrestrained
desintegración *nf, pl* **-ciones** : disintegration
desintegrar *vt* : to disintegrate, to break up — **desintegrarse** *vr*
desinterés *nm* **1** : lack of interest, indifference **2** : unselfishness
desinteresado, -da *adj* GENEROSO : unselfish
desintoxicar {72} *vt* : to detoxify, to detox

desistir *vi* **1** : to desist, to stop **2 ~ de** : to give up, to relinquish
deslave *nm Mex* : landslide
desleal *adj* INFIEL : disloyal — **deslealmente** *adv*
deslealtad *nf* : disloyalty
desleír {66} *vt* : to dilute, to dissolve
desligar {52} *vt* **1** : to separate, to undo **2** : to free (from an obligation) — **desligarse** *vr* **~ de** : to extricate oneself from
deslindar *vt* **1** : to mark the limits of, to demarcate **2** : to define, to clarify
deslinde *nm* : demarcation
desliz *nm, pl* **deslices** : error, mistake, slip <desliz de la lengua : slip of the tongue>
deslizar {21} *vt* **1** : to slide, to slip **2** : to slip in — **deslizarse** *vr* **1** : to slide, to glide **2** : to slip away
deslucido, -da *adj* **1** : unimpressive, dull **2** : faded, dingy, tarnished
deslucir {45} *vt* **1** : to spoil **2** : to fade, to dull, to tarnish **3** : to discredit
deslumbrar *vt* : to dazzle — **deslumbrante** *adj*
deslustrado, -da *adj* : dull, lusterless
deslustrar *vt* : to tarnish, to dull
deslustre *nm* : tarnish
desmán *nm, pl* **desmanes** **1** : outrage, abuse **2** : misfortune
desmandarse *vr* : to behave badly, to get out of hand
desmantelar *vt* DESMONTAR : to dismantle
desmañado, -da *adj* : clumsy, awkward
desmayado, -da *adj* **1** : fainting, weak **2** : dull, pale
desmayar *vi* : to lose heart, to falter — **desmayarse** *vr* DESVANECERSE : to faint, to swoon
desmayo *nm* **1** : faint, fainting **2 sufrir un desmayo** : to faint
desmedido, -da *adj* DESMESURADO : excessive, undue
desmejorar *vt* : to weaken, to make worse — *vi* : to decline (in health), to get worse
desmembramiento *nm* : dismemberment
desmembrar {55} *vt* **1** : to dismember **2** : to break up
desmemoriado, -da *adj* : absentminded, forgetful
desmentido *nm* : denial
desmentir {76} *vt* **1** NEGAR : to deny, to refute **2** CONTRADECIR : to contradict
desmenuzar {21} *vt* **1** : to break down, to scrutinize **2** : to crumble, to shred — **desmenuzarse** *vr*
desmerecer {53} *vt* : to be unworthy of — *vi* **1** : to decline in value **2 ~ de** : to compare unfavorably with
desmesurado, -da *adj* DESMEDIDO : excessive, inordinate — **desmesuradamente** *adv*
desmigajar *vt* : to crumble — **desmigajarse** *vr*
desmilitarizado, -da *adj* : demilitarized
desmontar *vt* **1** : to clear, to level off **2** DESMANTELAR : to dismantle, to take apart — *vi* : to dismount
desmonte *nm* : clearing, leveling
desmoralizador, -dora *adj* : demoralizing
desmoralizar {21} *vt* DESALENTAR : to demoralize, to discourage
desmoronamiento *nm* : crumbling, falling apart
desmoronar *vt* : to wear away, to erode — **desmoronarse** *vr* : to crumble, to deteriorate, to fall apart
desmotadora *nf* : gin, cotton gin
desmovilizar {21} *vt* : to demobilize — **desmovilización** *nf*
desnaturalizar {21} *vt* **1** : to denature **2** : to distort, to alter
desnivel *nm* **1** : disparity, difference **2** : unevenness (of a surface)
desnivelado, -da *adj* **1** : uneven **2** : unbalanced
desnudar *vt* **1** : to undress **2** : to strip, to lay bare — **desnudarse** *vr* : to undress, to strip off one's clothing
desnudez *nf, pl* **-deces** : nudity, nakedness
desnudismo → **nudismo**
desnudista → **nudista**
desnudo[1], **-da** *adj* : nude, naked, bare
desnudo[2] *nm* : nude
desnutrición *nf, pl* **-ciones** MALNUTRICIÓN : malnutrition, undernourishment
desnutrido, -da *adj* MALNUTRIDO : malnourished, undernourished
desobedecer {53} *v* : to disobey
desobediencia *nf* : disobedience — **desobediente** *adj*
desocupación *nf, pl* **-ciones** : unemployment
desocupado, -da *adj* **1** : vacant, empty **2** : free, unoccupied **3** : unemployed
desocupar *vt* **1** : to empty **2** : to vacate, to move out of — **desocuparse** *vr* : to leave, to quit (a job)
desodorante *adj & nm* : deodorant
desolación *nf, pl* **-ciones** : desolation
desolado, -da *adj* **1** : desolate **2** : devastated, distressed
desolador, -dora *adj* **1** : devastating **2** : bleak, desolate
desollar *vt* : to skin, to flay
desorbitado, -da *adj* **1** : excessive, exorbitant **2 con los ojos desorbitados** : with eyes popping out of one's head
desorden *nm, pl* **desórdenes** **1** DESBARAJUSTE : disorder, mess **2** : disorder, disturbance, upset
desordenado, -da *adj* **1** : untidy, messy **2** : disorderly, unruly
desordenar *vt* : to mess up — **desordenarse** *vr* : to get messed up
desorganización *nf, pl* **-ciones** : disorganization
desorganizar {21} *vt* : to disrupt, to disorganize

desorientación *nf, pl* **-ciones** : disorientation, confusion

desorientar *vt* : to disorient, to mislead, to confuse — **desorientarse** *vr* : to become disoriented, to lose one's way

desovar *vi* : to spawn

despachar *vt* **1** : to complete, to conclude **2** : to deal with, to take care of, to handle **3** : to dispatch, to send off **4** *fam* : to finish off, to kill — **despacharse** *vr fam* : to gulp down, to polish off

despacho *nm* **1** : dispatch, shipment **2** OFICINA : office, study

despacio *adv* LENTAMENTE, LENTO : slowly, slow ⟨¡despacio! : take it easy!, easy does it!⟩

desparasitar *vt* : to worm (an animal), to delouse

desparpajo *nm fam* **1** : self-confidence, nerve **2** *CA* : confusion, muddle

desparramar *vt* **1** : to spill, to splatter **2** : to spread, to scatter

despatarrarse *vr* : to sprawl (out)

despavorido, -da *adj* : terrified, horrified

despecho *nm* **1** : spite **2 a despecho de** : despite, in spite of

despectivo, -va *adj* **1** : contemptuous, disparaging **2** : derogatory, pejorative

despedazar {21} *vt* : to cut to pieces, to tear apart

despedida *nf* **1** : farewell, good-bye **2 despedida de soltera** : bridal shower

despedir {54} *vt* **1** : to see off, to show out **2** : to dismiss, to fire **3** EMITIR : to give off, to emit ⟨despedir un olor : to give off an odor⟩ — **despedirse** *vr* : to take one's leave, to say good-bye

despegado, -da *adj* **1** : separated, detached **2** : cold, distant

despegar {52} *vt* : to remove, to detach — *vi* : to take off, to lift off, to blast off

despegue *nm* : takeoff, liftoff

despeinado, -da *adj* : disheveled, tousled ⟨estoy despeinada : my hair's a mess⟩

despeinarse *vr* **1** : to mess up one's hair **2** : to become disheveled ⟨me despeiné : my hair got messed up⟩

despejado, -da *adj* **1** : clear, fair **2** : alert, clear-headed **3** : uncluttered, unobstructed

despejar *vt* **1** : to clear, to free **2** : to clarify — *vi* **1** : to clear up **2** : to punt (in sports)

despeje *nm* **1** : clearing **2** : punt (in sports)

despellejar *vt* : to skin (an animal)

despenalizar {21} *vt* : to legalize — **despenalización** *nf*

despensa *nf* **1** : pantry, larder **2** PROVISIONES : provisions *pl*, supplies *pl*

despeñar *vt* : to hurl down

despepitar *vt* : to seed, to remove the seeds from

desperdiciar *vt* **1** DESAPROVECHAR, MALGASTAR : to waste **2** : to miss, to miss out on

desperdicio *nm* **1** : waste **2 desperdicios** *nmpl* RESIDUOS : refuse, scraps, rubbish

desperdigar {52} *vt* DISPERSAR : to disperse, to scatter

desperfecto *nm* **1** DEFECTO : flaw, defect **2** : damage

despertador *nm* : alarm clock

despertar {55} *vi* : to awaken, to wake up — *vt* **1** : to arouse, to wake **2** EVOCAR : to elicit, to evoke — **despertarse** *vr* : to wake (oneself) up

despiadado, -da *adj* CRUEL : cruel, merciless, pitiless — **despiadadamente** *adv*

despido *nm* : dismissal, layoff

despierto, -ta *adj* **1** : awake, alert **2** LISTO : clever, sharp ⟨con la mente despierta : with a sharp mind⟩

despilfarrador[1], -dora *adj* : extravagant, wasteful

despilfarrador[2], -dora *n* : spendthrift, prodigal

despilfarrar *vt* MALGASTAR : to squander, to waste

despilfarro *nm* : extravagance, wastefulness

despintar *vt* : to strip the paint from — **despintarse** *vr* : to fade, to wash off, to peel off

despistado[1], -da *adj* **1** DISTRAÍDO : absentminded, forgetful **2** CONFUSO : confused, bewildered

despistado[2], -da *n* : scatterbrain, absentminded person

despistar *vt* : to throw off the track, to confuse — **despistarse** *vr*

despiste *nm* **1** : absentmindedness **2** : mistake, slip

desplantador *nm* : garden trowel

desplante *nm* : insolence, rudeness

desplazamiento *nm* **1** : movement, displacement **2** : journey

desplazar {21} *vt* **1** : to replace, to displace **2** TRASLADAR : to move, to shift

desplegar {49} *vt* **1** : to display, to show, to manifest **2** DESDOBLAR : to unfold, to unfurl **3** : to spread (out) **4** : to deploy

despliegue *nm* **1** : display **2** : deployment

desplomarse *vr* **1** : to plummet, to fall **2** DERRUMBARSE : to collapse, to break down

desplome *nm* **1** : fall, drop **2** : collapse

desplumar *vt* : to pluck (a chicken, etc.)

despoblado[1], -da *adj* : uninhabited, deserted

despoblado[2] *nm* : open country, deserted area

despoblar {19} *vt* : to depopulate

despojar *vt* **1** : to strip, to clear **2** : to divest, to deprive — **despojarse** *vr* **1 ~ de** : to remove (clothing) **2 ~ de** : to relinquish, to renounce

despojos *nmpl* **1** : remains, scraps **2** : plunder, spoils
desportilladura *nf* : chip, nick
desportillar *vt* : to chip — **desportillarse** *vr*
desposeer {20} *vt* : to dispossess
déspota *nmf* : despot, tyrant
despotismo *nm* : despotism — **despótico, -ca** *adj*
despotricar {72} *vi* : to rant and rave, to complain excessively
despreciable *adj* **1** : despicable, contemptible **2** : negligible ⟨nada despreciable : not inconsiderable, significant⟩
despreciar *vt* DESDEÑAR, MENOSPRECIAR : to despise, to scorn, to disdain
despreciativo, -va *adj* : scornful, disdainful
desprecio *nm* DESDÉN, MENOSPRECIO : disdain, contempt, scorn
desprender *vt* **1** SOLTAR : to detach, to loosen, to unfasten **2** EMITIR : to emit, to give off — **desprenderse** *vr* **1** : to come off, to come undone **2** : to be inferred, to follow **3** ~ **de** : to part with, to get rid of
desprendido, -da *adj* : generous, unselfish, disinterested
desprendimiento *nm* **1** : detachment **2** GENEROSIDAD : generosity **3 desprendimiento de tierras** : landslide
despreocupación *nf, pl* **-ciones** : indifference, lack of concern
despreocupado, -da *adj* : carefree, easygoing, unconcerned
desprestigiar *vt* DESACREDITAR : to discredit, to disgrace — **desprestigiarse** *vr* : to lose prestige
desprestigio *nm* DESCRÉDITO : discredit, disrepute
desprevenido, -da *adj* DESAPERCIBIDO : unprepared, off guard, unsuspecting
desproporción *nf, pl* **-ciones** : disproportion, disparity
desproporcionado, -da : out of proportion
despropósito *nm* : piece of nonsense, absurdity
desprotegido, -da *adj* : unprotected, vulnerable
desprovisto, -ta *adj* ~ **de** : devoid of, lacking in
después *adv* **1** : afterward, later **2** : then, next **3** ~ **de** : after, next after ⟨después de comer : after eating⟩ **4 después (de) que** : after ⟨después que lo acabé : after I finished it⟩ **5 después de todo** : after all **6 poco después** : shortly after, soon thereafter
despuntado, -da *adj* : blunt, dull
despuntar *vt* : to blunt — *vi* **1** : to dawn **2** : to sprout **3** : to excel, to stand out
desquiciar *vt* **1** : to unhinge (a door) **2** : to drive crazy — **desquiciarse** *vr* : to go crazy
desquitarse *vr* **1** : to get even, to retaliate **2** ~ **con** : to take it out on
desquite *nm* : revenge
desregulación *nf, pl* **-ciones** : deregulation
desregular *vt* : to deregulate
desregularización *nf* → **desregulación**
destacadamente *adv* : outstandingly, prominently
destacado, -da *adj* **1** : outstanding, prominent **2** : stationed, posted
destacamento *nm* : detachment (of troops)
destacar {72} *vt* **1** ENFATIZAR, SUBRAYAR : to emphasize, to highlight, to stress **2** : to station, to post — *vi* : to stand out
destajo *nm* **1** : piecework **2 a** ~ : by the item, by the job
destapador *nm* : bottle opener
destapar *vt* **1** : to open, to take the top off **2** DESCUBRIR : to reveal, to uncover **3** : to unblock, to unclog
destape *nm* : uncovering, revealing
destartalado, -da *adj* : dilapidated, tumbledown
destellar *vi* **1** : to sparkle, to flash, to glint **2** : to twinkle
destello *nm* **1** : flash, sparkle, twinkle **2** : glimmer, hint
destemplado, -da *adj* **1** : out of tune **2** : irritable, out of sorts **3** : unpleasant (of weather)
desteñir {67} *vi* : to run, to fade — **desteñirse** *vr* DESCOLORARSE : to fade
desterrado[1], **-da** *adj* : banished, exiled
desterrado[2], **-da** *n* : exile
desterrar {55} *vt* **1** EXILIAR : to banish, to exile **2** ERRADICAR : to eradicate, to do away with
destetar *vt* : to wean
destiempo *adv* **a** ~ : at the wrong time
destierro *nm* EXILIO : exile
destilación *nf, pl* **-ciones** : distillation
destilador, -dora *n* : distiller
destilar *vt* **1** : to exude **2** : to distill
destilería *nf* : distillery
destinación *nf, pl* **-ciones** DESTINO : destination
destinado, -da *adj* : destined, bound
destinar *vt* **1** : to appoint, to assign **2** ASIGNAR : to earmark, to allot
destinatario, -ria *n* **1** : addressee **2** : payee
destino *nm* **1** : destiny, fate **2** DESTINACIÓN : destination **3** : use **4** : assignment, post
destitución *nf, pl* **-ciones** : dismissal, removal from office
destituir {41} *vt* : to dismiss, to remove from office
destorcer {14} *vt* : to untwist
destornillador *nm* : screwdriver
destornillar *vt* : to unscrew
destrabar *vt* **1** : to untie, to undo, to ease up **2** : to separate
destreza *nf* HABILIDAD : dexterity, skill
destronar *vt* : to depose, to dethrone
destrozado, -da *adj* **1** : ruined, destroyed **2** : devastated, brokenhearted

destrozar {21} *vt* **1** : to smash, to shatter **2** : to destroy, to wreck — **destrozarse** *vr*

destrozo *nm* **1** DAÑO : damage **2** : havoc, destruction

destrucción *nf, pl* **-ciones** : destruction

destructivo, -va *adj* : destructive

destructor[1], **-tora** *adj* : destructive

destructor[2] *nm* : destroyer (ship)

destruir {41} *vt* : to destroy — **destruirse** *vr*

desubicado, -da *adj* **1** : out of place **2** : confused, disoriented

desunión *nf, pl* **-niones** : disunity

desunir *vt* : to split, to divide

desusado, -da *adj* **1** INSÓLITO : unusual **2** OBSOLETO : obsolete, disused, antiquated

desuso *nm* : disuse, obsolescence ⟨caer en desuso : to fall into disuse⟩

desvaído, -da *adj* **1** : pale, washed-out **2** : vague, blurred

desvainar *vt* : to shell

desvalido, -da *adj* DESAMPARADO : destitute, helpless

desvalijar *vt* **1** : to ransack **2** : to rob

desvalorización *nf, pl* **-ciones** **1** DEVALUACIÓN : devaluation **2** : depreciation

desvalorizar {21} *vt* : to devalue

desván *nm, pl* **desvanes** ÁTICO, BUHARDILLA : attic

desvanecer {53} *vt* **1** DISIPAR : to make disappear, to dispel **2** : to fade, to blur — **desvanecerse** *vr* **1** : to vanish, to disappear **2** : to fade **3** DESMAYARSE : to faint, to swoon

desvanecimiento *nm* **1** : disappearance **2** DESMAYO : faint **3** : fading

desvariar {85} *vi* **1** DELIRAR : to be delirious **2** : to rave, to talk nonsense

desvarío *nm* DELIRIO : delirium

desvelado, -da *adj* : sleepless

desvelar *vt* **1** : to keep awake **2** REVELAR : to reveal, to disclose — **desvelarse** *vr* **1** : to stay awake **2** : to do one's utmost

desvelo *nm* **1** : sleeplessness **2 desvelos** *nmpl* : efforts, pains

desvencijado, -da *adj* : dilapidated, rickety

desventaja *nf* : disadvantage, drawback

desventajoso, -sa *adj* : disadvantageous, unfavorable

desventura *nf* INFORTUNIO : misfortune

desventurado, -da *adj* : unfortunate, ill-fated

desvergonzado, -da *adj* : shameless, impudent

desvergüenza *nf* : shamelessness, impudence

desvestir {54} *vt* : to undress — **desvestirse** *vr* : to get undressed

desviación *nf, pl* **-ciones** **1** : deviation, departure **2** : detour, diversion

desviar {85} *vt* **1** : to change the course of, to divert **2** : to turn away, to deflect — **desviarse** *vr* **1** : to branch off **2** APARTARSE : to stray

desvinculación *nf, pl* **-ciones** : dissociation

desvincular *vt* **~ de** : to separate from, to dissociate from — **desvincularse** *vr*

desvío *nm* **1** : diversion, detour **2** : deviation

desvirtuar {3} *vt* **1** : to impair, to spoil **2** : to detract from **3** : to distort, to misrepresent

detalladamente *adv* : in detail, at great length

detallar *vt* : to detail

detalle *nm* **1** : detail **2 al detalle** : retail

detallista[1] *adj* **1** : meticulous **2** : retail

detallista[2] *nmf* **1** : perfectionist **2** : retailer

detección *nf, pl* **-ciones** : detection

detectar *vt* : to detect — **detectable** *adj*

detective *nmf* : detective

detector *nm* : detector ⟨detector de mentiras : lie detector⟩

detención *nf, pl* **-ciones** **1** ARRESTO : detention, arrest **2** : stop, halt **3** : delay, holdup

detener {80} *vt* **1** ARRESTAR : to arrest, to detain **2** PARAR : to stop, to halt **3** : to keep, to hold back — **detenerse** *vr* **1** : to stop **2** : to delay, to linger

detenidamente *adv* : thoroughly, at length

detenimiento *nm* **con ~** : carefully, in detail

detentar *vt* : to hold, to retain

detergente *nm* : detergent

deteriorado, -da *adj* : damaged, worn

deteriorar *vt* ESTROPEAR : to damage, to spoil — **deteriorarse** *vr* **1** : to get damaged, to wear out **2** : to deteriorate, to worsen

deterioro *nm* **1** : deterioration, wear **2** : worsening, decline

determinación *nf, pl* **-ciones** **1** : determination, resolve **2 tomar una determinación** : to make a decision

determinado, -da *adj* **1** : certain, particular **2** : determined, resolute

determinante[1] *adj* : determining, deciding

determinante[2] *nm* : determinant

determinar *vt* **1** : to determine **2** : to cause, to bring about — **determinarse** *vr* : to make up one's mind, to decide

detestar *vt* : to detest — **detestable** *adj*

detonación *nf, pl* **-ciones** : detonation

detonador *nm* : detonator

detonante[1] *adj* : detonating, explosive

detonante[2] *nm* **1** → **detonador** **2** : catalyst, cause

detonar *vi* : to detonate, to explode

detractor, -tora *n* : detractor, critic

detrás *adv* **1** : behind **2 ~ de** : in back of **3 por ~** : from behind

detrimento *nm* : detriment ⟨en detrimento de : to the detriment of⟩

detuvo, etc. → **detener**

deuda *nf* **1** DÉBITO : debt **2 en deuda con** : indebted to
deudo, **-da** *n* : relative
deudor[1], **-dora** *adj* : indebted
deudor[2], **-dora** *n* : debtor
devaluación *nf, pl* **-ciones** DESVALORIZACIÓN : devaluation
devaluar {3} *vt* : to devalue — **devaluarse** *vr* : to depreciate
devanarse *vr* **devanarse los sesos** : to rack one's brains
devaneo *nm* **1** : flirtation, fling **2** : idle pursuit
devastador, **-dora** *adj* : devastating
devastar *vt* : to devastate — **devastación** *nf*
devenir {87} *vi* **1** : to come about **2 ~ en** : to become, to turn into
devoción *nf, pl* **-ciones** : devotion
devolución *nf, pl* **-ciones** REEMBOLSO : return, refund
devolver {89} *vt* **1** : to return, to give back **2** REEMBOLSAR : to refund, to pay back **3** : to vomit, to bring up — *vi* : to vomit, to throw up — **devolverse** *vr* : to return, to come back, to go back
devorar *vt* **1** : to devour **2** : to consume
devoto[1], **-ta** *adj* : devout — **devotamente** *adv*
devoto[2], **-ta** *n* : devotee, admirer
di → **dar, decir**
día *nm* **1** : day ⟨todos los días : every day⟩ **2** : daytime, daylight ⟨de día : by day, in the daytime⟩ ⟨en pleno día : in broad daylight⟩ **3 al día** : up-to-date **4 en su día** : in due time
diabetes *nf* : diabetes
diabético, **-ca** *adj & n* : diabetic
diablillo *nm* : little devil, imp
diablo *nm* DEMONIO : devil
diablura *nf* **1** : prank **2 diabluras** *nfpl* : mischief
diabólico, **-ca** *adj* : diabolical, diabolic, devilish
diaconisa *nf* : deaconess
diácono *nm* : deacon
diacrítico, **-ca** *adj* : diacritic, diacritical
diadema *nf* : diadem, crown
diáfano, **-na** *adj* : diaphanous
diafragma *nm* : diaphragm
diagnosticar {72} *vt* : to diagnose
diagnóstico[1], **-ca** *adj* : diagnostic
diagnóstico[2] *nm* : diagnosis
diagonal *adj & nf* : diagonal — **diagonalmente** *adv*
diagrama *nm* **1** : diagram **2 diagrama de flujo** ORGANIGRAMA : flowchart
dial *nm* : dial (on a radio, etc.)
dialecto *nm* : dialect
dialogar {52} *vi* : to have a talk, to converse
diálogo *nm* : dialogue
diamante *nm* : diamond
diametral *adj* : diametric, diametrical — **diametralmente** *adv*
diámetro *nm* : diameter
diana *nf* **1** : target, bull's-eye **2** *or* **toque de diana** : reveille
diapositiva *nf* : slide, transparency
diario[1] *adv Mex* : every day, daily
diario[2], **-ria** *adj* : daily, everyday — **diariamente** *adv*
diario[3] *nm* **1** : diary **2** PERIÓDICO : newspaper
diarrea *nf* : diarrhea
diatriba *nf* : diatribe, tirade
dibujante *nmf* **1** : draftsman *m*, draftswoman *f* **2** CARICATURISTA : cartoonist
dibujar *vt* **1** : to draw, to sketch **2** : to portray, to depict
dibujo *nm* **1** : drawing **2** : design, pattern **3 dibujos animados** : (animated) cartoons
dicción *nf, pl* **-ciones** : diction
diccionario *nm* : dictionary
dícese → **decir**
dicha *nf* **1** SUERTE : good luck **2** FELICIDAD : happiness, joy
dicho[1] *pp* → **decir**
dicho[2], **-cha** *adj* : said, aforementioned
dicho[3] *nm* DECIR : saying, proverb
dichoso, **-sa** *adj* **1** : blessed **2** FELIZ : happy **3** AFORTUNADO : fortunate, lucky
diciembre *nm* : December
diciendo → **decir**
dictado *nm* : dictation
dictador, **-dora** *n* : dictator
dictadura *nf* : dictatorship
dictamen *nm, pl* **dictámenes** **1** : report **2** : judgment, opinion
dictaminar *vt* : to report — *vi* : to give an opinion, to pass judgment
dictar *vt* **1** : to dictate **2** : to pronounce (a judgment) **3** : to give, to deliver ⟨dictar una conferencia : to give a lecture⟩
dictatorial *adj* : dictatorial
didáctico, **-ca** *adj* : didactic
diecinueve *adj & nm* : nineteen
diecinueveavo[1], **-va** *adj* : nineteenth
diecinueveavo[2] *nm* : nineteenth (fraction)
dieciocho *adj & nm* : eighteen
dieciochoavo[1], **-va** *or* **dieciochavo**, **-va** *adj* : eighteenth
dieciochoavo[2] *or* **dieciochavo** *nm* : eighteenth (fraction)
dieciséis *adj & nm* : sixteen
dieciseisavo[1], **-va** *adj* : sixteenth
dieciseisavo[2] *nm* : sixteenth (fraction)
diecisiete *adj & nm* : seventeen
diecisieteavo[1], **-va** *adj* : seventeenth
diecisieteavo[2] *nm* : seventeenth
diente *nm* **1** : tooth ⟨diente canino : eyetooth, canine tooth⟩ **2** : tusk, fang **3** : prong, tine **4 diente de león** : dandelion
dieron, etc. → **dar**
diesel ['disɛl] *nm* : diesel
diestra *nf* : right hand
diestramente *adv* : skillfully, adroitly
diestro[1], **-tra** *adj* **1** : right **2** : skillful, accomplished
diestro[2] *nm* : bullfighter, matador
dieta *nf* : diet

dietética *nf* : dietetics
dietético, -ca *adj* : dietetic
dietista *nmf* : dietitian
diez *adj & nm, pl* **dieces** : ten
difamación *nf, pl* **-ciones** : defamation, slander
difamar *vt* : to defame, to slander
difamatorio, -ria *adj* : slanderous, defamatory, libelous
diferencia *nf* **1** : difference **2 a diferencia de** : unlike, in contrast to
diferenciación *nf, pl* **-ciones** : differentiation
diferenciar *vt* : to differentiate between, to distinguish — **diferenciarse** *vr* : to differ
diferendo *nm* : dispute, conflict
diferente *adj* DISTINTO : different — **diferentemente** *adv*
diferir {76} *vt* DILATAR, POSPONER : to postpone, to put off — *vi* : to differ
difícil *adj* : difficult, hard
difícilmente *adv* **1** : with difficulty **2** : hardly
dificultad *nf* : difficulty
dificultar *vt* : to make difficult, to obstruct
dificultoso, -sa *adj* : difficult, hard
difteria *nf* : diphtheria
difundir *vt* **1** : to diffuse, to spread out **2** : to broadcast, to spread
difunto, -ta *adj & n* FALLECIDO : deceased
difusión *nf, pl* **-siones 1** : spreading **2** : diffusion (of heat, etc.) **3** : broadcast, broadcasting ⟨los medios de difusión : the media⟩
difuso, -sa *adj* : diffuse, widespread
diga, etc. → **decir**
digerir {76} *vt* : to digest — **digerible** *adj*
digestión *nf, pl* **-tiones** : digestion
digestivo, -va *adj* : digestive
digital[1] *adj* : digital — **digitalmente** *adv*
digital[2] *nf* **1** DEDALERA : foxglove **2** : digitalis
dígito *nm* : digit
dignarse *vr* : to deign, to condescend ⟨no se dignó contestar : he didn't deign to answer⟩
dignatario, -ria *n* : dignitary
dignidad *nf* **1** : dignity **2** : dignitary
dignificar {72} *vt* : to dignify
digno, -na *adj* **1** HONORABLE : honorable **2** : worthy — **dignamente** *adv*
digresión *nf, pl* **-ciones** : digression
dije *nm* : charm (on a bracelet)
dijo, etc. → **decir**
dilación *nf, pl* **-ciones** : delay
dilapidar *vt* : to waste, to squander
dilatar *vt* **1** : to dilate, to widen, to expand **2** DIFERIR, POSPONER : to put off, to postpone — **dilatarse** *vr* **1** : to expand (of gases, metals, etc.) **2** *Mex* : to take long, to be long
dilatorio, -ria *adj* : dilatory, delaying
dilema *nm* : dilemma
diletante *nmf* : dilettante
diligencia *nf* **1** : diligence, care **2** : promptness, speed **3** : action, step **4** : task, errand **5** : stagecoach **6 diligencias** *nfpl* : judicial procedures, formalities
diligente *adj* : diligent — **diligentemente** *adv*
dilucidar *vt* : to elucidate, to clarify
dilución *nf, pl* **-ciones** : dilution
diluir {41} *vt* : to dilute
diluviar *v impers* : to pour (with rain), to pour down
diluvio *nm* **1** : flood **2** : downpour
dimensión *nf, pl* **-siones** : dimension — **dimensional** *adj*
dimensionar *vt* : to measure, to gauge
diminutivo[1], **-va** *adj* : diminutive
diminutivo[2] *nm* : diminutive
diminuto, -ta *adj* : minute, tiny
dimisión *nf, pl* **-siones** : resignation
dimitir *vi* : to resign, to step down
dimos → **dar**
dinámica *nf* : dynamics
dinámico, -ca *adj* : dynamic — **dinámicamente** *adv*
dinamismo *nm* : energy, vigor
dinamita *nf* : dynamite
dinamitar *vt* : to dynamite
dínamo *or* **dinamo** *nm* : dynamo
dinastía *nf* : dynasty
dineral *nm* : fortune, large sum of money
dinero *nm* : money
dinosaurio *nm* : dinosaur
dintel *nm* : lintel
dio, etc. → **dar**
diocesano, -na *adj* : diocesan
diócesis *nfs & pl* : diocese
dios, diosa *n* : god, goddess *f*
Dios *nm* : God
diploma *nm* : diploma
diplomacia *nf* : diplomacy
diplomado[1], **-da** *adj* : qualified, trained
diplomado[2] *nm Mex* : seminar
diplomático[1], **-ca** *adj* : diplomatic — **diplomáticamente** *adv*
diplomático[2], **-ca** *n* : diplomat
diptongo *nm* : diphthong
diputación *nf, pl* **-ciones** : deputation, delegation
diputado, -da *n* : delegate, representative
dique *nm* : dike
dirá, etc. → **decir**
dirección *nf, pl* **-ciones 1** : address **2** : direction **3** : management, leadership **4** : steering (of an automobile)
direccional[1] *adj* : directional
direccional[2] *nf* : directional, turn signal
directa *nf* : high gear
directamente *adv* : straight, directly
directiva *nf* **1** ORDEN : directive **2** DIRECTORIO, JUNTA : board of directors
directivo[1], **-va** *adj* : executive, managerial
directivo[2], **-va** *n* : executive, director
directo, -ta *adj* **1** : direct, straight, immediate **2 en ~** : live (in broadcasting)

director, -tora *n* **1** : director, manager, head **2** : conductor (of an orchestra)
directorial *adj* : managing, executive
directorio *nm* **1** : directory **2** DIRECTIVA, JUNTA : board of directors
directriz *nf, pl* **-trices** : guideline
dirigencia *nf* : leaders *pl,* leadership
dirigente[1] *adj* : directing, leading
dirigente[2] *nmf* : director, leader
dirigible *nm* : dirigible, blimp
dirigir {35} *vt* **1** : to direct, to lead **2** : to address **3** : to aim, to point **4** : to conduct (music) — **dirigirse** *vr* ~ **a 1** : to go towards **2** : to speak to, to address
dirimir *vt* **1** : to resolve, to settle **2** : to annul, to dissolve (a marriage)
discapacidad *nf* MINUSVALÍA : disability, handicap
discapacitado[1], **-da** *adj* : disabled, handicapped
discapacitado[2], **-da** *n* : disabled person, handicapped person
discar {72} *v* : to dial
discernimiento *nm* : discernment
discernir {25} *v* : to discern, to distinguish
disciplina *nf* : discipline
disciplinar *vt* : to discipline — **disciplinario, -ria** *adj*
discípulo, -la *n* : disciple, follower
disc jockey [ˌdiskˈjoke, -ˈʤo-] *nmf* : disc jockey
disco *nm* **1** : phonograph record **2** : disc, disk ⟨disco compacto : compact disc⟩ **3** : discus
díscolo, -la *adj* : unruly, disobedient
disconforme *adj* : in disagreement
discontinuidad *nf* : discontinuity
discontinuo, -nua *adj* : discontinuous
discordancia *nf* DESAVENENCIA : conflict, disagreement
discordante *adj* **1** : discordant **2** : conflicting
discordia *nf* : discord
discoteca *nf* **1** : disco, discotheque **2** *CA, Mex* : record store
discreción *nf, pl* **-ciones** : discretion
discrecional *adj* : discretionary
discrepancia *nf* : discrepancy
discrepar *vi* **1** : to disagree **2** : to differ
discreto, -ta *adj* : discreet — **discretamente** *adv*
discriminación *nf, pl* **-ciones** : discrimination
discriminar *vt* **1** : to discriminate against **2** : to distinguish, to differentiate
discriminatorio, -ria *adj* : discriminatory
disculpa *nf* **1** : apology **2** : excuse
disculpable *adj* : excusable
disculpar *vt* : to excuse, to pardon — **disculparse** *vr* : to apologize
discurrir *vi* **1** : to flow **2** : to pass, to go by **3** : to ponder, to reflect
discurso *nm* **1** ORACIÓN : speech, address **2** : discourse, treatise
discusión *nf, pl* **-siones 1** : discussion **2** ALTERCADO, DISPUTA : argument
discutible *adj* : arguable, debatable
discutidor, -dora *adj* : argumentative
discutir *vt* **1** : to discuss **2** : to dispute — *vi* ALTERCAR : to argue, to quarrel
disecar {72} *vt* **1** : to dissect **2** : to stuff (for preservation)
disección *nf, pl* **-ciones** : dissection
diseminación *nf, pl* **-ciones** : dissemination, spreading
diseminar *vt* : to disseminate, to spread
disensión *nf, pl* **-siones** : dissension, disagreement
disentería *nf* : dysentery
disentir {76} *vi* : to dissent, to disagree
diseñador, -dora *n* : designer
diseñar *vt* **1** : to design, to plan **2** : to lay out, to outline
diseño *nm* : design
disentimiento *nm* : dissent
disertación *nf, pl* **-ciones 1** : lecture, talk **2** : dissertation
disertar *vi* : to lecture, to give a talk
disfraz *nm, pl* **disfraces 1** : disguise **2** : costume **3** : front, pretense
disfrazar {21} *vt* **1** : to disguise **2** : to mask, to conceal — **disfrazarse** *vr* : to wear a costume, to be in disguise
disfrutar *vt* : to enjoy — *vi* : to enjoy oneself, to have a good time
disfrute *nm* : enjoyment
disfunción *nf, pl* **-ciones** : dysfunction — **disfuncional** *adj*
disgresión → **digresión**
disgustar *vt* : to upset, to displease, to make angry — **disgustarse** *vr*
disgusto *nm* **1** : annoyance, displeasure **2** : argument, quarrel **3** : trouble, misfortune
disidencia *nf* : dissidence, dissent
disidente *adj & nmf* : dissident
disímbolo, -la *adj Mex* : dissimilar
disímil *adj* : dissimilar
disimulado, -da *adj* **1** : concealed, disguised **2** : furtive, sly
disimular *vi* : to dissemble, to pretend — *vt* : to conceal, to hide
disimulo *nm* **1** : dissembling, pretense **2** : slyness, furtiveness **3** : tolerance
disipar *vt* **1** : to dissipate, to dispel **2** : to squander — **disiparse** *vr*
diskette [diˈskɛt] *nm* : floppy disk, diskette
dislocar {72} *vt* : to dislocate — **dislocación** *nf*
disminución *nf, pl* **-ciones** : decrease, drop, fall
disminuir {41} *vt* REDUCIR : to reduce, to decrease, to lower — *vi* **1** : to lower **2** : to drop, to fall
disociación *nf, pl* **-ciones** : dissociation
disociar *vt* : to dissociate, to separate
disolución *nf, pl* **-ciones 1** : dissolution, dissolving **2** : breaking up **3** : dissipation
disoluto, -ta *adj* : dissolute, dissipated

disolver {89} *vt* **1** : to dissolve **2** : to break up — **disolverse** *vr*
disonancia *nf* : dissonance — **disonante** *adj*
dispar *adj* **1** : different, disparate **2** DIVERSO : diverse **3** DESIGUAL : inconsistent
disparado, -da *adj* **salir disparado** *fam* : to take off in a hurry, to rush away
disparar *vi* **1** : to shoot, to fire **2** *Mex fam* : to pay — *vt* **1** : to shoot **2** *Mex fam* : to treat to, to buy — **dispararse** *vr* : to shoot up, to skyrocket
disparatado, -da *adj* ABSURDO, RIDÍCULO : absurd, ridiculous, crazy
disparate *nm* : silliness, stupidity ⟨decir disparates : to talk nonsense⟩
disparejo, -ja *adj* DESIGUAL : uneven
disparidad *nf* : disparity
disparo *nm* TIRO : shot
dispendio *nm* : wastefulness, extravagance
dispendioso, -sa *adj* : wasteful, extravagant
dispensa *nf* : dispensation
dispensable *adj* **1** : dispensable **2** : excusable
dispensar *vt* **1** : to dispense, to give, to grant **2** EXCUSAR : to excuse, to forgive **3** EXIMIR : to exempt
dispensario *nm* **1** : dispensary, clinic **2** *Mex* : dispenser
dispersar *vt* DESPERDIGAR : to disperse, to scatter
dispersión *nf, pl* **-siones** : dispersion
disperso, -sa *adj* : dispersed, scattered
displicencia *nf* : indifference, coldness, disdain
displicente *adj* : indifferent, cold, disdainful
disponer {60} *vt* **1** : to arrange, to lay out **2** : to stipulate, to order **3** : to prepare — *vi* **~ de** : to have at one's disposal — **disponerse** *vr* **~ a** : to prepare to, to be about to
disponibilidad *nf* : availability
disponible *adj* : available
disposición *nf, pl* **-ciones** **1** : disposition **2** : aptitude, talent **3** : order, arrangement **4** : willingness, readiness **5 última disposición** : last will and testament
dispositivo *nm* **1** APARATO, MECANISMO : device, mechanism **2** : force, detachment
dispuesto[1] *pp* → **disponer**
dispuesto[2], **-ta** *adj* PREPARADO : ready, prepared, disposed
dispuso, etc. → **disponer**
disputa *nf* ALTERCADO, DISCUSIÓN : dispute, argument
disputar *vi* : to argue, to contend, to vie — *vt* : to dispute, to question — **disputarse** *vr* : to be in competition for ⟨se disputan la corona : they're fighting for the crown⟩
disquera *nf* : record label, recording company
disquete → **diskette**
disquisición *nf, pl* **-ciones** **1** : formal discourse **2 disquisiciones** *nfpl* : digressions
distancia *nf* : distance
distanciamiento *nm* **1** : distancing **2** : rift, estrangement
distanciar *vt* **1** : to space out **2** : to draw apart — **distanciarse** *vr* : to grow apart, to become estranged
distante *adj* **1** : distant, far-off **2** : aloof
distar *vi* **~ de** : to be far from ⟨dista de ser perfecto : he is far from perfect⟩
diste → **dar**
distender {56} *vt* : to distend, to stretch
distensión *nf, pl* **-siones** : distension
distinción *nf, pl* **-ciones** : distinction
distinguible *adj* : distinguishable
distinguido, -da *adj* : distinguished, refined
distinguir {26} *vt* **1** : to distinguish **2** : to honor — **distinguirse** *vr*
distintivo, -va *adj* : distinctive, distinguishing
distinto, -ta *adj* **1** DIFERENTE : different **2** CLARO : distinct, clear, evident
distorsión *nf, pl* **-siones** : distortion
distorsionar *vt* : to distort
distracción *nf, pl* **-ciones** **1** : distraction, amusement **2** : forgetfulness **3** : oversight
distraer {81} *vt* **1** : to distract **2** ENTRETENER : to entertain, to amuse — **distraerse** *vr* **1** : to get distracted **2** : to amuse oneself
distraídamente *adv* : absentmindedly
distraído[1] *pp* → **distraer**
distraído[2], **-da** *adj* **1** : distracted, preoccupied **2** DESPISTADO : absentminded
distribución *nf, pl* **-ciones** : distribution
distribuidor, -dora *n* : distributor
distribuir {41} *vt* : to distribute
distributivo, -va *adj* : distributive
distrital *adj* : district, of the district
distrito *nm* : district
distrofia *nf* : dystrophy ⟨distrofia muscular : muscular dystrophy⟩
disturbio *nm* : disturbance
disuadir *vt* : to dissuade, to discourage
disuasión *nf, pl* **-siones** : dissuasion
disuasivo, -va *adj* : deterrent, discouraging
disuasorio, -ria *adj* : discouraging
disuelto *pp* → **disolver**
disyuntiva *nf* : dilemma
DIU [ˈdiu] *nm* (*d*ispositivo *i*ntra*u*terino) : IUD, intrauterine device
diurético[1], **-ca** *adj* : diuretic
diurético[2] *nm* : diuretic
diurno, -na *adj* : day, daytime
diva *nf* → **divo**
divagar {52} *vi* : to digress
diván *nm, pl* **divanes** : divan
divergencia *nf* : divergence, difference
divergente *adj* : divergent, differing
divergir {35} *vi* **1** : to diverge **2** : to differ, to disagree

diversidad *nf* : diversity, variety
diversificación *nf, pl* **-ciones** : diversification
diversificar {72} *vt* : to diversify
diversión *nf, pl* **-siones** ENTRETENIMIENTO : fun, amusement, diversion
diverso, **-sa** *adj* : diverse, various
divertido, **-da** *adj* **1** : amusing, funny **2** : entertaining, enjoyable
divertir {76} *vt* ENTRETENER : to amuse, to entertain — **divertirse** *vr* : to have fun, to have a good time
dividendo *nm* : dividend
dividir *vt* **1** : to divide, to split **2** : to distribute, to share out — **dividirse** *vr*
divieso *nm* : boil
divinidad *nf* : divinity
divino, **-na** *adj* : divine
divisa *nf* **1** : currency **2** LEMA : motto **3** : emblem, insignia
divisar *vt* : to discern, to make out
divisible *adj* : divisible
división *nf, pl* **-siones** : division
divisionismo *nm* : factionalism
divisivo, **-va** *adj* : divisive
divisor *nm* : denominator
divisorio, **-ria** *adj* : dividing
divo, **-va** *n* **1** : prima donna **2** : celebrity, star
divorciado[1], **-da** *adj* **1** : divorced **2** : split, divided
divorciado[2], **-da** *n* : divorcé *m*, divorcée *f*
divorciar *vt* : to divorce — **divorciarse** *vr* : to get a divorce
divorcio *nm* : divorce
divulgación *nf, pl* **-ciones** **1** : spreading, dissemination **2** : popularization
divulgar {52} *vt* **1** : to spread, to circulate **2** REVELAR : to divulge, to reveal **3** : to popularize — **divulgarse** *vr*
dizque *adv* : supposedly, apparently
dobladillar *vt* : to hem
dobladillo *nm* : hem
doblar *vt* **1** : to double **2** PLEGAR : to fold, to bend **3** : to turn ⟨doblar la esquina : to turn the corner⟩ **4** : to dub — *vi* **1** : to turn **2** : to toll, to ring — **doblarse** *vr* **1** : to fold up, to double over **2** : to give in, to yield
doble[1] *adj* : double — **doblemente** *adv*
doble[2] *nm* **1** : double **2** : toll (of a bell), knell
doble[3] *nmf* : stand-in, double
doblegar {52} *vt* **1** : to fold, to crease **2** : to force to yield — **doblegarse** *vr* : to yield, to bow
doblez[1] *nm, pl* **dobleces** : fold, crease
doblez[2] *nmf* : duplicity, deceitfulness
doce *adj & nm* : twelve
doceavo[1], **-va** *adj* : twelfth
doceavo[2] *nm* : twelfth (fraction)
docena *nf* **1** : dozen **2 docena de fraile** : baker's dozen
docencia *nf* : teaching
docente[1] *adj* : educational, teaching
docente[2] *n* : teacher, lecturer
dócil *adj* : docile — **dócilmente** *adv*
docilidad *nf* : docility
docto, **-ta** *adj* : learned, erudite
doctor, **-tora** *n* : doctor
doctorado *nm* : doctorate
doctrina *nf* : doctrine — **doctrinal** *adj*
documentación *nf, pl* **-ciones** : documentation
documental *adj & nm* : documentary
documentar *vt* : to document
documento *nm* : document
dogma *nm* : dogma
dogmático, **-ca** *adj* : dogmatic
dogmatismo *nm* : dogmatism
dólar *nm* : dollar
dolencia *nf* : ailment, malaise
doler {47} *vi* **1** : to hurt, to ache **2** : to grieve — **dolerse** *vr* **1** : to be distressed **2** : to complain
doliente *nmf* : mourner, bereaved
dolor *nm* **1** : pain, ache ⟨dolor de cabeza : headache⟩ **2** PENA, TRISTEZA : grief, sorrow
dolorido, **-da** *adj* **1** : sore, aching **2** : hurt, upset
doloroso, **-sa** *adj* **1** : painful **2** : distressing — **dolorosamente** *adv*
doloso, **-sa** *adj* : fraudulent — **dolosamente** *adv*
domador, **-dora** *n* : tamer
domar *vt* : to tame, to break in
domesticado, **-da** *adj* : domesticated, tame
domesticar {72} *vt* : to domesticate, to tame
doméstico, **-ca** *adj* : domestic, household
domiciliado, **-da** *adj* : residing
domiciliario, **-ria** *adj* **1** : home **2 arresto domiciliario** : house arrest
domiciliarse *vr* RESIDIR : to reside
domicilio *nm* : home, residence ⟨cambio de domicilio : change of address⟩
dominación *nf, pl* **-ciones** : domination
dominancia *nf* : dominance
dominante *adj* **1** : dominant **2** : domineering
dominar *vt* **1** : to dominate **2** : to master, to be proficient at — *vi* : to predominate, to prevail — **dominarse** *vr* : to control oneself
domingo *nm* : Sunday
dominical *adj* : Sunday ⟨periódico dominical : Sunday newspaper⟩
dominicano, **-na** *adj & n* : Dominican
dominio *nm* **1** : dominion, power **2** : mastery **3** : domain, field
dominó *nm, pl* **-nós** **1** : domino (tile) **2** : dominoes *pl* (game)
domo *nm* : dome
don[1] *nm* **1** : gift, present **2** : talent
don[2] *nm* **1** : title of courtesy preceding a man's first name **2 don nadie** : nobody, insignificant person
dona *nf Mex* : doughnut, donut
donación *nf, pl* **-ciones** : donation
donador, **-dora** *n* : donor
donaire *nm* **1** GARBO : grace, poise **2** : witticism

donante *nf* → **donador**
donar *vt* : to donate
donativo *nm* : donation
doncella *nf* : maiden, damsel
doncellez *nf* : maidenhood
donde[1] *conj* : where, in which ⟨el pueblo donde vivo : the town where I live⟩
donde[2] *prep* : over by ⟨lo encontré donde la silla : I found it over by the chair⟩
dónde *adv* : where ⟨¿dónde está su casa? : where is your house?⟩
dondequiera *adv* **1** : anywhere, no matter where **2 dondequiera que** : wherever, everywhere
doña *nf* : title of courtesy preceding a woman's first name
doquier *adv* **por ～** : everywhere, all over
dorado[1], **-da** *adj* : gold, golden
dorado[2], **-da** *nm* : gilt
dorar *vt* **1** : to gild **2** : to brown (food)
dormido, -da *adj* **1** : asleep **2** : numb ⟨tiene el pie dormido : her foot's numb, her foot's gone to sleep⟩
dormilón, -lona *n* : sleepyhead, late riser
dormir {27} *vt* : to put to sleep — *vi* : to sleep — **dormirse** *vr* : to fall asleep
dormitar *vi* : to snooze, to doze
dormitorio *nm* **1** : bedroom **2** : dormitory
dorsal[1] *adj* : dorsal
dorsal[2] *nm* : number (worn in sports)
dorso *nm* **1** : back ⟨el dorso de la mano : the back of the hand⟩ **2** *Mex* : backstroke
dos *adj & nm* : two
doscientos[1], **-tas** *adj* : two hundred
doscientos[2] *nms & pl* : two hundred
dosel *nm* : canopy
dosificación *nf, pl* **-ciones** : dosage
dosis *nfs & pl* **1** : dose **2** : amount, quantity
dossier *nm* : dossier
dotación *nf, pl* **-ciones 1** : endowment, funding **2** : staff, personnel
dotado, -da *adj* **1** : gifted **2 ～ de** : endowed with, equipped with
dotar *vt* **1** : to provide, to equip **2** : to endow
dote *nf* **1** : dowry **2 dotes** *nfpl* : talent, gift
doy → **dar**
draga *nf* : dredge
dragado *nm* : dredging
dragar {52} *vt* : to dredge
dragón *nm, pl* **dragones 1** : dragon **2** : snapdragon
drague, etc. → **dragar**
drama *nm* : drama
dramático, -ca *adj* : dramatic — **dramáticamente** *adv*
dramatizar {21} *vt* : to dramatize — **dramatización** *nf*
dramaturgo, -ga *n* : dramatist, playwright
drástico, -ca *adj* : drastic — **drásticamente** *adv*
drenaje *nm* : drainage
drenar *vt* : to drain
drene *nm Mex* : drain
driblar *vi* : to dribble (in basketball)
drible *nm* : dribble (in basketball)
droga *nf* : drug
drogadicción *nf, pl* **-ciones** : drug addiction
drogadicto, -ta *n* : drug addict
drogar {52} *vt* : to drug — **drogarse** *vr* : to take drugs
drogue, etc. → **drogar**
droguería *nf* FARMACIA : drugstore
dromedario *nm* : dromedary
dual *adj* : dual
dualidad *nf* : duality
dualismo *nm* : dualism
ducha *nf* : shower ⟨darse una ducha : to take a shower⟩
ducharse *vr* : to take a shower
ducho, -cha *adj* : experienced, skilled, expert
dúctil *adj* : ductile
ducto *nm* **1** : duct, shaft **2** : pipeline
duda *nf* : doubt ⟨no cabe duda : there's no doubt about it⟩
dudar *vt* : to doubt — *vi* **～ en** : to hesitate to ⟨no dudes en pedirme ayuda : don't hesitate to ask me for help⟩
dudoso, -sa *adj* **1** : doubtful **2** : dubious, questionable — **dudosamente** *adv*
duele, etc. → **doler**
duelo *nm* **1** : duel **2** LUTO : mourning
duende *nm* **1** : elf, goblin **2** ENCANTO : magic, charm ⟨una bailarina que tiene duende : a dancer with a certain magic⟩
dueño, -ña *n* **1** : owner, proprietor, proprietress *f* **2** : landlord, landlady *f*
duerme, etc. → **dormir**
dueto *nm* : duet
dulce[1] *adv* : sweetly, softly
dulce[2] *adj* **1** : sweet **2** : mild, gentle, mellow — **dulcemente** *adv*
dulce[3] *nm* : candy, sweet
dulcería *nf* : candy store
dulcificante *nm* : sweetener
dulzura *nf* **1** : sweetness **2** : gentleness, mellowness
duna *nf* : dune
dúo *nm* : duo, duet
duodécimo[1], **-ma** *adj* : twelfth
duodécimo[2], **-ma** *nm* : twelfth (in a series)
dúplex *nms & pl* : duplex apartment
duplicación *nf, pl* **-ciones** : duplication, copying
duplicado *nm* : duplicate, copy
duplicar {72} *vt* **1** : to double **2** : to duplicate, to copy
duplicidad *nf* : duplicity
duque *nm* : duke
duquesa *nf* : duchess
durabilidad *nf* : durability
durable → **duradero**

duración *nf, pl* **-ciones** : duration, length
duradero, -ra *adj* : durable, lasting
duramente *adv* **1** : harshly, severely **2** : hard
durante *prep* : during ⟨durante todo el día : all day long⟩ ⟨trabajó durante tres horas : he worked for three hours⟩
durar *vi* : to last, to endure
durazno *nm* **1** : peach **2** : peach tree
dureza *nf* **1** : hardness, toughness **2** : severity, harshness
durmiente[1] *adj* : sleeping
durmiente[2] *nmf* : sleeper
durmió, etc. → **dormir**
duro[1] *adv* : hard ⟨trabajé tan duro : I worked so hard⟩
duro[2], **-ra** *adj* **1** : hard, tough **2** : harsh, severe

E

e[1] *nf* : fifth letter of the Spanish alphabet
e[2] *conj (used instead of* **y** *before words beginning with i- or hi-)* : and
ebanista *nmf* : cabinetmaker
ebanistería *nf* : cabinetmaking
ébano *nm* : ebony
ebriedad *nf* EMBRIAGUEZ : inebriation, drunkenness
ebrio, -bria *adj* EMBRIAGADO : inebriated, drunk
ebullición *nf, pl* **-ciones** : boiling
eccéntrico → **excéntrico**
echar *vt* **1** LANZAR : to throw, to cast, to hurl **2** EXPULSAR : to throw out, to expel **3** EMITIR : to emit, give off **4** BROTAR : to sprout, to put forth **5** DESPEDIR : to fire, to dismiss **6** : to put in, to add **7 echar a perder** : to spoil, to ruin **8 echar de menos** : to miss ⟨echan de menos a su madre : they miss their mother⟩ — *vi* **1** : to start off **2 ∼ a** : to begin to — **echarse** *vr* **1** : to throw oneself **2** : to lie down **3** : to put on **4 ∼ a** : to start to **5 echarse a perder** : to go bad, to spoil **6 echárselas de** : to pose as
ecléctico, -ca *adj* : eclectic
eclesiástico[1], **-ca** *adj* : ecclesiastical, ecclesiastic
eclesiástico[2] *nm* CLÉRIGO : cleric, clergyman
eclipsar *vt* **1** : to eclipse **2** : to outshine, to surpass
eclipse *nm* : eclipse
eco *nm* : echo
ecografía *nf* : ultrasound scanning
ecología *nf* : ecology
ecológico, -ca *adj* : ecological — **ecológicamente** *adv*
ecologista *nmf* : ecologist, environmentalist
ecólogo, -ga *n* : ecologist
economía *nf* **1** : economy **2** : economics
económicamente *adv* : financially
económico, -ca *adj* : economic, economical
economista *nmf* : economist
economizar {21} *vt* : to save, to economize on — *vi* : to save up, to be frugal
ecosistema *nm* : ecosystem
ecuación *nf, pl* **-ciones** : equation
ecuador *nm* : equator
ecuánime *adj* **1** : even-tempered **2** : impartial
ecuanimidad *nf* **1** : equanimity **2** : impartiality
ecuatorial *adj* : equatorial
ecuatoriano, -na *adj & n* : Ecuadorian
ecuestre *adj* : equestrian
ecuménico, -ca *adj* : ecumenical
eczema *nm* : eczema
edad *nf* **1** : age ⟨¿qué edad tiene? : how old is she?⟩ **2** ÉPOCA, ERA : epoch, era
edema *nm* : edema
Edén *nm, pl* **Edenes** : Eden, paradise
edición *nf, pl* **-ciones 1** : edition **2** : publication, publishing
edicto *nm* : edict, proclamation
edificación *nf, pl* **-ciones 1** : edification **2** : construction, building
edificante *adj* : edifying
edificar {72} *vt* **1** : to edify **2** CONSTRUIR : to build, to construct
edificio *nm* : building, edifice
editar *vt* **1** : to edit **2** PUBLICAR : to publish
editor[1], **-tora** *adj* : publishing ⟨casa editora : publishing house⟩
editor[2], **-tora** *n* **1** : editor **2** : publisher
editora *nf* : publisher, publishing company
editorial[1] *adj* **1** : publishing **2** : editorial
editorial[2] *nm* : editorial
editorial[3] *nf* : publishing house
editorializar {21} *vi* : to editorialize
edredón *nm, pl* **-dones** COBERTOR, COLCHA : comforter, eiderdown, quilt
educable *adj* : educable, teachable
educación *nf, pl* **-ciones 1** ENSEÑANZA : education **2** : manners *pl* — **educacional** *adj*
educado, -da *adj* : polite, well-mannered
educador, -dora *n* : educator
educando, -da *n* ALUMNO, PUPILO : pupil, student
educar {72} *vt* **1** : to educate **2** CRIAR : to bring up, to raise **3** : to train — **educarse** *vr* : to be educated
educativo, -va *adj* : educational
efectista *adj* : dramatic, sensational
efectivamente *adv* : really, actually
efectividad *nf* : effectiveness

efectivo[1], **-va** *adj* **1** : effective **2** : real, actual **3** : permanent, regular (of employment)

efectivo[2] *nm* : cash

efecto *nm* **1** : effect **2 en ~** : actually, in fact **3 efectos** *nmpl* : goods, property ⟨efectos personales : personal effects⟩

efectuar {3} *vt* : to carry out, to bring about

efervescencia *nf* **1** : effervescence **2** : vivacity, high spirits *pl*

efervescente *adj* **1** : effervescent **2** : vivacious

eficacia *nf* **1** : effectiveness, efficacy **2** : efficiency

eficaz *adj, pl* **-caces 1** : effective **2** EFICIENTE : efficient — **eficazmente** *adv*

eficiencia *nf* : efficiency

eficiente *adj* EFICAZ : efficient — **eficientemente** *adv*

eficientizar {21} *vt Mex* : to streamline, to make more efficient

efigie *nf* : effigy

efímera *nf* : mayfly

efímero, -ra *adj* : ephemeral

efusión *nf, pl* **-siones 1** : effusion **2** : warmth, effusiveness **3 con ~** : effusively

efusivo, -va *adj* : effusive — **efusivamente** *adv*

egipcio, -cia *adj & n* : Egyptian

eglefino *nm* : haddock

ego *nm* : ego

egocéntrico, -ca *adj* : egocentric, self-centered

egoísmo *nm* : selfishness, egoism

egoísta[1] *adj* : selfish, egoistic

egoísta[2] *nmf* : egoist, selfish person

egotismo *nm* : egotism, conceit

egotista[1] *adj* : egotistic, egotistical, conceited

egotista[2] *nmf* : egotist, conceited person

egresado, -da *n* : graduate

egresar *vi* : to graduate

egreso *nm* **1** : graduation **2 ingresos y egresos** : income and expenditure

eh *interj* **1** : hey! **2** : eh?, huh?

eje *nm* **1** : axle **2** : axis

ejecución *nf, pl* **-ciones** : execution

ejecutante *nmf* : performer

ejecutar *vt* **1** : to execute, to put to death **2** : to carry out, to perform

ejecutivo, -va *adj & n* : executive

ejecutor, -tora *n* : executor

ejemplar[1] *adj* : exemplary, model

ejemplar[2] *nm* **1** : copy (of a book, magazine, etc.) **2** : specimen, example

ejemplificar {72} *vt* : to exemplify, to illustrate

ejemplo *nm* **1** : example **2 por ~** : for example **3 dar ejemplo** : to set an example

ejercer {86} *vi* **~ de** : to practice as, to work as — *vt* **1** : to practice **2** : exercise (a right) **3** : to exert

ejercicio *nm* **1** : exercise **2** : practice

ejercitar *vt* **1** : to exercise **2** ADIESTRAR : to drill, to train

ejército *nm* : army

ejidal *adj Mex* : cooperative

ejido *nm* **1** : common land **2** *Mex* : cooperative

ejote *nm Mex* : green bean

el[1] *pron* (*referring to masculine nouns*) **1** : the one ⟨tengo mi libro y el tuyo : I have my book and yours⟩ ⟨de los cantantes me gusta el de México : I prefer the singer from México⟩ **2 el que** : he who, whoever, the one that ⟨el que vino ayer : the one who came yesterday⟩ ⟨el que trabaja duro estará contento : he who works hard will be happy⟩

el[2], **la** *art, pl* **los, las** : the ⟨los niños están en la casa : the boys are in the house⟩ ⟨me duele el pie : my foot hurts⟩

él *pron* : he, him ⟨él es mi amigo : he's my friend⟩ ⟨hablaremos con él : we will speak with him⟩

elaboración *nf, pl* **-ciones 1** PRODUCCIÓN : production, making **2** : preparation, devising

elaborado, -da *adj* : elaborate

elaborar *vt* **1** : to make, to produce **2** : to devise, to draw up

elasticidad *nf* : elasticity

elástico[1], **-ca** *adj* **1** FLEXIBLE : flexible **2** : elastic

elástico[2] *nm* **1** : elastic (material) **2** : rubber band

elección *nf, pl* **-ciones 1** SELECCIÓN : choice, selection **2** : election

electivo, -va *adj* : elective

electo, -ta *adj* : elect ⟨el presidente electo : the president-elect⟩

elector, -tora *n* : elector, voter

electorado *nm* : electorate

electoral *adj* : electoral, election

electricidad *nf* : electricity

electricista *nmf* : electrician

eléctrico, -ca *adj* : electric, electrical

electrificar {72} *vt* : to electrify — **electrificación** *nf*

electrizar {21} *vt* : to electrify, to thrill — **electrizante** *adj*

electrocardiógrafo *nm* : electrocardiograph

electrocardiograma *nm* : electrocardiogram

electrocutar *vt* : to electrocute — **electrocución** *nf*

electrodo *nm* : electrode

electrodoméstico *nm* : electric appliance

electroimán *nm, pl* **-manes** : electromagnet

electrólisis *nfs & pl* : electrolysis

electrolito *nm* : electrolyte

electromagnético, -ca *adj* : electromagnetic

electromagnetismo *nm* : electromagnetism

electrón *nm, pl* **-trones** : electron

electrónica *nf* : electronics

electrónico, -ca *adj* : electronic — **electrónicamente** *adv*

elefante, -ta *n* : elephant
elegancia *nf* : elegance
elegante *adj* : elegant, smart — **elegantemente** *adv*
elegía *nf* : elegy
elegíaco, -ca *adj* : elegiac
elegibilidad *nf* : eligibility
elegible *adj* : eligible
elegido, -da *adj* **1** : chosen, selected **2** : elected
elegir {28} *vt* **1** ESCOGER, SELECCIONAR : to choose, to select **2** : to elect
elemental *adj* **1** : elementary, basic **2** : fundamental, essential
elemento *nm* : element
elenco *nm* : cast (of actors)
elepé *nm* : long-playing record
elevación *nf, pl* **-ciones** : elevation, height
elevado, -da *adj* **1** : elevated, lofty **2** : high
elevador *nm* ASCENSOR : elevator
elevar *vt* **1** ALZAR : to raise, to lift **2** AUMENTAR : to raise, to increase **3** : to elevate (in a hierarchy), to promote **4** : to present, to submit — **elevarse** *vr* : to rise
elfo *nm* : elf
eliminación *nf, pl* **-ciones** : elimination, removal
eliminar *vt* **1** : to eliminate, to remove **2** : to do in, to kill
elipse *nf* : ellipse
elipsis *nf* : ellipsis
elíptico, -ca *adj* : elliptical, elliptic
elite *or* **élite** *nf* : elite
elixir *or* **elíxir** *nm* : elixir
ella *pron* : she, her ⟨ella es mi amiga : she is my friend⟩ ⟨nos fuimos con ella : we left with her⟩
ello *pron* : it ⟨es por ello que me voy : that's why I'm going⟩
ellos, ellas *pron pl* **1** : they, them **2 de ellos, de ellas** : theirs
elocución *nf, pl* **-ciones** : elocution
elocuencia *nf* : eloquence
elocuente *adj* : eloquent — **elocuentemente** *adv*
elogiar *vt* ENCOMIAR : to praise
elogio *nm* : praise
elote *nm* **1** *Mex* : corn, maize **2** *CA, Mex* : corncob
elucidación *nf, pl* **-ciones** ESCLARECIMIENTO : elucidation
elucidar *vt* ESCLARECER : to elucidate
eludir *vt* EVADIR : to evade, to avoid, to elude
emanación *nf, pl* **-ciones** : emanation
emanar *vi* **∼ de** : to emanate from — *vt* : to exude
emancipar *vt* : to emancipate — **emancipación** *nf*
embadurnar *vt* EMBARRAR : to smear, to daub
embajada *nf* : embassy
embajador, -dora *n* : ambassador
embalaje *nm* : packing, packaging
embalar *vt* EMPAQUETAR : to pack
embaldosar *vt* : to tile, to pave with tiles
embalsamar *vt* : to embalm
embalsar *vt* : to dam, to dam up
embalse *nm* : dam, reservoir
embarazada *adj* ENCINTA, PREÑADA : pregnant, expecting
embarazar {21} *vt* **1** : to obstruct, to hamper **2** PREÑAR : to make pregnant
embarazo *nm* : pregnancy
embarazoso, -sa *adj* : embarrassing, awkward
embarcación *nf, pl* **-ciones** : boat, craft
embarcadero *nm* : wharf, pier, jetty
embarcar {72} *vi* : to embark, to board — *vt* : to load
embarco *nm* : embarkation
embargar {52} *vt* **1** : to seize, to impound **2** : to overwhelm
embargo *nm* **1** : seizure **2** : embargo **3 sin ∼** : however, nevertheless
embarque *nm* **1** : embarkation **2** : shipment
embarrancar {72} *vi* **1** : to run aground **2** : to get bogged down
embarrar *vt* **1** : to cover with mud **2** EMBADURNAR : to smear
embarullar *vt fam* : to muddle, to confuse — **embarullarse** *vr fam* : to get mixed up
embate *nm* **1** : onslaught **2** : battering (of waves or wind)
embaucador, -dora *n* : swindler, deceiver
embaucar {72} *vt* : to trick, to swindle
embeber *vt* : to absorb, to soak up — *vi* : to shrink
embelesado, -da *adj* : spellbound
embelesar *vt* : to enchant, to captivate
embellecer {53} *vt* : to embellish, to beautify
embellecimiento *nm* : beautification, embellishment
embestida *nf* **1** : charge (of a bull) **2** ARREMETIDA : attack, onslaught
embestir {54} *vt* : to hit, to run into, to charge at — *vi* ARREMETER : to charge, to attack
emblanquecer {53} *vt* BLANQUEAR : to bleach, to whiten — **emblanquecerse** *vr* : to turn white
emblema *nm* : emblem
emblemático, -ca *adj* : emblematic
embolia *nf* : embolism
émbolo *nm* : piston
embolsarse *vr* **1** : to pocket (money) **2** : to collect (payment)
emborracharse *vr* EMBRIAGARSE : to get drunk
emborronar *vt* **1** : to blot, to smudge **2** GARABATEAR : to scribble
emboscada *nf* : ambush
emboscar {72} *vt* : to ambush — **emboscarse** *vr* : to lie in ambush
embotadura *nf* : bluntness, dullness
embotar *vt* **1** : to dull, to blunt **2** : to weaken, to enervate
embotellamiento *nm* ATASCO : traffic jam

embotellar *vt* ENVASAR : to bottle

embragar {52} *vi* : to engage the clutch

embrague *nm* : clutch

embravecerse {53} *vr* **1** : to get furious **2** : to get rough ⟨el mar se embraveció : the sea became tempestuous⟩

embriagado, -da *adj* : inebriated, drunk

embriagador, -dora *adj* : intoxicating

embriagarse {52} *vr* EMBORRACHARSE : to get drunk

embriaguez *nf* EBRIEDAD : drunkenness, inebriation

embrión *nm, pl* **embriones** : embryo

embrionario, -ria *adj* : embryonic

embrollo *nm* ENREDO : imbroglio, confusion

embrujar *vt* HECHIZAR : to bewitch

embrujo *nm* : spell, curse

embudo *nm* : funnel

embuste *nm* **1** MENTIRA : lie, fib **2** ENGAÑO : trick, hoax

embustero[1], **-ra** *adj* : lying, deceitful

embustero[2], **-ra** *n* : liar, cheat

embutido *nm* **1** : sausage **2** : inlaid work

embutir *vt* **1** : to cram, to stuff, to jam **2** : to inlay

emergencia *nf* **1** : emergency **2** : emergence

emergente *adj* **1** : emergent **2** : consequent, resultant

emerger {15} *vi* : to emerge, to surface

emético[1], **-ca** *adj* : emetic

emético[2] *nm* : emetic

emigración *nf, pl* **-ciones** **1** : emigration **2** : migration

emigrante *adj & nmf* : emigrant

emigrar *vi* **1** : to emigrate **2** : to migrate

eminencia *nf* : eminence

eminente *adj* : eminent, distinguished

eminentemente *adv* : basically, essentially

emisario[1], **-ria** *n* : emissary

emisario[2] *nm* : outlet (of a body of water)

emisión *nf, pl* **-siones** **1** : emission **2** : broadcast **3** : issue ⟨emisión de acciones : stock issue⟩

emisor *nm* TRANSMISOR : television or radio transmitter

emisora *nf* : radio station

emitir *vt* **1** : to emit, to give off **2** : to broadcast **3** : to issue **4** : to cast (a vote)

emoción *nf, pl* **-ciones** : emotion — **emocional** *adj* — **emocionalmente** *adv*

emocionado, -da *adj* **1** : moved, affected by emotion **2** ENTUSIASMADO : excited

emocionante *adj* **1** CONMOVEDOR : moving, touching **2** EXCITANTE : exciting, thrilling

emocionar *vt* **1** CONMOVER : to move, to touch **2** : to excite, to thrill — **emocionarse** *vr*

emotivo, -va *adj* : emotional, moving

empacador, -dora *n* : packer

empacar {72} *vt* **1** EMPAQUETAR : to pack **2** : to bale — *vi* : to pack — **empacarse** *vr* **1** : to balk, to refuse to budge **2** *Col, Mex fam* : to eat ravenously, to devour

empachar *vt* **1** ESTORBAR : to obstruct **2** : to give indigestion to **3** DISFRAZAR : to disguise, to mask — **empacharse** *vr* **1** INDIGESTARSE : to get indigestion **2** AVERGONZARSE : to be embarrassed

empacho *nm* **1** INDIGESTIÓN : indigestion **2** VERGÜENZA : embarrassment **3** **no tener empacho en** : to have no qualms about

empadronarse *vr* : to register to vote

empalagar {52} *vt* **1** : to cloy, to surfeit **2** FASTIDIAR : to annoy, to bother

empalagoso, -sa *adj* MELOSO : cloying, excessively sweet

empalar *vt* : to impale

empalizada *nf* : palisade (fence)

empalmar *vt* **1** : to splice, to link **2** : to combine — *vi* : to meet, to converge

empalme *nm* **1** CONEXIÓN : connection, link **2** : junction

empanada *nf* : pie, turnover

empanadilla *nf* : meat or seafood pie

empanar *vt* : to bread

empantanado, -da *adj* : bogged down, delayed

empañar *vt* **1** : to steam up **2** : to tarnish, to sully

empapado, -da *adj* : soggy, sodden

empapar *vt* MOJAR : to soak, to drench — **empaparse** *vr* **1** : to get soaking wet **2** **~ de** : to absorb, to be imbued with

empapelar *vt* : to wallpaper

empaque *nm fam* **1** : presence, bearing **2** : pomposity **3** DESCARO : impudence, nerve

empaquetar *vt* EMBALAR : to pack, to package — **empaquetarse** *vr fam* : to dress up

emparedado *nm* : sandwich

emparedar *vt* : to wall in, to confine

emparejar *vt* **1** : to pair, to match up **2** : to make even — *vi* : to catch up — **emparejarse** *vr* : to pair up

emparentado, -da *adj* : related

emparentar {55} *vi* : to become related by marriage

emparrillado *nm Mex* : gridiron (in football)

empastar *vt* **1** : to fill (a tooth) **2** : to bind (a book)

empaste *nm* : filling (of a tooth)

empatar *vt* : to tie, to connect — *vi* : to result in a draw, to be tied — **empatarse** *vr Ven* : to hook up, to link together

empate *nm* : draw, tie

empatía *nf* : empathy

empecinado, -da *adj* TERCO : stubborn

empecinarse *vr* OBSTINARSE : to be stubborn, to persist

empedernido, -da *adj* INCORREGIBLE : hardened, inveterate

empedrado *nm* : paving, pavement

empedrar {55} *vt* : to pave (with stones)
empeine *nm* : instep
empellón *nm, pl* **-llones** : shove, push
empelotado, -da *adj* **1** *Mex fam* : madly in love **2** *fam* : stark naked
empeñado, -da *adj* : determined, committed
empeñar *vt* **1** : to pawn **2** : to pledge, to give (one's word) — **empeñarse** *vr* **1** : to insist stubbornly **2** : to make an effort
empeño *nm* **1** : pledge, commitment **2** : insistence **3** ESFUERZO : effort, determination **4** : pawning <casa de empeños : pawnshop>
empeoramiento *nm* : worsening, deterioration
empeorar *vi* : to deteriorate, to get worse — *vt* : to make worse
empequeñecer {53} *vi* : to diminish, to become smaller — *vt* : to minimize, to make smaller
emperador *nm* : emperor
emperatriz *nf, pl* **-trices** : empress
empero *conj* : however, nevertheless
empezar {29} *v* COMENZAR : to start, to begin
empinado, -da *adj* : steep
empinar *vt* ELEVAR : to lift, to raise — **empinarse** *vr* : to stand on tiptoe
empírico, -ca *adj* : empirical — **empíricamente** *adv*
emplasto *nm* : poultice, dressing
emplazamiento *nm* **1** : location, site **2** CITACIÓN : summons, subpoena
emplazar {21} *vt* **1** CONVOCAR : to convene, to summon **2** : to subpoena **3** UBICAR : to place, to position
empleado, -da *n* : employee
empleador, -dora *n* PATRÓN : employer
emplear *vt* **1** : to employ **2** USAR : to use — **emplearse** *vr* **1** : to get a job **2** : to occupy oneself
empleo *nm* **1** OCUPACIÓN : employment, occupation, job **2** : use, usage
empobrecer {53} *vt* : to impoverish — *vi* : to become poor — **empobrecerse** *vr*
empobrecimiento *nm* : impoverishment
empollar *vi* : to brood eggs — *vt* : to incubate
empolvado, -da *adj* **1** : dusty **2** : powdered, powdery
empolvar *vt* **1** : to cover with dust **2** : to powder — **empolvarse** *vr* **1** : to gather dust **2** : to powder one's face
emporio *nm* **1** : center, capital, empire <un emporio cultural : a cultural center> <un emporio financiero : a financial empire> **2** : department store
empotrado, -da *adj* : built-in <armarios empotrados : built-in cabinets>
empotrar *vt* : to build into, to embed
emprendedor, -dora *adj* : enterprising
emprender *vt* : to undertake, to begin
empresa *nf* **1** COMPAÑÍA, FIRMA : company, corporation, firm **2** : undertaking, venture
empresariado *nm* **1** : business world **2** : management, managers *pl*
empresarial *adj* : business, managerial, corporate
empresario, -ria *n* **1** : manager **2** : businessman *m,* businesswoman *f* **3** : impresario
empréstito *nm* : loan
empujar *vi* : to push, to shove — *vt* **1** : to push **2** PRESIONAR : to spur on, to press
empuje *nm* : impetus, drive
empujón *nm, pl* **-jones** : push, shove
empuñadura *nf* MANGO : hilt, handle
empuñar *vt* **1** ASIR : to grasp **2** **empuñar las armas** : to take up arms
emú *nm* : emu
emular *vt* IMITAR : to emulate — **emulación** *nf*
emulsión *nf, pl* **-siones** : emulsion
emulsionante *nm* : emulsifier
emulsionar *vt* : to emulsify
en *prep* **1** : in <en el bolsillo : in one's pocket> <en una semana : in a week> **2** : on <en la mesa : on the table> **3** : at <en casa : at home> <en el trabajo : at work> <en ese momento : at that moment>
enagua *nf* : petticoat, slip
enajenación *nf, pl* **-ciones** **1** : transfer (of property) **2** : alienation **3** : absentmindedness
enajenado, -da *adj* : out of one's mind
enajenar *vt* **1** : to transfer (property) **2** : to alienate **3** : to enrapture — **enajenarse** *vr* **1** : to become estranged **2** : to go mad
enaltecer {53} *vt* : to praise, to extol
enamorado[1], **-da** *adj* : in love
enamorado[2], **-da** *n* : lover, sweetheart
enamoramiento *nm* : infatuation, crush
enamorar *vt* : to enamor, to win the love of — **enamorarse** *vr* : to fall in love
enamoriscarse {72} *vr fam* : to have a crush, to be infatuated
enamorizado, -da *adj* : amorous, passionate
enano[1], **-na** *adj* : tiny, minute
enano[2], **-na** *n* : dwarf, midget
enarbolar *vt* **1** : to hoist, to raise **2** : to brandish
enarcar {72} *vt* : to arch, to raise
enardecer {53} *vt* **1** : to arouse (anger, passions) **2** : to stir up, to excite — **enardecerse** *vr*
encabezado *nm Mex* : headline
encabezamiento *nm* **1** : heading **2** : salutation, opening
encabezar {21} *vt* **1** : to head, to lead **2** : to put a heading on
encabritarse *vr* **1** : to rear up **2** *fam* : to get angry
encadenar *vt* **1** : to chain **2** : to connect, to link **3** INMOVILIZAR : to immobilize

encajar *vi* : to fit, to fit together, to fit in — *vt* **1** : to insert, to stick **2** : to take, to cope with <encajó el golpe : he withstood the blow>

encaje *nm* **1** : lace **2** : financial reserve

encajonar *vt* **1** : to box, to crate **2** : to cram in

encalar *vt* : to whitewash

encallar *vi* **1** : to run aground **2** : to get stuck

encallecido, -da *adj* : callused

encamar *vt* : to confine to a bed

encaminado, -da *adj* **1** : on the right track **2 ~ a** : aimed at, designed to

encaminar *vt* **1** : to direct, to channel **2** : to head in the right direction — **encaminarse** *vr* **~ a** : to head for, to aim at

encandilar *vt* : to dazzle

encanecer {53} *vi* : to gray, to go gray

encantado, -da *adj* **1** : charmed, bewitched **2** : delighted

encantador[1]**, -dora** *adj* : charming, delightful

encantador[2]**, -dora** *n* : magician

encantamiento *nm* : enchantment, spell

encantar *vt* **1** : to enchant, to bewitch **2** : to charm, to delight <me encanta esta canción : I love this song>

encanto *nm* **1** : charm, fascination **2** HECHIZO : spell **3** : delightful person or thing

encañonar *vt* : to point (a gun) at, to hold up

encapotado, -da *adj* : cloudy, overcast

encapotarse *vr* : to cloud over, to become overcast

encaprichado, -da *adj* : infatuated

encaprichamiento *nm* : infatuation

encapuchado, -da *adj* : hooded

encarado, -da *adj* **estar mal encarado** *fam* : to be ugly-looking, to look mean

encaramar *vt* : to raise, to lift up — **encaramarse** *vr* : to perch

encarar *vt* CONFRONTAR : to face, to confront

encarcelación *nf* → **encarcelamiento**

encarcelamiento *nm* : incarceration, imprisonment

encarcelar *vt* : to incarcerate, to imprison

encarecer {53} *vt* **1** : to increase, to raise (price, value) **2** : to beseech, to entreat — **encarecerse** *vr* : to become more expensive

encarecidamente *adv* : insistently, urgently

encarecimiento *nm* : increase, rise (in price)

encargado[1]**, -da** *adj* : in charge

encargado[2]**, -da** *n* : manager, person in charge

encargar {52} *vt* **1** : to put in charge of **2** : to recommend, to advise **3** : to order, to request — **encargarse** *vr* **~ de** : to take charge of

encargo *nm* **1** : errand **2** : job assignment **3** : order <hecho de encargo : custom-made, made to order>

encariñarse *vr* **~ con** : to become fond of, to grow attached to

encarnación *nf, pl* **-ciones** : incarnation, embodiment

encarnado[1]**, -da** *adj* **1** : incarnate **2** : flesh-colored **3** : red **4** : ingrown

encarnado[2] *nm* : red

encarnar *vt* : to incarnate, to embody — **encarnarse** *vr* **encarnarse una uña** : to have an ingrown nail

encarnizado, -da *adj* **1** : bloodshot, inflamed **2** : fierce, bloody

encarnizar {21} *vt* : to enrage, to infuriate — **encarnizarse** *vr* : to be brutal, to attack viciously

encarrilar *vt* : to guide, to put on the right track

encasillar *vt* CLASIFICAR : to classify, to pigeonhole, to categorize

encausar *vt* : to prosecute, to charge

encauzar {21} *vt* : to channel, to guide — **encauzarse** *vr*

encebollado, -da *adj* : cooked with onions

encefalitis *nms & pl* : encephalitis

enceguecedor, -dora *n* : blinding

encendedor *nm* : lighter

encender {56} *vi* : to light — *vt* **1** : to light, to set fire to **2** PRENDER : to switch on **3** : to start (a motor) **4** : to arouse, to kindle — **encenderse** *vr* **1** : to get excited **2** : to blush

encendido[1]**, -da** *adj* **1** : burning **2** : flushed **3** : fiery, passionate

encendido[2] *nm* : ignition

encerado *nm* **1** : waxing, polishing **2** : blackboard

encerar *vt* : to wax, to polish

encerrar {55} *vt* **1** : to lock up, to shut away **2** : to contain, to include **3** : to involve, to entail

encerrona *nf* **1** TRAMPA : trap, setup **2** **prepararle una encerrona a alguien** : to set a trap for someone, to set someone up

encestar *vi* : to make a basket (in basketball)

enchapado *nm* : plating, coating (of metal)

encharcamiento *nm* : flood, flooding

encharcar {72} *vt* : to flood, to swamp — **encharcarse** *vr*

enchilada *nf* : enchilada

enchilar *vt Mex* : to season with chili

enchuecar {72} *vt Chile, Mex fam* : to make crooked, to twist

enchufar *vt* **1** : to plug in **2** : to connect, to fit together

enchufe *nm* **1** : connection **2** : plug, socket

encía *nf* : gum (tissue)

encíclica *nf* : encyclical

enciclopedia *nf* : encyclopedia

enciclopédico, -ca *adj* : encyclopedic

encierro *nm* **1** : confinement **2** : enclosure

encima *adv* **1** : on top, above **2** ADEMÁS : as well, besides **3 ~ de** : on, on top of, over **4 por encima de** : above, beyond <por encima de la ley : above the law> **5 echarse encima** : to take upon oneself **6 estar encima de** *fam* : to nag, to criticize **7 quitarse de encima** : to get rid of

encina *nf* : evergreen oak

encinta *adj* EMBARAZADA, PREÑADA : pregnant, expecting

enclaustrado, -da *adj* : cloistered, shut away

enclavado, -da *adj* : buried

enclenque *adj* : weak, sickly

encoger {15} *vt* **1** : to shrink, to make smaller **2** : to intimidate — *vi* : to shrink, to contract — **encogerse** *vr* **1** : to shrink **2** : to be intimidated, to cower, to cringe **3 encogerse de hombros** : to shrug (one's shoulders)

encogido, -da *adj* **1** : shriveled, shrunken **2** TÍMIDO : shy, inhibited

encogimiento *nm* **1** : shrinking, shrinkage **2** : shrug **3** TIMIDEZ : shyness

encolar *vt* : to paste, to glue

encolerizar {21} *vt* ENFURECER : to enrage, to infuriate — **encolerizarse** *vr*

encomendar {55} *vt* CONFIAR : to entrust, to commend — **encomendarse** *vr*

encomiable *adj* : commendable, praiseworthy

encomiar *vt* ELOGIAR : to praise, to pay tribute to

encomienda *nf* **1** : charge, mission **2** : royal land grant **3** : parcel

encomio *nm* : praise, eulogy

encomioso, -sa *adj* : eulogistic, laudatory

enconar *vt* **1** : to irritate, to anger **2** : to inflame — **enconarse** *vr* **1** : to become heated **2** : to fester

encono *nm* **1** RENCOR : animosity, rancor **2** : inflammation, infection

encontrado, -da *adj* : contrary, opposing

encontrar {19} *vt* **1** HALLAR : to find **2** : to encounter, to meet — **encontrarse** *vr* **1** REUNIRSE : to meet **2** : to clash, to conflict **3** : to be <su abuelo se encuentra mejor : her grandfather is doing better>

encorvar *vt* : to bend, to curve — **encorvarse** *vr* : to hunch over, to stoop

encrespar *vt* **1** : to curl, to ruffle, to ripple **2** : to annoy, to irritate — **encresparse** *vr* **1** : to curl one's hair **2** : to become choppy **3** : to get annoyed

encrucijada *nf* : crossroads

encuadernación *nf, pl* **-ciones** : bookbinding

encuadernar *vt* EMPASTAR : to bind (a book)

encuadrar *vt* **1** ENMARCAR : to frame **2** ENCAJAR : to fit, to insert **3** COMPRENDER : to contain, to include

encubierto *pp* → **encubrir**

encubrimiento *nm* : cover-up

encubrir {2} *vt* : to cover up, to conceal

encuentro *nm* **1** : meeting, encounter **2** : conference, congress

encuerado, -da *adj fam* : naked

encuerar *vt fam* : to undress

encuesta *nf* **1** INVESTIGACIÓN, PESQUISA : inquiry, investigation **2** SONDEO : survey

encuestador, -dora *n* : pollster

encuestar *vt* : to poll, to take a survey of

encumbrado, -da *adj* **1** : lofty, high **2** : eminent, distinguished

encumbrar *vt* **1** : to exalt, to elevate **2** : to extol — **encumbrarse** *vr* : to reach the top

encurtir *vt* ESCABECHAR : to pickle

ende *adv* **por ~** : therefore, consequently

endeble *adj* : feeble, weak

endeblez *nf* : weakness, frailty

endémico, -ca *adj* : endemic

endemoniado, -da *adj* : fiendish, diabolical

endentecer {53} *vi* : to teethe

enderezar {21} *vt* **1** : to straighten (out) **2** : to stand on end, to put upright

endeudado, -da *adj* : in debt, indebted

endeudamiento *nm* : indebtedness

endeudarse *vr* **1** : to go into debt **2** : to feel obliged

endiabladamente *adv* : extremely, diabolically

endiablado, -da *adj* **1** : devilish, diabolical **2** : complicated, difficult

endibia *or* **endivia** *nf* : endive

endilgar {52} *vt fam* : to spring, to foist <me endilgó la responsabilidad : he saddled me with the responsibility>

endocrino, -na *adj* : endocrine

endogamia *nf* : inbreeding

endosar *vt* : to endorse

endoso *nm* : endorsement

endulzante *nm* : sweetener

endulzar {21} *vt* **1** : to sweeten **2** : to soften, to mellow — **endulzarse** *vr*

endurecer {53} *vt* : to harden, to toughen — **endurecerse** *vr*

enebro *nm* : juniper

eneldo *nm* : dill

enema *nm* : enema

enemigo, -ga *adj & n* : enemy

enemistad *nf* : enmity, hostility

enemistar *vt* : to make enemies of — **enemistarse** *vr* **~ con** : to fall out with

energía *nf* : energy

enérgico, -ca *adj* **1** : energetic, vigorous **2** : forceful, emphatic — **enérgicamente** *adv*

energúmeno, -na *n fam* : lunatic, crazy person

enero *nm* : January

enervar *vt* **1** : to enervate **2** *fam* : to annoy, to get on one's nerves — **enervante** *adj*

enésimo, -ma *adj* : umpteenth, nth

enfadar *vt* **1** : to annoy, to make angry **2** *Mex fam* : to bore — **enfadarse** *vr* : to get angry, to get annoyed

enfado *nm* : anger, annoyance

enfadoso, -sa *adj* : irritating, annoying

enfardar *vt* : to bale

énfasis *nms & pl* : emphasis

enfático, -ca *adj* : emphatic — **enfáticamente** *adv*

enfatizar {21} *vt* DESTACAR, SUBRAYAR : to emphasize

enfermar *vt* : to make sick — *vi* : to fall ill, to get sick — **enfermarse** *vr*

enfermedad *nf* **1** INDISPOSICIÓN : sickness, illness **2** : disease

enfermería *nf* : infirmary

enfermero, -ra *n* : nurse

enfermizo, -za *adj* : sickly

enfermo[1], **-ma** *adj* : sick, ill

enfermo[2], **-ma** *n* **1** : sick person, invalid **2** PACIENTE : patient

enfilar *vt* **1** : to take, to go along ⟨enfiló la carretera de Montevideo : she went up the road to Montevideo⟩ **2** : to line up, to put in a row **3** : to string, to thread **4** : to aim, to direct — *vi* : to make one's way

enflaquecer {53} *vi* : to lose weight, to become thin — *vt* : to emaciate

enfocar {72} *vt* **1** : to focus (on) **2** : to consider, to look at

enfoque *nm* : focus

enfrascamiento *nm* : immersion, absorption

enfrascarse {72} *vr* **~ en** : to immerse oneself in, to get caught up in

enfrentamiento *nm* : clash, confrontation

enfrentar *vt* : to confront, to face — **enfrentarse** *vr* **1 ~ con** : to clash with **2 ~ a** : to face up to

enfrente *adv* **1** DELANTE : in front **2** : opposite

enfriamiento *nm* **1** CATARRO : chill, cold **2** : cooling off, damper

enfriar {85} *vt* **1** : to chill, to cool **2** : to cool down, to dampen — *vi* : to get cold — **enfriarse** *vr* : to get chilled, to catch a cold

enfundar *vt* : to sheathe, to encase

enfurecer {53} *vt* ENCOLERIZAR : to infuriate — **enfurecerse** *vr* : to fly into a rage

enfurecido, -da *adj* : furious, raging

enfurruñarse *vr fam* : to sulk

engalanar *vt* : to decorate, to deck out — **engalanarse** *vr* : to dress up

enganchar *vt* **1** : to hook, to snag **2** : to attach, to hitch up — **engancharse** *vr* **1** : to get snagged, to get hooked **2** : to enlist

enganche *nm* **1** : hook **2** : coupling, hitch **3** *Mex* : down payment

engañar *vt* **1** EMBAUCAR : to trick, to deceive, to mislead **2** : to cheat on, to be unfaithful to — **engañarse** *vr* **1** : to be mistaken **2** : to deceive oneself

engaño *nm* **1** : deception, trick **2** : fake, feint (in sports)

engañoso, -sa *adj* **1** : deceitful **2** : misleading, deceptive

engarrotarse *vr* : to stiffen up, to go numb

engatusamiento *nm* : cajolery

engatusar *vt* : to coax, to cajole

engendrar *vt* **1** : to beget, to father **2** : to give rise to, to engender

engentarse *vr Mex* : to be in a daze

englobar *vt* : to include, to embrace

engomar *vt* : to glue

engordar *vt* : to fatten, to fatten up — *vi* : to gain weight

engorro *nm* : nuisance, bother

engorroso, -sa *adj* : bothersome

engranaje *nm* : gears *pl*, cogs *pl*

engranar *vt* : to mesh, to engage — *vi* : to mesh gears

engrandecer {53} *vt* **1** : to enlarge **2** : to exaggerate **3** : to exalt

engrandecimiento *nm* **1** : enlargement **2** : exaggeration **3** : exaltation

engrane *nm Mex* : cogwheel

engrapadora *nf* : stapler

engrapar *vt* : to staple

engrasar *vt* : to grease, to lubricate

engrase *nm* : greasing, lubrication

engreído, -da *adj* PRESUMIDO, VANIDOSO : vain, conceited, stuck-up

engreimiento *nm* ARROGANCIA : arrogance, conceit

engreír {66} *vt* ENVANECER : to make vain — **engreírse** *vr* : to become conceited

engrosar {19} *vt* : to enlarge, to increase, to swell — *vi* ENGORDAR : to gain weight

engrudo *nm* : paste

engullir {38} *vt* : to gulp down, to gobble up — **engullirse** *vr*

enharinar *vt* : to flour

enhebrar *vt* ENSARTAR : to string, to thread

enhiesto, -ta *adj* **1** : erect, upright **2** : lofty, towering

enhilar *vt* : to thread (a needle, etc.)

enhorabuena *nf* FELICIDADES : congratulations *pl*

enigma *nm* : enigma, mystery

enigmático, -ca *adj* : enigmatic — **enigmáticamente** *adv*

enjabonar *vt* : to soap up, to lather — **enjabonarse** *vr*

enjaezar {21} *vt* : to harness

enjalbegar {52} *vt* : to whitewash

enjambrar *vi* : to swarm

enjambre *nm* **1** : swarm **2** MUCHEDUMBRE : crowd, mob

enjaular *vt* **1** : to cage **2** *fam* : to jail, to lock up

enjuagar {52} *vt* : to rinse — **enjuagarse** *vr* : to rinse out

enjuague *nm* **1** : rinse **2 enjuague bucal** : mouthwash

enjugar {52} *vt* : to wipe away (tears)

enjuiciar *vt* **1** : to indict, to prosecute **2** JUZGAR : to try

enjundioso, -sa *adj* : substantial, weighty

enjuto, -ta *adj* : lean, gaunt

enlace *nm* **1** : bond, link, connection **2** : liaison
enladrillado *nm* : brick paving
enladrillar *vt* : to pave with bricks
enlatar *vt* ENVASAR : to can
enlazar {21} *v* : to join, to link, to fit together
enlistar *vt* : to list — **enlistarse** *vr* : to enlist
enlodado, -da *adj* BARROSO : muddy
enlodar *vt* **1** : to cover with mud **2** : to stain, to sully — **enlodarse** *vr*
enlodazar → **enlodar**
enloquecedor, -dora *adj* : maddening
enloquecer {53} *vt* ALOCAR : to drive crazy — **enloquecerse** *vr* : to go crazy
enlosado *nm* : flagstone pavement
enlosar *vt* : to pave with flagstone
enlutarse *vr* : to go into mourning
enmaderado *nm* **1** : wood paneling **2** : hardwood floor
enmarañar *vt* **1** : to tangle **2** : to complicate **3** : to confuse, to mix up — **enmarañarse** *vr*
enmarcar {72} *vt* **1** ENCUADRAR : to frame **2** : to provide the setting for
enmascarar *vt* : to mask, to disguise
enmasillar *vt* : to putty, to caulk
enmendar {55} *vt* **1** : to amend **2** CORREGIR : to emend, to correct **3** COMPENSAR : to compensate for — **enmendarse** *vr* : to mend one's ways
enmienda *nf* **1** : amendment **2** : correction, emendation
enmohecerse {53} *vr* **1** : to become moldy **2** OXIDARSE : to rust, to become rusty
enmudecer {53} *vt* : to mute, to silence — *vi* : to fall silent
enmugrar *vt* : to soil, to make dirty — **enmugrarse** *vr* : to get dirty
ennegrecer {53} *vt* : to blacken, to darken — **ennegrecerse** *vr*
ennoblecer {53} *vt* **1** : to ennoble **2** : to embellish
enojadizo, -za *adj* IRRITABLE : irritable, cranky
enojado, -da *adj* **1** : annoyed **2** : angry, mad
enojar *vt* **1** : to anger **2** : to annoy, to upset — **enojarse** *vr*
enojo *nm* **1** CÓLERA : anger **2** : annoyance
enojón, -jona *adj, pl* **-jones** *Chile, Mex fam* : irritable, cranky
enojoso, -sa *adj* FASTIDIOSO, MOLESTOSO : annoying, irritating
enorgullecer {53} *vt* : to make proud — **enorgullecerse** *vr* : to pride oneself
enorme *adj* INMENSO : enormous, huge — **enormemente** *adv*
enormidad *nf* **1** : enormity, seriousness **2** : immensity, hugeness
enraizado, -da *adj* : deep-seated, deeply rooted
enraizar {30} *vi* : to take root
enramada *nf* : arbor, bower
enramar *vt* : to cover with branches
enrarecer {53} *vt* : to rarefy — **enrarecerse** *vr*
enredadera *nf* : climbing plant, vine
enredar *vt* **1** : to tangle up, to entangle **2** : to confuse, to complicate **3** : to involve, to implicate — **enredarse** *vr*
enredo *nm* **1** EMBROLLO : muddle, confusion **2** MARAÑA : tangle
enredoso, -sa *adj* : complicated, tricky
enrejado *nm* **1** : railing **2** : grating, grille **3** : trellis, lattice
enrevesado, -da *adj* : complicated, involved
enriquecer {53} *vt* : to enrich — **enriquecerse** *vr* : to get rich
enriquecido, -da *adj* : enriched
enriquecimiento *nm* : enrichment
enrojecer {53} *vt* : to make red, to redden — **enrojecerse** *vr* : to blush
enrolar *vt* RECLUTAR : to recruit — **enrolarse** *vr* INSCRIBIRSE : to enlist, to sign up
enrollar *vt* : to roll up, to coil — **enrollarse** *vr*
enronquecerse {53} *vr* : to become hoarse
enroscar {72} *vt* TORCER : to twist — **enroscarse** *vr* : to coil, to twine
ensacar {72} *vt* : to bag (up)
ensalada *nf* : salad
ensaladera *nf* : salad bowl
ensalmo *nm* : incantation, spell
ensalzar {21} *vt* **1** : to praise, to extol **2** EXALTAR : to exalt
ensamblaje *nm* : assembly
ensamblar *vt* **1** : to assemble **2** : to join, to fit together
ensanchar *vt* **1** : to widen **2** : to expand, to extend — **ensancharse** *vr*
ensanche *nm* **1** : widening **2** : expansion, development
ensangrentado, -da *adj* : bloody, bloodstained
ensañarse *vr* : to act cruelly, to be merciless
ensartar *vt* **1** ENHEBRAR : to string, to thread **2** : to skewer, to pierce
ensayar *vi* : to rehearse — *vt* **1** : to try out, to test **2** : to assay
ensayista *nmf* : essayist
ensayo *nm* **1** : essay **2** : trial, test **3** : rehearsal **4** : assay (of metals)
enseguida *adv* INMEDIATAMENTE : right away, immediately, at once
ensenada *nf* : cove, inlet
enseña *nf* **1** INSIGNIA : emblem, insignia **2** : standard, banner
enseñanza *nf* **1** EDUCACIÓN : education **2** : teaching
enseñar *vt* **1** : to teach **2** MOSTRAR : to show, to display — **enseñarse** *vr* **~ a** : to learn to, to get used to
enseres *nmpl* : equipment, furnishings *pl* 〈enseres domésticos : household goods〉
ensillar *vt* : to saddle (up)
ensimismado, -da *adj* : absorbed, engrossed

ensimismarse *vr* : to lose oneself in thought

ensoberbecerse {53} *vr* : to become haughty

ensombrecer {53} *vt* : to cast a shadow over, to darken — **ensombrecerse** *vr*

ensoñación *nf, pl* **-ciones** : fantasy

ensopar *vt* **1** : to drench **2** : to dunk, to dip

ensordecedor, -dora *adj* : deafening, thunderous

ensordecer {53} *vt* : to deafen — *vi* : to go deaf

ensuciar *vt* : to soil, to dirty — **ensuciarse** *vr*

ensueño *nm* **1** : daydream, revery **2** FANTASÍA : illusion, fantasy

entablar *vt* **1** : to cover with boards **2** : to initiate, to enter into, to start

entallar *vt* AJUSTAR : to tailor, to fit, to take in — *vi* QUEDAR : to fit

ente *nm* **1** : being, entity **2** : body, organization ⟨ente rector : ruling body⟩ **3** *fam* : eccentric, crackpot

enteco, -ca *adj* : gaunt, frail

entenado, -da *n Mex* : stepchild, stepson *m,* stepdaughter *f*

entender[1] {56} *vt* **1** COMPRENDER : to understand **2** OPINAR : to think, to believe **3** : to mean, to intend **4** DEDUCIR : to infer, to deduce — *vi* **1** : to understand ⟨¡ya entiendo! : now I understand!⟩ **2 ~ de** : to know about, to be good at **3 ~ en** : to be in charge of — **entenderse** *vr* **1** : to be understood **2** : to get along well, to understand each other **3 ~ con** : to deal with

entender[2] *nm* **a mi entender** : in my opinion

entendible *adj* : understandable

entendido[1], **-da** *adj* **1** : skilled, expert **2 tener entendido** : to understand, to be under the impression ⟨teníamos entendido que vendrías : we were under the impression you would come⟩ **3 darse por entendido** : to go without saying

entendido[2] *nm* : expert, authority, connoisseur

entendimiento *nm* **1** : intellect, mind **2** : understanding, agreement

enterado, -da *adj* : aware, well-informed ⟨estar enterado de : to be privy to⟩

enteramente *adv* : entirely, completely

enterar *vt* INFORMAR : to inform — **enterarse** *vr* INFORMARSE : to find out, to learn

entereza *nf* **1** INTEGRIDAD : integrity **2** FORTALEZA : fortitude **3** FIRMEZA : resolve

enternecedor, -dora *adj* CONMOVEDOR : touching, moving

enternecer {53} *vt* CONMOVER : to move, to touch

entero[1], **-ra** *adj* **1** : entire, whole **2** : complete, absolute **3** : intact — **enteramente** *adv*

entero[2] *nm* **1** : integer, whole number **2** : point (in finance)

enterramiento *nm* : burial

enterrar {55} *vt* : to bury

entibiar *vt* : to cool (down) — **entibiarse** *vr* : to become lukewarm

entidad *nf* **1** ENTE : entity **2** : body, organization **3** : firm, company **4** : importance, significance

entierro *nm* **1** : burial **2** : funeral

entintar *vt* : to ink

entoldado *nm* : awning

entomología *nf* : entomology

entomólogo, -ga *n* : entomologist

entonación *nf, pl* **-ciones** : intonation

entonar *vi* : to be in tune — *vt* **1** : to intone **2** : to tone up

entonces *adv* **1** : then **2 desde ~** : since then **3 en aquel entonces** : in those days

entornado, -da *adj* ENTREABIERTO : half-closed, ajar

entornar *vt* ENTREABRIR : to leave ajar

entorno *nm* : surroundings *pl,* environment

entorpecer {53} *vt* **1** : to hinder, to obstruct **2** : to dull — **entorpecerse** *vr* : to dull the senses

entrada *nf* **1** : entrance, entry **2** : ticket, admission **3** : beginning, onset **4** : entrée **5** : cue (in music) **6 entradas** *nfpl* : income ⟨entradas y salidas : income and expenditures⟩ **7 tener entradas** : to have a receding hairline

entrado, -da *adj* **entrado en años** : elderly

entramado *nm* : framework

entrampar *vt* **1** ATRAPAR : to entrap, to ensnare **2** ENGAÑAR : to deceive, to trick

entrante *adj* **1** : next, upcoming ⟨el año entrante : next year⟩ **2** : incoming, new ⟨el presidente entrante : the president elect⟩

entraña *nf* **1** MEOLLO : core, heart, crux **2 entrañas** *nfpl* VÍSCERAS : entrails

entrañable *adj* : close, intimate

entrañar *vt* : to entail, to involve

entrar *vi* **1** : to enter, to go in, to come in **2** : to begin — *vt* **1** : to bring in, to introduce **2** : to access

entre *prep* **1** : between **2** : among

entreabierto[1] *pp* → **entreabrir**

entreabierto[2], **-ta** *adj* ENTORNADO : half-open, ajar

entreabrir {2} *vt* ENTORNAR : to leave ajar

entreacto *nm* : intermission, interval

entrecano, -na *adj* : grayish, graying

entrecejo *nm* **fruncir el entrecejo** : to knit one's brows

entrecomillar *vt* : to place in quotation marks

entrecortado, -da *adj* **1** : labored, difficult ⟨respiración entrecortada : shortness of breath⟩ **2** : faltering, hesitant ⟨con la voz entrecortada : with a catch in his voice⟩

entrecruzar {21} *vt* ENTRELAZAR : to interweave, to intertwine — **entrecruzarse** *vr*
entredicho *nm* **1** DUDA : doubt, question **2** : prohibition
entrega *nf* **1** : delivery **2** : handing over, surrender **3** : installment <entrega inicial : down payment>
entregar {52} *vt* **1** : to deliver **2** DAR : to give, to present **3** : to hand in, to hand over — **entregarse** *vr* **1** : to surrender, to give in **2** : to devote oneself
entrelazar {21} *vt* ENTRECRUZAR : to interweave, to intertwine
entremedias *adv* **1** : in between, halfway **2** : in the meantime
entremés *nm, pl* **-meses** **1** APERITIVO : appetizer, hors d'oeuvre **2** : interlude, short play
entremeterse → **entrometerse**
entremetido *nm* → **entrometido**
entremezclar *vt* : to intermingle
entrenador, -dora *n* : trainer, coach
entrenamiento *nm* : training, drill, practice
entrenar *vt* : to train, to drill, to practice — **entrenarse** *vr* : to train, to spar (in boxing)
entreoír {50} *vt* : to hear indistinctly
entrepierna *nf* **1** : inner thigh **2** : crotch **3** : inseam
entrepiso *nm* ENTRESUELO : mezzanine
entresacar {72} *vt* **1** SELECCIONAR : to pick out, to select **2** : to thin out
entresuelo *nm* ENTREPISO : mezzanine
entretanto[1] *adv* : meanwhile
entretanto[2] *nm* **en el entretanto** : in the meantime
entretejer *vt* : to interweave
entretela *nf* : facing (of a garment)
entretener {80} *vt* **1** DIVERTIR : to entertain, to amuse **2** DISTRAER : to distract **3** DEMORAR : to delay, to hold up — **entretenerse** *vr* **1** : to amuse oneself **2** : to dally
entretenido, -da *adj* DIVERTIDO : entertaining, amusing
entretenimiento *nm* **1** : entertainment, pastime **2** DIVERSIÓN : fun, amusement
entrever {88} *vt* **1** : to catch a glimpse of **2** : to make out, to see indistinctly
entreverar *vt* : to mix, to intermingle
entrevero *nm* : confusion, disorder
entrevista *nf* : interview
entrevistador, -dora *n* : interviewer
entrevistar *vt* : to interview — **entrevistarse** *vr* REUNIRSE **~ con** : to meet with
entristecer {53} *vt* : to sadden
entrometerse *vr* : to interfere, to meddle
entrometido, -da *n* : meddler, busybody
entroncar {72} *vt* RELACIONAR : to establish a relationship between, to connect — *vi* **1** : to be related **2** : to link up, to be connected
entronque *nm* **1** : kinship **2** VÍNCULO : link, connection
entuerto *nm* : wrong, injustice
entumecer {53} *vt* : to make numb, to be numb — **entumecerse** *vr* : to go numb, to fall asleep
entumecido, -da *adj* **1** : numb **2** : stiff (of muscles, joints, etc.)
entumecimiento *nm* : numbness
enturbiar *vt* **1** : to cloud **2** : to confuse — **enturbiarse** *vr*
entusiasmar *vt* : to excite, to fill with enthusiasm — **entusiasmarse** *vr* : to get excited
entusiasmo *nm* : enthusiasm
entusiasta[1] *adj* : enthusiastic
entusiasta[2] *nmf* AFICIONADO : enthusiast
enumerar *vt* : to enumerate — **enumeración** *nf*
enunciación *nf, pl* **-ciones** : enunciation, statement
enunciar *vt* : to enunciate, to state
envainar *vt* : to sheathe
envalentonar *vt* : to make bold, to encourage — **envalentonarse** *vr*
envanecer {53} *vt* ENGREÍR : to make vain — **envanecerse** *vr*
envasar *vt* **1** EMBOTELLAR : to bottle **2** ENLATAR : to can **3** : to pack in a container
envase *nm* **1** : packaging, packing **2** : container **3** LATA : can **4** : empty bottle
envejecer {53} *vt* : to age, to make look old — *vi* : to age, to grow old
envejecido, -da *adj* : aged, old-looking
envejecimiento *nm* : aging
envenenamiento *nm* : poisoning
envenenar *vt* **1** : to poison **2** : to embitter
envergadura *nf* **1** : span, breadth, spread **2** : importance, scope
envés *nm, pl* **enveses** : reverse, opposite side
enviado, -da *n* : envoy, correspondent
enviar {85} *vt* **1** : to send **2** : to ship
envidia *nf* : envy, jealousy
envidiar *vt* : to envy — **envidiable** *adj*
envidioso, -sa *adj* : envious, jealous
envilecer {53} *vt* : to degrade, to debase
envilecimiento *nm* : degradation, debasement
envío *nm* **1** : shipment **2** : remittance
enviudar *vi* : to be widowed, to become a widower
envoltorio *nm* **1** : bundle, package **2** : wrapping, wrapper
envoltura *nf* : wrapper, wrapping
envolver {89} *vt* **1** : to wrap **2** : to envelop, to surround **3** : to entangle, to involve — **envolverse** *vr* **1** : to become involved **2** : to wrap oneself (up)
envuelto *pp* → **envolver**
enyerbar *vt Mex* : to bewitch
enyesar *vt* **1** : to plaster **2** ESCAYOLAR : to put in a plaster cast
enzima *nf* : enzyme
éon *nm, pl* **eones** : aeon
eperlano *nm* : smelt (fish)

épico, -ca *adj* : epic
epicúreo[1], **-rea** *adj* : epicurean
epicúreo[2], **-rea** *n* : epicure
epidemia *nf* : epidemic
epidémico, -ca *adj* : epidemic
epidermis *nf* : epidermis
epifanía *nf* : feast of the Epiphany (January 6th)
epigrama *nm* : epigram
epilepsia *nf* : epilepsy
epiléptico, -ca *adj & n* : epileptic
epílogo *nm* : epilogue
episcopal *adj* : episcopal
episcopaliano, -na *adj & n* : Episcopalian
episódico, -ca *adj* : episodic
episodio *nm* : episode
epístola *nf* : epistle
epitafio *nm* : epitaph
epíteto *nm* : epithet, name
epítome *nm* : summary, abstract
época *nf* **1** EDAD, ERA, PERÍODO : epoch, age, period **2** : time of year, season **3 de ~** : vintage, antique
epopeya *nf* : epic poem
equidad *nf* JUSTICIA : equity, justice, fairness
equilátero, -ra *adj* : equilateral
equilibrado, -da *adj* : well-balanced
equilibrar *vt* : to balance — **equilibrarse** *vr*
equilibrio *nm* **1** : balance, equilibrium ⟨perder el equilibrio : to lose one's balance⟩ ⟨equilibrio político : balance of power⟩ **2** : poise, aplomb
equilibrista *nmf* ACRÓBATA, FUNÁMBULO : acrobat, tightrope walker
equino, -na *adj* : equine
equinoccio *nm* : equinox
equipaje *nm* BAGAJE : baggage, luggage
equipamiento *nm* : equipping, equipment
equipar *vt* : to equip — **equiparse** *vr*
equiparable *adj* : comparable
equiparar *vt* **1** IGUALAR : to put on a same level, to make equal **2** COMPARAR : to compare
equipo *nm* **1** : team, crew **2** : gear, equipment
equitación *nf, pl* **-ciones** : horseback riding, horsemanship
equitativo, -va *adj* JUSTO : equitable, fair, just — **equitativamente** *adv*
equivalencia *nf* : equivalence
equivalente *adj & nm* : equivalent
equivaler {84} *vi* : to be equivalent
equivocación *nf, pl* **-ciones** ERROR : error, mistake
equivocado, -da *adj* : mistaken, wrong — **equivocadamente** *adv*
equivocar {72} *vt* : to mistake, to confuse — **equivocarse** *vr* : to make a mistake, to be wrong
equívoco[1], **-ca** *adj* AMBIGUO : ambiguous, equivocal
equívoco[2] *nm* : misunderstanding
era[1], **etc.** → **ser**
era[2] *nf* EDAD, ÉPOCA : era, age
erario *nm* : public treasury
erección *nf, pl* **-ciones** : erection, raising
eremita *nmf* ERMITAÑO : hermit
ergonomía *nf* : ergonomics
erguido, -da *adj* : erect, upright
erguir {31} *vt* : to raise, to lift up — **erguirse** *vr* : to straighten up
erial *nm* : uncultivated land
erigir {35} *vt* : to build, to erect — **erigirse** *vr* **~ en** : to set oneself up as
erizado, -da *adj* : bristly
erizarse {21} *vr* : to bristle, to stand on end
erizo *nm* **1** : hedgehog **2 erizo de mar** : sea urchin
ermitaño[1], **-ña** *n* EREMITA : hermit, recluse
ermitaño[2] *nm* : hermit crab
erogación *nf, pl* **-ciones** : expenditure
erogar {52} *vt* **1** : to pay out **2** : to distribute
erosión *nf, pl* **-siones** : erosion
erosionar *vt* : to erode
erótico, -ca *adj* : erotic
erotismo *nm* : eroticism
errabundo, -da *adj* ERRANTE, VAGABUNDO : wandering
erradicar {72} *vt* : to eradicate — **erradicación** *nf*
errado, -da *adj* : wrong, mistaken
errante *adj* ERRABUNDO, VAGABUNDO : errant, wandering
errar {32} *vt* FALLAR : to miss — *vi* **1** DESACERTAR : to be wrong, to be mistaken **2** VAGAR : to wander
errata *nf* : misprint, error
errático, -ca *adj* : erratic — **erráticamente** *adv*
erróneo, -nea *adj* EQUIVOCADO : erroneous, wrong — **erróneamente** *adv*
error *nm* EQUIVOCACIÓN : error, mistake
eructar *vi* : to belch, to burp
eructo *nm* : belch, burp
erudición *nf, pl* **-ciones** : erudition, learning
erudito[1], **-ta** *adj* LETRADO : erudite, learned
erudito[2], **-ta** *n* : scholar
erupción *nf, pl* **-ciones** **1** : eruption **2** SARPULLIDO : rash
eruptivo, -va *adj* : eruptive
es → **ser**
esbelto, -ta *adj* DELGADO : slender, slim
esbirro *nm* : henchman
esbozar {21} *vt* BOSQUEJAR : to sketch, to outline
esbozo *nm* **1** : sketch **2** : rough draft
escabechar *vt* **1** ENCURTIR : to pickle **2** *fam* : to kill, to rub out
escabeche *nm* : brine (for pickling)
escabechina *nf* MASACRE : massacre, bloodbath
escabel *nm* : footstool
escabroso, -sa *adj* **1** : rugged, rough **2** : difficult, tough **3** : risqué
escabullirse {38} *vr* : to slip away, to escape

escala *nf* **1** : scale **2** ESCALERA : ladder **3** : stopover

escalada *nf* : ascent, climb

escalador, -dora *n* ALPINISTA : mountain climber

escalafón *nm, pl* **-fones** **1** : list of personnel **2** : salary scale, rank

escalar *vt* : to climb, to scale — *vi* **1** : to go climbing **2** : to escalate

escaldar *vt* : to scald

escalera *nf* **1** : ladder ⟨escalera de tijera : stepladder⟩ **2** : stairs *pl,* staircase **3 escalera mecánica** : escalator

escalfador *nm* : chafing dish

escalfar *vt* : to poach (eggs)

escalinata *nf* : flight of stairs

escalofriante *adj* : horrifying, bloodcurdling

escalofrío *nm* : shiver, chill, shudder

escalón *nm, pl* **-lones** **1** : echelon **2** : step, rung

escalonado, -da *adj* GRADUAL : gradual, staggered

escalonar *vt* **1** : to terrace **2** : to stagger, to alternate

escalpelo *nm* BISTURÍ : scalpel

escama *nf* **1** : scale (of fish or reptiles) **2** : flake (of skin)

escamar *vt* **1** : to scale (fish) **2** : to make suspicious

escamocha *nf Mex* : fruit salad

escamoso, -sa *adj* : scaly

escamotear *vt* **1** : to palm, to conceal **2** *fam* : to lift, to swipe **3** : to hide, to cover up

escandalizar {21} *vt* : to shock, to scandalize — *vi* : to make a fuss — **escandalizarse** *vr* : to be shocked

escándalo *nm* **1** : scandal **2** : scene, commotion

escandaloso, -sa *adj* **1** : shocking, scandalous **2** RUIDOSO : noisy, rowdy **3** : flagrant, outrageous — **escandalosamente** *adv*

escandinavo, -va *adj & n* : Scandinavian

escandir *vt* : to scan (poetry)

escanear *vt* : to scan

escáner *nm* : scanner, scan

escaño *nm* **1** : seat (in a legislative body) **2** BANCO : bench

escapada *nf* HUIDA : flight, escape

escapar *vi* HUIR : to escape, to flee, to run away — **escaparse** *vr* : to escape notice, to leak out

escaparate *nm* **1** : shop window **2** : showcase

escapatoria *nf* **1** : loophole, excuse, pretext ⟨no tener escapatoria : to have no way out⟩ **2** ESCAPADA : escape, flight

escape *nm* **1** FUGA : escape **2** : exhaust (from a vehicle)

escapismo *nm* : escapism

escápula *nf* OMÓPLATO : scapula, shoulder blade

escapulario *nm* : scapular

escarabajo *nm* : beetle

escaramuza *nf* **1** : skirmish **2** : scrimmage

escaramuzar {21} *vi* : to skirmish

escarapela *nf* : rosette (ornament)

escarbar *vt* **1** : to dig, to scratch up **2** : to poke, to pick **3 ~ en** : to investigate, to pry into

escarcha *nf* **1** : frost **2** *Mex, PRi* : glitter

escarchar *vt* **1** : to frost (a cake) **2** : to candy (fruit)

escardar *vt* **1** : to weed, to hoe **2** : to weed out

escariar *vt* : to ream

escarlata *adj & nf* : scarlet

escarlatina *nf* : scarlet fever

escarmentar {55} *vt* : to punish, to teach a lesson to — *vi* : to learn one's lesson

escarmiento *nm* **1** : lesson, warning **2** CASTIGO : punishment

escarnecer {53} *vt* RIDICULIZAR : to ridicule, to mock

escarnio *nm* : ridicule, mockery

escarola *nf* : escarole

escarpa *nf* : escarpment, steep slope

escarpado, -da *adj* : steep, sheer

escarpia *nf* : hook, spike

escasamente *adv* : scarcely, barely

escasear *vi* : to be scarce, to run short

escasez *nf, pl* **-seces** : shortage, scarcity

escaso, -sa *adj* **1** : scarce, scant **2 ~ de** : short of

escatimar *vt* : to skimp on, to be sparing with ⟨no escatimar esfuerzos : to spare no effort⟩

escayola *nf* **1** : plaster (for casts) **2** : plaster cast

escayolar *vt* : to put in a plaster cast

escena *nf* **1** : scene **2** : stage

escenario *nm* **1** ESCENA : stage **2** : setting, scene ⟨el escenario del crimen : the scene of the crime⟩

escénico, -ca *adj* **1** : scenic **2** : stage

escenificar {72} *vt* : to stage, to dramatize

escepticismo *nm* : skepticism

escéptico[1], **-ca** *adj* : skeptical

escéptico[2], **-ca** *n* : skeptic

escindirse *vr* **1** : to split **2** : to break away

escisión *nf, pl* **-siones** **1** : split, division **2** : excision

esclarecer {53} *vt* **1** ELUCIDAR : to elucidate, to clarify **2** ILUMINAR : to illuminate, to light up

esclarecimiento *nm* ELUCIDACIÓN : elucidation, clarification

esclavitud *nf* : slavery

esclavización *nf, pl* **-ciones** : enslavement

esclavizar {21} *vt* : to enslave

esclavo, -va *n* : slave

esclerosis *nf* **esclerosis múltiple** : multiple sclerosis

esclusa *nf* : floodgate, lock (of a canal)

escoba *nf* : broom

escobilla *nf* : small broom, brush, whisk broom

escobillón *nm, pl* **-llones** : swab

escocer {14} *vi* ARDER : to smart, to sting — **escocerse** *vr* : to be sore

escocés[1], **-cesa** *adj, mpl* **-ceses** **1** : Scottish **2** : tartan, plaid

escocés[2], **-cesa** *n, mpl* **-ceses** : Scottish person, Scot

escocés[3] *nm* **1** : Scots (language) **2** *pl* **-ceses** : Scotch (whiskey)

escofina *nf* : file, rasp

escoger {15} *vt* ELEGIR, SELECCIONAR : to choose, to select

escogido, -da *adj* : choice, select

escolar[1] *adj* : school

escolar[2] *nmf* : student, pupil

escolaridad *nf* : schooling ⟨escolaridad obligatoria : compulsory education⟩

escolarización *nf, pl* **-ciones** : education, schooling

escollo *nm* **1** : reef **2** OBSTÁCULO : obstacle

escolta *nmf* : escort

escoltar *vt* : to escort, to accompany

escombro *nm* **1** : debris, rubbish **2 escombros** *nmpl* : ruins, rubble

esconder *vt* OCULTAR : to hide, to conceal

escondidas *nfpl* **1** : hide-and-seek **2 a ~** : secretly, in secret

escondimiento *nm* : concealment

escondite *nm* **1** ENCONDRIJO : hiding place **2** ESCONDIDAS : hide-and-seek

escondrijo *nm* ESCONDITE : hiding place

escopeta *nf* : shotgun

escoplear *vt* : to chisel (out)

escoplo *nm* : chisel

escora *nf* : list, heeling

escorar *vi* : to list, to heel (of a boat)

escorbuto *nm* : scurvy

escoria *nf* **1** : slag, dross **2** HEZ : dregs *pl*, scum ⟨la escoria de la sociedad : the dregs of society⟩

Escorpio *or* **Escorpión** *nmf* : Scorpio

escorpión *nm, pl* **-piones** ALACRÁN : scorpion

escote *nm* **1** : low neckline **2 pagar a escote** : to go dutch

escotilla *nf* : hatch, hatchway

escotillón *nf, pl* **-llones** : trapdoor

escozor *nm* : smarting, stinging

escriba *nm* : scribe

escribano, -na *n* **1** : court clerk **2** NOTARIO : notary public

escribir {33} *v* **1** : to write **2** : to spell — **escribirse** *vr* CARTEARSE : to write to one another, to correspond

escrito[1] *pp* → **escribir**

escrito[2], **-ta** *adj* : written

escrito[3] *nm* **1** : written document **2 escritos** *nmpl* : writings, works

escritor, -tora *n* : writer

escritorio *nm* : desk

escritorzuelo, -la *n* : hack (writer)

escritura *nf* **1** : writing, handwriting **2** : deed **3 las Escrituras** : the Scriptures

escroto *nm* : scrotum

escrúpulo *nm* : scruple

escrupuloso, -sa *adj* **1** : scrupulous **2** METICULOSO : exact, meticulous — **escrupulosamente** *adv*

escrutador, -dora *adj* : penetrating, searching

escrutar *vt* ESCUDRIÑAR : to scrutinize, to examine closely

escrutinio *nm* : scrutiny

escuadra *nf* **1** : square (instrument) **2** : fleet, squadron

escuadrilla *nf* : squadron, formation, flight

escuadrón *nm, pl* **-drones** : squadron

escuálido, -da *adj* **1** : skinny, scrawny **2** INMUNDO : filthy, squalid

escuchar *vt* **1** : to listen to **2** : to hear — *vi* : to listen — **escucharse** *vr*

escudar *vt* : to shield — **escudarse** *vr* **~ en** : to hide behind

escudero *nm* : squire

escudo *nm* **1** : shield **2 escudo de armas** : coat of arms

escudriñar *vt* **1** ESCRUTAR : to scrutinize **2** : to inquire into, to investigate

escuela *nf* : school

escueto, -ta *adj* **1** : plain, simple **2** : succinct, concise — **escuetamente** *adv*

escuincle, -cla *n Mex fam* : child, kid

esculcar {72} *vt* : to search

esculpir *vt* **1** : to sculpt **2** : to carve, to engrave — *vi* : to sculpt

escultor, -tora *n* : sculptor

escultórico, -ca *adj* : sculptural

escultura *nf* : sculpture

escultural *adj* : statuesque

escupidera *nf* : spittoon, cuspidor

escupir *v* : to spit

escupitajo *nm* : spit

escurridizo, -za *adj* : slippery, elusive

escurridor *nm* **1** : dish rack **2** : colander

escurrir *vt* **1** : to wring out **2** : to drain — *vi* **1** : to drain **2** : to drip, to drip-dry — **escurrirse** *vr* : to slip away

ese, esa *adj, mpl* **esos** : that, those

ése, ésa *pron, mpl* **ésos** : that one, those ones *pl*

esencia *nf* : essence

esencial *adj* : essential — **esencialmente** *adv*

esfera *nf* **1** : sphere **2** : face, dial (of a watch)

esférico[1], **-ca** *adj* : spherical

esférico[2] *nm* : ball (in sports)

esfinge *nf* : sphinx

esforzado, -da *adj* **1** : energetic, vigorous **2** VALIENTE : courageous, brave

esforzar {36} *vt* : to strain — **esforzarse** *vr* : to make an effort

esfuerzo *nm* **1** : effort **2** ÁNIMO, VIGOR : spirit, vigor **3 sin ~** : effortlessly

esfumar *vt* : to tone down, to soften — **esfumarse** *vr* **1** : to fade away, to vanish **2** *fam* : to take off, to leave

esgrima *nf* : fencing (sport)

esgrimidor, -dora *n* : fencer

esgrimir *vt* **1** : to brandish, to wield **2** : to use, to resort to — *vi* : to fence

esguince *nm* : sprain, strain (of a muscle)
eslabón *nm, pl* **-bones** : link
eslabonar *vt* : to link, to connect, to join
eslavo[1], **-va** *adj* : Slavic
eslavo[2], **-va** *n* : Slav
eslogan *nm, pl* **-lóganes** : slogan
eslovaco, **-ca** *adj & n* : Slovakian, Slovak
esloveno, **-na** *adj & nm* : Slovene, Slovenian
esmaltar *vt* : to enamel
esmalte *nm* **1** : enamel **2 esmalte de uñas** : nail polish
esmerado, **-da** *adj* : careful, painstaking
esmeralda *nf* : emerald
esmerarse *vr* : to take great pains, to do one's utmost
esmeril *nm* : emery
esmero *nm* : meticulousness, great care
esmoquin *nm, pl* **-quins** : tuxedo
esnob[1] *adj, pl* **esnobs** : snobbish
esnob[2] *nmf, pl* **esnobs** : snob
esnobismo *nm* : snobbery, snobbishness
eso *pron* (*neuter*) **1** : that ⟨eso no me gusta : I don't like that⟩ **2 ¡eso es!** : that's it!, that's right! **3 a eso de** : around ⟨a eso de las tres : around three o'clock⟩ **4 en ~** : at that point, just then
esófago *nm* : esophagus
esos → **ese**
ésos → **ése**
esotérico, **-ca** *adj* : esoteric — **esotéricamente** *adv*
espabilado, **-da** *adj* : bright, smart
espabilarse *vr* **1** : to awaken **2** : to get a move on **3** : to get smart, to wise up
espacial *adj* **1** : space **2** : spatial
espaciar *vt* DISTANCIAR : to space out, to spread out
espacio *nm* **1** : space, room **2** : period, length (of time) **3 espacio exterior** : outer space
espacioso, **-sa** *adj* : spacious, roomy
espada[1] *nf* **1** : sword **2 espadas** *nfpl* : spades (in playing cards)
espada[2] *nm* MATADOR, TORERO : bullfighter, matador
espadaña *nf* **1** : belfry **2** : cattail
espadilla *nf* : scull, oar
espagueti *nm or* **espaguetis** *nmpl* : spaghetti
espalda *nf* **1** : back **2 espaldas** *nfpl* : shoulders, back **3 por la espalda** : from behind
espaldarazo *nm* **1** : recognition, support **2** : slap on the back
espaldera *nf* : trellis
espantajo *nm* : scarecrow
espantapájaros *nms & pl* : scarecrow
espantar *vt* ASUSTAR : to scare, to frighten — **espantarse** *vr*
espanto *nm* : fright, fear, horror
espantoso, **-sa** *adj* **1** : frightening, terrifying **2** : frightful, dreadful
español[1], **-ñola** *adj* : Spanish
español[2], **-ñola** *n* : Spaniard
español[3] *nm* CASTELLANO : Spanish (language)
esparadrapo *nm* : adhesive bandage, Band-Aid™
esparcimiento *nm* **1** DIVERSIÓN, RECREO : entertainment, recreation **2** DESCANSO : relaxation **3** DISEMINACIÓN : dissemination, spreading
esparcir {83} *vt* DISPERSAR : to scatter, to spread — **esparcirse** *vr* **1** : to spread out **2** DESCANSARSE : to take it easy **3** DIVERTIRSE : to amuse oneself
espárrago *nm* : asparagus
espartano, **-na** *adj* : severe, austere
espasmo *nm* : spasm
espasmódico, **-ca** *adj* : spasmodic
espástico, **-ca** *adj* : spastic
espátula *nf* : spatula
especia *nf* : spice
especial *adj & nm* : special
especialidad *nf* : specialty
especialista *nmf* : specialist, expert
especialización *nf, pl* **-ciones** : specialization
especializarse {21} *vr* : to specialize
especialmente *adv* : especially, particularly
especie *nf* **1** : species **2** CLASE, TIPO : type, kind, sort
especificación *nf, pl* **-ciones** : specification
especificar {72} *vt* : to specify
específico, **-ca** *adj* : specific — **específicamente** *adv*
espécimen *nm, pl* **especímenes** : specimen
especioso, **-sa** *adj* : specious
espectacular *adj* : spectacular — **espectacularmente** *adv*
espectáculo *nm* **1** : spectacle, sight **2** : show, performance
espectador, **-dora** *n* : spectator, onlooker
espectro *nm* **1** : ghost, specter **2** : spectrum
especulación *nf, pl* **-ciones** : speculation
especulador, **-dora** *n* : speculator
especular *vi* : to speculate
especulativo, **-va** *adj* : speculative
espejismo *nm* **1** : mirage **2** : illusion
espejo *nm* : mirror
espejuelos *nmpl* ANTEOJOS : spectacles, glasses
espeluznante *adj* : hair-raising, terrifying
espera *nf* : wait
esperado, **-da** *adj* : anticipated
esperanza *nf* : hope, expectation
esperanzado, **-da** *adj* : hopeful
esperanzador, **-dora** *adj* : encouraging, promising
esperanzar {21} *vt* : to give hope to
esperar *vt* **1** AGUARDAR : to wait for, to await **2** : to expect **3** : to hope ⟨espero poder trabajar : I hope to be able to work⟩ ⟨espero que sí : I hope so⟩ — *vi*

: to wait — **esperarse** *vr* **1** : to expect, to be hoped <como podría esperarse : as would be expected> **2** : to hold on, to hang on <espérate un momento : hold on a minute>
esperma *nmf* : sperm
esperpéntico, -ca *adj* GROTESCO : grotesque
esperpento *nm fam* MAMARRACHO : sight, fright <voy hecha un esperpento : I really look a sight>
espesante *nm* : thickener
espesar *vt* : to thicken — **espesarse** *vr*
espeso, -sa *adj* : thick, heavy, dense
espesor *nm* : thickness, density
espesura *nf* **1** : thickness **2** : thicket
espetar *vt* **1** : to blurt out **2** : to skewer
espía *nmf* : spy
espiar {85} *vt* : to spy on, to observe — *vi* : to spy
espiga *nf* **1** : ear (of wheat) **2** : spike (of flowers)
espigado, -da *adj* : willowy, slender
espigar {52} *vt* : to glean, to gather — **espigarse** *vr* : to grow quickly, to shoot up
espigón *nm, pl* **-gones** : breakwater
espina *nf* **1** : thorn **2** : spine <espina dorsal : spinal column> **3** : fish bone
espinaca *nf* **1** : spinach (plant) **2 espinacas** *nfpl* : spinach (food)
espinal *adj* : spinal
espinazo *nm* : backbone
espineta *nf* : spinet
espinilla *nf* **1** BARRO, GRANO : pimple **2** : shin
espino *nm* : hawthorn
espinoso, -sa *adj* **1** : thorny, prickly **2** : bony (of fish) **3** : knotty, difficult
espionaje *nm* : espionage
espiración *nf, pl* **-ciones** : exhalation
espiral *adj & nf* : spiral
espirar *vt* EXHALAR : to breathe out, to give off — *vi* : to exhale
espiritismo *nm* : spiritualism
espiritista *nmf* : spiritualist
espíritu *nm* **1** : spirit **2** ÁNIMO : state of mind, spirits *pl* **3 el Espíritu Santo** : the Holy Ghost
espiritual *adj* : spiritual — **espiritualmente** *adv*
espiritualidad *nf* : spirituality
espita *nf* : spigot, tap
esplendidez *nf, pl* **-deces** ESPLENDOR : magnificence, splendor
espléndido, -da *adj* **1** : splendid, magnificent **2** : generous, lavish — **espléndidamente** *adv*
esplendor *nm* ESPLENDIDEZ : splendor
esplendoroso, -sa *adj* MAGNÍFICO : magnificent, grand
espliego *nm* LAVANDA : lavender
espolear *vt* : to spur on
espoleta *nf* **1** DETONADOR : detonator, fuse **2** : wishbone
espolón *nm, pl* **-lones** : spur (of poultry), fetlock (of a horse)
espolvorear *vt* : to sprinkle, to dust
esponja *nf* **1** : sponge **2 tirar la esponja** : to throw in the towel
esponjado, -da *adj* : spongy
esponjoso, -sa *adj* **1** : spongy **2** : soft, fluffy
esponsales *nmpl* : betrothal, engagement
espontaneidad *nf* : spontaneity
espontáneo, -nea *adj* : spontaneous — **espontáneamente** *adv*
espora *nf* : spore
esporádico, -ca *adj* : sporadic — **esporádicamente** *adv*
esposar *vt* : to handcuff
esposas *nfpl* : handcuffs
esposo, -sa *n* : spouse, wife *f*, husband *m*
esprint *nm* : sprint
esprintar *vi* : to sprint
esprínter *nmf* : sprinter
espuela *nf* : spur
espuerta *nf* : two-handled basket
espulgar {52} *vt* **1** : to delouse **2** : to scrutinize
espuma *nf* **1** : foam **2** : lather **3** : froth, head (on beer)
espumar *vi* : to foam, to froth — *vt* : to skim off
espumoso, -sa *adj* : foamy, frothy
espurio, -ria *adj* : spurious
esputar *v* : to expectorate, to spit
esputo *nm* : spit, sputum
esqueje *nm* : cutting (from a plant)
esquela *nf* **1** : note **2** : notice, announcement
esquelético, -ca *adj* : emaciated, skeletal
esqueleto *nm* **1** : skeleton **2** ARMAZÓN : framework
esquema *nf* BOSQUEJO : outline, sketch, plan
esquemático, -ca *adj* : schematic
esquí *nm* **1** : ski **2 esquí acuático** : water ski, waterskiing
esquiador, -dora *n* : skier
esquiar {85} *vi* : to ski
esquife *nm* : skiff
esquila *nf* **1** CENCERRO : cowbell **2** : shearing
esquilar *vt* TRASQUILAR : to shear
esquimal *adj & nmf* : Eskimo
esquina *nf* : corner
esquinazo *nm* **1** : corner **2 dar esquinazo a** *fam* : to stand up, to give the slip to
esquirla *nf* : splinter (of bone, glass, etc.)
esquirol *nm* ROMPEHUELGAS : strikebreaker, scab
esquisto *nm* : shale
esquivar *vt* **1** EVADIR : to dodge, to evade **2** EVITAR : to avoid
esquivez *nf, pl* **-veces** **1** : aloofness **2** TIMIDEZ : shyness
esquivo, -va *adj* **1** HURAÑO : aloof, unsociable **2** : shy **3** : elusive, evasive
esquizofrenia *nf* : schizophrenia
esquizofrénico, -ca *adj & n* : schizophrenic

esta *adj* → **este**[1]

ésta → **éste**

estabilidad *nf* : stability

estabilización *nf, pl* **-ciones** : stabilization

estabilizador *nm* : stabilizer

estabilizar {21} *vt* : to stabilize — **estabilizarse** *vr*

estable *adj* : stable, steady

establecer {53} *vt* FUNDAR, INSTITUIR : to establish, to found, to set up — **establecerse** *vr* INSTALARSE : to settle, to establish oneself

establecimiento *nm* **1** : establishing **2** : establishment, institution, office

establo *nm* : stable

estaca *nf* : stake, picket, post

estacada *nf* **1** : picket fence **2** : stockade

estacar {72} *vt* **1** : to stake out **2** : to fasten down with stakes — **estacarse** *vr* : to remain rigid

estación *nf, pl* **-ciones** **1** : station ⟨estación de servicio : service station, gas station⟩ **2** : season

estacional *adj* : seasonal

estacionamiento *nm* **1** : parking **2** : parking lot

estacionar *vt* **1** : to place, to station **2** : to park — **estacionarse** *vr* **1** : to park **2** : to remain stationary

estacionario, -ria *adj* **1** : stationary **2** : stable

estada *nf* : stay

estadía *nf* ESTANCIA : stay, sojourn

estadio *nm* **1** : stadium **2** : phase, stage

estadista *nmf* : statesman

estadística *nf* **1** : statistic, figure **2** : statistics

estadístico[1], **-ca** *adj* : statistical — **estadísticamente** *adv*

estadístico[2], **-ca** *n* : statistician

estado *nm* **1** : state **2** : status ⟨estado civil : marital status⟩ **3** CONDICIÓN : condition

estadounidense *adj & nmf* AMERICANO, NORTEAMERICANO : American

estafa *nf* : swindle, fraud

estafador, -dora *n* : cheat, swindler

estafar *vt* DEFRAUDAR : to swindle, to defraud

estalactita *nf* : stalactite

estalagmita *nf* : stalagmite

estallar *vi* **1** REVENTAR : to burst, to explode, to erupt **2** : to break out

estallido *nm* **1** EXPLOSIÓN : explosion **2** : report (of a gun) **3** : outbreak, outburst

estambre *nm* **1** : worsted (fabric) **2** : stamen

estampa *nf* **1** ILUSTRACIÓN, IMAGEN : printed image, illustration **2** ASPECTO : appearance, demeanor

estampado[1], **-da** *adj* : patterned, printed

estampado[2] *nm* : print, pattern

estampar *vt* : to stamp, to print, to engrave

estampida *nf* : stampede

estampilla *nf* **1** : rubber stamp **2** SELLO, TIMBRE : postage stamp

estancado, -da *adj* : stagnant

estancamiento *nm* : stagnation

estancar {72} *vt* **1** : to dam up, to hold back **2** : to bring to a halt, to deadlock — **estancarse** *vr* **1** : to stagnate **2** : to be brought to a standstill, to be deadlocked

estancia *nf* **1** ESTADÍA : stay, sojourn **2** : ranch, farm

estanciero, -ra *n* : rancher, farmer

estanco, -ca *adj* : watertight

estándar *adj & nm* : standard

estandarización *nf, pl* **-ciones** : standardization

estandarizar {21} *vt* : to standardize

estandarte *nm* : standard, banner

estanque *nm* **1** : pool, pond **2** : tank, reservoir

estante *nm* REPISA : shelf

estantería *nf* : shelves *pl,* bookcase

estaño *nm* : tin

estaquilla *nf* **1** : peg **2** ESPIGA : spike

estar {34} *v aux* : to be ⟨estoy aprendiendo inglés : I'm learning English⟩ ⟨está terminado : it's finished⟩ — *vi* **1** (*indicating a state or condition*) : to be ⟨está muy alto : he's so tall, he's gotten very tall⟩ ⟨¿ya estás mejor? : are you feeling better now?⟩ ⟨estoy casado : I'm married⟩ **2** (*indicating location*) : to be ⟨están en la mesa : they're on the table⟩ ⟨estamos en la página 2 : we're on page 2⟩ **3** : to be at home ⟨¿está María? : is Maria in?⟩ **4** : to remain ⟨estaré aquí 5 días : I'll be here for 5 days⟩ **5** : to be ready, to be done ⟨estará para las diez : it will be ready by ten o'clock⟩ **6** : to agree ⟨¿estamos? : are we in agreement?⟩ ⟨estoy contigo : I'm with you⟩ **7 ¿cómo estás?** : how are you? **8 ¡está bien!** : all right!, that's fine! **9 ~ a** : to cost **10 ~ a** : to be ⟨¿a qué día estamos? : what's today's date?⟩ **11 ~ con** : to have ⟨está con fiebre : she has a fever⟩ **12 ~ de** : to be ⟨estoy de vacaciones : I'm on vacation⟩ ⟨está de director hoy : he's acting as director today⟩ **13 estar bien (mal)** : to be well (sick) **14 ~ para** : to be in the mood for **15 ~ por** : to be in favor of **16 ~ por** : to be about to ⟨está por cerrar : it's on the verge of closing⟩ **17 estar de más** : to be unnecessary **18 estar que** : to be (in a state or condition) ⟨está que echa chispas : he's hopping mad⟩ — **estarse** *vr* QUEDARSE : to stay, to remain ⟨¡estáte quieto! : be still!⟩

estarcir {83} *vt* : to stencil

estatal *adj* : state, national

estática *nf* : static

estático, -ca *adj* : static

estatizar {21} *vt* : to nationalize — **estatización** *nf*

estatua *nf* : statue

estatuilla *nf* : statuette, figurine
estatura *nf* : height, stature ⟨de mediana estatura : of medium height⟩
estatus *nm* : status, prestige
estatutario, -ria *adj* : statutory
estatuto *nm* : statute
este[1], **esta** *adj, mpl* **estos** : this, these
este[2] *adj* : eastern, east
este[3] *nm* **1** ORIENTE : east **2** : east wind **3 el Este** : the East, the Orient
éste, ésta *pron, mpl* **éstos** **1** : this one, these ones *pl* **2** : the latter
estela *nf* **1** : wake (of a ship) **2** RASTRO : trail (of dust, smoke, etc.)
estelar *adj* : stellar
estelarizar {21} *vt Mex* : to star in, to be the star of
esténcil *nm* : stencil
estentóreo, -rea *adj* : loud, thundering
estepa *nf* : steppe
éster *nf* : ester
estera *nf* : mat
estercolero *nm* : dunghill
estéreo *adj & nm* : stereo
estereofónico, -ca *adj* : stereophonic
estereotipado, -da *adj* : stereotyped
estereotipar *vt* : to stereotype
estereotipo *nm* : stereotype
estéril *adj* **1** : sterile, germ-free **2** : infertile, barren **3** : futile, vain
esterilidad *nf* **1** : sterility **2** : infertility
esterilizar {21} *vt* **1** : to sterilize, to disinfect **2** : to sterilize (a person), to spay (an animal) — **esterilización** *nf*
esterlina *adj* : sterling
esternón *nm, pl* **-nones** : sternum
estero *nm* : estuary
estertor *nm* : death rattle
estética *nf* : aesthetics
estético, -ca *adj* : aesthetic — **estéticamente** *adv*
estetoscopio *nm* : stethoscope
estibador, -dora *n* : longshoreman, stevedore
estibar *vt* : to load (freight)
estiércol *nm* : dung, manure
estigma *nm* : stigma
estigmatizar {21} *vt* : to stigmatize, to brand
estilarse *vr* : to be in fashion
estilete *nm* : stiletto
estilista *nmf* : stylist
estilizar {21} *vt* : to stylize
estilo *nm* **1** : style **2** : fashion, manner **3** : stylus
estima *nf* ESTIMACIÓN : esteem, regard
estimable *adj* **1** : considerable **2** : estimable, esteemed
estimación *nf, pl* **-ciones** **1** ESTIMA : esteem, regard **2** : estimate
estimado, -da *adj* : esteemed, dear ⟨Estimado señor Ortiz : Dear Mr. Ortiz⟩
estimar *vt* **1** APRECIAR : to esteem, to respect **2** EVALUAR : to estimate, to appraise **3** OPINAR : to consider, to deem
estimulación *nf, pl* **-ciones** : stimulation
estimulante[1] *adj* : stimulating
estimulante[2] *nm* : stimulant
estimular *vt* **1** : to stimulate **2** : to encourage
estímulo *nm* **1** : stimulus **2** INCENTIVO : incentive, encouragement
estío *nm* : summertime
estipendio *nm* **1** : salary **2** : stipend, remuneration
estipular *vt* : to stipulate — **estipulación** *nf*
estirado, -da *adj* **1** : stretched, extended **2** PRESUMIDO : stuck-up, conceited
estiramiento *nm* **1** : stretching **2 estiramiento facial** : face-lift
estirar *vt* : to stretch (out), to extend — **estirarse** *vr*
estirón *nm, pl* **-rones** **1** : pull, tug **2 dar un estirón** : to grow quickly, to shoot up
estirpe *nf* LINAJE : lineage, stock
estival *adj* VERANIEGO : summer
esto *pron (neuter)* **1** : this ⟨¿qué es esto? : what is this?⟩ **2 en ~** : at this point **3 por ~** : for this reason
estocada *nf* **1** : final thrust (in bullfighting) **2** : thrust, lunge (in fencing)
estofa *nf* CLASE : class, quality ⟨de baja estofa : low-class, poor-quality⟩
estofado *nm* COCIDO, GUISADO : stew
estofar *vt* GUISAR : to stew
estoicismo *nm* : stoicism
estoico[1], **-ca** *adj* : stoic, stoical
estoico[2], **-ca** *n* : stoic
estola *nf* : stole
estomacal *adj* GÁSTRICO : stomach, gastric
estómago *nm* : stomach
estoniano, -na *adj & n* : Estonian
estonio, -nia *adj & n* : Estonian
estopa *nf* **1** : tow (yarn or cloth) **2** : burlap
estopilla *nf* : cheesecloth
estoque *nm* : rapier, sword
estorbar *vt* OBSTRUIR : to obstruct, to hinder — *vi* : to get in the way
estorbo *nm* **1** : obstacle, hindrance **2** : nuisance
estornino *nm* : starling
estornudar *vi* : to sneeze
estornudo *nm* : sneeze
estos *adj* → **este**[1]
éstos → **éste**
estoy → **estar**
estrabismo *nm* : squint
estrado *nm* **1** : dais, platform, bench (of a judge) **2 estrados** *nmpl* : courts of law
estrafalario, -ria *adj* ESTRAMBÓTICO, EXCÉNTRICO : eccentric, bizarre
estragar {52} *vt* DEVASTAR : to ruin, to devastate
estragón *nm* : tarragon
estragos *nmpl* **1** : ravages, destruction, devastation ⟨los estragos de la guerra : the ravages of war⟩ **2 hacer estragos en** *or* **causar estragos entre** : to play havoc with
estrambótico, -ca *adj* ESTRAFALARIO, EXCÉNTRICO : eccentric, bizarre

estrangulamiento *nm* : strangling, strangulation
estrangular *vt* AHOGAR : to strangle — **estrangulación** *nf*
estratagema *nf* ARTIMAÑA : stratagem, ruse
estratega *nmf* : strategist
estrategia *nf* : strategy
estratégico, -ca *adj* : strategic, tactical — **estratégicamente** *adv*
estratificación *nf, pl* **-ciones** : stratification
estratificado, -da *adj* : stratified
estrato *nm* : stratum, layer
estratosfera *nf* : stratosphere
estratosférico, -ca *adj* **1** : stratospheric **2** : astronomical, exorbitant
estrechamiento *nm* **1** : narrowing **2** : narrow point **3** : tightening, strengthening (of relations)
estrechar *vt* **1** : to narrow **2** : to tighten, to strengthen (a bond) **3** : to hug, to embrace **4 estrechar la mano de** : to shake hands with — **estrecharse** *vr*
estrechez *nf, pl* **-checes 1** : tightness, narrowness **2 estrecheces** *nfpl* : financial problems
estrecho[1], **-cha** *adj* **1** : tight, narrow **2** ÍNTIMO : close — **estrechamente** *adv*
estrecho[2] *nm* : strait, narrows
estrella *nf* **1** ASTRO : star ⟨estrella fugaz : shooting star⟩ **2** : destiny ⟨tener buena estrella : to be born lucky⟩ **3** : movie star **4 estrella de mar** : starfish
estrellado, -da *adj* **1** : starry **2** : star-shaped **3 huevos estrellados** : fried eggs
estrellamiento *nm* : crash, collision
estrellar *vt* : to smash, to crash — **estrellarse** *vr* : to crash, to collide
estrellato *nm* : stardom
estremecedor, -dora *adj* : horrifying
estremecer {53} *vt* : to cause to shake — *vi* : to tremble, to shake — **estremecerse** *vr* : to shudder, to shiver (with emotion)
estremecimiento *nm* : trembling, shaking, shivering
estrenar *vt* **1** : to use for the first time **2** : to premiere, to open — **estrenarse** *vr* : to make one's debut
estreno *nm* DEBUT : debut, premiere
estreñimiento *nm* : constipation
estreñirse {67} *vr* : to be constipated
estrépito *nm* ESTRUENDO : clamor, din
estrepitoso, -sa *adj* : clamorous, noisy — **estrepitosamente** *adv*
estrés *nm, pl* **estreses** : stress
estresante *adj* : stressful
estresar *vt* : to stress, to stress out
estría *nf* : fluting, groove
estribación *nf, pl* **-ciones 1** : spur, ridge **2 estribaciones** *nfpl* : foothills
estribar *vi* FUNDARSE **~ en** : to be due to, to stem from
estribillo *nm* : refrain, chorus
estribo *nm* **1** : stirrup **2** : abutment, buttress **3 perder los estribos** : to lose one's temper
estribor *nm* : starboard
estricnina *nf* : strychnine
estricto, -ta *adj* SEVERO : strict, severe — **estrictamente** *adv*
estridente *adj* : strident, shrill, loud — **estridentemente** *adv*
estrofa *nf* : stanza, verse
estrógeno *nm* : estrogen
estropajo *nm* : scouring pad
estropear *vt* **1** ARRUINAR : to ruin, to spoil **2** : to break, to damage — **estropearse** *vr* **1** : to spoil, to go bad **2** : to break down
estropicio *nm* DAÑO : damage, breakage
estructura *nf* : structure, framework
estructuración *nf, pl* **-ciones** : structuring, structure
estructural *adj* : structural — **estructuralmente** *adv*
estructurar *vt* : to structure, to organize
estruendo *nm* ESTRÉPITO : racket, din, roar
estruendoso, -sa *adj* : resounding, thunderous
estrujar *vt* APRETAR : to press, to squeeze
estuario *nm* : estuary
estuche *nm* : kit, case
estuco *nm* : stucco
estudiado, -da *adj* : affected, mannered
estudiantado *nm* : student body, students *pl*
estudiante *nmf* : student
estudiantil *adj* : student ⟨la vida estudiantil : student life⟩
estudiar *v* : to study
estudio *nm* **1** : study **2** : studio **3 estudios** *nmpl* : studies, education
estudioso, -sa *adj* : studious
estufa *nf* **1** : stove, heater **2** *Col, Mex* : cooking stove, range
estupefacción *nf, pl* **-ciones** : stupefaction, astonishment
estupefaciente[1] *adj* : narcotic
estupefaciente[2] *nm* DROGA, NARCÓTICO : drug, narcotic
estupefacto, -ta *adj* : astonished, stunned
estupendo, -da *adj* MARAVILLOSO : stupendous, marvelous — **estupendamente** *adv*
estupidez *nf, pl* **-deces 1** : stupidity **2** : nonsense
estúpido[1], **-da** *adj* : stupid — **estúpidamente** *adj*
estúpido[2], **-da** *n* IDIOTA : idiot, fool
estupor *nm* **1** : stupor **2** : amazement
esturión *nm, pl* **-riones** : sturgeon
estuvo, etc. → **estar**
etano *nm* : ethane
etanol *nm* : ethanol
etapa *nf* FASE : stage, phase
etcétera[1] : et cetera, and so on
etcétera[2] *nmf* : et cetera
éter *nm* : ether

etéreo, **-rea** *adj* : ethereal, heavenly
eternidad *nf* : eternity
eternizar {21} *vt* PERPETUAR : to make eternal, to perpetuate — **eternizarse** *vr fam* : to take forever
eterno, **-na** *adj* : eternal, endless — **eternamente** *adv*
ética *nf* : ethics
ético, **-ca** *adj* : ethical — **éticamente** *adv*
etimología *nf* : etymology
etimológico, **-ca** *adj* : etymological
etimólogo, **-ga** *n* : etymologist
etíope *adj & nmf* : Ethiopian
etiqueta *nf* **1** : etiquette **2** : tag, label **3 de ~** : formal, dressy
etiquetar *vt* : to label
étnico, **-ca** *adj* : ethnic
etnología *nf* : ethnology
etnólogo, **-ga** *n* : ethnologist
eucalipto *nm* : eucalyptus
Eucaristía *nf* : Eucharist, communion
eucarístico, **-ca** *adj* : eucharistic
eufemismo *nm* : euphemism
eufemístico, **-ca** *adj* : euphemistic
eufonía *nf* : euphony
eufónico, **-ca** *adj* : euphonious
euforia *nf* : euphoria, joyousness
eufórico, **-ca** *adj* : euphoric, exuberant, joyous — **eufóricamente** *adv*
eunuco *nm* : eunuch
europeo, **-pea** *adj & n* : European
euskera *nm* : Basque (language)
eutanasia *nf* : euthanasia
evacuación *nf, pl* **-ciones** : evacuation
evacuar *vt* **1** : to evacuate, to vacate **2** : to carry out — *vi* : to have a bowel movement
evadir *vt* ELUDIR : to evade, to avoid — **evadirse** *vr* : to escape, to slip away
evaluación *nf, pl* **-ciones** : assessment, evaluation
evaluador, **-dora** *n* : assessor
evaluar {3} *vt* : to evaluate, to assess, to appraise
evangélico, **-ca** *adj* : evangelical — **evangélicamente** *adv*
evangelio *nm* : gospel
evangelismo *nm* : evangelism
evangelista *nm* : evangelist
evangelizador, **-dora** *n* : evangelist, missionary
evaporación *nf, pl* **-ciones** : evaporation
evaporar *vt* : to evaporate — **evaporarse** *vr* ESFUMARSE : to disappear, to vanish
evasión *nf, pl* **-siones** **1** : escape, flight **2** : evasion, dodge
evasiva *nf* : excuse, pretext
evasivo, **-va** *adj* : evasive
evento *nm* : event
eventual *adj* **1** : possible **2** : temporary ⟨trabajadores eventuales : temporary workers⟩ — **eventualmente** *adv*
eventualidad *nf* : possibility, eventuality
evidencia *nf* **1** : evidence, proof **2 poner en evidencia** : to demonstrate, to make clear
evidenciar *vt* : to demonstrate, to show — **evidenciarse** *vr* : to be evident
evidente *adj* : evident, obvious, clear — **evidentemente** *adv*
eviscerar *vt* : to eviscerate
evitable *adj* : avoidable, preventable
evitar *vt* **1** : to avoid **2** PREVENIR : to prevent **3** ELUDIR : to escape, to elude
evocación *nf, pl* **-ciones** : evocation
evocador, **-dora** *adj* : evocative
evocar {72} *vt* **1** : to evoke **2** RECORDAR : to recall
evolución *nf, pl* **-ciones** **1** : evolution **2** : development, progress
evolucionar *vi* **1** : to evolve **2** : to change, to develop
evolutivo, **-va** *adj* : evolutionary
exabrupto *nm* : pointed remark
exacción *nf, pl* **-ciones** : levying, exaction
exacerbar *vt* **1** : to exacerbate, to aggravate **2** : to irritate, to exasperate
exactamente *adv* : exactly
exactitud *nf* PRECISIÓN : accuracy, precision, exactitude
exacto, **-ta** *adj* PRECISO : accurate, precise, exact
exageración *nf, pl* **-ciones** : exaggeration
exagerado, **-da** *adj* **1** : exaggerated **2** : excessive — **exageradamente** *adv*
exagerar *v* : to exaggerate
exaltación *nf, pl* **-ciones** **1** : exaltation **2** : excitement, agitation
exaltado[1], **-da** *adj* : excitable, hotheaded
exaltado[2], **-da** *n* : hothead
exaltar *vt* **1** ENSALZAR : to exalt, to extol **2** : to excite, to agitate — **exaltarse** *vr* ACALORARSE : to get overexcited
ex–alumno → **alumno**
examen *nm, pl* **exámenes** **1** : examination, test **2** : consideration, investigation
examinar *vt* **1** : to examine **2** INSPECCIONAR : to inspect — **examinarse** *vr* : to take an exam
exánime *adj* **1** : lifeless **2** : exhausted
exasperante *adj* : exasperating
exasperar *vt* IRRITAR : to exasperate, to irritate — **exasperación** *nf*
excavación *nf, pl* **-ciones** : excavation
excavadora *nf* : excavator
excavar *v* : to excavate, to dig
excedente[1] *adj* **1** : excessive **2** : excess, surplus
excedente[2] *nm* : surplus, excess
exceder *vt* : to exceed, to surpass — **excederse** *vr* : to go too far
excelencia *nf* **1** : excellence **2** : excellency ⟨Su Excelencia : His Excellency⟩
excelente *adj* : excellent — **excelentemente** *adv*
excelso, **-sa** *adj* : lofty, sublime
excentricidad *nf* : eccentricity
excéntrico, **-ca** *adj & n* : eccentric
excepción *nf, pl* **-ciones** : exception
excepcional *adj* EXTRAORDINARIO : exceptional, extraordinary, rare

excepto *prep* SALVO : except
exceptuar {3} *vt* EXCLUIR : to except, to exclude
excesivo, -va *adj* : excessive — **excesivamente** *adv*
exceso *nm* **1** : excess **2 excesos** *nmpl* : excesses, abuses **3 exceso de velocidad** : speeding
excitabilidad *nf* : excitability
excitación *nf, pl* **-ciones** : excitement
excitante *adj* : exciting
excitar *vt* : to excite, to arouse — **excitarse** *vr*
exclamación *nf, pl* **-ciones** : exclamation
exclamar *v* : to exclaim
excluir {41} *vt* EXCEPTUAR : to exclude, to leave out
exclusión *nf, pl* **-siones** : exclusion
exclusividad *nf* **1** : exclusiveness **2** : exclusive rights *pl*
exclusivista *adj & nmf* : exclusivist
exclusivo, -va *adj* : exclusive — **exclusivamente** *adv*
excomulgar {52} *vt* : to excommunicate
excomunión *nf, pl* **-niones** : excommunication
excreción *nf, pl* **-ciones** : excretion
excremento *nm* : excrement
excretar *vt* : to excrete
exculpar *vt* : to exonerate, to exculpate — **exculpación** *nf*
excursión *nf, pl* **-siones** : excursion, outing
excursionista *nmf* **1** : sightseer, tourist **2** : hiker
excusa *nf* **1** PRETEXTO : excuse **2** DISCULPA : apology
excusado *nm Mex* : toilet
excusar *vt* **1** : to excuse **2** : to exempt — **excusarse** *vr* : to apologize, to send one's regrets
execrable *adj* : detestable, abominable
exención *nf, pl* **-ciones** : exemption
exento, -ta *adj* **1** : exempt, free **2 exento de impuestos** : tax-exempt
exequias *nfpl* FUNERALES : funeral rites
exhalación *nf, pl* **-ciones** **1** : exhalation **2** : shooting star ⟨salió como una exhalación : he took off like a shot⟩
exhalar *vt* ESPIRAR : to exhale, to give off
exhaustivo, -va *adj* : exhaustive — **exhaustivamente** *adv*
exhausto, -ta *adj* AGOTADO : exhausted, worn-out
exhibición *nf, pl* **-ciones** **1** : exhibition, show **2** : showing
exhibir *vt* : to exhibit, to show, to display — **exhibirse** *vr*
exhortación *nf, pl* **-ciones** : exhortation
exhortar *vt* : to exhort
exhumar *vt* DESENTERRAR : to exhume — **exhumación** *nf*
exigencia *nf* : demand, requirement
exigente *adj* : demanding, exacting
exigir {35} *vt* **1** : to demand, to require **2** : to exact, to levy
exiguo, -gua *adj* : meager
exiliado[1]**, -da** *adj* : exiled, in exile
exiliado[2]**, -da** *n* : exile
exiliar *vt* DESTERRAR : to exile, to banish — **exiliarse** *vr* : to go into exile
exilio *nm* DESTIERRO : exile
eximio, -mia *adj* : distinguished, eminent
eximir *vt* EXONERAR : to exempt
existencia *nf* **1** : existence **2 existencias** *nfpl* MERCANCÍA : goods, stock
existente *adj* **1** : existing, in existence **2** : in stock
existir *vi* : to exist
éxito *nm* **1** TRIUNFO : success, hit **2 tener éxito** : to be successful
exitoso, -sa *adj* : successful — **exitosamente** *adv*
éxodo *nm* : exodus
exoneración *nf, pl* **-ciones** EXENCIÓN : exoneration, exemption
exonerar *vt* **1** EXIMIR : to exempt, to exonerate **2** DESPEDIR : to dismiss
exorbitante *adj* : exorbitant
exorcismo *nm* : exorcism — **exorcista** *nmf*
exorcizar {21} *vt* : to exorcise
exótico, -ca *adj* : exotic
expandir *vt* EXPANSIONAR : to expand — **expandirse** *vr* : to spread
expansión *nf, pl* **-siones** **1** : expansion, spread **2** DIVERSIÓN : recreation, relaxation
expansionar *vt* EXPANDIR : to expand — **expansionarse** *vr* **1** : to expand **2** DIVERTIRSE : to amuse oneself, to relax
expansivo, -va *adj* : expansive
expatriado, -da *adj & n* : expatriate
expatriarse {85} *vr* **1** EMIGRAR : to emigrate **2** : to go into exile
expectación *nf, pl* **-ciones** : expectation, anticipation
expectante *adj* : expectant
expectativa *nf* **1** : expectation, hope **2 expectativas** *nfpl* : prospects
expedición *nf, pl* **-ciones** : expedition
expediente *nm* **1** : expedient, means **2** ARCHIVO : file, dossier, record
expedir {54} *vt* **1** EMITIR : to issue **2** DESPACHAR : to dispatch, to send
expedito, -ta *adj* **1** : free, clear **2** : quick, easy
expeler *vt* : to expel, to eject
expendedor, -dora *n* : dealer, seller
expendio *nm* TIENDA : store, shop
expensas *nfpl* **1** : expenses, costs **2 a expensas de** : at the expense of
experiencia *nf* **1** : experience **2** EXPERIMENTO : experiment
experimentación *nf, pl* **-ciones** : experimentation
experimental *adj* : experimental
experimentar *vi* : to experiment — *vt* **1** : to experiment with, to test out **2** : to experience
experimento *nm* EXPERIENCIA : experiment

experto, -ta *adj & n* : expert

expiación *nf, pl* **-ciones** : expiation, atonement

expiar {85} *vt* : to expiate, to atone for

expiración *nf, pl* **-ciones** VENCIMIENTO : expiration

expirar *vi* **1** FALLECER, MORIR : to pass away, to die **2** : to expire

explanada *nf* : esplanade, promenade

explayar *vt* : to extend — **explayarse** *vr* : to expound, to speak at length

explicable *adj* : explicable, explainable

explicación *nf, pl* **-ciones** : explanation

explicar {72} *vt* : to explain — **explicarse** *vr* : to understand

explicativo, -va *adj* : explanatory

explicitar *vt* : to state explicitly, to specify

explícito, -ta *adj* : explicit — **explícitamente** *adv*

exploración *nf, pl* **-ciones** : exploration

explorador, -dora *n* : explorer, scout

explorar *vt* : to explore — **exploratorio, -ria** *adj*

explosión *nf, pl* **-siones** **1** ESTALLIDO : explosion **2** : outburst ⟨una explosión de ira : an outburst of anger⟩

explosioniar *vi* : to explode

explosivo, -va *adj* : explosive

explotación *nf, pl* **-ciones** **1** : exploitation **2** : operation, running

explotar *vt* **1** : to exploit **2** : to operate, to run — *vi* ESTALLAR, REVENTAR : to explode — **explotable** *adj*

exponencial *adj* : exponential — **exponencialmente** *adv*

exponente *nm* : exponent

exponer {60} *vt* **1** : to exhibit, to show, to display **2** : to explain, to present, to set forth **3** : to expose, to risk — *vi* : to exhibit

exportación *nf, pl* **-ciones** **1** : exportation **2** **exportaciones** *nfpl* : exports

exportador, -dora *n* : exporter

exportar *vt* : to export — **exportable** *adj*

exposición *nf, pl* **-ciones** **1** EXHIBICIÓN : exposition, exhibition **2** : exposure **3** : presentation, statement

expositor, -tora *n* **1** : exhibitor **2** : exponent

exprés *nms & pl* **1** : express, express train **2** : espresso

expresamente *adv* : expressly, on purpose

expresar *vt* : to express — **expresarse** *vr*

expresión *nf, pl* **-siones** : expression

expresivo, -va *adj* **1** : expressive **2** CARIÑOSO : affectionate — **expresivamente** *adv*

expreso[1], -sa *adj* : express, specific

expreso[2] *nm* : express train, express

exprimidor *nm* : squeezer, juicer

exprimir *vt* **1** : to squeeze **2** : to exploit

expropiar *vt* : to expropriate, to commandeer — **expropiación** *nf*

expuesto[1] *pp* → **exponer**

expuesto[2], -ta *adj* **1** : exposed **2** : hazardous, risky

expulsar *vt* : to expel, to eject

expulsión *nf, pl* **-siones** : expulsion

expurgar {52} *vt* : to expurgate

expuso, etc. → **exponer**

exquisitez *nf, pl* **-teces** **1** : exquisiteness, refinement **2** : delicacy, special dish

exquisito, -ta *adj* **1** : exquisite **2** : delicious

extasiarse {85} *vr* : to be in ecstasy, to be enraptured

éxtasis *nms & pl* : ecstasy, rapture

extático, -ca *adj* : ecstatic

extemporáneo, -nea *adj* **1** : unseasonable **2** : untimely

extender {56} *vt* **1** : to spread out, to stretch out **2** : to broaden, to expand ⟨extender la influencia : to broaden one's influence⟩ **3** : to draw up (a document), to write out (a check) — **extenderse** *vr* **1** : to spread **2** : to last

extendido, -da *adj* **1** : outstretched **2** : widespread

extensamente *adv* : extensively, at length

extensible *adj* : extensible, extendable

extensión *nf, pl* **-siones** **1** : extension, stretching **2** : expanse, spread **3** : extent, range **4** : length, duration

extensivo, -va *adj* **1** : extensive **2** **hacer extensivo** : to extend

extenso, -sa *adj* **1** : extensive, detailed **2** : spacious, vast

extenuar {3} *vt* : to exhaust, to tire out — **extenuarse** *vr* — **extenuante** *adj*

exterior[1] *adj* **1** : exterior, external **2** : foreign ⟨asuntos exteriores : foreign affairs⟩

exterior[2] *nm* **1** : outside **2** : abroad

exteriorizar {21} *vt* : to express, to reveal

exteriormente *adv* : outwardly

exterminar *vt* : to exterminate — **exterminación** *nf*

exterminio *nm* : extermination

externar *vt Mex* : to express, to display

externo, -na *adj* : external, outward

extinción *nf, pl* **-ciones** : extinction

extinguidor *nm* : fire extinguisher

extinguir {26} *vt* **1** APAGAR : to extinguish, to put out **2** : to wipe out — **extinguirse** *vr* **1** APAGARSE : to go out, to fade out **2** : to die out, to become extinct

extinto, -ta *adj* : extinct

extintor *nm* : extinguisher

extirpación *n, pl* **-ciones** : removal, excision

extirpar *vt* : to eradicate, to remove, to excise — **extirparse** *vr*

extorsión *nf, pl* **-siones** **1** : extortion **2** : harm, trouble

extorsionar *vt* : to extort

extra[1] *adv* : extra

extra[2] *adj* **1** : additional, extra **2** : superior, top-quality

extra[3] *nmf* : extra (in movies)

extra[4] *nm* : extra expense <paga extra : bonus>
extracción *nf, pl* **-ciones** : extraction
extracto *nm* **1** : extract <extracto de vainilla : vanilla extract> **2** : abstract, summary
extractor *nm* : extractor
extracurricular *adj* : extracurricular
extradición *nf, pl* **-ciones** : extradition
extraditar *vt* : to extradite
extraer {81} *vt* : to extract
extraído *pp* → **extraer**
extrajudicial *adj* : out-of-court
extramatrimonial *adj* : extramarital
extranjerizante *adj* : foreign-sounding, foreign-looking
extranjero[1], **-ra** *adj* : foreign
extranjero[2], **-ra** *n* : foreigner
extranjero[3] *nm* : foreign countries *pl* <viajó al extranjero : he traveled abroad> <trabajan en el extranjero : they work overseas>
extrañamente *adv* : strangely, oddly
extrañamiento *nm* ASOMBRO : amazement, surprise, wonder
extrañar *vt* : to miss (someone) — **extrañarse** *vr* : to be surprised
extrañeza *nf* **1** : strangeness, oddness **2** : surprise
extraño[1], **-ña** *adj* **1** RARO : strange, odd **2** EXTRANJERO : foreign
extraño[2], **-ña** *n* DESCONOCIDO : stranger
extraoficial *adj* OFICIOSO : unofficial — **extraoficialmente** *adv*
extraordinario, -ria *adj* EXCEPCIONAL : extraordinary — **extraordinariamente** *adv*
extrasensorial *adj* : extrasensory <percepción extrasensorial : extrasensory perception>
extraterrestre *adj & nmf* : extraterrestrial, alien
extravagancia *nf* : extravagance, outlandishness, flamboyance
extravagante *adj* : extravagant, outrageous, flamboyant
extraviar {85} *vt* **1** : to mislead, to lead astray **2** : to misplace, to lose — **extraviarse** *vr* : to get lost, to go astray
extravío *nm* **1** PÉRDIDA : loss, misplacement **2** : misconduct
extremado, -da *adj* : extreme — **extremadamente** *adv*
extremar *vt* : to carry to extremes — **extremarse** *vr* : to do one's utmost
extremidad *nf* **1** : extremity, tip, edge **2 extremidades** *nfpl* : extremities
extremista *adj & nmf* : extremist
extremo[1], **-ma** *adj* **1** : extreme, utmost **2** EXCESIVO : excessive **3 en caso extremo** : as a last resort
extremo[2] *nm* **1** : extreme, end **2 al extremo de** : to the point of **3 en ~** : in the extreme
extrovertido[1], **-da** *adj* : extroverted, outgoing
extrovertido[2], **-da** *n* : extrovert
extrudir *vt* : to extrude
exuberancia *nf* **1** : exuberance **2** : luxuriance, lushness
exuberante *adj* : exuberant, luxuriant — **exuberantemente** *adv*
exudar *vt* : to exude
exultación *nf, pl* **-ciones** : exultation, elation
exultante *adj* : exultant, elated — **exultantemente** *adv*
exultar *vi* : to exult, to rejoice
eyacular *vi* : to ejaculate — **eyaculación** *nf*
eyección *nf, pl* **-ciones** : ejection, expulsion
eyectar *vt* : to eject, to expel — **eyectarse** *vr*

F

f *nf* : sixth letter of the Spanish alphabet
fábrica *nf* FACTORÍA : factory
fabricación *nf, pl* **-ciones** : manufacture
fabricante *nmf* : manufacturer
fabricar {72} *vt* MANUFACTURAR : to manufacture, to make
fabril *adj* INDUSTRIAL : industrial, manufacturing
fábula *nf* **1** : fable **2** : fabrication, fib
fabuloso, -sa *adj* **1** : fabulous, fantastic **2** : mythical, fabled
facción *nf, pl* **facciones 1** : faction **2 facciones** *nfpl* RASGOS : features
faccioso, -sa *adj* : factious
faceta *nf* : facet
facha *nf* : appearance, look <estar hecho una facha : to look a sight>
fachada *nf* : facade
facial *adj* : facial
fácil *adj* **1** : easy **2** : likely, probable <es fácil que no pase : it probably won't happen>
facilidad *nf* **1** : facility, ease **2 facilidades** *nfpl* : facilities, services **3 facilidades** *nfpl* : opportunities
facilitar *vt* **1** : to facilitate **2** : to provide, to supply
fácilmente *adv* : easily, readily
facsímil *or* **facsímile** *nm* **1** : facsimile, copy **2** : fax
facsimilar *adj* : facsimile
factibilidad *nf* : feasibility
factible *adj* : feasible, practicable
facticio, -cia *adj* : artificial, factitious
factor[1], **-tora** *n* **1** : agent, factor **2** : baggage clerk
factor[2] *nm* ELEMENTO : factor, element
factoría *nf* FÁBRICA : factory
factótum *nm* : factotum

factura *nf* **1** : making, manufacturing **2** : bill, invoice

facturación *nf, pl* **-ciones** **1** : invoicing, billing **2** : check-in

facturar *vt* **1** : to bill, to invoice **2** : to register, to check in

facultad *nf* **1** : faculty, ability ⟨facultades mentales : mental faculties⟩ **2** : authority, power **3** : school (of a university) ⟨facultad de derecho : law school⟩

facultar *vt* : to authorize, to empower

facultativo, -va *adj* **1** OPTATIVO : voluntary, optional **2** : medical ⟨informe facultativo : medical report⟩

faena *nf* : task, job, work ⟨faenas domésticas : housework⟩

faenar *vi* **1** : to work, to labor **2** PESCAR : to fish

fagot *nm* : bassoon

faisán *nm, pl* **faisanes** : pheasant

faja *nf* **1** : sash, belt **2** : girdle **3** : strip (of land)

fajar *vt* **1** : to wrap (a sash or girdle) around **2** : to hit, to thrash — **fajarse** *vr* **1** : to put on a sash or girdle **2** : to come to blows

fajín *nm, pl* **-jines** : sash, belt

fajo *nm* : bundle, sheaf ⟨un fajo de billetes : a wad of cash⟩

falacia *nf* : fallacy

falaz, -laza *adj, mpl* **falaces** FALSO : fallacious, false

falda *nf* **1** : skirt ⟨falda escocesa : kilt⟩ **2** REGAZO : lap (of the body) **3** VERTIENTE : side, slope

faldón *nm, pl* **-dones** **1** : tail (of a shirt, etc.) **2** : full skirt **3 faldón bautismal** : christening gown

falible *adj* : fallible

fálico, -ca *adj* : phallic

falla *nf* **1** : flaw, defect **2** : (geological) fault **3** : fault, failing

fallar *vi* **1** FRACASAR : to fail, to go wrong **2** : to rule (in a court of law) — *vt* **1** ERRAR : to miss (a target) **2** : to pronounce judgment on

fallecer {53} *vi* MORIR : to pass away, to die

fallecido, -da *adj & n* DIFUNTO : deceased

fallecimiento *nm* : demise, death

fallido, -da *adj* : failed, unsuccessful

fallo *nm* **1** SENTENCIA : sentence, judgment, verdict **2** : error, fault

falo *nm* : phallus, penis

falsamente *adv* : falsely

falsear *vt* **1** : to falsify, to fake **2** : to distort — *vi* **1** CEDER : to give way **2** : to be out of tune

falsedad *nf* **1** : falseness, hypocrisy **2** MENTIRA : falsehood, lie

falsete *nm* : falsetto

falsificación *nf, pl* **-ciones** **1** : counterfeit, forgery **2** : falsification

falsificador, -dora *n* : counterfeiter, forger

falsificar {72} *vt* **1** : to counterfeit, to forge **2** : to falsify

falso, -sa *adj* **1** FALAZ : false, untrue **2** : counterfeit, forged

falta *nf* **1** CARENCIA : lack ⟨hacer falta : to be lacking, to be needed⟩ **2** DEFECTO : defect, fault, error **3** : offense, misdemeanor **4** : foul (in basketball), fault (in tennis)

faltar *vi* **1** : to be lacking, to be needed ⟨me falta tiempo : I don't have enough time⟩ **2** : to be absent, to be missing **3** QUEDAR : to remain, to be left ⟨faltan pocos días para la fiesta : the party is just a few days away⟩ **4 ¡no faltaba más!** : don't mention it!, you're welcome!

falto, -ta *adj* **~ de** : lacking (in), short of

fama *nf* **1** : fame **2** REPUTACIÓN : reputation **3 de mala fama** : disreputable

famélico, -ca *adj* HAMBRIENTO : starving, famished

familia *nf* **1** : family **2 familia política** : in-laws

familiar[1] *adj* **1** CONOCIDO : familiar **2** : familial, family **3** INFORMAL : informal

familiar[2] *nmf* PARIENTE : relation, relative

familiaridad *nf* **1** : familiarity **2** : informality

familiarizarse {21} *vr* **~ con** : to familiarize oneself with

famoso[1], **-sa** *adj* CÉLEBRE : famous

famoso[2], **-sa** *n* : celebrity

fanal *nm* **1** : beacon, signal light **2** *Mex* : headlight

fanático, -ca *adj & n* : fanatic

fanatismo *nm* : fanaticism

fandango *nm* : fandango

fanfarria *nf* **1** : (musical) fanfare **2** : pomp, ceremony

fanfarrón[1], **-rrona** *adj, mpl* **-rrones** *fam* : bragging, boastful

fanfarrón[2], **-rrona** *n, mpl* **-rrones** *fam* : braggart

fanfarronada *nf* : boast, bluster

fanfarronear *vi* : to brag, to boast

fango *nm* LODO : mud, mire

fangosidad *nf* : muddiness

fangoso, -sa *adj* LODOSO : muddy

fantasear *vi* : to fantasize, to daydream

fantasía *nf* **1** : fantasy **2** : imagination

fantasioso, -sa *adj* : fanciful

fantasma *nm* : ghost, phantom

fantasmagórico, -ca *adj* : phantasmagoric

fantasmal *adj* : ghostly

fantástico, -ca *adj* **1** : fantastic, imaginary, unreal **2** *fam* : great, fantastic

faquir *nm* : fakir

farándula *nf* : show business, theater

faraón *nm, pl* **faraones** : pharaoh

fardo *nm* **1** : bale **2** : bundle

farfulla *nf* : jabbering

farfullar *v* : to jabber, to gabble

faringe *nf* : pharynx

faríngeo, -gea *adj* : pharyngeal
fariña *nf* : coarse manioc flour
farmacéutico[1], **-ca** *adj* : pharmaceutical
farmacéutico[2], **-ca** *n* : pharmacist
farmacia *nf* : drugstore, pharmacy
fármaco *nm* : medicine, drug
farmacodependencia *nf* : drug addiction
farmacología *nf* : pharmacology
faro *nm* **1** : lighthouse **2** : headlight
farol *nm* **1** : streetlight **2** : lantern, lamp **3** *fam* : bluff **4** *Mex* : headlight
farola *nf* **1** : lamppost **2** : streetlight
farolero, -ra *n fam* : bluffer
farra *nf* : spree, revelry
fárrago *nm* REVOLTIJO : hodgepodge, jumble
farsa *nf* **1** : farce **2** : fake, sham
farsante *nmf* CHARLATÁN : charlatan, fraud, phony
fascículo *nm* : fascicle, part (of a publication)
fascinación *nf, pl* **-ciones** : fascination
fascinante *adj* : fascinating
fascinar *vt* **1** : to fascinate **2** : to charm, to captivate
fascismo *nm* : fascism
fascista *adj & nmf* : fascist
fase *nf* : phase, stage
fastidiar *vt* **1** MOLESTAR : to annoy, to bother, to hassle **2** ABURRIR : to bore — *vi* : to be annoying or bothersome
fastidio *nm* **1** MOLESTIA : annoyance, nuisance, hassle **2** ABURRIMIENTO : boredom
fastidioso, -sa *adj* **1** MOLESTO : annoying, bothersome **2** ABURRIDO : boring
fatal *adj* **1** MORTAL : fatal **2** *fam* : awful, terrible **3** : fateful, unavoidable
fatalidad *nf* **1** : fatality **2** DESGRACIA : misfortune, bad luck
fatalismo *nm* : fatalism
fatalista[1] *adj* : fatalistic
fatalista[2] *nmf* : fatalist
fatalmente *adv* **1** : unavoidably **2** : unfortunately
fatídico, -ca *adj* : fateful, momentous
fatiga *nf* CANSANCIO : fatigue
fatigado, -da *adj* AGOTADO : weary, tired
fatigar {52} *vt* CANSAR : to fatigue, to tire — **fatigarse** *vr* : to wear oneself out
fatigoso, -sa *adj* : fatiguing, tiring
fatuidad *nf* **1** : fatuousness **2** VANIDAD : vanity, conceit
fatuo, -tua *adj* **1** : fatuous **2** PRESUMIDO : vain
fauces *nfpl* : jaws *pl,* maw
faul *nm, pl* **fauls** : foul, foul ball
fauna *nf* : fauna
fausto *nm* : splendor, magnificence
favor *nm* **1** : favor **2 a favor de** : in favor of **3 por ~** : please
favorable *adj* : favorable — **favorablemente** *adv*
favorecedor, -dora *adj* : becoming, flattering
favorecer {53} *vt* **1** : to favor **2** : to look well on, to suit
favorecido, -da *adj* **1** : flattering **2** : fortunate
favoritismo *nm* : favoritism
favorito, -ta *adj & n* : favorite
fax *nm* : fax, facsimile
fayuca *nf Mex* **1** : contraband **2** : black market
fayuquero *nm Mex* : smuggler, black marketeer
faz *nf* **1** : face, countenance ⟨la faz de la tierra : the face of the earth⟩ **2** : side (of coins, fabric, etc.)
fe *nf* **1** : faith **2** : assurance, testimony ⟨dar fe de : to bear witness to⟩ **3** : intention, will ⟨de buena fe : bona fide, in good faith⟩
fealdad *nf* : ugliness
febrero *nm* : February
febril *adj* : feverish — **febrilmente** *adv*
fecal *adj* : fecal
fecha *nf* **1** : date **2 fecha de caducidad** *or* **fecha de vencimiento** : expiration date **3 fecha límite** : deadline
fechar *vt* : to date, to put a date on
fechoría *nf* : misdeed
fécula *nf* : starch
fecundar *vt* : to fertilize (an egg) — **fecundación** *nf*
fecundidad *nf* **1** : fecundity, fertility **2** : productiveness
fecundo, -da *adj* FÉRTIL : fertile, fecund
federación *nf, pl* **-ciones** : federation
federal *adj* : federal
federalismo *nm* : federalism
federalista *adj & nmf* : federalist
federar *vt* : to federate
fehaciente *adj* : reliable, irrefutable — **fehacientemente** *adv*
feldespato *nm* : feldspar
felicidad *nf* **1** : happiness **2 ¡felicidades!** : best wishes!, congratulations!, happy birthday!
felicitación *nf, pl* **-ciones** **1** : congratulation ⟨¡felicitaciones! : congratulations!⟩ **2** : greeting card
felicitar *vt* CONGRATULAR : to congratulate — **felicitarse** *vr* **~ de** : to be glad about
feligrés, -gresa *n, mpl* **-greses** : parishioner
feligresía *nf* : parish
felino, -na *adj & n* : feline
feliz *adj, pl* **felices** **1** : happy **2 Feliz Navidad** : Merry Christmas
felizmente *adv* **1** : happily **2** : fortunately, luckily
felonía *nf* : felony
felpa *nf* **1** : terry cloth **2** : plush
felpudo *nm* : doormat
femenil *adj* : women's, girls' ⟨futbol femenil : women's soccer⟩
femenino, -na *adj* **1** : feminine **2** : women's ⟨derechos femeninos : women's rights⟩ **3** : female
femineidad *nf* : femininity
feminidad *nf* : femininity
feminismo *nm* : feminism
feminista *adj & nmf* : feminist

femoral *adj* : femoral
fémur *nm* : femur, thighbone
fenecer {53} *vi* **1** : to die, to pass away **2** : to come to an end, to cease
fénix *nm* : phoenix
fenomenal *adj* **1** : phenomenal **2** *fam* : fantastic, terrific — **fenomenalmente** *adv*
fenómeno *nm* **1** : phenomenon **2** : prodigy, genius
feo[1] *adv* : badly, bad
feo[2], **fea** *adj* **1** : ugly **2** : unpleasant, nasty
féretro *nm* ATAÚD : coffin, casket
feria *nf* **1** : fair, market **2** : festival, holiday **3** *Mex* : change (money)
feriado, -da *adj* **día feriado** : public holiday
ferial *nm* : fairground
fermentar *v* : to ferment — **fermentación** *nf*
fermento *nm* : ferment
ferocidad *nf* : ferocity, fierceness
feroz *adj, pl* **feroces** FIERO : ferocious, fierce — **ferozmente** *adv*
férreo, -rrea *adj* **1** : iron **2** : strong, steely <una voluntad férrea : an iron will> **3** : strict, severe **4 vía férrea** : railroad track
ferretería *nf* **1** : hardware store **2** : hardware **3** : foundry, ironworks
férrico, -ca *adj* : ferric
ferrocarril *nm* : railroad, railway
ferrocarrilero → **ferroviario**
ferroso, -sa *adj* : ferrous
ferroviario, -ria *adj* : rail, railroad
ferry *nm, pl* **ferrys** : ferry
fértil *adj* FECUNDO : fertile, fruitful
fertilidad *nf* : fertility
fertilizante[1] *adj* : fertilizing <droga fertilizante : fertility drug>
fertilizante[2] *nm* ABONO : fertilizer
fertilizar *vt* ABONAR : to fertilize — **fertilización** *nf*
ferviente *adj* FERVOROSO : fervent
fervor *nm* : fervor, zeal
fervoroso, -sa *adj* FERVIENTE : fervent, zealous
festejar *vt* **1** CELEBRAR : to celebrate **2** AGASAJAR : to entertain, to wine and dine **3** *Mex fam* : to thrash, to beat
festejo *nm* : celebration, festivity
festín *nm, pl* **festines** : banquet, feast
festinar *vt* : to hasten, to hurry up
festival *nm* : festival
festividad *nf* **1** : festivity **2** : (religious) feast, holiday
festivo, -va *adj* **1** : festive **2 día festivo** : holiday — **festivamente** *adv*
fetal *adj* : fetal
fetiche *nm* : fetish
fétido, -da *adj* : fetid, foul
feto *nm* : fetus
feudal *adj* : feudal — **feudalismo** *nm*
feudo *nm* **1** : fief **2** : domain, territory
fiabilidad *nf* : reliability, trustworthiness
fiable *adj* : trustworthy, reliable
fiado, -da *adj* : on credit
fiador, -dora *n* : bondsman, guarantor
fiambrería *nf* : delicatessen
fiambres *nfpl* : cold cuts
fianza *nf* **1** CAUCIÓN : bail, bond **2** : surety, deposit
fiar {85} *vt* **1** : to sell on credit **2** : to guarantee — **fiarse** *vr* **~ de** : to place trust in
fiasco *nm* FRACASO : fiasco, failure
fibra *nf* **1** : fiber **2 fibra de vidrio** : fiberglass
fibrilar *vi* : to fibrillate — **fibrilación** *nf*
fibroso, -sa *adj* : fibrous
ficción *nf, pl* **ficciones** **1** : fiction **2** : fabrication, lie
ficha *nf* **1** : index card **2** : file, record **3** : token **4** : domino, checker, counter, poker chip
fichar *vt* **1** : to open a file on **2** : to sign up — *vi* : to punch in, to punch out
fichero *nm* **1** : card file **2** : filing cabinet
ficticio, -cia *adj* : fictitious
fidedigno, -na *adj* FIABLE : reliable, trustworthy
fideicomisario, -ria *n* : trustee
fideicomiso *nm* : trusteeship, trust <guardar en fideicomiso : to hold in trust>
fidelidad *nf* : fidelity, faithfulness
fideo *nm* : noodle
fiduciario[1], **-ria** *adj* : fiduciary
fiduciario[2], **-ria** *n* : trustee
fiebre *nf* **1** CALENTURA : fever, temperature <fiebre amarilla : yellow fever> <fiebre palúdica : malaria> **2** : fever, excitement
fiel[1] *adj* **1** : faithful, loyal **2** : accurate — **fielmente** *adv*
fiel[2] *nm* **1** : pointer (of a scale) **2 los fieles** : the faithful
fieltro *nm* : felt
fiera *nf* **1** : wild animal, beast **2** : fiend, demon <una fiera para el trabajo : a demon for work>
fiereza *nf* : fierceness, ferocity
fiero, -ra *adj* FEROZ : fierce, ferocious
fierro *nm* HIERRO : iron
fiesta *nf* **1** : party, fiesta **2** : holiday, feast day
figura *nf* **1** : figure **2** : shape, form **3 figura retórica** : figure of speech
figurado, -da *adj* : figurative — **figuradamente** *adv*
figurar *vi* **1** : to figure, to be included <Rivera figura entre los más grandes pintores de México : Rivera is among Mexico's greatest painters> **2** : to be prominent, to stand out — *vt* : to represent <esta línea figura el horizonte : this line represents the horizon> — **figurarse** *vr* : to imagine, to think <¡figúrate el lío en que se metió! : imagine the mess she got into!>
fijación *nf, pl* **-ciones** **1** : fixation, obsession **2** : fixing, establishing **3** : fastening, securing
fijador *nm* **1** : fixative **2** : hair spray

fijamente *adv* : fixedly
fijar *vt* **1** : to fasten, to affix **2** ESTABLECER : to establish, to set up **3** CONCRETAR : to set, to fix ⟨fijar la fecha : to set the date⟩ — **fijarse** *vr* **1** : to settle, to become fixed **2 ~ en** : to notice, to pay attention to
fijeza *nf* **1** : firmness (of convictions) **2** : persistence, constancy ⟨mirar con fijeza a : to stare at⟩
fijiano, -na *adj & n* : Fijian
fijo, -ja *adj* **1** : fixed, firm, steady **2** PERMANENTE : permanent
fila *nf* **1** HILERA : line, file ⟨ponerse en fila : to get in line⟩ **2** : rank, row **3 filas** *nfpl* : ranks ⟨cerrar filas : to close ranks⟩
filamento *nm* : filament
filantropía *nf* : philanthropy
filantrópico, -ca *adj* : philanthropic
filántropo, -pa *n* : philanthropist
filatelia *nf* : philately, stamp collecting
filatelista *nmf* : stamp collector, philatelist
fildeador, -dora *n* : fielder
filete *nm* **1** : fillet **2** SOLOMILLO : sirloin **3** : thread (of a screw)
filiación *nf, pl* **-ciones 1** : affiliation, connection **2** : particulars *pl,* (police) description
filial[1] *adj* : filial
filial[2] *nf* : affiliate, subsidiary
filibustero *nm* : freebooter, pirate
filigrana *nf* **1** : filigree **2** : watermark (on paper)
filipino, -na *adj & n* : Filipino
filmación *nf, pl* **-ciones** : filming, shooting
filmar *vt* : to film, to shoot
filme *or* **film** *nm* PELÍCULA : film, movie
filmina *nf* : slide, transparency
filo *nm* **1** : cutting edge, blade **2** : edge ⟨al filo del escritorio : at the edge of the desk⟩ ⟨al filo de la medianoche : at the stroke of midnight⟩
filología *nf* : philology
filólogo, -ga *n* : philologist
filón *nm, pl* **filones 1** : seam, vein (of minerals) **2** *fam* : successful business, gold mine
filoso, -sa *adj* : sharp
filosofar *vi* : to philosophize
filosofía *nf* : philosophy
filosófico, -ca *adj* : philosophic, philosophical — **filosóficamente** *adv*
filósofo, -fa *n* : philosopher
filtración *nf* : seepage, leaking
filtrar *v* : to filter — **filtrarse** *vr* : to seep through, to leak
filtro *nm* : filter
filudo, -da *adj* : sharp
fin *nm* **1** : end **2** : purpose, aim, objective **3 en ~** : in short **4 fin de semana** : weekend **5 por ~** : finally, at last
finado, -da *adj & n* DIFUNTO : deceased
final[1] *adj* : final, ultimate — **finalmente** *adv*
final[2] *nm* : end, conclusion, finale
final[3] *nf* : final, play-off
finalidad *nf* **1** : purpose, aim **2** : finality
finalista *nmf* : finalist
finalización *nf* : completion, end
finalizar {21} *v* : to finish, to end
financiación *nf, pl* **-ciones** : financing, funding
financiamiento *nm* → **financiación**
financiar *vt* : to finance, to fund
financiero[1], **-ra** *adj* : financial
financiero[2], **-ra** *n* : financier
financista *nmf* : financier
finanzas *nfpl* : finances, finance ⟨altas finanzas : high finance⟩
finca *nf* **1** : farm, ranch **2** : country house
fineza *nf* FINURA, REFINAMIENTO : refinement
fingido, -da *adj* : false, feigned
fingimiento *nm* : pretense
fingir {35} *v* : to feign, to pretend
finiquitar *vt* **1** : to settle (an account) **2** : to conclude, to bring to an end
finiquito *nm* : settlement (of an account)
finito, -ta *adj* : finite
finja, etc. → **fingir**
finlandés, -desa *adj & n* : Finnish
fino, -na *adj* **1** : fine, excellent **2** : delicate, slender **3** REFINADO : refined **4** : sharp, acute ⟨olfato fino : keen sense of smell⟩ **5** : subtle
finta *nf* : feint
fintar *or* **fintear** *vi* : to feint
finura *nf* **1** : fineness, high quality **2** FINEZA, REFINAMIENTO : refinement
fiordo *nm* : fjord
fique *nm* : sisal
firma *nf* **1** : signature **2** : signing **3** EMPRESA : firm, company
firmamento *nm* : firmament, sky
firmante *nmf* : signer, signatory
firmar *v* : to sign
firme *adj* **1** : firm, resolute **2** : steady, stable
firmemente *adv* : firmly
firmeza *nf* **1** : firmness, stability **2** : strength, resolve
firuletes *nmpl* : frills, adornments
fiscal[1] *adj* : fiscal — **fiscalmente** *adv*
fiscal[2] *nmf* : district attorney, prosecutor
fiscalizar {21} *vt* **1** : to audit, to inspect **2** : to oversee **3** : to criticize
fisco *nm* : national treasury, exchequer
fisgar {52} *vt* HUSMEAR : to pry into, to snoop on
fisgón, -gona *n, mpl* **fisgones** : snoop, busybody
fisgonear *vi* : to snoop, to pry
fisgue, etc. → **fisgar**
física *nf* : physics
físico[1], **-ca** *adj* : physical — **físicamente** *adv*
físico[2], **-ca** *n* : physicist
físico[3] *nm* : physique, figure
fisiología *nf* : physiology

fisiológico, -ca *adj* : physiological, physiologic
fisiólogo, -ga *n* : physiologist
fisión *nf, pl* **fisiones** : fission — **fisionable** *adj*
fisionomía → **fisonomía**
fisioterapeuta *nmf* : physical therapist
fisioterapia *nf* : physical therapy
fisonomía *nf* : physiognomy, features *pl*
fistol *nm Mex* : tie clip
fisura *nf* : fissure, crevasse
fláccido, -da *or* **flácido, -da** *adj* : flaccid, flabby
flaco, -ca *adj* **1** DELGADO : thin, skinny **2** : feeble, weak ⟨una flaca excusa : a feeble excuse⟩
flagelar *vt* : to flagellate — **flagelación** *nf*
flagelo *nm* **1** : scourge, whip **2** : calamity
flagrante *adj* : flagrant, glaring, blatant — **flagrantemente** *adv*
flama *nf* LLAMA : flame
flamante *adj* **1** : bright, brilliant **2** : brand-new
flamear *vi* **1** LLAMEAR : to flame, to blaze **2** ONDEAR : to flap, to flutter
flamenco[1], -ca *adj* **1** : flamenco **2** : Flemish
flamenco[2], -ca *n* : Fleming, Flemish person
flamenco[3] *nm* **1** : Flemish (language) **2** : flamingo **3** : flamenco (music or dance)
flanco *nm* : flank, side
flanquear *vt* : to flank
flaquear *vi* DECAER : to flag, to weaken
flaqueza *nf* **1** DEBILIDAD : frailty, feebleness **2** : thinness **3** : weakness, failing
flato *nm* : gloom, melancholy
flatulento, -ta *adj* : flatulent — **flatulencia** *nf*
flauta *nf* **1** : flute **2** **flauta dulce** : recorder
flautín *nm, pl* **flautines** : piccolo
flautista *nmf* : flute player, flutist
flebitis *nf* : phlebitis
flecha *nf* : arrow
fleco *nm* **1** : bangs *pl* **2** : fringe
flema *nf* : phlegm
flemático, -ca *adj* : phlegmatic, stolid, impassive
flequillo *nm* : bangs *pl*
fletar *vt* **1** : to charter, to hire **2** : to load (freight)
flete *nm* **1** : charter fee **2** : shipping cost **3** : freight, cargo
fletero *nm* : shipper, carrier
flexibilidad *nf* : flexibility
flexibilizar {21} *vt* : to make more flexible
flexible[1] *adj* : flexible
flexible[2] *nm* **1** : flexible electrical cord **2** : soft hat
flirtear *vi* : to flirt
flojear *vi* **1** DEBILITARSE : to weaken, to flag **2** : to idle, to loaf around
flojedad *nf* : weakness
flojera *nf fam* **1** : lethargy, feeling of weakness **2** : laziness
flojo, -ja *adj* **1** SUELTO : loose, slack **2** : weak, poor ⟨está flojo en las ciencias : he's weak in science⟩ **3** PEREZOSO : lazy
flor *nf* **1** : flower **2** **flor de Pascua** : poinsettia
flora *nf* : flora
floración *nf* : flowering ⟨en plena floración : in full bloom⟩
floral *adj* : floral
floreado, -da *adj* : flowered, flowery
florear *vi* FLORECER : to flower, to bloom — *vt* **1** : to adorn with flowers **2** *Mex* : to flatter, to compliment
florecer {53} *vi* **1** : to bloom, to blossom **2** : to flourish, to thrive
floreciente *adj* **1** : flowering **2** PRÓSPERO : flourishing, thriving
florecimiento *nm* : flowering
floreo *nm* : flourish
florería *nf* : flower shop, florist's
florero[1], -ra *n* : florist
florero[2] *nm* JARRÓN : vase
floresta *nf* **1** : glade, grove **2** BOSQUE : woods
florido, -da *adj* **1** : full of flowers **2** : florid, flowery ⟨escritos floridos : flowery prose⟩
florista *nmf* : florist
floritura *nf* : frill, embellishment
flota *nf* : fleet
flotabilidad *nf* : buoyancy
flotación *nf, pl* **-ciones** : flotation
flotador *nm* **1** : float **2** : life preserver
flotante *adj* : floating, buoyant
flotar *vi* : to float
flote *nm* **a ~** : afloat
flotilla *nf* : flotilla, fleet
fluctuar {3} *vi* **1** : to fluctuate **2** VACILAR : to vacillate — **fluctuación** *nf* — **fluctuante** *adj*
fluidez *nf* **1** : fluency **2** : fluidity
fluido[1], -da *adj* **1** : flowing **2** : fluent **3** : fluid
fluido[2] *nm* : fluid
fluir {41} *vi* : to flow
flujo *nm* **1** : flow **2** : discharge
flúor *nm* : fluorine
fluoración *nf, pl* **-ciones** : fluoridation
fluorescencia *nf* : fluorescence — **fluorescente** *adj*
fluorizar {21} *vt* : to fluoridate
fluoruro *nm* : fluoride
fluvial *adj* : fluvial, river
fluye, etc. → **fluir**
fobia *nf* : phobia
foca *nf* : seal (animal)
focal *adj* : focal
focha *nf* : coot
foco *nm* **1** : focus **2** : center, pocket **3** : lightbulb **4** : spotlight **5** : headlight
fofo, -fa *adj* **1** ESPONJOSO : soft, spongy **2** : flabby
fogaje *nm* **1** FUEGO : skin eruption, cold sore **2** BOCHORNO : hot and humid weather

fogata *nf* : bonfire
fogón *nm, pl* **fogones** : bonfire
fogonazo *nm* : flash, explosion
fogonero, -ra *n* : stoker (of a furnace), fireman
fogoso, -sa *adj* ARDIENTE : ardent
foguear *vt* : to inure, to accustom
foja *nf* : sheet (of paper)
folículo *nm* : follicle
folio *nm* : folio, leaf
folklore *nm* : folklore
folklórico, -ca *adj* : folk, traditional
follaje *nm* : foliage
folleto *nm* : pamphlet, leaflet, circular
fomentar *vt* **1** : to foment, to stir up **2** PROMOVER : to promote, to foster
fomento *nm* : promotion, encouragement
fonda *nf* **1** POSADA : inn **2** : small restaurant
fondeado, -da *adj fam* : rich, in the money
fondear *vt* **1** : to sound **2** : to sound out, to examine **3** *Mex* : to fund, to finance — *vi* ANCLAR : to anchor — **fondearse** *vr fam* : to get rich
fondeo *nm* **1** : anchoring **2** *Mex* : funding, financing
fondillos *mpl* : seat, bottom (of clothing)
fondo *nm* **1** : bottom **2** : rear, back, end **3** : depth **4** : background **5** : sea bed **6** : fund ⟨fondo de inversiones : investment fund⟩ **7** *Mex* : slip, petticoat **8 fondos** *nmpl* : funds, resources ⟨cheque sin fondos : bounced check⟩ **9 a ~** : thoroughly, in depth **10 en ~** : abreast
fonema *nm* : phoneme
fonética *nf* : phonetics
fonético, -ca *adj* : phonetic
fontanería *nf* PLOMERÍA : plumbing
fontanero, -ra *n* PLOMERO : plumber
footing ['fu,tɪŋ] *nm* : jogging ⟨hacer footing : to jog⟩
foque *nm* : jib
forajido, -da *n* : bandit, fugitive, outlaw
foráneo, -nea *adj* : foreign, strange
forastero, -ra *n* : stranger, outsider
forcejear *vi* : to struggle
forcejeo *nm* : struggle
fórceps *nms & pl* : forceps *pl*
forense *adj* : forensic, legal
forestal *adj* : forest
forja *nf* FRAGUA : forge
forjar *vt* **1** : to forge **2** : to shape, to create ⟨forjar un compromiso : to hammer out a compromise⟩ **3** : to invent, to concoct
forma *nf* **1** : form, shape **2** MANERA, MODO : manner, way **3** : fitness ⟨estar en forma : to be fit, to be in shape⟩ **4 formas** *nfpl* : appearances, conventions
formación *nf, pl* **-ciones 1** : formation **2** : training ⟨formación profesional : vocational training⟩
formal *adj* **1** : formal **2** : serious, dignified **3** : dependable, reliable
formaldehído *nm* : formaldehyde
formalidad *nf* **1** : formality **2** : seriousness, dignity **3** : dependability, reliability
formalizar {21} *vt* : to formalize, to make official
formalmente *adv* : formally
formar *vt* **1** : to form, to make **2** CONSTITUIR : to constitute, to make up **3** : to train, to educate — **formarse** *vr* **1** DESARROLLARSE : to develop, to take shape **2** EDUCARSE : to be educated
formatear *vt* : to format
formativo, -va *adj* : formative
formato *nm* : format
formidable *adj* **1** : formidable, tremendous **2** *fam* : fantastic, terrific
formón *nm, pl* **formones** : chisel
fórmula *nf* : formula
formulación *nf, pl* **-ciones** : formulation
formular *vt* **1** : to formulate, to draw up **2** : to make, to lodge (a protest or complaint)
formulario *nm* : form ⟨rellenar un formulario : to fill out a form⟩
fornicar {72} *vi* : to fornicate — **fornicación** *nf*
fornido, -da *adj* : well-built, burly, hefty
foro *nm* **1** : forum **2** : public assembly, open discussion
forraje *nm* **1** : forage, fodder **2** : foraging **3** *fam* : hodgepodge
forrajear *vi* : to forage
forrar *vt* **1** : to line (a garment) **2** : to cover (a book)
forro *nm* **1** : lining **2** CUBIERTA : book cover
forsitia *nf* : forsythia
fortachón, -chona *adj, pl* **-chones** *fam* : brawny, strong, tough
fortalecer {53} *vt* : to strengthen, to fortify — **fortalecerse** *vr*
fortalecimiento *nm* **1** : strengthening, fortifying **2** : fortifications
fortaleza *nf* **1** : fortress **2** FUERZA : strength **3** : resolution, fortitude
fortificación *nf, pl* **-ciones** : fortification
fortificar {72} *vt* **1** : to fortify **2** : to strengthen
fortín *nm, pl* **fortines** : small fort
fortuito, -ta *adj* : fortuitous
fortuna *nf* **1** SUERTE : fortune, luck **2** RIQUEZA : wealth, fortune
forzar {36} *vt* **1** OBLIGAR : to force, to compel **2** : to force open **3** : to strain ⟨forzar los ojos : to strain one's eyes⟩
forzosamente *adv* **1** : forcibly, by force **2** : necessarily, inevitably ⟨forzosamente tendrán que pagar : they'll have no choice but to pay⟩
forzoso, -sa *adj* **1** : forced, compulsory **2** : necessary, inevitable
fosa *nf* **1** : ditch, pit ⟨fosa séptica : septic tank⟩ **2** TUMBA : grave **3** : cavity ⟨fosas nasales : nasal cavities, nostrils⟩
fosfato *nm* : phosphate

fosforescencia *nf* : phosphorescence — **fosforescente** *adj*
fósforo *nm* 1 CERILLA : match 2 : phosphorus
fósil[1] *adj* : fossilized, fossil
fósil[2] *nm* : fossil
fosilizarse {21} *vr* : to fossilize, to become fossilized
foso *nm* 1 FOSA, ZANJA : ditch 2 : pit (of a theater) 3 : moat
foto *nf* : photo, picture
fotocopia *nf* : photocopy — **fotocopiar** *vt*
fotocopiadora *nf* COPIADORA : photocopier
fotoeléctrico, -ca *adj* : photoelectric
fotogénico, -ca *adj* : photogenic
fotografía *nf* 1 : photograph 2 : photography
fotografiar {85} *vt* : to photograph
fotográfico, -ca *adj* : photographic — **fotográficamente** *adv*
fotógrafo, -fa *n* : photographer
fotosíntesis *nf* : photosynthesis
fotosintético, -ca *adj* : photosynthetic
fracasado[1], **-da** *adj* : unsuccessful, failed
fracasado[2], **-da** *n* : failure
fracasar *vi* 1 FALLAR : to fail 2 : to fall through
fracaso *nm* FIASCO : failure
fracción *nf, pl* **fracciones** 1 : fraction 2 : part, fragment 3 : faction, splinter group
fraccionamiento *nm* 1 : division, breaking up 2 *Mex* : residential area, housing development
fraccionar *vt* : to divide, to break up
fraccionario, -ria *adj* : fractional
fractura *nf* 1 : fracture 2 **fractura complicada** : compound fracture
fracturarse *vr* QUEBRARSE, ROMPERSE : to fracture, to break ‹fracturarse el brazo : to break one's arm›
fragancia *nf* : fragrance, scent
fragante *adj* : fragrant
fragata *nf* : frigate
frágil *adj* 1 : fragile 2 : frail, delicate
fragilidad *nf* 1 : fragility 2 : frailty, delicacy
fragmentar *vt* : to fragment — **fragmentación** *nf*
fragmentario, -ria *adj* : fragmentary, sketchy
fragmento *nm* 1 : fragment, shard 2 : bit, snippet 3 : excerpt, passage
fragor *nm* : clamor, din, roar
fragoroso, -sa *adj* : thunderous, deafening
fragoso, -sa *adj* 1 : rough, uneven 2 : thick, dense
fragua *nf* FORJA : forge
fraguar {10} *vt* 1 : to forge 2 : to conceive, to concoct, to hatch — *vi* : to set, to solidify
fraile *nm* : friar, monk
frambuesa *nf* : raspberry
francamente *adv* 1 : frankly, candidly 2 REALMENTE : really ‹es francamente admirable : it's really impressive›
francés[1], **-cesa** *adj, mpl* **franceses** : French
francés[2], **-cesa** *n, mpl* **franceses** : French person, Frenchman *m*, Frenchwoman *f*
francés[3] *nm* : French (language)
franciscano, -na *adj & n* : Franciscan
francmasón, -sona *n, mpl* **-sones** : Freemason — **francmasonería** *nf*
franco[1], **-ca** *adj* 1 CÁNDIDO : frank, candid 2 PATENTE : clear, obvious 3 : free ‹franco a bordo : free on board›
franco[2] *nm* : franc
francotirador, -dora *n* : sniper
franela *nf* : flannel
franja *nf* 1 : stripe, band 2 : border, fringe
franquear *vt* 1 : to clear 2 ATRAVESAR : to cross, to go through 3 : to pay the postage on
franqueo *nm* : postage
franqueza *nf* : frankness
franquicia *nf* 1 EXENCIÓN : exemption 2 : franchise
frasco *nm* : small bottle, flask, vial
frase *nf* 1 : phrase 2 ORACIÓN : sentence
frasear *vt* : to phrase
fraternal *adj* : fraternal, brotherly
fraternidad *nf* 1 : brotherhood 2 : fraternity
fraternizar {21} *vi* : to fraternize — **fraternización** *nf*
fraterno, -na *adj* : fraternal, brotherly
fratricida *adj* : fratricidal
fratricidio *nm* : fratricide
fraude *nm* : fraud
fraudulento, -ta *adj* : fraudulent — **fraudulentamente** *adv*
fray *nm* : brother (title of a friar) ‹Fray Bartolomé : Brother Bartholomew›
frazada *nf* COBIJA, MANTA : blanket
frecuencia *nf* : frequency
frecuentar *vt* : to frequent, to haunt
frecuente *adj* : frequent — **frecuentemente** *adv*
fregadera *nf fam* : hassle, pain in the neck
fregadero *nm* : kitchen sink
fregado[1], **-da** *adj fam* : annoying, bothersome
fregado[2] *nm* 1 : scrubbing, scouring 2 *fam* : mess, muddle
fregar {49} *vt* 1 : to scrub, to scour, to wash ‹fregar los trastes : to do the dishes› ‹fregar el suelo : to scrub the floor› 2 *fam* : to annoy — *vi* 1 : to wash the dishes 2 : to clean, to scrub 3 *fam* : to be annoying
freidera *nf Mex* : frying pan
freír {37} *vt* : to fry — **freírse** *vr*
frenar *vt* 1 : to brake 2 DETENER : to curb, to check — *vi* : to apply the brakes — **frenarse** *vr* : to restrain oneself

frenesí *nm* : frenzy
frenético, -ca *adj* : frantic, frenzied — **frenéticamente** *adv*
freno *nm* **1** : brake **2** : bit (of a bridle) **3** : check, restraint **4 frenos** *nmpl Mex* : braces (for teeth)
frente[1] *nm* **1** : front ⟨al frente de : at the head of⟩ ⟨en frente : in front, opposite⟩ **2** : facade **3** : front line, sphere of activity **4** : front (in meteorology) ⟨frente frío : cold front⟩ **5 hacer frente a** : to face up to, to brave
frente[2] *nf* **1** : forehead, brow **2 frente a frente** : face to face
fresa *nf* **1** : strawberry **2** : drill (in dentistry)
fresco[1], **-ca** *adj* **1** : fresh **2** : cool **3** *fam* : insolent, nervy
fresco[2] *nm* **1** : coolness **2** : fresh air ⟨al fresco : in the open air, outdoors⟩ **3** : fresco
frescor *nm* : cool air ⟨el frescor de la noche : the cool of the evening⟩
frescura *nf* **1** : freshness **2** : coolness **3** : calmness **4** DESCARO : nerve, audacity
fresno *nm* : ash (tree)
freza *nf* : spawn, roe
frezar {21} *vi* DESOVAR : to spawn
friable *adj* : friable
frialdad *nf* **1** : coldness **2** INDIFERENCIA : indifference, unconcern
fríamente *adv* : coldly, indifferently
fricasé *nm* : fricassee
fricción *nf, pl* **fricciones** **1** : friction **2** : rubbing, massage **3** : discord, disagreement ⟨fricción entre los hermanos : friction between the brothers⟩
friccionar *vt* **1** FROTAR : to rub **2** : to massage
friega[1], **friegue, etc.** → **fregar**
friega[2] *nf* **1** FRICCIÓN : rubdown, massage **2** : annoyance, bother
frigidez *nf* : (sexual) frigidity
frigorífico *nm Spain* : refrigerator
frijol *nm* : bean ⟨frijoles refritos : refried beans⟩
frío[1], **fría** *adj* **1** : cold **2** INDIFERENTE : cool, indifferent
frío[2] *nm* **1** : cold ⟨hace mucho frío esta noche : it's very cold tonight⟩ **2** INDIFERENCIA : coldness, indifference **3 tener frío** : to feel cold ⟨tengo frío : I'm cold⟩ **4 tomar frío** RESFRIARSE : to catch a cold
friolento, -ta *adj* : sensitive to cold
friolera *nf* (*used ironically or humorously*) : trifling amount ⟨una friolera de mil dólares : a mere thousand dollars⟩
friso *nm* : frieze
fritar *vt* : to fry
frito[1] *pp* → **freír**
frito[2], **-ta** *adj* **1** : fried **2** *fam* : worn-out, fed up ⟨tener frito a alguien : to get on someone's nerves⟩ **3** *fam* : fast asleep ⟨se quedó frito en el sofá : she fell asleep on the couch⟩
fritura *nf* **1** : frying **2** : fried food
frivolidad *nf* : frivolity
frívolo, -la *adj* : frivolous — **frívolamente** *adv*
fronda *nf* **1** : frond **2 frondas** *nfpl* : foliage
frondoso, -sa *adj* : leafy, luxuriant
frontal *adj* : frontal, head-on ⟨un choque frontal : a head-on collision⟩
frontalmente *adv* : head-on
frontera *nf* : border, frontier
fronterizo, -za *adj* : border, on the border ⟨estados fronterizos : neighboring states⟩
frontispicio *nm* : frontispiece
frotar *vt* **1** : to rub **2** : to strike (a match) — **frotarse** *vr* : to rub (together)
frote *nm* : rubbing, rub
fructífero, -ra *adj* : fruitful, productive
fructificar {72} *vi* **1** : to bear or produce fruit **2** : to be productive
fructuoso, -sa *adj* : fruitful
frugal *adj* : frugal, thrifty — **frugalmente** *adv*
frugalidad *adj* : frugality
frunce *nm* : gather (in cloth), pucker
fruncido *nm* : gathering, shirring
fruncir {83} *vt* **1** : to gather, to shirr **2 fruncir el ceño** : to knit one's brow, to frown **3 fruncir la boca** : to pucker up, to purse one's lips
frunza, etc. → **fruncir**
frustración *nf, pl* **-ciones** : frustration
frustrado, -da *adj* **1** : frustrated **2** : failed, unsuccessful
frustrante *adj* : frustrating
frustrar *vt* : to frustrate, to thwart — **frustrarse** *vr* FRACASAR : to fail, to come to nothing ⟨se frustraron sus esperanzas : his hopes were dashed⟩
fruta *nf* : fruit
frutal[1] *adj* : fruit, fruit-bearing
frutal[2] *nm* : fruit tree
frutilla *nf* : South American strawberry
fruto *nm* **1** : fruit, agricultural product ⟨los frutos de la tierra : the fruits of the earth⟩ **2** : result, consequence ⟨los frutos de su trabajo : the fruits of his labor⟩
fucsia *adj & nm* : fuchsia
fue, etc. → **ir, ser**
fuego *nm* **1** : fire **2** : light ⟨¿tienes fuego? : have you got a light?⟩ **3** : flame, burner (on a stove) **4** : ardor, passion **5** FOGAJE : skin eruption, cold sore **6 fuegos artificiales** *nmpl* : fireworks
fuelle *nm* : bellows
fuente *nf* **1** MANANTIAL : spring **2** : fountain **3** ORIGEN : source ⟨fuentes informativas : sources of information⟩ **4** : platter, serving dish
fuera *adv* **1** : outside, out **2** : abroad, away **3 ~ de** : outside of, out of, beyond **4 ~ de** : besides, in addition to ⟨fuera de eso : aside from that⟩ **5 fuera de lugar** : out of place, amiss
fuerce, fuerza etc. → **forzar**

fuero *nm* **1** JURISDICCIÓN : jurisdiction **2** : privilege, exemption **3 fuero interno** : conscience, heart of hearts

fuerte[1] *adv* **1** : strongly, tightly, hard **2** : loudly **3** : abundantly

fuerte[2] *adj* **1** : strong **2** : intense ⟨un fuerte dolor : an intense pain⟩ **3** : loud **4** : extreme, excessive

fuerte[3] *nm* **1** : fort, stronghold **2** : forte, strong point

fuerza *nf* **1** : strength, vigor ⟨fuerza de voluntad : willpower⟩ **2** : force ⟨fuerza bruta : brute force⟩ **3** : power, might ⟨fuerza de brazos : manpower⟩ **4 fuerzas** *nfpl* : forces ⟨fuerzas armadas : armed forces⟩ **5 a fuerza de** : by, by dint of

fuetazo *nm* : lash

fuga *nf* **1** HUIDA : flight, escape **2** : fugue **3** : leak ⟨fuga de gas : gas leak⟩

fugarse {52} *vr* **1** : to escape **2** HUIR : to flee, to run away **3** : to elope

fugaz *adj, pl* **fugaces** : brief, fleeting

fugitivo, -va *adj & n* : fugitive

fulana *nf* : hooker, slut

fulano, -na *n* : so-and-so, what's-his-name, what's-her-name ⟨fulano, mengano, y zutano : Tom, Dick, and Harry⟩ ⟨señora fulana de tal : Mrs. so-and-so⟩

fulcro *nm* : fulcrum

fulgor *nm* : brilliance, splendor

fulgurar *vi* : to shine brightly, to gleam, to glow

fulminante *adj* **1** : fulminating, explosive **2** : devastating, terrible ⟨una mirada fulminante : a withering look⟩

fulminar *vt* **1** : to strike with lightning **2** : to strike down ⟨fulminar a alguien con la mirada : to look daggers at someone⟩

fumador, -dora *n* : smoker

fumar *v* : to smoke

fumble *nm* : fumble (in football)

fumblear *vt* : to fumble (in football)

fumigante *nm* : fumigant

fumigar {52} *vt* : to fumigate — **fumigación** *nf*

funámbulo, -la *n* EQUILIBRISTA : tightrope walker

función *nf, pl* **funciones** **1** : function **2** : duty **3** : performance, show

funcional *adj* : functional — **funcionalmente** *adv*

funcionamiento *nm* **1** : functioning **2 en ~** : in operation

funcionar *vi* **1** : to function **2** : to run, to work

funcionario, -ria *n* : civil servant, official

funda *nf* **1** : case, cover, sheath **2** : pillowcase

fundación *nf, pl* **-ciones** : foundation, establishment

fundado, -da *adj* : well-founded, justified

fundador, -dora *n* : founder

fundamental *adj* BÁSICO : fundamental, basic — **fundamentalmente** *adv*

fundamentalismo *nm* : fundamentalism

fundamentalista *nmf* : fundamentalist

fundamentar *vt* **1** : to lay the foundations for **2** : to support, to back up **3** : to base, to found

fundamento *nm* : basis, foundation, groundwork

fundar *vt* **1** ESTABLECER, INSTITUIR : to found, to establish **2** BASAR : to base — **fundarse** *vr* **~ en** : to be based on, to stem from

fundición *nf, pl* **-ciones** **1** : founding, smelting **2** : foundry

fundir *vt* **1** : to melt down, to smelt **2** : to fuse, to merge **3** : to burn out (a lightbulb) — **fundirse** *vr* **1** : to fuse together, to blend, to merge **2** : to melt, to thaw **3** : to fade (in television or movies)

fúnebre *adj* **1** : funeral, funereal **2** LÚGUBRE : gloomy, mournful

funeral[1] *adj* : funeral, funerary

funeral[2] *nm* **1** : funeral **2 funerales** *nmpl* EXEQUIAS : funeral rites

funeraria *nf* **1** : funeral home, funeral parlor **2 director de funeraria** : funeral director, undertaker

funerario, -ria *adj* : funeral

funesto, -ta *adj* : terrible, disastrous ⟨consecuencias funestas : disastrous consequences⟩

fungicida[1] *adj* : fungicidal

fungicida[2] *nm* : fungicide

fungir {35} *vi* : to act, to function ⟨fungir de asesor : to act as a consultant⟩

fungoso, -sa *adj* : fungous

funja, etc. → **fungir**

furgón *nm, pl* **furgones** **1** : van, truck **2** : freight car, boxcar **3 furgón de cola** : caboose

furgoneta *nf* : van

furia *nf* **1** CÓLERA, IRA : fury, rage **2** : violence, fury ⟨la furia de la tormenta : the fury of the storm⟩

furibundo, -da *adj* : furious

furiosamente *adv* : furiously, frantically

furioso, -sa *adj* **1** AIRADO : furious, irate **2** : intense, violent

furor *nm* **1** : fury, rage **2** : violence (of the elements) **3** : passion, frenzy **4** : enthusiasm ⟨hacer furor : to be all the rage⟩

furtivo, -va *adj* : furtive — **furtivamente** *adv*

furúnculo *nm* DIVIESO : boil

fuselaje *nm* : fuselage

fusible *nm* : (electrical) fuse

fusil *nm* : rifle

fusilar *vt* **1** : to shoot, to execute (by firing squad) **2** *fam* : to plagiarize, to pirate

fusilería *nf* **1** : rifles *pl,* rifle fire **2 descarga de fusilería** : fusillade

fusión *nf, pl* **fusiones** **1** : fusion **2** : union, merger

fusionar *vt* **1** : to fuse **2** : to merge, to amalgamate — **fusionarse** *vr*
fusta *nf* : riding crop
fustigar {52} *vt* **1** AZOTAR : to whip, to lash **2** : to upbraid, to berate
futbol *or* **fútbol** *nm* **1** : soccer **2 futbol americano** : football
futbolista *nmf* : soccer player
futesa *nf* **1** : small thing, trifle **2 futesas** *nfpl* : small talk
fútil *adj* : trifling, trivial
futurista *adj* : futuristic
futuro[1], **-ra** *adj* : future
futuro[2] *nm* PORVENIR : future

G

g *nf* : seventh letter of the Spanish alphabet
gabán *nm, pl* **gabanes** : topcoat, overcoat
gabardina *nf* **1** : gabardine **2** : trench coat, raincoat
gabarra *nf* : barge
gabinete *nm* **1** : cabinet (in government) **2** : study, office (in the home) **3** : (professional) office
gablete *nm* : gable
gabonés, **-nesa** *adj & n, mpl* **-neses** : Gabonese
gacela *nf* : gazelle
gaceta *nf* : gazette, newspaper
gachas *nfpl* : porridge
gacho, **-cha** *adj* **1** : drooping, turned downward **2** *Mex fam* : nasty, awful **3 ir a gachas** *fam* : to go on all fours
gaélico[1], **-ca** *adj* : Gaelic
gaélico[2] *nm* : Gaelic (language)
gafas *nfpl* ANTEOJOS : eyeglasses, glasses
gaita *nf* : bagpipes *pl*
gajes *nmpl* **gajes del oficio** : occupational hazards
gajo *nm* **1** : broken branch (of a tree) **2** : cluster, bunch (of fruit) **3** : segment (of citrus fruit)
gala *nf* **1** : gala ⟨vestido de gala : formal dress⟩ ⟨tener algo a gala : to be proud of something⟩ **2 galas** *nfpl* : finery, attire
galáctico, **-ca** *adj* : galactic
galán *nm, pl* **galanes** **1** : ladies' man, gallant **2** : leading man, hero **3** : boyfriend, suitor
galano, **-na** *adj* **1** : elegant **2** *Mex* : mottled
galante *adj* : gallant, attentive — **galantemente** *adv*
galantear *vt* **1** CORTEJAR : to court, to woo **2** : to flirt with
galanteo *nm* **1** CORTEJO : courtship **2** : flirtation, flirting
galantería *nf* **1** : gallantry, attentiveness **2** : compliment
galápago *nm* : aquatic turtle
galardón *nm, pl* **-dones** : award, prize
galardonado, **-da** *adj* : prize-winning
galardonar *vt* : to give an award to
galaxia *nf* : galaxy
galeno *nm fam* : physician, doctor
galeón *nm, pl* **galeones** : galleon
galera *nf* : galley
galería *nf* **1** : gallery, balcony (in a theater) ⟨galería comercial : shopping mall⟩ **2** : corridor, passage
galerón *n, mpl* **-rones** *Mex* : large hall
galés[1], **-lesa** *adj* : Welsh
galés[2], **-lesa** *n, mpl* **galeses** **1** : Welshman *m*, Welshwoman *f* **2 los galeses** : the Welsh
galés[3] *nm* : Welsh (language)
galgo *nm* : greyhound
galimatías *nms & pl* : gibberish, nonsense
galio *nm* : gallium
gallardete *nm* : pennant, streamer
gallardía *nf* **1** VALENTÍA : bravery **2** APOSTURA : elegance, gracefulness
gallardo, **-da** *adj* **1** VALIENTE : brave **2** APUESTO : elegant, graceful
gallear *vi* : to show off, to strut around
gallego[1], **-ga** *adj* **1** : Galician **2** *fam* : Spanish
gallego[2], **-ga** *n* **1** : Galician **2** *fam* : Spaniard
galleta *nf* **1** : cookie **2** : cracker
gallina *nf* **1** : hen **2 gallina de Guinea** : guinea fowl
gallinazo *nm* : vulture, buzzard
gallinero *nm* : chicken coop, henhouse
gallito, **-ta** *adj fam* : cocky, belligerent
gallo *nm* **1** : rooster, cock **2** *fam* : squeak or crack in the voice **3** *Mex* : serenade **4 gallo de pelea** : gamecock
galo[1], **-la** *adj* **1** : Gaulish **2** : French
galo[2], **-la** *n* : Frenchman *m*, Frenchwoman *f*
galocha *nf* : galosh
galón *nm, pl* **galones** **1** : gallon **2** : stripe (military insignia)
galopada *nf* : gallop
galopante *adj* : galloping ⟨inflación galopante : galloping inflation⟩
galopar *vi* : to gallop
galope *nm* : gallop
galpón *nm, pl* **galpones** : shed, storehouse
galvanizar {21} *vt* : to galvanize — **galvanización** *nf*
gama *nf* **1** : range, spectrum, gamut **2** → **gamo**
gamba *nf* : large shrimp, prawn
gamberro, **-rra** *n Spain* : hooligan, troublemaker
gambiano, **-na** *adj & n* : Gambian
gambito *nm* : gambit (in chess)
gameto *nm* : gamete

gamo, -ma *n* : fallow deer

gamuza *nf* **1** : suede **2** : chamois

gana *nf* **1** : desire, inclination **2 de buena gana** : willingly, readily, gladly **3 de mala gana** : reluctantly, halfheartedly **4 tener ganas de** : to feel like, to be in the mood for ⟨tengo ganas de bailar : I feel like dancing⟩ **5 ponerle ganas a algo** : to put effort into something

ganadería *nf* **1** : cattle raising, stockbreeding **2** : cattle ranch **3** GANADO : cattle *pl,* livestock

ganadero[1], -ra *adj* : cattle, ranching

ganadero[2], -ra *n* : rancher, stockbreeder

ganado *nm* **1** : cattle *pl,* livestock **2 ganado ovino** : sheep *pl* **3 ganado porcino** : swine *pl*

ganador[1], -dora *adj* : winning

ganador[2], -dora *n* : winner

ganancia *nf* **1** : profit **2 ganancias** *nfpl* : winnings, gains

ganancioso, -sa *adj* : profitable

ganar *vt* **1** : to win **2** : to gain ⟨ganar tiempo : to buy time⟩ **3** : to earn ⟨ganar dinero : to make money⟩ **4** : to acquire, to obtain — *vi* **1** : to win **2** : to profit ⟨salir ganando : to come out ahead⟩ — **ganarse** *vr* **1** : to gain, to win ⟨ganarse a alguien : to win someone over⟩ **2** : to earn ⟨ganarse la vida : to make a living⟩ **3** : to deserve

gancho *nm* **1** : hook **2** : clothes hanger **3** : hairpin, bobby pin **4** *Col* : safety pin

gandul[1] *nm CA, Car, Col* : pigeon pea

gandul[2], -dula *n fam* : idler, lazybones

gandulear *vi* : to idle, to loaf, to lounge about

ganga *nf* : bargain

ganglio *nm* **1** : ganglion **2** : gland

gangrena *nf* : gangrene — **gangrenoso, -sa** *adj*

gángster *nmf, pl* **gángsters** : gangster

gansada *nf* : silly thing, nonsense

ganso, -sa *n* **1** : goose, gander *m* **2** : idiot, fool

gañido *nm* : yelp (of a dog)

gañir {38} *vi* : to yelp

garabatear *v* : to scribble, to scrawl, to doodle

garabato *nm* **1** : doodle **2 garabatos** *nmpl* : scribble, scrawl

garaje *nm* : garage

garante *nmf* : guarantor

garantía *nf* **1** : guarantee, warranty **2** : security ⟨garantía de trabajo : job security⟩

garantizar {21} *vt* : to guarantee

garapiña *nf* : pineapple drink

garapiñar *vt* : to candy

garbanzo *nm* : chickpea, garbanzo

garbo *nm* **1** DONAIRE : grace, poise **2** : jauntiness

garboso, -sa *adj* **1** : graceful **2** : elegant, stylish

garceta *nf* : egret

gardenia *nf* : gardenia

garfio *nm* : hook, gaff, grapnel

gargajo *nm fam* : phlegm

garganta *nf* **1** : throat **2** : neck (of a person or a bottle) **3** : ravine, narrow pass

gargantilla *nf* : choker, necklace

gárgara *nf* **1** : gargle, gargling **2 hacer gárgaras** : to gargle

gargarizar *vi* : to gargle

gárgola *nf* : gargoyle

garita *nf* **1** : cabin, hut **2** : sentry box, lookout post

garoso, -sa *adj Col, Ven* : gluttonous, greedy

garra *nf* **1** : claw **2** : hand, paw **3 garras** *nfpl* : claws, clutches ⟨caer en las garras de alguien : to fall into someone's clutches⟩

garrafa *nf* : decanter, carafe

garrafal *adj* : terrible, monstrous

garrafón *nm, pl* **-fones** : large decanter, large bottle

garrapata *nf* : tick

garrobo *nm CA* : large lizard, iguana

garrocha *nf* **1** PICA : lance, pike **2** : pole ⟨salto con garrocha : pole vault⟩

garrotazo *nm* : blow (with a club)

garrote *nm* **1** : club, stick **2** *Mex* : brake

garúa *nf* : drizzle

garuar {3} *v impers* LLOVIZNAR : to drizzle

garza *nf* : heron

gas *nm* : gas, vapor, fumes *pl* ⟨gas lagrimógeno : tear gas⟩

gasa *nf* : gauze

gasear *vt* **1** : to gas **2** : to aerate (a liquid)

gaseosa *nf* REFRESCO : soda, soft drink

gaseoso, -sa *adj* **1** : gaseous **2** : carbonated, fizzy

gasoducto *nm* : gas pipeline

gasolina *nf* : gasoline, gas

gasolinera *nf* : gas station, service station

gastado, -da *adj* **1** : spent **2** : worn, worn-out

gastador[1], -dora *adj* : extravagant, spendthrift

gastador[2], -dora *n* : spendthrift

gastar *vt* **1** : to spend **2** CONSUMIR : to consume, to use up **3** : to squander, to waste **4** : to wear ⟨gasta un bigote : he sports a mustache⟩ — **gastarse** *vr* **1** : to spend, to expend **2** : to run down, to wear out

gasto *nm* **1** : expense, expenditure **2** DETERIORO : wear **3 gastos generales** *or* **gastos indirectos** : overhead

gástrico, -ca *adj* : gastric

gastritis *nf* : gastritis

gastronomía *nf* : gastronomy

gastronómico, -ca *adj* : gastronomic

gastrónomo, -ma *n* : gourmet

gatas *adv* **andar a gatas** : to crawl, to go on all fours

gatear *vi* **1** : to crawl **2** : to climb, to clamber (up)

gatillero *nm Mex* : gunman
gatillo *nm* : trigger
gatito, -ta *n* : kitten
gato[1], -ta *n* : cat
gato[2] *nm* : jack (for an automobile)
gauchada *nf Arg, Uru* : favor, kindness
gaucho *nm* : gaucho
gaveta *nf* **1** CAJÓN : drawer **2** : till
gavilla *nf* **1** : gang, band **2** : sheaf
gaviota *nf* : gull, seagull
gay ['ge, 'gai] *adj* : gay (homosexual)
gaza *nf* : loop
gazapo *nm* **1** : young rabbit **2** : misprint, error
gazmoñería *nf* MOJIGATERÍA : prudery, primness
gazmoño[1], -ña *adj* : prudish, prim
gazmoño[2], -ña *n* MOJIGATO : prude, prig
gaznate *nm* : throat, gullet
gazpacho *nm* : gazpacho
géiser *or* **géyser** *nm* : geyser
gel *nm* : gel
gelatina *nf* : gelatin
gélido, -da *adj* : icy, freezing cold
gelificarse *vr* : to jell
gema *nf* : gem
gemelo[1], -la *adj & n* MELLIZO : twin
gemelo[2] *nm* **1** : cuff link **2 gemelos** *nmpl* BINOCULARES : binoculars
gemido *nm* : moan, groan, wail
Géminis *nmf* : Gemini
gemir {54} *vi* : to moan, to groan, to wail
gen *or* **gene** *nm* : gene
gendarme *nmf* POLICÍA : police officer, policeman *m*, policewoman *f*
gendarmería *nf* : police
genealogía *nf* : genealogy
genealógico, -ca *adj* : genealogical
generación *nf, pl* **-ciones 1** : generation ⟨tercera generación : third generation⟩ **2** : generating, creating **3** : class ⟨la generación del '97 : the class of '97⟩
generacional *adj* : generation, generational
generador *nm* : generator
general[1] *adj* **1** : general **2 en ~** *or* **por lo general** : in general, generally
general[2] *nmf* **1** : general **2 general de división** : major general
generalidad *nf* **1** : generality, generalization **2** : majority
generalización *nf, pl* **-ciones 1** : generalization **2** : escalation, spread
generalizado, -da *adj* : generalized, widespread
generalizar {21} *vi* : to generalize — *vt* : to spread, to spread out — **generalizarse** *vr* : to become widespread
generalmente *adv* : usually, generally
generar *vt* : to generate — **generarse** *vr*
genérico, -ca *adj* : generic
género *nm* **1** : genre, class, kind ⟨el género humano : the human race, mankind⟩ **2** : gender (in grammar) **3 géneros** *nmpl* : goods, commodities
generosidad *nf* : generosity
generoso, -sa *adj* **1** : generous, unselfish **2** : ample — **generosamente** *adv*
genética *nf* : genetics
genético, -ca *adj* : genetic — **genéticamente** *adv*
genetista *nmf* : geneticist
genial *adj* **1** AGRADABLE : genial, pleasant **2** : brilliant ⟨una obra genial : a work of genius⟩ **3** *fam* FORMIDABLE : fantastic, terrific
genialidad *nf* **1** : genius **2** : stroke of genius **3** : eccentricity
genio *nm* **1** : genius **2** : temper, disposition ⟨de mal genio : bad-tempered⟩ **3** : genie
genital *adj* : genital
genitales *nmpl* : genitals, genitalia
genocidio *nm* : genocide
genotipo *nm* : genotype
gente *nf* **1** : people **2** : relatives *pl*, folks *pl* **3 gente menuda** *fam* : children, kids *pl* **4 ser buena gente** : to be nice, to be kind
gentil[1] *adj* **1** AMABLE : kind **2** : gentile
gentil[2] *nmf* : gentile
gentileza *nf* **1** AMABILIDAD : kindness **2** CORTESÍA : courtesy
gentilicio, -cia *adj* **1** : national, tribal **2** : family
gentío *nm* MUCHEDUMBRE, MULTITUD : crowd, mob
gentuza *nf* CHUSMA : riffraff, rabble
genuflexión *nf, pl* **-xiones 1** : genuflection **2 hacer una genuflexión** : to genuflect
genuino, -na *adj* : genuine — **genuinamente** *adv*
geofísica *nf* : geophysics
geofísico, -ca *adj* : geophysical
geografía *nf* : geography
geográfico, -ca *adj* : geographic, geographical — **geográficamente** *adv*
geógrafo, -fa *n* : geographer
geología *nf* : geology
geológico, -ca *adj* : geologic, geological — **geológicamente** *adv*
geólogo, -ga *n* : geologist
geometría *nf* : geometry
geométrico, -ca *adj* : geometric, geometrical — **geométricamente** *adv*
geopolítica *nf* : geopolitics
geopolítico, -ca *adj* : geopolitical
georgiano, -na *adj & n* : Georgian
geranio *nm* : geranium
gerbo *nm* : gerbil
gerencia *nf* : management, administration
gerencial *adj* : managerial
gerente *nmf* : manager, director
geriatría *nf* : geriatrics
geriátrico, -ca *adj* : geriatric
germanio *nm* : germanium
germano, -na *adj* : Germanic, German
germen *nm, pl* **gérmenes** : germ
germicida *nf* : germicide
germinación *nf, pl* **-ciones** : germination
germinar *vi* : to germinate, to sprout
gerontología *nf* : gerontology
gerundio *nm* : gerund

gesta *nf* : deed, exploit

gestación *nf, pl* **-ciones** : gestation

gesticulación *nf, pl* **-ciones** : gesturing, gesticulation

gesticular *vi* : to gesticulate, to gesture

gestión *nf, pl* **gestiones** **1** TRÁMITE : procedure, step **2** ADMINISTRACIÓN : management **3** **gestiones** *nfpl* : negotiations

gestionar *vt* **1** : to negotiate, to work towards **2** ADMINISTRAR : to manage, to handle

gesto *nm* **1** ADEMÁN : gesture **2** : facial expression **3** MUECA : grimace

gestor[1], **-tora** *adj* : facilitating, negotiating, managing

gestor[2], **-tora** *n* : facilitator, manager

géyser → **géiser**

ghanés, **-nesa** *adj & n, mpl* **ghaneses** : Ghanaian

ghetto → **gueto**

giba *nf* **1** : hump (of an animal) **2** : hunchback (of a person)

gibón *nm, pl* **gibones** : gibbon

giboso[1], **-sa** *adj* : hunchbacked, humpbacked

giboso[2], **-sa** *n* : hunchback, humpback

gigabyte *nm* : gigabyte

gigante[1] *adj* : giant, gigantic

gigante[2], **-ta** *n* : giant

gigantesco, **-ca** *adj* : gigantic, huge

gime, etc. → **gemir**

gimnasia *nf* : gymnastics

gimnasio *nm* : gymnasium, gym

gimnasta *nmf* : gymnast

gimnástico, **-ca** *adj* : gymnastic

gimotear *vi* LLORIQUEAR : to whine, to whimper

gimoteo *nm* : whimpering

ginebra *nf* : gin

ginecología *nf* : gynecology

ginecológico, **-ca** *adj* : gynecologic, gynecological

ginecólogo, **-ga** *n* : gynecologist

ginseng *nm* : ginseng

gira *nf* : tour

giralda *nf* : weather vane

girar *vi* **1** : to turn around, to revolve **2** : to swing around, to swivel — *vt* **1** : to turn, to twist, to rotate **2** : to draft (checks) **3** : to transfer (funds)

girasol *nm* MIRASOL : sunflower

giratorio, **-ria** *adj* : revolving

giro *nm* **1** VUELTA : turn, rotation **2** : change of direction ⟨giro de 180 grados : U-turn, about-face⟩ **3** **giro bancario** : bank draft **4** **giro postal** : money order

giroscopio *or* **giróscopo** *nm* : gyroscope

gis *nm Mex* : chalk

gitano, **-na** *adj & n* : Gypsy

glacial *adj* : glacial, icy — **glacialmente** *adv*

glaciar *nm* : glacier

gladiador *nm* : gladiator

gladiolo *or* **gladíolo** *nm* : gladiolus

glándula *nf* : gland — **glandular** *adj*

glaseado *nm* : glaze, icing

glasear *vt* : to glaze

glaucoma *nm* : glaucoma

glicerina *nf* : glycerin, glycerol

glicinia *nf* : wisteria

global *adj* **1** : global, worldwide **2** : full, comprehensive **3** : total, overall

globalizar {21} *vt* **1** ABARCAR : to include, to encompass **2** : to extend worldwide

globalmente *adv* : globally, as a whole

globo *nm* **1** : globe, sphere **2** : balloon **3** **globo ocular** : eyeball

glóbulo *nm* **1** : globule **2** : blood cell, corpuscle

gloria *nf* **1** : glory **2** : fame, renown **3** : delight, enjoyment **4** : star, legend ⟨las glorias del cine : the great names in motion pictures⟩

glorieta *nf* **1** : rotary, traffic circle **2** : bower, arbor

glorificar {72} *vt* ALABAR : to glorify — **glorificación** *nf*

glorioso, **-sa** *adj* : glorious — **gloriosamente** *adv*

glosa *nf* **1** : gloss **2** : annotation, commentary

glosar *vt* **1** : to gloss **2** : to annotate, to comment on (a text)

glosario *nm* : glossary

glotis *nf* : glottis

glotón[1], **-tona** *adj, mpl* **glotones** : gluttonous

glotón[2], **-tona** *n, mpl* **glotones** : glutton

glotón[3] *nm, pl* **glotones** : wolverine

glotonería *nf* GULA : gluttony

glucosa *nf* : glucose

glutinoso, **-sa** *adj* : glutinous

gnomo [ˈnomo] *nm* : gnome

gobernación *nf, pl* **-ciones** : governing, government

gobernador, **-dora** *n* : governor

gobernante[1] *adj* : ruling, governing

gobernante[2] *nmf* : ruler, leader, governor

gobernar {55} *vt* **1** : to govern, to rule **2** : to steer, to sail (a ship) — *vi* **1** : to govern **2** : to steer

gobierno *nm* : government

goce[1], **etc.** → **gozar**

goce[2] *nm* **1** PLACER : enjoyment, pleasure **2** : use, possession

gol *nm* : goal (in soccer)

golear *vt* : to rout, to score many goals against (in soccer)

goleta *nf* : schooner

golf *nm* : golf

golfista *nmf* : golfer

golfo *nm* : gulf, bay

golondrina *nf* **1** : swallow (bird) **2** **golondrina de mar** : tern

golosina *nf* : sweet, snack

goloso, **-sa** *adj* : fond of sweets ⟨ser goloso : to have a sweet tooth⟩

golpazo *nm* : heavy blow, bang, thump

golpe *nm* **1** : blow ⟨caerle a golpes a alguien : to give someone a beating⟩ **2** : knock **3** **de ～** : suddenly **4** **de un**

golpe : all at once, in one fell swoop **5 golpe de estado** : coup, coup d'etat **6 golpe de suerte** : stroke of luck

golpeado, -da *adj* **1** : beaten, hit **2** : bruised (of fruit) **3** : dented

golpear *vt* **1** : to beat (up), to hit **2** : to slam, to bang, to strike — *vi* **1** : to knock (at a door) **2** : to beat ⟨la lluvia golpeaba contra el tejado : the rain beat against the roof⟩ — **golpearse** *vr*

golpetear *v* : to knock, to rattle, to tap

golpeteo *nm* : banging, knocking, tapping

goma *nf* **1** : gum ⟨goma de mascar : chewing gum⟩ **2** CAUCHO : rubber ⟨goma espuma : foam rubber⟩ **3** PEGAMENTO : glue **4** : rubber band **5** *Arg* : tire **6** *or* **goma de borrar** : eraser

gomita *nf* : rubber band

gomoso, -sa *adj* : gummy, sticky

góndola *nf* : gondola

gong *nm* : gong

gonorrea *nf* : gonorrhea

gorda *nf Mex* : thick corn tortilla

gordinflón[1]**, -flona** *adj, mpl* **-flones** *fam* : chubby, pudgy

gordinflón[2]**, -flona** *n, mpl* **-flones** *fam* : chubby person

gordo[1]**, -da** *adj* **1** : fat **2** : thick **3** : fatty, greasy, oily **4** : unpleasant ⟨me cae gorda tu tía : I can't stand your aunt⟩

gordo[2]**, -da** *n* : fat person

gordo[3] *nm* **1** GRASA : fat **2** : jackpot

gordura *nf* : fatness, flab

gorgojo *nm* : weevil

gorgotear *vi* : to gurgle, to bubble

gorgoteo *nm* : gurgle

gorila *nm* : gorilla

gorjear *vi* **1** : to chirp, to tweet, to warble **2** : to gurgle

gorjeo *nm* **1** : chirping, warbling **2** : gurgling

gorra *nf* **1** : bonnet **2** : cap **3 de ~** *fam* : for free, at someone else's expense ⟨vivir de gorra : to sponge, to freeload⟩

gorrear *vt fam* : to bum, to scrounge — *vi fam* : to freeload

gorrero, -ra *n fam* : freeloader, sponger

gorrión *nm, pl* **gorriones** : sparrow

gorro *nm* **1** : cap **2 estar hasta el gorro** : to be fed up

gorrón, -rrona *n, mpl* **gorrones** *fam* : freeloader, scrounger

gorronear *vt fam* : to bum, to scrounge — *vi fam* : to freeload

gota *nf* **1** : drop ⟨una gota de sudor : a bead of sweat⟩ ⟨como dos gotas de agua : like two peas in a pod⟩ ⟨sudar la gota gorda : to sweat buckets, to work very hard⟩ **2** : gout

gotear *v* **1** : to drip **2** : to leak — *v impers* LLOVIZNAR : to drizzle

goteo *nm* : drip, dripping

gotera *nf* **1** : leak **2** : stain (from dripping water)

gotero *nm* : (medicine) dropper

gótico, -ca *adj* : Gothic

gourmet *nmf* : gourmet

gozar {21} *vi* **1** : to enjoy oneself, to have a good time **2 ~ de** : to enjoy, to have, to possess ⟨gozar de buena salud : to enjoy good health⟩ **3 ~ con** : to take delight in

gozne *nm* BISAGRA : hinge

gozo *nm* **1** : joy **2** PLACER : enjoyment, pleasure

gozoso, -sa *adj* : joyful

grabación *nf, pl* **-ciones** : recording

grabado *nm* **1** : engraving **2 grabado al aguafuerte** : etching

grabador, -dora *n* : engraver

grabadora *nf* : tape recorder

grabar *vt* **1** : to engrave **2** : to record, to tape — *vi* **grabar al aguafuerte** : to etch — **grabarse** *vr* **grabársele a alguien en la memoria** : to become engraved on someone's mind

gracia *nf* **1** : grace **2** : favor, kindness **3** : humor, wit ⟨su comentario no me hizo gracia : I wasn't amused by his remark⟩ **4 gracias** *nfpl* : thanks ⟨¡gracias! : thank you!⟩ ⟨dar gracias : to give thanks⟩

grácil *adj* **1** : graceful **2** : delicate, slender, fine

gracilidad *nm* : gracefulness

gracioso, -sa *adj* **1** CHISTOSO : funny, amusing **2** : cute, attractive

grada *nf* **1** : harrow **2** PELDAÑO : step, stair **3 gradas** *nfpl* : bleachers, grandstand

gradación *nf, pl* **-ciones** : gradation, scale

gradar *vt* : to harrow, to hoe

gradería *nf* : tiers *pl*, stands *pl*, rows *pl* (in a theater)

gradiente *nf* : gradient, slope

grado *nm* **1** : degree (in meteorology and mathematics) ⟨grado centígrado : degree centigrade⟩ **2** : extent, level, degree ⟨en grado sumo : greatly, to the highest degree⟩ **3** RANGO : rank **4** : year, class (in education) **5 de buen grado** : willingly, readily

graduable *adj* : adjustable

graduación *nf, pl* **-ciones** **1** : graduation (from a school) **2** GRADO : rank **3** : alcohol content, proof

graduado[1]**, -da** *adj* **1** : graduated **2 lentes graduados** : prescription lenses

graduado[2]**, -da** *n* : graduate

gradual *adj* : gradual — **gradualmente** *adv*

graduar {3} *v* **1** : to regulate, to adjust **2** CALIBRAR : to calibrate, to gauge — **graduarse** *vr* : to graduate (from a school)

graffiti *or* **grafiti** *nmpl* : graffiti *pl*

gráfica *nf* → **gráfico**[2]

gráfico[1]**, -ca** *adj* : graphic — **gráficamente** *adv*

gráfico[2] *nm* **1** : graph, chart **2** : graphic (for a computer, etc.) **3 gráfico de barras** : bar graph

grafismo *nm* : graphics *pl*

grafito *nm* : graphite
gragea *nf* **1** : coated pill or tablet **2 grageas** *nfpl* : sprinkles, jimmies
grajo *nm* : rook (bird)
grama *nf* : grass
gramática *nf* : grammar
gramatical *adj* : grammatical — **gramaticalmente** *adv*
gramo *nm* : gram
gran → **grande**
grana *nf* : scarlet, deep red
granada *nf* **1** : pomegranate **2** : grenade ⟨granada de mano : hand grenade⟩
granadero *nm* **1** : grenadier **2 granaderos** *nmpl Mex* : riot squad
granadino, -na *adj & n* : Grenadian
granado, -da *adj* **1** DISTINGUIDO : distinguished **2** : choice, select
granate *nm* **1** : garnet **2** : deep red, maroon
grande *adj* (**gran** *before singular nouns*) **1** : large, big ⟨un libro grande : a big book⟩ **2** ALTO : tall **3** NOTABLE : great ⟨un gran autor : a great writer⟩ **4** (*indicating intensity*) : great ⟨con gran placer : with great pleasure⟩ **5** : old, grown-up ⟨hijos grandes : grown children⟩
grandeza *nf* **1** MAGNITUD : greatness, size **2** : nobility **3** : generosity, graciousness **4** : grandeur, magnificence
grandilocuencia *nf* : grandiloquence — **grandilocuente** *adj*
grandiosidad *nf* : grandeur
grandioso, -sa *adj* **1** MAGNÍFICO : grand, magnificent **2** : grandiose
granel *adv* **1 a ~** : galore, in great quantities **2 a ~** : in bulk ⟨vender a granel : to sell in bulk⟩
granero *nm* : barn, granary
granito *nm* : granite
granizada *nf* : hailstorm
granizar {21} *v impers* : to hail
granizo *nm* : hail
granja *nf* : farm
granjear *vt* : to earn, to win — **granjearse** *vr* : to gain, to earn
granjero, -ra *n* : farmer
grano *nm* **1** PARTÍCULA : grain, particle ⟨un grano de arena : a grain of sand⟩ **2** : grain (of rice, etc.), bean (of coffee), seed **3** : grain (of wood or rock) **4** BARRO, ESPINILLA : pimple **5 ir al grano** : to get to the point
granuja *nmf* PILLUELO : rascal, urchin
granular[1] *vt* : to granulate — **granularse** *vr* : to break out in spots
granular[2] *adj* : granular, grainy
granza *nf* : chaff
grapa *nf* **1** : staple **2** : clamp
grapadora *nf* ENGRAPADORA : stapler
grapar *vt* ENGRAPAR : to staple
grasa *nf* **1** : grease **2** : fat **3** *Mex* : shoe polish
grasiento, -ta *adj* : greasy, oily
graso, -sa *adj* **1** : fatty **2** : greasy, oily
grasoso, -sa *adj* GRASIENTO : greasy, oily
gratificación *nf, pl* **-ciones** **1** SATISFACCIÓN : gratification **2** : bonus **3** RECOMPENSA : recompense, reward
gratificar {72} *vt* **1** SATISFACER : to satisfy, to gratify **2** RECOMPENSAR : to reward **3** : to give a bonus to
gratinado, -da *adj* : au gratin
gratis[1] *adv* GRATUITAMENTE : free, for free, gratis
gratis[2] *adj* GRATUITO : free, gratis
gratitud *nf* : gratitude
grato, -ta *adj* AGRADABLE, PLACENTERO : pleasant, agreeable — **gratamente** *adv*
gratuitamente *adv* **1** : gratuitously **2** GRATIS : free, for free, gratis
gratuito, -ta *adj* **1** : gratuitous, unwarranted **2** GRATIS : free, gratis
grava *nf* : gravel
gravamen *nm, pl* **-vámenes** **1** : burden, obligation **2** : (property) tax
gravar *vt* **1** : to burden, to encumber **2** : to levy (a tax)
grave *adj* **1** : grave, important **2** : serious, somber **3** : serious (of an illness)
gravedad *nf* **1** : gravity ⟨centro de gravedad : center of gravity⟩ **2** : seriousness, severity
gravemente *adv* : gravely, seriously
gravilla *nf* : (fine) gravel
gravitación *nf, pl* **-ciones** : gravitation
gravitacional *adj* : gravitational
gravitar *vi* **1** : to gravitate **2 ~ sobre** : to rest on **3 ~ sobre** : to loom over
gravoso, -sa *adj* **1** ONEROSO : burdensome, onerous **2** : costly
graznar *vi* : to caw, to honk, to quack, to squawk
graznido *nm* : cawing, honking, quacking, squawking
gregario, -ria *adj* : gregarious
gregoriano, -na *adj* : Gregorian
gremial *adj* SINDICAL : union, labor
gremio *nm* SINDICATO : union, guild
greña *nf* **1** : mat, tangle **2 greñas** *nfpl* MELENAS : shaggy hair, mop
greñudo, -da *n* HIPPIE, MELENUDO : longhair, hippie
grey *nf* : congregation, flock
griego[1], **-ga** *adj & n* : Greek
griego[2] *nm* : Greek (language)
grieta *nf* : crack, crevice
grifo *nm* **1** : faucet ⟨agua del grifo : tap water⟩ **2** : griffin
grillete *nm* : shackle
grillo *nm* **1** : cricket **2 grillos** *nmpl* : fetters, shackles
grima *nf* **1** : disgust, uneasiness **2 darle grima a alguien** : to get on someone's nerves
gringo, -ga *adj & n* YANQUI : Yankee, gringo
gripa *nf Col, Mex* : flu
gripe *nf* : flu
gris *adj* **1** : gray **2** : overcast, cloudy
grisáceo, -cea *adj* : grayish
gritar *v* : to shout, to scream, to cry
gritería *nf* : shouting, clamor

grito *nm* : shout, scream, cry ⟨a grito pelado : at the top of one's voice⟩
groenlandés, **-desa** *adj & n* : Greenlander
grogui *adj fam* : dazed, groggy
grosella *nf* **1** : currant **2 grosella espinosa** : gooseberry
grosería *nf* **1** : insult, coarse language **2** : rudeness, discourtesy
grosero[1], **-ra** *adj* **1** : rude, fresh **2** : coarse, vulgar
grosero[2], **-ra** *n* : rude person
grosor *nm* : thickness
grosso *adj* **a grosso modo** : roughly, broadly, approximately
grotesco, **-ca** *adj* : grotesque, hideous
grúa *nf* **1** : crane (machine) **2** : tow truck
gruesa *nf* : gross
grueso[1], **-sa** *adj* **1** : thick, bulky **2** : heavy, big **3** : heavyset, stout
grueso[2] *nm* **1** : thickness **2** : main body, mass **3 en ~** : in bulk
grulla *nf* : crane (bird)
grumo *nm* : lump, glob
gruñido *nm* : growl, grunt
gruñir {38} *vi* **1** : to growl, to grunt **2** : to grumble
gruñón[1], **-ñona** *adj, mpl* **gruñones** *fam* : grumpy, crabby
gruñón[2], **-ñona** *n, mpl* **gruñones** *fam* : grumpy person, nag
grupa *nf* : rump, hindquarters *pl*
grupo *nm* : group
gruta *nf* : grotto, cave
guacal *nm Col, Mex, Ven* : crate
guacamayo *nm* : macaw
guacamole *or* **guacamol** *nm* : guacamole
guacamote *nm Mex* : yuca, cassava
guachinango → **huachinango**
guacho, **-cha** *adj* **1** *Arg, Col, Chile, Peru* : orphaned **2** *Chile, Peru* : odd, unmatched
guadaña *nf* : scythe
guagua *nf* **1** *Arg, Col, Chile, Peru* : baby **2** *Cuba, PRi* : bus
guaira *nf* **1** *CA* : traditional flute **2** *Peru* : smelting furnace
guajiro, **-ra** *n Cuba* : peasant
guajolote *nm Mex* : turkey
guanábana *nf* : guanabana, soursop (fruit)
guanaco *nm* : guanaco
guandú *nm CA, Car, Col* : pigeon pea
guango, **-ga** *adj Mex* **1** : loose-fitting, baggy **2** : slack, loose
guano *nm* : guano
guante *nm* **1** : glove ⟨guante de boxeo : boxing glove⟩ **2 arrojarle el guante (a alguien)** : to throw down the gauntlet (to someone)
guantelete *nm* : gauntlet
guapo, **-pa** *adj* **1** : handsome, good-looking, attractive **2** : elegant, smart **3** *fam* : bold, dashing
guapura *nf fam* : handsomeness, attractiveness, good looks *pl* ⟨¡qué guapura! : what a vision!⟩
guarache → **huarache**
guarachear *vi Cuba, PRi fam* : to go on a spree, to go out on the town
guaraní[1] *adj & nmf* : Guarani
guaraní[2] *nm* : Guarani (language of Paraguay)
guarda *nmf* **1** GUARDIÁN : security guard **2** : keeper, custodian
guardabarros *nms & pl* : fender, mudguard
guardabosque *nmf* : forest ranger, gamekeeper
guardacostas[1] *nmfs & pl* : coastguardsman
guardacostas[2] *nms & pl* : coast guard vessel
guardaespaldas *nmfs & pl* : bodyguard
guardafangos *nms & pl* : fender, mudguard
guardameta *nmf* ARQUERO, PORTERO : goalkeeper, goalie
guardapelo *nm* : locket
guardapolvo *nm* **1** : dustcover **2** : duster, housecoat
guardar *vt* **1** : to guard **2** : to maintain, to preserve **3** CONSERVAR : to put away **4** RESERVAR : to save **5** : to keep (a secret or promise) — **guardarse** *vr* **1 ~ de** : to refrain from **2 ~ de** : to guard against, to be careful not to
guardarropa *nm* **1** : cloakroom, checkroom **2** ARMARIO : closet, wardrobe
guardería *nf* : nursery, day-care center
guardia[1] *nf* **1** : guard, defense **2** : guard duty, watch **3 en ~** : on guard
guardia[2] *nmf* **1** : sentry, guardsman, guard **2** : police officer, policeman *m*, policewoman *f*
guardiamarina *nmf* : midshipman
guardián, **-diana** *n, mpl* **guardianes 1** GUARDA : security guard, watchman **2** : guardian, keeper **3 perro guardián** : watchdog
guarecer {53} *vt* : to shelter, to protect — **guarecerse** *vr* : to take shelter
guarida *nf* **1** : den, lair **2** : hideout
guarismo *nm* : figure, numeral
guarnecer {53} *vt* **1** : to adorn **2** : to garnish **3** : to garrison
guarnición *nf, pl* **-ciones 1** : garnish **2** : garrison **3** : decoration, trimming, setting (of a jewel)
guaro *nm CA* : liquor distilled from sugarcane
guasa *nf fam* **1** : joking, fooling around **2 de ~** : in jest, as a joke
guasón[1], **-sona** *adj, mpl* **guasones** *fam* : funny, witty
guasón[2], **-sona** *n, mpl* **guasones** *fam* : joker, clown
guatemalteco, **-ca** *adj & n* : Guatemalan
guau *interj* : wow!
guayaba *nf* : guava (fruit)
gubernamental *adj* : governmental
gubernativo, **-va** → **gubernamental**
gubernatura *nf Mex* : governing body
guepardo *nm* : cheetah
güero, **-ra** *adj Mex* : blond, fair

guerra *nf* **1** : war ⟨declarar la guerra : to declare war⟩ ⟨guerra sin cuartel : all-out war⟩ **2** : warfare **3** LUCHA : conflict, struggle

guerrear *vi* : to wage war

guerrero[1], **-ra** *adj* **1** : war, fighting **2** : warlike

guerrero[2], **-ra** *n* : warrior

guerrilla *nf* : guerrilla warfare

guerrillero, -ra *adj & n* : guerrilla

gueto *nm* : ghetto

guía[1] *nf* **1** : directory, guidebook **2** ORIENTACIÓN : guidance, direction ⟨la conciencia me sirve como guía : conscience is my guide⟩

guía[2] *nmf* : guide, leader ⟨guía de turismo : tour guide⟩

guiar {85} *vt* **1** : to guide, to lead **2** CONDUCIR : to manage — **guiarse** *vr* : to be guided by, to go by

guija *nf* : pebble

guijarro *nm* : pebble

guillotina *nf* : guillotine — **guillotinar** *vt*

guinda[1] *adj & nm Mex* : burgundy (color)

guinda[2] *nf* : morello (cherry)

guineo *nm Car* : banana

guinga *nf* : gingham

guiñada → **guiño**

guiñar *vi* : to wink

guiño *nm* : wink

guión *nm, pl* **guiones** **1** : script, screenplay **2** : hyphen, dash **3** ESTANDARTE : standard, banner

guirnalda *nf* : garland

guisa *nf* **1** : manner, fashion **2 a guisa de** : like, by way of **3 de tal guisa** : in such a way

guisado ESTOFADO *nm* : stew

guisante *nm* : pea

guisar *vt* **1** ESTOFAR : to stew **2** *Spain* : to cook

guiso *nm* **1** : stew **2** : casserole

güisqui → **whisky**

guita *nf* : string, twine

guitarra *nf* : guitar

guitarrista *nmf* : guitarist

gula *nf* GLOTONERÍA : gluttony, greed

gusano *nm* **1** LOMBRIZ : worm, earthworm ⟨gusano de seda : silkworm⟩ **2** : caterpillar, maggot, grub

gustar *vt* **1** : to taste **2** : to like ⟨¿gustan pasar? : would you like to come in?⟩ — *vi* **1** : to be pleasing ⟨me gustan los dulces : I like sweets⟩ ⟨a María le gusta Carlos : Maria is attracted to Carlos⟩ ⟨no me gusta que me griten : I don't like to be yelled at⟩ **2 ~ de** : to like, to enjoy ⟨no gusta de chismes : she doesn't like gossip⟩ **3 como guste** : as you wish, as you like

gustativo, -va *adj* : taste ⟨papilas gustativas : taste buds⟩

gusto *nm* **1** : flavor, taste **2** : taste, style **3** : pleasure, liking **4** : whim, fancy ⟨a gusto : at will⟩ **5 a ~** : comfortable, at ease **6 al gusto** : to taste, as one likes **7 mucho gusto** : pleased to meet you

gustosamente *adv* : gladly

gustoso, -sa *adj* **1** : willing, glad ⟨nuestra empresa participará gustosa : our company will be pleased to participate⟩ **2** : zesty, tasty

gutural *adj* : guttural

H

h *nf* : eighth letter of the Spanish alphabet

ha → **haber**

haba *nf* : broad bean

habanero[1], **-ra** *adj* : of or from Havana

habanero[2], **-ra** *n* : native or resident of Havana

haber[1] {39} *v aux* **1** : have, has ⟨no ha llegado el envío : the shipment hasn't arrived⟩ **2 ~ de** : must ⟨ha de ser tarde : it must be late⟩ — *v impers* **1 hay** : there is, there are ⟨hay dos mensajes : there are two messages⟩ ⟨¿qué hay de nuevo? : what's new?⟩ **2 hay que** : it is necessary ⟨hay que trabajar más rápido : you have to work faster⟩

haber[2] *nm* **1** : assets *pl* **2** : credit, credit side **3 haberes** *nmpl* : salary, income, remuneration

habichuela *nf* **1** : bean, kidney bean **2** : green bean

hábil *adj* **1** : able, skillful **2** : working ⟨días hábiles : working days⟩

habilidad *nf* CAPACIDAD : ability, skill

habilidoso, -sa *adj* : skillful, clever

habilitación *nf, pl* **-ciones** **1** : authorization **2** : furnishing, equipping

habilitar *vt* **1** : to enable, to authorize, to empower **2** : to equip, to furnish

hábilmente *adv* : skillfully, expertly

habitable *adj* : habitable, inhabitable

habitación *nf, pl* **-ciones** **1** CUARTO : room **2** DORMITORIO : bedroom **3** : habitation, occupancy

habitante *nmf* : inhabitant, resident

habitar *vt* : to inhabit — *vi* : to reside, to dwell

hábitat *nm, pl* **-tats** : habitat

hábito *nm* **1** : habit, custom **2** : habit (of a monk or nun)

habitual *adj* : habitual, customary — **habitualmente** *adv*

habituar {3} *vt* : to accustom, to habituate — **habituarse** *vr* **~ a** : to get used to, to grow accustomed to

habla *nf* **1** : speech **2** : language, dialect **3 de ~** : speaking ⟨de habla inglesa : English-speaking⟩

hablado, -da *adj* **1** : spoken **2 mal hablado** : foulmouthed

hablador[1], **-dora** *adj* : talkative
hablador[2], **-dora** *n* : chatterbox
habladuría *nf* **1** : rumor **2 habladurías** *nfpl* : gossip, scandal
hablante *nmf* : speaker
hablar *vi* **1** : to speak, to talk ⟨hablar en broma : to be joking⟩ **2 ~ de** : to mention, to talk about **3 dar que hablar** : to make people talk — *vt* **1** : to speak (a language) **2** : to talk about, to discuss ⟨háblalo con tu jefe : discuss it with your boss⟩ — **hablarse** *vr* **1** : to speak to each other, to be on speaking terms **2 se habla inglés (etc.)** : English (etc.) spoken
habrá, etc. → **haber**
hacedor, **-dora** *n* : creator, maker, doer
hacendado, **-da** *n* : landowner
hacer {40} *vt* **1** : to make **2** : to do, to perform **3** : to force, to oblige ⟨los hice esperar : I made them wait⟩ — *vi* : to act ⟨haces bien : you're doing the right thing⟩ — *v impers* **1** (*referring to weather*) ⟨hacer frío : to be cold⟩ ⟨hace viento : it's windy⟩ **2 hace** : ago ⟨hace mucho tiempo : a long time ago, for a long time⟩ **3 no le hace** : it doesn't matter, it makes no difference **4 hacer falta** : to be necessary, to be needed — **hacerse** *vr* **1** : to become **2** : to pretend, to act, to play ⟨hacerse el tonto : to play dumb⟩ **3** : to seem ⟨el examen se me hizo difícil : the exam seemed difficult to me⟩ **4** : to get, to grow ⟨se hace tarde : it's growing late⟩
hacha *nf* : hatchet, ax
hachazo *nm* : blow, chop (with an ax)
hachís *nm* : hashish
hacia *prep* **1** : toward, towards ⟨hacia abajo : downward⟩ ⟨hacia adelante : forward⟩ **2** : near, around, about ⟨hacia las seis : about six o'clock⟩
hacienda *nf* **1** : estate, ranch, farm **2** : property **3** : livestock **4 la Hacienda** : department of revenue, tax office
hacinar *vt* **1** : to pile up, to stack **2** : to overcrowd — **hacinarse** *vr* : to crowd together
hada *nf* : fairy
hado *nm* : destiny, fate
haga, etc. → **hacer**
haitiano, **-na** *adj & n* : Haitian
hala *interj Spain* **1** (*expressing encouragement or disbelief*) : come on! **2** (*expressing surprise*) : wow! **3** (*expressing protest*) : hey!
halagador[1], **-dora** *adj* : flattering
halagador[2], **-dora** *n* : flatterer
halagar {52} *vt* : to flatter, to compliment
halago *nm* : flattery, praise
halagüeño, **-ña** *adj* **1** : flattering **2** : encouraging, promising
halar *vt CA, Car* → **jalar**
halcón *nm, pl* **halcones** : hawk, falcon
halibut *nm, pl* **-buts** : halibut
hálito *nm* **1** : breath **2** : gentle breeze
hallar *vt* **1** ENCONTRAR : to find **2** DESCUBRIR : to discover, to find out — **hallarse** *vr* **1** : to be situated, to find oneself **2** : to feel ⟨no se halla bien : he doesn't feel comfortable, he feels out of place⟩
hallazgo *nm* **1** : discovery **2** : find ⟨¡es un verdadero hallazgo! : it's a real find!⟩
halo *nm* **1** : halo **2** : aura
halógeno *nm* : halogen
hamaca *nf* : hammock
hambre *nf* **1** : hunger **2** : starvation **3 tener hambre** : to be hungry **4 dar hambre** : to make hungry
hambriento, **-ta** *adj* : hungry, starving
hambruna *nf* : famine
hamburguesa *nf* : hamburger
hampa *nf* : criminal underworld
hampón, **-pona** *n, mpl* **hampones** : criminal, thug
hámster [ˈxamster] *nm, pl* **hámsters** : hamster
han → **haber**
handicap *or* **hándicap** [ˈhandiˌkap] *nm, pl* **-caps** : handicap (in sports)
hangar *nm* : hangar
hará, etc. → **hacer**
haragán[1], **-gana** *adj, mpl* **-ganes** : lazy, idle
haragán[2], **-gana** *n, mpl* **-ganes** HOLGAZÁN : slacker, good-for-nothing
haraganear *vi* : to be lazy, to waste one's time
haraganería *nf* : laziness
harapiento, **-ta** *adj* : ragged, tattered
harapos *nmpl* ANDRAJOS : rags, tatters
hardware [ˈhardˌwɛr] *nm* : computer hardware
harén *nm, pl* **harenes** : harem
harina *nf* **1** : flour **2 harina de maíz** : cornmeal
hartar *vt* **1** : to glut, to satiate **2** FASTIDIAR : to tire, to irritate, to annoy — **hartarse** *vr* : to be weary, to get fed up
harto[1] *adv* : most, extremely, very
harto[2], **-ta** *adj* **1** : full, satiated **2** : fed up
hartura *nf* **1** : surfeit **2** : abundance, plenty
has → **haber**
hasta[1] *adv* : even
hasta[2] *prep* **1** : until, up until ⟨hasta entonces : until then⟩ ⟨¡hasta luego! : see you later!⟩ **2** : as far as ⟨nos fuimos hasta Managua : we went all the way to Managua⟩ **3** : up to ⟨hasta cierto punto : up to a certain point⟩ **4 hasta que** : until
hastiar {85} *vt* **1** : to make weary, to bore **2** : to disgust, to sicken — **hastiarse** *vr* **~ de** : to get tired of
hastío *nm* **1** TEDIO : tedium **2** REPUGNANCIA : disgust
hato *nm* **1** : flock, herd **2** : bundle (of possessions)
hawaiano, **-na** *adj & n* : Hawaiian
hay → **haber**[1]

haya[1], **etc.** → **haber**
haya[2] *nf* : beech (tree and wood)
hayuco *nm* : beechnut
haz[1] → **hacer**
haz[2] *nm, pl* **haces** **1** FARDO : bundle **2** : beam (of light)
haz[3] *nf, pl* **haces** **1** : face **2 haz de la tierra** : surface of the earth
hazaña *nf* PROEZA : feat, exploit
hazmerreír *nm fam* : laughingstock
he[1] {39} → **haber**
he[2] *v impers* **he aquí** : here is, here are, behold
hebilla *nf* : buckle, clasp
hebra *nf* : strand, thread
hebreo[1], **-brea** *adj & n* : Hebrew
hebreo[2] *nm* : Hebrew (language)
hecatombe *nf* **1** MATANZA : massacre **2** : disaster
heces → **hez**
hechicería *nf* **1** BRUJERÍA : sorcery, witchcraft **2** : curse, spell
hechicero[1], **-ra** *adj* : bewitching, enchanting
hechicero[2], **-ra** *n* : sorcerer, sorceress *f*
hechizar {21} *vt* **1** EMBRUJAR : to bewitch **2** CAUTIVAR : to charm
hechizo *nm* **1** SORTILEGIO : spell, enchantment **2** ENCANTO : charm, fascination
hecho[1] *pp* → **hacer**
hecho[2], **-cha** *adj* **1** : made, done **2** : ready-to-wear **3** : complete, finished ⟨hecho y derecho : full-fledged⟩
hecho[3] *nm* **1** : fact **2** : event ⟨hechos históricos : historic events⟩ **3** : act, action **4 de ~** : in fact, in reality
hechura *nf* **1** : style **2** : craftsmanship, workmanship **3** : product, creation
hectárea *nf* : hectare
heder {56} *vi* : to stink, to reek
hediondez *nf, pl* **-deces** : stink, stench
hediondo, -da *adj* MALOLIENTE : foul-smelling, stinking
hedor *nm* : stench, stink
hegemonía *nf* **1** : dominance **2** : hegemony (in politics)
helada *nf* : frost (in meteorology)
heladería *nf* : ice-cream parlor, ice-cream stand
helado[1], **-da** *adj* **1** GÉLIDO : icy, freezing cold **2** CONGELADO : frozen
helado[2] *nm* : ice cream
heladora *nf* CONGELADOR : freezer
helar {55} *v* CONGELAR : to freeze — *v impers* : to produce frost ⟨anoche heló : there was frost last night⟩ — **helarse** *vr*
helecho *nm* : fern, bracken
hélice *nf* **1** : spiral, helix **2** : propeller
helicóptero *nm* : helicopter
helio *nm* : helium
helipuerto *nm* : heliport
hembra *adj & nf* : female
hemisférico, -ca *adj* : hemispheric, hemispherical
hemisferio *nm* : hemisphere
hemofilia *nf* : hemophilia
hemofílico, -ca *adj & n* : hemophiliac
hemoglobina *nf* : hemoglobin
hemorragia *nf* **1** : hemorrhage **2 hemorragia nasal** : nosebleed
hemorroides *nfpl* ALMORRANAS : hemorrhoids, piles
hemos → **haber**
henchido, -da *adj* : swollen, bloated
henchir {54} *vt* **1** : to stuff, to fill **2** : to swell, to swell up — **henchirse** *vr* **1** : to stuff oneself **2** LLENARSE : to fill up, to be full
hender {56} *vt* : to cleave, to split
hendidura *nf* : crack, crevice, fissure
henequén *nm, pl* **-quenes** : sisal hemp
heno *nm* : hay
hepatitis *nf* : hepatitis
heráldica *nf* : heraldry
heráldico, -ca *adj* : heraldic
heraldo *nm* : herald
herbario, -ria *adj* : herbal
herbicida *nm* : herbicide, weed killer
herbívoro[1], **-ra** *adj* : herbivorous
herbívoro[2] *nm* : herbivore
herbolario, -ria *n* : herbalist
hercio *nm* : hertz
hercúleo, -lea *adj* : herculean
heredar *vt* : to inherit
heredero, -ra *n* : heir, heiress *f*
hereditario, -ria *adj* : hereditary
hereje *nmf* : heretic
herejía *nf* : heresy
herencia *nf* **1** : inheritance **2** : heritage **3** : heredity
herético, -ca *adj* : heretical
herida *nf* : injury, wound
herido[1], **-da** *adj* **1** : injured, wounded **2** : hurt, offended
herido[2], **-da** *n* : injured person, casualty
herir {76} *vt* **1** : to injure, to wound **2** : to hurt, to offend
hermafrodita *nmf* : hermaphrodite
hermanar *vt* **1** : to unite, to bring together **2** : to match up, to twin (cities)
hermanastro, -tra *n* : half brother *m*, half sister *f*
hermandad *nf* **1** FRATERNIDAD : brotherhood ⟨hermandad de mujeres : sisterhood, sorority⟩ **2** : association
hermano, -na *n* : sibling, brother *m*, sister *f*
hermético, -ca *adj* : hermetic, watertight — **herméticamente** *adv*
hermoso, -sa *adj* BELLO : beautiful, lovely — **hermosamente** *adv*
hermosura *nf* BELLEZA : beauty, loveliness
hernia *nf* : hernia
héroe *nm* : hero
heroicidad *nf* : heroism, heroic deed
heroico, -ca *adj* : heroic — **heroicamente** *adv*
heroína *nf* **1** : heroine **2** : heroin
heroísmo *nm* : heroism
herpes *nms & pl* **1** : herpes **2** : shingles
herradura *nf* : horseshoe
herraje *nm* : ironwork

herramienta *nf* : tool
herrar {55} *vt* : to shoe (a horse)
herrería *nf* : blacksmith's shop
herrero, -ra *n* : blacksmith
herrumbre *nf* ORÍN : rust
herrumbroso, -sa *adj* OXIDADO : rusty
hertzio *nm* : hertz
hervidero *nm* **1** : mass, swarm **2** : hotbed (of crime, etc.)
hervidor *nm* : kettle
hervir {76} *vi* **1** BULLIR : to boil, to bubble **2 ~ de** : to teem with, to be swarming with — *vt* : to boil
hervor *nm* **1** : boiling **2** : fervor, ardor
heterogeneidad *nf* : heterogeneity
heterogéneo, -nea *adj* : heterogeneous
heterosexual *adj & nmf* : heterosexual
heterosexualidad *nf* : heterosexuality
hexágono *nm* : hexagon — **hexagonal** *adj*
hez *nf, pl* **heces** **1** ESCORIA : scum, dregs *pl* **2** : sediment, lees *pl* **3 heces** *nfpl* : feces, excrement
hiato *nm* : hiatus
hibernar *vi* : to hibernate — **hibernación** *nf*
híbrido[1], -da *adj* : hybrid
híbrido[2] *nm* : hybrid
hicieron, etc. → **hacer**
hidalgo, -ga *n* : nobleman *m,* noblewoman *f*
hidrante *nm CA, Col* : hydrant
hidratar *vt* : to moisturize — **hidratante** *adj*
hidrato *nm* **1** : hydrate **2 hidrato de carbono** : carbohydrate
hidráulico, -ca *adj* : hydraulic
hidroavión *nm, pl* **-viones** : seaplane
hidrocarburo *nm* : hydrocarbon
hidroeléctrico, -ca *adj* : hydroelectric
hidrofobia *nf* RABIA : hydrophobia, rabies
hidrófugo, -ga *adj* : water-repellent
hidrógeno *nm* : hydrogen
hidroplano *nm* : hydroplane
hiede, etc. → **heder**
hiedra *nf* **1** : ivy **2 hiedra venenosa** : poison ivy
hiel *nf* **1** BILIS : bile **2** : bitterness
hiela, etc. → **helar**
hielo *nm* **1** : ice **2** : coldness, reserve ⟨romper el hielo : to break the ice⟩
hiena *nf* : hyena
hiende, etc. → **hender**
hierba *nf* **1** : herb **2** : grass **3 mala hierba** : weed
hierbabuena *nf* : mint, spearmint
hiere, etc. → **herir**
hierra, etc. → **herrar**
hierro *nm* **1** : iron ⟨hierro fundido : cast iron⟩ **2** : branding iron
hierve, etc. → **hervir**
hígado *nm* : liver
higiene *nf* : hygiene
higiénico, -ca *adj* : hygienic — **higiénicamente** *adv*
higienista *nmf* : hygienist
higo *nm* **1** : fig **2 higo chumbo** : prickly pear (fruit)
higrómetro *nm* : hygrometer
higuera *nf* : fig tree
hijastro, -tra *n* : stepson *m,* stepdaughter *f*
hijo, -ja *n* **1** : son *m,* daughter *f* **2 hijos** *nmpl* : children, offspring
híjole *interj Mex* : wow!, good grief!
hilacha *nf* **1** : ravel, loose thread **2 mostrar la hilacha** : to show one's true colors
hilado *nm* **1** : spinning **2** HILO : yarn, thread
hilar *vt* **1** : to spin (thread) **2** : to consider, to string together (ideas) — *vi* **1** : to spin **2 hilar delgado** : to split hairs
hilarante *adj* **1** : humorous, hilarious **2 gas hilarante** : laughing gas
hilaridad *nf* : hilarity
hilera *nf* FILA : file, row, line
hilo *nm* **1** : thread ⟨colgar de un hilo : to hang by a thread⟩ ⟨hilo dental : dental floss⟩ **2** LINO : linen **3** : (electric) wire **4** : theme, thread (of a discourse) **5** : trickle (of water, etc.)
hilvanar *vt* **1** : to baste, to tack **2** : to piece together
himnario *nm* : hymnal
himno *nm* **1** : hymn **2 himno nacional** : national anthem
hincapié *nm* **hacer hincapié en** : to emphasize, to stress
hincar {72} *vt* CLAVAR : to stick, to plunge — **hincarse** *vr* **hincarse de rodillas** : to kneel down, to fall to one's knees
hinchado, -da *adj* **1** : swollen, inflated **2** : pompous, overblown
hinchar *vt* **1** INFLAR : to inflate **2** : to exaggerate — **hincharse** *vr* **1** : to swell up **2** : to become conceited, to swell with pride
hinchazón *nf, pl* **-zones** : swelling
hinche, etc. → **henchir**
hindi *nm* : Hindi
hindú *adj & nmf* : Hindu
hinduismo *nm* : Hinduism
hiniesta *nf* : broom (plant)
hinojo *nm* **1** : fennel **2 de hinojos** : on bended knee
hinque, etc. → **hincar**
hipar *vi* : to hiccup
hiperactividad *nf* : hyperactivity
hiperactivo, -va *adj* : hyperactive, overactive
hipérbole *nf* : hyperbole
hiperbólico, -ca *adj* : hyperbolic, exaggerated
hipercrítico, -ca *adj* : hypercritical
hipermetropía *nf* : farsightedness
hipersensibilidad *nf* : hypersensitivity
hipersensible *adj* : hypersensitive
hipertensión *nf, pl* **-siones** : hypertension, high blood pressure
hip–hop [ˌxipˈxop] *nm* : hip-hop (music)
hípico, -ca *adj* : equestrian ⟨concurso hípico : horse show⟩
hipil → **huipil**
hipnosis *nfs & pl* : hypnosis

hipnótico, -ca *adj* : hypnotic
hipnotismo *nm* : hypnotism
hipnotizador[1], **-dora** *adj* **1** : hypnotic **2** : spellbinding, mesmerizing
hipnotizador[2], **-dora** *n* : hypnotist
hipnotizar {21} *vt* : to hypnotize
hipo *nm* : hiccup, hiccups *pl*
hipocampo *nm* : sea horse
hipocondría *nf* : hypochondria
hipocondríaco, -ca *adj & n* : hypochondriac
hipocresía *nf* : hypocrisy
hipócrita[1] *adj* : hypocritical — **hipócritamente** *adv*
hipócrita[2] *nmf* : hypocrite
hipodérmico, -ca *adj* **aguja hipodérmica** : hypodermic needle
hipódromo *nm* : racetrack
hipopótamo *nm* : hippopotamus
hipoteca *nf* : mortgage
hipotecar {72} *vt* **1** : to mortgage **2** : to compromise, to jeopardize
hipotecario, -ria *adj* : mortgage
hipotensión *nf* : low blood pressure
hipotenusa *nf* : hypotenuse
hipótesis *nfs & pl* : hypothesis
hipotético, -ca *adj* : hypothetical — **hipotéticamente** *adv*
hippie *or* **hippy** ['hipi] *nmf, pl* **hippies** [-pis] : hippie
hiriente *adj* : hurtful, offensive
hirió, etc. → **herir**
hirsuto, -ta *adj* **1** : hirsute, hairy **2** : bristly, wiry
hirviente *adj* : boiling
hirvió, etc. → **hervir**
hisopo *nm* **1** : hyssop **2** : cotton swab
hispánico, -ca *adj & n* : Hispanic
hispano[1], **-na** *adj* : Hispanic ⟨de habla hispana : Spanish-speaking⟩
hispano[2], **-na** *n* : Hispanic (person)
hispanoamericano[1], **-na** *adj* LATINOAMERICANO : Latin-American
hispanoamericano[2], **-na** *n* LATINOAMERICANO : Latin American
hispanohablante[1] *adj* : Spanish-speaking
hispanohablante[2] *nmf* : Spanish speaker
histerectomía *nf* : hysterectomy
histeria *nf* **1** : hysteria **2** : hysterics
histérico, -ca *adj* : hysterical — **histéricamente** *adv*
histerismo *nm* **1** : hysteria **2** : hysterics
historia *nf* **1** : history **2** NARRACIÓN, RELATO : story
historiador, -dora *n* : historian
historial *nm* **1** : record, document **2** CURRÍCULUM : résumé, curriculum vitae
histórico, -ca *adj* **1** : historical **2** : historic, important — **históricamente** *adv*
historieta *nf* : comic strip
histrionismo *nm* : histrionics, acting
hit ['hit] *nm, pl* **hits 1** ÉXITO : hit, popular song **2** : hit (in baseball)
hito *nm* : milestone, landmark
hizo → **hacer**
hobby ['hɔbi] *nm, pl* **hobbies** [-bis] : hobby
hocico *nm* : snout, muzzle
hockey ['hɔke, -ki] *nm* : hockey
hogar *nm* **1** : home **2** : hearth, fireplace
hogareño, -ña *adj* **1** : home-loving **2** : domestic, homelike
hogaza *nf* : large loaf (of bread)
hoguera *nf* **1** FOGATA : bonfire **2 morir en la hoguera** : to burn at the stake
hoja *nf* **1** : leaf, petal, blade (of grass) **2** : sheet (of paper), page (of a book) ⟨hoja de cálculo : spreadsheet⟩ **3** FORMULARIO : form ⟨hoja de pedido : order form⟩ **4** : blade (of a knife) ⟨hoja de afeitar : razor blade⟩
hojalata *nf* : tinplate
hojaldre *nm* : puff pastry
hojarasca *nf* : fallen leaves *pl*
hojear *vt* : to leaf through (a book or magazine)
hojuela *nf* **1** : leaflet, young leaf **2** : flake
hola *interj* : hello!, hi!
holandés[1], **-desa** *adj, mpl* **-deses** : Dutch
holandés[2], **-desa** *n, mpl* **-deses** : Dutch person, Dutchman *m*, Dutchwoman *f* ⟨los holandeses : the Dutch⟩
holandés[3] *nm* : Dutch (language)
holgadamente *adv* : comfortably, easily ⟨vivir holgadamente : to be well-off⟩
holgado, -da *adj* **1** : loose, baggy **2** : at ease, comfortable
holganza *nf* : leisure, idleness
holgazán[1], **-zana** *adj, mpl* **-zanes** : lazy
holgazán[2], **-zana** *n, mpl* **-zanes** HARAGÁN : slacker, idler
holgazanear *vi* HARAGANEAR : to laze around, to loaf
holgazanería *nf* PEREZA : idleness, laziness
holgura *nf* **1** : looseness **2** COMODIDAD : comfort, ease
holístico, -ca *adj* : holistic
hollar {19} *vt* : to tread on, to trample
hollín *nm, pl* **hollines** TIZNE : soot
holocausto *nm* : holocaust
holograma *nm* : hologram
hombre *nm* **1** : man ⟨el hombre : man, mankind⟩ **2 hombre de estado** : statesman **3 hombre de negocios** : businessman **4 hombre lobo** : werewolf
hombrera *nf* **1** : shoulder pad **2** : epaulet
hombría *nf* : manliness
hombro *nm* : shoulder ⟨encogerse de hombros : to shrug one's shoulders⟩
hombruno, -na *adj* : mannish
homenaje *nm* : homage, tribute ⟨rendir homenaje a : to pay tribute to⟩
homenajear *vt* : to pay homage to, to honor
homeopatía *nf* : homeopathy
homicida[1] *adj* : homicidal, murderous
homicida[2] *nmf* ASESINO : murderer
homicidio *nm* ASESINATO : homicide, murder

homilía *nf* : homily, sermon

homófono *nm* : homophone

homogeneidad *nf* : homogeneity

homogeneización *nf* : homogenization

homogeneizar {21} *vt* : to homogenize

homogéneo, -nea *adj* : homogeneous

homógrafo *nm* : homograph

homologación *nf, pl* **-ciones** **1** : sanctioning, approval **2** : parity

homologar {52} *vt* **1** : to sanction **2** : to bring into line

homólogo[1], **-ga** *adj* : homologous, equivalent

homólogo[2], **-ga** *n* : counterpart

homónimo[1], **-ma** *n* TOCAYO : namesake

homónimo[2] *nm* : homonym

homosexual *adj & nmf* : homosexual

homosexualidad *nf* : homosexuality

honda *nf* : sling

hondo[1] *adv* : deeply

hondo[2], **-da** *adj* PROFUNDO : deep ⟨en lo más hondo de : in the depths of⟩ — **hondamente** *adv*

hondonada *nf* **1** : hollow, depression **2** : ravine, gorge

hondura *nf* : depth

hondureño, -ña *adj & n* : Honduran

honestidad *nf* **1** : decency, modesty **2** : honesty, uprightness

honesto, -ta *adj* **1** : decent, virtuous **2** : honest, honorable — **honestamente** *adv*

hongo *nm* **1** : fungus **2** : mushroom

honor *nm* **1** : honor ⟨en honor a la verdad : to be quite honest⟩ **2 honores** *nmpl* : honors ⟨hacer los honores : to do the honors⟩

honorable *adj* HONROSO : honorable — **honorablemente** *adv*

honorario, -ria *adj* : honorary

honorarios *nmpl* : payment, fees (for professional services)

honorífico, -ca *adj* : honorary ⟨mención honorífica : honorable mention⟩

honra *nf* **1** : dignity, self-respect ⟨tener a mucha honra : to take great pride in⟩ **2** : good name, reputation

honradamente *adv* : honestly, decently

honradez *nf, pl* **-deces** : honesty, integrity, probity

honrado, -da *adj* **1** HONESTO : honest, upright **2** : honored

honrar *vt* **1** : to honor **2** : to be a credit to ⟨su generosidad lo honra : his generosity does him credit⟩

honroso, -sa *adj* HONORABLE : honorable — **honrosamente** *adv*

hora *nf* **1** : hour ⟨media hora : half an hour⟩ ⟨a la última hora : at the last minute⟩ ⟨a la hora en punto : on the dot⟩ ⟨horas de oficina : office hours⟩ **2** : time ⟨¿qué hora es? : what time is it?⟩ **3** CITA : appointment

horario *nm* : schedule, timetable, hours *pl* ⟨horario de visita : visiting hours⟩

horca *nf* **1** : gallows *pl* **2** : pitchfork

horcajadas *nfpl* **a ~** : astride, astraddle

horcón *nm, pl* **horcones** : wooden post, prop

horda *nf* : horde

horizontal *adj* : horizontal — **horizontalmente** *adv*

horizonte *nm* : horizon, skyline

horma *nf* **1** : shoe tree **2** : shoemaker's last

hormiga *nf* : ant

hormigón *nm, pl* **-gones** CONCRETO : concrete

hormigonera *nf* : cement mixer

hormigueo *nm* **1** : tingling, pins and needles *pl* **2** : uneasiness

hormiguero *nm* **1** : anthill **2** : swarm (of people)

hormona *nf* : hormone — **hormonal** *adj*

hornacina *nf* : niche, recess

hornada *nf* : batch

hornear *vt* : to bake

hornilla *nf* : burner (of a stove)

horno *nm* **1** : oven ⟨horno crematorio : crematorium⟩ ⟨horno de microondas : microwave oven⟩ **2** : kiln

horóscopo *nm* : horoscope

horqueta *nf* **1** : fork (in a river or road) **2** : crotch (in a tree) **3** : small pitchfork

horquilla *nf* **1** : hairpin, bobby pin **2** : pitchfork

horrendo, -da *adj* : horrendous, horrible

horrible *adj* : horrible, dreadful — **horriblemente** *adv*

horripilante *adj* : horrifying, hair-raising

horripilar *vt* : to horrify, to terrify

horror *nm* : horror, dread

horrorizado, -da *adj* : terrified

horrorizar {21} *vt* : to horrify, to terrify — **horrorizarse** *vr*

horroroso, -sa *adj* **1** : horrifying, terrifying **2** : dreadful, bad

hortaliza *nf* **1** : vegetable **2 hortalizas** *nfpl* : garden produce

hortera *adj Spain fam* : tacky, gaudy

hortícola *adj* : horticultural

horticultor, -ra *n* : horticulturist

horticultura *nf* : horticulture

hosco, -ca *adj* : sullen, gloomy

hospedaje *nm* : lodging, accommodations *pl*

hospedar *vt* : to provide with lodging, to put up — **hospedarse** *vr* : to stay, to lodge

hospicio *nm* : orphanage

hospital *nm* : hospital

hospitalario, -ria *adj* : hospitable

hospitalidad *nf* : hospitality

hospitalización *nf, pl* **-ciones** : hospitalization

hospitalizar {21} *vt* : to hospitalize — **hospitalizarse** *vr*

hostería *nf* POSADA : inn

hostia *nf* : host, Eucharist

hostigamiento *nm* : harassment

hostigar {52} *vt* ACOSAR, ASEDIAR : to harass, to pester

hostil *adj* : hostile

hostilidad *nf* **1** : hostility, antagonism **2 hostilidades** *nfpl* : (military) hostilities
hostilizar {21} *vt* : to harass
hotel *nm* : hotel
hotelero[1], **-ra** *adj* : hotel ⟨la industria hotelera : the hotel business⟩
hotelero[2], **-ra** *n* : hotel manager, hotelier
hoy *adv* **1** : today ⟨hoy mismo : right now, this very day⟩ **2** : now, nowadays ⟨de hoy en adelante : from now on⟩
hoyo *nm* AGUJERO : hole
hoyuelo *nm* : dimple
hoz *nf, pl* **hoces** : sickle
hozar {21} *vi* : to root (of a pig)
huachinango *nm Mex* : red snapper
huarache *nm* : huarache sandal
hubo, etc. → **haber**
hueco[1], **-ca** *adj* **1** : hollow, empty **2** : soft, spongy **3** : hollow-sounding, resonant **4** : proud, conceited **5** : superficial
hueco[2] *nm* **1** : hole, hollow, cavity **2** : gap, space **3** : recess, alcove
huele, etc. → **oler**
huelga *nf* **1** PARO : strike **2 hacer huelga** : to strike, to go on strike
huelguista *nmf* : striker
huella[1], **etc.** → **hollar**
huella[2] *nf* **1** : footprint ⟨seguir las huellas de alguien : to follow in someone's footsteps⟩ **2** : mark, impact ⟨dejar huella : to leave one's mark⟩ ⟨sin dejar huella : without a trace⟩ **3 huella digital** *or* **huella dactilar** : fingerprint
huérfano[1], **-na** *adj* **1** : orphan, orphaned **2** : defenseless **3 ~ de** : lacking, devoid of
huérfano[2], **-na** *n* : orphan
huerta *nf* **1** : large vegetable garden, truck farm **2** : orchard **3** : irrigated land
huerto *nm* **1** : vegetable garden **2** : orchard
hueso *nm* **1** : bone **2** : pit, stone (of a fruit)
huésped[1], **-peda** *n* INVITADO : guest
huésped[2] *nm* : host ⟨organismo huésped : host organism⟩
huestes *nfpl* **1** : followers **2** : troops, army
huesudo, -da *adj* : bony
hueva *nf* : roe, spawn
huevo *nm* : egg ⟨huevos revueltos : scrambled eggs⟩
huida *nf* : flight, escape
huidizo, -za *adj* **1** ESCURRIDIZO : elusive, slippery **2** : shy, evasive
huipil *nm CA, Mex* : traditional sleeveless blouse or dress
huir {41} *vi* **1** ESCAPAR : to escape, to flee **2 ~ de** : to avoid
huiro *nm Chile, Peru* : seaweed
huizache *nm* : huisache, acacia
hule *nm* **1** : oilcloth, oilskin **2** *Mex* : rubber **3 hule espuma** *Mex* : foam rubber
humanidad *nf* **1** : humanity, mankind **2** : humaneness **3 humanidades** *nfpl* : humanities *pl*
humanismo *nm* : humanism
humanista *nmf* : humanist
humanístico, -ca *adj* : humanistic
humanitario, -ria *adj & n* : humanitarian
humano[1], **-na** *adj* **1** : human **2** BENÉVOLO : humane, benevolent — **humanamente** *adv*
humano[2] *nm* : human being, human
humareda *nf* : cloud of smoke
humeante *adj* **1** : smoky **2** : smoking, steaming
humear *vi* **1** : to smoke **2** : to steam
humectante[1] *adj* : moisturizing
humectante[2] *nm* : moisturizer
humedad *nf* **1** : humidity **2** : dampness, moistness
humedecer {53} *vt* **1** : to humidify **2** : to moisten, to dampen
húmedo, -da *adj* **1** : humid **2** : moist, damp
humidificador *nm* : humidifier
humidificar {72} *vt* : to humidify
humildad *nf* **1** : humility **2** : lowliness
humilde *adj* **1** : humble **2** : lowly ⟨gente humilde : poor people⟩
humildemente *adv* : meekly, humbly
humillación *nf, pl* **-ciones** : humiliation
humillante *adj* : humiliating
humillar *vt* : to humiliate — **humillarse** *vr* : to humble oneself ⟨humillarse a hacer algo : to stoop to doing something⟩
humo *nm* **1** : smoke, steam, fumes **2 humos** *nmpl* : airs *pl,* conceit
humor *nm* **1** : humor **2** : mood, temper ⟨está de buen humor : she's in a good mood⟩
humorada *nf* **1** BROMA : joke, witticism **2** : whim, caprice
humorismo *nm* : humor, wit
humorista *nmf* : humorist, comedian, comedienne *f*
humorístico, -ca *adj* : humorous — **humorísticamente** *adv*
humoso, -sa *adj* : smoky, steamy
humus *nm* : humus
hundido, -da *adj* **1** : sunken **2** : depressed
hundimiento *nm* **1** : sinking **2** : collapse, ruin
hundir *vt* **1** : to sink **2** : to destroy, to ruin — **hundirse** *vr* **1** : to sink down **2** : to cave in **3** : to break down, to go to pieces
húngaro[1], **-ra** *adj & n* : Hungarian
húngaro[2] *nm* : Hungarian (language)
huracán *nm, pl* **-canes** : hurricane
huraño, -ña *adj* **1** : unsociable, aloof **2** : timid, skittish (of an animal)
hurgar {52} *vt* : to poke, to jab, to rake (a fire) — *vi* **~ en** : to rummage in, to poke through
hurgue, etc. → **hurgar**
hurón *nm, pl* **hurones** : ferret
huronear *vi* : to pry, to snoop

hurra *interj* : hurrah!, hooray!
hurtadillas *nfpl* **a ~** : stealthily, on the sly
hurtar *vt* ROBAR : to steal
hurto *nm* **1** : theft, robbery **2** : stolen property, loot
husmear *vt* **1** : to follow the scent of, to track **2** : to sniff out, to pry into — *vi* **1** : to pry, to snoop **2** : to sniff around (of an animal)
huso *nm* **1** : spindle **2 huso horario** : time zone
huy *interj* : ow!, ouch!
huye, etc. → **huir**

I

i *nf* : ninth letter of the Spanish alphabet
iba, etc. → **ir**
ibérico, -ca *adj* : Iberian
ibero, -ra *or* **íbero, -ra** *adj & n* : Iberian
iberoamericano, -na *adj* HISPANOAMERICANO, LATINOAMERICANO : Latin-American
ibis *nfs & pl* : ibis
ice, etc. → **izar**
iceberg *nm, pl* **icebergs** : iceberg
icono *nm* : icon
iconoclasia *nf* : iconoclasm
iconoclasta *nmf* : iconoclast
ictericia *nf* : jaundice
ida *nf* **1** : going, departure **2 ida y vuelta** : round-trip **3 idas y venidas** : comings and goings
idea *nf* **1** : idea, notion **2** : opinion, belief **3** PROPÓSITO : intention
ideal *adj & nm* : ideal — **idealmente** *adv*
idealismo *nm* : idealism
idealista[1] *adj* : idealistic
idealista[2] *nmf* : idealist
idealizar {21} *vt* : to idealize — **idealización** *nf*
idear *vt* : to devise, to think up
ideario *nm* : ideology
ídem *nm* : idem, the same, ditto
idéntico, -ca *adj* : identical, alike — **idénticamente** *adv*
identidad *nf* : identity
identificable *adj* : identifiable
identificación *nf, pl* **-ciones** **1** : identification, identifying **2** : identification document, ID
identificar {72} *vt* : to identify — **identificarse** *vr* **1** : to identify oneself **2 ~ con** : to identify with
ideología *nf* : ideology — **ideológicamente** *adv*
ideológico, -ca *adj* : ideological
idílico, -ca *adj* : idyllic
idilio *nm* : idyll
idioma *nm* : language <el idioma inglés : the English language>
idiomático, -ca *adj* : idiomatic — **idiomáticamente** *adv*
idiosincrasia *nf* : idiosyncrasy
idiosincrásico, -ca *adj* : idiosyncratic
idiota[1] *adj* : idiotic, stupid, foolish
idiota[2] *nmf* : idiot, foolish person
idiotez *nf, pl* **-teces** **1** : idiocy **2** : idiotic act or remark <¡no digas idioteces! : don't talk nonsense!>
ido *pp* → **ir**
idólatra[1] *adj* : idolatrous
idólatra[2] *nmf* : idolater
idolatrar *vt* : to idolize
idolatría *nf* : idolatry
ídolo *nm* : idol
idoneidad *nf* : suitability
idóneo, -nea *adj* ADECUADO : suitable, fitting
iglesia *nf* : church
iglú *nm* : igloo
ignición *nf, pl* **-ciones** : ignition
ignífugo, -ga *adj* : fire-resistant, fireproof
ignominia *nf* : ignominy, disgrace
ignominioso, -sa *adj* : ignominious, shameful
ignorancia *nf* : ignorance
ignorante[1] *adj* : ignorant
ignorante[2] *nmf* : ignorant person, ignoramus
ignorar *vt* **1** : to ignore **2** DESCONOCER : to be unaware of <lo ignoramos por absoluto : we have no idea>
ignoto, -ta *adj* : unknown
igual[1] *adv* **1** : in the same way **2 por ~** : equally
igual[2] *adj* **1** : equal **2** IDÉNTICO : the same, alike **3** : even, smooth **4** SEMEJANTE : similar **5** CONSTANTE : constant
igual[3] *nmf* : equal, peer
igualación *nf* **1** : equalization **2** : leveling, smoothing **3** : equating (in mathematics)
igualado, -da *adj* **1** : even (of a score) **2** : level **3** *Mex* : disrespectful
igualar *vt* **1** : to equalize **2** : to tie <igualar el marcador : to even the score>
igualdad *nf* **1** : equality **2** UNIFORMIDAD : evenness, uniformity
igualmente *adv* **1** : equally **2** ASIMISMO : likewise
iguana *nf* : iguana
ijada *nf* : flank, loin, side
ijar *nm* → **ijada**
ilegal[1] *adj* : illegal, unlawful — **ilegalmente** *adv*
ilegal[2] *nmf CA, Mex* : illegal alien
ilegalidad *nf* : illegality, unlawfulness
ilegibilidad *nf* : illegibility
ilegible *adj* : illegible — **ilegiblemente** *adv*
ilegitimidad *nf* : illegitimacy
ilegítimo, -ma *adj* : illegitimate, unlawful

ileso, -sa *adj* : uninjured, unharmed
ilícito, -ta *adj* : illicit — **ilícitamente** *adv*
ilimitado, -da *adj* : unlimited
ilógico, -ca *adj* : illogical — **ilógicamente** *adv*
iluminación *nf, pl* **-ciones 1** : illumination **2** ALUMBRADO : lighting
iluminado, -da *adj* : illuminated, lighted
iluminar *vt* **1** : to illuminate, to light (up) **2** : to enlighten
ilusión *nf, pl* **-siones 1** : illusion, delusion **2** ESPERANZA : hope ⟨hacerse ilusiones : to get one's hopes up⟩
ilusionado, -da *adj* ESPERANZADO : hopeful, eager
ilusionar *vt* : to build up hope, to excite — **ilusionarse** *vr* : to get one's hopes up
iluso[1], -sa *adj* : naive, gullible
iluso[2], -sa *n* SOÑADOR : dreamer, visionary
ilusorio, -ria *adj* ENGAÑOSO : illusory, misleading
ilustración *nf, pl* **-ciones 1** : illustration **2** : erudition, learning ⟨la Ilustración : the Enlightenment⟩
ilustrado, -da *adj* **1** : illustrated **2** DOCTO : learned, erudite
ilustrador, -dora *n* : illustrator
ilustrar *vt* **1** : to illustrate **2** ACLARAR, CLARIFICAR : to explain
ilustrativo, -va *adj* : illustrative
ilustre *adj* : illustrious, eminent
imagen *nf, pl* **imágenes** : image, picture
imaginable *adj* : imaginable, conceivable
imaginación *nf, pl* **-ciones** : imagination
imaginar *vt* : to imagine — **imaginarse** *vr* **1** : to suppose, to imagine **2** : to picture
imaginario, -ria *adj* : imaginary
imaginativo, -va *adj* : imaginative — **imaginativamente** *adv*
imaginería *nf* **1** : imagery **2** : image making (in religion)
imán *nm, pl* **imanes** : magnet
imantar *vt* : to magnetize
imbatible *adj* : unbeatable
imbécil[1] *adj* : stupid, idiotic
imbécil[2] *nmf* **1** : imbecile **2** *fam* : idiot, dope
imborrable *adj* : indelible
imbuir {41} *vt* : to imbue — **imbuirse** *vr*
imitación *nf, pl* **-ciones 1** : imitation **2** : mimicry, impersonation
imitador[1], -dora *adj* : imitative
imitador[2], -dora *n* **1** : imitator **2** : mimic
imitar *vt* **1** : to imitate, to copy **2** : to mimic, to impersonate
imitativo, -va *adj* → **imitador[1]**
impaciencia *nf* : impatience
impacientar *vt* : to make impatient, to exasperate — **impacientarse** *vr*
impaciente *adj* : impatient — **impacientemente** *adv*
impactado, -da *adj* : shocked, stunned
impactante *adj* **1** : shocking **2** : impressive, powerful
impactar *vt* **1** GOLPEAR : to hit **2** IMPRESIONAR : to impact, to affect — **impactarse** *vr*
impacto *nm* **1** : impact, effect **2** : shock, collision
impagable *adj* **1** : unpayable **2** : priceless
impago *nm* : nonpayment
impalpable *adj* INTANGIBLE : impalpable, intangible
impar[1] *adj* : odd ⟨números impares : odd numbers⟩
impar[2] *nm* : odd number
imparable *adj* : unstoppable
imparcial *adj* : impartial — **imparcialmente** *adv*
imparcialidad *nf* : impartiality
impartir *vt* : to impart, to give
impasible *adj* : impassive, unmoved — **impasiblemente** *adv*
impasse *nm* : impasse
impávido, -da *adj* : undaunted, unperturbed
impecable *adj* INTACHABLE : impeccable, faultless — **impecablemente** *adv*
impedido, -da *adj* : disabled, crippled
impedimento *nm* **1** : impediment, obstacle **2** : disability
impedir {54} *vt* **1** : to prevent, to block **2** : to impede, to hinder
impeler *vt* **1** : to drive, to propel **2** : to impel
impenetrable *adj* : impenetrable — **impenetrabilidad** *nf*
impenitente *adj* : unrepentant, impenitent
impensable *adj* : unthinkable
impensado, -da *adj* : unforeseen, unexpected
imperante *adj* : prevailing
imperar *vi* **1** : to reign, to rule **2** PREDOMINAR : to prevail
imperativo[1], -va *adj* : imperative
imperativo[2] *nm* : imperative
imperceptible *adj* : imperceptible — **imperceptiblemente** *adv*
imperdible *nm Spain* : safety pin
imperdonable *adj* : unpardonable, unforgivable
imperecedero, -ra *adj* **1** : imperishable **2** INMORTAL : immortal, everlasting
imperfección *nf, pl* **-ciones 1** : imperfection **2** DEFECTO : defect, flaw
imperfecto[1], -ta *adj* : imperfect, flawed
imperfecto[2] *nm* : imperfect tense
imperial *adj* : imperial
imperialismo *nm* : imperialism
imperialista *adj & nmf* : imperialist
impericia *nf* : lack of skill, incompetence
imperio *nm* : empire
imperioso, -sa *adj* **1** : imperious **2** : pressing, urgent — **imperiosamente** *adv*
impermeabilizante *adj* : water-repellent
impermeabilizar {21} *vt* : to waterproof
impermeable[1] *adj* **1** : impervious **2** : impermeable, waterproof
impermeable[2] *nm* : raincoat

impersonal *adj* : impersonal — **impersonalmente** *adv*
impertinencia *nf* INSOLENCIA : impertinence, insolence
impertinente *adj* **1** INSOLENTE : impertinent, insolent **2** INOPORTUNO : inappropriate, uncalled-for **3** IRRELEVANTE : irrelevant
imperturbable *adj* : imperturbable, impassive, stolid
ímpetu *nm* **1** : impetus, momentum **2** : vigor, energy **3** : force, violence
impetuoso, -sa *adj* : impetuous, impulsive — **impetuosamente** *adv*
impiedad *nf* : impiety
impío, -pía *adj* : impious, ungodly
implacable *adj* : implacable, relentless — **implacablemente** *adv*
implantación *nf, pl* **-ciones 1** : implantation **2** ESTABLECIMIENTO : establishment, introduction
implantado, -da *adj* : well-established
implantar *vt* **1** : to implant **2** ESTABLECER : to establish, to introduce — **implantarse** *vr*
implante *nm* : implant
implementar *vt* : to implement — **implementarse** *vr* — **implementación** *nf*
implemento *nm* : implement, tool
implicación *nf, pl* **-ciones** : implication
implicar {72} *vt* **1** ENREDAR, ENVOLVER : to involve, to implicate **2** : to imply
implícito, -ta *adj* : implied, implicit — **implícitamente** *adv*
implorar *vt* : to implore
implosión *nf, pl* **-siones** : implosion — **implosivo, -va** *adj*
implosionar *vi* : to implode
imponderable *adj & nm* : imponderable
imponente *adj* : imposing, impressive
imponer {60} *vt* **1** : to impose **2** : to confer — *vi* : to be impressive, to command respect — **imponerse** *vr* **1** : to take on (a duty) **2** : to assert oneself **3** : to prevail
imponible *adj* : taxable
impopular *adj* : unpopular — **impopularidad** *nf*
importación *nf, pl* **-ciones 1** : importation **2 importaciones** *nfpl* : imports
importado, -da *adj* : imported
importador[1], **-dora** *adj* : importing
importador[2], **-dora** *n* : importer
importancia *nf* : importance
importante *adj* : important — **importantemente** *adv*
importar *vi* : to matter, to be important ⟨no le importa lo que piensen : she doesn't care what they think⟩ — *vt* : to import
importe *nm* **1** : price, cost **2** : sum, amount
importunar *vt* : to bother, to inconvenience — *vi* : to be inconvenient
importuno, -na *adj* **1** : inopportune, inconvenient **2** : bothersome, annoying
imposibilidad *nf* : impossibility
imposibilitado, -da *adj* **1** : disabled, crippled **2 verse imposibilitado** : to be unable (to do something)
imposibilitar *vt* **1** : to make impossible **2** : to disable, to incapacitate — **imposibilitarse** *vr* : to become disabled
imposible *adj* : impossible
imposición *nf, pl* **-ciones 1** : imposition **2** EXIGENCIA : demand, requirement **3** : tax **4** : deposit
impositivo, -va *adj* : tax ⟨tasa impositiva : tax rate⟩
impostor, -tora *n* : impostor
impostura *nf* **1** : fraud, imposture **2** CALUMNIA : slander
impotencia *nf* **1** : impotence, powerlessness **2** : impotence (in medicine)
impotente *adj* **1** : powerless **2** : impotent
impracticable *adj* : impracticable
imprecisión *nf, pl* **-siones 1** : imprecision, vagueness **2** : inaccuracy
impreciso, -sa *adj* **1** : imprecise, vague **2** : inaccurate
impredecible *adj* : unpredictable
impregnar *vt* : to impregnate
imprenta *nf* **1** : printing **2** : printing shop, press
imprescindible *adj* : essential, indispensable
impresentable *adj* : unpresentable, unfit
impresión *nf, pl* **-siones 1** : print, printing **2** : impression, feeling
impresionable *adj* : impressionable
impresionante *adj* : impressive, incredible, amazing — **impresionantemente** *adv*
impresionar *vt* **1** : to impress, to strike **2** : to affect, to move — *vi* : to make an impression — **impresionarse** *vr* : to be affected, to be removed
impresionismo *nm* : impressionism
impresionista[1] *adj* : impressionist, impressionistic
impresionista[2] *nmf* : impressionist
impreso[1] *pp* → **imprimir**
impreso[2], **-sa** *adj* : printed
impreso[3] *nm* PUBLICACIÓN : printed matter, publication
impresor, -sora *n* : printer
impresora *nf* : (computer) printer
imprevisible *adj* : unforeseeable
imprevisión *nf, pl* **-siones** : lack of foresight, thoughtlessness
imprevisto[1], **-ta** *adj* : unexpected, unforeseen
imprevisto[2] *nm* : unexpected occurrence, contingency
imprimir {42} *vt* **1** : to print **2** : to imprint, to stamp, to impress
improbabilidad *nf* : improbability
improbable *adj* : improbable, unlikely
improcedente *adj* **1** : inadmissible **2** : inappropriate, improper
improductivo, -va *adj* : unproductive
improperio *nm* : affront, insult
impropiedad *nf* : impropriety

impropio, -pia *adj* **1** : improper, incorrect **2** INADECUADO : unsuitable, inappropriate
improvisación *nf, pl* **-ciones** : improvisation, ad-lib
improvisado, -da *adj* : improvised, ad-lib
improvisar *v* : to improvise, to ad-lib
improviso *adj* **de ~** : all of a sudden, unexpectedly
imprudencia *nf* INDISCRECIÓN : imprudence, indiscretion
imprudente *adj* INDISCRETO : imprudent, indiscreet — **imprudentemente** *adv*
impúdico, -ca *adj* : shameless, indecent
impuesto[1] *pp* → **imponer**
impuesto[2] *nm* : tax
impugnar *vt* : to challenge, to contest
impulsar *vt* : to propel, to drive
impulsividad *nf* : impulsiveness
impulsivo, -va *adj* : impulsive — **impulsivamente** *adv*
impulso *nm* **1** : drive, thrust **2** : impulse, urge
impune *adj* : unpunished
impunemente *adv* : with impunity
impunidad *nf* : impunity
impureza *nf* : impurity
impuro, -ra *adj* : impure
impuso, etc. → **imponer**
imputable *adj* ATRIBUIBLE : attributable
imputación *nf, pl* **-ciones** **1** : attribution, imputation **2** : accusation
imputar *vt* ATRIBUIR : to impute, to attribute
inacabable *adj* : endless
inacabado, -da *adj* INCONCLUSO : unfinished
inaccesibilidad *nf* : inaccessibility
inaccesible *adj* **1** : inaccessible **2** : unattainable
inacción *nf, pl* **-ciones** : inactivity, inaction
inaceptable *adj* : unacceptable
inactividad *nf* : inactivity, idleness
inactivo, -va *adj* : inactive, idle
inadaptado[1], **-da** *adj* : maladjusted
inadaptado[2], **-da** *n* : misfit
inadecuación *nf, pl* **-ciones** : inadequacy
inadecuado, -da *adj* **1** : inadequate **2** IMPROPIO : inappropriate — **inadecuadamente** *adv*
inadmisible *adj* **1** : inadmissible **2** : unacceptable
inadvertencia *nf* : oversight
inadvertidamente *adv* : inadvertently
inadvertido, -da *adj* **1** : unnoticed ⟨pasar inadvertido : to go unnoticed⟩ **2** DESPISTADO, DISTRAÍDO : inattentive, distracted
inagotable *adj* : inexhaustible
inaguantable *adj* INSOPORTABLE : insufferable, unbearable
inalámbrico, -ca *adj* : wireless, cordless
inalcanzable *adj* : unreachable, unattainable
inalienable *adj* : inalienable
inalterable *adj* **1** : unalterable, unchangeable **2** : impassive **3** : colorfast
inamovible *adj* : immovable, fixed
inanición *nf, pl* **-ciones** : starvation
inanimado, -da *adj* : inanimate
inapelable *adj* : indisputable
inapetencia *nf* : lack of appetite
inaplicable *adj* : inapplicable
inapreciable *adj* **1** : imperceptible, negligible **2** : invaluable
inapropiado, -da *adj* : inappropriate, unsuitable
inarticulado, -da *adj* : inarticulate, unintelligible — **inarticuladamente** *adv*
inasequible *adj* : unattainable, inaccessible
inasistencia *nf* AUSENCIA : absence
inatacable *adj* : unassailable, indisputable
inaudible *adj* : inaudible
inaudito, -ta *adj* : unheard-of, unprecedented
inauguración *nf, pl* **-ciones** : inauguration
inaugural *adj* : inaugural, opening
inaugurar *vt* **1** : to inaugurate **2** : to open
inca *adj & nmf* : Inca
incalculable *adj* : incalculable
incalificable *adj* : indescribable
incandescencia *nf* : incandescence — **incandescente** *adj*
incansable *adj* INFATIGABLE : tireless — **incansablemente** *adv*
incapacidad *nf* **1** : inability, incapacity **2** : disability, handicap
incapacitado, -da *adj* **1** : disqualified **2** : disabled, handicapped
incapacitar *vt* **1** : to incapacitate, to disable **2** : to disqualify
incapaz *adj, pl* **-paces** **1** : incapable, unable **2** : incompetent, inept
incautación *nf, pl* **-ciones** : seizure, confiscation
incautar *vt* CONFISCAR : to confiscate, to seize — **incautarse** *vr*
incauto, -ta *adj* : unwary, unsuspecting
incendiar *vt* : to set fire to, to burn (down) — **incendiarse** *vr* : to catch fire
incendiario[1], **-ria** *adj* : incendiary, inflammatory
incendiario[2], **-ria** *n* : arsonist
incendio *nm* **1** : fire **2 incendio premeditado** : arson
incensario *nm* : censer
incentivar *vt* : to encourage, to stimulate
incentivo *nm* : incentive
incertidumbre *nf* : uncertainty, suspense
incesante *adj* : incessant — **incesantemente** *adv*
incesto *nm* : incest
incestuoso, -sa *adj* : incestuous
incidencia *nf* **1** : incident **2** : effect, impact **3 por ~** : by chance, accidentally

incidental *adj* : incidental

incidentalmente *adv* : by chance

incidente *nm* : incident, occurrence

incidir *vi* **1** ∼ **en** : to fall into, to enter into ⟨incidimos en el mismo error : we fell into the same mistake⟩ **2** ∼ **en** : to affect, to influence, to have a bearing on

incienso *nm* : incense

incierto, -ta *adj* **1** : uncertain **2** : untrue **3** : unsteady, insecure

incineración *nf, pl* **-ciones 1** : incineration **2** : cremation

incinerador *nm* : incinerator

incinerar *vt* **1** : to incinerate **2** : to cremate

incipiente *adj* : incipient

incisión *nf, pl* **-siones** : incision

incisivo[1], **-va** *adj* : incisive

incisivo[2] *nm* : incisor

inciso *nm* : digression, aside

incitación *nf, pl* **-ciones** : incitement

incitador[1], **-dora** *n* : instigator, agitator

incitador[2], **-dora** *adj* : provocative

incitante *adj* : provocative

incitar *vt* : to incite, to rouse

incivilizado, -da *adj* : uncivilized

inclemencia *nf* : inclemency, severity

inclemente *adj* : inclement

inclinación *nf, pl* **-ciones 1** PROPENSIÓN : inclination, tendency **2** : incline, slope

inclinado, -da *adj* **1** : sloping **2** : inclined, apt

inclinar *vt* : to tilt, to lean, to incline ⟨inclinar la cabeza : to bow one's head⟩ — **inclinarse** *vr* **1** : to lean, to lean over **2** ∼ **a** : to be inclined to

incluir {41} *vt* : to include

inclusión *nf, pl* **-siones** : inclusion

inclusive *adv* : inclusively, up to and including

inclusivo, -va *adj* : inclusive

incluso *adv* **1** AUN : even, in fact ⟨es importante e incluso crucial : it is important and even crucial⟩ **2** : inclusively

incógnita *nf* **1** : unknown quantity (in mathematics) **2** : mystery

incógnito, -ta *adj* **1** : unknown **2 de incógnito** : incognito

incoherencia *nf* : incoherence

incoherente *adj* : incoherent — **incoherentemente** *adv*

incoloro, -ra *adj* : colorless

incombustible *adj* : fireproof

incomible *adj* : inedible

incomodar *vt* **1** : to make uncomfortable **2** : to inconvenience — **incomodarse** *vr* : to put oneself out, to take the trouble

incomodidad *nf* **1** : discomfort, awkwardness **2** MOLESTIA : inconvenience, bother

incómodo, -da *adj* **1** : uncomfortable, awkward **2** INCONVENIENTE : inconvenient

incomparable *adj* : incomparable

incompatibilidad *nf* : incompatibility

incompatible *adj* : incompatible, uncongenial

incompetencia *nf* : incompetence

incompetente *adj & nmf* : incompetent

incompleto, -ta *adj* : incomplete

incomprendido, -da *adj* : misunderstood

incomprensible *adj* : incomprehensible

incomprensión *nf, pl* **-siones** : lack of understanding, incomprehension

incomunicación *nf, pl* **-ciones** : lack of communication

incomunicado, -da *adj* **1** : cut off, isolated **2** : in solitary confinement

inconcebible *adj* : inconceivable, unthinkable — **inconcebiblemente** *adv*

inconcluso, -sa *adj* INACABADO : unfinished

incondicional *adj* : unconditional — **incondicionalmente** *adv*

inconexo, -xa *adj* : unconnected, disconnected

inconfesable *adj* : unspeakable, shameful

inconforme *adj & nmf* : nonconformist

inconformidad *nf* : nonconformity

inconformista *adj & nmf* : nonconformist

inconfundible *adj* : unmistakable, obvious — **inconfundiblemente** *adv*

incongruencia *nf* : incongruity

incongruente *adj* : incongruous

inconmensurable *adj* : vast, immeasurable

inconquistable *adj* : unyielding

inconsciencia *nf* **1** : unconsciousness, unawareness **2** : irresponsibility

inconsciente[1] *adj* **1** : unconscious, unaware **2** : reckless, needless — **inconscientemente** *adv*

inconsciente[2] *nm* **el inconsciente** : the unconscious

inconsecuente *adj* : inconsistent — **inconsecuencia** *nf*

inconsiderado, -da *adj* : inconsiderate, thoughtless

inconsistencia *nf* : inconsistency

inconsistente *adj* **1** : weak, flimsy **2** : inconsistent, weak (of an argument)

inconsolable *adj* : inconsolable — **inconsolablemente** *adv*

inconstancia *nf* : inconstancy

inconstante *adj* : inconstant, fickle, changeable

inconstitucional *adj* : unconstitutional

inconstitucionalidad *nf* : unconstitutionality

incontable *adj* INNUMERABLE : countless, innumerable

incontenible *adj* : uncontrollable, unstoppable

incontestable *adj* INCUESTIONABLE, INDISCUTIBLE : irrefutable, indisputable

incontinencia *nf* : incontinence — **incontinente** *adj*

incontrolable *adj* : uncontrollable

incontrolado, -da *adj* : uncontrolled, out of control

incontrovertible *adj* : indisputable
inconveniencia *nf* **1** : inconvenience, trouble **2** : unsuitability, inappropriateness **3** : tactless remark
inconveniente[1] *adj* **1** INCÓMODO : inconvenient **2** INAPROPIADO : improper, unsuitable
inconveniente[2] *nm* : obstacle, problem, snag ⟨no tengo inconveniente en hacerlo : I don't mind doing it⟩
incorporación *nf, pl* **-ciones** : incorporation
incorporar *vt* **1** : to incorporate **2** : to add, to include — **incorporarse** *vr* **1** : to sit up **2 ~ a** : to join
incorpóreo, -rea *adj* : incorporeal, bodiless
incorrección *n, pl* **-ciones** : impropriety, improper word or action
incorrecto, -ta *adj* : incorrect — **incorrectamente** *adv*
incorregible *adj* : incorrigible — **incorregibilidad** *nf*
incorruptible *adj* : incorruptible
incredulidad *nf* : incredulity, skepticism
incrédulo[1], **-la** *adj* : incredulous, skeptical
incrédulo[2], **-la** *n* : skeptic
increíble *adj* : incredible, unbelievable — **increíblemente** *adv*
incrementar *vt* : to increase — **incrementarse** *vr*
incremento *nm* AUMENTO : increase
incriminar *vt* : to incriminate — **incriminación** *nf*
incriminatorio, -ria *adj* : incriminating, incriminatory
incruento, -ta *adj* : bloodless
incrustación *nf, pl* **-ciones** : inlay
incrustar *vt* **1** : to embed **2** : to inlay — **incrustarse** *vr* : to become embedded
incubación *nf, pl* **-ciones** : incubation
incubadora *nf* : incubator
incubar *v* : to incubate
incuestionable *adj* INCONTESTABLE, INDISCUTIBLE : unquestionable, indisputable — **incuestionablemente** *adv*
inculcar {72} *vt* : to inculcate, to instill
inculpar *vt* ACUSAR : to accuse, to charge
inculto, -ta *adj* **1** : uncultured, ignorant **2** : uncultivated, fallow
incumbencia *nf* : obligation, responsibility
incumbir *vi* (*3rd person only*) **~ a** : to be incumbent upon, to be of concern to ⟨a mí no me incumbe : it's not my concern⟩
incumplido, -da *adj* : irresponsible, unreliable
incumplimiento *nm* **1** : nonfulfillment, neglect **2 incumplimiento de contrato** : breach of contract
incumplir *vt* : to fail to carry out, to break (a promise, a contract)
incurable *adj* : incurable
incurrir *vi* **1 ~ en** : to incur ⟨incurrir en gastos : to incur expenses⟩ **2 ~ en** : to fall into, to commit ⟨incurrió en un error : he made a mistake⟩
incursión *nf, pl* **-siones** : incursion, raid
incursionar *vi* **1** : to raid **2 ~ en** : to go into, to enter ⟨el actor incursionó en el baile : the actor worked in dance for awhile⟩
indagación *nf, pl* **-ciones** : investigation, inquiry
indagar {52} *vt* : to inquire into, to investigate
indebido, -da *adj* : improper, undue — **indebidamente** *adv*
indecencia *nf* : indecency, obscenity
indecente *adj* : indecent, obscene
indecible *adj* : indescribable, inexpressible
indecisión *nf, pl* **-siones** : indecision
indeciso, -sa *adj* **1** IRRESOLUTO : indecisive **2** : undecided
indeclinable *adj* : unavoidable
indecoro *nm* : impropriety, indecorousness
indecoroso, -sa *adj* : indecorous, unseemly
indefectible *adj* : unfailing, sure
indefendible *adj* : indefensible
indefenso, -sa *adj* : defenseless, helpless
indefinible *adj* : indefinable
indefinido, -da *adj* **1** : undefined, vague **2** INDETERMINADO : indefinite — **indefinidamente** *adv*
indeleble *adj* : indelible — **indeleblemente** *adv*
indelicado, -da *adj* : indelicate, tactless
indemnización *nf, pl* **-ciones** **1** : indemnity **2 indemnización por despido** : severance pay
indemnizar {21} *vt* : to indemnify, to compensate
independencia *nf* : independence
independiente *adj* : independent — **independientemente** *adv*
independizarse {21} *vr* : to become independent, to gain independence
indescifrable *adj* : indecipherable
indescriptible *adj* : indescribable — **indescriptiblemente** *adv*
indeseable *adj & nmf* : undesirable
indestructible *adj* : indestructible
indeterminación *nf, pl* **-ciones** : indeterminacy
indeterminado, -da *adj* **1** INDEFINIDO : indefinite **2** : indeterminate
indexar *vt* INDICIAR : to index (wages, prices, etc.)
indicación *nf, pl* **-ciones** **1** : sign, signal **2** : direction, instruction **3** : suggestion, hint
indicado, -da *adj* **1** APROPIADO : appropriate, suitable **2** : specified, indicated ⟨al día indicado : on the specified day⟩
indicador *nm* **1** : gauge, dial, meter **2** : indicator ⟨indicadores económicos : economic indicators⟩
indicar {72} *vt* **1** SEÑALAR : to indicate **2** ENSEÑAR, MOSTRAR : to show
indicativo[1], **-va** *adj* : indicative
indicativo[2] *nm* : indicative (mood)

índice *nm* **1** : index **2** : index finger, forefinger **3** INDICIO : indication
indiciar *vt* : to index (prices, wages, etc.)
indicio *nm* : indication, sign
indiferencia *nf* : indifference
indiferente *adj* **1** : indifferent, unconcerned **2 ser indiferente** : to be of no concern ⟨me es indiferente : it doesn't matter to me⟩
indígena[1] *adj* : indigenous, native
indígena[2] *nmf* : native
indigencia *nf* MISERIA : poverty, destitution
indigente *adj & nmf* : indigent
indigestarse *vr* **1** EMPACHARSE : to have indigestion **2** *fam* : to nauseate, to disgust ⟨ese tipo se me indigesta : that guy makes me sick⟩
indigestión *nf, pl* **-tiones** EMPACHO : indigestion
indigesto, -ta *adj* : indigestible, difficult to digest
indignación *nf, pl* **-ciones** : indignation
indignado, -da *adj* : indignant
indignante *adj* : outrageous, infuriating
indignar *vt* : to outrage, to infuriate — **indignarse** *vr*
indignidad *nf* : indignity
indigno, -na *adj* : unworthy
índigo *nm* : indigo
indio[1], -dia *adj* **1** : American Indian, Indian, Amerindian **2** : Indian (from India)
indio[2], -dia *n* **1** : American Indian **2** : Indian (from India)
indirecta *nf* **1** : hint, innuendo **2 echar indirectas** *or* **lanzar indirectas** : to drop a hint, to insinuate
indirecto, -ta *adj* : indirect — **indirectamente** *adv*
indisciplina *nf* : indiscipline, unruliness
indisciplinado, -da *adj* : undisciplined, unruly
indiscreción *nf, pl* **-ciones** **1** IMPRUDENCIA : indiscretion **2** : tactless remark
indiscreto, -ta *adj* IMPRUDENTE : indiscreet, imprudent — **indiscretamente** *adv*
indiscriminado, -da *adj* : indiscriminate — **indiscriminadamente** *adv*
indiscutible *adj* INCONTESTABLE, INCUESTIONABLE : indisputable, unquestionable — **indiscutiblemente** *adv*
indispensable *adj* : indispensable — **indispensablemente** *adv*
indisponer {60} *vt* **1** : to spoil, to upset **2** : to make ill — **indisponerse** *vr* **1** : to become ill **2 ~ con** : to fall out with
indisposición *nf, pl* **-ciones** : indisposition, illness
indispuesto, -ta *adj* : unwell, indisposed
indistinguible *adj* : indistinguishable
indistintamente *adv* **1** : indistinctly **2** : indiscriminately
indistinto, -ta *adj* : indistinct, vague, faint
individual *adj* : individual — **individualmente** *adv*
individualidad *nf* : individuality
individualismo *nm* : individualism
individualista[1] *adj* : individualistic
individualista[2] *nmf* : individualist
individualizar {21} *vt* : to individualize
individuo *nm* : individual, person
indivisible *adj* : indivisible — **indivisibilidad** *nf*
indocumentado, -da *n* : illegal immigrant
índole *nf* **1** : nature, character **2** CLASE, TIPO : sort, kind
indolencia *nf* : indolence, laziness
indolente *adj* : indolent, lazy
indoloro, -ra *adj* : painless
indomable *adj* **1** : indomitable **2** : unruly, unmanageable
indómito, -ta *adj* : indomitable
indonesio, -sia *adj & n* : Indonesian
inducción *nf, pl* **-ciones** : induction
inducir {61} *vt* **1** : to induce, to cause **2** : to infer, to deduce
inductivo, -va *adj* : inductive
indudable *adj* : unquestionable, beyond doubt
indudablemente *adv* : undoubtedly, unquestionably
indulgencia *nf* **1** : indulgence, leniency **2** : indulgence (in religion)
indulgente *adj* : indulgent, lenient
indultar *vt* : to pardon, to reprieve
indulto *nm* : pardon, reprieve
indumentaria *nf* : clothing, attire
industria *nf* : industry
industrial[1] *adj* : industrial
industrial[2] *nmf* : industrialist, manufacturer
industrialización *nf, pl* **-ciones** : industrialization
industrializar {21} *vt* : to industrialize
industrioso, -sa *adj* : industrious
inédito, -ta *adj* **1** : unpublished **2** : unprecedented
inefable *adj* : ineffable
ineficacia *nf* **1** : inefficiency **2** : ineffectiveness
ineficaz *adj, pl* **-caces** **1** : inefficient **2** : ineffective — **ineficazmente** *adv*
ineficiencia *nf* : inefficiency
ineficiente *adj* : inefficient — **ineficientemente** *adv*
inelegancia *nf* : inelegance — **inelegante** *adj*
inelegible *adj* : ineligible — **inelegibilidad** *nf*
ineludible *adj* : inescapable, unavoidable — **ineludiblemente** *adv*
ineptitud *nf* : ineptitude, incompetence
inepto, -ta *adj* : inept, incompetent
inequidad *nf* : inequity
inequitativo, -va *adj* : inequitable
inequívoco, -ca *adj* : unequivocal, unmistakable — **inequívocamente** *adv*
inercia *nf* **1** : inertia **2** : apathy, passivity **3 por ~** : out of habit
inerme *adj* : unarmed, defenseless

inerte *adj* : inert
inescrupuloso, -sa *adj* : unscrupulous
inescrutable *adj* : inscrutable
inesperado, -da *adj* : unexpected — **inesperadamente** *adv*
inestabilidad *nf* : instability, unsteadiness
inestable *adj* : unstable, unsteady
inestimable *adj* : inestimable, invaluable
inevitabilidad *nf* : inevitability
inevitable *adj* : inevitable, unavoidable — **inevitablemente** *adv*
inexactitud *nf* : inaccuracy
inexacto, -ta *adj* : inexact, inaccurate
inexcusable *adj* : inexcusable, unforgivable
inexistencia *nf* : lack, nonexistence
inexistente *adj* : nonexistent
inexorable *adj* : inexorable — **inexorablemente** *adv*
inexperiencia *nf* : inexperience
inexperto, -ta *adj* : inexperienced, unskilled
inexplicable *adj* : inexplicable — **inexplicablemente** *adv*
inexplorado, -da *adj* : unexplored
inexpresable *adj* : inexpressible
inexpresivo, -va *adj* : inexpressive, expressionless
inexpugnable *adj* : impregnable
inextinguible *adj* **1** : inextinguishable **2** : unquenchable
inextricable *adj* : inextricable — **inextricablemente** *adv*
infalibilidad *nf* : infallibility
infalible *adj* : infallible — **infaliblemente** *adv*
infame *adj* **1** : infamous **2** : loathsome, vile ⟨tiempo infame : terrible weather⟩
infamia *nf* : infamy, disgrace
infancia *nf* **1** NIÑEZ : infancy, childhood **2** : children *pl* **3** : beginnings *pl*
infante *nm* **1** : infante, prince **2** : infantryman
infantería *nf* : infantry
infantil *adj* **1** : childish, infantile **2** : child's, children's
infantilismo *nm* **1** : infantilism **2** INMADUREZ : childishness
infarto *nm* : heart attack
infatigable *adj* : indefatigable, tireless — **infatigablemente** *adv*
infección *nf, pl* **-ciones** : infection
infeccioso, -sa *adj* : infectious
infectar *vt* : to infect — **infectarse** *vr*
infecto, -ta *adj* **1** : infected **2** : repulsive, sickening
infecundidad *nf* : infertility
infecundo, -da *adj* : infertile, barren
infelicidad *nf* : unhappiness
infeliz[1] *adj, pl* **-lices 1** : unhappy **2** : hapless, unfortunate, wretched
infeliz[2] *nmf, pl* **-lices** : wretch
inferencia *nf* : inference
inferior[1] *adj* : inferior, lower
inferior[2] *nmf* : inferior, underling
inferioridad *nf* : inferiority
inferir {76} *vt* **1** DEDUCIR : to infer, to deduce **2** : to cause (harm or injury), to inflict
infernal *adj* : infernal, hellish
infestación *n, pl* **-ciones** : infestation
infestar *vt* **1** : to infest **2** : to overrun, to invade
inficíón *nf, pl* **-ciones** *Mex* : pollution
infidelidad *nf* : unfaithfulness, infidelity
infiel[1] *adj* : unfaithful, disloyal
infiel[2] *nmf* : infidel, heathen
infierno *nm* **1** : hell **2 el quinto infierno** : the middle of nowhere
infiltrar *vt* : to infiltrate — **infiltrarse** *vr* — **infiltración** *nf*
infinidad *nf* **1** : infinity **2** SINFÍN : great number, huge quantity ⟨una infinidad de veces : countless times⟩
infinitesimal *adj* : infinitesimal
infinitivo *nm* : infinitive
infinito[1] *adv* : infinitely, vastly
infinito[2], **-ta** *adj* **1** : infinite **2** : limitless, endless **3 hasta lo infinito** : ad infinitum — **infinitamente** *adv*
infinito[3] *nm* : infinity
inflable *adj* : inflatable
inflación *nf, pl* **-ciones** : inflation
inflacionario, -ria *adj* : inflationary
inflacionista → **inflacionario**
inflamable *adj* : flammable
inflamación *nf, pl* **-ciones** : inflammation
inflamar *vt* : to inflame
inflamatorio, -ria *adj* : inflammatory
inflar *vt* HINCHAR : to inflate — **inflarse** *vr* **1** : to swell **2** : to become conceited
inflexibilidad *nf* : inflexibility
inflexible *adj* : inflexible, unyielding
inflexión *nf, pl* **-xiones** : inflection
infligir {35} *vt* : to inflict
influencia *nf* INFLUJO : influence
influenciable *adj* : easily influenced, suggestible
influenciar *vt* : to influence
influenza *nf* : influenza
influir {41} *vt* : to influence — *vi* **~ en** *or* **~ sobre** : to have an influence on, to affect
influjo *nm* INFLUENCIA : influence
influyente *adj* : influential
información *nf, pl* **-ciones 1** : information **2** INFORME : report, inquiry **3** NOTICIAS : news
informado, -da *adj* : informed ⟨bien informado : well-informed⟩
informador, -dora *n* : informer, informant
informal *adj* **1** : unreliable (of persons) **2** : informal, casual — **informalmente** *adv*
informalidad *nf* : informality
informante *nmf* : informant
informar *vt* ENTERAR : to inform — *vi* : to report — **informarse** *vr* ENTERARSE : to get information, to find out
informática *nf* : computer science, computing

informativo[1], **-va** *adj* : informative

informativo[2] *nm* : news program, news

informatización *nf, pl* **-ciones** : computerization

informatizar {21} *vt* : to computerize

informe[1] *adj* AMORFO : shapeless, formless

informe[2] *nm* **1** : report **2** : reference (for employment) **3 informes** *nmpl* : information, data

infortunado, **-da** *adj* : unfortunate, unlucky

infortunio *nm* **1** DESGRACIA : misfortune **2** CONTRATIEMPO : mishap

infracción *nf, pl* **-ciones** : violation, offense, infraction

infractor, **-tora** *n* : offender

infraestructura *nf* : infrastructure

infrahumano, **-na** *adj* : subhuman

infranqueable *adj* **1** : impassable **2** : insurmountable

infrarrojo, **-ja** *adj* : infrared

infrecuente *adj* : infrequent

infringir {35} *vt* : to infringe, to breach

infructuoso, **-sa** *adj* : fruitless — **infructuosamente** *adv*

ínfulas *nfpl* **1** : conceit **2 darse ínfulas** : to put on airs

infundado, **-da** *adj* : unfounded, baseless

infundio *nm* : false story, lie, tall tale ⟨todo eso son infundios : that's a pack of lies⟩

infundir *vt* **1** : to instill **2 infundir ánimo a** : to encourage **3 infundir miedo a** : to intimidate

infusión *nf, pl* **-siones** : infusion

ingeniar *vt* : to devise, to think up — **ingeniarse** *vr* : to manage, to find a way

ingeniería *nf* : engineering

ingeniero, **-ra** *n* : engineer

ingenio *nm* **1** : ingenuity **2** CHISPA : wit, wits **3** : device, apparatus **4 ingenio azucarero** : sugar refinery

ingenioso, **-sa** *adj* **1** : ingenious **2** : clever, witty — **ingeniosamente** *adv*

ingente *adj* : huge, enormous

ingenuidad *nf* : naïveté, ingenuousness

ingenuo[1], **-nua** *adj* CÁNDIDO : naive — **ingenuamente** *adv*

ingenuo[2], **-nua** *n* : naive person

ingerencia → **injerencia**

ingerir {76} *vt* : to ingest, to consume

ingestión *nf, pl* **-tiones** : ingestion

ingle *nf* : groin

inglés[1], **-glesa** *adj, mpl* **ingleses** : English

inglés[2], **-glesa** *n, mpl* **ingleses** : Englishman *m,* Englishwoman *f*

inglés[3] *nm* : English (language)

inglete *nm* : miter joint

ingobernable *adj* : ungovernable, lawless

ingratitud *nf* : ingratitude

ingrato[1], **-ta** *adj* **1** : ungrateful **2** : thankless

ingrato[2], **-ta** *n* : ingrate

ingrediente *nm* : ingredient

ingresar *vt* **1** : to admit ⟨ingresaron a Luis al hospital : Luis was admitted into the hospital⟩ **2** : to deposit — *vi* **1** : to enter, to go in **2 ~ en** : to join, to enroll in

ingreso *nm* **1** : entrance, entry **2** : admission **3 ingresos** *nmpl* : income, earnings *pl*

íngrimo, **-ma** *adj* : all alone, all by oneself

inhábil *adj* : unskillful, clumsy

inhabilidad *nf* **1** : unskillfulness **2** : unfitness

inhabilitar *vt* **1** : to disqualify, to bar **2** : to disable

inhabitable *adj* : uninhabitable

inhabituado, **-da** *adj* **~ a** : unaccustomed to

inhalador *nm* : inhaler

inhalante *nm* : inhalant

inhalar *vt* : to inhale — **inhalación** *nf*

inherente *adj* : inherent

inhibición *nf, pl* **-ciones** COHIBICIÓN : inhibition

inhibir *vt* : to inhibit — **inhibirse** *vr*

inhóspito, **-ta** *adj* : inhospitable

inhumación *nf, pl* **-ciones** : interment, burial

inhumanidad *nf* : inhumanity

inhumano, **-na** *adj* : inhuman, cruel, inhumane

inhumar *vt* : to inter, to bury

iniciación *nf, pl* **-ciones 1** : initiation **2** : introduction

iniciado, **-da** *n* : initiate

iniciador[1], **-dora** *adj* : initiatory

iniciador[2], **-dora** *n* : initiator, originator

inicial[1] *adj* : initial, original — **inicialmente** *adv*

inicial[2] *nf* : initial (letter)

iniciar *vt* COMENZAR : to initiate, to begin — **iniciarse** *vr*

iniciativa *nf* : initiative

inicio *nm* COMIENZO : beginning

inicuo, **-cua** *adj* : iniquitous, wicked

inigualado, **-da** *adj* : unequaled

inimaginable *adj* : unimaginable

inimitable *adj* : inimitable

ininteligible *adj* : unintelligible

ininterrumpido, **-da** *adj* : uninterrupted, continuous — **ininterrumpidamente** *adv*

iniquidad *nf* : iniquity, wickedness

injerencia *nf* : interference

injerirse {76} *vr* ENTROMETERSE, INMISCUIRSE : to meddle, to interfere

injertar *vt* : to graft

injerto *nm* : graft ⟨injerto de piel : skin graft⟩

injuria *nf* AGRAVIO : affront, insult

injuriar *vt* INSULTAR : to insult, to revile

injurioso, **-sa** *adj* : insulting, abusive

injusticia *nf* : injustice, unfairness

injustificable *adj* : unjustifiable

injustificadamente *adv* : unjustifiably, unfairly

injustificado, **-da** *adj* : unjustified, unwarranted

injusto, -ta *adj* : unfair, unjust — **injustamente** *adv*
inmaculado, -da *adj* : immaculate, spotless
inmadurez *nf, pl* **-reces** : immaturity
inmaduro, -ra *adj* **1** : immature **2** : unripe
inmediaciones *nfpl* : environs, surrounding area
inmediatamente *adv* ENSEGUIDA : immediately
inmediatez *nf, pl* **-teces** : immediacy
inmediato, -ta *adj* **1** : immediate **2** CONTIGUO : adjoining **3 de ~** : immediately, right away **4 ~ a** : next to, close to
inmejorable *adj* : excellent, unbeatable
inmemorial *adj* : immemorial ⟨tiempos inmemoriales : time immemorial⟩
inmensidad *nf* : immensity, vastness
inmenso, -sa *adj* ENORME : immense, huge, vast — **inmensamente** *adv*
inmensurable *adj* : boundless, immeasurable
inmerecido, -da *adj* : undeserved — **inmerecidamente** *adv*
inmersión *nf, pl* **-siones** : immersion
inmerso, -sa *adj* **1** : immersed **2** : involved, absorbed
inmigración *nf, pl* **-ciones** : immigration
inmigrado, -da *adj & n* : immigrant
inmigrante *adj & nmf* : immigrant
inmigrar *vi* : to immigrate
inminencia *nf* : imminence
inminente *adj* : imminent — **inminentemente** *adv*
inmiscuirse {41} *vr* ENTROMETERSE, INJERIRSE : to meddle, to interfere
inmobiliario, -ria *adj* : real estate, property
inmoderación *n, pl* **-ciones** : immoderation, intemperance
inmoderado, -da *adj* : immoderate, excessive — **inmoderamente** *adv*
inmodestia *nf* : immodesty — **inmodesto, -ta** *adj*
inmolar *vt* : to immolate — **inmolación** *nf*
inmoral *adj* : immoral
inmoralidad *nf* : immorality
inmortal *adj & nmf* : immortal
inmortalidad *nf* : immortality
inmortalizar {21} *vt* : to immortalize
inmotivado, -da *adj* **1** : unmotivated **2** : groundless
inmovible *adj* : immovable, fixed
inmóvil *adj* **1** : still, motionless **2** : steadfast
inmovilidad *nf* : immobility
inmovilizar {21} *vt* : to immobilize
inmueble *nm* : building, property
inmundicia *nf* : dirt, filth, trash
inmundo, -da *adj* : dirty, filthy, nasty
inmune *adj* : immune
inmunidad *nf* : immunity
inmunizar {21} *vt* : to immunize — **inmunización** *nf*
inmunología *nf* : immunology
inmunológico, -ca *adj* : immune ⟨sistema inmunológico : immune system⟩
inmutabilidad *nf* : immutability
inmutable *adj* : immutable, unchangeable
innato, -ta *adj* : innate, inborn
innecesario, -ria *adj* : unnecessary — **innecesariamente** *adv*
innegable *adj* : undeniable
innoble *adj* : ignoble — **innoblemente** *adv*
innovación *nf, pl* **-ciones** : innovation
innovador, -dora *adj* : innovative
innovar *vt* : to introduce — *vi* : to innovate
innumerable *adj* INCONTABLE : innumerable, countless
inobjetable *adj* : indisputable, unobjectionable
inocencia *nf* : innocence
inocente[1] *adj* **1** : innocent **2** INGENUO : naive — **inocentemente** *adv*
inocente[2] *nmf* : innocent person
inocentón[1], **-tona** *adj, mpl* **-tones** : naive, gullible
inocentón[2], **-tona** *n, mpl* **-tones** : simpleton, dupe
inocuidad *nf* : harmlessness
inocular *vt* : to inoculate, to vaccinate — **inoculación** *nf*
inocuo, -cua *adj* : innocuous, harmless
inodoro[1], **-ra** *adj* : odorless
inodoro[2] *nm* : toilet
inofensivo, -va *adj* : inoffensive, harmless
inolvidable *adj* : unforgettable
inoperable *adj* : inoperable
inoperante *adj* : ineffective, inoperative
inopinado, -da *adj* : unexpected — **inopinadamente** *adv*
inoportuno, -na *adj* : untimely, inopportune, inappropriate
inorgánico, -ca *adj* : inorganic
inoxidable *adj* **1** : rustproof **2 acero inoxidable** : stainless steel
inquebrantable *adj* : unshakable, unwavering
inquietante *adj* : disturbing, worrisome
inquietar *vt* PREOCUPAR : to disturb, to upset, to worry — **inquietarse** *vr*
inquieto, -ta *adj* **1** : anxious, uneasy, worried **2** : restless
inquietud *nf* **1** : anxiety, uneasiness, worry **2** AGITACIÓN : restlessness
inquilinato *nm* : tenancy
inquilino, -na *n* : tenant, occupant
inquina *nf* **1** : aversion, dislike **2** : ill will ⟨tener inquina a alguien : to have a grudge against someone⟩
inquirir {4} *vi* : to make inquiries — *vt* : to investigate
inquisición *nf, pl* **-ciones** : investigation, inquiry
inquisidor, -dora *adj* : inquisitive
inquisitivo, -va *adj* : inquisitive, curious — **inquisitivamente** *adv*
insaciable *adj* : insatiable
insalubre *adj* **1** : unhealthy **2** ANTIHIGIÉNICO : unsanitary

insalubridad *nf* : unhealthiness
insalvable *adj* : insuperable, insurmountable
insano, -na *adj* **1** LOCO : insane, mad **2** INSALUBRE : unhealthy
insatisfacción *nf, pl* **-ciones** : dissatisfaction
insatisfactorio *nm* : unsatisfactory
insatisfecho, -cha *adj* **1** : dissatisfied **2** : unsatisfied
inscribir {33} *vt* **1** MATRICULAR : to enroll, to register **2** GRABAR : to engrave — **inscribirse** *vr* : to register, to sign up
inscripción *nf, pl* **-ciones 1** MATRÍCULA : enrollment, registration **2** : inscription
inscrito *pp* → **inscribir**
insecticida[1] *adj* : insecticidal
insecticida[2] *nm* : insecticide
insecto *nm* : insect
inseguridad *nf* **1** : insecurity **2** : lack of safety **3** : uncertainty
inseguro, -ra *adj* **1** : insecure **2** : unsafe **3** : uncertain
inseminar *vt* : to inseminate — **inseminación** *nf*
insensatez *nf, pl* **-teces** : foolishness, stupidity
insensato[1], **-ta** *adj* : foolish, senseless
insensato[2], **-ta** *n* : fool
insensibilidad *nf* : insensitivity
insensible *adj* : insensitive, unfeeling
inseparable *adj* : inseparable — **inseparablemente** *adv*
inserción *nf, pl* **-ciones** : insertion
insertar *vt* : to insert
inservible *adj* INÚTIL : useless, unusable
insidia *nf* **1** : snare, trap **2** : malice
insidioso, -sa *adj* : insidious
insigne *adj* : noted, famous
insignia *nf* ENSEÑA : insignia, emblem, badge
insignificancia *nf* **1** : insignificance **2** NIMIEDAD : trifle, triviality
insignificante *adj* : insignificant
insincero, -ra *adj* : insincere — **insinceridad** *nf*
insinuación *nf, pl* **-ciones** : insinuation, hint
insinuante *adj* : suggestive
insinuar {3} *vt* : to insinuate, to hint at — **insinuarse** *vr* **1 ~ a** : to make advances to **2 ~ en** : to worm one's way into
insipidez *nf, pl* **-deces** : insipidness, blandness
insípido, -da *adj* : insipid, bland
insistencia *nf* : insistence
insistente *adj* : insistent — **insistentemente** *adv*
insistir *v* : to insist
insociable *adj* : unsociable
insolación *nf, pl* **-ciones** : sunstroke
insolencia *nf* IMPERTINENCIA : insolence
insolente *adj* IMPERTINENTE : insolent
insólito, -ta *adj* : rare, unusual
insoluble *adj* : insoluble — **insolubilidad** *nf*
insolvencia *nf* : insolvency, bankruptcy
insolvente *adj* : insolvent, bankrupt
insomne *adj & nmf* : insomniac
insomnio *nm* : insomnia
insondable *adj* : fathomless, deep
insonorizado, -da *adj* : soundproof
insoportable *adj* INAGUANTABLE : unbearable, intolerable
insoslayable *adj* : unavoidable, inescapable
insospechado, -da *adj* : unexpected, unforeseen
insostenible *adj* : untenable
inspección *nf, pl* **-ciones** : inspection
inspeccionar *vt* : to inspect
inspector, -tora *n* : inspector
inspiración *nf, pl* **-ciones 1** : inspiration **2** INHALACIÓN : inhalation
inspirador, -dora *adj* : inspiring
inspirar *vt* : to inspire — *vi* INHALAR : to inhale
instalación *nf, pl* **-ciones** : installation
instalar *vt* **1** : to install **2** : to instate — **instalarse** *vr* ESTABLECERSE : to settle, to establish oneself
instancia *nf* **1** : petition, request **2 en última instancia** : as a last resort
instantánea *nf* : snapshot
instantáneo, -nea *adj* : instantaneous — **instantáneamente** *adv*
instante *nm* **1** : instant, moment **2 al instante** : immediately **3 a cada instante** : frequently, all the time **4 por instantes** : constantly, incessantly
instar *vt* APREMIAR : to urge, to press — *vi* URGIR : to be urgent or pressing ⟨insta que vayamos pronto : it is imperative that we leave soon⟩
instauración *nf, pl* **-ciones** : establishment
instaurar *vt* : to establish
instigador, -dora *n* : instigator
instigar {52} *vt* : to instigate, to incite
instintivo, -va *adj* : instinctive — **instintivamente** *adv*
instinto *nm* : instinct
institución *nf, pl* **-ciones** : institution
institucional *adj* : institutional — **institucionalmente** *adv*
institucionalización *nf, pl* **-ciones** : institutionalization
institucionalizar {21} *vt* : to institutionalize
instituir {41} *vt* ESTABLECER, FUNDAR : to institute, to establish, to found
instituto *nm* : institute
institutriz *nf, pl* **-trices** : governess *f*
instrucción *nf, pl* **-ciones 1** EDUCACIÓN : education **2 instrucciones** *nfpl* : instructions, directions
instructivo, -va *adj* : instructive, educational
instructor, -tora *n* : instructor
instruir {41} *vt* **1** ADIESTRAR : to instruct, to train **2** ENSEÑAR : to educate, to teach

instrumentación *nf, pl* **-ciones** : orchestration
instrumental *adj* : instrumental
instrumentar *vt* : to orchestrate
instrumentista *nmf* : instrumentalist
instrumento *nm* : instrument
insubordinado, -da *adj* : insubordinate — **insubordinación** *nf*
insubordinarse *vr* : to rebel
insuficiencia *nf* **1** : insufficiency, inadequacy **2 insuficiencia cardíaca** : heart failure
insuficiente *adj* : insufficient, inadequate — **insuficientemente** *adv*
insufrible *adj* : insufferable
insular *adj* : insular
insularidad *nf* : insularity
insulina *nf* : insulin
insulso, -sa *adj* **1** INSÍPIDO : insipid, bland **2** : dull
insultante *adj* : insulting
insultar *vt* : to insult
insulto *nm* : insult
insumos *nmpl* : supplies ⟨insumos agrícolas : agricultural supplies⟩
insuperable *adj* : insuperable, insurmountable
insurgente *adj & nmf* : insurgent — **insurgencia** *nf*
insurrección *nf, pl* **-ciones** : insurrection, uprising
insustancial *adj* : insubstantial, flimsy
insustituible *adj* : irreplaceable
intachable *adj* : irreproachable, faultless
intacto, -ta *adj* : intact
intangible *adj* IMPALPABLE : intangible, impalpable
integración *nf, pl* **-ciones** : integration
integral *adj* **1** : integral, essential **2 pan integral** : whole grain bread
integrante[1] *adj* : integrating, integral
integrante[2] *nmf* : member
integrar *vt* : to make up, to compose — **integrarse** *vr* : to integrate, to fit in
integridad *nf* **1** RECTITUD : integrity, honesty **2** : wholeness, completeness
integrismo *nm* : fundamentalism
integrista *adj & nmf* : fundamentalist
íntegro, -gra *adj* **1** : honest, upright **2** ENTERO : whole, complete **3** : unabridged
intelecto *nm* : intellect
intelectual *adj & nmf* : intellectual — **intelectualmente** *adv*
intelectualidad *nf* : intelligentsia
inteligencia *nf* : intelligence
inteligente *adj* : intelligent — **inteligentemente** *adv*
inteligible *adj* : intelligible — **inteligibilidad** *nf*
intemperancia *adj* : intemperance, excess
intemperie *nf* **1** : bad weather, elements *pl* **2 a la intemperie** : in the open air, outside
intempestivo, -va *adj* : inopportune, untimely — **intempestivamente** *adv*
intención *nf, pl* **-ciones** : intention, plan
intencionado, -da → **intencional**
intencional *adj* : intentional — **intencionalmente** *adv*
intendencia *nf* : management, administration
intendente *nmf* : quartermaster
intensidad *nf* : intensity
intensificación *nf, pl* **-ciones** : intensification
intensificar {72} *vt* : to intensify — **intensificarse** *vr*
intensivo, -va *adj* : intensive — **intensivamente** *adv*
intenso, -sa *adj* : intense — **intensamente** *adv*
intentar *vt* : to attempt, to try
intento *nm* **1** PROPÓSITO : intent, intention **2** TENTATIVA : attempt, try
interacción *nf, pl* **-ciones** : interaction
interactivo, -va *adj* : interactive
interactuar {3} *vi* : to interact
intercalar *vt* : to intersperse, to insert
intercambiable *adj* : interchangeable
intercambiar *vt* CANJEAR : to exchange, to trade
intercambio *nm* CANJE : exchange, trade
interceder *vi* : to intercede
intercepción *nf, pl* **-ciones** : interception
interceptar *vt* **1** : to intercept, to block **2 interceptar las líneas** : to wiretap
intercesión *nf, pl* **-siones** : intercession
intercomunicación *nf, pl* **-ciones** : intercommunication
interconexión *nf, pl* **-xiones** : interconnection
interconfesional *adj* : interdenominational
interdepartamental *adj* : interdepartmental
interdependencia *nf* : interdependence — **interdependiente** *adj*
interdicción *nf, pl* **-ciones** : interdiction, prohibition
interés *nm, pl* **-reses** : interest
interesado, -da *adj* **1** : interested **2** : selfish, self-seeking
interesante *adj* : interesting
interesar *vt* : to interest — *vi* : to be of interest, to be interesting — **interesarse** *vr*
interestatal *adj* : interstate ⟨autopista interestatal : interstate highway⟩
interestelar *adj* : interstellar
interfase → **interfaz**
interfaz *nf, pl* **-faces** : interface
interferencia *nf* : interference, static
interferir {76} *vi* : to interfere, to meddle — *vt* : to interfere with, to obstruct
intergaláctico, -ca *adj* : intergalactic
intergubernamental *adj* : intergovernmental
interín[1] *or* **ínterin** *adv* : meanwhile
interín[2] *or* **ínterin** *nm, pl* **-rines** : meantime, interim ⟨en el interín : in the meantime⟩

interinamente *adv* : temporarily
interino, -na *adj* : acting, temporary, interim
interior[1] *adj* : interior, inner
interior[2] *nm* **1** : interior, inside **2** : inland region
interiormente *adv* : inwardly
interjección *nf, pl* **-ciones** : interjection
interlocutor, -tora *n* : interlocutor, speaker
interludio *nm* : interlude
intermediario, -ria *adj & n* : intermediary, go-between
intermedio[1], **-dia** *adj* : intermediate
intermedio[2] *nm* **1** : intermission **2 por intermedio de** : by means of
interminable *adj* : interminable, endless — **interminablemente** *adv*
intermisión *nf, pl* **-siones** : intermission, pause
intermitente[1] *adj* **1** : intermittent **2** : flashing, blinking (of a light) — **intermitentemente** *adv*
intermitente[2] *nm* : blinker, turn signal
internacional *adj* : international — **internacionalmente** *adv*
internacionalismo *nm* : internationalism
internacionalizar {21} *vt* : to internationalize
internado *nm* : boarding school
internar *vt* : to commit, to confine — **internarse** *vr* **1** : to penetrate, to advance into **2 ~ en** : to go into, to enter
internista *nmf* : internist
interno[1], **-na** *adj* : internal — **internamente** *adv*
interno[2], **-na** *n* **1** : intern **2** : inmate, internee
interpelación *nf, pl* **-ciones** : appeal, plea
interpelar *vt* : to question (formally)
interpersonal *adj* : interpersonal
interpolar *vt* : to insert, to interpolate
interponer {60} *vt* : to interpose — **interponerse** *vr* : to intervene
interpretación *nf, pl* **-ciones** : interpretation
interpretar *vt* **1** : to interpret **2** : to play, to perform
interpretativo, -va *adj* : interpretive
intérprete *nmf* **1** TRADUCTOR : interpreter **2** : performer
interpuesto *pp* → **interponer**
interracial *adj* : interracial
interrelación *nf, pl* **-ciones** : interrelationship
interrelacionar *vi* : to interrelate
interrogación *nf, pl* **-ciones** **1** : interrogation, questioning **2 signo de interrogación** : question mark
interrogador, -dora *n* : interrogator, questioner
interrogante[1] *adj* : questioning
interrogante[2] *nm* **1** : question mark **2** : query
interrogar {52} *vt* : to interrogate, to question
interrogativo, -va *adj* : interrogative
interrogatorio *nm* : interrogation, questioning
interrumpir *v* : to interrupt
interrupción *nf, pl* **-ciones** : interruption
interruptor *nm* **1** : (electrical) switch **2** : circuit breaker
intersección *nf, pl* **-ciones** : intersection
intersticio *nm* : interstice — **intersticial** *adj*
interuniversitario, -ria *adj* : intercollegiate
interurbano, -na *adj* **1** : intercity **2** : long-distance ⟨llamadas interurbanas : long-distance calls⟩
intervalo *nm* : interval
intervención *nf, pl* **-ciones** **1** : intervention **2** : audit **3 intervención quirúrgica** : operation
intervencionista *adj & nmf* : interventionist
intervenir {87} *vi* **1** : to take part **2** INTERCEDER : to intervene, to intercede — *vt* **1** : to control, to supervise **2** : to audit **3** : to operate on **4** : to tap (a telephone)
interventor, -tora *n* **1** : inspector **2** : auditor, comptroller
intestado, -da *adj* : intestate
intestinal *adj* : intestinal
intestino *nm* : intestine
intimar *vi* **~ con** : to become friendly with — *vt* : to require, to call on
intimidación *nf, pl* **-ciones** : intimidation
intimidad *nf* **1** : intimacy **2** : privacy, private life
intimidar *vt* ACOBARDAR : to intimidate
íntimo, -ma *adj* **1** : intimate, close **2** PRIVADO : private — **íntimamente** *adv*
intitular *vt* : to entitle, to title
intocable *adj* : untouchable
intolerable *adj* : intolerable, unbearable
intolerancia *nf* : intolerance
intolerante[1] *adj* : intolerant
intolerante[2] *nmf* : intolerant person, bigot
intoxicación *nf, pl* **-ciones** : poisoning
intoxicante *nm* : poison
intoxicar {72} *vt* : to poison
intranquilidad *nf* PREOCUPACIÓN : worry, anxiety
intranquilizar {21} *vt* : to upset, to make uneasy — **intranquilizarse** *vr* : to get worried, to be anxious
intranquilo, -la *adj* PREOCUPADO : uneasy, worried
intransigencia *nf* : intransigence
intransigente *adj* : intransigent, unyielding
intransitable *adj* : impassable
intransitivo, -va *adj* : intransitive
intrascendente *adj* : unimportant, insignificant
intratable *adj* **1** : intractable **2** : awkward **3** : unsociable
intravenoso, -sa *adj* : intravenous

intrepidez *nf* : fearlessness
intrépido, -da *adj* : intrepid, fearless
intriga *nf* : intrigue
intrigante *nmf* : schemer
intrigar {52} *v* : to intrigue — **intrigante** *adj*
intrincado, -da *adj* : intricate, involved
intrínseco, -ca *adj* : intrinsic — **intrínsecamente** *adv*
introducción *nf, pl* **-ciones** : introduction
introducir {61} *vt* **1** : to introduce **2** : to bring in **3** : to insert **4** : to input, to enter — **introducirse** *vr* : to penetrate, to get into
introductorio, -ria *adj* : introductory
intromisión *nf, pl* **-siones** : interference, meddling
introspección *nf, pl* **-ciones** : introspection
introspectivo, -va *adj* : introspective
introvertido[1], **-da** *adj* : introverted
introvertido[2], **-da** *n* : introvert
intrusión *nf, pl* **-siones** : intrusion
intruso[1], **-sa** *adj* : intrusive
intruso[2], **-sa** *n* : intruder
intuición *nf, pl* **-ciones** : intuition
intuir {41} *vt* : to intuit, to sense
intuitivo, -va *adj* : intuitive — **intuitivamente** *adv*
inundación *nf, pl* **-ciones** : flood, inundation
inundar *vt* : to flood, to inundate
inusitado, -da *adj* : unusual, uncommon — **inusitadamente** *adv*
inusual *adj* : unusual, uncommon — **inusualmente** *adv*
inútil[1] *adj* INSERVIBLE : useless — **inútilmente** *adv*
inútil[2] *nmf* : good-for-nothing
inutilidad *nf* : uselessness
inutilizar {21} *vt* **1** : to make useless **2** INCAPACITAR : to disable, to put out of commission
invadir *vt* : to invade
invalidar *vt* : to nullify, to invalidate
invalidez *nf, pl* **-deces 1** : invalidity **2** : disablement
inválido, -da *adj & n* : invalid
invalorable *adj* : invaluable
invariable *adj* : invariable — **invariablemente** *adv*
invasión *nf, pl* **-siones** : invasion
invasivo, -va *adj* : invasive
invasor[1], **-sora** *adj* : invading
invasor[2], **-sora** *n* : invader
invectiva *nf* : invective, abuse
invencibilidad *nf* : invincibility
invencible *adj* **1** : invincible **2** : insurmountable
invención *nf, pl* **-ciones 1** INVENTO : invention **2** MENTIRA : fabrication, lie
inventar *vt* **1** : to invent **2** : to fabricate, to make up
inventariar {85} *vt* : to inventory
inventario *nm* : inventory
inventiva *nf* : ingenuity, inventiveness
inventivo, -va *adj* : inventive
invento *nm* INVENCIÓN : invention
inventor, -tora *n* : inventor
invernadero *nm* : greenhouse, hothouse
invernal *adj* : winter, wintry
invernar {55} *vi* **1** : to spend the winter **2** HIBERNAR : to hibernate
inverosímil *adj* : unlikely, far-fetched
inversión *nf, pl* **-siones 1** : inversion **2** : investment
inversionista *nmf* : investor
inverso[1], **-sa** *adj* **1** : inverse, inverted **2** CONTRARIO : opposite **3 a la inversa** : on the contrary, vice versa **4 en orden inverso** : in reverse order — **inversamente** *adv*
inverso[2] *n* : inverse
inversor, -sora *n* : investor
invertebrado[1], **-da** *adj* : invertebrate
invertebrado[2] *nm* : invertebrate
invertir {76} *vt* **1** : to invert, to reverse **2** : to invest — *vi* : to make an investment — **invertirse** *vr* : to be reversed
investidura *nf* : investiture, inauguration
investigación *nf, pl* **-ciones 1** ENCUESTA, INDAGACIÓN : investigation, inquiry **2** : research
investigador[1], **-dora** *adj* : investigative
investigador[2], **-dora** *n* **1** : investigator **2** : researcher
investigar {52} *vt* **1** INDAGAR : to investigate **2** : to research — *vi* **~ sobre** : to do research into
investir {54} *vt* **1** : to empower **2** : to swear in, to inaugurate
inveterado, -da *adj* : inveterate, deep-seated
invicto, -ta *adj* : undefeated
invidente[1] *adj* CIEGO : blind, sightless
invidente[2] *nmf* CIEGO : blind person
invierno *nm* : winter, wintertime
inviolable *adj* : inviolable — **inviolabilidad** *nf*
inviolado, -da *adj* : inviolate, pure
invisibilidad *nf* : invisibility
invisible *adj* : invisible — **invisiblemente** *adv*
invitación *nf, pl* **-ciones** : invitation
invitado, -da *n* : guest
invitar *vt* : to invite
invocación *nf, pl* **-ciones** : invocation
invocar {72} *vt* : to invoke, to call on
involucramiento *nm* : involvement
involucrar *vt* : to implicate, to involve — **involucrarse** *vr* : to get involved
involuntario, -ria *adj* : involuntary — **involuntariamente** *adv*
invulnerable *adj* : invulnerable
inyección *nf, pl* **-ciones** : injection, shot
inyectado, -da *adj* **ojos inyectados** : bloodshot eyes
inyectar *vt* : to inject
ion *nm* : ion
iónico, -ca *adj* : ionic
ionizar {21} *vt* : to ionize — **ionización** *nf*
ionosfera *nf* : ionosphere
ir {43} *vi* **1** : to go ⟨ir a pie : to go on foot, to walk⟩ ⟨ir a caballo : to ride

horseback⟩ ⟨ir a casa : to go home⟩ **2** : to lead, to extend, to stretch ⟨el camino va de Cali a Bogotá : the road goes from Cali to Bogotá⟩ **3** FUNCIONAR : to work, to function ⟨esta computadora ya no va : this computer doesn't work anymore⟩ **4** : to get on, to get along ⟨¿cómo te va? : how are you?, how's it going?⟩ ⟨el negocio no va bien : the business isn't doing well⟩ **5** : to suit ⟨ese vestido te va bien : that dress really suits you⟩ **6 ~ con** : to be ⟨ir con prisa : to be in a hurry⟩ **7 ~ por** : to follow, to go along ⟨fueron por la costa : they followed the shoreline⟩ **8 dejarse ir** : to let oneself go **9 ir a parar** : to end up **10 vamos a ver** : let's see — *v aux* **1** (*with present participle*) ⟨ir caminando : to walk⟩ ⟨¡voy corriendo! : I'll be right there!⟩ **2 ~ a** : to be going to ⟨voy a hacerlo : I'm going to do it⟩ ⟨el avión va a despegar : the plane is about to take off⟩ — **irse** *vr* **1** : to leave, to go ⟨¡vámonos! : let's go!⟩ ⟨todo el mundo se fue : everyone left⟩ **2** ESCAPARSE : to leak **3** GASTARSE : to be used up, to be gone

ira *nf* CÓLERA, FURIA : wrath, anger

iracundo, -da *adj* : irate, angry

iraní *adj & nmf* : Iranian

iraquí *adj & nmf* : Iraqi

irascible *adj* : irascible, irritable — **irascibilidad** *nf*

irga, irgue etc. → **erguir**

iridio *nm* : iridium

iridiscencia *nf* : iridescence — **iridiscente** *adj*

iris *nms & pl* **1** : iris **2 arco iris** : rainbow

irlandés[1], **-desa** *adj, mpl* **-deses** : Irish

irlandés[2], **-desa** *n, pl* **-deses** : Irish person, Irishman *m,* Irishwoman *f*

irlandés[3] *nm* : Irish (language)

ironía *nf* : irony

irónico, -ca *adj* : ironic, ironical — **irónicamente** *adv*

irracional *adj* : irrational — **irracionalmente** *adv*

irracionalidad *nf* : irrationality

irradiación *nf, pl* **-ciones** : irradiation

irradiar *vt* : to radiate, to irradiate

irrazonable *adj* : unreasonable

irreal *adj* : unreal

irrebatible *adj* : unanswerable, irrefutable

irreconciliable *adj* : irreconcilable

irreconocible *adj* : unrecognizable

irrecuperable *adj* : irrecoverable, irretrievable

irredimible *adj* : irredeemable

irreductible *adj* : unyielding

irreemplazable *adj* : irreplaceable

irreflexión *nf, pl* **-xiones** : thoughtlessness, impetuosity

irreflexivo, -va *adj* : rash, unthinking — **irreflexivamente** *adv*

irrefrenable *adj* : uncontrollable, unstoppable ⟨un impulso irrefrenable : an irresistible urge⟩

irrefutable *adj* : irrefutable

irregular *adj* : irregular — **irregularmente** *adv*

irregularidad *nf* : irregularity

irrelevante *adj* : irrelevant — **irrelevancia** *nf*

irreligioso, -sa *adj* : irreligious

irremediable *adj* : incurable — **irremediablemente** *adv*

irreparable *adj* : irreparable

irreprimible *adj* : irrepressible

irreprochable *adj* : irreproachable

irresistible *adj* : irresistible — **irresistiblemente** *adv*

irresolución *nf, pl* **-ciones** : indecision, hesitation

irresoluto, -ta *adj* INDECISO : undecided

irrespeto *nm* : disrespect

irrespetuoso, -sa *adj* : disrespectful — **irrespetuosamente** *adv*

irresponsabilidad *nf* : irresponsibility

irresponsable *adj* : irresponsible — **irresponsablemente** *adv*

irrestricto, -ta *adj* : unrestricted, unconditional

irreverencia *nf* : disrespect

irreverente *adj* : disrespectful

irreversible *adj* : irreversible

irrevocable *adj* : irrevocable — **irrevocablemente** *adv*

irrigar {52} *vt* : to irrigate — **irrigación** *nf*

irrisible *adj* : laughable

irrisión *nf, pl* **-siones** : derision, ridicule

irrisorio, -ria *adj* RISIBLE : ridiculous, ludicrous

irritabilidad *nf* : irritability

irritable *adj* : irritable

irritación *nf, pl* **-ciones** : irritation

irritante *adj* : irritating

irritar *vt* : to irritate — **irritación** *nf*

irrompible *adj* : unbreakable

irrumpir *vi* **~ en** : to burst into

irrupción *nf, pl* **-ciones** **1** : irruption **2** : invasion

isla *nf* : island

islámico, -ca *adj* : Islamic, Muslim

islandés[1], **-desa** *adj, mpl* **-deses** : Icelandic

islandés[2], **-desa** *n, mpl* **-deses** : Icelander

islandés[3] *nm* : Icelandic (language)

isleño, -ña *n* : islander

islote *nm* : islet

isometría *nfs & pl* : isometrics

isométrico, -ca *adj* : isometric

isósceles *adj* : isosceles ⟨triángulo isósceles : isosceles triangle⟩

isótopo *nm* : isotope

israelí *adj & nmf* : Israeli

istmo *nm* : isthmus

itacate *nm Mex* : pack, provisions *pl*

italiano[1], **-na** *adj & n* : Italian

italiano[2] *nm* : Italian (language)

iterbio *nm* : ytterbium

itinerante *adj* AMBULANTE : traveling, itinerant

itinerario *nm* : itinerary, route

itrio *nm* : yttrium
izar {21} *vt* : to hoist, to raise ⟨izar la bandera : to raise the flag⟩
izquierda *nf* : left
izquierdista *adj & nmf* : leftist
izquierdo, -da *adj* : left

J

j *nf* : tenth letter of the Spanish alphabet
ja *interj* **1** : ha! **2 ja, ja** : ha-ha!
jabalí *nm* : wild boar
jabalina *nf* : javelin
jabón *nm, pl* **jabones** : soap
jabonar *vt* ENJABONAR : to soap up, to lather — **jabonarse** *vr*
jabonera *nf* : soap dish
jabonoso, -sa *adj* : soapy
jaca *nf* **1** : pony **2** YEGUA : mare
jacal *nm Mex* : shack, hut
jacinto *nm* : hyacinth
jactancia *nf* **1** : boastfulness **2** : boasting, bragging
jactancioso[1], **-sa** *adj* : boastful
jactancioso[2], **-sa** *n* : boaster, braggart
jactarse *vr* : to boast, to brag
jade *nm* : jade
jadear *vi* : to pant, to gasp, to puff — **jadeante** *adj*
jadeo *nm* : panting, gasping, puffing
jaez *nm, pl* **jaeces 1** : harness **2** : kind, sort, ilk **3 jaeces** *nmpl* : trappings
jaguar *nm* : jaguar
jai alai *nm* : jai alai
jaiba *nf* CANGREJO : crab
jalapeño *nm Mex* : jalapeño pepper
jalar *vt* **1** : to pull, to tug **2** *fam* : to attract, to draw in ⟨las ideas nuevas lo jalan : new ideas appeal to him⟩ — *vi* **1** : to pull, to pull together **2** *fam* : to hurry up, to get going **3** *Mex fam* : to be in working order ⟨esta máquina no jala : this machine doesn't work⟩
jalbegue *nm* : whitewash
jalea *nf* : jelly
jalear *vt* : to encourage, to urge on
jaleo *nm* **1** *fam* : uproar, ruckus, racket **2** *fam* : confusion, hassle **3** : cheering and clapping (for a dance)
jalón *nm, pl* **jalones 1** : milestone, landmark **2** TIRÓN : pull, tug
jalonar *vt* : to mark, to stake out
jalonear *vt Mex, Peru fam* : to tug at — *vi* **1** *fam* : to pull, to tug **2** *CA fam* : to haggle
jamaica *nf* : hibiscus
jamaicano, -na → **jamaiquino**
jamaiquino, -na *adj & n* : Jamaican
jamás *adv* **1** NUNCA : never **2 nunca jamás** *or* **jamás de los jamases** : never ever **3 para siempre jamás** : for ever and ever
jamba *nf* : jamb
jamelgo *nm* : nag (horse)
jamón *nm, pl* **jamones** : ham
Januká *nmf* : Hanukkah
japonés[1], **-nesa** *adj & n, mpl* **-neses** : Japanese
japonés[2] *nm, pl* **-neses** : Japanese (language)
jaque *nm* **1** : check (in chess) ⟨jaque mate : checkmate⟩ **2 tener en jaque** : to intimidate, to bully
jaqueca *nf* : headache, migraine
jarabe *nm* **1** : syrup **2** : Mexican folk dance
jarana *nf* **1** *fam* : revelry, partying, spree **2** *fam* : joking, fooling around **3** : small guitar
jaranear *vi fam* : to go on a spree, to party
jarcia *nf* **1** : rigging **2** : fishing tackle
jardín *nm, pl* **jardines 1** : garden **2 jardín de niños** : kindergarten **3 los jardines** *nmpl* : the outfield
jardinería *nf* : gardening
jardinero, -ra *n* **1** : gardener **2** : outfielder (in baseball)
jarra *nf* **1** : pitcher, jug **2** : stein, mug **3 de jarras** *or* **en jarras** : akimbo
jarrete *nm* **1** : back of the knee **2** CORVEJÓN : hock
jarro *nm* **1** : pitcher, jug **2** : mug
jarrón *nm, pl* **jarrones** FLORERO : vase
jaspe *nm* : jasper
jaspeado, -da *adj* **1** VETEADO : streaked, veined **2** : speckled, mottled
jaula *nf* : cage
jauría *nf* : pack of hounds
javanés, -nesa *adj & n* : Javanese
jazmín *nm, pl* **jazmines** : jasmine
jazz [ˈjas, ˈdʒas] *nm* : jazz
jeans [ˈjins, ˈdʒins] *nmpl* : jeans
jeep [ˈjip, ˈdʒip] *nm, pl* **jeeps** : jeep
jefatura *nf* **1** : leadership **2** : headquarters ⟨jefatura de policía : police headquarters⟩
jefe, -fa *n* **1** : chief, head, leader ⟨jefe de bomberos : fire chief⟩ **2** : boss
Jehová *nm* : Jehovah
jején *nm, pl* **jejenes** : gnat, small mosquito
jengibre *nm* : ginger
jeque *nm* : sheikh, sheik
jerarca *nmf* : leader, chief
jerarquía *nf* **1** : hierarchy **2** RANGO : rank
jerárquico, -ca *adj* : hierarchical
jerbo *nm* : gerbil
jerez *nm, pl* **jereces** : sherry
jerga *nf* **1** : jargon, slang **2** : coarse cloth
jerigonza *nf* GALIMATÍAS : mumbo jumbo, gibberish
jeringa *nf* : syringe
jeringar {52} *vt* **1** : to inject **2** *fam* JOROBAR : to annoy, to pester — *vi fam*

JOROBAR : to be annoying, to be a nuisance
jeringuear → **jeringar**
jeringuilla → **jeringa**
jeroglífico *nm* : hieroglyphic
jersey *nm, pl* **jerseys** **1** : jersey (fabric) **2** *Spain* : sweater
Jesucristo *nm* : Jesus Christ
jesuita *adj & nm* : Jesuit
Jesús *nm* **1** : Jesus **2 ¡Jesús!** : goodness!, good heavens!
jeta *nf* **1** : snout **2** *fam* : face, mug
jíbaro, -ra *adj* **1** : Jivaro **2** : rustic, rural
jibia *nf* : cuttlefish
jícama *nf* : jicama
jícara *nf Mex* : calabash
jilguero *nm* : European goldfinch
jinete *nmf* : horseman, horsewoman *f*, rider
jinetear *vt* **1** : to ride, to perform (on horseback) **2** DOMAR : to break in (a horse) — *vi* CABALGAR : to ride horseback
jingoísmo [ˌjɪŋgoˈizmo, ˌʤɪŋ-] *nm* : jingoism
jingoísta *adj* : jingoist, jingoistic
jiote *nm Mex* : rash
jira *nf* : outing, picnic
jirafa *nf* **1** : giraffe **2** : boom microphone
jirón *nm, pl* **jirones** : shred, rag ⟨hecho jirones : in tatters⟩
jitomate *nm Mex* : tomato
jockey [ˈjɔki, ˈʤɔ-] *nmf, pl* **jockeys** [-kis] : jockey
jocosidad *nf* : humor, jocularity
jocoso, -sa *adj* : playful, jocular — **jocosamente** *adv*
jofaina *nf* : washbowl
jogging [ˈjɔgɪŋ, ˈʤɔ-] *nm* : jogging
jolgorio *nm* : merrymaking, fun
jonrón *nm, pl* **jonrones** : home run
jordano, -na *adj & n* : Jordanian
jornada *nf* **1** : expedition, day's journey **2 jornada de trabajo** : working day **3 jornadas** *nfpl* : conference, congress
jornal *nm* **1** : day's pay **2 a ～** : by the day
jornalero, -ra *n* : day laborer
joroba *nf* **1** GIBA : hump **2** *fam* : nuisance, pain in the neck
jorobado[1], -da *adj* GIBOSO : hunchbacked, humpbacked
jorobado[2], -da *n* GIBOSO : hunchback, humpback
jorobar *vt fam* JERINGAR : to bother, to annoy — *vi fam* JERINGAR : to be annoying, to be a nuisance
jorongo *nm Mex* : full-length poncho
jota *nf* **1** : jot, bit ⟨no entiendo ni jota : I don't understand a word of it⟩ ⟨no se ve ni jota : you can't see a thing⟩ **2** : jack (in playing cards)
joven[1] *adj, pl* **jóvenes** **1** : young **2** : youthful
joven[2] *nmf, pl* **jóvenes** : young man *m*, young woman *f*, young person
jovial *adj* : jovial, cheerful — **jovialmente** *adv*
jovialidad *nf* : joviality, cheerfulness
joya *nf* **1** : jewel, piece of jewelry **2** : treasure, gem ⟨la nueva empleada es una joya : the new employee is a real gem⟩
joyería *nf* **1** : jewelry store **2** : jewelry **3 joyería de fantasía** : costume jewelry
joyero, -ra *n* : jeweler
juanete *nm* : bunion
jubilación *nf, pl* **-ciones** **1** : retirement **2** PENSIÓN : pension
jubilado[1], -da *adj* : retired, in retirement
jubilado[2], -da *nmf* : retired person, retiree
jubilar *vt* **1** : to retire, to pension off **2** *fam* : to get rid of, to discard — **jubilarse** *vr* : to retire
jubileo *nm* : jubilee
júbilo *nm* : jubilation, joy
jubiloso, -sa *adj* : jubilant, joyous
judaico, -ca *adj* : Judaic, Jewish
judaísmo *nm* : Judaism
judía *nf* **1** : bean **2** *or* **judía verde** : green bean, string bean
judicatura *nf* **1** : judiciary, judges *pl* **2** : office of judge
judicial *adj* : judicial — **judicialmente** *adv*
judío[1], -día *adj* : Jewish
judío[2], -día *n* : Jewish person, Jew
judo [ˈjuðo, ˈʤu-] *nm* : judo
juega, juegue, etc. → **jugar**
juego *nm* **1** : play, playing ⟨poner en juego : to bring into play⟩ **2** : game, sport ⟨juego de cartas : card game⟩ ⟨Juegos Olímpicos : Olympic Games⟩ **3** : gaming, gambling ⟨estar en juego : to be at stake⟩ **4** : set ⟨un juego de llaves : a set of keys⟩ **5 hacer juego** : to go together, to match **6 juego de manos** : conjuring trick, sleight of hand
juerga *nf* : partying, binge ⟨irse de juerga : to go on a spree⟩
juerguista *nmf* : reveler, carouser
jueves *nms & pl* : Thursday
juez[1] *nmf, pl* **jueces** **1** : judge **2** ÁRBITRO : umpire, referee
juez[2], jueza *n* → **juez[1]**
jugada *nf* **1** : play, move **2** : trick ⟨hacer una mala jugada : to play a dirty trick⟩
jugador, -dora *n* **1** : player **2** : gambler
jugar {44} *vi* **1** : to play ⟨jugar a la pelota : to play ball⟩ **2** APOSTAR : to gamble, to bet **3** : to joke, to kid — *vt* **1** : to play ⟨jugar un papel : to play a role⟩ ⟨jugar una carta : to play a card⟩ **2** : to bet — **jugarse** *vr* **1** : to risk, to gamble away ⟨jugarse la vida : to risk one's life⟩ **2 jugarse el todo por el todo** : to risk everything
jugarreta *nf fam* : prank, dirty trick
juglar *nm* : minstrel

jugo *nm* **1** : juice **2** : substance, essence ⟨sacarle el jugo a algo : to get the most out of something⟩

jugosidad *nf* : juiciness, succulence

jugoso, -sa *adj* : juicy

juguete *nm* : toy

juguetear *vi* **1** : to play, to cavort, to frolic **2** : to toy, to fiddle

juguetería *nf* : toy store

juguetón, -tona *adj, mpl* **-tones** : playful — **juguetonamente** *adv*

juicio *nm* **1** : good judgment, reason, sense **2** : opinion ⟨a mi juicio : in my opinion⟩ **3** : trial ⟨llevar a juicio : to take to court⟩

juicioso, -sa *adj* : judicious, wise — **juiciosamente** *adv*

julio *nm* : July

juncia *nf* : sedge

junco *nm* **1** : reed, rush **2** : junk (boat)

jungla *nf* : jungle

junio *nm* : June

junquillo *nm* : jonquil

junta *nf* **1** : board, committee ⟨junta directiva : board of directors⟩ **2** REUNIÓN : meeting, session **3** : junta **4** : joint, gasket

juntamente *adv* **1** : jointly, together ⟨juntamente con : together with⟩ **2** : at the same time

juntar *vt* **1** UNIR : to unite, to combine, to put together **2** REUNIR : to collect, to gather together, to assemble **3** : to close partway ⟨juntar la puerta : to leave the door ajar⟩ — **juntarse** *vr* **1** : to join together **2** : to socialize, to get together

junto, -ta *adj* **1** UNIDO : joined, united **2** : close, adjacent ⟨colgaron los dos retratos juntos : they hung the two paintings side by side⟩ **3** (*used adverbially*) : together ⟨llegamos juntos : we arrived together⟩ **4 ~ a** : next to, alongside of **5 ~ con** : together with, along with

juntura *nf* : joint, coupling

Júpiter *nm* : Jupiter

jura *nf* : oath, pledge ⟨jura de bandera : pledge of allegiance⟩

jurado[1] *nm* : jury

jurado[2], **-da** *n* : juror

juramento *nm* **1** : oath ⟨juramento hipocrático : Hippocratic oath⟩ **2** : swearword, oath

jurar *vt* **1** : to swear ⟨jurar lealtad : to swear loyalty⟩ **2** : to take an oath ⟨el alcalde juró su cargo : the mayor took the oath of office⟩ — *vi* : to curse, to swear

jurídico, -ca *adj* : legal

jurisdicción *nf, pl* **-ciones** : jurisdiction

jurisdiccional *adj* : jurisdictional, territorial

jurisprudencia *nf* : jurisprudence, law

jurista *nmf* : jurist

justa *nf* **1** : joust **2** TORNEO : tournament, competition

justamente *adv* **1** PRECISAMENTE : precisely, exactly **2** : justly, fairly

justar *vi* : to joust

justicia *nf* **1** : justice, fairness ⟨hacerle justicia a : to do justice to⟩ ⟨ser de justicia : to be only fair⟩ **2 la justicia** : the law ⟨tomarse la justicia por su mano : to take the law into one's own hands⟩

justiciero, -ra *adj* : righteous, avenging

justificable *adj* : justifiable

justificación *nf, pl* **-ciones** : justification

justificante *nm* **1** : justification **2** : proof, voucher

justificar {72} *vt* **1** : to justify **2** : to excuse, to vindicate

justo[1] *adv* **1** : justly **2** : right, exactly ⟨justo a tiempo : just in time⟩ **3** : tightly

justo[2], **-ta** *adj* **1** : just, fair **2** : right, exact **3** : tight ⟨estos zapatos me quedan muy justos : these shoes are too tight⟩

justo[3], **-ta** *n* : just person ⟨los justos : the just⟩

juvenil *adj* **1** : juvenile, young, youthful **2** ADOLESCENTE : teenage

juventud *nf* **1** : youth **2** : young people

juzgado *nm* TRIBUNAL : court, tribunal

juzgar {52} *vt* **1** : to try, to judge (a case in court) **2** : to pass judgment on **3** CONSIDERAR : to consider, to deem

juzgue, etc. → **juzgar**

K

k *nf* : eleventh letter of the Spanish alphabet

káiser *nm* : kaiser

kaki → **caqui**

kaleidoscopio → **caleidoscopio**

kamikaze *adj & nm* : kamikaze

kampucheano, -na *adj & n* : Kampuchean

kan *nm* : khan

karaoke *nm* : karaoke

karate *or* **kárate** *nm* : karate

kayac *or* **kayak** *nm, pl* **kayacs** *or* **kayaks** : kayak

keniano, -na *adj & n* : Kenyan

kepí *nm* : kepi

kermesse *or* **kermés** [kɛrˈmɛs] *nf, pl* **kermesses** *or* **kermeses** [-ˈmɛsɛs] : charity fair, bazaar

kerosene *or* **kerosén** *or* **keroseno** *nm* : kerosene, paraffin

kibutz *or* **kibbutz** *nms & pl* : kibbutz

kilo *nm* **1** : kilo, kilogram **2** *fam* : large amount

kilobyte [ˌkiloˈbait] *nm* : kilobyte

kilociclo *nm* : kilocycle

kilogramo *nm* : kilogram

kilohertzio *nm* : kilohertz
kilometraje *nm* : distance in kilometers, mileage
kilométrico, -ca *adj fam* : endless, very long
kilómetro *nm* : kilometer
kilovatio *nm* : kilowatt
kimono *nm* : kimono
kinder [ˈkɪndɛr] → **kindergarten**
kindergarten [ˌkɪndɛrˈgartɛn] *nm, pl* **kindergartens** [-tɛns] : kindergarten, nursery school
kinesiología *nf* : physical therapy
kinesiólogo, -ga *n* : physical therapist
kiosco → **quiosco**
kit *nm, pl* **kits** : kit
kiwi [ˈkiwi] *nm* **1** : kiwi (bird) **2** : kiwifruit
klaxon → **claxon**
knockout [nɔˈkaut] → **nocaut**
koala *nm* : koala bear
kriptón *nm* : krypton
kurdo[1], **-da** *adj* : Kurdish
kurdo[2], **-da** *n* : Kurd
kuwaití [kuˌwaiˈti] *adj & nmf* : Kuwaiti

L

l *nf* : twelfth letter of the Spanish alphabet
la[1] *pron* **1** : her, it <llámala hoy : call her today> <sacó la botella y la abrió : he took out the bottle and opened it> **2** (*formal*) : you <no la vi a usted, Señora Díaz : I didn't see you, Mrs. Díaz> **3** : the one <mi casa y la de la puerta roja : my house and the one with the red door> **4 la que** : the one who
la[2] *art* → **el**[2]
laberíntico, -ca *adj* : labyrinthine
laberinto *nm* : labyrinth, maze
labia *nf fam* : gift of gab <tu amigo tiene labia : your friend has a way with words>
labial *adj* : labial, lip <lápiz labial : lipstick>
labio *nm* **1** : lip **2 labio leporino** : harelip
labor *nf* : work, labor
laborable *adj* **1** : arable **2 día laborable** : workday, business day
laboral *adj* : work, labor <costos laborales : labor costs>
laborar *vi* : to work
laboratorio *nm* : laboratory, lab
laboriosidad *nf* : industriousness, diligence
laborioso, -sa *adj* **1** : laborious, hard **2** : industrious, hardworking
labrado[1], **-da** *adj* **1** : cultivated, tilled **2** : carved, wrought
labrado[2] *nm* : cultivated field
labrador, -dora *n* : farmer
labranza *nf* : farming
labrar *vt* **1** : to carve, to work (metal) **2** : to cultivate, to till **3** : to cause, to bring about
laca *nf* **1** : lacquer, shellac **2** : hair spray **3 laca de uñas** : nail polish
lacayo *nm* : lackey
lace, etc. → **lazar**
lacear *vt* : to lasso
laceración *nf, pl* **-ciones** : laceration
lacerante *adj* : hurtful, wounding
lacerar *vt* **1** : to lacerate, to cut **2** : to hurt, to wound (one's feelings)
lacio, -cia *adj* **1** : limp, lank **2 pelo lacio** : straight hair
lacónico, -ca *adj* : laconic — **lacónicamente** *adv*
lacra *nf* **1** : scar, mark (on the skin) **2** : stigma, blemish
lacrar *vt* : to seal (with wax)
lacrimógeno, -na *adj* **gas lacrimógeno** : tear gas
lacrimoso, -sa *adj* : tearful, moving
lactancia *nf* **1** : lactation **2** : breastfeeding
lactante *nmf* : nursing infant, suckling
lactar *v* : to breast-feed
lácteo, -tea *adj* **1** : dairy **2 Vía Láctea** : Milky Way
láctico, -ca *adj* : lactic
lactosa *nf* : lactose
ladeado, -da *adj* : crooked, tilted, lopsided
ladear *vt* : to tilt, to tip — **ladearse** *vr* : to bend (over)
ladera *nf* : slope, hillside
ladino[1], **-na** *adj* **1** : cunning, shrewd **2** *CA, Mex* : mestizo
ladino[2], **-na** *n* **1** : trickster **2** *CA, Mex* : Spanish-speaking Indian **3** *CA, Mex* : mestizo
lado *nm* **1** : side **2** PARTE : place <miró por todos lados : he looked everywhere> **3 al lado de** : next to, beside **4 de ~** : tilted, sideways <está de lado : it's lying on its side> **5 hacerse a un lado** : to step aside **6 lado a lado** : side by side **7 por otro lado** : on the other hand
ladrar *vi* : to bark
ladrido *nm* : bark (of a dog), barking
ladrillo *nm* **1** : brick **2** AZULEJO : tile
ladrón, -drona *n, mpl* **ladrones** : robber, thief, burglar
lagartija *nf* : small lizard
lagarto *nm* **1** : lizard **2 lagarto de Indias** : alligator
lago *nm* : lake
lágrima *nf* : tear, teardrop
lagrimear *vi* **1** : to water (of eyes) **2** : to weep easily
laguna *nf* **1** : lagoon **2** : lacuna, gap
laicado *nm* : laity
laico[1], **-ca** *adj* : lay, secular
laico[2], **-ca** *n* : layman *m*, laywoman *f*

laja *nf* : slab
lama[1] *nf* : slime, ooze
lama[2] *nm* : lama
lamber *vt* : to lick
lamé *nm* : lamé
lamentable *adj* **1** : unfortunate, lamentable **2** : pitiful, sad
lamentablemente *adv* : unfortunately, regrettably
lamentación *nf, pl* **-ciones** : lamentation, groaning, moaning
lamentar *vt* **1** : to lament **2** : to regret ⟨lo lamento : I'm sorry⟩ — **lamentarse** *vr* : to grumble, to complain
lamento *nm* : lament, groan, cry
lamer *vt* **1** : to lick **2** : to lap against
lamida *nf* : lick
lámina *nf* **1** PLANCHA : sheet, plate **2** : plate, illustration
laminado[1], **-da** *adj* : laminated
laminado[2] *nm* : laminate
laminar *vt* : to laminate — **laminación** *nf*
lámpara *nf* : lamp
lampiño, -ña *adj* : hairless
lamprea *nf* : lamprey
lana *nf* **1** : wool ⟨lana de acero : steel wool⟩ **2** *Mex fam* : money, dough
lance[1], **etc.** → **lanzar**
lance[2] *nm* **1** INCIDENTE : event, incident **2** RIÑA : quarrel **3** : throw, cast (of a net, etc.) **4** : move, play (in a game), throw (of dice)
lancear *vt* : to spear
lanceta *nf* : lancet
lancha *nf* **1** : small boat, launch **2 lancha motora** : motorboat, speedboat
langosta *nf* **1** : lobster **2** : locust
langostino *nm* : prawn, crayfish
languidecer {53} *vi* : to languish
languidez *nf, pl* **-deces** : languor, listlessness
lánguido, -da *adj* : languid, listless — **lánguidamente** *adv*
lanolina *nf* : lanolin
lanudo, -da *adj* : woolly
lanza *nf* : spear, lance
lanzadera *nf* **1** : shuttle (for weaving) **2 lanzadera espacial** : space shuttle
lanzado, -da *adj* **1** : impulsive, brazen **2** : forward, determined ⟨ir lanzado : to hurtle along⟩
lanzador, -dora *n* : thrower, pitcher
lanzallamas *nms & pl* : flamethrower
lanzamiento *nm* **1** : throw **2** : pitch (in baseball) **3** : launching, launch
lanzar {21} *vt* **1** : to throw, to hurl **2** : to pitch **3** : to launch — **lanzarse** *vr* **1** : to throw oneself (at, into) **2 ~ a** : to embark upon, to undertake
laosiano, -na *adj & n* : Laotian
lapicero *nm* **1** : mechanical pencil **2** *CA, Peru* : ballpoint pen
lápida *nf* : marker, tombstone
lapidar *vt* APEDREAR : to stone
lapidario, -ria *adj & n* : lapidary
lápiz *nm, pl* **lápices** **1** : pencil **2 lápiz de labios** *or* **lápiz labial** : lipstick
lapón, -pona *adj & n, mpl* **lapones** : Lapp
lapso *nm* : lapse, space (of time)
lapsus *nms & pl* : error, slip
laptop *nm, pl* **laptops** : laptop
laquear *vt* : to lacquer, to varnish, to shellac
largamente *adv* **1** : at length, extensively **2** : easily, comfortably **3** : generously
largar {52} *vt* **1** SOLTAR : to let loose, to release **2** AFLOJAR : to loosen, to slacken **3** *fam* : to give, to hand over **4** *fam* : to hurl, to let fly (insults, etc.) — **largarse** *vr fam* : to scram, to beat it
largo[1], **-ga** *adj* **1** : long **2 a lo largo** : lengthwise **3 a lo largo de** : along **4 a la larga** : in the long run
largo[2] *nm* : length ⟨tres metros de largo : three meters long⟩
largometraje *nm* : feature film
largue, etc. → **largar**
larguero *nm* : crossbeam
largueza *nf* : generosity, largesse
larguirucho, -cha *adj fam* : lanky
largura *nf* : length
laringe *nf* : larynx
laringitis *nfs & pl* : laryngitis
larva *nf* : larva — **larval** *adj*
las → **el**[2], **los**[1]
lasaña *nf* : lasagna
lasca *nf* : chip, chipping
lascivia *nf* : lasciviousness, lewdness
lascivo, -va *adj* : lascivious, lewd — **lascivamente** *adv*
láser *nm* : laser
lasitud *nf* : lassitude, weariness
laso, -sa *adj* : languid, weary
lástima *nf* **1** : compassion, pity **2** PENA : shame, pity ⟨¡qué lástima! : what a shame!⟩
lastimadura *nf* : injury, wound
lastimar *vt* **1** DAÑAR, HERIR : to hurt, to injure **2** AGRAVIAR : to offend — **lastimarse** *vr* : to hurt oneself
lastimero, -ra *adj* : pitiful, wretched
lastimoso, -sa *adj* **1** : shameful **2** : pitiful, terrible
lastrar *vt* **1** : to ballast **2** : to burden, to encumber
lastre *nm* **1** : burden **2** : ballast
lata *nf* **1** : tinplate **2** : tin can **3** *fam* : pest, bother, nuisance **4 dar lata** *fam* : to bother, to annoy
latencia *nf* : latency
latente *adj* : latent
lateral[1] *adj* **1** : lateral, side **2** : indirect — **lateralmente** *adv*
lateral[2] *nm* : end piece, side
látex *nms & pl* : latex
latido *nm* : beat, throb ⟨latido del corazón : heartbeat⟩
latifundio *nm* : large estate
latigazo *nm* : lash (with a whip)
látigo *nm* AZOTE : whip
latín *nm* : Latin (language)
latino[1], **-na** *adj* **1** : Latin **2** *fam* : Latin-American

latino[2], -na *n fam* : Latin American

latinoamericano[1], -na *adj* HISPANOAMERICANO : Latin American

latinoamericano, -na *n* : Latin American

latir *vi* **1** : to beat, to throb **2 latirle a uno** *Mex fam* : to have a hunch ⟨me late que no va a venir : I have a feeling he's not going to come⟩

latitud *nf* **1** : latitude **2** : breadth

lato, -ta *adj* **1** : extended, lengthy **2** : broad (in meaning)

latón *nm, pl* **latones** : brass

latoso[1], -sa *adj fam* : annoying, bothersome

latoso[2], -sa *n fam* : pest, nuisance

latrocinio *nm* : larceny

laúd *nm* : lute

laudable *adj* : laudable, praiseworthy

laudo *nm* : findings, decision

laureado, -da *adj & n* : laureate

laurear *vt* : to award, to honor

laurel *nm* **1** : laurel **2** : bay leaf **3 dormirse en sus laureles** : to rest on one's laurels

lava *nf* : lava

lavable *adj* : washable

lavabo *nm* **1** LAVAMANOS : sink, washbowl **2** : lavatory, toilet

lavadero *nm* : laundry room

lavado *nm* **1** : laundry, wash **2** : laundering ⟨lavado de dinero : money laundering⟩

lavadora *nf* : washing machine

lavamanos *nms & pl* LAVABO : sink, washbowl

lavanda *nf* ESPLIEGO : lavender

lavandería *nf* : laundry (service)

lavandero, -ra *n* : launderer, laundress *f*

lavaplatos *nms & pl* **1** : dishwasher **2** *Chile, Col, Mex* : kitchen sink

lavar *vt* **1** : to wash, to clean **2** : to launder (money) **3 lavar en seco** : to dry-clean — **lavarse** *vr* **1** : to wash oneself **2 lavarse las manos de** : to wash one's hands of

lavativa *nf* : enema

lavatorio *nm* : lavatory, washroom

lavavajillas *nms & pl* : dishwasher

laxante *adj & nm* : laxative

laxitud *nf* : laxity, slackness

laxo, -xa *adj* : lax, slack

lazada *nf* : bow, loop

lazar {21} *vt* : to rope, to lasso

lazo *nm* **1** VÍNCULO : link, bond **2** : bow, ribbon **3** : lasso, lariat

le *pron* **1** : to her, to him, to it ⟨¿qué le dijiste? : what did you tell him?⟩ **2** : from her, from him, from it ⟨el ladrón le robó la cartera : the thief stole his wallet⟩ **3** : for her, for him, for it ⟨cómprale flores a tu mamá : buy your mom some flowers⟩ **4** (*formal*) : to you, for you ⟨le traje un regalo : I brought you a gift⟩

leal *adj* : loyal, faithful — **lealmente** *adv*

lealtad *nf* : loyalty, allegiance

lebrel *nm* : hound

lección *nf, pl* **lecciones** : lesson

lechada *nf* **1** : whitewash **2** : grout

lechal *adj* : suckling, unweaned ⟨cordero lechal : suckling lamb⟩

leche *nf* **1** : milk ⟨leche en polvo : powdered milk⟩ ⟨leche de magnesia : milk of magnesia⟩ **2** : milky sap

lechera *nf* **1** : milk jug **2** : dairymaid *f*

lechería *nf* : dairy store

lechero[1], -ra *adj* : dairy

lechero[2], -ra *n* : milkman *m*, milk dealer

lecho *nm* **1** : bed ⟨un lecho de rosas : a bed of roses⟩ ⟨lecho de muerte : deathbed⟩ **2** : riverbed **3** : layer, stratum (in geology)

lechón, -chona *n, mpl* **lechones** : suckling pig

lechoso, -sa *adj* : milky

lechuga *nf* : lettuce

lechuza *nf* BÚHO : owl, barn owl

lectivo, -va *adj* : school ⟨año lectivo : school year⟩

lector[1], -tora *adj* : reading ⟨nivel lector : reading level⟩

lector[2], -tora *n* : reader

lector[3] *nm* : scanner, reader ⟨lector óptico : optical scanner⟩

lectura *nf* **1** : reading **2** : reading matter

leer {20} *v* : to read

legación *nf, pl* **-ciones** : legation

legado *nm* **1** : legacy, bequest **2** : legate, emissary

legajo *nm* : dossier, file

legal *adj* : legal, lawful — **legalmente** *adv*

legalidad *nf* : legality, lawfulness

legalista *adj* : legalistic

legalizar {21} *vt* : to legalize — **legalización** *nf*

legar {52} *vt* **1** : to bequeath, to hand down **2** DELEGAR : to delegate

legendario, -ria *adj* : legendary

legible *adj* : legible

legión *nf, pl* **legiones** : legion

legionario, -ria *n* : legionnaire

legislación *nf* **1** : legislation, lawmaking **2** : laws *pl*, legislation

legislador[1], -dora *adj* : legislative

legislador[2], -dora *n* : legislator

legislar *vi* : to legislate

legislativo, -va *adj* : legislative

legislatura *nf* **1** : legislature **2** : term of office

legitimar *vt* **1** : to legitimize **2** : to authenticate — **legitimación** *nf*

legitimidad *nf* : legitimacy

legítimo, -ma *adj* **1** : legitimate **2** : genuine, authentic — **legítimamente** *adv*

lego[1], -ga *adj* **1** : secular, lay **2** : uninformed, ignorant

lego[2], -ga *n* : layperson, layman *m*, laywoman *f*

legua *nf* **1** : league **2 notarse a leguas** : to be very obvious ⟨se notaba a leguas : you could tell from a mile away⟩

legue, etc. → **legar**

legumbre *nf* **1** HORTALIZA : vegetable **2** : legume

leíble *adj* : readable

leída *nf* : reading, read ⟨de una leída : in one reading, at one go⟩

leído[1] *pp* → **leer**

leído[2], **-da** *adj* : well-read

lejanía *nf* : remoteness, distance

lejano, -na *adj* : remote, distant, far away

lejía *nf* **1** : lye **2** : bleach

lejos *adv* **1** : far away, distant ⟨a lo lejos : in the distance, far off⟩ ⟨desde lejos : from a distance⟩ **2** : long ago, a long way off ⟨está lejos de los 50 años : he's a long way from 50 years old⟩ **3 de ~** : by far ⟨esta decisión fue de lejos la más fácil : this decision was by far the easiest⟩ **4 ~ de** : far from ⟨lejos de ser reprobado, recibió una nota de B : far from failing, he got a B⟩

lelo, -la *adj* : silly, stupid

lema *nm* : motto, slogan

lencería *nf* : lingerie

lengua *nf* **1** : tongue ⟨morderse la lengua : to bite one's tongue⟩ **2** IDIOMA : language ⟨lengua materna : mother tongue, native language⟩ ⟨lengua muerta : dead language⟩

lenguado *nm* : sole, flounder

lenguaje *nm* **1** : language, speech **2 lenguaje gestual** *or* **lenguaje de gestos** : sign language **3 lenguaje de programación** : programming language

lengüeta *nf* **1** : tongue (of a shoe), tab, flap **2** : reed (of a musical instrument) **3** : barb, point

lengüetada *nf* **beber a lengüetadas** : to lap (up)

lenidad *nf* : leniency

lenitivo, -va *adj* : soothing

lente *nmf* **1** : lens ⟨lentes de contacto : contact lenses⟩ **2 lentes** *nmpl* ANTEOJOS : eyeglasses ⟨lentes de sol : sunglasses⟩

lenteja *nf* : lentil

lentejuela *nf* : sequin, spangle

lentitud *nf* : slowness

lento[1] *adv* DESPACIO : slowly

lento[2], **-ta** *adj* **1** : slow **2** : slow-witted, dull — **lentamente** *adv*

leña *nf* : wood, firewood

leñador, -dora *n* : lumberjack, woodcutter

leñera *nf* : woodshed

leño *nm* : log

leñoso, -sa *adj* : woody

Leo *nmf* : Leo

león, -ona *n, mpl* **leones** **1** : lion, lioness *f* **2** (*in various countries*) : puma, cougar

leonado, -da *adj* : tawny

leonino, -na *adj* **1** : leonine **2** : one-sided, unfair

leopardo *nm* : leopard

leotardo *nm* MALLA : leotard, tights *pl*

leperada *nf Mex* : obscenity

lépero, -ra *adj Mex* : vulgar, coarse

lepra *nf* : leprosy

leproso[1], **-sa** *adj* : leprous

leproso[2], **-sa** *n* : leper

lerdo, -da *adj* **1** : clumsy **2** : dull, oafish, slow-witted

les *pron* **1** : to them ⟨dales una propina : give them a tip⟩ **2** : from them ⟨se les privó de su herencia : they were deprived of their inheritance⟩ **3** : for them ⟨les hice sus tareas : I did their homework for them⟩ **4** : to you *pl*, for you *pl* ⟨les compré un regalo : I bought you all a present⟩

lesbiana *nf* : lesbian — **lesbiano, -na** *adj*

lesbianismo *nm* : lesbianism

lesión *nf, pl* **lesiones** HERIDA : lesion, wound, injury ⟨una lesión grave : a serious injury⟩

lesionado, -da *adj* HERIDO : injured, wounded

lesionar *vt* : to injure, to wound — **lesionarse** *vr* : to hurt oneself

lesivo, -va *adj* : harmful, damaging

letal *adj* MORTÍFERO : deadly, lethal — **letalmente** *adv*

letanía *nf* **1** : litany **2** *fam* : spiel, song and dance

letárgico, -ca *adj* : lethargic

letargo *nm* : lethargy, torpor

letón[1], **-tona** *adj & n, mpl* **letones** : Latvian

letón[2] *nm* : Latvian (language)

letra *nf* **1** : letter **2** CALIGRAFÍA : handwriting, lettering **3** : lyrics *pl* **4 al pie de la letra** : word for word, by the book **5 letras** *nfpl* : arts (in education)

letrado[1], **-da** *adj* ERUDITO : learned, erudite

letrado[2], **-da** *n* : attorney-at-law, lawyer

letrero *nm* RÓTULO : sign, notice

letrina *nf* : latrine

letrista *nmf* : lyricist, songwriter

leucemia *nf* : leukemia

leva *nf* : cam

levadizo, -za *adj* **1** : liftable **2 puente levadizo** : drawbridge

levadura *nf* **1** : yeast, leavening **2 levadura en polvo** : baking powder

levantamiento *nm* **1** ALZAMIENTO : uprising **2** : raising, lifting ⟨levantamiento de pesas : weight lifting⟩

levantar *vt* **1** ALZAR : to lift, to raise **2** : to put up, to erect **3** : to call off, to adjourn **4** : to give rise to, to arouse ⟨levantar sospechas : to arouse suspicion⟩ — **levantarse** *vr* **1** : to rise, to stand up **2** : to get out of bed

levar *vt* **levar anclas** : to weigh anchor

leve *adj* **1** : light, slight **2** : trivial, unimportant — **levemente** *adv*

levedad *nf* : lightness

levemente *adv* LIGERAMENTE : lightly, softly

leviatán *nm, pl* **-tanes** : leviathan

léxico[1], **-ca** *adj* : lexical

léxico[2] *nm* : lexicon, glossary

lexicografía *nf* : lexicography

lexicográfico, -ca *adj* : lexicographical, lexicographic

lexicógrafo, -fa *n* : lexicographer

ley *nf* **1** : law ⟨fuera de la ley : outside the law⟩ ⟨la ley de gravedad : the law of gravity⟩ **2** : purity (of metals) ⟨oro de ley : pure gold⟩

leyenda *nf* **1** : legend **2** : caption, inscription

leyó, etc. → **leer**

liar {85} *vt* **1** ATAR : to bind, to tie (up) **2** : to roll (a cigarette) **3** : to confuse — **liarse** *vr* : to get mixed up

libanés, -nesa *adj & n, mpl* **-neses** : Lebanese

libar *vt* **1** : to suck (nectar) **2** : to sip, to swig (liquor, etc.)

libelo *nm* **1** : libel, lampoon **2** : petition (in court)

libélula *nf* : dragonfly

liberación *nf, pl* **-ciones** : liberation, deliverance ⟨liberación de la mujer : women's liberation⟩

liberado, -da *adj* **1** : liberated ⟨una mujer liberada : a liberated woman⟩ **2** : freed, delivered

liberal *adj & nmf* : liberal

liberalidad *nf* : generosity, liberality

liberalismo *nm* : liberalism

liberalizar {21} *vt* : to liberalize — **liberalización** *nf*

liberar *vt* : to liberate, to free — **liberarse** *vr* : to get free of

liberiano, -na *adj & n* : Liberian

libertad *nf* **1** : freedom, liberty ⟨tomarse la libertad de : to take the liberty of⟩ **2 libertad bajo fianza** : bail **3 libertad condicional** : parole

libertador[1], **-dora** *adj* : liberating

libertador[2], **-dora** *n* : liberator

libertar *vt* LIBRAR : to set free

libertario, -ria *adj & n* : libertarian

libertinaje *nm* : licentiousness, dissipation

libertino[1], **-na** *adj* : licentious, dissolute

libertino[2], **-na** *n* : libertine

libidinoso, -sa *adj* : lustful, lewd

libido *nf* : libido

libio, -bia *adj & n* : Libyan

libra *nf* **1** : pound **2 libra esterlina** : pound sterling

Libra *nmf* : Libra

libramiento *nm* **1** : liberating, freeing **2** LIBRANZA : order of payment **3** *Mex* : beltway

libranza *nf* : order of payment

librar *vt* **1** LIBERTAR : to deliver, to set free **2** : to wage ⟨librar batalla : to do battle⟩ **3** : to issue ⟨librar una orden : to issue an order⟩ — **librarse** *vr* **~ de** : to free oneself from, to get out of

libre[1] *adj* **1** : free ⟨un país libre : a free country⟩ ⟨libre de : free from, exempt from⟩ ⟨libre albedrío : free will⟩ **2** DESOCUPADO : vacant **3 día libre** : day off

libre[2] *nm Mex* : taxi

librea *nf* : livery

librecambio *nm* : free trade

libremente *adv* : freely

librería *nf* : bookstore

librero[1], **-ra** *n* : bookseller

librero[2] *nm Mex* : bookcase

libresco, -ca *adj* : bookish

libreta *nf* CUADERNO : notebook

libretista *nmf* **1** : librettist **2** : scriptwriter

libreto *nm* : libretto, script

libro *nm* **1** : book ⟨libro de texto : textbook⟩ **2 libros** *nmpl* : books (in bookkeeping), accounts ⟨llevar los libros : to keep the books⟩

licencia *nf* **1** : permission **2** : leave, leave of absence **3** : permit, license ⟨licencia de conducir : driver's license⟩

licenciado, -da *n* **1** : university graduate **2** ABOGADO : lawyer

licenciar *vt* **1** : to license, to permit, to allow **2** : to discharge **3** : to grant a university degree to — **licenciarse** *vr* : to graduate

licenciatura *nf* **1** : college degree **2** : course of study (at a college or university)

licencioso, -sa *adj* : licentious, lewd

liceo *nm* : secondary school, high school

licitación *nf, pl* **-ciones** : bid, bidding

licitar *vt* : to bid on

lícito, -ta *adj* **1** : lawful, licit **2** JUSTO : just, fair

licor *nm* **1** : liquor **2** : liqueur

licorera *nf* : decanter

licuado *nm* BATIDO : milk shake

licuadora *nf* : blender

licuar {3} *vt* : to liquefy — **licuarse** *vr*

lid *nf* **1** : fight, combat **2** : argument, dispute **3 lides** *nfpl* : matters, affairs **4 en buena lid** : fair and square

líder[1] *adj* : leading, foremost

líder[2] *nmf* : leader

liderar *vt* DIRIGIR : to lead, to head

liderato *nm* : leadership, leading

liderazgo → **liderato**

lidiar *vt* : to fight — *vi* BATALLAR, LUCHAR : to struggle, to battle, to wrestle

liebre *nf* : hare

liendre *nf* : nit

lienzo *nm* **1** : linen **2** : canvas, painting **3** : stretch of wall or fencing

liga *nf* **1** ASOCIACIÓN : league **2** GOMITA : rubber band **3** : garter

ligado, -da *adj* : linked, connected

ligadura *nf* **1** ATADURA : tie, bond **2** : ligature

ligamento *nm* : ligament

ligar {52} *vt* : to bind, to tie (up)

ligeramente *adv* **1** : slightly **2** LEVEMENTE : lightly, gently **3** : casually, flippantly

ligereza *nf* **1** : lightness **2** : flippancy **3** : agility

ligero, -ra *adj* **1** : light, lightweight **2** : slight, minor **3** : agile, quick **4** : lighthearted, superficial

lignito *nm* : lignite

ligue, etc. → **ligar**
lija *nf or* **papel de lija** : sandpaper
lijar *vt* : to sand
lila[1] *adj* : lilac, light purple
lila[2] *nf* : lilac
lima *nf* **1** : lime (fruit) **2** : file ⟨lima de uñas : nail file⟩
limadora *nf* : polisher
limar *vt* **1** : to file **2** : to polish, to put the final touch on **3** : to smooth over ⟨limar las diferencias : to iron out differences⟩
limbo *nm* **1** : limbo **2** : limb (in botany and astronomy)
limeño[1], **-ña** *adj* : of or from Lima, Peru
limeño[2], **-ña** *n* : person from Lima, Peru
limero *nm* : lime tree
limitación *nf, pl* **-ciones** **1** : limitation **2** : limit, restriction ⟨sin limitación : unlimited⟩
limitado, -da *adj* **1** RESTRINGIDO : limited **2** : dull, slow-witted
limitar *vt* RESTRINGIR : to limit, to restrict — *vi* **~ con** : to border on — **limitarse** *vr* **~ a** : to limit oneself to
límite *nm* **1** : boundary, border **2** : limit ⟨el límite de mi paciencia : the limit of my patience⟩ ⟨límite de velocidad : speed limit⟩ **3 fecha límite** : deadline
limítrofe *adj* LINDANTE, LINDERO : bordering, adjoining
limo *nm* : slime, mud
limón *nm, pl* **limones** **1** : lemon **2** : lemon tree **3 limón verde** *Mex* : lime
limonada *nf* : lemonade
limosna *nf* : alms, charity
limosnear *vi* : to beg (for alms)
limosnero, -ra *n* MENDIGO : beggar
limoso, -sa *adj* : slimy
limpiabotas *nmfs & pl* : bootblack
limpiador[1], **-dora** *adj* : cleaning
limpiador[2], **-dora** *n* : cleaning person, cleaner
limpiamente *adv* : cleanly, honestly, fairly
limpiaparabrisas *nms & pl* : windshield wiper
limpiar *vt* **1** : to clean, to cleanse **2** : to clean up, to remove defects **3** *fam* : to clean out (in a game) **4** *fam* : to swipe, to pinch — *vi* : to clean — **limpiarse** *vr*
limpiavidrios *nmfs & pl Mex* : windshield wiper
límpido, -da *adj* : limpid
limpieza *nf* **1** : cleanliness, tidiness **2** : cleaning **3** HONRADEZ : integrity, honesty **4** DESTREZA : skill, dexterity
limpio[1] *adv* : fairly
limpio[2], **-pia** *adj* **1** : clean, neat **2** : honest ⟨un juego limpio : a fair game⟩ **3** : free ⟨limpio de impurezas : pure, free from impurities⟩ **4** : clear, net ⟨ganancia limpia : clear profit⟩
limusina *nf* : limousine
linaje *nm* ABOLENGO : lineage, ancestry
linaza *nf* : linseed
lince *nm* : lynx
linchamiento *nm* : lynching
linchar *vt* : to lynch
lindante *adj* LIMÍTROFE, LINDERO : bordering, adjoining
lindar *vi* **1 ~ con** : to border, to skirt **2 ~ con** BORDEAR : to border on, to verge on
linde *nmf* : boundary, limit
lindero[1], **-ra** *adj* LIMÍTROFE, LINDANTE : bordering, adjoining
lindero[2] *nm* : boundary, limit
lindeza *nf* **1** : prettiness **2** : clever remark **3 lindezas** *nfpl, (used ironically)* : insults
lindo[1] *adv* **1** : beautifully, wonderfully ⟨canta lindo tu mujer : your wife sings beautifully⟩ **2 de lo lindo** : a lot, a great deal ⟨los zancudos nos picaban de lo lindo : the mosquitoes were biting away at us⟩
lindo[2], **-da** *adj* **1** BONITO : pretty, lovely **2** MONO : cute
línea *nf* **1** : line ⟨línea divisoria : dividing line⟩ ⟨línea de banda : sideline⟩ **2** : line, course, position ⟨línea de conducta : course of action⟩ ⟨en líneas generales : in general terms, along general lines⟩ **3** : line, service ⟨línea aérea : airline⟩ ⟨línea telefónica : telephone line⟩
lineal *adj* : linear
linfa *nf* : lymph
linfático, -ca *adj* : lymphatic
lingote *nm* : ingot
lingüista *nmf* : linguist
lingüística *nf* : linguistics
lingüístico, -ca *adj* : linguistic
linimento *nm* : liniment
lino *nm* **1** : linen **2** : flax
linóleo *nm* : linoleum
linterna *nf* **1** : lantern **2** : flashlight
lío *nm fam* **1** : confusion, mess **2** : hassle, trouble, jam ⟨meterse en un lío : to get into a jam⟩ **3** : affair, liaison
liofilizar {21} *vt* : to freeze-dry
lioso, -sa *adj fam* **1** : confusing, muddled **2** : troublemaking
liquen *nm* : lichen
liquidación *nf, pl* **-ciones** **1** : liquidation **2** : clearance sale **3** : settlement, payment
liquidar *vt* **1** : to liquefy **2** : to liquidate **3** : to settle, to pay off **4** *fam* : to rub out, to kill
liquidez *nf, pl* **-deces** : liquidity
líquido[1], **-da** *adj* **1** : liquid, fluid **2** : net ⟨ingresos líquidos : net income⟩
líquido[2] *nm* **1** : liquid, fluid ⟨líquido de frenos : brake fluid⟩ **2** : ready cash, liquid assets
lira *nf* : lyre
lírica *nf* : lyric poetry
lírico, -ca *adj* : lyric, lyrical
lirio *nm* **1** : iris **2 lirio de los valles** MUGUETE : lily of the valley
lirismo *nm* : lyricism
lirón *nm, pl* **lirones** : dormouse
lisiado[1], **-da** *adj* : disabled, crippled

lisiado[2], **-da** *n* : disabled person, cripple

lisiar *vt* : to cripple, to disable — **lisiarse** *vr*

liso, **-sa** *adj* **1** : smooth **2** : flat **3** : straight ⟨pelo liso : straight hair⟩ **4** : plain, unadorned ⟨liso y llano : plain and simple⟩

lisonja *nf* : flattery

lisonjear *vt* ADULAR : to flatter

lista *nf* **1** : list **2** : roster, roll ⟨pasar lista : to take attendance⟩ **3** : stripe, strip **4** : menu

listado[1], **-da** *adj* : striped

listado[2] *nm* : listing

listar *vt* : to list

listeza *nf* : smartness, alertness

listo, **-ta** *adj* **1** DISPUESTO, PREPARADO : ready ⟨¿estás listo? : are you ready?⟩ **2** : clever, smart

listón *nm, pl* **listones 1** : ribbon **2** : strip (of wood), lath **3** : high bar (in sports)

lisura *nf* : smoothness

litera *nf* : bunk bed, berth

literal *adj* : literal — **literalmente** *adv*

literario, **-ria** *adj* : literary

literato, **-ta** *n* : writer, author

literatura *nf* : literature

litigante *adj & nmf* : litigant

litigar {52} *vi* : to litigate, to be in litigation

litigio *nm* **1** : litigation, lawsuit **2 en ~** : in dispute

litigioso, **-sa** *adj* : litigious

litio *nm* : lithium

litografía *nf* **1** : lithography **2** : lithograph

litógrafo, **-fa** *n* : lithographer

litoral[1] *adj* : coastal

litoral[2] *nm* : shore, seaboard

litosfera *nf* : lithosphere

litro *nm* : liter

lituano[1], **-na** *adj & n* : Lithuanian

lituano[2] *nm* : Lithuanian (language)

liturgia *nf* : liturgy

litúrgico, **-ca** *adj* : liturgical — **litúrgicamente** *adv*

liviandad *nf* LIGEREZA : lightness

liviano, **-na** *adj* **1** : light, slight **2** INCONSTANTE : fickle

lividez *nf* PALIDEZ : pallor

lívido, **-da** *adj* **1** AMORATADO : livid **2** PÁLIDO : pallid, extremely pale

living *nm* : living room

llaga *nf* : sore, wound

llama *nf* **1** : flame **2** : llama

llamada *nf* : call ⟨llamada a larga distancia : long-distance call⟩ ⟨llamada al orden : call to order⟩

llamado[1], **-da** *adj* : named, called ⟨una mujer llamada Rosa : a woman called Rosa⟩

llamado[2] → **llamamiento**

llamador *nm* : door knocker

llamamiento *nm* : call, appeal

llamar *vt* **1** : to name, to call **2** : to call, to summon **3** : to phone, to call up — **llamarse** *vr* : to be called, to be named ⟨¿cómo te llamas? : what's your name?⟩

llamarada *nf* **1** : flare-up, sudden blaze **2** : flushing (of the face)

llamativo, **-va** *adj* : flashy, showy, striking

llameante *adj* : flaming, blazing

llamear *vi* : to flame, to blaze

llana *nf* **1** : trowel **2** → **llano**[2]

llanamente *adv* : simply, plainly, straightforwardly

llaneza *nf* : simplicity, naturalness

llano[1], **-na** *adj* **1** : even, flat **2** : frank, open **3** LISO : plain, simple

llano[2] *nm* : plain

llanta *nf* **1** NEUMÁTICO : tire **2** : rim

llantén *nm, pl* **llantenes** : plantain (weed)

llanto *nm* : crying, weeping

llanura *nf* : plain, prairie

llave *nf* **1** : key **2** : faucet **3** INTERRUPTOR : switch **4** : brace (punctuation mark) **5 llave inglesa** : monkey wrench

llavero *nm* : key chain, key ring

llegada *nf* : arrival

llegar {52} *vi* **1** : to arrive, to come **2 ~ a** : to arrive at, to reach, to amount to **3 ~ a** : to manage to ⟨llegó a terminar la novela : she managed to finish the novel⟩ **4 llegar a ser** : to become ⟨llegó a ser un miembro permanente : he became a permanent member⟩

llegue, **etc.** → **llegar**

llenar *vt* **1** : to fill, to fill up, to fill in **2** : to meet, to fulfill ⟨los regalos no llenaron sus expectativas : the gifts did not meet her expectations⟩ — **llenarse** *vr* : to fill up, to become full

llenito, **-ta** *adj fam* REGORDETE : chubby, plump

lleno[1], **-na** *adj* **1** : full, filled **2 de ~** : completely, fully **3 estar lleno de sí mismo** : to be full of oneself

lleno[2] *nm* **1** *fam* : plenty, abundance **2** : full house, sellout

llevadero, **-ra** *adj* : bearable

llevar *vt* **1** : to take away, to carry ⟨me gusta, me lo llevo : I like it, I'll take it⟩ **2** : to wear **3** : to take, to lead ⟨llevamos a Pedro al cine : we took Pedro to the movies⟩ **4 llevar a cabo** : to carry out **5 llevar adelante** : to carry on, to keep going — *vi* : to lead ⟨un problema lleva al otro : one problem leads to another⟩ — *v aux* : to have ⟨llevo mucho tiempo buscándolo : I've been looking for it for a long time⟩ ⟨lleva leído medio libro : he's halfway through the book⟩ — **llevarse** *vr* **1** : to take away, to carry off **2** : to get along ⟨siempre nos llevábamos bien : we always got along well⟩

llorar *vi* : to cry, to weep — *vt* : to mourn, to bewail

lloriquear *vi* : to whimper, to whine

lloriqueo *nm* : whimpering, whining

llorón, **-rona** *n, mpl* **llorones** : crybaby, whiner

lloroso, **-sa** *adj* : tearful, sad

llovedizo, -za *adj* : rain ⟨agua llovediza : rainwater⟩

llover {47} *v impers* : to rain ⟨está lloviendo : it's raining⟩ ⟨llover a cántaros : to rain cats and dogs⟩ — *vi* : to rain down, to shower ⟨le llovieron regalos : he was showered with gifts⟩

llovizna *nf* : drizzle, sprinkle

lloviznar *v impers* : to drizzle, to sprinkle

llueve, etc. → **llover**

lluvia *nf* **1** : rain, rainfall **2** : barrage, shower

lluvioso, -sa *adj* : rainy

lo[1] *pron* **1** : him, it ⟨lo vi ayer : I saw him yesterday⟩ ⟨lo entiendo : I understand it⟩ ⟨no lo creo : I don't believe so⟩ **2** (*formal, masculine*) : you ⟨disculpe, señor, no lo oí : excuse me sir, I didn't hear you⟩ **3 lo que** : what, that which ⟨eso es lo que más le gusta : that's what he likes the most⟩

lo[2] *art* **1** : the ⟨lo mejor : the best, the best thing⟩ **2** : how ⟨sé lo bueno que eres : I know how good you are⟩

loa *nf* : praise

loable *adj* : laudable, praiseworthy — **loablemente** *adv*

loar *vt* : to praise, to laud

lobato, -ta *n* : wolf cub

lobby *nm* : lobby, pressure group

lobo, -ba *n* : wolf

lóbrego, -ga *adj* SOMBRÍO : gloomy, dark

lobulado, -da *adj* : lobed

lóbulo *nm* : lobe ⟨lóbulo de la oreja : earlobe⟩

locación *nf, pl* **-ciones** **1** : location (in moviemaking) **2** *Mex* : place

local[1] *adj* : local — **localmente** *adv*

local[2] *nm* : premises *pl*

localidad *nf* : town, locality

localización *nf, pl* **-ciones** **1** : locating, localization **2** : location

localizar {21} *vt* **1** UBICAR : to locate, to find **2** : to localize — **localizarse** *vr* UBICARSE : to be located ⟨se localiza en el séptimo piso : it is located on the seventh floor⟩

locatario, -ria *n* : tenant

loción *nf, pl* **lociones** : lotion

lócker *nm, pl* **lóckers** : locker

loco[1], **-ca** *adj* **1** DEMENTE : crazy, insane, mad **2 a lo loco** : wildly, recklessly **3 volverse loco** : to go mad

loco[2], **-ca** *n* **1** : crazy person, lunatic **2 hacerse el loco** : to act the fool

locomoción *nf, pl* **-ciones** : locomotion

locomotor, -tora *adj* : locomotive

locomotora *nf* **1** : locomotive **2** : driving force

locuacidad *nf* : loquacity, talkativeness

locuaz *adj, pl* **locuaces** : loquacious, talkative

locución *nf, pl* **-ciones** : locution, phrase ⟨locución adverbial : adverbial phrase⟩

locura *nf* **1** : insanity, madness **2** : crazy thing, folly

locutor, -tora *n* : announcer

lodazal *nm* : bog, quagmire

lodo *nm* BARRO : mud, mire

lodoso, -sa *adj* : muddy

logaritmo *nm* : logarithm

logia *nf* : lodge ⟨logia masónica : Masonic lodge⟩

lógica *nf* : logic

lógico, -ca *adj* : logical — **lógicamente** *adv*

logística *nf* : logistics *pl*

logístico, -ca *adj* : logistic, logistical

logo → **logotipo**

logotipo *nm* : logo

logrado, -da *adj* : successful, well done

lograr *vt* **1** : to get, to obtain **2** : to achieve, to attain — **lograrse** *vr* : to be successful

logro *nm* : achievement, attainment

loma *nf* : hill, hillock

lombriz *nf, pl* **lombrices** : worm ⟨lombriz de tierra : earthworm, night crawler⟩ ⟨lombriz solitaria : tapeworm⟩ ⟨tener lombrices : to have worms⟩

lomo *nm* **1** : back (of an animal) **2** : loin ⟨lomo de cerdo : pork loin⟩ **3** : spine (of a book) **4** : blunt edge (of a knife)

lona *nf* : canvas

loncha *nf* LONJA, REBANADA : slice

lonche *nm* **1** ALMUERZO : lunch **2** *Mex* : submarine sandwich

lonchería *nf Mex* : luncheonette

londinense[1] *adj* : of or from London

londinense[2] *nmf* : Londoner

longaniza *nf* : spicy pork sausage

longevidad *nf* : longevity

longevo, -va *adj* : long-lived

longitud *nf* **1** LARGO : length ⟨longitud de onda : wavelength⟩ **2** : longitude

longitudinal *adj* : longitudinal

lonja *nf* LONCHA, REBANADA : slice

lontananza *nf* : background ⟨en lontananza : in the distance, far away⟩

lord *nm, pl* **lores** (*title in England*) : lord

loro *nm* : parrot

los[1], **las** *pron* **1** : them ⟨hice galletas y se las di a los nuevos vecinos : I made cookies and gave them to the new neighbors⟩ **2** : you ⟨voy a llevarlos a los dos : I am going to take both of you⟩ **3 los que, las que** : those, who, the ones ⟨los que van a cantar deben venir temprano : those who are singing must come early⟩ **4** (*used with* **haber**) ⟨los hay en varios colores : they come in various colors⟩

los[2] *art* → **el**[2]

losa *nf* : flagstone, paving stone

loseta *nf* BALDOSA : floor tile

lote *nm* **1** : part, share **2** : batch, lot **3** : plot of land, lot

lotería *nf* : lottery

loto *nm* : lotus

loza *nf* **1** : crockery, earthenware **2** : china

lozanía *nf* **1** : healthiness, robustness **2** : luxuriance, lushness

lozano, -na *adj* **1** : robust, healthy-looking ⟨un rostro lozano : a smooth, fresh face⟩ **2** : lush, luxuriant
LSD *nm* : LSD
lubricante[1] *adj* : lubricating
lubricante[2] *nm* : lubricant
lubricar {72} *vt* : to lubricate, to oil — **lubricación** *nf*
lucero *nm* : bright star ⟨lucero del alba : morning star⟩
lucha *nf* **1** : struggle, fight **2** : wrestling
luchador, -dora *n* **1** : fighter **2** : wrestler
luchar *vi* **1** : to fight, to struggle **2** : to wrestle
luchón, -chona *adj, mpl* **luchones** *Mex* : industrious, hardworking
lucidez *nf, pl* **-deces** : lucidity, clarity
lucido, -da *adj* MAGNÍFICO : magnificent, splendid
lúcido, -da *adj* : lucid
luciérnaga *nf* : firefly, glowworm
lucimiento *nm* **1** : brilliance, splendor, sparkle **2** : triumph, success ⟨salir con lucimiento : to succeed with flying colors⟩
lucio *nm* : pike (fish)
lucir {45} *vi* **1** : to shine **2** : to look good, to stand out **3** : to seem, to appear ⟨ahora luce contento : he looks happy now⟩ — *vt* **1** : to wear, to sport **2** : to flaunt, to show off — **lucirse** *vr* **1** : to distinguish oneself, to excel **2** : to show off
lucrarse *vr* : to make a profit
lucrativo, -va *adj* : lucrative, profitable — **lucrativamente** *adv*
lucro *nm* GANANCIA : profit, gain
luctuoso, -sa *adj* : mournful, tragic
luego[1] *adv* **1** DESPUÉS : then, afterwards **2** : later (on) **3 desde ~** : of course **4 ¡hasta luego!** : see you later! **5 luego que** : as soon as **6 luego luego** *Mex fam* : right away, immediately
luego[2] *conj* : therefore ⟨pienso, luego existo : I think, therefore I am⟩
lugar *nm* **1** : place, position ⟨se llevó el primer lugar en su división : she took first place in her division⟩ **2** ESPACIO : space, room **3 dar lugar a** : to give rise to, to lead to **4 en lugar de** : instead of **5 lugar común** : cliché, platitude **6 tener lugar** : to take place
lugareño[1], **-ña** *adj* : village, rural
lugareño[2], **-ña** *n* : villager
lugarteniente *nmf* : lieutenant, deputy
lúgubre *adj* : gloomy, lugubrious
lujo *nm* **1** : luxury **2 de ~** : deluxe
lujoso, -sa *adj* : luxurious
lujuria *nf* : lust, lechery
lujurioso, -sa *adj* : lustful, lecherous
lumbago *nm* : lumbago
lumbar *adj* : lumbar
lumbre *nf* **1** FUEGO : fire **2** : brilliance, splendor **3 poner en la lumbre** : to put on the stove, to warm up
lumbrera *nf* **1** : skylight **2** : vent, port **3** : brilliant person, luminary
luminaria *nf* **1** : altar lamp **2** LUMBRERA : luminary, celebrity
luminiscencia *nf* : luminescence — **luminiscente** *adj*
luminosidad *nf* : luminosity, brightness
luminoso, -sa *adj* : shining, luminous
luna *nf* **1** : moon **2 luna de miel** : honeymoon
lunar[1] *adj* : lunar
lunar[2] *nm* **1** : mole, beauty spot **2** : defect, blemish **3** : polka dot
lunático, -ca *adj & n* : lunatic
lunes *nms & pl* : Monday
luneta *nf* **1** : lens (of eyeglasses) **2** : windshield (of an automobile) **3** : crescent
lupa *nf* : magnifying glass
lúpulo *nm* : hops (plant)
lustrar *vt* : to shine, to polish
lustre *nm* **1** BRILLO : luster, shine **2** : glory, distinction
lustroso, -sa *adj* BRILLOSO : lustrous, shiny
luto *nm* : mourning ⟨estar de luto : to be in mourning⟩
luz *nf, pl* **luces 1** : light **2** : lighting **3** *fam* : electricity **4** : window, opening **5** : light, lamp **6** : span, spread (between supports) **7 a la luz de** : in light of **8 dar a luz** : to give birth **9 traje de luces** : matador's costume
luzca, etc. → **lucir**

M

m *nf* : thirteenth letter of the Spanish alphabet
macabro, -bra *adj* : macabre
macaco[1], **-ca** *adj* : ugly, misshapen
macaco[2], **-ca** *n* : macaque
macadán *nm, pl* **-danes** : macadam
macana *nf* **1** : club, cudgel **2** *fam* : nonsense, silliness **3** *fam* : lie, fib
macanudo, -da *adj fam* : great, fantastic
macarrón *nm, pl* **-rrones 1** : macaroon **2 macarrones** *nmpl* : macaroni
maceta *nf* **1** : flowerpot **2** : mallet **3** *Mex fam* : head
macetero *nm* **1** : plant stand **2** TIESTO : flowerpot, planter
machacar {72} *vt* **1** : to crush, to grind **2** : to beat, to pound — *vi* : to insist, to go on (about)
machacón, -cona *adj, mpl* **-cones** : insistent, tiresome
machete *nm* : machete
machetear *vt* : to hack with a machete — *vi Mex fam* : to plod, to work tirelessly
machismo *nm* **1** : machismo **2** : male chauvinism
machista *nm* : male chauvinist

macho[1] *adj* **1** : male **2** : macho, virile, tough
macho[2] *nm* **1** : male **2** : he-man
machote *nm* **1** *fam* : tough guy, he-man **2** *CA, Mex* : rough draft, model **3** *Mex* : blank form
machucar {72} *vt* **1** : to pound, to beat, to crush **2** : to bruise
machucón *nm, pl* **-cones** **1** MORETÓN : bruise **2** : smashing, pounding
macilento, -ta *adj* : gaunt, wan
macis *nm* : mace (spice)
macizo, -za *adj* **1** : solid ⟨oro macizo : solid gold⟩ **2** : strong, strapping **3** : massive
macrocosmo *nm* : macrocosm
mácula *nf* : blemish, stain
madeja *nf* **1** : skein, hank **2** : tangle (of hair)
madera *nf* **1** : wood **2** : lumber, timber **3 madera dura** *or* **madera noble** : hardwood
maderero, -ra *adj* : timber, lumber
madero *nm* : piece of lumber, plank
madrastra *nf* : stepmother
madrazo *nm Mex fam* : punch, blow ⟨se agarraron a madrazos : they beat each other up⟩
madre *nf* **1** : mother **2 madre política** : mother-in-law **3 la Madre Patria** : the mother country (said of Spain)
madrear *vt Mex fam* : to beat up
madreperla *nf* NÁCAR : mother-of-pearl
madreselva *nf* : honeysuckle
madriguera *nf* : burrow, den, lair
madrileño[1], **-ña** *adj* : of or from Madrid
madrileño[2], **-ña** *n* : person from Madrid
madrina *nf* **1** : godmother **2** : bridesmaid **3** : sponsor
madrugada *nf* **1** : early morning, wee hours **2** ALBA : dawn, daybreak
madrugador, -dora *n* : early riser
madrugar {52} *vi* **1** : to get up early **2** : to get a head start
madurar *v* **1** : to ripen **2** : to mature
madurez *nf, pl* **-reces** **1** : maturity **2** : ripeness
maduro, -ra *adj* **1** : mature **2** : ripe
maestría *nf* **1** : mastery, skill **2** : master's degree
maestro[1], **-tra** *adj* **1** : masterly, skilled **2** : chief, main **3** : trained ⟨un elefante maestro : a trained elephant⟩
maestro[2], **-tra** *n* **1** : teacher (in grammar school) **2** : expert, master **3** : maestro
Mafia *nf* : Mafia
mafioso, -sa *n* : mafioso, gangster
magdalena *nf* : bun, muffin
magenta *adj & n* : magenta
magia *nf* : magic
mágico, -ca *adj* : magic, magical — **mágicamente** *adv*
magisterio *nm* **1** : teaching **2** : teachers *pl,* teaching profession
magistrado, -da *n* : magistrate, judge
magistral *adj* **1** : masterful, skillful **2** : magisterial
magistralmente *adv* : masterfully, brilliantly
magistratura *nf* : judgeship, magistracy
magma *nm* : magma
magnanimidad *nf* : magnanimity
magnánimo, -ma *adj* GENEROSO : magnanimous — **magnánimamente** *adv*
magnate *nmf* : magnate, tycoon
magnesia *nf* : magnesia
magnesio *nm* : magnesium
magnético, -ca *adj* : magnetic
magnetismo *nm* : magnetism
magnetizar {21} *vt* : to magnetize
magnetófono *nm* : tape recorder
magnetofónico, -ca *adj* **cinta magnetofónica** : magnetic tape
magnificar {72} *vt* **1** : to magnify **2** EXAGERAR : to exaggerate **3** ENSALZAR : to exalt, to extol, to praise highly
magnificencia *nf* : magnificence, splendor
magnífico, -ca *adj* ESPLENDOROSO : magnificent, splendid — **magníficamente** *adv*
magnitud *nf* : magnitude
magnolia *nf* : magnolia (flower)
magnolio *nm* : magnolia (tree)
mago, -ga *n* **1** : magician **2** : wizard (in folk tales, etc.) **3 los Reyes Magos** : the Magi
magro, -gra *adj* **1** : lean (of meat) **2** : meager
maguey *nm* : maguey
magulladura *nf* MORETÓN : bruise
magullar *vt* : to bruise — **magullarse** *vr*
mahometano[1], **-na** *adj* ISLÁMICO : Islamic, Muslim
mahometano[2], **-na** *n* : Muslim
mahonesa → **mayonesa**
maicena *nf* : cornstarch
mainframe [ˈmein,freim] *nm* : mainframe
maíz *nm* : corn, maize
maizal *nm* : cornfield
maja *nf* : pestle
majadería *nf* **1** TONTERÍA : stupidity, foolishness **2** *Mex* LEPERADA : insult, obscenity
majadero[1], **-ra** *adj* **1** : foolish, silly **2** *Mex* LÉPERO : crude, vulgar
majadero[2], **-ra** *n* **1** TONTO : fool **2** *Mex* : rude person, boor
majar *vt* : to crush, to mash
majestad *nf* : majesty ⟨Su Majestad : Your Majesty⟩
majestuosamente *adv* : majestically
majestuosidad *nf* : majesty, grandeur
majestuoso, -sa *adj* : majestic, stately
majo, -ja *adj Spain* **1** : nice, likeable **2** GUAPO : attractive, good-looking
mal[1] *adv* **1** : badly, poorly ⟨baila muy mal : he dances very badly⟩ **2** : wrong, incorrectly ⟨me entendió mal : she misunderstood me⟩ **3** : with difficulty, hardly ⟨mal puedo oírte : I can hardly hear you⟩ **4 de mal en peor** : from bad to worse **5 menos mal** : it could have been worse

mal[2] *adj* → **malo**

mal[3] *nm* **1** : evil, wrong **2** DAÑO : harm, damage **3** DESGRACIA : misfortune **4** ENFERMEDAD : illness, sickness

malabar *adj* **juegos malabares** : juggling

malabarista *nmf* : juggler

malaconsejado, -da *adj* : ill-advised

malacostumbrado, -da *adj* CONSENTIDO : spoiled, pampered

malacostumbrar *vt* : to spoil

malagradecido, -da *adj* INGRATO : ungrateful

malaisio → **malasio**

malaquita *nf* : malachite

malaria *nf* PALUDISMO : malaria

malasio, -sia *adj & n* : Malaysian

malauiano, -na *adj & n* : Malawian

malaventura *nf* : misadventure, misfortune

malaventurado, -da *adj* MALHADADO : ill-fated, unfortunate

malayo, -ya *adj & n* : Malay, Malayan

malbaratar *vt* **1** MALGASTAR : to squander **2** : to undersell

malcriado[1], **-da** *adj* **1** : ill-bred, ill-mannered **2** : spoiled, pampered

malcriado[2], **-da** *n* : spoiled brat

maldad *nf* **1** : evil, wickedness **2** : evil deed

maldecir {11} *vt* : to curse, to damn — *vi* **1** : to curse, to swear **2** **~ de** : to speak ill of, to slander, to defame

maldición *nf, pl* **-ciones** : curse

maldiga, maldijo etc. → **maldecir**

maldito, -ta *adj* **1** : cursed, damned ⟨¡maldita sea! : damn it all!⟩ **2** : wicked

maldoso, -sa *adj Mex* : mischievous

maleable *adj* : malleable

maleante *nmf* : crook, thug

malecón *nm, pl* **-cones** : jetty, breakwater

maleducado, -da *adj* : ill-mannered, rude

maleficio *nm* : curse, hex

maléfico, -ca *adj* : evil, harmful

malentender {56} *vt* : to misunderstand

malentendido *nm* : misunderstanding

malestar *nm* **1** : discomfort **2** IRRITACIÓN : annoyance **3** INQUIETUD : uneasiness, unrest

maleta *nf* : suitcase, bag ⟨haz tus maletas : pack your bags⟩

maletero[1], **-ra** *n* : porter

maletero[2] *nm* : trunk (of an automobile)

maletín *nm, pl* **-tines** **1** PORTAFOLIO : briefcase **2** : overnight bag, satchel

malevolencia *nf* : malevolence, wickedness

malévolo, -la *adj* : malevolent, wicked

maleza *nf* **1** : thicket, underbrush **2** : weeds *pl*

malformación *nf, pl* **-ciones** : malformation

malgache *adj & nmf* : Madagascan

malgastar *vt* : to squander (resources), to waste (time, effort)

malhablado, -da *adj* : foul-mouthed

malhadado, -da *adj* MALAVENTURADO : ill-fated

malhechor, -chora *n* : criminal, delinquent, wrongdoer

malherir {76} *vt* : to injure seriously

malhumor *nm* : bad mood, sullenness

malhumorado, -da *adj* : bad-tempered, cross

malicia *nf* **1** : wickedness, malice **2** : mischief, naughtiness **3** : cunning, craftiness

malicioso, -sa *adj* **1** : malicious **2** PÍCARO : mischievous

malignidad *nf* **1** : malignancy **2** MALDAD : evil

maligno, -na *adj* **1** : malignant ⟨un tumor maligno : a malignant tumor⟩ **2** : evil, harmful, malign

malinchismo *nm Mex* : preference for foreign goods or people — **malinchista** *adj*

malintencionado, -da *adj* : malicious, spiteful

malinterpretar *vt* : to misinterpret

malla *nf* **1** : mesh **2** LEOTARDO : leotard, tights *pl* **3** **malla de baño** : bathing suit

mallorquín, -quina *adj & n* : Majorcan

malnutrición *nf, pl* **-ciones** DESNUTRICIÓN : malnutrition

malnutrido, -da *adj* DESNUTRIDO : malnourished, undernourished

malo[1], **-la** *adj* (**mal** *before masculine singular nouns*) **1** : bad ⟨mala suerte : bad luck⟩ **2** : wicked, naughty **3** : cheap, poor (quality) **4** : harmful ⟨malo para la salud : bad for one's health⟩ **5** (*using the form* **mal**) : unwell ⟨estar mal del corazón : to have heart trouble⟩ **6** **estar de malas** : to be in a bad mood

malo[2], **-la** *n* : villain, bad guy (in novels, movies, etc.)

malogrado, -da *adj* : failed, unsuccessful

malograr *vt* **1** : to spoil, to ruin **2** : to waste (an opportunity, time) — **malograrse** *vr* **1** FRACASAR : to fail **2** : to die young

malogro *nm* **1** : untimely death **2** FRACASO : failure

maloliente *adj* HEDIONDO : foul-smelling, smelly

malparado, -da *adj* **salir malparado** *or* **quedar malparado** : to come out of (something) badly, to end up in a bad state

malpensado, -da *adj* : distrustful, suspicious, nasty-minded

malquerencia *nf* AVERSIÓN : ill will, dislike

malquerer {64} *vt* : to dislike

malquiso, etc. → **malquerer**

malsano, -na *adj* : unhealthy

malsonante *adj* : rude, offensive ⟨palabras malsonantes : foul language⟩

malta *nf* : malt

malteada *nf* : malted milk ⟨malteada de chocolate : chocolate malt⟩

maltés, **-tesa** *adj & n, mpl* **malteses** : Maltese
maltratar *vt* **1** : to mistreat, to abuse **2** : to damage, to spoil
maltrato *nm* : mistreatment, abuse
maltrecho, **-cha** *adj* : battered, damaged
malucho, **-cha** *adj fam* : sick, under the weather
malva *adj & nm* : mauve
malvado[1], **-da** *adj* : evil, wicked
malvado[2], **-da** *n* : evildoer, wicked person
malvavisco *nm* : marshmallow
malvender *vt* : to sell at a loss
malversación *nf, pl* **-ciones** : misappropriation (of funds), embezzlement
malversador, **-dora** *n* : embezzler
malversar *vt* : to embezzle
malvivir *vi* : to live badly, to just scrape by
mamá *nf fam* : mom, mama
mamar *vi* **1** : to suckle **2 darle de mamar a** : to breast-feed — *vt* **1** : to suckle, to nurse **2** : to learn from childhood, to grow up with — **mamarse** *vr fam* : to get drunk
mamario, **-ria** *adj* : mammary
mamarracho *nm fam* **1** ESPERPENTO : mess, sight **2** : laughingstock, fool **3** : rubbish, junk
mambo *nm* : mambo
mami *nf fam* : mommy
mamífero[1], **-ra** *adj* : mammalian
mamífero[2] *nm* : mammal
mamila *nf* **1** : nipple **2** *Mex* : baby bottle, pacifier
mamografía *nf* : mammogram
mamola *nf* : pat, chuck under the chin
mamotreto *nm fam* **1** : huge book, tome **2** ARMATOSTE : hulk, monstrosity
mampara *nf* BIOMBO : screen, room divider
mamparo *nm* : bulkhead
mampostería *nf* : masonry, stonemasonry
mampostero *nm* : mason, stonemason
mamut *nm, pl* **mamuts** : mammoth
maná *nm* : manna
manada *nf* **1** : flock, herd, pack **2** *fam* : horde, mob ⟨llegaron en manada : they came in droves⟩
manantial *nm* **1** FUENTE : spring **2** : source
manar *vi* **1** : to flow **2** : to abound
manatí *nm* : manatee
mancha *nf* **1** : stain, spot, mark ⟨mancha de sangre : bloodstain⟩ **2** : blemish, blot ⟨una mancha en su reputación : a blemish on his reputation⟩ **3** : patch
manchado, **-da** *adj* : stained
manchar *vt* **1** ENSUCIAR : to stain, to soil **2** DESHONRAR : to sully, to tarnish — **mancharse** *vr* : to get dirty
mancillar *vt* : to sully, to besmirch
manco, **-ca** *adj* : one-armed, one-handed
mancomunar *vt* : to combine, to pool — **mancomunarse** *vr* : to unite, to join together
mancomunidad *nf* **1** : commonwealth **2** : association, confederation
mancuernas *nfpl* : cuff links
mancuernillas *nf Mex* : cuff links
mandadero, **-ra** *n* : errand boy *m*, errand girl *f*, messenger
mandado *nm* **1** : order, command **2** : errand ⟨hacer los mandados : to run errands, to go shopping⟩
mandamás *nmf, pl* **-mases** *fam* : boss, bigwig, honcho
mandamiento *nm* **1** : commandment **2** : command, order, warrant ⟨mandamiento judicial : warrant, court order⟩
mandar *vt* **1** ORDENAR : to command, to order **2** ENVIAR : to send ⟨te manda saludos : he sends you his regards⟩ **3** ECHAR : to hurl, to throw **4 ¿mande?** *Mex* : yes?, pardon? — *vi* : to be the boss, to be in charge — **mandarse** *vr Mex* : to take liberties, to take advantage
mandarín *nm* : Mandarin
mandarina *nf* : mandarin orange, tangerine
mandatario, **-ria** *n* **1** : leader (in politics) ⟨primer mandatario : head of state⟩ **2** : agent (in law)
mandato *nm* **1** : term of office **2** : mandate
mandíbula *nf* **1** : jaw **2** : mandible
mandil *nm* **1** DELANTAL : apron **2** : horse blanket
mandilón *nm, pl* **-lones** *fam* : wimp, coward
mandioca *nf* **1** : manioc, cassava **2** : tapioca
mando *nm* **1** : command, leadership **2** : control (for a device) ⟨mando a distancia : remote control⟩ **3 al mando de** : in charge of **4 al mando de** : under the command of
mandolina *nf* : mandolin
mandón, **-dona** *adj, mpl* **mandones** : bossy, domineering
mandonear *vt fam* MANGONEAR : to boss around
mandrágora *nf* : mandrake
manecilla *nf* : hand (of a clock), pointer
manejable *adj* **1** : manageable **2** : docile, easily led
manejar *vt* **1** CONDUCIR : to drive (a car) **2** OPERAR : to handle, to operate **3** : to manage **4** : to manipulate (a person) — *vi* : to drive — **manejarse** *vr* **1** COMPORTARSE : to behave **2** : to get along, to manage
manejo *nm* **1** : handling, operation **2** : management
manera *nf* **1** MODO : way, manner, fashion **2 de cualquier manera** *or* **de todas maneras** : anyway, anyhow **3 de manera que** : so, in order that **4 de ninguna manera** : by no means, absolutely not **5 manera de ser** : personality, demeanor

manga *nf* **1** : sleeve **2** MANGUERA : hose
manganeso *nm* : manganese
mangle *nm* : mangrove
mango *nm* **1** : hilt, handle **2** : mango
mangonear *vt fam* : to boss around, to bully — *vi* **1** : to be bossy **2** : to loaf, to fool around
mangosta *nf* : mongoose
manguera *nf* : hose
manguito *nm* **1** : muff **2** : sleeve (of a pipe, etc.), hose (of a car)
maní *nm, pl* **maníes** : peanut
manía *nf* **1** OBSESIÓN : mania, obsession **2** : craze, fad **3** : odd habit, peculiarity **4** : dislike, aversion
maníaco[1], **-ca** *adj* : maniacal
maníaco[2], **-ca** *n* : maniac
maniatar *vt* : to tie the hands of, to manacle
maniático[1], **-ca** *adj* **1** MANÍACO : maniacal **2** : obsessive **3** : fussy, finicky
maniático[2], **-ca** *n* **1** MANÍACO : maniac, lunatic **2** : obsessive person, fanatic **3** : eccentric, crank
manicomio *nm* : insane asylum, madhouse
manicura *nf* : manicure
manicuro, -ra *n* : manicurist
manido, -da *adj* : hackneyed, stale, trite
manifestación *nf, pl* **-ciones** **1** : manifestation, sign **2** : demonstration, rally
manifestante *nmf* : demonstrator
manifestar {55} *vt* **1** : to demonstrate, to show **2** : to declare — **manifestarse** *vr* **1** : to be or become evident **2** : to state one's position ⟨se han manifestado a favor del acuerdo : they have declared their support for the agreement⟩ **3** : to demonstrate, to rally
manifiesto[1], **-ta** *adj* : manifest, evident, clear — **manifiestamente** *adv*
manifiesto[2] *nm* : manifesto
manija *nf* MANGO : handle
manilla → **manecilla**
manillar *nm* : handlebars *pl*
maniobra *nf* : maneuver, stratagem
maniobrar *v* : to maneuver
manipulación *nf, pl* **-ciones** : manipulation
manipulador[1], **-dora** *adj* : manipulating, manipulative
manipulador[2], **-dora** *n* : manipulator
manipular *vt* **1** : to manipulate **2** MANEJAR : to handle
maniquí[1] *nmf, pl* **-quíes** : mannequin, model
maniquí[2] *nm, pl* **-quíes** : mannequin, dummy
manirroto[1], **-ta** *adj* : extravagant
manirroto[2], **-ta** *n* : spendthrift
manivela *nf* : crank
manjar *nm* : delicacy, special dish
mano[1] *nf* **1** : hand **2** : coat (of paint or varnish) **3 a ~** : by hand **4 a ~** *or* **a la mano** : handy, at hand, nearby **5 darse la mano** : to shake hands **6 de la mano** : hand in hand ⟨la política y la economía van de la mano : politics and economics go hand in hand⟩ **7 de primera mano** : firsthand, at firsthand **8 de segunda mano** : secondhand ⟨ropa de segunda mano : secondhand clothing⟩ **9 mano a mano** : one-on-one **10 mano de obra** : labor, manpower **11 mano de mortero** : pestle **12 echar una mano** : to lend a hand **13 mano negra** *Mex fam* : shady dealings *pl*
mano[2], **-na** *n Mex fam* : buddy, pal ⟨¡oye, mano! : hey man!⟩
manojo *nm* PUÑADO : handful, bunch
manopla *nf* **1** : mitten, mitt **2** : brass knuckles *pl*
manosear *vt* **1** : to handle or touch excessively **2** ACARICIAR : to fondle, to caress
manotazo *nm* : slap, smack, swipe
manotear *vi* : to wave one's hands, to gesticulate
mansalva *adv* **a ~** : at close range
mansarda *nf* BUHARDILLA : attic
mansedumbre *nf* **1** : gentleness, meekness **2** : tameness
mansión *nf, pl* **-siones** : mansion
manso, -sa *adj* **1** : gentle, meek **2** : tame — **mansamente** *adv*
manta *nf* **1** COBIJA, FRAZADA : blanket **2** : poncho **3** *Mex* : coarse cotton fabric
manteca *nf* **1** GRASA : lard, fat **2** : butter
mantecoso, -sa *adj* : buttery
mantel *nm* **1** : tablecloth **2** : altar cloth
mantelería *nf* : table linen
mantener {80} *vt* **1** SUSTENTAR : to support, to feed ⟨mantener uno su familia : to support one's family⟩ **2** CONSERVAR : to keep, to preserve **3** CONTINUAR : to keep up, to sustain ⟨mantener una correspondencia : to keep up a correspondence⟩ **4** AFIRMAR : to maintain, to affirm — **mantenerse** *vr* **1** : to support oneself, to subsist **2 mantenerse firme** : to hold one's ground
mantenimiento *nm* **1** : maintenance, upkeep **2** : sustenance, food **3** : preservation
mantequera *nf* **1** : churn **2** : butter dish
mantequería *nf* **1** : creamery, dairy **2** : grocery store
mantequilla *nf* : butter
mantilla *nf* : mantilla
mantis *nf* **mantis religiosa** : praying mantis
manto *nm* **1** : cloak **2** : mantle (in geology)
mantón *nm, pl* **-tones** CHAL : shawl
mantuvo, etc. → **mantener**
manual[1] *adj* **1** : manual ⟨trabajo manual : manual labor⟩ **2** : handy, manageable — **manualmente** *adv*
manual[2] *nm* : manual, handbook
manualidades *nfpl* : handicrafts (in schools)
manubrio *nm* **1** : handle, crank **2** : handlebars *pl*

manufactura *nf* **1** FABRICACIÓN : manufacture **2** : manufactured item, product **3** FÁBRICA : factory

manufacturar *vt* FABRICAR : to manufacture

manufacturero[1], -ra *adj* : manufacturing

manufacturero[2], -ra *n* FABRICANTE : manufacturer

manuscrito[1], -ta *adj* : handwritten

manuscrito[2] *nm* : manuscript

manutención *nf, pl* **-ciones** : maintenance, support

manzana *nf* **1** : apple **2** CUADRA : block (enclosed by streets or buildings) **3** *or* **manzana de Adán** : Adam's apple

manzanal *nm* **1** : apple orchard **2** MANZANO : apple tree

manzanar *nm* : apple orchard

manzanilla *nf* **1** : chamomile **2** : chamomile tea

manzano *nm* : apple tree

maña *nf* **1** : dexterity, skill **2** : cunning, guile **3 mañas** *or* **malas mañas** *nfpl* : bad habits, vices

mañana *nf* **1** : morning **2** : tomorrow

mañanero, -ra *adj* MATUTINO : morning ⟨rocío mañanero : morning dew⟩

mañanitas *nfpl Mex* : birthday serenade

mañoso, -sa *adj* **1** HÁBIL : skillful **2** ASTUTO : cunning, crafty **3** : fussy, finicky

mapa *nm* CARTA : map

mapache *nm* : raccoon

mapamundi *nm* : map of the world

maqueta *nf* : model, mock-up

maquillador, -dora *n* : makeup artist

maquillaje *nm* : makeup

maquillarse *vr* : to put on makeup, to make oneself up

máquina *nf* **1** : machine ⟨máquina de coser : sewing machine⟩ ⟨máquina de escribir : typewriter⟩ **2** LOCOMOTORA : engine, locomotive **3** : machine (in politics) **4 a toda máquina** : at full speed

maquinación *nf, pl* **-ciones** : machination, scheme, plot

maquinal *adj* : mechanical, automatic — **maquinalmente** *adv*

maquinar *vt* : to plot, to scheme

maquinaria *nf* **1** : machinery **2** : mechanism, works *pl*

maquinilla *nf* **1** : small machine or device **2** *CA, Car* : typewriter

maquinista *nmf* **1** : machinist **2** : railroad engineer

mar *nmf* **1** : sea ⟨un mar agitado : a rough sea⟩ ⟨hacerse a la mar : to set sail⟩ **2 alta mar** : high seas

maraca *nf* : maraca

maraña *nf* **1** : thicket **2** ENREDO : tangle, mess

marasmo *nm* : paralysis, stagnation

maratón *nm, pl* **-tones** : marathon

maravilla *nf* **1** : wonder, marvel ⟨a las mil maravillas : wonderfully, marvelously⟩ ⟨hacer maravillas : to work wonders⟩ **2** : marigold

maravillar *vt* ASOMBRAR : to astonish, to amaze — **maravillarse** *vr* : to be amazed, to marvel

maravilloso, -sa *adj* ESTUPENDO : wonderful, marvelous — **maravillosamente** *adv*

marbete *nm* **1** ETIQUETA : label, tag **2** *PRi* : registration sticker (of a car)

marca *nf* **1** : mark **2** : brand, make **3** : trademark ⟨marca registrada : registered trademark⟩ **4** : record (in sports) ⟨batir la marca : to beat the record⟩

marcado, -da *adj* : marked ⟨un marcado contraste : a marked contrast⟩

marcador *nm* **1** TANTEADOR : scoreboard **2** : marker, felt-tipped pen **3 marcador de libros** : bookmark

marcaje *nm* **1** : scoring (in sports) **2** : guarding (in sports)

marcapasos *nms & pl* : pacemaker

marcar {72} *vt* **1** : to mark **2** : to brand (livestock) **3** : to indicate, to show **4** RESALTAR : to emphasize **5** : to dial (a telephone) **6** : to guard (an opponent) **7** ANOTAR : to score (a goal, a point) — *vi* **1** ANOTAR : to score **2** : to dial

marcha *nf* **1** : march **2** : hike, walk ⟨ir de marcha : to go hiking⟩ **3** : pace, speed ⟨a toda marcha : at top speed⟩ **4** : gear (of an automobile) ⟨marcha atrás : reverse, reverse gear⟩ **5 en ~** : in motion, in gear, under way

marchar *vi* **1** IR : to go, to travel **2** ANDAR : to walk **3** FUNCIONAR : to work, to go **4** : to march — **marcharse** *vr* : to leave

marchitar *vi* : to make wither, to wilt — **marchitarse** *vr* **1** : to wither, to shrivel up, to wilt **2** : to languish, to fade away

marchito, -ta *adj* : withered, faded

marcial *adj* : martial, military

marco *nm* **1** : frame, framework **2** : goalposts *pl* **3** AMBIENTE : setting, atmosphere **4** : mark (unit of currency)

marea *nf* : tide

mareado, -da *adj* **1** : dizzy, lightheaded **2** : queasy, nauseous **3** : seasick

marear *vt* **1** : to make sick ⟨los gases me marearon : the fumes made me sick⟩ **2** : to bother, to annoy — **marearse** *vr* **1** : to get sick, to become nauseated **2** : to feel dizzy **3** : to get tipsy

marejada *nf* **1** : surge, swell (of the sea) **2** : undercurrent, ferment, unrest

maremoto *nm* : tidal wave

mareo *nm* **1** : dizzy spell **2** : nausea **3** : seasickness, motion sickness **4** : annoyance, vexation

marfil *nm* : ivory

margarina *nf* : margarine

margarita *nf* **1** : daisy **2** : margarita (cocktail)

margen[1] *nf, pl* **márgenes** : bank (of a river), side (of a street)

margen[2] *nm, pl* **márgenes** **1** : edge, border **2** : margin ⟨margen de ganancia : profit margin⟩
marginación *nf, pl* **-ciones** : marginalization, exclusion
marginado[1], **-da** *adj* **1** DESHEREDADO : outcast, alienated, dispossessed **2 clases marginadas** : underclass
marginado[2], **-da** *n* : outcast, misfit
marginal *adj* : marginal, fringe
marginalidad *nf* : marginality
marginar *vt* : to ostracize, to exclude
mariachi *nm* : mariachi musician or band
maridaje *nm* : marriage, union
maridar *vt* UNIR : to marry, to unite
marido *nm* ESPOSO : husband
marihuana *or* **mariguana** *or* **marijuana** *nf* : marihuana
marimacho *nmf fam* **1** : mannish woman **2** : tomboy
marimba *nf* : marimba
marina *nf* **1** : coast, coastal area **2** : navy, fleet ⟨marina mercante : merchant marine⟩
marinada *nf* : marinade
marinar *vt* : to marinate
marinero[1], **-ra** *adj* **1** : seaworthy **2** : sea, marine
marinero[2] *nm* : sailor
marino[1], **-na** *adj* : marine, sea
marino[2] *nm* : sailor, seaman
marioneta *nf* TÍTERE : puppet, marionette
mariposa *nf* **1** : butterfly **2 mariposa nocturna** : moth
mariquita[1] *nf* : ladybug
mariquita[2] *nm fam* : sissy, wimp
mariscal *nm* **1** : marshal **2 mariscal de campo** : field marshal (in the military), quarterback (in football)
marisco *nm* **1** : shellfish **2 mariscos** *nmpl* : seafood
marisma *nf* : marsh, salt marsh
marital *adj* : marital, married ⟨la vida marital : married life⟩
marítimo, -ma *adj* : maritime, shipping ⟨la industria marítima : the shipping industry⟩
marmita *nf* : (cooking) pot
mármol *nm* : marble
marmóreo, -rea *adj* : marble, marmoreal
marmota *nf* **1** : marmot **2 marmota de América** : woodchuck, groundhog
maroma *nf* **1** : rope **2** : acrobatic stunt **3** *Mex* : somersault
marque, etc. → **marcar**
marqués, -quesa *n, mpl* **marqueses** : marquis *m,* marquess *m,* marquise *f,* marchioness *f*
marquesina *nf* : marquee, canopy
marqueta *nf Mex* : block (of chocolate), lump (of sugar or salt)
marranada *nf* **1** : disgusting thing **2** : dirty trick
marrano[1], **-na** *adj* : filthy, disgusting
marrano[2], **-na** *n* **1** CERDO : pig, hog **2** : dirty pig, slob
marrar *vt* : to miss (a target) — *vi* : to fail, to go wrong
marras *adv* **1** : long ago **2 de ~** : said, aforementioned ⟨el individuo de marras : the individual in question⟩
marrasquino *nm* : maraschino
marrón *adj & nm, pl* **marrones** CASTAÑO : brown
marroquí *adj & nmf, pl* **-quíes** : Moroccan
marsopa *nf* : porpoise
marsupial *nm* : marsupial
marta *nf* **1** : marten **2 marta cebellina** : sable (animal)
Marte *nm* : Mars
martes *nms & pl* : Tuesday
martillar *v* : to hammer
martillazo *nm* : blow with a hammer
martillo *nm* **1** : hammer **2 martillo neumático** : jackhammer
martinete *nm* **1** : heron **2** : pile driver
mártir *nmf* : martyr
martirio *nm* **1** : martyrdom **2** : ordeal, torment
martirizar {21} *vt* **1** : to martyr **2** ATORMENTAR : to torment
marxismo *nm* : Marxism
marxista *adj & nmf* : Marxist
marzo *nm* : March
mas *conj* PERO : but
más[1] *adv* **1** : more ⟨¿hay algo más grande? : is there anything bigger?⟩ **2** : most ⟨Luis es el más alto : Luis is the tallest⟩ **3** : longer ⟨el sabor dura más : the flavor lasts longer⟩ **4** : rather ⟨más querría andar : I would rather walk⟩ **5 a ~** : besides, in addition **6 más allá** : further **7 qué . . . más . . .** : what . . ., what a . . . ⟨¡qué día más bonito! : what a beautiful day!⟩
más[2] *adj* **1** : more ⟨dáme dos kilos más : give me two more kilos⟩ **2** : most ⟨la que ganó más dinero : the one who earned the most money⟩ **3** : else ⟨¿quién más quiere vino? : who else wants wine?⟩
más[3] *n* : plus sign
más[4] *prep* : plus ⟨tres más dos es igual a cinco : three plus two equals five⟩
más[5] *pron* **1** : more ⟨¿tienes más? : do you have more?⟩ **2 a lo más** : at most **3 de ~** : extra, excess **4 más o menos** : more or less, approximately **5 por más que** : no matter how much ⟨por más que corras no llegarás a tiempo : no matter how fast you run you won't arrive on time⟩
masa *nf* **1** : mass, volume ⟨masa atómica : atomic mass⟩ ⟨producción en masa : mass production⟩ **2** : dough, batter **3 masas** *nfpl* : people, masses ⟨las masas populares : the common people⟩ **4 masa harina** *Mex* : corn flour (for tortillas, etc.)
masacrar *vt* : to massacre
masacre *nf* : massacre
masaje *nm* : massage
masajear *vt* : to massage

masajista *nmf* : masseur *m,* masseuse *f*

mascar {72} *v* MASTICAR : to chew

máscara *nf* **1** CARETA : mask **2** : appearance, pretense **3 máscara antigás** : gas mask

mascarada *nf* : masquerade

mascarilla *nf* **1** : mask (in medicine) ⟨mascarilla de oxígeno : oxygen mask⟩ **2** : facial mask (in cosmetology)

mascota *nf* : mascot

masculinidad *nf* : masculinity

masculino, -na *adj* **1** : masculine, male **2** : manly **3** : masculine (in grammar)

mascullar *v* : to mumble, to mutter

masificado, -da *adj* : overcrowded

masilla *nf* : putty

masivamente *adv* : en masse

masivo, -va *adj* : mass ⟨comunicación masiva : mass communication⟩

masón *nm, pl* **masones** FRANCMASÓN : Mason, Freemason

masonería *nf* FRANCMASONERÍA : Masonry, Freemasonry

masónico, -ca *adj* : Masonic

masoquismo *nm* : masochism

masoquista[1] *adj* : masochistic

masoquista[2] *nmf* : masochist

masque, etc. → **mascar**

masticar {72} *v* MASCAR : to chew, to masticate

mástil *nm* **1** : mast **2** ASTA : flagpole **3** : neck (of a stringed instrument)

mastín *nm, pl* **mastines** : mastiff

mástique *nm* : putty, filler

mastodonte *nm* : mastodon

masturbación *nf, pl* **-ciones** : masturbation

masturbarse *vr* : to masturbate

mata *nf* **1** ARBUSTO : bush, shrub **2** : plant ⟨mata de tomate : tomato plant⟩ **3** : sprig, tuft **4 mata de pelo** : mop of hair

matadero *nm* : slaughterhouse, abattoir

matado, -da *adj Mex* : strenuous, exhausting

matador *nm* TORERO : matador, bullfighter

matamoscas *nms & pl* : flyswatter

matanza *nf* MASACRE : slaughter, butchering

matar *vt* **1** : to kill **2** : to slaughter, to butcher **3** APAGAR : to extinguish, to put out (fire, light) **4** : to tone down (colors) **5** : to pass, to waste (time) **6** : to trump (in card games) — *vi* : to kill — **matarse** *vr* **1** : to be killed **2** SUICIDARSE : to commit suicide **3** *fam* : to exhaust oneself ⟨se mató tratando de terminarlo : he knocked himself out trying to finish it⟩

matasanos *nms & pl fam* : quack

matasellar *vt* : to cancel (a stamp), to postmark

matasellos *nms & pl* : postmark

matatena *nf Mex* : jacks

mate[1] *adj* : matte, dull

mate[2] *nm* **1** : maté **2 jaque mate** : checkmate ⟨darle mate a *or* darle jaque mate a : to checkmate⟩

matemática → **matemáticas**

matemáticas *nfpl* : mathematics, math

matemático[1], **-ca** *adj* : mathematical — **matemáticamente** *adv*

matemático[2], **-ca** *n* : mathematician

materia *nf* **1** : matter ⟨materia gris : gray matter⟩ **2** : material ⟨materia prima : raw material⟩ **3** : (academic) subject **4 en materia de** : on the subject of, concerning

material[1] *adj* **1** : material, physical, real **2 daños materiales** : property damage

material[2] *nm* **1** : material ⟨material de construcción : building material⟩ **2** EQUIPO : equipment, gear

materialismo *nm* : materialism

materialista[1] *adj* : materialistic

materialista[2] *nmf* **1** : materialist **2** *Mex* : truck driver

materializar {21} *vt* : to bring to fruition, to realize — **materializarse** *vr* : to materialize, to come into being

materialmente *adv* **1** : materially, physically ⟨materialmente imposible : physically impossible⟩ **2** : really, absolutely

maternal *adj* : maternal, motherly

maternidad *nf* **1** : maternity, motherhood **2** : maternity hospital, maternity ward

materno, -na *adj* : maternal

matinal *adj* MATUTINO : morning ⟨la pálida luz matinal : the pale morning light⟩

matinée *or* **matiné** *nf* : matinee

matiz *nm, pl* **matices** **1** : hue, shade **2** : nuance

matización *nf, pl* **-ciones** **1** : tinting, toning, shading **2** : clarification (of a statement)

matizar {21} *vt* **1** : to tinge, to tint (colors) **2** : to vary, to modulate (sounds) **3** : to qualify (statements)

matón *nm, pl* **matones** : thug, bully

matorral *nm* **1** : thicket **2** : scrub, scrubland

matraca *nf* **1** : rattle, noisemaker **2 dar la matraca a** : to pester, to nag

matriarca *nf* : matriarch

matriarcado *nm* : matriarchy

matrícula *nf* **1** : list, roll, register **2** INSCRIPCIÓN : registration, enrollment **3** : license plate, registration number

matriculación *nf, pl* **-ciones** : matriculation, registration

matricular *vt* **1** INSCRIBIR : to enroll, to register (a person) **2** : to register (a vehicle) — **matricularse** *vr* : to matriculate

matrimonial *adj* : marital, matrimonial ⟨la vida matrimonial : married life⟩

matrimonio *nm* **1** : marriage, matrimony **2** : married couple

matriz *nf, pl* **matrices** **1** : uterus, womb **2** : original, master copy **3** : main office, headquarters **4** : stub (of a check) **5** : matrix ⟨matriz de puntos : dot matrix⟩

matrona *nf* : matron

matronal *adj* : matronly

matutino[1], **-na** *adj* : morning ⟨la edición matutina : the morning edition⟩

matutino[2] *nm* : morning paper

maullar {8} *vi* : to meow

maullido *nm* : meow

mauritano, -na *adj & n* : Mauritanian

mausoleo *nm* : mausoleum

maxilar *nm* : jaw, jawbone

máxima *nf* : maxim

máxime *adv* ESPECIALMENTE : especially, principally

maximizar {21} *vt* : to maximize

máximo[1], **-ma** *adj* : maximum, greatest, highest

máximo[2] *nm* **1** : maximum **2 al máximo** : to the utmost **3 como ~** : at the most, at the latest

maya[1] *adj & nmf* : Mayan

maya[2] *nmf* : Maya, Mayan

mayo *nm* : May

mayonesa *nf* : mayonnaise

mayor[1] *adj* **1** (*comparative of* **grande**) : bigger, larger, greater, elder, older **2** (*superlative of* **grande**) : biggest, largest, greatest, eldest, oldest **3** : grown-up, mature **4** : main, major **5 mayor de edad** : of (legal) age **6 al por mayor** *or* **por ~** : wholesale

mayor[2] *nmf* **1** : major (in the military) **2** : adult

mayoral *nm* CAPATAZ : foreman, overseer

mayordomo *nm* : butler, majordomo

mayoreo *nm* : wholesale

mayores *nmpl* : grown-ups, elders

mayoría *nf* **1** : majority **2 en su mayoría** : on the whole

mayorista[1] *adj* ALMACENISTA : wholesale

mayorista[2] *nmf* : wholesaler

mayoritariamente *adv* : primarily, chiefly

mayoritario, -ria *adj & n* : majority ⟨un consenso mayoritario : a majority consensus⟩

mayormente *adv* : primarily, chiefly

mayúscula *nf* : capital letter

mayúsculo, -la *adj* **1** : capital, uppercase **2** : huge, terrible ⟨un problema mayúsculo : a huge problem⟩

maza *nf* **1** : mace (weapon) **2** : drumstick **3** *fam* : bore, pest

mazacote *nm* **1** : concrete **2** : lumpy mess (of food) **3** : eyesore, crude work of art

mazapán *nm, pl* **-panes** : marzipan

mazmorra *nf* CALABOZO : dungeon

mazo *nm* **1** : mallet **2** : pestle **3** MANOJO : handful, bunch

mazorca *nf* **1** CHOCLO : cob, ear of corn **2 pelar la mazorca** *Mex fam* : to smile from ear to ear

me *pron* **1** : me ⟨me vieron : they saw me⟩ **2** : to me, for me, from me ⟨dame el libro : give me the book⟩ ⟨me lo compró : he bought it for me⟩ ⟨me robaron la cartera : they stole my pocketbook⟩ **3** : myself, to myself, for myself, from myself ⟨me preparé una buena comida : I cooked myself a good dinner⟩ ⟨me equivoqué : I made a mistake⟩

mecánica *nf* : mechanics

mecánico[1], **-ca** *adj* : mechanical — **mecánicamente** *adv*

mecánico[2], **-ca** *n* **1** : mechanic **2** : technician ⟨mecánico dental : dental technician⟩

mecanismo *nm* : mechanism

mecanización *nf, pl* **-ciones** : mechanization

mecanizar {21} *vt* : to mechanize

mecanografía *nf* : typing

mecanografiar {85} *vt* : to type

mecanógrafo, -fa *n* : typist

mecate *nm CA, Mex, Ven* : rope, twine, cord

mecedor *nm* : glider (seat)

mecedora *nf* : rocking chair

mecenas *nmfs & pl* : patron (of the arts), sponsor

mecenazgo *nm* PATROCINIO : sponsorship, patronage

mecer {86} *vt* **1** : to rock **2** COLUMPIAR : to push (on a swing) — **mecerse** *vr* : to rock, to swing, to sway

mecha *nf* **1** : fuse **2** : wick **3 mechas** *nfpl* : highlights (in hair)

mechero *nm* **1** : burner **2** *Spain* : lighter

mechón *nm, pl* **mechones** : lock (of hair)

medalla *nf* : medal, medallion

medallista *nmf* : medalist

medallón *nm, pl* **-llones 1** : medallion **2** : locket

media *nf* **1** CALCETÍN : sock **2** : average, mean **3 medias** *nfpl* : stockings, hose, tights **4 a medias** : by halves, half and half, halfway ⟨ir a medias : to go halves⟩ ⟨verdad a medias : half-truth⟩

mediación *nf, pl* **-ciones** : mediation

mediado, -da *adj* **1** : half full, half empty, half over **2** : halfway through ⟨mediada la tarea : halfway through the job⟩

mediador, -dora *n* : mediator

mediados *nmpl* **a mediados de** : halfway through, in the middle of ⟨a mediados del mes : towards the middle of the month, mid-month⟩

medialuna *nf* **1** : crescent **2** : croissant, crescent roll

medianamente *adv* : fairly, moderately

medianero, -ra *adj* **1** : dividing **2** : mediating

medianía *nf* **1** : middle position **2** : mediocre person, mediocrity

mediano, -na *adj* **1** : medium, average ⟨la mediana edad : middle age⟩ **2** : mediocre

medianoche *nf* : midnight

mediante *prep* : through, by means of ⟨Dios mediante : God willing⟩

mediar *vi* **1** : to mediate **2** : to be in the middle, to be halfway through **3** : to elapse, to pass ⟨mediaron cinco años entre el inicio de la guerra y el armisticio : five years passed between the start of the war and the armistice⟩ **4** : to be a consideration ⟨media el hecho de que cuesta mucho : one must take into account that it is costly⟩ **5** : to come up, to happen ⟨medió algo urgente : something pressing came up⟩

mediatizar {21} *vt* : to influence, to interfere with

medicación *nf, pl* **-ciones** : medication, treatment

medicamento *nm* : medication, medicine, drug

medicar {72} *vt* : to medicate — **medicarse** *vr* : to take medicine

medicina *nf* : medicine

medicinal *adj* **1** : medicinal **2** : medicated

medicinar *vt* : to give medication to, to dose

medición *nf, pl* **-ciones** : measuring, measurement

médico¹, -ca *adj* : medical ⟨una receta médica : a doctor's prescription⟩

médico², -ca *n* DOCTOR : doctor, physician

medida *nf* **1** : measurement, measure ⟨hecho a medida : custom-made⟩ **2** : measure, step ⟨tomar medidas : to take steps⟩ **3** : moderation, prudence ⟨sin medida : immoderately⟩ **4** : extent, degree ⟨en gran medida : to a great extent⟩

medidor *nm* : meter, gauge

medieval *adj* : medieval — **medievalista** *nmf*

medievo → **medioevo**

medio¹ *adv* **1** : half ⟨está medio dormida : she's half asleep⟩ **2** : rather, kind of ⟨está medio aburrida esta fiesta : this party is rather boring⟩

medio², -dia *adj* **1** : half ⟨una media hora : half an hour⟩ ⟨medio hermano : half brother⟩ ⟨a media luz : in the half-light⟩ ⟨son las tres y media : it's half past three, it's three-thirty⟩ **2** : midway, halfway ⟨a medio camino : halfway there⟩ **3** : middle ⟨la clase media : the middle class⟩ **4** : average ⟨la temperatura media : the average temperature⟩

medio³ *nm* **1** CENTRO : middle, center ⟨en medio de : in the middle of, amid⟩ **2** AMBIENTE : milieu, environment **3** : medium, spiritualist **4** : means *pl*, way ⟨por medio de : by means of⟩ ⟨los medios de comunicación : the media⟩ **5 medios** *nmpl* : means, resources

mediocampista *nmf* : midfielder

mediocre *adj* : mediocre, average

mediocridad *nf* : mediocrity

mediodía *nm* : noon, midday

medioevo *nm* : Middle Ages

medir {54} *vt* **1** : to measure **2** : to weigh, to consider ⟨medir los riesgos : to weigh the risks⟩ — *vi* : to measure — **medirse** *vr* : to be moderate, to exercise restraint

meditabundo, -da *adj* PENSATIVO : pensive, thoughtful

meditación *nf, pl* **-ciones** : meditation, thought

meditar *vi* : to meditate, to think ⟨meditar sobre la vida : to contemplate life⟩ — *vt* **1** : to think over, to consider **2** : to plan, to work out

meditativo, -va *adj* : pensive

mediterráneo, -nea *adj* : Mediterranean

medrar *vi* **1** PROSPERAR : to prosper, to thrive **2** AUMENTAR : to increase, to grow

medro *nm* PROSPERIDAD : prosperity, growth

medroso, -sa *adj* : fainthearted, fearful

médula *nf* **1** : marrow, pith **2 médula espinal** : spinal cord

medular *adj* : fundamental, core ⟨el punto medular : the crux of the matter⟩

medusa *nf* : jellyfish, medusa

megabyte *nm* : megabyte

megáfono *nm* : megaphone

megahercio *nm* : megahertz

megahertzio *nm* : megahertz

megatón *nm, pl* **-tones** : megaton

megavatio *nm* : megawatt

mejicano → **mexicano**

mejilla *nf* : cheek

mejillón *nm, pl* **-llones** : mussel

mejor¹ *adv* **1** : better ⟨Carla cocina mejor que Ana : Carla cooks better than Ann⟩ **2** : best ⟨ella es la que lo hace mejor : she's the one who does it best⟩ **3** : rather ⟨mejor morir que rendirme : I'd rather die than give up⟩ **4** : it's better that . . . ⟨mejor te vas : you'd better go⟩ **5 a lo mejor** : maybe, perhaps

mejor² *adj* **1** (*comparative of* **bueno**) : better ⟨a falta de algo mejor : for lack of something better⟩ **2** (*comparative of* **bien**) : better ⟨está mucho mejor : he's much better⟩ **3** (*superlative of* **bueno**) : best, the better ⟨mi mejor amigo : my best friend⟩ **4** (*superlative of* **bien**) : best, the better ⟨duermo mejor en un clima seco : I sleep best in a dry climate⟩ **5** PREFERIBLE : preferable, better **6 lo mejor** : the best thing, the best part

mejor³ *nmf* (*with definite article*) : the better (one), the best (one)

mejora *nf* : improvement

mejoramiento *nm* : improvement

mejorana *nf* : marjoram

mejorar *vt* : to improve, to make better — *vi* : to improve, to get better — **mejorarse** *vr*

mejoría *nf* : improvement, betterment

mejunje *nm* : concoction, brew

melancolía *nf* : melancholy, sadness

melancólico, -ca *adj* : melancholy, sad

melanoma *nm* : melanoma

melaza *nf* : molasses

melena *nf* **1** : mane **2** : long hair **3 melenas** *nfpl* GREÑAS : shaggy hair, mop

melenudo[1], **-da** *adj fam* : longhaired
melenudo[2], **-da** *n* GREÑUDO : longhair, hippie
melindres *nmpl* **1** : affectation, airs *pl* **2** : finickiness
melindroso[1], **-sa** *adj* **1** : affected **2** : fussy, finicky
melindroso[2], **-sa** *n* : finicky person, fussbudget
melisa *nf* : lemon balm
mella *nf* **1** : dent, nick **2 hacer mella en** : to have an effect on, to make an impression on
mellado, **-da** *adj* **1** : chipped, dented **2** : gap-toothed
mellar *vt* : to dent, to nick
mellizo, **-za** *adj & n* GEMELO : twin
melocotón *nm, pl* **-tones** : peach
melodía *nf* : melody, tune
melódico, **-ca** *adj* : melodic
melodioso, **-sa** *adj* : melodious
melodrama *nm* : melodrama
melodramático, **-ca** *adj* : melodramatic
melón *nm, pl* **melones** : melon, cantaloupe
meloso, **-sa** *adj* **1** : honeyed, sweet **2** EMPALAGOSO : cloying, saccharine
membrana *nf* **1** : membrane **2 membrana interdigital** : web, webbing (of a bird's foot) — **membranoso**, **-sa** *adj*
membresía *nf* : membership, members *pl*
membrete *nm* : letterhead, heading
membrillo *nm* : quince
membrudo, **-da** *adj* FORNIDO : muscular, well-built
memez *nf, pl* **memeces** : stupid thing
memo, **-ma** *adj* : silly, stupid
memorabilia *nf* : memorabilia
memorable *adj* : memorable
memorándum *or* **memorando** *nm, pl* **-dums** *or* **-dos** **1** : memorandum, memo **2** : memo book, appointment book
memoria *nf* **1** : memory ⟨de memoria : by heart⟩ ⟨hacer memoria : to try to remember⟩ ⟨traer a la memoria : to call to mind⟩ **2** RECUERDO : remembrance, memory ⟨su memoria perdurará para siempre : his memory will live forever⟩ **3** : report ⟨memoria annual : annual report⟩ **4 memorias** *nfpl* : memoirs
memorizar {21} *vt* : to memorize — **memorización** *nf*
mena *nf* : ore
menaje *nm* : household goods *pl*, furnishings *pl*
mención *nf, pl* **-ciones** : mention
mencionar *vt* : to mention, to refer to
mendaz *adj, pl* **mendaces** : mendacious, lying
mendicidad *nf* : begging
mendigar {52} *vi* : to beg — *vt* : to beg for
mendigo, **-ga** *n* LIMOSNERO : beggar
mendrugo *nm* : crust (of bread)
menear *vt* **1** : to shake (one's head) **2** : to sway, to wiggle (one's hips) **3** : to wag (a tail) **4** : to stir (a liquid) — **menearse** *vr* **1** : to wiggle one's hips **2** : to fidget
meneo *nm* **1** : movement **2** : shake, toss **3** : swaying, wagging, wiggling **4** : stir, stirring
menester *nm* **1** : activity, occupation, duties *pl* **2 ser menester** : to be necessary ⟨es menester que vengas : you must come⟩
mengano, **-na** → **fulano**
mengua *nf* **1** : decrease, decline **2** : lack, want **3** : discredit, dishonor
menguar *vt* : to diminish, to lessen — *vi* **1** : to decline, to decrease **2** : to wane — **menguante** *adj*
meningitis *nf* : meningitis
menisco *nm* : meniscus, cartilage
menjurje → **mejunje**
menopausia *nf* : menopause
menor[1] *adj* **1** (*comparative of* **pequeño**) : smaller, lesser, younger **2** (*superlative of* **pequeño**) : smallest, least, youngest **3** : minor **4 al por menor** : retail **5 ser menor de edad** : to be a minor, to be underage
menor[2] *nmf* : minor, juvenile
menos[1] *adv* **1** : less ⟨llueve menos en agosto : it rains less in August⟩ **2** : least ⟨el coche menos caro : the least expensive car⟩ **3 ~ de** : less than, fewer than
menos[2] *adj* **1** : less, fewer ⟨tengo más trabajo y menos tiempo : I have more work and less time⟩ **2** : least, fewest ⟨la clase que tiene menos estudiantes : the class that has the fewest students⟩
menos[3] *prep* **1** SALVO, EXCEPTO : except **2** : minus ⟨quince menos cuatro son once : fifteen minus four is eleven⟩
menos[4] *pron* **1** : less, fewer ⟨no deberías aceptar menos : you shouldn't accept less⟩ **2 al menos** *or* **por lo menos** : at least **3 a menos que** : unless
menoscabar *vt* **1** : to lessen, to diminish **2** : to disgrace, to discredit **3** PERJUDICAR : to harm, to damage
menoscabo *nm* **1** : lessening, diminishing **2** : disgrace, discredit **3** : harm, damage
menospreciar *vt* **1** DESPRECIAR : to scorn, to look down on **2** : to underestimate, to undervalue
menosprecio *nm* DESPRECIO : contempt, scorn
mensaje *nm* : message
mensajero, **-ra** *n* : messenger
menso, **-sa** *adj Mex fam* : foolish, stupid
menstrual *adj* : menstrual
menstruar {3} *vi* : to menstruate — **menstruación** *nf*
mensual *adj* : monthly
mensualidad *nf* **1** : monthly payment, installment **2** : monthly salary
mensualmente *adv* : every month, monthly

mensurable *adj* : measurable

menta *nf* **1** : mint, peppermint **2 menta verde** : spearmint

mentado, -da *adj* **1** : aforementioned **2** FAMOSO : renowned, famous

mental *adj* : mental, intellectual — **mentalmente** *adv*

mentalidad *nf* : mentality

mentar {55} *vt* **1** : to mention, to name **2 mentar la madre a** *fam* : to insult, to swear at

mente *nf* : mind ⟨tener en mente : to have in mind⟩

mentecato[1], -ta *adj* : foolish, simple

mentecato[2], -ta *n* : fool, idiot

mentir {76} *vi* : to lie

mentira *nf* : lie

mentiroso[1], -sa *adj* EMBUSTERO : lying, untruthful

mentiroso[2], -sa *n* EMBUSTERO : liar

mentís *nm, pl* **mentises** : denial, repudiation ⟨dar el mentís a : to deny, to refute⟩

mentol *nm* : menthol

mentón *nm, pl* **mentones** BARBILLA : chin

mentor *nm* : mentor, counselor

menú *nm, pl* **menús** : menu

menudear *vi* : to occur frequently — *vt* : to do repeatedly

menudencia *nf* **1** : trifle **2 menudencias** *nfpl* : giblets

menudeo *nm* : retail, retailing

menudillos *nmpl* : giblets

menudo[1], -da *adj* **1** : minute, small **2 a ~** FRECUENTEMENTE : often, frequently

menudo[2] *nm* **1** *Mex* : tripe stew **2 menudos** *nmpl* : giblets

meñique *nm or* **dedo meñique** : little finger, pinkie

meollo *nm* **1** MÉDULA : marrow **2** SESO : brains *pl* **3** ENTRAÑA : essence, core ⟨el meollo del asunto : the heart of the matter⟩

mequetrefe *nm fam* : good-for-nothing

mercachifle *nm* : peddler, hawker

mercadeo *nm* : marketing

mercadería *nf* : merchandise, goods *pl*

mercado *nm* : market ⟨mercado de trabajo *or* mercado laboral : labor market⟩ ⟨mercado de valores *or* mercado bursátil : stock market⟩

mercadotecnia *nf* : marketing

mercancía *nf* : merchandise, goods *pl*

mercante *nmf* : merchant, dealer

mercantil *adj* COMERCIAL : commercial, mercantile

merced *nf* **1** : favor **2 ~ a** : thanks to, due to **3 a merced de** : at the mercy of

mercenario, -ria *adj & n* : mercenary

mercería *nf* : notions store

Mercosur *nm* : economic community consisting of Argentina, Brazil, Paraguay, and Uruguay

mercurio *nm* : mercury

Mercurio *nm* : Mercury (planet)

merecedor, -dora *adj* : deserving, worthy

merecer {53} *vt* : to deserve, to merit — *vi* : to be worthy

merecidamente *adv* : rightfully, deservedly

merecido *nm* : something merited, due ⟨recibieron su merecido : they got their just deserts⟩

merecimiento *nm* : merit, worth

merendar {55} *vi* : to have an afternoon snack — *vt* : to have as an afternoon snack

merendero *nm* **1** : lunchroom, snack bar **2** : picnic area

merengue *nm* **1** : meringue **2** : merengue (dance)

meridiano[1], -na *adj* **1** : midday **2** : crystal clear

meridiano[2] *nm* : meridian

meridional *adj* SUREÑO : southern

merienda *nf* : afternoon snack, tea

mérito *nm* : merit

meritorio[1], -ria *adj* : deserving, meritorious

meritorio[2], -ria *n* : intern, trainee

merluza *nf* : hake

merma *nf* **1** : decrease, cut **2** : waste, loss

mermar *vi* : to decrease, to diminish — *vt* : to reduce, to cut down

mermelada *nf* : marmalade, jam

mero[1], -ra *adv Mex fam* **1** : nearly, almost ⟨ya mero me caí : I almost fell⟩ **2** : just, exactly ⟨aquí mero : right here⟩

mero[2], -ra *adj* **1** : mere, simple **2** *Mex fam (used as an intensifier)* : very ⟨en el mero centro : in the very center of town⟩

mero[3] *nm* : grouper

merodeador, -dora *n* **1** : marauder **2** : prowler

merodear *vi* **1** : to maraud, to pillage **2** : to prowl around, to skulk

mes *nm* : month

mesa *nf* **1** : table **2** : committee, board

mesada *nf* : allowance, pocket money

mesarse *vr* : to pull at ⟨mesarse los cabellos : to tear one's hair⟩

mesero, -ra *n* CAMARERO : waiter, waitress *f*

meseta *nf* : plateau, tableland

Mesías *nm* : Messiah

mesón *nm, pl* **mesones** : inn

mesonero, -ra *nm* : innkeeper

mestizo[1], -za *adj* **1** : of mixed ancestry **2** HÍBRIDO : hybrid

mestizo[2], -za *n* : person of mixed ancestry

mesura *nf* **1** MODERACIÓN : moderation, discretion **2** CORTESÍA : courtesy **3** GRAVEDAD : seriousness, dignity

mesurado, -da *adj* COMEDIDO : moderate, restrained

mesurar *vt* : to moderate, to restrain, to temper — **mesurarse** *vr* : to restrain oneself

meta *nf* : goal, objective

metabólico, -ca *adj* : metabolic
metabolismo *nm* : metabolism
metabolizar {21} *vt* : to metabolize
metafísica *nf* : metaphysics
metafísico, -ca *adj* : metaphysical
metáfora *nf* : metaphor
metafórico, -ca *adj* : metaphoric, metaphorical
metal *nm* **1** : metal **2** : brass section (in an orchestra)
metálico, -ca *adj* : metallic, metal
metalistería *nf* : metalworking
metalurgia *nf* : metallurgy
metalúrgico[1], **-ca** *adj* : metallurgical
metalúrgico[2], **-ca** *n* : metallurgist
metamorfosis *nfs & pl* : metamorphosis
metano *nm* : methane
metedura *nf* **metedura de pata** : blunder, faux pas
meteórico, -ca *adj* : meteoric
meteorito *nm* : meteorite
meteoro *nm* : meteor
meteorología *nf* : meteorology
meteorológico, -ca *adj* : meteorologic, meteorological
meteorólogo, -ga *n* : meteorologist
meter *vt* **1** : to put (in) ⟨metieron su dinero en el banco : they put their money in the bank⟩ **2** : to fit, to squeeze ⟨puedes meter dos líneas más en esa página : you can fit two more lines on that page⟩ **3** : to place (in a job) ⟨lo metieron de barrendero : they got him a job as a street sweeper⟩ **4** : to involve ⟨lo metió en un buen lío : she got him in an awful mess⟩ **5** : to make, to cause ⟨meten demasiado ruido : they make too much noise⟩ **6** : to spread (a rumor) **7** : to strike (a blow) **8** : to take up, to take in (clothing) **9 a todo meter** : at top speed — **meterse** *vr* **1** : to get into, to enter **2** *fam* : to meddle ⟨no te metas en lo que no te importa : mind your own business⟩ **3 ~ con** *fam* : to pick a fight with, to provoke ⟨no te metas conmigo : don't mess with me⟩
metiche[1] *adj Mex fam* : nosy
metiche[2] *nmf Mex fam* : busybody
meticulosidad *nf* : thoroughness, meticulousness
meticuloso, -sa *adj* : meticulous, thorough — **meticulosamente** *adv*
metida *nf* **metida de pata** *fam* : blunder, gaffe, blooper
metódico, -ca *adj* : methodical — **metódicamente** *adv*
metodista *adj & nmf* : Methodist
método *nm* : method
metodología *nf* : methodology
metomentodo *nmf fam* : busybody
metraje *nm* : length (of a film) ⟨de largo metraje : feature-length⟩
metralla *nf* : shrapnel
metralleta *nf* : submachine gun
métrico, -ca *adj* **1** : metric **2 cinta métrica** : tape measure
metro *nm* **1** : meter **2** : subway
metrónomo *nm* : metronome
metrópoli *nf or* **metrópolis** *nfs & pl* : metropolis
metropolitano, -na *adj* : metropolitan
mexicanismo *nm* : Mexican word or expression
mexicano, -na *adj & n* : Mexican
mexicoamericano, -na *adj & n* : Mexican-American
meza, etc. → **mecer**
mezcla *nf* **1** : mixing **2** : mixture, blend **3** : mortar (masonry material)
mezclar *vt* **1** : to mix, to blend **2** : to mix up, to muddle **3** INVOLUCRAR : to involve — **mezclarse** *vr* **1** : to get mixed up (in) **2** : to mix, to mingle (socially)
mezclilla *nf Chile, Mex* : denim ⟨pantalones de mezclilla : jeans⟩
mezcolanza *nf* : jumble, hodgepodge
mezquindad *nf* **1** : meanness, stinginess **2** : petty deed, mean action
mezquino[1], **-na** *adj* **1** : mean, petty **2** : stingy **3** : paltry
mezquino[2] *nm Mex* : wart
mezquita *nf* : mosque
mezquite *nm* : mesquite
mi *adj* : my
mí *pron* **1** : me ⟨es para mí : it's for me⟩ ⟨a mí no me importa : it doesn't matter to me⟩ **2 mí mismo, mí misma** : myself
miasma *nm* : miasma
miau *nm* : meow
mica *nf* : mica
mico *nm* : monkey, long-tailed monkey
micra *nf* : micron
microbio *nm* : microbe, germ
microbiología *nf* : microbiology
microbiológico, -ca *adj* : microbiological
microbús *nm, pl* **-buses** : minibus
microcomputadora *nf* : microcomputer
microcosmos *nms & pl* : microcosm
microficha *nf* : microfiche
microfilm *nm, pl* **-films** : microfilm
micrófono *nm* : microphone
micrómetro *nm* : micrometer
microonda *nf* : microwave
microondas *nms & pl* : microwave, microwave oven
microordenador *nm Spain* : microcomputer
microorganismo *nm* : microorganism
microprocesador *nm* : microprocessor
microscópico, -ca *adj* : microscopic
microscopio *nm* : microscope
mide, etc. → **medir**
miedo *nm* **1** TEMOR : fear ⟨le tiene miedo al perro : he's scared of the dog⟩ ⟨tenían miedo de hablar : they were afraid to speak⟩ **2 dar miedo** : to frighten
miedoso, -sa *adj* TEMEROSO : fearful
miel *nf* : honey
miembro *nm* **1** : member **2** EXTREMIDAD : limb, extremity
mienta, etc. → **mentar**
miente, etc. → **mentir**

mientras[1] *adv* **1** *or* **mientras tanto** : meanwhile, in the meantime **2 mientras más** : the more ⟨mientras más como, más quiero : the more I eat, the more I want⟩

mientras[2] *conj* **1** : while, as ⟨roncaba mientras dormía : he snored while he was sleeping⟩ **2** : as long as ⟨luchará mientras pueda : he will fight as long as he is able⟩ **3 mientras que** : while, whereas ⟨él es alto mientras que ella es muy baja : he is tall, whereas she is very short⟩

miércoles *nms & pl* : Wednesday

miga *nf* **1** : crumb **2 hacer buenas (malas) migas con** : to get along well (poorly) with

migaja *nf* **1** : crumb **2 migajas** *nfpl* SOBRAS : leftovers, scraps

migración *nf, pl* **-ciones** : migration

migrante *nmf* : migrant

migraña *nf* : migraine

migratorio, -ria *adj* : migratory

mijo *nm* : millet

mil[1] *adj* : thousand

mil[2] *nm* : one thousand, a thousand

milagro *nm* : miracle ⟨de milagro : miraculously⟩

milagroso, -sa *adj* : miraculous, marvelous — **milagrosamente** *adv*

milenio *nm* : millennium

milésimo, -ma *adj* : thousandth — **milésimo** *nm*

milicia *nf* **1** : militia **2** : military service

miligramo *nm* : milligram

mililitro *nm* : milliliter

milímetro *nm* : millimeter

militancia *nf* : militancy

militante[1] *adj* : militant

militante[2] *nmf* : militant, activist

militar[1] *vi* **1** : to serve (in the military) **2** : to be active (in politics)

militar[2] *adj* : military

militar[3] *nmf* SOLDADO : soldier

militarismo *nm* : militarism

militarista *adj & nmf* : militarist

militarizar {21} *vt* : to militarize

milla *nf* : mile

millar *nm* : thousand

millón *nm, pl* **millones** : million

millonario, -ria *n* : millionaire

millonésimo[1], **-ma** *adj* : millionth

millonésimo[2] *nm* : millionth

mil millones *nms & pl* : billion

milpa *nf CA, Mex* : cornfield

milpiés *nms & pl* : millipede

mimar *vt* CONSENTIR : to pamper, to spoil

mimbre *nm* : wicker

mimeógrafo *nm* : mimeograph

mímica *nf* **1** : mime, sign language **2** IMITACIÓN : mimicry

mimo *nm* **1** : pampering, indulgence ⟨hacerle mimos a alguien : to pamper someone⟩ **2** : mime

mimoso, -sa *adj* **1** : fussy, finicky **2** : affectionate, clinging

mina *nf* **1** : mine **2** : lead (for pencils)

minar *vt* **1** : to mine **2** DEBILITAR : to undermine

minarete *nm* ALMINAR : minaret

mineral *adj & nm* : mineral

minería *nf* : mining

minero[1], **-ra** *adj* : mining

minero[2], **-ra** *n* : miner, mine worker

miniatura *nf* : miniature

minicomputadora *nf* : minicomputer

minifalda *nf* : miniskirt

minifundio *nm* : small farm

minimizar {21} *vt* : to minimize

mínimo[1], **-ma** *adj* **1** : minimum ⟨salario mínimo : minimum wage⟩ **2** : least, smallest **3** : very small, minute

mínimo[2] *nm* **1** : minimum, least amount **2** : modicum, small amount **3 como ~** : at least

minino, -na *n fam* : pussy, pussycat

miniserie *nf* : miniseries

ministerial *adj* : ministerial

ministerio *nm* : ministry, department

ministro, -tra *n* : minister, secretary ⟨primer ministro : prime minister⟩ ⟨Ministro de Defensa : Secretary of Defense⟩

minivan [ˌmini'ban, -'van] *nf, pl* **-vanes** : minivan

minoría *nf* : minority

minorista[1] *adj* : retail

minorista[2] *nmf* : retailer

minoritario, -ria *adj* : minority

mintió, etc. → **mentir**

minuciosamente *adv* **1** : minutely **2** : in great detail **3** : thoroughly, meticulously

minucioso, -sa *adj* **1** : minute **2** DETALLADO : detailed **3** : thorough, meticulous

minué *nm* : minuet

minúsculo, -la *adj* DIMINUTO : tiny, miniscule

minusvalía *nf* : disability, handicap

minusválido[1], **-da** *adj* : handicapped, disabled

minusválido[2], **-da** *n* : handicapped person

minuta *nf* **1** BORRADOR : rough draft **2** : bill, fee

minutero *nm* : minute hand

minuto *nm* : minute

mío[1], **mía** *adj* **1** : my, of mine ⟨¡Dios mío! : my God!, good heavens!⟩ ⟨una amiga mía : a friend of mine⟩ **2** : mine ⟨es mío : it's mine⟩

mío[2], **mía** *pron* (*with definite article*) : mine, my own ⟨tus zapatos son iguales a los míos : your shoes are just like mine⟩

miope *adj* : nearsighted, myopic

miopía *nf* : myopia, nearsightedness

mira *nf* **1** : sight (of a firearm or instrument) **2** : aim, objective ⟨con miras a : with the intention of, with a view to⟩ ⟨de amplias miras : broad-minded⟩ ⟨poner la mira en : to aim at, to aspire to⟩

mirada *nf* **1** : look, glance, gaze **2** EXPRESIÓN : look, expression ⟨una mirada de sorpresa : a look of surprise⟩

mirado, -da *adj* **1** : cautious, careful **2** : considerate **3 bien mirado** : well thought of **4 mal mirado** : disliked, disapproved of

mirador *nm* : balcony, lookout, vantage point

miramiento *nm* **1** CONSIDERACIÓN : consideration, respect **2 sin miramientos** : without due consideration, carelessly

mirar *vt* **1** : to look at **2** OBSERVAR : to watch **3** REFLEXIONAR : to consider, to think over — *vi* **1** : to look **2** : to face, to overlook **3 ~ por** : to look after, to look out for — **mirarse** *vr* **1** : to look at oneself **2** : to look at each other

mirasol *nm* GIRASOL : sunflower

miríada *nf* : myriad

mirlo *nm* : blackbird

mirra *nf* : myrrh

mirto *nm* ARRAYÁN : myrtle

misa *nf* : Mass

misantropía *nf* : misanthropy

misantrópico, -ca *adj* : misanthropic

misántropo, -pa *n* : misanthrope

miscelánea *nf* : miscellany

misceláneo, -nea *adj* : miscellaneous

miserable *adj* **1** LASTIMOSO : miserable, wretched **2** : paltry, meager **3** MEZQUINO : stingy, miserly **4** : despicable, vile

miseria *nf* **1** POBREZA : poverty **2** : misery, suffering **3** : pittance, meager amount

misericordia *nf* COMPASIÓN : mercy, compassion

misericordioso, -sa *adj* : merciful

mísero, -ra *adj* **1** : wretched, miserable **2** : stingy **3** : paltry, meager

misil *nm* : missile

misión *nf, pl* **misiones** : mission

misionero, -ra *adj & n* : missionary

misiva *nf* : missive, letter

mismísimo, -ma *adj* (*used as an intensifier*) : very, selfsame ⟨el mismísimo día : that very same day⟩

mismo[1] *adv* (*used as an intensifier*) : right, exactly ⟨hazlo ahora mismo : do it right now⟩ ⟨te llamará hoy mismo : he'll definitely call you today⟩

mismo[2]**, -ma** *adj* **1** : same **2** (*used as an intensifier*) : very ⟨en ese mismo momento : at that very moment⟩ **3** : oneself ⟨lo hizo ella misma : she made it herself⟩ **4 por lo mismo** : for that reason

misoginia *nf* : misogyny

misógino *nm* : misogynist

misterio *nm* : mystery

misterioso, -sa *adj* : mysterious — **misteriosamente** *adv*

misticismo *nm* : mysticism

místico[1]**, -ca** *adj* : mystic, mystical

místico[2]**, -ca** *n* : mystic

mitad *nf* **1** : half ⟨mitad y mitad : half and half⟩ **2** MEDIO : middle ⟨a mitad de : halfway through⟩ ⟨por la mitad : in half⟩

mítico, -ca *adj* : mythical, mythic

mitigar {52} *vt* ALIVIAR : to mitigate, to alleviate — **mitigación** *nf*

mitin *nm, pl* **mítines** : (political) meeting, rally

mito *nm* LEYENDA : myth, legend

mitología *nf* : mythology

mitológico, -ca *adj* : mythological

mitosis *nfs & pl* : mitosis

mitra *nf* : miter (bishop's hat)

mixto, -ta *adj* **1** : mixed, joint **2** : coeducational

mixtura *nf* : mixture, blend

mnemónico, -ca *adj* : mnemonic

mobiliario *nm* : furniture

mocasín *nm, pl* **-sines** : moccasin

mocedad *nf* **1** JUVENTUD : youth **2** : youthful prank

mochila *nf* MORRAL : backpack, knapsack

moción *nf, pl* **-ciones 1** MOVIMIENTO : motion, movement **2** : motion (to a court or assembly)

moco *nm* **1** : mucus **2** *fam* : snot ⟨limpiarse los mocos : to wipe one's (runny) nose⟩

mocoso, -sa *n* : kid, brat

moda *nf* **1** : fashion, style **2 a la moda** *or* **de ~** : in style, fashionable **3 moda pasajera** : fad

modales *nmpl* : manners

modalidad *nf* **1** CLASE : kind, type **2** MANERA : way, manner

modelar *vt* : to model, to mold — **modelarse** *vr* : to model oneself after, to emulate

modelo[1] *adj* : model ⟨una casa modelo : a model home⟩

modelo[2] *nm* : model, example, pattern

modelo[3] *nmf* : model, mannequin

módem *or* **modem** [ˈmoðɛm] *nm* : modem

moderación *nf, pl* **-ciones** MESURA : moderation

moderado, -da *adj & n* : moderate — **moderadamente** *adv*

moderador, -dora *n* : moderator, chair

moderar *vt* **1** TEMPERAR : to temper, to moderate **2** : to curb, to reduce ⟨moderar gastos : to curb spending⟩ **3** PRESIDIR : to chair (a meeting) — **moderarse** *vr* **1** : to restrain oneself **2** : to diminish, to calm down

modernidad *nf* **1** : modernity, modernness **2** : modern age

modernismo *nm* : modernism

modernista[1] *adj* : modernist, modernistic

modernista[2] *nmf* : modernist

modernizar {21} *vt* : to modernize — **modernización** *nf*

moderno, -na *adj* : modern, up-to-date

modestia *nf* : modesty

modesto, -ta *adj* : modest — **modestamente** *adv*
modificación *nf, pl* **-ciones** : alteration
modificador[1], -dora *adj* : modifying, moderating
modificador[2] → **modificante**
modificante *nm* : modifier
modificar {72} *vt* ALTERAR : to modify, to alter, to adapt
modismo *nm* : idiom
modista *nmf* **1** : dressmaker **2** : fashion designer
modo *nm* **1** MANERA : way, manner, mode ⟨de un modo u otro : one way or another⟩ ⟨a mi modo de ver : to my way of thinking⟩ **2** : mood (in grammar) **3** : mode (in music) **4 a modo de** : by way of, in the manner of, like ⟨a modo de ejemplo : by way of example⟩ **5 de cualquier modo** : in any case, anyway **6 de modo que** : so, in such a way that **7 de todos modos** : in any case, anyway **8 en cierto modo** : in a way, to a certain extent
modorra *nf* : drowsiness, lethargy
modular[1] *v* : to modulate — **modulación** *nf*
modular[2] *adj* : modular
módulo *nm* : module, unit
mofa *nf* **1** : mockery, ridicule **2 hacer mofa de** : to make fun of, to ridicule
mofarse *vr* **~ de** : to scoff at, to make fun of
mofeta *nf* ZORRILLO : skunk
mofle *nm CA, Mex* : muffler (of a car)
moflete *nm fam* : fat cheek
mofletudo, -da *adj fam* : fat-cheeked, chubby
mohín *nm, pl* **mohines** : grimace, face
mohino, -na *adj* : gloomy, melancholy
moho *nm* **1** : mold, mildew **2** : rust
mohoso, -sa *adj* **1** : moldy **2** : rusty
moisés *nm, pl* **moiseses** : bassinet, cradle
mojado[1], -da *adj* : wet
mojado[2], -da *n Mex fam* : illegal immigrant
mojar *vt* **1** : to wet, to moisten **2** : to dunk — **mojarse** *vr* : to get wet
mojigatería *nf* **1** : hypocrisy **2** GAZMOÑERÍA : primness, prudery
mojigato[1], -ta *adj* : prudish, prim — **mojigatamente** *adv*
mojigato[2], -ta *n* : prude, prig
mojón *nm, pl* **mojones** : boundary stone, marker
molar *nm* MUELA : molar
molcajete *nm Mex* : mortar
molde *nm* **1** : mold, form **2 letras de molde** : printing, block lettering
moldear *vt* **1** FORMAR : to mold, to shape **2** : to cast
moldura *nf* : molding
mole[1] *nm Mex* **1** : spicy sauce made with chilies and usually chocolate **2** : meat served with mole sauce
mole[2] *nf* : mass, bulk
molécula *nf* : molecule — **molecular** *adj*
moler {47} *vt* **1** : to grind, to crush **2** CANSAR : to exhaust, to wear out
molestar *vt* **1** FASTIDIAR : to annoy, to bother **2** : to disturb, to disrupt — *vi* : to be a nuisance — **molestarse** *vr* **~ en** : to take the trouble to
molestia *nf* **1** FASTIDIO : annoyance, bother, nuisance **2** : trouble ⟨se tomó la molestia de investigar : she took the trouble to investigate⟩ **3** MALESTAR : discomfort
molesto, -ta *adj* **1** ENOJADO : bothered, annoyed **2** FASTIDIOSO : bothersome, annoying
molestoso, -sa *adj* : bothersome, annoying
molido, -da *adj* **1** MACHACADO : ground, crushed **2 estar molido** : to be exhausted
molienda *nf* : milling, grinding
molinero, -ra *n* : miller
molinillo *nm* : grinder, mill ⟨molinillo de café : coffee grinder⟩
molino *nm* **1** : mill **2 molino de viento** : windmill
molla *nf* : soft fleshy part, flesh (of fruit), lean part (of meat)
molleja *nf* : gizzard
molusco *nm* : mollusk
momentáneamente *adv* : momentarily
momentáneo, -nea *adj* **1** : momentary **2** TEMPORARIO : temporary
momento *nm* **1** : moment, instant ⟨espera un momentito : wait just a moment⟩ **2** : time, period of time ⟨momentos difíciles : hard times⟩ **3** : present, moment ⟨los atletas del momento : the athletes of the moment, today's popular athletes⟩ **4** : momentum **5 al momento** : right away, at once **6 de ~** : at the moment, for the moment **7 de un momento a otro** : any time now **8 por momentos** : at times
momia *nf* : mummy
monaguillo *nm* ACÓLITO : altar boy
monarca *nmf* : monarch
monarquía *nf* : monarchy
monárquico, -ca *n* : monarchist
monasterio *nm* : monastery
monástico, -ca *adj* : monastic
mondadientes *nms & pl* PALILLO : toothpick
mondar *vt* : to peel
mondongo *nm* ENTRAÑAS : innards *pl*, insides *pl*, guts *pl*
moneda *nf* **1** : coin **2** : money, currency
monedero *nm* : change purse
monetario, -ria *adj* : monetary, financial
mongol, -gola *adj & n* : Mongol, Mongolian
monitor[1], -tora *n* : instructor (in sports)
monitor[2] *nm* : monitor ⟨monitor de televisión : television monitor⟩
monitorear *vt* : to monitor
monja *nf* : nun
monje *nm* : monk
mono[1], -na *adj fam* : lovely, pretty, cute, darling

mono[2], **-na** *n* : monkey
monóculo *nm* : monocle
monogamia *nf* : monogamy
monógamo, **-ma** *adj* : monogamous
monografía *nf* : monograph
monograma *nm* : monogram
monolingüe *adj* : monolingual
monolítico, **-ca** *adj* : monolithic
monolito *nm* : monolith
monólogo *nm* : monologue
monomanía *nf* : obsession
monopatín *nm, pl* **-tines** **1** : scooter **2** : skateboard
monopolio *nm* : monopoly
monopolizar {21} *vt* : to monopolize — **monopolización** *nf*
monosilábico, **-ca** *adj* : monosyllabic
monosílabo *nm* : monosyllable
monoteísmo *nm* : monotheism
monoteísta[1] *adj* : monotheistic
monoteísta[2] *nmf* : monotheist
monotonía *nf* **1** : monotony **2** : monotone
monótono, **-na** *adj* : monotonous — **monótonamente** *adv*
monóxido *nm* : monoxide ⟨monóxido de carbono : carbon monoxide⟩
monserga *nf* : gibberish, drivel
monstruo *nm* : monster
monstruosidad *nf* : monstrosity
monstruoso, **-sa** *adj* : monstrous — **monstruosamente** *adv*
monta *nf* **1** : sum, total **2** : importance, value ⟨de poca monta : unimportant, insignificant⟩
montaje *nm* **1** : assembling, assembly **2** : montage
montante *nm* : transom, fanlight
montaña *nf* **1** MONTE : mountain **2 montaña rusa** : roller coaster
montañero, **-ra** *n* : mountaineer, mountain climber
montañoso, **-sa** *adj* : mountainous
montar *vt* **1** : to mount **2** ESTABLECER : to set up, to establish **3** ARMAR : to assemble, to put together **4** : to edit (a film) **5** : to stage, to put on (a show) **6** : to cock (a gun) **7 montar en bicicleta** : to get on a bicycle **8 montar a caballo** CABALGAR : to ride horseback
monte *nm* **1** MONTAÑA : mountain, mount **2** : woodland, scrubland ⟨monte bajo : underbrush⟩ **3** : outskirts (of a town), surrounding country **4 monte de piedad** : pawnshop
montés *adj, pl* **monteses** : wild (of animals or plants)
montículo *nm* **1** : mound, heap **2** : hillock, knoll
monto *nm* : amount, total
montón *nm, pl* **-tones** **1** : heap, pile **2** *fam* : ton, load ⟨un montón de preguntas : a ton of questions⟩ ⟨montones de gente : loads of people⟩
montura *nf* **1** : mount (horse) **2** : saddle, tack **3** : setting, mounting (of jewelry) **4** : frame (of glasses)
monumental *adj fam* **1** : tremendous, terrific **2** : massive, huge
monumento *nm* : monument
monzón *nm, pl* **monzones** : monsoon
moño *nm* **1** : bun (chignon) **2** LAZO : bow, knot ⟨corbata de moño : bow tie⟩
moquear *vi* : to snivel
moquillo *nm* : distemper
mora *nf* **1** : blackberry **2** : mulberry
morada *nf* RESIDENCIA : dwelling, abode
morado[1], **-da** *adj* : purple
morado[2] *nm* : purple
morador, **-dora** *n* : dweller, inhabitant
moral[1] *adj* : moral — **moralmente** *adv*
moral[2] *nf* **1** MORALIDAD : ethics, morality, morals *pl* **2** ÁNIMO : morale, spirits *pl*
moraleja *nf* : moral (of a story)
moralidad *nf* : morality
moralista[1] *adj* : moralistic
moralista[2] *nmf* : moralist
morar *vi* : to dwell, to reside
moratoria *nf* : moratorium
mórbido, **-da** *adj* : morbid
morboso, **-sa** *adj* : morbid — **morbosidad** *nf*
morcilla *nf* : blood sausage, blood pudding
mordacidad *nf* : bite, sharpness
mordaz *adj* : caustic, scathing
mordaza *nf* **1** : gag **2** : clamp
mordedura *nf* : bite (of an animal)
morder {47} *v* : to bite
mordida *nf* **1** : bite **2** *CA, Mex* : bribe, payoff
mordisco *nm* : bite, nibble
mordisquear *vt* : to nibble (on), to bite
morena *nf* **1** : moraine **2** : moray (eel)
moreno[1], **-na** *adj* **1** : brunette **2** : dark, dark-skinned
moreno[2], **-na** *n* **1** : brunette **2** : dark-skinned person
moretón *nm, pl* **-tones** : bruise
morfina *nf* : morphine
morfología *nf* : morphology
morgue *nf* : morgue
moribundo[1], **-da** *adj* : dying, moribund
moribundo[2], **-da** *n* : dying person
morillo *nm* : andiron
morir {46} *vi* **1** FALLECER : to die **2** APAGARSE : to die out, to go out
mormón, **-mona** *adj & n, pl* **mormones** : Mormon
moro[1], **-ra** *adj* : Moorish
moro[2], **-ra** *n* **1** : Moor **2** : Muslim
morosidad *nf* **1** : delinquency (in payment) **2** : slowness
moroso, **-sa** *adj* **1** : delinquent, in arrears ⟨cuentas morosas : delinquent accounts⟩ **2** : slow, sluggish
morral *nm* MOCHILA : backpack, knapsack
morralla *nf* **1** : small fish **2** : trash, riffraff **3** *Mex* : small change
morriña *nf* : homesickness
morro *nm* HOCICO : snout

morsa *nf* : walrus
morse *nm* : Morse code
mortaja *nf* SUDARIO : shroud
mortal[1] *adj* **1** : mortal **2** FATAL : fatal, deadly — **mortalmente** *adv*
mortal[2] *nmf* : mortal
mortalidad *nf* : mortality
mortandad *nf* **1** : loss of life, death toll **2** : carnage, slaughter
mortero *nm* : mortar (bowl, cannon, or building material)
mortífero, -ra *adj* LETAL : deadly, fatal
mortificación *nf, pl* **-ciones** **1** : mortification **2** TORMENTO : anguish, torment
mortificar {72} *vt* **1** : to mortify **2** TORTURAR : to trouble, to torment — **mortificarse** *vr* : to be mortified, to feel embarrassed
mosaico *nm* : mosaic
mosca *nf* **1** : fly **2 mosca común** : housefly
moscada *adj* **nuez moscada** : nutmeg
moscovita *adj & nmf* : Muscovite
mosquearse *vr* **1** : to become suspicious **2** : to take offense
mosquete *nm* : musket
mosquetero *nm* : musketeer
mosquitero *nm* : mosquito net
mosquito *nm* ZANCUDO : mosquito
mostachón *nm, pl* **-chones** : macaroon
mostaza *nf* : mustard
mostrador *nm* : counter (in a store)
mostrar {19} *vt* **1** : to show **2** EXHIBIR : to exhibit, to display — **mostrarse** *vr* : to show oneself, to appear
mota *nf* **1** : fleck, speck **2** : defect, blemish
mote *nm* SOBRENOMBRE : nickname
moteado, -da *adj* : dotted, spotted, dappled
motel *nm* : motel
motín *nm, pl* **motines** **1** : riot **2** : rebellion, mutiny
motivación *nf, pl* **-ciones** : motivation — **motivacional** *adj*
motivar *vt* **1** CAUSAR : to cause **2** IMPULSAR : to motivate
motivo *nm* **1** MÓVIL : motive **2** CAUSA : cause, reason **3** TEMA : theme, motif
moto *nf* : motorcycle, motorbike
motocicleta *nf* : motorcycle
motociclismo *nm* : motorcycling
motociclista *nmf* : motorcyclist
motor[1], -ra *adj* MOTRIZ : motor
motor[2] *nm* **1** : motor, engine **2** : driving force, cause
motorista *nmf* : motorist
motriz *adj, pl* **motrices** : driving
motu proprio *adv* **de motu proprio** [de ˈmotuˈproprio] : voluntarily, of one's own accord
mousse [ˈmus] *nmf* : mousse
mover {47} *vt* **1** TRASLADAR : to move, to shift **2** AGITAR : to shake, to nod (the head) **3** ACCIONAR : to power, to drive **4** INDUCIR : to provoke, to cause **5** : to excite, to stir — **moverse** *vr* **1** : to move, to move over **2** : to hurry, to get a move on **3** : to get moving, to make an effort
movible *adj* : movable
movida *nf* : move (in a game)
móvil[1] *adj* : mobile
móvil[2] *nm* **1** MOTIVO : motive **2** : mobile
movilidad *nf* : mobility
movilizar {21} *vt* : to mobilize — **movilización** *nf*
movimiento *nm* : movement, motion ⟨movimiento del cuerpo : bodily movement⟩ ⟨movimiento sindicalista : labor movement⟩
mozo[1], -za *adj* : young, youthful
mozo[2], -za *n* **1** JOVEN : young man *m,* young woman *f,* youth **2** : helper, servant **3** *Arg, Chile, Col, Peru* : waiter *m,* waitress *f*
mucamo, -ma *n* : servant, maid *f*
muchacha *nf* : maid
muchacho, -cha *n* **1** : kid, boy *m,* girl *f* **2** JOVEN : young man *m,* young woman *f*
muchedumbre *nf* MULTITUD : crowd, multitude
mucho[1] *adv* **1** : much, a lot ⟨mucho más : much more⟩ ⟨le gusta mucho : he likes it a lot⟩ **2** : long, a long time ⟨tardó mucho en venir : he was a long time getting here⟩ **3 por mucho que** : no matter how much
mucho[2], -cha *adj* **1** : a lot of, many, much ⟨mucha gente : a lot of people⟩ ⟨hace mucho tiempo que no lo veo : I haven't seen him in ages⟩ **2 muchas veces** : often
mucho[3], -cha *pron* **1** : a lot, many, much ⟨hay mucho que hacer : there is a lot to do⟩ ⟨muchas no vinieron : many didn't come⟩ **2 cuando ~** *or* **como ~** : at most **3 con ~** : by far **4 ni mucho menos** : not at all, far from it
mucílago *nm* : mucilage
mucosidad *nf* : mucus
mucoso, -sa *adj* : mucous, slimy
muda *nf* **1** : change ⟨muda de ropa : change of clothes⟩ **2** : molt, molting
mudanza *nf* **1** CAMBIO : change **2** TRASLADO : move, moving
mudar *v* **1** CAMBIAR : to change **2** : to molt, to shed — **mudarse** *vr* **1** TRASLADARSE : to move (one's residence) **2** : to change (clothes)
mudo[1], -da *adj* **1** SILENCIOSO : silent ⟨el cine mudo : silent films⟩ **2** : mute, dumb
mudo[2], -da *n* : mute
mueble *nm* **1** : piece of furniture **2 muebles** *nmpl* : furniture, furnishings
mueblería *nf* : furniture store
mueca *nf* : grimace, face
muela *nf* **1** : tooth, molar ⟨dolor de muelas : toothache⟩ ⟨muela de juicio : wisdom tooth⟩ **2** : millstone **3** : whetstone
muele, etc. → **moler**

muelle[1] *adj* : soft, comfortable, easy

muelle[2] *nm* **1** : wharf, dock **2** RESORTE : spring

muérdago *nm* : mistletoe

muerde, etc. → **morder**

muere, etc. → **morir**

muerte *nf* : death

muerto[1] *pp* → **morir**

muerto[2], **-ta** *adj* **1** : dead **2** : lifeless, flat, dull **3 ~ de** : dying of ⟨estoy muerto de hambre : I'm dying of hunger⟩

muerto[3], **-ta** *nm* DIFUNTO : dead person, deceased

muesca *nf* : nick, notch

muestra[1], **etc.** → **mostrar**

muestra[2] *nf* **1** : sample **2** SEÑAL : sign, show ⟨una muestra de respeto : a show of respect⟩ **3** EXPOSICIÓN : exhibition, exposition **4** : pattern, model

mueve, etc. → **mover**

mugido *nm* : moo, lowing, bellow

mugir {35} *vi* : to moo, to low, to bellow

mugre *nf* SUCIEDAD : grime, filth

mugriento, -ta *adj* : filthy

muguete *nm* : lily of the valley

muja, etc. → **mugir**

mujer *nf* **1** : woman **2** ESPOSA : wife

mulato, -ta *adj & n* : mulatto

muleta *nf* : crutch

mullido, -da *adj* **1** : soft, fluffy **2** : spongy, springy

mulo, -la *n* : mule

multa *nf* : fine

multar *vt* : to fine

multicolor *adj* : multicolored

multicultural *adj* : multicultural

multidisciplinario, -ria *adj* : multidisciplinary

multifacético, -ca *adj* : multifaceted

multifamiliar *adj* : multifamily

multilateral *adj* : multilateral

multimedia *nf* : multimedia

multimillonario, -ria *n* : multimillionaire

multinacional *adj* : multinational

múltiple *adj* : multiple

multiplicación *nf, pl* **-ciones** : multiplication

multiplicar {72} *v* **1** : to multiply **2** : to increase — **multiplicarse** *vr* : to multiply, to reproduce

multiplicidad *nf* : multiplicity

múltiplo *nm* : multiple

multitud *nf* MUCHEDUMBRE : crowd, multitude

multiuso, -sa *adj* : multipurpose

multivitamínico, -ca *adj* : multivitamin

mundano, -na *adj* : worldly, earthly

mundial *adj* : world, worldwide

mundialmente *adv* : worldwide, all over the world

mundo *nm* **1** : world **2 todo el mundo** : everyone, everybody

municiones *nfpl* : ammunition, munitions

municipal *adj* : municipal

municipio *nm* **1** : municipality **2** AYUNTAMIENTO : town council

muñeca *nf* **1** : doll **2** MANIQUÍ : mannequin **3** : wrist

muñeco *nm* **1** : doll, boy doll **2** MARIONETA : puppet

muñón *nm, pl* **muñones** : stump (of an arm or leg)

mural *adj & nm* : mural

muralista *nmf* : muralist

muralla *nf* : rampart, wall

murciélago *nm* : bat (animal)

murga *nf* : band of street musicians

murió, etc. → **morir**

murmullo *nm* **1** : murmur, murmuring **2** : rustling, rustle ⟨el murmullo de las hojas : the rustling of the leaves⟩

murmurar *vt* **1** : to murmur, to mutter **2** : to whisper (gossip) — *vi* **1** : to murmur **2** CHISMEAR : to gossip

muro *nm* : wall

musa *nf* : muse

musaraña *nf* : shrew

muscular *adj* : muscular

musculatura *nf* : muscles *pl*, musculature

músculo *nm* : muscle

musculoso, -sa *adj* : muscular, brawny

muselina *nf* : muslin

museo *nm* : museum

musgo *nm* : moss

musgoso, -sa *adj* : mossy

música *nf* : music

musical *adj* : musical — **musicalmente** *adv*

músico[1], **-ca** *adj* : musical

músico[2], **-ca** *n* : musician

musitar *vt* : to mumble, to murmur

muslo *nm* : thigh

musulmán, -mana *adj & n, mpl* **-manes** : Muslim

mutación *nf, pl* **-ciones** : mutation

mutante *adj & nm* : mutant

mutar *v* : to mutate

mutilar *vt* : to mutilate — **mutilación** *nf*

mutis *nm* **1** : exit (in theater) **2** : silence

mutual *adj* : mutual

mutuo, -tua *adj* : mutual, reciprocal — **mutuamente** *adv*

muy *adv* **1** : very, quite ⟨es muy inteligente : she's very intelligent⟩ ⟨muy bien : very well, fine⟩ ⟨eso es muy americano : that's typically American⟩ **2** : too ⟨es muy grande para él : it's too big for him⟩

N

n *nf* : fourteenth letter of the Spanish alphabet

nabo *nm* : turnip

nácar *nm* MADREPERLA : nacre, mother-of-pearl

nacarado, -da *adj* : pearly

nacer {48} *vi* **1** : to be born ⟨nací en Guatemala : I was born in Guatemala⟩ ⟨no nació ayer : he wasn't born yesterday⟩ **2** : to hatch **3** : to bud, to sprout **4** : to rise, to originate **5 nacer para algo** : to be born to be something **6 volver a nacer** : to have a lucky escape

nacido[1], -da *adj* **1** : born **2 recién nacido** : newborn

nacido[2], -da *n* **1 los nacidos** : those born (at a particular time) **2 recién nacido** : newborn baby

naciente *adj* **1** : newfound, growing **2** : rising ⟨el sol naciente : the rising sun⟩

nacimiento *nm* **1** : birth **2** : source (of a river) **3** : beginning, origin **4** BELÉN : Nativity scene, crèche

nación *nf, pl* **naciones** : nation, country, people (of a country)

nacional[1] *adj* : national

nacional[2] *nmf* CIUDADANO : national, citizen

nacionalidad *nf* : nationality

nacionalismo *nm* : nationalism

nacionalista[1] *adj* : nationalist, nationalistic

nacionalista[2] *nmf* : nationalist

nacionalización *nf, pl* **-ciones** **1** : nationalization **2** : naturalization

nacionalizar {21} *vt* **1** : to nationalize **2** : to naturalize (as a citizen) — **nacionalizarse** *vr*

naco, -ca *adj Mex* : trashy, vulgar, common

nada[1] *adv* : not at all, not in the least ⟨no estamos nada cansados : we are not at all tired⟩

nada[2] *nf* **1** : nothingness **2** : smidgen, bit ⟨una nada le disgusta : the slightest thing upsets him⟩

nada[3] *pron* **1** : nothing ⟨no estoy haciendo nada : I'm not doing anything⟩ **2 casi nada** : next to nothing **3 de ~** : you're welcome **4 dentro de nada** : very soon, in no time **5 nada más** : nothing else, nothing more

nadador, -dora *n* : swimmer

nadar *vi* **1** : to swim **2 ~ en** : to be swimming in, to be rolling in — *vt* : to swim

nadería *nf* : small thing, trifle

nadie *pron* : nobody, no one ⟨no vi a nadie : I didn't see anyone⟩

nadir *nm* : nadir

nado *nm* **1** *Mex* : swimming **2 a ~** : swimming ⟨cruzó el río a nado : he swam across the river⟩

nafta *nf* **1** : naphtha **2** (*in various countries*) : gasoline

naftalina *nf* : naphthalene, mothballs *pl*

náhuatl[1] *adj & nmf, pl* **nahuas** : Nahuatl

náhuatl[2] *nm* : Nahuatl (language)

nailon → **nilón**

naipe *nm* : playing card

nalga *nf* **1** : buttock **2 nalgas** *nfpl* : buttocks, bottom

nalgada *nf* : smack on the bottom, spanking

namibio, -bia *adj & n* : Namibian

nana *nf* **1** : lullaby **2** *fam* : grandma **3** *CA, Col, Mex, Ven* : nanny

nanay *interj fam* : no way!, not likely!

naranja[1] *adj & nm* : orange (color)

naranja[2] *nf* : orange (fruit)

naranjal *nm* : orange grove

naranjo *nm* : orange tree

narcisismo *nm* : narcissism

narcisista[1] *adj* : narcissistic

narcisista[2] *nmf* : narcissist

narciso *nm* : narcissus, daffodil

narcótico[1], -ca *adj* : narcotic

narcótico[2] *nm* : narcotic

narcotizar {21} *vt* : to drug, to dope

narcotraficante *nmf* : drug trafficker

narcotráfico *nm* : drug trafficking

narigón, -gona *adj, mpl* **-gones** : big-nosed

narigudo → **narigón**

nariz *nf, pl* **narices** **1** : nose ⟨sonar(se) la nariz : to blow one's nose⟩ **2** : sense of smell

narración *nf, pl* **-ciones** : narration, account

narrador, -dora *n* : narrator

narrar *vt* : to narrate, to tell

narrativa *nf* : narrative, story

narrativo, -va *adj* : narrative

narval *nm* : narwhal

nasa *nf* : creel

nasal *adj* : nasal

nata *nf* **1** : cream ⟨nata batida : whipped cream⟩ **2** : skin (on boiled milk)

natación *nf, pl* **-ciones** : swimming

natal *adj* : native, natal

natalicio *nm* : birthday ⟨el natalicio de George Washington : George Washington's birthday⟩

natalidad *nf* : birthrate

natillas *nfpl* : custard

natividad *nf* : birth, nativity

nativo, -va *adj & n* : native

nato, -ta *adj* : born, natural

natural[1] *adj* **1** : natural **2** : normal ⟨como es natural : naturally, as expected⟩ **3 ~ de** : native of, from **4 de tamaño natural** : life-size

natural[2] *nm* **1** CARÁCTER : disposition, temperament **2** : native ⟨un natural de Venezuela : a native of Venezuela⟩

naturaleza *nf* **1** : nature ⟨la madre naturaleza : mother nature⟩ **2** ÍNDOLE : nature, disposition, constitution ⟨la naturaleza humana : human nature⟩ **3 naturaleza muerta** : still life

naturalidad *nf* : simplicity, naturalness
naturalismo *nm* : naturalism
naturalista[1] *adj* : naturalistic
naturalista[2] *nmf* : naturalist
naturalización *nf, pl* **-ciones** : naturalization
naturalizar {21} *vt* : to naturalize — **naturalizarse** *vr* NACIONALIZARSE : to become naturalized
naturalmente *adv* **1** : naturally, inherently **2** : of course
naufragar {52} *vi* **1** : to be shipwrecked **2** FRACASAR : to fail, to collapse
naufragio *nm* **1** : shipwreck **2** FRACASO : failure, collapse
náufrago[1], **-ga** *adj* : shipwrecked, castaway
náufrago[2], **-ga** *n* : shipwrecked person, castaway
náusea *nf* **1** : nausea **2 dar náuseas** : to nauseate, to disgust **3 náuseas matutinas** : morning sickness
nauseabundo, **-da** *adj* : nauseating, sickening
náutica *nf* : navigation
náutico, **-ca** *adj* : nautical
nautilo *nm* : nautilus
navaja *nf* **1** : pocketknife, penknife ⟨navaja de muelle : switchblade⟩ **2 navaja de afeitar** : straight razor, razor blade
navajo, **-ja** *adj & n* : Navajo
naval *adj* : naval
nave *nf* **1** : ship ⟨nave capitana : flagship⟩ ⟨nave espacial : spaceship⟩ **2** : nave ⟨nave lateral : aisle⟩ **3 quemar uno sus naves** : to burn one's bridges
navegabilidad *nf* : navigability
navegable *adj* : navigable
navegación *nf, pl* **-ciones** : navigation
navegante[1] *adj* : sailing, seafaring
navegante[2] *nmf* : navigator
navegar {52} *v* : to navigate, to sail
Navidad *nf* : Christmas, Christmastime ⟨Feliz Navidad : Merry Christmas⟩
navideño, **-ña** *adj* : Christmas
naviero, **-ra** *adj* : shipping
náyade *nf* : naiad
nazca, etc. → **nacer**
nazi *adj & nmf* : Nazi
nazismo *nm* : Nazism
nébeda *nf* : catnip
neblina *nf* : light fog, mist
neblinoso, **-sa** *adj* : misty, foggy
nebulosa *nf* : nebula
nebulosidad *nf* : mistiness, haziness
nebuloso, **-sa** *adj* **1** : hazy, misty **2** : nebulous, vague
necedad *nf* : stupidity, foolishness ⟨decir necedades : to talk nonsense⟩
necesariamente *adv* : necessarily
necesario, **-ria** *adj* **1** : necessary **2 si es necesario** : if need be **3 hacerse necesario** : to be required
neceser *nm* : toilet kit, vanity case
necesidad *nf* **1** : need, necessity **2** : poverty, want **3 necesidades** *nfpl* : hardships **4 hacer sus necesidades** : to relieve oneself
necesitado, **-da** *adj* : needy
necesitar *vt* **1** : to need **2** : to necessitate, to require — *vi* **~ de** : to have need of
necio[1], **-cia** *adj* **1** : foolish, silly, dumb **2** *fam* : naughty
necio[2], **-cia** *n* ESTÚPIDO : fool, idiot
necrología *nf* : obituary
necrópolis *nfs & pl* : cemetery
néctar *nm* : nectar
nectarina *nf* : nectarine
neerlandés[1], **-desa** *adj, mpl* **-deses** HOLANDÉS : Dutch
neerlandés[2], **-desa** *n, mpl* **-deses** HOLANDÉS : Dutch person, Dutchman *m*
nefando, **-da** *adj* : unspeakable, heinous
nefario, **-ria** *adj* : nefarious
nefasto, **-ta** *adj* **1** : ill-fated, unlucky **2** : disastrous, terrible
negación *nf, pl* **-ciones** **1** : negation, denial **2** : negative (in grammar)
negar {49} *vt* **1** : to deny **2** REHUSAR : to refuse **3** : to disown — **negarse** *vr* **1** : to refuse **2** : to deny oneself
negativa *nf* **1** : denial **2** : refusal
negativo[1], **-va** *adj* : negative
negativo[2] *nm* : negative (of a photograph)
negligé *nm* : negligee
negligencia *nf* : negligence
negligente *adj* : neglectful, negligent — **negligentemente** *adv*
negociable *adj* : negotiable
negociación *nf, pl* **-ciones** **1** : negotiation **2 negociación colectiva** : collective bargaining
negociador, **-dora** *n* : negotiator
negociante *nmf* : businessman *m*, businesswoman *f*
negociar *vt* : to negotiate — *vi* : to deal, to do business
negocio *nm* **1** : business, place of business **2** : deal, transaction **3 negocios** *nmpl* : commerce, trade, business
negrero, **-ra** *n* **1** : slave trader **2** *fam* : slave driver, brutal boss
negrita *nf* : boldface (type)
negro[1], **-gra** *adj* **1** : black, dark **2** BRONCEADO : suntanned **3** : gloomy, awful, desperate ⟨la cosa se está poniendo negra : things are looking bad⟩ **4 mercado negro** : black market
negro[2], **-gra** *n* **1** : dark-skinned person, black person **2** *fam* : darling, dear
negro[3] *nm* : black (color)
negrura *nf* : blackness
negruzco, **-ca** *adj* : blackish
nene, **-na** *n* : baby, small child
nenúfar *nm* : water lily
neocelandés → **neozelandés**
neoclasicismo *nm* : neoclassicism
neoclásico, **-ca** *adj* : neoclassical
neófito, **-ta** *n* : neophyte, novice
neologismo *nm* : neologism
neón *nm, pl* **neones** : neon
neoyorquino[1], **-na** *adj* : of or from New York

neoyorquino[2], **-na** *n* : New Yorker

neozelandés[1], **-desa** *adj, mpl* **-deses** : of or from New Zealand

neozelandés[2], **-desa** *n, mpl* **-deses** : New Zealander

nepalés, **-lesa** *adj & n, mpl* **-leses** : Nepali

nepotismo *nm* : nepotism

neptunio *nm* : neptunium

Neptuno *nm* : Neptune

nervio *nm* **1** : nerve **2** : tendon, sinew, gristle (in meat) **3** : energy, drive **4** : rib (of a vault) **5 nervios** *nmpl* : nerves ⟨estar mal de los nervios : to be a bundle of nerves⟩ ⟨ataque de nervios : nervous breakdown⟩

nerviosamente *adv* : nervously

nerviosidad → **nerviosismo**

nerviosismo *nf* : nervousness, anxiety

nervioso, -sa *adj* **1** : nervous, nerve ⟨sistema nervioso : nervous system⟩ **2** : high-strung, restless, anxious ⟨ponerse nervioso : to get nervous⟩ **3** : vigorous, energetic

nervudo, **-da** *adj* : sinewy, wiry

neta *nf Mex fam* : truth ⟨la neta es que me cae mal : the truth is, I don't like her⟩

netamente *adv* : clearly, obviously

neto, **-ta** *adj* **1** : net ⟨peso neto : net weight⟩ **2** : clear, distinct

neumático[1], **-ca** *adj* : pneumatic

neumático[2] *nm* LLANTA : tire

neumonía *nf* PULMONÍA : pneumonia

neural *adj* : neural

neuralgia *nf* : neuralgia

neuritis *nf* : neuritis

neurología *nf* : neurology

neurológico, **-ca** *adj* : neurological, neurologic

neurólogo, **-ga** *n* : neurologist

neurosis *nfs & pl* : neurosis

neurótico, **-ca** *adj & n* : neurotic

neutral *adj* : neutral

neutralidad *nf* : neutrality

neutralizar {21} *vt* : to neutralize — **neutralización** *nf*

neutro, **-tra** *adj* **1** : neutral **2** : neuter

neutrón *nm, pl* **neutrones** : neutron

nevada *nf* : snowfall

nevado, **-da** *adj* **1** : snowcapped **2** : snow-white

nevar {55} *v impers* : to snow

nevasca *nf* : snowstorm, blizzard

nevera *nf* REFRIGERADOR : refrigerator

nevería *nf Mex* : ice cream parlor

nevisca *nf* : light snowfall, flurry

nevoso, **-sa** *adj* : snowy

nexo *nm* VÍNCULO : link, connection, nexus

ni *conj* **1** : neither, nor ⟨afuera no hace ni frío ni calor : it's neither cold nor hot outside⟩ **2 ni que** : not even if, not as if ⟨ni que me pagaran : not even if they paid me⟩ ⟨ni que fuera (yo) su madre : it's not as if I were his mother⟩ **3 ni siquiera** : not even ⟨ni siquiera nos llamaron : they didn't even call us⟩

nicaragüense *adj & nmf* : Nicaraguan

nicho *nm* : niche

nicotina *nf* : nicotine

nido *nm* **1** : nest **2** : hiding place, den

niebla *nf* : fog, mist

niega, niegue etc. → **negar**

nieto, **-ta** *n* **1** : grandson *m*, granddaughter *f* **2 nietos** *nmpl* : grandchildren

nieva, etc. → **nevar**

nieve *nf* **1** : snow **2** *Cuba, Mex, PRi* : sherbet

nigeriano, **-na** *adj & n* : Nigerian

nigua *nf* : sand flea, chigger

nihilismo *nm* : nihilism

nilón *or* **nilon** *nm, pl* **nilones** : nylon

nimbo *nm* **1** : halo **2** : nimbus

nimiedad *nf* INSIGNIFICANCIA : trifle, triviality

nimio, **-mia** *adj* INSIGNIFICANTE : insignificant, trivial

ninfa *nf* : nymph

ningunear *vt Mex fam* : to disrespect

ninguno[1], **-na** (**ningún** *before masculine singular nouns*) *adj, mpl* **ningunos** : no, none ⟨no es ninguna tonta : she's no fool⟩ ⟨no debe hacerse en ningún momento : that should never be done⟩

ninguno[2], **-na** *pron* **1** : neither, none ⟨ninguno de los dos ha vuelto aún : neither one has returned yet⟩ **2** : no one, no other ⟨te quiero más que a ninguna : I love you more than any other⟩

niña *nf* **1** PUPILA : pupil (of the eye) **2 la niña de los ojos** : the apple of one's eye

niñada *nf* **1** : childishness **2** : trifle, silly thing

niñería → **niñada**

niñero, **-ra** *n* : baby-sitter, nanny

niñez *nf, pl* **niñeces** INFANCIA : childhood

niño, **-ña** *n* : child, boy *m*, girl *f*

niobio *nm* : niobium

nipón, **-pona** *adj & n, mpl* **nipones** JAPONÉS : Japanese

níquel *nm* : nickel

nitidez *nf, pl* **-deces** CLARIDAD : clarity, vividness, sharpness

nítido, **-da** *adj* CLARO : clear, vivid, sharp

nitrato *nm* : nitrate

nítrico, **-ca** *adj* **ácido nítrico** : nitric acid

nitrito *nm* : nitrite

nitrógeno *nm* : nitrogen

nitroglicerina *nf* : nitroglycerin

nivel *nm* **1** : level, height ⟨nivel del mar : sea level⟩ **2** : level, standard ⟨nivel de vida : standard of living⟩

nivelar *vt* : to level (out)

nixtamal *nm Mex* : limed corn used for tortillas

no *adv* **1** : no ⟨¿quieres ir al mercado? no, voy más tarde : do you want to go shopping? no, I'm going later⟩ **2** : not ⟨¡no hagas eso! : don't do that!⟩ ⟨creo que no : I don't think so⟩ **3** : non- ⟨no fumador : non-smoker⟩ **4 ¡como no!** : of course! **5 no bien** : as soon as, no sooner

nobelio *nm* : nobelium
noble[1] *adj* : noble — **noblemente** *adv*
noble[2] *nmf* : nobleman *m,* noblewoman *f*
nobleza *nf* **1** : nobility **2** HONRADEZ : honesty, integrity
nocaut *nm* : knockout, KO
noche *nf* **1** : night, nighttime, evening **2 buenas noches** : good evening, good night **3 de noche** *or* **por la noche** : at night **4 hacerse de noche** : to get dark
Nochebuena *nf* : Christmas Eve
nochecita *nf* : dusk
Nochevieja *nf* : New Year's Eve
noción *nf, pl* **nociones** **1** CONCEPTO : notion, concept **2 nociones** *nfpl* : smattering, rudiments *pl*
nocivo, -va *adj* DAÑINO : harmful, noxious
noctámbulo, -la *n* **1** : sleepwalker **2** : night owl
nocturno[1], **-na** *adj* : night, nocturnal
nocturno[2] *nm* : nocturne
nodriza *nf* : wet nurse
nódulo *nm* : nodule
nogal *nm* **1** : walnut tree **2** *Mex* : pecan tree **3 nogal americano** : hickory
nómada[1] *adj* : nomadic
nómada[2] *nmf* : nomad
nomás *adv* : only, just ⟨lo hice nomás porque sí : I did it just because⟩ ⟨nomás de recordarlo me enojo : I get angry just remembering it⟩ ⟨nomás faltan dos semanas para Navidad : there are only two weeks left till Christmas⟩
nombradía *nf* RENOMBRE : fame, renown
nombrado, -da *adj* : famous, well-known
nombramiento *nm* : appointment, nomination
nombrar *vt* **1** : to appoint **2** : to mention, to name
nombre *nm* **1** : name ⟨nombre de pluma : pseudonym, pen name⟩ ⟨en nombre : on behalf of⟩ ⟨sin nombre : nameless⟩ **2** : noun ⟨nombre propio : proper noun⟩ **3** : fame, renown
nomenclatura *nf* : nomenclature
nomeolvides *nmfs & pl* : forget-me-not
nómina *nf* : payroll
nominación *nf, pl* **-ciones** : nomination
nominal *adj* : nominal — **nominalmente** *adv*
nominar *vt* : to nominate
nominativo[1], **-va** *adj* : nominative
nominativo[2] *nm* : nominative (case)
nomo *nm* : gnome
non[1] *adj* IMPAR : odd, not even
non[2] *nm* : odd number
nonagésimo[1], **-ma** *adj* : ninetieth, ninety-
nonagésimo[2], **-ma** *n* : ninetieth, ninety- (in a series)
nono, -na *adj* : ninth — **nono** *nm*
nopal *nm* : nopal, cactus
nopalitos *nmpl Mex* : pickled cactus leaves
noquear *vt* : to knock out, to KO
norcoreano, -na *adj & n* : North Korean
nordeste[1] *or* **noreste** *adj* **1** : northeastern **2** : northeasterly
nordeste[2] *or* **noreste** *nm* : northeast
nórdico, -ca *adj & n* **1** ESCANDINAVO : Scandinavian **2** : Norse
noreste → **nordeste**
noria *nf* **1** : waterwheel **2** : Ferris wheel
norirlandés[1], **-desa** *adj, mpl* **-deses** : Northern Irish
norirlandés[2], **-desa** *n, mpl* **-deses** : person from Northern Ireland
norma *nf* **1** : rule, regulation **2** : norm, standard
normal *adj* **1** : normal, usual **2** : standard **3 escuela normal** : teacher-training college
normalidad *nf* : normality, normalcy
normalización *nf, pl* **-ciones** *nf* **1** REGULARIZACIÓN : normalization **2** ESTANDARIZACIÓN : standardization
normalizar {21} *vt* **1** REGULARIZAR : to normalize **2** ESTANDARIZAR : to standardize — **normalizarse** *vr* : to return to normal
normalmente *adv* GENERALMENTE : ordinarily, generally
noroeste[1] *adj* **1** : northwestern **2** : northwesterly
noroeste[2] *nm* : northwest
norte[1] *adj* : north, northern
norte[2] *nm* **1** : north **2** : north wind **3** META : aim, objective
norteamericano, -na *adj & n* **1** : North American **2** AMERICANO, ESTADOUNIDENSE : American, native or inhabitant of the United States
norteño[1], **-ña** *adj* : northern
norteño[2], **-ña** *n* : Northerner
noruego[1], **-ga** *adj & n* : Norwegian
noruego[2] *nm* : Norwegian (language)
nos *pron* **1** : us ⟨nos enviaron a la frontera : they sent us to the border⟩ **2** : ourselves ⟨nos divertimos muchísimo : we enjoyed ourselves a great deal⟩ **3** : each other, one another ⟨nos vimos desde lejos : we saw each other from far away⟩ **4** : to us, for us, from us ⟨nos lo dio : he gave it to us⟩ ⟨nos lo compraron : they bought it from us⟩
nosotros, -tras *pron* **1** : we ⟨nosotros llegamos ayer : we arrived yesterday⟩ **2** : us ⟨ven con nosotros : come with us⟩ **3 nosotros mismos** : ourselves ⟨lo arreglamos nosotros mismos : we fixed it ourselves⟩
nostalgia *nf* **1** : nostalgia, longing **2** : homesickness
nostálgico, -ca *adj* **1** : nostalgic **2** : homesick
nota *nf* **1** : note, message **2** : announcement ⟨nota de prensa : press release⟩ **3** : grade, mark (in school) **4** : characteristic, feature, touch **5** : note (in music) **6** : bill, check (in a restaurant)

notable *adj* **1** : notable, noteworthy **2** : outstanding

notación *nf, pl* **-ciones** : notation

notar *vt* **1** : to notice ⟨hacer notar algo : to point out something⟩ **2** : to tell ⟨la diferencia se nota inmediatamente : you can tell the difference right away⟩ — **notarse** *vr* **1** : to be evident, to show **2** : to feel, to seem

notario, -ria *n* : notary, notary public

noticia *nf* **1** : news item, piece of news **2 noticias** *nfpl* : news

noticiero *nm* : news program, newscast

noticioso, -sa *adj* : news ⟨agencia noticiosa : news agency⟩

notificación *nf, pl* **-ciones** : notification

notificar {72} *vt* : to notify, to inform

notoriedad *nf* **1** : knowledge, obviousness **2** : fame, notoriety

notorio, -ria *adj* **1** OBVIO : obvious, evident **2** CONOCIDO : well-known

novato[1], -ta *adj* : inexperienced, new

novato[2], -ta *n* : beginner, novice

novecientos[1], -tas *adj* : nine hundred

novecientos[2] *nms & pl* : nine hundred

novedad *nf* **1** : newness, novelty **2** : innovation

novedoso, -sa *adj* : original, novel

novel *adj* NOVATO : inexperienced, new

novela *nf* **1** : novel **2** : soap opera

novelar *vt* : to fictionalize, to make a novel out of

novelesco, -ca *adj* **1** : fictional **2** : fantastic, fabulous

novelista *nmf* : novelist

novena *nf* : novena

noveno, -na *adj* : ninth — **noveno, -na** *n*

noventa *adj & nm* : ninety

noventavo[1], -va *adj* : ninetieth

noventavo[2] *nm* : ninetieth (fraction)

noviazgo *nm* **1** : courtship, relationship **2** : engagement, betrothal

novicio, -cia *n* **1** : novice (in religion) **2** PRINCIPIANTE : novice, beginner

noviembre *nm* : November

novilla *nf* : heifer

novillada *nf* : bullfight featuring young bulls

novillero, -ra *n* : apprentice bullfighter

novillo *nm* : young bull

novio, -via *n* **1** : boyfriend *m,* girlfriend *f* **2** PROMETIDO : fiancé *m,* fiancée *f* **3** : bridegroom *m,* bride *f*

novocaína *nf* : novocaine

nubarrón *nm, pl* **-rrones** : storm cloud

nube *nf* **1** : cloud ⟨andar en las nubes : to have one's head in the clouds⟩ ⟨por las nubes : sky-high⟩ **2** : cloud (of dust), swarm (of insects, etc.)

nublado[1], -da *adj* **1** NUBOSO : cloudy, overcast **2** : clouded, dim

nublado[2] *nm* **1** : storm cloud **2** AMENAZA : menace, threat

nublar *vt* **1** : to cloud **2** OSCURECER : to obscure — **nublarse** *vr* : to get cloudy

nubosidad *nf* : cloudiness

nuboso, -sa *adj* NUBLADO : cloudy

nuca *nf* : nape, back of the neck

nuclear *adj* : nuclear

núcleo *nm* **1** : nucleus **2** : center, heart, core

nudillo *nm* : knuckle

nudismo *nm* : nudism

nudista *adj & nmf* : nudist

nudo *nm* **1** : knot ⟨nudo de rizo : square knot⟩ ⟨un nudo en la garganta : a lump in one's throat⟩ **2** : node **3** : junction, hub ⟨nudo de comunicaciones : communication center⟩ **4** : crux, heart (of a problem, etc.)

nudoso, -sa *adj* : knotty, gnarled

nuera *nf* : daughter-in-law

nuestro[1], -tra *adj* : our

nuestro[2], -tra *pron* (*with definite article*) : ours, our own ⟨el nuestro es más grande : ours is bigger⟩ ⟨es de los nuestros : it's one of ours⟩

nuevamente *adv* : again, anew

nuevas *nfpl* : tidings *pl*

nueve *adj & nm* : nine

nuevecito, -ta *adj* : brand-new

nuevo, -va *adj* **1** : new ⟨una casa nueva : a new house⟩ ⟨¿qué hay de nuevo? : what's new?⟩ **2 de ~** : again, once more **3 Nuevo Testamento** : New Testament

nuez *nf, pl* **nueces** **1** : nut **2** : walnut **3** *Mex* : pecan **4 nuez de Adán** : Adam's apple **5 nuez moscada** : nutmeg

nulidad *nf* **1** : nullity **2** : incompetent person ⟨¡es una nulidad! : he's hopeless!⟩

nulo, -la *adj* **1** : null, null and void **2** INEPTO : useless, inept ⟨es nula para la cocina : she's hopeless at cooking⟩

numen *nm* : poetic muse, inspiration

numerable *adj* : countable

numeración *nf, pl* **-ciones** **1** : numbering **2** : numbers *pl,* numerals *pl* ⟨numeración romana : Roman numerals⟩

numerador *nm* : numerator

numeral *adj* : numeral

numerar *vt* : to number

numerario, -ria *adj* : long-standing, permanent ⟨profesor numerario : tenured professor⟩

numérico, -ca *adj* : numerical — **numéricamente** *adv*

número *nm* **1** : number ⟨número impar : odd number⟩ ⟨número ordinal : ordinal number⟩ ⟨número arábico : Arabic numeral⟩ ⟨número quebrado : fraction⟩ **2** : issue (of a publication) **3 sin ~** : countless

numeroso, -sa *adj* : numerous

numismática *nf* : numismatics

nunca *adv* **1** : never, ever ⟨nunca es tarde : it's never too late⟩ ⟨no trabaja casi nunca : he hardly ever works⟩ **2 nunca más** : never again **3 nunca jamás** : never ever

nuncio *nm* : harbinger, herald

nupcial *adj* : nuptial, wedding

nupcias *nfpl* : nuptials *pl,* wedding

nutria *nf* **1** : otter **2** : nutria

nutrición *nf, pl* **-ciones** : nutrition, nourishment

nutrido, -da *adj* **1** : nourished ⟨mal nutrido : undernourished, malnourished⟩ **2** : considerable, abundant ⟨de nutrido : full of, abounding in⟩

nutriente *nm* : nutrient

nutrimento *nm* : nutriment

nutrir *vt* **1** ALIMENTAR : to feed, to nourish **2** : to foster, to provide

nutritivo, -va *adj* : nourishing, nutritious

nylon → **nilón**

ñ *nf* : fifteenth letter of the Spanish alphabet

ñame *nm* : yam

ñandú *nm* : rhea

ñapa *nf* : extra amount ⟨de ñapa : for good measure⟩

ñoñear *vi fam* : to whine

ñoño, -ña *adj fam* : whiny, fussy ⟨no seas tan ñoño : don't be such a wimp⟩

ñoquis *nmpl* : gnocchi *pl*

ñu *nm* : gnu, wildebeest

O

o[1] *nf* : sixteenth letter of the Spanish alphabet

o[2] *conj* (**u** *before words beginning with o- or ho-*) **1** : or ⟨¿vienes con nosotros o te quedas? : are you coming with us or staying?⟩ **2** : either ⟨o vienes con nosotros o te quedas : either you come with us or you stay⟩ **3 o sea** : that is to say, in other words

oasis *nms & pl* : oasis

obcecado, -da *adj* **1** : blinded ⟨obcecado por la ira : blinded by rage⟩ **2** : stubborn, obstinate

obcecar {72} *vt* : to blind (by emotions) — **obcecarse** *vr* : to become stubborn

obedecer {53} *vt* : to obey ⟨obedecer órdenes : to obey orders⟩ ⟨obedece a tus padres : obey your parents⟩ — *vi* **1** : to obey **2 ~ a** : to respond to **3 ~ a** : to be due to, to result from

obediencia *nf* : obedience

obediente *adj* : obedient — **obedientemente** *adv*

obelisco *nm* : obelisk

obertura *nf* : overture

obesidad *nf* : obesity

obeso, -sa *adj* : obese

óbice *nm* : obstacle, impediment

obispado *nm* DIÓCESIS : bishopric, diocese

obispo *nm* : bishop

obituario *nm* : obituary

objeción *nf, pl* **-ciones** : objection ⟨ponerle objeciones a algo : to object to something⟩

objetar *v* : to object ⟨no tengo nada que objetar : I have no objections⟩

objetividad *nf* : objectivity

objetivo[1], **-va** *adj* : objective — **objetivamente** *adv*

objetivo[2] *nm* **1** META : objective, goal, target **2** : lens

objeto *nm* **1** COSA : object, thing **2** OBJETIVO : objective, purpose ⟨con objeto de : in order to, with the aim of⟩ **3 objeto volador no identificado** : unidentified flying object

objetor, -tora *n* : objector ⟨objetor de conciencia : conscientious objector⟩

oblea *nf* **1** : wafer **2 hecho una oblea** *fam* : skinny as a rail

oblicuo, -cua *adj* : oblique — **oblicuamente** *adv*

obligación *nf, pl* **-ciones** **1** DEBER : obligation, duty **2** : bond, debenture

obligado, -da *adj* **1** : obliged **2** : obligatory, compulsory **3** : customary

obligar {52} *vt* : to force, to require, to oblige — **obligarse** *vr* : to commit oneself, to undertake (to do something)

obligatorio, -ria *adj* : mandatory, required, compulsory

obliterar *vt* : to obliterate, to destroy — **obliteración** *nf*

oblongo, -ga *adj* : oblong

obnubilación *nf, pl* **-ciones** : bewilderment, confusion

obnubilar *vt* : to daze, to bewilder

oboe[1] *nm* : oboe

oboe[2] *nmf* : oboist

obra *nf* **1** : work ⟨obra de arte : work of art⟩ ⟨obra de teatro : play⟩ ⟨obra de consulta : reference work⟩ **2** : deed ⟨una buena obra : a good deed⟩ **3** : construction work **4 obra maestra** : masterpiece **5 obras públicas** : public works **6 por obra de** : thanks to, because of

obrar *vt* : to work, to produce ⟨obrar milagros : to work miracles⟩ — *vi* **1** : to act, to behave ⟨obrar con cautela : to act with caution⟩ **2 obrar en poder de** : to be in possession of

obrero[1], **-ra** *adj* : working ⟨la clase obrera : the working class⟩

obrero[2], **-ra** *n* : worker, laborer

obscenidad *nf* : obscenity

obsceno, -na *adj* : obscene

obscurecer, obscuridad, obscuro → **oscurecer, oscuridad, oscuro**

obsequiar *vt* REGALAR : to give, to present ⟨lo obsequiaron con una placa : they presented him with a plaque⟩

obsequio *nm* REGALO : gift, present

obsequiosidad *nf* : attentiveness, deference

obsequioso, -sa *adj* : obliging, attentive

observable *adj* : observable

observación *nf, pl* **-ciones** **1** : observation, watching **2** : remark, comment

observador[1], **-dora** *adj* : observant

observador[2], **-dora** *n* : observer, watcher
observancia *nf* : observance
observante *adj* : observant ⟨los judíos observantes : observant Jews⟩
observar *vt* **1** : to observe, to watch ⟨estábamos observando a los niños : we were watching the children⟩ **2** NOTAR : to notice **3** ACATAR : to obey, to abide by **4** COMENTAR : to remark, to comment
observatorio *nm* : observatory
obsesión *nf, pl* **-siones** : obsession
obsesionar *vt* : to obsess, to preoccupy excessively — **obsesionarse** *vr*
obsesivo, **-va** *adj* : obsessive
obseso, **-sa** *adj* : obsessed
obsolescencia *nf* DESUSO : obsolescence — **obsolescente** *adj*
obsoleto, **-ta** *adj* DESUSADO : obsolete
obstaculizar {21} *vt* IMPEDIR : to obstruct, to hinder
obstáculo *nm* IMPEDIMENTO : obstacle
obstante[1] *conj* **no obstante** : nevertheless, however
obstante[2] *prep* **no obstante** : in spite of, despite ⟨mantuvo su inocencia no obstante la evidencia : he maintained his innocence in spite of the evidence⟩
obstar *v impers* **~ a** *or* **~ para** : to hinder, to prevent ⟨eso no obsta para que me vaya : that doesn't prevent me from leaving⟩
obstetra *nmf* TOCÓLOGO : obstetrician
obstetricia *nf* : obstetrics
obstétrico, **-ca** *adj* : obstetric, obstetrical
obstinación *nf, pl* **-ciones** **1** TERQUEDAD : obstinacy, stubbornness **2** : perseverance, tenacity
obstinado, **-da** *adj* **1** TERCO : obstinate, stubborn **2** : persistent — **obstinadamente** *adv*
obstinarse *vr* EMPECINARSE : to be obstinate, to be stubborn
obstrucción *nf, pl* **-ciones** : obstruction, blockage
obstruccionismo *nm* : obstructionism, filibustering
obstruccionista *adj* : obstructionist, filibustering
obstructor, **-tora** *adj* : obstructive
obstruir {41} *vt* BLOQUEAR : to obstruct, to block, to clog — **obstruirse** *vr*
obtención *nf* : obtaining, procurement
obtener {80} *vt* : to obtain, to secure, to get — **obtenible** *adj*
obturador *nm* : shutter (of a camera)
obtuso, **-sa** *adj* : obtuse
obtuvo, etc. → **obtener**
obús *nm, pl* **obuses** **1** : mortar (weapon) **2** : mortar shell
obviar *vt* : to get around (a difficulty), to avoid
obvio, **-via** *adj* : obvious — **obviamente** *adv*
oca *nf* : goose
ocasión *nf, pl* **-siones** **1** : occasion, time **2** : opportunity, chance **3** : bargain **4 de ~** : secondhand **5 aviso de ocasión** *Mex* : classified ad
ocasional *adj* **1** : occasional **2** : chance, fortuitous
ocasionalmente *adv* **1** : occasionally **2** : by chance
ocasionar *vt* CAUSAR : to cause, to occasion
ocaso *nm* **1** ANOCHECER : sunset, sundown **2** DECADENCIA : decline, fall
occidental *adj* : western, occidental
occidente *nm* **1** OESTE, PONIENTE : west **2 el Occidente** : the West
oceánico, **-ca** *adj* : oceanic
océano *nm* : ocean
oceanografía *nf* : oceanography
oceanográfico, **-ca** *adj* : oceanographic
ocelote *nm* : ocelot
ochenta *adj & nm* : eighty
ochentavo[1], **-va** *adj* : eightieth
ochentavo[2] *nm* : eightieth (fraction)
ocho *adj & nm* : eight
ochocientos[1], **-tas** *adj* : eight hundred
ochocientos[2] *ms & pl* : eight hundred
ocio *nm* **1** : free time, leisure **2** : idleness
ociosidad *nf* : idleness, inactivity
ocioso, **-sa** *adj* **1** INACTIVO : idle, inactive **2** INÚTIL : pointless, useless
ocre *nm* : ocher
octágono *nm* : octagon — **octagonal** *adj*
octava *nf* : octave
octavo, **-va** *adj* : eighth — **octavo**, **-va** *n*
octeto *nm* **1** : octet **2** : byte
octogésimo[1], **-ma** *adj* : eightieth, eighty-
octogésimo[2], **-ma** *n* : eightieth, eighty- (in a series)
octubre *nm* : October
ocular *adj* **1** : ocular, eye ⟨músculos oculares : eye muscles⟩ **2 testigo ocular** : eyewitness
oculista *nmf* : oculist, ophthalmologist
ocultación *nf, pl* **-ciones** : concealment
ocultar *vt* ESCONDER : to conceal, to hide — **ocultarse** *vr*
oculto, **-ta** *adj* **1** ESCONDIDO : hidden, concealed **2** : occult
ocupación *nf, pl* **-ciones** **1** : occupation, activity **2** : occupancy **3** EMPLEO : employment, job
ocupacional *adj* : occupational, job-related
ocupado, **-da** *adj* **1** : busy **2** : taken ⟨este asiento está ocupado : this seat is taken⟩ **3** : occupied ⟨territorios ocupados : occupied territories⟩ **4 señal de ocupado** : busy signal
ocupante *nmf* : occupant
ocupar *vt* **1** : to occupy, to take possession of **2** : to hold (a position) **3** : to employ, to keep busy **4** : to fill (space, time) **5** : to inhabit (a dwelling) **6** : to bother, to concern — **ocuparse** *vr* **~ de 1** : to be concerned with **2** : to take care of

ocurrencia *nf* **1** : occurrence, event **2** : witticism **3** : bright idea
ocurrente *adj* **1** : witty **2** : clever, sharp
ocurrir *vi* : to occur, to happen — **ocurrirse** *vr* **~ a** : to occur to, to strike ⟨se me ocurrió una mejor idea : a better idea occurred to me⟩
oda *nf* : ode
odiar *vt* ABOMINAR, ABORRECER : to hate
odio *nm* : hate, hatred
odioso, -sa *adj* ABOMINABLE, ABORRECIBLE : hateful, detestable
odisea *nf* : odyssey
odontología *nf* : dentistry, dental surgery
odontólogo, -ga *n* : dentist, dental surgeon
oeste[1] *adj* **1** : west, western ⟨la región oeste : the western region⟩ **2** : westerly
oeste[2] *nm* **1** : west, West **2** : west wind
ofender *vt* AGRAVIAR : to offend, to insult — *vi* : to offend, to be insulting — **ofenderse** *vr* : to take offense
ofensa *nf* : offense, insult
ofensiva *nf* : offensive ⟨pasar a la ofensiva : to go on the offensive⟩
ofensivo, -va *adj* : offensive, insulting
ofensor, -sora *n* : offender
oferente *nmf* **1** : supplier **2** FUENTE : source ⟨un oferente no identificado : an unidentified source⟩
oferta *nf* **1** : offer **2** : sale, bargain ⟨las camisas están en oferta : the shirts are on sale⟩ **3 oferta y demanda** : supply and demand
ofertar *vt* OFRECER : to offer
oficial[1] *adj* : official — **oficialmente** *adv*
oficial[2] *nmf* **1** : officer, police officer, commissioned officer (in the military) **2** : skilled worker
oficializar {21} *vt* : to make official
oficiante *nmf* : celebrant
oficiar *vt* **1** : to inform officially **2** : to officiate at, to celebrate (Mass) — *vi* **~ de** : to act as
oficina *nf* : office
oficinista *nmf* : office worker
oficio *nm* **1** : trade, profession ⟨es electricista de oficio : he's an electrician by trade⟩ **2** : function, role **3** : official communication **4** : experience ⟨tener oficio : to be experienced⟩ **5** : religious ceremony
oficioso, -sa *adj* **1** EXTRAOFICIAL : unofficial **2** : officious — **oficiosamente** *adv*
ofrecer {53} *vt* **1** : to offer **2** : to provide, to give **3** : to present (an appearance, etc.) — **ofrecerse** *vr* **1** : to offer oneself, to volunteer **2** : to open up, to present itself
ofrecimiento *nm* : offer, offering
ofrenda *nf* : offering
oftalmología *nf* : ophthalmology
oftalmólogo, -ga *n* : ophthalmologist
ofuscación *nf, pl* **-ciones** : blindness, confusion
ofuscar {72} *vt* **1** : to blind, to dazzle **2** CONFUNDIR : to bewilder, to confuse — **ofuscarse** *vr* **~ con** : to be blinded by
ogro *nm* : ogre
ohm *nm, pl* **ohms** : ohm
ohmio → **ohm**
oídas *nfpl* **de ~** : by hearsay
oído *nm* **1** : ear ⟨oído interno : inner ear⟩ **2** : hearing ⟨duro de oído : hard of hearing⟩ **3 tocar de oído** : to play by ear
oiga, etc. → **oír**
oír {50} *vi* : to hear — *vt* **1** : to hear **2** ESCUCHAR : to listen to **3** : to pay attention to, to heed **4 ¡oye!** *or* **¡oiga!** : listen!, excuse me!, look here!
ojal *nm* : buttonhole
ojalá *interj* **1** : I hope so!, if only!, God willing! **2** : I hope, I wish, hopefully ⟨¡ojalá que le vaya bien! : I hope things go well for her!⟩ ⟨¡ojalá no llueva! : hopefully it won't rain!⟩
ojeada *nf* : glimpse, glance ⟨echar una ojeada : to have a quick look⟩
ojear *vt* : to eye, to have a look at
ojete *nm* : eyelet
ojiva *nf* : warhead
ojo *nm* **1** : eye **2** : judgment, sharpness ⟨tener buen ojo para : to be a good judge of, to have a good eye for⟩ **3** : hole (in cheese), eye (in a needle), center (of a storm) **4** : span (of a bridge) **5 a ojos vistas** : openly, publicly **6 andar con ojo** : to be careful **7 ojo de agua** *Mex* : spring, source **8 ¡ojo!** : look out!, pay attention!
ola *nf* **1** : wave **2 ola de calor** : heat wave
oleada *nf* : swell, wave ⟨una oleada de protestas : a wave of protests⟩
oleaje *nm* : waves *pl*, surf
óleo *nm* **1** : oil **2** : oil painting
oleoducto *nm* : oil pipeline
oleoso, -sa *adj* : oily
oler {51} *vt* **1** : to smell **2** INQUIRIR : to pry into, to investigate **3** AVERIGUAR : to smell out, to uncover — *vi* **1** : to smell ⟨huele mal : it smells bad⟩ **2 ~ a** : to smell like, to smell of ⟨huele a pino : it smells like pine⟩ — **olerse** *vr* : to have a hunch, to suspect
olfatear *vt* **1** : to sniff **2** : to sense, to sniff out
olfativo, -va *adj* : olfactory
olfato *nm* **1** : sense of smell **2** : nose, instinct
oligarquía *nf* : oligarchy
olimpiada *or* **olimpíada** *nf* **1** : Olympiad **2** *or* **olympiadas** *nfpl* : Olympics *pl*
olímpico, -ca *adj* : Olympic
olisquear *vt* : to sniff at
oliva *nf* ACEITUNA : olive ⟨aceite de oliva : olive oil⟩
olivo *nm* : olive tree
olla *nf* **1** : pot ⟨olla de presión : pressure cooker⟩ **2 olla podrida** : Spanish stew

olmeca *adj & nmf* : Olmec

olmo *nm* : elm

olor *nm* : smell, odor

oloroso, -sa *adj* : scented, fragrant

olote *nm Mex* : cob, corncob

olvidadizo, -za *adj* : forgetful, absent-minded

olvidar *vt* **1** : to forget, to forget about ⟨olvida lo que pasó : forget about what happened⟩ **2** : to leave behind ⟨olvidé mi chequera en la casa : I left my checkbook at home⟩ — **olvidarse** *vr* : to forget ⟨se me olvidó mi cuaderno : I forgot my notebook⟩ ⟨se le olvidó llamarme : he forgot to call me⟩

olvido *nm* **1** : forgetfulness **2** : oblivion **3** DESCUIDO : oversight

omaní *adj & nmf* : Omani

ombligo *nm* : navel, belly button

ombudsman *nmfs & pl* : ombudsman

omelette *nmf* : omelet

ominoso, -sa *adj* : ominous — **ominosamente** *adv*

omisión *nf, pl* **-siones** : omission, neglect

omiso, -sa *adj* **1** NEGLIGENTE : neglectful **2 hacer caso omiso de** : to ignore

omitir *vt* **1** : to omit, to leave out **2** : to fail to ⟨omitió dar su nombre : he failed to give his name⟩

ómnibus *n, pl* **-bus** *or* **-buses** : bus, coach

omnipotencia *nf* : omnipotence

omnipotente *adj* TODOPODEROSO : omnipotent, almighty

omnipresencia *nf* : ubiquity, omnipresence

omnipresente *adj* : ubiquitous, omnipresent

omnisciente *adj* : omniscient — **omnisciencia** *nf*

omnívoro, -ra *adj* : omnivorous

omóplato *or* **omoplato** *nm* : shoulder blade

once *adj & nm* : eleven

onceavo[1], **-va** *adj* : eleventh

onceavo[2] *nm* : eleventh (fraction)

onda *nf* **1** : wave, ripple, undulation ⟨onda sonora : sound wave⟩ **2** : wave (in hair) **3** : scallop (on clothing) **4** *fam* : wavelength, understanding ⟨agarrar la onda : to get the point⟩ ⟨en la onda : on the ball, with it⟩ **5 ¿qué onda?** *fam* : what's happening?, what's up?

ondear *vi* : to ripple, to undulate, to flutter

ondulación *nf, pl* **-ciones** : undulation

ondulado, -da *adj* **1** : wavy ⟨pelo ondulado : wavy hair⟩ **2** : undulating

ondulante *adj* : undulating

ondular *vt* : to wave (hair) — *vi* : to undulate, to ripple

oneroso, -sa *adj* GRAVOSO : onerous, burdensome

ónix *nm* : onyx

onza *nf* : ounce

opacar {72} *vt* **1** : to make opaque or dull **2** : to outshine, to overshadow

opacidad *nf* **1** : opacity **2** : dullness

opaco, -ca *adj* **1** : opaque **2** : dull

ópalo *nm* : opal

opción *nf, pl* **opciones 1** ALTERNATIVA : option, choice **2** : right, chance ⟨tener opción a : to be eligible for⟩

opcional *adj* : optional — **opcionalmente** *adv*

ópera *nf* : opera

operación *nf, pl* **-ciones 1** : operation **2** : transaction, deal

operacional *adj* : operational

operador, -dora *n* **1** : operator **2** : cameraman, projectionist

operante *adj* : operating, working

operar *vt* **1** : to produce, to bring about **2** INTERVENIR : to operate on **3** *Mex* : to operate, to run (a machine) — *vi* **1** : to operate, to function **2** : to deal, to do business — **operarse** *vr* **1** : to come about, to take place **2** : to have an operation

operario, -ria *n* : laborer, worker

operático, -ca → **operístico**

operativo[1], **-va** *adj* **1** : operating ⟨capacidad operativa : operating capacity⟩ **2** : operative

operativo[2] *nm* : operation ⟨operativo militar : military operation⟩

opereta *nf* : operetta

operístico, -ca *adj* : operatic

opiato *nm* : opiate

opinable *adj* : arguable

opinar *vi* **1** : to think, to have an opinion **2** : to express an opinion **3 opinar bien de** : to think highly of — *vt* : to think ⟨opinamos lo mismo : we're of the same opinion, we're in agreement⟩

opinión *nf, pl* **-niones** : opinion, belief

opio *nm* : opium

oponente *nmf* : opponent

oponer {60} *vt* **1** CONTRAPONER : to oppose, to place against **2 oponer resistencia** : to resist, to put up a fight — **oponerse** *vr* **~ a** : to object to, to be against

oporto *nm* : port (wine)

oportunamente *adv* **1** : at the right time, opportunely **2** : appropriately

oportunidad *nf* : opportunity, chance

oportunismo *nm* : opportunism

oportunista[1] *adj* : opportunistic

oportunista[2] *nmf* : opportunist

oportuno, -na *adj* **1** : opportune, timely **2** : suitable, appropriate

oposición *nf, pl* **-ciones** : opposition

opositor, -tora *n* ADVERSARIO : opponent

oposum *nm* ZARIGÜEYA : opossum

opresión *nf, pl* **-siones 1** : oppression **2 opresión de pecho** : tightness in the chest

opresivo, -va *adj* : oppressive

opresor[1], **-sora** *adj* : oppressive

opresor[2], **-sora** *n* : oppressor

oprimir *vt* **1** : to oppress **2** : to press, to squeeze ⟨oprima el botón : push the button⟩

oprobio *nm* : opprobrium, shame

optar *vi* **1 ~ por** : to opt for, to choose **2 ~ a** : to aspire to, to apply for ⟨dos candidatos optan a la presidencia : two candidates are running for president⟩

optativo, -va *adj* FACULTATIVO : optional

óptica *nf* **1** : optics **2** : optician's shop **3** : viewpoint

óptico[1], -ca *adj* : optical, optic

óptico[2], -ca *n* : optician

optimismo *nm* : optimism

optimista[1] *adj* : optimistic

optimista[2] *nmf* : optimist

óptimo, -ma *adj* : optimum, optimal

optometría *nf* : optometry — **optometrista** *nmf*

opuesto[1] *pp* → **oponer**

opuesto[2] *adj* **1** : opposite, contrary **2** : opposed

opulencia *nf* : opulence — **opulento, -ta** *adj*

opus *nm* : opus

opuso, etc. → **oponer**

ora *conj* : now ⟨los matices eran variados, ora verdes, ora ocres : the hues were varied, now green, now ocher⟩

oración *nf, pl* **-ciones 1** DISCURSO : oration, speech **2** PLEGARIA : prayer **3** FRASE : sentence, clause

oráculo *nm* : oracle

orador, -dora *n* : speaker, orator

oral *adj* : oral — **oralmente** *adv*

órale *interj Mex fam* **1** : sure!, OK! ⟨¿los dos por cinco pesos? ¡órale! : both for five pesos? you've got a deal!⟩ **2** : come on! ⟨¡órale, vámonos! : come on, let's go!⟩

orangután *nm, pl* **-tanes** : orangutan

orar *vi* REZAR : to pray

oratoria *nf* : oratory

oratorio *nm* **1** CAPILLA : oratory, chapel **2** : oratorio

orbe *nm* **1** : orb, sphere **2** GLOBO : globe, world

órbita *nf* **1** : orbit **2** : eye socket **3** ÁMBITO : sphere, field

orbitador *nm* : space shuttle, orbiter

orbital *adj* : orbital

orbitar *v* : to orbit

orden[1] *nm, pl* **órdenes 1** : order ⟨todo está en orden : everything's in order⟩ ⟨por orden cronológico : in chronological order⟩ **2 orden del día** : agenda (at a meeting) **3 orden público** : law and order

orden[2] *nf, pl* **órdenes 1** : order ⟨una orden religiosa : a religious order⟩ ⟨una orden de tacos : an order of tacos⟩ **2 orden de compra** : purchase order **3 estar a la orden del día** : to be the order of the day, to be prevalent

ordenación *nf, pl* **-ciones 1** : ordination **2** : ordering, organizing

ordenadamente *adv* : in an orderly fashion, neatly

ordenado, -da *adj* : orderly, neat

ordenador *nm Spain* : computer

ordenamiento *nm* **1** : ordering, organizing **2** : code (of laws)

ordenanza[1] *nf* REGLAMENTO : ordinance, regulation

ordenanza[2] *nm* : orderly (in the armed forces)

ordenar *vt* **1** MANDAR : to order, to command **2** ARREGLAR : to put in order, to arrange **3** : to ordain (a priest)

ordeñar *vt* : to milk

ordeño *nm* : milking

ordinal *nm* : ordinal (number)

ordinariamente *adv* **1** : usually **2** : coarsely

ordinariez *nf* : coarseness, vulgarity

ordinario, -ria *adj* **1** : ordinary **2** : coarse, common, vulgar **3 de ~** : usually

orear *vt* : to air

orégano *nm* : oregano

oreja *nf* : ear

orfanato *nm* : orphanage

orfanatorio *nm Mex* : orphanage

orfebre *nmf* : goldsmith, silversmith

orfebrería *nf* : articles of gold or silver

orfelinato *nm* : orphanage

orgánico, -ca *adj* : organic — **orgánicamente** *adv*

organigrama *nm* : organization chart, flowchart

organismo *nm* **1** : organism **2** : agency, organization

organista *nmf* : organist

organización *nf, pl* **-ciones** : organization

organizador[1], -dora *adj* : organizing

organizador[2], -dora *n* : organizer

organizar {21} *vt* : to organize, to arrange — **organizarse** *vr* : to get organized

organizativo, -va *adj* : organizational

órgano *nm* : organ

orgasmo *nm* : orgasm

orgía *nf* : orgy

orgullo *nm* : pride

orgulloso, -sa *adj* : proud — **orgullosamente** *adv*

orientación *nf, pl* **-ciones 1** : orientation **2** DIRECCIÓN : direction, course **3** GUÍA : guidance, direction

oriental[1] *adj* **1** : eastern **2** : oriental **3** *Arg, Uru* : Uruguayan

oriental[2] *nmf* **1** : Easterner **2** : Oriental **3** *Arg, Uru* : Uruguayan

orientar *vt* **1** : to orient, to position **2** : to guide, to direct — **orientarse** *vr* **1** : to orient oneself, to get one's bearings **2 ~ hacia** : to turn towards, to lean towards

oriente *nm* **1** : east, East **2 el Oriente** : the Orient

orífice *nmf* : goldsmith

orificio *nm* : orifice, opening

origen *nm, pl* **orígenes 1** : origin **2** : lineage, birth **3 dar origen a** : to give rise to **4 en su origen** : originally

original *adj & nm* : original — **originalmente** *adv*
originalidad *nf* : originality
originar *vt* : to originate, to give rise to — **originarse** *vr* : to originate, to begin
originario, -ria *adj* ~ **de** : native of
originariamente *adv* : originally
orilla *nf* 1 BORDE : border, edge 2 : bank (of a river) 3 : shore
orillar *vt* 1 : to skirt, to go around 2 : to trim, to edge (cloth) 3 : to settle, to wind up 4 *Mex* : to pull over (a vehicle)
orín *nm* 1 HERRUMBRE : rust 2 **orines** *nmpl* : urine
orina *nf* : urine
orinación *nf* : urination
orinal *nm* : urinal (vessel)
orinar *vi* : to urinate — **orinarse** *vr* : to wet oneself
oriol *nm* OROPÉNDOLA : oriole
oriundo, -da *adj* ~ **de** : native of
orla *nf* : border, edging
orlar *vt* : to edge, to trim
ornamentación *nf, pl* **-ciones** : ornamentation
ornamental *adj* : ornamental
ornamentar *vt* ADORNAR : to ornament, to adorn
ornamento *nm* : ornament, adornment
ornar *vt* : to adorn, to decorate
ornitología *nf* : ornithology
ornitólogo, -ga *n* : ornithologist
ornitorrinco *nm* : platypus
oro *nm* : gold
orondo, -da *adj* 1 : rounded, potbellied (of a container) 2 *fam* : smug, self-satisfied
oropel *nm* : glitz, glitter, tinsel
oropéndola *nf* : oriole
orquesta *nf* : orchestra — **orquestal** *adj*
orquestar *vt* : to orchestrate — **orquestación** *nf*
orquídea *nf* : orchid
ortiga *nf* : nettle
ortodoncia *nf* : orthodontics
ortodoncista *nmf* : orthodontist
ortodoxia *nf* : orthodoxy
ortodoxo, -xa *adj* : orthodox
ortografía *nf* : orthography, spelling
ortográfico, -ca *adj* : orthographic, spelling
ortopedia *nf* : orthopedics
ortopédico, -ca *adj* : orthopedic
ortopedista *nmf* : orthopedist
oruga *nf* 1 : caterpillar 2 : track (of a tank, etc.)
orzuelo *nm* : sty, stye (in the eye)
os *pron pl* (*objective form of* **vosotros**) *Spain* 1 : you, to you 2 : yourselves, to yourselves 3 : each other, to each other
osa *nf* → **oso**
osadía *nf* 1 VALOR : boldness, daring 2 AUDACIA : audacity, nerve
osado, -da *adj* 1 : bold, daring 2 : audacious, impudent — **osadamente** *adv*
osamenta *nf* : skeletal remains *pl*, bones *pl*
osar *vi* : to dare
oscilación *nf, pl* **-ciones** 1 : oscillation 2 : fluctuation 3 : vacillation, wavering
oscilar *vi* 1 BALANCEARSE : to swing, to sway, to oscillate 2 FLUCTUAR : to fluctuate 3 : to vacillate, to waver
oscuramente *adv* : obscurely
oscurecer {53} *vt* 1 : to darken 2 : to obscure, to confuse, to cloud 3 **al oscurecer** : at dusk, at nightfall — *v impers* : to grow dark, to get dark — **oscurecerse** *vr* : to darken, to dim
oscuridad *nf* 1 : darkness 2 : obscurity
oscuro, -ra *adj* 1 : dark 2 : obscure 3 **a oscuras** : in the dark, in darkness
óseo, ósea *adj* : skeletal, bony
ósmosis *or* **osmosis** *nf* : osmosis
oso, osa *n* 1 : bear 2 **Osa Mayor** : Big Dipper 3 **Osa Menor** : Little Dipper 4 **oso blanco** : polar bear 5 **oso hormiguero** : anteater 6 **oso de peluche** : teddy bear
ostensible *adj* : ostensible, apparent — **ostensiblemente** *adv*
ostentación *nf, pl* **-ciones** : ostentation, display
ostentar *vt* 1 : to display, to flaunt 2 POSEER : to have, to hold ⟨ostenta el récord mundial : he holds the world record⟩
ostentoso, -sa *adj* : ostentatious, showy — **ostentosamente** *adv*
osteópata *nmf* : osteopath
osteopatía *n* : osteopathy
osteoporosis *nf* : osteoporosis
ostión *nm, pl* **ostiones** 1 *Mex* : oyster 2 *Chile* : scallop
ostra *nf* : oyster
ostracismo *nm* : ostracism
otear *vt* : to scan, to survey, to look over
otero *nm* : knoll, hillock
otomana *nf* : ottoman (mueble)
otomano, -na *adj & n* : Ottoman
otoñal *adj* : autumn, autumnal
otoño *nm* : autumn, fall
otorgamiento *nm* : granting, awarding
otorgar {52} *vt* 1 : to grant, to award 2 : to draw up, to frame (a legal document)
otro[1], **otra** *adj* 1 : other 2 : another ⟨en otro juego, ellos ganaron : in another game, they won⟩ 3 **otra vez** : again 4 **de otra manera** : otherwise 5 **otra parte** : elsewhere 6 **en otro tiempo** : once, formerly
otro[2], **otra** *pron* 1 : another one ⟨dame otro : give me another⟩ 2 : other one ⟨el uno o el otro : one or the other⟩ 3 **los otros, las otras** : the others, the rest ⟨me dio una y se quedó con las otras : he gave me one and kept the rest⟩
ovación *nf, pl* **-ciones** : ovation
ovacionar *vt* : to cheer, to applaud

oval → **ovalado**
ovalado, -da *adj* : oval
óvalo *nm* : oval
ovárico, -ca *adj* : ovarian
ovario *nm* : ovary
oveja *nf* **1** : sheep, ewe **2 oveja negra** : black sheep
overol *nm* : overalls *pl*
ovillar *vt* : to roll into a ball
ovillo *nm* **1** : ball (of yarn) **2** : tangle
ovni *or* **OVNI** *nm* (*o*bjeto *v*olador *n*o *i*dentificado) : UFO
ovoide *adj* : ovoid, ovoidal
ovulación *nf, pl* **-ciones** : ovulation
ovular *vi* : to ovulate
óvulo *nm* : ovum
oxidación *nf, pl* **-ciones 1** : oxidation **2** : rusting
oxidado, -da *adj* : rusty
oxidar *vt* **1** : to cause to rust **2** : to oxidize — **oxidarse** *vr* : to rust, to become rusty
óxido *nm* **1** HERRUMBRE, ORÍN : rust **2** : oxide
oxigenar *vt* **1** : to oxygenate **2** : to bleach (hair)
oxígeno *nm* : oxygen
oxiuro *nm* : pinworm
oye, etc. → **oír**
oyente *nmf* **1** : listener **2** : auditor, auditing student
ozono *nm* : ozone

P

p *nf* : seventeenth letter of the Spanish alphabet
pabellón *nm, pl* **-llones 1** : pavilion **2** : summerhouse, lodge **3** : flag (of a vessel)
pabilo *nm* MECHA : wick
paca *nf* FARDO : bale
pacana *nf* : pecan
pacer {48} *v* : to graze, to pasture
paces → **paz**
pachanga *nf fam* : party, bash
paciencia *nf* : patience
paciente *adj & nmf* : patient — **pacientemente** *adv*
pacificación *nf, pl* **-ciones** : pacification
pacíficamente *adv* : peacefully, peaceably
pacificar {72} *vt* : to pacify, to calm — **pacificarse** *vr* : to calm down, to abate
pacífico, -ca *adj* : peaceful, pacific
pacifismo *nm* : pacifism
pacifista *adj & nmf* : pacifist
pacotilla *nf* **de ~** : shoddy, trashy
pactar *vt* : to agree on — *vi* : to come to an agreement
pacto *nm* CONVENIO : pact, agreement
padecer {53} *vt* : to suffer, to endure — *vi* ADOLECER **~ de** : to suffer from
padecimiento *nm* **1** : suffering **2** : ailment, condition
padrastro *nm* **1** : stepfather **2** : hangnail
padre[1] *adj Mex fam* : fantastic, great
padre[2] *nm* **1** : father **2 padres** *nmpl* : parents
padrenuestro *nm* : Lord's Prayer, paternoster
padrino *nm* **1** : godfather **2** : best man **3** : sponsor, patron
padrón *nm, pl* **padrones** : register, roll ⟨padrón municipal : city register⟩
paella *nf* : paella
paga *nf* **1** : payment **2** : pay, wages *pl*
pagadero, -ra *adj* : payable
pagado, -da *adj* **1** : paid **2 pagado de sí mismo** : self-satisfied, smug
pagador, -dora *n* : payer
paganismo *nm* : paganism
pagano, -na *adj & n* : pagan
pagar {52} *vt* : to pay, to pay for, to repay — *vi* : to pay
pagaré *nm* VALE : promissory note, IOU
página *nf* : page
pago *nm* **1** : payment **2 en pago de** : in return for
pagoda *nf* : pagoda
pague, etc. → **pagar**
país *nm* **1** NACIÓN : country, nation **2** REGIÓN : region, territory
paisaje *nm* : scenery, landscape
paisano, -na *n* COMPATRIOTA : compatriot, fellow countryman
paja *nf* **1** : straw **2** *fam* : trash, tripe
pajar *nm* : hayloft, haystack
pajarera *nf* : aviary
pájaro *nm* : bird ⟨pájaro cantor : songbird⟩ ⟨pájaro bobo : penguin⟩ ⟨pájaro carpintero : woodpecker⟩
pajita *nf* : (drinking) straw
pajote *nm* : straw, mulch
pala *nf* **1** : shovel, spade **2** : blade (of an oar or a rotor) **3** : paddle, racket
palabra *nf* **1** VOCABLO : word **2** PROMESA : word, promise ⟨un hombre de palabra : a man of his word⟩ **3** HABLA : speech **4** : right to speak ⟨tener la palabra : to have the floor⟩
palabrería *nf* : empty talk
palabrota *nf* : swearword
palacio *nm* **1** : palace, mansion **2 palacio de justicia** : courthouse
paladar *nm* **1** : palate **2** GUSTO : taste
paladear *vt* SABOREAR : to savor
paladín *nm, pl* **-dines** : champion, defender
palanca *nf* **1** : lever, crowbar **2** *fam* : leverage, influence **3 palanca de cambio** *or* **palanca de velocidad** : gearshift
palangana *nf* : washbowl
palanqueta *nf* : jimmy, small crowbar
palco *nm* : box (in a theater or stadium)
palear *vt* **1** : to shovel **2** : to paddle
palenque *nm* **1** ESTACADA : stockade, palisade **2** : arena, ring

paleontología *nf* : paleontology

paleontólogo, -ga *n* : paleontologist

palestino, -na *adj & n* : Palestinian

palestra *nf* : arena ⟨salir a la palestra : to join the fray⟩

paleta *nf* **1** : palette **2** : trowel **3** : spatula **4** : blade, vane **5** : paddle **6** *CA, Mex* : lollipop, Popsicle

paletilla *nf* : shoulder blade

paliar *vt* MITIGAR : to alleviate, to palliate

paliativo[1], **-va** *adj* : palliative

paliativo[2] *nm* : palliative

palidecer {53} *vi* : to turn pale

palidez *nf, pl* **-deces** : paleness, pallor

pálido, -da *adj* : pale

palillo *nm* **1** MONDADIENTES : toothpick **2 palillos** *nmpl* : chopsticks **3 palillo de tambor** : drumstick

paliza *nf* : beating, pummeling ⟨darle una paliza a : to beat, to thrash⟩

palma *nf* **1** : palm (of the hand) **2** : palm (tree or leaf) **3 batir palmas** : to clap, to applaud **4 llevarse la palma** *fam* : to take the cake

palmada *nf* **1** : pat **2** : slap **3** : clap

palmarés *nm* : record (of achievements)

palmario, -ria *adj* MANIFIESTO : clear, manifest

palmeado, -da *adj* : webbed

palmear *vt* : to slap on the back — *vi* : to clap, to applaud

palmera *nf* : palm tree

palmo *nm* **1** : span, small amount **2 palmo a palmo** : bit by bit, inch by inch **3 dejar con un palmo de narices** : to disappoint

palmotear *vi* : to applaud

palmoteo *nm* : clapping, applause

palo *nm* **1** : stick, pole, post **2** : shaft, handle ⟨palo de escoba : broomstick⟩ **3** : mast, spar **4** : wood **5** : blow (with a stick) **6** : suit (of cards)

paloma *nf* **1** : pigeon, dove **2 paloma mensajera** : carrier pigeon

palomilla *nf* : moth

palomitas *nfpl* : popcorn

palpable *adj* : palpable, tangible

palpar *vt* : to feel, to touch

palpitación *nf, pl* **-ciones** : palpitation

palpitar *vi* : to palpitate, to throb — **palpitante** *adj*

palta *nf* : avocado

paludismo *nm* MALARIA : malaria

palurdo, -da *n* : boor, yokel, bumpkin

pampa *nf* : pampa

pampeano, -na *adj* : pampean, pampas

pampero → **pampeano**

pan *nm* **1** : bread **2** : loaf of bread **3** : cake, bar ⟨pan de jabón : bar of soap⟩ **4 pan dulce** *CA, Mex* : traditional pastry **5 pan tostado** : toast **6 ser pan comido** *fam* : to be a piece of cake, to be a cinch

pana *nf* : corduroy

panacea *nf* : panacea

panadería *nf* : bakery, bread shop

panadero, -ra *n* : baker

panal *nm* : honeycomb

panameño, -ña *adj & n* : Panamanian

pancarta *nf* : placard, sign

pancita *nf Mex* : tripe

páncreas *nms & pl* : pancreas

panda *nmf* : panda

pandeado, -da *adj* : warped

pandearse *vr* **1** : to warp **2** : to bulge, to sag

pandemonio *or* **pandemónium** *nm* : pandemonium

pandereta *nf* : tambourine

pandero *nm* : tambourine

pandilla *nf* **1** : group, clique **2** : gang

panecito *nm* : roll, bread roll

panegírico[1], **-ca** *adj* : eulogistic, panegyrical

panegírico[2] *nm* : eulogy, panegyric

panel *nm* : panel — **panelista** *nmf*

panera *nf* : bread box

panfleto *nm* : pamphlet

pánico *nm* : panic

panorama *nm* **1** VISTA : panorama, view **2** : scene, situation ⟨el panorama nacional : the national scene⟩ **3** PERSPECTIVA : outlook

panorámico, -ca *adj* : panoramic

panqueque *nm* : pancake

pantaletas *nfpl* : panties

pantalla *nf* **1** : screen, monitor **2** : lampshade **3** : fan

pantalón *nm, pl* **-lones** **1** : pants *pl*, trousers *pl* **2 pantalones vaqueros** : jeans **3 pantalones de mezclilla** *Chile, Mex* : jeans **4 pantalones de montar** : jodhpurs

pantano *nm* **1** : swamp, marsh, bayou **2** : reservoir **3** : obstacle, difficulty

pantanoso, -sa *adj* **1** : marshy, swampy **2** : difficult, thorny

panteón *nm, pl* **-teones** **1** CEMENTERIO : cemetery **2** : pantheon, mausoleum

pantera *nf* : panther

pantimedias *nfpl Mex* : panty hose

pantomima *nf* : pantomime

pantorrilla *nf* : calf (of the leg)

pantufla *nf* ZAPATILLA : slipper

panza *nf* BARRIGA : belly, paunch

panzón, -zona *adj, mpl* **panzones** : potbellied, paunchy

pañal *nm* : diaper

pañería *nf* **1** : cloth, material **2** : fabric store

pañito *nm* : doily

paño *nm* **1** : cloth **2** : rag, dust cloth **3 paño de cocina** : dishcloth **4 paño higiénico** : sanitary napkin

pañuelo *nm* **1** : handkerchief **2** : scarf

papa[1] *nm* : pope

papa[2] *nf* **1** : potato **2 papa dulce** : sweet potato **3 papas fritas** : potato chips, french fries **4 papas a la francesa** *Mex* : french fries

papá *nm fam* **1** : dad, pop **2 papás** *nmpl* : parents, folks

papada *nf* **1** : double chin, jowl **2** : dewlap

papagayo *nm* LORO : parrot

papal *adj* : papal

papalote *nm Mex* : kite

papaya *nf* : papaya

papel *nm* **1** : paper, piece of paper **2** : role, part **3 papel de estaño** : tinfoil **4 papel de empapelar** *or* **papel pintado** : wallpaper **5 papel higiénico** : toilet paper **6 papel de lija** : sandpaper

papeleo *nm* : paperwork, red tape

papelera *nf* : wastebasket

papelería *nf* : stationery store

papelero, -ra *adj* : paper

papeleta *nf* **1** : ballot **2** : ticket, slip

paperas *nfpl* : mumps

papi *nm fam* : daddy, papa

papilla *nf* **1** : pap, mash **2 hacer papilla** : to beat to a pulp

papiro *nm* : papyrus

paquete *nm* BULTO : package, parcel

paquistaní *adj & nmf* : Pakistani

par[1] *adj* : even (in number)

par[2] *nm* **1** : pair, couple **2** : equal, peer ⟨sin par : matchless, peerless⟩ **3** : par (in golf) **4** : rafter **5 de par en par** : wide open

par[3] *nf* **1** : par ⟨por encima de la par : above par⟩ **2 a la par que** : at the same time as, as well as ⟨interesante a la par que instructivo : both interesting and informative⟩

para *prep* **1** : for ⟨para ti : for you⟩ ⟨alta para su edad : tall for her age⟩ ⟨una cita para el lunes : an appointment for Monday⟩ **2** : to, towards ⟨para la derecha : to the right⟩ ⟨van para el río : they're heading towards the river⟩ **3** : to, in order to ⟨lo hace para molestarte : he does it to annoy you⟩ **4** : around, by (a time) ⟨para mañana estarán listos : they'll be ready by tomorrow⟩ **5 para adelante** : forwards **6 para atrás** : backwards **7 para que** : so, so that, in order that ⟨te lo digo para que sepas : I'm telling you so you'll know⟩

parabién *nm, pl* **-bienes** : congratulations *pl*

parábola *nf* **1** : parable **2** : parabola

parabrisas *nms & pl* : windshield

paracaídas *nms & pl* : parachute

paracaidista *nmf* **1** : parachutist **2** : paratrooper

parachoques *nms & pl* : bumper

parada *nf* **1** : stop ⟨parada de autobús : bus stop⟩ **2** : catch, save, parry (in sports) **3** DESFILE : parade

paradero *nm* : whereabouts

paradigma *nm* : paradigm

paradisíaco, -ca *or* **paradisiaco, -ca** *adj* : heavenly

parado, -da *adj* **1** : motionless, idle, stopped **2** : standing (up) **3** : confused, bewildered **4 bien (mal) parado** : in good (bad) shape ⟨salió bien parado : it turned out well for him⟩

paradoja *nf* : paradox

paradójico, -ca *adj* : paradoxical

parafernalia *nf* : paraphernalia

parafina *nf* : paraffin

parafrasear *vt* : to paraphrase

paráfrasis *nfs & pl* : paraphrase

paraguas *nms & pl* : umbrella

paraguayo, -ya *adj & n* : Paraguayan

paraíso *nm* **1** : paradise, heaven **2 paraíso fiscal** : tax shelter

paraje *nm* : spot, place

paralelismo *nm* : parallelism, similarity

paralelo[1], **-la** *adj* : parallel

paralelo[2] *nm* : parallel

paralelogramo *nm* : parallelogram

parálisis *nfs & pl* **1** : paralysis **2** : standstill **3 parálisis cerebral** : cerebral palsy

paralítico, -ca *adj & n* : paralytic

paralizar {21} *vt* **1** : to paralyze **2** : to bring to a standstill — **paralizarse** *vr*

parámetro *nm* : parameter

páramo *nm* : barren plateau, moor

parangón *nm, pl* **-gones 1** : comparison **2 sin ~** : incomparable

paraninfo *nm* : auditorium, assembly hall

paranoia *nf* : paranoia

paranoico, -ca *adj & n* : paranoid

parapeto *nm* : parapet, rampart

parapléjico, -ca *adj & n* : paraplegic

parar *vt* **1** DETENER : to stop **2** : to stand, to prop — *vi* **1** CESAR : to stop **2** : to stay, to put up **3 ir a parar** : to end up, to wind up — **pararse** *vr* **1** : to stop **2** ATASCARSE : to stall (out) **3** : to stand up, to get up

pararrayos *nms & pl* : lightning rod

parasitario, -ria *adj* : parasitic

parasitismo *nm* : parasitism

parásito *nm* : parasite

parasol *nm* SOMBRILLA : parasol

parcela *nf* : parcel, tract of land

parcelar *vt* : to parcel (land)

parchar *vt* : to patch, to patch up

parche *nm* : patch

parcial *adj* : partial — **parcialmente** *adv*

parcialidad *nf* : partiality, bias

parco, -ca *adj* **1** : sparing, frugal **2** : moderate, temperate

pardo, -da *adj* : brownish grey

pardusco → **pardo**

parecer[1] {53} *vi* **1** : to seem, to look, to appear to be ⟨parece bien fácil : it looks very easy⟩ ⟨así parece : so it seems⟩ ⟨pareces una princesa : you look like a princess⟩ **2** : to think, to have an opinion ⟨me parece que sí : I think so⟩ **3** : to like, to be in agreement ⟨si te parece : if you like, if it's all right with you⟩ — **parecerse** *vr* **~ a** : to resemble

parecer[2] *nm* **1** OPINIÓN : opinion **2** ASPECTO : appearance ⟨al parecer : apparently⟩

parecido[1], **-da** *adj* **1** : similar, alike **2 bien parecido** : good-looking

parecido[2] *nm* : resemblance, similarity

pared *nf* : wall

pareja *nf* **1** : couple, pair **2** : partner, mate

parejo, -ja *adj* **1** : even, smooth, level **2** : equal, similar

parentela *nf* : relations *pl,* kinfolk

parentesco *nm* : relationship, kinship

paréntesis *nms & pl* **1** : parenthesis **2** : digression

parentético, -ca *adj* : parenthetic, parenthetical

paria *nmf* : pariah, outcast

paridad *nf* : parity, equality

pariente *nmf* : relative, relation

parir *vi* : to give birth — *vt* : to give birth to, to bear

parking *nm* : parking lot

parlamentar *vi* : to talk, to parley

parlamentario[1], -ria *adj* : parliamentary

parlamentario[2], -ria *n* : member of parliament

parlamento *nm* **1** : parliament **2** : negotiations *pl,* talks *pl*

parlanchín[1], -china *adj, mpl* **-chines** : chatty, talkative

parlanchín[2], -china *n, mpl* **-chines** : chatterbox

parlante *nm* ALTOPARLANTE : loudspeaker

parlotear *vi fam* : to gab, to chat, to prattle

parloteo *nm fam* : prattle, chatter

paro *nm* **1** HUELGA : strike **2** : stoppage, stopping **3 paro forzoso** : layoff

parodia *nf* : parody

parodiar *vt* : to parody

paroxismo *nm* **1** : fit, paroxysm **2** : peak, height ⟨llevaral paroxismo : to carry to the extreme⟩

parpadear *vi* **1** : to blink **2** : to flicker

parpadeo *nm* **1** : blink, blinking **2** : flickering

párpado *nm* : eyelid

parque *nm* **1** : park **2 parque de atracciones** : amusement park

parquear *vt* : to park — **parquearse** *vr*

parqueo *nm* : parking

parquet *or* **parqué** *nm* : parquet

parquímetro *nm* : parking meter

parra *nf* : vine, grapevine

párrafo *nm* : paragraph

parranda *nf fam* : party, spree

parrilla *nf* **1** : broiler, grill **2** : grate

parrillada *nf* BARBACOA : barbecue

párroco *nm* : parish priest

parroquia *nf* **1** : parish **2** : parish church **3** : customers *pl,* clientele

parroquial *adj* : parochial

parroquiano, -na *nm* **1** : parishioner **2** : customer, patron

parsimonia *nf* **1** : calm **2** : parsimony, thrift

parsimonioso, -sa *adj* **1** : calm, unhurried **2** : parsimonious, thrifty

parte[1] *nm* : report, dispatch

parte[2] *nf* **1** : part, share **2** : part, place ⟨en alguna parte : somewhere⟩ ⟨por todas partes : everywhere⟩ **3** : party (in negotiations, etc.) **4 de parte de** : on behalf of **5 ¿de parte de quién?** : may I ask who's calling? **6 tomar parte** : to take part

partero, -ra *n* : midwife

partición *nf, pl* **-ciones** : division, sharing

participación *nf, pl* **-ciones** **1** : participation **2** : share, interest **3** : announcement, notice

participante *nmf* **1** : participant **2** : competitor, entrant

participar *vi* **1** : to participate, to take part **2 ~ en** : to have a share in — *vt* : to announce, to notify

partícipe *nmf* : participant

participio *nm* : participle

partícula *nf* : particle

particular[1] *adj* **1** : particular, specific **2** : private, personal **3** : special, unique

particular[2] *nm* **1** : matter, detail **2** : individual

particularidad *nf* : characteristic, peculiarity

particularizar {21} *vt* **1** : to distinguish, to characterize **2** : to specify

partida *nf* **1** : departure **2** : item, entry **3** : certificate ⟨partida de nacimiento : birth certificate⟩ **4** : game, match, hand **5** : party, group

partidario, -ria *n* : follower, supporter

partido *nm* **1** : (political) party **2** : game, match ⟨partido de futbol : soccer game⟩ **3** APOYO : support, following **4** PROVECHO : profit, advantage ⟨sacar partido de : to profit from⟩

partir *vt* **1** : to cut, to split **2** : to break, to crack **3** : to share (out), to divide — *vi* **1** : to leave, to depart **2 ~ de** : to start from **3 a partir de** : as of, from ⟨a partir de hoy : as of today⟩ — **partirse** *vr* **1** : to smash, to split open **2** : to chap

partisano, -na *adj & n* : partisan

partitura *nf* : (musical) score

parto *nm* **1** : childbirth, delivery, labor ⟨estar de parto : to be in labor⟩ **2** : product, creation, brainchild

parvulario *nm* : nursery school

párvulo, -la *n* : toddler, preschooler

pasa *nf* **1** : raisin **2 pasa de Corinto** : currant

pasable *adj* : passable, tolerable — **pasablemente** *adv*

pasada *nf* **1** : passage, passing **2** : pass, wipe, coat (of paint) **3 de ~** : in passing **4 mala pasada** : dirty trick

pasadizo *nm* : passageway, corridor

pasado[1], -da *adj* **1** : past ⟨el año pasado : last year⟩ ⟨pasado mañana : the day after tomorrow⟩ ⟨pasadas las siete : after seven o'clock⟩ **2** : stale, bad, overripe **3** : old-fashioned, out-of-date **4** : overripe, slightly spoiled

pasado[2] *nm* : past

pasador *nm* **1** : bolt, latch **2** : barrette **3** *Mex* : bobby pin

pasaje *nm* **1** : ticket (for travel) **2** TARIFA : fare **3** : passageway **4** : passengers *pl*

pasajero[1], -ra *adj* : passing, fleeting

pasajero[2], -ra *n* : passenger

pasamanos *nms & pl* **1** : handrail **2** : bannister

pasante *nmf* : assistant

pasaporte *nm* : passport

pasar *vi* **1** : to pass, to go by, to come by **2** : to come in, to enter ⟨¿se puede pasar? : may we come in?⟩ **3** : to happen ⟨¿qué pasa? : what's happening?, what's going on?⟩ **4** : to manage, to get by **5** : to be over, to end **6 ~ de** : to exceed, to go beyond **7 ~ por** : to pretend to be — *vt* **1** : to pass, to give ⟨¿me pasas la sal? : would you pass me the salt?⟩ **2** : to pass (a test) **3** : to go over, to cross **4** : to spend (time) **5** : to tolerate **6** : to go through, to suffer **7** : to show (a movie, etc.) **8** : to overtake, to pass, to surpass **9** : to pass over, to wipe up **10 pasarlo bien** *or* **pasarla bien** : to have a good time **11 pasarlo mal** *or* **pasarla mal** : to have a bad time, to have a hard time **12 pasar por alto** : to overlook, to omit — **pasarse** *vr* **1** : to move, to pass, to go away **2** : to slip one's mind, to forget **3** : to go too far

pasarela *nf* **1** : gangplank **2** : footbridge **3** : runway, catwalk

pasatiempo *nm* : pastime, hobby

Pascua *nf* **1** : Easter **2** : Passover **3** : Christmas **4 Pascuas** *nfpl* : Christmas season

pase *nm* **1** PERMISO : pass, permit **2 pase de abordar** *Mex* : boarding pass

pasear *vi* : to take a walk, to go for a ride — *vt* **1** : to take for a walk **2** : to parade around, to show off — **pasearse** *vr* : to walk around

paseo *nm* **1** : walk, stroll **2** : ride **3** EXCURSIÓN : outing, trip **4** : avenue, walk **5** *or* **paseo marítimo** : boardwalk

pasiflora *nf* : passionflower

pasillo *nm* CORREDOR : hallway, corridor, aisle

pasión *nf, pl* **pasiones** : passion

pasional *adj* : passionate ⟨crimen pasional : crime of passion⟩

pasionaria → **pasiflora**

pasivo[1], **-va** *adj* : passive — **pasivamente** *adv*

pasivo[2] *nm* **1** : liability ⟨activos y pasivos : assets and liabilities⟩ **2** : debit side (of an account)

pasmado, -da *adj* : stunned, flabbergasted

pasmar *vt* : to amaze, to stun — **pasmarse** *vr*

pasmo *nm* **1** : shock, astonishment **2** : wonder, marvel

pasmoso, -sa *adj* : incredible, amazing — **pasmosamente** *adv*

paso[1], **-sa** *adj* : dried ⟨ciruela pasa : prune⟩

paso[2] *nm* **1** : passage, passing ⟨de paso : in passing, on the way⟩ **2** : way, path ⟨abrirse paso : to make one's way⟩ **3** : crossing ⟨paso de peatones : crosswalk⟩ ⟨paso a desnivel : underpass⟩ ⟨paso elevado : overpass⟩ **4** : step ⟨paso a paso : step by step⟩ **5** : pace, gait ⟨a buen paso : quickly, at a good rate⟩

pasta *nf* **1** : paste ⟨pasta de dientes *or* pasta dental : toothpaste⟩ **2** : pasta **3** : pastry dough **4 libro en pasta dura** : hardcover book **5 tener pasta de** : to have the makings of

pastar *vi* : to graze — *vt* : to put to pasture

pastel[1] *adj* : pastel

pastel[2] *nm* **1** : cake ⟨pastel de cumpleaños : birthday cake⟩ **2** : pie, turnover **3** : pastel

pastelería *nf* : pastry shop

pasteurización *nf, pl* **-ciones** : pasteurization

pasteurizar {21} *vt* : to pasteurize

pastilla *nf* **1** COMPRIMIDO, PÍLDORA : pill, tablet **2** : lozenge ⟨pastilla para la tos : cough drop⟩ **3** : cake (of soap), bar (of chocolate)

pastizal *nm* : pasture, grazing land

pasto *nm* **1** : pasture **2** HIERBA : grass, lawn

pastor, -tora *n* **1** : shepherd, shepherdess *f* **2** : minister, pastor

pastoral *adj & nf* : pastoral

pastorear *vt* : to shepherd, to tend

pastorela *nf* **1** : pastoral, pastourelle **2** *Mex* : a traditional Christmas play

pastoso, -sa *adj* **1** : pasty, doughy **2** : smooth, mellow (of sounds)

pata *nf* **1** : paw, leg (of an animal) **2** : foot, leg (of furniture) **3 patas de gallo** : crow's-feet **4 meter la pata** *fam* : to put one's foot in it, to make a blunder

patada *nf* **1** PUNTAPIÉ : kick **2** : stamp (of the foot)

patalear *vi* **1** : to kick **2** : to stamp one's feet

pataleta *nf fam* : tantrum

patán[1] *adj, pl* **patanes** : boorish, crude

patán[2] *nm, pl* **patanes** : boor, lout

patata *nf Spain* : potato

pateador, -dora *n* : kicker (in sports)

patear *vt* : to kick — *vi* : to stamp one's foot

patentar *vt* : to patent

patente[1] *adj* EVIDENTE : obvious, patent — **patentemente** *adv*

patente[2] *nf* : patent

paternal *adj* : fatherly, paternal

paternidad *nf* **1** : fatherhood, paternity **2** : parenthood **3** : authorship

paterno, -na *adj* : paternal ⟨abuela paterna : paternal grandmother⟩

patético, -ca *adj* : pathetic, moving

patetismo *nm* : pathos

patíbulo *nm* : gallows, scaffold

patillas *nfpl* : sideburns

patín *nm, pl* **patines** : skate ⟨patín de ruedas : roller skate⟩

patinador, -dora *n* : skater

patinaje *nm* : skating

patinar *vi* **1** : to skate **2** : to skid, to slip **3** *fam* : to slip up, to blunder

patinazo *nm* **1** : skid **2** *fam* : blunder, slipup

patineta *nf* **1** : scooter **2** : skateboard
patinete *nm* : scooter
patio *nm* **1** : courtyard, patio **2 patio de recreo** : playground
patito, -ta *n* : duckling
pato, -ta *n* **1** : duck **2 pato real** : mallard **3 pagar el pato** *fam* : to take the blame
patología *nf* : pathology
patológico, -ca *adj* : pathological
patólogo, -ga *n* : pathologist
patraña *nf* : tall tale, humbug, nonsense
patria *nf* : native land
patriarca *nm* : patriarch — **patriarcal** *adj*
patriarcado *nm* : patriarchy
patrimonio *nm* : patrimony, legacy
patrio, -tria *adj* **1** : native, home ⟨suelo patrio : native soil⟩ **2** : paternal
patriota[1] *adj* : patriotic
patriota[2] *nmf* : patriot
patriotería *nf* : jingoism, chauvinism
patriotero[1], **-ra** *adj* : jingoistic, chauvinistic
patriotero[2], **-ra** *n* : jingoist, chauvinist
patriótico, -ca *adj* : patriotic
patriotismo *nm* : patriotism
patrocinador, -dora *n* : sponsor, patron
patrocinar *vt* : to sponsor
patrocinio *nm* : sponsorship, patronage
patrón[1], **-trona** *n, mpl* **patrones 1** JEFE : boss **2** : patron saint
patrón[2] *nm, pl* **patrones 1** : standard **2** : pattern (in sewing)
patronal *adj* **1** : management, employers' ⟨sindicato patronal : employers' association⟩ **2** : pertaining to a patron saint ⟨fiesta patronal : patron saint's day⟩
patronato *nm* **1** : board, council **2** : foundation, trust
patrono, -na *n* **1** : employer **2** : patron saint
patrulla *nf* **1** : patrol **2** : police car, cruiser
patrullar *v* : to patrol
patrullero *nm* **1** : police car **2** : patrol boat
paulatino, -na *adj* : gradual
paupérrimo, -ma *adj* : destitute, poverty-stricken
pausa *nf* : pause, break
pausado[1] *adv* : slowly, deliberately ⟨habla más pausado : speak more slowly⟩
pausado[2], **-da** *adj* : slow, deliberate — **pausadamente** *adv*
pauta *nf* **1** : rule, guideline **2** : lines *pl* (on paper)
pava *nf Arg, Bol, Chile* : kettle
pavimentar *vt* : pave
pavimento *nm* : pavement
pavo, -va *n* **1** : turkey **2 pavo real** : peacock **3 comer pavo** : to be a wallflower
pavón *nm, pl* **pavones** : peacock
pavonearse *vr* : to strut, to swagger
pavoneo *nm* : strut, swagger
pavor *nm* TERROR : dread, terror
pavoroso, -sa *adj* ATERRADOR : dreadful, terrifying
payasada *nf* BUFONADA : antic, buffoonery
payasear *vi* : to clown around
payaso, -sa *n* : clown
paz *nf, pl* **paces 1** : peace **2 dejar en paz** : to leave alone **3 hacer las paces** : to make up, to reconcile
pazca, etc. → **pacer**
PC *nmf* : PC, personal computer
peaje *nm* : toll
peatón *nm, pl* **-tones** : pedestrian
peatonal *adj* : pedestrian
peca *nf* : freckle
pecado *nm* : sin
pecador[1], **-dora** *adj* : sinful, sinning
pecador[2], **-dora** *n* : sinner
pecaminoso, -sa *adj* : sinful
pecar {72} *vi* **1** : to sin **2 ~ de** : to be too much (something) ⟨no pecan de amabilidad : they're not overly friendly⟩
pécari *or* **pecarí** *nm* : peccary
pececillo *nm* : small fish
pecera *nf* : fishbowl, fish tank
pecho *nm* **1** : chest **2** SENO : breast, bosom **3** : heart, courage **4 dar el pecho** : to breast-feed **5 tomar a pecho** : to take to heart
pechuga *nf* : breast (of fowl)
pecoso, -sa *adj* : freckled
pectoral *adj* : pectoral
peculado *nm* : embezzlement
peculiar *adj* **1** CARACTERÍSTICO : particular, characteristic **2** RARO : peculiar, uncommon
peculiaridad *nf* : peculiarity
pecuniario, -ria *adj* : pecuniary
pedagogía *nf* : pedagogy
pedagógico, -ca *adj* : pedagogic, pedagogical
pedagogo, -ga *n* : educator, pedagogue
pedal *nm* : pedal
pedalear *vi* : to pedal
pedante[1] *adj* : pedantic
pedante[2] *nmf* : pedant
pedantería *nf* : pedantry
pedazo *nm* TROZO : piece, bit, chunk ⟨caerse a pedazos : to fall to pieces⟩ ⟨hacer pedazos : to tear into shreds, to smash to pieces⟩
pedernal *nm* : flint
pedestal *nm* : pedestal
pedestre *adj* : commonplace, pedestrian
pediatra *nmf* : pediatrician
pediatría *nf* : pediatrics
pediátrico, -ca *adj* : pediatric
pedido *nm* **1** : order (of merchandise) **2** : request
pedigrí *nm* : pedigree
pedir {54} *vt* **1** : to ask for, to request ⟨le pedí un préstamo a Claudia : I asked Claudia for a loan⟩ **2** : to order (food, merchandise) **3 pedir disculpas** *or* **pedir perdón** : to apologize — *vi* **1** : to order **2** : to beg

pedrada *nf* **1** : blow (with a rock or stone) ⟨la ventana se quebró de una pedrada : the window was broken by a rock⟩ **2** *fam* : cutting remark, dig

pedregal *nm* : rocky ground

pedregoso, -sa *adj* : rocky, stony

pedrera *nf* CANTERA : quarry

pedrería *nf* : precious stones *pl*, gems *pl*

pegado, -da *adj* **1** : glued, stuck, stuck together **2 ~ a** : right next to

pegajoso, -sa *adj* **1** : sticky, gluey **2** : catchy ⟨una tonada pegajosa : a catchy tune⟩

pegamento *nm* : adhesive, glue

pegar {52} *vt* **1** : to glue, to stick, to paste **2** : to attach, to sew on **3** : to infect with, to give ⟨me pegó el resfriado : he gave me his cold⟩ **4** GOLPEAR : to hit, to deal, to strike ⟨me pegaron un puntapié : they gave me a kick⟩ **5** : to give (out with) ⟨pegó un grito : she let out a yell⟩ — *vi* **1** : to adhere, to stick **2 ~ en** : to hit, to strike (against) **3 ~ con** : to match, to go with — **pegarse** *vr* **1** GOLPEARSE : to hit oneself, to hit each other **2** : to stick, to take hold **3** : to be contagious **4** *fam* : to tag along, to stick around

pegote *nm* **1** : sticky mess **2** *Mex* : sticker, adhesive label

pegue, etc. → **pegar**

peinado *nm* : hairstyle, hairdo

peinador, -dora *n* : hairdresser

peinar *vt* : to comb — **peinarse** *vr*

peine *nm* : comb

peineta *nf* : ornamental comb

peladez *nf, pl* **-deces** *Mex fam* : obscenity, bad language

pelado, -da *adj* **1** : bald, hairless **2** : peeled **3** : bare, barren **4** : broke, penniless **5** *Mex fam* : coarse, crude

pelador *nm* : peeler

pelagra *nf* : pellagra

pelaje *nm* : coat (of an animal), fur

pelar *vt* **1** : to peel, to shell **2** : to skin **3** : to pluck **4** : to remove hair from **5** *fam* : to clean out (of money) — **pelarse** *vr* **1** : to peel **2** *fam* : to get a haircut **3** *Mex fam* : to split, to leave

peldaño *nm* **1** : step, stair **2** : rung

pelea *nf* **1** LUCHA : fight **2** : quarrel

pelear *vi* **1** LUCHAR : to fight **2** DISPUTAR : to quarrel — **pelearse** *vr*

peleón, -ona *adj, mpl* **-ones** *Spain* : quarrelsome, argumentative

peleonero, -ra *adj Mex* : quarrelsome

peletería *nf* **1** : fur shop **2** : fur trade

peletero, -ra *n* : furrier

peliagudo, -da *adj* : tricky, difficult, ticklish

pelícano *nm* : pelican

película *nf* **1** : movie, film **2** : (photographic) film **3** : thin covering, layer

peligrar *vi* : to be in danger

peligro *nm* **1** : danger, peril **2** : risk ⟨correr peligro de : to run the risk of⟩

peligroso, -sa *adj* : dangerous, hazardous

pelirrojo[1], **-ja** *adj* : red-haired, redheaded

pelirrojo[2], **-ja** *n* : redhead

pellejo *nm* **1** : hide, skin **2 salvar el pellejo** : to save one's neck

pellizcar {72} *vt* **1** : to pinch **2** : to nibble on

pellizco *nm* : pinch

pelo *nm* **1** : hair **2** : fur **3** : pile, nap **4 a pelo** : bareback **5 con pelos y señales** : in great detail **6 no tener pelos en la lengua** : to not mince words, to be blunt **7 tomarle el pelo a alguien** : to tease someone, to pull someone's leg

pelón, -lona *adj, mpl* **pelones 1** : bald **2** *fam* : broke **3** *Mex fam* : tough, difficult

pelota *nf* **1** : ball **2** *fam* : head **3 en pelotas** *fam* : naked **4 pelota vasca** : jai alai **5 pasar la pelota** *fam* : to pass the buck

pelotón *nm, pl* **-tones** : squad, detachment

peltre *nm* : pewter

peluca *nf* : wig

peluche *nm* : plush (fabric)

peludo, -da *adj* : hairy, shaggy, bushy

peluquería *nf* **1** : hairdresser's, barber shop **2** : hairdressing

peluquero, -ra *n* : barber, hairdresser

peluquín *nm, pl* **-quines** TUPÉ : hairpiece, toupee

pelusa *nf* : lint, fuzz

pélvico, -ca *adj* : pelvic

pelvis *nfs & pl* : pelvis

pena *nf* **1** CASTIGO : punishment, penalty ⟨pena de muerte : death penalty⟩ **2** AFLICCIÓN : sorrow, grief ⟨morir de pena : to die of a broken heart⟩ ⟨¡qué pena! : what a shame!, how sad!⟩ **3** DOLOR : pain, suffering **4** DIFICULTAD : difficulty, trouble ⟨a duras penas : with great difficulty⟩ **5** VERGÜENZA : shame, embarrassment **6 valer la pena** : to be worthwhile

penacho *nm* **1** : crest, tuft **2** : plume (of feathers)

penal[1] *adj* : penal

penal[2] *nm* CÁRCEL : prison, penitentiary

penalidad *nf* **1** : hardship **2** : penalty, punishment

penalizar {21} *vt* : to penalize

penalty *nm* : penalty (in sports)

penar *vt* : to punish, to penalize — *vi* : to suffer, to grieve

pendenciero, -ra *adj* : argumentative, quarrelsome

pender *vi* **1** : to hang **2** : to be pending

pendiente[1] *adj* **1** : pending **2 estar pendiente de** : to be watchful of, to be on the lookout for

pendiente[2] *nm Spain* : earring

pendiente[3] *nf* : slope, incline

pendón *nm, pl* **pendones** : banner

péndulo *nm* : pendulum

pene *nm* : penis

penetración *nf, pl* **-ciones** **1** : penetration **2** : insight
penetrante *adj* **1** : penetrating, piercing **2** : sharp, acute **3** : deep (of a wound)
penetrar *vi* **1** : to penetrate, to sink in **2 ~ por** *or* **~ en** : to pierce, to go in, to enter into ⟨el frío penetra por la ventana : the cold comes right in through the window⟩ — *vt* **1** : to penetrate, to permeate **2** : to pierce ⟨el dolor penetró su corazón : sorrow pierced her heart⟩ **3** : to fathom, to understand
penicilina *nf* : penicillin
península *nf* : peninsula — **peninsular** *adj*
penitencia *nf* : penance, penitence
penitenciaría *nf* : penitentiary
penitente *adj & nmf* : penitent
penol *nm* : yardarm
penoso, -sa *adj* **1** : painful, distressing **2** : difficult, arduous **3** : shy, bashful
pensado, -da *adj* **1 bien pensado** : well thought-out **2 en el momento menos pensado** : when least expected **3 poco pensado** : badly thought-out **4 mal pensado** : evil-minded
pensador, -dora *n* : thinker
pensamiento *nm* **1** : thought **2** : thinking **3** : pansy
pensar {55} *vi* **1** : to think **2 ~ en** : to think about — *vt* **1** : to think **2** : to think about **3** : to intend, to plan on — **pensarse** *vr* : to think over
pensativo, -va *adj* : pensive, thoughtful
pensión *nf, pl* **pensiones** **1** JUBILACIÓN : pension **2** : boarding house **3 pensión alimenticia** : alimony
pensionado, -da *n* → **pensionista**
pensionista *nmf* **1** JUBILADO : pensioner, retiree **2** : boarder, lodger
pentágono *nm* : pentagon — **pentagonal** *adj*
pentagrama *nm* : staff (in music)
penúltimo, -ma *adj* : next to last, penultimate
penumbra *nf* : semidarkness
penuria *nf* **1** ESCASEZ : shortage, scarcity **2** : poverty
peña *nf* : rock, crag
peñasco *nm* : crag, large rock
peñón → **peñasco**
peón *nm, pl* **peones** **1** : laborer, peon **2** : pawn (in chess)
peonía *nf* : peony
peor[1] *adv* **1** (*comparative of* **mal**) : worse ⟨se llevan peor que antes : they get along worse than before⟩ **2** (*superlative of* **mal**) : worst ⟨me fue peor que a nadie : I did the worst of all⟩
peor[2] *adj* **1** (*comparative of* **malo**) : worse ⟨es peor que el original : it's worse than the original⟩ **2** (*superlative of* **malo**) : worst ⟨el peor de todos : the worst of all⟩
pepa *nf* : seed, pit (of a fruit)
pepenador, -dora *n CA, Mex* : scavenger
pepenar *vt CA, Mex* : to scavenge, to scrounge
pepinillo *nm* : pickle, gherkin
pepino *nm* : cucumber
pepita *nf* **1** : seed, pip **2** : nugget **3** *Mex* : dried pumpkin seed
peque, etc. → **pecar**
pequeñez *nf, pl* **-ñeces** **1** : smallness **2** : trifle, triviality **3 pequeñez de espíritu** : pettiness
pequeño[1], **-ña** *adj* **1** : small, little ⟨un libro pequeño : a small book⟩ **2** : young **3** BAJO : short
pequeño[2], **-ña** *n* : child, little one
pera *nf* : pear
peraltar *vt* : to bank (a road)
perca *nf* : perch (fish)
percal *nm* : percale
percance *nm* : mishap, misfortune
percatarse *vr* **~ de** : to notice, to become aware of
percebe *nm* : barnacle
percepción *nf, pl* **-ciones** **1** : perception **2** : idea, notion **3** COBRO : receipt (of payment), collection
perceptible *adj* : perceptible, noticeable — **perceptiblemente** *adv*
percha *nf* **1** : perch **2** : coat hanger **3** : coatrack, coat hook
perchero *nm* : coatrack
percibir *vt* **1** : to perceive, to notice, to sense **2** : to earn, to draw (a salary)
percudido, -da *adj* : grimy
percudir *vt* : to make grimy — **percudirse** *vr*
percusión *nf, pl* **-siones** : percussion
percusor *or* **percutor** *nm* : hammer (of a firearm)
perdedor[1], **-dora** *adj* : losing
perdedor[2], **-dora** *n* : loser
perder {56} *vt* **1** : to lose **2** : to miss ⟨perdimos la oportunidad : we missed the opportunity⟩ **3** : to waste (time) — *vi* : to lose — **perderse** *vr* EXTRAVIARSE : to get lost, to stray
perdición *nf, pl* **-ciones** : perdition, damnation
pérdida *nf* **1** : loss **2 pérdida de tiempo** : waste of time
perdidamente *adv* : hopelessly
perdido, -da *adj* **1** : lost **2** : inveterate, incorrigible ⟨es un caso perdido : he's a hopeless case⟩ **3** : in trouble, done for **4 de ~** *Mex fam* : at least
perdigón *nm, pl* **-gones** : shot, pellet
perdiz *nf, pl* **perdices** : partridge
perdón[1] *nm, pl* **perdones** : forgiveness, pardon
perdón[2] *interj* : excuse me!, sorry!
perdonable *adj* : forgivable
perdonar *vt* **1** DISCULPAR : to forgive, to pardon **2** : to exempt, to excuse
perdurable *adj* : lasting
perdurar *vi* : to last, to endure, to survive
perecedero, -ra *adj* : perishable
perecer {53} *vi* : to perish, to die
peregrinación *nf, pl* **-ciones** : pilgrimage
peregrinaje *nm* → **peregrinación**

peregrino[1], **-na** *adj* **1** : unusual, odd **2** MIGRATORIO : migratory
peregrino[2], **-na** *n* : pilgrim
perejil *nm* : parsley
perenne *adj* : perennial
perentorio, **-ria** *adj* **1** : peremptory **2** URGENTE : urgent **3** FIJO : fixed, set
pereza *nf* FLOJERA, HOLGAZANERÍA : laziness, idleness
perezoso[1], **-sa** *adj* FLOJO, HOLGAZÁN : lazy
perezoso[2] *nm* : sloth (animal)
perfección *nf, pl* **-ciones** : perfection
perfeccionamiento *nm* : perfecting, refinement
perfeccionar *vt* : to perfect, to refine
perfeccionismo *nm* : perfectionism
perfeccionista *nmf* : perfectionist
perfecto, **-ta** *adj* : perfect — **perfectamente** *adv*
perfidia *nf* : perfidy, treachery
pérfido, **-da** *adj* : perfidious
perfil *nm* **1** : profile **2 de ~** : sideways, from the side **3 perfiles** *nmpl* RASGOS : features, characteristics
perfilar *vt* : to outline, to define — **perfilarse** *vr* **1** : to be outlined, to be silhouetted **2** : to take shape
perforación *nf, pl* **-ciones 1** : perforation **2** : drilling
perforadora *nf* **1** : hole punch (for paper) **2** : drill (in mining, etc.)
perforar *vt* **1** : to perforate, to pierce **2** : to drill, to bore
perfumar *vt* : to perfume, to scent — **perfumarse** *vr*
perfume *nm* : perfume, scent
pergamino *nm* : parchment
pérgola *nf* : pergola, arbor
pericia *nf* : skill, expertise
pericial *adj* : expert ⟨testigo pericial : expert witness⟩
perico *nm* COTORRA : small parrot
periferia *nf* : periphery
periférico[1], **-ca** *adj* : peripheral
periférico[2] *nm* **1** *CA, Mex* : beltway **2** : peripheral
perilla *nf* **1** : goatee **2** : pommel (on a saddle) **3** *Col, Mex* : knob, handle **4 perilla de la oreja** : earlobe **5 de perillas** *fam* : handy, just right
perímetro *nm* : perimeter
periódico[1], **-ca** *adj* : periodic — **periódicamente** *adv*
periódico[2] *nm* DIARIO : newspaper
periodismo *nm* : journalism
periodista *nmf* : journalist
periodístico, **-ca** *adj* : journalistic, news
período *or* **periodo** *nm* : period
peripecia *nf* VICISITUD : vicissitude, reversal ⟨las peripecias de su carrera : the ups and downs of her career⟩
periquito *nm* **1** : parakeet **2 periquito australiano** : budgerigar
periscopio *nm* : periscope
perito, **-ta** *adj & n* : expert
perjudicar {72} *vt* : to harm, to be detrimental to
perjudicial *adj* : harmful, detrimental
perjuicio *nm* **1** : harm, damage **2 en perjuicio de** : to the detriment of
perjurar *vi* : to perjure oneself
perjurio *nm* : perjury
perjuro, **-ra** *n* : perjurer
perla *nf* **1** : pearl **2 de perlas** *fam* : wonderfully ⟨me viene de perlas : it suits me just fine⟩
permanecer {53} *vi* **1** QUEDARSE : to remain, to stay **2** SEGUIR : to remain, to continue to be
permanencia *nf* **1** : permanence, continuance **2** ESTANCIA : stay
permanente[1] *adj* **1** : permanent **2** : constant — **permanentemente** *adv*
permanente[2] *nf* : permanent (wave)
permeabilidad *nf* : permeability
permeable *adj* : permeable
permisible *adj* : permissible, allowable
permisividad *nf* : permissiveness
permisivo, **-va** *adv* : permissive
permiso *nm* **1** : permission **2** : permit, license **3** : leave, furlough **4 con ~** : excuse me, pardon me
permitir *vt* : to permit, to allow — **permitirse** *vr*
permuta *nf* : exchange
permutar *vt* INTERCAMBIAR : to exchange
pernicioso, **-sa** *adj* : pernicious, destructive
pernil *nm* **1** : haunch (of an animal) **2** : leg (of meat), ham **3** : trouser leg
perno *nm* : bolt, pin
pernoctar *vi* : to stay overnight, to spend the night
pero[1] *nm* **1** : fault, defect ⟨ponerle peros a : to find fault with⟩ **2** : objection
pero[2] *conj* : but
perogrullada *nf* : truism, platitude, cliché
peroné *nm* : fibula
perorar *vi* : to deliver a speech
perorata *nf* : oration, long-winded speech
peróxido *nm* : peroxide
perpendicular *adj & nf* : perpendicular
perpetrar *vt* : to perpetrate
perpetuar {3} *vt* ETERNIZAR : to perpetuate
perpetuidad *nf* : perpetuity
perpetuo, **-tua** *adj* : perpetual — **perpetuamente** *adv*
perplejidad *nf* : perplexity
perplejo, **-ja** *adj* : perplexed, puzzled
perrada *nf fam* : dirty trick
perrera *nf* : kennel, dog pound
perrero, **-ra** *n* : dogcatcher
perrito, **-ta** *n* CACHORRO : puppy, small dog
perro, **-rra** *n* **1** : dog, bitch *f* **2 perro caliente** : hot dog **3 perro salchicha** : dachshund **4 perro faldero** : lapdog **5 perro cobrador** : retriever
persa[1] *adj & nmf* : Persian
persa[2] *nm* : Persian (language)

persecución *nf, pl* **-ciones 1** : pursuit, chase **2** : persecution
perseguidor, -dora *n* **1** : pursuer **2** : persecutor
perseguir {75} *vt* **1** : to pursue, to chase **2** : to persecute **3** : to pester, to annoy
perseverancia *nf* : perseverance
perseverar *vi* : to persevere
persiana *nf* : blind, venetian blind
persignarse *vr* SANTIGUARSE : to cross oneself, to make the sign of the cross
persistir *vi* : to persist — **persistencia** *nf* — **persistente** *adj*
persona *nf* : person
personaje *nm* **1** : character (in drama or literature) **2** : personage, celebrity
personal[1] *adj* : personal — **personalmente** *adv*
personal[2] *nm* : personnel, staff
personalidad *nf* : personality
personalizar {21} *vt* : to personalize
personificar {72} *vi* : to personify — **personificación** *nf*
perspectiva *nf* **1** : perspective, view **2** : prospect, outlook
perspicacia *nf* : shrewdness, perspicacity, insight
perspicaz *adj, pl* **-caces** : shrewd, perspicacious
persuadir *vt* : to persuade — **persuadirse** *vr* : to become convinced
persuasión *nf, pl* **-siones** : persuasion
persuasivo, -va *adj* : persuasive
pertenecer {53} *vi* : to belong
perteneciente *adj* **∼ a** : belonging to
pertenencia *nf* **1** : membership **2** : ownership **3 pertenencias** *nfpl* : belongings, possessions
pértiga *nf* GARROCHA : pole ⟨salto de pértiga : pole vault⟩
pertinaz *adj, pl* **-naces 1** OBSTINADO : obstinate **2** PERSISTENTE : persistent
pertinencia *nf* : pertinence, relevance — **pertinente** *adj*
pertrechos *nmpl* : equipment, gear
perturbación *nf, pl* **-ciones** : disturbance, disruption
perturbador, -dora *adj* **1** INQUIETANTE : disturbing, troubling **2** : disruptive
perturbar *vt* **1** : to disturb, to trouble **2** : to disrupt
peruano, -na *adj & n* : Peruvian
perversidad *nf* : perversity, depravity
perversión *nf, pl* **-siones** : perversion
perverso, -sa *adj* : wicked, depraved
pervertido[1], **-da** *adj* DEPRAVADO : perverted, depraved
pervertido[2], **-da** *n* : pervert
pervertir {76} *vt* : to pervert, to corrupt
pesa *nf* **1** : weight **2 levantamiento de pesas** : weightlifting
pesadamente *adv* **1** : heavily **2** : slowly, clumsily
pesadez *nf, pl* **-deces 1** : heaviness **2** : slowness **3** : tediousness
pesadilla *nf* : nightmare
pesado[1], **-da** *adj* **1** : heavy **2** : slow **3** : irritating, annoying **4** : tedious, boring **5** : tough, difficult
pesado[2], **-da** *n fam* : bore, pest
pesadumbre *nf* AFLICCIÓN : grief, sorrow, sadness
pésame *nm* : condolences *pl* ⟨mi más sentido pésame : my heartfelt condolences⟩
pesar[1] *vt* **1** : to weigh **2** EXAMINAR : to consider, to think over — *vi* **1** : to weigh ⟨¿cuánto pesa? : how much does it weigh?⟩ **2** : to be heavy **3** : to weigh heavily, to be a burden ⟨no le pesa : it's not a burden on him⟩ ⟨pesa sobre mi corazón : it weighs upon my heart⟩ **4** INFLUIR : to carry weight, to have bearing **5** (*with personal pronouns*) : to grieve, to sadden ⟨me pesa mucho : I'm very sorry⟩ **6 pese a** : in spite of, despite
pesar[2] *nm* **1** AFLICCIÓN, PENA : sorrow, grief **2** REMORDIMIENTO : remorse **3 a pesar de** : in spite of, despite
pesaroso, -sa *adj* **1** : sad, mournful **2** ARREPENTIDO : sorry, regretful
pesca *nf* : fishing
pescadería *nf* : fish market
pescado *nm* : fish (as food)
pescador, -dora *n* : fisherman *m,* fisherwoman *f*
pescar {72} *vt* **1** : to fish for **2** : to catch **3** *fam* : to get a hold of, to land — *vi* : to fish, to go fishing
pescuezo *nm* : neck
pesebre *nm* : manger
pesero *nm Mex* : minibus
peseta *nf* : peseta (Spanish unit of currency)
pesimismo *nm* : pessimism
pesimista[1] *adj* : pessimistic
pesimista[2] *nmf* : pessimist
pésimo, -ma *adj* : dreadful, abominable
peso *nm* **1** : weight, heaviness **2** : burden, responsibility **3** : weight (in sports) **4** BÁSCULA : scales *pl* **5** : peso
pesque, etc. → pescar
pesquería *nf* : fishery
pesquero[1], **-ra** *adj* : fishing ⟨pueblo pesquero : fishing village⟩
pesquero[2] *nm* : fishing boat
pesquisa *nf* INVESTIGACIÓN : inquiry, investigation
pestaña *nf* **1** : eyelash **2** : flange, rim
pestañear *vi* : to blink
pestañeo *nm* : blink
peste *nf* **1** : plague, pestilence **2** : stench, stink **3** : nuisance, pest
pesticida *nm* : pesticide
pestilencia *nf* **1** : stench, foul odor **2** : pestilence
pestilente *adj* **1** : foul, smelly **2** : pestilent
pestillo *nm* CERROJO : bolt, latch
petaca *nf* **1** *Mex* : suitcase **2 petacas** *nfpl Mex fam* : bottom, behind
pétalo *nm* : petal
petardear *vi* : to backfire

petardeo *nm* : backfiring

petardo *nm* : firecracker

petate *nm Mex* : mat

petición *nf, pl* **-ciones** : petition, request

peticionar *vt* : to petition

peticionario, -ria *n* : petitioner

petirrojo *nm* : robin

peto *nm* : bib (of clothing)

pétreo, -trea *adj* : stone, stony

petrificar {72} *vt* : to petrify

petróleo *nm* : oil, petroleum

petrolero[1], **-ra** *adj* : oil ⟨industria petrolera : oil industry⟩

petrolero[2] *nm* : oil tanker

petrolífero, -ra *adj* → **petrolero**[1]

petulancia *nf* INSOLENCIA : insolence, petulance

petulante *adj* INSOLENTE : insolent, petulant — **petulantemente** *adv*

petunia *nf* : petunia

peyorativo, -va *adj* : pejorative

pez[1] *nm, pl* **peces** 1 : fish 2 **pez de colores** : goldfish 3 **pez espada** : swordfish 4 **pez gordo** : big shot

pez[2] *nf, pl* **peces** : pitch, tar

pezón *nm, pl* **pezones** : nipple

pezuña *nf* : hoof ⟨pezuña hendida : cloven hoof⟩

pi *nf* : pi

piadoso, -sa *adj* 1 : compassionate, merciful 2 DEVOTO : pious, devout

pianista *nmf* : pianist, piano player

piano *nm* : piano

piar {85} *vi* : to chirp, to cheep, to tweet

pibe, -ba *n Arg, Uru fam* : kid, child

pica *nf* 1 : pike, lance 2 : goad (in bullfighting) 3 : spade (in playing cards)

picada *nf* 1 : bite, sting (of an insect) 2 : sharp descent

picadillo *nm* 1 : minced meat, hash 2 **hacer picadillo a** : to beat to a pulp

picado, -da *adj* 1 : perforated 2 : minced, chopped 3 : decayed (of teeth) 4 : choppy, rough 5 *fam* : annoyed, miffed

picador *nm* : picador

picadura *nf* 1 : sting, bite 2 : prick, puncture 3 : decay, cavity

picaflor *nm* COLIBRÍ : hummingbird

picana *nf* : goad, prod

picante[1] *adj* 1 : hot, spicy 2 : sharp, cutting 3 : racy, risqué

picante[2] *nm* 1 : spiciness 2 : hot spices *pl*, hot sauce

picaporte *nm* 1 : latch 2 : door handle 3 ALDABA : door knocker

picar {72} *vt* 1 : to sting, to bite 2 : to peck at 3 : to nibble on 4 : to prick, to puncture, to punch (a ticket) 5 : to grind, to chop 6 : to goad, to incite 7 : to pique, to provoke — *vi* 1 : to itch 2 : to sting 3 : to be spicy 4 : to nibble 5 : to take the bait 6 **~ en** : to dabble in 7 **picar muy alto** : to aim too high — **picarse** *vr* 1 : to get a cavity, to decay 2 : to get annoyed, to take offense

picardía *nf* 1 : cunning, craftiness 2 : prank, dirty trick

picaresco, -ca *adj* 1 : picaresque 2 : rascally, roguish

pícaro[1], **-ra** *adj* 1 : mischievous 2 : cunning, sly 3 : off-color, risqué

pícaro[2], **-ra** *n* 1 : rogue, scoundrel 2 : rascal

picazón *nf, pl* **-zones** COMEZÓN : itch

picea *nf* : spruce (tree)

pichel *nm* : pitcher, jug

pichón, -chona *n, mpl* **pichones** 1 : young pigeon, squab 2 *Mex fam* : novice, greenhorn

picnic *nm* : picnic

pico *nm* 1 : peak 2 : point, spike 3 : beak, bill 4 : pick, pickax 5 **y pico** : and a little, and a bit ⟨las siete y pico : a little after seven⟩ ⟨dos metros y pico : a bit over two meters⟩

picor *nm* : itch, irritation

picoso, -sa *adj Mex* : very hot, spicy

picota *nf* 1 : pillory, stock 2 **poner a alguien en la picota** : to put someone on the spot

picotada *nf* → **picotazo**

picotazo *nm* : peck (of a bird)

picotear *vt* : to peck — *vi* : to nibble, to pick

pictórico, -ca *adj* : pictorial

picudo, -da *adj* 1 : pointy, sharp 2 **~ para** *Mex fam* : clever at, good at

pide, etc. → **pedir**

pie *nm* 1 : foot ⟨a pie : on foot⟩ ⟨de pie : on one's feet, standing⟩ 2 : base, bottom, stem, foot ⟨pie de la cama : foot of the bed⟩ ⟨pie de una lámpara : base of a lamp⟩ ⟨pie de la escalera : bottom of the stairs⟩ ⟨pie de una copa : stem of a glass⟩ 3 : foot (in measurement) ⟨pie cuadrado : square foot⟩ 4 : cue (in theater) 5 **dar pie a** : to give cause for, to give rise to 6 **en pie de igualdad** : on equal footing

piedad *nf* 1 COMPASIÓN : mercy, pity 2 DEVOCIÓN : piety, devotion

piedra *nf* 1 : stone 2 : flint (of a lighter) 3 : hailstone 4 **piedra de afilar** : whetstone, grindstone 5 **piedra angular** : cornerstone 6 **piedra arenisca** : sandstone 7 **piedra caliza** : limestone 8 **piedra imán** : lodestone 9 **piedra de molino** : millstone 10 **piedra de toque** : touchstone

piel *nf* 1 : skin 2 CUERO : leather, hide ⟨piel de venado : deerskin⟩ 3 : fur, pelt 4 CÁSCARA : peel, skin 5 **piel de gallina** : goose bumps *pl* ⟨me pone la piel de gallina : it gives me goose bumps⟩

piélago *nm* **el piélago** : the deep, the ocean

piensa, etc. → **pensar**

pienso *nm* : feed, fodder

pierde, etc. → **perder**

pierna *nf* : leg

pieza *nf* 1 ELEMENTO : piece, part, component ⟨vestido de dos piezas : two-piece dress⟩ ⟨pieza de recambio : spare part⟩ ⟨pieza clave : key element⟩ 2 : piece (in chess) 3 OBRA : piece, work

⟨pieza de teatro : play⟩ **4** : room, bedroom

pifia *nf fam* : goof, blunder

pigargo *nm* : osprey

pigmentación *nf, pl* **-ciones** : pigmentation

pigmento *nm* : pigment

pigmeo, -mea *adj & n* : pygmy, Pygmy

pijama *nm* : pajamas *pl*

pila *nf* **1** BATERÍA : battery ⟨pila de linterna : flashlight battery⟩ **2** MONTÓN : pile, heap **3** : sink, basin, font ⟨pila bautismal : baptismal font⟩ ⟨pila para pájaros : birdbath⟩

pilar *nm* **1** : pillar, column **2** : support, mainstay

píldora *nf* PASTILLA : pill

pillaje *nm* : pillage, plunder

pillar *vt* **1** *fam* : to catch ⟨¡cuidado! ¡nos pillarán! : watch out! they'll catch us!⟩ **2** *fam* : to grasp, to catch on ⟨¿no lo pillas? : don't you get it?⟩

pillo[1], **-lla** *adj* : cunning, crafty

pillo[2], **-lla** *n* **1** : rascal, brat **2** : rogue, scoundrel

pilluelo, -la *n* : urchin

pilón *nm, pl* **pilones** **1** PILA : basin **2** : pillar, tower (for cables), pylon (of a bridge) **3** *Mex* : extra, lagniappe

pilotar *vt* : to pilot, to drive

pilote *nm* : pile (stake)

pilotear → **pilotar**

piloto *nm* **1** : pilot, driver **2** : pilot light

piltrafa *nf* **1** : poor quality meat **2** : wretch **3 piltrafas** *nfpl* : food scraps

pimentero *nm* : pepper shaker

pimentón *nm, pl* **-tones** **1** : paprika **2** : cayenne pepper

pimienta *nf* **1** : pepper (condiment) **2 pimienta de Jamaica** : allspice

pimiento *nm* : pepper (fruit) ⟨pimiento verde : green pepper⟩

pináculo *nm* **1** : pinnacle (of a building) **2** : peak, acme

pincel *nm* : paintbrush

pincelada *nf* **1** : brushstroke **2 últimas pinceladas** : final touches

pinchar *vt* **1** PICAR : to puncture (a tire) **2** : to prick, to stick **3** : to goad, to tease, to needle — *vi* **1** : to be prickly **2** : to get a flat tire **3** *fam* : to get beaten, to lose out — **pincharse** *vr* : to give oneself an injection

pinchazo *nm* **1** : prick, jab **2** : puncture, flat tire

pingüe *adj* **1** : rich, huge (of profits) **2** : lucrative

pingüino *nm* : penguin

pininos *or* **pinitos** *nmpl* : first steps ⟨hacer pininos : to take one's first steps, to toddle⟩

pino *nm* : pine, pine tree

pinta *nf* **1** : dot, spot **2** : pint **3** *fam* : aspect, appearance ⟨las peras tienen buena pinta : the pears look good⟩ **4 pintas** *nfpl Mex* : graffiti

pintadas *nfpl* : graffiti

pintar *vt* **1** : to paint **2** : to draw, to mark **3** : to describe, to depict — *vi* **1** : to paint, to draw **2** : to look ⟨no pinta bien : it doesn't look good⟩ **3** *fam* : to count ⟨aquí no pinta nada : he has no say here⟩ — **pintarse** *vr* **1** MAQUILLARSE : to put on makeup **2 pintárselas solo** *fam* : to manage by oneself, to know it all

pintarrajear *vt* : to daub (with paint)

pinto, -ta *adj* : speckled, spotted

pintor, -tora *n* **1** : painter **2 pintor de brocha gorda** : housepainter, dauber

pintoresco, -ca *adj* : picturesque, quaint

pintura *nf* **1** : paint **2** : painting (art, work of art)

pinza *nf* **1** : clothespin **2** : claw, pincer **3** : pleat, dart **4 pinzas** *nfpl* : tweezers **5 pinzas** *nfpl* ALICATES : pliers, pincers

pinzón *nm, pl* **pinzones** : finch

piña *nf* **1** : pineapple **2** : pine cone

piñata *nf* : piñata

piñón *nm, pl* **piñones** **1** : pine nut **2** : pinion

pío[1], **pía** *adj* **1** DEVOTO : pious, devout **2** : piebald, pied, dappled

pío[2] *nm* : peep, tweet, cheep

piocha *nf* **1** : pickax **2** *Mex* : goatee

piojo *nm* : louse

piojoso, -sa *adj* **1** : lousy **2** : filthy

pionero[1], **-ra** *adj* : pioneering

pionero[2], **-ra** *n* : pioneer

pipa *nf* : pipe (for smoking)

pipián *nm, pl* **pipianes** *Mex* : a spicy sauce or stew

pipiolo, -la *n fam* **1** : greenhorn, novice **2** : kid, youngster

pique[1], **etc.** → **picar**

pique[2] *nm* **1** : pique, resentment **2** : rivalry, competition **3 a pique de** : about to, on the verge of **4 irse a pique** : to sink, to founder

piqueta *nf* : pickax

piquete *nm* **1** : picketers *pl*, picket line **2** : squad, detachment **3** *Mex* : prick, jab

piquetear *vt* **1** : to picket **2** *Mex* : to prick, to jab

pira *nf* : pyre

piragua *nf* : canoe — **piragüista** *nmf*

pirámide *nf* : pyramid

piraña *nf* : piranha

pirata[1] *adj* : bootleg, pirated

pirata[2] *nmf* **1** : pirate **2** : bootlegger **3 pirata aéreo** : hijacker

piratear *vt* **1** : to hijack, to commandeer **2** : to bootleg, to pirate

piratería *nf* : piracy, bootlegging

piromanía *nf* : pyromania

pirómano, -na *n* : pyromaniac

piropo *nm* : flirtatious compliment

pirotecnia *nf* : fireworks *pl*, pyrotechnics *pl*

pirotécnico, -ca *adj* : fireworks, pyrotechnic

pírrico, -ca *adj* : Pyrrhic

pirueta *nf* : pirouette

pirulí *nm* : cone-shaped lollipop

pisada *nf* **1** : footstep **2** HUELLA : footprint

pisapapeles *nms & pl* : paperweight

pisar *vt* **1** : to step on, to set foot in **2** : to walk all over, to mistreat — *vi* : to step, to walk, to tread

piscina *nf* **1** : swimming pool **2** : fish pond

Piscis *nmf* : Pisces

piso *nm* **1** PLANTA : floor, story **2** SUELO : floor **3** *Spain* : apartment

pisotear *vt* **1** : to stamp on, to trample **2** PISAR : to walk all over **3** : to flout, to disregard

pisotón *nm, pl* **-tones** : stamp, step ⟨sufrieron empujones y pisotones : they were pushed and stepped on⟩

pista *nf* **1** RASTRO : trail, track ⟨siguen la pista de los sospechosos : they're on the trail of the suspects⟩ **2** : clue **3** CAMINO : road, trail **4** : track, racetrack **5** : ring, arena, rink **6 pista de aterrizaje** : runway, airstrip **7 pista de baile** : dance floor

pistacho *nm* : pistachio

pistilo *nm* : pistil

pistola *nf* **1** : pistol, handgun **2** : spray gun

pistolera *nf* : holster

pistolero *nm* : gunman

pistón *nm, pl* **pistones** : piston

pita *nf* **1** : agave **2** : pita fiber **3** : twine

pitar *vi* **1** : to blow a whistle **2** : to whistle, to boo **3** : to beep, to honk, to toot — *vt* : to whistle at, to boo

pitido *nm* **1** : whistle, whistling **2** : beep, honk, toot

pito *nm* **1** SILBATO : whistle **2 no me importa un pito** *fam* : I don't give a damn

pitón *nm, pl* **pitones** **1** : python **2** : point of a bull's horn

pituitario, -ria *adj* : pituitary

pívot *nmf, pl* **pívots** : center (in basketball)

pivote *nm* : pivot

piyama *nmf* : pajamas *pl*

pizarra *nf* **1** : slate **2** : blackboard **3** : scoreboard

pizarrón *nm, pl* **-rrones** : blackboard, chalkboard

pizca *nf* **1** : pinch ⟨una pizca de canela : a pinch of cinnamon⟩ **2** : speck, trace ⟨ni pizca : not a bit⟩ **3** *Mex* : harvest

pizcar {72} *vt Mex* : to harvest

pizque, etc. → **pizcar**

pizza [ˈpitsa, ˈpisa] *nf* : pizza

pizzería *nf* : pizzeria, pizza parlor

placa *nf* **1** : sheet, plate **2** : plaque, nameplate **3** : plate (in photography) **4** : badge, insignia **5 placa de matrícula** : license plate, tag **6 placa dental** : plaque, tartar

placebo *nm* : placebo

placenta *nf* : placenta, afterbirth

placentero, -ra *adj* AGRADABLE, GRATO : pleasant, agreeable

placer[1] {57} *vi* GUSTAR : to be pleasing ⟨hazlo como te plazca : do it however you please⟩

placer[2] *nm* **1** : pleasure, enjoyment **2 a ~** : as much as one wants

plácido, -da *adj* TRANQUILO : placid, calm

plaga *nf* **1** : plague, infestation, blight **2** CALAMIDAD : disaster, scourge

plagado, -da *adj* **~ de** : filled with, covered with

plagar {52} *vt* : to plague

plagiar *vt* **1** : to plagiarize **2** SECUESTRAR : to kidnap, to abduct

plagiario, -ria *n* **1** : plagiarist **2** SECUESTRADOR : kidnapper, abductor

plagio *nm* **1** : plagiarism **2** SECUESTRO : kidnapping, abduction

plague, etc. → **plagar**

plan *nm* **1** : plan, strategy, program ⟨plan de inversiones : investment plan⟩ ⟨plan de estudios : curriculum⟩ **2** PLANO : plan, diagram **3** : attitude, intent, purpose ⟨ponte en plan serio : be serious⟩ ⟨estamos en plan de divertirnos : we're looking to have some fun⟩

plana *nf* **1** : page ⟨noticias en primera plana : front-page news⟩ **2 plana mayor** : staff (in the military)

plancha *nf* **1** : iron, ironing **2** : grill, griddle ⟨a la plancha : grilled⟩ **3** : sheet, plate ⟨plancha para hornear : baking sheet⟩ **4** *fam* : blunder, blooper

planchada *nf* : ironing, pressing

planchado *nm* → **planchada**

planchar *v* : to iron

planchazo *nm fam* : goof, blunder

plancton *nm* : plankton

planeación *nf* → **planeamiento**

planeador *nm* : glider (aircraft)

planeamiento *nm* : plan, planning

planear *vt* : to plan — *vi* : to glide (in the air)

planeo *nm* : gliding, soaring

planeta *nm* : planet

planetario[1], **-ria** *adj* **1** : planetary **2** : global, worldwide

planetario[2] *nm* : planetarium

planicie *nf* : plain

planificación *nf* : planning ⟨planificación familiar : family planning⟩

planificar {72} *vt* : to plan

planilla *nf* **1** LISTA : list **2** NÓMINA : payroll **3** TABLA : chart, table **4** *Mex* : slate, ticket (of candidates) **5 planilla de cálculo** *Arg, Chile* : spreadsheet

plano[1], **-na** *adj* : flat, level, plane

plano[2] *nm* **1** PLAN : map, plan **2** : plane (surface) **3** NIVEL : level ⟨en un plano personal : on a personal level⟩ **4** : shot (in photography) **5 de ~** : flatly, outright, directly ⟨se negó de plano : he flatly refused⟩

planta *nf* **1** : plant ⟨planta de interior : houseplant⟩ **2** FÁBRICA : plant, factory **3** PISO : floor, story **4** : staff, employees *pl* **5** : sole (of the foot)

plantación *nf, pl* **-ciones** **1** : plantation **2** : planting

plantado, -da *adj* **1** : planted **2 dejar plantado** : to stand up (a date), to dump (a lover)

plantar *vt* **1** : to plant, to sow ⟨plantar de flores : to plant with flowers⟩ **2** : to put in, to place **3** *fam* : to plant, to land ⟨plantar un beso : to plant a kiss⟩ **4** *fam* : to leave, to jilt — **plantarse** *vr* **1** : to stand firm **2** *fam* : to arrive, to show up **3** *fam* : to balk

planteamiento *nm* **1** : approach, position ⟨el planteamiento feminista : the feminist viewpoint⟩ **2** : explanation, exposition **3** : proposal, suggestion, plan

plantear *vt* **1** : to set forth, to bring up, to suggest **2** : to establish, to set up **3** : to create, to pose (a problem) — **plantearse** *vr* **1** : to think about **2** : to arise

plantel *nm* **1** : educational institution **2** : staff, team

planteo → **planteamiento**

plantilla *nf* **1** : insole **2** : pattern, template, stencil **3** *Mex, Spain* : staff, roster of employees

plantío *nm* : field (planted with a crop)

plantón *nm, pl* **plantones** **1** : seedling **2** : long wait ⟨darle a alguien un plantón : to stand someone up⟩

plañidero[1], **-ra** *adj* : mournful

plañidero[2], **-ra** *nf* : hired mourner

plañir {38} *v* : to mourn, to lament

plasma *nm* : plasma

plasmar *vt* : to express, to give form to — **plasmarse** *vr*

plasta *nf* : soft mass, lump

plástica *nf* : modeling, sculpture

plasticidad *nf* : plasticity

plástico[1], **-ca** *adj* : plastic

plástico[2] *nm* : plastic

plastificar {72} *vt* : to laminate

plata *nf* **1** : silver **2** : money

plataforma *nf* **1** ESTRADO, TARIMA : platform, dais **2** : platform (in politics) **3** : springboard, stepping stone **4 plataforma continental** : continental shelf **5 plataforma de lanzamiento** : launchpad **6 plataforma petrolífera** : oil rig (at sea)

platal *nm* : large sum of money, fortune

platanal *nm* : banana plantation

platanero[1], **-ra** *adj* : banana, banana-producing

platanero[2], **-ra** *n* : banana grower

plátano *nm* **1** : banana **2** : plantain **3 plátano macho** *Mex* : plantain

platea *nf* : orchestra, pit (in a theater)

plateado, -da *adj* **1** : silver, silvery **2** : silver-plated

plática *nf* **1** : talk, lecture **2** : chat, conversation

platicar {72} *vi* : to talk, to chat — *vt* *Mex* : to tell, to say

platija *nf* : flatfish, flounder

platillo *nm* **1** : saucer ⟨platillo volador : flying saucer⟩ **2** : cymbal **3** *Mex* : dish ⟨platillos típicos : local dishes⟩

platino *nm* : platinum

plato *nm* **1** : plate, dish ⟨lavar los platos : to do the dishes⟩ **2** : serving, helping **3** : course (of a meal) **4** : dish ⟨plato típico : typical dish⟩ **5** : home plate (in baseball) **6 plato hondo** : soup bowl

plató *nm* : set (in the movies)

platónico, -ca *adj* : platonic

playa *nf* : beach, seashore

playera *nf* **1** : canvas sneaker **2** *CA, Mex* : T-shirt

plaza *nf* **1** : square, plaza **2** : marketplace **3** : room, space, seat (in a vehicle) **4** : post, position **5 plaza fuerte** : stronghold, fortified city **6 plaza de toros** : bullring

plazca, etc. → **placer**

plazo *nm* **1** : period, term ⟨un plazo de cinco días : a period of five days⟩ ⟨a largo plazo : long-term⟩ **2** ABONO : installment ⟨pagar a plazos : to pay in installments⟩

pleamar *nf* : high tide

plebe *nf* : common people, masses *pl*

plebeyo[1], **-ya** *adj* : plebeian

plebeyo[2], **-ya** *n* : plebeian, commoner

plegable *adj* : folding, collapsible

plegadizo → **plegable**

plegar {49} *vt* DOBLAR : to fold, to bend — **plegarse** *vr* : to give in, to yield

plegaria *nf* ORACIÓN : prayer

pleito *nm* **1** : lawsuit **2** : fight, argument, dispute

plenamente *adv* COMPLETAMENTE : fully, completely

plenario, -ria *adj* : plenary, full

plenilunio *nm* : full moon

plenipotenciario, -ria *n* : plenipotentiary

plenitud *nf* : fullness, abundance

pleno, -na *adj* COMPLETO ((*often used as an intensifier*)) : full, complete ⟨en pleno uso de sus facultades : in full command of his faculties⟩ ⟨en plena noche : in the middle of the night⟩ ⟨en pleno corazón de la ciudad : right in the heart of the city⟩

plétora *nf* : plethora

pleuresía *nf* : pleurisy

pliega, pliegue etc. → **plegar**

pliego *nm* **1** HOJA : sheet of paper **2** : sealed document

pliegue *nm* **1** DOBLEZ : crease, fold **2** : pleat

plisar *vt* : to pleat

plomada *nf* **1** : plumb line **2** : sinker

plomería *nf* FONTANERÍA : plumbing

plomero, -ra *n* FONTANERO : plumber

plomizo, -za *adj* : leaden

plomo *nm* **1** : lead **2** : plumb line **3** : fuse **4** *fam* : bore, drag **5 a ~** : plumb, straight

plugo, etc. → **placer**

pluma *nf* **1** : feather **2** : pen **3 pluma fuente** : fountain pen

plumaje *nm* : plumage

plumero *nm* : feather duster

plumilla *nf* : nib

plumón *nm, pl* **plumones** : down

plumoso, -sa *adj* : feathery, downy

plural *adj & nm* : plural

pluralidad *nf* : plurality

pluralizar {21} *vt* : to pluralize

pluriempleado, -da *adj* : holding more than one job

pluriempleo *nm* : moonlighting

plus *nm* : bonus

plusvalía *nf* : appreciation, capital gain

Plutón *nm* : Pluto

plutocracia *nf* : plutocracy

plutonio *nm* : plutonium

población *nf, pl* **-ciones 1** : population **2** : city, town, village

poblado[1], **-da** *adj* **1** : inhabited, populated **2** : full, thick ⟨cejas pobladas : bushy eyebrows⟩

poblado[2] *nm* : village, settlement

poblador, -dora *n* : settler

poblar {19} *vt* **1** : to populate, to inhabit **2** : to settle, to colonize **3 ~ de** : to stock with, to plant with — **poblarse** *vr* : to fill up, to become crowded

pobre[1] *adj* **1** : poor, impoverished **2** : unfortunate ⟨¡pobre de mí! : poor me!⟩ **3** : weak, deficient ⟨una dieta pobre : a poor diet⟩

pobre[2] *nmf* : poor person ⟨los pobres : the poor⟩ ⟨¡pobre! : poor thing!⟩

pobremente *adv* : poorly

pobreza *nf* : poverty

pocilga *nf* CHIQUERO : pigsty, pigpen

pocillo *nm* : small coffee cup, demitasse

poción *nf, pl* **pociones** : potion

poco[1] *adv* **1** : little, not much ⟨poco probable : not very likely⟩ ⟨come poco : he doesn't eat much⟩ **2** : a short time, a while ⟨tardaremos poco : we won't be very long⟩ **3 poco antes** : shortly before **4 poco después** : shortly after

poco[2], **-ca** *adj* **1** : little, not much, (a) few ⟨tengo poco dinero : I don't have much money⟩ ⟨en no pocas ocasiones : on more than a few occasions⟩ ⟨poca gente : few people⟩ **2 pocas veces** : rarely

poco[3], **-ca** *pron* **1** : little, few ⟨le falta poco para terminar : he's almost finished⟩ ⟨uno de los pocos que quedan : one of the remaining few⟩ **2 un poco** : a little, a bit ⟨un poco de vino : a little wine⟩ ⟨un poco extraño : a bit strange⟩ **3 a ~** *Mex* (*used to express disbelief*) ⟨¿a poco no se te hizo difícil? : you mean you didn't find it difficult?⟩ **4 de a poco** : little by little **5 hace poco** : not long ago **6 poco a poco** : little by little **7 dentro de poco** : shortly, in a little while **8 por ~** : nearly, almost

podar *vt* : to prune, to trim

poder[1] {58} *v aux* **1** : to be able to, can ⟨no puede hablar : he can't speak⟩ **2** (*expressing possibility*) : might, may ⟨puede llover : it may rain at any moment⟩ ⟨¿cómo puede ser? : how can that be?⟩ **3** (*expressing permission*) : can, may ⟨¿puedo ir a la fiesta? : can I go to the party?⟩ ⟨¿se puede? : may I come in?⟩ — *vi* **1** : to beat, to defeat ⟨cree que le puede a cualquiera : he thinks he can beat anyone⟩ **2** : to be possible ⟨¿crees que vendrán? — puede (que sí) : do you think they'll come? — maybe⟩ **3 ~ con** : to cope with, to manage ⟨¡no puedo con estos niños! : I can't handle these children!⟩ **4 no poder más** : to have had enough ⟨no puede más : she can't take anymore⟩ **5 no poder menos que** : to not be able to help ⟨no pudo menos que asombrarse : she couldn't help but be amazed⟩

poder[2] *nm* **1** : control, power ⟨poder adquisitivo : purchasing power⟩ **2** : authority ⟨el poder legislativo : the legislature⟩ **3** : possession ⟨está en mi poder : it's in my hands⟩ **4** : strength, force ⟨poder militar : military might⟩

poderío *nm* **1** : power **2** : wealth, influence

poderoso, -sa *adj* **1** : powerful **2** : wealthy, influential **3** : effective

podiatría *nf* : podiatry

podio *nm* : podium

pódium → **podio**

podología *nf* : podiatry, chiropody

podólogo, -ga *n* : podiatrist, chiropodist

podrá, etc. → **poder**

podredumbre *nf* **1** : decay, rottenness **2** : corruption

podrido, -da *adj* **1** : rotten, decayed **2** : corrupt

podrir → **pudrir**

poema *nm* : poem

poesía *nf* **1** : poetry **2** POEMA : poem

poeta *nmf* : poet

poético, -ca *adj* : poetic, poetical

pogrom *nm* : pogrom

póker *or* **poker** *nm* : poker (card game)

polaco[1], **-ca** *adj* : Polish

polaco[2], **-ca** *n* : Pole, Polish person

polaco[3] *nm* : Polish (language)

polar *adj* : polar

polarizar {21} *vt* : to polarize — **polarizarse** *vr* — **polarización** *nf*

polea *nf* : pulley

polémica *nf* CONTROVERSIA : controversy, polemics

polémico, -ca *adj* CONTROVERTIDO : controversial, polemical

polen *nm, pl* **pólenes** : pollen

policía[1] *nf* : police

policía[2] *nmf* : police officer, policeman *m*, policewoman *f*

policíaco, -ca *or* **policiaco, -ca** *adj* : police ⟨novela policíaca : detective story⟩

policial *adj* : police

poliéster *nm* : polyester

poligamia *nf* : polygamy

polígamo[1], **-ma** *adj* : polygamous

polígamo[2], **-ma** *n* : polygamist

polígono *nm* : polygon — **polígonal** *adj*

poliinsaturado, -da *adj* : polyunsaturated

polilla *nf* : moth

polimerizar {21} *vt* : to polymerize

polímero *nm* : polymer

polinesio, -sia *adj & n* : Polynesian

polinizar {21} *vt* : to pollinate — **polinización** *nf*

polio *nf* : polio

poliomielitis *nf* : poliomyelitis, polio

polisón *nm, pl* **-sones** : bustle (on clothing)

politécnico, -ca *adj* : polytechnic

politeísmo *nm* : polytheism — **politeísta** *adj & nmf*

política *nf* **1** : politics **2** : policy

políticamente *adv* : politically

político[1], **-ca** *adj* **1** : political **2** : tactful, politic **3** : by marriage ⟨padre político : father-in-law⟩

político[2], **-ca** *n* : politician

póliza *nf* : policy ⟨póliza de seguros : insurance policy⟩

polizón *nm, pl* **-zones** : stowaway ⟨viajar de polizón : to stow away⟩

polka *nf* : polka

polla *nf* APUESTA : bet

pollera *nf* **1** : chicken coop **2** : skirt

pollero, -ra *n* **1** : poulterer **2** : poultry farm **3** *Mex fam* COYOTE : smuggler of illegal immigrants

pollito, -ta *n* : chick, young bird, fledgling

pollo, -lla *n* **1** : chicken **2** POLLITO : chick **3** JOVEN : young man *m*, young lady *f*

polluelo *nm* → **pollito**

polo *nm* **1** : pole ⟨el Polo Norte : the North Pole⟩ ⟨polo negativo : negative pole⟩ **2** : polo (sport) **3** : polo shirt **4** : focal point, center **5 polo opuesto** : exact opposite

polución *nf, pl* **-ciones** CONTAMINACIÓN : pollution

polvareda *nf* **1** : cloud of dust **2** : uproar, fuss

polvera *nf* : compact (for face powder)

polvo *nm* **1** : dust **2** : powder **3 polvos** *nmpl* : face powder **4 polvos de hornear** : baking powder **5 hacer polvo** *fam* : to crush, to shatter ⟨vas a hacer polvo el reloj : you're going to destroy your watch⟩

pólvora *nf* **1** : gunpowder **2** : fireworks *pl*

polvoriento, -ta *adj* : dusty, powdery

polvorín *nm, pl* **-rines** : magazine, storehouse (for explosives)

pomada *nf* : ointment, cream

pomelo *nm* : grapefruit

pómez *nf or* **piedra pómez** : pumice

pomo *nm* **1** : pommel (on a sword) **2** : knob, handle **3** : perfume bottle

pompa *nf* **1** : bubble **2** : pomp, splendor **3 pompas fúnebres** : funeral

pompón *nm, pl* **pompones** BORLA : pom-pom

pomposidad *nf* **1** : pomp, splendor **2** : pomposity, ostentation

pomposo, -sa *adj* : pompous — **pomposamente** *adv*

pómulo *nm* : cheekbone

pon → **poner**

ponchadura *nf Mex* : puncture, flat (tire)

ponchar *vt* **1** : to strike out (in baseball) **2** *Mex* : to puncture — **poncharse** *vr* **1** *Col, Ven* : to strike out (in baseball) **2** *Mex* : to blow out (of a tire)

ponche *nm* **1** : punch (drink) **2 ponche de huevo** : eggnog

poncho *nm* : poncho

ponderación *nf, pl* **-ciones** **1** : consideration, deliberation **2** : high praise

ponderar *vt* **1** : to weigh, to consider **2** : to speak highly of

pondrá, etc. → **poner**

ponencia *nf* **1** DISCURSO : paper, presentation, address **2** INFORME : report

ponente *nmf* : speaker, presenter

poner {60} *vt* **1** COLOCAR : to put, to place ⟨pon el libro en la mesa : put the book on the table⟩ **2** AGREGAR, AÑADIR : to put in, to add **3** : to put on (clothes) **4** CONTRIBUIR : to contribute **5** ESCRIBIR : to put in writing ⟨no le puso su nombre : he didn't put his name on it⟩ **6** IMPONER : to set, to impose **7** EXPONER : to put, to expose ⟨lo puso en peligro : she put him in danger⟩ **8** : to prepare, to arrange ⟨poner la mesa : to set the table⟩ **9** : to name ⟨le pusimos Ana : we called her Ana⟩ **10** ESTABLECER : to set up, to establish ⟨puso un restaurante : he opened up a restaurant⟩ **11** INSTALAR : to install, to put in **12** (*with an adjective or adverb*) : to make ⟨siempre lo pones de mal humor : you always put him in a bad mood⟩ **13** : to turn on, to switch on **14** SUPONER : to suppose ⟨pongamos que no viene : supposing he doesn't come⟩ **15** : to lay (eggs) **16 ~ a** : to start (someone doing something) ⟨lo puse a trabajar : I put him to work⟩ **17 ~ de** : to place as ⟨la pusieron de directora : they made her director⟩ **18 ~ en** : to put in (a state or condition) ⟨poner en duda : to call into question⟩ — *vi* **1** : to contribute **2** : to lay eggs — **ponerse** *vr* **1** : to move (into a position) ⟨ponerse de pie : to stand up⟩ **2** : to put on, to wear **3** : to become, to turn ⟨se puso colorado : he turned red⟩ **4** : to set (of the sun or moon)

poni *or* **poney** *nm* : pony

ponga, etc. → **poner**

poniente *nm* **1** OCCIDENTE : west **2** : west wind

ponqué *nm Col, Ven* : cake

pontifical *adj* : pontifical

pontificar {72} *vi* : to pontificate

pontífice *nm* : pontiff, pope

pontón *nm, pl* **pontones** : pontoon

ponzoña *nf* VENENO : poison — **ponzoñoso, -sa** *adj*

popa *nf* **1** : stern **2 a ~** : astern, abaft, aft

popelín *nm, pl* **-lines** : poplin

popelina *nf* : poplin

popote *nm Mex* : (drinking) straw

populachero, -ra *adj* : common, popular, vulgar

populacho *nm* : rabble, masses *pl*

popular *adj* **1** : popular **2** : traditional **3** : colloquial

popularidad *nf* : popularity

popularizar {21} *vt* : to popularize — **popularizarse** *vr*

populista *adj & nmf* : populist — **populismo** *nm*

populoso, -sa *adj* : populous

popurrí *nm* : potpourri

por *prep* **1** : for, during ⟨se quedaron allí por la semana : they stayed there during the week⟩ ⟨por el momento : for now, at the moment⟩ **2** : around, during ⟨por noviembre empieza a nevar : around November it starts to snow⟩ ⟨por la mañana : in the morning⟩ **3** : around (a place) ⟨debe estar por allí : it must be over there⟩ ⟨por todas partes : everywhere⟩ **4** : by, through, along ⟨por la puerta : through the door⟩ ⟨pasé por tu casa : I stopped by your house⟩ ⟨por la costa : along the coast⟩ **5** : for, for the sake of ⟨lo hizo por su madre : he did it for his mother⟩ ⟨¡por Dios! : for heaven's sake!⟩ **6** : because of, on account of ⟨llegué tarde por el tráfico : I arrived late because of the traffic⟩ ⟨dejar por imposible : to give up as impossible⟩ **7** : per ⟨60 millas por hora : 60 miles per hour⟩ ⟨por docena : by the dozen⟩ **8** : for, in exchange for, instead of ⟨su hermana habló por él : his sister spoke on his behalf⟩ **9** : by means of ⟨hablar por teléfono : to talk on the phone⟩ ⟨por escrito : in writing⟩ **10** : as for ⟨por mí : as far as I'm concerned⟩ **11** : times ⟨tres por dos son seis : three times two is six⟩ **12** SEGÚN : from, according to ⟨por lo que dices : judging from what you're telling me⟩ **13** : as, for ⟨por ejemplo : for example⟩ **14** : by ⟨hecho por mi abuela : made by my grandmother⟩ ⟨por correo : by mail⟩ **15** : for, in order to ⟨lucha por ganar su respeto : he struggles to win her respect⟩ **16 estar por** : to be about to **17 por ciento** : percent **18 por favor** : please **19 por lo tanto** : therefore, consequently **20 ¿por qué?** : why? **21 por que** → **porque 22 por . . . que** : no matter how ⟨por mucho que intente : no matter how hard I try⟩ **23 por si** *or* **por si acaso** : just in case

porcelana *nf* : china, porcelain

porcentaje *nm* : percentage

porche *nm* : porch

porción *nf, pl* **porciones 1** : portion **2** PARTE : part, share **3** RACIÓN : serving, helping

pordiosear *vi* MENDIGAR : beg

pordiosero, -ra *n* MENDIGO : beggar

porfiado, -da *adj* OBSTINADO, TERCO : obstinate, stubborn — **porfiadamente** *adv*

porfiar {85} *vi* : to insist, to persist

pormenor *nm* DETALLE : detail

pormenorizar {21} *vi* : to go into detail — *vt* : to tell in detail

pornografía *nf* : pornography

pornográfico, -ca *adj* : pornographic

poro *nm* : pore

poroso, -sa *adj* : porous — **porosidad** *nf*

poroto *nm Arg, Chile, Uru* : bean

porque *conj* **1** : because **2** *or* **por que** : in order that

porqué *nm* : reason, cause

porquería *nf* **1** SUCIEDAD : dirt, filth **2** : nastiness, vulgarity **3** : worthless thing, trifle **4** : junk food

porra *nf* **1** : nightstick, club **2** *Mex* : cheer, yell ⟨los aficionados le echaban porras : the fans cheered him on⟩

porrazo *nm* **1** : blow, whack **2 de golpe y porrazo** : suddenly

porrista *nmf* **1** : cheerleader **2** : fan, supporter

portaaviones *nms & pl* : aircraft carrier

portada *nf* **1** : title page **2** : cover **3** : facade, front

portador, -dora *n* : carrier, bearer

portafolio *or* **portafolios** *nm, pl* **-lios 1** MALETÍN : briefcase **2** : portfolio (of investments)

portal *nm* **1** : portal, doorway **2** VESTÍBULO : vestibule, hall

portar *vt* **1** : to carry, to bear **2** : to wear — **portarse** *vr* CONDUCIRSE : to behave ⟨pórtate bien : behave yourself⟩

portátil *adj* : portable

portaviandas *nms & pl* : lunch box

portaviones *nm* → **portaaviones**

portavoz *nmf, pl* **-voces** : spokesperson, spokesman *m*, spokeswoman *f*

portazo *nm* : slam (of a door)

porte *nm* **1** ASPECTO : bearing, demeanor **2** TRANSPORTE : transport, carrying ⟨porte pagado : postage paid⟩

portento *nm* MARAVILLA : marvel, wonder

portentoso, -sa *adj* MARAVILLOSO : marvelous, wonderful

porteño, -ña *adj* : of or from Buenos Aires

portería *nf* **1** ARCO : goal, goalposts *pl* **2** : superintendent's office

portero, -ra *n* **1** ARQUERO : goalkeeper, goalie **2** : doorman *m* **3** : janitor, superintendent

pórtico *nm* : portico

portilla *nf* : porthole

portón *nm, pl* **portones 1** : main door **2** : gate

portugués[1], **-guesa** *adj & n, mpl* **-gueses** : Portuguese

portugués[2] *nm* : Portuguese (language)

porvenir *nm* FUTURO : future
pos *adv* **en pos de** : in pursuit of
posada *nf* **1** : inn **2** *Mex* : Advent celebration
posadero, -ra *n* : innkeeper
posar *vi* : to pose — *vt* : to place, to lay — **posarse** *vr* **1** : to land, to light, to perch **2** : to settle, to rest
posavasos *nms & pl* : coaster (for drinks)
posdata → **postdata**
pose *nf* : pose
poseedor, -dora *n* : possessor, holder
poseer {20} *vt* : to possess, to hold, to have
poseído, -da *adj* : possessed
posesión *nf, pl* **-siones** : possession
posesionarse *vr* **~ de** : to take possession of, to take over
posesivo[1], **-va** *adj* : possessive
posesivo[2] *nm* : possessive case
posguerra *nf* : postwar period
posibilidad *nf* **1** : possibility **2 posibilidades** *nfpl* : means, income
posibilitar *vt* : to make possible, to permit
posible *adj* : possible — **posiblemente** *adv*
posición *nf, pl* **-ciones** **1** : position, place **2** : status, standing **3** : attitude, stance
posicionar *vt* **1** : to position, to place **2** : to establish — **posicionarse** *vr*
positivo[1], **-va** *adj* : positive
positivo[2] *nm* : print (in photography)
poso *nm* **1** : sediment, dregs *pl* **2** : grounds *pl* (of coffee)
posoperatorio, -ria *adj* : postoperative
posponer {60} *vt* **1** : to postpone **2** : to put behind, to subordinate
pospuso, etc. → **posponer**
posta *nf* : relay race
postal[1] *adj* : postal
postal[2] *nf* : postcard
postdata *nf* : postscript
poste *nm* : post, pole <poste de teléfonos : telephone pole>
póster *or* **poster** *nm, pl* **pósters** *or* **posters** : poster, placard
postergación *nf, pl* **-ciones** : postponement, deferring
postergar {52} *vt* **1** : to delay, to postpone **2** : to pass over (an employee)
posteridad *nf* : posterity
posterior *adj* **1** ULTERIOR : later, subsequent **2** TRASERO : back, rear
postgrado *nm* : graduate course
postgraduado, -da *n* : graduate student, postgraduate
postigo *nm* **1** CONTRAVENTANA : shutter **2** : small door, wicket gate
postilla *nf* : scab
postizo, -za *adj* : artificial, false <dentadura postiza : dentures>
postnatal *adj* : postnatal
postor, -tora *n* : bidder <mejor postor : highest bidder>
postración *nf, pl* **-ciones** **1** : prostration **2** ABATIMIENTO : depression
postrado, -da *adj* **1** : prostrate **2 postrado en cama** : bedridden
potranco, -ca *n* → **potro**[1]
postrar *vt* DEBILITAR : to debilitate, to weaken — **postrarse** *vr* : to prostrate oneself
postre *nm* : dessert
postrero, -ra *adj* (**postrer** *before masculine singular nouns*) ÚLTIMO : last
postulación *nf, pl* **-ciones** **1** : collection **2** : nomination (of a candidate)
postulado *nm* : postulate, assumption
postulante, -ta *n* **1** : postulant **2** : candidate, applicant
postular *vt* **1** : to postulate **2** : to nominate **3** : to propose — **postularse** *vr* : to run, to be a candidate
póstumo, -ma *adj* : posthumous — **póstumamente** *adv*
postura *nf* **1** : posture, position (of the body) **2** ACTITUD, POSICIÓN : position, stance
potable *adj* : drinkable, potable
potaje *nm* : thick vegetable soup, pottage
potasa *nf* : potash
potasio *nm* : potassium
pote *nm* **1** OLLA : pot **2** : jar, container
potencia *nf* **1** : power <potencias extranjeras : foreign powers> <elevado a la tercera potencia : raised to the third power> **2** : capacity, potency
potencial *adj & nm* : potential
potenciar *vt* : to promote, to foster
potenciómetro *nm* : dimmer, dimmer switch
potentado, -da *n* **1** SOBERANO : potentate, sovereign **2** MAGNATE : tycoon, magnate
potente *adj* **1** : powerful, strong **2** : potent, virile
potestad *nf* **1** AUTORIDAD : authority, jurisdiction **2 patria potestad** : custody, guardianship
potrero *nm* **1** : field, pasture **2** : cattle ranch
potro[1], **-tra** *n* : colt *m,* filly *f*
potro[2] *nm* **1** : rack (for torture) **2** : horse (in gymnastics)
pozo *nm* **1** : well <pozo de petróleo : oil well> **2** : deep pool (in a river) **3** : mine shaft **4** *Arg, Par, Uru* : pothole **5 pozo séptico** : cesspool
pozole *nm Mex* : spicy stew made with pork and hominy
práctica *nf* **1** : practice, experience **2** EJERCICIO : exercising <la práctica de la medicina : the practice of medicine> **3** APLICACIÓN : application, practice <poner en práctica : to put into practice> **4 prácticas** *nfpl* : training
practicable *adj* : practicable, feasible
prácticamente *adv* : practically
practicante[1] *adj* : practicing <católicos practicantes : practicing Catholics>

practicante[2] *nmf* : practicer, practitioner

practicar {72} *vt* **1** : to practice **2** : to perform, to carry out **3** : to exercise (a profession) — *vi* : to practice

práctico, -ca *adj* : practical, useful

pradera *nf* : grassland, prairie

prado *nm* **1** CAMPO : field, meadow **2** : park

pragmático, -ca *adj* : pragmatic — **pragmáticamente** *adv*

pragmatismo *nm* : pragmatism

preámbulo *nm* **1** INTRODUCCIÓN : preamble, introduction **2** RODEO : evasion ⟨gastar preámbulos : to beat around the bush⟩

prebélico, -ca *adj* : antebellum

prebenda *nf* : privilege, perquisite

precalentar {55} *vt* : to preheat

precariedad *nf* : precariousness

precario, -ria *adj* : precarious — **precariamente** *adv*

precaución *nf, pl* **-ciones 1** : precaution ⟨medidas de precaución : precautionary measures⟩ **2** PRUDENCIA : caution, care ⟨con precaución : cautiously⟩

precautorio, -ria *adj* : precautionary

precaver *vt* PREVENIR : to prevent, to guard against — **precaverse** *vr* PREVENIRSE : to take precautions, to be on guard

precavido, -da *adj* CAUTELOSO : cautious, prudent

precedencia *nf* : precedence, priority

precedente[1] *adj* : preceding, previous

precedente[2] *nm* : precedent

preceder *v* : to precede

precepto *nm* : rule, precept

preciado, -da *adj* : esteemed, prized, valuable

preciarse *vr* **1** JACTARSE : to boast, to brag **2** ~ **de** : to pride oneself on

precinto *nm* : seal

precio *nm* **1** : price **2** : cost, sacrifice ⟨a cualquier precio : whatever the cost⟩

preciosidad *nf* : beautiful thing ⟨este vestido es una preciosidad : this dress is lovely⟩

precioso, -sa *adj* **1** HERMOSO : beautiful, exquisite **2** VALIOSO : precious, valuable

precipicio *nm* **1** : precipice **2** RUINA : ruin

precipitación *nf, pl* **-ciones 1** PRISA : haste, hurry, rush **2** : precipitation, rain, snow

precipitado, -da *adj* **1** : hasty, sudden **2** : rash — **precipitadamente** *adv*

precipitar *vt* **1** APRESURAR : to hasten, to speed up **2** ARROJAR : to hurl, to throw — **precipitarse** *vr* **1** APRESURARSE : to rush **2** : to act rashly **3** ARROJARSE : to throw oneself

precisamente *adv* JUSTAMENTE : precisely, exactly

precisar *vt* **1** : to specify, to determine exactly **2** NECESITAR : to need, to require — *vi* : to be necessary

precisión *nf, pl* **-siones 1** EXACTITUD : precision, accuracy **2** CLARIDAD : clarity (of style, etc.) **3** NECESIDAD : necessity ⟨tener precisión de : to have need of⟩

preciso, -sa *adj* **1** EXACTO : precise **2** : very, exact ⟨en ese preciso instante : at that very instant⟩ **3** NECESARIO : necessary

precocidad *nf* : precocity

precocinar *vt* : to precook

preconcebir {54} *vt* : to preconceive

precondición *nf, pl* **-ciones** : precondition

preconizar {21} *vt* **1** : to recommend, to advocate **2** : to extol

precoz *adj, pl* **precoces 1** : precocious **2** : early, premature — **precozmente** *adv*

precursor, -sora *n* : forerunner, precursor

predecesor, -sora *n* ANTECESOR : predecessor

predecir {11} *vt* : to foretell, to predict

predestinado, -da *adj* : predestined, fated

predestinar *vt* : to predestine — **predestinación** *nf*

predeterminar *vt* : to predetermine

prédica *nf* SERMÓN : sermon

predicado *nm* : predicate

predicador, -dora *n* : preacher

predicar {72} *v* : to preach

predicción *nf, pl* **-ciones 1** : prediction **2** PRONÓSTICO : forecast ⟨predicción del tiempo : weather forecast⟩

prediga, predijo etc. → **predecir**

predilección *nf, pl* **-ciones** : predilection, preference

predilecto, -ta *adj* : favorite

predio *nm* : property, piece of land

predisponer {60} *vt* **1** : to predispose, to incline **2** : to prejudice, to bias

predisposición *nf, pl* **-ciones 1** : predisposition, tendency **2** : prejudice, bias

predominante *adj* : predominant — **predominantemente** *adv*

predominar *vi* PREVALECER : to predominate, to prevail

predominio *nm* : predominance, prevalence

preeminente *adj* : preeminent — **preeminencia** *nf*

preescolar *adj & nm* : preschool

preestreno *nm* : preview

prefabricado, -da *adj* : prefabricated

prefacio *nm* : preface

prefecto *nm* : prefect

preferencia *nf* **1** : preference **2** PRIORIDAD : priority **3 de** ~ : preferably

preferencial *adj* : preferential

preferente *adj* : preferential, special ⟨trato preferente : special treatment⟩

preferentemente *adv* : preferably

preferible *adj* : preferable

preferido, -da *adj & n* : favorite

preferir {76} *vt* : to prefer

prefigurar *vt* : foreshadow, prefigure

prefijo *nm* : prefix

pregonar *vt* **1** : to proclaim, to announce **2** : to hawk (merchandise) **3** : to extol **4** : to reveal, to disclose

pregunta *nf* **1** : question **2 hacer una pregunta** : to ask a question

preguntar *vt* : to ask, to question — *vi* : to ask, to inquire — **preguntarse** *vr* : to wonder

preguntón, -tona *adj, mpl* **-tones** : inquisitive

prehistórico, -ca *adj* : prehistoric

prejuiciado, -da *adj* : prejudiced

prejuicio *nm* : prejudice

prejuzgar {52} *vt* : to prejudge

prelado *nm* : prelate

preliminar *adj & nm* : preliminary

preludio *nm* : prelude

prematrimonial *adj* : premarital

prematuro, -ra *adj* : premature

premeditación *nf, pl* **-ciones** : premeditation

premeditar *vt* : to premeditate, to plan

premenstrual *adj* : premenstrual

premiado, -da *adj* : winning, prizewinning

premiar *vt* **1** : to award a prize to **2** : to reward

premier *nmf* : premier, prime minister

premio *nm* **1** : prize ⟨premio gordo : grand prize, jackpot⟩ **2** : reward **3** : premium

premisa *nf* : premise, basis

premolar *nm* : bicuspid (tooth)

premonición *nf, pl* **-ciones** : premonition

premura *nf* : haste, urgency

prenatal *adj* : prenatal

prenda *nf* **1** : piece of clothing **2** : security, pledge

prendar *vt* **1** : to charm, to captivate **2** : to pawn, to pledge — **prendarse** *vr* **~ de** : to fall in love with

prendedor *nm* : brooch, pin

prender *vt* **1** SUJETAR : to pin, to fasten **2** APRESAR : to catch, to apprehend **3** : to light (a cigarette, a match) **4** : to turn on ⟨prende la luz : turn on the light⟩ **5 prender fuego a** : to set fire to — *vi* **1** : to take root **2** : to catch fire **3** : to catch on

prensa *nf* **1** : printing press **2** : press ⟨conferencia de prensa : press conference⟩

prensar *vt* : to press

prensil *adj* : prehensile

preñado, -da *adj* **1** : pregnant **2 ~ de** : filled with

preñar *vt* EMBARAZAR : to make pregnant

preñez *nf, pl* **preñeces** : pregnancy

preocupación *nf, pl* **-ciones** INQUIETUD : worry, concern

preocupante *adj* : worrisome

preocupar *vt* INQUIETAR : to worry, to concern — **preocuparse** *vr* APURARSE : to worry, to be concerned

preparación *nf, pl* **-ciones 1** : preparation, readiness **2** : education, training **3** : (medicinal) preparation

preparado[1], **-da** *adj* **1** : ready, prepared **2** : trained

preparado[2] *nm* : preparation, mixture

preparar *vt* **1** : to prepare, to make ready **2** : to teach, to train, to coach — **prepararse** *vr*

preparativos *nmpl* : preparations

preparatoria *nf Mex* : high school

preparatorio, -ria *adj* : preparatory

preponderante *adj* : preponderant, predominant — **preponderancia** *nf* — **preponderantemente** *adv*

preposición *nf, pl* **-ciones** : preposition — **preposicional** *adj*

prepotente *adj* : arrogant, domineering, overbearing — **prepotencia** *nf*

prerrogativa *nf* : prerogative, privilege

presa *nf* **1** : capture, seizure ⟨hacer presa de : to seize⟩ **2** : catch, prey ⟨presa de : prey to, seized with⟩ **3** : claw, fang **4** DIQUE : dam **5** : morsel, piece (of food)

presagiar *vt* : to presage, to portend

presagio *nm* : omen, portent

presbiterio *nm* : presbytery, sanctuary (of a church)

presbítero *nm* : presbyter

presciencia *nf* : prescience

prescindible *adj* : expendable, dispensable

prescindir *vi* **1 ~ de** : to do without, to dispense with **2** DESATENDER : to ignore, to disregard **3** OMITIR : to omit, to skip

prescribir {33} *vt* : to prescribe

prescripción *nf, pl* **-ciones** : prescription

prescrito *pp* → **prescribir**

presencia *nf* **1** : presence **2** ASPECTO : appearance

presenciar *vt* : to be present at, to witness

presentable *adj* : presentable

presentación *nf, pl* **-ciones 1** : presentation **2** : introduction **3** : appearance

presentador, -dora *n* : newscaster, anchorman *m*, anchorwoman *f*

presentar *vt* **1** : to present, to show **2** : to offer, to give **3** : to submit (a document), to launch (a product) **4** : to introduce (a person) — **presentarse** *vr* **1** : to show up, to appear **2** : to arise, to come up **3** : to introduce oneself

presente[1] *adj* **1** : present, in attendance **2** : present, current **3 tener presente** : to keep in mind

presente[2] *nm* **1** : present (time, tense) **2** : one present ⟨entre los presentes se encontraban . . . : those present included . . .⟩

presentimiento *nm* : premonition, hunch, feeling

presentir {76} *vt* : to sense, to intuit ⟨presentía lo que iba a pasar : he sensed what was going to happen⟩
preservación *nf, pl* **-ciones** : preservation
preservar *vt* **1** : to preserve **2** : to protect
preservativo *nm* CONDÓN : condom
presidencia *nf* **1** : presidency **2** : chairmanship
presidencial *adj* : presidential
presidente, -ta *n* **1** : president **2** : chair, chairperson **3** : presiding judge
presidiario, -ria *n* : convict, prisoner
presidio *nm* : prison, penitentiary
presidir *vt* **1** MODERAR : to preside over, to chair **2** : to dominate, to rule over
presilla *nf* : eye, loop, fastener
presión *nf, pl* **presiones 1** : pressure **2 presión arterial** : blood pressure
presionar *vt* **1** : to pressure **2** : to press, to push — *vi* : to put on the pressure
preso[1], **-sa** *adj* : imprisoned
preso[2], **-sa** *n* : prisoner
prestado, -da *adj* **1** : borrowed, on loan **2 pedir prestado** : to borrow
prestamista *nmf* : moneylender, pawnbroker
préstamo *nm* : loan
prestar *vt* **1** : to lend, to loan **2** : to render (a service), to give (aid) **3 prestar atención** : to pay attention **4 prestar juramento** : to take an oath — **prestarse** *vr* : to lend oneself ⟨se presta a confusiones : it lends itself to confusion⟩
prestatario, -ria *n* : borrower
presteza *nf* : promptness, speed
prestidigitación *nf, pl* **-ciones** : sleight of hand, prestidigitation
prestidigitador, -dora *n* : conjurer, magician
prestigio *nm* : prestige — **prestigioso, -sa** *adj*
presto[1] *adv* : promptly, at once
presto[2], **-ta** *adj* **1** : quick, prompt **2** DISPUESTO, PREPARADO : ready
presumido, -da *adj* VANIDOSO : conceited, vain
presumir *vt* SUPONER : to presume, to suppose — *vi* **1** ALARDEAR : to boast, to show off **2 ~ de** : to consider oneself ⟨presume de inteligente : he thinks he's intelligent⟩
presunción *nf, pl* **-ciones 1** SUPOSICIÓN : presumption, supposition **2** VANIDAD : conceit, vanity
presunto, -ta *adj* : presumed, supposed, alleged — **presuntamente** *adv*
presuntuoso, -sa *adj* : conceited
presuponer {60} *vt* : to presuppose
presupuestal *adj* : budget, budgetary
presupuestar *vi* : to budget — *vt* : to budget for
presupuestario, -ria *adj* : budget, budgetary
presupuesto *nm* **1** : budget, estimate **2** : assumption, supposition
presurizar {21} *vt* : to pressurize
presuroso, -sa *adj* : hasty, quick
pretencioso, -sa *adj* : pretentious
pretender *vt* **1** INTENTAR : to attempt, to try ⟨pretendo estudiar : I'm trying to study⟩ **2** AFIRMAR : to claim ⟨pretende ser pobre : he claims he's poor⟩ **3** : to seek, to aspire to ⟨¿qué pretendes tú? : what are you after?⟩ **4** CORTEJAR : to court **5 pretender que** : to expect ⟨¿pretendes que lo crea? : do you expect me to believe you?⟩
pretendiente[1] *nmf* **1** : candidate, applicant **2** : pretender, claimant (to a throne, etc.)
pretendiente[2] *nm* : suitor
pretensión *nf, pl* **-siones 1** : intention, hope, plan **2** : pretension ⟨sin pretensiones : unpretentious⟩
pretexto *nm* EXCUSA : pretext, excuse
pretil *nm* : parapet, railing
prevalecer {53} *vi* : to prevail, to triumph
prevaleciente *adj* : prevailing, prevalent
prevalerse {84} *vr* **~ de** : to avail oneself of, to take advantage of
prevención *nf, pl* **-ciones 1** : prevention **2** : preparation, readiness **3** : precautionary measure **4** : prejudice, bias
prevenido, -da *adj* **1** PREPARADO : prepared, ready **2** ADVERTIDO : forewarned **3** CAUTELOSO : cautious
prevenir {87} *vt* **1** : to prevent **2** : to warn — **prevenirse** *vr* **~ contra** *or* **~ de** : to take precautions against
preventivo, -va *adj* : preventive, precautionary
prever {88} *vt* ANTICIPAR : to foresee, to anticipate
previo, -via *adj* **1** : previous, prior **2** : after, upon ⟨previo pago : after paying, upon payment⟩
previsible *adj* : foreseeable
previsión *nf, pl* **-siones 1** : foresight **2** : prediction, forecast **3** : precaution
previsor, -sora *adj* : farsighted, prudent
prieto, -ta *adj* **1** : blackish, dark **2** : dark-skinned, swarthy **3** : tight, compressed
prima *nf* **1** : premium **2** : bonus **3** → **primo**
primacía *nf* **1** : precedence, priority **2** : superiority, supremacy
primado *nm* : primate (bishop)
primario, -ria *adj* : primary
primate *nm* : primate
primavera *nf* **1** : spring (season) **2** PRÍMULA : primrose
primaveral *adj* : spring, springlike
primero[1] *adv* **1** : first **2** : rather, sooner
primero[2], **-ra** *adj* (**primer** *before masculine singular nouns*) **1** : first **2** : top, leading **3** : fundamental, basic **4 de primera** : first-rate
primero[3], **-ra** *n* : first
primicia *nf* **1** : first fruits **2** : scoop, exclusive

primigenio, -nia *adj* : original, primary

primitivo, -va *adj* **1** : primitive **2** ORIGINAL : original

primo, -ma *n* : cousin

primogénito, -ta *adj & n* : firstborn

primor *nm* **1** : skill, care **2** : beauty, elegance

primordial *adj* **1** : primordial **2** : basic, fundamental

primoroso, -sa *adj* **1** : exquisite, fine, delicate **2** : skillful

prímula *nf* : primrose

princesa *nf* : princess

principado *nm* : principality

principal[1] *adj* **1** : main, principal **2** : foremost, leading

principal[2] *nm* : capital, principal

príncipe *nm* : prince

principesco, -ca *adj* : princely

principiante[1] *adj* : beginning

principiante[2] *nmf* : beginner, novice

principiar *vt* EMPEZAR : to begin

principio *nm* **1** COMIENZO : beginning **2** : principle **3 al principio** : at first **4 a principios de** : at the beginning of ⟨a principios de agosto : at the beginning of August⟩ **5 en ~** : in principle

pringar {52} *vt* **1** : to dip (in grease) **2** : to soil, to spatter (with grease) — **pringarse** *vr*

pringoso, -sa *adj* : greasy

pringue[1], **etc.** → **pringar**

pringue[2] *nm* : grease, drippings *pl*

prior, priora *n* : prior *m,* prioress *f*

priorato *nm* : priory

prioridad *nf* : priority, precedence

prisa *nf* **1** : hurry, rush **2 a ~** *or* **de ~** : quickly, fast **3 a toda prisa** : as fast as possible **4 darse prisa** : to hurry **5 tener prisa** : to be in a hurry

prisión *nf, pl* **prisiones** **1** CÁRCEL : prison, jail **2** ENCARCELAMIENTO : imprisonment

prisionero, -ra *n* : prisoner

prisma *nm* : prism

prismáticos *nmpl* : binoculars

prístino, -na *adj* : pristine

privacidad *nf* : privacy

privación *nf, pl* **-ciones** **1** : deprivation **2** : privation, want

privado, -da *adj* : private — **privadamente** *adv*

privar *vt* **1** DESPOJAR : to deprive **2** : to stun, to knock out — **privarse** *vr* : to deprive oneself

privativo, -va *adj* : exclusive, particular

privilegiado, -da *adj* : privileged

privilegiar *vt* : to grant a privilege to, to favor

privilegio *nm* : privilege

pro[1] *nm* **1** : pro, advantage ⟨los pros y contras : the pros and cons⟩ **2 en pro de** : for, in favor of

pro[2] *prep* : for, in favor of ⟨grupos pro derechos humanos : groups supporting human rights⟩

proa *nf* : bow, prow

probabilidad *nf* : probability

probable *adj* : probable, likely

probablemente *adv* : probably

probar {19} *vt* **1** : to demonstrate, to prove **2** : to test, to try out **3** : to try on (clothing) **4** : to taste, to sample — *vi* : to try — **probarse** *vr* : to try on (clothing)

probeta *nf* : test tube

probidad *nf* : probity

problema *nm* : problem

problemática *nf* : set of problems ⟨la problemática que debemos enfrentar : the problems we must face⟩

probóscide *nf* : proboscis

problemático, -ca *adj* : problematic

procaz *adj, pl* **procaces** **1** : insolent, impudent **2** : indecent

procedencia *nf* : origin, source

procedente *adj* **1** : proper, fitting **2 ~ de** : coming from

proceder *vi* **1** AVANZAR : to proceed **2** : to act, to behave **3** : to be appropriate, to be fitting **4 ~ de** : to originate from, to come from

procedimiento *nm* : procedure, process

prócer *nmf* : eminent person, leader

procesado, -da *n* : accused, defendant

procesador *nm* : processor ⟨procesador de textos : word processor⟩

procesamiento *nm* : processing ⟨procesamiento de datos : data processing⟩

procesar *vt* **1** : to prosecute, to try **2** : to process

procesión *nf, pl* **-siones** : procession

proceso *nm* **1** : process **2** : trial, proceedings *pl*

proclama *nf* : proclamation

proclamación *nf, pl* **-ciones** : proclamation

proclamar *vt* : to proclaim — **proclamarse** *vr*

proclive *adj* **~ a** : inclined to, prone to

proclividad *nf* : proclivity, inclination

procrear *vi* : to procreate — **procreación** *nf*

procurador, -dora *n* ABOGADO : attorney

procurar *vt* **1** INTENTAR : to try, to endeavor **2** CONSEGUIR : to obtain, to procure **3 procurar hacer** : to manage to do

prodigar {52} *vt* : to lavish, to be generous with

prodigio *nm* : wonder, marvel

prodigioso, -sa *adj* : prodigious, marvelous

pródigo[1], **-ga** *adj* **1** : generous, lavish **2** : wasteful, prodigal

pródigo[2], **-ga** *n* : spendthrift, prodigal

producción *nf, pl* **-ciones** **1** : production **2 producción en serie** : mass production

producir {61} *vt* **1** : to produce, to make, to manufacture **2** : to cause, to bring about **3** : to bear (interest) — **producirse** *vr* : to take place, to occur

productividad *nf* : productivity

productivo, -va *adj* **1** : productive **2** LUCRATIVO : profitable

producto *nm* **1** : product **2** : proceeds *pl*, yield
productor, -tora *n* : producer
proeza *nf* HAZAÑA : feat, exploit
profanar *vt* : to profane, to desecrate — **profanación** *nf*
profano[1], -na *adj* **1** : profane **2** : worldly, secular
profano[2], -na *n* : nonspecialist
profecía *nf* : prophecy
proferir {76} *vt* **1** : to utter **2** : to hurl (insults)
profesar *vt* **1** : to profess, to declare **2** : to practice, to exercise
profesión *nf, pl* **-siones** : profession
profesional *adj & nmf* : professional — **profesionalmente** *adv*
profesionalismo *nm* : professionalism
profesionalizar {21} *vt* : to professionalize
profesionista *nmf Mex* : professional
profesor, -sora *n* **1** MAESTRO : teacher **2** : professor
profesorado *nm* **1** : faculty **2** : teaching profession
profeta *nm* : prophet
profético, -ca *adj* : prophetic
profetisa *nf* : prophetess, prophet
profetizar {21} *vt* : to prophesy
prófugo, -ga *adj & n* : fugitive
profundidad *nf* : depth, profundity
profundizar {21} *vt* **1** : to deepen **2** : to study in depth — *vi* **~ en** : to go deeply into, to study in depth
profundo, -da *adj* **1** HONDO : deep **2** : profound — **profundamente** *adv*
profusión *nf, pl* **-siones** : abundance, profusion
profuso, -sa *adj* : profuse, abundant, extensive
progenie *nf* : progeny, offspring
progenitor, -tora *n* ANTEPASADO : ancestor, progenitor
progesterona *nf* : progesterone
prognóstico *nm* : prognosis
programa *nm* **1** : program **2** : plan **3 programa de estudios** : curriculum
programable *adj* : programmable
programación *nf, pl* **-ciones** **1** : programming **2** : planning
programador, -dora *n* : programmer
programar *vt* **1** : to schedule, to plan **2** : to program (a computer, etc.)
progresar *vi* : to progress, to make progress
progresista *adj & nmf* : progressive
progresivo, -va *adj* : progressive, gradual
progreso *nm* : progress
prohibición *nf, pl* **-ciones** : ban, prohibition
prohibir {62} *vt* : to prohibit, to ban, to forbid
prohibitivo, -va *adj* : prohibitive
prohijar {5} *vt* ADOPTAR : to adopt
prójimo *nm* : neighbor, fellow man
prole *nf* : offspring, progeny
proletariado *nm* : proletariat, working class
proletario, -ria *adj & n* : proletarian
proliferar *vi* : to proliferate — **proliferación** *nf*
prolífico, -ca *adj* : prolific
prolijo, -ja *adj* : wordy, long-winded
prólogo *nm* : prologue, preface, foreword
prolongación *nf, pl* **-ciones** : extension, lengthening
prolongar {52} *vt* **1** : to prolong **2** : to extend, to lengthen — **prolongarse** *vr* CONTINUAR : to last, to continue
promediar *vt* **1** : to average **2** : to divide in half — *vi* : to be half over
promedio *nm* **1** : average **2** : middle, midpoint
promesa *nf* : promise
prometedor, -dora *adj* : promising, hopeful
prometer *vt* : to promise — *vi* : to show promise — **prometerse** *vr* COMPROMETERSE : to get engaged
prometido[1], -da *adj* : engaged
prometido[2], -da *n* NOVIO : fiancé *m*, fiancée *f*
prominente *adj* : prominent — **prominencia** *nf*
promiscuo, -cua *adj* : promiscuous — **promiscuidad** *nf*
promisorio, -ria *adj* **1** : promising **2** : promissory
promoción *nf, pl* **-ciones** **1** : promotion **2** : class, year **3** : play-off (in soccer)
promocionar *vt* : to promote — **promocional** *adj*
promontorio *nm* : promontory, headland
promotor, -tora *n* : promoter
promover {47} *vt* **1** : to promote, to advance **2** FOMENTAR : to foster, to encourage **3** PROVOCAR : to provoke, to cause
promulgación *nf, pl* **-ciones** **1** : enactment **2** : proclamation, enactment
promulgar {52} *vt* **1** : to promulgate, to proclaim **2** : to enact (a law or decree)
prono, -na *adj* : prone
pronombre *nm* : pronoun
pronosticar {72} *vt* : to predict, to forecast
pronóstico *nm* **1** PREDICCIÓN : forecast, prediction **2** : prognosis
prontitud *nf* **1** PRESTEZA : promptness, speed **2 con ~** : promptly, quickly
pronto[1] *adv* **1** : quickly, promptly **2** : soon **3 de ~** : suddenly **4 lo más pronto posible** : as soon as possible **5 tan pronto como** : as soon as
pronto[2], -ta *adj* **1** RÁPIDO : quick, speedy, prompt **2** PREPARADO : ready
pronunciación *nf, pl* **-ciones** : pronunciation
pronunciado, -da *adj* **1** : pronounced, sharp, steep **2** : marked, noticeable
pronunciamiento *nm* **1** : pronouncement **2** : military uprising
pronunciar *vt* **1** : to pronounce, to say **2** : to give, to deliver (a speech) **3 pro-**

nunciar un fallo : to pronounce sentence — **pronunciarse** *vr* : to declare oneself

propagación *nf, pl* **-ciones** : propagation, spreading

propaganda *nf* **1** : propaganda **2** PUBLICIDAD : advertising

propagar {52} *vt* **1** : to propagate **2** : to spread, to disseminate — **propagarse** *vr*

propalar *vt* **1** : to divulge **2** : to spread

propano *nm* : propane

propasarse *vr* : to go too far, to overstep one's bounds

propensión *nf, pl* **-siones** INCLINACIÓN : inclination, propensity

propenso, -sa *adj* : prone, susceptible

propiamente *adv* **1** : properly, correctly **2** : exactly, precisely ⟨propiamente dicho : strictly speaking⟩

propiciar *vt* **1** : to propitiate **2** : to favor, to foster

propicio, -cia *adj* : favorable, propitious

propiedad *nf* **1** : property ⟨propiedad privada : private property⟩ **2** : ownership **3** CUALIDAD : property, quality **4** : suitability, appropriateness

propietario[1]**, -ria** *adj* : proprietary

propietario[2]**, -ria** *n* DUEÑO : owner, proprietor

propina *nf* : tip, gratuity

propinar *vt* : to give, to strike ⟨propinar una paliza : to give a beating⟩

propio, -pia *adj* **1** : own ⟨su propia casa : his own house⟩ ⟨sus recursos propios : their own resources⟩ **2** APROPIADO : appropriate, suitable **3** CARACTERÍSTICO : characteristic, typical **4** MISMO : oneself ⟨el propio director : the director himself⟩

proponer {60} *vt* **1** : to propose, to suggest **2** : to nominate — **proponerse** *vr* : to intend, to plan, to set out ⟨lo que se propone lo cumple : he does what he sets out to do⟩

proporción *nf, pl* **-ciones 1** : proportion **2** : ratio (in mathematics) **3 proporciones** *nfpl* : proportions, size ⟨de grandes proporciones : very large⟩

proporcionado, -da *adj* **1** : proportionate **2** : proportioned ⟨bien proporcionado : well-proportioned⟩ — **proporcionadamente** *adv*

proporcional *adj* : proportional — **proporcionalmente** *adv*

proporcionar *vt* **1** : to provide, to give **2** : to proportion, to adapt

proposición *nf, pl* **-ciones** : proposal, proposition

propósito *nm* **1** INTENCIÓN : purpose, intention **2 a ~** : by the way **3 a ~** : on purpose, intentionally

propuesta *nf* PROPOSICIÓN : proposal

propulsar *vt* **1** IMPULSAR : to propel, to drive **2** PROMOVER : to promote, to encourage

propulsión *nf, pl* **-siones** : propulsion

propulsor *nm* : propellant

propuso, etc. → **proponer**

prorrata *nf* **1** : share, quota **2 a ~** : pro rata, proportionately

prórroga *nf* **1** : extension, deferment **2** : overtime (in sports)

prorrogar {52} *vt* **1** : to extend (a deadline) **2** : to postpone

prorrumpir *vi* : to burst forth, to break out ⟨prorrumpí en lágrimas : I burst into tears⟩

prosa *nf* : prose

prosaico, -ca *adj* : prosaic, mundane

proscribir {33} *v* **1** PROHIBIR : to prohibit, to ban, to proscribe **2** DESTERRAR : to banish, to exile

proscripción *nf, pl* **-ciones 1** PROHIBICIÓN : ban, proscription **2** DESTIERRO : banishment

proscrito[1] *pp* → **proscribir**

proscrito[2]**, -ta** *n* **1** DESTERRADO : exile **2** : outlaw

prosecución *nf, pl* **-ciones 1** : continuation **2** : pursuit

proseguir {75} *vt* **1** CONTINUAR : to continue **2** : to pursue (studies, goals) — *vi* : to continue, to go on

prosélito, -ta *n* : proselyte

prospección *nf, pl* **-ciones** : prospecting, exploration

prospectar *vi* : to prospect

prospecto *nm* : prospectus, leaflet, brochure

prosperar *vi* : to prosper, to thrive

prosperidad *nf* : prosperity

próspero, -ra *adj* : prosperous, flourishing

próstata *nf* : prostate

prostitución *nf, pl* **-ciones** : prostitution

prostituir {41} *vt* : to prostitute — **prostituirse** *vr* : to prostitute oneself

prostituto, -ta *n* : prostitute

protagonista *nmf* **1** : protagonist, main character **2** : leader

protagonizar {21} *vt* : to star in

protección *nf, pl* **-ciones** : protection

protector[1]**, -tora** *adj* : protective

protector[2]**, -tora** *n* **1** : protector, guardian **2** : patron

protector[3] *nm* : protector, guard ⟨chaleco protector : chest protector⟩

protectorado *nm* : protectorate

proteger {15} *vt* : to protect, to defend — **protegerse** *vr*

protegido, -da *n* : protégé

proteína *nf* : protein

prótesis *nfs & pl* : prosthesis

protesta *nf* **1** : protest **2** *Mex* : promise, oath

protestante *adj & nmf* : Protestant

protestantismo *nm* : Protestantism

protestar *vi* : to protest, to object — *vt* **1** : to protest, to object to **2** : to declare, to profess

protocolo *nm* : protocol

protón *nm, pl* **protones** : proton

protoplasma *nm* : protoplasm

prototipo *nm* : prototype

protozoario *or* **protozoo** *nm* : protozoan

protuberancia *nf* : protuberance — **protuberante** *adj*
provecho *nm* : benefit, advantage
provechoso, -sa *adj* BENEFICIOSO : beneficial, profitable, useful — **provechosamente** *adv*
proveedor, -dora *n* : provider, supplier
proveer {63} *vt* : to provide, to supply — **proveerse** *vr* ~ **de** : to obtain, to supply oneself with
provenir {87} *vi* ~ **de** : to come from
provenzal[1] *adj* : Provençal
provenzal[2] *nmf* : Provençal
provenzal[3] *nm* : Provençal (language)
proverbio *nm* REFRÁN : proverb — **proverbial** *adj*
providencia *nf* **1** : providence, foresight **2** : Providence, God **3 providencias** *nfpl* : steps, measures
providencial *adj* : providential
provincia *nf* : province — **provincial** *adj*
provinciano, -na *adj* : provincial, unsophisticated
provisión *nf, pl* **-siones** : provision
provisional *adj* : provisional, temporary
provisionalmente *adv* : provisionally, tentatively
provisorio, -ria *adj* : provisional, temporary
provisto *pp* → **proveer**
provocación *nf, pl* **-ciones** : provocation
provocador[1], **-dora** *adj* : provocative, provoking
provocador[2], **-dora** *n* AGITADOR : agitator
provocar {72} *vt* **1** CAUSAR : to provoke, to cause **2** IRRITAR : to provoke, to pique
provocativo, -va *adj* : provocative
proxeneta *nmf* : pimp *m*
próximamente *adv* : shortly, soon
proximidad *nf* **1** : nearness, proximity **2 proximidades** *nfpl* : vicinity
próximo, -ma *adj* **1** : near, close ⟨la Navidad está próxima : Christmas is almost here⟩ **2** SIGUIENTE : next, following ⟨la próxima semana : the following week⟩
proyección *nf, pl* **-ciones 1** : projection **2** : showing, screening (of a film) **3** : range, influence, diffusion
proyectar *vt* **1** : to plan **2** LANZAR : to throw, to hurl **3** : to project, to cast (light or shadow) **4** : to show, to screen (a film)
proyectil *nm* : projectile, missile
proyecto *nm* **1** : plan, project **2 proyecto de ley** : bill
proyector *nm* **1** : projector **2** : spotlight
prudencia *nf* : prudence, care, discretion
prudente *adj* : prudent, sensible, reasonable
prueba[1], **etc.** → **probar**
prueba[2] *nf* **1** : proof, evidence **2** : trial, test **3** : proof (in printing or photography) **4** : event, qualifying round (in sports) **5 a prueba de agua** : waterproof **6 prueba de fuego** : acid test **7 poner a prueba** : to put to the test
prurito *nm* **1** : itching **2** : desire, urge
psicoanálisis *nm* : psychoanalysis — **psicoanalista** *nmf*
psicoanalítico, -ca *adj* : psychoanalytic
psicoanalizar {21} *vt* : to psychoanalyze
psicología *nf* : psychology
psicológico, -ca *adj* : psychological — **psicológicamente** *adv*
psicólogo, -ga *n* : psychologist
psicópata *nmf* : psychopath
psicopático, -ca *adj* : psycopathic
psicosis *nfs & pl* : psychosis
psicosomático, -ca *adj* : psychosomatic
psicoterapeuta *nmf* : psychotherapist
psicoterapia *nf* : psychotherapy
psicótico, -ca *adj & n* : psychotic
psique *nf* : psyche
psiquiatra *nmf* : psychiatrist
psiquiatría *nf* : psychiatry
psiquiátrico[1], **-ca** *adj* : psychiatric
psiquiátrico[2] *nm* : mental hospital
psíquico, -ca *adj* : psychic
psiquis *nfs & pl* : psyche
psoriasis *nf* : psoriasis
ptomaína *nf* : ptomaine
púa *nf* **1** : barb ⟨alambre de púas : barbed wire⟩ **2** : tooth (of a comb) **3** : quill, spine
pubertad *nf* : puberty
pubiano → **púbico**
púbico, -ca *adj* : pubic
publicación *nf, pl* **-ciones** : publication
publicar {72} *vt* **1** : to publish **2** DIVULGAR : to divulge, to disclose
publicidad *nf* **1** : publicity **2** : advertising
publicista *nmf* : publicist
publicitar *vt* **1** : to publicize **2** : to advertise
publicitario, -ria *adj* : advertising, publicity ⟨agencia publicitaria : advertising agency⟩
público[1], **-ca** *adj* : public — **públicamente** *adv*
público[2] *nm* **1** : public **2** : audience, spectators *pl*
puchero *nm* **1** : pot **2** : stew **3** : pout ⟨hacer pucheros : to pout⟩
pucho *nm* **1** : waste, residue **2** : cigarette butt **3 a puchos** : little by little, bit by bit
púdico, -ca *adj* : chaste, modest
pudiente *adj* **1** : powerful **2** : rich, wealthy
pudín *nm, pl* **pudines** BUDÍN : pudding
pudo, etc. → **poder**
pudor *nm* : modesty, reserve
pudoroso, -sa *adj* : modest, reserved, shy
pudrir {59} *vt* **1** : to rot **2** *fam* : to annoy, to upset — **pudrirse** *vr* **1** : to rot **2** : to languish
pueblerino, -na *adj* : provincial, countrified

puebla, etc. → **poblar**

pueblo *nm* **1** NACIÓN : people **2** : common people **3** ALDEA, POBLADO : town, village

puede, etc. → **poder**

puente *nm* **1** : bridge ⟨puente levadizo : drawbridge⟩ **2** : denture, bridge **3 puente aéreo** : airlift

puerco[1], -ca *adj* : dirty, filthy

puerco[2], -ca *n* **1** CERDO, MARRANO : pig, hog **2** : pig, dirty or greedy person **3 puerco espín** : porcupine

pueril *adj* : childish, puerile

puerro *nm* : leek

puerta *nf* **1** : door, entrance, gate **2 a puerta cerrada** : behind closed doors

puerto *nm* **1** : port, harbor **2** : mountain pass **3 puerto marítimo** : seaport

puertorriqueño, -ña *adj & n* : Puerto Rican

pues *conj* **1** : since, because, for ⟨no puedo ir, pues no tengo plata : I can't go, since I don't have any money⟩ ⟨lo hace, pues a él le gusta : he does it because he likes to⟩ **2** (*used interjectionally*) : well, then ⟨¡pues claro que sí! : well, of course!⟩ ⟨¡pues no voy! : well then, I'm not going!⟩

puesta *nf* **1** : setting ⟨puesta del sol : sunset⟩ **2** : laying (of eggs) **3 puesta a punto** : tune-up **4 puesta en marcha** : start, starting up

puestero, -ra *n* : seller, vendor

puesto[1] *pp* → **poner**

puesto[2], -ta *adj* : dressed ⟨bien puesto : well-dressed⟩

puesto[3] *nm* **1** LUGAR, SITIO : place, position **2** : position, job **3** : kiosk, stand, stall **4 puesto que** : since, given that

pugilato *nm* BOXEO : boxing, pugilism

pugilista *nm* BOXEADOR : boxer, pugilist

pugna *nf* **1** CONFLICTO, LUCHA : conflict, struggle **2 en ~** : at odds, in conflict

pugnar *vi* LUCHAR : to fight, to strive, to struggle

pugnaz *adj* : pugnacious

pujante *adj* : mighty, powerful

pujanza *nf* : strength, vigor ⟨pujanza económica : economic strength⟩

pulcritud *nf* **1** : neatness, tidiness **2** ESMERO : meticulousness

pulcro, -cra *adj* **1** : clean, neat **2** : exquisite, delicate, refined

pulga *nf* **1** : flea **2 tener malas pulgas** : to be bad-tempered

pulgada *nf* : inch

pulgar *nm* **1** : thumb **2** : big toe

pulir *vt* **1** : to polish, to shine **2** REFINAR : to refine, to perfect

pulla *nf* **1** : cutting remark, dig, gibe **2** : obscenity

pulmón *nm, pl* **pulmones** : lung

pulmonar *adj* : pulmonary

pulmonía *nf* NEUMONÍA : pneumonia

pulpa *nf* : pulp, flesh

pulpería *nf* : small grocery store

púlpito *nm* : pulpit

pulpo *nm* : octopus

pulsación *nf, pl* **-ciones** **1** : beat, pulsation, throb **2** : keystroke

pulsar *vt* **1** APRETAR : to press, to push **2** : to strike (a key) **3** : to assess — *vi* : to beat, to throb

pulsera *nf* : bracelet

pulso *nm* **1** : pulse ⟨tomarle el pulso a alguien : to take someone's pulse⟩ ⟨tomarle el pulso a la opinión : to sound out opinion⟩ **2** : steadiness (of hand) ⟨dibujo a pulso : freehand sketch⟩

pulular *vi* ABUNDAR : to abound, to swarm ⟨en el río pululan los peces : the river is teeming with fish⟩

pulverizador *nm* **1** : atomizer, spray **2** : spray gun

pulverizar {21} *vt* **1** : to pulverize, to crush **2** : to spray

puma *nf* : cougar, puma

puna *nf* : bleak Andean tableland

punción *nf, pl* **punciones** : puncture

punible *adj* : punishable

punitivo, -va *adj* : punitive

punce, etc. → **punzar**

punta *nf* **1** : tip, end ⟨punta del dedo : fingertip⟩ ⟨en la punta de la lengua : at the tip of one's tongue⟩ **2** : point (of a weapon or pencil) ⟨punta de lanza : spearhead⟩ **3** : point, headland **4** : bunch, lot ⟨una punta de ladrones : a bunch of thieves⟩ **5 a punta de** : by, by dint of

puntada *nf* **1** : stitch (in sewing) **2** PUNZADA : sharp pain, stitch, twinge **3** *Mex* : witticism, quip

puntal *nm* **1** : prop, support **2** : stanchion

puntapié *nm* PATADA : kick

puntazo *nm* CORNADA : wound (from a goring)

puntear *vt* **1** : to pluck (a guitar) **2** : to lead (in sports)

puntería *nf* : aim, marksmanship

puntero *nm* **1** : pointer **2** : leader

puntiagudo, -da *adj* : sharp, pointed

puntilla *nf* **1** : lace edging **2** : dagger (in bullfighting) **3 de puntillas** : on tiptoe

puntilloso, -sa *adj* : punctilious

punto *nm* **1** : dot, point **2** : period (in punctuation) **3** : item, question **4** : spot, place **5** : moment, stage, degree **6** : point (in a score) **7** : stitch **8 en ~** : on the dot, sharp ⟨a las dos en punto : at two o'clock sharp⟩ **9 al punto** : at once **10 a punto fijo** : exactly, certainly **11 dos puntos** : colon **12 hasta cierto punto** : up to a point **13 punto decimal** : decimal point **14 punto de vista** : point of view **15 punto y coma** : semicolon **16 y punto** : period ⟨es el mejor que hay y punto : it's the best there is, period⟩ **17 puntos cardinales** : points of the compass

puntuación *nf, pl* **-ciones** **1** : punctuation **2** : scoring, score, grade
puntual *adj* **1** : prompt, punctual **2** : exact, accurate — **puntualmente** *adv*
puntualidad *nf* **1** : promptness, punctuality **2** : exactness, accuracy
puntualizar {21} *vt* **1** : to specify, to state **2** : to point out
puntuar {3} *vt* : to punctuate — *vi* : to score points
punzada *nf* : sharp pain, twinge, stitch
punzante *adj* **1** : sharp **2** CÁUSTICO : biting, caustic
punzar {21} *vt* : to pierce, to puncture
punzón *nm, pl* **punzones** **1** : awl **2** : hole punch
puñado *nm* **1** : handful **2 a puñados** : lots of, by the handful
puñal *nm* DAGA : dagger
puñalada *nf* : stab, stab wound
puñetazo *nm* : punch (with the fist)
puño *nm* **1** : fist **2** : handful, fistful **3** : cuff (of a shirt) **4** : handle, hilt
pupila *nf* : pupil (of the eye)
pupilo, -la *n* **1** : pupil, student **2** : ward, charge
pupitre *nm* : writing desk
puré *nm* : purée ⟨puré de papas : mashed potatoes⟩
pureza *nf* : purity
purga *nf* **1** : laxative **2** : purge
purgante *adj & nm* : laxative, purgative
purgar {52} *vt* **1** : to purge, to cleanse **2** : to liquidate (in politics) **3** : to give a laxative to — **purgarse** *vr* **1** : to take a laxative **2 ~ de** : to purge oneself of
purgatorio *nm* : purgatory
purgue, etc. → **purgar**
purificador *nm* : purifier
purificar {72} *vt* : to purify — **purificación** *nf*
puritano[1], -na *adj* : puritanical, puritan
puritano[2], -na *n* **1** : Puritan **2** : puritan
puro[1] *adv* : sheer, much ⟨de puro terco : out of sheer stubbornness⟩
puro[2], -ra *adj* **1** : pure ⟨aire puro : fresh air⟩ **2** : plain, simple, sheer ⟨por pura curiosidad : from sheer curiosity⟩ **3** : only, just ⟨emplean puras mujeres : they only employ women⟩ **4 pura sangre** : Thoroughbred horse
puro[3] *nm* : cigar
púrpura *nf* : purple
purpúreo, -rea *adj* : purple
purpurina *nf* : glitter (for decoration)
pus *nm* : pus
pusilánime *adj* COBARDE : pusillanimous, cowardly
puso, etc. → **poner**
pústula *nf* : pustule, pimple
puta *nf* : whore, slut
putrefacción *nf, pl* **-ciones** : putrefaction
putrefacto, -ta *adj* **1** PODRIDO : putrid, rotten **2** : decayed
pútrido, -da *adj* : putrid, rotten
puya *nf* **1** : point (of a lance) **2 lanzar una puya** : to gibe, to taunt

Q

q *nf* : eighteenth letter of the Spanish alphabet
que[1] *conj* **1** : that ⟨dice que está listo : he says that he's ready⟩ ⟨espero que lo haga : I hope that he does it⟩ **2** : than ⟨más que nada : more than anything⟩ **3** (*implying permission or desire*) ⟨¡que entre! : send him in!⟩ ⟨¡que te vaya bien! : I wish you well!⟩ **4** (*indicating a reason or cause*) ⟨¡cuidado, que te caes! : be careful, you're about to fall!⟩ ⟨no provoques al perro, que te va a morder : don't provoke the dog or (else) he'll bite⟩ **5 es que** : the thing is that, I'm afraid that **6 yo que tú** : if I were you
que[2] *pron* **1** : who, that ⟨la niña que viene : the girl who is coming⟩ **2** : whom, that ⟨los alumnos que enseñé : the students that I taught⟩ **3** : that, which ⟨el carro que me gusta : the car that I like⟩ **4 el (la, lo, las, los) que** → **el[1], la[1], lo[1], los[1]**
qué[1] *adv* : how, what ⟨¡qué bonito! : how pretty!⟩
qué[2] *adj* : what, which ⟨¿qué hora es? : what time is it?⟩
qué[3] *pron* : what ⟨¿qué quieres? : what do you want?⟩
quebracho *nm* : quebracho (tree)
quebrada *nf* DESFILADERO : ravine, gorge
quebradizo, -za *adj* FRÁGIL : breakable, delicate, fragile
quebrado[1], -da *adj* **1** : bankrupt **2** : rough, uneven **3** ROTO : broken
quebrado[2] *nm* : fraction
quebrantamiento *nm* **1** : breaking **2** : deterioration, weakening
quebrantar *vt* **1** : to break, to split, to crack **2** : to weaken **3** : to violate (a law or contract)
quebranto *nm* **1** : break, breaking **2** AFLICCIÓN : affliction, grief **3** PÉRDIDA : loss
quebrar {55} *vt* **1** ROMPER : to break **2** DOBLAR : to bend, to twist — *vi* **1** : to go bankrupt **2** : to fall out, to break up — **quebrarse** *vr*
queda *nf* : curfew
quedar *vi* **1** PERMANECER : to remain, to stay **2** : to be ⟨quedamos contentos con las mejoras : we were pleased with the improvements⟩ **3** : to be situated ⟨queda muy lejos : it's very far, it's too far away⟩ **4** : to be left ⟨quedan sólo dos alternativas : there are only two options left⟩ **5** : to fit, to suit ⟨estos zap-

atos no me quedan : these shoes don't fit⟩ **6 quedar bien (mal)** : to turn out well (badly) **7 ~ en** : to agree, to arrange ⟨¿en qué quedamos? : what's the arrangement, then?⟩ — **quedarse** *vr* **1** : to stay ⟨se quedó en casa : she stayed at home⟩ **2** : to keep on ⟨se quedó esperando : he kept on waiting⟩ **3 quedarse atrás** : to stay behind ⟨no quedarse atrás : to be no slouch⟩ **4 ~ con** : to remain ⟨me quedé con hambre después de comer : I was still hungry after I ate⟩

quedo[1] *adv* : softly, quietly

quedo[2], **-da** *adj* : quiet, still

quehacer *nm* **1** : work **2 quehaceres** *nmpl* : chores

queja *nf* : complaint

quejarse *vr* **1** : to complain **2** : to groan, to moan

quejido *nm* **1** : groan, moan **2** : whine, whimper

quejoso, -sa *adj* : complaining, whining

quejumbroso, -sa *adj* : querulous, whining

quema *nf* **1** FUEGO : fire **2** : burning

quemado, -da *adj* **1** : burned, burnt **2** : annoyed **3** : burned-out

quemador *nm* : burner

quemadura *nf* : burn

quemar *vt* : to burn, to set fire to — *vi* : to be burning hot — **quemarse** *vr*

quemarropa *nf* **a ~** : point-blank

quemazón *nf, pl* **-zones** **1** : burning **2** : intense heat **3** : itch **4** : cutting remark

quena *nf* : Peruvian reed flute

quepa, etc. → **caber**

querella *nf* **1** : complaint **2** : lawsuit

querellante *nmf* : plaintiff

querellarse *vr* **~ contra** : to bring suit against, to sue

querer[1] {64} *vt* **1** DESEAR : to want, to desire ⟨quiere ser profesor : he wants to be a teacher⟩ ⟨¿cuánto quieres por esta computadora? : how much do you want for this computer?⟩ **2** : to love, to like, to be fond of ⟨te quiero : I love you⟩ **3** (*indicating a request*) ⟨¿quieres pasarme la leche? : please pass the milk⟩ **4 querer decir** : to mean **5 sin ~** : unintentionally — *vi* : like, want ⟨si quieras : if you like⟩

querer[2] *nm* : love, affection

querido[1], **-da** *adj* : dear, beloved

querido[2], **-da** *n* : dear, sweetheart

queroseno *nm* : kerosene

querrá, etc. → **querer**

querúbico, -ca *adj* : cherubic

querubín *nm, pl* **-bines** : cherub

quesadilla *nf* : quesadilla

quesería *nf* : cheese shop

queso *nm* : cheese

quetzal *nm* **1** : quetzal (bird) **2** : monetary unit of Guatemala

quicio *nm* **1 estar fuera de quicio** : to be beside oneself **2 sacar de quicio** : to exasperate, to drive crazy

quid *nm* : crux, gist ⟨el quid de la cuestión : the crux of the matter⟩

quiebra[1], **etc.** → **quebrar**

quiebra[2] *nf* **1** : break, crack **2** BANCARROTA : failure, bankruptcy

quien *pron, pl* **quienes** **1** : who, whom ⟨no sé quien ganará : I don't know who will win⟩ ⟨las personas con quienes trabajo : the people with whom I work⟩ **2** : whoever, whomever ⟨quien quiere salir que salga : whoever wants to can leave⟩ **3** : anyone, some people ⟨hay quienes no están de acuerdo : some people don't agree⟩

quién *pron, pl* **quiénes** **1** : who, whom ⟨¿quién sabe? : who knows?⟩ ⟨¿con quién hablo? : with whom am I speaking?⟩ **2 de ~** : whose ⟨¿de quién es este libro? : whose book is this?⟩

quienquiera *pron, pl* **quienesquiera** : whoever, whomever

quiere, etc. → **querer**

quieto, -ta *adj* **1** : calm, quiet **2** INMÓVIL : still

quietud *nf* **1** : calm, tranquility **2** INMOVILIDAD : stillness

quijada *nf* : jaw, jawbone

quijotesco, -ca *adj* : quixotic

quilate *nm* : karat

quilla *nf* : keel

quimera *nf* : chimera, illusion

quimérico, -ca *adj* : chimeric, fanciful

química *nf* : chemistry

químico[1], **-ca** *adj* : chemical

químico[2], **-ca** *n* : chemist

quimioterapia *nf* : chemotherapy

quimono *nm* : kimono

quince *adj & nm* : fifteen

quinceañero, -ra *n* : fifteen-year-old, teenager

quinceavo[1], **-va** *adj* : fifteenth

quinceavo[2] *nm* : fifteenth (fraction)

quincena *nf* : two week period, fortnight

quincenal *adj* : bimonthly, twice a month

quincuagésimo[1], **-ma** *adj* : fiftieth, fifty-

quincuagésimo[2], **-ma** *n* : fiftieth, fifty- (in a series)

quingombó *nm* : okra

quiniela *nf* : sports lottery

quinientos[1], **-tas** *adj* : five hundred

quinientos[2] *nms & pl* : five hundred

quinina *nf* : quinine

quino *nm* : cinchona

quinqué *nm* : oil lamp

quinquenal *adj* : five-year ⟨un plan quinquenal : a five-year plan⟩

quinta *nf* : country house, villa

quintaesencia *nf* : quintessence — **quintaesencial** *adj*

quintal *nm* : hundredweight

quinteto *nm* : quintet

quintillizo, -za *n* : quintuplet

quinto, -ta *adj* : fifth — **quinto, -ta** *n*

quíntuplo, -la *adj* : quintuple, five-fold

quiosco *nm* **1** : kiosk **2** : newsstand **3 quiosco de música** : bandstand

quirófano *nm* : operating room

quiromancia *nf* : palmistry
quiropráctica *nf* : chiropractic
quiropráctico, -ca *n* : chiropractor
quirúrgico, -ca *adj* : surgical — **quirúrgicamente** *adv*
quiso, etc. → **querer**
quisquilloso[1], **-sa** *adj* : fastidious, fussy
quisquilloso[2], **-sa** *n* : fussy person, fussbudget
quiste *nm* : cyst
quitaesmalte *nm* : nail polish remover
quitamanchas *nms & pl* : stain remover
quitanieves *nms & pl* : snowplow
quitar *vt* **1** : to remove, to take away **2** : to take off (clothes) **3** : to get rid of, to relieve — **quitarse** *vr* **1** : to withdraw, to leave **2** : to take off (one's clothes) **3** ~ **de** : to give up (a habit) **4 quitar de encima** : to get rid of
quitasol *nm* : parasol
quiteño[1], **-ña** *adj* : of or from Quito
quiteño[2], **-ña** *n* : person from Quito
quizá *or* **quizás** *adv* : maybe, perhaps
quórum *nm, pl* **quórums** : quorum

R

r *nf* : nineteenth letter of the Spanish alphabet
rábano *nm* **1** : radish **2 rábano picante** : horseradish
rabí *nmf, pl* **rabíes** : rabbi
rabia *nf* **1** HIDROFOBIA : rabies, hydrophobia **2** : rage, anger
rabiar *vi* **1** : to rage, to be furious **2** : to be in great pain **3 a** ~ *fam* : like crazy, like mad
rabieta *nf* BERRINCHE : tantrum
rabino, -na *n* : rabbi
rabioso, -sa *adj* **1** : enraged, furious **2** : rabid
rabo *nm* **1** COLA : tail **2 el rabo del ojo** : the corner of one's eye
racha *nf* **1** : gust of wind **2** : run, series, string <racha perdedora : losing streak>
racheado, -da *adj* : gusty, windy
racial *adj* : racial
racimo *nm* : bunch, cluster <un racimo de uvas : a bunch of grapes>
raciocinio *nm* : reason, reasoning
ración *nf, pl* **raciones** **1** : share, ration **2** PORCIÓN : portion, helping
racional *adj* : rational, reasonable — **racionalmente** *adv*
racionalidad *nf* : rationality
racionalización *nf, pl* **-ciones** : rationalization
racionalizar {21} *vt* **1** : to rationalize **2** : to streamline
racionamiento *nm* : rationing
racionar *vt* : to ration
racismo *nm* : racism
racista *adj & nmf* : racist
radar *nm* : radar
radiación *nf, pl* **-ciones** : radiation, irradiation
radiactividad *nf* : radioactivity
radiactivo, -va *adj* : radioactive
radiador *nm* : radiator
radial *adj* **1** : radial **2** : radio, broadcasting <emisora radial : radio transmitter>
radiante *adj* : radiant
radiar *vt* **1** : to radiate **2** : to irradiate **3** : to broadcast (on the radio)
radical[1] *adj* : radical, extreme — **radicalmente** *adv*
radical[2] *nmf* : radical
radicalismo *nm* : radicalism
radicar {72} *vi* **1** : to be found, to lie **2** ARRAIGAR : to take root — **radicarse** *vr* : to settle, to establish oneself
radio[1] *nm* **1** : radius **2** : radium
radio[2] *nmf* : radio
radioactividad *nf* : radioactivity
radioactivo, -va *adj* : radioactive
radioaficionado, -da *n* : ham radio operator
radiodifusión *nf, pl* **-siones** : radio broadcasting
radiodifusora *nf* : radio station
radioemisora *nf* : radio station
radiofaro *nm* : radio beacon
radiofónico, -ca *adj* : radio <estación radiofónica pública : public radio station>
radiofrecuencia *nf* : radio frequency
radiografía *nf* : X ray (photograph)
radiografiar {85} *vt* : to x-ray
radiología *nf* : radiology
radiólogo, -ga *n* : radiologist
radón *nm* : radon
raer {65} *vt* RASPAR : to scrape, to scrape off
ráfaga *nf* **1** : gust (of wind) **2** : flash, burst <una ráfaga de luz : a flash of light>
raid *nm CA, Mex fam* : lift, ride
raído, -da *adj* : worn, shabby
raiga, etc. → **raer**
raíz *nf, pl* **raíces** **1** : root **2** : origin, source **3 a raíz de** : following, as a result of **4 echar raíces** : to take root
raja *nf* **1** : crack, slit **2** : slice, wedge
rajá *nm* : raja
rajadura *nf* : crack, split
rajar *vt* HENDER : to crack, to split — *vi* **1** *fam* : to chatter **2** *fam* : to boast, to brag — **rajarse** *vr* **1** : to crack, to split open **2** *fam* : to back out
rajatabla *adv* **a** ~ : strictly, to the letter
ralea *nf* : kind, sort, ilk <son de la misma valea : they're two of a kind>
ralentí *nm* **dejar al ralentí** : to leave (a motor) idling
rallado, -da *adj* **1** : grated **2 pan rallado** : bread crumbs *pl*
rallador *nm* : grater

rallar *vt* : to grate
ralo, -la *adj* : sparse, thin
RAM *nf* : RAM, random-access memory
rama *nf* : branch
ramaje *nm* : branches *pl*
ramal *nm* **1** : branchline **2** : halter, strap
ramera *nf* : harlot, prostitute
ramificación *nf, pl* **-ciones** : ramification
ramificarse {72} *vr* : to branch out, to divide into branches
ramillete *nm* **1** RAMO : bouquet **2** : select group, cluster
ramo *nm* **1** : branch **2** RAMILLETE : bouquet **3** : division (of science or industry) **4 Domingo de Ramos** : Palm Sunday
rampa *nf* : ramp, incline
rana *nf* **1** : frog **2 rana toro** : bullfrog
ranchera *nf Mex* : traditional folk song
ranchería *nf* : settlement
ranchero, -ra *n* : rancher, farmer
rancho *nm* **1** : ranch, farm **2** : hut **3** : settlement, camp **4** : food, mess (for soldiers, etc.)
rancio, -cia *adj* **1** : aged, mellow (of wine) **2** : ancient, old **3** : rancid
rango *nm* **1** : rank, status **2** : high social standing **3** : pomp, splendor
ranúnculo *nm* : buttercup
ranura *nf* : groove, slot
rap *nm* : rap (music)
rapacidad *nf* : rapacity
rapar *vt* **1** : to crop **2** : to shave
rapaz[1] *adj, pl* **rapaces** : rapacious, predatory
rapaz[2], **-paza** *n, mpl* **rapaces** : youngster, child
rape *nm* : close haircut
rapé *nm* : snuff
rapero, -ra *n* : rapper, rap artist
rapidez *nf* : rapidity, speed
rápido[1] *adv* : quickly, fast ⟨¡manejas tan rápido! : you drive so fast!⟩
rápido[2], **-da** *adj* : rapid, quick — **rápidamente** *adv*
rápido[3] *nm* **1** : express train **2 rápidos** *nmpl* : rapids
rapiña *nf* **1** : plunder, pillage **2 ave de rapiña** : bird of prey
raposa *nf* : vixen (fox)
rapsodia *nf* : rhapsody
raptar *vt* SECUESTRAR : to abduct, to kidnap
rapto *nm* **1** SECUESTRO : kidnapping, abduction **2** ARREBATO : fit, outburst
raptor, -tora *n* SECUESTRADOR : kidnapper
raque *nm* : beachcombing
raquero, -ra *n* : beachcomber
raqueta *nf* **1** : racket (in sports) **2** : snowshoe
raquítico, -ca *adj* **1** : scrawny, weak **2** : measly, skimpy
raquitismo *nm* : rickets
raramente *adv* : seldom, rarely
rareza *nf* **1** : rarity **2** : peculiarity, oddity
raro, -ra *adj* **1** EXTRAÑO : odd, strange, peculiar **2** : unusual, rare **3** : exceptional **4 rara vez** : seldom, rarely
ras *nm* **a ras de** : level with
rasar *vt* **1** : to skim, to graze **2** : to level
rascacielos *nms & pl* : skyscraper
rascar {72} *vt* **1** : to scratch **2** : to scrape — **rascarse** *vr* : to scratch an itch
rasgadura *nf* : tear, rip
rasgar {52} *vt* : to rip, to tear — **rasgarse** *vr*
rasgo *nm* **1** : stroke (of a pen) ⟨a grandes rasgos : in broad outlines⟩ **2** CARACTERÍSTICA : trait, characteristic **3** : gesture, deed **4 rasgos** *nmpl* FACCIONES : features
rasgón *nm, pl* **rasgones** : rip, tear
rasgue, etc. → **rasgar**
rasguear *vt* : to strum
rasguñar *vt* **1** : to scratch **2** : to sketch, to outline
rasguño *nm* **1** : scratch **2** : sketch
raso[1], **-sa** *adj* **1** : level, flat **2 soldado raso** : private (in the army) ⟨los soldados rasos : the ranks⟩
raso[2] *nm* : satin
raspadura *nf* **1** : scratching, scraping **2 raspaduras** *nfpl* : scrapings
raspar *vt* **1** : to scrape **2** : to file down, to smooth — *vi* : to be rough
rasque, etc. → **rascar**
rastra *nf* **1** : harrow **2 a rastras** : by dragging, unwillingly
rastrear *vt* **1** : to track, to trace **2** : to comb, to search **3** : to trawl
rastrero, -ra *adj* **1** : creeping, crawling **2** : vile, despicable
rastrillar *vt* : to rake, to harrow
rastrillo *nm* **1** : rake **2** *Mex* : razor
rastro *nm* **1** PISTA : trail, track **2** VESTIGIO : trace, sign
rastrojo *nm* : stubble (of plants)
rasuradora *nf Mex, CA* : electric razor, shaver
rasurar *vt* AFEITAR : to shave — **rasurarse** *vr*
rata[1] *nm fam* : pickpocket, thief
rata[2] *nf* **1** : rat **2** *Col, Pan, Peru* : rate, percentage
ratear *vt* : to pilfer, to steal
ratero, -ra *n* : petty thief
ratificación *nf, pl* **-ciones** : ratification
ratificar {72} *vt* **1** : to ratify **2** : to confirm
rato *nm* **1** : while **2 pasar el rato** : to pass the time **3 a cada rato** : all the time, constantly ⟨les sacaba dinero a cada rato : he was always taking money from them⟩ **4 al poco rato** : later, shortly after
ratón[1], **-tona** *n, mpl* **ratones** **1** : mouse **2 ratón de biblioteca** *fam* : bookworm
ratón[2] *nm, pl* **ratones** **1** : (computer) mouse **2** *CoRi* : biceps
ratonera *nf* : mousetrap
raudal *nm* **1** : torrent **2 a raudales** : in abundance

raya[1], **etc.** → **raer**

raya[2] *nf* **1** : line **2** : stripe **3** : skate, ray **4** : part (in the hair) **5** : crease (in clothing)

rayar *vt* **1** ARAÑAR : to scratch **2** : to scrawl on, to mark up ⟨rayaron las paredes : they covered the walls with graffiti⟩ — *vi* **1** : to scratch **2** AMANECER : to dawn, to break ⟨al rayar el alba : at break of day⟩ **3 ~ con** : to be adjacent to, to be next to **4 ~ en** : to border on, to verge on ⟨su respuesta raya en lo ridículo : his answer borders on the ridiculous⟩ — **rayarse** *vr*

rayo *nm* **1** : ray, beam ⟨rayo láser : laser beam⟩ ⟨rayo de gamma : gamma ray⟩ ⟨rayo de sol : sunbeam⟩ **2** RELÁMPAGO : lightning bolt **3 rayo X** : X-ray

rayón *nm, pl* **rayones** : rayon

raza *nf* **1** : race ⟨raza humana : human race⟩ **2** : breed, strain **3 de ~** : thoroughbred, pedigreed

razón *nf, pl* **razones 1** MOTIVO : reason, motive ⟨en razón de : by reason of, because of⟩ **2** JUSTICIA : rightness, justice ⟨tener razón : to be right⟩ **3** : reasoning, sense ⟨perder la razón : to lose one's mind⟩ **4** : ratio, proportion

razonable *adj* : reasonable — **razonablemente** *adv*

razonado, -da *adj* : itemized, detailed

razonamiento *nm* : reasoning

razonar *v* : to reason, to think

reabastecimiento *nm* : replenishment

reabierto *pp* → **reabrir**

reabrir {2} *vt* : to reopen — **reabrirse** *vr*

reacción *nf, pl* **-ciones 1** : reaction **2 motor a reacción** : jet engine

reaccionar *vi* : to react, to respond

reaccionario, -ria *adj & n* : reactionary

reacio, -cia *adj* : resistant, opposed

reacondicionar *vt* : to recondition

reactivación *nf, pl* **-ciones** : reactivation, revival

reactivar *vt* : reactivate, revive

reactor *nm* **1** : reactor ⟨reactor nuclear : nuclear reactor⟩ **2** : jet engine **3** : jet airplane, jet

reafirmar *vt* : to reaffirm, to assert, to strengthen

reajustar *vt* : to readjust, to adjust

reajuste *nm* : readjustment ⟨reajuste de precios : price increase⟩

real *adj* **1** : real, true **2** : royal

realce *nm* **1** : embossing, relief **2 dar realce** : to highlight, to bring out

realeza *nf* : royalty

realidad *nf* **1** : reality **2 en ~** : in truth, actually

realinear *vt* : to realign

realismo *nm* **1** : realism **2** : royalism

realista[1] *adj* **1** : realistic **2** : realist **3** : royalist

realista[2] *nmf* **1** : realist **2** : royalist

realización *nf, pl* **-ciones** : execution, realization

realizar {21} *vt* **1** : to carry out, to execute **2** : to produce, to direct (a film or play) **3** : to fulfill, to achieve **4** : to realize (a profit) — **realizarse** *vr* **1** : to come true **2** : to fulfill oneself

realmente *adv* : really, in reality

realzar {21} *vt* **1** : to heighten, to raise **2** : to highlight, to enhance

reanimación *nf, pl* **-ciones** : revival, resuscitation

reanimar *vt* **1** : to revive, to restore **2** : to resuscitate — **reanimarse** *vr* : to come around, to recover

reanudación *nf, pl* **-ciones** : resumption, renewal

reanudar *vt* : to resume, to renew — **reanudarse** *vr* : to resume, to continue

reaparecer {53} *vi* **1** : to reappear **2** : to make a comeback

reaparición *nf, pl* **-ciones** : reappearance

reapertura *nf* : reopening

reata *nf* **1** : rope **2** *Mex* : lasso, lariat **3 de ~** : single file

reavivar *vt* : to revive, to reawaken

rebaja *nf* **1** : reduction **2** DESCUENTO : discount **3 rebajas** *nfpl* : sale

rebajar *vt* **1** : to reduce, to lower ⟨a precios rebajados : at reduced prices, on sale⟩ **2** : to lessen, to diminish **3** : to humiliate — **rebajarse** *vr* **1** : to humble oneself **2 rebajarse a** : to stoop to

rebanada *nf* : slice

rebañar *vt* : to mop up, to sop up

rebaño *nm* **1** : flock **2** : herd

rebasar *vt* **1** : to surpass, to exceed **2** *Mex* : to pass, to overtake

rebatiña *nf* : scramble, fight (over something)

rebatir *vt* REFUTAR : to refute

rebato *nm* **1** : surprise attack **2 tocar a rebato** : to sound the alarm

rebelarse *vr* : to rebel

rebelde[1] *adj* : rebellious, unruly

rebelde[2] *nmf* **1** : rebel **2** : defaulter

rebeldía *nf* **1** : rebelliousness **2 en ~** : in default

rebelión *nf, pl* **-liones** : rebellion

rebobinar *vt* : to rewind

reborde *nm* : border, flange, rim

rebosante *adj* : brimming, overflowing ⟨rebosante de salud : brimming with health⟩

rebosar *vi* **1** : to overflow **2 ~ de** : to abound in, to be bursting with — *vt* : to radiate

rebotar *vi* **1** : to bounce **2** : to ricochet, to rebound

rebote *nm* **1** : bounce **2** : rebound, ricochet

rebozar {21} *vt* : to coat in batter

rebozo *nm* **1** : shawl, wrap **2 sin ~** : frankly, openly

rebullir {38} *v* : to move, to stir — **rebullirse** *vr*

rebuscado, -da *adj* : affected, pretentious

rebuscar {72} *vi* : to search thoroughly

rebuznar *vi* : to bray
rebuzno *nm* : bray, braying
recabar *vt* **1** : to gather, to obtain, to collect **2 recabar fondos** : to raise money
recado *nm* **1** : message ⟨mandar recado : to send word⟩ **2** *Spain* : errand
recaer {13} *vi* **1** : to relapse **2 ~ en** *or* **~ sobre** : to fall on, to fall to
recaída *nf* : relapse
recaiga, etc. → **recaer**
recalar *vi* : to arrive
recalcar {72} *vt* : to emphasize, to stress
recalcitrante *adj* : recalcitrant
recalentar {55} *vt* **1** : to reheat, to warm up **2** : to overheat
recámara *nf* **1** *Col, Mex, Pan* : bedroom **2** : chamber (of a firearm)
recamarera *nf Mex* : chambermaid
recambio *nm* **1** : spare part **2** : refill (for a pen, etc.)
recapacitar *vi* **1** : to reconsider **2 ~ en** : to reflect on, to weigh
recapitular *v* : to recapitulate — **recapitulación** *nf*
recargable *adj* : rechargeable
recargado, -da *adj* : overly elaborate or ornate
recargar {52} *vt* **1** : to recharge **2** : to overload
recargo *nm* : surcharge
recatado, -da *adj* MODESTO : modest, demure
recato *nm* PUDOR : modesty
recaudación *nf, pl* **-ciones** **1** : collection **2** : earnings *pl*, takings *pl*
recaudador, -dora *n* **recaudador de impuestos** : tax collector
recaudar *vt* : to collect
recaudo *nm* : safe place ⟨a (buen) recaudo : in safe keeping⟩
recayó, etc. → **recaer**
rece, etc. → **rezar**
recelo *nm* : distrust, suspicion
receloso, -sa *adj* : distrustful, suspicious
recepción *nf, pl* **-ciones** : reception
recepcionista *nmf* : receptionist
receptáculo *nm* : receptacle
receptividad *nf* : receptivity, receptiveness
receptivo, -va *adj* : receptive
receptor[1], -tora *adj* : receiving
receptor[2], -tora *n* **1** : recipient **2** : catcher (in baseball), receiver (in football)
receptor[3] *nm* : receiver ⟨receptor de televisión : television set⟩
recesión *nf, pl* **-siones** : recession
recesivo, -va *adj* : recessive
receso *nm* : recess, adjournment
receta *nf* **1** : recipe **2** : prescription
recetar *vt* : to prescribe (medications)
rechazar {21} *vt* **1** : to reject **2** : to turn down, to refuse
rechazo *nm* : rejection, refusal
rechifla *nf* : booing, jeering
rechinar *vi* **1** : to squeak **2** : to grind, to gnash ⟨hacer rechinar los dientes : to grind one's teeth⟩
rechoncho, -cha *adj fam* : chubby, squat
recibidor *nm* : vestibule, entrance hall
recibimiento *nm* : reception, welcome
recibir *vt* **1** : to receive, to get **2** : to welcome — *vi* : to receive visitors — **recibirse** *vr* **~ de** : to qualify as
recibo *nm* : receipt
reciclable *adj* : recyclable
reciclado → **reciclaje**
reciclaje *nm* **1** : recycling **2** : retraining
reciclar *vt* **1** : to recycle **2** : to retrain
recién *adv* **1** : newly, recently ⟨recién nacido : newborn⟩ ⟨recién casados : newlyweds⟩ ⟨recién llegado : newcomer⟩ **2** : just, only just ⟨recién ahora me acordé : I just now remembered⟩
reciente *adj* : recent — **recientemente** *adv*
recinto *nm* **1** : enclosure **2** : site, premises *pl*
recio[1] *adv* **1** : strongly, hard **2** : loudly, loud
recio[2], -cia *adj* **1** : severe, harsh **2** : tough, strong
recipiente[1] *nm* : container, receptacle
recipiente[2] *nmf* : recipient
reciprocar {72} *vi* : to reciprocate
reciprocidad *nf* : reciprocity
recíproco, -ca *adj* : reciprocal, mutual
recitación *nf, pl* **-ciones** : recitation, recital
recital *nm* : recital
recitar *vt* : to recite
reclamación *nf, pl* **-ciones** **1** : claim, demand **2** QUEJA : complaint
reclamar *vt* **1** EXIGIR : to demand, to require **2** : to claim — *vi* : to complain
reclamo *nm* **1** : bird call, lure **2** : lure, decoy **3** : inducement, attraction **4** : advertisement **5** : complaint
reclinar *vt* : to rest, to lean — **reclinarse** *vr* : to recline, to lean back
recluir {41} *vt* : to confine, to lock up — **recluirse** *vr* : to shut oneself up, to withdraw
reclusión *nf, pl* **-siones** : imprisonment
recluso, -sa *n* **1** : inmate, prisoner **2** SOLITARIO : recluse
recluta *nmf* : recruit, draftee
reclutamiento *nm* : recruitment, recruiting
reclutar *vt* ENROLAR : to recruit, to enlist
recobrar *vt* : to recover, to regain — **recobrarse** *vr* : to recover, to recuperate
recocer {14} *vt* : to overcook, to cook again
recodo *nm* : bend
recogedor *nm* : dustpan
recoger {15} *vt* **1** : to collect, to gather **2** : to get, to retrieve, to pick up **3** : to clean up, to tidy (up)
recogido, -da *adj* : quiet, secluded
recogimiento *nm* **1** : collecting, gathering **2** : withdrawal **3** : absorption, concentration

recolección *nf, pl* **-ciones** **1** : collection ⟨recolección de basura : trash pickup⟩ **2** : harvest

recolectar *vt* **1** : to gather, to collect **2** : to harvest, to pick

recomendable *adj* : advisable, recommended

recomendación *nf, pl* **-ciones** : recommendation

recomendar {55} *vt* **1** : to recommend **2** ACONSEJAR : to advise

recompensa *nf* : reward, recompense

recompensar *vt* **1** PREMIAR : to reward **2** : to compensate

reconciliación *nf, pl* **-ciones** : reconciliation

reconciliar *vt* : to reconcile — **reconciliarse** *vr*

recóndito, -ta *adj* **1** : remote, isolated **2** : hidden, recondite **3 en lo más recóndito de** : in the depths of

reconfortar *vt* : to comfort — **reconfortante** *adj*

reconocer {18} *vt* **1** : to recognize **2** : to admit **3** : to examine

reconocible *adj* : recognizable

reconocido, -da *adj* **1** : recognized, accepted **2** : grateful

reconocimiento *nm* **1** : acknowledgment, recognition, avowal **2** : (medical) examination **3** : reconnaissance

reconquista *nf* : reconquest

reconquistar *vt* **1** : to reconquer, to recapture **2** RECUPERAR : to regain, to recover

reconsiderar *vt* : to reconsider — **reconsideración** *nf*

reconstrucción *nf, pl* **-ciones** : reconstruction

reconstruir {41} *vt* : to rebuild, to reconstruct

reconversión *nf, pl* **-siones** : restructuring

reconvertir {76} *vt* **1** : to restructure **2** : to retrain

recopilación *nf, pl* **-ciones** **1** : summary **2** : collection, compilation

recopilar *vt* : to compile, to collect

récord *or* **record** [ˈrɛkɔr] *nm, pl* **récords** *or* **records** [-kɔrs] : record ⟨record mundial : world record⟩ — **récord** *or* **record** *adj*

recordar {19} *vt* **1** : to recall, to remember **2** : to remind — *vi* **1** ACORDARSE : to remember **2** DESPERTAR : to wake up

recordatorio[1], **-ria** *adj* : commemorative

recordatorio[2] *nm* : reminder

recorrer *vt* **1** : to travel through, to tour **2** : to cover (a distance) **3** : to go over, to look over

recorrido *nm* **1** : journey, trip **2** : path, route, course **3** : round (in golf)

recortar *vt* **1** : to cut, to reduce **2** : to cut out **3** : to trim, to cut off **4** : to outline — **recortarse** *vr* : to stand out ⟨los árboles se recortaban en el horizonte : the trees were silhouetted against the horizon⟩

recorte *nm* **1** : cut, reduction **2** : clipping ⟨recortes de periódicos : newspaper clippings⟩

recostar {19} *vt* : to lean, to rest — **recostarse** *vr* : to lie down, recline

recoveco *nm* **1** VUELTA : bend, turn **2** : nook, corner **3 recovecos** *nmpl* : intricacies, ins and outs

recreación *nf, pl* **-ciones** **1** : re-creation **2** DIVERSIÓN : recreation, entertainment

recrear *vt* **1** : to re-create **2** : to entertain, to amuse — **recrearse** *vr* : to enjoy oneself

recreativo, -va *adj* : recreational

recreo *nm* **1** DIVERSIÓN : entertainment, amusement **2** : recess, break

recriminación *nf, pl* **-ciones** : reproach, recrimination

recriminar *vt* : to reproach — *vi* : to recriminate — **recriminarse** *vr*

recrudecer {53} *v* : to intensify, to worsen — **recrudecerse** *vr*

rectal *adj* : rectal

rectangular *adj* : rectangular

rectángulo *nm* : rectangle

rectificación *nf, pl* **-ciones** : rectification, correction

rectificar {72} *vt* **1** : to rectify, to correct **2** : to straighten (out)

rectitud *nf* **1** : straightness **2** : honesty, rectitude

recto[1] *adv* : straight

recto[2], **-ta** *adj* **1** : straight **2** : upright, honorable **3** : sound

recto[3] *nm* : rectum

rector[1], **-tora** *adj* : governing, managing

rector[2], **-tora** *n* : rector

rectoría *nf* : rectory

recubierto *pp* → **recubrir**

recubrir {2} *vt* : to cover, to coat

recuento *nm* : recount, count ⟨un recuento de los votos : a recount of the votes⟩

recuerdo *nm* **1** : memory **2** : souvenir, memento **3 recuerdos** *nmpl* : regards

recular *vi* **1** : to back up **2** REPLEGARSE : to retreat, to fall back **3** RETRACTARSE : to back down

recuperación *nf, pl* **-ciones** **1** : recovery, recuperation **2 recuperación de datos** : data retrieval

recuperar *vt* **1** : to recover, to get back, to retrieve **2** : to recuperate **3** : to make up for ⟨recuperar el tiempo perdido : to make up for lost time⟩ — **recuperarse** *vr* **∼ de** : to recover from, to get over

recurrente *adj* : recurrent, recurring

recurrir *vi* **1 ∼ a** : to turn to, to appeal to **2 ∼ a** : to resort to **3** : to appeal (in law)

recurso *nm* **1** : recourse ⟨el último recurso : the last resort⟩ **2** : appeal (in law) **3 recursos** *nmpl* : resources, means ⟨recursos naturales : natural resources⟩

red *nf* **1** : net, mesh **2** : network, system, chain **3** : trap, snare

redacción *nf, pl* **-ciones 1** : writing, composition **2** : editing

redactar *vt* **1** : to write, to draft **2** : to edit

redactor, -tora *n* : editor

redada *nf* **1** : raid **2** : catch, haul

redefinir *vt* : to redefine — **redefinición** *nf*

redención *nf, pl* **-ciones** : redemption

redentor[1], **-tora** *adj* : redeeming

redentor[2], **-tora** *n* : redeemer

redescubierto *pp* → **redescubrir**

redescubrir {2} *vt* : to rediscover

redicho, -cha *adj fam* : affected, pretentious

redil *nm* **1** : sheepfold **2 volver al redil** : to return to the fold

redimir *vt* : to redeem, to deliver (from sin)

rediseñar *vt* : to redesign

redistribuir {41} *vt* : to redistribute — **redistribución** *nf*

rédito *nm* : return, yield

redituar {3} *vt* : to produce, to yield

redoblar *vt* : to redouble, to strengthen — **redoblado, -da** *adj*

redoble *nm* : drum roll

redomado, -da *adj* **1** : sly, crafty **2** : utter, out-and-out

redonda *nf* **1** : region, surrounding area **2 a la redonda** ALREDEDOR : around ⟨de diez millas a la redonda : for ten miles around⟩

redondear *vt* : to round off, to round out

redondel *nm* **1** : ring, circle **2** : bullring, arena

redondez *nf* : roundness

redondo, -da *adj* **1** : round ⟨mesa redonda : round table⟩ **2** : great, perfect ⟨un negocio redondo : an excellent deal⟩ **3** : straightforward, flat ⟨un rechazo redondo : a flat refusal⟩ **4** *Mex* : round-trip **5 en ∼** : around

reducción *nf, pl* **-ciones** : reduction, decrease

reducido, -da *adj* **1** : reduced, limited **2** : small

reducir {61} *vt* **1** DISMINUIR : to reduce, to decrease, to cut **2** : to subdue **3** : to boil down — **reducirse** *vr* **∼ a** : to come down to, to be nothing more than

redundancia *nf* : redundancy

redundante *adj* : redundant

reedición *nf, pl* **-ciones** : reprint

reelegir {28} *vt* : to reelect — **reelección** *nf*

reembolsable *adj* : refundable

reembolsar *vt* **1** : to refund, to reimburse **2** : to repay

reembolso *nm* : refund, reimbursement

reemplazable *adj* : replaceable

reemplazar {21} *vt* : to replace, to substitute

reemplazo *nm* : replacement, substitution

reencarnación *nf, pl* **-ciones** : reincarnation

reencuentro *nm* : reunion

reestablecer {53} *vt* : to reestablish

reestructurar *vt* : to restructure

reexaminar *vt* : to reexamine

refaccionar *vt* : to repair, to renovate

refacciones *nfpl* : repairs, renovations

referencia *nf* **1** : reference **2 hacer referencia a** : to refer to

referendo → **referéndum**

referéndum *nm, pl* **-dums** : referendum

referente *adj* **∼ a** : concerning

réferi *or* **referi** [ˈrɛfɛri] *nmf* : referee

referir {76} *vt* **1** : to relate, to tell **2** : to refer ⟨nos refirió al diccionario : she referred us to the dictionary⟩ — **referirse** *vr* **∼ a 1** : to refer to **2 ∼ a** : to be concerned, to be in reference to ⟨en lo que se refiere a la educación : as far as education is concerned⟩

refinado[1], **-da** *adj* : refined

refinado[2] *nm* : refining

refinamiento *nm* **1** : refining **2** FINURA : refinement

refinanciar *vt* : to refinance

refinar *vt* : to refine

refinería *nf* : refinery

reflectante *adj* : reflective, reflecting

reflector[1], **-tora** *adj* : reflecting

reflector[2] *nm* **1** : spotlight, searchlight **2** : reflector

reflejar *vt* : to reflect — **reflejarse** *vr* : to be reflected ⟨la decepción se refleja en su rostro : the disappointment shows on her face⟩

reflejo *nm* **1** : reflection **2** : reflex **3 reflejos** *nmpl* : highlights, streaks (in hair)

reflexión *nf, pl* **-xiones** : reflection, thought

reflexionar *vi* : to reflect, to think

reflexivo, -va *adj* **1** : reflective, thoughtful **2** : reflexive

reflujo *nm* : ebb, ebb tide

reforma *nf* **1** : reform **2** : alteration, renovation

reformador, -dora *n* : reformer

reformar *vt* **1** : to reform **2** : to change, to alter **3** : to renovate, to repair — **reformarse** *vr* : to mend one's ways

reformatorio *nm* : reformatory

reformular *vt* : to reformulate — **reformulación** *nf*

reforzar {36} *vt* **1** : to reinforce, to strengthen **2** : to encourage, to support

refracción *nf, pl* **-ciones** : refraction

refractar *vt* : to refract — **refractarse** *vr*

refractario, -ria *adj* : refractory, obstinate

refrán *nm, pl* **refranes** ADAGIO : proverb, saying

refregar {49} *vt* : to scrub

refrenar *vt* **1** : to rein in (a horse) **2** : to restrain, to check — **refrenarse** *vr* : to restrain oneself

refrendar *vt* **1** : to countersign, to endorse **2** : to stamp (a passport)

refrescante *adj* : refreshing

refrescar {72} *vt* **1** : to refresh, to cool **2** : to brush up (on) **3 refrescar la memoria** : to refresh one's memory — *vi* : to turn cooler
refresco *nm* : refreshment, soft drink
refriega *nf* : skirmish, scuffle
refrigeración *nf, pl* **-ciones 1** : refrigeration **2** : air-conditioning
refrigerador *nmf* NEVERA : refrigerator
refrigeradora *nf Col, Peru* : refrigerator
refrigerante *nm* : coolant
refrigerar *vt* **1** : to refrigerate **2** : to air-condition
refrigerio *nm* : snack, refreshments *pl*
refrito[1], **-ta** *adj* : refried
refrito[2] *nm* : rehash
refuerzo *nm* : reinforcement, support
refugiado, -da *n* : refugee
refugiar *vt* : to shelter — **refugiarse** *vr* ACOGERSE : to take refuge
refugio *nm* : refuge, shelter
refulgencia *nf* : brilliance, splendor
refulgir {35} *vi* : to shine brightly
refundir *vt* **1** : to recast (metals) **2** : to revise, to rewrite
refunfuñar *vi* : to grumble, to groan
refutar *vt* : to refute — **refutación** *nf*
regadera *nf* **1** : watering can **2** : shower head, shower **3** : sprinkler
regaderazo *nm Mex* : shower
regalar *vt* **1** OBSEQUIAR : to present (as a gift), to give away **2** : to regale, to entertain **3** : to flatter, to make a fuss over — **regalarse** *vr* : to pamper oneself
regalía *nf* : royalty, payment
regaliz *nm, pl* **-lices** : licorice
regalo *nm* **1** OBSEQUIO : gift, present **2** : pleasure, comfort **3** : treat
regañadientes *mpl* **a ~** : reluctantly, unwillingly
regañar *vt* : to scold, to give a talking to — *vi* **1** QUEJARSE : to grumble, to complain **2** REÑIR : to quarrel, to argue
regaño *nm fam* : scolding
regañon, -ñona *adj, mpl* **-ñones** *fam* : grumpy, irritable
regar {49} *vt* **1** : to irrigate **2** : to water **3** : to wash, to hose down **4** : to spill, to scatter
regata *nf* : regatta, yacht race
regate *nm* : dodge, feint
regatear *vt* **1** : to haggle over **2** ESCATIMAR : to skimp on, to be sparing with — *vi* : to bargain, to haggle
regateo *nm* : bargaining, haggling
regatón *nm, pl* **-tones** : ferrule, tip
regazo *nm* : lap (of a person)
regencia *nf* : regency
regenerar *vt* : to regenerate — **regenerarse** *vr* — **regeneración** *nf*
regentar *vt* : to run, to manage
regente *nmf* : regent
regidor, -dora *n* : town councillor
régimen *nm, pl* **regímenes 1** : regime **2** : diet **3** : regimen, rules *pl* ⟨régimen de vida : lifestyle⟩
regimiento *nm* : regiment
regio, -gia *adj* **1** : great, magnificent **2** : regal, royal
región *nf, pl* **regiones** : region, area
regional *adj* : regional — **regionalmente** *adv*
regir {28} *vt* **1** : to rule **2** : to manage, to run **3** : to control, to govern ⟨las costumbres que rigen la conducta : the customs which govern behavior⟩ — *vi* : to apply, to be in force ⟨las leyes rigen en los tres países : the laws apply in all three countries⟩ — **regirse** *vr* **~ por** : to go by, to be guided by
registrador[1], **-dora** *adj* **caja registradora** : cash register
registrador[2], **-dora** *n* : registrar, recorder
registrar *vt* **1** : to register, to record **2** GRABAR : to record, to tape **3** : to search, to examine — **registrarse** *vr* **1** INSCRIBIRSE : to register **2** OCURRIR : to happen, to occur
registro *nm* **1** : register **2** : registration **3** : registry, record office **4** : range (of a voice or musical instrument) **5** : search
regla *nf* **1** NORMA : rule, regulation **2** : ruler ⟨regla de cálculo : slide rule⟩ **3** MENSTRUACIÓN : period, menstruation
reglamentación *nf, pl* **-ciones 1** : regulation **2** : rules *pl*
reglamentar *vt* : to regulate, to set rules for
reglamentario, -ria *adj* : regulation, official ⟨equipo reglamentario : standard equipment⟩
reglamento *nm* : regulations *pl*, rules *pl* ⟨reglamento de tráfico : traffic regulations⟩
regocijar *vt* : to gladden, to delight — **regocijarse** *vr* : to rejoice
regocijo *nm* : delight, rejoicing
regordete, -ta *adj fam* LLENITO : chubby
regresar *vt* DEVOLVER : to give back — *vi* : to return, to come back, to go back
regresión *nf, pl* **-siones** : regression, return
regresivo, -va *adj* : regressive
regreso *nm* **1** : return **2 estar de regreso** : to be back, to be home
reguero *nm* **1** : irrigation ditch **2** : trail, trace **3 propagarse como reguero de pólvora** : to spread like wildfire
regulable *adj* : adjustable
regulación *nf, pl* **-ciones** : regulation, control
regulador[1], **-dora** *adj* : regulating, regulatory
regulador[2] *nm* **1** : regulator, governor **2 regulador de tiro** : damper (in a chimney)
regular[1] *vt* : to regulate, to control
regular[2] *adj* **1** : regular **2** : fair, OK, so-so **3** : medium, average **4 por lo regular** : in general, generally
regularidad *nf* : regularity

regularización *nf, pl* **-ciones** NORMALIZACIÓN : normalization

regularizar {21} *vt* NORMALIZAR : to normalize, to make regular

regularmente *adv* : regularly

regusto *nm* : aftertaste

rehabilitar *vt* **1** : to rehabilitate **2** : to reinstate **3** : renovate, to restore — **rehabilitación** *nf*

rehacer {40} *vt* **1** : to redo **2** : to remake, to repair, to renew — **rehacerse** *vr* **1** : to recover **2 ~ de** : to get over

rehecho *pp* → **rehacer**

rehén *nm, pl* **rehenes** : hostage

rehicieron, etc. → **rehacer**

rehizo → **rehacer**

rehuir {41} *vt* : to avoid, to shun

rehusar {8} *v* : to refuse

reimprimir *vt* : to reprint

reina *nf* : queen

reinado *nm* : reign

reinante *adj* **1** : reigning **2** : prevailing, current

reinar *vi* **1** : to reign **2** : to prevail

reincidencia *nf* : recidivism, relapse

reincidente *nmf* : backslider, recidivist

reincidir *vi* : to backslide, to retrogress

reincorporar *vt* : to reinstate — **reincorporarse** *vr* **~ a** : to return to, to rejoin

reiniciar *vt* **1** : to resume, to restart **2** : to reboot (a computer)

reino *nm* : kingdom, realm ⟨reino animal : animal kingdom⟩

reinstalar *vt* **1** : to reinstall **2** : to reinstate

reintegración *nf, pl* **-ciones** **1** : reinstatement, reintegration **2** : refund, reimbursement

reintegrar *vt* **1** : to reintegrate, reinstate **2** : to refund, to reimburse — **reintegrarse** *vr* **~ a** : to return to, to rejoin

reír {66} *vi* : to laugh — *vt* : to laugh at — **reírse** *vr*

reiteración *nf, pl* **-ciones** : reiteration, repetition

reiterado, -da *adj* : repeated ⟨lo explicó en reiteradas ocasiones : he explained it repeatedly⟩ — **reiteradamente** *adv*

reiterar *vt* : to reiterate, to repeat

reiterativo, -va *adj* : repetitive, repetitious

reivindicación *nf, pl* **-ciones** **1** : demand, claim **2** : vindication

reivindicar {72} *vt* **1** : to vindicate **2** : to demand, to claim **3** : to restore

reja *nf* **1** : grille, grating ⟨entre rejas : behind bars⟩ **2** : plowshare

rejilla *nf* : grille, grate, screen

rejuvenecer {53} *vt* : to rejuvenate — *vi* : to be rejuvenated — **rejuvenecerse** *vr*

rejuvenecimiento *nm* : rejuvenation

relación *nf, pl* **-ciones** **1** : relation, connection, relevance **2** : relationship **3** RELATO : account **4** LISTA : list **5 con relación a** *or* **en relación con** : in relation to, concerning **6 relaciones públicas** : public relations

relacionar *vt* : to relate, to connect — **relacionarse** *vr* **~ con** : to be connected to, to be linked with

relajación *nf, pl* **-ciones** : relaxation

relajado, -da *adj* **1** : relaxed, loose **2** : dissolute, depraved

relajante *adj* : relaxing

relajar *vt* : to relax, to slacken — *vi* : to be relaxing — **relajarse** *vr*

relajo *nm* **1** : commotion, ruckus **2** : joke, laugh ⟨lo hizo de relajo : he did it for a laugh⟩

relamerse *vr* : to smack one's lips, to lick one's chops

relámpago *nm* : flash of lightning

relampaguear *vi* : to flash

relanzar {21} *vt* : to relaunch

relatar *vt* : to relate, to tell

relatividad *nf* : relativity

relativo, -va *adj* **1** : relative **2 en lo relativo a** : with regard to, concerning — **relativamente** *adv*

relato *nm* **1** : story, tale **2** : account

releer {20} *vt* : to reread

relegar {52} *vt* **1** : to relegate **2 relegar al olvido** : to consign to oblivion

relevante *adj* : outstanding, important

relevar *vt* **1** : to relieve, to take over from **2 ~ de** : to exempt from — **relevarse** *vr* : to take turns

relevo *nm* **1** : relief, replacement **2** : relay ⟨carrera de relevos : relay race⟩

relicario *nm* **1** : reliquary **2** : locket

relieve *nm* **1** : relief, projection ⟨mapa en relieve : relief map⟩ ⟨letras en relieve : embossed letters⟩ **2** : prominence, importance **3 poner en relieve** : to highlight, to emphasize

religión *nf, pl* **-giones** : religion

religiosamente *adv* : religiously, faithfully

religioso[1], **-sa** *adj* : religious

religioso[2], **-sa** *n* : monk *m*, nun *f*

relinchar *vi* : to neigh, to whinny

relincho *nm* : neigh, whinny

reliquia *nf* **1** : relic **2 reliquia de familia** : family heirloom

rellenar *vt* **1** : to refill **2** : to stuff, to fill **3** : to fill out

relleno[1], **-na** *adj* : stuffed, filled

relleno[2] *nm* : stuffing, filling

reloj *nm* **1** : clock **2** : watch **3 reloj de arena** : hourglass **4 reloj de pulsera** : wristwatch **5 como un reloj** : like clockwork

relojería *nf* **1** : watchmaker's shop **2** : watchmaking, clockmaking

reluciente *adj* : brilliant, shining

relucir {45} *vi* **1** : to glitter, to shine **2 salir a relucir** : to come to the surface **3 sacar a relucir** : to bring up, to mention

relumbrante *adj* : dazzling

relumbrar *vi* : to shine brightly

relumbrón *nm, pl* **-brones** **1** : flash, glare **2 de ~** : flashy, showy

remachar *vt* **1** : to rivet **2** : to clinch (a nail) **3** : to stress, to drive home — *vi* : to smash, to spike (a ball)

remache *nm* **1** : rivet **2** : smash, spike (in sports)

remanente *nm* **1** : remainder, balance **2** : surplus

remanso *nm* : pool

remar *vi* **1** : to row, to paddle **2** : to struggle, to toil

remarcar {72} *vt* : to emphasize, to stress

rematado, -da *adj* : utter, complete

rematador, -dora *n* : auctioneer

rematar *vt* **1** : to finish off **2** : to auction — *vi* **1** : to shoot **2** : to end

remate *nm* **1** : shot (in sports) **2** : auction **3** : end, conclusion **4 como ~** : to top it off **5 de ~** : completely, utterly

remecer {86} *vt* : to sway, to swing

remedar *vt* **1** IMITAR : to imitate, to copy **2** : to mimic, to ape

remediar *vt* **1** : to remedy, to repair **2** : to help out, to assist **3** EVITAR : to prevent, to avoid

remedio *nm* **1** : remedy, cure **2** : solution **3** : option ⟨no me quedó más remedio : I had no other choice⟩ ⟨no hay remedio : it can't be helped⟩ **4 poner remedio a** : to put a stop to **5 sin ~** : unavoidable, inevitable

remedo *nm* : imitation

rememorar *vi* : to recall ⟨rememorar los viejos tiempos : to reminisce⟩

remendar {55} *vt* **1** : to mend, to patch, to darn **2** : to correct

remero, -ra *n* : rower

remesa *nf* **1** : remittance **2** : shipment

remezón *nm, pl* **-zones** : mild earthquake, tremor

remiendo *nm* **1** : patch **2** : correction

remilgado, -da *adj* **1** : prim, prudish **2** : affected

remilgo *nm* : primness, affectation

reminiscencia *nf* : reminiscence

remisión *nf, pl* **-siones** **1** ENVÍO : sending, delivery **2** : remission **3** : reference, cross-reference

remiso, -sa *adj* **1** : lax, remiss **2** : reluctant

remitente[1] *nm* : return address

remitente[2] *nmf* : sender (of a letter, etc.)

remitir *vt* **1** : to send, to remit **2 ~ a** : to refer to, to direct to ⟨nos remitió al diccionario : he referred us to the dictionary⟩ — *vi* : to subside, to let up

remo *nm* **1** : paddle, oar **2** : rowing (sport)

remoción *nf, pl* **-ciones** **1** : removal **2** : dismissal

remodelación *nf, pl* **-ciones** **1** : remodeling **2** : reorganization, restructuring

remodelar *vt* **1** : to remodel **2** : to restructure

remojar *vt* **1** : to soak, to steep **2** : to dip, to dunk **3** : to celebrate with a drink

remojo *nm* **1** : soaking, steeping **2 poner en remojo** : to soak, to leave soaking

remolacha *nf* : beet

remolcador *nm* : tugboat

remolcar {72} *vt* : to tow, to haul

remolino *nm* **1** : whirlwind **2** : eddy, whirlpool **3** : crowd, throng **4** : cowlick

remolque *nm* **1** : towing, tow **2** : trailer **3 a ~** : in tow

remontar *vt* **1** : to overcome **2** SUBIR : to go up — **remontarse** *vr* **1** : to soar **2 ~ a** : to date from, to go back to

rémora *nf* : obstacle, hindrance

remorder {47} *vt* INQUIETAR : to trouble, to distress

remordimiento *nm* : remorse

remotamente *adv* : remotely, vaguely

remoto, -ta *adj* **1** : remote, unlikely ⟨hay una posibilidad remota : there is a slim possibility⟩ **2** : distant, far-off

remover {47} *vt* **1** : to stir **2** : to move around, to turn over **3** : to stir up **4** : to remove **5** : to dismiss

remozamiento *nm* : renovation

remozar {21} *vt* **1** : to renew, to brighten up **2** : to redo, to renovate

remuneración *nf, pl* **-ciones** : remuneration, pay

remunerar *vt* : to pay, to remunerate

remunerativo, -va *adj* : remunerative

renacer {48} *vi* : to be reborn, to revive

renacimiento *nm* **1** : rebirth, revival **2 el Renacimiento** : the Renaissance

renacuajo *nm* : tadpole, pollywog

renal *adj* : renal, kidney

rencilla *nf* : quarrel

renco, -ca *adj* : lame

rencor *nm* **1** : rancor, enmity, hostility **2 guardar rencor** : to hold a grudge

rencoroso, -sa *adj* : resentful, rancorous

rendición *nf, pl* **-ciones** **1** : surrender, submission **2** : yield, return

rendido, -da *adj* **1** : submissive **2** : worn-out, exhausted **3** : devoted

rendija *nf* GRIETA : crack, split

rendimiento *nm* **1** : performance **2** : yield

rendir {54} *vt* **1** : to render, to give ⟨rendir las gracias : to give thanks⟩ ⟨rendir homenaje a : to pay homage to⟩ **2** : to yield **3** CANSAR : to exhaust — *vi* **1** CUNDIR : to progress, to make headway **2** : to last, to go a long way — **rendirse** *vr* : to surrender, to give up

renegado, -da *n* : renegade

renegar {49} *vi* **1 ~ de** : to renounce, to disown, to give up **2 ~ de** : to complain about — *vt* **1** : to deny vigorously **2** : to abhor, to hate

renegociar *vt* : to renegotiate — **renegociación** *nf*

renglón *nm, pl* **renglones** **1** : line (of writing) **2** : merchandise, line (of products)

rengo, -ga *adj* : lame

renguear *vi* : to limp

reno *nm* : reindeer

renombrado, -da *adj* : renowned, famous

renombre *nm* NOMBRADÍA : renown, fame

renovable *adj* : renewable

renovación *nf, pl* **-ciones 1** : renewal ⟨renovación de un contrato : renewal of a contract⟩ **2** : change, renovation

renovar {19} *vt* **1** : to renew, to restore **2** : to renovate

renquear *vi* : to limp, to hobble

renquera *nf* COJERA : limp, lameness

renta *nf* **1** : income **2** : rent **3 impuesto sobre la renta** : income tax

rentable *adj* : profitable

rentar *vt* **1** : to produce, to yield **2** ALQUILAR : to rent

renuencia *nf* : reluctance, unwillingness

renuente *adj* : reluctant, unwilling

renuncia *nf* **1** : resignation **2** : renunciation **3** : waiver

renunciar *vi* **1** : to resign **2 ~ a** : to renounce, to relinquish ⟨renunció al título : herelinquished the title⟩

reñido, -da *adj* **1** : tough, hard-fought **2** : at odds, on bad terms

reñir {67} *vi* **1** : to argue **2 ~ con** : to fall out with, to go up against — *vt* : to scold, to reprimand

reo, rea *n* **1** : accused, defendant **2** : offender, culprit

reojo *nm* **de ~** : out of the corner of one's eye ⟨una mirada de reojo : a sidelong glance⟩

reorganizar {21} *vt* : to reorganize — **reorganización** *nf*

repantigarse {52} *vr* : to slouch, to loll about

reparación *nf, pl* **-ciones 1** : reparation, amends **2** : repair

reparar *vt* **1** : to repair, to fix, to mend **2** : to make amends for **3** : to correct **4** : to restore, to refresh — *vi* **1 ~ en** : to observe, to take notice of **2 ~ en** : to consider, to think about

reparo *nm* **1** : repair, restoration **2** : reservation, qualm ⟨no tuvieron reparos en decírmelo : they didn't hesitate to tell me⟩ **3 poner reparos a** : to find fault with, to object to

repartición *nf, pl* **-ciones 1** : distribution **2** : department, division

repartidor[1], **-dora** *adj* : delivery ⟨camión repartidor : delivery truck⟩

repartidor[2], **-dora** *n* : delivery person, distributor

repartimiento *nm* → **repartición**

repartir *vt* **1** : to allocate **2** DISTRIBUIR : to distribute, to hand out **3** : to spread

reparto *nm* **1** : allocation **2** : distribution **3** : cast (of characters)

repasar *vt* **1** : to pass by again **2** : to review, to go over **3** : to mend

repaso *nm* **1** : review **2** : mending **3** : checkup, overhaul

repatriar {85} *vt* : to repatriate — **repatriación** *nf*

repavimentar *vt* : to resurface

repelente[1] *adj* : repellent, repulsive

repelente[2] *nm* : repellent ⟨repelente de insectos : insect repellent⟩

repeler *vt* **1** : to repel, to resist, to repulse **2** : to reject **3** : to disgust ⟨el sabor me repele : I find the taste repulsive⟩

repensar {55} *v* : to rethink, to reconsider

repente *nm* **1** : sudden movement, start ⟨de repente : suddenly⟩ **2** : fit, outburst ⟨un repente de ira : a fit of anger⟩

repentino, -na *adj* : sudden — **repentinamente** *adv*

repercusión *nf, pl* **-siones** : repercussion

repercutir *vi* **1** : to reverberate, to echo **2 ~ en** : to have effects on, to have repercussions on

repertorio *nm* : repertoire

repetición *nf, pl* **-ciones 1** : repetition **2** : rerun, repeat

repetidamente *adv* : repeatedly

repetido, -da *adj* **1** : repeated, numerous **2 repetidas veces** : repeatedly, time and again

repetir {54} *vt* **1** : to repeat **2** : to have a second helping of — **repetirse** *vr* **1** : to repeat oneself **2** : to recur

repetitivo, -va *adj* : repetitive, repetitious

repicar {72} *vt* : to ring — *vi* : to ring out, to peal

repique *nm* : ringing, pealing

repisa *nf* : shelf, ledge ⟨repisa de chimenea : mantelpiece⟩ ⟨repisa de ventana : windowsill⟩

replantear *vt* : to redefine, to restate — **replantearse** *vr* : to reconsider

replegar {49} *vt* : to fold — **replegarse** *vr* RETIRARSE : to retreat, to withdraw

repleto, -ta *adj* **1** : replete, full **2 ~ de** : packed with, crammed with

réplica *nf* **1** : reply **2** : replica, reproduction **3** *Chile, Mex* : aftershock

replicación *nf, pl* **-ciones** : replication

replicar {72} *vi* **1** : to reply, to retort **2** : to argue, to answer back

repliegue *nm* **1** : fold **2** : retreat, withdrawal

repollo *nm* COL : cabbage

reponer {60} *vt* **1** : to replace, to put back **2** : to reinstate **3** : to reply — **reponerse** *vr* : to recover

reportaje *nm* : article, story, report

reportar *vt* **1** : to check, to restrain **2** : to bring, to carry, to yield ⟨me reportó numerosos beneficios : it brought me many benefits⟩ **3** : to report — **reportarse** *vr* **1** CONTENERSE : to control oneself **2** PRESENTARSE : to report, to show up

reporte *nm* : report

reportear *vt* : to report on, to cover

reportero, -ra *n* **1** : reporter **2 reportero gráfico** : photojournalist
reposado, -da *adj* : calm
reposar *vi* **1** : to rest, to repose **2** : to stand, to settle ⟨deje reposar la masa media hora : let the dough stand for half an hour⟩ **3** : to lie, to be buried — **reposarse** *vr* : to settle
reposición *nf, pl* **-ciones** **1** : replacement **2** : reinstatement **3** : revival
repositorio *nm* : repository
reposo *nm* : repose, rest
repostar *vi* **1** : to stock up **2** : to refuel
repostería *nf* **1** : confectioner's shop **2** : pastry-making
repostero, -ra *n* : confectioner
repreguntar *vt* : to cross-examine
repreguntas *nfpl* : cross-examination
reprender *vt* : to reprimand, to scold
reprensible *adj* : reprehensible
represa *nf* : dam
represalia *nf* **1** : reprisal, retaliation **2 tomar represalias** : to retaliate
represar *vt* : to dam
representación *nf, pl* **-ciones** **1** : representation **2** : performance **3 en representación de** : on behalf of
representante *nmf* **1** : representative **2** : performer
representar *vt* **1** : to represent, to act for **2** : to perform **3** : to look, to appear as **4** : to symbolize, to stand for **5** : to signify, to mean — **representarse** *vr* : to imagine, to picture
representativo, -va *adj* : representative
represión *nf, pl* **-siones** : repression
represivo, -va *adj* : repressive
reprimenda *nf* : reprimand
reprimir *vt* **1** : to repress **2** : to suppress, to stifle
reprobable *adj* : reprehensible, culpable
reprobación *nf* : disapproval
reprobar {19} *vt* **1** DESAPROBAR : to condemn, to disapprove of **2** : to fail (a course)
reprobatorio, -ria *adj* : disapproving, admonitory
reprochable *adj* : reprehensible, reproachable
reprochar *vt* : to reproach — **reprocharse** *vr*
reproche *nm* : reproach
reproducción *nf, pl* **-ciones** : reproduction
reproducir {61} *vt* : to reproduce — **reproducirse** *vr* **1** : to breed, to reproduce **2** : to recur
reproductor, -tora *adj* : reproductive
reptar *vi* : to crawl, to slither
reptil^{1} *adj* : reptilian
reptil^{2} *nm* : reptile
república *nf* : republic
republicanismo *nm* : republicanism
republicano, -na *adj & n* : republican
repudiar *vt* : to repudiate — **repudiación** *nf*
repudio *nm* : repudiation
repuesto^{1} *pp* → **reponer**
repuesto^{2} *nm* **1** : spare part **2 de ~** : spare ⟨rueda de repuesto : spare wheel⟩
repugnancia *nf* : repugnance
repugnante *adj* : repulsive, repugnant, revolting
repugnar *vt* : to cause repugnance, to disgust — **repugnarse** *vr*
repujar *vt* : to emboss
repulsivo, -va *adj* : repulsive
repuntar *vt Arg, Chile* : to round up (cattle) — *vi* : to begin to appear — **repuntarse** *vr* : to fall out, to quarrel
repuso, etc. → **reponer**
reputación *nf, pl* **-ciones** : reputation
reputar *vt* : to consider, to deem
requerir {76} *vt* **1** : to require, to call for **2** : to summon, to send for
requesón *nm, pl* **-sones** : curd cheese, cottage cheese
réquiem *nm* : requiem
requisa *nf* **1** : requisition **2** : seizure **3** : inspection
requisar *vt* **1** : to requisition **2** : to seize **3** INSPECCIONAR : to inspect
requisito *nm* **1** : requirement **2 requisito previo** : prerequisite
res *nf* **1** : beast, animal **2** *CA, Mex* : beef **3 reses** *nfpl* : cattle ⟨60 reses : 60 head of cattle⟩
resabio *nm* **1** VICIO : bad habit, vice **2** DEJO : aftertaste
resaca *nf* **1** : undertow **2** : hangover
resaltar *vi* **1** SOBRESALIR : to stand out **2 hacer resaltar** : to bring out, to highlight — *vt* : to stress, to emphasize
resarcimiento *nm* **1** : compensation **2** : reimbursement
resarcir {83} *vt* : to compensate, to indemnify — **resarcirse** *vr* **~ de** : to make up for
resbaladizo, -za *adj* **1** RESBALOSO : slippery **2** : tricky, ticklish, delicate
resbalar *vi* **1** : to slip, to slide **2** : to slip up, to make a mistake **3** : to skid — **resbalarse** *vr*
resbalón *nm, pl* **-lones** : slip
resbaloso, -sa *adj* : slippery
rescatar *vt* **1** : to rescue, to save **2** : to recover, to get back
rescate *nm* **1** : rescue **2** : recovery **3** : ransom
rescindir *vt* : to rescind, to annul, to cancel
rescisión *nf, pl* **-siones** : annulment, cancellation
rescoldo *nm* : embers *pl*
resecar {72} *vt* : to make dry, to dry up — **resecarse** *vr* : to dry up
reseco, -ca *adj* : dry, dried-up
resentido, -da *adj* : resentful
resentimiento *nm* : resentment
resentirse {76} *vr* **1** : to suffer, to be weakened **2** OFENDERSE : to be upset ⟨se resintió porque la insultaron : she got upset when they insulted her, she resented being insulted⟩ **3 ~ de** : to feel the effects of

reseña *nf* **1** : report, summary, review **2** : description

reseñar *vt* **1** : to review **2** DESCRIBIR : to describe

reserva *nf* **1** : reservation **2** : reserve **3** : confidence, privacy ⟨con la mayor reserva : in strictest confidence⟩ **4 de ~** : spare, in reserve **5 reservas** *nfpl* : reservations, doubts

reservación *nf, pl* **-ciones** : reservation

reservado, -da *adj* **1** : reserved, reticent **2** : confidential

reservar *vt* : to reserve — **reservarse** *vr* **1** : to save oneself **2** : to conceal, to keep to oneself

reservorio *nm* : reservoir, reserve

resfriado *nm* CATARRO : cold

resfriar {85} *vt* : to cool — **resfriarse** *vr* **1** : to cool off **2** : to catch a cold

resfrío *nm* : cold

resguardar *vt* : to safeguard, to protect — **resguardarse** *vr*

resguardo *nm* **1** : safeguard, protection **2** : receipt, voucher **3** : border guard, coast guard

residencia *nf* **1** : residence **2** : boarding house

residencial *adj* : residential

residente *adj & nmf* : resident

residir *vi* **1** VIVIR : to reside, to dwell **2 ~ en** : to lie in, to consist of

residual *adj* : residual

residuo *nm* **1** : residue **2** : remainder **3 residuos** *nmpl* : waste ⟨residuos nucleares : nuclear waste⟩

resignación *nf, pl* **-ciones** : resignation

resignar *vt* : to resign — **resignarse** *vr* **~ a** : to resign oneself to

resina *nf* **1** : resin **2 resina epoxídica** : epoxy

resistencia *nf* **1** : resistance **2** AGUANTE : endurance, strength, stamina

resistente *adj* **1** : resistant **2** : strong, tough

resistir *vt* **1** : to stand, to bear, to tolerate **2** : to withstand — *vi* : to resist ⟨resistió hasta el último minuto : he held out until the last minute⟩ — **resistirse** *vr* **~ a** : to be resistant to, to be reluctant

resollar {19} *vi* : to breathe heavily, to wheeze

resolución *nf, pl* **-ciones** **1** : resolution, settlement **2** : decision **3** : determination, resolve

resolver {89} *vt* **1** : to resolve, to settle **2** : to decide — **resolverse** *vr* : to make up one's mind

resonancia *nf* **1** : resonance **2** : impact, repercussions *pl*

resonante *adj* **1** : resonant **2** : tremendous, resounding ⟨un éxito resonante : a resounding success⟩

resonar {19} *vi* : to resound, to ring

resoplar *vi* **1** : to puff, to pant **2** : to snort

resoplo *nm* **1** : puffing, panting **2** : snort

resorte *nm* **1** MUELLE : spring **2** : elasticity **3** : influence, means *pl* ⟨tocar resortes : to pull strings⟩

resortera *nf Mex* : slingshot

respaldar *vt* : to back, to support, to endorse — **respaldarse** *vr* : to lean back

respaldo *nm* **1** : back (of an object) **2** : support, backing

respectar *vt* : to concern, to relate to ⟨por lo que a mí respecta : as far as I'm concerned⟩

respectivo, -va *adj* : respective — **respectivamente** *adv*

respecto *nm* **1 ~ a** : in regard to, concerning **2 al respecto** : on this matter, in this respect

respetable *adj* : respectable — **respetabilidad** *nf*

respetar *vt* : to respect

respeto *nm* **1** : respect, consideration **2 respetos** *nmpl* : respects ⟨presentar sus respetos : to pay one's respects⟩

respetuosidad *nf* : respectfulness

respetuoso, -sa *adj* : respectful — **respetuosamente** *adv*

respingo *nm* : start, jump

respiración *nf, pl* **-ciones** : respiration, breathing

respiradero *nm* : vent, ventilation shaft

respirador *nm* : respirator

respirar *v* : to breathe

respiratorio, -ria *adj* : respiratory

respiro *nm* **1** : breath **2** : respite, break

resplandecer {53} *vi* **1** : to shine **2** : to stand out

resplandeciente *adj* **1** : resplendent, shining **2** : radiant

resplandor *nm* **1** : brightness, brilliance, radiance **2** : flash

responder *vt* : to answer — *vi* **1** : to answer, to reply, to respond **2 ~ a** : to respond to ⟨responder al tratamiento : to respond to treatment⟩ **3 ~ de** : to answer for, to vouch for (something) **4 ~ por** : to vouch for (someone)

responsabilidad *nf* : responsibility

responsable *adj* : responsible — **responsablemente** *adv*

respuesta *nf* : answer, response

resquebrajar *vt* : to split, to crack — **resquebrajarse** *vr*

resquemor *nm* : resentment, bitterness

resquicio *nm* **1** : crack **2** : opportunity, chance **3** : trace ⟨sin un resquicio de remordimiento : without a trace of remorse⟩ **4 resquicio legal** : loophole

resta *nf* SUSTRACCIÓN : subtraction

restablecer {53} *vt* : to reestablish, to restore — **restablecerse** *vr* : to recover

restablecimiento *nm* **1** : reestablishment, restoration **2** : recovery

restallar *vi* : to crack, to crackle, to click

restallido *nm* : crack, crackle

restante *adj* **1** : remaining **2 lo restante, los restantes** : the rest

restañar *vt* : to stanch

restar *vt* **1** : to deduct, to subtract ⟨restar un punto : to deduct a point⟩

2 : to minimize, to play down — *vi* : to remain, to be left
restauración *nf, pl* **-ciones** **1** : restoration **2** : catering, food service
restaurante *nm* : restaurant
restaurar *vt* : to restore
restitución *nf, pl* **-ciones** : restitution, return
restituir {41} *vt* : to return, to restore, to reinstate
resto *nm* **1** : rest, remainder **2 restos** *nmpl* : remains ⟨restos de comida : leftovers⟩ ⟨restos arqueológicos : archeological ruins⟩ **3 restos mortales** : mortal remains
restorán *nm, pl* **-ranes** : restaurant
restregadura *nf* : scrub, scrubbing
restregar {49} *vt* **1** : to rub **2** : to scrub — **restregarse** *vr*
restricción *nf, pl* **-ciones** : restriction, limitation
restrictivo, -va *adj* : restrictive
restringido, -da *adj* LIMITADO : limited, restricted
restringir {35} *vt* LIMITAR : to restrict, to limit
restructuración *nf* : restructuring
restructurar *vt* : to restructure
resucitación *nf* : resuscitation ⟨resucitación cardiopulmonar : CPR, cardiopulmonary resuscitation⟩
resucitar *vt* **1** : to resuscitate, to revive, to resurrect **2** : to revitalize
resuello *nm* **1** : puffing, heavy breathing, wheezing **2** : break, breather
resuelto[1] *pp* → **resolver**
resuelto[2], **-ta** *adj* : determined, resolved, resolute
resulta *nf* **1** : consequence, result **2 a resultas de** *or* **de resultas de** : as a result of
resultado *nm* : result, outcome
resultante *adj & nf* : resultant
resultar *vi* **1** : to work, to work out ⟨mi idea no resultó : my idea didn't work out⟩ **2** : to prove, to turn out to be ⟨resultó bien simpático : he turned out to be very nice⟩ **3 ~ en** : to lead to, to result in **4 ~ de** : to be the result of
resumen *nm, pl* **-súmenes** **1** : summary, summation **2 en ~** : in summary, in short
resumidero *nm* : drain
resumir *v* : to summarize, to sum up
resurgimiento *nm* : resurgence
resurgir {35} *vi* : to reappear, to revive
resurrección *nf, pl* **-ciones** : resurrection
retablo *nm* **1** : tableau **2** : altarpiece
retador, -dora *n* : challenger (in sports)
retaguardia *nf* : rear guard
retahíla *nf* : string, series ⟨una retahíla de insultos : a volley of insults⟩
retaliación *nf, pl* **-ciones** : retaliation
retama *nf* : broom (plant)
retar *vt* DESAFIAR : to challenge, to defy
retardante *adj* : retardant
retardar *vt* **1** RETRASAR : to delay, to retard **2** : to postpone
retazo *nm* **1** : remnant, scrap **2** : fragment, piece ⟨retazos de su obra : bits and pieces from his writings⟩
retención *nf, pl* **-ciones** **1** : retention **2** : deduction, withholding
retener {80} *vt* **1** : to retain, to keep **2** : to withhold **3** : to detain
retentivo, -va *adj* : retentive
reticencia *nf* **1** : reluctance, reticence **2** : insinuation
reticente *adj* **1** : reluctant, reticent **2** : insinuating, misleading
retina *nf* : retina
retintín *nm, pl* **-tines** **1** : jingle, jangle **2 con ~** : sarcastically
retirada *nf* **1** : retreat ⟨batirse en retirada : to withdraw, to beat a retreat⟩ **2** : withdrawal (of funds) **3** : retirement **4** : refuge, haven
retirado, -da *adj* **1** : remote, distant, far off **2** : secluded, quiet
retirar *vt* **1** : to remove, to take away, to recall **2** : to withdraw, to take out — **retirarse** *vr* **1** REPLEGARSE : to retreat, to withdraw **2** JUBILARSE : to retire
retiro *nm* **1** JUBILACIÓN : retirement **2** : withdrawal, retreat **3** : seclusion
reto *nm* DESAFÍO : challenge, dare
retocar {72} *vt* : to touch up
retoñar *vi* : to sprout
retoño *nm* : sprout, shoot
retoque *nm* : retouching
retorcer {14} *vt* **1** : to twist **2** : to wring — **retorcerse** *vr* **1** : to get twisted, to get tangled up **2** : to squirm, to writhe, to wiggle about
retorcijón *nm, pl* **-jones** : cramp, sharp pain
retorcimiento *nm* **1** : twisting, wringing **2** : deviousness
retórica *nf* : rhetoric
retórico, -ca *adj* : rhetorical — **retóricamente** *adv*
retornar *v* : to return
retorno *nm* : return
retozar {21} *vi* : to frolic, to romp
retozo *nm* : frolicking
retozón, -zona *adj, mpl* **-zones** : playful
retracción *nf, pl* **-ciones** : retraction, withdrawal
retractable *adj* : retractable
retractación *nf, pl* **-ciones** : retraction (of a statement, etc.)
retractarse *vr* **1** : to withdraw, to back down **2 ~ de** : to take back, to retract
retraer {81} *vt* **1** : to bring back **2** : to dissuade — **retraerse** *vr* **1** RETIRARSE : to withdraw, to retire **2** REFUGIARSE : to take refuge
retraído, -da *adj* : withdrawn, retiring, shy
retraimiento *nm* **1** : shyness, timidity **2** : withdrawal
retrasado, -da *adj* **1** : retarded, mentally slow **2** : behind, in arrears **3**

: backward (of a country) **4** : slow (of a watch)
retrasar *vt* **1** DEMORAR, RETARDAR : to delay, to hold up **2** : to put off, to postpone — **retrasarse** *vr* **1** : to be late **2** : to fall behind
retraso *nm* **1** ATRASO : delay, lateness **2 retraso mental** : mental retardation
retratar *vt* **1** : to portray, to depict **2** : to photograph **3** : to paint a portrait of
retrato *nm* **1** : depiction, portrayal **2** : portrait, photograph
retrete *nm* : restroom, toilet
retribución *nf, pl* **-ciones 1** : pay, payment **2** : reward
retribuir {41} *vt* **1** : to pay **2** : to reward
retroactivo, -va *adj* : retroactive — **retroactivamente** *adv*
retroalimentación *nf, pl* **-ciones** : feedback
retroceder *vi* **1** : to move back, to turn back **2** : to back off, to back down **3** : to recoil (of a firearm)
retroceso *nm* **1** : backward movement **2** : backing down **3** : setback, relapse **4** : recoil
retrógrado, -da *adj* **1** : reactionary **2** : retrograde
retropropulsión *nf* : jet propulsion
retrospectiva *nf* : retrospective, hindsight
retrospectivo, -va *adj* **1** : retrospective **2 mirada retrospectiva** : backward glance
retrovisor *nm* : rearview mirror
retruécano *nm* : pun, play on words
retumbar *vi* **1** : to boom, to thunder **2** : to resound, to reverberate
retumbo *nm* : booming, thundering, roll
retuvo, etc. → **retener**
reubicar {72} *vt* : to relocate — **reubicación** *nf*
reuma *or* **reúma** *nmf* → **reumatismo**
reumático, -ca *adj* : rheumatic
reumatismo *nm* : rheumatism
reunión *nf, pl* **-niones 1** : meeting **2** : gathering, reunion
reunir {68} *vt* **1** : to unite, to join, to bring together **2** : to have, to possess <reunieron los requisitos necesarios : they fulfilled the necessary requirements> **3** : to gather, to collect, to raise (funds) — **reunirse** *vr* : to meet
reutilizable *adj* : reusable
reutilizar {21} *vt* : to recycle, to reuse
revalidar *vt* **1** : to confirm, to ratify **2** : to defend (a title)
revaluar {3} *vt* : to reevaluate — **revaluación** *n*
revancha *nf* **1** DESQUITE : revenge, requital **2** : rematch
revelación *nf, pl* **-ciones** : revelation
revelado *nm* : developing (of film)
revelador[1], -dora *adj* : revealing
revelador[2] *nm* : developer
revelar *vt* **1** : to reveal, to disclose **2** : to develop (film)
revendedor, -dora *n* **1** : scalper **2** DETALLISTA : retailer
revender *vt* **1** : to resell **2** : to scalp
reventa *nf* **1** : resale **2** : scalping
reventar {55} *vi* **1** ESTALLAR, EXPLOTAR : to burst, to blow up **2 ~ de** : to be bursting with — *vt* **1** : to burst **2** *fam* : to annoy, to rile
reventón *nm, pl* **-tones 1** : burst, bursting **2** : blowout, flat tire **3** *Mex fam* : bash, party
reverberar *vi* : to reverberate — **reverberación** *nf*
reverdecer {53} *vi* **1** : to grow green again **2** : to revive
reverencia *nf* **1** : reverence **2** : bow, curtsy
reverenciar *vt* : to revere, to venerate
reverendo[1], -da *adj* **1** : reverend **2** *fam* : total, absolute <es un reverendo imbécil : he is a complete idiot>
reverendo[2], -da *n* : reverend
reverente *adj* : reverent
reversa *nf Col, Mex* : reverse (gear)
reversible *adj* : reversible
reversión *nf, pl* **-siones** : reversion
reverso *nm* **1** : back, other side **2 el reverso de la medalla** : the complete opposite
revertir {76} *vi* **1** : to revert, to go back **2 ~ en** : to result in, to end up as
revés *nm, pl* **reveses 1** : back, wrong side **2** : setback, reversal **3** : backhand (in sports) **4 al revés** : the other way around, upside down, inside out **5 al revés de** : contrary to
revestimiento *nm* : covering, facing (of a building)
revestir {54} *vt* **1** : to coat, to cover, to surface **2** : to conceal, to disguise **3** : to take on, to assume <la reunión revistió gravedad : the meeting took on a serious note>
revisar *vt* **1** : to examine, to inspect, to check **2** : to check over, to overhaul (machinery) **3** : to revise
revisión *nf, pl* **-siones 1** : revision **2** : inspection, check
revisor, -sora *n* **1** : inspector **2** : conductor (on a train)
revista *nf* **1** : magazine, journal **2** : revue **3 pasar revista** : to review, to inspect
revistar *vt* : to review, to inspect
revitalizar {21} *vt* : to revitalize — **revitalización** *nf*
revivir *vi* : to revive, to come alive again — *vt* : to relive
revocación *nf, pl* **-ciones** : revocation, repeal
revocar {72} *vt* **1** : to revoke, to repeal **2** : to plaster (a wall)
revolcar {82} *vt* : to knock over, to knock down — **revolcarse** *vr* : to roll around, to wallow
revolcón *nm, pl* **-cones** *fam* : tumble, fall
revolotear *vi* : to flutter around, to flit
revoloteo *nm* : fluttering, flitting

revoltijo *nm* **1** FÁRRAGO : mess, jumble **2** *Mex* : traditional seafood dish

revoltoso, -sa *adj* : unruly, rebellious

revolución *nf, pl* **-ciones** : revolution

revolucionar *vt* : to revolutionize

revolucionario, -ria *adj & n* : revolutionary

revolver {89} *vt* **1** : to move about, to mix, to shake, to stir **2** : to upset (one's stomach) **3** : to mess up, to rummage through ⟨revolver la casa : to turn the house upside down⟩ — **revolverse** *vr* **1** : to toss and turn **2** VOLVERSE : to turn around

revólver *nm* : revolver

revoque *nm* : plaster

revuelo *nm* **1** : fluttering **2** : commotion, stir

revuelta *nf* : uprising, revolt

revuelto[1] *pp* → **revolver**

revuelto[2], **-ta** *adj* **1** : choppy, rough ⟨mar revuelto : rough sea⟩ **2** : untidy **3 huevos revueltos** : scrambled eggs

rey *nm* : king

reyerta *nf* : brawl, fight

rezagado, -da *n* : straggler, latecomer

rezagar {52} *vt* **1** : to leave behind **2** : to postpone — **rezagarse** *vr* : to fall behind, to lag

rezar {21} *vi* **1** : to pray **2** : to say ⟨como reza el refrán : as the saying goes⟩ **3 ~ con** : to concern, to have to do with — *vt* : to say, to recite ⟨rezar un Ave María : to say a Hail Mary⟩

rezo *nm* : prayer, praying

rezongar {52} *vi* : to gripe, to grumble

rezumar *v* : to ooze, to leak

ría[1], **etc.** → **reír**

ría[2] *nf* : estuary

riachuelo *nm* ARROYO : brook, stream

riada *nf* : flood

ribera *nf* : bank, shore

ribete *nm* **1** : border, trim **2** : frill, adornment **3 ribetes** *nmpl* : hint, touch ⟨tiene sus ribetes de genio : there's a touch of genius in him⟩

ribetear *vt* : to border, to edge, to trim

ricamente *adv* : richly, splendidly

rice, etc. → **rizar**

rico[1], **-ca** *adj* **1** : rich, wealthy **2** : fertile **3** : luxurious, valuable **4** : delicious **5** : adorable, lovely **6** : great, wonderful

rico[2], **-ca** *n* : rich person

ridiculez *nf, pl* **-leces** : ridiculousness, absurdity

ridiculizar {21} *vt* : to ridicule

ridículo[1], **-la** *adj* ABSURDO, DISPARATADO : ridiculous, ludicrous — **ridículamente** *adv*

ridículo[2], **-la** *n* **1 hacer el ridículo** : to make a fool of oneself **2 poner en ridículo** : to ridicule

ríe, etc. → **reír**

riega, riegue etc. → **regar**

riego *nm* : irrigation

riel *nm* : rail, track

rienda *nf* **1** : rein **2 dar rienda suelta a** : to give free rein to **3 llevar las riendas** : to be in charge **4 tomar las riendas** : to take control

riesgo *nm* : risk

riesgoso, -sa *adj* : risky

rifa *nf* : raffle

rifar *vt* : to raffle — *vi* : to quarrel, to fight

rifle *nm* : rifle

rige, rija etc. → **regir**

rigidez *nf, pl* **-deces** **1** : rigidity, stiffness ⟨rigidez cadavérica : rigor mortis⟩ **2** : inflexibility

rígido, -da *adj* **1** : rigid, stiff **2** : strict — **rígidamente** *adv*

rigor *nm* **1** : rigor, harshness **2** : precision, meticulousness **3 de ~** : usual ⟨la respuesta de rigor : the standard reply⟩ **4 de ~** : essential, obligatory **5 en ~** : strictly speaking, in reality

riguroso, -sa *adj* : rigorous — **rigurosamente** *adv*

rima *nf* **1** : rhyme **2 rimas** *nfpl* : verse, poetry

rimar *vi* : to rhyme

rimbombante *adj* **1** : grandiose, showy **2** : bombastic, pompous

rímel *or* **rimel** *nm* : mascara

rin *nm Col, Mex* : wheel, rim (of a tire)

rincón *nm, pl* **rincones** : corner, nook

rinde, etc. → **rendir**

rinoceronte *nm* : rhinoceros

riña *nf* **1** : fight, brawl **2** : dispute, quarrel

riñe, etc. → **reñir**

riñón *nm, pl* **riñones** : kidney

río[1] → **reír**

río[2] *nm* **1** : river **2** : torrent, stream ⟨un río de lágrimas : a flood of tears⟩

ripio *nm* **1** : debris, rubble **2** : gravel

riqueza *nf* **1** : wealth, riches *pl* **2** : richness **3 riquezas naturales** : natural resources

risa *nf* **1** : laughter, laugh **2 dar risa** : to make laugh ⟨me dio mucha risa : I found it very funny⟩ **3** *fam* **morirse de la risa** : to die laughing, to crack up

risco *nm* : crag, cliff

risible *adj* IRRISORIO : ludicrous, laughable

risita *nf* : giggle, titter, snicker

risotada *nf* : guffaw

ristra *nf* : string, series *pl*

risueño, -ña *adj* **1** : cheerful, pleasant **2** : promising

rítmico, -ca *adj* : rhythmical, rhythmic — **rítmicamente** *adv*

ritmo *nm* **1** : rhythm **2** : pace, tempo ⟨trabajó a ritmo lento : she worked at a slow pace⟩

rito *nm* : rite, ritual

ritual *adj & nm* : ritual — **ritualmente** *adv*

rival *adj & nmf* COMPETIDOR : rival

rivalidad *nf* : rivalry, competition

rivalizar {21} *vi* **~ con** : to rival, to compete with

rizado, -da *adj* **1** : curly **2** : ridged **3** : ripply, undulating

rizar {21} *vt* **1** : to curl **2** : to ripple, to ruffle (a surface) **3** : to crumple, to fold — **rizarse** *vr* **1** : to frizz **2** : to ripple

rizo *nm* **1** : curl **2** : loop (in aviation)

robalo *or* **róbalo** *nm* : sea bass

robar *vt* **1** : to steal **2** : to rob, to burglarize **3** SECUESTRAR : to abduct, to kidnap **4** : to captivate — *vi* **∼ en** : to break into

roble *nm* : oak

robo *nm* : robbery, theft

robot *nm, pl* **robots** : robot

robótica *nf* : robotics

robustecer {53} *vt* : to grow stronger, to strengthen

robustez *nf* : sturdiness, robustness

robusto, -ta *adj* : robust, sturdy

roca *nf* : rock, boulder

roce[1], **etc.** → **rozar**

roce[2] *nm* **1** : rubbing, chafing **2** : brush, graze, touch **3** : close contact, familiarity **4** : friction, disagreement

rociador *nm* : sprinkler

rociar {85} *vt* : to spray, to sprinkle

rocío *nm* **1** : dew **2** : shower, light rain

rock *or* **rock and roll** *nm* : rock, rock and roll

rocola *nf* : jukebox

rocoso, -sa *adj* : rocky

rodada *nf* : track (of a tire), rut

rodado, -da *adj* **1** : wheeled **2** : dappled (of a horse)

rodadura *nf* : rolling, taxiing

rodaja *nf* : round, slice

rodaje *nm* **1** : filming, shooting **2** : breaking in (of a vehicle)

rodamiento *nm* **1** : bearing ⟨rodamiento de bolas : ball bearings⟩ **2** : rolling

rodante *adj* : rolling

rodar {19} *vi* **1** : to roll, to roll down, to roll along ⟨rodé por la escalera : I tumbled down the stairs⟩ ⟨todo rodaba bien : everthing was going along well⟩ **2** GIRAR : to turn, to go around **3** : to move about, to travel ⟨andábamos rodando por todas partes : we drifted along from place to place⟩ — *vt* **1** : to film, to shoot **2** : to break in (a new vehicle)

rodear *vt* **1** : to surround **2** : to round up (cattle) — *vi* **1** : to go around **2** : to beat around the bush — **rodearse** *vr* **∼ de** : to surround oneself with

rodeo *nm* **1** : rodeo, roundup **2** DESVÍO : detour **3** : evasion ⟨andar con rodeos : to beat around the bush⟩ ⟨sin rodeos : without reservations⟩

rodilla *nf* : knee

rodillo *nm* **1** : roller **2** : rolling pin

rododendro *nm* : rhododendron

roedor[1], **-dora** *adj* : gnawing

roedor[2] *nm* : rodent

roer {69} *vt* **1** : to gnaw **2** : to eat away at, to torment

rogar {16} *vt* : to beg, to request — *vi* **1** : to beg, to plead **2** : to pray

roiga, etc. → **roer**

rojez *nf* : redness

rojizo, -za *adj* : reddish

rojo[1], **-ja** *adj* **1** : red **2 ponerse rojo** : to blush

rojo[2] *nm* : red

rol *nm* **1** : role **2** : list, roll

rollo *nm* **1** : roll, coil ⟨un rollo de cinta : a roll of tape⟩ ⟨en rollo : rolled up⟩ **2** *fam* : roll of fat **3** *fam* : boring speech, lecture

romance *nm* **1** : Romance language **2** : ballad **3** : romance **4 en buen romance** : simply stated, simply put

romano, -na *adj & n* : Roman

romanticismo *nm* : romanticism

romántico, -ca *adj* : romantic — **románticamente** *adv*

rombo *nm* : rhombus

romería *nf* **1** : pilgrimage, procession **2** : crowd, gathering

romero[1], **-ra** *n* PEREGRINO : pilgrim

romero[2] *nm* : rosemary

romo, -ma *adj* : blunt, dull

rompecabezas *nms & pl* : puzzle, riddle

rompehielos *nms & pl* : icebreaker (ship)

rompehuelgas *nmfs & pl* ESQUIROL : strikebreaker, scab

rompenueces *nms & pl* : nutcracker

rompeolas *ns & pl* : breakwater, jetty

romper {70} *vt* **1** : to break, to smash **2** : to rip, to tear **3** : to break off (relations), to break (a contract) **4** : to break through, to break down **5** GASTAR : to wear out — *vi* **1** : to break ⟨al romper del día : at the break of day⟩ **2 ∼ a** : to begin to, to burst out with ⟨romper a llorar : to burst into tears⟩ **3 ∼ con** : to break off with

rompope *nm CA, Mex* : drink similar to eggnog

ron *nm* : rum

roncar {72} *vi* **1** : to snore **2** : to roar

ronco, -ca *adj* **1** : hoarse **2** : husky (of the voice) — **roncamente** *adv*

ronda *nf* **1** : beat, patrol **2** : round (of drinks, of negotiations, of a game)

rondar *vt* **1** : to patrol **2** : to hang around ⟨siempre está rondando la calle : he's always hanging around the street⟩ **3** : to be approximately ⟨debe rondar los cincuenta : he must be about 50⟩ — *vi* **1** : to be on patrol **2** : to prowl around, to roam about

ronque, etc. → **roncar**

ronquera *nf* : hoarseness

ronquido *nm* **1** : snore **2** : roar

ronronear *vi* : to purr

ronroneo *nm* : purr, purring

ronzal *nm* : halter (for an animal)

ronzar {21} *v* : to munch, to crunch

roña *nf* **1** : mange **2** : dirt, filth **3** *fam* : stinginess

roñoso, -sa *adj* **1** : mangy **2** : dirty **3** *fam* : stingy

ropa *nf* **1** : clothes *pl,* clothing **2 ropa interior** : underwear

ropaje *nm* : apparel, garments *pl,* regalia
ropero *nm* ARMARIO, CLÓSET : wardrobe, closet
rosa[1] *adj* : rose-colored, pink
rosa[2] *nm* : rose, pink (color)
rosa[3] *nf* : rose (flower)
rosáceo, -cea *adj* : pinkish
rosado[1], **-da** *adj* **1** : pink **2 vino rosado** : rosé
rosado[2] *nm* : pink (color)
rosal *nm* : rosebush
rosario *nm* **1** : rosary **2** : series ‹un rosario de islas : a string of islands›
rosbif *nm* : roast beef
rosca *nf* **1** : thread (of a screw) ‹una tapa a rosca : a screw top› **2** : ring, coil
roseta *nf* : rosette
rosquilla *nf* : ring-shaped pastry, doughnut
rostro *nm* : face, countenance
rotación *nf, pl* **-ciones** : rotation
rotar *vt* : to rotate, to turn — *vi* : to turn, to spin
rotativo[1], **-va** *adj* : rotary
rotativo[2] *nm* : newspaper
rotatorio, -ria *adj* → **rotativo**[1]
roto[1] *pp* → **romper**
roto[2], **-ta** *adj* **1** : broken **2** : ripped, torn
rotonda *nf* **1** : traffic circle, rotary **2** : rotunda
rotor *nm* : rotor
rótula *nf* : kneecap
rotular *vt* **1** : to head, to entitle **2** : to label
rótulo *nm* **1** : heading, title **2** : label, sign
rotundo, -da *adj* **1** REDONDO : round **2** : categorical, absolute ‹un éxito rotundo : a resounding success› — **rotundamente** *adv*
rotura *nf* : break, tear, fracture
roya *nf* : plant rust
roya, etc. → **roer**
rozado, -da *adj* GASTADO : worn
rozadura *nf* **1** : scratch, abrasion **2** : rubbed spot, sore
rozar {21} *vt* **1** : to chafe, to rub against **2** : to border on, to touch on **3** : to graze, to touch lightly — **rozarse** *vr* **~ con** *fam* : to rub shoulders with
ruandés, -desa *adj & n* : Rwandan
ruano, -na *adj* : roan
rubí *nm, pl* **rubíes** : ruby
rubio, -bia *adj & n* : blond
rublo *nm* : ruble
rubor *nm* **1** : flush, blush **2** : rouge, blusher
ruborizarse {21} *vr* : to blush
rubrica *nf* : title, heading
rubricar {72} *vt* **1** : sign with a flourish ‹firmado y rubricado : signed and sealed› **2** : to endorse, to sanction
rubro *nm* **1** : heading, title **2** : line, area (in business)
rudeza *nf* ASPEREZA : roughness, coarseness
rudimentario, -ria *adj* : rudimentary — **rudimentariamente** *adv*
rudimento *nm* : rudiment, basics *pl*
rudo, -da *adj* **1** : rough, harsh **2** : coarse, unpolished — **rudamente** *adv*
rueda[1], **etc.** → **rodar**
rueda[2] *nf* **1** : wheel **2** RODAJA : round slice **3** : circle, ring **4 rueda de andar** : treadmill **5 rueda de prensa** : press conference **6 ir sobre ruedas** : to go smoothly
ruedita *nf* : caster (on furniture)
ruedo *nm* **1** : bullring, arena **2** : rotation, turn **3** : hem
ruega, ruegue etc. → **rogar**
ruego *nm* : request, appeal, plea
rugido *nm* : roar
rugir {35} *vi* : to roar
ruibarbo *nm* : rhubarb
ruido *nm* : noise, sound
ruidoso, -sa *adj* : loud, noisy — **ruidosamente** *adv*
ruin *adj* **1** : base, despicable **2** : mean, stingy
ruina *nf* **1** : ruin, destruction **2** : downfall, collapse **3 ruinas** *nfpl* : ruins, remains
ruinoso, -sa *adj* **1** : run-down, dilapidated **2** : ruinous, disastrous
ruiseñor *nm* : nightingale
ruja, etc. → **rugir**
ruleta *nf* : roulette
rulo *nm* : curler, roller
rumano, -na *n* : Romanian, Rumanian
rumbo *nm* **1** : direction, course ‹con rumbo a : bound for, heading for› ‹perder el rumbo : to go off course, to lose one's bearings› ‹sin rumbo : aimless, aimlessly› **2** : ostentation, pomp **3** : lavishness, generosity
rumiante *adj & nm* : ruminant
rumiar *vt* : to ponder, to mull over — *vi* **1** : to chew the cud **2** : to ruminate, to ponder
rumor *nm* **1** : rumor **2** : murmur
rumorearse *or* **rumorarse** *vr* : to be rumored ‹se rumorea que se va : rumor has it that she's leaving›
rumoroso, -sa *adj* : murmuring, babbling ‹un arroyo rumoroso : a babbling brook›
rupia *nf* : rupee
ruptura *nf* **1** : break **2** : breaking, breach (of a contract) **3** : breaking off, breakup
rural *adj* : rural
ruso[1], **-sa** *adj & n* : Russian
ruso[2] *nm* : Russian (language)
rústico[1], **-ca** *adj* : rural, rustic
rústico[2], **-ca** *n* : rustic, country dweller
ruta *nf* : route
rutina *nf* : routine, habit
rutinario, -ria *adj* : routine, ordinary ‹visita rutinaria : routine visit› — **rutinariamente** *adv*

S

s *nf* : twentieth letter of the Spanish alphabet
sábado *nm* **1** : Saturday **2** : Sabbath
sábalo *nm* : shad
sabana *nf* : savanna
sábana *nf* : sheet, bedsheet
sabandija *nf* BICHO : bug, small reptile, pesky creature
sabático, -ca *adj* : sabbatical
sabedor, -dora *adj* : aware, informed
sabelotodo *nmf fam* : know-it-all
saber[1] {71} *vt* **1** : to know **2** : to know how to, to be able to ⟨sabe tocar el violín : she can play the violin⟩ **3** : to learn, to find out **4 a ~** : to wit, namely — *vi* **1** : to know, to suppose **2** : to be informed ⟨supimos del desastre : we heard about the disaster⟩ **3** : to taste ⟨esto no sabe bien : this doesn't taste right⟩ **4 ~ a** : to taste like ⟨sabe a naranja : it tastes like orange⟩ — **saberse** *vr* : to know ⟨ese chiste no me lo sé : I don't know that joke⟩
saber[2] *nm* : knowledge, learning
sabiamente *adv* : wisely
sabido, -da *adj* : well-known
sabiduría *nf* **1** : wisdom **2** : learning, knowledge
sabiendas *adv* **1 a ~** : knowingly **2 a sabiendas de que** : knowing full well that
sabio[1], **-bia** *adj* **1** PRUDENTE : wise, sensible **2** DOCTO : learned
sabio[2], **-bia** *n* **1** : wise person **2** : savant, learned person
sable *nm* : saber, cutlass
sabor *nm* **1** : flavor, taste **2 sin ~** : flavorless
saborear *vt* **1** : to taste, to savor **2** : to enjoy, to relish
sabotaje *nm* : sabotage
saboteador, -dora *n* : saboteur
sabotear *vt* : to sabotage
sabrá, etc. → **saber**
sabroso, -sa *adj* **1** RICO : delicious, tasty **2** AGRADABLE : pleasant, nice, lovely
sabueso *nm* **1** : bloodhound **2** *fam* : detective, sleuth
sacacorchos *nms & pl* : corkscrew
sacapuntas *nms & pl* : pencil sharpener
sacar {72} *vt* **1** : to pull out, to take out ⟨saca el pollo del congelador : take the chicken out of the freezer⟩ **2** : to get, to obtain ⟨saqué un 100 en el examen : I got 100 on the exam⟩ **3** : to get out, to extract ⟨le saqué la información : I got the information from him⟩ **4** : to stick out ⟨sacar la lengua : to stick out one's tongue⟩ **5** : to bring out, to introduce ⟨sacar un libro : to publish a book⟩ ⟨sacaron una moda nueva : they introduced a new style⟩ **6** : to take (photos) **7** : to make (copies) — *vi* **1** : to kick off (in soccer or football) **2** : to serve (in sports)
sacarina *nf* : saccharin
sacarosa *nf* : sucrose
sacerdocio *nm* : priesthood
sacerdotal *adj* : priestly
sacerdote, -tisa *n* : priest *m*, priestess *f*
saciar *vt* **1** HARTAR : to sate, to satiate **2** SATISFACER : to satisfy
saciedad *nf* : satiety
saco *nm* **1** : bag, sack **2** : sac **3** : jacket, sport coat
sacramento *nm* : sacrament — **sacramental** *adj*
sacrificar {72} *vt* : to sacrifice — **sacrificarse** *vr* : to sacrifice oneself, to make sacrifices
sacrificio *nm* : sacrifice
sacrilegio *nm* : sacrilege
sacrílego, -ga *adj* : sacrilegious
sacristán *nm, pl* **-tanes** : sexton, sacristan
sacristía *nf* : sacristy, vestry
sacro, -cra *adj* SAGRADO : sacred ⟨arte sacro : sacred art⟩
sacrosanto, -ta *adj* : sacrosanct
sacudida *nf* **1** : shaking **2** : jerk, jolt, shock **3** : shake-up, upheaval
sacudir *vt* **1** : to shake, to beat **2** : to jerk, to jolt **3** : to dust off **4** CONMOVER : to shake up, to shock — **sacudirse** *vr* : to shake off
sacudón *nm, pl* **-dones** : intense jolt or shake-up
sádico[1], **-ca** *adj* : sadistic
sádico[2], **-ca** *n* : sadist
sadismo *nm* : sadism
safari *nm* : safari
saga *nf* : saga
sagacidad *nf* : sagacity, shrewdness
sagaz *adj, pl* **sagaces** PERSPICAZ : shrewd, discerning, sagacious
Sagitario *nmf* : Sagittarius, Sagittarian
sagrado, -da *adj* : sacred, holy
sainete *nm* : comedy sketch, one-act farce ⟨este proceso es un sainete : these proceedings are a farce⟩
sajar *vt* : to lance, to cut open
sal[1] → **salir**
sal[2] *nf* **1** : salt **2** *CA, Mex* : misfortune, bad luck
sala *nf* **1** : living room **2** : room, hall ⟨sala de conferencias : lecture hall⟩ ⟨sala de urgencias : emergency room⟩ ⟨sala de baile : ballroom⟩
salado, -da *adj* **1** : salty **2 agua salada** : salt water
salamandra *nf* : salamander
salami *nm* : salami
salar *vt* **1** : to salt **2** : to spoil, to ruin **3** *CoRi, Mex* : to jinx, to bring bad luck
salarial *adj* : salary, salary-related
salario *nm* **1** : salary **2 salario mínimo** : minimum wage
salaz *adj, pl* **salaces** : salacious, lecherous

salchicha *nf* **1** : sausage **2** : frankfurter, wiener

salchichón *nf, pl* **-chones** : a type of deli meat

salchichonería *nf Mex* **1** : delicatessen **2** : cold cuts *pl*

saldar *vt* : to settle, to pay off ⟨saldar una cuenta : to settle an account⟩

saldo *nm* **1** : settlement, payment **2** : balance ⟨saldo de cuenta : account balance⟩ **3** : remainder, leftover merchandise

saldrá, etc. → **salir**

salero *nm* **1** : saltshaker **2** : wit, charm

salga, etc. → **salir**

salida *nf* **1** : exit ⟨salida de emergencia : emergency exit⟩ **2** : leaving, departure **3** SOLUCIÓN : way out, solution **4** : start (of a race) **5** OCURRENCIA : wisecrack, joke **6 salida del sol** : sunrise

saliente[1] *adj* **1** : departing, outgoing **2** : projecting **3** DESTACADO : salient, prominent

saliente[2] *nm* **1** : projection, protrusion **2 ventana en saliente** : bay window

salinidad *nf* : salinity, saltiness

salino, -na *adj* : saline ⟨solución salina : saline solution⟩

salir {73} *vi* **1** : to go out, to come out, to get out ⟨salimos todas las noches : we go out every night⟩ ⟨su libro acaba de salir : her book just came out⟩ **2** PARTIR : to leave, to depart **3** APARECER : to appear ⟨salió en todos los diarios : it came out in all the papers⟩ **4** : to project, to stick out **5** : to cost, to come to **6** RESULTAR : to turn out, to prove **7** : to come up, to occur ⟨salga lo que salga : whatever happens⟩ ⟨salió una oportunidad : an opportunity came up⟩ **8 ~ a** : to take after, to look like, to resemble **9 ~ con** : to go out with, to date — **salirse** *vr* **1** : to escape, to get out, to leak out **2** : to come loose, to come off **3 salirse con la suya** : to get one's own way

saliva *nf* : saliva

salivar *vi* : to salivate

salmo *nm* : psalm

salmón[1] *adj* : salmon-colored

salmón[2] *nm, pl* **salmones** : salmon

salmuera *nf* : brine

salobre *adj* : brackish, briny

salón *nm, pl* **salones** **1** : hall, large room ⟨salón de clase : classroom⟩ ⟨salón de baile : ballroom⟩ **2** : salon ⟨salón de belleza : beauty salon⟩ **3** : parlor, sitting room

salpicadera *nf Mex* : fender

salpicadura *nf* : spatter, splash

salpicar {72} *vt* **1** : to spatter, to splash **2** : to sprinkle, to scatter about

salpimentar {55} *vt* **1** : to season (with salt and pepper) **2** : to spice up

salsa *nf* **1** : sauce ⟨salsa picante : hot sauce⟩ ⟨salsa inglesa : Worcestershire sauce⟩ ⟨salsa tártara : tartar sauce⟩ **2** : gravy **3** : salsa (music) **4 salsa mexicana** : salsa (sauce)

salsero, -ra *n* : salsa musician

saltador, -dora *n* : jumper

saltamontes *nms & pl* : grasshopper

saltar *vi* **1** BRINCAR : to jump, to leap **2** : to bounce **3** : to come off, to pop out **4** : to shatter, to break **5** : to explode, to blow up — *vt* **1** : to jump, to jump over **2** : to skip, to miss — **saltarse** *vr* OMITIR : to skip, to omit ⟨me salté ese capítulo : I skipped that chapter⟩

saltarín, -rina *adj, mpl* **-rines** : leaping, hopping ⟨frijol saltarín : jumping bean⟩

salteado, -da *adj* **1** : sautéed **2** : jumbled up ⟨los episodios se transmitieron salteados : the episodes were broadcast in random order⟩

salteador *nm* : highwayman

saltear *vt* **1** SOFREÍR : to sauté **2** : to skip around, to skip over

saltimbanqui *nmf* : acrobat

salto *nm* **1** BRINCO : jump, leap, skip **2** : jump, dive (in sports) **3** : gap, omission **4 dar saltos** : to jump up and down **5** *or* **salto de agua** CATARATA : waterfall

saltón, -tona *adj, mpl* **saltones** : bulging, protruding

salubre *adj* : healthful, salubrious

salubridad *nf* : healthfulness, health

salud *nf* **1** : health ⟨buena salud : good health⟩ **2 ¡salud!** : bless you! (when someone sneezes) **3 ¡salud!** : cheers!, to your health!

saludable *adj* **1** SALUBRE : healthful **2** SANO : healthy, well

saludar *vt* **1** : to greet, to say hello to **2** : to salute — **saludarse** *vr*

saludo *nm* **1** : greeting, regards *pl* **2** : salute

salutación *nf, pl* **-ciones** : salutation

salva *nf* **1** : salvo, volley **2 salva de aplausos** : round of applause

salvación *nf, pl* **-ciones** **1** : salvation **2** RESCATE : rescue

salvado *nm* : bran

salvador, -dora *n* **1** : savior, rescuer **2 el Salvador** : the Savior

salvadoreño, -ña *adj & n* : Salvadoran, El Salvadoran

salvaguardar *vt* : to safeguard

salvaguardia *or* **salvaguarda** *nf* : safeguard, defense

salvajada *nf* ATROCIDAD : atrocity, act of savagery

salvaje[1] *adj* **1** : wild ⟨animales salvajes : wild animals⟩ **2** : savage, cruel **3** : primitive, uncivilized

salvaje[2] *nmf* : savage

salvajismo *nm* : savagery

salvamento *nm* **1** : rescuing, lifesaving **2** : salvation **3** : refuge

salvar *vt* **1** : to save, to rescue **2** : to cover (a distance) **3** : to get around (an obstacle), to overcome (a difficulty) **4**

: to cross, to jump across **5 salvando** : except for, excluding — **salvarse** *vr* **1** : to survive, to escape **2** : to save one's soul
salvavidas[1] *nms & pl* **1** : life preserver **2 bote salvavidas** : lifeboat
salvavidas[2] *nmf* : lifeguard
salvedad *nf* **1** EXCEPCIÓN : exception **2** : proviso, stipulation
salvia *nf* : sage (plant)
salvo[1], **-va** *adj* **1** : unharmed, sound ⟨sano y salvo : safe and sound⟩ **2 a ~** : safe from danger
salvo[2] *prep* **1** EXCEPTO : except (for), save ⟨todos asistirán salvo Jaime : all will attend except for Jaime⟩ **2 salvo que** : unless ⟨salvo que llueva : unless it rains⟩
salvoconducto *nm* : safe-conduct
samba *nf* : samba
San *adj* → **santo**[1]
sanar *vt* : to heal, to cure — *vi* : to get well, to recover
sanatorio *nm* **1** : sanatorium **2** : clinic, private hospital
sanción *nf, pl* **sanciones** : sanction
sancionar *vt* **1** : to penalize, to impose a sanction on **2** : to sanction, to approve
sancochar *vt* : to parboil
sandalia *nf* : sandal
sándalo *nm* : sandalwood
sandez *nf, pl* **sandeces** ESTUPIDEZ : nonsense, silly thing to say
sandía *nf* : watermelon
sandwich [ˈsandwiʧ, ˈsaŋgwiʧ] *nm, pl* **sandwiches** [-dwiʧɛs, -gwi-] EMPAREDADO : sandwich
saneamiento *nm* **1** : cleaning up, sanitation **2** : reorganizing, streamlining
sanear *vt* **1** : to clean up, to sanitize **2** : to reorganize, to streamline
sangrante *adj* **1** : bleeding **2** : flagrant, blatant
sangrar *vi* : to bleed — *vt* : to indent (a paragraph, etc.)
sangre *nf* **1** : blood **2 a sangre fría** : in cold blood **3 a sangre y fuego** : by violent force **4 pura sangre** : thoroughbred
sangría *nf* **1** : bloodletting **2** : sangria (wine punch) **3** : drain, draining ⟨una sangría fiscal : a financial drain⟩ **4** : indentation, indenting
sangriento, **-ta** *adj* **1** : bloody **2** : cruel
sanguijuela *nf* **1** : leech, bloodsucker **2** : sponger, leech
sanguinario, **-ria** *adj* : bloodthirsty
sanguíneo, **-nea** *adj* **1** : blood ⟨vaso sanguíneo : blood vessel⟩ **2** : sanguine, ruddy
sanidad *nf* **1** : health **2** : public health, sanitation
sanitario[1], **-ria** *adj* **1** : sanitary **2** : health ⟨centro sanitario : health center⟩
sanitario[2], **-ria** *n* : sanitation worker
sanitario[3] *nm Col, Mex, Ven* : toilet ⟨los sanitarios : the toilets, the restroom⟩
sano, **-na** *adj* **1** SALUDABLE : healthy **2** : wholesome **3** : whole, intact
santiaguino, **-na** *adj* : of or from Santiago, Chile
santiamén *nm* **en un santiamén** : in no time at all
santidad *nf* : holiness, sanctity
santificar {72} *vt* : to sanctify, to consecrate, to hallow
santiguarse {10} *vr* PERSIGNARSE : to cross oneself
santo[1], **-ta** *adj* **1** : holy, saintly ⟨el Santo Padre : the Holy Father⟩ ⟨una vida santa : a saintly life⟩ **2 Santo, Santa (San** *before names of masculine saints except those beginning with D or T*) : Saint ⟨Santa Clara : Saint Claire⟩ ⟨Santo Tomás : Saint Thomas⟩ ⟨San Francisco : Saint Francis⟩
santo[2], **-ta** *n* : saint
santo[3] *nm* **1** : saint's day **2** CUMPLEAÑOS : birthday
santuario *nm* : sanctuary
santurrón, **-rrona** *adj, mpl* **-rrones** : overly pious, sanctimonious — **santurronamente** *adv*
saña *nf* **1** : fury, rage **2** : viciousness ⟨con saña : viciously⟩
sapo *nm* : toad
saque[1], **etc.** → **sacar**
saque[2] *nm* **1** : kickoff (in soccer or football) **2** : serve, service (in sports)
saqueador, **-dora** *n* DEPREDADOR : plunderer, looter
saquear *vt* : to sack, to plunder, to loot
saqueo *nm* DEPREDACIÓN : sacking, plunder, looting
sarampión *nm* : measles *pl*
sarape *nm CA, Mex* : serape, blanket
sarcasmo *nm* : sarcasm
sarcástico, **-ca** *adj* : sarcastic
sarcófago *nm* : sarcophagus
sardina *nf* : sardine
sardónico, **-ca** *adj* : sardonic
sarga *nf* : serge
sargento *nmf* : sergeant
sarna *nf* : mange
sarnoso, **-sa** *adj* : mangy
sarpullido *nm* ERUPCIÓN : rash
sarro *nm* **1** : deposit, coating **2** : tartar, plaque
sarta *nf* **1** : string, series (of insults, etc.) **2** : string (of pearls, etc.)
sartén *nmf, pl* **sartenes** **1** : frying pan **2 tener la sartén por el mango** : to call the shots, to be in control
sasafrás *nm* : sassafras
sastre, **-tra** *n* : tailor
sastrería *nf* **1** : tailoring **2** : tailor's shop
Satanás *or* **Satán** *nm* : Satan, the devil
satánico, **-ca** *adj* : satanic
satélite *nm* : satellite
satín *or* **satén** *nm, pl* **satines** *or* **satenes** : satin
satinado, **-da** *adj* : satiny, glossy
sátira *nf* : satire
satírico, **-ca** *adj* : satirical, satiric
satirizar {21} *vt* : to satirize

sátiro *nm* : satyr
satisfacción *nf, pl* **-ciones** : satisfaction
satisfacer {74} *vt* **1** : to satisfy **2** : to fulfill, to meet **3** : to pay, to settle — **satisfacerse** *vr* **1** : to be satisfied **2** : to take revenge
satisfactorio, -ria *adj* : satisfactory — **satisfactoriamente** *adv*
satisfecho, -cha *adj* : satisfied, content, pleased
saturación *nf, pl* **-ciones** : saturation
saturar *vt* **1** : to saturate, to fill up **2** : to satiate, to surfeit
saturnismo *nm* : lead poisoning
Saturno *nm* : Saturn
sauce *nm* : willow
saúco *nm* : elder (tree)
saudí *or* **saudita** *adj & nmf* : Saudi, Saudi Arabian
sauna *nmf* : sauna
savia *nf* : sap
saxofón *nm, pl* **-fones** : saxophone
sazón[1] *nf, pl* **sazones** **1** : flavor, seasoning **2** : ripeness, maturity ⟨en sazón : in season, ripe⟩ **3 a la sazón** : at that time, then
sazón[2] *nmf, pl* **sazones** *Mex* : flavor, seasoning
sazonar *vt* CONDIMENTAR : to season, to spice
scanner *nm* → **escáner**
sé → **saber, ser**
se *pron* **1** : to him, to her, to you, to them ⟨se los daré a ella : I'll give them to her⟩ **2** : each other, one another ⟨se abrazaron : they hugged each other⟩ **3** : himself, herself, itself, yourself, yourselves, themselves ⟨se afeitó antes de salir : he shaved before leaving⟩ **4** (*used in passive constructions*) ⟨se dice que es hermosa : they say she's beautiful⟩ ⟨se habla inglés : English spoken⟩
sea, etc. → **ser**
sebo *nm* **1** : grease, fat **2** : tallow **3** : suet
secado *nm* : drying
secador *nm* : hair dryer
secadora *nf* **1** : dryer, clothes dryer **2** *Mex* : hair dryer
secante *nm* : blotting paper, blotter
secar {72} *v* : to dry — **secarse** *vr* **1** : to get dry **2** : to dry up
sección *nf, pl* **secciones** **1** : section ⟨sección transversal : cross section⟩ **2** : department, division
seco, -ca *adj* **1** : dry **2** DISECADO : dried ⟨fruta seca : dried fruit⟩ **3** : thin, lean **4** : curt, brusque **5** : sharp ⟨un golpe seco : a sharp blow⟩ **6 a secas** : simply, just ⟨se llama Chico, a secas : he's just called Chico⟩ **7 en ~** : abruptly, suddenly ⟨frenar en seco : to make a sudden stop⟩
secoya *nf* : sequoia, redwood
secreción *nf, pl* **-ciones** : secretion
secretar *vt* : to secrete
secretaría *nf* **1** : secretariat, administrative department **2** *Mex* : ministry, cabinet office
secretariado *nm* **1** : secretariat **2** : secretarial profession
secretario, -ria *n* : secretary — **secretarial** *adj*
secreto[1], **-ta** *adj* **1** : secret **2** : secretive — **secretamente** *adv*
secreto[2] *nm* **1** : secret **2** : secrecy
secta *nf* : sect
sectario, -ria *adj & n* : sectarian
sector *nm* : sector
secuaz *nmf, pl* **secuaces** : follower, henchman, underling
secuela *nf* : consequence, sequel ⟨las secuelas de la guerra : the aftermath of the war⟩
secuencia *nf* : sequence
secuestrador, -dora *n* **1** : kidnapper, abductor **2** : hijacker
secuestrar *vt* **1** RAPTAR : to kidnap, to abduct **2** : to hijack, to commandeer **3** CONFISCAR : to confiscate, to seize
secuestro *nm* **1** RAPTO : kidnapping, abduction **2** : hijacking **3** : seizure, confiscation
secular *adj* : secular — **secularismo** *nm* — **secularización** *nf*
secundar *vt* : to support, to second
secundaria *nf* **1** : secondary education, high school **2** *Mex* : junior high school, middle school
secundario, -ria *adj* : secondary
secuoya *nf* : sequoia
sed *nf* **1** : thirst ⟨tener sed : to be thirsty⟩ **2 tener sed de** : to hunger for, to thirst for
seda *nf* : silk
sedación *nf, pl* **-ciones** : sedation
sedal *nm* : fishing line
sedán *nm, pl* **sedanes** : sedan
sedante *adj & nm* CALMANTE : sedative
sedar *vt* : to sedate
sede *nf* **1** : seat, headquarters **2** : venue, site **3 la Santa Sede** : the Holy See
sedentario, -ria *adj* : sedentary
sedición *nf, pl* **-ciones** : sedition — **sedicioso, -sa** *adj*
sediento, -ta *adj* : thirsty, thirsting
sedimentación *nf, pl* **-ciones** : sedimentation
sedimentario, -ria *adj* : sedimentary
sedimento *nm* : sediment
sedoso, -sa *adj* : silky, silken
seducción *nf, pl* **-ciones** : seduction
seducir {61} *vt* **1** : to seduce **2** : to captivate, to charm
seductivo, -va *adj* : seductive
seductor[1], **-tora** *adj* **1** SEDUCTIVO : seductive **2** ENCANTADOR : charming, alluring
seductor[2], **-tora** *n* : seducer
segador, -dora *n* : harvester
segar {49} *vt* **1** : to reap, to harvest, to cut **2** : to sever abruptly ⟨una vida segada por la enfermedad : a life cut short by illness⟩
seglar[1] *adj* LAICO : lay, secular
seglar[2] *nm* LAICO : layperson, layman *m*, laywoman *f*

segmentación *nf, pl* **-ciones** : segmentation

segmentado, -da *adj* : segmented

segmento *nm* : segment

segregar {52} *vt* **1** : to segregate **2** SECRETAR : to secrete

seguida *nf* **en ~** : right away, immediately ⟨vuelvo en seguida : I'll be right back⟩

seguidamente *adv* **1** : next, immediately after **2** : without a break, continuously

seguido[1] *adv* **1** RECTO : straight, straight ahead **2** : often, frequently

seguido[2], **-da** *adj* **1** CONSECUTIVO : consecutive, successive ⟨tres días seguidos : three days in a row⟩ **2** : straight, unbroken **3 ~ por** *or* **~ de** : followed by

seguidor, -dora *n* : follower, supporter

seguimiento *nm* **1** : following, pursuit **2** : continuation **3** : tracking, monitoring

seguir {75} *vt* **1** : to follow ⟨el sol sigue la lluvia : sunshine follows the rain⟩ ⟨seguiré tu consejo : I'll follow your advice⟩ ⟨me siguieron con la mirada : they followed me with their eyes⟩ **2** : to go along, to keep on ⟨seguimos toda la carretera panamericana : we continued along the PanAmerican Highway⟩ ⟨siguió hablando : he kept on talking⟩ ⟨seguir el curso : to stay on course⟩ **3** : to take (a course, a treatment) — *vi* **1** : to go on, to keep going ⟨sigue adelante : keep going, carry on⟩ **2** : to remain, to continue to be ⟨¿todavía sigues aquí? : you're still here?⟩ ⟨sigue con vida : she's still alive⟩ **3** : to follow, to come after ⟨la frase que sigue : the following sentence⟩

según[1] *adv* : it depends ⟨según y como : it all depends on⟩

según[2] *conj* **1** COMO, CONFORME : as, just as ⟨según lo dejé : just as I left it⟩ **2** : depending on how ⟨según se vea : depending on how one sees it⟩

según[3] *prep* **1** : according to ⟨según los rumores : according to the rumors⟩ **2** : depending on ⟨según los resultados : depending on the results⟩

segundo[1], **-da** *adj* : second ⟨el segundo lugar : second place⟩

segundo[2], **-da** *n* **1** : second (in a series) **2** : second (person), second-in-command

segundo[3] *nm* : second ⟨sesenta segundos : sixty seconds⟩

seguramente *adv* **1** : for sure, surely **2** : probably

seguridad *nf* **1** : safety, security **2** : (financial) security ⟨seguridad social : Social Security⟩ **3** CERTEZA : certainty, assurance ⟨con toda seguridad : with complete certainty⟩ **4** : confidence, self-confidence

seguro[1] *adv* : certainly, definitely ⟨va a llover, seguro : it's going to rain for sure⟩ ⟨¡seguro que sí! : of course!⟩

seguro[2], **-ra** *adj* **1** : safe, secure **2** : sure, certain ⟨estoy segura que es él : I'm sure that's him⟩ **3** : reliable, trustworthy **4** : self-assured

seguro[3] *nm* **1** : insurance ⟨seguro de vida : life insurance⟩ **2** : fastener, clasp **3** *Mex* : safety pin

seis *adj & nm* : six

seiscientos[1], **-tas** *adj* : six hundred

seiscientos[2] *nms & pl* : six hundred

selección *nf, pl* **-ciones** **1** ELECCIÓN : selection, choice **2 selección natural** : natural selection

seleccionar *vt* ELEGIR : to select, to choose

selectivo, -va *adj* : selective — **selectivamente** *adv*

selecto, -ta *adj* **1** : choice, select **2** EXCLUSIVO : exclusive

selenio *nm* : selenium

sellar *vt* **1** : to seal **2** : to stamp

sello *nm* **1** : seal **2** ESTAMPILLA, TIMBRE : postage stamp **3** : hallmark, characteristic

selva *nf* **1** BOSQUE : woods *pl,* forest ⟨selva húmeda : rain forest⟩ **2** JUNGLA : jungle

selvático, -ca *adj* **1** : forest, jungle ⟨sendero selvático : jungle path⟩ **2** : wild

semáforo *nm* **1** : traffic light **2** : stop signal

semana *nf* : week

semanal *adj* : weekly — **semanalmente** *adv*

semanario *nm* : weekly (publication)

semántica *nf* : semantics

semántico, -ca *adj* : semantic

semblante *nm* **1** : countenance, face **2** : appearance, look

semblanza *nf* : biographical sketch, profile

sembrado *nm* : cultivated field

sembrador, -dora *n* : planter, sower

sembradora *nf* : seeder (machine)

sembrar {55} *vt* **1** : to plant, to sow **2** : to scatter, to strew ⟨sembrar el pánico : to spread panic⟩

semejante[1] *adj* **1** PARECIDO : similar, alike **2** TAL : such ⟨nunca he visto cosa semejante : I have never seen such a thing⟩

semejante[2] *nm* PRÓJIMO : fellowman

semejanza *nf* PARECIDO : similarity, resemblance

semejar *vi* : to resemble, to look like — **semejarse** *vr* : to be similar, to look alike

semen *nm* : semen

semental *nm* : stud (animal) ⟨caballo semental : stallion⟩

semestre *nm* : semester

semicírculo *nm* : semicircle, half circle

semiconductor *nm* : semiconductor

semidiós *nm, pl* **-dioses** : demigod *m*

semifinal *nf* : semifinal

semifinalista[1] *adj* : semifinal

semifinalista[2] *nmf* : semifinalist

semiformal *adj* : semiformal

semilla *nf* : seed

semillero *nm* **1** : seedbed **2** : hotbed, breeding ground

seminario *nm* **1** : seminary **2** : seminar, graduate course

seminarista *nm* : seminarian

semiprecioso, -sa *adj* : semiprecious

semita[1] *adj* : Semitic

semita[2] *nmf* : Semite

sémola *nf* : semolina

sempiterno, -na *adj* ETERNO : eternal, everlasting

senado *nm* : senate

senador, -dora *n* : senator

sencillamente *adv* : simply, plainly

sencillez *nf* : simplicity

sencillo[1], **-lla** *adj* **1** : simple, easy **2** : plain, unaffected **3** : single

sencillo[2] *nm* **1** : single (recording) **2** : small change (coins) **3** : one-way ticket

senda *nf* CAMINO, SENDERO : path, way

sendero *nm* CAMINO, SENDA : path, way

sendos, -das *adj pl* : each, both ⟨llevaban sendos vestidos nuevos : they were each wearing a new dress⟩

senectud *nf* ANCIANIDAD : old age

senegalés, -lesa *adj & n, mpl* **-leses** : Senegalese

senil *adj* : senile — **senilidad** *nf*

seno *nm* **1** : breast, bosom ⟨los senos : the breasts⟩ ⟨el seno de la familia : the bosom of the family⟩ **2** : sinus **3 seno materno** : womb

sensación *nf, pl* **-ciones 1** IMPRESIÓN : feeling ⟨tener la sensación : to have a feeling⟩ **2** : sensation ⟨causar sensación : to cause a sensation⟩

sensacional *adj* : sensational

sensacionalista *adj* : sensationalistic, lurid

sensatez *nf* **1** : good sense **2 con ~** : sensibly

sensato, -ta *adj* : sensible, sound — **sensatamente** *adv*

sensibilidad *nf* **1** : sensitivity, sensibility **2** SENSACIÓN : feeling

sensibilizar {21} *vt* : to sensitize

sensible *adj* **1** : sensitive **2** APRECIABLE : considerable, significant

sensiblemente *adv* : considerably, significantly

sensiblería *nf* : sentimentality, mush

sensiblero, -ra *adj* : mawkish, sentimental, mushy

sensitivo, -va *adj* **1** : sense ⟨órganos sensitivos : sense organs⟩ **2** : sentient, capable of feeling

sensor *nm* : sensor

sensorial *adj* : sensory

sensual *adj* : sensual, sensuous — **sensualmente** *adv*

sensualidad *nf* : sensuality

sentado, -da *adj* **1** : sitting, seated **2** : established, settled ⟨dar por sentado : to take for granted⟩ ⟨dejar sentado : to make clear⟩ **3** : sensible, steady, judicious

sentar {55} *vt* **1** : to seat, to sit **2** : to establish, to set — *vi* **1** : to suit ⟨ese color te sienta : that color suits you⟩ **2** : to agree with (of food or drink) ⟨las cebollas no me sientan : onions don't agree with me⟩ **3** : to please ⟨le sentó mal el paseo : she didn't enjoy the trip⟩ — **sentarse** *vr* : to sit, to sit down ⟨siéntese, por favor : please have a seat⟩

sentencia *nf* **1** : sentence, judgment **2** : maxim, saying

sentenciar *vt* : to sentence

sentido[1], **-da** *adj* **1** : heartfelt, sincere ⟨mi más sentido pésame : my sincerest condolences⟩ **2** : touchy, sensitive **3** : offended, hurt

sentido[2] *nm* **1** : sense ⟨sentido común : common sense⟩ ⟨los cinco sentidos : the five senses⟩ ⟨sin sentido : senseless⟩ **2** CONOCIMIENTO : consciousness **3** SIGNIFICADO : meaning, sense ⟨doble sentido : double entendre⟩ **4** : direction ⟨calle de sentido único : one-way street⟩

sentimental[1] *adj* **1** : sentimental **2** : love, romantic ⟨vida sentimental : love life⟩

sentimental[2] *nmf* : sentimentalist

sentimentalismo *nm* : sentimentality, sentimentalism

sentimiento *nm* **1** : feeling, emotion **2** PESAR : regret, sorrow

sentir {76} *vt* **1** : to feel, to experience ⟨no siento nada de dolor : I don't feel any pain⟩ ⟨sentía sed : he was feeling thirsty⟩ ⟨sentir amor : to feel love⟩ **2** PERCIBIR : to perceive, to sense ⟨sentir un ruido : to hear a noise⟩ **3** LAMENTAR : to regret, to feel sorry for ⟨lo siento mucho : I'm very sorry⟩ — *vi* **1** : to have feeling, to feel **2 sin ~** : without noticing, inadvertently — **sentirse** *vr* **1** : to feel ⟨¿te sientes mejor? : are you feeling better?⟩ **2** *Chile, Mex* : to take offense

seña *nf* **1** : sign, signal **2 dar señas de** : to show signs of

señal *nf* **1** : signal **2** : sign ⟨señal de tráfico : traffic sign⟩ **3** INDICIO : indication ⟨en señal de : as a token of⟩ **4** VESTIGIO : trace, vestige **5** : scar, mark **6** : deposit, down payment

señalado, -da *adj* : distinguished, notable

señalador *nm* : marker ⟨señalador de libros : bookmark⟩

señalar *vt* **1** INDICAR : to indicate, to show **2** : to mark **3** : to point out, to stress **4** : to fix, to set — **señalarse** *vr* : to distinguish oneself

señor, -ñora *n* **1** : gentleman *m,* man *m,* lady *f,* woman *f,* wife *f* **2** : Sir *m,* Madam *f* ⟨estimados señores : Dear Sirs⟩ **3** : Mr. *m,* Mrs. *f* **4** : lord *m,* lady *f* ⟨el Señor : the Lord⟩

señoría *nf* **1** : lordship **2 Su Señoría** : Your Honor

señorial *adj* : stately, regal

señorío *nm* **1** : manor, estate **2** : dominion, power **3** : elegance, class
señorita *nf* **1** : young lady, young woman **2** : Miss
señuelo *nm* **1** : decoy **2** : bait
sépalo *nm* : sepal
sepa, etc. → **saber**
separación *nf, pl* **-ciones** **1** : separation, division **2** : gap, space
separadamente *adv* : separately, apart
separado, -da *adj* **1** : separated **2** : separate ⟨vidas separadas : separate lives⟩ **3 por ~** : separately
separar *vt* **1** : to separate, to divide **2** : to split up, to pull apart — **separarse** *vr*
sepelio *nm* : interment, burial
sepia[1] *adj & nm* : sepia
sepia[2] *nf* : cuttlefish
septentrional *adj* : northern
séptico, -ca *adj* : septic
septiembre *nm* : September
séptimo[1], **-ma** *adj* : seventh
séptimo[2] *nm* : seventh
septuagésimo[1], **-ma** *adj* : seventieth
septuagésimo[2] *nm* : seventieth
sepulcral *adj* **1** : sepulchral **2** : dismal, gloomy
sepulcro *nm* TUMBA : tomb, sepulchre
sepultar *vt* ENTERRAR : to bury
sepultura *nf* **1** : burial **2** TUMBA : grave, tomb
seque, etc. → **secar**
sequedad *nf* **1** : dryness **2** : brusqueness, curtness
sequía *nf* : drought
séquito *nm* : retinue, entourage
ser[1] {77} *vi* **1** : to be ⟨él es mi hermano : he is my brother⟩ ⟨Camila es linda : Camila is pretty⟩ **2** : to exist, to live ⟨ser, o no ser : to be or not to be⟩ **3** : to take place, to occur ⟨el concierto es el domingo : the concert is on Sunday⟩ **4** (*used with expressions of time, date, season*) ⟨son las diez : it's ten o'clock⟩ ⟨hoy es el 9 : today's the 9th⟩ **5** : to cost, to come to ⟨¿cuánto es? : how much is it?⟩ **6** (*with the future tense*) : to be able to be ⟨¿será posible? : can it be possible?⟩ **7 ~ de** : to come from ⟨somos de Managua : we're from Managua⟩ **8 ~ de** : to belong to ⟨ese lápiz es de Juan : that's Juan's pencil⟩ **9 es que** : the thing is that ⟨es que no lo conozco : it's just that I don't know him⟩ **10 ¡sea!** : agreed!, all right! **11 sea . . . sea** : either . . . or — *v aux* (*used in passive constructions*) : to be ⟨la cuenta ha sido pagada : the bill has been paid⟩ ⟨él fue asesinado : he was murdered⟩
ser[2] *nm* : being ⟨ser humano : human being⟩
seráfico, -ca *adj* : angelic, seraphic
serbio[1], **-bia** *adj & n* : Serb, Serbian
serbio[2] *nm* : Serbian (language)
serbocroata[1] *adj* : Serbo-Croatian
serbocroata[2] *nm* : Serbo-Croatian (language)
serenar *vt* : to calm, to soothe — **serenarse** *vr* CALMARSE : to calm down
serenata *nf* : serenade
serendipia *nf* : serendipity
serenidad *nf* : serenity, calmness
sereno[1], **-na** *adj* **1** SOSEGADO : serene, calm, composed **2** : fair, clear (of weather) **3** : calm, still (of the sea) — **serenamente** *adv*
sereno[2] *nm* : night watchman
seriado, -da *adj* : serial
serial *nm* : serial (on radio or television)
seriamente *adv* : seriously
serie *nf* **1** : series **2** SERIAL : serial **3 fabricación en serie** : mass production **4 fuera de serie** : extraordinary, amazing
seriedad *nf* **1** : seriousness, earnestness **2** : gravity, importance
serio, -ria *adj* **1** : serious, earnest **2** : reliable, responsible **3** : important **4 en ~** : seriously, in earnest — **seriamente** *adv*
sermón *nm, pl* **sermones** **1** : sermon **2** *fam* : harangue, lecture
sermonear *vt fam* : to harangue, to lecture
serpentear *vi* : to twist, to wind — **serpenteante** *adj*
serpentina *nf* : paper streamer
serpiente *nf* : serpent, snake
serrado, -da *adj* DENTADO : serrated
serranía *nf* : mountainous area
serrano, -na *adj* : from the mountains
serrar {55} *vt* : to saw
serrín *nm, pl* **serrines** : sawdust
serruchar *vt* : to saw up
serrucho *nm* : saw, handsaw
servicentro *nm Peru* : gas station
servicial *adj* : obliging, helpful
servicio *nm* **1** : service **2** SAQUE : serve (in sports) **3 servicios** *nmpl* : restroom
servidor, -dora *n* **1** : servant **2 su seguro servidor** : yours truly (in correspondence)
servidumbre *nf* **1** : servitude **2** : help, servants *pl*
servil *adj* **1** : servile, subservient **2** : menial
servilismo *nm* : servility, subservience
servilleta *nf* : napkin
servir {54} *vt* **1** : to serve, to be of use to **2** : to serve, to wait **3** SURTIR : to fill (an order) — *vi* **1** : to work ⟨mi radio no sirve : my radio isn't working⟩ **2** : to be of use, to be helpful ⟨esa computadora no sirve para nada : that computer's perfectly useless⟩ — **servirse** *vr* **1** : to help oneself to **2** : to be kind enough ⟨sírvase enviarnos un catálogo : please send us a catalog⟩
sésamo *nm* AJONJOLÍ : sesame, sesame seeds *pl*
sesenta *adj & nm* : sixty
sesentavo[1], **-va** *adj* : sixtieth
sesentavo[2] *n* : sixtieth (fraction)
sesgado, -da *adj* **1** : inclined, tilted **2** : slanted, biased

sesgar {52} *vt* **1** : to cut on the bias **2** : to tilt **3** : to bias, to slant
sesgo *nm* : bias
sesgue, etc. → **sesgar**
sesión *nf, pl* **sesiones** **1** : session **2** : showing, performance
sesionar *vi* REUNIRSE : to meet, to be in session
seso *nm* **1** : brains, intelligence **2 sesos** *nmpl* : brains (as food)
sesudo, -da *adj* **1** : prudent, sensible **2** : brainy
set *nm, pl* **sets** : set (in tennis)
seta *nf* : mushroom
setecientos[1], **-tas** *adj* : seven hundred
setecientos[2] *nms & pl* : seven hundred
setenta *adj & nm* : seventy
setentavo[1], **-va** *adj* : seventieth
setentavo[2] *nm* : seventieth
setiembre → **septiembre**
seto *nm* **1** : fence, enclosure **2 seto vivo** : hedge
seudónimo *nm* : pseudonym
severidad *nf* **1** : harshness, severity **2** : strictness
severo, -ra *adj* **1** : harsh, severe **2** ESTRICTO : strict — **severamente** *adv*
sexagésimo[1], **-ma** *adj* : sixtieth, sixty-
sexagésimo[2], **-ma** *n* : sixtieth, sixty- (in a series)
sexismo *nm* : sexism — **sexista** *adj & nmf*
sexo *nm* : sex
sextante *nm* : sextant
sexteto *nm* : sextet
sexto, -ta *adj* : sixth — **sexto, -ta** *n*
sexual *adj* : sexual, sex ⟨educación sexual : sex education⟩ — **sexualmente** *adv*
sexualidad *nf* : sexuality
sexy *adj, pl* **sexy** *or* **sexys** : sexy
shock [ˈʃɔk, ˈʧɔk] *nm* : shock ⟨estado de shock : state of shock⟩
short *nm, pl* **shorts** : shorts *pl*
show *nm, pl* **shows** : show
si *conj* **1** : if ⟨lo haré si me pagan : I'll do it if they pay me⟩ ⟨si lo supiera te lo diría : if I knew it I would tell you⟩ **2** : whether, if ⟨no importa si funciona o no : it doesn't matter whether it works (or not)⟩ **3** (*expressing desire, protest, or surprise*) ⟨si supiera la verdad : if only I knew the truth⟩ ⟨¡si no quiero! : but I don't want to!⟩ **4 si bien** : although ⟨si bien se ha progresado : although progress has been made⟩ **5 si no** : otherwise, or else ⟨si no, no voy : otherwise I won't go⟩
sí[1] *adv* **1** : yes ⟨sí, gracias : yes, please⟩ ⟨creo que sí : I think so⟩ **2 sí que** : indeed, absolutely ⟨esta vez sí que ganaré : this time I'm sure to win⟩ **3 porque sí** *fam* : because, just because ⟨lo hizo porque sí : she did it just because⟩
sí[2] *nm* : yes ⟨dar el sí : to say yes, to express consent⟩
sí[3] *pron* **1 de por sí** *or* **en sí** : by itself, in itself, per se **2 fuera de sí** : beside oneself **3 para sí (mismo)** : to himself, to herself, for himself, for herself **4 entre ~** : among themselves
siamés, -mesa *adj & n, mpl* **siameses** : Siamese
sibilante *adj & nf* : sibilant
siciliano, -na *adj & n* : Sicilian
sico- → **psico-**
sicomoro *or* **sicómoro** *nm* : sycamore
SIDA *or* **sida** *nm* (*s*índrome de *i*nmun*o*deficiencia *a*dquirida) : AIDS
siderurgia *nf* : iron and steel industry
siderúrgico, -ca *adj* : steel, iron ⟨la industria siderúrgica : the steel industry⟩
sidra *nf* : hard cider
siega[1], **siegue, etc.** → **segar**
siega[2] *nf* **1** : harvesting **2** : harvest time **3** : harvested crop
siembra[1], **etc.** → **sembrar**
siembra[2] *nf* **1** : sowing **2** : sowing season **3** SEMBRADO : cultivated field
siempre *adv* **1** : always ⟨siempre tienes hambre : you're always hungry⟩ **2** : still ⟨¿siempre te vas? : are you still going?⟩ **3** *Mex* : after all ⟨siempre no fui : I didn't go after all⟩ **4 siempre que** : whenever, every time ⟨siempre que pasa : every time he walks by⟩ **5 para ~** : forever, for good **6 siempre y cuando** : provided that
sien *nf* : temple (on the forehead)
sienta, etc. → **sentar**
siente, etc. → **sentir**
sierpe *nf* : serpent, snake
sierra[1], **etc.** → **serrar**
sierra[2] *nf* **1** : saw ⟨sierra de vaivén : jigsaw⟩ **2** CORDILLERA : mountain range **3** : mountains *pl* ⟨viven en la sierra : they live in the mountains⟩
siervo, -va *n* **1** : slave **2** : serf
siesta *nf* : nap, siesta
siete *adj & nm* : seven
sífilis *nf* : syphilis
sifón *nm, pl* **sifones** : siphon
siga, sigue etc. → **seguir**
sigilo *nm* : secrecy, stealth
sigiloso, -sa *adj* FURTIVO : furtive, stealthy — **sigilosamente** *adv*
sigla *nf* : acronym, abbreviation
siglo *nm* **1** : century **2** : age ⟨el Siglo de Oro : the Golden Age⟩ ⟨hace siglos que no te veo : I haven't seen you in ages⟩ **3** : world, secular life
signar *vt* : to sign (a treaty or agreement)
signatario, -ria *n* : signatory
significación *nf, pl* **-ciones** **1** : significance, importance **2** : signification, meaning
significado *nm* **1** : sense, meaning **2** : significance
significante *adj* : significant
significar {72} *vt* **1** : to mean, to signify **2** : to express, to make known — **significarse** *vr* **1** : to draw attention, to become known **2** : to take a stance
significativo, -va *adj* **1** : significant, important **2** : meaningful — **significativamente** *adv*

signo *nm* **1** : sign ⟨signo de igual : equal sign⟩ ⟨un signo de alegría : a sign of happiness⟩ **2** : (punctuation) mark ⟨signo de interrogación : question mark⟩ ⟨signo de admiración : exclamation point⟩ ⟨signo de intercalación : caret⟩

siguiente *adj* : next, following

sílaba *nf* : syllable

silábico, -ca *adj* : syllabic

silbar *v* : to whistle

silbato *nm* PITO : whistle

silbido *nm* : whistle, whistling

silenciador *nm* **1** : muffler (of an automobile) **2** : silencer

silenciar *vt* **1** : to silence **2** : to muffle

silencio *nm* **1** : silence, quiet ⟨¡silencio! : be quiet!⟩ **2** : rest (in music)

silencioso, -sa *adj* : silent, quiet — **silenciosamente** *adv*

sílice *nf* : silica

silicio *nm* : silicon

silla *nf* **1** : chair **2 silla de ruedas** : wheelchair

sillón *nm, pl* **sillones** : armchair, easy chair

silo *nm* : silo

silueta *nf* **1** : silhouette **2** : figure, shape

silvestre *adj* : wild ⟨flor silvestre : wildflower⟩

silvicultor, -tora *n* : forester

silvicultura *nf* : forestry

sima *nf* ABISMO : chasm, abyss

simbólico, -ca *adj* : symbolic — **simbólicamente** *adj*

simbolismo *nm* : symbolism

simbolizar {21} *vt* : to symbolize

símbolo *nm* : symbol

simetría *nf* : symmetry

simétrico, -ca *adj* : symmetrical, symmetric

simiente *nf* : seed

símil *nm* **1** : simile **2** : analogy, comparison

similar *adj* SEMEJANTE : similar, alike

similitud *nf* : similarity, resemblance

simio *nm* : ape

simpatía *nf* **1** : liking, affection ⟨tomarle simpatía a : to take a liking to⟩ **2** : warmth, friendliness **3** : support, solidarity

simpático, -ca *adj* : nice, friendly, likeable

simpatizante *nf* : sympathizer, supporter

simpatizar {21} *vi* **1** : to get along, to hit it off ⟨simpaticé mucho con él : I really liked him⟩ **2 ~ con** : to sympathize with, to support

simple[1] *adj* **1** SENCILLO : plain, simple, easy **2** : pure, mere ⟨por simple vanidad : out of pure vanity⟩ **3** : simpleminded, foolish

simple[2] *n* : fool, simpleton

simplemente *adv* : simply, merely, just

simpleza *nf* **1** : foolishness, simpleness **2** NECEDAD : nonsense

simplicidad *nf* : simplicity

simplificar {72} *vt* : to simplify — **simplificación** *nf*

simplista *adj* : simplistic

simposio *or* **simposium** *nm* : symposium

simulación *nf, pl* **-ciones** : simulation

simulacro *nm* : imitation, sham ⟨simulacro de juicio : mock trial⟩

simular *vt* **1** : to simulate **2** : to feign, to pretend

simultáneo, -nea *adj* : simultaneous — **simultáneamente** *adv*

sin *prep* **1** : without ⟨sin querer : unintentionally⟩ ⟨sin refinar : unrefined⟩ **2 sin que** : without ⟨lo hicimos sin que él se diera cuenta : we did it without him noticing⟩

sinagoga *nf* : synagogue

sinceridad *nf* : sincerity

sincero, -ra *adj* : sincere, honest, true — **sinceramente** *adv*

síncopa *nf* : syncopation

sincopar *vt* : to syncopate

sincronizar {21} *vt* : to synchronize — **sincronización** *nf*

sindical *adj* GREMIAL : union, labor ⟨representante sindical : union representative⟩

sindicalización *nf, pl* **-ciones** : unionizing, unionization

sindicalizar {21} *vt* : to unionize — **sindicalizarse** *vr* **1** : to form a union **2** : to join a union

sindicar → **sindicalizar**

sindicato *nm* GREMIO : union, guild

síndrome *nm* : syndrome

sinecura *nf* : sinecure

sinfín *nm* : endless number ⟨un sinfín de problemas : no end of problems⟩

sinfonía *nf* : symphony

sinfónica *nf* : symphony orchestra

sinfónico, -ca *adj* : symphonic, symphony

singular[1] *adj* **1** : singular, unique **2** PARTICULAR : peculiar, odd **3** : singular (in grammar) — **singularmente** *adv*

singular[2] *nm* : singular

singularidad *nf* : uniqueness, singularity

singularizar {21} *vt* : to make unique or distinct — **singularizarse** *vr* : to stand out, to distinguish oneself

siniestrado, -da *adj* : damaged, wrecked ⟨zona siniestrada : disaster zone⟩

siniestro[1], **-tra** *adj* **1** IZQUIERDO : left, left-hand **2** MALVADO : sinister, evil

siniestro[2] *nm* : accident, disaster

sinnúmero → **sinfín**

sino *conj* **1** : but, rather ⟨no será hoy, sino mañana : it won't be today, but tomorrow⟩ **2** EXCEPTO : but, except ⟨no hace sino despertar suspicacias : it does nothing but arouse suspicion⟩

sinónimo[1], **-ma** *adj* : synonymous

sinónimo[2] *nm* : synonym

sinopsis *nfs & pl* RESUMEN : synopsis, summary

sinrazón *nf, pl* **-zones** : wrong, injustice

sinsabores *nmpl* : woes, troubles
sinsonte *nm* : mockingbird
sintáctico, -ca *adj* : syntactic, syntactical
sintaxis *nfs & pl* : syntax
síntesis *nfs & pl* **1** : synthesis, fusion **2** SINOPSIS : synopsis, summary
sintético, -ca *adj* : synthetic — **sintéticamente** *adv*
sintetizar {21} *vt* **1** : to synthesize **2** RESUMIR : to summarize
sintió, etc. → **sentir**
síntoma *nm* : symptom
sintomático, -ca *adj* : symptomatic
sintonía *nf* **1** : tuning in (of a radio) **2 en sintonía con** : in tune with, attuned to
sintonizador *nm* : tuner, knob for tuning (of a radio, etc.)
sintonizar {21} *vt* : to tune (in) to — *vi* **1** : to tune in **2 ~ con** : to be in tune with, to empathize with
sinuosidad *nf* : sinuosity
sinuoso, -sa *adj* **1** : winding, sinuous **2** : devious
sinvergüenza[1] *adj* **1** DESCARADO : shameless, brazen, impudent **2** TRAVIESO : naughty
sinvergüenza[2] *nmf* **1** : rogue, scoundrel **2** : brat, rascal
sionista *adj & nmf* : Zionist — **sionismo** *nm*
siqui- → **psiqui-**
siquiera *adv* **1** : at least ⟨dame siquiera un poquito : at least give me a little bit⟩ **2** (*in negative constructions*) : not even ⟨ni siquiera nos saludaron : they didn't even say hello to us⟩
sirena *nf* **1** : mermaid **2** : siren ⟨sirena de niebla : foghorn⟩
sirio, -ria *adj & n* : Syrian
sirope *nm* : syrup
sirve, etc. → **servir**
sirviente, -ta *n* : servant, maid *f*
sisal *nm* : sisal
sisear *vi* : to hiss
siseo *nm* : hiss
sísmico, -ca *adj* : seismic
sismo *nm* **1** TERREMOTO : earthquake **2** TEMBLOR : tremor
sismógrafo *nm* : seismograph
sistema *nm* : system
sistemático, -ca *adj* : systematic — **sistemáticamente** *adv*
sistematizar {21} *vt* : to systematize
sistémico, -ca *adj* : systemic
sitiar *vt* ASEDIAR : to besiege
sitio *nm* **1** LUGAR : place, site ⟨vámonos a otro sitio : let's go somewhere else⟩ **2** ESPACIO : room, space ⟨hacer sitio a : to make room for⟩ **3** : siege ⟨estado de sitio : state of siege⟩ **4** *Mex* : taxi stand
situación *nf, pl* **-ciones** : situation
situado, -da *adj* : situated, placed
situar {3} *vt* UBICAR : to situate, to place, to locate — **situarse** *vr* **1** : to be placed, to be located **2** : to make a place for oneself, to do well
sketch *nm* : sketch, skit
slip *nm* : briefs *pl*, underpants *pl*
smog *nm* : smog
smoking *nm* ESMOQUIN : tuxedo
snob → **esnob**
so *prep* : under ⟨so pena de : under penalty of⟩
sobaco *nm* : armpit
sobado, -da *adj* **1** : worn, shabby **2** : well-worn, hackneyed
sobar *vt* **1** : to finger, to handle **2** : to knead **3** : to rub, to massage **4** *fam* : to beat, to pummel
soberanía *nf* : sovereignty
soberano, -na *adj & n* : sovereign
soberbia *nf* **1** ORGULLO : pride, arrogance **2** MAGNIFICENCIA : magnificence
soberbio, -bia *adj* **1** : proud, arrogant **2** : grand, magnificent
sobornable *adv* : venal, bribable
sobornar *vt* : to bribe
soborno *nm* **1** : bribery **2** : bribe
sobra *nf* **1** : excess, surplus **2 de ~** : extra, to spare **3 sobras** *nfpl* : leftovers, scraps
sobrado, -da *adj* : abundant, excessive, more than enough
sobrante[1] *adj* : remaining, superfluous
sobrante[2] *nm* : remainder, surplus
sobrar *vi* : to be in excess, to be superfluous ⟨más vale que sobre a que falte : it's better to have too much than not enough⟩
sobre[1] *nm* **1** : envelope **2** : packet ⟨un sobre de sazón : a packet of seasoning⟩
sobre[2] *prep* **1** : on, on top of ⟨sobre la mesa : on the table⟩ **2** : over, above **3** : about ⟨¿tiene libros sobre Bolivia? : do you have books on Bolivia?⟩ **4 sobre todo** : especially, above all
sobrealimentar *vt* : to overfeed
sobrecalentar {55} *vt* : to overheat — **sobrecalentarse** *vr*
sobrecama *nmf* : bedspread
sobrecargar {52} *vt* : to overload, to overburden, to weigh down
sobrecoger {15} *vt* **1** : to surprise, to startle **2** : to scare — **sobrecogerse** *vr*
sobrecubierta *nf* : dust jacket
sobredosis *nfs & pl* : overdose
sobreentender {56} *vt* : to infer, to understand
sobreestimar *vt* : to overestimate, to overrate
sobreexcitado, -da *adj* : overexcited
sobreexponer {60} *vt* : to overexpose
sobregirar *vt* : to overdraw
sobregiro *nm* : overdraft
sobrehumano, -na *adj* : superhuman
sobrellevar *vt* : to endure, to bear
sobremanera *adv* : exceedingly
sobremesa *nf* : after-dinner conversation
sobrenatural *adj* : supernatural
sobrenombre *nm* APODO : nickname
sobrentender → **sobreentender**

sobrepasar *vt* : to exceed, to surpass — **sobrepasarse** *vr* PASARSE : to go too far

sobrepelliz *nf, pl* **-pellices** : surplice

sobrepeso *nm* **1** : excess weight **2** : overweight, obesity

sobrepoblación, sobrepoblado → **superpoblación, superpoblado**

sobreponer {60} *vt* **1** SUPERPONER : to superimpose **2** ANTEPONER : to put first, to give priority to — **sobreponerse** *vr* **1** : to pull oneself together **2** **~ a** : to overcome

sobreprecio *nm* : surcharge

sobreproducción *nf, pl* **-ciones** : overproduction

sobreproducir {61} *vt* : to overproduce

sobreprotector, -tora *adj* : overprotective

sobreproteger {15} *vt* : to overprotect

sobresaliente[1] *adj* **1** : protruding, projecting **2** : outstanding, noteworthy **3** : significant, salient

sobresaliente[2] *nmf* : understudy

sobresalir {73} *vi* **1** : to protrude, to jut out, to project **2** : to stand out, to excel

sobresaltar *vt* : to startle, to frighten — **sobresaltarse** *vr*

sobresalto *nm* : start, fright

sobresueldo *nm* : bonus, additional pay

sobretasa *nf* : surcharge ⟨sobretasa a la gasolina : gas tax⟩

sobretodo *nm* : overcoat

sobrevalorar *or* **sobrevaluar** {3} *vt* : to overvalue, to overrate

sobrevender *vt* : to oversell

sobrevenir {87} *vi* ACAECER : to take place, to come about ⟨podrían sobrevenir complicaciones : complications could occur⟩

sobrevivencia → **supervivencia**

sobreviviente → **superviviente**

sobrevivir *vi* : to survive — *vt* : to outlive, to outlast

sobrevolar {19} *vt* : to fly over, to overfly

sobriedad *nf* : sobriety, moderation

sobrino, -na *n* : nephew *m*, niece *f*

sobrio, -bria *adj* : sober — **sobriamente** *adv*

socarrón, -rrona *adj, mpl* **-rrones** **1** : sly, cunning **2** : sarcastic

socavar *vt* : to undermine

sociabilidad *nf* : sociability

sociable *adj* : sociable

social *adj* : social — **socialmente** *adv*

socialista *adj & nmf* : socialist — **socialismo** *nm*

sociedad *nf* **1** : society **2** : company, enterprise **3** **sociedad anónima** : incorporated company

socio, -cia *n* **1** : member **2** : partner

socioeconómico, -ca *adj* : socioeconomic

sociología *nf* : sociology

sociológico, -ca *adj* : sociological — **sociológicamente** *adv*

sociólogo, -ga *n* : sociologist

socorrer *vt* : to assist, to come to the aid of

socorrido, -da *adj* ÚTIL : handy, practical

socorrista *nmf* **1** : rescue worker **2** : lifeguard

socorro *nm* AUXILIO **1** : aid, help ⟨equipo de socorro : rescue team⟩ **2** **¡socorro!** : help!

soda *nf* : soda, soda water

sodio *nf* : sodium

soez *adj, pl* **soeces** GROSERO : rude, vulgar — **soezmente** *adv*

sofá *nm* : couch, sofa

sofistería *nf* : sophistry — **sofista** *nmf*

sofisticación *nf, pl* **-ciones** : sophistication

sofisticado, -da *adj* : sophisticated

sofocante *adj* : suffocating, stifling

sofocar {72} *vt* **1** AHOGAR : to suffocate, to smother **2** EXTINGUIR : to extinguish, to put out (a fire) **3** APLASTAR : to crush, to put down ⟨sofocar una rebelión : to crush a rebellion⟩ — **sofocarse** *vr* **1** : to suffocate **2** *fam* : to get upset, to get mad

sofreír {66} *vt* : to sauté

sofrito[1]**, -ta** *adj* : sautéed

sofrito[2] *nm* : seasoning sauce

softbol *nm* : softball

software *nm* : software

soga *nf* : rope

soja → **soya**

sojuzgar *vt* : to subdue, to conquer, to subjugate

sol *nm* **1** : sun **2** : Peruvian unit of currency

solamente *adv* SÓLO : only, just

solapa *nf* **1** : lapel (of a jacket) **2** : flap (of an envelope)

solapado, -da *adj* : secret, underhanded

solapar *vt* : to cover up, to keep secret — **solaparse** *vr* : to overlap

solar[1] {19} *vt* : to floor, to tile

solar[2] *adj* : solar, sun

solar[3] *nm* **1** TERRENO : lot, piece of land, site **2** *Cuba, Peru* : tenement building

solariego, -ga *adj* : ancestral

solaz *nm, pl* **solaces** **1** CONSUELO : solace, comfort **2** DESCANSO : relaxation, recreation

solazarse {21} *vr* : to relax, to enjoy oneself

soldado *nm* **1** : soldier **2** **soldado raso** : private, enlisted man

soldador[1]**, -dora** *n* : welder

soldador[2] *nm* : soldering iron

soldadura *nf* **1** : welding **2** : soldering, solder

soldar {19} *vt* **1** : to weld **2** : to solder

soleado, -da *adj* : sunny

soledad *nf* : loneliness, solitude

solemne *adj* : solemn — **solemnemente** *adv*

solemnidad *nf* : solemnity

soler {78} *vi* : to be in the habit of, to tend to ⟨solía tomar café por la tarde : she usually drank coffee in the afternoon⟩ ⟨eso suele ocurrir : that frequently happens⟩
solera *nf* **1** : prop, support **2** : tradition
solicitante *nmf* : applicant
solicitar *vt* **1** : to request, to solicit **2** : to apply for ⟨solicitar empleo : to apply for employment⟩
solícito, -ta *adj* : solicitous, attentive, obliging
solicitud *nf* **1** : solicitude, concern **2** : request **3** : application
solidaridad *nf* : solidarity
solidario, -ria *adj* : supportive, united in support ⟨se declararon solidarios con la nueva ley : they declared their support for the new law⟩ ⟨espíritu solidario : spirit of solidarity⟩
solidarizar {21} *vi* : to be in solidarity ⟨solidarizamos con la huelga : we support the strike⟩
solidez *nf* **1** : solidity, firmness **2** : soundness (of an argument, etc.)
solidificar {72} *vt* : to solidify, to make solid — **solidificarse** *vr* — **solidificación** *nf*
sólido[1], **-da** *adj* **1** : solid, firm **2** : sturdy, well-made **3** : sound, well-founded — **sólidamente** *adv*
sólido[2] *nm* : solid
soliloquio *nm* : soliloquy
solista *nmf* : soloist
solitaria *nf* TENIA : tapeworm
solitario[1], **-ria** *adj* **1** : lonely **2** : lone, solitary **3** DESIERTO : deserted, lonely ⟨una calle solitaria : a deserted street⟩
solitario[2], **-ria** *n* : recluse, loner
solitario[3] *nm* : solitaire
sollozar {21} *vi* : to sob
sollozo *nm* : sob
solo[1], **-la** *adj* **1** : alone, by oneself **2** : lonely **3** ÚNICO : only, sole, unique ⟨hay un solo problema : there's only one problem⟩ **4 a solas** : alone
solo[2] *nm* : solo
sólo *adv* SOLAMENTE : just, only ⟨sólo quieren comer : they just want to eat⟩
solomillo *nm* : sirloin, loin
solsticio *nm* : solstice
soltar {19} *vt* **1** : to let go of, to drop **2** : to release, to set free **3** AFLOJAR : to loosen, to slacken
soltería *nf* : bachelorhood, spinsterhood
soltero[1], **-ra** *adj* : single, unmarried
soltero[2], **-ra** *n* **1** : bachelor *m*, single man *m*, single woman *f* **2 apellido de soltera** : maiden name
soltura *nf* **1** : looseness, slackness **2** : fluency (of language) **3** : agility, ease of movement
soluble *adj* : soluble — **solubilidad** *nf*
solución *nf, pl* **-ciones** **1** : solution (in a liquid) **2** : answer, solution
solucionar *vt* RESOLVER : to solve, to resolve — **solucionarse** *vr*
solvencia *nf* **1** : solvency **2** : settling, payment (of debts) **3** : reliability ⟨solvencia moral : trustworthiness⟩
solvente[1] *adj* **1** : solvent **2** : reliable, trustworthy
solvente[2] *nm* : solvent
somalí *adj & nmf* : Somalian
sombra *nf* **1** : shadow **2** : shade **3 sombras** *nfpl* : darkness, shadows *pl* **4 sin sombra de duda** : without a shadow of a doubt
sombreado, -da *adj* **1** : shady **2** : shaded, darkened
sombrear *vt* : to shade
sombrerero, -ra *n* : milliner, hatter
sombrero *nm* **1** : hat **2 sin ～** : bareheaded **3 sombrero hongo** : derby
sombrilla *nf* : parasol, umbrella
sombrío, -bría *adj* LÓBREGO : dark, somber, gloomy — **sombríamente** *adv*
someramente *adv* : cursorily, summarily
somero, -ra *adj* : superficial, cursory, shallow
someter *vt* **1** : to subjugate, to conquer **2** : to subordinate **3** : to subject (to treatment or testing) **4** : to submit, to present — **someterse** *vr* **1** : to submit, to yield **2** : to undergo
sometimiento *nm* **1** : submission, subjection **2** : presentation
somnífero[1], **-ra** *adj* : soporific
somnífero[2] *nm* : sleeping pill
somnolencia *nf* : drowsiness, sleepiness
somnoliento, -ta *adj* : drowsy, sleepy
somorgujo *or* **somormujo** *nm* : loon, grebe
somos → **ser**[1]
son[1] → **ser**
son[2] *nm* **1** : sound ⟨al son de la trompeta : at the sound of the trumpet⟩ **2** : news, rumor **3 en son de** : as, in the manner of, by way of ⟨en son de broma : as a joke⟩ ⟨en son de paz : in peace⟩
sonado, -da *adj* : celebrated, famous, much-discussed
sonaja *nf* : rattle
sonajero *nm* : rattle (toy)
sonámbulo, -la *n* : sleepwalker
sonar[1] {19} *vi* **1** : to sound ⟨suena bien : it sounds good⟩ **2** : to ring (bells) **3** : to look or sound familiar ⟨me suena ese nombre : that name rings a bell⟩ **4 ～ a** : to sound like — *vt* **1** : to ring **2** : to blow (a trumpet, a nose) — **sonarse** *vr* : to blow one's nose
sonar[2] *nm* : sonar
sonata *nf* : sonata
sonda *nf* **1** : sounding line **2** : probe **3** CATÉTER : catheter
sondar *vt* **1** : to sound, to probe (in medicine, drilling, etc.) **2** : to probe, to explore (outer space)
sondear *vt* **1** : to sound **2** : to probe **3** : to sound out, to test (opinions, markets)

sondeo *nm* **1** : sounding, probing **2** : drilling **3** ENCUESTA : survey, poll
soneto *nm* : sonnet
sónico, -ca *adj* : sonic
sonido *nm* : sound
sonoridad *nf* : sonority, resonance
sonoro, -ra *adj* **1** : resonant, sonorous, voiced (in linguistics) **2** : resounding, loud **3 banda sonora** : soundtrack
sonreír {66} *vi* : to smile
sonriente *adj* : smiling
sonrisa *nf* : smile
sonrojar *vt* : to cause to blush — **sonrojarse** *vr* : to blush
sonrojo *nm* RUBOR : blush
sonrosado, -da *adj* : rosy, pink
sonsacar {72} *vt* : to wheedle, to extract
sonsonete *nm* **1** : tapping **2** : drone **3** : mocking tone
soñador[1], **-dora** *adj* : dreamy
soñador[2], **-dora** *n* : dreamer
soñar {19} *v* **1** : to dream **2 ~ con** : to dream about **3 soñar despierto** : to daydream
soñoliento, -ta *adj* : sleepy, drowsy
sopa *nf* **1** : soup **2 estar hecho una sopa** : to be soaked to the bone
sopera *nf* : soup tureen
sopesar *vt* : to weigh, to evaluate
soplar *vi* : to blow — *vt* : to blow on, to blow out, to blow off
soplete *nm* : blowtorch
soplido *nm* : puff
soplo *nm* : puff, gust
soplón, -plona *n, mpl* **soplones** *fam* : tattletale, sneak
sopor *nm* SOMNOLENCIA : drowsiness, sleepiness
soporífero, -ra *adj* : soporific
soportable *adj* : bearable, tolerable
soportar *vt* **1** SOSTENER : to support, to hold up **2** RESISTIR : to withstand, to resist **3** AGUANTAR : to bear, to tolerate
soporte *nm* : base, stand, support
soprano *nmf* : soprano
sor *nf* : Sister (religious title)
sorber *vt* **1** : to sip, to suck in **2** : to absorb, to soak up
sorbete *nm* : sherbet
sorbo *nm* **1** : sip, gulp, swallow **2 beber a sorbos** : to sip
sordera *nf* : deafness
sordidez *nf, pl* **-deces** : sordidness, squalor
sórdido, -da *adj* : sordid, dirty, squalid
sordina *nf* : mute (for a musical instrument)
sordo, -da *adj* **1** : deaf **2** : muted, muffled
sordomudo, -da *n* : deaf-mute
sorgo *nm* : sorghum
soriasis *nfs & pl* : psoriasis
sorna *nf* : sarcasm, mocking tone
sorprendente *adj* : surprising — **sorprendentemente** *adv*
sorprender *vt* : to surprise — **sorprenderse** *vr*
sorpresa *nf* : surprise
sorpresivo, -va *adj* **1** : surprising, surprise **2** IMPREVISTO : sudden, unexpected
sortear *vt* **1** RIFAR : to raffle, to draw lots for **2** : to dodge, to avoid
sorteo *nm* : drawing, raffle
sortija *nf* **1** ANILLO : ring **2** : curl, ringlet
sortilegio *nm* **1** HECHIZO : spell, charm **2** HECHICERÍA : sorcery
SOS *nm* : SOS
sosegado, -da *adj* SERENO : calm, tranquil, serene
sosegar {49} *vt* : to calm, to pacify — **sosegarse** *vr*
sosiego *nm* : tranquillity, serenity, calm
soslayar *vt* ESQUIVAR : to dodge, to evade
soslayo *nm* **de ~** : obliquely, sideways <mirar de soslayo : to look askance>
soso, -sa *adj* **1** INSÍPIDO : bland, flavorless **2** ABURRIDO : dull, boring
sospecha *nf* : suspicion
sospechar *vt* : to suspect — *vi* : to be suspicious
sospechosamente *adv* : suspiciously
sospechoso[1], **-sa** *adj* : suspicious, suspect
sospechoso[2], **-sa** *n* : suspect
sostén *nm, pl* **sostenes 1** APOYO : support **2** : sustenance **3** : brassiere, bra
sostener {80} *vt* **1** : to support, to hold up **2** : to hold <sostenme la puerta : hold the door for me> <sostener una conversación : to hold a conversation> **3** : to sustain, to maintain — **sostenerse** *vr* **1** : to stand, to hold oneself up **2** : to continue, to remain
sostenible *adj* : sustainable, tenable
sostenido[1], **-da** *adj* **1** : sustained, prolonged **2** : sharp (in music)
sostenido[2] *nm* : sharp (in music)
sostuvo, etc. → **sostener**
sotana *nf* : cassock
sótano *nm* : basement
sotavento *nm* : lee <a sotavento : leeward>
soterrar {55} *vt* **1** : to bury **2** : to conceal, to hide away
soto *nm* : grove, copse
souvenir *nm, pl* **-nirs** RECUERDO : souvenir, memento
soviético, -ca *adj* : Soviet
soy → **ser**
soya *nf* : soy, soybean
spaghetti → **espagueti**
sport [ɛ'spor] *adj* : sport, casual
sprint [ɛ'sprin, -'sprint] *nm* : sprint — **sprinter** *nmf*
squash [ɛ'skwaʃ, -'skwatʃ] *nm* : squash (sport)
Sr. *nm* : Mr.
Sra. *nf* : Mrs., Ms.
Srta. *or* **Srita.** *nf* : Miss, Ms.
standard → **estándar**
stress → **estrés**
su *adj* **1** : his, her, its, their, one's <su libro : her book> <sus consecuencias

: its consequences⟩ **2** (*formal*) : your ⟨tómese su medicina, señor : take your medicine, sir⟩

suave *adj* **1** BLANDO : soft **2** LISO : smooth **3** : gentle, mild **4** *Mex fam* : great, fantastic

suavemente *adj* : smoothly, gently, softly

suavidad *nf* : softness, smoothness, mellowness

suavizante *nm* : softener, fabric softener

suavizar {21} *vt* **1** : to soften, to smooth out **2** : to tone down — **suavizarse** *vr*

subacuático, -ca *adj* : underwater

subalterno[1], **-na** *adj* **1** SUBORDINADO : subordinate **2** SECUNDARIO : secondary

subalterno[2], **-na** *n* SUBORDINADO : subordinate

subarrendar {55} *vt* : to sublet

subasta *nf* : auction

subastador, -dora *n* : auctioneer

subastar *vt* : to auction, to auction off

subcampeón, -peona *n, mpl* **-peones** : runner-up

subcomité *nm* : subcommittee

subconsciente *adj & nm* : subconscious — **subconscientemente** *adv*

subcontratar *vt* : to subcontract

subcontratista *nmf* : subcontractor

subcultura *nf* : subculture

subdesarrollado, -da *adj* : underdeveloped

subdirector, -tora *n* : assistant manager

súbdito, -ta *n* : subject (of a monarch)

subdividir *vt* : to subdivide

subdivisión *nf, pl* **-siones** : subdivision

subestimar *vt* : to underestimate, to undervalue

subexponer {60} *vt* : to underexpose

subexposición *nf, pl* **-ciones** : underexposure

subgrupo *nm* : subgroup

subibaja *nm* : seesaw

subida *nf* **1** : ascent, climb **2** : rise, increase **3** : slope, hill ⟨ir de subida : to go uphill⟩

subido, -da *adj* **1** : intense, strong ⟨amarillo subido : bright yellow⟩ **2 subido de tono** : risqué

subir *vt* **1** : to bring up, to take up **2** : to climb, to go up **3** : to raise — *vi* **1** : to go up, to come up **2** : to rise, to increase **3** : to be promoted **4 ~ a** : to get on, to mount ⟨subir a un tren : to get on a train⟩ — **subirse** *vr* **1** : to climb (up) **2** : to pull up (clothing) **3 subirse a la cabeza** : to go to one's head

súbito, -ta *adj* **1** REPENTINO : sudden **2 de ~** : all of a sudden, suddenly — **súbitamente** *adv*

subjetivo, -va *adj* : subjective — **subjetivamente** *adv* — **subjetividad** *nf*

subjuntivo[1], **-va** *adj* : subjunctive

subjuntivo[2] *nm* : subjunctive

sublevación *nf, pl* **-ciones** ALZAMIENTO : uprising, rebellion

sublevar *vt* : to incite to rebellion — **sublevarse** *vr* : to rebel, to rise up

sublimar *vt* : to sublimate — **sublimación** *nf*

sublime *adj* : sublime

submarinismo *nm* : scuba diving

submarinista *nmf* : scuba diver

submarino[1], **-na** *adj* : submarine, undersea

submarino[2] *nm* : submarine

suboficial *nmf* : noncommissioned officer, petty officer

subordinado, -da *adj & n* : subordinate

subordinar *vt* : to subordinate — **subordinarse** *vr* — **subordinación** *nf*

subproducto *nm* : by-product

subrayar *vt* **1** : to underline, to underscore **2** ENFATIZAR : to highlight, to emphasize

subrepticio, -cia *adj* : surreptitious — **subrepticiamente** *adv*

subsahariano, -na *adj* : sub-Saharan

subsanar *vt* **1** RECTIFICAR : to rectify, to correct **2** : to overlook, to excuse **3** : to make up for

subscribir → **suscribir**

subsecretario, -ria *n* : undersecretary

subsecuente *adj* : subsequent — **subsecuentemente** *adv*

subsidiar *vt* : to subsidize

subsidiaria *nf* : subsidiary

subsidio *nm* : subsidy

subsiguiente *adj* : subsequent

subsistencia *nf* **1** : subsistence **2** : sustenance

subsistir *vi* **1** : to subsist, to live **2** : to endure, to survive

substancia → **sustancia**

subteniente *nmf* : second lieutenant

subterfugio *nm* : subterfuge

subterráneo[1], **-nea** *adj* : underground, subterranean

subterráneo[2] *nm* **1** : underground passage, tunnel **2** *Arg, Uru* : subway

subtítulo *nm* : subtitle, subheading

subtotal *nm* : subtotal

suburbano, -na *adj* : suburban

suburbio *nm* **1** : suburb **2** : slum (outside a city)

subvención *nf, pl* **-ciones** : subsidy, grant

subvencionar *vt* : to subsidize

subversivo, -va *adj & n* : subversive — **subversión** *nf*

subvertir {76} *vt* : to subvert

subyacente *adj* : underlying

subyugar {52} *vt* : to subjugate — **subyugación** *nf*

succión *nf, pl* **succiones** : suction

succionar *vt* : to suck up, to draw in

sucedáneo *nm* : substitute ⟨sucedáneo de azucar : sugar substitute⟩

suceder *vi* **1** OCURRIR : to happen, to occur ⟨¿qué sucede? : what's going on?⟩ ⟨suceda lo que suceda : come what may⟩ **2 ~ a** : to follow, to succeed ⟨suceder al trono : to succeed to the throne⟩ ⟨a la primavera sucede el verano : summer follows spring⟩

sucesión *nf, pl* **-siones 1** : succession **2** : sequence, series **3** : issue, heirs *pl*

sucesivamente *adv* : successively, consecutively ⟨y así sucesivamente : and so on⟩

sucesivo, -va *adj* : successive ⟨en los días sucesivos : in the days that followed⟩

suceso *nm* **1** : event, happening, occurrence **2** : incident, crime

sucesor, -sora *n* : successor

suciedad *nf* **1** : dirtiness, filthiness **2** MUGRE : dirt, filth

sucinto, -ta *adj* CONCISO : succinct, concise — **sucintamente** *adv*

sucio, -cia *adj* : dirty, filthy

sucre *nm* : Ecuadoran unit of currency

suculento, -ta *adj* : succulent

sucumbir *vi* : to succumb

sucursal *nf* : branch (of a business)

sudadera *nf* : sweatshirt

sudado, -da → **sudoroso**

sudafricano, -na *adj & n* : South African

sudamericano, -na *adj & n* : South American

sudanés, -nesa *adj & n, mpl* **-neses** : Sudanese

sudar *vi* TRANSPIRAR : to sweat, to perspire

sudario *nm* : shroud

sudeste → **sureste**

sudoeste → **suroeste**

sudor *nm* TRANSPIRACIÓN : sweat, perspiration

sudoroso, -sa *adj* : sweaty

sueco[1], -ca *adj* : Swedish

sueco[2], -ca *n* : Swede

sueco[3] *nm* : Swedish (language)

suegro, -gra *n* **1** : father-in-law *m*, mother-in-law *f* **2 suegros** *nmpl* : in-laws

suela *nf* : sole (of a shoe)

suelda, etc. → **soldar**

sueldo *nm* : salary, wage

suele, etc. → **soler**

suelo *nm* **1** : ground ⟨caerse al suelo : to fall down, to hit the ground⟩ **2** : floor, flooring **3** TIERRA : soil, land

suelta, etc. → **soltar**

suelto[1], -ta *adj* : loose, free, unattached

suelto[2] *nm* : loose change

suena, etc. → **sonar**

sueña, etc. → **soñar**

sueño *nm* **1** : dream **2** : sleep ⟨perder el sueño : to lose sleep⟩ **3** : sleepiness ⟨tener sueño : to be sleepy⟩

suero *nm* **1** : serum **2** : whey

suerte *nf* **1** FORTUNA : luck, fortune ⟨tener suerte : to be lucky⟩ ⟨por suerte : luckily⟩ **2** DESTINO : fate, destiny, lot **3** CLASE, GÉNERO : sort, kind ⟨toda suerte de cosas : all kinds of things⟩

suertudo, -da *adj fam* : lucky

suéter *nm* : sweater

suficiencia *nf* **1** : adequacy, sufficiency **2** : competence, fitness **3** : smugness, self-satisfaction

suficiente *adj* **1** BASTANTE : enough, sufficient ⟨tener suficiente : to have enough⟩ **2** : suitable, fit **3** : smug, complacent

suficientemente *adv* : sufficiently, enough

sufijo *nm* : suffix

suflé *nm* : soufflé

sufragar {52} *vt* **1** AYUDAR : to help out, to support **2** : to defray (costs) — *vi* : to vote

sufragio *nm* : suffrage, vote

sufrido, -da *adj* **1** : long-suffering, patient **2** : sturdy, serviceable (of clothing)

sufrimiento *nm* : suffering

sufrir *vt* **1** : to suffer ⟨sufrir una pérdida : to suffer a loss⟩ **2** : to tolerate, to put up with ⟨ella no lo puede sufrir : she can't stand him⟩ — *vi* : to suffer

sugerencia *nf* : suggestion

sugerir {76} *vt* **1** PROPONER, RECOMENDAR : to suggest, to recommend, to propose **2** : to suggest, to bring to mind

sugestión *nf, pl* **-tiones** : suggestion, prompting ⟨poder de sugestión : power of suggestion⟩

sugestionable *adj* : suggestible, impressionable

sugestionar *vt* : to influence, to sway — **sugestionarse** *vr* **~ con** : to talk oneself into, to become convinced of

sugestivo, -va *adj* **1** : suggestive **2** : interesting, stimulating

suicida[1] *adj* : suicidal

suicida[2] *nmf* : suicide victim, suicide

suicidarse *vr* : to commit suicide

suicidio *nm* : suicide

suite *nf* : suite

suizo, -za *adj & n* : Swiss

sujeción *nf, pl* **-ciones 1** : holding, fastening **2** : subjection

sujetador *nm* **1** : fastener **2** : holder ⟨sujetador de tazas : cup holder⟩

sujetalibros *nms & pl* : bookend

sujetapapeles *nms & pl* CLIP : paper clip

sujetar *vt* **1** : to hold on to, to steady, to hold down **2** FIJAR : to fasten, to attach **3** DOMINAR : to subdue, to conquer — **sujetarse** *vr* **1** : to hold on, to hang on **2 ~ a** : to abide by

sujeto[1], -ta *adj* **1** : secure, fastened **2 ~ a** : subject to

sujeto[2] *nm* **1** INDIVIDUO : individual, character **2** : subject (in grammar)

sulfúrico, -ca *adj* : sulfuric

sulfuro *nm* : sulfur

sultán *nm, pl* **sultanes** : sultan

suma *nf* **1** CANTIDAD : sum, quantity **2** : addition

sumamente *adv* : extremely, exceedingly

sumar *vt* **1** : to add, to add up **2** : to add up to, to total — *vi* : to add up — **sumarse** *vr* **~ a** : to join

sumario[1], -ria *adj* SUCINTO : succinct, summary — **sumariamente** *adv*

sumario[2] *nm* : summary

sumergir {35} *vt* : to submerge, to immerse, to plunge — **sumergirse** *vr*
sumersión *nf, pl* **-siones** : submersion, immersion
sumidero *nm* : drain, sewer
suministrar *vt* : to supply, to provide
suministro *nm* : supply, provision
sumir *vt* SUMERGIR : to plunge, to immerse, to sink — **sumirse** *vr*
sumisión *nf, pl* **-siones 1** : submission **2** : submissiveness
sumiso, -sa *adj* : submissive, acquiescent, docile
sumo, -ma *adj* **1** : extreme, great, high ⟨la suma autoridad : the highest authority⟩ **2 a lo sumo** : at the most — **sumamente** *adv*
suntuoso, -sa *adj* : sumptuous, lavish — **suntuosamente** *adv*
supeditar *vt* SUBORDINAR : to subordinate — **supeditación** *nf*
super[1] *or* **súper** *adj fam* : super, great
super[2] *nm* SUPERMERCADO : market, supermarket
superable *adj* : surmountable
superabundancia *nf* : overabundance, superabundance — **superabundante** *adj*
superar *vt* **1** : to surpass, to exceed **2** : to overcome, to surmount — **superarse** *vr* : to improve oneself
superávit *nm, pl* **-vit** *or* **-vits** : surplus
superchería *nf* : trickery, fraud
supercomputadora *nf* : supercomputer
superestructura *nf* : superstructure
superficial *adj* : superficial — **superficialmente** *adv*
superficialidad *nf* : superficiality
superficie *nf* **1** : surface **2** : area ⟨la superficie de un triángulo : the area of a triangle⟩
superfluidad *nf* : superfluity
superfluo, -flua *adj* : superfluous
superintendente *nmf* : supervisor, superintendent
superior[1] *adj* **1** : superior **2** : upper ⟨nivel superior : upper level⟩ **3** : higher ⟨educación superior : higher education⟩ **4 ~ a** : above, higher than, in excess of
superior[2] *nm* : superior
superioridad *nf* : superiority
superlativo[1], **-va** *adj* : superlative
superlativo[2] *nm* : superlative
supermercado *nm* : supermarket
superpoblación *nf, pl* **-ciones** : overpopulation
superpoblado, -da *adj* : overpopulated
superponer {60} *vt* : to superimpose
superpotencia *nf* : superpower
superproducción → **sobreproducción**
supersónico, -ca *adj* : supersonic
superstición *nf, pl* **-ciones** : superstition
supersticioso, -sa *adj* : superstitious
supervisar *vt* : to supervise, to oversee
supervisión *nf, pl* **-siones** : supervision
supervisor, -sora *n* : supervisor, overseer
supervivencia *nf* : survival
superviviente *nmf* : survivor
supino, -na *adj* : supine
suplantar *vt* : to supplant, to replace
suplemental → **suplementario**
suplementario, -ria *adj* : supplementary, additional, extra
suplemento *nm* : supplement
suplencia *nf* : substitution, replacement
suplente *adj & nmf* : substitute ⟨equipo suplente : replacement team⟩
supletorio, -ria *adj* : extra, additional ⟨teléfono supletorio : extension phone⟩ ⟨cama supletoria : spare bed⟩
súplica *nf* : plea, entreaty
suplicar {72} *vt* IMPLORAR, ROGAR : to entreat, to implore, to supplicate
suplicio *nm* TORMENTO : ordeal, torture
suplir *vt* **1** COMPENSAR : to make up for, to compensate for **2** REEMPLAZAR : to replace, to substitute
supo, etc. → **saber**
suponer {60} *vt* **1** PRESUMIR : to suppose, to assume ⟨supongo que sí : I guess so, I suppose so⟩ ⟨se supone que van a llegar mañana : they're supposed to arrive tomorrow⟩ **2** : to imply, to suggest **3** : to involve, to entail ⟨el éxito supone mucho trabajo : success involves a lot of work⟩
suposición *nf, pl* **-ciones** PRESUNCIÓN : supposition, assumption
supositorio *nm* : suppository
supremacía *nf* : supremacy
supremo, -ma *adj* : supreme
supresión *nf, pl* **-siones 1** : suppression, elimination **2** : deletion
suprimir *vt* **1** : to suppress, to eliminate **2** : to delete
supuestamente *adv* : supposedly, allegedly
supuesto, -ta *adj* **1** : supposed, alleged **2 por ~** : of course, absolutely
supurar *vi* : to ooze, to discharge
supuso, etc. → **suponer**
sur[1] *adj* : southern, southerly, south
sur[2] *nm* **1** : south, South **2** : south wind
surafricano, -na → **sudafricano**
suramericano, -na → **sudamericano**
surcar {72} *vt* **1** : to plow (through) **2** : to groove, to score, to furrow
surco *nm* : groove, furrow, rut
sureño[1], **-ña** *adj* : southern, Southern
sureño[2], **-ña** *n* : Southerner
sureste[1] *adj* **1** : southeast, southeastern **2** : southeasterly
sureste[2] *nm* : southeast, Southeast
surf *nm* : surfing
surfear *vi* : to surf
surfing → **surf**
surfista *nmf* : surfer
surgimiento *nm* : rise, emergence
surgir {35} *vi* : to rise, to arise, to emerge
suroeste[1] *adj* **1** : southwest, southwestern **2** : southwesterly
suroeste[2] *nm* : southwest, Southwest
surtido[1], **-da** *adj* **1** : assorted, varied **2** : stocked, provisioned

surtido[2] *nm* : assortment, selection

surtidor *nm* **1** : jet, spout **2** *Arg, Chile, Spain* : gas pump

surtir *vt* **1** : to supply, to provide ⟨surtir un pedido : to fill an order⟩ **2 surtir efecto** : to have an effect — *vi* : to spout, to spurt up — **surtirse** *vr* : to stock up

susceptible *adj* : susceptible, sensitive — **susceptibilidad** *nf*

suscitar *vt* : to provoke, to give rise to

suscribir {33} *vt* **1** : to sign (a formal document) **2** : to endorse, to sanction — **suscribirse** *vr* **~ a** : to subscribe to

suscripción *nf, pl* **-ciones 1** : subscription **2** : endorsement, sanction **3** : signing

suscriptor, -tora *n* : subscriber

susodicho, -cha *adj* : aforementioned, aforesaid

suspender *vt* **1** COLGAR : to suspend, to hang **2** : to suspend, to discontinue **3** : to suspend, to dismiss

suspensión *nf, pl* **-siones** : suspension

suspenso *nm* : suspense

suspicacia *nf* : suspicion, mistrust

suspicaz *adj, pl* **-caces** DESCONFIADO : suspicious, wary

suspirar *vi* : to sigh

suspiro *nm* : sigh

surque, etc. → **surcar**

suscrito *pp* → **suscribir**

sustancia *nf* **1** : substance **2 sin ~** : shallow, lacking substance

sustancial *adj* **1** : substantial **2** ESENCIAL, FUNDAMENTAL : essential, fundamental — **sustancialmente** *adv*

sustancioso, -sa *adj* **1** NUTRITIVO : hearty, nutritious **2** : substantial, solid

sustantivo *nm* : noun

sustentación *nf, pl* **-ciones** SOSTÉN : support

sustentar *vt* **1** : to support, to hold up **2** : to sustain, to nourish **3** : to maintain, to hold (an opinion) — **sustentarse** *vr* : to support oneself

sustento *nm* **1** : means of support, livelihood **2** : sustenance, food

sustitución *nf, pl* **-ciones** : replacement, substitution

sustituir {41} *vt* **1** : to replace, to substitute for **2** : to stand in for

sustituto, -ta *n* : substitute, stand-in

susto *nm* : fright, scare

sustracción *nf, pl* **-ciones 1** RESTA : subtraction **2** : theft

sustraer {81} *vt* **1** : to remove, to take away **2** RESTAR : to subtract **3** : to steal — **sustraerse** *vr* **~ a** : to avoid, to evade

susurrar *vi* **1** : to whisper **2** : to murmur **3** : to rustle (leaves, etc.) — *vt* : to whisper

susurro *nm* **1** : whisper **2** : murmur **3** : rustle, rustling

sutil *adj* **1** : delicate, thin, fine **2** : subtle

sutileza *nf* **1** : delicacy **2** : subtlety

sutura *nf* : suture

suturar *vt* : to suture

suyo[1], **-ya** *adj* **1** : his, her, its, theirs ⟨los libros suyos : his books⟩ ⟨un amigo suyo : a friend of hers⟩ ⟨esta casa es suya : this house is theirs⟩ **2** (*formal*) : yours ⟨¿este abrigo es suyo, señor? : is this your coat, sir?⟩

suyo[2], **-ya** *pron* **1** : his, hers, theirs ⟨mi guitarra y la suya : my guitar and hers⟩ ⟨ellos trajeron las suyas : they brought theirs, they brought their own⟩ **2** (*formal*) : yours ⟨usted olvidó la suya : you forgot yours⟩

switch *nm* : switch

T

t *nf* : twenty-first letter of the Spanish alphabet

taba *nf* : anklebone

tabacalero[1], **-ra** *adj* : tobacco ⟨industria tabacalera : tobacco industry⟩

tabacalero[2], **-ra** *n* : tobacco grower

tabaco *nm* : tobacco

tábano *nm* : horsefly

taberna *nf* : tavern, bar

tabernáculo *nm* : tabernacle

tabicar {72} *vt* : to wall up

tabique *nm* : thin wall, partition

tabla *nf* **1** : table, list ⟨tabla de multiplicar : multiplication table⟩ **2** : board, plank, slab ⟨tabla de planchar : ironing board⟩ **3** : plot, strip (of land) **4 tablas** *nfpl* : stage, boards *pl*

tablado *nm* **1** : floor **2** : platform, scaffold **3** : stage

tablero *nm* **1** : bulletin board **2** : board (in games) ⟨tablero de ajedrez : chessboard⟩ ⟨tablero de damas : checkerboard⟩ **3** PIZARRA : blackboard **4** : switchboard **5 tablero de instrumentos** : dashboard, instrument panel

tableta *nf* **1** COMPRIMIDO, PÍLDORA : tablet, pill **2** : bar (of chocolate)

tabletear *vi* : to rattle, to clack

tableteo *nm* : clack, rattling

tablilla *nf* **1** : small board or tablet **2** : bulletin board **3** : splint

tabloide *nm* : tabloid

tablón *nm, pl* **tablones 1** : plank, beam **2 tablón de anuncios** : bulletin board

tabú[1] *adj* : taboo

tabú[2] *nm, pl* **tabúes** *or* **tabús** : taboo

tabulador *nm* : tabulator

tabular[1] *vt* : to tabulate

tabular[2] *adj* : tabular

taburete *nm* : footstool, stool

tacañería *nf* : miserliness, stinginess

tacaño[1], **-ña** *adj* MEZQUINO : stingy, miserly

tacaño[2], **-ña** *n* : miser, tightwad

tacha *nf* **1** : flaw, blemish, defect **2 poner tacha a** : to find fault with **3 sin ~** : flawless

tachadura *nf* : erasure, correction

tachar *vt* **1** : to cross out, to delete **2 ~ de** : to accuse of, to label as ⟨lo tacharon de mentiroso : they accused him of being a liar⟩

tachón *nm, pl* **tachones** : stud, hobnail

tachonar *vt* : to stud

tachuela *nf* : tack, hobnail, stud

tácito, -ta *adj* : tacit, implicit — **tácitamente** *adv*

taciturno, -na *adj* **1** : taciturn **2** : sullen, gloomy

tacle *nm* : tackle

taclear *vt* : to tackle (in football)

taco *nm* **1** : wad, stopper, plug **2** : pad (of paper) **3** : cleat **4** : heel (of a shoe) **5** : cue (in billiards) **6** : light snack, bite **7** : taco

tacón *nm, pl* **tacones** : heel (of a shoe) ⟨de tacón alto : high-heeled⟩

táctica *nf* : tactic, tactics *pl*

táctico[1], **-ca** *adj* : tactical

táctico[2], **-ca** *n* : tactician

táctil *adj* : tactile

tacto *nm* **1** : touch, touching, feel **2** DELICADEZA : tact

tafetán *nm, pl* **-tanes** : taffeta

tahúr *nm, pl* **tahúres** : gambler

tailandés[1], **-desa** *adj & n, pl* **-deses** : Thai

tailandés[2] *nm* : Thai (language)

taimado, -da *adj* **1** : crafty, sly **2** *Chile* : sullen, sulky

tajada *nf* **1** : slice **2 sacar tajada** *fam* : to get one's share

tajante *adj* **1** : cutting, sharp **2** : decisive, categorical

tajantemente *adj* : emphatically, categorically

tajar *vt* : to cut, to slice

tajo *nm* **1** : cut, slash, gash **2** ESCARPA : steep cliff

tal[1] *adv* **1** : so, in such a way **2 tal como** : just as ⟨tal como lo hice : just the way I did it⟩ **3 con tal que** : provided that, as long as **4 ¿qué tal?** : how are you?, how's it going?

tal[2] *adj* **1** : such, such a **2 tal vez** : maybe, perhaps

tal[3] *pron* **1** : such a one, someone **2** : such a thing, something **3 tal para cual** : two of a kind

tala *nf* : felling (of trees)

taladrar *vt* : to drill

taladro *nm* : drill, auger ⟨taladro eléctrico : power drill⟩

talante *nm* **1** HUMOR : mood, disposition **2** VOLUNTAD : will, willingness

talar *vt* **1** : to cut down, to fell **2** DEVASTAR : to devastate, to destroy

talco *nm* **1** : talc **2** : talcum powder

talego *nm* : sack

talento *nm* : talent, ability

talentoso, -sa *adj* : talented, gifted

talismán *nm, pl* **-manes** AMULETO : talisman, charm

talla *nf* **1** ESTATURA : height **2** : size (in clothing) **3** : stature, status **4** : sculpture, carving

tallar *vt* **1** : to sculpt, to carve **2** : to measure (someone's height) **3** : to deal (cards)

tallarín *nf, pl* **-rines** : noodle

talle *nm* **1** : size **2** : waist, waistline **3** : figure, shape

taller *nm* **1** : shop, workshop **2** : studio (of an artist)

tallo *nm* : stalk, stem ⟨tallo de maíz : cornstalk⟩

talón *nm, pl* **talones** **1** : heel (of the foot) **2** : stub (of a check) **3 talón de Aquiles** : Achilles' heel

talud *nm* : slope, incline

tamal *nm* : tamale

tamaño[1], **-ña** *adj* : such a big ⟨¿crees tamaña mentira? : do you believe such a lie?⟩

tamaño[2] *nm* **1** : size **2 de tamaño natural** : life-size

tamarindo *nm* : tamarind

tambalearse *vr* **1** : to teeter **2** : to totter, to stagger, to sway — **tambaleante** *adj*

tambaleo *nm* : staggering, lurching, swaying

también *adv* : too, as well, also

tambor *nm* : drum

tamborilear *vi* : to drum, to tap

tamborileo *nm* : tapping, drumming

tamiz *nm* : sieve

tamizar {21} *vt* : to sift

tampoco *adv* : neither, not either ⟨ni yo tampoco : me neither⟩

tampón *nm, pl* **tampones** **1** : ink pad **2** : tampon

tam–tam *nm* : tom-tom

tan *adv* **1** : so, so very ⟨no es tan difícil : it is not that difficult⟩ **2** : as ⟨tan pronto como : as soon as⟩ **3 tan siquiera** : at least, at the least **4 tan sólo** : only, merely

tanda *nf* **1** : turn, shift **2** : batch, lot, series

tándem *nm* **1** : tandem (bicycle) **2** : duo, pair

tangente *adj & nf* : tangent — **tangencial** *adj*

tangible *adj* : tangible

tango *nm* : tango

tanino *nm* : tannin

tanque *nm* **1** : tank, reservoir **2** : tanker, tank (vehicle)

tanteador *nm* MARCADOR : scoreboard

tantear *vt* **1** : to feel, to grope **2** : to size up, to weigh — *vi* **1** : to keep score **2** : to feel one's way

tanteo *nm* **1** : estimate, rough calculation **2** : testing, sizing up **3** : scoring

tanto[1] *adv* **1** : so much ⟨tanto mejor : so much the better⟩ **2** : so long ⟨¿por qué te tardaste tanto? : why did you take so long?⟩

tanto[2], -ta *adj* **1** : so much, so many, such ⟨no hagas tantas preguntas : don't ask so many questions⟩ ⟨tiene tanto encanto : he has such charm, he's so charming⟩ **2** : as much, as many ⟨come tantos dulces como yo : she eats as many sweets as I do⟩ **3** : odd, however many ⟨cuarenta y tantos años : forty-odd years⟩

tanto[3] *nm* **1** : certain amount **2** : goal, point (in sports) **3 al tanto** : abreast, in the picture **4 un tanto** : somewhat, rather ⟨un tanto cansado : rather tired⟩

tanto[4], -ta *pron* **1** : so much, so many ⟨tiene tanto que hacer : she has so much to do⟩ ⟨¡no me des tantos! : don't give me so many!⟩ **2 entre ~** : meanwhile **3 por lo tanto** : therefore

tañer {79} *vt* **1** : to ring (a bell) **2** : to play (a musical instrument)

tañido *nm* **1** CAMPANADA : ring, peal, toll **2** : sound (of an instrument)

tapa *nf* **1** : cover, top, lid **2** *Spain* : bar snack

tapacubos *nms & pl* : hubcap

tapadera *nf* **1** : cover, lid **2** : front, cover (for an organization or person)

tapar *vt* **1** CUBRIR : to cover, to cover up **2** OBSTRUIR : to block, to obstruct — **taparse** *vr*

tapete *nm* **1** : small rug, mat **2** : table cover **3 poner sobre el tapete** : to bring up for discussion

tapia *nf* : (adobe) wall, garden wall

tapiar *vt* **1** : to wall in **2** : to enclose, to block off

tapicería *nf* **1** : upholstery **2** TAPIZ : tapestry

tapicero, -ra *n* : upholsterer

tapioca *nf* : tapioca

tapir *nm* : tapir

tapiz *nm, pl* **tapices** : tapestry

tapizar {21} *vt* **1** : to upholster **2** : to cover, to carpet

tapón *nm, pl* **tapones** **1** : cork **2** : bottle cap **3** : plug, stopper

tapujo *nm* **1** : deceit, pretension **2 sin tapujos** : openly, frankly

taquigrafía *nf* : stenography, shorthand

taquigráfico, -ca *adj* : stenographic

taquígrafo, -fa *n* : stenographer

taquilla *nf* **1** : box office, ticket office **2** : earnings *pl*, take

taquillero, -ra *adj* : box-office, popular ⟨un éxito taquillero : a box-office success⟩

tarántula *nf* : tarantula

tararear *vt* : to hum

tardanza *nf* : lateness, delay

tardar *vi* **1** : to delay, to take a long time **2** : to be late **3 a más tardar** : at the latest — *vt* DEMORAR : to take (time) ⟨tarda una hora : it takes an hour⟩

tarde[1] *adv* **1** : late **2 tarde o temprano** : sooner or later

tarde[2] *nf* **1** : afternoon, evening **2 ¡buenas tardes!** : good afternoon!, good evening! **3 en la tarde** *or* **por la tarde** : in the afternoon, in the evening

tardío, -día *adj* : late, tardy

tardo, -da *adj* : slow

tarea *nf* **1** : task, job **2** : homework

tarifa *nf* **1** : rate ⟨tarifas postales : postal rates⟩ **2** : fare (for transportation) **3** : price list **4** ARANCEL : duty

tarima *nf* PLATAFORMA : dais, platform, stage

tarjeta *nf* : card ⟨tarjeta de crédito : credit card⟩ ⟨tarjeta postal : postcard⟩

tarro *nm* **1** : jar, pot **2** *Arg, Chile* : can, tin

tarta *nf* **1** : tart **2** : cake

tartaleta *nf* : tart

tartamudear *vi* : to stammer, to stutter

tartamudeo *nm* : stutter, stammer

tartán *nm, pl* **tartanes** : tartan, plaid

tártaro *nm* : tartar

tasa *nf* **1** : rate ⟨tasa de desempleo : unemployment rate⟩ **2** : tax, fee **3** : appraisal, valuation

tasación *nf, pl* **-ciones** : appraisal, assessment

tasador, -dora *n* : assessor, appraiser

tasar *vt* **1** VALORAR : to appraise, to value **2** : to set the price of **3** : to ration, to limit

tasca *nf* : cheap bar, dive

tatuaje *nm* : tattoo, tattooing

tatuar {3} *vt* : to tattoo

taurino, -na *adj* : bull, bullfighting

Tauro *nmf* : Taurus

tauromaquia *nf* : (art of) bullfighting

taxi *nm, pl* **taxis** : taxi, taxicab

taxidermia *nf* : taxidermy

taxidermista *nmf* : taxidermist

taxímetro *nm* : taximeter

taxista *nmf* : taxi driver

taza *nf* **1** : cup **2** : cupful **3** : (toilet) bowl **4** : basin (of a fountain)

tazón *nm, pl* **tazones** **1** : bowl **2** : large cup, mug

te *pron* **1** : you ⟨te quiero : I love you⟩ **2** : for you, to you, from you ⟨me gustaría dártelo : I would like to give it to you⟩ **3** : yourself, for yourself, to yourself, from yourself ⟨¡cálmate! : calm yourself!⟩ ⟨¿te guardaste uno? : did you keep one for yourself?⟩ **4** : thee

té *nm* **1** : tea **2** : tea party

tea *nf* : torch

teatral *adj* : theatrical — **teatralmente** *adv*

teatro *nm* **1** : theater **2 hacer teatro** : to put on an act, to exaggerate

teca *nf* : teak

techado *nm* **1** : roof **2 bajo techado** : under cover, indoors

techar *vt* : to roof, to shingle

techo *nm* **1** TEJADO : roof **2** : ceiling **3** : upper limit, ceiling

techumbre *nf* : roofing

tecla *nf* **1** : key (of a musical instrument or a machine) **2 dar en la tecla** : to hit the nail on the head

teclado *nm* : keyboard
teclear *vt* : to type in, to enter
técnica *nf* **1** : technique, skill **2** : technology
técnico[1], **-ca** *adj* : technical — **técnicamente** *adv*
técnico[2], **-ca** *n* : technician, expert, engineer
tecnología *nf* : technology
tecnológico, -ca *adj* : technological — **tecnológicamente** *adv*
tecolote *nm Mex* : owl
tedio *nm* : tedium, boredom
tedioso, -sa *adj* : tedious, boring — **tediosamente** *adv*
teja *nf* : tile
tejado *nm* TECHO : roof
tejedor, -dora *n* : weaver
tejer *vt* **1** : to knit, to crochet **2** : to weave **3** FABRICAR : to concoct, to make up, to fabricate
tejido *nm* **1** TELA : fabric, cloth **2** : weave, texture **3** : tissue ⟨tejido muscular : muscle tissue⟩
tejo *nm* **1** : yew **2** : hopscotch (children's game)
tejón *nm, pl* **tejones** : badger
tela *nf* **1** : fabric, cloth, material **2 tela de araña** : spiderweb **3 poner en tela de juicio** : to call into question, to doubt
telar *nm* : loom
telaraña *nf* : spiderweb, cobweb
tele *nf fam* : TV, television
telecomunicación *nf, pl* **-ciones** : telecommunication
teleconferencia *nf* : teleconference
teledifusión *nf, pl* **-siones** : television broadcasting
teledirigido, -da *adj* : remote-controlled
telefonear *v* : to telephone, to call
telefónico, -ca *adj* : phone, telephone ⟨llamada telefónica : phone call⟩
telefonista *nmf* : telephone operator
teléfono *nm* **1** : telephone **2 llamar por teléfono** : to telephone, to make a phone call
telegrafiar {85} *v* : to telegraph
telegráfico, -ca *adj* : telegraphic
telégrafo *nm* : telegraph
telegrama *nm* : telegram
telenovela *nf* : soap opera
telepatía *nf* : telepathy
telepático, -ca *adj* : telepathic — **telepáticamente** *adv*
telescópico, -ca *adj* : telescopic
telescopio *nm* : telescope
telespectador, -dora *n* : television viewer
telesquí *nm, pl* **-squís** : ski lift
televidente *nmf* : television viewer
televisar *vt* : to televise
televisión *nf, pl* **-siones** : television, TV
televisivo, -va *adj* : television ⟨serie televisiva : television series⟩
televisor *nm* : television set
telón *nm, pl* **telones** **1** : curtain (in theater) **2 telón de fondo** : backdrop, background
tema *nm* **1** ASUNTO : theme, topic, subject **2** MOTIVO : motif, central theme
temario *nm* **1** : set of topics (for study) **2** : agenda
temática *nf* : subject matter
temático, -ca *adj* : thematic
temblar {55} *vi* **1** : to tremble, to shake, to shiver ⟨le temblaban las rodillas : his knees were shaking⟩ **2** : to shudder, to be afraid ⟨tiemblo con sólo pensarlo : I shudder to think of it⟩
temblor *nm* **1** : shaking, trembling **2** : tremor, earthquake
tembloroso, -sa *adj* : tremulous, trembling, shaking ⟨con la voz temblorosa : with a shaky voice⟩
temer *vt* : to fear, to dread — *vi* : to be afraid
temerario, -ria *adj* : reckless, rash — **temerariamente** *adv*
temeridad *nf* **1** : temerity, recklessness, rashness **2** : rash act
temeroso, -sa *adj* MIEDOSO : fearful, frightened
temible *adj* : fearsome, dreadful
temor *nm* MIEDO : fear, dread
témpano *nm* : ice floe
temperamento *nm* : temperament — **temperamental** *adj*
temperancia *nf* : temperance
temperar *vt* MODERAR : to temper, to moderate — *vi* : to have a change of air
temperatura *nf* : temperature
tempestad *nf* **1** : storm, tempest **2 tempestad de arena** : sandstorm
tempestuoso, -sa *adj* : tempestuous, stormy
templado, -da *adj* **1** : temperate, mild **2** : moderate, restrained **3** : warm, lukewarm **4** VALIENTE : courageous, bold
templanza *nf* **1** : temperance, moderation **2** : mildness (of weather)
templar *vt* **1** : to temper (steel) **2** : to restrain, to moderate **3** : to tune (a musical instrument) **4** : to warm up, to cool down — **templarse** *vr* **1** : to be moderate **2** : to warm up, to cool down
temple *nm* **1** : temper (of steel, etc.) **2** HUMOR : mood ⟨de buen temple : in a good mood⟩ **3** : tuning **4** VALOR : courage
templo *nm* **1** : temple **2** : church, chapel
tempo *nm* : tempo (in music)
temporada *nf* **1** : season, time ⟨temporada de béisbol : baseball season⟩ **2** : period, spell ⟨por temporadas : on and off⟩
temporal[1] *adj* **1** : temporal **2** : temporary
temporal[2] *nm* **1** : storm **2 capear el temporal** : to weather the storm
temporalmente *adv* : temporarily
temporario, -ria *adj* : temporary — **temporariamente** *adv*
temporero[1], **-ra** *adj* : temporary, seasonal

temporero², **-ra** *n* : temporary or seasonal worker
temporizador *nm* : timer
tempranero, **-ra** *adj* **1** : early **2** : early-rising
temprano¹ *adv* : early ‹lo más temprano posible : as soon as possible›
temprano², **-na** *adj* : early ‹la parte temprana del siglo : the early part of the century›
ten → **tener**
tenacidad *nf* : tenacity, perseverance
tenaz *adj, pl* **tenaces** **1** : tenacious, persistent **2** : strong, tough
tenaza *nf, or* **tenazas** *nfpl* **1** : pliers, pincers **2** : tongs **3** : claw (of a crustacean)
tenazmente *adv* : tenaciously
tendedero *nm* : clothesline
tendencia *nf* **1** PROPENSIÓN : tendency, inclination **2** : trend
tendencioso, **-sa** *adj* : tendentious, biased
tendente → **tendiente**
tender {56} *vt* **1** EXTENDER : to spread out, to lay out **2** : to hang out (clothes) **3** : to lay (cables, etc.) **4** : to set (a trap) — *vi* **~ a** : to tend to, to have a tendency towards — **tenderse** *vr* : to stretch out, to lie down
tendero, **-ra** *n* : shopkeeper, storekeeper
tendido *nm* **1** : laying (of cables, etc.) **2** : seats *pl,* section (at a bullfight)
tendiente *adj* **~ a** : aimed at, designed to
tendón *nm, pl* **tendones** : tendon
tenebrosidad *nf* : darkness, gloom
tendrá, etc. → **tener**
tenebroso, **-sa** *adj* **1** OSCURO : gloomy, dark **2** SINIESTRO : sinister
tenedor¹, **-dora** *n* **1** : holder **2** **tenedor de libros, tenedora de libros** : bookkeeper
tenedor² *nm* : table fork
tenencia *nf* **1** : possession, holding **2** : tenancy **3** : tenure
tener {80} *vt* **1** : to have ‹tiene ojos verdes : she has green eyes› ‹tengo mucho que hacer : I have a lot to do› ‹tiene veinte años : he's twenty years old› ‹tiene un metro de largo : it's one meter long› **2** : to hold ‹ten esto un momento : hold this for a moment› **3** : to feel, to make ‹tengo frío : I'm cold› ‹eso nos tiene contentos : that makes us happy› **4** **~ por** : to think, to consider ‹me tienes por loco : you think I'm crazy› — *v aux* **1** **tener que** : to have to ‹tengo que salir : I have to leave› ‹tiene que estar aquí : it has to be here, it must be here› **2** (*with past participle*) ‹tenía pensado escribirte : I've been thinking of writing to you› — **tenerse** *vr* **1** : to stand up **2** **~ por** : to consider oneself ‹me tengo por afortunado : I consider myself lucky›
tenería *nf* CURTIDURÍA : tannery
tenga, etc. → **tener**
tenia *nf* SOLITARIA : tapeworm
teniente *nmf* **1** : lieutenant **2** **teniente coronel** : lieutenant colonel
tenis *nms & pl* **1** : tennis **2** **tenis** *nmpl* : sneakers *pl*
tenista *nmf* : tennis player
tenor *nm* **1** : tenor **2** : tone, sense
tensar *vt* **1** : to tense, to make taut **2** : to draw (a bow) — **tensarse** *vr* : to become tense
tensión *nf, pl* **tensiones** **1** : tension, tautness **2** : stress, strain **3** **tensión arterial** : blood pressure
tenso, **-sa** *adj* : tense
tentación *nf, pl* **-ciones** : temptation
tentáculo *nm* : tentacle, feeler
tentador¹, **-dora** *adj* : tempting
tentador², **-dora** *n* : tempter, temptress *f*
tentar {55} *vt* **1** TOCAR : to feel, to touch **2** PROBAR : to test, to try **3** ATRAER : to tempt, to entice
tentativa *nf* : attempt, try
tentempié *nm fam* : snack, bite
tenue *adj* **1** : tenuous **2** : faint, weak, dim **3** : light, fine **4** : thin, slender
teñir {67} *vt* **1** : to dye **2** : to stain
teodolito *nm* : theodolite, transit (for surveying)
teología *nf* : theology
teológico, **-ca** *adj* : theological
teólogo, **-ga** *n* : theologian
teorema *nm* : theorem
teoría *nf* : theory
teórico¹, **-ca** *adj* : theoretical — **teóricamente** *adv*
teórico², **-ca** *n* : theorist
teorizar {21} *vi* : to theorize
tepe *nm* : sod, turf
teponaztle *nm Mex* : traditional drum
tequila *nm* : tequila
terapeuta *nmf* : therapist
terapéutica *nf* : therapeutics
terapéutico, **-ca** *adj* : therapeutic
terapia *nf* **1** : therapy **2** **terapia intensiva** : intensive care
tercer → **tercero**
tercermundista *adj* : third-world
tercero¹, **-ra** *adj* (**tercer** *before masculine singular nouns*) **1** : third **2** **el Tercer Mundo** : the Third World
tercero², **-ra** *n* : third (in a series)
terceto *nm* **1** : tercet, triplet (in literature) **2** : trio (in music)
terciar *vt* **1** : to place diagonally **2** : to divide into three parts — *vi* **1** : to mediate **2** **~ en** : to take part in
terciario, **-ria** *adj* : tertiary
tercio¹, **-cia** → **tercero**
tercio² *nm* : third ‹dos tercios : two thirds›
terciopelo *nm* : velvet
terco, **-ca** *adj* OBSTINADO : obstinate, stubborn
tergiversación *nf, pl* **-ciones** : distortion
tergiversar *vt* : to distort, to twist
termal *adj* : thermal, hot
termas *nfpl* : hot springs
térmico, **-ca** *adj* : thermal, heat ‹energía térmica : thermal energy›

terminación *nf, pl* **-ciones** : termination, conclusion
terminal[1] *adj* : terminal — **terminalmente** *adv*
terminal[2] *nm* (*in some regions f*) : (electric or electronic) terminal
terminal[3] *nf* (*in some regions m*) : terminal, station
terminante *adj* : final, definitive, categorical — **terminantemente** *adv*
terminar *vt* **1** CONCLUIR : to end, to conclude **2** ACABAR : to complete, to finish off — *vi* **1** : to finish **2** : to stop, to end — **terminarse** *vr* **1** : to run out **2** : to come to an end
término *nm* **1** CONCLUSIÓN : end, conclusion **2** : term, expression **3** : period, term of office **4 término medio** : happy medium **5 términos** *nmpl* : terms, specifications ⟨los términos del acuerdo : the terms of the agreement⟩
terminología *nf* : terminology
termita *nf* : termite
termo *nm* : thermos
termodinámica *nf* : thermodynamics
termómetro *nm* : thermometer
termostato *nm* : thermostat
ternera *nf* : veal
ternero, -ra *n* : calf
terno *nm* **1** : set of three **2** : three-piece suit
ternura *nf* : tenderness
terquedad *nf* OBSTINACIÓN : obstinacy, stubbornness
terracota *nf* : terra-cotta
terraplén *nm, pl* **-plenes** : terrace, embankment
terráqueo, -quea *adj* **1** : earth **2 globo terráqueo** : the earth, globe (of the earth)
terrateniente *nmf* : landowner
terraza *nf* **1** : terrace, veranda **2** : balcony (in a theater) **3** : terrace (in agriculture)
terremoto *nm* : earthquake
terrenal *adj* : worldly, earthly
terreno *nm* **1** : terrain **2** SUELO : earth, ground **3** : plot, tract of land **4 perder terreno** : to lose ground **5 preparar el terreno** : to pave the way
terrestre *adj* : terrestrial
terrible *adj* : terrible, horrible — **terriblemente** *adv*
terrier *nmf* : terrier
territorial *adj* : territorial
territorio *nm* : territory
terrón *nm, pl* **terrones 1** : clod (of earth) **2 terrón de azúcar** : lump of sugar
terror *nm* : terror
terrorífico, -ca *adj* : horrific, terrifying
terrorismo *nm* : terrorism
terrorista *adj & nmf* : terrorist
terroso, -sa *adj* : earthy ⟨colores terrosos : earthy colors⟩
terruño *nm* : native land, homeland
terso, -sa *adj* **1** : smooth **2** : glossy, shiny **3** : polished, flowing (of a style)
tersura *nf* **1** : smoothness **2** : shine
tertulia *nf* : gathering, group ⟨tertulia literaria : literary circle⟩
tesauro *nm* : thesaurus
tesis *nfs & pl* : thesis
tesón *nm* : persistence, tenacity
tesonero, -ra *adj* : persistent, tenacious
tesorería *nf* : treasurer's office
tesorero, -ra *n* : treasurer
tesoro *nm* **1** : treasure **2** : thesaurus
test *nm* : test
testaferro *nm* : figurehead
testamentario[1], **-ria** *adj* : testamentary
testamentario[2], **-ria** *n* ALBACEA : executor, executrix *f*
testamento *nm* : testament, will
testar *vi* : to draw up a will
testarudo, -da *adj* : stubborn, pigheaded
testículo *nm* : testicle
testificar {72} *v* : to testify
testigo *nmf* : witness
testimonial *adj* **1** : testimonial **2** : token
testimoniar *vi* : to testify
testimonio *nm* : testimony, statement
teta *nf* : teat
tétano *or* **tétanos** *nm* : tetanus, lockjaw
tetera *nf* **1** : teapot **2** : teakettle
tetilla *nf* **1** : teat **2** : nipple
tetina *nf* : nipple (on a bottle)
tétrico, -ca *adj* : somber, gloomy
textil *adj & nm* : textile
texto *nm* : text
textual *adj* : literal, exact — **textualmente** *adv*
textura *nf* : texture
tez *nf, pl* **teces** : complexion, coloring
ti *pron* **1** : you ⟨es para ti : it's for you⟩ **2 ti mismo, ti misma** : yourself **3** : thee
tía → **tío**
tiamina *nf* : thiamine
tianguis *nm Mex* : open-air market
tibetano[1], **-na** *adj & n* : Tibetan
tibetano[2] *nm* : Tibetan (language)
tibia *nf* : tibia
tibieza *nf* **1** : tepidness **2** : halfheartedness
tibio, -bia *adj* **1** : lukewarm, tepid **2** : cool, unenthusiastic
tiburón *nm, pl* **-rones 1** : shark **2** : raider (in finance)
tic *nm* **1** : click, tick **2 tic nervioso** : tic
tico, -ca *adj & n fam* : Costa Rican
tictac *nm* **1** : ticking, tick-tock **2 hacer tictac** : to tick
tiembla, etc. → **temblar**
tiempo *nm* **1** : time ⟨justo a tiempo : just in time⟩ ⟨perder tiempo : to waste time⟩ ⟨tiempo libre : spare time⟩ **2** : period, age ⟨en los tiempos que corren : nowadays⟩ **3** : season, moment ⟨antes de tiempo : prematurely⟩ **4** : weather ⟨hace buen tiempo : the weather is fine, it's nice outside⟩ **5** : tempo (in music) **6** : half (in sports) **7** : tense (in grammar)
tienda *nf* **1** : store, shop **2** *or* **tienda de campaña** : tent
tiende, etc. → **tender**

tiene, etc. → **tener**

tienta[1], **etc.** → **tentar**

tienta[2] *nf* **andar a tientas** : to feel one's way, to grope around

tiernamente *adv* : tenderly

tierno, -na *adj* **1** : affectionate, tender **2** : tender, young

tierra *nf* **1** : land **2** SUELO : ground, earth **3** : country, homeland, soil **4** **tierra natal** : native land **5** **tierras altas** : highlands **6** **la Tierra** : the Earth

tieso, -sa *adj* **1** : stiff, rigid **2** : upright, erect

tiesto *nm* **1** : potsherd **2** MACETA : flowerpot

tiesura *nf* : stiffness, rigidity

tifoidea *nf* : typhoid

tifoideo, -dea *adj* : typhoid ⟨fiebre tifoidea : typhoid fever⟩

tifón *nm, pl* **tifones** : typhoon

tifus *nm* : typhus

tigre, -gresa *n* **1** : tiger, tigress *f* **2** : jaguar

tijera *nf* **1** *or* **tijeras** *nfpl* : scissors **2** **de ~** : folding ⟨escalera de tijera : stepladder⟩

tijereta *nf* : earwig

tijeretada *nf or* **tijeretazo** *nm* : cut, snip

tildar *vt* **~ de** : to brand as, to call ⟨lo tildaron de traidor : they branded him as a traitor⟩

tilde *nf* **1** : accent mark **2** : tilde (accent over *ñ*)

tilo *nm* : linden (tree)

timador, -dora *n* : swindler

timar *vt* : to swindle, to cheat

timbal *nm* **1** : kettledrum **2** **timbales** *nmpl* : timpani

timbre *nm* **1** : bell ⟨tocar el timbre : to ring the doorbell⟩ **2** : tone, timbre **3** SELLO : seal, stamp **4** *CA, Mex* : postage stamp

timidez *nf* : timidity, shyness

tímido, -da *adj* : timid, shy — **tímidamente** *adv*

timo *nm fam* : swindle, trick, hoax

timón *nm, pl* **timones** : rudder ⟨estar al timón : to beat the helm⟩

timonel *nm* : helmsman, coxswain

timorato, -ta *adj* **1** : timorous **2** : sanctimonious

tímpano *nm* **1** : eardrum **2** **tímpanos** *nmpl* : timpani, kettledrums

tina *nf* **1** BAÑERA : tub, bathtub **2** : vat

tinaco *nm Mex* : water tank

tinieblas *nfpl* **1** OSCURIDAD : darkness **2** : ignorance

tino *nm* **1** : good judgment, sense **2** : tact, sensitivity, insight

tinta *nf* : ink

tinte *nm* **1** : dye, coloring **2** : overtone ⟨tintes raciales : racial overtones⟩

tintero *nm* **1** : inkwell **2** **quedarse en el tintero** : to remain unsaid

tintinear *vt* : to jingle, to clink, to tinkle

tintineo *nm* : clink, jingle, tinkle

tinto, -ta *adj* **1** : dyed, stained ⟨tinto en sangre : bloodstained⟩ **2** : red (of wine)

tintorería *nf* : dry cleaner (service)

tintura *nf* **1** : dye, tint **2** : tincture ⟨tintura de yodo : tincture of iodine⟩

tiña *nf* : ringworm

tiñe, etc. → **teñir**

tío, tía *n* : uncle *m,* aunt *f*

tiovivo *nm* : merry-go-round

tipi *nm* : tepee

típico, -ca *adj* : typical — **típicamente** *adv*

tipificar {72} *vt* **1** : to classify, to categorize **2** : to typify

tiple *nm* : soprano

tipo[1] *nm* **1** CLASE : type, kind, sort **2** : figure, build, appearance **3** : rate ⟨tipo de interés : interest rate⟩ **4** : (printing) type, typeface **5** : style, model ⟨un vestido tipo 60's : a 60's-style dress⟩

tipo[2], **-pa** *n fam* : guy *m,* gal *f,* character

tipografía *nf* : typography, printing

tipográfico, -ca *adj* : typographic, typographical

tipográfo, -fa *n* : printer, typographer

tique *or* **tiquet** *nm* **1** : ticket **2** : receipt

tira *nf* **1** : strip, strap **2** **tira cómica** : comic, comic strip

tirabuzón *nf, pl* **-zones** : corkscrew

tirada *nf* **1** : throw **2** : distance, stretch **3** IMPRESIÓN : printing, issue

tiradero *nm Mex* **1** : dump **2** : mess, clutter

tirador[1] *nm* : handle, knob

tirador[2], **-dora** *n* : marksman *m,* markswoman *f*

tiragomas *nms & pl* : slingshot

tiranía *nf* : tyranny

tiránico, -ca *adj* : tyrannical

tiranizar {21} *vt* : to tyrannize

tirano[1], **-na** *adj* : tyrannical, despotic

tirano[2], **-na** *n* : tyrant

tirante[1] *adj* **1** : tense, strained **2** : taut

tirante[2] *nm* **1** : shoulder strap **2** **tirantes** *nmpl* : suspenders

tirantez *nf* **1** : tautness **2** : tension, friction, strain

tirar *vt* **1** : to throw, to hurl, to toss **2** BOTAR : to throw away, to throw out, to waste **3** DERRIBAR : to knock down **4** : to shoot, to fire, to launch **5** : to take (a photo) **6** : to print, to run off — *vi* **1** : to pull, to draw **2** : to shoot **3** : to attract **4** : to get by, to manage ⟨va tirando : he's getting along, he's managing⟩ **5** **~ a** : to tend towards, to be rather ⟨tira a picante : it's a bit spicy⟩ — **tirarse** *vr* **1** : to throw oneself **2** *fam* : to spend (time)

tiritar *vi* : to shiver, to tremble

tiro *nm* **1** BALAZO, DISPARO : shot, gunshot **2** : shot, kick (in sports) **3** : flue **4** : team (of horses, etc.) **5** **a ~** : within range **6** **al tiro** : right away **7** **tiro de gracia** : coup de grace, death blow

tiroideo, -dea *adj* : thyroid

tiroides *nmf* : thyroid, thyroid gland — **tiroides** *adj*

tirolés, -lesa *adj* : Tyrolean

tirón *nm, pl* **tirones** **1** : pull, tug, yank **2 de un tirón** : all at once, in one go

tiroteo *nm* **1** : shooting **2** : gunfight, shoot-out

tirria *nf* **tener tirria a** *fam* : to have a grudge against

titánico, -ca *adj* : titanic, huge

titanio *nm* : titanium

títere *nm* : puppet

tití *nm* : marmoset

titilar *vi* : to twinkle, to flicker

titileo *nm* : twinkle, flickering

titiritero, -ra *n* **1** : puppeteer **2** : acrobat

titubear *vi* **1** : to hesitate **2** : to stutter, to stammer — **titubeante** *adj*

titubeo *nm* **1** : hesitation **2** : stammering

titulado, -da *adj* **1** : titled, entitled **2** : qualified

titular[1] *vt* : to title, to entitle — **titularse** *vr* **1** : to be called, to be entitled **2** : to receive a degree

titular[2] *adj* : titular, official

titular[3] *nm* : headline

titular[4] *nmf* **1** : owner, holder **2** : officeholder, incumbent

titularidad *nf* **1** : ownership, title **2** : position, office (with a title) **3** : starting position (in sports)

título *nm* **1** : title **2** : degree, qualification **3** : security, bond **4 a título de** : by way of, in the capacity of

tiza *nf* : chalk

tiznar *vt* : to blacken (with soot, etc.)

tizne *nm* HOLLÍN : soot

tiznón *nm, pl* **tiznones** : stain, smudge

tlapalería *nf Mex* : hardware store

TNT *nm* (*tri*nitro*t*olueno) : TNT

toalla *nf* : towel

toallita *nf* : washcloth

tobillo *nm* : ankle

tobogán *nm, pl* **-ganes** **1** : toboggan, sled **2** : slide, chute

tocadiscos *nms & pl* : record player, phonograph

tocado[1], **-da** *adj* **1** : bad, bruised (of fruit) **2** *fam* : touched, not all there

tocado[2] *nm* : headdress

tocador[1] *nm* **1** : dressing table, vanity table **2 artículos de tocador** : toiletries

tocador[2], **-dora** *n* : player (of music)

tocante *adj* **~ a** : with regard to, regarding

tocar {72} *vt* **1** : to touch, to feel, to handle **2** : to touch on, to refer to **3** : to concern, to affect **4** : to play (a musical instrument) — *vi* **1** : to knock, to ring ⟨tocar a la puerta : to rap on the door⟩ **2 ~ en** : to touch on, to border on ⟨eso toca en lo ridículo : that's almost ludicrous⟩ **3 tocarle a** : to fall to, to be up to, to be one's turn ⟨¿a quién le toca manejar? : whose turn is it to drive?⟩

tocayo, -ya *n* : namesake

tocineta *nf Col, Ven* : bacon

tocino *nm* **1** : bacon **2** : salt pork

tocología *nf* OBSTETRICIA : obstetrics

tocólogo, -ga *n* OBSTETRA : obstetrician

tocón *nm, pl* **tocones** CEPA : stump (of a tree)

todavía *adv* **1** AÚN : still, yet ⟨todavía puedes verlo : you can still see it⟩ **2** : even ⟨todavía más rápido : even faster⟩ **3 todavía no** : not yet

todo[1], **-da** *adj* **1** : all, whole, entire ⟨con toda sinceridad : with all sincerity⟩ ⟨toda la comunidad : the whole community⟩ **2** : every, each ⟨a todo nivel : at every level⟩ **3** : maximum ⟨a toda velocidad : at top speed⟩ **4 todo el mundo** : everyone, everybody

todo[2] *nm* : whole

todo[3], **-da** *pron* **1** : everything, all, every bit ⟨lo sabe todo : he knows it all⟩ ⟨es todo un soldado : he's every inch a soldier⟩ **2 todos, -das** *pl* : everybody, everyone, all

todopoderoso, -sa *adj* OMNIPOTENTE : almighty, all-powerful

toga *nf* **1** : toga **2** : gown, robe (for magistrates, etc.)

toldo *nm* : awning, canopy

tolerable *adj* : tolerable — **tolerablemente** *adv*

tolerancia *nf* : tolerance, toleration

tolerante *adj* : tolerant — **tolerantemente** *adv*

tolerar *vt* : to tolerate

tolete *nm* : oarlock

tolva *nf* : hopper (container)

toma *nf* **1** : taking, seizure, capture **2** DOSIS : dose **3** : take, shot **4 toma de corriente** : wall socket, outlet **5 toma y daca** : give-and-take

tomar *vt* **1** : to take ⟨tomé el libro : I took the book⟩ ⟨tomar un taxi : to take a taxi⟩ ⟨tomar una foto : to take a photo⟩ ⟨toma dos años : it takes two years⟩ ⟨tomaron medidas drásticas : they took drastic measures⟩ **2** BEBER : to drink **3** CAPTURAR : to capture, to seize **4 tomar el sol** : to sunbathe **5 tomar tierra** : to land — *vi* : to drink (alcohol) — **tomarse** *vr* **1** : to take ⟨tomarse la molestia de : to take the trouble to⟩ **2** : to drink, to eat, to have

tomate *nm* : tomato

tomillo *nm* : thyme

tomo *nm* : volume, tome

ton *nm* **sin ton ni son** : without rhyme or reason

tonada *nf* **1** : tune, song **2** : accent

tonalidad *nf* : tonality

tonel *nm* BARRICA : barrel, cask

tonelada *nf* : ton

tonelaje *nm* : tonnage

tónica *nf* **1** : tonic (water) **2** : tonic (in music) **3** : trend, tone ⟨dar la tónica : to set the tone⟩

tónico[1], **-ca** *adj* : tonic

tónico[2] *nm* : tonic ⟨tónico capilar : hair tonic⟩

tono *nm* **1** : tone ⟨tono muscular : muscle tone⟩ **2** : shade (of colors) **3** : key (in music)

tontamente *adv* : foolishly, stupidly

tontear *vi* **1** : to fool around, to play the fool **2** : to flirt

tontería *nf* **1** : foolishness **2** : stupid remark or action **3 decir tonterías** : to talk nonsense

tonto[1], -ta *adj* **1** : dumb, stupid **2** : silly **3 a tontas y a locas** : without thinking, haphazardly

tonto[2], -ta *n* : fool, idiot

topacio *nm* : topaz

toparse *vr* **~ con** : to bump into, to run into, to come across ⟨me topé con algunas dificultades : I ran into some problems⟩

tope *nm* **1** : limit, end ⟨hasta el tope : to the limit, to the brim⟩ **2** : stop, check, buffer ⟨tope de puerta : doorstop⟩ **3** : bump, collision **4** *Mex* : speed bump

tópico[1], -ca *adj* **1** : topical, external **2** : trite, commonplace

tópico[2] *nm* **1** : topic, subject **2** : cliché, trite expression

topo *nm* **1** : mole (animal) **2** *fam* : clumsy person, blunderer

topografía *nf* : topography

topográfico, -ca *adj* : topographic, topographical

topógrafo, -fa *n* : topographer

toque[1], etc. → **tocar**

toque[2] *nm* **1** : touch ⟨el último toque : the finishing touch⟩ ⟨un toque de color : a touch of color⟩ **2** : ringing, peal, chime **3** *Mex* : shock, jolt **4 toque de queda** : curfew **5 toque de diana** : reveille

toquetear *vt* : to touch, to handle, to finger

tórax *nm* : thorax

torbellino *nm* : whirlwind

torcedura *nf* **1** : twisting, buckling **2** : sprain

torcer {14} *vt* **1** : to bend, to twist **2** : to sprain **3** : to turn (a corner) **4** : to wring, to wring out **5** : to distort — *vi* : to turn — **torcerse** *vr*

torcido, -da *adj* **1** : twisted, crooked **2** : devious

tordo *nm* ZORZAL : thrush

torear *vt* **1** : to fight (bulls) **2** : to dodge, to sidestep

toreo *nm* : bullfighting

torero, -ra *n* MATADOR : bullfighter, matador

tormenta *nf* **1** : storm ⟨tormenta de nieve : snowstorm⟩ **2** : turmoil, frenzy

tormento *nm* **1** : torment, anguish **2** : torture

tormentoso, -sa *adj* : stormy, turbulent

tornado *nm* : tornado

tornamesa *nmf* : turntable

tornar *vt* **1** : to return, to give back **2** : to make, to render — *vi* : to go back — **tornarse** *vr* : to become, to turn into

tornasol *nm* **1** : reflected light **2** : sunflower **3** : litmus

tornear *vt* : to turn (in carpentry)

torneo *nm* : tournament

tornillo *nm* **1** : screw **2 tornillo de banco** : vise

torniquete *nm* **1** : tourniquet **2** : turnstile

torno *nm* **1** : lathe **2** : winch **3 torno de banco** : vise **4 en torno a** : around, about ⟨en torno a este asunto : about this issue⟩ ⟨en torno suyo : around him⟩

toro *nm* : bull

toronja *nf* : grapefruit

toronjil *nm* : balm, lemon balm

torpe *adj* **1** DESMAÑADO : clumsy, awkward **2** : stupid, dull — **torpemente** *adv*

torpedear *vt* : to torpedo

torpedo *nm* : torpedo

torpeza *nf* **1** : clumsiness, awkwardness **2** : stupidity **3** : blunder

torre *nf* **1** : tower ⟨torre de perforación : oil rig⟩ **2** : turret **3** : rook, castle (in chess)

torrencial *adj* : torrential — **torrencialmente** *adv*

torrente *nm* **1** : torrent **2 torrente sanguíneo** : bloodstream

torreón *nm, pl* **-rreones** : tower (of a castle)

torreta *nf* : turret (of a tank, ship, etc.)

tórrido, -da *adj* : torrid

torsión *nf, pl* **torsiones** : torsion — **torsional** *adj*

torso *nm* : torso, trunk

torta *nf* **1** : torte, cake **2** *Mex* : sandwich

tortazo *nm fam* : blow, wallop

tortilla *nf* **1** : tortilla **2** *or* **tortilla de huevo** : omelet

tórtola *nf* : turtledove

tortuga *nf* **1** : turtle, tortoise **2 tortuga de agua dulce** : terrapin **3 tortuga boba** : loggerhead

tortuoso, -sa *adj* : tortuous, winding

tortura *nf* : torture

torturador, -dora *n* : torturer

torturar *vt* : to torture, to torment

torvo, -va *adj* : grim, stern, baleful

torzamos, etc. → **torcer**

tos *nf* **1** : cough **2 tos ferina** : whooping cough

tosco, -ca *adj* : rough, coarse

toser *vi* : to cough

tosquedad *nf* : crudeness, coarseness, roughness

tostada *nf* **1** : piece of toast **2** : tostada

tostador *nm* **1** : toaster **2** : roaster (for coffee)

tostar {19} *vt* **1** : to toast **2** : to roast (coffee) **3** : to tan — **tostarse** *vr* : to get a tan

tostón *nm, pl* **tostones** *Car* : fried plantain chip

total[1] *adv* : in the end, so ⟨total, que no fui : in short, I didn't go⟩

total[2] *adj & nm* : total — **totalmente** *adv*

totalidad *nf* : totality, whole

totalitario, -ria *adj & n* : totalitarian

totalitarismo *nm* : totalitarianism

totalizar {21} *vt* : total, to add up to
tótem *nm, pl* **tótems** : totem
totopo *nm CA, Mex* : tortilla chip
totuma *nf* : calabash
tour [ˈtur] *nm, pl* **tours** : tour, excursion
toxicidad *nf* : toxicity
tóxico[1], **-ca** *adj* : toxic, poisonous
tóxico[2] *nm* : poison
toxicomanía *nf* : drug addiction
toxicómano, -na *n* : drug addict
toxina *nf* : toxin
tozudez *nf* : stubbornness, obstinacy
tozudo, -da *adj* : stubborn, obstinate — **tozudamente** *adv*
traba *nf* **1** : tie, bond **2** : obstacle, hindrance
trabajador[1], **-dora** *adj* : hardworking
trabajador[2], **-dora** *n* : worker
trabajar *vi* **1** : to work ⟨trabaja mucho : he works hard⟩ ⟨trabajo de secretaria : I work as a secretary⟩ **2** : to strive ⟨trabajan por mejores oportunidades : they're striving for better opportunities⟩ **3** : to act, to perform ⟨trabajar en una película : to be in a movie⟩ — *vt* **1** : to work (metal) **2** : to knead **3** : to till **4** : to work on ⟨tienes que trabajar el español : you need to work on your Spanish⟩
trabajo *nm* **1** : work, job **2** LABOR : labor, work ⟨tengo mucho trabajo : I have a lot of work to do⟩ **3** TAREA : task **4** ESFUERZA : effort **5 costar trabajo** : to be difficult **6 tomarse el trabajo** : to take the trouble **7 trabajo en equipo** : teamwork **8 trabajos** *nmpl* : hardships, difficulties
trabajoso, -sa *adj* LABORIOSO : laborious — **trabajosamente** *adv*
trabalenguas *nms & pl* : tongue twister
trabar *vt* **1** : to join, to connect **2** : to impede, to hold back **3** : to strike up (a conversation), to form (a friendship) **4** : to thicken (sauces) — **trabarse** *vr* **1** : to jam **2** : to become entangled **3** : to be tongue-tied, to stammer
trabucar {72} *vt* : to confuse, to mix up
trabuco *nm* : blunderbuss
tracalero, -ra *adj Mex* : dishonest, tricky
tracción *nf* : traction
trace, etc. → **trazar**
tracto *nm* : tract
tractor *nm* : tractor
tradición *nf, pl* **-ciones** : tradition
tradicional *adj* : traditional — **tradicionalmente** *adv*
traducción *nf, pl* **-ciones** : translation
traducible *adj* : translatable
traducir {61} *vt* **1** : to translate **2** : to convey, to express — **traducirse** *vr* **~ en** : to result in
traductor, -tora *n* : translator
traer {81} *vt* **1** : to bring ⟨trae una ensalada : bring a salad⟩ **2** CAUSAR : to cause, to bring about ⟨el problema puede traer graves consecuencias : the problem could have serious consequences⟩ **3** : to carry, to have ⟨todos los periódicos traían las mismas noticias : all of the newspapers carried the same news⟩ **4** LLEVAR : to wear — **traerse** *vr* **1** : to bring along **2 traérselas** : to be difficult
traficante *nmf* : dealer, trafficker
traficar {72} *vi* **1** : to trade, to deal **2 ~ con** : to traffic in
tráfico *nm* **1** : trade **2** : traffic
tragaluz *nf, pl* **-luces** : skylight, fanlight
tragar {52} *v* : to swallow — **tragarse** *vr*
tragedia *nf* : tragedy
trágico, -ca *adj* : tragic — **trágicamente** *adv*
trago *nm* **1** : swallow, swig **2** : drink, liquor **3 trago amargo** : hard time
trague, etc. → **tragar**
traición *nf, pl* **traiciones** **1** : treason **2** : betrayal, treachery
traicionar *vt* : to betray
traicionero, -ra → **traidor**
traidor[1], **-dora** *adj* : traitorous, treasonous
traidor[2], **-dora** *n* : traitor
traiga, etc. → **traer**
tráiler *or* **trailer** *nm* : trailer
traílla *nf* **1** : leash **2** : harrow
traje *nm* **1** : suit **2** : dress **3** : costume **4 traje de baño** : bathing suit
trajín *nm, pl* **trajines** **1** : transport **2** *fam* : hustle and bustle
trajinar *vt* : to transport, to carry — *vi* : to rush around
trajo, etc. → **traer**
trama *nf* **1** : plot **2** : weave, weft (fabric)
tramar *vt* **1** : to plot, to plan **2** : to weave
tramitar *vt* : to transact, to negotiate, to handle
trámite *nm* : procedure, step
tramo *nm* **1** : stretch, section **2** : flight (of stairs)
trampa *nf* **1** : trap **2 hacer trampas** : to cheat
trampear *vt* : to cheat
trampero, -ra *n* : trapper
trampilla *nf* : trapdoor
trampolín *nm, pl* **-lines** **1** : diving board **2** : trampoline **3** : springboard ⟨un trampolín al éxito : a springboard to success⟩
tramposo[1], **-sa** *adj* : crooked, cheating
tramposo[2], **-sa** *n* : cheat, swindler
tranca *nf* **1** : stick, club **2** : bar, crossbar
trancar {72} *vt* : to bar (a door or window)
trancazo *nm* GOLPE : blow, hit
trance *nm* **1** : critical juncture, tough time **2** : trance **3 en trance de** : in the process of ⟨en trance de extinción : on the verge of extinction⟩
tranco *nm* **1** : stride **2** UMBRAL : threshold
tranque, etc. → **trancar**
tranquilidad *nf* : tranquility, peace
tranquilizador, -dora *adj* **1** : soothing **2** : reassuring
tranquilizante[1] *adj* **1** : reassuring **2** : tranquilizing

tranquilizante[2] *nm* : tranquilizer

tranquilizar {21} *vt* CALMAR : to calm down, to soothe ⟨tranquilizar la conciencia : to ease the conscience⟩ — **tranquilizarse** *vr*

tranquilo, -la *adj* CALMO : calm, tranquil ⟨una vida tranquila : a quiet life⟩ — **tranquilamente** *adv*

transacción *nf, pl* **-ciones** : transaction

transar *vi* TRANSIGIR : to give way, to compromise — *vt* : to buy and sell

transatlántico[1], **-ca** *adj* : transatlantic

transatlántico[2] *nm* : ocean liner

transbordador *nm* **1** : ferry **2 transbordador espacial** : space shuttle

transbordar *v* : to transfer

transbordo *nm* : transfer

transcendencia → **trascendencia**

transcender → **trascender**

transcribir {33} *vt* : to transcribe

transcrito *pp* → **transcribir**

transcripción *nf, pl* **-ciones** : transcription

transcurrir *vi* : to elapse, to pass

transcurso *nm* : course, progression ⟨en el transcurso de cien años : over the course of a hundred years⟩

transeúnte *nmf* **1** : passerby **2** : transient

transferencia *nf* : transfer, transference

transferir {76} *vt* TRASLADAR : to transfer — **transferible** *adj*

transfigurar *vt* : to transfigure, to transform — **transfiguración** *nf*

transformación *nf, pl* **-ciones** : transformation, conversion

transformador *nm* : transformer

transformar *vt* **1** CONVERTIR : to convert **2** : to transform, to change, to alter — **transformarse** *vr*

transfusión *nf, pl* **-siones** : transfusion

transgredir {1} *vt* : to transgress — **transgresión** *nf*

transgresor, -sora *n* : transgressor

transición *nf, pl* **-ciones** : transition ⟨período de transición : transition period⟩

transido, -da *adj* : overcome, beset ⟨transido de dolor : racked with pain⟩

transigir {35} *vi* **1** : to give in, to compromise **2 ~ con** : to tolerate, to put up with

transistor *nm* : transistor

transitable *adj* : passable

transitar *vi* : to go, to pass, to travel ⟨transitar por la ciudad : to travel through the city⟩

transitivo, -va *adj* : transitive

tránsito *nm* **1** TRÁFICO : traffic ⟨hora de máximo tránsito : rush hour⟩ **2** : transit, passage, movement **3** : death, passing

transitorio, -ria *adj* **1** : transitory **2** : provisional, temporary — **transitoriamente** *adv*

translúcido, -da *adj* : translucent

translucir → **traslucir**

transmisible *adj* : transmissible

transmisión *nf, pl* **-siones 1** : transmission, broadcast **2** : transfer **3** : transmission (of an automobile)

transmisor *nm* : transmitter

transmitir *vt* **1** : to transmit, to broadcast **2** : to pass on, to transfer — *vi* : to transmit, to broadcast

transparencia *nf* : transparency

transparentar *vt* : to reveal, to betray — **transparentarse** *vr* **1** : to be transparent **2** : to show through

transparente[1] *adj* : transparent — **transparentemente** *adv*

transparente[2] *nm* : shade, blind

transpiración *nf, pl* **-ciones** SUDOR : perspiration, sweat

transpirado, -da *adj* : sweaty

transpirar *vi* **1** SUDAR : to perspire, to sweat **2** : to transpire

transplantar, transplante → **trasplantar, trasplante**

transponer {60} *vt* **1** : to transpose, to move about **2** TRASPLANTAR : to transplant — **transponerse** *vr* **1** OCULTARSE : to hide **2** PONERSE : to set, to go down (of the sun or moon) **3** DORMITAR : to doze off

transportación *nf, pl* **-ciones** : transportation

transportador *nm* **1** : protractor **2** : conveyor

transportar *vt* **1** : to transport, to carry **2** : to transmit **3** : to transpose (music) — **transportarse** *vr* : to get carried away

transporte *nm* : transport, transportation

transportista *nmf* : hauler, carrier, trucker

transpuso, etc. → **transponer**

transversal *adj* : transverse, cross ⟨corte transversal : cross section⟩

transversalmente *adv* : obliquely

transverso, -sa *adj* : transverse

tranvía *nm* : streetcar, trolley

trapeador *nm* : mop

trapear *vt* : to mop

trapecio *nm* **1** : trapezoid **2** : trapeze

trapezoide *nm* : trapezoid

trapo *nm* **1** : cloth, rag ⟨trapo de polvo : dust cloth⟩ **2 soltar el trapo** : to burst into tears **3 trapos** *nmpl fam* : clothes

tráquea *nf* : trachea, windpipe

traquetear *vi* : to clatter, to jolt

traqueteo *nm* **1** : jolting **2** : clattering, clatter

tras *prep* **1** : after ⟨día tras día : day after day⟩ ⟨uno tras otro : one after another⟩ **2** : behind ⟨tras la puerta : behind the door⟩

trasbordar, trasbordo → **transbordar, transbordo**

trascendencia *nf* **1** : importance, significance **2** : transcendence

trascendental *adj* **1** : transcendental **2** : important, momentous

trascendente *adj* **1** : important, significant **2** : transcendent

trascender {56} *vi* **1** : to leak out, to become known **2** : to spread, to have a wide effect **3 ~ a** : to smell of ⟨la casa trascendía a flores : the house smelled of flowers⟩ **4 ~ de** : to transcend, to go beyond — *vt* : to transcend

trasero[1], **-ra** *adj* POSTERIOR : rear, back

trasero[2] *nm* : buttocks

trasfondo *nm* **1** : background, backdrop **2** : undertone, undercurrent

trasformación → **transformación**

trasgo *nm* : goblin, imp

trasgredir → **transgredir**

trasladar *vt* **1** TRANSFERIR : to transfer, to move **2** POSPONER : to postpone **3** TRADUCIR : to translate **4** COPIAR : to copy, to transcribe — **trasladarse** *vr* MUDARSE : to move, to relocate

traslado *nm* **1** : transfer, move **2** : copy

traslapar *vt* : to overlap — **traslaparse** *vr*

traslapo *nm* : overlap

traslúcido, -da → **translúcido**

traslucir {45} *vi* : to reveal, to show — **traslucirse** *vr* : to show through

trasmano *nm* **a ~** : out of the way, out of reach

trasmisión, trasmitir → **transmisión, transmitir**

trasnochar *vi* : to stay up all night

trasparencia *nf* **trasparente** → **transparencia, transparente**

traspasar *vt* **1** PERFORAR : to pierce, to go through **2** : to go beyond ⟨traspasar los límites : to overstep the limits⟩ **3** ATRAVESAR : to cross, to go across **4** : to sell, to transfer

traspaso *nm* : transfer, sale

traspié *nm* **1** : stumble **2** : blunder

traspiración → **transpiración**

trasplantar *vt* : to transplant

trasplante *nm* : transplant

trasponer → **transponer**

trasportar → **transportar**

trasquilar *vt* ESQUILAR : to shear

traste *nm* **1** : fret (on a guitar) **2** *CA, Mex, PRi* : kitchen utensil ⟨lavar los trastes : to do the dishes⟩ **3 dar al traste con** : to ruin, to destroy **4 irse al traste** : to fall through

trastornar *vt* : to disturb, to upset, to disrupt — **trastornarse** *vr*

trastorno *nm* **1** : disorder ⟨trastorno mental : mental disorder⟩ **2** : disturbance, upset

trastos *nmpl* **1** : implements, utensils **2** *fam* : pieces of junk, stuff

trasunto *nm* : image, likeness

tratable *adj* **1** : friendly, sociable **2** : treatable

tratado *nm* **1** : treatise **2** : treaty

tratamiento *nm* : treatment

tratante *nmf* : dealer, trader

tratar *vi* **1 ~ con** : to deal with, to have contact with ⟨no trato mucho con los clientes : I don't have much contact with customers⟩ **2 ~ de** : to try to ⟨estoy tratando de comer : I am trying to eat⟩ **3 ~ de** *or* **~ sobre** : to be about, to concern ⟨el libro trata de las plantas : the book is about plants⟩ **4 ~ en** : to deal in ⟨trata en herramientas : he deals in tools⟩ — *vt* **1** : to treat ⟨tratan bien a sus empleados : they treat their employees well⟩ **2** : to handle ⟨trató el tema con delicadeza : he handled the subject tactfully⟩ — **tratarse** *vr* **~ de** : to be about, to concern

trato *nm* **1** : deal, agreement **2** : relationship, dealings *pl* **3** : treatment ⟨malos tratos : ill-treatment⟩

trauma *nm* : trauma

traumático, -ca *adj* : traumatic — **traumáticamente** *adv*

traumatismo *nm* : injury ⟨traumatismo cervical : whiplash⟩

través *nm* **1 a través de** : across, through **2 al través** : crosswise, across **3 de través** : sideways

travesaño *nm* **1** : crossbar **2** : crossbeam, crosspiece, transom (of a window)

travesía *nf* : voyage, crossing (of the sea)

travesura *nf* **1** : prank, mischievous act **2 travesuras** *nfpl* : mischief

travieso, -sa *adj* : mischievous, naughty — **traviesamente** *adv*

trayecto *nm* **1** : journey **2** : route **3** : trajectory, path

trayectoria *nf* : course, path, trajectory

trayendo → **traer**

traza *nf* **1** DISEÑO : design, plan **2** : appearance

trazado *nm* **1** BOSQUEJO : outline, sketch **2** PLAN : plan, layout

trazar {21} *vt* **1** : to trace **2** : to draw up, to devise **3** : to outline, to sketch

trazo *nm* **1** : stroke, line **2** : sketch, outline

trébol *nm* **1** : clover, shamrock **2** : club (playing card)

trece *adj & nm* : thirteen

treceavo[1], **-va** *adj* : thirteenth

treceavo[2] *nm* : thirteenth (fraction)

trecho *nm* **1** : stretch, period ⟨de trecho en trecho : at intervals⟩ **2** : distance, space

tregua *nf* **1** : truce **2** : lull, respite **3 sin ~** : relentless, unrelenting

treinta *adj & nm* : thirty

treintavo[1], **-va** *adj* : thirtieth

treintavo[2] *nm* : thirtieth (fraction)

tremendo, -da *adj* **1** : tremendous, enormous **2** : terrible, dreadful **3** *fam* : great, super

trementina *nf* AGUARRÁS : turpentine

trémulo, -la *adj* **1** : trembling, shaky **2** : flickering

tren *nm* **1** : train **2** : set, assembly ⟨tren de aterrizaje : landing gear⟩ **3** : speed, pace ⟨a todo tren : at top speed⟩

trence, etc. → **trenzar**

trenza *nf* : braid, pigtail

trenzar {21} *vt* : to braid — **trenzarse** *vr* : to get involved

trepador, -dora *adj* : climbing ⟨rosal trepador : rambling rose⟩

trepadora *nf* **1** : climbing plant, climber **2** : nuthatch
trepar *vi* **1** : to climb ⟨trepar a un árbol : to climb up a tree⟩ **2** : to creep, to spread (of a plant)
trepidación *nf, pl* **-ciones** : vibration
trepidante *adj* **1** : vibrating **2** : fast, frantic
trepidar *vi* **1** : to shake, to vibrate **2** : to hesitate, to waver
tres *adj & nm* : three
trescientos[1], **-tas** *adj* : three hundred
trescientos[2] *nms & pl* : three hundred
treta *nf* : trick, ruse
tríada *nf* : triad
triángulo *nm* : triangle — **triangular** *adj*
tribal *adj* : tribal
tribu *nf* : tribe
tribulación *nf, pl* **-ciones** : tribulation
tribuna *nf* **1** : dais, platform **2** : stands *pl*, bleachers *pl*, grandstand
tribunal *nm* : court, tribunal
tributar *vt* : to pay, to render — *vi* : to pay taxes
tributario[1], **-ria** *adj* : tax ⟨evasión tributaria : tax evasion⟩
tributario[2] *nm* : tributary
tributo *nm* **1** : tax **2** : tribute
triciclo *nm* : tricycle
tricolor *adj* : tricolor, tricolored
tridente *nm* : trident
tridimensional *adj* : three-dimensional, 3-D
trienal *adj* : triennial
trifulca *nf fam* : row, ruckus
trigésimo[1], **-ma** *adj* : thirtieth, thirty-
trigésimo[2], **-ma** *n* : thirtieth, thirty- (in a series)
trigo *nm* **1** : wheat **2 trigo rubión** : buckwheat
trigonometría *nf* : trigonometry
trigueño, -ña *adj* **1** : light brown (of hair) **2** MORENO : dark, olive-skinned
trillado, -da *adj* : trite, hackneyed
trilladora *nf* : thresher, threshing machine
trillar *vt* : to thresh
trillizo, -za *n* : triplet
trilogía *nf* : trilogy
trimestral *adj* : quarterly — **trimestralmente** *adv*
trinar *vi* **1** : to thrill **2** : to warble
trinchar *vt* : to carve, to cut up
trinchera *nf* **1** : trench, ditch **2** : trench coat
trineo *nm* : sled, sleigh
trinidad *nf* **la Trinidad** : the Trinity
trino *nm* : trill, warble
trinquete *nm* : ratchet
trío *nm* : trio
tripa *nf* **1** INTESTINO : gut, intestine **2 tripas** *nfpl fam* : belly, tummy, insides *pl* ⟨dolerle a uno las tripas : to have a stomach ache⟩
tripartito, -ta *adj* : tripartite
triple *adj & nm* : triple
triplicado *nm* : triplicate
triplicar {72} *vt* : to triple, to treble
trípode *nm* : tripod
tripulación *nf, pl* **-ciones** : crew
tripulante *nmf* : crew member
tripular *vt* : to man
tris *nm* **estar en un tris de** : to be within an inch of, to be very close to
triste *adj* **1** : sad, gloomy ⟨ponerse triste : to become sad⟩ **2** : desolate, dismal ⟨una perspectiva triste : a dismal outlook⟩ **3** : sorry, sorry-looking ⟨la triste verdad : the sorry truth⟩
tristeza *nf* DOLOR : sadness, grief
tristón, -tona *adj, mpl* **-tones** : melancholy, downhearted
tritón *nm, pl* **tritones** : newt
triturar *vt* : to crush, to grind
triunfal *adj* : triumphal, triumphant — **triunfalmente** *adv*
triunfante *adj* : triumphant, victorious
triunfar *vi* : to triumph, to win
triunfo *nm* **1** : triumph, victory **2** ÉXITO : success **3** : trump (in card games)
triunvirato *nm* : triumvirate
trivial *adj* **1** : trivial **2** : trite, commonplace
trivialidad *nf* : triviality
triza *nf* **1** : shred, bit **2 hacer trizas** : to tear into shreds, to smash to pieces
trocar {82} *vt* **1** CAMBIAR : to exchange, to trade **2** CAMBIAR : to change, to alter, to transform **3** CONFUNDIR : to confuse, to mix up
trocha *nf* : path, trail
troce, etc. → **trozar**
trofeo *nm* : trophy
tromba *nf* **1** : whirlwind **2 tromba de agua** : downpour, cloudburst
trombón *nm, pl* **trombones** **1** : trombone **2** : trombonist — **trombonista** *nmf*
trombosis *nf* : thrombosis
trompa *nf* **1** : trunk (of an elephant), proboscis (of an insect) **2** : horn ⟨trompa de caza : hunting horn⟩ **3** : tube, duct (in the body)
trompada *nf fam* **1** : punch, blow **2** : bump, collision (of persons)
trompeta *nf* : trumpet
trompetista *nmf* : trumpet player, trumpeter
trompo *nm* : spinning top
tronada *nf* : thunderstorm
tronar {19} *vi* **1** : to thunder, to roar **2** : to be furious, to rage **3** *CA, Mex fam* : to shoot — *v impers* : to thunder ⟨está tronando : it's thundering⟩
tronchar *vt* **1** : to snap, to break off **2** : to cut off (relations)
tronco *nm* **1** : trunk (of a tree) **2** : log **3** : torso
trono *nm* **1** : throne **2** *fam* : toilet
tropa *nf* **1** : troop, soldiers *pl* **2** : crowd, mob **3** : herd (of livestock)
tropel *nm* : mob, swarm
tropezar {29} *vi* **1** : to trip, to stumble **2** : to slip up, to blunder **3 ~ con** : to run into, to bump into **4 ~ con** : to come up against (a problem)

tropezón *nm, pl* **-zones** **1** : stumble **2** : mistake, slip
tropical *adj* : tropical
trópico *nm* **1** : tropic ⟨trópico de Cáncer : tropic of Cancer⟩ **2 el trópico** : the tropics
tropiezo *nm* **1** CONTRATIEMPO : snag, setback **2** EQUIVOCACIÓN : mistake, slip
troqué, etc. → **trocar**
troquel *nm* : die (for stamping)
trotamundos *nmf* : globe-trotter
trotar *vi* **1** : to trot **2** : to jog **3** *fam* : to rush about
trote *nm* **1** : trot **2** *fam* : rush, bustle **3 de ~** : durable, for everyday use
trovador, -dora *n* : troubadour
trozar {21} *vt* : to cut up, to dice
trozo *nm* **1** PEDAZO : piece, bit, chunk **2** : passage, extract
trucha *nf* : trout
truco *nm* **1** : trick **2** : knack
truculento, -ta *adj* : horrifying, gruesome
trueca, trueque etc. → **trocar**
truena, etc. → **tronar**
trueno *nm* : thunder
trueque *nm* : barter, exchange
trufa *nf* : truffle
truncar {72} *vt* **1** : to truncate, to cut short **2** : to thwart, to frustrate ⟨truncó sus esperanzas : she shattered their hopes⟩
trunco, -ca *adj* **1** : truncated **2** : unfinished, incomplete
trunque, etc. → **truncar**
tu *adj* **1** : your ⟨tu vestido : your dress⟩ ⟨toma tus vitaminas : take your vitamins⟩ **2** : thy
tú *pron* **1** : you ⟨tú eres mi hijo : you are my son⟩ **2** : thou
tuba *nf* : tuba
tubérculo *nm* : tuber
tuberculosis *nf* : tuberculosis
tuberculoso, -sa *adj* : tuberculous, tubercular
tubería *nf* : pipes *pl*, tubing
tuberoso, -sa *adj* : tuberous
tubo *nm* **1** : tube ⟨tubo de ensayo : test tube⟩ **2** : pipe ⟨tubo de desagüe : drainpipe⟩ **3 tubo digestivo** : alimentary canal
tubular *adj* : tubular
tuerca *nf* : nut ⟨tuercas y tornillos : nuts and bolts⟩
tuerce, etc. → **torcer**
tuerto, -ta *adj* : one-eyed, blind in one eye
tuerza, etc. → **torcer**
tuesta, etc. → **tostar**
tuétano *nm* : marrow
tufo *nm* **1** : fume, vapor **2** *fam* : stench, stink
tugurio *nm* : hovel
tulipán *nm, pl* **-panes** : tulip
tumba *nf* **1** SEPULCRO : tomb **2** FOSA : grave **3** : felling of trees
tumbar *vt* **1** : to knock down **2** : to fell, to cut down — *vi* : to fall down — **tumbarse** *vr* ACOSTARSE : to lie down
tumbo *nm* **1** : tumble, fall **2 dar tumbos** : to jolt, to bump around
tumor *nm* : tumor
túmulo *nm* : burial mound
tumulto *nm* **1** ALBOROTO : commotion, tumult **2** MOTÍN : riot **3** MULTITUD : crowd
tumultuoso, -sa *adj* : tumultuous
tuna *nf* : prickly pear (fruit)
tundra *nf* : tundra
tunecino, -na *adj & n* : Tunisian
túnel *nm* : tunnel
tungsteno *nm* : tungsten
túnica *nf* : tunic
tupé *nm* PELUQUÍN : toupee
tupido, -da *adj* **1** DENSO : dense, thick **2** OBSTRUIDO : obstructed, blocked up
turba *nf* **1** : peat **2** : mob, throng
turbación *nf, pl* **-ciones** **1** : disturbance **2** : alarm, concern **3** : confusion
turbante *nm* : turban
turbar *vt* **1** : to disturb, to disrupt **2** : to worry, to upset **3** : to confuse
turbina *nf* : turbine
turbio, -bia *adj* **1** : cloudy, murky, turbid **2** : dim, blurred **3** : shady, crooked
turbopropulsor *nm* : turboprop
turborreactor *nm* : turbojet
turbulencia *nf* : turbulence
turbulento, -ta *adj* : turbulent
turco[1], **-ca** *adj* : Turkish
turco[2], **-ca** *n* : Turk
turco[3] *nm* : Turkish (language)
turgente *adj* : turgid, swollen
turismo *nm* : tourism, tourist industry
turista *nmf* : tourist, vacationer
turístico, -ca *adj* : tourist, travel
turnar *vi* : to take turns, to alternate
turno *nm* **1** : turn ⟨ya te tocará tu turno : you'll get your turn⟩ **2** : shift, duty ⟨turno de noche : night shift⟩ **3 por turno** : alternately
turón *nm, pl* **turones** : polecat
turquesa *nf* : turquoise
turrón *nm, pl* **turrones** : nougat
tusa *nf* : corn husk
tutear *vt* : to address as *tú*
tutela *nf* **1** : guardianship **2** : tutelage, protection
tuteo *nm* : addressing as *tú*
tutor, -tora *n* **1** : tutor **2** : guardian
tuvo, etc. → **tener**
tuyo[1], **-ya** *adj* : yours, of yours ⟨un amigo tuyo : a friend of yours⟩ ⟨¿es tuya esta casa? : is this house yours?⟩
tuyo[2], **-ya** *pron* **1** : yours ⟨ése es el tuyo : that one is yours⟩ ⟨trae la tuya : bring your own⟩ **2 los tuyos** : your relations, your friends ⟨¿vendrán los tuyos? : are your folks coming?⟩
tweed ['twið] *nm* : tweed

U

u[1] *nf* : twenty-second letter of the Spanish alphabet

u[2] *conj* (*used instead of* **o** *before words beginning with o- or ho-*) : or

ualabí *nm* : wallaby

uapití *nm* : American elk, wapiti

ubicación *nf, pl* **-ciones** : location, position

ubicar {72} *vt* **1** SITUAR : to place, to put, to position **2** LOCALIZAR : to locate, to find — **ubicarse** *vr* **1** LOCALIZARSE : to be placed, to be located **2** SITUARSE : to position oneself

ubicuidad *nf* OMNIPRESENCIA : ubiquity

ubicuo, -cua *adj* OMNIPRESENTE : ubiquitous

ubre *nf* : udder

ucraniano[1], -na *adj & n* : Ukranian

ucraniano[2] *nm* : Ukranian (language)

Ud., Uds. → **usted**

ufanarse *vr* **~ de** : to boast about, to pride oneself on

ufano, -na *adj* **1** ORGULLOSO : proud **2** : self-satisfied, smug

ugandés, -desa *adj & n, mpl* **-deses** : Ugandan

ukelele *nm* : ukulele

úlcera *nf* : ulcer — **ulceroso, -sa** *adj*

ulcerar *vt* : to ulcerate — **ulcerarse** *vr* — **ulceración** *nf*

ulceroso, -sa *adj* : ulcerous

ulterior *adj* : later, subsequent — **ulteriormente** *adv*

últimamente *adv* : lately, recently

ultimar *vt* **1** CONCLUIR : to complete, to finish, to finalize **2** MATAR : to kill

ultimátum *nm, pl* **-tums** : ultimatum

último, -ma *adj* **1** : last, final ⟨la última galleta : the last cookie⟩ ⟨en último caso : as a last resort⟩ **2** : last, latest, most recent ⟨su último viaje a España : her last trip to Spain⟩ ⟨en los últimos años : in recent years⟩ **3 por ~** : finally

ultrajar *vt* INSULTAR : to offend, to outrage, to insult

ultraje *nm* INSULTO : outrage, insult

ultramar *nm* **de ~** *or* **en ~** : overseas, abroad

ultranza *nf* **1 a ~** : to the extreme ⟨lo defendió a ultranza : she defended him fiercely⟩ **2 a ~** : extreme, out-and-out ⟨perfeccionismo a ultranza : rabid perfectionism⟩

ultrarrojo, -ja *adj* : infrared

ultravioleta *adj* : ultraviolet

ulular *vi* **1** : to hoot **2** : to howl, to wail

ululato *nm* : hoot (of an owl), wail (of a person)

umbilical *adj* : umbilical ⟨cordón umbilical : umbilical cord⟩

umbral *nm* : threshold, doorstep

un[1] *adj* → **uno[1]**

un[2], una *art, mpl* **unos 1** : a, an **2 unos** *or* **unas** *pl* : some, a few ⟨hace unas semanas : a few weeks ago⟩ **3 unos** *or* **unas** *pl* : about, approximately ⟨unos veinte años antes : about twenty years before⟩

unánime *adj* : unanimous — **unánimemente** *adv*

unanimidad *nf* **1** : unanimity **2 por ~** : unanimously

unción *nf, pl* **-ciones** : unction

uncir {83} *vt* : to yoke

undécimo[1], -ma *adj* : eleventh

undécimo[2], -ma *n* : eleventh (in a series)

ungir {35} *vt* : to anoint

ungüento *nm* : ointment, salve

únicamente *adv* : only, solely

unicelular *adj* : unicellular

único[1], -ca *adj* **1** : only, sole **2** : unique, extraordinary

único[2], -ca *n* : only one ⟨los únicos que vinieron : the only ones who showed up⟩

unicornio *nm* : unicorn

unidad *nf* **1** : unity **2** : unit

unidireccional *adj* : unidirectional

unido, -da *adj* **1** : joined, united **2** : close ⟨unos amigos muy unidos : very close friends⟩

unificar {72} *vt* : to unify — **unificación** *nf*

uniformado, -da *adj* : uniformed

uniformar *vt* ESTANDARIZAR : to standardize, to make uniform

uniforme[1] *adj* : uniform — **uniformemente** *adv*

uniforme[2] *nm* : uniform

uniformidad *nf* : uniformity

unilateral *adj* : unilateral — **unilateralmente** *adv*

unión *nf, pl* **uniones 1** : union **2** JUNTURA : joint, coupling

unir *vt* **1** JUNTAR : to unite, to join, to link **2** COMBINAR : to combine, to blend — **unirse** *vr* **1** : to join together **2** : to combine, to mix together **3 ~ a** : to join ⟨se unieron al grupo : they joined the group⟩

unísono *nm* : unison ⟨al unísono : in unison⟩

unitario, -ria *adj* : unitary, unit ⟨precio unitario : unit price⟩

universal *adj* : universal — **universalmente** *adv*

universidad *nf* : university

universitario[1], -ria *adj* : university, college

universitario[2], -ria *n* : university student, college student

universo *nm* : universe

unja, etc. → **ungir**

uno[1], una *adj* (**un** *before masculine singular nouns*) : one ⟨una silla : one chair⟩ ⟨tiene treinta y un años : he's thirty-one years old⟩ ⟨el tomo uno : volume one⟩

uno[2] *nm* : one, number one

uno[3], **una** *pron* **1** : one (number) ⟨uno por uno : one by one⟩ ⟨es la una : it's one o'clock⟩ **2** : one (person or thing) ⟨una es mejor que las otras : one (of them) is better than the others⟩ ⟨hacerlo uno mismo : to do it oneself⟩ **3 unos, unas** *pl* : some (ones), some people **4 uno y otro** : both **5 unos y otros** : all of them **6 el uno al otro** : one another, each other ⟨se enseñaron los unos a los otros : they taught each other⟩
untar *vt* **1** : to anoint **2** : to smear, to grease **3** : to bribe
unza, etc. → **uncir**
uña *nf* **1** : fingernail, toenail **2** : claw, hoof, stinger
uranio *nm* : uranium
Urano *nm* : Uranus
urbanidad *nf* : urbanity, courtesy
urbanización *nf, pl* **-ciones** : housing development, residential area
urbanizar {21} *vt* : to develop (an area)
urbano, -na *adj* **1** : urban **2** CORTÉS : urbane, polite
urbe *nf* : large city, metropolis
urdimbre *nf* : warp (in a loom)
urdu *nm* : Urdu
uretra *nf* : urethra
urgencia *nf* **1** : urgency **2** EMERGENCIA : emergency
urgente *adj* : urgent — **urgentemente** *adv*
urgir {35} *v impers* : to be urgent, to be pressing ⟨me urge localizarlo : I urgently need to find him⟩ ⟨el tiempo urge : time is running out⟩
urinario[1], **-ria** *adj* : urinary
urinario[2] *nm* : urinal (place)
urja, etc. → **urgir**
urna *nf* **1** : urn **2** : ballot box ⟨acudir a las urnas : to go to the polls⟩
urogallo *nm* : grouse (bird)
urraca *nf* **1** : magpie **2 urraca de América** : blue jay
urticaria *nf* : hives
uruguayo, -ya *adj & n* : Uruguayan
usado, -da *adj* **1** : used, secondhand **2** : worn, worn-out
usanza *nf* : custom, usage
usar *vt* **1** EMPLEAR, UTILIZAR : to use, to make use of **2** CONSUMIR : to consume, to use (up) **3** LLEVAR : to wear **4 de usar y tirar** : disposable — **usarse** *vr* **1** : to be used **2** : to be in fashion
uso *nm* **1** EMPLEO, UTILIZACIÓN : use ⟨de uso personal : for personal use⟩ ⟨hacer uso de : to make use of⟩ **2** : wear ⟨uso y desgaste : wear and tear⟩ **3** USANZA : custom, usage, habit ⟨al uso de : in the manner of, in the style of⟩
usted *pron* **1** (*formal form of address in most countries; often written as* **Ud.** *or* **Vd.**) : you **2 ustedes** *pl* (*often written as* **Uds.** *or* **Vds.**) : you, all of you
usual *adj* : usual, common, normal ⟨poco usual : not very common⟩ — **usualmente** *adv*
usuario, -ria *n* : user
usura *nf* : usury — **usurario, -ria** *adj*
usurero, -ra *n* : usurer
usurpador, -dora *n* : usurper
usurpar *vt* : to usurp — **usurpación** *nf*
utensilio *nm* : utensil, tool
uterino, -na *adj* : uterine
útero *nm* : uterus, womb
útil *adj* : useful, handy, helpful
útiles *nmpl* : implements, tools
utilidad *nf* **1** : utility, usefulness **2 utilidades** *nfpl* : profits
utilitario, -ria *adj* : utilitarian
utilizable *adj* : usable, fit for use
utilización *nf, pl* **-ciones** : utilization, use
utilizar {21} *vt* : to use, to utilize
útilmente *adv* : usefully
utopía *nf* : utopia
utópico, -ca *adj* : utopian
uva *nf* : grape
uvular *adj* : uvular

V

v *nf* : twenty-third letter of the Spanish alphabet
va → **ir**
vaca *nf* : cow
vacación *nf, pl* **-ciones 1** : vacation ⟨dos semanas de vacaciones : two weeks of vacation⟩ **2 estar de vacaciones** : to be on vacation **3 irse de vacaciones** : to go on vacation
vacacionar *vi Mex* : to vacation
vacacionista *nmf CA, Mex* : vacationer
vacante[1] *adj* : vacant, empty
vacante[2] *nf* : vacancy (for a job)
vaciado *nm* : cast, casting ⟨vaciado de yeso : plaster cast⟩
vaciar {85} *vt* **1** : to empty, to empty out, to drain **2** AHUECAR : to hollow out **3** : to cast (in a mold) — *vi* **~ en** : to flow into, to empty into
vacilación *nf, pl* **-ciones** : hesitation, vacillation
vacilante *adj* **1** : hesitant, unsure **2** : shaky, unsteady **3** : flickering
vacilar *vi* **1** : to hesitate, to vacillate, to waver **2** : to be unsteady, to wobble **3** : to flicker **4** *fam* : to joke, to fool around
vacío[1], **-cía** *adj* **1** : vacant **2** : empty **3** : meaningless
vacío[2] *nm* **1** : emptiness, void **2** : space, gap **3** : vacuum **4 hacerle el vacío a alguien** : to ostracize someone, to give someone the cold shoulder
vacuidad *nf* : vacuity, vacuousness

vacuna *nf* : vaccine
vacunación *nf, pl* **-ciones** INOCULACIÓN : vaccination, inoculation
vacunar *vt* INOCULAR : to vaccinate, to inoculate
vacuno[1], **-na** *adj* : bovine ⟨ganado vacuno : beef cattle⟩
vacuno[2] *nm* : bovine
vacuo, -cua *adj* : empty, shallow, inane
vadear *vt* : to ford, to wade across
vado *nm* : ford
vagabundear *vi* : to wander, to roam about
vagabundo[1], **-da** *adj* **1** ERRANTE : wandering **2** : stray
vagabundo[2], **-da** *n* : vagrant, bum, vagabond
vagamente *adv* : vaguely
vagancia *nf* **1** : vagrancy **2** PEREZA : laziness, idleness
vagar {52} *vi* ERRAR : to roam, to wander
vagina *nf* : vagina — **vaginal** *adj*
vago[1], **-ga** *adj* **1** : vague **2** PEREZOSO : lazy, idle
vago[2], **-ga** *n* **1** : idler, loafer **2** VAGABUNDO : vagrant, bum
vagón *nm, pl* **vagones** : car (of a train)
vague, etc. → **vagar**
vaguear *vi* **1** : to loaf, to lounge around **2** VAGAR : to wander
vaguedad *nf* : vagueness
vahído *nm* : dizzy spell
vaho *nm* **1** : breath **2** : vapor, steam (on glass, etc.)
vaina *nf* **1** : sheath, scabbard **2** : pod (of a pea or bean) **3** *fam* : nuisance, bother
vainilla *nf* : vanilla
vaivén *nm, pl* **vaivenes** **1** : swinging, swaying, rocking **2** : change, fluctuation ⟨los vaivenes de la vida : life's ups and downs⟩
vajilla *nf* : dishes *pl*, set of dishes
valdrá, etc. → **valer**
vale *nm* **1** : voucher **2** PAGARÉ : promissory note, IOU
valedero, -ra *adj* : valid
valentía *nf* : courage, valor
valer {84} *vt* **1** : to be worth ⟨valen una fortuna : they're worth a fortune⟩ ⟨no vale protestar : there's no point in protesting⟩ ⟨valer la pena : to be worth the trouble⟩ **2** : to cost ⟨¿cuánto vale? : how much does it cost?⟩ **3** : to earn, to gain ⟨le valió una reprimenda : it earned him a reprimand⟩ **4** : to protect, to aid ⟨¡válgame Dios! : God help me!⟩ **5** : to be equal to — *vi* **1** : to have value ⟨sus consejos no valen para nada : his advice is worthless⟩ **2** : to be valid, to count ⟨¡eso no vale! : that doesn't count!⟩ **3 hacerse valer** : to assert oneself **4 más vale** : it's better ⟨más vale que te vayas : you'd better go⟩ — **valerse** *vr* **1 ~ de** : to take advantage of **2 valerse solo** *or* **valerse por sí mismo** : to look after oneself **3** *Mex* : to be fair ⟨no se vale : it's not fair⟩
valeroso, -sa *adj* : brave, valiant
valet [ˈbalɛt, -ˈle] *nm* : jack (in playing cards)
valga, etc. → **valer**
valía *nf* : value, worth
validar *vt* : to validate — **validación** *nf*
validez *nf* : validity
válido, -da *adj* : valid
valiente *adj* **1** : brave, valiant **2** (*used ironically*) : fine, great ⟨¡valiente amiga! : what a fine friend!⟩ — **valientemente** *adv*
valija *nf* : suitcase, valise
valioso, -sa *adj* PRECIOSO : valuable, precious
valla *nf* **1** : fence, barricade **2** : hurdle (in sports) **3** : obstacle, hindrance
vallar *vt* : to fence, to put a fence around
valle *nm* : valley, vale
valor *nm* **1** : value, worth, importance **2** CORAJE : courage, valor **3 valores** *nmpl* : values, principles **4 valores** *nmpl* : securities, bonds **5 sin ~** : worthless
valoración *nf, pl* **-ciones** **1** EVALUACIÓN : valuation, appraisal, assessment **2** APRECIACIÓN : appreciation
valorar *vt* **1** EVALUAR : to evaluate, to appraise, to assess **2** APRECIAR : to value, to appreciate
valorizarse {21} *vr* : to appreciate, to increase in value — **valorización** *nf*
vals *nm* : waltz
valsar *vi* : to waltz
valuación *nf, pl* **-ciones** : valuation, appraisal
valuar {3} *vt* : to value, to appraise, to assess
válvula *nf* **1** : valve **2 válvula reguladora** : throttle
vamos → **ir**
vampiro *nm* : vampire
van → **ir**
vanadio *nm* : vanadium
vanagloriarse *vr* : to boast, to brag
vanamente *adv* : vainly, in vain
vandalismo : vandalism
vándalo *nm* : vandal — **vandalismo** *nm*
vanguardia *nf* **1** : vanguard **2** : avantegarde **3 a la vanguardia** : at the forefront
vanidad *nf* : vanity
vanidoso, -sa *adj* PRESUMIDO : vain, conceited
vano, -na *adj* **1** INÚTIL : vain, useless **2** : vain, worthless ⟨vanas promesas : empty promises⟩ **3 en ~** : in vain, of no avail
vapor *nm* **1** : vapor, steam **2** : steamer, steamship **3 al vapor** : steamed
vaporizador *nm* : vaporizer
vaporizar {21} *vt* : to vaporize — **vaporizarse** *vr* — **vaporización** *nf*
vaporoso, -sa *adj* **1** : vaporous **2** : sheer, airy
vapulear *vt* : to beat, to thrash
vaquero[1], **-ra** *adj* : cowboy ⟨pantalón vaquero : jeans⟩

vaquero[2], **-ra** *n* : cowboy *m,* cowgirl *f*
vaqueros *nmpl* JEANS : jeans
vaquilla *nf* : heifer
vara *nf* **1** : pole, stick, rod **2** : staff (of office) **3** : lance, pike (in bullfighting) **4** : yardstick **5 vara de oro** : goldenrod
varado, -da *adj* **1** : beached, aground **2** : stranded
varar *vt* : to beach (a ship), to strand — *vi* : to run aground
variable *adj & nf* : variable — **variabilidad** *nf*
variación *nf, pl* **-ciones** : variation
variado, -da *adj* : varied, diverse
variante *adj & nf* : variant
varianza *nf* : variance
variar {85} *vt* **1** : to change, to alter **2** : to diversify — *vi* **1** : to vary, to change **2 variar de opinión** : to change one's mind
varicela *nf* : chicken pox
varices *or* **várices** *nfpl* : varicose veins
varicoso, -sa *adj* : varicose
variedad *nf* DIVERSIDAD : variety, diversity
varilla *nf* **1** : rod, bar **2** : spoke (of a wheel) **3** : rib (of an umbrella)
vario, -ria *adj* **1** : varied, diverse **2** : variegated, motley **3** : changeable **4 varios, varias** *pl* : various, several
variopinto, -ta *adj* : diverse, assorted, motley
varita *nf* : wand ⟨varita mágica : magic wand⟩
varón *nm, pl* **varones 1** HOMBRE : man, male **2** NIÑO : boy
varonil *adj* **1** : masculine, manly **2** : mannish
vas → **ir**
vasallo *nm* : vassal — **vasallaje** *nm*
vasco[1], **-ca** *adj & n* : Basque
vasco[2] *nm* : Basque (language)
vascular *adj* : vascular
vasija *nf* : container, vessel
vaso *nm* **1** : glass, tumbler **2** : glassful **3** : vessel ⟨vaso sanguíneo : blood vessel⟩
vástago *nm* **1** : offspring, descendant **2** : shoot (of a plant)
vastedad *nf* : vastness, immensity
vasto, -ta *adj* : vast, immense
vataje *nm* : wattage
vaticinar *vt* : to predict, to foretell
vaticinio *nm* : prediction, prophecy
vatio *nm* : watt
vaya, etc. → **ir**
Vd., Vds. → **usted**
ve, etc. → **ir, ver**
vea, etc. → **ver**
vecinal *adj* : local
vecindad *nf* **1** : neighborhood, vicinity **2 casa de vecindad** : tenement
vecindario *nm* **1** : neighborhood, area **2** : residents *pl*
vecino, -na *n* **1** : neighbor **2** : resident, inhabitant
veda *nf* **1** PROHIBICIÓN : prohibition **2** : closed season (for hunting or fishing)
vedar *vt* **1** : to prohibit, to ban **2** IMPEDIR : to impede, to prevent
vega *nf* : fertile lowland
vegetación *nf, pl* **-ciones 1** : vegetation **2 vegetaciones** *nfpl* : adenoids
vegetal *adj & nm* : vegetable, plant
vegetar *vi* : to vegetate
vegetarianismo *nm* : vegetarianism
vegetariano, -na *adj & n* : vegetarian
vegetativo, -va *adj* : vegetative
vehemente *adj* : vehement — **vehemencia** *nf*
vehículo *nm* : vehicle — **vehicular** *adj*
veía, etc. → **ver**
veinte *adj & nm* : twenty
veinteavo[1], **-va** *adj* : twentieth
veinteavo[2] *nm* : twentieth (fraction)
veintena *nf* : group of twenty, score ⟨una veintena de participantes : about twenty participants⟩
vejación *nf, pl* **-ciones** : ill-treatment, humiliation
vejar *vt* : to mistreat, to ridicule, to harass
vejete *nm* : old fellow, codger
vejez *nf* : old age
vejiga *nf* **1** : bladder **2** AMPOLLA : blister
vela *nf* **1** VIGILIA : wakefulness ⟨pasé la noche en vela : I stayed awake all night⟩ **2** : watch, vigil, wake **3** : candle **4** : sail
velada *nf* : evening party, soirée
velado, -da *adj* **1** : veiled, hidden **2** : blurred **3** : muffled
velador[1], **-dora** *n* : guard, night watchman
velador[2] *nm* **1** : candlestick **2** : night table
velar *vt* **1** : to hold a wake over **2** : to watch over, to sit up with **3** : to blur, to expose (a photo) **4** : to veil, to conceal — *vi* **1** : to stay awake **2 ~ por** : to watch over, to look after
velatorio *nm* VELORIO : wake (for the dead)
veleidad *nf* **1** : fickleness **2** : whim, caprice
veleidoso, -sa : fickle, capricious
velero *nm* **1** : sailing ship **2** : sailboat
veleta *nf* : weather vane
vello *nm* **1** : body hair **2** : down, fuzz
vellocino *nm* : fleece
vellón *nm, pl* **vellones 1** : fleece, sheepskin **2** *PRi* : nickel (coin)
vellosidad *nf* : downiness, hairiness
velloso, -sa *adj* : downy, fluffy, hairy
velo *nm* : veil
velocidad *nf* **1** : speed, velocity ⟨velocidad máxima : speed limit⟩ **2** MARCHA : gear (of an automobile)
velocímetro *nm* : speedometer
velocista *nmf* : sprinter
velorio *nm* VELATORIO : wake (for the dead)
velour *nm* : velour, velours
veloz *adj, pl* **veloces** : fast, quick, swift — **velozmente** *adv*
ven → **venir**

vena *nf* **1** : vein ⟨vena yugular : jugular vein⟩ **2** : vein, seam, lode **3** : grain (of wood) **4** : style ⟨en vena lírica : in a lyrical vein⟩ **5** : strain, touch ⟨una vena de humor : a touch of humor⟩ **6** : mood

venado *nm* **1** : deer **2** : venison

venal *adj* : venal — **venalidad** *nf*

vencedor, -dora *n* : winner, victor

vencejo *nm* : swift (bird)

vencer {86} *vt* **1** DERROTAR : to vanquish, to defeat **2** SUPERAR : to overcome, to surmount — *vi* **1** GANAR : to win, to triumph **2** CADUCAR : to expire ⟨el plazo vence el jueves : the deadline is Thursday⟩ **3** : to fall due, to mature — **vencerse** *vr* **1** DOMINARSE : to control oneself **2** : to break, to collapse

vencido, -da *adj* **1** : defeated **2** : expired **3** : due, payable **4 darse por vencido** : to give up

vencimiento *nm* **1** : defeat **2** : expiration **3** : maturity (of a loan)

venda *nf* : bandage

vendaje *nm* : bandage, dressing

vendar *vt* **1** : to bandage **2 vendar los ojos** : to blindfold

vendaval *nm* : gale, strong wind

vendedor, -dora *n* : salesperson, salesman *m*, saleswoman *f*

vender *vt* **1** : to sell **2** : to sell out, to betray — **venderse** *vr* **1** : to be sold ⟨se vende : for sale⟩ **2** : to sell out

vendetta *nf* : vendetta

vendible *adj* : salable, marketable

vendimia *nf* : grape harvest

vendrá, etc. → **venir**

veneno *nm* **1** : poison **2** : venom

venenoso, -sa *adj* : poisonous, venomous

venerable *adj* : venerable

veneración *nf, pl* **-ciones** : veneration, reverence

venerar *vt* : to venerate, to revere

venéreo, -rea *adj* : venereal

venero *nm* **1** VENA : seam, lode, vein **2** MANANTIAL : spring **3** FUENTE : origin, source

venezolano, -na *adj & n* : Venezuelan

venga, etc. → **venir**

vengador, -dora *n* : avenger

venganza *nf* : vengeance, revenge

vengar {52} *vt* : to avenge — **vengarse** *vr* : to get even, to revenge oneself

vengativo, -va *adj* : vindictive, vengeful

vengue, etc. → **vengar**

venia *nf* **1** PERMISO : permission, leave **2** PERDÓN : pardon **3** : bow (of the head)

venial *adj* : venial

venida *nf* **1** LLEGADA : arrival, coming **2** REGRESO : return **3 idas y venidas** : comings and goings

venidero, -ra *adj* : coming, future

venir {87} *vi* **1** : to come ⟨lo vi venir : I saw him coming⟩ ⟨¡venga! : come on!⟩ **2** : to arrive ⟨vinieron en coche : they came by car⟩ **3** : to come, to originate ⟨sus zapatos vienen de Italia : her shoes are from Italy⟩ **4** : to come, to be available ⟨viene envuelto en plástico : it comes wrapped in plastic⟩ **5** : to come back, to return **6** : to affect, to overcome ⟨me vino un vahído : a dizzy spell came over me⟩ **7** : to fit ⟨te viene un poco grande : it's a little big for you⟩ **8** (*with the present participle*) : to have been ⟨viene entrenando diariamente : he's been training daily⟩ **9 ~ a** (*with the infinitive*) : to end up, to turn out ⟨viene a ser lo mismo : it comes out the same⟩ **10 que viene** : coming, next ⟨el año que viene : next year⟩ **11 venir bien** : to be suitable, to be just right — **venirse** *vr* **1** : to come, to arrive **2** : to come back **3 venirse abajo** : to fall apart, to collapse

venta *nf* **1** : sale **2 venta al por menor** *or* **venta al detalle** : retail sales

ventaja *nf* **1** : advantage **2** : lead, head start **3 ventajas** *nfpl* : perks, extras

ventajoso, -sa *adj* **1** : advantageous **2** : profitable — **ventajosamente** *adv*

ventana *nf* **1** : window (of a building) **2 ventana de la nariz** : nostril

ventanal *nm* : large window

ventanilla *nf* **1** : window (of a vehicle or airplane) **2** : ticket window, box office

ventero, -ra *n* : innkeeper

ventilación *nf, pl* **-ciones** : ventilation

ventilador *nm* **1** : ventilator **2** : fan

ventilar *vt* **1** : to ventilate, to air out **2** : to air, to discuss **3** : to make public, to reveal — **ventilarse** *vr* : to get some air

ventisca *nf* : snowstorm, blizzard

ventisquero *nm* : snowdrift

ventosear *vi* : to break wind

ventosidad *nf* : wind, flatulence

ventoso, -sa *adj* : windy

ventrículo *nm* : ventricle

ventrílocuo, -cua *n* : ventriloquist

ventriloquia *nf* : ventriloquism

ventura *nf* **1** : fortune, luck, chance **2** : happiness **3 a la ventura** : at random, as it comes

venturoso, -sa *adj* **1** AFORTUNADO : fortunate, lucky **2** : successful

Venus *nm* : Venus

venza, etc. → **vencer**

ver[1] {88} *vt* **1** : to see ⟨vimos la película : we saw the movie⟩ **2** ENTENDER : to understand ⟨ya lo veo : now I get it⟩ **3** EXAMINAR : to examine, to look into ⟨lo veré : I'll take a look at it⟩ **4** JUZGAR : to see, to judge ⟨a mi manera de ver : to my way of thinking⟩ **5** VISITAR : to meet with, to visit **6** AVERIGUAR : to find out **7 a ver** *or* **vamos a ver** : let's see — *vi* **1** : to see **2** ENTERARSE : to learn, to find out **3** ENTENDER : to understand — **verse** *vr* **1** HALLARSE : to find oneself **2** PARECER : to look, to appear **3** ENCONTRARSE : to see each other, to meet

ver[2] *nm* **1** : looks *pl*, appearance **2** : opinion ⟨a mi ver : in my view⟩

vera *nf* : side ⟨a la vera del camino : alongside the road⟩

veracidad *nf* : truthfulness, veracity

veranda *nf* : veranda

veraneante *nmf* : summer vacationer

veranear *vi* : to spend the summer

veraniego, -ga *adj* **1** ESTIVAL : summer ⟨el sol veraniego : the summer sun⟩ **2** : summery

verano *nm* : summer

veras *nfpl* **de ~** : really, truly

veraz *adj, pl* **veraces** : truthful, veracious

verbal *adj* : verbal — **verbalmente** *adv*

verbalizar {21} *vt* : to verbalize, to express

verbena *nf* **1** FIESTA : festival, fair **2** : verbena, vervain

verbigracia *adv* : for example

verbo *nm* : verb

verborrea *nf* : verbiage

verbosidad *nf* : verbosity, wordiness

verboso, -sa *adj* : verbose, wordy

verdad *nf* **1** : truth **2 de ~** : really, truly **3 ¿verdad?** : right?, isn't that so?

verdaderamente *adv* : really, truly

verdadero, -dera *adj* **1** REAL, VERÍDICO : true, real **2** AUTÉNTICO : genuine

verde[1] *adj* **1** : green (in color) **2** : green, unripe **3** : inexperienced, green **4** : dirty, risqué

verde[2] *nm* : green

verdear *vi* : to turn green, to become verdant

verdín *nm, pl* **verdines** : slime, scum

verdor *nm* **1** : greenness **2** : verdure

verdoso, -sa *adj* : greenish

verdugo *nm* **1** : executioner, hangman **2** : tyrant

verdugón *nm, pl* **-gones** : welt, wheal

verdura *nf* : vegetable(s), green(s)

vereda *nf* **1** SENDA : path, trail **2** : sidewalk, pavement

veredicto *nm* : verdict

verga *nf* : spar, yard (of a ship)

vergonzoso, -sa *adj* **1** : disgraceful, shameful **2** : bashful, shy — **vergonzosamente** *adv*

vergüenza *nf* **1** : disgrace, shame **2** : embarrassment **3** : bashfulness, shyness

vericueto *nm* : rough terrain

verídico, -ca *adj* **1** REAL, VERDADERO : true, real **2** VERAZ : truthful

verificación *nf, pl* **-ciones 1** : verification **2** : testing, checking

verificador, -dora *n* : inspector, tester

verificar {72} *vt* **1** : to verify, to confirm **2** : to test, to check **3** : to carry out, to conduct — **verificarse** *vr* **1** : to take place, to occur **2** : to come true

verja *nf* **1** : rails *pl* (of a fence) **2** : grating, grille **3** : gate

vermut *nm, pl* **vermuts** : vermouth

vernáculo, -la *adj* : vernacular

vernal *adj* : vernal, spring

verosímil *adj* **1** : probable, likely **2** : credible, realistic

verosimilitud *nf* **1** : probability, likeliness **2** : verisimilitude

verraco *nm* : boar

verruga *nf* : wart

versado, -da *adj* **~ en** : versed in, knowledgeable about

versar *vi* **~ sobre** : to deal with, to be about

versátil *adj* **1** : versatile **2** : fickle

versatilidad *nf* **1** : versatility **2** : fickleness

versículo *nm* : verse (in the Bible)

versión *nf, pl* **versiones 1** : version **2** : translation

verso *nm* : verse

versus *prep* : versus, against

vértebra *nf* : vertebra — **vertebral** *adj*

vertebrado[1], **-da** *adj* : vertebrate

vertebrado[2] *nm* : vertebrate

vertedero *nm* **1** : garbage dump **2** DESAGÜE : drain, outlet

verter {56} *vt* **1** : to pour **2** : to spill, to shed **3** : to empty out **4** : to express, to voice **5** : to translate, to render — *vi* : to flow

vertical *adj & nf* : vertical — **verticalmente** *adv*

vértice *nm* : vertex, apex

vertido *nm* : spilling, spill

vertiente *nf* **1** : slope **2** : aspect, side, element

vertiginoso, -sa *adj* : vertiginous — **vertiginosamente** *adv*

vértigo *nm* : vertigo, dizziness

vesícula *nf* **1** : vesicle **2 vesícula biliar** : gallbladder

vesicular *adj* : vesicular

vestíbulo *nm* : vestibule, hall, lobby, foyer

vestido *nm* **1** : dress, costume, clothes *pl* **2** : dress (garment)

vestidor *nm* : dressing room

vestiduras *nfpl* **1** : clothing, raiment, regalia **2** *or* **vestiduras sacerdotales** : vestments

vestigio *nm* : vestige, sign, trace

vestimenta *nf* ROPA : clothing, clothes *pl*

vestir {54} *vt* **1** : to dress, to clothe **2** LLEVAR : to wear **3** ADORNAR : to decorate, to dress up — *vi* **1** : to dress ⟨vestir bien : to dress well⟩ **2** : to look good, to suit the occasion — **vestirse** *vr* **1** : to get dressed **2 ~ de** : to dress up as ⟨se vistieron de soldados : they dressed up as soldiers⟩ **3 ~ de** : to wear, to dress in

vestuario *nm* **1** : wardrobe **2** : dressing room, locker room

veta *nf* **1** : grain (in wood) **2** : vein, seam, lode **3** : trace, streak ⟨una veta de terco : a stubborn streak⟩

vetar *vt* : to veto

veteado, -da *adj* : streaked, veined

veterano, -na *adj & n* : veteran

veterinaria *nf* : veterinary medicine

veterinario[1], **-ria** *adj* : veterinary

veterinario[2], **-ria** *n* : veterinarian

veto *nm* : veto
vetusto, -ta *adj* ANTIGUO : ancient, very old
vez *nf, pl* **veces 1** : time, occasion ⟨a la vez : at the same time⟩ ⟨a veces : at times, occasionally⟩ ⟨de vez en cuando : from time to time⟩ **2** (*with numbers*) : time ⟨una vez : once⟩ ⟨de una vez : all at once⟩ ⟨de una vez para siempre : once and for all⟩ ⟨dos veces : twice⟩ **3** : turn ⟨a su vez : in turn⟩ ⟨en vez de : instead of⟩ ⟨hacer las veces de : to act as, to stand in for⟩
vía[1] *nf* **1** RUTA, CAMINO : road, route, way ⟨Vía Láctea : Milky Way⟩ **2** MEDIO : means, way ⟨por vía oficial : through official channels⟩ **3** : track, line (of a railroad) **4** : tract, passage ⟨por vía oral : orally⟩ **5 en vías de** : in the process of ⟨en vías de solución : on the road to a solution⟩ **6 por ~** : by (in transportation) ⟨por vía aérea : by air, airmail⟩
vía[2] *prep* : via
viable *adj* : viable, feasible — **viabilidad** *nf*
viaducto *nm* : viaduct
viajante *mf* : traveling salesman, traveling saleswoman
viajar *vi* : to travel, to journey
viaje *nm* : trip, journey ⟨viaje de negocios : business trip⟩
viajero[1], **-ra** *adj* : traveling
viajero[2], **-ra** *n* **1** : traveler **2** PASAJERO : passenger
vial *adj* : road, traffic
viático *nm* : travel allowance, travel expenses *pl*
víbora *nf* : viper
vibración *nf, pl* **-ciones** : vibration
vibrador *nm* : vibrator
vibrante *adj* **1** : vibrant **2** : vibrating
vibrar *vi* : to vibrate
vibratorio, -ria *adj* : vibratory
vicario, -ria *n* : vicar
vicealmirante *nmf* : vice admiral
vicepresidente, -ta *n* : vice president — **vicepresidencia** *nf*
viceversa *adv* : vice versa, conversely
viciado, -da *adj* : stuffy, close
viciar *vt* **1** : to corrupt **2** : to invalidate **3** FALSEAR : to distort **4** : to pollute, to adulterate
vicio *nm* **1** : vice, depravity **2** : bad habit **3** : defect, blemish
vicioso, -sa *adj* : depraved, corrupt
vicisitud *nf* : vicissitude
víctima *nf* : victim
victimario, -ria *n* ASESINO : killer, murderer
victimizar {21} *vt Arg, Mex* : to victimize
victoria *nf* : victory — **victorioso, -sa** *adj* — **victoriosamente** *adv*
victoriano, -na *adj* : Victorian
vid *nf* : vine, grapevine
vida *nf* **1** : life ⟨la vida cotidiana : everyday life⟩ **2** : life span, lifetime **3** BIOGRAFÍA : biography, life **4** : way of life, lifestyle **5** : livelihood ⟨ganarse la vida : to earn one's living⟩ **6** VIVEZA : liveliness **7 media vida** : half-life
vidente *nmf* **1** : psychic, clairvoyant **2** : sighted person
video *or* **vídeo** *nm* : video
videocasete *or* **videocassette** *nm* : videocassette
videocasetera *or* **videocassettera** *nf* : videocassette recorder, VCR
videocinta *nf* : videotape
videograbar *vt* : to videotape
vidriado *nm* : glaze
vidriar *vt* : to glaze (pottery, tile, etc.)
vidriera *nf* **1** : stained-glass window **2** : glass door or window **3** : store window
vidriero, -ra *n* : glazier
vidrio *nm* **1** : glass, piece of glass **2** : windowpane
vidrioso, -sa *adj* **1** : brittle, fragile **2** : slippery **3** : glassy, glazed (of eyes) **4** : touchy, delicate
vieira *nf* **1** : scallop **2** : scallop shell
viejo[1], **-ja** *adj* **1** ANCIANO : old, elderly **2** ANTIGUO : former, longstanding ⟨viejas tradiciones : old traditions⟩ ⟨viejos amigos : old friends⟩ **3** GASTADO : old, worn, worn-out
viejo[2], **-ja** *n* ANCIANO : old man *m,* old woman *f*
viene, etc. → **venir**
viento *nm* **1** : wind **2 hacer viento** : to be windy **3 contra viento y marea** : against all odds **4 viento alisio** : trade wind **5 viento en popa** : splendidly, successfully
vientre *nm* **1** : abdomen, belly **2** : womb **3** : bowels *pl*
viernes *nms & pl* : Friday
vierte, etc. → **verter**
vietnamita[1] *adj & nmf* : Vietnamese
vietnamita[2] *nm* : Vietnamese (language)
viga *nf* **1** : beam, rafter, girder **2 viga voladiza** : cantilever
vigencia *nf* **1** : validity **2** : force, effect ⟨entrar en vigencia : to go into effect⟩
vigente *adj* : valid, in force
vigésimo[1], **-ma** *adj* : twentieth, twenty- ⟨la vigésima segunda edición : the twenty-second edition⟩
vigésimo[2], **-ma** *n* : twentieth, twenty- (in a series)
vigía *nmf* : lookout
vigilancia *nf* : vigilance, watchfulness ⟨bajo vigilancia : under surveillance⟩
vigilante[1] *adj* : vigilant, watchful
vigilante[2] *nmf* : watchman, guard
vigilar *vt* **1** CUIDAR : to look after, to keep an eye on **2** GUARDAR : to watch over, to guard — *vi* **1** : to be watchful **2** : to keep watch
vigilia *nf* **1** VELA : wakefulness **2** : night work **3** : vigil (in religion)
vigor *nm* **1** : vigor, energy, strength **2** VIGENCIA : force, effect
vigorizante *adj* : invigorating

vigorizar {21} *vt* : to strengthen, to invigorate

vigoroso, -sa *adj* : vigorous — **vigorosamente** *adv*

VIH *nm* (*v*irus de *i*nmunodeficiencia *h*umana) : HIV

vikingo, -ga *adj & n* : Viking

vil *adj* : vile, despicable

vileza *nf* **1** : vileness **2** : despicable action, villainy

vilipendiar *vt* : to vilify, to revile

villa *nf* **1** : town, village **2** : villa

villancico *nm* : carol, Christmas carol

villano, -na *n* **1** : villain **2** : peasant

vilo *nm* **1 en ~** : in the air **2 en ~** : uncertain, in suspense

vinagre *nm* : vinegar

vinagrera *nf* : cruet (for vinegar)

vinatería *nf* : wine shop

vinculación *nf, pl* **-ciones 1** : linking **2** RELACIÓN : bond, link, connection

vincular *vt* CONECTAR, RELACIONAR : to tie, to link, to connect

vínculo *nm* LAZO : tie, link, bond

vindicación *nf, pl* **-ciones** : vindication

vindicar *vt* **1** : to vindicate **2** : to avenge

vinilo *nm* : vinyl

vino[1], **etc.** → **venir**

vino[2] *nm* : wine

viña *nf* : vineyard

viñedo *nm* : vineyard

vio, etc. → **ver**

viola *nf* : viola

violación *nf, pl* **-ciones 1** : violation, offense **2** : rape

violador[1], **-dora** *n* : violator, offender

violador[2] *nm* : rapist

violar *vt* **1** : to rape **2** : to violate (a law or right) **3** PROFANAR : to desecrate

violencia *nf* : violence

violentamente *adv* : by force, violently

violentar *vt* **1** FORZAR : to break open, to force **2** : to distort (words or ideas) — **violentarse** *vr* : to force oneself

violento, -ta *adj* **1** : violent **2** EMBARAZOSO, INCÓMODO : awkward, embarassing

violeta[1] *adj & nm* : violet (color)

violeta[2] *nf* : violet (flower)

violín *nm, pl* **-lines** : violin

violinista *nmf* : violinist

violonchelista *nmf* : cellist

violonchelo *nm* : cello, violoncello

VIP *nmf, pl* **VIPs** : VIP

vira *nf* : welt (of a shoe)

virago *nf* : virago, shrew

viraje *nm* **1** : turn, swerve **2** : change

viral *adj* : viral

virar *vi* : to tack, to turn, to veer

virgen[1] *adj* : virgin ⟨lana virgen : virgin wool⟩

virgen[2] *nmf, pl* **vírgenes** : virgin ⟨la Santísima Virgen : the Blessed Virgin⟩

virginal *adj* : virginal, chaste

virginidad *nf* : virginity

Virgo *nmf* : Virgo

vírico, -ca *adj* : viral

viril *adj* : virile — **virilidad** *nf*

virrey, -rreina *n* : viceroy *m,* vicereine *f*

virtual *adj* : virtual — **virtualmente** *adv*

virtud *nf* **1** : virtue **2 en virtud de** : by virtue of

virtuosismo *nm* : virtuosity

virtuoso[1], **-sa** *adj* : virtuous — **virtuosamente** *adv*

virtuoso[2], **-sa** *n* : virtuoso

viruela *nf* **1** : smallpox **2** : pockmark

virulencia *nf* : virulence

virulento, -ta *adj* : virulent

virus *nm* : virus

viruta *nf* : shaving

visa *nf* : visa

visado *nm Spain* : visa

visaje *nm* : face, grimace ⟨hacer visajes : to make faces⟩

visceral *adj* : visceral

vísceras *nfpl* : viscera, entrails

visconde, -desa *n* : viscount *m,* viscountess *f*

viscosidad *nf* : viscosity

viscoso, -sa *adj* : viscous

visera *nf* : visor

visibilidad *nf* : visibility

visible *adj* : visible — **visiblemente** *adv*

visión *nf, pl* **visiones 1** : vision, eyesight **2** : view, perspective **3** : vision, illusion ⟨ver visiones : to be seeing things⟩

visionario, -ria *adj & n* : visionary

visita *nf* **1** : visit, call **2** : visitor **3 ir de visita** : to go visiting

visitador, -dora *n* : visitor, frequent caller

visitante[1] *adj* : visiting

visitante[2] *nmf* : visitor

visitar *vt* : to visit

vislumbrar *vt* **1** : to discern, to make out **2** : to begin to see, to have an inkling of

vislumbre *nf* : glimmer, gleam

viso *nm* **1** APARIENCIA : appearance ⟨tener visos de : to seem, to show signs of⟩ **2** DESTELLO : glint, gleam **3** : sheen, iridescence

visón *nm, pl* **visones** : mink

víspera *nf* **1** : eve, day before **2 vísperas** *nfpl* : vespers

vista *nf* **1** VISIÓN : vision, eyesight **2** MIRADA : look, gaze, glance **3** PANORAMA : view, vista, panorama **4** : hearing (in court) **5 a primera vista** : at first sight **6 en vista de** : in view of **7 hacer la vista gorda** : to turn a blind eye **8 ¡hasta la vista!** : so long!, see you! **9 perder de vista** : to lose sight of **10 punto de vista** : point of view

vistazo *nm* : glance, look

viste, etc. → **ver**[1], **vestir**

visto[1] *pp* → **ver**

visto[2], **-ta** *adj* **1** : obvious, clear **2** : in view of, considering **3 estar bien visto** : to be approved of **4 estar mal visto** : to be frowned upon **5 por lo visto** : apparently **6 nunca visto** : unheard-of **7 visto que** : since, given that

visto[3] *nm* **visto bueno** : approval

vistoso, -sa *adj* : colorful, bright
visual *adj* : visual — **visualmente** *adv*
visualización *nf, pl* **-ciones** : visualization
visualizar {21} *vt* **1** : to visualize **2** : to display (on a screen)
vital *adj* **1** : vital **2** : lively, dynamic
vitalicio, -cia *adj* : life, lifetime
vitalidad *nf* : vitality
vitamina *nf* : vitamin
vitamínico, -ca *adj* : vitamin ⟨complejos vitamínicos : vitamin compounds⟩
vitorear *vt* : to cheer, to acclaim
vitral *nm* : stained-glass window
vítreo, -rea *adj* : vitreous, glassy
vitrina *nf* **1** : showcase, display case **2** : store window
vitriolo *nm* : vitriol
vituperar *vt* : to condemn, to vituperate against
vituperio *nm* : vituperation, censure
viudez *nf* : widowerhood, widowhood
viudo, -da *n* : widower *m,* widow *f*
vivacidad *nf* VIVEZA : vivacity, liveliness
vivamente *adv* **1** : in a lively manner **2** : vividly **3** : strongly, acutely ⟨lo recomendamos vivamente : we strongly recommend it⟩
vivaque *nm* : bivouac
vivaquear *vi* : to bivouac
vivar *vi* : to cheer
vivaz *adj, pl* **vivaces** **1** : lively, vivacious **2** : clever, sharp **3** : perennial
víveres *nmpl* : provisions, supplies, food
vivero *nm* **1** : nursery (for plants) **2** : hatchery, fish farm
viveza *nf* **1** VIVACIDAD : liveliness **2** BRILLO : vividness, brightness **3** ASTUCIA : cleverness, sharpness
vívido, -da *adj* : vivid, lively
vividor, -dora *n* : sponger, parasite
vivienda *nf* **1** : housing **2** MORADA : dwelling, home
viviente *adj* : living
vivificar {72} *vt* : to vivify, to give life to
vivir[1] *vi* **1** : to live, to be alive **2** SUBSISTIR : to subsist, to make a living **3** RESIDIR : to reside **4** : to spend one's life ⟨vive para trabajar : she lives to work⟩ **5 ~ de** : to live on — *vt* **1** : to live ⟨vivir su vida : to live one's life⟩ **2** EXPERIMENTAR : to go through, to experience
vivir[2] *nm* **1** : life, lifestyle **2 de mal vivir** : disreputable
vivisección *nf, pl* **-ciones** : vivisection
vivo, -va *adj* **1** : alive **2** INTENSO : vivid, bright, intense **3** ANIMADO : lively, vivacious **4** ASTUTO : sharp, clever **5 en ~** : live ⟨transmisión en vivo : live broadcast⟩ **6 al rojo vivo** : red-hot
vizconde, -desa *n* : viscount *m,* viscountess *f*
vocablo *nm* PALABRA : word
vocabulario *nm* : vocabulary
vocación *nf, pl* **-ciones** : vocation
vocacional *adj* : vocational
vocal[1] *adj* : vocal
vocal[2] *nmf* : member (of a committee, board, etc.)
vocal[3] *nf* : vowel
vocalista *nmf* CANTANTE : singer, vocalist
vocalizar {21} *vi* : to vocalize
vocear *v* : to shout
vocerío *nm* : clamor, shouting
vocero, -ra *n* PORTAVOZ : spokesperson, spokesman *m,* spokeswoman *f*
vociferante *adj* : vociferous
vociferar *vi* GRITAR : to shout, to yell
vodevil *nm* : vaudeville
vodka *nm* : vodka
voladizo[1], **-za** *adj* : projecting
voladizo[2] *nm* : projection
volador, -dora *adj* : flying
volando *adv* : quickly, in a hurry
volante[1] *adj* : flying
volante[2] *nm* **1** : steering wheel **2** FOLLETO : flier, circular **3** : shuttlecock **4** : flywheel **5** : balance wheel (of a watch) **6** : ruffle, flounce
volar {19} *vi* **1** : to fly **2** CORRER : to hurry, to rush ⟨el tiempo vuela : time flies⟩ ⟨pasar volando : to fly past⟩ **3** DIVULGARSE : to spread ⟨unos rumores volaban : rumors were spreading around⟩ **4** DESAPARECER : to disappear ⟨el dinero ya voló : the money's already gone⟩ — *vt* **1** : to blow up, to demolish **2** : to irritate
volátil *adj* : volatile — **volatilidad** *nf*
volatilizar {21} *vt* : to volatize — **volatilizarse** *vr*
volcán *nm, pl* **volcanes** : volcano
volcánico, -ca *adj* : volcanic
volcar {82} *vt* **1** : to upset, to knock over, to turn over **2** : to empty out **3** : to make dizzy **4** : to cause a change of mind in **5** : to irritate — *vi* **1** : to overturn, to tip over **2** : to capsize — **volcarse** *vr* **1** : to overturn **2** : to do one's utmost
volea *nf* : volley (in sports)
volear *vi* : to volley (in sports)
voleibol *nm* : volleyball
voleo *nm* **al voleo** : haphazardly, at random
volframio *nm* : wolfram, tungsten
volición *nf, pl* **-ciones** : volition
volqué, etc. → **volcar**
voltaje *nm* : voltage
voltear *vt* **1** : to turn over, to turn upside down **2** : to reverse, to turn inside out **3** : to turn ⟨voltear la cara : to turn one's head⟩ **4** : to knock down — *vi* **1** : to roll over, to do somersaults **2** : to turn ⟨volteó a la izquierda : he turned left⟩ — **voltearse** *vr* **1** : to turn around **2** : to change one's allegiance
voltereta *nf* : somersault, tumble
voltio *nm* : volt
volubilidad *nf* : fickleness, changeableness
voluble *adj* : fickle, changeable
volumen *nm, pl* **-lúmenes** **1** TOMO : volume, book **2** : capacity, size, bulk **3** CANTIDAD : amount ⟨el volumen de

ventas : the volume of sales⟩ **4** : volume, loudness
voluminoso, -sa *adj* : voluminous, massive, bulky
voluntad *nf* **1** : will, volition **2** DESEO : desire, wish **3** INTENCIÓN : intention **4 a voluntad** : at will **5 buena voluntad** : good will **6 mala voluntad** : ill will **7 fuerza de voluntad** : willpower
voluntario[1], -ria *adj* : voluntary — **voluntariamente** *adv*
voluntario[2], -ria *n* : volunteer
voluntarioso, -sa *adj* **1** : stubborn **2** : willing, eager
voluptuosidad *nf* : voluptuousness
voluptuoso, -sa *adj* : voluptuous — **voluptuosamente** *adv*
voluta *nf* : spiral, column (of smoke)
volver {89} *vi* **1** : to return, to come or go back ⟨volver a casa : to return home⟩ **2** : to revert ⟨volver al tema : to get back to the subject⟩ **3 ~ a** : to do again ⟨volvieron a llamar : they called again⟩ **4 volver en sí** : to come to, to regain consciousness — *vt* **1** : to turn, to turn over, to turn inside out **2** : to return, to repay, to restore **3** : to cause, to make ⟨la volvía loca : it was driving her crazy⟩ — **volverse** *vr* **1** : to become ⟨se volvió deprimido : he became depressed⟩ **2** : to turn around
vomitar *vi* : to vomit — *vt* **1** : to vomit **2** : to spew out (lava, etc.)
vómito *nm* **1** : vomiting **2** : vomit
voracidad *nf* : voracity
vorágine *nf* : whirlpool, maelstrom
voraz *adj, pl* **voraces** : voracious — **vorazmente** *adv*
vórtice *nm* **1** : whirlpool, vortex **2** TORBELLINO : whirlwind
vos *pron* (*in some regions of Latin America*) : you
vosear *vt* : to address as *vos*
vosotros, -tras *pron pl Spain* **1** : you, yourselves **2** : ye
votación *nf, pl* **-ciones** : vote, voting
votante *nmf* : voter
votar *vi* : to vote — *vt* : to vote for
votivo, -va *adj* : votive
voto *nm* **1** : vote **2** : vow (in religion) **3 votos** *nmpl* : good wishes
voy → **ir**
voz *nf, pl* **voces 1** : voice **2** : opinion, say **3** GRITO : shout, yell **4** : sound **5** VOCABLO : word, term **6** : rumor **7 a voz en cuello** : at the top of one's lungs **8 dar voces** : to shout **9 en voz alta** : aloud, in a loud voice **10 en voz baja** : softly, in a low voice
vudú *nm* : voodoo
vuelco *nm* : upset, overturning ⟨me dio un vuelco el corazón : my heart skipped a beat⟩
vuela, etc. → **volar**
vuelca, vuelque etc. → **volcar**
vuelo *nm* **1** : flight, flying ⟨alzar el vuelo : to take flight⟩ **2** : flight (of an aircraft) ⟨vuelo espacial : space flight⟩ **3** : flare, fullness (of clothing) **4 al vuelo** : on the wing
vuelta *nf* **1** GIRO : turn ⟨se dio la vuelta : he turned around⟩ **2** REVOLUCIÓN : circle, revolution ⟨dio la vuelta al mundo : she went around the world⟩ ⟨las ruedas daban vueltas : the wheels were spinning⟩ **3** : flip, turn ⟨le dio la vuelta : she flipped it over⟩ **4** : bend, curve ⟨a la vuelta de la esquina : around the corner⟩ **5** REGRESO : return ⟨de ida y vuelta : round trip⟩ ⟨a vuelta de correo : return mail⟩ **6** : round, lap (in sports or games) **7** PASEO : walk, drive, ride ⟨dio una vuelta : he went for a walk⟩ **8** DORSO, REVÉS : back, other side ⟨a la vuelta : on the back⟩ **9** : cuff (of pants) **10 darle vueltas** : to think over **11 estar de vuelta** : to be back
vuelto *pp* → **volver**
vuelve, etc. → **volver**
vuestro[1], -stra *adj Spain* : your, of yours ⟨vuestros coches : your cars⟩ ⟨una amiga vuestra : a friend of yours⟩
vuestro[2], -stra *pron Spain,* (*with definite article*) : yours ⟨la vuestra es más grande : yours is bigger⟩ ⟨esos son los vuestros : those are yours⟩
vulcanizar {21} *vt* : to vulcanize
vulgar *adj* **1** : common **2** : vulgar
vulgaridad *nf* : vulgarity
vulgarismo *nm* : vulgarism
vulgarizar {21} *vt* : to vulgarize, to popularize
vulgarmente *adv* : vulgarly, popularly
vulgo *nm* **el vulgo** : the masses, common people
vulnerable *adj* : vulnerable — **vulnerabilidad** *nf*
vulnerar *vt* **1** : to injure, to damage (one's reputation or honor) **2** : to violate, to break (a law or contract)

w *nf* : twenty-fourth letter of the Spanish alphabet
wafle *nm* : waffle
waflera *nf* : waffle iron
wapití *nm* : wapiti, elk
whisky *nm, pl* **whiskys** *or* **whiskies** : whiskey
wigwam *nm* : wigwam

X

x *nf* : twenty-fifth letter of the Spanish alphabet
xenofobia *nf* : xenophobia
xenófobo[1], **-ba** *adj* : xenophobic
xenófobo[2], **-ba** *n* : xenophobe
xenón *nm* : xenon
xerocopiar *vt* : to photocopy, to xerox
xilófono *nm* : xylophone

Y

y[1] *nf* : twenty-sixth letter of the Spanish alphabet
y[2] *conj* (**e** *before words beginning with i- or hi-*) **1** : and ⟨mi hermano y yo : my brother and I⟩ ⟨¿y los demás? : and (what about) the others?⟩ **2** (*used in numbers*) ⟨cincuenta y cinco : fifty-five⟩ **3** *fam* : well ⟨y por supuesto : well, of course⟩
ya[1] *adv* **1** : already ⟨ya terminó : she's finished already⟩ **2** : now, right now ⟨¡hazlo ya! : do it now!⟩ ⟨ya mismo : right away⟩ **3** : later, soon ⟨ya iremos : we'll go later on⟩ **4** : no longer, anymore ⟨ya no fuma : he no longer smokes⟩ **5** (*used for emphasis*) ⟨¡ya lo sé! : I know!⟩ ⟨ya lo creo : of course⟩ **6 no ya** : not only ⟨no ya lloran sino gritan : they're not only crying but screaming⟩ **7 ya que** : now that, since ⟨ya que sabe la verdad : now that she knows the truth⟩
ya[2] *conj* **ya . . . ya** : whether . . . or, first . . . then ⟨ya le gusta, ya no : first he likes it, then he doesn't⟩
yac *nm* : yak
yacer {90} *vi* : to lie ⟨en esta tumba yacen sus abuelos : his grandparents lie in this grave⟩
yacimiento *nm* : bed, deposit ⟨yacimiento petrolífero : oil field⟩
yaga, etc. → **yacer**
yanqui *adj & nmf* : Yankee
yarda *nf* : yard
yate *nm* : yacht
yaz, yazca, yazga etc. → **yacer**
yedra *nf* : ivy
yegua *nf* : mare
yelmo *nm* : helmet
yema *nf* **1** : bud, shoot **2** : yolk (of an egg) **3 yema del dedo** : fingertip
yemenita *adj & nmf* : Yemenite
yen *nm* : yen (currency)
yendo → **ir**
yerba *nf* **1** *or* **yerba mate** : maté **2** → **hierba**
yerga, yergue etc. → **erguir**
yermo[1], **-ma** *adj* : barren, deserted
yermo[2] *nm* : wasteland
yerno *nm* : son-in-law
yerra, etc. → **errar**
yerro *nm* : blunder, mistake
yerto, -ta *adj* : rigid, stiff
yesca *nf* : tinder
yeso *nm* **1** : plaster **2** : gypsum
yo[1] *nm* : ego, self
yo[2] *pron* **1** : I **2** : me ⟨todos menos yo : everyone except me⟩ ⟨tan bajo como yo : as short as me⟩ **3 soy yo** : it is I, it's me
yodado, -da *adj* : iodized
yodo *nm* : iodine
yoduro *nm* : iodide
yoga *nm* : yoga
yogui *nm* : yogi
yogurt *or* **yogur** *nm* : yogurt
yola *nf* : yawl
yoyo *or* **yoyó** *nm* : yo-yo
yuca *nf* **1** : yucca (plant) **2** : cassava, manioc
yucateco[1], **-ca** *adj* : of or from the Yucatán
yucateco[2], **-ca** *n* : person from the Yucatán
yudo → **judo**
yugo *nm* : yoke
yugoslavo, -va *adj & n* : Yugoslavian
yugular *adj* : jugular ⟨vena yugular : jugular vein⟩
yungas *nfpl Bol, Chile, Peru* : warm tropical valleys
yunque *nm* : anvil
yunta *nf* : yoke, team (of oxen)
yuppy *nmf, pl* **yuppies** : yuppie
yute *nm* : jute
yuxtaponer {60} *vt* : to juxtapose — **yuxtaposición** *nf*

Z

z *nf* : twenty-seventh letter of the Spanish alphabet
zacate *nm CA, Mex* **1** : grass, forage **2** : hay
zafacón *nm, pl* **-cones** *Car* : wastebasket
zafar *vt* : to loosen, to untie — **zafarse** *vr* **1** : to loosen up, to come undone **2** : to get free of
zafio, -fia *adj* : coarse, crude
zafiro *nm* : sapphire
zaga *nf* **1** : defense (in sports) **2 a la zaga** *or* **en ∼** : behind, in the rear
zagual *nm* : paddle (of a canoe)

zaguán *nm, pl* **zaguanes** : front hall, vestibule
zaherir {76} *vt* **1** : to criticize sharply **2** : to wound, to mortify
zahones *nmpl* : chaps
zaino, -na *adj* : chestnut (color)
zalamería *nf* : flattery, sweet talk
zalamero[1], **-ra** *adj* : flattering, fawning
zalamero[2], **-ra** *n* : flatterer
zambiano, -na *adj & nmf* : Zambian
zambullida *nf* : dive, plunge
zambullirse {38} *vr* : to dive, to plunge
zanahoria *nf* : carrot
zancada *nf* : stride, step
zancadilla *nf* **1** : trip, stumble **2** *fam* : trick, ruse
zancos *nmpl* : stilts
zancuda *nf* : wading bird
zancudo *nm* MOSQUITO : mosquito
zángano *nm* : drone, male bee
zanja *nf* : ditch, trench
zanjar *vt* ACLARAR : to settle, to clear up, to resolve
zapallo *nm Arg, Chile, Peru, Uru* : pumpkin
zapapico *nm* : pickax
zapata *nf* : brake shoe
zapatería *nf* **1** : shoemaker's, shoe factory **2** : shoe store
zapatero[1], **-ra** *adj* : dry, tough, poorly cooked
zapatero[2], **-ra** *n* : shoemaker, cobbler
zapatilla *nf* **1** PANTUFLA : slipper **2** *or* **zapatilla de deporte** : sneaker
zapato *nm* : shoe
zar, zarina *n* : czar *m*, czarina *f*
zarandear *vt* **1** : to sift, to sieve **2** : to shake, to jostle, to jiggle
zarapito *nm* : curlew
zarcillo *nm* **1** : earring **2** : tendril (of a plant)
zarigüeya *nf* : opossum
zarista *adj & nmf* : czarist
zarpa *nf* : paw
zarpar *vi* : to set sail, to raise anchor
zarza *nf* : bramble, blackberry bush
zarzamora *nf* **1** : blackberry **2** : bramble, blackberry bush
zarzaparrilla *nf* : sarsaparilla
zepelín *nm, pl* **-lines** : zeppelin
zigoto *nm* : zygote
zigzag *nm, pl* **zigzags** *or* **zigzagues** : zigzag
zigzaguear *vi* : to zigzag
zimbabuense *adj & nmf* : Zimbabwean
zinc *nm* : zinc
zinnia *nf* : zinnia
zíper *nm CA, Mex* : zipper
zircón *nm, pl* **zircones** : zircon
zócalo *nm Mex* : main square
zodíaco *or* **zodiaco** *nm* : zodiac — **zodíacal** *adj*
zombi *or* **zombie** *nmf* : zombie
zona *nf* : zone, district, area
zonzo[1], **-za** *adj* : stupid, silly
zonzo[2], **-za** *n* : idiot, nitwit
zoo *nm* : zoo
zoología *nf* : zoology
zoológico[1], **-ca** *adj* : zoological
zoológico[2] *nm* : zoo
zoólogo, -ga *n* : zoologist
zoom *nm* : zoom lens
zopilote *nm CA, Mex* : buzzard
zoquete *nmf fam* : oaf, blockhead
zorrillo *nm* MOFETA : skunk
zorro[1], **-rra** *adj* : sly, crafty
zorro[2], **-rra** *n* **1** : fox, vixen **2** : sly crafty person
zorzal *nm* : thrush
zozobra *nf* : anxiety, worry
zozobrar *vi* : to capsize
zueco *nm* : clog (shoe)
zulú[1] *adj & nmf* : Zulu
zulú[2] *nm* : Zulu (language)
zumaque *nm* : sumac
zumbar *vi* : to buzz, to hum — *vt fam* **1** : to hit, to thrash **2** : to make fun of
zumbido *nm* : buzzing, humming
zumo *nf* JUGO : juice
zurcir {83} *vt* : to darn, to mend
zurdo[1], **-da** *adj* : left-handed
zurdo[2], **-da** *n* : left-handed person
zurza, etc. → **zurcir**
zutano, -na → **fulano**

English–Spanish Dictionary

A

a[1] [ˈeɪ] *n, pl* **a's** *or* **as** [ˈeɪz] : primera letra del alfabeto inglés

a[2] [ə, ˈeɪ] *art* (**an** [ən, ˈæn] before vowel or silent h*)* **1** : un *m*, una *f* ⟨a house : una casa⟩ ⟨half an hour : media hora⟩ ⟨what a surprise! : ¡qué sorpresa!⟩ **2** PER : por, a la, al ⟨30 kilometers an hour : 30 kilómetros por hora⟩ ⟨twice a month : dos veces al mes⟩

aardvark [ˈɑrdˌvɑrk] *n* : oso *m* hormiguero

aback [əˈbæk] *adv* **1** : por sorpresa **2 to be taken aback** : quedarse desconcertado

abacus [ˈæbəkəs] *n, pl* **abaci** [ˈæbəˌsaɪ, -ˌki:] *or* **abacuses** : ábaco *m*

abaft [əˈbæft] *adv* : a popa

abalone [ˌæbəˈlo:ni] *n* : abulón *m*, oreja *f* marina

abandon[1] [əˈbændən] *vt* **1** DESERT, FORSAKE : abandonar, desamparar (a alguien), desertar de (algo) **2** GIVE UP, SUSPEND : renunciar a, suspender ⟨he abandoned the search : suspendió la búsqueda⟩ **3** EVACUATE, LEAVE : abandonar, evacuar, dejar ⟨to abandon ship : abandonar el buque⟩ **4 to abandon oneself** : entregarse, abandonarse

abandon[2] *n* : desenfreno *m* ⟨with wild abandon : desenfrenadamente⟩

abandoned [əˈbændənd] *adj* **1** DESERTED : abandonado **2** UNRESTRAINED : desenfrenado, desinhibido

abandonment [əˈbændənmənt] *n* : abandono *m*, desamparo *m*

abase [əˈbeɪs] *vt* **abased; abasing** : degradar, humillar, rebajar

abash [əˈbæʃ] *vt* : avergonzar, abochornar

abashed [əˈbæʃt] *adj* : avergonzado

abate [əˈbeɪt] *vi* **abated; abating** : amainar, menguar, disminuir

abattoir [ˈæbəˌtwɑr] *n* : matadero *m*

abbess [ˈæbɪs, -ˌbɛs, -bəs] *n* : abadesa *f*

abbey [ˈæbi] *n, pl* **-beys** : abadía *f*

abbot [ˈæbət] *n* : abad *m*

abbreviate [əˈbri:viˌeɪt] *vt* **-ated; -ating** : abreviar

abbreviation [əˌbri:viˈeɪʃən] *n* : abreviación *f*, abreviatura *f*

ABC's [ˌeɪˌbi:ˈsi:z] *npl* : abecé *m*

abdicate [ˈæbdɪˌkeɪt] *v* **-cated; -cating** : abdicar

abdication [ˌæbdɪˈkeɪʃən] *n* : abdicación *f*

abdomen [ˈæbdəmən, æbˈdo:mən] *n* : abdomen *m*, vientre *m*

abdominal [æbˈdɑmənəl] *adj* : abdominal — **abdominally** *adv*

abduct [æbˈdʌkt] *vt* : raptar, secuestrar

abduction [æbˈdʌkʃən] *n* : rapto *m*, secuestro *m*

abductor [æbˈdʌktər] *n* : raptor *m*, -tora *f*; secuestrador *m*, -dora *f*

abed [əˈbɛd] *adv & adj* : en cama

aberrant [æˈbɛrənt, ˈæbərənt] *adj* **1** ABNORMAL : anormal, aberrante **2** ATYPICAL : anómalo, atípico

aberration [ˌæbəˈreɪʃən] *n* **1** : aberración *f* **2** DERANGEMENT : perturbación *f* mental

abet [əˈbɛt] *vt* **abetted; abetting** ASSIST : ayudar ⟨to aid and abet : ser cómplice de⟩

abeyance [əˈbeɪən*t*s] *n* : desuso *m*, suspensión *f*

abhor [əbˈhɔr, æb-] *vt* **-horred; -horring** : abominar, aborrecer

abhorrence [əbˈhɔrən*t*s, æb-] *n* : aborrecimiento *m*, odio *m*

abhorrent [əbˈhɔrənt, æb-] *adj* : abominable, aborrecible, odioso

abide [əˈbaɪd] *v* **abode** [əˈbo:d] *or* **abided; abiding** *vt* STAND : soportar, tolerar ⟨I can't abide them : no los puedo ver⟩ — *vi* **1** ENDURE : quedar, permanecer **2** DWELL : morar, residir **3 to abide by** : atenerse a

ability [əˈbɪləṭi] *n, pl* **-ties** **1** CAPABILITY : aptitud *f*, capacidad *f*, facultad *f* **2** COMPETENCE : competencia *f* **3** TALENT : talento *m*, don *m*, habilidad *f*

abject [ˈæbˌdʒɛkt, æbˈ-] *adj* **1** WRETCHED : miserable, desdichado **2** HOPELESS : abatido, desesperado **3** SERVILE : servil ⟨abject flattery : halagos serviles⟩ — **abjectly** *adv*

abjure [æbˈdʒʊr] *vt* **-jured; -juring** : abjurar de

ablaze [əˈbleɪz] *adj* **1** BURNING : ardiendo, en llamas **2** RADIANT : resplandeciente, radiante

able [ˈeɪbəl] *adj* **abler; ablest** **1** CAPABLE : capaz, hábil **2** COMPETENT : competente

ablution [əˈblu:ʃən] *n* : ablución *f* ⟨to perform one's ablutions : lavarse⟩

ably [ˈeɪbəli] *adv* : hábilmente, eficientemente

abnormal [æbˈnɔrməl] *adj* : anormal — **abnormally** *adv*

abnormality [ˌæbnərˈmæləṭi, -nɔr-] *n, pl* **-ties** : anormalidad *f*

aboard[1] [əˈbord] *adv* : a bordo

aboard[2] *prep* : a bordo de

abode[1] → **abide**

abode[2] [əˈbo:d] *n* : morada *f*, residencia *f*, vivienda *f*

abolish [əˈbɑlɪʃ] *vt* : abolir, suprimir

abolition [ˌæbəˈlɪʃən] *n* : abolición *f*, supresión *f*

abominable [əˈbɑmənəbəl] *adj* DETESTABLE : abominable, aborrecible, espantoso

abominate [əˈbɑməˌneɪt] *vt* **-nated; -nating** : abominar, aborrecer

abomination [əˌbɑməˈneɪʃən] *n* : abominación *f*

aboriginal [ˌæbəˈrɪdʒənəl] *adj* : aborigen, indígena

aborigine [ˌæbəˈrɪdʒəni] *n* NATIVE : aborigen *mf*, indígena *mf*

abort [ə'bɔrt] *vt* **1** : abortar (en medicina) **2** CALL OFF : suspender, abandonar — *vi* : abortar, hacerse un aborto

abortion [ə'bɔrʃən] *n* : aborto *m*

abortive [ə'bɔrt̬ɪv] *adj* UNSUCCESSFUL : fracasado, frustrado, malogrado

abound [ə'baʊnd] *vi* **to abound in** : abundar en, estar lleno de

about[1] [ə'baʊt] *adv* **1** APPROXIMATELY : aproximadamente, casi, más o menos **2** AROUND : por todas partes, alrededor ⟨the children are running about : los niños están corriendo por todas partes⟩ **3 to be about to** : estar a punto de **4 to be up and about** : estar levantado

about[2] *prep* **1** AROUND : alrededor de **2** CONCERNING : de, acerca de, sobre ⟨he always talks about politics : siempre habla de política⟩

above[1] [ə'bʌv] *adv* **1** OVERHEAD : por encima, arriba **2** : más arriba ⟨as stated above : como se indica más arriba⟩

above[2] *adj* : anterior, antedicho ⟨for the above reasons : por las razones antedichas⟩

above[3] *prep* **1** OVER : encima de, arriba de, sobre **2** : superior a, por encima de ⟨he's above those things : él está por encima de esas cosas⟩ **3** : más de, superior a ⟨he earns above $50,000 : gana más de $50,000⟩ ⟨a number above 10 : un número superior a 10⟩ **4 above all** : sobre todo

aboveboard[1] [ə'bʌv'bord, -ˌbord] *adv* **open and aboveboard** : sin tapujos

aboveboard[2] *adj* : legítimo, sincero

abrade [ə'breɪd] *vt* **abraded; abrading** **1** ERODE : erosionar, corroer **2** SCRAPE : escoriar, raspar

abrasion [ə'breɪʒən] *n* **1** SCRAPE, SCRATCH : raspadura *f*, rasguño *m* **2** EROSION : erosión *f*

abrasive[1] [ə'breɪsɪv] *adj* **1** ROUGH : abrasivo, áspero **2** BRUSQUE, IRRITATING : brusco, irritante

abrasive[2] *n* : abrasivo *m*

abreast [ə'brɛst] *adv* **1** : en fondo, al lado ⟨to march three abreast : marchar de tres en fondo⟩ **2 to keep abreast** : mantenerse al día

abridge [ə'brɪʤ] *vt* **abridged; abridging** : compendiar, resumir

abridgment *or* **abridgement** [ə'brɪʤmənt] *n* : compendio *m*, resumen *m*

abroad [ə'brɔd] *adv* **1** ABOUT, WIDELY : por todas partes, en todas direcciones ⟨the news spread abroad : la noticia corrió por todas partes⟩ **2** OVERSEAS : en el extranjero, en el exterior

abrogate ['æbrəˌgeɪt] *vt* **-gated; -gating** : abrogar

abrupt [ə'brʌpt] *adj* **1** SUDDEN : abrupto, repentino, súbito **2** BRUSQUE, CURT : brusco, cortante — **abruptly** *adv*

abscess ['æbˌsɛs] *n* : absceso *m*

abscond [æb'skɑnd] *vi* : huir, fugarse

absence ['æbsənts] *n* **1** : ausencia *f* (de una persona) **2** LACK : falta *f*, carencia *f*

absent[1] [æb'sɛnt] *vt* **to absent oneself** : ausentarse

absent[2] ['æbsənt] *adj* : ausente

absentee [ˌæbsən'tiː] *n* : ausente *mf*

absentminded [ˌæbsənt'maɪndəd] *adj* : distraído, despistado

absentmindedly [ˌæbsənt'maɪndədli] *adv* : distraídamente

absentmindedness [ˌæbsənt'maɪndədnəs] *n* : distracción *f*, despiste *m*

absolute ['æbsəˌluːt, ˌæbsə'luːt] *adj* **1** COMPLETE, PERFECT : completo, pleno, perfecto **2** UNCONDITIONAL : absoluto, incondicional **3** DEFINITE : categórico, definitivo

absolutely ['æbsəˌluːtli, ˌæbsə'luːtli] *adv* **1** COMPLETELY : completamente, absolutamente **2** CERTAINLY : desde luego ⟨do you agree? absolutely! : ¿estás de acuerdo? ¡desde luego!⟩

absolution [ˌæbsə'luːʃən] *n* : absolución *f*

absolutism ['æbsəˌluːˌtɪzəm] *n* : absolutismo *m*

absolve [əb'zɑlv, æb-, -'sɑlv] *vt* **-solved; -solving** : absolver, perdonar

absorb [əb'zɔrb, æb-, -'sɔrb] *vt* **1** : absorber, embeber (un líquido), amortiguar (un golpe, la luz) **2** ENGROSS : absorber **3** ASSIMILATE : asimilar

absorbed [əb'zɔrbd, æb-, -'sɔrbd] *adj* ENGROSSED : absorto, ensimismado

absorbency [əb'zɔrbəntsi, æb-, -'sɔr-] *n* : absorbencia *f*

absorbent [əb'zɔrbənt, æb-, -'sɔr-] *adj* : absorbente

absorbing [əb'zɔrbɪŋ, æb-, -'sɔr-] *adj* : absorbente, fascinante

absorption [əb'zɔrpʃən, æb-, -'sɔrp-] *n* **1** : absorción *f* **2** CONCENTRATION : concentración *f*

abstain [əb'steɪn, æb-] *vi* : abstenerse

abstainer [əb'steɪnər, æb-] *n* : abstemio *m*, -mia *f*

abstemious [æb'stiːmiəs] *adj* : abstemio, sobrio — **abstemiously** *adv*

abstention [əb'stɛnʧən, æb-] *n* : abstención *f*

abstinence ['æbstənənts] *n* : abstinencia *f*

abstract[1] [æb'strækt, 'æbˌ-] *vt* **1** EXTRACT : abstraer, extraer **2** SUMMARIZE : compendiar, resumir

abstract[2] *adj* : abstracto — **abstractly** [æb'stræktli, 'æbˌ-] *adv*

abstract[3] ['æbˌstrækt] *n* : resumen *m*, compendio *m*, sumario *m*

abstraction [æb'strækʃən] *n* **1** : abstracción *f*, idea *f* abstracta **2** ABSENTMINDEDNESS : distracción *f*

abstruse [əb'struːs, æb-] *adj* : abstruso, recóndito — **abstrusely** *adv*

absurd [əb'sərd, -'zərd] *adj* : absurdo, ridículo, disparatado — **absurdly** *adv*

absurdity [əbˈsərdət̬i, -ˈzər-] *n, pl* **-ties** **1** : absurdo *m* **2** NONSENSE : disparate *m*, despropósito *m*

abundance [əˈbʌndənts] *n* : abundancia *f*

abundant [əˈbʌndənt] *adj* : abundante, cuantioso, copioso

abundantly [əˈbʌndəntli] *adv* : abundantemente, en abundancia

abuse[1] [əˈbju:z] *vt* **abused; abusing** **1** MISUSE : abusar de **2** MISTREAT : maltratar **3** REVILE : insultar, injuriar, denostar

abuse[2] [əˈbju:s] *n* **1** MISUSE : abuso *m* **2** MISTREATMENT : abuso *m*, maltrato *m* **3** INSULTS : insultos *mpl*, improperios *mpl* ⟨a string of abuse : una serie de improperios⟩

abuser [əˈbju:zər] *n* : abusador *m*, -dora *f*

abusive [əˈbju:sɪv] *adj* **1** ABUSING : abusivo **2** INSULTING : ofensivo, injurioso, insultante — **abusively** *adv*

abut [əˈbʌt] *v* **abutted; abutting** *vt* : bordear — *vi* **to abut on** : colindar con

abutment [əˈbʌtmənt] *n* **1** BUTTRESS : contrafuerte *m*, estribo *m* **2** CLOSENESS : contigüidad *f*

abysmal [əˈbɪzməl] *adj* **1** DEEP : abismal, insondable **2** TERRIBLE : atroz, desastroso

abysmally [əˈbɪzməli] *adv* : desastrosamente, terriblemente

abyss [əˈbɪs, ˈæbɪs] *n* : abismo *m*, sima *f*

acacia [əˈkeɪʃə] *n* : acacia *f*

academic[1] [ˌækəˈdɛmɪk] *adj* **1** : académico **2** THEORETICAL : teórico — **academically** [-mɪkli] *adv*

academic[2] *n* : académico *m*, -ca *f*

academician [ˌækədəˈmɪʃən] *n* → **academic**

academy [əˈkædəmi] *n, pl* **-mies** : academia *f*

acanthus [əˈkæntθəs] *n* : acanto *m*

accede [ækˈsi:d] *vi* **-ceded; -ceding** **1** AGREE : acceder, consentir **2** ASCEND : subir, acceder ⟨he acceded to the throne : subió al trono⟩

accelerate [ɪkˈsɛləˌreɪt, æk-] *v* **-ated; -ating** *vt* : acelerar, apresurar — *vi* : acelerar (dícese de un carro)

acceleration [ɪkˌsɛləˈreɪʃən, æk-] *n* : aceleración *f*

accelerator [ɪkˈsɛləˌreɪt̬ər, æk-] *n* : acelerador *m*

accent[1] [ˈækˌsɛnt, ækˈsɛnt] *vt* : acentuar

accent[2] [ˈækˌsɛnt, -sənt] *n* **1** : acento *m* **2** EMPHASIS, STRESS : énfasis *m*, acento *m*

accentuate [ɪkˈsɛntʃʊˌeɪt, æk-] *vt* **-ated; -ating** : acentuar, poner énfasis en

accept [ɪkˈsɛpt, æk-] *vt* **1** : aceptar **2** ACKNOWLEDGE : admitir, reconocer

acceptability [ɪkˌsɛptəˈbɪlət̬i, æk-] *n* : aceptabilidad *f*

acceptable [ɪkˈsɛptəbəl, æk-] *adj* : aceptable, admisible — **acceptably** [-bli] *adv*

acceptance [ɪkˈsɛptənts, æk-] *n* : aceptación *f*, aprobación *f*

access[1] [ˈækˌsɛs] *vt* : obtener acceso a, entrar a

access[2] *n* : acceso *m*

accessibility [ɪkˌsɛsəˈbɪlət̬i] *n, pl* **-ties** : accesibilidad *f*

accessible [ɪkˈsɛsəbəl, æk-] *adj* : accesible, asequible

accession [ɪkˈsɛʃən, æk-] *n* **1** : ascenso *f*, subida *f* (al trono, etc.) **2** ACQUISITION : adquisición *f*

accessory[1] [ɪkˈsɛsəri, æk-] *adj* : auxiliar

accessory[2] *n, pl* **-ries** **1** : accesorio *m*, complemento *m* **2** ACCOMPLICE : cómplice *mf*

accident [ˈæksədənt] *n* **1** MISHAP : accidente *m* **2** CHANCE : casualidad *f*

accidental [ˌæksəˈdɛntəl] *adj* : accidental, casual, imprevisto, fortuito

accidentally [ˌæksəˈdɛntəli, -ˈdɛntli] *adv* **1** BY CHANCE : por casualidad **2** UNINTENTIONALLY : sin querer, involuntariamente

acclaim[1] [əˈkleɪm] *vt* : aclamar, elogiar

acclaim[2] *n* : aclamación *f*, elogio *m*

acclamation [ˌækləˈmeɪʃən] *n* : aclamación *f*

acclimate [ˈækləˌmeɪt, əˈklaɪmət] → **acclimatize**

acclimatize [əˈklaɪməˌtaɪz] *v* **-tized; -tizing** *vt* **1** : aclimatar **2 to acclimatize oneself** : aclimatarse

accolade [ˈækəˌleɪd, -ˌlɑd] *n* **1** PRAISE : elogio *m* **2** AWARD : galardón *m*

accommodate [əˈkɑməˌdeɪt] *vt* **-dated; -dating** **1** ADAPT : acomodar, adaptar **2** SATISFY : tener en cuenta, satisfacer **3** HOLD : dar cabida a, tener cabida para

accommodation [əˌkɑməˈdeɪʃən] *n* **1** : adaptación *f*, adecuación *f* **2 accommodations** *npl* LODGING : alojamiento *m*, hospedaje *m*

accompaniment [əˈkʌmpənəmənt, -ˈkɑm-] *n* : acompañamiento *m*

accompanist [əˈkʌmpənɪst, -ˈkɑm-] *n* : acompañante *mf*

accompany [əˈkʌmpəni, -ˈkɑm-] *vt* **-nied; -nying** : acompañar

accomplice [əˈkɑmpləs, -ˈkʌm-] *n* : cómplice *mf*

accomplish [əˈkɑmplɪʃ, -ˈkʌm-] *vt* : efectuar, realizar, lograr, llevar a cabo

accomplished [əˈkɑmplɪʃt, -ˈkʌm-] *adj* : consumado, logrado

accomplishment [əˈkɑmplɪʃmənt, -ˈkʌm-] *n* **1** ACHIEVEMENT : logro *m*, éxito *m* **2** SKILL : destreza *f*, habilidad *f*

accord[1] [əˈkɔrd] *vt* GRANT : conceder, otorgar — *vi* **to accord with** : concordar con, conformarse con

accord[2] *n* **1** AGREEMENT : acuerdo *m*, convenio *m* **2** VOLITION : voluntad *f*

⟨on one's own accord : voluntariamente, de motu proprio⟩
accordance [ə'kɔrdənts] *n* **1** ACCORD : acuerdo *m*, conformidad *f* **2 in accordance with** : conforme a, según, de acuerdo con
accordingly [ə'kɔrdɪŋli] *adv* **1** CORRESPONDINGLY : en consecuencia **2** CONSEQUENTLY : por consiguiente, por lo tanto
according to [ə'kɔrdɪŋ] *prep* : según, de acuerdo con, conforme a
accordion [ə'kɔrdiən] *n* : acordeón *m*
accordionist [ə'kɔrdiənɪst] *n* : acordeonista *mf*
accost [ə'kɔst] *vt* : abordar, dirigirse a
account[1] [ə'kaʊnt] *vt* : considerar, estimar ⟨he accounts himself lucky : se considera afortunado⟩ — *vi* **to account for** : dar cuenta de, explicar
account[2] *n* **1** : cuenta *f* ⟨savings account : cuenta de ahorros⟩ **2** EXPLANATION : versión *f*, explicación *f* **3** REPORT : relato *m*, informe *m* **4** IMPORTANCE : importancia *f* ⟨to be of no account : no tener importancia⟩ **5 on account of** BECAUSE OF : a causa de, debido a, por **6 on no account** : de ninguna manera
accountability [ə,kaʊntə'bɪləṭi] *n* : responsabilidad *f*
accountable [ə'kaʊntəbəl] *adj* : responsable
accountant [ə'kaʊntənt] *n* : contador *m*, -dora *f*; contable *mf Spain*
accounting [ə'kaʊntɪŋ] *n* : contabilidad *f*
accoutrements *or* **accouterments** [ə'ku:trəmənts, -'ku:ṭər-] *npl* **1** EQUIPMENT : equipo *m*, avíos *mpl* **2** ACCESSORIES : accesorios *mpl* **3** TRAPPINGS : símbolos *mpl* ⟨the accoutrements of power : los símbolos del poder⟩
accredit [ə'krɛdət] *vt* : acreditar, autorizar
accreditation [ə,krɛdə'teɪʃən] *n* : acreditación *f*, homologación *f*
accretion [ə'kri:ʃən] *n* **1** : acrecentamiento *m* (proceso) **2** : acreción *f*, acrecencia *f* (producto)
accrual [ə'kru:əl] *n* : incremento *m*, acumulación *f*
accrue [ə'kru:] *vi* **-crued; -cruing** : acumularse, aumentarse
accumulate [ə'kju:mjə,leɪt] *v* **-lated; -lating** *vt* : acumular, amontonar — *vi* : acumularse, amontonarse
accumulation [ə,kju:mjə'leɪʃən] *n* : acumulación *f*, amontonamiento *m*
accuracy ['ækjərəsi] *n* : exactitud *f*, precisión *f*
accurate ['ækjərət] *adj* : exacto, correcto, fiel, preciso — **accurately** *adv*
accusation [,ækjə'zeɪʃən] *n* : acusación *f*
accusatory [ə'kju:zə,tori] *adj* : acusatorio
accuse [ə'kju:z] *vt* **-cused; -cusing** : acusar, delatar, denunciar
accused [ə'kju:zd] *ns & pl* DEFENDANT : acusado *m*, -da *f*
accuser [ə'kju:zər] *n* : acusador *m*, -dora *f*
accustom [ə'kʌstəm] *vt* : acostumbrar, habituar
ace ['eɪs] *n* : as *m*
acerbic [ə'sərbɪk, æ-] *adj* : acerbo, mordaz
acetate ['æsə,teɪt] *n* : acetato *m*
acetic [ə'si:ṭɪk] *adj* : acético
acetone ['æsə,to:n] *n* : acetona *f*
acetylene [ə'sɛṭələn, -ṭə,li:n] *n* : acetileno *m*
ache[1] ['eɪk] *vi* **ached; aching 1** : doler **2 to ache for** : anhelar, ansiar
ache[2] *n* : dolor *m*
achieve [ə'ʧi:v] *vt* **achieved; achieving** : lograr, alcanzar, conseguir, realizar
achievement [ə'ʧi:vmənt] *n* : logro *m*, éxito *m*, realización *f*
acid[1] ['æsəd] *adj* **1** SOUR : ácido, agrio **2** CAUSTIC, SHARP : acerbo, mordaz — **acidly** *adv*
acid[2] *n* : ácido *m*
acidic [ə'sɪdɪk, æ-] *adj* : ácido
acidity [ə'sɪdəṭi, æ-] *n, pl* **-ties** : acidez *f*
acknowledge [ɪk'nɑlɪʤ, æk-] *vt* **-edged; -edging 1** ADMIT : reconocer, admitir **2** RECOGNIZE : reconocer **3 to acknowledge receipt of** : acusar recibo de
acknowledgment [ɪk'nɑlɪʤmənt, æk-] *n* **1** RECOGNITION : reconocimiento *m* **2** THANKS : agradecimiento *m*
acme ['ækmi] *n* : colmo *m*, apogeo *m*, cúspide *f*
acne ['ækni] *n* : acné *m*
acolyte ['ækə,laɪt] *n* : acólito *m*
acorn ['eɪ,kɔrn, -kərn] *n* : bellota *f*
acoustic [ə'ku:stɪk] *or* **acoustical** [-stɪkəl] *adj* : acústico — **acoustically** *adv*
acoustics [ə'ku:stɪks] *ns & pl* : acústica *f*
acquaint [ə'kweɪnt] *vt* **1** INFORM : enterar, informar **2** FAMILIARIZE : familiarizar **3 to be acquainted with** : conocer a (una persona), estar al tanto de (un hecho)
acquaintance [ə'kweɪntənts] *n* **1** KNOWLEDGE : conocimiento *m* **2** : conocido *m*, -da *f* ⟨friends and acquaintances : amigos y conocidos⟩
acquiesce [,ækwi'ɛs] *vi* **-esced; -escing** : consentir, conformarse
acquiescence [,ækwi'ɛsənts] *n* : consentimiento *m*, aquiescencia *f*
acquire [ə'kwaɪr] *vt* **-quired; -quiring** : adquirir, obtener
acquisition [,ækwə'zɪʃən] *n* : adquisición *f*
acquisitive [ə'kwɪzəṭɪv] *adj* : adquisitivo, codicioso
acquit [ə'kwɪt] *vt* **-quitted; -quitting 1** : absolver, exculpar **2 to acquit oneself** : comportarse, defenderse
acquittal [ə'kwɪṭəl] *n* : absolución *f*, exculpación *f*

acre ['eɪkər] *n* : acre *m*

acreage ['eɪkərɪʤ] *n* : superficie *f* en acres

acrid ['ækrəd] *adj* **1** BITTER : acre **2** CAUSTIC : acre, mordaz — **acridly** *adv*

acrimonious [ˌækrə'mo:niəs] *adj* : áspero, cáustico, sarcástico

acrimony ['ækrəˌmo:ni] *n, pl* **-nies** : acrimonia *f*

acrobat ['ækrəˌbæt] *n* : acróbata *mf*, saltimbanqui *mf*

acrobatic [ˌækrə'bæt̬ɪk] *adj* : acrobático

acrobatics [ˌækrə'bæt̬ɪks] *ns & pl* : acrobacia *f*

acronym ['ækrəˌnɪm] *n* : acrónimo *m*

across[1] [ə'krɔs] *adv* **1** CROSSWISE : al través **2** : a través, del otro lado ⟨he's already across : ya está del otro lado⟩ **3** : de ancho ⟨40 feet across : 40 pies de ancho⟩

across[2] *prep* **1** : al otro lado de ⟨across the street : al otro lado de la calle⟩ **2** : a través de ⟨a log across the road : un tronco a través del camino⟩

acrylic [ə'krɪlɪk] *n* : acrílico *m*

act[1] ['ækt] *vi* **1** PERFORM : actuar, interpretar **2** FEIGN, PRETEND : fingir, simular **3** BEHAVE : comportarse **4** FUNCTION : actuar, servir, funcionar **5** : tomar medidas ⟨he acted to save the business : tomó medidas para salvar el negocio⟩ **6 to act as** : servir de, hacer de

act[2] *n* **1** DEED : acto *m*, hecho *m*, acción *f* **2** DECREE : ley *f*, decreto *m* **3** : acto *m* (en una obra de teatro), número *m* (en un espectáculo) **4** PRETENSE : fingimiento *m*

action ['ækʃən] *n* **1** DEED : acción *f*, acto *m*, hecho *m* **2** BEHAVIOR : actuación *f*, comportamiento *m* **3** LAWSUIT : demanda *f* **4** MOVEMENT : movimiento *m* **5** COMBAT : combate *m* **6** PLOT : acción *f*, trama *f* **7** MECHANISM : mecanismo *m*

activate ['æktəˌveɪt] *vt* **-vated; -vating** : activar

activation [ˌæktə'veɪʃən] *n* : activación *f*

active ['æktɪv] *adj* **1** MOVING : activo, en movimiento **2** LIVELY : vigoroso, enérgico **3** : en actividad ⟨an active volcano : un volcán en actividad⟩ **4** OPERATIVE : vigente

actively ['æktɪvli] *adv* : activamente, enérgicamente

activist ['æktɪvɪst] *n* : activista *mf* — **activist** *adj*

activity [æk'tɪvət̬i] *n, pl* **-ties** **1** MOVEMENT : actividad *f*, movimiento *m* **2** VIGOR : vigor *m*, energía *f* **3** OCCUPATION : actividad *f*, ocupación *f*

actor ['æktər] *n* : actor *m*, artista *mf*

actress ['æktrəs] *n* : actriz *f*

actual ['ækʧʊəl] *adj* : real, verdadero

actuality [ˌækʧʊ'æləti] *n, pl* **-ties** : realidad *f*

actually ['ækʧʊəli, -ʃəli] *adv* : realmente, en realidad

actuary ['ækʧʊˌɛri] *n, pl* **-aries** : actuario *m*, -ria *f* de seguros

acumen [ə'kju:mən] *n* : perspicacia *f*

acupuncture ['ækjʊˌpʌŋkʧər] *n* : acupuntura *f*

acute [ə'kju:t] *adj* **acuter; acutest** **1** SHARP : agudo **2** PERCEPTIVE : perspicaz, sagaz **3** KEEN : fino, muy desarrollado, agudo ⟨an acute sense of smell : un fino olfato⟩ **4** SEVERE : grave **5 acute angle** : ángulo *m* agudo

acutely [ə'kju:tli] *adv* : intensamente ⟨to be acutely aware : estar perfectamente consciente⟩

acuteness [ə'kju:tnəs] *n* : agudeza *f*

ad ['æd] → **advertisement**

adage ['ædɪʤ] *n* : adagio *m*, refrán *m*, dicho *m*

adamant ['ædəmənt, -ˌmænt] *adj* : firme, categórico, inflexible — **adamantly** *adv*

Adam's apple ['ædəmz] *n* : nuez *f* de Adán

adapt [ə'dæpt] *vt* : adaptar, ajustar — *vi* : adaptarse

adaptability [əˌdæptə'bɪlət̬i] *n* : adaptabilidad *f*, flexibilidad *f*

adaptable [ə'dæptəbəl] *adj* : adaptable, amoldable

adaptation [ˌæˌdæp'teɪʃən, -dəp-] *n* **1** : adaptación *f*, modificación *f* **2** VERSION : versión *f*

adapter [ə'dæptər] *n* : adaptador *m*

add ['æd] *vt* **1** : añadir, agregar ⟨to add a comment : añadir una observación⟩ **2** : sumar ⟨add these numbers : suma estos números⟩ — *vi* : sumar (en total)

adder ['ædər] *n* : víbora *f*

addict[1] [ə'dɪkt] *vt* : causar adicción en

addict[2] ['ædɪkt] *n* **1** : adicto *m*, -ta *f* **2** **drug addict** : drogadicto *m*, -ta *f*; toxicómano *m*, -na *f*

addiction [ə'dɪkʃən] *n* **1** : adicción *f*, dependencia *f* **2** **drug addiction** : drogadicción *f*

addictive [ə'dɪktɪv] *adj* : adictivo

addition [ə'dɪʃən] *n* **1** : adición *f*, añadidura *f* **2 in ~** : además, también

additional [ə'dɪʃənəl] *adj* : extra, adicional, de más

additionally [ə'dɪʃənəli] *adv* : además, adicionalmente

additive ['ædət̬ɪv] *n* : aditivo *m*

addle ['ædəl] *vt* **-dled; -dling** : confundir, enturbiar

address[1] [ə'drɛs] *vt* **1** : dirigirse a, pronunciar un discurso ante ⟨to address a jury : dirigirse a un jurado⟩ **2** : dirigir, ponerle la dirección a ⟨to address a letter : dirigir una carta⟩

address[2] [ə'drɛs, 'æˌdrɛs] *n* **1** SPEECH : discurso *m*, alocución *f* **2** : dirección *f* (de una residencia, etc.)

addressee [ˌæˌdrɛ'si:, ə-] *n* : destinatario *m*, -ria *f*

adduce [ə-ˈduːs, ˈdjuːs] *vt* **-duced; -ducing** : aducir
adenoids [ˈædˌnɔɪd, -dənˌɔɪd] *npl* : adenoides *fpl*
adept [əˈdɛpt] *adj* : experto, hábil — **adeptly** *adv*
adequacy [ˈædɪkwəsi] *n, pl* **-cies** : cantidad *f* suficiente
adequate [ˈædɪkwət] *adj* **1** SUFFICIENT : adecuado, suficiente **2** ACCEPTABLE, PASSABLE : adecuado, aceptable
adequately [ˈædɪkwətli] *adv* : suficientemente, apropiadamente
adhere [ædˈhɪr, əd-] *vi* **-hered; -hering** **1** STICK : pegarse, adherirse **2 to adhere to** : adherirse a (una política, etc.), cumplir con (una promesa)
adherence [ædˈhɪrənts, əd-] *n* : adhesión *f*, adherencia *f*, observancia *f* (de una ley, etc.)
adherent[1] [ædˈhɪrənt, əd-] *adj* : adherente, adhesivo, pegajoso
adherent[2] *n* : adepto *m*, -ta *f*; partidario *m*, -ria *f*
adhesion [ædˈhiːʒən, əd-] *n* : adhesión *f*
adhesive[1] [ædˈhiːsɪv, əd-, -zɪv] *adj* : adhesivo
adhesive[2] *n* : adhesivo *m*, pegamento *m*
adjacent [əˈdʒeɪsənt] *adj* : adyacente, colindante, contiguo
adjective [ˈædʒɪktɪv] *n* : adjetivo *m* — **adjectival** [ˌædʒɪkˈtaɪvəl] *adj*
adjoin [əˈdʒɔɪn] *vt* : lindar con, colindar con
adjoining [əˈdʒɔɪnɪŋ] *adj* : contiguo, colindante
adjourn [əˈdʒərn] *vt* : levantar, suspender ⟨the meeting is adjourned : se levanta la sesión⟩ — *vi* : aplazarse
adjournment [əˈdʒərnmənt] *n* : suspensión *f*, aplazamiento *m*
adjudicate [əˈdʒuːdɪˌkeɪt] *vt* **-cated; -cating** : juzgar, arbitrar
adjudication [əˌdʒuːdɪˈkeɪʃən] *n* **1** JUDGING : arbitrio *m* (judicial) **2** JUDGMENT : fallo *m*
adjunct [ˈæˌdʒʌŋkt] *n* : adjunto *m*, complemento *m*
adjust [əˈdʒʌst] *vt* : ajustar, arreglar, regular — *vi* **to adjust to** : adaptarse a
adjustable [əˈdʒʌstəbəl] *adj* : ajustable, regulable, graduable
adjustment [əˈdʒʌstmənt] *n* : ajuste *m*, modificación *f*
ad–lib[1] [ˈædˈlɪb] *v* **-libbed; -libbing** : improvisar
ad–lib[2] *adj* : improvisado
administer [ædˈmɪnəstər, əd-] *vt* : administrar
administration [ædˌmɪnəˈstreɪʃən, əd-] *n* **1** MANAGING : administración *f*, dirección *f* **2** GOVERNMENT, MANAGEMENT : administración *f*, gobierno *m*
administrative [ædˈmɪnəˌstreɪtɪv, əd-] *adj* : administrativo — **administratively** *adv*
administrator [ædˈmɪnəˌstreɪtər, əd-] *n* : administrador *m*, -dora *f*
admirable [ˈædmərəbəl] *adj* : admirable, loable — **admirably** *adv*
admiral [ˈædmərəl] *n* : almirante *mf*
admiration [ˌædməˈreɪʃən] *n* : admiración *f*
admire [ædˈmaɪr] *vt* **-mired; -miring** : admirar
admirer [ædˈmaɪrər] *n* : admirador *m*, -dora *f*
admiring [ædˈmaɪrɪŋ] *adj* : admirativo, de admiración
admiringly [ædˈmaɪrɪŋli] *adv* : con admiración
admissible [ædˈmɪsəbəl] *adj* : admisible, aceptable
admission [ædˈmɪʃən] *n* **1** ADMITTANCE : entrada *f*, admisión *f* **2** ACKNOWLEDGMENT : reconocimiento *m*, admisión *f*
admit [ædˈmɪt, əd-] *vt* **-mitted; -mitting** **1** : admitir, dejar entrar ⟨the museum admits children : el museo deja entrar a los niños⟩ **2** ACKNOWLEDGE : reconocer, admitir
admittance [ædˈmɪtənts, əd-] *n* : admisión *f*, entrada *f*, acceso *m*
admittedly [ædˈmɪtədli, əd-] *adv* : la verdad es que, lo cierto es que ⟨admittedly we went too fast : la verdad es que fuimos demasiado de prisa⟩
admonish [ædˈmɑnɪʃ, əd-] *vt* : amonestar, reprender
admonition [ˌædməˈnɪʃən] *n* : admonición *f*
ado [əˈduː] *n* **1** FUSS : ruido *m*, alboroto *m* **2** TROUBLE : dificultad *f*, lío *m* **3 without further ado** : sin más preámbulos
adobe [əˈdoːbi] *n* : adobe *m*
adolescence [ˌædəlˈɛsənts] *n* : adolescencia *f*
adolescent[1] [ˌædəlˈɛsənt] *adj* : adolescente, de adolescencia
adolescent[2] *n* : adolescente *mf*
adopt [əˈdɑpt] *vt* : adoptar
adoption [əˈdɑpʃən] *n* : adopción *f*
adoptive [əˈdɑptɪv] *adj* : adoptivo
adorable [əˈdorəbəl] *adj* : adorable, encantador
adorably [əˈdorəbli] *adv* : de manera adorable
adoration [ˌædəˈreɪʃən] *n* : adoración *f*
adore [əˈdor] *vt* **adored; adoring** **1** WORSHIP : adorar **2** LOVE : querer, adorar **3** LIKE : encantarle (algo a uno), gustarle mucho (algo a uno) ⟨I adore your new dress : me encanta tu vestido nuevo⟩
adorn [əˈdɔrn] *vt* : adornar, ornar, engalanar
adornment [əˈdɔrnmənt] *n* : adorno *m*, decoración *f*
adrenaline [əˈdrɛnələn] *n* : adrenalina *f*
adrift [əˈdrɪft] *adj & adv* : a la deriva
adroit [əˈdrɔɪt] *adj* : diestro, hábil — **adroitly** *adv*
adroitness [əˈdrɔɪtnəs] *n* : destreza *f*, habilidad *f*

adult[1] [əˈdʌlt, ˈæˌdʌlt] *adj* : adulto

adult[2] *n* : adulto *m*, -ta *f*

adulterate [əˈdʌltəˌreɪt] *vt* **-ated; -ating** : adulterar

adulterous [əˈdʌltərəs] *adj* : adúltero

adultery [əˈdʌltəri] *n, pl* **-teries** : adulterio *m*

adulthood [əˈdʌltˌhʊd] *n* : adultez *f*, edad *f* adulta

advance[1] [ædˈvænts, əd-] *v* **-vanced; -vancing** *vt* **1** : avanzar, adelantar ⟨to advance troops : avanzar las tropas⟩ **2** PROMOTE : ascender, promover **3** PROPOSE : proponer, presentar **4** : adelantar, anticipar ⟨they advanced me next month's salary : me adelantaron el sueldo del próximo mes⟩ — *vi* **1** PROCEED : avanzar, adelantarse **2** PROGRESS : progresar

advance[2] *adj* : anticipado ⟨advance notice : previo aviso⟩

advance[3] *n* **1** PROGRESSION : avance *m* **2** PROGRESS : adelanto *m*, mejora *f*, progreso *m* **3** RISE : aumento *m*, alza *f* **4** LOAN : anticipo *m*, préstamo *m* **5** **in ~** : por adelantado

advanced [ædˈvæntst, əd-] *adj* **1** DEVELOPED : avanzado, desarrollado **2** PRECOCIOUS : adelantado, precoz **3** HIGHER : superior

advancement [ædˈvæntsmənt, əd-] *n* **1** FURTHERANCE : fomento *m*, adelantamiento *m*, progreso *m* **2** PROMOTION : ascenso *m*

advantage [ədˈvæntɪʤ, æd-] *n* **1** SUPERIORITY : ventaja *f*, superioridad *f* **2** GAIN : provecho *m*, partido *m* **3** **to take advantage of** : aprovecharse de

advantageous [ˌædˌvænˈteɪʤəs, -vən-] *adj* : ventajoso, provechoso — **advantageously** *adv*

advent [ˈædˌvɛnt] *n* **1** **Advent** : Adviento *m* **2** ARRIVAL : advenimiento *m*, venida *f*

adventure [ædˈvɛnʧər, əd-] *n* : aventura *f*

adventurer [ædˈvɛnʧərər, əd-] *n* : aventurero *m*, -ra *f*

adventurous [ædˈvɛnʧərəs, əd-] *adj* **1** : intrépido, aventurero ⟨an adventurous traveler : un viajero intrépido⟩ **2** RISKY : arriesgado, aventurado

adverb [ˈædˌvərb] *n* : adverbio *m* — **adverbial** [ædˈvərbiəl] *adj*

adversary [ˈædvərˌsɛri] *n, pl* **-saries** : adversario *m*, -ria *f*

adverse [ædˈvərs, ˈædˌ] *adj* **1** OPPOSING : opuesto, contrario **2** UNFAVORABLE : adverso, desfavorable — **adversely** *adv*

adversity [ædˈvərsət̬i, əd-] *n, pl* **-ties** : adversidad *f*

advertise [ˈædvərˌtaɪz] *v* **-tised; -tising** *vt* : anunciar, hacerle publicidad a — *vi* : hacer publicidad, hacer propaganda

advertisement [ˈædvərˌtaɪzmənt; æd ˈvərt̬əzmənt] *n* : anuncio *m*

advertiser [ˈædvərˌtaɪzər] *n* : anunciante *mf*

advertising [ˈædvərˌtaɪzɪŋ] *n* : publicidad *f*, propaganda *f*

advice [ædˈvaɪs] *n* : consejo *m*, recomendación *f* ⟨take my advice : sigue mis consejos⟩

advisability [ædˌvaɪzəˈbɪlət̬i, əd-] *n* : conveniencia *f*

advisable [ædˈvaɪzəbəl, əd-] *adj* : aconsejable, recomendable, conveniente

advise [ædˈvaɪz, əd-] *v* **-vised; -vising** *vt* **1** COUNSEL : aconsejar, asesorar **2** RECOMMEND : recomendar **3** INFORM : informar, notificar — *vi* : dar consejo

adviser *or* **advisor** [ædˈvaɪzər, əd-] *n* : consejero *m*, -ra *f*; asesor *m*, -sora *f*

advisory [ædˈvaɪzəri, əd-] *adj* **1** : consultivo **2** **in an advisory capacity** : como asesor

advocacy [ˈædvəkəsi] *n* : promoción *f*, apoyo *m*

advocate[1] [ˈædvəˌkeɪt] *vt* **-cated; -cating** : recomendar, abogar por, ser partidario de

advocate[2] [ˈædvəkət] *n* : defensor *m*, -sora *f*; partidario *m*, -ria *f*

adze [ˈædz] *n* : azuela *f*

aeon [ˈiːən, ˈiːˌɑn] *n* : eón *m*, siglo *m*, eternidad *f*

aerate [ˈærˌeɪt] *vt* **-ated; -ating** : gasear (un líquido), oxigenar (la sangre)

aerial[1] [ˈæriəl] *adj* : aéreo

aerial[2] *n* : antena *f*

aerie [ˈæri, ˈɪri, ˈeɪəri] *n* : aguilera *f*

aerobic [ˌærˈoːbɪk] *adj* : aerobio, aeróbico ⟨aerobic exercises : ejercicios aeróbicos⟩

aerobics [ˌærˈoːbɪks] *ns & pl* : aeróbic *m*

aerodynamic [ˌæroːdaɪˈnæmɪk] *adj* : aerodinámico — **aerodynamically** [-mɪkli] *adv*

aerodynamics [ˌæroːdaɪˈnæmɪks] *n* : aerodinámica *f*

aeronautical [ˌærəˈnɔt̬ɪkəl] *adj* : aeronáutico

aeronautics [ˌærəˈnɔt̬ɪks] *n* : aeronáutica *f*

aerosol [ˈærəˌsɔl] *n* : aerosol *m*

aerospace[1] [ˈæroˌspeɪs] *adj* : aeroespacial

aerospace[2] *n* : espacio *m*

aesthetic [ɛsˈθɛt̬ɪk] *adj* : estético — **aesthetically** [-t̬ɪkli] *adv*

aesthetics [ɛsˈθɛt̬ɪks] *n* : estética *f*

afar [əˈfɑr] *adv* : lejos, a lo lejos

affability [ˌæfəˈbɪlət̬i] *n* : afabilidad *f*

affable [ˈæfəbəl] *adj* : afable — **affably** *adv*

affair [əˈfær] *n* **1** MATTER : asunto *m*, cuestión *f*, caso *m* **2** EVENT : ocasión *f*, acontecimiento *m* **3** LIAISON : amorío *m*, aventura *f* **4** **business affairs** : negocios *mpl* **5** **current affairs** : actualidades *fpl*

affect [əˈfɛkt, æ-] *vt* **1** INFLUENCE, TOUCH : afectar, tocar **2** FEIGN : fingir

affectation [ˌæˌfɛk'teɪʃən] *n* : afectación *f*
affected [ə'fɛktəd, æ-] *adj* **1** FEIGNED : afectado, fingido **2** MOVED : conmovido
affecting [ə'fɛktɪŋ, æ-] *adj* : conmovedor
affection [ə'fɛkʃən] *n* : afecto *m*, cariño *m*
affectionate [ə'fɛkʃənət] *adj* : afectuoso, cariñoso — **affectionately** *adv*
affidavit [ˌæfə'deɪvət, 'æfəˌ-] *n* : declaración *f* jurada, affidávit *m*
affiliate[1] [ə'fɪliˌeɪt] *v* **-ated; -ating** *vt* : afiliar, asociar ⟨to be affiliated with : estar afiliado a⟩
affiliate[2] [ə'fɪliət] *n* : afiliado *m*, -da *f* (persona), filial *f* (organización)
affiliation [əˌfɪli'eɪʃən] *n* : afiliación *f*, filiación *f*
affinity [ə'fɪnət̬i] *n, pl* **-ties** : afinidad *f*
affirm [ə'fərm] *vt* : afirmar, aseverar, declarar
affirmation [ˌæfər'meɪʃən] *n* : afirmación *f*, aserto *m*, declaración *f*
affirmative[1] [ə'fərmət̬ɪv] *adj* : afirmativo ⟨affirmative action : acción afirmativa⟩
affirmative[2] *n* **1** : afirmativa *f* **2 to answer in the affirmative** : responder afirmativamente, dar una respuesta afirmativa
affix [ə'fɪks] *vt* : fijar, poner, pegar
afflict [ə'flɪkt] *vt* **1** : afligir, aquejar **2 to be afflicted with** : padecer de, sufrir de
affliction [ə'flɪkʃən] *n* **1** TRIBULATION : aflicción *f*, tribulación *f* **2** AILMENT : enfermedad *f*, padecimiento *m*
affluence ['æˌflu:əns; æ'flu:-, ə-] *n* : afluencia *f*, abundancia *f*, prosperidad *f*
affluent ['æˌflu:ənt; æ'flu:-, ə-] *adj* : próspero, adinerado
afford [ə'ford] *vt* **1** : tener los recursos para, permitirse el lujo de ⟨I can afford it : puedo permitírmelo, tengo con que comprarlo⟩ **2** PROVIDE : ofrecer, proporcionar, dar
affront[1] [ə'frʌnt] *vt* : afrentar, insultar, ofender
affront[2] *n* : afrenta *f*, insulto *m*, ofensa *f*
Afghan ['æfˌgæn, -gən] *n* : afgano *m*, -na *f* — **Afghan** *adj*
afire [ə'faɪr] *adj* : ardiendo, en llamas
aflame [ə'fleɪm] *adj* : llameante, en llamas
afloat [ə'flo:t] *adv & adj* : a flote
afoot [ə'fʊt] *adj* **1** WALKING : a pie, andando **2** UNDER WAY : en marcha ⟨something suspicious is afoot : algo sospechoso se está tramando⟩
aforementioned [ə'for'mentʃənd] *adj* : antedicho, susodicho
aforesaid [ə'forˌsɛd] *adj* : antes mencionado, antedicho
afraid [ə'freɪd] *adj* **1 to be afraid** : tener miedo **2 to be afraid that** : temerse que ⟨I'm afraid not : me temo que no⟩
afresh [ə'frɛʃ] *adv* **1** : de nuevo, otra vez **2 to start afresh** : volver a empezar
African ['æfrɪkən] *n* : africano *m*, -na *f* — **African** *adj*
Afro–American[1] [ˌæfroə'mɛrɪkən] *adj* : afroamericano *m*, -na *f*
Afro–American[2] *n* : afroamericano
aft ['æft] *adv* : a popa
after[1] ['æftər] *adv* **1** AFTERWARD : después **2** BEHIND : detrás, atrás
after[2] *adj* : posterior, siguiente ⟨in after years : en los años posteriores⟩
after[3] *conj* : después de, después de que ⟨after we ate : después de que comimos, después de comer⟩
after[4] *prep* **1** FOLLOWING : después de, tras ⟨after Saturday : después del sábado⟩ ⟨day after day : día tras día⟩ **2** BEHIND : tras de, después de ⟨I ran after the dog : corrí tras del perro⟩ **3** CONCERNING : por ⟨they asked after you : preguntaron por ti⟩ **4 after all** : después de todo
aftereffect ['æftərɪˌfɛkt] *n* : efecto *m* secundario
afterlife ['æftərˌlaɪf] *n* : vida *f* venidera, vida *f* después de la muerte
aftermath ['æftərˌmæθ] *n* : consecuencias *fpl*, resultados *mpl*
afternoon [ˌæftər'nu:n] *n* : tarde *f*
aftertaste ['æftərˌteɪst] *n* : resabio *m*, regusto *m*
afterthought ['æftərˌθɔt] *n* : ocurrencia *f* tardía, idea *f* tardía
afterward ['æftərwərd] *or* **afterwards** [-wərdz] *adv* : después, luego ⟨soon afterward : poco después⟩
again [ə'gɛn, -'gɪn] *adv* **1** ANEW, OVER : de nuevo, otra vez **2** BESIDES : además **3 then again** : por otra parte ⟨I may stay, then again I may not : puede ser que me quede, por otra parte, puede que no⟩
against [ə'gɛntst, -'gɪntst] *prep* **1** TOUCHING : contra ⟨against the wall : contra la pared⟩ **2** OPPOSING : contra, en contra de ⟨I will vote against the proposal : votaré en contra de la propuesta⟩ ⟨against the grain : a contrapelo⟩
agape [ə'geɪp] *adj* : boquiabierto
agate ['ægət] *n* : ágata *f*
age[1] ['eɪʤ] *vi* **aged; aging** : envejecer, madurar
age[2] *n* **1** : edad *f* ⟨ten years of age : diez años de edad⟩ ⟨to be of age : ser mayor de edad⟩ **2** PERIOD : era *f*, siglo *m*, época *f* **3 old age** : vejez *f* **4 ages** *npl* : siglos *mpl*, eternidad *f*
aged *adj* **1** ['eɪʤəd, 'eɪʤd] OLD : anciano, viejo, vetusto **2** ['eɪʤd] (*indicating a specified age*) ⟨a girl aged 10 : una niña de 10 años de edad⟩
ageless ['eɪʤləs] *adj* **1** YOUTHFUL : eternamente joven **2** TIMELESS : eterno, perenne
agency ['eɪʤəntsi] *n, pl* **-cies** **1** : agencia *f*, oficina *f* ⟨travel agency : agencia

de viajes⟩ **2 through the agency of** : a través de, por medio de

agenda [ə'ʤɛndə] *n* : agenda *f*, orden *m* del día

agent ['eɪʤənt] *n* **1** MEANS : agente *m*, medio *m*, instrumento *m* **2** REPRESENTATIVE : agente *mf*, representante *mf*

aggravate ['ægrəˌveɪt] *vt* **-vated; -vating 1** WORSEN : agravar, empeorar **2** ANNOY : irritar, exasperar

aggravation [ˌægrə'veɪʃən] *n* **1** WORSENING : empeoramiento *m* **2** ANNOYANCE : molestia *f*, irritación *f*, exasperación *f*

aggregate[1] ['ægrɪˌgeɪt] *vt* **-gated; -gating** : juntar, sumar

aggregate[2] ['ægrɪgət] *adj* : total, global, conjunto

aggregate[3] ['ægrɪgət] *n* **1** CONGLOMERATE : agregado *m*, conglomerado *m* **2** WHOLE : total *m*, conjunto *m*

aggression [ə'grɛʃən] *n* **1** ATTACK : agresión *f* **2** AGGRESSIVENESS : agresividad *f*

aggressive [ə'grɛsɪv] *adj* : agresivo — **aggressively** *adv*

aggressiveness [ə'grɛsɪvnəs] *n* : agresividad *f*

aggressor [ə'grɛsər] *n* : agresor *m*, -sora *f*

aggrieved [ə'gri:vd] *adj* : ofendido, herido

aghast [ə'gæst] *adj* : espantado, aterrado, horrorizado

agile ['æʤəl] *adj* : ágil

agility [ə'ʤɪləṭi] *n, pl* **-ties** : agilidad *f*

agitate ['æʤəˌteɪt] *v* **-tated; -tating** *vt* **1** SHAKE : agitar **2** UPSET : inquietar, perturbar — *vi* **to agitate against** : hacer campaña en contra de

agitation [ˌæʤə'teɪʃən] *n* : agitación *f*, inquietud *f*

agitator ['æʤəˌteɪṭər] *n* : agitador *m*, -dora *f*

agnostic [æg'nɑstɪk] *n* : agnóstico *m*, -ca *f*

ago [ə'go:] *adv* : hace ⟨two years ago : hace dos años⟩ ⟨long ago : hace tiempo, hace mucho tiempo⟩

agog [ə'gɑg] *adj* : ansioso, curioso

agonize ['ægəˌnaɪz] *vi* **-nized; -nizing** : tormentarse, angustiarse

agonizing ['ægəˌnaɪzɪŋ] *adj* : angustioso, terrible — **agonizingly** [-zɪŋli] *adv*

agony ['ægəni] *n, pl* **-nies 1** PAIN : dolor *m* **2** ANGUISH : angustia *f*

agrarian [ə'grɛriən] *adj* : agrario

agree [ə'gri:] *v* **agreed; agreeing** *vt* ACKNOWLEDGE : estar de acuerdo ⟨he agreed that I was right : estuvo de acuerdo en que tenía razón⟩ — *vi* **1** CONCUR : estar de acuerdo **2** CONSENT : ponerse de acuerdo **3** TALLY : concordar **4 to agree with** : sentarle bien (a alguien) ⟨this climate agrees with me : este clima me sienta bien⟩

agreeable [ə'gri:əbəl] *adj* **1** PLEASING : agradable, simpático **2** WILLING : dispuesto **3** AGREEING : de acuerdo, conforme

agreeably [ə'gri:əbli] *adv* : agradablemente

agreement [ə'gri:mənt] *n* **1** : acuerdo *m*, conformidad *f* ⟨in agreement with : de acuerdo con⟩ **2** CONTRACT, PACT : acuerdo *m*, pacto *m*, convenio *m* **3** CONCORD, HARMONY : concordia *f*

agriculture ['ægrɪˌkʌlʧər] *n* : agricultura *f* — **agricultural** [ˌægrɪ'kʌlʧərəl] *adj*

aground [ə'graʊnd] *adj* : encallado, varado

ahead [ə'hɛd] *adv* **1** : al frente, delante, adelante ⟨he walked ahead : caminó delante⟩ **2** BEFOREHAND : por adelantado, con antelación **3** LEADING : a la delantera **4 to get ahead** : adelantar, progresar

ahead of *prep* **1** : al frente de, delante de, antes de **2 to get ahead of** : adelantarse a

ahoy [ə'hɔɪ] *interj* **ship ahoy!** : ¡barco a la vista!

aid[1] ['eɪd] *vt* : ayudar, auxiliar

aid[2] *n* **1** HELP : ayuda *f*, asistencia *f* **2** ASSISTANT : asistente *mf*

aide ['eɪd] *n* : ayudante *mf*

AIDS ['eɪdz] *n* : SIDA *m*, sida *m*

ail ['eɪl] *vt* : molestar, afligir — *vi* : sufrir, estar enfermo

aileron ['eɪləˌrɑn] *n* : alerón *m*

ailment ['eɪlmənt] *n* : enfermedad *f*, dolencia *f*, achaque *m*

aim[1] ['eɪm] *vt* **1** : apuntar (un arma), dirigir (una observación) **2** INTEND : proponerse, querer ⟨he aims to do it tonight : se propone hacerlo esta noche⟩ — *vi* **1** POINT : apuntar **2 to aim at** : aspirar a

aim[2] *n* **1** MARKSMANSHIP : puntería *f* **2** GOAL : propósito *m*, objetivo *m*, fin *m*

aimless ['eɪmləs] *adj* : sin rumbo, sin objeto

aimlessly ['eɪmləsli] *adv* : sin rumbo, sin objeto

air[1] ['ær] *vt* **1** : airear, ventilar ⟨to air out a mattress : airear un colchón⟩ **2** EXPRESS : airear, manifestar, comunicar **3** BROADCAST : transmitir, emitir

air[2] *n* **1** : aire *m* **2** MELODY : aire *m* **3** APPEARANCE : aire *m*, aspecto *m* **4 airs** *npl* : aires *mpl*, afectación *f* **5 by ~** : por avión (dícese de una carta), en avión (dícese de una persona) **6 to be on the air** : estar en el aire, estar emitiendo

airborne ['ærˌborn] *adj* **1** : aerotransportado ⟨airborne troops : tropas aerotransportadas⟩ **2** FLYING : volando, en el aire

air–condition [ˌærkən'dɪʃən] *vt* : climatizar, condicionar con el aire

air conditioner [ˌærkən'dɪʃənər] *n* : acondicionador *m* de aire

air–conditioning [ˌærkənˈdɪʃənɪŋ] *n* : aire *m* acondicionado
aircraft [ˈærˌkræft] *ns & pl* **1** : avión *m*, aeronave *f* **2 aircraft carrier** : portaaviones *m*
airfield [ˈærˌfiːld] *n* : aeródromo *m*, campo *m* de aviación
air force *n* : fuerza *f* aérea
airlift [ˈærˌlɪft] *n* : puente *m* aéreo, transporte *m* aéreo
airline [ˈærˌlaɪn] *n* : aerolínea *f*, línea *f* aérea
airliner [ˈærˌlaɪnər] *n* : avión *m* de pasajeros
airmail[1] [ˈærˌmeɪl] *vt* : enviar por vía aérea
airmail[2] *n* : correo *m* aéreo
airman [ˈærmən] *n, pl* **-men** [-mən, -ˌmɛn] **1** AVIATOR : aviador *m*, -dora *f* **2** : soldado *m* de la fuerza aérea
airplane [ˈærˌpleɪn] *n* : avión *m*
airport [ˈærˌport] *n* : aeropuerto *m*
airship [ˈærˌʃɪp] *n* : dirigible *m*, zepelín *m*
airstrip [ˈærˌstrɪp] *n* : pista *f* de aterrizaje
airtight [ˈærˈtaɪt] *adj* : hermético, herméticamente cerrado
airwaves [ˈærˌweɪvz] *npl* : radio *m*, televisión *f*
airy [ˈæri] *adj* **airier** [-iər]; **-est** **1** DELICATE, LIGHT : delicado, ligero **2** BREEZY : aireado, bien ventilado
aisle [ˈaɪl] *n* : pasillo *m*, nave *f* lateral (de una iglesia)
ajar [əˈdʒɑr] *adj* : entreabierto, entornado
akimbo [əˈkɪmbo] *adj & adv* : en jarras
akin [əˈkɪn] *adj* **1** RELATED : emparentado **2** SIMILAR : semejante, parecido
alabaster [ˈæləˌbæstər] *n* : alabastro *m*
alacrity [əˈlækrət̬i] *n* : presteza *f*, prontitud *f*
alarm[1] [əˈlɑrm] *vt* **1** WARN : alarmar, alertar **2** FRIGHTEN : asustar
alarm[2] *n* **1** WARNING : alarma *f*, alerta *f* **2** APPREHENSION, FEAR : aprensión *f*, inquietud *f*, temor *m* **3 alarm clock** : despertador *m*
alarming [əˈlɑrmɪŋ] *adj* : alarmante
alas [əˈlæs] *interj* : ¡ay!
Albanian [ælˈbeɪniən] *n* : albanés *m*, -nesa *f* — **Albanian** *adj*
albatross [ˈælbəˌtrɔs] *n, pl* **-tross** *or* **-trosses** : albatros *m*
albeit [ɔlˈbiːət, æl-] *conj* : aunque
albino [ælˈbaɪno] *n, pl* **-nos** : albino *m*, -na *f*
album [ˈælbəm] *n* : álbum *m*
albumen [ælˈbjuːmən] *n* **1** : clara *f* de huevo **2** → **albumin**
albumin [ælˈbjuːmən] *n* : albúmina *f*
alchemist [ˈælkəmɪst] *n* : alquimista *mf*
alchemy [ˈælkəmi] *n, pl* **-mies** : alquimia *f*
alcohol [ˈælkəˌhɔl] *n* **1** ETHANOL : alcohol *m*, etanol *m* **2** LIQUOR : alcohol *m*, bebidas *fpl* alcohólicas
alcoholic[1] [ˌælkəˈhɔlɪk] *adj* : alcohólico
alcoholic[2] *n* : alcohólico *m*, -ca *f*
alcoholism [ˈælkəhɔˌlɪzəm] *n* : alcoholismo *m*
alcove [ˈælˌkoːv] *n* : nicho *m*, hueco *m*
alderman [ˈɔldərmən] *n, pl* **-men** [-mən, -ˌmɛn] : concejal *mf*
ale [ˈeɪl] *n* : cerveza *f*
alert[1] [əˈlərt] *vt* : alertar, poner sobre aviso
alert[2] *adj* **1** WATCHFUL : alerta, vigilante **2** QUICK : listo, vivo
alert[3] *n* : alerta *f*, alarma *f*
alertly [əˈlərtli] *adv* : con listeza
alertness [əˈlərtnəs] *n* **1** WATCHFULNESS : vigilancia *f* **2** ASTUTENESS : listeza *f*, viveza *f*
alfalfa [ælˈfælfə] *n* : alfalfa *f*
alga [ˈælgə] *n, pl* **-gae** [ˈælˌdʒiː] : alga *f*
algebra [ˈældʒəbrə] *n* : álgebra *m*
algebraic [ˌældʒəˈbreɪɪk] *adj* : algebraico — **algebraically** [-ɪkli] *adv*
Algerian [ælˈdʒɪriən] *n* : argelino *m*, -na *f* — **Algerian** *adj*
algorithm [ˈælgəˌrɪðəm] *n* : algoritmo *m*
alias[1] [ˈeɪliəs] *adv* : alias
alias[2] *n* : alias *m*
alibi[1] [ˈæləˌbaɪ] *vi* : ofrecer una coartada
alibi[2] *n* **1** : coartada *f* **2** EXCUSE : pretexto *m*, excusa *f*
alien[1] [ˈeɪliən] *adj* **1** STRANGE : ajeno, extraño **2** FOREIGN : extranjero, foráneo **3** EXTRATERRESTRIAL : extraterrestre
alien[2] *n* **1** FOREIGNER : extranjero *m*, -ra *f*; forastero *m*, -ra *f* **2** EXTRATERRESTRIAL : extraterrestre *mf*
alienate [ˈeɪliəˌneɪt] *vt* **-ated; -ating** **1** ESTRANGE : alienar, enajenar **2 to alienate oneself** : alejarse, distanciarse
alienation [ˌeɪliəˈneɪʃən] *n* : alienación *f*, enajenación *f*
alight [əˈlaɪt] *vi* **1** DISMOUNT : bajarse, apearse **2** LAND : posarse, aterrizar
align [əˈlaɪn] *vt* : alinear
alignment [əˈlaɪnmənt] *n* : alineación *f*, alineamiento *m*
alike[1] [əˈlaɪk] *adv* : igual, del mismo modo
alike[2] *adj* : igual, semejante, parecido
alimentary [ˌæləˈmɛntəri] *adj* **1** : alimenticio **2 alimentary canal** : tubo *m* digestivo
alimony [ˈæləˌmoːni] *n, pl* **-nies** : pensión *f* alimenticia
alive [əˈlaɪv] *adj* **1** LIVING : vivo, viviente **2** LIVELY : animado, activo **3** ACTIVE : vigente, en uso **4** AWARE : consciente ⟨alive to the danger : consciente del peligro⟩
alkali [ˈælkəˌlaɪ] *n, pl* **-lies** [-ˌlaɪz] *or* **-lis** [-ˌlaɪz] : álcali *m*
alkaline [ˈælkələn, -ˌlaɪn] *adj* : alcalino
all[1] [ˈɔl] *adv* **1** COMPLETELY : todo, completamente **2** : igual ⟨the score is 14 all : es 14 iguales, están empatados a 14⟩

3 all the better : tanto mejor **4 all the more** : aún más, todavía más
all[2] *adj* : todo ⟨all the children : todos los niños⟩ ⟨in all likelihood : con toda probabilidad, con la mayor probabilidad⟩
all[3] *pron* **1** : todo, -da ⟨they ate it all : lo comieron todo⟩ ⟨that's all : eso es todo⟩ ⟨enough for all : suficiente para todos⟩ **2 all in all** : en general **3 not at all** (*in negative constructions*) : en absoluto, para nada
Allah [ˈɑlɑ, ɑˈlɑ] *n* : Alá *m*
all–around [ˌɔləˈraʊnd] *adj* : completo, amplio
allay [əˈleɪ] *vt* **1** ALLEVIATE : aliviar, mitigar **2** CALM : aquietar, calmar
allegation [ˌælɪˈgeɪʃən] *n* : alegato *m*, acusación *f*
allege [əˈlɛʤ] *vt* **-leged; -leging 1** : alegar, afirmar **2 to be alleged** : decirse, pretenderse ⟨she is alleged to be wealthy : se dice que es adinerada⟩
alleged [əˈlɛʤd, əˈlɛʤəd] *adj* : presunto, supuesto
allegedly [əˈlɛʤədli] *adv* : supuestamente, según se alega
allegiance [əˈli:ʤən*t*s] *n* : lealtad *f*, fidelidad *f*
allegorical [ˌæləˈgɔrɪkəl] *adj* : alegórico
allegory [ˈæləˌgori] *n, pl* **-ries** : alegoría *f*
alleluia [ˌɑləˈlu:jə, ˌæ-] → **hallelujah**
allergen [ˈælərʤən] *n* : alérgeno *m*
allergic [əˈlərʤɪk] *adj* : alérgico
allergy [ˈælərʤi] *n, pl* **-gies** : alergia *f*
alleviate [əˈli:viˌeɪt] *vt* **-ated; -ating** : aliviar, mitigar, paliar
alleviation [əˌli:viˈeɪʃən] *n* : alivio *m*
alley [ˈæli] *n, pl* **-leys 1** : callejón *m* **2 bowling alley** : bolera *f*
alliance [əˈlaɪən*t*s] *n* : alianza *f*, coalición *f*
alligator [ˈæləˌgeɪt̬ər] *n* : caimán *m*
alliteration [əˌlɪt̬əˈreɪʃən] *n* : aliteración *f*
allocate [ˈæləˌkeɪt] *vt* **-cated; -cating** : asignar, adjudicar
allocation [ˌæləˈkeɪʃən] *n* : asignación *f*, reparto *m*, distribución *f*
allot [əˈlɑt] *vt* **-lotted; -lotting** : repartir, distribuir, asignar
allotment [əˈlɑtmənt] *n* : reparto *m*, asignación *f*, distribución *f*
allow [əˈlaʊ] *vt* **1** PERMIT : permitir, dejar **2** ALLOT : conceder, dar **3** ADMIT, CONCEDE : admitir, conceder — *vi* **to allow for** : tener en cuenta
allowable [əˈlaʊəbəl] *adj* **1** PERMISSIBLE : permisible, lícito **2** : deducible ⟨allowable expenditure : gasto deducible⟩
allowance [əˈlaʊən*t*s] *n* **1** : complemento *m* (para gastos, etc.), mesada *f* (para niños) **2 to make allowance(s)** : tener en cuenta, disculpar
alloy [ˈæˌlɔɪ] *n* : aleación *f*
all–purpose [ˈɔlˈpərpəs] *adj* : multiuso ⟨all-purpose flour : harina común⟩
all right[1] *adv* **1** YES : sí, por supuesto **2** WELL : bien ⟨I did all right : me fue bien⟩ **3** DEFINITELY : bien, ciertamente, sin duda ⟨he's sick all right : está bien enfermo⟩
all right[2] *adj* **1** OK : bien ⟨are you all right? : ¿estás bien?⟩ **2** SATISFACTORY : bien, bueno ⟨your work is all right : tu trabajo es bueno⟩
all–round [ˌɔlˈraʊnd] → **all–around**
allspice [ˈɔlspaɪs] *n* : pimienta *f* de Jamaica
allude [əˈlu:d] *vi* **-luded; -luding** : aludir, referirse
allure[1] [əˈlʊr] *vt* **-lured; -luring** : cautivar, atraer
allure[2] *n* : atractivo *m*, encanto *m*
allusion [əˈlu:ʒən] *n* : alusión *f*
ally[1] [əˈlaɪ, ˈæˌlaɪ] *vi* **-lied; -lying** : aliarse
ally[2] [ˈæˌlaɪ, əˈlaɪ] *n* : aliado *m*, -da *f*
almanac [ˈɔlməˌnæk, ˈæl-] *n* : almanaque *m*
almighty [ɔlˈmaɪt̬i] *adj* : omnipotente, todopoderoso
almond [ˈɑmənd, ˈɑl-, ˈæ-, ˈæl-] *n* : almendra *f*
almost [ˈɔlˌmo:st, ɔlˈmo:st] *adv* : casi, prácticamente
alms [ˈɑmz, ˈɑlmz, ˈælmz] *ns & pl* : limosna *f*, caridad *f*
aloe [ˈælo:] *n* : áloe *m*
aloft [əˈlɔft] *adv* : en alto, en el aire
alone[1] [əˈlo:n] *adv* : sólo, solamente, únicamente
alone[2] *adj* : solo ⟨they're alone in the house : están solos en la casa⟩
along[1] [əˈlɔŋ] *adv* **1** FORWARD : adelante ⟨farther along : más adelante⟩ ⟨move along! : ¡circulen, por favor!⟩ **2 to bring along** : traer **3 ~ with** : con, junto con **4 all along** : desde el principio
along[2] *prep* **1** : por, a lo largo de ⟨along the coast : a lo largo de la costa⟩ **2** : en, en el curso de, por ⟨along the way : en el curso del viaje⟩
alongside[1] [əˌlɔŋˈsaɪd] *adv* : al costado, al lado
alongside[2] *or* **alongside of** *prep* : junto a, al lado de
aloof [əˈlu:f] *adj* : distante, reservado
aloofness [əˈlu:fnəs] *n* : reserva *f*, actitud *f* distante
aloud [əˈlaʊd] *adv* : en voz alta
alpaca [ælˈpækə] *n* : alpaca *f*
alphabet [ˈælfəˌbɛt] *n* : alfabeto *m*
alphabetical [ˌælfəˈbɛt̬ɪkəl] *or* **alphabetic** [-ˈbɛt̬ɪk] *adj* : alfabético — **alphabetically** [-t̬ɪkli] *adv*
alphabetize [ˈælfəbəˌtaɪz] *vt* **-ized; -izing** : alfabetizar, poner en orden alfabético
alpine [ˈælˌpaɪn] *adj* : alpino
already [ɔlˈrɛdi] *adv* : ya
also [ˈɔlˌso:] *adv* : también, además
altar [ˈɔltər] *n* : altar *m*
alter [ˈɔltər] *vt* : alterar, cambiar, modificar

alteration [ˌɔltəˈreɪʃən] *n* : alteración *f*, cambio *m*, modificación *f*
altercation [ˌɔltərˈkeɪʃən] *n* : altercado *m*, disputa *f*
alternate[1] [ˈɔltərˌneɪt] *v* **-nated; -nating** : alternar
alternate[2] [ˈɔltərnət] *adj* **1** : alterno ⟨alternate cycles of inflation and depression : ciclos alternos de inflación y depresión⟩ **2** : uno sí y otro no ⟨he cooks on alternate days : cocina un día sí y otro no⟩
alternate[3] [ˈɔltərnət] *n* : suplente *mf*; sustituto *m*, -ta *f*
alternately [ˈɔltərnətli] *adv* : alternativamente, por turno
alternating current [ˈɔltərˌneɪt̬ɪŋ] *n* : corriente *f* alterna
alternation [ˌɔltərˈneɪʃən] *n* : alternancia *f*, rotación *f*
alternative[1] [ɔlˈtərnət̬ɪv] *adj* : alternativo
alternative[2] *n* : alternativa *f*
alternator [ˈɔltərˌneɪt̬ər] *n* : alternador *m*
although [ɔlˈðoː] *conj* : aunque, a pesar de que
altitude [ˈæltəˌtuːd, -ˌtjuːd] *n* : altitud *f*, altura *f*
alto [ˈælˌtoː] *n, pl* **-tos** : alto *mf*, contralto *mf*
altogether [ˌɔltəˈgɛðər] *adv* **1** COMPLETELY : completamente, totalmente, del todo **2** ON THE WHOLE : en suma, en general
altruism [ˈæltrʊˌɪzəm] *n* : altruismo *m*
altruistic [ˌæltrʊˈɪstɪk] *adj* : altruista — **altruistically** [-tɪkli] *adv*
alum [ˈæləm] *n* : alumbre *m*
aluminum [əˈluːmənəm] *n* : aluminio *m*
alumna [əˈlʌmnə] *n, pl* **-nae** [-ˌniː] : exalumna *f*
alumnus [əˈlʌmnəs] *n, pl* **-ni** [-ˌnaɪ] : exalumno *m*
always [ˈɔlwiz, -ˌweɪz] *adv* **1** INVARIABLY : siempre, invariablemente **2** FOREVER : para siempre
am → **be**
amalgam [əˈmælgəm] *n* : amalgama *f*
amalgamate [əˈmælgəˌmeɪt] *vt* **-ated; -ating** : amalgamar, unir, fusionar
amalgamation [əˌmælgəˈmeɪʃən] *n* : fusión *f*, unión *f*
amaryllis [ˌæməˈrɪləs] *n* : amarilis *f*
amass [əˈmæs] *vt* : amasar, acumular
amateur [ˈæmətʃər, -tər, -ˌtʊr, -ˌtjʊr] *n* **1** : amateur *mf* **2** BEGINNER : principiante *mf*; aficionado *m*, -da *f*
amateurish [ˈæməˌtʃərɪʃ, -ˌtər-, -ˌtʊr-, -ˌtjʊr-] *adj* : amateur, inexperto
amaze [əˈmeɪz] *vt* **amazed; amazing** : asombrar, maravillar, pasmar
amazement [əˈmeɪzmənt] *n* : asombro *m*, sorpresa *f*
amazing [əˈmeɪzɪŋ] *adj* : asombroso, sorprendente — **amazingly** [-zɪŋli] *adv*
Amazon [ˈæməˌzɑn] *n* : amazona *f* (en mitología)
Amazonian [ˌæməˈzoːniən] *adj* : amazónico
ambassador [æmˈbæsədər] *n* : embajador *m*, -dora *f*
amber [ˈæmbər] *n* : ámbar *m*
ambergris [ˈæmbərˌgrɪs, -ˌgriːs] *n* : ámbar *m* gris
ambidextrous [ˌæmbɪˈdɛkstrəs] *adj* : ambidextro — **ambidextrously** *adv*
ambience *or* **ambiance** [ˈæmbiənts, ˈɑmbiˌɑnts] *n* : ambiente *m*, atmósfera *f*
ambiguity [ˌæmbəˈgjuːət̬i] *n, pl* **-ties** : ambigüedad *f*
ambiguous [æmˈbɪgjʊəs] *adj* : ambiguo
ambition [æmˈbɪʃən] *n* : ambición *f*
ambitious [æmˈbɪʃəs] *adj* : ambicioso — **ambitiously** *adv*
ambivalence [æmˈbɪvələnts] *n* : ambivalencia *f*
ambivalent [æmˈbɪvələnt] *adj* : ambivalente
amble[1] [ˈæmbəl] *vi* **-bled; -bling** : ir tranquilamente, pasearse despreocupadamente
amble[2] *n* : paseo *m* tranquilo
ambulance [ˈæmbjələnts] *n* : ambulancia *f*
ambush[1] [ˈæmˌbʊʃ] *vt* : emboscar
ambush[2] *n* : emboscada *f*, celada *f*
ameliorate [əˈmiːljəˌreɪt] *v* **-rated; -rating** IMPROVE : mejorar
amelioration [əˌmiːljəˈreɪʃən] *n* : mejora *f*
amen [ˈeɪˈmɛn, ˈɑ-] *interj* : amén
amenable [əˈmiːnəbəl, -ˈmɛ-] *adj* RESPONSIVE : susceptible, receptivo, sensible
amend [əˈmɛnd] *vt* **1** IMPROVE : mejorar, enmendar **2** CORRECT : enmendar, corregir
amendment [əˈmɛndmənt] *n* : enmienda *f*
amends [əˈmɛndz] *ns & pl* : compensación *f*, reparación *f*, desagravio *m*
amenity [əˈmɛnət̬i, -ˈmiː-] *n, pl* **-ties 1** PLEASANTNESS : lo agradable, amenidad *f* **2 amenities** *npl* : servicios *mpl*, comodidades *fpl*
American [əˈmɛrɪkən] *n* : americano *m*, -na *f* — **American** *adj*
American Indian *n* : indio *m* (americano), india *f* (americana)
amethyst [ˈæməθəst] *n* : amatista *f*
amiability [ˌeɪmiːəˈbɪlət̬i] *n* : amabilidad *f*, afabilidad *f*
amiable [ˈeɪmiːəbəl] *adj* : amable, afable — **amiably** [-bli] *adv*
amicable [ˈæmɪkəbəl] *adj* : amigable, amistoso, cordial — **amicably** [-bli] *adv*
amid [əˈmɪd] *or* **amidst** [əˈmɪdst] *prep* : en medio de, entre
amino acid [əˈmiːno] *n* : aminoácido *m*
amiss[1] [əˈmɪs] *adv* : mal, fuera de lugar ⟨to take amiss : tomar a mal, llevar a mal⟩
amiss[2] *adj* **1** WRONG : malo, inoportuno **2 there's something amiss** : pasa algo, algo anda mal
ammeter [ˈæˌmiːt̬ər] *n* : amperímetro *m*

ammonia [ə'mo:njə] *n* : amoníaco *m*
ammunition [ˌæmjə'nɪʃən] *n* **1** : municiones *fpl* **2** ARGUMENTS : argumentos *mpl*
amnesia [æm'ni:ʒə] *n* : amnesia *f*
amnesty ['æmnəsti] *n, pl* **-ties** : amnistía *f*
amoeba [ə'mi:bə] *n, pl* **-bas** *or* **-bae** [-ˌbi:] : ameba *f*
amoebic [ə'mi:bɪk] *adj* : amébico
amok [ə'mʌk, -'mɑk] *adv* **to run amok** : correr a ciegas, enloquecerse, desbocarse (dícese de la economía, etc.)
among [ə'mʌŋ] *prep* : entre
amoral [eɪ'mɔrəl] *adj* : amoral
amorous ['æmərəs] *adj* **1** PASSIONATE : enamoradizo, apasionado **2** ENAMORED : enamorado **3** LOVING : amoroso, cariñoso
amorously ['æmərəsli] *adv* : con cariño
amorphous [ə'mɔrfəs] *adj* : amorfo, informe
amortize ['æmərˌtaɪz, ə'mɔr-] *vt* **-tized; -tizing** : amortizar
amount[1] [ə'maʊnt] *vi* **to amount to 1** : equivaler a, significar ⟨that amounts to treason : eso equivale a la traición⟩ **2** : ascender (a) ⟨my debts amount to $2000 : mis deudas ascienden a $2000⟩
amount[2] *n* : cantidad *f*, suma *f*
ampere ['æmˌpɪr] *n* : amperio *m*
ampersand ['æmpərˌsænd] *n* : el signo &
amphetamine [æm'fɛt̬əˌmi:n] *n* : anfetamina *f*
amphibian [æm'fɪbiən] *n* : anfibio *m*
amphibious [æm'fɪbiəs] *adj* : anfibio
amphitheater ['æmfəˌθi:ət̬ər] *n* : anfiteatro *m*
ample ['æmpəl] *adj* **-pler; -plest 1** LARGE, SPACIOUS : amplio, extenso, grande **2** ABUNDANT : abundante, generoso
amplifier ['æmpləˌfaɪər] *n* : amplificador *m*
amplify ['æmpləˌfaɪ] *vt* **-fied; -fying** : amplificar
amply ['æmpli] *adv* : ampliamente, abundantemente, suficientemente
amputate ['æmpjəˌteɪt] *vt* **-tated; -tating** : amputar
amputation [ˌæmpjə'teɪʃən] *n* : amputación *f*
amuck [ə'mʌk] → **amok**
amulet ['æmjələt] *n* : amuleto *m*, talismán *m*
amuse [ə'mju:z] *vt* **amused; amusing 1** ENTERTAIN : entretener, distraer **2** : hacer reír, divertir ⟨the joke amused us : la broma nos hizo reír⟩
amusement [ə'mju:zmənt] *n* **1** ENTERTAINMENT : diversión *f*, entretenimiento *m*, pasatiempo *m* **2** LAUGHTER : risa *f*
an *art* → **a[2]**
anachronism [ə'nækrəˌnɪzəm] *n* : anacronismo *m*
anachronistic [əˌnækrə'nɪstɪk] *adj* : anacrónico
anaconda [ˌænə'kɑndə] *n* : anaconda *f*
anagram ['ænəˌgræm] *n* : anagrama *m*
anal ['eɪnəl] *adj* : anal
analgesic [ˌænəl'ʤi:zɪk, -sɪk] *n* : analgésico *m*
analog ['ænəˌlɔg] *adj* : analógico
analogical [ˌænə'lɑʤɪkəl] *adj* : analógico — **analogically** [-kli] *adv*
analogous [ə'næləgəs] *adj* : análogo
analogy [ə'næləʤi] *n, pl* **-gies** : analogía *f*
analysis [ə'næləsəs] *n, pl* **-yses** [-ˌsi:z] **1** : análisis *m* **2** PSYCHOANALYSIS : psicoanálisis *m*
analyst ['ænəlɪst] *n* **1** : analista *mf* **2** PSYCHOANALYST : psicoanalista *mf*
analytic [ˌænə'lɪt̬ɪk] *or* **analytical** [-t̬ɪkəl] *adj* : analítico — **analytically** [-t̬ɪkli] *adv*
analyze ['ænəˌlaɪz] *vt* **-lyzed; -lyzing** : analizar
anarchic [æ'nɑrkɪk] *adj* : anárquico — **anarchically** [-kɪkli] *adv*
anarchism ['ænərˌkɪzəm, -nɑr-] *n* : anarquismo *m*
anarchist ['ænərkɪst, -nɑr-] *n* : anarquista *mf*
anarchy ['ænərki, -nɑr-] *n* : anarquía *f*
anathema [ə'næθəmə] *n* : anatema *m*
anatomic [ˌænə'tɑmɪk] *or* **anatomical** [-mɪkəl] *adj* : anatómico — **anatomically** [-mɪkli] *adv*
anatomy [ə'næt̬əmi] *n, pl* **-mies** : anatomía *f*
ancestor ['ænˌsɛstər] *n* : antepasado *m*, -da *f*; antecesor *m*, -sora *f*
ancestral [æn'sɛstrəl] *adj* : ancestral, de los antepasados
ancestry ['ænˌsɛstri] *n* **1** DESCENT : ascendencia *f*, linaje *m*, abolengo *m* **2** ANCESTORS : antepasados *mpl*, -das *fpl*
anchor[1] ['æŋkər] *vt* **1** MOOR : anclar, fondear **2** FASTEN : sujetar, asegurar, fijar
anchor[2] *n* **1** : ancla *f* **2** : presentador *m*, -dora *f* (en televisión)
anchorage ['æŋkərɪʤ] *n* : anclaje *m*
anchovy ['ænˌʧo:vi, æn'ʧo:-] *n, pl* **-vies** *or* **-vy** : anchoa *f*
ancient ['eɪntʃənt] *adj* **1** : antiguo ⟨ancient history : historia antigua⟩ **2** OLD : viejo
ancients ['eɪntʃənts] *npl* : los antiguos *mpl*
and ['ænd] *conj* **1** : y (**e** *before words beginning with i- or hi-*) **2** : con ⟨ham and eggs : huevos con jamón⟩ **3** : a ⟨go and see : ve a ver⟩ **4** : de ⟨try and finish it soon : trata de terminarlo pronto⟩
Andalusian [ˌændə'lu:ʒən] *n* : andaluz *m*, -luza *f* — **Andalusian** *adj*
Andean ['ændiən] *adj* : andino
andiron ['ænˌdaɪərn] *n* : morillo *m*
Andorran [æn'dɔrən] *n* : andorrano *m*, -na *f* — **Andorran** *adj*
androgynous [æn'drɑʤənəs] *adj* : andrógino
anecdotal [ˌænɪk'do:t̬əl] *adj* : anecdótico

anecdote [ˈænɪkˌdo:t] *n* : anécdota *f*
anemia [əˈni:miə] *n* : anemia *f*
anemic [əˈni:mɪk] *adj* : anémico
anemone [əˈnɛməni] *n* : anémona *f*
anesthesia [ˌænəsˈθi:ʒə] *n* : anestesia *f*
anesthetic[1] [ˌænəsˈθɛṭɪk] *adj* : anestésico
anesthetic[2] *n* : anestésico *m*
anesthetist [əˈnɛsθəṭɪst] *n* : anestesista *mf*
anesthetize [əˈnɛsθəˌtaɪz] *vt* **-tize; -tized** : anestesiar
aneurysm [ˈænjəˌrɪzəm] *n* : aneurisma *mf*
anew [əˈnu:, -ˈnju:] *adv* : de nuevo, otra vez, nuevamente
angel [ˈeɪnʤəl] *n* : ángel *m*
angelic [ænˈʤɛlɪk] *or* **angelical** [-lɪkəl] *adj* : angélico, angelical — **angelically** [-lɪkli] *adv*
anger[1] [ˈæŋgər] *vt* : enojar, enfadar
anger[2] *n* : enojo *m*, enfado *m*, ira *f*, cólera *f*, rabia *f*
angina [ænˈʤaɪnə] *n* : angina *f*
angle[1] [ˈæŋgəl] *v* **angled; angling** *vt* DIRECT, SLANT : orientar, dirigir — *vi* FISH : pescar (con caña)
angle[2] *n* **1** : ángulo *m* **2** POINT OF VIEW : perspectiva *f*, punto *m* de vista
angler [ˈæŋglər] *n* : pescador *m*, -dora *f*
Anglican [ˈæŋglɪkən] *n* : anglicano *m*, -na *f* — **Anglican** *adj*
Anglo–Saxon[1] [ˌæŋgloˈsæksən] *adj* : anglosajón
Anglo–Saxon[2] *n* : anglosajón *m*, -jona *f*
Angolan [æŋˈgo:lən, æn-] *n* : angoleño *m*, -ña *f* — **Angolan** *adj*
angora [æŋˈgorə, æn-] *n* : angora *f*
angrily [ˈæŋgrəli] *adv* : furiosamente, con ira
angry [ˈæŋgri] *adj* **-grier; -est** : enojado, enfadado, furioso
anguish [ˈæŋgwɪʃ] *n* : angustia *f*, congoja *f*
anguished [ˈæŋgwɪʃt] *adj* : angustiado, acongojado
angular [ˈæŋgjələr] *adj* : angular (dícese de las formas), anguloso (dícese de las caras)
animal [ˈænəməl] *n* **1** : animal *m* **2** BRUTE : bruto *m*, -ta *f*
animate[1] [ˈænəˌmeɪt] *vt* **-mated; -mating** : animar
animate[2] [ˈænəmət] *adj* : animado
animated [ˈænəˌmeɪṭəd] *adj* **1** LIVELY : animado, vivo, vivaz **2 animated cartoon** : dibujos *mpl* animados
animation [ˌænəˈmeɪʃən] *n* : animación *f*
animosity [ˌænəˈmɑsəṭi] *n, pl* **-ties** : animosidad *f*, animadversión *f*
anise [ˈænəs] *n* : anís *m*
aniseed [ˈænəsˌsi:d] *n* : anís *m*, semilla *f* de anís
ankle [ˈæŋkəl] *n* : tobillo *m*
anklebone [ˈæŋkəlˌbo:n] *n* : taba *f*
annals [ˈænəlz] *npl* : anales *mpl*, crónica *f*
anneal [əˈni:l] *vt* **1** TEMPER : templar **2** STRENGTHEN : fortalecer
annex[1] [əˈnɛks, ˈæˌnɛks] *vt* : anexar
annex[2] [ˈæˌnɛks, -nɪks] *n* : anexo *m*, anejo *m*
annexation [ˌæˌnɛkˈseɪʃən] *n* : anexión *f*
annihilate [əˈnaɪəˌleɪt] *vt* **-lated; -lating** : aniquilar
annihilation [əˌnaɪəˈleɪʃən] *n* : aniquilación *f*, aniquilamiento *m*
anniversary [ˌænəˈvərsəri] *n, pl* **-ries** : aniversario *m*
annotate [ˈænəˌteɪt] *vt* **-tated; -tating** : anotar
annotation [ˌænəˈteɪʃən] *n* : anotación *f*
announce [əˈnaʊnts] *vt* **-nounced; -nouncing** : anunciar
announcement [əˈnaʊntsmənt] *n* : anuncio *m*
announcer [əˈnaʊntsər] *n* : anunciador *m*, -dora *f*; comentarista *mf*; locutor *m*, -tora *f*
annoy [əˈnɔɪ] *vt* : molestar, fastidiar, irritar
annoyance [əˈnɔɪənts] *n* **1** IRRITATION : irritación *f*, fastidio *m* **2** NUISANCE : molestia *f*, fastidio *m*
annoying [əˈnɔɪɪŋ] *adj* : molesto, fastidioso, engorroso — **annoyingly** [-ɪŋli] *adv*
annual[1] [ˈænjʊəl] *adj* : anual — **annually** *adv*
annual[2] *n* **1** : planta *f* anual **2** YEARBOOK : anuario *m*
annuity [əˈnu:əṭi] *n, pl* **-ties** : anualidad *f*
annul [əˈnʌl] *vt* **anulled; anulling** : anular, invalidar
annulment [əˈnʌlmənt] *n* : anulación *f*
anode [ˈæˌno:d] *n* : ánodo
anoint [əˈnɔɪnt] *vt* : ungir
anomalous [əˈnɑmələs] *adj* : anómalo
anomaly [əˈnɑməli] *n, pl* **-lies** : anomalía *f*
anonymity [ˌænəˈnɪməṭi] *n* : anonimato *m*
anonymous [əˈnɑnəməs] *adj* : anónimo — **anonymously** *adv*
anorexia [ˌænəˈrɛksiə] *n* : anorexia *f*
anorexic [ˌænəˈrɛksɪk] *adj* : anoréxico
another[1] [əˈnʌðər] *adj* : otro
another[2] *pron* : otro, otra
answer[1] [ˈæntsər] *vt* **1** : contestar (a), responder (a) ⟨to answer the telephone : contestar el teléfono⟩ **2** FULFILL : satisfacer **3 to answer for** : ser responsable de, pagar por ⟨she'll answer for that mistake : pagará por ese error⟩ — *vi* : contestar, responder
answer[2] *n* **1** REPLY : respuesta *f*, contestación *f* **2** SOLUTION : solución *f*
answerable [ˈæntsərəbəl] *adj* : responsable
ant [ˈænt] *n* : hormiga *f*
antacid [æntˈæsəd, ˈænˌtæ-] *n* : antiácido *m*
antagonism [ænˈtægəˌnɪzəm] *n* : antagonismo *m*, hostilidad *f*
antagonist [ænˈtægənɪst] *n* : antagonista *mf*

antagonistic [æn,tægə'nɪstɪk] *adj* : antagonista, hostil
antagonize [æn'tægə,naɪz] *vt* **-nized; -nizing** : antagonizar
antarctic [ænt'ɑrktɪk, -'ɑrṭɪk] *adj* : antártico
antarctic circle *n* : círculo *m* antártico
anteater ['ænt,i:ṭər] *n* : oso *m* hormiguero
antebellum [,æntɪ'bɛləm] *adj* : prebélico
antecedent[1] [,æntə'si:dənt] *adj* : antecedente, precedente
antecedent[2] *n* : antecedente *mf*; precursor *m*, -sora *f*
antelope ['æntəl,o:p] *n, pl* **-lope** *or* **-lopes** : antílope *m*
antenna [æn'tɛnə] *n, pl* **-nae** [-,ni:, -,naɪ] *or* **-nas** : antena *f*
anterior [æn'tɪriər] *adj* : anterior
anthem ['ænθəm] *n* : himno *m* ⟨national anthem : himno nacional⟩
anther ['ænθər] *n* : antera *f*
anthill ['ænt,hɪl] *n* : hormiguero *m*
anthology [æn'θɑləʤi] *n, pl* **-gies** : antología *f*
anthracite ['ænθrə,saɪt] *n* : antracita *f*
anthropoid[1] ['ænθrə,pɔɪd] *adj* : antropoide
anthropoid[2] *n* : antropoide *mf*
anthropological [,ænθrəpə'lɑʤɪkəl] *adj* : antropológico
anthropologist [,ænθrə'pɑləʤɪst] *n* : antropólogo *m*, -ga *f*
anthropology [,ænθrə'pɑləʤi] *n* : antropología *f*
antiabortion [,æntiə'bɔrʃən, ,æntaɪ-] *adj* : antiaborto
antiaircraft [,ænti'ær,kræft, ,æntaɪ-] *adj* : antiaéreo
anti–American [,æntiə'mɛrɪkən, ,æntaɪ-] *adj* : antiamericano
antibiotic[1] [,æntibaɪ'ɑṭɪk, ,æntaɪ-, -bi-] *adj* : antibiótico
antibiotic[2] *n* : antibiótico *m*
antibody ['ænti,bɑdi] *n, pl* **-bodies** : anticuerpo *m*
antic[1] ['æntɪk] *adj* : extravagante, juguetón
antic[2] *n* : payasada *f*, travesura *f*
anticipate [æn'tɪsə,peɪt] *vt* **-pated; -pating 1** FORESEE : anticipar, prever **2** EXPECT : esperar, contar con
anticipation [æn,tɪsə'peɪʃən] *n* **1** FORESIGHT : previsión *f* **2** EXPECTATION : anticipación *f*, expectación *f*, esperanza *f*
anticipatory [æn'tɪsəpə,tori] *adj* : en anticipación, en previsión
anticlimactic [,æntiklaɪ'mæktɪk] *adj* : anticlimático, decepcionante
anticlimax [,ænti'klaɪ,mæks] *n* : anticlímax *m*
anticommunism [,ænti'kɑmjə,nɪzəm, ,æntaɪ-] *n* : anticomunismo *m*
anticommunist[1] [,ænti'kɑmjənɪst, ,æntaɪ-] *adj* : anticomunista
anticommunist[2] *n* : anticomunista *mf*
antidemocratic [,ænti,dɛmə'kræṭɪk, ,æntaɪ-] *adj* : antidemocrático
antidepressant [,æntidi'prɛsənt] *n* : antidepresivo *m* — **antidepressant** *adj*
antidote ['æntɪ,do:t] *n* : antídoto *m*
antidrug [,ænti'drʌg, ,æntaɪ-; 'ænti ,drʌg, 'æntaɪ-] *adj* : antidrogas
antifascist [,ænti'fæʃɪst, ,æntaɪ-] *adj* : antifascista
antifeminist [,ænti'fɛmənɪst, ,æntaɪ-] *adj* : antifeminista
antifreeze ['ænti,fri:z] *n* : anticongelante *m*
antigen ['æntɪʤən, -,ʤɛn] *n* : antígeno *m*
antihistamine [,ænti'hɪstə,mi:n, -mən] *n* : antihistamínico *m*
anti–imperialism [,æntiɪm'pɪriə,lɪzəm, ,æntaɪ-] *n* : antiimperialismo *m*
anti–imperialist [,æntiɪm'pɪriəlɪst, ,æntaɪ-] *adj* : antiimperialista
anti–inflammatory [,ætiɪn'flæmətori] *adj* : antiinflamatorio
anti–inflationary [,æntiɪn'fleɪʃə,nɛri, ,æntaɪ-] *adj* : antiinflacionario
antimony ['æntə,mo:ni] *n* : antimonio *m*
antipathy [æn'tɪpəθi] *n, pl* **-thies** : antipatía *f*, aversión *f*
antiperspirant [,ænti'pərspərənt, ,æntaɪ-] *n* : antitranspirante *m*
antiquarian[1] [,æntə'kwɛriən] *adj* : antiguo, anticuario ⟨an antiquarian book : un libro antiguo⟩
antiquarian[2] *n* : anticuario *m*, -ria *f*
antiquary ['æntə,kwɛri] *n* → **antiquarian**[2]
antiquated ['æntə,kweɪṭəd] *adj* : anticuado, pasado de moda
antique[1] [æn'ti:k] *adj* **1** OLD : antiguo, de época ⟨an antique mirror : un espejo antiguo⟩ **2** OLD-FASHIONED : anticuado, pasado de moda
antique[2] *n* : antigüedad *f*
antiquity [æn'tɪkwəṭi] *n, pl* **-ties** : antigüedad
antirevolutionary [,ænti,rɛvə'lu:ʃə,nɛri, ,æntaɪ-] *adj* : antirrevolucionario
anti–Semitic [,æntisə'mɪṭɪk, ,æntaɪ-] *adj* : antisemita
anti–Semitism [,ænti'sɛmə,tɪzəm, ,æntaɪ-] *n* : antisemitismo *m*
antiseptic[1] [,æntə'sɛptɪk] *adj* : antiséptico — **antiseptically** [-tɪkli] *adv*
antiseptic[2] *n* : antiséptico *m*
antismoking [,ænti'smo:kɪŋ, ,æntaɪ-] *adj* : antitabaco
antisocial [,ænti'so:ʃəl, ,æntaɪ-] *adj* **1** : antisocial **2** UNSOCIABLE : poco sociable
antitheft [,ænti'θɛft, ,æntaɪ-] *adj* : antirrobo
antithesis [æn'tɪθəsɪs] *n, pl* **-eses** [-,si:z] : antítesis *f*
antitoxin [,ænti'tɑksən, ,æntaɪ-] *n* : antitoxina *f*
antitrust [,ænti'trʌst, ,æntaɪ-] *adj* : antimonopolista
antler ['æntlər] *n* : asta *f*, cuerno *m*

antonym ['æntə,nɪm] *n* : antónimo *m*
anus ['eɪnəs] *n* : ano *m*
anvil ['ænvəl, -vɪl] *n* : yunque *m*
anxiety [æŋ*k*'zaɪət̬i] *n, pl* **-eties** **1** UNEASINESS : inquietud *f*, preocupación *f*, ansiedad *f* **2** APPREHENSION : ansiedad *f*, angustia *f*
anxious ['æŋ*k*ʃəs] *adj* **1** WORRIED : inquieto, preocupado, ansioso **2** WORRISOME : preocupante, inquietante **3** EAGER : ansioso, deseoso
anxiously ['æŋ*k*ʃəsli] *adv* : con inquietud, con ansiedad
any[1] ['ɛni] *adv* **1** : algo ⟨is it any better? : ¿está (algo) mejor?⟩ **2** : para nada ⟨it is not any good : no sirve para nada⟩
any[2] *adj* **1** : alguno ⟨is there any doubt? : ¿hay alguna duda?⟩ ⟨call me if you have any questions : llámeme si tiene alguna pregunta⟩ **2** : cualquier ⟨I can answer any question : puedo responder a cualquier pregunta⟩ **3** : todo ⟨in any case : en todo caso⟩ **4** : ningún ⟨he would not accept it under any circumstances : no lo aceptaría bajo ninguna circunstancia⟩
any[3] *pron* **1** : alguno *m*, -na *f* ⟨are there any left? : ¿queda alguno?⟩ **2** : ninguno *m*, -na *f* ⟨I don't want any : no quiero ninguno⟩
anybody ['ɛni,bʌdi, -,bɑ-] → **anyone**
anyhow ['ɛni,haʊ] *adv* **1** HAPHAZARDLY : de cualquier manera **2** IN ANY CASE : de todos modos, en todo caso
anymore [,ɛni'mor] *adv* **1** : ya, ya más ⟨he doesn't dance anymore : ya no baila más⟩ **2** : todavía ⟨do they sing anymore? : ¿cantan todavía?⟩
anyone ['ɛni,wʌn] *pron* **1** : alguien ⟨is anyone here? : ¿hay alguien aquí?⟩ ⟨if anyone wants to come : si alguno quiere venir⟩ **2** : cualquiera ⟨anyone can play : cualquiera puede jugar⟩ **3** : nadie ⟨I don't want anyone here : no quiero a nadie aquí⟩
anyplace ['ɛni,pleɪs] → **anywhere**
anything ['ɛni,θɪŋ] *pron* **1** : algo, alguna cosa ⟨do you want anything? : ¿quieres algo?, ¿quieres alguna cosa?⟩ **2** : nada ⟨hardly anything : casi nada⟩ **3** : cualquier cosa ⟨I eat anything : como de todo⟩
anytime ['ɛni,taɪm] *adv* : en cualquier momento, a cualquier hora, cuando sea
anyway ['ɛni,weɪ] → **anyhow**
anywhere ['ɛni,*h*wɛr] *adv* **1** : en algún sitio, en alguna parte ⟨do you see it anywhere? : ¿lo ves en alguna parte?⟩ **2** : en ningún sitio, por ninguna parte ⟨I can't find it anywhere : no puedo encontrarlo por ninguna parte⟩ **3** : en cualquier parte, dondequiera, donde sea ⟨put it anywhere : ponlo dondequiera⟩
aorta [eɪ'ɔrt̬ə] *n, pl* **-tas** *or* **-tae** [-t̬i, -t̬aɪ] : aorta *f*
Apache [ə'pætʃi] *n, pl* **Apache** *or* **Apaches** : apache *mf*
apart [ə'pɑrt] *adv* **1** SEPARATELY : aparte, separadamente **2** ASIDE : aparte, a un lado **3 to fall apart** : deshacerse, hacerse pedazos **4 to take apart** : desmontar, desmantelar
apartheid [ə'pɑr,teɪt, -,taɪt] *n* : apartheid *m*
apartment [ə'pɑrtmənt] *n* : apartamento *m*, departamento *m*, piso *m Spain*
apathetic [,æpə'θɛt̬ɪk] *adj* : apático, indiferente — **apathetically** [-t̬ɪkli] *adv*
apathy ['æpəθi] *n* : apatía *f*, indiferencia *f*
ape[1] ['eɪp] *vt* **aped; aping** : imitar, remedar
ape[2] *n* : simio *m*; mono *m*, -na *f*
aperitif [ə,pɛrə'ti:f] *n* : aperitivo *m*
aperture ['æpərtʃər, -,tʃʊr] *n* : abertura *f*, rendija *f*, apertura *f* (en fotografía)
apex ['eɪ,pɛks] *n, pl* **apexes** *or* **apices** ['eɪpə,si:z, 'æ-] : ápice *m*, cúspide *f*, cima *f*
aphid ['eɪfɪd, 'æ-] *n* : áfido *m*
aphorism ['æfə,rɪzəm] *n* : aforismo *m*
aphrodisiac [,æfrə'di:zi,æk, -'dɪ-] *n* : afrodisíaco *m*
apiary ['eɪpi,ɛri] *n, pl* **-aries** : apiario *m*, colmenar *m*
apiece [ə'pi:s] *adv* : cada uno
aplenty [ə'plɛnti] *adj* : en abundancia
aplomb [ə'plɑm, -'plʌm] *n* : aplomo *m*
apocalypse [ə'pɑkə,lɪps] *n* : apocalipsis *m*
apocalyptic [ə,pɑkə'lɪptɪk] *adj* : apocalíptico
apocrypha [ə'pɑkrəfə] *n* : textos *mpl* apócrifos
apocryphal [ə'pɑkrəfəl] *adj* : apócrifo
apologetic [ə,pɑlə'dʒɛt̬ɪk] *adj* : lleno de disculpas
apologetically [ə,pɑlə'dʒɛt̬ɪkli] *adv* : disculpándose, con aire de disculpas
apologize [ə'pɑlə,dʒaɪz] *vi* **-gized; -gizing** : disculparse, pedir perdón
apology [ə'pɑlədʒi] *n, pl* **-gies** : disculpa *f*, excusa *f*
apoplectic [,æpə'plɛktɪk] *adj* : apoplético
apoplexy ['æpə,plɛksi] *n* : apoplejía *f*
apostasy [ə'pɑstəsi] *n, pl* **-sies** : apostasía *f*
apostate [ə'pɑs,teɪt] *n* : apóstata *mf*
apostle [ə'pɑsəl] *n* : apóstol *m*
apostolic [,æpə'stɑlɪk] *adj* : apostólico
apostrophe [ə'pɑstrə,fi:] *n* : apóstrofo *m* (ortográfico)
apothecary [ə'pɑθə,kɛri] *n, pl* **-caries** : boticario *m*, -ria *f*
appall [ə'pɔl] *vt* : consternar, horrorizar
apparatus [,æpə'ræt̬əs, -'reɪ-] *n, pl* **-tuses** *or* **-tus** : aparato *m*, equipo *m*
apparel [ə'pærəl] *n* : atavío *m*, ropa *f*
apparent [ə'pærənt] *adj* **1** VISIBLE : visible **2** OBVIOUS : claro, evidente, manifiesto **3** SEEMING : aparente, ostensible

apparently [ə'pærəntli] *adv* : aparentemente, al parecer
apparition [ˌæpə'rɪʃən] *n* : aparición *f*, visión *f*
appeal[1] [ə'pi:l] *vt* : apelar ⟨to appeal a decision : apelar contra una decisión⟩ — *vi* **1 to appeal for** : pedir, solicitar **2 to appeal to** : atraer a ⟨that doesn't appeal to me : eso no me atrae⟩
appeal[2] *n* **1** : apelación *f* (en derecho) **2** PLEA : ruego *m*, súplica *f* **3** ATTRACTION : atracción *f*, atractivo *m*, interés *m*
appear [ə'pɪr] *vi* **1** : aparecer, aparecerse, presentarse ⟨he suddenly appeared : apareció de repente⟩ **2** COME OUT : aparecer, salir, publicarse **3** : comparecer (ante el tribunal), actuar (en el teatro) **4** SEEM : parecer
appearance [ə'pɪrənts] *n* **1** APPEARING : aparición *f*, presentación *f*, comparecencia *f* (ante un tribunal), publicación *f* (de un libro) **2** LOOK : apariencia *f*, aspecto *m*
appease [ə'pi:z] *vt* **-peased; -peasing 1** CALM, PACIFY : aplacar, apaciguar, sosegar **2** SATISFY : satisfacer, mitigar
appeasement [ə'pi:zmənt] *n* : aplacamiento *m*, apaciguamiento *m*
append [ə'pɛnd] *vt* : agregar, añadir, adjuntar
appendage [ə'pɛndɪʤ] *n* **1** ADDITION : apéndice *m*, añadidura *f* **2** LIMB : miembro *m*, extremidad *f*
appendectomy [ˌæpən'dɛktəmi] *n, pl* **-mies** : apendicectomía *f*
appendicitis [əˌpɛndə'saɪt̬əs] *n* : apendicitis *f*
appendix [ə'pɛndɪks] *n, pl* **-dixes** *or* **-dices** [-dəˌsi:z] : apéndice *m*
appetite ['æpəˌtaɪt] *n* **1** CRAVING : apetito *m*, deseo *m*, ganas *fpl* **2** PREFERENCE : gusto *m*, preferencia *f* ⟨the cultural appetites of today : los gustos culturales de hoy⟩
appetizer ['æpəˌtaɪzər] *n* : aperitivo *m*, entremés *m*, botana *f Mex*, tapa *f Spain*
appetizing ['æpəˌtaɪzɪŋ] *adj* : apetecible, apetitoso — **appetizingly** [-zɪŋli] *adv*
applaud [ə'plɔd] *v* : aplaudir
applause [ə'plɔz] *n* : aplauso *m*
apple ['æpəl] *n* : manzana *f*
appliance [ə'plaɪənts] *n* **1** : aparato *m* **2 household appliance** : electrodoméstico *m*, aparato *m* electrodoméstico
applicability [ˌæplɪkə'bɪləti, əˌplɪkə-] *n* : aplicabilidad *f*
applicable ['æplɪkəbəl, ə'plɪkə-] *adj* : aplicable, pertinente
applicant ['æplɪkənt] *n* : solicitante *mf*, aspirante *mf*, postulante *mf*; candidato *m*, -ta *f*
application [ˌæplə'keɪʃən] *n* **1** USE : aplicación *f*, empleo *m*, uso *m* **2** DILIGENCE : aplicación *f*, diligencia *f*, dedicación *f* **3** REQUEST : solicitud *f*, petición *f*, demanda *f*
applicator ['æpləˌkeɪt̬ər] *n* : aplicador *m*
appliqué[1] [ˌæplə'keɪ] *vt* : decorar con apliques
appliqué[2] *n* : aplique *m*
apply [ə'plaɪ] *v* **-plied; -plying** *vt* **1** : aplicar (una sustancia, los frenos, el conocimiento) **2 to apply oneself** : dedicarse, aplicarse — *vi* **1** : aplicarse, referirse ⟨the rules apply to everyone : las reglas se aplican a todos⟩ **2 to apply for** : solicitar, pedir
appoint [ə'pɔɪnt] *vt* **1** NAME : nombrar, designar **2** FIX, SET : fijar, señalar, designar ⟨to appoint a date : fijar una fecha⟩ **3** EQUIP : equipar ⟨a well-appointed office : una oficina bien equipada⟩
appointee [əˌpɔɪn'ti:, ˌæ-] *n* : persona *f* designada
appointment [ə'pɔɪntmənt] *n* **1** APPOINTING : nombramiento *m*, designación *f* **2** ENGAGEMENT : cita *f*, hora *f* **3** POST : puesto *m*
apportion [ə'porʃən] *vt* : distribuir, repartir
apportionment [ə'porʃənmənt] *n* : distribución *f*, repartición *f*, reparto *m*
apposite ['æpəzət] *adj* : apropiado, oportuno, pertinente — **appositely** *adv*
appraisal [ə'preɪzəl] *n* : evaluación *f*, valoración *f*, tasación *f*, apreciación *f*
appraise [ə'preɪz] *vt* **-praised; -praising** : evaluar, valorar, tasar, apreciar
appraiser [ə'preɪzər] *n* : tasador *m*, -dora *f*
appreciable [ə'pri:ʃəbəl, -'prɪʃiə-] *adj* : apreciable, sensible, considerable — **appreciably** [-bli] *adv*
appreciate [ə'pri:ʃiˌeɪt, -'prɪ-] *v* **-ated; -ating** *vt* **1** VALUE : apreciar, valorar **2** : agradecer ⟨we appreciate his frankness : agradecemos su franqueza⟩ **3** UNDERSTAND : darse cuenta de, entender — *vi* : apreciarse, valorizarse
appreciation [əˌpri:ʃi'eɪʃən, -ˌprɪ-] *n* **1** GRATITUDE : agradecimiento *m*, reconocimiento *m* **2** VALUING : apreciación *f*, valoración *f*, estimación *f* ⟨art appreciation : apreciación artística⟩ **3** UNDERSTANDING : comprensión *f*, entendimiento *m*
appreciative [ə'pri:ʃət̬ɪv, -'prɪ-; ə'pri:ʃiˌeɪ-] *adj* **1** : apreciativo ⟨an appreciative audience : un público apreciativo⟩ **2** GRATEFUL : agradecido **3** ADMIRING : de admiración
apprehend [ˌæprɪ'hɛnd] *vt* **1** ARREST : aprehender, detener, arrestar **2** DREAD : temer **3** COMPREHEND : comprender, entender
apprehension [ˌæprɪ'hɛntʃən] *n* **1** ARREST : arresto *m*, detención *f*, aprehensión *f* **2** ANXIETY : aprensión *f*, ansiedad *f*, temor *m* **3** UNDERSTANDING : comprensión *f*, percepción *f*
apprehensive [ˌæprɪ'hɛntsɪv] *adj* : aprensivo, inquieto — **apprehensively** *adv*

apprentice[1] [ə'prɛntɪs] *vt* **-ticed; -ticing** : colocar de aprendiz
apprentice[2] *n* : aprendiz *m*, -diza *f*
apprenticeship [ə'prɛntɪs,ʃɪp] *n* : aprendizaje *f*
apprise [ə'praɪz] *vt* **-prised; -prising** : informar, avisar
approach[1] [ə'pro:ʧ] *vt* **1** NEAR : acercarse a **2** APPROXIMATE : aproximarse a **3** : abordar, dirigirse a ‹I approached my boss with the proposal : me dirigí a mi jefe con la propuesta› **4** TACKLE : abordar, enfocar, considerar — *vi* : acercarse, aproximarse
approach[2] *n* **1** NEARING : acercamiento *m*, aproximación *f* **2** POSITION : enfoque *m*, planteamiento *m* **3** OFFER : propuesta *f*, oferta *f* **4** ACCESS : acceso *m*, vía *f* de acceso
approachable [ə'pro:ʧəbəl] *adj* : accesible, asequible
approbation [,æprə'beɪʃən] *n* : aprobación *f*
appropriate[1] [ə'pro:pri,eɪt] *vt* **-ated; -ating 1** SEIZE : apropiarse de **2** ALLOCATE : destinar, asignar
appropriate[2] [ə'pro:priət] *adj* : apropiado, adecuado, idóneo — **appropriately** *adv*
appropriateness [ə'pro:priətnəs] *n* : idoneidad *f*, propiedad *f*
appropriation [ə,pro:pri'eɪʃən] *n* **1** SEIZURE : apropiación *f* **2** ALLOCATION : asignación *f*
approval [ə'pru:vəl] *n* **1** : aprobación *f*, visto *m* bueno **2 on approval** : a prueba
approve [ə'pru:v] *vt* **-proved; -proving 1** : aprobar, sancionar, darle el visto bueno a **2 to approve of** : consentir en, aprobar ‹he doesn't approve of smoking : está en contra del tabaco›
approximate[1] [ə'prɑksə,meɪt] *vt* **-mated; -mating** : aproximarse a, acercarse a
approximate[2] [ə'prɑksəmət] *adj* : aproximado
approximately [ə'prɑksəmətli] *adv* : aproximadamente, más o menos
approximation [ə,prɑksə'meɪʃən] *n* : aproximación *f*
appurtenance [ə'pərtənənts] *n* : accesorio *m*
apricot ['æprə,kɑt, 'eɪ-] *n* : albaricoque *m*, chabacano *m Mex*
April ['eɪprəl] *n* : abril *m*
apron ['eɪprən] *n* : delantal *m*, mandil *m*
apropos[1] [,æprə'po:, 'æprə,po:] *adv* : a propósito
apropos[2] *adj* : pertinente, oportuno, acertado
apropos of *prep* : a propósito de
apt ['æpt] *adj* **1** FITTING : apto, apropiado, acertado, oportuno **2** LIABLE : propenso, inclinado **3** CLEVER, QUICK : listo, despierto
aptitude ['æptə,tu:d, -,tju:d] *n* **1** : aptitud *f*, capacidad *f* ‹aptitude test : prueba de aptitud› **2** TALENT : talento *m*, facilidad *f*
aptly ['æptli] *adv* : acertadamente
aqua ['ækwə, 'ɑ-] *n* : color *m* aguamarina
aquarium [ə'kwæriəm] *n, pl* **-iums** *or* **-ia** [-iə] : acuario *m*
Aquarius [ə'kwæriəs] *n* : Acuario *mf*
aquatic [ə'kwɑtɪk, -'kwæ-] *adj* : acuático
aqueduct ['ækwə,dʌkt] *n* : acueducto *m*
aqueous ['eɪkwiəs, 'æ-] *adj* : acuoso
aquiline ['ækwə,laɪn, -lən] *adj* : aguileño
Arab[1] ['ærəb] *adj* : árabe
Arab[2] *n* : árabe *mf*
arabesque [,ærə'bɛsk] *n* : arabesco *m*
Arabian[1] [ə'reɪbiən] *adj* : árabe
Arabian[2] *n* → **Arab**[2]
Arabic[1] ['ærəbɪk] *adj* : árabe
Arabic[2] *n* : árabe *m* (idioma)
arable ['ærəbəl] *adj* : arable, cultivable
arbiter ['ɑrbəţər] *n* : árbitro *m*, -tra *f*
arbitrary ['ɑrbə,trɛri] *adj* : arbitrario — **arbitrarily** [,ɑrbə'trɛrəli] *adv*
arbitrate ['ɑrbə,treɪt] *v* **-trated; -trating** : arbitrar
arbitration [,ɑrbə'treɪʃən] *n* : arbitraje *m*
arbitrator ['ɑrbə,treɪţər] *n* : árbitro *m*, -tra *f*
arbor ['ɑrbər] *n* : cenador *m*, pérgola *f*
arboreal [ɑr'boriəl] *adj* : arbóreo
arc[1] ['ɑrk] *vi* **arced; arcing** : formar un arco
arc[2] *n* : arco *m*
arcade [ɑr'keɪd] *n* **1** ARCHES : arcada *f* **2** MALL : galería *f* comercial
arcane [ɑr'keɪn] *adj* : arcano, secreto, misterioso
arch[1] ['ɑrʧ] *vt* : arquear, enarcar — *vi* : formar un arco, arquearse
arch[2] *adj* **1** CHIEF : principal **2** MISCHIEVOUS : malicioso, pícaro
arch[3] *n* : arco *m*
archaeological [,ɑrkiə'lɑʤɪkəl] *adj* : arqueológico
archaeologist [,ɑrki'ɑləʤɪst] *n* : arqueólogo *m*, -ga *f*
archaeology *or* **archeology** [,ɑrki'ɑləʤi] *n* : arqueología *f*
archaic [ɑr'keɪɪk] *adj* : arcaico — **archaically** [-ɪkli] *adv*
archangel ['ɑrk,eɪnʤəl] *n* : arcángel *m*
archbishop [ɑrʧ'bɪʃəp] *n* : arzobispo *m*
archdiocese [ɑrʧ'daɪəsəs, -,si:z, -,si:s] *n* : archidiócesis *f*
archer ['ɑrʧər] *n* : arquero *m*, -ra *f*
archery ['ɑrʧəri] *n* : tiro *m* al arco
archetypal [,ɑrkɪ'taɪpəl] *adj* : arquetípico
archetype ['ɑrkɪ,taɪp] *n* : arquetipo *m*
archipelago [,ɑrkə'pɛlə,go:, ,ɑrʧə-] *n, pl* **-goes** *or* **-gos** [-go:z] : archipiélago *m*
architect ['ɑrkə,tɛkt] *n* : arquitecto *m*, -ta *f*
architectural [,ɑrkə'tɛktʃərəl] *adj* : arquitectónico — **architecturally** *adv*
architecture ['ɑrkə,tɛktʃər] *n* : arquitectura *f*
archive ['ɑr,kaɪv] *n or* **archives** ['ɑr,kaɪvz] *npl* : archivo *m*

archivist [ˈɑrkəvɪst, -ˌkaɪ-] *n* : archivero *m*, -ra *f*; archivista *mf*

archway [ˈɑrʧˌweɪ] *n* : arco *m*, pasadizo *m* abovedado

arctic [ˈɑrktɪk, ˈɑrt̬-] *adj* **1** : ártico ⟨arctic regions : zonas árticas⟩ **2** FRIGID : glacial

arctic circle *n* : círculo *m* ártico

ardent [ˈɑrdənt] *adj* **1** PASSIONATE : ardiente, fogoso, apasionado **2** FERVENT : ferviente, fervoroso — **ardently** *adv*

ardor [ˈɑrdər] *n* : ardor *m*, pasión *f*, fervor *m*

arduous [ˈɑrʤʊəs] *adj* : arduo, duro, riguroso — **arduously** *adv*

arduousness [ˈɑrʤʊəsnəs] *n* : dureza *f*, rigor *m*

are → **be**

area [ˈæriə] *n* **1** SURFACE : área *f*, superficie *f* **2** REGION : área *f*, región *f*, zona *f* **3** FIELD : área *f*, terreno *m*, campo *m* (de conocimiento)

area code *n* : código *m* de la zona, prefijo *m Spain*

arena [əˈriːnə] *n* **1** : arena *f*, estadio *m* ⟨sports arena : estadio deportivo⟩ **2** : arena *f*, ruedo *m* ⟨the political arena : el ruedo político⟩

Argentine [ˈɑrʤənˌtaɪn, -ˌtiːn] *or* **Argentinean** *or* **Argentinian** [ˌɑrʤənˈtɪniən] *n* : argentino *m*, -na *f* — **Argentine** *or* **Argentinean** *or* **Argentinian** *adj*

argon [ˈɑrˌgɑn] *n* : argón *m*

argot [ˈɑrgət, -ˌgoː] *n* : argot *m*

arguable [ˈɑrgjʊəbəl] *adj* : discutible

argue [ˈɑrˌgjuː] *v* **-gued; -guing** *vi* **1** REASON : argüir, argumentar, razonar **2** DISPUTE : discutir, pelear(se), alegar — *vt* **1** SUGGEST : sugerir **2** MAINTAIN : alegar, argüir, sostener **3** DISCUSS : discutir, debatir

argument [ˈɑrgjəmənt] *n* **1** REASONING : argumento *m*, razonamiento *m* **2** DISCUSSION : discusión *f*, debate *m* **3** QUARREL : pelea *f*, riña *f*, disputa *f*

argumentative [ˌɑrgjəˈmɛnt̬ət̬ɪv] *adj* : discutidor

argyle [ˈɑrˌgaɪl] *n* : diseño *m* de rombos

aria [ˈɑriə] *n* : aria *f*

arid [ˈærəd] *adj* : árido

aridity [əˈrɪdət̬i, æ-] *n* : aridez *f*

Aries [ˈɛriːz, -iˌiːz] *n* : Aries *mf*

arise [əˈraɪz] *vi* **arose** [əˈroːz]; **arisen** [əˈrɪzən]; **arising 1** ASCEND : ascender, subir, elevarse **2** ORIGINATE : originarse, surgir, presentarse **3** GET UP : levantarse

aristocracy [ˌærəˈstɑkrəsi] *n, pl* **-cies** : aristocracia *f*

aristocrat [əˈrɪstəˌkræt] *n* : aristócrata *mf*

aristocratic [əˌrɪstəˈkræt̬ɪk] *adj* : aristocrático, noble

arithmetic¹ [ˌærɪθˈmɛt̬ɪk] *or* **arithmetical** [-t̬ɪkəl] *adj* : aritmético

arithmetic² [əˈrɪθməˌtɪk] *n* : aritmética *f*

ark [ˈɑrk] *n* : arca *f*

arm¹ [ˈɑrm] *vt* : armar — *vi* : armarse

arm² *n* **1** : brazo *m* (del cuerpo o de un sillón), manga *f* (de una prenda) **2** BRANCH : rama *f*, sección *f* **3** WEAPON : arma *f* ⟨to take up arms : tomar las armas⟩ **4** → **coat of arms**

armada [ɑrˈmɑdə, -ˈmeɪ-] *n* : armada *f*, flota *f*

armadillo [ˌɑrməˈdɪlo] *n, pl* **-los** : armadillo *m*

armament [ˈɑrməmənt] *n* : armamento *m*

armchair [ˈɑrmˌʧɛr] *n* : butaca *f*, sillón *m*

armed [ˈɑrmd] *adj* **1** : armado ⟨armed robbery : robo a mano armada⟩ **2** **armed forces** : fuerzas *fpl* armadas

Armenian [ɑrˈmiːniən] *n* : armenio *m*, -nia *f* — **Armenian** *adj*

armistice [ˈɑrməstɪs] *n* : armisticio *m*

armor [ˈɑrmər] *n* : armadura *f*, coraza *f*

armored [ˈɑrmərd] *adj* : blindado, acorazado

armory [ˈɑrməri] *n, pl* **-mories** : arsenal *m* (almacén), armería *f* (museo), fábrica *f* de armas

armpit [ˈɑrmˌpɪt] *n* : axila *f*, sobaco *m*

army [ˈɑrmi] *n, pl* **-mies 1** : ejército *m* (militar) **2** MULTITUDE : legión *f*, multitud *f*, ejército *m*

aroma [əˈroːmə] *n* : aroma *f*

aromatic [ˌærəˈmæt̬ɪk] *adj* : aromático

around¹ [əˈraʊnd] *adv* **1** : de circunferencia ⟨a tree three feet around : un árbol de tres pies de circunferencia⟩ **2** : alrededor, a la redonda ⟨for miles around : por millas a la redonda⟩ ⟨all around : por todos lados, todo alrededor⟩ **3** : por ahí ⟨they're somewhere around : deben estar por ahí⟩ **4** APPROXIMATELY : más o menos, aproximadamente ⟨around 5 o'clock : a eso de las 5⟩ **5** **to turn around** : darse la vuelta, voltearse

around² *prep* **1** SURROUNDING : alrededor de, en torno a **2** THROUGH : por, en ⟨he traveled around Mexico : viajó por México⟩ ⟨around the house : en casa⟩ **3** : a la vuelta de ⟨around the corner : a la vuelta de la esquina⟩ **4** NEAR : alrededor de, cerca de

arousal [əˈraʊzəl] *n* : excitación *f*

arouse [əˈraʊz] *vt* **aroused; arousing 1** AWAKE : despertar **2** EXCITE : despertar, suscitar, excitar

arraign [əˈreɪn] *vt* : hacer comparecer (ante un tribunal)

arraignment [əˈreɪnmənt] *n* : orden *m* de comparecencia, acusación *f*

arrange [əˈreɪnʤ] *vt* **-ranged; -ranging 1** ORDER : arreglar, poner en orden, disponer **2** SETTLE : arreglar, fijar, concertar **3** ADAPT : arreglar, adaptar

arrangement [əˈreɪnʤmənt] *n* **1** ORDER : arreglo *m*, orden *m* **2** ARRANGING : disposición *f* ⟨floral arrangement : arreglo floral⟩ **3** AGREEMENT : arreglo *m*, acuerdo *m*, convenio *m* **4 arrange-**

ments *npl* : preparativos *mpl*, planes *mpl*
array[1] [əˈreɪ] *vt* **1** ORDER : poner en orden, presentar, formar **2** GARB : vestir, ataviar, engalanar
array[2] *n* **1** ORDER : orden *m*, formación *f* **2** ATTIRE : atavío *m*, galas *mpl* **3** RANGE, SELECTION : selección *f*, serie *f*, gama *f* ⟨an array of problems : una serie de problemas⟩
arrears [əˈrɪrz] *npl* : atrasos *mpl* ⟨to be in arrears : estar atrasado en los pagos⟩
arrest[1] [əˈrɛst] *vt* **1** APPREHEND : arrestar, detener **2** CHECK, STOP : detener, parar
arrest[2] *n* **1** APPREHENSION : arresto *m*, detención *f* ⟨under arrest : detenido⟩ **2** STOPPING : paro *m*
arrival [əˈraɪvəl] *n* : llegada *f*, venida *f*, arribo *m*
arrive [əˈraɪv] *vi* **-rived; -riving** **1** COME : llegar, arribar **2** SUCCEED : triunfar, tener éxito
arrogance [ˈærəgənts] *n* : arrogancia *f*, soberbia *f*, altanería *f*, altivez *f*
arrogant [ˈærəgənt] *adj* : arrogante, soberbio, altanero, altivo — **arrogantly** *adv*
arrogate [ˈærəˌgeɪt] *vt* **-gated; -gating** **to arrogate to oneself** : arrogarse
arrow [ˈæro] *n* : flecha *f*
arrowhead [ˈæroˌhɛd] *n* : punta *f* de flecha
arroyo [əˈrɔɪo] *n* : arroyo *m*
arsenal [ˈɑrsənəl] *n* : arsenal *m*
arsenic [ˈɑrsənɪk] *n* : arsénico *m*
arson [ˈɑrsən] *n* : incendio *m* premeditado
arsonist [ˈɑrsənɪst] *n* : incendiario *m*, -ria *f*; pirómano *m*, -na *f*
art [ˈɑrt] *n* **1** : arte *m* **2** SKILL : destreza *f*, habilidad *f*, maña *f* **3** **arts** *npl* : letras *fpl* (en la educación) **4** **fine arts** : bellas artes *fpl*
arterial [ɑrˈtɪriəl] *adj* : arterial
arteriosclerosis [ɑrˌtɪriosklə'ro:sɪs] *n* : arteriosclerosis *f*
artery [ˈɑrt̬əri] *n, pl* **-teries** **1** : arteria *f* **2** THOROUGHFARE : carretera *f* principal, arteria *f*
artesian well [ɑrˈti:ʒən] *n* : pozo *m* artesiano
artful [ˈɑrtfəl] *adj* **1** INGENIOUS : ingenioso, diestro **2** CRAFTY : astuto, taimado, ladino, artero — **artfully** *adv*
arthritic [ɑrˈθrɪt̬ɪk] *adj* : artrítico
arthritis [ɑrˈθraɪt̬əs] *n, pl* **-tides** [ɑrˈθrɪt̬əˌdi:z] : artritis *f*
arthropod [ˈɑrθrəˌpɑd] *n* : artrópodo *m*
artichoke [ˈɑrt̬əˌʧo:k] *n* : alcachofa *f*
article [ˈɑrtɪkəl] *n* **1** ITEM : artículo *m*, objeto *m* **2** ESSAY : artículo *m* **3** CLAUSE : artículo *m*, cláusula *f* **4** : artículo *m* ⟨definite article : artículo determinado⟩
articulate[1] [ɑrˈtɪkjəˌleɪt] *vt* **-lated; -lating** **1** UTTER : articular, enunciar, expresar **2** CONNECT : articular (en anatomía)
articulate[2] [ɑrˈtɪkjələt] *adj* **to be articulate** : poder articular palabras, expresarse bien
articulately [ɑrˈtɪkjələtli] *adv* : elocuentemente, con fluidez
articulateness [ɑrˈtɪkjələtnəs] *n* : elocuencia *f*, fluidez *f*
articulation [ɑrˌtɪkjəˈleɪʃən] *n* **1** JOINT : articulación *f* **2** UTTERANCE : articulación *f*, declaración *f* **3** ENUNCIATION : articulación *f*, pronunciación *f*
artifact [ˈɑrt̬əˌfækt] *n* : artefacto *m*
artifice [ˈɑrt̬əfəs] *n* : artificio *m*
artificial [ˌɑrt̬əˈfɪʃəl] *adj* **1** SYNTHETIC : artificial, sintético **2** FEIGNED : artificial, falso, afectado
artificially [ˌɑrt̬əˈfɪʃəli] *adv* : artificialmente, con afectación
artillery [ɑrˈtɪləri] *n, pl* **-leries** : artillería *f*
artisan [ˈɑrt̬əzən, -sən] *n* : artesano *m*, -na *f*
artist [ˈɑrt̬ɪst] *n* : artista *mf*
artistic [ɑrˈtɪstɪk] *adj* : artístico — **artistically** [-tɪkli] *adv*
artistry [ˈɑrt̬əstri] *n* : maestría *f*, arte *m*
artless [ˈɑrtləs] *adj* : sencillo, natural, ingenuo, cándido — **artlessly** *adv*
artlessness [ˈɑrtləsnəs] *n* : ingenuidad *f*, candidez *f*
arty [ˈɑrt̬i] *adj* **artier; -est** : pretenciosamente artístico
as[1] [ˈæz] *adv* **1** : tan, tanto ⟨this one's not as difficult : éste no es tan difícil⟩ **2** : como ⟨some trees, as oak and pine : algunos árboles, como el roble y el pino⟩
as[2] *conj* **1** LIKE : como, igual que **2** WHEN, WHILE : cuando, mientras, a la vez que **3** BECAUSE : porque **4** THOUGH : aunque, por más que ⟨strange as it may appear : por extraño que parezca⟩ **5** **as is** : tal como está
as[3] *prep* **1** : de ⟨I met her as a child : la conocí de pequeña⟩ **2** LIKE : como ⟨behave as a man : compórtate como un hombre⟩
as[4] *pron* : que ⟨in the same building as my brother : en el mismo edificio que mi hermano⟩
asbestos [æzˈbɛstəs, æs-] *n* : asbesto *m*, amianto *m*
ascend [əˈsɛnd] *vi* : ascender, subir — *vt* : subir, subir a, escalar
ascendancy [əˈsɛndəntsi] *n* : ascendiente *m*, predominio *m*
ascendant[1] [əˈsɛndənt] *adj* **1** RISING : ascendente **2** DOMINANT : superior, dominante
ascendant[2] *n* **to be in the ascendant** : estar en alza, ir ganando predominio
ascension [əˈsɛntʃən] *n* : ascensión *f*
ascent [əˈsɛnt] *n* **1** RISE : ascensión *f*, subida *f*, ascenso *m* **2** SLOPE : cuesta *f*, pendiente *f*
ascertain [ˌæsərˈteɪn] *vt* : determinar, establecer, averiguar
ascertainable [ˌæsərˈteɪnəbəl] *adj* : determinable, averiguable

ascetic[1] [əˈsɛt̬ɪk] *adj* : ascético

ascetic[2] *n* : asceta *mf*

asceticism [əˈsɛt̬əˌsɪzəm] *n* : ascetismo *m*

ascribable [əˈskraɪbəbəl] *adj* : atribuible, imputable

ascribe [əˈskraɪb] *vt* **-cribed; -cribing** : atribuir, imputar

aseptic [eɪˈsɛptɪk] *adj* : aséptico

asexual [ˌeɪˈsɛkʃuəl] *adj* : asexual

as for *prep* CONCERNING : en cuanto a, respecto a, para

ash [ˈæʃ] *n* **1** : ceniza *f* ⟨to reduce to ashes : reducir a cenizas⟩ **2** : fresno *m* (árbol)

ashamed [əˈʃeɪmd] *adj* : avergonzado, abochornado, apenado — **ashamedly** [əˈʃeɪmədli] *adv*

ashen [ˈæʃən] *adj* : lívido, ceniciento, pálido

ashore [əˈʃor] *adv* **1** : en tierra **2 to go ashore** : desembarcar

ashtray [ˈæʃˌtreɪ] *n* : cenicero *m*

Asian[1] [ˈeɪʒən, -ʃən] *adj* : asiático

Asian[2] *n* : asiático *m*, -ca *f*

aside [əˈsaɪd] *adv* **1** : a un lado ⟨to step aside : hacerse a un lado⟩ **2** : de lado, aparte ⟨jesting aside : bromas aparte⟩ **3 to set aside** : guardar, apartar, reservar

aside from *prep* **1** BESIDES : además de **2** EXCEPT : aparte de, menos

as if *conj* : como si

asinine [ˈæsənˌaɪn] *adj* : necio, estúpido

ask [ˈæsk] *vt* **1** : preguntar ⟨ask him if he's coming : pregúntale si viene⟩ **2** REQUEST : pedir, solicitar ⟨to ask a favor : pedir un favor⟩ **3** INVITE : invitar — *vi* **1** INQUIRE : preguntar ⟨I asked about her children : pregunté por sus niños⟩ **2** REQUEST : pedir ⟨we asked for help : pedimos ayuda⟩

askance [əˈskæn*t*s] *adv* **1** SIDELONG : de reojo, de soslayo **2** SUSPICIOUSLY : con recelo, con desconfianza

askew [əˈskjuː] *adj* : torcido, ladeado

asleep [əˈsliːp] *adj* **1** : dormido, durmiendo **2 to fall asleep** : quedarse dormido

as of *prep* : desde, a partir de

asparagus [əˈspærəgəs] *n* : espárrago *m*

aspect [ˈæˌspɛkt] *n* : aspecto *m*

aspen [ˈæspən] *n* : álamo *m* temblón

asperity [æˈspɛrət̬i, ə-] *n, pl* **-ties** : aspereza *f*

aspersion [əˈspərʒən] *n* : difamación *f*, calumnia *f*

asphalt [ˈæsˌfɔlt] *n* : asfalto *m*

asphyxia [æˈsfɪksiə, ə-] *n* : asfixia *f*

asphyxiate [æˈsfɪksiˌeɪt] *v* **-ated; -ating** *vt* : asfixiar — *vi* : asfixiarse

asphyxiation [æˌsfɪksiˈeɪʃən] *n* : asfixia *f*

aspirant [ˈæspərənt, əˈspaɪrənt] *n* : aspirante *mf*, pretendiente *mf*

aspiration [ˌæspəˈreɪʃən] *n* **1** DESIRE : aspiración *f*, anhelo *m*, ambición *f* **2** BREATHING : aspiración *f*

aspire [əˈspaɪr] *vi* **-pired; -piring** : aspirar

aspirin [ˈæsprən, ˈæspə-] *n, pl* **aspirin** *or* **aspirins** : aspirina *f*

ass [ˈæs] *n* **1** : asno *m* **2** IDIOT : imbécil *mf*, idiota *mf*

assail [əˈseɪl] *vt* : atacar, asaltar

assailant [əˈseɪlənt] *n* : asaltante *mf*, atacante *mf*

assassin [əˈsæsən] *n* : asesino *m*, -na *f*

assassinate [əˈsæsənˌeɪt] *vt* **-nated; -nating** : asesinar

assassination [əˌsæsənˈeɪʃən] *n* : asesinato *m*

assault[1] [əˈsɔlt] *vt* : atacar, asaltar, agredir

assault[2] *n* : ataque *m*, asalto *m*, agresión *f*

assay[1] [æˈseɪ, ˈæˌseɪ] *vt* : ensayar

assay[2] [ˈæˌseɪ, æˈseɪ] *n* : ensayo *m*

assemble [əˈsɛmbəl] *v* **-bled; -bling** *vt* **1** GATHER : reunir, recoger, juntar **2** CONSTRUCT : ensamblar, montar, construir — *vi* : reunirse, congregarse

assembly [əˈsɛmbli] *n, pl* **-blies** **1** MEETING : reunión *f* **2** CONSTRUCTING : ensamblaje *m*, montaje *m*

assemblyman [əˈsɛmblimən] *n, pl* **-men** [-mən, -ˌmɛn] : asambleísta *m*

assemblywoman [əˈsɛmbliˌwʊmən] *n, pl* **-women** [-ˌwɪmən] : asambleísta *f*

assent[1] [əˈsɛnt] *vi* : asentir, consentir

assent[2] *n* : asentimiento *m*, aprobación *f*

assert [əˈsərt] *vt* **1** AFFIRM : afirmar, aseverar, mantener **2 to assert oneself** : imponerse, hacerse valer

assertion [əˈsərʃən] *n* : afirmación *f*, aseveración *f*, aserto *m*

assertive [əˈsərt̬ɪv] *adj* : firme, enérgico

assertiveness [əˈsərt̬ɪvnəs] *n* : seguridad *f* en sí mismo

assess [əˈsɛs] *vt* **1** IMPOSE : gravar (un impuesto), imponer **2** EVALUATE : evaluar, valorar, aquilatar

assessment [əˈsɛsmənt] *n* : evaluación *f*, valoración *f*

assessor [əˈsɛsər] *n* : evaluador *m*, -dora *f*; tasador *m*, -dora *f*

asset [ˈæˌsɛt] *n* **1** : ventaja *f*, recurso *m* **2 assets** *npl* : bienes *mpl*, activo *m* ⟨assets and liabilities : activo y pasivo⟩

assiduous [əˈsɪʤuəs] *adj* : diligente, aplicado, asiduo — **assiduously** *adv*

assign [əˈsaɪn] *vt* **1** APPOINT : designar, nombrar **2** ALLOT : asignar, señalar **3** ATTRIBUTE : atribuir, dar, conceder

assignment [əˈsaɪnmənt] *n* **1** TASK : función *f*, tarea *f*, misión *f* **2** HOMEWORK : tarea *f*, asignación *f PRi*, deberes *mpl Spain* **3** APPOINTMENT : nombramiento *m* **4** ALLOCATION : asignación *f*

assimilate [əˈsɪməˌleɪt] *v* **-lated; -lating** *vt* : asimilar — *vi* : adaptarse, integrarse

assimilation [əˌsɪməˈleɪʃən] *n* : asimilación *f*

assist[1] [əˈsɪst] *vt* : asistir, ayudar

assist[2] *n* : asistencia *f*, contribución *f*

assistance [əˈsɪstənts] *n* : asistencia *f*, ayuda *f*, auxilio *m*

assistant [əˈsɪstənt] *n* : ayudante *mf*, asistente *mf*

associate[1] [əˈsoːʃiˌeɪt, -si-] *v* **-ated; -ating** *vt* **1** CONNECT, RELATE : asociar, relacionar **2 to be associated with** : estar relacionado con, estar vinculado a — *vi* **to associate with** : relacionarse con, frecuentar

associate[2] [əˈsoːʃiət, -siət] *n* : asociado *m*, -da *f*; colega *mf*; socio *m*, -cia *f*

association [əˌsoːʃiˈeɪʃən, -si-] *n* **1** ORGANIZATION : asociación *f*, sociedad *f* **2** RELATIONSHIP : asociación *f*, relación *f*

as soon as *conj* : en cuanto, tan pronto como

assorted [əˈsɔrt̬əd] *adj* : surtido

assortment [əˈsɔrtmənt] *n* : surtido *m*, variedad *f*, colección *f*

assuage [əˈsweɪʤ] *vt* **-suaged; -suaging 1** EASE : aliviar, mitigar **2** CALM : calmar, aplacar **3** SATISFY : saciar, satisfacer

assume [əˈsuːm] *vt* **-sumed; -suming 1** SUPPOSE : suponer, asumir **2** UNDERTAKE : asumir, encargarse de **3** TAKE ON : adquirir, adoptar, tomar ⟨to assume importance : tomar importancia⟩ **4** FEIGN : adoptar, afectar, simular

assumption [əˈsʌmpʃən] *n* : asunción *f*, presunción *f*

assurance [əˈʃʊrənts] *n* **1** CERTAINTY : certidumbre *f*, certeza *f* **2** CONFIDENCE : confianza *f*, aplomo *m*, seguridad *f*

assure [əˈʃʊr] *vt* **-sured; -suring** : asegurar, garantizar ⟨I assure you that I'll do it : te aseguro que lo haré⟩

assured [əˈʃʊrd] *adj* **1** CERTAIN : seguro, asegurado **2** CONFIDENT : confiado, seguro de sí mismo

aster [ˈæstər] *n* : aster *m*

asterisk [ˈæstəˌrɪsk] *n* : asterisco *m*

astern [əˈstərn] *adv* **1** BEHIND : detrás, a popa **2** BACKWARDS : hacia atrás

asteroid [ˈæstəˌrɔɪd] *n* : asteroide *m*

asthma [ˈæzmə] *n* : asma *m*

asthmatic [æzˈmæt̬ɪk] *adj* : asmático

as though → **as if**

astigmatism [əˈstɪgməˌtɪzəm] *n* : astigmatismo *m*

as to *prep* **1** ABOUT : sobre, acerca de **2** → **according to**

astonish [əˈstɑnɪʃ] *vt* : asombrar, sorprender, pasmar

astonishing [əˈstɑnɪʃɪŋ] *adj* : asombroso, sorprendente, increíble — **astonishingly** *adv*

astonishment [əˈstɑnɪʃmənt] *n* : asombro *m*, estupefacción *f*, sorpresa *f*

astound [əˈstaʊnd] *vt* : asombrar, pasmar, dejar estupefacto

astounding [əˈstaʊndɪŋ] *adj* : asombroso, pasmoso — **astoundingly** *adv*

astraddle [əˈstrædəl] *adv* : a horcajadas

astral [ˈæstrəl] *adj* : astral

astray [əˈstreɪ] *adv & adj* : perdido, extraviado, descarriado

astride [əˈstraɪd] *adv* : a horcajadas

astringency [əˈstrɪnʤəntsi] *n* : astringencia *f*

astringent[1] [əˈstrɪnʤənt] *adj* : astringente

astringent[2] *n* : astringente *m*

astrologer [əˈstrɑləʤər] *n* : astrólogo *m*, -ga *f*

astrological [ˌæstrəˈlɑʤɪkəl] *adj* : astrológico

astrology [əˈstrɑləʤi] *n* : astrología *f*

astronaut [ˈæstrəˌnɔt] *n* : astronauta *mf*

astronautic [ˌæstrəˈnɔt̬ɪk] *or* **astronautical** [-t̬ɪkəl] *adj* : astronáutico

astronautics [ˌæstrəˈnɔt̬ɪks] *ns & pl* : astronáutica *f*

astronomer [əˈstrɑnəmər] *n* : astrónomo *m*, -ma *f*

astronomical [ˌæstrəˈnɑmɪkəl] *adj* **1** : astronómico **2** ENORMOUS : astronómico, enorme, gigantesco

astronomy [əˈstrɑnəmi] *n, pl* **-mies** : astronomía *f*

astute [əˈstuːt, -ˈstjuːt] *adj* : astuto, sagaz, perspicaz — **astutely** *adv*

astuteness [əˈstuːtnəs, -ˈstjuːt-] *n* : astucia *f*, sagacidad *f*, perspicacia *f*

asunder [əˈsʌndər] *adv* : en dos, en pedazos ⟨to tear asunder : hacer pedazos⟩

as well as[1] *conj* : tanto como

as well as[2] *prep* BESIDES : además de, aparte de

as yet *adv* : aún, todavía

asylum [əˈsaɪləm] *n* **1** REFUGE : refugio *m*, santuario *m*, asilo *m* **2 insane asylum** : manicomio *m*

asymmetrical [ˌeɪsəˈmɛtrɪkəl] *or* **asymmetric** [-ˈmɛtrɪk] *adj* : asimétrico

asymmetry [ˌeɪˈsɪmətri] *n* : asimetría *f*

at [ˈæt] *prep* **1** : en ⟨at the top : en lo alto⟩ ⟨at peace : en paz⟩ ⟨at Ann's house : en casa de Ana⟩ **2** : a ⟨at the rear : al fondo⟩ ⟨at 10 o'clock : a las diez⟩ **3** : por ⟨at last : por fin⟩ ⟨to be surprised at something : sorprenderse por algo⟩ **4** : de ⟨he's laughing at you : está riéndose de ti⟩ **5** : para ⟨you're good at this : eres bueno para esto⟩

at all *adv* : en absoluto, para nada

ate → **eat**

atheism [ˈeɪθiˌɪzəm] *n* : ateísmo *m*

atheist [ˈeɪθiɪst] *n* : ateo *m*, atea *f*

atheistic [ˌeɪθiˈɪstɪk] *adj* : ateo

athlete [ˈæθˌliːt] *n* : atleta *mf*

athletic [æθˈlɛt̬ɪk] *adj* : atlético

athletics [æθˈlɛt̬ɪks] *ns & pl* : atletismo *m*

Atlantic [ətˈlæntɪk, æt-] *adj* : atlántico

atlas [ˈætləs] *n* : atlas *m*

ATM [ˌeɪˌtiːˈɛm] *n* : cajero *m* automático

atmosphere [ˈætməˌsfɪr] *n* **1** AIR : atmósfera *f*, aire *m* **2** AMBIENCE : ambiente *m*, atmósfera *f*, clima *m*

atmospheric [ˌætməˈsfɪrɪk, -ˈsfɛr-] *adj* : atmosférico — **atmospherically** [-ɪkli] *adv*

atoll [ˈæˌtɔl, ˈeɪ-, -ˌtɑl] *n* : atolón *m*
atom [ˈæṭəm] *n* **1** : átomo *m* **2** SPECK : ápice *m*, pizca *f*
atomic [əˈtɑmɪk] *adj* : atómico
atomic bomb *n* : bomba *f* atómica
atomizer [ˈæṭəˌmaɪzər] *n* : atomizador *m*, pulverizador *m*
atone [əˈtoːn] *vt* **atoned; atoning to atone for** : expiar
atonement [əˈtoːnmənt] *n* : expiación *f*, desagravio *m*
atop[1] [əˈtɑp] *adj* : encima
atop[2] *prep* : encima de, sobre
atrium [ˈeɪtriəm] *n, pl* **atria** [-triə] *or* **atriums** **1** : atrio *m* **2** : aurícula *f* (del corazón)
atrocious [əˈtroːʃəs] *adj* : atroz — **atrociously** *adv*
atrocity [əˈtrɑsəṭi] *n, pl* **-ties** : atrocidad *f*
atrophy[1] [ˈætrəfi] *vt* **-phied; -phying** : atrofiar
atrophy[2] *n, pl* **-phies** : atrofia *f*
attach [əˈtæʧ] *vt* **1** FASTEN : sujetar, atar, amarrar, pegar **2** JOIN : juntar, adjuntar **3** ATTRIBUTE : dar, atribuir ⟨I attached little importance to it : le di poca importancia⟩ **4** SEIZE : embargar **5 to become attached to someone** : encariñarse con alguien
attaché [ˌæṭəˈʃeɪ, ˌæˌtæ-, əˌtæ-] *n* : agregado *m*, -da *f*
attachment [əˈtæʧmənt] *n* **1** ACCESSORY : accesorio *m* **2** CONNECTION : conexión *f*, acoplamiento *m* **3** FONDNESS : apego *m*, cariño *m*, afición *f*
attack[1] [əˈtæk] *vt* **1** ASSAULT : atacar, asaltar, agredir **2** TACKLE : acometer, combatir, enfrentarse con
attack[2] *n* **1** : ataque *m*, asalto *m*, acometida *f* ⟨to launch an attack : lanzar un ataque⟩ **2** : ataque *m*, crisis *f* ⟨heart attack : ataque cardíaco, infarto⟩ ⟨attack of nerves : crisis nerviosa⟩
attacker [əˈtækər] *n* : asaltante *mf*
attain [əˈteɪn] *vt* **1** ACHIEVE : lograr, conseguir, alcanzar, realizar **2** REACH : alcanzar, llegar a
attainable [əˈteɪnəbəl] *adj* : alcanzable, realizable, asequible
attainment [əˈteɪnmənt] *n* : logro *m*, consecución *f*, realización *f*
attempt[1] [əˈtɛmpt] *vt* : intentar, tratar de
attempt[2] *n* : intento *m*, tentativa *f*
attend [əˈtɛnd] *vt* **1** : asistir a ⟨to attend a meeting : asistir a una reunión⟩ **2** : atender, ocuparse de, cuidar ⟨to attend a patient : atender a un paciente⟩ **3** HEED : atender a, hacer caso de **4** ACCOMPANY : acompañar
attendance [əˈtɛndənts] *n* **1** ATTENDING : asistencia *f* **2** TURNOUT : concurrencia *f*
attendant[1] [əˈtɛndənt] *adj* : concomitante, inherente
attendant[2] *n* : asistente *mf*, acompañante *mf*, guarda *mf*
attention [əˈtɛnʧən] *n* **1** : atención *f* **2 to pay attention** : prestar atención, hacer caso **3 to stand at attention** : estar firme
attentive [əˈtɛntɪv] *adj* : atento — **attentively** *adv*
attentiveness [əˈtɛntɪvnəs] *n* **1** THOUGHTFULNESS : cortesía *f*, consideración *f* **2** CONCENTRATION : atención *f*, concentración *f*
attest [əˈtɛst] *vt* : atestiguar, dar fe de
attestation [ˌæˌtsˈteɪʃən] *n* : testimonio *m*
attic [ˈæṭɪk] *n* : ático *m*, desván *m*, buhardilla *f*
attire[1] [əˈtaɪr] *vt* **-tired; -tiring** : ataviar
attire[2] *n* : atuendo *m*, atavío *m*
attitude [ˈæṭəˌtuːd, -ˌtjuːd] *n* **1** FEELING : actitud *f* **2** POSTURE : postura *f*
attorney [əˈtərni] *n, pl* **-neys** : abogado *m*, -da *f*
attract [əˈtrækt] *vt* **1** : atraer **2 to attract attention** : llamar la atención
attraction [əˈtrækʃən] *n* : atracción *f*, atractivo *m*
attractive [əˈtræktɪv] *adj* : atractivo, atrayente
attractively [əˈtræktɪvli] *adv* : de manera atractiva, de buen gusto, hermosamente
attractiveness [əˈtræktɪvnəs] *n* : atractivo *m*
attributable [əˈtrɪbjʊṭəbəl] *adj* : atribuible, imputable
attribute[1] [əˈtrɪˌbjuːt] *vt* **-tributed; -tributing** : atribuir
attribute[2] [ˈætrəˌbjuːt] *n* : atributo *m*, cualidad *f*
attribution [ˌætrəˈbjuːʃən] *n* : atribución *f*
attune [əˈtuːn, -ˈtjuːn] *vt* **-tuned; -tuning** **1** ADAPT : adaptar, adecuar **2 to be attuned to** : estar en armonía con
atypical [ˌeɪˈtɪpɪkəl] *adj* : atípico
auburn [ˈɔbərn] *adj* : castaño rojizo
auction[1] [ˈɔkʃən] *vt* : subastar, rematar
auction[2] *n* : subasta *f*, remate *m*
auctioneer [ˌɔkʃəˈnɪr] *n* : subastador *m*, -dora *f*; rematador *m*, -dora *f*
audacious [ɔˈdeɪʃəs] *adj* : audaz, atrevido
audacity [ɔˈdæsəṭi] *n, pl* **-ties** : audacia *f*, atrevimiento *m*, descaro *m*
audible [ˈɔdəbəl] *adj* : audible — **audibly** [-bli] *adv*
audience [ˈɔdiənts] *n* **1** INTERVIEW : audiencia *f* **2** PUBLIC : audiencia *f*, público *m*, auditorio *m*, espectadores *mpl*
audio[1] [ˈɔdiˌoː] *adj* : de sonido, de audio
audio[2] *n* : audio *m*
audiovisual [ˌɔdioˈvɪʒʊəl] *adj* : audiovisual
audit[1] [ˈɔdət] *vt* **1** : auditar (finanzas) **2** : asistir como oyente a (una clase o un curso)
audit[2] *n* : auditoría *f*
audition[1] [ɔˈdɪʃən] *vi* : hacer una audición

audition[2] *n* : audición *f*
auditor [ˈɔdət̬ər] *n* **1** : auditor *m*, -tora *f* (de finanzas) **2** STUDENT : oyente *mf*
auditorium [ˌɔdəˈtoriəm] *n, pl* **-riums** *or* **-ria** [-riə] : auditorio *m*, sala *f*
auditory [ˈɔdəˌtori] *adj* : auditivo
auger [ˈɔgər] *n* : taladro *m*, barrena *f*
augment [ɔgˈmɛnt] *vt* : aumentar, incrementar
augmentation [ˌɔgmənˈteɪʃən] *n* : aumento *m*, incremento *m*
augur[1] [ˈɔgər] *vt* : augurar, presagiar — *vi* **to augur well** : ser de buen agüero
augur[2] *n* : augur *m*
augury [ˈɔgjʊri, -gər-] *n, pl* **-ries** : augurio *m*, presagio *m*, agüero *m*
august [ɔˈgʌst] *adj* : augusto
August [ˈɔgəst] *n* : agosto *m*
auk [ˈɔk] *n* : alca *f*
aunt [ˈænt, ˈant] *n* : tía *f*
aura [ˈɔrə] *n* : aura *f*
aural [ˈɔrəl] *adj* : auditivo
auricle [ˈɔrɪkəl] *n* : aurícula *f*
aurora borealis [əˈrorəˌboriˈæləs] *n* : aurora *f* boreal
auspices [ˈɔspəsəz, -ˌsi:z] *npl* : auspicios *mpl*
auspicious [ɔˈspɪʃəs] *adj* : prometedor, propicio, de buen augurio
austere [ɔˈstɪr] *adj* : austero, severo, adusto — **austerely** *adv*
austerity [ɔˈstɛrət̬i] *n, pl* **-ties** : austeridad *f*
Australian [ɔˈstreɪljən] *n* : australiano *m*, -na *f* — **Australian** *adj*
Austrian [ˈɔstriən] *n* : austriaco *m*, -ca *f* — **Austrian** *adj*
authentic [əˈθɛntɪk, ɔ-] *adj* : auténtico, genuino — **authentically** [-tɪkli] *adv*
authenticate [əˈθɛntɪˌkeɪt, ɔ-] *vt* **-cated; -cating** : autenticar, autentificar
authenticity [ɔˌθɛnˈtɪsət̬i] *n* : autenticidad *f*
author [ˈɔθər] *n* **1** WRITER : escritor *m*, -tora *f*; autor *m*, -tora *f* **2** CREATOR : autor *m*, -tora *f*; creador *m*, -dora *f*; artífice *mf*
authoritarian [ɔˌθɔrəˈtɛriən, ə-] *adj* : autoritario
authoritative [əˈθɔrəˌteɪt̬ɪv, ɔ-] *adj* **1** RELIABLE : fidedigno, autorizado **2** DICTATORIAL : autoritario, dictatorial, imperioso
authoritatively [əˈθɔrəˌteɪt̬ɪvli, ɔ-] *adv* **1** RELIABLY : con autoridad **2** DICTATORIALLY : de manera autoritaria
authority [əˈθɔrət̬i, ɔ-] *n, pl* **-ties** **1** EXPERT : autoridad *f*; experto *m*, -ta *f* **2** POWER : autoridad *f*, poder *m* **3** AUTHORIZATION : autorización *f*, licencia *f* **4 the authorities** : las autoridades **5 on good authority** : de buena fuente
authorization [ˌɔθərəˈzeɪʃən] *n* : autorización *f*
authorize [ˈɔθəˌraɪz] *vt* **-rized; -rizing** : autorizar, facultar
authorship [ˈɔθərˌʃɪp] *n* : autoría *f*
autism [ˈɔˌtɪzəm] *n* : autismo *m*
autistic [ɔˈtɪstɪk] *adj* : autista
auto [ˈɔt̬o] → **automobile**
autobiographical [ˌɔt̬oˌbaɪəˈgræfɪkəl] *adj* : autobiográfico
autobiography [ˌɔt̬obaɪˈɑgrəfi] *n, pl* **-phies** : autobiografía *f*
autocracy [ɔˈtɑkrəsi] *n, pl* **-cies** : autocracia *f*
autocrat [ˈɔt̬əˌkræt] *n* : autócrata *mf*
autocratic [ˌɔt̬əˈkræt̬ɪk] *adj* : autocrático — **autocratically** [-t̬ɪkli] *adv*
autograph[1] [ˈɔt̬əˌgræf] *vt* : autografiar
autograph[2] *n* : autógrafo *m*
automaker [ˈɔt̬o:meɪkər] *n* : fabricante *mf* de autos, automotriz *f*
automate [ˈɔt̬əˌmeɪt] *vt* **-mated; -mating** : automatizar
automatic [ˌɔt̬əˈmæt̬ɪk] *adj* : automático — **automatically** [-t̬ɪkli] *adv*
automation [ˌɔt̬əˈmeɪʃə n] *n* : automatización *f*
automaton [ɔˈtɑməˌtɑn] *n, pl* **-atons** *or* **-ata** [-t̬ə, -ˌtɑ] : autómata *m*
automobile [ˌɔt̬əmoˈbi:l, -ˈmo:ˌbi:l] *n* : automóvil *m*, auto *m*, carro *m*, coche *m*
automotive [ˌɔt̬əˈmo:t̬ɪv] *adj* : automotor
autonomous [ɔˈtɑnəməs] *adj* : autónomo — **autonomously** *adv*
autonomy [ɔˈtɑnəmi] *n, pl* **-mies** : autonomía *f*
autopsy [ˈɔˌtɑpsi, -təp-] *n, pl* **-sies** : autopsia *f*
autumn [ˈɔt̬əm] *n* : otoño *m*
autumnal [ɔˈtʌmnəl] *adj* : otoñal
auxiliary[1] [ɔgˈzɪljəri, -ˈzɪləri] *adj* : auxiliar
auxiliary[2] *n, pl* **-ries** : auxiliar *mf*, ayudante *mf*
avail[1] [əˈveɪl] *vt* **to avail oneself** : aprovecharse, valerse
avail[2] *n* **1** : provecho *m*, utilidad *f* **2 to no avail** : en vano **3 to be of no avail** : no servir de nada, ser inútil
availability [əˌveɪləˈbɪlət̬i] *n, pl* **-ties** : disponibilidad *f*
available [əˈveɪləbəl] *adj* : disponible
avalanche [ˈævəˌlæntʃ] *n* : avalancha *f*, alud *m*
avarice [ˈævərəs] *n* : avaricia *f*, codicia *f*
avaricious [ˌævəˈrɪʃəs] *adj* : avaricioso, codicioso
avenge [əˈvɛndʒ] *vt* **avenged; avenging** : vengar
avenger [əˈvɛndʒər] *n* : vengador *m*, -dora *f*
avenue [ˈævəˌnu:, -ˌnju:] *n* **1** : avenida *f* **2** MEANS : vía *f*, camino *m*
average[1] [ˈævrɪdʒ, ˈævə-] *vt* **-aged; -aging** **1** : hacer un promedio de ⟨he averages 8 hours a day : hace un promedio de 8 horas diarias⟩ **2** : calcular el promedio de, promediar (en matemáticas)
average[2] *adj* **1** MEAN : medio ⟨the average temperature : la temperatura media⟩ **2** ORDINARY : común, ordinario ⟨the average man : el hombre común⟩

average[3] *n* : promedio *m*
averse [ə'vərs] *adj* : reacio, opuesto
aversion [ə'vərʒən] *n* : aversión *f*
avert [ə'vərt] *vt* **1** : apartar, desviar ⟨he averted his eyes from the scene : apartó los ojos de la escena⟩ **2** AVOID, PREVENT : evitar, prevenir
aviary ['eɪvi,ɛri] *n, pl* **-aries** : pajarera *f*
aviation [,eɪvi'eɪʃən] *n* : aviación *f*
aviator ['eɪvi,eɪt̬ər] *n* : aviador *m*, -dora *f*
avid ['ævɪd] *adj* **1** GREEDY : ávido, codicioso **2** ENTHUSIASTIC : ávido, entusiasta, ferviente — **avidly** *adv*
avocado [,ævə'kado, ,ɑvə-] *n, pl* **-dos** : aguacate *m*, palta *f*
avocation [,ævə'keɪʃən] *n* : pasatiempo *m*, afición *f*
avoid [ə'vɔɪd] *vt* **1** SHUN : evitar, eludir **2** FORGO : evitar, abstenerse de ⟨I always avoided gossip : siempre evitaba los chismes⟩ **3** EVADE : evitar ⟨if I can avoid it : si puedo evitarlo⟩
avoidable [ə'vɔɪdəbəl] *adj* : evitable
avoidance [ə'vɔɪdənts] *n* : el evitar
avoirdupois [,ævərdə'pɔɪz] *n* : sistema *m* inglés de pesos y medidas
avow [ə'vaʊ] *vt* : reconocer, confesar
avowal [ə'vaʊəl] *n* : reconocimiento *m*, confesión *f*
await [ə'weɪt] *vt* : esperar
awake[1] [ə'weɪk] *v* **awoke** [ə'wo:k]; **awoken** [ə'wo:kən] *or* **awaked; awaking** : despertar
awake[2] *adj* : despierto
awaken [ə'weɪkən] → **awake**[1]
award[1] [ə'wɔrd] *vt* : otorgar, conceder, conferir
award[2] *n* **1** PRIZE : premio *m*, galardón *m* **2** MEDAL : condecoración *f*
aware [ə'wær] *adj* : consciente ⟨to be aware of : darse cuenta de, estar consciente de⟩
awareness [ə'wærnəs] *n* : conciencia *f*, conocimiento *m*
awash [ə'wɔʃ] *adj* : inundado
away[1] [ə'weɪ] *adv* **1** : de aquí ⟨go away! : ¡fuera de aquí!, ¡vete!⟩ **2** : de distancia ⟨10 miles away : 10 millas de distancia, queda a 10 millas⟩ **3 far away** : lejos, a lo lejos **4 right away** : en seguida, ahora mismo **5 to be away** : estar ausente, estar de viaje **6 to give away** : regalar (una posesión), revelar (un secreto) **7 to go away** : irse, largarse **8 to put away** : guardar **9 to turn away** : volver la cara
away[2] *adj* **1** ABSENT : ausente ⟨away for the week : ausente por la semana⟩ **2 away game** : partido *m* que se juega fuera
awe[1] ['ɔ] *vt* **awed; awing** : abrumar, asombrar, impresionar
awe[2] *n* : asombro *m*
awesome ['ɔsəm] *adj* **1** IMPOSING : imponente, formidable **2** AMAZING : asombroso
awestruck ['ɔ,strʌk] *adj* : asombrado
awful ['ɔfəl] *adj* **1** AWESOME : asombroso **2** DREADFUL : horrible, terrible, atroz **3** ENORMOUS : enorme, tremendo ⟨an awful lot of people : muchísima gente, la mar de gente⟩
awfully ['ɔfəli] *adv* **1** EXTREMELY : terriblemente, extremadamente **2** BADLY : muy mal, espantosamente
awhile [ə'*h*waɪl] *adv* : un rato, algún tiempo
awkward ['ɔkwərd] *adj* **1** CLUMSY : torpe, desmañado **2** EMBARRASSING : embarazoso, delicado — **awkwardly** *adv*
awkwardness ['ɔkwərdnəs] *n* **1** CLUMSINESS : torpeza *f* **2** INCONVENIENCE : incomodidad *f*
awl ['ɔl] *n* : punzón *m*
awning ['ɔnɪŋ] *n* : toldo *m*
awry [ə'raɪ] *adj* **1** ASKEW : torcido **2 to go awry** : salir mal, fracasar
ax *or* **axe** ['æks] *n* : hacha *m*
axiom ['æksiəm] *n* : axioma *m*
axiomatic [,æksiə'mæt̬ɪk] *adj* : axiomático
axis ['æksɪs] *n, pl* **axes** [-,si:z] : eje *m*
axle ['æksəl] *n* : eje *m*
aye[1] ['aɪ] *adv* : sí
aye[2] *n* : sí *m*
azalea [ə'zeɪljə] *n* : azalea *f*
azimuth ['æzəməθ] *n* : azimut *m*, acimut *m*
Aztec ['æz,tɛk] *n* : azteca *mf*
azure[1] ['æʒər] *adj* : azur, celeste
azure[2] *n* : azur *m*

B

b ['bi:] *n, pl* **b's** *or* **bs** ['bi:z] : segunda letra del alfabeto inglés
babble[1] ['bæbəl] *vi* **-bled; -bling** **1** PRATTLE : balbucear **2** CHATTER : charlatanear, parlotear *fam* **3** MURMUR : murmurar
babble[2] *n* : balbuceo *m* (de bebé), parloteo *m* (de adultos), murmullo *m* (de voces, de un arroyo)
babe ['beɪb] *n* → **baby**[3]
babel ['beɪbəl, 'bæ-] *n* : babel *f*, caos *m*
baboon [bæ'bu:n] *n* : babuino *m*
baby[1] ['beɪbi] *vt* **-bied; -bying** : mimar, consentir
baby[2] *adj* **1** : de niño ⟨a baby carriage : un cochecito⟩ ⟨baby talk : habla infantil⟩ **2** TINY : pequeño, minúsculo
baby[3] *n, pl* **-bies** : bebé *m*; niño *m*, -ña *f*
babyhood ['beɪbi,hʊd] *n* : niñez *f*, primera infancia *f*
babyish ['beɪbiɪʃ] *adj* : infantil, pueril

baby–sit [ˈbeɪbiˌsɪt] *vi* **-sat** [-ˌsæt]; **-sitting** : cuidar niños, hacer de canguro *Spain*

baby–sitter [ˈbeɪbiˌsɪtər] *n* : niñero *m*, -ra *f*; canguro *mf Spain*

baccalaureate [ˌbækəˈlɔriət] *n* : licenciatura *f*

bachelor [ˈbætʃələr] *n* **1** : soltero *m* **2** : licenciado *m*, -da *f* <bachelor of arts degree : licenciatura en filosofía y letras>

bacillus [bəˈsɪləs] *n, pl* **-li** [-ˌlaɪ] : bacilo *m*

back[1] [ˈbæk] *vt* **1** *or* **to back up** SUPPORT : apoyar, respaldar **2** *or* **to back up** REVERSE : darle marcha atrás a (un vehículo) **3** : estar detrás de, formar el fondo de <trees back the garden : unos árboles están detrás del jardín> — *vi* **1** *or* **to back up** : retroceder **2 to back away** : echarse atrás **3 to back down** *or* **to back out** : volverse atrás, echarse para atrás

back[2] *adv* **1** : atrás, hacia atrás, detrás <to move back : moverse atrás> <back and forth : de acá para allá> **2** AGO : atrás, antes, ya <some years back : unos años atrás, ya unos años> <10 months back : hace diez meses> **3** : de vuelta, de regreso <we're back : estamos de vuelta> <she ran back : volvió corriendo> <to call back : llamar de nuevo>

back[3] *adj* **1** REAR : de atrás, posterior, trasero **2** OVERDUE : atrasado **3 back pay** : atrasos *mpl*

back[4] *n* **1** : espalda *f* (de un ser humano), lomo *m* (de un animal) **2** : respaldo *m* (de una silla), espalda *f* (de ropa) **3** REVERSE : reverso *m*, dorso *m*, revés *m* **4** REAR : fondo *m*, parte *f* de atrás **5** : defensa *mf* (en deportes)

backache [ˈbækˌeɪk] *n* : dolor *m* de espalda

backbite [ˈbækˌbaɪt] *v* **-bit** [-ˌbɪt]; **-bitten** [-ˌbɪtən]; **-biting** *vt* : calumniar, hablar mal de — *vi* : murmurar

backbiter [ˈbækˌbaɪt̬ər] *n* : calumniador *m*, -dora *f*

backbone [ˈbækˌboːn] *n* **1** : columna *f* vertebral **2** FIRMNESS : firmeza *f*, carácter *m*

backdrop [ˈbækˌdrɑp] *n* : telón *m* de fondo

backer [ˈbækər] *n* **1** SUPPORTER : partidario *m*, -ria *f* **2** SPONSOR : patrocinador *m*, -dora *f*

backfire[1] [ˈbækˌfaɪr] *vi* **-fired; -firing 1** : petardear (dícese de un automóvil) **2** FAIL : fallar, salir el tiro por la culata

backfire[2] *n* : petardeo *m*, explosión *f*

background [ˈbækˌgraʊnd] *n* **1** : fondo *m* (de un cuadro, etc.), antecedentes *mpl* (de una situación) **2** EXPERIENCE, TRAINING : experiencia *f* profesional, formación *f*

backhand[1] [ˈbækˌhænd] *adv* : de revés, con el revés

backhand[2] *n* : revés *m*

backhanded [ˈbækˌhændəd] *adj* **1** : dado con el revés, de revés **2** INDIRECT : indirecto, ambiguo

backing [ˈbækɪŋ] *n* **1** SUPPORT : apoyo *m*, respaldo *m* **2** REINFORCEMENT : refuerzo *m* **3** SUPPORTERS : partidarios *mpl*, -rias *fpl*

backlash [ˈbækˌlæʃ] *n* : reacción *f* violenta

backlog [ˈbækˌlɔg] *n* : atraso *m*, trabajo *m* acumulado

backpack[1] [ˈbækˌpæk] *vi* : viajar con mochila

backpack[2] *n* : mochila *f*

backrest [ˈbækˌrɛst] *n* : respaldo *m*

backside [ˈbækˌsaɪd] *n* : trasero *m*

backslide [ˈbækˌslaɪd] *vi* **-slid** [-ˌslɪd]; **-slid** *or* **-slidden** [-ˌslɪdən]; **-sliding** : recaer, reincidir

backstage [ˌbækˈsteɪdʒ, ˈbækˌ-] *adv & adj* : entre bastidores

backtrack [ˈbækˌtræk] *vi* : dar marcha atrás, volverse atrás

backup [ˈbækˌʌp] *n* **1** SUPPORT : respaldo *m*, apoyo *m* **2** : copia *f* de seguridad (para computadoras)

backward[1] [ˈbækwərd] *or* **backwards** [-wərdz] *adv* **1** : hacia atrás **2** : de espaldas <he fell backwards : se cayó de espaldas> **3** : al revés <you're doing it backwards : lo estás haciendo al revés> **4 to bend over backwards** : hacer todo lo posible

backward[2] *adj* **1** : hacia atrás <a backward glance : una mirada hacia atrás> **2** RETARDED : retrasado **3** SHY : tímido **4** UNDERDEVELOPED : atrasado

backwardness [ˈbækwərdnəs] *n* : atraso *m* (dícese de una región), retraso *m* (dícese de una persona)

backwoods [ˌbækˈwʊdz] *npl* : monte *m*, región *f* alejada

bacon [ˈbeɪkən] *n* : tocino *m*, tocineta *f Col, Ven*, bacon *m Spain*

bacterial [bækˈtɪriəl] *adj* : bacteriano

bacteriologist [bækˌtɪriˈɑlədʒɪst] *n* : bacteriólogo *m*, -ga *f*

bacteriology [bækˌtɪriˈɑlədʒi] *n* : bacteriología *f*

bacterium [bækˈtɪriəm] *n, pl* **-ria** [-iə] : bacteria *f*

bad[1] [ˈbæd] *adv* → **badly**

bad[2] *adj* **1** : malo **2** ROTTEN : podrido **3** SERIOUS, SEVERE : grave **4** DEFECTIVE : defectuoso <a bad check : un cheque sin fondos> **5** HARMFUL : perjudicial **6** CORRUPT, EVIL : malo, corrompido **7** NAUGHTY : travieso **8 from bad to worse** : de mal en peor **9 too bad!** : ¡qué lástima!

bad[3] *n* : lo malo <the good and the bad : lo bueno y lo malo>

bade → **bid**

badge [ˈbædʒ] *n* : insignia *f*, botón *m*, chapa *f*

badger[1] [ˈbædʒər] *vt* : fastidiar, acosar, importunar

badger[2] *n* : tejón *m*
badly [ˈbædli] *adv* **1** : mal **2** URGENTLY : mucho, con urgencia **3** SEVERELY : gravemente
badminton [ˈbædˌmɪntən, -ˌmɪt-] *n* : bádminton *m*
badness [ˈbædnəs] *n* : maldad *f*
baffle[1] [ˈbæfəl] *vi* **-fled; -fling 1** PERPLEX : desconcertar, confundir **2** FRUSTRATE : frustrar
baffle[2] *n* : deflector *m*, bafle *m* (acústico)
bafflement [ˈbæfəlmənt] *n* : desconcierto *m*, confusión *f*
bag[1] [ˈbæg] *v* **bagged; bagging** *vi* SAG : formar bolsas — *vt* **1** : ensacar, poner en una bolsa **2** : cobrar (en la caza), cazar
bag[2] *n* **1** : bolsa *f*, saco *m* **2** HANDBAG : cartera *f*, bolso *m*, bolsa *f Mex* **3** SUITCASE : maleta *f*, valija *f*
bagatelle [ˌbægəˈtɛl] *n* : bagatela *f*
bagel [ˈbeɪgəl] *n* : rosquilla *f* de pan
baggage [ˈbægɪʤ] *n* : equipaje *m*
baggy [ˈbægi] *adj* **-gier; -est** : holgado, ancho
bagpipe [ˈbægˌpaɪp] *n or* **bagpipes** [ˈbægˌpaɪps] *npl* : gaita *f*
bail[1] [ˈbeɪl] *vt* **1** : achicar (agua de un bote) **2 to bail out** : poner en libertad (de una cárcel) bajo fianza **3 to bail out** EXTRICATE : sacar de apuros
bail[2] *n* : fianza *f*, caución *f*
bailiff [ˈbeɪləf] *n* : alguacil *mf*
bailiwick [ˈbeɪliˌwɪk] *n* : dominio *m*
bailout [ˈbeɪlˌaʊt] *n* : rescate *m* (financiero)
bait[1] [ˈbeɪt] *vt* **1** : cebar (un anzuelo o cepo) **2** HARASS : acosar
bait[2] *n* : cebo *m*, carnada *f*
bake[1] [ˈbeɪk] *vt* **baked; baking** : hornear, hacer al horno
bake[2] *n* : fiesta con platos hechos al horno
baker [ˈbeɪkər] *n* : panadero *m*, -ra *f*
baker's dozen *n* : docena *f* de fraile
bakery [ˈbeɪkəri] *n, pl* **-ries** : panadería *f*
bakeshop [ˈbeɪkˌʃɑp] *n* : pastelería *f*, panadería *f*
baking powder *n* : levadura *f* en polvo
baking soda → sodium bicarbonate
balance[1] [ˈbælənts] *v* **-anced; -ancing** *vt* **1** : hacer el balance de (una cuenta) ⟨to balance the books : cuadrar las cuentas⟩ **2** EQUALIZE : balancear, equilibrar **3** HARMONIZE : armonizar — *vi* : balancearse
balance[2] *n* **1** SCALES : balanza *f*, báscula *f* **2** COUNTERBALANCE : contrapeso *m* **3** EQUILIBRIUM : equilibrio *m* **4** REMAINDER : balance *m*, resto *m*
balanced [ˈbæləntst] *adj* : equilibrado, balanceado
balcony [ˈbælkəni] *n, pl* **-nies 1** : balcón *m*, terraza *f* (de un edificio) **2** : galería *f* (de un teatro)
bald [ˈbɔld] *adj* **1** : calvo, pelado, pelón **2** PLAIN : simple, puro ⟨the bald truth : la pura verdad⟩
balding [ˈbɔldɪŋ] *adj* : quedándose calvo
baldly [ˈbɔldli] *adv* : sin reparos, sin rodeos, francamente
baldness [ˈbɔldnəs] *n* : calvicie *f*
bale[1] [ˈbeɪl] *vt* **baled; baling** : empacar, hacer balas de
bale[2] *n* : bala *f*, fardo *m*, paca *f*
baleful [ˈbeɪlfəl] *adj* **1** DEADLY : mortífero **2** SINISTER : siniestro, funesto, torvo ⟨a baleful glance : una mirada torva⟩
balk[1] [ˈbɔk] *vt* : obstaculizar, impedir — *vi* **1** : plantarse *fam* (dícese de un caballo, etc.) **2 to balk at** : resistarse a, mostrarse reacio a
balk[2] *n* : obstáculo *m*
Balkan [ˈbɔlkən] *adj* : balcánico
balky [ˈbɔki] *adj* **balkier; -est** : reacio, obstinado, terco
ball[1] [ˈbɔl] *vt* : apelotonar, ovillar
ball[2] *n* **1** : pelota *f*, bola *f*, balón *m*, ovillo *m* (de lana) **2** : juego *m* con pelota o bola **3** DANCE : baile *m*, baile *m* de etiqueta
ballad [ˈbæləd] *n* : romance *m*, balada *f*
balladeer [ˌbæləˈdɪr] *n* : cantante *mf* de baladas
ballast[1] [ˈbæləst] *vt* : lastrar
ballast[2] *n* : lastre *m*
ball bearing *n* : cojinete *m* de bola
ballerina [ˌbæləˈriːnə] *n* : bailarina *f*
ballet [bæˈleɪ, ˈbæˌleɪ] *n* : ballet *m*
ballistic [bəˈlɪstɪk] *adj* : balístico
ballistics [bəˈlɪstɪks] *ns & pl* : balística *f*
balloon[1] [bəˈluːn] *vi* **1** : viajar en globo **2** SWELL : hincharse, inflarse
balloon[2] *n* : globo *m*
balloonist [bəˈluːnɪst] *n* : aeróstata *mf*
ballot[1] [ˈbælət] *vi* : votar
ballot[2] *n* **1** : papeleta *f* (de voto) **2** BALLOTING : votación *f* **3** VOTE : voto *m*
ballpoint pen [ˈbɔlˌpɔɪnt] *n* : bolígrafo *m*
ballroom [ˈbɔlˌruːm, -ˌrʊm] *n* : sala *f* de baile
ballyhoo [ˈbæliˌhuː] *n* : propaganda *f*, publicidad *f*, bombo *m fam*
balm [ˈbɑm, ˈbɑlm] *n* : bálsamo *m*, ungüento *m*
balmy [ˈbɑmi, ˈbɑl-] *adj* **balmier; -est 1** MILD : templado, agradable **2** SOOTHING : balsámico **3** CRAZY : chiflado *fam*, chalado *fam*
baloney [bəˈloːni] *n* NONSENSE : tonterías *fpl*, estupideces *fpl*
balsa [ˈbɔlsə] *n* : balsa *f*
balsam [ˈbɔlsəm] *n* **1** : bálsamo *m* **2** *or* **balsam fir** : abeto *m* balsámico
Baltic [ˈbɔltɪk] *adj* : báltico
baluster [ˈbæləstər] *n* : balaustre *m*
balustrade [ˈbæləˌstreɪd] *n* : balaustrada *f*
bamboo [bæmˈbuː] *n* : bambú *m*
bamboozle [bæmˈbuːzəl] *vt* **-zled; -zling** : engañar, embaucar

ban[1] [ˈbæn] *vt* **banned; banning** : prohibir, proscribir

ban[2] *n* : prohibición *f*, proscripción *f*

banal [bəˈnɑl, bəˈnæl, ˈbeɪnəl] *adj* : banal, trivial

banality [bəˈnæləṯi] *n, pl* **-ties** : banalidad *f*, trivialidad *f*

banana [bəˈnænə] *n* : banano *m*, plátano *m*, banana *f*, cambur *m Ven*, guineo *m Car*

band[1] [ˈbænd] *vt* **1** BIND : fajar, atar **2 to band together** : unirse, juntarse

band[2] *n* **1** STRIP : banda *f*, cinta *f* (de un sombrero, etc.) **2** STRIPE : franja *f* **3** : banda *f* (de radiofrecuencia) **4** RING : anillo *m* **5** GROUP : banda *f*, grupo *m*, conjunto *m* <jazz band : conjunto de jazz>

bandage[1] [ˈbændɪʤ] *vt* **-daged; -daging** : vendar

bandage[2] *n* : vendaje *m*, venda *f*

bandanna *or* **bandana** [bænˈdænə] *n* : pañuelo *m* (de colores)

bandit [ˈbændət] *n* : bandido *m*, -da *f*; bandolero *m*, -ra *f*

banditry [ˈbændətri] *n* : bandolerismo *m*, bandidaje *m*

bandstand [ˈbændˌstænd] *n* : quiosco *m* de música

bandwagon [ˈbændˌwægən] *n* **1** : carroza *f* de músicos **2 to jump on the bandwagon** : subirse al carro, seguir la moda

bandy[1] [ˈbændi] *vt* **-died; -dying 1** EXCHANGE : intercambiar **2 to bandy about** : circular, propagar

bandy[2] *adj* : arqueado, torcido <bandy-legged : de piernas arqueadas>

bane [ˈbeɪn] *n* **1** POISON : veneno *m* **2** RUIN : ruina *f*, pesadilla *f*

baneful [ˈbeɪnfəl] *adj* : nefasto, funesto

bang[1] [ˈbæŋ] *vt* **1** STRIKE : golpear, darse <he banged his elbow against the door : se dio con el codo en la puerta> **2** SLAM : cerrar (la puerta) con un portazo — *vi* **1** SLAM : cerrarse de un golpe **2 to bang on** : aporrear, golpear <she was banging on the table : aporreaba la mesa>

bang[2] *adv* : directamente, exactamente

bang[3] *n* **1** BLOW : golpe *m*, porrazo *m*, trancazo *m* **2** EXPLOSION : explosión *f*, estallido *m* **3** SLAM : portazo *m* **4 bangs** *npl* : flequillo *m*, fleco *m*

Bangladeshi [ˌbɑŋgləˈdɛʃi, ˌbæŋ-, ˌbʌŋ-, -ˈdeɪ-] *n* : bangladesí *mf* — **Bangladeshi** *adj*

bangle [ˈbæŋgəl] *n* : brazalete *m*, pulsera *f*

banish [ˈbænɪʃ] *vt* **1** EXILE : desterrar, exiliar **2** EXPEL : expulsar

banishment [ˈbænɪʃmənt] *n* **1** EXILE : destierro *m*, exilio *m* **2** EXPULSION : expulsión *f*

banister [ˈbænəstər] *n* **1** BALUSTER : balaustre *m* **2** HANDRAIL : pasamanos *m*, barandilla *f*, barandal *m*

banjo [ˈbænˌʤoː] *n, pl* **-jos** : banjo *m*

bank[1] [ˈbæŋk] *vt* **1** TILT : peraltar (una carretera), ladear (un avión) **2** HEAP : amontonar **3** : cubrir (un fuego) **4** : depositar (dinero en un banco) — *vi* **1** : ladearse (dícese de un avión) **2** : tener una cuenta (en un banco) **3 to bank on** : contar con

bank[2] *n* **1** MASS : montón *m*, montículo *m*, masa *f* **2** : orilla *f*, ribera *f* (de un río) **3** : peralte *m* (de una carretera) **4** : banco *m* <World Bank : Banco Mundial> <banco de sangre : blood bank>

bankbook [ˈbæŋkˌbʊk] *n* : libreta *f* bancaria, libreta *f* de ahorros

banker [ˈbæŋkər] *n* : banquero *m*, -ra *f*

banking [ˈbæŋkɪŋ] *n* : banca *f*

bankrupt[1] [ˈbæŋˌkrʌpt] *vt* : hacer quebrar, llevar a la quiebra, arruinar

bankrupt[2] *adj* **1** : en bancarrota, en quiebra **2 ~ of** LACKING : carente de, falto de

bankrupt[3] *n* : fallido *m*, -da *f*; quebrado *m*, -da *f*

bankruptcy [ˈbæŋˌkrʌptsi] *n, pl* **-cies** : ruina *f*, quiebra *f*, bancarrota *f*

banner[1] [ˈbænər] *adj* : excelente

banner[2] *n* : estandarte *m*, bandera *f*

banns [ˈbænz] *npl* : amonestaciones *fpl*

banquet[1] [ˈbæŋkwət] *vi* : celebrar un banquete

banquet[2] *n* : banquete *m*

banter[1] [ˈbæntər] *vi* : bromear, hacer bromas

banter[2] *n* : bromas *fpl*

baptism [ˈbæpˌtɪzəm] *n* : bautismo *m*

baptismal [bæpˈtɪzməl] *adj* : bautismal

Baptist [ˈbæptɪst] *n* : bautista *mf* — **Baptist** *adj*

baptize [bæpˈtaɪz, ˈbæpˌtaɪz] *vt* **-tized; -tizing** : bautizar

bar[1] [ˈbɑr] *vt* **barred; barring 1** OBSTRUCT : obstruir, bloquear **2** EXCLUDE : excluir **3** PROHIBIT : prohibir **4** SECURE : atrancar, asegurar <bar the door! : ¡atranca la puerta!>

bar[2] *n* **1** : barra *f*, barrote *m* (de una ventana), tranca *f* (de una puerta) **2** BARRIER : barrera *f*, obstáculo *m* **3** LAW : abogacía *f* **4** STRIPE : franja *f* **5** COUNTER : mostrador *m*, barra *f* **6** TAVERN : bar *m*, taberna *f*

bar[3] *prep* **1** : excepto, con excepción de **2 bar none** : sin excepción

barb [ˈbɑrb] *n* **1** POINT : púa *f*, lengüeta *f* **2** GIBE : pulla *f*

barbarian[1] [bɑrˈbæriən] *adj* **1** : bárbaro **2** CRUDE : tosco, bruto

barbarian[2] *n* : bárbaro *m*, -ra *f*

barbaric [bɑrˈbærɪk] *adj* **1** PRIMITIVE : primitivo **2** CRUEL : brutal, cruel

barbarity [bɑrˈbærəṯi] *n, pl* **-ties** : barbaridad *f*

barbarous [ˈbɑrbərəs] *adj* **1** UNCIVILIZED : bárbaro **2** MERCILESS : despiadado, cruel

barbarously [ˈbɑrbərəsli] *adv* : bárbaramente

barbecue[1] [ˈbɑrbɪˌkjuː] *vt* **-cued; -cuing** : asar a la parrilla
barbecue[2] *n* : barbacoa *f*, parrillada *f*
barbed [ˈbɑrbd] *adj* **1** : con púas ⟨barbed wire : alambre de púas⟩ **2** BITING : mordaz
barber [ˈbɑrbər] *n* : barbero *m*, -ra *f*
barbiturate [bɑrˈbɪʧərət] *n* : barbitúrico *m*
bard [ˈbɑrd] *n* : bardo *m*
bare[1] [ˈbær] *vt* **bared; baring** : desnudar
bare[2] *adj* **1** NAKED : desnudo **2** EXPOSED : descubierto, sin protección **3** EMPTY : desprovisto, vacío **4** MINIMUM : mero, mínimo ⟨the bare necessities : las necesidades mínimas⟩ **5** PLAIN : puro, sencillo
bareback [ˈbærˌbæk] *or* **barebacked** [-ˌbækt] *adv & adj* : a pelo
barefaced [ˈbærˌfeɪst] *adj* : descarado
barefoot [ˈbærˌfʊt] *or* **barefooted** [-ˌfʊt̬əd] *adv & adj* : descalzo
bareheaded [ˈbærˈhɛdəd] *adv & adj* : sin sombrero, con la cabeza descubierta
barely [ˈbærli] *adv* : apenas, por poco
bareness [ˈbærnəs] *n* : desnudez *f*
bargain[1] [ˈbɑrgən] *vi* HAGGLE : regatear, negociar — *vt* BARTER : trocar, cambiar
bargain[2] *n* **1** AGREEMENT : acuerdo *m*, convenio *m* ⟨to strike a bargain : cerrar un trato⟩ **2** : ganga *f* ⟨bargain price : precio de ganga⟩
barge[1] [ˈbɑrʤ] *vi* **barged; barging 1** : mover con torpeza **2 to barge in** : entrometerse, interrumpir
barge[2] *n* : barcaza *f*, gabarra *f*
bar graph *n* : gráfico *m* de barras
baritone [ˈbærəˌtoːn] *n* : barítono *m*
barium [ˈbæriəm] *n* : bario *m*
bark[1] [ˈbɑrk] *vi* : ladrar — *vt or* **to bark out** : gritar ⟨to bark out an order : dar una orden a gritos⟩
bark[2] *n* **1** : ladrido *m* (de un perro) **2** : corteza *f* (de un árbol) **3** *or* **barque** : tipo de embarcación con velas de proa y popa
barley [ˈbɑrli] *n* : cebada *f*
barn [ˈbɑrn] *n* : granero *m* (para cosechas), establo *m* (para ganado)
barnacle [ˈbɑrnɪkəl] *n* : percebe *m*
barnyard [ˈbɑrnˌjɑrd] *n* : corral *m*
barometer [bəˈrɑmət̬ər] *n* : barómetro *m*
barometric [ˌbærəˈmɛtrɪk] *adj* : barométrico
baron [ˈbærən] *n* **1** : barón *m* **2** TYCOON : magnate *mf*
baroness [ˈbærənɪs, -nəs, -ˌnɛs] *n* : baronesa *f*
baronet [ˌbærəˈnɛt, ˈbærənət] *n* : baronet *m*
baronial [bəˈroːniəl] *adj* **1** : de barón **2** STATELY : señorial, majestuoso
baroque [bəˈroːk, -ˈrɑk] *adj* : barroco
barracks [ˈbærəks] *ns & pl* : cuartel *m*
barracuda [ˌbærəˈkuːdə] *n, pl* **-da** *or* **-das** : barracuda *f*
barrage [bəˈrɑʒ, -ˈrɑʤ] *n* **1** : descarga *f* (de artillería) **2** DELUGE : aluvión *m* ⟨a barrage of questions : un aluvión de preguntas⟩
barred [ˈbɑrd] *adj* : excluido, prohibido
barrel[1] [ˈbærəl] *v* **-reled** *or* **-relled; -reling** *or* **-relling** *vt* : embarrilar — *vi* : ir disparado
barrel[2] *n* **1** : barril *m*, tonel *m* **2** : cañón *m* (de un arma de fuego), cilindro *m* (de una cerradura)
barren [ˈbærən] *adj* **1** STERILE : estéril (dícese de las plantas o la mujer), árido (dícese del suelo) **2** DESERTED : yermo, desierto
barrette [bɑˈrɛt, bə-] *n* : pasador *m*, broche *m* para el cabello
barricade[1] [ˈbærəˌkeɪd, ˌbærəˈ-] *vt* **-caded; -cading** : cerrar con barricadas
barricade[2] *n* : barricada *f*
barrier [ˈbæriər] *n* **1** : barrera *f* **2** OBSTACLE : obstáculo *m*, impedimento *m*
barring [ˈbɑrɪŋ] *prep* : excepto, salvo, a excepción de
barrio [ˈbɑrio, ˈbær-] *n* : barrio *m*
barroom [ˈbɑrˌruːm, -ˌrʊm] *n* : bar *m*
barrow [ˈbærˌoː] → **wheelbarrow**
bartender [ˈbɑrˌtɛndər] *n* : camarero *m*, -ra *f*; barman *m*
barter[1] [ˈbɑrt̬ər] *vt* : cambiar, trocar
barter[2] *n* : trueque *m*, permuta *f*
basalt [bəˈsɔlt, ˈbeɪˌ-] *n* : basalto *m*
base[1] [ˈbeɪs] *vt* **based; basing** : basar, fundamentar, establecer
base[2] *adj* **baser; basest 1** : de baja ley (dícese de un metal) **2** CONTEMPTIBLE : vil, despreciable
base[3] *n, pl* **bases** : base *f*
baseball [ˈbeɪsˌbɔl] *n* : beisbol *m*, béisbol *m*
baseless [ˈbeɪsləs] *adj* : infundado
basely [ˈbeɪsli] *adv* : vilmente
basement [ˈbeɪsmənt] *n* : sótano *m*
baseness [ˈbeɪsnəs] *n* : vileza *f*, bajeza *f*
bash[1] [ˈbæʃ] *vt* : golpear violentamente
bash[2] *n* **1** BLOW : golpe *m*, porrazo *m*, madrazo *m Mex fam* **2** PARTY : fiesta *f*, juerga *f fam*
bashful [ˈbæʃfəl] *adj* : tímido, vergonzoso, penoso
bashfulness [ˈbæʃfəlnəs] *n* : timidez *f*
basic[1] [ˈbeɪsɪk] *adj* **1** FUNDAMENTAL : básico, fundamental **2** RUDIMENTARY : básico, elemental **3** : básico (en química)
basic[2] *n* : fundamento *m*, rudimento *m*
basically [ˈbeɪsɪkli] *adv* : fundamentalmente
basil [ˈbeɪzəl, ˈbæzəl] *n* : albahaca *f*
basilica [bəˈsɪlɪkə] *n* : basílica *f*
basin [ˈbeɪsən] *n* **1** WASHBOWL : palangana *f*, lavamanos *m*, lavabo *m* **2** : cuenca *f* (de un río)
basis [ˈbeɪsəs] *n, pl* **bases** [-ˌsiːz] **1** BASE : base *f*, pilar *m* **2** FOUNDATION : fundamento *m*, base *f* **3 on a weekly basis** : semanalmente

bask ['bæsk] *vi* : disfrutar, deleitarse ‹to bask in the sun : disfrutar del sol›
basket ['bæskət] *n* : cesta *f*, cesto *m*, canasta *f*
basketball ['bæskət,bɔl] *n* : baloncesto *m*, basquetbol *m*
bas–relief [,bɑrɪ'li:f] *n* : bajorrelieve *m*
bass[1] ['bæs] *n, pl* **bass** *or* **basses** : róbalo *m* (pesca)
bass[2] ['beɪs] *n* : bajo *m* (tono, voz, cantante)
bass drum *n* : bombo *m*
basset hound ['bæsət,haʊnd] *n* : basset *m*
bassinet [,bæsə'nɛt] *n* : moisés *m*, cuna *f*
bassist ['beɪsɪst] *n* : bajista *mf*
bassoon [bə'su:n, bæ-] *n* : fagot *m*
bass viol ['beɪs'vaɪəl, -,o:l] → **double bass**
bastard[1] ['bæstərd] *adj* : bastardo
bastard[2] *n* : bastardo *m*, -da *f*
bastardize ['bæstər,daɪz] *vt* **-ized; -izing** DEBASE : degradar, envilecer
baste ['beɪst] *vt* **basted; basting 1** STITCH : hilvanar **2** : bañar (con su jugo durante la cocción)
bastion ['bæstʃən] *n* : bastión *m*, baluarte *m*
bat[1] ['bæt] *vt* **batted; batting 1** HIT : batear **2 without batting an eye** : sin pestañear
bat[2] *n* **1** : murciélago *m* (animal) **2** : bate *m* ‹baseball bat : bate de beisbol›
batch ['bætʃ] *n* : hornada *f*, tanda *f*, grupo *m*, cantidad *f*
bate ['beɪt] *vt* **bated; bating 1** : aminorar, reducir **2 with bated breath** : con ansiedad, aguantando la respiración
bath ['bæθ, 'baθ] *n, pl* **baths** ['bæðz, 'bæθs, 'baðz, 'baθs] **1** BATHING : baño *m* ‹to take a bath : bañarse› **2** : baño *m* (en fotografía, etc.) **3** BATHROOM : baño *m*, cuarto *m* de baño **4** SPA : balneario *m* **5** LOSS : pérdida *f*
bathe ['beɪð] *v* **bathed; bathing** *vt* **1** WASH : bañar, lavar **2** SOAK : poner en remojo **3** FLOOD : inundar ‹to bathe with light : inundar de luz› — *vi* : bañarse, ducharse
bather ['beɪðər] *n* : bañista *mf*
bathrobe ['bæθ,ro:b] *n* : bata *f* (de baño)
bathroom ['bæθ,ru:m, -,rʊm] *n* : baño *m*, cuarto *m* de baño
bathtub ['bæθ,tʌb] *n* : bañera *f*, tina *f* (de baño)
batiste [bə'ti:st] *n* : batista *f*
baton [bə'tɑn] *n* : batuta *f*, bastón *m*
battalion [bə'tæljən] *n* : batallón *m*
batten ['bætən] *vt* **to batten down the hatches** : cerrar las escotillas
batter[1] ['bæṭər] *vt* **1** BEAT : aporrear, golpear **2** MISTREAT : maltratar
batter[2] *n* **1** : masa *f* para rebozar **2** HITTER : bateador *m*, -dora *f*
battering ram *n* : ariete *m*
battery ['bæṭəri] *n, pl* **-teries 1** : lesiones *fpl* ‹assault and battery : agresión con lesiones› **2** ARTILLERY : batería *f* **3** : batería *f*, pila *f* (de electricidad) **4** SERIES : serie *f*
batting ['bæṭɪŋ] *n* **1** *or* **cotton batting** : algodón *m* en láminas **2** : bateo *m* (en beisbol)
battle[1] ['bæṭəl] *vi* **-tled; -tling** : luchar, pelear
battle[2] *n* : batalla *f*, lucha *f*, pelea *f*
battle–ax ['bæṭəl,æks] *n* : hacha *f* de guerra
battlefield ['bæṭəl,fɪ:ld] *n* : campo *m* de batalla
battlements ['bæṭəlmənts] *npl* : almenas *fpl*
battleship ['bæṭəl,ʃɪp] *n* : acorazado *m*
batty ['bæṭi] *adj* **-tier; -est** : chiflado *fam*, chalado *fam*
bauble ['bɔbəl] *n* : chuchería *f*, baratija *f*
Bavarian [bə'vɛriən] *n* : bávaro *m*, -ra *f* — **Bavarian** *adj*
bawdiness ['bɔdinəs] *n* : picardía *f*
bawdy ['bɔdi] *adj* **bawdier; -est** : subido de tono, verde, colorado *Mex*
bawl[1] ['bɔl] *vi* : llorar a gritos
bawl[2] *n* : grito *m*, alarido *m*
bawl out *vt* SCOLD : regañar
bay[1] ['beɪ] *vi* HOWL : aullar
bay[2] *adj* : castaño, zaino (dícese de los caballos)
bay[3] *n* **1** : bahía *f* ‹Bay of Campeche : Bahía de Campeche› **2** *or* **bay horse** : caballo *m* castaño **3** LAUREL : laurel *m* **4** HOWL : aullido *m* **5** : saliente *m* ‹bay window : ventana en saliente› **6** COMPARTMENT : área *f*, compartimento *m* **7 at ∼** : acorralado
bayberry ['beɪ,bɛri] *n, pl* **-ries** : arrayán *m* brabántico
bayonet[1] [,beɪə'nɛt, 'beɪə,nɛt] *vt* **-neted; -neting** : herir *o* matar) con bayoneta
bayonet[2] *n* : bayoneta *f*
bayou ['baɪ,u:, -,o:] *n* : pantano *m*
bazaar [bə'zɑr] *n* **1** : bazar *m* **2** SALE : venta *f* benéfica
bazooka [bə'zu:kə] *n* : bazuca *f*
BB ['bi:bi] *n* : balín *m*
be ['bi:] *v* **was** ['wəz, 'wɑz]; **were** ['wər]; **been** ['bɪn]; **being; am** ['æm]; **is** ['ɪz]; **are** ['ɑr] *vi* **1** (*expressing equality*) : ser ‹José is a doctor : José es doctor› ‹I'm Ann's sister : soy la hermana de Ana› **2** (*expressing quality*) : ser ‹the tree is tall : el árbol es alto› ‹you're silly! : ¡eres tonto!› **3** (*expressing origin or possession*) : ser ‹she's from Managua : es de Managua› ‹it's mine : es mío› **4** (*expressing location*) : estar ‹my mother is at home : mi madre está en casa› ‹the cups are on the table : las tazas están en la mesa› **5** (*expressing existence*) : ser, existir ‹to be or not to be : ser, o no ser› ‹I think, therefore I am : pienso, luego existo› **6** (*expressing a state of being*) : estar, tener ‹how are you? : ¿cómo estás?› ‹I'm cold : tengo frío› ‹she's 10 years old : tiene 10 años› ‹they're both sick : están en-

fermos los dos> — *v impers* **1** (*indicating time*) : ser <it's eight o'clock : son las ocho> <it's Friday : hoy es viernes> **2** (*indicating a condition*) : hacer, estar <it's sunny : hace sol> <it's very dark outside : está bien oscuro afuera> — *v aux* **1** (*expressing progression*) : estar <what are you doing?—I'm working : ¿qué haces?—estoy trabajando> **2** (*expressing occurrence*) : ser <it was finished yesterday : fue acabado ayer, se acabó ayer> <it was cooked in the oven : se cocinó en el horno> **3** (*expressing possibility*) : poderse <can she be trusted? : ¿se puede confiar en ella?> **4** (*expressing obligation*) : deber <you are to stay here : debes quedarte aquí> <he was to come yesterday : se esperaba que viniese ayer>

beach[1] [ˈbiːtʃ] *vt* : hacer embarrancar, hacer varar, hacer encallar

beach[2] *n* : playa *f*

beachcomber [ˈbiːtʃˌkoːmər] *n* : raquero *m*, -ra *f*

beachhead [ˈbiːtʃˌhɛd] *n* : cabeza *f* de playa

beacon [ˈbiːkən] *n* : faro *m*

bead[1] [ˈbiːd] *vi* : formarse en gotas

bead[2] *n* **1** : cuenta *f* **2** DROP : gota *f* **3 beads** *npl* NECKLACE : collar *m*

beady [ˈbiːdi] *adj* **beadier; -est 1** : de forma de cuenta **2 beady eyes** : ojos *mpl* pequeños y brillantes

beagle [ˈbiːgəl] *n* : beagle *m*

beak [ˈbiːk] *n* : pico *m*

beaker [ˈbiːkər] *n* **1** CUP : taza *f* alta **2** : vaso *m* de precipitados (en un laboratorio)

beam[1] [ˈbiːm] *vi* **1** SHINE : brillar **2** SMILE : sonreír radiantemente — *vt* BROADCAST : transmitir, emitir

beam[2] *n* **1** : viga *f*, barra *f* **2** RAY : rayo *m*, haz *m* de luz **3** : haz *m* de radiofaro (para guiar pilotos, etc.)

bean [ˈbiːn] *n* **1** : habichuela *f*, frijol *m* **2 broad bean** : haba *f* **3 string bean** : judía *f*

bear[1] [ˈbær] *v* **bore** [ˈbor]; **borne** [ˈbɔrn]; **bearing** *vt* **1** CARRY : llevar, portar **2** : dar a luz a (un niño) **3** PRODUCE : dar (frutas, cosechas) **4** ENDURE, SUPPORT : soportar, resistir, aguantar — *vi* **1** TURN : doblar, dar la vuelta <bear right : doble a la derecha> **2 to bear up** : resistir

bear[2] *n, pl* **bears** *or* **bear** : oso *m*, osa *f*

bearable [ˈbærəbəl] *adj* : soportable

beard [ˈbɪrd] *n* **1** : barba *f* **2** : arista *f* (de plantas)

bearded [ˈbɪrdəd] *adj* : barbudo, de barba

bearer [ˈbærər] *n* : portador *m*, -dora *f*

bearing [ˈbærɪŋ] *n* **1** CONDUCT, MANNERS : comportamiento *m*, modales *mpl* **2** SUPPORT : soporte *f* **3** SIGNIFICANCE : relación *f*, importancia *f* <to have no bearing on : no tener nada que ver con> **4** : cojinete *m*, rodamiento *m* (de una máquina) **5** COURSE, DIRECTION : dirección *f*, rumbo *m* <to get one's bearings : orientarse>

beast [ˈbiːst] *n* **1** : bestia *f*, fiera *f* <beast of burden : animal de carga> **2** BRUTE : bruto *m*, -ta *f*; bestia *mf*

beastly [ˈbiːstli] *adj* : detestable, repugnante

beat[1] [ˈbiːt] *v* **beat; beaten** [ˈbiːtən] *or* **beat; beating** *vt* **1** STRIKE : golpear, pegar, darle una paliza (a alguien) **2** DEFEAT : vencer, derrotar **3** AVOID : anticiparse a, evitar <to beat the crowd : evitar el gentío> **4** MASH, WHIP : batir — *vi* THROB : palpitar, latir

beat[2] *adj* EXHAUSTED : derrengado, muy cansado <I'm beat! : ¡estoy molido!>

beat[3] *n* **1** : golpe *m*, redoble *m* (de un tambor), latido *m* (del corazón) **2** RHYTHM : ritmo *m*, tiempo *m*

beater [ˈbiːt̬ər] *n* **1** : batidor *m*, -dora *f* **2** EGGBEATER : batidor *m*

beatific [ˌbiːəˈtɪfɪk] *adj* : beatífico

beatitude [biˈæt̬əˌtuːd] *n* **1** : beatitud *f* **2 the Beatitudes** : las bienaventuranzas

beau [ˈboː] *n, pl* **beaux** *or* **beaus** : pretendiente *m*, galán *m*

beautification [ˌbjuːt̬əfəˈkeɪʃən] *n* : embellecimiento *m*

beautiful [ˈbjuːt̬ɪfəl] *adj* : hermoso, bello, lindo, precioso

beautifully [ˈbjuːt̬ɪfəli] *adv* **1** ATTRACTIVELY : hermosamente **2** EXCELLENTLY : maravillosamente, excelentemente

beauty [ˈbjuːt̬i] *n, pl* **-ties** : belleza *f*, hermosura *f*, beldad *f*

beauty shop *or* **beauty salon** *n* : salón *m* de belleza

beaver [ˈbiːvər] *n* : castor *m*

because [bɪˈkʌz, -ˈkɔz] *conj* : porque

because of *prep* : por, a causa de, debido a

beck [ˈbɛk] *n* **to be at the beck and call of** : estar a la entera disposición de, estar sometido a la voluntad de

beckon [ˈbɛkən] *vi* **to beckon to someone** : hacerle señas a alguien

become [bɪˈkʌm] *v* **-came** [-ˈkeɪm]; **-come; -coming** *vi* : hacerse, volverse, ponerse <he became famous : se hizo famoso> <to become sad : ponerse triste> <to become accustomed to : acostumbrarse a> — *vt* **1** BEFIT : ser apropiado para **2** SUIT : favorecer, quedarle bien (a alguien) <that dress becomes you : ese vestido te favorece>

becoming [bɪˈkʌmɪŋ] *adj* **1** SUITABLE : apropiado **2** FLATTERING : favorecedor

bed[1] [ˈbɛd] *v* **bedded; bedding** *vt* : acostar — *vi* : acostarse

bed[2] *n* **1** : cama *f*, lecho *m* **2** : cauce *m* (de un río), fondo *m* (del mar) **3** : arriate *m* (para plantas) **4** LAYER, STRATUM : estrato *m*, capa *f*

bedbug ['bɛd,bʌg] *n* : chinche *f*
bedclothes ['bɛd,klo:ðz, -,klo:z] *npl* : ropa *f* de cama, sábanas *fpl*
bedding ['bɛdɪŋ] *n* **1** → **bedclothes 2** : cama *f* (para animales)
bedeck [bɪ'dɛk] *vt* : adornar, engalanar
bedevil [bɪ'dɛvəl] *vt* **-iled** *or* **-illed; -iling** *or* **-illing** : acosar, plagar
bedlam ['bɛdləm] *n* : locura *f*, caos *m*, alboroto *m*
bedraggled [bɪ'drægəld] *adj* : desaliñado, despeinado
bedridden ['bɛd,rɪdən] *adj* : postrado en cama
bedrock ['bɛd,rɑk] *n* : lecho *m* de roca
bedroom ['bɛd,ru:m, -,rʊm] *n* : dormitorio *m*, habitación *f*, pieza *f*, recámara *f Col, Mex, Pan*
bedspread ['bɛd,sprd] *n* : cubrecama *m*, colcha *f*, cobertor *m*
bee ['bi:] *n* **1** : abeja *f* (insecto) **2** GATHERING : círculo *m*, reunión *f*
beech ['bi:ʧ] *n, pl* **beeches** *or* **beech** : haya *f*
beechnut ['bi:ʧ,nʌt] *n* : hayuco *m*
beef[1] ['bi:f] *vt* **to beef up** : fortalecer, reforzar — *vi* COMPLAIN : quejarse
beef[2] *n, pl* **beefs** ['bi:fs] *or* **beeves** ['bi:vz] : carne *f* de vaca, carne *f* de res *CA, Mex*
beefsteak ['bi:f,steɪk] *n* : filete *m*, bistec *m*
beehive ['bi:,haɪv] *n* : colmena *f*
beekeeper ['bi:,ki:pər] *n* : apicultor *m*, -tora *f*
beeline ['bi:,laɪn] *n* **to make a beeline for** : ir derecho a, ir directo hacia
been → **be**
beep[1] ['bi:p] *v* : pitar
beep[2] *n* : pitido *m*
beeper ['bi:pər] *n* : busca *m*, buscapersonas *m*
beer ['bɪr] *n* : cerveza *f*
beeswax ['bi:z,wæks] *n* : cera *f* de abejas
beet ['bi:t] *n* : remolacha *f*, betabel *m Mex*
beetle ['bi:ţəl] *n* : escarabajo *m*
befall [bɪ'fɔl] *v* **-fell** [-'fl]; **-fallen** [-'fɔlən] *vt* : sucederle a, acontecerle a — *vi* : acontecer
befit [bɪ'fɪt] *vt* **-fitted; -fitting** : convenir a, ser apropiado para
before[1] [bɪ'for] *adv* **1** : antes ⟨before and after : antes y después⟩ **2** : anterior ⟨the month before : el mes anterior⟩
before[2] *conj* : antes que ⟨he would die before surrendering : moriría antes que rendirse⟩
before[3] *prep* **1** : antes de ⟨before eating : antes de comer⟩ **2** : delante de, ante ⟨I stood before the house : estaba parada delante de la casa⟩ ⟨before the judge : ante el juez⟩
beforehand [bɪ'for,hænd] *adv* : antes, por adelantado, de antemano, con anticipación
befriend [bɪ'frɛnd] *vt* : hacerse amigo de
befuddle [bɪ'fʌdəl] *vt* **-dled; -dling** : aturdir, ofuscar, confundir
beg ['bɛg] *v* **begged; begging** *vt* : pedir, mendigar, suplicar ⟨I begged him to go : le supliqué que fuera⟩ — *vi* : mendigar, pedir limosna
beget [bɪ'gɛt] *vt* **-got** [-'gɑt]; **-gotten** [-'gɑtən] *or* **-got; -getting** : engendrar
beggar ['bɛgər] *n* : mendigo *m*, -ga *f*; pordiosero *m*, -ra *f*
begin [bɪ'gɪn] *v* **-gan** [-'gæn]; **-gun** [-'gʌn]; **-ginning** *vt* : empezar, comenzar, iniciar — *vi* **1** START : empezar, comenzar, iniciarse **2** ORIGINATE : nacer, originarse **3 to begin with** : en primer lugar, para empezar
beginner [bɪ'gɪnər] *n* : principiante *mf*
beginning [bɪ'gɪnɪŋ] *n* : principio *m*, comienzo *m*
begone [bi'gɔn] *interj* : ¡fuera de aquí!
begonia [bɪ'go:njə] *n* : begonia *f*
begrudge [bɪ'grʌʤ] *vt* **-grudged; -grudging 1** : dar de mala gana **2** ENVY : envidiar, resentir
beguile [bɪ'gaɪl] *vt* **-guiled; -guiling 1** DECEIVE : engañar **2** AMUSE : divertir, entretener
behalf [bɪ'hæf, -'haf] *n* **1** : favor *m*, beneficio *m*, parte *f* **2 on behalf of** *or* **in behalf of** : de parte de, en nombre de
behave [bɪ'heɪv] *vi* **-haved; -having** : comportarse, portarse
behavior [bɪ'heɪvjər] *n* : comportamiento *m*, conducta *f*
behead [bɪ'hd] *vt* : decapitar
behest [bɪ'hɛst] *n* **1** : mandato *m*, orden *f* **2 at the behest of** : a instancia de
behind[1] [bɪ'haɪnd] *adv* : atrás, detrás ⟨to fall behind : quedarse atrás⟩
behind[2] *prep* **1** : atrás de, detrás de, tras ⟨behind the house : detrás de la casa⟩ ⟨one behind another : uno tras otro⟩ **2** : atrasado con, después de ⟨behind schedule : atrasado con el trabajo⟩ ⟨I arrived behind the others : llegué después de los otros⟩ **3** SUPPORTING : en apoyo de, detrás
behind[3] [bɪ'haɪnd, 'bi:,haɪnd] *n* : trasero *m*
behold [bɪ'ho:ld] *vt* **-held; -holding** : contemplar
beholder [bɪ'ho:ldər] *n* : observador *m*, -dora *f*
behoove [bɪ'hu:v] *vt* **-hooved; -hooving** : convenirle a, corresponderle a ⟨it behooves us to help him : nos conviene ayudarlo⟩
beige[1] ['beɪʒ] *adj* : beige
beige[2] *n* : beige *m*
being ['bi:ɪŋ] *n* **1** EXISTENCE : ser *m*, existencia *f* **2** CREATURE : ser *m*, ente *m*
belabor [bɪ'leɪbər] *vt* **to belabor the point** : extenderse sobre el tema
belated [bɪ'leɪţəd] *adj* : tardío, retrasado
belch[1] ['bɛlʧ] *vi* **1** BURP : eructar **2** EXPEL : expulsar, arrojar
belch[2] *n* : eructo *m*

beleaguer [bɪˈliːgər] *vt* **1** BESIEGE : asediar, sitiar **2** HARASS : fastidiar, molestar
belfry [ˈbɛlfri] *n, pl* **-fries** : campanario *m*
Belgian [ˈbɛlʤən] *n* : belga *mf* — **Belgian** *adj*
belie [bɪˈlaɪ] *vt* **-lied; -lying 1** MISREPRESENT : falsear, ocultar **2** CONTRADICT : contradecir, desmentir
belief [bəˈliːf] *n* **1** TRUST : confianza *f* **2** CONVICTION : creencia *f*, convicción *f* **3** FAITH : fe *f*
believable [bəˈliːvəbəl] *adj* : verosímil, creíble
believe [bəˈliːv] *v* **-lieved; -lieving** : creer
believer [bəˈliːvər] *n* **1** : creyente *mf* **2** : partidario *m*, -ria *f*; entusiasta *mf* ⟨she's a great believer in vitamins : ella es una gran partidaria de las vitaminas⟩
belittle [bɪˈlɪt̬əl] *vt* **-littled; -littling 1** DISPARAGE : menospreciar, denigrar, rebajar **2** MINIMIZE : minimizar, quitar importancia a
Belizean [bəˈliːziən] *n* : beliceño *m*, -ña *f* — **Belizean** *adj*
bell[1] [ˈbɛl] *vt* : ponerle un cascabel a
bell[2] *n* : campana *f*, cencerro *m* (para una vaca o cabra), cascabel *m* (para un gato), timbre *m* (de teléfono, de la puerta)
belle [ˈbɛl] *n* : belleza *f*, beldad *f*
bellhop [ˈbɛlˌhɑp] *n* : botones *m*
bellicose [ˈbɛlɪˌkoːs] *adj* : belicoso *m* — **bellicosity** [ˌbɛlɪˈkɑsət̬i] *n*
belligerence [bəˈlɪʤərənts] *n* : agresividad *f*, beligerancia *f*
belligerent[1] [bəˈlɪʤərənt] *adj* : agresivo, beligerante
belligerent[2] *n* : beligerante *mf*
bellow[1] [ˈbɛˌloː] *vi* : bramar, mugir — *vt* : gritar
bellow[2] *n* : bramido *m*, grito *m*
bellows [ˈbɛˌloːz] *ns & pl* : fuelle *m*
bellwether [ˈbɛlˌwɛðər] *n* : líder *mf*
belly[1] [ˈbɛli] *vi* **-lied; -lying** SWELL : hincharse, inflarse
belly[2] *n, pl* **-lies** : abdomen *m*, vientre *m*, barriga *f*, panza *f*
belong [bɪˈlɔŋ] *vi* **1** : pertenecer (a), ser propiedad (de) ⟨it belongs to her : pertenece a ella, es suyo, es de ella⟩ **2** : ser parte (de), ser miembro (de) ⟨he belongs to the club : es miembro del club⟩ **3** : deber estar, ir ⟨your coat belongs in the closet : tu abrigo va en el ropero⟩
belongings [bɪˈlɔŋɪŋz] *npl* : pertenencias *fpl*, efectos *mpl* personales
beloved[1] [bɪˈlʌvəd, -ˈlʌvd] *adj* : querido, amado
beloved[2] *n* : amado *m*, -da *f*; enamorado *m*, -da *f*; amor *m*
below[1] [bɪˈloː] *adv* : abajo
below[2] *prep* **1** : abajo de, debajo de ⟨below the window : debajo de la ventana⟩ **2** : por debajo de, bajo ⟨below average : por debajo del promedio⟩ ⟨5 degrees below zero : 5 grados bajo cero⟩
belt[1] [ˈbɛlt] *vt* **1** : ceñir con un cinturón, ponerle un cinturón a **2** THRASH : darle una paliza a, darle un trancazo a
belt[2] *n* **1** : cinturón *m*, cinto *m* (para el talle) **2** BAND, STRAP : cinta *f*, correa *f*, banda *f Mex* **3** AREA : frente *m*, zona *f*
beltway [ˈbɛltˌweɪ] *n* : carretera *f* de circunvalación; periférico *m CA, Mex*; libramiento *m Mex*
bemoan [bɪˈmoːn] *vt* : lamentarse de
bemuse [bɪˈmjuːz] *vt* **-mused; -musing 1** BEWILDER : confundir, desconcertar **2** ENGROSS : absorber
bench [ˈbɛntʃ] *n* **1** SEAT : banco *m*, escaño *m*, banca *f* **2** : estrado *m* (de un juez) **3** COURT : tribunal *m*
bend[1] [ˈbɛnd] *v* **bent** [ˈbnt;]; **bending** *vt* : torcer, doblar, curvar, flexionar — *vi* **1** : torcerse, agacharse ⟨to bend over : inclinarse⟩ **2** TURN : torcer, hacer una curva
bend[2] *n* **1** TURN : vuelta *f*, recodo *m* **2** CURVE : curva *f*, ángulo *m*, codo *m*
beneath[1] [bɪˈniːθ] *adv* : bajo, abajo, debajo
beneath[2] *prep* : bajo de, abajo de, por debajo de
benediction [ˌbɛnəˈdɪkʃən] *n* : bendición *f*
benefactor [ˈbɛnəˌfæktər] *n* : benefactor *m*, -tora *f*
beneficence [bəˈnɛfəsənts] *n* : beneficencia *f*
beneficent [bəˈnɛfəsənt] *adj* : benéfico, caritativo
beneficial [ˌbɛnəˈfɪʃəl] *adj* : beneficioso, provechoso — **beneficially** *adv*
beneficiary [ˌbɛnəˈfɪʃiˌɛri, -ˈfɪʃəri] *n, pl* **-ries** : beneficiario *m*, -ria *f*
benefit[1] [ˈbɛnəfɪt] *vt* : beneficiar — *vi* : beneficiarse
benefit[2] *n* **1** ADVANTAGE : beneficio *m*, ventaja *f*, provecho *m* **2** AID : asistencia *f*, beneficio *m* **3** : función *f* benéfica (para recaudar fondos)
benevolence [bəˈnɛvələnts] *n* : bondad *f*, benevolencia *f*
benevolent [bəˈnɛvələnt] *adj* : benévolo, bondadoso — **benevolently** *adv*
Bengali [bɛnˈgɔli, bɛŋ-] *n* **1** : bengalí *mf* **2** : bengalí *m* (idioma) — **Bengali** *adj*
benign [bɪˈnaɪn] *adj* **1** GENTLE, KIND : benévolo, amable **2** FAVORABLE : propicio, favorable **3** MILD : benigno ⟨a benign tumor : un tumor benigno⟩
Beninese [bəˌnɪˈniːz, -ˌniː-, -ˈniːs; ˌbnɪˈ-] *n* : beninés *m*, -nesa *f* — **Beninese** *adj*
bent [ˈbɛnt] *n* : aptitud *f*, inclinación *f*
benumb [bɪˈnʌm] *vt* : entumecer
benzene [ˈbɛnˌziːn] *n* : benceno *m*
bequeath [bɪˈkwiːθ, -ˈkwiːð] *vt* : legar, dejar en testamento
bequest [bɪˈkwɛst] *n* : legado *m*
berate [bɪˈreɪt] *vt* **-rated; -rating** : reprender, regañar
bereaved[1] [bɪˈriːvd] *adj* : que está de luto, afligido (por la muerte de alguien)

bereaved[2] *n* **the bereaved** : los deudos del difunto (o de la difunta)

bereavement [bɪˈriːvmənt] *n* **1** SORROW : dolor *m*, pesar *m* **2** LOSS : pérdida *f*

bereft [bɪˈrɛft] *adj* : privado, desprovisto

beret [bəˈreɪ] *n* : boina *f*

beriberi [ˌbɛriˈbɛri] *n* : beriberi *m*

berm [ˈbərm] *n* : arcén *m*

berry [ˈbɛri] *n, pl* **-ries** : baya *f*

berserk [bərˈsərk, -ˈzərk] *adj* **1** : enloquecido **2 to go beserk** : volverse loco

berth[1] [ˈbərθ] *vi* : atracar

berth[2] *n* **1** DOCK : atracadero *m* **2** ACCOMMODATION : litera *f*, camarote *m* **3** POSITION : trabajo *m*, puesto *m*

beryl [ˈbɛrəl] *n* : berilo *m*

beseech [bɪˈsiːʧ] *vt* **-seeched** *or* **-sought** [-ˈsɔt]; **-seeching** : suplicar, implorar, rogar

beset [bɪˈsɛt] *vt* **-set; -setting 1** HARASS : acosar **2** SURROUND : rodear

beside [bɪˈsaɪd] *prep* : al lado de, junto a

besides[1] [bɪˈsaɪdz] *adv* **1** ALSO : además, también, aparte **2** MOREOVER : además, por otra parte

besides[2] *prep* **1** : además de, aparte de ⟨six others besides you : seis otros además de ti⟩ **2** EXCEPT : excepto, fuera de, aparte de

besiege [bɪˈsiːʤ] *vt* **-sieged; -sieging** : asediar, sitiar, cercar

besmirch [bɪˈsmərʧ] *vt* : ensuciar, mancillar

best[1] [ˈbɛst] *vt* : superar, ganar a

best[2] *adv* (*superlative* of **well**) : mejor ⟨as best I can : lo mejor que puedo⟩

best[3] *adj* (*superlative* of **good**) : mejor ⟨my best friend : mi mejor amigo⟩

best[4] *n* **1 the best** : lo mejor, el mejor, la mejor, los mejores, las mejores **2 at ~** : a lo más **3 to do one's best** : hacer todo lo posible

bestial [ˈbɛsʧəl, ˈbiːs-] *adj* **1** : bestial **2** BRUTISH : brutal, salvaje

best man *n* : padrino *m*

bestow [bɪˈstoː] *vt* : conferir, otorgar, conceder

bestowal [bɪˈstoːəl] *n* : concesión *f*, otorgamiento *m*

bet[1] [ˈbɛt] *v* **bet; betting** *vt* : apostar — *vi* **to bet on** : apostarle a

bet[2] *n* : apuesta *f*

betoken [bɪˈtoːkən] *vt* : denotar, ser indicio de

betray [bɪˈtreɪ] *vt* **1** : traicionar ⟨to betray one's country : traicionar uno a su patria⟩ **2** DIVULGE, REVEAL : delatar, revelar ⟨to betray a secret : revelar un secreto⟩

betrayal [bɪˈtreɪəl] *n* : traición *f*, delación *f*, revelación *f* ⟨betrayal of trust : abuso de confianza⟩

betrothal [bɪˈtroːðəl, -ˈtrɔ-] *n* : esponsales *mpl*, compromiso *m*

betrothed [bɪˈtroːðd, -ˈtrɔθt] *n* FIANCÉ : prometido *m*, -da *f*

better[1] [ˈbɛt̬ər] *vt* **1** IMPROVE : mejorar **2** SURPASS : superar

better[2] *adv* (*comparative* of **well**) **1** : mejor **2** MORE : más ⟨better than 50 miles : más de 50 millas⟩

better[3] *adj* (*comparative* of **good**) **1** : mejor ⟨the weather is better today : hace mejor tiempo hoy⟩ ⟨I was sick, but now I'm better : estuve enfermo, pero ahora estoy mejor⟩ **2** : mayor ⟨the better part of a month : la mayor parte de un mes⟩

better[4] *n* **1** : el mejor, la mejor ⟨the better of the two : el mejor de los dos⟩ **2 to get the better of** : vencer a, quedar por encima de, superar

betterment [ˈbɛt̬ərmənt] *n* : mejoramiento *m*, mejora *f*

bettor *or* **better** [ˈbɛt̬ər] *n* : apostador *m*, -dora *f*

between[1] [bɪˈtwiːn] *adv* **1** : en medio, por lo medio **2 in ~** : intermedio

between[2] *prep* : entre

bevel[1] [ˈbɛvəl] *v* **-eled** *or* **-elled; -eling** *or* **-elling** *vt* : biselar — *vi* INCLINE : inclinarse

bevel[2] *n* : bisel *m*

beverage [ˈbɛvrɪʤ, ˈbɛvə-] *n* : bebida *f*

bevy [ˈbɛvi] *n, pl* **bevies** : grupo *m* (de personas), bandada *f* (de pájaros)

bewail [bɪˈweɪl] *vt* : lamentarse de, llorar

beware [bɪˈwær] *vi* **to beware of** : tener cuidado con ⟨beware of the dog! : ¡cuidado con el perro!⟩ — *vt* : guardarse de, cuidarse de

bewilder [bɪˈwɪldər] *vt* : desconcertar, dejar perplejo

bewilderment [bɪˈwɪldərmənt] *n* : desconcierto *m*, perplejidad *f*

bewitch [bɪˈwɪʧ] *vt* **1** : hechizar, embrujar **2** CHARM : cautivar, encantar

bewitchment [bɪˈwɪʧmənt] *n* : hechizo *m*

beyond[1] [biˈjɑnd] *adv* **1** FARTHER, LATER : más allá, más lejos (en el espacio), más adelante (en el tiempo) **2** MORE : más ⟨$50 and beyond : $50 o más⟩

beyond[2] *n* **the beyond** : el más allá, lo desconocido

beyond[3] *prep* **1** : más allá de ⟨beyond the frontier : más allá de la frontera⟩ **2** : fuera de ⟨beyond one's reach : fuera de su alcance⟩ **3** BESIDES : además de

biannual [ˌbaɪˈænjuəl] *adj* : bianual — **biannually** *adv*

bias[1] [ˈbaɪəs] *vt* **-ased** *or* **-assed; -asing** *or* **-assing 1** : predisponer, sesgar, influir en, afectar **2 to be biased against** : tener prejuicio contra

bias[2] *n* **1** : sesgo *m*, bies *m* (en la costura) **2** PREJUDICE : prejuicio *m* **3** TENDENCY : inclinación *f*, tendencia *f*

biased [ˈbaɪəst] *adj* : tendencioso, parcial

bib [ˈbɪb] *n* **1** : peto *m* **2** : babero *m* (para niños)

Bible [ˈbaɪbəl] *n* : Biblia *f*

biblical [ˈbɪblɪkəl] *adj* : bíblico

bibliographer [ˌbɪbliˈɑgrəfər] *n* : bibliógrafo *m*, -fa *f*

bibliographic [ˌbɪbliəˈgræfɪk] *adj* : bibliográfico

bibliography [ˌbɪbliˈɑgrəfi] *n, pl* **-phies** : bibliografía *f*

bicameral [ˌbaɪˈkæmərəl] *adj* : bicameral

bicarbonate [ˌbaɪˈkɑrbənət, -ˌneɪt] *n* : bicarbonato *m*

bicentennial [ˌbaɪsɛnˈtɛniəl] *n* : bicentenario *m*

biceps [ˈbaɪˌsɛps] *ns & pl* : bíceps *m*

bicker[1] [ˈbɪkər] *vi* : pelear, discutir, reñir

bicker[2] *n* : pelea *f*, riña *f*, discusión *f*

bicuspid [baɪˈkʌspɪd] *n* : premolar *m*, diente *m* bicúspide

bicycle[1] [ˈbaɪsɪkəl, -ˌsɪ-] *vi* **-cled; -cling** : ir en bicicleta

bicycle[2] *n* : bicicleta *f*

bicycling [ˈbaɪsɪkəlɪŋ] *n* : ciclismo *m*

bicyclist [ˈbaɪsɪkəlɪst] *n* : ciclista *mf*

bid[1] [ˈbɪd] *vt* **bade** [ˈbæd, ˈbeɪd] *or* **bid; bidden** [ˈbɪdən] *or* **bid; bidding 1** ORDER : pedir, mandar **2** INVITE : invitar **3** SAY : dar, decir ⟨to bid good evening : dar las buenas noches⟩ ⟨to bid farewell to : decir adiós a⟩ **4** : ofrecer (en una subasta), declarar (en juegos de cartas)

bid[2] *n* **1** OFFER : oferta *f* (en una subasta), declaración *f* (en juegos de cartas) **2** INVITATION : invitación *f* **3** ATTEMPT : intento *m*, tentativa *f*

bidder [ˈbɪdər] *n* : postor *m*, -tora *f*

bide [ˈbaɪd] *v* **bode** [ˈboːd] *or* **bided; bided; biding** *vt* : esperar, aguardar ⟨to bide one's time : esperar el momento oportuno⟩ — *vi* DWELL : morar, vivir

biennial [baɪˈɛniəl] *adj* : bienal — **biennially** *adv*

bier [ˈbɪr] *n* **1** STAND : andas *fpl* **2** COFFIN : ataúd *m*, féretro *m*

bifocals [ˈbaɪˌfoːkəlz] *npl* : lentes *mpl* bifocales, bifocales *mpl*

big [ˈbɪg] *adj* **bigger; biggest 1** LARGE : grande **2** PREGNANT : embarazada **3** IMPORTANT, MAJOR : importante, grande ⟨a big decision : una gran decisión⟩ **4** POPULAR : popular, famoso, conocido

bigamist [ˈbɪgəmɪst] *n* : bígamo *m*, -ma *f*

bigamous [ˈbɪgəməs] *adj* : bígamo

bigamy [ˈbɪgəmi] *n* : bigamia *f*

Big Dipper → **dipper**

bighorn [ˈbɪgˌhɔrn] *n, pl* **-horn** *or* **-horns** *or* **bighorn sheep** : oveja *f* salvaje de las montañas

bight [ˈbaɪt] *n* : bahía *f*, ensenada *f*, golfo *m*

bigot [ˈbɪgət] *n* : intolerante *mf*

bigoted [ˈbɪgət̬əd] *adj* : intolerante, prejuiciado, fanático

bigotry [ˈbɪgətri] *n, pl* **-tries** : intolerancia *f*

big shot *n* : pez *m* gordo *fam*, mandamás *mf*

bigwig [ˈbɪgˌwɪg] → **big shot**

bike [ˈbaɪk] *n* **1** : bicicleta *f*, bici *f fam* **2** : motocicleta *f*, moto *f*

bikini [bəˈkiːni] *n* : bikini *m*

bilateral [baɪˈlæt̬ərəl] *adj* : bilateral — **bilaterally** *adv*

bile [ˈbaɪl] *n* **1** : bilis *f* **2** IRRITABILITY : mal genio *m*

bilingual [baɪˈlɪŋgwəl] *adj* : bilingüe

bilious [ˈbɪliəs] *adj* **1** : bilioso **2** IRRITABLE : bilioso, colérico

bilk [ˈbɪlk] *vt* : burlar, estafar, defraudar

bill[1] [ˈbɪl] *vt* : pasarle la cuenta a — *vi* : acariciar ⟨to bill and coo : acariciarse⟩

bill[2] *n* **1** LAW : proyecto *m* de ley, ley *f* **2** INVOICE : cuenta *f*, factura *f* **3** POSTER : cartel *m* **4** PROGRAM : programa *m* (del teatro) **5** : billete *m* ⟨a five-dollar bill : un billete de cinco dólares⟩ **6** BEAK : pico *m*

billboard [ˈbɪlˌbɔrd] *n* : cartelera *f*

billet[1] [ˈbɪlət] *vt* : acuartelar, alojar

billet[2] *n* : alojamiento *m*

billfold [ˈbɪlˌfoːld] *n* : billetera *f*, cartera *f*

billiards [ˈbɪljərdz] *n* : billar *m*

billion [ˈbɪljən] *n, pl* **billions** *or* **billion** : mil millones *mpl*

billow[1] [ˈbɪlo] *vi* : hincharse, inflarse

billow[2] *n* **1** WAVE : ola *f* **2** CLOUD : nube *f* ⟨a billow of smoke : un nube de humo⟩

billowy [ˈbɪlowi] *adj* : ondulante

billy goat [ˈbɪliˌgoːt] *n* : macho *m* cabrío

bin [ˈbɪn] *n* : cubo *m*, cajón *m*

binary [ˈbaɪnəri, -ˌnɛri] *adj* : binario *m*

bind [ˈbaɪnd] *vt* **bound** [ˈbaʊnd]; **binding 1** TIE : atar, amarrar **2** OBLIGATE : obligar **3** UNITE : aglutinar, ligar, unir **4** BANDAGE : vendar **5** : encuadernar (un libro)

binder [ˈbaɪndər] *n* **1** FOLDER : carpeta *f* **2** : encuadernador *m*, -dora *f* (de libros)

binding [ˈbaɪndɪŋ] *n* **1** : encuadernación *f* (de libros) **2** COVER : cubierta *f*, forro *m*

binge [ˈbɪndʒ] *n* : juerga *f*, parranda *f fam*

bingo [ˈbɪŋˌgoː] *n, pl* **-gos** : bingo *m*

binocular [baɪˈnɑkjələr, bə-] *adj* : binocular

binoculars [bəˈnɑkjələrz, baɪ-] *npl* : binoculares *mpl*

biochemical[1] [ˌbaɪoˈkɛmɪkəl] *adj* : bioquímico

biochemical[2] *n* : bioquímico *m*

biochemist [ˌbaɪoˈkɛmɪst] *n* : bioquímico *m*, -ca *f*

biochemistry [ˌbaɪoˈkɛməstri] *n* : bioquímica *f*

biodegradable [ˌbaɪodɪˈgreɪdəbəl] *adj* : biodegradable

biodegradation [ˌbaɪodɛgrəˈdeɪʃən] *n* : biodegradación *f*

biodegrade [ˌbaɪodɪˈgreɪd] *vi* **-graded; -grading** : biodegradarse

biodiversity [ˌbaɪodəˈvərsət̬i, -daɪ-] *n, pl* **-ties** : biodiversidad *f*

biographer [baɪˈɑgrəfər] *n* : biógrafo *m*, -fa *f*

biographical [ˌbaɪəˈgræfɪkəl] *adj* : biográfico

biography [baɪˈɑgrəfi, biː-] *n, pl* **-phies** : biografía *f*

biologic [ˌbaɪəˈlɑʤɪk] *or* **biological** [-ʤɪkəl] *adj* : biológico

biologist [baɪˈɑləʤɪst] *n* : biólogo *m*, -ga *f*

biology [baɪˈɑləʤi] *n* : biología *f*

biophysical [ˌbaɪoˈfɪzɪkəl] *adj* : biofísico

biophysicist [ˌbaɪoˈfɪzəsɪst] *n* : biofísico *m*, -ca *f*

biophysics [ˌbaɪoˈfɪzɪks] *ns & pl* : biofísica *f*

biopsy [ˈbaɪˌɑpsi] *n, pl* **-sies** : biopsia *f*

biosphere [ˈbaɪəˌsfɪr] *n* : biosfera *f*, biósfera *f*

biotechnology [ˌbaɪotɛkˈnɑləʤi] *n* : biotecnología *f*

biotic [baɪˈɑtɪk] *adj* : biótico

bipartisan [baɪˈpɑrt̬əzən, -sən] *adj* : bipartidista, de dos partidas

biped [ˈbaɪˌpɛd] *n* : bípedo *m*

birch [ˈbərʧ] *n* : abedul *m*

bird [ˈbərd] *n* : pájaro *m* (pequeño), ave *f* (grande)

birdbath [ˈbərdˌbæθ, -ˌbaθ] *n* : pila *f* para pájaros

bird dog *n* : perro *m*, -rra *f* de caza

bird of prey *n* : ave *f* rapaz, ave *f* de presa

birdseed [ˈbərdˌsiːd] *n* : alpiste *m*

bird's–eye [ˈbərdzˌaɪ] *adj* **1** : visto desde arriba ⟨bird's-eye view : vista aérea⟩ **2** CURSORY : rápido, somero

birth [ˈbərθ] *n* **1** : nacimiento *m*, parto *m* **2** ORIGIN : origen *m*, nacimiento *m*

birthday [ˈbərθˌdeɪ] *n* : cumpleaños *m*, aniversario *m*

birthmark [ˈbərθˌmɑrk] *n* : mancha *f* de nacimiento

birthplace [ˈbərθˌpleɪs] *n* : lugar *m* de nacimiento

birthrate [ˈbərθˌreɪt] *n* : índice *m* de natalidad

birthright [ˈbərθˌraɪt] *n* : derecho *m* de nacimiento

biscuit [ˈbɪskət] *n* : bizcocho *m*

bisect [ˈbaɪˌsɛkt, ˌbaɪˈ-] *vt* : bisecar

bisexual [ˌbaɪˈsekʃʊəl] *adj* : bisexual

bishop [ˈbɪʃəp] *n* **1** : obispo *m* **2** : alfil *m* (en ajedrez)

bismuth [ˈbɪzməθ] *n* : bismuto *m*

bison [ˈbaɪzən, -sən] *ns & pl* : bisonte *m*

bistro [ˈbiːstro, ˈbɪs-] *n, pl* **-tros** : bar *m*, restaurante *m* pequeño

bit [ˈbɪt] *n* **1** FRAGMENT, PIECE : pedazo *m*, trozo *m* ⟨a bit of luck : un poco de suerte⟩ **2** : freno *m*, bocado *m* (de una brida) **3** : broca *f* (de un taladro) **4** : bit *m* (de información)

bitch[1] [ˈbɪʧ] *vi* COMPLAIN : quejarse, reclamar

bitch[2] *n* : perra *f*

bite[1] [ˈbaɪt] *v* **bit** [ˈbɪt]; **bitten** [ˈbɪtən]; **biting** *vt* **1** : morder **2** STING : picar **3** PUNCTURE : punzar, pinchar **4** GRIP : agarrar — *vi* **1** : morder ⟨that dog bites : ese perro muerde⟩ **2** STING : picar (dícese de un insecto), cortar (dícese del viento) **3** : picar ⟨the fish are biting now : ya están picando los peces⟩ **4** GRAB : agarrarse

bite[2] *n* **1** BITING : mordisco *m*, dentellada *f* **2** SNACK : bocado *m* ⟨a bite to eat : algo de comer⟩ **3** : picadura *f* (de un insecto), mordedura *f* (de un animal) **4** SHARPNESS : mordacidad *f*, penetración *f*

biting *adj* **1** PENETRATING : cortante, penetrante **2** CAUSTIC : mordaz, sarcástico

bitter [ˈbɪt̬ər] *adj* **1** ACRID : amargo, acre **2** PENETRATING : cortante, penetrante ⟨bitter cold : frío glacial⟩ **3** HARSH : duro, amargo ⟨to the bitter end : hasta el final⟩ **4** INTENSE, RELENTLESS : intenso, extremo, implacable ⟨bitter hatred : odio implacable⟩

bitterly [ˈbɪt̬ərli] *adv* : amargamente

bitterness [ˈbɪt̬ərnəs] *n* : amargura *f*

bittersweet [ˈbɪt̬ərˌswiːt] *adj* : agridulce

bivalve [ˈbaɪˌvælv] *n* : bivalvo *m* — **bivalve** *adj*

bivouac[1] [ˈbɪvəˌwæk, ˈbɪvˌwæk] *vi* **-ouacked; -ouacking** : acampar, vivaquear

bivouac[2] *n* : vivaque *m*

bizarre [bəˈzɑr] *adj* : extraño, singular, estrafalario, estrambótico — **bizarrely** *adv*

blab [ˈblæb] *vi* **blabbed; blabbing** : parlotear *fam*, cotorrear *fam*

black[1] [ˈblæk] *vt* : ennegrecer

black[2] *adj* **1** : negro (color, raza) **2** SOILED : sucio **3** DARK : oscuro, negro **4** WICKED : malvado, perverso, malo **5** GLOOMY : negro, sombrío, deprimente

black[3] *n* **1** : negro *m* (color) **2** : negro *m*, -gra *f* (persona)

black–and–blue [ˌblækənˈbluː] *adj* : amoratado

blackball [ˈblækˌbɔl] *vt* **1** OSTRACIZE : hacerle el vacío a, aislar **2** BOYCOTT : boicotear

blackberry [ˈblækˌbɛri] *n, pl* **-ries** : mora *f*

blackbird [ˈblækˌbərd] *n* : mirlo *m*

blackboard [ˈblækˌbɔrd] *n* : pizarra *f*, pizarrón *m*

blacken [ˈblækən] *vt* **1** BLACK : ennegrecer **2** DEFAME : deshonrar, difamar, manchar

blackhead [ˈblækˌhɛd] *n* : espinilla *f*, punto *m* negro

black hole *n* : agujero *m* negro

blackjack [ˈblækˌjæk] *n* **1** : cachiporra *f* (arma) **2** : veintiuna *f* (juego de cartas)

blacklist[1] [ˈblækˌlɪst] *vt* : poner en la lista negra

blacklist[2] *n* : lista *f* negra

blackmail[1] ['blæk,meɪl] *vt* : chantajear, hacer chantaje a

blackmail[2] *n* : chantaje *m*

blackmailer ['blæk,meɪlər] *n* : chantajista *mf*

blackout ['blæk,aʊt] *n* **1** : apagón *m* (de poder eléctrico) **2** FAINT : desmayo *m*, desvanecimiento *m*

black out *vt* : dejar sin luz — *vi* FAINT : perder el conocimiento, desmayarse

blacksmith ['blæk,smɪθ] *n* : herrero *m*

blacktop ['blæk,tɑp] *n* : asfalto *m*

bladder ['blædər] *n* : vejiga *f*

blade ['bleɪd] *n* : hoja *f* (de un cuchillo), cuchilla *f* (de un patín), pala *f* (de un remo o una hélice), brizna *f* (de hierba)

blamable ['bleɪməbəl] *adj* : culpable

blame[1] ['bleɪm] *vt* **blamed; blaming** : culpar, echar la culpa a

blame[2] *n* : culpa *f*

blameless ['bleɪmləs] *adj* : intachable, sin culpa, inocente — **blamelessly** *adv*

blameworthiness ['bleɪm,wərðinəs] *n* : culpa *f*, culpabilidad *f*

blameworthy ['bleɪm,wərði] *adj* : culpable, reprochable, censurable

blanch ['blæntʃ] *vt* WHITEN : blanquear — *vi* PALE : palidecer

bland ['blænd] *adj* : soso, insulso, desabrido ⟨a bland smile : una sonrisa insulsa⟩ ⟨a bland diet : una dieta fácil de digerir⟩

blandishments ['blændɪʃmənts] *npl* : lisonjas *fpl*, halagos *mpl*

blandly ['blændli] *adv* : de manera insulsa

blandness ['blændnəs] *n* : lo insulso, lo desabrido

blank[1] ['blæŋk] *vt* OBLITERATE : borrar

blank[2] *adj* **1** DAZED : perplejo, desconcertado **2** EXPRESSIONLESS : sin expresión, inexpresivo **3** : en blanco (dícese de un papel), liso (dícese de una pared) **4** EMPTY : vacío, en blanco ⟨a blank stare : una mirada vacía⟩ ⟨his mind went blank : se quedó en blanco⟩

blank[3] *n* **1** SPACE : espacio *m* en blanco **2** FORM : formulario *m* **3** CARTRIDGE : cartucho *m* de fogueo **4** *or* **blank key** : llave *f* ciega

blanket[1] [blæŋkət] *vt* : cubrir

blanket[2] *adj* : global

blanket[3] *n* : manta *f*, cobija *f*, frazada *f*

blankly ['blænkli] *adv* : sin comprender

blankness ['blænknəs] *n* **1** PERPLEXITY : desconcierto *m*, perplejidad *f* **2** EMPTINESS : vacío *m*, vacuidad *f*

blare[1] ['blær] *vi* **blared; blaring** : resonar

blare[2] *n* : estruendo *m*

blarney ['blɑrni] *n* : labia *f fam*

blasé [blɑ'zeɪ] *adj* : displicente, indiferente

blaspheme [blæs'fi:m, 'blæs,-] *vi* **-phemed; -pheming** : blasfemar

blasphemer [blæs'fi:mər, 'blæs,-] *n* : blasfemo *m*, -ma *f*

blasphemous ['blæsfəməs] *adj* : blasfemo

blasphemy ['blæsfəmi] *n, pl* **-mies** : blasfemia *f*

blast[1] ['blæst] *vt* **1** BLOW UP : volar, hacer volar **2** ATTACK : atacar, arremeter contra

blast[2] *n* **1** GUST : ráfaga *f* **2** EXPLOSION : explosión *f*

blast–off ['blæst,ɔf] *n* : despegue *m*

blast off *vi* : despegar

blatant ['bleɪtənt] *adj* : descarado — **blatantly** ['bleɪtəntli] *adv*

blaze[1] ['bleɪz] *v* **blazed; blazing** *vi* SHINE : arder, brillar, resplandecer — *vt* MARK : marcar, señalar ⟨to blaze a trail : abrir un camino⟩

blaze[2] *n* **1** FIRE : fuego *m* **2** BRIGHTNESS : resplandor *m*, brillantez *f* **3** OUTBURST : arranque *m* ⟨a blaze of anger : un arranque de cólera⟩ **4** DISPLAY : alarde *m*, llamarada *f* ⟨a blaze of color : un derroche de color⟩

blazer ['bleɪzər] *n* : chaqueta *f* deportiva, blazer *m*

bleach[1] ['bli:tʃ] *vt* : blanquear, decolorar

bleach[2] *n* : lejía *f*, blanqueador *m*

bleachers ['bli:tʃərz] *ns & pl* : gradas *fpl*, tribuna *f* descubierta

bleak ['bli:k] *adj* **1** DESOLATE : inhóspito, sombrío, desolado **2** DEPRESSING : deprimente, triste, sombrío

bleakly ['bli:kli] *adv* : sombríamente

bleakness ['bli:knəs] *n* : lo inhóspito, lo sombrío

blear ['blɪr] *adj* : empañado, nublado

bleary ['blɪri] *adj* **1** : adormilado, fatigado **2** **bleary–eyed** : con los ojos nublados

bleat[1] ['bli:t] *vi* : balar

bleat[2] *n* : balido *m*

bleed ['bli:d] *v* **bled** ['bɛld]; **bleeding** *vi* **1** : sangrar **2** GRIEVE : sufrir, afligirse **3** EXUDE : exudar (dícese de una planta), correrse (dícese de los colores) — *vt* **1** : sangrar (a una persona), purgar (frenos) **2** **to bleed someone dry** : sacarle todo el dinero a alguien

blemish[1] ['blɛmɪʃ] *vt* : manchar, marcar

blemish[2] *n* : imperfección *f*, mancha *f*, marca *f*

blend[1] ['blɛnd] *vt* **1** MIX : mezclar **2** COMBINE : combinar, aunar

blend[2] *n* : mezcla *f*, combinación *f*

blender ['blɛndər] *n* : licuadora *f*

bless ['blɛs] *vt* **blessed** ['blɛst]; **blessing** **1** CONSECRATE : bendecir, consagrar **2** : bendecir ⟨may God bless you! : ¡que Dios te bendiga!⟩ **3** **to bless with** : dotar de **4** **to bless oneself** : santiguarse

blessed ['blɛsəd] *or* **blest** ['blɛst] *adj* : bienaventurado, bendito, dichoso

blessedly ['blɛsədli] *adv* : felizmente, alegremente, afortunadamente

blessing ['blɛsɪŋ] *n* **1** : bendición *f* **2** APPROVAL : aprobación *f*, consentimiento *m*

blew → **blow**
blight[1] [ˈblaɪt] *vt* : arruinar, infestar
blight[2] *n* **1** : añublo *m* **2** PLAGUE : peste *f*, plaga *f* **3** DECAY : deterioro *m*, ruina *f*
blimp [ˈblɪmp] *n* : dirigible *m*
blind[1] [ˈblaɪnd] *vt* **1** : cegar, dejar ciego **2** DAZZLE : deslumbrar
blind[2] *adj* **1** SIGHTLESS : ciego **2** INSENSITIVE : ciego, insensible, sin razón **3** CLOSED : sin salida ⟨blind alley : callejón sin salida⟩
blind[3] *n* **1** : persiana *f* (para una ventana) **2** COVER : escondite *m*, escondrijo *m*
blinders [ˈblaɪndərz] *npl* : anteojeras *fpl*
blindfold[1] [ˈblaɪnd,fo:ld] *vt* : vendar los ojos
blindfold[2] *n* : venda *f* (para los ojos)
blinding [ˈblaɪndɪŋ] *adj* : enceguecedor, cegador ⟨with blinding speed : con una rapidez inusitada⟩
blindly [ˈblaɪndli] *adv* : a ciegas, ciegamente
blindness [ˈblaɪndnəs] *n* : ceguera *f*
blink[1] [ˈblɪŋk] *vi* **1** WINK : pestañear, parpadear **2** : brillar intermitentemente
blink[2] *n* : pestañeo *m*, parpadeo *m*
blinker [ˈblɪŋkər] *n* : intermitente *m*, direccional *f*
bliss [ˈblɪs] *n* **1** HAPPINESS : dicha *f*, felicidad *f* absoluta **2** PARADISE : paraíso *m*
blissful [ˈblɪsfəl] *adj* : dichoso, feliz — **blissfully** *adv*
blister[1] [ˈblɪstər] *vi* : ampollarse
blister[2] *n* : ampolla *f* (en la piel o una superficie), burbuja *f* (en una superficie)
blithe [ˈblaɪθ, ˈblaɪð] *adj* **blither; blithest** **1** CAREFREE : despreocupado **2** CHEERFUL : alegre, risueño — **blithely** *adv*
blitz[1] [ˈblɪts] *vt* **1** BOMBARD : bombardear **2** : atacar con rapidez
blitz[2] *n* **1** : bombardeo *m* aéreo **2** CAMPAIGN : ataque *m*, acometida *f*
blizzard [ˈblɪzərd] *n* : tormenta *f* de nieve, ventisca *f*
bloat [ˈblo:t] *vi* : hincharse, inflarse
blob [ˈblɑb] *n* : gota *f*, mancha *f*, borrón *m*
bloc [ˈblɑk] *n* : bloque *m*
block[1] [ˈblɑk] *vt* **1** OBSTRUCT : obstruir, bloquear **2** CLOG : atascar, atorar
block[2] *n* **1** PIECE : bloque *m* ⟨building blocks : cubos de construcción⟩ ⟨auction block : plataforma de subastas⟩ ⟨starting block : taco de salida⟩ **2** OBSTRUCTION : obstrucción *f*, bloqueo *m* **3** : cuadra *f*, manzana *f* (de edificios) ⟨to go around the block : dar la vuelta a la cuadra⟩ **4** BUILDING : edificio *m* (de apartamentos, oficinas, etc.) **5** GROUP, SERIES : serie *f*, grupo *m* ⟨a block of tickets : una serie de entradas⟩ **6 block and tackle** : aparejo *m* de poleas
blockade[1] [blɑˈkeɪd] *vt* **-aded; -ading** : bloquear
blockade[2] *n* : bloqueo *m*
blockage [ˈblɑkɪʤ] *n* : bloqueo *m*, obstrucción *f*
blockhead [ˈblɑk,hɛd] *n* : bruto *m*, -ta *f*; estúpido *m*, -da *f*
blond[1] *or* **blonde** [ˈblɑnd] *adj* : rubio, güero *Mex*, claro (dícese de la madera)
blond[2] *or* **blonde** *n* : rubio *m*, -bia *f*; güero *m*, -ra *f Mex*
blood [ˈblʌd] *n* **1** : sangre *f* **2** LIFEBLOOD : vida *f*, alma *f* **3** LINEAGE : linaje *m*, sangre *f*
blood bank *n* : banco *m* de sangre
bloodcurdling [ˈblʌd,kərdəlɪŋ] *adj* : espeluznante, aterrador
blooded [ˈblʌdəd] *adj* : de sangre ⟨cold-blooded animal : animal de sangre fría⟩
bloodhound [ˈblʌd,haʊnd] *n* : sabueso *m*
bloodless [ˈblʌdləs] *adj* **1** : incruento, sin derramamiento de sangre **2** LIFELESS : desanimado, insípido, sin vida
bloodmobile [ˈblʌdmo,bi:l] *n* : unidad *f* móvil para donantes de sangre
blood pressure *n* : tensión *f*, presión *f* (arterial)
bloodshed [ˈblʌd,ʃɛd] *n* : derramamiento *m* de sangre
bloodshot [ˈblʌd,ʃɑt] *adj* : inyectado de sangre
bloodstain [ˈblʌd,steɪn] *n* : mancha *f* de sangre
bloodstained [ˈblʌd,steɪnd] *adj* : manchado de sangre
bloodstream [ˈblʌd,stri:m] *n* : torrente *m* sanguíneo, corriente *f* sanguínea
bloodsucker [ˈblʌd,sʌkər] *n* : sanguijuela *f*
bloodthirsty [ˈblʌd,θərsti] *adj* : sanguinario
blood vessel *n* : vaso *m* sanguíneo
bloody [ˈblʌdi] *adj* **bloodier; -est** : ensangrentado, sangriento
bloom[1] [ˈblu:m] *vi* **1** FLOWER : florecer **2** MATURE : madurar
bloom[2] *n* **1** FLOWER : flor *f* ⟨to be in bloom : estar en flor⟩ **2** FLOWERING : floración *f* ⟨in full bloom : en plena floración⟩ **3** : rubor *m* (de la tez) ⟨in the bloom of youth : en plena juventud, en la flor de la vida⟩
bloomers [ˈblu:mərz] *npl* : bombachos *mpl*
blooper [ˈblu:pər] *n* : metedura *f* de pata *fam*
blossom[1] [ˈblɑsəm] *vi* : florecer, dar flor
blossom[2] *n* : flor *f*
blot[1] [ˈblɑt] *vt* **blotted; blotting** **1** SPOT : emborronar, borronear **2** DRY : secar
blot[2] *n* **1** STAIN : mancha *f*, borrón *m* **2** BLEMISH : mancha *f*, tacha *f*
blotch[1] [ˈblɑʧ] *vt* : emborronar, borronear
blotch[2] *n* : mancha *f*, borrón *m*
blotchy [ˈblɑʧi] *adj* **blotchier; -est** : lleno de manchas

blotter ['blɑt̬ər] *n* : hoja *f* de papel secante, secante *m*
blouse ['blaʊs, 'blaʊz] *n* : blusa *f*
blow[1] ['blo:] *v* **blew** ['blu:]; **blown** ['blo:n]; **blowing** *vi* **1** : soplar, volar ⟨the wind is blowing hard : el viento está soplando con fuerza⟩ ⟨it blew out the door : voló por la puerta⟩ ⟨the window blew shut : se cerró la ventana⟩ **2** SOUND : sonar ⟨the whistle blew : sonó el silbato⟩ **3 to blow out** : fundirse (dícese de un fusible eléctrico), reventarse (dícese de una llanta) **4 to blow off** : dejar plantado (a alguien), flatar a (una cita, etc.) — *vt* **1** : soplar, echar ⟨to blow smoke : echar humo⟩ **2** SOUND : tocar, sonar **3** SHAPE : soplar, dar forma a ⟨to blow glass : soplar vidrio⟩ **4** BUNGLE : echar a perder
blow[2] *n* **1** PUFF : soplo *m*, soplido *m* **2** GALE : vendaval *f* **3** HIT, STROKE : golpe *m* **4** CALAMITY : golpe *m*, desastre *m* **5 to come to blows** : llegar a las manos
blower ['blo:ər] *n* FAN : ventilador *m*
blowout ['blo:ˌaʊt] *n* : reventón *m*
blowtorch ['blo:ˌtɔrtʃ] *n* : soplete *m*
blow up *vi* EXPLODE : estallar, hacer explosión — *vt* BLAST : volar, hacer volar
blubber[1] ['blʌbər] *vi* : lloriquear
blubber[2] *n* : esperma *f* de ballena
bludgeon ['blʌdʒən] *vt* : aporrear
blue[1] ['blu:] *adj* **bluer; bluest 1** : azul **2** MELANCHOLY : melancólico, triste
blue[2] *n* : azul *m*
blueberry ['blu:ˌbɛri] *n, pl* **-ries** : arándano *m*
bluebird ['blu:ˌbərd] *n* : azulejo *m*
blue cheese *n* : queso *m* azul
blueprint ['blu:ˌprɪnt] *n* **1** : plano *m*, proyecto *m*, cianotipo *m* **2** PLAN : anteproyecto *m*, programa *m*
blues ['blu:z] *npl* **1** DEPRESSION : depresión *f*, melancolía *f* **2** : blues *m* ⟨to sing the blues : cantar blues⟩
bluff[1] ['blʌf] *vi* : hacer un farol, blofear *Col, Mex*
bluff[2] *adj* **1** STEEP : escarpado **2** FRANK : campechano, franco, directo
bluff[3] *n* **1** : farol *m*, blof *m Col, Mex* **2** CLIFF : acantilado *m*, risco *m*
bluing *or* **blueing** ['blu:ɪŋ] *n* : añil *m*, azulete *m*
bluish ['blu:ɪʃ] *adj* : azulado
blunder[1] ['blʌndər] *vi* **1** STUMBLE : tropezar, dar traspiés **2** ERR : cometer un error, tropezar, meter la pata *fam*
blunder[2] *n* : error *m*, fallo *m* garrafal, metedura *f* de pata *fam*
blunderbuss ['blʌndərˌbʌs] *n* : trabuco *m*
blunt[1] ['blʌnt] *vt* : despuntar (aguja o lápiz), desafilar (cuchillo o tijeras), suavizar (crítica)
blunt[2] *adj* **1** DULL : desafilado, despuntado **2** DIRECT : directo, franco, categórico
bluntly ['blʌntli] *adv* : sin rodeos, francamente, bruscamente
bluntness ['blʌntnəs] *n* **1** DULLNESS : falta *f* de filo, embotadura *f* **2** FRANKNESS : franqueza *f*
blur[1] ['blər] *vt* **blurred; blurring** : desdibujar, hacer borroso
blur[2] *n* **1** SMEAR : mancha *f*, borrón *m* **2** : aspecto *m* borroso ⟨everything was just a blur : todo se volvió borroso⟩
blurb ['blərb] *n* : propaganda *f*, nota *f* publicitaria
blurry ['bləri] *adj* : borroso
blurt ['blərt] *vt* : espetar, decir impulsivamente
blush[1] ['blʌʃ] *vi* : ruborizarse, sonrojarse, hacerse colorado
blush[2] *n* : rubor *m*, sonrojo *m*
bluster[1] ['blʌstər] *vi* **1** BLOW : soplar con fuerza **2** BOAST : fanfarronear, echar bravatas
bluster[2] *n* : fanfarronada *f*, bravatas *fpl*
blustery ['blʌstəri] *adj* : borrascoso, tempestuoso
boa ['bo:ə] *n* : boa *f*
boar ['bor] *n* : cerdo *m* macho, verraco *m*
board[1] ['bord] *vt* **1** : embarcarse en, subir a bordo de (una nave o un avión), subir a (un tren o carro) **2** LODGE : hospedar, dar hospedaje con comidas a **3 to board up** : cerrar con tablas
board[2] *n* **1** PLANK : tabla *f*, tablón *m* **2** : tablero *m* ⟨chessboard : tablero de ajedrez⟩ **3** MEALS : comida *f* ⟨board and lodging : comida y alojamiento⟩ **4** COMMITTEE, COUNCIL : junta *f*, consejo *m*
boarder ['bordər] *n* LODGER : huésped *m*, -peda *f*
boardinghouse ['bordɪŋˌhaʊs] *n* : casa *f* de huéspedes
boarding school *n* : internado *m*
boardwalk ['bordˌwɔk] *n* : paseo *m* marítimo
boast[1] ['bo:st] *vi* : alardear, presumir, jactarse
boast[2] *n* : jactancia *f*, alarde *m*
boaster ['bo:stər] *n* : presumido *m*, -da *f*; fanfarrón *m*, -rrona *f fam*
boastful ['bo:stfəl] *adj* : jactancioso, fanfarrón *fam*
boastfully ['bo:stfəli] *adv* : de manera jactanciosa
boat[1] ['bo:t] *vt* : transportar en barco, poner a bordo
boat[2] *n* : barco *m*, embarcación *f*, bote *m*, barca *f*
boatman ['bo:tmən] *n, pl* **-men** [-mən, -ˌmɛn] : barquero *m*
boatswain ['bo:sən] *n* : contramaestre *m*
bob[1] ['bɑb] *v* **bobbed; bobbing** *vi* **1** : balancearse, mecerse ⟨to bob up and down : subir y bajar⟩ **2** *or* **to bob up** APPEAR : presentarse, surgir — *vt* **1** : inclinar (la cabeza o el cuerpo) **2** CUT : cortar, recortar ⟨she bobbed her hair : se cortó el pelo⟩

bob[2] *n* **1** : inclinación *f* (de la cabeza, del cuerpo), sacudida *f* **2** FLOAT : flotador *m*, corcho *m* (de pesca) **3** : pelo *m* corto

bobbin [ˈbɑbən] *n* : bobina *f*, carrete *m*

bobby pin [ˈbɑbiˌpɪn] *n* : horquilla *f*

bobcat [ˈbɑbˌkæt] *n* : lince *m* rojo

bobolink [ˈbɑbəˌlɪŋk] *n* : tordo *m* arrocero

bobsled [ˈbɑbˌslɛd] *n* : bobsleigh *m*

bobwhite [ˈbɑbˈhwaɪt] *n* : codorniz *m* (del Nuevo Mundo)

bode[1] [ˈboːd] *v* **boded; boding** *vt* : presagiar, augurar — *vi* **to bode well** : ser de buen agüero

bode[2] → **bide**

bodice [ˈbɑdəs] *n* : corpiño *m*

bodied [ˈbɑdid] *adj* : de cuerpo ⟨lean-bodied : de cuerpo delgado⟩ ⟨able-bodied : no discapacitado⟩

bodiless [ˈbɑdiləs, ˈbɑdələs] *adj* : incorpóreo

bodily[1] [ˈbɑdəli] *adv* : en peso ⟨to lift someone bodily : levantar a alguien en peso⟩

bodily[2] *adj* : corporal, del cuerpo ⟨bodily harm : daños corporales⟩

body [ˈbɑdi] *n, pl* **bodies** **1** : cuerpo *m*, organismo *m* **2** CORPSE : cadáver *m* **3** PERSON : persona *f*, ser *m* humano **4** : nave *f* (de una iglesia), carrocería (de un automóvil), fuselaje *m* (de un avión), casco *m* (de una nave) **5** COLLECTION, MASS : conjunto *m*, grupo *m*, masa *f* ⟨in a body : todos juntos, en masa⟩ **6** ORGANIZATION : organismo *m*, organización *f*

bodyguard [ˈbɑdiˌgɑrd] *n* : guardaespaldas *mf*

bog[1] [ˈbɑg, ˈbɔg] *vt* **bogged; bogging** : empantanar, inundar ⟨to get bogged down : empantanarse⟩

bog[2] *n* : lodazal *m*, ciénaga *f*, cenagal *m*

bogey [ˈbʊgi, ˈboː-] *n, pl* **-geys** : terror *m*, coco *m fam*

boggle [ˈbɑgəl] *vi* **-gled; -gling** : quedarse atónito, quedarse pasmado ⟨the mind boggles! : ¡es increíble!⟩

boggy [ˈbɑgi, ˈbɔ-] *adj* **boggier; -est** : cenagoso

bogus [ˈboːgəs] *adj* : falso, fingido, falaz

bohemian [boːˈhiːmiən] *n* : bohemio *m*, -mia *f* — **bohemian** *adj*

boil[1] [ˈbɔɪl] *vi* **1** : hervir **2 to make one's blood boil** : hervirle la sangre a uno — *vt* **1** : hervir, hacer hervir ⟨to boil water : hervir agua⟩ **2** : cocer, hervir ⟨to boil potatoes : cocer papas⟩

boil[2] *n* **1** BOILING : hervor *m* **2** : furúnculo *m*, divieso *m* (en medicina)

boiler [ˈbɔɪlər] *n* : caldera *f*

boisterous [ˈbɔɪstərəs] *adj* : bullicioso, escandaloso — **boisterously** *adv*

bold [ˈboːld] *adj* **1** COURAGEOUS : valiente **2** INSOLENT : insolente, descarado **3** DARING : atrevido, audaz — **boldly** *adv*

boldface [ˈboːldˌfeɪs] *or* **boldface type** *n* : negrita *f*

boldness [ˈboːldnəs] *n* **1** COURAGE : valor *m*, coraje *m* **2** INSOLENCE : atrevimiento *m*, insolencia *f*, descaro *m* **3** DARING : audacia *f*

bolero [bəˈlɛro] *n, pl* **-ros** : bolero *m*

Bolivian [bəˈlɪviən] *n* : boliviano *m*, -na *f* — **Bolivian** *adj*

boll [ˈboːl] *n* : cápsula *f* (del algodón)

boll weevil *n* : gorgojo *m* del algodón

bologna [bəˈloːni] *n* : salchicha *f* ahumada

bolster[1] [ˈboːlstər] *vt* **-stered; -stering** : reforzar, reafirmar ⟨to bolster morale : levantar la moral⟩

bolster[2] *n* : cabezal *m*, almohadón *m*

bolt[1] [ˈboːlt] *vt* **1** : atornillar, sujetar con pernos ⟨bolted to the floor : sujetado con pernos al suelo⟩ **2** : cerrar con pestillo, echar el cerrojo a ⟨to bolt the door : echar el cerrojo a la puerta⟩ **3 to bolt down** : engullir ⟨she bolted down her dinner : engulló su comida⟩ — *vi* : echar a correr, salir corriendo ⟨he bolted from the room : salió corriendo de la sala⟩

bolt[2] *n* **1** LATCH : pestillo *m*, cerrojo *m* **2** : tornillo *m*, perno *m* ⟨nuts and bolts : tuercas y tornillos⟩ **3** : rollo *m* ⟨a bolt of cloth : un rollo de tela⟩ **4 lightning bolt** : relámpago *m*, rayo *m*

bomb[1] [ˈbɑm] *vt* : bombardear

bomb[2] *n* : bomba *f*

bombard [bɑmˈbɑrd, bəm-] *vt* : bombardear

bombardier [ˌbɑmbəˈdɪr] *n* : bombardero *m*, -ra *f*

bombardment [bɑmˈbɑrdmənt] *n* : bombardeo *m*

bombast [ˈbɑmˌbæst] *n* : grandilocuencia *f*, ampulosidad *f*

bombastic [bɑmˈbæstɪk] *adj* : grandilocuente, ampuloso, bombástico

bomber [ˈbɑmər] *n* : bombardero *m*

bombproof [ˈbɑmˌpruːf] *adj* : a prueba de bombas

bombshell [ˈbɑmˌʃɛl] *n* : bomba *f* ⟨a political bombshell : una bomba política⟩

bona fide [ˈboːnəˌfaɪd, ˈbɑ-; ˌboːnəˈfaɪdi] *adj* **1** : de buena fe ⟨a bona fide offer : una oferta de buena fe⟩ **2** GENUINE : genuino, auténtico

bonanza [bəˈnænzə] *n* : bonanza *f*

bonbon [ˈbɑnˌbɑn] *n* : bombón *m*

bond[1] [ˈbɑnd] *vt* **1** INSURE : dar fianza a, asegurar **2** STICK : adherir, pegar — *vi* : adherirse, pegarse

bond[2] *n* **1** LINK, TIE : vínculo *m*, lazo *m* **2** BAIL : fianza *f*, caución *f* **3** : bono *m* ⟨stocks and bonds : acciones y bonos⟩ **4 bonds** *npl* FETTERS : cadenas *fpl*

bondage [ˈbɑndɪʤ] *n* : esclavitud *f*

bondholder [ˈbɑndˌhoːldər] *n* : tenedor *m*, -dora *f* de bonos

bondsman [ˈbɑndzmən] *n, pl* **-men** [-mən, -ˌmɛn] **1** SLAVE : esclavo *m* **2** SURETY : fiador *m*, -dora *f*

bone[1] [ˈboːn] *vt* **boned; boning** : deshuesar

bone[2] *n* : hueso *m*
boneless [ˈbo:nləs] *adj* : sin huesos, sin espinas
boner [ˈbo:nər] *n* : metedura *f* de pata, metida *f* de pata
bonfire [ˈbɑnˌfaɪr] *n* : hoguera *f*, fogata *f*, fogón *m*
bonito [bəˈni:t̬o] *n, pl* **-tos** *or* **-to** : bonito *m*
bonnet [ˈbɑnət] *n* : sombrero *m* (de mujer), gorra *f* (de niño)
bonus [ˈbo:nəs] *n* **1** : prima *f*, bonificación *f* (pagado al empleado) **2** ADVANTAGE, BENEFIT : beneficio *m*, provecho *m*
bony [ˈbo:ni] *adj* **bonier; -est** : huesudo
boo[1] [ˈbu:] *vt* : abuchear
boo[2] *n, pl* **boos** : abucheo *m*
booby [ˈbu:bi] *n, pl* **-bies** : bobo *m*, -ba *f*; tonto *m*, -ta *f*
book[1] [ˈbʊk] *vt* : reservar ⟨to book a flight : reservar un vuelo⟩
book[2] *n* **1** : libro *m* **2 the Book** : la Biblia **3 by the book** : según las reglas
bookcase [ˈbʊkˌkeɪs] *n* : estantería *f*, librero *m Mex*
bookend [ˈbʊkˌɛnd] *n* : sujetalibros *m*
bookie [ˈbʊki] → **bookmaker**
bookish [ˈbʊkɪʃ] *adj* : libresco
bookkeeper [ˈbʊkˌki:pər] *n* : tenedor *m*, -dora *f* de libros; contable *mf Spain*
bookkeeping [ˈbʊkˌki:pɪŋ] *n* : contabilidad *f*, teneduría *f* de libros
booklet [ˈbʊklət] *n* : folleto *m*
bookmaker [ˈbʊkˌmeɪkər] *n* : corredor *m*, -dora *f* de apuestas
bookmark [ˈbʊkˌmɑrk] *n* : señalador *m* de libros, marcador *m* de libros
bookseller [ˈbʊkˌslər] *n* : librero *m*, -ra *f*
bookshelf [ˈbʊkˌʃɛlf] *n, pl* **-shelves 1** : estante *m* **2 bookshelves** *npl* : estantería *f*
bookstore [ˈbʊkˌstor] *n* : librería *f*
bookworm [ˈbʊkˌwərm] *n* : ratón *m* de biblioteca *fam*
boom[1] [ˈbu:m] *vi* **1** THUNDER : tronar, resonar **2** FLOURISH, PROSPER : estar en auge, prosperar
boom[2] *n* **1** BOOMING : bramido *m*, estruendo *m* **2** FLOURISHING : auge *m* ⟨population boom : auge de población⟩
boomerang [ˈbu:məˌræŋ] *n* : bumerán *m*
boon[1] [ˈbu:n] *adj* **boon companion** : amigo *m*, -ga *f* del alma
boon[2] *n* : ayuda *f*, beneficio *m*, adelanto *m*
boondocks [ˈbu:nˌdɑks] *npl* : área *f* rural remota, región *f* alejada
boor [ˈbʊr] *n* : grosero *m*, -ra *f*
boorish [ˈbʊrɪʃ] *adj* : grosero
boost[1] [ˈbu:st] *vt* **1** LIFT : levantar, alzar **2** INCREASE : aumentar, incrementar **3** PROMOTE : promover, fomentar, hacer publicidad por
boost[2] *n* **1** THRUST : impulso *m*, empujón *m* **2** ENCOURAGEMENT : estímulo *m*, aliento *m* **3** INCREASE : aumento *m*, incremento *m*
booster [ˈbu:stər] *n* **1** SUPPORTER : partidario *m*, -ria *f* **2 booster rocket** : cohete *m* propulsor **3 booster shot** : vacuna *f* de refuerzo
boot[1] [ˈbu:t] *vt* KICK : dar una patada a, patear
boot[2] *n* **1** : bota *f*, botín *m* **2** KICK : puntapié *m*, patada *f*
bootee *or* **bootie** [ˈbu:t̬i] *n* : botita *f*, botín *m*
booth [ˈbu:θ] *n, pl* **booths** [ˈbu:ðz, ˈbu:θs] : cabina *f* (de teléfono, de votar), caseta *f* (de información), barraca *f* (a una feria)
bootlegger [ˈbu:tˌlɛgər] *n* : contrabandista *mf* del alcohol
booty [ˈbu:t̬i] *n, pl* **-ties** : botín *m*
booze [ˈbu:z] *n fam* : alcohol *m*
borax [ˈbɔrˌæks] *n* : bórax *m*
border[1] [ˈbɔrdər] *vt* **1** EDGE : ribetear, bordear **2** BOUND : limitar con, lindar con — *vi* VERGE : rayar, lindar ⟨that borders on absurdity : eso raya en el absurdo⟩
border[2] *n* **1** EDGE : borde *m*, orilla *f* **2** TRIM : ribete *m* **3** FRONTIER : frontera *f*
bore[1] [ˈbor] *vt* **bored; boring 1** PIERCE : taladrar, perforar ⟨to bore metals : taladrar metales⟩ **2** OPEN : hacer, abrir ⟨to bore a tunnel : abrir un túnel⟩ **3** WEARY : aburrir
bore[2] → **bear**[1]
bore[3] *n* **1** : pesado *m*, -da *f* (persona aburrida) **2** TEDIOUSNESS : pesadez *f*, lo aburrido **3** DIAMETER : calibre *m*
boredom [ˈbordəm] *n* : aburrimiento *m*
boring [ˈborɪŋ] *adj* : aburrido, pesado
born [ˈbɔrn] *adj* **1** : nacido **2** : nato ⟨she's a born singer : es una cantante nata⟩ ⟨he's a born leader : nació para mandar⟩
borne *pp* → **bear**[1]
boron [ˈborˌɑn] *n* : boro *m*
borough [ˈbəro] *n* : distrito *m* municipal
borrow [ˈbɑro] *vt* **1** : pedir prestado, tomar prestado **2** APPROPRIATE : apropiarse de, adoptar
borrower [ˈbɑrəwər] *n* : prestatario *m*, -ria *f*
Bosnian [ˈbɑzniən, ˈbɔz-] *n* : bosnio *m*, -nia *f* — **Bosnian** *adj*
bosom[1] [ˈbʊzəm, ˈbu:-] *adj* : íntimo
bosom[2] *n* **1** CHEST : pecho *m* **2** BREAST : pecho *m*, seno *m* **3** CLOSENESS : seno *m* ⟨in the bosom of her family : en el seno de su familia⟩
bosomed [ˈbʊzəmd, ˈbu:-] *adj* : con busto ⟨big-bosomed : con mucho busto⟩
boss[1] [ˈbɔs] *vt* **1** SUPERVISE : dirigir, supervisar **2 to boss around** : mandonear *fam*, mangonear *fam*
boss[2] *n* : jefe *m*, -fa *f*; patrón *m*, -trona *f*
bossy [ˈbɔsi] *adj* **bossier; -est** : mandón *fam*, autoritario, dominante

botanist [ˈbɑtənɪst] *n* : botánico *m*, -ca *f*

botany [ˈbɑtəni] *n* : botánica *f* — **botanical** [bəˈtænɪkəl] *adj*

botch[1] [ˈbɑtʃ] *vt* : hacer una chapuza de, estropear

botch[2] *n* : chapuza *f*

both[1] [ˈboːθ] *adj* : ambos, los dos, las dos ⟨both books : ambos libros, los dos libros⟩

both[2] *conj* : tanto como ⟨both Ann and her mother are tall : tanto Ana como su madre son altas⟩

both[3] *pron* : ambos *m*, -bas *f*; los dos, las dos

bother[1] [ˈbɑðər] *vt* **1** IRK : preocupar ⟨nothing's bothering me : nada me preocupa⟩ ⟨what's bothering him? : ¿qué le pasa?⟩ **2** PESTER : molestar, fastidiar — *vi* **to bother to** : molestarse en, tomar la molestia de

bother[2] *n* **1** TROUBLE : molestia *f*, problemas *mpl* **2** ANNOYANCE : molestia *f*, fastidio *m*

bothersome [ˈbɑðərsəm] *adj* : molesto, fastidioso

bottle[1] [ˈbɑtəl] *vt* **bottled; bottling** : embotellar, envasar

bottle[2] *n* : botella *f*, frasco *m*

bottleneck [ˈbɑtəlˌnɛk] *n* **1** : cuello *m* de botella (en un camino) **2** : embotellamiento *m*, atasco *m* (de tráfico) **3** OBSTACLE : obstáculo *m*

bottom[1] [ˈbɑtəm] *adj* : más bajo, inferior, de abajo

bottom[2] *n* **1** : fondo *m* (de una caja, de una taza, del mar), pie *m* (de una escalera, una página, una montaña), asiento *m* (de una silla), parte *f* de abajo (de una pila) **2** CAUSE : origen *m*, causa *f* ⟨to get to the bottom of : llegar al fondo de⟩ **3** BUTTOCKS : trasero *m*, nalgas *fpl*

bottomless [ˈbɑtəmləs] *adj* : sin fondo, sin límites

botulism [ˈbɑtʃəˌlɪzəm] *n* : botulismo *m*

boudoir [bəˈdwɑr, bʊ-; ˈbuːˌ-, ˈbʊ-] *n* : tocador *m*

bough [ˈbaʊ] *n* : rama *f*

bought → **buy[1]**

bouillon [ˈbuːˌjɑn; ˈbʊlˌjɑn, -jən] *n* : caldo *m*

boulder [ˈboːldər] *n* : canto *m* rodado, roca *f* grande

boulevard [ˈbʊləˌvɑrd, ˈbuː-] *n* : bulevar *m*, boulevard *m*

bounce[1] [ˈbaʊnts] *v* **bounced; bouncing** *vt* : hacer rebotar — *vi* : rebotar

bounce[2] *n* : rebote *m*

bouncy [ˈbaʊntsi] *adj* **bouncier; -est** **1** LIVELY : vivo, exuberante, animado **2** RESILIENT : elástico, flexible **3** : que rebota (dícese de una pelota)

bound[1] [ˈbaʊnd] *vt* : delimitar, rodear — *vi* LEAP : saltar, dar brincos

bound[2] *adj* **1** OBLIGED : obligado **2** : encuadernado, empastado ⟨a book bound in leather : un libro encuadernado en cuero⟩ **3** DETERMINED : decidido, empeñado **4** **to be bound to** : ser seguro que, tener que, no caber duda que ⟨it was bound to happen : tenía que suceder⟩ **5** **bound for** : con rumbo a ⟨bound for Chicago : con rumbo a Chicago⟩ ⟨to be homeward bound : ir camino a casa⟩

bound[3] *n* **1** LIMIT : límite *m* **2** LEAP : salto *m*, brinco *m*

boundary [ˈbaʊndri, -dəri] *n, pl* **-aries** : límite *m*, línea *f* divisoria, linde *mf*

boundless [ˈbaʊndləs] *adj* : sin límites, infinito

bounteous [ˈbaʊntiəs] *adj* **1** GENEROUS : generoso **2** ABUNDANT : copioso, abundante — **bounteously** *adv*

bountiful [ˈbaʊntɪfəl] *adj* **1** GENEROUS, LIBERAL : munificente, pródigo, generoso **2** ABUNDANT : copioso, abundante

bounty [ˈbaʊnti] *n, pl* **-ties** **1** GENEROSITY : generosidad *f*, munificencia *f* **2** REWARD : recompensa *f*

bouquet [boːˈkeɪ, buː-] *n* **1** : ramo *m*, ramillete *m* **2** FRAGRANCE : bouquet *m*, aroma *m*

bourbon [ˈbərbən, ˈbʊr-] *n* : bourbon *m*, whisky *m* americano

bourgeois[1] [ˈbʊrʒˌwɑ, bʊrʒˈwɑ] *adj* : burgués

bourgeois[2] *n* : burgués *m*, -guesa *f*

bourgeoisie [ˌbʊrʒˌwɑˈzi] *n* : burguesía *f*

bout [ˈbaʊt] *n* **1** : encuentro *m*, combate *m* (en deportes) **2** ATTACK : ataque *m* (de una enfermedad) **3** PERIOD, SPELL : período *m* (de actividad)

boutique [buːˈtiːk] *n* : boutique *f*

bovine[1] [ˈboːˌvaɪn, -ˌviːn] *adj* : bovino, vacuno

bovine[2] *n* : bovino *m*

bow[1] [ˈbaʊ] *vi* **1** : hacer una reverencia, inclinarse **2** SUBMIT : ceder, resignarse, someterse — *vt* **1** LOWER : inclinar, bajar **2** BEND : doblar

bow[2] [ˈbaʊː] *n* **1** BOWING : reverencia *f*, inclinación *f* **2** : proa *f* (de un barco)

bow[3] [ˈboː] *vi* CURVE : arquearse, doblarse

bow[4] [ˈboː] *n* **1** ARCH, CURVE : arco *m*, curva *f* **2** : arco *m* (arma o vara para tocar varios instrumentos de música) **3** : lazo *m*, moño *m* ⟨to tie a bow : hacer un moño⟩

bowels [ˈbaʊəls] *npl* **1** INTESTINES : intestinos *mpl* **2** : entrañas *fpl* ⟨in the bowels of the earth : en las entrañas de la tierra⟩

bower [ˈbaʊər] *n* : enramada *f*

bowl[1] [ˈboːl] *vi* : jugar a los bolos

bowl[2] *n* : tazón *m*, cuenco *m*

bowler [ˈboːlər] *n* : jugador *m*, -dora *f* de bolos

bowling [ˈboːlɪŋ] *n* : bolos *mpl*

box[1] [ˈbɑks] *vt* **1** PACK : empaquetar, embalar, encajonar **2** SLAP : bofetear, cachetear — *vi* : boxear

box[2] *n* **1** CONTAINER : caja *f*, cajón *m* **2** COMPARTMENT : compartimento *m*, palco *m* (en el teatro) **3** SLAP : bofetada *f*, cachetada *f* **4** : boj *m* (planta)

boxcar [ˈbɑksˌkɑr] *n* : vagón *m* de carga, furgón *m*

boxer [ˈbɑksər] *n* : boxeador *m*, -dora *f*

boxing [ˈbɑksɪŋ] *n* : boxeo *m*

box office *n* : taquilla *f*, boletería *f*

boxwood [ˈbɑksˌwʊd] *n* : boj *m*

boy [ˈbɔɪ] *n* **1** : chico *m*, muchacho *m* **2** *or* **little boy** : niño *m*, chico *m* **3** SON : hijo *m*

boycott[1] [ˈbɔɪˌkɑt] *vt* : boicotear

boycott[2] *n* : boicot *m*

boyfriend [ˈbɔɪˌfrɛnd] *n* **1** FRIEND : amigo *m* **2** SWEETHEART : novio *m*

boyhood [ˈbɔɪˌhʊd] *n* : niñez *f*

boyish [ˈbɔɪɪʃ] *adj* : de niño, juvenil

bra [ˈbrɑ] → **brassiere**

brace[1] [ˈbreɪs] *v* **braced; bracing** *vt* **1** PROP UP, SUPPORT : apuntalar, apoyar, sostener **2** INVIGORATE : vigorizar **3** REINFORCE : reforzar — *vi* **to brace oneself** PREPARE : prepararse

brace[2] *n* **1** : berbiquí *m* ⟨brace and bit : berbiquí y barrena⟩ **2** CLAMP, REINFORCEMENT : abrazadera *f*, refuerzo *m* **3** : llave *f* (signo de puntuación) **4 braces** *npl* : aparatos *mpl* (de ortodoncia), frenos *mpl Mex*

bracelet [ˈbreɪslət] *n* : brazalete *m*, pulsera *f*

bracken [ˈbrækən] *n* : helecho *m*

bracket[1] [ˈbrækət] *vt* **1** SUPPORT : asegurar, apuntalar **2** : poner entre corchetes **3** CATEGORIZE, GROUP : catalogar, agrupar

bracket[2] *n* **1** SUPPORT : soporte *m* **2** : corchete *m* (marca de puntuación) **3** CATEGORY, CLASS : clase *f*, categoría *f*

brackish [ˈbrækɪʃ] *adj* : salobre

brad [ˈbræd] *n* : clavo *m* con cabeza pequeña, clavito *m*

brag[1] [ˈbræg] *vi* **bragged; bragging** : alardear, fanfarronear, jactarse

brag[2] *n* : alarde *m*, jactancia *f*, fanfarronada *f*

braggart [ˈbrægərt] *n* : fanfarrón *m*, -rrona *f fam*; jactancioso *m*, -sa *f*

braid[1] [ˈbreɪd] *vt* : trenzar

braid[2] *n* : trenza *f*

braille [ˈbreɪl] *n* : braille *m*

brain[1] [ˈbreɪn] *vt* : romper la crisma a, aplastar el cráneo a

brain[2] *n* **1** : cerebro *m* **2 brains** *npl* INTELLECT : inteligencia *f*, sesos *mpl*

brainless [ˈbreɪnləs] *adj* : estúpido, tonto

brainstorm [ˈbreɪnˌstɔrm] *n* : idea *f* brillante, idea *f* genial

brainy [ˈbreɪni] *adj* **brainier; -est** : inteligente, listo

braise [ˈbreɪz] *vt* **braised; braising** : cocer a fuego lento, estofar

brake[1] [ˈbreɪk] *v* **braked; braking** : frenar

brake[2] *n* : freno *m*

bramble [ˈbræmbəl] *n* : zarza *f*, zarzamora *f*

bran [ˈbræn] *n* : salvado *m*

branch[1] [ˈbræntʃ] *vi* **1** : echar ramas (dícese de una planta) **2** DIVERGE : ramificarse, separarse

branch[2] *n* **1** : rama *f* (de una planta) **2** EXTENSION : ramal *m* (de un camino, un ferrocarril, un río), rama *f* (de una familia o un campo de estudiar), sucursal *f* (de una empresa), agencia *f* (del gobierno)

brand[1] [ˈbrænd] *vt* **1** : marcar (ganado) **2** LABEL : tachar, tildar ⟨they branded him as a liar : lo tacharon de mentiroso⟩

brand[2] *n* **1** : marca *f* (de ganado) **2** STIGMA : estigma *m* **3** MAKE : marca *f* ⟨brand name : marca de fábrica⟩

brandish [ˈbrændɪʃ] *vt* : blandir

brand–new [ˈbrændˈnuː, -ˈnjuː] *adj* : nuevo, flamante

brandy [ˈbrændi] *n, pl* **-dies** : brandy *m*

brash [ˈbræʃ] *adj* **1** IMPULSIVE : impulsivo, impetuoso **2** BRAZEN : excesivamente desenvuelto, descarado

brass [ˈbræs] *n* **1** : latón *m* **2** GALL, NERVE : descaro *m*, cara *f fam* **3** OFFICERS : mandamases *mpl fam*

brassiere [brəˈzɪr, brɑ-] *n* : sostén *m*, brasier *m Col, Mex*

brassy [ˈbræsi] *adj* **brassier; -est** : dorado

brat [ˈbræt] *n* : mocoso *m*, -sa *f*; niño *m* mimado, niña *f* mimada

bravado [brəˈvɑdo] *n, pl* **-does** *or* **-dos** : bravuconadas *fpl*, bravatas *fpl*

brave[1] [ˈbreɪv] *vt* **braved; braving** : afrontar, hacer frente a

brave[2] *adj* **braver; bravest** : valiente, valeroso — **bravely** *adv*

brave[3] *n* : guerrero *m* indio

bravery [ˈbreɪvəri] *n* : valor *m*, valentía *f*

bravo [ˈbrɑˌvoː] *n, pl* **-vos** : bravo *m*

brawl[1] [ˈbrɔl] *vi* : pelearse, pegarse

brawl[2] *n* : pelea *f*, reyerta *f*

brawn [ˈbrɔn] *n* : fuerza *f* muscular

brawny [ˈbrɔni] *adj* **brawnier; -est** : musculoso

bray[1] [ˈbreɪ] *vi* : rebuznar

bray[2] *n* : rebuzno *m*

brazen [ˈbreɪzən] *adj* **1** : de latón **2** BOLD : descarado, directo

brazenly [ˈbreɪzənli] *adv* : descaradamente, insolentemente

brazenness [ˈbreɪzənnəs] *n* : descaro *m*, atrevimiento *m*

brazier [ˈbreɪʒər] *n* : brasero *m*

Brazilian [brəˈzɪljən] *n* : brasileño *m*, -ña *f* — **Brazilian** *adj*

Brazil nut [brəˈzɪlˌnʌt] *n* : nuez *f* de Brasil

breach[1] [ˈbriːtʃ] *vt* **1** PENETRATE : abrir una brecha en, penetrar **2** VIOLATE : infringir, violar

breach[2] *n* **1** VIOLATION : infracción *f*, violación *f* ⟨breach of trust : abuso de confianza⟩ **2** GAP, OPENING : brecha *f*

bread[1] [ˈbrɛd] *vt* : empanar

bread[2] *n* : pan *m*

breadth [ˈbrɛtθ] *n* : ancho *m*, anchura *f*

breadwinner [ˈbrɛd,wɪnər] *n* : sostén *m* de la familia

break[1] [ˈbreɪk] *v* **broke** [ˈbro:k]; **broken** [ˈbro:kən]; **breaking** *vt* **1** SMASH : romper, quebrar **2** VIOLATE : infringir, violar, romper **3** SURPASS : batir, superar **4** CRUSH, RUIN : arruinar, deshacer, destrozar ⟨to break one's spirit : quebrantar su espíritu⟩ **5** : dar, comunicar ⟨to break the news : dar las noticias⟩ **6** INTERRUPT : cortar, interrumpir — *vi* **1** : romperse, quebrarse ⟨my calculator broke : se me rompió la calculadora⟩ **2** DISPERSE : dispersarse, despejarse **3** : estallar (dícese de una tormenta), romper (dícese del día) **4** CHANGE : cambiar (dícese del tiempo o de la voz) **5** DECREASE : bajar ⟨my fever broke : me bajó la fiebre⟩ **6** : divulgarse, revelarse ⟨the news broke : la noticia se divulgó⟩ **7 to break into** : forzar, abrir **8 to break out of** : escaparse de **9 to break through** : penetrar

break[2] *n* **1** : ruptura *f*, rotura *f*, fractura *f* (de un hueso), claro *m* (entre las nubes), cambio *m* (del tiempo) **2** CHANCE : oportunidad *f* ⟨a lucky break : un golpe de suerte⟩ **3** REST : descanso *m* ⟨to take a break : tomar(se) un descanso⟩

breakable [ˈbreɪkəbəl] *adj* : quebradizo, frágil

breakage [ˈbreɪkɪʤ] *n* **1** BREAKING : rotura *f* **2** DAMAGE : destrozos *mpl*, daños *mpl*

breakdown [ˈbreɪk,daʊn] *n* **1** : avería *f* (de máquinas), interrupción *f* (de comunicaciones), fracaso *m* (de negociaciones) **2** ANALYSIS : análisis *m*, desglose *m* **3** *or* **nervous breakdown** : crisis *f* nerviosa

break down *vi* **1** : estropearse, descomponerse ⟨the machine broke down : la máquina se descompuso⟩ **2** FAIL : fracasar **3** CRY : echarse a llorar — *vt* **1** DESTROY : derribar, echar abajo **2** OVERCOME : vencer (la resistencia), disipar (sospechas) **3** ANALYZE : analizar, descomponer

breaker [ˈbreɪkər] *n* **1** WAVE : ola *f* grande **2** : interruptor *m* automático (de electricidad)

breakfast[1] [ˈbrɛkfəst] *vi* : desayunar

breakfast[2] *n* : desayuno *m*

breakneck [ˈbreɪk,nɛk] *adj* **at breakneck speed** : a una velocidad vertiginosa

break out *vi* **1** : salirse ⟨she broke out in spots : le salieron granos⟩ **2** ERUPT : estallar (dícese de una guerra, la violencia, etc.) **3** ESCAPE : fugarse, escaparse

breakup [ˈbreɪk,əp] *n* **1** DIVISION : desintegración *f* **2** : ruptura *f*

break up *vt* **1** DIVIDE : dividir **2** : disolver (una muchedumbre, una pelea, etc.) — *vi* **1** BREAK : romperse **2** SEPARATE : deshacerse, separarse ⟨I broke up with him : terminé con él⟩

breast [ˈbrɛst] *n* **1** : pecho *m*, seno *m* (de una mujer) **2** CHEST : pecho *m*

breastbone [ˈbrɛst,bo:n] *n* : esternón *m*

breast–feed [ˈbrɛst,fi:d] *vt* **-fed** [-,fɛd]; **-feeding** : amamantar, darle de mamar (a un niño)

breath [ˈbrɛθ] *n* **1** BREATHING : aliento *m* ⟨to hold one's breath : aguantar la respiración⟩ **2** BREEZE : soplo *m* ⟨a breath of fresh air : un soplo de aire freso⟩

breathe [ˈbri:ð] *v* **breathed; breathing** *vi* **1** : respirar **2** LIVE : vivir, respirar — *vt* **1** : respirar, aspirar ⟨to breathe fresh air : respirar el aire fresco⟩ **2** UTTER : decir ⟨I won't breathe a word of this : no diré nada de esto⟩

breathless [ˈbrɛθləs] *adj* : sin aliento, jadeante

breathlessly [ˈbrɛθləsli] *adv* : entrecortadamente, jadeando

breathlessness [ˈbrɛθləsnəs] *n* : dificultad *f* al respirar

breathtaking [ˈbrɛθ,teɪkɪŋ] *adj* IMPRESSIVE : impresionante, imponente

breeches [ˈbrɪʧəz, ˈbri:-] *npl* : pantalones *mpl*, calzones *mpl*, bombachos *mpl*

breed[1] [ˈbri:d] *v* **bred** [ˈbrɛd]; **breeding** *vt* **1** : criar (animales) **2** ENGENDER : engendrar, producir ⟨familiarity breeds contempt : la confianza hace perder el respeto⟩ **3** RAISE, REAR : criar, educar — *vi* REPRODUCE : reproducirse

breed[2] *n* **1** : variedad *f* (de plantas), raza *f* (de animales) **2** CLASS : clase *f*, tipo *m*

breeder [ˈbri:dər] *n* : criador *m*, -dora *f* (de animales); cultivador *m*, -dora *f* (de plantas)

breeze[1] [ˈbri:z] *vi* **breezed; breezing** : pasar con ligereza ⟨to breeze in : entrar como si nada⟩

breeze[2] *n* : brisa *f*, soplo *m* (de aire)

breezy [ˈbri:zi] *adj* **breezier; -est 1** AIRY, WINDY : aireado, ventoso **2** LIVELY : animado, alegre **3** NONCHALANT : despreocupado

brethren → **brother**

brevity [ˈbrɛvəṭi] *n, pl* **-ties** : brevedad *f*, concisión *f*

brew[1] [ˈbru:] *vt* **1** : fabricar, elaborar (cerveza) **2** FOMENT : tramar, maquinar, fomentar — *vi* **1** : fabricar cerveza **2** : amenazar ⟨a storm is brewing : una tormenta amenaza⟩

brew[2] *n* **1** BEER : cerveza *f* **2** POTION : brebaje *m*

brewer [ˈbru:ər] *n* : cervecero *m*, -ra *f*

brewery [ˈbru:əri, ˈbrʊri] *n, pl* **-eries** : cervecería *f*

briar [ˈbraɪər] → **brier**

bribe[1] [ˈbraɪb] *vt* **bribed; bribing** : sobornar, cohechar, coimear *Arg, Chile, Peru*

bribe[2] *n* : soborno *m*, cohecho *m*, coima *f Arg, Chile, Peru*, mordida *f CA, Mex*

bribery [ˈbraɪbəri] *n, pl* **-eries** : soborno *m*, cohecho *m*, coima *f*, mordida *f CA, Mex*

bric–a–brac [ˈbrɪkəˌbræk] *npl* : baratijas *fpl*, chucherías *fpl*

brick[1] [ˈbrɪk] *vt* **to brick up** : tabicar, tapiar

brick[2] *n* : ladrillo *m*

bricklayer [ˈbrɪkˌleɪər] *n* : albañil *mf*

bricklaying [ˈbrɪkˌleɪɪŋ] *n* : albañilería *f*

bridal [ˈbraɪdəl] *adj* : nupcial, de novia

bride [ˈbraɪd] *n* : novia *f*

bridegroom [ˈbraɪdˌgru:m] *n* : novio *m*

bridesmaid [ˈbraɪdzˌmeɪd] *n* : dama *f* de honor

bridge[1] [ˈbrɪʤ] *vt* **bridged; bridging 1** : tender un puente sobre **2 to bridge the gap** : salvar las diferencias

bridge[2] *n* **1** : puente *m* **2** : caballete *m* (de la nariz) **3** : puente *m* de mando (de un barco) **4** DENTURE : puente *m* (dental) **5** : bridge *m* (juego de naipes)

bridle[1] [ˈbraɪdəl] *v* **-dled; -dling** *vt* **1** : embridar (un caballo) **2** RESTRAIN : refrenar, dominar, contener — *vi* **to bridle at** : molestarse por, picarse por

bridle[2] *n* : brida *f*

brief[1] [ˈbri:f] *vt* : dar órdenes a, instruir

brief[2] *adj* : breve, sucinto, conciso

brief[3] *n* **1** : resumen *m*, sumario *m* **2 briefs** *npl* : calzoncillos *mpl*

briefcase [ˈbri:fˌkeɪs] *n* : portafolio *m*, maletín *m*

briefly [ˈbri:fli] *adv* : brevemente, por poco tiempo ⟨to speak briefly : discursar en pocas palabras⟩

brier [ˈbraɪər] *n* **1** BRAMBLE : zarza *f*, rosal *m* silvestre **2** HEATH : brezo *m* veteado

brig [ˈbrɪg] *n* **1** : bergantín *m* (barco) **2** : calabozo *m* (en un barco)

brigade [brɪˈgeɪd] *n* : brigada *f*

brigadier general [ˌbrɪgəˈdɪr] *n* : general *m* de brigada

brigand [ˈbrɪgənd] *n* : bandolero *m*, -ra *f*; forajido *m*, -da *f*

bright [ˈbraɪt] *adj* **1** : brillante (dícese del sol, de los ojos), vivo (dícese de un color), claro, fuerte **2** CHEERFUL : alegre, animado ⟨bright and early : muy temprano⟩ **3** INTELLIGENT : listo, inteligente ⟨a bright idea : una idea luminosa⟩

brighten [ˈbraɪtən] *vt* **1** ILLUMINATE : iluminar **2** ENLIVEN : alegrar, animar — *vi* **1** : hacerse más brillante **2 to brighten up** : animarse, alegrarse, mejorar

brightly [ˈbraɪtli] *adv* : vivamente, intensamente, alegremente

brightness [ˈbraɪtnəs] *n* **1** LUMINOSITY : luminosidad *f*, brillantez *f*, resplandor *m*, brillo *m* **2** CHEERFULNESS : alegría *f*, ánimo *m*

brilliance [ˈbrɪljənts] *n* **1** BRIGHTNESS : resplandor *m*, fulgor *m*, brillo *m*, brillantez *f* **2** INTELLIGENCE : inteligencia *f*, brillantez *f*

brilliancy [ˈbrɪljəntsi] → **brilliance**

brilliant [ˈbrɪljənt] *adj* : brillante

brilliantly [ˈbrɪljəntli] *adv* : brillantemente, con brillantez

brim[1] [ˈbrɪm] *vi* **brimmed; brimming 1** *or* **to brim over** : desbordarse, rebosar **2 to brim with tears** : llenarse de lágrimas

brim[2] *n* **1** : ala *f* (de un sombrero) **2** : borde *m* (de una taza o un vaso)

brimful [ˈbrɪmˈfʊl] *adj* : lleno hasta el borde, repleto, rebosante

brimless [ˈbrɪmləs] *adj* : sin ala

brimstone [ˈbrɪmˌsto:n] *n* : azufre *m*

brindled [ˈbrɪndəld] *adj* : manchado, pinto

brine [ˈbraɪn] *n* **1** : salmuera *f*, escabeche *m* (para encurtir) **2** OCEAN : océano *m*, mar *m*

bring [ˈbrɪŋ] *vt* **brought** [ˈbrɔt]; **bringing 1** CARRY : traer ⟨bring me some coffee : tráigame un café⟩ **2** PRODUCE : traer, producir, conseguir ⟨his efforts will bring him success : sus esfuerzos le conseguirán el éxito⟩ **3** PERSUADE : convencer, persuadir **4** YIELD : rendir, alcanzar, venderse por ⟨to bring a good price : alcanzar un precio alto⟩ **5 to bring to an end** : terminar (con) **6 to bring to light** : sacar a la luz

bring about *vt* : ocasionar, provocar, determinar

bring forth *vt* PRODUCE : producir

bring out *vt* : sacar, publicar (un libro, etc.)

bring to *vt* REVIVE : resucitar

bring up *vt* **1** REAR : criar **2** MENTION : sacar, mencionar

brininess [ˈbraɪninəs] *n* : salinidad *f*

brink [ˈbrɪŋk] *n* : borde *m*

briny [ˈbraɪni] *adj* **brinier; -est** : salobre

briquette *or* **briquet** [brɪˈkɛt] *n* : briqueta *f*

brisk [ˈbrɪsk] *adj* **1** LIVELY : rápido, enérgico, brioso **2** INVIGORATING : fresco, estimulante

brisket [ˈbrɪskət] *n* : falda *f*

briskly [ˈbrɪskli] *adv* : rápidamente, enérgicamente, con brío

briskness [ˈbrɪsknəs] *n* : brío *m*, rapidez *f*

bristle[1] [ˈbrɪsəl] *vi* **-tled; -tling 1** : erizarse, ponerse de punta **2** : enfurecerse, enojarse ⟨she bristled at the suggestion : se enfureció ante tal sugerencia⟩ **3** : estar plagado, estar repleto ⟨a city bristling with tourists : una ciudad repleta de turistas⟩

bristle[2] *n* : cerda *f* (de un animal), pelo *m* (de una planta)

bristly [ˈbrɪsəli] *adj* **bristlier; -est** : áspero y erizado

British[1] [ˈbrɪţɪʃ] *adj* : británico

British[2] *n* **the British** *npl* : los británicos

brittle [ˈbrɪtəl] *adj* **-tler; -tlest** : frágil, quebradizo
brittleness [ˈbrɪtəlnəs] *n* : fragilidad *f*
broach [ˈbroːtʃ] *vt* BRING UP : mencionar, abordar, sacar
broad [ˈbrɔd] *adj* **1** WIDE : ancho **2** SPACIOUS : amplio, extenso **3** FULL : pleno ⟨in broad daylight : en pleno día⟩ **4** OBVIOUS : claro, evidente **5** TOLERANT : tolerante, liberal **6** GENERAL : general **7** ESSENTIAL : principal, esencial ⟨the broad outline : los rasgos esenciales⟩
broadcast[1] [ˈbrɔdˌkæst] *vt* **-cast; -casting** **1** SCATTER : esparcir, diseminar **2** CIRCULATE, SPREAD : divulgar, difundir, propagar **3** TRANSMIT : transmitir, emitir
broadcast[2] *n* **1** TRANSMISSION : transmisión *f*, emisión *f* **2** PROGRAM : programa *m*, emisión *f*
broadcaster [ˈbrɔdˌkæstər] *n* : presentador *m*, -dora *f*; locutor *m*, -tora *f*
broadcloth [ˈbrɔdˌklɔθ] *n* : paño *m* fino
broaden [ˈbrɔdən] *vt* : ampliar, ensanchar — *vi* : ampliarse, ensancharse
broadloom [ˈbrɔdˌluːm] *adj* : tejido en telar ancho
broadly [ˈbrɔdli] *adv* **1** GENERALLY : en general, aproximadamente **2** WIDELY : extensivamente
broad–minded [ˈbrɔdˈmaɪndəd] *adj* : tolerante, de amplias miras
broad–mindedness [brɔdˈmaɪndədnəs] *n* : tolerancia *f*
broadside [ˈbrɔdˌsaɪd] *n* **1** VOLLEY : andanada *f* **2** ATTACK : ataque *m*, invectiva *f*, andanada *f*
brocade [broˈkeɪd] *n* : brocado *m*
broccoli [ˈbrɑkəli] *n* : brócoli *m*, brécol *m*
brochure [broˈʃʊr] *n* : folleto *m*
brogue [ˈbroːg] *n* : acento *m* irlandés
broil[1] [ˈbrɔɪl] *vt* : asar a la parrilla
broil[2] *n* : asado *m*
broiler [ˈbrɔɪlər] *n* **1** GRILL : parrilla *f* **2** : pollo *m* para asar
broke[1] [ˈbroːk] → **break**[1]
broke[2] *adj* : pelado, arruinado ⟨to go broke : arruinarse, quebrar⟩
broken [ˈbroːkən] *adj* **1** DAMAGED, SHATTERED : roto, quebrado, fracturado **2** IRREGULAR, UNEVEN : accidentado, irregular, recortado **3** VIOLATED : roto, quebrantado **4** INTERRUPTED : interrumpido, descontinuo **5** CRUSHED : abatido, quebrantado ⟨a broken man : un hombre destrozado⟩ **6** IMPERFECT : mal ⟨to speak broken English : hablar el inglés con dificultad⟩
brokenhearted [ˌbroːkənˈhɑrṭəd] *adj* : descorazonado, desconsolado
broker[1] [ˈbroːkər] *vt* : hacer corretaje de
broker[2] *n* **1** : agente *mf*; corredor *m*, -dora *f* **2** → **stockbroker**
brokerage [ˈbroːkərɪdʒ] *n* : corretaje *m*, agencia *f* de corredores
bromine [ˈbroːˌmiːn] *n* : bromo *m*
bronchitis [brɑnˈkaɪṭəs, brɑŋ-] *n* : bronquitis *f*
bronze[1] [ˈbrɑnz] *vt* **bronzed; bronzing** : broncear
bronze[2] *n* : bronce *m*
brooch [ˈbroːtʃ, ˈbruːtʃ] *n* : broche *m*, prendedor *m*
brood[1] [ˈbruːd] *vt* **1** INCUBATE : empollar, incubar **2** PONDER : sopesar, considerar — *vi* **1** INCUBATE : empollar **2** REFLECT : rumiar, reflexionar **3** WORRY : ponerse melancólico, inquietarse
brood[2] *adj* : de cría
brood[3] *n* : nidada *f* (de pájaros), camada *f* (de mamíferos)
brooder [ˈbruːdər] *n* **1** THINKER : pensador *m*, -dora *f* **2** INCUBATOR : incubadora *f*
brook[1] [ˈbrʊk] *vt* TOLERATE : tolerar, admitir
brook[2] *n* : arroyo *m*
broom [ˈbruːm, ˈbrʊm] *n* **1** : retama *f*, hiniesta *f* **2** : escoba *f* (para barrer)
broomstick [ˈbruːmˌstɪk, ˈbrʊm-] *n* : palo *m* de escoba
broth [ˈbrɔθ] *n, pl* **broths** [ˈbrɔθs, ˈbrɔðz] : caldo *m*
brothel [ˈbrɑθəl, ˈbrɔ-] *n* : burdel *m*
brother [ˈbrʌðər] *n, pl* **brothers** *also* **brethren** [ˈbrðrən, -ðərn] **1** : hermano *m* **2** KINSMAN : pariente *m*, familiar *m*
brotherhood [ˈbrʌðərˌhʊd] *n* **1** FELLOWSHIP : fraternidad *f* **2** ASSOCIATION : hermandad *f*
brother–in–law [ˈbrʌðərɪnˌlɔ] *n, pl* **brothers–in–law** : cuñado *m*
brotherly [ˈbrʌðərli] *adj* : fraternal
brought → **bring**
brow [ˈbraʊ] *n* **1** EYEBROW : ceja *f* **2** FOREHEAD : frente *f* **3** : cima *f* ⟨the brow of a hill : la cima de una colina⟩
browbeat [ˈbraʊˌbiːt] *vt* **-beat; -beaten** [-ˌbiːtən] *or* **-beat; -beating** : intimidar
brown[1] [ˈbraʊn] *vt* **1** : dorar (en cocina) **2** TAN : broncear — *vi* **1** : dorarse (en cocina) **2** TAN : broncearse
brown[2] *adj* : marrón, café, castaño (dícese del pelo), moreno (dícese de la piel)
brown[3] *n* : marrón *m*, café *m*
brownish [ˈbraʊnɪʃ] *adj* : pardo
browse [ˈbraʊz] *vi* **browsed; browsing** **1** GRAZE : pacer **2** LOOK : mirar, echar un vistazo
bruin [ˈbruːɪn] *n* BEAR : oso *m*
bruise[1] [ˈbruːz] *vt* **bruised; bruising** **1** : contusionar, machucar, magullar (a una persona) **2** DAMAGE : magullar, dañar (frutas) **3** CRUSH : majar **4** HURT : herir (los sentimientos)
bruise[2] *n* : moretón *m*, cardenal *m*, magulladura *f* (dícese de frutas)
brunch [ˈbrʌntʃ] *n* : combinación *f* de desayuno y almuerzo
brunet[1] *or* **brunette** [bruːˈnɛt] *adj* : moreno
brunet[2] *or* **brunette** *n* : moreno *m*, -na *f*

brunt ['brʌnt] *n* **to bear the brunt of** : llevar el peso de, aguantar el mayor impacto de

brush[1] ['brʌʃ] *vt* **1** : cepillar ⟨to brush one's teeth : cepillarse uno los dientes⟩ **2** SWEEP : barrer, quitar con un cepillo **3** GRAZE : rozar **4 to brush off** DISREGARD : hacer caso omiso de, ignorar — *vi* **to brush up on** : repasar, refrescar, dar un repaso a

brush[2] *n* **1** *or* **brushwood** ['brʌʃ,wʊd] : broza *f* **2** SCRUB, UNDERBRUSH : maleza *f* **3** : cepillo *m*, pincel *m* (de artista), brocha *f* (de pintor) **4** TOUCH : roce *m* **5** SKIRMISH : escaramuza *f*

brush–off ['brʌʃ,ɔf] *n* **to give the brush–off to** : dar calabazas a

brusque ['brʌsk] *adj* : brusco — **brusquely** *adv*

brussels sprout ['brʌsəlz,spraʊt] *n* : col *f* de Bruselas

brutal ['bru:ṭəl] *adj* : brutal, cruel, salvaje — **brutally** *adv*

brutality [bru:'tæləṭi] *n, pl* **-ties** : brutalidad *f*

brutalize ['bru:ṭəl,aɪz] *vt* **-ized; -izing** : brutalizar, maltratar

brute[1] ['bru:t] *adj* : bruto ⟨brute force : fuerza bruta⟩

brute[2] *n* **1** BEAST : bestia *f*, animal *m* **2** : bruto *m*, -ta *f*; bestia *mf* (persona)

brutish ['bru:ṭɪʃ] *adj* **1** : de animal **2** CRUEL : brutal, salvaje **3** STUPID : bruto, estúpido

bubble[1] ['bʌbəl] *vi* **-bled; -bling** : burbujear ⟨to bubble over with joy : rebosar de alegría⟩

bubble[2] *n* : burbuja *f*

bubbly ['bʌbəli] *adj* **bubblier; -est** **1** BUBBLING : burbujeante **2** LIVELY : vivaz, lleno de vida

bubonic plague [bu:'bɑnɪk, 'bju:-] *n* : peste *f* bubónica

buccaneer [,bʌkə'nɪr] *n* : bucanero *m*

buck[1] ['bʌk] *vi* **1** : corcovear (dícese de un caballo o un burro) **2** JOLT : dar sacudidas **3 to buck against** : resistirse a, rebelarse contra **4 to buck up** : animarse, levantar el ánimo — *vt* OPPOSE : oponerse a, ir en contra de

buck[2] *n, pl* **buck** *or* **bucks** **1** : animal *m* macho, ciervo *m* (macho) **2** DOLLAR : dólar *m* **3 to pass the buck** *fam* : pasar la pelota *fam*

bucket ['bʌkət] *n* : balde *m*, cubo *m*, cubeta *f Mex*

bucketful ['bʌkət,fʊl] *n* : balde *m* lleno

buckle[1] ['bʌkəl] *v* **-led; -ling** *vt* **1** FASTEN : abrochar **2** BEND, TWIST : combar, torcer — *vi* **1** BEND, TWIST : combarse, torcerse, doblarse (dícese de las rodillas) **2 to buckle down** : ponerse a trabajar con esmero **3 to buckle up** : abrocharse

buckle[2] *n* **1** : hebilla *f* **2** TWISTING : torcedura *f*

buckshot ['bʌk,ʃɑt] *n* : perdigón *m*

buckskin ['bʌk,skɪn] *n* : gamuza *f*

bucktooth ['bʌk,tu:θ] *n* : diente *m* saliente, diente *m* salido

buckwheat ['bʌk,*h*wi:t] *n* : trigo *m* rubión, alforfón *m*

bucolic [bju:'kɑlɪk] *adj* : bucólico

bud[1] ['bʌd] *v* **budded; budding** *vt* GRAFT : injertar — *vi* : brotar, hacer brotes

bud[2] *n* : brote *m*, yema *f*, capullo *m* (de una flor)

Buddhism ['bu:,dɪzəm, 'bʊ-] *n* : budismo *m*

Buddhist ['bu:dɪst, 'bʊ-] *n* : budista *mf* — **Buddhist** *adj*

buddy ['bʌdi] *n, pl* **-dies** : amigo *m*, -ga *f*; compinche *mf fam*; cuate *m*, -ta *f Mex fam*

budge ['bʌʤ] *vi* **budged; budging** **1** MOVE : moverse, desplazarse **2** YIELD : ceder

budget[1] ['bʌʤət] *vt* : presupuestar (gastos), asignar (dinero) — *vi* : presupuestar, planear el presupuesto

budget[2] *n* : presupuesto

budgetary ['bʌʤə,tɛri] *adj* : presupuestario

buff[1] ['bʌf] *vt* POLISH : pulir, sacar brillo a, lustrar

buff[2] *adj* : beige, amarillento

buff[3] *n* **1** : beige *m*, amarillento *m* **2** ENTHUSIAST : aficionado *m*, -da *f*; entusiasta *mf*

buffalo ['bʌfə,lo:] *n, pl* **-lo** *or* **-loes** **1** : búfalo *m* **2** BISON : bisonte *m*

buffer ['bʌfər] *n* **1** BARRIER : barrera *f* ⟨buffer state : estado tapón⟩ **2** SHOCK ABSORBER : amortiguador *m*

buffet[1] ['bʌfət] *vt* : golpear, zarandear, sacudir

buffet[2] *n* BLOW : golpe *m*

buffet[3] [,bʌ'feɪ, ,bu:-] *n* **1** : bufete *m*, bufé *m* (comida) **2** SIDEBOARD : aparador *m*

buffoon [,bʌ'fu:n] *n* : bufón *m*, -fona *f*; payaso *m*, -sa *f*

buffoonery [,bʌ'fu:nəri] *n, pl* **-eries** : bufonada *f*, payasada *f*

bug[1] ['bʌg] *vt* **bugged; bugging** **1** PESTER : fastidiar, molestar **2** : ocultar micrófonos en

bug[2] *n* **1** INSECT : bicho *m*, insecto *m* **2** DEFECT : defecto *m*, falla *f*, problema *m* **3** GERM : microbio *m*, virus *m* **4** MICROPHONE : micrófono *m*

bugaboo ['bʌgə,bu:] → **bogey**

bugbear ['bʌg,bær] *n* : pesadilla *f*, coco *m*

buggy ['bʌgi] *n, pl* **-gies** : calesa *f* (tirada por caballos), cochecito *m* (para niños)

bugle ['bju:gəl] *n* : clarín *m*, corneta *f*

bugler ['bju:gələr] *n* : corneta *mf*

build[1] ['bɪld] *v* **built** ['bɪlt]; **building** *vt* **1** CONSTRUCT : construir, edificar, ensamblar, levantar **2** DEVELOP : desarrollar, elaborar, forjar **3** INCREASE : incrementar, aumentar — *vi* **to build up** : aumentar, intensificar

build[2] *n* PHYSIQUE : físico *m*, complexión *f*

builder [ˈbɪldər] *n* : constructor *m*, -tora *f*; contratista *mf*
building [ˈbɪldɪŋ] *n* **1** EDIFICE : edificio *m* **2** CONSTRUCTION : construcción *f*
built–in [ˈbɪltˈɪn] *adj* **1** : empotrado <built-in cabinets : armarios empotrados> **2** INHERENT : incorporado, intrínseco
bulb [ˈbʌlb] *n* **1** : bulbo *m* (de una planta), cabeza *f* (de ajo), cubeta *f* (de un termómetro) **2** LIGHTBULB : bombilla *f*, foco *m*, bombillo *m CA, Col, Ven*
bulbous [ˈbʌlbəs] *adj* : bulboso
Bulgarian [bʌlˈgæriən, bʊl-] *n* **1** : búlgaro *m*, -ra *f* **2** : búlgaro *m* (idioma) — **Bulgarian** *adj*
bulge[1] [ˈbʌlʤ] *vi* **bulged; bulging** : abultar, sobresalir
bulge[2] *n* : bulto *m*, protuberancia *f*
bulk[1] [ˈbʌlk] *vt* : hinchar — *vi* EXPAND, SWELL : ampliarse, hincharse
bulk[2] *n* **1** SIZE, VOLUME : volumen *m*, tamaño *m* **2** FIBER : fibra *f* **3** MASS : mole *f* **4 the bulk of** : la mayor parte de **5 in ~** : en grandes cantidades
bulkhead [ˈbʌlkˌhɛd] *n* : mamparo *m*
bulky [ˈbʌlki] *adj* **bulkier; -est** : voluminoso, grande
bull[1] [ˈbʊl] *adj* : macho
bull[2] *n* **1** : toro *m*, macho *m* (de ciertas especies) **2** : bula *f* (papal) **3** DECREE : decreto *m*, edicto *m*
bulldog [ˈbʊlˌdɔg] *n* : bulldog *m*
bulldoze [ˈbʊlˌdo:z] *vt* **-dozed; -dozing 1** LEVEL : nivelar (el terreno), derribar (un edificio) **2** FORCE : forzar <he bulldozed his way through : se abrió paso a codazos>
bulldozer [ˈbʊlˌdo:zər] *n* : bulldozer *m*
bullet [ˈbʊlət] *n* : bala *f*
bulletin [ˈbʊlətən, -lətən] *n* **1** NOTICE : comunicado *m*, anuncio *m*, boletín *m* **2** NEWSLETTER : boletín *m* (informativo)
bulletin board *n* : tablón *m* de anuncios
bulletproof [ˈbʊlətˌpru:f] *adj* : antibalas, a prueba de balas
bullfight [ˈbʊlˌfaɪt] *n* : corrida *f* (de toros)
bullfighter [ˈbʊlˌfaɪtər] *n* : torero *m*, -ra *f*; matador *m*
bullfrog [ˈbʊlˌfrɔg] *n* : rana *f* toro
bullheaded [ˈbʊlˈhɛdəd] *adj* : testarudo
bullion [ˈbʊljən] *n* : oro *m* en lingotes, plata *f* en lingotes
bullock [ˈbʊlək] *n* **1** STEER : buey *m*, toro *m* castrado **2** : toro *m* joven, novillo *m*
bull's–eye [ˈbʊlzˌaɪ] *n, pl* **bull's–eyes** : diana *f*, blanco *m*
bully[1] [ˈbʊli] *vt* **-lied; -lying** : intimidar, amedrentar, mangonear
bully[2] *n, pl* **-lies** : matón *m*; bravucón *m*, -cona *f*
bulrush [ˈbʊlˌrʌʃ] *n* : especie *f* de junco
bulwark [ˈbʊlˌwərk, -ˌwɔrk; ˈbʌlˌwərk] *n* : baluarte *m*, bastión *f*
bum[1] [ˈbʌm] *v* **bummed; bumming** *vi* **to bum around** : vagabundear, vagar — *vt* : gorronear *fam*, sablear *fam*
bum[2] *adj* : inútil, malo <a bum rap : una acusación falsa>
bum[3] *n* **1** LOAFER : vago *m*, -ga *f* **2** HOBO, TRAMP : vagabundo *m*, -da *f*
bumblebee [ˈbʌmbəlˌbi:] *n* : abejorro *m*
bump[1] [ˈbʌmp] *vt* : chocar contra, golpear contra, dar <to bump one's head : darse (un golpe) en la cabeza> — *vi* **to bump into** MEET : encontrarse con, tropezarse con
bump[2] *n* **1** BULGE : bulto *m*, protuberancia *f* **2** IMPACT : golpe *m*, choque *m* **3** JOLT : sacudida *f*
bumper[1] [ˈbʌmpər] *adj* : extraordinario, récord <a bumper crop : una cosecha abundante>
bumper[2] *n* : parachoques *mpl*
bumpkin [ˈbʌmpkən] *n* : palurdo *m*, -da *f*
bumpy [ˈbʌmpi] *adj* **bumpier; -est** : desigual, lleno de baches (dícese de un camino), agitado (dícese de un vuelo en avión)
bun [ˈbʌn] *n* : bollo *m*
bunch[1] [ˈbʌntʃ] *vt* : agrupar, amontonar — *vi* **to bunch up** : amontonarse, agruparse, fruncirse (dícese de una tela)
bunch[2] *n* : grupo *m*, montón *m*, ramo *m* (de flores)
bundle[1] [ˈbʌndəl] *vt* **-dled; -dling** : liar, atar
bundle[2] *n* **1** : fardo *m*, atado *m*, bulto *m*, haz *m* (de palos) **2** PARCEL : paquete *m* **3** LOAD : montón *m* <a bundle of money : un montón de dinero>
bungalow [ˈbʌŋgəˌlo:] *n* : tipo de casa de un solo piso
bungle[1] [ˈbʌŋgəl] *vt* **-gled; -gling** : echar a perder, malograr
bungle[2] *n* : chapuza *f*, desatino *m*
bungler [ˈbʌŋgələr] *n* : chapucero *m*, -ra *f*; inepto *m*, -ta *f*
bunion [ˈbʌnjən] *n* : juanete *m*
bunk[1] [ˈbʌŋk] *vi* : dormir (en una litera)
bunk[2] *n* **1** *or* **bunk bed** : litera *f* **2** NONSENSE : tonterías *fpl*, bobadas *fpl*
bunker [ˈbʌŋkər] *n* **1** : carbonera *f* (en un barco) **2** SHELTER : búnker *m*
bunny [ˈbʌni] *n, pl* **-nies** : conejo *m*, -ja *f*
buoy[1] [ˈbu:i, ˈbɔɪ] *vt* **to buoy up 1** : mantener a flote **2** CHEER, HEARTEN : animar, levantar el ánimo a
buoy[2] *n* : boya *f*
buoyancy [ˈbɔɪəntsi, ˈbu:jən-] *n* **1** : flotabilidad *f* **2** OPTIMISM : confianza *f*, optimismo *m*
buoyant [ˈbɔɪənt, ˈbu:jənt] *adj* : boyante, flotante
bur *or* **burr** [ˈbər] *n* : abrojo *m* (de una planta)
burden[1] [ˈbərdən] *vt* : cargar, oprimir
burden[2] *n* : carga *f*, peso *m*
burdensome [ˈbərdənsəm] *adj* : oneroso
burdock [ˈbərˌdɑk] *n* : bardana *f*
bureau [ˈbjʊro] *n* **1** CHEST OF DRAWERS : cómoda *f* **2** DEPARTMENT : departamento *m* (del gobierno) **3** AGENCY

: agencia *f* ⟨travel bureau : agencia de viajes⟩

bureaucracy [bjʊˈrɑkrəsi] *n, pl* **-cies** : burocracia *f*

bureaucrat [ˈbjʊrəˌkræt] *n* : burócrata *mf*

bureaucratic [ˌbjʊrəˈkræṭɪk] *adj* : burocrático

burgeon [ˈbərdʒən] *vi* : florecer, retoñar, crecer

burglar [ˈbərglər] *n* : ladrón *m*, -drona *f*

burglarize [ˈbərgləˌraɪz] *vt* **-ized; -izing** : robar

burglary [ˈbərgləri] *n, pl* **-glaries** : robo *m*

burgle [ˈbərgəl] *vt* **-gled; -gling** : robar

burgundy [ˈbərgəndi] *n, pl* **-dies** : borgoña *m*, vino *m* de Borgoña

burial [ˈbɛriəl] *n* : entierro *m*, sepelio *m*

burlap [ˈbərˌlæp] *n* : arpillera *f*

burlesque[1] [bərˈlɛsk] *vt* **-lesqued; -lesquing** : parodiar

burlesque[2] *n* **1** PARODY : parodia *f* **2** REVUE : revista *f* (musical)

burly [ˈbərli] *adj* **-lier; -liest** : fornido, corpulento, musculoso

Burmese [ˌbərˈmiːz, -ˈmiːs] *n* : birmano *m*, -na *f* — **Burmese** *adj*

burn[1] [ˈbərn] *v* **burned** [ˈbərnd, ˈbərnt] *or* **burnt** [ˈbərnt]; **burning** *vt* **1** : quemar, incendiar ⟨to burn a building : incendiar un edificio⟩ ⟨I burned my hand : me quemé la mano⟩ **2** CONSUME : usar, gastar, consumir — *vi* **1** : arder (dícese de un fuego o un edificio), quemarse (dícese de la comida, etc.) **2** : estar prendido, estar encendido ⟨we left the lights burning : dejamos las luces encendidas⟩ **3 to burn out** : consumirse, apagarse **4 to burn with** : arder de ⟨he was burning with jealousy : ardía de celos⟩

burn[2] *n* : quemadura *f*

burner [ˈbərnər] *n* : quemador *m*

burnish [ˈbərnɪʃ] *vt* : bruñir

burp[1] [ˈbərp] *vi* : eructar — *vt* : hacer eructar

burp[2] *n* : eructo *m*

burr → **bur**

burro [ˈbəro, ˈbʊr-] *n, pl* **-os** : burro *m*

burrow[1] [ˈbəro] *vi* **1** : cavar, hacer una madriguera **2 to burrow into** : hurgar en — *vt* : cavar, excavar

burrow[2] *n* : madriguera *f*, conejera *f* (de un conejo)

bursar [ˈbərsər] *n* : administrador *m*, -dora *f*

bursitis [bərˈsaɪṭəs] *n* : bursitis *f*

burst[1] [ˈbərst] *v* **burst; bursting** *vi* **1** : reventarse (dícese de una llanta o un globo), estallar (dícese de obuses o fuegos artificiales), romperse (dícese de un dique) **2 to burst in** : irrumpir en **3 to burst into** : empezar a, echar a ⟨to burst into tears : echarse a llorar⟩ — *vt* : reventar

burst[2] *n* **1** EXPLOSION : estallido *m*, explosión *f*, reventón *m* (de una llanta) **2** OUTBURST : arranque *m* (de actividad, de velocidad), arrebato *m* (de ira), salva *f* (de aplausos)

Burundian [bʊˈruːndiən, -ˈrʊn-] *n* : burundés *m*, -desa *f* — **Burundian** *adj*

bury [ˈbɛri] *vt* **buried; burying 1** INTER : enterrar, sepultar **2** HIDE : esconder, ocultar **3 to bury oneself in** : enfrascarse en

bus[1] [ˈbʌs] *v* **bused** *or* **bussed** [ˈbʌst]; **busing** *or* **bussing** [ˈbʌsɪŋ] *vt* : transportar en autobús — *vi* : viajar en autobús

bus[2] *n* : autobús *m*, bus *m*, camión *m Mex*, colectivo *m Arg, Bol, Peru*

busboy [ˈbʌsˌbɔɪ] *n* : ayudante *mf* de camarero

bush [ˈbʊʃ] *n* **1** SHRUB : arbusto *m*, mata *f* **2** THICKET : maleza *f*, matorral *m*

bushel [ˈbʊʃəl] *n* : medida de áridos igual a 35.24 litros

bushing [ˈbʊʃɪŋ] *n* : cojinete *m*

bushy [ˈbʊʃi] *adj* **bushier; -est** : espeso, poblado ⟨bushy eyebrows : cejas pobladas⟩

busily [ˈbɪzəli] *adv* : afanosamente, diligentemente

business [ˈbɪznəs, -nəz] *n* **1** OCCUPATION : ocupación *f*, oficio *m* **2** DUTY, MISSION : misión *f*, deber *m*, responsabilidad *f* **3** ESTABLISHMENT, FIRM : empresa *f*, firma *f*, negocio *m*, comercio *m* **4** COMMERCE : negocios *mpl*, comercio *m* **5** AFFAIR, MATTER : asunto *m*, cuestión *f*, cosa *f* ⟨it's none of your business : no es asunto tuyo⟩

businessman [ˈbɪznəsˌmæn, -nəz-] *n, pl* **-men** [-mən, -ˌmɛn] : empresario *m*, hombre *m* de negocios

businesswoman [ˈbɪznəsˌwʊmən, -nəz-] *n, pl* **-women** [-ˌwɪmən] : empresaria *f*, mujer *f* de negocios

bust[1] [ˈbʌst] *vt* **1** BREAK, SMASH : romper, estropear, destrozar **2** TAME : domar, amansar (un caballo) — *vi* : romperse, estropearse

bust[2] *n* **1** : busto *m* (en la escultura) **2** BREASTS : pecho *m*, senos *mpl*, busto *m*

bustle[1] [ˈbʌsəl] *vi* **-tled; -tling to bustle about** : ir y venir, trajinar, ajetrearse

bustle[2] *n* **1** *or* **hustle and bustle** : bullicio *m*, ajetreo *m* **2** : polisón *m* (en la ropa feminina)

busy[1] [ˈbɪzi] *vt* **busied; busying to busy oneself with** : ocuparse con, ponerse a, entretenerse con

busy[2] *adj* **busier; -est 1** OCCUPIED : ocupado, atareado ⟨he's busy working : está ocupado en su trabajo⟩ ⟨the telephone was busy : el teléfono estaba ocupado⟩ **2** BUSTLING : concurrido, animado ⟨a busy street : una calle concurrida, una calle con mucho tránsito⟩

busybody [ˈbɪziˌbɑdi] *n, pl* **-bodies** : entrometido *m*, -da *f*; metiche *mf fam*; metomentodo *mf*

but[1] [ˈbʌt] *conj* **1** THAT : que ⟨there is no doubt but he is lazy : no cabe duda que sea perezoso⟩ **2** WITHOUT : sin que **3** NEVERTHELESS : pero, no obstante, sin embargo ⟨I called her but she didn't answer : la llamé pero no contestó⟩ **4** YET : pero ⟨he was poor but proud : era pobre pero orgulloso⟩

but[2] *prep* EXCEPT : excepto, menos ⟨everyone but Carlos : todos menos Carlos⟩ ⟨the last but one : el penúltimo⟩

butcher[1] [ˈbʊtʃər] *vt* **1** SLAUGHTER : matar (animales) **2** KILL : matar, asesinar, masacrar **3** BOTCH : estropear, hacer una chapuza

butcher[2] *n* **1** : carnicero *m*, -ra *f* **2** KILLER : asesino *m*, -na *f* **3** BUNGLER : chapucero *m*, -ra *f*

butler [ˈbʌtlər] *n* : mayordomo *m*

butt[1] [ˈbʌt] *vt* **1** : embestir (con los cuernos), darle un cabezazo a **2** ABUT : colindar con, bordear — *vi* **to butt in 1** INTERRUPT : interrumpir **2** MEDDLE : entrometerse, meterse

butt[2] *n* **1** BUTTING : embestida *f* (de cuernos), cabezazo *m* **2** TARGET : blanco *m* ⟨the butt of their jokes : el blanco de sus bromas⟩ **3** BOTTOM, END : extremo *m*, culata *f* (de un rifle), colilla *f* (de un cigarrillo)

butte [ˈbjuːt] *n* : colina *f* empinada y aislada

butter[1] [ˈbʌt̬ər] *vt* **1** : untar con mantequilla **2 to butter up** : halagar

butter[2] *n* : mantequilla *f*

buttercup [ˈbʌt̬ərˌkʌp] *n* : ranúnculo *m*

butterfat [ˈbʌt̬ərˌfæt] *n* : grasa *f* de la leche

butterfly [ˈbʌt̬ərˌflaɪ] *n, pl* **-flies** : mariposa *f*

buttermilk [ˈbʌt̬ərˌmɪlk] *n* : suero *m* de la leche

butternut [ˈbʌt̬ərˌnʌt] *n* : nogal *m* ceniciento (árbol)

butterscotch [ˈbʌt̬ərˌskɑtʃ] *n* : caramelo *m* duro hecho con mantequilla

buttery [ˈbʌt̬əri] *adj* : mantecoso

buttocks [ˈbʌt̬əks, -ˌtɑks] *npl* : nalgas *fpl*, trasero *m*

button[1] [ˈbʌtən] *vt* : abrochar, abotonar — *vi* : abrocharse, abotonarse

button[2] *n* : botón *m*

buttonhole[1] [ˈbʌtənˌhoːl] *vt* **-holed; -holing** : acorralar

buttonhole[2] *n* : ojal *m*

buttress[1] [ˈbʌtrəs] *vt* : apoyar, reforzar

buttress[2] *n* **1** : contrafuerte *m* (en la arquitectura) **2** SUPPORT : apoyo *m*, sostén *m*

buxom [ˈbʌksəm] *adj* : con mucho busto, con mucho pecho

buy[1] [ˈbaɪ] *vt* **bought** [ˈbɔt]; **buying** : comprar

buy[2] *n* BARGAIN : compra *f*, ganga *f*

buyer [ˈbaɪər] *n* : comprador *m*, -dora *f*

buzz[1] [ˈbʌz] *vi* : zumbar (dícese de un insecto), sonar (dícese de un teléfono o un despertador)

buzz[2] *n* **1** : zumbido *m* (de insectos) **2** : murmullo *m*, rumor *m* (de voces)

buzzard [ˈbʌzərd] *n* VULTURE : buitre *m*, zopilote *m CA, Mex*

buzzer [ˈbʌzər] *n* : timbre *m*, chicharra *f*

buzzword [ˈbʌzˌwərd] *n* : palabra *f* de moda

by[1] [ˈbaɪ] *adv* **1** NEAR : cerca ⟨he lives close by : vive muy cerca⟩ **2 to stop by** : pasar por casa, hacer una visita **3 to go by** : pasar ⟨they rushed by : pasaron corriendo⟩ **4 to put by** : reservar, poner a un lado **5 by and by** : poco después, dentro de poco **6 by and large** : en general

by[2] *prep* **1** NEAR : cerca de, al lado de, junto a **2** VIA : por ⟨she left by the door : salió por la puerta⟩ **3** PAST : por, por delante de ⟨they walked by him : pasaron por delante de él⟩ **4** DURING : de, durante ⟨by night : de noche⟩ **5** (*in expressions of time*) : para ⟨we'll be there by ten : estaremos allí para las diez⟩ ⟨by then : para entonces⟩ **6** (*indicating cause or agent*) : por, de, a ⟨built by the Romans : construido por los romanos⟩ ⟨a book by Borges : un libro de Borges⟩ ⟨made by hand : hecho a mano⟩

by and by *adv* : dentro de poco

bygone[1] [ˈbaɪˌgɔn] *adj* : pasado

bygone[2] *n* **let bygones be bygones** : lo pasado, pasado está

bylaw *or* **byelaw** [ˈbaɪˌlɔ] *n* : norma *f*, reglamento *m*

by–line [ˈbaɪˌlaɪn] *n* : data *f*

bypass[1] [ˈbaɪˌpæs] *vt* : evitar

bypass[2] *n* **1** BELTWAY : carretera *f* de circunvalación **2** DETOUR : desvío *m*

by–product [ˈbaɪˌprɑdəkt] *n* : subproducto *m*, producto *m* derivado

bystander [ˈbaɪˌstændər] *n* : espectador *m*, -dora *f*

byte [ˈbaɪt] *n* : byte *m*

byway [ˈbaɪˌweɪ] *n* : camino *m* (apartado), carretera *f* secundaria

byword [ˈbaɪˌwərd] *n* **1** PROVERB : proverbio *m*, refrán *m* **2 to be a byword for** : estar sinónimo de

C

c ['siː] *n, pl* **c's** *or* **cs** : tercera letra del alfabeto inglés
cab ['kæb] *n* **1** TAXI : taxi *m* **2** : cabina *f* (de un camión o una locomotora) **3** CARRIAGE : coche *m* de caballos
cabal [kə'bɑl, -'bæl] *n* **1** INTRIGUE, PLOT : conspiración *f*, complot *m*, intriga *f* **2** : grupo *m* de conspiradores
cabaret [ˌkæbə'reɪ] *n* : cabaret *m*
cabbage ['kæbɪʤ] *n* : col *f*, repollo *m*
cabbie *or* **cabby** ['kæbi] *n* : taxista *mf*
cabin ['kæbən] *n* **1** HUT : cabaña *f*, choza *f*, barraca *f* **2** STATEROOM : camarote *m* **3** : cabina *f* (de un automóvil o avión)
cabinet ['kæbnət] *n* **1** CUPBOARD : armario *m* **2** : gabinete *m*, consejo *m* de ministros **3 medicine cabinet** : botiquín *m*
cabinetmaker ['kæbnətˌmeɪkər] *n* : ebanista *mf*
cabinetmaking ['kæbnətˌmeɪkɪŋ] *n* : ebanistería *f*
cable[1] ['keɪbəl] *vt* **-bled; -bling** : enviar un cable, telegrafiar
cable[2] *n* **1** : cable *m* (para colgar o sostener algo) **2** : cable *m* eléctrico **3** → **cablegram**
cablegram ['keɪbəlˌgræm] *n* : telegrama *m*, cable *m*
caboose [kə'buːs] *n* : furgón *m* de cola, cabús *m Mex*
cabstand ['kæbˌstænd] *n* : parada *f* de taxis
cacao [kə'kaʊ, -'keɪo] *n, pl* **cacaos** : cacao *m*
cache[1] ['kæʃ] *vt* **cached; caching** : esconder, guardar en un escondrijo
cache[2] *n* **1** : escondite *m*, escondrijo *m* ⟨cache of weapons : escondite de armas⟩ **2** : cache *m* ⟨cache memory : memoria cache⟩
cachet [kæ'ʃeɪ] *n* : caché *m*, prestigio *m*
cackle[1] ['kækəl] *vi* **-led; -ling 1** CLUCK : cacarear **2** : reírse o carcajearse estridentemente ⟨he was cackling with delight : estaba carcajeándose de gusto⟩
cackle[2] *n* **1** : cacareo *m* (de una polla) **2** LAUGH : risa *f* estridente
cacophony [kæ'kɑfəni, -'kɔ-] *n, pl* **-nies** : cacofonía *f*
cactus ['kæktəs] *n, pl* **cacti** [-ˌtaɪ] *or* **-tuses** : cacto *m*, cactus *m*
cadaver [kə'dævər] *n* : cadáver *m*
cadaverous [kə'dævərəs] *adj* : cadavérico
caddie[1] *or* **caddy** ['kædi] *vi* **caddied; caddying** : trabajar de caddie, hacer de caddie
caddie[2] *or* **caddy** *n, pl* **-dies** : caddie *mf*
caddy ['kædi] *n, pl* **-dies** : cajita *f* para té
cadence ['keɪdənts] *n* : cadencia *f*, ritmo *m*
cadenced ['keɪdəntst] *adj* : cadencioso, rítmico
cadet [kə'dɛt] *n* : cadete *mf*
cadmium ['kædmiəm] *n* : cadmio *m*
cadre ['kæˌdreɪ, 'kɑ-, -ˌdriː] *n* : cuadro *m* (de expertos)
café [kæ'feɪ, kə-] *n* : café *m*, cafetería *f*
cafeteria [ˌkæfə'tɪriə] *n* : cafetería *f*, restaurante *m* de autoservicio
caffeine [kæ'fiːn] *n* : cafeína *f*
cage[1] ['keɪʤ] *vt* **caged; caging** : enjaular
cage[2] *n* : jaula *f*
cagey ['keɪʤi] *adj* **-gier; -est 1** CAUTIOUS : cauteloso, reservado **2** SHREWD : astuto, vivo — **cagily** [-ʤəli] *adv*
caisson ['keɪˌsɑn, -sən] *n* **1** : cajón *m* de municiones **2** : cajón *m* hidráulico
cajole [kə'ʤoːl] *vt* **-joled; -joling** : engatusar
cajolery [kə'ʤoːləri] *n* : engatusamiento *m*
cake[1] ['keɪk] *v* **caked; caking** *vt* : cubrir ⟨caked with mud : cubierto de barro⟩ — *vi* : endurecerse
cake[2] *n* **1** : torta *f*, bizcocho *m*, pastel *m* **2** : pastilla *f* (de jabón) **3 to take the cake** : llevarse la palma, ser el colmo
calabash ['kæləˌbæʃ] *n* : calabaza *f*
calamari [ˌkɑlə'mɑri] *ns & pl* : calamares *mpl*
calamine ['kæləˌmaɪn] *n* : calamina *f* ⟨calamine lotion : loción de calamina⟩
calamitous [kə'læmət̬əs] *adj* : desastroso, catastrófico, calamitoso — **calamitously** *adv*
calamity [kə'læmət̬i] *n, pl* **-ties** : desastre *m*, desgracia *f*, calamidad *f*
calcium ['kælsiəm] *n* : calcio *m*
calcium carbonate ['kɑrbəˌneɪt, -nət] *n* : carbonato *m* de calcio
calculable ['kælkjələbəl] *adj* : calculable, computable
calculate ['kælkjəˌleɪt] *v* **-lated; -lating** *vt* **1** COMPUTE : calcular, computar **2** ESTIMATE : calcular, creer **3** INTEND : planear, tener la intención de ⟨I calculated on spending $100 : planeaba gastar $100⟩ — *vi* : calcular, hacer cálculos
calculated ['kælkjəˌleɪt̬əd] *adj* **1** ESTIMATED : calculado **2** DELIBERATE : intencional, premeditado, deliberado
calculating ['kælkjəˌleɪt̬ɪŋ] *adj* SHREWD : calculador, astuto
calculation [ˌkælkjə'leɪʃən] *n* : cálculo *m*
calculator ['kælkjəˌleɪt̬ər] *n* : calculadora *f*
calculus ['kælkjələs] *n, pl* **-li** [-ˌlaɪ] **1** : cálculo *m* ⟨differential calculus : cálculo diferencial⟩ **2** TARTAR : sarro *m* (dental)
caldron ['kɔldrən] → **cauldron**
calendar ['kæləndər] *n* **1** : calendario *m* **2** SCHEDULE : calendario *m*, programa *m*, agenda *f*

calf [ˈkæf, ˈkaf] *n, pl* **calves** [ˈkævz, ˈkavz] **1** : becerro *m*, -rra *f*; ternero *m*, -ra *f* (de vacunos) **2** : cría *f* (de otros mamíferos) **3** : pantorrilla *f* (de la pierna)
calfskin [ˈkæfˌskɪn] *n* : piel *f* de becerro
caliber *or* **calibre** [ˈkæləbər] *n* **1** : calibre *m* ⟨a .38 caliber gun : una pistola de calibre .38⟩ **2** ABILITY : calibre *m*, valor *m*, capacidad *f*
calibrate [ˈkæləˌbreɪt] *vt* **-brated; -brating** : calibrar (armas), graduar (termómetros)
calibration [ˌkæləˈbreɪʃən] *n* : calibrado *m*, calibración *f*
calico [ˈkælɪˌkoː] *n, pl* **-coes** *or* **-cos** **1** : calicó *m*, percal *m* **2** *or* **calico cat** : gato *m* manchado
calipers [ˈkæləpərz] *npl* : calibrador *m*
caliph *or* **calif** [ˈkeɪləf, ˈkæ-] *n* : califa *m*
calisthenics [ˌkæləsˈθɛnɪks] *ns & pl* : calistenia *f*
calk [ˈkɔk] → **caulk**
call[1] [ˈkɔl] *vi* **1** CRY, SHOUT : gritar, vociferar **2** VISIT : hacer (una) visita, visitar **3 to call for** : exigir, requerir, necesitar ⟨it calls for patience : requiere mucha paciencia⟩ — *vt* **1** SUMMON : llamar, convocar **2** TELEPHONE : llamar por teléfono, telefonear **3** NAME : llamar, apodar
call[2] *n* **1** SHOUT : grito *m*, llamada *f* **2** : grito *m* (de un animal), reclamo *m* (de un pájaro) **3** SUMMONS : llamada *f* **4** DEMAND : llamado *m*, petición *f* **5** VISIT : visita *f* **6** DECISION : decisión *f* (en deportes) **7** *or* **telephone call** : llamada *f* (telefónica)
call down *vt* REPRIMAND : reprender, reñir
caller [ˈkɔlər] *n* **1** VISITOR : visita *f* **2** : persona *f* que llama (por teléfono)
calligraphy [kəˈlɪgrəfi] *n, pl* **-phies** : caligrafía *f*
calling [ˈkɔlɪŋ] *n* : vocación *f*, profesión *f*
calliope [kəˈlaɪəˌpiː, ˈkæliˌoːp] *n* : órgano *m* de vapor
call off *vt* CANCEL : cancelar, suspender
callous[1] [ˈkæləs] *vt* : encallecer
callous[2] *adj* **1** CALLUSED : calloso, encallecido **2** UNFEELING : insensible, desalmado, cruel
callously [ˈkæləsli] *adv* : cruelmente, insensiblemente
callousness [ˈkæləsnəs] *n* : insensibilidad *f*, crueldad *f*
callow [ˈkælo] *adj* : inexperto, inmaduro
callus [ˈkæləs] *n* : callo *m*
callused [ˈkæləst] *adj* : encallecido, calloso
calm[1] [ˈkɑm, ˈkɑlm] *vt* : tranquilizar, calmar, sosegar — *vi* : tranquilizarse, calmarse ⟨calm down! : ¡tranquilízate!⟩
calm[2] *adj* **1** TRANQUIL : calmo, tranquilo, sereno, ecuánime **2** STILL : en calma (dícese del mar), sin viento (dícese del aire)
calm[3] *n* : tranquilidad *f*, calma *f*
calmly [ˈkɑmli, ˈkɑlm-] *adv* : con calma, tranquilamente
calmness [ˈkɑmnəs, ˈkɑlm-] *n* : calma *f*, tranquilidad *f*
caloric [kəˈlɔrɪk] *adj* : calórico (dícese de los alimentos), calorífico (dícese de la energía)
calorie [ˈkæləri] *n* : caloría *f*
calumniate [kəˈlʌmniˌeɪt] *vt* **-ated; -ating** : calumniar, difamar
calumny [ˈkæləmni] *n, pl* **-nies** : calumnia *f*, difamación *f*
calve [ˈkæv, ˈkav] *vi* **calved; calving** : parir (dícese de los mamíferos)
calves → **calf**
calypso [kəˈlɪpˌsoː] *n, pl* **-sos** : calipso *m*
calyx [ˈkeɪlɪks, ˈkæ-] *n, pl* **-lyxes** *or* **-lyces** [-ləˌsiːz] : cáliz *m*
cam [ˈkæm] *n* : leva *f*
camaraderie [ˌkɑmˈrɑdəri, ˌkæm-; ˌkɑməˈrɑ-] *n* : compañerismo *m*, camaradería *f*
Cambodian [kæmˈboːdiən] *n* : camboyano *m*, -na *f* — **Cambodian** *adj*
came → **come**
camel [ˈkæməl] *n* : camello *m*
camellia [kəˈmiːljə] *n* : camelia *f*
cameo [ˈkæmiˌoː] *n, pl* **-eos** **1** : camafeo *m* **2** *or* **cameo performance** : actuación *f* especial
camera [ˈkæmrə, ˈkæmərə] *n* : cámara *f*, máquina *f* fotográfica
Cameroonian [ˌkæməˈruːniən] *n* : camerunés *m*, -nesa *f*
camouflage[1] [ˈkæməˌflɑʒ, -ˌflɑʤ] *vt* **-flaged; -flaging** : camuflajear, camuflar
camouflage[2] *n* : camuflaje *m*
camp[1] [ˈkæmp] *vi* : acampar, ir de camping
camp[2] *n* **1** : campamento *m* **2** FACTION : campo *m*, bando *m* ⟨in the same camp : del mismo bando⟩ **3 to pitch camp** : acampar, poner el campamento **4 to break camp** : levantar el campamento
campaign[1] [kæmˈpeɪn] *vi* : hacer (una) campaña
campaign[2] *n* : campaña *f*
campanile [ˌkæmpəˈniːˌliː, -ˈniːl] *n, pl* **-niles** *or* **-nili** [-ˈniːˌliː] : campanario *m*
camper [ˈkæmpər] *n* **1** : campista *mf* (persona) **2** : cámper *m* (vehículo)
campground [ˈkæmpˌgraʊnd] *n* : campamento *m*, camping *m*
camphor [ˈkæmpfər] *n* : alcanfor *m*
campsite [ˈkæmpˌsaɪt] *n* : campamento *m*, camping *m*
campus [ˈkæmpəs] *n* : campus *m*, recinto *m* universitario
can[1] [ˈkæn] *v aux, past* **could** [ˈkʊd]; *present s & pl* **can** **1** : poder ⟨could you help me? : ¿podría ayudarme?⟩ **2** : saber ⟨she can't drive yet : todavía no sabe manejar⟩ **3** MAY : poder, tener permiso para ⟨can I sit down? : ¿puedo sentarme?⟩ **4** : poder ⟨it can't be! : ¡no

puede ser!⟩ ⟨where can they be? : ¿dónde estarán?⟩

can[2] [ˈkæn] *vt* **canned; canning 1** : enlatar, envasar ⟨to can tomatoes : enlatar tomates⟩ **2** DISMISS, FIRE : despedir, echar

can[3] *n* : lata *f*, envase *m*, cubo *m* ⟨a can of beer : una lata de cerveza⟩ ⟨garbage can : cubo de basura⟩

Canadian [kəˈneɪdiən] *n* : canadiense *mf* — **Canadian** *adj*

canal [kəˈnæl] *n* **1** : canal *m*, tubo *m* ⟨alimentary canal : tubo digestivo⟩ **2** : canal *m* ⟨Panama Canal : Canal de Panamá⟩

canapé [ˈkænəpi, -ˌpeɪ] *n* : canapé *m*

canary [kəˈnɛri] *n, pl* **-naries** : canario *m*

cancel [ˈkæntsəl] *vt* **-celed** *or* **-celled; -celing** *or* **-celling** : cancelar

cancellation [ˌkæntsəˈleɪʃən] *n* : cancelación *f*

cancer [ˈkæntsər] *n* : cáncer *m*

Cancer *n* : Cáncer *mf*

cancerous [ˈkæntsərəs] *adj* : canceroso

candelabrum [ˌkændəˈlɑbrəm, -ˈlæ-] *or* **candelabra** [-brə] *n, pl* **-bra** *or* **-bras** : candelabro *m*

candid [ˈkændɪd] *adj* **1** FRANK : franco, sincero, abierto **2** : natural, espontáneo (en la fotografía)

candidacy [ˈkændədəsi] *n, pl* **-cies** : candidatura *f*

candidate [ˈkændəˌdeɪt, -dət] *n* : candidato *m*, -ta *f*

candidly [ˈkændɪdli] *adv* : con franqueza

candied [ˈkændid] *adj* : confitado

candle [ˈkændəl] *n* : vela *f*, candela *f*, cirio *m* (ceremonial)

candlestick [ˈkændəlˌstɪk] *n* : candelero *m*

candor [ˈkændər] *n* : franqueza *f*

candy [ˈkændi] *n, pl* **-dies** : dulce *m*, caramelo *m*

cane[1] [ˈkeɪn] *vt* **caned; caning 1** : tapizar (muebles) con mimbre **2** FLOG : azotar con una vara

cane[2] *n* **1** : bastón *m* (para andar), vara *f* (para castigar) **2** REED : caña *f*, mimbre *m* (para muebles)

canine[1] [ˈkeɪˌnaɪn] *adj* : canino

canine[2] *n* **1** DOG : canino *m*; perro *m*, -rra *f* **2** *or* **canine tooth** : colmillo *m*, diente *m* canino

canister [ˈkænəstər] *n* : lata *f*, bote *m*

canker [ˈkæŋkər] *n* : úlcera *f* bucal

cannery [ˈkænəri] *n, pl* **-ries** : fábrica *f* de conservas

cannibal [ˈkænəbəl] *n* : caníbal *mf*; antropófago *m*, -ga *f*

cannibalism [ˈkænəbəˌlɪzəm] *n* : canibalismo *m*, antropofagia *f*

cannibalize [ˈkænəbəˌlaɪz] *vt* **-ized; -izing** : canibalizar

cannily [ˈkænəli] *adv* : astutamente, sagazmente

cannon [ˈkænən] *n, pl* **-nons** *or* **-non** : cañón *m*

cannot (can not) [ˈkænˌɑt, kəˈnɑt] → **can**[1]

canny [ˈkæni] *adj* **-nier; -est** SHREWD : astuto, sagaz

canoe[1] [kəˈnuː] *vi* **-noed; -noeing** : ir en canoa

canoe[2] *n* : canoa *f*, piragua *f*

canon [ˈkænən] *n* **1** : canon *m* ⟨canon law : derecho canónico⟩ **2** WORKS : canon *m* ⟨the canon of American literature : el canon de la literatura americana⟩ **3** : canónigo *m* (de una catedral) **4** STANDARD : canon *m*, norma *f*

canonical [kəˈnɑnɪkəl] *adj* : canónico

canonize [ˈkænəˌnaɪz] *vt* **-ized; -izing** : canonizar

canopy [ˈkænəpi] *n, pl* **-pies** : dosel *m*, toldo *m*

cant[1] [ˈkænt] *vt* TILT : ladear, inclinar — *vi* **1** SLANT : ladearse, inclinarse, escorar (dícese de un barco) **2** : hablar insinceramente

cant[2] *n* **1** SLANT : plano *m* inclinado **2** JARGON : jerga *f* **3** : palabras *fpl* insinceras

can't [ˈkænt, ˈkant] (*contraction* of **can not**) → **can**[1]

cantaloupe [ˈkæntəlˌoːp] *n* : melón *m*, cantalupo *m*

cantankerous [kænˈtæŋkərəs] *adj* : irritable, irascible — **cantankerously** *adv*

cantankerousness [kænˈtæŋkərəsnəs] *n* : irritabilidad *f*, irascibilidad *f*

cantata [kənˈtɑt̬ə] *n* : cantata *f*

canteen [kænˈtiːn] *n* **1** FLASK : cantimplora *f* **2** CAFETERIA : cantina *f*, comedor *m* **3** : club *m* para actividades sociales y recreativas

canter[1] [ˈkæntər] *vi* : ir a medio galope

canter[2] *n* : medio galope *m*

cantilever [ˈkæntəˌliːvər, -ˌlɛvər] *n* **1** : viga *f* voladiza **2 cantilever bridge** : puente *m* voladizo

canto [ˈkænˌtoː] *n, pl* **-tos** : canto *m*

canton [ˈkæntən, -ˌtɑn] *n* : cantón *m*

Cantonese [ˌkæntənˈiːz, -ˈiːs] *n* **1** : cantonés *m*, -nesa *f* **2** : cantonés *m* (idioma) — **Cantonese** *adj*

cantor [ˈkæntər] *n* : solista *mf*

canvas [ˈkænvəs] *n* **1** : lona *f* **2** SAILS : velas *fpl* (de un barco) **3** : lienzo *m*, tela *f* (de pintar) **4** PAINTING : pintura *f*, óleo *m*, cuadro *m*

canvass[1] [ˈkænvəs] *vt* **1** SOLICIT : solicitar votos o pedidos de, hacer campaña entre **2** SOUND OUT : sondear (opiniones, etc.)

canvass[2] *n* SURVEY : sondeo *m*, encuesta *f*

canyon [ˈkænjən] *n* : cañón *m*

cap[1] [ˈkæp] *vt* **capped; capping 1** COVER : tapar (un recipiente), enfundar (un diente), cubrir (una montaña) **2** CLIMAX : coronar, ser el punto culminante de ⟨to cap it all off : para colmo⟩ **3** LIMIT : limitar, poner un tope a

cap[2] *n* **1** : gorra *f*, gorro *m*, cachucha *f* *Mex* ⟨baseball cap : gorra de béisbol⟩

2 COVER, TOP : tapa *f*, tapón *m* (de botellas), corcholata *f Mex* **3** LIMIT : tope *m*, límite *m*
capability [ˌkeɪpəˈbɪləṭi] *n, pl* **-ties** : capacidad *f*, habilidad *f*, competencia *f*
capable [ˈkeɪpəbəl] *adj* : competente, capaz, hábil — **capably** [-bli] *adv*
capacious [kəˈpeɪʃəs] *adj* : amplio, espacioso, de gran capacidad
capacity[1] [kəˈpæsəṭi] *adj* : completo, total ⟨a capacity crowd : un lleno completo⟩
capacity[2] *n, pl* **-ties 1** ROOM, SPACE : capacidad *f*, cabida *f*, espacio *m* **2** CAPABILITY : habilidad *f*, competencia *f* **3** FUNCTION, ROLE : calidad *f*, función *f* ⟨in his capacity as ambassador : en su calidad de embajador⟩
cape [ˈkeɪp] *n* **1** : capa *f* **2** : cabo *m* ⟨Cape Horn : el Cabo de Hornos⟩
caper[1] [ˈkeɪpər] *vi* : dar saltos, correr y brincar
caper[2] *n* **1** : alcaparra *f* ⟨olives and capers : aceitunas y alcaparras⟩ **2** ANTIC, PRANK : broma *f*, travesura *f* **3** LEAP : brinco *m*, salto *m*
Cape Verdean [ˈkeɪpˈvərdiən] *n* : caboverdiano *m*, -na *f* — **Cape Verdean** *adj*
capful [ˈkæpˌfʊl] *n* : tapa *f*, tapita *f*
capillary[1] [ˈkæpəˌlɛri] *adj* : capilar
capillary[2] *n, pl* **-ries** : capilar *m*
capital[1] [ˈkæpəṭəl] *adj* **1** : capital ⟨capital punishment : pena capital⟩ **2** : mayúsculo (dícese de las letras) **3** : de capital ⟨capital assets : activo fijo⟩ ⟨capital gain : ganancia de capital, plusvalía⟩ **4** EXCELLENT : excelente, estupendo
capital[2] *n* **1** *or* **capital city** : capital *f*, sede *f* del gobierno **2** WEALTH : capital *m* **3** *or* **capital letter** : mayúscula *f* **4** : capitel *m* (de una columna)
capitalism [ˈkæpəṭəlˌɪzəm] *n* : capitalismo *m*
capitalist[1] [ˈkæpəṭəlɪst] *or* **capitalistic** [ˌkæpəṭəlˈɪstɪk] *adj* : capitalista
capitalist[2] *n* : capitalista *mf*
capitalization [ˌkæpəṭələˈzeɪʃən] *n* : capitalización *f*
capitalize [ˈkæpəṭəlˌaɪz] *v* **-ized; -izing** *vt* **1** FINANCE : capitalizar, financiar **2** : escribir con mayúscula — *vi* **to capitalize on** : sacar partido de, aprovechar
capitol [ˈkæpəṭəl] *n* : capitolio *m*
capitulate [kəˈpɪʧəˌleɪt] *vi* **-lated; -lating** : capitular
capitulation [kəˌpɪʧəˈleɪʃən] *n* : capitulación *f*
capon [ˈkeɪˌpɑn, -pən] *n* : capón *m*
cappuccino [ˌkɑpəˈʧiːnoː] *n* : capuchino *m* (café)
caprice [kəˈpriːs] *n* : capricho *m*, antojo *m*
capricious [kəˈprɪʃəs, -ˈpriː-] *adj* : caprichoso — **capriciously** *adv*
Capricorn [ˈkæprɪˌkɔrn] *n* : Capricornio *mf*
capsize [ˈkæpˌsaɪz, kæpˈsaɪz] *v* **-sized; -sizing** *vi* : volcar, volcarse — *vt* : hacer volcar
capstan [ˈkæpstən, -ˌstæn] *n* : cabrestante *m*
capsule [ˈkæpsəl, -ˌsuːl] *n* **1** : cápsula *f* (en la farmacéutica y botánica) **2 space capsule** : cápsula *f* espacial
captain[1] [ˈkæptən] *vt* : capitanear
captain[2] *n* **1** : capitán *m*, -tana *f* **2** HEADWAITER : jefe *m*, -fa *f* de comedor **3 captain of industry** : magnate *mf*
caption[1] [ˈkæpʃən] *vt* : ponerle una leyenda a (una ilustración), titular (un artículo), subtitular (una película)
caption[2] *n* **1** HEADING : titular *m*, encabezamiento *m* **2** : leyenda *f* (al pie de una ilustración) **3** SUBTITLE : subtítulo *m*
captivate [ˈkæptəˌveɪt] *vt* **-vated; -vating** CHARM : cautivar, hechizar, encantar
captivating [ˈkæptəˌveɪṭɪŋ] *adj* : cautivador, hechicero, encantador
captive[1] [ˈkæptɪv] *adj* : cautivo
captive[2] *n* : cautivo *m*, -va *f*
captivity [kæpˈtɪvəṭi] *n* : cautiverio *m*
captor [ˈkæptər] *n* : captor *m*, -tora *f*
capture[1] [ˈkæpʃər] *vt* **-tured; -turing 1** SEIZE : capturar, apresar **2** CATCH : captar ⟨to capture one's interest : captar el interés de uno⟩
capture[2] *n* : captura *f*, apresamiento *m*
car [ˈkɑr] *n* **1** AUTOMOBILE : automóvil *m*, coche *m*, carro *m* **2** : vagón *m*, coche *m* (de un tren) **3** : cabina *f* (de un ascensor)
carafe [kəˈræf, -ˈrɑf] *n* : garrafa *f*
caramel [ˈkɑrməl; ˈkærəməl, -ˌmɛl] *n* **1** : caramelo *m*, azúcar *f* quemada **2** *or* **caramel candy** : caramelo *m*, dulce *m* de leche
carat [ˈkærət] *n* : quilate *m*
caravan [ˈkærəˌvæn] *n* : caravana *f*
caraway [ˈkærəˌweɪ] *n* : alcaravea *f*
carbine [ˈkɑrˌbaɪn, -ˌbiːn] *n* : carabina *f*
carbohydrate [ˌkɑrboˈhaɪˌdreɪt, -drət] *n* : carbohidrato *m*, hidrato *m* de carbono
carbon [ˈkɑrbən] *n* **1** : carbono *m* **2** → **carbon paper 3** → **carbon copy**
carbonated [ˈkɑrbəˌneɪṭəd] *adj* : carbonatado (dícese del agua), gaseoso (dícese de las bebidas)
carbon copy *n* **1** : copia *f* al carbón **2** DUPLICATE : duplicado *m*, copia *f* exacta
carbon paper *n* : papel *m* carbón
carbuncle [ˈkɑrˌbʌŋkəl] *n* : carbunco *m*
carburetor [ˈkɑrbəˌreɪṭər, -bjə-] *n* : carburador *m*
carcass [ˈkɑrkəs] *n* : cuerpo *m* (de un animal muerto)
carcinogen [kɑrˈsɪnəʤən, ˈkɑrsənəˌʤɛn] *n* : carcinógeno *m*, cancerígeno *m*
carcinogenic [ˌkɑrsənoˈʤɛnɪk] *adj* : carcinogénico
carcinoma [ˌkɑrsəˈnoːmə] *n* : carcinoma *m*

card[1] [ˈkɑrd] *vt* : cardar (fibras)
card[2] *n* **1** : carta *f*, naipe *m* ⟨to play cards : jugar a las cartas⟩ ⟨a deck of cards : una baraja⟩ **2** : tarjeta *f* ⟨birthday card : tarjeta de cumpleaños⟩ ⟨business card : tarjeta (de visita)⟩
cardboard [ˈkɑrdˌbord] *n* : cartón *m*, cartulina *f*
cardiac [ˈkɑrdiˌæk] *adj* : cardíaco, cardiaco
cardigan [ˈkɑrdɪgən] *n* : cárdigan *m*, chaqueta *f* de punto
cardinal[1] [ˈkɑrdənəl] *adj* FUNDAMENTAL : cardinal, fundamental
cardinal[2] *n* : cardenal *m*
cardinal number *n* : número *m* cardinal
cardinal point *n* : punto *m* cardinal
cardiologist [ˌkɑrdiˈɑləʤɪst] *n* : cardiólogo *m*, -ga *f*
cardiology [ˌkɑrdiˈɑləʤi] *n* : cardiología *f*
cardiovascular [ˌkɑrdioˈvæskjələr] *adj* : cardiovascular
care[1] [ˈkær] *v* **cared; caring** *vi* **1** : importarle a uno ⟨they don't care : no les importa⟩ **2** : preocuparse, inquietarse ⟨she cares about the poor : se preocupa por los pobres⟩ **3 to care for** TEND : cuidar (de), atender, encargarse de **4 to care for** CHERISH : querer, sentir cariño por **5 to care for** LIKE : gustarle (algo a uno) ⟨I don't care for your attitude : tu actitud no me agrada⟩ — *vt* WISH : desear, querer ⟨if you care to go : si deseas ir⟩
care[2] *n* **1** ANXIETY : inquietud *f*, preocupación *f* **2** CAREFULNESS : cuidado *m*, atención *f* ⟨handle with care : manejar con cuidado⟩ **3** CHARGE : cargo *m*, cuidado *m* **4 to take care of** : cuidar (de), atender, encargarse de
careen [kəˈri:n] *vi* **1** SWAY : oscilar, balancearse **2** CAREER : ir a toda velocidad
career[1] [kəˈrɪr] *vi* : ir a toda velocidad
career[2] *n* VOCATION : vocación *f*, profesión *f*, carrera *f*
carefree [ˈkærˌfri:, ˌkærˈ-] *adj* : despreocupado
careful [ˈkærfəl] *adj* **1** CAUTIOUS : cuidadoso, cauteloso **2** PAINSTAKING : cuidadoso, esmerado, meticuloso
carefully [ˈkærfəli] *adv* : con cuidado, cuidadosamente
carefulness [ˈkærfəlnəs] *n* **1** CAUTION : cuidado *m*, cautela *f* **2** METICULOUSNESS : esmero *m*, meticulosidad *f*
caregiver [ˈkærˌgɪvər] *n* : persona *f* que cuida a niños o enfermos
careless [ˈkærləs] *adj* : descuidado, negligente — **carelessly** *adv*
carelessness [ˈkærləsnəs] *n* : descuido *m*, negligencia *f*
caress[1] [kəˈrɛs] *vt* : acariciar
caress[2] *n* : caricia *f*
caret [ˈkærət] *n* : signo *m* de intercalación
caretaker [ˈkɛrˌteɪkər] *n* : conserje *mf*; velador *m*, -dora *f*
cargo [ˈkɑrˌgo:] *n, pl* **-goes** *or* **-gos** : cargamento *m*, carga *f*
Caribbean [kærəˈbi:ən, kəˈrɪbiən] *adj* : caribeño ⟨the Caribbean Sea : el mar Caribe⟩
caribou [ˈkærəˌbu:] *n, pl* **-bou** *or* **-bous** : caribú *m*
caricature[1] [ˈkærɪkəˌʧʊr] *vt* **-tured; -turing** : caricaturizar
caricature[2] *n* : caricatura *f*
caricaturist [ˈkærɪkəˌʧʊrɪst] *n* : caricaturista *mf*
caries [ˈkærˌi:z] *ns & pl* : caries *f*
carillon [ˈkærəˌlɑn] *n* : carillón *m*
carmine [ˈkɑrmən, -ˌmaɪn] *n* : carmín *m*
carnage [ˈkɑrnɪʤ] *n* : matanza *f*, carnicería *f*
carnal [ˈkɑrnəl] *adj* : carnal
carnation [kɑrˈneɪʃən] *n* : clavel *m*
carnival [ˈkɑrnəvəl] *n* : carnaval *m*, feria *f*
carnivore [ˈkɑrnəˌvor] *n* : carnívoro *m*
carnivorous [kɑrˈnɪvərəs] *adj* : carnívoro
carol[1] [ˈkærəl] *vi* **-oled** *or* **-olled; -oling** *or* **-olling** : cantar villancicos
carol[2] *n* : villancico *m*
caroler *or* **caroller** [ˈkærələr] *n* : persona *f* que canta villancicos
carom[1] [ˈkærəm] *vi* **1** REBOUND : rebotar ⟨the bullet caromed off the wall : la bala rebotó contra el muro⟩ **2** : hacer carambola (en billar)
carom[2] *n* : carambola *f*
carouse [kəˈraʊz] *vt* **-roused; -rousing** : irse de parranda, irse de juerga
carousel *or* **carrousel** [ˌkærəˈsɛl, ˈkærəˌ-] *n* : carrusel *m*, tiovivo *m*
carouser [kəˈraʊzər] *n* : juerguista *mf*
carp[1] [ˈkɑrp] *vi* **1** COMPLAIN : quejarse **2 to carp at** : criticar
carp[2] *n, pl* **carp** *or* **carps** : carpa *f*
carpel [ˈkɑrpəl] *n* : carpelo *m*
carpenter [ˈkɑrpəntər] *n* : carpintero *m*, -ra *f*
carpentry [ˈkɑrpəntri] *n* : carpintería *f*
carpet[1] [ˈkɑrpət] *vt* : alfombrar
carpet[2] *n* : alfombra *f*
carpeting [ˈkɑrpət̬ɪŋ] *n* : alfombrado *m*
carport [ˈkɑrˌpɔrt] *n* : cochera *f*, garaje *m* abierto
carriage [ˈkærɪʤ] *n* **1** TRANSPORT : transporte *m* **2** POSTURE : porte *m*, postura *f* **3 horse–drawn carriage** : carruaje *m*, coche *m* **4 baby carriage** : cochecito *m*
carrier [ˈkæriər] *n* **1** : transportista *mf*, empresa *f* de transportes **2** : portador *m*, -dora *f* (de una enfermedad) **3 aircraft carrier** : portaaviones *m*
carrier pigeon : paloma *f* mensajera
carrion [ˈkæriən] *n* : carroña *f*
carrot [ˈkærət] *n* : zanahoria *f*
carry [ˈkæri] *v* **-ried; -rying** *vt* **1** TRANSPORT : llevar, cargar, transportar (cargamento), conducir (electricidad), portar (un virus) ⟨to carry a bag : cargar una bolsa⟩ ⟨to carry money : llevar dinero encima, traer dinero consi-

go⟩ **2** BEAR : soportar, aguantar, resistir (peso) **3** STOCK : vender, tener en abasto **4** ENTAIL : llevar, implicar, acarrear **5** WIN : ganar (una elección o competición), aprobar (una moción) **6 to carry oneself** : portarse, comportarse ⟨he carried himself honorably : se comportó dignamente⟩ — *vi* : oírse, proyectarse ⟨her voice carries well : su voz se puede oír desde lejos⟩

carryall [ˈkæriˌɔl] *n* : bolsa *f* de viaje

carry away *vt* **to get carried away** : exaltarse, entusiasmarse

carry on *vt* CONDUCT : realizar, ejercer, mantener ⟨to carry on research : realizar investigaciones⟩ ⟨to carry on a correspondence : mantener una correspondencia⟩ — *vi* **1** : portarse de manera escandalosa o inapropiada ⟨it's embarrassing how he carries on : su manera de comportarse da vergüenza⟩ **2** CONTINUE : seguir, continuar

carry out *vt* **1** PERFORM : llevar a cabo, realizar **2** FULFILL : cumplir

cart[1] [ˈkɑrt] *vt* : acarrear, llevar

cart[2] *n* : carreta *f*, carro *m*

cartel [kɑrˈtɛl] *n* : cártel *m*

cartilage [ˈkɑrṭəlɪʤ] *n* : cartílago *m*

cartilaginous [ˌkɑrṭəlˈæʤənəs] *adj* : cartilaginoso

cartographer [kɑrˈtɑgrəfər] *n* : cartógrafo *m*, -fa *f*

cartography [kɑrˈtɑgrəfi] *n* : cartografía *f*

carton [ˈkɑrtən] *n* : caja *f* de cartón

cartoon [kɑrˈtuːn] *n* **1** : chiste *m* (gráfico), caricatura *f* ⟨a political cartoon : un chiste político⟩ **2** COMIC STRIP : tira *f* cómica, historieta *f* **3** *or* **animated cartoon** : dibujo *m* animado

cartoonist [kɑrˈtuːnɪst] *n* : caricaturista *mf*, dibujante *mf* (de chistes)

cartridge [ˈkɑrtrɪʤ] *n* : cartucho *m*

carve [ˈkɑrv] *vt* **carved; carving 1** : tallar (madera), esculpir (piedra), grabar ⟨he carved his name in the bark : grabó su nombre en la corteza⟩ **2** SLICE : cortar, trinchar (carne)

cascade[1] [kæsˈkeɪd] *vi* **-caded; -cading** : caer en cascada

cascade[2] *n* : cascada *f*, salto *m* de agua

case[1] [ˈkeɪs] *vt* **cased; casing 1** BOX, PACK : embalar, encajonar **2** INSPECT : observar, inspeccionar (antes de cometer un delito)

case[2] *n* **1** : caso *m* ⟨an unusual case : un caso insólito⟩ ⟨ablative case : caso ablativo⟩ ⟨a case of the flu : un caso de gripe⟩ **2** BOX : caja *f* **3** CONTAINER : funda *f*, estuche *m* **4 in any case** : de todos modos, en cualquier caso **5 in case** : como precaución ⟨just in case : por si acaso⟩ **6 in case of** : en caso de

casement [ˈkeɪsmənt] *n* : ventana *f* con bisagras

cash[1] [ˈkæʃ] *vt* : convertir en efectivo, cobrar, cambiar (un cheque)

cash[2] *n* : efectivo *m*, dinero *m* en efectivo

cashew [ˈkæˌʃuː, kəˈʃuː] *n* : anacardo *m*

cashier[1] [kæˈʃɪr] *vt* : destituir, despedir

cashier[2] *n* : cajero *m*, -ra *f*

cashmere [ˈkæʒˌmɪr, ˈkæʃ-] *n* : cachemir *m*

casino [kəˈsiːˌnoː] *n, pl* **-nos** : casino *m*

cask [ˈkæsk] *n* : tonel *m*, barrica *f*, barril *m*

casket [ˈkæskət] *n* COFFIN : ataúd *m*, féretro *m*

cassava [kəˈsɑvə] *n* : mandioca *f*, yuca *f*

casserole [ˈkæsəˌroːl] *n* **1** : cazuela *f* **2** : guiso *m*, guisado *m* ⟨tuna casserole : guiso de atún⟩

cassette [kəˈsɛt, kæ-] *n* : cassette *mf*

cassock [ˈkæsək] *n* : sotana *f*

cast[1] [ˈkæst] *vt* **cast; casting 1** THROW : tirar, echar, arrojar ⟨the die is cast : la suerte está echada⟩ **2** : depositar (un voto) **3** : asignar (papeles en una obra de teatro) **4** MOLD : moldear, fundir, vaciar **5 to cast off** ABANDON : desamparar, abandonar

cast[2] *n* **1** THROW : lance *m*, lanzamiento *m* **2** APPEARANCE : aspecto *m*, forma *f* **3** : elenco *m*, reparto *m* (de una obra de teatro) **4 plaster cast** : molde *m* de yeso, escayola *f*

castanets [ˌkæstəˈnɛts] *npl* : castañuelas *fpl*

castaway[1] [ˈkæstəˌweɪ] *adj* : náufrago

castaway[2] *n* : náufrago *m*, -ga *f*

caste [ˈkæst] *n* : casta *f*

caster [ˈkæstər] *n* : ruedita *f* (de un mueble)

castigate [ˈkæstəˌgeɪt] *vt* **-gated; -gating** : castigar severamente, censurar, reprobar

Castilian [kæˈstɪljən] *n* **1** : castellano *m*, -na *f* **2** : castellano *m* (idioma) — **Castilian** *adj*

cast iron *n* : hierro *m* fundido

castle [ˈkæsəl] *n* **1** : castillo *m* **2** : torre *f* (en ajedrez)

cast–off [ˈkæstˌɔf] *adj* : desechado

castoff [ˈkæstˌɔf] *n* : desecho *m*

castrate [ˈkæsˌtreɪt] *vt* **-trated; -trating** : castrar

castration [kæˈstreɪʃən] *n* : castración *f*

casual [ˈkæʒʊəl] *adj* **1** FORTUITOUS : casual, fortuito **2** INDIFFERENT : indiferente, despreocupado **3** INFORMAL : informal — **casually** [ˈkæʒʊəli, ˈkæʒəli] *adv*

casualness [ˈkæʒʊəlnəs] *n* **1** FORTUITOUSNESS : casualidad *f* **2** INDIFFERENCE : indiferencia *f*, despreocupación *f* **3** INFORMALITY : informalidad *f*

casualty [ˈkæʒʊəlti, ˈkæʒəl-] *n, pl* **-ties 1** ACCIDENT : accidente *m* serio, desastre *m* **2** VICTIM : víctima *f*; baja *f*; herido *m*, -da *f*

cat [ˈkæt] *n* : gato *m*, -ta *f*

cataclysm [ˈkæṭəˌklɪzəm] *n* : cataclismo *m*

cataclysmal [ˌkæt̬əˈklɪzməl] *or* **cataclysmic** [ˌkæt̬əˈklɪzmɪk] *adj* : catastrófico
catacombs [ˈkæt̬əˌkoːmz] *npl* : catacumbas *fpl*
Catalan [ˈkæt̬ələn, -ˌlæn] *n* **1** : catalán *m*, catalana *f* **2** : catalán *m* (idioma) — **Catalan** *adj*
catalog[1] *or* **catalogue** [ˈkæt̬əˌlɔg] *vt* **-loged** *or* **-logued; -loging** *or* **-loguing** : catalogar
catalog[2] *n* : catálogo *m*
catalyst [ˈkæt̬ələst] *n* : catalizador *m*
catalytic [ˌkæt̬əlˈɪtɪk] *adj* : catalítico
catamaran [ˌkæt̬əməˈræn, ˈkæt̬əməˌræn] *n* : catamarán *m*
catapult[1] [ˈkæt̬əˌpʌlt, -ˌpʊlt] *vt* : catapultar
catapult[2] *n* : catapulta *f*
cataract [ˈkæt̬əˌrækt] *n* : catarata *f*
catarrh [kəˈtɑr] *n* : catarro *m*
catastrophe [kəˈtæstrəˌfiː] *n* : catástrofe *f*
catastrophic [ˌkæt̬əˈstrɑfɪk] *adj* : catastrófico — **catastrophically** [-fɪkli] *adv*
catcall [ˈkætˌkɔl] *n* : rechifla *f*, abucheo *m*
catch[1] [ˈkætʃ, ˈkɛtʃ] *v* **caught** [ˈkɔt]; **catching** *vt* **1** CAPTURE, TRAP : capturar, agarrar, atrapar, coger **2** : agarrar, pillar *fam*, tomar de sorpresa ⟨they caught him red-handed : lo pillaron con las manos en la masa⟩ **3** GRASP : agarrar, captar **4** ENTANGLE : enganchar, enredar **5** : tomar (un tren, etc.) **6** : contagiarse de ⟨to catch a cold : contagiarse de un resfriado, resfriarse⟩ — *vi* **1** GRASP : agarrar **2** HOOK : engancharse **3** IGNITE : prender, agarrar
catch[2] *n* **1** CATCHING : captura *f*, atrapada *f*, parada *f* (de una pelota) **2** : redada *f* (de pescado), presa *f* (de caza) ⟨he's a good catch : es un buen partido⟩ **3** LATCH : pestillo *m*, pasador *m* **4** DIFFICULTY, TRICK : problema *m*, trampa *f*, truco *m*
catcher [ˈkætʃər, ˈkɛ-] *n* : catcher *mf*; receptor *m*, -tora *f* (en béisbol)
catching [ˈkætʃɪŋ, ˈkɛ-] *adj* : contagioso
catchup [ˈkætʃəp, ˈkɛ-] → **ketchup**
catchword [ˈkætʃˌwərd, ˈkɛtʃ-] *n* : eslogan *m*, lema *m*
catchy [ˈkætʃi, ˈkɛ-] *adj* **catchier; -est** : pegajoso ⟨a catchy song : una canción pegajosa⟩
catechism [ˈkæt̬əˌkɪzəm] *n* : catecismo *m*
categorical [ˌkæt̬əˈgɔrɪkəl] *adj* : categórico, absoluto, rotundo — **categorically** [-kli] *adv*
categorize [ˈkæt̬ɪgəˌraɪz] *vt* **-rized; -rizing** : clasificar, catalogar
category [ˈkæt̬əˌgori] *n, pl* **-ries** : categoría *f*, género *m*, clase *f*
cater [ˈkeɪt̬ər] *vi* **1** : proveer alimentos (para fiestas, bodas, etc.) **2 to cater to** : atender a ⟨to cater to all tastes : atender a todos los gustos⟩
catercorner[1] [ˈkæt̬iˌkɔrnər, ˈkæt̬ə-, ˈkɪt̬i-] *or* **cater–cornered** [-ˌkɔrnərd] *adv* : diagonalmente, en diagonal
catercorner[2] *or* **cater–cornered** *adj* : diagonal
caterer [ˈkeɪt̬ərər] *n* : proveedor *m*, -dora *f* de comida
caterpillar [ˈkæt̬ərˌpɪlər] *n* : oruga *f*
catfish [ˈkætˌfɪʃ] *n* : bagre *m*
catgut [ˈkætˌgʌt] *n* : cuerda *f* de tripa
catharsis [kəˈθɑrsɪs] *n, pl* **catharses** [-ˌsiːz] : catarsis *f*
cathartic[1] [kəˈθɑrt̬ɪk] *adj* : catártico
cathartic[2] *n* : purgante *m*
cathedral [kəˈθiːdrəl] *n* : catedral *f*
catheter [ˈkæθət̬ər] *n* : catéter *m*, sonda *f*
cathode [ˈkæˌθoːd] *n* : cátodo *m*
catholic [ˈkæθəlɪk] *adj* **1** BROAD, UNIVERSAL : liberal, universal **2 Catholic** : católico
Catholic *n* : católico *m*, -ca *f*
Catholicism [kəˈθɑləˌsɪzəm] *n* : catolicismo *m*
catlike [ˈkætˌlaɪk] *adj* : gatuno, felino
catnap[1] [ˈkætˌnæp] *vi* **-napped; -napping** : tomarse una siestecita
catnap[2] *n* : siesta *f* breve, siestecita *f*
catnip [ˈkætˌnɪp] *n* : nébeda *f*
catsup [ˈkɛtʃəp, ˈkætsəp] → **ketchup**
cattail [ˈkætˌteɪl] *n* : espadaña *f*, anea *f*
cattiness [ˈkæt̬inəs] *n* : malicia *f*
cattle [ˈkæt̬əl] *npl* : ganado *m*, reses *fpl*
cattleman [ˈkæt̬əlmən, -ˌmæn] *n, pl* **-men** [-mən, -ˌmɛn] : ganadero *m*
catty [ˈkæt̬i] *adj* **-tier; -est** : malicioso, malintencionado
catwalk [ˈkætˌwɔk] *n* : pasarela *f*
Caucasian[1] [kɔˈkeɪʒən] *adj* : caucásico
Caucasian[2] *n* : caucásico *m*, -ca *f*
caucus [ˈkɔkəs] *n* : junta *f* de políticos
caught → **catch**
cauldron [ˈkɔldrən] *n* : caldera *f*
cauliflower [ˈkɑlɪˌflaʊər, ˈkɔ-] *n* : coliflor *f*
caulk[1] [ˈkɔk] *vt* : calafatear (un barco), enmasillar (una grieta)
caulk[2] *n* : masilla *f*
causal [ˈkɔzəl] *adj* : causal
causality [kɔˈzæləţi] *n* : causalidad *f*
cause[1] [ˈkɔz] *vt* **caused; causing** : causar, provocar, ocasionar
cause[2] *n* **1** ORIGIN : causa *f*, origen *m* **2** REASON : causa *f*, razón *f*, motivo *m* **3** LAWSUIT : litigio *m*, pleito *m* **4** MOVEMENT : causa *f*, movimiento *m*
causeless [ˈkɔzləs] *adj* : sin causa
causeway [ˈkɔzˌweɪ] *n* : camino *m* elevado
caustic [ˈkɔstɪk] *adj* **1** CORROSIVE : cáustico, corrosivo **2** BITING : mordaz, sarcástico
cauterize [ˈkɔt̬əˌraɪz] *vt* **-ized; -izing** : cauterizar
caution[1] [ˈkɔʃən] *vt* : advertir
caution[2] *n* **1** WARNING : advertencia *f*, aviso *m* **2** CARE, PRUDENCE : precaución *f*, cuidado *m*, cautela *f*

cautionary [ˈkɔʃəˌnɛri] *adv* : admonitorio ⟨cautionary tale : cuento moral⟩
cautious [ˈkɔʃəs] *adj* : cauteloso, cuidadoso, precavido
cautiously [ˈkɔʃəsli] *adv* : cautelosamente, con precaución
cautiousness [ˈkɔʃəsnəs] *n* : cautela *f*, precaución *f*
cavalcade [ˌkævəlˈkeɪd, ˈkævəlˌ-] *n* **1** : cabalgata *f* **2** SERIES : serie *f*
cavalier[1] [ˌkævəˈlɪr] *adj* : altivo, desdeñoso — **cavalierly** *adv*
cavalier[2] *n* : caballero *m*
cavalry [ˈkævəlri] *n, pl* **-ries** : caballería *f*
cave[1] [ˈkeɪv] *vi* **caved; caving** *or* **to cave in** : derrumbarse
cave[2] *n* : cueva *f*
cavern [ˈkævərn] *n* : caverna *f*
cavernous [ˈkævərnəs] *adj* : cavernoso — **cavernously** *adv*
caviar *or* **caviare** [ˈkæviˌɑr, ˈkɑ-] *n* : caviar *m*
cavity [ˈkævət̬i] *n, pl* **-ties 1** HOLE : cavidad *f*, hueco *m* **2** CARIES : caries *f*
cavort [kəˈvɔrt] *vi* : brincar, hacer cabriolas
caw[1] [ˈkɔ] *vi* : graznar
caw[2] *n* : graznido *m*
cayenne pepper [ˌkaɪˈɛn, ˌkeɪ-] *n* : pimienta *f* cayena, pimentón *m*
CD [ˌsiːˈdiː] *n* : CD *m*, disco *m* compacto
CD–ROM [ˌsiːˌdiːˈram] *n* : CD-ROM *m*
cease [ˈsiːs] *v* **ceased; ceasing** *vt* : dejar de ⟨they ceased bickering : dejaron de discutir⟩ — *vi* : cesar, pasarse
ceaseless [ˈsiːsləs] *adj* : incesante, continuo
cedar [ˈsiːdər] *n* : cedro *m*
cede [ˈsiːd] *vt* **ceded; ceding** : ceder, conceder
ceiling [ˈsiːlɪŋ] *n* **1** : techo *m*, cielo *m* raso **2** LIMIT : límite *m*, tope *m*
celebrant [ˈsɛləbrənt] *n* : celebrante *mf*, oficiante *mf*
celebrate [ˈsɛləˌbreɪt] *v* **-brated; -brating** *vt* **1** : celebrar, oficiar ⟨to celebrate Mass : celebrar la misa⟩ **2** : celebrar, festejar ⟨we're celebrating our anniversary : estamos celebrando nuestro aniversario⟩ **3** EXTOL : alabar, ensalzar, exaltar — *vi* : estar de fiesta, divertirse
celebrated [ˈsɛləˌbreɪt̬əd] *adj* : célebre, famoso, renombrado
celebration [ˌsɛləˈbreɪʃən] *n* : celebración *f*, festejos *mpl*
celebrity [səˈlɛbrət̬i] *n, pl* **-ties 1** RENOWN : fama *f*, renombre *m*, celebridad *f* **2** PERSONALITY : celebridad *f*, personaje *m*
celery [ˈsɛləri] *n, pl* **-eries** : apio *m*
celestial [səˈlɛstʃəl, -ˈlstiəl] *adj* **1** : celeste **2** HEAVENLY : celestial, paradisiaco
celibacy [ˈsɛləbəsi] *n* : celibato *m*
celibate[1] [ˈsɛləbət] *adj* : célibe
celibate[2] *n* : célibe *mf*
cell [ˈsɛl] *n* **1** : célula *f* (de un organismo) **2** : celda *f* (en una cárcel, etc.) **3** : elemento *m* (de una pila)
cellar [ˈsɛlər] *n* **1** BASEMENT : sótano *m* **2** : bodega *f* (de vinos)
cellist [ˈtʃɛlɪst] *n* : violonchelista *mf*
cello [ˈtʃɛˌloː] *n, pl* **-los** : violonchelo *m*
cellophane [ˈsɛləˌfeɪn] *n* : celofán *m*
cell phone *n* : teléfono *m* celular
cellular [ˈsɛljələr] *adj* : celular
celluloid [ˈsɛljəˌlɔɪd] *n* : celuloide
cellulose [ˈsɛljəˌloːs] *n* : celulosa *f*
Celsius [ˈsɛlsiəs] *adj* : centígrado ⟨100 degrees Celsius : 100 grados centígrados⟩
Celt [ˈkɛlt, ˈsɛlt] *n* : celta *mf*
Celtic[1] [ˈkɛltɪk, ˈsɛl-] *adj* : celta
Celtic[2] *n* : celta *m*
cement[1] [sɪˈmɛnt] *vi* : unir o cubrir algo con cemento, cementar
cement[2] *n* **1** : cemento *m* **2** GLUE : pegamento *m*
cemetery [ˈsɛməˌtɛri] *n, pl* **-teries** : cementerio *m*, panteón *m*
censer [ˈsɛntsər] *n* : incensario *m*
censor[1] [ˈsɛntsər] *vt* : censurar
censor[2] *n* : censor *m*, -sora *f*
censorious [sɛnˈsoriəs] *adj* : de censura, crítico
censorship [ˈsɛntsərˌʃɪp] *n* : censura *f*
censure[1] [ˈsɛntʃər] *vt* **-sured; -suring** : censurar, criticar, reprobar — **censurable** [-tʃərəbəl] *adj*
censure[2] *n* : censura *f*, reproche *m* oficial
census [ˈsɛntsəs] *n* : censo *m*
cent [ˈsɛnt] *n* : centavo *m*
centaur [ˈsɛnˌtɔr] *n* : centauro *m*
centennial[1] [sɛnˈtɛniəl] *adj* : del centenario
centennial[2] *n* : centenario *m*
center[1] [ˈsɛntər] *vt* **1** : centrar **2** CONCENTRATE : concentrar, fijar, enfocar — *vi* : centrarse, enfocarse
center[2] *n* **1** : centro *m* ⟨center of gravity : centro de gravedad⟩ **2** : centro *mf* (en futbol americano), pívot *mf* (en basquetbol)
centerpiece [ˈsɛntərˌpiːs] *n* : centro *m* de mesa
centigrade [ˈsɛntəˌgreɪd, ˈsɑn-] *adj* : centígrado
centigram [ˈsɛntəˌgræm, ˈsɑn-] *n* : centigramo *m*
centimeter [ˈsɛntəˌmiːt̬ər, ˈsɑn-] *n* : centímetro *m*
centipede [ˈsɛntəˌpiːd] *n* : ciempiés *m*
central [ˈsɛntrəl] *adj* **1** : céntrico, central ⟨in a central location : en un lugar céntrico⟩ **2** MAIN, PRINCIPAL : central, fundamental, principal
Central American[1] *adj* : centroamericano
Central American[2] *n* : centroamericano *m*, -na *f*
centralization [ˌsɛntrələˈzeɪʃən] *n* : centralización *f*
centralize [ˈsɛntrəˌlaɪz] *vt* **-ized; -izing** : centralizar

centrally [ˈsɛntrəli] *adv* **1 centrally heated** : con calefacción central **2 centrally located** : céntrico, en un lugar céntrico
centre [ˈsɛntər] → **center**
centrifugal [sɛnˈtrɪfjəgəl, -ˈtrɪfɪ-] *adj* : centrífugo
centrifugal force *n* : fuerza *f* centrífuga
century [ˈsɛntʃəri] *n, pl* **-ries** : siglo *m*
ceramic[1] [səˈræmɪk] *adj* : de cerámica
ceramic[2] *n* **1** : objeto *m* de cerámica, cerámica *f* **2 ceramics** *npl* : cerámica *f*
cereal[1] [ˈsɪriəl] *adj* : cereal
cereal[2] *n* : cereal *m*
cerebellum [ˌsɛrəˈbɛləm] *n, pl* **-bellums** *or* **-bella** [-ˈbɛlə] : cerebelo *m*
cerebral [səˈriːbrəl, ˈsɛrə-] *adj* : cerebral
cerebral palsy *n* : parálisis *f* cerebral
cerebrum [səˈriːbrəm, ˈsɛrə-] *n, pl* **-brums** *or* **-bra** [-brə] : cerebro *m*
ceremonial[1] [ˌsɛrəˈmoːniəl] *adj* : ceremonial
ceremonial[2] *n* : ceremonial *m*
ceremonious [ˌsɛrəˈmoːniəs] *adj* **1** FORMAL : ceremonioso, formal **2** CEREMONIAL : ceremonial
ceremony [ˈsɛrəˌmoːni] *n, pl* **-nies** : ceremonia *f*
cerise [səˈriːs] *n* : rojo *m* cereza
certain[1] [ˈsərtən] *adj* **1** DEFINITE : cierto, determinado ⟨a certain percentage : un porcentaje determinado⟩ **2** TRUE : cierto, con certeza ⟨I don't know for certain : no sé exactamente⟩ **3** : cierto, alguno ⟨it has a certain charm : tiene cierta gracia⟩ **4** INEVITABLE : seguro, inevitable **5** ASSURED : seguro, asegurado ⟨she's certain to do well : seguro que le irá bien⟩
certain[2] *pron* : ciertos *pl*, algunos *pl* ⟨certain of my friends : algunos de mis amigos⟩
certainly [ˈsərtənli] *adv* **1** DEFINITELY : ciertamente, seguramente **2** OF COURSE : por supuesto
certainty [ˈsərtənti] *n, pl* **-ties** : certeza *f*, certidumbre *f*, seguridad *f*
certifiable [ˌsərt̬əˈfaɪəbəl] *adj* : certificable
certificate [sərˈtɪfɪkət] *n* : certificado *m*, acta *f* ⟨birth certificate : acta de nacimiento⟩
certification [ˌsərt̬əfəˈkeɪʃən] *n* : certificación *f*
certify [ˈsərt̬əˌfaɪ] *vt* **-fied; -fying 1** VERIFY : certificar, verificar, confirmar **2** ENDORSE : endosar, aprobar oficialmente
certitude [ˈsərt̬əˌtuːd, -ˌtjuːd] *n* : certeza *f*, certidumbre *f*
cervical [ˈsərvɪkəl] *adj* **1** : cervical (dícese del cuello) **2** : del cuello del útero
cervix [ˈsərvɪks] *n, pl* **-vices** [-vəˌsiːz] *or* **-vixes 1** NECK : cerviz *f* **2** *or* **uterine cervix** : cuello *m* del útero
cesarean[1] [sɪˈzæriən] *adj* : cesáreo
cesarean[2] *n* : cesárea *f*
cesium [ˈsiːziəm] *n* : cesio *m*
cessation [sˈseɪʃən] *n* : cesación *f*, cese *m*
cesspool [ˈsɛsˌpuːl] *n* : pozo *m* séptico
Chadian [ˈtʃædiən] *n* : chadiano *m*, -na *f* — **Chadian** *adj*
chafe [ˈtʃeɪf] *v* **chafed; chafing** *vi* : enojarse, irritarse — *vt* : rozar
chaff [ˈtʃæf] *n* **1** : barcia *f*, granzas *fpl* **2 to separate the wheat from the chaff** : separar el grano de la paja
chafing dish [ˈtʃeɪfɪŋˌdɪʃ] *n* : escalfador *m*
chagrin[1] [ʃəˈgrɪn] *vt* : desilusionar, avergonzar
chagrin[2] *n* : desilusión *f*, disgusto *m*
chain[1] [ˈtʃeɪn] *vt* : encadenar
chain[2] *n* **1** : cadena *f* ⟨steel chain : cadena de acero⟩ ⟨restaurant chain : cadena de restaurantes⟩ **2** SERIES : serie *f* ⟨chain of events : serie de eventos⟩ **3 chains** *npl* FETTERS : grillos *mpl*
chair[1] [ˈtʃɛr] *vt* : presidir, moderar
chair[2] *n* **1** : silla *f* **2** CHAIRMANSHIP : presidencia *f* **3** → **chairman, chairwoman**
chairman [ˈtʃɛrmən] *n, pl* **-men** [-mən, -ˌmɛn] : presidente *m*
chairmanship [ˈtʃɛrmənˌʃɪp] *n* : presidencia *f*
chairwoman [ˈtʃɛrˌwʊmən] *n, pl* **-women** [-ˌwɪmən] : presidenta *f*
chaise longue [ˈʃeɪzˈlɔŋ] *n, pl* **chaise longues** [-lɔŋ, -ˈlɔŋz] : chaise longue *f*
chalet [ʃæˈleɪ] *n* : chalet *m*, chalé *m*
chalice [ˈtʃælɪs] *n* : cáliz *m*
chalk[1] [ˈtʃɔk] *vt* : escribir con tiza
chalk[2] *n* **1** LIMESTONE : creta *f*, caliza *f* **2** : tiza *f*, gis *m Mex* (para escribir)
chalkboard [ˈtʃɔkˌbord] → **blackboard**
chalk up *vt* **1** ASCRIBE : atribuir, adscribir **2** SCORE : apuntarse, anotarse (una victoria, etc.)
chalky [ˈtʃɔki] *adj* **chalkier; -est 1** : calcáreo **2** PALE : pálido **3** POWDERY : polvoriento
challenge[1] [ˈtʃælɪndʒ] *vt* **-lenged; -lenging 1** DISPUTE : disputar, cuestionar, poner en duda **2** DARE : desafiar, retar **3** STIMULATE : estimular, incentivar
challenge[2] *n* : reto *m*, desafío *m*
challenger [ˈtʃælɪndʒər] *n* : retador *m*, -dora *f*; contendiente *mf*
chamber [ˈtʃeɪmbər] *n* **1** ROOM : cámara *f*, sala *f* ⟨the senate chamber : la cámara del senado⟩ **2** : recámara *f* (de un arma de fuego), cámara *f* (de combustión) **3** : cámara *f* ⟨chamber of commerce : cámara de comercio⟩ **4 chambers** *npl or* **judge's chambers** : despacho *m* del juez
chambermaid [ˈtʃeɪmbərˌmeɪd] *n* : camarera *f*
chamber music *n* : música *f* de cámara
chameleon [kəˈmiːljən, -liən] *n* : camaleón *m*

chamois [ˈʃæmi] *n, pl* **chamois** [-mi, -miz] : gamuza *f*
champ¹ [ˈʧæmp, ˈʧɑmp] *vi* **1** : masticar ruidosamente **2 to champ at the bit** : impacientarse, comerle a uno la impaciencia
champ² [ˈʧæmp] *n* : campeón *m*, -peona *f*
champagne [ʃæmˈpeɪn] *n* : champaña *m*, champán *m*
champion¹ [ˈʧæmpiən] *vt* : defender, luchar por (una causa)
champion² *n* **1** ADVOCATE, DEFENDER : paladín *m*; campeón *m*, -peona *f*; defensor *m*, -sora *f* **2** WINNER : campeón *m*, -peona *f* ⟨world champion : campeón mundial⟩
championship [ˈʧæmpiən,ʃɪp] *n* : campeonato *m*
chance¹ [ˈʧænts] *v* **chanced; chancing** *vi* **1** HAPPEN : ocurrir por casualidad **2 to chance upon** : encontrar por casualidad — *vt* RISK : arriesgar
chance² *adj* : fortuito, casual ⟨a chance encounter : un encuentro casual⟩
chance³ *n* **1** FATE, LUCK : azar *m*, suerte *f*, fortuna *f* **2** OPPORTUNITY : oportunidad *f*, ocasión *f* **3** PROBABILITY : probabilidad *f*, posibilidad *f* **4** RISK : riesgo *m* **5** : boleto *m* (de una rifa o lotería) **6 by chance** : por casualidad
chancellor [ˈʧæntsələr] *n* **1** : canciller *m* **2** : rector *m*, -tora *f* (de una universidad)
chancre [ˈʃæŋkər] *n* : chancro *m*
chancy [ˈʧæntsi] *adj* **chancier; -est** : riesgoso, arriesgado
chandelier [,ʃændəˈlɪr] *n* : araña *f* de luces
change¹ [ˈʧeɪnʤ] *v* **changed; changing** *vt* **1** ALTER : cambiar, alterar, modificar **2** EXCHANGE : cambiar de, intercambiar ⟨to change places : cambiar de sitio⟩ — *vi* **1** VARY : cambiar, variar, transformarse ⟨you haven't changed : no has cambiado⟩ **2** *or* **to change clothes** : cambiarse (de ropa)
change² *n* **1** ALTERATION : cambio *m* **2** : cambio *m*, vuelto *m* ⟨two dollars change : dos dólares de vuelto⟩ **3** COINS : cambio *m*, monedas *fpl*
changeable [ˈʧeɪnʤəbəl] *adj* : cambiante, variable
changeless [ˈʧeɪnʤləs] *adj* : invariable, constante
changer [ˈʧeɪnʤər] *n* **1** : cambiador *m* ⟨record changer : cambiador de discos⟩ **2** *or* **money changer** : cambista *mf* (de dinero)
channel¹ [ˈʧænəl] *vt* **-neled** *or* **-nelled; -neling** *or* **-nelling** : encauzar, canalizar
channel² *n* **1** RIVERBED : cauce *m* **2** STRAIT : canal *m*, estrecho *m* ⟨English Channel : Canal de la Mancha⟩ **3** COURSE, MEANS : vía *f*, conducto *m* ⟨the usual channels : las vías normales⟩ **4** : canal *m* (de televisión)
chant¹ [ˈʧænt] *v* : salmodiar, cantar
chant² *n* **1** : salmodia *f* **2 Gregorian chant** : canto *m* gregoriano
Chanukah [ˈxɑnəkə, ˈhɑ-] → **Hanukkah**
chaos [ˈkeɪ,ɑs] *n* : caos *m*
chaotic [keɪˈɑt̬ɪk] *adj* : caótico — **chaotically** [-t̬ɪkli] *adv*
chap¹ [ˈʧæp] *vi* **chapped; chapping** : partirse, agrietarse
chap² *n* FELLOW : tipo *m*, hombre *m*
chapel [ˈʧæpəl] *n* : capilla *f*
chaperon¹ *or* **chaperone** [ˈʃæpə,ro:n] *vt* **-oned; -oning** : ir de chaperón, acompañar
chaperon² *or* **chaperone** *n* : chaperón *m*, -rona *f*; acompañante *mf*
chaplain [ˈʧæplɪn] *n* : capellán *m*
chapter [ˈʧæptər] *n* **1** : capítulo *m* (de un libro) **2** BRANCH : sección *f*, división *f* (de una organización)
char [ˈʧɑr] *vt* **charred; charring 1** BURN : carbonizar **2** SCORCH : chamuscar
character [ˈkærɪktər] *n* **1** LETTER, SYMBOL : carácter *m* ⟨Chinese characters : caracteres chinos⟩ **2** DISPOSITION : carácter *m*, personalidad *f* ⟨of good character : de buena reputación⟩ **3** : tipo *m*, personaje *m* peculiar ⟨he's quite a character! : ¡él es algo serio!⟩ **4** : personaje *m* (ficticio)
characteristic¹ [,kærɪktəˈrɪstɪk] *adj* : característico, típico — **characteristically** [-tɪkli] *adv*
characteristic² *n* : característica *f*
characterization [,kærɪktərəˈzeɪʃən] *n* : caracterización *f*
characterize [ˈkærɪktə,raɪz] *vt* **-ized; -izing** : caracterizar
charades [ʃəˈreɪdz] *ns & pl* : charada *f*
charcoal [ˈʧɑr,ko:l] *n* : carbón *m*
chard [ˈʧɑrd] → **Swiss chard**
charge¹ [ˈʧɑrʤ] *v* **charged; charging** *vt* **1** : cargar ⟨to charge the batteries : cargar las pilas⟩ **2** ENTRUST : encomendar, encargar **3** COMMAND : ordenar, mandar **4** ACCUSE : acusar ⟨charged with robbery : acusado de robo⟩ **5** : cargar a una cuenta, comprar a crédito — *vi* **1** : cargar (contra el enemigo) ⟨charge! : ¡a la carga!⟩ **2** : cobrar ⟨they charge too much : cobran demasiado⟩
charge² *n* **1** : carga *f* (eléctrica) **2** BURDEN : carga *f*, peso *m* **3** RESPONSIBILITY : cargo *m*, responsabilidad *f* ⟨to take charge of : hacerse cargo de⟩ **4** ACCUSATION : cargo *m*, acusación *f* **5** COST : costo *m*, cargo *m*, precio *m* **6** ATTACK : carga *f*, ataque *m*
charge card → **credit card**
chargeable [ˈʧɑrʤəbəl] *adj* **1** : acusable, perseguible (dícese de un delito) **2 ~ to** : a cargo de (una cuenta)
charger [ˈʧɑrʤər] *n* : corcel *m*, caballo *m* (de guerra)
chariot [ˈʧæriət] *n* : carro *m* (de guerra)
charisma [kəˈrɪzmə] *n* : carisma *m*
charismatic [,kærəzˈmætɪk] *adj* : carismático

charitable [ˈʧærəṯəbəl] *adj* **1** GENEROUS : caritativo ⟨a charitable organization : una organización benéfica⟩ **2** KIND, UNDERSTANDING : generoso, benévolo, comprensivo — **charitably** [-bli] *adv*

charitableness [ˈʧærəṯəbəlnəs] *n* : caridad *f*

charity [ˈʧærəṯi] *n, pl* **-ties 1** GENEROSITY : caridad *f* **2** ALMS : caridad *f*, limosna *f* **3** : organización *f* benéfica, obra *f* de beneficencia

charlatan [ˈʃɑrlətən] *n* : charlatán *m*, -tana *f*; farsante *mf*

charley horse [ˈʧɑrliˌhɔrs] *n* : calambre *m*

charm[1] [ˈʧɑrm] *vt* : encantar, cautivar, fascinar

charm[2] *n* **1** AMULET : amuleto *m*, talismán *m* **2** ATTRACTION : encanto *m*, atractivo *m* ⟨it has a certain charm : tiene cierto atractivo⟩ **3** : dije *m*, colgante *m* ⟨charm bracelet : pulsera de dijes⟩

charmer [ˈʧɑrmər] *n* : persona *f* encantadora

charming [ˈʧɑrmɪŋ] *adj* : encantador, fascinante

chart[1] [ˈʧɑrt] *vt* **1** : trazar un mapa de, hacer un gráfico de **2** PLAN : trazar, planear ⟨to chart a course : trazar un derrotero⟩

chart[2] *n* **1** MAP : carta *f*, mapa *m* **2** DIAGRAM : gráfico *m*, cuadro *m*, tabla *f*

charter[1] [ˈʧɑrṯər] *vt* **1** : establecer los estatutos de (una organización) **2** RENT : alquilar, fletar

charter[2] *n* **1** STATUTES : estatutos *mpl* **2** CONSTITUTION : carta *f*, constitución *f*

chartreuse [ʃɑrˈtruːz, -ˈtruːs] *n* : color *m* verde-amarillo intenso

chary [ˈʧæri] *adj* **charier; -est 1** WARY : cauteloso, precavido **2** SPARING : parco

chase[1] [ˈʧeɪs] *vt* **chased; chasing 1** PURSUE : perseguir, ir a la caza de **2** DRIVE : ahuyentar, echar ⟨he chased the dog from the garden : ahuyentó al perro del jardín⟩ **3** : grabar (metales)

chase[2] *n* **1** PURSUIT : persecución *f*, caza *f* **2 the chase** HUNTING : caza *f*

chaser [ˈʧeɪsər] *n* **1** PURSUER : perseguidor *m*, -dora *f* **2** : bebida *f* que se toma después de un trago de licor

chasm [ˈkæzəm] *n* : abismo *m*, sima *f*

chassis [ˈʧæsi, ˈʃæsi] *n, pl* **chassis** [-siz] : chasis *m*, armazón *m*

chaste [ˈʧeɪst] *adj* **chaster; -est 1** : casto **2** MODEST : modesto, puro **3** AUSTERE : austero, sobrio

chastely [ˈʧeɪstli] *adv* : castamente

chasten [ˈʧeɪsən] *vt* : castigar, sancionar

chasteness [ˈʧeɪstnəs] *n* **1** MODESTY : modestia *f*, castidad *f* **2** AUSTERITY : sobriedad *f*, austeridad *f*

chastise [ˈʧæsˌtaɪz, ʧæsˈ-] *vt* **-tised; -tising 1** REPRIMAND : reprender, corregir, reprobar **2** PUNISH : castigar

chastisement [ˈʧæsˌtaɪzmənt, ʧæsˈtaɪz-, ˈʧæstəz-] *n* : castigo *m*, corrección *f*

chastity [ˈʧæstəṯi] *n* : castidad *f*, decencia *f*, modestia *f*

chat[1] [ˈʧæt] *vi* **chatted; chatting** : charlar, platicar

chat[2] *n* : charla *f*, plática *f*

château [ʃæˈtoː] *n, pl* **-teaus** [-ˈtoːz] *or* **-teaux** [-ˈtoː, -ˈtoːz] : mansión *f* campestre

chattel [ˈʧæṯəl] *n* : bienes *fpl* muebles, enseres *mpl*

chatter[1] [ˈʧæṯər] *vi* **1** : castañetear (dícese de los dientes) **2** GAB : parlotear *fam*, cotorrear *fam*

chatter[2] *n* **1** CHATTERING : castañeteo *m* (de dientes) **2** GABBING : parloteo *m fam*, cotorreo *m fam*, cháchara *f fam*

chatterbox [ˈʧæṯərˌbɑks] *n* : parlanchín *m*, -china *f*; charlatán *m*, -tana *f*; hablador *m*, -dora *f*

chatty [ˈʧæṯi] *adj* **chattier; chattiest 1** TALKATIVE : parlanchín, charlatán **2** CONVERSATIONAL : familiar, conversador ⟨a chatty letter : una carta llena de noticias⟩

chauffeur[1] [ˈʃoːfər, ʃoˈfər] *vi* : trabajar de chofer privado — *vt* : hacer de chofer para

chauffeur[2] *n* : chofer *m* privado

chauvinism [ˈʃoːvəˌnɪzəm] *n* : chauvinismo *m*, patriotería *f*

chauvinist [ˈʃoːvənɪst] *n* : chauvinista *mf*; patriotero *m*, -ra *f*

chauvinistic [ˌʃoːvəˈnɪstɪk] *adj* : chauvinista, patriotero

cheap[1] [ˈʧiːp] *adv* : barato ⟨to sell cheap : vender barato⟩

cheap[2] *adj* **1** INEXPENSIVE : barato, económico **2** SHODDY : barato, mal hecho **3** STINGY : tacaño, agarrado *fam*, codo *Mex*

cheapen [ˈʧiːpən] *vt* : degradar, rebajar

cheaply [ˈʧiːpli] *adv* : barato, a precio bajo

cheapness [ˈʧiːpnəs] *n* **1** : baratura *f*, precio *m* bajo **2** STINGINESS : tacañería *f*

cheapskate [ˈʧiːpˌskeɪt] *n* : tacaño *m*, -ña *f*; codo *m*, -da *f Mex*

cheat[1] [ˈʧiːt] *vt* : defraudar, estafar, engañar — *vi* : hacer trampa

cheat[2] *n* **1** CHEATING : engaño *m*, fraude *m*, trampa *f* **2** → **cheater**

cheater [ˈʧiːṯər] *n* : estafador *m*, -dora *f*; tramposo *m*, -sa *f*

check[1] [ˈʧɛk] *vt* **1** HALT : frenar, parar, detener **2** RESTRAIN : refrenar, contener, reprimir **3** VERIFY : verificar, comprobar **4** INSPECT : revisar, chequear, inspeccionar **5** MARK : marcar, señalar **6** : chequear, facturar (maletas, equipaje) **7** CHECKER : marcar con cuadros **8 to check in** : registrarse en un hotel **9 to check out** : irse de un hotel

check[2] *n* **1** HALT : detención *f* súbita, parada *f* **2** RESTRAINT : control *m*, freno *m* **3** INSPECTION : inspección *f*, verificación *f*, chequeo *m* **4** : cheque *m* ⟨to pay by check : pagar con cheque⟩ **5** VOUCHER : resguardo *m*, comprobante *m* **6** BILL : cuenta *f* (en un restaurante) **7** SQUARE : cuadro *m* **8** MARK : marca *f* **9** : jaque *m* (en ajedrez)

checkbook [ˈʧɛkˌbʊk] *n* : chequera *f*

checker[1] [ˈʧɛkər] *vt* : marcar con cuadros

checker[2] *n* **1** : pieza *f* (en el juego de damas) **2** : verificador *m*, -dora *f* **3** CASHIER : cajero *m*, -ra *f*

checkerboard [ˈʧɛkərˌbord] *n* : tablero *m* de damas

checkers [ˈʧɛkərz] *n* : damas *fpl*

checkmate[1] [ˈʧɛkˌmeɪt] *vt* **-mated; -mating** **1** : dar jaque mate a (en ajedrez) **2** THWART : frustrar, arruinar

checkmate[2] *n* : jaque mate *m*

checkout [ˈʧɛkˌaʊt] *n or* **checkout counter** : caja *f*

checkpoint [ˈʧɛkˌpɔɪnt] *n* : puesto *m* de control

checkup [ˈʧɛkˌʌp] *n* : examen *m* médico, chequeo *m*

cheddar [ˈʧɛdər] *n* : queso *m* Cheddar

cheek [ˈʧi:k] *n* **1** : mejilla *f*, cachete *m* **2** IMPUDENCE : insolencia *f*, descaro *m*

cheekbone [ˈʧi:kˌbo:n] *n* : pómulo *m*

cheeky [ˈʧi:ki] *adj* **cheekier; -est** : descarado, insolente, atrevido

cheep[1] [ˈʧi:p] *vi* : piar

cheep[2] *n* : pío *m*

cheer[1] [ˈʧɪr] *vt* **1** ENCOURAGE : alentar, animar **2** GLADDEN : alegrar, levantar el ánimo a **3** ACCLAIM : aclamar, vitorear, echar porras a

cheer[2] *n* **1** CHEERFULNESS : alegría *f*, buen humor *m*, jovialidad *f* **2** APPLAUSE : aclamación *f*, ovación *f*, aplausos *mpl* ⟨three cheers for the chief! : ¡viva el jefe!⟩ **3 cheers!** : ¡salud!

cheerful [ˈʧɪrfəl] *adj* : alegre, de buen humor

cheerfully [ˈʧɪrfəli] *adv* : alegremente, jovialmente

cheerfulness [ˈʧɪrfəlnəs] *n* : buen humor *m*, alegría *f*

cheerily [ˈʧɪrəli] *adv* : alegremente

cheeriness [ˈʧɪrinəs] *n* : buen humor *m*, alegría *f*

cheerleader [ˈʧɪrˌli:dər] *n* : porrista *mf*

cheerless [ˈʧɪrləs] *adj* BLEAK : triste, sombrío

cheerlessly [ˈʧɪrləsli] *adv* : desanimadamente

cheery [ˈʧɪri] *adj* **cheerier; -est** : alegre, de buen humor

cheese [ˈʧi:z] *n* : queso *m*

cheesecloth [ˈʧi:zˌklɔθ] *n* : estopilla *f*

cheesy [ˈʧi:zi] *adj* **cheesier; -est** **1** : a queso **2** : que contiene queso **3** CHEAP : barato, de mala calidad

cheetah [ˈʧi:t̬ə] *n* : guepardo *m*

chef [ˈʃɛf] *n* : chef *m*

chemical[1] [ˈkɛmɪkəl] *adj* : químico — **chemically** [-mɪkli] *adv*

chemical[2] *n* : sustancia *f* química

chemise [ʃəˈmi:z] *n* **1** : camiseta *f*, prenda *f* interior de una pieza **2** : vestido *m* holgado

chemist [ˈkɛmɪst] *n* : químico *m*, -ca *f*

chemistry [ˈkɛmɪstri] *n, pl* **-tries** : química *f*

chemotherapy [ˌki:moˈθɛrəpi, ˌkɛmo-] *n, pl* **-pies** : quimioterapia *f*

chenille [ʃəˈni:l] *n* : felpilla *f*

cherish [ˈʧɛrɪʃ] *vt* **1** VALUE : apreciar, valorar **2** HARBOR : abrigar, albergar

cherry [ˈʧɛri] *n, pl* **-ries** **1** : cereza *f* (fruta) **2** : cerezo *m* (árbol)

cherub [ˈʧɛrəb] *n* **1** *pl* **-ubim** [ˈʧɛrəˌbɪm, ˈʧɛrjə-] ANGEL : ángel *m*, querubín *m* **2** *pl* **-ubs** : niño *m* regordete, niña *f* regordeta

cherubic [ʧəˈru:bɪk] *adj* : querúbico, angelical

chess [ˈʧɛs] *n* : ajedrez *m*

chessboard [ˈʧɛsˌbord] *n* : tablero *m* de ajedrez

chessman [ˈʧɛsmən, -ˌmæn] *n, pl* **-men** [-mən, -ˌmɛn] : pieza *f* de ajedrez

chest [ˈʧɛst] *n* **1** : cofre *m*, baúl *m* **2** : pecho *m* ⟨chest pains : dolores de pecho⟩

chestnut [ˈʧɛstˌnʌt] *n* **1** : castaña *f* (fruto) **2** : castaño *m* (árbol)

chest of drawers *n* : cómoda *f*

chevron [ˈʃɛvrən] *n* : galón *m* (de un oficial militar)

chew[1] [ˈʧu:] *vt* : masticar, mascar

chew[2] *n* : algo que se masca (como tabaco)

chewable [ˈʧu:əbəl] *adj* : masticable

chewing gum *n* : goma *f* de mascar, chicle *m*

chewy [ˈʧu:i] *adj* **chewier; -est** **1** : fibroso (dícese de las carnes o los vegetales) **2** : pegajoso, chicloso (dícese de los dulces)

chic[1] [ˈʃi:k] *adj* : chic, elegante, de moda

chic[2] *n* : chic *m*, elegancia *f*

Chicano [ʧɪˈkɑno] *n* : chicano *m*, -na *f* — **Chicano** *adj*

chick [ˈʧɪk] *n* : pollito *m*, -ta *f*; polluelo *m*, -la *f*

chicken [ˈʧɪkən] *n* **1** FOWL : pollo *m* **2** COWARD : cobarde *mf*

chickenhearted [ˈʧɪkənˌhɑrt̬əd] *n* : miedoso, cobarde

chicken pox *n* : varicela *f*

chickpea [ˈʧɪkˌpi:] *n* : garbanzo *m*

chicle [ˈʧɪkəl] *n* : chicle *m* (resina)

chicory [ˈʧɪkəri] *n, pl* **-ries** **1** : endibia *f* (para ensaladas) **2** : achicoria *f* (aditivo de café)

chide [ˈʧaɪd] *vt* **chid** [ˈʧɪd] *or* **chided; chid** *or* **chidden** [ˈʧɪdən] *or* **chided; chiding** [ˈʧaɪdɪŋ] : regañar, reprender

chief[1] [ˈʧi:f] *adj* : principal, capital ⟨chief negotiator : negociador en jefe⟩ — **chiefly** *adv*

chief[2] *n* : jefe *m*, -fa *f*

chieftain [ˈʧiːftən] *n* : jefe *m*, -fa *f* (de una tribu)

chiffon [ʃɪˈfɑn, ˈʃɪˌ-] *n* : chifón *m*

chigger [ˈʧɪgər] *n* : nigua *f*

chignon [ˈʃiːnˌjɑn, -ˌjɔn] *n* : moño *m*, chongo *m Mex*

chilblain [ˈʧɪlˌbleɪn] *n* : sabañón *m*

child [ˈʧaɪld] *n, pl* **children** [ˈʧɪldrən] **1** BABY, YOUNGSTER : niño *m*, -ña *f*; criatura *f* **2** OFFSPRING : hijo *m*, -ja *f*; progenie *f*

childbearing[1] [ˈʧaɪlbɛrɪŋ] *adj* : relativo al parto ⟨of childbearing age : en edad fértil⟩

childbearing[2] → **childbirth**

childbirth [ˈʧaɪldˌbərθ] *n* : parto *m*

childhood [ˈʧaɪldˌhʊd] *n* : infancia *f*, niñez *f*

childish [ˈʧaɪldɪʃ] *adj* : infantil, inmaduro — **childishly** *adv*

childishness [ˈʧaɪldɪʃnəs] *n* : infantilismo *m*, inmadurez *f*

childless [ˈʧaɪldləs] *adj* : sin hijos

childlike [ˈʧaɪldˌlaɪk] *adj* : infantil, inocente ⟨a childlike imagination : una imaginación infantil⟩

childproof [ˈʧaɪldˌpruːf] *adj* : a prueba de niños

Chilean [ˈʧɪliən, ʧɪˈleɪən] *n* : chileno *m*, -na *f* — **Chilean** *adj*

chili *or* **chile** *or* **chilli** [ˈʧɪli] *n, pl* **chilies** *or* **chiles** *or* **chillies** **1** *or* **chili pepper** : chile *m*, ají *m* **2** : chile *m* con carne

chill[1] [ˈʧɪl] *v* : enfriar

chill[2] *adj* : frío, gélido ⟨a chill wind : un viento frío⟩

chill[3] *n* **1** CHILLINESS : fresco *m*, frío *m* **2** SHIVER : escalofrío *m* **3** DAMPER : enfriamiento *m*, frío *m* ⟨to cast a chill over : enfriar⟩

chilliness [ˈʧɪlinəs] *n* : frío *m*, fresco *m*

chilly [ˈʧɪli] *adj* **chillier; -est** : frío ⟨it's chilly tonight : hace frío esta noche⟩

chime[1] [ˈʧaɪm] *v* **chimed; chiming** *vt* : hacer sonar (una campana) — *vi* : sonar una campana, dar campanadas

chime[2] *n* **1** BELLS : juego *m* de campanitas sintonizadas, carillón *m* **2** PEAL : tañido *m*, campanada *f*

chime in *vi* : meterse en una conversación

chimera *or* **chimaera** [kaɪˈmɪrə, kə-] *n* : quimera *f*

chimney [ˈʧɪmni] *n, pl* **-neys** : chimenea *f*

chimney sweep *n* : deshollinador *m*, -dora *f*

chimp [ˈʧɪmp, ˈʃɪmp] → **chimpanzee**

chimpanzee [ˌʧɪmˌpænˈziː, ˌʃɪm-; ʧɪm ˈpænzi, ʃɪm-] *n* : chimpancé *m*

chin [ˈʧɪn] *n* : barbilla *f*, mentón *m*, barba *f*

china [ˈʧaɪnə] *n* **1** PORCELAIN : porcelana *f*, loza *f* **2** CROCKERY, TABLEWARE : loza *f*, vajilla *f*

chinchilla [ʧɪnˈʧɪlə] *n* : chinchilla *f*

Chinese [ˈʧaɪˈniːz, -ˈniːs] *n* **1** : chino *m*, -na *f* **2** : chino *m* (idioma) — **Chinese** *adj*

chink [ˈʧɪŋk] *n* : grieta *f*, abertura *f*

chintz [ˈʧɪnts] *n* : chintz *m*, chinz *m*

chip[1] [ˈʧɪp] *v* **chipped; chipping** *vt* : desportillar, desconchar, astillar (madera) — *vi* : desportillarse, desconcharse, descascararse (dícese de la pintura, etc.)

chip[2] *n* **1** : astilla *f* (de madera o vidrio), lasca *f* (de piedra) ⟨he's a chip off the old block : de tal palo, tal astilla⟩ **2** : bocado *m* pequeño (en rodajas o rebanadas) ⟨tortilla chips : totopos, tortillitas tostadas⟩ **3** : ficha *f* (de póker, etc.) **4** NICK : desportilladura *f*, mella *f* **5** : chip *m* ⟨memory chip : chip de memoria⟩

chip in *v* CONTRIBUTE : contribuir

chipmunk [ˈʧɪpˌmʌŋk] *n* : ardilla *f* listada

chipper [ˈʧɪpər] *adj* : alegre y vivaz

chiropodist [kəˈrɑpədɪst, ʃə-] *n* : podólogo *m*, -ga *f*

chiropody [kəˈrɑpədi, ʃə-] *n* : podología *f*

chiropractic [ˈkaɪrəˌpræktɪk] *n* : quiropráctica *f*

chiropractor [ˈkaɪrəˌpræktər] *n* : quiropráctico *m*, -ca *f*

chirp[1] [ˈʧərp] *vi* : gorjear (dícese de los pájaros), chirriar (dícese de los grillos)

chirp[2] *n* : gorjeo *m* (de un pájaro), chirrido *m* (de un grillo)

chisel[1] [ˈʧɪzəl] *vt* **-eled** *or* **-elled; -eling** *or* **-elling** **1** : cincelar, tallar, labrar **2** CHEAT : estafar, defraudar

chisel[2] *n* : cincel *m* (para piedras y metales), escoplo *m* (para madera), formón *m*

chiseler [ˈʧɪzələr] *n* SWINDLER : estafador *m*, -dora *f*; fraude *mf*

chit [ˈʧɪt] *n* : resguardo *m*, recibo *m*

chitchat [ˈʧɪtˌʧæt] *n* : cotorreo *m*, charla *f*

chivalric [ʃəˈvælrɪk] → **chivalrous**

chivalrous [ˈʃɪvəlrəs] *adj* **1** KNIGHTLY : caballeresco, relativo a la caballería **2** GENTLEMANLY : caballeroso, honesto, cortés

chivalrousness [ˈʃɪvəlrəsnəs] *n* : caballerosidad *f*, cortesía *f*

chivalry [ˈʃɪvəlri] *n, pl* **-ries** **1** KNIGHTHOOD : caballería *f* **2** CHIVALROUSNESS : caballerosidad *f*, nobleza *f*, cortesía *f*

chive [ˈʧaɪv] *n* : cebollino *m*

chloride [ˈklorˌaɪd] *n* : cloruro *m*

chlorinate [ˈklorəˌneɪt] *vt* **-nated; -nating** : clorar

chlorination [ˌklorəˈneɪʃən] *n* : cloración *f*

chlorine [ˈklorˌiːn] *n* : cloro *m*

chloroform [ˈklorəˌfɔrm] *n* : cloroformo *m*

chlorophyll [ˈklorəˌfɪl] *n* : clorofila *f*

chock–full [ˈʧɑkˈfʊl, ˈʧʌk-] *adj* : colmado, repleto

chocolate [ˈʧɑkələt, ˈʧɔk-] *n* **1** : chocolate *m* **2** BONBON : bombón *m* **3** : color *m* chocolate, marrón *m*

choice[1] ['ʧɔɪs] *adj* **choicer; -est** : selecto, escogido, de primera calidad
choice[2] *n* **1** CHOOSING : elección *f*, selección *f* **2** OPTION : elección *f*, opción *f* ⟨I have no choice : no tengo alternativa⟩ **3** PREFERENCE : preferencia *f*, elección *f* **4** VARIETY : surtido *m*, selección *f* ⟨a wide choice : un gran surtido⟩
choir ['kwaɪr] *n* : coro *m*
choirboy ['kwaɪr,bɔɪ] *n* : niño *m* de coro
choke[1] ['ʧo:k] *v* **choked; choking** *vt* **1** ASPHYXIATE, STRANGLE : sofocar, asfixiar, ahogar, estrangular **2** BLOCK : tapar, obstruir — *vi* **1** SUFFOCATE : asfixiarse, sofocarse, ahogarse, atragantarse (con comida) **2** CLOG : taparse, obstruirse
choke[2] *n* **1** CHOKING : estrangulación *f* **2** : choke *m* (de un motor)
choker ['ʧo:kər] *n* : gargantilla *f*
cholera ['kɑlərə] *n* : cólera *m*
cholesterol [kə'lɛstə,rɔl] *n* : colesterol *m*
choose ['ʧu:z] *v* **chose** ['ʧo:z]; **chosen** ['ʧo:zən]; **choosing** *vt* **1** SELECT : escoger, elegir ⟨choose only one : escoja sólo uno⟩ **2** DECIDE : decidir ⟨he chose to leave : decidió irse⟩ **3** PREFER : preferir ⟨which one do you choose? : ¿cuál prefiere?⟩ — *vi* : escoger ⟨much to choose from : mucho de donde escoger⟩
choosy *or* **choosey** ['ʧu:zi] *adj* **choosier; -est** : exigente, remilgado
chop[1] ['ʧɑp] *vt* **chopped; chopping 1** MINCE : picar, cortar, moler (carne) **2 to chop down** : cortar, talar (un árbol)
chop[2] *n* **1** CUT : hachazo *m* (con una hacha), tajo *m* (con una cuchilla) **2** BLOW : golpe *m* (penetrante) ⟨karate chop : golpe de karate⟩ **3** : chuleta *f* ⟨pork chops : chuletas de cerdo⟩
chopper ['ʧɑpər] → **helicopter**
choppy ['ʧɑpi] *adj* **choppier; -est 1** : agitado, picado (dícese del mar) **2** DISCONNECTED : incoherente, inconexo
chops ['ʧɑps] *npl* **1** : quijada *f*, mandíbula *f*, boca *f* (de una persona) **2 to lick one's chops** : relamerse
chopsticks ['ʧɑp,stɪks] *npl* : palillos *mpl*
choral ['korəl] *adj* : coral
chorale [kə'ræl, -'rɑl] *n* **1** : coral *f* (composición musical vocal) **2** CHOIR, CHORUS : coral *f*, coro *m*
chord ['kɔrd] *n* **1** : acorde *m* (en música) **2** : cuerda *f* (en anatomía o geometría)
chore ['ʧor] *n* **1** TASK : tarea *f* rutinaria **2** BOTHER, NUISANCE : lata *f fam*, fastidio *m* **3 chores** *npl* WORK : quehaceres *mpl*, faenas *fpl*
choreograph ['koriə,græf] *vt* : coreografiar
choreographer [,kori'ɑgrəfər] *n* : coreógrafo *m*, -fa *f*
choreographic [,koriə'græfɪk] *adj* : coreográfico
choreography [,kori'ɑgrəfi] *n, pl* **-phies** : coreografía *f*
chorister ['korəstər] *n* : corista *mf*
chortle[1] ['ʧɔrtəl] *vi* **-tled; -tling** : reírse (con satisfacción o júbilo)
chortle[2] *n* : risa *f* (de satisfacción o júbilo)
chorus[1] ['korəs] *vt* : corear
chorus[2] *n* **1** : coro *m* (grupo o composición musical) **2** REFRAIN : coro *m*, estribillo *m*
chose → **choose**
chosen ['ʧo:zən] *adj* : elegido, selecto
chow ['ʧaʊ] *n* **1** FOOD : comida *f* **2** : chow-chow *m* (perro)
chowder ['ʧaʊdər] *n* : sopa *f* de pescado
Christ ['kraɪst] *n* **1** : Cristo *m* **2 for Christ's sake** : ¡por Dios!
christen ['krɪsən] *vt* **1** BAPTIZE : bautizar **2** NAME : bautizar con el nombre de
Christendom ['krɪsəndəm] *n* : cristiandad *f*
christening ['krɪsənɪŋ] *n* : bautismo *m*, bautizo *m*
Christian[1] ['krɪsʧən] *adj* : cristiano
Christian[2] *n* : cristiano *m*, -na *f*
Christianity [,krɪsʧi'ænəti, ,krɪs'ʧæ-] *n* : cristianismo *m*
Christian name *n* : nombre *m* de pila
Christmas ['krɪsməs] *n* : Navidad *f* ⟨Christmas season : las Navidades⟩
chromatic [kro:'mætɪk] *adj* : cromático ⟨chromatic scale : escala cromática⟩
chrome ['kro:m] *n* : cromo *m* (metal)
chromium ['kro:miəm] *n* : cromo *m* (elemento)
chromosome ['kro:mə,so:m, -,zo:m] *n* : cromosoma *m*
chronic ['krɑnɪk] *adj* : crónico — **chronically** [-nɪkli] *adv*
chronicle[1] ['krɑnɪkəl] *vt* **-cled; -cling** : escribir (una crónica o historia)
chronicle[2] *n* : crónica *f*, historia *f*
chronicler ['krɑnɪklər] *n* : historiador *m*, -dora *f*; cronista *mf*
chronological [,krɑnəl'ɑʤɪkəl] *adj* : cronológico — **chronologically** [-kli] *adv*
chronology [krə'nɑləʤi] *n, pl* **-gies** : cronología *f*
chronometer [krə'nɑmətər] *n* : cronómetro *m*
chrysalis ['krɪsələs] *n, pl* **chrysalides** [krɪ'sælə,di:z] *or* **chrysalises** : crisálida *f*
chrysanthemum [krɪ'sæntθəməm] *n* : crisantemo *m*
chubbiness ['ʧʌbinəs] *n* : gordura *f*
chubby ['ʧʌbi] *adj* **-bier; -est** : gordito, regordete, rechoncho
chuck[1] ['ʧʌk] *vt* **1** TOSS : tirar, lanzar, aventar *Col, Mex* **2 to chuck under the chin** : hacer la mamola
chuck[2] *n* **1** PAT : mamola *f*, palmada *f* **2** TOSS : lanzamiento *m* **3** *or* **chuck steak** : corte *m* de carne de res
chuckle[1] ['ʧʌkəl] *vi* **-led; -ling** : reírse entre dientes
chuckle[2] *n* : risita *f*, risa *f* ahogada

chug[1] ['ʧʌg] *vi* **chugged; chugging** : resoplar, traquetear
chug[2] *n* : resoplido *m*, traqueteo *m*
chum[1] ['ʧʌm] *vi* **chummed; chumming** : ser camaradas, ser cuates *Mex fam*
chum[2] *n* : amigo *m*, -ga *f*; camarada *mf*; compinche *mf fam*
chummy ['ʧʌmi] *adj* **-mier; -est** : amistoso ⟨they're very chummy : son muy amigos⟩
chump ['ʧʌmp] *n* : tonto *m*, -ta *f*; idiota *mf*
chunk ['ʧʌnk] *n* **1** PIECE : cacho *m*, pedazo *m*, trozo *m* **2** : cantidad *f* grande ⟨a chunk of money : mucho dinero⟩
chunky ['ʧʌnki] *adj* **chunkier; -est 1** STOCKY : fornido, robusto **2** : que contiene pedazos
church ['ʧərʧ] *n* **1** : iglesia *f* ⟨to go to church : ir a la iglesia⟩ **2** CHRISTIANS : iglesia *f*, conjunto *m* de fieles cristianos **3** DENOMINATION : confesión *f*, secta *f* **4** CONGREGATION : feligreses *mpl*, fieles *mpl*
churchgoer ['ʧərʧˌgo:ər] *n* : practicante *mf*
churchyard ['ʧərʧˌjɑrd] *n* : cementerio *m* (junto a una iglesia)
churn[1] ['ʧərn] *vt* **1** : batir (crema), hacer (mantequilla) **2** : agitar con fuerza, revolver — *vi* : agitarse, arremolinarse
churn[2] *n* : mantequera *f*
chute ['ʃu:t] *n* : conducto *m* inclinado, vertedero *m* (para basuras)
chutney ['ʧʌtni] *n, pl* **-neys** : chutney *m*
chutzpah ['hʊtspə, 'xʊt-, -ˌspɑ] *n* : descaro *m*, frescura *f*, cara *f fam*
cicada [sə'keɪdə, -'kɑ-] *n* : cigarra *f*, chicharra *f*
cider ['saɪdər] *n* **1** : jugo *m* (de manzana, etc.) **2 hard cider** : sidra *f*
cigar [sɪ'gɑr] *n* : puro *m*, cigarro *m*
cigarette [ˌsɪgə'rɛt, 'sɪgəˌrɛt] *n* : cigarrillo *m*, cigarro *m*
cilantro [sɪ'lɑntro:, -'læn-] *n* : cilantro *m*
cinch[1] ['sɪnʧ] *vt* **1** : cinchar (un caballo) **2** ASSURE : asegurar
cinch[2] *n* **1** : cincha *f* (para caballos) **2** : algo fácil o seguro ⟨it's a cinch : es bien fácil, es pan comido⟩
cinchona [sɪŋ'ko:nə] *n* : quino *m*
cinder ['sɪndər] *n* **1** EMBER : brasa *f*, ascua *f* **2 cinders** *npl* ASHES : cenizas *fpl*
cinema ['sɪnəmə] *n* : cine *m*
cinematic [ˌsɪnə'mæṭɪk] *adj* : cinematográfico
cinnamon ['sɪnəmən] *n* : canela *f*
cipher ['saɪfər] *n* **1** ZERO : cero *m* **2** CODE : cifra *f*, clave *f*
circa ['sərkə] *prep* : alrededor de, hacia ⟨circa 1800 : hacia el año 1800⟩
circle[1] ['sərkəl] *v* **-cled; -cling** *vt* **1** : encerrar en un círculo, poner un círculo alrededor de **2** : girar alrededor de, dar vueltas a ⟨we circled the building twice : le dimos vueltas al edificio dos veces⟩ — *vi* : dar vueltas
circle[2] *n* **1** : círculo *m* **2** CYCLE : ciclo *m* ⟨to come full circle : volver al punto de partida⟩ **3** GROUP : círculo *m*, grupo *m* (social)
circuit ['sərkət] *n* **1** BOUNDARY : circuito *m*, perímetro *m* (de una zona o un territorio) **2** TOUR : circuito *m*, recorrido *m*, tour *m* **3** : circuito *m* (eléctrico) ⟨a short circuit : un cortocircuito⟩
circuitous [ˌsər'kju:əṭəs] *adj* : sinuoso, tortuoso
circuitry ['sərkətri] *n, pl* **-ries** : sistema *m* de circuitos
circular[1] ['sərkjələr] *adj* ROUND : circular, redondo
circular[2] *n* : circular *f*
circulate ['sərkjəˌleɪt] *v* **-lated; -lating** *vi* : circular — *vt* **1** : circular (noticias, etc.) **2** DISSEMINATE : hacer circular, divulgar
circulation [ˌsərkjə'leɪʃən] *n* : circulación *f*
circulatory ['sərkjələˌtori] *adj* : circulatorio
circumcise ['sərkəmˌsaɪz] *vt* **-cised; -cising** : circuncidar
circumcision [ˌsərkəm'sɪʒən, 'sərkəmˌ-] *n* : circuncisión *f*
circumference [sər'kʌmpfrənts] *n* : circunferencia *f*
circumflex ['sərkəmˌflɛks] *n* : acento *m* circunflejo
circumlocution [ˌsərkəmlo'kju:ʃən] *n* : circunlocución *f*
circumnavigate [ˌsərkəm'nævəˌgeɪt] *vt* **-gated; -gating** : circunnavegar
circumscribe ['sərkəmˌskraɪb] *vt* **-scribed; -scribing 1** : circunscribir, trazar una figura alrededor de **2** LIMIT : circunscribir, limitar
circumspect ['sərkəmˌspɛkt] *adj* : circunspecto, prudente, cauto
circumspection [ˌsərkəm'spɛkʃən] *n* : circunspección *f*, cautela *f*
circumstance ['sərkəmˌstænts] *n* **1** EVENT : circunstancia *f*, acontecimiento *m* **2 circumstances** *npl* SITUATION : circunstancias *fpl*, situación *f* ⟨under the circumstances : dadas las circunstancias⟩ ⟨under no circumstances : de ninguna manera, bajo ningún concepto⟩ **3 circumstances** *npl* : situación *f* económica
circumstantial [ˌsərkəm'stænʧəl] *adj* : circunstancial
circumvent [ˌsərkəm'vɛnt] *vt* : evadir, burlar (una ley o regla), sortear (una responsabilidad o dificultad)
circumvention [ˌsərkəm'vɛnʧən] *n* : evasión *f*
circus ['sərkəs] *n* : circo *m*
cirrhosis [sə'ro:sɪs] *n, pl* **-rhoses** [-'ro:ˌsi:z] : cirrosis *f*
cirrus ['sɪrəs] *n, pl* **-ri** ['sɪrˌaɪ] : cirro *m*
cistern ['sɪstərn] *n* : cisterna *f*, aljibe *m*
citadel ['sɪṭədəl, -ˌdɛl] *n* FORTRESS : ciudadela *f*, fortaleza *f*

citation [saɪˈteɪʃən] *n* **1** SUMMONS : emplazamiento *m*, citación *f*, convocatoria *f* (judicial) **2** QUOTATION : cita *f* **3** COMMENDATION : elogio *m*, mención *f* (de honor)

cite [ˈsaɪt] *vt* **cited; citing 1** ARRAIGN, SUBPOENA : emplazar, citar, hacer comparecer (ante un tribunal) **2** QUOTE : citar **3** COMMEND : elogiar, honrar (oficialmente)

citizen [ˈsɪt̬əzən] *n* : ciudadano *m*, -na *f*

citizenry [ˈsɪt̬əzənri] *n, pl* **-ries** : ciudadanía *f*, conjunto *m* de ciudadanos

citizenship [ˈsɪt̬əzənˌʃɪp] *n* : ciudadanía *f* ⟨Nicaraguan citizenship : ciudadanía nicaragüense⟩

citron [ˈsɪtrən] *n* : cidra *f*

citrus [ˈsɪtrəs] *n, pl* **-rus** *or* **-ruses** : cítrico *m*

city [ˈsɪt̬i] *n, pl* **cities** : ciudad *f*

civic [ˈsɪvɪk] *adj* : cívico

civics [ˈsɪvɪks] *ns & pl* : civismo *m*

civil [ˈsɪvəl] *adj* **1** : civil ⟨civil law : derecho civil⟩ **2** POLITE : civil, cortés

civilian [səˈvɪljən] *n* : civil *mf* ⟨soldiers and civilians : soldados y civiles⟩

civility [səˈvɪlət̬i] *n, pl* **-ties** : cortesía *f*, educación *f*

civilization [ˌsɪvələˈzeɪʃən] *n* : civilización *f*

civilize [ˈsɪvəˌlaɪz] *vt* **-lized; -lizing** : civilizar — **civilized** *adj*

civil liberties *npl* : derechos *mpl* civiles

civilly [ˈsɪvəli] *adv* : cortésmente

civil rights *npl* : derechos *mpl* civiles

civil service *n* : administración *f* pública

civil war *n* : guerra *f* civil

clack[1] [ˈklæk] *vi* : tabletear

clack[2] *n* : tableteo *m*

clad [ˈklæd] *adj* **1** CLOTHED : vestido **2** COVERED : cubierto

claim[1] [ˈkleɪm] *vt* **1** DEMAND : reclamar, reivindicar ⟨she claimed her rights : reclamó sus derechos⟩ **2** MAINTAIN : afirmar, sostener ⟨they claim it's theirs : sostienen que es suyo⟩

claim[2] *n* **1** DEMAND : demanda *f*, reclamación *f* **2** DECLARATION : declaración *f*, afirmación *f* **3 to stake a claim** : reclamar, reivindicar

claimant [ˈkleɪmənt] *n* : demandante *mf* (ante un juez), pretendiente *mf* (al trono, etc.)

clairvoyance [klærˈvɔɪənts] *n* : clarividencia *f*

clairvoyant[1] [klærˈvɔɪənt] *adj* : clarividente

clairvoyant[2] *n* : clarividente *mf*

clam [ˈklæm] *n* : almeja *f*

clamber [ˈklæmbər] *vi* : treparse o subirse torpemente

clammy [ˈklæmi] *adj* **-mier; -est** : húmedo y algo frío

clamor[1] [ˈklæmər] *vi* : gritar, clamar

clamor[2] *n* : clamor *m*

clamorous [ˈklæmərəs] *adj* : clamoroso, ruidoso, estrepitoso

clamp[1] [ˈklæmp] *vt* : sujetar con abrazaderas

clamp[2] *n* : abrazadera *f*

clan [ˈklæn] *n* : clan *m*

clandestine [klænˈdɛstɪn] *adj* : clandestino, secreto

clang[1] [ˈklæŋ] *vi* : hacer resonar (dícese de un objeto metálico)

clang[2] *n* : ruido *m* metálico fuerte

clangor [ˈklæŋər, -gər] *n* : estruendo *m* metálico

clank[1] [ˈklæŋk] *vi* : producir un ruido metálico seco

clank[2] *n* : ruido *m* metálico seco

clannish [ˈklænɪʃ] *adj* : exclusivista

clap[1] [ˈklæp] *v* **clapped; clapping** *vt* **1** SLAP, STRIKE : golpear ruidosamente, dar una palmada ⟨to clap one's hands : batir palmas, dar palmadas⟩ **2** APPLAUD : aplaudir — *vi* APPLAUD : aplaudir

clap[2] *n* **1** SLAP : palmada *f*, golpecito *m* **2** NOISE : ruido *m* seco ⟨a clap of thunder : un trueno⟩

clapboard [ˈklæbərd, ˈklæpˌbord] *n* : tabla *f* de madera (para revestir muros)

clapper [ˈklæpər] *n* : badajo *m* (de una campana)

clarification [ˌklærəfəˈkeɪʃən] *n* : clarificación *f*

clarify [ˈklærəˌfaɪ] *vt* **-fied; -fying 1** EXPLAIN : aclarar **2** : clarificar (un líquido)

clarinet [ˌklærəˈnɛt] *n* : clarinete *m*

clarion [ˈklæriən] *adj* : claro y sonoro

clarity [ˈklærət̬i] *n* : claridad *f*, nitidez *f*

clash[1] [ˈklæʃ] *vi* **1** : sonar, chocarse ⟨the cymbals clashed : los platillos sonaron⟩ **2** : chocar, enfrentarse ⟨the students clashed with the police : los estudiantes se enfrentaron con la policía⟩ **3** CONFLICT : estar en conflicto, oponerse **4** : desentonar (dícese de los colores), coincidir (dícese de los datos)

clash[2] *n* **1** : ruido *m* (producido por un choque) **2** CONFLICT, CONFRONTATION : enfrentamiento *m*, conflicto *m*, choque *m* **3** : desentono *m* (de colores), coincidencia *f* (de datos)

clasp[1] [ˈklæsp] *vt* **1** FASTEN : sujetar, abrochar **2** EMBRACE, GRASP : agarrar, sujetar, abrazar

clasp[2] *n* **1** FASTENING : broche *m*, cierre *m* **2** EMBRACE, SQUEEZE : apretón *m*, abrazo *m*

class[1] [ˈklæs] *vt* : clasificar, catalogar

class[2] *n* **1** KIND, TYPE : clase *f*, tipo *m*, especie *f* **2** : clase *f*, rango *m* social ⟨the working class : la clase obrera⟩ **3** LESSON : clase *f*, curso *m* ⟨English class : clase de inglés⟩ **4** : conjunto *m* de estudiantes, clase *f* ⟨the class of '97 : la promoción del 97⟩

classic[1] [ˈklæsɪk] *adj* : clásico

classic[2] *n* : clásico *m*, obra *f* clásica

classical [ˈklæsɪkəl] *adj* : clásico — **classically** [-kli] *adv*

classicism [ˈklæsəˌsɪzəm] *n* : clasicismo *m*

classification [ˌklæsəfəˈkeɪʃən] *n* : clasificación *f*

classified [ˈklæsəˌfaɪd] *adj* **1** : clasificado ⟨classified ads : avisos clasificados⟩ **2** RESTRICTED : confidencial, secreto ⟨classified documents : documentos secretos⟩

classify [ˈklæsəˌfaɪ] *vt* **-fied; -fying** : clasificar, catalogar

classless [ˈklæsləs] *adj* : sin clases

classmate [ˈklæsˌmeɪt] *n* : compañero *m*, -ra *f* de clase

classroom [ˈklæsˌruːm] *n* : aula *f*, salón *m* de clase

clatter[1] [ˈklæt̬ər] *vi* : traquetear, hacer ruido

clatter[2] *n* : traqueteo *m*, ruido *m*, estrépito *m*

clause [ˈklɔz] *n* : cláusula *f*

claustrophobia [ˌklɔstrəˈfoːbiə] *n* : claustrofobia *f*

claustrophobic [ˌklɔstrəˈfoːbɪk] *adj* : claustrofóbico

clavicle [ˈklævɪkəl] *n* : clavícula *f*

claw[1] [ˈklɔ] *v* : arañar

claw[2] *n* : garra *f*, uña *f* (de un gato), pinza *f* (de un crustáceo)

clay [ˈkleɪ] *n* : arcilla *f*, barro *m*

clayey [ˈkleɪi] *adj* : arcilloso

clean[1] [ˈkliːn] *vt* : limpiar, lavar, asear

clean[2] *adv* : limpio, limpiamente ⟨to play clean : jugar limpio⟩

clean[3] *adj* **1** : limpio **2** UNADULTERATED : puro **3** IRREPROACHABLE : intachable, sin mancha ⟨to have a clean record : no tener antecedentes penales⟩ **4** DECENT : decente **5** COMPLETE : completo, absoluto ⟨a clean break with the past : un corte radical con el pasado⟩

cleaner [ˈkliːnər] *n* **1** : limpiador *m*, -dora *f* **2** : producto *m* de limpieza **3** DRY CLEANER : tintorería *f* (servicio)

cleanliness [ˈklɛnlinəs] *n* : limpieza *f*, aseo *m*

cleanly[1] [ˈkliːnli] *adv* : limpiamente, con limpieza

cleanly[2] [ˈklɛnli] *adj* **-lier; -est** : limpio, pulcro

cleanness [ˈkliːnnəs] *n* : limpieza *f*

cleanse [ˈklɛnz] *vt* **cleansed; cleansing** : limpiar, purificar

cleanser [ˈklɛnzər] *n* : limpiador *m*, purificador *m*

clear[1] [ˈklɪr] *vt* **1** CLARIFY : aclarar, clarificar (un líquido) **2** : despejar (una superficie), desatascar (un tubo), desmontar (una selva) ⟨to clear the table : levantar la mesa⟩ ⟨to clear one's throat : carraspear, aclararse la voz⟩ **3** EXONERATE : absolver, limpiar el nombre de **4** EARN : ganar, sacar (una ganancia de) **5** : pasar sin tocar ⟨he cleared the hurdle : saltó por encima de la valla⟩ **6 to clear up** RESOLVE : aclarar, resolver, esclarecer — *vi* **1** DISPERSE : irse, despejarse, disiparse **2** : ser compensado (dícese de un cheque) **3 to clear up** : despejar (dícese del tiempo), mejorarse (dícese de una enfermedad)

clear[2] *adv* : claro, claramente

clear[3] *adj* **1** BRIGHT : claro, lúcido **2** FAIR : claro, despejado **3** TRANSPARENT : transparente, translúcido **4** EVIDENT, UNMISTAKABLE : evidente, claro, obvio **5** CERTAIN : seguro **6** UNOBSTRUCTED : despejado, libre

clear[4] *n* **1 in the clear** : inocente, libre de toda sospecha **2 in the clear** SAFE : fuera de peligro

clearance [ˈklɪrən*t*s] *n* **1** CLEARING : despeje *m* **2** SPACE : espacio *m* (libre), margen *m* **3** AUTHORIZATION : autorización *f*, despacho *m* (de la aduana)

clearing [ˈklɪrɪŋ] *n* : claro *m* (de un bosque)

clearly [ˈklɪrli] *adv* **1** DISTINCTLY : claramente, directamente **2** OBVIOUSLY : obviamente, evidentemente

cleat [ˈkliːt] *n* **1** : taco *m* **2 cleats** *npl* : zapatos *mpl* deportivos (con tacos)

cleavage [ˈkliːvɪʤ] *n* **1** CLEFT : hendidura *f*, raja *f* **2** : escote *m* (del busto)

cleave[1] [ˈkliːv] *vi* **cleaved** [ˈkliːvd] *or* **clove** [ˈkloːv]; **cleaving** ADHERE : adherirse, unirse

cleave[2] *vt* **cleaved; cleaving** SPLIT : hender, dividir, partir

cleaver [ˈkliːvər] *n* : cuchilla *f* de carnicero

clef [ˈklɛf] *n* : clave *f*

cleft [ˈklɛft] *n* : hendidura *f*, raja *f*, grieta *f*

clemency [ˈklɛmən*t*si] *n* : clemencia *f*

clement [ˈklɛmənt] *adj* **1** MERCIFUL : clemente, piadoso **2** MILD : clemente, apacible

clench [ˈklɛnʧ] *vt* **1** CLUTCH : agarrar **2** TIGHTEN : apretar (el puño, los dientes)

clergy [ˈklərʤi] *n, pl* **-gies** : clero *m*

clergyman [ˈklərʤimən] *n, pl* **-men** [-mən, -ˌmɛn] : clérigo *m*

cleric [ˈklɛrɪk] *n* : clérigo *m*, -ga *f*

clerical [ˈklɛrɪkəl] *adj* **1** : clerical ⟨a clerical collar : un alzacuello⟩ **2** : de oficina ⟨clerical staff : personal de oficina⟩

clerk[1] [ˈklərk, *Brit* ˈklɑrk] *vi* : trabajar de oficinista, trabajar de dependiente

clerk[2] *n* **1** : funcionario *m*, -ria *f* (de una oficina gubernamental) **2** : oficinista *mf*, empleado *m*, -da *f* de oficina **3** SALESPERSON : dependiente *m*, -ta *f*

clever [ˈklɛvər] *adj* **1** SKILLFUL : ingenioso, hábil **2** SMART : listo, inteligente, astuto

cleverly [ˈklɛvərli] *adv* **1** SKILLFULLY : ingeniosamente, hábilmente **2** INTELLIGENTLY : inteligentemente

cleverness [ˈklɛvərnəs] *n* **1** SKILL : ingenio *m*, habilidad *f* **2** INTELLIGENCE : inteligencia *f*

clew ['klu:] → **clue**
cliché [kli'ʃeɪ] *n* : cliché *m*, tópico *m*
click[1] ['klɪk] *vt* **1** : chasquear (los dedos, etc.) ⟨to click one's heels : dar un taconazo⟩ **2** : hacer clic en (un botón, etc.) — *vi* **1** : hacer clic **2** SNAP : chasquear **3** SUCCEED : tener éxito **4** GET ALONG : congeniar, llevarse bien
click[2] *n* : chasquido *m* (de los dedos, etc.), clic *m* (de un botón, etc.)
client ['klaɪənt] *n* : cliente *m*, -ta *f*
clientele [ˌklaɪən'tɛl, ˌkli:-] *n* : clientela *f*
cliff ['klɪf] *n* : acantilado *m*, precipicio *m*, risco *m*
climate ['klaɪmət] *n* : clima *m*
climatic [klaɪ'mæṭɪk, klə-] *adj* : climático
climax[1] ['klaɪˌmæks] *vi* : llegar al punto culminante, culminar — *vt* : ser el punto culminante de
climax[2] *n* : clímax *m*, punto *m* culminante
climb[1] ['klaɪm] *vt* : escalar, trepar a, subir a ⟨to climb a mountain : escalar una montaña⟩ — *vi* **1** RISE : subir, ascender ⟨prices are climbing : los precios están subiendo⟩ **2** : subirse, treparse ⟨to climb up a tree : treparse a un árbol⟩
climb[2] *n* : ascenso *m*, subida *f*
climber ['klaɪmər] *n* **1** : escalador *m*, -dora *f* ⟨a mountain climber : un alpinista⟩ **2** : trepadora *f* (planta)
clinch[1] ['klɪntʃ] *vt* **1** FASTEN, SECURE : remachar (un clavo), afianzar, abrochar **2** SETTLE : decidir, cerrar ⟨to clinch the title : ganar el título⟩
clinch[2] *n* : abrazo *m*, clinch *m* (en el boxeo)
clincher ['klɪntʃər] *n* : argumento *m* decisivo
cling ['klɪŋ] *vi* **clung** ['klʌŋ]; **clinging** **1** STICK : adherirse, pegarse **2** : aferrarse, agarrarse ⟨he clung to the railing : se aferró a la barandilla⟩
clinic ['klɪnɪk] *n* : clínica *f*
clinical ['klɪnɪkəl] *adj* : clínico — **clinically** [-kli] *adv*
clink[1] ['klɪŋk] *vi* : tintinear
clink[2] *n* : tintineo *m*
clip[1] ['klɪp] *vt* **clipped; clipping** **1** CUT : cortar, recortar **2** HIT : golpear, dar un puñetazo a **3** FASTEN : sujetar (con un clip)
clip[2] *n* **1** → **clippers** **2** BLOW : golpe *m*, puñetazo *m* **3** PACE : paso *m* rápido **4** FASTENER : clip *m* ⟨a paper clip : un sujetapapeles⟩
clipper ['klɪpər] *n* **1** : clíper *m* (buque de vela) **2** **clippers** *npl* : tijeras *fpl* ⟨nail clippers : cortauñas⟩
clique ['kli:k, 'klɪk] *n* : grupo *m* exclusivo, camarilla *f* (de políticos)
clitoris ['klɪṭərəs, klɪ'tɔrəs] *n, pl* **clitorides** [-'tɔrəˌdi:z] : clítoris *m*
cloak[1] ['klo:k] *vt* : encubrir, envolver (en un manto de)
cloak[2] *n* : capa *f*, capote *m*, manto *m* ⟨under the cloak of darkness : al amparo de la oscuridad⟩
clobber ['klɑbər] *vt* : dar una paliza a
clock[1] ['klɑk] *vt* : cronometrar
clock[2] *n* **1** : reloj *m* (de pared), cronómetro *m* (en deportes o competencias) **2** **around the clock** : las veinticuatro horas
clockwise ['klɑkˌwaɪz] *adv & adj* : en la dirección de las manecillas del reloj
clockwork ['klɑkˌwərk] *n* : mecanismo *m* de relojería
clod ['klɑd] *n* **1** : terrón *m* **2** OAF : zoquete *mf*
clog[1] ['klɑg] *v* **clogged; clogging** *vt* **1** HINDER : estorbar, impedir **2** BLOCK : atascar, tapar — *vi* : atascarse, taparse
clog[2] *n* **1** OBSTACLE : traba *f*, impedimento *m*, estorbo *m* **2** : zueco *m* (zapato)
cloister[1] ['klɔɪstər] *vt* : enclaustrar
cloister[2] *n* : claustro *m*
clone ['klo:n] *n* **1** : clon *m* (de un organismo) **2** COPY : copia *f*, reproducción *f*
close[1] ['klo:z] *v* **closed; closing** *vt* : cerrar — *vi* **1** : cerrarse, cerrar **2** TERMINATE : concluirse, terminar **3** **to close in** APPROACH : acercarse, aproximarse
close[2] ['klo:s] *adv* : cerca, de cerca
close[3] *adj* **closer; closest** **1** CONFINING : restrictivo, estrecho **2** SECRETIVE : reservado **3** STRICT : estricto, detallado **4** STUFFY : cargado, bochornoso (dícese del tiempo) **5** TIGHT : apretado, entallado, ceñido ⟨it's a close fit : es muy apretado⟩ **6** NEAR : cercano, próximo **7** INTIMATE : íntimo ⟨close friends : amigos íntimos⟩ **8** ACCURATE : fiel, exacto **9** : reñido ⟨a close election : una elección muy reñida⟩
close[4] ['klo:z] *n* : fin *m*, final *m*, conclusión *f*
closely ['klo:sli] *adv* : cerca, de cerca
closeness ['klo:snəs] *n* **1** NEARNESS : cercanía *f*, proximidad *f* **2** INTIMACY : intimidad *f*
closet[1] ['klɑzət] *vt* **to be closeted with** : estar encerrado con
closet[2] *n* : armario *m*, guardarropa *f*, clóset *m*
closure ['klo:ʒər] *n* **1** CLOSING, END : cierre *m*, clausura *f*, fin *m* **2** FASTENER : cierre *m*
clot[1] ['klɑt] *v* **clotted; clotting** *vt* : coagular, cuajar — *vi* : cuajarse, coagularse
clot[2] *n* : coágulo *m*
cloth ['klɔθ] *n, pl* **cloths** ['klɔðz, 'klɔθs] **1** FABRIC : tela *f* **2** RAG : trapo *m* **3** TABLECLOTH : mantel *m*
clothe ['klo:ð] *vt* **clothed** *or* **clad** ['klæd]; **clothing** DRESS : vestir, arropar, ataviar
clothes ['klo:z, 'klo:ðz] *npl* **1** CLOTHING : ropa *f* **2** BEDCLOTHES : ropa *f* de cama
clothespin ['klo:zˌpɪn] *n* : pinza *f* (para la ropa)

clothing ['klo:ðɪŋ] *n* : ropa *f*, indumentaria *f*
cloud[1] ['klaʊd] *vt* : nublar, oscurecer — *vi* **to cloud over** : nublarse
cloud[2] *n* : nube *f*
cloudburst ['klaʊd,bərst] *n* : chaparrón *m*, aguacero *m*
cloudless ['klaʊdləs] *adj* : despejado, claro
cloudy ['klaʊdi] *adj* **cloudier; -est** : nublado, nuboso
clout[1] ['klaʊt] *vt* : bofetear, dar un tortazo a
clout[2] *n* **1** BLOW : golpe *m*, tortazo *m fam* **2** INFLUENCE : influencia *f*, palanca *f fam*
clove[1] ['klo:v] *n* **1** : diente *m* (de ajo) **2** : clavo *m* (especia)
clove[2] → **cleave**
cloven hoof ['klo:vən] *n* : pezuña *f* hendida
clover ['klo:vər] *n* : trébol *m*
cloverleaf ['klo:vər,li:f] *n, pl* **-leafs** *or* **-leaves** [-,li:vz] : intersección *f* en trébol
clown[1] ['klaʊn] *vi* : payasear, bromear <stop clowning around : déjate de payasadas>
clown[2] *n* : payaso *m*, -sa *f*
clownish ['klaʊnɪʃ] *adj* **1** : de payaso **2** BOORISH : grosero — **clownishly** *adv*
cloying ['klɔɪɪŋ] *adj* : empalagoso, meloso
club[1] ['klʌb] *vt* **clubbed; clubbing** : aporrear, dar garrotazos a
club[2] *n* **1** CUDGEL : garrote *m*, porra *f* **2** : palo *m* <golf club : palo de golf> **3** : trébol *m* (naipe) **4** ASSOCIATION : club *m*
clubfoot ['klʌb,fʊt] *n, pl* **-feet** : pie *m* deforme
clubhouse ['klʌb,haʊs] *n* : sede *f* de un club
cluck[1] ['klʌk] *vi* : cloquear, cacarear
cluck[2] *n* : cloqueo *m*, cacareo *m*
clue[1] ['klu:] *vt* **clued; clueing** *or* **cluing** *or* **to clue in** : dar una pista a, informar
clue[2] *n* : pista *f*, indicio *m*
clump[1] ['klʌmp] *vi* **1** : caminar con pisadas fuertes **2** LUMP : agruparse, aglutinarse — *vt* : amontonar
clump[2] *n* **1** : grupo *m* (de arbustos o árboles), terrón *m* (de tierra) **2** : pisada *f* fuerte
clumsily ['klʌmzəli] *adv* : torpemente, sin gracia
clumsiness ['klʌmzinəs] *n* : torpeza *f*
clumsy ['klʌmzi] *adj* **-sier; -est** **1** AWKWARD : torpe, desmañado **2** TACTLESS : carente de tacto, poco delicado
clung → **cling**
clunky ['klʌŋki] *adj* : torpe, poco elegante
cluster[1] ['klʌstər] *vt* : agrupar, juntar — *vi* : agruparse, apiñarse, arracimarse
cluster[2] *n* : grupo *m*, conjunto *m*, racimo *m* (de uvas)
clutch[1] ['klʌʧ] *vt* : agarrar, asir — *vi* **to clutch at** : tratar de agarrar
clutch[2] *n* **1** GRASP, GRIP : agarre *m*, apretón *m* **2** : embrague *m*, clutch *m* (de una máquina) **3** **clutches** *npl* : garras *fpl* <he fell into their clutches : cayó en sus garras>
clutter[1] ['klʌtər] *vt* : atiborrar o atestar de cosas, llenar desordenadamente
clutter[2] *n* : desorden *m*, revoltijo *m*
coach[1] ['ko:ʧ] *vt* : entrenar (atletas, artistas), preparar (alumnos)
coach[2] *n* **1** CARRIAGE : coche *m*, carruaje *m*, carroza *f* **2** : vagón *m* de pasajeros (de un tren) **3** BUS : autobús *m*, ómnibus *m* **4** : pasaje *m* aéreo de segunda clase **5** TRAINER : entrenador *m*, -dora *f*
coagulate [ko'ægjə,leɪt] *v* **-lated; -lating** *vt* : coagular, cuajar — *vi* : coagularse, cuajarse
coal ['ko:l] *n* **1** EMBER : ascua *f*, brasa *f* **2** : carbón *m* <a coal mine : una mina de carbón>
coalesce [,ko:ə'lɛs] *vi* **-alesced; -alescing** : unirse
coalition [,ko:ə'lɪʃən] *n* : coalición *f*
coarse ['kors] *adj* **coarser; -est** **1** : grueso (dícese de la arena o la sal), basto (dícese de las telas), áspero (dícese de la piel) **2** CRUDE, ROUGH : basto, tosco, ordinario **3** VULGAR : grosero — **coarsely** *adv*
coarsen ['korsən] *vt* : hacer áspero o basto — *vi* : volverse áspero o basto
coarseness ['korsnəs] *n* : aspereza *f*, tosquedad *f*
coast[1] ['ko:st] *vi* : deslizarse, rodar sin impulso
coast[2] *n* : costa *f*, litoral *m*
coastal ['ko:stəl] *adj* : costero
coaster ['ko:stər] *n* : posavasos *m*
coast guard *n* : guardia *f* costera, guardacostas *mpl*
coastline ['ko:st,laɪn] *n* : costa *f*
coat[1] ['ko:t] *vt* : cubrir, revestir, bañar (en un líquido)
coat[2] *n* **1** : abrigo *m* <a sport coat : una chaqueta, un saco> **2** : pelaje *m* (de animales) **3** LAYER : capa *f*, mano *f* (de pintura)
coating ['ko:tɪŋ] *n* : capa *f*
coat of arms *n* : escudo *m* de armas
coax ['ko:ks] *vt* : engatusar, persuadir
cob ['kɑb] → **corncob**
cobalt ['ko:,bɔlt] *n* : cobalto *m*
cobble ['kɑbəl] *vt* **cobbled; cobbling** **1** : fabricar o remendar (zapatos) **2** **to cobble together** : improvisar, hacer apresuradamente
cobbler ['kɑblər] *n* **1** SHOEMAKER : zapatero *m*, -ra *f* **2** **fruit cobbler** : tarta *f* de fruta
cobblestone ['kɑbəl,sto:n] *n* : adoquín *m*
cobra ['ko:brə] *n* : cobra *f*
cobweb ['kɑb,wɛb] *n* : telaraña *f*
coca ['ko:kə] *n* : coca *f*

cocaine [koː'keɪn, 'koːˌkeɪn] *n* : cocaína *f*
cock[1] ['kɑk] *vt* **1** : ladear ⟨to cock one's head : ladear la cabeza⟩ **2** : montar, amartillar (un arma de fuego)
cock[2] *n* **1** ROOSTER : gallo *m* **2** FAUCET : grifo *m*, llave *f* **3** : martillo *m* (de un arma de fuego)
cockatoo ['kɑkəˌtuː] *n, pl* **-toos** : cacatúa *f*
cockeyed ['kɑkˌaɪd] *adj* **1** ASKEW : ladeado, torcido, chueco **2** ABSURD : disparatado, absurdo
cockfight ['kɑkˌfaɪt] *n* : pelea *f* de gallos
cockiness ['kɑkinəs] *n* : arrogancia *f*
cockle ['kɑkəl] *n* : berberecho *m*
cockpit ['kɑkˌpɪt] *n* : cabina *f*
cockroach ['kɑkˌroːʧ] *n* : cucaracha *f*
cocktail ['kɑkˌteɪl] *n* **1** : coctel *m*, cóctel *m* **2** APPETIZER : aperitivo *m*
cocky ['kɑki] *adj* **cockier; -est** : creído, engreído
cocoa ['koːˌkoː] *n* **1** CACAO : cacao *m* **2** : cocoa *f*, chocolate *m* (bebida)
coconut ['koːkəˌnʌt] *n* : coco *m*
cocoon [kə'kuːn] *n* : capullo *m*
cod ['kɑd] *n, pl* **cod** : bacalao *m*
coddle ['kɑdəl] *vt* **-dled; -dling** : mimar, consentir
code ['koːd] *n* **1** : código *m* ⟨civil code : código civil⟩ **2** : código *m*, clave *f* ⟨secret code : clave secreta⟩
codeine ['koːˌdiːn] *n* : codeína *f*
codex ['koːˌdɛks] *n, pl* **-dexes** [-ˌdɛksəz] *or* **-dices** [-dəˌsiːz] : códice *m*
codger ['kɑʤər] *n* : viejo *m*, vejete *m*
codify ['kɑdəˌfaɪ, 'koː-] *vt* **-fied; -fying** : codificar
coeducation [ˌkoːˌɛʤə'keɪʃən] *n* : coeducación *f*, enseñanza *f* mixta
coeducational [ˌkoːˌɛʤə'keɪʃənəl] *adj* : mixto
coefficient [ˌkoːə'fɪʃənt] *n* : coeficiente *m*
coerce [ko'ərs] *vt* **-erced; -ercing** : coaccionar, forzar, obligar
coercion [ko'ərʒən, -ʃən] *n* : coacción *f*
coercive [ko'ərsɪv] *adj* : coactivo
coexist [ˌkoːɪg'zɪst] *vi* : coexistir
coexistence [ˌkoːɪg'zɪstən*t*s] *n* : coexistencia *f*
coffee ['kɔfi] *n* : café *m*
coffeepot ['kɔfiˌpɑt] *n* : cafetera *f*
coffee table *n* : mesa *f* de centro
coffer ['kɔfər] *n* : cofre *m*
coffin ['kɔfən] *n* : ataúd *m*, féretro *m*
cog ['kɑg] *n* : diente *m* (de una rueda dentada)
cogent ['koːʤənt] *adj* : convincente, persuasivo
cogitate ['kɑʤəˌteɪt] *vi* **-tated; -tating** : reflexionar, meditar, discurrir
cogitation [ˌkɑʤə'teɪʃən] *n* : reflexión *f*, meditación *f*
cognac ['koːnˌjæk] *n* : coñac *m*
cognate ['kɑgˌneɪt] *adj* : relacionado, afín
cognition [kɑg'nɪʃən] *n* : cognición *f*
cognitive ['kɑgnəṭɪv] *adj* : cognitivo
cogwheel ['kɑgˌ*h*wiːl] *n* : rueda *f* dentada
cohabit [ˌkoː'hæbət] *vi* : cohabitar
cohere [ko'hɪr] *vi* **-hered; -hering 1** ADHERE : adherirse, pegarse **2** : ser coherente o congruente
coherence [ko'hɪrən*t*s] *n* : coherencia *f*, congruencia *f*
coherent [ko'hɪrənt] *adj* : coherente, congruente — **coherently** *adv*
cohesion [ko'hiːʒən] *n* : cohesión *f*
cohesive [koː'hiːsɪv, -zɪv] *adj* : cohesivo
cohort ['koːˌhɔrt] *n* **1** : cohorte *f* (de soldados) **2** COMPANION : compañero *m*, -ra *f*; colega *mf*
coiffure [kwɑ'fjʊr] *n* : peinado *m*
coil[1] ['kɔɪl] *vt* : enrollar — *vi* : enrollarse, enroscarse
coil[2] *n* : rollo *m* (de cuerda, etc.), espiral *f* (de humo)
coin[1] ['kɔɪn] *vt* **1** MINT : acuñar (moneda) **2** INVENT : acuñar, crear, inventar ⟨to coin a phrase : como se suele decir⟩
coin[2] *n* : moneda *f*
coincide [ˌkoːɪn'saɪd, 'koːɪnˌsaɪd] *vi* **-cided; -ciding** : coincidir
coincidence [ko'ɪn*t*sədən*t*s] *n* : coincidencia *f*, casualidad *f* ⟨what a coincidence! : ¡qué casualidad!⟩
coincident [ko'ɪn*t*sədənt] *adj* : coincidente, concurrente
coincidental [koˌɪn*t*sə'dɛntəl] *adj* : casual, accidental, fortuito
coitus ['koːəṭəs] *n* : coito *m*
coke ['koːk] *n* : coque *m*
colander ['kɑləndər, 'kʌ-] *n* : colador *m*
cold[1] ['koːld] *adj* : frío ⟨it's cold out : hace frío⟩ ⟨a cold reception : una fría recepción⟩ ⟨in cold blood : a sangre fría⟩
cold[2] *n* **1** : frío *m* ⟨to feel the cold : sentir frío⟩ **2** : resfriado *m*, catarro *m* ⟨to catch a cold : resfriarse⟩
cold–blooded ['koːld'blʌdəd] *adj* **1** CRUEL : cruel, despiadado **2** : de sangre fría (dícese de los reptiles, etc.)
coldly ['koːldli] *adv* : fríamente, con frialdad
coldness ['koːldnəs] *n* : frialdad *f* (de una persona o una actitud), frío *m* (de la temperatura)
coleslaw ['koːlˌslɔ] *n* : ensalada *f* de col
colic ['kɑlɪk] *n* : cólico *m*
coliseum [ˌkɑlə'siːəm] *n* : coliseo *m*, arena *f*
collaborate [kə'læbəˌreɪt] *vi* **-rated; -rating** : colaborar
collaboration [kəˌlæbə'reɪʃə n] *n* : colaboración *f*
collaborator [kə'læbəˌreɪṭər] *n* **1** COLLEAGUE : colaborador *m*, -dora *f* **2** TRAITOR : colaboracionista *mf*
collage [kə'lɑʒ] *n* : collage *m*
collapse[1] [kə'læps] *vi* **-lapsed; -lapsing 1** : derrumbarse, desplomarse, hundirse ⟨the building collapsed : el edificio

se derrumbó⟩ **2** FALL : desplomarse, caerse ⟨he collapsed on the bed : se desplomó en la cama⟩ ⟨to collapse with laughter : morirse de risa⟩ **3** FAIL : fracasar, quebrar, arruinarse **4** FOLD : plegarse

collapse[2] *n* **1** FALL : derrumbe *m*, desplome *m* **2** BREAKDOWN, FAILURE : fracaso *m*, colapso *m* (físico), quiebra *f* (económica)

collapsible [kə'læpsəbəl] *adj* : plegable

collar[1] ['kɑlər] *vt* : agarrar, atrapar

collar[2] *n* : cuello *m*

collarbone ['kɑlər,bo:n] *n* : clavícula *f*

collate [kə'leɪt; 'kɑ,leɪt, 'ko:-] *vt* **-lated; -lating 1** COMPARE : cotejar, comparar **2** : ordenar, recopilar (páginas)

collateral[1] [kə'lætərəl] *adj* : colateral

collateral[2] *n* : garantía *f*, fianza *f*, prenda *f*

colleague ['kɑ,li:g] *n* : colega *mf*; compañero *m*, -ra *f*

collect[1] [kə'lɛkt] *vt* **1** GATHER : recopilar, reunir, recoger ⟨she collected her thoughts : puso en orden sus ideas⟩ **2** : coleccionar, juntar ⟨to collect stamps : coleccionar timbres⟩ **3** : cobrar (una deuda), recaudar (un impuesto) **4** DRAW : cobrar, percibir (un sueldo, etc.) — *vi* **1** ACCUMULATE : acumularse, juntarse **2** CONGREGATE : congregarse, reunirse

collect[2] *adv & adj* : por cobrar, a cobro revertido

collectible *or* **collectable** [kə'lɛktəbəl] *adj* : coleccionable

collection [kə'lɛkʃən] *n* **1** COLLECTING : colecta *f* (de contribuciones), cobro *m* (de deudas), recaudación *f* (de impuestos) **2** GROUP : colección *f* (de objetos), grupo *m* (de personas)

collective[1] [kə'lɛktɪv] *adj* : colectivo — **collectively** *adv*

collective[2] *n* : colectivo *m*

collector [kə'lɛktər] *n* **1** : coleccionista *mf* (de objetos) **2** : cobrador *m*, -dora *f* (de deudas)

college ['kɑlɪʤ] *n* **1** : universidad *f* **2** : colegio *m* (de electores o profesionales)

collegiate [kə'li:ʤət] *adj* : universitario

collide [kə'laɪd] *vi* **-lided; -liding** : chocar, colisionar, estrellarse

collie ['kɑli] *n* : collie *mf*

collision [kə'lɪʒən] *n* : choque *m*, colisión *f*

colloquial [kə'lo:kwiəl] *adj* : coloquial

colloquialism [kə'lo:kwiə,lɪzəm] *n* : expresión *f* coloquial

collusion [kə'lu:ʒən] *n* : colusión *f*

cologne [kə'lo:n] *n* : colonia *f*

Colombian [kə'lʌmbiən] *n* : colombiano *m*, -na *f* — **Colombian** *adj*

colon[1] ['ko:lən] *n, pl* **colons** *or* **cola** [-lə] : colon *m* (de los intestinos)

colon[2] *n, pl* **colons** : dos puntos *mpl* (signo ortográfico)

colonel ['kərnəl] *n* : coronel *m*

colonial[1] [kə'lo:niəl] *adj* : colonial

colonial[2] *n* : colono *m*, -na *f*

colonist ['kɑlənɪst] *n* : colono *m*, -na *f*; colonizador *m*, -dora *f*

colonization [,kɑlənə'zeɪʃən] *n* : colonización *f*

colonize ['kɑlə,naɪz] *vt* **-nized; -nizing 1** : establecer una colonia en **2** SETTLE : colonizar

colonnade [,kɑlə'neɪd] *n* : columnata *f*

colony ['kɑləni] *n, pl* **-nies** : colonia *f*

color[1] ['kʌlər] *vt* **1** : colorear, pintar **2** INFLUENCE : influir en, influenciar — *vi* BLUSH : sonrojarse, ruborizarse

color[2] *n* **1** : color *m* ⟨primary colors : colores primarios⟩ **2** INTEREST, VIVIDNESS : color *m*, colorido *m* ⟨local color : color local⟩

coloration [kələ'reɪʃən] *n* : coloración *f*

color-blind ['kʌlər,blaɪnd] *adj* : daltónico

color blindness *n* : daltonismo *m*

colored ['kʌlərd] *adj* **1** : de color (dícese de los objetos) **2** : de color, negro (dícese de las personas)

colorfast ['kʌlər,fæst] *adj* : que no se destiñe

colorful ['kʌlərfəl] *adj* **1** : lleno de colorido, de colores vivos **2** PICTURESQUE, STRIKING : pintoresco, llamativo

coloring ['kələrɪŋ] *n* **1** : color *m*, colorido *m* **2 food coloring** : colorante *m*

colorless ['kʌlərləs] *adj* **1** : incoloro, sin color **2** DULL : soso, aburrido

colossal [kə'lɑsəl] *adj* : colosal

colossus [kə'lɑsəs] *n, pl* **-si** [-,saɪ] : coloso *m*

colt ['ko:lt] *n* : potro *m*, potranco *m*

column ['kɑləm] *n* : columna *f*

columnist ['kɑləmnɪst, -ləmɪst] *n* : columnista *mf*

coma ['ko:mə] *n* : coma *m*, estado *m* de coma

Comanche [kə'mænʧi] *n* : comanche *mf* — **Comanche** *adj*

comatose ['ko:mə,to:s, 'kɑ-] *adj* : comatoso, en estado de coma

comb[1] ['ko:m] *vt* **1** : peinar (el pelo) **2** SEARCH : peinar, rastrear, registrar a fondo

comb[2] *n* **1** : peine *m* **2** : cresta *f* (de un gallo)

combat[1] [kəm'bæt, 'kɑm,bæt] *vt* **-bated** *or* **-batted; -bating** *or* **-batting** : combatir, luchar contra

combat[2] ['kɑm,bæt] *n* : combate *m*, lucha *f*

combatant [kəm'bætənt] *n* : combatiente *mf*

combative [kəm'bætɪv] *adj* : combativo

combination [,kɑmbə'neɪʃən] *n* : combinación *f*

combine[1] [kəm'baɪn] *v* **-bined; -bining** *vt* : combinar, aunar — *vi* : combinarse, mezclarse

combine[2] ['kɑm,baɪn] *n* **1** ALLIANCE : alianza *f* comercial o política **2** HARVESTER : cosechadora *f*

combustible [kəm'bʌstəbəl] *adj* : inflamable, combustible

combustion [kəm'bʌsʧən] *n* : combustión *f*

come ['kʌm] *vi* **came** ['keɪm]; **come; coming 1** APPROACH : venir, aproximarse ⟨here they come : acá vienen⟩ **2** ARRIVE : venir, llegar, alcanzar ⟨they came yesterday : vinieron ayer⟩ **3** ORIGINATE : venir, provenir ⟨this wine comes from France : este vino viene de Francia⟩ **4** AMOUNT : llegar, ascender ⟨the investment came to two million : la inversión llegó a dos millones⟩ **5 to come clean** : confesar, desahogar la conciencia **6 to come into** ACQUIRE : adquirir ⟨to come into a fortune : heredar una fortuna⟩ **7 to come off** SUCCEED : tener éxito, ser un éxito **8 to come out** : salir, aparecer, publicarse **9 to come to** REVIVE : recobrar el conocimiento, volver en sí **10 to come to pass** HAPPEN : acontecer **11 to come to terms** : llegar a un acuerdo

comeback ['kʌm,bæk] *n* **1** RETORT : réplica *f*, respuesta *f* **2** RETURN : retorno *m*, regreso *m* ⟨the champion announced his comeback : el campeón anunció su regreso⟩

come back *vi* **1** RETORT : replicar, contestar **2** RETURN : volver ⟨come back here! : ¡vuelve acá!⟩ ⟨that style's coming back : ese estilo está volviendo⟩

comedian [kə'mi:diən] *n* : cómico *m*, -ca *f*; humorista *mf*

comedienne [kə,mi:di'ɛn] *n* : cómica *f*, humorista *f*

comedy ['kɑmədi] *n, pl* **-dies** : comedia *f*

comely ['kʌmli] *adj* **-lier; -est** : bello, bonito

comet ['kɑmət] *n* : cometa *m*

comfort[1] ['kʌmpfərt] *vt* **1** CHEER : confortar, alentar **2** CONSOLE : consolar

comfort[2] *n* **1** CONSOLATION : consuelo *m* **2** WELL-BEING : confort *m*, bienestar *m* **3** CONVENIENCE : comodidad *f* ⟨the comforts of home : las comodidades del hogar⟩

comfortable ['kʌmpfərṭəbəl, 'kʌmpftə-] *adj* : cómodo, confortable — **comfortably** ['kʌmpfərṭəbli, 'kʌmpftə-] *adv*

comforter ['kʌmpfərṭər] *n* QUILT : edredón *m*, cobertor *m*

comic[1] ['kɑmɪk] *adj* : cómico, humorístico

comic[2] *n* **1** COMEDIAN : cómico *m*, -ca *f*; humorista *mf* **2** *or* **comic book** : historieta *f*, cómic *m*

comical ['kɑmɪkəl] *adj* : cómico, gracioso, chistoso

comic strip *n* : tira *f* cómica, historieta *f*

coming ['kʌmɪŋ] *adj* : siguiente, próximo, que viene

comma ['kɑmə] *n* : coma *f*

command[1] [kə'mænd] *vt* **1** ORDER : ordenar, mandar **2** CONTROL, DIRECT : comandar, tener el mando de — *vi* **1** : dar órdenes **2** GOVERN : estar al mando *m*, gobernar

command[2] *n* **1** CONTROL, LEADERSHIP : mando *m*, control *m*, dirección *f* **2** ORDER : orden *f*, mandato *m* **3** MASTERY : maestría *f*, destreza *f*, dominio *m* **4** : tropa *f* asignada a un comandante

commandant ['kɑmən,dɑnt, -,dænt] *n* : comandante *mf*

commandeer [,kɑmən'dɪr] *vt* : piratear, secuestrar (un vehículo, etc.)

commander [kə'mændər] *n* : comandante *mf*

commandment [kə'mændmənt] *n* : mandamiento *m*, orden *f* ⟨the Ten Commandments : los diez mandamientos⟩

commando [kə'mændo:] *n* : comando *m*

commemorate [kə'mɛmə,reɪt] *vt* **-rated; -rating** : conmemorar

commemoration [kə,mɛmə'reɪʃən] *n* : conmemoración *f*

commemorative [kə'mɛmrəṭɪv, -'mɛmə,reɪṭɪv] *adj* : conmemorativo

commence [kə'mɛnts] *v* **-menced; -mencing** *vt* : iniciar, comenzar — *vi* : iniciarse, comenzar

commencement [kə'mɛntsmənt] *n* **1** BEGINNING : inicio *m*, comienzo *m* **2** : ceremonia *f* de graduación

commend [kə'mɛnd] *vt* **1** ENTRUST : encomendar **2** RECOMMEND : recomendar **3** PRAISE : elogiar, alabar

commendable [kə'mɛndəbəl] *adj* : loable, meritorio, encomiable

commendation [,kɑmən'deɪʃən, -,mɛn-] *n* : elogio *m*, encomio *m*

commensurate [kə'mɛntsərət, -'mɛnʧʊrət] *adj* : proporcionado ⟨commensurate with : en proporción a⟩

comment[1] ['kɑ,mɛnt] *vi* **1** : hacer comentarios **2 to comment on** : comentar, hacer observaciones sobre

comment[2] *n* : comentario *m*, observación *f*

commentary ['kɑmən,tɛri] *n, pl* **-taries** : comentario *m*, crónica *f* (deportiva)

commentator ['kɑmən,teɪṭər] *n* : comentarista *mf*, cronista *mf* (de deportes)

commerce ['kɑmərs] *n* : comercio *m*

commercial[1] [kə'mərʃəl] *adj* : comercial — **commercially** *adv*

commercial[2] *n* : comercial *m*

commercialize [kə'mərʃə,laɪz] *vt* **-ized; -izing** : comercializar

commiserate [kə'mɪzə,reɪt] *vi* **-ated; -ating** : compadecerse, consolarse

commiseration [kə,mɪzə'reɪʃən] *n* : conmiseración *f*

commission[1] [kə'mɪʃən] *vt* **1** : nombrar (un oficial) **2** : comisionar, encargar ⟨to commission a painting : encargar una pintura⟩

commission² *n* **1** : nombramiento *m* (al grado de oficial) **2** COMMITTEE : comisión *f*, comité *m* **3** COMMITTING : comisión *f*, realización *f* (de un acto) **4** PERCENTAGE : comisión *f* ⟨sales commissions : comisiones de venta⟩
commissioned officer *n* : oficial *mf*
commissioner [kəˈmɪʃənər] *n* **1** : comisionado *m*, -da *f*; miembro *m* de una comisión **2** : comisario *m*, -ria *f* (de policía, etc.)
commit [kəˈmɪt] *vt* **-mitted; -mitting 1** ENTRUST : encomendar, confiar **2** CONFINE : internar (en un hospital), encarcelar (en una prisión) **3** PERPETRATE : cometer ⟨to commit a crime : cometer un crimen⟩ **4 to commit oneself** : comprometerse
commitment [kəˈmɪtmənt] *n* **1** RESPONSIBILITY : compromiso *m*, responsabilidad *f* **2** DEDICATION : dedicación *f*, devoción *f* ⟨commitment to the cause : devoción a la causa⟩
committee [kəˈmɪt̬i] *n* : comité *m*
commodious [kəˈmo:diəs] *adj* SPACIOUS : amplio, espacioso
commodity [kəˈmɑdət̬i] *n, pl* **-ties** : artículo *m* de comercio, mercancía *f*, mercadería *f*
commodore [ˈkɑməˌdor] *n* : comodoro *m*
common¹ [ˈkɑmən] *adj* **1** PUBLIC : común, público ⟨the common good : el bien común⟩ **2** SHARED : común ⟨a common interest : un interés común⟩ **3** GENERAL : común, general ⟨it's common knowledge : todo el mundo lo sabe⟩ **4** ORDINARY : ordinario, común y corriente ⟨the common man : el hombre medio, el hombre de la calle⟩
common² *n* **1** : tierra *f* comunal **2 in ~** : en común
common cold *n* : resfriado *m* común
common denominator *n* : denominador *m* común
commoner [ˈkɑmənər] *n* : plebeyo *m*, -ya *f*
commonly [ˈkɑmənli] *adv* **1** FREQUENTLY : comúnmente, frecuentemente **2** USUALLY : normalmente
common noun *n* : nombre *m* común
commonplace¹ [ˈkɑmənˌpleɪs] *adj* : común, ordinario
commonplace² *n* : cliché *m*, tópico *m*
common sense *n* : sentido *m* común
commonwealth [ˈkɑmənˌwɛlθ] *n* : entidad *f* política ⟨the British Commonwealth : la Mancomunidad Británica⟩
commotion [kəˈmo:ʃən] *n* **1** RUCKUS : alboroto *m*, jaleo *m*, escándalo *m* **2** STIR, UPSET : revuelo *m*, conmoción *f*
communal [kəˈmju:nəl] *adj* : comunal
commune¹ [kəˈmju:n] *vi* **-muned; -muning** : estar en comunión
commune² [ˈkɑˌmju:n, kəˈmju:n] *n* : comuna *f*
communicable [kəˈmju:nɪkəbəl] *adj* CONTAGIOUS : transmisible, contagioso
communicate [kəˈmju:nəˌkeɪt] *v* **-cated; -cating** *vt* **1** CONVEY : comunicar, expresar, hacer saber **2** TRANSMIT : transmitir (una enfermedad), contagiar — *vi* : comunicarse, expresarse
communication [kəˌmju:nəˈkeɪʃən] *n* : comunicación *f*
communicative [kəˈmju:nɪˌkeɪt̬ɪv, -kət̬ɪv] *adj* : comunicativo
communion [kəˈmju:njən] *n* **1** SHARING : comunión *f* **2 Communion** : comunión *f*, eucaristía *f*
communiqué [kəˈmju:nəˌkeɪ, -ˌmju:nəˈkeɪ] *n* : comunicado *m*
communism *or* **Communism** [ˈkɑmjəˌnɪzəm] *n* : comunismo *m*
communist¹ *or* **Communist** [ˈkɑmjəˌnɪst] *adj* : comunista ⟨the Communist Party : el Partido Comunista⟩
communist² *or* **Communist** *n* : comunista *mf*
communistic *or* **Communistic** [ˌkɑmjəˈnɪstɪk] *adj* : comunista
community [kəˈmju:nət̬i] *n, pl* **-ties** : comunidad *f*
commute [kəˈmju:t] *v* **-muted; -muting** *vt* REDUCE : conmutar, reducir (una sentencia) — *vi* : viajar de la residencia al trabajo
commuter [kəˈmju:t̬ər] *n* : persona *f* que viaja diariamente al trabajo
compact¹ [kəmˈpækt, ˈkɑmˌpækt] *vt* : compactar, consolidar, comprimir
compact² [kəmˈpækt, ˈkɑmˌpækt] *adj* **1** DENSE, SOLID : compacto, macizo, denso **2** CONCISE : breve, conciso
compact³ [ˈkɑmˌpækt] *n* **1** AGREEMENT : acuerdo *m*, pacto *m* **2** : polvera *f*, estuche *m* de maquillaje **3** *or* **compact car** : auto *m* compacto
compact disc [ˈkɑmˌpæktˈdɪsk] *n* : disco *m* compacto, compact disc *m*
compactly [kəmˈpæktli, ˈkɑmˌpækt-] *adv* **1** DENSELY : densamente, macizamente **2** CONCISELY : concisamente, brevemente
companion [kəmˈpænjən] *n* **1** COMRADE : compañero *m*, -ra *f*; acompañante *mf* **2** MATE : pareja *f* (de un zapato, etc.)
companionable [kəmˈpænjənəbəl] *adj* : sociable, amigable
companionship [kəmˈpænjənˌʃɪp] *n* : compañerismo *m*, camaradería *f*
company [ˈkʌmpəni] *n, pl* **-nies 1** FIRM : compañía *f*, empresa *f* **2** GROUP : compañía *f* (de actores o soldados) **3** GUESTS : visita *f* ⟨we have company : tenemos visita⟩
comparable [ˈkɑmpərəbəl] *adj* : comparable, parecido
comparative¹ [kəmˈpærət̬ɪv] *adj* RELATIVE : comparativo, relativo — **comparatively** *adv*
comparative² *n* : comparativo *m*

compare[1] [kəm'pær] *v* **-pared; -paring** *vt* : comparar — *vi* **to compare with** : poder comparar con, tener comparación con
compare[2] *n* : comparación *f* ⟨beyond compare : sin igual, sin par⟩
comparison [kəm'pærəsən] *n* : comparación *f*
compartment [kəm'pɑrtmənt] *n* : compartimento *m*, compartimiento *m*
compass ['kʌmpəs, 'kɑm-] *n* **1** RANGE, SCOPE : alcance *m*, extensión *f*, límites *mpl* **2** : compás *m* (para trazar circunferencias) **3** : compás *m*, brújula *f* ⟨the points of the compass : los puntos cardinales⟩
compassion [kəm'pæʃən] *n* : compasión *f*, piedad *f*, misericordia *f*
compassionate [kəm'pæʃənət] *adj* : compasivo
compatibility [kəm,pæt̬ə'bɪlət̬i] *n* : compatibilidad *f*
compatible [kəm'pæt̬əbəl] *adj* : compatible, afín
compatriot [kəm'peɪtriət, -'pæ-] *n* : compatriota *mf*; paisano *m*, -na *f*
compel [kəm'pɛl] *vt* **-pelled; -pelling** : obligar, compeler
compelling [kəm'pɛlɪŋ] *adj* **1** FORCEFUL : fuerte **2** ENGAGING : absorbente **3** PERSUASIVE : persuasivo, convincente
compendium [kəm'pɛndiəm] *n, pl* **-diums** *or* **-dia** [-diə] : compendio *m*
compensate ['kɑmpən,seɪt] *v* **-sated; -sating** *vi* **to compensate for** : compensar — *vt* : indemnizar, compensar
compensation [,kɑmpən'seɪʃən] *n* : compensación *f*, indemnización *f*
compensatory [kəm'pɛntsə,tori] *adj* : compensatorio
compete [kəm'pi:t] *vi* **-peted; -peting** : competir, contender, rivalizar
competence ['kɑmpətənts] *n* : competencia *f*, aptitud *f*
competency ['kɑmpətəntsi] → **competence**
competent ['kɑmpətənt] *adj* : competente, capaz
competition [,kɑmpə'tɪʃən] *n* : competencia *f*, concurso *m*
competitive [kəm'pɛt̬ət̬ɪv] *adj* : competitivo
competitor [kəm'pɛt̬ət̬ər] *n* : competidor *m*, -dora *f*
compilation [,kɑmpə'leɪʃən] *n* : recopilación *f*, compilación *f*
compile [kəm'paɪl] *vt* **-piled; -piling** : compilar, recopilar
complacency [kəm'pleɪsəntsi] *n* : satisfacción *f* consigo mismo, suficiencia *f*
complacent [kəm'pleɪsənt] *adj* : satisfecho de sí mismo, suficiente
complain [kəm'pleɪn] *vi* **1** GRIPE : quejarse, regañar, rezongar **2** PROTEST : reclamar, protestar
complaint [kəm'pleɪnt] *n* **1** GRIPE : queja *f* **2** AILMENT : afección *f*, dolencia *f* **3** ACCUSATION : reclamo *m*, acusación *f*
complement[1] ['kɑmplə,mɛnt] *vt* : complementar
complement[2] ['kɑmpləmənt] *n* : complemento *m*
complementary [,kɑmplə'mɛntəri] *adj* : complementario
complete[1] [kəm'pli:t] *vt* **-pleted; -pleting** **1** : completar, hacer entero ⟨this piece completes the collection : esta pieza completa la colección⟩ **2** FINISH : completar, acabar, terminar ⟨she completed her studies : completó sus estudios⟩
complete[2] *adj* **-pleter; -est** **1** WHOLE : completo, entero, íntegro **2** FINISHED : terminado, acabado **3** TOTAL : completo, total, absoluto
completely [kəm'pli:tli] *adv* : completamente, totalmente
completion [kəm'pli:ʃən] *n* : finalización *f*, cumplimiento *m*
complex[1] [kɑm'plɛks, kəm-; 'kɑm-,plɛks] *adj* : complejo, complicado
complex[2] ['kɑm,plɛks] *n* : complejo *m*
complexion [kəm'plɛkʃən] *n* : cutis *m*, tez *f* ⟨of dark complexion : de tez morena⟩
complexity [kəm'plɛksət̬i, kɑm-] *n, pl* **-ties** : complejidad *f*
compliance [kəm'plaɪənts] *n* : conformidad *f* ⟨in compliance with the law : conforme a la ley⟩
compliant [kəm'plaɪənt] *adj* : dócil, sumiso
complicate ['kɑmplə,keɪt] *vt* **-cated; -cating** : complicar
complicated ['kɑmplə,keɪt̬əd] *adj* : complicado
complication [,kɑmplə'keɪʃən] *n* : complicación *f*
complicity [kəm'plɪsət̬i] *n, pl* **-ties** : complicidad *f*
compliment[1] ['kɑmplə,mɛnt] *vt* : halagar, florear *Mex*
compliment[2] ['kɑmpləmənt] *n* **1** : halago *m*, cumplido *m* **2 compliments** *npl* : saludos *mpl* ⟨give them my compliments : déles saludos de mi parte⟩
complimentary [,kɑmplə'mɛntəri] *adj* **1** FLATTERING : halagador, halagüeño **2** FREE : de cortesía, gratis
comply [kəm'plaɪ] *vi* **-plied; -plying** : cumplir, acceder, obedecer
component[1] [kəm'po:nənt, 'kɑm-,po:-] *adj* : componente
component[2] *n* : componente *m*, elemento *m*, pieza *f*
compose [kəm'po:z] *vt* **-posed; -posing** **1** : componer, crear ⟨to compose a melody : componer una melodía⟩ **2** CALM : calmar, serenar ⟨to compose oneself : serenarse⟩ **3** CONSTITUTE : constar, componer ⟨to be composed of : constar de⟩ **4** : componer (un texto a imprimirse)
composer [kəm'po:zər] *n* : compositor *m*, -tora *f*

composite[1] [kɑm'pɑzət, kəm-; 'kɑmpəzət] *adj* : compuesto (de varias partes)
composite[2] *n* : compuesto *m*, mezcla *f*
composition [ˌkɑmpə'zɪʃən] *n* **1** MAKEUP : composición *f* **2** ESSAY : ensayo *m*, trabajo *m*
compost ['kɑmˌpo:st] *n* : abono *m* vegetal
composure [kəm'po:ʒər] *n* : compostura *f*, serenidad *f*
compound[1] [kɑm'paʊnd, kəm-; 'kɑmˌpaʊnd] *vt* **1** COMBINE, COMPOSE : combinar, componer **2** AUGMENT : agravar, aumentar ⟨to compound a problem : agravar un problema⟩
compound[2] ['kɑmˌpaʊnd; kɑm'paʊnd, kəm-] *adj* : compuesto ⟨compound interest : interés compuesto⟩
compound[3] ['kɑmˌpaʊnd] *n* **1** MIXTURE : compuesto *m*, mezcla *f* **2** ENCLOSURE : recinto *m* (de residencias, etc.)
compound fracture *n* : fractura *f* complicada
comprehend [ˌkɑmprɪ'hɛnd] *vt* **1** UNDERSTAND : comprender, entender **2** INCLUDE : comprender, incluir, abarcar
comprehensible [ˌkɑmprɪ'hɛn*t*səbəl] *adj* : comprensible
comprehension [ˌkɑmprɪ'hɛnʧən] *n* : comprensión *f*
comprehensive [ˌkɑmprɪ'hɛn*t*sɪv] *adj* **1** INCLUSIVE : inclusivo, exhaustivo **2** BROAD : extenso, amplio
compress[1] [kəm'prɛs] *vt* : comprimir
compress[2] ['kɑmˌprɛs] *n* : compresa *f*
compression [kəm'prɛʃən] *n* : compresión *f*
compressor [kəm'prɛsər] *n* : compresor *m*
comprise [kəm'praɪz] *vt* **-prised; -prising** **1** INCLUDE : comprender, incluir **2** : componerse de, constar de ⟨the installation comprises several buildings : la instalación está compuesta de varios edificios⟩
compromise[1] ['kɑmprəˌmaɪz] *v* **-mised; -mising** *vi* : transigir, avenirse — *vt* JEOPARDIZE : comprometer, poner en peligro
compromise[2] *n* : acuerdo *m* mutuo, compromiso *m*
comptroller [kən'tro:lər, 'kɑmp-ˌtro:-] *n* : contralor *m*, -lora *f*; interventor *m*, -tora *f*
compulsion [kəm'pʌlʃən] *n* **1** COERCION : coacción *f* **2** URGE : compulsión *f*, impulso *m*
compulsive [kəm'pʌlsɪv] *adj* : compulsivo
compulsory [kəm'pʌlsəri] *adj* : obligatorio
compunction [kəm'pʌŋkʃən] *n* **1** QUALM : reparo *m*, escrúpulo *m* **2** REMORSE : remordimiento *m*
computation [ˌkɑmpjʊ'teɪʃən] *n* : cálculo *m*, cómputo *m*
compute [kəm'pju:t] *vt* **-puted; -puting** : computar, calcular
computer [kəm'pju:ţər] *n* : computadora *f*, computador *m*, ordenador *m Spain*
computerize [kəm'pju:ţəˌraɪz] *vt* **-ized; -izing** : computarizar, informatizar
comrade ['kɑmˌræd] *n* : camarada *mf*; compañero *m*, -ra *f*
con[1] ['kɑn] *vt* **conned; conning** SWINDLE : estafar, timar
con[2] *adv* : contra
con[3] *n* : contra *m* ⟨the pros and cons : los pros y los contras⟩
concave [kɑn'keɪv, 'kɑnˌkeɪv] *adj* : cóncavo
conceal [kən'si:l] *vt* : esconder, ocultar, disimular
concealment [kən'si:lmənt] *n* : escondimiento *m*, ocultación *f*
concede [kən'si:d] *vt* **-ceded; -ceding** **1** ALLOW, GRANT : conceder **2** ADMIT : conceder, reconocer ⟨to concede defeat : reconocer la derrota⟩
conceit [kən'si:t] *n* : engreimiento *m*, presunción *f*
conceited [kən'si:ţəd] *adj* : presumido, engreído, presuntuoso
conceivable [kən'si:vəbəl] *adj* : concebible, imaginable
conceivably [kən'si:vəbli] *adv* : posiblemente, de manera concebible
conceive [kən'si:v] *v* **-ceived; -ceiving** *vi* : concebir, embarazarse — *vt* IMAGINE : concebir, imaginar
concentrate[1] ['kɑn*t*sənˌtreɪt] *v* **-trated; -trating** *vt* : concentrar — *vi* : concentrarse
concentrate[2] *n* : concentrado *m*
concentration [ˌkɑn*t*sən'treɪʃən] *n* : concentración *f*
concentric [kən'sɛntrɪk] *adj* : concéntrico
concept ['kɑnˌsɛpt] *n* : concepto *m*, idea *f*
conception [kən'sɛpʃən] *n* **1** : concepción *f* (de un bebé) **2** IDEA : concepto *m*, idea *f*
concern[1] [kən'sərn] *vt* **1** : tratarse de, tener que ver con ⟨the novel concerns a sailor : la novela se trata de un marinero⟩ **2** INVOLVE : concernir, incumbir a, afectar ⟨that does not concern me : eso no me incumbe⟩
concern[2] *n* **1** AFFAIR : asunto *m* **2** WORRY : inquietud *f*, preocupación *f* **3** BUSINESS : negocio *m*
concerned [kən'sərnd] *adj* **1** ANXIOUS : preocupado, ansioso **2** INTERESTED, INVOLVED : interesado, afectado
concerning [kən'sərnɪŋ] *prep* REGARDING : con respecto a, acerca de, sobre
concert ['kɑnˌsərt] *n* **1** AGREEMENT : concierto *m*, acuerdo *m* **2** : concierto *m* (musical)
concerted [kən'sərţəd] *adj* : concertado, coordinado ⟨to make a concerted effort : coordinar los esfuerzos⟩
concertina [ˌkɑn*t*sər'ti:nə] *n* : concertina *f*

concerto [kən'ʧɛrt̬o:] *n, pl* **-ti** [-t̬i, -ˌti:] *or* **-tos** : concierto *m* ⟨violin concerto : concierto para violín⟩

concession [kən'sɛʃən] *n* : concesión *f*

conch ['kaŋk, 'kanʧ] *n, pl* **conchs** ['kaŋks] *or* **conches** ['kanʧəz] : caracol *m* (animal), caracola *f* (concha)

conciliatory [kən'sɪliəˌtori] *adj* : conciliador, conciliatorio

concise [kən'saɪs] *adj* : conciso, breve — **concisely** *adv*

conclave ['kanˌkleɪv] *n* : cónclave *m*

conclude [kən'klu:d] *v* **-cluded; -cluding** *vt* **1** END : concluir, finalizar ⟨to conclude a meeting : concluir una reunión⟩ **2** DECIDE : concluir, llegar a la conclusión de — *vi* END : concluir, terminar

conclusion [kən'klu:ʒən] *n* **1** INFERENCE : conclusión *f* **2** END : fin *m*, final *m*

conclusive [kən'klu:sɪv] *adj* : concluyente, decisivo — **conclusively** *adv*

concoct [kən'kakt, kan-] *vt* **1** PREPARE : preparar, confeccionar **2** DEVISE : inventar, tramar

concoction [kən'kakʃən] *n* : invención *f*, mejunje *m*, brebaje *m*

concomitant [kən'kamət̬ənt] *adj* : concomitante

concord ['kanˌkɔrd, 'kaŋ-] *n* **1** HARMONY : concordia *f*, armonía *f* **2** AGREEMENT : acuerdo *m*

concordance [kən'kɔrdənts] *n* : concordancia *f*

concourse ['kanˌkors] *n* : explanada *f*, salón *m* (para pasajeros)

concrete[1] [kan'kri:t, 'kanˌkri:t] *adj* **1** REAL : concreto ⟨concrete objects : objetos concretos⟩ **2** SPECIFIC : determinado, específico **3** : de concreto, de hormigón ⟨concrete walls : paredes de concreto⟩

concrete[2] ['kanˌkri:t, kan'kri:t] *n* : concreto *m*, hormigón *m*

concur [kən'kər] *vi* **concurred; concurring** **1** COINCIDE : concurrir, coincidir **2** AGREE : concurrir, estar de acuerdo

concurrent [kən'kərənt] *adj* : concurrente, simultáneo

concussion [kən'kʌʃən] *n* : conmoción *f* cerebral

condemn [kən'dɛm] *vt* **1** CENSURE : condenar, reprobar, censurar **2** : declarar insalubre (alimentos), declarar ruinoso (un edificio) **3** SENTENCE : condenar ⟨condemned to death : condenado a muerte⟩

condemnation [ˌkanˌdɛm'neɪʃən] *n* : condena *f*, reprobación *f*

condensation [ˌkanˌdɛn'seɪʃən, -dən-] *n* : condensación *f*

condense [kən'dɛnts] *v* **-densed; -densing** *vt* **1** ABRIDGE : condensar, resumir **2** : condensar (vapor, etc.) — *vi* : condensarse

condescend [ˌkandɪ'sɛnd] *vi* **1** DEIGN : condescender, dignarse **2 to condescend to someone** : tratar a alguien con condescendencia

condescension [ˌkandɪ'sɛnʧən] *n* : condescendencia *f*

condiment ['kandəmənt] *n* : condimento *m*

condition[1] [kən'dɪʃən] *vt* **1** DETERMINE : condicionar, determinar **2** : acondicionar (el pelo o el aire), poner en forma (el cuerpo)

condition[2] *n* **1** STIPULATION : condición *f*, estipulación *f* ⟨on the condition that : a condición de que⟩ **2** STATE : condición *f*, estado *m* ⟨in poor condition : en malas condiciones⟩ **3 conditions** *npl* : condiciones *fpl*, situación *f* ⟨working conditions : condiciones del trabajo⟩

conditional [kən'dɪʃənəl] *adj* : condicional — **conditionally** *adv*

conditioner [kən'dɪʃənər] *n* : acondicionador *m*

condo ['kando:] → **condominium**

condolence [kən'do:lənts] *n* **1** SYMPATHY : condolencia *f* **2 condolences** *npl* : pésame *m*

condom ['kandəm] *n* : condón *m*

condominium [ˌkandə'mɪniəm] *n, pl* **-ums** : condominio *m*

condone [kən'do:n] *vt* **-doned; -doning** : aprobar, perdonar, tolerar

condor ['kandər, -ˌdɔr] *n* : cóndor *m*

conducive [kən'du:sɪv, -'dju:-] *adj* : propicio, favorable

conduct[1] [kən'dʌkt] *vt* **1** GUIDE : guiar, conducir ⟨to conduct a tour : guiar una visita⟩ **2** DIRECT : conducir, dirigir ⟨to conduct an orchestra : dirigir una orquesta⟩ **3** CARRY OUT : realizar, llevar a cabo ⟨to conduct an investigation : llevar a cabo una investigación⟩ **4** TRANSMIT : conducir, transmitir (calor, electricidad, etc.) **5 to conduct oneself** BEHAVE : conducirse, comportarse

conduct[2] ['kanˌdʌkt] *n* **1** MANAGEMENT : conducción *f*, dirección *f*, manejo *m* ⟨the conduct of foreign affairs : la conducción de asuntos exteriores⟩ **2** BEHAVIOR : conducta *f*, comportamiento *m*

conduction [kən'dʌkʃən] *n* : conducción *f*

conductivity [ˌkanˌdʌk'tɪvət̬i] *n, pl* **-ties** : conductividad *f*

conductor [kən'dʌktər] *n* **1** : conductor *m*, -tora *f*; revisor *m*, -sora *f* (en un tren); cobrador *m*, -dora *f* (en un bus); director *m*, -tora *f* (de una orquesta) **2** : conductor *m* (de electricidad, etc.)

conduit ['kanˌdu:ət, -ˌdju:-] *n* : conducto *m*, canal *m*, vía *f*

cone ['ko:n] *n* **1** : piña *f* (fruto de las coníferas) **2** : cono *m* (en geometría) **3 ice–cream cone** : cono *m*, barquillo *m*, cucurucho *m*

confection [kən'fɛkʃən] *n* : dulce *m*

confectioner [kən'fɛkʃənər] *n* : confitero *m*, -ra *f*
confederacy [kən'fɛdərəsi] *n, pl* **-cies** : confederación *f*
confederate[1] [kən'fɛdə,reɪt] *v* **-ated; -ating** *vt* : unir, confederar — *vi* : confederarse, aliarse
confederate[2] [kən'fɛdərət] *adj* : confederado
confederate[3] *n* : cómplice *mf*; aliado *m*, -da *f*
confederation [kən,fɛdə'reɪʃən] *n* : confederación *f*, alianza *f*
confer [kən'fər] *v* **-ferred; -ferring** *vt* : conferir, otorgar — *vi* **to confer with** : consultar
conference ['kɑnfrənts, -fərənts] *n* : conferencia *f* ⟨press conference : conferencia de prensa⟩
confess [kən'fɛs] *vt* : confesar — *vi* **1** : confesar ⟨the prisoner confessed : el detenido confesó⟩ **2** : confesarse (en religión)
confession [kən'fɛʃən] *n* : confesión *f*
confessional [kən'fɛʃənəl] *n* : confesionario *m*
confessor [kən'fɛsər] *n* : confesor *m*
confetti [kən'fɛṭi] *n* : confeti *m*
confidant ['kɑnfə,dɑnt, -,dænt] *n* : confidente *mf*
confide [kən'faɪd] *v* **-fided; -fiding** : confiar
confidence ['kɑnfədənts] *n* **1** TRUST : confianza *f* **2** SELF-ASSURANCE : confianza *f* en sí mismo, seguridad *f* en sí mismo **3** SECRET : confidencia *f*, secreto *m*
confident ['kɑnfədənt] *adj* **1** SURE : seguro **2** SELF-ASSURED : confiado, seguro de sí mismo
confidential [,kɑnfə'dɛntʃəl] *adj* : confidencial — **confidentially** [,kɑnfə'dɛntʃəli] *adv*
confidently ['kɑnfədəntli] *adv* : con seguridad, con confianza
configuration [kən,fɪgjə'reɪʃən] *n* : configuración *f*
confine [kən'faɪn] *vt* **-fined; -fining 1** LIMIT : confinar, restringir, limitar **2** IMPRISON : recluir, encarcelar, encerrar
confinement [kən'faɪnmənt] *n* : confinamiento *m*, reclusión *f*, encierro *m*
confines ['kɑn,faɪnz] *npl* : límites *mpl*, confines *mpl*
confirm [kən'fərm] *vt* **1** RATIFY : ratificar **2** VERIFY : confirmar, verificar **3** : confirmar (en religión)
confirmation [,kɑnfər'meɪʃən] *n* : confirmación *f*
confiscate ['kɑnfə,skeɪt] *vt* **-cated; -cating** : confiscar, incautar, decomisar
confiscation [,kɑnfə'skeɪʃən] *n* : confiscación *f*, incautación *f*, decomiso *m*
conflagration [,kɑnflə'greɪʃən] *n* : conflagración *f*
conflict[1] [kən'flɪkt] *vi* : estar en conflicto, oponerse
conflict[2] ['kɑn,flɪkt] *n* : conflicto *m* ⟨to be in conflict : estar en desacuerdo⟩
confluence ['kɑn,flu:ənts, kən'flu:ənts] *n* : confluencia *f*
conform [kən'fɔrm] *vi* **1** ACCORD, COMPLY : ajustarse, adaptarse, conformarse ⟨it conforms with our standards : se ajusta a nuestras normas⟩ **2** CORRESPOND : corresponder, encajar ⟨to conform to the truth : corresponder a la verdad⟩
conformity [kən'fɔrməṭi] *n, pl* **-ties** : conformidad *f*
confound [kən'faʊnd, kɑn-] *vt* : confundir, desconcertar
confront [kən'frʌnt] *vt* : afrontar, enfrentarse a, encarar
confrontation [,kɑnfrən'teɪʃən] *n* : enfrentamiento *m*, confrontación *f*
confuse [kən'fju:z] *vt* **-fused; -fusing 1** PUZZLE : confundir, enturbiar **2** COMPLICATE : confundir, enredar, complicar ⟨to confuse the issue : complicar las cosas⟩
confusing [kən'fju:zɪŋ] *adj* : complicado, que confunde
confusion [kən'fju:ʒən] *n* **1** PERPLEXITY : confusión *f* **2** MESS, TURMOIL : confusión *f*, embrollo *m*, lío *m fam*
congeal [kən'ʤi:l] *vi* **1** FREEZE : congelarse **2** COAGULATE, CURDLE : coagularse, cuajarse
congenial [kən'ʤi:niəl] *adj* : agradable, simpático
congenital [kən'ʤɛnəṭəl] *adj* : congénito
congest [kən'ʤɛst] *vt* **1** : congestionar (en la medicina) **2** OVERCROWD : abarrotar, atestar, congestionar (el tráfico) — *vi* : congestionarse
congestion [kən'ʤɛstʃən] *n* : congestión *f*
conglomerate[1] [kən'glɑmərət] *adj* : conglomerado
conglomerate[2] [kən'glɑmərət] *n* : conglomerado *m*
conglomeration [kən,glɑmə'reɪʃən] *n* : conglomerado *m*, acumulación *f*
Congolese [,kɑŋgə'li:z, -'li:s] *n* : congoleño *m*, -ña *f* — **Congolese** *adj*
congratulate [kən'græʤə,leɪt, -'grætʃə-] *vt* **-lated; -lating** : felicitar
congratulation [kən,græʤə'leɪʃən, -,grætʃə-] *n* : felicitación *f* ⟨congratulations! : ¡felicidades!, ¡enhorabuena!⟩
congregate ['kɑŋgrɪ,geɪt] *v* **-gated; -gating** *vt* : congregar, reunir — *vi* : congregarse, reunirse
congregation [,kɑŋgrɪ'geɪʃən] *n* **1** GATHERING : congregación *f*, fieles *mpl* (a un servicio religioso) **2** PARISHIONERS : feligreses *mpl*
congress ['kɑŋgrəs] *n* : congreso *m*
congressional [kən'grɛʃənəl, kɑn-] *adj* : del congreso
congressman ['kɑŋgrəsmən] *n, pl* **-men** [-mən, -,mɛn] : congresista *m*, diputado *m*

congresswoman [ˈkɑŋgrəsˌwʊmən] *n, pl* **-women** [-ˌwɪmən] : congresista *f*, diputada *f*
congruence [kənˈgruːənts, ˈkɑŋgrʊənts] *n* : congruencia *f*
congruent [kənˈgruːənt, ˈkɑŋgrʊənt] *adj* : congruente
conic [ˈkɑnɪk] → **conical**
conical [ˈkɑnɪkəl] *adj* : cónico
conifer [ˈkɑnəfər, ˈkoː-] *n* : conífera *f*
coniferous [koːˈnɪfərəs, kə-] *adj* : conífero
conjecture[1] [kənˈʤɛkʧər] *v* **-tured; -turing** : conjeturar
conjecture[2] *n* : conjetura *f*, presunción *f*
conjugal [ˈkɑnʤɪgəl, kənˈʤuː-] *adj* : conyugal
conjugate [ˈkɑnʤəˌgeɪt] *vt* **-gated; -gating** : conjugar
conjugation [ˌkɑnʤəˈgeɪʃən] *n* : conjugación *f*
conjunction [kənˈʤʌŋkʃən] *n* : conjunción *f* ⟨in conjunction with : en combinación con⟩
conjure [ˈkɑnʤər, ˈkʌn-] *v* **-jured; -juring** *vt* **1** ENTREAT : rogar, suplicar **2 to conjure up** : hacer aparecer (apariciones), evocar (memorias, etc.) — *vi* : practicar la magia
conjurer *or* **conjuror** [ˈkɑnʤərər, ˈkʌn-] *n* : mago *m*, -ga *f*; prestidigitador *m*, -dora *f*
connect [kəˈnɛkt] *vi* : conectar, enlazar, empalmar, comunicarse — *vt* **1** JOIN, LINK : conectar, unir, juntar, vincular **2** RELATE : relacionar, asociar (ideas)
connection [kənˈnɛkʃən] *n* : conexión *f*, enlace *m* ⟨professional connections : relaciones profesionales⟩
connective [kəˈnɛktɪv] *adj* : conectivo, conjuntivo ⟨connective tissue : tejido conjuntivo⟩
connector [kəˈnɛktər] *n* : conector *m*
connivance [kəˈnaɪvənts] *n* : connivencia *f*, complicidad *f*
connive [kəˈnaɪv] *vi* **-nived; -niving** CONSPIRE, PLOT : actuar en connivencia, confabularse, conspirar
connoisseur [ˌkɑnəˈsər, -ˈsʊr] *n* : conocedor *m*, -dora *f*; entendido *m*, -da *f*
connotation [ˌkɑnəˈteɪʃən] *n* : connotación *f*
connote [kəˈnoːt] *vt* **-noted; -noting** : connotar
conquer [ˈkɑŋkər] *vt* : conquistar, vencer
conqueror [ˈkɑŋkərər] *n* : conquistador *m*, -dora *f*
conquest [ˈkɑnˌkwɛst, ˈkɑŋ-] *n* : conquista *f*
conscience [ˈkɑnʧənts] *n* : conciencia *f*, consciencia *f* ⟨to have a clear conscience : tener la conciencia limpia⟩
conscientious [ˌkɑnʧiˈɛnʧəs] *adj* : concienzudo — **conscientiously** *adv*
conscious [ˈkɑnʧəs] *adj* **1** AWARE : consciente ⟨to become conscious of : darse cuenta de⟩ **2** ALERT, AWAKE : consciente **3** INTENTIONAL : intencional, deliberado
consciously [ˈkɑnʧəsli] *adv* INTENTIONALLY : intencionalmente, deliberadamente, a propósito
consciousness [ˈkɑnʧəsnəs] *n* **1** AWARENESS : conciencia *f*, consciencia *f* **2** : conocimiento *m* ⟨to lose consciousness : perder el conocimiento⟩
conscript[1] [kənˈskrɪpt] *vt* : reclutar, alistar, enrolar
conscript[2] [ˈkɑnˌskrɪpt] *n* : conscripto *m*, -ta *f*; recluta *mf*
consecrate [ˈkɑntsəˌkreɪt] *vt* **-crated; -crating** : consagrar
consecration [ˌkɑntsəˈkreɪʃən] *n* : consagración *f*, dedicación *f*
consecutive [kənˈsɛkjət̬ɪv] *adj* : consecutivo, seguido ⟨on five consecutive days : cinco días seguidos⟩
consecutively [kənˈsɛkjət̬ivli] *adv* : consecutivamente
consensus [kənˈsɛntsəs] *n* : consenso *m*
consent[1] [kənˈsɛnt] *vi* **1** AGREE : acceder, ponerse de acuerdo **2 to consent to do something** : consentir en hacer algo
consent[2] *n* : consentimiento *m*, permiso *m* ⟨by common consent : de común acuerdo⟩
consequence [ˈkɑntsəˌkwɛnts, -kwənts] *n* **1** RESULT : consecuencia *f*, secuela *f* **2** IMPORTANCE : importancia *f*, trascendencia *f*
consequent [ˈkɑntsəkwənt, -ˌkwɛnt] *adj* : consiguiente
consequential [ˌkɑntsəˈkwɛnʧəl] *adj* **1** CONSEQUENT : consiguiente **2** IMPORTANT : importante, trascendente, trascendental
consequently [ˈkɑntsəkwəntli, -ˌkwɛnt-] *adv* : por consiguiente, por ende, por lo tanto
conservation [ˌkɑntsərˈveɪʃən] *n* : conservación *f*, protección *f*
conservationist [ˌkɑntsərˈveɪʃənɪst] *n* : conservacionista *mf*
conservatism [kənˈsərvəˌtɪzəm] *n* : conservadurismo *m*
conservative[1] [kənˈsərvət̬ɪv] *adj* **1** : conservador **2** CAUTIOUS : moderado, cauteloso ⟨a conservative estimate : un cálculo moderado⟩
conservative[2] *n* : conservador *m*, -dora *f*
conservatory [kənˈsərvəˌtori] *n, pl* **-ries** : conservatorio *m*
conserve[1] [kənˈsərv] *vt* **-served; -serving** : conservar, preservar
conserve[2] [ˈkɑnˌsərv] *n* PRESERVES : confitura *f*
consider [kənˈsɪdər] *vt* **1** CONTEMPLATE : considerar, pensar en ⟨we'd considered attending : habíamos pensado en asistir⟩ **2** : considerar, tener en cuenta ⟨consider the consequences : considera las consecuencias⟩ **3** JUDGE, REGARD : considerar, estimar

considerable [kən'sɪdərəbəl] *adj* : considerable — **considerably** [-bli] *adv*
considerate [kən'sɪdərət] *adj* : considerado, atento
consideration [kən,sɪdə'reɪʃən] *n* : consideración *f* ⟨to take into consideration : tener en cuenta⟩
considering [kən'sɪdərɪŋ] *prep* : teniendo en cuenta, visto
consign [kən'saɪn] *vt* **1** COMMIT, ENTRUST : confiar, encomendar **2** TRANSFER : consignar, transferir **3** SEND : consignar, enviar (mercancía)
consignment [kən'saɪnmənt] *n* **1** : envío *m*, remesa *f* **2 on ~** : en consignación
consist [kən'sɪst] *vi* **1** LIE : consistir ⟨success consists in hard work : el éxito consiste en trabajar duro⟩ **2** : constar, componerse ⟨the set consists of 5 pieces : el juego se compone de 5 piezas⟩
consistency [kən'sɪstəntsi] *n, pl* **-cies 1** : consistencia *f* (de una mezcla o sustancia) **2** COHERENCE : coherencia *f* **3** UNIFORMITY : regularidad *f*, uniformidad *f*
consistent [kən'sɪstənt] *adj* **1** COMPATIBLE : compatible, coincidente ⟨consistent with policy : coincidente con la política⟩ **2** UNIFORM : uniforme, constante, regular — **consistently** [kən'sɪstəntli] *adv*
consolation [,kɑntsə'leɪʃə n] *n* **1** : consuelo *m* **2 consolation prize** : premio *m* de consolación
console[1] [kən'so:l] *vt* **-soled; -soling** : consolar
console[2] ['kɑn,so:l] *n* : consola *f*
consolidate [kən'sɑlə,deɪt] *vt* **-dated; -dating** : consolidar, unir
consolidation [kən,sɑlə'deɪʃən] *n* : consolidación *f*
consommé [,kɑntsə'meɪ] *n* : consomé *m*
consonant ['kɑntsənənt] *n* : consonante *m*
consort[1] [kən'sɔrt] *vi* : asociarse, relacionarse, tener trato ⟨to consort with criminals : tener trato con criminales⟩
consort[2] ['kɑn,sɔrt] *n* : consorte *mf*
consortium [kən'sɔrʃəm] *n, pl* **-tia** [-ʃə] *or* **-tiums** [-ʃəmz] : consorcio *m*
conspicuous [kən'spɪkjʊəs] *adj* **1** OBVIOUS : visible, evidente **2** STRIKING : llamativo
conspicuously [kən'spɪkjʊəsli] *adv* : de manera llamativa
conspiracy [kən'spɪrəsi] *n, pl* **-cies** : conspiración *f*, complot *m*, confabulación *f*
conspirator [kən'spɪrət̬ər] *n* : conspirador *m*, -dora *f*
conspire [kən'spaɪr] *vi* **-spired; -spiring** : conspirar, confabularse
constable ['kɑntstəbəl, 'kʌntstə-] *n* : agente *mf* de policía (en un pueblo)
constancy ['kɑntstəntsi] *n, pl* **-cies** : constancia *f*
constant[1] ['kɑntstənt] *adj* **1** FAITHFUL : leal, fiel **2** INVARIABLE : constante, invariable **3** CONTINUAL : constante, continuo
constant[2] *n* : constante *f*
constantly ['kɑntstəntli] *adv* : constantemente, continuamente
constellation [,kɑntstə'leɪʃən] *n* : constelación *f*
consternation [,kɑntstər'neɪʃən] *n* : consternación *f*
constipate ['kɑntstə,peɪt] *vt* **-pated; -pating** : estreñir
constipation ['kɑntstə'peɪʃən] *n* : estreñimiento *m*, constipación *f* (de vientre)
constituency [kən'stɪtʃʊəntsi] *n, pl* **-cies 1** : distrito *m* electoral **2** : residentes *mpl* de un distrito electoral
constituent[1] [kən'stɪtʃʊənt] *adj* **1** COMPONENT : constituyente, componente **2** : constituyente, constitutivo ⟨a constituent assembly : una asamblea constituyente⟩
constituent[2] *n* **1** COMPONENT : componente *m* **2** ELECTOR, VOTER : elector *m*, -tora *f*; votante *mf*
constitute ['kɑntstə,tu:t, -,tju:t] *vt* **-tuted; -tuting 1** ESTABLISH : constituir, establecer **2** COMPOSE, FORM : constituir, componer
constitution [,kɑntstə'tu:ʃən, -'tju:-] *n* : constitución *f*
constitutional [,kɑntstə'tu:ʃənəl, -'tju:-] *adj* : constitucional
constitutionality [,kɑntstə,tu:ʃə'næləţi, -,tju:-] *n* : constitucionalidad *f*
constrain [kən'streɪn] *vt* **1** COMPEL : constreñir, obligar **2** CONFINE : constreñir, limitar, restringir **3** RESTRAIN : contener, refrenar
constraint [kən'streɪnt] *n* : restricción *f*, limitación *f*
constrict [kən'strɪkt] *vt* : estrechar, apretar, comprimir
constriction [kən'strɪkʃən] *n* : estrechamiento *m*, compresión *f*
construct [kən'strʌkt] *vt* : construir
construction [kən'strʌkʃən] *n* : construcción *f*
constructive [kən'strʌktɪv] *adj* : constructivo
construe [kən'stru:] *vt* **-strued; -struing** : interpretar
consul ['kɑntsəl] *n* : cónsul *mf*
consular ['kɑntsələr] *adj* : consular
consulate ['kɑntsələt] *n* : consulado *m*
consult [kən'sʌlt] *vt* : consultar — *vi* **to consult with** : consultar con, solicitar la opinión de
consultant [kən'sʌltənt] *n* : consultor *m*, -tora *f*; asesor *m*, -sora *f*
consultation [,kɑntsəl'teɪʃən] *n* : consulta *f*
consumable [kən'su:məbəl] *adj* : consumible
consume [kən'su:m] *vt* **-sumed; -suming** : consumir, usar, gastar

consumer [kən'su:mər] *n* : consumidor *m*, -dora *f*
consummate[1] ['kɑntsəˌmeɪt] *vt* **-mated; -mating** : consumar
consummate[2] [kən'sʌmət, 'kɑntsə-mət] *adj* : consumado, perfecto
consummation [ˌkɑntsə'meɪʃən] *n* : consumación *f*
consumption [kən'sʌmpʃən] *n* **1** USE : consumo *m*, uso *m* ⟨consumption of electricity : consumo de electricidad⟩ **2** TUBERCULOSIS : tisis *f*, consunción *f*
contact[1] ['kɑnˌtækt, kən'-] *vt* : ponerse en contacto con, contactar (con)
contact[2] ['kɑnˌtækt] *n* **1** TOUCHING : contacto *m* ⟨to come into contact with : entrar en contacto con⟩ **2** TOUCH : contacto *m*, comunicación *f* ⟨to lose contact with : perder contacto con⟩ **3** CONNECTION : contacto *m* (en negocios) **4** → **contact lens**
contact lens ['kɑnˌtækt'lɛnz] *n* : lente *mf* de contacto, pupilente *m Mex*
contagion [kən'teɪʤən] *n* : contagio *m*
contagious [kən'teɪʤəs] *adj* : contagioso
contain [kən'teɪn] *vt* **1** : contener **2 to contain oneself** : contenerse
container [kən'teɪnər] *n* : recipiente *m*, envase *m*
containment [kən'teɪnmənt] *n* : contención *f*
contaminant [kən'tæmənənt] *n* : contaminante *m*
contaminate [kən'tæməˌneɪt] *vt* **-nated; -nating** : contaminar
contamination [kənˌtæmə'neɪʃən] *n* : contaminación *f*
contemplate ['kɑntəmˌpleɪt] *v* **-plated; -plating** *vt* **1** VIEW : contemplar **2** PONDER : contemplar, considerar **3** CONSIDER, PROPOSE : proponerse, proyectar, pensar en ⟨to contemplate a trip : pensar en viajar⟩ — *vi* MEDITATE : meditar
contemplation [ˌkɑntəm'pleɪʃən] *n* : contemplación *f*
contemplative [kən'tɛmplət̬ɪv, 'kɑntəmˌpleɪt̬ɪv] *adj* : contemplativo
contemporaneous [kənˌtɛmpə'reɪniəs] *adj* → **contemporary**[1]
contemporary[1] [kən'tɛmpəˌrɛri] *adj* : contemporáneo
contemporary[2] *n, pl* **-raries** : contemporáneo *m*, -nea *f*
contempt [kən'tɛmpt] *n* **1** DISDAIN : desprecio *m*, desdén *m* ⟨to hold in contempt : despreciar⟩ **2** : desacato *m* (ante un tribunal)
contemptible [kən'tɛmptəbəl] *adj* : despreciable, vil
contemptuous [kən'tɛmpʧʊəs] *adj* : despectivo, despreciativo, desdeñoso
contemptuously [kən'tɛmpʧʊəsli] *adv* : despectivamente, con desprecio
contend [kən'tɛnd] *vi* **1** STRUGGLE : luchar, lidiar, contender ⟨to contend with a problem : lidiar con un problema⟩ **2** COMPETE : competir ⟨to contend for a position : competir por un puesto⟩ — *vt* **1** ARGUE, MAINTAIN : argüir, sostener, afirmar ⟨he contended that he was right : afirmó que tenía razón⟩ **2** CONTEST : protestar contra (una decisión, etc.), disputar
contender [kən'tɛndər] *n* : contendiente *mf*; aspirante *mf*; competidor *m*, -dora *f*
content[1] [kən'tɛnt] *vt* SATISFY : contentar, satisfacer
content[2] *adj* : conforme, contento, satisfecho
content[3] *n* CONTENTMENT : contento *m*, satisfacción *f* ⟨to one's heart's content : hasta quedar satisfecho, a más no poder⟩
content[4] ['kɑnˌtɛnt] *n* **1** MEANING : contenido *m*, significado *m* **2** PROPORTION : contenido *m*, proporción *f* ⟨fat content : contenido de grasa⟩ **3 contents** *npl* : contenido *m*, sumario *m* (de un libro) ⟨table of contents : índice de materias⟩
contented [kən'tɛntəd] *adj* : conforme, satisfecho ⟨a contented smile : una sonrisa de satisfacción⟩
contentedly [kən'tɛntədli] *adv* : con satisfacción
contention [kən'tɛnʧən] *n* **1** DISPUTE : disputa *f*, discusión *f* **2** COMPETITION : competencia *f*, contienda *f* **3** OPINION : argumento *m*, opinión *f*
contentious [kən'tɛnʧəs] *adj* : disputador, pugnaz, combativo
contentment [kən'tɛntmənt] *n* : satisfacción *f*, contento *m*
contest[1] [kən'tɛst] *vt* : disputar, cuestionar, impugnar ⟨to contest a will : impugnar un testamento⟩
contest[2] ['kɑnˌtɛst] *n* **1** STRUGGLE : lucha *f*, contienda *f* **2** GAME : concurso *m*, competencia *f*
contestable [kən'tɛstəbəl] *adj* : discutible, cuestionable
contestant [kən'tɛstənt] *n* : concursante *mf*; competidor *m*, -dora *f*
context ['kɑnˌtɛkst] *n* : contexto *m*
contiguous [kən'tɪgjʊəs] *adj* : contiguo
continence ['kɑntənənts] *n* : continencia *f*
continent[1] ['kɑntənənt] *adj* : continente
continent[2] *n* : continente *m* — **continental** [ˌkɑntən'ɛntəl] *adj*
contingency [kən'tɪnʤəntsi] *n, pl* **-cies** : contingencia *f*, eventualidad *f*
contingent[1] [kən'tɪnʤənt] *adj* **1** POSSIBLE : contingente, eventual **2** ACCIDENTAL : fortuito, accidental **3 to be contingent on** : depender de, estar sujeto a
contingent[2] *n* : contingente *m*
continual [kən'tɪnjʊəl] *adj* : continuo, constante — **continually** [kən-'tɪnjʊəli, -'tɪnjəli] *adv*
continuance [kən'tɪnjʊənts] *n* **1** CONTINUATION : continuación *f* **2** DURA-

TION : duración *f* **3** : aplazamiento *m* (de un proceso)

continuation [kən͵tɪnjʊ'eɪʃən] *n* : continuación *f*, prolongación *f*

continue [kən'tɪnju:] *v* **-tinued; -tinuing** *vi* **1** CARRY ON : continuar, seguir, proseguir ⟨please continue : continúe, por favor⟩ **2** ENDURE, LAST : continuar, prolongarse, durar **3** RESUME : continuar, reanudarse — *vt* **1** : continuar, seguir ⟨she continued writing : continuó escribiendo⟩ **2** RESUME : continuar, reanudar **3** EXTEND, PROLONG : continuar, prolongar

continuity [͵kɑntə-'nu:əţi, -'nju:-] *n, pl* **-ties** : continuidad *f*

continuous [kən'tɪnjʊəs] *adj* : continuo — **continuously** *adv*

contort [kən'tɔrt] *vt* : torcer, retorcer, contraer (el rostro) — *vi* : contraerse, demudarse

contortion [kən'tɔrʃən] *n* : contorsión *f*

contour ['kɑn͵tʊr] *n* **1** OUTLINE : contorno *m* **2 contours** *npl* SHAPE : forma *f*, curvas *fpl* **3 contour map** : mapa *m* topográfico

contraband ['kɑntrə͵bænd] *n* : contrabando *m*

contraception [͵kɑntrə'sɛpʃən] *n* : anticoncepción *f*, contracepción *f*

contraceptive[1] [͵kɑntrə'sɛptɪv] *adj* : anticonceptivo, contraceptivo

contraceptive[2] *n* : anticonceptivo *m*, contraceptivo *m*

contract[1] [kən'trækt, 1 *usu* 'kɑn-͵trækt] *vt* **1** : contratar (servicios profesionales) **2** : contraer (una enfermedad, una deuda) **3** TIGHTEN : contraer (un músculo) **4** SHORTEN : contraer (una palabra) — *vi* : contraerse, reducirse

contract[2] ['kɑn͵trækt] *n* : contrato *m*

contraction [kən'trækʃən] *n* : contracción *f*

contractor ['kɑn͵træktər, kən'træk-] *n* : contratista *mf*

contractual [kən'træktʃʊəl] *adj* : contractual — **contractually** *adv*

contradict [͵kɑntrə'dɪkt] *vt* : contradecir, desmentir

contradiction [͵kɑntrə'dɪkʃən] *n* : contradicción *f*

contradictory [͵kɑntrə'dɪktəri] *adj* : contradictorio

contralto [kən'træl͵to:] *n, pl* **-tos** : contralto *m* (voz), contralto *mf* (vocalista)

contraption [kən'træpʃən] *n* DEVICE : aparato *m*, artefacto *m*

contrary[1] ['kɑn͵trɛri, *2 often* kən-'trɛri] *adj* **1** OPPOSITE : contrario, opuesto **2** BALKY, STUBBORN : terco, testarudo **3 contrary to** : al contrario de, en contra de ⟨contrary to the facts : en contra de los hechos⟩

contrary[2] ['kɑn͵trɛri] *n, pl* **-traries** **1** OPPOSITE : lo contrario, lo opuesto **2 on the contrary** : al contrario, todo lo contrario

contrast[1] [kən'træst] *vi* DIFFER : contrastar, diferir — *vt* COMPARE : contrastar, comparar

contrast[2] ['kɑn͵træst] *n* : contraste *m*

contravene [͵kɑntrə'vi:n] *vt* **-vened; -vening** : contravenir, infringir

contribute [kən'trɪbjət] *v* **-uted; -uting** *vt* : contribuir, aportar (dinero, bienes, etc.) — *vi* : contribuir

contribution [͵kɑntrə'bju:ʃən] *n* : contribución *f*

contributor [kən'trɪbjəţər] *n* : contribuidor *m*, -dora *f*; colaborador *m*, -dora *f* (en periodismo)

contrite ['kɑn͵traɪt, kən'traɪt] *adj* REPENTANT : contrito, arrepentido

contrition [kən'trɪʃən] *n* : contrición *f*, arrepentimiento *m*

contrivance [kən'traɪvənts] *n* **1** DEVICE : aparato *m*, artefacto *m* **2** SCHEME : artimaña *f*, treta *f*, ardid *m*

contrive [kən'traɪv] *vt* **-trived; -triving** **1** DEVISE : idear, ingeniar, maquinar **2** MANAGE : lograr, ingeniárselas para ⟨she contrived a way out of the mess : se las ingenió para salir del enredo⟩

control[1] [kən'tro:l] *vt* **-trolled; -trolling** : controlar, dominar

control[2] *n* **1** : control *m*, dominio *m*, mando *m* ⟨to be under control : estar bajo control⟩ **2** RESTRAINT : control *m*, limitación *f* ⟨birth control : control natal⟩ **3** : control *m*, dispositivo *m* de mando ⟨remote control : control remoto⟩

controllable [kən'tro:ləbəl] *adj* : controlable

controller [kən'tro:lər, 'kɑn͵-] *n* **1** → **comptroller** **2** : controlador *m*, -dora *f* ⟨air traffic controller : controlador aéreo⟩

controversial [͵kɑntrə'vərʃəl, -siəl] *adj* : controvertido ⟨a controversial decision : una decisión controvertida⟩

controversy ['kɑntrə͵vərsi] *n, pl* **-sies** : controversia *f*

controvert ['kɑntrə͵vərt, ͵kɑntrə'-] *vt* : controvertir, contradecir

contusion [kən'tu:ʒən, -tju:-] *n* BRUISE : contusión *f*, moretón *m*

conundrum [kə'nʌndrəm] *n* RIDDLE : acertijo *m*, adivinanza *f*

convalesce [͵kɑnvə'lɛs] *vi* **-lesced; -lescing** : convalecer

convalescence [͵kɑnvə'lɛsənts] *n* : convalecencia *f*

convalescent[1] [͵kɑnvə'lɛsənt] *adj* : convaleciente

convalescent[2] *n* : convaleciente *mf*

convection [kən'vɛkʃən] *n* : convección *f*

convene [kən'vi:n] *v* **-vened; -vening** *vt* : convocar — *vi* : reunirse

convenience [kən'vi:njənts] *n* **1** : conveniencia *f* ⟨at your convenience : cuando le resulte conveniente⟩ **2** AMENITY : comodidad *f* ⟨modern conveniences : comodidades modernas⟩

convenience store *n* : tienda *f* de conveniencia
convenient [kən'vi:njənt] *adj* : conveniente, cómodo — **conveniently** *adv*
convent ['kɑnvənt, -ˌvɛnt] *n* : convento *m*
convention [kən'vɛntʃən] *n* **1** PACT : convención *f*, convenio *m*, pacto *m* ⟨the Geneva Convention : la Convención de Ginebra⟩ **2** MEETING : convención *f*, congreso *m* **3** CUSTOM : convención *f*, convencionalismo *m*
conventional [kən'vɛntʃənəl] *adj* : convencional — **conventionally** *adv*
converge [kən'vərʤ] *vi* **-verged; -verging** : converger, convergir
convergence [kən'vərʤənts] *n* : convergencia *f*
convergent [kən'vərʤənt] *adj* : convergente
conversant [kən'vərsənt] *adj* **conversant with** : versado con, experto en
conversation [ˌkɑnvər'seɪʃən] *n* : conversación *f*
conversational [ˌkɑnvər'seɪʃənəl] *adj* : familiar ⟨a conversational style : un estilo familiar⟩
converse[1] [kən'vərs] *vi* **-versed; -versing** : conversar
converse[2] [kən'vərs, 'kɑnˌvərs] *adj* : contrario, opuesto, inverso
conversely [kən'vərsli, 'kɑnˌvərs-] *adv* : a la inversa
conversion [kən'vərʒən] *n* **1** CHANGE : conversión *f*, transformación *f*, cambio *m* **2** : conversión *f* (a una religión)
convert[1] [kən'vərt] *vt* **1** : convertir (a una religión o un partido) **2** CHANGE : convertir, cambiar — *vi* : convertirse
convert[2] ['kɑnˌvərt] *n* : converso *m*, -sa *f*
converter *or* **convertor** [kən'vərṭər] *n* : convertidor *m*
convertible[1] [kən'vərṭəbəl] *adj* : convertible
convertible[2] *n* : convertible *m*, descapotable *m*
convex [kɑn'vɛks, 'kɑnˌ-, kən'-] *adj* : convexo
convey [kən'veɪ] *vt* **1** TRANSPORT : transportar, conducir **2** TRANSMIT : transmitir, comunicar, expresar (noticias, ideas, etc.)
conveyance [kən'veɪənts] *n* **1** TRANSPORT : transporte *m*, transportación *f* **2** COMMUNICATION : transmisión *f*, comunicación *f* **3** TRANSFER : transferencia *f*, traspaso *m* (de una propiedad)
conveyor [kən'veɪər] *n* : transportador *m*, -dora *f* ⟨conveyor belt : cinta transportadora⟩
convict[1] [kən'vɪkt] *vt* : declarar culpable
convict[2] ['kɑnˌvɪkt] *n* : preso *m*, -sa *f*; presidiario *m*, -ria *f*; recluso *m*, -sa *f*
conviction [kən'vɪkʃən] *n* **1** : condena *f* (de un acusado) **2** BELIEF : convicción *f*, creencia *f*
convince [kən'vɪnts] *vt* **-vinced; -vincing** : convencer
convincing [kən'vɪntsɪŋ] *adj* : convincente, persuasivo
convincingly [kən'vɪntsɪŋli] *adv* : de forma convincente
convivial [kən'vɪvjəl, -'vɪviəl] *adj* : jovial, festivo, alegre
conviviality [kənˌvɪvi'æləṭi] *n, pl* **-ties** : jovialidad *f*
convoke [kən'vo:k] *vt* **-voked; -voking** : convocar
convoluted ['kɑnvəˌlu:ṭəd] *adj* : intrincado, complicado
convoy ['kɑnˌvɔɪ] *n* : convoy *m*
convulse [kən'vʌls] *v* **-vulsed; -vulsing** *vt* : convulsionar ⟨convulsed with laughter : muerto de risa⟩ — *vi* : sufrir convulsiones
convulsion [kən'vʌlʃən] *n* : convulsión *f*
convulsive [kən'vʌlsɪv] *adj* : convulsivo — **convulsively** *adv*
coo[1] ['ku:] *vi* : arrullar
coo[2] *n* : arrullo *m* (de una paloma)
cook[1] ['kʊk] *vi* : cocinar — *vt* **1** : preparar (comida) **2 to cook up** CONCOCT : inventar, tramar
cook[2] *n* : cocinero *m*, -ra *f*
cookbook ['kʊkˌbʊk] *n* : libro *m* de cocina
cookery ['kʊkəri] *n, pl* **-eries** : cocina *f*
cookie *or* **cooky** ['kʊki] *n, pl* **-ies** : galleta *f* (dulce)
cooking ['kʊkɪŋ] *n* **1** COOKERY : cocina *f* **2** : cocción *f*, cocimiento *m* ⟨cooking time : tiempo de cocción⟩
cookout ['kʊkˌaʊt] *n* : comida *f* al aire libre
cool[1] ['ku:l] *vt* : refrescar, enfriar — *vi* **1** : refrescarse, enfriarse ⟨the pie is cooling : el pastel se está enfriando⟩ **2** : calmarse, tranquilizarse ⟨his anger cooled : su ira se calmó⟩
cool[2] *adj* **1** : fresco, frío ⟨cool weather : tiempo fresco⟩ **2** CALM : tranquilo, sereno **3** ALOOF : frío, distante
cool[3] *n* **1** : fresco *m* ⟨the cool of the evening : el fresco de la tarde⟩ **2** COMPOSURE : calma *f*, serenidad *f*
coolant ['ku:lənt] *n* : refrigerante *m*
cooler ['ku:lər] *n* : nevera *f* portátil
coolie ['ku:li] *n* : culi *m*
coolly ['ku:lli] *adv* **1** CALMLY : con calma, tranquilamente **2** COLDLY : fríamente, con frialdad
coolness ['ku:lnəs] *n* **1** : frescura *f*, frescor *m* ⟨the coolness of the evening : el frescor de la noche⟩ **2** CALMNESS : tranquilidad *f*, serenidad *f* **3** COLDNESS, INDIFFERENCE : frialdad *f*, indiferencia
coop[1] ['ku:p, 'kʊp] *vt or* **to coop up** : encerrar ⟨cooped up in the house : encerrado en la casa⟩
coop[2] *n* : gallinero *m*
co–op ['ko:ˌɑp] *n* → **cooperative**[2]
cooperate [ko'ɑpəˌreɪt] *vi* **-ated; -ating** : cooperar, colaborar

cooperation [ko,ɑpəˈreɪʃən] *n* : cooperación *f*, colaboración *f*
cooperative[1] [koˈɑpərət̬ɪv, -ˈɑpə,reɪt̬ɪv] *adj* : cooperativo
cooperative[2] [koˈɑpərət̬ɪv] *n* : cooperativa *f*
co–opt [koˈɑpt] *vt* **1** : nombrar como miembro, cooptar **2** APPROPRIATE : apropiarse de
coordinate[1] [koˈɔrdən,eɪt] *v* **-nated; -nating** *vt* : coordinar — *vi* : coordinarse, combinar, acordar
coordinate[2] [koˈɔrdənət] *adj* **1** COORDINATED : coordinado **2** EQUAL : igual, semejante
coordinate[3] [koˈɔrdənət] *n* : coordenada *f*
coordination [ko,ɔrdənˈeɪʃən] *n* : coordinación *f*
coordinator [koˈɔrdən,eɪt̬ər] *n* : coordinador *m*, -dora *f*
cop [ˈkɑp] → **police officer**
cope [ˈko:p] *vi* **coped; coping 1** : arreglárselas **2 to cope with** : hacer frente a, poder con ⟨I can't cope with all this! : ¡no puedo con todo esto!⟩
copier [ˈkɑpiər] *n* : copiadora *f*, fotocopiadora *f*
copilot [ˈko:,paɪlət] *n* : copiloto *m*
copious [ˈko:piəs] *adj* : copioso, abundante — **copiously** *adv*
copiousness [ˈko:piəsnəs] *n* : abundancia *f*
copper [ˈkɑpər] *n* : cobre *m*
coppery [ˈkɑpəri] *adj* : cobrizo
copra [ˈko:prə, ˈkɑ-] *n* : copra *f*
copse [ˈkɑps] *n* THICKET : soto *m*, matorral *m*
copulate [ˈkɑpjə,leɪt] *vi* **-lated; -lating** : copular
copulation [,kɑpjəˈleɪʃən] *n* : cópula *f*, relaciones *fpl* sexuales
copy[1] [ˈkɑpi] *vt* **copied; copying 1** DUPLICATE : hacer una copia de, duplicar, reproducir **2** IMITATE : copiar, imitar
copy[2] *n, pl* **copies 1** : copia *f*, duplicado *m* (de un documento), reproducción *f* (de una obra de arte) **2** : ejemplar *m* (de un libro), número *m* (de una revista) **3** TEXT : manuscrito *m*, texto *m*
copyright[1] [ˈkɑpi,raɪt] *vt* : registrar los derechos de
copyright[2] *n* : derechos *mpl* de autor
coral[1] [ˈkɔrəl] *adj* : de coral ⟨a coral reef : un arrecife de coral⟩
coral[2] *n* : coral *m*
coral snake *n* : serpiente *f* de coral
cord [ˈkɔrd] *n* **1** ROPE, STRING : cuerda *f*, cordón *m*, cordel *m* **2** : cuerda *f*, cordón *m*, médula *f* (en la anatomía) ⟨vocal cords : cuerdas vocales⟩ **3** : cuerda *f* ⟨a cord of firewood : una cuerda de leña⟩ **4** *or* **electric cord** : cable *m* eléctrico
cordial[1] [ˈkɔrʤəl] *adj* : cordial — **cordially** *adv*
cordial[2] *n* : cordial *m*
cordiality [,kɔrʤiˈæləṯi] *n* : cordialidad *f*
cordless [ˈkɔrdləs] *adj* : inalámbrico
cordon[1] [ˈkɔrdən] *vt* **to cordon off** : acordonar
cordon[2] *n* : cordón *m*
corduroy [ˈkɔrdə,rɔɪ] *n* **1** : pana *f* **2 corduroys** *npl* : pantalones *mpl* de pana
core[1] [ˈkor] *vt* **cored; coring** : quitar el corazón a (una fruta)
core[2] *n* **1** : corazón *m*, centro *m* (de algunas frutas) **2** CENTER : núcleo *m*, centro *m* **3** ESSENCE : núcleo *m*, meollo *m* ⟨to the core : hasta la médula⟩
coriander [ˈkori,ændər] *n* : cilantro *m*
cork[1] [ˈkɔrk] *vt* : ponerle un corcho a
cork[2] *n* : corcho *m*
corkscrew [ˈkɔrk,skru:] *n* : tirabuzón *m*, sacacorchos *m*
cormorant [ˈkɔrmərənt, -,rænt] *n* : cormorán *m*
corn[1] [ˈkɔrn] *vt* : conservar en salmuera ⟨corned beef : carne en conserva⟩
corn[2] *n* **1** GRAIN : grano *m* **2** : maíz *m*, elote *m Mex* ⟨corn tortillas : tortillas de maíz⟩ **3** : callo *m* ⟨corn plaster : emplasto para callos⟩
corncob [ˈkɔrn,kɑb] *n* : mazorca *f* (de maíz), choclo *m*, elote *m CA, Mex*
cornea [ˈkɔrniə] *n* : córnea *f*
corner[1] [ˈkɔrnər] *vt* **1** TRAP : acorralar, arrinconar **2** MONOPOLIZE : monopolizar, acaparar (un mercado) — *vi* : tomar una curva, doblar una esquina (en un automóvil)
corner[2] *n* **1** ANGLE : rincón *m*, esquina *f*, ángulo *m* ⟨the corner of a room : el rincón de una sala⟩ ⟨all corners of the world : todos los rincones del mundo⟩ ⟨to cut corners : atajar, economizar esfuerzos⟩ **2** INTERSECTION : esquina *f* **3** IMPASSE, PREDICAMENT : aprieto *m*, impasse *m* ⟨to be backed into a corner : estar acorralado⟩
cornerstone [ˈkɔrnər,sto:n] *n* : piedra *f* angular
cornet [kɔrˈnɛt] *n* : corneta *f*
cornfield [ˈkɔrn,fi:ld] *n* : maizal *m*; milpa *f CA, Mex*
cornice [ˈkɔrnɪs] *n* : cornisa *f*
cornmeal [ˈkɔrn,mi:l] *n* : harina *f* de maíz
cornstalk [ˈkɔrn,stɔk] *n* : tallo *m* del maíz
cornstarch [ˈkɔrn,stɑrʧ] *n* : maicena *f*, almidón *m* de maíz
cornucopia [,kɔrnəˈko:piə, -njə-] *n* : cornucopia *f*
corolla [kəˈrɑlə] *n* : corola *f*
corollary [ˈkɔrə,lɛri] *n, pl* **-laries** : corolario *m*
corona [kəˈro:nə] *n* : corona *f* (del sol)
coronary[1] [ˈkɔrə,nɛri] *adj* : coronario
coronary[2] *n, pl* **-naries 1** : trombosis *f* coronaria **2** HEART ATTACK : infarto *m*, ataque *m* al corazón
coronation [,kɔrəˈneɪʃən] *n* : coronación *f*

coroner ['kɔrənər] *n* : médico *m* forense
corporal[1] ['kɔrpərəl] *adj* : corporal <corporal punishment : castigos corporales>
corporal[2] *n* : cabo *m*
corporate ['kɔrpərət] *adj* : corporativo, empresarial
corporation [ˌkɔrpə'reɪʃən] *n* : sociedad *f* anónima, corporación *f*, empresa *f*
corporeal [kɔr'poriəl] *adj* **1** PHYSICAL : corpóreo **2** MATERIAL : material, tangible — **corporeally** *adv*
corps ['kor] *n, pl* **corps** ['korz] : cuerpo *m* <medical corps : cuerpo médico> <diplomatic corps : cuerpo diplomático>
corpse ['kɔrps] *n* : cadáver *m*
corpulence ['kɔrpjələn*t*s] *n* : obesidad *f*, gordura *f*
corpulent ['kɔrpjələnt] *adj* : obeso, gordo
corpuscle ['kɔrˌpʌsəl] *n* : corpúsculo *m*, glóbulo *m* (sanguíneo)
corral[1] [kə'ræl] *vt* **-ralled; -ralling** : acorralar, encorralar (ganado)
corral[2] *n* : corral *m*
correct[1] [kə'rɛkt] *vt* **1** RECTIFY : corregir, rectificar **2** REPRIMAND : corregir, reprender
correct[2] *adj* **1** ACCURATE, RIGHT : correcto, exacto <to be correct : estar en lo cierto> **2** PROPER : correcto, apropiado
correction [kə'rɛkʃən] *n* : corrección *f*
corrective [kə'rɛktɪv] *adj* : correctivo
correctly [kə'rɛktli] *adv* : correctamente
correctness [kə'rɛk(t)nəs] *n* **1** ACCURACY : exactitud *f* **2** PROPRIETY : corrección *f*
correlate ['kɔrəˌleɪt] *vt* **-lated; -lating** : relacionar, poner en correlación
correlation [ˌkɔrə'leɪʃən] *n* : correlación *f*
correspond [ˌkɔrə'spɑnd] *vi* **1** MATCH : corresponder, concordar, coincidir **2** WRITE : corresponderse, escribirse
correspondence [ˌkɔrə'spɑndən*t*s] *n* : correspondencia *f*
correspondent [ˌkɔrə'spɑndənt] *n* : corresponsal *mf*
corresponding [kɔrə'spɑndɪŋ, kɑr-] *adj* : correspondiente
correspondingly [ˌkɔrə'spɑndɪŋli] *adv* : en consecuencia, de la misma manera
corridor ['kɔrədər, -ˌdɔr] *n* : corredor *m*, pasillo *m*
corroborate [kə'rɑbəˌreɪt] *vt* **-rated; -rating** : corroborar
corroboration [kəˌrɑbə'reɪʃən] *n* : corroboración *f*
corrode [kə'ro:d] *v* **-roded; -roding** *vt* : corroer — *vi* : corroerse
corrosion [kə'ro:ʒən] *n* : corrosión *f*
corrosive [kə'ro:sɪv] *adj* : corrosivo
corrugate ['kɔrəˌgeɪt] *vt* **-gated; -gating** : ondular, acanalar, corrugar
corrugated ['kɔrəˌgeɪt̬əd] *adj* : ondulado, acanalado <corrugated cardboard : cartón ondulado>
corrupt[1] [kə'rʌpt] *vt* **1** PERVERT : corromper, pervertir, degradar (información) **2** BRIBE : sobornar
corrupt[2] *adj* : corrupto, corrompido
corruptible [kə'rʌptəbəl] *adj* : corruptible
corruption [kə'rʌpʃən] *n* : corrupción *f*
corsage [kɔr'sɑʒ, -'sɑʤ] *n* : ramillete *m* que se lleva como adorno
corset ['kɔrsət] *n* : corsé *m*
cortex ['kɔrˌtɛks] *n, pl* **-tices** ['kɔrt̬əˌsi:z] *or* **-texes** : corteza *f* <cerebral cortex : corteza cerebral>
cortisone ['kɔrt̬əˌso:n, -zo:n] *n* : cortisona *f*
cosmetic[1] [kɑz'mɛt̬ɪk] *adj* : cosmético
cosmetic[2] *n* : cosmético *m*
cosmic ['kɑzmɪk] *adj* **1** : cósmico <cosmic ray : rayo cósmico> **2** VAST : grandioso, inmenso, vasto
cosmonaut ['kɑzməˌnɔt] *n* : cosmonauta *mf*
cosmopolitan[1] [ˌkɑzmə'pɑlətən] *adj* : cosmopolita
cosmopolitan[2] *n* : cosmopolita *mf*
cosmos ['kɑzməs, -ˌmo:s, -ˌmɑs] *n* : cosmos *m*, universo *m*
cost[1] ['kɔst] *v* **cost; costing** *vt* : costar <how much does it cost? : ¿cuánto cuesta?, ¿cuánto vale?> — *vi* : costar <these cost more : éstos cuestan más>
cost[2] *n* : costo *m*, precio *m*, coste *m* <cost of living : costo de vida> <victory at all costs : victoria a toda costa>
Costa Rican[1] [ˌkɔstə'ri:kən] *adj* : costarricense
Costa Rican[2] *n* : costarricense *mf*
costly ['kɔstli] *adj* : costoso, caro
costume ['kɑsˌtu:m, -ˌtju:m] *n* **1** : traje *m* <national costume : traje típico> **2** : disfraz *m* <costume party : fiesta de disfraces> **3** OUTFIT : vestimenta *f*, traje *m*, conjunto *m*
cosy ['ko:zi] → **cozy**
cot ['kɑt] *n* : catre *m*
coterie ['ko:t̬əˌri, ˌko:t̬ə'-] *n* : tertulia *f*, círculo *m* (social)
cottage ['kɑt̬ɪʤ] *n* : casita *f* (de campo)
cottage cheese *n* : requesón *m*
cotton ['kɑtən] *n* : algodón *m*
cottonmouth ['kɑtənˌmaʊθ] → **moccasin**
cottonseed ['kɑtənˌsi:d] *n* : semilla *f* de algodón
cotton swab → **swab**
cottontail ['kɑtənˌteɪl] *n* : conejo *m* de cola blanca
couch[1] ['kaʊʧ] *vt* : expresar, formular <couched in strong language : expresado en lenguaje enérgico>
couch[2] *n* SOFA : sofá *m*
couch potato *n* : haragán *m*, -gana *f*; vago *m*, -ga *f*
cougar ['ku:gər] *n* : puma *m*
cough[1] ['kɔf] *vi* : toser

cough[2] *n* : tos *f*
could [ˈkʊd] → **can**
council [ˈkaʊntsəl] *n* **1** : concejo *m* ⟨city council : concejo municipal, ayuntamiento⟩ **2** MEETING : concejo *m*, junta *f* **3** BOARD : consejo *m* **4** : concilio *m* (eclesiástico)
councillor *or* **councilor** [ˈkaʊntsələr] *n* : concejal *m*, -jala *f*
councilman [ˈkaʊntsəlmən] *n, pl* **-men** [-mən, -ˌmɛn] : concejal *m*
councilwoman [ˈkaʊntsəlˌwʊmən] *n, pl* **-women** [-ˌwɪmən] : concejala *f*
counsel[1] [ˈkaʊntsəl] *v* **-seled** *or* **-selled**; **-seling** *or* **-selling** *vt* ADVISE : aconsejar, asesorar, recomendar — *vi* CONSULT : consultar
counsel[2] *n* **1** ADVICE : consejo *m*, recomendación *f* **2** CONSULTATION : consulta *f* **3 counsel** *ns & pl* LAWYER : abogado *m*, -da *f*
counselor *or* **counsellor** [ˈkaʊntsələr] *n* : consejero *m*, -ra *f*; consultor *m*, -tora *f*; asesor *m*, -sora *f*
count[1] [ˈkaʊnt] *vt* : contar, enumerar — *vi* **1** : contar ⟨to count out loud : contar en voz alta⟩ **2** MATTER : contar, valer, importar ⟨that's what counts : eso es lo que cuenta⟩ **3 to count on** : contar con
count[2] *n* **1** COMPUTATION : cómputo *m*, recuento *m*, cuenta *f* ⟨to lose count : perder la cuenta⟩ **2** CHARGE : cargo *m* ⟨two counts of robbery : dos cargos de robo⟩ **3** : conde *m* (noble)
countable [ˈkaʊntəbəl] *adj* : numerable
countdown [ˈkaʊntˌdaʊn] *n* : cuenta *f* atrás
countenance[1] [ˈkaʊntənənts] *vt* **-nanced; -nancing** : permitir, tolerar
countenance[2] *n* FACE : semblante *m*, rostro *m*
counter[1] [ˈkaʊntər] *vt* **1** → **counteract** **2** OPPOSE : oponerse a, resistir — *vi* RETALIATE : responder, contraatacar
counter[2] *adv* **counter to** : contrario a, en contra de
counter[3] *adj* : contrario, opuesto
counter[4] *n* **1** PIECE : ficha *f* (de un juego) **2** : mostrador *m* (de un negocio), ventanilla *f* (en un banco) **3** : contador *m* (aparato) **4** COUNTERBALANCE : fuerza *f* opuesta, contrapeso *m*
counteract [ˌkaʊntərˈækt] *vt* : contrarrestar
counterattack [ˈkaʊntərəˌtæk] *n* : contraataque *m*
counterbalance[1] [ˌkaʊntərˈbælənts] *vt* **-anced; -ancing** : contrapesar
counterbalance[2] [ˈkaʊntərˌbælənts] *n* : contrapeso *m*
counterclockwise [ˌkaʊntərˈklɑkˌwaɪz] *adv & adj* : en el sentido opuesto al de las manecillas del reloj
counterfeit[1] [ˈkaʊntərˌfɪt] *vt* **1** : falsificar (dinero) **2** PRETEND : fingir, aparentar
counterfeit[2] *adj* : falso, inauténtico
counterfeit[3] *n* : falsificación *f*
counterfeiter [ˈkaʊntərˌfɪt̬ər] *n* : falsificador *m*, -dora *f*
countermand [ˈkaʊntərˌmænd, ˌkaʊntərˈ-] *vt* : contramandar
countermeasure [ˈkaʊntərˌmɛʒər] *n* : contramedida *f*
counterpart [ˈkaʊntərˌpɑrt] *n* : homólogo *m*, contraparte *f Mex*
counterpoint [ˈkaʊntərˌpɔɪnt] *n* : contrapunto *m*
counterproductive [ˌkaʊntərprəˈdʌktɪv] *adj* : contraproducente
counterrevolution [ˌkaʊntərˌrɛvəˈluːʃən] *n* : contrarrevolución *f*
counterrevolutionary[1] [ˌkaʊntərˌrɛvəˈluːʃənˌɛri] *adj* : contrarrevolucionario
counterrevolutionary[2] *n, pl* **-ries** : contrarrevolucionario *m*, -ria *f*
countersign [ˈkaʊntərˌsaɪn] *n* : contraseña *f*
countess [ˈkaʊntɪs] *n* : condesa *f*
countless [ˈkaʊntləs] *adj* : incontable, innumerable
country[1] [ˈkʌntri] *adj* : campestre, rural
country[2] *n, pl* **-tries** **1** NATION : país *m*, nación *f*, patria *f* ⟨country of origin : país de origen⟩ ⟨love of one's country : amor a la patria⟩ **2** : campo *m* ⟨they left the city for the country : se fueron de la ciudad al campo⟩
countryman [ˈkʌntrimən] *n, pl* **-men** [-mən, -ˌmɛn] : compatriota *mf*; paisano *m*, -na *f*
countryside [ˈkʌntriˌsaɪd] *n* : campo *m*, campiña *f*
county [ˈkaʊnti] *n, pl* **-ties** : condado *m*
coup [ˈkuː] *n, pl* **coups** [ˈkuːz] **1** : golpe *m* maestro **2** *or* **coup d'etat** : golpe *m* (de estado), cuartelazo *m*
coupe [ˈkuːp] *n* : cupé *m*
couple[1] [ˈkʌpəl] *vt* **-pled; -pling** : acoplar, enganchar, conectar
couple[2] *n* **1** PAIR : par *m* ⟨a couple of hours : un par de horas, unas dos horas⟩ **2** : pareja *f* ⟨a young couple : una pareja joven⟩
coupling [ˈkʌplɪŋ] *n* : acoplamiento *m*
coupon [ˈkuːˌpɑn, ˈkjuː-] *n* : cupón *m*
courage [ˈkərɪʤ] *n* : valor *m*, valentía *f*, coraje *m*
courageous [kəˈreɪʤəs] *adj* : valiente, valeroso
courier [ˈkʊriər, ˈkəriər] *n* : mensajero *m*, -ra *f*
course[1] [ˈkors] *vi* **coursed; coursing** : correr (a toda velocidad)
course[2] *n* **1** PROGRESS : curso *m*, transcurso *m* ⟨to run its course : seguir su curso⟩ **2** DIRECTION : rumbo *m* (de un avión), derrota *f*, derrotero *m* (de un barco) **3** PATH, WAY : camino *m*, vía *f* ⟨course of action : línea de conducta⟩ **4** : plato *m* (de una cena) ⟨the main course : el plato principal⟩ **5** : curso *m* (académico) **6 of course** : desde luego, por supuesto ⟨yes, of course! : ¡claro que sí!⟩

court[1] [ˈkort] *vt* WOO : cortejar, galantear
court[2] *n* **1** PALACE : palacio *m* **2** RETINUE : corte *f*, séquito *m* **3** COURTYARD : patio *m* **4** : cancha *f* (de tenis, baloncesto, etc.) **5** TRIBUNAL : corte *f*, tribunal *m* ⟨the Supreme Court : la Corte Suprema⟩
courteous [ˈkərt̬iəs] *adj* : cortés, atento, educado — **courteously** *adv*
courtesan [ˈkort̬əzən, ˈkər-] *n* : cortesana *f*
courtesy [ˈkərt̬əsi] *n, pl* **-sies** : cortesía *f*
courthouse [ˈkortˌhaʊs] *n* : palacio *m* de justicia, juzgado *m*
courtier [ˈkort̬iər, ˈkortjər] *n* : cortesano *m*, -na *f*
courtly [ˈkortli] *adj* **-lier; -est** : distinguido, elegante, cortés
court–martial[1] [ˈkortˌmarʃəl] *vt* : someter a consejo de guerra
court–martial[2] *n, pl* **courts–martial** [ˈkortsˌmarʃəl] : consejo *m* de guerra
court order *n* : mandamiento *m* judicial
courtroom [ˈkortˌru:m] *n* : tribunal *m*, corte *f*
courtship [ˈkortˌʃɪp] *n* : cortejo *m*, noviazgo *m*
courtyard [ˈkortˌjard] *n* : patio *m*
cousin [ˈkʌzən] *n* : primo *m*, -ma *f*
couture [ku:ˈtʊr] *n* : industria *f* de la moda ⟨haute couture : alta costura⟩
cove [ˈko:v] *n* : ensenada *f*, cala *f*
covenant [ˈkʌvənənt] *n* : pacto *m*, contrato *m*
cover[1] [ˈkʌvər] *vt* **1** : cubrir, tapar ⟨cover your head : tápate la cabeza⟩ ⟨covered with mud : cubierto de lodo⟩ **2** HIDE, PROTECT : encubrir, proteger **3** TREAT : tratar **4** INSURE : asegurar, cubrir
cover[2] *n* **1** SHELTER : cubierta *f*, abrigo *m*, refugio *m* ⟨to take cover : ponerse a cubierto⟩ ⟨under cover of darkness : al amparo de la oscuridad⟩ **2** LID, TOP : cubierta *f*, tapa *f* **3** : cubierta *f* (de un libro), portada *f* (de una revista) **4 covers** *npl* BEDCLOTHES : ropa *f* de cama, cobijas *fpl*, mantas *fpl*
coverage [ˈkʌvərɪʤ] *n* : cobertura *f*
coverlet [ˈkʌvərlət] *n* : cobertor *m*
covert[1] [ˈko:ˌvərt, ˈkʌvərt] *adj* : encubierto, secreto ⟨covert operations : operaciones encubiertas⟩
covert[2] [ˈkʌvərt, ˈko:-] *n* THICKET : espesura *f*, maleza *f*
cover–up [ˈkʌvərˌʌp] *n* : encubrimiento *m* (de algo ilícito)
covet [ˈkʌvət] *vt* : codiciar
covetous [ˈkʌvət̬əs] *adj* : codicioso
covey [ˈkʌvi] *n, pl* **-eys 1** : bandada *f* pequeña (de codornices, etc.) **2** GROUP : grupo *m*
cow[1] [ˈkaʊ] *vt* : intimidar, acobardar
cow[2] *n* : vaca *f*, hembra *f* (de ciertas especies)
coward [ˈkaʊərd] *n* : cobarde *mf*
cowardice [ˈkaʊərdɪs] *n* : cobardía *f*
cowardly [ˈkaʊərdli] *adj* : cobarde
cowboy [ˈkaʊˌbɔɪ] *n* : vaquero *m*, cowboy *m*
cower [ˈkaʊər] *vi* : encogerse (de miedo), acobardarse
cowgirl [ˈkaʊˌgərl] *n* : vaquera *f*
cowherd [ˈkaʊˌhərd] *n* : vaquero *m*, -ra *f*
cowhide [ˈkaʊˌhaɪd] *n* : cuero *m*, piel *f* de vaca
cowl [ˈkaʊl] *n* : capucha *f* (de un monje)
cowlick [ˈkaʊˌlɪk] *n* : remolino *m*
cowpuncher [ˈkaʊˌpʌntʃər] → **cowboy**
cowslip [ˈkaʊˌslɪp] *n* : prímula *f*, primavera *f*
coxswain [ˈkaksən, -ˌsweɪn] *n* : timonel *m*
coy [ˈkɔɪ] *adj* **1** SHY : tímido, cohibido **2** COQUETTISH : coqueto
coyote [kaɪˈo:t̬i, ˈkaɪˌo:t] *n, pl* **coyotes** *or* **coyote** : coyote *m*
cozy [ˈko:zi] *adj* **-zier; -est** : acogedor, cómodo
CPU [ˌsi:ˌpi:ˈju:] *n* (*c*entral *p*rocessing *u*nit) : CPU *f*
crab [ˈkræb] *n* : cangrejo *m*, jaiba *f*
crabby [ˈkræbi] *adj* **-bier; -est** : gruñón, malhumorado
crabgrass [ˈkræbˌgræs] *n* : garranchuelo *m*
crack[1] [ˈkræk] *vi* **1** : chasquear, restallar ⟨the whip cracked : el látigo restalló⟩ **2** SPLIT : rajarse, resquebrajarse, agrietarse **3** : quebrarse (dícese de la voz) — *vt* **1** : restallar, chasquear (un látigo, etc.) **2** SPLIT : rajar, agrietar, resquebrajar **3** BREAK : romper (un huevo), cascar (nueces), forzar (una caja fuerte) **4** SOLVE : resolver, descifrar (un código)
crack[2] *adj* FIRST-RATE : buenísimo, de primera
crack[3] *n* **1** : chasquido *m*, restallido *m*, estallido *m* (de un arma de fuego), crujido *m* (de huesos) ⟨a crack of thunder : un trueno⟩ **2** WISECRACK : chiste *m*, ocurrencia *f*, salida *f* **3** CREVICE : raja *f*, grieta *f*, fisura *f* **4** BLOW : golpe *m* **5** ATTEMPT : intento *m*
crackdown [ˈkrækˌdaʊn] *n* : medidas *fpl* enérgicas
crack down *vt* : tomar medidas enérgicas
cracker [ˈkrækər] *n* : galleta *f* (de soda, etc.)
crackle[1] [ˈkrækəl] *vi* **-led; -ling** : crepitar, chisporrotear
crackle[2] *n* : crujido *m*, chisporroteo *m*
crackpot [ˈkrækˌpat] *n* : excéntrico *m*, -ca *f*; chiflado *m*, -da *f*
crack–up [ˈkrækˌʌp] *n* **1** CRASH : choque *m*, estrellamiento *m* **2** BREAKDOWN : crisis *f* nerviosa
crack up *vt* **1** : estrellar (un vehículo) **2** : hacer reír **3** : elogiar ⟨it isn't all that it's cracked up to be : no es tan bueno como se dice⟩ — *vi* **1** : estrellarse **2** LAUGH : echarse a reír

cradle[1] [ˈkreɪdəl] *vt* **-dled; -dling** : acunar, mecer (a un niño)
cradle[2] *n* : cuna *f*
craft [ˈkræft] *n* **1** TRADE : oficio *m* ⟨the craft of carpentry : el oficio de carpintero⟩ **2** CRAFTSMANSHIP, SKILL : arte *m*, artesanía *f*, destreza *f* **3** CRAFTINESS : astucia *f*, maña *f* **4** *pl usually* **craft** BOAT : barco *m*, embarcación *f* **5** *pl usually* **craft** AIRCRAFT : avión *m*, aeronave *f*
craftiness [ˈkræftinəs] *n* : astucia *f*, maña *f*
craftsman [ˈkræftsmən] *n, pl* **-men** [-mən, -ˌmɛn] : artesano *m*, -na *f*
craftsmanship [ˈkræftsmənˌʃɪp] *n* : artesanía *f*, destreza *f*
crafty [ˈkræfti] *adj* **craftier; -est** : astuto, taimado
crag [ˈkræg] *n* : peñasco *m*
craggy [ˈkrægi] *adj* **-gier; -est** : peñascoso
cram [ˈkræm] *v* **crammed; cramming** *vt* **1** JAM : embutir, meter **2** STUFF : atiborrar, abarrotar ⟨crammed with people : atiborrado de gente⟩ — *vi* : estudiar a última hora, memorizar (para un examen)
cramp[1] [ˈkræmp] *vt* **1** : dar calambre en **2** RESTRICT : limitar, restringir, entorpecer ⟨to cramp someone's style : cortarle el vuelo a alguien⟩ — *vi or* **to cramp up** : acalambrarse
cramp[2] *n* **1** SPASM : calambre *m*, espasmo *m* (de los músculos) **2** **cramps** *npl* : retorcijones *mpl* ⟨stomach cramps : retorcijones de estómago⟩
cranberry [ˈkrænˌbɛri] *n, pl* **-berries** : arándano *m* (rojo y agrio)
crane[1] [ˈkreɪn] *vt* **craned; craning** : estirar ⟨to crane one's neck : estirar el cuello⟩
crane[2] *n* **1** : grulla *f* (ave) **2** : grúa *f* (máquina)
cranial [ˈkreɪniəl] *adj* : craneal, craneano
cranium [ˈkreɪniəm] *n, pl* **-niums** *or* **-nia** [-niə] : cráneo *m*
crank[1] [ˈkræŋk] *vt or* **to crank up** : arrancar (con una manivela)
crank[2] *n* **1** : manivela *f*, manubrio *m* **2** ECCENTRIC : excéntrico *m*, -ca *f*
cranky [ˈkræŋki] *adj* **crankier; -est** : irritable, malhumorado, enojadizo
cranny [ˈkræni] *n, pl* **-nies** : grieta *f* ⟨every nook and cranny : todos los rincones⟩
crash[1] [ˈkræʃ] *vi* **1** SMASH : caerse con estrépito, estrellarse **2** COLLIDE : estrellarse, chocar **3** BOOM, RESOUND : retumbar, resonar — *vt* **1** SMASH : estrellar **2 to crash a party** : colarse en una fiesta **3 to crash one's car** : tener un accidente
crash[2] *n* **1** DIN : estrépito *m* **2** COLLISION : choque *m*, colisión *f* ⟨car crash : accidente automovilístico⟩ **3** FAILURE : quiebra *f* (de un negocio), crac *m* (de la bolsa)
crass [ˈkræs] *adj* : grosero, de mal gusto
crate[1] [ˈkreɪt] *vt* **crated; crating** : empacar en un cajón
crate[2] *n* : cajón *m* (de madera)
crater [ˈkreɪt̬ər] *n* : cráter *m*
cravat [krəˈvæt] *n* : corbata *f*
crave [ˈkreɪv] *vt* **craved; craving** : ansiar, apetecer, tener muchas ganas de
craven [ˈkreɪvən] *adj* : cobarde, pusilánime
craving [ˈkreɪvɪŋ] *n* : ansia *f*, antojo *m*, deseo *m*
crawfish [ˈkrɔˌfɪʃ] → **crayfish**
crawl[1] [ˈkrɔl] *vi* **1** CREEP : arrastrarse, gatear (dícese de un bebé) **2** TEEM : estar plagado
crawl[2] *n* : paso *m* lento
crayfish [ˈkreɪˌfɪʃ] *n* **1** : ástaco *m* (de agua dulce) **2** : langostino *m* (de mar)
crayon [ˈkreɪˌɑn, -ən] *n* : crayón *m*
craze [ˈkreɪz] *n* : moda *f* pasajera, manía *f*
crazed [ˈkreɪzd] *adj* : enloquecido
crazily [ˈkreɪzəli] *adv* : locamente, erráticamente, insensatamente
craziness [ˈkreɪzinəs] *n* : locura *f*, demencia *f*
crazy [ˈkreɪzi] *adj* **-zier; -est** **1** INSANE : loco, demente ⟨to go crazy : volverse loco⟩ **2** ABSURD, FOOLISH : loco, insensato, absurdo **3 like crazy** : como loco **4 to be crazy about** : estar loco por
creak[1] [ˈkriːk] *vi* : chirriar, rechinar, crujir
creak[2] *n* : chirrido *m*, crujido *m*
creaky [ˈkriːki] *adj* **creakier; -est** : chirriante, que cruje
cream[1] [ˈkriːm] *vt* **1** BEAT, MIX : batir, mezclar (azúcar y mantequilla, etc.) **2** : preparar (alimentos) con crema
cream[2] *n* **1** : crema *f* (de leche) **2** LOTION : crema *f*, loción *f* **3** ELITE : crema *f*, elite *f* ⟨the cream of the crop : la crema y nata, lo mejor⟩
creamery [ˈkriːməri] *n, pl* **-eries** : fábrica *f* de productos lácteos
creamy [ˈkriːmi] *adj* **creamier; -est** : cremoso
crease[1] [ˈkriːs] *vt* **creased; creasing** **1** : plegar, poner una raya en (pantalones) **2** WRINKLE : arrugar
crease[2] *n* : pliegue *m*, doblez *m*, raya *f* (de pantalones)
create [kriˈeɪt] *vt* **-ated; -ating** : crear, hacer
creation [kriˈeɪʃən] *n* : creación *f*
creative [kriˈeɪt̬ɪv] *adj* : creativo, original ⟨creative people : personas creativas⟩ ⟨a creative work : un obra original⟩
creatively [kriˈeɪt̬ɪvli] *adv* : creativamente, con originalidad
creativity [ˌkriːeɪˈtɪvət̬i] *n* : creatividad *f*
creator [kriˈeɪt̬ər] *n* : creador *m*, -dora *f*
creature [ˈkriːtʃər] *n* : ser *m* viviente, criatura *f*, animal *m*

credence ['kri:dənts] *n* : crédito *m*

credentials [krɪ'dɛntʃəlz] *npl* : referencias *fpl* oficiales, cartas *fpl* credenciales

credibility [ˌkrɛdə'bɪləṭi] *n* : credibilidad *f*

credible ['krɛdəbəl] *adj* : creíble

credit[1] ['krɛdɪt] *vt* **1** BELIEVE : creer, dar crédito a **2** : ingresar, abonar ⟨to credit $100 to an account : ingresar $100 en (una) cuenta⟩ **3** ATTRIBUTE : atribuir ⟨they credit the invention to him : a él se le atribuye el invento⟩

credit[2] *n* **1** : saldo *m* positivo, saldo *m* a favor (de una cuenta) **2** : crédito *m* ⟨to buy on credit : comprar a crédito⟩ ⟨credit card : tarjeta de crédito⟩ **3** CREDENCE : crédito *m* ⟨I gave credit to everything he said : di crédito a todo lo que dijo⟩ **4** RECOGNITION : reconocimiento *m* **5** : orgullo *m*, honor *m* ⟨she's a credit to the school : ella es el orgullo de la escuela⟩

creditable ['krɛdɪṭəbəl] *adj* : encomiable, loable — **creditably** [-bli] *adv*

credit card *n* : tarjeta de crédito

creditor ['krɛdɪṭər] *n* : acreedor *m*, -dora *f*

credo ['kri:do:, 'kreɪ-] *n* : credo *m*

credulity [krɪ'du:ləṭi, -'dju:-] *n* : credulidad *f*

credulous ['krɛdʒələs] *adj* : crédulo

creed ['kri:d] *n* : credo *m*

creek ['kri:k, 'krɪk] *n* : arroyo *m*, riachuelo *m*

creel ['kri:l] *n* : nasa *f*, cesta *f* (de pescador)

creep[1] ['kri:p] *vi* **crept** ['krɛpt]; **creeping** **1** CRAWL : arrastrarse, gatear **2** : moverse lentamente o sigilosamente ⟨he crept out of the house : salió sigilosamente de la casa⟩ **3** SPREAD : trepar (dícese de una planta)

creep[2] *n* **1** CRAWL : paso *m* lento **2** : asqueroso *m*, -sa *f* **3** **creeps** *npl* : escalofríos *mpl* ⟨that gives me the creeps : eso me da escalofríos⟩

creeper ['kri:pər] *n* : planta *f* trepadora, trepadora *f*

creepy ['kri:pi] *adj* **1** SPOOKY : espeluznante **2** UNPLEASANT : asqueroso

cremate ['kri:ˌmeɪt] *vt* **-mated; -mating** : cremar

cremation [krɪ'meɪʃən] *n* : cremación *f*

Creole ['kri:ˌo:l] *n* **1** : criollo *m*, criolla *f* **2** : criollo *m* (idioma) — **Creole** *adj*

creosote ['kri:əˌso:t] *n* : creosota *f*

crepe *or* **crêpe** ['kreɪp] *n* **1** : crespón *m* (tela) **2** PANCAKE : crepe *mf*, crepa *f* *Mex*

crescendo [krɪ'ʃɛnˌdo:] *n, pl* **-dos** *or* **-does** : crescendo *m*

crescent ['krɛsənt] *n* : creciente *m*

crest ['krɛst] *n* **1** : cresta *f*, penacho *m* (de un ave) **2** PEAK, TOP : cresta *f* (de una ola), cima *f* (de una colina) **3** : emblema *m* (sobre un escudo de armas)

crestfallen ['krɛstˌfɔlən] *adj* : alicaído, abatido

cretin ['kri:tən] *n* : cretino *m*, -na *f*

crevasse [krɪ'væs] *n* : grieta *f*, fisura *f*

crevice ['krɛvɪs] *n* : grieta *f*, hendidura *f*

crew ['kru:] *n* **1** : tripulación *f* (de una nave) **2** TEAM : equipo *m* (de trabajadores o atletas)

crib ['krɪb] *n* **1** MANGER : pesebre *m* **2** GRANARY : granero *m* **3** : cuna *f* (de un bebé)

crick ['krɪk] *n* : calambre *m*, espasmo *m* muscular

cricket ['krɪkət] *n* **1** : grillo *m* (insecto) **2** : críquet *m* (juego)

crime ['kraɪm] *n* **1** : crimen *m*, delito *m* ⟨to commit a crime : cometer un delito⟩ **2** : crimen *m*, delincuencia *f* ⟨organized crime : crimen organizado⟩

criminal[1] ['krɪmənəl] *adj* : criminal

criminal[2] *n* : criminal *mf*, delincuente *mf*

crimp ['krɪmp] *vt* : ondular, rizar (el pelo), arrugar (una tela, etc.)

crimson ['krɪmzən] *n* : carmesí *m*

cringe ['krɪndʒ] *vi* **cringed; cringing** : encogerse

crinkle[1] ['krɪŋkəl] *v* **-kled; -kling** *vt* : arrugar — *vi* : arrugarse

crinkle[2] *n* : arruga *f*

crinkly ['krɪŋkəli] *adj* : arrugado

cripple[1] ['krɪpəl] *vt* **-pled; -pling** **1** DISABLE : lisiar, dejar inválido **2** INCAPACITATE : inutilizar, incapacitar

cripple[2] *n* : lisiado *m*, -da *f*

crisis ['kraɪsɪs] *n, pl* **crises** [-ˌsi:z] : crisis *f*

crisp[1] ['krɪsp] *vt* : tostar, hacer crujiente

crisp[2] *adj* **1** CRUNCHY : crujiente, crocante **2** FIRM, FRESH : firme, fresco ⟨crisp lettuce : lechuga fresca⟩ **3** LIVELY : vivaz, alegre ⟨a crisp tempo : un ritmo alegre⟩ **4** INVIGORATING : fresco, vigorizante ⟨the crisp autumn air : el fresco aire otoñal⟩ — **crisply** *adv*

crisp[3] *n* : postre *m* de fruta (con pedacitos de masa dulce por encima)

crispy ['krɪspi] *adj* **crispier; -est** : crujiente ⟨crispy potato chips : papitas crujientes⟩

crisscross ['krɪsˌkrɔs] *vt* : entrecruzar

criterion [kraɪ'tɪriən] *n, pl* **-ria** [-iə] : criterio *m*

critic ['krɪṭɪk] *n* **1** : crítico *m*, -ca *f* (de las artes) **2** FAULTFINDER : detractor *m*, -tora *f*; criticón *m*, -cona *f*

critical ['krɪṭɪkəl] *adj* : crítico

critically ['krɪṭɪkli] *adv* : críticamente ⟨critically ill : gravemente enfermo⟩

criticism ['krɪṭəˌsɪzəm] *n* : crítica *f*

criticize ['krɪṭəˌsaɪz] *vt* **-cized; -cizing** **1** EVALUATE, JUDGE : criticar, analizar, evaluar **2** CENSURE : criticar, reprobar

critique [krɪ'ti:k] *n* : crítica *f*, evaluación *f*

croak[1] ['kro:k] *vi* : croar

croak[2] *n* : croar *m*, canto *m* (de la rana)

Croatian [kro'eɪʃən] *n* : croata *mf* — **Croatian** *adj*

crochet[1] [kroːˈʃeɪ] *v* : tejer al croché
crochet[2] *n* : croché *m*, crochet *m*
crock [ˈkrɑk] *n* : vasija *f* de barro
crockery [ˈkrɑkəri] *n* : vajilla *f* (de barro)
crocodile [ˈkrɑkəˌdaɪl] *n* : cocodrilo *m*
crocus [ˈkroːkəs] *n, pl* **-cuses** : azafrán *m*
croissant [krəˈsɑnt] *n* : croissant *m*
crone [ˈkroːn] *n* : vieja *f* arpía, vieja *f* bruja
crony [ˈkroːni] *n, pl* **-nies** : amigote *m fam*; compinche *mf fam*
crook[1] [ˈkrʊk] *vt* : doblar (el brazo o el dedo)
crook[2] *n* **1** STAFF : cayado *m* (de pastor), báculo *m* (de obispo) **2** THIEF : ratero *m*, -ra *f*; ladrón *m*, -drona *f*
crooked [ˈkrʊkəd] *adj* **1** BENT : chueco, torcido **2** DISHONEST : deshonesto
crookedness [ˈkrʊkədnəs] *n* **1** : lo torcido, lo chueco **2** DISHONESTY : falta *f* de honradez
croon [ˈkruːn] *v* : cantar suavemente
crop[1] [ˈkrɑp] *v* **cropped; cropping** *vt* TRIM : recortar, cortar — *vi* **to crop up** : aparecer, surgir ⟨these problems keep cropping up : estos problemas no cesan de surgir⟩
crop[2] *n* **1** : buche *m* (de un ave o insecto) **2** WHIP : fusta *f* (de jinete) **3** HARVEST : cosecha *f*, cultivo *m*
croquet [ˌkroːˈkeɪ] *n* : croquet *m*
croquette [ˌkroːˈkɛt] *n* : croqueta *f*
cross[1] [ˈkrɔs] *vt* **1** : cruzar, atravesar ⟨to cross the street : cruzar la calle⟩ ⟨several canals cross the city : varios canales atraviesan la ciudad⟩ **2** CANCEL : tachar, cancelar ⟨he crossed his name off the list : tachó su nombre de la planilla⟩ **3** INTERBREED : cruzar (en genética)
cross[2] *adj* **1** : que atraviesa ⟨cross ventilation : ventilación que atraviesa un cuarto⟩ **2** CONTRARY : contrario, opuesto ⟨cross purposes : objetivos opuestos⟩ **3** ANGRY : enojado, de mal humor
cross[3] *n* **1** : cruz *f* ⟨the sign of the cross : la señal de la cruz⟩ **2** : cruza *f* (en biología)
crossbones [ˈkrɔsˌboːnz] *npl* **1** : huesos *mpl* cruzados **2** → **skull**
crossbow [ˈkrɔsˌboː] *n* : ballesta *f*
crossbreed [ˈkrɔsˌbriːd] *vt* **-bred** [-ˌbrɛd]; **-breeding** : cruzar
crosscurrent [ˈkrɔsˌkərənt] *n* : contracorriente *f*
cross–examination [ˌkrɔsɪgˌzæməˈneɪʃən] *n* : repreguntas *fpl*, interrogatorio *m*
cross–examine [ˌkrɔsɪgˈzæmən] *vt* **-ined; -ining** : repreguntar
cross–eyed [ˈkrɔsˌaɪd] *adj* : bizco
crossing [ˈkrɔsɪŋ] *n* **1** INTERSECTION : cruce *m*, paso *m* ⟨pedestrian crossing : paso de peatones⟩ **2** VOYAGE : travesía *f* (del mar)
crossly [ˈkrɔsli] *adv* : con enojo, con enfado
cross–reference [ˌkrɔsˈrɛfrənts, -ˈrɛfərənts] *n* : referencia *f*, remisión *f*
crossroads [ˈkrɔsˌroːdz] *n* : cruce *m*, encrucijada *f*, crucero *m Mex*
cross section *n* **1** SECTION : corte *m* transversal **2** SAMPLE : muestra *f* representativa ⟨a cross section of the population : una muestra representativa de la población⟩
crosswalk [ˈkrɔsˌwɔk] *n* : cruce *m* peatonal, paso *m* de peatones
crossways [ˈkrɔsˌweɪz] → **crosswise**
crosswise[1] [ˈkrɔsˌwaɪz] *adv* : transversalmente, diagonalmente
crosswise[2] *adj* : transversal, diagonal
crossword puzzle [ˈkrɔsˌwərd] *n* : crucigrama *m*
crotch [ˈkrɑtʃ] *n* : entrepierna *f*
crotchety [ˈkrɑtʃət̬i] *adj* CRANKY : malhumorado, irritable, enojadizo
crouch [ˈkraʊtʃ] *vi* : agacharse, ponerse de cuclillas
croup [ˈkruːp] *n* : crup *m*
crouton [ˈkruːˌtɑn] *n* : crutón *m*
crow[1] [ˈkroː] *vi* **1** : cacarear, cantar (como un cuervo) **2** BRAG : alardear, presumir
crow[2] *n* **1** : cuervo *m* (ave) **2** : cantar *m* (del gallo)
crowbar [ˈkroːˌbɑr] *n* : palanca *f*
crowd[1] [ˈkraʊd] *vi* : aglomerarse, amontonarse — *vt* : atestar, atiborrar, llenar
crowd[2] *n* : multitud *f*, muchedumbre *f*, gentío *m*
crown[1] [ˈkraʊn] *vt* : coronar
crown[2] *n* : corona *f*
crow's nest *n* : cofa *f*
crucial [ˈkruːʃəl] *adj* : crucial, decisivo
crucible [ˈkruːsəbəl] *n* : crisol *m*
crucifix [ˈkruːsəˌfɪks] *n* : crucifijo *m*
crucifixion [ˌkruːsəˈfɪkʃən] *n* : crucifixión *f*
crucify [ˈkruːsəˌfaɪ] *vt* **-fied; -fying** : crucificar
crude [ˈkruːd] *adj* **cruder; -est** **1** RAW, UNREFINED : crudo, sin refinar ⟨crude oil : petróleo crudo⟩ **2** VULGAR : grosero, de mal gusto **3** ROUGH : tosco, burdo, rudo
crudely [ˈkruːdli] *adv* **1** VULGARLY : groseramente **2** ROUGHLY : burdamente, de manera rudimentaria
crudity [ˈkruːdət̬i] *n, pl* **-ties** **1** VULGARITY : grosería *f* **2** COARSENESS, ROUGHNESS : tosquedad *f*, rudeza *f*
cruel [ˈkruːəl] *adj* **-eler** *or* **-eller; -elest** *or* **-ellest** : cruel
cruelly [ˈkruːəli] *adv* : cruelmente
cruelty [ˈkruːəlti] *n, pl* **-ties** : crueldad *f*
cruet [ˈkruːɪt] *n* : vinagrera *f*, aceitera *f*
cruise[1] [ˈkruːz] *vi* **cruised; cruising** **1** : hacer un crucero **2** : navegar o conducir a una velocidad constante ⟨cruising speed : velocidad de crucero⟩
cruise[2] *n* : crucero *m*

cruiser [ˈkru:zər] *n* **1** WARSHIP : crucero *m*, buque *m* de guerra **2** : patrulla *f* (de policía)

crumb [ˈkrʌm] *n* : miga *f*, migaja *f*

crumble [ˈkrʌmbəl] *v* **-bled; -bling** *vt* : desmigajar, desmenuzar — *vi* : desmigajarse, desmoronarse, desmenuzarse

crumbly [ˈkrʌmbli] *adj* : que se desmenuza fácilmente, friable

crumple [ˈkrʌmpəl] *v* **-pled; -pling** *vt* RUMPLE : arrugar — *vi* **1** WRINKLE : arrugarse **2** COLLAPSE : desplomarse

crunch[1] [ˈkrʌntʃ] *vt* **1** : ronzar (con los dientes) **2** : hacer crujir (con los pies, etc.) — *vi* : crujir

crunch[2] *n* : crujido *m*

crunchy [ˈkrʌntʃi] *adj* **crunchier; -est** : crujiente

crusade[1] [kru:ˈseɪd] *vi* **-saded; -sading** : hacer una campaña (a favor de o contra algo)

crusade[2] *n* **1** : campaña *f* (de reforma, etc.) **2 Crusade** : cruzada *f*

crusader [kru:ˈseɪdər] *n* **1** : cruzado *m* (en la Edad Media) **2** : campeón *m*, -peona *f* (de una causa)

crush[1] [ˈkrʌʃ] *vt* **1** SQUASH : aplastar, apachurrar **2** GRIND, PULVERIZE : triturar, machacar **3** SUPPRESS : aplastar, suprimir

crush[2] *n* **1** CROWD, MOB : gentío *m*, multitud *f*, aglomeración *f* **2** INFATUATION : enamoramiento *m*

crushing [ˈkrʌʃɪŋ] *adj* : aplastante, abrumador

crust [ˈkrʌst] *n* **1** : corteza *f*, costra *f* (de pan) **2** : tapa *f* de masa, pasta *f* (de un pastel) **3** LAYER : capa *f*, corteza *f* ⟨the earth's crust : la corteza terrestre⟩

crustacean [ˌkrʌsˈteɪʃən] *n* : crustáceo *m*

crusty [ˈkrʌsti] *adj* **crustier; -est 1** : de corteza dura **2** CROSS, GRUMPY : enojado, malhumorado

crutch [ˈkrʌtʃ] *n* : muleta *f*

crux [ˈkrʌks, ˈkrʊks] *n, pl* **cruxes** : quid *m*, esencia *f*, meollo *m* ⟨the crux of the problem : el quid del problema⟩

cry[1] [ˈkraɪ] *vi* **cried; crying 1** SHOUT : gritar ⟨they cried for more : a gritos pidieron más⟩ **2** WEEP : llorar

cry[2] *n, pl* **cries 1** SHOUT : grito *m* **2** WEEPING : llanto *m* **3** : chillido *m* (de un animal)

crybaby [ˈkraɪˌbeɪbi] *n, pl* **-bies** : llorón *m*, -rona *f*

crypt [ˈkrɪpt] *n* : cripta *f*

cryptic [ˈkrɪptɪk] *adj* : enigmático, críptico

crystal [ˈkrɪstəl] *n* : cristal *m*

crystalline [ˈkrɪstəlɪn] *adj* : cristalino

crystallize [ˈkrɪstəˌlaɪz] *v* **-lized; -lizing** *vt* : cristalizar, materializar ⟨to crystallize one's thoughts : cristalizar uno sus pensamientos⟩ — *vi* : cristalizarse

cub [ˈkʌb] *n* : cachorro *m*

Cuban [ˈkju:bən] *n* : cubano *m*, -na *f* — **Cuban** *adj*

cubbyhole [ˈkʌbiˌho:l] *n* : chiribitil *m*

cube[1] [ˈkju:b] *vt* **cubed; cubing 1** : elevar (un número) al cubo **2** : cortar en cubos

cube[2] *n* **1** : cubo *m* **2 ice cube** : cubito *m* de hielo **3 sugar cube** : terrón *m* de azúcar

cubic [ˈkju:bɪk] *adj* : cúbico

cubicle [ˈkju:bɪkəl] *n* : cubículo *m*

cuckoo[1] [ˈku:ˌku:, ˈkʊ-] *adj* : loco, chiflado

cuckoo[2] *n, pl* **-oos** : cuco *m*, cuclillo *m*

cucumber [ˈkju:ˌkʌmbər] *n* : pepino *m*

cud [ˈkʌd] *n* **to chew the cud** : rumiar

cuddle [ˈkʌdəl] *v* **-dled; -dling** *vi* : abrazarse tiernamente, acurrucarse — *vt* : abrazar

cudgel[1] [ˈkʌdʒəl] *vt* **-geled** *or* **-gelled; -geling** *or* **-gelling** : apalear, aporrear

cudgel[2] *n* : garrote *m*, porra *f*

cue[1] [ˈkju:] *vt* **cued; cuing** *or* **cueing** : darle el pie a, darle la señal a

cue[2] *n* **1** SIGNAL : señal *f*, pie *m* (en teatro), entrada *f* (en música) **2** : taco *m* (de billar)

cuff[1] [ˈkʌf] *vt* : bofetear, cachetear

cuff[2] *n* **1** : puño *m* (de una camisa), vuelta *f* (de pantalones) **2** SLAP : bofetada *f*, cachetada *f* **3 cuffs** *npl* HANDCUFFS : esposas *fpl*

cuisine [kwɪˈzi:n] *n* : cocina *f* ⟨Mexican cuisine : la cocina mexicana⟩

culinary [ˈkʌləˌnɛri, ˈkju:lə-] *adj* : culinario

cull [ˈkʌl] *vt* : seleccionar, entresacar

culminate [ˈkʌlməˌneɪt] *vi* **-nated; -nating** : culminar

culmination [ˌkʌlməˈneɪʃən] *n* : culminación *f*, punto *m* culminante

culpable [ˈkʌlpəbəl] *adj* : culpable

culprit [ˈkʌlprɪt] *n* : culpable *mf*

cult [ˈkʌlt] *n* : culto *m*

cultivate [ˈkʌltəˌveɪt] *vt* **-vated; -vating 1** TILL : cultivar, labrar **2** FOSTER : cultivar, fomentar **3** REFINE : cultivar, refinar ⟨to cultivate the mind : cultivar la mente⟩

cultivation [ˌkʌltəˈveɪʃən] *n* **1** : cultivo *m* ⟨under cultivation : en cultivo⟩ **2** CULTURE, REFINEMENT : cultura *f*, refinamiento *m*

cultural [ˈkʌltʃərəl] *adj* : cultural — **culturally** *adv*

culture [ˈkʌltʃər] *n* **1** CULTIVATION : cultivo *m* **2** REFINEMENT : cultura *f*, educación *f*, refinamiento *m* **3** CIVILIZATION : cultura *f*, civilización *f* ⟨the Incan culture : la cultura inca⟩

cultured [ˈkʌltʃərd] *adj* **1** EDUCATED, REFINED : culto, educado, refinado **2** : de cultivo, cultivado ⟨cultured pearls : perlas de cultivo⟩

culvert [ˈkʌlvərt] *n* : alcantarilla *f*

cumbersome [ˈkʌmbərsəm] *adj* : torpe y pesado, difícil de manejar

cumin [ˈkʌmən] *n* : comino *m*

cumulative [ˈkju:mjələṭɪv, -ˌleɪṭɪv] *adj* : acumulativo

cumulus ['kju:mjələs] *n, pl* **-li** [-ˌlaɪ, -ˌli:] : cúmulo *m*
cunning[1] ['kʌnɪŋ] *adj* **1** CRAFTY : astuto, taimado **2** CLEVER : ingenioso, hábil **3** CUTE : mono, gracioso, lindo
cunning[2] *n* **1** SKILL : habilidad *f* **2** CRAFTINESS : astucia *f*, maña *f*
cup[1] ['kʌp] *vt* **cupped; cupping** : ahuecar (las manos)
cup[2] *n* **1** : taza *f* ⟨a cup of coffee : una taza de café⟩ **2** CUPFUL : taza *f* **3** : media pinta *f* (unidad de medida) **4** GOBLET : copa *f* **5** TROPHY : copa *f*, trofeo *m*
cupboard ['kʌbərd] *n* : alacena *f*, armario *m*
cupcake ['kʌpˌkeɪk] *n* : pastelito *m*
cupful ['kʌpˌfʊl] *n* : taza *f*
cupola ['kju:pələ, -ˌlo:] *n* : cúpula *f*
cur ['kər] *n* : perro *m* callejero, perro *m* corriente *Mex*
curate ['kjʊrət] *n* : cura *m*, párroco *m*
curator ['kjʊrˌeɪt̬ər, kjʊ'reɪt̬ər] *n* : conservador *m*, -dora *f* (de un museo); director *m*, -tora *f* (de un zoológico)
curb[1] ['kərb] *vt* : refrenar, restringir, controlar
curb[2] *n* **1** RESTRAINT : freno *m*, control *m* **2** : borde *m* de la acera
curd ['kərd] *n* : cuajada *f*
curdle ['kərdəl] *v* **-dled; -dling** *vi* : cuajarse — *vt* : cuajar ⟨to curdle one's blood : helarle la sangre a uno⟩
cure[1] ['kjʊr] *vt* **cured; curing** **1** HEAL : curar, sanar **2** REMEDY : remediar **3** PROCESS : curar (alimentos, etc.)
cure[2] *n* **1** RECOVERY : curación *f*, recuperación *f* **2** REMEDY : cura *f*, remedio *m*
curfew ['kərˌfju:] *n* : toque *m* de queda
curio ['kjʊriˌo:] *n, pl* **-rios** : curiosidad *f*, objeto *m* curioso
curiosity [ˌkjʊri'ɑsət̬i] *n, pl* **-ties** : curiosidad *f*
curious ['kjʊriəs] *adj* **1** INQUISITIVE : curioso **2** STRANGE : curioso, raro
curl[1] ['kərl] *vt* **1** : rizar, ondular (el pelo) **2** COIL : enrollar **3** TWIST : torcer ⟨to curl one's lip : hacer una mueca⟩ — *vi* **1** : rizarse, ondularse **2 to curl up** : acurrucarse (con un libro, etc.)
curl[2] *n* **1** RINGLET : rizo *m* **2** COIL : espiral *f*, rosca *f*
curler ['kərlər] *n* : rulo *m*
curlew ['kərˌlu:, 'kərlˌju:] *n, pl* **-lews** *or* **-lew** : zarapito *m*
curly ['kərli] *adj* **curlier; -est** : rizado, crespo
currant ['kərənt] *n* **1** : grosella *f* (fruta) **2** RAISIN : pasa *f* de Corinto
currency ['kərəntsi] *n, pl* **-cies** **1** PREVALENCE, USE : uso *m*, aceptación *f*, difusión *f* ⟨to be in currency : estar en uso⟩ **2** MONEY : moneda *f*, dinero *m*
current[1] ['kərənt] *adj* **1** PRESENT : actual ⟨current events : actualidades⟩ **2** PREVALENT : corriente, común — **currently** *adv*
current[2] *n* : corriente *f*
curriculum [kə'rɪkjələm] *n, pl* **-la** [-lə] : currículum *m*, currículo *m*, programa *m* de estudio
curriculum vitae ['vi:ˌtaɪ, 'vaɪt̬i] *n, pl* **curricula vitae** : currículum *m*, currículo *m*
curry[1] ['kəri] *vt* **-ried; -rying** **1** GROOM : almohazar (un caballo) **2** : condimentar con curry **3 to curry favor** : congraciarse (con alguien)
curry[2] *n, pl* **-ries** : curry *m*
curse[1] ['kərs] *v* **cursed; cursing** *vt* **1** DAMN : maldecir **2** INSULT : injuriar, insultar, decir malas palabras a **3** AFFLICT : afligir — *vi* : maldecir, decir malas palabras
curse[2] *n* **1** : maldición *f* ⟨to put a curse on someone : echarle una maldición a alguien⟩ **2** AFFLICTION : maldición *f*, aflicción *f*, cruz *f*
cursor ['kərsər] *n* : cursor *m*
cursory ['kərsəri] *adj* : rápido, superficial, somero
curt ['kərt] *adj* : cortante, brusco, seco — **curtly** *adv*
curtail [kər'teɪl] *vt* : acortar, limitar, restringir
curtailment [kər'teɪlmənt] *n* : restricción *f*, limitación *f*
curtain ['kərtən] *n* : cortina *f* (de una ventana), telón *m* (en un teatro)
curtness ['kərtnəs] *n* : brusquedad *f*, sequedad *f*
curtsy[1] *or* **curtsey** ['kərtsi] *vt* **-sied** *or* **-seyed; -sying** *or* **-seying** : hacer una reverencia
curtsy[2] *or* **curtsey** *n, pl* **-sies** *or* **-seys** : reverencia *f*
curvature ['kərvəˌʧʊr] *n* : curvatura *f*
curve[1] ['kərv] *v* **curved; curving** *vi* : torcerse, describir una curva — *vt* : encorvar
curve[2] *n* : curva *f*
cushion[1] ['kʊʃən] *vt* **1** : poner cojines o almohadones a **2** SOFTEN : amortiguar, mitigar, suavizar ⟨to cushion a blow : amortiguar un golpe⟩
cushion[2] *n* **1** : cojín *m*, almohadón *m* **2** PROTECTION : colchón *m*, protección *f*
cusp ['kʌsp] *n* : cúspide *f* (de un diente), cuerno *m* (de la luna)
cuspid ['kʌspɪd] *n* : diente *m* canino, colmillo *m*
custard ['kʌstərd] *n* : natillas *fpl*
custodian [ˌkʌ'sto:diən] *n* : custodio *m*, -dia *f*; guardián, -diana *f*
custody ['kʌstədi] *n, pl* **-dies** : custodia *f*, cuidado *m* ⟨to be in custody : estar detenido⟩
custom[1] ['kʌstəm] *adj* : a la medida, a la orden
custom[2] *n* **1** : costumbre *f*, tradición *f* **2 customs** *npl* : aduana *f*
customarily [ˌkʌstə'mɛrəli] *adv* : habitualmente, normalmente, de costumbre

customary [ˈkʌstəˌmɛri] *adj* **1** TRADITIONAL : tradicional **2** USUAL : habitual, de costumbre

customer [ˈkʌstəmər] *n* : cliente *m*, -ta *f*

custom–made [ˈkʌstəmˈmeɪd] *adj* : hecho a la medida

cut[1] [ˈkʌt] *v* **cut; cutting** *vt* **1** : cortar ⟨to cut paper : cortar papel⟩ **2** : cortarse ⟨to cut one's finger : cortarse uno el dedo⟩ **3** TRIM : cortar, recortar ⟨to have one's hair cut : cortarse el pelo⟩ **4** INTERSECT : cruzar, atravesar **5** SHORTEN : acortar, abreviar **6** REDUCE : reducir, rebajar ⟨to cut prices : rebajar los precios⟩ **7 to cut one's teeth** : salirle los dientes a uno — *vi* **1** : cortar, cortarse **2 to cut in** : entrometerse

cut[2] *n* **1** : corte *m* ⟨a cut of meat : un corte de carne⟩ **2** SLASH : tajo *m*, corte *m*, cortadura *f* **3** REDUCTION : rebaja *f*, reducción *f* ⟨a cut in the rates : una rebaja en las tarifas⟩

cute [ˈkju:t] *adj* **cuter; -est** : mono *fam*, lindo

cuticle [ˈkju:tɪkəl] *n* : cutícula *f*

cutlass [ˈkʌtləs] *n* : alfanje *m*

cutlery [ˈkʌtləri] *n* : cubiertos *mpl*

cutlet [ˈkʌtlət] *n* : chuleta *f*

cutter [ˈkʌt̬ər] *n* **1** : cortadora *f* (implemento) **2** : cortador *m*, -dora *f* (persona) **3** : cúter *m* (embarcación)

cutthroat [ˈkʌtˌθro:t] *adj* : despiadado, desalmado ⟨cutthroat competition : competencia feroz⟩

cutting[1] [ˈkʌt̬ɪŋ] *adj* **1** : cortante ⟨a cutting wind : un viento cortante⟩ **2** CAUSTIC : mordaz

cutting[2] *n* : esqueje *m* (de una planta)

cuttlefish [ˈkʌt̬əlˌfɪʃ] *n, pl* **-fish** *or* **-fishes** : jibia *f*, sepia *f*

cyanide [ˈsaɪəˌnaɪd, -nɪd] *n* : cianuro *m*

cycle[1] [ˈsaɪkəl] *vi* **-cled; -cling** : andar en bicicleta, ir en bicicleta

cycle[2] *n* **1** : ciclo *m* ⟨life cycle : ciclo de vida, ciclo vital⟩ **2** BICYCLE : bicicleta *f* **3** MOTORCYCLE : motocicleta *f*

cyclic [ˈsaɪklɪk, ˈsɪ-] *or* **cyclical** [-klɪkəl] *adj* : cíclico

cyclist [ˈsaɪklɪst] *n* : ciclista *mf*

cyclone [ˈsaɪˌklo:n] *n* **1** : ciclón *m* **2** TORNADO : tornado *m*

cyclopedia *or* **cyclopaedia** [ˌsaɪkləˈpi:diə] → **encyclopedia**

cylinder [ˈsɪləndər] *n* : cilindro *m*

cylindrical [səˈlɪndrɪkəl] *adj* : cilíndrico

cymbal [ˈsɪmbəl] *n* : platillo *m*, címbalo *m*

cynic [ˈsɪnɪk] *n* : cínico *m*, -ca *f*

cynical [ˈsɪnɪkəl] *adj* : cínico

cynicism [ˈsɪnəˌsɪzəm] *n* : cinismo *m*

cypress [ˈsaɪprəs] *n* : ciprés *m*

Cypriot [ˈsɪpriət, -ˌɑt] *n* : chipriota *mf* — **Cypriot** *adj*

cyst [ˈsɪst] *n* : quiste *m*

cytoplasm [ˈsaɪt̬oˌplæzəm] *n* : citoplasma *m*

czar [ˈzɑr, ˈsɑr] *n* : zar *m*

czarina [zɑˈri:nə, sɑ-] *n* : zarina *f*

Czech [ˈʧɛk] *n* **1** : checo *m*, -ca *f* **2** : checo *m* (idioma) — **Czech** *adj*

Czechoslovak [ˌʧɛkoˈslo:ˌvɑk, -ˌvæk] *or* **Czechoslovakian** [-sloˈvɑkiən, -ˈvæ-] *n* : checoslovaco *m*, -ca *f* — **Czechoslovak** *or* **Czechoslovakian** *adj*

D

d [ˈdi:] *n, pl* **d's** *or* **ds** [ˈdi:z] : cuarta letra del alfabeto inglés

dab[1] [ˈdæb] *vt* **dabbed; dabbing** : darle toques ligeros a, aplicar suavemente

dab[2] *n* **1** BIT : toque *m*, pizca *f*, poco *m* ⟨a dab of ointment : un toque de ungüento⟩ **2** PAT : toque *m* ligero, golpecito *m*

dabble [ˈdæbəl] *v* **-bled; -bling** *vt* SPATTER : salpicar — *vi* **1** SPLASH : chapotear **2** TRIFLE : jugar, interesarse superficialmente

dabbler [ˈdæbələr] *n* : diletante *mf*

dachshund [ˈdɑksˌhʊnt, -ˌhʊnd; ˈdɑksənt, -sənd] *n* : perro *m* salchicha

dad [ˈdæd] *n* : papá *m fam*

daddy [ˈdædi] *n, pl* **-dies** : papi *m fam*

daffodil [ˈdæfəˌdɪl] *n* : narciso *m*

daft [ˈdæft] *adj* : tonto, bobo

dagger [ˈdægər] *n* : daga *f*, puñal *m*

dahlia [ˈdæljə, ˈdɑl-, ˈdeɪl-] *n* : dalia *f*

daily[1] [ˈdeɪli] *adv* : a diario, diariamente

daily[2] *adj* : diario, cotidiano

daily[3] *n, pl* **-lies** : diario *m*, periódico *m*

daintily [ˈdeɪntəli] *adv* : delicadamente, con delicadeza

daintiness [ˈdeɪntinəs] *n* : delicadeza *f*, finura *f*

dainty[1] [ˈdeɪnti] *adj* **-tier; -est** **1** DELICATE : delicado **2** FASTIDIOUS : remilgado, melindroso **3** DELICIOUS : exquisito, sabroso

dainty[2] *n, pl* **-ties** DELICACY : exquisitez *f*, manjar *m*

dairy [ˈdæri] *n, pl* **-ies** **1** *or* **dairy store** : lechería *f* **2** *or* **dairy farm** : granja *f* lechera

dairymaid [ˈdæriˌmeɪd] *n* : lechera *f*

dairyman [ˈdærimən, -ˌmæn] *n, pl* **-men** [-mən, -ˌmɛn] : lechero *m*

dais [ˈdeɪəs] *n* : tarima *f*, estrado *m*

daisy [ˈdeɪzi] *n, pl* **-sies** : margarita *f*

dale [ˈdeɪl] *n* : valle *m*

dally [ˈdæli] *vi* **-lied; -lying** **1** TRIFLE : juguetear **2** DAWDLE : entretenerse, perder tiempo

dalmatian [dælˈmeɪʃən, dɔl-] *n* : dálmata *m*

dam[1] [ˈdæm] *vt* **dammed; damming** : represar, embalsar

dam[2] *n* **1** : represa *f*, dique *m* **2** : madre *f* (de animales domésticos)

damage[1] ['dæmɪʤ] *vt* **-aged; -aging** : dañar (un objeto o una máquina), perjudicar (la salud o una reputación)
damage[2] *n* **1** : daño *m*, perjuicio *m* **2 damages** *npl* : daños y perjuicios *mpl*
damaging ['dæməʤɪŋ] *adj* : perjudicial
damask ['dæməsk] *n* : damasco *m*
dame ['deɪm] *n* LADY : dama *f*, señora *f*
damn[1] ['dæm] *vt* **1** CONDEMN : condenar **2** CURSE : maldecir
damn[2] *or* **damned** ['dæmd] *adj* : condenado *fam*, maldito *fam*
damn[3] *n* : pito *m*, bledo *m*, comino *m* ⟨it's not worth a damn : no vale un pito⟩ ⟨I don't give a damn : me importa un comino⟩
damnable ['dæmnəbəl] *adj* : condenable, detestable
damnation [dæm'neɪʃən] *n* : condenación *f*
damned[1] ['dæmd] *adv* VERY : muy
damned[2] *adj* **1** → **damnable 2** REMARKABLE : extraordinario
damp[1] ['dæmp] *vt* → **dampen**
damp[2] *adj* : húmedo
damp[3] *n* MOISTURE : humedad *f*
dampen ['dæmpən] *vt* **1** MOISTEN : humedecer **2** DISCOURAGE : desalentar, desanimar
damper ['dæmpər] *n* **1** : regulador *m* de tiro (de una chimenea) **2** : sordina *f* (de un piano) **3 to put a damper on** : desanimar, apagar (el entusiasmo), enfriar
dampness ['dæmpnəs] *n* : humedad *f*
damsel ['dæmzəl] *n* : damisela *f*
dance[1] ['dænts] *v* **danced; dancing** : bailar
dance[2] *n* : baile *m*
dancer ['dæntsər] *n* : bailarín *m*, -rina *f*
dandelion ['dændəlˌaɪən] *n* : diente *m* de león
dandruff ['dændrəf] *n* : caspa *f*
dandy[1] ['dændi] *adj* **-dier; -est** : excelente, magnífico, macanudo *fam*
dandy[2] *n, pl* **-dies 1** FOP : dandi *m* **2** : algo *m* excelente ⟨this new program is a dandy : este programa nuevo es algo excelente⟩
Dane ['deɪn] *n* : danés *m*, -nesa *f*
danger ['deɪnʤər] *n* : peligro *m*
dangerous ['deɪnʤərəs] *adj* : peligroso
dangle ['dæŋgəl] *v* **-gled; -gling** *vi* HANG : colgar, pender — *vt* **1** SWING : hacer oscilar **2** PROFFER : ofrecer (como incentivo) **3 to keep someone dangling** : dejar a alguien en suspenso
Danish[1] ['deɪnɪʃ] *adj* : danés
Danish[2] *n* : danés *m* (idioma)
dank ['dæŋk] *adj* : frío y húmedo
dapper ['dæpər] *adj* : pulcro, atildado
dappled ['dæpəld] *adj* : moteado ⟨a dappled horse : un caballo rodado⟩
dare[1] ['dær] *v* **dared; daring** *vi* : osar, atreverse ⟨how dare you! : ¡cómo te atreves!⟩ — *vt* **1** CHALLENGE : desafiar, retar **2 to dare to do something** : atreverse a hacer algo, osar hacer algo
dare[2] *n* : desafío *m*, reto *m*
daredevil ['dærˌdɛvəl] *n* : persona *f* temeraria
daring[1] ['dærɪŋ] *adj* : osado, atrevido, audaz
daring[2] *n* : arrojo *m*, coraje *m*, audacia *f*
dark ['dɑrk] *adj* **1** : oscuro (dícese del ambiente o de los colores), moreno (dícese del pelo o de la piel) **2** SOMBER : sombrío, triste
darken ['dɑrkən] *vt* **1** DIM : oscurecer **2** SADDEN : entristecer — *vi* : ensombrecerse, nublarse
darkly ['dɑrkli] *adv* **1** DIMLY : oscuramente **2** GLOOMILY : tristemente **3** MYSTERIOUSLY : misteriosamente, enigmáticamente
darkness ['dɑrknəs] *n* : oscuridad *f*, tinieblas *f*
darling[1] ['dɑrlɪŋ] *adj* **1** BELOVED : querido, amado **2** CHARMING : encantador, mono *fam*
darling[2] *n* **1** BELOVED : querido *m*, -da *f*; amado *m*, -da *f*; cariño *m*, -ña *f* **2** FAVORITE : preferido *m*, -da *f*; favorito *m*, -ta *f*
darn[1] ['dɑrn] *vt* : zurcir
darn[2] *n* **1** : zurcido *m* **2** → **damn**[3]
dart[1] ['dɑrt] *vt* THROW : lanzar, tirar — *vi* DASH : lanzarse, precipitarse
dart[2] *n* **1** : dardo *m* **2 darts** *npl* : juego *m* de dardos
dash[1] ['dæʃ] *vt* **1** SMASH : romper, estrellar **2** HURL : arrojar, lanzar **3** SPLASH : salpicar **4** FRUSTRATE : frustrar **5 to dash off** : hacer (algo) rápidamente — *vi* **1** SMASH : romperse, estrellarse **2** DART : lanzarse, irse apresuradamente
dash[2] *n* **1** BURST, SPLASH : arranque *m*, salpicadura *f* (de aguas) **2** : guión *m* largo (signo de puntuación) **3** DROP : gota *f*, pizca *f* **4** VERVE : brío *m* **5** RACE : carrera *f* ⟨a 100-meter dash : una carrera de 100 metros⟩ **6 to make a dash for it** : precipitarse (hacia), echarse a correr **7** → **dashboard**
dashboard ['dæʃˌbord] *n* : tablero *m* de instrumentos
dashing ['dæʃɪŋ] *adj* : gallardo, apuesto
data ['deɪṭə, 'dæ-, 'dɑ-] *ns & pl* : datos *mpl*, información *f*
database ['deɪṭəˌbeɪs, 'dæ-, 'dɑ-] *n* : base *f* de datos
date[1] ['deɪt] *v* **dated; dating** *vt* **1** : fechar (una carta, etc.), datar (un objeto) ⟨it was dated June 9 : estaba fechada el 9 de junio⟩ **2** : salir con ⟨she's dating my brother : sale con mi hermano⟩ — *vi* : datar
date[2] *n* **1** : fecha *f* ⟨to date : hasta la fecha⟩ **2** EPOCH, PERIOD : época *f*, período *m* **3** APPOINTMENT : cita *f* **4** COMPANION : acompañante *mf* **5** : dátil *m* (fruta)
dated ['deɪṭəd] *adj* OUT-OF-DATE : anticuado, pasado de moda

datum [ˈdeɪṭəm, ˈdæ-, ˈdɑ-] *n, pl* **-ta** [-ṭə] *or* **-tums** : dato *m*
daub[1] [ˈdɔb] *vt* : embadurnar
daub[2] *n* : mancha *f*
daughter [ˈdɔṭər] *n* : hija *f*
daughter–in–law [ˈdɔṭərɪnˌlɔ] *n, pl* **daughters–in–law** : nuera *f*, hija *f* política
daunt [ˈdɔnt] *vt* : amilanar, acobardar, intimidar
dauntless [ˈdɔntləs] *adj* : intrépido, impávido
davenport [ˈdævənˌport] *n* : sofá *m*
dawdle [ˈdɔdəl] *vi* **-dled; -dling 1** DALLY : demorarse, entretenerse, perder tiempo **2** LOITER : vagar, holgazanear, haraganear
dawn[1] [ˈdɔn] *vi* **1** : amanecer, alborear, despuntar ⟨Saturday dawned clear and bright : el sábado amaneció claro y luminoso⟩ **2 to dawn on** : hacerse obvio ⟨it dawned on me that she was right : me di cuenta de que tenía razón⟩
dawn[2] *n* **1** DAYBREAK : amanecer *m*, alba *f* **2** BEGINNING : albor *m*, comienzo *m* ⟨the dawn of history : los albores de la historia⟩ **3 from dawn to dusk** : de sol a sol
day [ˈdeɪ] *n* **1** : día *m* **2** DATE : fecha *f* **3** TIME : día *m*, tiempo *m* ⟨in olden days : intaño⟩ **4** WORKDAY : jornada *f* laboral
daybreak [ˈdeɪˌbreɪk] *n* : alba *f*, amanecer *m*
day care *n* : servicio *m* de guardería infantil
daydream[1] [ˈdeɪˌdri:m] *vi* : soñar despierto, fantasear
daydream[2] *n* : ensueño *m*, ensoñación *f*, fantasía *f*
daylight [ˈdeɪˌlaɪt] *n* **1** : luz *f* del día ⟨in broad daylight : a plena luz del día⟩ **2** → **daybreak 3** → **daytime**
daylight saving time *n* : hora *f* de verano
daytime [ˈdeɪˌtaɪm] *n* : horas *fpl* diurnas, día *m*
daze[1] [ˈdeɪz] *vt* **dazed; dazing 1** STUN : aturdir **2** DAZZLE : deslumbrar, ofuscar
daze[2] *n* **1** : aturdimiento *m* **2 in a daze** : aturdido, atontado
dazzle[1] [ˈdæzəl] *vt* **-zled; -zling** : deslumbrar, ofuscar
dazzle[2] *n* : resplandor *m*, brillo *m*
DDT [ˌdi:ˌdi:ˈti:] *n* : DDT *m*
deacon [ˈdi:kən] *n* : diácono *m*
dead[1] [ˈdɛd] *adv* **1** ABRUPTLY : repentinamente, súbitamente ⟨to stop dead : parar en seco⟩ **2** ABSOLUTELY : absolutamente ⟨I'm dead certain : estoy absolutamente seguro⟩ **3** DIRECTLY : justo ⟨dead ahead : justo adelante⟩
dead[2] *adj* **1** LIFELESS : muerto **2** NUMB : entumecido **3** INDIFFERENT : indiferente, frío **4** INACTIVE : inactivo ⟨a dead volcano : un volcán inactivo⟩ **5** : desconectado (dícese del teléfono), descargado (dícese de una batería) **6** EXHAUSTED : agotado, derrengado, muerto **7** OBSOLETE : obsoleto, muerto ⟨a dead language : una lengua muerta⟩ **8** EXACT : exacto ⟨in the dead center : justo en el blanco⟩
dead[3] *n* **1 the dead** : los muertos **2 in the dead of night** : a las altas horas de la noche **3 in the dead of winter** : en pleno invierno
deadbeat [ˈdɛdˌbi:t] *n* **1** LOAFER : vago *m*, -ga *f*; holgazán *m*, -zana *f* **2** FREELOADER : gorrón *m*, -rrona *f fam*; gorrero *m*, -ra *f fam*
deaden [ˈdɛdən] *vt* **1** : atenuar (un dolor), entorpecer (sensaciones) **2** DULL : deslustrar **3** DISPIRIT : desanimar **4** MUFFLE : amortiguar, reducir (sonidos)
dead–end [ˈdɛdˈɛnd] *adj* **1** : sin salida ⟨dead-end street : calle sin salida⟩ **2** : sin futuro ⟨a dead-end job : un trabajo sin porvenir⟩
dead end *n* : callejón *m* sin salida
dead heat *n* : empate *m*
deadline [ˈdɛdˌlaɪn] *n* : fecha *f* límite, fecha *f* tope, plazo *m* (determinado)
deadlock[1] [ˈdɛdˌlɑk] *vt* : estancar — *vi* : estancarse, llegar a punto muerto
deadlock[2] *n* : punto *m* muerto, impasse *m*
deadly[1] [ˈdɛdli] *adv* : extremadamente, sumamente ⟨deadly serious : muy en serio⟩
deadly[2] *adj* **-lier; -est 1** LETHAL : mortal, letal, mortífero **2** ACCURATE : certero, preciso ⟨a deadly aim : una puntería infalible⟩ **3** CAPITAL : capital ⟨the seven deadly sins : los siete pecados capitales⟩ **4** DULL : funesto, aburrido **5** EXTREME : extremo, absoluto ⟨a deadly calm : una calma absoluta⟩
deadpan[1] [ˈdɛdˌpæn] *adv* : de manera inexpresiva, sin expresión
deadpan[2] *adj* : inexpresivo, impasible
deaf [ˈdɛf] *adj* : sordo
deafen [ˈdɛfən] *vt* **-ened; -ening** : ensordecer
deafening [ˈdɛfənɪŋ] *adj* : ensordecedor
deaf–mute [ˈdɛfˈmju:t] *n* : sordomudo *m*, -da *f*
deafness [ˈdɛfnəs] *n* : sordera *f*
deal[1] [ˈdi:l] *v* **dealt; dealing** *vt* **1** APPORTION : repartir ⟨to deal justice : repartir la justicia⟩ **2** DISTRIBUTE : repartir, dar (naipes) **3** DELIVER : asestar, propinar ⟨to deal a blow : asestar un golpe⟩ — *vi* **1** : dar, repartir (en juegos de naipes) **2 to deal in** : comerciar en, traficar con (drogas) **3 to deal with** CONCERN : tratar de, tener que ver con ⟨the book deals with poverty : el libro trata de la pobreza⟩ **4 to deal with** HANDLE : tratar (con), encargarse de **5 to deal with** TREAT : tratar ⟨the judge dealt with him severely : el juez lo trató con severidad⟩ **6 to deal with** ACCEPT : aceptar (una situación o desgracia)

deal[2] *n* **1** : reparto *m* (de naipes) **2** AGREEMENT, TRANSACTION : trato *m*, acuerdo *m*, transacción *f* **3** TREATMENT : trato *m* ⟨he got a raw deal : le hicieron una injusticia⟩ **4** BARGAIN : ganga *f*, oferta *f* **5 a good deal** *or* **a great deal** : mucho, una gran cantidad

dealer [ˈdiːlər] *n* : comerciante *mf*, traficante *mf*

dealership [ˈdiːlərˌʃɪp] *n* : concesión *f*

dealings [ˈdiːlɪŋz] *npl* **1** : relaciones *fpl* (personales) **2** TRANSACTIONS : negocios *mpl*, transacciones *fpl*

dean [ˈdiːn] *n* **1** : deán *m* (del clero) **2** : decano *m*, -na *f* (de una facultad o profesión)

dear[1] [ˈdɪr] *adj* **1** ESTEEMED, LOVED : querido, estimado ⟨a dear friend : un amigo querido⟩ ⟨Dear Sir : Estimado Señor⟩ **2** COSTLY : caro, costoso

dear[2] *n* : querido *m*, -da *f*; amado *m*, -da *f*

dearly [ˈdɪrli] *adv* **1** : mucho ⟨I love them dearly : los quiero mucho⟩ **2** : caro ⟨to pay dearly : pagar caro⟩

dearth [ˈdərθ] *n* : escasez *f*, carestía *f*

death [ˈdɛθ] *n* **1** : muerte *f*, fallecimiento *m* ⟨to be the death of : matar⟩ **2** FATALITY : víctima *f* (mortal); muerto *m*, -ta *f* **3** END : fin *m* ⟨the death of civilization : el fin de la civilización⟩

deathbed [ˈdɛθˌbɛd] *n* : lecho *m* de muerte

deathblow [ˈdɛθˌbloː] *n* : golpe *m* mortal

deathless [ˈdɛθləs] *adj* : eterno, inmortal

deathly [ˈdɛθli] *adj* : de muerte, sepulcral (dícese del silencio), cadavérico (dícese de la palidez)

debacle [dɪˈbɑkəl, -ˈbæ-] *n* : desastre *m*, debacle *m*, fiasco *m*

debar [diˈbɑr] *vt* **-barred; -barring** : excluir, prohibir

debase [diˈbeɪs] *vt* **-based; -basing** : degradar, envilecer

debasement [diˈbeɪsmənt] *n* : degradación *f*, envilecimiento *m*

debatable [diˈbeɪt̬əbəl] *adj* : discutible

debate[1] [diˈbeɪt] *vt* **-bated; -bating** : debatir, discutir

debate[2] *n* : debate *m*, discusión *f*

debauch [diˈbɔʧ] *vt* : pervertir, corromper

debauchery [diˈbɔʧəri] *n, pl* **-eries** : libertinaje *m*, disipación *f*, intemperancia *f*

debilitate [diˈbɪləˌteɪt] *vt* **-tated; -tating** : debilitar

debility [diˈbɪlət̬i] *n, pl* **-ties** : debilidad *f*

debit[1] [ˈdɛbɪt] *vt* : adeudar, cargar, debitar

debit[2] *n* : débito *m*, cargo *m*, debe *m*

debonair [ˌdɛbəˈnær] *adj* : elegante y desenvuelto, apuesto

debris [dəˈbriː, deɪ-; ˈdeɪˌbriː] *n, pl* **-bris** [-ˈbriːz, -ˌbriːz] **1** RUBBLE, RUINS : escombros *mpl*, ruinas *fpl*, restos *mpl* **2** RUBBISH : basura *f*, deshechos *mpl*

debt [ˈdɛt] *n* **1** : deuda *f* ⟨to pay a debt : saldar una deuda⟩ **2** INDEBTEDNESS : endeudamiento *m*

debtor [ˈdɛt̬ər] *n* : deudor *m*, -dora *f*

debunk [diˈbʌŋk] *vt* DISCREDIT : desacreditar, desprestigiar

debut[1] [deɪˈbjuː, ˈdeɪˌbjuː] *vi* : debutar

debut[2] *n* **1** : debut *m* (de un actor), estreno *m* (de una obra) **2** : debut *m*, presentación *f* (en sociedad)

debutante [ˈdɛbjʊˌtɑnt] *n* : debutante *f*

decade [ˈdɛˌkeɪd, dɛˈkeɪd] *n* : década *f*

decadence [ˈdɛkədən*t*s] *n* : decadencia *f*

decadent [ˈdɛkədənt] *adj* : decadente

decaf[1] [ˈdiːˌkæf] → **decaffeinated**

decaf[2] *n* : café *m* descafeinado

decaffeinated [diˈkæfəˌneɪt̬əd] *adj* : descafeinado

decal [ˈdiːˌkæl, diˈkæl] *n* : calcomanía *f*

decamp [diˈkæmp] *vi* : irse, largarse *fam*

decant [diˈkænt] *vt* : decantar

decanter [diˈkæntər] *n* : licorera *f*, garrafa *f*

decapitate [diˈkæpəˌteɪt] *vt* **-tated; -tating** : decapitar

decay[1] [diˈkeɪ] *vi* **1** DECOMPOSE : descomponerse, pudrirse **2** DETERIORATE : deteriorarse **3** : cariarse (dícese de los dientes)

decay[2] *n* **1** DECOMPOSITION : descomposición *f* **2** DECLINE, DETERIORATION : decadencia *f*, deterioro *m* **3** : caries *f* (de los dientes)

decease[1] [diˈsiːs] *vi* **-ceased; -ceasing** : morir, fallecer

decease[2] *n* : fallecimiento *m*, defunción *f*, deceso *m*

deceit [diˈsiːt] *n* **1** DECEPTION : engaño *m* **2** DISHONESTY : deshonestidad *f*

deceitful [diˈsiːtfəl] *adj* : falso, embustero, engañoso, mentiroso

deceitfully [diˈsiːtfəli] *adv* : con engaño, con falsedad

deceitfulness [diˈsiːtfəlnəs] *n* : falsedad *f*, engaño *m*

deceive [diˈsiːv] *vt* **-ceived; -ceiving** : engañar, burlar

deceiver [diˈsiːvər] *n* : impostor *m*, -tora *f*

decelerate [diˈsɛləˌreɪt] *vi* **-ated; -ating** : reducir la velocidad, desacelerar

December [diˈsɛmbər] *n* : diciembre *m*

decency [ˈdisən*t*si] *n, pl* **-cies** : decencia *f*, decoro *m*

decent [ˈdiːsənt] *adj* **1** CORRECT, PROPER : decente, decoroso, correcto **2** CLOTHED : vestido, presentable **3** MODEST : púdico, modesto **4** ADEQUATE : decente, adecuado ⟨decent wages : paga adecuada⟩

decently [ˈdiːsəntli] *adv* : decentemente

decentralize [diˈsɛntrəˌlaɪz] *v* **-lized** [-ˌlaɪzd]; **-lizing** [-ˌlaɪzɪŋ] *vt* : descentralizar — *vi* : descentralizarse

deception [diˈsɛpʃən] *n* : engaño *m*

deceptive [di'sɛptɪv] *adj* : engañoso, falaz — **deceptively** *adv*
decibel ['dɛsəbəl, -ˌbɛl] *n* : decibelio *m*
decide [di'saɪd] *v* **-cided; -ciding** *vt* **1** CONCLUDE : decidir, llegar a la conclusión de ⟨he decided what to do : decidió qué iba a hacer⟩ **2** DETERMINE : decidir, determinar ⟨one blow decided the fight : un solo golpe determinó la pelea⟩ **3** CONVINCE : decidir ⟨her pleas decided me to help : sus súplicas me decidieron a ayudarla⟩ **4** RESOLVE : resolver — *vi* : decidirse
decided [di'saɪdəd] *adj* **1** UNQUESTIONABLE : indudable **2** RESOLUTE : decidido, resuelto — **decidedly** *adv*
deciduous [di'sɪʤʊəs] *adj* : caduco, de hoja caduca
decimal[1] ['dɛsəməl] *adj* : decimal
decimal[2] *n* : número *m* decimal
decipher [di'saɪfər] *vt* : descifrar — **decipherable** [-əbəl] *adj*
decision [dɪ'sɪʒən] *n* : decisión *f*, determinación *f* ⟨to make a decision : tomar una decisión⟩
decisive [dɪ'saɪsɪv] *adj* **1** DECIDING : decisivo ⟨the decisive vote : el voto decisivo⟩ **2** CONCLUSIVE : decisivo, concluyente, contundente ⟨a decisive victory : una victoria contundente⟩ **3** RESOLUTE : decidido, resuelto, firme
decisively [dɪ'saɪsɪvli] *adv* : con decisión, de manera decisiva
decisiveness [dɪ'saɪsɪvnəs] *n* **1** FORCEFULNESS : contundencia *f* **2** RESOLUTION : firmeza *f*, decisión *f*, determinación *f*
deck[1] ['dɛk] *vt* **1** FLOOR : tumbar, derribar ⟨she decked him with one blow : lo tumbó de un solo golpe⟩ **2 to deck out** : adornar, engalanar
deck[2] *n* **1** : cubierta *f* (de un barco) **2** *or* **deck of cards** : baraja *f* (de naipes)
declaim [di'kleɪm] *v* : declamar
declaration [ˌdɛklə'reɪʃən] *n* : declaración *f*, pronunciamiento *m* (oficial)
declare [di'klær] *vt* **-clared; -claring** : declarar, manifestar ⟨to declare war : declarar la guerra⟩ ⟨they declared their support : manifestaron su apoyo⟩
decline[1] [di'klaɪn] *v* **-clined; -clining** *vi* **1** DESCEND : descender **2** DETERIORATE : deteriorarse, decaer ⟨her health is declining : su salud se está deteriorando⟩ **3** DECREASE : disminuir, decrecer, decaer **4** REFUSE : rehusar — *vt* **1** INFLECT : declinar **2** REFUSE, TURN DOWN : declinar, rehusar
decline[2] *n* **1** DETERIORATION : decadencia *f*, deterioro *m* **2** DECREASE : disminución *f*, descenso *m* **3** SLOPE : declive *m*, pendiente *f*
decode [di'ko:d] *vt* **-coded; -coding** : descifrar (un mensaje), descodificar (una señal)
decoder [di'ko:dər] *n* : descodificador *m*
decompose [ˌdi:kəm'po:z] *v* **-posed; -posing** *vt* **1** BREAK DOWN : descomponer **2** ROT : descomponer, pudrir — *vi* : descomponerse, pudrirse
decomposition [ˌdi:ˌkɑmpə'zɪʃən] *n* : descomposición *f*
decongestant [ˌdi:kən'ʤɛstənt] *n* : descongestionante *m*
decor *or* **décor** [deɪ'kɔr, 'deɪˌkɔr] *n* : decoración *f*
decorate ['dɛkəˌreɪt] *vt* **-rated; -rating** **1** ADORN : decorar, adornar **2** : condecorar ⟨he was decorated for bravery : lo condecoraron por valor⟩
decoration [ˌdɛkə'reɪʃən] *n* **1** ADORNMENT : decoración *f*, adorno *m* **2** : condecoración *f* (de honor)
decorative ['dɛkərət̬ɪv, -ˌreɪ-] *adj* : decorativo, ornamental, de adorno
decorator ['dɛkəˌreɪt̬ər] *n* : decorador *m*, -dora *f*
decorum [di'korəm] *n* : decoro *m*
decoy[1] ['di:ˌkɔɪ, di'-] *vt* : atraer (con señuelo)
decoy[2] *n* : señuelo *m*, reclamo *m*, cimbel *m*
decrease[1] [di'kri:s] *v* **-creased; -creasing** *vi* : decrecer, disminuir, bajar — *vt* : reducir, disminuir
decrease[2] ['di:ˌkri:s] *n* : disminución *f*, descenso *m*, bajada *f*
decree[1] [di'kri:] *vt* **-creed; -creeing** : decretar
decree[2] *n* : decreto *m*
decrepit [di'krɛpɪt] *adj* **1** FEEBLE : decrépito, débil **2** DILAPIDATED : deteriorado, ruinoso
decry [di'kraɪ] *vt* **-cried; -crying** : censurar, criticar
dedicate ['dɛdɪˌkeɪt] *vt* **-cated; -cating** **1** : dedicar ⟨she dedicated the book to Carlos : le dedicó el libro a Carlos⟩ **2** : consagrar, dedicar ⟨to dedicate one's life : consagrar uno su vida⟩
dedication [ˌdɛdɪ'keɪʃən] *n* **1** DEVOTION : dedicación *f*, devoción *f* **2** : dedicatoria *f* (de un libro, una canción, etc.) **3** CONSECRATION : dedicación *f*
deduce [di'du:s, -'dju:s] *vt* **-duced; -ducing** : deducir, inferir
deduct [di'dʌkt] *vt* : deducir, descontar, restar
deductible [di'dʌktəbəl] *adj* : deducible
deduction [di'dʌkʃən] *n* : deducción *f*
deed[1] ['di:d] *vt* : ceder, transferir
deed[2] *n* **1** ACT : acto *m*, acción *f*, hecho *m* ⟨a good deed : una buena acción⟩ **2** FEAT : hazaña *f*, proeza *f* **3** TITLE : escritura *f*, título *m*
deem ['di:m] *vt* : considerar, juzgar
deep[1] ['di:p] *adv* : hondo, profundamente ⟨to dig deep : cavar hondo⟩
deep[2] *adj* **1** : hondo, profundo ⟨the deep end : la parte honda⟩ ⟨a deep wound : una herida profunda⟩ **2** WIDE : ancho **3** INTENSE : profundo, intenso **4** DARK : intenso, subido ⟨deep red : rojo subido⟩ **5** LOW : profundo ⟨a deep tone

: un tono profundo> 6 ABSORBED : absorto <deep in thought : absorto en la meditación>

deep[3] *n* **1 the deep** : lo profundo, el piélago **2 the deep of night** : lo más profundo de la noche

deepen [ˈdi:pən] *vt* **1** : ahondar, profundizar **2** INTENSIFY : intensificar — *vi* **1** : hacerse más profundo **2** INTENSIFY : intensificarse

deeply [ˈdi:pli] *adv* : hondo, profundamente <I'm deeply sorry : lo siento sinceramente>

deep–seated [ˈdi:pˈsi:t̬əd] *adj* : profundamente arraigado, enraizado

deer [ˈdɪr] *ns & pl* : ciervo *m*, venado *m*

deerskin [ˈdɪrˌskɪn] *n* : piel *f* de venado

deface [diˈfeɪs] *vt* **-faced; -facing** MAR : desfigurar

defacement [diˈfeɪsmənt] *n* : desfiguración *f*

defamation [ˌdɛfəˈmeɪʃən] *n* : difamación *f*

defamatory [diˈfæməˌtori] *adj* : difamatorio

defame [diˈfeɪm] *vt* **-famed; -faming** : difamar, calumniar

default[1] [diˈfɔlt, ˈdi:ˌfɔlt] *vi* **1** : no cumplir (con una obligación), no pagar **2** : no presentarse (en un tribunal)

default[2] *n* **1** NEGLECT : omisión *f*, negligencia *f* **2** NONPAYMENT : impago *m*, falta *f* de pago **3 to win by default** : ganar por abandono

defaulter [diˈfɔltər] *n* : moroso *m*, -sa *f*; rebelde *mf* (en un tribunal)

defeat[1] [diˈfi:t] *vt* **1** FRUSTRATE : frustrar **2** BEAT : vencer, derrotar

defeat[2] *n* : derrota *f*, rechazo *m* (de legislación), fracaso *m* (de planes, etc.)

defecate [ˈdɛfɪˌkeɪt] *vi* **-cated; -cating** : defecar

defect[1] [diˈfɛkt] *vi* : desertar

defect[2] [ˈdi:ˌfɛkt, diˈfɛkt] *n* : defecto *m*

defection [diˈfɛkʃən] *n* : deserción *f*, defección *f*

defective [diˈfɛktɪv] *adj* **1** FAULTY : defectuoso **2** DEFICIENT : deficiente

defector [diˈfɛktər] *n* : desertor *m*, -tora *f*

defend [diˈfɛnd] *vt* : defender

defendant [diˈfɛndənt] *n* : acusado *m*, -da *f*; demandado *m*, -da *f*

defender [diˈfɛndər] *n* **1** ADVOCATE : defensor *m*, -sora *f* **2** : defensa *mf* (en deportes)

defense [diˈfɛnts, ˈdi:ˌfɛnts] *n* : defensa *f*

defenseless [diˈfɛntsləs] *adj* : indefenso

defensive[1] [diˈfɛntsɪv] *adj* : defensivo

defensive[2] *n* **on the defensive** : a la defensiva

defer [diˈfər] *v* **-ferred; -ferring** *vt* POSTPONE : diferir, aplazar, posponer — *vi* **to defer to** : deferir a

deference [ˈdɛfərənts] *n* : deferencia *f*

deferential [ˌdɛfəˈrɛntʃəl] *adj* : respetuoso

deferment [diˈfərmənt] *n* : aplazamiento *m*

defiance [diˈfaɪənts] *n* : desafío *m*

defiant [diˈfaɪənt] *adj* : desafiante, insolente

deficiency [diˈfɪʃəntsi] *n, pl* **-cies** : deficiencia *f*, carencia *f*

deficient [diˈfɪʃənt] *adj* : deficiente, carente

deficit [ˈdɛfəsɪt] *n* : déficit *m*

defile [diˈfaɪl] *vt* **-filed; -filing 1** DIRTY : ensuciar, manchar **2** CORRUPT : corromper **3** DESECRATE, PROFANE : profanar **4** DISHONOR : deshonrar

defilement [diˈfaɪlmənt] *n* **1** DESECRATION : profanación *f* **2** CORRUPTION : corrupción *f* **3** CONTAMINATION : contaminación *f*

define [diˈfaɪn] *vt* **-fined; -fining 1** BOUND : delimitar, demarcar **2** CLARIFY : aclarar, definir **3** : definir <to define a word : definir una palabra>

definite [ˈdɛfənɪt] *adj* **1** CERTAIN : definido, determinado **2** CLEAR : claro, explícito **3** UNQUESTIONABLE : seguro, incuestionable

definite article *n* : artículo *m* definido

definitely [ˈdɛfənɪtli] *adv* **1** DOUBTLESSLY : indudablemente, sin duda **2** DEFINITIVELY : definitivamente, seguramente

definition [ˌdɛfəˈnɪʃən] *n* : definición *f*

definitive [diˈfɪnət̬ɪv] *adj* **1** CONCLUSIVE : definitivo, decisivo **2** AUTHORITATIVE : de autoridad, autorizado

deflate [diˈfleɪt] *v* **-flated; -flating** *vt* **1** : desinflar (una llanta, etc.) **2** REDUCE : rebajar <to deflate one's ego : bajarle los humos a uno> — *vi* : desinflarse

deflation [diˈfleɪʃən] *n* **1** : desinflación *f* (de una llanta, etc.) **2** : deflación *f* (económica)

deflect [diˈflɛkt] *vt* : desviar — *vi* : desviarse

defoliant [diˈfo:liənt] *n* : defoliante *m*

deforestation [diˌfɔrəˈsteɪʃən] *n* : deforestación *f*, desforestación *f*

deform [diˈfɔrm] *vt* : deformar

deformation [ˌdi:ˌfɔrˈmeɪʃən] *n* : deformación *f*

deformed [diˈfɔrmd] *adj* : deforme

deformity [diˈfɔrmət̬i] *n, pl* **-ties** : deformidad *f*

defraud [diˈfrɔd] *vt* : estafar, defraudar

defray [diˈfreɪ] *vt* : sufragar, costear

defrost [diˈfrɔst] *vt* : descongelar, deshelar — *vi* : descongelarse, deshelarse

deft [ˈdɛft] *adj* : hábil, diestro — **deftly** *adv*

defunct [diˈfʌŋkt] *adj* **1** DECEASED : difunto, fallecido **2** EXTINCT : extinto, fenecido

defuse [diˈfju:z] *vt* : desactivar <to defuse the situation : reducir las tensiones>

defy [diˈfaɪ] *vt* **-fied; -fying 1** CHALLENGE : desafiar, retar **2** DISOBEY : desobedecer **3** RESIST : resistir, hacer imposible, hacer inútil

degenerate[1] [di'ʤɛnəˌreɪt] *vi* **-ated; -ating** : degenerar

degenerate[2] [di'ʤɛnərət] *adj* : degenerado

degeneration [diˌʤɛnə'reɪʃən] *n* : degeneración *f*

degenerative [di'ʤɛnərətɪv] *adj* : degenerative

degradation [ˌdɛgrə'deɪʃən] *n* : degradación *f*

degrade [di'greɪd] *vt* **-graded; -grading** **1** : degradar, envilecer **2 to degrade oneself** : rebajarse

degrading [di'greɪdɪŋ] *adj* : degradante

degree [di'gri:] *n* **1** EXTENT : grado *m* ⟨a third degree burn : una quemadura de tercer grado⟩ **2** : título *m* (de enseñanza superior) **3** : grado *m* (de un círculo, de la temperatura) **4 by degrees** : gradualmente, poco a poco

dehydrate [di'haɪˌdreɪt] *v* **-drated; -drating** *vt* : deshidratar — *vi* : deshidratarse

dehydration [ˌdi:haɪ'dreɪʃən] *n* : deshidratación *f*

deice [ˌdi:'aɪs] *vt* **-iced; -icing** : deshelar, descongelar

deify ['di:əˌfaɪ, 'deɪ-] *vt* **-fied; -fying** : deificar

deign ['deɪn] *vi* : dignarse, condescender

deity ['di:əṯi, 'deɪ-] *n, pl* **-ties** **1 the Deity** : Dios *m* **2** GOD, GODDESS : deidad *f*; dios *m*, diosa *f*

dejected [di'ʤɛktəd] *adj* : abatido, desalentado, desanimado

dejection [di'ʤɛkʃən] *n* : abatimiento *m*, desaliento *m*, desánimo *m*

delay[1] [di'leɪ] *vt* **1** POSTPONE : posponer, postergar **2** HOLD UP : retrasar, demorar — *vi* : tardar, demorar

delay[2] *n* **1** LATENESS : tardanza *f* **2** HOLDUP : demora *f*, retraso *m*

delectable [di'lɛktəbəl] *adj* **1** DELICIOUS : delicioso, exquisito **2** DELIGHTFUL : encantador

delegate[1] ['dɛlɪˌgeɪt] *v* **-gated; -gating** : delegar

delegate[2] ['dɛlɪgət, -ˌgeɪt] *n* : delegado *m*, -da *f*

delegation [ˌdɛlɪ'geɪʃən] *n* : delegación *f*

delete [di'li:t] *vt* **-leted; -leting** : suprimir, tachar, eliminar

deletion [di'li:ʃən] *n* : supresión *f*, tachadura *f*, eliminación *f*

deli ['dɛli] → **delicatessen**

deliberate[1] [dɪ'lɪbəˌreɪt] *v* **-ated; -ating** *vt* : deliberar sobre, reflexionar sobre, considerar — *vi* : deliberar

deliberate[2] [dɪ'lɪbərət] *adj* **1** CONSIDERED : reflexionado, premeditado **2** INTENTIONAL : deliberado, intencional **3** SLOW : lento, pausado

deliberately [dɪ'lɪbərətli] *adv* **1** INTENTIONALLY : adrede, a propósito **2** SLOWLY : pausadamente, lentamente

deliberation [dɪˌlɪbə'reɪʃən] *n* **1** CONSIDERATION : deliberación *f*, consideración *f* **2** SLOWNESS : lentitud *f*

delicacy ['dɛlɪkəsi] *n, pl* **-cies** **1** : manjar *m*, exquisitez *f* ⟨caviar is a real delicacy : el caviar es un verdadero manjar⟩ **2** FINENESS : delicadeza *f* **3** FRAGILITY : fragilidad *f*

delicate ['dɛlɪkət] *adj* **1** SUBTLE : delicado ⟨a delicate fragrance : una fragancia delicada⟩ **2** DAINTY : delicado, primoroso, fino **3** FRAGILE : frágil **4** SENSITIVE : delicado ⟨a delicate matter : un asunto delicado⟩

delicately ['dɛlɪkətli] *adv* : delicadamente, con delicadeza

delicatessen [ˌdɛlɪkə'tɛsən] *n* : charcutería *f*, fiambrería *f*, salchichonería *f* *Mex*

delicious [di'lɪʃəs] *adj* : delicioso, exquisito, rico — **deliciously** *adv*

delight[1] [dɪ'laɪt] *vt* : deleitar, encantar — *vi* **to delight in** : deleitarse con, complacerse en

delight[2] *n* **1** JOY : placer *m*, deleite *m*, gozo *m* **2** : encanto *m* ⟨your garden is a delight : su jardín es un encanto⟩

delightful [dɪ'laɪtfəl] *adj* : delicioso, encantador

delightfully [dɪ'laɪtfəli] *adv* : de manera encantadora, de maravilla

delineate [di'lɪniˌeɪt] *vt* **-eated; -eating** : delinear, trazar, bosquejar

delinquency [di'lɪŋkwən*t*si] *n, pl* **-cies** : delincuencia *f*

delinquent[1] [di'lɪŋkwənt] *adj* **1** : delincuente **2** OVERDUE : vencido y sin pagar, moroso

delinquent[2] *n* : delincuente *mf* ⟨juvenile delinquent : delincuente juvenil⟩

delirious [di'lɪriəs] *adj* : delirante ⟨delirious with joy : loco de alegría⟩

delirium [di'lɪriəm] *n* : delirio *m*, desvarío *m*

deliver [di'lɪvər] *vt* **1** FREE : liberar, librar **2** DISTRIBUTE, HAND : entregar, repartir **3** : asistir en el parto de (un niño) **4** : pronunciar ⟨to deliver a speech : pronunciar un discurso⟩ **5** PROJECT : despachar, lanzar ⟨he delivered a fast ball : lanzó un pelota rápida⟩ **6** DEAL : propinar, asestar ⟨to deliver a blow : asestar un golpe⟩

deliverance [di'lɪvərən*t*s] *n* : liberación *f*, rescate *m*, salvación *f*

deliverer [di'lɪvərər] *n* RESCUER : libertador *m*, -dora *f*; salvador *m*, -dora *f*

delivery [di'lɪvəri] *n, pl* **-eries** **1** LIBERATION : liberación *f* **2** : entrega *f*, reparto *m* ⟨cash on delivery : entrega contra reembolso⟩ ⟨home delivery : servicio a domicilio⟩ **3** CHILDBIRTH : parto *m*, alumbramiento *m* **4** SPEECH : expresión *f* oral, modo *m* de hablar **5** THROW : lanzamiento *m*

dell ['dɛl] *n* : hondonada *f*, valle *m* pequeño

delta ['dɛltə] *n* : delta *m*

delude [di'lu:d] *vt* **-luded; -luding** **1** : engañar **2 to delude oneself** : engañarse

deluge[1] [ˈdɛlˌju:ʤ, -ˌju:ʒ] *vt* **-uged; -uging 1** FLOOD : inundar **2** OVERWHELM : abrumar ⟨deluged with requests : abrumado de pedidos⟩

deluge[2] *n* **1** FLOOD : inundación *f* **2** DOWNPOUR : aguacero *m* **3** BARRAGE : aluvión *m*

delusion [diˈlu:ʒən] *n* **1** : ilusión *f* (falsa) **2 delusions of grandeur** : delirios *mpl* de grandeza

deluxe [diˈlʌks, -ˈlʊks] *adj* : de lujo

delve [ˈdɛlv] *vi* **delved; delving 1** DIG : escarbar **2 to delve into** PROBE : cavar en, ahondar en

demagogue [ˈdɛməˌgɑg] *n* : demagogo *m*, demagoga *f*

demand[1] [diˈmænd] *vt* : demandar, exigir, reclamar

demand[2] *n* **1** REQUEST : petición *f*, pedido *m*, demanda *f* ⟨by popular demand : a petición del público⟩ **2** CLAIM : reclamación *f*, exigencia *f* **3** MARKET : demanda *f* ⟨supply and demand : la oferta y la demanda⟩

demanding [diˈmændɪŋ] *adj* : exigente

demarcation [ˌdi:ˌmɑrˈkeɪʃən] *n* : demarcación *f*, deslinde *m*

demean [diˈmi:n] *vt* : degradar, rebajar

demeanor [diˈmi:nər] *n* : comportamiento *m*, conducta *f*

demented [diˈmɛntəd] *adj* : demente, loco

dementia [diˈmɛntʃə] *n* : demencia *f*

demerit [diˈmɛrət] *n* : demérito *m*

demigod [ˈdɛmiˌgɑd, -ˌgɔd] *n* : semidiós *m*

demise [dɪˈmaɪz] *n* **1** DEATH : fallecimiento *m*, deceso *m* **2** END : hundimiento *m*, desaparición *f* (de una institución, etc.)

demitasse [ˈdɛmiˌtæs, -ˌtɑs] *n* : taza *f* pequeña (de café)

demobilization [diˌmo:bələˈzeɪʃən] *n* : desmovilización *f*

demobilize [diˈmo:bəˌlaɪz] *vt* **-lized; -lizing** : desmovilizar

democracy [diˈmɑkrəsi] *n, pl* **-cies** : democracia *f*

democrat [ˈdɛməˌkræt] *n* : demócrata *mf*

democratic [ˌdɛməˈkræt̬ɪk] *adj* : democrático — **democratically** [-t̬ɪkli] *adv*

demographic [dɛməˈgræfɪk] *adj* : demográfico

demolish [diˈmɑlɪʃ] *vt* **1** RAZE : demoler, derribar, arrasar **2** DESTROY : destruir, destrozar

demolition [ˌdɛməˈlɪʃən, ˌdi:-] *n* : demolición *f*, derribo *m*

demon [ˈdi:mən] *n* : demonio *m*, diablo *m*

demonstrably [diˈmɑntstrəbli] *adv* : manifiestamente, claramente

demonstrate [ˈdɛmənˌstreɪt] *vt* **-strated; -strating 1** SHOW : demostrar **2** PROVE : probar, demostrar **3** EXPLAIN : explicar, ilustrar

demonstration [ˌdɛmənˈstreɪʃən] *n* **1** SHOW : muestra *f*, demostración *f* **2** RALLY : manifestación *f*

demonstrative [diˈmɑntstrət̬ɪv] *adj* **1** EFFUSIVE : efusivo, expresivo, demostrativo **2** : demostrativo (en lingüística) ⟨demonstrative pronoun : pronombre demostrativo⟩

demonstrator [ˈdɛmənˌstreɪt̬ər] *n* **1** : demostrador *m*, -dora *f* (de productos) **2** PROTESTER : manifestante *mf*

demoralize [diˈmɔrəˌlaɪz] *vt* **-ized; -izing** : desmoralizar

demote [diˈmo:t] *vt* **-moted; -moting** : degradar, bajar de categoría

demotion [diˈmo:ʃən] *n* : degradación *f*, descenso *m* de categoría

demur [diˈmər] *vi* **-murred; -murring 1** OBJECT : oponerse **2 to demur at** : ponerle objeciones a (algo)

demure [diˈmjʊr] *adj* : recatado, modesto — **demurely** *adv*

den [ˈdɛn] *n* **1** LAIR : cubil *m*, madriguera *f* **2** HIDEOUT : guarida *f* **3** STUDY : estudio *m*, gabinete *m*

denature [diˈneɪtʃər] *vt* **-tured; -turing** : desnaturalizar

denial [diˈnaɪəl] *n* **1** REFUSAL : rechazo *m*, denegación *f*, negativa *f* **2** REPUDIATION : negación *f* (de una creencia, etc.), rechazo *m*

denigrate [ˈdɛnɪˌgreɪt] *vt* **-grated; -grating** : denigrar

denim [ˈdɛnəm] *n* **1** : tela *f* vaquera, mezclilla *f Chile, Mex* **2 denims** *npl* → **jeans**

denizen [ˈdɛnəzən] *n* : habitante *mf*; morador *m*, -dora *f*

denomination [dɪˌnɑməˈneɪʃən] *n* **1** FAITH : confesión *f*, fe *f* **2** VALUE : denominación *f*, valor *m* (de una moneda)

denominator [dɪˈnɑməˌneɪt̬ər] *n* : denominador *m*

denote [diˈno:t] *vt* **-noted; -noting 1** INDICATE, MARK : indicar, denotar, señalar **2** MEAN : significar

denouement [ˌdeɪˌnu:ˈmɑ] *n* : desenlace *m*

denounce [diˈnaʊnts] *vt* **-nounced; -nouncing 1** CENSURE : denunciar, censurar **2** ACCUSE : denunciar, acusar, delatar

dense [ˈdɛnts] *adj* **denser; -est 1** THICK : espeso, denso ⟨dense vegetation : vegetación densa⟩ ⟨a dense fog : una niebla espesa⟩ **2** STUPID : estúpido, burro *fam*

densely [ˈdɛntsli] *adv* **1** THICKLY : densamente **2** STUPIDLY : torpemente

denseness [ˈdɛntsnəs] *n* **1** → **density 2** STUPIDITY : estupidez *f*

density [ˈdɛntsət̬i] *n, pl* **-ties** : densidad *f*

dent[1] [ˈdɛnt] *vt* : abollar, mellar

dent[2] *n* : abolladura *f*, mella *f*

dental [ˈdɛntəl] *adj* : dental

dental floss *n* : hilo *m* dental

dentifrice [ˈdɛntəfrɪs] *n* : dentífrico *m*, pasta *f* de dientes

dentist [ˈdɛntɪst] *n* : dentista *mf*

dentistry [ˈdɛntɪstri] *n* : odontología *f*

dentures [ˈdɛnʧərz] *npl* : dentadura *f* postiza

denude [diˈnu:d, -ˈnju:d] *vt* **-nuded; -nuding** STRIP : desnudar, despojar

denunciation [di,nʌntsiˈeɪʃən] *n* : denuncia *f*, acusación *f*

deny [diˈnaɪ] *vt* **-nied; -nying 1** REFUTE : desmentir, negar **2** DISOWN, REPUDIATE : negar, renegar de **3** REFUSE : denegar **4 to deny oneself** : privarse, sacrificarse

deodorant [diˈo:dərənt] *n* : desodorante *m*

deodorize [diˈo:də,raɪz] *vt* **-ized; -izing** : desodorizar

depart [diˈpɑrt] *vt* : salirse de — *vi* **1** LEAVE : salir, partir, irse **2** DIE : morir

department [diˈpɑrtmənt] *n* **1** DIVISION : sección *f* (de una tienda, una organización, etc.), departamento *m* (de una empresa, una universidad, etc.), ministerio *m* (del gobierno) **2** PROVINCE, SPHERE : esfera *f*, campo *m*, competencia *f*

departmental [di,pɑrtˈmɛntəl, ,di:-] *adj* : departamental

department store *n* : grandes almacenes *mpl*

departure [diˈpɑrʧər] *n* **1** LEAVING : salida *f*, partida *f* **2** DEVIATION : desviación *f*

depend [diˈpɛnd] *vi* **1** RELY : contar (con), confiar (en) ⟨depend on me! : ¡cuenta conmigo!⟩ **2 to depend on** : depender de ⟨success depends on hard work : el éxito depende de trabajar duro⟩ **3 that depends** : según, eso depende

dependable [diˈpɛndəbəl] *adj* : responsable, digno de confianza, fiable

dependence [diˈpɛndənts] *n* : dependencia *f*

dependency [diˈpɛndəntsi] *n, pl* **-cies 1** → **dependence 2** : posesión *f* (de una unidad política)

dependent[1] [diˈpɛndənt] *adj* : dependiente

dependent[2] *n* : persona *f* a cargo de alguien

depict [diˈpɪkt] *vt* **1** PORTRAY : representar **2** DESCRIBE : describir

depiction [diˈpɪkʃən] *n* : representación *f*, descripción *f*

deplete [diˈpli:t] *vt* **-pleted; -pleting 1** EXHAUST : agotar **2** REDUCE : reducir

depletion [diˈpli:ʃən] *n* **1** EXHAUSTION : agotamiento *m* **2** REDUCTION : reducción *f*, disminución *f*

deplorable [diˈplorəbəl] *adj* **1** CONTEMPTIBLE : deplorable, despreciable **2** LAMENTABLE : lamentable

deplore [diˈplor] *vt* **-plored; -ploring 1** REGRET : deplorar, lamentar **2** CONDEMN : condenar, deplorar

deploy [diˈplɔɪ] *vt* : desplegar

deployment [diˈplɔɪmənt] *n* : despliegue *m*

deport [diˈport] *vt* **1** EXPEL : deportar, expulsar (de un país) **2 to deport oneself** BEHAVE : comportarse

deportation [,di:,porˈteɪʃən] *n* : deportación *f*

depose [diˈpo:z] *vt* **-posed; -posing** : deponer

deposit[1] [diˈpɑzət] *vt* **-ited; -iting** : depositar

deposit[2] *n* **1** : depósito *m* (en el banco) **2** DOWN PAYMENT : entrega *f* inicial **3** : depósito *m*, yacimiento *m* (en geología)

deposition [,dɛpəˈzɪʃən] *n* TESTIMONY : deposición *f*

depositor [diˈpɑzəṱər] *n* : depositante *mf*

depository [diˈpɑzə,tori] *n, pl* **-ries** : almacén *m*, depósito *m*

depot [*in sense 1 usu* ˈdɛ,po:, *2 usu* ˈdi:-] *n* **1** STOREHOUSE : almacén *m*, depósito *m* **2** STATION, TERMINAL : terminal *mf*, estación *f* (de autobuses, ferrocarriles, etc.)

deprave [diˈpreɪv] *vt* **-praved; -praving** : depravar, pervertir

depraved [diˈpreɪvd] *adj* : depravado, degenerado

depravity [diˈprævəṱi] *n, pl* **-ties** : depravación *f*

depreciate [diˈpri:ʃi,eɪt] *v* **-ated; -ating** *vt* **1** DEVALUE : depreciar, devaluar **2** DISPARAGE : menospreciar, despreciar — *vi* : depreciarse, devaluarse

depreciation [di,pri:ʃiˈeɪʃən] *n* : depreciación *f*, devaluación *f*

depress [diˈprɛs] *vt* **1** PRESS, PUSH : apretar, presionar, pulsar **2** REDUCE : reducir, hacer bajar (precios, ventas, etc.) **3** SADDEN : deprimir, abatir, entristecer **4** DEVALUE : depreciar

depressant[1] [diˈprɛsənt] *adj* : depresivo

depressant[2] *n* : depresivo *m*

depressed [diˈprɛst] *adj* **1** DEJECTED : deprimido, abatido **2** : deprimido, en crisis (dícese de la economía)

depressing [diˈprɛsɪŋ] *adj* : deprimente, triste

depression [diˈprɛʃən] *n* **1** DESPONDENCY : depresión *f*, abatimiento *m* **2** : depresión (en una superficie) **3** RECESSION : depresión *f* económica, crisis *f*

deprivation [,dɛprəˈveɪʃən] *n* : privación *f*

deprive [diˈpraɪv] *vt* **-prived; -priving** : privar

depth [ˈdɛpθ] *n, pl* **depths** [ˈdɛpθs, ˈdɛps] : profundidad *f*, fondo *m* ⟨to study in depth : estudiar a fondo⟩ ⟨in the depths of winter : en pleno invierno⟩

deputize [ˈdɛpjʊ,taɪz] *vt* **-tized; -tizing** : nombrar como segundo

deputy [ˈdɛpjʊṱi] *n, pl* **-ties** : suplente *mf*; sustituto *m*, -ta *f*

derail [diˈreɪl] *v* : descarrilar

derailment [di'reɪlmənt] *n* : descarrilamiento *m*

derange [di'reɪndʒ] *vt* **-ranged; -ranging** **1** DISARRANGE : desarreglar, desordenar **2** DISTURB, UPSET : trastornar, perturbar **3** MADDEN : enloquecer, volver loco

derangement [di'reɪndʒmənt] *n* **1** DISTURBANCE, UPSET : trastorno *m* **2** INSANITY : locura *f*, perturbación *f* mental

derby ['dərbi] *n, pl* **-bies** **1** : derby *m* ⟨the Kentucky Derby : el Derby de Kentucky⟩ **2** : sombrero *m* hongo

deregulate [di'rɛgjʊˌleɪt] *vt* **-lated; -lating** : desregular

deregulation [diˌrɛgjʊ'leɪʃən] *n* : desregulación *f*

derelict[1] ['dɛrəˌlɪkt] *adj* **1** ABANDONED : abandonado, en ruinas **2** REMISS : negligente, remiso

derelict[2] *n* **1** : propiedad *f* abandonada **2** VAGRANT : vagabundo *m*, -da *f*

deride [di'raɪd] *vt* **-rided; -riding** : ridiculizar, burlarse de

derision [di'rɪʒən] *n* : escarnio *m*, irrisión *f*, mofa *f*

derisive [di'raɪsɪv] *adj* : burlón

derivation [ˌdɛrə'veɪʃən] *n* : derivación *f*

derivative[1] [di'rɪvəṭɪv] *adj* **1** DERIVED : derivado **2** BANAL : carente de originalidad, banal

derivative[2] *n* : derivado *m*

derive [di'raɪv] *v* **-rived; -riving** *vt* **1** OBTAIN : obtener, sacar **2** DEDUCE : deducir, inferir — *vi* : provenir, derivar, proceder

dermatologist [ˌdərmə'tɑlədʒɪst] *n* : dermatólogo *m*, -ga *f*

dermatology [ˌdərmə'tɑlədʒi] *n* : dermatología *f*

derogatory [di'rɑgəˌtori] *adj* : despectivo, despreciativo

derrick ['dɛrɪk] *n* **1** CRANE : grúa *f* **2** : torre *f* de perforación (sobre un pozo de petróleo)

descend [di'sɛnd] *vt* : descender, bajar — *vi* **1** : descender, bajar ⟨he descended from the platform : descendió del estrado⟩ **2** DERIVE : descender, provenir **3** STOOP : rebajarse ⟨I descended to his level : me rebajé a su nivel⟩ **4 to descend upon** : caer sobre, invadir

descendant[1] [di'sɛndənt] *adj* : descendente

descendant[2] *n* : descendiente *mf*

descent [di'sɛnt] *n* **1** : bajada *f*, descenso *m* ⟨the descent from the mountain : el descenso de la montaña⟩ **2** ANCESTRY : ascendencia *f*, linaje *f* **3** SLOPE : pendiente *f*, cuesta *f* **4** FALL : caída *f* **5** ATTACK : incursión *f*, ataque *m*

describe [di'skraɪb] *vt* **-scribed; -scribing** : describir

description [di'skrɪpʃən] *n* : descripción *f*

descriptive [di'skrɪptɪv] *adj* : descriptivo ⟨descriptive adjective : adjetivo calificativo⟩

desecrate ['dɛsɪˌkreɪt] *vt* **-crated; -crating** : profanar

desecration [ˌdɛsɪ'kreɪʃən] *n* : profanación *f*

desegregate [di'sɛgrəˌgeɪt] *vt* **-gated; -gating** : eliminar la segregación racial de

desegregation [diˌsɛgrə'geɪʃən] *n* : eliminación *f* de la segregación racial

desert[1] [di'zərt] *vt* : abandonar (una persona o un lugar), desertar de (una causa, etc.) — *vi* : desertar

desert[2] ['dɛzərt] *adj* : desierto ⟨a desert island : una isla desierta⟩

desert[3] *n* **1** ['dɛzərt] : desierto *m* (en geografía) **2** [di'zərt] → **deserts**

deserter [di'zərṭər] *n* : desertor *m*, -tora *f*

desertion [di'zərʃən] *n* : abandono *m*, deserción *f* (militar)

deserts [di'zərts] *npl* : merecido *m* ⟨to get one's just deserts : llevarse uno su merecido⟩

deserve [di'zərv] *vt* **-served; -serving** : merecer, ser digno de

deserving [di'zərvɪŋ] *adj* : meritorio ⟨deserving of : digno de⟩

desiccate ['dɛsɪˌkeɪt] *vt* **-cated; -cating** : desecar, deshidratar

design[1] [di'zaɪn] *vt* **1** DEVISE : diseñar, concebir, idear **2** PLAN : proyectar **3** SKETCH : trazar, bosquejar

design[2] *n* **1** PLAN, SCHEME : plan *m*, proyecto *m* ⟨by design : a propósito, intencionalmente⟩ **2** SKETCH : diseño *m*, bosquejo *m* **3** PATTERN, STYLE : diseño *m*, estilo *m* **4 designs** *npl* INTENTIONS : propósitos *mpl*, designios *mpl*

designate ['dɛzɪgˌneɪt] *vt* **-nated; -nating** **1** INDICATE, SPECIFY : indicar, especificar **2** APPOINT : nombrar, designar

designation [ˌdɛzɪg'neɪʃən] *n* **1** NAMING : designación *f* **2** NAME : denominación *f*, nombre *m* **3** APPOINTMENT : designación *f*, nombramiento *m*

designer [di'zaɪnər] *n* : diseñador *m*, -dora *f*

desirability [diˌzaɪrə'bɪləṭi] *n, pl* **-ties** **1** ADVISABILITY : conveniencia *f* **2** ATTRACTIVENESS : atractivo *m*

desirable [di'zaɪrəbəl] *adj* **1** ADVISABLE : conveniente, aconsejable **2** ATTRACTIVE : deseable, atractivo

desire[1] [di'zaɪr] *vt* **-sired; -siring** **1** WANT : desear **2** REQUEST : rogar, solicitar

desire[2] *n* : deseo *m*, anhelo *m*, ansia *m*

desist [di'sɪst, -'zɪst] *vi* **to desist from** : desistir de, abstenerse de

desk ['dɛsk] *n* : escritorio *m*, pupitre *m* (en la escuela)

desktop ['dɛskˌtɑp] *adj* : de escritorio

desolate[1] ['dɛsəˌleɪt, -zə-] *vt* **-lated; -lating** : devastar, desolar

desolate[2] [ˈdɛsələt, -zə-] *adj* 1 BARREN : desolado, desierto, yermo 2 DISCONSOLATE : desconsolado, desolado
desolation [ˌdɛsəˈleɪʃən, -zə-] *n* : desolación *f*
despair[1] [diˈspær] *vi* : desesperar, perder las esperanzas
despair[2] *n* : desesperación *f*, desesperanza *f*
desperate [ˈdɛspərət] *adj* 1 HOPELESS : desesperado, sin esperanzas 2 RASH : desesperado, precipitado 3 SERIOUS, URGENT : grave, urgente, apremiante ⟨a desperate need : una necesidad apremiante⟩
desperately [ˈdɛspərətli] *adv* : desesperadamente, urgentemente
desperation [ˌdɛspəˈreɪʃən] *n* : desesperación *f*
despicable [diˈspɪkəbəl, ˈdɛspɪ-] *adj* : vil, despreciable, infame
despise [diˈspaɪz] *vt* **-spised; -spising** : despreciar
despite [dəˈspaɪt] *prep* : a pesar de, aún con
despoil [diˈspɔɪl] *vt* : saquear
despondency [diˈspɑndəntsi] *n* : desaliento *m*, desánimo *m*, depresión *f*
despondent [diˈspɑndənt] *adj* : desalentado, desanimado
despot [ˈdɛspət, -ˌpɑt] *n* : déspota *mf*; tirano *m*, -na *f*
despotic [dɛsˈpɑt̬ɪk] *adj* : despótico
despotism [ˈdɛspəˌtɪzəm] *n* : despotismo *m*
dessert [diˈzərt] *n* : postre *m*
destination [ˌdɛstəˈneɪʃən] *n* : destino *m*, destinación *f*
destined [ˈdɛstənd] *adj* 1 FATED : predestinado 2 BOUND : destinado, con destino (a), con rumbo (a)
destiny [ˈdɛstəni] *n, pl* **-nies** : destino *m*
destitute [ˈdɛstəˌtuːt, -ˌtjuːt] *adj* 1 LACKING : carente, desprovisto 2 POOR : indigente, en miseria
destitution [ˌdɛstəˈtuːʃən, -ˈtjuː-] *n* : indigencia *f*, miseria *f*
destroy [diˈstrɔɪ] *vt* 1 KILL : matar 2 DEMOLISH : destruir, destrozar
destroyer [diˈstrɔɪər] *n* : destructor *m* (buque)
destructible [diˈstrʌktəbəl] *adj* : destructible
destruction [diˈstrʌkʃən] *n* : destrucción *f*, ruina *f*
destructive [diˈstrʌktɪv] *adj* : destructor, destructivo
desultory [ˈdɛsəlˌtori] *adj* 1 AIMLESS : sin rumbo, sin objeto 2 DISCONNECTED : inconexo
detach [diˈtætʃ] *vt* : separar, quitar, desprender
detached [diˈtætʃt] *adj* 1 SEPARATE : separado, suelto 2 ALOOF : distante, indiferente 3 IMPARTIAL : imparcial, objetivo
detachment [diˈtætʃmənt] *n* 1 SEPARATION : separación *f* 2 DETAIL : destacamento *m* (de tropas) 3 ALOOFNESS : reserva *f*, indiferencia *f* 4 IMPARTIALITY : imparcialidad *f*
detail[1] [diˈteɪl, ˈdiːˌteɪl] *vt* : detallar, exponer en detalle
detail[2] *n* 1 : detalle *m*, pormenor *m* 2 : destacamento *m* (de tropas)
detailed [diˈteɪld, ˈdiːˌteɪld] *adj* : detallado, minucioso
detain [diˈteɪn] *vt* 1 HOLD : detener 2 DELAY : entretener, demorar, retrasar
detect [diˈtɛkt] *vt* : detectar, descubrir
detection [diˈtɛkʃən] *n* : descubrimiento *m*
detective [diˈtɛktɪv] *n* : detective *mf* ⟨private detective : detective privado⟩
detector [diˈtɛktər] *n* : detector *m*
detention [diˈtɛntʃən] *n* : detención *m*
deter [diˈtər] *vt* **-terred; -terring** : disuadir, impedir
detergent [diˈtərdʒənt] *n* : detergente *m*
deteriorate [diˈtɪriəˌreɪt] *vi* **-rated; -rating** : deteriorarse, empeorar
deterioration [diˌtɪriəˈreɪʃən] *n* : deterioro *m*, empeoramiento *m*
determinant[1] [diˈtərmənənt] *adj* : determinante
determinant[2] *n* 1 : factor *m* determinante 2 : determinante *m* (en matemáticas)
determination [dɪˌtərməˈneɪʃən] *n* 1 DECISION : determinación *f*, decisión *f* 2 RESOLUTION : resolución *f*, determinación *f* ⟨with grim determination : con una firme resolución⟩
determine [diˈtərmən] *vt* **-mined; -mining** 1 ESTABLISH : determinar, establecer 2 SETTLE : decidir 3 FIND OUT : averiguar 4 BRING ABOUT : determinar
determined [diˈtərmənd] *adj* RESOLUTE : decidido, resuelto
deterrent [diˈtərənt] *n* : medida *f* disuasiva
detest [diˈtɛst] *vt* : detestar, odiar, aborrecer
detestable [diˈtɛstəbəl] *adj* : detestable, odioso, aborrecible
dethrone [diˈθroːn] *vt* **-throned; -throning** : destronar
detonate [ˈdɛtənˌeɪt] *v* **-nated; -nating** *vt* : hacer detonar — *vi* : detonar, estallar
detonation [ˌdɛt̬əˈneɪʃən] *n* : detonación *f*
detour[1] [ˈdiːˌtʊr, diˈtʊr] *vi* : desviarse
detour[2] *n* : desvío *m*, rodeo *m*
detract [diˈtrækt] *vi* **to detract from** : restarle valor a, quitarle méritos a
detractor [diˈtræktər] *n* : detractor *m*, -tora *f*
detriment [ˈdɛtrəmənt] *n* : detrimento *m*, perjuicio *m*
detrimental [ˌdɛtrəˈmɛntəl] *adj* : perjudicial — **detrimentally** *adv*
devaluation [diˌvæljʊˈeɪʃən] *n* : devaluación *f*
devalue [diˈvælˌjuː] *vt* **-ued; -uing** : devaluar, depreciar

devastate [ˈdɛvəˌsteɪt] *vt* **-tated; -tating** : devastar, arrasar, asolar

devastation [ˌdɛvəˈsteɪʃən] *n* : devastación *f*, estragos *mpl*

develop [diˈvɛləp] *vt* **1** FORM, MAKE : desarrollar, elaborar, formar **2** : revelar (en fotografía) **3** FOSTER : desarrollar, fomentar **4** EXPLOIT : explotar (recursos), urbanizar (un área) **5** ACQUIRE : adquirir ⟨to develop an interest : adquirir un interés⟩ **6** CONTRACT : contraer (una enfermedad) — *vi* **1** GROW : desarrollarse **2** ARISE : aparecer, surgir

developed [diˈvɛləpt] *adj* : avanzado, desarrollado

developer [diˈvɛləpər] *n* **1** : inmobiliaria *f*, urbanizadora *f* **2** : revelador *m* (en fotografía)

development [diˈvɛləpmənt] *n* **1** : desarrollo *m* ⟨physical development : desarrollo físico⟩ **2** : urbanización *f* (de un área), explotación *f* (de recursos), creación *f* (de inventos) **3** EVENT : acontecimiento *m*, suceso *m* ⟨to await developments : esperar acontecimientos⟩

deviant [ˈdiːviənt] *adj* : desviado, anormal

deviate [ˈdiːviˌeɪt] *v* **-ated; -ating** *vi* : desviarse, apartarse — *vt* : desviar

deviation [ˌdiːviˈeɪʃən] *n* : desviación *f*

device [diˈvaɪs] *n* **1** MECHANISM : dispositivo *m*, aparato *m*, mecanismo *m* **2** EMBLEM : emblema *m*

devil[1] [ˈdɛvəl] *vt* **-iled** *or* **-illed; -iling** *or* **-illing 1** : sazonar con picante y especias **2** PESTER : molestar

devil[2] *n* **1** SATAN : el diablo, Satanás *m* **2** DEMON : diablo *m*, demonio *m* **3** FIEND : persona *f* diabólica; malvado *m*, -da *f*

devilish [ˈdɛvəlɪʃ] *adj* : diabólico

devilry [ˈdɛvəlri] *n, pl* **-ries** : diabluras *fpl*, travesuras *fpl*

devious [ˈdiːviəs] *adj* **1** CRAFTY : taimado, artero **2** WINDING : tortuoso, sinuoso

devise [diˈvaɪz] *vt* **-vised; -vising 1** INVENT : idear, concebir, inventar **2** PLOT : tramar

devoid [diˈvɔɪd] *adj* **~ of** : carente de, desprovisto de

devote [diˈvoːt] *vt* **-voted; -voting 1** DEDICATE : consagrar, dedicar ⟨to devote one's life : dedicar uno su vida⟩ **2 to devote oneself** : dedicarse

devoted [diˈvoːt̬əd] *adj* **1** FAITHFUL : leal, fiel **2 to be devoted to someone** : tenerle mucho cariño a alguien

devotee [ˌdɛvəˈtiː, -ˈteɪ] *n* : devoto *m*, -ta *f*

devotion [diˈvoːʃən] *n* **1** DEDICATION : dedicación *f*, devoción *f* **2 devotions** PRAYERS : oraciones *fpl*, devociones *fpl*

devour [diˈvaʊər] *vt* : devorar

devout [diˈvaʊt] *adj* **1** PIOUS : devoto, piadoso **2** EARNEST, SINCERE : sincero, ferviente — **devoutly** *adv*

devoutness [diˈvaʊtnəs] *n* : devoción *f*, piedad *f*

dew [ˈduː, ˈdjuː] *n* : rocío *m*

dewlap [ˈduˌlæp, ˈdju-] *n* : papada *f*

dew point *n* : punto *m* de condensación

dewy [ˈduːi, ˈdjuːi] *adj* **dewier; -est** : cubierto de rocío

dexterity [dɛkˈstɛrət̬i] *n, pl* **-ties** : destreza *f*, habilidad *f*

dexterous [ˈdɛkstrəs] *adj* : diestro, hábil

dexterously [ˈdɛkstrəsli] *adv* : con destreza, con habilidad, hábilmente

dextrose [ˈdɛkˌstroːs] *n* : dextrosa *f*

diabetes [ˌdaɪəˈbiːt̬iz] *n* : diabetes *f*

diabetic[1] [ˌdaɪəˈbɛt̬ɪk] *adj* : diabético

diabetic[2] *n* : diabético *m*, -ca *f*

diabolic [ˌdaɪəˈbɑlɪk] *or* **diabolical** [-lɪkəl] *adj* : diabólico, satánico

diacritical mark [ˌdaɪəˈkrɪt̬ɪkəl] *n* : signo *m* diacrítico

diadem [ˈdaɪəˌdɛm, -dəm] *n* : diadema *f*

diagnose [ˈdaɪɪgˌnoːs, ˌdaɪɪgˈnoːs] *vt* **-nosed; -nosing** : diagnosticar

diagnosis [ˌdaɪɪgˈnoːsɪs] *n, pl* **-noses** [-ˈnoːˌsiːz] : diagnóstico *m*

diagnostic [ˌdaɪɪgˈnɑstɪk] *adj* : diagnóstico

diagonal[1] [daɪˈægənəl] *adj* : diagonal, en diagonal

diagonal[2] *n* : diagonal *f*

diagonally [daɪˈægənəli] *adv* : diagonalmente, en diagonal

diagram[1] [ˈdaɪəˌgræm] *vt* **-gramed** *or* **-grammed; -graming** *or* **-gramming** : hacer un diagrama de

diagram[2] *n* : diagrama *m*, gráfico *m*, esquema *m*

dial[1] [ˈdaɪl] *v* **dialed** *or* **dialled; dialing** *or* **dialling** : marcar, discar

dial[2] *n* : esfera *f* (de un reloj), dial *m* (de un radio), disco *m* (de un teléfono)

dialect [ˈdaɪəˌlɛkt] *n* : dialecto *m*

dialogue [ˈdaɪəˌlɔg] *n* : diálogo *m*

diameter [daɪˈæmət̬ər] *n* : diámetro *m*

diamond [ˈdaɪmənd, ˈdaɪə-] *n* **1** : diamante *m*, brillante *m* ⟨a diamond necklace : un collar de brillantes⟩ **2** : rombo *m*, forma *f* de rombo **3** : diamante *m* (en naipes) **4** INFIELD : cuadro *m*, diamante *m* (en béisbol)

diaper [ˈdaɪpər, ˈdaɪə-] *n* : pañal *m*

diaphragm [ˈdaɪəˌfræm] *n* : diafragma *m*

diarrhea [ˌdaɪəˈriːə] *n* : diarrea *f*

diary [ˈdaɪəri] *n, pl* **-ries** : diario *m*

diatribe [ˈdaɪəˌtraɪb] *n* : diatriba *f*

dice[1] [ˈdaɪs] *vt* **diced; dicing** : cortar en cubos

dice[2] *ns & pl* **1** → **die**[2] **2** : dados *mpl* (juego)

dicker [ˈdɪkər] *vt* : regatear

dictate[1] [ˈdɪkˌteɪt, dɪkˈteɪt] *v* **-tated; -tating** *vt* **1** : dictar ⟨to dictate a letter : dictar una carta⟩ **2** ORDER : mandar, ordenar — *vi* : dar órdenes

dictate[2] [ˈdɪkˌteɪt] *n* **1** : mandato *m*, orden *f* **2 dictates** *npl* : dictados *mpl* ⟨the dictates of conscience : los dictados de la conciencia⟩
dictation [dɪkˈteɪʃən] *n* : dictado *m*
dictator [ˈdɪkˌteɪt̬ər] *n* : dictador *m*, -dora *f*
dictatorial [ˌdɪktəˈtoriəl] *adj* : dictatorial — **dictatorially** *adv*
dictatorship [dɪkˈteɪt̬ərˌʃɪp, ˈdɪkˌ-] *n* : dictadura *f*
diction [ˈdɪkʃən] *n* **1** : lenguaje *m*, estilo *m* **2** ENUNCIATION : dicción *f*, articulación *f*
dictionary [ˈdɪkʃəˌnɛri] *n, pl* **-naries** : diccionario *m*
did → **do**
didactic [daɪˈdæktɪk] *adj* : didáctico
die[1] [ˈdaɪ] *vi* **died** [ˈdaɪd]; **dying** [ˈdaɪɪŋ] **1** : morir **2** CEASE : morir, morirse ⟨a dying civilization : una civilización moribunda⟩ **3** STOP : apagarse, dejar de funcionar ⟨the motor died : el motor se apagó⟩ **4 to die down** SUBSIDE : amainar, disminuir **5 to die out** : extinguirse **6 to be dying for** *or* **to be dying to** : morirse por ⟨I'm dying to leave : me muero por irme⟩
die[2] [ˈdaɪ] *n, pl* **dice** [ˈdaɪs] : dado *m*
die[3] *n, pl* **dies** [ˈdaɪz] **1** STAMP : troquel *m*, cuño *m* **2** MOLD : matriz *f*, molde *m*
diesel [ˈdiːzəl, -səl] *n* : diesel *m*
diet[1] [ˈdaɪət] *vi* : ponerse a régimen, hacer dieta
diet[2] *n* : régimen *m*, dieta *f*
dietary [ˈdaɪəˌtɛri] *adj* : alimenticio, dietético
dietitian *or* **dietician** [ˌdaɪəˈtɪʃən] *n* : dietista *mf*
differ [ˈdɪfər] *vi* **-ferred; -ferring 1** : diferir, diferenciarse **2** VARY : variar **3** DISAGREE : discrepar, diferir, no estar de acuerdo
difference [ˈdɪfrənts, ˈdɪfərənts] *n* : diferencia *f*
different [ˈdɪfrənt, ˈdɪfərənt] *adj* : distinto, diferente
differentiate [ˌdɪfəˈrɛntʃiˌeɪt] *v* **-ated; -ating** *vt* **1** : hacer diferente **2** DISTINGUISH : distinguir, diferenciar — *vi* : distinguir
differentiation [ˌdɪfəˌrɛntʃiˈeɪʃən] *n* : diferenciación *f*
differently [ˈdɪfrəntli, ˈdɪfərənt-] *adv* : de otra manera, de otro modo, distintamente
difficult [ˈdɪfɪˌkʌlt] *adj* : difícil
difficulty [ˈdɪfɪˌkʌlti] *n, pl* **-ties 1** : dificultad *f* **2** PROBLEM : problema *f*, dificultad *f*
diffidence [ˈdɪfədənts] *n* **1** SHYNESS : retraimiento *m*, timidez *f*, apocamiento *m* **2** RETICENCE : reticencia *f*
diffident [ˈdɪfədənt] *adj* **1** SHY : tímido, apocado, inseguro **2** RESERVED : reservado
diffuse[1] [dɪˈfjuːz] *v* **-fused; -fusing** *vt* : difundir, esparcir — *vi* : difundirse, esparcirse
diffuse[2] [dɪˈfjuːs] *adj* **1** WORDY : prolijo, verboso **2** WIDESPREAD : difuso
diffusion [dɪˈfjuːʒən] *n* : difusión *f*
dig[1] [ˈdɪg] *v* **dug** [ˈdʌg]; **digging** *vt* **1** : cavar, excavar ⟨to dig a hole : cavar un hoyo⟩ **2** EXTRACT : sacar ⟨to dig up potatoes : sacar papas del suelo⟩ **3** POKE, THRUST : clavar, hincar ⟨he dug me in the ribs : me dio un codazo en las costillas⟩ **4 to dig up** DISCOVER : descubrir, sacar a luz — *vi* : cavar, excavar
dig[2] *n* **1** POKE : codazo *m* **2** GIBE : pulla *f* **3** EXCAVATION : excavación *f*
digest[1] [daɪˈdʒɛst, dɪ-] *vt* **1** ASSIMILATE : digerir, asimilar **2** : digerir (comida) **3** SUMMARIZE : compendiar, resumir
digest[2] [ˈdaɪˌdʒɛst] *n* : compendio *m*, resumen *m*
digestible [daɪˈdʒɛstəbəl, dɪ-] *adj* : digerible
digestion [daɪˈdʒɛstʃən, dɪ-] *n* : digestión *f*
digestive [daɪˈdʒɛstɪv, dɪ-] *adj* : digestivo ⟨the digestive system : el sistema digestivo⟩
digit [ˈdɪdʒət] *n* **1** NUMERAL : dígito *m*, número *m* **2** FINGER, TOE : dedo *m*
digital [ˈdɪdʒət̬əl] *adj* : digital — **digitally** *adv*
dignified [ˈdɪgnəˌfaɪd] *adj* : digno, decoroso
dignify [ˈdɪgnəˌfaɪ] *vt* **-fied; -fying** : dignificar, honrar
dignitary [ˈdɪgnəˌtɛri] *n, pl* **-taries** : dignatario *m*, -ria *f*
dignity [ˈdɪgnət̬i] *n, pl* **-ties** : dignidad *f*
digress [daɪˈgrɛs, də-] *vi* : desviarse del tema, divagar
digression [daɪˈgrɛʃən, də-] *n* : digresión *f*
dike *or* **dyke** [ˈdaɪk] *n* : dique *m*
dilapidated [dəˈlæpəˌdeɪt̬əd] *adj* : ruinoso, desvencijado, destartalado
dilapidation [dəˌlæpəˈdeɪʃən] *n* : deterioro *m*, estado *m* ruinoso
dilate [daɪˈleɪt, ˈdaɪˌleɪt] *v* **-lated; -lating** *vt* : dilatar — *vi* : dilatarse
dilemma [dɪˈlɛmə] *n* : dilema *m*
dilettante [ˈdɪləˌtɑnt, -ˌtænt] *n, pl* **-tantes** [-ˌtɑnts, -ˌtænts] *or* **-tanti** [ˌdɪləˈtɑnti, -ˈtæn-] : diletante *mf*
diligence [ˈdɪlədʒənts] *n* : diligencia *f*, aplicación *f*
diligent [ˈdɪlədʒənt] *adj* : diligente ⟨a diligent search : una búsqueda minuciosa⟩ — **diligently** *adv*
dill [ˈdɪl] *n* : eneldo *m*
dillydally [ˈdɪliˌdæli] *vi* **-lied; lying** : demorarse, perder tiempo
dilute [daɪˈluːt, də-] *vt* **-luted; -luting** : diluir, aguar
dilution [daɪˈluːʃən, də-] *n* : dilución *f*
dim[1] [ˈdɪm] *v* **dimmed; dimming** *vt* : atenuar (la luz), nublar (la vista), bo-

rrar (la memoria), opacar (una superficie) — *vi* : oscurecerse, apagarse

dim[2] *adj* **dimmer; dimmest** **1** FAINT : oscuro, tenue (dícese de la luz), nublado (dícese de la vista), borrado (dícese de la memoria) **2** DULL : deslustrado **3** STUPID : tonto, torpe

dime ['daɪm] *n* : moneda *f* de diez centavos

dimension [də'mɛntʃən, daɪ-] *n* **1** : dimensión *f* **2 dimensions** *npl* EXTENT, SCOPE : dimensiones *fpl*, extensión *f*, medida *f*

diminish [də'mɪnɪʃ] *vt* LESSEN : disminuir, reducir, amainar — *vi* DWINDLE, WANE : menguar, reducirse

diminutive [də'mɪnjʊt̬ɪv] *adj* : diminutivo, minúsculo

dimly ['dɪmli] *adv* : indistintamente, débilmente

dimmer ['dɪmər] *n* : potenciómetro *m*, conmutador *m* de luces (en automóviles)

dimness ['dɪmnəs] *n* : oscuridad *f*, debilidad *f* (de la vista), imprecisión *f* (de la memoria)

dimple ['dɪmpəl] *n* : hoyuelo *m*

din ['dɪn] *n* : estrépito *m*, estruendo *m*

dine ['daɪn] *vi* **dined; dining** : cenar

diner ['daɪnər] *n* **1** : comensal *mf* (persona) **2** : vagón *m* restaurante (en un tren) **3** : cafetería *f*, restaurante *m* barato

dinghy ['dɪŋi, 'dɪŋgi, 'dɪŋki] *n, pl* **-ghies** : bote *m*

dinginess ['dɪndʒinəs] *n* **1** DIRTINESS : suciedad *f* **2** SHABBINESS : lo gastado, lo deslucido

dingy ['dɪndʒi] *adj* **-gier; -est** **1** DIRTY : sucio **2** SHABBY : gastado, deslucido

dinner ['dɪnər] *n* : cena *f*, comida *f*

dinosaur ['daɪnəˌsɔr] *n* : dinosaurio *m*

dint ['dɪnt] *n* **by dint of** : a fuerza de

diocese ['daɪəsəs, -ˌsiːz, -ˌsiːs] *n, pl* **-ceses** ['daɪəsəsəz] : diócesis *f*

dip[1] ['dɪp] *v* **dipped; dipping** *vt* **1** DUNK, PLUNGE : sumergir, mojar, meter **2** LADLE : servir con cucharón **3** LOWER : bajar, arriar (una bandera) — *vi* **1** DESCEND, DROP : bajar en picada, descender **2** SLOPE : bajar, inclinarse

dip[2] *n* **1** SWIM : chapuzón *m* **2** DROP : descenso *m*, caída *f* **3** SLOPE : cuesta *f*, declive *m* **4** SAUCE : salsa *f*

diphtheria [dɪf'θɪriə] *n* : difteria *f*

diphthong ['dɪfˌθɔŋ] *n* : diptongo *m*

diploma [də'ploːmə] *n, pl* **-mas** : diploma *m*

diplomacy [də'ploːməsi] *n* **1** : diplomacia *f* **2** TACT : tacto *m*, discreción *f*

diplomat ['dɪpləˌmæt] *n* **1** : diplomático *m*, -ca *f* (en relaciones internacionales) **2** : persona *f* diplomática

diplomatic [ˌdɪplə'mæt̬ɪk] *adj* : diplomático ⟨diplomatic immunity : inmunidad diplomática⟩

dipper ['dɪpər] *n* **1** LADLE : cucharón *m*, cazo *m* **2 Big Dipper** : Osa *f* Mayor **3 Little Dipper** : Osa *f* Menor

dire ['daɪr] *adj* **direr; direst** **1** HORRIBLE : espantoso, terrible, horrendo **2** EXTREME : extremo ⟨dire poverty : pobreza extrema⟩

direct[1] [də'rɛkt, daɪ-] *vt* **1** ADDRESS : dirigir, mandar **2** AIM, POINT : dirigir **3** GUIDE : indicarle el camino (a alguien), orientar **4** MANAGE : dirigir ⟨to direct a film : dirigir una película⟩ **5** COMMAND : ordenar, mandar

direct[2] *adv* : directamente

direct[3] *adj* **1** STRAIGHT : directo **2** FRANK : franco

direct current *n* : corriente *f* continua

direction [də'rɛkʃən, daɪ-] *n* **1** SUPERVISION : dirección *f* **2** INSTRUCTION, ORDER : instrucción *f*, orden *f* **3** COURSE : dirección *f*, rumbo *m* ⟨to change direction : cambiar de dirección⟩ **4 to ask directions** : pedir indicaciones

directional [də'rɛkʃənəl, daɪ-] *adj* : direccional

directive [də'rɛktɪv, daɪ-] *n* : directiva *f*

directly [də'rɛktli, daɪ-] *adv* **1** STRAIGHT : directamente ⟨directly north : directamente al norte⟩ **2** FRANKLY : francamente **3** EXACTLY : exactamente, justo ⟨directly opposite : justo enfrente⟩ **4** IMMEDIATELY : en seguida, inmediatamente

directness [də'rɛktnəs, daɪ-] *n* : franqueza *f*

director [də'rɛktər, daɪ-] *n* **1** : director *m*, -tora *f* **2 board of directors** : junta *f* directiva, directorio *m*

directory [də'rɛktəri, daɪ-] *n, pl* **-ries** : guía *f*, directorio *m* ⟨telephone directory : directorio telefónico⟩

dirge ['dərdʒ] *n* : canto *m* fúnebre

dirigible ['dɪrədʒəbəl, də'rɪdʒə-] *n* : dirigible *m*, zepelín *m*

dirt ['dərt] *n* **1** FILTH : suciedad *f*, mugre *f*, porquería *f* **2** SOIL : tierra *f*

dirtiness ['dərt̬inəs] *n* : suciedad *f*

dirty[1] ['dərt̬i] *vt* **dirtied; dirtying** : ensuciar, manchar

dirty[2] *adj* **dirtier; -est** **1** SOILED, STAINED : sucio, manchado **2** DISHONEST : sucio, deshonesto ⟨a dirty player : un jugador tramposo⟩ ⟨a dirty trick : una mala pasada⟩ **3** INDECENT : indecente, cochino ⟨a dirty joke : un chiste verde⟩

disability [ˌdɪsə'bɪlət̬i] *n, pl* **-ties** : minusvalía *f*, discapacidad *f*, invalidez *f*

disable [dɪs'eɪbəl] *vt* **-abled; -abling** : dejar inválido, inutilizar, incapacitar

disabled [dɪs'eɪbəld] *adj* : minusválido, discapacitado

disabuse [ˌdɪsə'bjuːz] *vt* **-bused; -busing** : desengañar, sacar del error

disadvantage [ˌdɪsəd'væntɪdʒ] *n* : desventaja *f*

disadvantageous [ˌdɪsˌædˌvæn'teɪ-dʒəs] *adj* : desventajoso, desfavorable

disagree [ˌdɪsəˈgriː] *vi* **1** DIFFER : discrepar, no coincidir **2** DISSENT : disentir, discrepar, no estar de acuerdo
disagreeable [ˌdɪsəˈgriːəbəl] *adj* : desagradable
disagreement [ˌdɪsəˈgriːmənt] *n* **1** : desacuerdo *m* **2** DISCREPANCY : discrepancia *f* **3** ARGUMENT : discusión *f*, altercado *m*, disputa *f*
disappear [ˌdɪsəˈpɪr] *vi* : desaparecer, desvanecerse ⟨to disappear from view : perderse de vista⟩
disappearance [ˌdɪsəˈpɪrənts] *n* : desaparición *f*
disappoint [ˌdɪsəˈpɔɪnt] *vt* : decepcionar, defraudar, fallar
disappointing [ˌdɪsəˈpɔɪntɪŋ] *adj* : decepcionante
disappointment [ˌdɪsəˈpɔɪntmənt] *n* : decepción *f*, desilusión *f*, chasco *m*
disapproval [ˌdɪsəˈpruːvəl] *n* : desaprobación *f*
disapprove [ˌdɪsəˈpruːv] *vi* **-proved; -proving** : desaprobar, estar en contra
disapprovingly [ˌdɪsəˈpruːvɪŋli] *adv* : con desaprobación
disarm [dɪsˈɑrm] *vt* : desarmar
disarmament [dɪsˈɑrməmənt] *n* : desarme *m* ⟨nuclear disarmament : desarme nuclear⟩
disarrange [ˌdɪsəˈreɪndʒ] *vt* **-ranged; -ranging** : desarreglar, desordenar
disarray [ˌdɪsəˈreɪ] *n* : desorden *m*, confusión *f*, desorganización *f*
disaster [dɪˈzæstər] *n* : desastre *m*, catástrofe *f*
disastrous [dɪˈzæstrəs] *adj* : desastroso
disband [dɪsˈbænd] *vt* : disolver — *vi* : disolverse, dispersarse
disbar [dɪsˈbɑr] *vt* **-barred; -barring** : prohibir de ejercer la abogacía
disbelief [ˌdɪsbɪˈliːf] *n* : incredulidad *f*
disbelieve [ˌdɪsbɪˈliːv] *v* **-lieved; -lieving** : no creer, dudar
disburse [dɪsˈbərs] *vt* **-bursed; -bursing** : desembolsar
disbursement [dɪsˈbərsmənt] *n* : desembolso *m*
disc → **disk**
discard [dɪsˈkɑrd, ˈdɪsˌkɑrd] *vt* : desechar, deshacerse de, botar — *vi* : descartarse (en juegos de naipes)
discern [dɪˈsərn, -ˈzərn] *vt* : discernir, distinguir, percibir
discernible [dɪˈsərnəbəl, -ˈzər-] *adj* : perceptible, visible
discernment [dɪˈsərnmənt, -ˈzərn-] *n* : discernimiento *m*, criterio *m*
discharge[1] [dɪsˈtʃɑrdʒ, ˈdɪsˌ-] *v* **-charged; -charging 1** UNLOAD : descargar (carga), desembarcar (pasajeros) **2** SHOOT : descargar, disparar **3** FREE : liberar, poner en libertad **4** DISMISS : despedir **5** EMIT : despedir (humo, etc.), descargar (electricidad) **6** : cumplir con (una obligación), saldar (una deuda) — *vi* **1** : descargarse (dícese de una batería) **2** OOZE : supurar
discharge[2] [ˈdɪsˌtʃɑrdʒ, dɪsˈ-] *n* **1** EMISSION : descarga *f* (de electricidad), emisión *f* (de gases) **2** DISMISSAL : despido *m* (del empleo), baja *f* (del ejército) **3** SECRETION : secreción *f*
disciple [dɪˈsaɪpəl] *n* : discípulo *m*, -la *f*
discipline[1] [ˈdɪsəplən] *vt* **-plined; -plining 1** PUNISH : castigar, sancionar (a los empleados) **2** CONTROL : disciplinar **3 to discipline oneself** : disciplinarse
discipline[2] *n* **1** FIELD : disciplina *f*, campo *m* **2** TRAINING : disciplina *f* **3** PUNISHMENT : castigo *m* **4** SELF-CONTROL : dominio *m* de sí mismo
disc jockey *n* : disc jockey *mf*
disclaim [dɪsˈkleɪm] *vt* DENY : negar
disclose [dɪsˈkloːz] *vt* **-closed; -closing** : revelar, poner en evidencia
disclosure [dɪsˈkloːʒər] *n* : revelación *f*
disco [ˈdɪskoː] *n* **1** → **discotheque 2** *or* **disco music** : disco *f*, música *f* disco
discolor [dɪsˈkʌlər] *vt* **1** BLEACH : decolorar **2** FADE : desteñir **3** STAIN : manchar — *vi* : decolorarse, desteñirse
discoloration [dɪsˌkʌləˈreɪʃən] *n* **1** FADING : decoloración *f* **2** STAIN : mancha *f*
discomfort [dɪsˈkʌmfərt] *n* **1** PAIN : molestia *f*, malestar *m* **2** UNEASINESS : inquietud *f*
disconcert [ˌdɪskənˈsərt] *vt* : desconcertar
disconcerting [ˌdɪskənˈsərṭɪŋ] *adj* : desconcertante
disconnect [ˌdɪskəˈnɛkt] *vt* : desconectar
disconnected [ˌdɪskəˈnɛktəd] *adj* : inconexo
disconsolate [dɪsˈkɑntsələt] *adj* : desconsolado
discontent [ˌdɪskənˈtɛnt] *n* : descontento *m*
discontented [ˌdɪskənˈtɛntəd] *adj* : descontento
discontinue [ˌdɪskənˈtɪnˌjuː] *vt* **-ued; -uing** : suspender, descontinuar
discontinuity [dɪsˌkɑntəˈnuːəṭi, -ˈnjuː-] *n, pl* **-ties** : discontinuidad *f*
discontinuous [ˌdɪskənˈtɪnjəwəs] *adj* : discontinuo
discord [ˈdɪsˌkɔrd] *n* **1** STRIFE : discordia *f*, discordancia *f* **2** : disonancia *f* (en música)
discordant [dɪsˈkɔrdənt] *adj* : discordante, discorde — **discordantly** *adv*
discotheque [ˈdɪskəˌtɛk, ˌdɪskəˈtɛk] *n* : discoteca *f*
discount[1] [ˈdɪsˌkaʊnt, dɪsˈ-] *vt* **1** REDUCE : descontar, rebajar (precios) **2** DISREGARD : descartar, ignorar
discount[2] [ˈdɪsˌkaʊnt] *n* : descuento *m*, rebaja *f*
discourage [dɪsˈkərɪdʒ] *vt* **-aged; -aging 1** DISHEARTEN : desalentar, desanimar **2** DISSUADE : disuadir
discouragement [dɪsˈkərɪdʒmənt] *n* : desánimo *m*, desaliento *m*

discouraging [dɪsˈkərəʤɪŋ] *adj* : desalentador
discourse[1] [dɪsˈkors] *vi* **-coursed; -coursing** : disertar, conversar
discourse[2] [ˈdɪsˌkors] *n* **1** TALK : conversación *f* **2** SPEECH, TREATISE : discurso *m*, tratado *m*
discourteous [dɪsˈkərt̬iəs] *adj* : descortés — **discourteously** *adv*
discourtesy [dɪsˈkərt̬əsi] *n, pl* **-sies** : descortesía *f*
discover [dɪsˈkʌvər] *vt* : descubrir
discoverer [dɪsˈkʌvərər] *n* : descubridor *m*, -dora *f*
discovery [dɪsˈkʌvəri] *n, pl* **-ries** : descubrimiento *m*
discredit[1] [dɪsˈkrɛdət] *vt* **1** DISBELIEVE : no creer, dudar **2** : desacreditar, desprestigiar, poner en duda 〈they discredited his research : desacreditaron sus investigaciones〉
discredit[2] *n* **1** DISREPUTE : descrédito *m*, desprestigio *m* **2** DOUBT : duda *f*
discreet [dɪsˈkriːt] *adj* : discreto — **discreetly** *adv*
discrepancy [dɪsˈkrɛpəntsi] *n, pl* **-cies** : discrepancia *f*
discretion [dɪsˈkrɛʃən] *n* **1** CIRCUMSPECTION : discreción *f*, circunspección *f* **2** JUDGMENT : discernimiento *m*, criterio *m*
discretionary [dɪsˈkrɛʃəˌnɛri] *adj* : discrecional
discriminate [dɪsˈkrɪməˌneɪt] *v* **-nated; -nating** *vt* DISTINGUISH : distinguir, discriminar, diferenciar — *vi* : discriminar 〈to discriminate against women : discriminar a las mujeres〉
discrimination [dɪsˌkrɪməˈneɪʃən] *n* **1** PREJUDICE : discriminación *f* **2** DISCERNMENT : discernimiento *m*
discriminatory [dɪsˈkrɪmənəˌtori] *adj* : discriminatorio
discus [ˈdɪskəs] *n, pl* **-cuses** [-kəsəz] : disco *m*
discuss [dɪsˈkʌs] *vt* : hablar de, discutir, tratar (de)
discussion [dɪsˈkʌʃən] *n* : discusión *f*, debate *m*, conversación *f*
disdain[1] [dɪsˈdeɪn] *vt* : desdeñar, despreciar 〈they disdained to reply : no se dignaron a responder〉
disdain[2] *n* : desdén *m*
disdainful [dɪsˈdeɪnfəl] *adj* : desdeñoso — **disdainfully** *adv*
disease [dɪˈziːz] *n* : enfermedad *f*, mal *m*, dolencia *f*
diseased [dɪˈziːzd] *adj* : enfermo
disembark [ˌdɪsɪmˈbɑrk] *v* : desembarcar
disembarkation [dɪsˌɛmˌbɑrˈkeɪʃən] *n* : desembarco *m*, desembarque *m*
disembodied [ˌdɪsɪmˈbɑdid] *adj* : incorpóreo
disenchant [ˌdɪsɪnˈʧænt] *vt* : desilusionar, desencantar, desengañar
disenchantment [ˌdɪsɪnˈʧæntmənt] *n* : desencanto *m*, desilusión *f*
disengage [ˌdɪsɪnˈgeɪʤ] *vt* **-gaged; -gaging 1** : soltar, desconectar (un mecanismo) **2 to disengage the clutch** : desembragar
disentangle [ˌdɪsɪnˈtæŋgəl] *vt* **-gled; -gling** UNTANGLE : desenredar, desenmarañar
disfavor [dɪsˈfeɪvər] *n* : desaprobación *f*
disfigure [dɪsˈfɪgjər] *vt* **-ured; -uring** : desfigurar (a una persona), afear (un edificio, un área)
disfigurement [dɪsˈfɪgjərmənt] *n* : desfiguración *f*, afeamiento *m*
disfranchise [dɪsˈfrænˌʧaɪz] *vt* **-chised; -chising** : privar del derecho a votar
disgrace[1] [dɪˈskreɪs] *vt* **-graced; -gracing** : deshonrar
disgrace[2] *n* **1** DISHONOR : desgracia *f*, deshonra *f* **2** SHAME : vergüenza *f* 〈he's a disgrace to his family : es una vergüenza para su familia〉
disgraceful [dɪˈskreɪsfəl] *adj* : vergonzoso, deshonroso, ignominioso
disgracefully [dɪˈskreɪsfəli] *adv* : vergonzosamente
disgruntle [dɪsˈgrʌntəl] *vt* **-tled; -tling** : enfadar, contrariar
disguise[1] [dɪˈskaɪz] *vt* **-guised; -guising 1** : disfrazar, enmascarar (el aspecto) **2** CONCEAL : encubrir, disimular
disguise[2] *n* : disfraz *m*
disgust[1] [dɪˈskʌst] *vt* : darle asco (a alguien), asquear, repugnar 〈that disgusts me : eso me da asco〉
disgust[2] *n* : asco *m*, repugnancia *f*
disgusting [dɪˈskʌstɪŋ] *adj* : asqueroso, repugnante — **disgustingly** *adv*
dish[1] [ˈdɪʃ] *vt* SERVE : servir
dish[2] *n* **1** : plato *m* 〈the national dish : el plato nacional〉 **2** PLATE : plato *m* 〈to wash the dishes : lavar los platos〉 **3 serving dish** : fuente *f*
dishcloth [ˈdɪʃˌklɔth] *n* : paño *m* de cocina (para secar), trapo *m* de fregar (para lavar)
dishearten [dɪsˈhɑrtən] *vt* : desanimar, desalentar
dishevel [dɪˈʃɛvəl] *vt* **-eled** *or* **-elled; -eling** *or* **-elling** : desarreglar, despeinar (el pelo)
disheveled *or* **dishevelled** [dɪˈʃɛvəld] *adj* : despeinado (dícese del pelo), desarreglado, desaliñado
dishonest [dɪˈsɑnəst] *adj* : deshonesto, fraudulento — **dishonestly** *adv*
dishonesty [dɪˈsɑnəsti] *n, pl* **-ties** : deshonestidad *f*, falta *f* de honradez
dishonor[1] [dɪˈsɑnər] *vt* : deshonrar
dishonor[2] *n* : deshonra *f*
dishonorable [dɪˈsɑnərəbəl] *adj* : deshonroso — **dishonorably** [-bli] *adv*
dishrag [ˈdɪʃˌræg] → **dishcloth**
dishwasher [ˈdɪʃˌwɔʃər] *n* : lavaplatos *m*, lavavajillas *m*
disillusion [ˌdɪsəˈluːʒən] *vt* : desilusionar, desencantar, desengañar
disillusionment [ˌdɪsəˈluːʒənmənt] *n* : desilusión *f*, desencanto *m*

disinclination [dɪsˌɪnklə'neɪʃən, -ˌɪŋ-] *n* : aversión *f*
disinclined [ˌdɪsɪn'klaɪnd] *adv* : poco dispuesto
disinfect [ˌdɪsɪn'fɛkt] *vt* : desinfectar
disinfectant[1] [ˌdɪsɪn'fɛktənt] *adj* : desinfectante
disinfectant[2] *n* : desinfectante *m*
disinherit [ˌdɪsɪn'hɛrət] *vt* : desheredar
disintegrate [dɪs'ɪntəˌgreɪt] *v* **-grated; -grating** *vt* : desintegrar, deshacer — *vi* : desintegrarse, deshacerse
disintegration [dɪsˌɪntə'greɪʃən] *n* : desintegración *f*
disinterested [dɪs'ɪntərəstəd, -ˌrɛs-] *adj* **1** INDIFFERENT : indiferente **2** IMPARTIAL : imparcial, desinteresado
disinterestedness [dɪs'ɪntərəstədnəs, -ˌrɛs-] *n* : desinterés *m*
disjointed [dɪs'ʤɔɪntəd] *adj* : inconexo, incoherente
disk *or* **disc** ['dɪsk] *n* : disco *m*
disk drive *n* : unidad *f* de disco
diskette [ˌdɪs'kɛt] *n* : diskette *m*, disquete *m*
dislike[1] [dɪs'laɪk] *vt* **-liked; -liking** : tenerle aversión a (algo), tenerle antipatía (a alguien), no gustarle (algo a uno)
dislike[2] *n* : aversión *f*, antipatía *f*
dislocate ['dɪsloˌkeɪt, dɪs'lo:-] *vt* **-cated; -cating** : dislocar
dislocation [ˌdɪslo'keɪʃən] *n* : dislocación *f*
dislodge [dɪs'lɑʤ] *vt* **-lodged; -lodging** : sacar, desalojar, desplazar
disloyal [dɪs'lɔɪəl] *adj* : desleal
disloyalty [dɪs'lɔɪəlti] *n, pl* **-ties** : deslealtad *f*
dismal ['dɪzməl] *adj* **1** GLOOMY : sombrío, lúgubre, tétrico **2** DEPRESSING : deprimente, triste
dismantle [dɪs'mæntəl] *vt* **-tled; -tling** : desmantelar, desmontar, desarmar
dismay[1] [dɪs'meɪ] *vt* : consternar
dismay[2] *n* : consternación *f*
dismember [dɪs'mɛmbər] *vt* : desmembrar
dismiss [dɪs'mɪs] *vt* **1** : dejar salir, darle permiso (a alguien) para retirarse **2** DISCHARGE : despedir, destituir **3** REJECT : descartar, desechar, rechazar
dismissal [dɪs'mɪsəl] *n* **1** : permiso *m* para retirarse **2** DISCHARGE : despido *m* (de un empleado), destitución *f* (de un funcionario) **3** REJECTION : rechazo *m*
dismount [dɪs'maʊnt] *vi* : desmontar, bajarse, apearse
disobedience [ˌdɪsə'bi:diənts] *n* : desobediencia *f* — **disobedient** [-ənt] *adj*
disobey [ˌdɪsə'beɪ] *v* : desobedecer
disorder[1] [dɪs'ɔrdər] *vt* : desordenar, desarreglar
disorder[2] *n* **1** DISARRAY : desorden *m* **2** UNREST : disturbios *mpl*, desórdenes *mpl* **3** AILMENT : afección *f*, indisposición *f*, dolencia *f*
disorderly [dɪs'ɔrdərli] *adj* **1** UNTIDY : desordenado, desarreglado **2** UNRULY : indisciplinado, alborotado **3** **disorderly conduct** : conducta *f* escandalosa
disorganization [dɪsˌɔrgənə'zeɪʃən] *n* : desorganización *f*
disorganize [dɪs'ɔrgəˌnaɪz] *vt* **-nized; -nizing** : desorganizar
disorient [dɪs'oriˌɛnt] *vt* : desorientar
disown [dɪs'o:n] *vt* : renegar de, repudiar
disparage [dɪs'pærɪʤ] *vt* **-aged; -aging** : menospreciar, denigrar
disparagement [dɪs'pærɪʤmənt] *n* : menosprecio *m*
disparate ['dɪspərət, dɪs'pærət] *adj* : dispar, diferente
disparity [dɪs'pærəṭi] *n, pl* **-ties** : disparidad *f*
dispassionate [dɪs'pæʃənət] *adj* : desapasionado, imparcial — **dispassionately** *adv*
dispatch[1] [dɪs'pæʧ] *vt* **1** SEND : despachar, enviar **2** KILL : despachar, matar **3** HANDLE : despachar
dispatch[2] *n* **1** SENDING : envío *m*, despacho *m* **2** MESSAGE : despacho *m*, reportaje *m* (de un periodista), parte *m* (en el ejército) **3** PROMPTNESS : prontitud *f*, rapidez *f*
dispel [dɪs'pɛl] *vt* **-pelled; -pelling** : disipar, desvanecer
dispensable [dɪ'spɛntsəbəl] *adj* : prescindible
dispensation [ˌdɪspɛn'seɪʃən] *n* EXEMPTION : exención *m*, dispensa *f*
dispense [dɪs'pɛnts] *v* **-pensed; -pensing** *vt* **1** DISTRIBUTE : repartir, distribuir, dar **2** ADMINISTER, BESTOW : administrar (justicia), conceder (favores, etc.) **3** : preparar y despachar (medicamentos) — *vi* **to dispense with** : prescindir de
dispenser [dɪs'pɛntsər] *n* : dispensador *m*, distribuidor *m* automático
dispersal [dɪs'pərsəl] *n* : dispersión *f*
disperse [dɪs'pərs] *v* **-persed; -persing** *vt* : dispersar, diseminar — *vi* : dispersarse
dispersion [dɪ'spərʒən] *n* : dispersión *f*
dispirit [dɪ'spɪrət] *vt* : desalentar, desanimar
displace [dɪs'pleɪs] *vt* **-placed; -placing** **1** : desplazar (un líquido, etc.) **2** REPLACE : reemplazar
displacement [dɪs'pleɪsmənt] *n* **1** : desplazamiento *m* (de personas) **2** REPLACEMENT : sustitución *f*, reemplazo *m*
display[1] [dɪs'pleɪ] *vt* : exponer, exhibir, mostrar
display[2] *n* **1** : muestra *f*, exposición *f*, alarde *m* **2** : visualizador *m* (de una computadora)
displease [dɪs'pli:z] *vt* **-pleased; -pleasing** : desagradar a, disgustar, contrariar

displeasure [dɪsˈplɛʒər] *n* : desagrado *m*
disposable [dɪsˈpoːzəbəl] *adj* **1** : desechable ⟨disposable diapers : pañales desechables⟩ **2** AVAILABLE : disponible
disposal [dɪsˈpoːzəl] *n* **1** PLACEMENT : disposición *f*, colocación *f* **2** REMOVAL : eliminación *f* **3 to have at one's disposal** : disponer de, tener a su disposición
dispose [dɪsˈpoːz] *v* **-posed; -posing** *vt* **1** ARRANGE : disponer, colocar **2** INCLINE : predisponer — *vi* **1 to dispose of** DISCARD : desechar, deshacerse de **2 to dispose of** HANDLE : despachar
disposition [ˌdɪspəˈzɪʃən] *n* **1** ARRANGEMENT : disposición *f* **2** TENDENCY : predisposición *f*, inclinación *f* **3** TEMPERAMENT : temperamento *m*, carácter *m*
dispossess [ˌdɪspəˈzɛs] *vt* : deposeer
disproportion [ˌdɪsprəˈporʃən] *n* : desproporción *f*
disproportionate [ˌdɪsprəˈporʃənət] *adj* : desproporcionado — **disproportionately** *adv*
disprove [dɪsˈpruːv] *vt* **-proved; -proving** : rebatir, refutar
disputable [dɪsˈpjuːt̬əbəl, ˈdɪspjʊt̬əbəl] *adj* : disputable, discutible
dispute[1] [dɪsˈpjuːt] *v* **-puted; -puting** *vt* **1** QUESTION : discutir, cuestionar **2** OPPOSE : combatir, resistir — *vi* ARGUE, DEBATE : discutir
dispute[2] *n* **1** DEBATE : debate *m*, discusión *f* **2** QUARREL : disputa *f*, discusión *f*
disqualification [dɪsˌkwɑləfəˈkeɪʃən] *n* : descalificación *f*
disqualify [dɪsˈkwɑləˌfaɪ] *vt* **-fied; -fying** : descalificar, inhabilitar
disquiet[1] [dɪsˈkwaɪət] *vt* : inquietar
disquiet[2] *n* : ansiedad *f*, inquietud *f*
disregard[1] [ˌdɪsrɪˈgɑrd] *vt* : ignorar, no prestar atención a
disregard[2] *n* : indiferencia *f*
disrepair [ˌdɪsrɪˈpær] *n* : mal estado *m*
disreputable [dɪsˈrɛpjʊt̬əbəl] *adj* : de mala fama (dícese de una persona o un lugar), vergonzoso (dícese de la conducta)
disreputably [dɪsˈrɛpjʊt̬əbli] *adv* : vergonzosamente
disrepute [ˌdɪsrɪˈpjuːt] *n* : descrédito *m*, mala fama *f*, deshonra *f*
disrespect [ˌdɪsrɪˈspɛkt] *n* : falta *f* de respeto
disrespectful [ˌdɪsrɪˈspɛktfəl] *adj* : irrespetuoso — **disrespectfully** *adv*
disrobe [dɪsˈroːb] *v* **-robed; -robing** *vt* : desvestir, desnudar — *vi* : desvestirse, desnudarse
disrupt [dɪsˈrʌpt] *vt* : trastornar, perturbar
disruption [dɪsˈrʌpʃən] *n* : trastorno *m*
disruptive [dɪsˈrʌptɪv] *adj* : perjudicial, perturbador — **disruptively** *adv*
dissatisfaction [dɪsˌsæt̬əsˈfækʃən] *n* : descontento *m*, insatisfacción *f*
dissatisfied [dɪsˈsæt̬əsˌfaɪd] *adj* : descontento, insatisfecho
dissatisfy [dɪsˈsæt̬əsˌfaɪ] *vt* **-fied; -fying** : no contentar, no satisfacer
dissect [dɪˈsɛkt] *vt* : disecar
dissection [dɪˈsɛkʃən] *n* : disección *f*
dissemble [dɪˈsɛmbəl] *v* **-bled; -bling** *vt* HIDE : ocultar, disimular — *vi* PRETEND : fingir, disimular
disseminate [dɪˈsɛməˌneɪt] *vt* **-nated; -nating** : diseminar, difundir, divulgar
dissemination [dɪˌsɛməˈneɪʃən] *n* : diseminación *f*, difusión *f*
dissension [dɪˈsɛntʃən] *n* : disensión *f*, desacuerdo *m*
dissent[1] [dɪˈsɛnt] *vi* : disentir
dissent[2] *n* : disentimiento *m*, disensión *f*
dissertation [ˌdɪsərˈteɪʃən] *n* **1** DISCOURSE : disertación *f*, discurso *m* **2** THESIS : tesis *f*
disservice [dɪsˈsərvɪs] *n* : perjuicio *m*
dissident[1] [ˈdɪsədənt] *adj* : disidente
dissident[2] *n* : disidente *mf*
dissimilar [dɪˈsɪmələr] *adj* : distinto, diferente, disímil
dissipate [ˈdɪsəˌpeɪt] *vt* **-pated; -pating** **1** DISPERSE : disipar, dispersar **2** SQUANDER : malgastar, desperdiciar, derrochar, disipar
dissipation [ˌdɪsəˈpeɪʃən] *n* : disipación *f*, libertinaje *m*
dissociate [dɪˈsoːʃiˌeɪt, -si-] *v* **-ated** [-ˌeɪt̬əd]; **-ating** [-ˌeɪt̬ɪŋ] *vt* : disociar ⟨to disassociate oneself : disociarse⟩ — *vi* : disociarse
dissociation [dɪˌsoːʃiˈeɪʃən, -si-] *n* : disociación *f*
dissolute [ˈdɪsəˌluːt] *adj* : disoluto
dissolution [ˌdɪsəˈluːʃən] *n* : disolución *f*
dissolve [dɪˈzɑlv] *v* **-solved; -solving** *vt* : disolver — *vi* : disolverse
dissonance [ˈdɪsənənts] *n* : disonancia *f*
dissuade [dɪˈsweɪd] *vt* **-suaded; -suading** : disuadir
distance[1] [ˈdɪstənts] *vt* **-tanced** [-təntst]; **-tancing** [-təntsɪŋ] **to distance oneself** : distanciarse
distance[2] *n* **1** : distancia *f* ⟨the distance between two points : la distancia entre dos puntos⟩ ⟨in the distance : a lo lejos⟩ **2** RESERVE : actitud *f* distante, reserva *f* ⟨to keep one's distance : guardar las distancias⟩
distant [ˈdɪstənt] *adj* **1** FAR : distante, lejano **2** REMOTE : distante, lejano, remoto **3** ALOOF : distante, frío
distantly [ˈdɪstəntli] *adv* **1** LOOSELY : aproximadamente, vagamente **2** COLDLY : fríamente, con frialdad
distaste [dɪsˈteɪst] *n* : desagrado *m*, aversión *f*
distasteful [dɪsˈteɪstfəl] *adj* : desagradable, de mal gusto
distemper [dɪsˈtɛmpər] *n* : moquillo *m*
distend [dɪsˈtɛnd] *vt* : dilatar, hinchar — *vi* : dilatarse, hincharse

distill [dɪˈstɪl] *vt* : destilar
distillation [ˌdɪstəˈleɪʃən] *n* : destilación *f*
distiller [dɪˈstɪlər] *n* : destilador *m*, -dora *f*
distillery [dɪˈstɪləri] *n, pl* **-ries** [-riz] : destilería *f*
distinct [dɪˈstɪŋkt] *adj* **1** DIFFERENT : distinto, diferente **2** CLEAR, UNMISTAKABLE : marcado, claro, evidente ⟨a distinct possibility : una clara posibilidad⟩
distinction [dɪˈstɪŋkʃən] *n* **1** DIFFERENTIATION : distinción *f* **2** DIFFERENCE : diferencia *f* **3** EXCELLENCE : distinción *f*, excelencia *f* ⟨a writer of distinction : un escritor destacado⟩
distinctive [dɪˈstɪŋktɪv] *adj* : distintivo, característico — **distinctively** *adv*
distinctiveness [dɪˈstɪŋktɪvnəs] *n* : peculiaridad *f*
distinctly [dɪˈstɪŋktli] *adv* : claramente, con claridad
distinguish [dɪsˈtɪŋgwɪʃ] *vt* **1** DIFFERENTIATE : distinguir, diferenciar **2** DISCERN : distinguir ⟨he distinguished the sound of the piano : distinguió el sonido del piano⟩ **3 to distinguish oneself** : señalarse, distinguirse — *vi* DISCRIMINATE : distinguir
distinguishable [dɪsˈtɪŋgwɪʃəbəl] *adj* : distinguible
distinguished [dɪsˈtɪŋgwɪʃt] *adj* : distinguido
distort [dɪˈstɔrt] *vt* **1** MISREPRESENT : distorsionar, tergiversar **2** DEFORM : distorsionar, deformar
distortion [dɪˈstɔrʃən] *n* : distorsión *f*, deformación *f*, tergiversación *f*
distract [dɪˈstrækt] *vt* : distraer, entretener
distracted [dɪˈstræktəd] *adj* : distraído
distraction [dɪˈstrækʃən] *n* **1** INTERRUPTION : distracción *f*, interrupción *f* **2** CONFUSION : confusión *f* **3** AMUSEMENT : diversión *f*, entretenimiento *m*, distracción *f*
distraught [dɪˈstrɔt] *adj* : afligido, turbado
distress[1] [dɪˈstɛrs] *vt* : afligir, darle pena (a alguien), hacer sufrir
distress[2] *n* **1** SORROW : dolor *m*, angustia *f*, aflicción *f* **2** PAIN : dolor *m* **3 in ∼** : en peligro
distressful [dɪˈstrɛsfəl] *adj* : doloroso, penoso
distribute [dɪˈstrɪˌbjuːt, -bjʊt] *vt* **-uted; -uting** : distribuir, repartir
distribution [ˌdɪstrəˈbjuːʃən] *n* : distribución *f*, reparto *m*
distributive [dɪˈstrɪbjʊt̬ɪv] *adj* : distributivo
distributor [dɪˈstrɪbjʊt̬ər] *n* : distribuidor *m*, -dora *f*
district [ˈdɪsˌtrɪkt] *n* **1** REGION : región *f*, zona *f*, barrio *m* (de una ciudad) **2** : distrito *m* (zona política)
distrust[1] [dɪsˈtrʌst] *vt* : desconfiar de
distrust[2] *n* : desconfianza *f*, recelo *m*
distrustful [dɪsˈtrʌstfəl] *adj* : desconfiado, receloso, suspicaz
disturb [dɪˈstərb] *vt* **1** BOTHER : molestar, perturbar ⟨sorry to disturb you : perdone la molestia⟩ **2** DISARRANGE : desordenar **3** WORRY : inquietar, preocupar **4 to disturb the peace** : alterar el orden público
disturbance [dɪˈstərbənts] *n* **1** COMMOTION : alboroto *m*, disturbio *m* **2** INTERRUPTION : interrupción *f*
disuse [dɪsˈjuːs] *n* : desuso *m*
ditch[1] [ˈdɪʧ] *vt* **1** : cavar zanjas en **2** DISCARD : deshacerse de, botar
ditch[2] *n* : zanja *f*, fosa *f*, cuneta *f* (en una carretera)
dither [ˈdɪðər] *n* **to be in a dither** : estar nervioso, ponerse como loco
ditto [ˈdɪt̬oː] *n, pl* **-tos 1** : lo mismo, ídem *m* **2 ditto marks** : comillas *fpl*
ditty [ˈdɪt̬i] *n, pl* **-ties** : canción *f* corta y simple
diurnal [daɪˈərnəl] *adj* **1** DAILY : diario, cotidiano **2** : diurno ⟨a diurnal animal : un animal diurno⟩
divan [ˈdaɪˌvæn, dɪˈ-] *n* : diván *m*
dive[1] [ˈdaɪv] *vi* **dived** *or* **dove** [ˈdoːv]; **dived; diving 1** PLUNGE : tirarse al agua, zambullirse, dar un clavado **2** SUBMERGE : sumergirse **3** DROP : bajar en picada (dícese de un avión), caer en picada
dive[2] *n* **1** PLUNGE : zambullida *f*, clavado *m* (en el agua) **2** DESCENT : descenso *m* en picada **3** BAR, JOINT : antro *m*
diver [ˈdaɪvər] *n* : saltador *m*, -dora *f*; clavadista *mf*
diverge [dəˈvərʤ, daɪ-] *vi* **-verged; -verging 1** SEPARATE : divergir, separarse **2** DIFFER : divergir, discrepar
divergence [dəˈvərʤənts, daɪ-] *n* : divergencia *f* — **divergent** [-ənt] *adj*
diverse [daɪˈvərs, də-, ˈdaɪˌvərs] *adj* : diverso, variado
diversification [daɪˌvərsəfəˈkeɪʃən, də-] *n* : diversificación *f*
diversify [daɪˈvərsəˌfaɪ, də-] *vt* **-fied; -fying** : diversificar, variar
diversion [daɪˈvərʒən, də-] *n* **1** DEVIATION : desviación *f* **2** AMUSEMENT, DISTRACTION : diversión *f*, distracción *f*, entretenimiento *m*
diversity [daɪˈvərsət̬i, də-] *n, pl* **-ties** : diversidad *f*
divert [dəˈvərt, daɪ-] *vt* **1** DEFLECT : desviar **2** DISTRACT : distraer **3** AMUSE : divertir, entretener
divest [daɪˈvɛst, də-] *vt* **1** UNDRESS : desnudar, desvestir **2 to divest of** : despojar de
divide [dəˈvaɪd] *v* **-vided; -viding** *vt* **1** HALVE : dividir, partir por la mitad **2** SHARE : repartir, dividir **3** : dividir (números) — *vi* : dividirse, dividir (en matemáticas)

dividend [ˈdɪvəˌdɛnd, -dənd] *n* **1** : dividendo *m* (en finanzas) **2** BONUS : beneficio *m*, provecho *m* **3** : dividendo *m* (en matemáticas)

divider [dɪˈvaɪdər] *n* **1** : separador *m* (para ficheros, etc.) **2** *or* **room divider** : mampara *f*, biombo *m*

divination [ˌdɪvəˈneɪʃən] *n* : adivinación *f*

divine[1] [dəˈvaɪn] *adj* **-viner; -est 1** : divino **2** SUPERB : divino, espléndido — **divinely** *adv*

divine[2] *n* : clérigo *m*, eclesiástico *m*

divinity [dəˈvɪnət̮i] *n, pl* **-ties** : divinidad *f*

divisible [dɪˈvɪzəbəl] *adj* : divisible

division [dɪˈvɪʒən] *n* **1** DISTRIBUTION : división *f*, reparto *m* ⟨division of labor : distribución del trabajo⟩ **2** PART : división *f*, sección *f* **3** : división *f* (en matemáticas)

divisive [dəˈvaɪsɪv] *adj* : divisivo

divisor [dɪˈvaɪzər] *n* : divisor *m*

divorce[1] [dəˈvors] *v* **-vorced; -vorcing** *vt* : divorciar — *vi* : divorciarse

divorce[2] *n* : divorcio *m*

divorcé [dɪˌvorˈseɪ, -ˈsiː; -ˈvorˌ-] *n* : divorciado *m*

divorcée [dɪˌvorˈseɪ, -ˈsiː; -ˈvorˌ-] *n* : divorciada *f*

divulge [dəˈvʌlʤ, daɪ-] *vt* **-vulged; -vulging** : revelar, divulgar

dizzily [ˈdɪzəli] *adv* : vertiginosamente

dizziness [ˈdɪzinəs] *n* : mareo *m*, vahído *m*, vértigo *m*

dizzy [ˈdɪzi] *adj* **dizzier; -est 1** : mareado ⟨I feel dizzy : estoy mareado⟩ **2** : vertiginoso ⟨a dizzy speed : una velocidad vertiginosa⟩

DNA [ˌdiːˌɛnˈeɪ] *n* : ADN *m*

do [ˈduː] *v* **did** [ˈdɪd]; **done** [ˈdʌn]; **doing; does** [ˈdʌz] *vt* **1** CARRY OUT, PERFORM : hacer, realizar, llevar a cabo ⟨she did her best : hizo todo lo posible⟩ **2** PREPARE : preparar, hacer ⟨do your homework : haz tu tarea⟩ **3** ARRANGE : arreglar, peinar (el pelo) **4 to do in** RUIN : estropear, arruinar **5 to do in** KILL : matar, liquidar *fam* — *vi* **1** : hacer ⟨you did well : hiciste bien⟩ **2** FARE : estar, ir, andar ⟨how are you doing? : ¿cómo estás?, ¿cómo te va?⟩ **3** FINISH : terminar ⟨now I'm done : ya terminé⟩ **4** SERVE : servir, ser suficiente, alcanzar ⟨this will do for now : esto servirá por el momento⟩ **5 to do away with** ABOLISH : abolir, suprimir **6 to do away with** KILL : eliminar, matar **7 to do by** TREAT : tratar ⟨he does well by her : él la trata bien⟩ — *v aux* **1** (*used in interrogative sentences and negative statements*) ⟨do you know her? : ¿la conoces?⟩ ⟨I don't like that : a mí no me gusta eso⟩ **2** (*used for emphasis*) ⟨I do hope you'll come : espero que vengas⟩ **3** (*used as a substitute verb to avoid repetition*) ⟨do you speak English? yes, I do : ¿habla inglés? sí⟩

docile [ˈdɑsəl] *adj* : dócil, sumiso

dock[1] [ˈdɑk] *vt* **1** CUT : cortar **2** : descontar dinero de (un sueldo) — *vi* ANCHOR, LAND : fondear, atracar

dock[2] *n* **1** PIER : atracadero *m* **2** WHARF : muelle *m* **3** : banquillo *m* de los acusados (en un tribunal)

doctor[1] [ˈdɑktər] *vt* **1** TREAT : tratar, curar **2** ALTER : adulterar, alterar, falsificar (un documento)

doctor[2] *n* **1** : doctor *m*, -tora *f* ⟨Doctor of Philosophy : doctor en filosofía⟩ **2** PHYSICIAN : médico *m*, -ca *f*; doctor *m*, -tora *f*

doctorate [ˈdɑktərət] *n* : doctorado *m*

doctrine [ˈdɑktrɪn] *n* : doctrina *f*

document[1] [ˈdɑkjʊˌmɛnt] *vt* : documentar

document[2] [ˈdɑkjʊmənt] *n* : documento *m*

documentary[1] [ˌdɑkjʊˈmɛntəri] *adj* : documental

documentary[2] *n, pl* **-ries** : documental *m*

documentation [ˌdɑkjʊmənˈteɪʃən] *n* : documentación *f*

dodge[1] [ˈdɑʤ] *v* **dodged; dodging** *vt* : esquivar, eludir, evadir (impuestos) — *vi* : echarse a un lado

dodge[2] *n* **1** RUSE : truco *m*, treta *f*, artimaña *f* **2** EVASION : regate *m*, evasión *f*

dodo [ˈdoːˌdoː] *n, pl* **-does** *or* **-dos** : dodo *m*

doe [ˈdoː] *n, pl* **does** *or* **doe** : gama *f*, cierva *f*

doer [ˈduːər] *n* : hacedor *m*, -dora *f*

does → **do**

doff [ˈdɑf, ˈdɔf] *vt* : quitarse ⟨to doff one's hat : quitarse el sombrero⟩

dog[1] [ˈdɔg, ˈdɑg] *vt* **dogged; dogging** : seguir de cerca, perseguir, acosar ⟨to dog someone's footsteps : seguir los pasos de alguien⟩ ⟨dogged by bad luck : perseguido por la mala suerte⟩

dog[2] *n* : perro *m*, -rra *f*

dogcatcher [ˈdɔgˌkæʧər] *n* : perrero *m*, -ra *f*

dog–eared [ˈdɔgˌɪrd] *adj* : con las esquinas dobladas

dogged [ˈdɔgəd] *adj* : tenaz, terco, obstinado

doggy [ˈdɔgi] *n, pl* **doggies** : perrito *m*, -ta *f*

doghouse [ˈdɔgˌhaʊs] *n* : casita *f* de perro

dogma [ˈdɔgmə] *n* : dogma *m*

dogmatic [dɔgˈmæt̮ɪk] *adj* : dogmático

dogmatism [ˈdɔgməˌtɪzəm] *n* : dogmatismo *m*

dogwood [ˈdɔgˌwʊd] *n* : cornejo *m*

doily [ˈdɔɪli] *n, pl* **-lies** : pañito *m*

doings [ˈduːɪŋz] *npl* : eventos *mpl*, actividades *fpl*

doldrums [ˈdoːldrəmz, ˈdɑl-] *npl* **1** : zona *f* de las calmas ecuatoriales **2 to be in the doldrums** : estar abatido (dícese de una persona), estar estancado (dícese de una empresa)

dole [ˈdoːl] *n* **1** ALMS : distribución *f* a los necesitados, limosna *f* **2** : subsidios *mpl* de desempleo
doleful [ˈdoːlfəl] *adj* : triste, lúgubre
dolefully [ˈdoːlfəli] *adv* : con pesar, de manera triste
dole out *vt* **doled out; doling out** : repartir
doll [ˈdɑl, ˈdɔl] *n* : muñeco *m*, -ca *f*
dollar [ˈdɑlər] *n* : dólar *m*
dolly [ˈdɑli] *n, pl* **-lies** **1** → **doll** **2** : plataforma *f* rodante
dolphin [ˈdɑlfən, ˈdɔl-] *n* : delfín *m*
dolt [ˈdoːlt] *n* : imbécil *mf*; tonto *m*, -ta *f*
domain [doˈmeɪn, də-] *n* **1** TERRITORY : dominio *m*, territorio *m* **2** FIELD : campo *m*, esfera *f*, ámbito *m* ⟨the domain of art : el ámbito de las artes⟩
dome [ˈdoːm] *n* : cúpula *f*, bóveda *f*
domestic[1] [dəˈmɛstɪk] *adj* **1** HOUSEHOLD : doméstico, casero **2** : nacional, interno ⟨domestic policy : política interna⟩ **3** TAME : domesticado
domestic[2] *n* : empleado *m* doméstico, empleada *f* doméstica
domestically [dəˈmɛstɪkli] *adv* : domésticamente
domesticate [dəˈmɛstɪˌkeɪt] *vt* **-cated; -cating** : domesticar
domicile [ˈdɑməˌsaɪl, ˈdoː-; ˈdɑməsɪl] *n* : domicilio *m*
dominance [ˈdɑmənənts] *n* : dominio *m*, dominación *f*
dominant [ˈdɑmənənt] *adj* : dominante
dominate [ˈdɑməˌneɪt] *v* **-nated; -nating** : dominar
domination [ˌdɑməˈneɪʃən] *n* : dominación *f*
domineer [ˌdɑməˈnɪr] *vt* : dominar sobre, avasallar, tiranizar
Dominican [dəˈmɪnɪkən] *n* : dominicano *m*, -na *f* — **Dominican** *adj*
dominion [dəˈmɪnjən] *n* **1** POWER : dominio *m* **2** DOMAIN, TERRITORY : dominio *m*, territorio *m*
domino [ˈdɑməˌnoː] *n, pl* **-noes** *or* **-nos** **1** : dominó *m* **2 dominoes** *npl* : dominó *m* (juego)
don [ˈdɑn] *vt* **donned; donning** : ponerse
donate [ˈdoːˌneɪt, doːˈ-] *vt* **-nated; -nating** : donar, hacer un donativo de
donation [doːˈneɪʃən] *n* : donación *f*, donativo *m*
done[1] [ˈdʌn] → **do**
done[2] *adj* **1** FINISHED : terminado, acabado, concluido **2** COOKED : cocinado
donkey [ˈdɑŋki, ˈdʌŋ-] *n, pl* **-keys** : burro *m*, asno *m*
donor [ˈdoːnər] *n* : donante *mf*; donador *m*, -dora *f*
don't [ˈdoːnt] (*contraction* of **do not**) → **do**
doodle[1] [ˈduːdəl] *v* **-dled; -dling** : garabatear
doodle[2] *n* : garabato *m*
doom[1] [ˈduːm] *vt* : condenar
doom[2] *n* **1** JUDGMENT : sentencia *f*, condena *f* **2** DEATH : muerte *f* **3** FATE : destino *m* **4** RUIN : perdición *f*, ruina *f*
door [ˈdor] *n* : puerta *f*
doorbell [ˈdorˌbɛl] *n* : timbre *m*
doorknob [ˈdorˌnɑb] *n* : pomo *m*, perilla *f*
doorman [ˈdormən] *n, pl* **-men** [-mən, -ˌmɛn] : portero *m*
doormat [ˈdorˌmæt] : felpudo *m*
doorstep [ˈdorˌstɛp] *n* : umbral *m*
doorway [ˈdorˌweɪ] *n* : entrada *f*, portal *m*
dope[1] [ˈdoːp] *vt* **doped; doping** : drogar, narcotizar
dope[2] *n* **1** DRUG : droga *f*, estupefaciente *m*, narcótico *m* **2** IDIOT : idiota *mf*; tonto *m*, -ta *f* **3** INFORMATION : información *f*
dormant [ˈdɔrmənt] *adj* : inactivo, latente
dormer [ˈdɔrmər] *n* : buhardilla *f*
dormitory [ˈdɔrməˌtori] *n, pl* **-ries** : dormitorio *m*, residencia *f* de estudiantes
dormouse [ˈdɔrˌmaʊs] *n* : lirón *m*
dorsal [ˈdɔrsəl] *adj* : dorsal — **dorsally** *adv*
dory [ˈdori] *n, pl* **-ries** : bote *m* de fondo plano
dosage [ˈdoːsɪʤ] *n* : dosis *f*
dose[1] [ˈdoːs] *vt* **dosed; dosing** : medicinar
dose[2] *n* : dosis *f*
dossier [ˈdɔsˌjeɪ, ˈdɑs-] *n* : dossier *m*
dot[1] [ˈdɑt] *vt* **dotted; dotting** **1** : poner el punto sobre (una letra) **2** SCATTER : esparcir, salpicar
dot[2] *n* : punto *m* ⟨at six on the dot : a las seis en punto⟩ ⟨dots and dashes : puntos y rayas⟩
dote [ˈdoːt] *vi* **doted; doting** : chochear
double[1] [ˈdʌbəl] *v* **-bled; -bling** *vt* **1** : doblar, duplicar (una cantidad), redoblar (esfuerzos) **2** FOLD : doblar, plegar **3 to double one's fist** : apretar el puño — *vi* **1** : doblarse, duplicarse **2 to double over** : retorcerse
double[2] *adj* : doble — **doubly** *adv*
double[3] *n* : doble *mf*
double bass *n* : contrabajo *m*
double–cross [ˌdʌbəlˈkrɔs] *vt* : traicionar
double–crosser [ˌdʌbəlˈkrɔsər] *n* : traidor *m*, -dora *f*
double–jointed [ˌdʌbəlˈʤɔintəd] *adj* : con articulaciones dobles
double–talk [ˈdʌbəlˌtɔk] *n* : ambigüedades *fpl*, lenguaje *m* con doble sentido
doubt[1] [ˈdaʊt] *vt* **1** QUESTION : dudar de, cuestionar **2** DISTRUST : desconfiar de **3** : dudar, creer poco probable ⟨I doubt it very much : lo dudo mucho⟩
doubt[2] *n* **1** UNCERTAINTY : duda *f*, incertidumbre *f* **2** DISTRUST : desconfianza *f* **3** SKEPTICISM : duda *f*, escepticismo *m*

doubtful [ˈdaʊtfəl] *adj* **1** QUESTIONABLE : dudoso **2** UNCERTAIN : dudoso, incierto

doubtfully [ˈdaʊtfəli] *adv* : dudosamente, sin estar convencido

doubtless [ˈdaʊtləs] *or* **doubtlessly** *adv* : sin duda

douche[1] [ˈduːʃ] *vt* **douched; douching** : irrigar

douche[2] *n* : ducha *f*, irrigación *f*

dough [ˈdoː] *n* : masa *f*

doughnut *or* **donut** [ˈdoːˌnʌt] *n* : rosquilla *f*, dona *f Mex*

doughty [ˈdaʊt̬i] *adj* **-tier; -est** : fuerte, valiente

dour [ˈdaʊər, ˈdʊr] *adj* **1** STERN : severo, adusto **2** SULLEN : hosco, taciturno — **dourly** *adv*

douse [ˈdaʊs, ˈdaʊz] *vt* **doused; dousing 1** DRENCH : empapar, mojar **2** EXTINGUISH : extinguir, apagar

dove[1] [ˈdoːv] → **dive**

dove[2] [ˈdʌv] *n* : paloma *f*

dovetail [ˈdʌvˌteɪl] *vi* : encajar, enlazar

dowdy [ˈdaʊdi] *adj* **dowdier; -est** : sin gracia, poco elegante

dowel [ˈdaʊəl] *n* : clavija *f*

down[1] [ˈdaʊn] *vt* **1** FELL : tumbar, derribar, abatir **2** DEFEAT : derrotar

down[2] *adv* **1** DOWNWARD : hacia abajo **2 to lie down** : acostarse, echarse **3 to put down (money)** : pagar un depósito (de dinero) **4 to sit down** : sentarse **5 to take down, to write down** : apuntar, anotar

down[3] *adj* **1** DESCENDING : de bajada ⟨the down elevator : el ascensor de bajada⟩ **2** REDUCED : reducido, rebajado ⟨attendance is down : la concurrencia ha disminuido⟩ **3** DOWNCAST : abatido, deprimido

down[4] *n* **1** : plumón *m* **2** : down *m* (en deportes) **3 ups and downs** : altibajos *mpl*

down[5] *prep* **1** : (hacia) abajo ⟨down the mountain : montaña abajo⟩ ⟨I walked down the stairs : bajé por la escalera⟩ **2** ALONG : por, a lo largo de ⟨we ran down the beach : corrimos por la playa⟩ **3** : a través de ⟨down the years : a través de los años⟩

downcast [ˈdaʊnˌkæst] *adj* **1** SAD : triste, abatido **2 with downcast eyes** : con los ojos bajos, con los ojos mirando al suelo

downfall [ˈdaʊnˌfɔl] *n* : ruina *f*, perdición *f*

downgrade[1] [ˈdaʊnˌgreɪd] *vt* **-graded; -grading** : bajar de categoría

downgrade[2] *n* : bajada *f*

downhearted [ˈdaʊnˌhɑrt̬əd] *adj* : desanimado, descorazonado

downhill [ˈdaʊnˈhɪl] *adv & adj* : cuesta abajo

download[1] [ˈdaʊnˌloːd] *vt* : descargar (un archivo)

download[2] *n* : descarga *f* (de archivos, etc.)

down payment *n* : entrega *f* inicial

downplay [ˈdaʊnˌpleɪ] *vt* : minimizar

downpour [ˈdaʊnˌpor] *n* : aguacero *m*, chaparrón *m*

downright[1] [ˈdaʊnˌraɪt] *adv* THOROUGHLY : absolutamente, completamente

downright[2] *adj* : patente, manifiesto, absoluto ⟨a downright refusal : un rechazo categórico⟩

downside [ˈdaʊnˌsaɪd] *n* : desventaja *f*

downstairs[1] [ˈdaʊnˈstærz] *adv* : abajo

downstairs[2] [ˈdaʊnˌstærz] *adj* : del piso de abajo

downstairs[3] [ˈdaʊnˈstærz, -ˌstærz] *n* : planta *f* baja

downstream [ˈdaʊnˈstriːm] *adv* : río abajo

down–to–earth [ˌdaʊntuˈərth] *adj* : práctico, realista

downtown[1] [ˌdaʊnˈtaʊn] *adv* : hacia el centro, al centro, en el centro (de la ciudad)

downtown[2] *adj* : del centro (de la ciudad) ⟨downtown Chicago : el centro de Chicago⟩

downtown[3] [ˌdaʊnˈtaʊn, ˈdaʊnˌtaʊn] *n* : centro *m* (de la ciudad)

downtrodden [ˈdaʊnˌtrɑdən] *adj* : oprimido

downward [ˈdaʊnwərd] *or* **downwards** [-wərdz] *adv & adj* : hacia abajo

downwind [ˈdaʊnˈwɪnd] *adv & adj* : en la dirección del viento

downy [ˈdaʊni] *adj* **downier; -est 1** : cubierto de plumón, plumoso **2** VELVETY : aterciopelado, velloso

dowry [ˈdaʊri] *n, pl* **-ries** : dote *f*

doze[1] [ˈdoːz] *vi* **dozed; dozing** : dormitar

doze[2] *n* : sueño *m* ligero, cabezada *f*

dozen [ˈdʌzən] *n, pl* **dozens** *or* **dozen** : docena *f*

drab [ˈdræb] *adj* **drabber; drabbest 1** BROWNISH : pardo **2** DULL, LACKLUSTER : monótono, gris, deslustrado

draft[1] [ˈdræft, ˈdraft] *vt* **1** CONSCRIPT : reclutar **2** COMPOSE, SKETCH : hacer el borrador de, redactar

draft[2] *adj* **1** : de barril ⟨draft beer : cerveza de barril⟩ **2** : de tiro ⟨draft horses : caballos de tiro⟩

draft[3] *n* **1** HAULAGE : tiro *m* **2** DRINK, GULP : trago *m* **3** OUTLINE, SKETCH : bosquejo *m*, borrador *m*, versión *f* **4** : corriente *f* de aire, chiflón *m*, tiro *m* (de una chimenea) **5** CONSCRIPTION : conscripción *f* **6 bank draft** : giro *m* bancario, letra *f* de cambio

draftee [dræfˈtiː] *n* : recluta *mf*

draftsman [ˈdræftsmən] *n, pl* **-men** [-mən, -ˌmɛn] : dibujante *mf*

drafty [ˈdræfti] *adj* **draftier; -est** : con corrientes de aire

drag[1] [ˈdræg] *v* **dragged; dragging** *vt* **1** HAUL : arrastrar, jalar **2** DREDGE : dragar — *vi* **1** TRAIL : arrastrarse **2** LAG : rezagarse **3** : hacerse pesado, hacerse largo ⟨the day dragged on : el día se hizo largo⟩

drag[2] *n* **1** RESISTANCE : resistencia *f* (aerodinámica) **2** HINDRANCE : traba *f*, estorbo *m* **3** BORE : pesadez *f*, plomo *m fam*

dragnet ['dræg,nɛt] *n* **1** : red *f* barredera (en pesca) **2** : operativo *m* policial de captura

dragon ['drægən] *n* : dragón *m*

dragonfly ['drægən,flaɪ] *n, pl* **-flies** : libélula *f*

drain[1] ['dreɪn] *vt* **1** EMPTY : vaciar, drenar **2** EXHAUST : agotar, consumir — *vi* **1** : escurrir, escurrirse ⟨the dishes are draining : los platos están escurriéndose⟩ **2** EMPTY : desaguar **3 to drain away** : irse agotando

drain[2] *n* **1** : desagüe *m* **2** SEWER : alcantarilla *f* **3** GRATING : sumidero *m*, resumidero *m*, rejilla *f* **4** EXHAUSTION : agotamiento *m*, disminución *f* (de energía, etc.) ⟨to be a drain on : agotar, consumir⟩ **5 to throw down the drain** : tirar por la ventana

drainage ['dreɪnɪʤ] *n* : desagüe *m*, drenaje *m*

drainpipe ['dreɪn,paɪp] *n* : tubo *m* de desagüe, caño *m*

drake ['dreɪk] *n* : pato *m* (macho)

drama ['drɑmə, 'dræ-] *n* **1** THEATER : drama *m*, teatro *m* **2** PLAY : obra *f* de teatro, drama *m*

dramatic [drə'mæt̬ɪk] *adj* : dramático — **dramatically** [-t̬ɪkli] *adv*

dramatist ['dræmət̬ɪst, 'drɑ-] *n* : dramaturgo *m*, -ga *f*

dramatization [,dræmət̬ə'zeɪʃən, ,drɑ-] *n* : dramatización *f*

dramatize ['dræmə,taɪz, 'drɑ-] *vt* **-tized; -tizing** : dramatizar

drank → **drink**

drape[1] ['dreɪp] *vt* **draped; draping 1** COVER : cubrir (con tela) **2** HANG : drapear, disponer los pliegues de

drape[2] *n* **1** HANG : caída *f* **2 drapes** *npl* : cortinas *fpl*

drapery ['dreɪpəri] *n, pl* **-eries 1** CLOTH : pañería *f*, tela *f* para cortinas **2 draperies** *npl* : cortinas *fpl*

drastic ['dræstɪk] *adj* **1** HARSH, SEVERE : drástico, severo **2** EXTREME : radical, excepcional — **drastically** [-tɪkli] *adv*

draught ['dræft, 'draft] *n* → **draft[3]**

draughty ['drafti] → **drafty**

draw[1] ['drɔ] *v* **drew** ['dru:]; **drawn** ['drɔn]; **drawing** *vt* **1** PULL : tirar de, jalar, correr (cortinas) **2** ATTRACT : atraer **3** PROVOKE : provocar, suscitar **4** INHALE : aspirar ⟨to draw breath : respirar⟩ **5** EXTRACT : sacar, extraer **6** TAKE : sacar ⟨to draw a number : sacar un número⟩ **7** COLLECT : cobrar, percibir (un sueldo, etc.) **8** BEND : tensar (un arco) **9** TIE : empatar (en deportes) **10** SKETCH : dibujar, trazar **11** FORMULATE : sacar, formular, llegar a ⟨to draw a conclusion : llegar a una conclusión⟩ **12 to draw out** : hacer hablar (sobre algo), hacer salir de sí mismo **13 to draw up** DRAFT : redactar — *vi* **1** SKETCH : dibujar **2** TUG : tirar, jalar **3 to draw near** : acercarse **4 to draw to a close** : terminar, finalizar **5 to draw up** STOP : parar

draw[2] *n* **1** DRAWING, RAFFLE : sorteo *m* **2** TIE : empate *m* **3** ATTRACTION : atracción *f* **4** PUFF : chupada *f* (de un cigarrillo, etc.)

drawback ['drɔ,bæk] *n* : desventaja *f*, inconveniente *m*

drawbridge ['drɔ,brɪʤ] *n* : puente *m* levadizo

drawer ['drɔr, 'drɔər] *n* **1** ILLUSTRATOR : dibujante *mf* **2** : gaveta *f*, cajón *m* (en un mueble) **3 drawers** *npl* UNDERPANTS : calzones *mpl*

drawing ['drɔɪŋ] *n* **1** LOTTERY : sorteo *m*, lotería *f* **2** SKETCH : dibujo *m*, bosquejo *m*

drawl[1] ['drɔl] *vi* : hablar arrastrando las palabras

drawl[2] *n* : habla *f* lenta y con vocales prolongadas

dread[1] ['drɛd] *vt* : tenerle pavor a, temer

dread[2] *adj* : pavoroso, aterrado

dread[3] *n* : pavor *m*, temor *m*

dreadful ['drɛdfəl] *adj* **1** DREAD : pavoroso **2** TERRIBLE : espantoso, atroz, terrible — **dreadfully** *adv*

dream[1] ['dri:m] *v* **dreamed** ['drɛmpt, 'dri:md] *or* **dreamt** ['drɛmpt]; **dreaming** *vi* **1** : soñar ⟨to dream about : soñar con⟩ **2** FANTASIZE : fantasear — *vt* **1** : soñar **2** IMAGINE : imaginarse **3 to dream up** : inventar, idear

dream[2] *n* **1** : sueño *m*, ensueño *m* **2 bad dream** NIGHTMARE : pesadilla *f*

dreamer ['dri:mər] *n* : soñador *m*, -dora *f*

dreamlike ['dri:m,laɪk] *adj* : de ensueño

dreamy ['dri:mi] *adj* **dreamier; -est 1** DISTRACTED : soñador, distraído **2** DREAMLIKE : de ensueño **3** MARVELOUS : maravilloso

drearily ['drɪrəli] *adv* : sombríamente

dreary ['drɪri] *adj* **-rier; -est** : deprimente, lóbrego, sombrío

dredge[1] ['drɛʤ] *vt* **dredged; dredging 1** DIG : dragar **2** COAT : espolvorear, enharinar

dredge[2] *n* : draga *f*

dredger ['drɛʤər] *n* : draga *f*

dregs ['drɛgz] *npl* **1** LEES : posos *mpl*, heces *fpl* (de un líquido) **2** : heces *fpl*, escoria *f* ⟨the dregs of society : la escoria de la sociedad⟩

drench ['drɛnʧ] *vt* : empapar, mojar, calar

dress[1] ['drɛs] *vt* **1** CLOTHE : vestir **2** DECORATE : decorar, adornar **3** : preparar (pollo o pescado), aliñar (ensalada) **4** : curar, vendar (una herida) **5** FERTILIZE : abonar (la tierra) — *vi* **1** : vestirse **2 to dress up** : ataviarse, engalanarse, ponerse de etiqueta

dress[2] *n* **1** APPAREL : indumentaria *f*, ropa *f* **2** : vestido *m*, traje *m* (de mujer)

dresser [ˈdrɛsər] *n* : cómoda *f* con espejo

dressing [ˈdrɛsɪŋ] *n* **1** : vestirse *m* **2** : aderezo *m*, aliño *m* (de ensalada), relleno *m* (de pollo) **3** BANDAGE : vendaje *m*, gasa *f*

dressmaker [ˈdrɛsˌmeɪkər] *n* : modista *mf*

dressmaking [ˈdrɛsˌmeɪkɪŋ] *n* : costura *f*

dressy [ˈdrɛsi] *adj* **dressier; -est** : de mucho vestir, elegante

drew → **draw**

dribble[1] [ˈdrɪbəl] *vi* **-bled; -bling 1** DRIP : gotear **2** DROOL : babear **3** : driblar (en basquetbol)

dribble[2] *n* **1** TRICKLE : goteo *m*, hilo *m* **2** DROOL : baba *f* **3** : drible *m* (en basquetbol)

drier → **dry**[2], **dryer**

driest *adj* → **dry**[2]

drift[1] [ˈdrɪft] *vi* **1** : dejarse llevar por la corriente, ir a la deriva (dícese de un bote), ir sin rumbo (dícese de una persona) **2** ACCUMULATE : amontonarse, acumularse, apilarse

drift[2] *n* **1** DRIFTING : deriva *f* **2** HEAP, MASS : montón *m* (de arena, etc.), ventisquero *m* (de nieve) **3** MEANING : sentido *m*

drifter [ˈdrɪftər] *n* : vagabundo *m*, -da *f*

driftwood [ˈdrɪftˌwʊd] *n* : madera *f* flotante

drill[1] [ˈdrɪl] *vt* **1** BORE : perforar, taladrar **2** INSTRUCT : instruir por repetición — *vi* **1** TRAIN : entrenarse **2 to drill for oil** : perforar en busca de petróleo

drill[2] *n* **1** : taladro *m*, barrena *f* **2** EXERCISE, PRACTICE : ejercicio *m*, instrucción *f*

drily → **dryly**

drink[1] [ˈdrɪŋk] *v* **drank** [ˈdræŋk]; **drunk** [ˈdrʌŋk] *or* **drank; drinking** *vt* **1** IMBIBE : beber, tomar **2 to drink up** ABSORB : absorber — *vi* **1** : beber **2** : beber alcohol, tomar

drink[2] *n* **1** : bebida *f* **2** : bebida *f* alcohólica

drinkable [ˈdrɪŋkəbəl] *adj* : potable

drinker [ˈdrɪŋkər] *n* : bebedor *m*, -dora *f*

drip[1] [ˈdrɪp] *vi* **dripped; dripping** : gotear, chorrear

drip[2] *n* **1** DROP : gota *f* **2** DRIPPING : goteo *m*

drive[1] [ˈdraɪv] *v* **drove** [ˈdro:v]; **driven** [ˈdrɪvən]; **driving** *vt* **1** IMPEL : impeler, impulsar **2** OPERATE : guiar, conducir, manejar (un vehículo) **3** COMPEL : obligar, forzar **4** : clavar, hincar ⟨to drive a stake : clavar una estaca⟩ **5** *or* **to drive away** : ahuyentar, echar **6 to drive crazy** : volver loco — *vi* : manejar, conducir ⟨do you know how to drive? : ¿sabes manejar?⟩

drive[2] *n* **1** RIDE : paseo *m* en coche **2** CAMPAIGN : campaña *f* ⟨fund-raising drive : campaña para recaudar fondos⟩ **3** DRIVEWAY : camino *m* de entrada, entrada *f* **4** TRANSMISSION : transmisión *f* ⟨front-wheel drive : tracción delantera⟩ **5** ENERGY : dinamismo *m*, energía *f* **6** INSTINCT, NEED : instinto *m*, necesidad *f* básica **7** → **disk drive**

drivel [ˈdrɪvəl] *n* : tontería *f*, estupidez *f*

driver [ˈdraɪvər] *n* : conductor *m*, -tora *f*; chofer *m*

driveway [ˈdraɪvˌweɪ] *n* : camino *m* de entrada, entrada *f* (para coches)

drizzle[1] [ˈdrɪzəl] *vi* **-zled; -zling** : lloviznar, garuar

drizzle[2] *n* : llovizna *f*, garúa *f*

droll [ˈdro:l] *adj* : cómico, gracioso, chistoso — **drolly** *adv*

dromedary [ˈdrɑməˌdɛri] *n, pl* **-daries** : dromedario *m*

drone[1] [ˈdro:n] *vi* **droned; droning 1** BUZZ : zumbar **2** MURMUR : hablar con monotonía, murmurar

drone[2] *n* **1** : zángano *m* (abeja) **2** FREELOADER : gorrón *m*, -rrona *f fam*; parásito *m*, -ta *f* **3** BUZZ, HUM : zumbido *m*, murmullo *m*

drool[1] [ˈdru:l] *vi* : babear

drool[2] *n* : baba *f*

droop[1] [ˈdru:p] *vi* **1** HANG : inclinarse (dícese de la cabeza), encorvarse (dícese de los escombros), marchitarse (dícese de las flores) **2** FLAG : decaer, flaquear ⟨his spirits drooped : se desanimó⟩

droop[2] *n* : inclinación *f*, caída *f*

drop[1] [ˈdrɑp] *v* **dropped; dropping** *vt* **1** : dejar caer, soltar ⟨she dropped the glass : se le cayó el vaso⟩ ⟨to drop a hint : dejar caer una indirecta⟩ **2** SEND : mandar ⟨drop me a line : mándame unas líneas⟩ **3** ABANDON : abandonar, dejar ⟨to drop the subject : cambiar de tema⟩ **4** LOWER : bajar ⟨he dropped his voice : bajó la voz⟩ **5** OMIT : omitir **6 to drop off** : dejar — *vi* **1** DRIP : gotear **2** FALL : caer(se) **3** DECREASE, DESCEND : bajar, descender ⟨the wind dropped : amainó el viento⟩ **4 to drop back** *or* **to drop behind** : rezagarse, quedarse atrás **5 to drop by** *or* **to drop in** : pasar

drop[2] *n* **1** : gota *f* (de líquido) **2** DECLINE : caída *f*, bajada *f*, descenso *m* **3** INCLINE : caída *f*, pendiente *f* ⟨a 20-foot drop : una caída de 20 pies⟩ **4** SWEET : pastilla *f*, dulce *m* **5 drops** *npl* : gotas *fpl* (de medicina)

droplet [ˈdrɑplət] *n* : gotita *f*

dropper [ˈdrɑpər] *n* : gotero *m*, cuentagotas *m*

dross [ˈdrɑs, ˈdrɔs] *n* : escoria *f*

drought [ˈdraʊt] *n* : sequía *f*

drove[1] → **drive**

drove[2] [ˈdro:v] *n* : multitud *f*, gentío *m*, manada *f* (de ganado) ⟨in droves : en manada⟩

drown ['draʊn] *vt* **1** : ahogar **2** INUNDATE : anegar, inundar **3 to drown out** : ahogar — *vi* : ahogarse
drowse[1] ['draʊz] *vi* **drowsed; drowsing** DOZE : dormitar
drowse[2] *n* : sueño *m* ligero, cabezada *f*
drowsiness ['draʊzinəs] *n* : somnolencia *f*, adormecimiento *m*
drowsy ['draʊzi] *adj* **drowsier; -est** : somnoliento, soñoliento
drub ['drʌb] *vt* **drubbed; drubbing 1** BEAT, THRASH : golpear, apalear **2** DEFEAT : derrotar por completo
drudge[1] ['drʌʤ] *vi* **drudged; drudging** : trabajar como esclavo, trabajar duro
drudge[2] *n* : esclavo *m*, -va *f* del trabajo
drudgery ['drʌʤəri] *n, pl* **-eries** : trabajo *m* pesado
drug[1] ['drʌg] *vt* **drugged; drugging** : drogar, narcotizar
drug[2] *n* **1** MEDICATION : droga *f*, medicina *f*, medicamento *m* **2** NARCOTIC : narcótico *m*, estupefaciente *m*, droga *f*
druggist ['drʌgɪst] *n* : farmacéutico *m*, -ca *f*
drugstore ['drʌgˌstor] *n* : farmacia *f*, botica *f*, droguería *f*
drum[1] ['drʌm] *v* **drummed; drumming** *vt* : meter a fuerza ⟨he drummed it into my head : me lo metió en la cabeza a fuerza⟩ — *vi* : tocar el tambor
drum[2] *n* **1** : tambor *m* **2** : bidón *m* ⟨oil drum : bidón de petróleo⟩
drummer ['drʌmər] *n* : baterista *mf*
drumstick ['drʌmˌstɪk] *n* **1** : palillo *m* (de tambor), baqueta *f* **2** : muslo *m* de pollo
drunk[1] *pp* → **drink**[1]
drunk[2] ['drʌŋk] *adj* : borracho, embriagado, ebrio
drunk[3] *n* : borracho *m*, -cha *f*
drunkard ['drʌŋkərd] *n* : borracho *m*, -cha *f*
drunken ['drʌŋkən] *adj* : borracho, ebrio ⟨drunken driver : conductor ebrio⟩ ⟨drunken brawl : pleito de borrachos⟩
drunkenly ['drʌŋkənli] *adv* : como un borracho
drunkenness ['drʌŋkənnəs] *n* : borrachera *f*, embriaguez *f*, ebriedad *f*
dry[1] ['draɪ] *v* **dried; drying** *vt* : secar — *vi* : secarse
dry[2] *adj* **drier; driest 1** : seco **2** THIRSTY : sediento **3** : donde la venta de bebidas alcohólicas está prohibida ⟨a dry county : un condado seco⟩ **4** DULL : aburrido, árido **5** : seco (dícese del vino), brut (dícese de la champaña)
dry–clean ['draɪˌkli:n] *v* : limpiar en seco
dry cleaner *n* : tintorería *f* (servicio)
dry cleaning *n* : limpieza *f* en seco
dryer ['draɪər] *n* **1 hair dryer** : secador *m* **2 clothes dryer** : secadora *f*
dry goods *npl* : artículos *mpl* de confección
dry ice *n* : hielo *m* seco
dryly ['draɪli] *adv* : secamente
dryness ['draɪnəs] *n* : sequedad *f*, aridez *f*
dual ['du:əl, 'dju:-] *adj* : doble
dualism ['du:əˌlɪzəm] *n* : dualismo *m*
dub ['dʌb] *vt* **dubbed; dubbing 1** CALL : apodar **2** : doblar (una película), mezclar (una grabación)
dubious ['du:biəs, 'dju:-] *adj* **1** UNCERTAIN : dudoso, indeciso **2** QUESTIONABLE : sospechoso, dudoso, discutible
dubiously ['du:biəsli, 'dju:-] *adv* **1** UNCERTAINLY : dudosamente, con desconfianza **2** SUSPICIOUSLY : de modo sospechoso, con recelo
duchess ['dʌʧəs] *n* : duquesa *f*
duck[1] ['dʌk] *vt* **1** LOWER : agachar, bajar (la cabeza) **2** PLUNGE : zambullir **3** EVADE : eludir, evadir — *vi* **to duck down** : agacharse
duck[2] *n, pl* **duck** *or* **ducks** : pato *m*, -ta *f*
duckling ['dʌklɪŋ] *n* : patito *m*, -ta *f*
duct ['dʌkt] *n* : conducto *m*
ductile ['dʌktəl] *adj* : dúctil
dude ['du:d, 'dju:d] *n* **1** DANDY : dandi *m*, dandy *m* **2** GUY : tipo *m*
due[1] ['du:, 'dju:] *adv* : justo a, derecho hacia ⟨due north : derecho hacia el norte⟩
due[2] *adj* **1** PAYABLE : pagadero, sin pagar **2** APPROPRIATE : debido, apropiado ⟨after due consideration : con las debidas consideraciones⟩ **3** EXPECTED : esperado ⟨the train is due soon : esperamos el tren muy pronto, el tren debe llegar pronto⟩ **4 due to** : debido a, por
due[3] *n* **1 to give someone his (her) due** : darle a alguien su merecido **2 dues** *npl* : cuota *f*
duel[1] ['du:əl, 'dju:-] *vi* : batirse en duelo
duel[2] *n* : duelo *m*
duet [du'ɛt, dju-] *n* : dúo *m*
due to *prep* : debido a
dug → **dig**
dugout ['dʌgˌaʊt] *n* **1** CANOE : piragua *f* **2** SHELTER : refugio *m* subterráneo
duke ['du:k, 'dju:k] *n* : duque *m*
dull[1] ['dʌl] *vt* **1** DIM : opacar, quitar el brillo a, deslustrar **2** BLUNT : embotar (un filo), entorpecer (los sentidos), aliviar (el dolor), amortiguar (sonidos)
dull[2] *adj* **1** STUPID : torpe, lerdo, lento **2** BLUNT : desafilado, despuntado **3** LACKLUSTER : sin brillo, deslustrado **4** BORING : aburrido, soso, pesado — **dully** *adv*
dullness ['dʌlnəs] *n* **1** STUPIDITY : estupidez *f* **2** : embotamiento *m* (de los sentidos) **3** MONOTONY : monotonía *f*, insipidez *f* **4** : falta *f* de brillo **5** BLUNTNESS : falta *f* de filo, embotadura *f*
duly ['du:li, 'dju:-] *adv* PROPERLY : debidamente, a su debido tiempo
dumb ['dʌm] *adj* **1** MUTE : mudo **2** STUPID : estúpido, tonto, bobo — **dumbly** *adv*

dumbbell [ˈdʌmˌbɛl] *n* **1** WEIGHT : pesa *f* **2** : estúpido *m*, -da *f*
dumbfound *or* **dumfound** [ˌdʌm-ˈfaʊnd] *vt* : dejar atónito, dejar sin habla
dummy [ˈdʌmi] *n, pl* **-mies** **1** SHAM : imitación *f*, sustituto *m* **2** PUPPET : muñeco *m* **3** MANNEQUIN : maniquí *m* **4** IDIOT : tonto *m*, -ta *f*; idiota *mf*
dump[1] [ˈdʌmp] *vt* : descargar, verter
dump[2] *n* **1** : vertedero *m*, tiradero *m* *Mex* **2 down in the dumps** : triste, deprimido
dumpling [ˈdʌmplɪŋ] *n* : bola *f* de masa hervida
dumpy [ˈdʌmpi] *adj* **dumpier; -est** : rechoncho, regordete
dun[1] [ˈdʌn] *vt* **dunned; dunning** : apremiar (a un deudor)
dun[2] *adj* : pardo (color)
dunce [ˈdʌn*t*s] *n* : estúpido *m*, -da *f*; burro *m*, -rra *f fam*
dune [ˈdu:n, ˈdju:n] *n* : duna *f*
dung [ˈdʌŋ] *n* **1** FECES : excrementos *mpl* **2** MANURE : estiércol *m*
dungaree [ˌdʌŋgəˈri:] *n* **1** DENIM : tela *f* vaquera, mezclilla *f Chile, Mex* **2 dungarees** *npl* : pantalones *mpl* de trabajo hechos de tela vaquera
dungeon [ˈdʌndʒən] *n* : mazmorra *f*, calabozo *m*
dunk [ˈdʌŋk] *vt* : mojar, ensopar
duo [ˈdu:o:, ˈdju:-] *n, pl* **duos** : dúo *m*, par *m*
dupe[1] [ˈdu:p, dju:p] *vt* **duped; duping** : engañar, embaucar
dupe[2] *n* : inocentón *m*, -tona *f*; simple *mf*
duplex[1] [ˈdu:ˌplɛks, ˈdju:-] *adj* : doble
duplex[2] *n* : casa *f* de dos viviendas, dúplex *m*
duplicate[1] [ˈdu:plɪˌkeɪt, ˈdju:-] *vt* **-cated; -cating** **1** COPY : duplicar, hacer copias de **2** REPEAT : repetir, reproducir
duplicate[2] [ˈdu:plɪkət, ˈdju:-] *adj* : duplicado ⟨a duplicate invoice : una factura por duplicado⟩
duplicate[3] [ˈdu:plɪkət, ˈdju:-] *n* : duplicado *m*, copia *f*
duplication [ˌdu:plɪˈkeɪʃən, ˌdju:-] *n* **1** DUPLICATING : duplicación *f*, repetición *f* (de esfuerzos) **2** DUPLICATE : copia *f*, duplicado *m*
duplicity [dʊˈplɪsət̬i, ˌdju:-] *n, pl* **-ties** : duplicidad *f*
durability [ˌdʊrəˈbɪlət̬i, ˌdjʊr-] *n* : durabilidad *f* (de un producto) permanencia *f*
durable [ˈdʊrəbəl, ˈdjʊr-] *adj* : duradero
duration [dʊˈreɪʃən, djʊ-] *n* : duración *f*
duress [dʊˈrɛs, djʊ-] *n* : coacción *f*
during [ˈdʊrɪŋ, ˈdjʊr-] *prep* : durante
dusk [ˈdʌsk] *n* : anochecer *m*, crepúsculo *m*
dusky [ˈdʌski] *adj* **duskier; -est** : oscuro (dícese de los colores)
dust[1] [ˈdʌst] *vt* **1** : quitar el polvo de **2** SPRINKLE : espolvorear
dust[2] *n* : polvo *m*
duster [ˈdʌstər] *n* **1** *or* **dust cloth** : trapo *m* de polvo **2** HOUSECOAT : guardapolvo *m* **3 feather duster** : plumero *m*
dustpan [ˈdʌstˌpæn] *n* : recogedor *m*
dusty [ˈdʌsti] *adj* **dustier; -est** : cubierto de polvo, polvoriento
Dutch[1] [ˈdʌtʃ] *adj* : holandés
Dutch[2] *n* **1** : holandés *m* (idioma) **2 the Dutch** *npl* : los holandeses
Dutch treat *n* : invitación o pago a escote
dutiful [ˈdu:t̬ɪfəl, ˈdju:-] *adj* : motivado por sus deberes, responsable
duty [ˈdu:t̬i, ˈdju:-] *n, pl* **-ties** **1** OBLIGATION : deber *m*, obligación *f*, responsabilidad *f* **2** TAX : impuesto *m*, arancel *m*
DVD [ˌdi:ˌvi:ˈdi:] *n* : DVD *m*
dwarf[1] [ˈdwɔrf] *vt* **1** STUNT : arrestar el crecimiento de **2** : hacer parecer pequeño
dwarf[2] *n, pl* **dwarfs** [ˈdwɔrfs] *or* **dwarves** [ˈdwɔrvz] : enano *m*, -na *f*
dwell [ˈdwɛl] *vi* **dwelled** *or* **dwelt** [ˈdwɛlt]; **dwelling** **1** RESIDE : residir, morar, vivir **2 to dwell on** : pensar demasiado en, insistir en
dweller [ˈdwɛlər] *n* : habitante *mf*
dwelling [ˈdwɛlɪŋ] *n* : morada *f*, vivienda *f*, residencia *f*
dwindle [ˈdwɪndəl] *vi* **-dled; -dling** : menguar, reducirse, disminuir
dye[1] [ˈdaɪ] *vt* **dyed; dyeing** : teñir
dye[2] *n* : tintura *f*, tinte *m*
dying → **die**
dyke → **dike**
dynamic [daɪˈnæmɪk] *adj* : dinámico
dynamics [daɪˈnæmɪks] *npl* : dinámica *f*
dynamite[1] [ˈdaɪnəˌmaɪt] *vt* **-mited; -miting** : dinamitar
dynamite[2] *n* : dinamita *f*
dynamo [ˈdaɪnəˌmo:] *n, pl* **-mos** : dínamo *m*, generador *m* de electricidad
dynasty [ˈdaɪnəsti, -ˌnæs-] *n, pl* **-ties** : dinastía *f*
dysentery [ˈdɪsənˌtɛri] *n, pl* **-teries** : disentería *f*
dysfunction [dɪsˈfʌŋ*k*ʃən] *n* : disfunción *f*
dystrophy [ˈdɪstrəfi] *n, pl* **-phies** **1** : distrofia *f* **2** → **muscular dystrophy**

E

e [ˈiː] *n, pl* **e's** *or* **es** [ˈiːz] : quinta letra del alfabeto inglés
each[1] [ˈiːʧ] *adv* : cada uno, por persona ⟨they cost $10 each : costaron $10 cada uno⟩
each[2] *adj* : cada ⟨each student : cada estudiante⟩ ⟨each and every one : todos sin excepción⟩
each[3] *pron* **1** : cada uno *m*, cada una *f* ⟨each of us : cada uno de nosotros⟩ **2 each other** : el uno al otro, mutuamente ⟨we are helping each other : nos ayudamos el uno al otro⟩ ⟨they love each other : se aman⟩
eager [ˈiːgər] *adj* **1** ENTHUSIASTIC : entusiasta, ávido, deseoso **2** ANXIOUS : ansioso, impaciente
eagerly [ˈiːgərli] *adv* : con entusiasmo, ansiosamente
eagerness [ˈiːgərnəs] *n* : entusiasmo *m*, deseo *m*, impaciencia *f*
eagle [ˈiːgəl] *n* : águila *f*
ear [ˈɪr] *n* **1** : oído *m*, oreja *f* ⟨inner ear : oído interno⟩ ⟨big ears : orejas grandes⟩ **2 ear of corn** : mazorca *f*, choclo *m*
earache [ˈɪrˌeɪk] *n* : dolor *m* de oído
eardrum [ˈɪrˌdrʌm] *n* : tímpano *m*
earl [ˈərl] *n* : conde *m*
earlobe [ˈɪrˌloːb] *n* : lóbulo *m* de la oreja, perilla *f* de la oreja
early[1] [ˈərli] *adv* **earlier; -est** : temprano, pronto ⟨he arrived early : llegó temprano⟩ ⟨as early as possible : lo más pronto posible, cuanto antes⟩ ⟨ten minutes early : diez minutos de adelanto⟩
early[2] *adj* **earlier; -est 1** (*referring to a beginning*) : primero ⟨the early stages : las primeras etapas⟩ ⟨in early May : a principios de mayo⟩ **2** (*referring to antiquity*) : primitivo, antiguo ⟨early man : el hombre primitivo⟩ ⟨early painting : la pintura antigua⟩ **3** (*referring to a designated time*) : temprano, antes de la hora, prematuro ⟨he was early : llegó temprano⟩ ⟨early fruit : frutas tempraneras⟩ ⟨an early death : una muerte prematura⟩
earmark [ˈɪrˌmɑrk] *vt* : destinar ⟨earmarked funds : fondos destinados⟩
earn [ˈərn] *vt* **1** : ganar ⟨to earn money : ganar dinero⟩ **2** DESERVE : ganarse, merecer
earnest[1] [ˈərnəst] *adj* : serio, sincero
earnest[2] *n* **in ∼** : en serio, de verdad ⟨we began in earnest : empezamos de verdad⟩
earnestly [ˈərnəstli] *adv* **1** SERIOUSLY : con seriedad, en serio **2** FERVENTLY : de todo corazón
earnestness [ˈərnəstnəs] *n* : seriedad *f*, sinceridad *f*
earnings [ˈərnɪŋz] *npl* : ingresos *mpl*, ganancias *fpl*, utilidades *fpl*
earphone [ˈɪrˌfoːn] *n* : audífono *m*
earring [ˈɪrˌrɪŋ] *n* : zarcillo *m*, arete *m*, aro *m Arg, Chile, Uru*, pendiente *m Spain*
earshot [ˈɪrˌʃɑt] *n* : alcance *m* del oído
earth [ˈərθ] *n* **1** LAND, SOIL : tierra *f*, suelo *m* **2 the Earth** : la Tierra
earthen [ˈərθən, -ðən] *adj* : de tierra, de barro
earthenware [ˈərθənˌwær, -ðən-] *n* : loza *f*, vajillas *fpl* de barro
earthly [ˈərθli] *adj* : terrenal, mundano
earthquake [ˈərθˌkweɪk] *n* : terremoto *m*, temblor *m*
earthworm [ˈərθˌwərm] *n* : lombriz *f* (de tierra)
earthy [ˈərθi] *adj* **earthier; -est 1** : terroso ⟨earthy colors : colores terrosos⟩ **2** DOWN-TO-EARTH : realista, práctico, llano **3** COARSE, CRUDE : basto, grosero, tosco ⟨earthy jokes : chistes groseros⟩
earwax [ˈɪrˌwæks] *n* → **wax**[2]
earwig [ˈɪrˌwɪg] *n* : tijereta *f*
ease[1] [ˈiːz] *v* **eased; easing** *vt* **1** ALLEVIATE : aliviar, calmar, hacer disminuir **2** LOOSEN, RELAX : aflojar (una cuerda), relajar (restricciones), descargar (tensiones) **3** FACILITATE : facilitar — *vi* : calmarse, relajarse
ease[2] *n* **1** CALM, RELIEF : tranquilidad *f*, comodidad *f*, desahogo *m* **2** FACILITY : facilidad *f* **3 at ∼** : relajado, cómodo ⟨to put someone at ease : tranquilizar a alguien⟩
easel [ˈiːzəl] *n* : caballete *m*
easily [ˈiːzəli] *adv* **1** : fácilmente, con facilidad **2** UNQUESTIONABLY : con mucho, de lejos
easiness [ˈiːzinəs] *n* : facilidad *f*, soltura *f*
east[1] [ˈiːst] *adv* : al este
east[2] *adj* : este, del este, oriental ⟨east winds : vientos del este⟩
east[3] *n* **1** : este *m* **2 the East** : el Oriente
Easter [ˈiːstər] *n* : Pascua *f* (de Resurrección)
easterly [ˈiːstərli] *adv & adj* : del este
eastern [ˈiːstərn] *adj* **1** : Oriental, del Este ⟨Eastern Europe : Europa del Este⟩ **2** : oriental, este
Easterner [ˈiːstərnər] *n* : habitante *mf* del este
eastward [ˈiːstwərd] *adv & adj* : hacia el este
easy [ˈiːzi] *adj* **easier; -est 1** : fácil **2** LENIENT : indulgente
easygoing [ˌiːziˈgoːɪŋ] *adj* : acomodaticio, tolerante, poco exigente
eat [ˈiːt] *v* **ate** [ˈeɪt]; **eaten** [ˈiːtən]; **eating** *vt* **1** : comer **2** CONSUME : consumir, gastar, devorar ⟨expenses ate up profits : los gastos devoraron las ganancias⟩ **3** CORRODE : corroer — *vi* **1** : comer **2 to eat away at** *or* **to eat into** : comerse **3 to eat out** : comer fuera

eatable[1] [ˈiːt̬əbəl] *adj* : comestible, comible *fam*
eatable[2] *n* **1** : algo para comer **2 eatables** *npl* : comestibles *mpl*, alimentos *mpl*
eater [ˈiːt̬ər] *n* : comedor *m*, -dora *f*
eaves [ˈiːvz] *npl* : alero *m*
eavesdrop [ˈiːvz,drɑp] *vi* **-dropped; -dropping** : escuchar a escondidas
eavesdropper [ˈiːvz,drɑpər] *n* : persona *f* que escucha a escondidas
ebb[1] [ˈɛb] *vi* **1** : bajar, menguar (dícese de la marea) **2** DECLINE : decaer, disminuir
ebb[2] *n* **1** : reflujo *m* (de una marea) **2** DECLINE : decadencia *f*, declive *m*, disminución *f*
ebony[1] [ˈɛbəni] *adj* **1** : de ébano **2** BLACK : de color ébano, negro
ebony[2] *n, pl* **-nies** : ébano *m*
ebullience [ɪˈbʊljənts, -ˈbʌl-] *n* : efervescencia *f*, vivacidad *f*
ebullient [ɪˈbʊljənt, -ˈbʌl-] *adj* : efervescente, vivaz
eccentric[1] [ɪkˈsɛntrɪk] *adj* **1** : excéntrico <an eccentric wheel : una rueda excéntrica> **2** ODD, SINGULAR : excéntrico, extraño, raro — **eccentrically** [-trɪkli] *adv*
eccentric[2] *n* : excéntrico *m*, -ca *f*
eccentricity [,ɛk,sɛnˈtrɪsət̬i] *n, pl* **-ties** : excentricidad *f*
ecclesiastic [ɪ,kliːziˈæstɪk] *n* : eclesiástico *m*, clérigo *m*
ecclesiastical [ɪ,kliːziˈæstɪkəl] *or* **ecclesiastic** *adj* : eclesiástico — **ecclesiastically** *adv*
echelon [ˈɛʃə,lɑn] *n* **1** : escalón *m* (de tropas o aviones) **2** LEVEL : nivel *m*, esfera *f*, estrato *m*
echo[1] [ˈɛ,koː] *v* **echoed; echoing** *vi* : hacer eco, resonar — *vt* : repetir
echo[2] *n, pl* **echoes** : eco *m*
éclair [eɪˈklær, i-] *n* : pastel *m* relleno de crema
eclectic [ɛˈklɛktɪk, ɪ-] *adj* : ecléctico
eclipse[1] [ɪˈklɪps] *vt* **eclipsed; eclipsing** : eclipsar
eclipse[2] *n* : eclipse *m*
ecological [,iːkəˈlɑʤɪkəl, ,ɛkə-] *adj* : ecológico — **ecologically** *adv*
ecologist [iˈkɑləʤɪst, ɛ-] *n* : ecólogo *m*, -ga *f*
ecology [iˈkɑləʤi, ɛ-] *n, pl* **-gies** : ecología *f*
economic [,iːkəˈnɑmɪk, ,ɛkə-] *adj* : económico
economical [,iːkəˈnɑmɪkəl, ,ɛkə-] *adj* : económico — **economically** *adv*
economics [,iːkəˈnɑmɪks, ,ɛkə-] *n* : economía *f*
economist [iˈkɑnəmɪst] *n* : economista *mf*
economize [iˈkɑnə,maɪz] *v* **-mized; -mizing** : economizar, ahorrar
economy [iˈkɑnəmi] *n, pl* **-mies** **1** : economía *f*, sistema *m* económico **2** THRIFT : economía *f*, ahorro *m*
ecosystem [ˈiːko,sɪstəm] *n* : ecosistema *m*
ecru [ˈɛ,kruː, ˈeɪ-] *n* : color *m* crudo
ecstasy [ˈɛkstəsi] *n, pl* **-sies** : éxtasis *m*
ecstatic [ɛkˈstæt̬ɪk, ɪk-] *adj* : extático
ecstatically [ɛkˈstæt̬ɪkli, ɪk-] *adv* : con éxtasis, con gran entusiasmo
Ecuadoran [,ɛkwəˈdorən] *or* **Ecuadorean** *or* **Ecuadorian** [-ˈdoriən] *n* : ecuatoriano *m*, -na *f* — **Ecuadorean** *or* **Ecuadorian** *adj*
ecumenical [,ɛkjʊˈmnɪkəl] *adj* : ecuménico
eczema [ɪgˈziːmə, ˈɛgzəmə, ˈɛksə-] *n* : eczema *m*
eddy[1] [ˈɛdi] *vi* **eddied; eddying** : arremolinarse, hacer remolinos
eddy[2] *n, pl* **-dies** : remolino *m*
edema [ɪˈdiːmə] *n* : edema *m*
Eden [ˈiːdən] *n* : Edén *m*
edge[1] [ˈɛʤ] *v* **edged; edging** *vt* **1** BORDER : bordear, ribetear, orlar **2** SHARPEN : afilar, aguzar **3** *or* **to edge one's way** : avanzar poco a poco **4 to edge out** : derrotar por muy poco — *vi* ADVANCE : ir avanzando (poco a poco)
edge[2] *n* **1** : filo *m* (de un cuchillo) **2** BORDER : borde *m*, orilla *f*, margen *m* **3** ADVANTAGE : ventaja *f*
edger [ˈɛʤər] *n* : cortabordes *m*
edgewise [ˈɛʤ,waɪz] *adv* SIDEWAYS : de lado, de canto
edginess [ˈɛʤinəs] *n* : tensión *f*, nerviosismo *m*
edgy [ˈɛʤi] *adj* **edgier; -est** : tenso, nervioso
edible [ˈɛdəbəl] *adj* : comestible
edict [ˈiː,dɪkt] *n* : edicto *m*, mandato *m*, orden *f*
edification [,ɛdəfəˈkeɪʃən] *n* : edificación *f*, instrucción *f*
edifice [ˈɛdəfɪs] *n* : edificio *m*
edify [ˈɛdə,faɪ] *vt* **-fied; -fying** : edificar
edit [ˈɛdɪt] *vt* **1** : editar, redactar, corregir **2** *or* **to edit out** DELETE : recortar, cortar
edition [ɪˈdɪʃən] *n* : edición *f*
editor [ˈɛdɪt̬ər] *n* : editor *m*, -tora *f*; redactor *m*, -tora *f*
editorial[1] [,ɛdɪˈtoriəl] *adj* **1** : de redacción **2** : editorial <an editorial comment : un comentario editorial>
editorial[2] *n* : editorial *m*
editorship [ˈɛdət̬ər,ʃɪp] *n* : dirección *f*
educable [ˈɛʤəkəbəl] *adj* : educable
educate [ˈɛʤə,keɪt] *vt* **-cated; -cating** **1** TEACH : educar, enseñar **2** INSTRUCT : formar, educar, instruir **3** INFORM : informar, concientizar
education [,ɛʤəˈkeɪʃən] *n* : educación *f*
educational [,ɛʤəˈkeɪʃənəl] *adj* **1** : docente, de enseñanza <an educational institution : una institución docente> **2** PEDAGOGICAL : pedagógico **3** INSTRUCTIONAL : educativo, instructivo
educator [ˈɛʤə,keɪt̬ər] *n* : educador *m*, -dora *f*
eel [ˈiːl] *n* : anguila *f*

eerie [ˈɪri] *adj* **-rier; -est 1** SPOOKY : que da miedo, espeluznante **2** GHOSTLY : fantasmagórico
eerily [ˈɪrəli] *adv* : de manera extraña y misteriosa
efface [ɪˈfeɪs, -] *vt* **-faced; -facing** : borrar
effect[1] [ɪˈfɛkt] *vt* **1** CARRY OUT : efectuar, llevar a cabo **2** ACHIEVE : lograr, realizar
effect[2] *n* **1** RESULT : efecto *m*, resultado *m*, consecuencia *f* ⟨to no effect : sin resultado⟩ **2** MEANING : sentido *m* ⟨something to that effect : algo por el estilo⟩ **3** INFLUENCE : efecto *m*, influencia *f* **4 effects** *npl* BELONGINGS : efectos *mpl*, pertenencias *fpl* **5 to go into effect** : entrar en vigor **6 in ~** REALLY : en realidad, efectivamente
effective [ɪˈfɛktɪv] *adj* **1** EFFECTUAL : efectivo, eficaz **2** OPERATIVE : vigente — **effectively** *adv*
effectiveness [ɪˈfɛktɪvnəs] *n* : eficacia *f*, efectividad *f*
effectual [ɪˈfɛkʧʊəl] *adj* : eficaz, efectivo — **effectually** *adv*
effeminate [əˈfɛmənət] *adj* : afeminado
effervesce [ˌɛfərˈvɛs] *vi* **-vesced; -vescing 1** : estar en efervescencia, burbujear (dícese de líquidos) **2** : estar eufórico, estar muy animado (dícese de las personas)
effervescence [ˌɛfərˈvɛsənts] *n* **1** : efervescencia *f* **2** LIVELINESS : vivacidad *f*
effervescent [ˌɛfərˈvɛsənt] *adj* **1** : efervescente **2** LIVELY, VIVACIOUS : vivaz, animado
effete [ˈɛfiːt, ɪ-] *adj* **1** WORN-OUT : desgastado, agotado **2** DECADENT : decadente **3** EFFEMINATE : afeminado
efficacious [ˌɛfəˈkeɪʃəs] *adj* : eficaz, efectivo
efficacy [ˈɛfɪkəsi] *n, pl* **-cies** : eficacia *f*
efficiency [ɪˈfɪʃəntsi] *n, pl* **-cies** : eficiencia *f*
efficient [ɪˈfɪʃənt] *adj* : eficiente — **efficiently** *adv*
effigy [ˈɛfəʤi] *n, pl* **-gies** : efigie *f*
effluent [ˈɛˌfluːənt, ɛˈfluː-] *n* : efluente *m* — **effluent** *adj*
effort [ˈɛfərt] *n* **1** EXERTION : esfuerzo *m* **2** ATTEMPT : tentativa *f*, intento *m* ⟨it's not worth the effort : no vale la pena⟩
effortless [ˈɛfərtləs] *adj* : fácil, sin esfuerzo
effortlessly [ˈɛfərtləsli] *adv* : sin esfuerzo, fácilmente
effrontery [ɪˈfrʌntəri] *n, pl* **-teries** : insolencia *f*, desfachatez *f*, descaro *m*
effusion [ɪˈfjuːʒən, ɛ-] *n* : efusión *f*
effusive [ɪˈfjuːsɪv, ɛ-] *adj* : efusivo — **effusively** *adv*
egg[1] [ˈɛg] *vt* **to egg on** : incitar, azuzar, provocar
egg[2] *n* **1** : huevo *m* **2** OVUM : óvulo *m*
eggbeater [ˈɛgˌbiːṭər] *n* : batidor *m* (de huevos)
eggnog [ˈɛgˌnɑg] *n* : ponche *m* de huevo, rompope *m CA, Mex*
eggplant [ˈɛgˌplænt] *n* : berenjena *f*
eggshell [ˈɛgˌʃɛl] *n* : cascarón *m*
ego [ˈiːˌgoː] *n, pl* **egos 1** SELF-ESTEEM : amor *m* propio **2** SELF : ego *m*, yo *m*
egocentric [ˌiːgoˈsɛntrɪk] *adj* : egocéntrico
egoism [ˈiːgoˌwɪzəm] *n* : egoísmo *m*
egoist [ˈiːgowɪst] *n* : egoísta *mf*
egoistic [ˌiːˌgoˈwɪstɪk] *adj* : egoísta
egotism [ˈiːgəˌtɪzəm] *n* : egotismo *m*
egotist [ˈiːgətɪst] *n* : egotista *mf*
egotistic [ˌiːgəˈtɪstɪk] *or* **egotistical** [-ˈtɪstɪkəl] *adj* : egotista — **egotistically** *adv*
egregious [ɪˈgriːʤəs] *adj* : atroz, flagrante, mayúsculo — **egregiously** *adv*
egress [ˈiːˌgrɛs] *n* : salida *f*
egret [ˈiːgrət, -ˌgrɛt] *n* : garceta *f*
Egyptian [ɪˈʤɪpʃən] *n* **1** : egipcio *m*, -cia *f* **2** : egipcio *m* (idioma) — **Egyptian** *adj*
eiderdown [ˈaɪdərˌdaʊn] *n* **1** : plumón *m* **2** COMFORTER : edredón *m*
eight[1] [ˈeɪt] *adj* : ocho
eight[2] *n* : ocho *m*
eight hundred[1] *adj* : ochocientos
eight hundred[2] *n* : ochocientos *m*
eighteen[1] [eitˈtiːn] *adj* : dieciocho
eighteen[2] *n* : dieciocho *m*
eighteenth[1] [eɪtˈtiːnθ] *adj* : decimoctavo
eighteenth[2] *n* **1** : decimoctavo *m*, -va *f* (en una serie) **2** : dieciochoavo *m*, dieciochoava parte *f*
eighth[1] [ˈeɪtθ] *adj* : octavo
eighth[2] *n* **1** : octavo *m*, -va *f* (en una serie) **2** : octavo *m*, octava parte *f*
eightieth[1] [ˈeɪṭiəθ] *adj* : octogésimo
eightieth[2] *n* **1** : octogésimo *m*, -ma *f* (en una serie) **2** : ochentavo *m*, ochentava parte *f*
eighty[1] [ˈeɪṭi] *adj* : ochenta
eighty[2] *n, pl* **eighties 1** : ochenta *m* **2 the eighties** : los ochenta *mpl*
either[1] [ˈiːðər, ˈaɪ-] *adj* **1** : cualquiera (de los dos) ⟨we can watch either movie : podemos ver cualquiera de las dos películas⟩ **2** : ninguno de los dos ⟨she wasn't in either room : no estaba en ninguna de las dos salas⟩ **3** EACH : cada ⟨on either side of the street : a cada lado de la calle⟩
either[2] *pron* **1** : cualquiera *mf* (de los dos) ⟨either is fine : cualquiera de los dos está bien⟩ **2** : ninguno *m*, -na *f* (de los dos) ⟨I don't like either : no me gusta ninguno⟩ **3** : algún *m*, alguna *f* ⟨is either of you interested? : ¿está alguno de ustedes (dos) interesado?⟩
either[3] *conj* **1** : o, u ⟨either David or Daniel could go : puede ir (o) David o Daniel⟩ **2** : ni ⟨we won't watch either this movie or the other : no veremos ni esta película ni la otra⟩
ejaculate [iˈʤækjəˌleɪt] *v* **-lated; -lating** *vt* **1** : eyacular **2** EXCLAIM : exclamar — *vi* : eyacular

ejaculation [iˌʤækjəˈleɪʃən] *n* **1** : eyaculación *f* (en fisiología) **2** EXCLAMATION : exclamación *f*
eject [iˈʤɛkt] *vt* : expulsar, expeler
ejection [iˈʤɛkʃən] *n* : expulsión *f*
eke [ˈiːk] *vt* **eked; eking** *or* **to eke out** : ganar a duras penas
elaborate[1] [iˈlæbəˌreɪt] *v* **-rated; -rating** *vt* : elaborar, idear, desarrollar — *vi* **to elaborate on** : ampliar, entrar en detalles
elaborate[2] [iˈlæbərət] *adj* **1** DETAILED : detallado, minucioso, elaborado **2** COMPLICATED : complicado, intrincado, elaborado — **elaborately** *adv*
elaboration [iˌlæbəˈreɪʃən] *n* : elaboración *f*
elapse [iˈlæps] *vi* **elapsed; elapsing** : transcurrir, pasar
elastic[1] [iˈlæstɪk] *adj* : elástico
elastic[2] *n* **1** : elástico *m* **2** RUBBER BAND : goma *f*, gomita *f*, elástico *m*, liga *f*
elasticity [iˌlæsˈtɪsəṯi, ˌiːˌlæs-] *n, pl* **-ties** : elasticidad *f*
elate [iˈleɪt] *vt* **elated; elating** : alborozar, regocijar
elation [iˈleɪʃən] *n* : euforia *f*, júbilo *m*, alborozo *m*
elbow[1] [ˈɛlˌboː] *vt* : darle un codazo a
elbow[2] *n* : codo *m*
elder[1] [ˈɛldər] *adj* : mayor
elder[2] *n* **1 to be someone's elder** : ser mayor que alguien **2** : anciano *m*, -na *f* (de un pueblo o una tribu) **3** : miembro *m* del consejo (en varias religiones)
elderberry [ˈɛldərˌbɛri] *n, pl* **-berries** : baya *f* de saúco (fruta), saúco *m* (árbol)
elderly [ˈɛldərli] *adj* : mayor, de edad, anciano
eldest [ˈɛldəst] *adj* : mayor, de más edad
elect[1] [iˈlɛkt] *vt* : elegir
elect[2] *adj* : electo <the president-elect : el presidente electo>
elect[3] *npl* **the elect** : los elegidos *mpl*
election [iˈlɛkʃən] *n* : elección *f*
elective[1] [iˈlɛktɪv] *adj* **1** : electivo **2** OPTIONAL : facultativo, optativo
elective[2] *n* : asignatura *f* electiva
elector [iˈlɛktər] *n* : elector *m*, -tora *f*
electoral [iˈlɛktərəl] *adj* : electoral
electorate [iˈlɛktərət] *n* : electorado *m*
electric [iˈlɛktrɪk] *adj* **1** *or* **electrical** [-trɪkəl] : eléctrico **2** THRILLING : electrizante, emocionante
electrician [iˌlɛkˈtrɪʃən] *n* : electricista *mf*
electricity [iˌlɛkˈtrɪsəṯi] *n, pl* **-ties** **1** : electricidad *f* **2** CURRENT : corriente *m* eléctrica
electrification [iˌlɛktrəfəˈkeɪʃən] *n* : electrificación *f*
electrify [iˈlɛktrəˌfaɪ] *vt* **-fied; -fying** **1** : electrificar **2** THRILL : electrizar, emocionar
electrocardiogram [iˌlɛktroˈkɑrdiəˌgræm] *n* : electrocardiograma *m*
electrocardiograph [iˌlɛktroˈkɑrdiəˌgræf] *n* : electrocardiógrafo *m*
electrocute [iˈlɛktrəˌkjuːt] *vt* **-cuted; -cuting** : electrocutar
electrocution [iˌlɛktrəˈkjuːʃən] *n* : electrocución *f*
electrode [iˈlɛkˌtroːd] *n* : electrodo *m*
electrolysis [iˌlɛkˈtrɑləsɪs] *n* : electrólisis *f*
electrolyte [iˈlɛktrəˌlaɪt] *n* : electrolito *m*
electromagnet [iˌlɛktroˈmægnət] *n* : electroimán *m*
electromagnetic [iˌlɛktromægˈnɛṯɪk] *adj* : electromagnético — **electromagnetically** [-ṯɪkli] *adv*
electromagnetism [iˌlɛktroˈmægnəˌtɪzəm] *n* : electromagnetismo *m*
electron [iˈlɛkˌtrɑn] *n* : electrón *m*
electronic [iˌlɛkˈtrɑnɪk] *adj* : electrónico — **electronically** [-nɪkli] *adv*
electronic mail *n* : correo *m* electrónico
electronics [iˌlɛkˈtrɑnɪks] *n* : electrónica *f*
electroplate [iˈlɛktrəˌpleɪt] *vt* **-plated; plating** : galvanizar mediante electrólisis
elegance [ˈɛlɪgənts] *n* : elegancia *f*
elegant [ˈɛlɪgənt] *adj* : elegante — **elegantly** *adv*
elegy [ˈɛləʤi] *n, pl* **-gies** : elegía *f*
element [ˈɛləmənt] *n* **1** COMPONENT : elemento *m*, factor *m* **2** : elemento *m* (en la química) **3** MILIEU : elemento *m*, medio *m* <to be in one's element : estar en su elemento> **4 elements** *npl* RUDIMENTS : elementos *mpl*, rudimentos *mpl*, bases *fpl* **5 the elements** WEATHER : los elementos *mpl*
elemental [ˌɛləˈmɛntəl] *adj* **1** BASIC : elemental, primario **2** : elemental (dícese de los elementos químicos)
elementary [ˌɛləˈmɛntri] *adj* **1** SIMPLE : elemental, simple, fundamental **2** : de enseñanza primaria
elementary school *n* : escuela *f* primaria
elephant [ˈɛləfənt] *n* : elefante *m*, -ta *f*
elevate [ˈɛləˌveɪt] *vt* **-vated; -vating** **1** RAISE : elevar, levantar, alzar **2** EXALT, PROMOTE : elevar, exaltar, ascender **3** ELATE : alborozar, regocijar
elevation [ˌɛləˈveɪʃən] *n* **1** : elevación *f* **2** ALTITUDE : altura *f*, altitud *f* **3** PROMOTION : ascenso *m*
elevator [ˈɛləˌveɪṯər] *n* : ascensor *m*, elevador *m*
eleven[1] [ɪˈlɛvən] *adj* : once
eleven[2] *n* : once *m*
eleventh[1] [ɪlɛvəntθ] *adj* : undécimo
eleventh[2] *n* **1** : undécimo *m*, -ma *f* (en una serie) **2** : onceavo *m*, onceava parte *f*
elf [ˈɛlf] *n, pl* **elves** [ˈɛlvz] : elfo *m*, geniecillo *m*, duende *m*
elfin [ˈɛlfən] *adj* **1** : de elfo, menudo **2** ENCHANTING, MAGIC : mágico, encantador
elfish [ˈɛlfɪʃ] *adj* **1** : de elfo **2** MISCHIEVOUS : travieso
elicit [ɪˈlɪsət] *vt* : provocar

eligibility [ˌɛlədʒəˈbɪləṭi] *n, pl* **-ties** : elegibilidad *f*
eligible [ˈɛlədʒəbəl] *adj* **1** QUALIFIED : elegible **2** SUITABLE : idóneo
eliminate [ɪˈlɪməˌneɪt] *vt* **-nated; -nating** : eliminar
elimination [ɪˌlɪməˈneɪʃən] *n* : eliminación *f*
elite [eɪˈli:t, i-] *n* : elite *f*
elixir [iˈlɪksər] *n* : elixir *m*
elk [ˈɛlk] *n* : alce *m* (de Europa), uapití *m* (de América)
ellipse [ɪˈlɪps, -] *n* : elipse *f*
ellipsis [ɪˈlɪpsəs, -] *n, pl* **-lipses** [-ˌsi:z] **1** : elipsis *f* **2** : puntos *mpl* suspensivos (en la puntuación)
elliptical [ɪˈlɪptɪkəl, -] *or* **elliptic** [-tɪk] *adj* : elíptico
elm [ˈɛlm] *n* : olmo *m*
elocution [ˌɛləˈkju:ʃən] *n* : elocución *f*
elongate [iˈlɔŋˌgeɪt] *vt* **-gated; -gating** : alargar
elongation [ˌi:ˌlɔŋˈgeɪʃən] *n* : alargamiento *m*
elope [iˈlo:p] *vi* **eloped; eloping** : fugarse
elopement [iˈlo:pmənt] *n* : fuga *f*
eloquence [ˈɛləkwənts] *n* : elocuencia *f*
eloquent [ˈɛləkwənt] *adj* : elocuente — **eloquently** *adv*
El Salvadoran [ˌɛlˌsælvəˈdorən] *n* : salvadoreño *m*, -ña *f* — **El Salvadoran** *adj*
else[1] [ˈɛls] *adv* **1** DIFFERENTLY : de otro modo, de otra manera ⟨how else? : ¿de qué otro modo?⟩ **2** ELSEWHERE : de otro sitio, de otro lugar ⟨where else? : ¿en qué otro sitio?⟩ **3 or else** OTHERWISE : si no, de lo contrario
else[2] *adj* **1** OTHER : otro ⟨anyone else : cualquier otro⟩ ⟨everyone else : todos los demás⟩ ⟨nobody else : ningún otro, nadie más⟩ ⟨somebody else : otra persona⟩ **2** MORE : más ⟨nothing else : nada más⟩ ⟨what else? : ¿qué más?⟩
elsewhere [ˈɛlsˌhwɛr] *adv* : en otra parte, en otro sitio, en otro lugar
elucidate [iˈlu:səˌdeɪt] *vt* **-dated; -dating** : dilucidar, elucidar, esclarecer
elucidation [iˌlu:səˈdeɪʃən] *n* : elucidación *f*, esclarecimiento *m*
elude [iˈlu:d] *vt* **eluded; eluding** : eludir, evadir
elusive [iˈlu:sɪv] *adj* **1** EVASIVE : evasivo, esquivo **2** SLIPPERY : huidizo, escurridizo **3** FLEETING, INTANGIBLE : impalpable, fugaz
elusively [iˈlu:sɪvli] *adv* : de manera esquiva
elves → **elf**
emaciate [iˈmeɪʃiˌeɪt] *vt* **-ated; -ating** : enflaquecer
emaciation [iˌmeɪsiˈeɪʃən, -ʃi-] *n* : enflaquecimiento *m*, escualidez *f*, delgadez *f* extrema
e–mail [ˈi:ˌmeɪl] *n* : e-mail *m*
emanate [ˈɛməˌneɪt] *v* **-nated; -nating** *vi* : emanar, provenir, proceder — *vt* : emanar
emanation [ˌɛməˈneɪʃən] *n* : emanación *f*
emancipate [iˈmæntsəˌpeɪt] *vt* **-pated; -pating** : emancipar
emancipation [iˌmæntsəˈpeɪʃən] *n* : emancipación *f*
emasculate [iˈmæskjəˌleɪt] *vt* **-lated; -lating** **1** CASTRATE : castrar, emascular **2** WEAKEN : debilitar
embalm [ɪmˈbɑm, ɛm-, -ˈbɑlm] *vt* : embalsamar
embankment [ɪmˈbæŋkmənt, ɛm-] *n* : terraplén *m*, muro *m* de contención
embargo[1] [ɪmˈbɑrgo, ɛm-] *vt* **-goed; -going** : imponer un embargo sobre
embargo[2] *n, pl* **-goes** : embargo *m*
embark [ɪmˈbɑrk, ɛm-] *vt* : embarcar — *vi* **1** : embarcarse **2 to embark on** START : emprender, embarcarse en
embarkation [ˌɛmˌbɑrˈkeɪʃən] *n* : embarque *m*, embarco *m*
embarrass [ɪmˈbærəs, ɛm-] *vt* : avergonzar, abochornar
embarrassing [ɪmˈbærəsɪŋ, ɛm-] *adj* : embarazoso, violento
embarrassment [ɪmˈbærəsmənt, ɛm-] *n* : vergüenza *f*, pena *f*
embassy [ˈɛmbəsi] *n, pl* **-sies** : embajada *f*
embed [ɪmˈbɛd, ɛm-] *vt* **-bedded; -bedding** : incrustar, empotrar, grabar (en la memoria)
embellish [ɪmˈbɛlɪʃ, ɛm-] *vt* : adornar, embellecer
embellishment [ɪmˈbɛlɪʃmənt, ɛm-] *n* : adorno *m*
ember [ˈɛmbər] *n* : ascua *f*, brasa *f*
embezzle [ɪmˈbɛzəl, ɛm-] *vt* **-zled; -zling** : desfalcar, malversar
embezzlement [ɪmˈbɛzəlmənt, ɛm-] *n* : desfalco *m*, malversación *f*
embezzler [ɪmˈbɛzələr, ɛm-] *n* : desfalcador *m*, -dora *f*; malversador *m*, -dora *f*
embitter [ɪmˈbɪṭər, ɛm-] *vt* : amargar
emblem [ˈɛmbləm] *n* : emblema *m*, símbolo *m*
emblematic [ˌɛmbləˈmæṭɪk] *adj* : emblemático, simbólico
embodiment [ɪmˈbɑdɪmənt, ɛm-] *n* : encarnación *f*, personificación *f*
embody [ɪmˈbɑdi, ɛm-] *vt* **-bodied; -bodying** : encarnar, personificar
emboss [ɪmˈbɑs, ɛm-, -ˈbɔs] *vt* : repujar, grabar en relieve
embrace[1] [ɪmˈbreɪs, ɛm-] *vt* **-braced; -bracing** **1** HUG : abrazar **2** ADOPT, TAKE ON : adoptar, aceptar **3** INCLUDE : abarcar, incluir
embrace[2] *n* : abrazo *m*
embroider [ɪmˈbrɔɪdər, ɛm-] *vt* : bordar (una tela), adornar (una historia)
embroidery [ɪmˈbrɔɪdəri, ɛm-] *n, pl* **-deries** : bordado *m*
embroil [ɪmˈbrɔɪl, ɛm-] *vt* : embrollar, enredar
embryo [ˈɛmbriˌo:] *n, pl* **embryos** : embrión *m*

embryonic [ˌɛmbriˈɑnɪk] *adj* : embrionario
emend [iˈmɛnd] *vt* : enmendar, corregir
emendation [ˌiːˌmɛnˈdeɪʃən] *n* : enmienda *f*
emerald[1] [ˈɛmrəld, ˈɛmə-] *adj* : verde esmeralda
emerald[2] *n* : esmeralda *f*
emerge [iˈmərʤ] *vi* **emerged; emerging** : emerger, salir, aparecer, surgir
emergence [iˈmərʤənts] *n* : aparición *f*, surgimiento *m*
emergency [iˈmərʤəntsi] *n, pl* **-cies** : emergencia *f*
emergent [iˈmərʤənt] *adj* : emergente
emery [ˈɛməri] *n, pl* **-eries** : esmeril *m*
emetic[1] [iˈmɛt̬ɪk] *adj* : vomitivo, emético
emetic[2] *n* : vomitivo *m*, emético *m*
emigrant [ˈɛmɪgrənt] *n* : emigrante *mf*
emigrate [ˈɛməˌgreɪt] *vi* **-grated; -grating** : emigrar
emigration [ˌɛməˈgreɪʃən] *n* : emigración *f*
eminence [ˈɛmənənts] *n* **1** PROMINENCE : eminencia *f*, prestigio *m*, renombre *m* **2** DIGNITARY : eminencia *f*; dignatario *m*, -ria *f* ⟨Your Eminence : Su Eminencia⟩
eminent [ˈɛmənənt] *adj* : eminente, ilustre
eminently [ˈɛmənəntli] *adv* : sumamente
emissary [ˈɛməˌsɛri] *n, pl* **-saries** : emisario *m*, -ria *f*
emission [iˈmɪʃən] *n* : emisión *f*
emit [iˈmɪt] *vt* **emitted; emitting** : emitir, despedir, producir
emote [iˈmoːt] *vi* **emoted; emoting** : exteriorizar las emociones
emotion [iˈmoːʃən] *n* : emoción *f*, sentimiento *m*
emotional [iˈmoːʃənəl] *adj* **1** : emocional, afectivo ⟨an emotional reaction : una reacción emocional⟩ **2** MOVING : emocionante, emotivo, conmovedor
emotionally [iˈmoːʃənəli] *adv* : emocionalmente
empathy [ˈɛmpəθi] *n* : empatía *f*
emperor [ˈɛmpərər] *n* : emperador *m*
emphasis [ˈɛmfəsɪs] *n, pl* **-phases** [-ˌsiːz] : énfasis *m*, hincapié *m*
emphasize [ˈɛmfəˌsaɪz] *vt* **-sized; -sizing** : enfatizar, destacar, subrayar, hacer hincapié en
emphatic [ɪmˈfætɪk, ɛm-] *adj* : enfático, enérgico, categórico — **emphatically** [-ɪkli] *adv*
empire [ˈɛmˌpaɪr] *n* : imperio *m*
empirical [ɪmˈpɪrɪkəl, ɛm-] *adj* : empírico — **empirically** [-ɪkli] *adv*
employ[1] [ɪmˈplɔɪ, ɛm-] *vt* **1** USE : usar, utilizar **2** HIRE : contratar, emplear **3** OCCUPY : ocupar, dedicar, emplear
employ[2] [ɪmˈplɔɪ, ɛm-; ˈɪmˌ-, ˈɛmˌ-] *n* **1** : puesto *m*, cargo *m*, ocupación *f* **2 to be in the employ of** : estar al servicio de, trabajar para
employee [ɪmˌplɔɪˈiː, ɛm-, -ˈplɔɪˌiː] *n* : empleado *m*, -da *f*
employer [ɪmˈplɔɪər, ɛm-] *n* : patrón *m*, -trona *f*; empleador *m*, -dora *f*
employment [ɪmˈplɔɪmənt, ɛm-] *n* : trabajo *m*, empleo *m*
empower [ɪmˈpaʊər, ɛm-] *vt* : facultar, autorizar, conferirle poder a
empowerment [ɪmˈpaʊərmənt, ɛm-] *n* : autorización *f*
empress [ˈɛmprəs] *n* : emperatriz *f*
emptiness [ˈɛmptinəs] *n* : vacío *m*, vacuidad *f*
empty[1] [ˈɛmpti] *v* **-tied; -tying** *vt* : vaciar — *vi* : desaguar (dícese de un río)
empty[2] *adj* **emptier; -est 1** : vacío **2** VACANT : desocupado, libre **3** MEANINGLESS : vacío, hueco, vano
empty–handed [ˌɛmptiˈhændəd] *adj* : con las manos vacías
empty–headed [ˌɛmptiˈhɛdəd] *adj* : cabeza hueca, tonto
emu [ˈiːˌmjuː] *n* : emú *m*
emulate [ˈɛmjəˌleɪt] *vt* **-lated; -lating** : emular
emulation [ˌɛmjəˈleɪʃən] *n* : emulación *f*
emulsifier [ɪˈmʌlsəˌfaɪər] *n* : emulsionante *m*
emulsify [ɪˈmʌlsəˌfaɪ] *vt* **-fied; -fying** : emulsionar
emulsion [ɪˈmʌlʃən] *n* : emulsión *f*
enable [ɪˈneɪbəl, ɛ-] *vt* **-abled; -abling 1** EMPOWER : habilitar, autorizar, facultar **2** PERMIT : hacer posible, posibilitar, permitir
enact [ɪˈnækt, ɛ-] *vt* **1** : promulgar (un ley o decreto) **2** : representar (un papel en el teatro)
enactment [ɪˈnæktmənt, ɛ-] *n* : promulgación *f*
enamel[1] [ɪˈnæməl] *vt* **-eled** *or* **-elled; -eling** *or* **-elling** : esmaltar
enamel[2] *n* : esmalte *m*
enamor [ɪˈnæmər] *vt* **1** : enamorar **2 to be enamored of** : estar enamorado de (una persona), estar entusiasmado con (algo)
encamp [ɪnˈkæmp, ɛn-] *vi* : acampar
encampment [ɪnˈkæmpmənt, ɛn-] *n* : campamento *m*
encase [ɪnˈkeɪs, ɛn-] *vt* **-cased; -casing** : encerrar, revestir
encephalitis [ɪnˌsɛfəˈlaɪt̬əs, ɛn-] *n, pl* **-litides** [ˈlɪt̬əˌdiːz] : encefalitis *f*
enchant [ɪnˈʧænt, ɛn-] *vt* **1** BEWITCH : hechizar, encantar, embrujar **2** CHARM, FASCINATE : cautivar, fascinar, encantar
enchanting [ɪnˈʧæntɪŋ, ɛn-] *adj* : encantador
enchanter [ɪnˈʧæntər, ɛn-] *n* SORCERER : mago *m*, encantador *m*
enchantment [ɪnˈʧæntmənt, ɛn-] *n* **1** SPELL : encanto *m*, hechizo *m* **2** CHARM : encanto *m*
enchantress [ɪnˈʧæntrəs, ɛn-] *n* **1** SORCERESS : maga *f*, hechicera *f* **2** CHARMER : mujer *f* cautivadora
encircle [ɪnˈsərkəl, ɛn-] *vt* **-cled; -cling** : rodear, ceñir, cercar

enclose [ɪn'klo:z, ɛn-] *vt* **-closed; -closing 1** SURROUND : encerrar, cercar, rodear **2** INCLUDE : incluir, adjuntar, acompañar ⟨please find enclosed : le enviamos adjunto⟩

enclosure [ɪn'klo:ʒər, ɛn-] *n* **1** ENCLOSING : encierro *m* **2** : cercado *m* (de terreno), recinto *m* ⟨an enclosure for the press : un recinto para la prensa⟩ **3** ADJUNCT : anexo *m* (con una carta), documento *m* adjunto

encode [ɪn'ko:d, ɛn-] *vt* : cifrar (mensajes, etc.), codificar (en informática)

encompass [ɪn'kʌmpəs, ɛn-, -'kɑm-] *vt* **1** SURROUND : circundar, rodear **2** INCLUDE : abarcar, comprender

encore ['ɑn,kor] *n* : bis *m*, repetición *f*

encounter[1] [ɪn'kaʊntər, ɛn-] *vt* **1** MEET : encontrar, encontrarse con, toparse con, tropezar con **2** FIGHT : combatir, luchar contra

encounter[2] *n* : encuentro *m*

encourage [ɪn'kərɪʤ, ɛn-] *vt* **-aged; -aging 1** HEARTEN, INSPIRE : animar, alentar **2** FOSTER : fomentar, promover

encouragement [ɪn'kərɪʤmənt, ɛn-] *n* : ánimo *m*, aliento *m*

encouraging [ɪn'kərəʤɪŋ, ɛn-] *adj* : alentador, esperanzador

encroach [ɪn'kro:ʧ, ɛn-] *vi* **to encroach on** : invadir, abusar (derechos), quitar (tiempo)

encroachment [ɪn'kro:ʧmənt, ɛn-] *n* : invasión *f*, usurpación *f*

encrust [ɪn'krʌst, ɛn-] *vt* **1** : recubrir con una costra **2** INLAY : incrustar ⟨encrusted with gems : incrustado de gemas⟩

encumber [ɪn'kʌmbər, ɛn-] *vt* **1** BLOCK : obstruir, estorbar **2** BURDEN : cargar, gravar

encumbrance [ɪn'kʌmbrənts, ɛn-] *n* : estorbo *m*, carga *f*, gravamen *m*

encyclopedia [ɪn,saɪklə'pi:diə, ɛn-] *n* : enciclopedia *f*

encyclopedic [ɪn,saɪklə'pi:dɪk, ɛn-] *adj* : enciclopédico

end[1] ['ɛnd] *vt* **1** STOP : terminar, poner fin a **2** CONCLUDE : concluir, terminar — *vi* : terminar(se), acabar, concluir(se)

end[2] *n* **1** EXTREMITY : extremo *m*, final *m*, punta *f* **2** CONCLUSION : fin *m*, final *m* **3** AIM : fin *m*

endanger [ɪn'deɪnʤər, ɛn-] *vt* : poner en peligro

endear [ɪn'dɪr, ɛn-] *vt* **to endear oneself to** : ganarse la simpatía de, granjearse el cariño de

endearment [ɪn'dɪrmənt, ɛn-] *n* : expresión *f* de cariño

endeavor[1] [ɪn'dɛvər, ɛn-] *vt* : intentar, esforzarse por ⟨he endeavored to improve his work : intentó por mejorar su trabajo⟩

endeavor[2] *n* : intento *m*, esfuerzo *m*

endemic [ɛn'dɛmɪk, ɪn-] *adj* : endémico

ending ['ɛndɪŋ] *n* **1** CONCLUSION : final *m*, desenlace *m* **2** SUFFIX : sufijo *m*, terminación *f*

endive ['ɛn,daɪv, ,ɑn'di:v] *n* : endibia *f*, endivia *f*

endless ['ɛndləs] *adj* **1** INTERMINABLE : interminable, inacabable, sin fin **2** INNUMERABLE : innumerable, incontable

endlessly ['ɛndləsli] *adv* : interminablemente, eternamente, sin parar

endocrine ['ɛndəkrən, -,kraɪn, -,kri:n] *adj* : endocrino

endorse [ɪn'dɔrs, ɛn-] *vt* **-dorsed; -dorsing 1** SIGN : endosar, firmar **2** APPROVE : aprobar, sancionar

endorsement [ɪn'dɔrsmənt, ɛn-] *n* **1** SIGNATURE : endoso *m*, firma *f* **2** APPROVAL : aprobación *f*, aval *m*

endow [ɪn'daʊ, ɛn-] *vt* : dotar

endowment [ɪn'daʊmənt, ɛn-] *n* **1** FUNDING : dotación *f* **2** DONATION : donación *f*, legado *m* **3** ATTRIBUTE, GIFT : atributo *m*, dotes *fpl*

endurable [ɪn'dʊrəbəl, ɛn-, -'djʊr-] *adj* : tolerable, soportable

endurance [ɪn'dʊrənts, ɛn-, -'djʊr-] *n* : resistencia *f*, aguante *m*

endure [ɪn'dʊr, ɛn-, -'djʊr] *v* **-dured; -during** *vt* **1** BEAR : resistir, soportar, aguantar **2** TOLERATE : tolerar, soportar — *vi* LAST : durar, perdurar

enema ['ɛnəmə] *n* : enema *m*, lavativa *f*

enemy ['ɛnəmi] *n, pl* **-mies** : enemigo *m*, -ga *f*

energetic [,ɛnər'ʤɛṭɪk] *adj* : enérgico, vigoroso — **energetically** [-ṭɪkli] *adv*

energize ['ɛnər,ʤaɪz] *vt* **-gized; -gizing 1** ACTIVATE : activar **2** INVIGORATE : vigorizar

energy ['ɛnərʤi] *n, pl* **-gies 1** VITALITY : energía *f*, vitalidad *f* **2** EFFORT : esfuerzo *m*, energías *fpl* **3** POWER : energía *f* ⟨atomic energy : energía atómica⟩

enervate ['ɛnər,veɪt] *vt* **-vated; -vating** : enervar, debilitar

enfold [ɪn'fo:ld, ɛn-] *vt* : envolver

enforce [ɪn'fors, ɛn-] *vt* **-forced; -forcing 1** : hacer respetar, hacer cumplir (una ley, etc.) **2** IMPOSE : imponer ⟨to enforce obedience : imponer la obediencia⟩

enforcement [ɪn'forsmənt, ɛn-] *n* : imposición *f*

enfranchise [ɪn'fræn,ʧaɪz, ɛn-] *vt* **-chised; -chising** : conceder el voto a

enfranchisement [ɪn'fræn,ʧaɪzmənt, ɛn-] *n* : concesión *f* del voto

engage [ɪn'geɪʤ, ɛn-] *v* **-gaged; -gaging** *vt* **1** ATTRACT : captar, atraer, llamar ⟨to engage one's attention : captar la atención⟩ **2** MESH : engranar ⟨to engage the clutch : embragar⟩ **3** COMMIT : comprometer ⟨to get engaged : comprometerse⟩ **4** HIRE : contratar **5** : entablar combate con (un enemigo)

— *vi* **1** PARTICIPATE : participar **2 to engage in combat** : entrar en combate
engagement [ɪnˈgeɪʤmənt, ɛn-] *n* **1** APPOINTMENT : cita *f*, hora *f* **2** BETROTHAL : compromiso *m*
engaging [ɪnˈgeɪʤɪŋ, ɛn-] *adj* : atractivo, encantador, interesante
engender [ɪnˈʤndər, ɛn-] *vt* **-dered; -dering** : engendrar
engine [ˈɛnʤən] *n* **1** MOTOR : motor *m* **2** LOCOMOTIVE : locomotora *f*, máquina *f*
engineer[1] [ˌɛnʤəˈnɪr] *vt* **1** : diseñar, construir (un sistema, un mecanismo, etc.) **2** CONTRIVE : maquinar, tramar, fraguar
engineer[2] *n* **1** : ingeniero *m*, -ra *f* **2** : maquinista *mf* (de locomotoras)
engineering [ˌɛnʤəˈnɪrɪŋ] *n* : ingeniería *f*
English[1] [ˈɪŋglɪʃ, ˈŋlɪʃ] *adj* : inglés
English[2] *n* **1** : inglés *m* (idioma) **2 the English** : los ingleses
Englishman [ˈɪŋglɪʃmən, ˈɪŋlɪʃ-] *n, pl* **-men** [-mən, -ˌmɛn] : inglés *m*
Englishwoman [ˈɪŋglɪʃˌwʊmən, ˈɪŋlɪʃ-] *n, pl* **-women** [-ˌwɪmən] : inglesa *f*
engrave [ɪnˈgreɪv, ɛn-] *vt* **-graved; -graving** : grabar
engraver [ɪnˈgreɪvər, ɛn-] *n* : grabador *m*, -dora *f*
engraving [ɪnˈgreɪvɪŋ, ɛn-] *n* : grabado *m*
engross [ɪnˈgro:s, ɛn-] *vt* : absorber
engrossed [ɪnˈgro:st, ɛn-] *adj* : absorto
engrossing [ɪnˈgro:sɪŋ, ɛn-] *adj* : fascinante, absorbente
engulf [ɪnˈgʌlf, ɛn-] *vt* : envolver, sepultar
enhance [ɪnˈhænts, ɛn-] *vt* **-hanced; -hancing** : realzar, aumentar, mejorar
enhancement [ɪnˈhæntsmənt, ɛn-] *n* : mejora *f*, realce *m*, aumento *m*
enigma [ɪˈnɪgmə] *n* : enigma *m*
enigmatic [ˌɛnɪgˈmæṯɪk, ˌi:nɪg-] *adj* : enigmático — **enigmatically** [-ṯɪkli] *adv*
enjoin [ɪnˈʤɔɪn, ɛn-] *vt* **1** COMMAND : ordenar, imponer **2** FORBID : prohibir, vedar
enjoy [ɪnˈʤɔɪ, ɛn-] *vt* **1** : disfrutar, gozar de ⟨did you enjoy the book? : ¿te gustó el libro?⟩ ⟨to enjoy good health : gozar de buena salud⟩ **2 to enjoy oneself** : divertirse, pasarlo bien
enjoyable [ɪnˈʤɔɪəbəl, ɛn-] *adj* : agradable, placentero, divertido
enjoyment [ɪnˈʤɔɪmənt, ɛn-] *n* : placer *m*, goce *m*, disfrute *m*, deleite *m*
enlarge [ɪnˈlɑrʤ, ɛn-] *v* **-larged; -larging** *vt* : extender, agrandar, ampliar — *vi* **1** : ampliarse **2 to enlarge upon** : extenderse sobre, entrar en detalles sobre
enlargement [ɪnˈlɑrʤmənt, ɛn-] *n* : expansión *f*, ampliación *f* (dícese de fotografías)
enlarger [ɪnˈlɑrʤər, ɛn-] *n* : ampliadora *f*
enlighten [ɪnˈlaɪtən, ɛn-] *vt* : iluminar, aclarar
enlightenment [ɪnˈlaɪtənmənt, ɛn-] *n* **1** : ilustración *f* ⟨the Enlightenment : la Ilustración⟩ **2** CLARIFICATION : aclaración *f*
enlist [ɪnˈlɪst, ɛn-] *vt* **1** ENROLL : alistar, reclutar **2** SECURE : conseguir ⟨to enlist the support of : conseguir el apoyo de⟩ — *vi* : alistarse
enlisted man [ɪnˈlɪstəd, ɛn-] *n* : soldado *m* raso
enlistment [ɪnˈlɪstmənt, ɛn-] *n* : alistamiento *m*, reclutamiento *m*
enliven [ɪnˈlaɪvən, ɛn-] *vt* : animar, alegrar, darle vida a
enmity [ˈɛnməṯi] *n, pl* **-ties** : enemistad *f*, animadversión *f*
ennoble [ɪˈno:bəl, ɛ-] *vt* **-bled; -bling** : ennoblecer
ennui [ˌɑnˈwi:] *n* : hastío *m*, tedio *m*, fastidio *m*, aburrimiento *m*
enormity [ɪˈnɔrməṯi] *n, pl* **-ties 1** ATROCITY : atrocidad *f*, barbaridad *f* **2** IMMENSITY : enormidad *f*, inmensidad *f*
enormous [ɪˈnɔrməs] *adj* : enorme, inmenso, tremendo — **enormously** *adv*
enough[1] [ɪˈnʌf] *adv* **1** : bastante, suficientemente **2 fair enough!** : ¡está bien!, ¡de acuerdo! **3 strangely enough** : por extraño que parezca **4 sure enough** : en efecto, sin duda alguna **5 well enough** : muy bien, bastante bien
enough[2] *adj* : bastante, suficiente ⟨do we have enough chairs? : ¿tenemos suficientes sillas?⟩
enough[3] *pron* : (lo) suficiente, (lo) bastante ⟨enough to eat : lo suficiente para comer⟩ ⟨it's not enough : no basta⟩ ⟨I've had enough! : ¡estoy harto!, ¡está bueno ya!⟩
enquire [ɪnˈkwaɪr, ɛn-] **enquiry** [ˈɪnˌkwaɪri, ˈɛn-, -kwəri; ɪnˈkwaɪri, ɛnˈ-] → **inquire, inquiry**
enrage [ɪnˈreɪʤ, ɛn-] *vt* **-raged; -raging** : enfurecer, encolerizar
enraged [ɪnˈreɪʤd, ɛn-] *adj* : enfurecido, furioso
enrich [ɪnˈrɪʧ, ɛn-] *vt* : enriquecer
enrichment [ɪnˈrɪʧmənt, ɛn-] *n* : enriquecimiento *m*
enroll *or* **enrol** [ɪnˈro:l, ɛn-] *v* **-rolled; -rolling** *vt* : matricular, inscribir — *vi* : matricularse, inscribirse
enrollment [ɪnˈro:lmənt, ɛn-] *n* : matrícula *f*, inscripción *f*
en route [ɑˈru:t, ɛnˈraʊt] *adv* : de camino, por el camino
ensconce [ɪnˈskɑnts, ɛn-] *vt* **-sconced; -sconcing** : acomodar, instalar, establecer cómodamente
ensemble [ɑnˈsɑmbəl] *n* : conjunto *m*
enshrine [ɪnˈʃraɪn, ɛn-] *vt* **-shrined; -shrining** : conservar religiosamente, preservar
ensign [ˈntsən, ˈɛnˌsaɪn] *n* **1** FLAG : enseña *f*, pabellón *m* **2** : alférez *mf* (de fragata)

enslave [ɪn'sleɪv, ɛn-] *vt* **-slaved; -slaving** : esclavizar

enslavement [ɪn'sleɪvmənt, ɛn-] *n* : esclavización *f*

ensnare [ɪn'snær, ɛn-] *vt* **-snared; -snaring** : atrapar

ensue [ɪn'su:, ɛn-] *vi* **-sued; -suing** : seguir, resultar

ensure [ɪn'ʃʊr, ɛn-] *vt* **-sured; -suring** : asegurar, garantizar

entail [ɪn'teɪl, ɛn-] *vt* : implicar, suponer, conllevar

entangle [ɪn'tæŋgəl, ɛn-] *vt* **-gled; -gling** : enredar

entanglement [ɪn'tæŋgəlmənt, ɛn-] *n* : enredo *m*

enter ['ɛntər] *vt* **1** : entrar en, entrar a **2** BEGIN : entrar en, comenzar, iniciar **3** RECORD : anotar, inscribir, dar entrada a <to enter data : introducir datos> **4** JOIN : entrar en, alistarse en, hacerse socio de — *vi* **1** : entrar **2 to enter into** : entrar en, firmar (un acuerdo), entablar (negociaciones, etc.)

enterprise ['ɛntər,praɪz] *n* **1** UNDERTAKING : empresa *f* **2** BUSINESS : empresa *f*, firma *f* **3** INITIATIVE : iniciativa *f*, empuje *m*

enterprising ['ɛntər,praɪzɪŋ] *adj* : emprendedor

entertain [,ɛntər'teɪn] *vt* **1** : recibir, agasajar <to entertain guests : tener invitados> **2** CONSIDER : considerar, contemplar **3** AMUSE : entretener, divertir

entertainer [,ɛntər'teɪnər] *n* : artista *mf*

entertaining [,ɛntər'teɪnɪŋ] *adj* : entretenido, divertido

entertainment [,ɛntər'teɪnmənt] *n* : entretenimiento *m*, diversión *f*

enthrall *or* **enthral** [ɪn'θrɔl, ɛn-] *vt* **-thralled; -thralling** : cautivar, embelesar

enthuse [ɪn'θuiz, ɛn-] *v* **-thused; -thusing** *vt* **1** EXCITE : entusiasmar **2** : decir con entusiasmo — *vi* **to enthuse over** : hablar con entusiasmo sobre

enthusiasm [ɪn'θu:zi,æzəm, ɛn-, -'θju:-] *n* : entusiasmo *m*

enthusiast [ɪn'θu:zi,æst, ɛn-, -'θju:-, -əst] *n* : entusiasta *mf*; aficionado *m*, -da *f*

enthusiastic [ɪn,θu:zi'æstɪk, ɛn-, -,θju:-] *adj* : entusiasta, aficionado

enthusiastically [ɪn,θu:zi'æstɪkli, ɛn-, -,θju:-] *adv* : con entusiasmo

entice [ɪn'taɪs, ɛn-] *vt* **-ticed; -ticing** : atraer, tentar

enticement [ɪn'taɪsmənt, ɛn-] *n* : tentación *f*, atracción *f*, señuelo *m*

entire [ɪn'taɪr, ɛn-] *adj* : entero, completo

entirely [ɪn'taɪrli, ɛn-] *adv* : completamente, totalmente

entirety [ɪn'taɪrti, ɛn-, -'taɪrəti] *n, pl* **-ties** : totalidad *f*

entitle [ɪn'taɪtəl, ɛn-] *vt* **-tled; -tling** **1** NAME : titular, intitular **2** : dar derecho a <it entitles you to enter free : le da derecho a entrar gratis> **3 to be entitled to** : tener derecho a

entitlement [ɪn'taɪtəlmənt, ɛn-] *n* RIGHT : derecho *m*

entity ['ɛntəti] *n, pl* **-ties** : entidad *f*, ente *m*

entomologist [,ɛntə'mɑləʤɪst] *n* : entomólogo *m*, -ga *f*

entomology [,ɛntə'mɑləʤi] *n* : entomología *f*

entourage [,ɑntʊ'rɑʒ] *n* : séquito *m*

entrails ['ɛn,treɪlz, -trəlz] *npl* : entrañas *fpl*, vísceras *fpl*

entrance[1] [ɪn'træn*t*s, ɛn-] *vt* **-tranced; -trancing** : encantar, embelesar, fascinar

entrance[2] ['ɛntrən*t*s] *n* **1** ENTERING : entrada *f* <to make an entrance : entrar en escena> **2** ENTRY : entrada *f*, puerta *f* **3** ADMISSION : entrada *f*, ingreso *m* <entrance examination : examen de ingreso>

entrant ['ɛntrənt] *n* : candidato *m*, -ta *f* (en un examen); participante *mf* (en un concurso)

entrap [ɪn'træp, ɛn-] *vt* **-trapped; -trapping** : atrapar, entrampar, hacer caer en una trampa

entrapment [ɪn'træpmənt, ɛn-] *n* : captura *f*

entreat [ɪn'tri:t, ɛn-] *vt* : suplicar, rogar

entreaty [ɪn'tri:ti, ɛn-] *n, pl* **-treaties** : ruego *m*, súplica *f*

entrée *or* **entree** ['ɑn,treɪ, ,ɑn'-] *n* : plato *m* principal

entrench [ɪn'trɛntʃ, ɛn-] *vt* **1** FORTIFY : atrincherar (una posición militar) **2** : consolidar, afianzar <firmly entrenched in his job : afianzado en su puesto>

entrepreneur [,ɑntrəprə'nər, -'njʊr] *n* : empresario *m*, -ria *f*

entrust [ɪn'trʌst, ɛn-] *vt* : confiar, encomendar

entry ['ɛntri] *n, pl* **-tries** **1** ENTRANCE : entrada *f* **2** NOTATION : entrada *f*, anotación *f*

entwine [ɪn'twaɪn, ɛn-] *vt* **-twined; -twining** : entrelazar, entretejer, entrecruzar

enumerate [ɪ'nu:mə,reɪt, ɛ-, -'nju:-] *vt* **-ated; -ating** **1** LIST : enumerar **2** COUNT : contar, enumerar

enumeration [ɪ,nu:mə'reɪʃən, ɛ-, -,nju:-] *n* : enumeración *f*, lista *f*

enunciate [i'nʌn*t*si,eɪt, ɛ-] *vt* **-ated; -ating** **1** STATE : enunciar, decir **2** PRONOUNCE : articular, pronunciar

enunciation [i,nʌn*t*si'eɪʃən, ɛ-] *n* **1** STATEMENT : enunciación *f*, declaración *f* **2** ARTICULATION : articulación *f*, pronunciación *f*, dicción *f*

envelop [ɪn'vɛləp, ɛn-] *vt* : envolver, cubrir

envelope ['ɛnvə,lo:p, 'ɑn-] *n* : sobre *m*

enviable ['ɛnviəbəl] *adj* : envidiable

envious ['ɛnviəs] *adj* : envidioso — **enviously** *adv*

environment [ɪnˈvaɪrənmənt, ɛn-, -ˈvaɪərn-] *n* : medio *m* (ambiente), ambiente *m*, entorno *m*
environmental [ɪnˌvaɪrənˈmɛntəl, ɛn-, -ˌvaɪərn-] *adj* : ambiental
environmentalist [ɪnˌvaɪrənˈmɛntəlɪst, ɛn-, -ˌvaɪərn-] *n* : ecologista *mf*
environs [ɪnˈvaɪrənz, ɛn-, -ˈvaɪərnz] *npl* : alrededores *mpl*, entorno *m*, inmediaciones *fpl*
envisage [ɪnˈvɪzɪʤ, ɛn-] *vt* **-aged; -aging 1** IMAGINE : imaginarse, concebir **2** FORESEE : prever
envision [ɪnˈvɪʒən, ɛn-] *vt* : imaginar
envoy [ˈɛnˌvɔɪ, ˈɑn-] *n* : enviado *m*, -da *f*
envy[1] [ˈɛnvi] *vt* **-vied; -vying** : envidiar
envy[2] *n, pl* **envies** : envidia *f*
enzyme [ˈɛnˌzaɪm] *n* : enzima *f*
eon [ˈiːən, iːˌɑn] → **aeon**
epaulet [ˌɛpəˈlɛt] *n* : charretera *f*
ephemeral [ɪˈfɛmərəl, -ˈfiː-] *adj* : efímero, fugaz
epic[1] [ˈɛpɪk] *adj* : épico
epic[2] *n* : poema *m* épico, epopeya *f*
epicure [ˈɛpɪˌkjʊr] *n* : epicúreo *m*, -rea *f*; gastrónomo *m*, -ma *f*
epicurean [ˌɛpɪkjʊˈriːən, -ˈkjʊriən] *adj* : epicúreo
epidemic[1] [ˌɛpəˈdɛmɪk] *adj* : epidémico
epidemic[2] *n* : epidemia *f*
epidermis [ˌɛpəˈdərməs] *n* : epidermis *f*
epigram [ˈɛpəˌgræm] *n* : epigrama *m*
epilepsy [ˈɛpəˌlɛpsi] *n, pl* **-sies** : epilepsia *f*
epileptic[1] [ˌɛpəˈlɛptɪk] *adj* : epiléptico
epileptic[2] *n* : epiléptico *m*, -ca *f*
epilogue [ˈɛpəˌlɔg, -ˌlɑg] *n* : epílogo *m*
epiphany [ɪˈpɪfəni] *n, pl* **-nies 1 Epiphany** : Epifanía *f* **2 to have an epiphany** : tener una revelación
episcopal [ɪˈpɪskəpəl] *adj* : episcopal
Episcopalian [ɪˌpɪskəˈpeɪljən] *n* : episcopalista *mf*; episcopaliano *m*, -na *f*
episode [ˈɛpəˌsoːd] *n* : episodio *m*
episodic [ˌɛpəˈsɑdɪk] *adj* : episódico
epistle [ɪˈpɪsəl] *n* : epístola *f*, carta *f*
epitaph [ˈɛpəˌtæf] *n* : epitafio *m*
epithet [ˈɛpəˌθɛt, -θət] *n* : epíteto *m*
epitome [ɪˈpɪṭəmi] *n* **1** SUMMARY : epítome *m*, resumen *m* **2** EMBODIMENT : personificación *f*
epitomize [ɪˈpɪṭəˌmaɪz] *vt* **-mized; -mizing 1** SUMMARIZE : resumir **2** EMBODY : ser la personificación de, personificar
epoch [ˈɛpək, ˈɛˌpɑk, ˈiːˌpɑk] *n* : época *f*, era *f*
epoxy [ɪˈpɑksi] *n, pl* **epoxies** : resina *f* epoxídica
equable [ˈɛkwəbəl, ˈiː-] *adj* **1** CALM, STEADY : ecuánime **2** UNIFORM : estable (dícese de la temperatura), constante (dícese del clima), uniforme
equably [ˈɛkwəbli, ˈiː-] *adv* : con ecuanimidad
equal[1] [ˈiːkwəl] *vt* **equaled** *or* **equalled; equaling** *or* **equalling 1** : ser igual a <two plus three equals five : dos más tres es igual a cinco> **2** MATCH : igualar
equal[2] *adj* **1** SAME : igual **2** ADEQUATE : adecuado, capaz
equal[3] *n* : igual *mf*
equality [ɪˈkwɑləṭi] *n, pl* **-ties** : igualdad *f*
equalize [ˈiːkwəˌlaɪz] *vt* **-ized; -izing** : igualar, equiparar
equally [ˈiːkwəli] *adv* : igualmente, por igual
equanimity [ˌiːkwəˈnɪməṭi, ˌɛ-] *n, pl* **-ties** : ecuanimidad *f*
equate [ɪˈkweɪt] *vt* **equated; equating** : equiparar, identificar
equation [ɪˈkweɪʒən] *n* : ecuación *f*
equator [ɪˈkweɪṭər] *n* : ecuador *m*
equatorial [ˌiːkwəˈtoriəl, ˌɛ-] *adj* : ecuatorial
equestrian[1] [ɪˈkwɛstriən, ɛ-] *adj* : ecuestre
equestrian[2] *n* : jinete *mf*, caballista *mf*
equilateral [ˌiːkwəˈlæṭərəl, ˌɛ-] *adj* : equilátero
equilibrium [ˌiːkwəˈlɪbriəm, ˌɛ-] *n, pl* **-riums** *or* **-ria** [-briə] : equilibrio *m*
equine [ˈiːˌkwaɪn, ˈɛ-] *adj* : equino, hípico
equinox [ˈiːkwəˌnɑks, ˈɛ-] *n* : equinoccio *m*
equip [ɪˈkwɪp] *vt* **equipped; equipping 1** FURNISH : equipar **2** PREPARE : preparar
equipment [ɪˈkwɪpmənt] *n* : equipo *m*
equitable [ˈɛkwəṭəbəl] *adj* : equitativo, justo, imparcial
equity [ˈɛkwəṭi] *n, pl* **-ties 1** FAIRNESS : equidad *f*, imparcialidad *f* **2** VALUE : valor *m* líquido
equivalence [ɪˈkwɪvələnts] *n* : equivalencia *f*
equivalent[1] [ɪˈkwɪvələnt] *adj* : equivalente
equivalent[2] *n* : equivalente *m*
equivocal [ɪˈkwɪvəkəl] *adj* **1** AMBIGUOUS : equívoco, ambiguo **2** QUESTIONABLE : incierto, dudoso, sospechoso
equivocate [ɪˈkwɪvəˌkeɪt] *vi* **-cated; -cating** : usar lenguaje equívoco, andarse con evasivas
equivocation [ɪˌkwɪvəˈkeɪʃən] *n* : evasiva *f*, subterfugio *m*
era [ˈɪrə, ˈɛrə, ˈiːrə] *n* : era *f*, época *f*
eradicate [ɪˈrædəˌkeɪt] *vt* **-cated; -cating** : erradicar
erase [ɪˈreɪs] *vt* **erased; erasing** : borrar
eraser [ɪˈreɪsər] *n* : goma *f* de borrar, borrador *m*
erasure [ɪˈreɪʃər] *n* : tachadura *f*
ere[1] [ˈɛr] *conj* : antes de que
ere[2] *prep* **1** : antes de **2 ere long** : dentro de poco
erect[1] [ɪˈrɛkt] *vt* **1** CONSTRUCT : erigir, construir **2** RAISE : levantar **3** ESTABLISH : establecer
erect[2] *adj* : erguido, derecho, erecto

erection [ɪˈrɛkʃən] *n* **1** : erección *f* (en fisiología) **2** BUILDING : construcción *f*

ergonomics [ˌərgəˈnɑmɪks] *npl* : ergonomía *f*

ermine [ˈərmən] *n* : armiño *m*

erode [ɪˈro:d] *vt* **eroded; eroding** : erosionar (el suelo), corroer (metales)

erosion [ɪˈro:ʒən] *n* : erosión *f*, corrosión *f*

erotic [ɪˈrɑt̬ɪk] *adj* : erótico — **erotically** [-t̬ɪkli] *adv*

eroticism [ɪˈrɑt̬əˌsɪzəm] *n* : erotismo *m*

err [ˈɛr, ˈər] *vi* : cometer un error, equivocarse, errar

errand [ˈɛrənd] *n* : mandado *m*, encargo *m*, recado *m Spain* ⟨an errand of mercy : una misión de caridad⟩

errant [ˈɛrənt] *adj* **1** WANDERING : errante **2** ASTRAY : descarriado

erratic [ɪˈræt̬ɪk] *adj* **1** INCONSISTENT : errático, irregular, inconsistente **2** ECCENTRIC : excéntrico, raro

erratically [ɪˈræt̬ɪkli] *adv* : erráticamente, de manera irregular

erroneous [ɪˈro:niəs, ɛ-] *adj* : erróneo — **erroneously** *adv*

error [ˈɛrər] *n* : error *m*, equivocación *f* ⟨to be in error : estar equivocado⟩

ersatz [ˈɛrˌsɑts, ˈərˌsæts] *adj* : artificial, sustituto

erstwhile [ˈərstˌ*h*waɪl] *adj* : antiguo

erudite [ˈɛrəˌdaɪt, ˈɛrjʊ-] *adj* : erudito, letrado

erudition [ˌɛrəˈdɪʃən, ˌɛrjʊ-] *n* : erudición *f*

erupt [ɪˈrʌpt] *vi* **1** : hacer erupción (dícese de un volcán o un sarpullido) **2** : estallar (dícese de la cólera o la violencia)

eruption [ɪˈrʌpʃən] *n* : erupción *f*, estallido *m*

eruptive [ɪˈrʌptɪv] *adj* : eruptivo

escalate [ˈɛskəˌleɪt] *v* **-lated; -lating** *vt* : intensificar (un conflicto), aumentar (precios) — *vi* : intensificarse, aumentarse

escalation [ˌɛskəˈleɪʃən] *n* : intensificación *f*, escalada *f*, aumento *m*, subida *f*

escalator [ˈɛskəˌleɪtər] *n* : escalera *f* mecánica

escapade [ˈɛskəˌpeɪd] *n* : aventura *f*

escape[1] [ɪˈskeɪp, ɛ-] *v* **-caped; -caping** *vt* : escaparse de, librarse de, evitar — *vi* : escaparse, fugarse, huir

escape[2] *n* **1** FLIGHT : fuga *f*, huida *f*, escapada *f* **2** LEAKAGE : escape *m*, fuga *f* **3** : escapatoria *f*, evasión *f* ⟨to have no escape : no tener escapatoria⟩ ⟨escape from reality : evasión de la realidad⟩

escapee [ɪˌskeɪˈpi:, ˌɛ-] *n* : fugitivo *m*, -va *f*

escarole [ˈɛskəˌro:l] *n* : escarola *f*

escarpment [ɪsˈkɑrpmənt, ɛs-] *n* : escarpa *f*, escarpadura *f*

eschew [ɛˈʃu:, ɪsˈʧu:] *vt* : evitar, rehuir, abstenerse de

escort[1] [ɪˈskɔrt, ɛ-] *vt* **1** : escoltar ⟨to escort a ship : escoltar un barco⟩ **2** ACCOMPANY : acompañar

escort[2] [ˈɛsˌkɔrt] *n* **1** : escolta *f* ⟨armed escort : escolta armada⟩ **2** COMPANION : acompañante *mf*; compañero *m*, -ra *f*

escrow [ˈɛsˌkro:] *n* **in escrow** : en depósito, en custodia de un tercero

Eskimo [ˈɛskəˌmo:] *n* **1** : esquimal *mf* **2** : esquimal *m* (idioma) — **Eskimo** *adj*

esophagus [ɪˈsɑfəgəs, i:-] *n, pl* **-gi** [-ˌgaɪ, -ˌʤaɪ] : esófago *m*

esoteric [ˌɛsəˈtɛrɪk] *adj* : esotérico, hermético

especially [ɪˈspɛʃəli] *adv* : especialmente, particularmente

espionage [ˈɛspiəˌnɑʒ, -ˌnɑʤ] *n* : espionaje *m*

espouse [ɪˈspaʊz, ɛ-] *vt* **espoused; espousing** **1** MARRY : casarse con **2** ADOPT, ADVOCATE : apoyar, adherirse a, adoptar

espresso [ˈɛsprɛˌso:] *n, pl* **-sos** : café *m* exprés

essay[1] [ˈɛseɪ, ˈɛˌseɪ] *vt* : intentar, tratar

essay[2] [ˈɛˌseɪ] *n* **1** COMPOSITION : ensayo *m*, trabajo *m* **2** ATTEMPT : intento *m*

essayist [ˈɛˌseɪɪst] *n* : ensayista *mf*

essence [ˈɛsənts] *n* **1** CORE : esencia *f*, núcleo *m*, meollo *m* ⟨in essence : esencialmente⟩ **2** EXTRACT : esencia *f*, extracto *m* **3** PERFUME : esencia *f*, perfume *m*

essential[1] [ɪˈsɛnʧəl] *adj* : esencial, imprescindible, fundamental — **essentially** *adv*

essential[2] *n* : elemento *m* esencial, lo imprescindible

establish [ɪˈstæblɪʃ, ɛ-] *vt* **1** FOUND : establecer, fundar **2** SET UP : establecer, instaurar, instituir **3** PROVE : demostrar, probar

establishment [ɪˈstæblɪʃmənt, ɛ-] *n* **1** ESTABLISHING : establecimiento *m*, fundación *f*, instauración *f* **2** BUSINESS : negocio *m*, establecimiento *m* **3 the Establishment** : la clase dirigente

estate [ɪˈsteɪt, ɛ-] *n* **1** POSSESSIONS : bienes *mpl*, propiedad *f*, patrimonio *m* **2** PROPERTY : hacienda *f*, finca *f*, propiedad *f*

esteem[1] [ɪˈsti:m, ɛ-] *vt* : estimar, apreciar

esteem[2] *n* : estima *f*, aprecio *m*

ester [ˈɛstər] *n* : éster *m*

esthetic [ɛsˈθɛt̬ɪk] → **aesthetic**

estimable [ˈɛstəməbəl] *adj* : estimable

estimate[1] [ˈɛstəˌmeɪt] *vt* **-mated; -mating** : calcular, estimar

estimate[2] [ˈɛstəmət] *n* **1** : cálculo *m* aproximado ⟨to make an estimate : hacer un cálculo⟩ **2** ASSESSMENT : valoración *f*, estimación *f*

estimation [ˌɛstəˈmeɪʃən] *n* **1** JUDGMENT : juicio *m*, opinión *f* ⟨in my estimation : en mi opinión, según mis cálculos⟩ **2** ESTEEM : estima *f*, aprecio *m*

estimator [ˈɛstəˌmeɪt̬ər] *n* : tasador *m*, -dora *f*
Estonian [ɛˈsto:niən] *n* : estonio *m*, -nia *f* — **Estonian** *adj*
estrange [ɪˈstreɪndʒ, ɛ-] *vt* **-tranged; -tranging** : enajenar, apartar, alejar
estrangement [ɪˈstreɪndʒmənt, ɛ-] *n* : alejamiento *m*, distanciamiento *m*
estrogen [ˈɛstrədʒən] *n* : estrógeno *m*
estrus [ˈɛstrəs] *n* : celo *m*
estuary [ˈɛstʃʊˌwɛri] *n, pl* **-aries** : estuario *m*, -ría *f*
et cetera [ɛtˈsɛt̬ərə, -ˈsɛtrə] : etcétera
etch [ˈɛtʃ] *v* : grabar al aguafuerte
etching [ˈɛtʃɪŋ] *n* : aguafuerte *m*, grabado *m* al aguafuerte
eternal [ɪˈtərnəl, i:-] *adj* **1** EVERLASTING : eterno **2** INTERMINABLE : constante, incesante
eternally [ɪˈtərnəli, i:-] *adv* : eternamente, para siempre
eternity [ɪˈtərnət̬i, i:-] *n, pl* **-ties** : eternidad *f*
ethane [ˈɛˌθeɪn] *n* : etano *m*
ethanol [ˈɛθəˌnɔl, -ˌno:l] *n* : etanol *m*
ether [ˈi:θər] *n* : éter *m*
ethereal [ɪˈθɪriəl, i:-] *adj* **1** CELESTIAL : etéreo, celeste **2** DELICATE : delicado
ethical [ˈɛθɪkəl] *adj* : ético — **ethically** *adv*
ethics [ˈɛθɪks] *ns & pl* **1** : ética *f* **2** MORALITY : ética *f*, moral *f*, moralidad *f*
Ethiopian [ˌi:θiˈo:piən] *n* : etíope *mf* — **Ethiopian** *adj*
ethnic [ˈɛθnɪk] *adj* : étnico
ethnologist [ɛθˈnɑlədʒɪst] *n* : etnólogo *m*, -ga *f*
ethnology [ɛθˈnɑlədʒi] *n* : etnología *f*
etiquette [ˈɛt̬ɪkət, -ˌkɛt] *n* : etiqueta *f*, protocolo *m*
etymological [ˌɛt̬əməˈlɑdʒɪkəl] *adj* : etimológico
etymology [ˌɛt̬əˈmɑlədʒi] *n, pl* **-gies** : etimología *f*
eucalyptus [ˌju:kəˈlɪptəs] *n, pl* **-ti** [-ˌtaɪ] *or* **-tuses** [-təsəz] : eucalipto *m*
Eucharist [ˈju:kərɪst] *n* : Eucaristía *f*
eulogize [ˈju:ləˌdʒaɪz] *vt* **-gized; -gizing** : elogiar, encomiar
eulogy [ˈju:lədʒi] *n, pl* **-gies** : elogio *m*, encomio *m*, panegírico *m*
eunuch [ˈju:nək] *n* : eunuco *m*
euphemism [ˈju:fəˌmɪzəm] *n* : eufemismo *m*
euphemistic [ˌju:fəˈmɪstɪk] *adj* : eufemístico
euphony [ˈju:fəni] *n, pl* **-nies** : eufonía *f*
euphoria [jʊˈforiə] *n* : euforia *f*
euphoric [jʊˈforɪk] *adj* : eufórico
European [ˌjʊrəˈpi:ən] *n* : europeo *m*, europea *f* — **European** *adj*
euthanasia [ˌju:θəˈneɪʒə, -ʒiə] *n* : eutanasia *f*
evacuate [ɪˈvækjʊˌeɪt] *v* **-ated; -ating** *vt* VACATE : evacuar, desalojar — *vi* WITHDRAW : retirarse
evacuation [ɪˌvækjʊˈeɪʃən] *n* : evacuación *f*, desalojo *m*
evade [ɪˈveɪd] *vt* **evaded; evading** : evadir, eludir, esquivar
evaluate [ɪˈvæljʊˌeɪt] *vt* **-ated; -ating** : evaluar, valorar, tasar
evaluation [ɪˌvæljʊˈeɪʃən] *n* : evaluación *f*, valoración *f*, tasación *f*
evangelical [ˌi:ˌvænˈdʒɛlɪkəl, ˌɛvən-] *adj* : evangélico
evangelist [ɪˈvændʒəlɪst] *n* **1** : evangelista *m* **2** PREACHER : predicador *m*, -dora *f*
evaporate [ɪˈvæpəˌreɪt] *vi* **-rated; -rating** **1** VAPORIZE : evaporarse **2** VANISH : evaporarse, desvanecerse, esfumarse
evaporation [ɪˌvæpəˈreɪʃən] *n* : evaporación *f*
evasion [ɪˈveɪʒən] *n* : evasión *f*
evasive [ɪˈveɪsɪv] *adj* : evasivo
evasiveness [ɪˈveɪsɪvnəs] *n* : carácter *m* evasivo
eve [ˈi:v] *n* **1** : víspera *f* ⟨on the eve of the festivities : en vísperas de las festividades⟩ **2** → **evening**
even[1] [ˈi:vən] *vt* **1** LEVEL : allanar, nivelar, emparejar **2** EQUALIZE : igualar, equilibrar — *vi* **to even out** : nivelarse, emparejarse
even[2] *adv* **1** : hasta, incluso ⟨even a child can do it : hasta un niño puede hacerlo⟩ ⟨he looked content, even happy : se le veía satisfecho, incluso feliz⟩ **2** (*in negative constructions*) : ni siquiera ⟨he didn't even try : ni siquiera lo intentó⟩ **3** (*in comparisons*) : aún, todavía ⟨even better : aún mejor, todavía mejor⟩ **4** **even if** : aunque **5** **even so** : aun así **6** **even though** : aun cuando, a pesar de que
even[3] *adj* **1** SMOOTH : uniforme, liso, parejo **2** FLAT : plano, llano **3** EQUAL : igual, igualado ⟨an even score : un marcador igualado⟩ **4** REGULAR : regular, constante ⟨an even pace : un ritmo constante⟩ **5** EXACT : exacto, justo **6** : par ⟨even number : número par⟩ **7** **to be even** : estar en paz, estar a mano **8** **to get even** : desquitarse, vengarse
evening [ˈi:vnɪŋ] *n* : tarde *f*, noche *f* ⟨in the evening : por la noche⟩
evenly [ˈi:vənli] *adv* **1** UNIFORMLY : de modo uniforme, de manera constante **2** FAIRLY : igualmente, equitativamente
evenness [ˈi:vənnəs] *n* : uniformidad *f*, igualdad *f*, regularidad *f*
event [ɪˈvɛnt] *n* **1** : acontecimiento *m*, suceso *m*, prueba *f* (en deportes) **2** **in the event that** : en caso de que
eventful [ɪˈvɛntfəl] *adj* : lleno de incidentes, memorable
eventual [ɪˈvɛntʃʊəl] *adj* : final, consiguiente
eventuality [ɪˌvɛntʃʊˈælət̬i] *n, pl* **-ties** : eventualidad *f*
eventually [ɪˈvɛntʃʊəli] *adv* : al fin, con el tiempo, algún día

ever [ˈɛvər] *adv* **1** ALWAYS : siempre ⟨as ever : como siempre⟩ ⟨ever since : desde entonces⟩ **2** (*in questions*) : alguna vez, algún día ⟨have you ever been to Mexico? : ¿has estado en México alguna vez?⟩ **3** (*in negative constructions*) : nunca ⟨doesn't he ever work? : ¿es que nunca trabaja?⟩ ⟨nobody ever helps me : nadie nunca me ayuda⟩ **4** (*in comparisons*) : nunca ⟨better than ever : mejor que nunca⟩ **5** (*as intensifier*) ⟨I'm ever so happy! : ¡estoy tan y tan feliz!⟩ ⟨he looks ever so angry : parece estar muy enojado⟩
evergreen[1] [ˈɛvərˌgri:n] *adj* : de hoja perenne
evergreen[2] *n* : planta *f* de hoja perenne
everlasting [ˌɛvərˈlæstɪŋ] *adj* : eterno, perpetuo, imperecedero
evermore [ˌɛvərˈmor] *adv* : eternamente
every [ˈɛvri] *adj* **1** EACH : cada ⟨every time : cada vez⟩ ⟨every other house : cada dos casas⟩ **2** ALL : todo ⟨every month : todos los meses⟩ ⟨every woman : toda mujer, todas las mujeres⟩ **3** COMPLETE : pleno, entero ⟨to have every confidence : tener plena confianza⟩
everybody [ˈɛvriˌbʌdi, -ˌbɑ-] *pron* : todos *mpl*, -das *fpl*; todo el mundo
everyday [ˌɛvriˈdeɪ, ˈɛvriˌ-] *adj* : cotidiano, diario, corriente ⟨everyday clothes : ropa de todos los días⟩
everyone [ˈɛvriˌwʌn] → **everybody**
everything [ˈɛvriˌθɪŋ] *pron* : todo
everywhere [ˈɛvriˌ*h*wɛr] *adv* : en todas partes, por todas partes, dondequiera ⟨I looked everywhere : busqué en todas partes⟩ ⟨everywhere we go : dondequiera que vayamos⟩
evict [ɪˈvɪkt] *vt* : desalojar, desahuciar
eviction [ɪˈvɪkʃən] *n* : desalojo *m*, desahucio *m*
evidence [ˈɛvədən*t*s] *n* **1** INDICATION : indicio *m*, señal *m* ⟨to be in evidence : estar a la vista⟩ **2** PROOF : evidencia *f*, prueba *f* **3** TESTIMONY : testimonio *m*, declaración *f* ⟨to give evidence : declarar como testigo, prestar declaración⟩
evident [ˈɛvidənt] *adj* : evidente, patente, manifiesto
evidently [ˈɛvidəntli, ˌɛviˈdɛntli] *adv* **1** CLEARLY : claramente, obviamente **2** APPARENTLY : aparentemente, evidentemente, al parecer
evil[1] [ˈi:vəl, -vɪl] *adj* **eviler** *or* **eviller**; **evilest** *or* **evillest** **1** WICKED : malvado, malo, maligno **2** HARMFUL : nocivo, dañino, pernicioso **3** UNPLEASANT : desagradable ⟨an evil odor : un olor horrible⟩
evil[2] *n* **1** WICKEDNESS : mal *m*, maldad *f* **2** MISFORTUNE : desgracia *f*, mal *m*
evildoer [ˌi:vəlˈdu:ər, ˌi:vɪl-] *n* : malvado *m*, -da *f*
evince [ɪˈvɪn*t*s] *vt* **evinced; evincing** : mostrar, manifestar, revelar
eviscerate [ɪˈvɪsəˌreɪt] *vt* **-ated; -ating** : eviscerar, destripar (un pollo, etc.)
evocation [ˌi:voˈkeɪʃən, ˌɛ-] *n* : evocación *f*
evocative [iˈvɑkət̬ɪv] *adj* : evocador
evoke [iˈvo:k] *vt* **evoked; evoking** : evocar, provocar
evolution [ˌɛvəˈlu:ʃən, ˌi:-] *n* : evolución *f*, desarrollo *m*
evolutionary [ˌɛvəˈlu:ʃəˌnɛri, ˌi:-] *adj* : evolutivo
evolve [iˈvɑlv] *vi* **evolved; evolving** : evolucionar, desarrollarse
ewe [ˈju:] *n* : oveja *f*
exacerbate [ɪgˈzæsərˌbeɪt] *vt* **-bated; -bating** : exacerbar
exact[1] [ɪgˈzækt, ɛ-] *vt* : exigir, imponer, arrancar
exact[2] *adj* : exacto, preciso — **exactly** *adv*
exacting [ɪˈzæktɪŋ, ɛg-] *adj* : exigente, riguroso
exactitude [ɪgˈzæktəˌtu:d, ɛg-, -ˌtju:d] *n* : exactitud *f*, precisión *f*
exaggerate [ɪgˈzæʤəˌreɪt, ɛg-] *v* **-ated; -ating** : exagerar
exaggerated [ɪgˈzæʤəˌreɪt̬əd, ɛg-] *adj* : exagerado — **exaggeratedly** *adv*
exaggeration [ɪgˌzæʤəˈreɪʃən, ɛg-] *n* : exageración *f*
exalt [ɪgˈzɔlt, ɛg-] *vt* : exaltar, ensalzar, glorificar
exaltation [ˌɛgˌzɔlˈteɪʃən, ˌɛkˌsɔl-] *n* : exaltación *f*
exam [ɪgˈzæm, ɛg-] → **examination**
examination [ɪgˌzæməˈneɪʃən, ɛg-] *n* **1** TEST : examen *m* **2** INSPECTION : inspección *f*, revisión *f* **3** INVESTIGATION : examen *m*, estudio *m*
examine [ɪgˈzæmən, ɛg-] *vt* **-ined; -ining** **1** TEST : examinar **2** INSPECT : inspeccionar, revisar **3** STUDY : examinar
example [ɪgˈzæmpəl, ɛg-] *n* : ejemplo *m* ⟨for example : por ejemplo⟩ ⟨to set an example : dar ejemplo⟩
exasperate [ɪgˈzæspəˌreɪt, ɛg-] *vt* **-ated; -ating** : exasperar, sacar de quicio
exasperation [ɪgˌzæspəˈreɪʃən, ɛg-] *n* : exasperación *f*
excavate [ˈɛkskəˌveɪt] *vt* **-vated; -vating** : excavar
excavation [ˌɛkskəˈveɪʃən] *n* : excavación *f*
exceed [ɪkˈsi:d, ɛk-] *vt* **1** SURPASS : exceder, rebasar, sobrepasar **2** : exceder de, sobrepasar ⟨not exceeding two months : que no exceda de dos meses⟩
exceedingly [ɪkˈsi:dɪŋli, ɛk-] *adv* : extremadamente, sumamente
excel [ɪkˈsɛl, ɛk-] *v* **-celled; -celling** *vi* : sobresalir, descollar, lucirse — *vt* : superar
excellence [ˈɛksələn*t*s] *n* : excelencia *f*
excellency [ˈɛksələn*t*si] *n, pl* **-cies** : excelencia *f* ⟨His Excellency : Su Excelencia⟩
excellent [ˈɛksələnt] *adj* : excelente, sobresaliente — **excellently** *adv*

except[1] [ɪk'sɛpt] *vt* : exceptuar, excluir

except[2] *conj* : pero, si no fuera por

except[3] *prep* : excepto, menos, salvo ⟨everyone except Carlos : todos menos Carlos⟩

exception [ɪk'sɛpʃən] *n* **1** : excepción *f* **2 to take exception to** : ofenderse por, objetar a

exceptional [ɪk'sɛpʃənəl] *adj* : excepcional, extraordinario — **exceptionally** *adv*

excerpt[1] [ɛk'sərpt, ɛg'zərpt, 'ɛk,-, 'g,-] *vt* : escoger, seleccionar

excerpt[2] ['ɛk,sərpt, 'ɛg,zərpt] *n* : pasaje *m*, selección *f*

excess[1] ['ɛk,sɛs, ɪk'sɛs] *adj* **1** : excesivo, de sobra **2 excess baggage** : exceso *m* de equipaje

excess[2] [ɪk'sɛs, 'ɛk,sɛs] *n* **1** SUPERFLUITY : exceso *m*, superfluidad *f* ⟨an excess of energy : un exceso de energía⟩ **2** SURPLUS : excedente *m*, sobrante *m* ⟨in excess of : superior a⟩

excessive [ɪk'sɛsɪv, ɛk-] *adj* : excesivo, exagerado, desmesurado — **excessively** *adv*

exchange[1] [ɪks'ʧeɪnʤ, ɛks-; 'ɛks-,ʧeɪnʤ] *vt* **-changed; -changing** : cambiar, intercambiar, canjear

exchange[2] *n* **1** : cambio *m*, intercambio *m*, canje *m* **2 stock exchange** : bolsa *f* (de valores)

exchangeable [ɪks'ʧeɪnʤəbəl, ɛks-] *adj* : canjeable

excise[1] [ɪk'saɪz, ɛk-] *vt* **-cised; -cising** : extirpar

excise[2] ['ɛk,saɪz] *n* **excise tax** : impuesto *m* interno, impuesto *m* sobre el consumo

excision [ɪk'sɪʒən, ɛk-] *n* : extirpación *f*, excisión *f*

excitability [ɪk,saɪtə'bɪləṭi, ɛk-] *n* : excitabilidad *f*

excitable [ɪk'saɪṭəbəl, ɛk-] *adj* : excitable

excitation [,ɛk,saɪ'teɪʃən] *n* : excitación *f*

excite [ɪk'saɪt, ɛk-] *vt* **-cited; -citing** **1** AROUSE, STIMULATE : excitar, mover, estimular **2** ANIMATE : entusiasmar, animar **3** EVOKE, PROVOKE : provocar, despertar, suscitar ⟨to excite curiosity : despertar la curiosidad⟩

excited [ɪk'saɪṭəd, ɛk-] *adj* **1** STIMULATED : excitado, estimulado **2** ENTHUSIASTIC : entusiasmado, emocionado

excitedly [ɪk'saɪṭədli, ɛk-] *adv* : con excitación, con entusiasmo

excitement [ɪk'saɪtmənt, ɛk-] *n* **1** ENTHUSIASM : entusiasmo *m*, emoción *f* **2** AGITATION : agitación *f*, alboroto *m*, conmoción *f* **3** AROUSAL : excitación *f*

exciting [ɪk'saɪṭɪŋ, ɛk-] *adj* **1** : emocionante **2** AROUSING : excitante

exclaim [ɪks'kleɪm, ɛk-] *v* : exclamar

exclamation [,ɛksklə'meɪʃən] *n* : exclamación *f*

exclamation point *n* : signo *m* de admiración

exclamatory [ɪks'klæmə,tori, ɛks-] *adj* : exclamativo

exclude [ɪks'klu:d, ɛks-] *vt* **-cluded; -cluding** **1** BAR : excluir, descartar, no admitir **2** EXPEL : expeler, expulsar

exclusion [ɪks'klu:ʒən, ɛks-] *n* : exclusión *f*

exclusive[1] [ɪks'klu:sɪv, ɛks-] *adj* **1** SOLE : exclusivo, único **2** SELECT : exclusivo, selecto

exclusive[2] *n* : exclusiva *f*

exclusively [ɪks'klu:sɪvli, ɛks-] *adv* : exclusivamente, únicamente

exclusiveness [ɪks'klu:sɪvnəs, ɛks-] *n* : exclusividad *f*

excommunicate [,ɛkskə'mju:nə,keɪt] *vt* **-cated; -cating** : excomulgar

excommunication [,ɛkskə,mju:nə'keɪʃən] *n* : excomunión *f*

excrement ['ɛkskrəmənt] *n* : excremento *m*

excrete [ɪk'skri:t, ɛk-] *vt* **-creted; -creting** : excretar

excretion [ɪk'skri:ʃən, ɛk-] *n* : excreción *f*

excruciating [ɪk'skru:ʃi,eɪṭɪŋ, ɛk-] *adj* : insoportable, atroz, terrible — **excruciatingly** *adv*

exculpate ['ɛkskəl,peɪt] *vt* **-pated; -pating** : exculpar

excursion [ɪk'skərʒən, ɛk-] *n* **1** OUTING : excursión *f*, paseo *m* **2** DIGRESSION : digresión *f*

excuse[1] [ɪk'skju:z, ɛk-] *vt* **-cused; -cusing** **1** PARDON : disculpar, perdonar ⟨excuse me : con permiso, perdóneme, perdón⟩ **2** EXEMPT : eximir, disculpar **3** JUSTIFY : excusar, justificar

excuse[2] [ɪk'skju:s, ɛk-] *n* **1** JUSTIFICATION : excusa *f*, justificación *f* **2** PRETEXT : pretexto *m* **3 to make one's excuses to someone** : pedirle disculpas a alguien

execute ['ɛksɪ,kju:t] *vt* **-cuted; -cuting** **1** CARRY OUT : ejecutar, llevar a cabo, desempeñar **2** ENFORCE : ejecutar, cumplir (un testamento, etc.) **3** KILL : ejecutar, ajusticiar

execution [,ɛksɪ'kju:ʃən] *n* **1** PERFORMANCE : ejecución *f*, desempeño *m* **2** IMPLEMENTATION : cumplimiento *m* **3** : ejecución *f* (por un delito)

executioner [,ɛksɪ'kju:ʃənər] *n* : verdugo *m*

executive[1] [ɪg'zɛkjəṭɪv, ɛg-] *adj* : ejecutivo

executive[2] *n* : ejecutivo *m*, -va *f*

executor [ɪg'zɛkjəṭər, ɛg-] *n* : albacea *m*, testamentario *m*

executrix [ɪg'zɛkjə,trɪks, ɛg-] *n, pl* **executrices** [-,zɛkjə'traɪ,si:z] *or* **executrixes** [-'zɛkjə,trɪksəz] : albacea *f*, testamentaria *f*

exemplary [ɪg'zɛmpləri, ɛg-] *adj* : ejemplar

exemplify [ɪg'zɛmplə,faɪ, ɛg-] *vt* **-fied; -fying** : ejemplificar, ilustrar, demostrar

exempt[1] [ɪg'zɛmpt, ɛg-] *vt* : eximir, dispensar, exonerar
exempt[2] *adj* : exento, eximido
exemption [ɪg'zɛmpʃən, ɛg-] *n* : exención *f*
exercise[1] ['ɛksər,saɪz] *v* **-cised; -cising** *vt* **1** : ejercitar (el cuerpo) **2** USE : ejercer, hacer uso de — *vi* : hacer ejercicio
exercise[2] *n* **1** : ejercicio *m* **2 exercises** *npl* WORKOUT : ejercicios *mpl* físicos **3 exercises** *npl* CEREMONY : ceremonia *f*
exert [ɪg'zərt, ɛg-] *vt* **1** : ejercer, emplear **2 to exert oneself** : esforzarse
exertion [ɪg'zərʃən, ɛg-] *n* **1** USE : ejercicio *m* (de autoridad, etc.), uso *m* (de fuerza, etc.) **2** EFFORT : esfuerzo *m*, empeño *m*
exhalation [,ɛksə'leɪʃən, ,ɛkshə-] *n* : exhalación *f*, espiración *f*
exhale [ɛks'heɪl] *v* **-haled; -haling** *vt* **1** : exhalar, espirar **2** EMIT : exhalar, despedir, emitir — *vi* : espirar
exhaust[1] [ɪg'zɔst, ɛg-] *vt* **1** DEPLETE : agotar **2** TIRE : cansar, fatigar, agotar **3** EMPTY : vaciar
exhaust[2] *n* **1 exhaust fumes** : gases *mpl* de escape **2 exhaust pipe** : tubo *m* de escape **3 exhaust system** : sistema *m* de escape
exhausted [ɪg'zɔstəd, ɛg-] *adj* : agotado, derrengado
exhausting [ɪg'zɔstɪŋ, ɛg-] *adj* : extenuante, agotador
exhaustion [ɪg'zɔstʃən, ɛg-] *n* : agotamiento *m*
exhaustive [ɪg'zɔstɪv, ɛg-] *adj* : exhaustivo
exhibit[1] [ɪg'zɪbət, ɛg-] *vt* **1** DISPLAY : exhibir, exponer **2** PRODUCE, SHOW : mostrar, presentar
exhibit[2] *n* **1** OBJECT : objeto *m* expuesto **2** EXHIBITION : exposición *f*, exhibición *f* **3** EVIDENCE : prueba *f* instrumental
exhibition [,ɛksə'bɪʃən] *n* **1** : exposición *f*, exhibición *f* **2 to make an exhibition of oneself** : dar el espectáculo, hacer el ridículo
exhibitor [ɪg'zɪbət̬ər] *n* : expositor *m*, -tora *f*
exhilarate [ɪg'zɪlə,reɪt, ɛg-] *vt* **-rated; -rating** : alegrar, levantar el ánimo de
exhilaration [ɪg,zɪlə'reɪʃən, ɛg-] *n* : alegría *f*, regocijo *m*, júbilo *m*
exhort [ɪg'zɔrt, ɛg-] *vt* : exhortar
exhortation [,ɛk,sɔr'teɪʃən, -sər-; ,ɛg-,zɔr-] *n* : exhortación *f*
exhumation [,ɛksju'meɪʃən, -hju-; ,ɛgzu-, -zju-] *n* : exhumación *f*
exhume [ɪg'zu:m, -'zju:m; ɪks'ju:m, -'hju:m] *vt* **-humed; -huming** : exhumar, desenterrar
exigencies ['ɛksɪdʒəntsiz, ɪg'zɪdʒən,si:z] *npl* : exigencias *fpl*
exile[1] ['ɛg,zaɪl, 'ɛk,saɪl] *vt* **exiled; exiling** : exiliar, desterrar
exile[2] *n* **1** BANISHMENT : exilio *m*, destierro *m* **2** OUTCAST : exiliado *m*, -da *f*; desterrado *m*, -da *f*
exist [ɪg'zɪst, ɛg-] *vi* **1** BE : existir **2** LIVE : subsistir, vivir
existence [ɪg'zɪstənts, ɛg-] *n* : existencia *f*
existent [ɪg'zɪstənt, ɛg-] *adj* : existente
existing [ɪg'zɪstɪŋ] *adj* : existente
exit[1] ['ɛgzət, 'ɛksət] *vi* : salir, hacer mutis (en el teatro) — *vt* : salir de
exit[2] *n* **1** DEPARTURE : salida *f*, partida *f* **2** EGRESS : salida *f* ‹emergency exit : salida de emergencia›
exodus ['ɛksədəs] *n* : éxodo *m*
exonerate [ɪg'zɑnə,reɪt, ɛg-] *vt* **-ated; -ating** : exonerar, disculpar, absolver
exoneration [ɪg,zɑnə'reɪʃən, ɛg-] *n* : exoneración *f*
exorbitant [ɪg'zɔrbətənt, ɛg-] *adj* : exorbitante, excesivo
exorcise ['ɛk,sɔr,saɪz, -sər-] *vt* **-cised; -cising** : exorcizar
exorcism ['ɛksər,sɪzəm] *n* : exorcismo *m*
exotic[1] [ɪg'zɑtɪk, ɛg-] *adj* : exótico — **exotically** [-ɪkli] *adv*
exotic[2] *n* : planta *f* exótica
expand [ɪk'spænd, ɛk-] *vt* **1** ENLARGE : expandir, dilatar, aumentar, ampliar **2** EXTEND : extender — *vi* **1** ENLARGE : ampliarse, extenderse **2** : expandirse, dilatarse (dícese de los metales, gases, etc.)
expanse [ɪk'spænts, ɛk-] *n* : extensión *f*
expansion [ɪk'spæntʃən, ɛk-] *n* **1** ENLARGEMENT : expansión *f*, ampliación *f* **2** EXPANSE : extensión *f*
expansive [ɪk'spæntsɪv, ɛk-] *adj* **1** : expansivo **2** OUTGOING : expansivo, comunicativo **3** AMPLE : ancho, amplio — **expansively** *adv*
expansiveness [ɪk'spæntsɪvnəs, ɛk-] *n* : expansibilidad *f*
expatriate[1] [ɛks'peɪtri,eɪt] *vt* **-ated; -ating** : expatriar
expatriate[2] [ɛks'peɪtriət, -,eɪt] *adj* : expatriado
expatriate[3] [ɛks'peɪtriət, -,eɪt] *n* : expatriado *m*, -da *f*
expect [ɪk'spkt, ɛk-] *vt* **1** SUPPOSE : suponer, imaginarse **2** ANTICIPATE : esperar **3** COUNT ON, REQUIRE : contar con, esperar — *vi* **to be expecting** : estar embarazada
expectancy [ɪk'spɛktəntsi, ɛk-] *n, pl* **-cies** : expectativa *f*, esperanza *f*
expectant [ɪk'spɛktənt, ɛk-] *adj* **1** ANTICIPATING : expectante **2** EXPECTING : futuro ‹expectant mother : futura madre›
expectantly [ɪk'spɛktəntli, ɛk-] *adv* : con expectación
expectation [,ɛk,spɛk'teɪʃən] *n* **1** ANTICIPATION : expectación *f* **2** EXPECTANCY : expectativa *f*
expedient[1] [ɪk'spi:diənt, ɛk-] *adj* : conveniente, oportuno
expedient[2] *n* : expediente *m*, recurso *m*

expedite ['ɛkspə,daɪt] *vt* **-dited; -diting** **1** FACILITATE : facilitar, dar curso a **2** HASTEN : acelerar
expedition [,ɛkspə'dɪʃən] *n* : expedición *f*
expeditious [,ɛkspə'dɪʃəs] *adj* : pronto, rápido
expel [ɪk'spɛl, ɛk-] *vt* **-pelled; -pelling** : expulsar, expeler
expend [ɪk'spɛnd, ɛk-] *vt* **1** DISBURSE : gastar, desembolsar **2** CONSUME : consumir, agotar
expendable [ɪk'spɛndəbəl, ɛk-] *adj* : prescindible
expenditure [ɪk'spɛndɪʧər, ɛk-, -,ʧʊr] *n* : gasto *m*
expense [ɪk'spɛnts, ɛk-] *n* **1** COST : gasto *m* **2 expenses** *npl* : gastos *mpl*, expensas *fpl* **3 at the expense of** : a expensas de
expensive [ɪk'spɛntsɪv, ɛk-] *adj* : costoso, caro — **expensively** *adv*
experience[1] [ɪk'spɪriənts, ɛk-] *vt* **-enced; -encing** : experimentar (sentimientos), tener (dificultades), sufrir (una pérdida)
experience[2] *n* : experiencia *f*
experienced [ɪk'spɪriəntst, ɛk-] *adj* : con experiencia, experimentado
experiment[1] [ɪk'spɛrəmənt, ɛk-, -'spɪr-] *vi* : experimentar, hacer experimentos
experiment[2] *n* : experimento *m*
experimental [ɪk,spɛrə'mntəl, ɛk-, -,spɪr-] *adj* : experimental — **experimentally** *adv*
experimentation [ɪk,spɛrəmən'teɪʃən, ɛk-, -,spɪr-] *n* : experimentación *f*
expert[1] ['ɛk,spərt, ɪk'spərt] *adj* : experto, de experto, pericial (dícese de un testigo) — **expertly** *adv*
expert[2] ['ɛk,spərt] *n* : experto *m*, -ta *f*; perito *m*, -ta *f*; especialista *mf*
expertise [,ɛkspər'ti:z] *n* : pericia *f*, competencia *f*
expiate ['ɛkspi,eɪt] *vt* **-ated; -ating** : expiar
expiation [,ɛkspi'eɪʃən] *n* : expiación *f*
expiration [,ɛkspə'reɪʃən] *n* **1** EXHALATION : exhalación *f*, espiración *f* **2** DEATH : muerte *f* **3** TERMINATION : vencimiento *m*, caducidad *f*
expire [ɪk'spaɪr, ɛk-] *vi* **-pired; -piring** **1** EXHALE : espirar **2** DIE : expirar, morir **3** TERMINATE : caducar, vencer
explain [ɪk'spleɪn, ɛk-] *vt* : explicar
explanation [,ɛksplə'neɪʃən] *n* : explicación *f*
explanatory [ɪk'splænə,tori, ɛk-] *adj* : explicativo, aclaratorio
expletive ['ɛkspləṭɪv] *n* : improperio *m*, palabrota *f fam*, grosería *f*
explicable [ɛk'splɪkəbəl, 'ɛksplɪ-] *adj* : explicable
explicit [ɪk'splɪsət, ɛk-] *adj* : explícito, claro, categórico, rotundo — **explicitly** *adv*
explicitness [ɪk'splɪsətnəs, ɛk-] *n* : claridad *f*, carácter *m* explícito
explode [ɪk'splo:d, ɛk-] *v* **-ploded; -ploding** *vt* **1** BURST : hacer explosionar, hacer explotar **2** REFUTE : rebatir, refutar, desmentir — *vi* **1** BURST : explotar, estallar, reventar **2** SKYROCKET : dispararse
exploit[1] [ɪk'splɔɪt, ɛk-] *vt* : explotar, aprovecharse de
exploit[2] ['ɛk,splɔɪt] *n* : hazaña *f*, proeza *f*
exploitation [,ɛk,splɔɪ'teɪʃən] *n* : explotación *f*
exploration [,ɛksplə'reɪʃən] *n* : exploración *f*
exploratory [ɪk'splorə,tori, ɛk-] *adj* : exploratorio
explore [ɪk'splor, ɛk-] *vt* **-plored; -ploring** : explorar, investigar, examinar
explorer [ɪk'splorər, ɛk-] *n* : explorador *m*, -dora *f*
explosion [ɪk'splo:ʒən, ɛk-] *n* : explosión *f*, estallido *m*
explosive[1] [ɪk'splo:sɪv, ɛk-] *adj* : explosivo, fulminante — **explosively** *adv*
explosive[2] *n* : explosivo *m*
exponent [ɪk'spo:nənt, 'ɛk,spo:-] *n* **1** : exponente *m* **2** ADVOCATE : defensor *m*, -sora *f*; partidario *m*, -ria *f*
exponential [,ɛkspə'nɛnʧəl] *adj* : exponencial — **exponentially** *adv*
export[1] [ɛk'sport, 'ɛk,sport] *vt* : exportar
export[2] ['ɛk,sport] *n* **1** : artículo *m* de exportación **2** → **exportation**
exportation [,ɛk,spor'teɪʃən] *n* : exportación *f*
exporter [ɛk'sporṭər, 'ɛk,spor-] *n* : exportador *m*, -dora *f*
expose [ɪk'spo:z, ɛk-] *vt* **-posed; -posing** **1** : exponer (al peligro, a los elementos, a una enfermedad) **2** : exponer (una película a la luz) **3** DISCLOSE : descubrir, revelar, poner en evidencia **4** UNMASK : desenmascarar
exposé *or* **expose** [,ɛkspo'zeɪ] *n* : exposición *f* (de hechos), revelación *f* (de un escándalo)
exposed [ɪk'spo:zd, ɛk-] *adj* : descubierto, sin protección
exposition [,ɛkspə'zɪʃən] *n* : exposición *f*
exposure [ɪk'spo:ʒər, ɛk-] *n* **1** : exposición *f* **2** CONTACT : exposición *f*, experiencia *f*, contacto *m* **3** UNMASKING : desenmascaramiento *m* **4** ORIENTATION : orientación *f* ⟨a room with a northern exposure : una sala orientada al norte⟩
expound [ɪk'spaʊnd, ɛk-] *vt* : exponer, explicar — *vi* : hacer comentarios detallados
express[1] [ɪk'sprɛs, ɛk-] *vt* **1** SAY : expresar, comunicar **2** SHOW : expresar, manifestar, externar *Mex* **3** SQUEEZE : exprimir ⟨to express the juice from a lemon : exprimir el jugo de un limón⟩
express[2] *adv* : por correo exprés, por correo urgente

express[3] *adj* **1** EXPLICIT : expreso, manifiesto **2** SPECIFIC : específico ⟨for that express purpose : con ese fin específico⟩ **3** RAPID : expreso, rápido
express[4] *n* **1** : correo *m* exprés, correo *m* urgente **2** : expreso *m* (tren)
expression [ɪk'sprɛʃən, ɛk-] *n* **1** UTTERANCE : expresión *f* ⟨freedom of expression : libertad de expresión⟩ **2** : expresión *f* (en la matemática) **3** PHRASE : frase *f*, expresión *f* **4** LOOK : expresión *f*, cara *f*, gesto *m* ⟨with a sad expression : con un gesto de tristeza⟩
expressionless [ɪk'sprɛʃənləs, ɛk-] *adj* : inexpresivo
expressive [ɪk'sprɛsɪv, ɛk-] *adj* : expresivo
expressway [ɪk'sprɛs͵weɪ, ɛk-] *n* : autopista *f*
expulsion [ɪk'spʌlʃən, ɛk-] *n* : expulsión *f*
expurgate ['ɛkspər͵geɪt] *vt* **-gated; -gating** : expurgar
exquisite [ɛk'skwɪzət, 'ɛk͵skwɪ-] *adj* **1** FINE : exquisito, delicado, primoroso **2** INTENSE : intenso, extremo
extant ['ɛkstənt, ɛk'stænt] *adj* : existente
extemporaneous [ɛk͵stɛmpə'reɪniəs] *adj* : improvisado — **extemporaneously** *adv*
extend [ɪk'stɛnd, ɛk-] *vt* **1** STRETCH : extender, tender **2** PROLONG : prolongar, prorrogar **3** ENLARGE : agrandar, ampliar, aumentar **4** PROFFER : extender, dar, ofrecer — *vi* : extenderse
extended [ɪk'stɛndəd, ɛk-] *adj* LENGTHY : prolongado, largo
extension [ɪk'stɛntʃən, ɛk-] *n* **1** EXTENDING : extensión *f*, ampliación *f*, prórroga *f*, prolongación *f* **2** ANNEX : ampliación *f*, anexo *m* **3** : extensión *f* (de teléfono)
extensive [ɪk'stɛntsɪv, ɛk-] *adj* : extenso, vasto, amplio — **extensively** *adv*
extent [ɪk'stɛnt, ɛk-] *n* **1** SIZE : extensión *f*, magnitud *f* **2** DEGREE, SCOPE : alcance *m*, grado *m* ⟨to a certain extent : hasta cierto punto⟩
extenuate [ɪk'stɛnjə͵weɪt, ɛk-] *vt* **-ated; -ating** : atenuar, aminorar, mitigar ⟨extenuating circumstances : circunstancias atenuantes⟩
extenuation [ɪk͵stɛnjə'weɪʃən, ɛk-] *n* : atenuación *f*, aminoración *f*
exterior[1] [ɛk'stɪriər] *adj* : exterior
exterior[2] *n* : exterior *m*
exterminate [ɪk'stərmə͵neɪt, ɛk-] *vt* **-nated; -nating** : exterminar
extermination [ɪk͵stərmə'neɪʃən, ɛk-] *n* : exterminación *f*, exterminio *m*
exterminator [ɪk'stərmə͵neɪt̬ər, ɛk-] *n* : exterminador *m*, -dora *f*
external [ɪk'stərnəl, ɛk-] *adj* : externo, exterior — **externally** *adv*
extinct [ɪk'stɪŋkt, ɛk-] *adj* : extinto
extinction [ɪk'stɪŋkʃən, ɛk-] *n* : extinción *f*
extinguish [ɪk'stɪŋgwɪʃ, ɛk-] *vt* : extinguir, apagar
extinguisher [ɪk'stɪŋgwɪʃər, ɛk-] *n* : extinguidor *m*, extintor *m*
extirpate ['ɛkstər͵peɪt] *vt* **-pated; -pating** : extirpar, exterminar
extol [ɪk'sto:l, ɛk-] *vt* **-tolled; -tolling** : exaltar, ensalzar, alabar
extort [ɪk'stɔrt, ɛk-] *vt* : extorsionar
extortion [ɪk'stɔrʃən, ɛk-] *n* : extorsión *f*
extra[1] ['ɛkstrə] *adv* : extra, más, extremadamente, super ⟨extra special : súper especial⟩
extra[2] *adj* **1** ADDITIONAL : adicional, suplementario, de más **2** SUPERIOR : superior
extra[3] *n* : extra *m*
extract[1] [ɪk'strækt, ɛk-] *vt* : extraer, sacar
extract[2] ['ɛk͵strækt] *n* **1** EXCERPT : pasaje *m*, selección *f*, trozo *m* **2** : extracto *m* ⟨vanilla extract : extracto de vainilla⟩
extraction [ɪk'strækʃən, ɛk-] *n* : extracción *f*
extractor [ɪk'stræktər, ɛk-] *n* : extractor *m*
extracurricular [͵ɛkstrəkə'rɪkjələr] *adj* : extracurricular
extradite ['ɛkstrə͵daɪt] *vt* **-dited; -diting** : extraditar
extradition [͵ɛkstrə'dɪʃən] *n* : extradición *f*
extramarital [͵ɛkstrə'mærət̬əl] *adj* : extramatrimonial
extraneous [ɛk'streɪniəs] *adj* **1** OUTSIDE : extrínseco, externo **2** SUPERFLUOUS : superfluo, ajeno — **extraneously** *adv*
extraordinary [ɪk'strɔrdən͵ɛri, ͵ɛkstrə'ɔrd-] *adj* : extraordinario, excepcional — **extraordinarily** [ɪk͵strɔrdən'ɛrəli, ͵kstrə͵ɔrd-] *adv*
extrasensory [͵ɛkstrə'sɛntsəri] *adj* : extrasensorial
extraterrestrial[1] [͵ɛkstrətə'rɛstriəl] *adj* : extraterrestre
extraterrestrial[2] *n* : extraterrestre *mf*
extravagance [ɪk'strævɪgənts, ɛk-] *n* **1** EXCESS : exceso *m*, extravagancia *f* **2** WASTEFULNESS : derroche *m*, despilfarro *m* **3** LUXURY : lujo *m*
extravagant [ɪk'strævɪgənt, ɛk-] *adj* **1** EXCESSIVE : excesivo, extravagante **2** WASTEFUL : despilfarrador, derrochador, gastador **3** EXORBITANT : costoso, exorbitante
extravagantly [ɪk'strævɪgəntli, ɛk-] *adv* **1** LAVISHLY : a lo grande **2** EXCESSIVELY : exageradamente, desmesuradamente
extravaganza [ɪk͵strævə'gænzə, ɛk-] *n* : gran espectáculo *m*
extreme[1] [ɪk'stri:m, ɛk-] *adj* **1** UTMOST : extremo, sumo ⟨of extreme importance : de suma importancia⟩ **2** INTENSE : intenso, extremado ⟨extreme cold : frío extremado⟩ **3** EXCESSIVE : excesivo, extremo ⟨extreme views : opiniones extremas⟩ ⟨extreme measures : medidas excepcionales, medi-

das drásticas⟩ **4** OUTERMOST : extremo ⟨the extreme north : el norte extremo⟩

extreme[2] *n* **1** : extremo *m* **2 in the extreme** : en extremo, en sumo grado

extremely [ɪk'stri:mli, ɛk-] *adv* : sumamente, extremadamente, terriblemente

extremist [ɪk'stri:mɪst, ɛk-] *n* : extremista *mf* — **extremist** *adj*

extremity [ɪk'strɛməṭi, ɛk-] *n, pl* **-ties** **1** EXTREME : extremo *m* **2 extremities** *npl* LIMBS : extremidades *fpl*

extricate ['ɛkstrə,keɪt] *vt* **-cated; -cating** : librar, sacar

extrinsic [ɪk'strɪnzɪk, -'strɪntsɪk] *adj* : extrínseco

extrovert ['ɛkstrə,vərt] *n* : extrovertido *m*, -da *f*

extroverted ['ɛkstrə,vərṭəd] *adj* : extrovertido

extrude [ɪk'stru:d, ɛk-] *vt* **-truded; -truding** : extrudir, expulsar

exuberance [ɪg'zu:bərənts, ɛg-] *n* **1** JOYOUSNESS : euforia *f*, exaltación *f* **2** VIGOR : exuberancia *f*, vigor *m*

exuberant [ɪg'zu:bərənt, ɛg-] *adj* **1** JOYOUS : eufórico **2** LUSH : exuberante — **exuberantly** *adv*

exude [ɪg'zu:d, ɛg-] *vt* **-uded; -uding** **1** OOZE : rezumar, exudar **2** EMANATE : emanar, irradiar

exult [ɪg'zʌlt, ɛg-] *vi* : exultar, regocijarse

exultant [ɪg'zʌltənt, ɛg-] *adj* : exultante, jubiloso — **exultantly** *adv*

exultation [,ɛksəl'teɪʃən, ,ɛgzəl-] *n* : exultación *f*, júbilo *m*, alborozo *m*

eye[1] ['aɪ] *vt* **eyed; eyeing** *or* **eying** : mirar, observar

eye[2] *n* **1** : ojo *m* **2** VISION : visión *f*, vista *f*, ojo *m* ⟨a good eye for bargains : un buen ojo para las gangas⟩ **3** GLANCE : mirada *f*, ojeada *f* **4** ATTENTION : atención *f* ⟨to catch one's eye : llamar la atención⟩ **5** POINT OF VIEW : punto *m* de vista ⟨in the eyes of the law : según la ley⟩ **6** : ojo *m* (de una aguja, una papa, una tormenta)

eyeball ['aɪ,bɔl] *n* : globo *m* ocular

eyebrow ['aɪ,braʊ] *n* : ceja *f*

eyedropper ['aɪ,drɑpər] *n* : cuentagotas *f*

eyeglasses ['aɪ,glæsəz] *npl* : anteojos *mpl*, lentes *mpl*, espejuelos *mpl*, gafas *fpl*

eyelash ['aɪ,læʃ] *n* : pestaña *f*

eyelet ['aɪlət] *n* : ojete *m*

eyelid ['aɪ,lɪd] *n* : párpado *m*

eye–opener ['aɪ,o:pənər] *n* : revelación *f*, sorpresa *f*

eye–opening ['aɪ,o:pənɪŋ] *adj* : revelador

eyepiece ['aɪ,pi:s] *n* : ocular *m*

eyesight ['aɪ,saɪt] *n* : vista *f*, visión *f*

eyesore ['aɪ,sor] *n* : monstruosidad *f*, adefesio *m*

eyestrain ['aɪ,streɪn] *n* : fatiga *f* visual, vista *f* cansada

eyetooth ['aɪ,tu:θ] *n* : colmillo *m*

eyewitness ['aɪ'wɪtnəs] *n* : testigo *mf* ocular, testigo *mf* presencial

eyrie ['aɪri] → **aerie**

F

f ['ɛf] *n, pl* **f's** *or* **fs** ['ɛfs] : sexta letra del alfabeto inglés

fable ['feɪbəl] *n* : fábula *f*

fabled ['feɪbəld] *adj* : legendario, fabuloso

fabric ['fæbrɪk] *n* **1** MATERIAL : tela *f*, tejido *m* **2** STRUCTURE : estructura *f* ⟨the fabric of society : la estructura de la sociedad⟩

fabricate ['fæbrɪ,keɪt] *vt* **-cated; -cating** **1** CONSTRUCT, MANUFACTURE : construir, fabricar **2** INVENT : inventar (excusas o mentiras)

fabrication [,fæbrɪ'keɪʃən] *n* **1** LIE : mentira *f*, invención *f* **2** MANUFACTURE : fabricación *f*

fabulous ['fæbjələs] *adj* **1** LEGENDARY : fabuloso, legendario **2** INCREDIBLE : increíble, fabuloso ⟨fabulous wealth : riqueza fabulosa⟩ **3** WONDERFUL : magnífico, estupendo, fabuloso — **fabulously** *adv*

facade [fə'sɑd] *n* : fachada *f*

face[1] ['feɪs] *v* **faced; facing** *vt* **1** LINE : recubrir (una superficie), forrar (ropa) **2** CONFRONT : enfrentarse a, afrontar, hacer frente a ⟨to face the music : afrontar las consecuencias⟩ ⟨to face the facts : aceptar la realidad⟩ **3** : estar de cara a, estar enfrente de ⟨she's facing her brother : está de cara a su hermano⟩ **4** OVERLOOK : dar a — *vi* : mirar (hacia), estar orientado (a)

face[2] *n* **1** : cara *f*, rostro *m* ⟨he told me to my face : me lo dijo a la cara⟩ **2** EXPRESSION : cara *f*, expresión *f* ⟨to pull a long face : poner mala cara⟩ **3** GRIMACE : mueca *f* ⟨to make faces : hacer muecas⟩ **4** APPEARANCE : fisonomía *f*, aspecto *m* ⟨the face of society : la fisonomía de la sociedad⟩ **5** EFFRONTERY : desfachatez *f* **6** PRESTIGE : prestigio *m* ⟨to lose face : desprestigiarse⟩ **7** FRONT, SIDE : cara *f* (de una moneda), esfera *f* (de un reloj), fachada *f* (de un edificio), pared *f* (de una montaña) **8** SURFACE : superficie *f*, faz *f* (de la tierra), cara *f* (de la luna) **9 in the face of** DESPITE : en medio de, en visto de, ante

facedown ['feɪs,daʊn] *adv* : boca abajo

faceless ['feɪsləs] *adj* ANONYMOUS : anónimo

face–lift ['feɪs,lɪft] *n* **1** : estiramiento *m*

facial 2 RENOVATION : renovación *f*, remozamiento *m*

facet [ˈfæsət] *n* **1** : faceta *f* (de una piedra) **2** ASPECT : faceta *f*, aspecto *m*

facetious [fəˈsiːʃəs] *adj* : gracioso, burlón, bromista

facetiously [fəˈsiːʃəsli] *adv* : en tono de burla

facetiousness [fəˈsiːʃəsnəs] *n* : jocosidad *f*

face–to–face *adv & adj* : cara a cara

faceup [ˈfeɪsˈʌp] *adv* : boca arriba

face value *n* : valor *m* nominal

facial[1] [ˈfeɪʃəl] *adj* : de la cara, facial

facial[2] *n* : tratamiento *m* facial, limpieza *f* de cutis

facile [ˈfæsəl] *adj* SUPERFICIAL : superficial, simplista

facilitate [fəˈsɪləˌteɪt] *vt* **-tated; -tating** : facilitar

facility [fəˈsɪləṭi] *n, pl* **-ties 1** EASE : facilidad *f* **2** CENTER, COMPLEX : centro *m*, complejo *m* **3 facilities** *npl* AMENITIES : comodidades *fpl*, servicios *mpl*

facing [ˈfeɪsɪŋ] *n* **1** LINING : entretela *f* (de una prenda) **2** : revestimiento *m* (de un edificio)

facsimile [fækˈsɪməli] *n* : facsímile *m*, facsímil *m*

fact [ˈfækt] *n* **1** : hecho *m* ⟨as a matter of fact : de hecho⟩ **2** INFORMATION : información *f*, datos *mpl* ⟨facts and figures : datos y cifras⟩ **3** REALITY : realidad *f* ⟨in fact : en realidad⟩

faction [ˈfækʃən] *n* : facción *m*, bando *m*

factional [ˈfækʃənəl] *adj* : entre facciones

factious [ˈfækʃəs] *adj* : faccioso, contencioso

factitious [fækˈtɪʃəs] *adj* : artificial, facticio

factor [ˈfæktər] *n* : factor *m*

factory [ˈfæktəri] *n, pl* **-ries** : fábrica *f*

factual [ˈfækʧʊəl] *adj* : basado en hechos, objetivo

factually [ˈfækʧʊəli] *adv* : en cuanto a los hechos

faculty [ˈfækəlti] *n, pl* **-ties 1** : facultad *f* ⟨the faculty of sight : las facultades visuales, el sentido de la vista⟩ **2** APTITUDE : aptitud *f*, facilidad *f* **3** TEACHERS : cuerpo *m* docente

fad [ˈfæd] *n* : moda *f* pasajera, manía *f*

fade [ˈfeɪd] *v* **faded; fading** *vi* **1** WITHER : debilitarse (dícese de las personas), marchitarse (dícese de las flores y las plantas) **2** DISCOLOR : desteñirse, decolorarse **3** DIM : apagarse (dícese de la luz), perderse (dícese de los sonidos), fundirse (dícese de las imágenes) **4** VANISH : desvanecerse, decaer — *vt* DISCOLOR : desteñir

fag [ˈfæg] *vt* **fagged; fagging** EXHAUST : cansar, fatigar

fagot *or* **faggot** [ˈfægət] *n* : haz *m* de leña

Fahrenheit [ˈfærənˌhaɪt] *adj* : Fahrenheit

fail[1] [ˈfeɪl] *vi* **1** WEAKEN : fallar, deteriorarse **2** STOP : fallar, detenerse ⟨his heart failed : le falló el corazón⟩ **3** : fracasar, fallar ⟨her plan failed : su plan fracasó⟩ ⟨the crops failed : se perdió la cosecha⟩ **4** : quebrar ⟨a business about to fail : una empresa a punto de quebrar⟩ **5 to fail in** : faltar a, no cumplir con ⟨to fail in one's duties : faltar a sus deberes⟩ — *vt* **1** FLUNK : reprobar (un examen) **2** : fallar ⟨words fail me : las palabras me fallan, no encuentro palabras⟩ **3** DISAPPOINT : fallar, decepcionar ⟨don't fail me! : ¡no me falles!⟩

fail[2] *n* : fracaso *m*

failing [ˈfeɪlɪŋ] *n* : defecto *m*

failure [ˈfeɪljər] *n* **1** : fracaso *m*, malogro *m* ⟨crop failure : pérdida de la cosecha⟩ ⟨heart failure : insuficiencia cardíaca⟩ ⟨engine failure : falla mecánica⟩ **2** BANKRUPTCY : bancarrota *f*, quiebra *f* **3** : fracaso *m* (persona) ⟨he was a failure as a manager : como gerente, fue un fracaso⟩

faint[1] [ˈfeɪnt] *vi* : desmayarse

faint[2] *adj* **1** COWARDLY, TIMID : cobarde, tímido **2** DIZZY : mareado ⟨faint with hunger : desfallecido de hambre⟩ **3** SLIGHT : leve, ligero, vago ⟨I haven't the faintest idea : no tengo la más mínima idea⟩ **4** INDISTINCT : tenue, indistinto, apenas perceptible

faint[3] *n* : desmayo *m*

fainthearted [ˈfeɪntˈhɑrṭəd] *adj* : cobarde, pusilánime

faintly [ˈfeɪntli] *adv* : débilmente, ligeramente, levemente

faintness [ˈfeɪntnəs] *n* **1** INDISTINCTNESS : lo débil, falta *f* de claridad **2** FAINTING : desmayo *m*, desfallecimiento *m*

fair[1] [ˈfær] *adj* **1** ATTRACTIVE, BEAUTIFUL : bello, hermoso, atractivo **2** (*relating to weather*) : bueno, despejado ⟨fair weather : tiempo despejado⟩ **3** JUST : justo, imparcial **4** ALLOWABLE : permisible **5** BLOND, LIGHT : rubio (dícese del pelo), blanco (dícese de la tez) **6** ADEQUATE : bastante, adecuado ⟨fair to middling : mediano, regular⟩ **7 fair game** : presa *f* fácil **8 to play fair** : jugar limpio

fair[2] *n* : feria *f*

fairground [ˈfærˌgraʊnd] *n* : parque *m* de diversiones

fairly [ˈfærli] *adv* **1** IMPARTIALLY : imparcialmente, limpiamente, equitativamente **2** QUITE : bastante **3** MODERATELY : medianamente

fairness [ˈfærnəs] *n* **1** IMPARTIALITY : imparcialidad *f*, justicia *f* **2** LIGHTNESS : blancura *f* (de la piel), lo rubio (del pelo)

fairy [ˈfæri] *n, pl* **fairies 1** : hada *f* **2 fairy tale** : cuento *m* de hadas

fairyland [ˈfæriˌlænd] *n* **1** : país *m* de las hadas **2** : lugar *m* encantador

faith [ˈfeɪθ] *n, pl* **faiths** [ˈfeɪθs, ˈfeɪðz] **1** BELIEF : fe *f* **2** ALLEGIANCE : lealtad *f* **3** CONFIDENCE, TRUST : confianza *f*, fe *f* **4** RELIGION : religión *f*

faithful [ˈfeɪθfəl] *adj* : fiel — **faithfully** *adv*

faithfulness [ˈfeɪθfəlnəs] *n* : fidelidad *f*

faithless [ˈfeɪθləs] *adj* **1** DISLOYAL : desleal **2** : infiel (en la religión) — **faithlessly** *adv*

faithlessness [ˈfeɪθləsnəs] *n* : deslealtad *f*

fake[1] [ˈfeɪk] *v* **faked; faking** *vt* **1** FALSIFY : falsificar, falsear **2** FEIGN : fingir — *vi* **1** PRETEND : fingir **2** : hacer un engaño, hacer una finta (en deportes)

fake[2] *adj* : falso, fingido, postizo

fake[3] *n* **1** IMITATION : imitación *f*, falsificación *f* **2** IMPOSTOR : impostor *m*, -tora *f*; charlatán *m*, -tana *f*; farsante *mf* **3** FEINT : engaño *m*, finta *f* (en deportes)

faker [ˈfeɪkər] *n* : impostor *m*, -tora *f*; charlatán *m*, -tana *f*; farsante *mf*

fakir [fəˈkɪr, ˈfeɪkər] *n* : faquir *m*

falcon [ˈfælkən, ˈfɔl-] *n* : halcón *m*

falconry [ˈfælkənri, ˈfɔl-] *n* : cetrería *f*

fall[1] [ˈfɔl] *vi* **fell** [ˈfl]; **fallen** [fɔlən]; **falling** **1** : caer, caerse ⟨to fall out of bed : caer de la cama⟩ ⟨to fall down : caerse⟩ **2** HANG : caer **3** DESCEND : caer (dícese de la lluvia o de la noche), bajar (dícese de los precios), descender (dícese de la temperatura) **4** : caer (a un enemigo), rendirse ⟨the city fell : la ciudad se rindió⟩ **5** OCCUR : caer ⟨Christmas falls on a Friday : la Navidad cae en viernes⟩ **6 to fall asleep** : dormirse, quedarse dormido **7 to fall from grace** SIN : perder la gracia **8 to fall sick** : caer enfermo, enfermarse **9 to fall through** : fracasar, caer en la nada **10 to fall to** : tocar a, corresponder a ⟨the task fell to him : le tocó hacerlo⟩

fall[2] *n* **1** TUMBLE : caída *f* ⟨to break one's fall : frenar uno su caída⟩ ⟨a fall of three feet : una caída de tres pies⟩ **2** FALLING : derrumbe *m* (de rocas), aguacero *m* (de lluvia), nevada *f* (de nieve), bajada *f* (de precios), disminución *f* (de cantidades) **3** AUTUMN : otoño *m* **4** DOWNFALL : caída *f*, ruina *f* **5 falls** *npl* WATERFALL : cascada *f*, catarata *f*

fallacious [fəˈleɪʃəs] *adj* : erróneo, engañoso, falaz

fallacy [ˈfæləsi] *n, pl* **-cies** : falacia *f*

fall back *vi* **1** RETREAT : retirarse, replegarse **2 to fall back on** : recurrir a

fall guy *n* SCAPEGOAT : chivo *m* expiatorio

fallible [ˈfæləbəl] *adj* : falible

fallout [ˈfɔlˌaʊt] *n* **1** : lluvia *f* radioactiva **2** CONSEQUENCES : secuelas *fpl*, consecuencias *fpl*

fallow[1] [ˈfælo] *vt* : barbechar

fallow[2] *adj* **to lie fallow** : estar en barbecho

fallow[3] *n* : barbecho *m*

false [ˈfɔls] *adj* **falser; falsest** **1** UNTRUE : falso **2** ERRONEOUS : erróneo, equivocado **3** FAKE : falso, postizo **4** UNFAITHFUL : infiel **5** FRAUDULENT : fraudulento ⟨under false pretenses : por fraude⟩

falsehood [ˈfɔlsˌhʊd] *n* : mentira *f*, falsedad *f*

falsely [ˈfɔlsli] *adv* : falsamente, con falsedad

falseness [ˈfɔlsnəs] *n* : falsedad *f*

falsetto [fɔlˈsɛt̬oː] *n, pl* **-tos** : falsete *m*

falsification [ˌfɔlsəfəˈkeɪʃən] *n* : falsificación *f*, falseamiento *m*

falsify [ˈfɔlsəˌfaɪ] *vt* **-fied; fying** : falsificar, falsear

falsity [ˈfɔlsət̬i] *n, pl* **-ties** : falsedad *f*

falter [ˈfɔltər] *vi* **-tered; -tering** **1** TOTTER : tambalearse **2** STAMMER : titubear, tartamudear **3** WAVER : vacilar

faltering [ˈfɔltərɪŋ] *adj* : titubeante, vacilante

fame [ˈfeɪm] *n* : fama *f*

famed [ˈfeɪmd] *adj* : famoso, célebre, afamado

familial [fəˈmɪljəl, -liəl] *adj* : familiar

familiar[1] [fəˈmɪljər] *adj* **1** KNOWN : familiar, conocido ⟨to be familiar with : estar familiarizado con⟩ **2** INFORMAL : familiar, informal **3** INTIMATE : íntimo, de confianza **4** FORWARD : confianzudo, atrevido — **familiarly** *adv*

familiar[2] *n* : espíritu *m* guardián

familiarity [fəˌmɪliˈærət̬i, -ˌmɪlˈjær-] *n, pl* **-ties** **1** KNOWLEDGE : conocimiento *m*, familiaridad *f* **2** INFORMALITY, INTIMACY : confianza *f*, familiaridad *f* **3** FORWARDNESS : exceso *m* de confianza, descaro *m*

familiarize [fəˈmɪljəˌraɪz] *vt* **-ized; -izing** **1** : familiarizar **2 to familiarize oneself** : familiarizarse

family [ˈfæmli, ˈfæmə-] *n, pl* **-lies** : familia *f*

family room *n* : living *m*, sala *f* (informal)

family tree *n* : árbol *m* genealógico

famine [ˈfæmən] *n* : hambre *f*, hambruna *f*

famish [ˈfæmɪʃ] *vi* **to be famished** : estar famélico, estar hambriento, morir de hambre *fam*

famous [ˈfeɪməs] *adj* : famoso

famously [ˈfeɪməsli] *adv* **to get on famously** : llevarse de maravilla

fan[1] [ˈfæn] *vt* **fanned; fanning** **1** : abanicar (a una persona), avivar (un fuego) **2** STIMULATE : avivar, estimular

fan[2] *n* **1** : ventilador *m*, abanico *m* **2** ADMIRER, ENTHUSIAST : aficionado *m*, -da *f*; entusiasta *mf*; admirador *m*, -dora *f*

fanatic[1] [fəˈnæt̬ɪk] *or* **fanatical** [-t̬ɪ-kəl] *adj* : fanático

fanatic[2] *n* : fanático *m*, -ca *f*

fanaticism [fəˈnæt̬əˌsɪzəm] *n* : fanatismo *m*

fanciful [ˈfæntsɪfəl] *adj* **1** CAPRICIOUS : caprichoso, fantástico, extravagante **2** IMAGINATIVE : imaginativo — **fancifully** *adv*

fancy[1] [ˈfæntsi] *vt* **-cied; -cying 1** IMAGINE : imaginarse, figurarse ⟨fancy that! : ¡figúrate!, ¡imagínate!⟩ **2** CRAVE : apetecer, tener ganas de

fancy[2] *adj* **-cier; -est 1** ELABORATE : elaborado **2** LUXURIOUS : lujoso, elegante — **fancily** [ˈfæntsəli] *adv*

fancy[3] *n, pl* **-cies 1** LIKING : gusto *m*, afición *f* **2** WHIM : antojo *m*, capricho *m* **3** IMAGINATION : fantasía *f*, imaginación *f*

fandango [fænˈdæŋgo] *n, pl* **-gos** : fandango *m*

fanfare [ˈfænˌfær] *n* : fanfarria *f*

fang [ˈfæŋ] *n* : colmillo *m* (de un animal), diente *m* (de una serpiente)

fanlight [ˈfænˌlaɪt] *n* : tragaluz *m*

fantasia [fænˈteɪʒə, -ziə; ˌfæntəˈziːə] *n* : fantasía *f*

fantasize [ˈfæntəˌsaɪz] *vi* **-sized; -sizing** : fantasear

fantastic [fænˈtæstɪk] *adj* **1** UNBELIEVABLE : fantástico, increíble, extraño **2** ENORMOUS : fabuloso, inmenso ⟨fantastic sums : sumas fabulosas⟩ **3** WONDERFUL : estupendo, fantástico, bárbaro *fam*, macanudo *fam* — **fantastically** [-tɪkli] *adv*

fantasy [ˈfæntəsi] *n, pl* **-sies** : fantasía *f*

far[1] [ˈfɑr] *adv* **farther** [ˈfɑrðər] *or* **further** [ˈfər-]; **farthest** *or* **furthest** [-ðəst] **1** : lejos ⟨far from here : lejos de aquí⟩ ⟨to go far : llegar lejos⟩ ⟨as far as Chicago : hasta Chicago⟩ ⟨far away : a lo lejos⟩ **2** MUCH : muy, mucho ⟨far bigger : mucho más grande⟩ ⟨far superior : muy superior⟩ ⟨it's by far the best : es con mucho el mejor⟩ **3** (*expressing degree or extent*) ⟨the results are far off : salieron muy inexactos los resultados⟩ ⟨to go so far as : decir tanto como⟩ ⟨to go far enough : tener el alcance necesario⟩ **4** (*expressing progress*) ⟨the work is far advanced : el trabajo está muy avanzado⟩ ⟨to take (something) too far : llevar (algo) demasiado lejos⟩ **5 far and wide** : por todas partes **6 far from it!** : ¡todo lo contrario! **7 so far** : hasta ahora, todavía

far[2] *adj* **farther** *or* **further; farthest** *or* **furthest 1** REMOTE : lejano, remoto ⟨the Far East : el Lejano Oriente, el Extremo Oriente⟩ ⟨a far country : un país lejano⟩ **2** LONG : largo ⟨a far journey : un viaje largo⟩ **3** EXTREME : extremo ⟨the far right : la extrema derecha⟩ ⟨at the far end of the room : en el otro extremo de la sala⟩

faraway [ˈfɑrəˌweɪ] *adj* : remoto, lejano

farce [ˈfɑrs] *n* : farsa *f*

farcical [ˈfɑrsɪkəl] *adj* : absurdo, ridículo

fare[1] [ˈfær] *vi* **fared; faring** : ir, salir ⟨how did you fare? : ¿cómo te fue?⟩

fare[2] *n* **1** : pasaje *m*, billete *m*, boleto *m* ⟨half fare : medio pasaje⟩ **2** FOOD : comida *f*

farewell[1] [færˈwɛl] *adj* : de despedida

farewell[2] *n* : despedida *f*

far–fetched [ˈfɑrˈfɛtʃt] *adj* : improbable, exagerado

farina [fəˈriːnə] *n* : harina *f*

farm[1] [ˈfɑrm] *vt* **1** : cultivar, labrar **2** : criar (animales) — *vi* : ser agricultor

farm[2] *n* : granja *f*, hacienda *f*, finca *f*, estancia *f*

farmer [ˈfɑrmər] *n* : agricultor *m*, granjero *m*

farmhand [ˈfɑrmˌhænd] *n* : peón *m*

farmhouse [ˈfɑrmˌhaʊs] *n* : granja *f*, vivienda *f* del granjero, casa *f* de hacienda

farming [ˈfɑrmɪŋ] *n* : labranza *f*, cultivo *m*, crianza *f* (de animales)

farmland [ˈfɑrmˌlænd] *n* : tierras *fpl* de labranza

farmyard [ˈfɑrmˌjɑrd] *n* : corral *m*

far–off [ˈfɑrˌɔf, -ˈɔf] *adj* : remoto, distante, lejano

far–reaching [ˈfɑrˈriːtʃɪŋ] *adj* : de gran alcance

farsighted [ˈfɑrˌsaɪt̬əd] *adj* **1** : hipermétrope **2** JUDICIOUS : con visión de futuro, previsor, precavido

farsightedness [ˈfɑrˌsaɪt̬ədnəs] *n* **1** : hipermetropía *f* **2** PRUDENCE : previsión *f*

farther[1] [ˈfɑrðər] *adv* **1** AHEAD : más lejos (en el espacio), más adelante (en el tiempo) **2** MORE : más

farther[2] *adj* : más lejano, más remoto

farthermost [ˈfɑrðərˌmoːst] *adj* : (el) más lejano

farthest[1] [ˈfɑrðəst] *adv* **1** : lo más lejos ⟨I jumped farthest : salté lo más lejos⟩ **2** : lo más avanzado ⟨he progressed farthest : progresó al punto más avanzado⟩ **3** : más ⟨the farthest developed plan : el plan más desarrollado⟩

farthest[2] *adj* : más lejano

fascicle [ˈfæsɪkəl] *n* : fascículo *m*

fascinate [ˈfæsənˌeɪt] *vt* **-nated; -nating** : fascinar, cautivar

fascinating [ˈfæsənˌeɪt̬ɪŋ] *adj* : fascinante

fascination [ˌfæsənˈeɪʃən] *n* : fascinación *f*

fascism [ˈfæʃˌɪzəm] *n* : fascismo *m*

fascist[1] [ˈfæʃɪst] *adj* : fascista

fascist[2] *n* : fascista *mf*

fashion[1] [ˈfæʃən] *vt* : formar, moldear

fashion[2] *n* **1** MANNER : manera *f*, modo *m* **2** CUSTOM : costumbre *f* **3** STYLE : moda *f*

fashionable [ˈfæʃənəbəl] *adj* : de moda, chic

fashionably [ˈfæʃənəbli] *adv* : a la moda

fast[1] [ˈfæst] *vi* : ayunar

fast[2] *adv* **1** SECURELY : firmemente, seguramente ⟨to hold fast : agarrarse bien⟩ **2** RAPIDLY : rápidamente, rápido, de prisa **3 to run fast** : ir adelantado (dícese de un reloj) **4** SOUNDLY : profundamente ⟨fast asleep : profundamente dormido⟩

fast[3] *adj* **1** SECURE : firme, seguro ⟨to make fast : amarrar (un barco)⟩ **2** FAITHFUL : leal ⟨fast friends : amigos leales⟩ **3** RAPID : rápido, veloz **4** : adelantado ⟨my watch is fast : tengo el reloj adelantado⟩ **5** DEEP : profundo ⟨a fast sleep : un sueño profundo⟩ **6** COLORFAST : inalterable, que no destiñe **7** DISSOLUTE : extravagante, disipado, disoluto

fast[4] *n* : ayuno *m*

fasten [ˈfæsən] *vt* **1** ATTACH : sujetar, atar **2** FIX : fijar ⟨to fasten one's eyes on : fijar los ojos en⟩ **3** SECURE : abrochar (ropa o cinturones), atar (cordones), cerrar (una maleta) — *vi* : abrocharse, cerrar

fastener [ˈfæsənər] *n* : cierre *m*, sujetador *m*

fastening [ˈfæsənɪŋ] *n* : cierre *m*, sujetador *m*

fast food *n* : comida *f* rápida

fastidious [fæsˈtɪdiəs] *adj* : quisquilloso, exigente — **fastidiously** *adv*

fat[1] [ˈfæt] *adj* **fatter; fattest 1** OBESE : gordo, obeso **2** THICK : grueso

fat[2] *n* : grasa *f*

fatal [ˈfeɪt̬əl] *adj* **1** DEADLY : mortal **2** ILL-FATED : malhadado, fatal **3** MOMENTOUS : fatídico

fatalism [ˈfeɪt̬əlˌɪzəm] *n* : fatalismo *m*

fatalist [ˈfeɪt̬əlɪst] *n* : fatalista *mf*

fatalistic [ˌfeɪt̬əlˈɪstɪk] *adj* : fatalista

fatality [feɪˈtæləţi, fə-] *n, pl* **-ties** : víctima *f* mortal

fatally [ˈfeɪt̬əli] *adv* : mortalmente

fate [ˈfeɪt] *n* **1** DESTINY : destino *m* **2** END, LOT : final *m*, suerte *f*

fated [ˈfeɪt̬əd] *adj* : predestinado

fateful [ˈfeɪtfəl] *adj* **1** MOMENTOUS : fatídico, aciago **2** PROPHETIC : profético — **fatefully** *adv*

father[1] [ˈfɑðər] *vt* : engendrar

father[2] *n* **1** : padre *m* ⟨my father and my mother : mi padre y mi madre⟩ ⟨Father Smith : el padre Smith⟩ **2 the Father** GOD : el Padre, Dios *m*

fatherhood [ˈfɑðərˌhʊd] *n* : paternidad *f*

father–in–law [ˈfɑðərɪnˌlɔ] *n, pl* **fathers–in–law** : suegro *m*

fatherland [ˈfɑðərˌlænd] *n* : patria *f*

fatherless [ˈfɑðərləs] *adj* : huérfano de padre, sin padre

fatherly [ˈfɑðərli] *adj* : paternal

fathom[1] [ˈfæðəm] *vt* UNDERSTAND : entender, comprender

fathom[2] *n* : braza *f*

fatigue[1] [fəˈtiːg] *vt* **-tigued; -tiguing** : fatigar, cansar

fatigue[2] *n* : fatiga *f*

fatness [ˈfætnəs] *n* : gordura *f* (de una persona o un animal), grosor *m* (de un objeto)

fatten [ˈfætən] *vt* : engordar, cebar

fatty [ˈfæţi] *adj* **fattier; -est** : graso, grasoso, adiposo (dícese de los tejidos)

fatuous [ˈfætʃʊəs] *adj* : necio, fatuo — **fatuously** *adv*

faucet [ˈfɔsət] *n* : llave *f*, canilla *f Arg, Uru*, grifo *m*

fault[1] [ˈfɔlt] *vt* : encontrar defectos a

fault[2] *n* **1** SHORTCOMING : defecto *m*, falta *f* **2** DEFECT : falta *f*, defecto *m*, falla *f* **3** BLAME : culpa *f* **4** FRACTURE : falla *f* (geológica)

faultfinder [ˈfɔltˌfaɪndər] *n* : criticón *m*, -cona *f*

faultfinding [ˈfɔltˌfaɪndɪŋ] *n* : crítica *f*

faultless [ˈfɔltləs] *adj* : sin culpa, sin imperfecciones, impecable

faultlessly [ˈfɔltləsli] *adv* : impecablemente, perfectamente

faulty [ˈfɔlti] *adj* **faultier; -est** : defectuoso, imperfecto — **faultily** [ˈfɔltəli] *adv*

fauna [ˈfɔnə] *n* : fauna *f*

faux [ˈfoː] *adj* : de imitación

faux pas [ˌfoːˈpɑ] *n, pl* **faux pas** [*same or* -ˈpɑz] : metedura *f* de pata *fam*

favor[1] [ˈfeɪvər] *vt* **1** SUPPORT : estar a favor de, ser partidario de, apoyar **2** OBLIGE : hacerle un favor a **3** PREFER : preferir **4** RESEMBLE : parecerse a, salir a

favor[2] *n* : favor *m* ⟨in favor of : a favor de⟩ ⟨an error in his favor : un error a su favor⟩

favorable [ˈfeɪvərəbəl] *adj* : favorable, propicio

favorably [ˈfeɪvərəbli] *adv* : favorablemente, bien

favorite[1] [ˈfeɪvərət] *adj* : favorito, preferido

favorite[2] *n* : favorito *m*, -ta *f*; preferido *m*, -da *f*

favoritism [ˈfeɪvərəˌtɪzəm] *n* : favoritismo *m*

fawn[1] [ˈfɔn] *vi* : adular, lisonjear

fawn[2] *n* : cervato *m*

fax [ˈfæks] *n* : facsímil *m*, facsímile *m*

faze [ˈfeɪz] *vt* **fazed; fazing** : desconcertar, perturbar

fear[1] [ˈfɪr] *vt* : temer, tener miedo de — *vi* : temer

fear[2] *n* : miedo *m*, temor *m* ⟨for fear of : por temor a⟩

fearful [ˈfɪrfəl] *adj* **1** FRIGHTENING : espantoso, aterrador, horrible **2** FRIGHTENED : temeroso, miedoso

fearfully [ˈfɪrfəli] *adv* **1** EXTREMELY : extremadamente, terriblemente **2** TIMIDLY : con temor

fearless [ˈfɪrləs] *adj* : intrépido, impávido

fearlessly [ˈfɪrləsli] *adv* : sin temor

fearlessness [ˈfɪrləsnəs] *n* : intrepidez *f*, impavidez *f*

fearsome [ˈfɪrsəm] *adj* : aterrador

feasibility [ˌfiːzəˈbɪləţi] *n* : viabilidad *f*, factibilidad *f*

feasible [ˈfiːzəbəl] *adj* : viable, factible, realizable

feast[1] [ˈfi:st] *vi* : banquetear — *vt* **1** : agasajar, festejar **2 to feast one's eyes on** : regalarse la vista con
feast[2] *n* **1** BANQUET : banquete *m*, festín *m* **2** FESTIVAL : fiesta *f*
feat [ˈfi:t] *n* : proeza *f*, hazaña *f*
feather[1] [ˈfɛðər] *vt* **1** : emplumar **2 to feather one's nest** : hacer su agosto
feather[2] *n* **1** : pluma *f* **2 a feather in one's cap** : un triunfo personal
feathered [ˈfɛðərd] *adj* : con plumas
feathery [ˈfɛðəri] *adj* **1** DOWNY : plumoso **2** LIGHT : liviano
feature[1] [ˈfi:ʧər] *v* **-tured; -turing** *vt* **1** IMAGINE : imaginarse **2** PRESENT : presentar — *vi* : figurar
feature[2] *n* **1** CHARACTERISTIC : característica *f*, rasgo *m* **2** : largometraje *m* (en el cine), artículo *m* (en un periódico), documental *m* (en la televisión) **3 features** *npl* : rasgos *mpl*, facciones *fpl* ⟨delicate features : facciones delicadas⟩
February [ˈfɛbjʊˌri, ˈfɛbʊ-, ˈfbrʊ-] *n* : febrero *m*
fecal [ˈfi:kəl] *adj* : fecal
feces [ˈfi:ˌsi:z] *npl* : heces *fpl*, excrementos *mpl*
feckless [ˈfɛkləs] *adj* : irresponsable
fecund [ˈfɛkənd, ˈfi:-] *adj* : fecundo
fecundity [fɪˈkʌndəṭi, fɛ-] *n* : fecundidad *f*
federal [ˈfɛdrəl, -dərəl] *adj* : federal
federalism [ˈfɛdrəˌlɪzəm, -dərə-] *n* : federalismo *m*
federalist[1] [ˈfɛdrəlɪst, -dərə-] *adj* : federalista
federalist[2] *n* : federalista *mf*
federate [ˈfɛdəˌreɪt] *vt* **-ated; -ating** : federar
federation [ˌfɛdəˈreɪʃən] *n* : federación *f*
fedora [fɪˈdorə] *n* : sombrero *m* flexible de fieltro
fed up *adj* : harto
fee [ˈfi:] *n* **1** : honorarios *mpl* (a un médico, un abogado, etc.) **2 entrance fee** : entrada *f*
feeble [ˈfi:bəl] *adj* **-bler; -blest 1** WEAK : débil, endeble **2** INEFFECTIVE : flojo, pobre, poco convincente
feebleminded [ˌfi:bəlˈmaɪndəd] *adj* **1** : débil mental **2** FOOLISH, STUPID : imbécil, tonto
feebleness [ˈfi:bəlnəs] *n* : debilidad *f*
feebly [ˈfi:bli] *adv* : débilmente
feed[1] [ˈfi:d] *v* **fed** [ˈfɛd]; **feeding** *vt* **1** : dar de comer a, nutrir, alimentar (a una persona) **2** : alimentar (un fuego o una máquina), proveer (información), introducir (datos) — *vi* : comer, alimentarse
feed[2] *n* **1** NOURISHMENT : alimento *m* **2** FODDER : pienso *m*
feedback [ˈfi:dˌbæk] *n* **1** : realimentación *f* (electrónica) **2** RESPONSE : reacción *f*
feeder [ˈfi:dər] *n* : comedero *m* (para animales)
feel[1] [ˈfi:l] *v* **felt** [ˈflt]; **feeling** *vi* **1** : sentirse, encontrarse ⟨I feel tired : me siento cansada⟩ ⟨he feels hungry : tiene hambre⟩ ⟨she feels like a fool : se siente como una idiota⟩ ⟨to feel like doing something : tener ganas de hacer algo⟩ **2** SEEM : parecer ⟨it feels like spring : parece primavera⟩ **3** THINK : parecerse, opinar, pensar ⟨how does he feel about that? : ¿qué opina él de eso?⟩ — *vt* **1** TOUCH : tocar, palpar **2** SENSE : sentir ⟨to feel the cold : sentir el frío⟩ **3** CONSIDER : sentir, creer, considerar ⟨to feel (it) necessary : creer necesario⟩
feel[2] *n* **1** SENSATION, TOUCH : sensación *f*, tacto *m* **2** ATMOSPHERE : ambiente *m*, atmósfera *f* **3 to have a feel for** : tener un talento especial para
feeler [ˈfi:lər] *n* : antena *f*, tentáculo *m*
feeling [ˈfi:lɪŋ] *n* **1** SENSATION : sensación *f*, sensibilidad *f* **2** EMOTION : sentimiento *m* **3** OPINION : opinión *f* **4 feelings** *npl* SENSIBILITIES : sentimientos *mpl* ⟨to hurt someone's feelings : herir los sentimientos de alguien⟩
feet → **foot**
feign [ˈfeɪn] *vt* : simular, aparentar, fingir
feint[1] [ˈfeɪnt] *vi* : fintar, fintear
feint[2] *n* : finta *f*
feldspar [ˈfɛldˌspɑr] *n* : feldespato *m*
felicitate [fɪˈlɪsəˌteɪt] *vt* **-tated; -tating** : felicitar, congratular
felicitation [fɪˌlɪsəˈteɪʃən] *n* : felicitación *f*
felicitous [fɪˈlɪsəṭəs] *adj* : acertado, oportuno
feline[1] [ˈfi:ˌlaɪn] *adj* : felino
feline[2] *n* : felino *m*, -na *f*
fell[1] [ˈfɛl] *vt* : talar (un árbol), derribar (a una persona)
fell[2] → **fall**
fellow [ˈfɛˌlo:] *n* **1** COMPANION : compañero *m*, -ra *f*; camarada *mf* **2** ASSOCIATE : socio *m*, -cia *f* **3** MAN : tipo *m*, hombre *m*
fellowman [ˌfɛloˈmæn] *n, pl* **-men** : prójimo *m*, semejante *m*
fellowship [ˈfɛloˌʃɪp] *n* **1** COMPANIONSHIP : camaradería *f*, compañerismo *m* **2** ASSOCIATION : fraternidad *f* **3** GRANT : beca *f* (de investigación)
felon [ˈfɛlən] *n* : malhechor *m*, -chora *f*; criminal *mf*
felonious [fəˈlo:niəs] *adj* : criminal
felony [ˈfɛləni] *n, pl* **-nies** : delito *m* grave
felt[1] [ˈfɛlt] *n* : fieltro *m*
felt[2] → **feel**
female[1] [ˈfi:ˌmeɪl] *adj* : femenino
female[2] *n* **1** : hembra *f* (de animal) **2** WOMAN : mujer *f*
feminine [ˈfɛmənən] *adj* : femenino
femininity [ˌfɛməˈnɪnəṭi] *n* : feminidad *f*, femineidad *f*
feminism [ˈfɛməˌnɪzəm] *n* : feminismo *m*
feminist[1] [ˈfɛmənɪst] *adj* : feminista
feminist[2] *n* : feminista *mf*

femoral [ˈfɛmərəl] *adj* : femoral
femur [ˈfiːmər] *n, pl* **femurs** *or* **femora** [ˈfɛmərə] : fémur *m*
fence[1] [ˈfɛnts] *v* **fenced; fencing** *vt* : vallar, cercar — *vi* : hacer esgrima
fence[2] *n* : cerca *f*, valla *f*, cerco *m*
fencer [ˈfɛntsər] *n* : esgrimista *mf*; esgrimidor *m*, -dora *f*
fencing [ˈfɛntsɪŋ] *n* **1** : esgrima *m* (deporte) **2** : materiales *mpl* para cercas **3** ENCLOSURE : cercado *m*
fend [ˈfɛnd] *vt* **to fend off** : rechazar (un enemigo), parar (un golpe), eludir (una pregunta) — *vi* **to fend for oneself** : arreglárselas sólo, valerse por sí mismo
fender [ˈfɛndər] *n* : guardabarros *mpl*, salpicadera *f Mex*
fennel [ˈfɛnəl] *n* : hinojo *m*
ferment[1] [fərˈmɛnt] *v* : fermentar
ferment[2] [ˈfərˌmɛnt] *n* **1** : fermento *m* (en la química) **2** TURMOIL : agitación *f*, conmoción *f*
fermentation [ˌfərmənˈteɪʃən, -ˌmɛn-] *n* : fermentación *f*
fern [ˈfərn] *n* : helecho *m*
ferocious [fəˈroːʃəs] *adj* : feroz — **ferociously** *adv*
ferociousness [fəˈroːʃəsnəs] *n* : ferocidad *f*
ferocity [fəˈrɑsət̬i] *n* : ferocidad *f*
ferret[1] [ˈfɛrət] *vi* SNOOP : hurgar, husmear — *vt* **to ferret out** : descubrir
ferret[2] *n* : hurón *m*
ferric [ˈfɛrɪk] *or* **ferrous** [ˈfɛrəs] *adj* : férrico
Ferris wheel [ˈfɛrɪs] *n* : noria *f*
ferry[1] [ˈfɛri] *vt* **-ried; -rying** : llevar, transportar
ferry[2] *n, pl* **-ries** : transbordador *m*, ferry *m*
ferryboat [ˈfɛriˌboːt] *n* : transbordador *m*, ferry *m*
fertile [ˈfərt̬əl] *adj* : fértil, fecundo
fertility [fərˈtɪlət̬i] *n* : fertilidad *f*
fertilization [ˌfərt̬ələˈzeɪʃən] *n* : fertilización *f* (del suelo), fecundación (de un huevo)
fertilize [ˈfərt̬əlˌaɪz] *vt* **-ized; -izing 1** : fecundar (un huevo) **2** : fertilizar, abonar (el suelo)
fertilizer [ˈfərt̬əlˌaɪzər] *n* : fertilizante *m*, abono *m*
fervent [ˈfərvənt] *adj* : ferviente, fervoroso, ardiente — **fervently** *adv*
fervid [ˈfərvɪd] *adj* : ardiente, apasionado — **fervidly** *adv*
fervor [ˈfərvər] *n* : fervor *m*, ardor *m*
fester [ˈfɛstər] *vi* : enconarse, supurar
festival [ˈfɛstəvəl] *n* : fiesta *f*, festividad *f*, festival *m*
festive [ˈfɛstɪv] *adj* : festivo — **festively** *adv*
festivity [fɛsˈtɪvət̬i] *n, pl* **-ties** : festividad *f*, celebración *f*
festoon[1] [fɛsˈtuːn] *vt* : adornar, engalanar
festoon[2] *n* GARLAND : guirnalda *f*
fetal [ˈfiːt̬əl] *adj* : fetal
fetch [ˈfɛʧ] *vt* **1** BRING : traer, recoger, ir a buscar **2** REALIZE : realizar, venderse por <the jewelry fetched $10,000 : las joyas se vendieron por $10,000>
fetching [ˈfɛʧɪŋ] *adj* : atractivo, encantador
fête[1] [ˈfeɪt, ˈfɛt] *vt* **fêted; fêting** : festejar, agasajar
fête[2] *n* : fiesta *f*
fetid [ˈfɛt̬əd] *adj* : fétido
fetish [ˈfɛt̬ɪʃ] *n* : fetiche *m*
fetlock [ˈfɛtˌlɑk] *n* : espolón *m*
fetter [ˈfɛt̬ər] *vt* : encadenar, poner grillos a
fetters [ˈfɛt̬ərz] *npl* : grillos *mpl*, grilletes *mpl*, cadenas *fpl*
fettle [ˈfɛt̬əl] *n* **in fine fettle** : en buena forma, en plena forma
fetus [ˈfiːt̬əs] *n* : feto *m*
feud[1] [ˈfjuːd] *vi* : pelear, contender
feud[2] *n* : contienda *f*, enemistad *f* (heredada)
feudal [ˈfjuːdəl] *adj* : feudal
feudalism [ˈfjuːdəlˌɪzəm] *n* : feudalismo *m*
fever [ˈfiːvər] *n* : fiebre *f*, calentura *f*
feverish [ˈfiːvərɪʃ] *adj* **1** : afiebrado, con fiebre, febril **2** FRANTIC : febril, frenético
few[1] [ˈfjuː] *adj* : pocos <with few exceptions : con pocas excepciones> <a few times : varias veces>
few[2] *pron* **1** : pocos <few (of them) were ready : pocos estaban listos> **2 a few** : algunos, unos cuantos **3 few and far between** : contados
fewer [ˈfjuːər] *pron* : menos <the fewer the better : cuantos menos mejor>
fez [ˈfɛz] *n, pl* **fezzes** : fez *m*
fiancé [ˌfiːˌɑnˈseɪ, ˌfiːˈɑnˌseɪ] *n* : prometido *m*, novio *m*
fiancée [ˌfiːˌɑnˈseɪ, ˌfiːˈɑnˌseɪ] *n* : prometida *f*, novia *f*
fiasco [fiˈæsˌkoː] *n, pl* **-coes** : fiasco *m*, fracaso *m*
fiat [ˈfiːˌɑt, -ˌæt, -ət; ˈfaɪət, -ˌæt] *n* : decreto *m*, orden *m*
fib[1] [ˈfɪb] *vi* **fibbed; fibbing** : decir mentirillas
fib[2] *n* : mentirilla *f*, bola *f fam*
fibber [ˈfɪbər] *n* : mentirosillo *m*, -lla *f*; cuentista *mf fam*
fiber *or* **fibre** [ˈfaɪbər] *n* : fibra *f*
fiberboard [ˈfaɪbərˌbord] *n* : cartón *m* madera
fiberglass [ˈfaɪbərˌglæs] *n* : fibra *f* de vidrio
fibrillate [ˈfɪbrəˌleɪt, ˈfaɪ-] *vi* **-lated; -lating** : fibrilar
fibrillation [ˌfɪbrəˈleɪʃən, ˌfaɪ-] *n* : fibrilación *f*
fibrous [ˈfaɪbrəs] *adj* : fibroso
fibula [ˈfɪbjələ] *n, pl* **-lae** [-ˌliː, -ˌlaɪ] *or* **-las** : peroné *m*
fickle [ˈfɪkəl] *adj* : inconstante, voluble, veleidoso
fickleness [ˈfɪkəlnəs] *n* : volubilidad *f*, inconstancia *f*, veleidad *f*

fiction [ˈfɪkʃən] *n* : ficción *f*

fictional [ˈfɪkʃənəl] *adj* : ficticio

fictitious [fɪkˈtɪʃəs] *adj* **1** IMAGINARY : ficticio, imaginario **2** FALSE : falso, ficticio

fiddle[1] [ˈfɪdəl] *vi* **-dled; -dling** **1** : tocar el violín **2 to fiddle with** : juguetear con, toquetear

fiddle[2] *n* : violín *m*

fiddler [ˈfɪdlər, ˈfɪdələr] *n* : violinista *mf*

fiddlesticks [ˈfɪdəlˌstɪks] *interj* : ¡tonterías!

fidelity [fəˈdɛləṭi, faɪ-] *n, pl* **-ties** : fidelidad *f*

fidget[1] [ˈfɪʤət] *vi* **1** : moverse, estarse inquieto **2 to fidget with** : juguetear con

fidget[2] *n* **1** : persona *f* inquieta **2 fidgets** *npl* RESTLESSNESS : inquietud *f*

fidgety [ˈfɪʤəṭi] *adj* : inquieto

fiduciary[1] [fəˈduːʃiˌɛri, -ˈdjuː-, -ʃəri] *adj* : fiduciario

fiduciary[2] *n, pl* **-ries** : fiduciario *m*, -ria *f*

field[1] [ˈfiːld] *vt* : interceptar y devolver (una pelota), presentar (un candidato), sortear (una pregunta)

field[2] *adj* : de campaña, de campo ⟨field hospital : hospital de campaña⟩ ⟨field goal : gol de campo⟩ ⟨field trip : viaje de estudio⟩

field[3] *n* **1** : campo *m* (de cosechas, de batalla, de magnetismo) **2** : campo *m*, cancha *f* (en deportes) **3** : campo *m* (de trabajo), esfera *f* (de actividades)

fielder [ˈfiːldər] *n* : jugador *m*, -dora *f* de campo; fildeador *m*, -dora *f*

field glasses *n* : binoculares *mpl*, gemelos *mpl*

fiend [ˈfiːnd] *n* **1** DEMON : demonio *m* **2** EVILDOER : persona *f* maligna; malvado *m*, -da *f* **3** FANATIC : fanático *m*, -ca *f*

fiendish [ˈfiːndɪʃ] *adj* : diabólico — **fiendishly** *adv*

fierce [ˈfɪrs] *adj* **fiercer; -est** **1** FEROCIOUS : fiero, feroz **2** HEATED : acalorado **3** INTENSE : intenso, violento, fuerte — **fiercely** *adv*

fierceness [ˈfɪrsnəs] *n* **1** FEROCITY : ferocidad *f*, fiereza *f* **2** INTENSITY : intensidad *f*, violencia *f*

fieriness [ˈfaɪərinəs] *n* : pasión *f*, ardor *m*

fiery [ˈfaɪəri] *adj* **fierier; -est** **1** BURNING : ardiente, llameante **2** GLOWING : encendido **3** PASSIONATE : acalorado, ardiente, fogoso

fiesta [fiˈɛstə] *n* : fiesta *f*

fife [ˈfaɪf] *n* : pífano *m*

fifteen[1] [fɪfˈtiːn] *adj* : quince

fifteen[2] *n* : quince *m*

fifteenth[1] [fɪfˈtiːnθ] *adj* : decimoquinto

fifteenth[2] *n* **1** : decimoquinto *m*, -ta *f* (en una serie) **2** : quinceavo *m*, quinceava parte *f*

fifth[1] [ˈfɪfθ] *adj* : quinto

fifth[2] *n* **1** : quinto *m*, -ta *f* (en una serie) **2** : quinto *m*, quinta parte *f* **3** : quinta *f* (en la música)

fiftieth[1] [ˈfɪftiəθ] *adj* : quincuagésimo

fiftieth[2] *n* **1** : quincuagésimo *m*, -ma *f* (en una serie) **2** : cincuentavo *m*, cincuentava parte *f*

fifty[1] [ˈfɪfti] *adj* : cincuenta

fifty[2] *n, pl* **-ties** : cincuenta *m*

fifty–fifty[1] [ˌfɪftiˈfɪfti] *adv* : a medias, mitad y mitad

fifty–fifty[2] *adj* **to have a fifty–fifty chance** : tener un cincuenta por ciento de posibilidades

fig [ˈfɪg] *n* : higo *m*

fight[1] [ˈfaɪt] *v* **fought** [ˈfɔt]; **fighting** *vi* : luchar, combatir, pelear — *vt* : luchar contra, combatir contra

fight[2] *n* **1** COMBAT : lucha *f*, pelea *f*, combate *m* **2** MATCH : pelea *f*, combate *m* (en boxeo) **3** QUARREL : disputa *f*, pelea *f*, pleito *m*

fighter [ˈfaɪṭər] *n* **1** COMBATANT : luchador *m*, -dora *f*; combatiente *mf* **2** BOXER : boxeador *m*, -dora *f*

figment [ˈfɪgmənt] *n* **figment of the imagination** : producto *m* de la imaginación

figurative [ˈfɪgjərəṭɪv, -gə-] *adj* : figurado, metafórico

figuratively [ˈfɪgjərəṭɪvli, -gə-] *adv* : en sentido figurado, de manera metafórica

figure[1] [ˈfɪgjər, -gər] *v* **-ured; -uring** *vt* **1** CALCULATE : calcular **2** ESTIMATE : figurarse, calcular ⟨he figured it was possible : se figuró que era posible⟩ — *vi* **1** FEATURE, STAND OUT : figurar, destacar **2 that figures!** : ¡obvio!, ¡no me extraña nada!

figure[2] *n* **1** DIGIT : número *m*, cifra *f* **2** PRICE : precio *m*, cifra *f* **3** PERSONAGE : figura *f*, personaje *m* **4** : figura *f*, tipo *m*, físico *m* ⟨to have a good figure : tener buen tipo, tener un buen físico⟩ **5** DESIGN, OUTLINE : figura *f* **6 figures** *npl* : aritmética *f*

figurehead [ˈfɪgjərˌhɛd, -gər-] *n* : testaferro *m*, líder *mf* sin poder

figure of speech *n* : figura *f* retórica, figura *f* de hablar

figure out *vt* **1** UNDERSTAND : entender **2** RESOLVE : resolver (un problema, etc.)

figurine [ˌfɪgjəˈriːn] *n* : estatuilla *f*

Fijian [ˈfiːʤiən, fɪˈjiːən] *n* : fijiano *m*, -na *f* — **Fijian** *adj*

filament [ˈfɪləmənt] *n* : filamento *m*

filbert [ˈfɪlbərt] *n* : avellana *f*

filch [ˈfɪlʧ] *vt* : hurtar, birlar *fam*

file[1] [ˈfaɪl] *v* **filed; filing** *vt* **1** CLASSIFY : clasificar **2** : archivar (documentos) **3** SUBMIT : presentar ⟨to file charges : presentar cargos⟩ **4** SMOOTH : limar — *vi* : desfilar, entrar (o salir) en fila

file[2] *n* **1** : lima *f* ⟨nail file : lima de uñas⟩ **2** DOCUMENTS : archivo *m* **3** LINE : fila *f*

filial [ˈfɪliəl, ˈfɪljəl] *adj* : filial
filibuster[1] [ˈfɪləˌbʌstər] *vi* : practicar el obstruccionismo
filibuster[2] *n* : obstruccionismo *m*
filibusterer [ˈfɪləˌbʌstərər] *n* : obstruccionista *mf*
filigree [ˈfɪləˌgriː] *n* : filigrana *f*
Filipino [ˌfɪləˈpiːnoː] *n* : filipino *m*, -na *f* — **Filipino** *adj*
fill[1] [ˈfɪl] *vt* **1** : llenar, ocupar ‹to fill a cup : llenar una taza› ‹to fill a room : ocupar una sala› **2** STUFF : rellenar **3** PLUG : tapar, rellenar, empastar (un diente) **4** SATISFY : cumplir con, satisfacer **5** *or* **to fill out** : llenar, re- llenar ‹to fill out a form : rellenar un formulario›
fill[2] *n* **1** FILLING, STUFFING : relleno *m* **2 to eat one's fill** : comer lo suficiente **3 to have one's fill of** : estar harto de
filler [ˈfɪlər] *n* : relleno *m*
fillet[1] [ˈfɪlət, fɪˈleɪ, ˈfɪˌleɪ] *vt* : cortar en filetes
fillet[2] *n* : filete *m*
fill in *vt* INFORM : informar, poner al corriente — *vi* **to fill in for** : reemplazar a
filling [ˈfɪlɪŋ] *n* **1** : relleno *m* **2** : empaste *m* (de un diente)
filling station → **gas station**
filly [ˈfɪli] *n, pl* **-lies** : potra *f*, potranca *f*
film[1] [ˈfɪlm] *vt* : filmar — *vi* : rodar
film[2] *n* **1** COATING : capa *f*, película *f* **2** : película *f* (fotográfica) **3** MOVIE : película *f*, filme *m*
filmmaker [ˈfɪlmˌmeɪkər] *n* : cineasta *mf*
filmy [ˈfɪlmi] *adj* **filmier; -est 1** GAUZY : diáfano, vaporoso **2** : cubierto de una película
filter[1] [ˈfɪltər] *vt* : filtrar
filter[2] *n* : filtro *m*
filth [ˈfɪlθ] *n* : mugre *f*, porquería *f*, roña *f*
filthiness [ˈfɪlθinəs] *n* : suciedad *f*
filthy [ˈfɪlθi] *adj* **filthier; -est 1** DIRTY : mugriento, sucio **2** OBSCENE : obsceno, indecente
filtration [fɪlˈtreɪʃən] *n* : filtración *f*
fin [ˈfɪn] *n* **1** : aleta *f* **2** : alerón *m* (de un automóvil o un avión)
finagle [fəˈneɪgəl] *vt* **-gled; -gling** : arreglárselas para conseguir
final[1] [ˈfaɪnəl] *adj* **1** DEFINITIVE : definitivo, final, inapelable **2** ULTIMATE : final **3** LAST : último, final
final[2] *n* **1** : final *f* (en deportes) **2 finals** *npl* : exámenes *mpl* finales
finale [fɪˈnæli, -ˈnɑ-] *n* : final *m* ‹grand finale : final triunfal›
finalist [ˈfaɪnəlɪst] *n* : finalista *mf*
finality [faɪˈnæləṭi, fə-] *n, pl* **-ties** : finalidad *f*
finalize [ˈfaɪnəlˌaɪz] *vt* **-ized; -izing** : finalizar
finally [ˈfaɪnəli] *adv* **1** LASTLY : por último, finalmente **2** EVENTUALLY : por fin, al final **3** DEFINITIVELY : definitivamente
finance[1] [fəˈnænts, ˈfaɪˌnænts] *vt* **-nanced; -nancing** : financiar
finance[2] *n* **1** : finanzas *fpl* **2 finances** *npl* RESOURCES : recursos *mpl* financieros
financial [fəˈnæntʃəl, faɪ-] *adj* : financiero, económico
financially [fəˈnæntʃəli, faɪ-] *adv* : económicamente
financier [ˌfɪnənˈsɪr, ˌfaɪˌnæn-] *n* : financiero *m*, -ra *f*; financista *mf*
financing [fəˈnæntsɪŋ, ˈfæɪˌnæntsɪŋ] *n* : financiación *f*, financiamiento *m*
finch [ˈfɪntʃ] *n* : pinzón *m*
find[1] [ˈfaɪnd] *vt* **found** [ˈfaʊnd]; **finding 1** LOCATE : encontrar, hallar ‹I can't find it : no lo encuentro› ‹to find one's way : encontrar el camino, orientarse› **2** DISCOVER, REALIZE : descubrir, darse cuenta de ‹he found it difficult : descubrió que era difícil› **3** DECLARE : declarar, hallar ‹they found him guilty : lo declararon culpable›
find[2] *n* : hallazgo *m*
finder [ˈfaɪndər] *n* : descubridor *m*, -dora *f*
finding [ˈfaɪndɪŋ] *n* **1** FIND : hallazgo *m* **2 findings** *npl* : conclusiones *fpl*
find out *vt* DISCOVER : descubrir, averiguar — *vi* LEARN : enterarse
fine[1] [ˈfaɪn] *vt* **fined; fining** : multar
fine[2] *adj* **finer; -est 1** PURE : puro (dícese del oro y de la plata) **2** THIN : fino, delgado **3** : fino ‹fine sand : arena fina› **4** SMALL : pequeño, minúsculo ‹fine print : letras minúsculas› **5** SUBTLE : sutil, delicado **6** EXCELLENT : excelente, magnífico, selecto **7** FAIR : bueno ‹it's a fine day : hace buen tiempo› **8** EXQUISITE : exquisito, delicado, fino **9 fine arts** : bellas artes *fpl*
fine[3] *n* : multa *f*
finely [ˈfaɪnli] *adv* **1** EXCELLENTLY : con arte **2** ELEGANTLY : elegantemente **3** PRECISELY : con precisión **4 to chop finely** : picar muy fino, picar en trozos pequeños
fineness [ˈfaɪnnəs] *n* **1** EXCELLENCE : excelencia *f* **2** ELEGANCE : elegancia *f*, refinamiento *m* **3** DELICACY : delicadeza *f*, lo fino **4** PRECISION : precisión *f* **5** SUBTLETY : sutileza *f* **6** PURITY : ley *f* (de oro y plata)
finery [ˈfaɪnəri] *n* : galas *fpl*, adornos *mpl*
finesse[1] [fəˈnɛs] *vt* **-nessed; -nessing** : ingeniar
finesse[2] *n* **1** REFINEMENT : refinamiento *m*, finura *f* **2** TACT : delicadeza *f*, tacto *m*, diplomacia *f* **3** CRAFTINESS : astucia *f*
finger[1] [ˈfɪŋgər] *vt* **1** HANDLE : tocar, toquetear **2** ACCUSE : acusar, delatar
finger[2] *n* : dedo *m*
fingerling [ˈfɪŋgərlɪŋ] *n* : pez *m* pequeño y joven
fingernail [ˈfɪŋgərˌneɪl] *n* : uña *f*
fingerprint[1] [ˈfɪŋgərˌprɪnt] *vt* : tomar las huellas digitales a

fingerprint[2] *n* : huella *f* digital
fingertip ['fɪŋgər,tɪp] *n* : punta *f* del dedo, yema *f* del dedo
finicky ['fɪnɪki] *adj* : maniático, melindroso, mañoso
finish[1] ['fɪnɪʃ] *vt* **1** COMPLETE : acabar, terminar **2** : aplicar un acabado a (muebles, etc.)
finish[2] *n* **1** END : fin *m*, final *m* **2** REFINEMENT : refinamiento *m* **3** : acabado *m* ⟨a glossy finish : un acabado brillante⟩
finite ['faɪ,naɪt] *adj* : finito
fink ['fɪŋk] *n* : mequetrefe *mf fam*
Finn ['fɪn] *n* : finlandés *m*, -desa *f*
Finnish[1] ['fɪnɪʃ] *adj* : finlandés
Finnish[2] *n* : finlandés *m* (idioma)
fiord [fi'ɔrd] → **fjord**
fir ['fər] *n* : abeto *m*
fire[1] ['faɪr] *vt* **fired; firing** **1** IGNITE, KINDLE : encender **2** ENLIVEN : animar, avivar **3** DISMISS : despedir **4** SHOOT : disparar **5** BAKE : cocer (cerámica)
fire[2] *n* **1** : fuego *m* **2** BURNING : incendio *m* ⟨fire alarm : alarma contra incendios⟩ ⟨to be on fire : estar en llamas⟩ **3** ENTHUSIASM : ardor *m*, entusiasmo *m* **4** SHOOTING : disparos *mpl*, fuego *m*
firearm ['faɪr,ɑrm] *n* : arma *f* de fuego
fireball ['faɪr,bɔl] *n* **1** : bola *f* de fuego **2** METEOR : bólido *m*
firebreak ['faɪr,breɪk] *n* : cortafuegos *m*
firebug ['faɪr,bʌg] *n* : pirómano *m*, -na *f*; incendiario *m*, -ria *f*
firecracker ['faɪr,krækər] *n* : petardo *m*
fire escape *n* : escalera *f* de incendios
firefighter ['faɪr,faɪt̬ər] *n* : bombero *m*, -ra *f*
firefly ['faɪr,flaɪ] *n, pl* **-flies** : luciérnaga *f*
fireman ['faɪrmən] *n, pl* **-men** [-mən, -,mɛn] **1** FIREFIGHTER : bombero *m*, -ra *f* **2** STOKER : fogonero *m*, -ra *f*
fireplace ['faɪr,pleɪs] *n* : hogar *m*, chimenea *f*
fireproof[1] ['faɪr,pru:f] *vt* : hacer incombustible
fireproof[2] *adj* : incombustible, ignífugo
fireside[1] ['faɪr,saɪd] *adj* : informal ⟨fireside chat : charla informal⟩
fireside[2] *n* **1** HEARTH : chimenea *f*, hogar *m* **2** HOME : hogar *m*, casa *f*
firewall ['faɪr,wɔl] *n* : cortafuegos *m*
firewood ['faɪr,wʊd] *n* : leña *f*
fireworks ['faɪr,wərks] *npl* : fuegos *mpl* artificiales, pirotecnia *f*
firm[1] ['fərm] *vt or* **to firm up** : endurecer
firm[2] *adj* **1** VIGOROUS : fuerte, vigoroso **2** SOLID, UNYIELDING : firme, duro, sólido **3** UNCHANGING : firme, inalterable **4** RESOLUTE : firme, resuelto
firm[3] *n* : empresa *f*, firma *f*, compañía *f*
firmament ['fərməmənt] *n* : firmamento *m*
firmly ['fərmli] *adv* : firmemente
firmness ['fərmnəs] *n* : firmeza *f*
first[1] ['fərst] *adv* **1** : primero ⟨finish your homework first : primero termina tu tarea⟩ ⟨first and foremost : ante todo⟩ ⟨first of all : en primer lugar⟩ **2** : por primera vez ⟨I saw it first in Boston : lo vi por primera vez en Boston⟩
first[2] *adj* **1** : primero ⟨the first time : la primera vez⟩ ⟨at first sight : a primera vista⟩ ⟨in the first place : en primer lugar⟩ ⟨the first ten applicants : los diez primeros candidatos⟩ **2** FOREMOST : principal, primero ⟨first tenor : tenor principal⟩
first[3] *n* **1** : primero *m*, -ra *f* **2** *or* **first gear** : primera *f* **3 at ~** : al principio
first aid *n* : primeros auxilios *mpl*
first–class[1] ['fərst'klæs] *adv* : en primera ⟨to travel first-class : viajar en primera⟩
first–class[2] *adj* : de primera
first class *n* : primera clase *f*
firsthand[1] ['fərst'hænd] *adv* : directamente
firsthand[2] *adj* : de primera mano
first lieutenant *n* : teniente *mf*; teniente primero *m*, teniente primera *f*
firstly ['fərstli] *adv* : primeramente, principalmente, en primer lugar
first–rate[1] ['fərst'reɪt] *adv* : muy bien
first–rate[2] *adj* : de primera, de primera clase
first sergeant *n* : sargento *mf*
firth ['fərθ] *n* : estuario *m*
fiscal ['fɪskəl] *adj* : fiscal — **fiscally** *adv*
fish[1] ['fɪʃ] *vi* **1** : pescar **2 to fish for** SEEK : buscar, rebuscar ⟨to fish for compliments : andar a la caza de cumplidos⟩ — *vt* : pescar
fish[2] *n, pl* **fish** *or* **fishes** : pez *m* (vivo), pescado *m* (para comer)
fisherman ['fɪʃərmən] *n, pl* **-men** [-mən, -,mɛn] : pescador *m*, -dora *f*
fishery ['fɪʃəri] *n, pl* **-eries** **1** → **fishing** **2** : zona *f* pesquera, pesquería *f*
fishhook ['fɪʃ,hʊk] *n* : anzuelo *m*
fishing ['fɪʃɪŋ] *n* : pesca *f*, industria *f* pesquera
fishing pole *n* : caña *f* de pescar
fish market *n* : pescadería *f*
fishy ['fɪʃi] *adj* **fishier; -est** **1** : a pescado ⟨a fishy taste : un sabor a pescado⟩ **2** QUESTIONABLE : dudoso, sospechoso ⟨there's something fishy going on : aquí hay gato encerrado⟩
fission ['fɪʃən, -ʒən] *n* : fisión *f*
fissure ['fɪʃər] *n* : fisura *f*, hendidura *f*
fist ['fɪst] *n* : puño *m*
fistful ['fɪst,fʊl] *n* : puñado *m*
fisticuffs ['fɪstɪ,kʌfs] *npl* : lucha *f* a puñetazos
fit[1] ['fɪt] *v* **fitted; fitting** *vt* **1** MATCH : corresponder a, coincidir con ⟨the punishment fits the crime : el castigo corresponde al crimen⟩ **2** : quedar ⟨the dress doesn't fit me : el vestido no me queda⟩ **3** GO : caber, encajar en ⟨her key fits the lock : su llave encaja en la cerradura⟩ **4** INSERT, INSTALL : poner, colocar **5** ADAPT : adecuar, ajustar, adaptar **6** *or* **to fit out** EQUIP : equipar

— *vi* **1** : quedar, entallar ⟨these pants don't fit : estos pantalones no me quedan⟩ **2** CONFORM : encajar, cuadrar **3 to fit in** : encajar, estar integrado

fit[2] *adj* **fitter; fittest** **1** SUITABLE : adecuado, apropiado, conveniente **2** QUALIFIED : calificado, competente **3** HEALTHY : sano, en forma

fit[3] *n* **1** ATTACK : ataque *m*, acceso *m*, arranque *m* **2 to be a good fit** : quedar bien **3 to be a tight fit** : ser muy entallado (de ropa), estar apretado (de espacios)

fitful [ˈfɪtfəl] *adj* : irregular, intermitente — **fitfully** *adv*

fitness [ˈfɪtnəs] *n* **1** HEALTH : salud *f*, buena forma *f* (física) **2** SUITABILITY : idoneidad *f*

fitting[1] [ˈfɪṭɪŋ] *adj* : adecuado, apropiado

fitting[2] *n* : accesorio *m*

five[1] [ˈfaɪv] *adj* : cinco

five[2] *n* : cinco *m*

five hundred[1] *adj* : quinientos

five hundred[2] *n* : quinientos *m*

fix[1] [ˈfɪks] *vt* **1** ATTACH, SECURE : sujetar, asegurar, fijar **2** ESTABLISH : fijar, concretar, establecer **3** REPAIR : arreglar, reparar **4** PREPARE : preparar ⟨to fix dinner : preparar la cena⟩ **5** : arreglar, amañar ⟨to fix a race : arreglar una carrera⟩ **6** RIVET : fijar (los ojos, la mirada, etc.)

fix[2] *n* **1** PREDICAMENT : aprieto *m*, apuro *m* **2** : posición *f* ⟨to get a fix on : establecer la posición de⟩

fixate [ˈfɪkˌseɪt] *vi* **-ated; -ating** : obsesionarse

fixation [fɪkˈseɪʃən] *n* : fijación *f*, obsesión *f*

fixed [ˈfɪkst] *adj* **1** STATIONARY : estacionario, inmóvil **2** UNCHANGING : fijo, inalterable **3** INTENT : fijo ⟨a fixed stare : una mirada fija⟩ **4 to be comfortably fixed** : estar en posición acomodada

fixedly [ˈfɪksədli] *adv* : fijamente

fixedness [ˈfɪksədnəs, ˈfikst-] *n* : rigidez *f*

fixture [ˈfɪkstʃər] *n* **1** : parte *f* integrante, elemento *m* fijo **2 fixtures** *npl* : instalaciones *fpl* (de una casa)

fizz[1] [ˈfɪz] *vi* : burbujear

fizz[2] *n* : efervescencia *f*, burbujeo *m*

fizzle[1] [ˈfɪzəl] *vi* **-zled; -zling** **1** FIZZ : burbujear **2** FAIL : fracasar

fizzle[2] *n* : fracaso *m*, fiasco *m*

fjord [fiˈɔrd] *n* : fiordo *m*

flab [ˈflæb] *n* : gordura *f*

flabbergast [ˈflæbərˌgæst] *vt* : asombrar, pasmar, dejar atónito

flabby [ˈflæbi] *adj* **-bier; -est** : blando, fofo, aguado *CA, Col, Mex*

flaccid [ˈflæksəd, ˈflæsəd] *adj* : fláccido

flag[1] [ˈflæg] *vi* **flagged; flagging** **1** : hacer señales con banderas **2** WEAKEN : flaquear, desfallecer

flag[2] *n* : bandera *f*, pabellón *m*, estandarte *m*

flagon [ˈflægən] *n* : jarra *f* grande

flagpole [ˈflægˌpoːl] *n* : asta *f*, mástil *m*

flagrant [ˈfleɪgrənt] *adj* : flagrante — **flagrantly** *adv*

flagship [ˈflægˌʃɪp] *n* : buque *m* insignia

flagstaff [ˈflægˌstæf] → **flagpole**

flagstone [ˈflægˌstoːn] *n* : losa *f*, piedra *f*

flail[1] [ˈfleɪl] *vt* **1** : trillar (grano) **2** : sacudir, agitar (los brazos)

flail[2] *n* : mayal *m*

flair [ˈflær] *n* : don *m*, facilidad *f*

flak [ˈflæk] *ns & pl* **1** : fuego *m* antiaéreo **2** CRITICISM : críticas *fpl*

flake[1] [ˈfleɪk] *vi* **flaked; flaking** : desmenuzarse, pelarse (dícese de la piel)

flake[2] *n* : copo *m* (de nieve), escama *f* (de la piel), astilla *f* (de madera)

flamboyance [flæmˈbɔɪənts] *n* : extravagancia *f*, rimbombancia *f*

flamboyant [flæmˈbɔɪənt] *adj* : exuberante, extravagante, rimbombante

flame[1] [ˈfleɪm] *vi* **flamed; flaming** **1** BLAZE : arder, llamear **2** GLOW : brillar, encenderse

flame[2] *n* BLAZE : llama *f* ⟨to burst into flames : estallar en llamas⟩ ⟨to go up in flame : incendiarse⟩

flamethrower [ˈfleɪmˌθroːər] *n* : lanzallamas *m*

flamingo [fləˈmɪŋgo] *n, pl* **-gos** : flamenco *m*

flammable [ˈflæməbəl] *adj* : inflamable, flamable

flange [ˈflænʤ] *n* : reborde *m*, pestaña *f*

flank[1] [ˈflæŋk] *vt* **1** : flanquear (para defender o atacar) **2** BORDER, LINE : bordear

flank[2] *n* : ijada *f* (de un animal), costado *m* (de una persona), falda *f* (de una colina), flanco *m* (de un cuerpo de soldados)

flannel [ˈflænəl] *n* : franela *f*

flap[1] [ˈflæp] *v* **flapped; flapping** *vi* **1** : aletear ⟨the bird was flapping (its wings) : el pájaro aleteaba⟩ **2** FLUTTER : ondear, agitarse — *vt* : batir, agitar

flap[2] *n* **1** FLAPPING : aleteo *m*, aletazo *m* (de alas) **2** : soplada *f* (de un sobre), hoja *f* (de una mesa), faldón *m* (de una chaqueta)

flapjack [ˈflæpˌʤæk] → **pancake**

flare[1] [ˈflær] *vi* **flared; flaring** **1** FLAME, SHINE : llamear, brillar **2 to flare up** : estallar, explotar (de cólera)

flare[2] *n* **1** FLASH : destello *m* **2** SIGNAL : (luz *f* de) bengala *f* **3 solar flare** : erupción *f* solar

flash[1] [ˈflæʃ] *vi* **1** SHINE, SPARKLE : destellar, brillar, relampaguear **2** : pasar como un relámpago ⟨an idea flashed through my mind : una idea me cruzó la mente como un relámpago⟩ — *vt* : despedir, lanzar (una luz), transmitir (un mensaje)

flash[2] *adj* SUDDEN : repentino
flash[3] *n* **1** : destello *m* (de luz), fogonazo *m* (de una explosión) **2 flash of lightning** : relámpago *m* **3 in a flash** : de repente, de un abrir y cerrar los ojos
flashback [ˈflæʃˌbæk] *n* : flashback *m*
flashiness [ˈflæʃinəs] *n* : ostentación *f*
flashlight [ˈflæʃˌlaɪt] *n* : linterna *f*
flashy [ˈflæʃi] *adj* **flashier; -est** : llamativo, ostentoso
flask [ˈflæsk] *n* : frasco *m*
flat[1] [ˈflæt] *vt* **flatted; flatting 1** FLATTEN : aplanar, achatar **2** : bajar de tono (en música)
flat[2] *adv* **1** EXACTLY : exactamente ⟨in ten minutes flat : en diez minutos exactos⟩ **2** : desafinado, demasiado bajo (en la música)
flat[3] *adj* **flatter; flattest 1** EVEN, LEVEL : plano, llano **2** SMOOTH : liso **3** DEFINITE : categórico, rotundo, explícito ⟨a flat refusal : una negativa categórica⟩ **4** DULL : aburrido, soso, monótono (dícese la voz) **5** DEFLATED : desinflado, pinchado, ponchado *Mex* **6** : bemol (en música) ⟨to sing flat : cantar desafinado⟩
flat[4] *n* **1** PLAIN : llano *m*, terreno *m* llano **2** : bemol *m* (en la música) **3** APARTMENT : apartamento *m*, departamento *m* **4** *or* **flat tire** : pinchazo *m*, ponchadura *f Mex*
flatbed [ˈflætˌbɛd] *n* : camión *m* de plataforma
flatcar [ˈflætˌkɑr] *n* : vagón *m* abierto
flatfish [ˈflætˌfɪʃ] *n* : platija *f*
flat-footed [ˈflætˌfʊt̬əd, ˌflætˈ-] *adj* : de pies planos
flatly [ˈflætli] *adv* DEFINITELY : categóricamente, rotundamente
flatness [ˈflætnəs] *n* **1** EVENNESS : lo llano, lisura *f*, uniformidad *f* **2** DULLNESS : monotonía *f*
flat-out [ˈflætˈaʊt] *adj* **1** : frenético, a toda máquina ⟨a flat-out effort : un esfuerzo frenético⟩ **2** CATEGORICAL : descarado, rotundo, categórico
flatten [ˈflætən] *vt* : aplanar, achatar
flatter [ˈflæt̬ər] *vt* **1** OVERPRAISE : adular **2** COMPLIMENT : halagar **3** : favorecer ⟨the photo flatters you : la foto te favorece⟩
flatterer [ˈflæt̬ərər] *n* : adulador *m*, -dora *f*
flattering [ˈflæt̬ərɪŋ] *adj* **1** COMPLIMENTARY : halagador **2** BECOMING : favorecedor
flattery [ˈflæt̬əri] *n, pl* **-ries** : halagos *mpl*
flatulence [ˈflætʃələnts] *n* : flatulencia *f*, ventosidad *f*
flatulent [ˈflætʃələnt] *adj* : flatulento
flatware [ˈflætˌwær] *n* : cubertería *f*, cubiertos *mpl*
flaunt[1] [ˈflɔnt] *vt* : alardear, hacer alarde de
flaunt[2] *n* : alarde *m*, ostentación *f*
flavor[1] [ˈfleɪvər] *vt* : dar sabor a, sazonar
flavor[2] *n* **1** : gusto *m*, sabor *m* **2** FLAVORING : sazón *f*, condimento *m*
flavorful [ˈfleɪvərfəl] *adj* : sabroso
flavoring [ˈfleɪvərɪŋ] *n* : condimento *m*, sazón *f*
flavorless [ˈfleɪvərləs] *adj* : sin sabor
flaw [ˈflɔ] *n* : falla *f*, defecto *m*, imperfección *f*
flawed [ˈflɔd] *adj* : imperfecto, con defectos
flawless [ˈflɔləs] *adj* : impecable, perfecto — **flawlessly** *adv*
flax [ˈflæks] *n* : lino *m*
flaxen [ˈflæksən] *adj* : rubio, blondo (dícese del pelo)
flay [ˈfleɪ] *vt* **1** SKIN : desollar, despellejar **2** VILIFY : criticar con dureza, vilipendiar
flea [ˈfliː] *n* : pulga *f*
fleck[1] [ˈflɛk] *vt* : salpicar
fleck[2] *n* : mota *f*, pinta *f*
fledgling [ˈflɛdʒlɪŋ] *n* : polluelo *m*, pollito *m*
flee [ˈfliː] *v* **fled** [ˈflɛd]; **fleeing** *vi* : huir, escapar(se) — *vt* : huir de
fleece[1] [ˈfliːs] *vt* **fleeced; fleecing 1** SHEAR : esquilar, trasquilar **2** SWINDLE : estafar, defraudar
fleece[2] *n* : lana *f*, vellón *m*
fleet[1] [ˈfliːt] *vi* : moverse con rapidez
fleet[2] *adj* SWIFT : rápido, veloz
fleet[3] *n* : flota *f*
fleet admiral *n* : almirante *mf*
fleeting [ˈfliːt̬ɪŋ] *adj* : fugaz, breve
flesh [ˈflɛʃ] *n* **1** : carne *f* (de seres humanos y animales) **2** : pulpa *f* (de frutas)
flesh out *vt* : desarrollar, darle cuerpo a
fleshy [ˈflɛʃi] *adj* **fleshier; -est** : gordo (dícese de las personas), carnoso (dícese de la fruta)
flew → **fly**
flex [ˈflɛks] *vt* : doblar, flexionar
flexibility [ˌflɛksəˈbɪlət̬i] *n, pl* **-ties** : flexibilidad *f*, elasticidad *f*
flexible [ˈflɛksəbəl] *adj* : flexible — **flexibly** [-bli] *adv*
flick[1] [ˈflɪk] *vt* : dar un capirotazo a (con el dedo) ⟨to flick a switch : darle al interruptor⟩ — *vi* **1** FLIT : revolotear **2 to flick through** : hojear (un libro)
flick[2] *n* : coletazo *m* (de una cola), capirotazo *m* (de un dedo)
flicker[1] [ˈflɪkər] *vi* **1** FLUTTER : revolotear, aletear **2** BLINK, TWINKLE : parpadear, titilar
flicker[2] *n* **1** : parpadeo *m*, titileo *m* **2** HINT, TRACE : indicio *m*, rastro *m* ⟨a flicker of hope : un rayo de esperanza⟩
flier [ˈflaɪər] *n* **1** AVIATOR : aviador *m*, -dora *f* **2** CIRCULAR : folleto *m* publicitario, circular *f*
flight [ˈflaɪt] *n* **1** : vuelo *m* (de aves o aviones), trayectoria *f* (de proyectiles) **2** TRIP : vuelo *m* **3** FLOCK, SQUADRON : bandada *f* (de pájaros), escuadrilla *f* (de aviones) **4** ESCAPE : huida *f*, fuga

f **5 flight of fancy** : ilusiones *fpl*, fantasía *f* **6 flight of stairs** : tramo *m*
flight attendant *n* : auxiliar *mf* de vuelo
flightless [ˈflaɪtləs] *adj* : no volador
flighty [ˈflaɪt̬i] *adj* **flightier; -est** : caprichoso, frívolo
flimsy [flɪmzi] *adj* **flimsier; -est 1** LIGHT, THIN : ligero, fino **2** WEAK : endeble, poco sólido **3** IMPLAUSIBLE : pobre, flojo, poco convincente ⟨a flimsy excuse : una excusa floja⟩
flinch [ˈflɪntʃ] *vi* **1** WINCE : estremecerse **2** RECOIL : recular, retroceder
fling[1] [ˈflɪŋ] *vt* **flung** [ˈflʌŋ]; **flinging 1** THROW : lanzar, tirar, arrojar **2 to fling oneself** : lanzarse, tirarse, precipitarse
fling[2] *n* **1** THROW : lanzamiento *m* **2** ATTEMPT : intento *m* **3** AFFAIR : aventura *f* **4** BINGE : juerga *f*
flint [ˈflɪnt] *n* : pedernal *m*
flinty [ˈflɪnti] *adj* **flintier; -est 1** : de pedernal **2** STERN, UNYIELDING : severo, inflexible
flip[1] [ˈflɪp] *v* **flipped; flipping** *vt* **1** TOSS : tirar ⟨to flip a coin : echar a cara o cruz⟩ **2** OVERTURN : dar la vuelta a, voltear — *vi* **1** : moverse bruscamente **2 to flip through** : hojear (un libro)
flip[2] *adj* : insolente, descarado
flip[3] *n* **1** FLICK : capirotazo *m*, golpe *m* ligero **2** SOMERSAULT : voltereta *f*
flip–flop [ˈflɪpˌflɑp] *n* **1** REVERSAL : giro *m* radical **2** THONG : chancla *f*, chancleta *f*
flippancy [ˈflɪpəntsi] *n, pl* **-cies** : ligereza *f*, falta *f* de seriedad
flippant [ˈflɪpənt] *adj* : ligero, frívolo, poco serio
flipper [ˈflɪpər] *n* : aleta *f*
flirt[1] [ˈflərt] *vi* **1** : coquetear, flirtear **2** TRIFLE : jugar ⟨to flirt with death : jugar con la muerte⟩
flirt[2] *n* : coqueto *m*, -ta *f*
flirtation [ˌflərˈteɪʃən] *n* : devaneo *m*, coqueteo *m*
flirtatious [ˌflərˈteɪʃəs] *adj* : insinuante, coqueto
flit [ˈflɪt] *vi* **flitted; flitting 1** : revolotear **2 to flit about** : ir y venir rápidamente
float[1] [ˈflo:t] *vi* **1** : flotar **2** WANDER : vagar, errar — *vt* **1** : poner a flote, hacer flotar (un barco) **2** LAUNCH : hacer flotar (una empresa) **3** ISSUE : emitir (acciones en la bolsa)
float[2] *n* **1** : flotador *m*, corcho *m* (para pescar) **2** BUOY : boya *f* **3** : carroza *f* (en un desfile)
floating [ˈflo:t̬ɪŋ] *adj* : flotante
flock[1] [ˈflɑk] *vi* **1** : moverse en rebaño **2** CONGREGATE : congregarse, reunirse
flock[2] *n* : rebaño *m* (de ovejas), bandada *f* (de pájaros)
floe [ˈflo:] *n* : témpano *m* de hielo
flog [ˈflɑg] *vt* **flogged; flogging** : azotar, fustigar
flood[1] [ˈflʌd] *vt* : inundar, anegar
flood[2] *n* **1** INUNDATION : inundación *f* **2** TORRENT : avalancha *f*, diluvio *m*, torrente *m* ⟨a flood of tears : un mar de lágrimas⟩
floodlight [ˈflʌdˌlaɪt] *n* : foco *m*
floodwater [ˈflʌdˌwɔt̬ər] *n* : crecida *f*, creciente *f*
floor[1] [ˈflor] *vt* **1** : solar, poner suelo a (una casa o una sala) **2** KNOCK DOWN : derribar, echar al suelo **3** NONPLUS : desconcertar, confundir, dejar perplejo
floor[2] *n* **1** : suelo *m*, piso *m* ⟨dance floor : pista de baile⟩ **2** STORY : piso *m*, planta *f* ⟨ground floor : planta baja⟩ ⟨second floor : primer piso⟩ **3** : mínimo *m* (de sueldos, precios, etc.)
floorboard [ˈflorˌbord] *n* : tabla *f* del suelo, suelo *m*, piso *m*
flooring [ˈflorɪŋ] *n* : entarimado *m*
flop[1] [ˈflɑp] *vi* **flopped; flopping 1** FLAP : golpearse, agitarse **2** COLLAPSE : dejarse caer, desplomarse **3** FAIL : fracasar
flop[2] *n* **1** FAILURE : fracaso *m* **2 to take a flop** : caerse
floppy [ˈflɑpi] *adj* **-pier; -est 1** : blando, flexible **2 floppy disk** : diskette *m*, disquete *m*
flora [ˈflorə] *n* : flora *f*
floral [ˈflorəl] *adj* : floral, floreado
florid [ˈflorɪd] *adj* **1** FLOWERY : florido **2** REDDISH : rojizo
florist [ˈflorɪst] *n* : florista *mf*
floss[1] [ˈflɔs] *vi* : limpiarse los dientes con hilo dental
floss[2] *n* **1** : hilo *m* de seda (de bordar) **2 → dental floss**
flotation [floˈteɪʃən] *n* : flotación *f*
flotilla [floˈtɪlə] *n* : flotilla *f*
flotsam [ˈflɑtsəm] *n* **1** : restos *mpl* flotantes (en el mar) **2 flotsam and jetsam** : desechos *mpl*, restos *mpl*
flounce[1] [ˈflaʊnts] *vi* **flounced; flouncing** : moverse haciendo aspavientos ⟨she flounced into the room : entró en la sala haciendo aspavientos⟩
flounce[2] *n* **1** RUFFLE : volante *m* **2** FLOURISH : aspaviento *m*
flounder[1] [ˈflaʊndər] *vi* **1** STRUGGLE : forcejear **2** STUMBLE : no saber qué hacer o decir, perder el hilo (en un discurso)
flounder[2] *n, pl* **flounder** *or* **flounders** : platija *f*
flour[1] [ˈflaʊər] *vt* : enharinar
flour[2] *n* : harina *f*
flourish[1] [ˈflərɪʃ] *vi* THRIVE : florecer, prosperar, crecer (dícese de las plantas) — *vt* BRANDISH : blandir
flourish[2] *n* : floritura *f*, floreo *m*
flourishing [ˈflərɪʃɪŋ] *adj* : floreciente, próspero
flout [ˈflaʊt] *vt* : desacatar, burlarse de
flow[1] [ˈflo:] *vi* **1** COURSE : fluir, manar, correr **2** CIRCULATE : circular, correr ⟨traffic is flowing smoothly : el tránsito está circulando con fluidez⟩

flow[2] *n* **1** FLOWING : flujo *m*, circulación *f* **2** STREAM : corriente *f*, chorro *m*
flower[1] [ˈflaʊər] *vi* : florecer, florear
flower[2] *n* : flor *f*
flowered [ˈflaʊərd] *adj* : florido, floreado
floweriness [ˈflaʊərinəs] *n* : floritura *f*
flowering[1] [ˈflaʊərɪŋ] *adj* : floreciente
flowering[2] *n* : floración *f*, florecimiento *m*
flowerpot [ˈflaʊərˌpɑt] *n* : maceta *f*, tiesto *m*, macetero *m*
flowery [ˈflaʊəri] *adj* **1** : florido **2** FLOWERED : floreado, de flores
flowing [ˈfloːɪŋ] *adj* : fluido, corriente
flown → **fly**
flu [ˈfluː] *n* : gripe *f*, gripa *f Col, Mex*
fluctuate [ˈflʌktʃʊˌeɪt] *vi* **-ated; -ating** : fluctuar
fluctuation [ˌflʌktʃʊˈeɪʃən] *n* : fluctuación *f*
flue [ˈfluː] *n* : tiro *m*, salida *f* de humos
fluency [ˈfluːən*t*si] *n* : fluidez *f*, soltura *f*
fluent [ˈfluːənt] *adj* : fluido
fluently [ˈfluːəntli] *adv* : con soltura, con fluidez
fluff[1] [ˈflʌf] *vt* **1** : mullir ⟨to fluff up the pillows : mullir las almohadas⟩ **2** BUNGLE : echar a perder, equivocarse
fluff[2] *n* **1** FUZZ : pelusa *f* **2** DOWN : plumón *m*
fluffy [ˈflʌfi] *adj* **fluffier; -est** **1** DOWNY : lleno de pelusa, velloso **2** SPONGY : esponjoso
fluid[1] [ˈfluːɪd] *adj* : fluido
fluid[2] *n* : fluido *m*, líquido *m*
fluidity [fluˈɪdət̬i] *n* : fluidez *f*
fluid ounce *n* : onza *f* líquida (29.57 mililitros)
fluke [ˈfluːk] *n* : golpe *m* de suerte, chiripa *f*, casualidad *f*
flung → **fling**
flunk [ˈflʌŋk] *vt* FAIL : reprobar — *vi* : salir reprobando
fluorescence [ˌflʊrˈɛsən*t*s, ˌflɔr-] *n* : fluorescencia *f*
fluorescent [ˌflʊrˈɛsənt, ˌflɔr-] *adj* : fluorescente
fluoridate [ˈflɔrəˌdeɪt, ˈflʊr-] *vt* **-dated; -dating** : fluorizar
fluoridation [ˌflɔrəˈdeɪʃən, ˌflʊr-] *n* : fluorización *f*, fluoración *f*
fluoride [ˈflɔrˌaɪd, ˈflʊr-] *n* : fluoruro *m*
fluorine [ˈflʊrˌiːn] *n* : flúor *m*
fluorocarbon [ˌflɔroˈkɑrbən, ˌflʊr-] *n* : fluorocarbono *m*
flurry [ˈfləri] *n, pl* **-ries** **1** GUST : ráfaga *f* **2** SNOWFALL : nevisca *f* **3** BUSTLE : frenesí *m*, bullicio *m* **4** BARRAGE : aluvión *m*, oleada *f* ⟨a flurry of questions : un aluvión de preguntas⟩
flush[1] [ˈflʌʃ] *vt* **1** : limpiar con agua ⟨to flush the toilet : jalar la cadena⟩ **2** RAISE : hacer salir, levantar (en la caza) — *vi* BLUSH : ruborizarse, sonrojarse
flush[2] *adv* : al mismo nivel, a ras
flush[3] *adj* **1** *or* **flushed** [ˈflʌʃt] : colorado, rojo, encendido (dícese de la cara) **2** FILLED : lleno a rebosar **3** ABUNDANT : copioso, abundante **4** AFFLUENT : adinerado **5** ALIGNED, SMOOTH : alineado, liso **6 flush against** : pegado a, contra
flush[4] *n* **1** FLOW, JET : chorro *m*, flujo *m* rápido **2** SURGE : arrebato *m*, arranque *m* ⟨a flush of anger : un arrebato de cólera⟩ **3** BLUSH : rubor *m*, sonrojo *m* **4** GLOW : resplandor *m*, flor *f* ⟨the flush of youth : la flor de la juventud⟩ ⟨in the flush of victory : en la euforia del triunfo⟩
fluster[1] [ˈflʌstər] *vt* : poner nervioso, aturdir
fluster[2] *n* : agitación *f*, confusión *f*
flute [ˈfluːt] *n* : flauta *f*
fluted [ˈfluːt̬əd] *adj* **1** GROOVED : estriado, acanalado **2** WAVY : ondulado
fluting [ˈfluːt̬ɪŋ] *n* : estrías *fpl*
flutist [ˈfluːt̬ɪst] *n* : flautista *mf*
flutter[1] [ˈflʌt̬ər] *vi* **1** : revolotear (dícese de un pájaro), ondear (dícese de una bandera), palpitar con fuerza (dícese del corazón) **2 to flutter about** : ir y venir, revolotear — *vt* : sacudir, batir
flutter[2] *n* **1** FLUTTERING : revoloteo *m*, aleteo *m* **2** COMMOTION, STIR : revuelo *m*, agitación *f*
flux [ˈflʌks] *n* **1** : flujo *m* (en física y medicina) **2** CHANGE : cambio *m* ⟨to be in a state of flux : estar cambiando continuamente⟩
fly[1] [ˈflaɪ] *v* **flew** [ˈfluː]; **flown** [ˈfloːn]; **flying** *vi* **1** : volar (dícese de los pájaros, etc.) **2** TRAVEL : volar (dícese de los aviones), ir en avión (dícese de los pasajeros) **3** FLOAT : flotar, ondear **4** FLEE : huir, escapar **5** RUSH : correr, irse volando **6** PASS : pasar (volando) ⟨how time flies! : ¡cómo pasa el tiempo!⟩ **7 to fly open** : abrir de golpe — *vt* : pilotar (un avión), hacer volar (una cometa)
fly[2] *n, pl* **flies** **1** : mosca *f* ⟨to drop like flies : caer como moscas⟩ **2** : bragueta *f* (de pantalones, etc.)
flyer → **flier**
flying saucer *n* : platillo *m* volador
flypaper [ˈflaɪˌpeɪpər] *n* : papel *m* matamoscas
flyspeck [ˈflaɪˌspɛk] *n* **1** : excremento *m* de mosca **2** SPECK : motita *f*, puntito *m*
flyswatter [ˈflaɪˌswɑt̬ər] *n* : matamoscas *m*
flywheel [ˈflaɪˌ*h*wiːl] *n* : volante *m*
foal[1] [ˈfoːl] *vi* : parir
foal[2] *n* : potro *m*, -tra *f*
foam[1] [ˈfoːm] *vi* : hacer espuma
foam[2] *n* : espuma *f*
foamy [ˈfoːmi] *adj* **foamier; -est** : espumoso
focal [ˈfoːkəl] *adj* **1** : focal, central **2 focal point** : foco *m*, punto *m* de referencia
fo'c'sle [ˈfoːksəl] → **forecastle**

focus[1] [ˈfoːkəs] *v* **-cused** *or* **-cussed; -cusing** *or* **-cussing** *vt* **1** : enfocar (un instrumento) **2** CONCENTRATE : concentrar, centrar — *vi* : enfocar, fijar la vista

focus[2] *n, pl* **-ci** [ˈfoːˌsaɪ, -ˌkaɪ] **1** : foco *m* ⟨to be in focus : estar enfocado⟩ **2** FOCUSING : enfoque *m* **3** CENTER : centro *m*, foco *m*

fodder [ˈfɑdər] *n* : pienso *m*, forraje *m*

foe [ˈfoː] *n* : enemigo *m*, -ga *f*

fog[1] [ˈfɔg, ˈfɑg] *v* **fogged; fogging** *vt* : empañar — *vi* **to fog up** : empañarse

fog[2] *n* : niebla *f*, neblina *f*

foggy [ˈfɔgi, ˈfɑ-] *adj* **foggier; -est** : nebuloso, brumoso

foghorn [ˈfɔgˌhɔrn, ˈfɑg-] *n* : sirena *f* de niebla

fogy [ˈfoːgi] *n, pl* **-gies** : carca *mf fam*, persona *f* chapada a la antigua

foible [ˈfɔɪbəl] *n* : flaqueza *f*, debilidad *f*

foil[1] [ˈfɔɪl] *vt* : frustrar, hacer fracasar

foil[2] *n* **1** : lámina *f* de metal, papel *m* de aluminio **2** CONTRAST : contraste *m*, complemento *m* **3** SWORD : florete *m* (en esgrima)

foist [ˈfɔɪst] *vt* : encajar, endilgar *fam*, colocar

fold[1] [ˈfoːld] *vt* **1** BEND : doblar, plegar **2** CLASP : cruzar (brazos), enlazar (manos), plegar (alas) **3** EMBRACE : estrechar, abrazar **4 to fold in** : incorporar ⟨fold in the cream : incorpore la crema⟩ — *vi* **1** FAIL : fracasar **2 to fold up** : doblarse, plegarse

fold[2] *n* **1** SHEEPFOLD : redil *m* (para ovejas) **2** FLOCK : rebaño *m* ⟨to return to the fold : volver al redil⟩ **3** CREASE : pliegue *m*, doblez *m*

folder [ˈfoːldər] *n* **1** CIRCULAR : circular *f*, folleto *m* **2** BINDER : carpeta *f*

foliage [ˈfoːliɪʤ, -lɪʤ] *n* : follaje *m*

folio [ˈfoːliˌoː] *n, pl* **-lios** : folio *m*

folk[1] [ˈfoːk] *adj* : popular, folklórico ⟨folk customs : costumbres populares⟩ ⟨folk dance : danza folklórica⟩

folk[2] *n, pl* **folk** *or* **folks** **1** PEOPLE : gente *f* **2 folks** *npl* : familia *f*, padres *mpl*

folklore [ˈfoːkˌlor] *n* : folklore *m*

folklorist [ˈfoːkˌlorɪst] *n* : folklorista *mf*

folksy [ˈfoːksi] *adj* **folksier; -est** : campechano

follicle [ˈfɑlɪkəl] *n* : folículo *m*

follow [ˈfɑlo] *vt* **1** : seguir ⟨follow the guide : siga al guía⟩ ⟨she followed the road : siguió el camino, continuó por el camino⟩ **2** PURSUE : perseguir, seguir **3** OBEY : seguir, cumplir, observar **4** UNDERSTAND : entender — *vi* **1** : seguir **2** UNDERSTAND : entender **3 it follows that . . .** : se deduce que . . .

follower [ˈfɑloər] *n* : seguidor *m*, -dora *f*

following[1] [ˈfɑloɪŋ] *adj* NEXT : siguiente

following[2] *n* FOLLOWERS : seguidores *mpl*

following[3] *prep* AFTER : después de

follow through *vi* **to follow through with** : continuar con, realizar

follow up *vt* : seguir (una sugerencia, etc.), investigar (una huella)

folly [ˈfɑli] *n, pl* **-lies** : locura *f*, desatino *m*

foment [foˈmɛnt] *vt* : fomentar

fond [ˈfɑnd] *adj* **1** LOVING : cariñoso, tierno **2** PARTIAL : aficionado **3** FERVENT : ferviente, fervoroso

fondle [ˈfɑndəl] *vt* **-dled; -dling** : acariciar

fondly [ˈfɑndli] *adv* : cariñosamente, afectuosamente

fondness [ˈfɑndnəs] *n* **1** LOVE : cariño *m* **2** LIKING : afición *f*

fondue [fɑnˈduː, -ˈdjuː] *n* : fondue *f*

font [ˈfɑnt] *n* **1** *or* **baptismal font** : pila *f* bautismal **2** FOUNTAIN : fuente *f*

food [ˈfuːd] *n* : comida *f*, alimento *m*

food chain *n* : cadena *f* alimenticia

foodstuffs [ˈfuːdˌstʌfs] *npl* : comestibles *mpl*

fool[1] [ˈfuːl] *vi* **1** JOKE : bromear, hacer el tonto **2** TOY : jugar, juguetear ⟨don't fool with the computer : no juegues con la computadora⟩ **3 to fool around** : perder el tiempo ⟨he fools around instead of working : pierde el tiempo en vez de trabajar⟩ — *vt* DECEIVE : engañar, burlar

fool[2] *n* **1** IDIOT : idiota *mf*; tonto *m*, -ta *f*; bobo *m*, -ba *f* **2** JESTER : bufón *m*, -fona *f*

foolhardiness [ˈfuːlˌhɑrdinəs] *n* : imprudencia *f*

foolhardy [ˈfuːlˌhɑrdi] *adj* RASH : imprudente, temerario, precipitado

foolish [ˈfuːlɪʃ] *adj* **1** STUPID : insensato, estúpido **2** SILLY : idiota, tonto

foolishly [ˈfuːlɪʃli] *adv* : tontamente

foolishness [ˈfuːlɪʃnəs] *n* : insensatez *f*, estupidez *f*, tontería *f*

foolproof [ˈfuːlˌpruːf] *adj* : infalible

foot [ˈfʊt] *n, pl* **feet** [ˈfiːt] : pie *m*

footage [ˈfʊṭɪʤ] *n* : medida *f* en pies, metraje *m* (en el cine)

football [ˈfʊtˌbɔl] *n* : futbol *m* americano, fútbol *m* americano

footbridge [ˈfʊtˌbrɪʤ] *n* : pasarela *f*, puente *m* peatonal

foothills [ˈfʊtˌhɪlz] *npl* : estribaciones *fpl*

foothold [ˈfʊtˌhoːld] *n* **1** : punto *m* de apoyo **2 to gain a foothold** : afianzarse en una posición

footing [ˈfʊṭɪŋ] *n* **1** BALANCE : equilibrio *m* **2** FOOTHOLD : punto *m* de apoyo **3** BASIS : base *f* ⟨on an equal footing : en igualdad⟩

footlights [ˈfʊtˌlaɪts] *npl* : candilejas *fpl*

footlocker [ˈfʊtˌlɑkər] *n* : baúl *m* pequeño, cofre *m*

footloose [ˈfʊtˌluːs] *adj* : libre y sin compromiso

footman [ˈfʊtmən] *n, pl* **-men** [-mən, -ˌmɛn] : lacayo *m*

footnote [ˈfʊtˌnoːt] *n* : nota *f* al pie de la página

footpath [ˈfʊtˌpæθ] *n* : sendero *m*, senda *f*, vereda *f*

footprint [ˈfʊtˌprɪnt] *n* : huella *f*
footrace [ˈfʊtˌreɪs] *n* : carrera *f* pedestre
footrest [ˈfʊtˌrɛst] *n* : apoyapiés *m*, reposapiés *m*
footstep [ˈfʊtˌstɛp] *n* **1** STEP : paso *m* **2** FOOTPRINT : huella *f*
footstool [ˈfʊtˌstuːl] *n* : taburete *m*, escabel *m*
footwear [ˈfʊtˌwær] *n* : calzado *m*
footwork [ˈfʊtˌwərk] *n* : juego *m* de piernas, juego *m* de pies
fop [ˈfɑp] *n* : petimetre *m*, dandi *m*
for[1] [ˈfɔr] *conj* : puesto que, porque
for[2] *prep* **1** (*indicating purpose*) : para, de ⟨clothes for children : ropa para niños⟩ ⟨it's time for dinner : es la hora de comer⟩ **2** BECAUSE OF : por ⟨for fear of : por miedo de⟩ **3** (*indicating a recipient*) : para, por ⟨a gift for you : un regalo para ti⟩ **4** (*indicating support*) : por ⟨he fought for his country : luchó por su patria⟩ **5** (*indicating a goal*) : por, para ⟨a cure for cancer : una cura para el cáncer⟩ ⟨for your own good : por tu propio bien⟩ **6** (*indicating correspondence or exchange*) : por, para ⟨I bought it for $5 : lo compré por $5⟩ ⟨a lot of trouble for nothing : mucha molestia para nada⟩ **7** AS FOR : para, con respecto a **8** (*indicating duration*) : durante, por ⟨he's going for two years : se va por dos años⟩ ⟨I spoke for ten minutes : hablé (durante) diez minutos⟩ ⟨she has known it for three months : lo sabe desde hace tres meses⟩
forage[1] [ˈfɔrɪʤ] *v* **-aged; -aging** *vi* : hurgar (en busca de alimento) — *vt* : buscar (provisiones)
forage[2] *n* : forraje *m*
foray [ˈfɔrˌeɪ] *n* : incursión *f*
forbear[1] [fɔrˈbær] *vi* **-bore** [-ˈbor]; **-borne** [-ˈborn]; **-bearing** **1** ABSTAIN : abstenerse **2** : tener paciencia
forbear[2] → **forbear**
forbearance [fɔrˈbærənts] *n* **1** ABSTAINING : abstención *f* **2** PATIENCE : paciencia *f*
forbid [fərˈbɪd] *vt* **-bade** [-ˈbæd, -ˈbeɪd]; **-bidden** [-ˈbɪdən]; **-bidding** **1** PROHIBIT : prohibir **2** PREVENT : impedir
forbidding [fərˈbɪdɪŋ] *adj* **1** IMPOSING : imponente **2** DISAGREEABLE : desagradable, ingrato **3** GRIM : severo
force[1] [ˈfors] *vt* **forced; forcing** **1** COMPEL : obligar, forzar **2** : forzar ⟨to force open the window : forzar la ventana⟩ ⟨to force a lock : forzar una cerradura⟩ **3** IMPOSE : imponer, obligar
force[2] *n* **1** : fuerza *f* **2 by force** : por la fuerza **3 in force** : en vigor, en vigencia
forced [ˈforst] *adj* : forzado, forzoso
forceful [ˈforsfəl] *adj* : fuerte, energético, contundente
forcefully [ˈforsfəli] *adv* : con energía, con fuerza
forcefulness [ˈforsfəlnəs] *n* : contundencia *f*, fuerza *f*
forceps [ˈfɔrsəps, -ˌsɛps] *ns & pl* : fórceps *m*
forcible [ˈforsəbəl] *adj* **1** FORCED : forzoso **2** CONVINCING : contundente, convincente — **forcibly** [-bli] *adv*
ford[1] [ˈford] *vt* : vadear
ford[2] *n* : vado *m*
fore[1] [ˈfor] *adv* **1** FORWARD : hacia adelante **2 fore and aft** : de popa a proa
fore[2] *adj* **1** FORWARD : delantero, de adelante **2** FORMER : anterior
fore[3] *n* **1** : frente *m*, delantera *f* **2 to come to the fore** : empezar a destacar, saltar a primera plana
fore–and–aft [ˈforənˈæft, -ənd-] *adj* : longitudinal
forearm [ˈforˌɑrm] *n* : antebrazo *m*
forebear [ˈforˌbær] *n* : antepasado *m*, -da *f*
foreboding [forˈboːdɪŋ] *n* : premonición *f*, presentimiento *m*
forecast[1] [ˈforˌkæst] *vt* **-cast; -casting** : pronosticar, predecir
forecast[2] *n* : predicción *f*, pronóstico *m*
forecastle [ˈfoːksəl] *n* : castillo *m* de proa
foreclose [forˈkloːz] *vt* **-closed; -closing** : ejecutar (una hipoteca)
forefather [ˈforˌfɑðər] *n* : antepasado *m*, ancestro *m*
forefinger [ˈforˌfɪŋgər] *n* : índice *m*, dedo *m* índice
forefoot [ˈforˌfʊt] *n* : pata *f* delantera
forefront [ˈforˌfrʌnt] *n* : frente *m*, vanguardia *f* ⟨in the forefront : a la vanguardia⟩
forego [forˈgoː] *vt* **-went; -gone; -going** **1** PRECEDE : preceder **2** → **forgo**
foregoing [forˈgoːɪŋ] *adj* : precedente, anterior
foregone [forˈgɔn] *adj* : previsto ⟨a foregone conclusion : un resultado inevitable⟩
foreground [ˈforˌgraʊnd] *n* : primer plano *m*
forehand[1] [ˈforˌhænd] *adj* : directo, derecho
forehand[2] *n* : golpe *m* del derecho
forehead [ˈfɔrəd, ˈforˌhɛd] *n* : frente *f*
foreign [ˈfɔrən] *adj* **1** : extranjero, exterior ⟨foreign countries : países extranjeros⟩ ⟨foreign trade : comercio exterior⟩ **2** ALIEN : ajeno, extraño ⟨foreign to their nature : ajeno a su carácter⟩ ⟨a foreign body : un cuerpo extraño⟩
foreigner [ˈfɔrənər] *n* : extranjero *m*, -ra *f*
foreknowledge [forˈnɑlɪʤ] *n* : conocimiento *m* previo
foreleg [ˈforˌlɛg] *n* : pata *f* delantera
foreman [ˈformən] *n, pl* **-men** [-mən, -ˌmɛn] : capataz *mf* ⟨foreman of the jury : presidente del jurado⟩
foremost[1] [ˈforˌmoːst] *adv* : en primer lugar
foremost[2] *adj* : más importante, principal, grande
forenoon [ˈforˌnuːn] *n* : mañana *m*

forensic [fəˈrɛntsɪk] *adj* **1** RHETORICAL : retórico, de argumentación **2** : forense ⟨forensic medicine : medicina forense⟩
foreordain [ˌforɔrˈdeɪn] *vt* : predestinar, predeterminar
forequarter [ˈforˌkwɔrt̬ər] *n* : cuarto *m* delantero
forerunner [ˈforˌrʌnər] *n* : precursor *m*, -sora *f*
foresee [forˈsiː] *vt* **-saw; -seen; -seeing** : prever
foreseeable [forˈsiːəbəl] *adj* : previsible ⟨in the foreseeable future : en el futuro inmediato⟩
foreshadow [forˈʃædoː] *vt* : anunciar, prefigurar
foresight [ˈforˌsaɪt] *n* : previsión *f*
foresighted [ˈforˌsaɪt̬əd] *adj* : previsto
forest [ˈfɔrəst] *n* : bosque *m* (en zonas templadas), selva *f* (en zonas tropicales)
forestall [forˈstɔl] *vt* **1** PREVENT : prevenir, impedir **2** PREEMPT : adelantarse a
forested [ˈfɔrəstəd] *adj* : arbolado
forester [ˈfɔrəstər] *n* : silvicultor *m*, -tora *f*
forestland [ˈfɔrəstˌlænd] *n* : zona *f* boscosa
forest ranger → **ranger**
forestry [ˈfɔrəstri] *n* : silvicultura *f*, ingeniería *f* forestal
foreswear → **forswear**
foretaste[1] [ˈforˌteɪst] *vt* **-tasted; -tasting** : anticipar
foretaste[2] *n* : anticipo *m*
foretell [forˈtɛl] *vt* **-told; -telling** : predecir, pronosticar, profetizar
forethought [ˈforˌθɔt] *n* : previsión *f*, reflexión *f* previa
forever [fɔrˈɛvər] *adv* **1** PERPETUALLY : para siempre, eternamente **2** CONTINUALLY : siempre, constantemente
forevermore [fɔrˌɛvərˈmor] *adv* : por siempre jamás
forewarn [forˈwɔrn] *vt* : prevenir, advertir
foreword [ˈforwərd] *n* : prólogo *m*
forfeit[1] [ˈfɔrfət] *vt* : perder el derecho a
forfeit[2] *n* **1** FINE, PENALTY : multa *f* **2** : prenda *f* (en un juego)
forge[1] [ˈforʤ] *v* **forged; forging** *vt* **1** : forjar (metal o un plan) **2** COUNTERFEIT : falsificar — *vi* **to forge ahead** : avanzar, seguir adelante
forge[2] *n* : forja *f*
forger [ˈforʤər] *n* : falsificador *m*, -dora *f*
forgery [ˈforʤəri] *n, pl* **-eries** : falsificación *f*
forget [fərˈgɛt] *v* **-got** [-ˈgɑt]; **-gotten** [-ˈgɑtən] *or* **-got; -getting** *vt* : olvidar — *vi* **to forget about** : olvidarse de, no acordarse de
forgetful [fərˈgɛtfəl] *adj* : olvidadizo
forget-me-not [fərˈgɛtmiˌnɑt] *n* : nomeolvides *mf*
forgettable [fərˈgɛt̬əbəl] *adj* : poco memorable
forgivable [fərˈgɪvəbəl] *adj* : perdonable
forgive [fərˈgɪv] *vt* **-gave** [-ˈgeɪv]; **-given** [-ˈgɪvən]; **-giving** : perdonar
forgiveness [fərˈgɪvnəs] *n* : perdón *m*
forgiving [fərˈgɪvɪŋ] *adj* : indulgente, comprensivo, clemente
forgo *or* **forego** [forˈgoː] *vt* **-went; -gone; -going** : privarse de, renunciar a
fork[1] [ˈfɔrk] *vi* : ramificarse, bifurcarse — *vt* **1** : levantar (con un tenedor, una horca, etc.) **2 to fork over** : desembolsar
fork[2] *n* **1** : tenedor *m* (utensilio de cocina) **2** PITCHFORK : horca *f*, horquilla *f* **3** : bifurcación *f* (de un río o camino), horqueta *f* (de un árbol)
forked [ˈfɔrkt, ˈfɔrkəd] *adj* : bífido, ahorquillado
forklift [ˈfɔrkˌlɪft] *n* : carretilla *f* elevadora
forlorn [fɔrˈlɔrn] *adj* **1** DESOLATE : abandonado, desolado, desamparado **2** SAD : triste **3** DESPERATE : desesperado
forlornly [fɔrˈlɔrnli] *adv* **1** SADLY : con tristeza **2** HALFHEARTEDLY : sin ánimo
form[1] [ˈfɔrm] *vt* **1** FASHION, MAKE : formar **2** DEVELOP : moldear, desarrollar **3** CONSTITUTE : constituir, formar **4** ACQUIRE : adquirir (un hábito), formar (una idea) — *vi* : tomar forma, formarse
form[2] *n* **1** SHAPE : forma *f*, figura *f* **2** MANNER : manera *f*, forma *f* **3** DOCUMENT : formulario *m* **4** : forma *f* ⟨in good form : en buena forma⟩ ⟨true to form : en forma consecuente⟩ **5** MOLD : molde *m* **6** KIND, VARIETY : clase *f*, tipo *m* **7** : forma *f* (en gramática) ⟨plural forms : formas plurales⟩
formal[1] [ˈfɔrməl] *adj* **1** CEREMONIOUS : formal, de etiqueta, ceremonioso **2** OFFICIAL : formal, oficial, de forma
formal[2] *n* **1** BALL : baile *m* formal, baile *m* de etiqueta **2** *or* **formal dress** : traje *m* de etiqueta
formaldehyde [fɔrˈmældəˌhaɪd] *n* : formaldehído *m*
formality [fɔrˈmæləti] *n, pl* **-ties** : formalidad *f*
formalize [ˈfɔrməˌlaɪz] *vt* **-ized; -izing** : formalizar
formally [ˈfɔrməli] *adv* : formalmente
format[1] [ˈfɔrˌmæt] *vt* **-matted; -matting** : formatear
format[2] *n* : formato *m*
formation [fɔrˈmeɪʃən] *n* **1** FORMING : formación *f* **2** SHAPE : forma *f* **3 in formation** : en formación
formative [ˈfɔrmət̬ɪv] *adj* : formativo
former [ˈfɔrmər] *adj* **1** PREVIOUS : antiguo, anterior ⟨the former president : el antiguo presidente⟩ **2** : primero (de dos)
formerly [ˈfɔrmərli] *adv* : anteriormente, antes

formidable [ˈfɔrmədəbəl, fɔrˈmɪdə-] *adj* : formidable — **formidably** *adv*
formless [ˈfɔrmləs] *adj* : informe, amorfo
formula [ˈfɔrmjələ] *n, pl* **-las** *or* **-lae** [-ˌliː, -ˌlaɪ] **1** : fórmula *f* **2 baby formula** : preparado *m* para biberón
formulate [ˈfɔrmjəˌleɪt] *vt* **-lated; -lating** : formular, hacer
formulation [ˌfɔrmjəˈleɪʃən] *n* : formulación *f*
fornicate [ˈfɔrnəˌkeɪt] *vi* **-cated; -cating** : fornicar
fornication [ˌfɔrnəˈkeɪʃən] *n* : fornicación *f*
forsake [fərˈseɪk] *vt* **-sook** [-ˈsʊk]; **-saken** [-ˈseɪkən]; **-saking 1** ABANDON : abandonar, desamparar **2** RELINQUISH : renunciar a
forswear [fɔrˈswær] *v* **-swore; -sworn; -swearing** *vt* RENOUNCE : renunciar a — *vi* : perjurar
forsythia [fərˈsɪθiə] *n* : forsitia *f*
fort [ˈfort] *n* **1** STRONGHOLD : fuerte *m*, fortaleza *f*, fortín *m* **2** BASE : base *f* militar
forte [ˈfort, ˈforˌteɪ] *n* : fuerte *m*
forth [ˈforθ] *adv* **1** : adelante ⟨from this day forth : de hoy en adelante⟩ **2 and so forth** : etcétera
forthcoming [forθˈkʌmɪŋ, ˈforθˌ-] *adj* **1** COMING : próximo **2** DIRECT, OPEN : directo, franco, comunicativo
forthright [ˈforθˌraɪt] *adj* : directo, franco — **forthrightly** *adv*
forthrightness [ˈforθˌraɪtnəs] *n* : franqueza *f*
forthwith [forθˈwɪθ, -ˈwɪð] *adv* : inmediatamente, en el acto, enseguida
fortieth[1] [ˈfɔrt̬iəθ] *adj* : cuadragésimo
fortieth[2] *n* **1** : cuadragésimo *m*, -ma *f* (en una serie) **2** : cuarentavo *m*, cuarentava parte *f*
fortification [ˌfɔrt̬əfəˈkeɪʃən] *n* : fortificación *f*
fortify [ˈfɔrt̬əˌfaɪ] *vt* **-fied; -fying** : fortificar
fortitude [ˈfɔrt̬əˌtuːd, -ˌtjuːd] *n* : fortaleza *f*, valor *m*
fortnight [ˈfortˌnaɪt] *n* : quince días *mpl*, dos semanas *fpl*
fortnightly[1] [ˈfortˌnaɪtli] *adv* : cada quince días
fortnightly[2] *adj* : quincenal
fortress [ˈfɔrtrəs] *n* : fortaleza *f*
fortuitous [fɔrˈtuːət̬əs, -ˈtjuː-] *adj* : fortuito, accidental
fortunate [ˈfɔrtʃənət] *adj* : afortunado
fortunately [ˈfɔrtʃənətli] *adv* : afortunadamente, con suerte
fortune [ˈfɔrtʃən] *n* **1** : fortuna *f* ⟨to seek one's fortune : buscar uno su fortuna⟩ **2** LUCK : suerte *f*, fortuna *f* **3** DESTINY, FUTURE : destino *m*, buenaventura *f* **4** : dineral *m*, platal *m* ⟨she spent a fortune : se gastó un dineral⟩
fortune–teller [ˈfɔrtʃənˌtɛlər] *n* : adivino *m*, -na *f*
fortune–telling [ˈfɔrtʃənˌtɛlɪŋ] *n* : adivinación *f*
forty[1] [ˈfɔrt̬i] *adj* : cuarenta
forty[2] *n, pl* **forties** : cuarenta *m*
forum [ˈforəm] *n, pl* **-rums** : foro *m*
forward[1] [ˈfɔrwərd] *vt* **1** PROMOTE : promover, adelantar, fomentar **2** SEND : remitir, enviar
forward[2] *adv* **1** : adelante, hacia adelante ⟨to go forward : irse adelante⟩ **2 from this day forward** : de aquí en adelante
forward[3] *adj* **1** : hacia adelante, delantero **2** BRASH : atrevido, descarado
forward[4] *n* : delantero *m*, -ra *f* (en deportes)
forwarder [ˈfɔrwərdər] *n* : agencia *f* de transportes, agente *mf* expedidor
forwardness [ˈfɔrwərdnəs] *n* : atrevimiento *m*, descaro *m*
forwards [ˈfɔrwərdz] *adv* → **forward**[2]
fossil[1] [ˈfɑsəl] *adj* : fósil
fossil[2] *n* : fósil *m*
fossilize [ˈfɑsəˌlaɪz] *vt* **-ized; -izing** : fosilizar — *vi* : fosilizarse
foster[1] [ˈfɔstər] *vt* : promover, fomentar
foster[2] *adj* : adoptivo ⟨foster child : niño adoptivo⟩
fought → **fight**
foul[1] [ˈfaʊl] *vi* : cometer faltas (en deportes) — *vt* **1** DIRTY, POLLUTE : contaminar, ensuciar **2** TANGLE : enredar
foul[2] *adv* **1** → **foully 2** : contra las reglas
foul[3] *adj* **1** REPULSIVE : asqueroso, repugnante **2** CLOGGED : atascado, obstruido **3** TANGLED : enredado **4** OBSCENE : obsceno **5** BAD : malo ⟨foul weather : mal tiempo⟩ **6** : antirreglamentario (en deportes)
foul[4] *n* : falta *f*, faul *m*
foully [ˈfaʊli] *adv* : asquerosamente
foulmouthed [ˈfaʊlˌmæʊːðd, -ˌmaʊθt] *adj* : malhablado
foulness [ˈfaʊlnəs] *n* **1** DIRTINESS : suciedad *f* **2** INCLEMENCY : inclemencia *f* **3** OBSCENITY : obscenidad *f*, grosería *f*
foul play *n* : actos *mpl* criminales
foul–up [ˈfaʊlˌʌp] *n* : lío *m*, confusión *f*, desastre *m*
foul up *vt* SPOIL : estropear, arruinar — *vi* BUNGLE : echar todo a perder
found[1] → **find**
found[2] [ˈfaʊnd] *vt* : fundar, establecer
foundation [faʊnˈdeɪʃən] *n* **1** FOUNDING : fundación *f* **2** BASIS : fundamento *m*, base *f* **3** INSTITUTION : fundación *f* **4** : cimientos *mpl* (de un edificio)
founder[1] [ˈfaʊndər] *vi* SINK : hundirse, irse a pique
founder[2] *n* : fundador *m*, -dora *f*
founding [ˈfaʊndɪŋ] *adj* : fundador ⟨the founding fathers : los fundadores⟩
foundling [ˈfaʊndlɪŋ] *n* : expósito *m*, -ta *f*
foundry [ˈfaʊndri] *n, pl* **-dries** : fundición *f*

fount ['faʊnt] *n* SOURCE : fuente *f*, origen *m*
fountain ['faʊntən] *n* **1** SPRING : fuente *f*, manantial *m* **2** SOURCE : fuente *f*, origen *m* **3** JET : chorro *m* (de agua), surtidor *m*
fountain pen *n* : pluma *f* fuente
four[1] ['for] *adj* : cuatro
four[2] *n* **1** : cuatro *m* **2 on all fours** : a gatas
fourfold ['for,fo:ld, -'fo:ld] *adj* : cuadruple
four hundred[1] *adj* : cuatrocientos
four hundred[2] *n* : cuatrocientos *m*
fourscore ['for'skor] *adj* EIGHTY : ochenta *m*
fourteen[1] [for'ti:n] *adj* : catorce
fourteen[2] *n* : catorce *m*
fourteenth[1] [for'ti:nθ] *adj* : decimocuarto
fourteenth[2] *n* **1** : decimocuarto *m*, -ta *f* (en una serie) **2** : catorceavo *m*, catorceava parte *f*
fourth[1] ['forθ] *adj* : cuarto
fourth[2] *n* **1** : cuarto *m*, -ta *f* (en una serie) **2** : cuarto *m*, cuarta parte *f*
fowl ['faʊl] *n, pl* **fowl** *or* **fowls** **1** BIRD : ave *f* **2** CHICKEN : pollo *m*
fox[1] ['fɑks] *vt* **1** TRICK : engañar **2** BAFFLE : confundir
fox[2] *n, pl* **foxes** : zorro *m*, -ra *f*
foxglove ['fɑks,glʌv] *n* : dedalera *f*, digital *f*
foxhole ['fɑks,ho:l] *n* : hoyo *m* para atrincherarse, trinchera *f* individual
foxy ['fɑksi] *adj* **foxier; -est** SHREWD : astuto
foyer ['fɔɪər, 'fɔɪ,jeɪ] *n* : vestíbulo *m*
fracas ['freɪkəs, 'fræ-] *n, pl* **-cases** [-kəsəz] : altercado *m*, pelea *f*, reyerta *f*
fraction ['frækʃən] *n* **1** : fracción *f*, quebrado *m* **2** PORTION : porción *f*, parte *f*
fractional ['frækʃənəl] *adj* **1** : fraccionario **2** TINY : minúsculo, mínimo, insignificante
fractious ['frækʃəs] *adj* **1** UNRULY : rebelde **2** IRRITABLE : malhumorado, irritable
fracture[1] ['frækʧər] *vt* **-tured; -turing** : fracturar
fracture[2] *n* **1** : fractura *f* (de un hueso) **2** CRACK : fisura *f*, grieta *f*, falla *f* (geológica)
fragile ['frædʒəl, -,dʒaɪl] *adj* : frágil
fragility [frə'dʒɪləṭi] *n, pl* **-ties** : fragilidad *f*
fragment[1] ['fræg,mɛnt] *vt* : fragmentar — *vi* : fragmentarse, hacerse añicos
fragment[2] ['frægmənt] *n* : fragmento *m*, trozo *m*, pedazo *m*
fragmentary ['frægmən,tɛri] *adj* : fragmentario, incompleto
fragmentation [,frægmən'teɪʃən, -,mn-] *n* : fragmentación *f*
fragrance ['freɪgrənts] *n* : fragancia *f*, aroma *m*
fragrant ['freɪgrənt] *adj* : fragante, aromático — **fragrantly** *adv*
frail ['freɪl] *adj* : débil, delicado
frailty ['freɪlti] *n, pl* **-ties** : debilidad *f*, flaqueza *f*
frame[1] ['freɪm] *vt* **framed; framing** **1** FORMULATE : formular, elaborar **2** BORDER : enmarcar, encuadrar **3** INCRIMINATE : incriminar
frame[2] *n* **1** BODY : cuerpo *m* **2** : armazón *f* (de un edificio, un barco, o un avión), bastidor *m* (de un automóvil), cuadro *m* (de una bicicleta), marco *m* (de un cuadro, una ventana, una puerta, etc.) **3 frames** *npl* : armazón *mf*, montura *f* (para anteojos) **4 frame of mind** : estado *m* de ánimo
framework ['freɪm,wərk] *n* **1** SKELETON, STRUCTURE : armazón *f*, estructura *f* **2** BASIS : marco *m*
franc ['fræŋk] *n* : franco *m*
franchise ['fræn,ʧaɪz] *n* **1** LICENSE : licencia *f* exclusiva, concesión *f* (en comercio) **2** SUFFRAGE : sufragio *m*
franchisee [,fræn,ʧaɪ'zi:, -ʧə-] *n* : concesionario *m*, -ria *f*
Franciscan [fræn'sɪskən] *n* : franciscano *m*, -na *f* — **Franciscan** *adj*
frank[1] ['fræŋk] *vt* : franquear
frank[2] *adj* : franco, sincero, cándido — **frankly** *adv*
frank[3] *n* : franqueo *m* (de correo)
frankfurter ['fræŋkfərṭər, -,fər-] *or* **frankfurt** [-fərt] *n* : salchicha *f* (de Frankfurt, de Viena), perro *m* caliente
frankincense ['fræŋkən,sɛnts] *n* : incienso *m*
frankness ['fræŋknəs] *n* : franqueza *f*, sinceridad *f*, candidez *f*
frantic ['fræntɪk] *adj* : frenético, desesperado — **frantically** *adv*
fraternal [frə'tərnəl] *adj* : fraterno, fraternal
fraternity [frə'tərnəṭi] *n, pl* **-ties** : fraternidad *f*
fraternization [,fræṭərnə'zeɪʃən] *n* : fraternización *f*, confraternización *f*
fraternize ['fræṭər,naɪz] *vi* **-nized; -nizing** : fraternizar, confraternizar
fratricidal [,frætrə'saɪdəl] *adj* : fratricida
fratricide ['frætrə,saɪd] *n* : fratricidio *m*
fraud ['frɔd] *n* **1** DECEPTION, SWINDLE : fraude *m*, estafa *f*, engaño *m* **2** IMPOSTOR : impostor *m*, -tora *f*; farsante *mf*
fraudulent ['frɔdʒələnt] *adj* : fraudulento — **fraudulently** *adv*
fraught ['frɔt] *adj* **fraught with** : lleno de, cargado de
fray[1] ['freɪ] *vt* **1** WEAR : desgastar, deshilachar **2** IRRITATE : crispar, irritar (los nervios) — *vi* : desgastarse, deshilacharse
fray[2] *n* : pelea *f* ⟨to join the fray : salir a la palestra⟩ ⟨to return to the fray : volver a la carga⟩

frazzle[1] [ˈfræzəl] *vt* **-zled; -zling 1** FRAY : desgastar, deshilachar **2** EXHAUST : agotar, fatigar

frazzle[2] *n* EXHAUSTION : agotamiento *m*

freak [ˈfri:k] *n* **1** ODDITY : ejemplar *m* anormal, fenómeno *m*, rareza *f* **2** ENTHUSIAST : entusiasta *mf*

freakish [ˈfri:kɪʃ] *adj* : extraño, estrafalario, raro

freak out *vi* : ponerse como loco — *vt* : darle un ataque (a alguien)

freckle[1] [ˈfrɛkəl] *vi* **-led; -ling** : cubrirse de pecas

freckle[2] *n* : peca *f*

free[1] [ˈfri:] *vt* **freed; freeing 1** LIBERATE : libertar, liberar, poner en libertad **2** RELIEVE, RID : librar, eximir **3** RELEASE, UNTIE : desatar, soltar **4** UNCLOG : desatascar, destapar

free[2] *adv* **1** FREELY : libremente **2** GRATIS : gratuitamente, gratis

free[3] *adj* **freer; freest 1** : libre ⟨free as a bird : libre como un pájaro⟩ **2** EXEMPT : libre ⟨tax-free : libre de impuestos⟩ **3** GRATIS : gratuito, gratis **4** VOLUNTARY : espontáneo, voluntario, libre **5** UNOCCUPIED : desocupado, libre **6** LOOSE : suelto

freebooter [ˈfri:ˌbu:t̬ər] *n* : pirata *mf*

freeborn [ˈfri:ˈbɔrn] *adj* : nacido libre

freedom [ˈfri:dəm] *n* : libertad *f*

free–for–all [ˈfri:fərˌɔl] *n* : pelea *f*, batalla *f* campal

freelance[1] [ˈfri:ˌlænts] *vi* **-lanced; -lancing** : trabajar por cuenta propia

freelance[2] *adj* : por cuenta propia, independiente

freeload [ˈfri:ˌlo:d] *vi* : gorronear *fam*, gorrear *fam*

freeloader [ˈfri:ˌlo:dər] *n* : gorrón *m*, -rrona *f*; gorrero *m*, -ra *f*; vividor *m*, -dora *f*

freely [ˈfri:li] *adv* **1** FREE : libremente **2** GRATIS : gratis, gratuitamente

freestanding [ˈfri:ˈstændɪŋ] *adj* : de pie, no empotrado, independiente

freeway [ˈfri:ˌweɪ] *n* : autopista *f*

freewill [ˈfri:ˌwɪl] *adj* : de propia voluntad

free will *n* : libre albedrío *m*, propia voluntad *f*

freeze[1] [ˈfri:z] *v* **froze** [ˈfro:z]; **frozen** [ˈfro:zən]; **freezing** *vi* **1** : congelarse, helarse ⟨the water froze in the lake : el agua se congeló en el lago⟩ ⟨my blood froze : se me heló la sangre⟩ ⟨I'm freezing : me estoy helando⟩ **2** STOP : quedarse inmóvil — *vt* : helar, congelar (líquidos), congelar (alimentos, precios, activos)

freeze[2] *n* **1** FROST : helada *f* **2** FREEZING : congelación *f*, congelamiento *m*

freeze–dried [ˈfri:zˈdraɪd] *adj* : liofilizado

freeze–dry [ˈfri:zˈdraɪ] *vt* **-dried; -drying** : liofilizar

freezer [ˈfri:zər] *n* : congelador *m*

freezing [ˈfri:zɪŋ] *adj* : helando ⟨it's freezing! : ¡hace un frío espantoso!⟩

freezing point *n* : punto *m* de congelación

freight[1] [ˈfreɪt] *vt* : enviar como carga

freight[2] *n* **1** SHIPPING, TRANSPORT : transporte *m*, porte *m*, flete *m* **2** GOODS : mercancías *fpl*, carga *f*

freighter [ˈfreɪt̬ər] *n* : carguero *m*, buque *m* de carga

French[1] [ˈfrɛntʃ] *adj* : francés

French[2] *n* **1** : francés *m* (idioma) **2 the French** *npl* : los franceses

french fries [ˈfrɛntʃˌfraɪz] *npl* : papas *fpl* fritas

Frenchman [ˈfrɛntʃmən] *n, pl* **-men** [-mən, -ˌmɛn] : francés *m*

Frenchwoman [ˈfrɛntʃˌwʊmən] *n, pl* **-women** [-ˌwɪmən] : francesa *f*

frenetic [frɪˈnɛt̬ɪk] *adj* : frenético — **frenetically** [-t̬ɪkli] *adv*

frenzied [ˈfrɛnzid] *adj* : frenético

frenzy [ˈfrɛnzi] *n, pl* **-zies** : frenesí *m*

frequency [ˈfri:kwəntsi] *n, pl* **-cies** : frecuencia *f*

frequent[1] [friˈkwɛnt, ˈfri:kwənt] *vt* : frecuentar

frequent[2] [ˈfri:kwənt] *adj* : frecuente — **frequently** *adv*

fresco [ˈfrɛsˌko:] *n, pl* **-coes** : fresco *m*

fresh [ˈfrɛʃ] *adj* **1** : dulce ⟨freshwater : agua dulce⟩ **2** PURE : puro **3** : fresco ⟨fresh fruits : frutas frescas⟩ **4** CLEAN, NEW : limpio, nuevo ⟨fresh clothes : ropa limpia⟩ ⟨fresh evidence : evidencia nueva⟩ **5** REFRESHED : fresco, descansado **6** IMPERTINENT : descarado, impertinente

freshen [ˈfrɛʃən] *vt* : refrescar, arreglar — *vi* **to freshen up** : arreglarse, lavarse

freshet [ˈfrɛʃət] *n* : arroyo *m* desbordado

freshly [ˈfrɛʃli] *adv* : recientemente, recién

freshman [ˈfrɛʃmən] *n, pl* **-men** [-mən, -ˌmɛn] : estudiante *mf* de primer año universitario

freshness [ˈfrɛʃnəs] *n* : frescura *f*

freshwater [ˈfrɛʃˌwɔt̬ər] *n* : agua *f* dulce

fret[1] [ˈfrɛt] *vi* **fretted; fretting** : preocuparse, inquietarse

fret[2] *n* **1** VEXATION : irritación *f*, molestia *f* **2** WORRY : preocupación *f* **3** : traste *m* (de un instrumento musical)

fretful [ˈfrɛtfəl] *adj* : fastidioso, quejoso, neurótico

fretfully [ˈfrɛtfəli] *adv* : ansiosamente, fastidiosamente, inquieto

fretfulness [ˈfrɛtfəlnəs] *n* : inquietud *f*, irritabilidad *f*

friable [ˈfraɪəbəl] *adj* : friable, pulverizable

friar [ˈfraɪər] *n* : fraile *m*

fricassee[1] [ˈfrɪkəˌsi:, ˌfrɪkəˈsi:] *vt* **-seed; -seeing** : cocinar al fricasé

fricassee[2] *n* : fricasé *m*

friction [ˈfrɪkʃən] *n* **1** RUBBING : fricción *f* **2** CONFLICT : fricción *f*, roce *m*

Friday [ˈfraɪˌdeɪ, -di] *n* : viernes *m*

fridge [ˈfrɪʤ] → **refrigerator**

friend [ˈfrɛnd] *n* : amigo *m*, -ga *f*
friendless [ˈfrɛndləs] *adj* : sin amigos
friendliness [ˈfrɛndlinəs] *n* : simpatía *f*, amabilidad *f*
friendly [ˈfrɛndli] *adj* **-lier; -est 1** : simpático, amable, de amigo ⟨a friendly child : un niño simpático⟩ ⟨friendly advice : consejo de amigo⟩ **2** : agradable, acogedor ⟨a friendly atmosphere : un ambiente agradable⟩ **3** GOOD-NATURED : amigable, amistoso ⟨friendly competition : competencia amistosa⟩
friendship [frɛndˌʃɪp] *n* : amistad *f*
frieze [ˈfriːz] *n* : friso *m*
frigate [ˈfrɪgət] *n* : fragata *f*
fright [ˈfraɪt] *n* : miedo *m*, susto *m*
frighten [ˈfraitən] *vt* : asustar, espantar
frightened [ˈfraitənd] *adj* : asustado, temeroso
frightening [ˈfraitənɪŋ] *adj* : espantoso, aterrador
frightful [ˈfraɪtfəl] *adj* **1** → **frightening 2** TREMENDOUS : espantoso, tremendo
frightfully [ˈfraɪtfəli] *adv* : terriblemente, tremendamente
frigid [ˈfrɪʤɪd] *adj* : glacial, extremadamente frío
frigidity [frɪˈʤɪdət̬i] *n* **1** COLDNESS : frialdad *f* **2** : frigidez *f* (sexual)
frill [ˈfrɪl] *n* **1** RUFFLE : volante *m* **2** EMBELLISHMENT : floritura *f*, adorno *m*
frilly [ˈfrɪli] *adj* **frillier; -est 1** RUFFLY : con volantes **2** OVERDONE : recargado
fringe[1] [ˈfrɪnʤ] *vt* **fringed; fringing** : orlar, bordear
fringe[2] *n* **1** BORDER : fleco *m*, orla *f* **2** EDGE : periferia *f*, margen *m* **3 fringe benefits** : incentivos *mpl*, extras *mpl*
frisk [ˈfrɪsk] *vi* FROLIC : retozar, juguetear — *vt* SEARCH : cachear, registrar
friskiness [ˈfrɪskinəs] *n* : vivacidad *f*
frisky [ˈfrɪski] *adj* **friskier; -est** : retozón, juguetón
fritter[1] [ˈfrɪt̬ər] *vt* : desperdiciar, malgastar ⟨I frittered away the money : malgasté el dinero⟩
fritter[2] *n* : buñuelo *m*
frivolity [frɪˈvɑlət̬i] *n, pl* **-ties** : frivolidad *f*
frivolous [ˈfrɪvələs] *adj* : frívolo, de poca importancia
frivolously [ˈfrɪvələsli] *adv* : frívolamente, a la ligera
frizz[1] [ˈfrɪz] *vi* : rizarse, encresparse, ponerse chino *Mex*
frizz[2] *n* : rizos *mpl* muy apretados
frizzy [ˈfrɪzi] *adj* **frizzier; -est** : rizado, crespo, chino *Mex*
fro [ˈfroː] *adv* **to and fro** : de aquí para allá, de un lado para otro
frock [ˈfrɑk] *n* DRESS : vestido *m*
frog [ˈfrɔg, ˈfrɑg] *n* **1** : rana *f* **2** FASTENER : alamar *m* **3 to have a frog in one's throat** : tener carraspera
frogman [ˈfrɔgˌmæn, ˈfrɑg-, -mən] *n, pl* **-men** [-mən, -ˌmɛn] : hombre *m* rana, submarinista *mf*
frolic[1] [ˈfrɑlɪk] *vi* **-icked; -icking** : retozar, juguetear
frolic[2] *n* FUN : diversión *f*
frolicsome [ˈfrɑlɪksəm] *adj* : juguetón
from [ˈfrʌm, ˈfrɑm] *prep* **1** (*indicating a starting point*) : desde, de, a partir de ⟨from Cali to Bogota : de Cali a Bogotá⟩ ⟨where are you from? : ¿de dónde eres?⟩ ⟨from that time onward : desde entonces⟩ ⟨from tomorrow : a partir de mañana⟩ **2** (*indicating a source or sender*) : de ⟨a letter from my friend : una carta de mi amiga⟩ ⟨a quote from Shakespeare : una cita de Shakespeare⟩ **3** (*indicating distance*) : de ⟨10 feet from the entrance : a 10 pies de la entrada⟩ **4** (*indicating a cause*) : de ⟨red from crying : rojos de llorar⟩ ⟨he died from the cold : murió del frío⟩ **5** OFF, OUT OF : de ⟨she took it from the drawer : lo sacó del cajón⟩ **6** (*with adverbs or adverbial phrases*) : de, desde ⟨from above : desde arriba⟩ ⟨from among : de entre⟩
frond [ˈfrɑnd] *n* : fronda *f*, hoja *f*
front[1] [ˈfrʌnt] *vi* **1** FACE : dar, estar orientado ⟨the house fronts north : la casa da al norte⟩ **2** : servir de pantalla ⟨he fronts for his boss : sirve de pantalla para su jefe⟩
front[2] *adj* : delantero, de adelante, primero ⟨the front row : la primera fila⟩
front[3] *n* **1** : frente *m*, parte *f* de adelante, delantera *f* ⟨the front of the class : el frente de la clase⟩ ⟨at the front of the train : en la parte delantera del tren⟩ **2** AREA, ZONE : frente *m*, zona *f* ⟨the Eastern front : el frente oriental⟩ ⟨on the educational front : en el frente de la enseñanza⟩ **3** FACADE : fachada *f* (de un edificio o una persona) **4** : frente *m* (en meteorología)
frontage [ˈfrʌntɪʤ] *n* : fachada *f*, frente *m*
frontal [ˈfrʌntəl] *adj* : frontal, de frente
frontier [ˌfrʌnˈtɪr] *n* : frontera *f*
frontiersman [ˌfrʌnˈtɪrzmən] *n, pl* **-men** [-mən, -ˌmɛn] : hombre *m* de la frontera
frontispiece [ˈfrʌntəsˌpiːs] *n* : frontispicio *m*
frost[1] [ˈfrɔst] *vt* **1** FREEZE : helar **2** ICE : escarchar (pasteles)
frost[2] *n* **1** : helada *f* (en meteorología) **2** : escarcha *f* ⟨frost on the window : escarcha en la ventana⟩
frostbite [ˈfrɔstˌbaɪt] *n* : congelación *f*
frostbitten [ˈfrɔstˌbɪtən] *adj* : congelado (dícese de una persona), quemado (dícese de una planta)
frosting [ˈfrɔstɪŋ] *n* ICING : glaseado *m*, betún *m Mex*
frosty [ˈfrɔsti] *adj* **frostier; -est 1** CHILLY : helado, frío **2** COOL, UNFRIENDLY : frío, glacial
froth [ˈfrɔθ] *n, pl* **froths** [ˈfrɔθs, ˈfrɔðz] : espuma *f*

frothy ['frɔθi] *adj* **frothier; -est** : espumoso
frown[1] ['fraʊn] *vi* **1** : fruncir el ceño, fruncir el entrecejo **2 to frown at** : mirar (algo) con ceño, mirar (a alguien) con ceño
frown[2] *n* : ceño *m* (fruncido)
frowsy *or* **frowzy** ['fraʊzi] *adj* **frowsier** *or* **frowzier; -est** : desaliñado, desaseado
froze → **freeze**
frozen → **freeze**
frugal ['fru:gəl] *adj* : frugal, ahorrativo, parco — **frugally** *adv*
frugality [fru'gæləṭi] *n* : frugalidad *f*
fruit[1] ['fru:t] *vi* : dar fruto
fruit[2] *n* **1** : fruta *f* (término genérico), fruto *m* (término particular) **2 fruits** *npl* REWARDS : frutos *mpl* ⟨the fruits of his labor : los frutos de su trabajo⟩
fruitcake ['fru:t,keɪk] *n* : pastel *m* de frutas
fruitful ['fru:tfəl] *adj* : fructífero, provechoso
fruition [fru'ɪʃən] *n* **1** : cumplimiento *m*, realización *f* **2 to bring to fruition** : realizar
fruitless ['fru:tləs] *adj* : infructuoso, inútil — **fruitlessly** *adv*
fruity ['fru:ṭi] *adj* **fruitier; -est** : (con sabor) a fruta
frumpy ['frʌmpi] *adj* **frumpier; -est** : anticuado y sin atractivo
frustrate ['frʌs,treɪt] *vt* **-trated; -trating** : frustrar
frustrating ['frʌs,treɪṭɪŋ] *adj* : frustrante — **frustratingly** *adv*
frustration [,frʌs'treɪʃən] *n* : frustración *f*
fry[1] ['fraɪ] *vt* **fried; frying** : freír
fry[2] *n, pl* **fries 1** : fritura *f*, plato *m* frito **2** : fiesta *f* en que se sirven frituras **3** *pl* **fry** : alevín *m* (pez)
frying pan *n* : sartén *mf*
fuchsia ['fju:ʃə] *n* **1** : fucsia *f* (planta) **2** : fucsia *m* (color)
fuddle ['fʌdəl] *vt* **-dled; -dling** : confundir, atontar
fuddy–duddy ['fʌdi,dʌdi] *n, pl* **-dies** : persona *f* chapada a la antigua, carca *mf*
fudge[1] ['fʌʤ] *vt* **fudged; fudging 1** FALSIFY : amañar, falsificar **2** DODGE : esquivar
fudge[2] *n* : dulce *m* blando de chocolate y leche
fuel[1] ['fju:əl] *vt* **-eled** *or* **-elled; -eling** *or* **-elling 1** : abastecer de combustible **2** STIMULATE : estimular
fuel[2] *n* : combustible *m*, carburante *m* (para motores)
fugitive[1] ['fju:ʤəṭɪv] *adj* **1** RUNAWAY : fugitivo **2** FLEETING : efímero, pasajero, fugaz
fugitive[2] *n* : fugitivo *m*, -va *f*
fugue ['fju:g] *n* : fuga *f*
fulcrum ['fʊlkrəm, 'fʌl-] *n, pl* **-crums** *or* **-cra** [-krə] : fulcro *m*
fulfill *or* **fulfil** [fʊl'fɪl] *vt* **-filled; -filling 1** PERFORM : cumplir con, realizar, llevar a cabo **2** SATISFY : satisfacer
fulfillment [fʊl'fɪlmənt] *n* **1** PERFORMANCE : cumplimiento *m*, ejecución *f* **2** SATISFACTION : satisfacción *f*, realización *f*
full[1] ['fʊl, 'fʌl] *adv* **1** VERY : muy ⟨full well : muy bien, perfectamente⟩ **2** ENTIRELY : completamente ⟨she swung full around : giró completamente⟩ **3** DIRECTLY : de lleno, directamente ⟨he looked me full in the face : me miró directamente a la cara⟩
full[2] *adj* **1** FILLED : lleno **2** COMPLETE : completo, detallado **3** MAXIMUM : todo, pleno ⟨at full speed : a toda velocidad⟩ ⟨in full bloom : en plena flor⟩ **4** PLUMP : redondo, llenito *fam*, regordete *fam* ⟨a full face : una cara redonda⟩ ⟨a full figure : un cuerpo llenito⟩ **5** AMPLE : amplio ⟨a full skirt : una falda amplia⟩
full[3] *n* **1 to pay in full** : pagar en su totalidad **2 to the full** : al máximo
full–fledged ['fʊl'flɛʤd] *adj* : hecho y derecho
fullness ['fʊlnəs] *n* **1** ABUNDANCE : plenitud *f*, abundancia *f* **2** : amplitud *f* (de una falda)
fully ['fʊli] *adv* **1** COMPLETELY : completamente, totalmente **2** : al menos, por lo menos ⟨fully half of them : al menos la mitad de ellos⟩
fulsome ['fʊlsəm] *adj* : excesivo, exagerado, efusivo
fumble[1] ['fʌmbəl] *v* **-bled; -bling** *vt* **1** : dejar caer, fumblear **2 to fumble one's way** : ir a tientas — *vi* **1** GROPE : hurgar, tantear **2 to fumble with** : manejar con torpeza
fumble[2] *n* : fumble *m* (en futbol americano)
fume[1] ['fju:m] *vi* **fumed; fuming 1** SMOKE : echar humo, humear **2** : estar furioso
fume[2] *n* : gas *m*, humo *m*, vapor *m*
fumigate ['fju:mə,geɪt] *vt* **-gated; -gating** : fumigar
fumigation [,fju:mə'geɪʃən] *n* : fumigación *m*
fun[1] ['fʌn] *adj* : divertido, entretenido
fun[2] *n* **1** AMUSEMENT : diversión *f*, entretenimiento *m* **2** ENJOYMENT : disfrute *m* **3 to have fun** : divertirse **4 to make fun of** : reírse de, burlarse de
function[1] ['fʌŋkʃən] *vi* : funcionar, desempeñarse, servir
function[2] *n* **1** PURPOSE : función *f* **2** GATHERING : reunión *f* social, recepción *f* **3** CEREMONY : ceremonia *f*, acto *m*
functional ['fʌŋkʃənəl] *adj* : funcional — **functionally** *adv*
functionary ['fʌŋkʃə,nɛri] *n, pl* **-aries** : funcionario *m*, -ria *f*
fund[1] ['fʌnd] *vt* : financiar

fund[2] *n* **1** SUPPLY : reserva *f*, cúmulo *m* **2** : fondo *m* ⟨investment fund : fondo de inversiones⟩ **3 funds** *npl* RESOURCES : fondos *mpl*

fundamental[1] [ˌfʌndəˈmɛntəl] *adj* **1** BASIC : fundamental, básico **2** PRINCIPAL : esencial, principal **3** INNATE : innato, intrínseco

fundamental[2] *n* : fundamento *m*

fundamentalism [ˌfʌndəˈmɛntəlˌɪzəm] *n* : integrismo *m*, fundamentalismo *m*

fundamentalist [ˌfʌndəˈmɛntəlɪst] *n* : integrista *mf*, fundamentalista *mf* — **fundamentalist** *adj*

fundamentally [ˌfʌndəˈmɛntəli] *adv* : fundamentalmente, básicamente

funding [ˈfʌndɪŋ] *n* : financiación *f*

fund–raiser [ˈfʌndˌreɪzər] *n* : función *f* para recaudar fondos

funeral[1] [ˈfjuːnərəl] *adj* **1** : funeral, funerario, fúnebre ⟨funeral procession : cortejo fúnebre⟩ **2 funeral home** : funeraria *f*

funeral[2] *n* : funeral *m*, funerales *mpl*

funereal [fjuːˈnɪriəl] *adj* : fúnebre

fungal [ˈfʌŋgəl] *adj* : de hongos, micótico

fungicidal [ˌfʌnʤəˈsaɪdəl, ˌfʌngə-] *adj* : fungicida

fungicide [ˈfʌnʤəˌsaɪd, ˈfʌŋgə-] *n* : fungicida *m*

fungous [ˈfʌŋgəs] *adj* : fungoso

fungus [ˈfʌŋgəs] *n, pl* **fungi** [ˈfʌnˌʤaɪ, ˈfʌŋˌgaɪ] : hongo *m*

funk [ˈfʌŋk] *n* **1** FEAR : miedo *m* **2** DEPRESSION : depresión *f*

funky [ˈfʌŋki] *adj* **funkier; -est** ODD, QUAINT : raro, extraño, original

funnel[1] [ˈfʌnəl] *vt* **-neled; -neling** CHANNEL : canalizar, encauzar

funnel[2] *n* **1** : embudo *m* **2** SMOKESTACK : chimenea *f* (de un barco o vapor)

funnies [ˈfʌniz] *npl* : tiras *fpl* cómicas

funny [ˈfʌni] *adj* **funnier; -est 1** AMUSING : divertido, cómico **2** STRANGE : extraño, raro

fur[1] [ˈfər] *adj* : de piel

fur[2] *n* **1** : pelaje *m*, piel *f* **2** : prenda *f* de piel

furbish [ˈfərbɪʃ] *vt* : pulir, limpiar

furious [ˈfjʊriəs] *adj* **1** ANGRY : furioso **2** FRANTIC : violento, frenético, vertiginoso (dícese de la velocidad)

furiously [ˈfjʊriəsli] *adv* **1** ANGRILY : furiosamente **2** FRANTICALLY : frenéticamente

furlong [ˈfərˌlɔŋ] *n* : estadio *m* (201.2 m)

furlough[1] [ˈfərˌloː] *vt* : dar permiso a, dar licencia a

furlough[2] *n* LEAVE : permiso *m*, licencia *f*

furnace [ˈfərnəs] *n* : horno *m*

furnish [ˈfərnɪʃ] *vt* **1** SUPPLY : proveer, suministrar **2** : amueblar ⟨furnished apartment : departamento amueblado⟩

furnishings [ˈfərnɪʃɪŋz] *npl* **1** ACCESSORIES : accesorios *mpl* **2** FURNITURE : muebles *mpl*, mobiliario *m*

furniture [ˈfərnɪʧər] *n* : muebles *mpl*, mobiliario *m*

furor [ˈfjʊrˌɔr, -ər] *n* **1** RAGE : furia *f*, rabia *f* **2** UPROAR : escándalo *m*, jaleo *m*, alboroto *m*

furrier [ˈfəriər] *n* : peletero *m*, -ra *f*

furrow[1] [ˈfəroː] *vt* **1** : surcar **2 to furrow one's brow** : fruncir el ceño

furrow[2] *n* **1** GROOVE : surco *m* **2** WRINKLE : arruga *f*, surco *m*

furry [ˈfəri] *adj* **furrier; -est** : peludo (dícese de un animal), peluche (dícese de un objeto)

further[1] [ˈfərðər] *vt* : promover, fomentar

further[2] *adv* **1** FARTHER : más lejos, más adelante **2** MOREOVER : además **3** MORE : más ⟨I'll consider it further in the morning : lo consideraré más en la mañana⟩

further[3] *adj* **1** FARTHER : más lejano **2** ADDITIONAL : adicional, más

furtherance [ˈfərðərənts] *n* : promoción *f*, fomento *m*, adelantamiento *m*

furthermore [ˈfərðərˌmor] *adv* : además

furthermost [ˈfərðərˌmoːst] *adj* : más lejano, más distante

furthest [ˈfərðəst] → **farthest**[1], **farthest**[2]

furtive [ˈfərt̬ɪv] *adj* : furtivo, sigiloso — **furtively** *adv*

furtiveness [ˈfərt̬ɪvnəs] *n* STEALTH : sigilo *m*

fury [ˈfjʊri] *n, pl* **-ries 1** RAGE : furia *f*, ira *f* **2** VIOLENCE : furia *f*, furor *m*

fuse[1] [ˈfjuːz] *or* **fuze** *vt* **fused** *or* **fuzed; fusing** *or* **fuzing** : equipar con un fusible

fuse[2] *v* **fused; fusing** *vt* **1** SMELT : fundir **2** MERGE : fusionar, fundir — *vi* : fundirse, fusionarse

fuse[3] *n* : fusible *m*

fuselage [ˈfjuːsəˌlɑʒ, -zə-] *n* : fuselaje *m*

fusillade [ˈfjuːsəˌlɑd, -ˌleɪd, ˌfjuːsəˈ-, -zə-] *n* : descarga *f* de fusilería

fusion [ˈfjuːʒən] *n* : fusión *f*

fuss[1] [ˈfʌs] *vi* **1** WORRY : preocuparse **2 to fuss with** : juguetear con, toquetear **3 to fuss over** : mimar

fuss[2] *n* **1** COMMOTION : alboroto *m*, escándalo *m* **2** ATTENTION : atenciones *fpl* **3** COMPLAINT : quejas *fpl*

fussbudget [ˈfʌsˌbʌʤət] *n* : quisquilloso *m*, -sa *f*; melindroso *m*, -sa *f*

fussiness [ˈfʌsinəs] *n* **1** IRRITABILITY : irritabilidad *f* **2** ORNATENESS : lo recargado **3** METICULOUSNESS : meticulosidad *f*

fussy [ˈfʌsi] *adj* **fussier; -est 1** IRRITABLE : irritable, nervioso **2** OVERELABORATE : recargado **3** METICULOUS : meticuloso **4** FASTIDIOUS : quisquilloso, exigente

futile [ˈfjuːt̬əl, ˈfjuːˌtaɪl] *adj* : inútil, vano

futility [fjuˈtɪlət̬i] *n, pl* **-ties** : inutilidad *f*

future[1] [ˈfjuːʧər] *adj* : futuro

future[2] *n* : futuro *m*

futuristic [ˌfjuːʧəˈrɪstɪk] *adj* : futurista

fuze → **fuse**[1]

fuzz [ˈfʌz] *n* : pelusa *f*
fuzziness [ˈfʌzinəs] *n* **1** DOWNINESS : vellosidad *f* **2** INDISTINCTNESS : falta *f* de claridad
fuzzy [ˈfʌzi] *adj* **fuzzier; -est 1** FLUFFY, FURRY : con pelusa, peludo **2** INDISTINCT : indistinto ⟨a fuzzy image : una imagen borrosa⟩

G

g [ˈʤiː] *n, pl* **g's** *or* **gs** [ˈʤiːz] : séptima letra del alfabeto inglés
gab[1] [ˈgæb] *vi* **gabbed; gabbing** : charlar, cotorrear *fam*, parlotear *fam*
gab[2] *n* CHATTER : cotorreo *m fam*, parloteo *m fam*
gabardine [ˈgæbərˌdiːn] *n* : gabardina *f*
gabby [ˈgæbi] *adj* **gabbier; -est** : hablador, parlanchín
gable [ˈgeɪbəl] *n* : hastial *m*, aguilón *m*
Gabonese [ˌgæbəˈniːz, -ˈniːs] *n* : gabonés *m*, -nesa *f* — **Gabonese** *adj*
gad [ˈgæd] *vi* **gadded; gadding** WANDER : deambular, vagar, callejear
gadfly [ˈgædˌflaɪ] *n, pl* **-flies 1** : tábano *m* (insecto) **2** FAULTFINDER : criticón *m*, -cona *f fam*
gadget [ˈgæʤət] *n* : artilugio *m*, aparato *m*
gadgetry [ˈgæʤətri] *n* : artilugios *mpl*, aparatos *mpl*
Gaelic [ˈgeɪlɪk, ˈgæ] *n* : gaélico *m* (idioma) — **Gaelic** *adj*
gaff [ˈgæf] *n* **1** : garfio *m* **2** → **gaffe**
gaffe [ˈgæf] *n* : metedura *f* de pata *fam*
gag[1] [ˈgæg] *v* **gagged; gagging** *vt* : amordazar ⟨to tie up and gag : atar y amordazar⟩ — *vi* **1** CHOKE : atragantarse **2** RETCH : hacer arcadas
gag[2] *n* **1** : mordaza *f* (para la boca) **2** JOKE : chiste *m*
gage → **gauge**
gaggle [ˈgægəl] *n* : bandada *f*, manada *f* (de gansos)
gaiety [ˈgeɪəṭi] *n, pl* **-eties 1** MERRYMAKING : juerga *f* **2** MERRIMENT : alegría *f*, regocijo *m*
gaily [ˈgeɪli] *adv* : alegremente
gain[1] [ˈgeɪn] *vt* **1** ACQUIRE, OBTAIN : ganar, obtener, adquirir, conseguir ⟨to gain knowledge : adquirir conocimientos⟩ ⟨to gain a victory : obtener una victoria⟩ **2** REACH : alcanzar, llegar a **3** INCREASE : ganar, aumentar ⟨to gain weight : aumentar de peso⟩ **4** : adelantarse, ganar ⟨the watch gains two minutes a day : el reloj se adelanta dos minutos por día⟩ — *vi* **1** PROFIT : beneficiarse **2** INCREASE : aumentar
gain[2] *n* **1** PROFIT : beneficio *m*, ganancia *f*, lucro *m*, provecho *m* **2** INCREASE : aumento *m*
gainful [ˈgeɪnfəl] *adj* : lucrativo, beneficioso, provechoso ⟨gainful employment : trabajo remunerado⟩
gait [ˈgeɪt] *n* : paso *m*, andar *m*, manera *f* de caminar
gal [ˈgæl] *n* : muchacha *f*
gala[1] [ˈgeɪlə, ˈgæ-, ˈgɑ-] *adj* : de gala
gala[2] *n* : gala *f*, fiesta *f*
galactic [gəˈlæktɪk] *adj* : galáctico
galaxy [ˈgæləksi] *n, pl* **-axies** : galaxia *f*
gale [ˈgeɪl] *n* **1** WIND : vendaval *f*, viento *m* fuerte **2 gales of laughter** : carcajadas *fpl*
gall[1] [ˈgɔl] *vt* **1** CHAFE : rozar **2** IRRITATE, VEX : irritar, molestar
gall[2] *n* **1** BILE : bilis *f*, hiel *f* **2** INSOLENCE : audacia *f*, insolencia *f*, descaro *m* **3** SORE : rozadura *f* (de un caballo) **4** : agalla *f* (de una planta)
gallant [ˈgælənt] *adj* **1** BRAVE : valiente, gallardo **2** CHIVALROUS, POLITE : galante, cortés
gallantry [ˈgæləntri] *n, pl* **-ries** : galantería *f*, caballerosidad *f*
gallbladder [ˈgɔlˌblædər] *n* : vesícula *f* biliar
galleon [ˈgæljən] *n* : galeón *m*
gallery [ˈgæləri] *n, pl* **-leries 1** BALCONY : galería *f* (para espectadores) **2** CORRIDOR : pasillo *m*, galería *f*, corredor *m* **3** : galería *f* (para exposiciones)
galley [ˈgæli] *n, pl* **-leys** : galera *f*
gallium [ˈgæliəm] *n* : galio *m*
gallivant [ˈgæləˌvænt] *vi* : callejear
gallon [ˈgælən] *n* : galón *m*
gallop[1] [ˈgæləp] *vi* : galopar
gallop[2] *n* : galope *m*
gallows [ˈgæˌloːz] *n, pl* **-lows** *or* **-lowses** [-ˌloːzəz] : horca *f*
gallstone [ˈgɔlˌstoːn] *n* : cálculo *m* biliar
galore [gəˈlor] *adj* : en abundancia ⟨bargains galore : muchísimas gangas⟩
galoshes [gəˈlɑʃəz] *npl* : galochas *fpl*, chanclos *mpl*
galvanize [ˈgælvənˌaɪz] *vt* **-nized; -nizing 1** STIMULATE : estimular, excitar, impulsar **2** : galvanizar (metales)
Gambian [ˈgæmbiən] *n* : gambiano *m*, -na *f* — **Gambian** *adj*
gambit [ˈgæmbɪt] *n* **1** : gambito *m* (en ajedrez) **2** STRATAGEM : estratagema *f*, táctica *f*
gamble[1] [ˈgæmbəl] *v* **-bled; -bling** *vi* : jugar, arriesgarse — *vt* **1** BET, WAGER : apostar, jugarse **2** RISK : arriesgar
gamble[2] *n* **1** BET : apuesta *f* **2** RISK : riesgo *m*
gambler [ˈgæmbələr] *n* : jugador *m*, -dora *f*
gambling [ˈgæmbəlɪŋ] *n* : juego *m*
gambol [ˈgæmbəl] *vi* **-boled** *or* **-bolled; -boling** *or* **-bolling** FROLIC : retozar, juguetear
game[1] [ˈgeɪm] *adj* **1** READY : listo, dispuesto ⟨we're game for anything : es-

tamos listos para lo que sea⟩ **2** LAME : cojo

game[2] *n* **1** AMUSEMENT : juego *m*, diversión *f* **2** CONTEST : juego *m*, partido *m*, concurso *m* **3** : caza *f* ⟨big game : caza mayor⟩

gamecock [ˈgeɪm,kɑk] *n* : gallo *m* de pelea

gamekeeper [ˈgeɪm,ki:pər] *n* : guardabosque *mf*

gamely [ˈgeɪmli] *adv* : animosamente

gamma ray [ˈgæmə] *n* : rayo *m* gamma

gamut [ˈgæmət] *n* : gama *f*, espectro *m* ⟨to run the gamut : pasar por toda la gama⟩

gamy *or* **gamey** [ˈgeɪmi] *adj* **gamier; -est** : con sabor de animal de caza, fuerte

gander [ˈgændər] *n* **1** : ganso *m* (animal) **2** GLANCE : mirada *f*, vistazo *m*, ojeada *f*

gang[1] [ˈgæŋ] *vi* **to gang up** : agruparse, unirse

gang[2] *n* : banda *f*, pandilla *f*

gangling [ˈgæŋglɪŋ] *adj* LANKY : larguirucho *fam*

ganglion [ˈgæŋgliən] *n, pl* **-glia** [-gliə] : ganglio *m*

gangplank [ˈgæŋ,plæŋk] *n* : pasarela *f*

gangrene [ˈgæŋ,gri:n, ˈgæn-; gæŋˈ-, gænˈ-] *n* : gangrena *f*

gangrenous [ˈgæŋgrənəs] *adj* : gangrenoso

gangster [ˈgæŋstər] *n* : gángster *mf*

gangway [ˈgæŋ,weɪ] *n* **1** : pasarela *f* **2** **gangway!** : ¡abran paso!

gap [ˈgæp] *n* **1** BREACH, OPENING : espacio *m*, brecha *f*, abertura *f* **2** GORGE : desfiladero *m*, barranco *m* **3** : laguna *f* ⟨a gap in my education : una laguna en mi educación⟩ **4** INTERVAL : pausa *f*, intervalo *m* **5** DISPARITY : brecha *f*, disparidad *f*

gape[1] [ˈgeɪp] *vi* **gaped; gaping 1** OPEN : abrirse, estar abierto **2** STARE : mirar fijamente con la boca abierta, mirar boquiabierto

gape[2] *n* **1** OPENING : abertura *f*, brecha *f* **2** STARE : mirada *f* boquiabierta

garage[1] [gəˈrɑʒ, -ˈrɑʤ] *vt* **-raged; -raging** : dejar en un garaje

garage[2] *n* : garaje *m*, cochera *f*

garb[1] [ˈgɑrb] *vt* : vestir, ataviar

garb[2] *n* : vestimenta *f*, atuendo *f*

garbage [ˈgɑrbɪʤ] *n* : basura *f*, desechos *mpl*

garbageman [ˈgɑrbɪʤmən] *n, pl* **-men** [-mən, -,mɛn] : basurero *m*

garble [ˈgɑrbəl] *vt* **-bled; -bling** : tergiversar, distorsionar

garbled [ˈgɑrbəld] *adj* : incoherente, incomprensible

garden[1] [ˈgɑrdən] *vi* : trabajar en el jardín

garden[2] *n* : jardín *m*

gardener [ˈgɑrdənər] *n* : jardinero *m*, -ra *f*

gardenia [gɑrˈdi:njə] *n* : gardenia *f*

gardening [ˈgɑrdənɪŋ] *n* : jardinería *f*

gargantuan [gɑrˈgænʧʊən] *adj* : gigantesco, colosal

gargle[1] [ˈgɑrgəl] *vi* **-gled; -gling** : hacer gárgaras, gargarizar

gargle[2] *n* : gárgara *f*

gargoyle [ˈgɑr,gɔɪl] *n* : gárgola *f*

garish [ˈgærɪʃ] *adj* GAUDY : llamativo, chillón, charro — **garishly** *adv*

garland[1] [ˈgɑrlənd] *vt* : adornar con guirnaldas

garland[2] *n* : guirnalda *f*

garlic [ˈgɑrlɪk] *n* : ajo *m*

garment [ˈgɑrmənt] *n* : prenda *f*

garner [ˈgɑrnər] *vt* : recoger, cosechar

garnet [ˈgɑrnət] *n* : granate *m*

garnish[1] [ˈgɑrnɪʃ] *vt* : aderezar, guarnecer

garnish[2] *n* : aderezo *m*, guarnición *f*

garret [ˈgærət] *n* : buhardilla *f*, desván *m*

garrison[1] [ˈgærəsən] *vt* **1** QUARTER : acuartelar (tropas) **2** OCCUPY : guarnecer, ocupar (con tropas)

garrison[2] *n* **1** : guarnición *f* (ciudad) **2** FORT : fortaleza *f*, poste *m* militar

garrulous [ˈgærələs] *adj* : charlatán, parlanchín, garlero *Col fam*

garter [ˈgɑrţər] *n* : liga *f*

gas[1] [ˈgæs] *v* **gassed; gassing** *vt* : gasear — *vi* **to gas up** : llenar el tanque con gasolina

gas[2] *n, pl* **gases** [ˈgæsəz] **1** : gas *m* ⟨tear gas : gas lacrimógeno⟩ **2** GASOLINE : gasolina *f*

gaseous [ˈgæʃəs, ˈgæsiəs] *adj* : gaseoso

gash[1] [ˈgæʃ] *vt* : hacer un tajo en, cortar

gash[2] *n* : cuchillada *f*, tajo *m*

gasket [ˈgæskət] *n* : junta *f*

gas mask *n* : máscara *f* antigás

gasoline [ˈgæsə,li:n, ,gæsəˈ-] *n* : gasolina *f*, nafta *f*

gasp[1] [ˈgæsp] *vi* **1** : boquear ⟨to gasp with surprise : gritar de asombro⟩ **2** PANT : jadear, respirar con dificultad

gasp[2] *n* **1** : boqueada *f* ⟨a gasp of surprise : un grito sofocado⟩ **2** PANTING : jadeo *m*

gas station *n* : estación *f* de servicio, gasolinera *f*

gastric [ˈgæstrɪk] *adj* : gástrico ⟨gastric juice : jugo gástrico⟩

gastronomic [,gæstrəˈnɑmɪk] *adj* : gastronómico

gastronomy [gæsˈtrɑnəmi] *n* : gastronomía *f*

gate [ˈgeɪt] *n* : portón *m*, verja *f*, puerta *f*

gatekeeper [ˈgeɪt,ki:pər] *n* : guarda *mf*; guardián *m*, -diana *f*

gateway [ˈgeɪt,weɪ] *n* : puerta *f* (de acceso), entrada *f*

gather [ˈgæðər] *vt* **1** ASSEMBLE : juntar, recoger, reunir **2** HARVEST : recoger, cosechar **3** : fruncir (una tela) **4** INFER : deducir, suponer

gathering [ˈgæðərɪŋ] *n* : reunión *f*

gauche [ˈgo:ʃ] *adj* : torpe, falto de tacto

gaudy ['gɔdi] *adj* **gaudier; -est** : chillón, llamativo
gauge[1] ['geɪʤ] *vt* **gauged; gauging 1** MEASURE : medir **2** ESTIMATE, JUDGE : estimar, evaluar, juzgar
gauge[2] *n* **1** : indicador *m* ⟨pressure gauge : indicador de presión⟩ **2** CALIBER : calibre *m* **3** INDICATION : indicio *m*, muestra *f*
gaunt ['gɔnt] *adj* : demacrado, enjuto, descarnado
gauntlet ['gɔntlət] *n* : guante *m* ⟨to run the gauntlet of : exponerse a⟩
gauze ['gɔz] *n* : gasa *f*
gauzy ['gɔzi] *adj* **gauzier; -est** : diáfano, vaporoso
gave → **give**
gavel ['gævəl] *n* : martillo *m* (de un juez, un subastador, etc.)
gawk ['gɔk] *vi* GAPE : mirar boquiabierto
gawky ['gɔki] *adj* **gawkier; -est** : desmañado, torpe, desgarbado
gay ['geɪ] *adj* **1** MERRY : alegre **2** BRIGHT, COLORFUL : vistoso, vivo **3** HOMOSEXUAL : homosexual
gaze[1] ['geɪz] *vi* **gazed; gazing** : mirar (fijamente)
gaze[2] *n* : mirada *f* (fija)
gazelle [gə'zɛl] *n* : gacela *f*
gazette [gə'zɛt] *n* : gaceta *f*
gazetteer [ˌgæzə'tɪr] *n* : diccionario *m* geográfico
gear[1] ['gɪr] *vt* ADAPT, ORIENT : adaptar, ajustar, orientar ⟨a book geared to children : un libro adaptado a los niños⟩ — *vi* **to gear up** : prepararse
gear[2] *n* **1** CLOTHING : ropa *f* **2** BELONGINGS : efectos *mpl* personales **3** EQUIPMENT, TOOLS : equipo *m*, aparejo *m*, herramientas *fpl* ⟨fishing gear : aparejo de pescar⟩ ⟨landing gear : tren de aterrizaje⟩ **4** COGWHEEL : rueda *f* dentada **5** : marcha *f*, velocidad *f* (de un vehículo) ⟨to put in gear : poner en marcha⟩ ⟨to change gear(s) : cambiar de velocidad⟩
gearshift ['gɪrˌʃɪft] *n* : palanca *f* de cambio, palanca *f* de velocidad
geek ['gi:k] *n fam* : intelectual *mf*
geese → **goose**
Geiger counter ['gaɪgərˌkaʊntər] *n* : contador *m* Geiger
gel ['ʤɛl] *n* : gel *m*
gelatin ['ʤɛlətən] *n* : gelatina *f*
gem ['ʤɛm] *n* : joya *f*, gema *f*, alhaja *f*
Gemini ['ʤɛməˌnaɪ] *n* : Géminis *mf*
gemstone ['ʤɛmˌsto:n] *n* : piedra *f* (semipreciosa o preciosa), gema *f*
gender ['ʤɛndər] *n* **1** SEX : sexo *m* **2** : género *m* (en la gramática)
gene ['ʤi:n] *n* : gen *m*, gene *m*
genealogical [ˌʤi:niə'lɑʤɪkəl] *adj* : genealógico
genealogy [ˌʤi:ni'ɑləʤi, ˌʤɛ-, -'æ-] *n, pl* **-gies** : genealogía *f*
genera → **genus**
general[1] ['ʤɛnrəl, 'ʤɛnə-] *adj* : general ⟨in general : en general, por lo general⟩
general[2] *n* : general *mf*
generality [ˌʤɛnə'ræləṭi] *n, pl* **-ties** : generalidad *f*
generalization [ˌʤɛnrələ'zeɪʃən, ˌʤɛnərə-] *n* : generalización *f*
generalize ['ʤɛnrəˌlaɪz, 'ʤɛnərə-] *v* **-ized; -izing** : generalizar
generally ['ʤɛnrəli, 'ʤɛnərə-] *adv* : generalmente, por lo general, en general
generate ['ʤɛnəˌreɪt] *vt* **-ated; -ating** : generar, producir
generation [ˌʤɛnə'reɪʃən] *n* : generación *f*
generator ['ʤɛnəˌreɪṭər] *n* : generador *m*
generic [ʤə'nɛrɪk] *adj* : genérico
generosity [ˌʤɛnə'rɑsəṭi] *n, pl* **-ties** : generosidad *f*
generous ['ʤɛnərəs] *adj* **1** OPENHANDED : generoso, dadivoso, desprendido **2** ABUNDANT, AMPLE : abundante, amplio, generoso — **generously** *adv*
genetic [ʤə'nɛṭɪk] *adj* : genético — **genetically** [-ṭɪkli] *adv*
geneticist [ʤə'nɛṭəsɪst] *n* : genetista *mf*
genetics [ʤə'nɛṭɪks] *n* : genética *f*
genial ['ʤi:niəl] *adj* GRACIOUS : simpático, cordial, afable — **genially** *adv*
geniality [ˌʤi:ni'æləṭi] *n* : simpatía *f*, afabilidad *f*
genie ['ʤi:ni] *n* : genio *m*
genital ['ʤɛnəṭəl] *adj* : genital
genitals ['ʤɛnəṭəlz] *npl* : genitales *mpl*
genius ['ʤi:njəs] *n* : genio *m*
genocide ['ʤɛnəˌsaɪd] *n* : genocidio *m*
genre ['ʒɑnrə, 'ʒɑr] *n* : género *m*
genteel [ʤɛn'ti:l] *adj* : cortés, fino, refinado
gentile[1] ['ʤɛnˌtaɪl] *adj* : gentil
gentile[2] *n* : gentil *mf*
gentility [ʤɛn'tɪləṭi] *n, pl* **-ties 1** : nobleza *f* (de nacimiento) **2** POLITENESS, REFINEMENT : cortesía *f*, refinamiento *m*
gentle ['ʤɛntəl] *adj* **-tler; -tlest 1** NOBLE : bien nacido, noble **2** DOCILE : dócil, manso **3** KINDLY : bondadoso, amable **4** MILD : suave, apacible ⟨a gentle breeze : una brisa suave⟩ **5** SOFT : suave (dícese de un sonido), ligero (dícese del tacto) **6** MODERATE : moderado, gradual ⟨a gentle slope : una cuesta gradual⟩
gentleman ['ʤɛntəlmən] *n, pl* **-men** [-mən, -ˌmɛn] : caballero *m*, señor *m*
gentlemanly ['ʤɛntəlmənli] *adj* : caballeroso
gentleness ['ʤɛntəlnəs] *n* : delicadeza *f*, suavidad *f*, ternura *f*
gentlewoman ['ʤɛntəlˌwʊmən] *n, pl* **-women** [-ˌwɪmən] : dama *f*, señora *f*
gently ['ʤɛntli] *adv* **1** CAREFULLY, SOFTLY : con cuidado, suavemente, ligeramente **2** KINDLY : amablemente, con delicadeza

gentry [ˈʤɛntri] *n, pl* **-tries** : aristocracia *f*

genuflect [ˈʤɛnjʊˌflɛkt] *vi* : doblar la rodilla, hacer una genuflexión

genuflection [ˌʤɛnjʊˈflɛkʃən] *n* : genuflexión *f*

genuine [ˈʤɛnjʊwən] *adj* **1** AUTHENTIC, REAL : genuino, verdadero, auténtico **2** SINCERE : sincero — **genuinely** *adv*

genus [ˈʤiːnəs] *n, pl* **genera** [ˈʤ-nərə] : género *m*

geographer [ʤiˈɑgrəfər] *n* : geógrafo *m*, -fa *f*

geographical [ˌʤiːəˈgræfɪkəl] *or* **geographic** [-fɪk] *adj* : geográfico — **geographically** [-fɪkli] *adv*

geography [ʤiˈɑgrəfi] *n, pl* **-phies** : geografía *f*

geologic [ˌʤiːəˈlɑʤɪk] *or* **geological** [-ʤɪkəl] *adj* : geológico — **geologically** [-ʤɪkli] *adv*

geologist [ʤiˈɑləʤɪst] *n* : geólogo *m*, -ga *f*

geology [ʤiˈɑləʤi] *n* : geología *f*

geometric [ˌʤiːəˈmɛtrɪk] *or* **geometrical** [-trɪkəl] *adj* : geométrico

geometry [ʤiˈɑmətri] *n, pl* **-tries** : geometría *f*

geopolitical [ˌʤiːopəˈlɪt̬ɪkəl] *adj* : geopolítico

Georgian [ˈʤɔrʤən] *n* **1** : georgiano *m* (idioma) **2** : georgiano *m*, -na *f* — **Georgian** *adj*

geranium [ʤəˈreɪniəm] *n* : geranio *m*

gerbil [ˈʤərbəl] *n* : jerbo *m*, gerbo *m*

geriatric [ˌʤɛriˈætrɪk] *adj* : geriátrico

geriatrics [ˌʤɛriˈætrɪks] *n* : geriatría *f*

germ [ˈʤərm] *n* **1** MICROORGANISM : microbio *m*, germen *m* **2** BEGINNING : germen *m*, principio *m* ⟨the germ of a plan : el germen de un plan⟩

German [ˈʤərmən] *n* **1** : alemán *m*, -mana *f* **2** : alemán *m* (idioma) — **German** *adj*

germane [ʤərˈmeɪn] *adj* : relevante, pertinente

Germanic[1] [ʤərˈmænɪk] *adj* : germánico, germano

Germanic[2] *n* : germánico *m* (idioma)

germanium [ʤərˈmeɪniəm] *n* : germanio *m*

germ cell *n* : célula *f* germen

germicide [ˈʤərməˌsaɪd] *n* : germicida *m*

germinate [ˈʤərməˌneɪt] *v* **-nated; -nating** *vi* : germinar — *vt* : hacer germinar

germination [ˌʤərməˈneɪʃən] *n* : germinación *f*

gerund [ˈʤɛrənd] *n* : gerundio *m*

gestation [ʤɛˈsteɪʃən] *n* : gestación *f*

gesture[1] [ˈʤɛsʧər] *vi* **-tured; -turing** : gesticular, hacer gestos

gesture[2] *n* **1** : gesto *m*, ademán *m* **2** SIGN, TOKEN : gesto *m*, señal *f* ⟨a gesture of friendship : una señal de amistad⟩

get [ˈgɛt] *v* **got** [ˈgɑt]; **got** *or* **gotten** [ˈgɑtən]; **getting** *vt* **1** OBTAIN : conseguir, obtener, adquirir **2** RECEIVE : recibir ⟨to get a letter : recibir una carta⟩ **3** EARN : ganar ⟨he gets $10 an hour : gana $10 por hora⟩ **4** FETCH : traer ⟨get me my book : tráigame el libro⟩ **5** CATCH : tomar (un tren, etc.), agarrar (una pelota, una persona, etc.) **6** CONTRACT : contagiarse de, contraer ⟨she got the measles : le dio el sarampión⟩ **7** PREPARE : preparar (una comida) **8** PERSUADE : persuadir, mandar a hacer ⟨I got him to agree : logré convencerlo⟩ **9** (*to cause to be*) ⟨to get one's hair cut : cortarse el pelo⟩ **10** UNDERSTAND : entender ⟨now I get it! : ¡ya entiendo!⟩ **11 to have got** : tener ⟨I've got a headache : tengo un dolor de cabeza⟩ **12 to have got to** : tener que ⟨you've got to come : tienes que venir⟩ — *vi* **1** BECOME : ponerse, volverse, hacerse ⟨to get angry : ponerse furioso, enojarse⟩ **2** GO, MOVE : ir, avanzar ⟨he didn't get far : no avanzó mucho⟩ **3** ARRIVE : llegar ⟨to get home : llegar a casa⟩ **4 to get to be** : llegar a ser ⟨she got to be the director : llegó a ser directora⟩ **5 to get ahead** : adelantarse, progresar **6 to get along** : llevarse bien (con alguien), congeniar **7 to get by** MANAGE : arreglárselas **8 to get over** OVERCOME : superar, consolarse de **9 to get together** MEET : reunirse **10 to get up** : levantarse

getaway [ˈgɛt̬əˌweɪ] *n* ESCAPE : fuga *f*, huida *f*, escapada *f*

geyser [ˈgaɪzər] *n* : géiser *m*

Ghanaian [ˈgɑniən, ˈgæ-] *n* : ghanés *m*, -nesa *f* — **Ghanaian** *adj*

ghastly [ˈgæstli] *adj* **-lier; -est** **1** HORRIBLE : horrible, espantoso **2** PALE : pálido, cadavérico

gherkin [ˈgərkən] *n* : pepinillo *m*

ghetto [ˈgɛt̬oː] *n, pl* **-tos** *or* **-toes** : gueto *m*

ghost [ˈgoːst] *n* **1** : fantasma *f*, espectro *m* **2 the Holy Ghost** : el Espíritu Santo

ghostly [ˈgoːstli] *adv* : fantasmal

ghoul [ˈguːl] *n* **1** : demonio *m* necrófago **2** : persona *f* de gustos macabros

GI [ˌʤiːˈaɪ] *n, pl* **GI's** *or* **GIs** : soldado *m* estadounidense

giant[1] [ˈʤaɪənt] *adj* : gigante, gigantesco, enorme

giant[2] *n* : gigante *m*, -ta *f*

gibberish [ˈʤɪbərɪʃ] *n* : galimatías *m*, jerigonza *f*

gibbon [ˈgɪbən] *n* : gibón *m*

gibe[1] [ˈʤaɪb] *vi* **gibed; gibing** : mofarse, burlarse

gibe[2] *n* : pulla *f*, burla *f*, mofa *f*

giblets [ˈʤɪbləts] *npl* : menudos *mpl*, menudencias *fpl*

giddiness [ˈgɪdinəs] *n* **1** DIZZINESS : vértigo *m*, mareo *m* **2** SILLINESS : frivolidad *f*, estupidez *f*

giddy [ˈgɪdi] *adj* **-dier; -est 1** DIZZY : mareado, vertiginoso **2** FRIVOLOUS, SILLY : frívolo, tonto

gift [ˈgɪft] *n* **1** TALENT : don *m*, talento *m*, dotes *fpl* **2** PRESENT : regalo *m*, obsequio *m*

gifted [ˈgɪftəd] *adj* TALENTED : talentoso

gig [ˈgɪg] *vi* : trabajo *m* (de duración limitada) ⟨to play a gig : tocar en un concierto⟩

gigabyte [ˈʤɪgəˌbaɪt, ˈgɪ-] *n* : gigabyte *m*

gigantic [ʤaɪˈgæntɪk] *adj* : gigantesco, enorme, colosal

giggle[1] [ˈgɪgəl] *vi* **-gled; -gling** : reírse tontamente

giggle[2] *n* : risita *f*, risa *f* tonta

gild [ˈgɪld] *vt* **gilded** *or* **gilt** [ˈgɪlt]; **gilding** : dorar

gill [ˈgɪl] *n* : agalla *f*, branquia *f*

gilt[1] [ˈgɪlt] *adj* : dorado

gilt[2] *n* : dorado *m*

gimlet [ˈgɪmlət] *n* **1** : barrena *f* (herramienta) **2** : bebida *f* de vodka o ginebra y limón

gimmick [ˈgɪmɪk] *n* **1** GADGET : artilugio *m* **2** CATCH : engaño *m*, trampa *f* **3** SCHEME, TRICK : ardid *m*, truco *m*

gin [ˈʤɪn] *n* **1** : desmotadora *f* (de algodón) **2** : ginebra *f* (bebida alcohólica)

ginger [ˈʤɪnʤər] *n* : jengibre *m*

ginger ale *n* : ginger ale *m*, gaseosa *f* de jengibre

gingerbread [ˈʤɪnʤərˌbrɛd] *n* : pan *m* de jengibre

gingerly [ˈʤɪnʤərli] *adv* : con cuidado, cautelosamente

gingham [ˈgɪŋəm] *n* : guinga *f*

ginseng [ˈʤɪnˌsɪŋ, -ˌsɛŋ] *n* : ginseng *m*

giraffe [ʤəˈræf] *n* : jirafa *f*

gird [ˈgərd] *vt* **girded** *or* **girt** [ˈgərt]; **girding 1** BIND : ceñir, atar **2** ENCIRCLE : rodear **3 to gird oneself** : prepararse

girder [ˈgərdər] *n* : viga *f*

girdle[1] [ˈgərdəl] *vt* **-dled; -dling 1** GIRD : ceñir, atar **2** SURROUND : rodear, circundar

girdle[2] *n* : faja *f*

girl [ˈgərl] *n* **1** : chica *f*, muchacha *f* **2** *or* **little girl** : niña *f*, chica *f* **3** SWEETHEART : novia *f* **4** DAUGHTER : hija *f*

girlfriend [ˈgərlˌfrɛnd] *n* : novia *f*, amiga *f*

girlhood [ˈgərlˌhʊd] *n* : niñez *f*, juventud *f* (de una muchacha)

girlish [ˈgərlɪʃ] *adj* : de niña

girth [ˈgərθ] *n* **1** : circunferencia *f* (de un árbol, etc.), cintura *f* (de una persona) **2** CINCH : cincha *f* (para caballos, etc.)

gist [ˈʤɪst] *n* : quid *m*, meollo *m*

give[1] [ˈgɪv] *v* **gave** [ˈgeɪv]; **given** [ˈgɪvən]; **giving** *vt* **1** HAND, PRESENT : dar, regalar, obsequiar ⟨give it to me : dámelo⟩ ⟨they gave him a gold watch : le regalaron un reloj de oro⟩ **2** PAY : dar, pagar ⟨I'll give you $10 for this one : te daré $10 por éste⟩ **3** UTTER : dar, pronunciar ⟨to give a shout : dar un grito⟩ ⟨to give a speech : pronunciar un discurso⟩ ⟨to give a verdict : dictar sentencia⟩ **4** PROVIDE : dar ⟨to give one's word : dar uno su palabra⟩ ⟨to give a party : dar una fiesta⟩ **5** CAUSE : dar, causar, ocasionar ⟨to give trouble : causar problemas⟩ ⟨to give someone to understand : darle a entender a alguien⟩ **6** GRANT : dar, otorgar ⟨to give permission : dar permiso⟩ — *vi* **1** : hacer regalos **2** YIELD : ceder, romperse ⟨it gave under the weight of the crowd : cedió bajo el peso de la muchedumbre⟩ **3 to give in** *or* **to give up** SURRENDER : rendirse, entregarse **4 to give out** : agotarse, acabarse ⟨the supplies gave out : las provisiones se agotaron⟩

give[2] *n* FLEXIBILITY : flexibilidad *f*, elasticidad *f*

giveaway [ˈgɪvəˌweɪ] *n* **1** : revelación *f* involuntaria **2** GIFT : regalo *m*, obsequio *m*

given [ˈgɪvən] *adj* **1** INCLINED : dado, inclinado ⟨he's given to quarreling : es muy dado a discutir⟩ **2** SPECIFIC : dado, determinado ⟨at a given time : en un momento dado⟩

given name *n* : nombre *m* de pila

give up *vt* : dejar, renunciar a, abandonar ⟨to give up smoking : dejar de fumar⟩

gizzard [ˈgɪzərd] *n* : molleja *f*

glacial [ˈgleɪʃəl] *adj* : glacial — **glacially** *adv*

glacier [ˈgleɪʃər] *n* : glaciar *m*

glad [ˈglæd] *adj* **gladder; gladdest 1** PLEASED : alegre, contento ⟨she was glad I came : se alegró de que haya venido⟩ ⟨glad to meet you! : ¡mucho gusto!⟩ **2** HAPPY, PLEASING : feliz, agradable ⟨glad tidings : buenas nuevas⟩ **3** WILLING : dispuesto, gustoso ⟨I'll be glad to do it : lo haré con mucho gusto⟩

gladden [ˈglædən] *vt* : alegrar

glade [ˈgleɪd] *n* : claro *m*

gladiator [ˈglædiˌeɪṭər] *n* : gladiador *m*

gladiolus [ˌglædiˈoːləs] *n, pl* **-li** [-li, -ˌlaɪ] : gladiolo *m*, gladíolo *m*

gladly [ˈglædli] *adv* : con mucho gusto

gladness [ˈglædnəs] *n* : alegría *f*, gozo *m*

glamor *or* **glamour** [ˈglæmər] *n* : atractivo *m*, hechizo *m*, encanto *m*

glamorous [ˈglæmərəs] *adj* : atractivo, encantador

glance[1] [ˈglænts] *vi* **glanced; glancing 1** RICOCHET : rebotar ⟨it glanced off the wall : rebotó en la pared⟩ **2 to glance at** : mirar, echar un vistazo a **3 to glance away** : apartar los ojos

glance[2] *n* : mirada *f*, vistazo *m*, ojeada *f*

gland [ˈglænd] *n* : glándula *f*

glandular [ˈglænʤʊlər] *adj* : glandular

glare[1] [ˈglær] *vi* **glared; glaring 1** SHINE : brillar, relumbrar **2** STARE : mirar con ira, lanzar una mirada feroz

glare[2] *n* **1** BRIGHTNESS : resplandor *m*, luz *f* deslumbrante **2** : mirada *f* feroz
glaring [ˈglærɪŋ] *adj* **1** BRIGHT : deslumbrante, brillante **2** FLAGRANT, OBVIOUS : flagrante, manifiesto ⟨a glaring error : un error que salta a la vista⟩
glass [ˈglæs] *n* **1** : vidrio *m*, cristal *m* ⟨stained glass : vidrio de color⟩ **2** : vaso *m* ⟨a glass of milk : un vaso de leche⟩ **3 glasses** *npl* SPECTACLES : gafas *fpl*, anteojos *mpl*, lentes *mpl*, espejuelos *mpl*
glassblowing [ˈglæsˌbloːɪŋ] *n* : soplado *m* del vidrio
glassful [ˈglæsˌfʊl] *n* : vaso *m*, copa *f*
glassware [ˈglæsˌwær] *n* : cristalería *f*
glassy [ˈglæsi] *adj* **glassier; -est 1** VITREOUS : vítreo **2** : vidrioso ⟨glassy eyes : ojos vidriosos⟩
glaucoma [glaʊˈkoːmə, glɔ-] *n* : glaucoma *m*
glaze[1] [ˈgleɪz] *vt* **glazed; glazing 1** : ponerle vidrios a (una ventana, etc.) **2** : vidriar (cerámica) **3** : glasear (papel, verduras, etc.)
glaze[2] *n* : vidriado *m*, glaseado *m*, barniz *m*
glazier [ˈgleɪʒər] *n* : vidriero *m*, -ra *f*
gleam[1] [ˈgliːm] *vi* : brillar, destellar, relucir
gleam[2] *n* **1** LIGHT : luz *f* (oscura) **2** GLINT : destello *m* **3** GLIMMER : rayo *m*, vislumbre *f* ⟨a gleam of hope : un rayo de esperanza⟩
glean [ˈgliːn] *vt* : recoger, espigar
glee [ˈgliː] *n* : alegría *f*, júbilo *m*, regocijo *m*
gleeful [ˈgliːfəl] *adj* : lleno de alegría
glen [ˈglɛn] *n* : cañada *f*
glib [ˈglɪb] *adj* **glibber; glibbest 1** : simplista ⟨a glib reply : una respuesta simplista⟩ **2** : con mucha labia (dícese de una persona)
glibly [ˈglɪbli] *adv* : con mucha labia
glide[1] [ˈglaɪd] *vi* **glided; gliding** : deslizarse (en una superficie), planear (en el aire)
glide[2] *n* : planeo *m*
glider [ˈglaɪdər] *n* **1** : planeador *m* (aeronave) **2** : mecedor *m* (tipo de columpio)
glimmer[1] [ˈglɪmər] *vi* : brillar con luz trémula
glimmer[2] *n* **1** : luz *f* trémula, luz *f* tenue **2** GLEAM : rayo *m*, vislumbre *f* ⟨a glimmer of understanding : un rayo de entendimiento⟩
glimpse[1] [ˈglɪmps] *vt* **glimpsed; glimpsing** : vislumbrar, entrever
glimpse[2] *n* : mirada *f* breve ⟨to catch a glimpse of : alcanzar a ver, vislumbrar⟩
glint[1] [ˈglɪnt] *vi* GLEAM, SPARKLE : destellar, fulgurar
glint[2] *n* **1** SPARKLE : destello *m*, centelleo *m* **2 to have a glint in one's eye** : chispearle los ojos a uno
glisten[1] [ˈglɪsən] *vi* : brillar, centellear
glisten[2] *n* : brillo *m*, centelleo *m*
glitch [ˈglɪʧ] *n* **1** MALFUNCTION : mal funcionamiento *m* **2** SNAG : problema *m*, complicación *f*
glitter[1] [ˈglɪt̬ər] *vi* **1** SPARKLE : destellar, relucir, brillar **2** FLASH : relampaguear ⟨his eyes glittered in anger : le relampagueaban los ojos de ira⟩
glitter[2] *n* **1** BRIGHTNESS : brillo *m* **2** : purpurina *f* (para decoración)
glitz [ˈglɪts] *n* : oropel *m*
gloat [ˈgloːt] *vi* **to gloat over** : regodearse en
glob [ˈglɑb] *n* : plasta *f*, masa *f*, grumo *m*
global [ˈgloːbəl] *adj* **1** SPHERICAL : esférico **2** WORLDWIDE : global, mundial — **globally** *adv*
globe [ˈgloːb] *n* **1** SPHERE : esfera *f*, globo *m* **2** EARTH : globo *m*, Tierra *f* **3** : globo *m* terráqueo (modelo de la Tierra)
globe–trotter [ˈgloːbˌtrɑt̬ər] *n* : trotamundos *mf*
globular [ˈglɑbjʊlər] *adj* : globular
globule [ˈglɑˌbjuːl] *n* : glóbulo *m*
gloom [ˈgluːm] *n* **1** DARKNESS : penumbra *f*, oscuridad *f* **2** MELANCHOLY : melancolía *f*, tristeza *f*
gloomily [ˈgluːməli] *adv* : tristemente
gloomy [ˈgluːmi] *adj* **gloomier; -est 1** DARK : oscuro, tenebroso ⟨gloomy weather : tiempo gris⟩ **2** MELANCHOLY : melancólico **3** PESSIMISTIC : pesimista **4** DEPRESSING : deprimente, lúgubre
glorification [ˌglorəfəˈkeɪʃən] *n* : glorificación *f*
glorify [ˈglorəˌfaɪ] *vt* **-fied; -fying** : glorificar
glorious [ˈgloriəs] *adj* **1** ILLUSTRIOUS : glorioso, ilustre **2** MAGNIFICENT : magnífico, espléndido, maravilloso — **gloriously** *adv*
glory[1] [ˈglori] *vi* **-ried; -rying** EXULT : exultar, regocijarse
glory[2] *n, pl* **-ries 1** RENOWN : gloria *f*, fama *f*, honor *m* **2** PRAISE : gloria *f* ⟨glory to God : gloria a Dios⟩ **3** MAGNIFICENCE : magnificencia *f*, esplendor *m*, gloria *f* **4 to be in one's glory** : estar uno en su gloria
gloss[1] [ˈglɔs, ˈglɑs] *vt* **1** EXPLAIN : glosar, explicar **2** POLISH : lustrar, pulir **3 to gloss over** : quitarle importancia a, minimizar
gloss[2] *n* **1** SHINE : lustre *m*, brillo *m* **2** EXPLANATION : glosa *f*, explicación *f* breve **3** → **glossary**
glossary [ˈglɔsəri, ˈglɑ-] *n, pl* **-ries** : glosario *m*
glossy [ˈglɔsi, ˈglɑ-] *adj* **glossier; -est** : brillante, lustroso, satinado (dícese del papel)
glove [ˈglʌv] *n* : guante *m*
glow[1] [ˈgloː] *vi* **1** SHINE : brillar, resplandecer **2** BRIM : rebosar ⟨to glow with health : rebosar de salud⟩

glow[2] *n* **1** BRIGHTNESS : resplandor *m*, brillo *m*, luminosidad *f* **2** FEELING : sensación *f* (de bienestar), oleada *f* (de sentimiento) **3** INCANDESCENCE : incandescencia *f*

glower [ˈglaʊər] *vi* : fruncir el ceño

glowworm [ˈglo:ˌwərm] *n* : luciérnaga *f*

glucose [ˈglu:ˌko:s] *n* : glucosa *f*

glue[1] [ˈglu:] *vt* **glued; gluing** *or* **glueing** : pegar, encolar

glue[2] *n* : pegamento *m*, cola *f*

gluey [ˈglu:i] *adj* **gluier; -est** : pegajoso

glum [ˈglʌm] *adj* **glummer; glummest** **1** SULLEN : hosco, sombrío **2** DREARY, GLOOMY : sombrío, triste, melancólico

glut[1] [ˈglʌt] *vt* **glutted; glutting** **1** SATIATE : saciar, hartar **2** : inundar (el mercado)

glut[2] *n* : exceso *m*, superabundancia *f*

glutinous [ˈglu:tənəs] *adj* STICKY : pegajoso, glutinoso

glutton [ˈglʌtən] *n* : glotón *m*, -tona *f*

gluttonous [ˈglʌtənəs] *adj* : glotón

gluttony [ˈglʌtəni] *n, pl* **-tonies** : glotonería *f*, gula *f*

gnarled [ˈnɑrld] *adj* **1** KNOTTY : nudoso **2** TWISTED : retorcido

gnash [ˈnæʃ] *vt* : hacer rechinar (los dientes)

gnat [ˈnæt] *n* : jején *m*

gnaw [ˈnɔ] *vt* : roer

gnome [ˈno:m] *n* : gnomo *m*

gnu [ˈnu:, ˈnju:] *n, pl* **gnu** *or* **gnus** : ñu *m*

go[1] [ˈgo:] *v* **went** [ˈwɛnt]; **gone** [ˈgɔn, ˈgɑn]; **going; goes** [ˈgo:z] *vi* **1** PROCEED : ir ⟨to go slow : ir despacio⟩ ⟨to go shopping : ir de compras⟩ **2** LEAVE : irse, marcharse, salir ⟨let's go! : ¡vámonos!⟩ ⟨the train went on time : el tren salió a tiempo⟩ **3** DISAPPEAR : desaparecer, pasarse, irse ⟨her fear is gone : se le ha pasado el miedo⟩ ⟨my pen is gone! : ¡mi pluma desapareció!⟩ **4** EXTEND : ir, extenderse, llegar ⟨this road goes to the river : este camino se extiende hasta el río⟩ ⟨to go from top to bottom : ir de arriba abajo⟩ **5** FUNCTION : funcionar, marchar ⟨the car won't go : el coche no funciona⟩ ⟨to get something going : poner algo en marcha⟩ **6** SELL : venderse ⟨it goes for $15 : se vende por $15⟩ **7** PROGRESS : ir, andar, seguir ⟨my exam went well : me fue bien en el examen⟩ ⟨how did the meeting go? : ¿qué tal la reunión?⟩ **8** BECOME : volverse, quedarse ⟨he's going crazy : está volviéndose loco⟩ ⟨the tire went flat : la llanta se desinfló⟩ **9** FIT : caber ⟨it will go through the door : cabe por la puerta⟩ **10 anything goes!** : ¡todo vale! **11 to go** : faltar ⟨only 10 days to go : faltan sólo 10 días⟩ **12 to go back on** : faltar uno a (su promesa) **13 to go bad** SPOIL : estropearse, echarse a perder **14 to go for** : interesarse uno en, gustarle a uno (algo, alguien) ⟨I don't go for that : eso no me interesa⟩ **15 to go off** EXPLODE : estallar **16 to go with** MATCH : armonizar con, hacer juego con — *v aux* **to be going to** : ir a ⟨I'm going to write a letter : voy a escribir una carta⟩ ⟨it's not going to last : no va a durar⟩

go[2] *n, pl* **goes** **1** ATTEMPT : intento *m* ⟨to have a go at : intentar, probar⟩ **2** SUCCESS : éxito *m* **3** ENERGY : energía *f*, empuje *m* ⟨to be on the go : no parar, no descansar⟩

goad[1] [ˈgo:d] *vt* : aguijonear (un animal), incitar (a una persona)

goad[2] *n* : aguijón *m*

goal [ˈgo:l] *n* **1** : gol *m* (en deportes) ⟨to score a goal : anotar un gol⟩ **2** *or* **goalposts** : portería *f* **3** AIM, OBJECTIVE : meta *m*, objetivo *m*

goalie [ˈgo:li] → **goalkeeper**

goalkeeper [ˈgo:lˌki:pər] *n* : portero *m*, -ra *f*; guardameta *mf*; arquero *m*, -ra *f*

goaltender [ˈgo:lˌtɛndər] → **goalkeeper**

goat [ˈgo:t] *n* **1** : cabra *f* (hembra) **2 billy goat** : macho *m* cabrío, chivo *m*

goatee [go:ˈti:] *n* : barbita *f* de chivo, piocha *f Mex*

goatskin [ˈgo:tˌskɪn] *n* : piel *f* de cabra

gob [ˈgɑb] *n* : masa *f*, grumo *m*

gobble [ˈgɑbəl] *v* **-bled; -bling** *vt* **to gobble up** : tragar, engullir — *vi* : hacer ruidos de pavo

gobbledygook [ˈgɑbəldiˌgʊk, -ˌgu:k] *n* GIBBERISH : jerigonza *f*

go–between [ˈgo:bɪˌtwi:n] *n* : intermediario *m*, -ria *f*; mediador *m*, -dora *f*

goblet [ˈgɑblət] *n* : copa *f*

goblin [ˈgɑblən] *n* : duende *m*, trasgo *m*

god [ˈgɑd, ˈgɔd] *n* **1** : dios *m* **2 God** : Dios *m*

godchild [ˈgɑdˌʧaɪld, ˈgɔd-] *n, pl* **-children** : ahijado *m*, -da *f*

goddess [ˈgɑdəs, ˈgɔ-] *n* : diosa *f*

godfather [ˈgɑdˌfɑðər, ˈgɔd-] *n* : padrino *m*

godless [ˈgɑdləs, ˈgɔd-] *adj* : ateo

godlike [ˈgɑdˌlaɪk, ˈgɔd-] *adj* : divino

godly [ˈgɑdli, ˈgɔd-] *adj* **-lier; -est** **1** DIVINE : divino **2** DEVOUT, PIOUS : piadoso, devoto, beato

godmother [ˈgɑdˌmʌðər, ˈgɔd-] *n* : madrina *f*

godparents [ˈgɑdˌpærənts, ˈgɔd-] *npl* : padrinos *mpl*

godsend [ˈgɑdˌsɛnd, ˈgɔd-] *n* : bendición *f*, regalo *m* divino

goes → **go**

go–getter [ˈgo:ˌgɛt̬ər] *n* : persona *f* ambiciosa, buscavidas *mf fam*

goggle [ˈgɑgəl] *vi* **-gled; -gling** : mirar con ojos desorbitados

goggles [ˈgɑgəlz] *npl* : gafas *fpl* (protectoras), anteojos *mpl*

goings–on [ˌgo:ɪŋzˈɑn, -ˈɔn] *npl* : sucesos *mpl*, ocurrencias *fpl*

goiter [ˈgɔɪt̬ər] *n* : bocio *m*

gold [ˈgo:ld] *n* : oro *m*

golden [ˈgo:ldən] *adj* **1** : (hecho) de oro **2** : dorado, de color oro ⟨golden hair

: pelo rubio⟩ **3** FLOURISHING, PROSPEROUS : dorado, próspero ⟨golden years : años dorados⟩ **4** FAVORABLE : favorable, excelente ⟨a golden opportunity : una excelente oportunidad⟩

goldenrod [ˈgoːldənˌrɑd] *n* : vara *f* de oro

golden rule *n* : regla *f* de oro

goldfinch [ˈgoːldˌfɪntʃ] *n* : jilguero *m*

goldfish [ˈgoːldˌfɪʃ] *n* : pez *m* de colores

goldsmith [ˈgoːldˌsmɪθ] *n* : orífice *mf*, orfebre *mf*

golf[1] [ˈgɑlf, ˈgɔlf] *vi* : jugar (al) golf

golf[2] *n* : golf *m*

golfer [ˈgɑlfər, ˈgɔl-] *n* : golfista *mf*

gondola [ˈgɑndələ, gɑnˈdoːlə] *n* : góndola *f*

gone [ˈgɔn] *adj* **1** DEAD : muerto **2** PAST : pasado, ido **3** LOST : perdido, desaparecido **4 to be far gone** : estar muy avanzado **5 to be gone on** : estar loco por

goner [ˈgɔnər] *n* **to be a goner** : estar en las últimas

gong [ˈgɔŋ, ˈgɑŋ] *n* : gong *m*

gonorrhea [ˌgɑnəˈriːə] *n* : gonorrea *f*

good[1] [ˈgʊd] *adv* **1** (*used as an intensifier*) : bien ⟨a good strong rope : una cuerda bien fuerte⟩ **2** WELL : bien

good[2] *adj* **better** [ˈbɛt̬ər]; **best** [ˈbɛst] **1** PLEASANT : bueno, agradable ⟨good news : buenas noticias⟩ ⟨to have a good time : divertirse⟩ **2** BENEFICIAL : bueno, beneficioso ⟨good for a cold : beneficioso para los resfriados⟩ ⟨it's good for you : es bueno para uno⟩ **3** FULL : completo, entero ⟨a good hour : una hora entera⟩ **4** CONSIDERABLE : bueno, bastante ⟨a good many people : muchísima gente, un buen número de gente⟩ **5** ATTRACTIVE, DESIRABLE : bueno, bien ⟨a good salary : un buen sueldo⟩ ⟨to look good : quedar bien⟩ **6** KIND, VIRTUOUS : bueno, amable ⟨she's a good person : es buena gente⟩ ⟨that's good of you! : ¡qué amable!⟩ ⟨good deeds : buenas obras⟩ **7** SKILLED : bueno, hábil ⟨to be good at : tener facilidad para⟩ **8** SOUND : bueno, sensato ⟨good advice : buenos consejos⟩ **9** (*in greetings*) : bueno ⟨good morning : buenos días⟩ ⟨good afternoon (evening) : buenas tardes⟩ ⟨good night : buenas noches⟩

good[3] *n* **1** RIGHT : bien *m* ⟨to do good : hacer el bien⟩ **2** GOODNESS : bondad *f* **3** BENEFIT : bien *m*, provecho *m* ⟨it's for your own good : es por tu propio bien⟩ **4 goods** *npl* PROPERTY : efectos *mpl* personales, posesiones *fpl* **5 goods** *npl* WARES : mercancía *f*, mercadería *f*, artículos *mpl* **6 for ~** : para siempre

good–bye *or* **good–by** [gʊdˈbaɪ] *n* : adiós *m*

good–for–nothing [ˈgʊdfərˌnʌθɪŋ] *n* : inútil *mf*; haragán *m*, -gana *f*; holgazán *m*, -zana *f*

Good Friday *n* : Viernes *m* Santo

good–hearted [ˈgʊdˈhɑrt̬əd] *adj* : bondadoso, benévolo, de buen corazón

good–looking [ˈgʊdˈlʊkɪŋ] *adj* : bello, bonito, guapo

goodly [ˈgʊdli] *adj* **-lier; -est** : considerable, importante ⟨a goodly number : un número considerable⟩

good–natured [ˈgʊdˈneɪtʃərd] *adj* : amigable, amistoso, bonachón *fam*

goodness [ˈgʊdnəs] *n* **1** : bondad *f* **2 thank goodness!** : ¡gracias a Dios!, ¡menos mal!

good–tempered [ˈgʊdˈtɛmpərd] *adj* : de buen genio

goodwill [ˌgʊdˈwɪl] *n* **1** BENEVOLENCE : benevolencia *f*, buena voluntad *f* **2** : buen nombre *m* (de comercios), renombre *m* comercial

goody [ˈgʊdi] *n, pl* **goodies** : cosa *f* rica para comer, golosina *f*

gooey [ˈguːi] *adj* **gooier; gooiest** : pegajoso

goof[1] [ˈguːf] *vi* **1 to goof off** : holgazanear **2 to goof around** : hacer tonterías **3 to goof up** BLUNDER : cometer un error

goof[2] *n* **1** : bobo *m*, -ba *f*; tonto *m*, -ta *f* **2** BLUNDER : error *m*, planchazo *m fam*

goofy [ˈguːfi] *adj* **goofier; -est** SILLY : tonto, bobo

goose [ˈguːs] *n, pl* **geese** [ˈgiːs] : ganso *m*, -sa *f*; ánsar *m*; oca *f*

gooseberry [ˈguːsˌbɛriː, ˈguːz-] *n, pl* **-berries** : grosella *f* espinosa

goose bumps *npl* : carne *f* de gallina

gooseflesh [ˈguːsˌflɛʃ] → **goose bumps**

goose pimples → **goose bumps**

gopher [ˈgoːfər] *n* : taltuza *f*

gore[1] [ˈgor] *vt* **gored; goring** : cornear

gore[2] *n* BLOOD : sangre *f*

gorge[1] [ˈgɔrdʒ] *vt* **gorged; gorging 1** SATIATE : saciar, hartar **2 to gorge oneself** : hartarse, atiborrarse, atracarse *fam*

gorge[2] *n* RAVINE : desfiladero *m*

gorgeous [ˈgɔrdʒəs] *adj* : hermoso, espléndido, magnífico

gorilla [gəˈrɪlə] *n* : gorila *m*

gory [ˈgori] *adj* **gorier; -est** BLOODY : sangriento

gosling [ˈgɑzlɪŋ, ˈgɔz-] *n* : ansarino *m*

gospel [ˈgɑspəl] *n* **1** *or* **Gospel** : evangelio *m* ⟨the four Gospels : los cuatro evangelios⟩ **2 the gospel truth** : el evangelio, la pura verdad

gossamer [ˈgɑsəmər, ˈgɑzə-] *adj* : tenue, sutil ⟨gossamer wings : alas tenues⟩

gossip[1] [ˈgɑsɪp] *vi* : chismear, contar chismes

gossip[2] *n* **1** : chismoso *m*, -sa *f* (persona) **2** RUMOR : chisme *m*, rumor *m*

gossipy [ˈgɑsɪpi] *adj* : chismoso

got → **get**

Gothic [ˈgɑθɪk] *adj* : gótico

gotten → **get**

gouge[1] [ˈgaʊdʒ] *vt* **gouged; gouging 1** : excavar, escoplear (con una gubia) **2** SWINDLE : estafar, extorsionar

gouge[2] *n* **1** CHISEL : gubia *f*, formón *m* **2** GROOVE : ranura *f*, hoyo *m* (hecho por un formón)

goulash [ˈguːˌlɑʃ, -ˌlæʃ] *n* : estofado *m*, guiso *m* al estilo húngaro

gourd [ˈgord, ˈgʊrd] *n* : calabaza *f*

gourmand [ˈgʊrˌmɑnd] *n* **1** GLUTTON : glotón *m*, -tona *f* **2** → **gourmet**

gourmet [ˈgʊrˌmeɪ, gʊrˈmeɪ] *n* : gourmet *mf*; gastrónomo *m*, -ma *f*

gout [ˈgaʊt] *n* : gota *f*

govern [ˈgʌvərn] *vt* **1** RULE : gobernar **2** CONTROL, DETERMINE : determinar, controlar, guiar **3** RESTRAIN : dominar (las emociones, etc.) — *vi* : gobernar

governess [ˈgʌvərnəs] *n* : institutriz *f*

government [ˈgʌvərmənt] *n* : gobierno *m*

governmental [ˌgʌvərˈmɛntəl] *adj* : gubernamental, gubernativo

governor [ˈgʌvənər, ˈgʌvərnər] *n* **1** : gobernador *m*, -dora *f* (de un estado, etc.) **2** : regulador *m* (de una máquina)

governorship [ˈgʌvənərˌʃɪp, ˈgʌvərnər-] *n* : cargo *m* de gobernador

gown [ˈgaʊn] *n* **1** : vestido *m* ⟨evening gown : traje de fiesta⟩ **2** : toga *f* (de magistrados, clérigos, etc.)

grab[1] [ˈgræb] *v* **grabbed; grabbing** *vt* SNATCH : agarrar, arrebatar — *vi* : agarrarse

grab[2] *n* **1 to make a grab for** : tratar de agarrar **2 up for grabs** : disponible, libre

grace[1] [ˈgreɪs] *vt* **graced; gracing 1** HONOR : honrar **2** ADORN : adornar, embellecer

grace[2] *n* **1** : gracia *f* ⟨by the grace of God : por la gracia de Dios⟩ **2** BLESSING : bendición *f* (de la mesa) **3** RESPITE : plazo *m*, gracia *f* ⟨a five days' grace (period) : un plazo de cinco días⟩ **4** GRACIOUSNESS : gentileza *f*, cortesía *f* **5** ELEGANCE : elegancia *f*, gracia *f* **6 to be in the good graces of** : estar en buenas relaciones con **7 with good grace** : de buena gana

graceful [ˈgreɪsfəl] *adj* : lleno de gracia, garboso, grácil

gracefully [ˈgreɪsfəli] *adv* : con gracia, con garbo

gracefulness [ˈgreɪsfəlnəs] *n* : gracilidad *f*, apostura *f*, gallardía *f*

graceless [ˈgreɪsləs] *adj* **1** DISCOURTEOUS : descortés **2** CLUMSY, INELEGANT : torpe, desgarbado, poco elegante

gracious [ˈgreɪʃəs] *adj* : cortés, gentil, cordial

graciously [ˈgreɪʃəsli] *adv* : gentilmente

graciousness [ˈgreɪʃəsnəs] *n* : gentileza *f*

gradation [greɪˈdeɪʃən, grə-] *n* : gradación *f*

grade[1] [ˈgreɪd] *vt* **graded; grading 1** SORT : clasificar **2** LEVEL : nivelar **3** : calificar (exámenes, alumnos)

grade[2] *n* **1** QUALITY : categoría *f*, calidad *f* **2** RANK : grado *m*, rango *m* (militar) **3** YEAR : grado *m*, curso *m*, año *m* ⟨sixth grade : el sexto grado⟩ **4** MARK : nota *f*, calificación *f* (en educación) **5** SLOPE : cuesta *f*, pendiente *f*, gradiente *f*

grade school → **elementary school**

gradient [ˈgreɪdiənt] *n* : gradiente *f*

gradual [ˈgrædʒʊəl] *adj* : gradual, paulatino

gradually [ˈgrædʒʊəli, ˈgrædʒəli] *adv* : gradualmente, poco a poco

graduate[1] [ˈgrædʒʊˌeɪt] *v* **-ated; -ating** *vi* : graduarse, licenciarse — *vt* : graduar ⟨a graduated thermometer : un termómetro graduado⟩

graduate[2] [ˈgrædʒʊət] *adj* : de postgrado ⟨graduate course : curso de postgrado⟩

graduate[3] *n* **1** : licenciado *m*, -da *f*; graduado *m*, -da *f* (de la universidad) **2** : bachiller *mf* (de la escuela secundaria)

graduate student *n* : postgraduado *m*, -da *f*

graduation [ˌgrædʒʊˈeɪʃən] *n* : graduación *f*

graffiti [grəˈfiːţi, græ-] *npl* : pintadas *fpl*, graffiti *mpl*

graft[1] [ˈgræft] *vt* : injertar

graft[2] *n* **1** : injerto *m* ⟨skin graft : injerto cutáneo⟩ **2** CORRUPTION : soborno *m* (político), ganancia *f* ilegal

grain [ˈgreɪn] *n* **1** : grano *m* ⟨a grain of corn : un grano de maíz⟩ ⟨like a grain of sand : como grano de arena⟩ **2** CEREALS : cereales *mpl* **3** : veta *f*, vena *f*, grano *m* (de madera) **4** SPECK, TRACE : pizca *f*, ápice *m* ⟨a grain of truth : una pizca de verdad⟩ **5** grano *m* (unidad de peso)

gram [ˈgræm] *n* : gramo *m*

grammar [ˈgræmər] *n* : gramática *f*

grammar school → **elementary school**

grammatical [grəˈmæţɪkəl] *adj* : gramatical — **grammatically** [-kli] *adv*

granary [ˈgreɪnəri, ˈgræ-] *n, pl* **-ries** : granero *m*

grand [ˈgrænd] *adj* **1** FOREMOST : grande **2** IMPRESSIVE : impresionante, magnífico ⟨a grand view : una vista magnífica⟩ **3** LAVISH : grandioso, suntuoso, lujoso ⟨to live in a grand manner : vivir a lo grande⟩ **4** FABULOUS : fabuloso, magnífico ⟨to have a grand time : pasarlo estupendamente, pasarlo en grande⟩ **5 grand total** : total *m*, suma *f* total

grandchild [ˈgrændˌtʃaɪld] *n, pl* **-children** : nieto *m*, -ta *f*

granddaughter [ˈgrændˌdɔţər] *n* : nieta *f*

grandeur [ˈgrændʒər] *n* : grandiosidad *f*, esplendor *m*

grandfather [ˈgrændˌfɑðər] *n* : abuelo *m*

grandiose [ˈgrændiˌoːs, ˌgrændiˈ-] *adj* **1** IMPOSING : imponente, grandioso **2** POMPOUS : pomposo, presuntuoso

grandma [ˈgrænˌmɑ, -ˌmɔ] *n* : abuelita *f*, nana *f*

grandmother [ˈgrænd,mʌðər] *n* : abuela *f*

grandpa [ˈgræm,pɑ, -,pɔ] *n* : abuelito *m*

grandparents [ˈgrænd,pærənts] *npl* : abuelos *mpl*

grandson [ˈgrænd,sʌn] *n* : nieto *m*

grandstand [ˈgrænd,stænd] *n* : tribuna *f*

granite [ˈgrænɪt] *n* : granito *m*

grant[1] [ˈgrænt] *vt* **1** ALLOW : conceder ⟨to grant a request : conceder una petición⟩ **2** BESTOW : conceder, dar, otorgar ⟨to grant a favor : otorgar un favor⟩ **3** ADMIT : reconocer, admitir ⟨I'll grant that he's clever : reconozco que es listo⟩ **4 to take for granted** : dar (algo) por sentado

grant[2] *n* **1** GRANTING : concesión *f*, otorgamiento *m* **2** SCHOLARSHIP : beca *f* **3** SUBSIDY : subvención *f*

granular [ˈgrænjʊlər] *adj* : granular

granulated [ˈgrænjʊ,leɪṭəd] *adj* : granulado

grape [ˈgreɪp] *n* : uva *f*

grapefruit [ˈgreɪp,fru:t] *n* : toronja *f*, pomelo *m*

grapevine [ˈgreɪp,vaɪn] *n* **1** : vid *f*, parra *f* **2 through the grapevine** : por vías secretas ⟨I heard it through the grapevine : me lo contaron⟩

graph [ˈgræf] *n* : gráfica *f*, gráfico *m*

graphic [ˈgræfɪk] *adj* **1** VIVID : vívido, gráfico **2 graphic arts** : artes gráficas

graphically [ˈgræfɪkli] *adv* : gráficamente

graphite [ˈgræ,faɪt] *n* : grafito *m*

grapnel [ˈgræpnəl] *n* : rezón *m*

grapple [ˈgræpəl] *v* **-pled; -pling** *vt* GRIP : agarrar (con un garfio) — *vi* STRUGGLE : forcejear, luchar (con un problema, etc.)

grasp[1] [ˈgræsp] *vt* **1** GRIP, SEIZE : agarrar, asir **2** COMPREHEND : entender, comprender — *vi* **to grasp at** : aprovechar

grasp[2] *n* **1** GRIP : agarre *m* **2** CONTROL : control *m*, garras *fpl* **3** REACH : alcance *m* ⟨within your grasp : a su alcance⟩ **4** UNDERSTANDING : comprensión *f*, entendimiento *m*

grass [ˈgræs] *n* **1** : hierba *f* (planta) **2** PASTURE : pasto *m*, zacate *m CA, Mex* **3** LAWN : césped *m*, pasto *m*

grasshopper [ˈgræs,hɑpər] *n* : saltamontes *m*

grassland [ˈgræs,lænd] *n* : pradera *f*

grassy [ˈgræsi] *adj* **grassier; -est** : cubierto de hierba

grate[1] [ˈgreɪt] *v* **grated; -ing** *vt* **1** : rallar (en cocina) **2** SCRAPE : rascar **3 to grate one's teeth** : hacer rechinar los dientes — *vi* **1** RASP, SQUEAK : chirriar **2** IRRITATE : irritar ⟨to grate on one's nerves : crisparle los nervios a uno⟩

grate[2] *n* **1** : parrilla *f* (para cocinar) **2** GRATING : reja *f*, rejilla *f*, verja *f* (en una ventana)

grateful [ˈgreɪtfəl] *adj* : agradecido

gratefully [ˈgreɪtfəli] *adv* : con agradecimiento

gratefulness [ˈgreɪtfəlnəs] *n* : gratitud *f*, agradecimiento *m*

grater [ˈgreɪṭər] *n* : rallador *m*

gratification [,græṭəfəˈkeɪʃən] *n* : gratificación *f*

gratify [ˈgræṭə,faɪ] *vt* **-fied; -fying** **1** PLEASE : complacer **2** SATISFY : satisfacer, gratificar

grating [ˈgreɪṭɪŋ] *n* : reja *f*, rejilla *f*

gratis[1] [ˈgræṭəs, ˈgreɪ-] *adv* : gratis, gratuitamente

gratis[2] *adj* : gratis, gratuito

gratitude [ˈgræṭə,tu:d, -,tju:d] *n* : gratitud *f*, agradecimiento *m*

gratuitous [grəˈtu:əṭəs] *adj* : gratuito

gratuity [grəˈtu:əṭi] *n, pl* **-ities** TIP : propina *f*

grave[1] [ˈgreɪv] *adj* **graver; -est** **1** IMPORTANT : grave, de mucha gravedad **2** SERIOUS, SOLEMN : grave, serio

grave[2] *n* : tumba *f*, sepultura *f*

gravel [ˈgrævəl] *n* : grava *f*, gravilla *f*

gravelly [ˈgrævəli] *adj* **1** : de grava **2** HARSH : áspero (dícese de la voz)

gravely [ˈgreɪvli] *adv* : gravemente

gravestone [ˈgreɪv,sto:n] *n* : lápida *f*

graveyard [ˈgreɪv,jɑrd] *n* CEMETERY : cementerio *m*, panteón *m*, camposanto *m*

gravitate [ˈgrævə,teɪt] *vi* **-tated; -tating** : gravitar

gravitation [,grævəˈteɪʃən] *n* : gravitación *f*

gravitational [,grævəˈteɪʃənəl] *adj* : gravitacional

gravity [ˈgrævəṭi] *n, pl* **-ties** **1** SERIOUSNESS : gravedad *f*, seriedad *f* **2** : gravedad *f* ⟨the law of gravity : la ley de la gravedad⟩

gravy [ˈgreɪvi] *n, pl* **-vies** : salsa *f* (preparada con el jugo de la carne asada)

gray[1] [ˈgreɪ] *vt* : hacer gris — *vi* : encanecer, ponerse gris

gray[2] *adj* **1** : gris (dícese del color) **2** : cano, canoso ⟨gray hair : pelo canoso⟩ ⟨to go gray : volverse cano⟩ **3** DISMAL, GLOOMY : gris, triste

gray[3] *n* : gris *m*

grayish [ˈgreɪɪʃ] *adj* : grisáceo

graze [ˈgreɪz] *v* **grazed; grazing** *vi* : pastar, pacer — *vt* **1** : pastorear (ganado) **2** BRUSH : rozar **3** SCRATCH : raspar

grease[1] [ˈgri:s, ˈgri:z] *vt* **greased; greasing** : engrasar, lubricar

grease[2] [ˈgri:s] *n* : grasa *f*

greasy [ˈgri:si, -zi] *adj* **greasier; -est** **1** : grasiento **2** OILY : graso, grasoso

great [ˈgreɪt] *adj* **1** LARGE : grande ⟨a great mountain : una montaña grande⟩ ⟨a great crowd : una gran muchedumbre⟩ **2** INTENSE : intenso, fuerte, grande ⟨great pain : gran dolor⟩ **3** EMINENT : grande, eminente, distinguido ⟨a great poet : un gran poeta⟩ **4** EXCELLENT, TERRIFIC : excelente, estupendo, fabuloso ⟨to have a great time : pasarlo en grande⟩ **5 a great while** : mucho tiempo

great–aunt [ˌgreɪtˈænt, -ˈant] *n* : tía *f* abuela

greater [ˈgreɪt̬ər] (*comparative* of **great**) : mayor

greatest [ˈgreɪt̬əst] (*superlative* of **great**) : el mayor, la mayor

great–grandchild [ˌgreɪtˈgrænd-ˌʧaɪld] *n, pl* **-children** [-ˌʧɪldrən] : bisnieto *m*, -ta *f*

great–grandfather [ˌgreɪtˈgrænd-ˌfɑðər] *n* : bisabuelo *m*

great–grandmother [ˌgreɪtˈgrænd-ˌmʌðər] *n* : bisabuela *f*

greatly [ˈgreɪtli] *adv* **1** MUCH : mucho, sumamente ⟨to be greatly improved : haber mejorado mucho⟩ **2** VERY : muy ⟨greatly superior : muy superior⟩

greatness [ˈgreɪtnəs] *n* : grandeza *f*

great–uncle [ˌgreɪtˈʌŋkəl] *n* : tío *m* abuelo

grebe [ˈgri:b] *n* : somorgujo *m*

greed [ˈgri:d] *n* **1** AVARICE : avaricia *f*, codicia *f* **2** GLUTTONY : glotonería *f*, gula *f*

greedily [ˈgri:dəli] *adv* : con avaricia, con gula

greediness [ˈgri:dinəs] → **greed**

greedy [ˈgri:di] *adj* **greedier**; **-est** **1** AVARICIOUS : codicioso, avaricioso **2** GLUTTONOUS : glotón

Greek [ˈgri:k] *n* **1** : griego *m*, -ga *f* **2** : griego *m* (idioma) — **Greek** *adj*

green[1] [ˈgri:n] *adj* **1** : verde (dícese del color) **2** UNRIPE : verde, inmaduro **3** INEXPERIENCED : verde, novato

green[2] *n* **1** : verde *m* **2 greens** *npl* VEGETABLES : verduras *fpl*

greenery [ˈgri:nəri] *n, pl* **-eries** : plantas *fpl* verdes, vegetación *f*

greenhorn [ˈgri:nˌhɔrn] *n* : novato *m*, -ta *f*

greenhouse [ˈgri:nˌhaʊs] *n* : invernadero *m*

greenhouse effect : efecto *m* invernadero

greenish [ˈgri:nɪʃ] *adj* : verdoso

Greenlander [ˈgri:nləndər, -ˌlæn-] *n* : groenlandés *m*, -desa *f*

greenness [ˈgri:nnəs] *n* **1** : verdor *m* **2** INEXPERIENCE : inexperiencia *f*

green thumb *n* **to have a green thumb** : tener buena mano para las plantas

greet [ˈgri:t] *vt* **1** : saludar ⟨to greet a friend : saludar a un amigo⟩ **2** : acoger, recibir ⟨they greeted him with boos : lo recibieron con abucheos⟩

greeting [ˈgri:t̬ɪŋ] *n* **1** : saludo *m* **2 greetings** *npl* REGARDS : saludos *mpl*, recuerdos *mpl*

gregarious [grɪˈgæriəs] *adj* : gregario (dícese de los animales), sociable (dícese de las personas) — **gregariously** *adv*

gregariousness [grɪˈgæriəsnəs] *n* : sociabilidad *f*

gremlin [ˈgrɛmlən] *n* : duende *m*

grenade [grəˈneɪd] *n* : granada *f*

Grenadian [grəˈneɪdiən] *n* : granadino *m*, -na *f* — **Grenadian** *adj*

grew → **grow**

grey → **gray**

greyhound [ˈgreɪˌhaʊnd] *n* : galgo *m*

grid [ˈgrɪd] *n* **1** GRATING : rejilla *f* **2** NETWORK : red *f* (de electricidad, etc.) **3** : cuadriculado *m* (de un mapa)

griddle [ˈgrɪdəl] *n* : plancha *f*

griddle cake → **pancake**

gridiron [ˈgrɪdˌaɪərn] *n* **1** GRILL : parrilla *f* **2** : campo *m* de futbol americano

gridlock [ˈgrɪdˌlɑk] *n* : atasco *m* completo (de una red de calles)

grief [ˈgri:f] *n* **1** SORROW : dolor *m*, pena *f* **2** ANNOYANCE, TROUBLE : problemas *mpl*, molestia *f*

grievance [ˈgri:vənts] *n* COMPLAINT : queja *f*

grieve [ˈgri:v] *v* **grieved**; **grieving** *vt* DISTRESS : afligir, entristecer, apenar — *vi* **1** : sufrir, afligirse **2 to grieve for** *or* **to grieve over** : llorar, lamentar

grievous [ˈgri:vəs] *adj* **1** OPPRESSIVE : gravoso, opresivo, severo **2** GRAVE, SERIOUS : grave, severo, doloroso

grievously [ˈgri:vəsli] *adv* : gravemente, de gravedad

grill[1] [ˈgrɪl] *vt* **1** : asar (a la parrilla) **2** INTERROGATE : interrogar

grill[2] *n* **1** : parrilla *f* (para cocinar) **2** : parrillada *f* (comida) **3** RESTAURANT : grill *m*

grille *or* **grill** [ˈgrɪl] *n* : reja *f*, enrejado *m*

grim [ˈgrɪm] *adj* **grimmer**; **grimmest** **1** CRUEL : cruel, feroz **2** STERN : adusto, severo ⟨a grim expression : un gesto severo⟩ **3** GLOOMY : sombrío, deprimente **4** SINISTER : macabro, siniestro **5** UNYIELDING : inflexible, persistente ⟨with grim determination : con una voluntad de hierro⟩

grimace[1] [ˈgrɪməs, grɪˈmeɪs] *vi* **-maced**; **-macing** : hacer muecas

grimace[2] *n* : mueca *f*

grime [ˈgraɪm] *n* : mugre *f*, suciedad *f*

grimly [ˈgrɪmli] *adv* **1** STERNLY : severamente **2** RESOLUTELY : inexorablemente

grimy [ˈgraɪmi] *adj* **grimier**; **-est** : mugriento, sucio

grin[1] [ˈgrɪn] *vi* **grinned**; **grinning** : sonreír abiertamente

grin[2] *n* : sonrisa *f* abierta

grind[1] [ˈgraɪnd] *v* **ground** [ˈgraʊnd]; **grinding** *vt* **1** CRUSH : moler, machacar, triturar **2** SHARPEN : afilar **3** POLISH : pulir, esmerilar (lentes, espejos) **4 to grind one's teeth** : rechinarle los dientes a uno **5 to grind down** OPPRESS : oprimir, agobiar — *vi* **1** : funcionar con dificultad, rechinar ⟨to grind to a halt : pararse poco a poco, llegar a un punto muerto⟩ **2** STUDY : estudiar mucho

grind[2] *n* : trabajo *m* pesado ⟨the daily grind : la rutina diaria⟩
grinder [ˈgraɪndər] *n* : molinillo *m* ⟨coffee grinder : molinillo de café⟩
grindstone [ˈgraɪndˌsto:n] *n* : piedra *m* de afilar
grip[1] [ˈgrɪp] *vt* **gripped; gripping 1** GRASP : agarrar, asir **2** HOLD, INTEREST : captar el interés de
grip[2] *n* **1** GRASP : agarre *m*, asidero *m* ⟨to have a firm grip on something : agarrarse bien de algo⟩ **2** CONTROL, HOLD : control *m*, dominio *m* ⟨to lose one's grip on : perder el control de⟩ ⟨inflation tightened its grip on the economy : la inflación se afianzó en su dominio de la economía⟩ **3** UNDERSTANDING : comprensión *f*, entendimiento *m* ⟨to come to grips with : llegar a entender⟩ **4** HANDLE : asidero *m*, empuñadura *f* (de un arma)
gripe[1] [ˈgraɪp] *v* **griped; griping** *vt* IRRITATE, VEX : irritar, fastidiar, molestar — *vi* COMPLAIN : quejarse, rezongar
gripe[2] *n* : queja *f*
grippe [ˈgrɪp] *n* : influenza *f*, gripe *f*, gripa *f Col, Mex*
grisly [ˈgrɪzli] *adj* **-lier; -est** : horripilante, horroroso, truculento
grist [ˈgrɪst] *n* : molienda *f* ⟨it's all grist for the mill : todo ayuda, todo es provechoso⟩
gristle [ˈgrɪsəl] *n* : cartílago *m*
gristly [ˈgrɪsli] *adj* **-tlier; -est** : cartilaginoso
grit[1] [ˈgrɪt] *vt* **gritted; gritting** : hacer rechinar (los dientes, etc.)
grit[2] *n* **1** SAND : arena *f* **2** GRAVEL : grava *f* **3** COURAGE : valor *m*, coraje *m* **4** **grits** *npl* : sémola *f* de maíz
gritty [ˈgrɪti] *adj* **-tier; -est 1** : arenoso ⟨a gritty surface : una superficie arenosa⟩ **2** PLUCKY : valiente
grizzled [ˈgrɪzəld] *adj* : entrecano
grizzly bear [ˈgrɪzli] *n* : oso *m* pardo
groan[1] [ˈgro:n] *vi* **1** MOAN : gemir, quejarse **2** CREAK : crujir
groan[2] *n* **1** MOAN : gemido *m*, quejido *m* **2** CREAK : crujido *m*
grocer [ˈgro:sər] *n* : tendero *m*, -ra *f*
grocery [ˈgro:səri, -ʃəri] *n, pl* **-ceries 1** *or* **grocery store** : tienda *f* de comestibles, tienda *f* de abarrotes **2 groceries** *npl* : comestibles *mpl*, abarrotes *mpl*
groggy [ˈgrɑgi] *adj* **-gier; -est** : atontado, grogui, tambaleante
groin [ˈgrɔɪn] *n* : ingle *f*
grommet [ˈgrɑmət, ˈgrʌ-] *n* : arandela *f*
groom[1] [ˈgru:m, ˈgrʊm] *vt* **1** : cepillar, almohazar (un animal) **2** : arreglar, cuidar ⟨well-groomed : bien arreglado⟩ **3** PREPARE : preparar
groom[2] *n* **1** : mozo *m*, -za *f* de cuadra **2** BRIDEGROOM : novio *m*
groove[1] [ˈgru:v] *vt* **grooved; grooving** : acanalar, hacer ranuras en, surcar
groove[2] *n* **1** FURROW, SLOT : ranura *f*, surco *m* **2** RUT : rutina *f*
grope [ˈgro:p] *v* **groped; groping** *vi* : andar a tientas, tantear ⟨he groped for the switch : buscó el interruptor a tientas⟩ — *vt* **to grope one's way** : avanzar a tientas
gross[1] [ˈgro:s] *vt* : tener entrada bruta de, recaudar en bruto
gross[2] *adj* **1** FLAGRANT : flagrante, grave ⟨a gross error : un error flagrante⟩ ⟨a gross injustice : una injusticia grave⟩ **2** FAT : muy gordo, obeso **3** : bruto ⟨gross national product : producto nacional bruto⟩ **4** COARSE, VULGAR : grosero, basto
gross[3] *n* **1** *pl* **gross** : gruesa *f* (12 docenas) **2** *or* **gross income** : ingresos *mpl* brutos
grossly [ˈgro:sli] *adv* **1** EXTREMELY : extremadamente ⟨grossly unfair : totalmente injusto⟩ **2** CRUDELY : groseramente
grotesque [gro:ˈtɛsk] *adj* : grotesco
grotesquely [gro:ˈtɛskli] *adv* : de forma grotesca
grotto [ˈgrɑto:] *n, pl* **-toes** : gruta *f*
grouch[1] [ˈgraʊtʃ] *vi* : refunfuñar, rezongar
grouch[2] *n* **1** COMPLAINT : queja *f* **2** GRUMBLER : gruñón *m*, -ñona *f*; cascarrabias *mf fam*
grouchy [ˈgraʊtʃi] *adj* **grouchier; -est** : malhumorado, gruñón
ground[1] [ˈgraʊnd] *vt* **1** BASE : fundar, basar **2** INSTRUCT : enseñar los conocimientos básicos a ⟨to be well grounded in : ser muy entendido en⟩ **3** : conectar a tierra (un aparato eléctrico) **4** : varar, hacer encallar (un barco) **5** : restringir (un avión o un piloto) a la tierra
ground[2] *n* **1** EARTH, SOIL : suelo *m*, tierra *f* ⟨to dig (in) the ground : cavar la tierra⟩ ⟨to fall to the ground : caerse al suelo⟩ **2** LAND, TERRAIN : terreno *m* ⟨hilly ground : terreno alto⟩ ⟨to lose ground : perder terreno⟩ **3** BASIS, REASON : razón *f*, motivo *m* ⟨grounds for complaint : motivos de queja⟩ **4** BACKGROUND : fondo *m* **5** FIELD : campo *m*, plaza *f* ⟨parade ground : plaza de armas⟩ **6** : tierra *f* (para electricidad) **7 grounds** *npl* PREMISES : recinto *m*, terreno *m* **8 grounds** *npl* DREGS : posos *mpl* (de café)
ground[3] → **grind**
groundhog [ˈgraʊndˌhɔg] *n* : marmota *f* (de América)
groundless [ˈgraʊndləs] *adj* : infundado
groundwork [ˈgraʊndˌwərk] *n* **1** FOUNDATION : fundamento *m*, base *f* **2** PREPARATION : trabajo *m* preparatorio
group[1] [ˈgru:p] *vt* : agrupar
group[2] *n* : grupo *m*, agrupación *f*, conjunto *m*, compañía *f*
grouper [ˈgru:pər] *n* : mero *m*

grouse[1] [ˈgraʊs] *vi* **groused; grousing** : quejarse, rezongar, refunfuñar
grouse[2] *n, pl* **grouse** *or* **grouses** : urogallo *m* (ave)
grout [ˈgraʊt] *n* : lechada *f*
grove [ˈgroːv] *n* : bosquecillo *m*, arboleda *f*, soto *m*
grovel [ˈgrɑvəl, ˈgrʌ-] *vi* **-eled** *or* **-elled; -eling** *or* **-elling 1** CRAWL : arrastrarse **2** : humillarse, postrarse ⟨to grovel before someone : postrarse ante alguien⟩
grow [ˈgroː] *v* **grew** [ˈgruː]; **grown** [ˈgroːn]; **growing** *vi* **1** : crecer ⟨palm trees grow on the islands : las palmas crecen en las islas⟩ ⟨my hair grows very fast : mi pelo crece muy rápido⟩ **2** DEVELOP, MATURE : desarrollarse, madurar **3** INCREASE : crecer, aumentar **4** BECOME : hacerse, volverse, ponerse ⟨she was growing angry : se estaba poniendo furiosa⟩ ⟨to grow dark : oscurecerse⟩ **5 to grow up** : hacerse mayor ⟨grow up! : ¡no seas niño!⟩ — *vt* **1** CULTIVATE, RAISE : cultivar **2** : dejar crecer ⟨to grow one's hair : dejarse crecer el pelo⟩
grower [ˈgroːər] *n* : cultivador *m*, -dora *f*
growl[1] [ˈgraʊl] *vi* : gruñir (dícese de un animal), refunfuñar (dícese de una persona)
growl[2] *n* : gruñido *m*
grown-up[1] [ˈgroːnˌəp] *adj* : adulto, mayor
grown-up[2] *n* : adulto *m*, -ta *f*; persona *f* mayor
growth [ˈgroːθ] *n* **1** : crecimiento *m* ⟨to stunt one's growth : detener el crecimiento⟩ **2** INCREASE : aumento *m*, crecimiento *m*, expansión *f* **3** DEVELOPMENT : desarrollo *m* ⟨economic growth : desarrollo económico⟩ ⟨a five days' growth of beard : una barba de cinco días⟩ **4** LUMP, TUMOR : bulto *m*, tumor *m*
grub[1] [ˈgrʌb] *vi* **grubbed; grubbing 1** DIG : escarbar **2** RUMMAGE : hurgar, buscar **3** DRUDGE : trabajar duro
grub[2] *n* **1** : larva *f* ⟨beetle grub : larva del escarabajo⟩ **2** DRUDGE : esclavo *m*, -va *f* del trabajo **3** FOOD : comida *f*
grubby [ˈgrʌbi] *adj* **grubbier; -est** : mugriento, sucio
grudge[1] [ˈgrʌʤ] *vt* **grudged; grudging** : resentir, envidiar
grudge[2] *n* : rencor *m*, resentimiento *m* ⟨to hold a grudge : guardar rencor⟩
grueling *or* **gruelling** [ˈgruːlɪŋ, ˈgruːə-] *adj* : extenuante, agotador, duro
gruesome [ˈgruːsəm] *adj* : horripilante, truculento, horroroso
gruff [ˈgrʌf] *adj* **1** BRUSQUE : brusco ⟨a gruff reply : una respuesta brusca⟩ **2** HOARSE : ronco — **gruffly** *adv*
grumble[1] [ˈgrʌmbəl] *vi* **-bled; -bling 1** COMPLAIN : refunfuñar, rezongar, quejarse **2** RUMBLE : hacer un ruido sordo, retumbar (dícese del trueno)
grumble[2] *n* **1** COMPLAINT : queja *f* **2** RUMBLE : ruido *m* sordo, estruendo *m*
grumbler [ˈgrʌmbələr] *n* : gruñón *m*, -ñona *f*
grumpy [ˈgrʌmpi] *adj* **grumpier; -est** : malhumorado, gruñón
grungy [ˈgrʌnʤi] *adj* : sucio
grunt[1] [ˈgrʌnt] *vi* : gruñir
grunt[2] *n* : gruñido *m*
guacamole [ˌgwɑkəˈmoːli] *n* : guacamole *m*, guacamol *m*
guarantee[1] [ˌgærənˈtiː] *vt* **-teed; -teeing 1** PROMISE : asegurar, prometer **2** : poner bajo garantía, garantizar (un producto o servicio)
guarantee[2] *n* **1** PROMISE : garantía *f*, promesa *f* ⟨lifetime guarantee : garantía de por vida⟩ **2** → **guarantor**
guarantor [ˌgærənˈtɔr] *n* : garante *mf*; fiador *m*, -dora *f*
guaranty [ˌgærənˈtiː] → **guarantee**
guard[1] [ˈgɑrd] *vt* **1** DEFEND, PROTECT : defender, proteger **2** : guardar, vigilar, custodiar ⟨to guard the frontier : vigilar la frontera⟩ ⟨she guarded my secret well : guardó bien mi secreto⟩ — *vi* **to guard against** : protegerse contra, evitar
guard[2] *n* **1** WATCHMAN : guarda *mf* ⟨security guard : guarda de seguridad⟩ **2** VIGILANCE : guardia *f*, vigilancia *f* ⟨to be on guard : estar en guardia⟩ ⟨to let one's guard down : bajar la guardia⟩ **3** SAFEGUARD : salvaguardia *f*, dispositivo *m* de seguridad (en una máquina) **4** PRECAUTION : precaución *f*, protección *f*
guardhouse [ˈgɑrdˌhaʊs] *n* : cuartel *m* de la guardia
guardian [ˈgɑrdiən] *n* **1** PROTECTOR : guardián *m*, -diana *f*; custodio *m*, -dia *f* **2** : tutor *m*, -tora *f* (de un niño)
guardianship [ˈgɑrdiənˌʃɪp] *n* : custodia *f*, tutela *f*
Guatemalan [ˌgwɑt̬əˈmɑlən] *n* : guatemalteco *m*, -ca *f* — **Guatemalan** *adj*
guava [ˈgwɑvə] *n* : guayaba *f*
gubernatorial [ˌguːbənəˈtoriːəl, ˌgjuː-] *adj* : del gobernador
guerrilla *or* **guerilla** [gəˈrɪlə] *n* : guerrillero *m*, -ra *f*
guess[1] [ˈgɛs] *vt* **1** CONJECTURE : adivinar, conjeturar ⟨guess what happened! : ¡adivina lo que pasó!⟩ **2** SUPPOSE : pensar, creer, suponer ⟨I guess so : supongo que sí⟩ **3** : adivinar correctamente, acertar ⟨to guess the answer : acertar la respuesta⟩ — *vi* : adivinar
guess[2] *n* : conjetura *f*, suposición *f*
guesswork [ˈgɛsˌwərk] *n* : suposiciones *fpl*, conjeturas *fpl*
guest [ˈgɛst] *n* : huésped *mf*; invitado *m*, -da *f*
guffaw[1] [gəˈfɔ] *vi* : reírse a carcajadas, carcajearse *fam*
guffaw[2] [gəˈfɔ, ˈgʌˌfɔ] *n* : carcajada *f*, risotada *f*

guidance [ˈgaɪdənts] *n* : orientación *f*, consejos *mpl*

guide[1] [ˈgaɪd] *vt* **guided; guiding 1** DIRECT, LEAD : guiar, dirigir, conducir **2** ADVISE, COUNSEL : aconsejar, orientar

guide[2] *n* : guía *f*

guidebook [ˈgaɪdˌbʊk] *n* : guía *f* (para viajeros)

guideline [ˈgaɪdˌlaɪn] *n* : pauta *f*, directriz *f*

guild [ˈgɪld] *n* : gremio *m*, sindicato *m*, asociación *f*

guile [ˈgaɪl] *n* : astucia *f*, engaño *m*

guileless [ˈgaɪlləs] *adj* : inocente, cándido, sin malicia

guillotine[1] [ˈgɪləˌtiːn, ˈgiːjəˌ-] *vt* **-tined; -tining** : guillotinar

guillotine[2] *n* : guillotina *f*

guilt [ˈgɪlt] *n* : culpa *f*, culpabilidad *f*

guilty [ˈgɪlti] *adj* **guiltier; -est** : culpable

guinea fowl [ˈgɪni] *n* : gallina *f* de Guinea

guinea pig *n* : conejillo *m* de Indias, cobaya *f*

guise [ˈgaɪz] *n* : apariencia *f*, aspecto *m*, forma *f*

guitar [gəˈtɑr, gɪ-] *n* : guitarra *f*

guitarist [gəˈtɑrɪst, gɪ-] *n* : guitarrista *mf*

gulch [ˈgʌltʃ] *n* : barranco *m*, quebrada *f*

gulf [ˈgʌlf] *n* **1** : golfo *m* ⟨the Gulf of Mexico : el Golfo de México⟩ **2** GAP : brecha *f* ⟨the gulf between generations : la brecha entre las generaciones⟩ **3** CHASM : abismo *m*

gull [ˈgʌl] *n* : gaviota *f*

gullet [ˈgʌlət] *n* : garganta *f*

gullible [ˈgʌlɪbəl] *adj* : crédulo

gully [ˈgʌli] *n, pl* **-lies** : barranco *m*, hondonada *f*

gulp[1] [ˈgʌlp] *vt* **1** : engullir, tragar ⟨he gulped down the whiskey : engulló el whisky⟩ **2** SUPPRESS : suprimir, reprimir, tragar ⟨to gulp down a sob : reprimir un sollozo⟩ — *vi* : tragar saliva, tener un nudo en la garganta

gulp[2] *n* : trago *m*

gum [ˈgʌm] *n* **1** CHEWING GUM : goma *f* de mascar, chicle *m* **2 gums** *npl* : encías *fpl*

gumbo [ˈgʌmˌboː] *n* : sopa *f* de quingombó

gumdrop [ˈgʌmˌdrɑp] *n* : pastilla *f* de goma

gummy [ˈgʌmi] *adj* **gummier; -est** : gomoso

gumption [ˈgʌmpʃən] *n* : iniciativa *f*, agallas *fpl fam*

gun[1] [ˈgʌn] *vt* **gunned; gunning 1** *or* **to gun down** : matar a tiros, asesinar **2** : acelerar (rápidamente) ⟨to gun the engine : acelerar el motor⟩

gun[2] *n* **1** CANNON : cañón *m* **2** FIREARM : arma *f* de fuego **3** SPRAY GUN : pistola *f* **4 to jump the gun** : adelantarse, salir antes de tiempo

gunboat [ˈgʌnˌboːt] *n* : cañonero *m*

gunfight [ˈgʌnˌfaɪt] *n* : tiroteo *m*, balacera *f*

gunfire [ˈgʌnˌfaɪr] *n* : disparos *mpl*

gunman [ˈgʌnmən] *n, pl* **-men** [-mən, -ˌmɛn] : pistolero *m*, gatillero *m Mex*

gunner [ˈgʌnər] *n* : artillero *m*, -ra *f*

gunnysack [ˈgʌniˌsæk] *n* : saco *m* de yute

gunpowder [ˈgʌnˌpaʊdər] *n* : pólvora *f*

gunshot [ˈgʌnˌʃɑt] *n* : disparo *m*, tiro *m*, balazo *m*

gunwale [ˈgʌnəl] *n* : borda *f*

guppy [ˈgʌpi] *n, pl* **-pies** : lebistes *m*

gurgle[1] [ˈgərgəl] *vi* **-gled; -gling 1** : borbotar, gorgotear (dícese de un líquido) **2** : gorjear (dícese de un niño)

gurgle[2] *n* **1** : borboteo *m*, gorgoteo *m* (de un líquido) **2** : gorjeo *m* (de un niño)

gush [ˈgʌʃ] *vi* **1** SPOUT : surgir, salir a chorros, chorrear **2** : hablar con entusiasmo efusivo ⟨she gushed with praise : se deshizo en elogios⟩

gust [ˈgʌst] *n* : ráfaga *f*, racha *f*

gusto [ˈgʌsˌtoː] *n, pl* **gustoes** : entusiasmo *m* ⟨with gusto : con deleite, con ganas⟩

gusty [ˈgʌsti] *adj* **gustier; -est** : racheado

gut[1] [ˈgʌt] *vt* **gutted; gutting 1** EVISCERATE : destripar (un pollo, etc.), limpiar (un pescado) **2** : destruir el interior de (un edificio)

gut[2] *n* **1** INTESTINE : intestino *m* **2 guts** *npl* INNARDS : tripas *fpl fam*, entrañas *fpl* **3 guts** *npl* COURAGE : valentía *f*, agallas *fpl*

gutter [ˈgʌt̬ər] *n* **1** : canal *mf*, canaleta *f* (de un techo) **2** : cuneta *f*, arroyo *m* (de una calle)

guttural [ˈgʌt̬ərəl] *adj* : gutural

guy [ˈgaɪ] *n* **1** *or* **guyline** : cuerda *f* tensora, cable *m* **2** FELLOW : tipo *m*, hombre *m*

guzzle [ˈgʌzəl] *vt* **-zled; -zling** : chupar, tragarse

gym [ˈdʒɪm] → **gymnasium**

gymnasium [dʒɪmˈneɪziəm, -ʒəm] *n, pl* **-siums** *or* **-sia** [-ziːə, -ʒə] : gimnasio *m*

gymnast [ˈdʒɪmnəst, -ˌnæst] *n* : gimnasta *mf*

gymnastic [dʒɪmˈnæstɪk] *adj* : gimnástico

gymnastics [dʒɪmˈnæstɪks] *ns & pl* : gimnasia *f*

gynecologist [ˌgaɪnəˈkɑlədʒɪst, ˌdʒɪnə-] *n* : ginecólogo *m*, -ga *f*

gynecology [ˌgaɪnəˈkɑlədʒi, ˌdʒɪnə-] *n* : ginecología *f*

gyp[1] [ˈdʒɪp] *vt* **gypped; gypping** : estafar, timar

gyp[2] *n* **1** SWINDLER : estafador *m*, -dora *f* **2** FRAUD, SWINDLE : estafa *f*, timo *m fam*

gypsum [ˈdʒɪpsəm] *n* : yeso *m*

Gypsy [ˈdʒɪpsi] *n, pl* **-sies** : gitano *m*, -na *f*

gyrate [ˈdʒaɪˌreɪt] *vi* **-rated; -rating** : girar, rotar

gyration [dʒaɪˈreɪʃən] *n* : giro *m*, rotación *f*

gyroscope [ˈdʒaɪrəˌskoːp] *n* : giroscopio *m*, giróscopo *m*

H

h [ˈeɪʧ] *n, pl* **h's** *or* **hs** [ˈeɪʧəz] : octava letra del alfabeto inglés

ha [ˈhɑ] *interj* : ¡ja!

haberdashery [ˈhæbərˌdæʃəri] *n, pl* **-eries** : tienda *f* de ropa para caballeros

habit [ˈhæbɪt] *n* **1** CUSTOM : hábito *m*, costumbre *f* **2** : hábito *m* (de un monje o una religiosa) **3** ADDICTION : dependencia *f*, adicción *f*

habitable [ˈhæbɪṭəbəl] *adj* : habitable

habitat [ˈhæbɪˌtæt] *n* : hábitat *m*

habitation [ˌhæbɪˈteɪʃən] *n* **1** OCCUPANCY : habitación *f* **2** RESIDENCE : residencia *f*, morada *f*

habit–forming [ˈhæbɪtˌfɔrmɪŋ] *adj* : que crea dependencia

habitual [həˈbɪʧʊəl] *adj* **1** CUSTOMARY : habitual, acostumbrado **2** INVETERATE : incorregible, empedernido — **habitually** *adv*

habituate [həˈbɪʧʊˌeɪt] *vt* **-ated; -ating** : habituar, acostumbrar

hack[1] [ˈhæk] *vt* : cortar, tajear (a hachazos, etc.) ⟨to hack one's way : abrirse paso⟩ — *vi* **1** : hacer tajos **2** COUGH : toser

hack[2] *n* **1** CHOP : hachazo *m*, tajo *m* **2** HORSE : caballo *m* de alquiler **3** WRITER : escritor *m*, -tora *f* a sueldo; escritorzuelo *m*, -la *f* **4** COUGH : tos *f* seca

hackles [ˈhækəlz] *npl* **1** : pluma *f* erizada (de un ave), pelo *m* erizado (de un perro, etc.) **2 to get one's hackles up** : ponerse furioso

hackney [ˈhækni] *n, pl* **-neys** : caballo *m* de silla, caballo *m* de tiro

hackneyed [ˈhæknid] *adj* TRITE : trillado, gastado

hacksaw [ˈhækˌsɔ] *n* : sierra *f* para metales

had → **have**

haddock [ˈhædək] *ns & pl* : eglefino *m*

hadn't [ˈhædənt] (*contraction* of **had not**) → **have**

haft [ˈhæft] *n* : mango *m*, empuñadura *f*

hag [ˈhæg] *n* **1** WITCH : bruja *f*, hechicera *f* **2** CRONE : vieja *f* fea

haggard [ˈhægərd] *adj* : demacrado, macilento — **haggardly** *adv*

haggle [ˈhægəl] *vi* **-gled; -gling** : regatear

ha–ha [ˌhɑˈhɑ, ˈhɑˈhɑ] *interj* : ¡ja, ja!

hail[1] [ˈheɪl] *vt* **1** GREET : saludar **2** SUMMON : llamar ⟨to hail a taxi : llamar un taxi⟩ — *vi* : granizar (en meteorología)

hail[2] *n* **1** : granizo *m* **2** BARRAGE : aluvión *m*, lluvia *f*

hail[3] *interj* : ¡salve!

hailstone [ˈheɪlˌstoːn] *n* : granizo *m*, piedra *f* de granizo

hailstorm [ˈheɪlˌstɔrm] *n* : granizada *f*

hair [ˈhær] *n* **1** : pelo *m*, cabello *m* ⟨to get one's hair cut : cortarse el pelo⟩ **2** : vello *m* (en las piernas, etc.)

hairbreadth [ˈhærˌbrɛdθ] *or* **hairsbreadth** [ˈhærz-] *n* **by a hairbreadth** : por un pelo

hairbrush [ˈhærˌbrʌʃ] *n* : cepillo *m* (para el pelo)

haircut [ˈhærˌkʌt] *n* : corte *m* de pelo

hairdo [ˈhærˌduː] *n, pl* **-dos** : peinado *m*

hairdresser [ˈhærˌdrɛsər] *n* : peluquero *m*, -ra *f*

hairiness [ˈhærinəs] *n* : vellosidad *f*

hairless [ˈhærləs] *adj* : sin pelo, calvo, pelón

hairline [ˈhærˌlaɪn] *n* **1** : línea *f* delgada **2** : nacimiento *m* del pelo ⟨to have a receding hairline : tener entradas⟩

hairpin [ˈhærˌpɪn] *n* : horquilla *f*

hair–raising [ˈhærˌreɪzɪŋ] *adj* : espeluznante

hair spray *n* : laca *f*, fijador *m* (para el pelo)

hairstyle [ˈhærˌstaɪl] *n* : peinado *m*

hairy [ˈhæri] *adj* **hairier; -est** : peludo, velludo

Haitian [ˈheɪʃən, ˈheɪṭiən] *n* : haitiano *m*, -na *f* — **Haitian** *adj*

hake [ˈheɪk] *n* : merluza *f*

hale[1] [ˈheɪl] *vt* **haled; haling** : arrastrar, halar ⟨to hale to court : arrastrar al tribunal⟩

hale[2] *adj* : saludable, robusto

half[1] [ˈhæf, ˈhaf] *adv* : medio, a medias ⟨half cooked : medio cocido⟩

half[2] *adj* : medio, a medias ⟨a half hour : una media hora⟩ ⟨a half truth : una verdad a medias⟩

half[3] *n, pl* **halves** [ˈhævz, ˈhavz] **1** : mitad *f* ⟨half of my friends : la mitad de mis amigos⟩ ⟨in half : por la mitad⟩ **2** : tiempo *m* (en deportes)

half brother *n* : medio hermano *m*, hermanastro *m*

halfhearted [ˈhæfˈhɑrṭəd] *adj* : sin ánimo, poco entusiasta

halfheartedly [ˈhæfˈhɑrṭədli] *adv* : con poco entusiasmo, sin ánimo

half–life [ˈhæfˌlaɪf] *n, pl* **half–lives** : media vida *f*

half sister *n* : media hermana *f*, hermanastra *f*

halfway[1] [ˈhæfˈweɪ] *adv* : a medio camino, a mitad de camino

halfway[2] *adj* : medio, intermedio ⟨a halfway point : un punto intermedio⟩

half–wit [ˈhæfˌwɪt] *n* : tonto *m*, -ta *f*; imbécil *mf*

half–witted [ˈhæfˌwɪṭəd] *adj* : estúpido

halibut [ˈhælɪbət] *ns & pl* : halibut *m*

hall [ˈhɔl] *n* **1** BUILDING : residencia *f* estudiantil, facultad *f* (de una universidad) **2** VESTIBULE : entrada *f*, vestíbulo *m*, zaguán *m* **3** CORRIDOR : corredor *m*, pasillo *m* **4** AUDITORIUM : sala *f*, salón *m* ⟨concert hall : sala de conciertos⟩ **5 city hall** : ayuntamiento *m*

hallelujah [ˌhæləˈluːjə, ˌhɑ-] *interj* : ¡aleluya!

hallmark [ˈhɔlˌmɑrk] *n* : sello *m* (distintivo)

hallow [ˈhæˌlo:] *vt* : santificar, consagrar

hallowed [ˈhæˌlo:d, ˈhæˌlo:əd, ˈhɑˌlo:d] *adj* : sagrado

Halloween [ˌhæləˈwi:n, ˌhɑ-] *n* : víspera *f* de Todos los Santos

hallucinate [hæˈlu:sənˌeɪt] *vi* **-nated; -nating** : alucinar

hallucination [həˌlu:sənˈeɪʃən] *n* : alucinación *f*

hallucinatory [həˈlu:sənəˌtori] *adj* : alucinante

hallucinogen [həˈlu:sənəʤən] *n* : alucinógeno *m*

hallucinogenic [həˌlu:sənəˈʤɛnɪk] *adj* : alucinógeno

hallway [ˈhɔlˌweɪ] *n* **1** ENTRANCE : entrada *f* **2** CORRIDOR : corredor *m*, pasillo *m*

halo [ˈheɪˌlo:] *n, pl* **-los** *or* **-loes** : aureola *f*, halo *m*

halt[1] [ˈhɔlt] *vi* : detenerse, pararse — *vt* **1** STOP : detener, parar (a una persona) **2** INTERRUPT : interrumpir (una actividad)

halt[2] *n* **1** : alto *m*, parada *f* **2 to come to a halt** : pararse, detenerse

halter [ˈhɔltər] *n* **1** : cabestro *m*, ronzal *m* (para un animal) **2** : blusa *f* sin espalda

halting [ˈhɔltɪŋ] *adj* HESITANT : vacilante, titubeante — **haltingly** *adv*

halve [ˈhæv, ˈhav] *vt* **halved; halving 1** DIVIDE : partir por la mitad **2** REDUCE : reducir a la mitad

halves → **half**

ham [ˈhæm] *n* **1** : jamón *m* **2** *or* **ham actor** : comicastro *m*, -tra *f* **3** *or* **ham radio operator** : radioaficionado *m*, -da *f* **4 hams** *npl* HAUNCHES : ancas *fpl*

hamburger [ˈhæmˌbərgər] *or* **hamburg** [-ˌbərg] *n* **1** : carne *f* molida **2** : hamburguesa *f* (emparedado)

hamlet [ˈhæmlət] *n* VILLAGE : aldea *f*, poblado *m*

hammer[1] [ˈhæmər] *vt* **1** STRIKE : clavar, golpear **2** NAIL : clavar, martillar **3 to hammer out** NEGOTIATE : elaborar, negociar, llegar a — *vi* : martillar, golpear

hammer[2] *n* **1** : martillo *m* **2** : percusor *m*, percutor *m* (de un arma de fuego)

hammock [ˈhæmək] *n* : hamaca *f*

hamper[1] [ˈhæmpər] *vt* : obstaculizar, dificultar

hamper[2] *n* : cesto *m*, canasta *f*

hamster [ˈhæm*p*stər] *n* : hámster *m*

hamstring [ˈhæmˌstrɪŋ] *vt* **-strung** [-ˌstrʌŋ]; **-stringing 1** : cortarle el tendón del corvejón a (un animal) **2** INCAPACITATE : incapacitar, inutilizar

hand[1] [ˈhænd] *vt* : pasar, dar, entregar

hand[2] *n* **1** : mano *f* ⟨made by hand : hecho a mano⟩ **2** POINTER : manecilla *f*, aguja *f* (de un reloj o instrumento) **3** SIDE : lado *m* ⟨on the other hand : por otro lado⟩ **4** HANDWRITING : letra *f*, escritura *f* **5** APPLAUSE : aplauso *m* **6** : mano *f*, cartas *fpl* (en juegos de naipes) **7** WORKER : obrero *m*, -ra *f*; trabajador *m*, -dora *f* **8 to ask for someone's hand (in marriage)** : pedir la mano de alguien **9 to lend a hand** : echar una mano

handbag [ˈhændˌbæg] *n* : cartera *f*, bolso *m*, bolsa *f Mex*

handball [ˈhændˌbɔl] *n* : frontón *m*, pelota *f*

handbill [ˈhændˌbɪl] *n* : folleto *m*, volante *m*

handbook [ˈhændˌbʊk] *n* : manual *m*

handcuff [ˈhændˌkʌf] *vt* : esposar, ponerle esposas (a alguien)

handcuffs [ˈhændˌkʌfs] *npl* : esposas *fpl*

handful [ˈhændˌfʊl] *n* : puñado *m*

handgun [ˈhændˌgʌn] *n* : pistola *f*, revólver *m*

handheld [ˈhændˌhɛld] *adj* : de mano

handicap[1] [ˈhændiˌkæp] *vt* **-capped; -capping 1** : asignar un handicap a (en deportes) **2** HAMPER : obstaculizar, poner en desventaja

handicap[2] *n* **1** DISABILITY : minusvalía *f*, discapacidad *f* **2** DISADVANTAGE : desventaja *f*, handicap *m* (en deportes)

handicapped [ˈhændiˌkæpt] *adj* DISABLED : minusválido, discapacitado

handicraft [ˈhændiˌkræft] *n* : artesanía *f*

handily [ˈhændəli] *adv* EASILY : fácilmente, con facilidad

handiwork [ˈhændiˌwərk] *n* **1** WORK : trabajo *m* **2** CRAFTS : artesanías *fpl*

handkerchief [ˈhæŋkərʧəf, -ˌʧi:f] *n, pl* **-chiefs** : pañuelo *m*

handle[1] [ˈhændəl] *v* **-dled; -dling** *vt* **1** TOUCH : tocar **2** MANAGE : tratar, manejar, despachar **3** SELL : comerciar con, vender — *vi* : responder, conducirse (dícese de un vehículo)

handle[2] *n* : asa *m*, asidero *m*, mango *m* (de un cuchillo, etc.), pomo *m* (de una puerta), tirador *m* (de un cajón)

handlebars [ˈhændəlˌbɑrz] *npl* : manubrio *m*, manillar *m*

handler [ˈhændələr] *n* : cuidador *m*, -dora *f*

handling [ˈhændəlɪŋ] *n* **1** MANAGEMENT : manejo *m* **2** TOUCHING : manoseo *m* **3 shipping and handling** : porte *m*, transporte *m*

handmade [ˈhændˌmeɪd] *adj* : hecho a mano

hand–me–downs [ˈhænd*d*miˌdaʊnz] *npl* : ropa *f* usada

handout [ˈhændˌaʊt] *n* **1** AID : dádiva *f*, limosna *f* **2** LEAFLET : folleto *m*

handpick [ˈhændˈpɪk] *vt* : seleccionar con cuidado

handrail [ˈhændˌreɪl] *n* : pasamanos *m*, barandilla *f*, barandal *m*

handsaw [ˈhændˌsɔ] *n* : serrucho *m*

hands down *adv* **1** EASILY : con facilidad **2** UNQUESTIONABLY : con mucho, de lejos

handshake [ˈhændˌʃeɪk] *n* : apretón *m* de manos

handsome [ˈhæntsəm] *adj* **-somer; -est** **1** ATTRACTIVE : apuesto, guapo, atractivo **2** GENEROUS : generoso **3** SIZABLE : considerable
handsomely [ˈhæntsəmli] *adv* **1** ELEGANTLY : elegantemente **2** GENEROUSLY : con generosidad
handspring [ˈhændˌsprɪŋ] *n* : voltereta *f*
handstand [ˈhændˌstænd] *n* **to do a handstand** : pararse de manos
hand–to–hand [ˈhændtəˈhænd] *adj* : cuerpo a cuerpo
handwriting [ˈhændˌraɪt̬ɪŋ] *n* : letra *f*, escritura *f*
handwritten [ˈhændˌrɪtən] *adj* : escrito a mano
handy [ˈhændi] *adj* **handier; -est** **1** NEARBY : a mano, cercano **2** USEFUL : útil, práctico **3** DEXTEROUS : hábil
hang[1] [ˈhæŋ] *v* **hung** [ˈhʌŋ]; **hanging** *vt* **1** SUSPEND : colgar, tender, suspender **2** *past tense often* **hanged** EXECUTE : colgar, ahorcar **3 to hang one's head** : bajar la cabeza — *vi* **1** FALL : caer (dícese de las telas y la ropa) **2** DANGLE : colgar **3** HOVER : flotar, sostenerse en el aire **4** : ser ahorcado **5** DROOP : inclinarse **6 to hang up** : colgar ⟨he hung up on me : me colgó⟩
hang[2] *n* **1** DRAPE : caída *f* **2 to get the hang of something** : agarrarle la onda a algo
hangar [ˈhæŋər, ˈhæŋgər] *n* : hangar *m*
hanger [ˈhæŋər] *n* : percha *f*, gancho *m* (para ropa)
hangman [ˈhæŋmən] *n, pl* **-men** [-mən, -ˌmɛn] : verdugo *m*
hangnail [ˈhæŋˌneɪl] *n* : padrastro *m*
hangout [ˈhæŋˌaʊt] *n* : lugar *m* popular, sitio *m* muy frecuentado
hangover [ˈhæŋˌoːvər] *n* : resaca *f*
hank [ˈhæŋk] *n* : madeja *f*
hanker [ˈhæŋkər] *vi* **to hanker for** : tener ansias de, tener ganas de
hankering [ˈhæŋkərɪŋ] *n* : ansia *f*, anhelo *m*
hansom [ˈhæntsəm] *n* : coche *m* de caballos
Hanukkah [ˈxɑnəkə, ˈhɑ-] *n* : Januká, Hanukkah
haphazard [hæpˈhæzərd] *adj* : casual, fortuito, al azar — **haphazardly** *adv*
hapless [ˈhæpləs] *adj* UNFORTUNATE : desafortunado, desventurado — **haplessly** *adv*
happen [ˈhæpən] *vi* **1** OCCUR : pasar, ocurrir, suceder, tener lugar **2** BEFALL : pasar, acontecer ⟨what happened to her? : ¿qué le ha pasado?⟩ **3** CHANCE : resultar, ocurrir por casualidad ⟨it happened that I wasn't home : resulta que estaba fuera de casa⟩ ⟨he happens to be right : da la casualidad de que tiene razón⟩
happening [ˈhæpənɪŋ] *n* : suceso *m*, acontecimiento *m*
happiness [ˈhæpinəs] *n* : felicidad *f*, dicha *f*
happy [ˈhæpi] *adj* **-pier; -est** **1** JOYFUL : feliz, contento, alegre **2** FORTUNATE : afortunado, feliz — **happily** [-pəli] *adv*
happy–go–lucky [ˈhæpigoːˈlʌki] *adj* : despreocupado
harangue[1] [həˈræŋ] *vt* **-rangued; -ranguing** : arengar
harangue[2] *n* : arenga *f*
harass [həˈræs, ˈhærəs] *vt* **1** BESIEGE, HOUND : acosar, asediar, hostigar **2** ANNOY : molestar
harassment [həˈræsmənt, ˈhærəsmənt] *n* : acoso *m*, hostigamiento *m* ⟨sexual harrassment : acoso sexual⟩
harbinger [ˈhɑrbɪndʒər] *n* **1** HERALD : heraldo *m*, precursor *m* **2** OMEN : presagio *m*
harbor[1] [ˈhɑrbər] *vt* **1** SHELTER : dar refugio a, albergar **2** CHERISH, KEEP : abrigar, guardar, albergar ⟨to harbor doubts : guardar dudas⟩
harbor[2] *n* **1** REFUGE : refugio *m* **2** PORT : puerto *m*
hard[1] [ˈhɑrd] *adv* **1** FORCEFULLY : fuerte, con fuerza ⟨the wind blew hard : el viento sopló fuerte⟩ **2** STRENUOUSLY : duro, mucho ⟨to work hard : trabajar duro⟩ **3 to take something hard** : tomarse algo muy mal, estar muy afectado por algo
hard[2] *adj* **1** FIRM, SOLID : duro, firme, sólido **2** DIFFICULT : difícil, arduo **3** SEVERE : severo, duro ⟨a hard winter : un invierno severo⟩ **4** UNFEELING : insensible, duro **5** DILIGENT : diligente ⟨to be a hard worker : ser muy trabajador⟩ **6 hard liquor** : bebidas *fpl* fuertes **7 hard water** : agua *f* dura
hardcover [ˈhɑrdˌkʌvər] *adj* : de pasta dura, de tapa dura
hard disk *n* : disco *m* duro
hard drive → **hard disk**
harden [ˈhɑrdən] *vt* : endurecer
hardheaded [ˌhɑrdˈhɛdəd] *adj* **1** STUBBORN : testarudo, terco **2** REALISTIC : realista, práctico — **hardheadedly** *adv*
hard–hearted [ˌhɑrdˈhɑrt̬əd] *adj* : despiadado, insensible — **hard–heartedly** *adv*
hard–heartedness [ˌhɑrdˈhɑrt̬ədnəs] *n* : dureza *f* de corazón
hardly [ˈhɑrdli] *adv* **1** SCARCELY : apenas, casi ⟨I hardly knew her : apenas la conocía⟩ ⟨hardly ever : casi nunca⟩ **2** NOT : difícilmente, poco, no ⟨they can hardly blame me! : ¡difícilmente pueden echarme la culpa!⟩ ⟨it's hardly likely : es poco probable⟩
hardness [ˈhɑrdnəs] *n* **1** FIRMNESS : dureza *f* **2** DIFFICULTY : dificultad *f* **3** SEVERITY : severidad *f*
hardship [ˈhɑrdˌʃɪp] *n* : dificultad *f*, privación *f*
hardware [ˈhɑrdˌwær] *n* **1** TOOLS : ferretería *f* **2** : hardware *m* (de una computadora)
hardwood [ˈhɑrdˌwʊd] *n* : madera *f* dura, madera *f* noble

hardworking [ˈhɑrdˈwərkɪŋ] *adj* : trabajador
hardy [ˈhɑrdi] *adj* **-dier; -est** : fuerte, robusto, resistente (dícese de las plantas) — **hardily** [-dəli] *adv*
hare [ˈhær] *n, pl* **hare** *or* **hares** : liebre *f*
harebrained [ˈhær,breɪnd] *adj* : estúpido, absurdo, disparatado
harelip [ˈhær,lɪp] *n* : labio *m* leporino
harem [ˈhærəm] *n* : harén *m*
hark [ˈhɑrk] *vi* **1** (*used only in the imperative*) LISTEN : escuchar **2 hark back** RETURN : volver **3 hark back** RECALL : recordar
harlequin [ˈhɑrlɪkən, -kwən] *n* : arlequín *m*
harm¹ [ˈhɑrm] *vt* : hacerle daño a, perjudicar
harm² *n* : daño *m*, perjuicio *m*
harmful [ˈhɑrmfəl] *adj* : dañino, perjudicial — **harmfully** *adv*
harmless [ˈhɑrmləs] *adj* : inofensivo, inocuo — **harmlessly** *adv*
harmlessness [ˈhɑrmləsnəs] *n* : inocuidad *f*
harmonic [hɑrˈmɑnɪk] *adj* : armónico — **harmonically** [-nɪkli] *adv*
harmonica [hɑrˈmɑnɪkə] *n* : armónica *f*
harmonious [hɑrˈmoːniəs] *adj* : armonioso — **harmoniously** *adv*
harmonize [ˈhɑrmə,naɪz] *v* **-nized; -nizing** : armonizar
harmony [ˈhɑrməni] *n, pl* **-nies** : armonía *f*
harness¹ [ˈhɑrnəs] *vt* **1** : enjaezar (un animal) **2** UTILIZE : utilizar, aprovechar
harness² *n* : arreos *mpl*, guarniciones *fpl*, arnés *m*
harp¹ [ˈhɑrp] *vi* **to harp on** : insistir sobre, machacar sobre
harp² *n* : arpa *m*
harpist [ˈhɑrpɪst] *n* : arpista *mf*
harpoon¹ [hɑrˈpuːn] *vt* : arponear
harpoon² *n* : arpón *m*
harpsichord [ˈhɑrpsɪ,kɔrd] *n* : clavicémbalo *m*
harrow¹ [ˈhær,oː] *vt* **1** CULTIVATE : gradar, labrar (la tierra) **2** TORMENT : atormentar
harrow² *n* : grada *f*, rastra *f*
harry [ˈhæri] *vt* **-ried; -rying** HARASS : acosar, hostigar
harsh [ˈhɑrʃ] *adj* **1** ROUGH : áspero **2** SEVERE : duro, severo **3** : discordante (dícese de los sonidos) — **harshly** *adv*
harshness [ˈhɑrʃnəs] *n* **1** ROUGHNESS : aspereza *f* **2** SEVERITY : dureza *f*, severidad *f*
harvest¹ [ˈhɑrvəst] *v* : cosechar
harvest² *n* **1** HARVESTING : siega *f*, recolección *f* **2** CROP : cosecha *f*
harvester [ˈhɑrvəstər] *n* : segador *m*, -dora *f*; cosechadora *f* (máquina)
has → **have**
hash¹ [ˈhæʃ] *vt* **1** MINCE : picar **2 to hash over** DISCUSS : discutir, repasar
hash² *n* **1** : picadillo *m* (comida) **2** JUMBLE : revoltijo *m*, fárrago *m*
hasn't [ˈhæzənt] (*contraction* of **has not**) → **has**
hasp [ˈhæsp] *n* : picaporte *m*, pestillo *m*
hassle¹ [ˈhæsəl] *vt* **-sled; -sling** : fastidiar, molestar
hassle² *n* **1** ARGUMENT : discusión *f*, disputa *f*, bronca *f* **2** FIGHT : pelea *f*, riña *f* **3** BOTHER, TROUBLE : problemas *mpl*, lío *m*
hassock [ˈhæsək] *n* **1** CUSHION : almohadón *m*, cojín *m* **2** FOOTSTOOL : escabel *m*
haste [ˈheɪst] *n* **1** : prisa *f*, apuro *m* **2 to make haste** : darse prisa, apurarse
hasten [ˈheɪsən] *vt* : acelerar, precipitar — *vi* : apresurarse, apurarse
hasty [ˈheɪsti] *adj* **hastier; -est 1** HURRIED, QUICK : rápido, apresurado, apurado **2** RASH : precipitado — **hastily** [-təli] *adv*
hat [ˈhæt] *n* : sombrero *m*
hatch¹ [ˈhætʃ] *vt* **1** : incubar, empollar (huevos) **2** DEVISE : idear, tramar — *vi* : salir del cascarón
hatch² *n* : escotilla *f*
hatchery [ˈhætʃəri] *n, pl* **-ries** : criadero *m*
hatchet [ˈhætʃət] *n* : hacha *f*
hatchway [ˈhætʃ,weɪ] *n* : escotilla *f*
hate¹ [ˈheɪt] *vt* **hated; hating** : odiar, aborrecer, detestar
hate² *n* : odio *m*
hateful [ˈheɪtfəl] *adj* : odioso, aborrecible, detestable — **hatefully** *adv*
hatred [ˈheɪtrəd] *n* : odio *m*
hatter [ˈhæt̬ər] *n* : sombrerero *m*, -ra *f*
haughtiness [ˈhɔt̬inəs] *n* : altanería *f*, altivez *f*
haughty [ˈhɔt̬i] *adj* **-tier; -est** : altanero, altivo — **haughtily** [-t̬əli] *adv*
haul¹ [ˈhɔl] *vt* **1** DRAG, PULL : arrastrar, jalar **2** TRANSPORT : transportar
haul² *n* **1** PULL : tirón *m*, jalón *m* **2** CATCH : redada *f* **3** JOURNEY : viaje *m*, trayecto *m* ⟨it's a long haul : es un trayecto largo⟩
haulage [ˈhɔlɪdʒ] *n* : transporte *m*, tiro *m*
hauler [ˈhɔlər] *n* : transportista *mf*
haunch [ˈhɔntʃ] *n* **1** HIP : cadera *f* **2 haunches** *npl* HINDQUARTERS : ancas *fpl*, cuartos *mpl* traseros
haunt¹ [ˈhɔnt] *vt* **1** : aparecer en (dícese de un fantasma) **2** FREQUENT : frecuentar, rondar **3** PREOCCUPY : perseguir, obsesionar
haunt² *n* : guarida *f* (de animales o ladrones), lugar *m* predilecto
haunting [ˈhɔntɪŋ] *adj* : obsesionante, evocador — **hauntingly** *adv*
haute [ˈoːt] *adj* **1** : de moda, de categoría **2 haute couture** [,oːtkʊˈtʊr] : alta costura *f* **3 haute cuisine** [,oːtkwɪˈziːn] : alta cocina *f*
have [ˈhæv, *in sense 3 as an auxiliary verb usu* ˈhæf] *v* **had** [ˈhæd]; **having; has** [ˈhæz, *in sense 3 as an auxiliary verb usu* ˈhæs] *vt* **1** POSSESS : tener ⟨do you have

change? : ¿tienes cambio?⟩ **2** EXPERIENCE, UNDERGO : tener, experimentar, sufrir ⟨I have a toothache : tengo un dolor de muelas⟩ **3** INCLUDE : tener, incluir ⟨April has 30 days : abril tiene 30 días⟩ **4** CONSUME : comer, tomar **5** RECEIVE : tener, recibir ⟨he had my permission : tenía mi permiso⟩ **6** ALLOW : permitir, dejar ⟨I won't have it! : ¡no lo permitiré!⟩ **7** HOLD : hacer ⟨to have a party : dar una fiesta⟩ ⟨to have a meeting : convocar una reunión⟩ **8** HOLD : tener ⟨he had me in his power : me tenía en su poder⟩ **9** BEAR : tener (niños) **10** (*indicating causation*) ⟨she had a dress made : mandó hacer un vestido⟩ ⟨to have one's hair cut : cortarse el pelo⟩ — *v aux* **1** : haber ⟨she has been very busy : ha estado muy ocupada⟩ ⟨I've lived here three years : hace tres años que vivo aquí⟩ **2** (*used in tags*) ⟨you've finished, haven't you? : ha terminado, ¿no?⟩ **3 to have to** : deber, tener que ⟨we have to leave : tenemos que salir⟩

haven [ˈheɪvən] *n* : refugio *m*

havoc [ˈhævək] *n* **1** DESTRUCTION : estragos *mpl*, destrucción *f* **2** CHAOS, DISORDER : desorden *m*, caos *m*

Hawaiian[1] [həˈwaɪən] *adj* : hawaiano

Hawaiian[2] *n* : hawaiano *m*, -na *f*

hawk[1] [ˈhɔk] *vt* : pregonar, vender (mercancías) en la calle

hawk[2] *n* : halcón *m*

hawker [ˈhɔkər] *n* : vendedor *m*, -dora *f* ambulante

hawthorn [ˈhɔˌθɔrn] *n* : espino *m*

hay [ˈheɪ] *n* : heno *m*

hay fever *n* : fiebre *f* del heno

hayloft [ˈheɪˌlɔft] *n* : pajar *m*

hayseed [ˈheɪˌsiːd] *n* : palurdo *m*, -da *f*

haystack [ˈheɪˌstæk] *n* : almiar *m*

haywire [ˈheɪˌwaɪr] *adj* : descompuesto, desbaratado ⟨to go haywire : estropearse⟩

hazard[1] [ˈhæzərd] *vt* : arriesgar, aventurar

hazard[2] *n* **1** DANGER : peligro *m*, riesgo *m* **2** CHANCE : azar *m*

hazardous [ˈhæzərdəs] *adj* : arriesgado, peligroso

haze[1] [ˈheɪz] *vt* **hazed; hazing** : abrumar, acosar

haze[2] *n* : bruma *f*, neblina *f*

hazel [ˈheɪzəl] *n* **1** : avellano *m* (árbol) **2** : color *m* avellana

hazelnut [ˈheɪzəlˌnʌt] *n* : avellana *f*

haziness [ˈheɪzinəs] *n* **1** MISTINESS : nebulosidad *f* **2** VAGUENESS : vaguedad *f*

hazy [ˈheɪzi] *adj* **hazier; -est 1** MISTY : brumoso, neblinoso, nebuloso **2** VAGUE : vago, confuso

he [ˈhiː] *pron* : él

head[1] [ˈhɛd] *vt* **1** LEAD : encabezar **2** DIRECT : dirigir — *vi* : dirigirse

head[2] *adj* MAIN : principal ⟨the head office : la oficina central, la sede⟩

head[3] *n* **1** : cabeza *f* ⟨from head to foot : de pies a cabeza⟩ **2** MIND : mente *f*, cabeza *f* **3** TIP, TOP : cabeza *f* (de un clavo, un martillo, etc.), cabecera *f* (de una mesa o un río), punta *f* (de una flecha), flor *m* (de un repollo, etc.), encabezamiento *m* (de una carta, etc.), espuma *f* (de cerveza) **4** DIRECTOR, LEADER : director *m*, -tora *f*; jefe *m*, -fa *f*; cabeza *f* (de una familia) **5** : cara *f* (de una moneda) ⟨heads or tails : cara o cruz⟩ **6** : cabeza *f* ⟨500 head of cattle : 500 cabezas de ganado⟩ ⟨$10 a head : $10 por cabeza⟩ **7 to come to a head** : llegar a un punto crítico

headache [ˈhɛdˌeɪk] *n* : dolor *m* de cabeza, jaqueca *f*

headband [ˈhɛdˌbænd] *n* : cinta *f* del pelo

headdress [ˈhɛdˌdrɛs] *n* : tocado *m*

headfirst [ˈhɛdˈfərst] *adv* : de cabeza

headgear [ˈhɛdˌgɪr] *n* : gorro *m*, casco *m*, sombrero *m*

heading [ˈhɛdɪŋ] *n* **1** DIRECTION : dirección *f* **2** TITLE : encabezamiento *m*, título *m* **3** : membrete *m* (de una carta)

headland [ˈhɛdlənd, -ˌlænd] *n* : cabo *m*

headlight [ˈhɛdˌlaɪt] *n* : faro *m*, foco *m*, farol *m Mex*

headline [ˈhɛdˌlaɪn] *n* : titular *m*

headlong[1] [ˈhɛdˈlɔŋ] *adv* **1** HEADFIRST : de cabeza **2** HASTILY : precipitadamente

headlong[2] [ˈhɛdˌlɔŋ] *adj* : precipitado

headmaster [ˈhɛdˌmæstər] *n* : director *m*

headmistress [ˈhɛdˌmɪstrəs, -ˈmɪs-] *n* : directora *f*

head–on [ˈhɛdˈɑn, -ˈɔn] *adv & adj* : de frente

headphones [ˈhɛdˌfoːnz] *npl* : audífonos *mpl*, cascos *mpl*

headquarters [ˈhɛdˌkwɔrt̬ərz] *ns & pl* **1** SEAT : oficina *f* central, sede *f* **2** : cuartel *m* general (de los militares)

headrest [ˈhɛdˌrɛst] *n* : apoyacabezas *m*

headship [ˈhɛdˌʃɪp] *n* : dirección *f*

head start *n* : ventaja *f*

headstone [ˈhɛdˌstoːn] *n* : lápida *f*

headstrong [ˈhɛdˈstrɔŋ] *adj* : testarudo, obstinado, empecinado

headwaiter [ˈhɛdˈweɪt̬ər] *n* : jefe *m*, -fa *f* de comedor

headwaters [ˈhɛdˌwɔt̬ərz, -ˌwɑ-] *npl* : cabecera *f*

headway [ˈhɛdˌweɪ] *n* : progreso *m* ⟨to make headway against : avanzar contra⟩

heady [ˈhɛdi] *adj* **headier; -est 1** INTOXICATING : embriagador, excitante **2** SHREWD : astuto, sagaz

heal [ˈhiːl] *vt* : curar, sanar — *vi* **1** : sanar, curarse **2 to heal up** : cicatrizarse

healer [ˈhiːlər] *n* **1** : curandero *m*, -dera *f* **2** : curador *m*, -dora *f* (cosa)

health [ˈhɛlθ] *n* : salud *f*

healthful [ˈhɛlθfəl] *adj* : saludable, salubre — **healthfully** *adv*

healthy [ˈhɛlθi] *adj* **healthier; -est** : sano, bien — **healthily** [-θəli] *adv*

heap[1] [ˈhi:p] *vt* **1** PILE : amontonar, apilar **2** SHOWER : colmar

heap[2] *n* : montón *m*, pila *f*

hear [ˈhɪr] *v* **heard** [ˈhərd]; **hearing** *vt* **1** : oír ⟨do you hear me? : ¿me oyes?⟩ **2** HEED : oír, prestar atención a **3** LEARN : oír, enterarse de — *vi* **1** : oír ⟨to hear about : oír hablar de⟩ **2 to hear from** : tener noticias de

hearing [ˈhɪrɪŋ] *n* **1** : oído *m* ⟨hard of hearing : duro de oído⟩ **2** : vista *f* (en un tribunal) **3** ATTENTION : consideración *f*, oportunidad *f* de expresarse **4** EARSHOT : alcance *m* del oído

hearing aid *n* : audífono *m*

hearken [ˈhɑrkən] *vt* : escuchar

hearsay [ˈhɪrˌseɪ] *n* : rumores *mpl*

hearse [ˈhərs] *n* : coche *m* fúnebre

heart [ˈhɑrt] *n* **1** : corazón *m* **2** CENTER, CORE : corazón *m*, centro *m* ⟨the heart of the matter : el meollo del asunto⟩ **3** FEELINGS : corazón *m*, sentimientos *mpl* ⟨a broken heart : un corazón destrozado⟩ ⟨to have a good heart : tener buen corazón⟩ ⟨to take something to heart : tomarse algo a pecho⟩ **4** COURAGE : valor *m*, corazón *m* ⟨to take heart : animarse, cobrar ánimos⟩ **5 hearts** *npl* : corazones *mpl* (en juegos de naipes) **6 by heart** : de memoria

heartache [ˈhɑrṭˌeɪk] *n* : pena *f*, angustia *f*

heart attack *n* : infarto *m*, ataque *m* al corazón

heartbeat [ˈhɑrtˌbi:t] *n* : latido *m* (del corazón)

heartbreak [ˈhɑrtˌbreɪk] *n* : congoja *f*, angustia *f*

heartbreaking [ˈhɑrtˌbreɪkɪŋ] *adj* : desgarrador, que parte el corazón

heartbroken [ˈhɑrtˌbro:kən] *adj* : desconsolado, destrozado

heartburn [ˈhɑrtˌbərn] *n* : acidez *f* estomacal

hearten [ˈhɑrtən] *vt* : alentar, animar

heartfelt [ˈhɑrtˌfɛlt] *adj* : sentido

hearth [ˈhɑrθ] *n* : hogar *m*, chimenea *f*

heartily [ˈhɑrṭəli] *adv* **1** ENTHUSIASTICALLY : de buena gana, con entusiasmo **2** TOTALLY : totalmente, completamente

heartless [ˈhɑrtləs] *adj* : desalmado, despiadado, cruel

heartsick [ˈhɑrtˌsɪk] *adj* : abatido, desconsolado

heartstrings [ˈhɑrtˌstrɪŋz] *npl* : fibras *fpl* del corazón

heartwarming [ˈhɑrtˌwɔrmɪŋ] *adj* : conmovedor, emocionante

hearty [ˈhɑrṭi] *adj* **heartier; -est 1** CORDIAL, WARM : cordial, caluroso **2** STRONG : fuerte ⟨to have a hearty appetite : ser de buen comer⟩ **3** SUBSTANTIAL : abundante, sustancioso ⟨a hearty breakfast : un desayuno abundante⟩

heat[1] [ˈhi:t] *vt* : calentar

heat[2] *n* **1** WARMTH : calor *m* **2** HEATING : calefacción *f* **3** EXCITEMENT : calor *m*, entusiasmo *m* ⟨in the heat of the moment : en el calor del momento⟩ **4** ESTRUS : celo *m*

heated [ˈhi:ṭəd] *adj* **1** WARMED : calentado **2** IMPASSIONED : acalorado, apasionado

heater [ˈhi:ṭər] *n* : calentador *m*, estufa *f*, calefactor *m*

heath [ˈhi:θ] *n* **1** MOOR : brezal *m*, páramo *m* **2** HEATHER : brezo *m*

heathen[1] [ˈhi:ðən] *adj* : pagano

heathen[2] *n, pl* **-thens** *or* **-then** : pagano *m*, -na *f*; infiel *mf*

heather [ˈhɛðər] *n* : brezo *m*

heave[1] [ˈhi:v] *v* **heaved** *or* **hove** [ˈho:v]; **heaving** *vt* **1** LIFT, RAISE : levantar con esfuerzo **2** HURL : lanzar, tirar **3 to heave a sigh** : echar un suspiro, suspirar — *vi* **1** : subir y bajar, palpitar (dícese del pecho) **2 to heave up** RISE : levantarse

heave[2] *n* **1** EFFORT : gran esfuerzo *m* (para levantar algo) **2** THROW : lanzamiento *m*

heaven [ˈhɛvən] *n* **1** : cielo *m* ⟨for heaven's sake : por Dios⟩ **2 heavens** *npl* SKY : cielo *m* ⟨the heavens opened up : empezó a llover a cántaros⟩

heavenly [ˈhɛvənli] *adj* **1** : celestial, celeste **2** DELIGHTFUL : divino, encantador

heavily [ˈhɛvəli] *adv* **1** : pesadamente, con mucho peso **2** LABORIOUSLY : trabajosamente, penosamente **3** : mucho

heaviness [ˈhɛvinəs] *n* : peso *m*, pesadez *f*

heavy [ˈhɛvi] *adj* **heavier; -est 1** WEIGHTY : pesado **2** DENSE, THICK : denso, espeso, grueso **3** BURDENSOME : oneroso, gravoso **4** PROFOUND : profundo **5** SLUGGISH : lento, tardo **6** STOUT : corpulento **7** SEVERE : severo, duro, fuerte

heavy–duty [ˈhɛviˈdu:ṭi, -ˈdju:-] *adj* : muy resistente, fuerte

heavyweight [ˈhɛviˌweɪt] *n* : peso *m* pesado (en deportes)

Hebrew[1] [ˈhi:ˌbru:] *adj* : hebreo

Hebrew[2] *n* **1** : hebreo *m*, -brea *f* **2** : hebreo *m* (idioma)

heck [ˈhɛk] *n* : ¡caramba!, ¡caray! ⟨a heck of a lot : un montón⟩ ⟨what the heck is . . . ? : ¿que diablos es . . . ?⟩

heckle [ˈhɛkəl] *vt* **-led; -ling** : interrumpir (a un orador)

hectare [ˈhɛkˌtær] *n* : hectárea *f*

hectic [ˈhɛktɪk] *adj* : agitado, ajetreado — **hectically** [-tɪkli] *adv*

he'd [ˈhi:d] (*contraction* of **he had** *or* **he would**) → **have, would**

hedge[1] [ˈhɛʤ] *v* **hedged; hedging** *vt* **1** : cercar con un seto **2 to hedge one's bet** : cubrirse — *vi* **1** : dar rodeos, con-

testar con evasivas **2 to hedge against** : cubrirse contra, protegerse contra
hedge[2] *n* **1** : seto *m* vivo **2** SAFEGUARD : salvaguardia *f*, protección *f*
hedgehog ['hɛʤ,hɔg, -hɑg] *n* : erizo *m*
heed[1] ['hi:d] *vt* : prestar atención a, hacer caso de
heed[2] *n* : atención *f*
heedless ['hi:dləs] *adj* : descuidado, despreocupado, inconsciente ⟨to be heedless of : hacer caso omiso de⟩ — **heedlessly** *adv*
heel[1] ['hi:l] *vi* : inclinarse
heel[2] *n* : talón *m* (del pie), tacón *m* (de calzado)
heft ['hɛft] *vt* : sopesar
hefty ['hɛfti] *adj* **heftier; -est** : robusto, fornido, pesado
hegemony [hɪ'ʤɛməni] *n, pl* **-nies** : hegemonía *f*
heifer ['hɛfər] *n* : novilla *f*
height ['haɪt] *n* **1** PEAK : cumbre *f*, cima *f*, punto *m* alto ⟨at the height of her career : en la cumbre de su carrera⟩ ⟨the height of stupidity : el colmo de la estupidez⟩ **2** TALLNESS : estatura *f* (de una persona), altura *f* (de un objeto) **3** ALTITUDE : altura *f*
heighten ['haɪtən] *vt* **1** : hacer más alto **2** INTENSIFY : aumentar, intensificar — *vi* : aumentarse, intensificarse
heinous ['heɪnəs] *adj* : atroz, abominable, nefando
heir ['ær] *n* : heredero *m*, -ra *f*
heiress ['ærəs] *n* : heredera *f*
heirloom ['ær,lu:m] *n* : reliquia *f* de familia
held → **hold**
helicopter ['hɛlə,kɑptər] *n* : helicóptero *m*
helium ['hi:liəm] *n* : helio *m*
helix ['hi:lɪks] *n, pl* **helices** ['hɛlə,si:z, 'hi:-] *or* **helixes** ['hi:lɪksəz] : hélice *f*
hell ['hɛl] *n* : infierno *m*
he'll ['hi:l, 'hɪl] (*contraction of* **he shall** *or* **he will**) → **shall, will**
hellish ['hɛlɪʃ] *adj* : horroroso, infernal
hello [hə'lo:, hɛ-] *interj* : ¡hola!
helm ['hɛlm] *n* **1** : timón *m* **2 to take the helm** : tomar el mando
helmet ['hɛlmət] *n* : casco *m*
help[1] ['hɛlp] *vt* **1** AID, ASSIST : ayudar, auxiliar, socorrer, asistir **2** ALLEVIATE : aliviar **3** SERVE : servir ⟨help yourself! : ¡sírvete!⟩ **4** AVOID : evitar ⟨it can't be helped : no lo podemos evitar, no hay más remedio⟩ ⟨I couldn't help smiling : no pude menos que sonreír⟩
help[2] *n* **1** ASSISTANCE : ayuda *f* ⟨help! : ¡socorro!, ¡auxilio!⟩ **2** STAFF : personal *m* (en una oficina), servicio *m* doméstico
helper ['hɛlpər] *n* : ayudante *mf*
helpful ['hɛlpfəl] *adj* **1** OBLIGING : servicial, amable, atento **2** USEFUL : útil, práctico — **helpfully** *adv*
helpfulness ['hɛlpfəlnəs] *n* **1** KINDNESS : bondad *f*, amabilidad *f* **2** USEFULNESS : utilidad *f*
helping ['hɛlpɪŋ] *n* : porción *f*
helpless ['hɛlpləs] *adj* **1** POWERLESS : incapaz, impotente **2** DEFENSELESS : indefenso
helplessly ['hɛlpləsli] *adv* : en vano, inútilmente
helplessness ['hɛlpləsnəs] *n* POWERLESSNESS : incapacidad *f*, impotencia *f*
helter–skelter [,hɛltər'skɛltər] *adv* : atropelladamente, precipitadamente
hem[1] ['hɛm] *vt* **hemmed; hemming 1** : dobladillar **2 to hem in** : encerrar
hem[2] *n* : dobladillo *m*, bastilla *f*
hemisphere ['hɛmə,sfɪr] *n* : hemisferio *m*
hemispheric [,hɛmə'sfɪrɪk, -'sfɛr-] *or* **hemispherical** [-ɪkəl] *adj* : hemisférico
hemlock ['hɛm,lɑk] *n* : cicuta *f*
hemoglobin ['hi:mə,glo:bən] *n* : hemoglobina *f*
hemophilia [,hi:mə'fɪliə] *n* : hemofilia *f*
hemorrhage[1] ['hɛmərɪʤ] *vi* **-rhaged; -rhaging** : sufrir una hemorragia
hemorrhage[2] *n* : hemorragia *f*
hemorrhoids ['hɛmə,rɔɪdz, 'hɛm-,rɔɪdz] *npl* : hemorroides *fpl*, almorranas *fpl*
hemp ['hɛmp] *n* : cáñamo *m*
hen ['hɛn] *n* : gallina *f*
hence ['hɛnts] *adv* **1** : de aquí, de ahí ⟨10 years hence : de aquí a 10 años⟩ ⟨a dog bit me, hence my dislike of animals : un perro me mordió, de ahí mi aversión a los animales⟩ **2** THEREFORE : por lo tanto, por consiguiente
henceforth ['hɛnts,forθ, ,hɛnts'-] *adv* : de ahora en adelante
henchman ['hɛntʃmən] *n, pl* **-men** [-mən, -,mɛn] : secuaz *mf*, esbirro *m*
henpeck ['hɛn,pk] *vt* : dominar (al marido)
hepatitis [,hɛpə'taɪt̬əs] *n, pl* **-titides** [-'tɪt̬ə,di:z] : hepatitis *f*
her[1] ['hər] *adj* : su, sus, de ella ⟨her house : su casa, la casa de ella⟩
her[2] ['hər, ər] *pron* **1** (*used as direct object*) : la ⟨I saw her yesterday : la vi ayer⟩ **2** (*used as indirect object*) : le, se ⟨he gave her the book : le dio el libro⟩ ⟨he sent it to her : se lo mandó⟩ **3** (*used as object of a preposition*) : ella ⟨we did it for her : lo hicimos por ella⟩ ⟨taller than her : más alto que ella⟩
herald[1] ['hɛrəld] *vt* ANNOUNCE : anunciar, proclamar
herald[2] *n* **1** MESSENGER : heraldo *m* **2** HARBINGER : precursor *m*
heraldic [hɛ'rældɪk, hə-] *adj* : heráldico
heraldry ['hɛrəldri] *n, pl* **-ries** : heráldica *f*
herb ['ərb, 'hərb] *n* : hierba *f*
herbal ['ərbəl, 'hər-] *adj* : herbario
herbicide ['ərbə,saɪd, 'hər-] *n* : herbicida *m*
herbivore ['ərbə,vor, 'hər-] *n* : herbívoro *m*
herbivorous [,ər'bɪvərəs, ,hər-] *adj* : herbívoro
herculean [,hərkjə'li:ən, ,hər'kju:-liən] *adj* : hercúleo, sobrehumano

herd[1] [ˈhərd] *vt* : reunir en manada, conducir en manada — *vi* : ir en manada (dícese de los animales), apiñarse (dícese de la gente)

herd[2] *n* : manada *f*

herder [ˈhərdər] → **herdsman**

herdsman [ˈhərdzmən] *n, pl* **-men** [-mən, -ˌmɛn] : vaquero *m* (de ganado), pastor *m* (de ovejas)

here [ˈhɪr] *adv* **1** : aquí, acá ⟨come here! : ¡ven acá!⟩ ⟨right here : aquí mismo⟩ **2** NOW : en este momento, ahora, ya ⟨here he comes : ya viene⟩ ⟨here it's three o'clock (already) : ahora son las tres⟩ **3** : en este punto ⟨here we agree : estamos de acuerdo en este punto⟩ **4** **here you are!** : ¡toma!

hereabouts [ˈhɪrəˌbaʊts] *or* **hereabout** [-ˌbaʊt] *adv* : por aquí (cerca)

hereafter[1] [hɪrˈæftər] *adv* **1** : de aquí en adelante, a continuación **2** : en el futuro

hereafter[2] *n* **the hereafter** : el más allá

hereby [hɪrˈbaɪ] *adv* : por este medio

hereditary [həˈrɛdəˌtɛri] *adj* : hereditario

heredity [həˈrɛdət̬i] *n* : herencia *f*

herein [hɪrˈɪn] *adv* : aquí

hereof [hɪrˈʌv] *adv* : de aquí

hereon [hɪrˈɑn, -ˈɔn] *adv* : sobre esto

heresy [ˈhɛrəsi] *n, pl* **-sies** : herejía *f*

heretic [ˈhɛrəˌtɪk] *n* : hereje *mf*

heretical [həˈrɛt̬ɪkəl] *adj* : herético

hereto [hɪrˈtuː] *adv* : a esto

heretofore [ˈhɪrt̬əˌfor] *adv* HITHERTO : hasta ahora

hereunder [hɪrˈʌndər] *adv* : a continuación, abajo

hereupon [hɪrəˈpɑn, -ˈpɔn] *adv* : con esto, en ese momento

herewith [hɪrˈwɪθ] *adv* : adjunto

heritage [ˈhɛrət̬ɪʤ] *n* : patrimonio *m* (nacional)

hermaphrodite [hərˈmæfrəˌdaɪt] *n* : hermafrodita *mf*

hermetic [hərˈmɛt̬ɪk] *adj* : hermético — **hermetically** [-t̬ɪkli] *adv*

hermit [ˈhərmət] *n* : ermitaño *m*, -ña *f*; eremita *mf*

hernia [ˈhərniə] *n, pl* **-nias** *or* **-niae** [-niˌiː, -niˌaɪ] : hernia *f*

hero [ˈhiːˌroː, ˈhɪrˌoː] *n, pl* **-roes** **1** : héroe *m* **2** PROTAGONIST : protagonista *mf*

heroic [hɪˈroːɪk] *adj* : heroico — **heroically** [-ɪkli] *adv*

heroics [hɪˈroːɪks] *npl* : actos *mpl* heroicos

heroin [ˈhɛroən] *n* : heroína *f*

heroine [ˈhɛroən] *n* **1** : heroína *f* **2** PROTAGONIST : protagonista *f*

heroism [ˈhɛroˌɪzəm] *n* : heroísmo *m*

heron [ˈhɛrən] *n* : garza *f*

herpes [ˈhərˌpiːz] *n* : herpes *m*

herring [ˈhɛrɪŋ] *n, pl* **-ring** *or* **-rings** : arenque *m*

hers [ˈhərz] *pron* : suyo, -ya; suyos, -yas; de ella ⟨these shoes are hers : estos zapatos son suyos⟩ ⟨hers are bigger : los de ella son más grandes⟩

herself [hərˈsɛlf] *pron* **1** (*used reflexively*) : se ⟨she dressed herself : se vistió⟩ **2** (*used emphatically*) : ella misma ⟨she fixed it herself : lo arregló ella misma, lo arregló por sí sola⟩

hertz [ˈhərts, ˈhɛrts] *ns & pl* : hercio *m*

he's [ˈhiːz] (*contraction of* **he is** *or* **he has**) → **be, have**

hesitancy [ˈhɛzət̬əntsi] *n, pl* **-cies** : vacilación *f*, titubeo *m*, indecisión *f*

hesitant [ˈhɛzət̬ənt] *adj* : titubeante, vacilante — **hesitantly** *adv*

hesitate [ˈhɛzəˌteɪt] *vi* **-tated; -tating** : vacilar, titubear

hesitation [ˌhɛzəˈteɪʃən] *n* : vacilación *f*, indecisión *f*, titubeo *m*

heterogeneous [ˌhɛt̬ərəˈʤiːniəs, -njəs] *adj* : heterogéneo

heterosexual[1] [ˌhɛt̬əroˈskʃuəl] *adj* : heterosexual

heterosexual[2] *n* : heterosexual *mf*

heterosexuality [ˌhɛt̬əroˌskʃuˈæləti] *n* : heterosexualidad *f*

hew [ˈhjuː] *v* **hewed; hewed** *or* **hewn** [ˈhjuːn]; **hewing** *vt* **1** CUT : cortar, talar (árboles) **2** SHAPE : labrar, tallar — *vi* CONFORM : conformarse, ceñirse

hex[1] [ˈhɛks] *vt* : hacerle un maleficio (a alguien)

hex[2] *n* : maleficio *m*

hexagon [ˈhɛksəˌgɑn] *n* : hexágono *m*

hexagonal [hɛkˈsægənəl] *adj* : hexagonal

hey [ˈheɪ] *interj* : ¡eh!, ¡oye!

heyday [ˈheɪˌdeɪ] *n* : auge *m*, apogeo *m*

hi [ˈhaɪ] *interj* : ¡hola!

hiatus [haɪˈeɪt̬əs] *n* **1** : hiato *m* **2** PAUSE : pausa *f*

hibernate [ˈhaɪbərˌneɪt] *vi* **-nated; -nating** : hibernar, invernar

hibernation [ˌhaɪbərˈneɪʃən] *n* : hibernación *f*

hiccup[1] [ˈhɪkəp] *vi* **-cuped; -cuping** : hipar, tener hipo

hiccup[2] *n* : hipo *m* ⟨to have the hiccups : tener hipo⟩

hick [ˈhɪk] *n* BUMPKIN : palurdo *m*, -da *f*

hickory [ˈhɪkəri] *n, pl* **-ries** : nogal *m* americano

hidden [ˈhɪdən] *adj* : oculto

hide[1] [ˈhaɪd] *v* **hid** [ˈhɪd]; **hidden** [ˈhɪdən] *or* **hid; hiding** *vt* **1** CONCEAL : esconder **2** : ocultar ⟨to hide one's motives : ocultar uno sus motivos⟩ **3** SCREEN : tapar, no dejar ver — *vi* : esconderse

hide[2] *n* : piel *f*, cuero *m* ⟨to save one's hide : salvar el pellejo⟩

hide–and–seek [ˈhaɪdəndˈsiːk] *n* **to play hide–and–seek** : jugar a las escondidas

hidebound [ˈhaɪdˌbaʊnd] *adj* : rígido, conservador

hideous [ˈhɪdiəs] *adj* : horrible, horroroso, espantoso — **hideously** *adv*

hideout [ˈhaɪdˌaʊt] *n* : guarida *f*, escondrijo *m*

hierarchical [ˌhaɪəˈrɑrkɪkəl] *adj* : jerárquico

hierarchy [ˈhaɪəˌrɑrki] *n, pl* **-chies** : jerarquía *f*
hieroglyphic [ˌhaɪərəˈglɪfɪk] *n* : jeroglífico *m*
hi–fi [ˈhaɪˈfaɪ] *n* **1** → **high fidelity 2** : equipo *m* de alta fidelidad
high[1] [ˈhaɪ] *adv* : alto
high[2] *adj* **1** TALL : alto ⟨a high wall : una pared alta⟩ **2** ELEVATED : alto, elevado ⟨high prices : precios elevados⟩ ⟨high blood pressure : presión alta⟩ **3** GREAT, IMPORTANT : grande, importante, alto ⟨a high number : un número grande⟩ ⟨high society : alta sociedad⟩ ⟨high hopes : grandes esperanzas⟩ **4** : alto (en música) **5** INTOXICATED : borracho, drogado
high[3] *n* **1** : récord *m*, punto *m* máximo ⟨to reach an all-time high : batir el récord⟩ **2** : zona *f* de alta presión (en meteorología) **3** *or* **high gear** : directa *f* **4 on high** : en las alturas
highbrow [ˈhaɪˌbraʊ] *n* : intelectual *mf*
higher [ˈhaɪər] *adj* : superior
high fidelity *n* : alta fidelidad *f*
high–flown [ˈhaɪˈflo:n] *adj* : altisonante
high–handed [ˈhaɪˈhændəd] *adj* : arbitrario
highlands [ˈhaɪləndz] *npl* : tierras *fpl* altas, altiplano *m*
highlight[1] [ˈhaɪˌlaɪt] *vt* **1** EMPHASIZE : destacar, poner en relieve, subrayar **2** : ser el punto culminante de
highlight[2] *n* : punto *m* culminante
highly [ˈhaɪli] *adv* **1** VERY : muy, sumamente **2** FAVORABLY : muy bien ⟨to speak highly of : hablar muy bien de⟩ ⟨to think highly of : tener en mucho a⟩
highness [ˈhaɪnəs] *n* **1** HEIGHT : altura *f* **2 Highness** : Alteza *f* ⟨Your Royal Highness : Su Alteza Real⟩
high–pitched [ˈhaɪˈpɪtʃt] *adj* : agudo
high–rise [ˈhaɪˌraɪz] *adj* : alto, de muchas plantas
high school *n* : escuela *f* superior, escuela *f* secundaria
high seas *npl* : alta mar *f*
high–spirited [ˈhaɪˈspɪrət̬əd] *adj* : vivaz, muy animado, brioso
high–strung [ˌhaɪˈstrʌŋ] *adj* : nervioso, excitable
highway [ˈhaɪˌweɪ] *n* : carretera *f*
highwayman [ˈhaɪˌweɪmən] *n, pl* **-men** [-mən, -ˌmɛn] : salteador *m* (de caminos), bandido *m*
hijack[1] [ˈhaɪˌdʒæk] *vt* : secuestrar
hijack[2] *n* : secuestro *m*
hijacker [ˈhaɪˌdʒækər] *n* : secuestrador *m*, -dora *f*
hike[1] [ˈhaɪk] *v* **hiked; hiking** *vi* : hacer una caminata — *vt* RAISE : subir
hike[2] *n* **1** : caminata *f*, excursión *f* **2** INCREASE : subida *f* (de precios)
hiker [ˈhaɪkər] *n* : excursionista *mf*
hilarious [hɪˈlæriəs, haɪˈ-] *adj* : muy divertido, hilarante
hilarity [hɪˈlærət̬i, haɪ-] *n* : hilaridad *f*
hill [ˈhɪl] *n* **1** : colina *f*, cerro *m* **2** SLOPE : cuesta *f*, pendiente *f*
hillbilly [ˈhɪlˌbɪli] *n, pl* **-lies** : palurdo *m*, -da *f* (de las montañas)
hillock [ˈhɪlək] *n* : loma *f*, altozano *m*, otero *m*
hillside [ˈhɪlˌsaɪd] *n* : ladera *f*, cuesta *f*
hilltop [ˈhɪlˌtɑp] *n* : cima *f*, cumbre *f*
hilly [ˈhɪli] *adj* **hillier; -est** : montañoso, accidentado
hilt [ˈhɪlt] *n* : puño *m*, empuñadura *f*
him [ˈhɪm, əm] *pron* **1** (*used as direct object*) : lo ⟨I found him : lo encontré⟩ **2** (*used as indirect object*) : le, se ⟨we gave him a present : le dimos un regalo⟩ ⟨I sent it to him : se lo mandé⟩ **3** (*used as object of a preposition*) : él ⟨she was thinking of him : pensaba en él⟩ ⟨younger than him : más joven que él⟩
himself [hɪmˈsɛlf] *pron* **1** (*used reflexively*) : se ⟨he washed himself : se lavó⟩ **2** (*used emphatically*) : él mismo ⟨he did it himself : lo hizo él mismo, lo hizo por sí solo⟩
hind[1] [ˈhaɪnd] *adj* : trasero, posterior ⟨hind legs : patas traseras⟩
hind[2] *n* : cierva *f*
hinder [ˈhɪndər] *vt* : dificultar, impedir, estorbar
Hindi [ˈhɪndi:] *n* : hindi *m*
hindquarters [ˈhaɪndˌkwɔrt̬ərz] *npl* : cuartos *mpl* traseros
hindrance [ˈhɪndrən*t*s] *n* : estorbo *m*, obstáculo *m*, impedimento *m*
hindsight [ˈhaɪndˌsaɪt] *n* : retrospectiva *f* ⟨with the benefit of hindsight : en retrospectiva, con la perspectiva que da la experiencia⟩
Hindu[1] [ˈhɪnˌdu:] *adj* : hindú
Hindu[2] *n* : hindú *mf*
Hinduism [ˈhɪndu:ˌɪzəm] *n* : hinduismo *m*
hinge[1] [ˈhɪndʒ] *v* **hinged; hinging** *vt* : unir con bisagras — *vi* **to hinge on** : depender de
hinge[2] *n* : bisagra *f*, gozne *m*
hint[1] [ˈhɪnt] *vt* : insinuar, dar a entender — *vi* : soltar indirectas
hint[2] *n* **1** INSINUATION : insinuación *f*, indirecta *f* **2** TIP : consejo *m*, sugerencia *f* **3** TRACE : pizca *f*, indicio *m*
hinterland [ˈhɪntərˌlænd, -lənd] *n* : interior *m* (de un país)
hip [ˈhɪp] *n* : cadera *f*
hip–hop [ˈhɪpˌhɑp] *n* : hip-hop *m*
hippie [ˈhɪpi] *n* : hippie *mf*, hippy *mf*
hippopotamus [ˌhɪpəˈpɑt̬əməs] *n, pl* **-muses** *or* **-mi** [-ˌmaɪ] : hipopótamo *m*
hippo [ˈhɪpo:] *n, pl* **hippos** → **hippopotamus**
hire[1] [ˈhaɪr] *vt* **hired; hiring 1** EMPLOY : contratar, emplear **2** RENT : alquilar, arrendar
hire[2] *n* **1** RENT : alquiler *m* ⟨for hire : se alquila⟩ **2** WAGES : paga *f*, sueldo *m* **3** EMPLOYEE : empleado *m*, -da *f*
his[1] [ˈhɪz, ɪz] *adj* : su, sus, de él ⟨his hat : su sombrero, el sombrero de él⟩
his[2] *pron* : suyo, -ya; suyos, suyas; de él ⟨the decision is his : la decisión es suya⟩ ⟨it's his, not hers : es de él, no de ella⟩

Hispanic[1] [hɪˈspænɪk] *adj* : hispano, hispánico
Hispanic[2] *n* : hispano *m*, -na *f*; hispánico *m*, -ca *f*
hiss[1] [ˈhɪs] *vi* : sisear, silbar — *vt* : decir entre dientes
hiss[2] *n* : siseo *m*, silbido *m*
historian [hɪˈstɔriən] *n* : historiador *m*, -dora *f*
historic [hɪˈstɔrɪk] *or* **historical** [-ɪkəl] *adj* : histórico — **historically** [-ɪkli] *adv*
history [ˈhɪstəri] *n, pl* **-ries** **1** : historia *f* **2** RECORD : historial *m*
histrionics [ˌhɪstriˈɑnɪks] *ns & pl* : histrionismo *m*
hit[1] [ˈhɪt] *v* **hit; hitting** *vt* **1** STRIKE : golpear, pegar, batear (una pelota) <he hit the dog : le pegó al perro> **2** : chocar contra, dar con, dar en (el blanco) <the car hit a tree : el coche chocó contra un árbol> **3** AFFECT : afectar <the news hit us hard : la noticia nos afectó mucho> **4** ENCOUNTER : tropezar con, toparse con <to hit a snag : tropezar con un obstáculo> **5** REACH : llegar a, alcanzar <the price hit $10 a pound : el precio alcanzó los $10 dólares por libra> <to hit town : llegar a la ciudad> <to hit the headlines : ser noticia> **6 to hit on** *or* **to hit upon** : dar con — *vi* : golpear
hit[2] *n* **1** BLOW : golpe *m* **2** : impacto *m* (de un arma) **3** SUCCESS : éxito *m*
hitch[1] [ˈhɪʧ] *vt* **1** : mover con sacudidas **2** ATTACH : enganchar, atar, amarrar **3** → **hitchhike** **4 to hitch up** : subirse (los pantalones, etc.)
hitch[2] *n* **1** JERK : tirón *m*, jalón *m* **2** OBSTACLE : obstáculo *m*, impedimento *m*, tropiezo *m*
hitchhike [ˈhɪʧˌhaɪk] *vi* **-hiked; -hiking** : hacer autostop, ir de aventón *Col, Mex fam*
hitchhiker [ˈhɪʧˌhaɪkər] *n* : autostopista *mf*
hither [ˈhɪðər] *adv* : acá, por aquí
hitherto [ˈhɪðərˌtuː, ˌhɪðərˈ-] *adv* : hasta ahora
hitter [ˈhɪt̬ər] *n* BATTER : bateador *m*, -dora *f*
HIV [ˌeɪʧˌaɪˈviː] *n* (*h*uman *i*mmunodeficiency *v*irus) : VIH *m*, virus *m* del sida
hive [ˈhaɪv] *n* **1** : colmena *f* **2** SWARM : enjambre *m* **3** : lugar *m* muy activo <a hive of activity : un hervidero de actividad>
hives [ˈhaɪvz] *ns & pl* : urticaria *f*
hoard[1] [ˈhord] *vt* : acumular, atesorar
hoard[2] *n* : tesoro *m*, reserva *f*, provisión *f*
hoarfrost [ˈhorˌfrɔst] *n* : escarcha *f*
hoarse [ˈhors] *adj* **hoarser; -est** : ronco — **hoarsely** *adv*
hoarseness [ˈhorsnəs] *n* : ronquera *f*
hoary [ˈhori] *adj* **hoarier; -est** **1** : cano, canoso **2** OLD : vetusto, antiguo
hoax[1] [ˈhoːks] *vt* : engañar, embaucar, bromear
hoax[2] *n* : engaño *m*, broma *f*
hobble[1] [ˈhɑbəl] *v* **-bled; -bling** *vi* LIMP : cojear, renguear — *vt* : manear (un animal)
hobble[2] *n* **1** LIMP : cojera *f*, rengo *m* **2** : maniota *f* (para un animal)
hobby [ˈhɑbi] *n, pl* **-bies** : pasatiempo *m*, afición *f*
hobgoblin [ˈhɑbˌgɑblən] *n* : duende *m*
hobnail [ˈhɑbˌneɪl] *n* : tachuela *f*
hobnob [ˈhɑbˌnɑb] *vi* **-nobbed; -nobbing** : codearse
hobo [ˈhoːˌboː] *n, pl* **-boes** : vagabundo *m*, -da *f*
hock[1] [ˈhɑk] *vt* PAWN : empeñar
hock[2] *n* **in hock** : empeñado
hockey [ˈhɑki] *n* : hockey *m*
hodgepodge [ˈhɑʤˌpɑʤ] *n* : mezcolanza *f*
hoe[1] [ˈhoː] *vt* **hoed; hoeing** : azadonar
hoe[2] *n* : azada *f*, azadón *m*
hog[1] [ˈhɔg, ˈhɑg] *vt* **hogged; hogging** : acaparar, monopolizar
hog[2] *n* **1** PIG : cerdo *m*, -da *f* **2** GLUTTON : glotón *m*, -tona *f*
hogshead [ˈhɔgzˌhɛd, ˈhɑgz-] *n* : tonel *m*
hoist[1] [ˈhɔɪst] *vt* : levantar, alzar, izar (una bandera, una vela)
hoist[2] *n* : grúa *f*
hold[1] [ˈhoːld] *v* **held** [ˈhɛld]; **holding** *vt* **1** POSSESS : tener <to hold office : ocupar un puesto> **2** RESTRAIN : detener, controlar <to hold one's temper : controlar su mal genio> **3** CLASP, GRASP : agarrar, coger <to hold hands : agarrarse de la mano> **4** : sujetar, mantener fijo <hold this nail for me : sujétame este clavo> **5** CONTAIN : contener, dar cabida a **6** SUPPORT : aguantar, sostener **7** REGARD : considerar, tener <he held me responsible : me consideró responsable> **8** CONDUCT : celebrar (una reunión), realizar (un evento), mantener (una conversación) — *vi* **1** : aguantar, resistir <the rope will hold : la cuerda resistirá> **2** : ser válido, valer <my offer still holds : mi oferta todavía es válida> **3 to hold forth** : perorar, arengar **4 to hold to** : mantenerse firme en **5 to hold with** : estar de acuerdo con
hold[2] *n* **1** GRIP : agarre *m*, llave *f* (en deportes) **2** CONTROL : control *m*, dominio *m* <to get hold of oneself : controlarse> **3** DELAY : demora *f* <to put on hold : suspender temporalmente> **4** : bodega *f* (en un barco o un avión) **5 to get hold of** : conseguir, localizar
holder [ˈhoːldər] *n* : poseedor *m*, -dora *f*; titular *mf*
holdings [ˈhoːldɪŋz] *npl* : propiedades *fpl*
hold out *vi* **1** LAST : aguantar, durar **2** RESIST : resistir
holdup [ˈhoːldˌʌp] *n* **1** ROBBERY : atraco *m* **2** DELAY : retraso *m*, demora *f*
hold up *vt* **1** ROB : robarle (a alguien), atracar, asaltar **2** DELAY : retrasar
hole [ˈhoːl] *n* : agujero *m*, hoyo *m*

holiday [ˈhɑləˌdeɪ] *n* **1** : día *m* feriado, fiesta *f* **2** VACATION : vacaciones *fpl*
holiness [ˈho:linəs] *n* **1** : santidad *f* **2 His Holiness** : Su Santidad
holistic [ho:ˈlɪstɪk] *adj* : holístico
holler1 [ˈhɑlər] *vi* : gritar, chillar
holler2 *n* : grito *m*, chillido *m*
hollow1 [ˈhɑˌlo:] *vt or* **to hollow out** : ahuecar
hollow2 *adj* **-lower; -est 1** : hueco, hundido (dícese de las mejillas, etc.), cavernoso (dícese de un sonido) **2** EMPTY, FALSE : vacío, falso
hollow3 *n* **1** CAVITY : hueco *m*, depresión *f*, cavidad *f* **2** VALLEY : hondonada *f*, valle *m*
hollowness [ˈhɑˌlo:nəs] *n* **1** HOLLOW : hueco *m*, cavidad *f* **2** FALSENESS : falsedad *f* **3** EMPTINESS : vacuidad *f*
holly [ˈhɑli] *n, pl* **-lies** : acebo *m*
hollyhock [ˈhɑliˌhɑk] *n* : malvarrosa *f*
holocaust [ˈhɑləˌkɔst, ˈho:-, ˈhɔ-] *n* : holocausto *m*
hologram [ˈho:ləˌgræm, ˈhɑ-] *n* : holograma *m*
holster [ˈho:lstər] *n* : pistolera *f*
holy [ˈho:li] *adj* **-lier; -est** : santo, sagrado
Holy Ghost → **Holy Spirit**
Holy Spirit *n* **the Holy Spirit** : el Espíritu Santo
homage [ˈɑmɪʤ, ˈhɑ-] *n* : homenaje *m*
home [ˈho:m] *n* **1** : casa *f*, hogar *m*, domicilio *m* ⟨to feel at home : sentirse en casa⟩ **2** INSTITUTION : residencia *f*, asilo *m*
homecoming [ˈho:mˌkʌmɪŋ] *n* : regreso *m* (a casa)
homegrown [ˈho:mˈgro:n] *adj* **1** : de cosecha propia **2** LOCAL : local
homeland [ˈho:mˌlænd] *n* : patria *f*, tierra *f* natal, terruño *m*
homeless [ˈho:mləs] *adj* : sin hogar, sin techo
homely [ˈho:mli] *adj* **-lier; -est 1** DOMESTIC : casero, hogareño **2** UGLY : feo, poco atractivo
homemade [ˈho:mˈmeɪd] *adj* : casero, hecho en casa
homemaker [ˈho:mˌmeɪkər] *n* : ama *f* de casa, persona *f* que se ocupa de la casa
home plate *n* : base *f* del bateador
home run *n* : jonrón *m*
homesick [ˈho:mˌsɪk] *adj* : nostálgico ⟨to be homesick : echar de menos a la familia⟩
homesickness [ˈho:mˌsɪknəs] *n* : nostalgia *f*, morriña *f*
homespun [ˈho:mˌspʌn] *adj* : simple, sencillo
homestead [ˈho:mˌstɛd] *n* : estancia *f*, hacienda *f*
homeward1 [ˈho:mwərd] *or* **homewards** [-wərdz] *adv* : de vuelta a casa, hacia casa
homeward2 *adj* : de vuelta, de regreso
homework [ˈho:mˌwərk] *n* : tarea *f*, deberes *mpl Spain*, asignación *f PRi*
homey [ˈho:mi] *adj* **homier; -est** : hogareño
homicidal [ˌhɑməˈsaɪdəl, ˌho:-] *adj* : homicida
homicide [ˈhɑməˌsaɪd, ˈho:-] *n* : homicidio *m*
hominy [ˈhɑməni] *n* : maíz *m* descascarillado
homogeneity [ˌho:məʤəˈni:əṭi, -ˈneɪ-] *n, pl* **-ties** : homogeneidad *f*
homogeneous [ˌho:məˈʤi:niəs, -njəs] *adj* : homogéneo — **homogeneously** *adv*
homogenize [ho:ˈmɑʤəˌnaɪz, hə-] *vt* **-nized; -nizing** : homogeneizar
homograph [ˈhɑməˌgræf, ˈho:-] *n* : homógrafo *m*
homologous [ho:ˈmɑləgəs, hə-] *adj* : homólogo
homonym [ˈhɑməˌnɪm, ˈho:-] *n* : homónimo *m*
homophone [ˈhɑməˌfo:n, ˈho:-] *n* : homófono *m*
homosexual1 [ˌho:məˈsɛkʃʊəl] *adj* : homosexual
homosexual2 *n* : homosexual *mf*
homosexuality [ˌho:məˌsɛkʃʊˈæləṭi] *n* : homosexualidad *f*
honcho [ˈhɑnˌʧo:] *n* : pez *m* gordo ⟨the head honcho : el jefe⟩
Honduran [hɑnˈdʊrən, -ˈdjʊr-] *n* : hondureño *m*, -ña *f* — **Honduran** *adj*
hone [ˈho:n] *vt* **honed; honing** : afilar
honest [ˈɑnəst] *adj* : honesto, honrado — **honestly** *adv*
honesty [ˈɑnəsti] *n, pl* **-ties** : honestidad *f*, honradez *f*
honey [ˈhʌni] *n, pl* **-eys** : miel *f*
honeybee [ˈhʌniˌbi:] *n* : abeja *f*
honeycomb [ˈhʌniˌko:m] *n* : panal *m*
honeymoon1 [ˈhʌniˌmu:n] *vi* : pasar la luna de miel
honeymoon2 *n* : luna *f* de miel
honeysuckle [ˈhʌniˌsʌkəl] *n* : madreselva *f*
honk1 [ˈhɑŋk, ˈhɔŋk] *vi* **1** : graznar (dícese del ganso) **2** : tocar la bocina (dícese de un vehículo), pitar
honk2 *n* : graznido *m* (del ganso), bocinazo *m* (de un vehículo)
honor1 [ˈɑnər] *vt* **1** RESPECT : honrar **2** : cumplir con ⟨to honor one's word : cumplir con su palabra⟩ **3** : aceptar (un cheque, etc.)
honor2 *n* **1** : honor *m* ⟨in honor of : en honor de⟩ **2 honors** *npl* AWARDS : honores *mpl*, condecoraciones *fpl* **3 Your Honor** : Su Señoría
honorable [ˈɑnərəbəl] *adj* : honorable, honroso — **honorably** [-bli] *adv*
honorary [ˈɑnəˌrɛri] *adj* : honorario
hood [ˈhʊd] *n* **1** : capucha *f* **2** : capó *m*, bonete *m Car* (de un automóvil)
hooded [ˈhʊdəd] *adj* : encapuchado
hoodlum [ˈhʊdləm, ˈhu:d-] *n* THUG : maleante *mf*, matón *m*
hoodwink [ˈhʊdˌwɪŋk] *vt* : engañar

hoof [ˈhʊf, ˈhu:f] *n, pl* **hooves** [ˈhʊvz, ˈhu:vz] *or* **hoofs** : pezuña *f*, casco *m*
hoofed [ˈhʊft, ˈhu:ft] *adj* : ungulado
hook[1] [ˈhʊk] *vt* : enganchar — *vi* : abrocharse, engancharse
hook[2] *n* : gancho *m*, percha *f*
hooked [ˈhʊkt] *adj* **1** : en forma de gancho **2 to be hooked on** : estar enganchado a
hooker [ˈhʊkər] *n* : prostituta *f*, fulana *f fam*
hookworm [ˈhʊk,wərm] *n* : anquilostoma *m*
hooligan [ˈhu:lɪgən] *n* : gamberro *m*, -rra *f*
hoop [ˈhu:p] *n* : aro *m*
hooray [hʊˈreɪ] → **hurrah**
hoot[1] [ˈhu:t] *vi* **1** SHOUT : gritar ⟨to hoot with laughter : morirse de risa, reírse a carcajadas⟩ **2** : ulular (dícese de un búho), tocar la bocina (dícese de un vehículo), silbar (dícese de un tren o un barco)
hoot[2] *n* **1** : ululato *m* (de un búho), silbido *m* (de un tren), bocinazo *m* (de un vehículo) **2** GUFFAW : carcajada *f*, risotada *f* **3 I don't give a hoot** : me vale un comino, me importa un pito
hop[1] [ˈhɑp] *vi* **hopped; hopping** : brincar, saltar
hop[2] *n* **1** LEAP : salto *m*, brinco *m* **2** FLIGHT : vuelo *m* corto **3** : lúpulo *m* (planta)
hope[1] [ˈho:p] *v* **hoped; hoping** *vi* : esperar — *vt* : esperar que ⟨we hope she comes : esperamos que venga⟩ ⟨I hope not : espero que no⟩
hope[2] *n* : esperanza *f*
hopeful [ˈho:pfəl] *adj* : esperanzado — **hopefully** *adv*
hopeless [ˈho:pləs] *adj* **1** DESPAIRING : desesperado **2** IMPOSSIBLE : imposible ⟨a hopeless case : un caso perdido⟩
hopelessly [ˈho:pləsli] *adv* **1** : sin esperanzas, desesperadamente **2** COMPLETELY : totalmente, completamente **3** IMPOSSIBLY : imposiblemente
hopelessness [ˈho:pləsnəs] *n* : desesperanza *f*
hopper [ˈhɑpər] *n* : tolva *f*
hopscotch [ˈhɑp,skɑʧ] *n* : tejo *m*
horde [ˈhord] *n* : horda *f*, multitud *f*
horizon [həˈraɪzən] *n* : horizonte *m*
horizontal [,hɔrəˈzɑntəl] *adj* : horizontal — **horizontally** *adv*
hormone [ˈhɔr,mo:n] *n* : hormona *f* — **hormonal** [hɔrˈmo:nəl] *adj*
horn [ˈhɔrn] *n* **1** : cuerno *m* (de un toro, una vaca, etc.) **2** : cuerno *m*, trompa *f* (instrumento musical) **3** : bocina *f*, claxon *m* (de un vehículo)
horned [ˈhɔrnd, ˈhɔrnəd] *adj* : cornudo, astado, con cuernos
hornet [ˈhɔrnət] *n* : avispón *m*
horny [ˈhɔrni] *adj* **hornier; -est 1** CALLOUS : calloso **2** LUSTFUL *fam* : caliente *fam*
horoscope [ˈhɔrə,sko:p] *n* : horóscopo *m*
horrendous [hɔˈrɛndəs] *adj* : horrendo, horroroso, atroz
horrible [ˈhɔrəbəl] *adj* : horrible, espantoso, horroroso — **horribly** [-bli] *adv*
horrid [ˈhɔrɪd] *adj* : horroroso, horrible — **horridly** *adv*
horrific [hɔˈrɪfɪk] *adj* : terrorífico, horroroso
horrify [ˈhɔrə,faɪ] *vt* **-fied; -fying** : horrorizar
horrifying [ˈhɔrə,faɪɪŋ] *adj* : horripilante, horroroso
horror [ˈhɔrər] *n* : horror *m*
hors d'oeuvre [ɔrˈdərv] *n, pl* **hors d'oeuvres** [-ˈdərvz] : entremés *m*
horse [ˈhɔrs] *n* : caballo *m*
horseback [ˈhɔrs,bæk] *n* **on ~** : a caballo
horse chestnut *n* : castaña *f* de Indias
horsefly [ˈhɔrs,flaɪ] *n, pl* **-flies** : tábano *m*
horsehair [ˈhɔrs,hær] *n* : crin *f*
horseman [ˈhɔrsmən] *n, pl* **-men** [-mən, -,mɛn] : jinete *m*, caballista *m*
horsemanship [ˈhɔrsmən,ʃɪp] *n* : equitación *f*
horseplay [ˈhɔrs,pleɪ] *n* : payasadas *fpl*
horsepower [ˈhɔrs,paʊər] *n* : caballo *m* de fuerza
horseradish [ˈhɔrs,rædɪʃ] *n* : rábano *m* picante
horseshoe [ˈhɔrs,ʃu:] *n* : herradura *f*
horsewhip [ˈhɔrs,*h*wɪp] *vt* **-whipped; -whipping** : azotar, darle fuetazos (a alguien)
horsewoman [ˈhɔrs,wʊmən] *n, pl* **-women** [-,wɪmən] : amazona *f*, jinete *f*, caballista *f*
horsey *or* **horsy** [ˈhɔrsi] *adj* **horsier; -est** : relacionado a los caballos, caballar
horticultural [,hɔrt̬əˈkʌlʧərəl] *adj* : hortícola
horticulture [ˈhɔrt̬ə,kʌlʧər] *n* : horticultura *f*
hose[1] [ˈho:z] *vt* **hosed; hosing** : regar o lavar con manguera
hose[2] *n* **1** *pl* **hose** SOCKS : calcetines *mpl*, medias *fpl* **2** *pl* **hose** STOCKINGS : medias *fpl* **3** *pl* **hoses** : manguera *f*, manga *f*
hosiery [ˈho:ʒəri, ˈho:zə-] *n* : calcetería *f*, medias *fpl*
hospice [ˈhɑspəs] *n* : hospicio *m*
hospitable [hɑˈspɪt̬əbəl, ˈhɑs,pɪ-] *adj* : hospitalario — **hospitably** [-bli] *adv*
hospital [ˈhɑs,pɪt̬əl] *n* : hospital *m*
hospitality [,hɑspəˈtælət̬i] *n, pl* **-ties** : hospitalidad *f*
hospitalization [,hɑs,pɪt̬ələˈzeɪʃən] *n* : hospitalización *f*
hospitalize [ˈhɑs,pɪt̬əl,aɪz] *vt* **-ized; -izing** : hospitalizar
host[1] [ˈho:st] *vt* : presentar (un programa de televisión, etc.)
host[2] *n* **1** : anfitrión *m*, -triona *f* (en la casa, a un evento); presentador *m*, -dora *f* (de un programa de televisión, etc.) **2** *or* **host organism** : huésped *m*

3 TROOPS : huestes *fpl* **4** MULTITUDE : multitud *f* ⟨for a host of reasons : por muchas razones⟩ **5** EUCHARIST : hostia *f*, Eucaristía *f*

hostage ['hɑstɪʤ] *n* : rehén *m*

hostel ['hɑstəl] *n* : albergue *m* juvenil

hostess ['ho:stɪs] *n* : anfitriona *f* (en la casa), presentadora *f* (de un programa)

hostile ['hɑstəl, -ˌtaɪl] *adj* : hostil — **hostilely** *adv*

hostility [hɑs'tɪləṭi] *n, pl* **-ties** : hostilidad *f*

hot ['hɑt] *adj* **hotter; hottest 1** : caliente, cálido, caluroso ⟨hot water : agua caliente⟩ ⟨a hot climate : un clima cálido⟩ ⟨a hot day : un día caluroso⟩ **2** ARDENT, FIERY : ardiente, acalorado ⟨to have a hot temper : tener mal genio⟩ **3** SPICY : picante **4** FRESH : reciente, nuevo ⟨hot news : noticias de última hora⟩ **5** EAGER : ávido **6** STOLEN : robado

hot air *n* : palabrería *f*

hotbed ['hɑtˌbɛd] *n* **1** : semillero *m* (de plantas) **2** : hervidero *m*, semillero *m* (de crimen, etc.)

hot dog *n* : perro *m* caliente

hotel [ho:'tɛl] *n* : hotel *m*

hothead ['hɑtˌhɛd] *n* : exaltado *m*, -da *f*

hotheaded ['hɑt'hɛdəd] *adj* : exaltado

hothouse ['hɑtˌhaʊs] *n* : invernadero *m*

hot plate *n* : placa *f* (de cocina)

hot rod *n* : coche *m* con motor modificado

hot water *n* **to get into hot water** : meterse en un lío

hound[1] ['haʊnd] *vt* : acosar, perseguir

hound[2] *n* : perro *m* (de caza)

hour ['aʊər] *n* : hora *f*

hourglass ['aʊərˌglæs] *n* : reloj *m* de arena

hourly ['aʊərli] *adv & adj* : cada hora, por hora

house[1] ['haʊz] *vt* **housed; housing** : albergar, alojar, hospedar

house[2] ['haʊs] *n, pl* **houses** ['haʊzəz, -səz] **1** HOME : casa *f* **2** : cámara *f* (del gobierno) **3** BUSINESS : casa *f*, empresa *f*

houseboat ['haʊsˌbo:t] *n* : casa *f* flotante

housebroken ['haʊsˌbro:kən] *adj* : enseñado

housefly ['haʊsˌflaɪ] *n, pl* **-flies** : mosca *f* común

household[1] ['haʊsˌho:ld] *adj* **1** DOMESTIC : doméstico, de la casa **2** FAMILIAR : conocido por todos

household[2] *n* : casa *f*, familia *f*

householder ['haʊsˌho:ldər] *n* : dueño *m*, -ña *f* de casa

housekeeper ['haʊsˌki:pər] *n* : ama *f* de llaves

housekeeping ['haʊsˌki:pɪŋ] *n* : gobierno *m* de la casa, quehaceres *mpl* domésticos

housemaid ['haʊsˌmeɪd] *n* : criada *f*, mucama *f*, muchacha *f*, sirvienta *f*

housewarming ['haʊsˌwɔrmɪŋ] *n* : fiesta *f* de estreno de una casa

housewife ['haʊsˌwaɪf] *n, pl* **-wives** : ama *f* de casa

housework ['haʊsˌwərk] *n* : faenas *fpl* domésticas, quehaceres *mpl* domésticos

housing ['haʊzɪŋ] *n* **1** HOUSES : vivienda *f* **2** COVERING : caja *f* protectora

hove → **heave**

hovel ['hʌvəl, 'hɑ-] *n* : casucha *f*, tugurio *m*

hover ['hʌvər, 'hɑ-] *vi* **1** : cernerse, sostenerse en el aire **2 to hover about** : rondar

how ['haʊ] *adv* **1** : cómo ⟨how are you? : ¿cómo estás?⟩ ⟨I don't know how to fix it : no se cómo arreglarlo⟩ **2** : qué ⟨how beautiful! : ¡qué bonito!⟩ **3** : cuánto ⟨how old are you? : ¿cuántos años tienes?⟩ **4 how about . . . ?** : ¿qué te parece . . . ?

however[1] [haʊ'ɛvər] *adv* **1** : por mucho que, por más que ⟨however hot it is : por mucho calor que haga⟩ **2** NEVERTHELESS : sin embargo, no obstante

however[2] *conj* : comoquiera que, de cualquier manera que

howl[1] ['haʊl] *vi* : aullar

howl[2] *n* : aullido *m*, alarido *m*

hub ['hʌb] *n* **1** CENTER : centro *m* **2** : cubo *m* (de una rueda)

hubbub ['hʌˌbʌb] *n* : algarabía *f*, alboroto *m*, jaleo *m*

hubcap ['hʌbˌkæp] *n* : tapacubos *m*

huckster ['hʌkstər] *n* : buhonero *m*, -ra *f*; vendedor *m*, -dora *f* ambulante

huddle[1] ['hʌdəl] *vi* **-dled; -dling 1** : apiñarse, amontonarse **2 to huddle together** : acurrucarse

huddle[2] *n* : grupo *m* (cerrado) ⟨to go into a huddle : conferenciar en secreto⟩

hue ['hju:] *n* : color *m*, tono *m*

huff ['hʌf] *n* : enojo *m*, enfado *m* ⟨to be in a huff : estar enojado⟩

huffy ['hʌfi] *adj* **huffier; -est** : enojado, enfadado

hug[1] ['hʌg] *vt* **hugged; hugging 1** EMBRACE : abrazar **2** : ir pegado a ⟨the road hugs the river : el camino está pegado al río⟩

hug[2] *n* : abrazo *m*

huge ['hju:ʤ] *adj* **huger; hugest** : inmenso, enorme — **hugely** *adv*

hulk ['hʌlk] *n* **1** : persona *f* fornida **2** : casco *m* (barco), armatoste *m* (edificio, etc.)

hulking ['hʌlkɪŋ] *adj* : grandote *fam*, pesado

hull[1] ['hʌl] *vt* : pelar

hull[2] *n* **1** HUSK : cáscara *f* **2** : casco *m* (de un barco, un avión, etc.)

hullabaloo ['hʌləbəˌlu:] *n, pl* **-loos** : alboroto *m*, jaleo *m*

hum[1] ['hʌm] *v* **hummed; humming** *vi* **1** BUZZ : zumbar **2** : estar muy activo, moverse ⟨to hum with activity : bullir de actividad⟩ — *vt* : tararear (una melodía)

hum[2] *n* : zumbido *m*, murmullo *m*
human[1] [ˈhjuːmən, ˈjuː-] *adj* : humano — **humanly** *adv*
human[2] *n* : ser *m* humano
humane [hjuːˈmeɪn, juː-] *adj* : humano, humanitario — **humanely** *adv*
humanism [ˈhjuːməˌnɪzəm, ˈjuː-] *n* : humanismo *m*
humanist[1] [ˈhjuːmənɪst, ˈjuː-] *n* : humanista *mf*
humanist[2] *or* **humanistic** [ˌhjuːməˈnɪstɪk, ˌjuː-] *adj* : humanístico
humanitarian[1] [hjuːˌmænəˈtriən, juː-] *adj* : humanitario
humanitarian[2] *n* : humanitario *m*, -ria *f*
humanity [hjuːˈmænəṯi, juː-] *n, pl* **-ties** : humanidad *f*
humankind [ˈhjuːmənˈkaɪnd, ˈjuː-] *n* : género *m* humano
humble[1] [ˈhʌmbəl] *vt* **-bled; -bling 1** : humillar **2 to humble oneself** : humillarse
humble[2] *adj* **-bler; -blest** : humilde, modesto — **humbly** [ˈhʌmbli] *adv*
humbug [ˈhʌmˌbʌg] *n* **1** FRAUD : charlatán *m*, -tana *f*; farsante *mf* **2** NONSENSE : patrañas *fpl*, tonterías *fpl*
humdrum [ˈhʌmˌdrʌm] *adj* : monótono, rutinario
humid [ˈhjuːməd, ˈjuː-] *adj* : húmedo
humidifier [hjuːˈmɪdəˌfaɪər, juː-] *n* : humidificador *m*
humidify [hjuːˈmɪdəˌfaɪ, juː-] *vt* **-fied; -fying** : humidificar
humidity [hjuːˈmɪdəṯi, juː-] *n, pl* **-ties** : humedad *f*
humiliate [hjuːˈmɪliˌeɪt, juː-] *vt* **-ated; -ating** : humillar
humiliating [hjuːˈmɪliˌeɪṯɪŋ, juː-] *adj* : humillante
humiliation [hjuːˌmɪliˈeɪʃən, juː-] *n* : humillación *f*
humility [hjuːˈmɪləṯi, juː-] *n* : humildad *f*
hummingbird [ˈhʌmɪŋˌbərd] *n* : colibrí *m*, picaflor *m*
hummock [ˈhʌmək] *n* : montículo *m*
humor[1] [ˈhjuːmər, ˈjuː-] *vt* : seguir el humor a, complacer
humor[2] *n* : humor *m*
humorist [ˈhjuːmərɪst, ˈjuː-] *n* : humorista *mf*
humorless [ˈhjuːmərləs, ˈjuː-] *adj* : sin sentido del humor ⟨a humorless smile : una sonrisa forzada⟩
humorous [ˈhjuːmərəs, ˈjuː-] *adj* : humorístico, cómico — **humorously** *adv*
hump [ˈhʌmp] *n* : joroba *f*, giba *f*
humpback [ˈhʌmpˌbæk] *n* **1** HUMP : joroba *f*, giba *f* **2** HUNCHBACK : jorobado *m*, -da *f*; giboso *m*, -sa *f*
humpbacked [ˈhʌmpˌbækt] *adj* : jorobado, giboso
humus [ˈhjuːməs, ˈjuː-] *n* : humus *m*
hunch[1] [ˈhʌntʃ] *vt* : encorvar — *vi or* **to hunch up** : encorvarse
hunch[2] *n* PREMONITION : presentimiento *m*
hunchback [ˈhʌntʃˌbæk] *n* **1** HUMP : joroba *f*, giba *f* **2** HUMPBACK : jorobado *m*, -da *f*; giboso *m*, -sa *f*
hunchbacked [ˈhʌntʃˌbækt] *adj* : jorobado, giboso
hundred[1] [ˈhʌndrəd] *adj* : cien, ciento
hundred[2] *n, pl* **-dreds** *or* **-dred** : ciento *m*
hundredth[1] [ˈhʌndrədθ] *adj* : centésimo
hundredth[2] *n* **1** : centésimo *m*, -ma *f* (en una serie) **2** : centésimo *m*, centésima parte *f*
hung → **hang**
Hungarian [hʌŋˈgæriən] *n* **1** : húngaro *m*, -ra *f* **2** : húngaro *m* (idioma) — **Hungarian** *adj*
hunger[1] [ˈhʌŋgər] *vi* **1** : tener hambre **2 to hunger for** : ansiar, anhelar
hunger[2] *n* : hambre *m*
hungrily [ˈhʌŋgrəli] *adv* : ávidamente
hungry [ˈhʌŋgri] *adj* **-grier; -est 1** : hambriento **2 to be hungry** : tener hambre
hunk [ˈhʌŋk] *n* : trozo *m*, pedazo *m*
hunt[1] [ˈhʌnt] *vt* **1** PURSUE : cazar **2 to hunt for** : buscar
hunt[2] *n* **1** PURSUIT : caza *f*, cacería *f* **2** SEARCH : búsqueda *f*, busca *f*
hunter [ˈhʌntər] *n* : cazador *m*, -dora *f*
hunting [ˈhʌntɪŋ] *n* : caza *f* ⟨to go hunting : ir de caza⟩
hurdle[1] [ˈhərdəl] *vt* **-dled; -dling** : saltar, salvar (un obstáculo)
hurdle[2] *n* : valla *f* (en deportes), obstáculo *m*
hurl [ˈhərl] *vt* : arrojar, tirar, lanzar
hurrah [hʊˈrɑ, -ˈrɔ] *interj* : ¡hurra!
hurricane [ˈhərəˌkeɪn] *n* : huracán *m*
hurried [ˈhərid] *adj* : apresurado, precipitado
hurriedly [ˈhərədli] *adv* : apresuradamente, de prisa
hurry[1] [ˈhəri] *v* **-ried; -rying** *vi* : apurarse, darse prisa, apresurarse — *vt* : apurar, darle prisa (a alguien)
hurry[2] *n* : prisa *f*, apuro *f*
hurt[1] [ˈhərt] *v* **hurt; hurting** *vt* **1** INJURE : hacer daño a, herir, lastimar ⟨to hurt oneself : hacerse daño⟩ **2** DISTRESS, OFFEND : hacer sufrir, ofender, herir — *vi* : doler ⟨my foot hurts : me duele el pie⟩
hurt[2] *n* **1** INJURY : herida *f* **2** DISTRESS, PAIN : dolor *m*, pena *f*
hurtful [ˈhərtfəl] *adj* : hiriente, doloroso
hurtle [ˈhərṯəl] *vi* **-tled; -tling** : lanzarse, precipitarse
husband[1] [ˈhʌzbənd] *vt* : economizar, bien administrar
husband[2] *n* : esposo *m*, marido *m*
husbandry [ˈhʌzbəndri] *n* **1** MANAGEMENT, THRIFT : economía *f*, buena administración *f* **2** AGRICULTURE : agricultura *f* ⟨animal husbandry : cría de animales⟩
hush[1] [ˈhʌʃ] *vt* **1** SILENCE : hacer callar, acallar **2** CALM : calmar, apaciguar
hush[2] *n* : silencio *m*

hush–hush [ˈhʌʃˌhʌʃ, ˌhʌʃˈhʌʃ] *adj* : muy secreto, confidencial
husk[1] [ˈhʌsk] *vt* : descascarar
husk[2] *n* : cáscara *f*
huskily [ˈhʌskəli] *adv* : con voz ronca
husky[1] [ˈhʌski] *adj* **-kier; -est 1** HOARSE : ronco **2** BURLY : fornido
husky[2] *n, pl* **-kies** : perro *m*, -rra *f* esquimal
hustle[1] [ˈhəsəl] *v* **-tled; -tling** *vt* : darle prisa (a alguien), apurar <they hustled me in : me hicieron entrar a empujones> — *vi* : apurarse, ajetrearse
hustle[2] *n* BUSTLE : ajetreo *m*
hut [ˈhʌt] *n* : cabaña *f*, choza *f*, barraca *f*
hutch [ˈhʌtʃ] *n* **1** CUPBOARD : alacena *f* **2 rabbit hutch** : conejera *f*
hyacinth [ˈhaɪəˌsɪnθ] *n* : jacinto *m*
hybrid[1] [ˈhaɪbrɪd] *adj* : híbrido
hybrid[2] *n* : híbrido *m*
hydrant [ˈhaɪdrənt] *n* : boca *f* de riego, hidrante *m CA, Col* <fire hydrant : boca de incendios>
hydraulic [haɪˈdrɔlɪk] *adj* : hidráulico — **hydraulically** *adv*
hydrocarbon [ˌhaɪdroˈkɑrbən] *n* : hidrocarburo *m*
hydrochloric acid [ˌhaɪdroˈklorɪk] *n* : ácido *m* clorhídrico
hydroelectric [ˌhaɪdroɪˈlɛktrɪk] *adj* : hidroeléctrico
hydrogen [ˈhaɪdrədʒən] *n* : hidrógeno *m*
hydrogen bomb *n* : bomba *f* de hidrógeno
hydrogen peroxide *n* : agua *f* oxigenada, peróxido *m* de hidrógeno
hydrophobia [ˌhaɪdrəˈfoːbiə] *n* : hidrofobia *f*, rabia *f*
hydroplane [ˈhaɪdrəˌpleɪn] *n* : hidroplano *m*
hyena [haɪˈiːnə] *n* : hiena *f*
hygiene [ˈhaɪˌdʒiːn] *n* : higiene *f*
hygienic [haɪˈdʒɛnɪk, -ˈdʒiː-; ˌhaɪ-dʒiˈnɪk] *adj* : higiénico — **hygienically** [-nɪkli] *adv*
hygienist [haɪˈdʒiːnɪst, -ˈdʒɛ-; ˈhaɪ-ˌdʒiː-] *n* : higienista *mf*
hygrometer [haɪˈgrɑmət̬ər] *n* : higrómetro *m*
hymn [ˈhɪm] *n* : himno *m*
hymnal [ˈhɪmnəl] *n* : himnario *m*
hype [ˈhaɪp] *n* : bombo *m* publicitario
hyperactive [ˌhaɪpərˈæktɪv] *adj* : hiperactivo
hyperactivity [ˌhaɪpərˌækˈtɪvət̬i] *n, pl* **-ties** : hiperactividad *f*
hyperbole [haɪˈpərbəli] *n* : hipérbole *f*
hyperbolic [ˌhaɪpərˈbɑlɪk] *adj* : hiperbólico
hypercritical [ˌhaɪpərˈkrɪt̬əkəl] *adj* : hipercrítico
hypersensitivity [ˌhaɪpərˌsɛntsəˈtɪ-vət̬i] *n* : hipersensibilidad *f*
hypertension [ˈhaɪpərˌtɛntʃən] *n* : hipertensión *f*
hyphen [ˈhaɪfən] *n* : guión *m*
hyphenate [ˈhaɪfənˌeɪt] *vt* **-ated; -ating** : escribir con guión
hypnosis [hɪpˈnoːsɪs] *n, pl* **-noses** [-ˌsiːz] : hipnosis *f*
hypnotic [hɪpˈnɑt̬ɪk] *adj* : hipnótico, hipnotizador
hypnotism [ˈhɪpnəˌtɪzəm] *n* : hipnotismo *m*
hypnotize [ˈhɪpnəˌtaɪz] *vt* **-tized; -tizing** : hipnotizar
hypochondria [ˌhaɪpəˈkɑndriə] *n* : hipocondría *f*
hypochondriac [ˌhaɪpəˈkɑndriˌæk] *n* : hipocondríaco *m*, -ca *f*
hypocrisy [hɪpˈɑkrəsi] *n, pl* **-sies** : hipocresía *f*
hypocrite [ˈhɪpəˌkrɪt] *n* : hipócrita *mf*
hypocritical [ˌhɪpəˈkrɪt̬ɪkəl] *adj* : hipócrita
hypodermic[1] [ˌhaɪpəˈdərmɪk] *adj* : hipodérmico
hypodermic[2] *n* : aguja *f* hipodérmica
hypotenuse [haɪˈpɑtənˌuːs, -ˌuːz, -ˌjuːs, -ˌjuːz] *n* : hipotenusa *f*
hypothesis [haɪˈpɑθəsɪs] *n, pl* **-eses** [-ˌsiːz] : hipótesis *f*
hypothetical [ˌhaɪpəˈθɛt̬ɪkəl] *adj* : hipotético — **hypothetically** [-t̬ɪkli] *adv*
hysteria [hɪsˈtɛriə, -tɪr-] *n* : histeria *f*, histerismo *m*
hysterical [hɪsˈtɛrɪkəl] *adj* : histérico — **hysterically** [-ɪkli] *adv*
hysterics [hɪsˈtɛrɪks] *n* : histeria *f*, histerismo *m*

I

i [ˈaɪ] *n, pl* **i's** *or* **is** [ˈaɪz] : novena letra del alfabeto inglés
I [ˈaɪ] *pron* : yo
Iberian [aɪˈbɪriən] *adj* : ibérico
ibis [ˈaɪbəs] *n, pl* **ibis** *or* **ibises** : ibis *f*
ice[1] [ˈaɪs] *v* **iced; icing** *vt* **1** FREEZE : congelar, helar **2** CHILL : enfriar **3 to ice a cake** : escarchar un pastel — *vi* : helarse, congelarse
ice[2] *n* **1** : hielo *m* **2** SHERBET : sorbete *m*, nieve *f Cuba, Mex, PRi*
iceberg [ˈaɪsˌbərg] *n* : iceberg *m*
icebox [ˈaɪsˌbɑks] → **refrigerator**
icebreaker [ˈaɪsˌbreɪkər] *n* : rompehielos *m*
ice cap *n* : casquete *m* glaciar
ice–cold [ˈaɪsˈkoːld] *adj* : helado
ice cream *n* : helado *m*, mantecado *m PRi*
Icelander [ˈaɪsˌlændər, -lən-] *n* : islandés *m*, -desa *f*
Icelandic[1] [aɪsˈlændɪk] *adj* : islandés

Icelandic² *n* : islandés *m* (idioma)
ice–skate [ˈaɪsˌskeɪt] *vi* **-skated; -skating** : patinar
ice skater *n* : patinador *m*, -dora *f*
ichthyology [ˌɪkthiˈɑləʤi] *n* : ictiología *f*
icicle [ˈaɪˌsɪkəl] *n* : carámbano *m*
icily [ˈaɪsəli] *adv* : fríamente, con frialdad ⟨he stared at me icily : me fijó la mirada con mucha frialdad⟩
icing [ˈaɪsɪŋ] *n* : glaseado *m*, betún *m Mex*
icon [ˈaɪˌkɑn, -kən] *n* : icono *m*
iconoclasm [aɪˈkɑnəˌklæzəm] *n* : iconoclasia *f*
iconoclast [aɪˈkɑnəˌklæst] *n* : iconoclasta *mf*
icy [ˈaɪsi] *adj* **icier; -est 1** : cubierto de hielo ⟨an icy road : una carretera cubierta de hielo⟩ **2** FREEZING : helado, gélido, glacial **3** ALOOF : frío, distante
id [ˈɪd] *n* : id *m*
I'd [ˈaɪd] (*contraction of* **I should** *or* **I would**) → **should, would**
idea [aɪˈdiːə] *n* : idea *f*
ideal¹ [aɪˈdiːəl] *adj* : ideal
ideal² *n* : ideal *m*
idealism [aɪˈdiːəˌlɪzəm] *n* : idealismo *m*
idealist [aɪˈdiːəlɪst] *n* : idealista *mf*
idealistic [aɪˌdiːəˈlɪstɪk] *adj* : idealista
idealistically [aɪˌdiːəˈlɪstɪkli] *adv* : con idealismo
idealization [aɪˌdiːələˈzeɪʃən] *n* : idealización *f*
idealize [aɪˈdiːəˌlaɪz] *vt* **-ized; -izing** : idealizar
ideally [aɪˈdiːəli] *adv* : perfectamente
identical [aɪˈdɛntɪkəl] *adj* : idéntico — **identically** [-tɪkli] *adv*
identifiable [aɪˌdɛntəˈfaɪəbəl] *adj* : identificable
identification [aɪˌdɛntəfəˈkeɪʃən] *n* **1** : identificación *f* **2 identification card** : carnet *m*, cédula *f* de identidad, identificación *f*
identify [aɪˈdɛntəˌfaɪ] *v* **-fied; -fying** *vt* : identificar — *vi* **to identify with** : identificarse con
identity [aɪˈdɛntət̬i] *n, pl* **-ties** : identidad *f*
ideological [ˌaɪdiəˈlɑʤɪkəl, ˌɪ-] *adj* : ideológico — **ideologically** [-ʤɪkli] *adv*
ideology [ˌaɪdiˈɑləʤi, ˌɪ-] *n, pl* **-gies** : ideología *f*
idiocy [ˈɪdiəsi] *n, pl* **-cies 1** : idiotez *f* **2** NONSENSE : estupidez *f*, tontería *f*
idiom [ˈɪdiəm] *n* **1** LANGUAGE : lenguaje *m* **2** EXPRESSION : modismo *m*, expresión *f* idiomática
idiomatic [ˌɪdiəˈmæt̬ɪk] *adj* : idiomático
idiosyncrasy [ˌɪdioˈsɪŋkrəsi] *n, pl* **-sies** : idiosincrasia *f*
idiosyncratic [ˌɪdiosɪnˈkræt̬ɪk] *adj* : idiosincrásico — **idiosyncratically** [-t̬ɪkli] *adv*
idiot [ˈɪdiət] *n* **1** : idiota *mf* (en medicina) **2** FOOL : idiota *mf*; tonto *m*, -ta *f*; imbécil *mf fam*
idiotic [ˌɪdiˈɑt̬ɪk] *adj* : estúpido, idiota
idiotically [ˌɪdiˈɑt̬ɪkli] *adv* : estúpidamente
idle¹ [ˈaɪdəl] *v* **idled; idling** *vi* **1** LOAF : holgazanear, flojear, haraganear **2** : andar al ralentí (dícese de un automóvil), marchar en vacío (dícese de una máquina) — *vt* : dejar sin trabajo
idle² *adj* **idler; idlest 1** VAIN : frívolo, vano, infundado ⟨idle curiosity : pura curiosidad⟩ **2** INACTIVE : inactivo, parado, desocupado **3** LAZY : holgazán, haragán, perezoso
idleness [ˈaɪdəlnəs] *n* **1** INACTIVITY : inactividad *f*, ociosidad *f* **2** LAZINESS : holgazanería *f*, flojera *f*, pereza *f*
idler [ˈaɪdələr] *n* : haragán *m*, -gana *f*; holgazán *m*, -zana *f*
idly [ˈaɪdəli] *adv* : ociosamente
idol [ˈaɪdəl] *n* : ídolo *m*
idolater *or* **idolator** [aɪˈdɑlət̬ər] *n* : idólatra *mf*
idolatrous [aɪˈdɑlətrəs] *adj* : idólatra
idolatry [aɪˈdɑlətri] *n, pl* **-tries** : idolatría *f*
idolize [ˈaɪdəlaɪz] *vt* **-ized; -izing** : idolatrar
idyll [ˈaɪdəl] *n* : idilio *m*
idyllic [aɪˈdɪlɪk] *adj* : idílico
if [ˈɪf] *conj* **1** : si ⟨I would do it if I could : lo haría si pudiera⟩ ⟨if so : si es así⟩ ⟨as if : como si⟩ ⟨if I were you : yo que tú⟩ **2** WHETHER : si ⟨I don't know if they're ready : no sé si están listos⟩ **3** THOUGH : aunque, si bien ⟨it's pretty, if somewhat old-fashioned : es lindo aunque algo anticuado⟩
igloo [ˈɪˌgluː] *n, pl* **-loos** : iglú *m*
ignite [ɪgˈnaɪt] *v* **-nited; -niting** *vt* : prenderle fuego a, encender — *vi* : prender, encenderse
ignition [ɪgˈnɪʃən] *n* **1** IGNITING : ignición *f*, encendido *m* **2** *or* **ignition switch** : encendido *m*, arranque *m* ⟨to turn on the ignition : arrancar el motor⟩
ignoble [ɪgˈnoːbəl] *adj* : innoble — **ignobly** *adv*
ignominious [ˌɪgnəˈmɪniəs] *adj* : ignominioso, deshonroso — **ignominiously** *adv*
ignominy [ˈɪgnəˌmɪni] *n, pl* **-nies** : ignominia *f*
ignoramus [ˌɪgnəˈreɪməs] *n* : ignorante *mf*; bestia *mf*; bruto *m*, -ta *f*
ignorance [ˈɪgnərənts] *n* : ignorancia *f*
ignorant [ˈɪgnərənt] *adj* **1** : ignorante **2 to be ignorant of** : no ser consciente de, desconocer, ignorar
ignorantly [ˈɪgnərəntli] *adv* : ignorantemente, con ignorancia
ignore [ɪgˈnor] *vt* **-nored; -noring** : ignorar, hacer caso omiso de, no hacer caso de
iguana [ɪˈgwɑnə] *n* : iguana *f*, garrobo *f CA*
ilk [ˈɪlk] *n* : tipo *m*, clase *f*, índole *f*
ill¹ [ˈɪl] *adv* **worse** [ˈwərs]; **worst** [ˈwərst] : mal ⟨to speak ill of : hablar mal de⟩

⟨he can ill afford to fail : mal puede permitirse el lujo de fracasar⟩
ill² *adj* **worse; worst 1** SICK : enfermo **2** BAD : malo ⟨ill luck : mala suerte⟩
ill³ *n* **1** EVIL : mal *m* **2** MISFORTUNE : mal *m*, desgracia *f* **3** AILMENT : enfermedad *f*
I'll [ˈaɪl] (*contraction of* **I shall** *or* **I will**) → **shall, will**
illegal [ɪlˈliːgəl] *adj* : ilegal — **illegally** *adv*
illegality [ɪliˈgæləṭi] *n* : ilegalidad *f*
illegibility [ɪlˌlɛʤəˈbɪləṭi] *n, pl* **-ties** : ilegibilidad *f*
illegible [ɪlˈlɛʤəbəl] *adj* : ilegible — **illegibly** [-bli] *adv*
illegitimacy [ˌɪlɪˈʤɪṭəməsi] *n* : ilegitimidad *f*
illegitimate [ˌɪlɪˈʤɪṭəmət] *adj* **1** BASTARD : ilegítimo, bastardo **2** UNLAWFUL : ilegítimo, ilegal — **illegitimately** *adv*
ill–fated [ˈɪlˈfeɪṭəd] *adj* : malhadado, infortunado, desventurado
illicit [ɪlˈlɪsət] *adj* : ilícito — **illicitly** *adv*
illiteracy [ɪlˈlɪṭərəsi] *n, pl* **-cies** : analfabetismo *m*
illiterate¹ [ɪlˈlɪṭərət] *adj* : analfabeto
illiterate² *n* : analfabeto *m*, -ta *f*
ill–mannered [ˌɪlˈmanərd] *adj* : descortés, maleducado
ill–natured [ˌɪlˈneɪʧərd] *adj* : desagradable, de mal genio
ill–naturedly [ˌɪlˈneɪʧərdli] *adv* : desagradablemente
illness [ˈɪlnəs] *n* : enfermedad *f*
illogical [ɪlˈlɑʤɪkəl] *adj* : ilógico — **illogically** [-kli] *adv*
ill–tempered [ˌɪlˈtempərd] → **ill–natured**
ill–treat [ˌɪlˈtriːt] *vt* : maltratar
ill–treatment [ˌɪlˈtriːtmənt] *n* : maltrato *m*
illuminate [ɪˈluːməˌneɪt] *vt* **-nated; -nating 1** : iluminar, alumbrar **2** ELUCIDATE : esclarecer, elucidar
illumination [ɪˌluːməˈneɪʃən] *n* **1** LIGHTING : iluminación *f*, luz *f* **2** ELUCIDATION : esclarecimiento *m*, elucidación *f*
ill–use [ˈɪlˈjuːz] → **ill–treat**
illusion [ɪˈluːʒən] *n* : ilusión *f*
illusory [ɪˈluːsəri, -zəri] *adj* : engañoso, ilusorio
illustrate [ˈɪləsˌtreɪt] *v* **-trated; -trating** : ilustrar
illustration [ˌɪləˈstreɪʃən] *n* **1** PICTURE : ilustración *f* **2** EXAMPLE : ejemplo *m*, ilustración *f*
illustrative [ɪˈlʌstrəṭɪv, ˈɪləˌstreɪṭɪv] *adj* : ilustrativo — **illustratively** *adv*
illustrator [ˈɪləˌstreɪṭər] *n* : ilustrador *m*, -dora *f*; dibujante *mf*
illustrious [ɪˈlʌstriəs] *adj* : ilustre, eminente, glorioso
illustriousness [ɪˈlʌstriəsnəs] *n* : eminencia *f*, prestigio *m*
ill will *n* : animosidad *f*, malquerencia *f*, mala voluntad *f*
I'm [ˈaɪm] (*contraction of* **I am**) → **be**
image¹ [ˈɪmɪʤ] *vt* **-aged; -aging** : imaginar, crear una imagen de
image² *n* : imagen *f*
imagery [ˈɪmɪʤri] *n, pl* **-eries 1** IMAGES : imágenes *fpl* **2** : imaginería *f* (en el arte)
imaginable [ɪˈmæʤənəbəl] *adj* : imaginable — **imaginably** [-bli] *adv*
imaginary [ɪˈmæʤəˌnɛri] *adj* : imaginario
imagination [ɪˌmæʤəˈneɪʃən] *n* : imaginación *f*
imaginative [ɪˈmæʤənəṭɪv, -əˌneɪṭɪv] *adj* : imaginativo — **imaginatively** *adv*
imagine [ɪˈmæʤən] *vt* **-ined; -ining** : imaginar(se)
imbalance [ɪmˈbælən*t*s] *n* : desajuste *m*, desbalance *m*, desequilibrio *m*
imbecile¹ [ˈɪmbəsəl, -ˌsɪl] *or* **imbecilic** [ˌɪmbəˈsɪlɪk] *adj* : imbécil, estúpido
imbecile² *n* **1** : imbécil *mf* (en medicina) **2** FOOL : idiota *mf*; imbécil *mf fam*; estúpido *m*, -da *f*
imbecility [ˌɪmbəˈsɪləṭi] *n, pl* **-ties** : imbecilidad *f*
imbibe [ɪmˈbaɪb] *v* **-bibed; -bibing** *vt* **1** DRINK : beber **2** ABSORB : absorber, embeber — *vi* : beber
imbue [ɪmˈbjuː] *vt* **-bued; -buing** : imbuir
imitate [ˈɪməˌteɪt] *vt* **-tated; -tating** : imitar, remedar
imitation¹ [ˌɪməˈteɪʃən] *adj* : de imitación, artificial
imitation² *n* : imitación *f*
imitative [ˈɪməˌteɪṭɪv] *adj* : imitativo, imitador, poco original
imitator [ˈɪməˌteɪṭər] *n* : imitador *m*, -dora *f*
immaculate [ɪˈmækjələt] *adj* **1** PURE : inmaculado, puro **2** FLAWLESS : impecable, intachable — **immaculately** *adv*
immaterial [ˌɪməˈtɪriəl] *adj* **1** INCORPOREAL : incorpóreo **2** UNIMPORTANT : irrelevante, sin importancia
immature [ˌɪməˈʧʊr, -ˈtjʊr, -ˈtʊr] *adj* : inmaduro, verde (dícese de la fruta)
immaturity [ˌɪməˈʧʊrəṭi, -ˈtjʊr-, -ˈtʊr-] *n, pl* **-ties** : inmadurez *f*, falta *f* de madurez
immeasurable [ɪˈmɛʒərəbəl] *adj* : inconmensurable, incalculable — **immeasurably** [-bli] *adv*
immediacy [ɪˈmiːdiəsi] *n* : inmediatez *f*
immediate [ɪˈmiːdiət] *adj* **1** INSTANT : inmediato, instantáneo ⟨immediate relief : alivio instantáneo⟩ **2** DIRECT : inmediato, directo ⟨the immediate cause of death : la causa directa de la muerte⟩ **3** URGENT : urgente, apremiante **4** CLOSE : cercano, próximo, inmediato ⟨her immediate family : sus familiares más cercanos⟩ ⟨in the immediate vicinity : en los alrededores, en las inmediaciones⟩
immediately [ɪˈmiːdiətli] *adv* : inmediatamente, enseguida

immemorial [ˌɪmə'moriəl] *adj* : inmemorial
immense [ɪ'mɛnts] *adj* : inmenso, enorme — **immensely** *adv*
immensity [ɪ'mɛntsət̬i] *n, pl* **-ties** : inmensidad *f*
immerse [ɪ'mərs] *vt* **-mersed; -mersing** **1** SUBMERGE : sumergir **2 to immerse oneself in** : enfrascarse en
immersion [ɪ'mərʒən] *n* **1** : inmersión *f* (en un líquido) **2** : enfrascamiento *m* (en una actividad)
immigrant ['ɪmɪgrənt] *n* : inmigrante *mf*
immigrate ['ɪməˌgreɪt] *vi* **-grated; -grating** : inmigrar
immigration [ˌɪmə'greɪʃən] *n* : inmigración *f*
imminence ['ɪmənənts] *n* : inminencia *f*
imminent ['ɪmənənt] *adj* : inminente — **imminently** *adv*
immobile [ɪm'oːbəl] *adj* **1** FIXED, IMMOVABLE : inmovible, fijo **2** MOTIONLESS : inmóvil
immobility [ˌɪmo'bɪlət̬i] *n, pl* **-ties** : inmovilidad *f*
immobilize [ɪ'moːbəˌlaɪz] *vt* **-lized; -lizing** : inmovilizar, paralizar
immoderate [ɪ'mɑdərət] *adj* : inmoderado, desmesurado, desmedido, excesivo — **immoderately** *adv*
immodest [ɪ'mɑdəst] *adj* **1** INDECENT : inmodesto, indecente, impúdico **2** CONCEITED : inmodesto, presuntuoso, engreído — **immodestly** *adv*
immodesty [ɪ'mɑdəsti] *n* : inmodestia *f*
immoral [ɪ'mɔrəl] *adj* : inmoral
immorality [ˌɪmɔ'rælət̬i, ˌɪmə-] *n, pl* **-ties** : inmoralidad *f*
immorally [ɪ'mɔrəli] *adv* : de manera inmoral
immortal[1] [ɪ'mɔrtəl] *adj* : inmortal
immortal[2] *n* : inmortal *mf*
immortality [ˌɪˌmɔr'tælət̬i] *n* : inmortalidad *f*
immortalize [ɪ'mɔrtəlˌaɪz] *vt* **-ized; -izing** : inmortalizar
immovable [ɪ'muːvəbəl] *adj* **1** FIXED : fijo, inmovible **2** UNYIELDING : inflexible
immune [ɪ'mjuːn] *adj* **1** : inmune ⟨immune to smallpox : inmune a la viruela⟩ **2** EXEMPT : exento, inmune
immune system *n* : sistema *m* inmunológico
immunity [ɪ'mjuːnət̬i] *n, pl* **-ties** **1** : inmunidad *f* **2** EXEMPTION : exención *f*
immunization [ˌɪmjʊnə'zeɪʃən] *n* : inmunización *f*
immunize ['ɪmjʊˌnaɪz] *vt* **-nized; -nizing** : inmunizar
immunology [ˌɪmjʊ'nɑləʤi] *n* : inmunología *f*
immutable [ɪ'mjuːt̬əbəl] *adj* : inmutable
imp ['ɪmp] *n* RASCAL : diablillo *m*; pillo *m*, -lla *f*
impact[1] [ɪm'pækt] *vt* **1** STRIKE : chocar con, impactar **2** AFFECT : afectar, impactar, impresionar — *vi* **1** STRIKE : hacer impacto, golpear **2 to impact on** : tener un impacto sobre
impact[2] ['ɪmˌpækt] *n* **1** COLLISION : impacto *m*, choque *m*, colisión *f* **2** EFFECT : efecto *m*, impacto *m*, consecuencias *fpl*
impacted [ɪm'pæktəd] *adj* : impactado, incrustado (dícese de los dientes)
impair [ɪm'pær] *vt* : perjudicar, dañar, afectar
impairment [ɪm'pærmənt] *n* : perjuicio *m*, daño *m*
impala [ɪm'pɑlə, -'pæ-] *n, pl* **impalas** *or* **impala** : impala *m*
impale [ɪm'peɪl] *vt* **-paled; -paling** : empalar
impanel [ɪm'pænəl] *vt* **-eled** *or* **-elled; -eling** *or* **-elling** : elegir (un jurado)
impart [ɪm'pɑrt] *vt* **1** CONVEY : impartir, dar, conferir **2** DISCLOSE : revelar, divulgar
impartial [ɪm'pɑrʃəl] *adj* : imparcial — **impartially** *adv*
impartiality [ɪmˌpɑrʃi'ælət̬i] *n, pl* **-ties** : imparcialidad *f*
impassable [ɪm'pæsəbəl] *adj* : infranqueable, intransitable — **impassably** [-bli] *adv*
impasse ['ɪmˌpæs] *n* **1** DEADLOCK : impasse *m*, punto *m* muerto **2** DEAD END : callejón *m* sin salida
impassioned [ɪm'pæʃənd] *adj* : apasionado, vehemente
impassive [ɪm'pæsɪv] *adj* : impasible, indiferente
impassively [ɪm'pæsɪvli] *adv* : impasiblemente, sin emoción
impatience [ɪm'peɪʃənts] *n* : impaciencia *f*
impatient [ɪm'peɪʃənt] *adj* : impaciente — **impatiently** *adv*
impeach [ɪm'piːʧ] *vt* : destituir (a un funcionario) de su cargo
impeachment [ɪm'piːʧmənt] *n* **1** ACCUSATION : acusación *f* **2** DISMISSAL : destitución *f*
impeccable [ɪm'pɛkəbəl] *adj* : impecable — **impeccably** [-bli] *adv*
impecunious [ˌɪmpɪ'kjuːniəs] *adj* : falto de dinero
impede [ɪm'piːd] *vt* **-peded; -peding** : impedir, dificultar, obstaculizar
impediment [ɪm'pɛdəmənt] *n* **1** HINDRANCE : impedimento *m*, obstáculo *m* **2 speech impediment** : defecto *m* del habla
impel [ɪm'pɛl] *vt* **-pelled; -pelling** : impeler
impend [ɪm'pɛnd] *vi* : ser inminente
impenetrable [ɪm'pɛnətrəbəl] *adj* **1** : impenetrable ⟨an impenetrable forest : una selva impenetrable⟩ **2** INSCRUTABLE : incomprensible, inescrutable, impenetrable — **impenetrably** [-bli] *adv*
impenitent [ɪm'pɛnətənt] *adj* : impenitente

imperative[1] [ɪm'pɛrət̬ɪv] *adj* **1** AUTHORITATIVE : imperativo, imperioso **2** NECESSARY : imprescindible — **imperatively** *adv*
imperative[2] *n* : imperativo *m*
imperceptible [ˌɪmpər'sɛptəbəl] *adj* : imperceptible — **imperceptibly** [-bli] *adv*
imperfect [ɪm'pərfɪkt] *adj* : imperfecto, defectuoso — **imperfectly** *adv*
imperfection [ɪmˌpər'fkʃən] *n* : imperfección *f*, defecto *m*
imperial [ɪm'pɪriəl] *adj* **1** : imperial **2** SOVEREIGN : soberano **3** IMPERIOUS : imperioso, señorial
imperialism [ɪm'pɪriəˌlɪzəm] *n* : imperialismo *m*
imperialist[1] [ɪm'pɪriəlɪst] *adj* : imperialista
imperialist[2] *n* : imperialista *mf*
imperialistic [ɪmˌpɪriːə'lɪstɪk] *adj* : imperialista
imperil [ɪm'pɛrəl] *vt* **-iled** *or* **-illed; -iling** *or* **-illing** : poner en peligro
imperious [ɪm'pɪriəs] *adj* : imperioso — **imperiously** *adv*
imperishable [ɪm'pɛrɪʃəbəl] *adj* : imperecedero
impermanent [ɪm'pərmənənt] *adj* : pasajero, inestable, efímero — **impermanently** *adv*
impermeable [ɪm'pərmiəbəl] *adj* : impermeable
impersonal [ɪm'pərsənəl] *adj* : impersonal — **impersonally** *adv*
impersonate [ɪm'pərsənˌeɪt] *vt* **-ated; -ating** : hacerse pasar por, imitar
impersonation [ɪmˌpərsən'eɪʃən] *n* : imitación *f*
impersonator [ɪm'pərsənˌeɪt̬ər] *n* : imitador *m*, -dora *f*
impertinence [ɪm'pərtənən*t*s] *n* : impertinencia *f*
impertinent [ɪm'pərtənənt] *adj* **1** IRRELEVANT : impertinente, irrelevante **2** INSOLENT : impertinente, insolente
impertinently [ɪm'pərtənəntli] *adv* : con impertinencia, impertinentemente
imperturbable [ˌɪmpər'tərbəbəl] *adj* : imperturbable
impervious [ɪm'pərviəs] *adj* **1** IMPENETRABLE : impermeable **2** INSENSITIVE : insensible ⟨impervious to criticism : insensible a la crítica⟩
impetuosity [ɪmˌpɛʧʊ'ɑsət̬i] *n, pl* **-ties** : impetuosidad *f*
impetuous [ɪm'pɛʧʊəs] *adj* : impetuoso, impulsivo
impetuously [ɪm'pɛʧʊəsli] *adv* : de manera impulsiva, impetuosamente
impetus ['ɪmpət̬əs] *n* : ímpetu *m*, impulso *m*
impiety [ɪm'paɪət̬i] *n, pl* **-ties** : impiedad *f*
impinge [ɪm'pɪnʤ] *vi* **-pinged; -pinging** **1 to impinge on** AFFECT : afectar a, incidir en **2 to impinge on** VIOLATE : violar, vulnerar
impious ['ɪmpiəs, ɪm'paɪəs] *adj* : impío, irreverente
impish ['ɪmpɪʃ] *adj* MISCHIEVOUS : pícaro, travieso
impishly ['ɪmpɪʃli] *adv* : con picardía
implacable [ɪm'plækəbəl] *adj* : implacable — **implacably** [-bli] *adv*
implant[1] [ɪm'plænt] *vt* **1** INCULCATE, INSTILL : inculcar, implantar **2** INSERT : implantar, insertar
implant[2] ['ɪmˌplænt] *n* : implante *m* (de pelo), injerto *m* (de piel)
implantation [ˌɪmˌplæn'teɪʃən] *n* : implantación *f*
implausibility [ɪmˌplɔzə'bɪlət̬i] *n, pl* **-ties** : inverosimilitud *f*
implausible [ɪm'plɔzəbəl] *adj* : inverosímil, poco convincente
implement[1] ['ɪmpləˌmnt] *vt* : poner en práctica, implementar
implement[2] ['ɪmpləmənt] *n* : utensilio *m*, instrumento *m*, implemento *m*
implementation [ˌɪmpləmən'teɪʃən] *n* : implementación *f*, ejecución *f*, cumplimiento *m*
implicate ['ɪmpləˌkeɪt] *vt* **-cated; -cating** : implicar, involucrar
implication [ˌɪmplə'keɪʃən] *n* **1** CONSEQUENCE : implicación *f*, consecuencia *f* **2** INFERENCE : insinuación *f*, inferencia *f*
implicit [ɪm'plɪsət] *adj* **1** IMPLIED : implícito, tácito **2** ABSOLUTE : absoluto, completo ⟨implicit faith : fe ciega⟩ — **implicitly** *adv*
implied [ɪm'plaɪd] *adj* : implícito, tácito
implode [ɪm'ploːd] *vi* **-ploded; -ploding** : implosionar
implore [ɪm'plor] *vt* **-plored; -ploring** : implorar, suplicar
implosion [ɪm'ploːʒən] *n* : implosión *f*
imply [ɪm'plaɪ] *vt* **-plied; -plying** **1** SUGGEST : insinuar, dar a entender **2** INVOLVE : implicar, suponer ⟨rights imply obligations : los derechos implican unas obligaciones⟩
impolite [ˌɪmpə'laɪt] *adj* : descortés, maleducado
impoliteness [ˌɪmpə'laɪtnəs] *n* : descortesía *f*, falta *f* de educación
impolitic [ɪm'pɑləˌtɪk] *adj* : imprudente, poco político
imponderable[1] [ɪm'pɑndərəbəl] *adj* : imponderable
imponderable[2] *n* : imponderable *m*
import[1] [ɪm'port] *vt* **1** SIGNIFY : significar **2** : importar ⟨to import foreign cars : importar autos extranjeros⟩
import[2] ['ɪmˌport] *n* **1** SIGNIFICANCE : importancia *f*, significación *f* **2** → **importation**
importance [ɪm'portən*t*s] *n* : importancia *f*
important [ɪm'pɔrtənt] *adj* : importante
importantly [ɪm'pɔrtəntli] *adv* **1** : con importancia **2 more importantly** : lo que es más importante
importation [ˌɪmˌpɔr'teɪʃən] *n* : importación *f*
importer [ɪm'port̬ər] *n* : importador *m*, -dora *f*

importunate [ɪm'pɔrʧənət] *adj* : importuno, insistente
importune [ˌɪmpər'tu:n, -'tju:n; ɪm'pɔrʧən] *vt* **-tuned; -tuning** : importunar, implorar
impose [ɪm'po:z] *v* **-posed; -posing** *vt* : imponer ⟨to impose a tax : imponer un impuesto⟩ — *vi* **to impose on** : abusar de, molestar ⟨to impose on her kindness : abusar de su bondad⟩
imposing [ɪm'po:zɪŋ] *adj* : imponente, impresionante
imposition [ˌɪmpə'zɪʃən] *n* : imposición *f*
impossibility [ɪmˌpɑsə'bɪləṭi] *n, pl* **-ties** : imposibilidad *f*
impossible [ɪm'pɑsəbəl] *adj* **1** : imposible ⟨an impossible task : una tarea imposible⟩ ⟨to make life impossible for : hacerle la vida imposible a⟩ **2** UNACCEPTABLE : inaceptable
impossibly [ɪm'pɑsəbli] *adv* : imposiblemente, increíblemente
impostor *or* **imposter** [ɪm'pɑstər] *n* : impostor *m*, -tora *f*
impotence ['ɪmpəṭəntˢ] *n* : impotencia *f*
impotency ['ɪmpəṭəntˢsi] → **impotence**
impotent ['ɪmpəṭənt] *adj* : impotente
impound [ɪm'paʊnd] *vt* : incautar, embargar, confiscar
impoverish [ɪm'pɑvərɪʃ] *vt* : empobrecer
impoverishment [ɪm'pɑvərɪʃmənt] *n* : empobrecimiento *m*
impracticable [ɪm'præktɪkəbəl] *adj* : impracticable
impractical [ɪm'præktɪkəl] *adj* : poco práctico
imprecise [ˌɪmprɪ'saɪs] *adj* : impreciso
imprecisely [ˌɪmprɪ'saɪsli] *adv* : con imprecisión
impreciseness [ˌɪmprɪ'saɪsnəs] → **imprecision**
imprecision [ˌɪmprɪ'sɪʒən] *n* : imprecisión *f*, falta de precisión *f*
impregnable [ɪm'prɛgnəbəl] *adj* : inexpugnable, impenetrable, inconquistable
impregnate [ɪm'prɛgˌneɪt] *vt* **-nated; -nating** **1** FERTILIZE : fecundar **2** PERMEATE, SATURATE : impregnar, empapar, saturar
impresario [ˌɪmprə'sɑriˌo, -'sær-] *n, pl* **-rios** : empresario *m*, -ria *f*
impress [ɪm'prɛs] *vt* **1** IMPRINT : imprimir, estampar **2** : impresionar, causar impresión a ⟨I was not impressed : no me hizo buena impresión⟩ **3 to impress (something) on someone** : recalcarle (algo) a alguien — *vi* : impresionar, hacer una impresión
impression [ɪm'prɛʃən] *n* **1** IMPRINT : marca *f*, huella *f*, molde *m* (de los dientes) **2** EFFECT : impresión *f*, efecto *m*, impacto *m* **3** PRINTING : impresión *f* **4** NOTION : impresión *f*, noción *f*
impressionable [ɪm'prɛʃənəbəl] *adj* : impresionable
impressionism [ɪm'prɛʃəˌnɪzəm] *n* : impresionismo *m*
impressionist [ɪm'prɛʃənɪst] *n* : impresionista *mf* — **impressionist** *adj*
impressive [ɪm'prɛsɪv] *adj* : impresionante — **impressively** *adv*
impressiveness [ɪm'prɛsɪvnəs] *n* : calidad de ser impresionante
imprint[1] [ɪm'prɪnt, 'ɪmˌ-] *vt* : imprimir, estampar
imprint[2] ['ɪmˌprɪnt] *n* : marca *f*, huella *f*
imprison [ɪm'prɪzən] *vt* **1** JAIL : encarcelar, aprisionar **2** CONFINE : recluir, encerrar
imprisonment [ɪm'prɪzənmənt] *n* : encarcelamiento *m*
improbability [ɪmˌprɑbə'bɪləṭi] *n, pl* **-ties** : improbabilidad *f*, inverosimilitud *f*
improbable [ɪm'prɑbəbəl] *adj* : improbable, inverosímil
impromptu[1] [ɪm'prɑmpˌtu:, -ˌtju:] *adv* : sin preparación, espontáneamente
impromptu[2] *adj* : espontáneo, improvisado
impromptu[3] *n* : improvisación *f*
improper [ɪm'prɑpər] *adj* **1** INCORRECT : incorrecto, impropio **2** INDECOROUS : indecoroso
improperly [ɪm'prɑpərli] *adv* : incorrectamente, indebidamente
impropriety [ˌɪmprə'praɪəṭi] *n, pl* **-eties** **1** INDECOROUSNESS : indecoro *m*, falta *f* de decoro **2** ERROR : impropiedad *f*, incorrección *f*
improve [ɪm'pru:v] *v* **-proved; -proving** : mejorar
improvement [ɪm'pru:vmənt] *n* : mejoramiento *m*, mejora *f*
improvidence [ɪm'prɑvədəntˢ] *n* : imprevisión *f*
improvisation [ɪmˌprɑvə'zeɪʃən, ˌɪmprəvə-] *n* : improvisación *f*
improvise ['ɪmprəˌvaɪz] *v* **-vised; -vising** : improvisar
imprudence [ɪm'pru:dəntˢ] *n* : imprudencia *f*, indiscreción *f*
imprudent [ɪm'pru:dənt] *adj* : imprudente, indiscreto
impudence ['ɪmpjədəntˢ] *n* : insolencia *f*, descaro *m*
impudent ['ɪmpjədənt] *adj* : insolente, descarado — **impudently** *adv*
impugn [ɪm'pju:n] *vt* : impugnar
impulse ['ɪmˌpʌls] *n* **1** : impulso *m* **2 on impulse** : sin reflexionar
impulsive [ɪm'pʌlsɪv] *adj* : impulsivo — **impulsively** *adv*
impulsiveness [ɪm'pʌlsɪvnəs] *n* : impulsividad *f*
impunity [ɪm'pju:nəṭi] *n* **1** : impunidad *f* **2 with impunity** : impunemente
impure [ɪm'pjʊr] *adj* **1** : impuro ⟨impure thoughts : pensamientos impuros⟩ **2** CONTAMINATED : con impurezas, impuro
impurity [ɪm'pjʊrəṭi] *n, pl* **-ties** : impureza *f*

impute [ɪm'pju:t] *vt* **-puted; -puting** ATTRIBUTE : imputar, atribuir

in[1] ['ɪn] *adv* **1** INSIDE : dentro, adentro ⟨let's go in : vamos adentro⟩ **2** HARVESTED : recogido ⟨the crops are in : las cosechas ya están recogidas⟩ **3 to be in** : estar ⟨is Linda in? : ¿está Linda?⟩ **4 to be in** : estar en poder ⟨the Democrats are in : los demócratas están en el poder⟩ **5 to be in for** : ser objeto de, estar a punto de ⟨they're in for a treat : los van a agasajar⟩ ⟨he's in for a surprise : se va a llevar una sorpresa⟩ **6 to be in on** : participar en, tomar parte en

in[2] *adj* **1** INSIDE : interior ⟨the in part : la parte interior⟩ **2** FASHIONABLE : de moda

in[3] *prep* **1** (*indicating location or position*) ⟨in the lake : en el lago⟩ ⟨a pain in the leg : un dolor en la pierna⟩ ⟨in the sun : al sol⟩ ⟨in the rain : bajo la lluvia⟩ ⟨the best restaurant in Buenos Aires : el mejor restaurante de Buenos Aires⟩ **2** INTO : en, a ⟨he broke it in pieces : lo rompió en pedazos⟩ ⟨she went in the house : se metió a la casa⟩ **3** DURING : por, durante ⟨in the afternoon : por la tarde⟩ **4** WITHIN : dentro de ⟨I'll be back in a week : vuelvo dentro de una semana⟩ **5** (*indicating manner*) : en, con, de ⟨in Spanish : en español⟩ ⟨written in pencil : escrito con lápiz⟩ ⟨in this way : de esta manera⟩ **6** (*indicating states or circumstances*) ⟨to be in luck : tener suerte⟩ ⟨to be in love : estar enamorado⟩ ⟨to be in a hurry : tener prisa⟩ **7** (*indicating purpose*) : en ⟨in reply : en respuesta, como réplica⟩

in[4] *n* **ins and outs** : pormenores *mpl*

inability [ˌɪnə'bɪləṯi] *n, pl* **-ties** : incapacidad *f*

inaccessibility [ˌɪnɪkˌsɛsə'bɪləṯi] *n, pl* **-ties** : inaccesibilidad *f*

inaccessible [ˌɪnɪk'sɛsəbəl] *adj* : inaccesible

inaccuracy [ɪn'ækjərəsi] *n, pl* **-cies 1** : inexactitud *f* **2** MISTAKE : error *m*

inaccurate [ɪn'ækjərət] *n* : inexacto, erróneo, incorrecto

inaccurately [ɪn'ækjərətli] *adv* : incorrectamente, con inexactitud

inaction [ɪn'ækʃən] *n* : inactividad *f*, inacción *f*

inactive [ɪn'æktɪv] *adj* : inactivo

inactivity [ˌɪnˌæk'tɪvəṯi] *n, pl* **-ties** : inactividad *f*, ociosidad *f*

inadequacy [ɪn'ædɪkwəsi] *n, pl* **-cies 1** INSUFFICIENCY : insuficiencia *f* **2** INCOMPETENCE : ineptitud *f*, incompetencia *f*

inadequate [ɪn'ædɪkwət] *adj* **1** INSUFFICIENT : insuficiente, inadecuado **2** INCOMPETENT : inepto, incompetente

inadmissible [ˌɪnæd'mɪsəbəl] *adj* : inadmisible

inadvertent [ˌɪnəd'vərtənt] *adj* : inadvertido, involuntario — **inadvertently** *adv*

inadvisable [ˌɪnæd'vaɪzəbəl] *adj* : desaconsejable

inalienable [ɪn'eɪljənəbəl, -'eɪliənə-] *adj* : inalienable

inane [ɪ'neɪn] *adj* **inaner; -est** : estúpido, idiota, necio

inanimate [ɪn'ænəmət] *adj* : inanimado, exánime

inanity [ɪ'nænəṯi] *n, pl* **-ties 1** STUPIDITY : estupidez *f* **2** NONSENSE : idiotez *f*, disparate *m*

inapplicable [ɪn'æplɪkəbəl, ˌɪnə-'plɪkəbəl] *adj* IRRELEVANT : inaplicable, irrelevante

inappreciable [ˌɪnə'pri:ʃəbəl] *adj* : inapreciable, imperceptible

inappropriate [ˌɪnə'pro:priət] *adj* : inapropiado, inadecuado, impropio

inappropriateness [ˌɪnə'pro:priətnəs] *n* : lo inapropiado, impropiedad *f*

inapt [ɪn'æpt] *adj* **1** UNSUITABLE : inadecuado, inapropiado **2** INEPT : inepto

inarticulate [ˌɪnɑr'tɪkjələt] *adj* : inarticulado, incapaz de expresarse

inarticulately [ˌɪnɑr'tɪkjələtli] *adv* : inarticuladamente

inasmuch as [ˌɪnæz'mʌʧæz] *conj* : ya que, dado que, puesto que

inattention [ˌɪnə'tɛnʧən] *n* : falta *f* de atención, distracción *f*

inattentive [ˌɪnə'tɛntɪv] *adj* : distraído, despistado

inattentively [ˌɪnə'tɛntɪvli] *adv* : distraídamente, sin prestar atención

inaudible [ɪn'ɔdəbəl] *adj* : inaudible

inaudibly [ɪn'ɔdəbli] *adv* : de forma inaudible

inaugural[1] [ɪ'nɔgjərəl, -gərəl] *adj* : inaugural, de investidura

inaugural[2] *n* **1** *or* **inaugural address** : discurso *m* de investidura **2** INAUGURATION : investidura *f* (de una persona)

inaugurate [ɪ'nɔgjəˌreɪt, -gə-] *vt* **-rated; -rating 1** BEGIN : inaugurar **2** INDUCT : investir ⟨to inaugurate the president : investir al presidente⟩

inauguration [ɪˌnɔgjə'reɪʃən, -gə-] *n* **1** : inauguración *f* (de un edificio, un sistema, etc.) **2** : investidura *f* (de una persona)

inauspicious [ˌɪnɔ'spɪʃəs] *adj* : desfavorable, poco propicio

inborn ['ɪnˌbɔrn] *adj* **1** CONGENITAL, INNATE : innato, congénito **2** HEREDITARY : hereditario

inbred ['ɪnˌbrɛd] *adj* **1** : engendrado por endogamia **2** INNATE : innato

inbreed ['ɪnˌbri:d] *vt* **-bred; -breeding** : engendrar por endogamia

inbreeding ['ɪnˌbri:dɪŋ] *n* : endogamia *f*

Inca ['ɪŋkə] *n* : inca *mf*

incalculable [ɪn'kælkjələbəl] *adj* : incalculable — **incalculably** [-bli] *adv*

incandescence [ˌɪnkənˈdɛsənts] *n* : incandescencia *f*
incandescent [ˌɪnkənˈdɛsənt] *adj* **1** : incandescente **2** BRILLIANT : brillante
incantation [ˌɪnˌkænˈteɪʃən] *n* : conjuro *m*, ensalmo *m*
incapable [ɪnˈkeɪpəbəl] *adj* : incapaz
incapacitate [ˌɪnkəˈpæsəˌteɪt] *vt* **-tated; -tating** : incapacitar
incapacity [ˌɪnkəˈpæsət̬i] *n, pl* **-ties** : incapacidad *f*
incarcerate [ɪnˈkɑrsəˌreɪt] *vt* **-ated; -ating** : encarcelar
incarceration [ɪnˌkɑrsəˈreɪʃən] *n* : encarcelamiento *m*, encarcelación *f*
incarnate[1] [ɪnˈkɑrˌneɪt] *vt* **-nated; -nating** : encarnar
incarnate[2] [ɪnˈkɑrnət, -ˌneɪt] *adj* : encarnado
incarnation [ˌɪnˌkɑrˈneɪʃən] *n* : encarnación *f*
incendiary[1] [ɪnˈsɛndiˌri] *adj* : incendiario
incendiary[2] *n, pl* **-aries** : incendiario *m*, -ria *f*; pirómano *m*, -na *f*
incense[1] [ɪnˈsɛnts] *vt* **-censed; -censing** : indignar, enfadar, enfurecer
incense[2] [ˈɪnˌsɛnts] *n* : incienso *m*
incentive [ɪnˈsɛntɪv] *n* : incentivo *m*, aliciente *m*, motivación *f*, acicate *m*
inception [ɪnˈsɛpʃən] *n* : comienzo *m*, principio *m*
incessant [ɪnˈsɛsənt] *adj* : incesante, continuo — **incessantly** *adv*
incest [ˈɪnˌsɛst] *n* : incesto *m*
incestuous [ɪnˈsɛsʧuəs] *adj* : incestuoso
inch[1] [ˈɪnʧ] *v* : avanzar poco a poco
inch[2] *n* **1** : pulgada *f* **2 every inch** : absoluto, seguro <every inch a winner : un seguro ganador> **3 within an inch of** : a punto de
incidence [ˈɪntsədənts] *n* **1** FREQUENCY : frecuencia *f*, índice *m* <a high incidence of crime : un alto índice de crímenes> **2 angle of incidence** : ángulo *m* de incidencia
incident[1] [ˈɪntsədənt] *adj* : incidente
incident[2] *n* : incidente *m*, incidencia *f*, episodio *m* (en una obra de ficción)
incidental[1] [ˌɪntsəˈdɛntəl] *adj* **1** SECONDARY : incidental, secundario **2** ACCIDENTAL : casual, fortuito
incidental[2] *n* **1** : algo incidental **2 incidentals** *npl* : imprevistos *mpl*
incidentally [ˌɪntsəˈdɛntəli, -ˈdɛntli] *adv* **1** BY CHANCE : incidentalmente, casualmente **2** BY THE WAY : a propósito, por cierto
incinerate [ɪnˈsɪnəˌreɪt] *vt* **-ated; -ating** : incinerar
incinerator [ɪnˈsɪnəˌreɪt̬ər] *n* : incinerador *m*
incipient [ɪnˈsɪpiənt] *adj* : incipiente, naciente
incise [ɪnˈsaɪz] *vt* **-cised; -cising 1** ENGRAVE : grabar, cincelar, inscribir **2** : hacer una incisión en
incision [ɪnˈsɪʒən] *n* : incisión *f*
incisive [ɪnˈsaɪsɪv] *adj* : incisivo, penetrante
incisively [ɪnˈsaɪsɪvli] *adv* : con agudeza
incisor [ɪnˈsaɪzər] *n* : incisivo *m*
incite [ɪnˈsaɪt] *vt* **-cited; -citing** : incitar, instigar
incitement [ɪnˈsaɪtmənt] *n* : incitación *f*
inclemency [ɪnˈklɛməntsi] *n, pl* **-cies** : inclemencia *f*
inclement [ɪnˈklɛmənt] *adj* : inclemente, tormentoso
inclination [ˌɪnkləˈneɪʃən] *n* **1** PROPENSITY : inclinación *f*, tendencia *f* **2** DESIRE : deseo *m*, ganas *fpl* **3** BOW : inclinación *f*
incline[1] [ɪnˈklaɪn] *v* **-clined; -clining** *vi* **1** SLOPE : inclinarse **2** TEND : inclinarse, tender <he is inclined to be late : tiende a llegar tarde> — *vt* **1** LOWER : inclinar, bajar <to incline one's head : bajar la cabeza> **2** SLANT : inclinar **3** PREDISPOSE : predisponer
incline[2] [ˈɪnˌklaɪn] *n* : inclinación *f*, pendiente *f*
inclined [ɪnˈklaɪnd] *adj* **1** SLOPING : inclinado **2** PRONE : prono, dispuesto, dado
inclose, inclosure → **enclose, enclosure**
include [ɪnˈkluːd] *vt* **-cluded; -cluding** : incluir, comprender
inclusion [ɪnˈkluːʒən] *n* : inclusión *f*
inclusive [ɪnˈkluːsɪv] *adj* : inclusivo
incognito [ˌɪnˌkɑgˈniːt̬o, ɪnˈkɑgnəˌtoː] *adv & adj* : de incógnito
incoherence [ˌɪnkoˈhɪrənts, -ˈhɛr-] *n* : incoherencia *f*
incoherent [ˌɪnkoˈhɪrənt, -ˈhɛr-] *adj* : incoherente — **incoherently** *adv*
incombustible [ˌɪnkəmˈbʌstəbəl] *adj* : incombustible
income [ˈɪnˌkʌm] *n* : ingresos *mpl*, entradas *fpl*
income tax *n* : impuesto *m* sobre la renta
incoming [ˈɪnˌkʌmɪŋ] *adj* **1** ARRIVING : que se recibe (dícese del correo), que llega (dícese de las personas), ascendente (dícese de la marea) **2** NEW : nuevo, entrante <the incoming president : el nuevo presidente> <the incoming year : el año entrante>
incommunicado [ˌɪnkəˌmjuːnəˈkɑdo] *adj* : incomunicado
incomparable [ɪnˈkɑmpərəbəl] *adj* : incomparable, sin igual
incompatible [ˌɪnkəmˈpæt̬əbəl] *adj* : incompatible
incompetence [ɪnˈkɑmpət̬ənts] *n* : incompetencia *f*, impericia *f*, ineptitud *f*
incompetent [ɪnˈkɑmpət̬ənt] *adj* : incompetente, inepto, incapaz
incomplete [ˌɪnkəmˈpliːt] *adj* : incompleto — **incompletely** *adv*
incomprehensible [ˌɪnˌkɑmpriˈhɛntsəbəl] *adj* : incomprensible
inconceivable [ˌɪnkənˈsiːvəbəl] *adj* **1** INCOMPREHENSIBLE : incomprensible **2** UNBELIEVABLE : inconcebible, increíble

inconceivably [ˌɪnkənˈsi:vəbli] *adv* : inconcebiblemente, increíblemente
inconclusive [ˌɪnkənˈklu:sɪv] *adj* : inconcluyente, no decisivo
incongruity [ˌɪnkənˈgru:əṭi, -ˌkɑn-] *n, pl* **-ties** : incongruencia *f*
incongruous [ɪnˈkɑŋgrʊəs] *adj* : incongruente, inapropiado, fuera de lugar
incongruously [ɪnˈkɑŋgrʊəsli] *adv* : de manera incongruente, inapropiadamente
inconsequential [ˌɪnˌkɑnsəˈkwɛnʧəl] *adj* : intrascendente, de poco importancia
inconsiderable [ˌɪnkənˈsɪdərəbəl] *adj* : insignificante
inconsiderate [ˌɪnkənˈsɪdərət] *adj* : desconsiderado, sin consideración — **inconsiderately** *adv*
inconsistency [ˌɪnkənˈsɪstən*t*si] *n, pl* **-cies** : inconsecuencia *f*, inconsistencia *f*
inconsistent [ˌɪnkənˈsɪstənt] *adj* : inconsecuente, inconsistente
inconsolable [ˌɪnkənˈso:ləbəl] *adj* : inconsolable — **inconsolably** [-bli] *adv*
inconspicuous [ˌɪnkənˈspɪkjʊəs] *adj* : discreto, no conspicuo, que no llama la atención
inconspicuously [ˌɪnkənˈspɪkjʊəsli] *adv* : discretamente, sin llamar la atención
incontestable [ˌɪnkənˈtɛstəbəl] *adj* : incontestable, indiscutible — **incontestably** [-bli] *adv*
incontinence [ɪnˈkɑntənən*t*s] *n* : incontinencia *f*
incontinent [ɪnˈkɑntənənt] *adj* : incontinente
inconvenience[1] [ˌɪnkənˈvi:njən*t*s] *vt* **-nienced; -niencing** : importunar, incomodar, molestar
inconvenience[2] *n* : incomodidad *f*, molestia *f*
inconvenient [ˌɪnkənˈvi:njənt] *adj* : inconveniente, importuno, incómodo — **inconveniently** *adv*
incorporate [ɪnˈkɔrpəˌreɪt] *vt* **-rated; -rating 1** INCLUDE : incorporar, incluir **2** : incorporar, constituir en sociedad (dícese de un negocio)
incorporation [ɪnˌkɔrpəˈreɪʃən] *n* : incorporación *f*
incorporeal [ˌɪnˌkɔrˈporiəl] *adj* : incorpóreo
incorrect [ˌɪnkəˈrɛkt] *adj* **1** INACCURATE : incorrecto **2** WRONG : equivocado, erróneo **3** IMPROPER : impropio — **incorrectly** *adv*
incorrigible [ɪnˈkɔrəʤəbəl] *adj* : incorregible
incorruptible [ˌɪnkəˈrʌptəbəl] *adj* : incorruptible
increase[1] [ɪnˈkri:s, ˈɪnˌkri:s] *v* **-creased; -creasing** *vi* GROW : aumentar, crecer, subir (dícese de los precios) — *vt* AUGMENT : aumentar, acrecentar
increase[2] [ˈɪnˌkri:s, ɪnˈkri:s] *n* : aumento *m*, incremento *m*, subida *f* (de precios)
increasing [ɪnˈkri:sɪŋ, ˈɪnˌkri:sɪŋ] *adj* : creciente
increasingly [ɪnˈkri:sɪŋli] *adv* : cada vez más
incredible [ɪnˈkrɛdəbəl] *adj* : increíble — **incredibly** [-bli] *adv*
incredulity [ˌɪnkrɪˈdu:ləṭi, -ˈdju:-] *n* : incredulidad *f*
incredulous [ɪnˈkrɛʤələs] *adj* : incrédulo, escéptico
incredulously [ɪnˈkrɛʤələsli] *adv* : con incredulidad
increment [ˈɪŋkrəmənt, ˈɪn-] *n* : incremento *m*, aumento *m*
incremental [ˌɪŋkrəˈmɛntəl, ˌɪn-] *adj* : de incremento
incriminate [ɪnˈkrɪməˌneɪt] *vt* **-nated; -nating** : incriminar
incrimination [ɪnˌkrɪməˈneɪʃən] *n* : incriminación *f*
incriminatory [ɪnˈkrɪmənəˌtori] *adj* : incriminatorio
incubate [ˈɪŋkjʊˌbeɪt, ˈɪn-] *v* **-bated; -bating** *vt* : incubar, empollar — *vi* : incubar(se), empollar
incubation [ˌɪŋkjʊˈbeɪʃən, ˌɪn-] *n* : incubación *f*
incubator [ˈɪŋkjʊˌbeɪṭər, ˈɪn-] *n* : incubadora *f*
inculcate [ɪnˈkʌlˌkeɪt, ˈɪnˌkʌl-] *vt* **-cated; -cating** : inculcar
incumbency [ɪnˈkʌmbən*t*si] *n, pl* **-cies 1** OBLIGATION : incumbencia *f* **2** : mandato *m* (en la política)
incumbent[1] [ɪnˈkʌmbənt] *adj* : obligatorio
incumbent[2] *n* : titular *mf*
incur [ɪnˈkər] *vt* **incurred; incurring** : provocar (al enojo), incurrir en (gastos, obligaciones)
incurable [ɪnˈkjʊrəbəl] *adj* : incurable, sin remedio
incursion [ɪnˈkərʒən] *n* : incursión *f*
indebted [ɪnˈdɛṭəd] *adj* **1** : endeudado **2 to be indebted to** : estar en deuda con, estarle agradecido a
indebtedness [ɪnˈdɛṭədnəs] *n* : endeudamiento *m*
indecency [ɪnˈdi:sən*t*si] *n, pl* **-cies** : indecencia *f*
indecent [ɪnˈdi:sənt] *adj* : indecente — **indecently** *adv*
indecipherable [ˌɪndɪˈsaɪfərəbəl] *adj* : indescifrable
indecision [ˌɪndɪˈsɪʒən] *n* : indecisión *f*, irresolución *f*
indecisive [ˌɪndɪˈsaɪsɪv] *adj* **1** INCONCLUSIVE : indeciso, que no es decisivo **2** IRRESOLUTE : indeciso, irresoluto, vacilante **3** INDEFINITE : indefinido — **indecisively** *adv*
indecorous [ɪnˈdɛkərəs, ˌɪndɪˈkorəs] *adj* : indecoroso — **indecorously** *adv*
indecorousness [ɪnˈdkərəsnəs, ˌɪndɪˈkorəs-] *n* : indecoro *m*
indeed [ɪnˈdi:d] *adv* **1** TRULY : verdaderamente, de veras **2** (*used as intensifier*) <thank you very much indeed

: muchísimas gracias⟩ **3** OF COURSE : claro, por supuesto

indefatigable [ˌɪndɪˈfæt̬ɪgəbəl] *adj* : incansable, infatigable — **indefatigably** [-bli] *adv*

indefensible [ˌɪndɪˈfɛntsəbəl] *adj* **1** VULNERABLE : indefendible, vulnerable **2** INEXCUSABLE : inexcusable

indefinable [ˌɪndɪˈfaɪnəbəl] *adj* : indefinible

indefinite [ɪnˈdɛfənət] *adj* **1** : indefinido, indeterminado ⟨indefinite pronouns : pronombres indefinidos⟩ **2** VAGUE : vago, impreciso

indefinitely [ɪnˈdɛfənətli] *adv* : indefinidamente, por un tiempo indefinido

indelible [ɪnˈdɛləbəl] *adj* : indeleble, imborrable — **indelibly** [-bli] *adv*

indelicacy [ɪnˈdɛləkəsi] *n* : falta *f* de delicadeza

indelicate [ɪnˈdɛlɪkət] *adj* **1** IMPROPER : indelicado, indecoroso **2** TACTLESS : indiscreto, falto de tacto

indemnify [ɪnˈdɛmnəˌfaɪ] *vt* **-fied; -fying** **1** INSURE : asegurar **2** COMPENSATE : indemnizar, compensar

indemnity [ɪnˈdɛmnət̬i] *n, pl* **-ties** **1** INSURANCE : indemnidad *f* **2** COMPENSATION : indemnización *f*

indent [ɪnˈdɛnt] *vt* : sangrar (un párrafo)

indentation [ˌɪnˌdɛnˈteɪʃən] *n* **1** NOTCH : muesca *f*, mella *f* **2** INDENTING : sangría *f* (de un párrafo)

indenture[1] [ɪnˈdɛntʃər] *vt* **-tured; -turing** : ligar por contrato

indenture[2] *n* : contrato de aprendizaje

independence [ˌɪndəˈpɛndənts] *n* : independencia *f*

Independence Day *n* : día *m* de la Independencia (4 de julio en los EE.UU.)

independent[1] [ˌɪndəˈpɛndənt] *adj* : independiente — **independently** *adv*

independent[2] *n* : independiente *mf*

indescribable [ˌɪndɪˈskraɪbəbəl] *adj* : indescriptible, incalificable — **indescribably** [-bli] *adv*

indestructibility [ˌɪndɪˌstrʌktəˈbɪlət̬i] *n* : indestructibilidad *f*

indestructible [ˌɪndɪˈstrʌktəbəl] *adj* : indestructible

indeterminate [ˌɪndɪˈtərmənət] *adj* **1** VAGUE : vago, impreciso, indeterminado **2** INDEFINITE : indeterminado, indefinido

index[1] [ˈɪnˌdɛks] *vt* **1** : ponerle un índice a (un libro o una revista) **2** : incluir en un índice ⟨all proper names are indexed : todos los nombres propios están incluidos en el índice⟩ **3** INDICATE : indicar, señalar **4** REGULATE : indexar, indiciar ⟨to index prices : indiciar los precios⟩

index[2] *n, pl* **-dexes** *or* **-dices** [ˈɪndəˌsiːz] **1** : índice *m* (de un libro, de precios) **2** INDICATION : indicio *m*, índice *m*, señal *f* ⟨an index of her character : una señal de su carácter⟩

index finger *n* FOREFINGER : dedo *m* índice

Indian [ˈɪndiən] *n* **1** : indio *m*, -dia *f* **2** → **American Indian** — **Indian** *adj*

indicate [ˈɪndəˌkeɪt] *vt* **-cated; -cating** **1** POINT OUT : indicar, señalar **2** SHOW, SUGGEST : ser indicio de, ser señal de **3** EXPRESS : expresar, señalar **4** REGISTER : marcar, poner (una medida, etc.)

indication [ˌɪndəˈkeɪʃən] *n* : indicio *m*, señal *f*

indicative [ɪnˈdɪkət̬ɪv] *adj* : indicativo

indicator [ˈɪndəˌkeɪt̬ər] *n* : indicador *m*

indict [ɪnˈdaɪt] *vt* : acusar, procesar (por un crímen)

indictment [ɪnˈdaɪtmənt] *n* : acusación *f*

indifference [ɪnˈdɪfrənts, -ˈdɪfə-] *n* : indiferencia *f*

indifferent [ɪnˈdɪfrənt, -ˈdɪfə-] *adj* **1** UNCONCERNED : indiferente **2** MEDIOCRE : mediocre

indifferently [ɪnˈdɪfrəntli, -ˈdɪfə-] *adv* **1** : con indiferencia, indiferentemente **2** SO-SO : de modo regular, más o menos

indigence [ˈɪndɪʤənts] *n* : indigencia *f*

indigenous [ɪnˈdɪʤənəs] *adj* : indígena, nativo

indigent [ˈɪndɪʤənt] *adj* : indigente, pobre

indigestible [ˌɪndaɪˈʤɛstəbəl, -dɪ-] *adj* : difícil de digerir

indigestion [ˌɪndaɪˈʤɛstʃən, -dɪ-] *n* : indigestión *f*, empacho *m*

indignant [ɪnˈdɪgnənt] *adj* : indignado

indignantly [ɪnˈdɪgnəntli] *adv* : con indignación

indignation [ˌɪndɪgˈneɪʃən] *n* : indignación *f*

indignity [ɪnˈdɪgnət̬i] *n, pl* **-ties** : indignidad *f*

indigo [ˈɪndɪˌgoː] *n, pl* **-gos** *or* **-goes** : añil *m*, índigo *m*

indirect [ˌɪndəˈrɛkt, -daɪ-] *adj* : indirecto — **indirectly** *adv*

indiscernible [ˌɪndɪˈsərnəbəl, -ˈzər-] *adj* : imperceptible

indiscreet [ˌɪndɪˈskriːt] *adj* : indiscreto, imprudente — **indiscreetly** *adv*

indiscretion [ˌɪndɪˈskrɛʃən] *n* : indiscreción *f*, imprudencia *f*

indiscriminate [ˌɪndɪˈskrɪmənət] *adj* : indiscriminado

indiscriminately [ˌɪndɪˈskrɪmənətli] *adv* : sin discriminación, sin discernimiento

indispensable [ˌɪndɪˈspɛntsəbəl] *adj* : indispensable, necesario, imprescindible — **indispensably** [-bli] *adv*

indisposed [ˌɪndɪˈspoːzd] *adj* **1** ILL : indispuesto, enfermo **2** AVERSE, DISINCLINED : opuesto, reacio ⟨to be indisposed toward working : no tener ganas de trabajar⟩

indisputable [ˌɪndɪˈspjuːt̬əbəl, ɪnˈdɪspjʊt̬ə-] *adj* : indiscutible, incuestionable, incontestable — **indisputably** [-bli] *adv*

indistinct [ˌɪndɪˈstɪŋkt] *adj* : indistinto — **indistinctly** *adv*
indistinctness [ˌɪndɪˈstɪŋktnəs] *n* : falta *f* de claridad
indistinguishable [ˌɪndɪˈstɪŋgwɪʃəbəl] *adj* : indistinguible
individual[1] [ˌɪndəˈvɪʤʊəl] *adj* **1** PERSONAL : individual, personal ⟨individual traits : características personales⟩ **2** SEPARATE : individual, separado **3** PARTICULAR : particular, propio
individual[2] *n* : individuo *m*
individualism [ˌɪndəˈvɪʤəwəˌlɪzəm] *n* : individualismo *m*
individualist [ˌɪndəˈvɪʤʊəlɪst] *n* : individualista *mf*
individuality [ˌɪndəˌvɪʤʊˈælət̬i] *n, pl* **-ties** : individualidad *f*
individually [ˌɪndəˈvɪʤʊəli, -ʤəli] *adv* : individualmente
indivisible [ˌɪndɪˈvɪzəbəl] *adj* : indivisible
indoctrinate [ɪnˈdɑktrəˌneɪt] *vt* **-nated; -nating 1** TEACH : enseñar, instruir **2** PROPAGANDIZE : adoctrinar
indoctrination [ɪnˌdɑktrəˈneɪʃən] *n* : adoctrinamiento *m*
indolence [ˈɪndələn*t*s] *n* : indolencia *f*
indolent [ˈɪndələnt] *adj* : indolente
indomitable [ɪnˈdɑmət̬əbəl] *adj* : invencible, indomable, indómito — **indomitably** [-bli] *adv*
Indonesian [ˌɪndoˈniːʒən, -ʃən] *n* : indonesio *m*, -sia *f* — **Indonesian** *adj*
indoor [ˈɪnˈdor] *adj* : interior (dícese de las plantas), para estar en casa (dícese de la ropa), cubierto (dícese de las piscinas, etc.), bajo techo (dícese de los deportes)
indoors [ˈɪnˈdorz] *adv* : adentro, dentro
indubitable [ɪnˈduːbət̬əbəl, -ˈdjuː-] *adj* : indudable, incuestionable, indiscutible
indubitably [ɪnˈduːbət̬əbli, -ˈdjuː-] *adv* : indudablemente
induce [ɪnˈduːs, -ˈdjuːs] *vt* **-duced; -ducing 1** PERSUADE : persuadir, inducir **2** CAUSE : inducir, provocar ⟨to induce labor : provocar un parto⟩
inducement [ɪnˈduːsmənt, -ˈdjuːs-] *n* **1** INCENTIVE : incentivo *m*, aliciente *m* **2** : inducción *f*, provocación *f* (de un parto)
induct [ɪnˈdʌkt] *vt* **1** INSTALL : instalar, investir **2** ADMIT : admitir (como miembro) **3** CONSCRIPT : reclutar (al servicio militar)
inductee [ˌɪnˌdʌkˈtiː] *n* : recluta *mf*, conscripto *m*, -ta *f*
induction [ɪnˈdʌkʃən] *n* **1** INTRODUCTION : iniciación *f*, introducción *f* **2** : inducción *f* (en la lógica o la electricidad)
inductive [ɪnˈdʌktɪv] *adj* : inductivo
indulge [ɪnˈdʌlʤ] *v* **-dulged; -dulging** *vt* **1** GRATIFY : gratificar, satisfacer **2** SPOIL : consentir, mimar — *vi* **to indulge in** : permitirse
indulgence [ɪnˈdʌlʤən*t*s] *n* **1** SATISFYING : satisfacción *f*, gratificación *f* **2** HUMORING : complacencia *f*, indulgencia *f* **3** SPOILING : consentimiento *m* **4** : indulgencia *f* (en la religión)
indulgent [ɪŋˈdʌlʤənt] *adj* : indulgente, consentido — **indulgently** *adv*
industrial [ɪnˈdʌstriəl] *adj* : industrial — **industrially** *adv*
industrialist [ɪnˈdʌstriəlɪst] *n* : industrial *mf*
industrialization [ɪnˌdʌstriələˈzeɪ-ʃən] *n* : industrialización *f*
industrialize [ɪnˈdʌstriəˌlaɪz] *vt* **-ized; -izing** : industrializar
industrious [ɪnˈdʌstriəs] *adj* : diligente, industrioso, trabajador
industriously [ɪnˈdʌstriəsli] *adv* : con diligencia, con aplicación
industriousness [ɪnˈdʌstriəsnəs] *n* : diligencia *f*, aplicación *f*
industry [ˈɪndəstri] *n, pl* **-tries 1** DILIGENCE : diligencia *f*, aplicación *f* **2** : industria *f* ⟨the steel industry : la industria siderúrgica⟩
inebriated [ɪˈniːbriˌeɪt̬əd] *adj* : ebrio, embriagado
inebriation [ɪˌniːbriˈeɪʃən] *n* : ebriedad *f*, embriaguez *f*
ineffable [ɪnˈɛfəbəl] *adj* : inefable — **ineffably** [-bli] *adv*
ineffective [ˌɪnɪˈfɛktɪv] *adj* **1** INEFFECTUAL : ineficaz, inútil **2** INCAPABLE : incompetente, ineficiente, incapaz
ineffectively [ˌɪnɪˈfɛktɪvli] *adv* : ineficazmente, infructuosamente
ineffectual [ˌɪnɪˈfɛk*t*ʃʊəl] *adj* : inútil, ineficaz — **ineffectually** *adv*
inefficiency [ˌɪnɪˈfɪʃən*t*si] *n, pl* **-cies** : ineficiencia *f*, ineficacia *f*
inefficient [ˌɪnɪˈfɪʃənt] *adj* **1** : ineficiente, ineficaz **2** INCAPABLE, INCOMPETENT : incompetente, incapaz — **inefficiently** *adv*
inelegance [ɪnˈɛləgən*t*s] *n* : inelegancia *f*
inelegant [ɪnˈɛləgənt] *adj* : inelegante, poco elegante
ineligibility [ɪnˌɛləʤəˈbɪlət̬i] *n* : inelegibilidad *f*
ineligible [ɪnˈɛləʤəbəl] *adj* : inelegible
inept [ɪˈɛnpt] *adj* : inepto ⟨inept at : incapaz para⟩
ineptitude [ɪˈɛnptəˌtuːd, -ˌtjuːd] *n* : ineptitud *f*, incompetencia *f*, incapacidad *f*
inequality [ˌɪnɪˈkwɑlət̬i] *n, pl* **-ties** : desigualdad *f*
inert [ɪˈnərt] *adj* **1** INACTIVE : inerte, inactivo **2** SLUGGISH : lento
inertia [ɪˈnərʃə] *n* : inercia *f*
inescapable [ˌɪnɪˈskeɪpəbəl] *adj* : inevitable, ineludible — **inescapably** [-bli] *adv*
inessential [ˌɪnɪˈsɛn*t*ʃəl] *adj* : que no es esencial, innecesario
inestimable [ɪnˈɛstəməbəl] *adj* : inestimable, inapreciable

inevitability [ɪn,ɛvət̬əˈbɪlət̬i] *n, pl* **-ties** : inevitabilidad *f*

inevitable [ɪnˈɛvət̬əbəl] *adj* : inevitable — **inevitably** [-bli] *adv*

inexact [,ɪnɪgˈzækt] *adj* : inexacto

inexactly [,ɪnɪgˈzæktli] *adv* : sin exactitud

inexcusable [,ɪnɪkˈskju:zəbəl] *adj* : inexcusable, imperdonable — **inexcusably** [-bli] *adv*

inexhaustible [,ɪnɪgˈzɔstəbəl] *adj* **1** INDEFATIGABLE : infatigable, incansable **2** ENDLESS : inagotable — **inexhaustibly** [-bli] *adv*

inexorable [ɪnˈɛksərəbəl] *adj* : inexorable — **inexorably** [-bli] *adv*

inexpensive [,ɪnɪkˈspɛntsɪv] *adj* : barato, económico

inexperience [,ɪnɪkˈspɪriənts] *n* : inexperiencia *f*

inexperienced [,ɪnɪkˈspɪriəntst] *adj* : inexperto, novato

inexplicable [,ɪnɪkˈsplɪkəbəl] *adj* : inexplicable — **inexplicably** [-bli] *adv*

inexpressible [,ɪnɪkˈsprɛsəbəl] *adj* : inexpresable, inefable

inextricable [,ɪnɪkˈstrɪkəbəl, ɪˈnɛk-,strɪ-] *adj* : inextricable — **inextricably** [-bli] *adv*

infallibility [ɪn,fæləˈbɪlət̬i] *n* : infalibilidad *f*

infallible [ɪnˈfæləbəl] *adj* : infalible — **infallibly** [-bli] *adv*

infamous [ˈɪnfəməs] *adj* : infame — **infamously** *adv*

infamy [ˈɪnfəmi] *n, pl* **-mies** : infamia *f*

infancy [ˈɪnfəntsi] *n, pl* **-cies** : infancia *f*

infant [ˈɪnfənt] *n* : bebé *m*; niño *m*, -ña *f*

infantile [ˈɪnfən,taɪl, -təl, -,ti:l] *adj* : infantil, pueril

infantile paralysis → **poliomyelitis**

infantry [ˈɪnfəntri] *n, pl* **-tries** : infantería *f*

infatuated [ɪnˈfætʃʊ,eɪt̬əd] *adj* **to be infatuated with** : estar encaprichado con

infatuation [ɪn,fætʃʊˈeɪʃən] *n* : encaprichamiento *m*, enamoramiento *m*

infect [ɪnˈfɛkt] *vt* : infectar, contagiar

infection [ɪnˈfɛkʃən] *n* : infección *f*, contagio *m*

infectious [ɪnˈfɛkʃəs] *adj* : infeccioso, contagioso

infer [ɪnˈfər] *vt* **inferred; inferring 1** DEDUCE : deducir, inferir **2** SURMISE : concluir, suponer, tener entendido **3** IMPLY : sugerir, insinuar

inference [ˈɪnfərənts] *n* : deducción *f*, inferencia *f*, conclusión *f*

inferior[1] [ɪnˈfɪriər] *adj* : inferior, malo

inferior[2] *n* : inferior *mf*

inferiority [ɪn,fɪriˈɔrət̬i] *n, pl* **-ties** : inferioridad *f* ⟨inferiority complex : complejo de inferioridad⟩

infernal [ɪnˈfərnəl] *adj* **1** : infernal ⟨infernal fires : fuegos infernales⟩ **2** DIABOLICAL : infernal, diabólico **3** DAMNABLE : maldito, condenado

inferno [ɪnˈfər,no:] *n, pl* **-nos** : infierno *m*

infertile [ɪnˈfərt̬əl, -,taɪl] *adj* : estéril, infecundo

infertility [,ɪnfərˈtɪlət̬i] *n* : esterilidad *f*, infecundidad *f*

infest [ɪnˈfɛst] *vt* : infestar, plagar

infestation [,ɪn,fɛsˈteɪʃən] *n* : infestación *f*, plaga *f*

infidel [ˈɪnfədəl, -,dɛl] *n* : infiel *mf*

infidelity [,ɪnfəˈdɛlət̬i, -faɪ-] *n, pl* **-ties 1** UNFAITHFULNESS : infidelidad *f* **2** DISLOYALTY : deslealtad *f*

infield [ˈɪn,fi:ld] *n* : cuadro *m*, diamante *m*

infiltrate [ɪnˈfɪl,treɪt, ˈɪnfɪl-] *v* **-trated; -trating** *vt* : infiltrar — *vi* : infiltrarse

infiltration [,ɪnfɪlˈtreɪʃən] *n* : infiltración *f*

infinite [ˈɪnfənət] *adj* **1** LIMITLESS : infinito, sin límites **2** VAST : infinito, vasto, extenso

infinitely [ˈɪnfənətli] *adv* : infinitamente

infinitesimal [,ɪn,fɪnəˈtɛsəməl] *adj* : infinitésimo, infinitesimal — **infinitesimally** *adv*

infinitive [ɪnˈfɪnət̬ɪv] *n* : infinitivo *m*

infinity [ɪnˈfɪnət̬i] *n, pl* **-ties 1** : infinito *m* (en matemáticas, etc.) **2** : infinidad *f* ⟨an infinity of stars : una infinidad de estrellas⟩

infirm [ɪnˈfərm] *adj* **1** FEEBLE : enfermizo, endeble **2** INSECURE : inseguro

infirmary [ɪnˈfərməri] *n, pl* **-ries** : enfermería *f*, hospital *m*

infirmity [ɪnˈfərmət̬i] *n, pl* **-ties 1** FRAILTY : debilidad *f*, endeblez *f* **2** AILMENT : enfermedad *f*, dolencia *f* ⟨the infirmities of age : los achaques de la vejez⟩

inflame [ɪnˈfleɪm] *v* **-flamed; -flaming** *vt* **1** KINDLE : inflamar, encender **2** : inflamar (una herida) **3** STIR UP : encender, provocar, inflamar — *vi* : inflamarse

inflammable [ɪnˈflæməbəl] *adj* **1** FLAMMABLE : inflamable **2** IRASCIBLE : irascible, explosivo

inflammation [,ɪnfləˈmeɪʃən] *n* : inflamación *f*

inflammatory [ɪnˈflæmə,tori] *adj* : inflamatorio, incendiario

inflatable [ɪnˈfleɪt̬əbəl] *adj* : inflable

inflate [ɪnˈfleɪt] *vt* **-flated; -flating** : inflar, hinchar

inflation [ɪnˈfleɪʃən] *n* : inflación *f*

inflationary [ɪnˈfleɪʃə,nɛri] *adj* : inflacionario, inflacionista

inflect [ɪnˈflɛkt] *vt* **1** CONJUGATE, DECLINE : conjugar, declinar **2** MODULATE : modular (la voz)

inflection [ɪnˈflɛkʃən] *n* : inflexión *f*

inflexibility [ɪn,flɛksəˈbɪlət̬i] *n, pl* **-ties** : inflexibilidad *f*

inflexible [ɪnˈflɛksɪbəl] *adj* : inflexible

inflict [ɪnˈflɪkt] *vt* **1** : infligir, causar, imponer **2 to inflict oneself on** : imponer uno su presencia (a alguien)

infliction [ɪnˈflɪkʃən] *n* : imposición *f*

influence[1] [ˈɪn͵flu:ənts, ɪnˈflu:ənts] *vt* **-enced; -encing** : influenciar, influir en

influence[2] *n* **1** : influencia *f*, influjo *m* ⟨to exert influence over : ejercer influencia sobre⟩ ⟨the influence of gravity : el influjo de la gravidad⟩ **2 under the influence** : bajo la influencia del alcohol, embriagado

influential [͵ɪnfluˈɛntʃəl] *adj* : influyente

influenza [͵ɪnfluˈɛnzə] *n* : gripe *f*, influenza *f*, gripa *f Col, Mex*

influx [ˈɪn͵flʌks] *n* : afluencia *f* (de gente), entrada *f* (de mercancías), llegada *f* (de ideas)

inform [ɪnˈfɔrm] *vt* : informar, notificar, avisar — *vi* **to inform on** : delatar, denunciar

informal [ɪnˈfɔrməl] *adj* **1** UNCEREMONIOUS : sin ceremonia, sin etiqueta **2** CASUAL : informal, familiar (dícese del lenguaje) **3** UNOFFICIAL : extraoficial

informality [͵ɪnfɔrˈmæləṭi, -fər-] *n, pl* **-ties** : informalidad *f*, familiaridad *f*, falta *f* de ceremonia

informally [ɪnˈfɔrməli] *adv* : sin ceremonias, de manera informal, informalmente

informant [ɪnˈfɔrmənt] *n* : informante *mf*; informador *m*, -dora *f*

information [͵ɪnfərˈmeɪʃən] *n* : información *f*

informative [ɪnˈfɔrməṭɪv] *adj* : informativo, instructivo

informer [ɪnˈfɔrmər] *n* : informante *mf*; informador *m*, -dora *f*

infraction [ɪnˈfrækʃən] *n* : infracción *f*, violación *f*, transgresión *f*

infrared [͵ɪnfrəˈrɛd] *adj* : infrarrojo

infrastructure [ˈɪnfrə͵strʌktʃər] *n* : infraestructura *f*

infrequent [ɪnˈfri:kwənt] *adj* : infrecuente, raro

infrequently [ɪnˈfri:kwəntli] *adv* : raramente, con poca frecuencia

infringe [ɪnˈfrɪndʒ] *v* **-fringed; -fringing** *vt* : infringir, violar — *vi* **to infringe on** : abusar de, violar

infringement [ɪnˈfrɪndʒmənt] *n* **1** VIOLATION : violación *f* (de la ley), incumplimiento *m* (de un contrato) **2** ENCROACHMENT : usurpación *f* (de derechos, etc.)

infuriate [ɪnˈfjʊri͵eɪt] *vt* **-ated; -ating** : enfurecer, poner furioso

infuriating [ɪnˈfjʊri͵eɪṭɪŋ] *adj* : indignante, exasperante

infuse [ɪnˈfju:z] *vt* **-fused; -fusing 1** INSTILL : infundir **2** STEEP : hacer una infusión de

infusion [ɪnˈfju:ʒən] *n* : infusión *f*

ingenious [ɪnˈdʒi:njəs] *adj* : ingenioso — **ingeniously** *adv*

ingenue *or* **ingénue** [ˈɑndʒə͵nu:, ˈæn-; ˈæʒə-, ˈɑ-] *n* : ingenua *f*

ingenuity [͵ɪndʒəˈnu:əṭi, -ˈnju:-] *n, pl* **-ities** : ingenio

ingenuous [ɪnˈdʒɛnjʊəs] *adj* **1** FRANK : cándido, franco **2** NAIVE : ingenuo — **ingenuously** *adv*

ingenuousness [ɪnˈdʒɛnjʊəsnəs] *n* **1** FRANKNESS : candidez *f*, candor *m* **2** NAÏVETÉ : ingenuidad *f*

ingest [ɪnˈdʒɛst] *vt* : ingerir

ingestion [ɪnˈdʒɛstʃən] *n* : ingestión *f*

inglorious [ɪnˈgloriəs] *adj* : deshonroso, ignominioso

ingot [ˈɪŋgət] *n* : lingote *m*

ingrained [ɪnˈgreɪnd] *adj* : arraigado

ingrate [ˈɪn͵greɪt] *n* : ingrato *m*, -ta *f*

ingratiate [ɪnˈgreɪʃi͵eɪt] *vt* **-ated; -ating** : conseguir la benevolencia de ⟨to ingratiate oneself with someone : congraciarse con alguien⟩

ingratiating [ɪnˈgreɪʃi͵eɪṭɪŋ] *adj* : halagador, zalamero, obsequioso

ingratitude [ɪnˈgræṭə͵tu:d, -͵tju:d] *n* : ingratitud *f*

ingredient [ɪnˈgri:diənt] *n* : ingrediente *m*, componente *m*

ingrown [ˈɪn͵gro:n] *adj* **1** : crecido hacia adentro **2 ingrown toenail** : uña *f* encarnada

inhabit [ɪnˈhæbət] *vt* : vivir en, habitar, ocupar

inhabitable [ɪnˈhæbəṭəbəl] *adj* : habitable

inhabitant [ɪnˈhæbəṭənt] *n* : habitante *mf*

inhalant [ɪnˈheɪlənt] *n* : inhalante *m*

inhalation [͵ɪnhəˈleɪʃən, ͵ɪnə-] *n* : inhalación *f*

inhale [ɪnˈheɪl] *v* **-haled; -haling** *vt* : inhalar, aspirar — *vi* : inspirar

inhaler [ɪnˈheɪlər] *n* : inhalador *m*

inhere [ɪnˈhɪr] *vi* **-hered; -hering** : ser inherente

inherent [ɪnˈhɪrənt, -ˈhɛr-] *adj* : inherente, intrínseco — **inherently** *adv*

inherit [ɪnˈhɛrət] *vt* : heredar

inheritance [ɪnˈhɛrəṭənts] *n* : herencia *f*

inheritor [ɪnˈhɛrəṭər] *n* : heredero *m*, -da *f*

inhibit [ɪnˈhɪbət] *vt* IMPEDE : inhibir, impedir

inhibition [͵ɪnhəˈbɪʃən, ͵ɪnə-] *n* : inhibición *f*, cohibición *f*

inhuman [ɪnˈhju:mən, -ˈju:-] *adj* : inhumano, cruel — **inhumanly** *adv*

inhumane [͵ɪnhjuˈmeɪn, -ju-] *adj* INHUMAN : inhumano, cruel

inhumanity [͵ɪnhjuˈmænəṭi, -ju-] *n, pl* **-ties** : inhumanidad *f*, crueldad *f*

inimical [ɪˈnɪmɪkəl] *adj* **1** UNFAVORABLE : adverso, desfavorable **2** HOSTILE : hostil — **inimically** *adv*

inimitable [ɪˈnɪməṭəbəl] *adj* : inimitable

iniquitous [ɪˈnɪkwəṭəs] *adj* : inicuo, malvado

iniquity [ɪˈnɪkwəṭi] *n, pl* **-ties** : iniquidad *f*

initial[1] [ɪˈnɪʃəl] *vt* **-tialed** *or* **-tialled; -tialing** *or* **-tialling** : poner las iniciales a, firmar con las iniciales

initial[2] *adj* : inicial, primero — **initially** *adv*

initial[3] *n* : inicial *f*
initiate[1] [ɪˈnɪʃiˌeɪt] *vt* **-ated; -ating 1** BEGIN : comenzar, iniciar **2** INDUCT : instruir **3** INTRODUCE : introducir, instruir
initiate[2] [ɪˈnɪʃiət] *n* : iniciado *m*, -da *f*
initiation [ɪˌnɪʃiˈeɪʃən] *n* : iniciación *f*
initiative [ɪˈnɪʃət̬ɪv] *n* : iniciativa *f*
initiatory [ɪˈnɪʃiəˌtori] *adj* **1** INTRODUCTORY : introductorio **2** : de iniciación ⟨initiatory rites : ritos de iniciación⟩
inject [ɪnˈʤɛkt] *vt* : inyectar
injection [ɪnˈʤɛkʃən] *n* : inyección *f*
injudicious [ˌɪnʤʊˈdɪʃəs] *adj* : imprudente, indiscreto, poco juicioso
injunction [ɪnˈʤʌŋkʃən] *n* **1** ORDER : orden *f*, mandato *m* **2** COURT ORDER : mandamiento *m* judicial
injure [ˈɪnʤər] *vt* **-jured; -juring 1** WOUND : herir, lesionar **2** HURT : lastimar, dañar, herir **3 to injure oneself** : hacerse daño
injurious [ɪnˈʤʊriəs] *adj* : perjudicial ⟨injurious to one's health : perjudicial a la salud⟩
injury [ˈɪnʤəri] *n, pl* **-ries 1** WRONG : mal *m*, injusticia *f* **2** DAMAGE, HARM : herida *f*, daño *m*, perjuicio *m*
injustice [ɪnˈʤʌstəs] *n* : injusticia *f*
ink[1] [ˈɪŋk] *vt* : entintar
ink[2] *n* : tinta *f*
inkling [ˈɪŋklɪŋ] *n* : presentimiento *m*, indicio *m*, sospecha *f*
inkwell [ˈɪŋkˌwɛl] *n* : tintero *m*
inky [ˈɪŋki] *adj* **1** : manchado de tinta **2** BLACK : negro, impenetrable ⟨inky darkness : negra oscuridad⟩
inland[1] [ˈɪnˌlænd, -lənd] *adv* : hacia el interior, tierra adentro
inland[2] *adj* : interior
inland[3] *n* : interior *m*
in–law [ˈɪnˌlɔ] *n* **1** : pariente *m* político **2 in–laws** *npl* : suegros *mpl*
inlay[1] [ɪnˈleɪ, ˈɪnˌleɪ] *vt* **-laid** [-ˈleɪd, -ˌleɪd]; **-laying** : incrustar, taracear
inlay[2] [ˈɪnˌleɪ] *n* **1** : incrustación *f* **2** : empaste *m* (de un diente)
inlet [ˈɪnˌlɛt, -lət] *n* : cala *f*, ensenada *f*
inmate [ˈɪnˌmeɪt] *n* : paciente *mf* (en un hospital); preso *m*, -sa *f* (en una prisión); interno *m*, -na *f* (en un asilo)
in memoriam [ˌɪnməˈmoriəm] *prep* : en memoria de
inmost [ˈɪnˌmoːst] → **innermost**
inn [ˈɪn] *n* **1** : posada *f*, hostería *f*, fonda *f* **2** TAVERN : taberna *f*
innards [ˈɪnərdz] *npl* : entrañas *fpl*, tripas *fpl fam*
innate [ɪˈneɪt] *adj* **1** INBORN : innato **2** INHERENT : inherente
inner [ˈɪnər] *adj* : interior, interno
innermost [ˈɪnərˌmoːst] *adj* : más íntimo, más profundo
innersole [ˈɪnərˈsoːl] → **insole**
inning [ˈɪnɪŋ] *n* : entrada *f*
innkeeper [ˈɪnˌkiːpər] *n* : posadero *m*, -ra *f*
innocence [ˈɪnəsənts] *n* : inocencia *f*
innocent[1] [ˈɪnəsənt] *adj* : inocente — **innocently** *adv*
innocent[2] *n* : inocente *mf*
innocuous [ɪˈnɑkjəwəs] *adj* **1** HARMLESS : inocuo **2** INOFFENSIVE : inofensivo
innovate [ˈɪnəˌveɪt] *vi* **-vated; -vating** : innovar
innovation [ˌɪnəˈveɪʃən] *n* : innovación *f*, novedad *f*
innovative [ˈɪnəˌveɪt̬ɪv] *adj* : innovador
innovator [ˈɪnəˌveɪt̬ər] *n* : innovador *m*, -dora *f*
innuendo [ˌɪnjʊˈɛndo] *n, pl* **-dos** *or* **-does** : insinuación *f*, indirecta *f*
innumerable [ɪˈnuːmərəbəl, -ˈnjuː-] *adj* : innumerable
inoculate [ɪˈnɑkjəˌleɪt] *vt* **-lated; -lating** : inocular
inoculation [ɪˌnɑkjəˈleɪʃən] *n* : inoculación *f*
inoffensive [ˌɪnəˈfɛntsɪv] *adj* : inofensivo
inoperable [ɪnˈɑpərəbəl] *adj* : inoperable
inoperative [ɪnˈɑpərət̬ɪv, -ˌreɪ-] *adj* : inoperante
inopportune [ɪnˌɑpərˈtuːn, -ˈtjuːn] *adj* : inoportuno — **inopportunely** *adv*
inordinate [ɪnˈɔrdənət] *adj* : excesivo, inmoderado, desmesurado — **inordinately** *adv*
inorganic [ˌɪnˌɔrˈgænɪk] *adj* : inorgánico
inpatient [ˈɪnˌpeɪʃənt] *n* : paciente *mf* hospitalizado
input[1] [ˈɪnˌpʊt] *vt* **inputted** *or* **input; inputting** : entrar (datos, información)
input[2] *n* **1** CONTRIBUTION : aportación *f*, contribución *f* **2** ENTRY : entrada *f* (de datos) **3** ADVICE, OPINION : consejos *mpl*, opinión *f*
inquest [ˈɪnˌkwɛst] *n* INQUIRY, INVESTIGATION : investigación *f*, averiguación *f*, pesquisa *f* (judicial)
inquire [ɪnˈkwaɪr] *v* **-quired; -quiring** *vt* : preguntar, informarse de, inquirir ⟨he inquired how to get in : preguntó como entrar⟩ — *vi* **1** ASK : preguntar, informarse ⟨to inquire about : informarse sobre⟩ ⟨to inquire after (someone) : preguntar por (alguien)⟩ **2 to inquire into** INVESTIGATE : investigar, inquirir sobre
inquiringly [ɪnˈkwaɪrɪŋli] *adv* : inquisitivamente
inquiry [ˈɪnˌkwaɪri, ɪnˈkwaɪri; ˈɪnkwəri, ˈɪŋ-] *n, pl* **-ries 1** QUESTION : pregunta *f* ⟨to make inquiries about : pedir información sobre⟩ **2** INVESTIGATION : investigación *f*, inquisición *f*, pesquisa *f*
inquisition [ˌɪnkwəˈzɪʃən, ˌɪŋ-] *n* **1** : inquisición *f*, interrogatorio *m*, investigación *f* **2 the Inquisition** : la Inquisición *f*
inquisitive [ɪnˈkwɪzət̬ɪv] *adj* : inquisidor, inquisitivo, curioso — **inquisitively** *adv*

inquisitiveness [ɪn'kwɪzət̬ɪvnəs] *n* : curiosidad *f*
inquisitor [ɪn'kwɪzət̬ər] *n* : inquisidor *m*, -dora *f*; interrogador *m*, -dora *f*
inroad ['ɪn,ro:d] *n* **1** ENCROACHMENT, INVASION : invasión *f*, incursión *f* **2 to make inroads into** : ocupar parte de (un tiempo), agotar parte de (ahorros, recursos), invadir (un territorio)
insane [ɪn'seɪn] *adj* **1** MAD : loco, demente ⟨to go insane : volverse loco⟩ **2** ABSURD : absurdo, insensato ⟨an insane scheme : un proyecto insensato⟩
insanely [ɪn'seɪnli] *adv* : como un loco ⟨insanely suspicious : loco de recelo⟩
insanity [ɪn'sænət̬i] *n, pl* **-ties 1** MADNESS : locura *f* **2** FOLLY : locura *f*, insensatez *f*
insatiable [ɪn'seɪʃəbəl] *adj* : insaciable — **insatiably** [-bli] *adv*
inscribe [ɪn'skraɪb] *vt* **-scribed; -scribing 1** ENGRAVE : inscribir, grabar **2** ENROLL : inscribir **3** DEDICATE : dedicar (un libro)
inscription [ɪn'skrɪpʃən] *n* : inscripción *f* (en un monumento), dedicación *f* (en un libro), leyenda *f* (de una ilustración, etc.)
inscrutable [ɪn'skru:t̬əbəl] *adj* : inescrutable, misterioso — **inscrutably** [-bli] *adv*
inseam ['ɪn,si:m] *n* : entrepierna *f*
insect ['ɪn,sɛkt] *n* : insecto *m*
insecticidal [ɪn,sɛktə'saɪdəl] *adj* : insecticida
insecticide [ɪn'sɛktə,saɪd] *n* : insecticida *m*
insecure [,ɪnsɪ'kjʊr] *adj* : inseguro, poco seguro — **insecurely** *adv*
insecurely [,ɪnsɪ'kjʊrli] *adv* : inseguramente
insecurity [,ɪnsɪ'kjʊrət̬i] *n, pl* **-ties** : inseguridad *f*
inseminate [ɪn'sɛmə,neɪt] *vt* **-nated; -nating** : inseminar
insemination [ɪn,sɛmə'neɪʃən] *n* : inseminación *f*
insensibility [ɪn,sɛntsə'bɪlət̬i] *n, pl* **-ties** : insensibilidad *f*
insensible [ɪn'sɛntsəbəl] *adj* **1** UNCONSCIOUS : inconsciente, sin conocimiento **2** NUMB : insensible, entumecido **3** UNAWARE : inconsciente
insensitive [ɪn'sɛntsət̬ɪv] *adj* : insensible
insensitivity [ɪn,sɛntsə'tɪvət̬i] *n, pl* **-ties** : insensibilidad *f*
inseparable [ɪn'sɛpərəbəl] *adj* : inseparable
insert[1] [ɪn'sərt] *vt* **1** : insertar, introducir, poner, meter ⟨insert your key in the lock : mete tu llave en la cerradura⟩ **2** INTERPOLATE : interpolar, intercalar
insert[2] ['ɪn,sərt] *n* : inserción *f*, hoja *f* insertada (en una revista, etc.)
insertion [ɪn'sərʃən] *n* : inserción *f*
inset ['ɪn,sɛt] *n* : página *f* intercalada (en un libro), entredós *m* (de encaje en la ropa)
inshore[1] ['ɪn'ʃor] *adv* : hacia la costa
inshore[2] *adj* : cercano a la costa, costero ⟨inshore fishing : pesca costera⟩
inside[1] [ɪn'saɪd, 'ɪn,saɪd] *adv* : adentro, dentro ⟨to run inside : correr para adentro⟩ ⟨inside and out : por dentro y por fuera⟩
inside[2] *adj* **1** : interior, de adentro, de dentro ⟨the inside lane : el carril interior⟩ **2** : confidencial ⟨inside information : información confidencial⟩
inside[3] *n* **1** : interior *m*, parte *f* de adentro **2 insides** *npl* BELLY, GUTS : tripas *fpl fam* **3 inside out** : al revés
inside[4] *prep* **1** INTO : al interior de **2** WITHIN : dentro de **3** (*referring to time*) : en menos de ⟨inside an hour : en menos de una hora⟩
inside of *prep* INSIDE : dentro de
insider [ɪn'saɪdər] *n* : persona *f* enterada
insidious [ɪn'sɪdiəs] *adj* : insidioso — **insidiously** *adv*
insidiousness [ɪn'sɪdiəsnəs] *n* : insidia *f*
insight ['ɪn,saɪt] *n* : perspicacia *f*, penetración *f*
insightful [ɪn'saɪtfəl] *adj* : perspicaz
insignia [ɪn'sɪgniə] *or* **insigne** [-,ni:] *n, pl* **-nia** *or* **-nias** : insignia *f*, enseña *f*
insignificance [,ɪnsɪg'nɪfɪkənts] *n* : insignificancia *f*
insignificant [,ɪnsɪg'nɪfɪkənt] *adj* : insignificante
insincere [,ɪnsɪn'sɪr] *adj* : insincero, poco sincero
insincerely [,ɪnsɪn'sɪrli] *adv* : con poca sinceridad
insincerity [,ɪnsɪn'sɛrət̬i, -'sɪr-] *n, pl* **-ties** : insinceridad *f*
insinuate [ɪn'sɪnjʊ,eɪt] *vt* **-ated; -ating** : insinuar
insinuation [ɪn,sɪnjʊ'eɪʃən] *n* : insinuación *f*
insipid [ɪn'sɪpəd] *adj* : insípido
insist [ɪn'sɪst] *v* : insistir
insistence [ɪn'sɪstənts] *n* : insistencia *f*
insistent [ɪn'sɪstənt] *adj* : insistente — **insistently** *adv*
insofar as [,ɪnso'fɑræz] *conj* : en la medida en que, en tanto que, en cuanto a
insole ['ɪn,so:l] *n* : plantilla *f*
insolence ['ɪntsələnts] *n* : insolencia *f*
insolent ['ɪntsələnt] *adj* : insolente
insolubility [ɪn,sɑljʊ'bɪlət̬i] *n* : insolubilidad *f*
insoluble [ɪn'sɑljʊbəl] *adj* : insoluble
insolvency [ɪn'sɑlvəntsi] *n, pl* **-cies** : insolvencia *f*
insolvent [ɪn'sɑlvənt] *adj* : insolvente
insomnia [ɪn'sɑmniə] *n* : insomnio *m*
insomuch as [,ɪnso'mʌtʃæz] → **inasmuch as**
insomuch that *conj* SO : así que, de manera que
inspect [ɪn'spɛkt] *vt* : inspeccionar, examinar, revisar
inspection [ɪn'spɛkʃən] *n* : inspección *f*, examen *m*, revisión *f*, revista *f* (de tropas)

inspector [ɪnˈspɛktər] *n* : inspector *m*, -tora *f*

inspiration [ˌɪntspəˈreɪʃən] *n* : inspiración *f*

inspirational [ˌɪntspəˈreɪʃənəl] *adj* : inspirador

inspire [ɪnˈspaɪr] *v* **-spired; -spiring** *vt* **1** INHALE : inhalar, aspirar **2** STIMULATE : estimular, animar, inspirar **3** INSTILL : inspirar, infundir — *vi* : inspirar

instability [ˌɪntstəˈbɪləti] *n, pl* **-ties** : inestabilidad *f*

install [ɪnˈstɔl] *vt* **-stalled; -stalling 1** : instalar ⟨to install the new president : instalar el presidente nuevo⟩ ⟨to install a fan : montar un abanico⟩ **2 to install oneself** : instalarse

installation [ˌɪntstəˈleɪʃən] *n* : instalación *f*

installment [ɪnˈstɔlmənt] *n* **1** : plazo *m*, cuota *f* ⟨to pay in four installments : pagar a cuatro plazos⟩ **2** : entrega *f* (de una publicación o telenovela) **3** INSTALLATION : instalación *f*

instance [ˈɪntstənts] *n* **1** INSTIGATION : instancia *f* **2** EXAMPLE : ejemplo *m* ⟨for instance : por ejemplo⟩ **3** OCCASION : instancia *f*, caso *m*, ocasión *f* ⟨he prefers, in this instance, to remain anonymous : en este caso prefiere quedarse anónimo⟩

instant¹ [ˈɪntstənt] *adj* **1** IMMEDIATE : inmediato, instantáneo ⟨an instant reply : una respuesta inmediata⟩ **2** : instantáneo ⟨instant coffee : café instantáneo⟩

instant² *n* : momento *m*, instante *m*

instantaneous [ˌɪntstənˈteɪniəs] *adj* : instantáneo

instantaneously [ˌɪntstənˈteɪniəsli] *adv* : instantáneamente, al instante

instantly [ˈɪntstəntli] *adv* : al instante, instantáneamente

instead [ɪnˈstɛd] *adv* **1** : en cambio, en lugar de eso, en su lugar ⟨Dad was going, but Mom went instead : papá iba a ir, pero mamá fue en su lugar⟩ **2** RATHER : al contrario

instead of *prep* : en vez de, en lugar de

instep [ˈɪnˌstɛp] *n* : empeine *m*

instigate [ˈɪntstəˌgeɪt] *vt* **-gated; -gating** INCITE, PROVOKE : instigar, incitar, provocar, fomentar

instigation [ˌɪntstəˈgeɪʃən] *n* : instancia *f*, incitación *f*

instigator [ˈɪntstəˌgeɪtər] *n* : instigador *m*, -dora *f*; incitador *m*, -dora *f*

instill [ɪnˈstɪl] *vt* **-stilled; -stilling** : inculcar, infundir

instinct [ˈɪnˌstɪŋkt] *n* **1** TALENT : instinto *m*, don *m* ⟨an instinct for the right word : un don para escoger la palabra apropiada⟩ **2** : instinto *m* ⟨maternal instincts : instintos maternales⟩

instinctive [ɪnˈstɪŋktɪv] *adj* : instintivo

instinctively [ɪnˈstɪŋktɪvli] *adv* : instintivamente, por instinto

instinctual [ɪnˈstɪŋktʃuəl] *adj* : instintivo

institute¹ [ˈɪntstəˌtuːt, -ˌtjuːt] *vt* **-tuted; -tuting 1** ESTABLISH : establecer, instituir, fundar **2** INITIATE : iniciar, empezar, entablar

institute² *n* : instituto *m*

institution [ˌɪntstəˈtuːʃən, -ˈtjuː-] *n* **1** ESTABLISHING : institución *f*, establecimiento *m* **2** CUSTOM : institución *f*, tradición *f* ⟨the institution of marriage : la institución del matrimonio⟩ **3** ORGANIZATION : institución *f*, organismo *m* **4** ASYLUM : asilo *m*

institutional [ˌɪntstəˈtuːʃənəl, -ˈtjuː-] *adj* : institucional

institutionalize [ˌɪntstəˈtuːʃənəˌlaɪz, -ˈtjuː-] *vt* **-ized; -izing 1** : institucionalizar ⟨institutionalized values : valores institucionalizados⟩ **2** : internar ⟨institutionalized orphans : huérfanos internados⟩

instruct [ɪnˈstrʌkt] *vt* **1** TEACH, TRAIN : instruir, adiestrar, enseñar **2** COMMAND : mandar, ordenar, dar instrucciones a

instruction [ɪnˈstrʌkʃən] *n* **1** TEACHING : instrucción *f*, enseñanza *f* **2** COMMAND : orden *f*, instrucción *f* **3 instructions** *npl* DIRECTIONS : instrucciones *fpl*, modo *m* de empleo

instructional [ɪnˈstrʌkʃənəl] *adj* : instructivo, educativo

instructive [ɪnˈstrʌktɪv] *adj* : instructivo

instructor [ɪnˈstrʌktər] *n* : instructor *m*, -tora *f*

instrument [ˈɪntstrəmənt] *n* : instrumento *m*

instrumental [ˌɪntstrəˈmɛntəl] *adj* : instrumental

instrumentalist [ˌɪntstrəˈmɛntəlɪst] *n* : instrumentista *mf*

insubordinate [ˌɪnsəˈbɔrdənət] *adj* : insubordinado

insubordination [ˌɪnsəˌbɔrdənˈeɪʃən] *n* : insubordinación *f*

insubstantial [ˌɪnsəbˈstæntʃəl] *adj* : insustancial, poco nutritivo (dícese de una comida), poco sólido (dícese de una estructura o un argumento)

insufferable [ɪnˈsʌfərəbəl] *adj* UNBEARABLE : insufrible, intolerable, inaguantable, insoportable — **insufferably** [-bli] *adv*

insufficiency [ˌɪnsəˈfɪʃəntsi] *n, pl* **-cies** : insuficiencia *f*

insufficient [ˌɪnsəˈfɪʃənt] *adj* : insuficiente — **insufficiently** *adv*

insular [ˈɪntsʊlər, -sjʊ-] *adj* **1** : isleño (dícese de la gente), insular (dícese del clima) ⟨insular residents : residentes de la isla⟩ **2** NARROW-MINDED : de miras estrechas

insularity [ˌɪntsʊˈlærəti, -sjʊ-] *n* : insularidad *f*

insulate [ˈɪntsəˌleɪt] *vt* **-lated; -lating** : aislar

insulation [ˌɪntsəˈleɪʃən] *n* : aislamiento *m*

insulator [ˈɪntsəˌleɪtər] *n* : aislador *m* (pieza), aislante *m* (material)

insulin ['ɪntsələn] *n* : insulina *f*
insult[1] [ɪn'sʌlt] *vt* : insultar, ofender, injuriar
insult[2] ['ɪn,sʌlt] *n* : insulto *m*, injuria *f*, agravio *m*
insulting [ɪn'sʌltɪŋ] *adj* : ofensivo, injurioso, insultante
insultingly [ɪn'sʌltɪŋli] *adv* : ofensivamente, de manera insultante
insuperable [ɪn'su:pərəbəl] *adj* : insuperable — **insuperably** [-bli] *adv*
insurable [ɪn'ʃʊrəbəl] *adj* : asegurable
insurance [ɪn'ʃʊrənts, 'ɪn,ʃʊr-] *n* : seguro *m* ⟨life insurance : seguro de vida⟩ ⟨insurance company : compañía de seguros⟩
insure [ɪn'ʃʊr] *vt* **-sured; -suring 1** UNDERWRITE : asegurar **2** ENSURE : asegurar, garantizar
insured [ɪn'ʃʊrd] *n* : asegurado *m*, -da *f*
insurer [ɪn'ʃʊrər] *n* : asegurador *m*, -dora *f*
insurgent[1] [ɪn'sərʤənt] *adj* : insurgente
insurgent[2] *n* : insurgente *mf*
insurmountable [,ɪnsər'maʊntəbəl] *adj* : insuperable, insalvable — **insurmountably** [-bli] *adv*
insurrection [,ɪnsə'rɛkʃən] *n* : insurrección *f*, levantamiento *m*, alzamiento *m*
intact [ɪn'tækt] *adj* : intacto
intake ['ɪn,teɪk] *n* **1** OPENING : entrada *f*, toma *f* ⟨fuel intake : toma de combustible⟩ **2** : entrada *f* (de agua o aire), consumo *m* (de sustancias nutritivas) **3 intake of breath** : inhalación *f*
intangible [ɪn'tænʤəbəl] *adj* : intangible, impalpable — **intangibly** [-bli] *adv*
integer ['ɪntɪʤər] *n* : entero *m*
integral ['ɪntɪgrəl] *adj* : integral, esencial
integrate ['ɪntə,greɪt] *v* **-grated; -grating** *vt* **1** UNITE : integrar, unir **2** DESEGREGATE : eliminar la segregación de — *vi* : integrarse
integration [,ɪntə'greɪʃən] *n* : integración *f*
integrity [ɪn'tɛgrət̬i] *n* : integridad *f*
intellect ['ɪntəl,ɛkt] *n* : intelecto *m*, inteligencia *f*, capacidad *f* intelectual
intellectual[1] [,ɪntə'lɛkʧʊəl] *adj* : intelectual — **intellectually** *adv*
intellectual[2] *n* : intelectual *mf*
intellectualism [,ɪntə'lɛkʧʊə,lɪzəm] *n* : intelectualismo *m*
intelligence [ɪn'tɛləʤənts] *n* **1** : inteligencia *f* **2** INFORMATION, NEWS : inteligencia *f*, información *f*, noticias *fpl*
intelligent [ɪn'tɛləʤənt] *adj* : inteligente — **intelligently** *adv*
intelligentsia [ɪn,tɛlə'ʤɛntsiə, -'gɛn-] *ns & pl* : intelectualidad *f*
intelligibility [ɪn,tɛləʤə'bɪlət̬i] *n* : inteligibilidad *f*
intelligible [ɪn'tɛləʤəbəl] *adj* : inteligible, comprensible — **intelligibly** [-bli] *adv*
intemperance [ɪn'tɛmpərənts] *n* : inmoderación *f*, intemperancia *f*
intemperate [ɪn'tɛmpərət] *adj* : excesivo, inmoderado, desmedido
intend [ɪn'tɛnd] *vt* **1** MEAN : querer decir ⟨that's not what I intended : eso no es lo que quería decir⟩ **2** PLAN : tener planeado, proyectar, proponerse ⟨I intend to finish by Thursday : me propongo acabar para el jueves⟩
intended [ɪn'tɛndəd] *adj* **1** PLANNED : previsto, proyectado **2** INTENTIONAL : intencional, deliberado
intense [ɪn'tɛnts] *adj* **1** EXTREME : intenso, extremo ⟨intense pain : dolor intenso⟩ **2** : profundo, intenso ⟨to my intense relief : para mi alivio profundo⟩ ⟨intense enthusiasm : entusiasmo ardiente⟩
intensely [ɪn'tɛntsli] *adv* : sumamente, profundamente, intensamente
intensification [ɪn,tɛntsəfə'keɪʃən] *n* : intensificación *f*
intensify [ɪn'tɛntsə,faɪ] *v* **-fied; -fying** *vt* **1** STRENGTHEN : intensificar, redoblar ⟨to intensify one's efforts : redoblar uno sus esfuerzos⟩ **2** SHARPEN : intensificar, agudizar (dolor, ansiedad) — *vi* : intensificarse, hacerse más intenso
intensity [ɪn'tɛntsət̬i] *n, pl* **-ties** : intensidad *f*
intensive [ɪn'tɛntsɪv] *adj* : intensivo — **intensively** *adv*
intent[1] [ɪn'tɛnt] *adj* **1** FIXED : concentrado, fijo ⟨an intent stare : una mirada fija⟩ **2 intent on** *or* **intent upon** : resuelto a, atento a
intent[2] *n* **1** PURPOSE : intención *f*, propósito *m* **2 for all intents and purposes** : a todos los efectos, prácticamente
intention [ɪn'tɛntʃən] *n* : intención *f*, propósito *m*
intentional [ɪn'tɛntʃənəl] *adj* : intencional, deliberado
intentionally [ɪn'tɛntʃənəli] *adv* : a propósito, adrede
intently [ɪn'tɛntli] *adv* : atentamente, fijamente
inter [ɪn'tər] *vt* **-terred; -terring** : enterrar, inhumar
interact [,ɪntər'ækt] *vi* : interactuar, actuar recíprocamente, relacionarse
interaction [,ɪntər'ækʃən] *n* : interacción *f*, interrelación *f*
interactive [,ɪntər'æktɪv] *adj* : interactivo
interbreed [,ɪntər'bri:d] *v* **-bred** [-'brɛd]; **-breeding** *vt* : cruzar — *vi* : cruzarse
intercalate [ɪn'tərkə,leɪt] *vt* **-lated; -lating** : intercalar
intercede [,ɪntər'si:d] *vi* **-ceded; -ceding** : interceder
intercept [,ɪntər'sɛpt] *vt* : interceptar
interception [,ɪntər'sɛpʃən] *n* : intercepción *f*
intercession [,ɪntər'sɛʃən] *n* : intercesión *f*

interchange[1] [ˌɪntərˈʧeɪnʤ] *vt* **-changed; -changing** : intercambiar

interchange[2] [ˈɪntərˌʧeɪnʤ] *n* **1** EXCHANGE : intercambio *m*, cambio *m* **2** JUNCTION : empalme *m*, enlace *m* de carreteras

interchangeable [ˌɪntərˈʧeɪnʤəbəl] *adj* : intercambiable

intercity [ˈɪntərˈsɪt̬i] *adj* : interurbano

intercollegiate [ˌɪntərkəˈliːʤət, -ʤiət] *adj* : interuniversitario

interconnect [ˌɪntərkəˈnɛkt] *vt* **1** : conectar, interconectar (en tecnología) **2** RELATE : interrelacionar — *vi* **1** : conectar **2** : interrelacionarse

intercontinental [ˌɪntərˌkɑntənˈnɛtəl] *adj* : intercontinental

intercourse [ˈɪntərˌkors] *n* **1** RELATIONS : relaciones *fpl*, trato *m* **2** COPULATION : acto *m* sexual, relaciones *fpl* sexuales, coito *m*

interdenominational [ˌɪntərdɪˌnɑməˈneɪʃənəl] *adj* : interconfesional

interdepartmental [ˌɪntərdɪˌpɑrtˈmɛntəl, -ˌdiː-] *adj* : interdepartamental

interdependence [ˌɪntərdɪˈpɛndənts] *n* : interdependencia *f*

interdependent [ˌɪntərdɪˈpɛndənt] *adj* : interdependiente

interdict [ˌɪntərˈdɪkt] *vt* **1** PROHIBIT : prohibir **2** : cortar (las líneas de comunicación o provisión del enemigo)

interest[1] [ˈɪntrəst, -təˌrɛst] *vt* : interesar

interest[2] *n* **1** SHARE, STAKE : interés *m*, participación *f* **2** BENEFIT : provecho *m*, beneficio *m*, interés *m* ⟨in the public interest : en el interés público⟩ **3** CHARGE : interés *m*, cargo *m* ⟨compound interest : interés compuesto⟩ **4** CURIOSITY : interés *m*, curiosidad *f* **5** COLOR : color *m*, interés *m* ⟨places of local interest : lugares de color local⟩ **6** HOBBY : afición *f*

interesting [ˈɪntrəstɪŋ, -təˌrɛstɪŋ] *adj* : interesante — **interestingly** *adv*

interface [ˈɪntərˌfeɪs] *n* **1** : punto *m* de contacto ⟨oil-water interface : punto de contacto entre el agua y el aceite⟩ **2** : interfaz *f* (de una computadora), interfase *f*

interfere [ˌɪntərˈfɪr] *vi* **-fered; -fering 1** INTERPOSE : interponerse, hacer interferencia ⟨to interfere with a play : obstruir una jugada⟩ **2** MEDDLE : entrometerse, interferir, intervenir **3 to interfere with** DISRUPT : afectar (una actividad), interferir (la radiotransmisión) **4 to interfere with** TOUCH : tocar ⟨someone interfered with my papers : alguien tocó mis papeles⟩

interference [ˌɪntərˈfɪrənts] *n* : interferencia *f*, intromisión *f*

intergalactic [ˌɪntərgəˈlæktɪk] *adj* : intergaláctico

intergovernmental [ˌɪntərˌgʌvər-ˈmɛntəl, -vərn-] *adj* : intergubernamental

interim[1] [ˈɪntərəm] *adj* : interino, provisional

interim[2] *n* **1** : interín *m*, intervalo *m* **2 in the interim** : en el interín, mientras tanto

interior[1] [ɪnˈtɪriər] *adj* : interior

interior[2] *n* : interior *m*

interject [ˌɪntərˈʤɛkt] *vt* : interponer, agregar

interjection [ˌɪntərˈʤɛkʃən] *n* **1** : interjección *f* (en lingüística) **2** EXCLAMATION : exclamación *f* **3** INTERPOSITION, INTERRUPTION : interposición *f*, interrupción *f*

interlace [ˌɪntərˈleɪs] *vt* **-laced; -lacing 1** INTERWEAVE : entrelazar **2** INTERSPERSE : intercalar

interlock [ˌɪntərˈlɑk] *vt* **1** UNITE : trabar, unir **2** ENGAGE, MESH : engranar — *vi* : entrelazarse, trabarse

interloper [ˌɪntərˈloːpər] *n* **1** INTRUDER : intruso *m*, -sa *f* **2** MEDDLER : entrometido *m*, -da *f*

interlude [ˈɪntərˌluːd] *n* **1** INTERVAL : intervalo *m*, intermedio *m* (en el teatro) **2** : interludio *m* (en música)

intermarriage [ˌɪntərˈmærɪʤ] *n* **1** : matrimonio *m* mixto (entre miembros de distintas razas o religiones) **2** : matrimonio *m* entre miembros del mismo grupo

intermarry [ˌɪntərˈmæri] *vi* **-married; -marrying 1** : casarse (con miembros de otros grupos) **2** : casarse entre sí (con miembros del mismo grupo)

intermediary[1] [ˌɪntərˈmiːdiˌɛri] *adj* : intermediario

intermediary[2] *n, pl* **-aries** : intermediario *m*, -ria *f*

intermediate[1] [ˌɪntərˈmiːdiət] *adj* : intermedio

intermediate[2] *n* GO-BETWEEN : intermediario *m*, -ria *f*; mediador *m*, -dora *f*

interment [ɪnˈtərmənt] *n* : entierro *m*

interminable [ɪnˈtərmənəbəl] *adj* : interminable, constante — **interminably** [-bli] *adv*

intermingle [ˌɪntərˈmɪŋgəl] *vt* **-mingled; -mingling** : entremezclar, mezclar — *vi* : entremezclarse

intermission [ˌɪntərˈmɪʃən] *n* : intermisión *f*, intervalo *m*, intermedio *m*

intermittent [ˌɪntərˈmɪtənt] *adj* : intermitente — **intermittently** *adv*

intermix [ˌɪntərˈmɪks] *vt* : entremezclar

intern[1] [ˈɪnˌtərn, ɪnˈtərn] *vt* : confinar (durante la guerra) — *vi* : servir de interno, hacer las prácticas

intern[2] [ˈɪnˌtərn] *n* : interno *m*, -na *f*

internal [ɪnˈtərnəl] *adj* : interno, interior ⟨internal bleeding : hemorragia interna⟩ ⟨internal affairs : asuntos interiores, asuntos domésticos⟩ — **internally** *adv*

international [ˌɪntərˈnæʃənəl] *adj* : internacional — **internationally** *adv*

internationalize [ˌɪntərˈnæʃənəˌlaɪz] *vt* **-ized; -izing** : internacionalizar

internee [ˌɪnˌtərˈniː] *n* : interno *m*, -na *f*

Internet [ˈɪntərˌnɛt] *n* : Internet *mf*

internist [ˈɪnˌtərnɪst] *n* : internista *mf*
interpersonal [ˌɪntərˈpərsənəl] *adj* : interpersonal
interplay [ˈɪntərˌpleɪ] *n* : interacción *f*, juego *m*
interpolate [ɪnˈtərpəˌleɪt] *vt* **-lated; -lating** : interpolar
interpose [ˌɪntərˈpoːz] *v* **-posed; -posing** *vt* : interponer, interrumpir con — *vi* : interponerse
interposition [ˌɪntərpəˈzɪʃən] *n* : interposición *f*
interpret [ɪnˈtərprət] *vt* : interpretar
interpretation [ɪnˌtərprəˈteɪʃən] *n* : interpretación *f*
interpretative [ɪnˈtərprəˌteɪt̬ɪv] *adj* : interpretativo
interpreter [ɪnˈtərprət̬ər] *n* : intérprete *mf*
interpretive [ɪnˈtərprət̬ɪv] *adj* : interpretativo
interracial [ˌɪntərˈreɪʃəl] *adj* : interracial
interrelate [ˌɪntərɪˈleɪt] *v* **-related; -relating** : interrelacionar
interrelationship [ˌɪntərɪˈleɪʃənˌʃɪp] *n* : interrelación *f*
interrogate [ɪnˈtɛrəˌgeɪt] *vt* **-gated; -gating** : interrogar, someter a un interrogatorio
interrogation [ɪnˌtɛrəˈgeɪʃən] *n* : interrogación *f*
interrogative[1] [ˌɪntəˈrɑgət̬ɪv] *adj* : interrogativo
interrogative[2] *n* : interrogativo *m*
interrogator [ɪnˈtɛrəˌgeɪt̬ər] *n* : interrogador *m*, -dora *f*
interrogatory [ˌɪntəˈrɑgəˌtori] *adj* → **interrogative**[1]
interrupt [ˌɪntəˈrʌpt] *v* : interrumpir
interruption [ˌɪntəˈrʌpʃən] *n* : interrupción *f*
intersect [ˌɪntərˈsɛkt] *vt* : cruzar, cortar — *vi* : cruzarse (dícese de los caminos), intersectarse (dícese de las líneas o figuras), cortarse
intersection [ˌɪntərˈsɛkʃən] *n* : intersección *f*, cruce *m*
intersperse [ˌɪntərˈspərs] *vt* **-spersed; -spersing** : intercalar, entremezclar
interstate [ˌɪntərˈsteɪt] *adj* : interestatal
interstellar [ˌɪntərˈstɛlər] *adj* : interestelar
interstice [ɪnˈtərstəs] *n, pl* **-stices** [-stəˌsiːz, -stəsəz] : intersticio *m*
intertwine [ˌɪntərˈtwaɪn] *vi* **-twined; -twining** : entrelazarse
interval [ˈɪntərvəl] *n* : intervalo *m*
intervene [ˌɪntərˈviːn] *vi* **-vened; -vening** **1** ELAPSE : transcurrir, pasar ⟨the intervening years : los años intermediarios⟩ **2** INTERCEDE : intervenir, interceder, mediar
intervention [ˌɪntərˈvɛntʃən] *n* : intervención *f*
interview[1] [ˈɪntərˌvjuː] *vt* : entrevistar — *vi* : hacer entrevistas
interview[2] *n* : entrevista *f*
interviewer [ˈɪntərˌvjuːər] *n* : entrevistador *m*, -dora *f*
interweave [ˌɪntərˈwiːv] *v* **-wove** [-ˈwoːv]; **-woven** [-ˈwoːvən]; **-weaving** *vt* : entretejer, entrelazar — *vi* INTERTWINE : entrelazarse, entretejerse
interwoven [ˌɪntərˈwoːvən] *adj* : entretejido
intestate [ɪnˈtɛsˌteɪt, -tət] *adj* : intestado
intestinal [ɪnˈtɛstənəl] *adj* : intestinal
intestine [ɪnˈtɛstən] *n* **1** : intestino *m* **2** **small intestine** : intestino *m* delgado **3** **large intestine** : intestino *m* grueso
intimacy [ˈɪntəməsi] *n, pl* **-cies** **1** CLOSENESS : intimidad *f* **2** FAMILIARITY : familiaridad *f*
intimate[1] [ˈɪntəˌmeɪt] *vt* **-mated; -mating** : insinuar, dar a entender
intimate[2] [ˈɪntəmət] *adj* **1** CLOSE : íntimo, de confianza ⟨intimate friends : amigos íntimos⟩ **2** PRIVATE : íntimo, privado ⟨intimate clubs : clubes íntimos⟩ **3** INNERMOST, SECRET : íntimo, secreto ⟨intimate fantasies : fantasías secretas⟩
intimate[3] *n* : amigo *m* íntimo, amiga *f* íntima
intimidate [ɪnˈtɪməˌdeɪt] *vt* **-dated; -dating** : intimidar
intimidation [ɪnˌtɪməˈdeɪʃən] *n* : intimidación *f*
into [ˈɪnˌtuː] *prep* **1** (*indicating motion*) : en, a, contra, dentro de ⟨she got into bed : se metió en la cama⟩ ⟨to get into a plane : subir a un avión⟩ ⟨he crashed into the wall : chocó contra la pared⟩ ⟨looking into the sun : mirando al sol⟩ **2** (*indicating state or condition*) : a, en ⟨to burst into tears : echarse a llorar⟩ ⟨the water turned into ice : el agua se convirtió en hielo⟩ ⟨to translate into English : traducir al inglés⟩ **3** (*indicating time*) ⟨far into the night : hasta bien entrada la noche⟩ ⟨he's well into his eighties : tiene los ochenta bien cumplidos⟩ **4** (*in mathematics*) ⟨3 into 12 is 4 : 12 dividido por 3 es 4⟩
intolerable [ɪnˈtɑlərəbəl] *adj* : intolerable — **intolerably** [-bli] *adv*
intolerance [ɪnˈtɑlərənts] *n* : intolerancia *f*
intolerant [ɪnˈtɑlərənt] *adj* : intolerante
intonation [ˌɪntoˈneɪʃən] *n* : entonación *f*
intone [ɪnˈtoːn] *vt* **-toned; -toning** : entonar
intoxicant [ɪnˈtɑksɪkənt] *n* : bebida *f* alcohólica
intoxicate [ɪnˈtɑksəˌkeɪt] *vt* **-cated; -cating** : emborrachar, embriagar
intoxicated [ɪnˈtɑksəˌkeɪt̬əd] *adj* : borracho, embriagado
intoxicating [ɪnˈtɑksəˌkeɪt̬ɪŋ] *adj* : embriagador
intoxication [ɪnˌtɑksəˈkeɪʃən] *n* : embriaguez *f*
intractable [ɪnˈtræktəbəl] *adj* : obstinado, intratable
intramural [ˌɪntrəˈmjʊrəl] *adj* : interno, dentro de la universidad

intransigence [ɪnˈtrænʦəʤənʦ, -ˈtrænzə-] *n* : intransigencia *f*
intransigent [ɪnˈtrænʦəʤənt, -ˈtrænzə-] *adj* : intransigente
intransitive [ɪnˈtrænʦəṭɪv, -ˈtrænzə-] *adj* : intransitivo
intravenous [ˌɪntrəˈviːnəs] *adj* : intravenoso — **intravenously** *adv*
intrepid [ɪnˈtrɛpəd] *adj* : intrépido
intricacy [ˈɪntrɪkəsi] *n, pl* **-cies** : complejidad *f*, lo intrincado
intricate [ˈɪntrɪkət] *adj* : intrincado, complicado — **intricately** *adv*
intrigue[1] [ɪnˈtriːg] *v* **-trigued; -triguing** : intrigar
intrigue[2] [ˈɪnˌtriːg, ɪnˈtriːg] *n* : intriga *f*
intriguing [ɪnˈtriːgɪŋ] *adj* : intrigante, fascinante
intrinsic [ɪnˈtrɪnzɪk, -ˈtrɪnʦɪk] *adj* : intrínseco, esencial — **intrinsically** [-zɪkli, -sɪ-] *adv*
introduce [ˌɪntrəˈduːs, -ˈdjuːs] *vt* **-duced; -ducing 1** : presentar ⟨let me introduce my father : permítame presentar a mi padre⟩ **2** : introducir (algo nuevo), lanzar (un producto), presentar (una ley), proponer (una idea o un tema)
introduction [ˌɪntrəˈdʌkʃən] *n* : introducción *f*, presentación *f*
introductory [ˌɪntrəˈdʌktəri] *adj* : introductorio, preliminar, de introducción
introspection [ˌɪntrəˈspɛkʃən] *n* : introspección *f*
introspective [ˌɪntrəˈspɛktɪv] *adj* : introspectivo — **introspectively** *adv*
introvert [ˈɪntrəˌvərt] *n* : introvertido *m*, -da *f*
introverted [ˈɪntrəˌvərṭəd] *adj* : introvertido
intrude [ɪnˈtruːd] *v* **-truded; -truding** *vi* **1** INTERFERE : inmiscuirse, entrometerse **2** DISTURB, INTERRUPT : molestar, estorbar, interrumpir — *vt* : introducir por fuerza
intruder [ɪnˈtruːdər] *n* : intruso *m*, -sa *f*
intrusion [ɪnˈtruːʒən] *n* : intrusión *f*
intrusive [ɪnˈtruːsɪv] *adj* : intruso
intuit [ɪnˈtuːɪt, -ˈtjuː-] *vt* : intuir
intuition [ˌɪntʊˈɪʃən, -tjʊ-] *n* : intuición *f*
intuitive [ɪnˈtuːəṭɪv, -ˈtjuː-] *adj* : intuitivo — **intuitively** *adv*
inundate [ˈɪnənˌdeɪt] *vt* **-dated; -dating** : inundar
inundation [ˌɪnənˈdeɪʃən] *n* : inundación *f*
inure [ɪˈnʊr, -ˈnjʊr] *vt* **-ured; -uring** : acostumbrar, habituar
invade [ɪnˈveɪd] *vt* **-vaded; -vading** : invadir
invader [ɪnˈveɪdər] *n* : invasor *m*, -sora *f*
invalid[1] [ɪnˈvæləd] *adj* : inválido, nulo
invalid[2] [ˈɪnvələd] *adj* : inválido, discapacitado
invalid[3] [ˈɪnvələd] *n* : inválido *m*, -da *f*
invalidate [ɪnˈvæləˌdeɪt] *vt* **-dated; -dating** : invalidar
invalidity [ˌɪnvəˈlɪdəṭi] *n, pl* **-ties** : invalidez *f*, falta de validez *f*
invaluable [ɪnˈvæljəbəl, -ˈvæljʊə-] *adj* : invalorable, inestimable, inapreciable
invariable [ɪnˈværiəbəl] *adj* : invariable, constante — **invariably** [-bli] *adv*
invasion [ɪnˈveɪʒən] *n* : invasión *f*
invasive [ɪnˈveɪsɪv] *adj* : invasivo
invective [ɪnˈvɛktɪv] *n* : invectiva *f*, improperio *m*, vituperio *m*
inveigh [ɪnˈveɪ] *vi* **to inveigh against** : arremeter contra, lanzar invectivas contra
inveigle [ɪnˈveɪgəl, -ˈviː-] *vt* **-gled; -gling** : engatusar, embaucar, persuadir con engaños
invent [ɪnˈvɛnt] *vt* : inventar
invention [ɪnˈvɛnʧən] *n* : invención *f*, invento *m*
inventive [ɪnˈvɛntɪv] *adj* : inventivo
inventiveness [ɪnˈvɛntɪvnəs] *n* : ingenio *m*, inventiva *f*
inventor [ɪnˈvɛntər] *n* : inventor *m*, -tora *f*
inventory[1] [ˈɪnvənˌtɔri] *vt* **-ried; -rying** : inventariar
inventory[2] *n, pl* **-ries 1** LIST : inventario *m* **2** STOCK : existencias *fpl*
inverse[1] [ɪnˈvərs, ˈɪnˌvərs] *adj* : inverso — **inversely** *adv*
inverse[2] *n* : inverso *m*
inversion [ɪnˈvɛrʒən] *n* : inversión *f*
invert [ɪnˈvərt] *vt* : invertir
invertebrate[1] [ɪnˈvərṭəbrət, -ˌbreɪt] *adj* : invertebrado
invertebrate[2] *n* : invertebrado *m*
invest [ɪnˈvɛst] *vt* **1** AUTHORIZE : investir, autorizar **2** CONFER : conferir **3** : invertir, dedicar ⟨he invested his savings in stocks : invirtió sus ahorros en acciones⟩ ⟨to invest one's time : dedicar uno su tiempo⟩
investigate [ɪnˈvɛstəˌgeɪt] *v* **-gated; -gating** : investigar
investigation [ɪnˌvɛstəˈgeɪʃən] *n* : investigación *f*, estudio *m*
investigative [ɪnˈvɛstəˌgeɪṭɪv] *adj* : investigador
investigator [ɪnˈvɛstəˌgeɪṭər] *n* : investigador *m*, -dora *f*
investiture [ɪnˈvɛstəˌʧʊr, -ʧər] *n* : investidura *f*
investment [ɪnˈvɛstmənt] *n* : inversión *f*
investor [ɪnˈvɛstər] *n* : inversor *m*, -sora *f*; inversionista *mf*
inveterate [ɪnˈvɛṭərət] *adj* **1** DEEP-SEATED : inveterado, enraizado **2** HABITUAL : empedernido, incorregible
invidious [ɪnˈvɪdiəs] *adj* **1** OBNOXIOUS : repugnante, odioso **2** UNJUST : injusto — **invidiously** *adv*
invigorate [ɪnˈvɪgəˌreɪt] *vt* **-rated; -rating** : vigorizar, animar
invigorating [ɪnˈvɪgəˌreɪṭɪŋ] *adj* : vigorizante, estimulante
invigoration [ɪnˌvɪgəˈreɪʃən] *n* : animación *f*
invincibility [ɪnˌvɪnʦəˈbɪləṭi] *n* : invencibilidad *f*

invincible [ɪnˈvɪntsəbəl] *adj* : invencible — **invincibly** [-bli] *adv*
inviolable [ɪnˈvaɪələbəl] *adj* : inviolable
inviolate [ɪnˈvaɪələt] *adj* : inviolado, puro
invisibility [ɪnˌvɪzəˈbɪləṭi] *n* : invisibilidad *f*
invisible [ɪnˈvɪzəbəl] *adj* : invisible — **invisibly** [-bli] *adv*
invitation [ˌɪnvəˈteɪʃən] *n* : invitación *f*
invite [ɪnˈvaɪt] *vt* **-vited; -viting 1** ATTRACT : atraer, tentar ⟨a book that invites interest : un libro que atrae el interés⟩ **2** PROVOKE : provocar, buscar ⟨to invite trouble : buscarse problemas⟩ **3** ASK : invitar ⟨we invited them for dinner : los invitamos acenar⟩ **4** SOLICIT : solicitar, buscar (preguntas, comentarios, etc.)
inviting [ɪnˈvaɪṭɪŋ] *adj* : atractivo, atrayente
invocation [ˌɪnvəˈkeɪʃən] *n* : invocación *f*
invoice[1] [ˈɪnˌvɔɪs] *vt* **-voiced; -voicing** : facturar
invoice[2] *n* : factura *f*
invoke [ɪnˈvoːk] *vt* **-voked; -voking 1** : invocar, apelar a ⟨she invoked our aid : apeló a nuestra ayuda⟩ **2** CITE : invocar, citar ⟨to invoke a precedent : invocar un precedente⟩ **3** CONJURE UP : hacer aparecer, invocar
involuntary [ɪnˈvɑlənˌtɛri] *adj* : involuntario — **involuntarily** [ɪn-ˌvɑlənˈtrəli] *adv*
involve [ɪnˈvɑlv] *vt* **-volved; -volving 1** ENGAGE : ocupar (con una tarea, etc.) **2** IMPLICATE : involucrar, enredar, implicar ⟨to be involved in a crime : estar involucrado en un crimen⟩ **3** CONCERN : concernir, afectar **4** CONNECT : conectar, relacionar **5** ENTAIL, INCLUDE : suponer, incluir, consistir en ⟨what does the job involve? : ¿en qué consiste el trabajo?⟩ **6 to be involved with someone** : tener una relación (amorosa) con alguien
involved [ɪnˈvɑlvd] *adj* **1** COMPLEX, INTRICATE : complicado, complejo **2** CONCERNED : interesado, afectado
involvement [ɪnˈvɑlvmənt] *n* **1** PARTICIPATION : participación *f*, complicidad *f* **2** RELATIONSHIP : relación *f*
invulnerable [ɪnˈvʌlnərəbəl] *adj* : invulnerable
inward[1] [ˈɪnwərd] *or* **inwards** [-wərdz] *adv* : hacia adentro, hacia el interior
inward[2] *adj* INSIDE : interior, interno
inwardly [ˈɪnwərdli] *adv* **1** MENTALLY, SPIRITUALLY : por dentro **2** INTERNALLY : internamente, interiormente **3** PRIVATELY : para sus adentros, para sí
iodide [ˈaɪəˌdaɪd] *n* : yoduro *m*
iodine [ˈaɪəˌdaɪn, -dən] *n* : yodo *m*, tintura *f* de yodo
iodize [ˈaɪəˌdaɪz] *vt* **-dized; -dizing** : yodar
ion [ˈaɪən, ˈaɪˌɑn] *n* : ion *m*
ionic [aɪˈɑnɪk] *adj* : iónico
ionize [ˈaɪəˌnaɪz] *v* **ionized; ionizing** : ionizar
ionosphere [aɪˈɑnəˌsfɪr] *n* : ionosfera *f*
iota [aɪˈoːṭə] *n* : pizca *f*, ápice *m*
IOU [ˌaɪˌoˈjuː] *n* : pagaré *m*, vale *m*
IPA [ˌaɪˌpiːˈeɪ] *n* *I*nternational *P*honetic *A*lphabet : AFI *m*
IQ [ˌaɪˈkjuː] *n* (*i*ntelligence *q*uotient) : CI *m*, coeficiente *m* intelectual
Iranian [ɪˈreɪniən, -ˈræ-, -ˈrɑ-; aɪˈ-] *n* : iraní *mf* — **Iranian** *adj*
Iraqi [ɪˈrɑkiː] *n* : iraquí *mf* — **Iraqi** *adj*
irascibility [ɪˌræsəˈbɪləṭi] *n* : irascibilidad *f*
irascible [ɪˈræsəbəl] *adj* : irascible
irate [aɪˈreɪt] *adj* : furioso, airado, iracundo — **irately** *adv*
ire [ˈaɪr] *n* : ira *f*, cólera *f*
iridescence [ˌɪrəˈdɛsənts] *n* : iridiscencia *f*
iridescent [ˌɪrəˈdɛsənt] *adj* : iridiscente
iridium [ɪˈrɪdiəm] *n* : iridio *m*
iris [ˈaɪrəs] *n, pl* **irises** *or* **irides** [ˈaɪrəˌdiːz, ˈɪr-] **1** : iris *m* (del ojo) **2** : lirio *m* (planta)
Irish[1] [ˈaɪrɪʃ] *adj* : irlandés
Irish[2] **1** : irlandés *m* (idioma) **2 the Irish** *npl* : los irlandeses
Irishman [ˈaɪrɪʃmən] *n, pl* **-men** : irlandés *m*
Irishwoman [ˈaɪrɪʃˌwʊmən] *n, pl* **-women** : irlandesa *f*
irk [ˈərk] *vt* : fastidiar, irritar, preocupar
irksome [ˈərksəm] *adj* : irritante, fastidioso — **irksomely** *adv*
iron[1] [ˈaɪərn] *v* : planchar
iron[2] *n* **1** : hierro *m*, fierro *m* ⟨a will of iron : una voluntad de hierro, una voluntad férrea⟩ **2** : plancha *f* (para planchar la ropa)
ironclad [ˈaɪərnˈklæd] *adj* **1** : acorazado, blindado **2** STRICT : riguroso, estricto
ironic [aɪˈrɑnɪk] *or* **ironical** [-nɪkəl] *adj* : irónico — **ironically** [-kli] *adv*
ironing [ˈaɪərnɪŋ] *n* **1** PRESSING : planchada *f* **2** : ropa *f* para planchar
ironing board *n* : tabla *f* (de planchar)
ironwork [ˈaɪərnˌwərk] *n* **1** : obra *f* de hierro **2 ironworks** *npl* : fundición *f*
ironworker [ˈaɪərnˌwərkər] *n* : fundidor *m*, -dora *f*
irony [ˈaɪrəni] *n, pl* **-nies** : ironía *f*
irradiate [ɪˈreɪdiˌeɪt] *vt* **-ated; -ating** : irradiar, radiar
irradiation [ɪˌreɪdiˈeɪʃən] *n* : irradiación *f*, radiación *f*
irrational [ɪˈræʃənəl] *adj* : irracional — **irrationally** *adv*
irrationality [ɪˌræʃəˈnæləṭi] *n, pl* **-ties** : irracionalidad *f*
irreconcilable [ɪˌrɛkənˈsaɪləbəl] *adj* : irreconciliable
irrecoverable [ˌɪrɪˈkʌvərəbəl] *adj* : irrecuperable — **irrecoverably** [-bli] *adv*

irredeemable [ˌɪrɪˈdiːməbəl] *adj* **1** : irredimible (dícese de un bono) **2** HOPELESS : irremediable, irreparable
irreducible [ˌɪrɪˈduːsəbəl, -ˈdjuː-] *adj* : irreducible — **irreducibly** [-bli] *adv*
irrefutable [ˌɪrɪˈfjuːt̬əbəl, ɪrˈrɛfjə-] *adj* : irrefutable
irregular[1] [ɪˈrɛgjələr] *adj* : irregular — **irregularly** *adv*
irregular[2] *n* **1** : soldado *m* irregular **2 irregulars** *npl* : artículos *mpl* defectuosos
irregularity [ɪˌrɛgjəˈlærət̬i] *n, pl* **-ties** : irregularidad *f*
irrelevance [ɪˈrɛləvənts] *n* : irrelevancia *f*
irrelevant [ɪˈrɛləvənt] *adj* : irrelevante
irreligious [ˌɪrɪˈlɪʤəs] *adj* : irreligioso
irreparable [ɪˈrɛpərəbəl] *adj* : irreparable
irreplaceable [ˌɪrɪˈpleɪsəbəl] *adj* : irreemplazable, insustituible
irrepressible [ˌɪrɪˈprɛsəbəl] *adj* : incontenible, incontrolable
irreproachable [ɪrɪˈproːʧəbəl] *adj* : irreprochable, intachable
irresistible [ˌɪrɪˈzɪst̬əbəl] *adj* : irresistible — **irresistibly** [-bli] *adv*
irresolute [ɪˈrɛzəˌluːt] *adj* : irresoluto, indeciso
irresolutely [ɪˈrɛzəˌluːtli, -ˌrzəˈluːt-] *adv* : de manera indecisa
irresolution [ɪˌrɛzəˈluːʃən] *n* : irresolución *f*
irrespective of [ˌɪrɪˈspɛktɪvəv] *prep* : sin tomar en consideración, sin tener en cuenta
irresponsibility [ˌɪrɪˌspɑntsəˈbɪlət̬i] *n, pl* **-ties** : irresponsabilidad *f*, falta *f* de responsabilidad
irresponsible [ˌɪrɪˈspɑntsəbəl] *adj* : irresponsable — **irresponsibly** [-bli] *adv*
irretrievable [ˌɪrɪˈtriːvəbəl] *adj* IRRECOVERABLE : irrecuperable
irreverence [ɪˈrɛvərənts] *n* : irreverencia *f*, falta *f* de respeto
irreverent [ɪˈrɛvərənt] *adj* : irreverente, irrespetuoso
irreversible [ˌɪrɪˈvərsəbəl] *adj* : irreversible
irrevocable [ɪˈrɛvəkəbəl] *adj* : irrevocable — **irrevocably** [-bli] *adv*
irrigate [ˈɪrəˌgeɪt] *vt* **-gated; -gating** : irrigar, regar
irrigation [ˌɪrəˈgeɪʃən] *n* : irrigación *f*, riego *m*
irritability [ˌɪrət̬əˈbɪlət̬i] *n, pl* **-ties** : irritabilidad *f*
irritable [ˈɪrət̬əbəl] *adj* : irritable, colérico
irritably [ˈɪrət̬əbli] *adv* : con irritación
irritant[1] [ˈɪrətənt] *adj* : irritante
irritant[2] *n* : agente *m* irritante
irritate [ˈɪrəˌteɪt] *vt* **-tated; -tating 1** ANNOY : irritar, molestar **2** : irritar (en medicina)
irritating [ˈɪrəˌteɪt̬ɪŋ] *adj* : irritante
irritatingly [ˈɪrəˌteɪt̬ɪŋli] *adv* : de modo irritante, fastidiosamente
irritation [ˌɪrəˈteɪʃən] *n* : irritación *f*
is → **be**
Islam [ɪsˈlɑm, ɪz-, -ˈlæm; ˈɪsˌlɑm, ˈɪz-, -ˌlæm] *n* : el Islam
Islamic [ɪsˈlɑmɪk, ɪz-, -ˈlæ-] *adj* : islámico
island [ˈaɪlənd] *n* : isla *f*
islander [ˈaɪləndər] *n* : isleño *m*, -ña *f*
isle [ˈaɪl] *n* : isla *f*, islote *m*
islet [ˈaɪlət] *n* : islote *m*
isolate [ˈaɪsəˌleɪt] *vt* **-lated; -lating** : aislar
isolated [ˈaɪsəˌleɪt̬əd] *adj* : aislado, solo
isolation [ˌaɪsəˈleɪʃən] *n* : aislamiento *m*
isometric [ˌaɪsəˈmɛtrɪk] *adj* : isométrico
isometrics [ˌaɪsəˈmɛtrɪks] *ns & pl* : isometría *f*
isosceles [aɪˈsɑsəˌliːz] *adj* : isósceles
isotope [ˈaɪsəˌtoːp] *n* : isótopo *m*
Israeli [ɪzˈreɪli] *n* : israelí *mf* — **Israeli** *adj*
issue[1] [ˈɪˌʃuː] *v* **-sued; -suing** *vi* **1** EMERGE : emerger, salir, fluir **2** DESCEND : descender (dícese de los padres o antepasados específicos) **3** EMANATE, RESULT : emanar, surgir, resultar — *vt* **1** EMIT : emitir **2** DISTRIBUTE : emitir, distribuir ⟨to issue a new stamp : emitir un sello nuevo⟩ **3** PUBLISH : publicar
issue[2] *n* **1** EMERGENCE, FLOW : emergencia *f*, flujo *m* **2** PROGENY : descendencia *f*, progenie *f* **3** OUTCOME, RESULT : desenlace *m*, resultado *m*, consecuencia *f* **4** MATTER, QUESTION : asunto *m*, cuestión *f* **5** PUBLICATION : publicación *f*, distribución *f*, emisión *f* **6** : número *m* (de un periódico o una revista)
isthmus [ˈɪsməs] *n* : istmo *m*
it [ˈɪt] *pron* **1** (*as subject; generally omitted*) : él, ella, ello ⟨it's a big building : es un edificio grande⟩ ⟨who was it? : ¿quién era?⟩ **2** (*as indirect object*) : le ⟨I'll give it some water : voy a darle agua⟩ **3** (*as direct object*) : lo, la ⟨give it to me : dámelo⟩ **4** (*as object of a preposition; generally omitted*) : él, ella, ello ⟨behind it : detrás, detrás de él⟩ **5** (*in impersonal constructions*) ⟨it's raining : está lloviendo⟩ ⟨it's 8 o'clock : son las ocho⟩ **6** (*as the implied subject or object of a verb*) ⟨it is necessary to study : es necesario estudiar⟩ ⟨to give it all one's got : dar lo mejor de sí⟩
Italian [ɪˈtæliən, aɪ-] *n* **1** : italiano *m*, -na *f* **2** : italiano *m* (idioma) — **Italian** *adj*
italic[1] [ɪˈtælɪk, aɪ-] *adj* : en cursiva, en bastardilla
italic[2] *n* : cursiva *f*, bastardilla *f*
italicize [ɪˈtæləˌsaɪz, aɪ-] *vt* **-cized; -cizing** : poner en cursiva
itch[1] [ˈɪʧ] *vi* **1** : picar ⟨her arm itched : le pica el brazo⟩ **2** : morirse ⟨they were itching to go outside : se morían por salir⟩ — *vt* : dar picazón, hacer picar

itch[2] *n* **1** ITCHING : picazón *f*, picor *m*, comezón *f* **2** RASH : sarpullido *m*, erupción *f* **3** DESIRE : ansia *f*, deseo *m*

itchy [ˈɪtʃi] *adj* **itchier; -est** : que pica, que da comezón

it'd [ˈɪt̬əd] (*contraction of* **it had** *or* **it would**) → **have, would**

item [ˈaɪt̬əm] *n* **1** OBJECT : artículo *m*, pieza *f* ⟨item of clothing : prenda de vestir⟩ **2** : punto *m* (en una agenda), número *m* (en el teatro), ítem *m* (en un documento) **3 news item** : noticia *f*

itemize [ˈaɪt̬əˌmaɪz] *vt* **-ized; -izing** : detallar, enumerar, listar

itinerant [aɪˈtɪnərənt] *adj* : itinerante, ambulante

itinerary [aɪˈtɪnəˌrɛri] *n, pl* **-aries** : itinerario *m*

it'll [ˈɪt̬əl] (*contraction of* **it shall** *or* **it will**) → **shall, will**

its [ˈɪts] *adj* : su, sus ⟨its kennel : su perrera⟩ ⟨a city and its inhabitants : una ciudad y sus habitantes⟩

it's [ˈɪts] (*contraction of* **it is** *or* **it has**) → **be, have**

itself [ɪtˈsɛlf] *pron* **1** (*used reflexively*) : se ⟨the cat gave itself a bath : el gato se bañó⟩ **2** (*used for emphasis*) : (él) mismo, (ella) misma, sí (mismo), solo ⟨he is courtesy itself : es la misma cortesía⟩ ⟨in and of itself : por sí mismo⟩ ⟨it opened by itself : se abrió solo⟩

IUD [ˌaɪˌjuːˈdiː] *n* *i*ntra*u*terine *d*evice : DIU *m*, dispositivo *m* intrauterino

I've [ˈaɪv] (*contraction of* **I have**) → **have**

ivory [ˈaɪvəri] *n, pl* **-ries** **1** : marfil *m* **2** : color *m* de marfil

ivy [ˈaɪvi] *n, pl* **ivies** **1** : hiedra *f*, yedra *f* **2** → **poison ivy**

J

j [ˈdʒeɪ] *n, pl* **j's** *or* **js** [ˈdʒeɪz] : décima letra del alfabeto inglés

jab[1] [ˈdʒæb] *v* **jabbed; jabbing** *vt* **1** PUNCTURE : clavar, pinchar **2** POKE : dar, golpear (con la punta de algo) ⟨he jabbed me in the ribs : me dio un codazo en las costillas⟩ — *vi* **to jab at** : dar, golpear

jab[2] *n* **1** PRICK : pinchazo *m* **2** POKE : golpe *m* abrupto

jabber[1] [ˈdʒæbər] *v* : farfullar

jabber[2] *n* : galimatías *m*, farfulla *f*

jack[1] [ˈdʒæk] *vt* **to jack up** **1** : levantar (con un gato) **2** INCREASE : subir, aumentar

jack[2] *n* **1** : gato *m*, cric *m* ⟨hydraulic jack : gato hidráulico⟩ **2** FLAG : pabellón *m* **3** SOCKET : enchufe *m* hembra **4** : jota *f*, valet *m* ⟨jack of hearts : jota de corazones⟩ **5 jacks** *npl* : cantillos *mpl*

jackal [ˈdʒækəl] *n* : chacal *m*

jackass [ˈdʒækˌæs] *n* : asno *m*, burro *m*

jacket [ˈdʒækət] *n* **1** : chaqueta *f* **2** COVER : sobrecubierta *f* (de un libro), carátula *f* (de un disco)

jackhammer [ˈdʒækˌhæmər] *n* : martillo *m* neumático

jack–in–the–box [ˈdʒækɪnðəˌbɑks] *n* : caja *f* de sorpresa

jackknife[1] [ˈdʒækˌnaɪf] *vi* **-knifed; -knifing** : doblarse como una navaja, plegarse

jackknife[2] *n* : navaja *f*

jack–of–all–trades *n* : persona *f* que sabe un poco de todo, persona *f* de muchos oficios

jack–o'–lantern [ˈdʒækəˌlæntərn] *n* : linterna *f* hecha de una calabaza

jackpot [ˈdʒækˌpɑt] *n* **1** : primer premio *m*, gordo *m* **2 to hit the jackpot** : sacarse la lotería, sacarse el gordo

jackrabbit [ˈdʒækˌræbət] *n* : liebre *f* grande de Norteamérica

jade [ˈdʒeɪd] *n* : jade *m*

jaded [ˈdʒeɪdəd] *adj* **1** TIRED : agotado **2** BORED : hastiado

jagged [ˈdʒægəd] *adj* : dentado, mellado

jaguar [ˈdʒægˌwɑr, ˈdʒægjʊˌwɑr] *n* : jaguar *m*

jai alai [ˈhaɪˌlaɪ] *n* : jai alai *m*, pelota *f* vasca

jail[1] [ˈdʒeɪl] *vt* : encarcelar

jail[2] *n* : cárcel *f*

jailbreak [ˈdʒeɪlˌbreɪk] *n* : fuga *f*, huida *f* (de la cárcel)

jailer *or* **jailor** [ˈdʒeɪlər] *n* : carcelero *m*, -ra *f*

jalapeño [ˌhɑləˈpeɪnjo, ˌhæ-, -ˈpiːno] *n* : jalapeño *m*

jalopy [dʒəˈlɑpi] *n, pl* **-lopies** : cacharro *m fam*, carro *m* destartalado

jalousie [ˈdʒæləsi] *n* : celosía *f*

jam[1] [ˈdʒæm] *v* **jammed; jamming** *vt* **1** CRAM : apiñar, embutir **2** BLOCK : atascar, atorar **3 to jam on the brakes** : frenar en seco — *vi* STICK : atascarse, atrancarse

jam[2] *n* **1** *or* **traffic jam** : atasco *m*, embotellamiento *m* (de tráfico) **2** PREDICAMENT : lío *m*, aprieto *m*, apuro *m* **3** : mermelada *f* ⟨strawberry jam : mermelada de fresa⟩

Jamaican [dʒəˈmeɪkən] *n* : jamaiquino *m*, -na *f*; jamaicano *m*, -na *f* — **Jamaican** *adj*

jamb [ˈdʒæm] *n* : jamba *f*

jamboree [ˌdʒæmbəˈriː] *n* : fiesta *f* grande

jangle[1] [ˈdʒæŋgəl] *v* **-gled; -gling** *vi* : hacer un ruido metálico — *vt* **1** : hacer sonar **2 to jangle one's nerves** : irritar, crispar

jangle[2] *n* : ruido *m* metálico

janitor [ˈdʒænət̬ər] *n* : portero *m*, -ra *f*; conserje *mf*

January [ˈdʒænjʊˌɛri] *n* : enero *m*

Japanese [ˌdʒæpəˈniːz, -ˈniːs] *n* **1**

: japonés *m*, -nesa *f* **2** : japonés *m* (idioma) — **Japanese** *adj*

jar[1] ['ʤɑr] *v* **jarred; jarring** *vi* **1** GRATE : chirriar **2** CLASH : desentonar **3** SHAKE : sacudirse **4 to jar on** : crispar, enervar — *vt* JOLT : sacudir

jar[2] *n* **1** GRATING : chirrido *m* **2** JOLT : vibración *f*, sacudida *f* **3** : tarro *m*, bote *m*, pote *m* ⟨a jar of honey : un tarro de miel⟩

jargon ['ʤɑrgən] *n* : jerga *f*

jasmine ['ʤæzmən] *n* : jazmín *m*

jasper ['ʤæspər] *n* : jaspe *m*

jaundice ['ʤɔndɪs] *n* : ictericia *f*

jaundiced ['ʤɔndɪst] *adj* **1** : ictérico **2** EMBITTERED, RESENTFUL : amargado, resentido, negativo ⟨with a jaundiced eye : con una actitud de cinismo⟩

jaunt ['ʤɔnt] *n* : excursión *f*, paseo *m*

jauntily ['ʤɔntəli] *adv* : animadamente

jauntiness ['ʤɔntinəs] *n* : animación *f*, vivacidad *f*

jaunty ['ʤɔnti] *adj* **-tier; -est** **1** SPRIGHTLY : animado, alegre **2** RAKISH : desenvuelto, desenfadado

Javanese [ˌʤævə'ni:z, ˌʤɑ-, -'ni:s] *n* **1** : javanés *m* (idioma) **2** : javanés *m*, -nesa *f* — **Javanese** *adj*

javelin ['ʤævələn] *n* : jabalina *f*

jaw[1] ['ʤɔ] *vi* GAB : cotorrear *fam*, parlotear *fam*

jaw[2] *n* **1** : mandíbula *f*, quijada *f* **2** : mordaza *f* (de una herramienta) **3 the jaws of death** : las garras *f* de la muerte

jawbone ['ʤɔˌbo:n] *n* : mandíbula *f*

jay ['ʤeɪ] *n* : arrendajo *m*, chara *f Mex*, azulejo *m Mex*

jaybird ['ʤeɪˌbərd] → **jay**

jaywalk ['ʤeɪˌwɔk] *vi* : cruzar la calle sin prudencia

jaywalker ['ʤeɪˌwɔkər] *n* : peatón *m* imprudente

jazz[1] ['ʤæz] *vt* **to jazz up** : animar, alegrar

jazz[2] *n* : jazz *m*

jazzy ['ʤæzi] *adj* **jazzier; -est** **1** : con ritmo de jazz **2** FLASHY, SHOWY : llamativo, ostentoso

jealous ['ʤɛləs] *adj* : celoso, envidioso — **jealously** *adv*

jealousy ['ʤɛləsi] *n* : celos *mpl*, envidia *f*

jeans ['ʤi:nz] *npl* : jeans *mpl*, vaqueros *mpl*

jeep ['ʤi:p] *n* : jeep *m*

jeer[1] ['ʤɪr] *vi* **1** BOO : abuchear **2** SCOFF : mofarse, burlarse — *vt* RIDICULE : mofarse de, burlarse de

jeer[2] *n* **1** : abucheo *m* **2** TAUNT : mofa *f*, burla *f*

Jehovah [ʤɪ'ho:və] *n* : Jehová *m*

jell ['ʤɛl] *vi* **1** SET : gelificarse, cuajar **2** FORM : cuajar, formarse (una idea, etc.)

jelly[1] ['ʤɛli] *v* **jellied; jellying** *vi* **1** JELL : gelificarse, cuajar **2** : hacer jalea — *vt* : gelificar

jelly[2] *n, pl* **-lies** **1** : jalea *f* **2** GELATIN : gelatina *f*

jellyfish ['ʤɛliˌfɪʃ] *n* : medusa *f*

jeopardize ['ʤɛpərˌdaɪz] *vt* **-dized; -dizing** : arriesgar, poner en peligro

jeopardy ['ʤɛpərdi] *n* : peligro *m*, riesgo *m*

jerk[1] ['ʤərk] *vt* **1** JOLT : sacudir **2** TUG, YANK : darle un tirón a — *vi* JOLT : dar sacudidas ⟨the train jerked along : el tren iba moviéndose a sacudidas⟩

jerk[2] *n* **1** TUG : tirón *m*, jalón *m* **2** JOLT : sacudida *f* brusca **3** FOOL : estúpido *m*, -da *f*; idiota *mf*

jerkin ['ʤərkən] *n* : chaqueta *f* sin mangas, chaleco *m*

jerky ['ʤərki] *adj* **jerkier; -est** **1** : espasmódico (dícese de los movimientos) **2** CHOPPY : inconexo (dícese de la prosa) — **jerkily** [-kəli] *adv*

jerry–built ['ʤɛriˌbɪlt] *adj* : mal construido, chapucero

jersey ['ʤərzi] *n, pl* **-seys** : jersey *m*

jest[1] ['ʤɛst] *vi* : bromear

jest[2] *n* : broma *f*, chiste *m*

jester ['ʤɛstər] *n* : bufón *m*, -fona *f*

Jesuit ['ʤɛzuət] *n* : jesuita *m* — **Jesuit** *adj*

Jesus ['ʤi:zəs, -zəz] *n* **1** : Jesús *m* **2** **Jesus Christ** : Jesucristo *m* **3 Jesus (Christ)!** *fam* : ¡por Dios!

jet[1] ['ʤɛt] *v* **jetted; jetting** *vt* SPOUT : arrojar a chorros — *vi* **1** GUSH : salir a chorros, chorrear **2** FLY : viajar en avión, volar

jet[2] *n* **1** STREAM : chorro *m* **2** *or* **jet airplane** : avión *m* a reacción, reactor *m* **3** : azabache *m* (mineral) **4 jet engine** : reactor *m*, motor *m* a reacción **5 jet lag** : desajuste *m* de horario (debido a un vuelo largo)

jet–propelled *adj* : a reacción

jetsam ['ʤɛtsəm] *n* **flotsam and jetsam** : restos *mpl*, desechos *mpl*

jettison ['ʤɛt̬əsən] *vt* **1** : echar al mar **2** DISCARD : desechar, deshacerse de

jetty ['ʤɛt̬i] *n, pl* **-ties** **1** PIER, WHARF : desembarcadero *m*, muelle *m* **2** BREAKWATER : malecón *m*, rompeolas *m*

Jew ['ʤu:] *n* : judío *m*, -día *f*

jewel ['ʤu:əl] *n* **1** : joya *f*, alhaja *f* **2** GEM : piedra *f* preciosa, gema *f* **3** : rubí *m* (de un reloj) **4** TREASURE : joya *f*, tesoro *m*

jeweler *or* **jeweller** ['ʤu:ələr] *n* : joyero *m*, -ra *f*

jewelry ['ʤu:əlri] *n* : joyas *fpl*, alhajas *fpl*

Jewish ['ʤu:ɪʃ] *adj* : judío

jib ['ʤɪb] *n* : foque *m* (de un barco)

jibe ['ʤaɪb] *vi* **jibed; jibing** AGREE : concordar

jiffy ['ʤɪfi] *n, pl* **-fies** : santiamén *m*, segundo *m*, momento *m*

jig[1] ['ʤɪg] *vi* **jigged; jigging** : bailar la giga

jig[2] *n* **1** : giga *f* **2 the jig is up** : se acabó la fiesta

jigger ['ʤɪgər] *n* : medida de 1 a 2 onzas (para licores)

jiggle[1] [ˈʤɪgəl] *v* **-gled; -gling** *vt* : agitar o sacudir ligeramente — *vi* : agitarse, vibrar

jiggle[2] *n* : sacudida *f*, vibración *f*

jigsaw [ˈʤɪgˌsɔ] *n* **1** : sierra *f* de vaivén **2 jigsaw puzzle** : rompecabezas *m*

jilt [ˈʤɪlt] *vt* : dejar plantado, dar calabazas a

jimmy[1] [ˈʤɪmi] *vt* **-mied; -mying** : forzar con una palanqueta

jimmy[2] *n, pl* **-mies** : palanqueta *f*

jingle[1] [ˈʤɪŋgəl] *v* **-gled; -gling** *vi* : tintinear — *vt* : hacer sonar

jingle[2] *n* **1** TINKLE : tintineo *m*, retintín *m* **2** : canción *f* rimada

jingoism [ˈʤɪŋgoˌɪzəm] *n* : jingoísmo *m*, patriotería *f*

jingoistic [ˌʤɪŋgoˈɪstɪk] *or* **jingoist** [ˈʤɪŋgoɪst] *adj* : jingoísta, patriotero

jinx[1] [ˈʤɪŋks] *vt* : traer mala suerte a, salar *CoRi, Mex*

jinx[2] *n* **1** : cenizo *m*, -za *f* **2 to put a jinx on** : echarle el mal de ojo a

jitters [ˈʤɪṱərz] *npl* : nervios *mpl* ⟨he got the jitters : se puso nervioso⟩

jittery [ˈʤɪṱəri] *adj* : nervioso

job [ˈʤɑb] *n* **1** : trabajo *m* ⟨he did odd jobs for her : le hizo algunos trabajos⟩ **2** CHORE, TASK : tarea *f*, quehacer *m* **3** EMPLOYMENT : trabajo *m*, empleo *m*, puesto *m*

jobber [ˈʤɑbər] *n* MIDDLEMAN : intermediario *m*, -ria *f*

jock [ˈʤɑk] *n* : deportista *mf*, atleta *mf*

jockey[1] [ˈʤɑki] *v* **-eyed; -eying** *vt* **1** MANIPULATE : manipular **2** MANEUVER : maniobrar — *vi* **to jockey for position** : maniobrar para conseguir algo

jockey[2] *n, pl* **-eys** : jockey *mf*

jocose [ʤoˈko:s] *adj* : jocoso

jocular [ˈʤɑkjʊlər] *adj* : jocoso — **jocularly** *adv*

jocularity [ˌʤɑkjʊˈlærəṱi] *n* : jocosidad *f*

jodhpurs [ˈʤɑdpərz] *npl* : pantalones *mpl* de montar

jog[1] [ˈʤɑg] *v* **jogged; jogging** *vt* **1** NUDGE : dar, empujar, codear **2 to jog one's memory** : refrescar la memoria — *vi* **1** RUN : correr despacio, trotar, hacer footing (como ejercicio) **2** TRUDGE : andar a trote corto

jog[2] *n* **1** PUSH, SHAKE : empujoncito *m*, sacudida *f* leve **2** TROT : trote *m* corto, footing *m* (en deportes) **3** TWIST : recodo *m*, vuelta *f*, curva *f*

jogger [ˈʤɑgər] *n* : persona *f* que hace footing

join [ˈʤɔɪn] *vt* **1** CONNECT, LINK : unir, juntar ⟨to join in marriage : unir en matrimonio⟩ **2** ADJOIN : lindar con, colindar con **3** MEET : reunirse con, encontrarse con ⟨we joined them for lunch : nos reunimos con ellos para almorzar⟩ **4** : hacerse socio de (una organización), afiliarse a (un partido), entrar en (una empresa) — *vi* **1** UNITE : unirse **2** MERGE : empalmar (dícese de las carreteras), confluir (dícese de los ríos) **3 to join up** : hacerse socio, enrolarse

joiner [ˈʤɔɪnər] *n* **1** CARPENTER : carpintero *m*, -ra *f* **2** : persona *f* que se une a varios grupos

joint[1] [ˈʤɔɪnt] *adj* : conjunto, colectivo, mutuo ⟨a joint effort : un esfuerzo conjunto⟩ — **jointly** *adv*

joint[2] *n* **1** : articulación *f*, coyuntura *f* ⟨out of joint : dislocado⟩ **2** ROAST : asado *m* **3** JUNCTURE : juntura *f*, unión *f* **4** DIVE : antro *m*, tasca *f*

joist [ˈʤɔɪst] *n* : viga *f*

joke[1] [ˈʤo:k] *vi* **joked; joking** : bromear

joke[2] *n* **1** STORY : chiste *m* **2** PRANK : broma *f*

joker [ˈʤo:kər] *n* **1** PRANKSTER : bromista *mf* **2** : comodín *m* (en los naipes)

jokingly [ˈʤo:kɪŋli] *adv* : en broma

jollity [ˈʤɑləṱi] *n, pl* **-ties** MERRIMENT : alegría *f*, regocijo *m*

jolly [ˈʤɑli] *adj* **-lier; -est** : alegre, jovial

jolt[1] [ˈʤo:lt] *vi* JERK : dar tumbos, dar sacudidas — *vt* : sacudir

jolt[2] *n* **1** JERK : sacudida *f* brusca **2** SHOCK : golpe *m* (emocional)

jonquil [ˈʤɑnkwɪl] *n* : junquillo *m*

Jordanian [ʤɔrˈdeɪniən] *n* : jordano *m*, -na *f* — **Jordanian** *adj*

josh [ˈʤɑʃ] *vt* TEASE : tomarle el pelo (a alguien) — *vi* JOKE : bromear

jostle [ˈʤɑsəl] *v* **-tled; -tling** *vi* **1** SHOVE : empujar, dar empellones **2** CONTEND : competir — *vt* **1** SHOVE : empujar **2 to jostle one's way** : abrirse paso a empellones

jot[1] [ˈʤɑt] *vt* **jotted; jotting** : anotar, apuntar ⟨jot it down : apúntalo⟩

jot[2] *n* BIT : ápice *m*, jota *f*, pizca *f*

jounce[1] [ˈʤæʊnts] *v* **jounced; jouncing** *vt* JOLT : sacudir — *vi* : dar tumbos, dar sacudidas

jounce[2] *n* JOLT : sacudida *f*, tumbo *m*

journal [ˈʤərnəl] *n* **1** DIARY : diario *m* **2** PERIODICAL : revista *f*, publicación *f* periódica **3** NEWSPAPER : periódico *m*, diario *m*

journalism [ˈʤərnəlˌɪzəm] *n* : periodismo *m*

journalist [ˈʤərnəlɪst] *n* : periodista *mf*

journalistic [ˌʤərnəlˈɪstɪk] *adj* : periodístico

journey[1] [ˈʤərni] *vi* **-neyed; -neying** : viajar

journey[2] *n, pl* **-neys** : viaje *m*

journeyman [ˈʤərnimən] *n, pl* **-men** [-mən, -ˌmɛn] : oficial *m*

joust[1] [ˈʤæʊst] *vi* : justar

joust[2] *n* : justa *f*

jovial [ˈʤo:viəl] *adj* : jovial — **jovially** *adv*

joviality [ˌʤo:viˈæləṱi] *n* : jovialidad *f*

jowl [ˈʤæʊl] *n* **1** JAW : mandíbula *f* **2** CHEEK : mejilla *f*, cachete *m*

joy [ˈʤɔɪ] *n* **1** HAPPINESS : gozo *m*, alegría *f*, felicidad *f* **2** DELIGHT : placer *m*, deleite *m* ⟨the child is a real joy : el niño es un verdadero placer⟩

joyful ['ʤɔɪfəl] *adj* : gozoso, alegre, feliz — **joyfully** *adv*
joyless ['ʤɔɪləs] *adj* : sin alegría, triste
joyous ['ʤɔɪəs] *adj* : alegre, feliz, eufórico — **joyously** *adv*
joyousness ['ʤɔɪəsnəs] *n* : alegría *f*, felicidad *f*, euforia *f*
joyride ['ʤɔɪˌraɪd] *n* : paseo *m* temerario e irresponsable (en coche)
joystick ['ʤɔɪˌstɪk] *n* : joystick *m*
jubilant ['ʤu:bələnt] *adj* : jubiloso, alborozado — **jubilantly** *adv*
jubilation [ˌʤu:bə'leɪʃən] *n* : júbilo *m*
jubilee ['ʤu:bəˌli:] *n* **1** : quincuagésimo aniversario *m* **2** CELEBRATION : celebración *f*, festejos *mpl*
Judaic [ʤʊ'deɪɪk] *adj* : judaico
Judaism ['ʤu:dəˌɪzəm, 'ʤu:di-, 'ʤu:ˌdeɪ-] *n* : judaísmo *m*
judge[1] ['ʤʌʤ] *vt* **judged; judging 1** ASSESS : evaluar, juzgar **2** DEEM : juzgar, considerar **3** TRY : juzgar (ante el tribunal) **4 judging by** : a juzgar por
judge[2] *n* **1** : juez *mf*, jueza *f* **2 to be a good judge of** : saber juzgar a, entender mucho de
judgment *or* **judgement** ['ʤʌʤ-mənt] *n* **1** RULING : fallo *m*, sentencia *f* **2** OPINION : opinión *f* **3** DISCERNMENT : juicio *m*, discernimiento *m*
judgmental [ˌʤʌʤ'mntəl] *adj* : crítico — **judgmentally** *adv*
judicature ['ʤu:dɪkəˌʧʊr] *n* : judicatura *f*
judicial [ʤʊ'dɪʃəl] *adj* : judicial — **judicially** *adv*
judiciary[1] [ʤʊ'dɪʃiˌri, -'dɪʃəri] *adj* : judicial
judiciary[2] *n* **1** JUDICATURE : judicatura *f* **2** : poder *m* judicial
judicious [ʤʊ'dɪʃəs] *adj* SOUND, WISE : juicioso, sensato — **judiciously** *adv*
judo ['ʤu:ˌdo:] *n* : judo *m*
jug ['ʤʌg] *n* **1** : jarra *f*, jarro *m*, cántaro *m* **2** JAIL : cárcel *f*, chirona *f fam*
juggernaut ['ʤʌgərˌnɔt] *n* : gigante *m*, fuerza *f* irresistible ⟨a political juggernaut : un gigante político⟩
juggle ['ʤʌgəl] *v* **-gled; -gling** *vt* **1** : hacer juegos malabares con **2** MANIPULATE : manipular, jugar con — *vi* : hacer juegos malabares
juggler ['ʤʌgələr] *n* : malabarista *mf*
jugular ['ʤʌgjʊlər] *adj* : yugular ⟨jugular vein : vena yugular⟩
juice ['ʤu:s] *n* **1** : jugo *m* (de carne, de frutas) *m*, zumo *m* (de frutas) **2** ELECTRICITY : electricidad *f*, luz *f*
juicer ['ʤu:sər] *n* : exprimidor *m*
juiciness ['ʤu:sinəs] *n* : jugosidad *f*
juicy ['ʤu:si] *adj* **juicier; -est 1** SUCCULENT : jugoso, suculento **2** PROFITABLE : jugoso, lucrativo **3** RACY : picante
jukebox ['ʤu:kˌbɑks] *n* : rocola *f*, máquina *f* de discos
julep ['ʤu:ləp] *n* : bebida *f* hecha con whisky americano y menta
July [ʤʊ'laɪ] *n* : julio *m*
jumble[1] ['ʤʌmbəl] *vt* **-bled; -bling** : mezclar, revolver
jumble[2] *n* : revoltijo *m*, fárrago *m*, embrollo *m*
jumbo[1] ['ʤʌmˌbo:] *adj* : gigante, enorme, de tamaño extra grande
jumbo[2] *n, pl* **-bos** : coloso *m*, cosa *f* de tamaño extra grande
jump[1] ['ʤʌmp] *vi* **1** LEAP : saltar, brincar **2** START : levantarse de un salto, sobresaltarse **3** MOVE, SHIFT : moverse, pasar ⟨to jump from job to job : pasar de un empleo a otro⟩ **4** INCREASE, RISE : dar un salto, aumentarse de golpe, subir bruscamente **5** BUSTLE : animarse, ajetrearse **6 to jump to conclusions** : sacar conclusiones precipitadas — *vt* **1** : saltar ⟨to jump a fence : saltar una valla⟩ **2** SKIP : saltarse **3** ATTACK : atacar, asaltar **4 to jump the gun** : precipitarse
jump[2] *n* **1** LEAP : salto *m* **2** START : sobresalto *m*, respingo *m* **3** INCREASE : subida *f* brusca, aumento *m* **4** ADVANTAGE : ventaja *f* ⟨we got the jump on them : les llevamos la ventaja⟩
jumper ['ʤʌmpər] *n* **1** : saltador *m*, -dora *f* (en deportes) **2** : jumper *m*, vestido *m* sin mangas
jumpy ['ʤʌmpi] *adj* **jumpier; -est** : asustadizo, nervioso
junction ['ʤʌŋkʃən] *n* **1** JOINING : unión *f* **2** : cruce *m* (de calles), empalme *m* (de un ferrocarril), confluencia *f* (de ríos)
juncture ['ʤʌŋkʧər] *n* **1** UNION : juntura *f*, unión *f* **2** MOMENT, POINT : coyuntura *f* ⟨at this juncture : en esta coyuntura, en este momento⟩
June ['ʤu:n] *n* : junio *m*
jungle ['ʤʌŋgəl] *n* : jungla *f*, selva *f*
junior[1] ['ʤu:njər] *adj* **1** YOUNGER : más joven ⟨John Smith, Junior : John Smith, hijo⟩ **2** SUBORDINATE : subordinado, subalterno
junior[2] *n* **1** : persona *f* de menor edad ⟨she's my junior : es menor que yo⟩ **2** SUBORDINATE : subalterno *m*, -na *f*; subordinado *m*, -da *f* **3** : estudiante *mf* de penúltimo año
juniper ['ʤu:nəpər] *n* : enebro *m*
junk[1] ['ʤʌŋk] *vt* : echar a la basura
junk[2] *n* **1** RUBBISH : desechos *mpl*, desperdicios *mpl* **2** STUFF : trastos *mpl fam*, cachivaches *mpl fam* **3 piece of junk** : cacharro *m*, porquería *f*
junket ['ʤʌŋkət] *n* : viaje *m* (pagado con dinero público)
junta ['hʊntə, 'ʤʌn-, 'hʌn-] *n* : junta *f* militar
Jupiter ['ʤu:pət̬ər] *n* : Júpiter *m*
jurisdiction [ˌʤʊrəs'dɪkʃən] *n* : jurisdicción *f*
jurisprudence [ˌʤʊrəs'pru:dən*t*s] *n* : jurisprudencia *f*
jurist ['ʤʊrɪst] *n* : jurista *mf*; magistrado *m*, -da *f*

juror [ˈʤʊrər] *n* : jurado *m*, -da *f*
jury [ˈʤʊri] *n, pl* **-ries** : jurado *m*
just[1] [ˈʤʌst] *adv* **1** EXACTLY : justo, precisamente, exactamente **2** POSSIBLY : posiblemente ⟨it just might work : tal vez resulte⟩ **3** BARELY : justo, apenas ⟨just in time : justo a tiempo⟩ **4** ONLY : sólo, solamente, nada más ⟨just us : sólo nosotros⟩ **5** QUITE : muy, simplemente ⟨it's just horrible! : ¡qué horrible!⟩ **6 to have just (done something)** : acabar de (hacer algo) ⟨he just called : acaba de llamar⟩
just[2] *adj* : justo — **justly** *adv*
justice [ˈʤʌstɪs] *n* **1** : justicia *f* **2** JUDGE : juez *mf*, jueza *f*
justification [ˌʤʌstəfəˈkeɪʃən] *n* : justificación *f*
justify [ˈʤʌstəˌfaɪ] *vt* **-fied; -fying** : justificar — **justifiable** [ˌʤʌstə-ˈfaɪəbəl] *adj*
jut [ˈʤʌt] *vi* **jutted; jutting** : sobresalir
jute [ˈʤuːt] *n* : yute *m*
juvenile[1] [ˈʤuːvəˌnaɪl, -vənəl] *adj* **1** : juvenil ⟨juvenile delinquent : delincuente juvenil⟩ ⟨juvenile court : tribunal de menores⟩ **2** CHILDISH : infantil
juvenile[2] *n* : menor *mf*
juxtapose [ˈʤʌkstəˌpoːz] *vt* **-posed; -posing** : yuxtaponer
juxtaposition [ˌʤʌkstəpəˈzɪʃən] *n* : yuxtaposición *f*

K

k [ˈkeɪ] *n, pl* **k's** *or* **ks** [ˈkeɪz] : undécima letra del alfabeto inglés
kaiser [ˈkaɪzər] *n* : káiser *m*
kale [ˈkeɪl] *n* : col *f* rizada
kaleidoscope [kəˈlaɪdəˌskoːp] *n* : calidoscopio *m*
kamikaze [ˌkɑmɪˈkɑzi] *n* : kamikaze *m* — **kamikaze** *adj*
kangaroo [ˌkæŋgəˈruː] *n, pl* **-roos** : canguro *m*
kaolin [ˈkeɪələn] *n* : caolín *m*
karaoke [ˌkæriˈoːki] *n* : karaoke *m*
karat [ˈkærət] *n* : quilate *m*
karate [kəˈrɑṭi] *n* : karate *m*
katydid [ˈkeɪṭiˌdɪd] *n* : saltamontes *m*
kayak [ˈkaɪˌæk] *n* : kayac *m*, kayak *m*
keel[1] [ˈkiːl] *vi* **to keel over** : volcar (dícese de un barco), desplomarse (dícese de una persona)
keel[2] *n* : quilla *f*
keen [ˈkiːn] *adj* **1** SHARP : afilado, filoso ⟨a keen blade : una hoja afilada⟩ **2** PENETRATING : cortante, penetrante ⟨a keen wind : un viento cortante⟩ **3** ENTHUSIASTIC : entusiasta **4** ACUTE : agudo, fino ⟨keen hearing : oído fino⟩ ⟨keen intelligence : inteligencia aguda⟩
keenly [ˈkiːnli] *adv* **1** ENTHUSIASTICALLY : con entusiasmo **2** INTENSELY : vivamente, profundamente ⟨keenly aware of : muy consciente de⟩
keenness [ˈkiːnnəs] *n* **1** SHARPNESS : lo afilado, lo filoso **2** ENTHUSIASM : entusiasmo *m* **3** ACUTENESS : agudeza *f*
keep[1] [ˈkiːp] *v* **kept** [ˈkpt]; **keeping** *vt* **1** : cumplir (la palabra a uno), acudir a (una cita) **2** OBSERVE : observar (una fiesta) **3** GUARD : guardar, cuidar **4** CONTINUE : mantener ⟨to keep silence : mantener silencio⟩ **5** SUPPORT : mantener (una familia) **6** RAISE : criar (animales) **7** : llevar, escribir (un diario, etc.) **8** RETAIN : guardar, conservar, quedarse con **9** STORE : guardar **10** DETAIN : hacer quedar, detener **11** PRESERVE : guardar ⟨to keep a secret : guardar un secreto⟩ — *vi* **1** : conservarse (dícese de los alimentos) **2** CONTINUE : seguir, no dejar ⟨he keeps on pestering us : no deja de molestarnos⟩ **3 to keep from** : abstenerse de ⟨I couldn't keep from laughing : no podía contener la risa⟩
keep[2] *n* **1** TOWER : torreón *m* (de un castillo), torre *f* del homenaje **2** SUSTENANCE : manutención *f*, sustento *m* **3 for keeps** : para siempre
keeper [ˈkiːpər] *n* **1** : guarda *mf* (en un zoológico); conservador *m*, -dora *f* (en un museo) **2** GAMEKEEPER : guardabosque *mf*
keeping [ˈkiːpɪŋ] *n* **1** CONFORMITY : conformidad *f*, acuerdo *m* ⟨in keeping with : de acuerdo con⟩ **2** CARE : cuidado *m* ⟨in the keeping of : al cuidado de⟩
keepsake [ˈkiːpˌseɪk] *n* : recuerdo *m*
keep up *vt* CONTINUE, MAINTAIN : mantener, seguir con — *vi* **1** : mantenerse al corriente ⟨he kept up with the news : se mantenía al tanto de las noticias⟩ **2** CONTINUE : continuar **3 to keep up with someone** : mantener contacto con alguien
keg [ˈkɛg] *n* : barril *m*
kelp [ˈkɛlp] *n* : alga *f* marina
ken [ˈkɛn] *n* **1** SIGHT : vista *f*, alcance *m* de la vista **2** UNDERSTANDING : comprensión *f*, alcance *m* del conocimiento ⟨it's beyond his ken : no lo puede entender⟩
kennel [ˈkɛnəl] *n* : caseta *f* para perros, perrera *f*
Kenyan [ˈkɛnjən, ˈkiːn-] *n* : keniano *m*, -na *f* — **Kenyan** *adj*
kept → **keep**
kerchief [ˈkərʧəf, -ˌʧiːf] *n* : pañuelo *m*
kernel [ˈkərnəl] *n* **1** : almendra *f* (de semillas y nueces) **2** : grano *m* (de cereales) **3** CORE : meollo *m* ⟨a kernel of truth : un fondo de verdad⟩
kerosene *or* **kerosine** [ˈkɛrəˌsiːn, ˌkɛrəˈ-] *n* : queroseno *m*, kerosén *m*, kerosene *m*

ketchup ['kɛtʃəp, 'kæ-] *n* : salsa *f* catsup
kettle ['kɛtəl] *n* **1** : hervidor *m*, pava *f Arg, Bol, Chile* **2** → **teakettle**
kettledrum ['kɛtəl,drʌm] *n* : timbal *m*
key[1] ['ki:] *vt* **1** ATTUNE : adaptar, adecuar **2 to key up** : poner nervioso, inquietar
key[2] *adj* : clave, fundamental
key[3] *n* **1** : llave *f* **2** SOLUTION : clave *f*, soluciones *fpl* **3** : tecla *f* (de un piano o una máquina) **4** : tono *m*, tonalidad *f* (en la música) **5** ISLET, REEF : cayo *m*, islote *m*
keyboard ['ki:,bord] *n* : teclado *m*
keyhole ['ki:,ho:l] *n* : bocallave *f*, ojo *m* (de una cerradura)
keynote[1] ['ki:,no:t] *vt* **-noted; -noting 1** : establecer la tónica de (en música) **2** : pronunciar el discurso principal de
keynote[2] *n* **1** : tónica *f* (en música) **2** : idea *f* fundamental
keystone ['ki:,sto:n] *n* : clave *f*, dovela *f*
keystroke ['ki:,stro:k] *n* : pulsación *f* (de tecla)
khaki ['kæki, 'kɑ-] *n* : caqui *m*
khan ['kɑn, 'kæn] *n* : kan *m*
kibbutz [kə'bʊts, -'bu:ts] *n, pl* **-butzim** [-,bʊt'si:m, -,bu:t-] : kibutz *m*
kibitz ['kɪbɪts] *vi* : dar consejos molestos
kibitzer ['kɪbɪtsər, kɪ'bɪt-] *n* : persona *f* que da consejos molestos
kick[1] ['kɪk] *vi* **1** : dar patadas (dícese de una persona), cocear (dícese de un animal) **2** PROTEST : patalear, protestar **3** RECOIL : dar un culatazo (dícese de un arma de fuego) — *vt* : patear, darle una patada (a alguien)
kick[2] *n* **1** : patada *f*, puntapié *m*, coz *f* (de un animal) **2** RECOIL : culatazo *m* (de un arma de fuego) **3** : fuerza *f* <a drink with a kick : una bebida fuerte>
kicker ['kɪkər] *n* : pateador *m*, -dora *f* (en deportes)
kickoff ['kɪk,ɔf] *n* : saque *m* (inicial)
kick off *vi* **1** : hacer el saque inicial (en deportes) **2** BEGIN : empezar — *vt* : empezar
kid[1] ['kɪd] *v* **kidded; kidding** *vt* **1** FOOL : engañar **2** TEASE : tomarle el pelo (a alguien) — *vi* JOKE : bromear <I'm only kidding : lo digo en broma>
kid[2] *n* **1** : chivo *m*, -va *f*; cabrito *m*, -ta *f* **2** CHILD : chico *m*, -ca *f*; niño *m*, -ña *f*
kidder ['kɪdər] *n* : bromista *mf*
kiddingly ['kɪdɪŋli] *adv* : en broma
kidnap ['kɪd,næp] *vt* **-napped** *or* **-naped** [-,næpt]; **-napping** *or* **-naping** [-,næpɪŋ] : secuestrar, raptar
kidnapper *or* **kidnaper** ['kɪd,næpər] *n* : secuestrador *m*, -dora *f*; raptor *m*, -tora *f*
kidnapping ['kɪd,næpɪŋ] *n* : secuestro *m*
kidney ['kɪdni] *n, pl* **-neys** : riñón *m*
kidney bean *n* : frijol *m*
kill[1] ['kɪl] *vt* **1** : matar **2** END : acabar con, poner fin a **3 to kill time** : matar el tiempo
kill[2] *n* **1** KILLING : matanza *f* **2** PREY : presa *f*
killer ['kɪlər] *n* : asesino *m*, -na *f*
killjoy ['kɪl,dʒɔɪ] *n* : aguafiestas *mf*
kiln ['kɪl, 'kɪln] *n* : horno *m*
kilo ['ki:,lo:] *n, pl* **-los** : kilo *m*
kilobyte ['kɪlə,baɪt] *n* : kilobyte *m*
kilocycle ['kɪlə,saɪkəl] *n* : kilociclo *m*
kilogram ['kɪlə,græm, 'ki:-] *n* : kilogramo *m*
kilohertz ['kɪlə,hərts] *n* : kilohertzio *m*
kilometer [kɪ'lɑmət̬ər, 'kɪlə,mi:-] *n* : kilómetro *m*
kilowatt ['kɪlə,wɑt] *n* : kilovatio *m*
kilt ['kɪlt] *n* : falda *f* escocesa
kilter ['kɪltər] *n* **1** ORDER : buen estado *m* **2 out of kilter** : descompuesto, estropeado
kimono [kə'mo:no, -nə] *n, pl* **-nos** : kimono *m*, quimono *m*
kin ['kɪn] *n* : familiares *mpl*, parientes *mpl*
kind[1] ['kaɪnd] *adj* : amable, bondadoso, benévolo
kind[2] *n* **1** ESSENCE : esencia *f* <a difference in degree, not in kind : una diferencia cuantitativa y no cualitativa> **2** CATEGORY : especie *f*, género *m* **3** TYPE : clase *f*, tipo *m*, índole *f*
kindergarten ['kɪndər,gɑrtən, -dən] *n* : kinder *m*, kindergarten *m*, jardín *m* de infantes, jardín *m* de niños *Mex*
kindhearted [,kaɪnd'hɑrt̬əd] *adj* : bondadoso, de buen corazón
kindle ['kɪndəl] *v* **-dled; -dling** *vt* **1** IGNITE : encender **2** AROUSE : despertar, suscitar — *vi* : encenderse
kindliness ['kaɪndlinəs] *n* : bondad *f*
kindling ['kɪndlɪŋ, 'kɪndlən] *n* : astillas *fpl*, leña *f*
kindly[1] ['kaɪndli] *adv* **1** AMIABLY : amablemente, bondadosamente **2** COURTEOUSLY : cortésmente, con cortesía <we kindly ask you not smoke : les rogamos que no fumen> **3** PLEASE : por favor **4 to take kindly to** : aceptar de buena gana
kindly[2] *adj* **-lier; -est** : bondadoso, amable
kindness ['kaɪndnəs] *n* : bondad *f*
kind of *adv* SOMEWHAT : un tanto, algo
kindred[1] ['kɪndrəd] *adj* SIMILAR : similar, afín <kindred spirits : almas gemelas>
kindred[2] *n* **1** FAMILY : familia *f*, parentela *f* **2** → **kin**
kinfolk ['kɪn,fo:k] *or* **kinfolks** [-,fo:ks] *npl* → **kin**
king ['kɪŋ] *n* : rey *m*
kingdom ['kɪŋdəm] *n* : reino *m*
kingfisher ['kɪŋ,fɪʃər] *n* : martín *m* pescador
kingly ['kɪŋli] *adj* **-lier; -est** : regio, real
king–size ['kɪŋ,saɪz] *or* **king–sized** [-,saɪzd] *adj* : de tamaño muy grande, extra largo (dícese de cigarrillos)
kink ['kɪŋk] *n* **1** : rizo *m* (en el pelo), vuelta *f* (en una cuerda) **2** CRAMP

: calambre *m* ⟨to have a kink in the neck : tener tortícolis⟩
kinky [ˈkɪŋki] *adj* **-kier; -est** : rizado (dícese del pelo), enroscado (dícese de una cuerda)
kinship [ˈkɪn,ʃɪp] *n* : parentesco *m*
kinsman [ˈkɪnzmən] *n, pl* **-men** [-mən, -ˌmɛn] : familiar *m*, pariente *m*
kinswoman [ˈkɪnzˌwʊmən] *n, pl* **-women** [-ˌwɪmən] : familiar *f*, pariente *f*
kiosk [ˈkiːˌɑsk] *n* : quiosco *m*
kipper [ˈkɪpər] *n* : arenque *m* ahumado
kiss[1] [ˈkɪs] *vt* : besar — *vi* : besarse
kiss[2] *n* : beso *m*
kit [ˈkɪt] *n* **1** SET : juego *m*, kit *m* **2** CASE : estuche *m*, caja *f* **3 first-aid kit** : botiquín *m* **4 tool kit** : caja *f* de herramientas **5 travel kit** : neceser *m*
kitchen [ˈkɪʧən] *n* : cocina *f*
kite [ˈkaɪt] *n* **1** : milano *m* (ave) **2** : cometa *f*, papalote *m Mex* ⟨to fly a kite : hacer volar una cometa⟩
kith [ˈkɪθ] *n* : amigos *mpl* ⟨kith and kin : amigos y parientes⟩
kitten [ˈkɪtən] *n* : gatito *m*, -ta *f*
kitty [ˈkɪt̬i] *n, pl* **-ties** **1** FUND, POOL : bote *m*, fondo *m* común **2** CAT : gato *m*, gatito *m*
kitty–corner [ˈkɪt̬iˌkɔrnər] *or* **kitty–cornered** [-nərd] → **catercorner**
kiwi [ˈkiːˌwiː] *n* : kiwi *m*
kleptomania [ˌklɛptəˈmeɪniə] *n* : cleptomanía *f*
kleptomaniac [ˌklɛptəˈmeɪniˌæk] *n* : cleptómano *m*, -na *f*
knack [ˈnæk] *n* : maña *f*, facilidad *f*
knapsack [ˈnæpˌsæk] *n* : mochila *f*, morral *m*
knave [ˈneɪv] *n* : bellaco *m*, pícaro *m*
knead [ˈniːd] *vt* **1** : amasar, sobar **2** MASSAGE : masajear
knee [ˈniː] *n* : rodilla *f*
kneecap [ˈniːˌkæp] *n* : rótula *f*
kneel [ˈniːl] *vi* **knelt** [ˈnɛlt] *or* **kneeled** [ˈniːld]; **kneeling** : arrodillarse, ponerse de rodillas
knell [ˈnɛl] *n* : doble *m*, toque *m* ⟨death knell : toque de difuntos⟩
knew → **know**
knickers [ˈnɪkərz] *npl* : pantalones *mpl* bombachos de media pierna
knickknack [ˈnɪkˌnæk] *n* : chuchería *f*, baratija *f*
knife[1] [ˈnaɪf] *vt* **knifed** [ˈnaɪft]; **knifing** : acuchillar, apuñalar
knife[2] *n, pl* **knives** [ˈnaɪvz] : cuchillo *m*
knight[1] [ˈnaɪt] *vt* : conceder el título de *Sir* a
knight[2] *n* **1** : caballero *m* ⟨knight errant : caballero andante⟩ **2** : caballo *m* (en ajedrez) **3** : uno que tiene el título de *Sir*
knighthood [ˈnaɪtˌhʊd] *n* **1** : caballería *f* **2** : título *m* de *Sir*
knightly [ˈnaɪtli] *adj* : caballeresco
knit[1] [ˈnɪt] *v* **knit** *or* **knitted** [ˈnɪt̬əd]; **knitting** *vt* **1** UNITE : unir, enlazar **2** : tejer ⟨to knit a sweater : tejer un suéter⟩ **3 to knit one's brows** : fruncir el ceño — *vi* **1** : tejer **2** : soldarse (dícese de los huesos)
knit[2] *n* : prenda *f* tejida
knitter [ˈnɪt̬ər] *n* : tejedor *m*, -dora *f*
knob [ˈnɑb] *n* **1** LUMP : bulto *m*, protuberancia *f* **2** HANDLE : perilla *f*, tirador *m*, botón *m*
knobbed [ˈnɑbd] *adj* **1** KNOTTY : nudoso **2** : que tiene perilla o botón
knobby [ˈnɑbi] *adj* **knobbier; -est** **1** KNOTTY : nudoso **2 knobby knees** : rodillas *fpl* huesudas
knock[1] [ˈnɑk] *vt* **1** HIT, RAP : golpear, golpetear **2** : hacer chocar ⟨they knocked heads : se dieron en la cabeza⟩ **3** CRITICIZE : criticar — *vi* **1** RAP : dar un golpe, llamar (a la puerta) **2** COLLIDE : darse, chocar
knock[2] *n* : golpe *m*, llamada *f* (a la puerta), golpeteo *m* (de un motor)
knock down *vt* : derribar, echar al suelo
knocker [ˈnɑkər] *n* : aldaba *f*, llamador *m*
knock–kneed [ˈnɑkˈniːd] *adj* : patizambo
knockout [ˈnɑkˌaʊt] *n* : nocaut *m*, knockout *m* (en deportes)
knock out *vt* : dejar sin sentido, poner fuera de combate (en el boxeo)
knoll [ˈnoːl] *n* : loma *f*, otero *m*, montículo *m*
knot[1] [ˈnɑt] *v* **knotted; knotting** *vt* : anudar — *vi* : anudarse
knot[2] *n* **1** : nudo *m* (en cordel o madera), nódulo *m* (en los músculos) **2** CLUSTER : grupo *m* **3** : nudo *m* (unidad de velocidad)
knotty [ˈnɑt̬i] *adj* **-tier; -est** **1** GNARLED : nudoso **2** COMPLEX : espinoso, enredado, complejo
know [ˈnoː] *v* **knew** [ˈnuː, ˈnjuː]; **known** [ˈnoːn]; **knowing** *vt* **1** : saber ⟨he knows the answer : sabe la respuesta⟩ **2** : conocer (a una persona, un lugar) ⟨do you know Julia? : ¿conoces a Julia?⟩ **3** RECOGNIZE : reconocer **4** DISCERN, DISTINGUISH : distinguir, discernir **5 to know how to** : saber ⟨I don't know how to dance : no sé bailar⟩ — *vi* : saber
knowable [ˈnoːəbəl] *adj* : conocible
knowing [ˈnoːɪŋ] *adj* **1** KNOWLEDGEABLE : informado ⟨a knowing look : una mirada de complicidad⟩ **2** ASTUTE : astuto **3** DELIBERATE : deliberado, intencional
knowingly [ˈnoːɪŋli] *adv* **1** : con complicidad ⟨she smiled knowingly : sonrió con una mirada de complicidad⟩ **2** DELIBERATELY : a sabiendas, adrede, a propósito
know–it–all [ˈnoːɪt̬ˌɔl] *n* : sabelotodo *mf fam*
knowledge [ˈnɑlɪʤ] *n* **1** AWARENESS : conocimiento *m* **2** LEARNING : conocimientos *mpl*, saber *m*
knowledgeable [ˈnɑlɪʤəbəl] *adj* : informado, entendido, enterado

known [ˈnoːn] *adj* : conocido, familiar
knuckle [ˈnʌkəl] *n* : nudillo *m*
koala [koˈwɑlə] *n* : koala *m*
kohlrabi [ˌkoːlˈrɑbi, -ˈræ-] *n, pl* **-bies** : colinabo *m*
Koran [kəˈrɑn, -ˈræn] *n* **the Koran** : el Corán
Korean [kəˈriːən] *n* **1** : coreano *m*, -na *f* **2** : coreano *m* (idioma) — **Korean** *adj*
kosher [ˈkoːʃər] *adj* : aprobado por la ley judía
kowtow [ˌkaʊˈtaʊ, ˈkaʊˌtaʊ] *vi* **to kowtow to** : humillarse ante, doblegarse ante
krypton [ˈkrɪpˌtɑn] *n* : criptón *m*
kudos [ˈkjuːˌdɑs, ˈkuː-, -ˌdoːz] *n* : fama *f*, renombre *m*
kumquat [ˈkʌmˌkwɑt] *n* : naranjita *f* china
Kurd [ˈkʊrd, ˈkərd] *n* : kurdo *m*, -da *f*
Kurdish [ˈkʊrdɪʃ, ˈkər-] *adj* : kurdo
Kuwaiti [kʊˈweɪt̬i] *n* : kuwaití *mf* — **Kuwaiti** *adj*

L

l [ˈɛl] *n, pl* **l's** *or* **ls** [ˈlz] : duodécima letra del alfabeto inglés
lab [ˈlæb] → **laboratory**
label[1] [ˈleɪbəl] *vt* **-beled** *or* **-belled; -beling** *or* **-belling** **1** : etiquetar, poner etiqueta a **2** BRAND, CATEGORIZE : calificar, tildar, tachar ⟨they labeled him as a fraud : lo calificaron de farsante⟩
label[2] *n* **1** : etiqueta *f*, rótulo *m* **2** DESCRIPTION : calificación *f*, descripción *f* **3** BRAND : marca *f*
labial [ˈleɪbiəl] *adj* : labial
labor[1] [ˈleɪbər] *vi* **1** WORK : trabajar **2** STRUGGLE : avanzar penosamente (dícese de una persona), funcionar con dificultad (dícese de un motor) **3 to labor under a delusion** : hacerse ilusiones, tener una falsa impresión — *vt* BELABOR : insistir en, extenderse sobre
labor[2] *n* **1** EFFORT, WORK : trabajo *m*, esfuerzos *mpl* **2** : parto *m* ⟨to be in labor : estar de parto⟩ **3** TASK : tarea *f*, labor *m* **4** WORKERS : mano *f* de obra
laboratory [ˈlæbrəˌtori, ləˈbɔrə-] *n, pl* **-ries** : laboratorio *m*
Labor Day *n* : Día *m* del Trabajo
laborer [ˈleɪbərər] *n* : peón *m*; trabajador *m*, -dora *f*
laborious [ləˈboriəs] *adj* : laborioso, difícil
laboriously [ləˈboriəsli] *adv* : laboriosamente, trabajosamente
labor union → **union**
labyrinth [ˈlæbəˌrɪnθ] *n* : laberinto *m*
lace[1] [ˈleɪs] *vt* **laced; lacing** **1** TIE : acordonar, atar los cordones de **2** : adornar de encaje ⟨I laced the dress in white : adorné el vestido de encaje blanco⟩ **3** SPIKE : echar licor a
lace[2] *n* **1** : encaje *m* **2** SHOELACE : cordón *m* (de zapatos), agujeta *f Mex*
lacerate [ˈlæsəˌreɪt] *vt* **-ated; -ating** : lacerar
laceration [ˌlæsəˈreɪʃən] *n* : laceración *f*
lack[1] [ˈlæk] *vt* : carecer de, no tener ⟨she lacks patience : carece de paciencia⟩ — *vi* : faltar ⟨they lack for nothing : no les falta nada⟩
lack[2] *n* : falta *f*, carencia *f*
lackadaisical [ˌlækəˈdeɪzɪkəl] *adj* : apático, indiferente, lánguido — **lackadaisically** [-kli] *adv*
lackey [ˈlæki] *n, pl* **-eys** **1** FOOTMAN : lacayo *m* **2** TOADY : adulador *m*, -dora *f*
lackluster [ˈlækˌlʌstər] *adj* **1** DULL : sin brillo, apagado, deslustrado **2** MEDIOCRE : deslucido, mediocre
laconic [ləˈkɑnɪk] *adj* : lacónico — **laconically** [-nɪkli] *adv*
lacquer[1] [ˈlækər] *vt* : laquear, pintar con laca
lacquer[2] *n* : laca *f*
lacrosse [ləˈkrɔs] *n* : lacrosse *f*
lactic acid [ˈlæktɪk] *n* : ácido *m* láctico
lacuna [ləˈkuːnə, -ˈkjuː-] *n, pl* **-nae** [-ˌniː, -ˌnaɪ] *or* **-nas** : laguna *f*
lacy [ˈleɪsi] *adj* **lacier; -est** : de encaje, como de encaje
lad [ˈlæd] *n* : muchacho *m*, niño *m*
ladder [ˈlædər] *n* : escalera *f*
laden [ˈleɪdən] *adj* : cargado
ladle[1] [ˈleɪdəl] *vt* **-dled; -dling** : servir con cucharón
ladle[2] *n* : cucharón *m*, cazo *m*
lady [ˈleɪdi] *n, pl* **-dies** **1** : señora *f*, dama *f* **2** WOMAN : mujer *f*
ladybird [ˈleɪdiˌbərd] → **ladybug**
ladybug [ˈleɪdiˌbʌg] *n* : mariquita *f*
lag[1] [ˈlæg] *vi* **lagged; lagging** : quedarse atrás, retrasarse, rezagarse
lag[2] *n* **1** DELAY : retraso *m*, demora *f* **2** INTERVAL : lapso *m*, intervalo *m*
lager [ˈlɑgər] *n* : cerveza *f* rubia
laggard[1] [ˈlægərd] *adj* : retardado, retrasado
laggard[2] *n* : rezagado *m*, -da *f*
lagoon [ləˈguːn] *n* : laguna *f*
laid → **lay**[1]
laid–back [ˈleɪdˈbæk] *adj* : tranquilo, relajado
lain *pp* → **lie**[1]
lair [ˈlær] *n* : guarida *f*, madriguera *f*
laissez–faire [ˌlɛˌseɪˈfær, ˌleɪˌzeɪ-] *n* : liberalismo *m* económico
laity [ˈleɪət̬i] *n* **the laity** : los laicos, el laicado
lake [ˈleɪk] *n* : lago *m*
lama [ˈlɑmə] *n* : lama *m*
lamb [ˈlæm] *n* **1** : cordero *m*, borrego *m* (animal) **2** : carne *f* de cordero

lambaste [læm'beɪst] *or* **lambast** [-'bæst] *vt* **-basted; -basting 1** BEAT, THRASH : golpear, azotar, darle una paliza (a alguien) **2** CENSURE : arremeter contra, censurar

lame[1] ['leɪm] *vt* **lamed; laming** : lisiar, hacer cojo

lame[2] *adj* **lamer; lamest 1** : cojo, renco, rengo **2** WEAK : pobre, débil, poco convincente ⟨a lame excuse : una excusa débil⟩

lamé [lɑ'meɪ, læ-] *n* : lamé *m*

lame duck *n* : persona *f* sin poder ⟨a lame-duck President : un presidente saliente⟩

lamely ['leɪmli] *adv* : sin convicción

lameness ['leɪmnəs] *n* **1** : cojera *f*, renquera *f* **2** : falta *f* de convicción, debilidad *f*, pobreza *f* ⟨the lameness of her response : la pobreza de su respuesta⟩

lament[1] [lə'mɛnt] *vt* **1** MOURN : llorar, llorar por **2** DEPLORE : lamentar, deplorar — *vi* : llorar

lament[2] *n* : lamento *m*

lamentable ['læməntəbəl, lə'mɛntə-] *adj* : lamentable, deplorable — **lamentably** [-bli] *adv*

lamentation [ˌlæmən'teɪʃən] *n* : lamentación *f*, lamento *m*

laminate[1] ['læməˌneɪt] *vt* **-nated; -nating** : laminar

laminate[2] ['læmənət] *n* : laminado *m*

laminated ['læməˌneɪt̬əd] *adj* : laminado

lamp ['læmp] *n* : lámpara *f*

lampoon[1] [læm'puːn] *vt* : satirizar

lampoon[2] *n* : sátira *f*

lamprey ['læmpri] *n, pl* **-preys** : lamprea *f*

lance[1] ['lænts] *vt* **lanced; lancing** : abrir con lanceta, sajar

lance[2] *n* : lanza *f*

lance corporal *n* : cabo *m* interino, soldado *m* de primera clase

lancet ['læntsət] *n* : lanceta *f*

land[1] ['lænd] *vt* **1** : desembarcar (pasajeros de un barco), hacer aterrizar (un avión) **2** CATCH : pescar, sacar (un pez) del agua **3** GAIN, SECURE : conseguir, ganar ⟨to land a job : conseguir empleo⟩ **4** DELIVER : dar, asestar ⟨he landed a punch : asestó un puñetazo⟩ — *vi* **1** : aterrizar, tomar tierra, atracar ⟨the plane just landed : el avión acaba de aterrizar⟩ ⟨the ship landed an hour ago : el barco atracó hace una hora⟩ **2** ALIGHT : posarse, aterrizar ⟨to land on one's feet : caer de pie⟩

land[2] *n* **1** GROUND : tierra *f* ⟨dry land : tierra firme⟩ **2** TERRAIN : terreno *m* **3** NATION : país *m*, nación *f* **4** DOMAIN : mundo *m*, dominio *m* ⟨the land of dreams : el mundo de los sueños⟩

landfill ['lændˌfɪl] *n* : vertedero *m* (de basuras)

landing ['lændɪŋ] *n* **1** : aterrizaje *m* (de aviones), desembarco *m* (de barcos) **2** : descansillo *m* (de una escalera)

landing field *n* : campo *m* de aterrizaje

landing strip → **airstrip**

landlady ['lændˌleɪdi] *n, pl* **-dies** : casera *f*, dueña *f*, arrendadora *f*

landless ['lændləs] *adj* : sin tierra

landlocked ['lændˌlɑkt] *adj* : sin salida al mar

landlord ['lændˌlɔrd] *n* : dueño *m*, casero *m*, arrendador *m*

landlubber ['lændˌlʌbər] *n* : marinero *m* de agua dulce

landmark ['lændˌmɑrk] *n* **1** : señal *f* (geográfica), punto *m* de referencia **2** MILESTONE : hito *m* ⟨a landmark in our history : un hito en nuestra historia⟩ **3** MONUMENT : monumento *m* histórico

landowner ['lændˌoːnər] *n* : hacendado *m*, -da *f*; terrateniente *mf*

landscape[1] ['lændˌskeɪp] *vt* **-scaped; -scaping** : ajardinar

landscape[2] *n* : paisaje *m*

landslide ['lændˌslaɪd] *n* **1** : desprendimiento *m* de tierras, derrumbe *m* **2** **landslide victory** : victoria *f* arrolladora

landward ['lændwərd] *adv* : en dirección de la tierra, hacia tierra

lane ['leɪn] *n* **1** PATH, WAY : camino *m*, sendero *m* **2** : carril *m* (de una carretera)

language ['læŋgwɪʤ] *n* **1** : idioma *m*, lengua *f* ⟨the English language : el idioma inglés⟩ **2** : lenguaje *m* ⟨body language : lenguaje corporal⟩

languid ['læŋgwɪd] *adj* : lánguido — **languidly** *adv*

languish ['læŋgwɪʃ] *vi* **1** WEAKEN : languidecer, debilitarse **2** PINE : consumirse, suspirar (por) ⟨to languish for love : suspirar por el amor⟩ ⟨he languished in prison : estuvo pudriéndose en la cárcel⟩

languor ['læŋgər] *n* : languidez *f*

languorous ['læŋgərəs] *adj* : lánguido — **languorously** *adv*

lank ['læŋk] *adj* **1** THIN : delgado, larguirucho *fam* **2** LIMP : lacio

lanky ['læŋki] *adj* **lankier; -est** : delgado, larguirucho *fam*

lanolin ['lænəlɪn] *n* : lanolina *f*

lantern ['læntərn] *n* : linterna *f*, farol *m*

Laotian [leɪ'oːʃən, 'laʊʃən] *n* : laosiano *m*, -na *f* — **Laotian** *adj*

lap[1] ['læp] *v* **lapped; lapping** *vt* **1** FOLD : plegar, doblar **2** WRAP : envolver **3** : lamer, besar ⟨waves were lapping the shore : las olas lamían la orilla⟩ **4 to lap up** : beber a lengüetadas (como un gato) — *vi* OVERLAP : traslaparse

lap[2] *n* **1** : falda *f*, regazo *m* (del cuerpo) **2** OVERLAP : traslapo *m* **3** : vuelta *f* (en deportes) **4** STAGE : etapa *f* (de un viaje)

lapdog ['læpˌdɔg] *n* : perro *m* faldero

lapel [lə'pɛl] *n* : solapa *f*

Lapp ['læp] *n* : lapón *m*, -pona *f* — **Lapp** *adj*

lapse[1] ['læps] *vi* **lapsed; lapsing 1** FALL, SLIP : caer ⟨to lapse into bad habits : caer en malos hábitos⟩ ⟨to lapse into unconsciousness : perder el conocimiento⟩ ⟨to lapse into silence : quedarse callado⟩ **2** FADE : decaer, desvanecerse ⟨her dedication lapsed : su dedicación se desvaneció⟩ **3** CEASE : cancelarse, perderse **4** ELAPSE : transcurrir, pasar **5** EXPIRE : caducar

lapse[2] *n* **1** SLIP : lapsus *m*, desliz *m*, falla *f* ⟨a lapse of memory : una falla de memoria⟩ **2** INTERVAL : lapso *m*, intervalo *m*, período *m* **3** EXPIRATION : caducidad *f*

laptop[1] [ˈlæpˌtɑp] *adj* : portátil, laptop

laptop[2] *n* : laptop *m*

larboard [ˈlɑrbərd] *n* : babor *m*

larcenous [ˈlɑrsənəs] *adj* : de robo

larceny [ˈlɑrsəni] *n, pl* **-nies** : robo *m*, hurto *m*

larch [ˈlɑrʧ] *n* : alerce *f*

lard [ˈlɑrd] *n* : manteca *f* de cerdo

larder [ˈlɑrdər] *n* : despensa *f*, alacena *f*

large [ˈlɑrʤ] *adj* **larger; largest** **1** BIG : grande **2** COMPREHENSIVE : amplio, extenso **3 by and large** : por lo general

largely [ˈlɑrʤli] *adv* : en gran parte, en su mayoría

largeness [ˈlɑrʤnəs] *n* : lo grande

largesse *or* **largess** [lɑrˈʒɛs, -ˈʤɛs] *n* : generosidad *f*, largueza *f*

lariat [ˈlæriət] *n* : lazo *m*

lark [ˈlɑrk] *n* **1** FUN : diversión *f* ⟨what a lark! : ¡qué divertido!⟩ **2** : alondra *f* (pájaro)

larva [ˈlɑrvə] *n, pl* **-vae** [-ˌviː, -ˌvaɪ] : larva *f* — **larval** [-vəl] *adj*

laryngitis [ˌlærənˈʤaɪţəs] *n* : laringitis *f*

larynx [ˈlærɪŋks] *n, pl* **-rynges** [ləˈrɪnˌʤiːz] *or* **-ynxes** [ˈlærɪŋksəz] : laringe *f*

lasagna [ləˈzɑnjə] *n* : lasaña *f*

lascivious [ləˈsɪviəs] *adj* : lascivo

lasciviousness [ləˈsɪviəsnəs] *n* : lascivia *f*, lujuria *f*

laser [ˈleɪzər] *n* : láser *m*

laser disc *n* : disco *m* láser

lash[1] [ˈlæʃ] *vt* **1** WHIP : azotar **2** BIND : atar, amarrar

lash[2] *n* **1** WHIP : látigo *m* **2** STROKE : latigazo *m* **3** EYELASH : pestaña *f*

lass [ˈlæs] *or* **lassie** [ˈlæsi] *n* : muchacha *f*, chica *f*

lassitude [ˈlæsəˌtuːd, -ˌtjuːd] *n* : lasitud *f*

lasso[1] [ˈlæˌsoː, læˈsuː] *vt* : lazar

lasso[2] *n, pl* **-sos** *or* **-soes** : lazo *m*, reata *f Mex*

last[1] [ˈlæst] *vi* **1** CONTINUE : durar ⟨how long will it last? : ¿cuánto durará?⟩ **2** ENDURE : aguantar, durar **3** SURVIVE : durar, sobrevivir **4** SUFFICE : durar, bastar — *vt* **1** : durar ⟨it will last a lifetime : durará toda la vida⟩ **2 to last out** : aguantar

last[2] *adv* **1** : en último lugar, al último ⟨we came in last : llegamos en último lugar⟩ **2** : por última vez, la última vez ⟨I saw him last in Bogota : lo vi por última vez en Bogotá⟩ **3** FINALLY : por último, en conclusión

last[3] *adj* **1** FINAL : último, final **2** PREVIOUS : pasado ⟨last year : el año pasado⟩

last[4] *n* **1** : el último, la última, lo último ⟨at last : por fin, al fin, finalmente⟩ **2** : horma *f* (de zapatero)

lasting [ˈlæstɪŋ] *adj* : perdurable, duradero, estable

lastly [ˈlæstli] *adv* : por último, finalmente

latch[1] [ˈlæʧ] *vt* : cerrar con picaporte

latch[2] *n* : picaporte *m*, pestillo *m*, pasador *m*

late[1] [ˈleɪt] *adv* **later; latest** **1** : tarde ⟨to arrive late : llegar tarde⟩ ⟨to sleep late : dormir hasta tarde⟩ **2** : a última hora, a finales ⟨late in the month : a finales del mes⟩ **3** RECENTLY : recién, últimamente ⟨as late as last year : todavía en el año pasado⟩

late[2] *adj* **later; latest** **1** TARDY : tardío, de retraso ⟨to be late : llegar tarde⟩ **2** : avanzado ⟨because of the late hour : a causa de la hora avanzada⟩ **3** DECEASED : difunto, fallecido **4** RECENT : reciente, último ⟨our late quarrel : nuestra última pelea⟩

latecomer [ˈleɪtˌkʌmər] *n* : rezagado *m*, -da *f*

lately [ˈleɪtli] *adv* : recientemente, últimamente

lateness [ˈleɪtnəs] *n* **1** DELAY : retraso *m*, atraso *m*, tardanza *f* **2** : lo avanzado (de la hora)

latent [ˈleɪtənt] *adj* : latente — **latently** *adv*

lateral [ˈlæţərəl] *adj* : lateral — **laterally** *adv*

latex [ˈleɪˌtɛks] *n, pl* **-tices** [ˈleɪţəˌsiːz, ˈlæţə-] *or* **-texes** : látex *m*

lath [ˈlæθ, ˈlæð] *n, pl* **laths** *or* **lath** : listón *m*

lathe [ˈleɪð] *n* : torno *m*

lather[1] [ˈlæðər] *vt* : enjabonar — *vi* : espumar, hacer espuma

lather[2] *n* **1** : espuma *f* (de jabón) **2** : sudor *m* (de caballo) **3 to get into a lather** : ponerse histérico

Latin[1] *adj* : latino

Latin[2] *n* **1** : latín *m* (idioma) **2** → **Latin American**

Latin–American [ˈlætənəˈmrikən] *adj* : latinoamericano

Latin American *n* : latinoamericano *m*, -na *f*

latitude [ˈlæţəˌtuːd, -ˌtjuːd] *n* : latitud *f*

latrine [ləˈtriːn] *n* : letrina *f*

latte [ˈlɑˌteɪ] *n* : café *m* con leche

latter[1] [ˈlæţər] *adj* **1** SECOND : segundo **2** LAST : último

latter[2] *pron* **the latter** : éste, ésta, éstos *pl*, éstas *pl*

lattice [ˈlæţəs] *n* : enrejado *m*, celosía *f*

Latvian [ˈlætviən] *n* : letón *m*, -tona *f* — **Latvian** *adj*

laud[1] [ˈlɔd] *vt* : alabar, loar

laud[2] *n* : alabanza *f*, loa *f*

laudable [ˈlɔdəbəl] *adj* : loable — **laudably** [-bli] *adv*

laugh[1] [ˈlæf] *vi* : reír, reírse

laugh[2] *n* **1** LAUGHTER : risa *f* **2** JOKE : chiste *m*, broma *f* ⟨he did it for a laugh : lo hizo en broma, lo hizo para divertirse⟩

laughable [ˈlæfəbəl] *adj* : risible, de risa

laughingstock [ˈlæfɪŋˌstɑk] *n* : hazmerreír *m*

laughter [ˈlæftər] *n* : risa *f*, risas *fpl*

launch[1] [ˈlɔntʃ] *vt* **1** HURL : lanzar **2** : botar (un barco) **3** START : iniciar, empezar

launch[2] *n* **1** : lancha *f* (bote) **2** LAUNCHING : lanzamiento *m*

launder [ˈlɔndər] *vt* **1** : lavar y planchar (ropa) **2** : blanquear, lavar (dinero)

launderer [ˈlɔndərər] *n* : lavandero *m*, -ra *f*

laundress [ˈlɔndrəs] *n* : lavandera *f*

laundry [ˈlɔndri] *n, pl* **laundries** **1** : ropa *f* sucia, ropa *f* para lavar ⟨to do the laundry : lavar la ropa⟩ **2** : lavandería *f* (servicio de lavar)

laureate [ˈlɔriət] *n* : laureado *m*, -da *f* ⟨poet laureate : poeta laureado⟩

laurel [ˈlɔrəl] *n* **1** : laurel *m* (planta) **2** **laurels** *npl* : laureles *mpl* ⟨to rest on one's laurels : dormirse uno en sus laureles⟩

lava [ˈlɑvə, ˈlæ-] *n* : lava *f*

lavatory [ˈlævəˌtori] *n, pl* **-ries** : baño *m*, cuarto *m* de baño

lavender [ˈlævəndər] *n* : lavanda *f*, espliego *m*

lavish[1] [ˈlævɪʃ] *vt* : prodigar (a), colmar (de)

lavish[2] *adj* **1** EXTRAVAGANT : pródigo, generoso, derrochador **2** ABUNDANT : abundante **3** LUXURIOUS : lujoso, espléndido

lavishly [ˈlævɪʃli] *adv* : con generosidad, espléndidamente ⟨to live lavishly : vivir a lo grande⟩

lavishness [ˈlævɪʃnəs] *n* : generosidad *f*, esplendidez *f*

law [ˈlɔ] *n* **1** : ley *f* ⟨to break the law : violar la ley⟩ **2** : derecho *m* ⟨criminal law : derecho criminal⟩ **3** : abogacía *f* ⟨to practice law : ejercer la abogacía⟩

law–abiding [ˈlɔəˌbaɪdɪŋ] *adj* : observante de la ley

lawbreaker [ˈlɔˌbreɪkər] *n* : infractor *m*, -tora *f* de la ley

lawful [ˈlɔfəl] *adj* : legal, legítimo, lícito — **lawfully** *adv*

lawgiver [ˈlɔˌgɪvər] *n* : legislador *m*, -dora *f*

lawless [ˈlɔləs] *adj* : anárquico, ingobernable — **lawlessly** *adv*

lawlessness [ˈlɔləsnəs] *n* : anarquía *f*, desorden *m*

lawmaker [ˈlɔˌmeɪkər] *n* : legislador *m*, -dora *f*

lawman [ˈlɔmən] *n, pl* **-men** [-mən, -ˌmɛn] : agente *m* del orden

lawn [ˈlɔn] *n* : césped *m*, pasto *m*

lawn mower *n* : cortadora *f* de césped

lawsuit [ˈlɔˌsu:t] *n* : pleito *m*, litigio *m*, demanda *f*

lawyer [ˈlɔɪər, ˈlɔjər] *n* : abogado *m*, -da *f*

lax [ˈlæks] *adj* : laxo, relajado — **laxly** *adv*

laxative [ˈlæksət̬ɪv] *n* : laxante *m*

laxity [ˈlæksət̬i] *n* : relajación *f*, descuido *m*, falta *f* de rigor

lay[1] [ˈleɪ] *vt* **laid** [ˈleɪd]; **laying** **1** PLACE, PUT : poner, colocar ⟨she laid it on the table : lo puso en la mesa⟩ ⟨to lay eggs : poner huevos⟩ **2** : hacer ⟨to lay a bet : hacer una apuesta⟩ **3** IMPOSE : imponer ⟨to lay a tax : imponer un impuesto⟩ ⟨to lay the blame on : echarle la culpa a⟩ **4 to lay out** PRESENT : presentar, exponer ⟨he laid out his plan : presentó su proyecto⟩ **5 to lay out** DESIGN : diseñar (el trazado de)

lay[2] → **lie**[1]

lay[3] *adj* SECULAR : laico, lego

lay[4] *n* **1** : disposición *f*, configuración *f* ⟨the lay of the land : la configuración del terreno⟩ **2** BALLAD : romance *m*, balada *f*

layer [ˈleɪər] *n* **1** : capa *f* (de pintura, etc.), estrato *m* (de roca) **2** : gallina *f* ponedora

layman [ˈleɪmən] *n, pl* **-men** [-mən, -ˌmɛn] : laico *m*, lego *m*

layoff [ˈleɪˌɔf] *n* : despido *m*

lay off *vt* : despedir

layout [ˈleɪˌaʊt] *n* : disposición *f*, distribución *f* (de una casa, etc.), trazado *m* (de una ciudad)

lay up *vt* **1** STORE : guardar, almacenar **2 to be laid up** : estar enfermo, tener que guardar cama

laywoman [ˈleɪˌwʊmən] *n, pl* **-women** [-ˌwɪmən] : laica *f*, lega *f*

laziness [ˈleɪzinəs] *n* : pereza *f*, flojera *f*

lazy [ˈleɪzi] *adj* **-zier**; **-est** : perezoso, holgazán — **lazily** [ˈleɪzəli] *adv*

leach [ˈli:tʃ] *vt* : filtrar

lead[1] [ˈli:d] *vt* **led** [ˈlɛd]; **leading** **1** GUIDE : conducir, llevar, guiar **2** DIRECT : dirigir **3** HEAD : encabezar, ir al frente de **4 to lead to** : resultar en, llevar a ⟨it only leads to trouble : sólo resulta en problemas⟩

lead[2] *n* : delantera *f*, primer lugar *m* ⟨to take the lead : tomar la delantera⟩

lead[3] [ˈlɛd] *n* **1** : plomo *m* (metal) **2** : mina *f* (de lápiz) **3 lead poisoning** : saturnismo *m*

leaden [ˈlɛdən] *adj* **1** : plomizo ⟨a leaden sky : un ciel plomizo⟩ **2** HEAVY : pesado

leader [ˈli:dər] *n* : jefe *m*, -fa *f*; líder *mf*; dirigente *mf*; gobernante *mf*

leadership [ˈli:dərˌʃɪp] *n* : mando *m*, dirección *f*

leaf[1] [ˈli:f] *vi* **1** : echar hojas (dícese de un árbol) **2 to leaf through** : hojear (un libro)

leaf[2] *n, pl* **leaves** [ˈli:vz] **1** : hoja *f* (de plantas o libros) **2 to turn over a new leaf** : hacer borrón y cuenta nueva

leafless [ˈli:fləs] *adj* : sin hojas, pelado

leaflet [ˈli:flət] *n* : folleto *m*

leafy [ˈli:fi] *adj* **leafier; -est** : frondoso

league[1] [ˈli:g] *v* **leagued; leaguing** *vt* : aliar, unir — *vi* : aliarse, unirse

league[2] *n* **1** : legua *f* (medida de distancia) **2** ASSOCIATION : alianza *f*, sociedad *f*, liga *f*

leak[1] [ˈli:k] *vt* **1** : perder, dejar escapar (un líquido o un gas) **2** : filtrar (información) — *vi* **1** : gotear, escaparse, fugarse (dícese de un líquido o un gas) **2** : hacer agua (dícese de un bote) **3** : filtrarse, divulgarse (dícese de información)

leak[2] *n* **1** HOLE : agujero *m* (en recipientes), gotera *f* (en un tejado) **2** ESCAPE : fuga *f*, escape *m* **3** : filtración *f* (de información)

leakage [ˈli:kɪʤ] *n* : escape *m*, fuga *f*

leaky [ˈli:ki] *adj* **leakier; -est** : agujereado (dícese de un recipiente), que hace agua (dícese de un bote), con goteras (dícese de un tejado)

lean[1] [ˈli:n] *vi* **1** BEND : inclinarse, ladearse **2** RECLINE : reclinarse **3** RELY : apoyarse (en), depender (de) **4** INCLINE, TEND : inclinarse, tender — *vt* : apoyar

lean[2] *adj* **1** THIN : delgado, flaco **2** : sin grasa, magro (dícese de la carne)

leanness [ˈli:nnəs] *n* : delgadez *f*

lean–to [ˈli:n,tu:] *n* : cobertizo *m*

leap[1] [ˈli:p] *vi* **leaped** [ˈli:pt, ˈlɛpt] *or* **leapt; leaping** : saltar, brincar

leap[2] *n* : salto *m*, brinco *m*

leap year *n* : año *m* bisiesto

learn [ˈlərn] *vt* **1** : aprender ⟨to learn to sing : aprender a cantar⟩ **2** MEMORIZE : aprender de memoria **3** DISCOVER : saber, enterarse de — *vi* **1** : aprender ⟨to learn from experience : aprender por experiencia⟩ **2** FIND OUT : enterarse, saber

learned [ˈlərnəd] *adj* : erudito

learner [ˈlərnər] *n* : principiante *mf*, estudiante *mf*

learning [ˈlərnɪŋ] *n* : erudición *f*, saber *m*

lease[1] [ˈli:s] *vt* **leased; leasing** : arrendar

lease[2] *n* : contrato *m* de arrendamiento

leash[1] [ˈli:ʃ] *vt* : atraillar (un animal)

leash[2] *n* : traílla *f*

least[1] [ˈli:st] *adv* : menos ⟨when least expected : cuando menos se espera⟩

least[2] *adj* (*superlative of* **little**) : menor, más mínimo

least[3] *n* **1** : lo menos ⟨at least : por lo menos⟩ **2 to say the least** : por no decir más

leather [ˈlɛðər] *n* : cuero *m*

leathery [ˈlɛðəri] *adj* : curtido (dícese de la piel), correoso (dícese de la carne)

leave[1] [ˈli:v] *v* **left** [ˈlɛft]; **leaving** *vt* **1** BEQUEATH : dejar, legar **2** DEPART : dejar, salir(se) de **3** ABANDON : abandonar, dejar **4** FORGET : dejar, olvidarse de ⟨I left the books at the library : dejé los libros en la biblioteca⟩ **5 to be left** : quedar ⟨it's all I have left : es todo lo que me queda⟩ **6 to be left over** : sobrar **7 to leave out** : omitir, excluir — *vi* : irse, salir, partir, marcharse ⟨she left yesterday morning : se fue ayer por la mañana⟩

leave[2] *n* **1** PERMISSION : permiso *m* ⟨by your leave : con su permiso⟩ **2** *or* **leave of absence** : permiso *m*, licencia *f* ⟨maternity leave : licencia por maternidad⟩ **3 to take one's leave** : despedirse

leaven [ˈlɛvən] *n* : levadura *f*

leaves → **leaf**[2]

leaving [ˈli:vɪŋ] *n* **1** : salida *f*, partida *f* **2 leavings** *npl* : restos *mpl*, sobras *fpl*

Lebanese [ˌlɛbəˈni:z, -ˈni:s] *n* : libanés *m*, -nesa *f* — **Lebanese** *adj*

lecherous [ˈlɛʧərəs] *adj* : lascivo, libidinoso — **lecherously** *adv*

lechery [ˈlɛʧəri] *n* : lascivia *f*, lujuria *f*

lecture[1] [ˈlɛkʧər] *v* **-tured; -turing** *vi* : dar clase, dictar clase, dar una conferencia — *vt* SCOLD : sermonear, echar una reprimenda a, regañar

lecture[2] *n* **1** : conferencia *f* **2** REPRIMAND : reprimenda *f*

lecturer [ˈlɛkʧərər] *n* **1** SPEAKER : conferenciante *mf* **2** TEACHER : profesor *m*, -sora *f*

led → **lead**[1]

ledge [ˈlɛʤ] *n* : repisa *f* (de una pared), antepecho *m* (de una ventana), saliente *m* (de una montaña)

ledger [ˈlɛʤər] *n* : libro *m* mayor, libro *m* de contabilidad

lee[1] [ˈli:] *adj* : de sotavento

lee[2] *n* : sotavento *m*

leech [ˈli:ʧ] *n* : sanguijuela *f*

leek [ˈli:k] *n* : puerro *m*

leer[1] [ˈlɪr] *vi* : mirar con lascivia

leer[2] *n* : mirada *f* lasciva

leery [ˈlɪri] *adj* : receloso

lees [ˈli:z] *npl* : posos *mpl*, heces *fpl*

leeward[1] [ˈli:wərd, ˈlu:ərd] *adj* : de sotavento

leeward[2] *n* : sotavento *m*

leeway [ˈli:ˌweɪ] *n* : libertad *f*, margen *m*

left[1] [ˈlɛft] *adv* : hacia la izquierda

left[2] → **leave**[1]

left[3] *adj* : izquierdo

left[4] *n* : izquierda *f* ⟨on the left : a la izquierda⟩

left–hand [ˈlɛftˈhand] *adj* **1** : de la izquierda **2** → **left–handed**

left–handed [ˈlɛftˈhandəd] *adj* **1** : zurdo (dícese de una persona) **2** : con doble sentido ⟨a left-handed compliment : un cumplido a medias⟩

leftist [ˈlɛftɪst] *n* : izquierdista *mf* — **leftist** *adj*

leftover [ˈlɛftˌo:vər] *adj* : sobrante, que sobra

leftovers [ˈlɛftˌoːvərz] *npl* : restos *mpl*, sobras *fpl*
left wing *n* **the left wing** : la izquierda
left–winger [ˈlɛftˈwɪŋər] *n* : izquierdista *mf*
leg [ˈlɛg] *n* **1** : pierna *f* (de una persona, de carne, de ropa), pata *f* (de un animal, de muebles) **2** STAGE : etapa *f* (de un viaje), vuelta *f* (de una carrera)
legacy [ˈlɛgəsi] *n, pl* **-cies** : legado *m*, herencia *f*
legal [ˈliːgəl] *adj* **1** : legal, jurídico ⟨legal advisor : asesor jurídico⟩ ⟨the legal profession : la abogacía⟩ **2** LAWFUL : legítimo, legal
legalistic [ˌliːgəˈlɪstɪk] *adj* : legalista
legality [liˈgæləṭi] *n, pl* **-ties** : legalidad *f*
legalize [ˈliːgəˌlaɪz] *vt* **-ized; -izing** : legalizar
legally [ˈliːgəli] *adv* : legalmente
legate [ˈlɛgət] *n* : legado *m*
legation [lɪˈgeɪʃən] *n* : legación *f*
legend [ˈlɛʤənd] *n* **1** STORY : leyenda *f* **2** INSCRIPTION : leyenda *f*, inscripción *f* **3** : signos *mpl* convencionales (en un mapa)
legendary [ˈlɛʤənˌdɛri] *adj* : legendario
legerdemain [ˌlɛʤərdəˈmeɪn] → **sleight of hand**
leggings [ˈlɛgɪŋz, ˈlɛgənz] *npl* : mallas *fpl*
legibility [ˌlɛʤəˈbɪləṭi] *n* : legibilidad *f*
legible [ˈlɛʤəbəl] *adj* : legible
legibly [ˈlɛʤəbli] *adv* : de manera legible
legion [ˈliːʤən] *n* : legión *f*
legionnaire [ˌliːʤəˈnær] *n* : legionario *m*, -ria *f*
legislate [ˈlɛʤəsˌleɪt] *vi* **-lated; -lating** : legislar
legislation [ˌlɛʤəsˈleɪʃən] *n* : legislación *f*
legislative [ˈlɛʤəsˌleɪṭɪv] *adj* : legislativo, legislador
legislator [ˈlɛʤəsˌleɪṭər] *n* : legislador *m*, -dora *f*
legislature [ˈlɛʤəsˌleɪʧər] *n* : asamblea *f* legislativa
legitimacy [lɪˈʤɪṭəməsi] *n* : legitimidad *f*
legitimate [lɪˈʤɪṭəmət] *adj* **1** VALID : legítimo, válido, justificado **2** LAWFUL : legítimo, legal
legitimately [lɪˈʤɪṭəmətli] *adv* : legítimamente
legitimize [lɪˈʤɪṭəˌmaɪz] *vt* **-mized; -mizing** : legitimar, hacer legítimo
legume [ˈlɛˌgjuːm, lɪˈgjuːm] *n* : legumbre *f*
leisure [ˈliːʒər, ˈlɛ-] *n* **1** : ocio *m*, tiempo *m* libre ⟨a life of leisure : una vida de ocio⟩ **2 to take one's leisure** : reposar **3 at your leisure** : cuando te venga bien, cuando tengas tiempo
leisurely [ˈliːʒərli, ˈlɛ-] *adj & adv* : lento, sin prisas
lemming [ˈlɛmɪŋ] *n* : lemming *m*
lemon [ˈlɛmən] *n* : limón *m*
lemonade [ˌlɛməˈneɪd] *n* : limonada *f*
lemony [ˈlɛməni] *adj* : a limón
lend [ˈlɛnd] *vt* **lent** [ˈlɛnt]; **lending 1** : prestar ⟨to lend money : prestar dinero⟩ **2** GIVE : dar ⟨it lends force to his criticism : da fuerza a su crítica⟩ **3 to lend oneself to** : prestarse a
length [ˈlɛŋkθ] *n* **1** : longitud *f*, largo *m* ⟨10 feet in length : 10 pies de largo⟩ **2** DURATION : duración *f* **3** : trozo *m* (de madera), corte *m* (de tela) **4 to go to any lengths** : hacer todo lo posible **5 at ~** : extensamente ⟨to speak at length : hablar largo y tendido⟩
lengthen [ˈlɛŋkθən] *vt* **1** : alargar ⟨can they lengthen the dress? : ¿se puede alargar el vestido?⟩ **2** EXTEND, PROLONG : prolongar, extender — *vi* : alargarse, crecer ⟨the days are lengthening : los días están creciendo⟩
lengthways [ˈlɛŋkθˌweɪz] → **lengthwise**
lengthwise [ˈlɛŋkθˌwaɪz] *adv* : a lo largo, longitudinalmente
lengthy [ˈlɛŋkθi] *adj* **lengthier; -est 1** OVERLONG : largo y pesado **2** EXTENDED : prolongado, largo
leniency [ˈliːniəntsi] *n, pl* **-cies** : lenidad *f*, indulgencia *f*
lenient [ˈliːniənt] *adj* : indulgente, poco severo
leniently [ˈliːniəntli] *adv* : con lenidad, con indulgencia
lens [ˈlɛnz] *n* **1** : cristalino *m* (del ojo) **2** : lente *mf* (de un instrumento o una cámara) **3** → **contact lens**
lent → **lend**
Lent [ˈlɛnt] *n* : Cuaresma *f*
lentil [ˈlɛntəl] *n* : lenteja *f*
Leo [ˈliːoː] *n* : Leo *mf*
leopard [ˈlɛpərd] *n* : leopardo *m*
leotard [ˈliːəˌtɑrd] *n* : leotardo *m*, malla *f*
leper [ˈlɛpər] *n* : leproso *m*, -sa *f*
leprechaun [ˈlɛprəˌkɑn] *n* : duende *m* (irlandés)
leprosy [ˈlɛprəsi] *n* : lepra *f* — **leprous** [ˈlɛprəs] *adj*
lesbian[1] [ˈlɛzbiən] *adj* : lesbiano
lesbian[2] *n* : lesbiana *f*
lesbianism [ˈlɛzbiəˌnɪzəm] *n* : lesbianismo *m*
lesion [ˈliːʒən] *n* : lesión *f*
less[1] [ˈlɛs] *adv* (*comparative of* **little**[1]) : menos ⟨the less you know, the better : cuanto menos sepas, mejor⟩ ⟨less and less : cada vez menos⟩
less[2] *adj* (*comparative of* **little**[2]) : menos ⟨less than three : menos de tres⟩ ⟨less money : menos dinero⟩ ⟨nothing less than perfection : nada menos que la perfección⟩
less[3] *pron* : menos ⟨I'm earning less : estoy ganando menos⟩
less[4] *prep* : menos ⟨one month less two days : un mes menos dos días⟩
lessee [lɛˈsiː] *n* : arrendatario *m*, -ria *f*
lessen [ˈlɛsən] *vt* : disminuir, reducir — *vi* : disminuir, reducirse

lesser ['lɛsər] *adj* : menor ⟨to a lesser degree : en menor grado⟩
lesson ['lɛsən] *n* **1** CLASS : clase *f*, curso *m* **2** : lección *f* ⟨the lessons of history : las lecciones de la historia⟩
lessor ['lɛˌsɔr, lɛ'sɔr] *n* : arrendador *m*, -dora *f*
lest ['lɛst] *conj* : para (que) no ⟨lest we forget : para que no olvidemos⟩
let ['lɛt] *vt* **let; letting 1** ALLOW : dejar, permitir ⟨let me see it : déjame verlo⟩ **2** MAKE : hacer ⟨let me know : házmelo saber, avísame⟩ ⟨let them wait : que esperen, haz que esperen⟩ **3** RENT : alquilar **4** (*used in the first person plural imperative*) ⟨let's go! : ¡vamos!, ¡vámonos!⟩ ⟨let us pray : oremos⟩ **5 to let down** DISAPPOINT : fallar **6 to let off** FORGIVE : perdonar **7 to let out** REVEAL : revelar **8 to let up** ABATE : amainar, disminuir ⟨the pace never lets up : el ritmo nunca disminuye⟩
letdown *n* : chasco *m*, decepción *f*
lethal ['li:θəl] *adj* : letal — **lethally** *adv*
lethargic [lɪ'θɑrʤɪk] *adj* : letárgico
lethargy ['lɛθərʤi] *n* : letargo *m*
let on *vi* **1** ADMIT : reconocer ⟨don't let on! : ¡no digas nada!⟩ **2** PRETEND : fingir
let's ['lɛts] (*contraction of* **let us**) → **let**
letter[1] ['lɛt̬ər] *vt* : marcar con letras, inscribir letras en
letter[2] *n* **1** : letra *f* (del alfabeto) **2** : carta *f* ⟨a letter to my mother : una carta a mi madre⟩ **3 letters** *npl* ARTS : letras *fpl* **4 to the letter** : al pie de la letra
lettering ['lɛt̬ərɪŋ] *n* : letra *f*
lettuce ['lɛt̬əs] *n* : lechuga *f*
leukemia [lu:'ki:miə] *n* : leucemia *f*
levee ['lɛvi] *n* : dique *m*
level[1] ['lɛvəl] *vt* **-eled** *or* **-elled; -eling** *or* **-elling 1** FLATTEN : nivelar, aplanar **2** AIM : apuntar (una pistola), dirigir (una acusación) **3** RAZE : rasar, arrasar
level[2] *adj* **1** EVEN : llano, plano, parejo **2** CALM : tranquilo ⟨to keep a level head : no perder la cabeza⟩
level[3] *n* : nivel *m*
leveler ['lɛvələr] *n* : nivelador *m*, -dora *f*
levelheaded ['lɛvəl'hɛdəd] *adj* : sensato, equilibrado
levelly ['lɛvəli] *adv* CALMLY : con ecuanimidad *f*, con calma
levelness ['lɛvəlnəs] *n* : uniformidad *f*
lever ['lɛvər, 'li:-] *n* : palanca *f*
leverage ['lɛvərɪʤ, 'li:-] *n* **1** : apalancamiento *m* (en física) **2** INFLUENCE : influencia *f*, palanca *f fam*
leviathan [lɪ'vaɪəθən] *n* : leviatán *m*, gigante *m*
levity ['lɛvət̬i] *n* : ligereza *f*, frivolidad *f*
levy[1] ['lɛvi] *vt* **levied; levying 1** IMPOSE : imponer, exigir, gravar (un impuesto) **2** COLLECT : recaudar (un impuesto)
levy[2] *n, pl* **levies** : impuesto *m*, gravamen *m*
lewd ['lu:d] *adj* : lascivo — **lewdly** *adv*
lewdness ['lu:dnəs] *n* : lascivia *f*
lexical ['lɛksɪkəl] *adj* : léxico
lexicographer [ˌlɛksə'kɑgrəfər] *n* : lexicógrafo *m*, -fa *f*
lexicographical [ˌlɛksəko'græfɪkəl] *or* **lexicographic** [-'græfɪk] *adj* : lexicográfico
lexicography [ˌlɛksə'kɑgrəfi] *n* : lexicografía *f*
lexicon ['lɛksɪˌkɑn] *n, pl* **-ica** [-kə] *or* **-icons** : léxico *m*, lexicón *m*
liability [ˌlaɪə'bɪlət̬i] *n, pl* **-ties 1** RESPONSIBILITY : responsabilidad *f* **2** SUSCEPTIBILITY : propensión *f* **3** DRAWBACK : desventaja *f* **4 liabilities** *npl* DEBTS : deudas *fpl*, pasivo *m*
liable ['laɪəbəl] *adj* **1** RESPONSIBLE : responsable **2** SUSCEPTIBLE : propenso **3** PROBABLE : probable ⟨it's liable to happen : es probable que suceda⟩
liaison ['li:əˌzɑn, li'eɪ-] *n* **1** CONNECTION : enlace *m*, relación *f* **2** AFFAIR : amorío *m*, aventura *f*
liar ['laɪər] *n* : mentiroso *m*, -sa *f*; embustero *m*, -ra *f*
libel[1] ['laɪbəl] *vt* **-beled** *or* **-belled; -beling** *or* **-belling** : difamar, calumniar
libel[2] *n* : difamación *f*, calumnia *f*
libeler ['laɪbələr] *n* : difamador *m*, -dora *f*; calumniador *m*, -dora *f*; libelista *mf*
libelous *or* **libellous** ['laɪbələs] *adj* : difamatorio, calumnioso, injurioso
liberal[1] ['lɪbrəl, 'lɪbərəl] *adj* **1** TOLERANT : liberal, tolerante **2** GENEROUS : generoso **3** ABUNDANT : abundante **4 liberal arts** : humanidades *fpl*, artes *fpl* liberales
liberal[2] *n* : liberal *mf*
liberalism ['lɪbrəˌlɪzəm, 'lɪbərə-] *n* : liberalismo *m*
liberality [ˌlɪbə'rælət̬i] *n, pl* **-ties** : liberalidad *f*, generosidad *f*
liberalize ['lɪbrəˌlaɪz, 'lɪbərə-] *vt* **-ized; -izing** : liberalizar
liberally ['lɪbrəli, 'lɪbərə-] *adv* **1** GENEROUSLY : generosamente **2** ABUNDANTLY : abundantemente **3** FREELY : libremente
liberate ['lɪbəˌreɪt] *vt* **-ated; -ating** : liberar, libertar
liberation [ˌlɪbə'reɪʃən] *n* : liberación *f*
liberator ['lɪbəˌreɪt̬ər] *n* : libertador *m*, -dora *f*
Liberian [laɪ'bɪriən] *n* : liberiano *m*, -na *f* — **Liberian** *adj*
libertine ['lɪbərˌti:n] *n* : libertino *m*, -na *f*
liberty ['lɪbərt̬i] *n, pl* **-ties 1** : libertad *f* **2 to take the liberty of** : tomarse la libertad de **3 to take liberties with** : tomarse confianzas con, tomarse libertades con
libido [lə'bi:do:, -'baɪ-] *n, pl* **-dos** : libido *f* — **libidinous** [lə'bɪdənəs] *adj*
Libra ['li:brə] *n* : Libra *mf*
librarian [laɪ'brɛriən] *n* : bibliotecario *m*, -ria *f*
library ['laɪˌbrɛri] *n, pl* **-braries** : biblioteca *f*

librettist [lɪˈbrɛt̬ɪst] *n* : libretista *mf*
libretto [lɪˈbrɛt̬o] *n, pl* **-tos** *or* **-ti** [-t̬iː] : libreto *m*
Libyan [ˈlɪbiən] *n* : libio *m*, -bia *f* — **Libyan** *adj*
lice → **louse**
license[1] [ˈlaɪsənts] *vt* **licensed; licensing** : licenciar, autorizar, dar permiso a
license[2] *or* **licence** *n* **1** PERMISSION : licencia *f*, permiso *m* **2** PERMIT : licencia *f*, carnet *m Spain* ⟨driver's license : licencia de conducir⟩ **3** FREEDOM : libertad *f* **4** LICENTIOUSNESS : libertinaje *m*
licentious [laɪˈsɛntʃəs] *adj* : licencioso, disoluto — **licentiously** *adv*
licentiousness [laɪˈsɛntʃəsnəs] *n* : libertinaje *m*
lichen [ˈlaɪkən] *n* : liquen *m*
licit [ˈlɪsət] *adj* : lícito
lick[1] [ˈlɪk] *vt* **1** : lamer **2** BEAT : darle una paliza (a alguien)
lick[2] *n* **1** : lamida *f*, lengüetada *f* ⟨a lick of paint : una mano de pintura⟩ **2** BIT : pizca *f*, ápice *m* **3 a lick and a promise** : una lavada a la carrera
licorice [ˈlɪkərɪʃ, -rəs] *n* : regaliz *m*, dulce *m* de regaliz
lid [ˈlɪd] *n* **1** COVER : tapa *f* **2** EYELID : párpado *m*
lie[1] [ˈlaɪ] *vi* **lay** [ˈleɪ]; **lain** [ˈleɪn]; **lying** [ˈlaɪɪŋ] **1** : acostarse, echarse ⟨I lay down : me acosté⟩ **2** : estar, estar situado, encontrarse ⟨the book lay on the table : el libro estaba en la mesa⟩ ⟨the city lies to the south : la ciudad se encuentra al sur⟩ **3** CONSIST : consistir **4 to lie in** : residir en ⟨the power lies in the people : el poder reside en el pueblo⟩
lie[2] *vi* **lied; lying** [ˈlaɪɪŋ] : mentir
lie[3] *n* **1** UNTRUTH : mentira *f* ⟨to tell lies : decir mentiras⟩ **2** POSITION : posición *f*
liege [ˈliːdʒ] *n* : señor *m* feudal
lien [ˈliːn, ˈliːən] *n* : derecho *m* de retención
lieutenant [luːˈtɛnənt] *n* : teniente *mf*
lieutenant colonel *n* : teniente *mf* coronel
lieutenant commander *n* : capitán *m*, -tana *f* de corbeta
lieutenant general *n* : teniente *mf* general
life [ˈlaɪf] *n, pl* **lives** [ˈlaɪvz] **1** : vida *f* ⟨plant life : la vida vegetal⟩ **2** EXISTENCE : vida *f*, existencia *f* **3** BIOGRAPHY : biografía *f*, vida *f* **4** DURATION : duración *f*, vida *f* **5** LIVELINESS : vivacidad *f*, animación *f*
lifeblood [ˈlaɪfˌblʌd] *n* : parte *f* vital, sustento *m*
lifeboat [ˈlaɪfˌboːt] *n* : bote *m* salvavidas
lifeguard [ˈlaɪfˌgɑrd] *n* : socorrista *mf*, salvavidas *mf*
lifeless [ˈlaɪfləs] *adj* : sin vida, muerto
lifelike [ˈlaɪfˌlaɪk] *adj* : que parece vivo, natural, verosímil
lifelong [ˈlaɪfˈlɔŋ] *adj* : de toda la vida ⟨a lifelong friend : un amigo de toda la vida⟩
life preserver *n* : salvavidas *m*
lifesaver [ˈlaɪfˌseɪvər] *n* **1** : salvación *f* **2** → **lifeguard**
lifesaving [ˈlaɪfˌseɪvɪŋ] *n* : socorrismo *m*
lifestyle [ˈlaɪfˌstaɪl] *n* : estilo *m* de vida
lifetime [ˈlaɪfˌtaɪm] *n* : vida *f*, curso *m* de la vida
lift[1] [ˈlɪft] *vt* **1** RAISE : levantar, alzar, subir **2** END : levantar ⟨to lift a ban : levantar una prohibición⟩ — *vi* **1** RISE : levantarse, alzarse **2** CLEAR UP : despejar ⟨the fog lifted : se disipó la niebla⟩
lift[2] *n* **1** LIFTING : levantamiento *m*, alzamiento *m* **2** BOOST : impulso *m*, estímulo *m* **3 to give someone a lift** : llevar en coche a alguien
liftoff [ˈlɪftˌɔf] *n* : despegue *m*
ligament [ˈlɪgəmənt] *n* : ligamento *m*
ligature [ˈlɪgəˌtʃʊr, -tʃər] *n* : ligadura *f*
light[1] [ˈlaɪt] *v* **lit** [ˈlɪt] *or* **lighted; lighting** *vt* **1** ILLUMINATE : iluminar, alumbrar **2** IGNITE : encender, prenderle fuego a — *vi* : encenderse, prender
light[2] *vi* **lighted** *or* **lit** [ˈlɪt]; **lighting** **1** LAND, SETTLE : posarse **2** DISMOUNT : bajarse, apearse
light[3] [ˈlaɪt] *adv* **1** LIGHTLY : suavemente, ligeramente **2 to travel light** : viajar con poco equipaje
light[4] *adj* **1** LIGHTWEIGHT : ligero, liviano, poco pesado **2** EASY : fácil, ligero, liviano ⟨light reading : lectura fácil⟩ ⟨light work : trabajo liviano⟩ **3** GENTLE, MILD : fino, suave, leve ⟨a light breeze : una brisa suave⟩ ⟨a light rain : una lluvia fina⟩ **4** FRIVOLOUS : de poca importancia, superficial **5** BRIGHT : bien iluminado, claro **6** PALE : claro (dícese de los colores), rubio (dícese del pelo)
light[5] *n* **1** ILLUMINATION : luz *f* **2** DAYLIGHT : luz *f* del día **3** DAWN : amanecer *m*, madrugada *f* **4** LAMP : lámpara *f* ⟨to turn on off the light : apagar la luz⟩ **5** ASPECT : aspecto *m* ⟨in a new light : con otros ojos⟩ ⟨in the light of : en vista de, a la luz de⟩ **6** MATCH : fósforo *m*, cerillo *m* **7 to bring to light** : sacar a (la) luz
lightbulb [ˈlaɪtˌbʌlb] *n* : bombilla *f*, foco *m*, bombillo *m CA, Col, Ven*
lighten [ˈlaɪtən] *vt* **1** ILLUMINATE : iluminar, dar más luz a **2** : aclararse (el pelo) **3** : aligerar (una carga, etc.) **4** RELIEVE : aliviar **5** GLADDEN : alegrar ⟨it lightened his heart : alegró su corazón⟩
lighter [ˈlaɪt̬ər] *n* : encendedor *m*
lighthearted [ˈlaɪtˈhɑrt̬əd] *adj* : alegre, despreocupado, desenfadado — **lightheartedly** *adv*
lightheartedness [ˈlaɪtˈhɑrt̬ədnəs] *n* : desenfado *m*, alegría *f*
lighthouse [ˈlaɪtˌhaʊs] *n* : faro *m*

lighting ['laɪţɪŋ] *n* : iluminación *f*

lightly ['laɪtli] *adv* **1** GENTLY : suavemente **2** SLIGHTLY : ligeramente **3** FRIVOLOUSLY : a la ligera **4 to let off lightly** : tratar con indulgencia

lightness ['laɪtnəs] *n* **1** BRIGHTNESS : luminosidad *f*, claridad *f* **2** GENTLENESS : ligereza *f*, suavidad *f*, delicadeza *f* **3** : ligereza *f*, liviandad *f* (de peso)

lightning ['laɪtnɪŋ] *n* : relámpago *m*, rayo *m*

lightning bug → **firefly**

lightproof ['laɪt,pru:f] *adj* : impenetrable por la luz, opaco

lightweight ['laɪt'weɪt] *adj* : ligero, liviano, de poco peso

light–year ['laɪt,jɪr] *n* : año *m* luz

lignite ['lɪg,naɪt] *n* : lignito *m*

likable *or* **likeable** ['laɪkəbəl] *adj* : simpático, agradable

like[1] ['laɪk] *v* **liked; liking** *vt* **1** : agradar, gustarle (algo a uno) ⟨he likes rice : le gusta el arroz⟩ ⟨she doesn't like flowers : a ella no le gustan las flores⟩ ⟨I like you : me caes bien⟩ **2** WANT : querer, desear ⟨I'd like a hamburger : quiero una hamburguesa⟩ ⟨he would like more help : le gustaría tener más ayuda⟩ — *vi* : querer ⟨do as you like : haz lo que quieras⟩

like[2] *adj* : parecido, semejante, similar

like[3] *n* **1** PREFERENCE : preferencia *f*, gusto *m* **2 the like** : cosa *f* parecida, cosas *fpl* por el estilo ⟨I've never seen the like : nunca he visto cosa parecida⟩

like[4] *conj* **1** AS IF : como si ⟨they looked at me like I was crazy : se me quedaron mirando como si estuviera loca⟩ **2** AS : como, igual que ⟨she doesn't love you like I do : ella no te quiere como yo⟩

like[5] *prep* **1** : como, parecido a ⟨she acts like my mother : se comporta como mi madre⟩ ⟨he looks like me : se parece a mí⟩ **2** : propio de, típico de ⟨that's just like her : eso es muy típico de ella⟩ **3** : como ⟨animals like cows : animales como vacas⟩ **4 like this, like that** : así ⟨do it like that : hazlo así⟩

likelihood ['laɪkli,hʊd] *n* : probabilidad *f* ⟨in all likelihood : con toda probabilidad⟩

likely[1] ['laɪkli] *adv* : probablemente ⟨most likely he's sick : lo más probable es que esté enfermo⟩ ⟨they're likely to come : es probable que vengan⟩

likely[2] *adj* **-lier; -est 1** PROBABLE : probable ⟨to be likely to : ser muy probable que⟩ **2** SUITABLE : apropiado, adecuado **3** BELIEVABLE : verosímil, creíble **4** PROMISING : prometedor

liken ['laɪkən] *vt* : comparar

likeness ['laɪknəs] *n* **1** SIMILARITY : semejanza *f*, parecido *m* **2** PORTRAIT : retrato *m*

likewise ['laɪk,waɪz] *adv* **1** SIMILARLY : de la misma manera, asimismo **2** ALSO : también, además, asimismo

liking ['laɪkɪŋ] *n* **1** FONDNESS : afición *f* (por una cosa), simpatía *f* (por una persona) **2** TASTE : gusto *m* ⟨is it to your liking? : ¿te gusta?⟩

lilac ['laɪlək, -,læk, -,lɑk] *n* : lila *f*

lilt ['lɪlt] *n* : cadencia *f*, ritmo *m* alegre

lily ['lɪli] *n, pl* **lilies 1** : lirio *m*, azucena *f* **2 lily of the valley** : lirio *m* de los valles, muguete *m*

lima bean ['laɪmə] *n* : frijol *m* de media luna

limb ['lɪm] *n* **1** APPENDAGE : miembro *m*, extremidad *f* **2** BRANCH : rama *f*

limber[1] ['lɪmbər] *vi or* **to limber up** : calentarse, prepararse

limber[2] *adj* : ágil (dícese de las personas), flexible (dícese de los objetos)

limbo ['lɪm,bo:] *n, pl* **-bos 1** : limbo *m* (en la religión) **2** OBLIVION : olvido *m* ⟨the project is in limbo : el proyecto ha caído en el olvido⟩

lime ['laɪm] *n* **1** : cal *f* (óxido) **2** : lima *f* (fruta), limón *m* verde *Mex*

limelight ['laɪm,laɪt] *n* **to be in the limelight** : ser el centro de atención, estar en el candelero

limerick ['lɪmərɪk] *n* : poema *m* jocoso de cinco versos

limestone ['laɪm,sto:n] *n* : piedra *f* caliza, caliza *f*

limit[1] ['lɪmət] *vt* : limitar, restringir

limit[2] *n* **1** MAXIMUM : límite *m*, máximo *m* ⟨speed limit : límite de velocidad⟩ **2 limits** *npl* : límites *mpl*, confines *mpl* ⟨city limits : límites de la ciudad⟩ **3 that's the limit!** : ¡eso es el colmo!

limitation [,lɪmə'teɪʃən] *n* : limitación *f*, restricción *f*

limited ['lɪməţəd] *adj* : limitado, restringido

limitless ['lɪmətləs] *adj* : ilimitado, sin límites

limousine ['lɪmə,zi:n, ,lɪmə'-] *n* : limusina *f*

limp[1] ['lɪmp] *vi* : cojear

limp[2] *adj* **1** FLACCID : fláccido **2** LANK : lacio (dícese del pelo) **3** WEAK : débil ⟨to feel limp : sentirse desfallecer, sentirse sin fuerzas⟩

limp[3] *n* : cojera *f*

limpid ['lɪmpəd] *adj* : límpido, claro

limply ['lɪmpli] *adv* : sin fuerzas

limpness ['lɪmpnəs] *n* : flaccidez *f*, debilidad *f*

linden ['lɪndən] *n* : tilo *m*

line[1] ['laɪn] *v* **lined; lining** *vt* **1** : forrar, cubrir ⟨to line a dress : forrar un vestido⟩ ⟨to line the walls : cubrir las paredes⟩ **2** MARK : rayar, trazar líneas en **3** BORDER : bordear **4** ALIGN : alinear — *vi* **to line up** : ponerse in fila, hacer cola

line[2] *n* **1** CORD, ROPE : cuerda *f* **2** WIRE : cable *m* ⟨power line : cable eléctrico⟩ **3** : línea *f* (de teléfono) **4** ROW : fila *f*, hilera *f* **5** NOTE : nota *f*, líneas *fpl* ⟨drop me a line : mándame unas líneas⟩ **6** COURSE : línea *f* ⟨line of inquiry : línea de investigación⟩ 7 AGREEMENT : conformidad *f* ⟨to be in line with : ser conforme a⟩ ⟨to fall into line : estar de acuerdo⟩ 8 OCCUPATION : ocupación *f*, rama *f*, especialidad *f* 9 LIMIT : línea *f*, límite *m* ⟨dividing line : línea divisoria⟩ ⟨to draw the line : fijar límites⟩ 10 SERVICE : línea *f* ⟨bus line : línea de autobuses⟩ 11 MARK : línea *f*, arruga *f* (de la cara)

lineage [ˈlɪniɪʤ] *n* : linaje *m*, abolengo *m*

lineal [ˈlɪniəl] *adj* : en línea directa

lineaments [ˈlɪniəmənts] *npl* : facciones *fpl* (de la cara), rasgos *mpl*

linear [ˈlɪniər] *adj* : lineal

linen [ˈlɪnən] *n* : lino *m*

liner [ˈlaɪnər] *n* 1 LINING : forro *m* 2 SHIP : buque *m*, transatlántico *m*

lineup [ˈlaɪnˌəp] *n* 1 : fila *f* de sospechosos 2 : formación *f* (en deportes) 3 ALIGNMENT : alineación *f*

linger [ˈlɪŋgər] *vi* 1 TARRY : quedarse, entretenerse, rezagarse 2 PERSIST : persistir, sobrevivir

lingerie [ˌlɑnʤəˈreɪ, ˌlænʒəˈriː] *n* : ropa *f* íntima femenina, lencería *f*

lingo [ˈlɪŋgo] *n, pl* **-goes** 1 LANGUAGE : idioma *m* 2 JARGON : jerga *f*

linguist [ˈlɪŋgwɪst] *n* : lingüista *mf*

linguistic [lɪŋˈgwɪstɪk] *adj* : lingüístico

linguistics [lɪŋˈgwɪstɪks] *n* : lingüística *f*

liniment [ˈlɪnəmənt] *n* : linimento *m*

lining [ˈlaɪnɪŋ] *n* : forro *m*

link[1] [ˈlɪŋk] *vt* : unir, enlazar, conectar — *vi* **to link up** : unirse, conectar

link[2] *n* 1 : eslabón *m* (de una cadena) 2 BOND : conexión *f*, lazo *m*, vínculo *m*

linkage [ˈlɪŋkɪʤ] *n* : conexión *f*, unión *f*, enlace *m*

linoleum [ləˈnoːliəm] *n* : linóleo *m*

linseed oil [ˈlɪnˌsiːd] *n* : aceite *m* de linaza

lint [ˈlɪnt] *n* : pelusa *f*

lintel [ˈlɪntəl] *n* : dintel *m*

lion [ˈlaɪən] *n* : león *m*

lioness [ˈlaɪənɪs] *n* : leona *f*

lionize [ˈlaɪəˌnaɪz] *vt* **-ized; -izing** : tratar a una persona como muy importante

lip [ˈlɪp] *n* 1 : labio *m* 2 EDGE, RIM : pico *m* (de una jarra), borde *m* (de una taza)

lipreading [ˈlɪpˌriːdɪŋ] *n* : lectura *f* de los labios

lipstick [ˈlɪpˌstɪk] *n* : lápiz *m* de labios, barra *f* de labios

liquefy [ˈlɪkwəˌfaɪ] *v* **-fied; -fying** *vt* : licuar — *vi* : licuarse

liqueur [lɪˈkʊr, -ˈkər, -ˈkjʊr] *n* : licor *m*

liquid[1] [ˈlɪkwəd] *adj* : líquido

liquid[2] *n* : líquido *m*

liquidate [ˈlɪkwəˌdeɪt] *vt* **-dated; -dating** : liquidar

liquidation [ˌlɪkwəˈdeɪʃən] *n* : liquidación *f*

liquidity [lɪkˈwɪdət̬i] *n* : liquidez *f*

liquor [ˈlɪkər] *n* : alcohol *m*, bebidas *fpl* alcohólicas, licor *m*

lisp[1] [ˈlɪsp] *vi* : cecear

lisp[2] *n* : ceceo *m*

lissome [ˈlɪsəm] *adj* 1 FLEXIBLE : flexible 2 LITHE : ágil y grácil

list[1] [ˈlɪst] *vt* 1 ENUMERATE : hacer una lista de, enumerar 2 INCLUDE : poner en una lista, incluir — *vi* : escorar (dícese de un barco)

list[2] *n* 1 ENUMERATION : lista *f* 2 SLANT : escora *f*, inclinación *f*

listen [ˈlɪsən] *vi* 1 : escuchar, oír 2 **to listen to** HEED : prestar atención a, hacer caso de, escuchar 3 **to listen to reason** : atender a razones

listener [ˈlɪsənər] *n* : oyente *mf*, persona *f* que sabe escuchar

listless [ˈlɪstləs] *adj* : lánguido, apático — **listlessly** *adv*

listlessness [ˈlɪstləsnəs] *n* : apatía *f*, languidez *f*, desgana *f*

lit [ˈlɪt] → **light**

litany [ˈlɪtəni] *n, pl* **-nies** : letanía *f*

liter [ˈliːt̬ər] *n* : litro *m*

literacy [ˈlɪt̬ərəsi] *n* : alfabetismo *m*

literal [ˈlɪt̬ərəl] *adj* : literal — **literally** *adv*

literary [ˈlɪt̬əˌrri] *adj* : literario

literate [ˈlɪt̬ərət] *adj* : alfabetizado

literature [ˈlɪt̬ərəˌʧʊr, -ʧər] *n* : literatura *f*

lithe [ˈlaɪð, ˈlaɪθ] *adj* : ágil y grácil

lithesome [ˈlaɪðsəm, ˈlaɪθ-] → **lissome**

lithium [ˈlɪθiəm] *n* : litio *m*

lithograph [ˈlɪθəˌgræf] *n* : litografía *f*

lithographer [lɪˈθɑgrəfər, ˈlɪθə-ˌgræfər] *n* : litógrafo *m*, -fa *f*

lithography [lɪˈθɑgrəfi] *n* : litografía *f*

lithosphere [ˈlɪθəˌsfɪr] *n* : litosfera *f*

Lithuanian [ˌlɪθəˈweɪniən] *n* 1 : lituano *m* (idioma) 2 : lituano *m*, -na *f* — **Lithuanian** *adj*

litigant [ˈlɪt̬ɪgənt] *n* : litigante *mf*

litigate [ˈlɪt̬əˌgeɪt] *vi* **-gated; -gating** : litigar

litigation [ˌlɪt̬əˈgeɪʃən] *n* : litigio *m*

litmus paper [ˈlɪtməs] *n* : papel *m* de tornasol

litter[1] [ˈlɪt̬ər] *vt* : tirar basura en, ensuciar — *vi* : tirar basura

litter[2] *n* 1 : camada *f*, cría *f* ⟨a litter of kittens : una cría de gatitos⟩ 2 STRETCHER : camilla *f* 3 RUBBISH : basura *f* 4 : arena *f* higiénica (para gatos)

little[1] [ˈlɪtəl] *adv* **less** [ˈlɛs]; **least** [ˈliːst] 1 : poco ⟨she sings very little : canta muy poco⟩ 2 **little did I know that . . .** : no tenía la menor idea de que . . . 3 **as little as possible** : lo menos posible

little[2] *adj* **littler** *or* **less** [ˈlɛs] *or* **lesser** [ˈlɛsər]; **littlest** *or* **least** [ˈliːst] 1 SMALL : pequeño 2 : poco ⟨they speak little Spanish : hablan poco español⟩ ⟨little by little : poco a poco⟩ 3 TRIVIAL : sin importancia, trivial

little[3] *n* 1 : poco *m* ⟨little has changed : poco ha cambiado⟩ 2 **a little** : un poco, algo ⟨it's a little surprising : es algo sorprendente⟩

Little Dipper → **dipper**

liturgical [ləˈtərʤɪkəl] *adj* : litúrgico — **liturgically** [-kli] *adv*

liturgy [ˈlɪt̬ərʤi] *n, pl* **-gies** : liturgia *f*

livable [ˈlɪvəbəl] *adj* : habitable

live[1] [ˈlɪv] *vi* **lived; living 1** EXIST : vivir ⟨as long as I live : mientras viva⟩ ⟨to live from day to day : vivir al día⟩ **2** : llevar una vida, vivir ⟨he lived simply : llevó una vida sencilla⟩ **3** SUBSIST : mantenerse, vivir **4** RESIDE : vivir, residir

live[2] [ˈlaɪv] *adj* **1** LIVING : vivo **2** BURNING : encendido ⟨a live coal : una brasa⟩ **3** : con corriente ⟨live wires : cables con corriente⟩ **4** : cargado, sin estallar ⟨a live bomb : una bomba sin estallar⟩ **5** CURRENT : de actualidad ⟨a live issue : un asunto de actualidad⟩ **6** : en vivo, en directo ⟨a live interview : una entrevista en vivo⟩

livelihood [ˈlaɪvliˌhʊd] *n* : sustento *m*, vida *f*, medio *m* de vida

liveliness [ˈlaɪvlinəs] *n* : animación *f*, vivacidad *f*

livelong [ˈlɪvˈlɔŋ] *adj* : entero, completo

lively [ˈlaɪvli] *adj* **-lier; -est** : animado, vivaz, vivo, enérgico

liven [ˈlaɪvən] *vt* : animar — *vi* : animarse

liver [ˈlɪvər] *n* : hígado *m*

livery [ˈlɪvəri] *n, pl* **-eries** : librea *f*

lives → **life**

livestock [ˈlaɪvˌstɑk] *n* : ganado *m*

live wire *n* : persona *f* vivaz y muy activa

livid [ˈlɪvəd] *adj* **1** BLACK-AND-BLUE : amoratado **2** PALE : lívido **3** ENRAGED : furioso

living[1] [ˈlɪvɪŋ] *adj* : vivo

living[2] *n* **to make a living** : ganarse la vida

living room *n* : living *m*, sala *f* de estar

lizard [ˈlɪzərd] *n* : lagarto *m*

llama [ˈlɑmə, ˈjɑ-] *n* : llama *f*

load[1] [ˈlo:d] *vt* : cargar, embarcar

load[2] *n* **1** CARGO : carga *f* **2** WEIGHT : peso *m* **3** BURDEN : carga *f*, peso *m* **4 loads** *npl* : montón *m*, pila *f*, cantidad *f* ⟨loads of work : un montón de trabajo⟩

loaf[1] [ˈlo:f] *vi* : holgazanear, flojear, haraganear

loaf[2] *n, pl* **loaves** [ˈlo:vz] **1** : pan *m*, pan *m* de molde, barra *f* de pan **2 meat loaf** : pan *m* de carne

loafer [ˈlo:fər] *n* : holgazán *m*, -zana *f*; haragán *m*, -gana *f*; vago *m*, -ga *f*

loam [ˈlo:m] *n* : marga *f*, suelo *m*

loan[1] [ˈlo:n] *vt* : prestar

loan[2] *n* : préstamo *m*, empréstito *m* (del banco)

loath [ˈlo:θ, ˈlo:ð] *adj* : poco dispuesto ⟨I am loath to say it : me resisto a decirlo⟩

loathe [ˈlo:ð] *vt* **loathed; loathing** : odiar, aborrecer

loathing [ˈlo:ðɪŋ] *n* : aversión *f*, odio *m*, aborrecimiento *m*

loathsome [ˈlo:θsəm, ˈlo:ð-] *adj* : odioso, repugnante

lob[1] [ˈlɑb] *vt* **lobbed; lobbing** : hacerle un globo (a otro jugador)

lob[2] *n* : globo *m* (en deportes)

lobby[1] [ˈlɑbi] *v* **-bied; -bying** *vt* : presionar, ejercer presión sobre — *vi* **to lobby for** : presionar para (lograr algo)

lobby[2] *n, pl* **-bies 1** FOYER : vestíbulo *m* **2** LOBBYISTS : grupo *m* de presión, lobby *m*

lobbyist [ˈlɑbiɪst] *n* : miembro *m* de un lobby

lobe [ˈlo:b] *n* : lóbulo *m*

lobed [ˈlo:bd] *adj* : lobulado

lobotomy [ləˈbɑt̬əmi, lo-] *n, pl* **-mies** : lobotomía *f*

lobster [ˈlɑbstər] *n* : langosta *f*

local[1] [ˈlo:kəl] *adj* : local

local[2] *n* **1** : anestesia *f* local **2 the locals** : los vecinos del lugar, los habitantes

locale [loˈkæl] *n* : lugar *m*, escenario *m*

locality [loˈkæləṭi] *n, pl* **-ties** : localidad *f*

localize [ˈlo:kəˌlaɪz] *vt* **-ized; -izing** : localizar

locally [ˈlo:kəli] *adv* : en la localidad, en la zona

locate [ˈlo:ˌkeɪt, loˈkeɪt] *v* **-cated; -cating** *vt* **1** POSITION : situar, ubicar **2** FIND : localizar, ubicar — *vi* SETTLE : establecerse

location [loˈkeɪʃən] *n* **1** POSITION : posición *f*, emplazamiento *m*, ubicación *f* **2** PLACE : lugar *m*, sitio *m*

lock[1] [ˈlɑk] *vt* **1** FASTEN : cerrar **2** CONFINE : encerrar ⟨they locked me in the room : me encerraron en la sala⟩ **3** IMMOBILIZE : bloquear (una rueda) — *vi* **1** : cerrarse (dícese de una puerta) **2** : trabarse, bloquearse (dícese de una rueda)

lock[2] *n* **1** : mechón *m* (de pelo) **2** FASTENER : cerradura *f*, cerrojo *m*, chapa *f* **3** : esclusa *f* (de un canal)

locker [ˈlɑkər] *n* : armario *m*, cajón *m* con llave, lócker *m*

locket [ˈlɑkət] *n* : medallón *m*, guardapelo *m*, relicario *m*

lockjaw [ˈlɑkˌʤɔ] *n* : tétano *m*

lockout [ˈlɑkˌaʊt] *n* : cierre *m* patronal, lockout *m*

locksmith [ˈlɑkˌsmɪθ] *n* : cerrajero *m*, -ra *f*

lockup [ˈlɑkˌʌp] *n* JAIL : cárcel *f*

locomotion [ˌlo:kəˈmo:ʃən] *n* : locomoción *f*

locomotive[1] [ˌlo:kəˈmo:t̬ɪv] *adj* : locomotor

locomotive[2] *n* : locomotora *f*

locust [ˈlo:kəst] *n* **1** : langosta *f*, chapulín *m CA, Mex* **2** CICADA : cigarra *f*, chicharra *f* **3** : acacia *f* blanca (árbol)

locution [loˈkju:ʃən] *n* : locución *f*

lode [ˈlo:d] *n* : veta *f*, vena *f*, filón *m*

lodestar [ˈlo:dˌstɑr] *n* : estrella *f* polar

lodestone [ˈlo:dˌsto:n] *n* : piedra *f* imán

lodge[1] [ˈlɑʤ] *v* **lodged; lodging** *vt* **1** HOUSE : hospedar, alojar **2** FILE : presentar ⟨to lodge a complaint : presentar una demanda⟩ — *vi* **1** : posarse, meterse ⟨the bullet lodged in the door

: la bala se incrustó en la puerta⟩ **2** STAY : hospedarse, alojarse

lodge[2] *n* **1** : pabellón *m*, casa *f* de campo ⟨hunting lodge : refugio de caza⟩ **2** : madriguera *f* (de un castor) **3** : logia *f* ⟨Masonic lodge : logia masónica⟩

lodger [ˈlɑʤər] *n* : inquilino *m*, -na *f*; huésped *m*, -peda *f*

lodging [ˈlɑʤɪŋ] *n* **1** : alojamiento *m* **2 lodgings** *npl* ROOMS : habitaciones *fpl*

loft [ˈlɔft] *n* **1** ATTIC : desván *m*, ático *m*, buhardilla *f* **2** : loft *m* (en un depósito comercial) **3** HAYLOFT : pajar *m* **4** : galería *f* ⟨choir loft : galería del coro⟩

loftily [ˈlɔftəli] *adv* : altaneramente, con altivez

loftiness [ˈlɔftinəs] *n* **1** NOBILITY : nobleza *f* **2** ARROGANCE : altanería *f*, arrogancia *f* **3** HEIGHT : altura *f*, elevación *f*

lofty [ˈlɔfti] *adj* **loftier; -est 1** NOBLE : noble, elevado **2** HAUGHTY : altivo, arrogante, altanero **3** HIGH : majestuoso, elevado

log[1] [ˈlɔg, ˈlɑg] *vi* **logged; logging 1** : talar (árboles) **2** RECORD : registrar, anotar **3 to log on** : entrar (al sistema) **4 to log off** : salir (del sistema)

log[2] *n* **1** : tronco *m*, leño *m* **2** RECORD : diario *m*

logarithm [ˈlɔgəˌrɪðəm, ˈlɑ-] *n* : logaritmo *m*

logger [ˈlɔgər, ˈlɑ-] *n* : leñador *m*, -dora *f*

loggerhead [ˈlɔgərˌhd, ˈlɑ-] *n* **1** : tortuga *f* boba **2 to be at loggerheads** : estar en pugna, estar en desacuerdo

logic [ˈlɑʤɪk] *n* : lógica *f* — **logical** [ˈlɑʤɪkəl] *adj* — **logically** [-kli] *adv*

logistic [ləˈʤɪstɪk, lo-] *adj* : logístico

logistics [ləˈʤɪstɪks, lo-] *ns & pl* : logística *f*

logo [ˈloːˌgoː] *n, pl* **logos** [-ˌgoːz] : logotipo *m*

loin [ˈlɔɪn] *n* **1** : lomo *m* ⟨pork loin : lomo de cerdo⟩ **2 loins** *npl* : lomos *mpl* ⟨to gird one's loins : prepararse para la lucha⟩

loiter [ˈlɔɪṭər] *vi* : vagar, perder el tiempo

loll [ˈlɑl] *vi* **1** SLOUCH : repantigarse **2** IDLE : holgazanear, hacer el vago

lollipop *or* **lollypop** [ˈlɑliˌpɑp] *n* : dulce *m* en palito, chupete *m Chile, Peru*, paleta *f CA, Mex*

lone [ˈloːn] *adj* **1** SOLITARY : solitario **2** ONLY : único

loneliness [ˈloːnlinəs] *n* : soledad *f*

lonely [ˈloːnli] *adj* **-lier; -est 1** SOLITARY : solitario, aislado **2** LONESOME : solo ⟨to feel lonely : sentirse muy solo⟩

loner [ˈloːnər] *n* : solitario *m*, -ria *f*; recluso *m*, -sa *f*

lonesome [ˈloːnsəm] *adj* : solo, solitario

long[1] [ˈlɔŋ] *vi* **1 to long for** : añorar, desear, anhelar **2 to long to** : anhelar, estar deseando ⟨they longed to see her : estaban deseando verla, tenían muchas ganas de verla⟩

long[2] *adv* **1** : mucho, mucho tiempo ⟨it didn't take long : no llevó mucho tiempo⟩ ⟨will it last long? : ¿va a durar mucho?⟩ **2 all day long** : todo el día **3 as long as** *or* **so long as** : mientras, con tal que **4 long before** : mucho antes **5 so long!** : ¡hasta luego!, ¡adiós!

long[3] *adj* **longer** [ˈlɔngər]; **longest** [ˈlɔŋgəst] **1** (*indicating length*)) : largo ⟨the dress is too long : el vestido es demasiado largo⟩ ⟨a long way from : bastante lejos de⟩ ⟨in the long run : a la larga⟩ **2** (*indicating time*)) : largo, prolongado ⟨a long illness : una enfermedad prolongada⟩ ⟨a long walk : un paseo largo⟩ ⟨at long last : por fin⟩ **3 to be long on** : estar cargado de

long[4] *n* **1 before long** : dentro de poco **2 the long and the short** : lo esencial, lo fundamental

longevity [lɑnˈʤɛvəṭi] *n* : longevidad *f*

longhand [ˈlɔŋˌhænd] *n* : escritura *f* a mano, escritura *f* cursiva

longhorn [ˈlɔŋˌhɔrn] *n* : longhorn *mf*

longing [lɔŋɪŋ] *n* : vivo deseo *m*, ansia *f*, anhelo *m*

longingly [lɔŋɪŋlli] *adv* : ansiosamente, con ansia

longitude [ˈlɑnʤəˌtuːd, -ˌtjuːd] *n* : longitud *f*

longitudinal [ˌlɑnʤəˈtuːdənəl, -ˈtjuː-] *adj* : longitudinal — **longitudinally** *adv*

long–lived [ˈlɔŋˈlɪvd, -ˈlaɪvd] *adj* : longevo

longshoreman [ˈlɔŋˈʃormən] *n, pl* **-men** [-mən, -ˌmɛn] : estibador *m*, -dora *f*

long–standing [ˈlɔŋˈstændɪŋ] *adj* : de larga data

long–suffering [ˈlɔŋˈsʌfərɪŋ] *adj* : paciente, sufrido

look[1] [ˈlʊk] *vi* **1** GLANCE : mirar ⟨to look out the window : mirar por la ventana⟩ **2** INVESTIGATE : buscar, mirar ⟨look in the closet : busca en el closet⟩ ⟨look before you leap : mira lo que haces⟩ **3** SEEM : parecer ⟨he looks happy : parece estar contento⟩ ⟨I look like my mother : me parezco a mi madre⟩ **4 to look after** : cuidar, cuidar de **5 to look for** EXPECT : esperar **6 to look for** SEEK : buscar — *vt* : mirar

look[2] *n* **1** GLANCE : mirada *f* **2** EXPRESSION : cara *f* ⟨a look of disapproval : una cara de desaprobación⟩ **3** ASPECT : aspecto *m*, apariencia *f*, aire *m* **4 looks** *npl* : belleza *f*

lookout [ˈlʊkˌaʊt] *n* **1** : centinela *mf*, vigía *mf* **2 to be on the lookout for** : estar al acecho de, andar a la caza de

loom[1] [ˈluːm] *vi* **1** : aparecer, surgir ⟨the city loomed up in the distance : la ciudad surgió en la distancia⟩ **2** IMPEND : amenazar, ser inminente **3 to loom large** : cobrar mucha importancia

loom[2] *n* : telar *m*

loon [ˈluːn] *n* : somorgujo *m*, somormujo *m*

loony *or* **looney** [ˈluːni] *adj* **-nier; -est** : loco, chiflado *fam*

loop[1] ['luːp] *vt* **1** : hacer lazadas con **2 to loop around** : pasar alrededor de — *vi* **1** : rizar el rizo (dícese de un avión) **2** : serpentear (dícese de una carretera)

loop[2] *n* **1** : lazada *f* (en hilo o cuerda) **2** BEND : curva *f* **3** CIRCUIT : circuito *m* cerrado **4** : rizo *m* (en la aviación) ⟨to loop the loop : rizar el rizo⟩

loophole ['luːpˌhoːl] *n* : escapatoria *f*, pretexto *m*

loose[1] ['luːs] *vt* **loosed; loosing 1** RELEASE : poner en libertad, soltar **2** UNTIE : deshacer, desatar **3** DISCHARGE, UNLEASH : descargar, desatar

loose[2] → **loosely**

loose[3] *adj* **looser; -est 1** INSECURE : flojo, suelto, poco seguro ⟨a loose tooth : un diente flojo⟩ **2** ROOMY : suelto, holgado ⟨loose clothing : ropa holgada⟩ **3** OPEN : suelto, abierto ⟨loose soil : suelo suelto⟩ ⟨a loose weave : una tejida abierta⟩ **4** FREE : suelto ⟨to break loose : soltarse⟩ **5** SLACK : flojo, flexible **6** APPROXIMATE : libre, aproximado ⟨a loose translation : una traducción aproximada⟩

loosely ['luːsli] *adv* **1** : sin apretar **2** ROUGHLY : aproximadamente, más o menos

loosen ['luːsən] *vt* : aflojar

loose–leaf ['luːs'liːf] *adj* : de hojas sueltas

looseness ['luːsnəs] *n* **1** : aflojamiento *m*, holgura *f* (de ropa) **2** IMPRECISION : imprecisión *f*

loot[1] ['luːt] *vt* : saquear, robar

loot[2] *n* : botín *m*

looter ['luːt̬ər] *n* : saqueador *m*, -dora *f*

lop ['lɑp] *vt* **lopped; lopping** : cortar, podar

lope[1] ['loːp] *vi* **loped; loping** : correr a paso largo

lope[2] *n* : paso *m* largo

lopsided ['lɑpˌsaɪdəd] *adj* **1** CROOKED : torcido, chueco, ladeado **2** ASYMETRICAL : asimétrico

loquacious [lo'kweɪʃəs] *adj* : locuaz

lord ['lɔrd] *n* **1** : señor *m*, noble *m* **2** : lord *m* (en la Gran Bretaña) **3 the Lord** : el Señor **4 good Lord!** : ¡Dios mío!

lordly ['lɔrdli] *adj* **-lier; -est** HAUGHTY : arrogante, altanero

lordship ['lɔrdˌʃɪp] *n* : señoría *f*

Lord's Supper *n* : Eucaristía *f*

lore ['lor] *n* : saber *m* popular, tradición *f*

lose ['luːz] *v* **lost** ['lɔst]; **losing** ['luː-zɪŋ] *vt* **1** : perder ⟨I lost my umbrella : perdí mi paraguas⟩ ⟨to lose blood : perder sangre⟩ ⟨to lose one's voice : quedarse fónico⟩ ⟨to have nothing to lose : no tener nada que perder⟩ ⟨to lose no time : no perder tiempo⟩ ⟨to lose weight : perder peso, adelgazar⟩ ⟨to lose one's temper : perder los estribos, enojarse, enfadarse⟩ ⟨to lose sight of : perder de vista⟩ **2** : costar, hacer perder ⟨the errors lost him his job : los errores le costaron su empleo⟩ **3** : atrasar ⟨my watch loses 5 minutes a day : mi reloj atrasa 5 minutos por día⟩ **4 to lose oneself** : perderse, ensimismarse — *vi* **1** : perder ⟨we lost to the other team : perdimos contra el otro equipo⟩ **2** : atrasarse ⟨the clock loses time : el reloj se atrasa⟩

loser ['luːzər] *n* : perdedor *m*, -dora *f*

loss ['lɔs] *n* **1** LOSING : pérdida *f* ⟨loss of memory : pérdida de memoria⟩ ⟨to sell at a loss : vender con pérdida⟩ ⟨to be at a loss to : no saber como⟩ **2** DEFEAT : derrota *f*, juego *m* perdido **3 losses** *npl* DEATHS : muertos *mpl*

lost ['lɔst] *adj* **1** : perdido ⟨a lost cause : una causa perdida⟩ ⟨lost in thought : absorto⟩ **2 to get lost** : perderse **3 to make up for lost time** : recuperar el tiempo perdido

lot ['lɑt] *n* **1** DRAWING : sorteo *m* ⟨by lot : por sorteo⟩ **2** SHARE : parte *f*, porción *f* **3** FATE : suerte *f* **4** LAND, PLOT : terreno *m*, solar *m*, lote *m*, parcela *f* ⟨parking lot : estacionamiento⟩ **5 a lot of** *or* **lots of** : mucho, un montón de, bastante ⟨lots of books : un montón de libros, muchos libros⟩ ⟨a lot of people : mucha gente⟩

loth ['loːθ, 'loːð] → **loath**

lotion ['loːʃən] *n* : loción *f*

lottery ['lɑt̬əri] *n, pl* **-teries** : lotería *f*

lotus ['loːt̬əs] *n* : loto *m*

loud[1] ['laʊd] *adv* : alto, fuerte ⟨out loud : en voz alta⟩

loud[2] *adj* **1** : alto, fuerte ⟨a loud voice : una voz alta⟩ **2** NOISY : ruidoso ⟨a loud party : una fiesta ruidosa⟩ **3** FLASHY : llamativo, chillón

loudly ['laʊdli] *adv* : alto, fuerte, en voz alta

loudness ['laʊdnəs] *n* : volumen *m*, fuerza *f* (del ruido)

loudspeaker ['laʊdˌspiːkər] *n* : altavoz *m*, altoparlante *m*

lounge[1] ['laʊndʒ] *vi* **lounged; lounging** : holgazanear, gandulear

lounge[2] *n* : salón *m*, sala *f* de estar

louse ['laʊs] *n, pl* **lice** ['laɪs] : piojo *m*

lousy ['laʊzi] *adj* **lousier; -est 1** : piojoso, lleno de piojos **2** BAD : pésimo, muy malo

lout ['laʊt] *n* : bruto *m*, patán *m*

louver *or* **louvre** ['luːvər] *n* : persiana *f*, listón *m* de persiana

lovable ['lʌvəbəl] *adj* : adorable, amoroso, encantador

love[1] ['lʌv] *v* **loved; loving** *vt* **1** : querer, amar ⟨I love you : te quiero⟩ **2** ENJOY : encantarle a alguien, ser (muy) aficionado a, gustarle mucho a uno (algo) ⟨she loves flowers : le encantan las flores⟩ ⟨he loves golf : es muy aficionado al golf⟩ ⟨I'd love to go with you : me gustaría mucho acompañarte⟩ — *vi* : querer, amar

love[2] *n* **1** : amor *m*, cariño *m* ⟨to be in love with : estar enamorado de⟩ ⟨to fall

in love with : enamorarse de⟩ **2** ENTHUSIASM, INTEREST : amor *m*, afición *m*, gusto *m* ⟨love of music : afición a la música⟩ **3** BELOVED : amor *m*; amado *m*, -da *f*; enamorado *m*, -da *f*
loveless [ˈlʌvləs] *adj* : sin amor
loveliness [ˈlʌvlinəs] *n* : belleza *f*, hermosura *f*
lovelorn [ˈlʌvˌlɔrn] *adj* : herido de amor, perdidamente enamorado
lovely [ˈlʌvli] *adj* **-lier; -est** : hermoso, bello, lindo, precioso
lover [ˈlʌvər] *n* : amante *mf* (de personas); aficionado *m*, -da *f* (a alguna actividad)
loving [ˈlʌvɪŋ] *adj* : amoroso, cariñoso
lovingly [ˈlʌvɪŋli] *adv* : cariñosamente
low[1] [ˈloː] *vi* : mugir
low[2] *adv* : bajo, profundo ⟨to aim low : apuntar bajo⟩ ⟨to lie low : mantenerse escondido⟩ ⟨to turn the lights down low : bajar las luces⟩
low[3] *adj* **lower** [ˈloːər]; **-est** **1** : bajo ⟨a low building : un edificio bajo⟩ ⟨a low bow : una profunda reverencia⟩ **2** SOFT : bajo, suave ⟨in a low voice : en voz baja⟩ **3** SHALLOW : bajo, poco profundo **4** HUMBLE : humilde, modesto **5** DEPRESSED : deprimido, bajo de moral **6** INFERIOR : bajo, inferior **7** UNFAVORABLE : mal ⟨to have a low opinion of him : tener un mal concepto de él⟩ **8 to be low on** : tener poco de, estar escaso de
low[4] *n* **1** : punto *m* bajo ⟨to reach an all-time low : estar más bajo que nunca⟩ **2** *or* **low gear** : primera velocidad *f* **3** : mugido *m* (de una vaca)
lowbrow [ˈloːˌbraʊ] *n* : persona *f* inculta
lower[1] [ˈloːər] *vt* **1** DROP : bajar ⟨to lower one's voice : bajar la voz⟩ **2** : arriar, bajar ⟨to lower the flag : arriar la bandera⟩ **3** REDUCE : reducir, bajar **4 to lower oneself** : rebajarse
lower[2] [ˈloːər] *adj* : inferior, más bajo, de abajo
lowland [ˈloːlənd, -ˌlænd] *n* : tierras *fpl* bajas
lowly [ˈloːli] *adj* **-lier; -est** : humilde, modesto
loyal [ˈlɔɪəl] *adj* : leal, fiel — **loyally** *adv*
loyalist [ˈlɔɪəlɪst] *n* : partidario *m*, -ria *f* del régimen
loyalty [ˈlɔɪəlti] *n, pl* **-ties** : lealtad *f*, fidelidad *f*
lozenge [ˈlɑzənʤ] *n* : pastilla *f*
LSD [ˌɛlˌɛsˈdiː] *n* : LSD *m*
lubricant [ˈluːbrɪkənt] *n* : lubricante *m*
lubricate [ˈluːbrɪˌkeɪt] *vt* **-cated; -cating** : lubricar — **lubrication** [ˌluːbrɪˈkeɪʃən] *n*
lucid [ˈluːsəd] *adj* : lúcido, claro — **lucidly** *adv*
lucidity [luːˈsɪdəṭi] *n* : lucidez *f*
luck [ˈlʌk] *n* **1** : suerte *f* **2 to have bad luck** : tener mala suerte **3 good luck!** : ¡(buena) suerte!
luckily [ˈlʌkəli] *adv* : afortunadamente, por suerte
luckless [ˈlʌkləs] *adj* : desafortunado
lucky [ˈlʌki] *adj* **luckier; -est** **1** : afortunado, que tiene suerte ⟨a lucky woman : una mujer afortunada⟩ **2** FORTUITOUS : fortuito, de suerte **3** OPPORTUNE : oportuno **4** : de (la) suerte ⟨lucky number : número de la suerte⟩
lucrative [ˈluːkrəṭɪv] *adj* : lucrativo, provechoso — **lucratively** *adv*
ludicrous [ˈluːdəkrəs] *adj* : ridículo, absurdo — **ludicrously** *adv*
ludicrousness [ˈluːdəkrəsnəs] *n* : ridiculez *f*, absurdo *m*
lug [ˈlʌg] *vt* **lugged; lugging** : arrastrar, transportar con dificultad
luggage [ˈlʌgɪʤ] *n* : equipaje *m*
lugubrious [lʊˈguːbriəs] *adj* : lúgubre — **lugubriously** *adv*
lukewarm [ˈluːkˈwɔrm] *adj* **1** TEPID : tibio **2** HALFHEARTED : poco entusiasta
lull[1] [ˈlʌl] *vt* **1** CALM, SOOTHE : calmar, sosegar **2 to lull to sleep** : arrullar, adormecer
lull[2] *n* : calma *f*, pausa *f*
lullaby [ˈlʌləˌbaɪ] *n, pl* **-bies** : canción *f* de cuna, arrullo *m*, nana *f*
lumber[1] [ˈlʌmbər] *vt* : aserrar (madera) — *vi* : moverse pesadamente
lumber[2] *n* : madera *f*
lumberjack [ˈlʌmbərˌʤæk] *n* : leñador *m*, -dora *f*
lumberyard [ˈlʌmbərˌjɑrd] *n* : almacén *m* de maderas
luminary [ˈluːməˌnɛri] *n, pl* **-naries** : lumbrera *f*, luminaria *f*
luminescence [ˌluːməˈnɛsənts] *n* : luminiscencia *f* — **luminescent** [-ˈnɛsənt] *adj*
luminosity [ˌluːməˈnɑsəṭi] *n, pl* **-ties** : luminosidad *f*
luminous [ˈluːmənəs] *adj* : luminoso — **luminously** *adv*
lump[1] [ˈlʌmp] *vt or* **to lump together** : juntar, agrupar, amontonar — *vi* CLUMP : agruparse, aglutinarse
lump[2] *n* **1** GLOB : grumo *m* **2** PIECE : pedazo *m*, trozo *m*, terrón *m* ⟨a lump of coal : un trozo de carbón⟩ ⟨a lump of sugar : un terrón de azúcar⟩ **3** SWELLING : bulto *m*, hinchazón *f*, protuberancia *f* **4 to have a lump in one's throat** : tener un nudo en la garganta
lumpy [ˈlʌmpi] *adj* **lumpier; -est** **1** : lleno de grumos (dícese de una salsa) **2** UNEVEN : desigual, disparejo
lunacy [ˈluːnəsi] *n, pl* **-cies** : locura *f*
lunar [ˈluːnər] *adj* : lunar
lunatic[1] [ˈluːnəˌtɪk] *adj* : lunático, loco
lunatic[2] *n* : loco *m*, -ca *f*
lunch[1] [ˈlʌnʧ] *vi* : almorzar, comer
lunch[2] *n* : almuerzo *m*, comida *f*, lonche *m*
luncheon [ˈlʌnʧən] *n* **1** : comida *f*, almuerzo *m* **2 luncheon meat** : fiambres *fpl*

lung [ˈlʌŋ] *n* : pulmón *m*
lunge¹ [ˈlʌndʒ] *vi* **lunged; lunging 1** THRUST : atacar (en la esgrima) **2 to lunge forward** : arremeter, lanzarse
lunge² *n* **1** : arremetida *f*, embestida *f* **2** : estocada *f* (en la esgrima)
lurch¹ [ˈlərtʃ] *vi* **1** PITCH : cabecear, dar bandazos, dar sacudidas **2** STAGGER : tambalearse
lurch² *n* **1** : sacudida *f*, bandazo *m* (de un vehículo) **2** : tambaleo *m* (de una persona)
lure¹ [ˈlʊr] *vt* **lured; luring** : atraer
lure² *n* **1** ATTRACTION : atractivo *m* **2** ENTICEMENT : señuelo *m*, aliciente *m* **3** BAIT : cebo *m* artificial (en la pesca)
lurid [ˈlʊrəd] *adj* **1** GRUESOME : espeluznante, horripilante **2** SENSATIONAL : sensacionalista, chocante **3** GAUDY : chillón
lurk [ˈlərk] *vi* : estar al acecho
luscious [ˈlʌʃəs] *adj* **1** DELICIOUS : delicioso, exquisito **2** SEDUCTIVE : seductor, cautivador
lush [ˈlʌʃ] *adj* **1** LUXURIANT : exuberante, lozano **2** LUXURIOUS : suntuoso, lujoso
lust¹ [ˈlʌst] *vi* **to lust after** : desear (a una persona), codiciar (riquezas, etc.)
lust² *n* **1** LASCIVIOUSNESS : lujuria *f*, lascivia *f* **2** CRAVING : deseo *m*, ansia *f*, anhelo *m*
luster *or* **lustre** [ˈlʌstər] *n* **1** GLOSS, SHEEN : lustre *m*, brillo *m* **2** SPLENDOR : lustre *m*, esplendor *m*
lusterless [ˈlʌstərləs] *adj* : deslustrado, sin brillo
lustful [ˈlʌstfəl] *adj* : lujurioso, lascivo, lleno de deseo
lustrous [ˈlʌstrəs] *adj* : brillante, brilloso, lustroso
lusty [ˈlʌsti] *adj* **lustier; -est** : fuerte, robusto, vigoroso — **lustily** [ˈlʌstəli] *adv*
lute [ˈlu:t] *n* : laúd *m*
luxuriant [ˌlʌgˈʒʊriənt, ˌlʌkˈʃʊr-] *adj* **1** : exuberante, lozano (dícese de las plantas) **2** : abundante y hermoso (dícese del pelo) — **luxuriantly** *adv*
luxuriate [ˌlʌgˈʒʊriˌeɪt, ˌlʌkˈʃʊr-] *vi* **-ated; -ating 1** : disfrutar **2 to luxuriate in** : deleitarse con
luxurious [ˌlʌgˈʒʊriəs, ˌlʌkˈʃʊr-] *adj* : lujoso, suntuoso — **luxuriously** *adv*
luxury [ˈlʌkʃəri, ˈlʌgʒə-] *n, pl* **-ries** : lujo *m*
lye [ˈlaɪ] *n* : lejía *f*
lying → **lie¹**, **lie²**
lymph [ˈlɪmpf] *n* : linfa *f*
lymphatic [lɪmˈfæt̬ɪk] *adj* : linfático
lynch [ˈlɪntʃ] *vt* : linchar
lynx [ˈlɪŋks] *n, pl* **lynx** *or* **lynxes** : lince *m*
lyre [ˈlaɪr] *n* : lira *f*
lyric¹ [ˈlɪrɪk] *adj* : lírico
lyric² *n* **1** : poema *m* lírico **2 lyrics** *npl* : letra *f* (de una canción)
lyrical [ˈlɪrɪkəl] *adj* : lírico, elocuente

M

m [ˈɛm] *n, pl* **m's** *or* **ms** [ˈɛmz] : decimotercera letra del alfabeto inglés
ma'am [ˈmæm] → **madam**
macabre [məˈkɑb, -ˈkɑbər, -ˈkɑbrə] *adj* : macabro
macadam [məˈkædəm] *n* : macadán *m*
macaroni [ˌmækəˈro:ni] *n* : macarrones *mpl*
macaroon [ˌmækəˈru:n] *n* : macarrón *m*, mostachón *m*
macaw [məˈkɔ] *n* : guacamayo *m*
mace [ˈmeɪs] *n* **1** : maza *f* (arma o símbolo) **2** : macis *f* (especia)
machete [məˈʃɛt̬i] *n* : machete *m*
machination [ˌmækəˈneɪʃən, ˌmæʃə-] *n* : maquinación *f*, intriga *f*
machine¹ [məˈʃi:n] *vt* **-chined; -chining** : trabajar a máquina
machine² *n* **1** : máquina *f* ⟨machine shop : taller de máquinas⟩ ⟨machine language : lenguaje de la máquina⟩ **2** : aparato *m*, maquinaria *f* (en política)
machine gun *n* : ametralladora *f*
machinery [məˈʃi:nəri] *n, pl* **-eries 1** : maquinaria *f* **2** WORKS : mecanismo *m*
machinist [məˈʃi:nɪst] *n* : maquinista *mf*
machismo [mɑˈtʃi:zmo:] *n* : machismo *m*, masculinidad *f*
macho [ˈmɑtʃo:] *adj* : machote, macho
mackerel [ˈmækərəl] *n, pl* **-el** *or* **-els** : caballa *f*
mackinaw [ˈmækəˌnɔ] *n* : chaqueta *f* escocesa de lana
mad [ˈmæd] *adj* **madder; maddest 1** INSANE : loco, demente **2** RABID : rabioso **3** FOOLISH : tonto, insensato **4** ANGRY : enojado, furioso **5** CRAZY : loco ⟨I'm mad about you : estoy loco por ti⟩
Madagascan [ˌmædəˈgæskən] *n* : malgache *mf* — **Madagascan** *adj*
madam [ˈmædəm] *n, pl* **mesdames** [meɪˈdɑm, -ˈdæm] : señora *f*
madcap¹ [ˈmædˌkæp] *adj* ZANY : alocado, disparatado
madcap² *n* : alocado *m*, -da *f*
madden [ˈmædən] *vt* : enloquecer, enfurecer
maddening [ˈmædənɪŋ] *adj* : enloquecedor, exasperante ⟨I find it maddening : me saca de quicio⟩
made → **make¹**
madhouse [ˈmædˌhaʊs] *n* : manicomio *m* ⟨the office was a madhouse : la oficina parecía una casa de locos⟩
madly [ˈmædli] *adv* : como un loco, locamente

madman [ˈmæd͵mæn, -mən] *n, pl* **-men** [-mən, -͵mɛn] : loco *m*, demente *m*

madness [ˈmædnəs] *n* : locura *f*, demencia *f*

madwoman [ˈmæd͵wʊmən] *n, pl* **-women** [-͵wɪmən] : loca *f*, demente *f*

maelstrom [ˈmeɪlstrəm] *n* : remolino *m*, vorágine *f*

maestro [ˈmaɪ͵stro:] *n, pl* **-stros** *or* **-stri** [-͵stri:] : maestro *m*

Mafia [ˈmɑfiə] *n* : Mafia *f*

magazine [ˈmægə͵zi:n] *n* **1** STOREHOUSE : almacén *m*, polvorín *m* (de explosivos) **2** PERIODICAL : revista *f* **3** : cargador *m* (de un arma de fuego)

magenta [məˈʤɛntə] *n* : magenta *f*, color *m* magenta

maggot [ˈmægət] *n* : gusano *m*

magic[1] [ˈmæʤɪk] *or* **magical** [ˈmæʤɪkəl] *adj* : mágico

magic[2] *n* : magia *f*

magically [ˈmæʤɪkli] *adv* : mágicamente ⟨they magically appeared : aparecieron como por arte de magia⟩

magician [məˈʤɪʃən] *n* **1** SORCERER : mago *m*, -ga *f* **2** CONJURER : prestidigitador *m*, -dora *f*; mago *m*, -ga *f*

magistrate [ˈmæʤə͵streɪt] *n* : magistrado *m*, -da *f*

magma [ˈmægmə] *n* : magma *m*

magnanimity [͵mægnəˈnɪməţi] *n, pl* **-ties** : magnanimidad *f*

magnanimous [mægˈnænəməs] *adj* : magnánimo, generoso — **magnanimously** *adv*

magnate [ˈmæg͵neɪt, -nət] *n* : magnate *mf*

magnesium [mægˈni:ziəm, -ʒəm] *n* : magnesio *m*

magnet [ˈmægnət] *n* : imán *m*

magnetic [mægˈnɛţɪk] *adj* : magnético — **magnetically** [-ţɪkli] *adv*

magnetic field *n* : campo *m* magnético

magnetism [ˈmægnə͵tɪzəm] *n* : magnetismo *m*

magnetize [ˈmægnə͵taɪz] *vt* **-tized; -tizing 1** : magnetizar, imantar **2** ATTRACT : magnetizar, atraer

magnification [͵mægnəfəˈkeɪʃən] *n* : aumento *m*, ampliación *f*

magnificence [mægˈnɪfəsənts] *n* : magnificencia *f*

magnificent [mægˈnɪfəsənt] *adj* : magnífico — **magnificently** *adv*

magnify [ˈmægnə͵faɪ] *vt* **-fied; -fying 1** ENLARGE : ampliar **2** EXAGGERATE : magnificar, exagerar

magnifying glass *n* : lupa *f*

magnitude [ˈmægnə͵tu:d, -͵tju:d] *n* **1** GREATNESS : magnitud *f*, grandeza *f* **2** QUANTITY : cantidad *f* **3** IMPORTANCE : magnitud *f*, envergadura *f*

magnolia [mægˈno:ljə] *n* : magnolia *f* (flor), magnolio *m* (árbol)

magpie [ˈmæg͵paɪ] *n* : urraca *f*

mahogany [məˈhɑgəni] *n, pl* **-nies** : caoba *f*

maid [ˈmeɪd] *n* **1** MAIDEN : doncella *f* **2** *or* **maidservant** [ˈmeɪd͵sərvənt] : sirvienta *f*, muchacha *f*, mucama *f*, criada *f*

maiden[1] [ˈmeɪdən] *adj* **1** UNMARRIED : soltera **2** FIRST : primero ⟨maiden voyage : primera travesía⟩

maiden[2] *n* : doncella *f*

maidenhood [ˈmeɪdən͵hʊd] *n* : doncellez *f*

maiden name *n* : nombre *m* de soltera

mail[1] [ˈmeɪl] *vt* : enviar por correo, echar al correo

mail[2] *n* **1** : correo *m* ⟨airmail : correo aéreo⟩ **2** : malla *f* ⟨coat of mail : cota de malla⟩

mailbox [ˈmeɪl͵bɑks] *n* : buzón *m*

mailman [ˈmeɪl͵mæn, -mən] *n, pl* **-men** [-mən, -͵mn] : cartero *m*

maim [ˈmeɪm] *vt* : mutilar, desfigurar, lisiar

main[1] [ˈmeɪn] *adj* : principal, central ⟨the main office : la oficina central⟩

main[2] *n* **1** HIGH SEAS : alta mar *f* **2** : tubería *f* principal (de agua o gas), cable *m* principal (de un circuito) **3 with might and main** : con todas sus fuerzas

mainframe [ˈmeɪn͵freɪm] *n* : mainframe *m*, computadora *f* central

mainland [ˈmeɪn͵lænd, -lənd] *n* : continente *m*

mainly [ˈmeɪnli] *adv* **1** PRINCIPALLY : principalmente, en primer lugar **2** MOSTLY : principalmente, en la mayor parte

mainstay [ˈmeɪn͵steɪ] *n* : pilar *m*, sostén *m* principal

mainstream[1] [ˈmeɪn͵stri:m] *adj* : dominante, corriente, convencional

mainstream[2] *n* : corriente *f* principal

maintain [meɪnˈteɪn] *vt* **1** SERVICE : dar mantenimiento a (una máquina) **2** PRESERVE : mantener, conservar ⟨to maintain silence : guardar silencio⟩ **3** SUPPORT : mantener, sostener **4** ASSERT : mantener, sostener, afirmar

maintenance [ˈmeɪntənənts] *n* : mantenimiento *m*

maize [ˈmeɪz] *n* : maíz *m*

majestic [məˈʤɛstɪk] *adj* : majestuoso — **majestically** [-tɪkli] *adv*

majesty [ˈmæʤəsti] *n, pl* **-ties 1** : majestad *f* ⟨Your Majesty : su Majestad⟩ **2** SPLENDOR : majestuosidad *f*, esplendor *m*

major[1] [ˈmeɪʤər] *vi* **-jored; -joring** : especializarse

major[2] *adj* **1** GREATER : mayor **2** NOTEWORTHY : mayor, notable **3** SERIOUS : grave **4** : mayor (en la música)

major[3] *n* **1** : mayor *mf*, comandante *mf* (en las fuerzas armadas) **2** : especialidad *f* (universitaria)

Majorcan [mɑˈʤɔrkən, mə-, -ˈjɔr-] *n* : mallorquín *m*, -quina *f* — **Majorcan** *adj*

major general *n* : general *mf* de división

majority [mə'ʤɔrəṯi] *n, pl* **-ties 1** ADULTHOOD : mayoría *f* de edad **2** : mayoría *f*, mayor parte *f* ⟨the vast majority : la inmensa mayoría⟩

make[1] ['meɪk] *v* **made** ['meɪd;]; **making** *vt* **1** CREATE : hacer ⟨to make noise : hacer ruido⟩ **2** FASHION, MANUFACTURE : hacer, fabricar ⟨she made a dress : hizo un vestido⟩ **3** DEVISE, FORM : desarrollar, elaborar, formar **4** CONSTITUTE : hacer, constituir ⟨made of stone : hecho de piedra⟩ **5** PREPARE : hacer, preparar **6** RENDER : hacer, poner ⟨it makes him nervous : lo pone nervioso⟩ ⟨to make someone happy : hacer feliz a alguien⟩ ⟨it made me sad : me dio pena⟩ **7** PERFORM : hacer ⟨to make a gesture : hacer un gesto⟩ **8** COMPEL : hacer, forzar, obligar **9** EARN : ganar ⟨to make a living : ganarse la vida⟩ — *vi* **1** HEAD : ir, dirigirse ⟨we made for home : nos fuimos a casa⟩ **2 to make do** : arreglárselas **3 to make good** REPAY : pagar **4 to make good** SUCCEED : tener éxito

make[2] *n* BRAND : marca *f*

make–believe[1] [ˌmeɪkbə'li:v] *adj* : imaginario

make–believe[2] *n* : fantasía *f*, invención *f* ⟨a world of make-believe : un mundo de ensueño⟩

make out *vt* **1** WRITE : hacer (un cheque) **2** DISCERN : distinguir, divisar **3** UNDERSTAND : comprender, entender — *vi* : arreglárselas ⟨how did you make out? : ¿qué tal te fue?⟩

maker ['meɪkər] *n* : fabricante *mf*

makeshift ['meɪkˌʃɪft] *adj* : provisional, improvisado

makeup ['meɪkˌʌp] *n* **1** COMPOSITION : composición *f* **2** CHARACTER : carácter *m*, temperamento *m* **3** COSMETICS : maquillaje *m*

make up *vt* **1** INVENT : inventar **2** : recuperar ⟨she made up the time : recuperó las horas perdidas⟩ — *vi* RECONCILE : hacer las paces, reconciliarse

making ['meɪkɪŋ] *n* **1** : creación *f*, producción *f* ⟨in the making : en ciernes⟩ **2 to have the makings of** : tener madera de (dícese de personas), tener los ingredientes para

maladjusted [ˌmælə'ʤʌstəd] *adj* : inadaptado

malady ['mælədi] *n, pl* **-dies** : dolencia *f*, enfermedad *f*, mal *m*

malaise [mə'leɪz, mæ-] *n* : malestar *m*

malapropism ['mæləˌprɑˌpɪzəm] *n* : uso *m* incorrecto y cómico de una palabra

malaria [mə'lɛriə] *n* : malaria *f*, paludismo *m*

malarkey [mə'lɑrki] *n* : tonterías *fpl*, estupideces *fpl*

Malawian [mə'lɑwiən] *n* : malauiano *m*, -na *f* — **Malawian** *adj*

Malay [mə'leɪ, 'meɪˌleɪ] *n* **1** *or* **Malayan** [mə'leɪən, meɪ-; 'meɪˌleɪən] : malayo *m*, -ya *f* **2** : malayo *m* (idioma) — **Malay** *or* **Malayan** *adj*

Malaysian [mə'leɪʒən, -ʃən] *n* : malasio *m*, -sia *f*; malaisio *m*, -sia *f* — **Malaysian** *adj*

male[1] ['meɪl] *adj* **1** : macho **2** MASCULINE : masculino

male[2] *n* : macho *m* (de animales o plantas), varón *m* (de personas)

malefactor ['mæləˌfæktər] *n* : malhechor *m*, -chora *f*

maleness ['meɪlnəs] *n* : masculinidad *f*

malevolence [mə'lɛvələn*t*s] *n* : malevolencia *f*

malevolent [mə'lɛvələnt] *adj* : malévolo

malformation [ˌmælfɔr'meɪʃən] *n* : malformación *f*

malformed [mæl'fɔrmd] *adj* : mal formado, deforme

malfunction[1] [mæl'fʌŋkʃən] *vi* : funcionar mal

malfunction[2] *n* : mal funcionamiento *m*

malice ['mælɪs] *n* **1** : malicia *f*, malevolencia *f* **2 with malice aforethought** : con premeditación

malicious [mə'lɪʃəs] *adj* : malicioso, malévolo — **maliciously** *adv*

malign[1] [mə'laɪn] *vt* : calumniar, difamar

malign[2] *adj* : maligno

malignancy [mə'lɪgnən*t*si] *n, pl* **-cies** : malignidad *f*

malignant [mə'lɪgnənt] *adj* : maligno

malinger [mə'lɪŋgər] *vi* : fingirse enfermo

malingerer [mə'lɪŋgərər] *n* : uno que se finge enfermo

mall ['mɔl] *n* **1** PROMENADE : alameda *f*, paseo *m* (arbolado) **2** : centro *m* comercial ⟨shopping mall : galería comercial⟩

mallard ['mælərd] *n, pl* **-lard** *or* **-lards** : pato *m* real, ánade *mf* real

malleable ['mæliəbəl] *adj* : maleable

mallet ['mælət] *n* : mazo *m*

malnourished [mæl'nərɪʃt] *adj* : desnutrido, malnutrido

malnutrition [ˌmælnʊ'trɪʃən, -njʊ-] *n* : desnutrición *f*, malnutrición *f*

malodorous [mæl'o:dərəs] *adj* : maloliente

malpractice [ˌmæl'præktəs] *n* : mala práctica *f*, negligencia *f*

malt ['mɔlt] *n* : malta *f*

maltreat [mæl'tri:t] *vt* : maltratar

mama *or* **mamma** ['mɑmə] *n* : mamá *f*

mammal ['mæməl] *n* : mamífero *m*

mammalian [mə'meɪliən, mæ-] *adj* : mamífero

mammary ['mæməri] *adj* **1** : mamario **2 mammary gland** : glándula mamaria

mammogram ['mæməˌgræm] *n* : mamografía *f*

mammoth[1] ['mæməθ] *adj* : colosal, gigantesco

mammoth[2] *n* : mamut *m*

man[1] ['mæn] *vt* **manned; manning** : tripular (un barco o avión), encargarse de (un servicio)

man² *n, pl* **men** [ˈmɛn] **1** PERSON : hombre *m*, persona *f* **2** MALE : hombre *m* **3** MANKIND : humanidad *f*
manacles [ˈmænɪkəlz] *npl* HANDCUFFS : esposas *fpl*
manage [ˈmænɪʤ] *v* **-aged; -aging** *vt* **1** HANDLE : controlar, manejar **2** DIRECT : administrar, dirigir **3** CONTRIVE : lograr, ingeniárselas para — *vi* COPE : arreglárselas
manageable [ˈmænɪʤəbəl] *adj* : manejable
management [ˈmænɪʤmənt] *n* **1** DIRECTION : administración *f*, gestión *f*, dirección *f* **2** HANDLING : manejo *m* **3** MANAGERS : dirección *f*, gerencia *f*
manager [ˈmænɪʤər] *n* : director *m*, -tora *f*; gerente *mf*; administrador *m*, -dora *f*
managerial [ˌmænəˈʤɪriəl] *adj* : directivo, gerencial
mandarin [ˈmændərən] *n* **1** : mandarín *m* **2** *or* **mandarin orange** : mandarina *f*
mandate [ˈmænˌdeɪt] *n* : mandato *m*
mandatory [ˈmændəˌtori] *adj* : obligatorio
mandible [ˈmændəbəl] *n* : mandíbula *f*
mandolin [ˌmændəˈlɪn, ˈmændələn] *n* : mandolina *f*
mane [ˈmeɪn] *n* : crin *f* (de un caballo), melena *f* (de un león o una persona)
maneuver¹ [məˈnuːvər, -ˈnjuː-] *vt* **1** PLACE, POSITION : maniobrar, posicionar, colocar **2** MANIPULATE : manipular, maniobrar — *vi* : maniobrar
maneuver² *n* : maniobra *f*
manfully [ˈmænfəli] *adj* : valientemente
manganese [ˈmæŋgəˌniːz, -ˌniːs] *n* : manganeso *m*
mange [ˈmeɪnʤ] *n* : sarna *f*
manger [ˈmeɪnʤər] *n* : pesebre *m*
mangle [ˈmæŋgəl] *vt* **-gled; -gling** **1** CRUSH, DESTROY : aplastar, despedazar, destrozar **2** MUTILATE : mutilar ⟨to mangle a text : mutilar un texto⟩
mango [ˈmæŋˌgoː] *n, pl* **-goes** : mango *m*
mangrove [ˈmænˌgroːv, ˈmæŋ-] *n* : mangle *m*
mangy [ˈmeɪnʤi] *adj* **mangier; -est** **1** : sarnoso **2** SHABBY : gastado
manhandle [ˈmænˌhændəl] *vt* **-dled; -dling** : maltratar, tratar con poco cuidado
manhole [ˈmænˌhoːl] *n* : boca *f* de alcantarilla
manhood [ˈmænˌhʊd] *n* **1** : madurez *f* (de un hombre) **2** COURAGE, MANLINESS : hombría *f*, valor *m* **3** MEN : hombres *mpl*
manhunt [ˈmænˌhʌnt] *n* : búsqueda *f* (de un criminal)
mania [ˈmeɪniə, -njə] *n* : manía *f*
maniac [ˈmeɪniˌæk] *n* : maníaco *m*, -ca *f*; maniático *m*, -ca *f*
maniacal [məˈnaɪəkəl] *adj* : maníaco, maniaco
manicure¹ [ˈmænəˌkjʊr] *vt* **-cured; -curing** **1** : hacer la manicura a **2** TRIM : recortar
manicure² *n* : manicura *f*
manicurist [ˈmænəˌkjʊrɪst] *n* : manicuro *m*, -ra *f*
manifest¹ [ˈmænəˌfɛst] *vt* : manifestar
manifest² *adj* : manifiesto, patente — **manifestly** *adv*
manifestation [ˌmænəfəˈsteɪʃən] *n* : manifestación *f*
manifesto [ˌmænəˈfɛsˌtoː] *n, pl* **-tos** *or* **-toes** : manifiesto *m*
manifold¹ [ˈmænəˌfoːld] *adj* : diverso, variado
manifold² *n* : colector *m* (de escape)
manipulate [məˈnɪpjəˌleɪt] *vt* **-lated; -lating** : manipular
manipulation [məˌnɪpjəˈleɪʃən] *n* : manipulación *f*
manipulative [məˈnɪpjəˌleɪtɪv, -lət̬ɪv] *adj* : manipulador
mankind [ˈmænˈkaɪnd, ˌkaɪnd] *n* : género *m* humano, humanidad *f*
manliness [ˈmænlinəs] *n* : hombría *f*, masculinidad *f*
manly [ˈmænli] *adj* **-lier; -est** : varonil, viril
man–made [ˈmænˈmeɪd] *adj* : artificial ⟨man-made fabrics : telas sintéticas⟩
manna [ˈmænə] *n* : maná *m*
mannequin [ˈmænɪkən] *n* **1** DUMMY : maniquí *m* **2** MODEL : modelo *mf*
manner [ˈmænər] *n* **1** KIND, SORT : tipo *m*, clase *f* **2** WAY : manera *f*, modo *m* **3** STYLE : estilo *m* (artístico) **4 manners** *npl* CUSTOMS : costumbres *fpl* ⟨Victorian manners : costumbres victorianas⟩ **5 manners** *npl* ETIQUETTE : modales *mpl*, educación *f*, etiqueta *f* ⟨good manners : buenos modales⟩
mannered [ˈmænərd] *adj* **1** AFFECTED, ARTIFICIAL : amanerado, afectado **2 well–mannered** : educado, cortés **3** → **ill–mannered**
mannerism [ˈmænəˌrɪzəm] *n* : peculiaridad *f*, gesto *m* particular
mannerly [ˈmænərli] *adj* : cortés, bien educado
mannish [ˈmænɪʃ] *adj* : masculino, hombruno
man–of–war [ˌmænəˈwɔr, -əvˈwɔr] *n, pl* **men–of–war** [ˌmɛn-] WARSHIP : buque *m* de guerra
manor [ˈmænər] *n* **1** : casa *f* solariega, casa *f* señorial **2** ESTATE : señorío *m*
manpower [ˈmænˌpaʊər] *n* : personal *m*, mano *f* de obra
mansion [ˈmænʧən] *n* : mansión *f*
manslaughter [ˈmænˌslɔt̬ər] *n* : homicidio *m* sin premeditación
mantel [ˈmæntəl] *n* : repisa *f* de chimenea
mantelpiece [ˈmæntəlˌpiːs] → **mantel**
mantis [ˈmæntəs] *n, pl* **-tises** *or* **-tes** [ˈmænˌtiːz] : mantis *f* religiosa
mantle [ˈmæntəl] *n* : manto *m*

manual[1] [ˈmænjʊəl] *adj* : manual — **manually** *adv*

manual[2] *n* : manual *m*

manufacture[1] [ˌmænjəˈfæktʃər] *vt* **-tured; -turing** : fabricar, manufacturar, confeccionar (ropa), elaborar (comestibles)

manufacture[2] *n* : manufactura *f*, fabricación *f*, confección *f* (de ropa), elaboración *f* (de comestibles)

manufacturer [ˌmænjəˈfæktʃərər] *n* : fabricante *m*; manufacturero *m*, -ra *f*

manure [məˈnʊr, -ˈnjʊr] *n* : estiércol *m*

manuscript [ˈmænjəˌskrɪpt] *n* : manuscrito *m*

many[1] [ˈmɛni] *adj* **more** [ˈmor]; **most** [ˈmoːst] : muchos

many[2] *pron* : muchos *pl*, -chas *pl*

map[1] [ˈmæp] *vt* **mapped; mapping 1** : trazar el mapa de **2** PLAN : planear, proyectar ⟨to map out a program : planear un programa⟩

map[2] *n* : mapa *m*

maple [ˈmeɪpəl] *n* : arce *m*

mar [ˈmɑr] *vt* **marred; marring 1** SPOIL : estropear, echar a perder **2** DEFACE : desfigurar

maraschino [ˌmærəˈskiːnoː, -ˈʃiː-] *n, pl* **-nos** : cereza *f* al marrasquino

marathon [ˈmærəˌθɑn] *n* **1** RACE : maratón *m* **2** CONTEST : competencia *f* de resistencia

maraud [məˈrɔd] *vi* : merodear

marauder [məˈrɔdər] *n* : merodeador *m*, -dora *f*

marble [ˈmɑrbəl] *n* **1** : mármol *m* **2** : canica *f* ⟨to play marbles : jugar a las canicas⟩

march[1] [ˈmɑrtʃ] *vi* **1** : marchar, desfilar ⟨they marched past the grandstand : desfilaron ante la tribuna⟩ **2** : caminar con resolución ⟨she marched right up to him : se le acercó sin vacilación⟩

march[2] *n* **1** MARCHING : marcha *f* **2** PASSAGE : paso *m* (del tiempo) **3** PROGRESS : avance *m*, progreso *m* **4** : marcha *f* (en música)

March [ˈmɑrtʃ] *n* : marzo *m*

marchioness [ˈmɑrʃənɪs] *n* : marquesa *f*

Mardi Gras [ˈmɑrdiˌgrɑ] *n* : martes *m* de Carnaval

mare [ˈmær] *n* : yegua *f*

margarine [ˈmɑrdʒərən] *n* : margarina *f*

margin [ˈmɑrdʒən] *n* : margen *m*

marginal [ˈmɑrdʒənəl] *adj* **1** : marginal **2** MINIMAL : mínimo — **marginally** *adv*

marigold [ˈmærəˌgoːld] *n* : maravilla *f*, caléndula *f*

marijuana [ˌmærəˈhwɑnə] *n* : marihuana *f*

marina [məˈriːnə] *n* : puerto *m* deportivo

marinade [ˌmærəˈnɑd] *n* : adobo *m*, marinada *f*

marinate [ˈmærəˌneɪt] *vt* **-nated; -nating** : marinar

marine[1] [məˈriːn] *adj* **1** : marino ⟨marine life : vida marina⟩ **2** NAUTICAL : náutico, marítimo **3** : de la infantería de marina

marine[2] *n* : soldado *m* de marina

mariner [ˈmærɪnər] *n* : marinero *m*, marino *m*

marionette [ˌmæriəˈnɛt] *n* : marioneta *f*, títere *m*

marital [ˈmærəṭəl] *adj* **1** : matrimonial **2 marital status** : estado *m* civil

maritime [ˈmærəˌtaɪm] *adj* : marítimo

marjoram [ˈmɑrdʒərəm] *n* : mejorana *f*

mark[1] [ˈmɑrk] *vt* **1** : marcar **2** CHARACTERIZE : caracterizar **3** SIGNAL : señalar **4** NOTICE : prestar atención a, hacer caso de **5 to mark off** : demarcar, delimitar

mark[2] *n* **1** TARGET : blanco *m* **2** : marca *f*, señal *f* ⟨put a mark where you left off : pon una señal donde terminaste⟩ **3** INDICATION : señal *f*, indicio *m* **4** GRADE : nota *f* **5** IMPRINT : huella *f*, marca *f* **6** BLEMISH : marca *f*, imperfección *f*

marked [ˈmɑrkt] *adj* : marcado, notable — **markedly** [ˈmɑrkədli] *adv*

marker [ˈmɑrkər] *n* : marcador *m*

market[1] [ˈmɑrkət] *vt* : poner en venta, comercializar

market[2] *n* **1** MARKETPLACE : mercado *m* ⟨the open market : el mercado libre⟩ **2** DEMAND : demanda *f*, mercado *m* **3** STORE : tienda *f* **4** → **stock market**

marketable [ˈmɑrkəṭəbəl] *adj* : vendible

marketing [ˈmɑrkəṭɪŋ] *n* : mercadotecnia *f*, mercadeo *m*

marketplace [ˈmɑrkətˌpleɪs] *n* : mercado *m*

marksman [ˈmɑrksmən] *n, pl* **-men** [-mən, -ˌmɛn] : tirador *m*

marksmanship [ˈmɑrksmənˌʃɪp] *n* : puntería *f*

marlin [ˈmɑrlɪn] *n* : marlín *m*

marmalade [ˈmɑrməˌleɪd] *n* : mermelada *f*

marmoset [ˈmɑrməˌsɛt] *n* : tití *m*

marmot [ˈmɑrmət] *n* : marmota *f*

maroon[1] [məˈruːn] *vt* : abandonar, aislar

maroon[2] *n* : rojo *m* oscuro, granate *m*

marquee [mɑrˈkiː] *n* : marquesina *f*

marquess [ˈmɑrkwɪs] *or* **marquis** [ˈmɑrkwɪs, mɑrˈkiː] *n, pl* **-quesses** *or* **-quises** [-ˈkiːz, -ˈkiːzəz] *or* **-quis** [-ˈkiː, -ˈkiːz] : marqués *m*

marquise [mɑrˈkiːz] → **marchioness**

marriage [ˈmærɪdʒ] *n* **1** : matrimonio *m* **2** WEDDING : casamiento *m*, boda *f*

marriageable [ˈmærɪdʒəbəl] *adj* **of marriageable age** : de edad de casarse

married [ˈmærid] *adj* **1** : casado **2 to get married** : casarse

marrow [ˈmæroː] *n* : médula *f*, tuétano *m*

marry [ˈmæri] *vt* **-ried; -rying 1** : casar ⟨the priest married them : el cura los casó⟩ **2** : casarse con ⟨she married John : se casó con John⟩

Mars ['mɑrz] *n* : Marte *m*
marsh ['mɑrʃ] *n* **1** : pantano *m* **2 salt marsh** : marisma *f*
marshal¹ ['mɑrʃəl] *vt* **-shaled** *or* **-shalled; -shaling** *or* **-shalling 1** : poner en orden, reunir **2** USHER : conducir
marshal² *n* **1** : maestro *m* de ceremonias **2** : mariscal *m* (en el ejército); jefe *m*, -fa *f* (de la policía, de los bomberos, etc.)
marshmallow ['mɑrʃ,mɛlo:, -,mælo:] *n* : malvavisco *m*
marshy ['mɑrʃi] *adj* **marshier; -est** : pantanoso
marsupial [mɑr'su:piəl] *n* : marsupial *m*
mart ['mɑrt] *n* MARKET : mercado *m*
marten ['mɑrtən] *n, pl* **-ten** *or* **-tens** : marta *f*
martial ['mɑrʃəl] *adj* : marcial
martin ['mɑrtən] *n* **1** SWALLOW : golondrina *f* **2** SWIFT : vencejo *m*
martyr¹ ['mɑrt̬ər] *vt* : martirizar
martyr² *n* : mártir *mf*
martyrdom ['mɑrt̬ərdəm] *n* : martirio *m*
marvel¹ ['mɑrvəl] *vi* **-veled** *or* **-velled; -veling** *or* **-velling** : maravillarse
marvel² *n* : maravilla *f*
marvelous ['mɑrvələs] *or* **marvellous** *adj* : maravilloso — **marvelously** *adv*
Marxism ['mɑrk,sɪzəm] *n* : marxismo *m*
Marxist¹ ['mɑrksɪst] *adj* : marxista
Marxist² *n* : marxista *mf*
mascara [mæs'kærə] *n* : rímel *m*, rimel *m*
mascot ['mæs,kɑt, -kət] *n* : mascota *f*
masculine ['mæskjələn] *adj* : masculino
masculinity [,mæskjə'lɪnət̬i] *n* : masculinidad *f*
mash¹ ['mæʃ] *vt* **1** : hacer puré de (papas, etc.) **2** CRUSH : aplastar, majar
mash² *n* **1** FEED : afrecho *m* **2** : malta *f* (para hacer bebidas alcohólicas) **3** PASTE, PULP : papilla *f*, pasta *f*
mask¹ ['mæsk] *vt* **1** CONCEAL, DISGUISE : enmascarar, ocultar **2** COVER : cubrir, tapar
mask² *n* : máscara *f*, careta *f*, mascarilla *f* (de un cirujano o dentista)
masochism ['mæsə,kɪzəm, 'mæzə-] *n* : masoquismo *m*
masochist ['mæsə,kɪst, 'mæzə-] *n* : masoquista *mf*
masochistic [,mæsə'kɪstɪk, ,mæzə-] *adj* : masoquista
mason ['meɪsən] *n* **1** BRICKLAYER : albañil *mf* **2** *or* **stonemason** ['sto:n,-] : mampostero *m*, cantero *m*
masonry ['meɪsənri] *n, pl* **-ries 1** BRICKLAYING : albañería *f* **2** *or* **stonemasonry** ['sto:n,-] : mampostería *f*
masquerade¹ [,mæskə'reɪd] *vi* **-aded; -ading 1** : disfrazarse (de), hacerse pasar (por) **2** : asistir a una mascarada
masquerade² *n* **1** : mascarada *f*, baile *m* de disfraces **2** FACADE : farsa *f*, fachada *f*
mass¹ ['mæs] *vi* : concentrarse, juntarse en masa — *vt* : concentrar
mass² *n* **1** : masa *f* <atomic mass : masa atómica> **2** BULK : mole *f*, volumen *m* **3** MULTITUDE : cantidad *f*, montón *m* (de cosas), multitud *f* (de gente) **4 the masses** : las masas, el pueblo, el populacho
Mass ['mæs] *n* : misa *f*
massacre¹ ['mæsɪkər] *vt* **-cred; -cring** : masacrar
massacre² *n* : masacre *f*
massage¹ [mə'sɑʒ, -'sɑʤ] *vt* **-saged; -saging** : masajear
massage² *n* : masaje *m*
masseur [mæ'sər] *n* : masajista *m*
masseuse [mæ'søz, -'su:z] *n* : masajista *f*
massive ['mæsɪv] *adj* **1** BULKY : voluminoso, macizo **2** HUGE : masivo, enorme — **massively** *adv*
mast ['mæst] *n* : mástil *m*, palo *m*
master¹ ['mæstər] *vt* **1** SUBDUE : dominar **2** : llegar a dominar <she mastered French : llegó a dominar el francés>
master² *n* **1** TEACHER : maestro *m*, profesor *m* **2** EXPERT : experto *m*, -ta *f*; maestro *m*, -tra *f* **3** : amo *m* (de animales o esclavos), señor *m* (de la casa) **4 master's degree** : maestría *f*
masterful ['mæstərfəl] *adj* **1** IMPERIOUS : autoritario, imperioso, dominante **2** SKILLFUL : magistral — **masterfully** *adv*
masterly ['mæstərli] *adj* : magistral
mastermind ['mæstər,maɪnd] *n* : cerebro *m*, artífice *mf*
masterpiece ['mæstər,pi:s] *n* : obra *f* maestra
masterwork ['mæstər,wərk] → **masterpiece**
mastery ['mæstəri] *n* **1** DOMINION : dominio *m*, autoridad *f* **2** SUPERIORITY : superioridad *f* **3** EXPERTISE : maestría *f*
masticate ['mæstə,keɪt] *v* **-cated; -cating** : masticar
mastiff ['mæstɪf] *n* : mastín *m*
mastodon ['mæstə,dɑn] *n* : mastodonte *m*
masturbate ['mæstər,beɪt] *v* **-bated; bating** *vi* : masturbarse — *vt* : masturbar
masturbation [,mæstər'beɪʃən] *n* : masturbación *f*
mat¹ ['mæt] *v* **matted; matting** *vt* TANGLE : enmarañar — *vi* : enmarañarse
mat² *n* **1** : estera *f* **2** TANGLE : maraña *f* **3** PAD : colchoneta *f* (de gimnasia) **4** *or* **matt** *or* **matte** ['mæt] FRAME : marco *m* (de cartón)
mat³ → **matte**
matador ['mæt̬ə,dɔr] *n* : matador *m*
match¹ ['mæʧ] *vt* **1** PIT : enfrentar, oponer **2** EQUAL, FIT : igualar, corresponder a, coincidir con **3** : combinar con, hacer juego con <her shoes match her dress : sus zapatos hacen juego con su vestido> — *vi* **1** CORRESPOND : concordar, coincidir **2** : hacer juego <with a tie to match : con una corbata que hace juego>

match[2] *n* **1** EQUAL : igual *mf* ⟨he's no match for her : no puede competir con ella⟩ **2** FIGHT, GAME : partido *m*, combate *m* (en boxeo) **3** MARRIAGE : matrimonio *m*, casamiento *m* **4** : fósforo *m*, cerilla *f*, cerillo *m in various countries*) ⟨he lit a match : encendió un fósforo⟩ **5 to be a good match** : hacer buena pareja (dícese de las personas), hacer juego (dícese de la ropa)

matchless [ˈmætʃləs] *adj* : sin igual, sin par

matchmaker [ˈmætʃˌmeɪkər] *n* : casamentero *m*, -ra *f*

mate[1] [ˈmeɪt] *v* **mated; mating** *vi* **1** FIT : encajar **2** PAIR : emparejarse **3** (*relating to animals*) : aparearse, copular — *vt* : aparear, acoplar (animales)

mate[2] *n* **1** COMPANION : compañero *m*, -ra *f*; camarada *mf* **2** : macho *m*, hembra *f* (de animales) **3** : oficial *mf* (de un barco) ⟨first mate : primer oficial⟩ **4** : compañero *m*, -ra *f*; pareja *f* (de un zapato, etc.)

material[1] [məˈtɪriəl] *adj* **1** PHYSICAL : material, físico ⟨the material world : el mundo material⟩ ⟨material needs : necesidades materiales⟩ **2** IMPORTANT : importante, esencial **3 material evidence** : prueba *f* sustancial

material[2] *n* **1** : material *m* **2** CLOTH : tejido *m*, tela *f*

materialism [məˈtɪriəˌlɪzəm] *n* : materialismo *m*

materialist [məˈtɪriəlɪst] *n* : materialista *mf*

materialistic [məˌtɪriəˈlɪstɪk] *adj* : materialista

materialize [məˈtɪriəˌlaɪz] *v* **-ized; -izing** *vt* : materializar, hacer aparecer — *vi* : materializarse, aparecer

maternal [məˈtərnəl] *adj* MOTHERLY : maternal — **maternally** *adv*

maternity[1] [məˈtərnəṭi] *adj* : de maternidad ⟨maternity clothes : ropa de futura mamá⟩ ⟨maternity leave : licencia por maternidad⟩

maternity[2] *n, pl* **-ties** : maternidad *f*

math [ˈmæθ] → **mathematics**

mathematical [ˌmæθəˈmæṭɪkəl] *adj* : matemático — **mathematically** *adv*

mathematician [ˌmæθəməˈtɪʃən] *n* : matemático *m*, -ca *f*

mathematics [ˌmæθəˈmæṭɪks] *ns & pl* : matemáticas *fpl*, matemática *f*

matinee *or* **matinée** [ˌmætənˈeɪ] *n* : matiné *f*

matriarch [ˈmeɪtriˌɑrk] *n* : matriarca *f*

matriarchy [ˈmeɪtriˌɑrki] *n, pl* **-chies** : matriarcado *m*

matriculate [məˈtrɪkjəˌleɪt] *v* **-lated; -lating** *vt* : matricular — *vi* : matricularse

matriculation [məˌtrɪkjəˈleɪʃən] *n* : matrícula *f*, matriculación *f*

matrimony [ˈmætrəˌmoːni] *n* : matrimonio *m* — **matrimonial** [ˌmætrəˈmoːniəl] *adj*

matrix [ˈmeɪtrɪks] *n, pl* **-trices** [ˈmeɪtrəˌsiːz, ˈmæ-] *or* **-trixes** [ˈmeɪtrɪksəz] : matriz *f*

matron [ˈmeɪtrən] *n* : matrona *f*

matronly [ˈmeɪtrənli] *adj* : de matrona, matronal

matte [ˈmæt] *adj* : mate, de acabado mate

matter[1] [ˈmæṭər] *vi* : importar ⟨it doesn't matter : no importa⟩

matter[2] *n* **1** QUESTION : asunto *m*, cuestión *f* ⟨a matter of taste : una cuestión de gusto⟩ **2** SUBSTANCE : materia *f*, sustancia *f* **3 matters** *npl* CIRCUMSTANCES : situación *f*, cosas *fpl* ⟨to make matters worse : para colmo de males⟩ **4 to be the matter** : pasar ⟨what's the matter? : ¿qué pasa?⟩ **5 as a matter of fact** : en efecto, en realidad **6 for that matter** : de hecho **7 no matter how much** : por mucho que

matter–of–fact [ˈmæṭərəvˈfækt] *adj* : práctico, realista

mattress [ˈmætrəs] *n* : colchón *m*

mature[1] [məˈtʊr, -ˈtjʊr, -ˈtʃʊr] *vi* **-tured; -turing 1** : madurar **2** : vencer ⟨when does the loan mature? : ¿cuándo vence el préstamo?⟩

mature[2] *adj* **-turer; -est 1** : maduro **2** DUE : vencido

maturity [məˈtʊrəṭi, -ˈtjʊr-, -ˈtʃʊr-] *n* : madurez *f*

maudlin [ˈmɔdlɪn] *adj* : sensiblero

maul[1] [ˈmɔl] *vt* **1** BEAT : golpear, pegar **2** MANGLE : mutilar **3** MANHANDLE : maltratar

maul[2] *n* MALLET : mazo *m*

Mauritanian [ˌmɔrəˈteɪniən] *n* : mauritano *m*, -na *f* — **Mauritanian** *adj*

mausoleum [ˌmɔsəˈliːəm, ˌmɔzə-] *n, pl* **-leums** *or* **-lea** [-ˈliːə] : mausoleo *m*

mauve [ˈmoːv, ˈmɔv] *n* : malva *m*

maven *or* **mavin** [ˈmeɪvən] *n* EXPERT : experto *m*, -ta *f*

maverick [ˈmævrɪk, ˈmævə-] *n* **1** : ternero *m* sin marcar **2** NONCONFORMIST : inconformista *mf*, disidente *mf*

mawkish [ˈmɔkɪʃ] *adj* : sensiblero

maxim [ˈmæksəm] *n* : máxima *f*

maximize [ˈmæksəˌmaɪz] *vt* **-mized; -mizing** : maximizar, llevar al máximo

maximum[1] [ˈmæksəməm] *adj* : máximo

maximum[2] *n, pl* **-ma** [ˈmæksəmə] *or* **-mums** : máximo *m*

may [ˈmeɪ] *v aux, past* **might** [ˈmaɪt] *present s & pl* **may 1** (*expressing permission*) : poder ⟨you may go : puedes ir⟩ **2** (*expressing possibility or probability*) : poder ⟨you may be right : puede que tengas razón⟩ ⟨it may happen occasionally : puede pasar de vez en cuando⟩ **3** (*expressing desires, intentions, or contingencies*) ⟨may the best man win : que gane el mejor⟩ ⟨I laugh that I may not weep : me río para no llorar⟩ ⟨come what may : pase lo que pase⟩

May [ˈmeɪ] *n* : mayo *m*

Maya [ˈmaɪə] *or* **Mayan** [ˈmaɪən] *n* : maya *mf* — **Maya** *or* **Mayan** *adj*
maybe [ˈmeɪbi] *adv* PERHAPS : quizás, tal vez
mayfly [ˈmeɪˌflaɪ] *n, pl* **-flies** : efímera *f*
mayhem [ˈmeɪˌhɛm, ˈmeɪəm] *n* **1** MUTILATION : mutilación *f* **2** DEVASTATION : estragos *mpl*
mayonnaise [ˈmeɪəˌneɪz] *n* : mayonesa *f*
mayor [ˈmeɪər, ˈmɛr] *n* : alcalde *m*, -desa *f*
mayoral [ˈmeɪərəl, ˈmɛrəl] *adj* : de alcalde
maze [ˈmeɪz] *n* : laberinto *m*
me [ˈmiː] *pron* **1** : me ⟨she called me : me llamó⟩ ⟨give it to me : dámelo⟩ **2** (*after a preposition*) : mí ⟨for me : para mí⟩ ⟨with me : conmigo⟩ **3** (*after conjunctions and verbs*) : yo ⟨it's me : soy yo⟩ ⟨as big as me : tan grande como yo⟩ **4** (*emphatic use*) : yo ⟨me, too! : ¡yo también!⟩ ⟨who, me? : ¿quién, yo?⟩
meadow [ˈmɛdoː] *n* : prado *m*, pradera *f*
meadowland [ˈmɛdoˌlænd] *n* : pradera *f*
meadowlark [ˈmɛdoˌlɑrk] *n* : pájaro *m* cantor con el pecho amarillo
meager *or* **meagre** [ˈmiːgər] *adj* **1** THIN : magro, flaco **2** POOR, SCANTY : exiguo, escaso, pobre
meagerly [ˈmiːgərli] *adv* : pobremente
meagerness [ˈmiːgərnəs] *n* : escasez *f*, pobreza *f*
meal [ˈmiːl] *n* **1** : comida *f* ⟨a hearty meal : una comida sustanciosa⟩ **2** : harina *f* (de maíz, etc.)
mealtime [ˈmiːlˌtaɪm] *n* : hora *f* de comer
mean[1] [ˈmiːn] *vt* **meant** [ˈmɛnt]; **meaning** **1** INTEND : querer, pensar, tener la intención de ⟨I didn't mean to do it : lo hice sin querer⟩ ⟨what do you mean to do? : ¿qué piensas hacer?⟩ **2** SIGNIFY : querer decir, significar ⟨what does that mean? : ¿qué quiere decir eso?⟩ **3** : importar ⟨health means everything : lo que más importa es la salud⟩
mean[2] *adj* **1** HUMBLE : humilde **2** NEGLIGIBLE : despreciable ⟨it's no mean feat : no es poca cosa⟩ **3** STINGY : mezquino, tacaño **4** CRUEL : malo, cruel ⟨to be mean to someone : tratar mal a alguien⟩ **5** AVERAGE, MEDIAN : medio
mean[3] *n* **1** MIDPOINT : término *m* medio **2** AVERAGE : promedio *m*, media *f* aritmética **3 means** *npl* WAY : medio *m*, manera *f*, vía *f* **4 means** *npl* RESOURCES : medios *mpl*, recursos *mpl* **5 by all means** : por supuesto, cómo no **6 by means of** : por medio de **7 by no means** : de ninguna manera, de ningún modo
meander [miˈændər] *vi* **-dered; -dering** **1** WIND : serpentear **2** WANDER : vagar, andar sin rumbo fijo
meaning [ˈmiːnɪŋ] *n* **1** : significado *m*, sentido *m* ⟨double meaning : doble sentido⟩ **2** INTENT : intención *f*, propósito *m*
meaningful [ˈmiːnɪŋfəl] *adj* : significativo — **meaningfully** *adv*
meaningless [ˈmiːnɪŋləs] *adj* : sin sentido
meanness [ˈmiːnnəs] *n* **1** CRUELTY : crueldad *f*, mezquindad *f* **2** STINGINESS : tacañería *f*
meantime[1] [ˈmiːnˌtaɪm] *adv* → **meanwhile**[1]
meantime[2] *n* **1** : interín *m* **2 in the meantime** : entretanto, mientras tanto
meanwhile[1] [ˈmiːnˌhwaɪl] *adv* : entretanto, mientras tanto
meanwhile[2] *n* → **meantime**[2]
measles [ˈmiːzəlz] *ns & pl* : sarampión *m*
measly [ˈmiːzli] *adj* **-slier; -est** : miserable, mezquino
measurable [ˈmɛʒərəbəl, ˈmeɪ-] *adj* : mensurable — **measurably** [-bli] *adv*
measure[1] [ˈmɛʒər, ˈmeɪ-] *v* **-sured; -suring** : medir ⟨he measured the table : midió la mesa⟩ ⟨it measures 15 feet tall : mide 15 pies de altura⟩
measure[2] *n* **1** AMOUNT : medida *f*, cantidad *f* ⟨in large measure : en gran medida⟩ ⟨a full measure : una cantidad exacta⟩ ⟨a measure of proficiency : una cierta competencia⟩ ⟨for good measure : de ñapa, por añadidura⟩ **2** DIMENSIONS, SIZE : medida *f*, tamaño *m* **3** RULER : regla *f* ⟨tape measure : cinta métrica⟩ **4** MEASUREMENT : medida *f* ⟨cubic measure : medida de capacidad⟩ **5** MEASURING : medición *f* **6 measures** *npl* : medidas *fpl* ⟨security measures : medidas de seguridad⟩
measureless [ˈmɛʒərləs, ˈmeɪ-] *adj* : inmensurable
measurement [ˈmɛʒərmənt, ˈmeɪ-] *n* **1** MEASURING : medición *f* **2** DIMENSION : medida *f*
measure up *vi* **to measure up to** : estar a la altura de
meat [ˈmiːt] *n* **1** FOOD : comida *f* **2** : carne *f* ⟨meat and fish : carne y pescado⟩ **3** SUBSTANCE : sustancia *f*, esencia *f* ⟨the meat of the story : la sustancia del cuento⟩
meatball [ˈmiːtˌbɔl] *n* : albóndiga *f*
meaty [ˈmiːt̬i] *adj* **meatier; -est** : con mucha carne, carnoso
mechanic [mɪˈkænɪk] *n* : mecánico *m*, -ca *f*
mechanical [mɪˈkænɪkəl] *adj* : mecánico — **mechanically** *adv*
mechanics [mɪˈkænɪks] *ns & pl* **1** : mecánica *f* ⟨fluid mechanics : la mecánica de fluidos⟩ **2** MECHANISMS : mecanismos *mpl*, aspectos *mpl* prácticos
mechanism [ˈmɛkəˌnɪzəm] *n* : mecanismo *m*
mechanization [ˌmɛkənəˈzeɪʃən] *n* : mecanización *f*

mechanize [ˈmɛkəˌnaɪz] *vt* **-nized; -nizing** : mecanizar

medal [ˈmɛdəl] *n* : medalla *f*, condecoración *f*

medalist [ˈmɛdəlɪst] *or* **medallist** *n* : medallista *mf*

medallion [məˈdæljən] *n* : medallón *m*

meddle [ˈmɛdəl] *vi* **-dled; -dling** : meterse, entrometerse

meddler [ˈmɛdələr] *n* : entrometido *m*, -da *f*

meddlesome [ˈmɛdəlsəm] *adj* : entrometido

media [ˈmi:diə] *npl* : medios *mpl* de comunicación

median[1] [ˈmi:diən] *adj* : medio

median[2] *n* : valor *m* medio

mediate [ˈmi:diˌeɪt] *vi* **-ated; -ating** : mediar

mediation [ˌmi:diˈeɪʃən] *n* : mediación *f*

mediator [ˈmi:diˌeɪt̬ər] *n* : mediador *m*, -dora *f*

medical [ˈmɛdɪkəl] *adj* : médico

medicate [ˈmɛdəˌkeɪt] *vt* **-cated; -cating** : medicar ⟨medicated powder : polvos medicinales⟩

medication [ˌmɛdəˈkeɪʃən] *n* **1** TREATMENT : tratamiento *m*, medicación *f* **2** MEDICINE : medicamento *m* ⟨to be on medication : estar medicado⟩

medicinal [məˈdɪsənəl] *adj* : medicinal

medicine [ˈmɛdəsən] *n* **1** MEDICATION : medicina *f*, medicamento *m* **2** : medicina *f* ⟨he's studying medicine : estudia medicina⟩

medicine man *n* : hechicero *m*

medieval *or* **mediaeval** [mɪˈdi:vəl, ˌmi:-, ˌmɛ-, -diˈi:vəl] *adj* : medieval

mediocre [ˌmi:diˈo:kər] *adj* : mediocre

mediocrity [ˌmi:diˈɑkrət̬i] *n, pl* **-ties** : mediocridad *f*

meditate [ˈmɛdəˌteɪt] *vi* **-tated; -tating** : meditar

meditation [ˌmɛdəˈteɪʃən] *n* : meditación *f*

meditative [ˈmɛdəˌteɪt̬ɪv] *adj* : meditabundo

medium[1] [ˈmi:diəm] *adj* : mediano ⟨of medium height : de estatura mediana, de estatura regular⟩

medium[2] *n, pl* **-diums** *or* **-dia** [ˈmi:-diə] **1** MEAN : punto *m* medio, término *m* medio ⟨happy medium : justo medio⟩ **2** MEANS : medio *m* **3** SUBSTANCE : medio *m*, sustancia *f* ⟨a viscous medium : un medio viscoso⟩ **4** : medio *m* de comunicación **5** : medio *m* (artístico)

medley [ˈmɛdli] *n, pl* **-leys** : popurrí *m* (de canciones)

meek [ˈmi:k] *adj* **1** LONG-SUFFERING : paciente, sufrido **2** SUBMISSIVE : sumiso, dócil, manso

meekly [ˈmi:kli] *adv* : dócilmente

meekness [ˈmi:knəs] *n* : mansedumbre *f*, docilidad *f*

meet[1] [ˈmi:t] *v* **met** [ˈmɛt]; **meeting** *vt* **1** ENCOUNTER : encontrarse con **2** JOIN : unirse con **3** CONFRONT : enfrentarse a **4** SATISFY : satisfacer, cumplir con ⟨to meet costs : pagar los gastos⟩ **5** : conocer ⟨I met his sister : conocí a su hermana⟩ — *vi* ASSEMBLE : reunirse, congregarse

meet[2] *n* : encuentro *m*

meeting [ˈmi:t̬ɪŋ] *n* **1** : reunión *f* ⟨to open the meeting : abrir la sesión⟩ **2** ENCOUNTER : encuentro *m* **3** : entrevista *f* (formal)

meetinghouse [ˈmi:t̬ɪŋˌhaʊs] *n* : iglesia *f* (de ciertas confesiones protestantes)

megabyte [ˈmɛgəˌbaɪt] *n* : megabyte *m*

megahertz [ˈmɛgəˌhərts, -ˌhrts] *n* : megahercio *m*

megaphone [ˈmɛgəˌfo:n] *n* : megáfono *m*

melancholy[1] [ˈmɛlənˌkɑli] *adj* : melancólico, triste, sombrío

melancholy[2] *n, pl* **-cholies** : melancolía *f*

melanoma [ˌmɛləˈno:mə] *n, pl* **-mas** : melanoma *m*

meld [ˈmɛld] *vt* : fusionar, unir — *vi* : fusionarse, unirse

melee [ˈmeɪˌleɪ, meɪˈleɪ] *n* BRAWL : reyerta *f*, riña *f*, pelea *f*

meliorate [ˈmi:ljəˌreɪt, ˈmi:liə-] → **ameliorate**

mellow[1] [ˈmɛlo:] *vt* : suavizar, endulzar — *vi* : suavizarse, endulzarse

mellow[2] *adj* **1** RIPE : maduro **2** MILD : apacible ⟨a mellow character : un carácter apacible⟩ ⟨mellow wines : vinos añejos⟩ **3** : suave, dulce ⟨mellow colors : colores suaves⟩ ⟨mellow tones : tonos dulces⟩

mellowness [ˈmɛlonəs] *n* : suavidad *f*, dulzura *f*

melodic [məˈlɑdɪk] *adj* : melódico — **melodically** [-dɪkli] *adv*

melodious [məˈlo:diəs] *adj* : melodioso — **melodiously** *adv*

melodiousness [məˈlo:diəsnəs] *n* : calidad *f* de melódico

melodrama [ˈmɛləˌdrɑmə, -ˌdræ-] *n* : melodrama *m*

melodramatic [ˌmɛlədrəˈmæt̬ɪk] *adj* : melodramático — **melodramatically** [-t̬ɪkli] *adv*

melody [ˈmɛlədi] *n, pl* **-dies** : melodía *f*, tonada *f*

melon [ˈmɛlən] *n* : melón *m*

melt [ˈmɛlt] *vt* **1** : derretir, disolver **2** SOFTEN : ablandar ⟨it melted his heart : ablandó su corazón⟩ — *vi* **1** : derretirse, disolverse **2** SOFTEN : ablandarse **3** DISAPPEAR : desvanecerse, esfumarse ⟨the clouds melted away : las nubes se desvanecieron⟩

melting point *n* : punto *m* de fusión

member [ˈmɛmbər] *n* **1** LIMB : miembro *m* **2** : miembro *m* (de un grupo); socio *m*, -cia *f* (de un club) **3** PART : miembro *m*, parte *f*

membership [ˈmɛmbərˌʃɪp] *n* **1** : membresía *f* ⟨application for membership

: solicitud de entrada⟩ **2** MEMBERS : membresía *f*, miembros *mpl*, socios *mpl*

membrane [ˈmɛmˌbreɪn] *n* : membrana *f* — **membranous** [ˈmɛmbrə-nəs] *adj*

memento [mɪˈmɛnˌto:] *n, pl* **-tos** *or* **-toes** : recuerdo *m*

memo [ˈmɛmo:] *n, pl* **memos** : memorándum *m*

memoirs [ˈmɛmˌwɑrz] *npl* : memorias *fpl*, autobiografía *f*

memorabilia [ˌmɛmərəˈbiliə, -ˈbɪljə] *npl* **1** : objetos *mpl* de interés histórico **2** MEMENTOS : recuerdos *mpl*

memorable [ˈmɛmərəbəl] *adj* : memorable, notable — **memorably** [-bli] *adv*

memorandum [ˌmɛməˈrændəm] *n, pl* **-dums** *or* **-da** [-də] : memorándum *m*

memorial[1] [məˈmoriəl] *adj* : conmemorativo

memorial[2] *n* : monumento *m* conmemorativo

Memorial Day *n* : el último lunes de mayo (observado en Estados Unidos como día feriado para conmemorar a los caídos en guerra)

memorialize [məˈmoriəˌlaɪz] *vt* **-ized; -izing** COMMEMORATE : conmemorar

memorization [ˌmɛmərəˈzeɪʃən] *n* : memorización *f*

memorize [ˈmɛməˌraɪz] *vt* **-rized; -rizing** : memorizar, aprender de memoria

memory [ˈmɛmri, ˈmɛmə-] *n, pl* **-ries** **1** : memoria *f* ⟨he has a good memory : tiene buena memoria⟩ **2** RECOLLECTION : recuerdo *m* **3** COMMEMORATION : memoria *f*, conmemoración *f*

men → **man**[2]

menace[1] [ˈmɛnəs] *vt* **-aced; -acing** **1** THREATEN : amenazar **2** ENDANGER : poner en peligro

menace[2] *n* : amenaza *f*

menacing [ˈmɛnəsɪŋ] *adj* : amenazador, amenazante

menagerie [məˈnæʤəri, -ˈnæʒəri] *n* : colección *f* de animales salvajes

mend[1] [ˈmɛnd] *vt* **1** CORRECT : enmendar, corregir ⟨to mend one's ways : enmendarse⟩ **2** REPAIR : remendar, arreglar, reparar — *vi* HEAL : curarse

mend[2] *n* : remiendo *m*

mendicant [ˈmɛndɪkənt] *n* BEGGAR : mendigo *m*, -ga *f*

menhaden [mɛnˈheɪdən, mən-] *ns & pl* : pez *m* de la misma familia que los arenques

menial[1] [ˈmi:niəl] *adj* : servil, bajo

menial[2] *n* : sirviente *m*, -ta *f*

meningitis [ˌmɛnənˈʤaɪṭəs] *n, pl* **-gitides** [-ˈʤɪṭəˌdi:z] : meningitis *f*

menopause [ˈmɛnəˌpɔz] *n* : menopausia *f*

menorah [məˈnorə] *n* : candelabro *m* (usado en los oficios religiosos judíos)

menstrual [ˈmɛntstruəl] *adj* : menstrual

menstruate [ˈmɛntstruˌeɪt] *vi* **-ated; -ating** : menstruar

menstruation [ˌmɛntstruˈeɪʃən] *n* : menstruación *f*

mental [ˈmɛntəl] *adj* : mental ⟨mental hospital : hospital psiquiátrico⟩ — **mentally** *adv*

mentality [mɛnˈtæləṭi] *n, pl* **-ties** : mentalidad *f*

menthol [ˈmɛnˌθɔl, -ˌθo:l] *n* : mentol *m*

mentholated [ˌmɛntθəˌleɪṭəd] *adj* : mentolado

mention[1] [ˈmɛntʃən] *vt* : mencionar, mentar, referirse a ⟨don't mention it! : ¡de nada!, ¡no hay de qué!⟩

mention[2] *n* : mención *f*

mentor [ˈmɛnˌtɔr, ˈmɛntər] *n* : mentor *m*

menu [ˈmɛnˌju:] *n* **1** : menú *m*, carta *f* (en un restaurante) **2** : menú *m* (de computadoras)

meow[1] [mi:ˈaʊ] *vi* : maullar

meow[2] *n* : maullido *m*, miau *m*

mercantile [ˈmərkənˌti:l, -ˌtaɪl] *adj* : mercantil

mercenary[1] [ˈmərsənɛˌri] *adj* : mercenario

mercenary[2] *n, pl* **-naries** : mercenario *m*, -ria *f*

merchandise [ˈmərtʃənˌdaɪz, -ˌdaɪs] *n* : mercancía *f*, mercadería *f*

merchandiser [ˈmərtʃənˌdaɪzər] *n* : comerciante *mf*; vendedor *m*, -dora *f*

merchant [ˈmərtʃənt] *n* : comerciante *mf*

merchant marine *n* : marina *f* mercante

merciful [ˈmərsɪfəl] *adj* : misericordioso, clemente

mercifully [ˈmərsɪfli] *adv* **1** : con misericordia, con compasión **2** FORTUNATELY : afortunadamente

merciless [ˈmərsɪləs] *adj* : despiadado — **mercilessly** *adv*

mercurial [ˌmərˈkjʊriəl] *adj* TEMPERAMENTAL : temperamental, volátil

mercury [ˈmərkjəri] *n, pl* **-ries** : mercurio *m*

Mercury *n* : Mercurio *m*

mercy [ˈmərsi] *n, pl* **-cies** **1** CLEMENCY : misericordia *f*, clemencia *f* **2** BLESSING : bendición *f*

mere [ˈmɪr] *adj, superlative* **merest** : mero, simple

merely [ˈmɪrli] *adv* : solamente, simplemente

merge [ˈmərʤ] *v* **merged; merging** *vi* : unirse, fusionarse (dícese de las compañías), confluir (dícese de los ríos, las calles, etc.) — *vt* : unir, fusionar, combinar

merger [ˈmərʤər] *n* : unión *f*, fusión *f*

meridian [məˈrɪdiən] *n* : meridiano *m*

meringue [məˈræŋ] *n* : merengue *m*

merino [məˈri:no] *n, pl* **-nos** **1** : merino *m*, -na *f* **2** *or* **merino wool** : lana *f* merino

merit[1] [ˈmɛrət] *vt* : merecer, ser digno de

merit[2] *n* : mérito *m*, valor *m*

meritorious [ˌmɛrəˈtoriəs] *adj* : meritorio

mermaid [ˈmərˌmeɪd] *n* : sirena *f*

merriment [ˈmɛrɪmənt] *n* : alegría *f*, júbilo *m*, regocijo *m*

merry [ˈmɛri] *adj* **-rier; -est** : alegre — **merrily** [ˈmɛrəli] *adv*
merry–go–round [ˈmɛrigo͵raʊnd] *n* : carrusel *m*, tiovivo *m*
merrymaker [ˈmɛri͵meɪkər] *n* : juerguista *mf*
merrymaking [ˈmɛri͵meɪkɪŋ] *n* : juerga *f*
mesa [ˈmeɪsə] *n* : mesa *f*
mesdames → **madam, Mrs.**
mesh[1] [ˈmɛʃ] *vi* **1** ENGAGE : engranar (dícese de las piezas mecánicas) **2** TANGLE : enredarse **3** COORDINATE : coordinarse, combinar
mesh[2] *n* **1** : malla *f* ⟨wire mesh : malla metálica⟩ **2** NETWORK : red *f* **3** MESHING : engranaje *m* ⟨in mesh : engranado⟩
mesmerize [ˈmɛzmə͵raɪz] *vt* **-ized; -izing 1** HYPNOTIZE : hipnotizar **2** FASCINATE : cautivar, embelesar, fascinar
mess[1] [ˈmɛs] *vt* **1** SOIL : ensuciar **2 to mess up** DISARRANGE : desordenar, desarreglar **3 to mess up** BUNGLE : echar a perder — *vi* **1** PUTTER : entretenerse **2** INTERFERE : meterse, entrometerse ⟨don't mess with me : no te metas conmigo⟩
mess[2] *n* **1** : rancho *m* (para soldados, etc.) **2** DISORDER : desorden *m* ⟨your room is a mess : tienes el cuarto hecho un desastre⟩ **3** CONFUSION, TURMOIL : confusión *f*, embrollo *m*, lío *m fam*
message [ˈmɛsɪʤ] *n* : mensaje *m*, recado *m*
messenger [ˈmɛsənʤər] *n* : mensajero *m*, -ra *f*
Messiah [məˈsaɪə] *n* : Mesías *m*
Messrs. → **Mr.**
messy [ˈmɛsi] *adj* **messier; -est** UNTIDY : desordenado, sucio
met → **meet**
metabolic [͵mɛt̬əˈbɑlɪk] *adj* : metabólico
metabolism [məˈtæbə͵lɪzəm] *n* : metabolismo *m*
metabolize [məˈtæbə͵laɪz] *vt* **-lized; -lizing** : metabolizar
metal [ˈmɛt̬əl] *n* : metal *m*
metallic [məˈtælɪk] *adj* : metálico
metallurgical [͵mɛt̬əlˈərʤɪkəl] *adj* : metalúrgico
metallurgy [ˈmɛt̬əl͵ərʤi] *n* : metalurgia *f*
metalwork [ˈmɛt̬əl͵wərk] *n* : objeto *m* de metal
metalworking [ˈmɛt̬əl͵wərkɪŋ] *n* : metalistería *f*
metamorphosis [͵mɛt̬əˈmɔrfəsɪs] *n, pl* **-phoses** [-͵si:z] : metamorfosis *f*
metaphor [ˈmɛt̬ə͵fɔr, -fər] *n* : metáfora *f*
metaphoric [͵mɛt̬əˈfɔrɪk] *or* **metaphorical** [-ɪkəl] *adj* : metafórico
metaphysical [͵mɛt̬əˈfɪzəkəl] *adj* : metafísico
metaphysics [͵mɛt̬əˈfɪzɪks] *n* : metafísica *f*
mete [ˈmi:t] *vt* **meted; meting** ALLOT : repartir, distribuir ⟨to mete out punishment : imponer castigos⟩
meteor [ˈmi:t̬iər, -t̬i:͵ɔr] *n* : meteoro *m*
meteoric [͵mi:t̬iˈɔrɪk] *adj* : meteórico
meteorite [ˈmi:t̬iə͵raɪt] *n* : meteorito *m*
meteorologic [͵mi:t̬i͵ɔrəˈlɑʤɪk] *or* **meteorological** [-ˈlɑʤɪkəl] *adj* : meteorológico
meteorologist [͵mi:t̬iəˈrɑləʤɪst] *n* : meteorólogo *m*, -ga *f*
meteorology [͵mi:t̬iəˈrɑləʤi] *n* : meteorología *f*
meter [ˈmi:t̬ər] *n* **1** : metro *m* ⟨it measures 2 meters : mide 2 metros⟩ **2** : contador *m*, medidor *m* (de electricidad, etc.) ⟨parking meter : parquímetro⟩ **3** : metro *m* (en literatura o música)
methane [ˈmɛ͵θeɪn] *n* : metano *m*
method [ˈmɛθəd] *n* : método *m*
methodical [məˈθɑdɪkəl] *adj* : metódico — **methodically** *adv*
Methodist [ˈmɛθədɪst] *n* : metodista *mf* — **Methodist** *adj*
methodology [͵mɛθəˈdɑləʤi] *n, pl* **-gies** : metodología *f*
meticulous [məˈtɪkjələs] *adj* : meticuloso — **meticulously** *adv*
meticulousness [məˈtɪkjələsnəs] *n* : meticulosidad *f*
metric [ˈmɛtrɪk] *or* **metrical** [-trɪkəl] *adj* : métrico
metric system *n* : sistema *m* métrico
metronome [ˈmɛtrə͵no:m] *n* : metrónomo *m*
metropolis [məˈtrɑpələs] *n* : metrópoli *f*, metrópolis *f*
metropolitan [͵mɛtrəˈpɑlətən] *adj* : metropolitano
mettle [ˈmɛt̬əl] *n* : temple *m*, valor *m* ⟨on one's mettle : dispuesto a mostrar su valía⟩
Mexican [ˈmɛksɪkən] *n* : mexicano *m*, -na *f* — **Mexican** *adj*
mezzanine [ˈmɛzə͵ni:n, ͵mɛzəˈni:n] *n* **1** : entrepiso *m*, entresuelo *m* **2** : primer piso *m* (de un teatro)
miasma [maɪˈæzmə] *n* : miasma *m*
mica [ˈmaɪkə] *n* : mica *f*
mice → **mouse**
micro [ˈmaɪkro] *adj* : muy pequeño, microscópico
microbe [ˈmaɪ͵kro:b] *n* : microbio *m*
microbiology [͵maɪkrobaɪˈɑləʤi] *n* : microbiología *f*
microchip [ˈmaɪkro͵ʧɪp] *n* : microchip *m*
microcomputer [ˈmaɪkrokəm͵pju:t̬ər] *n* : microcomputadora *f*
microcosm [ˈmaɪkro͵kɑzəm] *n* : microcosmo *m*
microfilm [ˈmaɪkro͵fɪlm] *n* : microfilm *m*
micrometer [maɪˈkrɑmət̬ər] *n* : micrómetro *m*
micron [ˈmaɪ͵krɑn] *n* : micrón *m*
microorganism [͵maɪkroˈɔrgə͵nɪzəm] *n* : microorganismo *m*, microbio *m*

microphone [ˈmaɪkrəˌfo:n] *n* : micrófono *m*
microprocessor [ˈmaɪkroˌprɑˌssər] *n* : microprocesador *m*
microscope [ˈmaɪkrəˌsko:p] *n* : microscopio *m*
microscopic [ˌmaɪkrəˈskɑpɪk] *adj* : microscópico
microscopy [maɪˈkrɑskəpi] *n* : microscopía *f*
microwave [ˈmaɪkrəˌweɪv] *n* **1** : microonda *f* **2** *or* **microwave oven** : microondas *m*
mid [ˈmɪd] *adj* : medio ⟨mid morning : a media mañana⟩ ⟨in mid-August : a mediados de agosto⟩ ⟨in mid ocean : en alta mar⟩
midair [ˈmɪdˈær] *n* **in ~** : en el aire ⟨to catch in midair : agarrar al vuelo⟩
midday [ˈmɪdˈdeɪ] *n* NOON : mediodía *m*
middle¹ [ˈmɪdəl] *adj* **1** CENTRAL : medio, del medio, de en medio **2** INTERMEDIATE : intermedio, mediano ⟨middle age : la mediana edad⟩
middle² *n* **1** CENTER : medio *m*, centro *m* ⟨fold it down the middle : dóblalo por la mitad⟩ **2 in the middle of** : en medio de (un espacio), a mitad de (una actividad) ⟨in the middle of the month : a mediados del mes⟩
Middle Ages *npl* : Edad *f* Media
middle class *n* : clase *f* media
middleman [ˈmɪdəlˌmæn] *n, pl* **-men** [-mən, -ˌmɛn] : intermediario *m*, -ria *f*
middling [ˈmɪdlɪŋ, -lən] *adj* **1** MEDIUM, MIDDLE : mediano **2** MEDIOCRE : mediocre, regular
midfielder [ˈmɪdˌfi:ldər] *n* : mediocampista *mf*
midge [ˈmɪʤ] *n* : mosca *f* pequeña
midget [ˈmɪʤət] *n* **1** : enano *m*, -na *f* (persona) **2** : cosa *f* diminuta
midland [ˈmɪdlənd, -ˌlænd] *n* : región *f* central (de un país)
midnight [ˈmɪdˌnaɪt] *n* : medianoche *f*
midpoint [ˈmɪdˌpɔɪnt] *n* : punto *m* medio, término *m* medio
midriff [ˈmɪdˌrɪf] *n* : diafragma *m*
midshipman [ˈmɪdˌʃɪpmən, ˌmɪdˈʃɪp-] *n, pl* **-men** [-mən, -ˌmɛn] : guardiamarina *m*
midst¹ [ˈmɪdst] *n* : medio *m* ⟨in our midst : entre nosotros⟩ ⟨in the midst of : en medio de⟩
midst² *prep* : entre
midstream [ˈmɪdˈstri:m, -ˌstri:m] *n* : medio *m* de la corriente ⟨in the midstream of his career : en medio de su carrera⟩
midsummer [ˈmɪdˈsʌmər, -ˌsʌ-] *n* : pleno verano *m*
midtown [ˈmɪdˌtaʊn] *n* : centro *m* (de una ciudad)
midway [ˈmɪdˌweɪ] *adv* HALFWAY : a mitad de camino
midweek [ˈmɪdˌwi:k] *n* : medio *m* de la semana ⟨in midweek : a media semana⟩
midwife [ˈmɪdˌwaɪf] *n, pl* **-wives** [-ˌwaɪvz] : partera *f*, comadrona *f*
midwinter [ˈmɪdˈwɪntər, -ˌwin-] *n* : pleno invierno *m*
midyear [ˈmɪdˌjɪr] *n* : medio *m* del año ⟨at midyear : a mediados del año⟩
mien [ˈmi:n] *n* : aspecto *m*, porte *m*, semblante *m*
miff [ˈmɪf] *vt* : ofender
might¹ [ˈmaɪt] (*used to express permission or possibility or as a polite alternative to* **may**) → **may** ⟨it might be true : podría ser verdad⟩ ⟨might I speak with Sarah? : ¿se puede hablar con Sarah?⟩
might² *n* : fuerza *f*, poder *m*
mightily [ˈmaɪt̬əli] *adv* : con mucha fuerza, poderosamente
mighty¹ [ˈmaɪt̬i] *adv* VERY : muy ⟨mighty good : muy bueno, buenísimo⟩
mighty² *adj* **mightier; -est 1** POWERFUL : poderoso, potente **2** GREAT : grande, imponente
migraine [ˈmaɪˌgreɪn] *n* : jaqueca *f*, migraña *f*
migrant [ˈmaɪgrənt] *n* : trabajador *m*, -dora *f* ambulante
migrate [ˈmaɪˌgreɪt] *vi* **-grated; -grating** : emigrar
migration [maɪˈgreɪʃən] *n* : migración *f*
migratory [ˈmaɪgrəˌtori] *adj* : migratorio
mild [ˈmaɪld] *adj* **1** GENTLE : apacible, suave ⟨a mild disposition : un temperamento suave⟩ **2** LIGHT : leve, ligero ⟨a mild punishment : un castigo leve, un castigo poco severo⟩ **3** TEMPERATE : templado (dícese del clima) — **mildly** *adv*
mildew¹ [ˈmɪlˌdu:, -ˌdju:] *vi* : enmohecerse
mildew² *n* : moho *m*
mildness [ˈmaɪldnəs] *n* : apacibilidad *f*, suavidad *f*
mile [ˈmaɪl] *n* : milla *f*
mileage [ˈmaɪlɪʤ] *n* **1** ALLOWANCE : viáticos *mpl* (pagados por milla recorrida) **2** : distancia *f* recorrida (en millas), kilometraje *m*
milestone [ˈmaɪlˌsto:n] *n* LANDMARK : hito *m*, jalón *m* ⟨a milestone in his life : un hito en su vida⟩
milieu [mi:lˈju:, -ˈjø] *n, pl* **-lieus** *or* **-lieux** [-ˈju:z, -ˈjø] SURROUNDINGS : entorno *m*, medio *m*, ambiente *m*
militant¹ [ˈmɪlətənt] *adj* : militante, combativo
militant² *n* : militante *mf*
militarism [ˈmɪlət̬əˌrɪzəm] *n* : militarismo *m*
militaristic [ˌmɪlət̬əˈrɪstɪk] *adj* : militarista
military¹ [ˈmɪləˌtɛri] *adj* : militar
military² *n* **the military** : las fuerzas armadas
militia [məˈlɪʃə] *n* : milicia *f*
milk¹ [ˈmɪlk] *vt* **1** : ordeñar (una vaca, etc.) **2** EXPLOIT : explotar

milk[2] *n* : leche *f*

milkman [ˈmɪlk,mæn, -mən] *n, pl* **-men** [-mən, -ˌmɛn] : lechero *m*

milk shake *n* : batido *m*, licuado *m*

milkweed [ˈmɪlk,wi:d] *n* : algodoncillo *m*

milky [ˈmɪlki] *adj* **milkier; -est** : lechoso

Milky Way *n* : Vía *f* Láctea

mill[1] [ˈmɪl] *vt* : moler (granos), fresar (metales), acordonar (monedas) — *vi* **to mill about** : arremolinarse

mill[2] *n* **1** : molino *m* (para moler granos) **2** FACTORY : fábrica *f* ⟨textile mill : fábrica textil⟩ **3** GRINDER : molinillo *m*

millennium [məˈlɛniəm] *n, pl* **-nia** [-niə] *or* **-niums** : milenio *m*

miller [ˈmɪlər] *n* : molinero *m*, -ra *f*

millet [ˈmɪlət] *n* : mijo *m*

milligram [ˈmɪlə,græm] *n* : miligramo *m*

milliliter [ˈmɪlə,li:tər] *n* : mililitro *m*

millimeter [ˈmɪlə,mi:ţər] *n* : milímetro *m*

milliner [ˈmɪlənər] *n* : sombrerero *m*, -ra *f* (de señoras)

millinery [ˈmɪlə,nɛri] *n* : sombreros *mpl* de señora

million[1] [ˈmɪljən] *adj* **a million** : un millón de

million[2] *n, pl* **millions** *or* **million** : millón *m*

millionaire [ˌmɪljəˈnær, ˈmɪljə,nær] *n* : millonario *m*, -ria *f*

millionth[1] [ˈmɪljənθ] *adj* : millonésimo

millionth[2] *n* : millonésimo *m*

millipede [ˈmɪlə,pi:d] *n* : milpiés *m*

millstone [ˈmɪl,sto:n] *n* : rueda *f* de molino, muela *f*

mime[1] [ˈmaɪm] *v* **mimed; miming** *vt* MIMIC : imitar, remedar — *vi* PANTOMIME : hacer la mímica

mime[2] *n* **1** : mimo *mf* **2** PANTOMIME : pantomima *f*

mimeograph [ˈmɪmiə,græf] *n* : mimeógrafo *m*

mimic[1] [ˈmɪmɪk] *vt* **-icked; -icking** : imitar, remedar

mimic[2] *n* : imitador *m*, -dora *f*

mimicry [ˈmɪmɪkri] *n, pl* **-ries** : mímica *f*, imitación *f*

minaret [ˌmɪnəˈrɛt] *n* : alminar *m*, minarete *m*

mince [ˈmɪnts] *v* **minced; mincing** *vt* **1** CHOP : picar, moler (carne) **2 not to mince one's words** : no tener uno pelos en la lengua — *vi* : caminar de manera afectada

mincemeat [ˈmɪnts,mi:t] *n* : mezcla *f* de fruta picada, sebo, y especias

mind[1] [ˈmaɪnd] *vt* **1** TEND : cuidar, atender ⟨mind the children : cuida a los niños⟩ **2** OBEY : obedecer **3** : preocuparse por, sentirse molestado por ⟨I don't mind his jokes : sus bromas no me molestan⟩ **4** : tener cuidado con ⟨mind the ladder! : ¡cuidado con la escalera!⟩ — *vi* **1** OBEY : obedecer **2** CARE : importarle a uno ⟨I don't mind : no me importa, me es igual⟩

mind[2] *n* **1** MEMORY : memoria *f*, recuerdo *m* ⟨keep it in mind : téngalo en cuenta⟩ **2** : mente *f* ⟨the mind and the body : la mente y el cuerpo⟩ **3** INTENTION : intención *f*, propósito *m* ⟨to have a mind to do something : tener intención de hacer algo⟩ **4** : razón *f* ⟨he's out of his mind : está loco⟩ **5** OPINION : opinión *f* ⟨to change one's mind : cambiar de opinión⟩ **6** INTELLECT : capacidad *f* intelectual

minded [ˈmaɪndəd] *adj* **1** (*used in combination*) ⟨narrow-minded : de mentalidad cerrada⟩ ⟨health-minded : preocupado por la salud⟩ **2** INCLINED : inclinado

mindful [ˈmaɪndfəl] *adj* AWARE : consciente — **mindfully** *adv*

mindless [ˈmaɪndləs] *adj* **1** SENSELESS : estúpido, sin sentido ⟨mindless violence : violencia sin sentido⟩ **2** HEEDLESS : inconsciente

mindlessly [ˈmaɪndləsli] *adv* **1** SENSELESSLY : sin sentido **2** HEEDLESSLY : inconscientemente

mine[1] [ˈmaɪn] *vt* **mined; mining 1** : extraer (oro, etc.) **2** : minar (con artefactos explosivos)

mine[2] *n* : mina *f* ⟨gold mine : mina de oro⟩

mine[3] *pron* : mío, mía ⟨that one's mine : ése es el mío⟩ ⟨some friends of mine : unos amigos míos⟩

minefield [ˈmaɪn:fi:ld] *n* : campo *m* de minas

miner [ˈmaɪnər] *n* : minero *m*, -ra *f*

mineral [ˈmɪnərəl] *n* : mineral *m* — **mineral** *adj*

mineralogy [ˌmɪnəˈrɑləʤi, -ˈræ-] *n* : mineralogía *f*

mingle [ˈmɪŋgəl] *v* **-gled; -gling** *vt* MIX : mezclar — *vi* **1** MIX : mezclarse **2** CIRCULATE : circular

miniature[1] [ˈmɪniə,ʧʊr, ˈmɪnɪ,ʧʊr, -ʧər] *adj* : en miniatura, diminuto

miniature[2] *n* : miniatura *f*

minibus [ˈmɪni,bʌs] *n* : microbús *m*, pesera *f Mex*

minicomputer [ˈmɪnikəm,pju:ţər] *n* : minicomputadora *f*

minimal [ˈmɪnəməl] *adj* : mínimo

minimally [ˈmɪnəməli] *adv* : en grado mínimo

minimize [ˈmɪnə,maɪz] *vt* **-mized; -mizing** : minimizar

minimum[1] [ˈmɪnəməm] *adj* : mínimo

minimum[2] *n, pl* **-ma** [ˈmɪnəmə] *or* **-mums** : mínimo *m*

miniseries [ˈmɪni,sɪri:z] *n* : miniserie *f*

miniskirt [ˈmɪni,skərt] *n* : minifalda *f*

minister[1] [ˈmɪnəstər] *vi* **to minister to** : cuidar (de), atender a

minister[2] *n* **1** : pastor *m*, -tora *f* (de una iglesia) **2** : ministro *m*, -tra *f* (en política)

ministerial [ˌmɪnəˈstɪriəl] *adj* : ministerial

ministry [ˈmɪnəstri] *n, pl* **-tries 1** : ministerio *m* (en política) **2** : sacerdocio *m* (en el catolicismo), clerecía *f* (en el protestantismo)

minivan ['mɪni,væn] *n* : minivan *f*
mink ['mɪŋk] *n, pl* **mink** *or* **minks** : visón *m*
minnow ['mɪno:] *n, pl* **-nows** : pececillo *m* de agua dulce
minor[1] ['maɪnər] *adj* : menor
minor[2] *n* **1** : menor *mf* (de edad) **2** : asignatura *f* secundaria (de estudios)
minority [mə'nɔrət̬i, maɪ-] *n, pl* **-ties** : minoría *f*
minstrel ['mɪntstrəl] *n* : juglar *m*, trovador *m* (en el medioevo)
mint[1] ['mɪnt] *vt* : acuñar
mint[2] *adj* : sin usar ⟨in mint condition : como nuevo⟩
mint[3] *n* **1** : menta *f* ⟨mint tea : té de menta⟩ **2** : pastilla *f* de menta **3** : casa *f* de la moneda ⟨the U.S. Mint : la casa de la moneda de los EE.UU.⟩ **4** FORTUNE : dineral *m*, fortuna *f*
minuet [,mɪnjʊ'ɛt] *n* : minué *m*
minus[1] ['maɪnəs] *n* **1** : cantidad *f* negativa **2 minus sign** : signo *m* de menos
minus[2] *prep* **1** : menos ⟨four minus two : cuatro menos dos⟩ **2** WITHOUT : sin ⟨minus his hat : sin su sombrero⟩
minuscule *or* **miniscule** ['mɪnəs,kju:l, mɪ'nʌs-] *adj* : minúsculo
minute[1] [maɪ'nu:t, mɪ-, -'nju:t] *adj* **-nuter; -est 1** TINY : diminuto, minúsculo **2** DETAILED : minucioso
minute[2] ['mɪnət] *n* **1** : minuto *m* ⟨ten minutes late : diez minutos de retraso⟩ **2** MOMENT : momento *m* **3 minutes** *npl* : actas *fpl* (de una reunión)
minutely [maɪ'nu:tli, mɪ-, -'nju:t-] *adv* : minuciosamente
miracle ['mɪrɪkəl] *n* : milagro *m*
miraculous [mə'rækjələs] *adj* : milagroso — **miraculously** *adv*
mirage [mɪ'rɑʒ, *chiefly Brit* 'mɪr,ɑʒ] *n* : espejismo *m*
mire[1] ['maɪr] *vi* **mired; miring** : atascarse
mire[2] *n* **1** MUD : barro *m*, lodo *m* **2** : atolladero *m* ⟨stuck in a mire of debt : agobiado por la deuda⟩
mirror[1] ['mɪrər] *vt* : reflejar
mirror[2] *n* : espejo *m*
mirth ['mərθ] *n* : alegría *f*, regocijo *m*
mirthful ['mərθfəl] *adj* : alegre, regocijado
misadventure [,mɪsəd'vɛntʃər] *n* : malaventura *f*, desventura *f*
misanthrope ['mɪsən,θro:p] *n* : misántropo *m*, -pa *f*
misanthropic [,mɪsən'θrɑpɪk] *adj* : misantrópico
misanthropy [mɪ'sænθrəpi] *n* : misantropía *f*
misapprehend [,mɪs,æprə'hɛnd] *vt* : entender mal
misapprehension [,mɪs,æprə'hɛntʃən] *n* : malentendido *m*
misappropriate [,mɪsə'pro:pri,eɪt] *vt* **-ated; -ating** : malversar
misbegotten [,mɪsbi'gɑtən] *adj* **1** ILLEGITIMATE : ilegítimo **2** : mal concebido ⟨misbegotten laws : leyes mal concebidas⟩
misbehave [,mɪsbi'heɪv] *vi* **-haved; -having** : portarse mal
misbehavior [,mɪsbi'heɪvjər] *n* : mala conducta *f*
miscalculate [mɪs'kælkjə,leɪt] *v* **-lated; -lating** : calcular mal
miscalculation [mɪs,kælkjə'leɪʃən] *n* : error *m* de cálculo, mal cálculo *m*
miscarriage [,mɪs'kærɪdʒ, 'mɪs,kærɪdʒ] *n* **1** : aborto *m* **2** FAILURE : fracaso *m*, malogro *m* ⟨a miscarriage of justice : una injusticia, un error judicial⟩
miscarry [,mɪs'kæri, 'mɪs,kæri] *vi* **-ried; -rying 1** ABORT : abortar **2** FAIL : malograrse, fracasar
miscellaneous [,mɪsə'leɪniəs] *adj* : misceláneo
miscellany ['mɪsə,leɪni] *n, pl* **-nies** : miscelánea *f*
mischance [mɪs'tʃænts] *n* : desgracia *f*, infortunio *m*, mala suerte *f*
mischief ['mɪstʃəf] *n* : diabluras *fpl*, travesuras *fpl*
mischievous ['mɪstʃəvəs] *adj* : travieso, pícaro
mischievously ['mɪstʃəvəsli] *adv* : de manera traviesa
misconception [,mɪskən'sɛpʃən] *n* : concepto *m* erróneo, idea *f* falsa
misconduct [mɪs'kɑndəkt] *n* : mala conducta *f*
misconstrue [,mɪskən'stru:] *vt* **-strued; -struing** : malinterpretar
misdeed [mɪs'di:d] *n* : fechoría *f*
misdemeanor [,mɪsdɪ'mi:nər] *n* : delito *m* menor
miser ['maɪzər] *n* : avaro *m*, -ra *f*; tacaño *m*, -ña *f*
miserable ['mɪzərəbəl] *adj* **1** UNHAPPY : triste, desdichado **2** WRETCHED : miserable, desgraciado ⟨a miserable hut : una choza miserable⟩ **3** UNPLEASANT : desagradable, malo ⟨miserable weather : tiempo malísimo⟩ **4** CONTEMPTIBLE : despreciable, mísero ⟨for a miserable $10 : por unos míseros diez dólares⟩
miserably ['mɪzərəbli] *adv* **1** SADLY : tristemente **2** WRETCHEDLY : miserablemente, lamentablemente **3** UNFORTUNATELY : desgraciadamente
miserly ['maɪzərli] *adj* : avaro, tacaño
misery ['mɪzəri] *n, pl* **-eries** : miseria *f*, sufrimiento *m*
misfire [mɪs'faɪr] *vi* **-fired; -firing** : fallar
misfit ['mɪs,fɪt] *n* : inadaptado *m*, -da *f*
misfortune [mɪs'fɔrtʃən] *n* : desgracia *f*, desventura *f*, infortunio *m*
misgiving [mɪs'gɪvɪŋ] *n* : duda *f*, recelo *m*
misguided [mɪs'gaɪdəd] *adj* : desacertado, equivocado, mal informado
mishap ['mɪs,hæp] *n* : contratiempo *m*, percance *m*, accidente *m*
misinform [,mɪsɪn'fɔrm] *vt* : informar mal
misinterpret [,mɪsɪn'tərprət] *vt* : malinterpretar

misinterpretation [ˌmɪsɪnˌtərprəˈteɪ-ʃən] *n* : mala interpretación *f*, malentendido *m*
misjudge [mɪsˈʤʌʤ] *vt* **-judged; -judging** : juzgar mal
mislay [mɪsˈleɪ] *vt* **-laid** [-leɪd]; **-laying** : extraviar, perder
mislead [mɪsˈli:d] *vt* **-led** [-ˈlɛd]; **-leading** : engañar
misleading [mɪsˈli:dɪŋ] *adj* : engañoso
mismanage [mɪsˈmænɪʤ] *vt* **-aged; -aging** : administrar mal
mismanagement [mɪsˈmænɪʤmənt] *n* : mala administración *f*
misnomer [mɪsˈno:mər] *n* : nombre *m* inapropiado
misogynist [mɪˈsɑʤənɪst] *n* : misógino *m*
misogyny [məˈsɑʤəni] *n* : misoginia *f*
misplace [mɪsˈpleɪs] *vt* **-placed; -placing** : extraviar, perder
misprint [ˈmɪsˌprɪnt, mɪsˈ-] *n* : errata *f*, error *m* de imprenta
mispronounce [ˌmɪsprəˈnaʊnts] *vt* **-nounced; -nouncing** : pronunciar mal
mispronunciation [ˌmɪsprəˌnʌntsiˈeɪʃən] *n* : pronunciación *f* incorrecta
misquote [mɪsˈkwo:t] *vt* **-quoted; -quoting** : citar incorrectamente
misread [mɪsˈri:d] *vt* **-read; -reading** **1** : leer mal ⟨she misread the sentence : leyó mal la frase⟩ **2** MISUNDERSTAND : malinterpretar ⟨they misread his intention : malinterpretaron su intención⟩
misrepresent [ˌmɪsˌrɛprɪˈzɛnt] *vt* : distorsionar, falsear, tergiversar
misrule[1] [mɪsˈru:l] *vt* **-ruled; -ruling** : gobernar mal
misrule[2] *n* : mal gobierno *m*
miss[1] [ˈmɪs] *vt* **1** : errar, faltar ⟨to miss the target : no dar en el blanco⟩ **2** : no encontrar, perder ⟨they missed each other : no se encontraron⟩ ⟨I missed the plane : perdí el avión⟩ **3** : echar de menos, extrañar ⟨we miss him a lot : lo echamos mucho de menos⟩ **4** OVERLOOK : pasar por alto, perder (una oportunidad, etc.) **5** AVOID : evitar ⟨they just missed hitting the tree : por muy poco chocan contra el árbol⟩ **6** OMIT : saltarse ⟨he missed breakfast : se saltó el desayuno⟩
miss[2] *n* **1** : fallo *m* (de un tiro, etc.) **2** FAILURE : fracaso *m* **3** : señorita *f* ⟨Miss Jones called us : nos llamó la señorita Jones⟩ ⟨excuse me, miss : perdone, señorita⟩
missal [ˈmɪsəl] *n* : misal *m*
misshapen [mɪˈʃeɪpən] *adj* : deforme
missile [ˈmɪsəl] *n* **1** : misil *m* ⟨guided missile : misil guiado⟩ **2** PROJECTILE : proyectil *m*
missing [ˈmɪsɪŋ] *adj* **1** ABSENT : ausente ⟨who's missing? : ¿quién falta?⟩ **2** LOST : perdido, desaparecido ⟨missing persons : los desaparecidos⟩
mission [ˈmɪʃən] *n* **1** : misión *f* (mandada por una iglesia) **2** DELEGATION : misión *f*, delegación *f*, embajada *f* **3** TASK : misión *f*
missionary[1] [ˈmɪʃəˌnɛri] *adj* : misionero
missionary[2] *n, pl* **-aries** : misionero *m*, -ra *f*
missive [ˈmɪsɪv] *n* : misiva *f*
misspell [mɪsˈspɛl] *vt* : escribir mal
misspelling [mɪsˈspɛlɪŋ] *n* : falta *f* de ortografía
misstep [ˈmɪsˌstɛp] *n* : traspié *m*, tropezón *m*
mist [ˈmɪst] *n* **1** HAZE : neblina *f*, niebla *f* **2** SPRAY : rocío *m*
mistake[1] [mɪˈsteɪk] *vt* **-took** [-ˈstʊk]; **-taken** [-ˈsteɪkən]; **-taking** **1** MISINTERPRET : malinterpretar **2** CONFUSE : confundir ⟨he mistook her for Clara : la confundió con Clara⟩
mistake[2] *n* **1** MISUNDERSTANDING : malentendido *m*, confusión *f* **2** ERROR : error *m* ⟨I made a mistake : me equivoqué, cometí un error⟩
mistaken [mɪˈsteɪkən] *adj* WRONG : equivocado — **mistakenly** *adv*
mister [ˈmɪstər] *n* : señor *m* ⟨watch out, mister : cuidado, señor⟩
mistiness [ˈmɪstinəs] *n* : nebulosidad *f*
mistletoe [ˈmɪsəlˌto:] *n* : muérdago *m*
mistreat [mɪsˈtri:t] *vt* : maltratar
mistreatment [mɪsˈtri:tmənt] *n* : maltrato *m*, abuso *m*
mistress [ˈmɪstrəs] *n* **1** : dueña *f*, señora *f* (de una casa) **2** LOVER : amante *f*
mistrust[1] [mɪsˈtrʌst] *vt* : desconfiar de
mistrust[2] *n* : desconfianza *f*
mistrustful [mɪsˈtrʌstfəl] *adj* : desconfiado
misty [ˈmɪsti] *adj* **mistier; -est** **1** : neblinoso, nebuloso **2** TEARFUL : lloroso
misunderstand [ˌmɪsˌʌndərˈstænd] *vt* **-stood** [-ˈstʊd]; **-standing** **1** : entender mal **2** MISINTERPRET : malinterpretar ⟨don't misunderstand me : no me malinterpretes⟩
misunderstanding [ˌmɪsˌʌndərˈstændɪŋ] *n* **1** MISINTERPRETATION : malentendido *m* **2** DISAGREEMENT, QUARREL : disputa *f*, discusión *f*
misuse[1] [mɪsˈju:z] *vt* **-used; -using** **1** : emplear mal **2** ABUSE, MISTREAT : abusar de, maltratar
misuse[2] [mɪsˈju:s] *n* **1** : mal empleo *m*, mal uso *m* **2** WASTE : derroche *m*, despilfarro *m* **3** ABUSE : abuso *m*
mite [ˈmaɪt] *n* **1** : ácaro *m* **2** BIT : poco *m* ⟨a mite tired : un poquito cansado⟩
miter *or* **mitre** [ˈmaɪt̬ər] *n* **1** : mitra *f* (de un obispo) **2** *or* **miter joint** : inglete *m*
mitigate [ˈmɪt̬əˌgeɪt] *vt* **-gated; -gating** : mitigar, aliviar
mitigation [ˌmɪt̬əˈgeɪʃən] *n* : mitigación *f*, alivio *m*
mitosis [maɪˈto:sɪs] *n, pl* **-toses** [-ˌsi:z] : mitosis *f*
mitt [ˈmɪt] *n* : manopla *f*, guante *m* (de béisbol)

mitten ['mɪtən] *n* : manopla *f*, mitón *m*
mix[1] ['mɪks] *vt* **1** COMBINE : mezclar **2** STIR : remover, revolver **3 to mix up** CONFUSE : confundir — *vi* : mezclarse
mix[2] *n* : mezcla *f*
mixer ['mɪksər] *n* **1** : batidora *f* (de la cocina) **2 cement mixer** : hormigonera *f*
mixture ['mɪkstʃər] *n* : mezcla *f*
mix–up ['mɪks,ʌp] *n* CONFUSION : confusión *f*, lío *m fam*
mnemonic [nɪ'manɪk] *adj* : mnemónico
moan[1] ['mo:n] *vi* : gemir
moan[2] *n* : gemido *m*
moat ['mo:t] *n* : foso *m*
mob[1] ['mab] *vt* **mobbed; mobbing 1** ATTACK : atacar en masa **2** HOUND : acosar, rodear
mob[2] *n* **1** THRONG : multitud *f*, turba *f*, muchedumbre *f* **2** GANG : pandilla *f*
mobile[1] ['mo:bəl, -ˌbi:l, -ˌbaɪl] *adj* : móvil ⟨mobile home : caravana, casa rodante⟩
mobile[2] ['moˌbi:l] *n* : móvil *m*
mobility [mo'bɪləṭi] *n* : movilidad *f*
mobilize ['mo:bəˌlaɪz] *vt* **-lized; -lizing** : movilizar
moccasin ['makəsən] *n* **1** : mocasín *m* **2** *or* **water moccasin** : serpiente *f* venenosa de Norteamérica
mocha ['mo:kə] *n* **1** : mezcla *f* de café y chocolate **2** : color *m* chocolate
mock[1] ['mak, 'mɔk] *vt* **1** RIDICULE : burlarse de, mofarse de **2** MIMIC : imitar, remedar (de manera burlona)
mock[2] *adj* **1** SIMULATED : simulado **2** PHONY : falso
mockery ['makəri, 'mɔ-] *n, pl* **-eries 1** JEER, TAUNT : burla *f*, mofa *f* ⟨to make a mockery of : burlarse de⟩ **2** FAKE : imitación *f* (burlona)
mockingbird ['makɪŋˌbərd, 'mɔ-] *n* : sinsonte *m*
mode ['mo:d] *n* **1** FORM : modo *m*, forma *f* **2** MANNER : modo *m*, manera *f*, estilo *m* **3** FASHION : moda *f*
model[1] ['madəl] *v* **-eled** *or* **-elled; -eling** *or* **-elling** *vt* SHAPE : modelar — *vi* : trabajar de modelo
model[2] *adj* **1** EXEMPLARY : modelo, ejemplar ⟨a model student : un estudiante modelo⟩ **2** MINIATURE : en miniatura
model[3] *n* **1** PATTERN : modelo *m* **2** MINIATURE : modelo *m*, miniatura *f* **3** EXAMPLE : modelo *m*, ejemplo *m* **4** MANNEQUIN : modelo *mf* **5** DESIGN : modelo *m* ⟨the '97 model : el modelo '97⟩
modem ['mo:dəm, -ˌdɛm] *n* : módem *m*
moderate[1] ['madəˌreɪt] *v* **-ated; -ating** *vt* : moderar, temperar — *vi* **1** CALM : moderarse, calmarse **2** : fungir como moderador (en un debate, etc.)
moderate[2] ['madərət] *adj* : moderado
moderate[3] ['madərət] *n* : moderado *m*, -da *f*
moderately ['madərətli] *adv* **1** : con moderación **2** FAIRLY : medianamente
moderation [ˌmadə'reɪʃən] *n* : moderación *f*
moderator ['madəˌreɪṭər] *n* : moderador *m*, -dora *f*
modern ['madərn] *adj* : moderno
modernism ['madərˌnɪzəm] *n* : modernismo *m*
modernist ['madərnɪst] *n* : modernista *mf* — **modernist** *adj*
modernity [mə'dərnəṭi] *n* : modernidad *f*
modernization [ˌmadərnə'zeɪʃən] *n* : modernización *f*
modernize ['madərˌnaɪz] *v* **-ized; -izing** *vt* : modernizar — *vi* : modernizarse
modest ['madəst] *adj* **1** HUMBLE : modesto **2** DEMURE : recatado, pudoroso **3** MODERATE : modesto, moderado — **modestly** *adv*
modesty ['madəsti] *n* : modestia *f*
modicum ['madɪkəm] *n* : mínimo *m*, pizca *f*
modification [ˌmadəfə'keɪʃən] *n* : modificación *f*
modifier ['madəˌfaɪər] *n* : modificante *m*, modificador *m*
modify ['madəˌfaɪ] *vt* **-fied; -fying** : modificar, calificar (en gramática)
modish ['mo:dɪʃ] *adj* STYLISH : a la moda, de moda
modular ['madʒələr] *adj* : modular
modulate ['madʒəˌleɪt] *vt* **-lated; -lating** : modular
modulation [ˌmadʒə'leɪʃən] *n* : modulación *f*
module ['maˌdʒu:l] *n* : módulo *m*
mogul ['mo:gəl] *n* : magnate *mf*; potentado *m*, -da *f*
mohair ['mo:ˌhær] *n* : mohair *m*
moist ['mɔɪst] *adj* : húmedo
moisten ['mɔɪsən] *vt* : humedecer
moistness ['mɔɪstnəs] *n* : humedad *f*
moisture ['mɔɪstʃər] *n* : humedad *f*
moisturize ['mɔɪstʃəˌraɪz] *vt* **-ized; -izing** : humedecer (el aire), humectar (la piel)
moisturizer ['mɔɪtʃəˌraɪzər] *n* : crema *f* hidratante, crema *f* humectante
molar ['mo:lər] *n* : muela *f*, molar *m*
molasses [mə'læsəz] *n* : melaza *f*
mold[1] ['mo:ld] *vt* : moldear, formar (carácter, etc.) — *vi* : enmohecerse ⟨the bread will mold : el pan se enmohecerá⟩
mold[2] *n* **1** *or* **leaf mold** : mantillo *m* **2** FORM : molde *m* ⟨to break the mold : romper el molde⟩ **3** FUNGUS : moho *m*
molder ['mo:ldər] *vi* CRUMBLE : desmoronarse
molding ['mo:ldɪŋ] *n* : moldura *f* (en arquitectura)
moldy ['mo:ldi] *adj* **moldier; -est** : mohoso
mole ['mo:l] *n* **1** : lunar *m* (en la piel) **2** : topo *m* (animal)

molecule ['mɑlɪ,kju:l] *n* : molécula *f* — **molecular** [mə'lɛkjələr] *adj*
molehill ['mo:l,hɪl] *n* : topera *f*
molest [mə'lɛst] *vt* **1** ANNOY, DISTURB : molestar **2** : abusar (sexualmente)
mollify ['mɑlə,faɪ] *vt* **-fied; -fying** : apaciguar, aplacar
mollusk *or* **mollusc** ['mɑləsk] *n* : molusco *m*
mollycoddle ['mɑli,kɑdəl] *vt* **-dled; -dling** PAMPER : consentir, mimar
molt ['mo:lt] *vi* : mudar, hacer la muda
molten ['mo:ltən] *adj* : fundido
mom ['mɑm, 'mʌm] *n* : mamá *f*
moment ['mo:mənt] *n* **1** INSTANT : momento *m* ⟨one moment, please : un momento, por favor⟩ **2** TIME : momento *m* ⟨at the moment : de momento, actualmente⟩ ⟨from that moment : desde entonces⟩ **3** IMPORTANCE : importancia *f* ⟨of great moment : de gran importancia⟩
momentarily [,mo:mən'tɛrəli] *adv* **1** : momentáneamente **2** SOON : dentro de poco, pronto
momentary ['mo:mən,tɛri] *adj* : momentáneo
momentous [mo'mɛntəs] *adj* : de suma importancia, fatídico
momentum [mo'mɛntəm] *n, pl* **-ta** [-tə] *or* **-tums 1** : momento *m* (en física) **2** IMPETUS : ímpetu *m*, impulso *m*
mommy ['mɑmi, 'mʌ-] *n* : mami *f*
monarch ['mɑ,nɑrk, -nərk] *n* : monarca *mf*
monarchism ['mɑ,nɑr,kɪzəm, -nər-] *n* : monarquismo *m*
monarchist ['mɑ,nɑrkɪst, -nər-] *n* : monárquico *m*, -ca *f*
monarchy ['mɑ,nɑrki, -nər-] *n, pl* **-chies** : monarquía *f*
monastery ['mɑnə,stɛri] *n, pl* **-teries** : monasterio *m*
monastic [mə'næstɪk] *adj* : monástico — **monastically** [-tɪkli] *adv*
Monday ['mʌn,deɪ, -di] *n* : lunes *m*
monetary ['mɑnə,tɛri, 'mʌnə-] *adj* : monetario
money ['mʌni] *n, pl* **-eys** *or* **-ies** ['mʌniz] : dinero *m*, plata *f*
moneyed ['mʌnid] *adj* : adinerado
moneylender ['mʌni,lɛndər] *n* : prestamista *mf*
money order *n* : giro *m* postal
Mongol ['mɑŋgəl, -,go:l] → **Mongolian**
Mongolian [mɑn'go:liən, mɑŋ-] *n* : mongol *m*, -gola *f* — **Mongolian** *adj*
mongoose ['mɑn,gu:s, 'mɑŋ-] *n, pl* **-gooses** : mangosta *f*
mongrel ['mɑŋgrəl, 'mʌŋ-] *n* **1** : perro *m* mestizo, perro *m* corriente *Mex* **2** HYBRID : híbrido *m*
monitor[1] ['mɑnət̬ər] *vt* : controlar, monitorear
monitor[2] *n* **1** : ayudante *mf* (en una escuela) **2** : monitor *m* (de una computadora, etc.)
monk ['mʌŋk] *n* : monje *m*
monkey[1] ['mʌŋki] *vi* **-keyed; -keying 1 to monkey around** : hacer payasadas, payasear **2 to monkey with** : juguetear con
monkey[2] *n, pl* **-keys** : mono *m*, -na *f*
monkeyshines ['mʌŋki,ʃaɪnz] *npl* PRANKS : picardías *fpl*, travesuras *fpl*
monkey wrench *n* : llave *f* inglesa
monocle ['mɑnɪkəl] *n* : monóculo *m*
monogamous [mə'nɑgəməs] *adj* : monógamo
monogamy [mə'nɑgəmi] *n* : monogamia *f*
monogram[1] ['mɑnə,græm] *vt* **-grammed; -gramming** : marcar con monograma ⟨monogrammed towels : toallas con monograma⟩
monogram[2] *n* : monograma *m*
monograph ['mɑnə,græf] *n* : monografía *f*
monolingual [,mɑnə'lɪŋgwəl] *adj* : monolingüe
monolith ['mɑnə,lɪθ] *n* : monolito *m*
monolithic [,mɑnə'lɪθɪk] *adj* : monolítico
monologue ['mɑnə,lɔg] *n* : monólogo *m*
monoplane ['mɑnə,pleɪn] *n* : monoplano *m*
monopolize [mə'nɑpə,laɪz] *vt* **-lized; -lizing** : monopolizar
monopoly [mə'nɑpəli] *n, pl* **-lies** : monopolio *m*
monosyllabic [,mɑnosə'læbɪk] *adj* : monosilábico
monosyllable ['mɑno,sɪləbəl] *n* : monosílabo *m*
monotheism ['mɑnoθi:,ɪzəm] *n* : monoteísmo *m*
monotheistic [,mɑnoθi:'ɪstɪk] *adj* : monoteísta
monotone ['mɑnə,to:n] *n* : voz *f* monótona
monotonous [mə'nɑtənəs] *adj* : monótono — **monotonously** *adv*
monotony [mə'nɑtəni] *n* : monotonía *f*, uniformidad *f*
monoxide [mə'nɑk,saɪd] *n* : monóxido *m*
monsoon [mɑn'su:n] *n* : monzón *m*
monster ['mɑntstər] *n* : monstruo *m*
monstrosity [mɑn'strɑsət̬i] *n, pl* **-ties** : monstruosidad *f*
monstrous ['mɑntstrəs] *adj* : monstruoso — **monstrously** *adv*
montage [mɑn'tɑʒ] *n* : montaje *m*
month ['mʌnθ] *n* : mes *m*
monthly[1] ['mʌnθli] *adv* : mensualmente
monthly[2] *adj* : mensual
monthly[3] *n, pl* **-lies** : publicación *f* mensual
monument ['mɑnjəmənt] *n* : monumento *m*
monumental [,mɑnjə'mɛntəl] *adj* : monumental — **monumentally** *adv*
moo[1] ['mu:] *vi* : mugir
moo[2] *n* : mugido *m*
mood ['mu:d] *n* : humor *m* ⟨to be in a good mood : estar de buen humor⟩ ⟨to

be in the mood for : tener ganas de⟩ ⟨to be in no mood for : no estar para⟩
moodiness [ˈmuːdinəs] *n* **1** SADNESS : melancolía *f*, tristeza *f* **2** : cambios *mpl* de humor, carácter *m* temperamental
moody [ˈmuːdi] *adj* **moodier; -est 1** GLOOMY : melancólico, deprimido **2** TEMPERAMENTAL : temperamental, de humor variable
moon [ˈmuːn] *n* : luna *f*
moonbeam [ˈmuːn,biːm] *n* : rayo *m* de luna
moonlight[1] [ˈmuːn,laɪt] *vi* : estar pluriempleado
moonlight[2] *n* : claro *m* de luna, luz *f* de la luna
moonlit [ˈmuːn,lɪt] *adj* : iluminado por la luna ⟨a moonlit night : una noche de luna⟩
moonshine [ˈmuːn,ʃaɪn] *n* **1** MOONLIGHT : luz *f* de la luna **2** NONSENSE : disparates *mpl*, tonterías *fpl* **3** : whisky *m* destilado ilegalmente
moor[1] [ˈmʊr, ˈmɔr] *vt* : amarrar
moor[2] *n* : brezal *m*, páramo *m*
Moor [ˈmʊr] *n* : moro *m*, -ra *f*
mooring [ˈmʊrɪŋ, ˈmɔr-] *n* DOCK : atracadero *m*
Moorish [ˈmʊrɪʃ] *adj* : moro
moose [ˈmuːs] *ns & pl* : alce *m* (norteamericano)
moot [ˈmuːt] *adj* DEBATABLE : discutible
mop[1] [ˈmɑp] *vt* **mopped; mopping** : trapear
mop[2] *n* : trapeador *m*
mope [ˈmoːp] *vi* **moped; moping** : andar deprimido, quedar abatido
moped [ˈmoː,pɛd] *n* : ciclomotor *m*
moraine [məˈreɪn] *n* : morena *f*
moral[1] [ˈmɔrəl] *adj* : moral ⟨moral judgment : juicio moral⟩ ⟨moral support : apoyo moral⟩ — **morally** *adv*
moral[2] *n* **1** : moraleja *f* (de un cuento, etc.) **2 morals** *npl* : moral *f*, moralidad *f*
morale [məˈræl] *n* : moral *f*
moralist [ˈmɔrəlɪst] *n* : moralista *mf*
moralistic [,mɔrəˈlɪstɪk] *adj* : moralista
morality [məˈrælət̬i] *n, pl* **-ties** : moralidad *f*
morass [məˈræs] *n* **1** SWAMP : ciénaga *f*, pantano *m* **2** CONFUSION, MESS : lío *m fam*, embrollo *m*
moratorium [,mɔrəˈtoriəm] *n, pl* **-riums** *or* **-ria** [-iə] : moratoria *f*
moray [ˈmɔr,eɪ, məˈreɪ] *n* : morena *f*
morbid [ˈmɔrbɪd] *adj* **1** : mórbido, morboso (en medicina) **2** GRUESOME : morboso, horripilante
morbidity [mɔrˈbɪdət̬i] *n, pl* **-ties** : morbosidad *f*
more[1] [ˈmor] *adv* : más ⟨what more can I say? : ¿qué más puedo decir?⟩ ⟨more important : más importante⟩ ⟨once more : una vez más⟩
more[2] *adj* : más ⟨nothing more than that : nada más que eso⟩ ⟨more work : más trabajo⟩
more[3] *n* : más *m* ⟨the more you eat, the more you want : cuanto más comes, tanto más quieres⟩
more[4] *pron* : más ⟨more were found : se encontraron más⟩
moreover [morˈoːvər] *adv* : además
mores [ˈmɔr,eɪz, -iːz] *npl* CUSTOMS : costumbres *fpl*, tradiciones *fpl*
morgue [ˈmɔrg] *n* : morgue *f*
moribund [ˈmɔrə,bʌnd] *adj* : moribundo
Mormon [ˈmɔrmən] *n* : mormón *m*, -mona *f* — **Mormon** *adj*
morn [ˈmɔrn] → **morning**
morning [ˈmɔrnɪŋ] *n* : mañana *f* ⟨good morning! : ¡buenos días!⟩
Moroccan [məˈrɑkən] *n* : marroquí *mf* — **Moroccan** *adj*
moron [ˈmor,ɑn] *n* **1** : retrasado *m*, -da *f* mental **2** DUNCE : estúpido *m*, -da *f*; tonto *m*, -ta *f*
morose [məˈroːs] *adj* : hosco, sombrío — **morosely** *adv*
moroseness [məˈroːsnəs] *n* : malhumor *m*
morphine [ˈmɔr,fiːn] *n* : morfina *f*
morphology [mɔrˈfɑləʤi] *n, pl* **-gies** : morfología *f*
morrow [ˈmɑroː] *n* : día *m* siguiente
Morse code [ˈmɔrs] *n* : código *m* morse
morsel [ˈmɔrsəl] *n* **1** BITE : bocado *m* **2** FRAGMENT : pedazo *m*
mortal[1] [ˈmɔrt̬əl] *adj* : mortal ⟨mortal blow : golpe mortal⟩ ⟨mortal fear : miedo mortal⟩ — **mortally** *adv*
mortal[2] *n* : mortal *mf*
mortality [mɔrˈtælət̬i] *n* : mortalidad *f*
mortar [ˈmɔrt̬ər] *n* **1** : mortero *m*, molcajete *m Mex* ⟨mortar and pestle : mortero y maja⟩ **2** : mortero *m* ⟨mortar shell : granada de mortero⟩ **3** CEMENT : mortero *m*, argamasa *f*
mortgage[1] [ˈmɔrgɪʤ] *vt* **-gaged; -gaging** : hipotecar
mortgage[2] *n* : hipoteca *f*
mortification [,mɔrt̬əfəˈkeɪʃən] *n* **1** : mortificación *f* **2** HUMILIATION : humillación *f*, vergüenza *f*
mortify [ˈmɔrt̬ə,faɪ] *vt* **-fied; -fying 1** : mortificar (en religión) **2** HUMILIATE : humillar, avergonzar
mortuary [ˈmɔrʧə,wɛri] *n, pl* **-aries** FUNERAL HOME : funeraria *f*
mosaic [moˈzeɪɪk] *n* : mosaico *m*
Moslem [ˈmɑzləm] → **Muslim**
mosque [ˈmɑsk] *n* : mezquita *f*
mosquito [məˈskiːt̬o] *n, pl* **-toes** : mosquito *m*, zancudo *m*
moss [ˈmɔs] *n* : musgo *m*
mossy [ˈmɔsi] *adj* **-ier; -est** : musgoso
most[1] [ˈmoːst] *adv* : más ⟨the most interesting book : el libro más interesante⟩
most[2] *adj* **1** : la mayoría de, la mayor parte de ⟨most people : la mayoría de la gente⟩ **2** GREATEST : más (dícese de los números), mayor (dícese de las cantidades) ⟨the most ability : la mayor capacidad⟩

most[3] *n* : más *m*, máximo *m* ⟨the most I can do : lo más que puedo hacer⟩ ⟨three weeks at the most : tres semanas como máximo⟩

most[4] *pron* : la mayoría, la mayor parte ⟨most will go : la mayoría irá⟩

mostly [ˈmoːstli] *adv* MAINLY : en su mayor parte, principalmente

mote [ˈmoːt] *n* SPECK : mota *f*

motel [moˈtɛl] *n* : motel *m*

moth [ˈmɔθ] *n* : palomilla *f*, polilla *f*

mother[1] [ˈmʌðər] *vt* **1** BEAR : dar a luz a **2** PROTECT : cuidar de, proteger

mother[2] *n* : madre *f*

motherhood [ˈmʌðərˌhʊd] *n* : maternidad *f*

mother–in–law [ˈmʌðərɪnˌlɔ] *n, pl* **mothers–in–law** : suegra *f*

motherland [ˈmʌðərˌlænd] *n* : patria *f*

motherly [ˈmʌðərli] *adj* : maternal

mother–of–pearl [ˌmʌðərəvˈpərl] *n* : nácar *m*, madreperla *f*

motif [moˈtiːf] *n* : motivo *m*

motion[1] [ˈmoːʃən] *vt* : hacerle señas (a alguien) ⟨she motioned us to come in : nos hizo señas para que entráramos⟩

motion[2] *n* **1** MOVEMENT : movimiento *m* ⟨to set in motion : poner en marcha⟩ **2** PROPOSAL : moción *f* ⟨to second a motion : apoyar una moción⟩

motionless [ˈmoːʃənləs] *adj* : inmóvil, quieto

motion picture *n* MOVIE : película *f*

motivate [ˈmoːt̬əˌveɪt] *vt* **-vated; -vating** : motivar, mover, inducir

motivation [ˌmoːt̬əˈveɪʃən] *n* : motivación *f*

motive[1] [ˈmoːt̬ɪv] *adj* : motor ⟨motive power : fuerza motriz⟩

motive[2] *n* : motivo *m*, móvil *m*

motley [ˈmɑtli] *adj* : abigarrado, variopinto

motor[1] [ˈmoːt̬ər] *vi* : viajar en coche

motor[2] *n* : motor *m*

motorbike [ˈmoːt̬ərˌbaɪk] *n* : motocicleta *f* (pequeña), moto *f*

motorboat [ˈmoːt̬ərˌboːt] *n* : bote *m* a motor, lancha *f* motora

motorcar [ˈmoːt̬ərˌkɑr] *n* : automóvil *m*

motorcycle [ˈmoːt̬ərˌsaɪkəl] *n* : motocicleta *f*

motorcyclist [ˈmoːt̬ərˌsaɪkəlɪst] *n* : motociclista *mf*

motorist [ˈmoːt̬ərɪst] *n* : automovilista *mf*, motorista *mf*

mottle [ˈmɑt̬əl] *vt* **-tled; -tling** : manchar, motear ⟨mottled skin : piel manchada⟩ ⟨a mottled surface : una superficie moteada⟩

motto [ˈmɑt̬oː] *n, pl* **-toes** : lema *m*

mould [ˈmoːld] → **mold**

mound [ˈmaʊnd] *n* **1** PILE : montón *m* **2** KNOLL : montículo *m* **3 burial mound** : túmulo *m*

mount[1] [ˈmaʊnt] *vt* **1** : montar a (un caballo), montar en (una bicicleta), subir a **2** : montar (artillería, etc.) — *vi* INCREASE : aumentar

mount[2] *n* **1** SUPPORT : soporte *m* **2** HORSE : caballería *f*, montura *f* **3** MOUNTAIN : monte *m*, montaña *f*

mountain [ˈmaʊntən] *n* : montaña *f*

mountaineer [ˌmaʊntənˈɪr] *n* : alpinista *mf*; montañero *m*, -ra *f*

mountaineering [ˌmaʊntənˈɪrɪŋ] *n* : alpinismo *m*

mountainous [ˈmaʊntənəs] *adj* : montañoso

mountaintop [ˈmaʊntənˌtɑp] *n* : cima *f*, cumbre *f*

mourn [ˈmorn] *vt* : llorar (por), lamentar ⟨to mourn the death of : llorar la muerte de⟩ — *vi* : llorar, estar de luto

mourner [ˈmornər] *n* : doliente *mf*

mournful [ˈmornfəl] *adj* **1** SORROWFUL : lloroso, plañidero, triste **2** GLOOMY : deprimente, entristecedor — **mournfully** *adv*

mourning [ˈmornɪŋ] *n* : duelo *m*, luto *m*

mouse [ˈmaʊs] *n, pl* **mice** [ˈmaɪs] **1** : ratón *m*, -tona *f* **2** : ratón *m* (de una computadora)

mousetrap [ˈmaʊsˌtræp] *n* : ratonera *f*

mousse [ˈmuːs] *n* : mousse *mf*

moustache [ˈmʌˌstæʃ, məˈstæʃ] → **mustache**

mouth[1] [ˈmaʊð] *vt* **1** : decir con poca sinceridad, repetir sin comprensión **2** : articular en silencio ⟨she mouthed the words : formó las palabras con los labios⟩

mouth[2] [ˈmaʊθ] *n* : boca *f* (de una persona o un animal), entrada *f* (de un túnel), desembocadura *f* (de un río)

mouthful [ˈmaʊθˌfʊl] *n* : bocado *m* (de comida), bocanada *f* (de líquido o humo)

mouthpiece [ˈmaʊθˌpiːs] *n* : boquilla *f* (de un instrumento musical)

mouthwash [ˈmaʊθˌwɔʃ, -ˌwɑʃ] *n* : enjuague *m* bucal

movable [ˈmuːvəbəl] *or* **moveable** *adj* : movible, móvil

move[1] [ˈmuːv] *v* **moved; moving** *vi* **1** GO : ir **2** RELOCATE : mudarse, trasladarse **3** STIR : moverse ⟨don't move! : ¡no te muevas!⟩ **4** ACT : actuar — *vt* **1** : mover ⟨move it over there : ponlo allí⟩ ⟨he kept moving his feet : no dejaba de mover los pies⟩ **2** INDUCE, PERSUADE : inducir, persuadir, mover **3** TOUCH : conmover ⟨it moved him to tears : lo hizo llorar⟩ **4** PROPOSE : proponer

move[2] *n* **1** MOVEMENT : movimiento *m* **2** RELOCATION : mudanza *f* (de casa), traslado *m* **3** STEP : paso *m* ⟨a good move : un paso acertado⟩

movement [ˈmuːvmənt] *n* : movimiento *m*

mover [ˈmuːvər] *n* : persona *f* que hace mudanzas

movie [ˈmuːvi] *n* **1** : película *f* **2 movies** *npl* : cine *m*

moving [ˈmuːvɪŋ] *adj* **1** : en movimiento ⟨a moving target : un blanco móvil⟩

2 TOUCHING : conmovedor, emocionante
mow[1] ['mo:] *vt* **mowed; mowed** *or* **mown** ['mo:n]; **mowing** : cortar (la hierba)
mow[2] ['maʊ] *n* : pajar *m*
mower ['mo:ər] → **lawn mower**
Mr. ['mɪstər] *n, pl* **Messrs.** ['mɛsərz] : señor *m*
Mrs. ['mɪsəz, -səs, *esp South* 'mɪzəz, -zəs] *n, pl* **Mesdames** [meɪ'dɑm, -'dæm] : señora *f*
Ms. ['mɪz] *n* : señora *f*, señorita *f*
much[1] ['mʌʧ] *adv* **more** ['mor]; **most** ['mo:st] : mucho ⟨I'm much happier : estoy mucho más contenta⟩ ⟨she talks as much as I do : habla tanto como yo⟩
much[2] *adj* **more; most** : mucho ⟨it has much validity : tiene mucha validez⟩ ⟨too much time : demasiado tiempo⟩
much[3] *pron* : mucho, -cha ⟨I don't need much : no necesito mucho⟩
mucilage ['mju:səlɪʤ] *n* : mucílago *m*
muck ['mʌk] *n* **1** MANURE : estiércol *m* **2** DIRT, FILTH : mugre *f*, suciedad *f* **3** MIRE, MUD : barro *m*, fango *m*, lodo *m*
mucous ['mju:kəs] *adj* : mucoso ⟨mucous membrane : membrana mucosa⟩
mucus ['mju:kəs] *n* : mucosidad *f*
mud ['mʌd] *n* : barro *m*, fango *m*, lodo *m*
muddle[1] ['mʌdəl] *v* **-dled; -dling** *vt* **1** CONFUSE : confundir **2** BUNGLE : echar a perder, malograr — *vi* : andar confundido ⟨to muddle through : arreglárselas⟩
muddle[2] *n* : confusión *f*, embrollo *m*, lío *m*
muddleheaded [ˌmʌdəl'hɛdəd, 'mʌdəlˌ-] *adj* CONFUSED : confuso, despistado
muddy[1] ['mʌdi] *vt* **-died; -dying** : llenar de barro
muddy[2] *adj* **-dier; -est** : barroso, fangoso, lodoso, enlodado ⟨you're all muddy : estás cubierto de barro⟩
muff[1] ['mʌf] *vt* BUNGLE : echar a perder, fallar (un tiro, etc.)
muff[2] *n* : manguito *m*
muffin ['mʌfən] *n* : magdalena *f*, mantecada *f Mex*
muffle ['mʌfəl] *vt* **-fled; -fling** **1** ENVELOP : cubrir, tapar **2** DEADEN : amortiguar (un sonido)
muffler ['mʌflər] *n* **1** SCARF : bufanda *f* **2** : silenciador *m*, mofle *m CA, Mex* (de un automóvil)
mug[1] ['mʌg] *v* **mugged; mugging** *vi* : posar (con afectación), hacer muecas ⟨mugging for the camera : haciendo muecas para la cámara⟩ — *vt* ASSAULT : asaltar, atracar
mug[2] *n* CUP : tazón *m*
mugger ['mʌgər] *n* : atracador *m*, -dora *f*
mugginess ['mʌginəs] *n* : bochorno *m*
muggy ['mʌgi] *adj* **-gier; -est** : bochornoso
mulatto [mʊ'lɑt̬o, -'læ-] *n, pl* **-toes** *or* **-tos** : mulato *m*, -ta *f*
mulberry ['mʌlˌbɛri] *n, pl* **-ries** : morera *f* (árbol), mora *f* (fruta)
mulch[1] ['mʌlʧ] *vt* : cubrir con pajote
mulch[2] *n* : pajote *m*
mule ['mju:l] *n* **1** : mula *f* **2** : obstinado *m*, -da *f*; terco *m*, -ca *f*
mulish ['mju:lɪʃ] *adj* : obstinado, terco
mull ['mʌl] *vt* **to mull over** : reflexionar sobre
mullet ['mʌlət] *n, pl* **-let** *or* **-lets** : mújol *m*, múgil *m*
multicolored [ˌmʌlti'kʌlərd, ˌmʌltaɪ-] *adj* : multicolor, abigarrado
multicultural [ˌmʌlti'kʌlʧərəl] *adj* : multicultural
multifaceted [ˌmʌlti'fæsət̬əd, ˌmʌltaɪ-] *adj* : multifacético
multifamily [ˌmʌlti'fæmli, ˌmʌltaɪ-] *adj* : multifamiliar
multifarious [ˌmʌltə'færiəs] *adj* DIVERSE : diverso, variado
multilateral [ˌmʌlti'læt̬ərəl, ˌmʌltaɪ-] *adj* : multilateral
multimedia [ˌmʌlti'mi:diə, ˌmʌltaɪ-] *adj* : multimedia
multimillionaire [ˌmʌltiˌmɪljə'nær, ˌmʌltaɪ-, -'mɪljəˌnær] *adj* : multimillonario
multinational [ˌmʌlti'næʃənəl, ˌmʌltaɪ-] *adj* : multinacional
multiple[1] ['mʌltəpəl] *adj* : múltiple
multiple[2] *n* : múltiplo *m*
multiple sclerosis [sklə'ro:sɪs] *n* : esclerosis *f* múltiple
multiplication [ˌmʌltəplə'keɪʃən] *n* : multiplicación *f*
multiplicity [ˌmʌltə'plɪsət̬i] *n, pl* **-ties** : multiplicidad *f*
multiplier ['mʌltəˌplaɪər] *n* : multiplicador *m* (en matemáticas)
multiply ['mʌltəˌplaɪ] *v* **-plied; -plying** *vt* : multiplicar — *vi* : multiplicarse
multipurpose [ˌmʌlti'pərpəs, ˌmʌltaɪ-] *adj* : multiuso
multitude ['mʌltəˌtu:d, -ˌtju:d] *n* **1** CROWD : multitud *f*, muchedumbre *f* **2** HOST : multitud *f*, gran cantidad *f* ⟨a multitude of ideas : numerosas ideas⟩
multivitamin [ˌmʌlti'vaɪt̬əmən, ˌmʌltaɪ-] *adj* : multivitamínico
mum[1] ['mʌm] *adj* SILENT : callado
mum[2] *n* → **chrysanthemum**
mumble[1] ['mʌmbəl] *v* **-bled; -bling** *vt* : mascullar, musitar — *vi* : mascullar, hablar entre dientes, murmurar
mumble[2] *n* **to speak in a mumble** : hablar entre dientes
mummy ['mʌmi] *n, pl* **-mies** : momia *f*
mumps ['mʌmps] *ns & pl* : paperas *fpl*
munch ['mʌnʧ] *v* : mascar, masticar
mundane [ˌmʌn'deɪn, 'mʌnˌ-] *adj* **1** EARTHLY, WORLDLY : mundano, terrenal **2** COMMONPLACE : rutinario, ordinario
municipal [mjʊ'nɪsəpəl] *adj* : municipal
municipality [mjʊˌnɪsə'pælət̬i] *n, pl* **-ties** : municipio *m*
munitions [mjʊ'nɪʃənz] *npl* : municiones *fpl*

mural[1] [ˈmjʊrəl] *adj* : mural
mural[2] [ˈmjʊrəlɪst] *n* : mural *m*
murder[1] [ˈmərdər] *vt* : asesinar, matar — *vi* : matar
murder[2] *n* : asesinato *m*, homicidio *m*
murderer [ˈmərdərər] *n* : asesino *m*, -na *f*; homicida *mf*
murderess [ˈmərdərɪs, -dəˌrɛs, -dərəs] *n* : asesina *f*, homicida *f*
murderous [ˈmərdərəs] *adj* : asesino, homicida
murk [ˈmərk] *n* DARKNESS : oscuridad *f*, tinieblas *fpl*
murkiness [ˈmərkinəs] *n* : oscuridad *f*, tenebrosidad *f*
murky [ˈmərki] *adj* **-kier; -est** : oscuro, tenebroso
murmur[1] [ˈmərmər] *vi* **1** DRONE : murmurar **2** GRUMBLE : refunfuñar, regañar, rezongar — *vt* MUMBLE : murmurar
murmur[2] *n* **1** COMPLAINT : queja *f* **2** DRONE : murmullo *m*, rumor *m*
muscle[1] [ˈmʌsəl] *vi* **-cled; -cling** : meterse <to muscle in on : meterse por la fuerza en, entrometerse en>
muscle[2] *n* **1** : músculo *m* **2** STRENGTH : fuerza *f*
muscular [ˈmʌskjələr] *adj* **1** : muscular <muscular tissue : tejido muscular> **2** BRAWNY : musculoso
muscular dystrophy *n* : distrofia *f* muscular
musculature [ˈmʌskjələˌʧʊr, -ʧər] *n* : musculatura *f*
muse[1] [ˈmju:z] *vi* **mused; musing** PONDER, REFLECT : cavilar, meditar, reflexionar
muse[2] *n* : musa *f*
museum [mjʊˈzi:əm] *n* : museo *m*
mush [ˈmʌʃ] *n* **1** : gachas *fpl* (de maíz) **2** SENTIMENTALITY : sensiblería *f*
mushroom[1] [ˈmʌʃˌru:m, -ˌrʊm] *vi* GROW, MULTIPLY : crecer rápidamente, multiplicarse
mushroom[2] *n* : hongo *m*, champiñón *m*, seta *f*
mushy [ˈmʌʃi] *adj* **mushier; -est 1** SOFT : blando **2** MAWKISH : sensiblero
music [ˈmju:zɪk] *n* : música *f*
musical[1] [ˈmju:zɪkəl] *adj* : musical, de música — **musically** *adv*
musical[2] *n* : comedia *f* musical
music box *n* : cajita *f* de música
musician [mjʊˈzɪʃən] *n* : músico *m*, -ca *f*
musk [ˈmʌsk] *n* : almizcle *m*
musket [ˈmʌskət] *n* : mosquete *m*
musketeer [ˌmʌskəˈtɪr] *n* : mosquetero *m*
muskrat [ˈmʌskˌræt] *n, pl* **-rat** *or* **-rats** : rata *f* almizclera
Muslim[1] [ˈmʌzləm, ˈmʊs-, ˈmʊz-] *adj* : musulmán
Muslim[2] *n* : musulmán *m*, -mana *f*
muslin [ˈmʌzlən] *n* : muselina *f*
muss[1] [ˈmʌs] *vt* : desordenar, despeinar (el pelo)
muss[2] *n* : desorden *m*
mussel [ˈmʌsəl] *n* : mejillón *m*
must[1] [ˈmʌst] *v aux* **1** (*expressing obligation or necessity*) : deber, tener que <you must stop : debes parar> <we must obey : tenemos que obedecer> **2** (*expressing probability*) : deber (de), haber de <you must be tired : debes de estar cansado> <it must be late : ha de ser tarde>
must[2] *n* : necesidad *f* <exercise is a must : el ejercicio es imprescindible>
mustache [ˈmʌˌstæʃ, mʌˈstæʃ] *n* : bigote *m*, bigotes *mpl*
mustang [ˈmʌˌstæŋ] *n* : mustang *m*
mustard [ˈmʌstərd] *n* : mostaza *f*
muster[1] [ˈmʌstər] *vt* **1** ASSEMBLE : reunir **2 to muster up** : armarse de, cobrar (valor, fuerzas, etc.)
muster[2] *n* **1** INSPECTION : revista *f* (de tropas) <it didn't pass muster : no resistió un examen minucioso> **2** COLLECTION : colección *f*
mustiness [ˈmʌstinəs] *n* : lo mohoso
musty [ˈmʌsti] *adj* **mustier; -est** : mohoso, que huele a moho, que huele a encerrado
mutant[1] [ˈmju:tənt] *adj* : mutante
mutant[2] *n* : mutante *m*
mutate [ˈmju:ˌteɪt] *vi* **-tated; -tating 1** : mutar (genéticamente) **2** CHANGE : transformarse
mutation [mju:ˈteɪʃən] *n* : mutación *f* (genética)
mute[1] [ˈmju:t] *vt* **muted; muting** MUFFLE : amortiguar, ponerle sordina a (un instrumento musical)
mute[2] *adj* **muter; mutest** : mudo — **mutely** *adv*
mute[3] *n* **1** : mudo *m*, -da *f* (persona) **2** : sordina *f* (para un instrumento musical)
mutilate [ˈmju:t̬əˌleɪt] *vt* **-lated; -lating** : mutilar
mutilation [ˌmju:t̬əˈleɪʃən] *n* : mutilación *f*
mutineer [ˌmju:tənˈɪr] *n* : amotinado *m*, -da *f*
mutinous [ˈmju:tənəs] *adj* : amotinado
mutiny[1] [ˈmju:təni] *vi* **-nied; -nying** : amotinarse
mutiny[2] *n, pl* **-nies** : amotinamiento *m*, motín *m*
mutt [ˈmʌt] *n* MONGREL : perro *m* mestizo, perro *m* corriente *Mex*
mutter [ˈmʌt̬ər] *vi* **1** MUMBLE : mascullar, hablar entre dientes, murmurar **2** GRUMBLE : refunfuñar, regañar, rezongar
mutton [ˈmʌtən] *n* : carne *f* de carnero
mutual [ˈmju:ʧʊəl] *adj* **1** : mutuo <mutual respect : respeto mutuo> **2** COMMON : común <a mutual friend : un amigo común>
mutually [ˈmju:ʧʊəli, -ʧəli] *adv* **1** : mutuamente <mutually beneficial : mutuamente beneficioso> **2** JOINTLY : conjuntamente

muzzle[1] ['mʌzəl] *vt* **-zled; -zling** : ponerle un bozal a (un animal), amordazar
muzzle[2] *n* **1** SNOUT : hocico *m* **2** : bozal *m* (para un perro, etc.) **3** : boca *f* (de un arma de fuego)
my[1] ['maɪ] *adj* : mi ⟨my parents : mis padres⟩
my[2] *interj* : ¡caramba!, ¡Dios mío!
myopia [maɪ'o:piə] *n* : miopía *f*
myopic [maɪ'o:pɪk, -'ɑ-] *adj* : miope
myriad[1] ['mɪriəd] *adj* INNUMERABLE : innumerable
myriad[2] *n* : miríada *f*
myrrh ['mər] *n* : mirra *f*
myrtle ['mərtəl] *n* : mirto *m*, arrayán *m*
myself [maɪ'sɛlf] *pron* **1** (*used reflexively*) : me ⟨I washed myself : me lavé⟩ **2** (*used for emphasis*) : yo mismo, yo misma ⟨I did it myself : lo hice yo mismo⟩
mysterious [mɪ'stɪriəs] *adj* : misterioso — **mysteriously** *adv*
mysteriousness [mɪ'stɪriəsnəs] *n* : lo misterioso
mystery ['mɪstəri] *n, pl* **-teries** : misterio *m*
mystic[1] ['mɪstɪk] *adj* : místico
mystic[2] *n* : místico *m*, -ca *f*
mystical ['mɪstɪkəl] *adj* : místico — **mystically** *adv*
mysticism ['mɪstəˌsɪzəm] *n* : misticismo *m*
mystify ['mɪstəˌfaɪ] *vt* **-fied; -fying** : dejar perplejo, confundir
mystique [mɪ'sti:k] *n* : aura *f* de misterio
myth ['mɪθ] *n* : mito *m*
mythic ['mɪθɪk] *adj* : mítico
mythical ['mɪθɪkəl] *adj* : mítico
mythological [ˌmɪθə'lɑʤɪkəl] *adj* : mitológico
mythology [mɪ'θɑləʤi] *n, pl* **-gies** : mitología *f*

N

n ['ɛn] *n, pl* **n's** *or* **ns** ['ɛnz] : decimocuarta letra del alfabeto inglés
nab ['næb] *vt* **nabbed; nabbing** : prender, pillar *fam*, pescar *fam*
nadir ['neɪdər, 'neɪˌdɪr] *n* : nadir *m*, punto *m* más bajo
nag[1] ['næg] *v* **nagged; nagging** *vi* **1** COMPLAIN : quejarse, rezongar **2 to nag at** HASSLE : molestar, darle (la) lata (a alguien) — *vt* **1** PESTER : molestar, fastidiar **2** SCOLD : regañar, estarle encima a *fam*
nag[2] *n* **1** GRUMBLER : gruñón *m*, -ñona *f* **2** HORSE : jamelgo *m*
naiad ['neɪəd, 'naɪ-, -ˌæd] *n, pl* **-iads** *or* **-iades** [-əˌdi:z] : náyade *f*
nail[1] ['neɪl] *vt* : clavar, sujetar con clavos
nail[2] *n* **1** FINGERNAIL : uña *f* ⟨nail file : lima (de uñas)⟩ ⟨nail polish : laca de uñas⟩ **2** : clavo *m* ⟨to hit the nail on the head : dar en el clavo⟩
naive *or* **naïve** [nɑ'i:v] *adj* **-iver; -est 1** INGENUOUS : ingenuo, cándido **2** GULLIBLE : crédulo
naively [nɑ'i:vli] *adv* : ingenuamente
naïveté [ˌnɑˌi:və'teɪ, nɑ'i:vəˌ-] *n* : ingenuidad *f*
naked ['neɪkəd] *adj* **1** UNCLOTHED : desnudo **2** UNCOVERED : desenvainado (dícese de una espada), pelado (dícese de los árboles), expuesto al aire (dícese de una llama) **3** OBVIOUS, PLAIN : manifiesto, puro, desnudo ⟨the naked truth : la pura verdad⟩ **4 to the naked eye** : a simple vista
nakedly ['neɪkədli] *adv* : manifiestamente
nakedness ['neɪkədnəs] *n* : desnudez *f*
name[1] ['neɪm] *vt* **named; naming 1** CALL : llamar, bautizar, ponerle nombre a **2** MENTION : mentar, mencionar, dar el nombre de ⟨they have named a suspect : han dado el nombre de un sospechoso⟩ **3** APPOINT : nombrar **4 to name a price** : fijar un precio
name[2] *adj* **1** KNOWN : de nombre ⟨name brand : marca conocida⟩ **2** PROMINENT : de renombre, de prestigio
name[3] *n* **1** : nombre *m* ⟨what is your name? : ¿cómo se llama?⟩ **2** SURNAME : apellido *m* **3** EPITHET : epíteto *m* ⟨to call somebody names : llamar a alguien de todo⟩ **4** REPUTATION : fama *f*, reputación *f* ⟨to make a name for oneself : darse a conocer, hacerse famoso⟩
nameless ['neɪmləs] *adj* **1** ANONYMOUS : anónimo **2** INDESCRIBABLE : indecible, indescriptible
namelessly ['neɪmləsli] *adv* : anónimamente
namely ['neɪmli] *adv* : a saber
namesake ['neɪmˌseɪk] *n* : tocayo *m*, -ya *f*; homónimo *m*, -ma *f*
Namibian [nə'mɪbiən] *n* : namibio *m*, -bia *f* — **Namibian** *adj*
nanny ['næni] *n, pl* **nannies** : niñera *f*; nana *f CA, Col, Mex, Ven*
nap[1] ['næp] *vi* **napped; napping 1** : dormir, dormir la siesta **2 to be caught napping** : estar desprevenido
nap[2] *n* **1** SLEEP : siesta *f* ⟨to take a nap : echarse una siesta⟩ **2** FUZZ, PILE : pelo *m*, pelusa *f* (de telas)
nape ['neɪp, 'næp] *n* : nuca *f*, cerviz *f*, cogote *m*
naphtha ['næfθə] *n* : nafta *f*
napkin ['næpkən] *n* : servilleta *f*
narcissism ['nɑrsəˌsɪzəm] *n* : narcisismo *m*
narcissist ['nɑrsəsɪst] *n* : narcisista *mf*
narcissistic [ˌnɑrsə'sɪstɪk] *adj* : narcisista
narcissus [nɑr'sɪsəs] *n, pl* **-cissus** *or*

-cissuses *or* **-cissi** [-ˈsɪˌsaɪ, -ˌsiː] : narciso *m*
narcotic[1] [nɑrˈkɑṯɪk] *adj* : narcótico
narcotic[2] *n* : narcótico *m*, estupefaciente *m*
narrate [ˈnærˌeɪt] *vt* **-rated; -rating** : narrar, relatar
narration [næˈreɪʃən] *n* : narración *f*
narrative[1] [ˈnærəṯɪv] *adj* : narrativo
narrative[2] *n* : narración *f*, narrativa *f*, relato *m*
narrator [ˈnærˌeɪṯər] *n* : narrador *m*, -dora *f*
narrow[1] [ˈnærˌoː] *vi* : estrecharse, angostarse ⟨the river narrowed : el río se estrechó⟩ — *vt* **1** : estrechar, angostar **2** LIMIT : restringir, limitar ⟨to narrow the search : limitar la búsqueda⟩
narrow[2] *adj* **1** : estrecho, angosto **2** LIMITED : estricto, limitado ⟨in the narrowest sense of the word : en el sentido más estricto de la palabra⟩ **3 to have a narrow escape** : escapar por un pelo
narrowly [ˈnæroli] *adv* **1** BARELY : por poco **2** CLOSELY : de cerca
narrow–minded [ˌnæroˈmaɪndəd] *adj* : de miras estrechas
narrowness [ˈnæronəs] *n* : estrechez *f*
narrows [ˈnæroːz] *npl* STRAIT : estrecho *m*
narwhal [ˈnɑrˌ*h*wɑl, ˈnɑrwəl] *n* : narval *m*
nasal [ˈneɪzəl] *adj* : nasal, gangoso ⟨a nasal voice : una voz gangosa⟩
nasally [ˈneɪzəli] *adv* **1** : por la nariz **2** : con voz gangosa
nastily [ˈnæstəli] *adv* : con maldad, cruelmente
nastiness [ˈnæstinəs] *n* : porquería *f*
nasturtium [nəˈstərʃəm, næ-] *n* : capuchina *f*
nasty [ˈnæsti] *adj* **-tier; -est** **1** FILTHY : sucio, mugriento **2** OBSCENE : obsceno **3** MEAN, SPITEFUL : malo, malicioso **4** UNPLEASANT : desagradable, feo **5** REPUGNANT : asqueroso, repugnante ⟨a nasty smell : un olor asqueroso⟩
natal [ˈneɪṯəl] *adj* : natal
nation [ˈneɪʃən] *n* : nación *f*
national[1] [ˈnæʃənəl] *adj* : nacional
national[2] *n* : ciudadano *m*, -na *f*; nacional *mf*
nationalism [ˈnæʃənəˌlɪzəm] *n* : nacionalismo *m*
nationalist[1] [ˈnæʃənəlɪst] *adj* : nacionalista
nationalist[2] *n* : nacionalista *mf*
nationalistic [ˌnæʃənəˈlɪstɪk] *adj* : nacionalista
nationality [ˌnæʃəˈnæləṯi] *n, pl* **-ties** : nacionalidad *f*
nationalization [ˌnæʃənələˈzeɪʃən] *n* : nacionalización *f*
nationalize [ˈnæʃənəˌlaɪz] *vt* **-ized; -izing** : nacionalizar
nationally [ˈnæʃənəli] *adv* : a escala nacional, a nivel nacional
nationwide [ˈneɪʃənˈwaɪd] *adj* : en toda la nación, por todo el país
native[1] [ˈneɪṯɪv] *adj* **1** INNATE : innato **2** : natal ⟨her native city : su ciudad natal⟩ **3** INDIGENOUS : indígena, autóctono
native[2] *n* **1** ABORIGINE : nativo *m*, -va *f*; indígena *mf* **2** : natural *m* ⟨he's a native of Mexico : es natural de México⟩
Native American → **American Indian**
nativity [nəˈtɪvəṯi, neɪ-] *n, pl* **-ties** **1** BIRTH : navidad *f* **2 the Nativity** : la Natividad, la Navidad
natty [ˈnæṯi] *adj* **-tier; -est** : elegante, garboso
natural[1] [ˈnætʃərəl] *adj* **1** : natural, de la naturaleza ⟨natural woodlands : bosques naturales⟩ ⟨natural childbirth : parto natural⟩ **2** INNATE : innato, natural **3** UNAFFECTED : natural, sin afectación **4** LIFELIKE : natural, vivo
natural[2] *n* **to be a natural** : tener un talento innato (para algo)
natural gas *n* : gas *m* natural
natural history *n* : historia *f* natural
naturalism [ˈnætʃərəˌlɪzəm] *n* : naturalismo *m*
naturalist [ˈnætʃərəlɪst] *n* : naturalista *mf* — **naturalist** *adj*
naturalistic [ˌnætʃərəˈlɪstɪk] *adj* : naturalista
naturalization [ˌnætʃərələˈzeɪʃən] *n* : naturalización *f*
naturalize [ˈnætʃərəˌlaɪz] *vt* **-ized; -izing** : naturalizar
naturally [ˈnætʃərəli] *adv* **1** INHERENTLY : naturalmente, intrínsecamente **2** UNAFFECTEDLY : de manera natural **3** OF COURSE : por supuesto, naturalmente
naturalness [ˈnætʃərəlnəs] *n* : naturalidad *f*
natural science *n* : ciencias *fpl* naturales
nature [ˈneɪtʃər] *n* **1** : naturaleza *f* ⟨the laws of nature : las leyes de la naturaleza⟩ **2** KIND, SORT : índole *f*, clase *f* ⟨things of this nature : cosas de esta índole⟩ **3** DISPOSITION : carácter *m*, natural *m*, naturaleza *f* ⟨it is his nature to be friendly : es de natural simpático⟩ ⟨human nature : la naturaleza humana⟩
naught [ˈnɔt] *n* **1** : nada *f* ⟨to come to naught : reducirse a nada, fracasar⟩ **2** ZERO : cero *m*
naughtily [ˈnɔṯəli] *adv* : traviesamente, con malicia
naughtiness [ˈnɔṯinəs] *n* : mala conducta *f*, travesuras *fpl*, malicia *f*
naughty [ˈnɔṯi] *adj* **-tier; -est** **1** MISCHIEVOUS : travieso, pícaro **2** RISQUÉ : picante, subido de tono
nausea [ˈnɔziə, ˈnɔʃə] *n* **1** SICKNESS : náuseas *fpl* **2** DISGUST : asco *m*
nauseate [ˈnɔziˌeɪt, -ʒi-, -si-, -ʃi-] *vt* **-ated; -ating** **1** SICKEN : darle náuseas (a alguien) **2** DISGUST : asquear, darle asco (a alguien)

nauseating *adj* : nauseabundo, repugnante
nauseatingly ['nɔzi,eɪt̬ɪŋli, -ʒi-, -si-, -ʃi-] *adv* : hasta el punto de dar asco ⟨nauseatingly sweet : tan dulce que da asco⟩
nauseous ['nɔʃəs, -ziəs] *adj* **1** SICK : mareado, con náuseas **2** SICKENING : nauseabundo
nautical ['nɔt̬ɪkəl] *adj* : náutico
nautilus ['nɔt̬ələs] *n, pl* **-luses** *or* **-li** [-,laɪ, -,li:] : nautilo *m*
Navajo ['nævə,ho:, 'nɑ-] *n* : navajo *m*, -ja *f* — **Navajo** *adj*
naval ['neɪvəl] *adj* : naval
nave ['neɪv] *n* : nave *f*
navel ['neɪvəl] *n* : ombligo *m*
navigability [,nævɪgə'bɪlət̬i] *n* : navegabilidad *f*
navigable ['nævɪgəbəl] *adj* : navegable
navigate ['nævə,geɪt] *v* **-gated; -gating** *vi* : navegar — *vt* **1** STEER : gobernar (un barco), pilotar (un avión) **2** : navegar por (un río, etc.)
navigation [,nævə'geɪʃən] *n* : navegación *f*
navigator ['nævə,geɪt̬ər] *n* : navegante *mf*
navy ['neɪvi] *n, pl* **-vies** **1** FLEET : flota *f* **2** : marina *f* de guerra, armada *f* ⟨the United States Navy : la armada de los Estados Unidos⟩ **3** *or* **navy blue** : azul *m* marino
nay[1] ['neɪ] *adv* : no
nay[2] *n* : no *m*, voto *m* en contra
Nazi ['nɑtsi, 'næt-] *n* : nazi *mf*
Nazism ['nɑt,sɪzəm, 'næt-] *or* **Naziism** ['nɑtsi,ɪzəm, 'næt-] *n* : nazismo *m*
Neanderthal man [ni'ændər,θɔl, -,tɔl] *n* : hombre *m* de Neanderthal
near[1] ['nɪr] *vt* **1** : acercarse a ⟨the ship is nearing port : el barco se está acercando al puerto⟩ **2** : estar a punto de ⟨she is nearing graduation : está a punto de graduarse⟩
near[2] *adv* **1** CLOSE : cerca ⟨my family lives quite near : mi familia vive muy cerca⟩ **2** NEARLY : casi ⟨I came near to finishing : casi terminé⟩
near[3] *adj* **1** CLOSE : cercano, próximo **2** SIMILAR : parecido, semejante
near[4] *prep* : cerca de
nearby[1] [nɪr'baɪ, 'nɪr,baɪ] *adv* : cerca
nearby[2] *adj* : cercano
nearly ['nɪrli] *adv* **1** ALMOST : casi ⟨nearly asleep : casi dormido⟩ **2 not nearly** : ni con mucho, ni mucho menos ⟨it was not nearly so bad as I had expected : no fue ni con mucho tan malo como esperaba⟩
nearness ['nɪrnəs] *n* : proximidad *f*
nearsighted ['nɪr,saɪt̬əd] *adj* : miope, corto de vista
nearsightedly ['nɪr,saɪt̬ədli] *adv* : con miopía
nearsightedness ['nɪr,saɪt̬ədnəs] *n* : miopía *f*
neat ['ni:t] *adj* **1** CLEAN, ORDERLY : ordenado, pulcro, limpio **2** UNDILUTED : solo, sin diluir **3** SIMPLE, TASTEFUL : sencillo y de buen gusto **4** CLEVER : hábil, ingenioso ⟨a neat trick : un truco ingenioso⟩
neatly ['ni:tli] *adv* **1** TIDILY : ordenadamente **2** CLEVERLY : ingeniosamente
neatness ['ni:tnəs] *n* : pulcritud *f*, limpieza *f*, orden *m*
nebula ['nɛbjʊlə] *n, pl* **-lae** [-,li:, -,laɪ] : nebulosa *f*
nebulous ['nɛbjʊləs] *adj* : nebuloso, vago
necessarily [,nɛsə'sɛrəli] *adv* : necesariamente, forzosamente
necessary[1] ['nɛsə,sɛri] *adj* **1** INEVITABLE : inevitable **2** COMPULSORY : necesario, obligatorio **3** ESSENTIAL : imprescindible, preciso, necesario
necessary[2] *n, pl* **-saries** : lo esencial, lo necesario
necessitate [nɪ'sɛsə,teɪt] *vt* **-tated; -tating** : necesitar, requerir
necessity [nɪ'sɛsət̬i] *n, pl* **-ties** **1** NEED : necesidad *f* **2** REQUIREMENT : requisito *m* indispensable **3** POVERTY : indigencia *f*, necesidad *f* **4** INEVITABILITY : inevitabilidad *f*
neck[1] ['nɛk] *vi* : besuquearse
neck[2] *n* **1** : cuello *m* (de una persona), pescuezo *m* (de un animal) **2** COLLAR : cuello *m* **3** : cuello *m* (de una botella), mástil *m* (de una guitarra)
neckerchief ['nɛkərtʃəf, -,tʃi:f] *n, pl* **-chiefs** [-tʃəfs, -,tʃi:fs] : pañuelo *m* (para el cuello), mascada *f Mex*
necklace ['nɛkləs] *n* : collar *m*
neckline ['nɛk,laɪn] *n* : escote *m*
necktie ['nɛk,taɪ] *n* : corbata *f*
nectar ['nɛktər] *n* : néctar *m*
nectarine [,nɛktə'ri:n] *n* : nectarina *f*
née *or* **nee** ['neɪ] *adj* : de soltera ⟨Mrs. Smith, née Whitman : la señora Smith, de soltera Whitman⟩
need[1] ['ni:d] *vt* **1** : necesitar ⟨I need your help : necesito su ayuda⟩ ⟨I need money : me falta dinero⟩ **2** REQUIRE : requerir, exigir ⟨that job needs patience : ese trabajo exige paciencia⟩ **3 to need to** : tener que ⟨he needs to study : tiene que estudiar⟩ ⟨they need to be scolded : hay que reprenderlos⟩ — *v aux* **1** MUST : tener que, deber ⟨need you shout? : ¿tienes que gritar?⟩ **2 to be needed** : hacer falta ⟨you needn't worry : no hace falta que te preocupes, no hay por qué preocuparse⟩
need[2] *n* **1** NECESSITY : necesidad *f* ⟨in case of need : en caso de necesidad⟩ **2** LACK : falta *f* ⟨the need for better training : la falta de mejor capacitación⟩ ⟨to be in need : necesitar⟩ **3** POVERTY : necesidad *f*, indigencia *f* **4 needs** *npl* : requisitos *mpl*, carencias *fpl*
needful ['ni:dfəl] *adj* : necesario
needle[1] ['ni:dəl] *vt* **-dled; -dling** : pinchar
needle[2] *n* **1** : aguja *f* ⟨to thread a needle : enhebrar una aguja⟩ ⟨knitting

needle : aguja de tejer⟩ **2** POINTER : aguja *f*, indicador *m*
needlepoint [ˈniːdəlˌpɔint] *n* **1** LACE : encaje *m* de mano **2** EMBROIDERY : bordado *m* en cañamazo
needless [ˈniːdləs] *adj* : innecesario
needlessly [ˈniːdləsli] *adv* : sin ninguna necesidad, innecesariamente
needlework [ˈniːdəlˌwərk] *n* : bordado *m*
needn't [ˈniːdənt] (*contraction of* **need not**) → **need**
needy[1] [ˈniːdi] *adj* **needier; -est** : necesitado
needy[2] *n* **the needy** : los necesitados *mpl*
nefarious [nɪˈfæriəs] *adj* : nefario, nefando, infame
negate [nɪˈgeɪt] *vt* **-gated; -gating** **1** DENY : negar **2** NULLIFY : invalidar, anular
negation [nɪˈgeɪʃən] *n* : negación *f*
negative[1] [ˈnɛgəṭɪv] *adj* : negativo
negative[2] *n* **1** : negación *f* (en lingüística) **2** : negativa *f* ⟨to answer in the negative : contestar con una negativa⟩ **3** : término *m* negativo (en matemáticas) **4** : negativo *m*, imagen *f* en negativo (en fotografía)
negatively [ˈnɛgəṭɪvli] *adv* : negativamente
neglect[1] [nɪˈglɛkt] *vt* **1** : desatender, descuidar ⟨to neglect one's health : descuidar la salud⟩ **2** : no cumplir con, faltar a ⟨to neglect one's obligations : faltar uno a sus obligaciones⟩ ⟨he neglected to tell me : omitió decírmelo⟩
neglect[2] *n* **1** : negligencia *f*, descuido *m*, incumplimiento *m* ⟨through neglect : por negligencia⟩ ⟨neglect of duty : incumplimiento del deber⟩ **2 in a state of neglect** : abandonado, descuidado
neglectful [nɪˈglɛktfəl] *adj* : descuidado *m*
negligee [ˌnɛgləˈʒeɪ] *n* : negligé *m*
negligence [ˈnɛglɪʤənts] *n* : descuido *m*, negligencia *f*
negligent [ˈnɛglɪʤənt] *adj* : negligente, descuidado — **negligently** *adv*
negligible [ˈnɛglɪʤəbəl] *adj* : insignificante, despreciable
negotiable [nɪˈgoːʃəbəl, -ʃiə-] *adj* : negociable
negotiate [nɪˈgoːʃiˌeɪt] *v* **-ated; -ating** *vi* : negociar — *vt* **1** : negociar, gestionar ⟨to negotiate a treaty : negociar un trato⟩ **2** : salvar, franquear ⟨they negotiated the obstacles : salvaron los obstáculos⟩ ⟨to negotiate a turn : tomar una curva⟩
negotiation [nɪˌgoːʃiˈeɪʃən, -siˈeɪ-] *n* : negociación *f*
negotiator [nɪˈgoːʃiˌeɪṭər, -siˌeɪ-] *n* : negociador *m*, -dora *f*
Negro [ˈniːˌgroː] *n, pl* **-groes** : negro *m*, -gra *f*
neigh[1] [ˈneɪ] *vi* : relinchar
neigh[2] *n* : relincho *m*
neighbor[1] [ˈneɪbər] *vt* : ser vecino de, estar junto a ⟨her house neighbors mine : su casa está junto a la mía⟩ — *vi* : estar cercano, lindar, colindar ⟨her land neighbors on mine : sus tierras lindan con las mías⟩
neighbor[2] *n* **1** : vecino *m*, -na *f* **2 love thy neighbor** : ama a tu prójimo
neighborhood [ˈneɪbərˌhʊd] *n* **1** : barrio *m*, vecindad *f*, vecindario *m* **2 in the neighborhood of** : alrededor de, cerca de
neighborly [ˈneɪbərli] *adv* : amable, de buena vecindad
neither[1] [ˈniːðər, ˈnaɪ-] *adj* : ninguno (de los dos)
neither[2] *conj* **1** : ni ⟨neither asleep nor awake : ni dormido ni despierto⟩ **2** NOR : ni (tampoco) ⟨I'm not asleep—neither am I : no estoy dormido—ni yo tampoco⟩
neither[3] *pron* : ninguno
nemesis [ˈnɛməsɪs] *n, pl* **-eses** [-ˌsiːz] **1** RIVAL : rival *mf* **2** RETRIBUTION : justo castigo *m*
Neoclassical [ˌniːoˈklæsɪkəl] *adj* : neoclásico
neologism [niˈɑləˌʤɪzəm] *n* : neologismo *m*
neon[1] [ˈniːˌɑn] *adj* : de neón ⟨neon sign : letrero de neón⟩
neon[2] *n* : neón *m*
neophyte [ˈniːəˌfaɪt] *n* : neófito *m*, -ta *f*
Nepali [nəˈpɔli, -ˈpɑ-, -ˈpæ-] *n* : nepalés *m*, -lesa *f* — **Nepali** *adj*
nephew [ˈnɛˌfjuː, *chiefly British* ˈnɛˌvjuː] *n* : sobrino *m*
nepotism [ˈnɛpəˌtɪzəm] *n* : nepotismo *m*
Neptune [ˈnɛpˌtuːn, -ˌtjuːn] *n* : Neptuno *m*
nerd [ˈnərd] *n* : ganso *m*, -sa *f*
nerve [ˈnərv] *n* **1** : nervio *m* **2** COURAGE : coraje *m*, valor *m*, fuerza *f* de la voluntad ⟨to lose one's nerve : perder el valor⟩ **3** AUDACITY, GALL : atrevimiento *m*, descaro *m* ⟨of all the nerve! : ¡qué descaro!⟩ **4 nerves** *npl* : nervios *mpl* ⟨a fit of nerves : un ataque de nervios⟩
nervous [ˈnərvəs] *adj* **1** : nervioso ⟨the nervous system : el sistema nervioso⟩ **2** EXCITABLE : nervioso, excitable ⟨to get nervous : excitarse, ponerse nervioso⟩ **3** FEARFUL : miedoso, temeroso
nervously [ˈnərvəsli] *adv* : nerviosamente
nervousness [ˈnərvəsnəs] *n* : nerviosismo *m*, nerviosidad *f*, ansiedad *f*
nervy [ˈnərvi] *adj* **nervier; -est** **1** COURAGEOUS : valiente **2** IMPUDENT : atrevido, descarado, fresco *fam* **3** NERVOUS : nervioso
nest[1] [ˈnɛst] *vi* : anidar
nest[2] *n* **1** : nido *m* (de un ave), avispero *m* (de una avispa), madriguera *f* (de un animal) **2** REFUGE : nido *m*, refugio *m* **3** SET : juego *m* ⟨a nest of tables : un juego de mesitas⟩
nestle [ˈnɛsəl] *vi* **-tled; -tling** : acurrucarse, arrimarse cómodamente

net¹ [ˈnɛt] *vt* **netted; netting 1** CATCH : pescar, atrapar con una red **2** CLEAR : ganar neto <they netted $5000 : ganaron $5000 netos> **3** YIELD : producir neto

net² *adj* : neto <net weight : peso neto> <net gain : ganancia neta>

net³ *n* : red *f*, malla *f*

nether [ˈnɛðər] *adj* **1** : inferior, más bajo **2 the nether regions** : el infierno

nettle¹ [ˈnɛtəl] *vt* **-tled; -tling** : irritar, provocar, molestar

nettle² *n* : ortiga *f*

network [ˈnɛtˌwərk] *n* **1** SYSTEM : red *f* **2** CHAIN : cadena *f* <a network of supermarkets : una cadena de supermercados>

neural [ˈnʊrəl, ˈnjʊr-] *adj* : neural

neuralgia [nʊˈrælʤə, njʊ-] *n* : neuralgia *f*

neuritis [nʊˈraɪtəs, njʊ-] *n, pl* **-ritides** [-ˈrɪtəˌdiːz] *or* **-ritises** : neuritis *f*

neurological [ˌnʊrəˈlɑʤɪkəl, ˌnjʊr-] *or* **neurologic** [ˌnʊrəˈlɑʤɪk, ˌnjʊr-] *adj* : neurológico

neurologist [nʊˈrɑləʤɪst, njʊ-] *n* : neurólogo *m*, -ga *f*

neurology [nʊˈrɑləʤi, njʊ-] *n* : neurología *f*

neurosis [nʊˈroːsɪs, njʊ-] *n, pl* **-roses** [-ˌsiːz] : neurosis *f*

neurotic¹ [nʊˈrɑtɪk, njʊ-] *adj* : neurótico

neurotic² *n* : neurótico *m*, -ca *f*

neuter¹ [ˈnuːtər, ˈnjuː-] *vt* : castrar

neuter² *adj* : neutro

neutral¹ [ˈnuːtrəl, ˈnjuː-] *adj* **1** IMPARTIAL : neutral, imparcial <to remain neutral : permanecer neutral> **2** : neutro <a neutral color : un color neutro> **3** : neutro (en la química o la electricidad)

neutral² *n* : punto *m* muerto (de un automóvil)

neutrality [nuːˈtrælət̬iː, njuː-] *n* : neutralidad *f*

neutralization [ˌnuːtrələˈzeɪʃən, ˌnjuː-] *n* : neutralización *f*

neutralize [ˈnuːtrəˌlaɪz, ˈnjuː-] *vt* **-ized; -izing** : neutralizar

neutron [ˈnuːˌtrɑn, ˈnjuː-] *n* : neutrón *m*

never [ˈnɛvər] *adv* **1** : nunca, jamás <he never studies : nunca estudia> **2 never again** : nunca más, nunca jamás **3 never mind** : no importa

nevermore [ˌnɛvərˈmor] *adv* : nunca más

nevertheless [ˌnɛvərðəˈlɛs] *adv* : sin embargo, no obstante

new [ˈnuː, ˈnjuː] *adj* **1** : nuevo <a new dress : un vestido nuevo> **2** RECENT : nuevo, reciente <what's new? : ¿qué hay de nuevo?> <a new arrival : un recién llegado> **3** DIFFERENT : nuevo, distinto <this problem is new : este problema es distinto> <new ideas : ideas nuevas> **4 like new** : como nuevo

newborn [ˈnuːˌbɔrn, ˈnjuː-] *adj* : recién nacido

newcomer [ˈnuːˌkʌmər, ˈnjuː-] *n* : recién llegado *m*, recién llegada *f*

newfangled [ˈnuːˈfæŋgəld, ˈnjuː-] *adj* : novedoso

newfound [ˈnuːˈfaʊnd, ˈnjuː-] *adj* : recién descubierto

newly [ˈnuːli, ˈnjuː-] *adv* : recién, recientemente

newlywed [ˈnuːliˌwɛd, ˈnjuː-] *n* : recién casado *m*, -da *f*

new moon *n* : luna *f* nueva

newness [ˈnuːnəs, ˈnjuː-] *n* : novedad *f*

news [ˈnuːz, ˈnjuːz] *n* : noticias *fpl*

newscast [ˈnuːzˌkæst, ˈnjuːz-] *n* : noticiero *m*, informativo *m*

newscaster [ˈnuːzˌkæstər, ˈnjuːz-] *n* : presentador *m*, -dora *f*; locutor *m*, -tora *f*

newsletter [ˈnuːzˌlɛt̬ər, ˈnjuːz-] *n* : boletín *m* informativo

newsman [ˈnuːzmən, ˈnjuːz-, -ˌmæn] *n, pl* **-men** [-mən, -ˌmɛn] : periodista *m*, reportero *m*

newspaper [ˈnuːzˌpeɪpər, ˈnjuːz-] *n* : periódico *m*, diario *m*

newspaperman [ˈnuːzˌpeɪpərˌmæn, ˈnjuːz-] *n, pl* **-men** [-mən, -ˌmɛn] **1** REPORTER : periodista *m*, reportero *m* **2** : dueño *m* de un periódico

newsprint [ˈnuːzˌprɪnt, ˈnjuːz-] *n* : papel *m* de prensa

newsstand [ˈnuːzˌstænd, ˈnjuːz-] *n* : quiosco *m*, puesto *m* de periódicos

newswoman [ˈnuːzˌwʊmən, ˈnjuːz-] *n, pl* **-women** [-ˌwɪmən] : periodista *f*, reportera *f*

newsworthy [ˈnuːzˌwərði, ˈnjuːz-] *adj* : de interés periodístico

newsy [ˈnuːziː, ˈnjuː-] *adj* **newsier; -est** : lleno de noticias

newt [ˈnuːt, ˈnjuːt] *n* : tritón *m*

New Testament *n* : Nuevo Testamento *m*

New Year *n* : Año *m* Nuevo

New Year's Day *n* : día *m* del Año Nuevo

New Yorker [nuːˈjɔrkər, njuː-] *n* : neoyorquino *m*, -na *f*

New Zealander [nuːˈziːləndər, njuː-] *n* : neozelandés *m*, -desa *f*

next¹ [ˈnɛkst] *adv* **1** AFTERWARD : después, luego <what will you do next? : ¿qué harás después?> **2** NOW : después, ahora, entonces <next I will sing a song : ahora voy a cantar una canción> **3** : la próxima vez <when next we meet : la próxima vez que nos encontremos>

next² *adj* **1** ADJACENT : contiguo, de al lado **2** COMING : que viene, próximo <next Friday : el viernes que viene> **3** FOLLOWING : siguiente <the next year : el año siguiente>

next–door [ˈnɛkstˈdor] *adj* : de al lado

next to¹ *adv* ALMOST : casi, prácticamente <next to impossible : casi imposible>

next to[2] *prep* : junto a, al lado de
nexus [ˈnɛksəs] *n* : nexo *m*
nib [ˈnɪb] *n* : plumilla *f*
nibble[1] [ˈnɪbəl] *v* **-bled; -bling** *vt* : pellizcar, mordisquear, picar — *vi* : picar
nibble[2] *n* : mordisco *m*
Nicaraguan [ˌnɪkəˈrɑgwən] *n* : nicaragüense *mf* — **Nicaraguan** *adj*
nice [ˈnaɪs] *adj* **nicer; nicest 1** REFINED : pulido, refinado **2** SUBTLE : fino, sutil **3** PLEASING : agradable, bueno, lindo ⟨nice weather : buen tiempo⟩ **4** RESPECTABLE : bueno, decente **5 nice and** : bien, muy ⟨nice and hot : bien caliente⟩ ⟨nice and slow : despacito⟩
nicely [ˈnaɪsli] *adv* **1** KINDLY : amablemente **2** POLITELY : con buenos modales **3** ATTRACTIVELY : de buen gusto
niceness [ˈnaɪsnəs] *n* : simpatía *f*, amabilidad *f*
nicety [ˈnaɪsət̬i] *n, pl* **-ties 1** DETAIL, SUBTLETY : sutileza *f*, detalle *m* **2 niceties** *npl* : lujos *mpl*, detalles *mpl*
niche [ˈnɪʧ] *n* **1** RECESS : nicho *m*, hornacina *f* **2** : nicho *m*, hueco *m* ⟨to make a niche for oneself : hacerse un hueco, encontrarse una buena posición⟩
nick[1] [ˈnɪk] *vt* : cortar, hacer una muesca en
nick[2] *n* **1** CUT : corte *m*, muesca *f* **2 in the nick of time** : en el momento crítico, justo a tiempo
nickel [ˈnɪkəl] *n* **1** : níquel *m* **2** : moneda *f* de cinco centavos
nickname[1] [ˈnɪkˌneɪm] *vt* **-named; -naming** : apodar
nickname[2] *n* : apodo *m*, mote *m*, sobrenombre *m*
nicotine [ˈnɪkəˌtiːn] *n* : nicotina *f*
niece [ˈniːs] *n* : sobrina *f*
Nigerian [naɪˈʤɪriən] *n* : nigeriano *m*, -na *f* — **Nigerian** *adj*
niggardly [ˈnɪgərdli] *adj* : mezquino, tacaño
niggling [ˈnɪgəlɪŋ] *adj* **1** PETTY : insignificante **2** PERSISTENT : constante, persistente ⟨a niggling doubt : una duda constante⟩
nigh[1] [ˈnaɪ] *adv* **1** NEARLY : casi **2 to draw nigh** : acercarse, avecinarse
nigh[2] *adj* : cercano, próximo
night[1] [ˈnaɪt] *adj* : nocturno, de la noche ⟨the night sky : el cielo nocturno⟩ ⟨night shift : turno de la noche⟩
night[2] *n* **1** EVENING : noche *f* ⟨at night : de noche⟩ ⟨last night : anoche⟩ ⟨tomorrow night : mañana por la noche⟩ **2** DARKNESS : noche *f*, oscuridad *f* ⟨night fell : cayó la noche⟩
nightclothes [ˈnaɪtˌkloːðz, -ˌkloːz] *npl* : ropa *f* de dormir
nightclub [ˈnaɪtˌklʌb] *n* : cabaret *m*, club *m* nocturno
night crawler [ˈnaɪtˌkrɔlər] *n* EARTHWORM : lombriz *f* (de tierra)
nightfall [ˈnaɪtˌfɔl] *n* : anochecer *m*
nightgown [ˈnaɪtˌgaʊn] *n* : camisón *m* (de noche)
nightingale [ˈnaɪtənˌgeɪl, ˈnaɪt̬ɪŋ-] *n* : ruiseñor *m*
nightly[1] [ˈnaɪtli] *adv* : cada noche, todas las noches
nightly[2] *adj* : de todas las noches
nightmare [ˈnaɪtˌmær] *n* : pesadilla *f*
nightmarish [ˈnaɪtˌmærɪʃ] *adj* : de pesadilla
night owl *n* : noctámbulo *m*, -la *f*
nightshade [ˈnaɪtˌʃeɪd] *n* : hierba *f* mora
nightshirt [ˈnaɪtˌʃərt] *n* : camisa *f* de dormir
nightstick [ˈnaɪtˌstɪk] *n* : porra *f*
nighttime [ˈnaɪtˌtaɪm] *n* : noche *f*
nihilism [ˈnaɪəˌlɪzəm] *n* : nihilismo *m*
nil [ˈnɪl] *n* : nada *f*, cero *m*
nimble [ˈnɪmbəl] *adj* **-bler; -blest 1** AGILE : ágil **2** CLEVER : hábil, ingenioso
nimbleness [ˈnɪmbəlnəs] *n* : agilidad *f*
nimbly [ˈnɪmbli] *adv* : con agilidad, ágilmente
nincompoop [ˈnɪnkəmˌpuːp, ˈnɪŋ-] *n* FOOL : tonto *m*, -ta *f*; bobo *m*, -ba *f*
nine[1] [ˈnaɪn] *adj* **1** : nueve **2 nine times out of ten** : casi siempre
nine[2] *n* : nueve *m*
nine hundred[1] *adj* : novecientos
nine hundred[2] *n* : novecientos *m*
ninepins [ˈnaɪnˌpɪnz] *n* : bolos *mpl*
nineteen[1] [naɪnˈtiːn] *adj* : diecinueve
nineteen[2] *n* : diecinueve *m*
nineteenth[1] [naɪnˈtiːnθ] *adj* : decimonoveno, decimonono ⟨the nineteenth century : el siglo diecinueve⟩
nineteenth[2] *n* **1** : decimonoveno *m*, -na *f*; decimonono *m*, -na *f* (en una serie) **2** : diecinueveavo *m*, diecinueveava parte *f*
ninetieth[1] [ˈnaɪnt̬iəθ] *adj* : nonagésimo
ninetieth[2] *n* **1** : nonagésimo *m*, -ma *f* (en una serie) **2** : noventavo *m*, noventava parte *f*
ninety[1] [ˈnaɪnt̬i] *adj* : noventa
ninety[2] *n, pl* **-ties** : noventa *m*
ninth[1] [ˈnaɪnθ] *adj* : noveno
ninth[2] *n* **1** : noveno *m*, -na *f* (en una serie) **2** : noveno *m*, novena parte *f*
ninny [ˈnɪni] *n, pl* **ninnies** FOOL : tonto *m*, -ta *f*; bobo *m*, -ba *f*
nip[1] [ˈnɪp] *vt* **nipped; nipping 1** PINCH : pellizcar **2** BITE : morder, mordisquear **3 to nip in the bud** : cortar de raíz
nip[2] *n* **1** TANG : sabor *m* fuerte **2** PINCH : pellizco *m* **3** NIBBLE : mordisco *m* **4** SWALLOW : trago *m*, traguito *m* **5 there's a nip in the air** : hace fresco
nipple [ˈnɪpəl] *n* : pezón *m* (de una mujer), tetilla *f* (de un hombre)
nippy [ˈnɪpi] *adj* **-pier; -est 1** SHARP : fuerte, picante **2** CHILLY : frío ⟨it's nippy today : hoy hace frío⟩
nit [ˈnɪt] *n* : liendre *f*
nitrate [ˈnaɪˌtreɪt] *n* : nitrato *m*
nitric acid [ˈnaɪtrɪk] *n* : ácido *m* nítrico
nitrite [ˈnaɪˌtraɪt] *n* : nitrito *m*
nitrogen [ˈnaɪtrəʤən] *n* : nitrógeno *m*
nitroglycerin *or* **nitroglycerine** [ˌnaɪtroˈglɪsərən] *n* : nitroglicerina *f*

nitwit ['nɪt,wɪt] *n* : zonzo *m*, -za *f*; bobo *m*, -ba *f*
no[1] ['no:] *adv* : no ⟨are you leaving?—no : ¿te vas?—no⟩ ⟨no less than : no menos de⟩ ⟨to say no : decir que no⟩ ⟨like it or no : quieras o no quieras⟩
no[2] *adj* **1** : ninguno ⟨it's no trouble : no es ningún problema⟩ ⟨she has no money : no tiene dinero⟩ **2** (*indicating a small amount*) ⟨we'll be there in no time : llegamos dentro de poco, no tardamos nada⟩ **3** (*expressing a negation*) ⟨he's no liar : no es mentiroso⟩
no[3] *n, pl* **noes** *or* **nos** ['no:z] **1** DENIAL : no *m* ⟨I won't take no for an answer : no aceptaré un no por respuesta⟩ **2** : voto *f* en contra ⟨the noes have it : se ha rechazado la moción⟩
nobility [no'bɪləţi] *n* : nobleza *f*
noble[1] ['no:bəl] *adj* **-bler; -blest** **1** ILLUSTRIOUS : noble, glorioso **2** ARISTOCRATIC : noble **3** STATELY : majestuoso, magnífico **4** LOFTY : noble, elevado ⟨noble sentiments : sentimientos elevados⟩
noble[2] *n* : noble *mf*, aristócrata *mf*
nobleman ['no:bəlmən] *n, pl* **-men** [-mən, -,mɛn] : noble *m*, aristócrata *m*
nobleness ['no:bəlnəs] *n* : nobleza *f*
noblewoman ['no:bəl,wʊmən] *n, pl* **-women** [-,wɪmən] : noble *f*, aristócrata *f*
nobly ['no:bli] *adv* : noblemente
nobody[1] ['no:bədi, -,bɑdi] *n, pl* **-bodies** : don nadie *m* ⟨he's a mere nobody : es un don nadie⟩
nobody[2] *pron* : nadie
nocturnal [nɑk'tərnəl] *adj* : nocturno
nocturne ['nɑk,tərn] *n* : nocturno *m*
nod[1] ['nɑd] *v* **nodded; nodding** *vi* **1** : saludar con la cabeza, asentir con la cabeza **2 to nod off** : dormirse, quedarse dormido — *vt* : inclinar (la cabeza) ⟨to nod one's head in agreement : asentir con la cabeza⟩
nod[2] *n* : saludo *m* con la cabeza, señal *m* con la cabeza, señal *m* de asentimiento
node ['no:d] *n* : nudo *m* (de una planta)
nodule ['nɑ,ʤu:l] *n* : nódulo *m*
noel [no'ɛl] *n* **1** CAROL : villancico *m* de Navidad **2 Noel** CHRISTMAS : Navidad *f*
noes → **no**[3]
noise[1] ['nɔɪz] *vt* **noised; noising** : rumorear, publicar
noise[2] *n* : ruido *m*
noiseless ['nɔɪzləs] *adj* : silencioso, sin ruido
noiselessly ['nɔɪzləsli] *adv* : silenciosamente
noisemaker ['nɔɪz,meɪkər] *n* : matraca *f*
noisiness ['nɔɪzinəs] *n* : ruido *m*
noisome ['nɔɪsəm] *adj* : maloliente, fétido
noisy ['nɔɪzi] *adj* **noisier; -est** : ruidoso — **noisily** ['nɔɪzəli] *adv*
nomad[1] ['no:,mæd] → **nomadic**
nomad[2] *n* : nómada *mf*
nomadic [no'mædɪk] *adj* : nómada
nomenclature ['no:mən,kleɪʧər] *n* : nomenclatura *f*
nominal ['nɑmənəl] *adj* **1** : nominal ⟨the nominal head of his party : el jefe nominal de su partido⟩ **2** TRIFLING : insignificante
nominally ['nɑmənəli] *adv* : sólo de nombre, nominalmente
nominate ['nɑmə,neɪt] *vt* **-nated; -nating** **1** PROPOSE : proponer (como candidato), nominar **2** APPOINT : nombrar
nomination [,nɑmə'neɪʃən] *n* **1** PROPOSAL : propuesta *f*, postulación *f* **2** APPOINTMENT : nombramiento *m*
nominative[1] ['nɑmənəţɪv] *adj* : nominativo
nominative[2] *n or* **nominative case** : nominativo *m*
nominee [,nɑmə'ni:] *n* : candidato *m*, -ta *f*
nonaddictive [,nɑnə'dɪktɪv] *adj* : que no crea dependencia
nonalcoholic [,nɑn,ælkə'hɔlɪk] *adj* : sin alcohol, no alcohólico
nonaligned [,nɑnə'laɪnd] *adj* : no alineado
nonbeliever [,nɑnbə'li:vər] *n* : no creyente *mf*
nonbreakable [,nɑn'breɪkəbəl] *adj* : irrompible
nonce ['nɑnts] *n* **for the nonce** : por el momento
nonchalance [,nɑnʃə'lɑnts] *n* : indiferencia *f*, despreocupación *f*
nonchalant [,nɑnʃə'lɑnt] *adj* : indiferente, despreocupado, impasible
nonchalantly [,nɑnʃə'lɑntli] *adv* : con aire despreocupado, con indiferencia
noncombatant [,nɑnkəm'bætənt, -'kɑmbə-] *n* : no combatiente *mf*
noncommissioned officer [,nɑnkə'mɪʃənd] *n* : suboficial *mf*
noncommittal [,nɑnkə'mɪţəl] *adj* : evasivo, que no se compromete
nonconductor [,nɑnkən'dʌktər] *n* : aislante *m*
nonconformist [,nɑnkən'fɔrmɪst] *n* : inconformista *mf*, inconforme *mf*
nonconformity [,nɑnkən'fɔrməţi] *n* : inconformidad *f*, no conformidad *f*
noncontagious [,nɑnkən'teɪʤəs] *adj* : no contagioso
nondenominational [,nɑndɪ,nɑmə'neɪʃənəl] *adj* : no sectario
nondescript [,nɑndɪ'skrɪpt] *adj* : anodino, soso
nondiscriminatory [,nɑndɪ'skrɪmənə,tori] *adj* : no discriminatorio
nondrinker [,nɑn'drɪŋkər] *n* : abstemio *m*, -mia *f*
none[1] ['nʌn] *adv* : de ninguna manera, de ningún modo, nada ⟨he was none too happy : no se sintió nada contento⟩ ⟨I'm none the worse for it : no estoy peor por ello⟩ ⟨none too soon : a buena hora⟩

none[2] *pron* : ninguno, ninguna
nonentity [ˌnɑnˈɛntət̬i] *n, pl* **-ties** : persona *f* insignificante, nulidad *f*
nonessential [ˌnɑnɪˈsɛntʃəl] *adj* : secundario, no esencial
nonessentials [ˌnɑnɪˈsɛntʃəlz] *npl* : cosas *fpl* secundarias, cosas *fpl* accesorias
nonetheless [ˌnʌnðəˈlɛs] *adv* : sin embargo, no obstante
nonexistence [ˌnɑnɪɡˈzɪstənts] *n* : inexistencia *f*
nonexistent [ˌnɑnɪɡˈzɪstənt] *adj* : inexistente
nonfat [ˌnɑnˈfæt] *adj* : sin grasa
nonfattening [ˌnɑnˈfætənɪŋ] *adj* : que no engorda
nonfiction [ˌnɑnˈfɪkʃən] *n* : no ficción *f*
nonflammable [ˌnɑnˈflæməbəl] *adj* : no inflamable
nonintervention [ˌnɑnˌɪntərˈvɛntʃən] *n* : no intervención *f*
nonmalignant [ˌnɑnməˈlɪɡnənt] *adj* : no maligno, benigno
nonnegotiable [ˌnɑnnɪˈɡoːʃəbəl, -ʃiə-] *adj* : no negociable
nonpareil[1] [ˌnɑnpəˈrɛl] *adj* : sin parangón, sin par
nonpareil[2] *n* : persona *f* sin igual, cosa *f* sin par
nonpartisan [ˌnɑnˈpɑrt̬əzən, -sən] *adj* : imparcial
nonpaying [ˌnɑnˈpeɪɪŋ] *adj* : que no paga
nonpayment [ˌnɑnˈpeɪmənt] *n* : impago *m*, falta *f* de pago
nonperson [ˌnɑnˈpərsən] *n* : persona *f* sin derechos
nonplus [ˌnɑnˈplʌs] *vt* **-plussed; -plussing** : confundir, desconcertar, dejar perplejo
nonprescription [ˌnɑnprɪˈskrɪpʃən] *adj* : disponible sin receta del médico
nonproductive [ˌnɑnprəˈdʌktɪv] *adj* : improductivo
nonprofit [ˌnɑnˈprɑfət] *adj* : sin fines lucrativos
nonproliferation [ˌnɑnprəˌlɪfəˈreɪʃən] *adj* : no proliferación
nonresident [ˌnɑnˈrɛzədənt, -ˌdɛnt] *n* : no residente *mf*
nonscheduled [ˌnɑnˈskɛˌdʒuːld] *adj* : no programado, no regular
nonsectarian [ˌnɑnˌsɛkˈtæriən] *adj* : no sectario
nonsense [ˈnɑnˌsɛnts, ˈnɑntsənts] *n* : tonterías *fpl*, disparates *mpl*
nonsensical [nɑnˈsɛntsɪkəl] *adj* ABSURD : absurdo, disparatado — **nonsensically** [-kli] *adv*
nonsmoker [ˌnɑnˈsmoːkər] *n* : no fumador *m*, -dora *f*; persona *f* que no fuma
nonstandard [ˌnɑnˈstændərd] *adj* : no regular, no estándar
nonstick [ˌnɑnˈstɪk] *adj* : antiadherente
nonstop[1] [ˌnɑnˈstɑp] *adv* : sin parar ⟨he talked nonstop : habló sin parar⟩
nonstop[2] *adj* : directo, sin escalas ⟨nonstop flight : vuelo directo⟩
nonsupport [ˌnɑnsəˈpɔrt] *n* : falta *f* de manutención
nontaxable [ˌnɑnˈtæksəbəl] *adj* : exento de impuestos
nontoxic [ˌnɑnˈtɑksɪk] *adj* : no tóxico
nonviolence [ˌnɑnˈvaɪlənts, -ˈvaɪə-] *n* : no violencia *f*
nonviolent [ˌnɑnˈvaɪlənt, -ˈvaɪə-] *adj* : pacífico, no violento
noodle [ˈnuːdəl] *n* : fideo *m*, tallarín *m*
nook [ˈnʊk] *n* : rincón *m*, recoveco *m*, escondrijo *m* ⟨in every nook and cranny : en todos los rincones⟩
noon [ˈnuːn] *n* : mediodía *m*
noonday [ˈnuːnˌdeɪ] *n* : mediodía *m* ⟨the noonday sun : el sol de mediodía⟩
no one *pron* NOBODY : nadie
noontime [ˈnuːnˌtaɪm] *n* : mediodía *m*
noose [ˈnuːs] *n* **1** LASSO : lazo *m* **2 hangman's noose** : dogal *m*, soga *f*
nor [ˈnɔr] *conj* : ni ⟨neither good nor bad : ni bueno ni malo⟩ ⟨nor I! : ¡ni yo tampoco!⟩
Nordic [ˈnɔrdɪk] *adj* : nórdico
norm [ˈnɔrm] *n* **1** STANDARD : norma *f*, modelo *m* **2** CUSTOM, RULE : regla *f* general, lo normal
normal [ˈnɔrməl] *adj* : normal — **normally** *adv*
normalcy [ˈnɔrməlsi] *n* : normalidad *f*
normality [nɔrˈmælət̬i] *n* : normalidad *f*
normalize [ˈnɔrməˌlaɪz] *vt* : normalizar
Norse [ˈnɔrs] *adj* : nórdico
north[1] [ˈnɔrθ] *adv* : al norte
north[2] *adj* : norte, del norte ⟨the north coast : la costa del norte⟩
north[3] *n* **1** : norte *m* **2 the North** : el Norte *m*
North American *n* : norteamericano *m*, -na *f* — **North American** *adj*
northbound [ˈnɔrθˌbaʊnd] *adv* : con rumbo al norte
northeast[1] [nɔrθˈiːst] *adv* : hacia el nordeste
northeast[2] *adj* : nordeste, del nordeste
northeast[3] *n* : nordeste *m*, noreste *m*
northeasterly[1] [nɔrθˈiːstərli] *adv* : hacia el nordeste
northeasterly[2] *adj* : nordeste, del nordeste
northeastern [nɔrθˈiːstərn] *adj* : nordeste, del nordeste
northerly[1] [ˈnɔrðərli] *adv* : hacia el norte
northerly[2] *adj* : del norte ⟨a northerly wind : un viento del norte⟩
northern [ˈnɔrðərn] *adj* : norte, norteño, septentrional
Northerner [ˈnɔrðərnər] *n* : norteño *m*, -ña *f*
northern lights → **aurora borealis**
North Pole : Polo *m* Norte
North Star *n* : estrella *f* polar
northward [ˈnɔrθwərd] *adv & adj* : hacia el norte
northwest[1] [nɔrθˈwɛst] *adv* : hacia el noroeste
northwest[2] *adj* : del noroeste
northwest[3] *n* : noroeste *m*

northwesterly[1] [nɔrθ'wɛstərli] *adv* : hacia el noroeste
northwesterly[2] *adj* : del noroeste
northwestern [nɔrθ'wɛstərn] *adj* : noroeste, del noroeste
Norwegian [nɔr'wi:ʤən] *n* **1** : noruego *m*, -ga *f* **2** : noruego *m* (idioma) — **Norwegian** *adj*
nose[1] ['no:z] *v* **nosed; nosing** *vt* **1** SMELL : olfatear **2** : empujar con el hocico ⟨the dog nosed open the bag : el perro abrió el saco con el hocico⟩ **3** EDGE, MOVE : mover poco a poco — *vi* **1** PRY : entrometerse, meter las narices **2** EDGE : avanzar poco a poco
nose[2] *n* **1** : nariz *f* (de una persona), hocico *m* (de un animal) ⟨to blow one's nose : sonarse las narices⟩ **2** SMELL : olfato *m*, sentido *m* del olfato **3** FRONT : parte *f* delantera, nariz *f* (de un avión), proa *f* (de un barco) **4 to follow one's nose** : dejarse guiar por el instinto
nosebleed ['no:z,bli:d] *n* : hemorragia *f* nasal
nosedive ['no:z,daɪv] *n* **1** : descenso *m* en picada (de un avión) **2** : caída *f* súbita (de precios, etc.)
nose–dive ['no:z,daɪv] *vi* : descender en picada, caer en picada
nostalgia [nɑ'stælʤə, nə-] *n* : nostalgia *f*
nostalgic [nɑ'stælʤɪk, nə-] *adj* : nostálgico
nostril ['nɑstrəl] *n* : ventana *f* de la nariz
nostrum ['nɑstrəm] *n* : panacea *f*
nosy *or* **nosey** ['no:zi] *adj* **nosier; -est** : entrometido
not ['nɑt] *adv* **1** (*used to form a negative*) : no ⟨she is not tired : no está cansada⟩ ⟨not to say something would be wrong : no decir nada sería injusto⟩ **2** (*used to replace a negative clause*) : no ⟨are we going or not? : ¿vamos a ir o no?⟩ ⟨of course not! : ¡claro que no!⟩
notable[1] ['no:t̬əbəl] *adj* **1** NOTEWORTHY : notable, de notar **2** DISTINGUISHED, PROMINENT : distinguido, destacado
notable[2] *n* : persona *f* importante, personaje *m*
notably ['no:t̬əbli] *adv* : notablemente, particularmente
notarize ['no:t̬ə,raɪz] *vt* **-rized; -rizing** : autenticar, autorizar
notary public ['no:t̬əri] *n, pl* **-ries public** *or* **-ry publics** : notario *m*, -ria *f*; escribano *m*, -na *f*
notation [no'teɪʃən] *n* **1** NOTE : anotación *f*, nota *f* **2** : notación *f* ⟨musical notation : notación musical⟩
notch[1] ['nɑʧ] *vt* : hacer una muesca en, cortar
notch[2] *n* : muesca *f*, corte *m*
note[1] ['no:t] *vt* **noted; noting** **1** NOTICE : notar, observar, tomar nota de **2** RECORD : anotar, apuntar
note[2] *n* **1** : nota *f* (musical) **2** COMMENT : nota *f*, comentario *m* **3** LETTER : nota *f*, cartita *f* **4** PROMINENCE : prestigio *m* ⟨a musician of note : un músico destacado⟩ **5** ATTENTION : atención *f* ⟨to take note of : prestar atención a⟩
notebook ['no:t,bʊk] *n* **1** : libreta *f*, cuaderno *m* **2** : notebook *m* (computadora)
noted ['no:t̬əd] *adj* EMINENT : renombrado, eminente, celebrado
noteworthy ['no:t,wərði] *adj* : notable, de notar, de interés
nothing[1] ['nʌθɪŋ] *adv* **1** : de ninguna manera ⟨nothing daunted, we carried on : sin amilanarnos, seguimos adelante⟩ **2 nothing like** : no . . . en nada ⟨he's nothing like his brother : no se parece en nada a su hermano⟩
nothing[2] *n* NOTHINGNESS : nada *f* **2** ZERO : cero *m* **3** : persona *f* de poca importancia, cero *m* **4** TRIFLE : nimiedad *f*
nothing[3] *pron* : nada ⟨there's nothing better : no hay nada mejor⟩ ⟨nothing else : nada más⟩ ⟨nothing but : solamente⟩ ⟨they mean nothing to me : ellos me son indiferentes⟩
nothingness ['nʌθɪŋnəs] *n* **1** VOID : vacío *m*, nada *f* **2** NONEXISTENCE : inexistencia *f* **3** TRIFLE : nimiedad *f*
notice[1] ['no:t̬ɪs] *vt* **-ticed; -ticing** : notar, observar, advertir, darse cuenta de
notice[2] *n* **1** NOTIFICATION : aviso *m*, notificación *f* **2** ATTENTION : atención *f* ⟨to take notice of : prestar atención a⟩
noticeable ['no:t̬ɪsəbəl] *adj* : evidente, perceptible — **noticeably** [-bli] *adv*
notification [,no:t̬əfə'keɪʃən] *n* : notificación *f*, aviso *m*
notify ['no:t̬ə,faɪ] *vt* **-fied; -fying** : notificar, avisar
notion ['no:ʃən] *n* **1** IDEA : idea *f*, noción *f* **2** WHIM : capricho *m*, antojo *m* **3 notions** *npl* : artículos *mpl* de mercería
notoriety [,no:t̬ə'raɪət̬i] *n* : mala fama *f*, notoriedad *f*
notorious [no'to:riəs] *adj* : de mala fama, célebre, bien conocido
notwithstanding[1] [,nɑtwɪθ'stændɪŋ, -wɪð-] *adv* NEVERTHELESS : no obstante, sin embargo
notwithstanding[2] *conj* : a pesar de que
notwithstanding[3] *prep* : a pesar de, no obstante
nougat ['nu:gət] *n* : turrón *m*
nought ['nɔt, 'nɑt] → **naught**
noun ['naʊn] *n* : nombre *m*, sustantivo *m*
nourish ['nərɪʃ] *vt* **1** FEED : alimentar, nutrir, sustentar **2** FOSTER : fomentar, alentar
nourishing ['nərɪʃɪŋ] *adj* : alimenticio, nutritivo
nourishment ['nərɪʃmənt] *n* : nutrición *f*, alimento *m*, sustento *m*
novel[1] ['nɑvəl] *adj* : original, novedoso

novel[2] *n* : novela *f*

novelist [ˈnɑvəlɪst] *n* : novelista *mf*

novelty [ˈnɑvəlt̬i] *n, pl* **-ties** **1** : novedad *f* **2 novelties** *npl* TRINKETS : baratijas *fpl*, chucherías *fpl*

November [noˈvɛmbər] *n* : noviembre *m*

novice [ˈnɑvɪs] *n* : novato *m*, -ta *f*; principiante *mf*; novicio *m*, -cia *f*

now[1] [ˈnaʊ] *adv* **1** PRESENTLY : ahora, ya, actualmente ⟨from now on : de ahora en adelante⟩ ⟨long before now : ya hace tiempo⟩ ⟨now and then : de vez en cuando⟩ **2** IMMEDIATELY : ahora (mismo), inmediatamente ⟨do it right now! : ¡hazlo ahora mismo!⟩ **3** THEN : ya, entonces ⟨now they were ready : ya estaban listos⟩ **4** (*used to introduce a statement, a question, a command, or a transition*) ⟨now hear this! : ¡presten atención!⟩ ⟨now what do you think of that? : ¿qué piensas de eso?⟩

now[2] *n* (*indicating the present time*) ⟨until now : hasta ahora⟩ ⟨by now : ya⟩ ⟨ten years from now : dentro de 10 años⟩

now[3] *conj* **now that** : ahora que, ya que

nowadays [ˈnaʊəˌdeɪz] *adv* : hoy en día, actualmente, en la actualidad

nowhere[1] [ˈnoːˌhwɛr] *adv* **1** : en ninguna parte, a ningún lado ⟨nowhere to be found : en ninguna parte, por ningún lado⟩ ⟨you're going nowhere : no estás yendo a ningún lado, no estás yendo a ninguna parte⟩ **2 nowhere near** : ni con mucho, nada cerca ⟨it's nowhere near here : no está nada cerca de aquí⟩

nowhere[2] *n* **1** : ninguna parte *f* **2 out of nowhere** : de la nada

noxious [ˈnɑkʃəs] *adj* : nocivo, dañino, tóxico

nozzle [ˈnɑzəl] *n* : boca *f*

nuance [ˈnuːˌɑnts, ˈnjuː-] *n* : matiz *m*

nub [ˈnʌb] *n* **1** KNOB, LUMP : protuberancia *f*, nudo *m* **2** GIST : quid *m*, meollo *m*

nuclear [ˈnuːkliər, ˈnjuː-] *adj* : nuclear

nucleus [ˈnuːkliəs, ˈnjuː-] *n, pl* **-clei** [-kliˌaɪ] : núcleo *m*

nude[1] [ˈnuːd, ˈnjuːd] *adj* **nuder; nudest** : desnudo

nude[2] *n* : desnudo *m*

nudge[1] [ˈnʌʤ] *vt* **nudged; nudging** : darle con el codo (a alguien)

nudge[2] *n* : toque *m* que se da con el codo

nudism [ˈnuːˌdɪzəm, ˈnjuː-] *n* : nudismo *m*

nudist [ˈnuːdɪst, ˈnjuː-] *n* : nudista *mf*

nudity [ˈnuːdət̬i, ˈnjuː-] *n* : desnudez *f*

nugget [ˈnʌgət] *n* : pepita *f*

nuisance [ˈnuːsənts, ˈnjuː-] *n* **1** BOTHER : fastidio *m*, molestia *f*, lata *f* **2** PEST : pesado *m*, -da *f fam*

null [ˈnʌl] *adj* : nulo ⟨null and void : nulo y sin efecto⟩

nullify [ˈnʌləˌfaɪ] *vt* **-fied; -fying** : invalidar, anular

nullity [ˈnələt̬i] *n, pl* **-ties** : nulidad *f*

numb[1] [ˈnʌm] *vt* : entumecer, adormecer

numb[2] *adj* : entumecido, dormido ⟨numb with fear : paralizado de miedo⟩

number[1] [ˈnʌmbər] *vt* **1** COUNT, INCLUDE : contar, incluir **2** : numerar ⟨number the pages : numera las páginas⟩ **3** TOTAL : ascender a, sumar

number[2] *n* **1** : número *m* ⟨in round numbers : en números redondos⟩ ⟨telephone number : número de teléfono⟩ **2 a number of** : varios, unos pocos, unos cuantos

numberless [ˈnʌmbərləs] *adj* : innumerable, sin número

numbness [ˈnʌmnəs] *n* : entumecimiento *m*

numeral [ˈnuːmərəl, ˈnjuː-] *n* : número *m* ⟨Roman numeral : número romano⟩

numerator [ˈnuːməˌreɪt̬ər, ˈnjuː-] *n* : numerador *m*

numeric [nʊˈmɛrɪk, njʊ-] *adj* : numérico

numerical [nʊˈmɛrɪkəl, njʊ-] *adj* : numérico — **numerically** [-kli] *adv*

numerous [ˈnuːmərəs, ˈnjuː-] *adj* : numeroso

numismatics [ˌnuːməzˈmæt̬ɪks, ˌnjuː-] *n* : numismática *f*

numskull [ˈnʌmˌskʌl] *n* : tonto *m*, -ta *f*; mentecato *m*, -ta *f*; zoquete *m fam*

nun [ˈnʌn] *n* : monja *f*

nuptial [ˈnʌpʃəl] *adj* : nupcial

nuptials [ˈnʌpʃəlz] *npl* WEDDING : nupcias *fpl*, boda *f*

nurse[1] [ˈnərs] *vt* **nursed; nursing** **1** SUCKLE : amamantar **2** : cuidar (de), atender ⟨to nurse the sick : cuidar a los enfermos⟩ ⟨to nurse a cold : curarse de un resfriado⟩

nurse[2] *n* **1** : enfermero *m*, -ra *f* **2** → **nursemaid**

nursemaid [ˈnərsˌmeɪd] *n* : niñera *f*

nursery [ˈnərsəri] *n, pl* **-eries** **1** *or* **day nursery** : guardería *f* **2** : vivero *m* (de plantas)

nursing home *n* : hogar *m* de ancianos, clínica *f* de reposo

nurture[1] [ˈnərʧər] *vt* **-tured; -turing** **1** FEED, NOURISH : nutrir, alimentar **2** EDUCATE : criar, educar **3** FOSTER : alimentar, fomentar

nurture[2] *n* **1** UPBRINGING : crianza *f*, educación *f* **2** FOOD : alimento *m*

nut [ˈnʌt] *n* **1** : nuez *f* **2** : tuerca *f* ⟨nuts and bolts : tuercas y tornillos⟩ **3** LUNATIC : loco *m*, -ca *f*; chiflado *m*, -da *f fam* **4** ENTHUSIAST : fanático *m*, -ca *f*; entusiasta *mf*

nutcracker [ˈnʌtˌkrækər] *n* : cascanueces *m*

nuthatch [ˈnʌtˌhæʧ] *n* : trepador *m*

nutmeg [ˈnʌtˌmɛg] *n* : nuez *f* moscada

nutrient [ˈnuːtriənt, ˈnjuː-] *n* : nutriente *m*, alimento *m* nutritivo

nutriment [ˈnuːtrəmənt, ˈnjuː-] *n* : nutrimento *m*

nutrition [nʊˈtrɪʃən, njʊ-] *n* : nutrición *f*

nutritional [nʊˈtrɪʃənəl, njʊ-] *adj* : alimenticio

nutritious [nʊˈtrɪʃəs, njʊ-] *adj* : nutritivo, alimenticio

nuts [ˈnʌts] *adj* **1** FANATICAL : fanático **2** CRAZY : loco, chiflado *fam*
nutshell [ˈnʌt,ʃɛl] *n* **1** : cáscara *f* de nuez **2 in a nutshell** : en pocas palabras
nutty [ˈnʌṭi] *adj* **-tier; -tiest** : loco, chiflado *fam*
nuzzle [ˈnʌzəl] *v* **-zled; -zling** *vi* NESTLE : acurrucarse, arrimarse — *vt* : acariciar con el hocico
nylon [ˈnaɪ,lɑn] *n* **1** : nilón *m* **2 nylons** *npl* : medias *fpl* de nilón
nymph [ˈnɪmpf] *n* : ninfa *f*

O

o [ˈo:] *n, pl* **o's** *or* **os** [ˈo:z] **1** : decimoquinta letra del alfabeto inglés **2** ZERO : cero *m*
O [ˈo:] → **oh**
oaf [ˈo:f] *n* : zoquete *m*; bruto *m*, -ta *f*
oafish [ˈo:fɪʃ] *adj* : torpe, lerdo
oak [ˈo:k] *n, pl* **oaks** *or* **oak** : roble *m*
oaken [ˈo:kən] *adj* : de roble
oar [ˈor] *n* : remo *m*
oarlock [ˈor,lɑk] *n* : tolete *m*, escálamo *m*
oasis [oˈeɪsɪs] *n, pl* **oases** [-,si:z] : oasis *m*
oat [ˈo:t] *n* : avena *f*
oath [ˈo:θ] *n, pl* **oaths** [ˈo:ðz, ˈo:θs] **1** : juramento *m* ⟨to take an oath : prestar juramento⟩ **2** SWEARWORD : mala palabra *f*, palabrota *f*
oatmeal [ˈo:t,mi:l] *n* : avena *f* ⟨instant oatmeal : avena instantánea⟩
obdurate [ˈɑbdʊrət, -djʊ-] *adj* : inflexible, firme, obstinado
obedience [oˈbi:diənts] *n* : obediencia *f*
obedient [oˈbi:diənt] *adj* : obediente — **obediently** *adv*
obelisk [ˈɑbə,lɪsk] *n* : obelisco *m*
obese [oˈbi:s] *adj* : obeso
obesity [oˈbi:səṭi] *n* : obesidad *f*
obey [oˈbeɪ] *v* **obeyed; obeying** : obedecer ⟨to obey the law : cumplir la ley⟩
obfuscate [ˈɑbfə,skeɪt] *vt* **-cated; -cating** : ofuscar, confundir
obituary [əˈbɪtʃʊ,ɛri] *n, pl* **-aries** : obituario *m*, necrología *f*
object[1] [əbˈdʒɛkt] *vt* : objetar — *vi* : oponerse, poner reparos, hacer objeciones
object[2] [ˈɑbdʒɪkt] *n* **1** : objeto *m* **2** OBJECTIVE, PURPOSE : objetivo *m*, propósito *m* **3** : complemento *m* (en gramática)
objection [əbˈdʒɛkʃən] *n* : objeción *f*
objectionable [əbˈdʒɛkʃənəbəl] *adj* : ofensivo, indeseable — **objectionably** [-bli] *adv*
objective[1] [əbˈdʒɛktɪv] *adj* **1** IMPARTIAL : objetivo, imparcial **2** : de complemento, directo (en gramática)
objective[2] *n* **1** : objetivo *m* **2** *or* **objective case** : acusativo *m*
objectively [əbˈdʒɛktɪvli] *adv* : objetivamente
objectivity [,ɑb,dʒɛkˈtɪvəṭi] *n, pl* **-ties** : objetividad *f*
obligate [ˈɑblə,geɪt] *vt* **-gated; -gating** : obligar
obligation [,ɑbləˈgeɪʃən] *n* : obligación *f*
obligatory [əˈblɪgə,tori] *adj* : obligatorio
oblige [əˈblaɪdʒ] *vt* **obliged; obliging** **1** COMPEL : obligar **2** : hacerle un favor (a alguien), complacer ⟨to oblige a friend : hacerle un favor a un amigo⟩ **3 to be much obliged** : estar muy agradecido
obliging [əˈblaɪdʒɪŋ] *adj* : servicial, complaciente — **obligingly** *adv*
oblique [oˈbli:k] *adj* **1** SLANTING : oblicuo **2** INDIRECT : indirecto — **obliquely** *adv*
obliterate [əˈblɪṭə,reɪt] *vt* **-ated; -ating** **1** ERASE : obliterar, borrar **2** DESTROY : destruir, eliminar
obliteration [ə,blɪṭəˈreɪʃən] *n* : obliteración *f*
oblivion [əˈblɪviən] *n* : olvido *m*
oblivious [əˈblɪviəs] *adj* : inconsciente — **obliviously** *adv*
oblong[1] [ˈɑ,blɔŋ] *adj* : oblongo
oblong[2] *n* : figura *f* oblonga, rectángulo *m*
obnoxious [ɑbˈnɑkʃəs, əb-] *adj* : repugnante, odioso — **obnoxiously** *adv*
oboe [ˈo:,bo:] *n* : oboe *m*
oboist [ˈo,boɪst] *n* : oboe *mf*
obscene [ɑbˈsi:n, əb-] *adj* : obsceno, indecente — **obscenely** *adv*
obscenity [ɑbˈsɛnəṭi, əb-] *n, pl* **-ties** : obscenidad *f*
obscure[1] [ɑbˈskjʊr, əb-] *vt* **-scured; -scuring** **1** CLOUD, DIM : oscurecer, nublar **2** HIDE : ocultar
obscure[2] *adj* **1** DIM : oscuro **2** REMOTE, SECLUDED : recóndito **3** VAGUE : oscuro, confuso, vago **4** UNKNOWN : desconocido ⟨an obscure poet : un poeta desconocido⟩ — **obscurely** *adv*
obscurity [ɑbˈskjʊrəṭi, əb-] *n, pl* **-ties** : oscuridad *f*
obsequious [əbˈsi:kwiəs] *adj* : servil, excesivamente atento
observable [əbˈzərvəbəl] *adj* : observable, perceptible
observance [əbˈzərvənts] *n* **1** FULFILLMENT : observancia *f*, cumplimiento *m* **2** PRACTICE : práctica *f*
observant [əbˈzərvənt] *adj* : observador
observation [,ɑbsərˈveɪʃən, -zər-] *n* : observación *f*
observatory [əbˈzərvə,tori] *n, pl* **-ries** : observatorio *m*
observe [əbˈzərv] *v* **-served; -serving** *vt* **1** OBEY : observar, obedecer **2** CELEBRATE : celebrar, guardar (una práctica religiosa) **3** WATCH : observar, mi-

rar **4** REMARK : observar, comentar — *vi* LOOK : mirar

observer [ɑbˈzərvər] *n* : observador *m*, -dora *f*

obsess [əbˈsɛs] *vt* : obsesionar

obsession [ɑbˈsɛʃən, əb-] *n* : obsesión *f*

obsessive [ɑbˈsɛsɪv, əb-] *adj* : obsesivo — **obsessively** *adv*

obsolescence [ˌɑbsəˈlɛsənts] *n* : obsolescencia *f*

obsolescent [ˌɑbsəˈlɛsənt] *adj* : obsolescente ⟨to become obsolescent : caer en desuso⟩

obsolete [ˌɑbsəˈliːt, ˈɑbsəˌ-] *adj* : obsoleto, anticuado

obstacle [ˈɑbstɪkəl] *n* : obstáculo *m*, impedimento *m*

obstetric [əbˈstɛtrɪk] *or* **obstetrical** [-trɪkəl] *adj* : obstétrico

obstetrician [ˌɑbstəˈtrɪʃən] *n* : obstetra *mf*; tocólogo *m*, -ga *f*

obstetrics [əbˈstɛtrɪks] *ns & pl* : obstetricia *f*, tocología *f*

obstinacy [ˈɑbstənəsi] *n, pl* **-cies** : obstinación *f*, terquedad *f*

obstinate [ˈɑbstənət] *adj* : obstinado, terco — **obstinately** *adv*

obstreperous [əbˈstrɛpərəs] *adj* **1** CLAMOROUS : ruidoso, clamoroso **2** UNRULY : rebelde, indisciplinado

obstruct [əbˈstrʌkt] *vt* : obstruir, bloquear

obstruction [əbˈstrʌkʃən] *n* : obstrucción *f*, bloqueo *m*

obstructive [əbˈstrəktɪv] *adj* : obstructor

obtain [əbˈteɪn] *vt* : obtener, conseguir — *vi* PREVAIL : imperar, prevalecer

obtainable [əbˈteɪnəbəl] *adj* : obtenible, asequible

obtrude [əbˈtruːd] *v* **-truded; -truding** *vt* **1** EXTRUDE : expulsar **2** IMPOSE : imponer — *vi* INTRUDE : inmiscuirse, entrometerse

obtrusive [əbˈtruːsɪv] *adj* **1** IMPERTINENT, MEDDLESOME : impertinente, entrometido **2** PROTRUDING : prominente

obtuse [ɑbˈtuːs, əb-, -ˈtjuːs] *adj* : obtuso, torpe

obtuse angle *n* : ángulo obtuso

obviate [ˈɑbviˌeɪt] *vt* **-ated; -ating** : obviar, evitar

obvious [ˈɑbviəs] *adj* : obvio, evidente, manifiesto

obviously [ˈɑbviəsli] *adv* **1** CLEARLY : obviamente, evidentemente **2** OF COURSE : claro, por supuesto

occasion[1] [əˈkeɪʒən] *vt* : ocasionar, causar

occasion[2] *n* **1** OPPORTUNITY : oportunidad *f*, ocasión *f* **2** CAUSE : motivo *m*, razón *f* **3** INSTANCE : ocasión *f* **4** EVENT : ocasión *f*, acontecimiento *m* **5 on ~** : de vez en cuando, ocasionalmente

occasional [əˈkeɪʒənəl] *adj* : ocasional

occasionally [əˈkeɪʒənəli] *adv* : de vez en cuando, ocasionalmente

occidental [ˌɑksəˈdɛntəl] *adj* : oeste, del oeste, occidental

occult[1] [əˈkʌlt, ˈɑˌkʌlt] *adj* **1** HIDDEN, SECRET : oculto, secreto **2** ARCANE : arcano, esotérico

occult[2] *n* **the occult** : las ciencias ocultas

occupancy [ˈɑkjəpəntsi] *n, pl* **-cies** : ocupación *f*, habitación *f*

occupant [ˈɑkjəpənt] *n* : ocupante *mf*

occupation [ˌɑkjəˈpeɪʃən] *n* : ocupación *f*, profesión *f*, oficio *m*

occupational [ˌɑkjəˈpeɪʃənəl] *adj* : ocupacional

occupy [ˈɑkjəˌpaɪ] *vt* **-pied; -pying** : ocupar

occur [əˈkər] *vi* **occurred; occurring 1** EXIST : encontrarse, existir **2** HAPPEN : ocurrir, acontecer, suceder, tener lugar **3** : ocurrirse ⟨it occurred to him that . . . : se le ocurrió que . . .⟩

occurrence [əˈkərənts] *n* : acontecimiento *m*, suceso *m*, ocurrencia *f*

ocean [ˈoːʃən] *n* : océano *m*

oceanic [ˌoːʃiˈænɪk] *adj* : oceánico

oceanography [ˌoːʃəˈnɑgrəfi] *n* : oceanografía *f*

ocelot [ˈɑsəˌlɑt, ˈoː-] *n* : ocelote *m*

ocher *or* **ochre** [ˈoːkər] *n* : ocre *m*

o'clock [əˈklɑk] *adv* (*used in telling time*) ⟨it's ten o'clock : son las diez⟩ ⟨at six o'clock : a las seis⟩

octagon [ˈɑktəˌgɑn] *n* : octágono *m*

octagonal [ɑkˈtægənəl] *adj* : octagonal

octave [ˈɑktɪv] *n* : octava *f*

October [ɑkˈtoːbər] *n* : octubre *m*

octopus [ˈɑktəˌpʊs, -pəs] *n, pl* **-puses** *or* **-pi** [-ˌpaɪ] : pulpo *m*

ocular [ˈɑkjələr] *adj* : ocular

oculist [ˈɑkjəlɪst] *n* **1** OPHTHALMOLOGIST : oftalmólogo *m*, -ga *f*; oculista *mf* **2** OPTOMETRIST : optometrista *mf*

odd [ˈɑd] *adj* **1** : sin pareja, suelto ⟨an odd sock : un calcetín sin pareja⟩ **2** UNEVEN : impar ⟨odd numbers : números impares⟩ **3** : y pico, y tantos ⟨forty odd years ago : hace cuarenta y pico años⟩ **4** : alguno, uno que otro ⟨odd jobs : algunos trabajos⟩ **5** STRANGE : extraño, raro

oddball [ˈɑdˌbɔl] *n* : excéntrico *m*, -ca *f*; persona *f* rara

oddity [ˈɑdəṭi] *n, pl* **-ties** : rareza *f*, cosa *f* rara

oddly [ˈɑdli] *adv* : de manera extraña

oddness [ˈɑdnəs] *n* : rareza *f*, excentricidad *f*

odds [ˈɑdz] *npl* **1** CHANCES : probabilidades *fpl* **2** : puntos *mpl* de ventaja (de una apuesta) **3 to be at odds** : estar en desacuerdo

odds and ends *npl* : costillas *fpl*, cosas *fpl* sueltas, cachivaches *mpl*

ode [ˈoːd] *n* : oda *f*

odious [ˈoːdiəs] *adj* : odioso — **odiously** *adv*

odor [ˈoːdər] *n* : olor *m*

odorless [ˈoːdərləs] *adj* : inodoro, sin olor

odorous [ˈoːdərəs] *adj* : oloroso

odyssey [ˈɑdəsi] *n, pl* **-seys** : odisea *f*

o'er [ˈor] → **over**

of [ˈʌv, ˈɑv] *prep* **1** FROM : de ⟨a man of the city : un hombre de la ciudad⟩ **2** (*indicating character or background*) : de ⟨a woman of great ability : una mujer de gran capacidad⟩ **3** (*indicating cause*) : de ⟨he died of the flu : murió de la gripe⟩ **4** BY : de ⟨the works of Shakespeare : las obras de Shakespeare⟩ **5** (*indicating contents, material, or quantity*) : de ⟨a house of wood : una casa de madera⟩ ⟨a glass of water : un vaso de agua⟩ **6** (*indicating belonging or connection*) : de ⟨the front of the house : el frente de la casa⟩ **7** ABOUT : sobre, de ⟨tales of the West : los cuentos del Oeste⟩ **8** (*indicating a particular example*) : de ⟨the city of Caracas : la ciudad de Caracas⟩ **9** FOR : por, a ⟨love of country : amor por la patria⟩ **10** (*indicating time or date*) ⟨five minutes of ten : las diez menos cinco⟩ ⟨the eighth of April : el ocho de abril⟩

off[1] [ˈɔf] *adv* **1** (*indicating change of position or state*) ⟨to march off : marcharse⟩ ⟨he dozed off : se puso a dormir⟩ **2** (*indicating distance in space or time*) ⟨some miles off : a varias millas⟩ ⟨the holiday is three weeks off : faltan tres semanas para la fiesta⟩ **3** (*indicating removal*) ⟨the knob came off : se le cayó el pomo⟩ **4** (*indicating termination*) ⟨shut the television off : apaga la televisión⟩ **5** (*indicating suspension of work*) ⟨to take a day off : tomarse un día de descanso⟩ **6 off and on** : de vez en cuando

off[2] *adj* **1** FARTHER : más remoto, distante ⟨the off side of the building : el lado distante del edificio⟩ **2** STARTED : empezado ⟨to be off on a spree : irse de juerga⟩ **3** OUT : apagado ⟨the light is off : la luz está apagada⟩ **4** CANCELED : cancelado, suspendido **5** INCORRECT : erróneo, incorrecto **6** REMOTE : remoto, lejano ⟨an off chance : una posibilidad remota⟩ **7** FREE : libre ⟨I'm off today : hoy estoy libre⟩ **8 to be well off** : vivir con desahogo, tener bastante dinero

off[3] *prep* **1** (*indicating physical separation*) : de ⟨she took it off the table : lo tomó de la mesa⟩ ⟨a shop off the main street : una tienda al lado de la calle principal⟩ **2** : a la costa de, a expensas de ⟨he lives off his sister : vive a expensas de su hermana⟩ **3** (*indicating the suspension of an activity*) ⟨to be off duty : estar libre⟩ ⟨he's off liquor : ha dejado el alcohol⟩ **4** BELOW : por debajo de ⟨he's off his game : está por debajo de su juego normal⟩

offal [ˈɔfəl] *n* **1** RUBBISH, WASTE : desechos *mpl*, desperdicios *mpl* **2** VISCERA : vísceras *fpl*, asaduras *fpl*

offend [əˈfɛnd] *vt* **1** VIOLATE : violar, atentar contra **2** HURT : ofender ⟨to be easily offended : ser muy susceptible⟩

offender [əˈfɛndər] *n* : delincuente *mf*; infractor *m*, -tora *f*

offense *or* **offence** [əˈfɛnts, ˈɔˌfɛnts] *n* **1** INSULT : ofensa *f*, injuria *f*, agravio *m* ⟨to take offense : ofenderse⟩ **2** ASSAULT : ataque *m* **3** : ofensiva *f* (en deportes) **4** CRIME, INFRACTION : infracción *f*, delito *m*

offensive[1] [əˈfɛntsɪv, ˈɔˌfɛnt-] *adj* : ofensivo — **offensively** *adv*

offensive[2] *n* : ofensiva *f*

offer[1] [ˈɔfər] *vt* **1** : ofrecer ⟨they offered him the job : le ofrecieron el puesto⟩ **2** PROPOSE : proponer, sugerir **3** SHOW : ofrecer, mostrar ⟨to offer resistance : ofrecer resistencia⟩

offer[2] *n* : oferta *f*, ofrecimiento *m*, propuesta *f*

offering [ˈɔfərɪŋ] *n* : ofrenda *f*

offhand[1] [ˈɔfˈhænd] *adv* : sin preparación, sin pensarlo

offhand[2] *adj* **1** IMPROMPTU : improvisado **2** ABRUPT : brusco

office [ˈɔfəs] *n* **1** : cargo *m* ⟨to run for office : presentarse como candidato⟩ **2** : oficina *f*, despacho *m*, gabinete *m* (en la casa) ⟨office hours : horas de oficina⟩

officeholder [ˈɔfəsˌhoːldər] *n* : titular *mf*

officer [ˈɔfəsər] *n* **1** *or* **police officer** : policía *mf*, agente *mf* de policía **2** OFFICIAL : oficial *mf*; funcionario *m*, -ria *f*; director *m*, -tora *f* (en una empresa) **3** COMMISSIONED OFFICER : oficial *mf*

official[1] [əˈfɪʃəl] *adj* : oficial — **officially** *adv*

official[2] *n* : funcionario *m*, -ria *f*; oficial *mf*

officiate [əˈfɪʃiˌeɪt] *v* **-ated; -ating** *vi* **1** : arbitrar (en deportes) **2 to officiate at** : oficiar, celebrar — *vt* : arbitrar

officious [əˈfɪʃəs] *adj* : oficioso

offing [ˈɔfɪŋ] *n* **in the offing** : en perspectiva

offset [ˈɔfˌsɛt] *vt* **-set; -setting** : compensar

offshoot [ˈɔfˌʃuːt] *n* **1** OUTGROWTH : producto *m*, resultado *m* **2** BRANCH, SHOOT : retoño *m*, rama *f*, vástago *m* (de una planta)

offshore[1] [ˈɔfˈʃor] *adv* : a una distancia de la costa

offshore[2] *adj* **1** : de (la) tierra ⟨an offshore wind : un viento que sopla de tierra⟩ **2** : (de) costa afuera, cercano a la costa ⟨an offshore island : una isla costera⟩

offspring [ˈɔfˌsprɪŋ] *ns & pl* **1** YOUNG : crías *fpl* (de los animales) **2** PROGENY : prole *f*, progenie *f*

off–white [ˈɔfˈhwaɪt] *adj* : blancuzco

often [ˈɔfən, ˈɔftən] *adv* : muchas veces, a menudo, seguido

oftentimes [ˈɔfən,taɪmz, ˈɔftən-] *or* **ofttimes** [ˈɔft,taɪms] → **often**

ogle [ˈoːgəl] *vt* **ogled; ogling** : comerse con los ojos, quedarse mirando a

ogre [ˈoːgər] *n* : ogro *m*

oh [ˈoː] *interj* : ¡oh!, ¡ah!, ¡ay! ⟨oh, of course : ah, por supuesto⟩ ⟨oh no! : ¡ay no!⟩ ⟨oh really? : ¿de veras?⟩

ohm [ˈoːm] *n* : ohm *m*, ohmio *m*

oil[1] [ˈɔɪl] *vt* : lubricar, engrasar, aceitar

oil[2] *n* **1** : aceite *m* **2** PETROLEUM : petróleo *m* **3** *or* **oil painting** : óleo *m*, pintura *f* al óleo **4** *or* **oil paint(s)** : óleo *m*

oilcloth [ˈɔɪl,klɔθ] *n* : hule *m*

oiliness [ˈɔɪlinəs] *n* : lo aceitoso

oilskin [ˈɔɪl,skɪn] *n* **1** : hule *m* **2 oilskins** *npl* : impermeable *m*

oily [ˈɔɪli] *adj* **oilier; -est** : aceitoso, grasiento, grasoso ⟨oily fingers : dedos grasientos⟩

ointment [ˈɔɪntmənt] *n* : ungüento *m*, pomada *f*

OK[1] [,oːˈkeɪ] *vt* **OK'd** *or* **okayed** [,oːˈkeɪd]; **OK'ing** *or* **okaying** APPROVE, AUTHORIZE : dar el visto bueno a, autorizar, aprobar

OK[2] *or* **okay** [,oːˈkeɪ] *adv* **1** WELL : bien **2** YES : sí, por supuesto

OK[3] *adj* : bien ⟨he's OK : está bien⟩ ⟨it's OK with me : estoy de acuerdo⟩

OK[4] *n* : autorización *f*, visto *m* bueno

okra [ˈoːkrə, *South also* -kri] *n* : quingombó *m*

old[1] [ˈoːld] *adj* **1** ANCIENT : antiguo ⟨old civilizations : civilizaciones antiguas⟩ **2** FAMILIAR : viejo ⟨old friends : viejos amigos⟩ ⟨the same old story : el mismo cuento⟩ **3** (*indicating a certain age*) ⟨he's ten years old : tiene diez años (de edad)⟩ **4** AGED : viejo, anciano ⟨an old woman : una anciana⟩ **5** FORMER : antiguo ⟨her old neighborhood : su antiguo barrio⟩ **6** WORN-OUT : viejo, gastado

old[2] *n* **1 the old** : los viejos, los ancianos **2 in the days of old** : antaño, en los tiempos antiguos

olden [ˈoːldən] *adj* : de antaño, de antigüedad

old–fashioned [ˈoːldˈfæʃənd] *adj* : anticuado, pasado de moda

old maid *n* **1** SPINSTER : soltera *f* **2** FUSSBUDGET : maniático *m*, -ca *f*; melindroso *m*, -sa *f*

Old Testament *n* : Antiguo Testamento *m*

old–time [ˈoːldˈtaɪm] *adj* : antiguo

old–timer [ˈoːldˈtaɪmər] *n* **1** VETERAN : veterano *m*, -na *f* **2** *or* **oldster** : anciano *m*, -na *f*

old–world [ˈoːldˈwərld] *adj* : pintoresco (de antaño)

oleander [ˈoːli,ændər] *n* : adelfa *f*

oleomargarine [,oːlioˈmɑrdʒərən] → **margarine**

olfactory [ɑlˈfæktəri, ol-] *adj* : olfativo

oligarchy [ˈɑlə,gɑrki, ˈoːlə-] *n, pl* **-chies** : oligarquía *f*

olive [ˈɑlɪv, -ləv] *n* **1** : aceituna *f*, oliva *f* (fruta) **2** : olivo *m* (árbol) **3** *or* **olive green** : color *m* aceituna, verde *m* oliva

Olmec [ˈɑl,mɛk, ˈoːl-] *n* : olmeca *mf* — **Olmec** *adj*

Olympic [əˈlɪmpɪk, o-] *adj* : olímpico

Olympic Games *npl* : Juegos *mpl* Olímpicos

Olympics [əˈlɪmpɪks, o-] *npl* : olimpiadas *fpl*

Omani [oˈmɑni, -ˈmæ-] *n* : omaní *mf* — **Omani** *adj*

ombudsman [ˈɑm,bʊdzmən, ɑmˈbʊdz-] *n, pl* **-men** [-mən, -,mɛn] : ombudsman *m*

omelet *or* **omelette** [ˈɑmlət, ˈɑmə-] *n* : omelette *mf*, tortilla *f* (de huevo)

omen [ˈoːmən] *n* : presagio *m*, augurio *m*, agüero *m*

ominous [ˈɑmənəs] *adj* : ominoso, agorero, de mal agüero

ominously [ˈɑmənəsli] *adv* : de manera amenazadora

omission [oˈmɪʃən] *n* : omisión *f*

omit [oˈmɪt] *vt* **omitted; omitting** **1** LEAVE OUT : omitir, excluir **2** NEGLECT : omitir ⟨they omitted to tell us : omitieron decírnoslo⟩

omnipotence [ɑmˈnɪpət̬ənts] *n* : omnipotencia *f* — **omnipotent** [ɑmˈnɪpət̬ənt] *adj*

omnipresent [,ɑmnɪˈprɛzənt] *adj* : omnipresente

omniscient [ɑmˈnɪʃənt] *adj* : omnisciente

omnivorous [ɑmˈnɪvərəs] *adj* **1** : omnívoro **2** AVID : ávido, voraz

on[1] [ˈɑn, ˈɔn] *adv* **1** (*indicating contact with a surface*) ⟨put the top on : pon la tapa⟩ ⟨he has a hat on : lleva un sombrero puesto⟩ **2** (*indicating forward movement*) ⟨from that moment on : a partir de ese momento⟩ ⟨farther on : más adelante⟩ **3** (*indicating operation or an operating position*) ⟨turn the light on : prende la luz⟩

on[2] *adj* **1** (*being in operation*) ⟨the radio is on : el radio está prendido⟩ **2** (*taking place*) ⟨the game is on : el juego ha comenzado⟩ **3 to be on to** : estar enterado de

on[3] *prep* **1** (*indicating position*) : en, sobre, encima de ⟨on the table : en (sobre, encima de) la mesa⟩ ⟨shadows on the wall : sombras en la pared⟩ ⟨on horseback : a caballo⟩ **2** AT, TO : a ⟨on the right : a la derecha⟩ **3** ABOARD, IN : en, a ⟨on the plane : en el avión⟩ ⟨he got on the train : subió al tren⟩ **4** (*indicating time*) ⟨she worked on Saturdays : trabajaba los sábados⟩ ⟨every hour on the hour : a la hora en punto⟩ **5** (*indicating means or agency*) : por ⟨he cut himself on a tin can : se cortó con una lata⟩ ⟨to talk on the telephone : hablar por teléfono⟩ **6** (*indicating a state or process*) : en ⟨on fire : en llamas⟩ ⟨on the increase : en aumento⟩ **7** (*indicating connection or membership*) : en ⟨on a committee : en una comisión⟩ **8** (*indicating an activity*) ⟨on vacation : de vacaciones⟩ ⟨on a diet : a dieta⟩ **9** ABOUT, CONCERNING : sobre ⟨a book on insects : un libro sobre insectos⟩ ⟨reflect on that : reflexiona sobre eso⟩

once[1] [ˈwʌnts] *adv* **1** : una vez ⟨once a month : una vez al mes⟩ ⟨once and for all : de una vez por todas⟩ **2** EVER : alguna vez **3** FORMERLY : antes, anteriormente

once[2] *adj* FORMER : antiguo

once[3] *n* **1** : una vez **2 at ~** SIMULTANEOUSLY : al mismo tiempo, simultáneamente **3 at ~** IMMEDIATELY : inmediatamente, en seguida

once[4] *conj* : una vez que, tan pronto como

once–over [ˌwʌntsˈoːvər, ˈwʌntsˌ-] *n* **to give someone the once–over** : echarle un vistazo a alguien

oncoming [ˈɑnˌkʌmɪŋ, ˈɔn-] *adj* : que viene

one[1] [ˈwʌn] *adj* **1** (*being a single unit*) : un, una ⟨he only wants one apple : sólo quiere una manzana⟩ **2** (*being a particular one*) : un, una ⟨he arrived early one morning : llegó temprano una mañana⟩ **3** (*being the same*) : mismo, misma ⟨they're all members of one team : todos son miembros del mismo equipo⟩ ⟨one and the same thing : la misma cosa⟩ **4** SOME : alguno, alguna; un, una ⟨I'll see you again one day : algún día te veré otra vez⟩ ⟨at one time or another : en una u otra ocasión⟩

one[2] *n* **1** : uno *m* (número) **2** (*indicating the first of a set or series*) ⟨from day one : desde el primer momento⟩ **3** (*indicating a single person or thing*) ⟨the one (girl) on the right : la de la derecha⟩ ⟨he has the one but needs the other : tiene uno pero necesita el otro⟩

one[3] *pron* **1** : uno, una ⟨one of his friends : una de sus amigas⟩ ⟨one never knows : uno nunca sabe, nunca se sabe⟩ ⟨to cut one's finger : cortarse el dedo⟩ **2 one and all** : todos, todo el mundo **3 one another** : el uno al otro, se ⟨they loved one another : se amaban⟩ **4 that one** : aquél, aquella **5 which one?** : ¿cuál?

one–on–one [wʌnɔnˈwʌn, -ɑn-] *adj* : uno a uno — **one–on–one** *adv*

onerous [ˈɑnərəs, ˈoːnə-] *adj* : oneroso, gravoso

oneself [ˌwʌnˈsɛlf] *pron* **1** (*used reflexively or for emphasis*) : se, sí mismo, uno mismo ⟨to control oneself : controlarse⟩ ⟨to talk to oneself : hablarse a sí mismo⟩ ⟨to do it oneself : hacérselo uno mismo⟩ **2 by ~** : solo

one–sided [ˈwʌnˈsaɪdəd] *adj* **1** : de un solo lado **2** LOPSIDED : asimétrico **3** BIASED : parcial, tendencioso **4** UNILATERAL : unilateral

onetime [ˈwʌnˈtaɪm] *adj* FORMER : antiguo

one–way [ˈwʌnˈweɪ] *adj* **1** : de sentido único, de una sola dirección ⟨a one-way street : una calle de sentido único⟩ **2** : de ida, sencillo ⟨a one-way ticket : un boleto de ida⟩

ongoing [ˈɑnˌgoːɪŋ] *adj* **1** CONTINUING : en curso, corriente **2** DEVELOPING : en desarrollo

onion [ˈʌnjən] *n* : cebolla *f*

online [ˈɔnˈlaɪn, ˈɑn-] *adj* : en línea

onlooker [ˈɔnˌlʊkər, ˈɑn-] *n* : espectador *m*, -dora *f*, circunstante *mf*

only[1] [ˈoːnli] *adv* **1** MERELY : sólo, solamente, nomás ⟨for only two dollars : por tan sólo dos dólares⟩ ⟨only once : sólo una vez, no más de una vez⟩ ⟨I only did it to help : lo hice por ayudar nomás⟩ **2** SOLELY : únicamente, sólo, solamente ⟨only he knows it : solamente él lo sabe⟩ **3** (*indicating a result*) ⟨it will only cause him problems : no hará más que crearle problemas⟩ **4 if only** : ojalá, por lo menos ⟨if only it were true! : ¡ojalá sea cierto!⟩ ⟨if he could only dance : si por lo menos pudiera bailar⟩

only[2] *adj* : único ⟨an only child : un hijo único⟩ ⟨the only chance : la única oportunidad⟩

only[3] *conj* BUT : pero ⟨I would go, only I'm sick : iría, pero estoy enfermo⟩

onset [ˈɑnˌsɛt] *n* : comienzo *m*, llegada *f*

onslaught [ˈɑnˌslɔt, ˈɔn-] *n* : arremetida *f*, embestida *f*, embate *m*

onto [ˈɑnˌtuː, ˈɔn-] *prep* : sobre

onus [ˈoːnəs] *n* : responsabilidad *f*, carga *f*

onward[1] [ˈɑnwərd, ˈɔn-] *or* **onwards** *adv* FORWARD : adelante, hacia adelante

onward[2] *adj* : hacia adelante

onyx [ˈɑnɪks] *n* : ónix *m*

ooze[1] [ˈuːz] *v* **oozed; oozing** *vi* : rezumar — *vt* **1** : rezumar **2** EXUDE : irradiar, rebosar ⟨to ooze confidence : irradiar confianza⟩

ooze[2] *n* SLIME : cieno *m*, limo *m*

opacity [oˈpæsət̬i] *n, pl* **-ties** : opacidad *f*

opal [ˈoːpəl] *n* : ópalo *m*

opaque [oˈpeɪk] *adj* **1** : opaco **2** UNCLEAR : poco claro

open[1] [ˈoːpən] *vt* **1** : abrir ⟨open the door : abre la puerta⟩ **2** UNCOVER : destapar **3** UNFOLD : desplegar, abrir **4** CLEAR : abrir (un camino, etc.) **5** INAUGURATE : abrir (una tienda), inaugurar (una exposición, etc.) **6** INITIATE : iniciar, entablar, abrir ⟨to open the meeting : abrir la sesión⟩ ⟨to open a discussion : entablar un debate⟩ — *vi* **1** : abrirse **2** BEGIN : empezar, comenzar

open[2] *adj* **1** : abierto ⟨an open window : una ventana abierta⟩ **2** FRANK : abierto, franco, directo **3** UNCOV-

ERED : descubierto, abierto **4** EXTENDED : extendido, abierto ⟨with open arms : con los brazos abiertos⟩ **5** UNRESTRICTED : libre, abierto **6** UNDECIDED : pendiente, por decidir, sin resolver ⟨an open question : una cuestión pendiente⟩ **7** AVAILABLE : vacante, libre ⟨the job is open : el puesto está vacante⟩

open[3] *n* **in the open 1** OUTDOORS : al aire libre **2** KNOWN : conocido, sacado a la luz

open–air [ˈo:pənˈær] *adj* OUTDOOR : al aire libre

open–and–shut [ˈo:pənəndˈʃʌt] *adj* : claro, evidente ⟨an open-and-shut case : un caso muy claro⟩

opener [ˈo:pənər] *n* : destapador *m*, abrelatas *m*, abridor *m*

openhanded [ˌo:pənˈhændəd] *adj* : generoso, liberal

openhearted [ˌo:pənˈhɑrt̬əd] *adj* **1** FRANK : franco, sincero **2** : generoso, de gran corazón

opening [ˈo:pənɪŋ] *n* **1** BEGINNING : comienzo *m*, principio *m*, apertura *f* **2** APERTURE : abertura *f*, brecha *f*, claro *m* (en el bosque) **3** OPPORTUNITY : oportunidad *f*

openly [ˈo:pənli] *adv* **1** FRANKLY : abiertamente, francamente **2** PUBLICLY : públicamente, declaradamente

openness [ˈo:pənnəs] *n* : franqueza *f*

opera [ˈɑprə, ˈɑpərə] *n* **1** : ópera *f* **2** → **opus**

opera glasses *npl* : gemelos *mpl* de teatro

operate [ˈɑpəˌreɪt] *v* **-ated; -ating** *vi* **1** ACT, FUNCTION : operar, funcionar, actuar **2 to operate on (someone)** : operar a (alguien) — *vt* **1** WORK : operar, manejar, hacer funcionar (una máquina) **2** MANAGE : manejar, administrar (un negocio)

operatic [ˌɑpəˈræt̬ɪk] *adj* : operístico

operation [ˌɑpəˈreɪʃən] *n* **1** FUNCTIONING : funcionamiento *m* **2** USE : uso *m*, manejo *m* (de máquinas) **3** SURGERY : operación *f*, intervención *f* quirúrgica

operational [ˌɑpəˈreɪʃənəl] *adj* : operacional, de operación

operative [ˈɑpərət̬ɪv, -ˌreɪ-] *adj* **1** OPERATING : vigente, en vigor **2** WORKING : operativo **3** SURGICAL : quirúrgico

operator [ˈɑpəˌreɪt̬ər] *n* : operador *m*, -dora *f*

operetta [ˌɑpəˈrɛt̬ə] *n* : opereta *f*

ophthalmologist [ˌɑfˌθælˈmɑləʤɪst, -θəˈmɑ-] *n* : oftalmólogo *m*, -ga *f*

ophthalmology [ˌɑfˌθælˈmɑləʤi, -θəˈmɑ-] *n* : oftalmología *f*

opiate [ˈo:piət, -piˌeɪt] *n* : opiato *m*

opinion [əˈpɪnjən] *n* : opinión *f*

opinionated [əˈpɪnjəˌneɪt̬əd] *adj* : testarudo, dogmático

opium [ˈo:piəm] *n* : opio *m*

opossum [əˈpɑsəm] *n* : zarigüeya *f*, oposum *m*

opponent [əˈpo:nənt] *n* : oponente *mf*; opositor *m*, -tora *f*; contrincante *mf* (en deportes)

opportune [ˌɑpərˈtu:n, -ˈtju:n] *adj* : oportuno — **opportunely** *adv*

opportunist [ˌɑpərˈtu:nɪst, -ˈtju:-] *n* : oportunista *mf*

opportunistic [ˌɑpərtuˈnɪstɪk, -tju-] *adj* : oportunista *mf*

opportunity [ˌɑpərˈtu:nət̬i, -ˈtju:-] *n, pl* **-ties** : oportunidad *f*, ocasión *f*, chance *m*, posibilidades *fpl*

oppose [əˈpo:z] *vt* **-posed; -posing 1** : ir en contra de, oponerse a ⟨good opposes evil : el bien se opone al mal⟩ **2** COMBAT : luchar contra, combatir, resistir

opposite[1] [ˈɑpəzət] *adv* : enfrente

opposite[2] *adj* **1** FACING : de enfrente ⟨the opposite side : el lado de enfrente⟩ **2** CONTRARY : opuesto, contrario ⟨in opposite directions : en direcciones contrarias⟩ ⟨the opposite sex : el sexo opuesto, el otro sexo⟩

opposite[3] *n* : lo contrario, lo opuesto

opposite[4] *prep* : enfrente de, frente a

opposition [ˌɑpəˈzɪʃən] *n* **1** : oposición *f*, resistencia *f* **2 in opposition to** AGAINST : en contra de

oppress [əˈprɛs] *vt* **1** PERSECUTE : oprimir, perseguir **2** BURDEN : oprimir, agobiar

oppression [əˈprɛʃən] *n* : opresión *f*

oppressive [əˈprɛsɪv] *adj* **1** HARSH : opresivo, severo **2** STIFLING : agobiante, sofocante ⟨oppressive heat : calor sofocante⟩

oppressor [əˈprɛsər] *n* : opresor *m*, -sora *f*

opprobrium [əˈpro:briəm] *n* : oprobio *m*

opt [ˈɑpt] *vi* : optar

optic [ˈɑptɪk] *or* **optical** [-tɪkəl] *adj* : óptico

optical disk *n* : disco *m* óptico

optician [ɑpˈtɪʃən] *n* : óptico *m*, -ca *f*

optics [ˈɑptɪks] *npl* : óptica *f*

optimal [ˈɑptəməl] *adj* : óptimo

optimism [ˈɑptəˌmɪzəm] *n* : optimismo *m*

optimist [ˈɑptəmɪst] *n* : optimista *mf*

optimistic [ˌɑptəˈmɪstɪk] *adj* : optimista

optimistically [ˌɑptəˈmɪstɪkli] *adv* : con optimismo, positivamente

optimum[1] [ˈɑptəməm] *adj* → **optimal**

optimum[2] *n, pl* **-ma** [ˈɑptəmə] : lo óptimo, lo ideal

option [ˈɑpʃən] *n* : opción *f* ⟨she has no option : no tiene más remedio⟩

optional [ˈɑpʃənəl] *adj* : facultativo, optativo

optometrist [ɑpˈtɑmətrɪst] *n* : optometrista *mf*

optometry [ɑpˈtɑmətri] *n* : optometría *f*

opulence [ˈɑpjələnts] *n* : opulencia *f*

opulent [ˈɑpjələnt] *adj* : opulento

opus [ˈo:pəs] *n, pl* **opera** [ˈo:pərə, ˈɑpə-] : opus *m*, obra *f* (de música)

or [ˈɔr] *conj* **1** (*indicating an alternative*) : o (**u** *before words beginning with o or ho*) ⟨coffee or tea : café o té⟩ ⟨one day

or another : un día u otro> 2 (*following a negative*) : ni <he didn't have his keys or his wallet : no llevaba ni sus llaves ni su billetera>
oracle [ˈɔrəkəl] *n* : oráculo *m*
oral [ˈorəl] *adj* : oral — **orally** *adv*
orange [ˈɔrɪndʒ] *n* **1** : naranja *f*, china *f PRi* (fruto) **2** : naranja *m* (color), color *m* de china *PRi*
orangeade [ˌɔrɪndʒˈeɪd] *n* : naranjada *f*
orangutan [əˈræŋəˌtæŋ, -ˈræŋgə-, -ˌtæn] *n* : orangután *m*
oration [əˈreɪʃən] *n* : oración *f*, discurso *m*
orator [ˈɔrət̬ər] *n* : orador *m*, -dora *f*
oratorio [ˌɔrəˈtoriˌo:] *n, pl* **-rios** : oratorio *m*
oratory [ˈɔrəˌtori] *n, pl* **-ries** : oratoria *f*
orb [ˈɔrb] *n* : orbe *m*
orbit[1] [ˈɔrbət] *vt* **1** CIRCLE : girar alrededor de, orbitar **2** : poner en órbita (un satélite, etc.) — *vi* : orbitar
orbit[2] *n* : órbita *f*
orbital [ˈɔrbət̬əl] *adj* : orbital
orchard [ˈɔrtʃərd] *n* : huerto *m*
orchestra [ˈɔrkəstrə] *n* : orquesta *f*
orchestral [ɔrˈkɛstrəl] *adj* : orquestal
orchestrate [ˈɔrkəˌstreɪt] *vt* **-trated; -trating** **1** : orquestar, instrumentar (en música) **2** ORGANIZE : arreglar, organizar
orchestration [ˌɔrkəˈstreɪʃən] *n* : orquestación *f*
orchid [ˈɔrkɪd] *n* : orquídea *f*
ordain [ɔrˈdeɪn] *vt* **1** : ordenar (en religión) **2** DECREE : decretar, ordenar
ordeal [ɔrˈdi:l, ˈɔrˌdi:l] *n* : prueba *f* dura, experiencia *f* terrible
order[1] [ˈɔrdər] *vt* **1** ORGANIZE : arreglar, ordenar, poner en orden **2** COMMAND : ordenar, mandar **3** REQUEST : pedir, encargar <to order a meal : pedir algo de comer> — *vi* : hacer un pedido
order[2] *n* **1** : orden *f* <a religious order : una orden religiosa> **2** COMMAND : orden *f*, mandato *m* <to give an order : dar una orden> **3** REQUEST : orden *f*, pedido *m* <purchase order : orden de compra> **4** ARRANGEMENT : orden *m* <in chronological order : por orden cronológico> **5** DISCIPLINE : orden *m* <law and order : el orden público> **6** **in order to** : para **7** **out of order** : descompuesto, averiado **8** **orders** *npl or* **holy orders** : órdenes *fpl* sagradas
orderliness [ˈɔrdərlinəs] *n* : orden *m*
orderly[1] [ˈɔrdərli] *adj* **1** METHODICAL : ordenado, metódico **2** PEACEFUL : pacífico, disciplinado
orderly[2] *n, pl* **-lies** **1** : ordenanza *m* (en el ejército) **2** : camillero *m* (en un hospital)
ordinal [ˈɔrdənəl] *n or* **ordinal number** : ordinal *m*, número *m* ordinal
ordinance [ˈɔrdənənts] *n* : ordenanza *f*, reglamento *m*
ordinarily [ˌɔrdənˈɛrəli] *adv* : ordinariamente, por lo general
ordinary [ˈɔrdənˌɛri] *adj* **1** NORMAL, USUAL : normal, usual **2** AVERAGE : común y corriente, normal **3** MEDIOCRE : mediocre, ordinario
ordination [ˌɔrdənˈeɪʃən] *n* : ordenación *f*
ordnance [ˈɔrdnənts] *n* : artillería *f*
ore [ˈor] *n* : mineral *m* (metalífero), mena *f*
oregano [əˈrɛgəˌno:] *n* : orégano *m*
organ [ˈɔrgən] *n* **1** : órgano *m* (instrumento) **2** : órgano *m* (del cuerpo) **3** PERIODICAL : publicación *f* periódica, órgano *m*
organic [ɔrˈgænɪk] *adj* : orgánico — **organically** *adv*
organism [ˈɔrgəˌnɪzəm] *n* : organismo *m*
organist [ˈɔrgənɪst] *n* : organista *mf*
organization [ˌɔrgənəˈzeɪʃən] *n* **1** ORGANIZING : organización *f* **2** BODY : organización *f*, organismo *m*
organizational [ˌɔrgənəˈzeɪʃənəl] *adj* : organizativo
organize [ˈɔrgəˌnaɪz] *vt* **-nized; -nizing** : organizar, arreglar, poner en orden
organizer [ˈɔrgəˌnaɪzər] *n* : organizador *m*, -dora *f*
orgasm [ˈɔrˌgæzəm] *n* : orgasmo *m*
orgy [ˈɔrdʒi] *n, pl* **-gies** : orgía *f*
orient [ˈoriˌɛnt] *vt* : orientar
Orient *n* **the Orient** : el Oriente
oriental [ˌoriˈɛntəl] *adj* : del Oriente, oriental
Oriental *n* : oriental *mf*
orientation [ˌoriənˈteɪʃən] *n* : orientación *f*
orifice [ˈɔrəfəs] *n* : orificio *m*
origin [ˈɔrədʒən] *n* **1** ANCESTRY : origen *m*, ascendencia *f* **2** SOURCE : origen *m*, raíz *f*, fuente *f*
original[1] [əˈrɪdʒənəl] *adj* : original
original[2] *n* : original *m*
originality [əˌrɪdʒəˈnæləṯi] *n* : originalidad *f*
originally [əˈrɪdʒənəli] *adv* **1** AT FIRST : al principio, originariamente **2** CREATIVELY : originalmente, con originalidad
originate [əˈrɪdʒəˌneɪt] *v* **-nated; -nating** *vt* : originar, iniciar, crear — *vi* **1** BEGIN : originarse, empezar **2** COME : provenir, proceder, derivarse
originator [əˈrɪdʒəˌneɪṯər] *n* : creador *m*, -dora *f*; inventor *m*, -tora *f*
oriole [ˈoriˌo:l, -iəl] *n* : oropéndola *f*
ornament[1] [ˈɔrnəmənt] *vt* : adornar, decorar, ornamentar
ornament[2] *n* : ornamento *m*, adorno *m*, decoración *f*
ornamental [ˌɔrnəˈmɛntəl] *adj* : ornamental, de adorno, decorativo
ornamentation [ˌɔrnəmənˈteɪʃən, -mɛn-] *n* : ornamentación *f*
ornate [ɔrˈneɪt] *adj* : elaborado, recargado
ornery [ˈɔrnəri, ˈɑrnəri] *adj* **ornerier; -est** : de mal genio, malhumorado
ornithologist [ˌɔrnəˈθɑlədʒɪst] *n* : ornitólogo *m*, -ga *f*

ornithology [ˌɔrnəˈθɑləʤi] *n, pl* **-gies** : ornitología *f*

orphan[1] [ˈɔrfən] *vt* : dejar huérfano

orphan[2] *n* : huérfano *m*, -na *f*

orphanage [ˈɔrfənɪʤ] *n* : orfelinato *m*, orfanato *m*

orthodontics [ˌɔrθəˈdɑntɪks] *n* : ortodoncia *f*

orthodontist [ˌɔrθəˈdɑntɪst] *n* : ortodoncista *mf*

orthodox [ˈɔrθəˌdɑks] *adj* : ortodoxo

orthodoxy [ˈɔrθəˌdɑksi] *n, pl* **-doxies** : ortodoxia *f*

orthographic [ˌɔrθəˈgræfɪk] *adj* : ortográfico

orthography [ɔrˈθɑgrəfi] *n, pl* **-phies** SPELLING : ortografía *f*

orthopedic [ˌɔrθəˈpiːdɪk] *adj* : ortopédico

orthopedics [ˌɔrθəˈpiːdɪks] *ns & pl* : ortopedia *f*

orthopedist [ˌɔrθəˈpiːdɪst] *n* : ortopedista *mf*

oscillate [ˈɑsəˌleɪt] *vi* **-lated; -lating** : oscilar

oscillation [ˌɑsəˈleɪʃən] *n* : oscilación *f*

osmosis [ɑzˈmoːsɪs, ɑs-] *n* : ósmosis *f*, osmosis *f*

osprey [ˈɑspri, -ˌpreɪ] *n* : pigargo *m*

ostensible [ɑˈstɛntsəbəl] *adj* APPARENT : aparente, ostensible — **ostensibly** [-bli] *adv*

ostentation [ˌɑstənˈteɪʃən] *n* : ostentación *f*, boato *m*

ostentatious [ˌɑstənˈteɪʃəs] *adj* : ostentoso — **ostentatiously** *adv*

osteopath [ˈɑstiəˌpæθ] *n* : osteópata *f*

osteopathy [ˌɑstiˈɑpəθi] *n* : osteopatía *f*

osteoporosis [ˌɑstiopəˈroːsɪs] *n, pl* **-roses** [-ˌsiːz] : osteoporosis *f*

ostracism [ˈɑstrəˌsɪzəm] *n* : ostracismo *m*

ostracize [ˈɑstrəˌsaɪz] *vt* **-cized; -cizing** : condenar al ostracismo, marginar, aislar

ostrich [ˈɑstrɪʧ, ˈɔs-] *n* : avestruz *m*

other[1] [ˈʌðər] *adv* **other than** : aparte de, fuera de

other[2] *adj* : otro ⟨the other boys : los otros muchachos⟩ ⟨smarter than other people : más inteligente que los demás⟩ ⟨on the other hand : por otra parte, por otro lado⟩ ⟨every other day : cada dos días⟩

other[3] *pron* : otro, otra ⟨one in front of the other : uno tras otro⟩ ⟨myself and three others : yo y tres otros, yo y tres más⟩ ⟨somewhere or other : en alguna parte⟩

otherwise[1] [ˈʌðərˌwaɪz] *adv* **1** DIFFERENTLY : de otro modo, de manera distinta ⟨he could not act otherwise : no pudo actuar de manera distinta⟩ **2** : eso aparte, por lo demás ⟨I'm dizzy, but otherwise I'm fine : estoy mareado pero, por lo demás, estoy bien⟩ **3** OR ELSE : de lo contrario, si no ⟨do what I tell you, otherwise you'll be sorry : haz lo que te digo, de lo contrario, te arrepentirás⟩

otherwise[2] *adj* : diferente, distinto ⟨the facts are otherwise : la realidad es diferente⟩

otter [ˈɑt̬ər] *n* : nutria *f*

Ottoman [ˈɑt̬əmən] *n* **1** : otomano *m*, -na *f* **2** : otomana *f* (mueble) — **Ottoman** *adj*

ouch [ˈaʊʧ] *interj* : ¡ay!, ¡huy!

ought [ˈɔt] *v aux* : deber ⟨you ought to take care of yourself : deberías cuidarte⟩

oughtn't [ˈɔtənt] (*contraction of* **ought not**) → **ought**

ounce [ˈaʊnts] *n* : onza *f*

our [ˈɑr, ˈaʊr] *adj* : nuestro

ours [ˈaʊrz, ˈɑrz] *pron* : nuestro, nuestra ⟨a cousin of ours : un primo nuestro⟩

ourselves [ɑrˈsɛlvz, aʊr-] *pron* **1** (*used reflexively*) : nos, nosotros ⟨we amused ourselves : nos divertimos⟩ ⟨we were always thinking of ourselves : siempre pensábamos en nosotros⟩ **2** (*used for emphasis*) : nosotros mismos, nosotras mismas ⟨we did it ourselves : lo hicimos nosotros mismos⟩

oust [ˈaʊst] *vt* : desbancar, expulsar

ouster [ˈaʊstər] *n* : expulsión *f* (de un país, etc.), destitución *f* (de un puesto)

out[1] [ˈaʊt] *vi* : revelarse, hacerse conocido

out[2] *adv* **1** (*indicating direction or movement*) : para afuera ⟨she opened the door and looked out : abrió la puerta y miró para afuera⟩ **2** (*indicating a location away from home or work*) : fuera, afuera ⟨to eat out : comer afuera⟩ **3** (*indicating loss of control or possession*) ⟨they let the secret out : sacaron el secreto a la luz⟩ **4** (*indicating completion or discontinuance*) ⟨his money ran out : se le acabó el dinero⟩ ⟨to turn out the light : apagar la luz⟩ **5** OUTSIDE : fuera, afuera ⟨out in the garden : afuera en el jardín⟩ **6** ALOUD : en voz alta, en alto ⟨to cry out : gritar⟩

out[3] *adj* **1** EXTERNAL : externo, exterior **2** OUTLYING : alejado, distante ⟨the out islands : las islas distantes⟩ **3** ABSENT : ausente **4** UNFASHIONABLE : fuera de moda **5** EXTINGUISHED : apagado

out[4] *prep* **1** (*used to indicate an outward movement*) : por ⟨I looked out the window : miré por la ventana⟩ ⟨she ran out the door : corrió por la puerta⟩ **2** → **out of**

out–and–out [ˈaʊtənˈaʊt] *adj* UTTER : redomado, absoluto

outboard motor [ˈaʊtˌbord] *n* : motor *m* fuera de borde

outbound [ˈaʊtˌbaʊnd] *adj* : que sale, de salida

outbreak [ˈaʊtˌbreɪk] *n* : brote *m* (de una enfermedad), comienzo *m* (de guerra), ola *f* (de violencia), erupción *f* (de granos)

outbuilding [ˈaʊtˌbɪldɪŋ] *n* : edificio *m* anexo

outburst [ˈaʊtˌbərst] *n* : arranque *m*, arrebato *m*

outcast [ˈaʊtˌkæst] *n* : marginado *m*, -da *f*; paria *mf*

outcome [ˈaʊtˌkʌm] *n* : resultado *m*, desenlace *m*, consecuencia *f*

outcrop [ˈaʊtˌkrɑp] *n* : afloramiento *m*

outcry [ˈaʊtˌkraɪ] *n, pl* **-cries** : clamor *m*, protesta *f*

outdated [ˌaʊtˈdeɪṭəd] *adj* : anticuado, fuera de moda

outdistance [ˌaʊtˈdɪstənts] *vt* **-tanced; -tancing** : aventajar, dejar atrás

outdo [ˌaʊtˈduː] *vt* **-did** [-ˈdɪd]; **-done** [-ˈdʌn]; **-doing; -does** [-ˈdʌz] : superar

outdoor [ˈaʊtˈdor] *adj* : al aire libre ⟨outdoor sports : deportes al aire libre⟩ ⟨outdoor clothing : ropa de calle⟩

outdoors[1] [ˈaʊtˈdorz] *adv* : afuera, al aire libre

outdoors[2] *n* : aire *m* libre

outer [ˈaʊṭər] *adj* **1** : exterior, externo **2 outer space** : espacio *m* exterior

outermost [ˈaʊṭərˌmoːst] *adj* : más remoto, más exterior, extremo

outfield [ˈaʊtˌfiːld] *n* **the outfield** : los jardines

outfielder [ˈaʊtˌfiːldər] *n* : jardinero *m*, -ra *f*

outfit[1] [ˈaʊtˌfɪt] *vt* **-fitted; -fitting** EQUIP : equipar

outfit[2] *n* **1** EQUIPMENT : equipo *m* **2** COSTUME, ENSEMBLE : traje *m*, conjunto *m* **3** GROUP : conjunto *m*

outgo [ˈaʊtˌgoː] *n, pl* **outgoes** : gasto *m*

outgoing [ˈaʊtˌgoːɪŋ] *adj* **1** OUTBOUND : que sale **2** DEPARTING : saliente ⟨an outgoing president : un presidente saliente⟩ **3** EXTROVERTED : extrovertido, expansivo

outgrow [ˌaʊtˈgroː] *vt* **-grew** [-ˈgruː]; **-grown** [-ˈgroːn]; **-growing** **1** : crecer más que ⟨that tree outgrew all the others : ese árbol creció más que todos los otros⟩ **2 to outgrow one's clothes** : quedarle pequeña la ropa a uno

outgrowth [ˈaʊtˌgroːθ] *n* **1** OFFSHOOT : brote *m*, vástago *m* (de una planta) **2** CONSEQUENCE : consecuencia *f*, producto *m*, resultado *m*

outing [ˈaʊṭɪŋ] *n* : excursión *f*

outlandish [aʊtˈlændɪʃ] *adj* : descabellado, muy extraño

outlast [ˌaʊtˈlæst] *vt* : durar más que

outlaw[1] [ˈaʊtˌlɔ] *vt* : hacerse ilegal, declarar fuera de la ley, prohibir

outlaw[2] *n* : bandido *m*, -da *f*; bandolero *m*, -ra *f*; forajido *m*, -da *f*

outlay [ˈaʊtˌleɪ] *n* : gasto *m*, desembolso *m*

outlet [ˈaʊtˌlɛt, -lət] *n* **1** EXIT : salida *f*, escape *m* ⟨electrical outlet : toma de corriente⟩ **2** RELIEF : desahogo *m* **3** MARKET : mercado *m*, salida *f*

outline[1] [ˈaʊtˌlaɪn] *vt* **-lined; -lining** **1** SKETCH : diseñar, esbozar, bosquejar **2** DEFINE, EXPLAIN : perfilar, delinear, explicar ⟨she outlined our responsibilities : delineó nuestras responsabilidades⟩

outline[2] *n* **1** PROFILE : perfil *m*, silueta *f*, contorno *m* **2** SKETCH : bosquejo *m*, boceto *m* **3** SUMMARY : esquema *m*, resumen *m*, sinopsis *m* ⟨an outline of world history : un esquema de la historia mundial⟩

outlive [ˌaʊtˈlɪv] *vt* **-lived; -living** : sobrevivir a

outlook [ˈaʊtˌlʊk] *n* **1** VIEW : vista *f*, panorama *f* **2** POINT OF VIEW : punto *m* de vista **3** PROSPECTS : perspectivas *fpl*

outlying [ˈaʊtˌlaɪɪŋ] *adj* : alejado, distante, remoto ⟨the outlying areas : las afueras⟩

outmoded [ˌaʊtˈmoːdəd] *adj* : pasado de moda, anticuado

outnumber [ˌaʊtˈnʌmbər] *vt* : superar en número a, ser más numeroso de

out of *prep* **1** (*indicating direction or movement from within*) : de, por ⟨we ran out of the house : salimos corriendo de la casa⟩ ⟨to look out of the window : mirar por la ventana⟩ **2** (*being beyond the limits of*) ⟨out of control : fuera de control⟩ ⟨to be out of sight : desaparecer de vista⟩ **3** OF : de ⟨one out of four : uno de cada cuatro⟩ **4** (*indicating absence or loss*) : sin ⟨out of money : sin dinero⟩ ⟨we're out of matches : nos hemos quedado sin fósforos⟩ **5** BECAUSE OF : por ⟨out of curiosity : por curiosidad⟩ **6** FROM : de ⟨made out of plastic : hecho de plástico⟩

out–of–date [ˌaʊṭəvˈdeɪt] *adj* : anticuado, obsoleto, pasado de moda

out–of–door [ˌaʊṭəvˈdor] *or* **out–of–doors** [-ˈdorz] → **outdoor**

out–of–doors *n* → **outdoors**[2]

outpatient [ˈaʊtˌpeɪʃənt] *n* : paciente *m* externo, paciente *f* externa

outpost [ˈaʊtˌpoːst] *n* : puesto *m* avanzado

output[1] [ˈaʊtˌpʊt] *vt* **-putted** *or* **-put; -putting** : producir

output[2] *n* : producción *f* (de una fábrica), rendimiento *m* (de una máquina), productividad *f* (de una persona)

outrage[1] [ˈaʊtˌreɪʤ] *vt* **-raged; -raging** **1** INSULT : ultrajar, injuriar **2** INFURIATE : indignar, enfurecer

outrage[2] *n* **1** ATROCITY : atropello *m*, atrocidad *f*, atentado *m* **2** SCANDAL : escándalo *m* **3** ANGER : ira *f*, furia *f*

outrageous [ˌaʊtˈreɪʤəs] *adj* **1** SCANDALOUS : escandaloso, ofensivo, atroz **2** UNCONVENTIONAL : poco convencional, extravagante **3** EXORBITANT : exorbitante, excesivo (dícese de los precios, etc.)

outright[1] [ˌaʊtˈraɪt] *adv* **1** COMPLETELY : por completo, totalmente ⟨to sell outright : vender por completo⟩ ⟨he refused it outright : lo rechazó rotundamente⟩ **2** DIRECTLY : directamente, sin reserva **3** INSTANTLY : al instante, en el acto

outright[2] [ˈaʊtˌraɪt] *adj* **1** COMPLETE : completo, absoluto, categórico ⟨an outright lie : una mentira absoluta⟩ **2** : sin reservas ⟨an outright gift : un regalo sin reservas⟩

outset [ˈaʊtˌsɛt] *n* : comienzo *m*, principio *m*

outshine [ˌaʊtˈʃaɪn] *vt* **-shone** [-ˈʃoːn, -ˈʃɑn] *or* **-shined; -shining** : eclipsar

outside[1] [ˌaʊtˈsaɪd, ˈaʊtˌ-] *adv* : fuera, afuera

outside[2] *adj* **1** : exterior, externo ⟨the outside edge : el borde exterior⟩ ⟨outside influences : influencias externas⟩ **2** REMOTE : remoto ⟨an outside chance : una posibilidad remota⟩

outside[3] *n* **1** EXTERIOR : parte *f* de afuera, exterior *m* **2** MOST : máximo *m* ⟨three weeks at the outside : tres semanas como máximo⟩ **3 from the outside** : desde afuera, desde fuera

outside[4] *prep* : fuera de, afuera de ⟨outside my window : fuera de mi ventana⟩ ⟨outside regular hours : fuera del horario normal⟩ ⟨outside the law : afuera de la ley⟩

outside of *prep* **1** → **outside**[4] **2** → **besides**[2]

outsider [ˌaʊtˈsaɪdər] *n* : forastero *m*, -ra *f*

outskirts [ˈaʊtˌskərts] *npl* : afueras *fpl*, alrededores *mpl*

outsmart [ˌaʊtˈsmɑrt] → **outwit**

outspoken [ˌaʊtˈspoːkən] *adj* : franco, directo

outstanding [ˌaʊtˈstændɪŋ] *adj* **1** UNPAID : pendiente **2** NOTABLE : destacado, notable, excepcional, sobresaliente

outstandingly [ˌaʊtˈstændɪŋli] *adv* : excepcionalmente

outstretched [ˌaʊtˈstrɛtʃt] *adj* : extendido

outstrip [ˌaʊtˈstrɪp] *vt* **-stripped** *or* **-stript** [-ˈstrɪpt]; **-stripping** **1** : aventajar, dejar atrás ⟨he outstripped the other runners : aventajó a los otros corredores⟩ **2** SURPASS : aventajar, sobrepasar

outward[1] [ˈaʊtwərd] *or* **outwards** [-wərdz] *adv* : hacia afuera, hacia el exterior

outward[2] *adj* **1** : hacia afuera ⟨an outward flow : un flujo hacia afuera⟩ **2** : externo ⟨outward beauty : belleza externa⟩

outwardly [ˈaʊtwərdli] *adv* **1** EXTERNALLY : exteriormente **2** APPARENTLY : aparentemente ⟨outwardly friendly : aparentemente simpático⟩

outwit [ˌaʊtˈwɪt] *vt* **-witted; -witting** : ser más listo que

ova → **ovum**

oval[1] [ˈoːvəl] *adj* : ovalado, oval

oval[2] *n* : óvalo *m*

ovarian [oˈværiən] *adj* : ovárico

ovary [ˈoːvəri] *n, pl* **-ries** : ovario *m*

ovation [oˈveɪʃən] *n* : ovación *f*

oven [ˈʌvən] *n* : horno *m*

over[1] [ˈoːvər] *adv* **1** (*indicating movement across*) ⟨he flew over to London : voló a Londres⟩ ⟨come on over! : ¡ven acá!⟩ **2** (*indicating an additional amount*) ⟨the show ran 10 minutes over : el espectáculo terminó 10 minutos de tarde⟩ **3** ABOVE, OVERHEAD : por encima **4** AGAIN : otra vez, de nuevo ⟨over and over : una y otra vez⟩ ⟨to start over : volver a empezar⟩ **5 all over** EVERYWHERE : por todas partes **6 to fall over** : caerse **7 to turn over** : poner boca abajo, voltear

over[2] *adj* **1** HIGHER, UPPER : superior **2** REMAINING : sobrante, que sobra **3** ENDED : terminado, acabado ⟨the work is over : el trabajo está terminado⟩

over[3] *prep* **1** ABOVE : encima de, arriba de, sobre ⟨over the fireplace : encima de la chimenea⟩ ⟨the hawk flew over the hills : el halcón voló sobre los cerros⟩ **2** : más de ⟨over $50 : más de $50⟩ **3** ALONG : por, sobre ⟨to glide over the ice : deslizarse sobre el hielo⟩ **4** (*indicating motion through a place or thing*) ⟨they showed me over the house : me mostraron la casa⟩ **5** ACROSS : por encima de, sobre ⟨he jumped over the ditch : saltó por encima de la zanja⟩ **6** UPON : sobre ⟨a cape over my shoulders : una capa sobre los hombros⟩ **7** ON : por ⟨to speak over the telephone : hablar por teléfono⟩ **8** DURING : en, durante ⟨over the past 25 years : durante los últimos 25 años⟩ **9** BECAUSE OF : por ⟨they fought over the money : se pelearon por el dinero⟩

overabundance [ˌoːvərəˈbʌndənts] *n* : superabundancia *f*

overabundant [ˌoːvərəˈbʌndənt] *adj* : superabundante

overactive [ˌoːvərˈæktɪv] *adj* : hiperactivo

overall [ˌoːvərˈɔl] *adj* : total, global, de conjunto

overalls [ˈoːvərˌɔlz] *npl* : overol *m*

overawe [ˌoːvərˈɔ] *vt* **-awed; -awing** : intimidar, impresionar

overbearing [ˌoːvərˈbærɪŋ] *adj* : dominante, imperioso, prepotente

overblown [ˌoːvərˈbloːn] *adj* **1** INFLATED : inflado, exagerado **2** BOMBASTIC : grandilocuente, rimbombante

overboard [ˈoːvərˌbord] *adv* : por la borda, al agua

overburden [ˌoːvərˈbərdən] *vt* : sobrecargar, agobiar

overcast [ˈoːvərˌkæst] *adj* CLOUDY : nublado

overcharge [ˌoːvərˈtʃɑrdʒ] *vt* **-charged; -charging** : cobrarle de más (a alguien)

overcoat [ˈoːvərˌkoːt] *n* : abrigo *m*

overcome [ˌoːvərˈkʌm] *v* **-came** [-ˈkeɪm]; **-come; -coming** *vt* **1** CON-

QUER : vencer, derrotar, superar **2** OVERWHELM : abrumar, agobiar — *vi* : vencer

overconfidence [ˌo:vərˈkɑnfədənts] *n* : exceso *m* de confianza

overconfident [ˌo:vərˈkɑnfədənt] *adj* : demasiado confiado

overcook [ˌo:vərˈkʊk] *vt* : recocer, cocer demasiado

overcrowded [ˌo:vərˈkraʊdəd] *adj* **1** PACKED : abarrotado, atestado de gente **2** OVERPOPULATED : superpoblado

overdo [ˌo:vərˈdu:] *vt* **-did** [-ˈdɪd]; **-done** [-ˈdʌn]; **-doing; -does** [-ˈdʌz] **1** : hacer demasiado **2** EXAGGERATE : exagerar **3** OVERCOOK : recocer

overdose [ˈo:vərˌdo:s] *n* : sobredosis *f*

overdraft [ˈo:vərˌdræft] *n* : sobregiro *m*, descubierto *m*

overdraw [ˌo:vərˈdrɔ] *vt* **-drew** [-ˈdru:]; **-drawn** [-ˈdrɔn]; **-drawing** **1** : sobregirar ⟨my account is overdrawn : tengo la cuenta en descubierto⟩ **2** EXAGGERATE : exagerar

overdue [ˌo:vərˈdu:] *adj* **1** UNPAID : vencido y sin pagar **2** TARDY : de retraso, tardío

overeat [ˌo:vərˈi:t] *vi* **-ate** [-ˈeɪt]; **-eaten** [-ˈi:tən]; **-eating** : comer demasiado

overelaborate [ˌo:vərɪˈlæbərət] *adj* : recargado

overestimate [ˌo:vərˈɛstəˌmeɪt] *vt* **-mated; -mating** : sobreestimar

overexcited [ˌo:vərɪkˈsaɪṭəd] *adj* : sobreexcitado

overexpose [ˌo:vərɪkˈspo:z] *vt* **-posed; -posing** : sobreexponer

overfeed [ˌo:vərˈfi:d] *vt* **-fed** [-ˈfɛd]; **-feeding** : sobrealimentar

overflow[1] [ˌo:vərˈflo:] *vt* **1** : desbordar **2** INUNDATE : inundar — *vi* : desbordarse, rebosar

overflow[2] [ˈo:vərˌflo:] *n* **1** : derrame *m*, desbordamiento *m* (de un río) **2** SURPLUS : exceso *m*, excedente *m*

overfly [ˌo:vərˈflaɪ] *vt* **-flew** [-ˈflu:]; **-flown** [-ˈflo:n]; **-flying** : sobrevolar

overgrown [ˌo:vərˈgro:n] *adj* **1** : cubierto ⟨overgrown with weeds : cubierto de malas hierbas⟩ **2** : demasiado grande

overhand[1] [ˈo:vərˌhænd] *adv* : por encima de la cabeza

overhand[2] *adj* : por lo alto (tirada)

overhang[1] [ˌo:vərˈhæŋ] *v* **-hung** [-ˈhʌŋ]; **-hanging** *vt* **1** : sobresalir por encima de **2** THREATEN : amenazar — *vi* : sobresalir

overhang[2] [ˈo:vərˌhæŋ] *n* : saliente *mf*

overhaul [ˌo:vərˈhɔl] *vt* **1** : revisar ⟨to overhaul an engine : revisar un motor⟩ **2** OVERTAKE : adelantar

overhead[1] [ˌo:vərˈhɛd] *adv* : por encima, arriba, por lo alto

overhead[2] [ˈo:vərˌhɛd] *adj* : de arriba

overhead[3] [ˈo:vərˌhɛd] *n* : gastos *mpl* generales

overhear [ˌo:vərˈhɪr] *vt* **-heard; -hearing** : oír por casualidad

overheat [ˌo:vərˈhi:t] *vt* : recalentar, sobrecalentar, calentar demasiado

overjoyed [ˌo:vərˈʤɔɪd] *adj* : rebosante de alegría

overkill [ˈo:vərˌkɪl] *n* : exceso *m*, excedente *m*

overland[1] [ˈo:vərˌlænd, -lənd] *adv* : por tierra

overland[2] *adj* : terrestre, por tierra

overlap[1] [ˌo:vərˈlæp] *v* **-lapped; -lapping** *vt* : traslapar — *vi* : traslaparse, solaparse

overlap[2] [ˈo:vərˌlæp] *n* : traslapo *m*

overlay[1] [ˌo:vərˈleɪ] *vt* **-laid** [-ˈleɪd]; **-laying** : recubrir, revestir

overlay[2] [ˈo:vərˌleɪ] *n* : revestimiento *m*

overload [ˌo:vərˈlo:d] *vt* : sobrecargar

overlong [ˌo:vərˈlɔŋ] *adj* : excesivamente largo, largo y pesado

overlook [ˌo:vərˈlʊk] *vt* **1** INSPECT : inspeccionar, revisar **2** : tener vista a, dar a ⟨a house overlooking the valley : una casa que tiene vista al valle⟩ **3** MISS : pasar por alto **4** EXCUSE : dejar pasar, disculpar

overly [ˈo:vərli] *adv* : demasiado

overnight[1] [ˌo:vərˈnaɪt] *adv* **1** : por la noche, durante la noche **2** : de la noche a la mañana ⟨we can't do it overnight : no podemos hacerlo de la noche a la mañana⟩

overnight[2] [ˈo:vərˈnaɪt] *adj* **1** : de noche ⟨an overnight stay : una estancia de una noche⟩ ⟨an overnight bag : una bolsa de viaje⟩ **2** SUDDEN : repentino

overpass [ˈo:vərˌpæs] *n* : paso *m* elevado, paso *m* a desnivel *Mex*

overpopulated [ˌo:vərˈpɑpjəˌleɪṭəd] *adj* : sobrepoblado

overpower [ˌo:vərˈpaʊər] *vt* **1** CONQUER, SUBDUE : vencer, superar **2** OVERWHELM : abrumar, agobiar ⟨overpowered by the heat : sofocado por el calor⟩

overpraise [ˌo:vərˈpreɪz] *vt* **-praised; -praising** : adular

overrate [ˌo:vərˈreɪt] *vt* **-rated; -rating** : sobrevalorar, sobrevaluar

override [ˌo:vərˈraɪd] *vt* **-rode** [-ˈro:d]; **-ridden** [-ˈrɪdən]; **-riding** **1** : predominar sobre, contar más que ⟨hunger overrode our manners : el hambre predominó sobre los modales⟩ **2** ANNUL : anular, invalidar ⟨to override a veto : anular un veto⟩

overrule [ˌo:vərˈru:l] *vt* **-ruled; -ruling** : anular (una decisión), desautorizar (una persona), denegar (un pedido)

overrun [ˌo:vərˈrʌn] *v* **-ran** [-ˈræn]; **-running** *vt* **1** INVADE : invadir **2** INFEST : infestar, plagar **3** EXCEED : exceder, rebasar — *vi* : rebasar el tiempo previsto

overseas[1] [ˌo:vərˈsi:z] *adv* : en el extranjero ⟨to travel overseas : viajar al extranjero⟩

overseas[2] [ˈoːvərˌsiːz] *adj* : extranjero, exterior
oversee [ˌoːvərˈsiː] *vt* **-saw** [-ˈsɔ]; **-seen** [-ˈsiːn]; **-seeing** SUPERVISE : supervisar
overseer [ˈoːvərˌsiːər] *n* : supervisor *m*, -sora *f*; capataz *mf*
overshadow [ˌoːvərˈʃæˌdoː] *vt* **1** DARKEN : oscurecer, ensombrecer **2** ECLIPSE, OUTSHINE : eclipsar
overshoe [ˈoːvərˌʃuː] *n* : chanclo *m*
overshoot [ˌoːvərˈʃuːt] *vt* **-shot** [-ˈʃɑt]; **-shooting** : pasarse de ⟨to overshoot the mark : pasarse de la raya⟩
oversight [ˈoːvərˌsaɪt] *n* : descuido *m*, inadvertencia *f*
oversleep [ˌoːvərˈsliːp] *vi* **-slept** [-ˈslɛpt]; **-sleeping** : no despertarse a tiempo, quedarse dormido
overspread [ˌoːvərˈsprɛd] *vt* **-spread; -spreading** : extenderse sobre
overstaffed [ˌoːvərˈstæft] *adj* : con exceso de personal
overstate [ˌoːvərˈsteɪt] *vt* **-stated; -stating** EXAGGERATE : exagerar
overstatement [ˌoːvərˈsteɪtmənt] *n* : exageración *f*
overstep [ˌoːvərˈstɛp] *vt* **-stepped; -stepping** EXCEED : sobrepasar, traspasar, exceder
overt [oˈvərt, ˈoːˌvərt] *adj* : evidente, manifiesto, patente
overtake [ˌoːvərˈteɪk] *vt* **-took** [-ˈtʊk]; **-taken** [-ˈteɪkən]; **-taking** : pasar, adelantar, rebasar *Mex*
overthrow[1] [ˌoːvərˈθroː] *vt* **-threw** [-ˈθruː]; **-thrown** [-ˈθroːn]; **-throwing** **1** OVERTURN : dar la vuelta a, volcar **2** DEFEAT, TOPPLE : derrocar, derribar, deponer
overthrow[2] [ˈoːvərˌθroː] *n* : derrocamiento *m*, caída *f*
overtime [ˈoːvərˌtaɪm] *n* **1** : horas *fpl* extras (de trabajo) **2** : prórroga *f* (en deportes)
overtly [oˈvərtli, ˈoːˌvərt-] *adv* OPENLY : abiertamente
overtone [ˈoːvərˌtoːn] *n* **1** : armónico *m* (en música) **2** HINT, SUGGESTION : tinte *m*, insinuación *f*
overture [ˈoːvərˌʧʊr, -ʧər] *n* **1** PROPOSAL : propuesta *f* **2** : obertura *f* (en música)
overturn [ˌoːvərˈtərn] *vt* **1** UPSET : dar la vuelta a, volcar **2** NULLIFY : anular, invalidar — *vi* TURN OVER : volcar, dar un vuelco
overuse [ˌoːvərˈjuːz] *vt* **-used; -using** : abusar de
overview [ˈoːvərˌvjuː] *n* : resumen *m*, visión *f* general
overweening [ˌoːvərˈwiːnɪŋ] *adj* **1** ARROGANT : arrogante, soberbio **2** IMMODERATE : desmesurado
overweight [ˌoːvərˈweɪt] *adj* : demasiado gordo, demasiado pesado
overwhelm [ˌoːvərˈhwɛlm] *vt* **1** CRUSH, DEFEAT : aplastar, arrollar **2** SUBMERGE : inundar, sumergir **3** OVERPOWER : abrumar, agobiar ⟨overwhelmed by remorse : abrumado de remordimiento⟩
overwhelming [ˌoːvərˈhwɛlmɪŋ] *adj* **1** CRUSHING : abrumador, apabullante **2** SWEEPING : arrollador, aplastante ⟨an overwhelming majority : una mayoría aplastante⟩
overwork [ˌoːvərˈwərk] *vt* **1** : hacer trabajar demasiado **2** OVERUSE : abusar de — *vi* : trabajar demasiado
overwrought [ˌoːvərˈrɔt] *adj* : alterado, sobreexcitado
ovoid [ˈoːˌvɔɪd] *or* **ovoidal** [oˈvɔɪdəl] *adj* : ovoide
ovulate [ˈɑvjəˌleɪt, ˈoː-] *vi* **-lated; -lating** : ovular
ovulation [ˌɑvjəˈleɪʃən, ˌoː-] *n* : ovulación *f*
ovum [ˈoːvəm] *n, pl* **ova** [-və] : óvulo *m*
owe [ˈoː] *vt* **owed; owing** : deber ⟨you owe me $10 : me debes $10⟩ ⟨he owes his wealth to his father : le debe su riqueza a su padre⟩
owing to *prep* : debido a
owl [ˈaʊl] *n* : búho *m*, lechuza *f*, tecolote *m Mex*
own[1] [ˈoːn] *vt* **1** POSSESS : poseer, tener, ser dueño de **2** ADMIT : reconocer, admitir — *vi* **to own up** : reconocer (algo), admitir (algo)
own[2] *adj* : propio, personal, particular ⟨his own car : su propio coche⟩
own[3] *pron* **my; (your, his/her, our, their); own** : el mío, la mía; el tuyo, la tuya; el suyo, la suya; el nuestro, la nuestra ⟨to each his own : cada uno a lo suyo⟩ ⟨money of my own : mi propio dinero⟩ ⟨to be on one's own : estar solo⟩
owner [ˈoːnər] *n* : dueño *m*, -ña *f*; propietario *m*, -ria *f*
ownership [ˈoːnərˌʃɪp] *n* : propiedad *f*
ox [ˈɑks] *n, pl* **oxen** [ˈɑksən] : buey *m*
oxidation [ˌɑksəˈdeɪʃən] *n* : oxidación *f*
oxide [ˈɑkˌsaɪd] *n* : óxido *m*
oxidize [ˈɑksəˌdaɪz] *vt* **-dized; -dizing** : oxidar
oxygen [ˈɑksɪʤən] *n* : oxígeno *m*
oyster [ˈɔɪstər] *n* : ostra *f*, ostión *m Mex*
ozone [ˈoːˌzoːn] *n* : ozono *m*

P

p [ˈpiː] *n, pl* **p's** *or* **ps** [ˈpiːz] : decimosexta letra del alfabeto inglés
pace[1] [ˈpeɪs] *v* **paced; pacing** *vi* : caminar, ir y venir — *vt* **1** : caminar por ⟨she paced the floor : caminaba de un lado a otro del cuarto⟩ **2 to pace a runner** : marcarle el ritmo a un corredor
pace[2] *n* **1** STEP : paso *m* **2** RATE : paso *m*, ritmo *m* ⟨to set the pace : marcar el paso, marcar la pauta⟩
pacemaker [ˈpeɪsˌmeɪkər] *n* : marcapasos *m*
pacific [pəˈsɪfɪk] *adj* : pacífico
pacifier [ˈpæsəˌfaɪər] *n* : chupete *m*, chupón *m*, mamila *f Mex*
pacifism [ˈpæsəˌfɪzəm] *n* : pacifismo *m*
pacifist [ˈpæsəfɪst] *n* : pacifista *mf*
pacify [ˈpæsəˌfaɪ] *vt* **-fied; -fying** **1** SOOTHE : apaciguar, pacificar **2** : pacificar (un país, una región, etc.)
pack[1] [ˈpæk] *vt* **1** PACKAGE : empaquetar, embalar, envasar **2** : empacar, meter (en una maleta) ⟨to pack one's bag : hacer la maleta⟩ **3** FILL : llenar, abarrotar ⟨a packed theater : un teatro abarrotado⟩ **4 to pack off** SEND : mandar — *vi* : empacar, hacer las maletas
pack[2] *n* **1** BUNDLE : bulto *m*, fardo *m* **2** BACKPACK : mochila *f* **3** PACKAGE : paquete *m*, cajetilla *f* (de cigarrillos, etc.) **4** : manada *f* (de lobos, etc.), jauría *f* (de perros) ⟨a pack of thieves : una pandilla de ladrones⟩
package[1] [ˈpækɪʤ] *vt* **-aged; -aging** : empaquetar, embalar
package[2] *n* : paquete *m*, bulto *m*
packaging [ˈpækɪʤɪŋ] *n* **1** : embalaje *m* **2** WRAPPING : envoltorio *m*
packer [ˈpækər] *n* : empacador *m*, -dora *f*
packet [ˈpækət] *n* : paquete *m*
packing [ˈpækɪŋ] *n* : embalaje *m*
pact [ˈpækt] *n* : pacto *m*, acuerdo *m*
pad[1] [ˈpæd] *vt* **padded; padding** **1** FILL, STUFF : rellenar, acolchar (una silla, una pared) **2** : meter paja en, rellenar ⟨to pad a speech : rellenar un discurso⟩
pad[2] *n* **1** CUSHION : almohadilla *f* ⟨a shoulder pad : una hombrera⟩ **2** TABLET : bloc *m* (de papel) **3** *or* **lily pad** : hoja *f* grande (de un nenúfar) **4** **ink pad** : tampón *m* **5 launching pad** : plataforma *f* (de lanzamiento)
padding [ˈpædɪŋ] *n* **1** FILLING : relleno *m* **2** : paja *f* (en un discurso, etc.)
paddle[1] [ˈpædəl] *v* **-dled; -dling** *vt* **1** : hacer avanzar (una canoa) con canalete **2** HIT : azotar, darle nalgadas a (con una pala o paleta) — *vi* **1** : remar (en una canoa) **2** SPLASH : chapotear, mojarse los pies
paddle[2] *n* **1** : canalete *m*, zagual *m* (de una canoa, etc.) **2** : pala *f*, paleta *f* (en deportes)
paddock [ˈpædək] *n* **1** PASTURE : potrero *m* **2** : paddock *m*, cercado *m* (en un hipódromo)
paddy [ˈpædi] *n, pl* **-dies** : arrozal *m*
padlock[1] [ˈpædˌlɑk] *vt* : cerrar con candado
padlock[2] *n* : candado *m*
pagan[1] [ˈpeɪgən] *adj* : pagano
pagan[2] *n* : pagano *m*, -na *f*
paganism [ˈpeɪgənˌɪzəm] *n* : paganismo *m*
page[1] [ˈpeɪʤ] *vt* **paged; paging** : llamar por altavoz
page[2] *n* **1** BELLHOP : botones *m* **2** : página *f* (de un libro, etc.)
pageant [ˈpæʤənt] *n* **1** SPECTACLE : espectáculo *m* **2** PROCESSION : desfile *m*
pageantry [ˈpæʤəntri] *n* : pompa *f*, fausto *m*
pager [ˈpeɪʤər] *n* BEEPER : buscapersonas *m*
pagoda [pəˈgoːdə] *n* : pagoda *f*
paid → **pay**
pail [ˈpeɪl] *n* : balde *m*, cubo *m*, cubeta *f Mex*
pailful [ˈpeɪlˌfʊl] *n* : balde *m*, cubo *m*, cubeta *f Mex*
pain[1] [ˈpeɪn] *vt* : doler
pain[2] *n* **1** PENALTY : pena *f* ⟨under pain of death : so pena de muerte⟩ **2** SUFFERING : dolor *m*, malestar *m*, pena *f* (mental) **3 pains** *npl* EFFORT : esmero *m*, esfuerzo *m* ⟨to take pains : esmerarse⟩
painful [ˈpeɪnfəl] *adj* : doloroso — **painfully** *adv*
painkiller [ˈpeɪnˌkɪlər] *n* : analgésico *m*
painless [ˈpeɪnləs] *adj* : indoloro, sin dolor
painlessly [ˈpeɪnləsli] *adv* : sin dolor
painstaking [ˈpeɪnˌsteɪkɪŋ] *adj* : esmerado, cuidadoso, meticuloso — **painstakingly** *adv*
paint[1] [ˈpeɪnt] *v* : pintar
paint[2] *n* : pintura *f*
paintbrush [ˈpeɪntˌbrʌʃ] *n* : pincel *m* (de un artista), brocha *f* (para pintar casas, etc.)
painter [ˈpeɪntər] *n* : pintor *m*, -tora *f*
painting [ˈpeɪntɪŋ] *n* : pintura *f*
pair[1] [ˈpær] *vt* : emparejar, poner en parejas — *vi* : emparejarse
pair[2] *n* : par *m* (de objetos), pareja *f* (de personas o animales) ⟨a pair of scissors : unas tijeras⟩
pajamas [pəˈʤɑməz, -ˈʤæ-] *npl* : pijama *m*, piyama *mf*
Pakistani [ˌpækɪˈstæni, ˌpɑkɪˈstɑni] *n* : paquistaní *mf* — **Pakistani** *adj*
pal [ˈpæl] *n* : amigo *m*, -ga *f*; compinche *mf fam*; chamo *m*, -ma *f Ven fam*; cuate *m*, -ta *f Mex*
palace [ˈpæləs] *n* : palacio *m*
palatable [ˈpælət̬əbəl] *adj* : sabroso
palate [ˈpælət] *n* **1** : paladar *m* (de la boca) **2** TASTE : paladar *m*, gusto *m*

palatial [pəˈleɪʃəl] *adj* : suntuoso, espléndido
palaver [pəˈlævər, -ˈlɑ-] *n* : palabrería *f*
pale[1] [ˈpeɪl] *v* **paled; paling** *vi* : palidecer — *vt* : hacer pálido
pale[2] *adj* **paler; palest** **1** : pálido ⟨to turn pale : palidecer, ponerse pálido⟩ **2** : claro (dícese de los colores)
paleness [ˈpeɪlnəs] *n* : palidez *f*
paleontologist [ˌpeɪliˌɑnˈtɑləʤɪst] *n* : paleontólogo *m*, -ga *f*
paleontology [ˌpeɪliˌɑnˈtɑləʤi] *n* : paleontología *f*
Palestinian [ˌpæləˈstɪniən] *n* : palestino *m*, -na *f* — **Palestinian** *adj*
palette [ˈpælət] *n* : paleta *f* (para mezclar pigmentos)
palisade [ˌpæləˈseɪd] *n* **1** FENCE : empalizada *f*, estacada *f* **2** CLIFFS : acantilado *m*
pall[1] [ˈpɔl] *vi* : perder su sabor, dejar de gustar
pall[2] *n* **1** : paño *m* mortuorio (sobre un ataúd) **2** COVER : cortina *f* (de humo, etc.) **3 to cast a pall over** : ensombrecer
pallbearer [ˈpɔlˌbɛrər] *n* : portador *m*, -dora *f* del féretro
pallet [ˈpælət] *n* **1** BED : camastro *m* **2** PLATFORM : plataforma *f* de carga
palliative [ˈpæliˌeɪt̬ɪv, ˈpæljət̬ɪv] *adj* : paliativo
pallid [ˈpæləd] *adj* : pálido
pallor [ˈpælər] *n* : palidez *f*
palm[1] [ˈpɑm, ˈpɑlm] *vt* **1** CONCEAL : escamotear (un naipe, etc.) **2 to palm off** : encajar, endilgar *fam* ⟨he palmed it off on me : me lo endilgó⟩
palm[2] *n* **1** *or* **palm tree** : palmera *f* **2** : palma *f* (de la mano)
Palm Sunday *n* : Domingo *m* de Ramos
palomino [ˌpæləˈmiːˌnoː] *n, pl* **-nos** : caballo *m* de color dorado
palpable [ˈpælpəbəl] *adj* : palpable — **palpably** [-bli] *adv*
palpitate [ˈpælpəˌteɪt] *vi* **-tated; -tating** : palpitar
palpitation [ˌpælpəˈteɪʃən] *n* : palpitación *f*
palsy [ˈpɔlzi] *n, pl* **-sies** **1** : parálisis *f* **2** → **cerebral palsy**
paltry [ˈpɔltri] *adj* **-trier; -est** : mísero, mezquino, insignificante ⟨a paltry excuse : una mala excusa⟩
pampas [ˈpæmpəz, ˈpɑmpəs] *npl* : pampa *f*
pamper [ˈpæmpər] *vt* : mimar, consentir, chiquear *Mex*
pamphlet [ˈpæmpflət] *n* : panfleto *m*, folleto *m*
pan[1] [ˈpæn] *vt* **panned; panning** CRITICIZE : poner por los suelos — *vi* **to pan for gold** : cribar el oro con batea, lavar oro
pan[2] *n* **1** : cacerola *f*, cazuela *f* **2 frying pan** : sartén *mf*, freidera *f Mex*
panacea [ˌpænəˈsiːə] *n* : panacea *f*
Panamanian [ˌpænəˈmeɪniən] *n* : panameño *m*, -ña *f* — **Panamanian** *adj*
pancake [ˈpænˌkeɪk] *n* : panqueque *m*
pancreas [ˈpæŋkriəs, ˈpæn-] *n* : páncreas *m*
panda [ˈpændə] *n* : panda *mf*
pandemonium [ˌpændəˈmoːniəm] *n* : pandemonio *m*, pandemónium *m*
pander [ˈpændər] *vi* **to pander to** : satisfacer, complacer (a alguien) ⟨to pander to popular taste : satisfacer el gusto popular⟩
pane [ˈpeɪn] *n* : cristal *m*, vidrio *m*
panel[1] [ˈpænəl] *vt* **-eled** *or* **-elled; -eling** *or* **-elling** : adornar con paneles
panel[2] *n* **1** : lista *f* de nombres (de un jurado, etc.) **2** GROUP : panel *m*, grupo *m* ⟨discussion panel : panel de discusión⟩ **3** : panel *m* (de una pared, etc.) **4 instrument panel** : tablero *m* de instrumentos
paneling [ˈpænəlɪŋ] *n* : paneles *mpl*
pang [ˈpæŋ] *n* : puntada *f*, punzada *f*
panic[1] [ˈpænɪk] *v* **-icked; -icking** *vt* : llenar de pánico — *vi* : ser presa de pánico
panic[2] *n* : pánico *m*
panicky [ˈpænɪki] *adj* : presa de pánico
panorama [ˌpænəˈræmə, -ˈrɑ-] *n* : panorama *m*
panoramic [ˌpænəˈræmɪk, -ˈrɑ-] *adj* : panorámico
pansy [ˈpænzi] *n, pl* **-sies** : pensamiento *m*
pant[1] [ˈpænt] *vi* : jadear, resoplar
pant[2] *n* : jadeo *m*, resoplo *m*
pantaloons [ˌpæntəˈluːnz] → **pants**
pantheon [ˈpæntθiˌɑn, -ən] *n* : panteón *m*
panther [ˈpænθər] *n* : pantera *f*
panties [ˈpæntiz] *npl* : calzones *mpl*; pantaletas *fpl Mex, Ven*; bragas *fpl Spain*
pantomime[1] [ˈpæntəˌmaɪm] *v* **-mimed; -miming** *vt* : representar mediante la pantomima — *vi* : hacer la mímica
pantomime[2] *n* : pantomima *f*
pantry [ˈpæntri] *n, pl* **-tries** : despensa *f*
pants [ˈpænts] *npl* **1** TROUSERS : pantalón *m*, pantalones *mpl* **2** → **panties**
panty hose [ˈpænti] *ns & pl* : medias *fpl*, panties *mfpl*, pantimedias *fpl Mex*
pap [ˈpæp] *n* : papilla *f* (para bebés, etc.)
papa [ˈpɑpə] *n* : papá *m*
papal [ˈpeɪpəl] *adj* : papal
papaya [pəˈpaɪə] *n* : papaya *f* (fruta)
paper[1] [ˈpeɪpər] *vt* WALLPAPER : empapelar
paper[2] *adj* : de papel
paper[3] *n* **1** : papel *m* ⟨a piece of paper : un papel⟩ **2** DOCUMENT : papel *m*, documento *m* **3** NEWSPAPER : periódico *m*, diario *m*
paperback [ˈpeɪpərˌbæk] *n* : libro *m* en rústica
paper clip *n* : clip *m*, sujetapapeles *m*
paperweight [ˈpeɪpərˌweɪt] *n* : pisapapeles *m*

paperwork [ˈpeɪpərˌwərk] *n* : papeleo *m*
papery [ˈpeɪpəri] *adj* : parecido al papel
papier–mâché [ˌpeɪpərməˈʃeɪ, ˌpæˌpjeɪmæˈʃeɪ] *n* : papel *m* maché
papoose [pæˈpu:s, pə-] *n* : niño *m*, -ña *f* de los indios norteamericanos
paprika [pəˈpri:kə, pæ-] *n* : pimentón *m*, paprika *f*
papyrus [pəˈpaɪrəs] *n, pl* **-ruses** *or* **-ri** [-ri, -ˌraɪ] : papiro *m*
par [ˈpɑr] *n* **1** VALUE : valor *m* (nominal), par *f* ⟨below par : debajo de la par⟩ **2** EQUALITY : igualdad *f* ⟨to be on a par with : estar al mismo nivel que⟩ **3** : par *m* (en golf)
parable [ˈpærəbəl] *n* : parábola *f*
parabola [pəˈræbələ] *n* : parábola *f* (en matemáticas)
parachute¹ [ˈpærəˌʃu:t] *vi* **-chuted; -chuting** : lanzarse en paracaídas
parachute² *n* : paracaídas *m*
parachutist [ˈpærəˌʃu:t̬ɪst] *n* : paracaidista *mf*
parade¹ [pəˈreɪd] *vi* **-raded; -rading 1** MARCH : desfilar **2** SHOW OFF : pavonearse, lucirse
parade² *n* **1** PROCESSION : desfile *m* **2** DISPLAY : alarde *m*
paradigm [ˈpærəˌdaɪm] *n* : paradigma *m*
paradise [ˈpærəˌdaɪs, -ˌdaɪz] *n* : paraíso *m*
paradox [ˈpærəˌdɑks] *n* : paradoja *f*
paradoxical [ˌpærəˈdɑksɪkəl] *adj* : paradójico — **paradoxically** *adv*
paraffin [ˈpærəfən] *n* : parafina *f*
paragon [ˈpærəˌgɑn, -gən] *n* : dechado *m*
paragraph¹ [ˈpærəˌgræf] *vt* : dividir en párrafos
paragraph² *n* : párrafo *m*, acápite *m*
Paraguayan [ˌpærəˈgwaɪən, -ˈgweɪ-] *n* : paraguayo *m*, -ya *f* — **Paraguayan** *adj*
parakeet [ˈpærəˌki:t] *n* : periquito *m*
paralegal [ˌpærəˈli:gəl] *n* : asistente *mf* de abogado
parallel¹ [ˈpærəˌlɛl, -ləl] *vt* **1** MATCH, RESEMBLE : ser paralelo a, ser análogo a, corresponder con **2** : extenderse en línea paralela con ⟨the road parallels the river : el camino se extiende a lo largo del río⟩
parallel² *adj* : paralelo
parallel³ *n* **1** : línea *f* paralela, superficie *f* paralela **2** : paralelo *m* (en geografía) **3** SIMILARITY : paralelismo *m*, semejanza *f*
parallelogram [ˌpærəˈlɛləˌgræm] *n* : paralelogramo *m*
paralysis [pəˈræləsɪs] *n, pl* **-yses** [-ˌsi:z] : parálisis *f*
paralyze [ˈpærəˌlaɪz] *vt* **-lyzed; -lyzing** : paralizar
parameter [pəˈræmət̬ər] *n* : parámetro *m*
paramount [ˈpærəˌmaʊnt] *adj* : supremo ⟨of paramount importance : de suma importancia⟩
paranoia [ˌpærəˈnɔɪə] *n* : paranoia *f*
paranoid [ˈpærəˌnɔɪd] *adj* : paranoico
parapet [ˈpærəpət, -ˌpɛt] *n* : parapeto *m*
paraphernalia [ˌpærəfəˈneɪljə, -fər-] *ns & pl* : parafernalia *f*
paraphrase¹ [ˈpærəˌfreɪz] *vt* **-phrased; -phrasing** : parafrasear
paraphrase² *n* : paráfrasis *f*
paraplegic¹ [ˌpærəˈpli:ʤɪk] *adj* : parapléjico
paraplegic² *n* : parapléjico *m*, -ca *f*
parasite [ˈpærəˌsaɪt] *n* : parásito *m*
parasitic [ˌpærəˈsɪt̬ɪk] *adj* : parasitario
parasol [ˈpærəˌsɔl] *n* : sombrilla *f*, quitasol *m*, parasol *m*
paratrooper [ˈpærəˌtru:pər] *n* : paracaidista *mf* (militar)
parboil [ˈpɑrˌbɔɪl] *vt* : sancochar, cocer a medias
parcel¹ [ˈpɑrsəl] *vt* **-celed** *or* **-celled; -celing** *or* **-celling** *or* **to parcel out** : repartir, parcelar (tierras)
parcel² *n* **1** LOT : parcela *f*, lote *m* **2** PACKAGE : paquete *m*, bulto *m*
parch [ˈpɑrʧ] *vt* : resecar
parchment [ˈpɑrʧmənt] *n* : pergamino *m*
pardon¹ [ˈpɑrdən] *vt* **1** FORGIVE : perdonar, disculpar ⟨pardon me! : ¡perdone!, ¡disculpe la molestia!⟩ **2** REPRIEVE : indultar (a un delincuente)
pardon² *n* **1** FORGIVENESS : perdón *m* **2** REPRIEVE : indulto *m*
pardonable [ˈpɑrdənəbəl] *adj* : perdonable, disculpable
pare [ˈpær] *vt* **pared; paring 1** PEEL : pelar **2** TRIM : recortar **3** REDUCE : reducir ⟨he pared it (down) to 50 pages : lo redujo a 50 páginas⟩
parent [ˈpærənt] *n* **1** : madre *f*, padre *m* **2 parents** *npl* : padres *mpl*
parentage [ˈpærəntɪʤ] *n* : linaje *m*, abolengo *m*, origen *m*
parental [pəˈrɛntəl] *adj* : de los padres
parenthesis [pəˈrɛnθəsɪs] *n, pl* **-theses** [-ˌsi:z] : paréntesis *m*
parenthetic [ˌpærənˈθɛt̬ɪk] *or* **parenthetical** [-t̬ɪkəl] *adj* : parentético — **parenthetically** [-t̬ɪkli] *adv*
parenthood [ˈpærəntˌhʊd] *n* : paternidad *f*
parfait [pɑrˈfeɪ] *n* : postre *m* elaborado con frutas y helado
pariah [pəˈraɪə] *n* : paria *mf*
parish [ˈpærɪʃ] *n* : parroquia *f*
parishioner [pəˈrɪʃənər] *n* : feligrés *m*, -gresa *f*
parity [ˈpærət̬i] *n, pl* **-ties** : paridad *f*
park¹ [ˈpɑrk] *vt* : estacionar, parquear, aparcar *Spain* — *vi* : estacionarse, parquearse, aparcar *Spain*
park² *n* : parque *m*
parka [ˈpɑrkə] *n* : parka *f*
parking [ˈpɑrkɪŋ] *n* : estacionamiento *m*, aparcamiento *m Spain*
parkway [ˈpɑrkˌweɪ] *n* : carretera *f* ajardinada, bulevar *m*
parley¹ [ˈpɑrli] *vi* : parlamentar, negociar

parley[2] *n, pl* **-leys** : negociación *f*, parlamento *m*
parliament [ˈpɑrləmənt, ˈpɑrljə-] *n* : parlamento *m*
parliamentary [ˌpɑrləˈmɛntəri, ˌpɑrljə-] *adj* : parlamentario
parlor [ˈpɑrlər] *n* **1** : sala *f*, salón *m* (en una casa) **2** : salón *m* ⟨beauty parlor : salón de belleza⟩ **3 funeral parlor** : funeraria *f*
parochial [pəˈroːkiəl] *adj* **1** : parroquial **2** PROVINCIAL : pueblerino, de miras estrechas
parody[1] [ˈpærədi] *vt* **-died; -dying** : parodiar
parody[2] *n, pl* **-dies** : parodia *f*
parole [pəˈroːl] *n* : libertad *f* condicional
paroxysm [ˈpærəkˌsɪzəm, pəˈrɑk-] *n* : paroxismo *m*
parquet [ˈpɑrˌkeɪ, pɑrˈkeɪ] *n* : parquet *m*, parqué *m*
parrakeet → **parakeet**
parrot [ˈpærət] *n* : loro *m*, papagayo *m*
parry[1] [ˈpæri] *v* **-ried; -rying** *vi* : parar un golpe — *vt* EVADE : esquivar (una pregunta, etc.)
parry[2] *n, pl* **-ries** : parada *f*
parsimonious [ˌpɑrsəˈmoːniəs] *adj* : tacaño, mezquino
parsley [ˈpɑrsli] *n* : perejil *m*
parsnip [ˈpɑrsnɪp] *n* : chirivía *f*
parson [ˈpɑrsən] *n* : pastor *m*, -tora *f*; clérigo *m*
parsonage [ˈpɑrsənɪʤ] *n* : rectoría *f*, casa *f* del párroco
part[1] [ˈpɑrt] *vi* **1** SEPARATE : separarse, despedirse ⟨we should part as friends : debemos separarnos amistosamente⟩ **2** OPEN : abrirse ⟨the curtains parted : las cortinas se abrieron⟩ **3 to part with** : deshacerse de — *vt* **1** SEPARATE : separar **2 to part one's hair** : hacerse la raya, peinarse con raya
part[2] *n* **1** SECTION, SEGMENT : parte *f*, sección *f* **2** PIECE : pieza *f* (de una máquina, etc.) **3** ROLE : papel *m* **4** : raya *f* (del pelo)
partake [pɑrˈteɪk, pər-] *vi* **-took** [-ˈtʊk]; **-taken** [-ˈteɪkən;]; **-taking 1 to partake of** CONSUME : comer, beber, tomar **2 to partake in** : participar en (una actividad, etc.)
partial [ˈpɑrʃəl] *adj* **1** BIASED : parcial, tendencioso **2** INCOMPLETE : parcial, incompleto **3 to be partial to** : ser aficionado a
partiality [ˌpɑrʃiˈæləṯi] *n, pl* **-ties** : parcialidad *f*
partially [ˈpɑrʃəli] *adv* : parcialmente
participant [pərˈtɪsəpənt, pɑr-] *n* : participante *mf*
participate [pərˈtɪsəˌpeɪt, pɑr-] *vi* **-pated; -pating** : participar
participation [pərˌtɪsəˈpeɪʃən, pɑr-] *n* : participación *f*
participle [ˈpɑrṯəˌsɪpəl] *n* : participio *m*
particle [ˈpɑrṯɪkəl] *n* : partícula *f*
particular[1] [pɑrˈtɪkjələr] *adj* **1** SPECIFIC : particular, en particular ⟨this particular person : esta persona en particular⟩ **2** SPECIAL : particular, especial ⟨with particular emphasis : con un énfasis especial⟩ **3** FUSSY : exigente, maniático ⟨to be very particular : ser muy especial⟩ ⟨I'm not particular : me da igual⟩
particular[2] *n* **1** DETAIL : detalle *m*, sentido *m* **2 in particular** : en particular, en especial
particularly [pɑrˈtɪkjələrli] *adv* **1** ESPECIALLY : particularmente, especialmente **2** SPECIFICALLY : específicamente, en especial
partisan [ˈpɑrṯəzən, -sən] *n* **1** ADHERENT : partidario *m*, -ria *f* **2** GUERRILLA : partisano *m*, -na *f*; guerrillero *m*, -ra *f*
partition[1] [pərˈtɪʃən, pɑr-] *vt* : dividir ⟨to partition off (a room) : dividir (una habitación) con un tabique⟩
partition[2] *n* **1** DISTRIBUTION : partición *f*, división *f*, reparto *m* **2** DIVIDER : tabique *m*, mampara *f*, biombo *m*
partly [ˈpɑrtli] *adv* : en parte, parcialmente
partner [ˈpɑrtnər] *n* **1** COMPANION : compañero *m*, -ra *f* **2** : pareja *f* (en un juego, etc.) ⟨dancing partner : pareja de baile⟩ **3** SPOUSE : cónyuge *mf* **4** *or* **business partner** : socio *m*, -cia *f*; asociado *m*, -da *f*
partnership [ˈpɑrtnərˌʃɪp] *n* **1** ASSOCIATION : asociación *f*, compañerismo *m* **2** : sociedad *f* (de negociantes) ⟨to form a partnership : asociarse⟩
part of speech : categoría *f* gramatical
partridge [ˈpɑrtrɪʤ] *n, pl* **-tridge** *or* **-tridges** : perdiz *f*
party [ˈpɑrṯi] *n, pl* **-ties 1** : partido *m* (político) **2** PARTICIPANT : parte *f*, participante *mf* **3** GROUP : grupo *m* (de personas) **4** GATHERING : fiesta *f* ⟨to throw a party : dar una fiesta⟩
parvenu [ˈpɑrvəˌnuː, -ˌnjuː] *n* : advenedizo *m*, -za *f*
pass[1] [ˈpæs] *vi* **1** : pasar, cruzarse ⟨a car passed by : pasó un coche⟩ ⟨we passed in the hallway : nos cruzamos en el pasillo⟩ **2** CEASE : pasarse ⟨the pain passed : se pasó el dolor⟩ **3** ELAPSE : pasar, transcurrir **4** PROCEED : pasar ⟨let me pass : déjame pasar⟩ **5** HAPPEN : pasar, ocurrir **6** : pasar, aprobar (en un examen) **7** RULE : fallar ⟨the jury passed on the case : el jurado falló en el caso⟩ **8** *or* **to pass down** : pasar ⟨the throne passed to his son : el trono pasó a su hijo⟩ **9 to let pass** OVERLOOK : pasar por alto **10 to pass as** : pasar por **11 to pass away** *or* **to pass on** DIE : fallecer, morir — *vt* **1** : pasar por ⟨they passed the house : pasaron por la casa⟩ **2** OVERTAKE : pasar, adelantar **3** SPEND : pasar (tiempo) **4** HAND : pasar ⟨pass me the salt : pásame la sal⟩ **5** : aprobar (un examen, una ley)

pass[2] *n* **1** CROSSING, GAP : paso *m*, desfiladero *m*, puerto *m* ⟨mountain pass : puerto de montaña⟩ **2** PERMIT : pase *m*, permiso *m* **3** : pase *m* (en deportes) **4** SITUATION : situación *f* (díficil) ⟨things have come to a pretty pass! : ¡hasta dónde hemos llegado!⟩

passable [ˈpæsəbəl] *adj* **1** ADEQUATE : adecuado, pasable **2** : transitable (dícese de un camino, etc.)

passably [ˈpæsəbli] *adv* : pasablemente

passage [ˈpæsɪʤ] *n* **1** PASSING : paso *m* ⟨the passage of time : el paso del tiempo⟩ **2** PASSAGEWAY : pasillo *m* (dentro de un edificio), pasaje *m* (entre edificios) **3** VOYAGE : travesía *f* (por el mar), viaje *m* ⟨to grant safe passage : dar un salvoconducto⟩ **4** SECTION : pasaje *m* (en música o literatura)

passageway [ˈpæsɪʤˌweɪ] *n* : pasillo *m*, pasadizo *m*, corredor *m*

passbook [ˈpæsˌbʊk] *n* BANKBOOK : libreta *f* de ahorros

passé [pæˈseɪ] *adj* : pasado de moda

passenger [ˈpæsənʤər] *n* : pasajero *m*, -ra *f*

passerby [ˌpæsərˈbaɪ, ˈpæsərˌ-] *n, pl* **passersby** : transeúnte *mf*

passing [ˈpæsɪŋ] *n* DEATH : fallecimiento *m*

passion [ˈpæʃən] *n* : pasión *f*, ardor *m*

passionate [ˈpæʃənət] *adj* **1** IRASCIBLE : irascible, iracundo **2** ARDENT : apasionado, ardiente, ferviente, fogoso

passionately [ˈpæʃənətli] *adv* : apasionadamente, fervientemente, con pasión

passive[1] [ˈpæsɪv] *adj* : pasivo — **passively** *adv*

passive[2] *n* : voz *f* pasiva (en gramática)

passivity [pæˈsɪvət̬i] *n* : pasividad *f*

Passover [ˈpæsˌoːvər] *n* : Pascua *f* (en el judaísmo)

passport [ˈpæsˌport] *n* : pasaporte *m*

password [ˈpæsˌwərd] *n* : contraseña *f*

past[1] [ˈpæst] *adv* : por delante ⟨he drove past : pasamos en coche⟩

past[2] *adj* **1** AGO : hace ⟨10 years past : hace 10 años⟩ **2** LAST : último ⟨the past few months : los últimos meses⟩ **3** BYGONE : pasado ⟨in past times : en tiempos pasados⟩ **4** : pasado (en gramática)

past[3] *n* : pasado *m*

past[4] *prep* **1** BY : por, por delante de ⟨he ran past the house : pasó por la casa corriendo⟩ **2** BEYOND : más allá de ⟨just past the corner : un poco más allá de la esquina⟩ ⟨we went past the exit : pasamos la salida⟩ **3** AFTER : después de ⟨past noon : después del mediodía⟩ ⟨half past two : las dos y media⟩

pasta [ˈpɑstə, ˈpæs-] *n* : pasta *f*

paste[1] [ˈpeɪst] *vt* **pasted; pasting** : pegar (con engrudo)

paste[2] *n* **1** : pasta *f* ⟨tomato paste : pasta de tomate⟩ **2** : engrudo *m* (para pegar)

pasteboard [ˈpeɪstˌbord] *n* : cartón *m*, cartulina *f*

pastel [pæˈstɛl] *n* : pastel *m* — **pastel** *adj*

pasteurization [ˌpæsʧərəˈzeɪʃən, ˌpæstjə-] *n* : pasteurización *f*

pasteurize [ˈpæsʧəˌraɪz, ˈpæstjə-] *vt* **-ized; -izing** : pasteurizar

pastime [ˈpæsˌtaɪm] *n* : pasatiempo *m*

pastor [ˈpæstər] *n* : pastor *m*, -tora *f*

pastoral [ˈpæstərəl] *adj* : pastoral

past participle *n* : participio *m* pasado

pastry [ˈpeɪstri] *n, pl* **-ries 1** DOUGH : pasta *f*, masa *f* **2 pastries** *npl* : pasteles *mpl*

pasture[1] [ˈpæsʧər] *v* **-tured; -turing** *vi* GRAZE : pacer, pastar — *vt* : apacentar, pastar

pasture[2] *n* : pastizal *m*, potrero *m*, pasto *m*

pasty [ˈpeɪsti] *adj* **pastier; -est 1** : pastoso (en consistencia) **2** PALLID : pálido

pat[1] [ˈpæt] *vt* **patted; patting** : dar palmaditas a, tocar

pat[2] *adv* : de memoria ⟨to have down pat : saberse de memoria⟩

pat[3] *adj* **1** APT : apto, apropiado **2** GLIB : fácil **3** UNYIELDING : firme ⟨to stand pat : mantenerse firme⟩

pat[4] *n* **1** TAP : golpecito *m*, palmadita *f* ⟨a pat on the back : una palmadita en la espalda⟩ **2** CARESS : caricia *f* **3** : porción *f* ⟨a pat of butter : una porción de mantequilla⟩

patch[1] [ˈpæʧ] *vt* **1** MEND, REPAIR : remendar, parchar, ponerle un parche a **2 to patch together** IMPROVISE : confeccionar, improvisar **3 to patch up** : arreglar ⟨they patched things up : hicieron las paces⟩

patch[2] *n* **1** : parche *m*, remiendo *m* (para la ropa) ⟨eye patch : parche para el ojo⟩ **2** PIECE : mancha *f*, trozo *m* ⟨a patch of sky : un trozo de cielo⟩ **3** PLOT : parcela *f*, terreno *m* ⟨cabbage patch : parcela de repollos⟩

patchwork [ˈpæʧˌwərk] *n* : labor *f* de retazos

patchy [ˈpæʧi] *adj* **patchier; -est 1** IRREGULAR : irregular, desigual **2** INCOMPLETE : parcial, incompleto

patent[1] [ˈpætənt] *vt* : patentar

patent[2] [ˈpætənt, ˈpeɪt-] *adj* **1** OBVIOUS : patente, evidente **2** [ˈpæt-] PATENTED : patentado

patent[3] [ˈpætənt] *n* : patente *f*

patently [ˈpætəntli] *adv* : patentemente, evidentemente

paternal [pəˈtərnəl] *adj* **1** FATHERLY : paternal **2** : paterno ⟨paternal grandfather : abuelo paterno⟩

paternity [pəˈtərnət̬i] *n* : paternidad *f*

path [ˈpæθ, ˈpɑθ] *n* **1** TRACK, TRAIL : camino *m*, sendero *m*, senda *f* **2** COURSE, ROUTE : recorrido *m*, trayecto *m*, trayectoria *f*

pathetic [pəˈθɛt̬ɪk] *adj* : patético — **pathetically** [-t̬ɪkli] *adv*

pathological [ˌpæθəˈlɑʤɪkəl] *adj* : patológico

pathologist [pəˈθɑləʤɪst] *n* : patólogo *m*, -ga *f*
pathology [pəˈθɑləʤi] *n, pl* **-gies** : patología *f*
pathos [ˈpeɪˌθɑs, ˈpæ-, -ˌθɔs] *n* : patetismo *m*
pathway [ˈpæθˌweɪ] *n* : camino *m*, sendero *m*, senda *f*, vereda *f*
patience [ˈpeɪʃənts] *n* : paciencia *f*
patient¹ [ˈpeɪʃənt] *adj* : paciente — **patiently** *adv*
patient² *n* : paciente *mf*
patio [ˈpæt̬iˌo:] *n, pl* **-tios** : patio *m*
patriarch [ˈpeɪtriˌɑrk] *n* : patriarca *m*
patriarchy [ˈpeɪtriˌɑrki] *n, pl* **-chies** : patriarcado *m*
patrimony [ˈpætrəˌmo:ni] *n, pl* **-nies** : patrimonio *m*
patriot [ˈpeɪtriət] *n* : patriota *mf*
patriotic [ˌpeɪtriˈɑt̬ɪk] *adj* : patriótico — **patriotically** *adv*
patriotism [ˈpeɪtriəˌtɪzəm] *n* : patriotismo *m*
patrol¹ [pəˈtro:l] *v* **-trolled; -trolling** : patrullar
patrol² *n* : patrulla *f*
patrolman [pəˈtro:lmən] *n, pl* **-men** [-mən, -ˌmɛn] : policía *mf*, guardia *mf*
patron [ˈpeɪtrən] *n* **1** SPONSOR : patrocinador *m*, -dora *f* **2** CUSTOMER : cliente *m*, -ta *f* **3** *or* **patron saint** : patrono *m*, -na *f*
patronage [ˈpeɪtrənɪʤ, ˈpæ-] *n* **1** SPONSORSHIP : patrocinio *m* **2** CLIENTELE : clientela *f* **3** : influencia *f* (política)
patronize [ˈpeɪtrəˌnaɪz, ˈpæ-] *vt* **-ized; -izing 1** SPONSOR : patrocinar **2** : ser cliente de (un negocio) **3** : tratar con condescendencia
patter¹ [ˈpæt̬ər] *vi* **1** TAP : golpetear, tamborilear (dícese de la lluvia) **2 to patter about** : corretear (con pasos ligeros)
patter² *n* **1** TAPPING : golpeteo *m*, tamborileo *m* (de la lluvia), correteo *m* (de pies) **2** CHATTER : palabrería *f*, parloteo *m fam*
pattern¹ [ˈpæt̬ərn] *vt* **1** BASE : basar (en un modelo) **2 to pattern after** : hacer imitación de
pattern² *n* **1** MODEL : modelo *m*, patrón *m* (de costura) **2** DESIGN : diseño *m*, dibujo *m*, estampado *m* (de tela) **3** NORM, STANDARD : pauta *f*, norma *f*, patrón *m*
patty [ˈpæt̬i] *n, pl* **-ties** : porción *f* de carne picada (u otro alimento) en forma de ruedita ⟨a hamburger patty : una hamburguesa⟩
paucity [ˈpɔsət̬i] *n* : escasez *f*
paunch [ˈpɔntʃ] *n* : panza *f*, barriga *f*
pauper [ˈpɔpər] *n* : pobre *mf*, indigente *mf*
pause¹ [ˈpɔz] *vi* **paused; pausing** : hacer una pausa, pararse (brevemente)
pause² *n* : pausa *f*
pave [ˈpeɪv] *vt* **paved; paving** : pavimentar ⟨to pave with stones : empedrar⟩
pavement [ˈpeɪvmənt] *n* : pavimento *m*, empedrado *m*
pavilion [pəˈvɪljən] *n* : pabellón *m*
paving [ˈpeɪvɪŋ] → **pavement**
paw¹ [ˈpɔ] *vt* : tocar, manosear, sobar
paw² *n* : pata *f*, garra *f*, zarpa *f*
pawn¹ [ˈpɔn] *vt* : empeñar, prendar
pawn² *n* **1** PLEDGE, SECURITY : prenda *f* **2** PAWNING : empeño *m* **3** : peón *m* (en ajedrez)
pawnbroker [ˈpɔnˌbro:kər] *n* : prestamista *mf*
pawnshop [ˈpɔnˌʃɑp] *n* : casa *f* de empeños, monte *m* de piedad
pay¹ [ˈpeɪ] *v* **paid** [ˈpeɪd]; **paying** *vt* **1** : pagar (una cuenta, a un empleado, etc.) **2 to pay attention** : poner atención, prestar atención, hacer caso **3 to pay back** : pagar, devolver ⟨she paid them back : les devolvió el dinero⟩ ⟨I'll pay you back for what you did! : ¡me las pagarás!⟩ **4 to pay off** SETTLE : saldar, cancelar (una deuda, etc.) **5 to pay one's respects** : presentar uno sus respetos **6 to pay a visit** : hacer una visita — *vi* : valer la pena ⟨crime doesn't pay : no hay crimen sin castigo⟩
pay² *n* : paga *f*
payable [ˈpeɪəbəl] *adj* DUE : pagadero
paycheck [ˈpeɪˌtʃɛk] *n* : sueldo *m*, cheque *m* del sueldo
payee [peɪˈi:] *n* : beneficiario *m*, -ria *f* (de un cheque, etc.)
payment [ˈpeɪmənt] *n* **1** : pago *m* **2** INSTALLMENT : plazo *m*, cuota *f* **3** REWARD : recompensa *f*
payoff [ˈpeɪˌɔf] *n* **1** REWARD : recompensa *f* **2** PROFIT : ganancia *f* **3** BRIBE : soborno *m*
payroll [ˈpeɪˌro:l] *n* : nómina *f*
PC [ˌpi:ˈsi:] *n, pl* **PCs** *or* **PC's** : PC *mf*, computadora *f* personal
pea [ˈpi:] *n* : chícharo *m*, guisante *m*, arveja *f*
peace [ˈpi:s] *n* **1** : paz *f* ⟨peace treaty : tratado de paz⟩ ⟨peace and tranquillity : paz y tranquilidad⟩ **2** ORDER : orden *m* (público)
peaceable [ˈpi:səbəl] *adj* : pacífico — **peaceably** [-bli] *adv*
peaceful [ˈpi:sfəl] *adj* **1** PEACEABLE : pacífico **2** CALM, QUIET : tranquilo, sosegado — **peacefully** *adv*
peacemaker [ˈpi:sˌmeɪkər] *n* : conciliador *m*, -dora *f*; mediador *m*, -dora *f*
peach [ˈpi:tʃ] *n* : durazno *m*, melocotón *m*
peacock [ˈpi:ˌkɑk] *n* : pavo *m* real
peak¹ [ˈpi:k] *vi* : alcanzar su nivel máximo
peak² *adj* : máximo
peak³ *n* **1** POINT : punta *f* **2** CREST, SUMMIT : cima *f*, cumbre *f* **3** APEX : cúspide *f*, apogeo *m*, nivel *m* máximo
peaked [ˈpi:kəd] *adj* SICKLY : pálido
peal¹ [ˈpi:l] *vi* : repicar
peal² *n* : repique *m*, tañido *m* (de campanada) ⟨peals of laughter : carcajadas⟩

peanut [ˈpi:ˌnʌt] *n* : maní *m*, cacahuate *m Mex*, cacahuete *m Spain*
pear [ˈpær] *n* : pera *f*
pearl [ˈpərl] *n* : perla *f*
pearly [ˈpərli] *adj* **pearlier; -est** : nacarado
peasant [ˈpɛzənt] *n* : campesino *m*, -na *f*
peat [ˈpi:t] *n* : turba *f*
pebble [ˈpɛbəl] *n* : guijarro *m*, piedrecita *f*, piedrita *f*
pecan [pɪˈkɑn, -ˈkæn, ˈpi:ˌkæn] *n* : pacana *f*, nuez *f Mex*
peccadillo [ˌpɛkəˈdɪlo] *n, pl* **-loes** *or* **-los** : pecadillo *m*
peccary [ˈpɛkəri] *n, pl* **-ries** : pécari *m*, pecarí *m*
peck[1] [ˈpɛk] *vt* : picar, picotear
peck[2] *n* **1** : medida *f* de áridos equivalente a 8.810 litros **2** : picotazo *m* (de un pájaro) ⟨a peck on the cheek : un besito en la mejilla⟩
pectoral [ˈpɛktərəl] *adj* : pectoral
peculiar [pɪˈkju:ljər] *adj* **1** DISTINCTIVE : propio, peculiar, característico ⟨peculiar to this area : propio de esta zona⟩ **2** STRANGE : extraño, raro — **peculiarly** *adv*
peculiarity [pɪˌkju:lˈjærət̬i, -ˌkju:liˈær-] *n, pl* **-ties** **1** DISTINCTIVENESS : peculiaridad *f* **2** ODDITY, QUIRK : rareza *f*, idiosincrasia *f*, excentricidad *f*
pecuniary [pɪˈkju:niˌɛri] *adj* : pecuniario
pedagogical [ˌpɛdəˈgɑdʒɪkəl, -ˈgo:-] *adj* : pedagógico
pedagogy [ˈpɛdəˌgo:dʒi, -ˌgɑ-] *n* : pedagogía *f*
pedal[1] [ˈpɛdəl] *v* **-aled** *or* **-alled; -aling** *or* **-alling** *vi* : pedalear — *vt* : darle a los pedales de
pedal[2] *n* : pedal *m*
pedant [ˈpɛdənt] *n* : pedante *mf*
pedantic [pɪˈdæntɪk] *adj* : pedante
pedantry [ˈpɛdəntri] *n, pl* **-ries** : pedantería *f*
peddle [ˈpɛdəl] *vt* **-dled; -dling** : vender (en las calles)
peddler [ˈpɛdlər] *n* : vendedor *m*, -dora *f* ambulante; mercachifle *m*
pedestal [ˈpɛdəstəl] *n* : pedestal *m*
pedestrian[1] [pəˈdɛstriən] *adj* **1** COMMONPLACE : pedestre, ordinario **2** : de peatón, peatonal ⟨pedestrian crossing : paso de peatones⟩
pedestrian[2] *n* : peatón *m*, -tona *f*
pediatric [ˌpi:diˈætrɪk] *adj* : pediátrico
pediatrician [ˌpi:diəˈtrɪʃən] *n* : pediatra *mf*
pediatrics [ˌpi:diˈætrɪks] *ns & pl* : pediatría *f*
pedigree [ˈpɛdəˌgri:] *n* **1** FAMILY TREE : árbol *m* genealógico **2** LINEAGE : pedigrí *m* (de un animal), linaje *m* (de una persona)
peek[1] [ˈpi:k] *vi* **1** PEEP : espiar, mirar furtivamente **2** GLANCE : echar un vistazo
peek[2] *n* **1** : miradita *f* (furtiva) **2** GLANCE : vistazo *m*, ojeada *f*
peel[1] [ˈpi:l] *vt* **1** : pelar (fruta, etc.) **2** *or* **to peel away** : quitar — *vi* : pelarse (dícese de la piel), desconcharse (dícese de la pintura)
peel[2] *n* : cáscara *f*
peep[1] [ˈpi:p] *vi* **1** PEEK : espiar, mirar furtivamente **2** CHEEP : piar **3 to peep out** SHOW : asomarse
peep[2] *n* **1** CHEEP : pío *m* (de un pajarito) **2** GLANCE : vistazo *m*, ojeada *f*
peer[1] [ˈpɪr] *vi* : mirar detenidamente, mirar con atención
peer[2] *n* **1** EQUAL : par *m*, igual *mf* **2** NOBLE : noble *mf*
peerage [ˈpɪrɪdʒ] *n* : nobleza *f*
peerless [ˈpɪrləs] *adj* : sin par, incomparable
peeve[1] [ˈpi:v] *vt* **peeved; peeving** : fastidiar, irritar, molestar
peeve[2] *n* : queja *f*
peevish [ˈpi:vɪʃ] *adj* : quejoso, fastidioso — **peevishly** *adv*
peevishness [ˈpi:vɪʃnəs] *n* : irritabilidad *f*
peg[1] [ˈpɛg] *vt* **pegged; pegging** **1** PLUG : tapar (con una clavija) **2** FASTEN, FIX : sujetar (con estaquillas) **3 to peg out** MARK : marcar (con estaquillas)
peg[2] *n* : estaquilla *f* (para clavar), clavija *f* (para tapar)
pejorative [pɪˈdʒɔrət̬ɪv] *adj* : peyorativo — **pejoratively** *adv*
pelican [ˈpɛlɪkən] *n* : pelícano *m*
pellagra [pəˈlægrə, -ˈleɪ-] *n* : pelagra *f*
pellet [ˈpɛlət] *n* **1** BALL : bolita *f* ⟨food pellet : bolita de comida⟩ **2** SHOT : perdigón *m*
pell–mell [ˈpɛlˈmɛl] *adv* : desordenadamente, atropelladamente
pelt[1] [ˈpɛlt] *vt* **1** THROW : lanzar, tirar (algo a alguien) **2 to pelt with stones** : apedrear — *vi* BEAT : golpear con fuerza ⟨the rain was pelting down : llovía a cántaros⟩
pelt[2] *n* : piel *f*, pellejo *m*
pelvic [ˈpɛlvɪk] *adj* : pélvico
pelvis [ˈpɛlvɪs] *n, pl* **-vises** *or* **-ves** [ˈpɛlˌvi:z] : pelvis *f*
pen[1] [ˈpɛn] *vt* **penned; penning** **1** *or* **pen in** : encerrar (animales) **2** WRITE : escribir
pen[2] *n* **1** CORRAL : corral *m*, redil *m* (para ovejas) **2** : pluma *f* ⟨fountain pen : pluma fuente⟩ ⟨ballpoint pen : bolígrafo⟩
penal [ˈpi:nəl] *adj* : penal
penalize [ˈpi:nəlˌaɪz, ˈpɛn-] *vt* **-ized; -izing** : penalizar, sancionar, penar
penalty [ˈpɛnəlti] *n, pl* **-ties** **1** PUNISHMENT : pena *f*, castigo *m* **2** DISADVANTAGE : desventaja *f*, castigo *m*, penalty *m* (en deportes) **3** FINE : multa *f*
penance [ˈpɛnənts] *n* : penitencia *f*
pence → **penny**
penchant [ˈpɛntʃənt] *n* : inclinación *f*, afición *f*

pencil[1] [ˈpɛntsəl] *vt* **-ciled** *or* **-cilled; -ciling** *or* **-cilling** : escribir con lápiz, dibujar con lápiz
pencil[2] *n* : lápiz *m*
pendant [ˈpɛndənt] *n* : colgante *m*
pending[1] [ˈpɛndɪŋ] *adj* : pendiente
pending[2] *prep* **1** DURING : durante **2** AWAITING : en espera de
pendulum [ˈpɛndʒələm, -djʊləm] *n* : péndulo *m*
penetrate [ˈpɛnəˌtreɪt] *vt* **-trated; -trating** : penetrar
penetrating [ˈpɛnəˌtreɪt̬ɪŋ] *adj* : penetrante, cortante
penetration [ˌpɛnəˈtreɪʃən] *n* : penetración *f*
penguin [ˈpɛŋgwɪn, ˈpɛn-] *n* : pingüino *m*
penicillin [ˌpɛnəˈsɪlən] *n* : penicilina *f*
peninsula [pəˈnɪntsələ, -ˈnɪntʃʊlə] *n* : península *f*
penis [ˈpiːnəs] *n, pl* **-nes** [-ˌniːz] *or* **-nises** : pene *m*
penitence [ˈpɛnət̬ənts] *n* : arrepentimiento *m*, penitencia *f*
penitent[1] [ˈpɛnət̬ənt] *adj* : arrepentido, penitente
penitent[2] *n* : penitente *mf*
penitentiary [ˌpɛnəˈtɛntʃəri] *n, pl* **-ries** : penitenciaría *f*, prisión *m*, presidio *m*
penmanship [ˈpɛnmənˌʃɪp] *n* : escritura *f*, caligrafía *f*
pen name *n* : seudónimo *m*
pennant [ˈpɛnənt] *n* : gallardete *m* (de un barco), banderín *m*
penniless [ˈpɛniləs] *adj* : sin un centavo
penny [ˈpɛni] *n, pl* **-nies** *or* **pence** [ˈpɛnts] **1** : penique *m* (del Reino Unido) **2** *pl* **-nies** CENT : centavo *m* (de los Estados Unidos)
pension[1] [ˈpɛntʃən] *vt or* **to pension off** : jubilar
pension[2] *n* : pensión *m*, jubilación *f*
pensive [ˈpɛntsɪv] *adj* : pensativo, meditabundo — **pensively** *adv*
pent [ˈpɛnt] *adj* : encerrado ⟨pent-up feelings : emociones reprimidas⟩
pentagon [ˈpɛntəˌgɑn] *n* : pentágono *m*
pentagonal [pɛnˈtægənəl] *adj* : pentagonal
penthouse [ˈpɛntˌhaʊs] *n* : ático *m*, penthouse *m*
penultimate [pɪˈnʌltəmət] *adj* : penúltimo
penury [ˈpɛnjəri] *n* : penuria *f*, miseria *f*
peon [ˈpiːˌɑn, -ən] *n, pl* **-ons** *or* **-ones** [peɪˈoːniːz] : peón *m*
peony [ˈpiːəni] *n, pl* **-nies** : peonía *f*
people[1] [ˈpiːpəl] *vt* **-pled; -pling** : poblar
people[2] *ns & pl* **1 people** *npl* : gente *f*, personas *fpl* ⟨people like him : él le cae bien a la gente⟩ ⟨many people : mucha gente, muchas personas⟩ **2** *pl* **peoples** : pueblo *m* ⟨the Cuban people : el pueblo cubano⟩
pep[1] [ˈpɛp] *vt* **pepped; pepping** *or* **to pep up** : animar
pep[2] *n* : energía *f*, vigor *m*
pepper[1] [ˈpɛpər] *vt* **1** : añadir pimienta a **2** RIDDLE : acribillar (a balazos) **3** SPRINKLE : salpicar ⟨peppered with quotations : salpicado de citas⟩
pepper[2] *n* **1** : pimienta *f* (condimento) **2** : pimiento *m*, pimentón *m* (fruta) **3** → **chili**
peppermint [ˈpɛpərˌmɪnt] *n* : menta *f*
peppery [ˈpɛpəri] *adj* : picante
peppy [ˈpɛpi] *adj* **peppier; -est** : lleno de energía, vivaz
peptic [ˈpɛptɪk] *adj* **peptic ulcer** : úlcera *f* estomacal
per [ˈpər] *prep* **1** : por ⟨miles per hour : millas por hora⟩ **2** ACCORDING TO : según ⟨per his specifications : según sus especificaciones⟩
per annum [pərˈænəm] *adv* : al año, por año
percale [ˌpərˈkeɪl, ˈpər-ˌ; ˌpərˈkæl] *n* : percal *m*
per capita [pərˈkæpɪt̬ə] *adv & adj* : per cápita
perceive [pərˈsiːv] *vt* **-ceived; -ceiving** **1** REALIZE : percatarse de, concientizarse de, darse cuenta de **2** NOTE : percibir, notar
percent[1] [pərˈsɛnt] *adv* : por ciento
percent[2] *n, pl* **-cent** *or* **-cents** **1** : por ciento ⟨10 percent of the population : el 10 por ciento de la población⟩ **2** → **percentage**
percentage [pərˈsɛntɪdʒ] *n* : porcentaje *m*
perceptible [pərˈsɛptəbəl] *adj* : perceptible — **perceptibly** [-bli] *adv*
perception [pərˈsɛpʃən] *n* **1** : percepción *f* ⟨color perception : la percepción de los colores⟩ **2** INSIGHT : perspicacia *f* **3** IDEA : idea *f*, imagen *f*
perceptive [pərˈsɛptɪv] *adj* : perspicaz
perceptively [pərˈsɛptɪvli] *adv* : con perspicacia
perch[1] [ˈpərtʃ] *vi* **1** ROOST : posarse **2** SIT : sentarse (en un sitio elevado) — *vt* PLACE : posar, colocar
perch[2] *n* **1** ROOST : percha *f* (para los pájaros) **2** *pl* **perch** *or* **perches** : perca *f* (pez)
percolate [ˈpərkəˌleɪt] *vi* **-lated; -lating** : colarse, filtrarse ⟨percolated coffee : café filtrado⟩
percolator [ˈpərkəˌleɪt̬ər] *n* : cafetera *f* de filtro
percussion [pərˈkʌʃən] *n* **1** STRIKING : percusión *f* **2** *or* **percussion instruments** : instrumentos *mpl* de percusión
peremptory [pəˈrɛmptəri] *adj* : perentorio
perennial[1] [pəˈrɛniəl] *adj* **1** : perenne, vivaz ⟨perennial flowers : flores perennes⟩ **2** RECURRENT : perenne, continuo ⟨a perennial problem : un problema eterno⟩
perennial[2] *n* : planta *f* perenne, planta *f* vivaz
perfect[1] [pərˈfɛkt] *vt* : perfeccionar

perfect[2] [ˈpərfɪkt] *adj* : perfecto — **perfectly** *adv*
perfection [pərˈfɛkʃən] *n* : perfección *f*
perfectionist [pərˈfɛkʃənɪst] *n* : perfeccionista *mf*
perfidious [pərˈfɪdiəs] *adj* : pérfido
perforate [ˈpərfəˌreɪt] *vt* **-rated; -rating** : perforar
perforation [ˌpərfəˈreɪʃən] *n* : perforación *f*
perform [pərˈfɔrm] *vt* **1** CARRY OUT : realizar, hacer, desempeñar **2** PRESENT : representar, dar (una obra teatral, etc.) — *vi* : actuar (en una obra teatral), cantar (en una ópera, etc.), tocar (en un concierto, etc.), bailar (en un ballet, etc.)
performance [pərˈfɔrmən*t*s] *n* **1** EXECUTION : ejecución *f*, realización *f*, desempeño *m*, rendimiento *m* **2** INTERPRETATION : interpretación *f* ⟨his performance of Hamlet : su interpretación de Hamlet⟩ **3** PRESENTATION : representación *f* (de una obra teatral), función *f*
performer [pərˈfɔrmər] *n* : artista *mf*; actor *m*, -triz *f*; intérprete *mf* (de música)
perfume[1] [pərˈfjuːm, ˈpərˌ-] *vt* **-fumed; -fuming** : perfumar
perfume[2] [ˈpərˌfjuːm, pərˈ-] *n* : perfume *m*
perfunctory [pərˈfʌŋktəri] *adj* : mecánico, superficial, somero
perhaps [pərˈhæps] *adv* : tal vez, quizá, quizás
peril [ˈpɛrəl] *n* : peligro *m*
perilous [ˈpɛrələs] *adj* : peligroso — **perilously** *adv*
perimeter [pəˈrɪmət̬ər] *n* : perímetro *m*
period [ˈpɪriəd] *n* **1** : punto *m* (en puntuación) **2** : período *m* ⟨a two-hour period : un período de dos horas⟩ **3** STAGE : época *f* (histórica), fase *f*, etapa *f*
periodic [ˌpɪriˈɑdɪk] *or* **periodical** [-dɪkəl] *adj* : periódico — **periodically** [-dɪkli] *adv*
periodical [ˌpɪriˈɑdɪkəl] *n* : publicación *f* periódica, revista *f*
peripheral [pəˈrɪfərəl] *adj* : periférico
periphery [pəˈrɪfəri] *n, pl* **-eries** : periferia *f*
periscope [ˈpɛrəˌskoːp] *n* : periscopio *m*
perish [ˈpɛrɪʃ] *vi* DIE : perecer, morirse
perishable[1] [ˈpɛrɪʃəbəl] *adj* : perecedero
perishable[2] *n* : producto *m* perecedero
perjure [ˈpərʤər] *vt* **-jured; -juring** (*used in law*) **to perjure oneself** : perjurar, perjurarse
perjury [ˈpərʤəri] *n* : perjurio *m*
perk[1] [ˈpərk] *vt* **1** : levantar (las orejas, etc.) **2** *or* **to perk up** FRESHEN : arreglar — *vi* **to perk up** : animarse, reanimarse
perk[2] *n* : extra *m*
perky [ˈpərki] *adj* **perkier; -est** : animado, alegre, lleno de vida
permanence [ˈpərmənən*t*s] *n* : permanencia *f*
permanent[1] [ˈpərmənənt] *adj* : permanente — **permanently** *adv*
permanent[2] *n* : permanente *f*
permeability [ˌpərmiəˈbɪlət̬i] *n* : permeabilidad *f*
permeable [ˈpərmiəbəl] *adj* : permeable
permeate [ˈpərmiˌeɪt] *v* **-ated; -ating** *vt* **1** PENETRATE : penetrar, impregnar **2** PERVADE : penetrar, difundirse por — *vi* : penetrar
permissible [pərˈmɪsəbəl] *adj* : permisible, lícito
permission [pərˈmɪʃən] *n* : permiso *m*
permissive [pərˈmɪsɪv] *adj* : permisivo
permit[1] [pərˈmɪt] *vt* **-mitted; -mitting** : permitir, dejar ⟨weather permitting : si el tiempo lo permite⟩
permit[2] [ˈpərˌmɪt, pərˈ-] *n* : permiso *m*, licencia *f*
pernicious [pərˈnɪʃəs] *adj* : pernicioso
peroxide [pəˈrɑkˌsaɪd] *n* **1** : peróxido *m* **2** → **hydrogen peroxide**
perpendicular[1] [ˌpərpənˈdɪkjələr] *adj* **1** VERTICAL : vertical **2** : perpendicular ⟨perpendicular lines : líneas perpendiculares⟩ — **perpendicularly** *adv*
perpendicular[2] *n* : perpendicular *f*
perpetrate [ˈpərpəˌtreɪt] *vt* **-trated; -trating** : perpetrar, cometer (un delito)
perpetrator [ˈpərpəˌtreɪt̬ər] *n* : autor *m*, -tora *f* (de un delito)
perpetual [pərˈpɛʧuəl] *adj* **1** EVERLASTING : perpetuo, eterno **2** CONTINUAL : perpetuo, continuo, constante
perpetually [pərˈpɛʧuəli, -ʧəli] *adv* : para siempre, eternamente
perpetuate [pərˈpɛʧuˌeɪt] *vt* **-ated; -ating** : perpetuar
perpetuity [ˌpərpəˈtuːət̬i, -ˈtjuː-] *n, pl* **-ties** : perpetuidad *f*
perplex [pərˈplɛks] *vt* : dejar perplejo, confundir
perplexed [pərˈplɛkst] *adj* : perplejo
perplexity [pərˈplɛksət̬i] *n, pl* **-ties** : perplejidad *f*, confusión *f*
persecute [ˈpərsɪˌkjuːt] *vt* **-cuted; -cuting** : perseguir
persecution [ˌpərsɪˈkjuːʃən] *n* : persecución *f*
perseverance [ˌpərsəˈvɪrən*t*s] *n* : perseverancia *f*
persevere [ˌpərsəˈvɪr] *vi* **-vered; -vering** : perseverar
Persian [ˈpərʒən] *n* **1** : persa *mf* **2** : persa *m* (idioma) — **Persian** *adj*
persist [pərˈsɪst] *vi* : persistir
persistence [pərˈsɪstən*t*s] *n* **1** CONTINUATION : persistencia *f* **2** TENACITY : perseverancia *f*, tenacidad *f*
persistent [pərˈsɪstənt] *adj* : persistente — **persistently** *adv*
person [ˈpərsən] *n* **1** HUMAN, INDIVIDUAL : persona *f*, individuo *m*, ser *m* humano **2** : persona *f* (en gramática) **3** **in person** : en persona
personable [ˈpərsənəbəl] *adj* : agradable

personage [ˈpərsənɪʤ] *n* : personaje *m*
personal [ˈpərsənəl] *adj* **1** OWN, PRIVATE : personal, particular, privado ⟨for personal reasons : por razones personales⟩ **2** : en persona ⟨to make a personal appearance : presentarse en persona, hacerse acto de presencia⟩ **3** : íntimo, personal ⟨personal hygiene : higiene personal⟩ **4** INDISCREET, PRYING : indiscreto, personal
personal computer *n* : computadora *f* personal, ordenador *m* personal *Spain*
personal digital assistant *n* : asistente *m* personal digital
personality [ˌpərsənˈæləṭi] *n, pl* **-ties** **1** DISPOSITION : personalidad *f*, temperamento *m* **2** CELEBRITY : personalidad *f*, personaje *m*, celebridad *f*
personalize [ˈpərsənəˌlaɪz] *vt* **-ized; -izing** : personalizar
personally [ˈpərsənəli] *adv* **1** : personalmente, en persona ⟨I'll do it personally : lo haré personalmente⟩ **2** : como persona ⟨personally she's very amiable : como persona es muy amable⟩ **3** : personalmente ⟨personally, I don't believe it : yo, personalmente, no me lo creo⟩
personification [pərˌsɑnəfəˈkeɪʃən] *n* : personificación *f*
personify [pərˈsɑnəˌfaɪ] *vt* **-fied; -fying** : personificar
personnel [ˌpərsənˈɛl] *n* : personal *m*
perspective [pərˈspɛktɪv] *n* : perspectiva *f*
perspicacious [ˌpərspəˈkeɪʃəs] *adj* : perspicaz
perspiration [ˌpərspəˈreɪʃən] *n* : transpiración *f*, sudor *m*
perspire [pərˈspaɪr] *vi* **-spired; -spiring** : transpirar, sudar
persuade [pərˈsweɪd] *vt* **-suaded; -suading** : persuadir, convencer
persuasion [pərˈsweɪʒən] *n* : persuasión *f*
persuasive [pərˈsweɪsɪv, -zɪv] *adj* : persuasivo — **persuasively** *adv*
persuasiveness [pərˈsweɪsɪvnəs, -zɪv-] *n* : persuasión *f*
pert [ˈpərt] *adj* **1** SAUCY : descarado, impertinente **2** JAUNTY : alegre, animado ⟨a pert little hat : un sombrero coqueto⟩
pertain [pərˈteɪn] *vi* **1** BELONG : pertenecer (a) **2** RELATE : estar relacionado (con)
pertinence [ˈpərtənənts] *n* : pertinencia *f*
pertinent [ˈpərtənənt] *adj* : pertinente
perturb [pərˈtərb] *vt* : perturbar
perusal [pəˈruːzəl] *n* : lectura *f* cuidadosa
peruse [pəˈruːz] *vt* **-rused; -rusing** **1** READ : leer con cuidado **2** SCAN : recorrer con la vista ⟨he perused the newspaper : echó un vistazo al periódico⟩
Peruvian [pəˈruːviən] *n* : peruano *m*, -na *f* — **Peruvian** *adj*
pervade [pərˈveɪd] *vt* **-vaded; -vading** : penetrar, difundirse por
pervasive [pərˈveɪsɪv, -zɪv] *adj* : penetrante
perverse [pərˈvərs] *adj* **1** CORRUPT : perverso, corrompido **2** STUBBORN : obstinado, porfiado, terco (sin razón) — **perversely** *adv*
perversion [pərˈvərʒən] *n* : perversión *f*
perversity [pərˈvərsəṭi] *n, pl* **-ties** **1** CORRUPTION : corrupción *f* **2** STUBBORNNESS : obstinación *f*, terquedad *f*
pervert[1] [pərˈvərt] *vt* **1** DISTORT : pervertir, distorsionar **2** CORRUPT : pervertir, corromper
pervert[2] [ˈpərˌvərt] *n* : pervertido *m*, -da *f*
pesky [ˈpɛski] *adj* : molestoso, molesto
peso [ˈpeɪˌsoː] *n, pl* **-sos** : peso *m*
pessimism [ˈpɛsəˌmɪzəm] *n* : pesimismo *m*
pessimist [ˈpɛsəmɪst] *n* : pesimista *mf*
pessimistic [ˌpɛsəˈmɪstɪk] *adj* : pesimista
pest [ˈpɛst] *n* **1** NUISANCE : peste *f*; latoso *m*, -sa *f fam* ⟨to be a pest : dar (la) lata⟩ **2** : insecto *m* nocivo, animal *m* nocivo ⟨the squirrels were pests : las ardillas eran una plaga⟩
pester [ˈpɛstər] *vt* **-tered; -tering** : molestar, fastidiar
pesticide [ˈpɛstəˌsaɪd] *n* : pesticida *m*
pestilence [ˈpɛstələnts] *n* : pestilencia *f*, peste *f*
pestle [ˈpɛsəl, ˈpɛstəl] *n* : mano *f* de mortero, mazo *m*, maja *f*
pet[1] [ˈpɛt] *vt* **petted; petting** : acariciar
pet[2] *n* **1** : animal *m* doméstico **2** FAVORITE : favorito *m*, -ta *f*
petal [ˈpɛṭəl] *n* : pétalo *m*
petite [pəˈtiːt] *adj* : pequeña, menuda, chiquita
petition[1] [pəˈtɪʃən] *vt* : peticionar
petition[2] *n* : petición *f*
petitioner [pəˈtɪʃənər] *n* : peticionario *m*, -ria *f*
petrify [ˈpɛtrəˌfaɪ] *vt* **-fied; -fying** : petrificar
petroleum [pəˈtroːliəm] *n* : petróleo *m*
petticoat [ˈpɛṭiˌkoːt] *n* : enagua *f*, fondo *m Mex*
pettiness [ˈpɛṭinəs] *n* **1** INSIGNIFICANCE : insignificancia *f* **2** MEANNESS : mezquindad *f*
petty [ˈpɛṭi] *adj* **-tier; -est** **1** MINOR : menor ⟨petty cash : dinero para gastos menores⟩ **2** INSIGNIFICANT : insignificante, trivial, nimio **3** MEAN : mezquino
petty officer *n* : suboficial *mf*
petulance [ˈpɛʧələnts] *n* : irritabilidad *f*, mal genio *m*
petulant [ˈpɛʧələnt] *adj* : irritable, de mal genio
petunia [pɪˈtuːnjə, -ˈtjuː-] *n* : petunia *f*
pew [ˈpjuː] *n* : banco *m* (de iglesia)

pewter ['pjuːt̬ər] *n* : peltre *m*
pH [ˌpiːˈeɪtʃ] *n* : pH *m*
phallic ['fælɪk] *adj* : fálico
phallus ['fæləs] *n, pl* **-li** ['fæˌlaɪ] *or* **-luses** : falo *m*
phantasy ['fæntəsi] → **fantasy**
phantom ['fæntəm] *n* : fantasma *m*
pharaoh ['fɛrˌoː, 'feɪˌroː] *n* : faraón *m*
pharmaceutical [ˌfɑrməˈsuːt̬ɪkəl] *adj* : farmacéutico
pharmacist ['fɑrməsɪst] *n* : farmacéutico *m*, -ca *f*
pharmacology [ˌfɑrməˈkɑləʤi] *n* : farmacología *f*
pharmacy ['fɑrməsi] *n, pl* **-cies** : farmacia *f*
pharynx ['færɪŋks] *n, pl* **pharynges** [fəˈrɪnˌʤiːz] : faringe *f*
phase[1] ['feɪz] *vt* **phased; phasing 1** SYNCHRONIZE : sincronizar, poner en fase **2** STAGGER : escalonar **3 to phase in** : introducir progresivamente **4 to phase out** : retirar progresivamente, dejar de producir
phase[2] *n* **1** : fase *f* (de la luna, etc.) **2** STAGE : fase *f*, etapa *f*
pheasant ['fɛzənt] *n, pl* **-ant** *or* **-ants** : faisán *m*
phenomenal [fɪˈnɑmənəl] *adj* : extraordinario, excepcional
phenomenon [fɪˈnɑməˌnɑn, -nən] *n, pl* **-na** [-nə] *or* **-nons 1** : fenómeno *m* **2** *pl* **-nons** PRODIGY : fenómeno *m*, prodigio *m*
philanthropic [ˌfɪlənˈθrɑpɪk] *adj* : filantrópico
philanthropist [fəˈlæntθrəpɪst] *n* : filántropo *m*, -pa *f*
philanthropy [fəˈlæntθrəpi] *n, pl* **-pies** : filantropía *f*
philately [fəˈlætəli] *n* : filatelia *f*
philodendron [ˌfɪləˈdɛndrən] *n, pl* **-drons** *or* **-dra** [-drə] : arácea *f*
philosopher [fəˈlɑsəfər] *n* : filósofo *m*, -fa *f*
philosophic [ˌfɪləˈsɑfɪk] *or* **philosophical** [-fɪkəl] *adj* : filosófico — **philosophically** [-kli] *adv*
philosophize [fəˈlɑsəˌfaɪz] *vi* **-phized; -phizing** : filosofar
philosophy [fəˈlɑsəfi] *n, pl* **-phies** : filosofía *f*
phlebitis [flɪˈbaɪt̬əs] *n* : flebitis *f*
phlegm ['flɛm] *n* : flema *f*
phlox ['flɑks] *n, pl* **phlox** *or* **phloxes** : polemonio *m*
phobia ['foːbiə] *n* : fobia *f*
phoenix ['fiːnɪks] *n* : fénix *m*
phone[1] ['foːn] *v* → **telephone**[1]
phone[2] *n* → **telephone**[2]
phoneme ['foːˌniːm] *n* : fonema *m*
phonetic [fəˈnɛt̬ɪk] *adj* : fonético
phonetics [fəˈnɛt̬ɪks] *n* : fonética *f*
phonics ['fɑnɪks] *n* : método *m* fonético de aprender a leer
phonograph ['foːnəˌgræf] *n* : fonógrafo *m*, tocadiscos *m*
phony[1] *or* **phoney** ['foːni] *adj* **-nier; -est** : falso
phony[2] *or* **phoney** *n, pl* **-nies** : farsante *mf*; charlatán *m*, -tana *f*
phosphate ['fɑsˌfeɪt] *n* : fosfato *m*
phosphorescence [ˌfɑsfəˈrɛsənts] *n* : fosforescencia *f*
phosphorescent [ˌfɑsfəˈrɛsənt] *adj* : fosforescente — **phosphorescently** *adv*
phosphorus ['fɑsfərəs] *n* : fósforo *m*
photo ['foːt̬oː] *n, pl* **-tos** : foto *f*
photocopier ['foːt̬oˌkɑpiər] *n* : fotocopiadora *f*
photocopy[1] ['foːt̬oˌkɑpi] *vt* **-copied; -copying** : fotocopiar
photocopy[2] *n, pl* **-copies** : fotocopia *f*
photoelectric [ˌfoːt̬oɪˈlɛktrɪk] *adj* : fotoeléctrico
photogenic [ˌfoːt̬əˈʤɛnɪk] *adj* : fotogénico
photograph[1] ['foːt̬əˌgræf] *vt* : fotografiar
photograph[2] *n* : fotografía *f*, foto *f* ⟨to take a photograph of : tomarle una fotografía a, tomar una fotografía de⟩
photographer [fəˈtɑgrəfər] *n* : fotógrafo *m*, -fa *f*
photographic [ˌfoːt̬əˈgræfɪk] *adj* : fotográfico — **photographically** [-fɪkli] *adv*
photography [fəˈtɑgrəfi] *n* : fotografía *f*
photosynthesis [ˌfoːt̬oˈsɪntθəsɪs] *n* : fotosíntesis *f*
photosynthetic [ˌfoːt̬osɪnˈθɛt̬ɪk] *adj* : fotosintético, de fotosíntesis
phrase[1] ['freɪz] *vt* **phrased; phrasing** : expresar
phrase[2] *n* : frase *f*, locución *f* ⟨to coin a phrase : para decirlo así⟩
phylum ['faɪləm] *n, pl* **-la** [-lə] : phylum *m*
physical[1] ['fɪzɪkəl] *adj* **1** : físico ⟨physical laws : leyes físicas⟩ **2** MATERIAL : material, físico **3** BODILY : físico, corpóreo — **physically** [-kli] *adv*
physical[2] *n* CHECKUP : chequeo *m*, reconocimiento *m* médico
physician [fəˈzɪʃən] *n* : médico *m*, -ca *f*
physicist ['fɪzəsɪst] *n* : físico *m*, -ca *f*
physics ['fɪzɪks] *ns & pl* : física *f*
physiognomy [ˌfɪziˈɑgnəmi] *n, pl* **-mies** : fisonomía *f*
physiological ['fɪziəˈlɑʤɪkəl] *or* **physiologic** [-ʤɪk] *adj* : fisiológico
physiologist [ˌfɪziˈɑləʤɪst] *n* : fisiólogo *m*, -ga *f*
physiology [ˌfɪziˈɑləʤi] *n* : fisiología *f*
physique [fəˈziːk] *n* : físico *m*
pi ['paɪ] *n, pl* **pis** ['paɪz] : pi *f*
pianist [piˈænɪst, 'piːənɪst] *n* : pianista *mf*
piano [piˈænoː] *n, pl* **-anos** : piano *m*
piazza [piˈæzə, -ˈɑtsə] *n, pl* **-zas** *or* **-ze** [-ˈɑtˌseɪ] : plaza *f*
picaresque [ˌpɪkəˈrɛsk, ˌpiː-] *adj* : picaresco
picayune [ˌpɪkiˈjuːn] *adj* : trivial, nimio, insignificante
piccolo ['pɪkəˌloː] *n, pl* **-los** : flautín *m*
pick[1] ['pɪk] *vt* **1** : picar, labrar (con un pico) ⟨he picked the hard soil : picó la

tierra dura⟩ **2** : quitar, sacar (poco a poco) ⟨to pick meat off the bones : quitar pedazos de carne de los huesos⟩ **3** : recoger, arrancar (frutas, flores, etc.) **4** SELECT : escoger, elegir **5** PROVOKE : provocar ⟨to pick a quarrel : buscar pleito, buscar pelea⟩ **6 to pick a lock** : forzar una cerradura **7 to pick someone's pocket** : robarle algo del bolsillo de alguien ⟨someone picked my pocket! : ¡me robaron la cartera del bolsillo!⟩ — *vi* **1** NIBBLE : picar, picotear **2 to pick and choose** : ser exigente **3 to pick at** : tocar, rascarse (una herida, etc.) **4 to pick on** TEASE : mofarse de, atormentar

pick[2] *n* **1** CHOICE : selección *f* **2** BEST : lo mejor ⟨the pick of the crop : la crema y nata⟩ **3** → **pickax**

pickax [ˈpɪkˌæks] *n* : pico *m*, zapapico *m*, piqueta *f*

pickerel [ˈpɪkərəl] *n, pl* **-el** *or* **-els** : lucio *m* pequeño

picket[1] [ˈpɪkət] *v* : piquetear

picket[2] *n* **1** STAKE : estaca *f* **2** STRIKER : huelguista *mf*, integrante *mf* de un piquete

pickle[1] [ˈpɪkəl] *vt* **-led; -ling** : encurtir, escabechar

pickle[2] *n* **1** BRINE : escabeche *m* **2** GHERKIN : pepinillo *m* (encurtido) **3** JAM, TROUBLE : lío *m*, apuro *m*

pickpocket [ˈpɪkˌpɑkət] *n* : carterista *mf*

pickup [ˈpɪkˌəp] *n* **1** IMPROVEMENT : mejora *f* **2** *or* **pickup truck** : camioneta *f*

pick up *vt* **1** LIFT : levantar **2** TIDY : arreglar, ordenar — *vi* IMPROVE : mejorar

picnic[1] [ˈpɪkˌnɪk] *vi* **-nicked; -nicking** : ir de picnic

picnic[2] *n* : picnic *m*

pictorial [pɪkˈtoriəl] *adj* : pictórico

picture[1] [ˈpɪktʃər] *vt* **-tured; -turing** **1** DEPICT : representar **2** IMAGINE : imaginarse ⟨can you picture it? : ¿te lo puedes imaginar?⟩

picture[2] *n* **1** : cuadro *m* (pintado o dibujado), ilustración *f*, fotografía *f* **2** DESCRIPTION : descripción *f* **3** IMAGE : imagen *f* ⟨he's the picture of his father : es la viva imagen de su padre⟩ **4** MOVIE : película *f*

picturesque [ˌpɪktʃəˈrɛsk] *adj* : pintoresco

pie [ˈpaɪ] *n* : pastel *m* (con fruta o carne), empanada *f* (con carne)

piebald [ˈpaɪˌbɔld] *adj* : picazo, pío

piece[1] [ˈpiːs] *vt* **pieced; piecing** **1** PATCH : parchar, arreglar **2 to piece together** : construir pieza por pieza

piece[2] *n* **1** FRAGMENT : trozo *m*, pedazo *m* **2** COMPONENT : pieza *f* ⟨a three-piece suit : un traje de tres piezas⟩ **3** UNIT : pieza *f* ⟨a piece of fruit : una (pieza de) fruta⟩ **4** WORK : obra *f*, pieza *f* (de música, etc.) **5** (*in board games*) : ficha *f*, pieza *f*, figura *f* (en ajedrez)

piecemeal[1] [ˈpiːsˌmiːl] *adv* : poco a poco, por partes

piecemeal[2] *adj* : hecho poco a poco, poco sistemático

pied [ˈpaɪd] *adj* : pío

pier [ˈpɪr] *n* **1** : pila *f* (de un puente) **2** WHARF : muelle *m*, atracadero *m*, embarcadero *m* **3** PILLAR : pilar *m*

pierce [ˈpɪrs] *vt* **pierced; piercing** **1** PENETRATE : atravesar, traspasar, penetrar (en) ⟨the bullet pierced his leg : la bala le atravesó la pierna⟩ ⟨to pierce one's heart : traspasarle el corazón a uno⟩ **2** PERFORATE : perforar, agujerear (las orejas, etc.) **3 to pierce the silence** : desgarrar el silencio

piety [ˈpaɪət̬i] *n, pl* **-eties** : piedad *f*

pig [ˈpɪg] *n* **1** HOG, SWINE : cerdo *m*, -da *f*; puerco *m*, -ca *f* **2** SLOB : persona *f* desaliñada; cerdo *m*, -da *f* **3** GLUTTON : glotón *m*, -tona *f* **4** *or* **pig iron** : lingote *m* de hierro

pigeon [ˈpɪdʒən] *n* : paloma *f*

pigeonhole [ˈpɪdʒənˌhoːl] *n* : casilla *f*

pigeon–toed [ˈpɪdʒənˌtoːd] *adj* : patituerto

piggish [ˈpɪgɪʃ] *adj* **1** GREEDY : glotón **2** DIRTY : cochino, sucio

piggyback [ˈpɪgiˌbæk] *adv & adj* : a cuestas

pigheaded [ˈpɪgˌhɛdəd] *adj* : terco, obstinado

piglet [ˈpɪglət] *n* : cochinillo *m*; lechón *m*, -chona *f*

pigment [ˈpɪgmənt] *n* : pigmento *m*

pigmentation [ˌpɪgmənˈteɪʃən] *n* : pigmentación *f*

pigmy → **pygmy**

pigpen [ˈpɪgˌpɛn] *n* : chiquero *m*, pocilga *f*

pigsty [ˈpɪgˌstaɪ] → **pigpen**

pigtail [ˈpɪgˌteɪl] *n* : coleta *f*, trenza *f*

pike [ˈpaɪk] *n, pl* **pike** *or* **pikes** **1** : lucio *m* (pez) **2** LANCE : pica *f* **3** → **turnpike**

pile[1] [ˈpaɪl] *v* **piled; piling** *vt* : amontonar, apilar — *vi* **to pile up** : amontonarse, acumularse

pile[2] *n* **1** STAKE : pilote *m* **2** HEAP : montón *m*, pila *f* **3** NAP : pelo *m* (de telas)

piles [ˈpaɪlz] *npl* HEMORRHOIDS : hemorroides *fpl*, almorranas *fpl*

pilfer [ˈpɪlfər] *vt* : robar (cosas pequeñas), ratear

pilgrim [ˈpɪlgrəm] *n* : peregrino *m*, -na *f*

pilgrimage [ˈpɪlgrəmɪdʒ] *n* : peregrinación *f*

pill [ˈpɪl] *n* : pastilla *f*, píldora *f*

pillage[1] [ˈpɪlɪdʒ] *vt* **-laged; -laging** : saquear

pillage[2] *n* : saqueo *m*

pillar [ˈpɪlər] *n* : pilar *m*, columna *f*

pillory [ˈpɪləri] *n, pl* **-ries** : picota *f*

pillow [ˈpɪˌloː] *n* : almohada *f*

pillowcase [ˈpɪˌloːˌkeɪs] *n* : funda *f*

pilot[1] [ˈpaɪlət] *vt* : pilotar, pilotear

pilot[2] *n* : piloto *mf*

pilot light *n* : piloto *m*

pimento [pəˈmɛnˌtoː] → **pimiento**

pimiento [pəˈmɛnˌto:, -ˈmjɛn-] *n, pl* **-tos** : pimiento *m* morrón

pimp [ˈpɪmp] *n* : proxeneta *m*

pimple [ˈpɪmpəl] *n* : grano *m*

pimply [ˈpɪmpəli] *adj* **-plier; -est** : cubierto de granos

pin[1] [ˈpɪn] *vt* **pinned; pinning 1** FASTEN : prender, sujetar (con alfileres) **2** HOLD, IMMOBILIZE : inmovilizar, sujetar **3 to pin one's hopes on** : poner sus esperanzas en

pin[2] *n* **1** : alfiler *m* ⟨safety pin : alfiler de gancho⟩ ⟨a bobby pin : una horquilla⟩ **2** BROOCH : alfiler *m*, broche *m*, prendedor *m* **3** *or* **bowling pin** : bolo *m*

pinafore [ˈpɪnəˌfor] *n* : delantal *m*

pincer [ˈpɪntsər] *n* **1** CLAW : pinza *f* (de una langosta, etc.) **2 pincers** *npl* : pinzas *fpl*, tenazas *fpl*, tenaza *f*

pinch[1] [ˈpɪntʃ] *vt* **1** : pellizcar ⟨she pinched my cheek : me pellizcó el cachete⟩ **2** STEAL : robar — *vi* : apretar ⟨my shoes pinch : me aprietan los zapatos⟩

pinch[2] *n* **1** EMERGENCY : emergencia *f* ⟨in a pinch : en caso necesario⟩ **2** PAIN : dolor *m*, tormento *m* **3** SQUEEZE : pellizco *m* (con los dedos) **4** BIT : pizca *f*, pellizco *m* ⟨a pinch of cinnamon : una pizca de canela⟩

pinch hitter *n* **1** SUBSTITUTE : sustituto *m*, -ta *f* **2** : bateador *m* emergente (en beisbol)

pincushion [ˈpɪnˌkʊʃən] *n* : acerico *m*, alfiletero *m*

pine[1] [ˈpaɪn] *vi* **pined; pining 1 to pine away** : languidecer, consumirse **2 to pine for** : añorar, suspirar por

pine[2] *n* **1** : pino *m* (árbol) **2** : madera *f* de pino

pineapple [ˈpaɪnˌæpəl] *n* : piña *f*, ananá *m*, ananás *m*

ping–pong [ˈpɪŋˌpɑŋ, -ˌpɔŋ] *n* : ping-pong *m*

pinion[1] [ˈpɪnjən] *vt* : sujetar los brazos de, inmovilizar

pinion[2] *n* : piñón *m*

pink[1] [ˈpɪŋk] *adj* : rosa, rosado

pink[2] *n* **1** : clavelito *m* (flor) **2** : rosa *m*, rosado *m* (color) **3 to be in the pink** : estar en plena forma, rebosar de salud

pinkeye [ˈpɪŋkˌaɪ] *n* : conjuntivitis *f* aguda

pinkish [ˈpɪŋkɪʃ] *adj* : rosáceo

pinnacle [ˈpɪnɪkəl] *n* **1** : pináculo *m* (de un edificio) **2** PEAK : cima *f*, cumbre *f* (de una montaña) **3** ACME : pináculo *m*, cúspide *f*, apogeo *m*

pinpoint [ˈpɪnˌpɔɪnt] *vt* : precisar, localizar con precisión

pint [ˈpaɪnt] *n* : pinta *f*

pinto [ˈpɪnˌto:] *n, pl* **pintos** : caballo *m* pinto

pinworm [ˈpɪnˌwərm] *n* : oxiuro *m*

pioneer[1] [ˌpaɪəˈnɪr] *vt* : promover, iniciar, introducir

pioneer[2] *n* : pionero *m*, -ra *f*

pious [ˈpaɪəs] *adj* **1** DEVOUT : piadoso, devoto **2** SANCTIMONIOUS : beato

piously [ˈpaɪəsli] *adv* **1** DEVOUTLY : piadosamente **2** SANCTIMONIOUSLY : santurronamente

pipe[1] [ˈpaɪp] *v* **piped; piping** *vi* : hablar en voz chillona — *vt* **1** PLAY : tocar (el caramillo o la flauta) **2** : conducir por tuberías ⟨to pipe water : transportar el agua por tubería⟩

pipe[2] *n* **1** : caramillo *m* (instrumento musical) **2** BAGPIPE : gaita *f* **3** : tubo *m*, caño *m* ⟨gas pipes : tubería de gas⟩ **4** : pipa *f* (para fumar)

pipeline [ˈpaɪpˌlaɪn] *n* **1** : conducto *m*, oleoducto *m* (para petróleo), gasoducto *m* (para gas) **2** CONDUIT : vía *f* (de información, etc.)

piper [ˈpaɪpər] *n* : músico *m*, -ca *f* que toca el caramillo o la gaita

piping [ˈpaɪpɪŋ] *n* **1** : música *f* del caramillo o de la gaita **2** TRIM : cordoncillo *m*, ribete *m* con cordón

piquant [ˈpi:kənt, ˈpɪkwənt] *adj* **1** SPICY : picante **2** INTRIGUING : intrigante, estimulante

pique[1] [ˈpi:k] *vt* **piqued; piquing 1** IRRITATE : picar, irritar **2** AROUSE : despertar (la curiosidad, etc.)

pique[2] *n* : pique *m*, resentimiento *m*

piracy [ˈpaɪrəsi] *n, pl* **-cies** : piratería *f*

piranha [pəˈrɑnə, -ˈrɑnjə, -ˈrænjə] *n* : piraña *f*

pirate[1] [ˈpaɪrət] *n* : pirata *mf*

pirate[2] *vt* **-rated; -rating** : piratear (software, etc.)

pirouette [ˌpɪrəˈwɛt] *n* : pirueta *f*

pis → **pi**

Pisces [ˈpaɪˌsi:z, ˈpɪ-; ˈpɪsˌkeɪs] *n* : Piscis *mf*

pistachio [pəˈstæʃiˌo:, -ˈstɑ-] *n, pl* **-chios** : pistacho *m*

pistil [ˈpɪstəl] *n* : pistilo *m*

pistol [ˈpɪstəl] *n* : pistola *f*

piston [ˈpɪstən] *n* : pistón *m*, émbolo *m*

pit[1] [ˈpɪt] *v* **pitted; pitting** *vt* **1** : marcar de hoyos, picar (una superficie) **2** : deshuesar (una fruta) **3 to pit against** : enfrentar a, oponer a — *vi* : quedar marcado

pit[2] *n* **1** HOLE : fosa *f*, hoyo *m* ⟨a bottomless pit : un pozo sin fondo⟩ **2** MINE : mina *f* **3** : foso *m* ⟨orchestra pit : foso orquestal⟩ **4** POCKMARK : marca *f* (en la cara), cicatriz *f* de viruela **5** STONE : hueso *m*, pepa *f* (de una fruta) **6 pit of the stomach** : boca *f* del estómago

pitch[1] [ˈpɪtʃ] *vt* **1** SET UP : montar, armar (una tienda) **2** THROW : lanzar, arrojar **3** ADJUST, SET : dar el tono de (un discurso, un instrumento musical) — *vi* **1** *or* **pitch forward** FALL : caerse **2** LURCH : cabecear (dícese de un barco o un avión), dar bandazos

pitch[2] *n* **1** LURCHING : cabezada *f*, cabeceo *m* (de un barco o un avión) **2** SLOPE : (grado de) inclinación *f*, pendiente *f* **3** : tono *m* (en música) ⟨perfect pitch : oído absoluto⟩ **4** THROW : lanzamiento *m* **5** DEGREE : grado *m*, nivel *m*, punto *m* ⟨the excitement reached a high pitch : la excitación llegó a un punto culminante⟩ **6** *or* **sales pitch** : presentación *f* (de un vendedor) **7** TAR : pez *f*, brea *f*

pitcher [ˈpɪʧər] *n* **1** JUG : jarra *f*, jarro *m*, cántaro *m*, pichel *m* **2** : lanzador *m*, -dora *f* (en béisbol, etc.)

pitchfork [ˈpɪʧˌfɔrk] *n* : horquilla *f*, horca *f*

piteous [ˈpɪt̬iəs] *adj* : lastimoso, lastimero — **piteously** *adv*

pitfall [ˈpɪtˌfɔl] *n* : peligro *m* (poco obvio), dificultad *f*

pith [ˈpɪθ] *n* **1** : médula *f* (de una planta) **2** CORE : meollo *m*, entraña *f*

pithy [ˈpɪθi] *adj* **pithier; -est** : conciso y sustancioso ⟨pithy comments : comentarios sucintos⟩

pitiable [ˈpɪt̬iəbəl] → **pitiful**

pitiful [ˈpɪt̬ɪfəl] *adj* **1** LAMENTABLE : lastimero, lastimoso, lamentable **2** CONTEMPTIBLE : despreciable, lamentable — **pitifully** [-fli] *adv*

pitiless [ˈpɪt̬ɪləs] *adj* : despiadado — **pitilessly** *adv*

pittance [ˈpɪtənts] *n* : miseria *f*

pituitary [pəˈtuːəˌtɛri, -ˈtjuː-] *adj* : pituitario

pity[1] [ˈpɪt̬i] *vt* **pitied; pitying** : compadecer, compadecerse de

pity[2] *n, pl* **pities** **1** COMPASSION : compasión *f*, piedad *f* **2** SHAME : lástima *f*, pena *f* ⟨what a pity! : ¡qué lástima!⟩

pivot[1] [ˈpɪvət] *vi* **1** : girar sobre un eje **2** **to pivot on** : girar sobre, depender de

pivot[2] *n* : pivote *m*

pivotal [ˈpɪvət̬əl] *adj* : fundamental, central

pixie *or* **pixy** [ˈpɪksi] *n, pl* **pixies** : elfo *m*, hada *f*

pizza [ˈpiːtsə] *n* : pizza *f*

pizzazz *or* **pizazz** [pəˈzæz] *n* **1** GLAMOR : encanto *m* **2** VITALITY : animación *f*, vitalidad *f*

placard [ˈplækərd, -ˌkɑrd] *n* POSTER : cartel *m*, póster *m*, afiche *m*

placate [ˈpleɪˌkeɪt, ˈplæ-] *vt* **-cated; -cating** : aplacar, apaciguar

place[1] [ˈpleɪs] *vt* **placed; placing** **1** PUT, SET : poner, colocar **2** SITUATE : situar, ubicar, emplazar ⟨to be well placed : estar bien situado⟩ ⟨to place in a job : colocar en un trabajo⟩ **3** IDENTIFY, RECALL : identificar, ubicar, recordar ⟨I can't place him : no lo ubico⟩ **4** **to place an order** : hacer un pedido

place[2] *n* **1** SPACE : sitio *m*, lugar *m* ⟨there's no place to sit : no hay sitio para sentarse⟩ **2** LOCATION, SPOT : lugar *m*, sitio *m*, parte *f* ⟨place of work : lugar de trabajo⟩ ⟨our summer place : nuestra casa de verano⟩ ⟨all over the place : por todas partes⟩ **3** RANK : lugar *m*, puesto *m* ⟨he took first place : ganó el primer lugar⟩ **4** POSITION : lugar *m* ⟨everything in its place : todo en su debido lugar⟩ ⟨to feel out of place : sentirse fuera de lugar⟩ **5** SEAT : asiento *m*, cubierto *m* (a la mesa) **6** JOB : puesto *m* **7** ROLE : papel *m*, lugar *m* ⟨to change places : cambiarse los papeles⟩ **8** **to take place** : tener lugar **9** **to take the place of** : sustituir a

placebo [pləˈsiːˌboː] *n, pl* **-bos** : placebo *m*

placement [ˈpleɪsmənt] *n* : colocación *f*

placenta [pləˈsɛntə] *n, pl* **-tas** *or* **-tae** [-ti, -ˌtaɪ] : placenta *f*

placid [ˈplæsəd] *adj* : plácido, tranquilo — **placidly** *adv*

plagiarism [ˈpleɪʤəˌrɪzəm] *n* : plagio *m*

plagiarist [ˈpleɪʤərɪst] *n* : plagiario *m*, -ria *f*

plagiarize [ˈpleɪʤəˌraɪz] *vt* **-rized; -rizing** : plagiar

plague[1] [ˈpleɪg] *vt* **plagued; plaguing** **1** AFFLICT : plagar, afligir **2** HARASS : acosar, atormentar

plague[2] *n* **1** : plaga *f* (de insectos, etc.) **2** : peste *f* (en medicina)

plaid[1] [ˈplæd] *adj* : escocés, de cuadros ⟨a plaid skirt : una falda escocesa⟩

plaid[2] *n* TARTAN : tela *f* escocesa, tartán *m*

plain[1] [ˈpleɪn] *adj* **1** SIMPLE, UNADORNED : liso, sencillo, sin adornos **2** CLEAR : claro ⟨in plain language : en palabras claras⟩ **3** FRANK : franco, puro ⟨the plain truth : la pura verdad⟩ **4** HOMELY : ordinario, poco atractivo **5** **in plain sight** : a la vista de todos

plain[2] *n* : llanura *f*, llano *m*, planicie *f*

plainly [ˈpleɪnli] *adv* **1** CLEARLY : claramente **2** FRANKLY : francamente, con franqueza **3** SIMPLY : sencillamente

plaintiff [ˈpleɪntɪf] *n* : demandante *mf*

plaintive [ˈpleɪntɪv] *adj* MOURNFUL : lastimero, plañidero

plait[1] [ˈpleɪt, ˈplæt] *vt* **1** PLEAT : plisar **2** BRAID : trenzar

plait[2] *n* **1** PLEAT : pliegue *m* **2** BRAID : trenza *f*

plan[1] [ˈplæn] *v* **planned; planning** *vt* **1** : planear, proyectar, planificar ⟨to plan a trip : planear un viaje⟩ ⟨to plan a city : planificar una ciudad⟩ **2** INTEND : tener planeado, proyectar — *vi* : hacer planes

plan[2] *n* **1** DIAGRAM : plano *m*, esquema *m* **2** SCHEME : plan *m*, proyecto *m*, programa *m* ⟨to draw up a plan : elaborar un proyecto⟩

plane[1] [ˈpleɪn] *vt* **planed; planing** : cepillar (madera)

plane[2] *adj* : plano

plane[3] *n* **1** : plano *m* (en matemáticas, etc.) **2** LEVEL : nivel *m* **3** : cepillo *m* (de carpintero) **4** → **airplane**

planet [ˈplænət] *n* : planeta *f*

planetarium [ˌplænəˈtɛriəm] *n, pl* **-iums** *or* **-ia** [-iə] : planetario *m*

planetary [ˈplænəˌtɛri] *adj* : planetario

plank [ˈplæŋk] *n* **1** BOARD : tablón *m*, tabla *f* **2** : artículo *m*, punto *m* (de una plataforma política)

plankton [ˈplæŋktən] *n* : plancton *m*
plant[1] [ˈplænt] *vt* **1** : plantar, sembrar (semillas) ⟨planted with flowers : plantado de flores⟩ **2** PLACE : plantar, colocar ⟨to plant an idea : inculcar una idea⟩
plant[2] *n* **1** : planta *f* ⟨leafy plants : plantas frondosas⟩ **2** FACTORY : planta *f*, fábrica *f* ⟨hydroelectric plant : planta hidroeléctrica⟩ **3** MACHINERY : maquinaria *f*, equipo *m*
plantain [ˈplæntən] *n* **1** : llantén *m* (mala hierba) **2** : plátano *m*, plátano *m* macho *Mex* (fruta)
plantation [plænˈteɪʃən] *n* : plantación *f*, hacienda *f* ⟨a coffee plantation : un cafetal⟩
planter [ˈplæntər] *n* **1** : hacendado *m*, -da *f* (de una hacienda) **2** FLOWERPOT : tiesto *m*, maceta *f*
plaque [ˈplæk] *n* **1** TABLET : placa *f* **2** : placa *f* (dental)
plasma [ˈplæzmə] *n* : plasma *m*
plaster[1] [ˈplæstər] *vt* **1** : enyesar, revocar (con yeso) **2** COVER : cubrir, llenar ⟨a wall plastered with notices : una pared cubierta de avisos⟩
plaster[2] *n* **1** : yeso *m*, revoque *m* (para paredes, etc.) **2** : escayola *f*, yeso *m* (en medicina) **3 plaster of Paris** [ˈpærɪs] : yeso *m* mate
plaster cast *n* : vaciado *m* de yeso
plasterer [ˈplæstərər] *n* : revocador *m*, -dora *f*
plastic[1] [ˈplæstɪk] *adj* **1** : de plástico **2** PLIABLE : plástico, flexible **3 plastic surgery** : cirugía *f* plástica
plastic[2] *n* : plástico *m*
plasticity [plæˈstɪsət̬i] *n, pl* **-ties** : plasticidad *f*
plate[1] [ˈpleɪt] *vt* **plated; plating** : chapar (en metal)
plate[2] *n* **1** PLAQUE, SHEET : placa *f* ⟨a steel plate : una placa de acero⟩ **2** UTENSILS : vajilla *f* (de metal) ⟨silver plate : vajilla de plata⟩ **3** DISH : plato *m* **4** DENTURES : dentadura *f* postiza **5** ILLUSTRATION : lámina *f* (en un libro) **6 license plate** : matrícula *f*, placa *f* de matrícula
plateau [plæˈtoː] *n, pl* **-teaus** *or* **-teaux** [-ˈtoːz] : meseta *f*
platform [ˈplætˌfɔrm] *n* **1** STAGE : plataforma *f*, estrado *m*, tribuna *f* **2** : andén *m* (de una estación de ferrocarril) **3 political platform** : plataforma *f* política, programa *m* electoral
plating [ˈpleɪt̬ɪŋ] *n* **1** : enchapado *m* **2 silver plating** : plateado *m*
platinum [ˈplætənəm] *n* : platino *m*
platitude [ˈplæt̬əˌtuːd, -ˌtjuːd] *n* : lugar *m* común, perogrullada *f*
platonic [pləˈtɑnɪk] *adj* : platónico
platoon [pləˈtuːn] *n* : sección *f* (en el ejército)
platter [ˈplæt̬ər] *n* : fuente *f*
platypus [ˈplæt̬ɪpəs, -ˌpʊs] *n, pl* **platypuses** *or* **platypi** [-ˌpaɪ, -ˌpiː] : ornitorrinco *m*
plausibility [ˌplɔzəˈbɪlət̬i] *n, pl* **-ties** : credibilidad *f*, verosimilitud *f*
plausible [ˈplɔzəbəl] *adj* : creíble, convincente, verosímil — **plausibly** [-bli] *adv*
play[1] [ˈpleɪ] *vi* **1** : jugar ⟨to play with a doll : jugar con una muñeca⟩ ⟨to play with an idea : darle vueltas a una idea⟩ **2** FIDDLE, TOY : jugar, juguetear ⟨don't play with your food : no juegues con la comida⟩ **3** : tocar ⟨to play in a band : tocar en un grupo⟩ **4** : actuar (en una obra de teatro) — *vt* **1** : jugar (un deporte, etc.), jugar a (un juego), jugar contra (un contrincante) **2** : tocar (música o un instrumento) **3** PERFORM : interpretar, hacer el papel de (un carácter), representar (una obra de teatro) ⟨she plays the lead : hace el papel principal⟩ **4 to play back** : poner (una grabación) **5 to play down** : minimizar **6 to play up** : resaltar
play[2] *n* **1** GAME, RECREATION : juego *m* ⟨children at play : niños jugando⟩ ⟨a play on words : un juego de palabras⟩ **2** ACTION : juego *m* ⟨the ball is in play : la pelota está en juego⟩ ⟨to bring into play : poner en juego⟩ **3** DRAMA : obra *f* de teatro, pieza *f* (de teatro) **4** MOVEMENT : juego *m* (de la luz, una brisa, etc.) **5** SLACK : juego *m* ⟨there's not enough play in the wheel : la rueda no da lo suficiente⟩
playacting [ˈpleɪˌæktɪŋ] *n* : actuación *f*, teatro *m*
player [ˈpleɪər] *n* **1** : jugador *m*, -dora *f* (en un juego) **2** ACTOR : actor *m*, actriz *f* **3** MUSICIAN : músico *m*, -ca *f*
playful [ˈpleɪfəl] *adj* **1** FROLICSOME : juguetón **2** JOCULAR : jocoso — **playfully** *adv*
playfulness [ˈpleɪfəlnəs] *n* : lo juguetón, jocosidad *f*, alegría *f*
playground [ˈpleɪˌgraʊnd] *n* : patio *m* de recreo, jardín *m* para jugar
playhouse [ˈpleɪˌhaʊs] *n* **1** THEATER : teatro *m* **2** : casita *f* de juguete
playing card *n* : naipe *m*, carta *f*
playmate [ˈpleɪˌmeɪt] *n* : compañero *m*, -ra *f* de juego
play–off [ˈpleɪˌɔf] *n* : desempate *m*
playpen [ˈpleɪˌpɛn] *n* : corral *m* (para niños)
plaything [ˈpleɪˌθɪŋ] *n* : juguete *m*
playwright [ˈpleɪˌraɪt] *n* : dramaturgo *m*, -ga *f*
plaza [ˈplæzə, ˈplɑ-] *n* **1** SQUARE : plaza *f* **2 shopping plaza** MALL : centro *m* comercial
plea [ˈpliː] *n* **1** : acto *m* de declararse ⟨he entered a plea of guilty : se declaró culpable⟩ **2** APPEAL : ruego *m*, súplica *f*
plead [ˈpliːd] *v* **pleaded** *or* **pled** [ˈplɛd]; **pleading** *vi* **1** : declararse (culpable o inocente) **2 to plead for** : suplicar, implorar — *vt* **1** : alegar, pretextar ⟨he pleaded illness : pretextó la enfermedad⟩ **2 to plead a case** : defender un caso

pleasant [ˈplɛzənt] *adj* : agradable, grato, bueno — **pleasantly** *adv*
pleasantness [ˈplɛzəntnəs] *n* : lo agradable, amenidad *f*
pleasantries [ˈplɛzəntriz] *npl* : cumplidos *mpl*, cortesías *fpl* ⟨to exchange pleasantries : intercambiar cumplidos⟩
please[1] [ˈpli:z] *v* **pleased; pleasing** *vt* **1** GRATIFY : complacer ⟨please yourself! : ¡cómo quieras!⟩ **2** SATISFY : contentar, satisfacer — *vi* **1** SATISFY : complacer, agradar ⟨anxious to please : deseoso de complacer⟩ **2** LIKE : querer ⟨do as you please : haz lo que quieras, haz lo que te parezca⟩
please[2] *adv* : por favor
pleased [ˈpli:zd] *adj* : contento, satisfecho, alegre
pleasing [ˈpli:zɪŋ] *adj* : agradable — **pleasingly** *adv*
pleasurable [ˈplɛʒərəbəl] *adj* PLEASANT : agradable
pleasure [ˈplɛʒər] *n* **1** WISH : deseo *m*, voluntad *f* ⟨at your pleasure : cuando guste⟩ **2** ENJOYMENT : placer *m*, disfrute *m*, goce *m* ⟨with pleasure : con mucho gusto⟩ **3** : placer *m*, gusto *m* ⟨it's a pleasure to be here : me da gusto estar aquí⟩ ⟨the pleasures of reading : los placeres de leer⟩
pleat[1] [ˈpli:t] *vt* : plisar
pleat[2] *n* : pliegue *m*
plebeian [plɪˈbiən] *adj* : ordinario, plebeyo
pledge[1] [ˈplɛʤ] *vt* **pledged; pledging 1** PAWN : empeñar, prendar **2** PROMISE : prometer, jurar
pledge[2] *n* **1** SECURITY : garantía *f*, prenda *f* **2** PROMISE : promesa *f*
plenteous [ˈplɛntiəs] *adj* : copioso, abundante
plentiful [ˈplɛntɪfəl] *adj* : abundante — **plentifully** [-fli] *adv*
plenty [ˈplɛnti] *n* : abundancia *f* ⟨plenty of time : tiempo de sobra⟩ ⟨plenty of visitors : muchos visitantes⟩
plethora [ˈplɛθərə] *n* : plétora *f*
pleurisy [ˈplʊrəsi] *n* : pleuresía *f*
pliable [ˈplaɪəbəl] *adj* : flexible, maleable
pliant [ˈplaɪənt] → **pliable**
pliers [ˈplaɪərz] *npl* : alicates *mpl*, pinzas *fpl*
plight [ˈplaɪt] *n* : situación *f* difícil, apuro *m*
plod [ˈplɑd] *vi* **plodded; plodding 1** TRUDGE : caminar pesadamente y lentamente **2** DRUDGE : trabajar laboriosamente
plot[1] [ˈplɑt] *v* **plotted; plotting** *vt* **1** DEVISE : tramar **2 to plot out** : trazar, determinar (una posición, etc.) — *vi* CONSPIRE : conspirar
plot[2] *n* **1** LOT : terreno *m*, parcela *f*, lote *m* **2** STORY : argumento *m* (en el teatro), trama *f* (en un libro, etc.) **3** CONSPIRACY, INTRIGUE : complot *m*, intriga *f*
plotter [ˈplɑt̬ər] *n* : conspirador *m*, -dora *f*; intrigante *mf*
plow[1] *or* **plough** [ˈplaʊ] *vt* **1** : arar (la tierra) **2 to plow the seas** : surcar los mares
plow[2] *or* **plough** *n* **1** : arado *m* **2** → **snowplow**
plowshare [ˈplaʊˌʃɛr] *n* : reja *f* del arado
ploy [ˈplɔɪ] *n* : estratagema *f*, maniobra *f*
pluck[1] [ˈplʌk] *vt* **1** PICK : arrancar **2** : desplumar (un pollo, etc.) — *vi* **to pluck at** : tirar de
pluck[2] *n* **1** TUG : tirón *m* **2** COURAGE, SPIRIT : valor *m*, ánimo *m*
plucky [ˈplʌki] *adj* **pluckier; -est** : valiente, animoso
plug[1] [ˈplʌg] *vt* **plugged; plugging 1** BLOCK : tapar **2** PROMOTE : hacerle publicidad a, promocionar **3 to plug in** : enchufar
plug[2] *n* **1** STOPPER : tapón *m* **2** : enchufe *m* (eléctrico) **3** ADVERTISEMENT : publicidad *f*, propaganda *f*
plum [ˈplʌm] *n* **1** : ciruela *f* (fruta) **2** : color *m* ciruela **3** PRIZE : premio *m*, algo muy atractivo
plumage [ˈplu:mɪʤ] *n* : plumaje *m*
plumb[1] [ˈplʌm] *vt* **1** : aplomar ⟨to plumb a wall : aplomar una pared⟩ **2** SOUND : sondear, sondar
plumb[2] *adv* **1** VERTICALLY : a plomo, verticalmente **2** EXACTLY : justo, exactamente **3** COMPLETELY : completamente, absolutamente ⟨plumb crazy : loco de remate⟩
plumb[3] *adj* : a plomo
plumb[4] *n or* **plumb line** : plomada *f*
plumber [ˈplʌmər] *n* : plomero *m*, -ra *f*; fontanero *m*, -ra *f*
plumbing [ˈplʌmɪŋ] *n* **1** : plomería *f*, fontanería *f* (trabajo del plomero) **2** PIPES : cañería *f*, tubería *f*
plume [ˈplu:m] *n* **1** FEATHER : pluma *f* **2** TUFT : penacho *m* (en un sombrero, etc.)
plumed [ˈplu:md] *adj* : con plumas ⟨white-plumed birds : aves de plumaje blanco⟩
plummet [ˈplʌmət] *vi* : caer en picada, desplomarse
plump[1] [ˈplʌmp] *vi or* **to plump down** : dejarse caer (pesadamente)
plump[2] *adv* **1** STRAIGHT : a plomo **2** DIRECTLY : directamente, sin rodeos ⟨he ran plump into the door : dio de cara con la puerta⟩
plump[3] *adj* : llenito *fam*, regordete *fam*, rechoncho *fam*
plumpness [ˈplʌmpnəs] *n* : gordura *f*
plunder[1] [ˈplʌndər] *vi* : saquear, robar
plunder[2] *n* : botín *m*
plunderer [ˈplʌndərər] *n* : saqueador *m*, -dora *f*
plunge[1] [ˈplʌnʤ] *v* **plunged; plunging** *vt* **1** IMMERSE : sumergir **2** THRUST : hundir, clavar — *vi* **1** DIVE : zambullirse (en el agua) **2** : meterse precipitadamente o violentamente ⟨they plunged into war : se enfrascaron en

una guerra⟩ ⟨he plunged into depression : cayó en la depresión⟩ **3** DESCEND : descender en picada ⟨the road plunges dizzily : la calle desciende vertiginosamente⟩

plunge[2] *n* **1** DIVE : zambullida *f* **2** DROP : descenso *m* abrupto ⟨the plunge in prices : el desplome de los precios⟩

plural[1] ['plʊrəl] *adj* : plural

plural[2] *n* : plural *m*

plurality [plʊ'ræləṭi] *n, pl* **-ties** : pluralidad *f*

pluralize ['plʊrəˌlaɪz] *vt* **-ized; -izing** : pluralizar

plus[1] ['plʌs] *adj* **1** POSITIVE : positivo ⟨a plus factor : un factor positivo⟩ **2** (*indicating a quantity in addition*) ⟨a grade of C plus : una calificación entre C y B⟩ ⟨a salary of $30,000 plus : un sueldo de más de $30,000⟩

plus[2] *n* **1** *or* **plus sign** : más *m*, signo *m* de más **2** ADVANTAGE : ventaja *f*

plus[3] *prep* : más (en matemáticas)

plus[4] *conj* AND : y

plush[1] ['plʌʃ] *adj* **1** : afelpado **2** LUXURIOUS : lujoso

plush[2] *n* : felpa *f*, peluche *m*

plushy ['plʌʃi] *adj* **plushier; -est** : lujoso

Pluto ['plu:ṭo:] *n* : Plutón *m*

plutocracy [plu:'tɑkrəsi] *n, pl* **-cies** : plutocracia *f*

plutonium [plu:'to:niəm] *n* : plutonio *m*

ply[1] ['plaɪ] *v* **plied; plying** *vt* **1** USE, WIELD : manejar ⟨to ply an ax : manejar un hacha⟩ **2** PRACTICE : ejercer ⟨to ply a trade : ejercer un oficio⟩ **3 to ply with questions** : acosar con preguntas

ply[2] *n, pl* **plies 1** LAYER : chapa *f* (de madera), capa *f* (de papel) **2** STRAND : cabo *m* (de hilo, etc.)

plywood ['plaɪˌwʊd] *n* : contrachapado *m*

pneumatic [nʊ'mæṭɪk, njʊ-] *adj* : neumático

pneumonia [nʊ'mo:njə, njʊ-] *n* : pulmonía *f*, neumonía *f*

poach ['po:ʧ] *vt* **1** : cocer a fuego lento ⟨to poach an egg : escalfar un huevo⟩ **2 to poach game** : cazar ilegalmente — *vi* : cazar ilegalmente

poacher ['po:ʧər] *n* : cazador *m* furtivo, cazadora *f* furtiva

pock ['pɑk] *n* **1** PUSTULE : pústula *f* **2** → **pockmark**

pocket[1] ['pɑkət] *vt* **1** : meterse en el bolsillo ⟨he pocketed the pen : se metió la pluma en el bolsillo⟩ **2** STEAL : embolsarse

pocket[2] *n* **1** : bolsillo *m*, bolsa *f Mex* ⟨a coat pocket : el bolsillo de un abrigo⟩ ⟨air pockets : bolsas de aire⟩ **2** CENTER : foco *m*, centro *m* ⟨a pocket of resistance : un foco de resistencia⟩

pocketbook ['pɑkətˌbʊk] *n* **1** PURSE : cartera *f*, bolso *m*, bolsa *f Mex* **2** MEANS : recursos *mpl*

pocketknife ['pɑkətˌnaɪf] *n, pl* **-knives** : navaja *f*

pocket–size ['pɑkət'saɪz] *adj* : de bolsillo

pockmark ['pɑkˌmɑrk] *n* : cicatriz *f* de viruela, viruela *f*

pod ['pɑd] *n* : vaina *f* ⟨pea pod : vaina de guisantes⟩

podiatrist [pə'daɪətrɪst, po-] *n* : podólogo *m*, -ga *f*

podiatry [pə'daɪətri, po-] *n* : podología *f*, podiatría *f*

podium ['po:diəm] *n, pl* **-diums** *or* **-dia** [-diə] : podio *m*, estrado *m*, tarima *f*

poem ['po:əm] *n* : poema *m*, poesía *f*

poet ['po:ət] *n* : poeta *mf*

poetic [po'ɛṭɪk] *or* **poetical** [-ṭɪkəl] *adj* : poético

poetry ['po:ətri] *n* : poesía *f*

pogrom ['po:grəm, pə'grɑm, 'pɑgrəm] *n* : pogrom *m*

poignancy ['pɔɪnjəntsi] *n, pl* **-cies** : lo conmovedor

poignant ['pɔɪnjənt] *adj* **1** PAINFUL : penoso, doloroso ⟨poignant grief : profundo dolor⟩ **2** TOUCHING : conmovedor, emocionante

poinsettia [pɔɪn'sɛṭiə, -'sɛṭə] *n* : flor *f* de Nochebuena

point[1] ['pɔɪnt] *vt* **1** SHARPEN : afilar (la punta de) **2** INDICATE : señalar, indicar ⟨to point the way : señalar el camino⟩ **3** AIM : apuntar **4 to point out** : señalar, indicar — *vi* **1 to point at** : señalar (con el dedo) **2 to point to** INDICATE : señalar, indicar

point[2] *n* **1** ITEM : punto *m* ⟨the main points : los puntos principales⟩ **2** QUALITY : cualidad *f* ⟨her good points : sus buenas cualidades⟩ ⟨it's not his strong point : no es su (punto) fuerte⟩ **3** (*indicating a chief idea or meaning*) ⟨it's beside the point : no viene al caso⟩ ⟨to get to the point : ir al grano⟩ ⟨to stick to the point : no salirse del tema⟩ **4** PURPOSE : fin *m*, propósito *m* ⟨there's no point to it : no vale la pena, no sirve para nada⟩ **5** PLACE : punto *m*, lugar *m* ⟨points of interest : puntos interesantes⟩ **6** : punto *m* (en una escala) ⟨boiling point : punto de ebullición⟩ **7** MOMENT : momento *m*, coyuntura *f* ⟨at this point : en este momento⟩ **8** TIP : punta *f* **9** HEADLAND : punta *f*, cabo *m* **10** PERIOD : punto *m* (marca de puntuación) **11** UNIT : punto *m* ⟨he scored 15 points : ganó 15 puntos⟩ ⟨shares fell 10 points : las acciones bajaron 10 enteros⟩ **12 compass points** : puntos *mpl* cardinales **13 decimal point** : punto *m* decimal, coma *f*

point–blank[1] ['pɔɪnt'blæŋk] *adv* **1** : a quemarropa ⟨to shoot point-blank : disparar a quemarropa⟩ **2** BLUNTLY, DIRECTLY : a bocajarro, sin rodeos, francamente

point–blank[2] *adj* **1** : a quemarropa ⟨point-blank shots : disparos a quemarropa⟩ **2** BLUNT, DIRECT : directo, franco

pointed [ˈpɔɪntəd] *adj* **1** POINTY : puntiagudo **2** PERTINENT : atinado **3** CONSPICUOUS : marcado, manifiesto
pointedly [ˈpɔɪntədli] *adv* : intencionadamente, directamente
pointer [ˈpɔɪntər] *n* **1** STICK : puntero *m* (para maestros, etc.) **2** INDICATOR, NEEDLE : indicador *m*, aguja *f* **3** : perro *m* de muestra **4** HINT, TIP : consejo *m*
pointless [ˈpɔɪntləs] *adj* : inútil, ocioso, vano ⟨it's pointless to continue : no tiene sentido continuar⟩
point of view *n* : perspectiva *f*, punto *m* de vista
pointy [ˈpɔɪnti] *adj* : puntiagudo
poise[1] [ˈpɔɪz] *vt* **poised; poising** BALANCE : equilibrar, balancear
poise[2] *n* : aplomo *m*, compostura *f*
poison[1] [ˈpɔɪzən] *vt* **1** : envenenar, intoxicar **2** CORRUPT : corromper
poison[2] *n* : veneno *m*
poison ivy *n* : hiedra *f* venenosa
poisonous [ˈpɔɪzənəs] *adj* : venenoso, tóxico, ponzoñoso
poke[1] [ˈpoːk] *v* **poked; poking** *vt* **1** JAB : golpear (con la punta de algo), dar ⟨he poked me with his finger : me dio con el dedo⟩ **2** THRUST : introducir, asomar ⟨I poked my head out the window : asomé la cabeza por la ventana⟩ — *vi* **1 to poke around** RUMMAGE : hurgar **2 to poke along** DAWDLE : demorarse, entretenerse
poke[2] *n* : golpe *m* abrupto (con la punta de algo)
poker [ˈpoːkər] *n* **1** : atizador *m* (para el fuego) **2** : póker *m*, poker *m* (juego de naipes)
polar [ˈpoːlər] *adj* : polar
polar bear *n* : oso *m* blanco
Polaris [poˈlærɪs, -ˈlɑr-] → **North Star**
polarize [ˈpoːləˌraɪz] *vt* **-ized; -izing** : polarizar
pole [ˈpoːl] *n* **1** : palo *m*, poste *m*, vara *f* ⟨telephone pole : poste de teléfonos⟩ **2** : polo *m* ⟨the South Pole : el Polo Sur⟩ **3** : polo *m* (eléctrico o magnético)
Pole [ˈpoːl] *n* : polaco *m*, -ca *f*
polecat [ˈpoːlˌkæt] *n, pl* **polecats** *or* **polecat 1** : turón *m* (de Europa) **2** SKUNK : mofeta *f*, zorrillo *m*
polemical [pəˈlɛmɪkəl] *adj* : polémico
polemics [pəˈlɛmɪks] *ns & pl* : polémica *f*
polestar [ˈpoːlˌstɑr] → **North Star**
police[1] [pəˈliːs] *vt* **-liced; -licing** : mantener el orden en ⟨to police the streets : patrullar las calles⟩
police[2] *ns & pl* **1** : policía *f* (organización) **2** POLICE OFFICERS : policías *mfpl*
policeman [pəˈliːsmən] *n, pl* **-men** [-mən, -ˌmɛn] : policía *m*
police officer *n* : policía *mf*, agente *mf* de policía
policewoman [pəˈliːsˌwʊmən] *n, pl* **-women** [-ˌwɪmən] : policía *f*, mujer *f* policía
policy [ˈpɑləsi] *n, pl* **-cies 1** : política *f* ⟨foreign policy : política exterior⟩ **2** *or* **insurance policy** : póliza *f* de seguros, seguro *m*
polio[1] [ˈpoːliˌoː] *adj* : de polio ⟨polio vaccine : vacuna contra la polio⟩
polio[2] *n* → **poliomyelitis**
poliomyelitis [ˌpoːliˌoːˌmaɪəˈlaɪt̬əs] *n* : poliomielitis *f*, polio *f*
polish[1] [ˈpɑlɪʃ] *vt* **1** : pulir, lustrar, sacar brillo a ⟨to polish one's nails : pintarse las uñas⟩ **2** REFINE : pulir, perfeccionar
polish[2] *n* **1** LUSTER : brillo *m*, lustre *m* **2** REFINEMENT : refinamiento *m* **3** : betún *m* (para zapatos), cera *f* (para suelos y muebles), esmalte *m* (para las uñas)
Polish[1] [ˈpoːlɪʃ] *adj* : polaco
Polish[2] *n* : polaco *m* (idioma)
polite [pəˈlaɪt] *adj* **-liter; -est** : cortés, correcto, educado
politely [pəˈlaɪtli] *adv* : cortésmente, correctamente, con buenos modales
politeness [pəˈlaɪtnəs] *n* : cortesía *f*
politic [ˈpɑləˌtɪk] *adj* : diplomático, prudente
political [pəˈlɪt̬ɪkəl] *adj* : político — **politically** [-t̬ɪkli] *adv*
politician [ˌpɑləˈtɪʃən] *n* : político *m*, -ca *f*
politics [ˈpɑləˌtɪks] *ns & pl* : política *f*
polka [ˈpoːlkə, ˈpoːkə] *n* : polka *f*
polka dot [ˈpoːkəˌdɑt] *n* : lunar *m* (en un diseño)
poll[1] [ˈpoːl] *vt* **1** : obtener (votos) ⟨she polled over 1000 votes : obtuvo más de 1000 votos⟩ **2** CANVASS : encuestar, sondear — *vi* : obtener votos
poll[2] *n* **1** SURVEY : encuesta *f*, sondeo *m* **2 polls** *npl* : urnas *fpl* ⟨to go to the polls : acudir a las urnas, ir a votar⟩
pollen [ˈpɑlən] *n* : polen *m*
pollinate [ˈpɑləˌneɪt] *vt* **-nated; -nating** : polinizar
pollination [ˌpɑləˈneɪʃən] *n* : polinización *f*
pollster [ˈpoːlstər] *n* : encuestador *m*, -dora *f*
pollutant [pəˈluːtənt] *n* : contaminante *m*
pollute [pəˈluːt] *vt* **-luted; -luting** : contaminar
pollution [pəˈluːʃən] *n* : contaminación *f*
pollywog *or* **polliwog** [ˈpɑliˌwɔg] *n* TADPOLE : renacuajo *m*
polo [ˈpoːˌloː] *n* : polo *m*
poltergeist [ˈpoːlt̬ərˌgaɪst] *n* : poltergeist *m*, fantasma *m* travieso
polyester [ˈpɑliˌɛstər, ˌpɑliˈ-] *n* : poliéster *m*
polygamous [pəˈlɪgəməs] *adj* : polígamo
polygamy [pəˈlɪgəmi] *n* : poligamia *f*
polygon [ˈpɑliˌgɑn] *n* : polígono *m*

polymer ['pαləmər] *n* : polímero *m*

Polynesian [ˌpαlə'ni:ʒən, -ʃən] *n* : polinesio *m*, -sia *f* — **Polynesian** *adj*

polyunsaturated [ˌpαliˌʌn'sæʧə-ˌreɪṭəd] *adj* : poliinsaturado

pomegranate ['pαməˌgrænət, 'pαmˌgrænət] *n* : granada *f* (fruta)

pommel[1] ['pʌməl] *vt* → **pummel**

pommel[2] ['pʌməl, 'pα-] *n* **1** : pomo *m* (de una espada) **2** : perilla *f* (de una silla de montar)

pomp ['pαmp] *n* **1** SPLENDOR : pompa *f*, esplendor *m* **2** OSTENTATION : boato *m*, ostentación *f*

pom–pom ['pαmˌpαm] *n* : borla *f*, pompón *m*

pomposity [pαm'pαsəṭi] *n, pl* **-ties** : pomposidad *f*

pompous ['pαmpəs] *adj* : pomposo — **pompously** *adv*

poncho ['pαnˌʧo:] *n, pl* **-chos** : poncho *m*

pond ['pαnd] *n* : charca *f* (natural), estanque *m* (artificial)

ponder ['pαndər] *vt* : reflexionar, considerar — *vi* **to ponder over** : reflexionar sobre, sopesar

ponderous ['pαndərəs] *adj* : pesado

pontiff ['pαntɪf] *n* POPE : pontífice *m*

pontificate [pαn'tɪfəˌkeɪt] *vi* **-cated; -cating** : pontificar

pontoon [pαn'tu:n] *n* : pontón *m*

pony ['po:ni] *n, pl* **-nies** : poni *m*, poney *m*, jaca *f*

ponytail ['po:niˌteɪl] *n* : cola *f* de caballo, coleta *f*

poodle ['pu:dəl] *n* : caniche *m*

pool[1] ['pu:l] *vt* : mancomunar, hacer un fondo común de

pool[2] *n* **1** : charca *f* ⟨a swimming pool : una piscina⟩ **2** PUDDLE : charco *m* **3** RESERVE, SUPPLY : fondo *m* común (de recursos), reserva *f* **4** : billar *m* (juego)

poor ['pʊr, 'por] *adj* **1** : pobre ⟨poor people : los pobres⟩ **2** SCANTY : pobre, escaso ⟨poor attendance : baja asistencia⟩ **3** UNFORTUNATE : pobre ⟨poor thing! : ¡pobrecito!⟩ **4** BAD : malo ⟨to be in poor health : estar mal de salud⟩

poorly ['pʊrli, 'por-] *adv* : mal

pop[1] ['pαp] *v* **popped; popping** *vi* **1** BURST : reventarse, estallar **2** : ir, venir, o aparecer abruptamente ⟨he popped into the house : se metió en la casa⟩ ⟨a menu pops up : aparece un menú⟩ **3 to pop out** PROTRUDE : salirse, saltarse ⟨my eyes popped out of my head : se me saltaban los ojos⟩ — *vt* **1** BURST : reventar **2** : hacer o meter abruptamente ⟨he popped it into his mouth : se lo metió en la boca⟩

pop[2] *adj* : popular ⟨pop music : música popular⟩

pop[3] *n* **1** : estallido *m* pequeño (de un globo, etc.) **2** SODA : refresco *m*, gaseosa *f*

popcorn ['pαpˌkɔrn] *n* : palomitas *fpl* (de maíz)

pope ['po:p] *n* : papa *m* ⟨Pope John : el Papa Juan⟩

poplar ['pαplər] *n* : álamo *m*

poplin ['pαplɪn] *n* : popelín *m*, popelina *f*

poppy ['pαpi] *n, pl* **-pies** : amapola *f*

populace ['pαpjələs] *n* **1** MASSES : pueblo *m* **2** POPULATION : población *f*

popular ['pαpjələr] *adj* **1** : popular ⟨the popular vote : el voto popular⟩ **2** COMMON : generalizado, común ⟨popular beliefs : creencias generalizadas⟩ **3** : popular, de gran popularidad ⟨a popular singer : un cantante popular⟩

popularity [ˌpαpjə'lærəṭi] *n* : popularidad *f*

popularize ['pαpjələˌraɪz] *vt* **-ized; -izing** : popularizar

popularly ['pαpjələrli] *adv* : popularmente, vulgarmente

populate ['pαpjəˌleɪt] *vt* **-lated; -lating** : poblar

population [ˌpαpjə'leɪʃən] *n* : población *f*

populist ['pαpjəlɪst] *n* : populista *mf* — **populist** *adj*

populous ['pαpjələs] *adj* : populoso

porcelain ['porsələn] *n* : porcelana *f*

porch ['porʧ] *n* : porche *m*

porcupine ['pɔrkjəˌpaɪn] *n* : puerco *m* espín

pore[1] ['por] *vi* **pored; poring 1** GAZE : mirar (con atención) **2 to pore over** : leer detenidamente, estudiar

pore[2] *n* : poro *m*

pork ['pork] *n* : carne *f* de cerdo, carne *f* de puerco

pornographic [ˌpɔrnə'græfɪk] *adj* : pornográfico

pornography [pɔr'nαgrəfi] *n* : pornografía *f*

porous ['porəs] *adj* : poroso

porpoise ['pɔrpəs] *n* **1** : marsopa *f* **2** DOLPHIN : delfín *m*

porridge ['pɔrɪʤ] *n* : sopa *f* espesa de harina, gachas *fpl*

port[1] ['port] *adj* : de babor ⟨on the port side : a babor⟩

port[2] *n* **1** HARBOR : puerto *m* **2** ORIFICE : orificio *m* (de una válvula, etc.) **3** : puerto *m* (de una computadora) **4** PORTHOLE : portilla *f* **5** *or* **port side** : babor *m* (de un barco) **6** : oporto *m* (vino)

portable ['porṭəbəl] *adj* : portátil

portal ['porṭəl] *n* : portal *m*

portend [pɔr'tɛnd] *vt* : presagiar, augurar

portent ['pɔrˌtɛnt] *n* : presagio *m*, augurio *m*

portentous [pɔr'tɛntəs] *adj* : profético, que presagia

porter ['porṭər] *n* : maletero *m*, mozo *m* (de estación)

portfolio [port'fo:liˌo] *n, pl* **-lios 1** FOLDER : cartera *f* (para llevar papeles), carpeta *f* **2** : cartera *f* (diplomática) **3 investment portfolio** : cartera de inversiones

porthole [ˈportˌho:l] *n* : portilla *f* (de un barco), ventanilla *f* (de un avión)

portico [ˈporṭɪˌko] *n, pl* **-coes** *or* **-cos** : pórtico *m*

portion¹ [ˈporʃən] *vt* DISTRIBUTE : repartir

portion² *n* PART, SHARE : porción *f*, parte *f*

portly [ˈportli] *adj* **-lier; -est** : corpulento

portrait [ˈportrət, -ˌtreɪt] *n* : retrato *m*

portray [porˈtreɪ] *vt* **1** DEPICT : representar, retratar **2** DESCRIBE : describir **3** PLAY : interpretar (un personaje)

portrayal [porˈtreɪəl] *n* **1** REPRESENTATION : representación *f* **2** PORTRAIT : retrato *m*

Portuguese [ˌporʧəˈgi:z, -ˈgi:s] *n* **1** : portugués *m*, -guesa *f* (persona) **2** : portugués *m* (idioma) — **Portuguese** *adj*

pose¹ [ˈpo:z] *v* **posed; posing** *vt* PRESENT : plantear (una pregunta, etc.), representar (una amenaza) — *vi* **1** : posar (para una foto, etc.) **2 to pose as** : hacerse pasar por

pose² *n* **1** : pose *f* ⟨to strike a pose : asumir una pose⟩ **2** PRETENSE : pose *f*, afectación *f*

posh [ˈpɑʃ] *adj* : elegante, de lujo

position¹ [pəˈzɪʃən] *vt* : colocar, situar, ubicar

position² *n* **1** APPROACH, STANCE : posición *f*, postura *f*, planteamiento *m* **2** LOCATION : posición *f*, ubicación *f* **3** STATUS : posición *f* (en una jerarquía) **4** JOB : puesto *m*

positive [ˈpɑzəṭɪv] *adj* **1** DEFINITE : incuestionable, inequívoco ⟨positive evidence : pruebas irrefutables⟩ **2** CONFIDENT : seguro **3** : positivo (en gramática, matemáticas, y física) **4** AFFIRMATIVE : positivo, afirmativo ⟨a positive response : una respuesta positiva⟩

positively [ˈpɑzəṭɪvli] *adv* **1** FAVORABLY : favorablemente **2** OPTIMISTICALLY : positivamente **3** DEFINITELY : definitivamente, en forma concluyente **4** (*used for emphasis*) : realmente, verdaderamente ⟨it's positively awful! : ¡es verdaderamente malo!⟩

possess [pəˈzɛs] *vt* **1** HAVE, OWN : poseer, tener **2** SEIZE : apoderarse de ⟨he was possessed by fear : el miedo se apoderó de él⟩

possession [pəˈzɛʃən] *n* **1** POSSESSING : posesión *f* **2** : posesión *f* (por un demonio, etc.) **3 possessions** *npl* PROPERTY : bienes *mpl*, propiedad *f*

possessive¹ [pəˈzɛsɪv] *adj* **1** : posesivo (en gramática) **2** JEALOUS : posesivo, celoso

possessive² *n or* **possessive case** : posesivo *m*

possessor [pəˈzɛsər] *n* : poseedor *m*, -dora *f*

possibility [ˌpɑsəˈbɪləṭi] *n, pl* **-ties** : posibilidad *f*

possible [ˈpɑsəbəl] *adj* : posible

possibly [ˈpɑsəbli] *adv* **1** CONCEIVABLY : posiblemente ⟨it can't possibly be true! : ¡no puede ser!⟩ **2** PERHAPS : quizás, posiblemente

possum [ˈpɑsəm] → **opossum**

post¹ [ˈpo:st] *vt* **1** MAIL : echar al correo, mandar por correo **2** ANNOUNCE : anunciar ⟨they've posted the grades : han anunciado las notas⟩ **3** AFFIX : fijar, poner (noticias, etc.) **4** STATION : apostar **5 to keep (someone) posted** : tener al corriente (a alguien)

post² *n* **1** POLE : poste *m*, palo *m* **2** STATION : puesto *m* **3** CAMP : puesto *m* (militar) **4** JOB, POSITION : puesto *m*, empleo *m*, cargo *m*

postage [ˈpo:stɪʤ] *n* : franqueo *m*

postal [ˈpo:stəl] *adj* : postal

postcard [ˈpo:stˌkɑrd] *n* : postal *f*, tarjeta *f* postal

poster [ˈpo:stər] *n* : póster *m*, cartel *m*, afiche *m*

posterior¹ [pɑˈstɪriər, po-] *adj* : posterior

posterior² *n* BUTTOCKS : trasero *m*, nalgas *fpl*, asentaderas *fpl*

posterity [pɑˈstɛrəṭi] *n* : posteridad *f*

postgraduate¹ [ˌpo:stˈgræʤʊət] *adj* : de postgrado

postgraduate² *n* : postgraduado *m*, -da *f*

posthaste [ˈpo:stˈheɪst] *adv* : a toda prisa

posthumous [ˈpɑsʧəməs] *adj* : póstumo — **posthumously** *adv*

postman [ˈpo:stmən, -ˌmæn] → **mailman**

postmark¹ [ˈpo:stˌmɑrk] *vt* : matasellar

postmark² *n* : matasellos *m*

postmaster [ˈpo:stˌmæstər] *n* : administrador *m*, -dora *f* de correos

postmodern [ˌpo:stˈmɑdərn] *adj* : posmoderno

postmortem [ˌpo:stˈmɔrṭəm] *n* : autopsia *f*

postnatal [ˌpo:stˈneɪṭəl] *adj* : postnatal ⟨postnatal depression : depresión posparto⟩

post office *n* : correo *m*, oficina *f* de correos

postoperative [ˌpo:stˈɑpərəṭɪv, -ˌreɪ-] *adj* : posoperatorio

postpaid [ˌpo:stˈpeɪd] *adv* : con franqueo pagado

postpone [ˌpo:stˈpo:n] *vt* **-poned; -poning** : postergar, aplazar, posponer

postponement [ˌpo:stˈpo:nmənt] *n* : postergación *f*, aplazamiento *m*

postscript [ˈpo:stˌskrɪpt] *n* : postdata *f*, posdata *f*

postulate [ˈpɑsʧəˌleɪt] *vt* **-lated; -lating** : postular

posture¹ [ˈpɑsʧər] *vi* **-tured; -turing** : posar, asumir una pose

posture² *n* : postura *f*

postwar [ˌpo:stˈwɔr] *adj* : de (la) posguerra

posy ['po:zi] *n, pl* **-sies 1** FLOWER : flor *f* **2** BOUQUET : ramo *m*, ramillete *m*
pot[1] ['pɑt] *vt* **potted; potting** : plantar (en una maceta)
pot[2] *n* **1** : olla *f* (de cocina) **2 pots and pans** : cacharros *mpl*
potable ['po:t̬əbəl] *adj* : potable
potash ['pɑt,æʃ] *n* : potasa *f*
potassium [pə'tæsiəm] *n* : potasio *m*
potato [pə'teɪt̬o] *n, pl* **-toes** : papa *f*, patata *f Spain*
potato chips *npl* : papas *fpl* fritas (de bolsa)
potbellied ['pɑt,bɛlid] *adj* : panzón, barrigón *fam*
potbelly ['pɑt,bɛli] *n* : panza *f*, barriga *f*
potency ['po:təntsi] *n, pl* **-cies 1** POWER : fuerza *f*, potencia *f* **2** EFFECTIVENESS : eficacia *f*
potent ['po:tənt] *adj* **1** POWERFUL : potente, poderoso **2** EFFECTIVE : eficaz ⟨a potent medicine : una medicina bien fuerte⟩
potential[1] [pə'tɛntʃəl] *adj* : potencial, posible
potential[2] *n* **1** : potencial *m* ⟨growth potential : potencial de crecimiento⟩ ⟨a child with potential : un niño que promete⟩ **2** : potencial *m* (eléctrico) — **potentially** *adv*
potful ['pɑt,fʊl] *n* : contenido *m* de una olla ⟨a potful of water : una olla de agua⟩
pothole ['pɑt,ho:l] *n* : bache *m*
potion ['po:ʃən] *n* : brebaje *m*, poción *f*
potluck ['pɑt,lʌk] *n* **to take potluck** : tomar lo que haya
potpourri [,po:pʊ'ri:] *n* : popurrí *m*
potshot ['pɑt,ʃɑt] *n* **1** : tiro *m* al azar ⟨to take potshots at : disparar al azar a⟩ **2** CRITICISM : crítica *f* (hecha al azar)
potter ['pɑt̬ər] *n* : alfarero *m*, -ra *f*
pottery ['pɑt̬əri] *n, pl* **-teries** : cerámica *f*
pouch ['paʊtʃ] *n* **1** BAG : bolsa *f* pequeña **2** : bolsa *f* (de un animal)
poultice ['po:lt̬əs] *n* : emplasto *m*, cataplasma *f*
poultry ['po:ltri] *n* : aves *fpl* de corral
pounce ['paʊnts] *vi* **pounced; pouncing** : abalanzarse
pound[1] ['paʊnd] *vt* **1** CRUSH : machacar, machucar, majar **2** BEAT : golpear, machacar ⟨she pounded the lessons into them : les machacaba las lecciones⟩ ⟨he pounded home his point : les hizo entender su razonamiento⟩ — *vi* **1** BEAT : palpitar (dícese del corazón) **2** RESOUND : retumbar, resonar **3** : andar con paso pesado ⟨we pounded through the mud : caminamos pesadamente por el barro⟩
pound[2] *n* **1** : libra *f* (unidad de peso) **2** : libra *f* (unidad monetaria) **3 dog pound** : perrera *f*
pour ['por] *vt* **1** : echar, verter, servir (bebidas) ⟨pour it into a pot : viértalo en una olla⟩ **2** : proveer con abundancia ⟨they poured money into it : le invirtieron mucho dinero⟩ **3 to pour out** : dar salida a ⟨he poured out his feelings to her : se desahogó con ella⟩ — *vi* **1** FLOW : manar, fluir, salir ⟨blood was pouring from the wound : la sangre le salía de la herida⟩ **2 it's pouring (outside)** : está lloviendo a cántaros
pout[1] ['paʊt] *vi* : hacer pucheros
pout[2] *n* : puchero *m*
poverty ['pɑvərt̬i] *n* : pobreza *f*, indigencia *f*
powder[1] ['paʊdər] *vt* **1** : empolvar ⟨to powder one's face : empolvarse la cara⟩ **2** PULVERIZE : pulverizar
powder[2] *n* : polvo *m*, polvos *mpl*
powdery ['paʊdəri] *adj* : polvoriento, como polvo
power[1] ['paʊər] *vt* : impulsar, propulsar
power[2] *n* **1** AUTHORITY : poder *m*, autoridad *f* ⟨executive powers : poderes ejecutivos⟩ **2** ABILITY : capacidad *f*, poder *m* **3** : potencia *f* (política) ⟨foreign powers : potencias extranjeras⟩ **4** STRENGTH : fuerza *f* **5** : potencia *f* (en física y matemáticas)
powerful ['paʊərfəl] *adj* : poderoso, potente — **powerfully** *adv*
powerhouse ['paʊər,haʊs] *n* : persona *f* dinámica
powerless ['paʊərləs] *adj* : impotente
power plant *n* : central *f* eléctrica
powwow ['paʊ,waʊ] *n* : conferencia *f*
pox ['pɑks] *n, pl* **pox** *or* **poxes 1** CHICKEN POX : varicela *f* **2** SYPHILIS : sífilis *f*
practicable ['præktɪkəbəl] *adj* : practicable, viable, factible
practical ['præktɪkəl] *adj* : práctico
practicality [,præktɪ'kæləṭi] *n, pl* **-ties** : factibilidad *f*, viabilidad *f*
practical joke *n* : broma *f* (pesada)
practically ['præktɪkli] *adv* **1** : de manera práctica **2** ALMOST : casi, prácticamente
practice[1] *or* **practise** ['præktəs] *vt* **-ticed** *or* **-tised; -ticing** *or* **-tising 1** : practicar ⟨he practiced his German on us : practicó el alemán con nosotros⟩ ⟨to practice politeness : practicar la cortesía⟩ **2** : ejercer ⟨to practice medicine : ejercer la medicina⟩
practice[2] *n* **1** USE : práctica *f* ⟨to put into practice : poner en práctica⟩ **2** CUSTOM : costumbre *f* ⟨it's a common practice here : por aquí se acostumbra hacerlo⟩ **3** TRAINING : práctica *f* **4** : ejercicio *m* (de una profesión)
practitioner [præk'tɪʃənər] *n* **1** : profesional *mf* **2 general practitioner** : médico *m*, -ca *f*
pragmatic [præg'mæt̬ɪk] *adj* : pragmático — **pragmatically** *adv*
pragmatism ['prægmə,tɪzəm] *n* : pragmatismo
prairie ['prɛri] *n* : pradera *f*, llanura *f*

praise[1] ['preɪz] *vt* **praised; praising** : elogiar, alabar ⟨to praise God : alabar a Dios⟩

praise[2] *n* : elogio *m*, alabanza *f*

praiseworthy ['preɪz,wərði] *adj* : digno de alabanza, loable

prance[1] ['prænts] *vi* **pranced; prancing** 1 : hacer cabriolas, cabriolar ⟨a prancing horse : un caballo haciendo cabriolas⟩ 2 SWAGGER : pavonearse

prance[2] *n* : cabriola *f*

prank ['præŋk] *n* : broma *f*, travesura *f*

prankster ['præŋkstər] *n* : bromista *mf*

prattle[1] ['prætəl] *vt* **-tled; -tling** : parlotear *fam*, cotorrear *fam*, balbucear (como un niño)

prattle[2] *n* : parloteo *m fam*, cotorreo *m fam*, cháchara *f fam*

prawn ['prɔn] *n* : langostino *m*, camarón *m*, gamba *f*

pray ['preɪ] *vt* ENTREAT : rogar, suplicar — *vi* : rezar

prayer ['prɛr] *n* 1 : plegaria *f*, oración *f* ⟨to say one's prayers : orar, rezar⟩ ⟨the Lord's Prayer : el Padrenuestro⟩ 2 PRAYING : rezo *m*, oración *f* ⟨to kneel in prayer : arrodillarse para rezar⟩

praying mantis → **mantis**

preach ['pri:ʧ] *vi* : predicar — *vt* ADVOCATE : abogar por ⟨to preach cooperation : promover la cooperación⟩

preacher ['pri:ʧər] *n* 1 : predicador *m*, -dora *f* 2 MINISTER : pastor *m*, -tora *f*

preamble ['pri:,æmbəl] *n* : preámbulo *m*

prearrange [,pri:ə'reɪnʤ] *vt* **-ranged; -ranging** : arreglar de antemano

precarious [pri'kæriəs] *adj* : precario — **precariously** *adv*

precariousness [pri'kæriəsnəs] *n* : precariedad *f*

precaution [pri'kɔʃən] *n* : precaución *f*

precautionary [pri'kɔʃə,nɛri] *adj* : preventivo, cautelar, precautorio

precede [pri'si:d] *v* **-ceded; -ceding** : preceder a

precedence ['prɛsədənts, prɪ'si:dənts] *n* : precedencia *f*

precedent ['prɛsədənt] *n* : precedente *m*

precept ['pri:,sɛpt] *n* : precepto *m*

precinct ['pri:,sɪŋkt] *n* 1 DISTRICT : distrito *m* (policial, electoral, etc.) 2 **precincts** *npl* PREMISES : recinto *m*, predio *m*, límites *mpl* (de una ciudad)

precious ['prɛʃəs] *adj* 1 : precioso ⟨precious gems : piedras preciosas⟩ 2 DEAR : querido 3 AFFECTED : afectado

precipice ['prɛsəpəs] *n* : precipicio *m*

precipitate [pri'sɪpə,teɪt] *v* **-tated; -tating** *vt* 1 HASTEN, PROVOKE : precipitar, provocar 2 HURL : arrojar 3 : precipitar (en química) — *vi* : precipitarse (en química), condensarse (en meteorología)

precipitation [pri,sɪpə'teɪʃən] *n* 1 HASTE : precipitación *f*, prisa *f* 2 : precipitaciones *fpl* (en meteorología)

precipitous [pri'sɪpət̬əs] *adj* 1 HASTY, RASH : precipitado 2 STEEP : escarpado, empinado ⟨a precipitous drop : una caída vertiginosa⟩

précis [preɪ'si:] *n, pl* **précis** [-'si:z] : resumen *m*

precise [pri'saɪs] *adj* 1 DEFINITE : preciso, explícito 2 EXACT : exacto, preciso ⟨precise calculations : cálculos precisos⟩ — **precisely** *adv*

preciseness [pri'saɪsnəs] *n* : precisión *f*, exactitud *f*

precision [pri'sɪʒən] *n* : precisión *f*

preclude [pri'klu:d] *vt* **-cluded; -cluding** : evitar, impedir, excluir (una posibilidad, etc.)

precocious [pri'ko:ʃəs] *adj* : precoz — **precociously** *adv*

precocity [pri'kɑsət̬i] *n* : precocidad *f*

preconceive [,pri:kən'si:v] *vt* **-ceived; -ceiving** : preconcebir

preconception [,pri:kən'spʃən] *n* : idea *f* preconcebida

precondition [,pri:kən'dɪʃən] *n* : precondición *f*, condición *f* previa

precook [,pri:'kʊk] *vt* : precocinar

precursor [pri'kərsər] *n* : precursor *m*, -sora *f*

predator ['prɛdət̬ər] *n* : depredador *m*, -dora *f*

predatory ['prɛdə,tori] *adj* : depredador

predecessor ['prɛdə,sɛsər, 'pri:-] *n* : antecesor *m*, -sora *f*; predecesor *m*, -sora *f*

predestination [pri,dɛstə'neɪʃən] *n* : predestinación *f*

predestine [pri'dɛstən] *vt* **-tined; -tining** : predestinar

predetermine [,pri:dɪ'tərmən] *vt* **-mined; -mining** : predeterminar

predicament [pri'dɪkəmənt] *n* : apuro *m*, aprieto *m*

predicate[1] ['prɛdə,keɪt] *vt* **-cated; -cating** 1 AFFIRM : afirmar, aseverar 2 **to be predicated on** : estar basado en

predicate[2] ['prɛdɪkət] *n* : predicado *m*

predict [pri'dɪkt] *vt* : pronosticar, predecir

predictable [pri'dɪktəbəl] *adj* : previsible — **predictably** [-bli] *adv*

prediction [pri'dɪkʃən] *n* : pronóstico *m*, predicción *f*

predilection [,prɛdəl'ɛkʃən, ,pri:-] *n* : predilección *f*

predispose [,pri:dɪ'spo:z] *vt* **-posed; -posing** : predisponer

predisposition [,pri:,dɪspə'zɪʃən] *n* : predisposición *f*

predominance [pri'dɑmənənts] *n* : predominio *m*

predominant [pri'dɑmənənt] *adj* : predominante — **predominantly** *adv*

predominate [pri'dɑmə,neɪt] *vi* **-nated; -nating** 1 : predominar (en cantidad) 2 PREVAIL : prevalecer

preeminence [pri'ɛmənənts] *n* : preeminencia *f*

preeminent [pri'ɛmənənt] *adj* : preeminente

preeminently [pri'ɛmənəntli] *adv* : especialmente

preempt [pri'ɛmpt] *vt* **1** APPROPRIATE : apoderarse de, apropiarse de **2** : reemplazar (un programa de televisión, etc.) **3** FORESTALL : adelantarse a (un ataque, etc.)

preen ['pri:n] *vt* : arreglarse (el pelo, las plumas, etc.)

prefabricated [ˌpri:'fæbrəˌkeɪt̬əd] *adj* : prefabricado

preface ['prɛfəs] *n* : prefacio *m*, prólogo *m*

prefatory ['prɛfəˌtori] *adj* : preliminar

prefer [pri'fər] *vt* **-ferred; -ferring 1** : preferir ⟨I prefer coffee : prefiero café⟩ **2 to prefer charges against** : presentar cargos contra

preferable ['prɛfərəbəl] *adj* : preferible

preferably ['prɛfərəbli] *adv* : preferentemente, de preferencia

preference ['prɛfrənts, 'prɛfər-] *n* : preferencia *f*, gusto *m*

preferential [ˌprɛfə'rɛntʃəl] *adj* : preferencial, preferente

prefigure [pri'fɪgjər] *vt* **-ured; -uring** FORESHADOW : prefigurar, anunciar

prefix ['pri:ˌfɪks] *n* : prefijo *m*

pregnancy ['prɛgnəntsi] *n, pl* **-cies** : embarazo *m*, preñez *f*

pregnant ['prɛgnənt] *adj* **1** : embarazada (dícese de una mujer), preñada (dícese de un animal) **2** MEANINGFUL : significativo

preheat [ˌpri:'hi:t] *vt* : precalentar

prehensile [pri'hɛntsəl, -'hɛnˌsaɪl] *adj* : prensil

prehistoric [ˌpri:hɪs'tɔrɪk] *or* **prehistorical** [-ɪkəl] *adj* : prehistórico

prejudge [ˌpri:'ʤʌʤ] *vt* **-judged; -judging** : prejuzgar

prejudice[1] ['prɛʤədəs] *vt* **-diced; -dicing 1** DAMAGE : perjudicar **2** BIAS : predisponer, influir en

prejudice[2] *n* **1** DAMAGE : perjuicio *m* (en derecho) **2** BIAS : prejuicio *m*

prelate ['prɛlət] *n* : prelado *m*

preliminary[1] [pri'lɪməˌnɛri] *adj* : preliminar

preliminary[2] *n, pl* **-naries 1** : preámbulo *m*, preludio *m* **2 preliminaries** *npl* : preliminares *mpl*

prelude ['prɛˌlu:d, 'prɛlˌju:d; 'preɪˌlu:d, 'pri:-] *n* : preludio *m*

premarital [ˌpri:'mærət̬əl] *adj* : prematrimonial

premature [ˌpri:mə'tʊr, -'tjʊr, -'tʃʊr] *adj* : prematuro — **prematurely** *adv*

premeditate [pri'mɛdəˌteɪt] *vt* **-tated; -tating** : premeditar

premeditation [priˌmɛdə'teɪʃən] *n* : premeditación *f*

premenstrual [pri'mɛntstruəl] *adj* : premenstrual

premier[1] [pri'mɪr, -'mjɪr; 'pri:miər] *adj* : principal

premier[2] *n* PRIME MINISTER : primer ministro *m*, primera ministra *f*

premiere[1] [prɪ'mjɛr, -'mɪr] *vt* **-miered; -miering** : estrenar

premiere[2] *n* : estreno *m*

premise ['prɛmɪs] *n* **1** : premisa *f* ⟨the premise of his arguments : la premisa de sus argumentos⟩ **2 premises** *npl* : recinto *m*, local *m*

premium ['pri:miəm] *n* **1** BONUS : prima *f* **2** SURCHARGE : recargo *m* ⟨to sell at a premium : vender (algo) muy caro⟩ **3 insurance premium** : prima *f* (de seguros) **4 to set a premium on** : darle un gran valor (a algo)

premonition [ˌpri:mə'nɪʃən, ˌprɛmə-] *n* : presentimiento *m*, premonición *f*

prenatal [ˌpri:'neɪt̬əl] *adj* : prenatal

preoccupation [priˌɑkjə'peɪʃən] *n* : preocupación *f*

preoccupied [pri'ɑkjəˌpaɪd] *adj* : abstraído, ensimismado, preocupado

preoccupy [pri'ɑkjəˌpaɪ] *vt* **-pied; -pying** : preocupar

preparation [ˌprɛpə'reɪʃən] *n* **1** PREPARING : preparación *f* **2** MIXTURE : preparado *m* ⟨a preparation for burns : un preparado para quemaduras⟩ **3 preparations** *npl* ARRANGEMENTS : preparativos *mpl*

preparatory [pri'pærəˌtori] *adj* : preparatorio

prepare [pri'pær] *v* **-pared; -paring** *vt* : preparar — *vi* : prepararse

prepay [ˌpri:'peɪ] *vt* **-paid; -paying** : pagar por adelantado

preponderance [pri'pɑndərənts] *n* : preponderancia *f*

preponderant [pri'pɑndərənt] *adj* : preponderante — **preponderantly** *adv*

preposition [ˌprɛpə'zɪʃən] *n* : preposición *f*

prepositional [ˌprɛpə'zɪʃənəl] *adj* : preposicional

prepossessing [ˌpri:pə'zɛsɪŋ] *adj* : atractivo, agradable

preposterous [pri'pɑstərəs] *adj* : absurdo, ridículo

prerequisite[1] [pri'rɛkwəzət] *adj* : necesario, esencial

prerequisite[2] *n* : condición *f* necesario, requisito *m* previo

prerogative [pri'rɑgət̬ɪv] *n* : prerrogativa *f*

presage ['prɛsɪʤ, pri'seɪʤ] *vt* **-saged; -saging** : presagiar

preschool ['pri:ˌsku:l] *adj* : preescolar ⟨preschool students : estudiantes de preescolar⟩

prescribe [pri'skraɪb] *vt* **-scribed; -scribing 1** ORDAIN : prescribir, ordenar **2** : recetar (medicinas, etc.)

prescription [pri'skrɪpʃən] *n* : receta *f*

presence ['prɛzənts] *n* : presencia *f*

present[1] [pri'zɛnt] *vt* **1** INTRODUCE : presentar ⟨to present oneself : presentarse⟩ **2** : presentar (una obra de teatro, etc.) **3** GIVE : entregar (un regalo, etc.), regalar, obsequiar **4** SHOW : presentar, ofrecer ⟨it presents a lovely view : ofrece una vista muy linda⟩

present[2] ['prɛzənt] *adj* **1** : actual ⟨present conditions : condiciones actuales⟩

2 : presente ⟨all the students were present : todos los estudiantes estaban presentes⟩

present[3] [ˈprɛzənt] *n* **1** GIFT : regalo *m*, obsequio *m* **2** : presente *m* ⟨at present : en este momento⟩ **3** *or* **present tense** : presente *m*

presentable [priˈzɛntəbəl] *adj* : presentable

presentation [ˌpriːˌzɛnˈteɪʃən, ˌprɛzən-] *n* : presentación *f* ⟨presentation ceremony : ceremonia de entrega⟩

presentiment [priˈzɛntəmənt] *n* : presentimiento *m*, premonición *f*

presently [ˈprɛzəntli] *adv* **1** SOON : pronto, dentro de poco **2** NOW : actualmente, ahora

present participle *n* : participio *m* presente, participio *m* activo

preservation [ˌprɛzərˈveɪʃən] *n* : conservación *f*, preservación *f*

preservative [priˈzərvət̬ɪv] *n* : conservante *m*

preserve[1] [priˈzərv] *vt* **-served; -serving** **1** PROTECT : proteger, preservar **2** : conservar (los alimentos, etc.) **3** MAINTAIN : conservar, mantener

preserve[2] *n* **1** *or* **preserves** *npl* : conserva *f* ⟨peach preserves : duraznos en conserva⟩ **2** : coto *m* ⟨game preserve : coto de caza⟩

preside [priˈzaɪd] *vi* **-sided; -siding** **1 to preside over** : presidir ⟨he presided over the meeting : presidió la reunión⟩ **2 to preside over** : supervisar ⟨she presides over the department : dirige el departamento⟩

presidency [ˈprɛzədəntsi] *n, pl* **-cies** : presidencia *f*

president [ˈprɛzədənt] *n* : presidente *m*, -ta *f*

presidential [ˌprɛzəˈdɛntʃəl] *adj* : presidencial

press[1] [ˈprɛs] *vt* **1** PUSH : apretar **2** SQUEEZE : apretar, prensar (frutas, flores, etc.) **3** IRON : planchar (ropa) **4** URGE : instar, apremiar ⟨he pressed me to come : insistió en que viniera⟩ — *vi* **1** PUSH : apretar ⟨press hard : aprieta con fuerza⟩ **2** CROWD : apiñarse **3** : abrirse paso ⟨I pressed through the crowd : me abrí paso entre el gentío⟩ **4** URGE : presionar

press[2] *n* **1** CROWD : multitud *f* **2** : imprenta *f*, prensa *f* ⟨to go to press : entrar en prensa⟩ **3** URGENCY : urgencia *f*, prisa *f* **4** PRINTER, PUBLISHER : imprenta *f*, editorial *f* **5 the press** : la prensa ⟨freedom of the press : libertad de prensa⟩

pressing [ˈprɛsɪŋ] *adj* URGENT : urgente

pressure[1] [ˈprɛʃər] *vt* **-sured; -suring** : presionar, apremiar

pressure[2] *n* **1** : presión *f* ⟨to be under pressure : estar bajo presión⟩ **2** → **blood pressure**

pressurize [ˈprɛʃəˌraɪz] *vt* **-ized; -izing** : presurizar

prestige [prɛˈstiːʒ, -ˈstiːdʒ] *n* : prestigio *m*

prestigious [prɛˈstɪdʒəs] *adj* : prestigioso

presto [ˈprɛsˌtoː] *adv* : de pronto

presumably [priˈzuːməbli] *adv* : es de suponer, supuestamente ⟨presumably, he's guilty : supone que es culpable⟩

presume [priˈzuːm] *vt* **-sumed; -suming** **1** ASSUME, SUPPOSE : suponer, asumir, presumir **2 to presume to** : atreverse a, osar

presumption [priˈzʌmpʃən] *n* **1** AUDACITY : atrevimiento *m*, osadía *f* **2** ASSUMPTION : presunción *f*, suposición *f*

presumptuous [priˈzʌmptʃʊəs] *adj* : descarado, atrevido

presuppose [ˌpriːsəˈpoːz] *vt* **-posed; -posing** : presuponer

pretend [priˈtɛnd] *vt* **1** CLAIM : pretender **2** FEIGN : fingir, simular — *vi* : fingir

pretender [priˈtɛndər] *n* : pretendiente *mf* (al trono, etc.)

pretense *or* **pretence** [ˈpriːˌtɛnts, priˈtɛnts] *n* **1** CLAIM : afirmación *f* (falsa), pretensión *f* **2** FEIGNING : fingimiento *m*, simulación *f* ⟨to make a pretense of doing something : fingir hacer algo⟩ ⟨a pretense of order : una apariencia de orden⟩ **3** PRETEXT : pretexto *m* ⟨under false pretenses : con pretextos falsos, de manera fraudulenta⟩

pretension [priˈtɛntʃən] *n* **1** CLAIM : pretensión *f*, afirmación *f* **2** ASPIRATION : aspiración *f*, ambición *f* **3** PRETENTIOUSNESS : pretensiones *fpl*, presunción *f*

pretentious [priˈtɛntʃəs] *adj* : pretencioso

pretentiousness [priˈtɛntʃəsnəs] *n* : presunción *f*, pretensiones *fpl*

pretext [ˈpriːˌtɛkst] *n* : pretexto *m*, excusa *f*

prettily [ˈprɪtəli] *adv* : atractivamente

prettiness [ˈprɪt̬inəs] *n* : lindeza *f*

pretty[1] [ˈprɪt̬i] *adv* : bastante, bien ⟨it's pretty obvious : está bien claro⟩ ⟨it's pretty much the same : es más o menos igual⟩

pretty[2] *adj* **-tier; -est** : bonito, lindo, guapo ⟨a pretty girl : una muchacha guapa⟩ ⟨what a pretty dress! : ¡qué vestido más lindo!⟩

pretzel [ˈprɛtsəl] *n* : galleta *f* salada (en forma de nudo)

prevail [priˈveɪl] *vi* **1** TRIUMPH : prevalecer **2** PREDOMINATE : predominar **3 to prevail upon** : persuadir, convencer ⟨I prevailed upon her to sing : la convencí para que cantara⟩

prevailing [priˈveɪlɪŋ] *adj* : imperante, prevaleciente

prevalence [ˈprɛvələnts] *n* : preponderancia *f*, predominio *m*

prevalent [ˈprɛvələnt] *adj* **1** COMMON : común y corriente, general **2** WIDESPREAD : extendido

prevaricate [pri'værə,keɪt] *vi* **-cated; -cating** LIE : mentir
prevarication [pri,værə'keɪʃən] *n* : mentira *f*
prevent [pri'vɛnt] *vt* **1** AVOID : prevenir, evitar ⟨steps to prevent war : medidas para evitar la guerra⟩ **2** HINDER : impedir
preventable [pri'vɛntəbəl] *adj* : evitable
preventative [pri'vɛntət̬ɪv] → **preventive**
prevention [pri'vɛntʃən] *n* : prevención *f*
preventive [pri'vɛntɪv] *adj* : preventivo
preview ['pri:,vju] *n* : preestreno *m*
previous ['pri:viəs] *adj* : previo, anterior ⟨previous knowledge : conocimientos previos⟩ ⟨the previous day : el día anterior⟩ ⟨in the previous year : en el año pasado⟩
previously ['pri:viəsli] *adv* : antes
prewar [,pri:'wɔr] *adj* : de antes de la guerra
prey ['preɪ] *n, pl* **preys** : presa *f*
prey on *vt* **1** : cazar, alimentarse de ⟨it preys on fish : se alimenta de peces⟩ **2 to prey on one's mind** : hacer presa en alguien, atormentar a alguien
price^{1} ['praɪs] *vt* **priced; pricing** : poner un precio a
price^{2} *n* : precio *m* ⟨peace at any price : la paz a toda costa⟩
priceless ['praɪsləs] *adj* : inestimable, inapreciable
pricey ['praɪsi] *adj* : caro
prick^{1} ['prɪk] *vt* **1** : pinchar **2 to prick up one's ears** : levantar las orejas — *vi* : pinchar
prick^{2} *n* **1** STAB : pinchazo *m* ⟨a prick of conscience : un remordimiento⟩ **2** → **pricker**
pricker ['prɪkər] *n* THORN : espina *f*
prickle^{1} ['prɪkəl] *vi* **-led; -ling** : sentir un cosquilleo, tener un hormigueo
prickle^{2} *n* **1** : espina *f* (de una planta) **2** TINGLE : cosquilleo *m*, hormigueo *m*
prickly ['prɪkəli] *adj* **1** THORNY : espinoso **2** : que pica ⟨a prickly sensation : un hormigueo⟩
prickly pear *n* : tuna *f*
pride^{1} ['praɪd] *vt* **prided; priding** : estar orgulloso de ⟨to pride oneself on : preciarse de, enorgullecerse de⟩
pride^{2} *n* : orgullo *m*
priest ['pri:st] *n* : sacerdote *m*, cura *m*
priestess ['pri:stɪs] *n* : sacerdotisa *f*
priesthood ['pri:st,hʊd] *n* : sacerdocio *m*
priestly ['pri:stli] *adj* : sacerdotal
prig ['prɪg] *n* : mojigato *m*, -ta *f*; gazmoño *m*, -ña *f*
prim ['prɪm] *adj* **primmer; primmest 1** PRISSY : remilgado **2** PRUDISH : mojigato, gazmoño
primarily [praɪ'mɛrəli] *adv* : principalmente, fundamentalmente
primary^{1} ['praɪ,mɛri, 'praɪməri] *adj* **1** FIRST : primario **2** PRINCIPAL : principal **3** BASIC : fundamental
primary^{2} *n, pl* **-ries** : elección *f* primaria
primary color *n* : color *m* primario
primary school → **elementary school**
primate *n* **1** ['praɪ,meɪt, -mət] : primado *m* (obispo) **2** [-,meɪt] : primate *m* (animal)
prime^{1} ['praɪm] *vt* **primed; priming 1** : cebar ⟨to prime a pump : cebar una bomba⟩ **2** PREPARE : preparar (una superficie para pintar) **3** COACH : preparar (a un testigo, etc.)
prime^{2} *adj* **1** CHIEF, MAIN : principal, primero **2** EXCELLENT : de primera (categoría), excelente
prime^{3} *n* **the prime of one's life** : la flor de la vida
prime minister *n* : primer ministro *m*, primera ministra *f*
primer^{1} ['prɪmər] *n* **1** READER : cartilla *f* **2** MANUAL : manual *m*
primer^{2} ['praɪmər] *n* **1** : cebo *m* (para explosivos) **2** : base *f* (de pintura)
prime time *n* : horas *fpl* de mayor audiencia
primeval [praɪ'mi:vəl] *adj* : primitivo, primigenio
primitive ['prɪmət̬ɪv] *adj* : primitivo
primly ['prɪmli] *adv* : mojigatamente
primness ['prɪmnəs] *n* : mojigatería *f*, gazmoñería *f*
primordial [praɪ'mɔrdiəl] *adj* : primordial, fundamental
primp ['prɪmp] *vi* : arreglarse, acicalarse
primrose ['prɪm,ro:z] *n* : primavera *f*, prímula *f*
prince ['prɪnts] *n* : príncipe *m*
princely ['prɪntsli] *adj* : principesco
princess ['prɪntsəs, 'prɪn,sɛs] *n* : princesa *f*
principal^{1} ['prɪntsəpəl] *adj* : principal — **principally** *adv*
principal^{2} *n* **1** PROTAGONIST : protagonista *mf* **2** : director *m*, -tora *f* (de una escuela) **3** CAPITAL : principal *m*, capital *m* (en finanzas)
principality [,prɪntsə'pæləṱi] *n, pl* **-ties** : principado *m*
principle ['prɪntsəpəl] *n* : principio *m*
print^{1} ['prɪnt] *vt* : imprimir (libros, etc.) — *vi* : escribir con letra de molde
print^{2} *n* **1** IMPRESSION : marca *f*, huella *f*, impresión *f* **2** : texto *m* impreso ⟨to be out of print : estar agotado⟩ **3** LETTERING : letra *f* **4** ENGRAVING : grabado *m* **5** : copia *f* (en fotografía) **6** : estampado *m* (de tela)
printer ['prɪntər] *n* **1** : impresor *m*, -sora *f* (persona) **2** : impresora *f* (máquina)
printing ['prɪntɪŋ] *n* **1** : impresión *f* (acto) ⟨the third printing : la tercera tirada⟩ **2** : imprenta *f* (profesión) **3** LETTERING : letras *fpl* de molde
printing press *n* : prensa *f*
print out *vt* : imprimir (de una computadora)
printout ['prɪnt,aʊt] *n* : copia *f* impresa (de una computadora)
prior ['praɪər] *adj* **1** : previo **2 prior to** : antes de

priority [praɪˈɔrət̬i] *n, pl* **-ties** : prioridad *f*
priory [ˈpraɪəri] *n, pl* **-ries** : priorato *m*
prism [ˈprɪzəm] *n* : prisma *m*
prison [ˈprɪzən] *n* : prisión *f*, cárcel *f*
prisoner [ˈprɪzənər] *n* : preso *m*, -sa *f*; recluso *m*, -sa *f* ⟨prisoner of war : prisionero de guerra⟩
prissy [ˈprɪsi] *adj* **-sier; -est** : remilgado, melindroso
pristine [ˈprɪsˌti:n, prɪsˈ-] *adj* : puro, prístino
privacy [ˈpraɪvəsi] *n, pl* **-cies** : privacidad *f*
private[1] [ˈpraɪvət] *adj* **1** PERSONAL : privado, particular ⟨private property : propiedad privada⟩ **2** INDEPENDENT : privado, independiente ⟨private studies : estudios privados⟩ **3** SECRET : secreto **4** SECLUDED : aislado, privado — **privately** *adv*
private[2] *n* : soldado *m* raso
privateer [ˌpraɪvəˈtɪr] *n* : corsario *m*
privation [praɪˈveɪʃən] *n* : privación *f*
privilege [ˈprɪvlɪʤ, ˈprɪvə-] *n* : privilegio *m*
privileged [ˈprɪvlɪʤd, ˈprɪvə-] *adj* : privilegiado
privy[1] [ˈprɪvi] *adj* **to be privy to** : estar enterado de
privy[2] *n, pl* **privies** : excusado *m*, retrete *m* (exterior)
prize[1] [ˈpraɪz] *vt* **prized; prizing** : valorar, apreciar
prize[2] *adj* **1** : premiado ⟨a prize stallion : un semental premiado⟩ **2** OUTSTANDING : de primera, excepcional
prize[3] *n* **1** AWARD : premio *m* ⟨third prize : el tercer premio⟩ **2** : joya *f*, tesoro *m* ⟨he's a real prize : es un tesoro⟩
prizefighter [ˈpraɪzˌfaɪt̬ər] *n* : boxeador *m*, -dora *f* profesional
prizewinning [ˈpraɪzˌwɪnɪŋ] *adj* : premiado
pro[1] [ˈpro:] *adv* : a favor
pro[2] *adj* → **professional**[1]
pro[3] *n* **1** : pro *m* ⟨the pros and cons : los pros y los contras⟩ **2** → **professional**[2]
probability [ˌprɑbəˈbɪlət̬i] *n, pl* **-ties** : probabilidad *f*
probable [ˈprɑbəbəl] *adj* : probable — **probably** [-bli] *adv*
probate[1] [ˈpro:ˌbeɪt] *vt* **-bated; -bating** : autenticar (un testamento)
probate[2] *n* : autenticación *f* (de un testamento)
probation [proˈbeɪʃən] *n* **1** : período *m* de prueba (para un empleado, etc.) **2** : libertad *f* condicional (para un preso)
probationary [proˈbeɪʃəˌnɛri] *adj* : de prueba
probe[1] [ˈpro:b] *vt* **probed; probing** **1** : sondar (en medicina y tecnología) **2** INVESTIGATE : investigar, sondear
probe[2] *n* **1** : sonda *f* (en medicina, etc.) ⟨space probe : sonda espacial⟩ **2** INVESTIGATION : investigación *f*, sondeo *m*
probity [ˈpro:bət̬i] *n* : probidad *f*
problem[1] [ˈprɑbləm] *adj* : difícil
problem[2] *n* : problema *m*
problematic [ˌprɑbləˈmæt̬ɪk] *or* **problematical** [-t̬ɪkəl] *adj* : problemático
proboscis [prəˈbɑsɪs] *n, pl* **-cises** *also* **-cides** [-səˌdi:z] : probóscide *f*
procedural [prəˈsi:ʤərəl] *adj* : de procedimiento
procedure [prəˈsi:ʤər] *n* : procedimiento *m* ⟨administrative procedures : trámites administrativos⟩
proceed [proˈsi:d] *vi* **1** : proceder ⟨to proceed to do something : proceder a hacer algo⟩ **2** CONTINUE : continuar, proseguir, seguir ⟨he proceeded to the next phase : pasó a la segunda fase⟩ **3** ADVANCE : avanzar ⟨as the conference proceeded : mientras seguía avanzando la conferencia⟩ ⟨the road proceeds south : la calle sigue hacia el sur⟩
proceeding [proˈsi:dɪŋ] *n* **1** PROCEDURE : procedimiento *m* **2** **proceedings** *npl* EVENTS : acontecimientos *mpl* **3** **proceedings** *npl* MINUTES : actas *fpl* (de una reunión, etc.)
proceeds [ˈpro:ˌsi:dz] *npl* : ganancias *fpl*
process[1] [ˈprɑˌsɛs, ˈpro:-] *vt* : procesar, tratar
process[2] *n, pl* **-cesses** [ˈprɑˌsɛsəz, ˈpro:-, -səsəz, -səˌsi:z] **1** : proceso *m* ⟨the process of elimination : el proceso de eliminación⟩ **2** METHOD : proceso *m*, método *m* ⟨manufacturing processes : procesos industriales⟩ **3** : acción *f* judicial ⟨due process of law : el debido proceso (de la ley)⟩ **4** SUMMONS : citación *f* **5** PROJECTION : protuberancia *f* (anatómica) **6** **in the process of** : en vías de ⟨in the process of repair : en reparaciones⟩
procession [prəˈsɛʃən] *n* : procesión *f*, desfile *m* ⟨a funeral procession : un cortejo fúnebre⟩
processional [prəˈsɛʃənəl] *n* : himno *m* para una procesión
processor [ˈprɑˌsɛsər, ˈpro:-, -səsər] *n* **1** : procesador *m* (de una computadora) **2** **food processor** : procesador *m* de alimentos
proclaim [proˈkleɪm] *vt* : proclamar
proclamation [ˌprɑkləˈmeɪʃən] *n* : proclamación *f*
proclivity [proˈklɪvət̬i] *n, pl* **-ties** : proclividad *f*
procrastinate [prəˈkræstəˌneɪt] *vi* **-nated; -nating** : demorar, aplazar las responsabilidades
procrastination [prəˌkræstəˈneɪʃən] *n* : aplazamiento *m*, demora *f*, dilación *f*
procreate [ˈpro:kriˌeɪt] *vi* **-ated; -ating** : procrear
procreation [ˌpro:kriˈeɪʃən] *n* : procreación *f*
proctor[1] [ˈprɑktər] *vt* : supervisar (un examen)
proctor[2] *n* : supervisor *m*, -sora *f* (de un examen)

procure [prə'kjʊr] *vt* **-cured; -curing 1** OBTAIN : procurar, obtener **2** BRING ABOUT : provocar, lograr, conseguir
procurement [prə'kjʊrmənt] *n* : obtención *f*
prod[1] ['prɑd] *vt* **prodded; prodding 1** JAB, POKE : pinchar, golpear (con la punta de algo) **2** GOAD : incitar, estimular
prod[2] *n* **1** JAB, POKE : golpe *m* (con la punta de algo), pinchazo *m* **2** STIMULUS : estímulo *m* **3 cattle prod** : picana *f*, aguijón *m*
prodigal[1] ['prɑdɪgəl] *adj* SPENDTHRIFT : pródigo, despilfarrador, derrochador
prodigal[2] *n* : pródigo *m*, -ga *f*; derrochador *m*, -dora *f*
prodigious [prə'dɪʤəs] *adj* **1** MARVELOUS : prodigioso, maravilloso **2** HUGE : enorme, vasto ⟨prodigious sums : muchísimo dinero⟩ — **prodigiously** *adv*
prodigy ['prɑdəʤi] *n, pl* **-gies** : prodigio *m* ⟨child prodigy : niño prodigio⟩
produce[1] [prə'du:s, -'dju:s] *vt* **-duced; -ducing 1** EXHIBIT : presentar, mostrar **2** YIELD : producir **3** CAUSE : producir, causar **4** CREATE : producir ⟨to produce a poem : escribir un poema⟩ **5** : poner en escena (una obra de teatro), producir (una película)
produce[2] ['prɑˌdu:s, 'pro:-, -ˌdju:s] *n* : productos *mpl* agrícolas
producer [prə'du:sər, -'dju:-] *n* : productor *m*, -tora *f*
product ['prɑˌdʌkt] *n* : producto *m*
production [prə'dʌkʃən] *n* : producción *f*
productive [prə'dʌktɪv] *adj* : productivo
productivity [ˌpro:ˌdʌk'tɪvəṯi, ˌprɑ-] *n* : productividad *f*
profane[1] [pro'feɪn] *vt* **-faned; -faning** : profanar
profane[2] *adj* **1** SECULAR : profano **2** IRREVERENT : irreverente, impío
profanity [pro'fænəṯi] *n, pl* **-ties 1** IRREVERENCE : irreverencia *f*, impiedad *f* **2** : blasfemias *fpl*, obscenidades *fpl* ⟨don't use profanity : no digas blasfemias⟩
profess [prə'fɛs] *vt* **1** DECLARE : declarar, manifestar **2** CLAIM : pretender **3** : profesar (una religión, etc.)
professedly [prə'fɛsədli] *adv* **1** OPENLY : declaradamente **2** ALLEGEDLY : supuestamente
profession [prə'fɛʃən] *n* : profesión *f*
professional[1] [prə'fɛʃənəl] *adj* : profesional — **professionally** *adv*
professional[2] *n* : profesional *mf*
professionalism [prə'fɛʃənəˌlizəm] *n* : profesionalismo *m*
professor [prə'fɛsər] *n* : profesor *m* (universitario), profesora *f* (universitaria); catedrático *m*, -ca *f*
proffer ['prɑfər] *vt* **-fered; -fering** : ofrecer, dar
proficiency [prə'fɪʃəntsi] *n* : competencia *f*, capacidad *f*
proficient [prə'fɪʃənt] *adj* : competente, experto — **proficiently** *adv*
profile ['pro:ˌfaɪl] *n* : perfil *m* ⟨a portrait in profile : un retrato de perfil⟩ ⟨to keep a low profile : no llamar la atención, hacerse pasar desapercibido⟩
profit[1] ['prɑfət] *vi* : sacar provecho (de), beneficiarse (de)
profit[2] *n* **1** ADVANTAGE : provecho *m*, partido *m*, beneficio *m* **2** GAIN : beneficio *m*, utilidad *f*, ganancia *f* ⟨to make a profit : sacar beneficios⟩
profitable ['prɑfəṯəbəl] *adj* : rentable, lucrativo — **profitably** [-bli] *adv*
profitless ['prɑfətləs] *adj* : infructuoso, inútil
profligate ['prɑflɪgət, -ˌgeɪt] *adj* **1** DISSOLUTE : disoluto, licencioso **2** SPENDTHRIFT : despilfarrador, derrochador, pródigo
profound [prə'faʊnd] *adj* : profundo
profoundly [prə'faʊndli] *adv* : profundamente, en profundidad
profundity [prə'fʌndəṯi] *n, pl* **-ties** : profundidad *f*
profuse [prə'fju:s] *adj* **1** COPIOUS : profuso, copioso **2** LAVISH : pródigo — **profusely** *adv*
profusion [prə'fju:ʒən] *n* : abundancia *f*, profusión *f*
progenitor [pro'ʤɛnəṯər] *n* : progenitor *m*, -tora *f*
progeny ['prɑʤəni] *n, pl* **-nies** : progenie *f*
progesterone [pro'ʤɛstəˌro:n] *n* : progesterona *f*
prognosis [prɑg'no:sɪs] *n, pl* **-noses** [-ˌsi:z] : pronóstico *m* (médico)
program[1] ['pro:ˌgræm, -grəm] *vt* **-grammed** *or* **-gramed; -gramming** *or* **-graming** : programar
program[2] *n* : programa *m*
programmable ['pro:ˌgræməbəl] *adj* : programable
programmer ['pro:ˌgræmər] *n* : programador *m*, -dora *f*
programming ['pro:ˌgræmɪŋ] *n* : programación *f*
progress[1] [prə'grɛs] *vi* **1** PROCEED : progresar, adelantar **2** IMPROVE : mejorar
progress[2] ['prɑgrəs, -ˌgrɛs] *n* **1** ADVANCE : progreso *m*, adelanto *m*, avance *m* ⟨to make progress : hacer progresos⟩ **2** BETTERMENT : mejora *f*, mejoramiento *m*
progression [prə'grɛʃən] *n* **1** ADVANCE : avance *m* **2** SEQUENCE : desarrollo *m* (de eventos)
progressive [prə'grɛsɪv] *adj* **1** : progresista ⟨a progressive society : una sociedad progresista⟩ **2** : progresivo ⟨a progressive disease : una enfermedad progresiva⟩ **3** *or* **Progressive** : progresista (en política) **4** : progresivo (en gramática)

progressively [prəˈgrɛsɪvli] *adv* : progresivamente, poco a poco

prohibit [proˈhɪbət] *vt* : prohibir

prohibition [ˌpro:əˈbɪʃən, ˌpro:hə-] *n* : prohibición *f*

prohibitive [proˈhɪbət̬ɪv] *adj* : prohibitivo

project[1] [prəˈʤɛkt] *vt* **1** PLAN : proyectar, planear **2** : proyectar (imágenes, misiles, etc.) — *vi* PROTRUDE : sobresalir, salir

project[2] [ˈprɑˌʤɛkt, -ʤɪkt] *n* : proyecto *m*, trabajo *m* (de un estudiante) ⟨research project : proyecto de investigación⟩

projectile [prəˈʤɛktəl, -ˌtaɪl] *n* : proyectil *m*

projection [prəˈʤɛkʃən] *n* **1** PLAN : plan *m*, proyección *f* **2** : proyección *f* (de imágenes, misiles, etc.) **3** PROTRUSION : saliente *m*

projector [prəˈʤɛktər] *n* : proyector *m*

proletarian[1] [ˌpro:ləˈtɛriən] *adj* : proletario

proletarian[2] *n* : proletario *m*, -ria *f*

proletariat [ˌpro:ləˈtɛriət] *n* : proletariado *m*

proliferate [prəˈlɪfəˌreɪt] *vi* **-ated; -ating** : proliferar

proliferation [prəˌlɪfəˈreɪʃən] *n* : proliferación *f*

prolific [prəˈlɪfɪk] *adj* : prolífico

prologue [ˈpro:ˌlɔg] *n* : prólogo *m*

prolong [prəˈlɔŋ] *vt* : prolongar

prolongation [ˌpro:ˌlɔŋˈgeɪʃən] *n* : prolongación *f*

prom [ˈprɑm] *n* : baile *m* formal (de un colegio)

promenade[1] [ˌprɑməˈneɪd, -ˈnɑd] *vi* **-naded; -nading** : pasear, pasearse, dar un paseo

promenade[2] *n* : paseo *m*

prominence [ˈprɑmənənts] *n* **1** PROJECTION : prominencia *f* **2** EMINENCE : eminencia *f*, prestigio *m*

prominent [ˈprɑmənənt] *adj* **1** OUTSTANDING : prominente, destacado **2** PROJECTING : prominente, saliente

prominently [ˈprɑmənəntli] *adv* : destacadamente, prominentemente

promiscuity [ˌprɑmɪsˈkju:ət̬i] *n, pl* **-ties** : promiscuidad *f*

promiscuous [prəˈmɪskjʊəs] *adj* : promiscuo — **promiscuously** *adv*

promise[1] [ˈprɑməs] *v* **-ised; -ising** : prometer

promise[2] *n* **1** : promesa *f* ⟨he kept his promise : cumplió su promesa⟩ **2 to show promise** : prometer

promising [ˈprɑməsɪŋ] *adj* : prometedor

promissory [ˈprɑməˌsori] *adj* : que promete ⟨a promissory note : un pagaré⟩

promontory [ˈprɑmənˌtori] *n, pl* **-ries** : promontorio *m*

promote [prəˈmo:t] *vt* **-moted; -moting** **1** : ascender (a un alumno o un empleado) **2** ADVERTISE : promocionar, hacerle publicidad a **3** FURTHER : promover, fomentar

promoter [prəˈmo:t̬ər] *n* : promotor *m*, -tora *f*; empresario *m*, -ria *f* (en deportes)

promotion [prəˈmo:ʃən] *n* **1** : ascenso *m* (de un alumno o un empleado) **2** FURTHERING : promoción *f*, fomento *m* **3** ADVERTISING : publicidad *f*, propaganda *f*

promotional [prəˈmo:ʃənəl] *adj* : promocional

prompt[1] [ˈprɑmpt] *vt* **1** INDUCE : provocar (una cosa), inducir (a una persona) ⟨curiosity prompted me to ask you : la curiosidad me indujo a preguntarle⟩ **2** : apuntar (a un actor, etc.)

prompt[2] *adj* : pronto, rápido ⟨prompt payment : pago puntual⟩

prompter [ˈprɑmptər] *n* : apuntador *m*, -dora *f* (en teatro)

promptly [ˈprɑmptli] *adv* : inmediatamente, rápidamente

promptness [ˈprɑmptnəs] *n* : prontitud *f*, rapidez *f*

promulgate [ˈprɑməlˌgeɪt] *vt* **-gated; -gating** : promulgar

prone [ˈpro:n] *adj* **1** LIABLE : propenso, proclive ⟨accident-prone : propenso a los accidentes⟩ **2** : boca abajo, decúbito prono ⟨in a prone position : en decúbito prono⟩

prong [ˈprɔŋ] *n* : punta *f*, diente *m*

pronoun [ˈpro:ˌnaʊn] *n* : pronombre *m*

pronounce [prəˈnaʊnts] *vt* **-nounced; -nouncing** **1** : pronunciar ⟨how do you pronounce your name? : ¿cómo se pronuncia su nombre?⟩ **2** DECLARE : declarar **3 to pronounce sentence** : dictar sentencia, pronunciar un fallo

pronounced [prəˈnaʊntst] *adj* MARKED : pronunciado, marcado

pronouncement [prəˈnaʊntsmənt] *n* : declaración *f*

pronunciation [prəˌnʌntsiˈeɪʃən] *n* : pronunciación *f*

proof[1] [ˈpru:f] *adj* : a prueba ⟨proof against tampering : a prueba de manipulación⟩

proof[2] *n* : prueba *f*

proofread [ˈpru:fˌri:d] *v* **-read; -reading** *vt* : corregir — *vi* : corregir pruebas

proofreader [ˈpru:fˌri:dər] *n* : corrector *m*, -tora *f* (de pruebas)

prop[1] [ˈprɑp] *vt* **propped; propping** **1 to prop against** : apoyar contra **2 to prop up** SUPPORT : apoyar, apuntalar, sostener **3 to prop up** SUSTAIN : alentar (a alguien), darle ánimo (a alguien)

prop[2] *n* **1** SUPPORT : puntal *m*, apoyo *m*, soporte *m* **2** : accesorio *m* (en teatro)

propaganda [ˌprɑpəˈgændə, ˌpro:-] *n* : propaganda *f*

propagandize [ˌprɑpəˈgænˌdaɪz, ˌpro:-] *v* **-dized; -dizing** *vt* : someter a propaganda — *vi* : hacer propaganda

propagate [ˈprɑpəˌgeɪt] *v* **-gated; -gating** *vi* : propagarse — *vt* : propagar
propagation [ˌprɑpəˈgeɪʃən] *n* : propagación *f*
propane [ˈpro:ˌpeɪn] *n* : propano *m*
propel [prəˈpɛl] *vt* **-pelled; -pelling** : impulsar, propulsar, impeler
propellant *or* **propellent** [prəˈpɛlənt] *n* : propulsor *m*
propeller [prəˈpɛlər] *n* : hélice *f*
propensity [prəˈpɛntsəṭi] *n, pl* **-ties** : propensión *f*, tendencia *f*, inclinación *f*
proper [ˈprɑpər] *adj* **1** RIGHT, SUITABLE : apropiado, adecuado **2** : propio, mismo ‹the city proper : la propia ciudad› **3** CORRECT : correcto **4** GENTEEL : fino, refinado, cortés **5** OWN, SPECIAL : propio ‹proper name : nombre propio› — **properly** *adv*
property [ˈprɑpərṭi] *n, pl* **-ties 1** CHARACTERISTIC : característica *f*, propiedad *f* **2** POSSESSIONS : propiedad *f* **3** BUILDING : inmueble *m* **4** LAND, LOT : terreno *m*, lote *m*, parcela *f* **5** PROP : accesorio *m* (en teatro)
prophecy [ˈprɑfəsi] *n, pl* **-cies** : profecía *f*, vaticinio *m*
prophesy [ˈprɑfəˌsaɪ] *v* **-sied; -sying** *vt* **1** FORETELL : profetizar (como profeta) **2** PREDICT : profetizar, predecir, vaticinar — *vi* : hacer profecías
prophet [ˈprɑfət] *n* : profeta *m*, profetisa *f*
prophetic [prəˈfɛṭɪk] *or* **prophetical** [-ṭɪkəl] *adj* : profético — **prophetically** [-ṭɪkli] *adv*
propitiate [proˈpɪʃiˌeɪt] *vt* **-ated; -ating** : propiciar
propitious [prəˈpɪʃəs] *adj* : propicio
proponent [prəˈpo:nənt] *n* : defensor *m*, -sora *f*; partidario *m*, -ria *f*
proportion¹ [prəˈporʃən] *vt* : proporcionar ‹well-proportioned : de buenas proporciones›
proportion² *n* **1** RATIO : proporción *f* **2** SYMMETRY : proporción *f*, simetría *f* ‹out of proportion : desproporcionado› **3** SHARE : parte *f* **4 proportions** *npl* SIZE : dimensiones *fpl*
proportional [prəˈporʃənəl] *adj* : proporcional — **proportionally** *adv*
proportionate [prəˈporʃənət] *adj* : proporcional — **proportionately** *adv*
proposal [prəˈpo:zəl] *n* **1** PROPOSITION : propuesta *f*, proposición *f* ‹marriage proposal : propuesta de matrimonio› **2** PLAN : proyecto *m*, propuesta *f*
propose [prəˈpo:z] *v* **-posed; -posing** *vi* : proponer matrimonio — *vt* **1** INTEND : pensar, proponerse **2** SUGGEST : proponer
proposition [ˌprɑpəˈzɪʃən] *n* **1** PROPOSAL : proposición *f*, propuesta *f* **2** STATEMENT : proposición *f*
propound [prəˈpaʊnd] *vt* : proponer, exponer
proprietary [prəˈpraɪəˌtɛri] *adj* : propietario, patentado
proprietor [prəˈpraɪəṭər] *n* : propietario *m*, -ria *f*
propriety [prəˈpraɪəṭi] *n, pl* **-eties 1** DECORUM : decencia *f*, decoro *m* **2 proprieties** *npl* CONVENTIONS : convenciones *fpl*, cánones *mpl* sociales
propulsion [prəˈpʌlʃən] *n* : propulsión *f*
prosaic [proˈzeɪɪk] *adj* : prosaico
proscribe [proˈskraɪb] *vt* **-scribed; -scribing** : proscribir
prose [ˈpro:z] *n* : prosa *f*
prosecute [ˈprɑsɪˌkju:t] *vt* **-cuted; -cuting 1** CARRY OUT : llevar a cabo **2** : procesar, enjuiciar ‹prosecuted for fraud : procesado por fraude›
prosecution [ˌprɑsɪˈkju:ʃən] *n* **1** : procesamiento *m* ‹the prosecution of forgers : el procesamiento de falsificadores› **2** PROSECUTORS : acusación *f* ‹witness for the prosecution : testigo de cargo›
prosecutor [ˈprɑsɪˌkju:ṭər] *n* : acusador *m*, -dora *f*; fiscal *mf*
prospect¹ [ˈprɑˌspɛkt] *vi* : prospectar (el terreno) ‹to prospect for gold : buscar oro›
prospect² *n* **1** VISTA : vista *f*, panorama *m* **2** POSSIBILITY : posibilidad *f* **3** OUTLOOK : perspectiva *f* **4** : posible cliente *m*, -ta *f* ‹a salesman looking for prospects : un vendedor buscando nuevos clientes›
prospective [prəˈspɛktɪv, ˈprɑˌspɛk-] *adj* **1** EXPECTANT : futuro ‹prospective mother : futura madre› **2** POTENTIAL : potencial, posible ‹prospective employee : posible empleado›
prospector [ˈprɑˌspɛktər, prɑˈspɛk-] *n* : prospector *m*, -tora *f*; explorador *m*, -dora *f*
prospectus [prəˈspɛktəs] *n* : prospecto *m*
prosper [ˈprɑspər] *vi* : prosperar
prosperity [prɑˈspɛrəṭi] *n* : prosperidad *f*
prosperous [ˈprɑspərəs] *adj* : próspero
prostate [ˈprɑˌsteɪt] *n* : próstata *f*
prosthesis [prɑsˈθi:sɪs, ˈprɑsθə-] *n, pl* **-theses** [-ˌsi:z] : prótesis *f*
prostitute¹ [ˈprɑstəˌtu:t, -ˌtju:t] *vt* **-tuted; -tuting 1** : prostituir **2 to prostitute oneself** : prostituirse
prostitute² *n* : prostituto *m*, -ta *f*
prostitution [ˌprɑstəˈtu:ʃən, -ˈtju:-] *n* : prostitución *f*
prostrate¹ [ˈprɑˌstreɪt] *vt* **-trated; -trating 1** : postrar **2 to prostrate oneself** : postrarse
prostrate² *adj* : postrado
prostration [prɑˈstreɪʃən] *n* : postración *f*
protagonist [proˈtægənɪst] *n* : protagonista *mf*
protect [prəˈtɛkt] *vt* : proteger
protection [prəˈtɛkʃən] *n* : protección *f*
protective [prəˈtɛktɪv] *adj* : protector
protector [prəˈtɛktər] *n* **1** : protector *m*, -tora *f* (persona) **2** GUARD : protector *m* (aparato)

protectorate [prə'tɛktərət] *n* : protectorado *m*

protégé ['pro:t̬əˌʒeɪ] *n* : protegido *m*, -da *f*

protein ['pro:ˌti:n] *n* : proteína *f*

protest[1] [pro'tɛst] *vt* **1** ASSERT : afirmar, declarar **2** : protestar ⟨they protested the decision : protestaron (por) la decisión⟩ — *vi* **to protest against** : protestar contra

protest[2] ['pro:ˌtɛst] *n* **1** DEMONSTRATION : manifestación *f* (de protesta) ⟨a public protest : una manifestación pública⟩ **2** COMPLAINT : queja *f*, protesta *f*

Protestant ['prɑt̬əstənt] *n* : protestante *mf*

Protestantism ['prɑt̬əstənˌtɪzəm] *n* : protestantismo *m*

protocol ['pro:t̬əˌkɔl] *n* : protocolo *m*

proton ['proˌtɑn] *n* : protón *m*

protoplasm ['pro:t̬əˌplæzəm] *n* : protoplasma *m*

prototype ['pro:t̬əˌtaɪp] *n* : prototipo *m*

protozoan [ˌpro:t̬ə'zo:ən] *n* : protozoario *m*, protozoo *m*

protract [pro'trækt] *vt* : prolongar

protractor [pro'træktər] *n* : transportador *m* (instrumento)

protrude [pro'tru:d] *vi* **-truded; -truding** : salir, sobresalir

protrusion [pro'tru:ʒən] *n* : protuberancia *f*, saliente *m*

protuberance [pro'tu:bərənts, -'tju:-] *n* : protuberancia *f*

proud ['praʊd] *adj* **1** HAUGHTY : altanero, orgulloso, arrogante **2** : orgulloso ⟨she was proud of her work : estaba orgullosa de su trabajo⟩ ⟨too proud to beg : demasiado orgulloso para rogar⟩ **3** GLORIOUS : glorioso — **proudly** *adv*

prove ['pru:v] *v* **proved; proved** *or* **proven** ['pru:vən]; **proving** *vt* **1** TEST : probar **2** DEMONSTRATE : probar, demostrar — *vi* : resultar ⟨it proved effective : resultó efectivo⟩

Provençal [ˌpro:vɑn'sɑl, ˌprɑvən-] *n* **1** : provenzal *mf* **2** : provenzal *m* (idioma) — **Provençal** *adj*

proverb ['prɑˌvərb] *n* : proverbio *m*, refrán *m*

proverbial [prə'vərbiəl] *adj* : proverbial

provide [prə'vaɪd] *v* **-vided; -viding** *vt* **1** STIPULATE : estipular **2 to provide with** : proveer de, proporcionar — *vi* **1** : proveer ⟨the Lord will provide : el Señor proveerá⟩ **2 to provide for** SUPPORT : mantener **3 to provide for** ANTICIPATE : hacer previsiones para, prever

provided [prə'vaɪdəd] *or* **provided that** *conj* : con tal (de) que, siempre que

providence ['prɑvədənts] *n* **1** PRUDENCE : previsión *f*, prudencia *f* **2** *or* **Providence** : providencia *f* ⟨divine providence : la Divina Providencia⟩ **3** **Providence** GOD : Providencia *f*

provident ['prɑvədənt] *adj* **1** PRUDENT : previsor, prudente **2** FRUGAL : frugal, ahorrativo

providential [ˌprɑvə'dɛntʃəl] *adj* : providencial

provider [prə'vaɪdər] *n* **1** PURVEYOR : proveedor *m*, -dora *f* **2** BREADWINNER : sostén *m* (económico)

providing that → **provided**

province ['prɑvɪnts] *n* **1** : provincia *f* (de un país) ⟨to live in the provinces : vivir en las provincias⟩ **2** FIELD, SPHERE : campo *m*, competencia *f* ⟨it's not in my province : no es de mi competencia⟩

provincial [prə'vɪntʃəl] *adj* **1** : provincial ⟨provincial government : gobierno provincial⟩ **2** : provinciano, pueblerino ⟨a provincial mentality : una mentalidad provinciana⟩

provision[1] [prə'vɪʒən] *vt* : aprovisionar, abastecer

provision[2] *n* **1** PROVIDING : provisión *f*, suministro *m* **2** STIPULATION : condición *f*, salvedad *f*, estipulación *f* **3 provisions** *npl* : despensa *f*, víveres *mpl*, provisiones *fpl*

provisional [prə'vɪʒənəl] *adj* : provisional, provisorio — **provisionally** *adv*

proviso [prə'vaɪˌzo:] *n, pl* **-sos** *or* **-soes** : condición *f*, salvedad *f*, estipulación *f*

provocation [ˌprɑvə'keɪʃən] *n* : provocación *f*

provocative [prə'vɑkət̬ɪv] *adj* : provocador, provocativo ⟨a provocative article : un artículo que hace pensar⟩

provoke [prə'vo:k] *vt* **-voked; -voking** : provocar

prow ['praʊ] *n* : proa *f*

prowess ['praʊəs] *n* **1** VALOR : valor *m*, valentía *f* **2** SKILL : habilidad *f*, destreza *f*

prowl ['praʊl] *vi* : merodear, rondar — *vt* : rondar por

prowler ['praʊlər] *n* : merodeador *m*, -dora *f*

proximity [prɑk'sɪmət̬i] *n* : proximidad *f*

proxy ['prɑksi] *n, pl* **proxies** **1** : poder *m* (de actuar en nombre de alguien) ⟨by proxy : por poder⟩ **2** AGENT : apoderado *m*, -da *f*; representante *mf*

prude ['pru:d] *n* : mojigato *m*, -ta *f*; gazmoño *m*, -ña *f*

prudence ['pru:dənts] *n* **1** SHREWDNESS : prudencia *f*, sagacidad *f* **2** CAUTION : prudencia *f*, cautela *f* **3** THRIFTINESS : frugalidad *f*

prudent ['pru:dənt] *adj* **1** SHREWD : prudente, sagaz **2** CAUTIOUS, FARSIGHTED : prudente, previsor, precavido **3** THRIFTY : frugal, ahorrativo — **prudently** *adv*

prudery ['pru:dəri] *n, pl* **-eries** : mojigatería *f*, gazmoñería *f*

prudish ['pru:dɪʃ] *adj* : mojigato, gazmoño

prune[1] [ˈpru:n] *vt* **pruned; pruning** : podar (arbustos, etc.), acortar (un texto), recortar (gastos, etc.)
prune[2] *n* : ciruela *f* pasa
prurient [ˈprʊriənt] *adj* : lascivo
pry [ˈpraɪ] *v* **pried; prying** *vi* : curiosear, huronear ⟨to pry into other people's business : meterse uno en lo que no le importa⟩ — *vt or* **to pry open** : abrir (con una palanca), apalancar
psalm [ˈsɑm, ˈsɑlm] *n* : salmo *m*
pseudonym [ˈsu:dəˌnɪm] *n* : seudónimo *m*
psoriasis [səˈraɪəsɪs] *n* : soriasis *f*, psoriasis *f*
psyche [ˈsaɪki] *n* : psique *f*, psiquis *f*
psychedelic[1] [ˌsaɪkəˈdɛlɪk] *adj* : psicodélico
psychedelic[2] *n* : droga *f* psicodélica
psychiatric [ˌsaɪkiˈætrɪk] *adj* : psiquiátrico, siquiátrico
psychiatrist [səˈkaɪətrɪst, saɪ-] *n* : psiquiatra *mf*, siquiatra *mf*
psychiatry [səˈkaɪətri, saɪ-] *n* : psiquiatría *f*, siquiatría *f*
psychic[1] [ˈsaɪkɪk] *adj* **1** : psíquico, síquico (en psicología) **2** CLAIRVOYANT : clarividente
psychic[2] *n* : vidente *mf*, clarividente *mf*
psychoanalysis [ˌsaɪkoəˈnæləsɪs] *n, pl* **-yses** : psicoanálisis *m*, sicoanálisis *m*
psychoanalyst [ˌsaɪkoˈænəlɪst] *n* : psicoanalista *mf*, sicoanalista *mf*
psychoanalytic [ˌsaɪkoˌænəlˈɪţɪk] *adj* : psicoanalítico, sicoanalítico
psychoanalyze [ˌsaɪkoˈænəlˌaɪz] *vt* **-lyzed; -lyzing** : psicoanalizar, sicoanalizar
psychological [ˌsaɪkəˈlɑʤɪkəl] *adj* : psicológico, sicológico — **psychologically** *adv*
psychologist [saɪˈkɑləʤɪst] *n* : psicólogo *m*, -ga *f*; sicólogo *m*, -ga *f*
psychology [saɪˈkɑləʤi] *n, pl* **-gies** : psicología *f*, sicología *f*
psychopath [ˈsaɪkəˌpæθ] *n* : psicópata *mf*, sicópata *mf*
psychopathic [ˌsaɪkəˈpæθɪk] *adj* : psicopático, sicopático
psychosis [saɪˈko:sɪs] *n, pl* **-choses** [-ˈko:ˌsi:z] : psicosis *f*, sicosis *f*
psychosomatic [ˌsaɪkəsəˈmæţɪk] *adj* : psicosomático, sicosomático
psychotherapist [ˌsaɪkoˈθɛrəpɪst] *n* : psicoterapeuta *mf*, sicoterapeuta *mf*
psychotherapy [ˌsaɪkoˈθɛrəpi] *n, pl* **-pies** : psicoterapia *f*, sicoterapia *f*
psychotic[1] [saɪˈkɑţɪk] *adj* : psicótico, sicótico
psychotic[2] *n* : psicótico *m*, -ca *f*; sicótico *m*, -ca *f*
puberty [ˈpju:bərţi] *n* : pubertad *f*
pubic [ˈpju:bɪk] *adj* : pubiano, púbico
public[1] [ˈpʌblɪk] *adj* : público — **publicly** *adv*
public[2] *n* : público *m*
publication [ˌpʌbləˈkeɪʃən] *n* : publicación *f*
publicist [ˈpʌbləsɪst] *n* : publicista *mf*
publicity [pəˈblɪsəţi] *n* : publicidad *f*
publicize [ˈpʌbləˌsaɪz] *vt* **-cized; -cizing** : publicitar
public school *n* : escuela *f* pública
publish [ˈpʌblɪʃ] *vt* : publicar
publisher [ˈpʌblɪʃər] *n* : casa *f* editorial (compañía); editor *m*, -tora *f* (persona)
publishing [ˈpʌblɪʃɪŋ] *n* : industria *f* editorial
pucker[1] [ˈpʌkər] *vt* : fruncir, arrugar — *vi* : arrugarse
pucker[2] *n* : arruga *f*, frunce *m*, fruncido *m*
pudding [ˈpʊdɪŋ] *n* : budín *m*, pudín *m*
puddle [ˈpʌdəl] *n* : charco *m*
pudgy [ˈpʌʤi] *adj* **pudgier; -est** : regordete *fam*, rechoncho *fam*, gordinflón *fam*
puerile [ˈpjʊrəl] *adj* : pueril
Puerto Rican[1] [ˌpwɛrţəˈri:kən, ˌporţə-] *adj* : puertorriqueño
Puerto Rican[2] *n* : puertorriqueño *m*, -ña *f*
puff[1] [ˈpʌf] *vi* **1** BLOW : soplar **2** PANT : resoplar, jadear **3 to puff up** SWELL : hincharse — *vt* **1** BLOW : soplar ⟨to puff smoke : echar humo⟩ **2** INFLATE : inflar, hinchar ⟨to puff out one's cheeks : inflar las mejillas⟩
puff[2] *n* **1** GUST : soplo *m*, ráfaga *f*, bocanada *f* (de humo) **2** DRAW : chupada *f* (a un cigarrillo) **3** SWELLING : hinchazón *f* **4 cream puff** : pastelito *m* de crema **5 powder puff** : borla *f*
puffy [ˈpʌfi] *adj* **puffier; -est 1** SWOLLEN : hinchado, inflado **2** SPONGY : esponjoso, suave
pug [ˈpʌg] *n* **1** : doguillo *m* (perro) **2** *or* **pug nose** : nariz *f* achatada
pugnacious [ˌpʌgˈneɪʃəs] *adj* : pugnaz, agresivo
puke [ˈpju:k] *vi* **puked; puking** : vomitar, devolver
pull[1] [ˈpʊl, ˈpʌl] *vt* **1** DRAW, TUG : tirar de, jalar **2** EXTRACT : sacar, extraer ⟨to pull teeth : sacar muelas⟩ ⟨to pull a gun on : amenazar a (alguien) con pistola⟩ **3** TEAR : desgarrarse (un músculo, etc.) **4 to pull down** : bajar, echar abajo, derribar (un edificio) **5 to pull in** ATTRACT : atraer (una muchedumbre, etc.) ⟨to pull in votes : conseguir votos⟩ **6 to pull off** REMOVE : sacar, quitar **7 to pull oneself together** : calmarse, tranquilizarse **8 to pull up** RAISE : levantar, subir — *vi* **1** DRAW, TUG : tirar, jalar **2** (*indicating movement in a specific direction*) ⟨they pulled in front of us : se nos metieron delante⟩ ⟨to pull to a stop : pararse⟩ **3 to pull through** RECOVER : recobrarse, reponerse **4 to pull together** COOPERATE : trabajar juntos, cooperar
pull[2] *n* **1** TUG : tirón *m*, jalón *m* ⟨he gave it a pull : le dio un tirón⟩ **2** ATTRACTION : atracción *f*, fuerza *f* ⟨the pull of gravity : la fuerza de la gravedad⟩ **3**

INFLUENCE : influencia *f* **4** HANDLE : tirador *m* (de un cajón, etc.) **5 bell pull** : cuerda *f*
pullet [ˈpʊlət] *n* : polla *f*, gallina *f* (joven)
pulley [ˈpʊli] *n, pl* **-leys** : polea *f*
pullover [ˈpʊlˌoːvər] *n* : suéter *m*
pulmonary [ˈpʊlməˌnɛri, ˈpʌl-] *adj* : pulmonar
pulp [ˈpʌlp] *n* **1** : pulpa *f* (de una fruta, etc.) **2** MASH : papilla *f*, pasta *f* ‹wood pulp : pasta de papel, pulpa de papel› ‹to beat to a pulp : hacer papilla (a alguien)› **3** : pulpa *f* (de los dientes)
pulpit [ˈpʊlˌpɪt] *n* : púlpito *m*
pulsate [ˈpʌlˌseɪt] *vi* **-sated; -sating 1** BEAT : latir, palpitar **2** VIBRATE : vibrar
pulsation [ˌpʌlˈseɪʃən] *n* : pulsación *f*
pulse [ˈpʌls] *n* : pulso *m*
pulverize [ˈpʌlvəˌraɪz] *vt* **-ized; -izing** : pulverizar
puma [ˈpuːmə, ˈpjuː-] *n* : puma *m*; león *m*, leona *f* (in various countries)
pumice [ˈpʌməs] *n* : piedra *f* pómez
pummel [ˈpʌməl] *vt* **-meled; -meling** : aporrear, apalear
pump[1] [ˈpʌmp] *vt* **1** : bombear ‹to pump water : bombear agua› ‹to pump (up) a tire : inflar una llanta› **2** : mover (una manivela, un pedal, etc.) de arriba abajo ‹to pump someone's hand : darle un fuerte apretón de manos (a alguien)› **3 to pump out** : sacar, vaciar (con una bomba)
pump[2] *n* **1** : bomba *f* ‹water pump : bomba de agua› **2** SHOE : zapato *m* de tacón
pumpernickel [ˈpʌmpərˌnɪkəl] *n* : pan *m* negro de centeno
pumpkin [ˈpʌmpkɪn, ˈpʌŋkən] *n* : calabaza *f*, zapallo *m Arg, Chile, Peru, Uru*
pun[1] [ˈpʌn] *vi* **punned; punning** : hacer juegos de palabras
pun[2] *n* : juego *m* de palabras, albur *m Mex*
punch[1] [ˈpʌntʃ] *vt* **1** HIT : darle un puñetazo (a alguien), golpear ‹she punched him in the nose : le dio un puñetazo en la nariz› **2** PERFORATE : perforar (papel, etc.), picar (un boleto)
punch[2] *n* **1** : perforadora *f* ‹paper punch : perforadora de papel› **2** BLOW : golpe *m*, puñetazo *m* **3** : ponche *m* ‹fruit punch : ponche de frutas›
punctilious [pəŋkˈtɪliəs] *adj* : puntilloso
punctual [ˈpʌŋktʃʊəl] *adj* : puntual
punctuality [ˌpʌŋktʃʊˈæləṭi] *n* : puntualidad *f*
punctually [ˈpʌŋktʃʊəli] *adv* : puntualmente, a tiempo
punctuate [ˈpʌŋktʃʊˌeɪt] *vt* **-ated; -ating** : puntuar
punctuation [ˌpʌŋktʃʊˈeɪʃən] *n* : puntuación *f*
puncture[1] [ˈpʌŋktʃər] *vt* **-tured; -turing** : pinchar, punzar, perforar, ponchar *Mex*
puncture[2] *n* : pinchazo *m*, ponchadura *f Mex*
pundit [ˈpʌndɪt] *n* : experto *m*, -ta *f*
pungency [ˈpʌndʒəntsi] *n* : acritud *f*, acrimonia *f*
pungent [ˈpʌndʒənt] *adj* : acre
punish [ˈpʌnɪʃ] *vt* : castigar
punishable [ˈpʌnɪʃəbəl] *adj* : punible
punishment [ˈpʌnɪʃmənt] *n* : castigo *m*
punitive [ˈpjuːnəṭɪv] *adj* : punitivo
punt[1] [ˈpʌnt] *vt* : impulsar (un barco) con una pértiga — *vi* : despejar (en deportes)
punt[2] *n* **1** : batea *f* (barco) **2** : patada *f* de despeje (en deportes)
puny [ˈpjuːni] *adj* **-nier; -est** : enclenque, endeble
pup [ˈpʌp] *n* : cachorro *m*, -rra *f* (de un perro); cría *f* (de otros animales)
pupa [ˈpjuːpə] *n, pl* **-pae** [-pi, -ˌpaɪ] *or* **-pas** : crisálida *f*, pupa *f*
pupil [ˈpjuːpəl] *n* **1** : alumno *m*, -na *f* (de colegio) **2** : pupila *f* (del ojo)
puppet [ˈpʌpət] *n* : títere *m*, marioneta *f*
puppy [ˈpʌpi] *n, pl* **-pies** : cachorro *m*, -rra *f*
purchase[1] [ˈpərtʃəs] *vt* **-chased; -chasing** : comprar
purchase[2] *n* **1** PURCHASING : compra *f*, adquisición *f* **2** : compra *f* ‹last-minute purchases : compras de última hora› **3** GRIP : agarre *m*, asidero *m* ‹she got a firm purchase on the wheel : se agarró bien del volante›
purchase order *n* : orden *f* de compra
pure [ˈpjʊr] *adj* **purer; purest** : puro
puree[1] [pjʊˈreɪ, -ˈriː] *vt* **-reed; -reeing** : hacer un puré con
puree[2] *n* : puré *m*
purely [ˈpjʊrli] *adv* **1** WHOLLY : puramente, completamente ‹purely by chance : por pura casualidad› **2** SIMPLY : sencillamente, meramente
purgative [ˈpərgəṭɪv] *n* : purgante *m*
purgatory [ˈpərgəˌtori] *n, pl* **-ries** : purgatorio *m*
purge[1] [ˈpərdʒ] *vt* **purged; purging** : purgar
purge[2] *n* : purga *f*
purification [ˌpjʊrəfəˈkeɪʃən] *n* : purificación *f*
purify [ˈpjʊrəˌfaɪ] *vt* **-fied; -fying** : purificar
puritan [ˈpjʊrətən] *n* : puritano *m*, -na *f* — **puritan** *adj*
puritanical [ˌpjuːrəˈtænɪkəl] *adj* : puritano
purity [ˈpjʊrəṭi] *n* : pureza *f*
purl[1] [ˈpərl] *v* : tejer al revés, tejer del revés
purl[2] *n* : punto *m* del revés
purloin [pərˈlɔɪn, ˈpərˌlɔɪn] *vt* : hurtar, robar
purple [ˈpərpəl] *n* : morado *m*, color *m* púrpura
purport [pərˈport] *vt* : pretender ‹to purport to be : pretender ser›
purpose [ˈpərpəs] *n* **1** INTENTION : propósito *m*, intención *f* ‹on purpose

: a propósito, adrede⟩ **2** FUNCTION : función *f* **3** RESOLUTION : resolución *f*, determinación *f*
purposeful [ˈpərpəsfəl] *adj* : determinado, decidido, resuelto
purposefully [ˈpərpəsfəli] *adv* : decididamente, resueltamente
purposely [ˈpərpəsli] *adv* : intencionadamente, a propósito, adrede
purr[1] [ˈpər] *vi* : ronronear
purr[2] *n* : ronroneo *m*
purse[1] [ˈpərs] *vt* **pursed; pursing** : fruncir ⟨to purse one's lips : fruncir la boca⟩
purse[2] *n* **1** HANDBAG : cartera *f*, bolso *m*, bolsa *f Mex* ⟨a change purse : un monedero⟩ **2** FUNDS : fondos *mpl* **3** PRIZE : premio *m*
pursue [pərˈsuː] *vt* **-sued; -suing 1** CHASE : perseguir **2** SEEK : buscar, tratar de encontrar ⟨to pursue pleasure : buscar el placer⟩ **3** FOLLOW : seguir ⟨the road pursues a northerly course : el camino sigue hacia el norte⟩ **4** : dedicarse a ⟨to pursue a hobby : dedicarse a un pasatiempo⟩
pursuer [pərˈsuːər] *n* : perseguidor *m*, -dora *f*
pursuit [pərˈsuːt] *n* **1** CHASE : persecución *f* **2** SEARCH : búsqueda *f*, busca *f* **3** ACTIVITY : actividad *f*, pasatiempo *m*
purveyor [pərˈveɪər] *n* : proveedor *m*, -dora *f*
pus [ˈpʌs] *n* : pus *m*
push[1] [ˈpʊʃ] *vt* **1** SHOVE : empujar **2** PRESS : apretar, pulsar ⟨push that button : aprieta ese botón⟩ **3** PRESSURE, URGE : presionar **4 to push around** BULLY : intimidar, mangonear — *vi* **1** SHOVE : empujar **2** INSIST : insistir, presionar **3 to push off** LEAVE : marcharse, irse, largarse *fam* **4 to push on** PROCEED : seguir
push[2] *n* **1** SHOVE : empujón *m* **2** DRIVE : empuje *m*, energía *f*, dinamismo *m* **3** EFFORT : esfuerzo *m*
push–button [ˈpʊʃˈbʌtən] *adj* : de botones
pushcart [ˈpʊʃˌkɑrt] *n* : carretilla *f* de mano
pushy [ˈpʊʃi] *adj* **pushier; -est** : mandón, prepotente
pussy [ˈpʊsi] *n, pl* **pussies** : gatito *m*, -ta *f*; minino *m*, -na *f*
pussy willow *n* : sauce *m* blanco
pustule [ˈpʌsˌtʃuːl] *n* : pústula *f*
put [ˈpʊt] *v* **put; putting** *vt* **1** PLACE : poner, colocar ⟨put it on the table : ponlo en la mesa⟩ **2** INSERT : meter **3** (*indicating causation of a state or feeling*) : poner ⟨it put her in a good mood : la puso de buen humor⟩ ⟨to put into effect : poner en práctica⟩ **4** IMPOSE : imponer ⟨they put a tax on it : lo gravaron con un impuesto⟩ **5** SUBJECT : someter, poner ⟨to put to the test : poner a prueba⟩ ⟨to put to death : ejecutar⟩ **6** EXPRESS : expresar, decir ⟨he put it simply : lo dijo sencillamente⟩ **7** APPLY : aplicar ⟨to put one's mind to something : proponerse hacer algo⟩ **8** SET : poner ⟨I put him to work : lo puse a trabajar⟩ **9** ATTACH : dar ⟨to put a high value on : dar gran valor a⟩ **10** PRESENT : presentar, exponer ⟨to put a question to someone : hacer una pregunta a alguien⟩ — *vi* **1 to put to sea** : hacerse a la mar **2 to put up with** : aguantar, soportar
put away *vt* **1** KEEP : guardar **2** *or* **to put aside** : dejar a un lado
put by *vt* SAVE : ahorrar
put down *vt* **1** SUPPRESS : aplastar, suprimir **2** ATTRIBUTE : atribuir ⟨she put it down to luck : lo atribuyó a la suerte⟩
put in *vi* : presentarse ⟨I've put in for the position : me presenté para el puesto⟩ — *vt* DEVOTE : dedicar (unas horas, etc.)
put off *vt* DEFER : aplazar, posponer
put on *vt* **1** ASSUME : afectar, adoptar **2** PRODUCE : presentar (una obra de teatro, etc.) **3** WEAR : ponerse
put out *vt* INCONVENIENCE : importunar, incomodar
putrefy [ˈpjuːtrəˌfaɪ] *v* **-fied; -fying** *vt* : pudrir — *vi* : pudrirse
putrid [ˈpjuːtrɪd] *adj* : putrefacto, pútrido
putter [ˈpʌṭər] *vi or* **to putter around** : entretenerse
putty[1] [ˈpʌṭi] *vt* **-tied; -tying** : poner masilla en
putty[2] *n, pl* **-ties** : masilla *f*
put up *vt* **1** LODGE : alojar **2** CONTRIBUTE : contribuir, pagar
puzzle[1] [ˈpʌzəl] *vt* **-zled; -zling 1** CONFUSE : confundir, dejar perplejo **2 to puzzle out** : dar vueltas a, tratar de resolver
puzzle[2] *n* **1** : rompecabezas *m* ⟨a crossword puzzle : un crucigrama⟩ **2** MYSTERY : misterio *m*, enigma *m*
puzzlement [ˈpʌzəlmənt] *n* : desconcierto *m*, perplejidad *f*
pygmy[1] [ˈpɪgmi] *adj* : enano, pigmeo
pygmy[2] *n, pl* **-mies 1** DWARF : enano *m*, -na *f* **2 Pygmy** : pigmeo *m*, -mea *f*
pylon [ˈpaɪˌlɑn, -lən] *n* **1** : torre *f* de conducta eléctrica **2** : pilón *m* (de un puente)
pyramid [ˈpɪrəˌmɪd] *n* : pirámide *f*
pyre [ˈpaɪr] *n* : pira *f*
pyromania [ˌpaɪroˈmeɪniə] *n* : piromanía *f*
pyromaniac [ˌpaɪroˈmeɪniˌæk] *n* : pirómano *m*, -na *f*
pyrotechnics [ˌpaɪrəˈtɛknɪks] *npl* **1** FIREWORKS : fuegos *mpl* artificiales **2** DISPLAY, SHOW : espectáculo *m*, muestra *f* de virtuosismo ⟨computer pyrotechnics : efectos especiales hechos por computadora⟩
python [ˈpaɪˌθɑn, -θən] *n* : pitón *f*, serpiente *f* pitón

Q

q [ˈkjuː] *n, pl* **q's** *or* **qs** [ˈkjuːz] : decimoséptima letra del alfabeto inglés
quack¹ [ˈkwæk] *vi* : graznar
quack² *n* **1** : graznido *m* (de pato) **2** CHARLATAN : curandero *m*, -ra *f*; matasanos *m fam*
quadrangle [ˈkwɑˌdræŋgəl] *n* **1** COURTYARD : patio *m* interior **2** → **quadrilateral**
quadrant [ˈkwɑdrənt] *n* : cuadrante *m*
quadrilateral [ˌkwɑdrəˈlæṭərəl] *n* : cuadrilátero *m*
quadruped [ˈkwɑdrəˌpɛd] *n* : cuadrúpedo *m*
quadruple [kwɑˈdruːpəl, -ˈdrʌ-; ˈkwɑdrə-] *v* **-pled; -pling** *vt* : cuadruplicar — *vi* : cuadruplicarse
quadruplet [kwɑˈdruːplət, -ˈdrʌ-; ˈkwɑdrə-] *n* : cuatrillizo *m*, -za *f*
quagmire [ˈkwægˌmaɪr, ˈkwɑg-] *n* **1** : lodazal *m*, barrizal *m* **2** PREDICAMENT : atolladero *m*
quail¹ [ˈkweɪl] *vi* : encogerse, acobardarse
quail² *n, pl* **quail** *or* **quails** : codorniz *f*
quaint [ˈkweɪnt] *adj* **1** ODD : extraño, curioso **2** PICTURESQUE : pintoresco — **quaintly** *adv*
quaintness [ˈkweɪntnəs] *n* : rareza *f*, lo curioso
quake¹ [ˈkweɪk] *vi* **quaked; quaking** : temblar
quake² *n* : temblor *m*, terremoto *m*
qualification [ˌkwɑləfəˈkeɪʃən] *n* **1** LIMITATION, RESERVATION : reserva *f*, limitación *f* ⟨without qualification : sin reservas⟩ **2** REQUIREMENT : requisito *m* **3 qualifications** *npl* ABILITY : aptitud *f*, capacidad *f*
qualified [ˈkwɑləˌfaɪd] *adj* : competente, capacitado
qualifier [ˈkwɑləˌfaɪər] *n* **1** : clasificado *m*, -da *f* (en deportes) **2** : calificativo *m* (en gramática)
qualify [ˈkwɑləˌfaɪ] *v* **-fied; -fying** *vt* **1** : matizar ⟨to qualify a statement : matizar una declaración⟩ **2** MODIFY : calificar (en gramática) **3** : habilitar ⟨the certificate qualified her to teach : el certificado la habilitó para enseñar⟩ — *vi* **1** : obtener el título, recibirse ⟨to qualify as an engineer : recibirse de ingeniero⟩ **2** : clasificarse (en deportes)
quality [ˈkwɑləṭi] *n, pl* **-ties** **1** NATURE : carácter *m* **2** ATTRIBUTE : cualidad *f* **3** GRADE : calidad *f* ⟨of good quality : de buena calidad⟩
qualm [ˈkwɑm, ˈkwɑlm, ˈkwɔm] *n* **1** MISGIVING : duda *f*, aprensión *f* **2** RESERVATION, SCRUPLE : escrúpulo *m*, reparo *m*
quandary [ˈkwɑndri] *n, pl* **-ries** : dilema *m*
quantitative [ˈkwɑntəˌteɪṭɪv] *adj* : cuantitativo
quantity [ˈkwɑntəṭi] *n, pl* **-ties** : cantidad *f*
quantum¹ [ˈkwɑntəm] *n* : cuanto *m* (en física)
quantum² *adj* : cuántico
quantum theory [ˈkwɑntəm] *n* : teoría *f* cuántica
quarantine¹ [ˈkwɔrənˌtiːn] *vt* **-tined; -tining** : poner en cuarentena
quarantine² *n* : cuarentena *f*
quarrel¹ [ˈkwɔrəl] *vi* **-reled** *or* **-relled; -reling** *or* **-relling** : pelearse, reñir, discutir
quarrel² *n* : pelea *f*, riña *f*, disputa *f*
quarrelsome [ˈkwɔrəlsəm] *adj* : pendenciero, discutidor
quarry¹ [ˈkwɔri] *vt* **quarried; quarrying** **1** EXTRACT : extraer, sacar ⟨to quarry marble : extraer mármol⟩ **2** EXCAVATE : excavar ⟨to quarry a hill : excavar un cerro⟩
quarry² *n, pl* **quarries** **1** PREY : presa *f* **2** *or* **stone quarry** : cantera *f*
quart [ˈkwɔrt] *n* : cuarto *m* de galón
quarter¹ [ˈkwɔrṭər] *vt* **1** : dividir en cuatro partes **2** LODGE : alojar, acuartelar (tropas)
quarter² *n* **1** : cuarto *m*, cuarta parte *f* ⟨a foot and a quarter : un pie y cuarto⟩ ⟨a quarter after three : las tres y cuarto⟩ **2** : moneda *f* de 25 centavos, cuarto *m* de dólar **3** DISTRICT : barrio *m* ⟨business quarter : barrio comercial⟩ **4** PLACE : parte *f* ⟨from all quarters : de todas partes⟩ ⟨at close quarters : de muy cerca⟩ **5** MERCY : clemencia *f*, cuartel *m* ⟨to give no quarter : no dar cuartel⟩ **6 quarters** *npl* LODGING : alojamiento *m*, cuartel *m* (militar)
quarterback [ˈkwɔrṭərˌbæk] *n* : mariscal *m* de campo
quarterly¹ [ˈkwɔrṭərli] *adv* : cada tres meses, trimestralmente
quarterly² *adj* : trimestral
quarterly³ *n, pl* **-lies** : publicación *f* trimestral
quartermaster [ˈkwɔrṭərˌmæstər] *n* : intendente *mf*
quartet [kwɔrˈtɛt] *n* : cuarteto *m*
quartz [ˈkwɔrts] *n* : cuarzo *m*
quash [ˈkwɑʃ, ˈkwɔʃ] *vt* **1** ANNUL : anular **2** QUELL : sofocar, aplastar
quaver¹ [ˈkweɪvər] *vi* **1** SHAKE : temblar ⟨her voice was quavering : le temblaba la voz⟩ **2** TRILL : trinar
quaver² *n* : temblor *m* (de la voz)
quay [ˈkiː, ˈkeɪ, ˈkweɪ] *n* : muelle *m*
queasiness [ˈkwiːzinəs] *n* : mareo *m*, náusea *f*
queasy [ˈkwiːzi] *adj* **-sier; -est** : mareado
queen [ˈkwiːn] *n* : reina *f*
queenly [ˈkwiːnli] *adj* **-lier; -est** : de reina, regio
queer [ˈkwɪr] *adj* : extraño, raro, curioso — **queerly** *adv*
quell [ˈkwl] *vt* : aplastar, sofocar

quench [ˈkwɛntʃ] *vt* **1** EXTINGUISH : apagar, sofocar **2** SATISFY : saciar, satisfacer (la sed)

querulous [ˈkwɛrələs, ˈkwɛrjələs, ˈkwɪr-] *adj* : quejumbroso, quejoso — **querulously** *adv*

query[1] [ˈkwɪri, ˈkwɛr-] *vt* **-ried; -rying 1** ASK : preguntar, interrogar ⟨we queried the professor : preguntamos al profesor⟩ **2** QUESTION : cuestionar, poner en duda ⟨to query a matter : cuestionar un asunto⟩

query[2] *n, pl* **-ries 1** QUESTION : pregunta *f* **2** DOUBT : duda *f*

quest[1] [ˈkwɛst] *v* : buscar

quest[2] *n* : búsqueda *f*

question[1] [ˈkwɛstʃən] *vt* **1** ASK : preguntar **2** DOUBT : poner en duda, cuestionar **3** INTERROGATE : interrogar — *vi* INQUIRE : inquirir, preguntar

question[2] *n* **1** QUERY : pregunta *f* **2** ISSUE : asunto *m*, problema *f*, cuestión *f* **3** POSSIBILITY : posibilidad *f* ⟨it's out of the question : es indiscutible⟩ **4** DOUBT : duda *f* ⟨to call into question : poner en duda⟩

questionable [ˈkwɛstʃənəbəl] *adj* : dudoso, discutible, cuestionable ⟨questionable results : resultados discutibles⟩ ⟨questionable motives : motivos sospechosos⟩

questioner [ˈkwɛstʃənər] *n* : interrogador *m*, -dora *f*

question mark *n* : signo *m* de interrogación

questionnaire [ˌkwɛstʃəˈnær] *n* : cuestionario *m*

queue[1] [ˈkju:] *vi* **queued; queuing** *or* **queueing** : hacer cola

queue[2] *n* **1** PIGTAIL : coleta *f*, trenza *f* **2** LINE : cola *f*, fila *f*

quibble[1] [ˈkwɪbəl] *vi* **-bled; -bling** : quejarse por nimiedades, andar con sutilezas

quibble[2] *n* : objeción *f* de poca monta, queja *f* insignificante

quick[1] [ˈkwɪk] *adv* : rápidamente

quick[2] *adj* **1** RAPID : rápido **2** ALERT, CLEVER : listo, vivo, agudo **3 a quick temper** : un genio vivo

quick[3] *n* **1** FLESH : carne *f* viva **2 to cut someone to the quick** : herir a alguien en lo más vivo

quicken [ˈkwɪkən] *vt* **1** REVIVE : resucitar **2** AROUSE : estimular, despertar **3** HASTEN : acelerar ⟨she quickened her pace : aceleró el paso⟩

quickly [ˈkwɪkli] *adv* : rápidamente, rápido, de prisa

quickness [ˈkwɪknəs] *n* : rapidez *f*

quicksand [ˈkwɪkˌsænd] *n* : arena *f* movediza

quicksilver [ˈkwɪkˌsɪlvər] *n* : mercurio *m*, azogue *m*

quick–tempered [ˈkwɪkˈtɛmpərd] *adj* : irascible, de genio vivo

quick–witted [ˈkwɪkˈwɪt̬əd] *adj* : agudo

quiet[1] [ˈkwaɪət] *vt* **1** SILENCE : hacer callar, acallar **2** CALM : calmar, tranquilizar — *vi* **to quiet down** : calmarse, tranquilizarse

quiet[2] *adv* : silenciosamente ⟨a quiet-running engine : un motor silencioso⟩

quiet[3] *adj* **1** CALM : tranquilo, calmoso **2** MILD : sosegado, suave ⟨a quiet disposition : un temperamento sosegado⟩ **3** SILENT : silencioso **4** UNOBTRUSIVE : discreto **5** SECLUDED : aislado ⟨a quiet nook : un rincón aislado⟩ — **quietly** *adv*

quiet[4] *n* **1** CALM : calma *f*, tranquilidad *f* **2** SILENCE : silencio *m*

quietness [ˈkwaɪətnəs] *n* : suavidad *f*, tranquilidad *f*, quietud *f*

quietude [ˈkwaɪəˌtu:d, -ˌtju:d] *n* : quietud *f*, reposo *m*

quill [ˈkwɪl] *n* **1** SPINE : púa *f* (de un puerco espín) **2** : pluma *f* (para escribir)

quilt[1] [ˈkwɪlt] *vt* : acolchar

quilt[2] *n* : colcha *f*, edredón *m*

quince [ˈkwɪnts] *n* : membrillo *m*

quinine [ˈkwaɪˌnaɪn] *n* : quinina *f*

quintessence [kwɪnˈtɛsənts] *n* : quintaesencia *f*

quintet [kwɪnˈtɛt] *n* : quinteto *m*

quintuple [kwɪnˈtu:pəl, -ˈtju:-, -ˈtʌ-; ˈkwɪntə-] *adj* : quíntuplo

quintuplet [kwɪnˈtʌplət, -ˈtu:-, -ˈtju:-; ˈkwɪntə-] *n* : quintillizo *m*, -za *f*

quip[1] [ˈkwɪp] *vi* **quipped; quipping** : bromear

quip[2] *n* : ocurrencia *f*, salida *f*

quirk [ˈkwərk] *n* : peculiaridad *f*, rareza *f* ⟨a quirk of fate : un capricho del destino⟩

quirky [ˈkwərki] *adj* **-kier; -est** : peculiar, raro

quit [ˈkwɪt] *v* **quit; quitting** *vt* : dejar, abandonar ⟨to quit smoking : dejar de fumar⟩ — *vi* **1** STOP : parar **2** RESIGN : dimitir, renunciar

quite [ˈkwaɪt] *adv* **1** COMPLETELY : completamente, totalmente **2** RATHER : bastante ⟨quite near : bastante cerca⟩

quits [ˈkwɪts] *adj* **to call it quits** : quedar en paz

quitter [ˈkwɪt̬ər] *n* : derrotista *mf*

quiver[1] [ˈkwɪvər] *vi* : temblar, estremecerse, vibrar

quiver[2] *n* **1** : carcaj *m*, aljaba *f* (para flechas) **2** TREMBLING : temblor *m*, estremecimiento *m*

quixotic [kwɪkˈsɑt̬ɪk] *adj* : quijotesco

quiz[1] [ˈkwɪz] *vt* **quizzed; quizzing** : interrogar, hacer una prueba a (en el colegio)

quiz[2] *n, pl* **quizzes** : examen *m* corto, prueba *f*

quizzical [ˈkwɪzɪkəl] *adj* **1** TEASING : burlón **2** CURIOUS : curioso, interrogativo

quorum [ˈkworəm] *n* : quórum *m*

quota [ˈkwoːt̬ə] *n* : cuota *f*, cupo *m*
quotable [ˈkwoːt̬əbəl] *adj* : citable
quotation [kwoˈteɪʃən] *n* **1** CITATION : cita *f* **2** ESTIMATE : presupuesto *m*, estimación *f* **3** PRICE : cotización *f*
quotation marks *npl* : comillas *fpl*
quote[1] [ˈkwoːt] *vt* **quoted; quoting 1** CITE : citar **2** VALUE : cotizar (en finanzas)
quote[2] *n* **1** → **quotation 2 quotes** *npl* → **quotation marks**
quotient [ˈkwoːʃənt] *n* : cociente *m*

R

r [ˈɑr] *n, pl* **r's** *or* **rs** [ˈɑrz] : decimoctava letra del alfabeto inglés
rabbi [ˈræˌbaɪ] *n* : rabino *m*, -na *f*
rabbit [ˈræbət] *n, pl* **-bit** *or* **-bits** : conejo *m*, -ja *f*
rabble [ˈræbəl] *n* **1** MASSES : populacho *m* **2** RIFFRAFF : chusma *f*, gentuza *f*
rabid [ˈræbɪd] *adj* **1** : rabioso, afectado con la rabia **2** FURIOUS : furioso **3** FANATIC : fanático
rabies [ˈreɪbiːz] *ns & pl* : rabia *f*
raccoon [ræˈkuːn] *n, pl* **-coon** *or* **-coons** : mapache *m*
race[1] [ˈreɪs] *vi* **raced; racing 1** : correr, competir (en una carrera) **2** RUSH : ir a toda prisa, ir corriendo
race[2] *n* **1** CURRENT : corriente *f* (de agua) **2** : carrera *f* ⟨dog race : carrera de perros⟩ ⟨the presidential race : la carrera presidential⟩ **3** : raza *f* ⟨the black race : la raza negra⟩ ⟨the human race : el género humano⟩
racecourse [ˈreɪsˌkors] *n* : pista *f* (de carreras)
racehorse [ˈreɪsˌhors] *n* : caballo *m* de carreras
racer [ˈreɪsər] *n* : corredor *m*, -dora *f*
racetrack [ˈreɪsˌtræk] *n* : pista *f* (de carreras)
racial [ˈreɪʃəl] *adj* : racial — **racially** *adv*
racism [ˈreɪˌsɪzəm] *n* : racismo *m*
racist [ˈreɪsɪst] *n* : racista *mf*
rack[1] [ˈræk] *vt* **1** : atormentar ⟨racked with pain : atormentado por el dolor⟩ **2 to rack one's brains** : devanarse los sesos
rack[2] *n* **1** SHELF, STAND : estante *m* ⟨a luggage rack : un portaequipajes⟩ ⟨a coatrack : un perchero, una percha⟩ **2** : potro *m* (instrumento de la tortura)
racket [ˈrækət] *n* **1** : raqueta *f* (en deportes) **2** DIN : estruendo *m*, bulla *f*, jaleo *m fam* **3** SWINDLE : estafa *f*, timo *m fam*
racketeer [ˌrækəˈtɪr] *n* : estafador *m*, -dora *f*
raconteur [ˌræˌkɑnˈtər] *n* : anecdotista *mf*
racy [ˈreɪsi] *adj* **racier; -est** : subido de tono, picante
radar [ˈreɪˌdɑr] *n* : radar *m*
radial [ˈreɪdiəl] *adj* : radial
radiance [ˈreɪdiənts] *n* : resplandor *m*
radiant [ˈreɪdiənt] *adj* : radiante — **radiantly** *adv*
radiate [ˈreɪdiˌeɪt] *v* **-ated; -ating** *vt* : irradiar, emitir ⟨to radiate heat : irradiar el calor⟩ ⟨to radiate happiness : rebosar de alegría⟩ — *vi* **1** : irradiar **2** SPREAD : salir, extenderse ⟨to radiate (out) from the center : salir del centro⟩
radiation [ˌreɪdiˈeɪʃən] *n* : radiación *f*
radiator [ˈreɪdiˌeɪt̬ər] *n* : radiador *m*
radical[1] [ˈrædɪkəl] *adj* : radical — **radically** [-kli] *adv*
radical[2] *n* : radical *mf*
radicalism [ˈrædɪkəˌlɪzəm] *n* : radicalismo *m*
radii → **radius**
radio[1] [ˈreɪdiˌoː] *v* : llamar por radio, transmitir por radio
radio[2] *n, pl* **-dios** : radio *m* (aparato), radio *f* (emisora, radiodifusión)
radioactive [ˈreɪdioˈæktɪv] *adj* : radiactivo, radioactivo
radioactivity [ˌreɪdioˌækˈtɪvət̬i] *n, pl* **-ties** : radiactividad *f*, radioactividad *f*
radiologist [ˌreɪdiˈɑləʤɪst] *n* : radiólogo *m*, -ga *f*
radiology [ˌreɪdiˈɑləʤi] *n* : radiología *f*
radish [ˈrædɪʃ] *n* : rábano *m*
radium [ˈreɪdiəm] *n* : radio *m*
radius [ˈreɪdiəs] *n, pl* **radii** [-diˌaɪ] : radio *m*
radon [ˈreɪˌdɑn] *n* : radón *m*
raffle[1] [ˈræfəl] *vt* **-fled; -fling** : rifar, sortear
raffle[2] *n* : rifa *f*, sorteo *m*
raft [ˈræft] *n* **1** : balsa *f* ⟨rubber rafts : balsas de goma⟩ **2** LOT, SLEW : montón *m* ⟨a raft of documents : un montón de documentos⟩
rafter [ˈræftər] *n* : par *m*, viga *f*
rag [ˈræg] *n* **1** CLOTH : trapo *m* **2 rags** *npl* TATTERS : harapos *mpl*, andrajos *mpl*
ragamuffin [ˈrægəˌmʌfən] *n* : pilluelo *m*, -la *f*
rage[1] [ˈreɪʤ] *vi* **raged; raging 1** : estar furioso, rabiar ⟨to fly into a rage : enfurecerse⟩ **2** : bramar, hacer estragos ⟨the wind was raging : el viento bramaba⟩ ⟨flu raged through the school : la gripe hizo estragos por el colegio⟩
rage[2] *n* **1** ANGER : furia *f*, ira *f*, cólera *f* **2** FAD : moda *f*, furor *m*
ragged [ˈrægəd] *adj* **1** UNEVEN : irregular, desigual **2** TORN : hecho jirones **3** TATTERED : andrajoso, harapiento
ragout [ræˈguː] *n* : ragú *m*, estofado *m*
ragtime [ˈrægˌtaɪm] *n* : ragtime *m*
ragweed [ˈrægˌwiːd] *n* : ambrosía *f*
raid[1] [ˈreɪd] *vt* **1** : invadir, hacer una incursión en ⟨raided by enemy troops

: invadido por tropas enemigas⟩ **2** : asaltar, atracar ⟨the gang raided the warehouse : la pandilla asaltó el almacén⟩ **3** : allanar, hacer una redada en ⟨police raided the house : la policía allanó la vivienda⟩

raid[2] *n* **1** : invasión *f* (militar) **2** : asalto *m* (por delincuentes) **3** : redada *f*, allanamiento *m* (por la policía)

raider [ˈreɪdər] *n* **1** ATTACKER : asaltante *mf*; invasor *m*, -sora *f* **2 corporate raider** : tiburón *m*

rail[1] [ˈreɪl] *vi* **1 to rail against** REVILE : denostar contra **2 to rail at** SCOLD : regañar, reprender

rail[2] *n* **1** BAR : barra *f*, barrera *f* **2** HANDRAIL : pasamanos *m*, barandilla *f* **3** TRACK : riel *m* (para ferrocarriles) **4** RAILROAD : ferrocarril *m*

railing [ˈreɪlɪŋ] *n* **1** : baranda *f* (de un balcón, etc.) **2** RAILS : verja *f*

raillery [ˈreɪləri] *n, pl* **-leries** : bromas *fpl*

railroad [ˈreɪlˌroːd] *n* : ferrocarril *m*

railway [ˈreɪlˌweɪ] → **railroad**

raiment [ˈreɪmənt] *n* : vestiduras *fpl*

rain[1] [ˈreɪn] *vi* **1** : llover ⟨it's raining : está lloviendo⟩ **2 to rain down** SHOWER : llover ⟨insults rained down on him : le llovieron los insultos⟩

rain[2] *n* : lluvia *f*

rainbow [ˈreɪnˌboː] *n* : arco *m* iris

raincoat [ˈreɪnˌkoːt] *n* : impermeable *m*

raindrop [ˈreɪnˌdrɑp] *n* : gota *f* de lluvia

rainfall [ˈreɪnˌfɔl] *n* : lluvia *f*, precipitación *f*

rainstorm [ˈreɪnˌstɔrm] *n* : temporal *m* (de lluvia)

rainwater [ˈreɪnˌwɔt̬ər] *n* : agua *f* de lluvia

rainy [ˈreɪni] *adj* **rainier; -est** : lluvioso

raise[1] [ˈreɪz] *vt* **raised; raising 1** LIFT : levantar, subir, alzar ⟨to raise one's spirits : levantarle el ánimo a alguien⟩ **2** ERECT : levantar, erigir **3** COLLECT : recaudar ⟨to raise money : recaudar dinero⟩ **4** REAR : criar ⟨to raise one's children : criar uno a sus niños⟩ **5** GROW : cultivar **6** INCREASE : aumentar, subir **7** PROMOTE : ascender **8** PROVOKE : provocar ⟨it raised a laugh : provocó una risa⟩ **9** BRING UP : sacar (temas, objeciones, etc.)

raise[2] *n* : aumento *m*

raisin [ˈreɪzən] *n* : pasa *f*

raja *or* **rajah** [ˈrɑʤə, -ˌʤɑ, -ˌʒɑ] *n* : rajá *m*

rake[1] [ˈreɪk] *v* **raked; raking** *vt* **1** : rastrillar ⟨to rake leaves : rastrillar las hojas⟩ **2** SWEEP : barrer ⟨raked with gunfire : barrido con metralla⟩ — *vi* **to rake through** : revolver, hurgar en

rake[2] *n* **1** : rastrillo *m* **2** LIBERTINE : libertino *m*, -na *f*; calavera *m*

rakish [ˈreɪkɪʃ] *adj* **1** JAUNTY : desenvuelto, desenfadado **2** DISSOLUTE : libertino, disoluto

rally[1] [ˈræli] *v* **-lied; -lying** *vi* **1** MEET, UNITE : reunirse, congregarse **2** RECOVER : recuperarse — *vt* **1** ASSEMBLE : reunir (tropas, etc.) **2** RECOVER : recobrar (la fuerza, el ánimo, etc.)

rally[2] *n, pl* **-lies** : reunión *f*, mitin *m*, manifestación *f*

ram[1] [ˈræm] *v* **rammed; ramming** *vt* **1** DRIVE : hincar, clavar ⟨he rammed it into the ground : lo hincó en la tierra⟩ **2** SMASH : estrellar, embestir — *vi* COLLIDE : chocar (contra), estrellarse

ram[2] *n* **1** : carnero *m* (animal) **2 battering ram** : ariete *m*

RAM [ˈræm] *n* : RAM *f*

ramble[1] [ˈræmbəl] *vi* **-bled; -bling 1** WANDER : pasear, deambular **2 to ramble on** : divagar, perder el hilo **3** SPREAD : trepar (dícese de una planta)

ramble[2] *n* : paseo *m*, excursión *f*

rambler [ˈræmblər] *n* **1** WALKER : excursionista *mf* **2** ROSE : rosa *f* trepadora

rambunctious [ræmˈbʌŋkʃəs] *adj* UNRULY : alborotado

ramification [ˌræməfəˈkeɪʃən] *n* : ramificación *f*

ramify [ˈræməˌfaɪ] *vi* **-fied; -fying** : ramificarse

ramp [ˈræmp] *n* : rampa *f*

rampage[1] [ˈræmˌpeɪʤ, ræmˈpeɪʤ] *vi* **-paged; -paging** : andar arrasando todo, correr destrozando

rampage[2] [ˈræmˌpeɪʤ] *n* : alboroto *m*, frenesí *m* (de violencia)

rampant [ˈræmpənt] *adj* : desenfrenado

rampart [ˈræmˌpɑrt] *n* : terraplén *m*, muralla *f*

ramrod [ˈræmˌrɑd] *n* : baqueta *f*

ramshackle [ˈræmˌʃækəl] *adj* : destartalado

ran → **run**

ranch [ˈrænʧ] *n* **1** : hacienda *f*, rancho *m*, finca *f* ganadera **2** FARM : granja *f* ⟨fruit ranch : granja de frutas⟩

rancher [ˈrænʧər] *n* : estanciero *m*, -ra *f*; ranchero *m*, -ra *f*

rancid [ˈræn*t*sɪd] *adj* : rancio

rancor [ˈræŋkər] *n* : rencor *m*

random [ˈrændəm] *adj* **1** : fortuito, aleatorio **2 at ~** : al azar — **randomly** *adv*

rang → **ring**

range[1] [ˈreɪnʤ] *v* **ranged; ranging** *vt* ARRANGE : alinear, ordenar, arreglar — *vi* **1** ROAM : deambular ⟨to range through the town : deambular por el pueblo⟩ **2** EXTEND : extenderse ⟨the results range widely : los resultados se extienden mucho⟩ **3** VARY : variar ⟨discounts range from 20% to 40% : los descuentos varían entre 20% y 40%⟩

range[2] *n* **1** ROW : fila *f*, hilera *f* ⟨a mountain range : una cordillera⟩ **2** GRASSLAND : pradera *f*, pampa *f* **3** STOVE : cocina *f* **4** VARIETY : variedad *f*, gama *f* **5** SPHERE : ámbito *m*, esfera *f*, campo *m* **6** REACH : registro *m* (de la voz), alcance *m* (de un arma de fuego) **7 shooting range** : campo *m* de tiro

ranger [ˈreɪndʒər] *n or* **forest ranger** : guardabosque *mf*

rangy [ˈreɪndʒi] *adj* **rangier; -est** : alto y delgado

rank[1] [ˈræŋk] *vt* **1** RANGE : alinear, ordenar, poner en fila **2** CLASSIFY : clasificar — *vi* **1 to rank above** : ser superior a **2 to rank among** : encontrarse entre, figurar entre

rank[2] *adj* **1** LUXURIANT : lozano, exuberante (dícese de una planta) **2** SMELLY : fétido, maloliente **3** OUTRIGHT : completo, absoluto ⟨a rank injustice : una injusticia manifiesta⟩

rank[3] *n* **1** LINE, ROW : fila *f* ⟨to close ranks : cerrar filas⟩ **2** GRADE, POSITION : grado *m*, rango *m* (militar) ⟨to pull rank : abusar de su autoridad⟩ **3** CLASS : categoría *f*, clase *f* **4 ranks** *npl* : soldados *mpl* rasos

rank and file *n* **1** RANKS : soldados *mpl* rasos **2** : bases *fpl* (de un partido, etc.)

rankle [ˈræŋkəl] *v* **-kled; -kling** *vi* : doler — *vt* : irritar, herir

ransack [ˈræn,sæk] *vt* : revolver, desvalijar, registrar de arriba abajo

ransom[1] [ˈræn*t*səm] *vt* : rescatar, pagar un rescate por

ransom[2] *n* : rescate *m*

rant [ˈrænt] *vi or* **to rant and rave** : despotricar, desvariar

rap[1] [ˈræp] *v* **rapped; rapping** *vt* **1** KNOCK : golpetear, dar un golpe en **2** CRITICIZE : criticar — *vi* **1** CHAT : charlar, cotorrear *fam* **2** KNOCK : dar un golpe

rap[2] *n* **1** BLOW, KNOCK : golpe *m*, golpecito *m* **2** CHAT : charla *f* **3** *or* **rap music** : rap *m* **4 to take the rap** : pagar el pato *fam*

rapacious [rəˈpeɪʃəs] *adj* **1** GREEDY : avaricioso, codicioso **2** PREDATORY : rapaz, de rapiña **3** RAVENOUS : voraz

rape[1] [ˈreɪp] *vt* **raped; raping** : violar

rape[2] *n* **1** : colza *f* (planta) **2** : violación *f* (de una persona)

rapid [ˈræpɪd] *adj* : rápido — **rapidly** *adv*

rapidity [rəˈpɪdəṭi] *n* : rapidez *f*

rapids [ˈræpɪdz] *npl* : rápidos *mpl*

rapier [ˈreɪpiər] *n* : estoque *m*

rapist [ˈreɪpɪst] *n* : violador *m*, -dora *f*

rapper [ˈræpər] *n* : cantante *mf* de rap; rapero *m*, -ra *f*

rapport [ræˈpor] *n* : relación *f* armoniosa, entendimiento *m*

rapt [ˈræpt] *adj* : absorto, embelesado

rapture [ˈræptʃər] *n* : éxtasis *m*

rapturous [ˈræptʃərəs] *adj* : extasiado, embelesado

rare [ˈrær] *adj* **rarer; rarest 1** RAREFIED : enrarecido **2** FINE : excelente, excepcional ⟨a rare talent : un talento excepcional⟩ **3** UNCOMMON : raro, poco común **4** : poco cocido (dícese de la carne)

rarefy [ˈrærə,faɪ] *vt* **-fied; -fying** : rarificar, enrarecer

rarely [ˈrærli] *adv* SELDOM : pocas veces, rara vez

raring [ˈrærən, -ɪŋ] *adj* : lleno de entusiasmo, con muchas ganas

rarity [ˈrærəṭi] *n, pl* **-ties** : rareza *f*

rascal [ˈræskəl] *n* : pillo *m*, -lla *f*; pícaro *m*, -ra *f*

rash[1] [ˈræʃ] *adj* : imprudente, precipitado — **rashly** *adv*

rash[2] *n* : sarpullido *m*, erupción *f*

rashness [ˈræʃnəs] *n* : precipitación *f*, impetuosidad *f*

rasp[1] [ˈræsp] *vt* **1** SCRAPE : raspar, escofinar **2 to rasp out** : decir en voz áspera

rasp[2] *n* : escofina *f*

raspberry [ˈræz,bɛri] *n, pl* **-ries** : frambuesa *f*

rat [ˈræt] *n* : rata *f*

ratchet [ˈrætʃət] *n* : trinquete *m*

rate[1] [ˈreɪt] *vt* **rated; rating 1** CONSIDER, REGARD : considerar, estimar **2** DESERVE : merecer

rate[2] *n* **1** PACE, SPEED : velocidad *f*, ritmo *m* ⟨at this rate : a este paso⟩ **2** : índice *m*, tasa *f* ⟨birth rate : índice de natalidad⟩ ⟨interest rate : tasa de interés⟩ **3** CHARGE, PRICE : precio *m*, tarifa *f*

rather [ˈræðər, ˈrʌ-, ˈrɑ-] *adv* **1** (*indicating preference*) ⟨she would rather stay in the house : preferiría quedarse en casa⟩ ⟨I'd rather not : mejor que no⟩ **2** (*indicating preciseness*) ⟨my father, or rather my stepfather : mi padre, o mejor dicho mi padrastro⟩ **3** INSTEAD : sino que, más que, al contrario ⟨I'm not pleased; rather I'm disappointed : no estoy satisfecho, sino desilusionado⟩ **4** SOMEWHAT : algo, un tanto ⟨rather strange : un poco extraño⟩ **5** QUITE : bastante ⟨rather difficult : bastante difícil⟩

ratification [,ræṭəfəˈkeɪʃən] *n* : ratificación *f*

ratify [ˈræṭə,faɪ] *vt* **-fied; -fying** : ratificar

rating [ˈreɪṭɪŋ] *n* **1** STANDING : clasificación *f*, posición *f* **2 ratings** *npl* : índice *m* de audiencia

ratio [ˈreɪʃio] *n, pl* **-tios** : proporción *f*, relación *f*

ration[1] [ˈræʃən, ˈreɪʃən] *vt* : racionar

ration[2] *n* **1** : ración *f* **2 rations** *npl* PROVISIONS : víveres *mpl*

rational [ˈræʃənəl] *adj* : racional, razonable, lógico — **rationally** *adv*

rationale [,ræʃəˈnæl] *n* **1** EXPLANATION : explicación *f* **2** BASIS : base *f*, razones *fpl*

rationality [,ræʃəˈnæləṭi] *n, pl* **-ties** : racionalidad *f*

rationalization [,ræʃənələˈzeɪʃən] *n* : racionalización *f*

rationalize [ˈræʃənə,laɪz] *vt* **-ized; -izing** : racionalizar

rattle[1] [ˈræṭəl] *v* **-tled; -tling** *vi* **1** CLATTER : traquetear, hacer ruido **2 to rattle on** CHATTER : parlotear *fam* — *vt*

1 : hacer sonar, agitar ⟨the wind rattled the door : el viento sacudió la puerta⟩ **2** DISCONCERT, WORRY : desconcertar, poner nervioso **3 to rattle off** : despachar, recitar, decir de corrido

rattle[2] *n* **1** CLATTER : traqueteo *m*, ruido *m* **2** *or* **baby's rattle** : sonajero *m* **3** : cascabel *m* (de una culebra)

rattler [ˈræt̬ələr] → **rattlesnake**

rattlesnake [ˈræt̬əlˌsneɪk] *n* : serpiente *f* de cascabel

ratty [ˈræt̬i] *adj* **rattier; -est** : raído, andrajoso

raucous [ˈrɔkəs] *adj* **1** HOARSE : ronco **2** BOISTEROUS : escandaloso, bullicioso — **raucously** *adv*

ravage[1] [ˈrævɪʤ] *vt* **-aged; -aging** : devastar, arrasar, hacer estragos

ravage[2] *n* : destrozo *m*, destrucción *f* ⟨the ravages of war : los estragos de la guerra⟩

rave [ˈreɪv] *vi* **raved; raving 1** : delirar, desvariar ⟨to rave like a maniac : desvariar como un loco⟩ **2 to rave about** : hablar con entusiasmo sobre, entusiasmarse por

ravel [ˈrævəl] *v* **-eled** *or* **-elled; -eling** *or* **-elling** *vt* UNRAVEL : desenredar, desenmarañar — *vi* FRAY : deshilacharse

raven [ˈreɪvən] *n* : cuervo *m*

ravenous [ˈrævənəs] *adj* : hambriento, voraz — **ravenously** *adv*

ravine [rəˈviːn] *n* : barranco *m*, quebrada *f*

ravish [ˈrævɪʃ] *vt* **1** PLUNDER : saquear **2** ENCHANT : embelesar, cautivar, encantar

raw [ˈrɔ] *adj* **rawer; rawest 1** UNCOOKED : crudo **2** UNTREATED : sin tratar, sin refinar, puro ⟨raw data : datos en bruto⟩ ⟨raw materials : materias primas⟩ **3** INEXPERIENCED : novato, inexperto **4** OPEN : abierto, en carne viva ⟨a raw sore : una llaga abierta⟩ **5** : frío y húmedo ⟨a raw day : un día crudo⟩ **6** UNFAIR : injusto ⟨a raw deal : un trato injusto, una injusticia⟩

rawhide [ˈrɔˌhaɪd] *n* : cuero *m* sin curtir

ray [ˈreɪ] *n* **1** : rayo *m* (de la luz, etc.) ⟨a ray of hope : un resquicio de esperanza⟩ **2** : raya *f* (pez)

rayon [ˈreɪˌɑn] *n* : rayón *m*

raze [ˈreɪz] *vt* **razed; razing** : arrasar, demoler

razor [ˈreɪzər] *n* **1** *or* **straight razor** : navaja *f* (de afeitar) **2** *or* **safety razor** : maquinilla *f* de afeitar, rastrillo *m Mex* **3** SHAVER : afeitadora *f*, rasuradora *f*

reach[1] [ˈriːʧ] *vt* **1** EXTEND : extender, alargar ⟨to reach out one's hand : extender la mano⟩ **2** : alcanzar ⟨I couldn't reach the apple : no pude alcanzar la manzana⟩ **3** : llegar a, llegar hasta ⟨the shadow reached the wall : la sombra llegó hasta la pared⟩ **4** CONTACT : contactar, ponerse en contacto con — *vi* **1** *or* **to reach out** : extender la mano **2** STRETCH : extenderse **3 to reach for** : tratar de agarrar

reach[2] *n* : alcance *m*, extensión *f*

react [riˈækt] *vi* : reaccionar

reaction [riˈækʃən] *n* : reacción *f*

reactionary[1] [riˈækʃəˌnɛri] *adj* : reaccionario

reactionary[2] *n, pl* **-ries** : reaccionario *m*, -ria *f*

reactor [riˈæktər] *n* : reactor *m* ⟨nuclear reactor : reactor nuclear⟩

read[1] [ˈriːd] *v* **read** [ˈrɛd]; **reading** *vt* **1** : leer ⟨to read a story : leer un cuento⟩ **2** INTERPRET : interpretar ⟨it can be read two ways : se puede interpretar de dos maneras⟩ **3** : decir, poner ⟨the sign read "No smoking" : el letrero decía "No Fumar"⟩ **4** : marcar ⟨the thermometer reads 70° : el termómetro marca 70°⟩ — *vi* **1** : leer ⟨he can read : sabe leer⟩ **2** SAY : decir ⟨the list reads as follows : la lista dice lo siguiente⟩

read[2] *n* **to be a good read** : ser una lectura amena

readable [ˈriːdəbəl] *adj* : legible — **readably** [-bli] *adv*

reader [ˈriːdər] *n* : lector *m*, -tora *f*

readily [ˈrɛdəli] *adv* **1** WILLINGLY : de buena gana, con gusto **2** EASILY : fácilmente, con facilidad

readiness [ˈrɛdinəs] *n* **1** WILLINGNESS : buena disposición *f* **2 to be in readiness** : estar preparado

reading [ˈriːdɪŋ] *n* : lectura *f*

readjust [ˌriːəˈʤʌst] *vt* : reajustar — *vi* : volverse a adaptar

readjustment [ˌriːəˈʤʌstmənt] *n* : reajuste *m*

ready[1] [ˈrɛdi] *vt* **readied; readying** : preparar

ready[2] *adj* **readier; -est 1** PREPARED : listo, preparado **2** WILLING : dispuesto **3** : a punto de ⟨ready to cry : a punto de llorar⟩ **4** AVAILABLE : disponible ⟨ready cash : efectivo⟩ **5** QUICK : vivo, agudo ⟨a ready wit : un ingenio agudo⟩

ready–made [ˈrɛdiˈmeɪd] *adj* : preparado, confeccionado

reaffirm [ˌriːəˈfərm] *vt* : reafirmar

real[1] [ˈriːl] *adv* VERY : muy ⟨we had a real good time : lo pasamos muy bien⟩

real[2] *adj* **1** : inmobiliario ⟨real property : bien inmueble, bien raíz⟩ **2** GENUINE : auténtico, genuino **3** ACTUAL, TRUE : real, verdadero ⟨a real friend : un verdadero amigo⟩ **4 for real** SERIOUSLY : de veras, de verdad

real estate *n* : propiedad *f* inmobiliaria, bienes *mpl* raíces

realign [ˌriːəˈlaɪn] *vt* : realinear

realignment [ˌriːəˈlaɪnmənt] *n* : realineamiento *m*

realism [ˈriːəˌlɪzəm] *n* : realismo *m*

realist [ˈriːəlɪst] *n* : realista *mf*

realistic [ˌriːəˈlɪstɪk] *adj* : realista

realistically [ˌriːəˈlɪstɪkli] *adv* : de manera realista

reality [ri'æləṭi] *n, pl* **-ties** : realidad *f*
realizable [ˌri:ə'laɪzəbəl] *adj* : realizable, alcanzable
realization [ˌri:ələ'zeɪʃən] *n* : realización *f*
realize ['ri:əˌlaɪz] *vt* **-ized; -izing 1** ACCOMPLISH : realizar, llevar a cabo **2** GAIN : obtener, realizar, sacar ‹to realize a profit : realizar beneficios› **3** UNDERSTAND : darse cuenta de, saber
really ['rɪli, 'ri:-] *adv* **1** ACTUALLY : de verdad, en realidad **2** TRULY : verdaderamente, realmente **3** FRANKLY : francamente, en serio
realm ['rɛlm] *n* **1** KINGDOM : reino *m* **2** SPHERE : esfera *f*, campo *m*
ream[1] ['ri:m] *vt* : escariar
ream[2] *n* **1** : resma *f* (de papel) **2 reams** *npl* LOADS : montones *mpl*
reap ['ri:p] *v* : cosechar
reaper ['ri:pər] *n* **1** : cosechador *m*, -dora *f* (persona) **2** : cosechadora *f* (máquina)
reappear [ˌri:ə'pɪr] *vi* : reaparecer
reappearance [ˌri:ə'pɪrənts] *n* : reaparición *f*
rear[1] ['rɪr] *vt* **1** LIFT, RAISE : levantar **2** BREED, BRING UP : criar — *vi or* **to rear up** : encabritarse
rear[2] *adj* : trasero, posterior, de atrás
rear[3] *n* **1** BACK : parte *f* de atrás ‹to bring up the rear : cerrar la marcha› **2** *or* **rear end** : trasero *m*
rear admiral *n* : contraalmirante *mf*
rearrange [ˌri:ə'reɪndʒ] *vt* **-ranged; -ranging** : colocar de otra manera, volver a arreglar, reorganizar
rearview mirror ['rɪrˌvju:-] *n* : retrovisor *m*
reason[1] ['ri:zən] *vt* THINK : pensar — *vi* : razonar ‹I can't reason with her : no puedo razonar con ella›
reason[2] *n* **1** CAUSE, GROUND : razón *f*, motivo *m* ‹the reason for his trip : el motivo de su viaje› ‹for this reason : por esta razón, por lo cual› ‹the reason why : la razón por la cual, el porqué› **2** SENSE : razón *f* ‹to lose one's reason : perder los sesos› ‹to listen to reason : avenirse a razones›
reasonable ['ri:zənəbəl] *adj* **1** SENSIBLE : razonable **2** INEXPENSIVE : barato, económico
reasonably ['ri:zənəbli] *adv* **1** SENSIBLY : razonablemente **2** FAIRLY : bastante
reasoning ['ri:zənɪŋ] *n* : razonamiento *m*, raciocinio *m*, argumentos *mpl*
reassess [ˌri:ə'sɛs] *vt* : revaluar, reconsiderar
reassurance [ˌri:ə'ʃʊrənts] *n* : consuelo *m*, palabras *fpl* alentadoras
reassure [ˌri:ə'ʃʊr] *vt* **-sured; -suring** : tranquilizar
reassuring [ˌri:ə'ʃʊrɪŋ] *adj* : tranquilizador
reawaken [ˌri:ə'weɪkən] *vt* : volver a despertar, reavivar
rebate ['ri:ˌbeɪt] *n* : reembolso *m*, devolución *f*
rebel[1] [rɪ'bɛl] *vi* **-belled; -belling** : rebelarse, sublevarse
rebel[2] ['rɛbəl] *adj* : rebelde
rebel[3] ['rɛbəl] *n* : rebelde *mf*
rebellion [rɪ'bɛljən] *n* : rebelión *f*
rebellious [rɪ'bɛljəs] *adj* : rebelde
rebelliousness [rɪ'bɛljəsnəs] *n* : rebeldía *f*
rebirth [ˌri:'bərθ] *n* : renacimiento *m*
reboot [ri'bu:t] *vt* : reiniciar (una computadora)
reborn [ri:'bɔrn] *adj* **to be reborn** : renacer
rebound[1] ['ri:ˌbaʊnd, ˌri:'baʊnd] *vi* : rebotar
rebound[2] ['ri:ˌbaʊnd] *n* : rebote *m*
rebuff[1] [ri'bʌf] *vt* : desairar, rechazar
rebuff[2] *n* : desaire *m*, rechazo *m*
rebuild [ˌri:'bɪld] *vt* **-built** [-'bɪlt]; **-building** : reconstruir
rebuke[1] [ri'bju:k] *vt* **-buked; -buking** : reprender, regañar
rebuke[2] *n* : reprimenda *f*, reproche *m*
rebut [ri'bʌt] *vt* **-butted; -butting** : rebatir, refutar
rebuttal [ri'bʌṭəl] *n* : refutación *f*
recalcitrant [ri'kælsətrənt] *adj* : recalcitrante
recall[1] [ri'kɔl] *vt* **1** : llamar, retirar ‹recalled to active duty : llamado al servicio activo› **2** REMEMBER : recordar, acordarse de **3** REVOKE : revocar
recall[2] [ri'kɔl, 'ri:ˌkɔl] *n* **1** : retirada *f* (de personas o mercancías) **2** MEMORY : memoria *f* ‹to have total recall : poder recordar todo›
recant [ri'kænt] *vt* : retractarse de — *vi* : retractarse, renegar
recapitulate [ˌri:kə'pɪtʃəˌleɪt] *v* **-lated; -lating** : resumir, recapitular
recapture [ˌri:'kæptʃər] *vt* **-tured; -turing 1** REGAIN : volver a tomar, reconquistar **2** RELIVE : revivir (la juventud, etc.)
recast [ri:'kæst] *vt* **-cast; -casting 1** : refundir (metales) **2** REWRITE : refundir, modificar
recede [ri'si:d] *vi* **-ceded; -ceding 1** WITHDRAW : retirarse, retroceder **2** FADE : desvanecerse, alejarse **3** SLANT : inclinarse **4 to have a receding hairline** : tener entradas
receipt [ri'si:t] *n* **1** : recibo *m* **2 receipts** *npl* : ingresos *mpl*, entradas *fpl*
receivable [ri'si:vəbəl] *adj* **accounts receivable** : cuentas por cobrar
receive [ri'si:v] *vt* **-ceived; -ceiving 1** GET : recibir ‹to receive a letter : recibir una carta› ‹to receive a blow : recibir un golpe› **2** WELCOME : acoger, recibir ‹to receive guests : tener invitados› **3** : recibir, captar (señales de radio)
receiver [ri'si:vər] *n* **1** : receptor *m*, -tora *f* (en futbol americano) **2** : receptor *m* (de radio o televisión) **3 telephone receiver** : auricular *m*
recent ['ri:sənt] *adj* : reciente — **recently** *adv*

receptacle [ri'sɛptɪkəl] *n* : receptáculo *m*, recipiente *m*

reception [ri'sɛpʃən] *n* : recepción *f*

receptionist [ri'sɛpʃənɪst] *n* : recepcionista *mf*

receptive [ri'sɛptɪv] *adj* : receptivo

receptivity [ˌri:ˌsɛp'tɪvət̬i] *n* : receptividad *f*

recess[1] ['ri:ˌsɛs, rɪ'sɛs] *vt* **1** : poner en un hueco ⟨recessed lighting : iluminación empotrada⟩ **2** ADJOURN : suspender, levantar

recess[2] *n* **1** ALCOVE : hueco *m*, nicho *m* **2** BREAK : receso *m*, descanso *m*, recreo *m* (en el colegio)

recession [ri'sɛʃən] *n* : recesión *f*, depresión *f* económica

recessive [ri'sɛsɪv] *adj* : recesivo

recharge [ˌri:'ʧɑrʤ] *vt* **-charged; -charging** : recargar

rechargeable [ˌri:'ʧɑrʤəbəl] *adj* : recargable

recipe ['rɛsəˌpi:] *n* : receta *f*

recipient [ri'sɪpiənt] *n* : recipiente *mf*

reciprocal [ri'sɪprəkəl] *adj* : recíproco

reciprocate [ri'sɪprəˌkeɪt] *vi* **-cated; -cating** : reciprocar

reciprocity [ˌrɛsə'prɑsət̬i] *n, pl* **-ties** : reciprocidad *f*

recital [ri'saɪt̬əl] *n* **1** PERFORMANCE : recital *m* **2** ENUMERATION : relato *m*, enumeración *f*

recitation [ˌrɛsə'teɪʃən] *n* : recitación *f*

recite [ri'saɪt] *vt* **-cited; -citing 1** : recitar (un poema, etc.) **2** RECOUNT : narrar, relatar, enumerar

reckless ['rɛkləs] *adj* : imprudente, temerario — **recklessly** *adv*

recklessness ['rɛkləsnəs] *n* : imprudencia *f*, temeridad *f*

reckon ['rɛkən] *vt* **1** CALCULATE : calcular, contar **2** CONSIDER : considerar

reckoning ['rɛkənɪŋ] *n* **1** CALCULATION : cálculo *m* **2** SETTLEMENT : ajuste *m* de cuentas ⟨day of reckoning : día del juicio final⟩

reclaim [ri'kleɪm] *vt* **1** : ganar, sanear ⟨to reclaim marshy land : sanear las tierras pantanosas⟩ **2** RECOVER : recobrar, reciclar ⟨to reclaim old tires : reciclar llantas desechadas⟩ **3** REGAIN : reclamar, recuperar ⟨to reclaim one's rights : reclamar uno sus derechos⟩

recline [ri'klaɪn] *vi* **-clined; -clining 1** LEAN : reclinarse **2** REPOSE : recostarse

recluse ['rɛˌklu:s, ri'klu:s] *n* : solitario *m*, -ria *f*

recognition [ˌrɛkɪg'nɪʃən] *n* : reconocimiento *m*

recognizable ['rɛkəgˌnaɪzəbəl] *adj* : reconocible

recognize ['rɛkɪgˌnaɪz] *vt* **-nized; -nizing** : reconocer

recoil[1] [ri'kɔɪl] *vi* : retroceder, dar un culatazo

recoil[2] ['ri:ˌkɔɪl, ri'-] *n* : retroceso *m*, culatazo *m*

recollect [ˌrɛkə'lɛkt] *v* : recordar

recollection [ˌrɛkə'lɛkʃən] *n* : recuerdo *m*

recommend [ˌrɛkə'mɛnd] *vt* **1** : recomendar ⟨she recommended the medicine : recomendó la medicina⟩ **2** ADVISE, COUNSEL : aconsejar, recomendar

recommendation [ˌrɛkəmən'deɪʃən] *n* : recomendación *f*

recompense[1] ['rɛkəmˌpɛnts] *vt* **-pensed; -pensing** : indemnizar, recompensar

recompense[2] *n* : indemnización *f*, compensación *f*

reconcile ['rɛkənˌsaɪl] *v* **-ciled; -ciling** *vt* **1** : reconciliar (personas), conciliar (ideas, etc.) **2 to reconcile oneself to** : resignarse a — *vi* MAKE UP : reconciliarse, hacer las paces

reconciliation [ˌrɛkənˌsɪli'eɪʃən] *n* : reconciliación *f* (con personas), conciliación *f* (con ideas, etc.)

recondite ['rɛkənˌdaɪt, ri'kɑn-] *adj* : recóndito, abstruso

recondition [ˌri:kən'dɪʃən] *vt* : reacondicionar

reconnaissance [ri'kɑnəzənts, -sənts] *n* : reconocimiento *m*

reconnoiter *or* **reconnoitre** [ˌri:kə'nɔɪt̬ər, ˌrɛkə-] *v* **-tered** *or* **-tred; -tering** *or* **-tring** *vt* : reconocer — *vi* : hacer un reconocimiento

reconsider [ˌri:kən'sɪdər] *vt* : reconsiderar, repensar

reconsideration [ˌri:kənˌsɪdə'reɪʃən] *n* : reconsideración *f*

reconstruct [ˌri:kən'strʌkt] *vt* : reconstruir

reconstruction [ˌri:kən'strʌkʃən] *n* : reconstrucción *f*

record[1] [ri'kɔrd] *vt* **1** WRITE DOWN : anotar, apuntar **2** REGISTER : registrar, hacer constar **3** INDICATE : marcar (una temperatura, etc.) **4** TAPE : grabar

record[2] ['rɛkərd] *n* **1** DOCUMENT : registro *m*, documento *m* oficial **2** HISTORY : historial *m* ⟨a good academic record : un buen historial académico⟩ ⟨criminal record : antecedentes penales⟩ **3** : récord *m* ⟨the world record : el récord mundial⟩ **4** : disco *m* (de música, etc.) ⟨to make a record : grabar un disco⟩

recorder [ri'kɔrdər] *n* **1** : flauta *f* dulce (instrumento de viento) **2 tape recorder** : grabadora *f*

recording [ri'kɔrdɪŋ] *n* : grabación *f*

recount[1] [ri'kaʊnt] *vt* **1** NARRATE : narrar, relatar **2** : volver a contar (votos, etc.)

recount[2] ['ri:ˌkaʊnt, ˌri'-] *n* : recuento *m*

recoup [ri'ku:p] *vt* : recuperar, recobrar

recourse ['ri:ˌkors, ri'-] *n* : recurso *m* ⟨to have recourse to : recurrir a⟩

recover [ri'kʌvər] *vt* REGAIN : recobrar — *vi* RECUPERATE : recuperarse

recovery [ri'kʌvəri] *n, pl* **-eries** : recuperación *f*
re–create [ˌri:kri'eɪt] *vt* **-ated; -ating** : recrear
recreation [ˌrɛkri'eɪʃən] *n* : recreo *m*, esparcimiento *m*, diversión *f*
recreational [ˌrɛkri'eɪʃənəl] *adj* : recreativo, de recreo
recrimination [riˌkrɪmə'neɪʃən] *n* : recriminación *f*
recruit[1] [ri'kru:t] *vt* : reclutar
recruit[2] *n* : recluta *mf*
recruitment [ri'kru:tmənt] *n* : reclutamiento *m*, alistamiento *m*
rectal ['rɛktəl] *adj* : rectal
rectangle ['rɛkˌtæŋgəl] *n* : rectángulo *m*
rectangular [rɛk'tæŋgjələr] *adj* : rectangular
rectify ['rɛktəˌfaɪ] *vt* **-fied; -fying** : rectificar
rectitude ['rktəˌtu:d, -ˌtju:d] *n* : rectitud *f*
rector ['rɛktər] *n* : rector *m*, -tora *f*
rectory ['rɛktəri] *n, pl* **-ries** : rectoría *f*
rectum ['rɛktəm] *n, pl* **-tums** *or* **-ta** [-tə] : recto *m*
recuperate [ri'ku:pəˌreɪt, -'kju:-] *v* **-ated; -ating** *vt* : recuperar — *vi* : recuperarse, restablecerse
recuperation [riˌku:pə'reɪʃən, -ˌkju:-] *n* : recuperación *f*
recur [ri'kər] *vi* **-curred; -curring** : volver a ocurrir, volver a producirse, repetirse
recurrence [ri'kərən*t*s] *n* : repetición *f*, reaparición *f*
recurrent [ri'kərənt] *adj* : recurrente, que se repite
recyclable [ri'saɪkələbəl] *adj* : reciclable
recycle [ri'saɪkəl] *vt* **-cled; -cling** : reciclar
recycling [ri'saɪkəlɪŋ] *n* : reciclaje *m*
red[1] ['rɛd] *adj* **1** : rojo, colorado ⟨to be red in the face : ponerse colorado⟩ ⟨to have red hair : ser pelirrojo⟩ **2** COMMUNIST : rojo, comunista
red[2] *n* **1** : rojo *m*, colorado *m* **2 Red** COMMUNIST : comunista *mf*
red blood cell *n* : glóbulo *m* rojo
red–blooded ['rɛd'blʌdəd] *adj* : vigoroso
redcap ['rɛdˌkæp] → **porter**
redden ['rɛdən] *vt* : enrojecer — *vi* BLUSH : enrojecerse, ruborizarse
reddish ['rɛdɪʃ] *adj* : rojizo
redecorate [ˌri:'dɛkəˌreɪt] *vt* **-rated; -rating** : renovar, pintar de nuevo
redeem [ri'di:m] *vt* **1** RESCUE, SAVE : rescatar, salvar **2** : desempeñar ⟨she redeemed it from the pawnshop : lo desempeñó de la casa de empeños⟩ **3** : redimir (en religión) **4** : canjear, vender ⟨to redeem coupons : canjear cupones⟩
redeemer [ri'di:mər] *n* : redentor *m*, -tora *f*
redefine [ˌri:dɪ'faɪn] *vt* : redefinir
redemption [ri'dɛmpʃən] *n* : redención *f*
redesign [ˌri:di'zaɪn] *vt* : rediseñar
red–handed ['rɛd'hændəd] *adj* : con las manos en la masa
redhead ['rɛdˌhɛd] *n* : pelirrojo *m*, -ja *f*
red–hot ['rɛd'hɑt] *adj* **1** : al rojo vivo, candente **2** CURRENT : de candente actualidad **3** POPULAR : de gran popularidad
rediscover [ˌri:di'skʌvər] *vt* : redescubrir
redistribute [ˌri:di'strɪˌbju:t] *vt* **-uted; -uting** : redistribuir
red–letter ['rɛd'lɛt̬ər] *adj* **red–letter day** : día *m* memorable
redness ['rɛdnəs] *n* : rojez *f*
redo [ˌri:'du:] *vt* **-did** [-dɪd]; **-done** [-'dʌn]; **-doing 1** : hacer de nuevo **2** → **redecorate**
redolence ['rɛdələn*t*s] *n* : fragancia *f*
redolent ['rɛdələnt] *adj* **1** FRAGRANT : fragante, oloroso **2** SUGGESTIVE : evocador
redouble [ri'dʌbəl] *vt* **-bled; -bling** : redoblar, intensificar (esfuerzos, etc.)
redoubtable [r'daʊt̬əbəl] *adj* : temible
redress [ri'drɛs] *vt* : reparar, remediar, enmendar
red snapper *n* : pargo *m*, huachinango *m Mex*
red tape *n* : papeleo *m*
reduce [ri'du:s, -'dju:s] *v* **-duced; -ducing** *vt* **1** LESSEN : reducir, disminuir, rebajar (precios) **2** DEMOTE : bajar de categoría, degradar **3 to be reduced to** : verse rebajado a, verse forzado a **4 to reduce someone to tears** : hacer llorar a alguien — *vi* SLIM : adelgazar
reduction [ri'dʌkʃən] *n* : reducción *f*, rebaja *f*
redundancy [ri'dʌndən*t*si] *n, pl* **-cies 1** : superfluidad *f* **2** REPETITION : redundancia *f*
redundant [ri'dʌndənt] *adj* : superfluo, redundante
redwood ['rɛdˌwʊd] *n* : secoya *f*
reed ['ri:d] *n* **1** : caña *f*, carrizo *m*, junco *m* **2** : lengüeta *f* (para instrumentos de viento)
reef ['ri:f] *n* : arrecife *m*, escollo *m*
reek[1] ['ri:k] *vi* : apestar
reek[2] *n* : hedor *m*
reel[1] ['ri:l] *vt* **1 to reel in** : enrollar, sacar (un pez) del agua **2 to reel off** : recitar de un tirón — *vi* **1** SPIN, WHIRL : girar, dar vueltas **2** STAGGER : tambalearse
reel[2] *n* **1** : carrete *m* (de pescar etc.), rollo *m* (de fotos) **2** : baile *m* escocés **3** STAGGER : tambaleo *m*
reelect [ˌri:ɪ'lɛkt] *vt* : reelegir
reenact [ˌri:ɪ'nækt] *vt* : representar de nuevo, reconstruir
reenter [ˌri:'ɛntər] *vt* : volver a entrar
reestablish [ˌri:ɪ'stæblɪʃ] *vt* : restablecer
reevaluate [ˌri:ɪ'væljʊˌeɪt] *vt* **-ated; -ating** : revaluar
reevaluation [ˌri:ɪˌvæljʊ'eɪʃən] *n* : revaluación *f*

reexamine [ˌriːɪg'zæmən, -g-] *vt* **-ined; -ining** : volver a examinar, reexaminar
refer [ri'fər] *v* **-ferred; -ferring** *vt* DIRECT, SEND : remitir, enviar ⟨to refer a patient to a specialist : enviar a un paciente a un especialista⟩ — *vi* **to refer to** MENTION : referirse a, aludir a
referee[1] [ˌrɛfə'riː] *v* **-eed; -eeing** : arbitrar
referee[2] *n* : árbitro *m*, -tra *f*; réferi *mf*
reference ['rɛfrənts, 'rɛfə-] *n* **1** ALLUSION : referencia *f*, alusión *f* ⟨to make reference to : hacer referencia a⟩ **2** CONSULTATION : consulta *f* ⟨for future reference : para futuras consultas⟩ **3** *or* **reference book** : libro *m* de consulta **4** TESTIMONIAL : informe *m*, referencia *f*, recomendación *f*
referendum [ˌrɛfə'rɛndəm] *n, pl* **-da** [-də] *or* **-dums** : referéndum *m*
refill[1] [ˌriː'fɪl] *vt* : rellenar
refill[2] ['riːˌfɪl] *n* : recambio *m*
refinance [ˌriː'faɪˌnænts] *vt* **-nanced; -nancing** : refinanciar
refine [ri'faɪn] *vt* **-fined; -fining** **1** : refinar (azúcar, petróleo, etc.) **2** PERFECT : perfeccionar, pulir
refined [ri'faɪnd] *adj* **1** : refinado (dícese del azúcar, etc.) **2** CULTURED : culto, educado, refinado
refinement [ri'faɪnmənt] *n* : refinamiento *m*, fineza *f*, finura *f*
refinery [ri'faɪnəri] *n, pl* **-eries** : refinería *f*
reflect [ri'flɛkt] *vt* **1** : reflejar ⟨to reflect light : reflejar la luz⟩ ⟨happiness is reflected in her face : la felicidad se refleja en su cara⟩ **2 to reflect that** : pensar que, considerar que — *vi* **1 to reflect on** : reflexionar sobre **2 to reflect badly on** : desacreditar, perjudicar
reflection [ri'flɛkʃən] *n* **1** : reflexión *f*, reflejo *m* (de la luz, de imágenes, etc.) **2** THOUGHT : reflexión *f*, meditación *f*
reflective [ri'flɛktɪv] *adj* **1** THOUGHTFUL : reflexivo, pensativo **2** : reflectante (en física)
reflector [ri'flɛktər] *n* : reflector *m*
reflex ['riːˌflɛks] *n* : reflejo *m*
reflexive [ri'flɛksɪv] *adj* : reflexivo ⟨a reflexive verb : un verbo reflexivo⟩
reform[1] [ri'fɔrm] *vt* : reformar — *vi* : reformarse
reform[2] *n* : reforma *f*
reformation [ˌrɛfər'meɪʃən] *n* : reforma *f* ⟨the Reformation : la Reforma⟩
reformatory [ri'fɔrməˌtori] *n, pl* **-ries** : reformatorio *m*
reformer [ri'fɔrmər] *n* : reformador *m*, -dora *f*
refract [ri'frækt] *vt* : refractar — *vi* : refractarse
refraction [ri'frækʃən] *n* : refracción *f*
refractory [ri'fræktəri] *adj* OBSTINATE : refractario, obstinado
refrain[1] [ri'freɪn] *vi* **to refrain from** : abstenerse de
refrain[2] *n* : estribillo *m* (en música)
refresh [ri'frɛʃ] *vt* : refrescar ⟨to refresh one's memory : refrescarle la memoria a uno⟩
refreshing [ri'frɛʃɪŋ] *adj* : refrescante ⟨a refreshing sleep : un sueño reparador⟩
refreshment [ri'frɛʃmənt] *n* **1** : refresco *m* **2 refreshments** *npl* : refrigerio *m*
refrigerate [ri'frɪʤəˌreɪt] *vt* **-ated; -ating** : refrigerar
refrigeration [riˌfrɪʤə'reɪʃən] *n* : refrigeración *f*
refrigerator [ri'frɪʤəˌreɪt̬ər] *n* : refrigerador *m*, -dora *f*, nevera *f*
refuel [riː'fjuːəl] *v* **-eled** *or* **-elled; -eling** *or* **-elling** *vi* : repostar — *vt* : llenar de combustible
refuge ['rɛˌfjuːʤ] *n* : refugio *m*
refugee [ˌrɛfjʊ'ʤiː] *n* : refugiado *m*, -da *f*
refund[1] [ri'fʌnd, 'riːˌfʌnd] *vt* : reembolsar, devolver
refund[2] ['riːˌfʌnd] *n* : reembolso *m*, devolución *f*
refundable [ri'fʌndəbəl] *adj* : reembolsable
refurbish [ri'fərbɪʃ] *vt* : renovar, restaurar
refusal [ri'fjuːzəl] *n* : negativa *f*, rechazo *m*, denegación *f* (de una petición)
refuse[1] [ri'fjuːz] *vt* **-fused; -fusing** **1** REJECT : rechazar, rehusar **2** DENY : negar, rehusar, denegar ⟨to refuse permission : negar el permiso⟩ **3 to refuse to** : negarse a
refuse[2] ['rɛˌfjuːs, -ˌfjuːz] *n* : basura *f*, desechos *mpl*, desperdicios *mpl*
refutation [ˌrɛfjʊ'teɪʃən] *n* : refutación *f*
refute [ri'fjuːt] *vt* **-futed; -futing** **1** DENY : desmentir, negar **2** DISPROVE : refutar, rebatir
regain [riː'geɪn] *vt* **1** RECOVER : recuperar, recobrar **2** REACH : alcanzar ⟨to regain the shore : llegar a la tierra⟩
regal ['riːgəl] *adj* : real, regio
regale [ri'geɪl] *vt* **-galed; -galing** **1** ENTERTAIN : agasajar, entretener **2** AMUSE, DELIGHT : deleitar, divertir
regalia [ri'geɪljə] *npl* : ropaje *m*, vestiduras *fpl*, adornos *mpl*
regard[1] [ri'gɑrd] *vt* **1** OBSERVE : observar, mirar **2** HEED : tener en cuenta, hacer caso de **3** CONSIDER : considerar **4** RESPECT : respetar ⟨highly regarded : muy estimado⟩ **5 as regards** : en cuanto a, en lo que se refiere a
regard[2] *n* **1** CONSIDERATION : consideración *f* **2** ESTEEM : respeto *m*, estima *f* **3** PARTICULAR : aspecto *m*, sentido *m* ⟨in this regard : en este sentido⟩ **4 regards** *npl* : saludos *mpl*, recuerdos *mpl* **5 with regard to** : con relación a, con respecto a
regarding [ri'gɑrdɪŋ] *prep* : con respecto a, en cuanto a
regardless [ri'gɑrdləs] *adv* : a pesar de todo

regardless of *prep* : a pesar de, sin tener en cuenta ⟨regardless of our mistakes : a pesar de nuestros errores⟩ ⟨regardless of age : sin tener en cuenta la edad⟩
regenerate [riˈʤɛnəˌreɪt] *v* **-ated; -ating** *vt* : regenerar — *vi* : regenerarse
regeneration [riˌʤɛnəˈreɪʃən] *n* : regeneración *f*
regent [ˈriːʤənt] *n* **1** RULER : regente *mf* **2** : miembro *m* de la junta directiva (de una universidad, etc.)
regime [reɪˈʒiːm, rɪ-] *n* : régimen *m*
regimen [ˈrɛʤəmən] *n* : régimen *m*
regiment[1] [ˈrɛʤəˌmɛnt] *vt* : reglamentar
regiment[2] [ˈrɛʤəmənt] *n* : regimiento *m*
region [ˈriːʤən] *n* **1** : región *f* **2 in the region of** : alrededor de
regional [ˈriːʤənəl] *adj* : regional — **regionally** *adv*
register[1] [ˈrɛʤəstər] *vt* **1** RECORD : registrar, inscribir **2** INDICATE : marcar (temperatura, medidas, etc.) **3** REVEAL : manifestar, acusar ⟨to register surprise : acusar sorpresa⟩ **4** : certificar (correo) — *vi* ENROLL : inscribirse, matricularse
register[2] *n* : registro *m*
registrar [ˈrɛʤəˌstrɑr] *n* : registrador *m*, -dora *f* oficial
registration [ˌrɛʤəˈstreɪʃən] *n* **1** REGISTERING : inscripción *f*, matriculación *f*, registro *m* **2** *or* **registration number** : matrícula *f*, número *m* de matrícula
registry [ˈrɛʤəstri] *n, pl* **-tries** : registro *m*
regress [riˈgrɛs] *vi* : retroceder
regression [riˈgrɛʃən] *n* : retroceso *m*, regresión *f*
regressive [riˈgrɛsɪv] *adj* : regresivo
regret[1] [riˈgrɛt] *vt* **-gretted; -gretting** : arrepentirse de, lamentar ⟨he regrets nothing : no se arrepiente de nada⟩ ⟨I regret to tell you : lamento decirle⟩
regret[2] *n* **1** REMORSE : arrepentimiento *m*, remordimientos *mpl* **2** SADNESS : pesar *m*, dolor *m* **3 regrets** *npl* : excusas *fpl* ⟨to send one's regrets : excusarse⟩
regretful [riˈgrɛtfəl] *adj* : arrepentido, pesaroso
regretfully [riˈgrɛtfəli] *adv* : con pesar
regrettable [riˈgrɛt̬əbəl] *adj* : lamentable — **regrettably** [-bli] *adv*
regular[1] [ˈrɛgjələr] *adj* **1** NORMAL : regular, normal, usual **2** STEADY : uniforme, regular ⟨a regular pace : un paso regular⟩ **3** CUSTOMARY, HABITUAL : habitual, de costumbre
regular[2] *n* : cliente *mf* habitual
regularity [ˌrɛgjəˈlærət̬i] *n, pl* **-ties** : regularidad *f*
regularly [ˈrɛgjələrli] *adv* : regularmente, con regularidad
regulate [ˈrɛgjəˌleɪt] *vt* **-lated; -lating** : regular
regulation [ˌrɛgjəˈleɪʃən] *n* **1** REGULATING : regulación *f* **2** RULE : regla *f*, reglamento *m*, norma *f* ⟨safety regulations : reglas de seguridad⟩
regulator [ˈrɛgjəˌleɪt̬ər] *n* **1** : regulador *m* (mecanismo) **2** : persona *f* que regula
regulatory [ˈrɛgjələˌtori] *adj* : regulador
regurgitate [riˈgərʤəˌteɪt] *v* **-tated; -tating** : regurgitar, vomitar
rehabilitate [ˌriːhəˈbɪləˌteɪt, ˌriːə-] *vt* **-tated; -tating** : rehabilitar
rehabilitation [ˌriːhəˌbɪləˈteɪʃən, ˌriːə-] *n* : rehabilitación *f*
rehearsal [riˈhərsəl] *n* : ensayo *m*
rehearse [riˈhərs] *v* **-hearsed; -hearsing** : ensayar
reheat [ˌriːˈhiːt] *vt* : recalentar
reign[1] [ˈreɪn] *vi* **1** RULE : reinar **2** PREVAIL : reinar, predominar ⟨the reigning champion : el actual campeón⟩
reign[2] *n* : reinado *m*
reimburse [ˌriːəmˈbərs] *vt* **-bursed; -bursing** : reembolsar
reimbursement [ˌriːəmˈbərsmənt] *n* : reembolso *m*
rein[1] [ˈreɪn] *vt* : refrenar (un caballo)
rein[2] *n* **1** : rienda *f* ⟨to give free rein to : dar rienda suelta a⟩ **2** CHECK : control *m* ⟨to keep a tight rein on : llevar un estricto control de⟩
reincarnation [ˌriːɪnˌkɑrˈneɪʃən] *n* : reencarnación *f*
reindeer [ˈreɪnˌdɪr] *n* : reno *m*
reinforce [ˌriːənˈfors] *vt* **-forced; -forcing** : reforzar
reinforcement [ˌriːənˈforsmənt] *n* : refuerzo *m*
reinstate [ˌriːənˈsteɪt] *vt* **-stated; -stating** **1** : reintegrar, restituir (una persona) **2** RESTORE : restablecer (un servicio, etc.)
reinstatement [ˌriːənˈsteɪtmənt] *n* : reintegración *f*, restitución *f*, restablecimiento *m*
reiterate [riˈɪt̬əˌreɪt] *vt* **-ated; -ating** : reiterar, repetir
reiteration [riˌɪt̬əˈreɪʃən] *n* : reiteración *f*, repetición *f*
reject[1] [riˈʤɛkt] *vt* : rechazar
reject[2] [ˈriːˌʤɛkt] *n* : desecho *m* (cosa), persona *f* rechazada
rejection [riˈʤɛkʃən] *n* : rechazo *m*
rejoice [riˈʤɔɪs] *vi* **-joiced; -joicing** : alegrarse, regocijarse
rejoin [ˌriːˈʤɔɪn] *vt* **1** : reincorporarse a, reintegrarse a ⟨he rejoined the firm : se reincorporó a la firma⟩ **2** [riˈ-] REPLY, RETORT : replicar
rejoinder [riˈʤɔɪndər] *n* : réplica *f*
rejuvenate [riˈʤuːvəˌneɪt] *vt* **-nated; -nating** : rejuvenecer
rejuvenation [riˌʤuːvəˈneɪʃən] *n* : rejuvenecimiento *m*
rekindle [ˌriːˈkɪndəl] *vt* **-dled; -dling** : reavivar
relapse[1] [riˈlæps] *vi* **-lapsed; -lapsing** : recaer, volver a caer
relapse[2] [ˈriːˌlæps, riˈlæps] *n* : recaída *f*

relate [ri'leɪt] *v* **-lated; -lating** *vt* **1** TELL : relatar, contar **2** ASSOCIATE : relacionar, asociar ‹to relate crime to poverty : relacionar la delincuencia a la pobreza› — *vi* **1** CONNECT : conectar, estar relacionado (con) **2** INTERACT : relacionarse (con), llevarse bien (con) **3 to relate to** UNDERSTAND : identificarse con, simpatizar con
related [ri'leɪt̬əd] *adj* : emparentado ‹to be related to : ser pariente de›
relation [ri'leɪʃən] *n* **1** NARRATION : relato *m*, narración *f* **2** RELATIVE : pariente *mf*, familiar *mf* **3** RELATIONSHIP : relación *f* ‹in relation to : en relación con, con relación a› **4 relations** *npl* : relaciones *fpl* ‹public relations : relaciones públicas›
relationship [ri'leɪʃən,ʃɪp] *n* **1** CONNECTION : relación *f* **2** KINSHIP : parentesco *m*
relative[1] ['rɛlət̬ɪv] *adj* : relativo — **relatively** *adv*
relative[2] *n* : pariente *mf*, familiar *mf*
relativism ['rɛlətɪ,vɪzəm] *n* : relativismo *m*
relativity [,rɛlə'tɪvət̬i] *n, pl* **-ties** : relatividad *f*
relax [ri'læks] *vt* : relajar, aflojar — *vi* : relajarse
relaxation [,ri:,læk'seɪʃən] *n* **1** RELAXING : relajación *f*, aflojamiento *m* **2** DIVERSION : esparcimiento *m*, distracción *f*
relaxing [ri'læksɪŋ] *adj* : relajante
relay[1] ['ri:,leɪ, ri'leɪ] *vt* **-layed; -laying** : transmitir
relay[2] ['ri:,leɪ] *n* **1** : relevo *m* **2** *or* **relay race** : carrera de relevos
release[1] [ri'li:s] *vt* **-leased; -leasing 1** FREE : liberar, poner en libertad **2** LOOSEN : soltar, aflojar ‹to release the brake : soltar el freno› **3** RELINQUISH : renunciar a, ceder **4** ISSUE : publicar (un libro), estrenar (una película), sacar (un disco)
release[2] *n* **1** LIBERATION : liberación *f*, puesta *f* en libertad **2** RELINQUISHMENT : cesión *f* (de propiedad, etc.) **3** ISSUE : estreno *m* (de una película), puesta *f* en venta (de un disco), publicación *f* (de un libro) **4** ESCAPE : escape *m*, fuga *f* (de un gas)
relegate ['rɛlə,geɪt] *vt* **-gated; -gating** : relegar
relent [ri'lɛnt] *vi* : ablandarse, ceder
relentless [ri'lɛntləs] *adj* : implacable, sin tregua
relentlessly [ri'lɛntləsli] *adv* : implacablemente
relevance ['rɛləvənts] *n* : pertinencia *f*, relación *f*
relevant ['rɛləvənt] *adj* : pertinente — **relevantly** *adv*
reliability [ri,laɪə'bɪlət̬i] *n, pl* **-ties 1** : fiabilidad *f*, seguridad *f* (de una cosa) **2** : formalidad *f*, seriedad *f* (de una persona)
reliable [ri'laɪəbəl] *adj* : confiable, fiable, fidedigno, seguro
reliably [ri'laɪəbli] *adv* : sin fallar ‹to be reliably informed : saber (algo) de fuentes fidedignas›
reliance [ri'laɪənts] *n* **1** DEPENDENCE : dependencia *f* **2** CONFIDENCE : confianza *f*
reliant [ri'laɪənt] *adj* : dependiente
relic ['rɛlɪk] *n* **1** : reliquia *f* **2** VESTIGE : vestigio *m*
relief [ri'li:f] *n* **1** : alivio *m*, desahogo *m* ‹relief from pain : alivio del dolor› **2** AID, WELFARE : ayuda *f* (benéfica), asistencia *f* social **3** : relieve *m* (en la escultura) ‹relief map : mapa en relieve› **4** REPLACEMENT : relevo *m*
relieve [ri'li:v] *vt* **-lieved; -lieving 1** ALLEVIATE : aliviar, mitigar ‹to feel relieved : sentirse aliviado› **2** FREE : liberar, eximir ‹to relieve someone of responsibility for : eximir a alguien de la responsabilidad de› **3** REPLACE : relevar (a un centinela, etc.) **4** BREAK : romper ‹to relieve the monotony : romper la monotonía›
religion [ri'lɪʤən] *n* : religión *f*
religious [ri'lɪʤəs] *adj* : religioso — **religiously** *adv*
relinquish [ri'lɪŋkwɪʃ, -'lɪn-] *vt* **1** GIVE UP : renunciar a, abandonar **2** RELEASE : soltar
relish[1] ['rɛlɪʃ] *vt* : saborear (comida), disfrutar con (una idea, una perspectiva, etc.)
relish[2] *n* **1** ENJOYMENT : gusto *m*, deleite *m* **2** : salsa *f* (condimento)
relive [,ri:'lɪv] *vt* **-lived; -living** : revivir
relocate [,ri:'lo:,keɪt, ,ri:lo'keɪt] *v* **-cated; -cating** *vt* : reubicar, trasladar — *vi* : trasladarse
relocation [,ri:lo'keɪʃən] *n* : reubicación *f*, traslado *m*
reluctance [ri'lʌktənts] *n* : renuencia *f*, reticencia *f*, desgana *f*
reluctant [ri'lʌktənt] *adj* : renuente, reacio, reticente
reluctantly [ri'lʌktəntli] *adv* : a regañadientes
rely [ri'laɪ] *vi* **-lied; -lying 1** DEPEND : depender (de), contar (con) **2** TRUST : confiar (en)
remain [ri'meɪn] *vi* **1** : quedar ‹very little remains : queda muy poco› ‹the remaining 10 minutes : los 10 minutos que quedan› **2** STAY : quedarse, permanecer **3** CONTINUE : continuar, seguir ‹to remain the same : continuar siendo igual› **4 to remain to** : quedar por ‹to remain to be done : quedar por hacer› ‹it remains to be seen : está por ver›
remainder [ri'meɪndər] *n* : resto *m*, remanente *m*
remains [ri'meɪnz] *npl* : restos *mpl* ‹mortal remains : restos mortales›
remake[1] [ri:'meɪk] *vt* **-made; -making 1** TRANSFORM : rehacer **2** : hacer una nueva versión de (una película, etc.)

remake[2] [ˈriːˌmeɪk] *n* : nueva versión *f*
remark[1] [riˈmɑrk] *vt* **1** NOTICE : observar **2** SAY : comentar, observar — *vi* **to remark on** : hacer observaciones sobre
remark[2] *n* : comentario *m*, observación *f*
remarkable [riˈmɑrkəbəl] *adj* : extraordinario, notable — **remarkably** [-bli] *adv*
rematch [ˈriːˌmætʃ] *n* : revancha *f*
remedial [riˈmiːdiəl] *adj* : correctivo ⟨remedial classes : clases para alumnos atrasados⟩
remedy[1] [ˈrɛmədi] *vt* **-died; -dying** : remediar
remedy[2] *n, pl* **-dies** : remedio *m*, medicamento *m*
remember [riˈmɛmbər] *vt* **1** RECOLLECT : acordarse de, recordar **2** : no olvidar ⟨remember my words : no olvides mis palabras⟩ ⟨to remember to : acordarse de⟩ **3** : dar saludos, dar recuerdos ⟨remember me to her : dale saludos de mi parte⟩ **4** COMMEMORATE : recordar, conmemorar
remembrance [riˈmɛmbrənts] *n* **1** RECOLLECTION : recuerdo *m* ⟨in remembrance of : en conmemoración de⟩ **2** MEMENTO : recuerdo *m*
remind [riˈmaɪnd] *vt* : recordar ⟨remind me to do it : recuérdame que lo haga⟩ ⟨she reminds me of Clara : me recuerda de Clara⟩
reminder [riˈmaɪndər] *n* : recuerdo *m*
reminisce [ˌrɛməˈnɪs] *vi* **-nisced; -niscing** : rememorar los viejos tiempos
reminiscence [ˌrɛməˈnɪsənts] *n* : recuerdo *m*, reminiscencia *f*
reminiscent [ˌrɛməˈnɪsənt] *adj* **1** NOSTALGIC : reminiscente, nostálgico **2** SUGGESTIVE : evocador, que recuerda — **reminiscently** *adv*
remiss [riˈmɪs] *adj* : negligente, descuidado, remiso
remission [riˈmɪʃən] *n* : remisión *f*
remit [riˈmɪt] *vt* **-mitted; -mitting** **1** PARDON : perdonar **2** SEND : remitir, enviar (dinero)
remittance [riˈmɪtənts] *n* : remesa *f*
remnant [ˈrɛmnənt] *n* : restos *mpl*, vestigio *m*
remodel [riˈmɑdəl] *vt* **-eled** *or* **-elled; -eling** *or* **-elling** : remodelar, reformar
remonstrate [riˈmɑnˌstreɪt] *vi* **-strated; -strating** : protestar ⟨to remonstrate with someone : quejarse a alguien⟩
remorse [riˈmɔrs] *n* : remordimiento *m*
remorseful [riˈmɔrsfəl] *adj* : arrepentido, lleno de remordimiento
remorseless [riˈmɔrsləs] *adj* **1** PITILESS : despiadado **2** RELENTLESS : implacable
remote [riˈmoːt] *adj* **-moter; -est** **1** FAR-OFF : lejano, remoto ⟨remote countries : países remotos⟩ ⟨in the remote past : en el pasado lejano⟩ **2** SECLUDED : recóndito **3** : a distancia, remoto ⟨remote control : control remoto⟩ **4** SLIGHT : remoto **5** ALOOF : distante
remotely [riˈmoːtli] *adv* **1** SLIGHTLY : remotamente **2** DISTANTLY : en un lugar remoto, muy lejos
remoteness [riˈmoːtnəs] *n* : lejanía *f*
removable [riˈmuːvəbəl] *adj* : removible
removal [riˈmuːvəl] *n* : separación *f*, extracción *f*, supresión *f* (en algo escrito), eliminación *f* (de problemas, etc.)
remove [riˈmuːv] *vt* **-moved; -moving** **1** : quitar, quitarse ⟨remove the lid : quite la tapa⟩ ⟨to remove one's hat : quitarse el sombrero⟩ **2** EXTRACT : sacar, extraer ⟨to remove the contents of : sacar el contenido de⟩ **3** ELIMINATE : eliminar, disipar
remunerate [riˈmjuːnəˌreɪt] *vt* **-ated; -ating** : remunerar
remuneration [riˌmjuːnəˈreɪʃən] *n* : remuneración *f*
remunerative [riˈmjuːnərətɪv, -ˌreɪ-] *adj* : remunerativo
renaissance [ˌrɛnəˈsɑnts, -ˈzɑnts; ˈrɛnə-ˌ-] *n* : renacimiento *m* ⟨the Renaissance : el Renacimiento⟩
renal [ˈriːnəl] *adj* : renal
rename [ˌriːˈneɪm] *vt* **-named; -naming** : ponerle un nombre nuevo a
rend [ˈrɛnd] *vt* **rent** [ˈrɛnt]; **rending** : desgarrar
render [ˈrɛndər] *vt* **1** : derretir ⟨to render lard : derretir la manteca⟩ **2** GIVE : prestar, dar ⟨to render aid : prestar ayuda⟩ **3** MAKE : hacer, volver, dejar ⟨it rendered him helpless : lo dejó incapacitado⟩ **4** TRANSLATE : traducir, verter ⟨to render into English : traducir al inglés⟩
rendezvous [ˈrɑndɪˌvuː, -deɪ-] *ns & pl* : encuentro *m*, cita *f*
rendition [rɛnˈdɪʃən] *n* : interpretación *f*
renegade [ˈrɛnɪˌgeɪd] *n* : renegado *m*, -da *f*
renege [riˈnɪg, -ˈnɛg] *vi* **-neged; -neging** : no cumplir con (una promesa, etc.)
renew [riˈnuː, -ˈnjuː] *vt* **1** REVIVE : renovar, reavivar ⟨to renew the sentiments of youth : renovar los sentimientos de la juventud⟩ **2** RESUME : reanudar **3** EXTEND : renovar ⟨to renew a subscription : renovar una suscripción⟩
renewable [riˈnuːəbəl, -ˈnjuː-] *adj* : renovable
renewal [riˈnuːəl, -ˈnjuː-] *n* : renovación *f*
renounce [riˈnaʊnts] *vt* **-nounced; -nouncing** : renunciar a
renovate [ˈrɛnəˌveɪt] *vt* **-vated; -vating** : restaurar, renovar
renovation [ˌrɛnəˈveɪʃən] *n* : restauración *f*, renovación *f*
renown [riˈnaʊn] *n* : renombre *m*, fama *f*, celebridad *f*
renowned [riˈnaʊnd] *adj* : renombrado, célebre, famoso
rent[1] [ˈrɛnt] *vt* : rentar, alquilar

rent[2] *n* **1** : renta *f*, alquiler *m* ⟨for rent : se alquila⟩ **2** RIP : rasgadura *f*
rental[1] [ˈrɛntəl] *adj* RENT : de alquiler
rental[2] *n* : alquiler *m*
renter [ˈrɛntər] *n* : arrendatario *m*, -ria *f*
renunciation [ri,nʌntsiˈeɪʃən] *n* : renuncia *f*
reopen [,ri:ˈo:pən] *vt* : volver a abrir
reorganization [,ri:,ɔrgənəˈzeɪʃən] *n* : reorganización *f*
reorganize [,ri:ˈɔrgən,aɪz] *vt* **-nized; -nizing** : reorganizar
repair[1] [riˈpær] *vt* : reparar, arreglar, refaccionar
repair[2] *n* **1** : reparación *f*, arreglo *m* **2** CONDITION : estado *m* ⟨in bad repair : en mal estado⟩
reparation [,rɛpəˈreɪʃən] *n* **1** AMENDS : reparación *f* **2 reparations** *npl* COMPENSATION : indemnización *f*
repartee [,rɛpərˈti:, -,pɑr-, -ˈteɪ] *n* : intercambio *m* de réplicas ingeniosas
repast [riˈpæst, ˈri:,pæst] *n* : comida *f*
repatriate [riˈpeɪtri,eɪt] *vt* **-ated; -ating** : repatriar
repay [riˈpeɪ] *vt* **-paid; -paying** : pagar, devolver, reembolsar
repeal[1] [riˈpi:l] *vt* : abrogar, revocar
repeal[2] *n* : abrogación *f*, revocación *f*
repeat[1] [riˈpi:t] *vt* : repetir
repeat[2] *n* : repetición *f*
repeatedly [riˈpi:t̬ədli] *adv* : repetidamente, repetidas veces
repel [riˈpɛl] *vt* **-pelled; -pelling** **1** REPULSE : repeler (un enemigo, etc.) **2** RESIST : repeler **3** REJECT : rechazar, repeler **4** DISGUST : repugnar, darle asco (a alguien)
repellent *or* **repellant** [riˈpɛlənt] *n* : repelente *m*
repent [riˈpɛnt] *vi* : arrepentirse
repentance [riˈpɛntənts] *n* : arrepentimiento *m*
repentant [riˈpɛntənt] *adj* : arrepentido
repercussion [,ri:pərˈkʌʃən, ,rɛpər-] *n* : repercusión *f*
repertoire [ˈrɛpər,twɑr] *n* : repertorio *m*
repertory [ˈrɛpər,tori] *n, pl* **-ries** : repertorio *m*
repetition [,rɛpəˈtɪʃən] *n* : repetición *f*
repetitious [,rɛpəˈtɪʃəs] *adj* : repetitivo, reiterativo — **repetitiously** *adv*
repetitive [riˈpt̬ət̬ɪv] *adj* : repetitivo, reiterativo
replace [riˈpleɪs] *vt* **-placed; -placing** **1** : volver a poner ⟨replace it in the drawer : vuelve a ponerlo en el cajón⟩ **2** SUBSTITUTE : reemplazar, sustituir **3** : reponer ⟨to replace the worn carpet : reponer la alfombra raída⟩
replaceable [riˈpleɪsəbəl] *adj* : reemplazable
replacement [riˈpleɪsmənt] *n* **1** SUBSTITUTION : reemplazo *m*, sustitución *f* **2** SUBSTITUTE : sustituto *m*, -ta *f*; suplente *mf* (persona) **3 replacement part** : repuesto *m*, pieza *f* de recambio
replenish [riˈplɛnɪʃ] *vt* : rellenar, llenar de nuevo
replenishment [riˈplɛnɪʃmənt] *n* : reabastecimiento *m*
replete [riˈpli:t] *adj* : repleto, lleno
replica [ˈrɛplɪkə] *n* : réplica *f*, reproducción *f*
replicate [ˈrɛplə,keɪt] *v* **-cated; -cating** *vt* : duplicar, repetir — *vi* : duplicarse
replication [,rɛpləˈkeɪʃən] *n* **1** REPRODUCTION : reproducción *f* **2** REPETITION : repetición *f* **3** : replicación *f* (celular)
reply[1] [riˈplaɪ] *vi* **-plied; -plying** : contestar, responder
reply[2] *n, pl* **-plies** : respuesta *f*, contestación *f*
report[1] [riˈport] *vt* **1** ANNOUNCE : relatar, anunciar **2** : dar parte de, informar de, reportar ⟨he reported an accident : dio parte de un accidente⟩ ⟨to report a crime : denunciar un delito⟩ **3** : informar acerca de (en un periódico, la televisión, etc.) — *vi* **1** : hacer un informe, informar **2 to report for duty** : presentarse, reportarse
report[2] *n* **1** RUMOR : rumor *m* **2** REPUTATION : reputación *f* ⟨people of evil report : personas de mala fama⟩ **3** ACCOUNT : informe *m*, reportaje *m* (en un periódico, etc.) **4** BANG : estallido *m* (de un arma de fuego)
report card *n* : boletín *m* de calificaciones, boletín *m* de notas
reportedly [riˈport̬ədli] *adv* : según se dice, según se informa
reporter [riˈport̬ər] *n* : periodista *mf*; reportero *m*, -ra *f*
repose[1] [riˈpo:z] *vi* **-posed; -posing** : reposar, descansar
repose[2] *n* **1** : reposo *m*, descanso *m* **2** CALM : calma *f*, tranquilidad *f*
repository [riˈpɑzə,tori] *n, pl* **-ries** : depósito *m*
repossess [,ri:pəˈzɛs] *vt* : recuperar, recobrar la posesión de
reprehensible [,rɛpriˈhɛntsəbəl] *adj* : reprensible — **reprehensibly** *adv*
represent [,rɛprɪˈzɛnt] *vt* **1** SYMBOLIZE : representar ⟨the flag represents our country : la bandera representa a nuestro país⟩ **2** : representar, ser un representante de ⟨an attorney who represents his client : un abogado que representa su cliente⟩ **3** PORTRAY : presentar ⟨he represents himself as a friend : se presenta como amigo⟩
representation [,rɛprɪ,zɛnˈteɪʃən, -zən-] *n* : representación *f*
representative[1] [,rɛprɪˈzɛntət̬ɪv] *adj* : representativo
representative[2] *n* **1** : representante *mf* **2** : diputado *m*, -da *f* (en la política)
repress [riˈprɛs] *vt* : reprimir
repression [riˈprɛʃən] *n* : represión *f*
repressive [riˈprɛsɪv] *adj* : represivo
reprieve[1] [riˈpri:v] *vt* **-prieved; -prieving** : indultar
reprieve[2] *n* : indulto *m*
reprimand[1] [ˈrɛprə,mænd] *vt* : reprender

reprimand[2] *n* : reprimenda *f*
reprint[1] [ri'prɪnt] *vt* : reimprimir
reprint[2] ['ri:ˌprɪnt, ri'prɪnt] *n* : reedición *f*
reprisal [ri'praɪzəl] *n* : represalia *f*
reproach[1] [ri'pro:ʧ] *vt* : reprochar
reproach[2] *n* **1** DISGRACE : deshonra *f* **2** REBUKE : reproche *m*, recriminación *f*
reproachful [ri'pro:ʧfəl] *adj* : de reproche
reproduce [ˌri:prə'du:s, -'dju:s] *v* **-duced; -ducing** *vt* : reproducir — *vi* BREED : reproducirse
reproduction [ˌri:prə'dʌkʃən] *n* : reproducción *f*
reproductive [ˌri:prə'dʌktɪv] *adj* : reproductor
reproof [ri'pru:f] *n* : reprobación *f*, reprimenda *f*, reproche *m*
reprove [ri'pru:v] *vt* **-proved; -proving** : reprender, censurar
reptile ['rɛpˌtaɪl] *n* : reptil *m*
republic [ri'pʌblɪk] *n* : república *f*
republican[1] [ri'pʌblɪkən] *adj* : republicano
republican[2] *n* : republicano *m*, -na *f*
repudiate [ri'pju:diˌeɪt] *vt* **-ated; -ating** **1** REJECT : rechazar **2** DISOWN : repudiar, renegar de
repudiation [riˌpju:di'eɪʃən] *n* : rechazo *m*, repudio *m*
repugnance [ri'pʌgnənts] *n* : repugnancia *f*
repugnant [ri'pʌgnənt] *adj* : repugnante, asqueroso
repulse[1] [ri'pʌls] *vt* **-pulsed; -pulsing** **1** REPEL : repeler **2** REBUFF : desairar, rechazar
repulse[2] *n* : rechazo *m*
repulsive [ri'pʌlsɪv] *adj* : repulsivo, repugnante, asqueroso — **repulsively** *adv*
reputable ['rɛpjət̬əbəl] *adj* : acreditado, de buena reputación
reputation [ˌrɛpjə'teɪʃən] *n* : reputación *f*, fama *f*
repute [ri'pju:t] *n* : reputación *f*, fama *f*
reputed [ri'pju:t̬əd] *adj* : reputado, supuesto ⟨she's reputed to be the best : tiene fama de ser la mejor⟩
reputedly [ri'pju:t̬ədli] *adv* : supuestamente, según se dice
request[1] [ri'kwɛst] *vt* : pedir, solicitar, rogar ⟨to request assistance : solicitar asistencia, pedir ayuda⟩ ⟨I requested him to do it : le pedí que lo hiciera⟩
request[2] *n* : petición *f*, solicitud *f*, pedido *m*
requiem ['rɛkwiəm, 'reɪ-] *n* : réquiem *m*
require [ri'kwaɪr] *vt* **-quired; -quiring** **1** CALL FOR, DEMAND : requerir, exigir ⟨if required : si se requiere⟩ ⟨to require that something be done : exigir que algo se haga⟩ **2** NEED : necesitar, requerir
requirement [ri'kwaɪrmənt] *n* **1** NECESSITY : necesidad *f* **2** DEMAND : requisito *m*, demanda *f*
requisite[1] ['rɛkwəzɪt] *adj* : esencial, necesario
requisite[2] *n* : requisito *m*, necesidad *f*
requisition[1] [ˌrɛkwə'zɪʃən] *vt* : requisar
requisition[2] *n* : requisición *f*, requisa *f*
reread [ˌri:'ri:d] *vt* **-read; -reading** : releer
reroute [ˌri:'ru:t, -'raʊt] *vt* **-routed; -routing** : desviar
rerun[1] [ri:'rʌn] *vt* **-ran; -run; -running** : reponer (un programa televisivo)
rerun[2] ['ri:ˌrʌn] *n* **1** : reposición *f* (de un programa televisivo) **2** REPEAT : repetición *f*
resale ['ri:ˌseɪl, ˌri:'seɪl] *n* : reventa *f* ⟨resale price : precio de venta⟩
rescind [ri'sɪnd] *vt* **1** CANCEL : rescindir, cancelar **2** REPEAL : abrogar, revocar
rescue[1] ['rɛsˌkju:] *vt* **-cued; -cuing** : rescatar, salvar
rescue[2] *n* : rescate *m*
rescuer ['rɛskjuər] *n* : salvador *m*, -dora *f*
research[1] [ri'sərʧ, 'ri:ˌsərʧ] *v* : investigar
research[2] *n* : investigación *f*
researcher [ri'sərʧər, 'ri:ˌ-] *n* : investigador *m*, -dora *f*
resemblance [ri'zɛmblənts] *n* : semejanza *f*, parecido *m*
resemble [ri'zɛmbəl] *vt* **-sembled; -sembling** : parecerse a, asemejarse a
resent [ri'zɛnt] *vt* : resentirse de, ofenderse por
resentful [ri'zɛntfəl] *adj* : resentido, rencoroso — **resentfully** *adv*
resentment [ri'zɛntmənt] *n* : resentimiento *m*
reservation [ˌrɛzər'veɪʃən] *n* **1** : reservación *f*, reserva *f* ⟨to make a reservation : hacer una reservación⟩ **2** DOUBT, MISGIVING : reserva *f*, duda *f* ⟨without reservations : sin reservas⟩ **3** : reserva *f* (de indios americanos)
reserve[1] [ri'zərv] *vt* **-served; -serving** : reservar
reserve[2] *n* **1** STOCK : reserva *f* ⟨to keep in reserve : guardar en reserva⟩ **2** RESTRAINT : reserva *f*, moderación *f* **3 reserves** *npl* : reservas *fpl* (militares)
reserved [ri'zərvd] *adj* : reservado
reservoir ['rɛzərˌvwɑr, -ˌvwɔr, -ˌvɔr] *n* : embalse *m*
reset [ˌri:'sɛt] *vt* **-set; -setting** : reajustar, poner en hora (un reloj), reiniciar (una computadora)
reside [ri'zaɪd] *vi* **-sided; -siding** **1** DWELL : residir **2** LIE : radicar, residir ⟨the power resides in the presidency : el poder radica en la presidencia⟩
residence ['rɛzədənts] *n* : residencia *f*
resident[1] ['rɛzədənt] *adj* : residente
resident[2] *n* : residente *mf*
residential [ˌrɛzə'dɛnʧəl] *adj* : residencial
residual [ri'zɪʤʊəl] *adj* : residual
residue ['rɛzəˌdu:, -ˌdju:] *n* : residuo *m*, resto *m*

resign [ri'zaɪn] *vt* **1** QUIT : dimitir, renunciar **2 to resign oneself** : aguantarse, resignarse
resignation [ˌrɛzɪg'neɪʃən] *n* : resignación *f*
resignedly [ri'zaɪnədli] *adv* : con resignación
resilience [ri'zɪljənts] *n* **1** : capacidad *f* de recuperación, adaptabilidad *f* **2** ELASTICITY : elasticidad *f*
resiliency [ri'zɪljəntsi] → **resilience**
resilient [ri'zɪljənt] *adj* **1** STRONG : resistente, fuerte **2** ELASTIC : elástico
resin ['rɛzən] *n* : resina *f*
resist [ri'zɪst] *vt* **1** WITHSTAND : resistir ⟨to resist heat : resistir el calor⟩ **2** OPPOSE : oponerse a
resistance [ri'zɪstənts] *n* : resistencia *f*
resistant [ri'zɪstənt] *adj* : resistente
resolute ['rɛzəˌlu:t] *adj* : firme, resuelto, decidido
resolutely ['rɛzəˌlu:tli, ˌrzə'-] *adv* : resueltamente, firmemente
resolution [ˌrɛzə'lu:ʃən] *n* **1** SOLUTION : solución *f* **2** RESOLVE : resolución *f*, determinación *f* **3** DECISION : propósito *m*, decisión *f* ⟨New Year's resolutions : propósitos para el Año Nuevo⟩ **4** MOTION, PROPOSAL : moción *f*, resolución *f* (legislativa)
resolve[1] [ri'zɑlv] *vt* **-solved; -solving 1** SOLVE : resolver, solucionar **2** DECIDE : resolver ⟨she resolved to get more sleep : resolvió dormir más⟩
resolve[2] *n* : resolución *f*, determinación *f*
resonance ['rɛzənənts] *n* : resonancia *f*
resonant ['rɛzənənt] *adj* : resonante, retumbante
resort[1] [ri'zɔrt] *vi* **to resort to** : recurrir ⟨to resort to force : recurrir a la fuerza⟩
resort[2] *n* **1** RECOURSE : recurso *m* ⟨as a last resort : como último recurso⟩ **2** HANGOUT : lugar *m* popular, lugar *m* muy frecuentado **3** : lugar *m* de vacaciones ⟨tourist resort : centro turístico⟩
resound [ri'zaʊnd] *vi* : retumbar, resonar
resounding [ri'zaʊndɪŋ] *adj* **1** RESONANT : retumbante, resonante **2** ABSOLUTE, CATEGORICAL : rotundo, tremendo ⟨a resounding success : un éxito rotundo⟩
resource ['ri:ˌsors, ri'sors] *n* **1** RESOURCEFULNESS : ingenio *m*, recursos *mpl* **2 resources** *npl* : recursos *mpl* ⟨natural resources : recursos naturales⟩ **3 resources** *npl* MEANS : recursos *mpl*, medios *mpl*, fondos *mpl*
resourceful [ri'sorsfəl, -'zors-] *adj* : ingenioso
resourcefulness [ri'sorsfəlnəs, -'zors-] *n* : ingenio *m*, recursos *mpl*, inventiva *f*
respect[1] [ri'spɛkt] *vt* : respetar, estimar
respect[2] *n* **1** REFERENCE : relación *f*, respeto *m* ⟨with respect to : en lo que respecta a⟩ **2** ESTEEM : respeto *m*, estima *f* **3** DETAIL, PARTICULAR : detalle *m*, sentido *m*, respeto *m* ⟨in some respects : en algunos sentidos⟩ **4 respects** *npl* : respetos *mpl* ⟨to pay one's respects : presentar uno susrespetos⟩
respectability [riˌspɛktə'bɪləṭi] *n* : respetabilidad *f*
respectable [ri'spɛktəbəl] *adj* **1** PROPER : respetable, decente **2** CONSIDERABLE : considerable, respetable ⟨a respectable amount : una cantidad respetable⟩ — **respectably** [-bli] *adv*
respectful [ri'spɛktfəl] *adj* : respetuoso — **respectfully** *adv*
respectfulness [ri'spɛktfəlnəs] *n* : respetuosidad *f*
respective [ri'spɛktɪv] *adj* : respectivo ⟨their respective homes : sus casas respectivas⟩ — **respectively** *adv*
respiration [ˌrɛspə'reɪʃən] *n* : respiración *f*
respirator ['rɛspəˌreɪṭər] *n* : respirador *m*
respiratory ['rɛspərəˌtori, rɪ'spaɪrə-] *adj* : respiratorio
respite ['rɛspɪt, rɪ'spaɪt] *n* : respiro *m*, tregua *f*
resplendent [ri'splɛndənt] *adj* : resplandeciente — **resplendently** *adv*
respond [ri'spɑnd] *vi* **1** ANSWER : contestar, responder **2** REACT : responder, reaccionar ⟨to respond to treatment : responder al tratamiento⟩
response [ri'spɑnts] *n* : respuesta *f*
responsibility [riˌspɑntsə'bɪləṭi] *n, pl* **-ties** : responsabilidad *f*
responsible [ri'spɑntsəbəl] *adj* : responsable — **responsibly** [-bli] *adv*
responsive [ri'spɑntsɪv] *adj* **1** ANSWERING : que responde **2** SENSITIVE : sensible, receptivo
responsiveness [ri'spɑntsɪvnəs] *n* : receptividad *f*, sensibilidad *f*
rest[1] ['rɛst] *vi* **1** REPOSE : reposar, descansar **2** RELAX : quedarse tranquilo **3** STOP : pararse, detenerse **4** DEPEND : basarse (en), descansar (sobre), depender (de) ⟨the decision rests with her : la decisión pesa sobre ella⟩ **5 to rest on** : apoyarse en, descansar sobre ⟨to rest on one's arm : apoyarse en el brazo⟩ — *vt* **1** RELAX : descansar **2** SUPPORT : apoyar **3 to rest one's eyes on** : fijar la mirada en
rest[2] *n* **1** RELAXATION, REPOSE : reposo *m*, descanso *m* **2** SUPPORT : soporte *m*, apoyo *m* **3** : silencio *m* (en música) **4** REMAINDER : resto *m* **5 to come to rest** : pararse
restart [ri'stɑrt] *vt* **1** : volver a empezar **2** RESUME : reanudar **3** : volver a arrancar (un motor), reiniciar (una computadora) — *vi* **1** : reanudarse **2** : volver a arrancar
restatement [ˌri:'steɪtmənt] *n* : repetición *f*
restaurant ['rɛstəˌrɑnt, -rənt] *n* : restaurante *m*

restful [ˈrɛstfəl] *adj* **1** RELAXING : relajante **2** PEACEFUL : tranquilo, sosegado
restitution [ˌrɛstəˈtuːʃən, -ˈtjuː-] *n* : restitución *f*
restive [ˈrɛstɪv] *adj* : inquieto, nervioso
restless [ˈrɛstləs] *adj* **1** FIDGETY : inquieto, agitado **2** IMPATIENT : impaciente **3** SLEEPLESS : desvelado ⟨a restless night : una noche en blanco⟩
restlessly [ˈrɛstləsli] *adv* : nerviosamente
restlessness [ˈrɛstləsnəs] *n* : inquietud *f*, agitación *f*
restoration [ˌrɛstəˈreɪʃən] *n* : restauración *f*, restablecimiento *m*
restore [riˈstor] *vt* **-stored; -storing 1** RETURN : volver **2** REESTABLISH : restablecer **3** REPAIR : restaurar
restrain [riˈstreɪn] *vt* **1** : refrenar, contener **2 to restrain oneself** : contenerse
restrained [riˈstreɪnd] *adj* : comedido, templado, contenido
restraint [riˈstreɪnt] *n* **1** RESTRICTION : restricción *f*, limitación *f*, control *m* **2** CONFINEMENT : encierro *m* **3** RESERVE : reserva *f*, control *m* de sí mismo
restrict [riˈstrɪkt] *vt* : restringir, limitar, constreñir
restricted [riˈstrɪktəd] *adj* **1** LIMITED : limitado, restringido **2** CLASSIFIED : secreto, confidencial
restriction [riˈstrɪkʃən] *n* : restricción *f*
restrictive [riˈstrɪktɪv] *adj* : restrictivo — **restrictively** *adv*
rest room *n* : servicios *mpl*, baño *m*
restructure [riˈstrʌkʧər] *vt* **-tured; -turing** : reestructurar
result[1] [riˈzʌlt] *vi* : resultar ⟨to result in : resultar en, tener por resultado⟩
result[2] *n* : resultado *m*, consecuencia *f* ⟨as a result of : como consecuencia de⟩
resultant [riˈzʌltənt] *adj* : resultante
resume [riˈzuːm] *v* **-sumed; -suming** *vt* : reanudar — *vi* : reanudarse
résumé *or* **resume** *or* **resumé** [ˈrɛzə ˌmeɪ, ˌrɛzəˈ-] *n* **1** SUMMARY : resumen *m* **2** CURRICULUM VITAE : currículum *m*, currículo *m*
resumption [riˈzʌmpʃən] *n* : reanudación *f*
resurface [ˌriːˈsərfəs] *v* **-faced; -facing** *vt* : pavimentar (una carretera) de nuevo — *vi* : volver a salir en la superficie
resurgence [riˈsərʤənts] *n* : resurgimiento *m*
resurrect [ˌrɛzəˈrɛkt] *vt* : resucitar, desempolvar
resurrection [ˌrɛzəˈrɛkʃən] *n* : resurrección *f*
resuscitate [riˈsʌsəˌteɪt] *vt* **-tated; -tating** : resucitar, revivir
resuscitation [riˌsʌsəˈteɪʃən] *n* : reanimación *f*, resucitación *f*
retail[1] [ˈriːˌteɪl] *vt* : vender al por menor, vender al detalle
retail[2] *adv* : al por menor, al detalle
retail[3] *adj* : detallista, minorista
retail[4] *n* : venta *f* al detalle, venta *f* al por menor
retailer [ˈriːˌteɪlər] *n* : detallista *mf*, minorista *mf*
retain [riˈteɪn] *vt* : retener, conservar, guardar
retainer [riˈteɪnər] *n* **1** SERVANT : criado *m*, -da *f* **2** ADVANCE : anticipo *m*
retaliate [riˈtæliˌeɪt] *vi* **-ated; -ating** : responder, contraatacar, tomar represalias
retaliation [riˌtæliˈeɪʃən] *n* : represalia *f*, retaliación *f*
retard [riˈtɑrd] *vt* : retardar, retrasar
retardation [ˌriːˌtɑrˈdeɪʃən] *n* **1** : retardación *f* **2** *or* **mental retardation** : retraso *m* mental
retarded [riˈtɑrdəd] *adj* : retrasado
retch [ˈrɛʧ] *vi* : hacer arcadas
retention [riˈtɛnʧən] *n* : retención *f*
retentive [riˈtɛntɪv] *adj* : retentivo
rethink [riːˈθɪŋk] *vt* **-thought; -thinking** : reconsiderar, repensar
reticence [ˈrɛt̬əsənts] *n* : reticencia *f*
reticent [ˈrɛt̬əsənt] *adj* : reticente
retina [ˈrɛtənə] *n, pl* **-nas** *or* **-nae** [-əni, -ənˌaɪ] : retina *f*
retinue [ˈrɛtənˌuː, -ˌjuː] *n* : séquito *m*, comitiva *f*, cortejo *m*
retire [riˈtaɪr] *vi* **-tired; -tiring 1** RETREAT, WITHDRAW : retirarse, retraerse **2** : retirarse, jubilarse (de su trabajo) **3** : acostarse, irse a dormir
retiree [riˌtaɪˈriː] *n* : jubilado *m*, -da *f*
retirement [riˈtaɪrmənt] *n* : jubilación *f*
retiring [riˈtaɪrɪŋ] *adj* SHY : retraído
retort[1] [riˈtɔrt] *vt* : replicar
retort[2] *n* : réplica *f*
retrace [ˌriːˈtreɪs] *vt* **-traced; -tracing** : volver sobre, desandar ⟨to retrace one's steps : volver uno sobre sus pasos⟩
retract [riˈtrækt] *vt* **1** TAKE BACK, WITHDRAW : retirar, retractarse de **2** : retraer (las garras) — *vi* : retractarse
retractable [riˈtræktəbəl] *adj* : retractable
retrain [ˌriːˈtreɪn] *vt* : reciclar, reconvertir
retreat[1] [riˈtriːt] *vi* : retirarse
retreat[2] *n* **1** WITHDRAWAL : retirada *f*, repliegue *m*, retiro *m* ⟨to beat a retreat : batirse en retirada⟩ **2** REFUGE : retiro *m*, refugio *m*
retrench [riˈtrɛnʧ] *vt* : reducir (gastos) — *vi* : economizar
retribution [ˌrɛtrəˈbjuːʃən] *n* PUNISHMENT : castigo *m*, pena *f* merecida
retrieval [riˈtriːvəl] *n* : recuperación *f* ⟨beyond retrieval : irrecuperable⟩ ⟨data retrieval : recuperación de datos⟩
retrieve [riˈtriːv] *vt* **-trieved; -trieving 1** : cobrar ⟨to retrieve game : cobrar la caza⟩ **2** RECOVER : recuperar
retriever [riˈtriːvər] *n* : perro *m* cobrador

retroactive [ˌrɛtro'æktɪv] *adj* : retroactivo — **retroactively** *adv*
retrograde ['rɛtrəˌgreɪd] *adj* : retrógrado
retrospect ['rɛtrəˌspɛkt] *n* **in retrospect** : mirando hacia atrás, retrospectivamente
retrospective [ˌrɛtrə'spɛktɪv] *adj* : retrospectivo
return[1] [ri'tərn] *vi* **1** : volver, regresar ⟨to return home : regresar a casa⟩ **2** REAPPEAR : reaparecer, resurgir **3** ANSWER : responder — *vt* **1** REPLACE, RESTORE : devolver, volver (a poner), restituir ⟨to return something to its place : volver a poner algo en su lugar⟩ **2** YIELD : producir, redituar, rendir **3** REPAY : pagar, devolver ⟨to return a compliment : devolver un cumplido⟩
return[2] *adj* : de vuelta
return[3] *n* **1** RETURNING : regreso *m*, vuelta *f*, retorno *m* **2** *or* **tax return** : declaración *f* de impuestos **3** YIELD : rédito *m*, rendimiento *m*, ganancia *f* **4 returns** *npl* DATA, RESULTS : resultados *mpl*, datos *mpl*
reunion [ri'ju:njən] *n* : reunión *f*, reencuentro *m*
reunite [ˌri:jʊ'naɪt] *v* **-nited; -niting** *vt* : (volver a) reunir — *vi* : (volver a) reunirse
reusable [ri'ju:zəbəl] *adj* : reutilizable
reuse [ri'ju:z] *vt* **-used; -using** : reutilizar, usar de nuevo
revamp [ˌri'væmp] *vt* : renovar
reveal [ri'vi:l] *vt* **1** DIVULGE : revelar, divulgar ⟨to reveal a secret : revelar un secreto⟩ **2** SHOW : manifestar, mostrar, dejar ver
revealing [ri'vi:lɪŋ] *adj* : revelador
reveille ['rɛvəli] *n* : toque *m* de diana
revel[1] ['rɛvəl] *vi* **-eled** *or* **-elled; -eling** *or* **-elling 1** CAROUSE : ir de juerga **2 to revel in** : deleitarse en
revel[2] *n* : juerga *f*, parranda *f fam*
revelation [ˌrɛvə'leɪʃən] *n* : revelación *f*
reveler *or* **reveller** ['rɛvələr] *n* : juerguista *mf*
revelry ['rɛvəlri] *n, pl* **–ries** : juerga *f*, parranda *f fam*, jarana *f fam*
revenge[1] [ri'vɛnʤ] *vt* **-venged; -venging** : vengar ⟨to revenge oneself on : vengarse de⟩
revenge[2] *n* : venganza *f*
revenue ['rɛvəˌnu:, -ˌnju:] *n* : ingresos *mpl*, rentas *fpl*
reverberate [ri'vərbəˌreɪt] *vi* **-ated; -ating** : reverberar
reverberation [riˌvərbə'reɪʃən] *n* : reverberación *f*
revere [ri'vɪr] *vt* **-vered; -vering** : reverenciar, venerar
reverence ['rɛvərən*t*s] *n* : reverencia *f*, veneración *f*
reverend ['rɛvərənd] *adj* : reverendo ⟨the Reverend John Chapin : el reverendo John Chapin⟩
reverent ['rɛvərənt] *adj* : reverente — **reverently** *adv*
reverie ['rɛvəri] *n, pl* **-eries** : ensueño *m*
reversal [ri'vərsəl] *n* **1** INVERSION : inversión *f* (del orden normal) **2** CHANGE : cambio *m* total **3** SETBACK : revés *m*, contratiempo *m*
reverse[1] [ri'vərs] *v* **-versed; -versing** *vt* **1** INVERT : invertir **2** CHANGE : cambiar totalmente **3** ANNUL : anular, revocar — *vi* : dar marcha atrás
reverse[2] *adj* **1** : inverso ⟨in reverse order : en orden inverso⟩ ⟨the reverse side : el reverso⟩ **2** OPPOSITE : contrario, opuesto
reverse[3] *n* **1** OPPOSITE : lo contrario, lo opuesto **2** SETBACK : revés *m*, contratiempo *m* **3** BACK : reverso *m*, dorso *m*, revés *m* **4** *or* **reverse gear** : marcha *f* atrás, reversa *f Col, Mex*
reversible [ri'vərsəbəl] *adj* : reversible
reversion [ri'vərʒən] *n* : reversión *f*, vuelta *f*
revert [ri'vərt] *vi* : revertir
review[1] [ri'vju:] *vt* **1** REEXAMINE : volver a examinar, repasar (una lección) **2** CRITICIZE : reseñar, hacer una crítica de **3** EXAMINE : examinar, analizar ⟨to review one's life : examinar su vida⟩ **4 to review the troops** : pasar revista a las tropas
review[2] *n* **1** INSPECTION : revista *f* (de tropas) **2** ANALYSIS, OVERVIEW : resumen *m*, análisis *m* ⟨a review of current affairs : un análisis de las actualidades⟩ **3** CRITICISM : reseña *f*, crítica *f* (de un libro, etc.) **4** : repaso *m* (para un examen) **5** REVUE : revista *f* (musical)
reviewer [ri'vju:ər] *n* : crítico *m*, -ca *f*
revile [ri'vaɪl] *vt* **-viled; -viling** : injuriar, denostar
revise [ri'vaɪz] *vt* **-vised; -vising** : revisar, corregir, refundir ⟨to revise a dictionary : corregir un diccionario⟩
revision [ri'vɪʒən] *n* : revisión *f*
revival [ri'vaɪvəl] *n* **1** : renacimiento *m* (de ideas, etc.), restablecimiento *m* (de costumbres, etc.), reactivación *f* (de la economía) **2** : reanimación *f*, resucitación *f* (en medicina) **3** *or* **revival meeting** : asamblea *f* evangelista
revive [ri'vaɪv] *v* **-vived; -viving** *vt* **1** REAWAKEN : reavivar, reanimar, reactivar (la economía), resucitar (a un paciente) **2** REESTABLISH : restablecer — *vi* **1** : renacer, reanimarse, reactivarse **2** COME TO : recobrar el sentido, volver en sí
revoke [ri'vo:k] *vt* **-voked; -voking** : revocar
revolt[1] [ri'vo:lt] *vi* **1** REBEL : rebelarse, sublevarse **2 to revolt at** : sentir repugnancia por — *vt* DISGUST : darle asco (a alguien), repugnar
revolt[2] *n* REBELLION : rebelión *f*, revuelta *f*, sublevación *f*
revolting [ri'vo:ltɪŋ] *adj* : asqueroso, repugnante

revolution [ˌrɛvəˈluːʃən] *n* : revolución *f*
revolutionary[1] [ˌrɛvəˈluːʃənɛˌri] *adj* : revolucionario
revolutionary[2] *n, pl* **-aries** : revolucionario *m*, -ria *f*
revolutionize [ˌrɛvəˈluːʃənˌaɪz] *vt* **-ized; -izing** : cambiar radicalmente, revolucionar
revolve [riˈvɑlv] *v* **-volved; -volving** *vt* ROTATE : hacer girar — *vi* **1** ROTATE : girar ⟨to revolve around : girar alrededor de⟩ **2 to revolve in one's mind** : darle vueltas en la cabeza a alguien
revolver [riˈvɑlvər] *n* : revólver *m*
revue [riˈvjuː] *n* : revista *f* (musical)
revulsion [riˈvʌlʃən] *n* : repugnancia *f*
reward[1] [riˈwɔrd] *vt* : recompensar, premiar
reward[2] *n* : recompensa *f*
rewrite [ˌriːˈraɪt] *vt* **-wrote; -written; -writing** : escribir de nuevo, volver a escribir
rhapsody [ˈræpsədi] *n, pl* **-dies** **1** : elogio *m* excesivo ⟨to go into rhapsodies over : extasiarse por⟩ **2** : rapsodia *f* (en música)
rhetoric [ˈrɛt̬ərɪk] *n* : retórica *f*
rhetorical [rɪˈtɔrɪkəl] *adj* : retórico
rheumatic [rʊˈmæt̬ɪk] *adj* : reumático
rheumatism [ˈruːməˌtɪzəm, ˈrʊ-] *n* : reumatismo *m*
rhinestone [ˈraɪnˌstoːn] *n* : diamante *m* de imitación
rhino [ˈraɪˌnoː] *n, pl* **rhino** *or* **rhinos** → **rhinoceros**
rhinoceros [raɪˈnɑsərəs] *n, pl* **-eroses** *or* **-eros** *or* **-eri** [-ˌraɪ] : rinoceronte *m*
rhododendron [ˌroːdəˈdɛndrən] *n* : rododendro *m*
rhombus [ˈrɑmbəs] *n, pl* **-buses** *or* **-bi** [-ˌbaɪ, -bi] : rombo *m*
rhubarb [ˈruːˌbɑrb] *n* : ruibarbo *m*
rhyme[1] [ˈraɪm] *vi* **rhymed; rhyming** : rimar
rhyme[2] *n* **1** : rima *f* **2** VERSE : verso *m* (en rima)
rhythm [ˈrɪðəm] *n* : ritmo *m*
rhythmic [ˈrɪðmɪk] *or* **rhythmical** [-mɪkəl] *adj* : rítmico — **rhythmically** [-mɪkli] *adv*
rib[1] [ˈrɪb] *vt* **ribbed; ribbing** **1** : hacer en canalé ⟨a ribbed sweater : un suéter en canalé⟩ **2** TEASE : tomarle el pelo (a alguien)
rib[2] *n* **1** : costilla *f* (de una persona o un animal) **2** : nervio *m* (de una bóveda o una hoja), varilla *f* (de un paraguas), canalé *m* (de una prenda tejida)
ribald [ˈrɪbəld] *adj* : escabroso, procaz
ribbon [ˈrɪbən] *n* **1** : cinta *f* **2 to tear to ribbons** : hacer jirones
rice [ˈraɪs] *n* : arroz *m*
rich [ˈrɪʧ] *adj* **1** WEALTHY : rico **2** SUMPTUOUS : suntuoso, lujoso **3** : pesado ⟨rich foods : comida pesada⟩ **4** ABUNDANT : abundante **5** : vivo, intenso ⟨rich colors : colores vivos⟩ **6** FERTILE : fértil, rico
riches [ˈrɪʧəz] *npl* : riquezas *fpl*
richly [ˈrɪʧli] *adv* **1** SUMPTUOUSLY : suntuosamente, ricamente **2** ABUNDANTLY : abundantemente **3 richly deserved** : bien merecido
richness [ˈrɪʧnəs] *n* : riqueza *f*
rickets [ˈrɪkəts] *n* : raquitismo *m*
rickety [ˈrɪkət̬i] *adj* : desvencijado, destartalado
ricksha *or* **rickshaw** [ˈrɪkˌʃɔ] *n* : cochecillo *m* tirado por un hombre
ricochet[1] [ˈrɪkəˌʃeɪ] *vi* **-cheted** [-ˌʃeɪd] *or* **-chetted** [-ˌʃɛt̬əd]; **-cheting** [-ˌʃeɪɪŋ] *or* **-chetting** [-ˌʃɛt̬ɪŋ] : rebotar
ricochet[2] *n* : rebote *m*
rid [ˈrɪd] *vt* **rid; ridding** **1** FREE : librar ⟨to rid the city of thieves : librar la ciudad de ladrones⟩ **2 to rid oneself of** : desembarazarse de
riddance [ˈrɪdənts] *n* : libramiento *m* ⟨good riddance! : ¡adiós y buen viaje!, ¡vete con viento fresco!⟩
riddle[1] [ˈrɪdəl] *vt* **-dled; -dling** : acribillar ⟨riddled with bullets : acribillado a balazos⟩ ⟨riddled with errors : lleno de errores⟩
riddle[2] *n* : acertijo *m*, adivinanza *f*
ride[1] [ˈraɪd] *v* **rode** [ˈroːd]; **ridden** [ˈrɪdən]; **riding** *vt* **1** : montar, ir, andar ⟨to ride a horse : montar a caballo⟩ ⟨to ride a bicycle : montar en bicicleta, andar en bicicleta⟩ ⟨to ride the bus : ir en autobús⟩ **2** TRAVERSE : recorrer ⟨he rode 5 miles : recorrió 5 millas⟩ **3** TEASE : burlarse de, ridiculizar **4** CARRY : llevar **5** WEATHER : capear ⟨they rode out the storm : capearon el temporal⟩ **6 to ride the waves** : surcar los mares — *vi* **1** : montar a caballo, cabalgar **2** TRAVEL : ir, viajar (en coche, en bicicleta, etc.) **3** RUN : andar, marchar ⟨the car rides well : el coche anda bien⟩ **4 to ride at anchor** : estar fondeado **5 to let things ride** : dejar pasar las cosas
ride[2] *n* **1** : paseo *m*, vuelta *f* (en coche, en bicicleta, a caballo) ⟨to go for a ride : dar una vuelta⟩ ⟨to give someone a ride : llevar en coche a alguien⟩ **2** : aparato *m* (en un parque de diversiones)
rider [ˈraɪdər] *n* **1** : jinete *mf* ⟨the rider fell off his horse : el jinete se cayó de su caballo⟩ **2** CYCLIST : ciclista *mf* **3** MOTORCYCLIST : motociclista *mf* **4** CLAUSE : cláusula *f* añadida
ridge [ˈrɪʤ] *n* **1** CHAIN : cadena *f* (de montañas o cerros) **2** : caballete *m* (de un techo), cresta *f* (de una ola o una montaña), cordoncillo *m* (de telas)
ridicule[1] [ˈrɪdəˌkjuːl] *vt* **-culed; -culing** : burlarse de, mofarse de, ridiculizar
ridicule[2] *n* : burlas *fpl*
ridiculous [rəˈdɪkjələs] *adj* : ridículo, absurdo
ridiculously [rəˈdɪkjələsli] *adv* : de forma ridícula
rife [ˈraɪf] *adj* : abundante, común ⟨to be rife with : estar plagado de⟩

riffraff ['rɪf,ræf] *n* : chusma *f*, gentuza *f*

rifle[1] ['raɪfəl] *v* **-fled; -fling** *vt* RANSACK : desvalijar, saquear — *vi* **to rifle through** : revolver

rifle[2] *n* : rifle *m*, fusil *m*

rift ['rɪft] *n* **1** FISSURE : grieta *f*, fisura *f* **2** BREAK : ruptura *f* (entre personas), división *f* (dentro de un grupo)

rig[1] ['rɪg] *vt* **rigged; rigging 1** : aparejar (un barco) **2** EQUIP : equipar **3** FIX : amañar (una elección, etc.) **4 to rig up** CONSTRUCT : construir, erigir **5 to rig oneself out as** : vestirse de

rig[2] *n* **1** : aparejo *m* (de un barco) **2** *or* **oil rig** : torre *f* de perforación, plataforma *f* petrolífera

rigging ['rɪgɪŋ, -gən] *n* : jarcia *f*, aparejo *m*

right[1] ['raɪt] *vt* **1** FIX, RESTORE : reparar ⟨to right the economy : reparar la economía⟩ **2** STRAIGHTEN : enderezar

right[2] *adv* **1** : bien ⟨to live right : vivir bien⟩ **2** PRECISELY : precisamente, justo ⟨right in the middle : justo en medio⟩ **3** DIRECTLY, STRAIGHT : derecho, directamente ⟨he went right home : fue derecho a casa⟩ **4** IMMEDIATELY : inmediatamente ⟨right after lunch : inmediatamente después del almuerzo⟩ **5** COMPLETELY : completamente ⟨he felt right at home : se sintió completamente cómodo⟩ **6** : a la derecha ⟨to look left and right : mirar a la izquierda y a la derecha⟩

right[3] *adj* **1** UPRIGHT : bueno, honrado ⟨right conduct : conducta honrada⟩ **2** CORRECT : correcto ⟨the right answer : la respuesta correcta⟩ **3** APPROPRIATE : apropiado, adecuado, debido ⟨the right man for the job : el hombre perfecto para el trabajo⟩ **4** STRAIGHT : recto ⟨a right line : una línea recta⟩ **5** : derecho ⟨the right hand : la mano derecha⟩ **6** SOUND : bien ⟨he's not in his right mind : no está bien de la cabeza⟩

right[4] *n* **1** GOOD : bien *m* ⟨to do right : hacer el bien⟩ **2** : derecha *f* ⟨on the right : a la derecha⟩ **3** *or* **right hand** : mano *f* derecha **4** ENTITLEMENT : derecho *m* ⟨the right to vote : el derecho a votar⟩ ⟨women's rights : los derechos de la mujer⟩ **5 the Right** : la derecha (en la política)

right angle *n* : ángulo *m* recto

right–angled ['raɪt̬'æŋgəld] *or* **right–angle** [-gəl] *adj* **1** : en ángulo recto **2 right–angled triangle** : triángulo *m* rectángulo

righteous ['raɪtʃəs] *adj* : recto, honrado — **righteously** *adv*

righteousness ['raɪtʃəsnəs] *n* : rectitud *f*, honradez *f*

rightful ['raɪtfəl] *adj* **1** JUST : justo **2** LAWFUL : legítimo — **rightfully** *adv*

right–hand ['raɪt'hænd] *adj* **1** : situado a la derecha **2** RIGHT-HANDED : para la mano derecha, con la mano derecha **3 right–hand man** : brazo *m* derecho

right–handed ['raɪt'hændəd] *adj* **1** : diestro ⟨a right-handed pitcher : un lanzador diestro⟩ **2** : para la mano derecha, con la mano derecha **3** CLOCKWISE : en la dirección de las manecillas del reloj

rightly ['raɪtli] *adv* **1** JUSTLY : justamente, con razón **2** PROPERLY : debidamente, apropiadamente **3** CORRECTLY : correctamente

right–of–way ['raɪt̬ə'weɪ, -əv-] *n, pl* **rights–of–way 1** : preferencia (del tráfico) **2** ACCESS : derecho *m* de paso

rightward ['raɪtwərd] *adj* : a la derecha, hacia la derecha

right–wing ['raɪt'wɪŋ] *adj* : derechista

right wing *n* **the right wing** : la derecha

right–winger ['raɪt'wɪŋər] *n* : derechista *mf*

rigid ['rɪʤɪd] *adj* : rígido — **rigidly** *adv*

rigidity [rɪ'ʤɪdət̬i] *n, pl* **-ties** : rigidez *f*

rigmarole ['rɪgmə,ro:l, 'rɪgə-] *n* **1** NONSENSE : galimatías *m*, disparates *mpl* **2** PROCEDURES : trámites *mpl*

rigor ['rɪgər] *n* : rigor *m*

rigor mortis [,rɪgər'mɔrt̬əs] *n* : rigidez *f* cadavérica

rigorous ['rɪgərəs] *adj* : riguroso — **rigorously** *adv*

rile ['raɪl] *vt* **riled; riling** : irritar

rill ['rɪl] *n* : riachuelo *m*

rim ['rɪm] *n* **1** EDGE : borde *m* **2** : llanta *f*, rin *m Col, Mex* (de una rueda) **3** FRAME : montura *f* (de anteojos)

rime ['raɪm] *n* : escarcha *f*

rind ['raɪnd] *n* : corteza *f*

ring[1] ['rɪŋ] *v* **rang** ['ræŋ]; **rung** ['rʌŋ]; **ringing** *vi* **1** : sonar ⟨the doorbell rang : el timbre sonó⟩ ⟨to ring for : llamar⟩ **2** RESOUND : resonar **3** SEEM : parecer ⟨to ring true : parecer cierto⟩ — *vt* **1** : tocar, hacer sonar (un timbre, una alarma, etc.) **2** SURROUND : cercar, rodear

ring[2] *n* **1** : anillo *m*, sortija *f* ⟨wedding ring : anillo de matrimonio⟩ **2** BAND : aro *m*, anillo *m* ⟨piston ring : aro de émbolo⟩ **3** CIRCLE : círculo *m* **4** ARENA : arena *f*, ruedo *m* ⟨a boxing ring : un cuadrilátero, un ring⟩ **5** GANG : banda *f* (de ladrones, etc.) **6** SOUND : timbre *m*, sonido *m* **7** CALL : llamada *f* (por teléfono)

ringer ['rɪŋər] *n* **to be a dead ringer for** : ser un vivo retrato de

ringleader ['rɪŋ,li:dər] *n* : cabecilla *mf*

ringlet ['rɪŋlət] *n* : sortija *f*, rizo *m*

ringworm ['rɪŋ,wərm] *n* : tiña *f*

rink ['rɪŋk] *n* : pista *f* ⟨skating rink : pista de patinaje⟩

rinse[1] ['rɪnts] *vt* **rinsed; rinsing** : enjuagar ⟨to rinse out one's mouth : enjuagarse la boca⟩

rinse[2] *n* : enjuague *m*

riot[1] ['raɪət] *vi* : amotinarse

riot[2] *n* : motín *m*, tumulto *m*, alboroto *m*

rioter [ˈraɪət̬ər] *n* : alborotador *m*, -dora *f*
riotous [ˈraɪət̬əs] *adj* **1** UNRULY, WILD : desenfrenado, alborotado **2** ABUNDANT : abundante
rip[1] [ˈrɪp] *v* **ripped; ripping** *vt* : rasgar, arrancar, desgarrar — *vi* : rasgarse, desgarrarse
rip[2] *n* : rasgón *m*, desgarrón *m*
ripe [ˈraɪp] *adj* **riper; ripest 1** MATURE : maduro ⟨ripe fruit : fruta madura⟩ **2** READY : listo, preparado
ripen [ˈraɪpən] *v* : madurar
ripeness [ˈraɪpnəs] *n* : madurez *f*
rip–off [ˈrɪp,ɔf] *n* **1** THEFT : robo *m* **2** SWINDLE : estafa *f*, timo *m fam*
rip off *vt* **1** : rasgar, arrancar, desgarrar **2** SWINDLE *fam* : estafar, tifar
ripple[1] [ˈrɪpəl] *v* **-pled; -pling** *vi* : rizarse, ondear, ondular — *vt* : rizar
ripple[2] *n* : onda *f*, ondulación *f*
rise[1] [ˈraɪz] *vi* **rose** [ˈro:z]; **risen** [ˈrɪz-ən]; **rising 1** GET UP : levantarse ⟨to rise to one's feet : ponerse de pie⟩ **2** : elevarse, alzarse ⟨the mountains rose to the west : las montañas se elevaron al oeste⟩ **3** : salir (dícese del sol y de la luna) **4** : subir (dícese de las aguas, del humo, etc.) ⟨the river rose : las aguas subieron de nivel⟩ **5** INCREASE : aumentar, subir **6** ORIGINATE : nacer, proceder **7 to rise in rank** : ascender **8 to rise up** REBEL : sublevarse, rebelarse
rise[2] *n* **1** ASCENT : ascensión *f*, subida *f* **2** ORIGIN : origen *m* **3** ELEVATION : elevación *f* **4** INCREASE : subida *f*, aumento *m*, alzamiento *m* **5** SLOPE : pendiente *f*, cuesta *f*
riser [ˈraɪzər] *n* **1** : contrahuella *f* (de una escalera) **2 early riser** : madrugador *m*, -dora *f* **3 late riser** : dormilón *m*, -lona *f*
risk[1] [ˈrɪsk] *vt* : arriesgar
risk[2] *n* : riesgo *m*, peligro *m* ⟨at risk : en peligro⟩ ⟨at your own risk : por su cuenta y riesgo⟩
risky [ˈrɪski] *adj* **riskier; -est** : arriesgado, peligroso, riesgoso
risqué [rɪˈskeɪ] *adj* : escabroso, picante, subido de tono
rite [ˈraɪt] *n* : rito *m*
ritual[1] [ˈrɪʧʊəl] *adj* : ritual — **ritually** *adv*
ritual[2] *n* : ritual *m*
rival[1] [ˈraɪvəl] *vt* **-valed** *or* **-valled; -valing** *or* **-valling** : rivalizar con, competir con
rival[2] *adj* : competidor, rival
rival[3] *n* : rival *mf*; competidor *m*, -dora *f*
rivalry [ˈraɪvəlri] *n, pl* **-ries** : rivalidad *f*, competencia *f*
river [ˈrɪvər] *n* : río *m*
riverbank [ˈrɪvər,bæŋk] *n* : ribera *f*, orilla *f*
riverbed [ˈrɪvər,bɛd] *n* : cauce *m*, lecho *m*
riverside [ˈrɪvər,saɪd] *n* : ribera *f*, orilla *f*
rivet[1] [ˈrɪvət] *vt* **1** : remachar **2** FIX : fijar (los ojos, etc.) **3** FASCINATE : fascinar, cautivar
rivet[2] *n* : remache *m*
rivulet [ˈrɪvjələt] *n* : arroyo *m*, riachuelo *m* ⟨rivulets of sweat : gotas de sudor⟩
roach [ˈro:ʧ] → **cockroach**
road [ˈro:d] *n* **1** : carretera *f*, calle *f*, camino *m* **2** PATH : camino *m*, sendero *m*, vía *f* ⟨on the road to a solution : en vías de una solución⟩
roadblock [ˈro:d,blɑk] *n* : control *m*
roadrunner [ˈro:d,rʌnər] *n* : correcaminos *m*
roadside [ˈro:d,saɪd] *n* : borde *m* de la carretera
roadway [ˈro:d,weɪ] *n* : carretera *f*, calzada *f*
roam [ˈro:m] *vi* : vagar, deambular, errar — *vt* : vagar por
roan[1] [ˈro:n] *adj* : ruano
roan[2] *n* : caballo *m* ruano
roar[1] [ˈror] *vi* : rugir, bramar ⟨to roar with laughter : reírse a carcajadas⟩ — *vt* : decir a gritos
roar[2] *n* **1** : rugido *m*, bramido *m* (de un animal) **2** DIN : clamor *m* (de gente), fragor *m* (del trueno), estruendo *m* (del tráfico, etc.)
roast[1] [ˈro:st] *vt* : asar (carne, papas), tostar (café, nueces) — *vi* : asarse
roast[2] *adj* **1** : asado ⟨roast chicken : pollo asado⟩ **2 roast beef** : rosbif *m*
roast[3] *n* : asado *m*
rob [ˈrɑb] *v* **robbed; robbing** *vt* **1** STEAL : robar **2** DEPRIVE : privar, quitar — *vi* : robar
robber [ˈrɑbər] *n* : ladrón *m*, -drona *f*
robbery [ˈrɑbəri] *n, pl* **-beries** : robo *m*
robe[1] [ˈro:b] *vt* **robed; robing** : vestirse
robe[2] *n* **1** : toga *f* (de magistrados, etc.), sotana *f* (de eclesiásticos) ⟨robe of office : traje de ceremonias⟩ **2** BATHROBE : bata *f*
robin [ˈrɑbən] *n* : petirrojo *m*
robot [ˈro:,bɑt, -bət] *n* : robot *m*
robotic [roˈbɑt̬ɪk] *adj* : robótico, robotizado
robotics [roˈbɑt̬ɪks] *ns & pl* : robótica *f*
robust [roˈbʌst, ˈro:,bʌst] *adj* : robusto, fuerte — **robustly** *adv*
rock[1] [ˈrɑk] *vt* **1** : acunar (a un niño), mecer (una cuna) **2** SHAKE : sacudir — *vi* SWAY : mecerse, balancearse
rock[2] *adj* : de rock
rock[3] *n* **1** ROCKING : balanceo *m* **2** *or* **rock music** : rock *m*, música *f* rock **3** : roca *f* (substancia) **4** STONE : piedra *f*
rock and roll *n* : rock and roll *m*
rocker [ˈrɑkər] *n* **1** : balancín *m* **2** *or* **rocking chair** : mecedora *f*, balancín *m* **3 to be off one's rocker** : estar chiflado, estar loco
rocket[1] [ˈrɑkət] *vi* : dispararse, subir rápidamente
rocket[2] *n* : cohete *m*

rocking horse *n* : caballito *m* (de balancín)
rock salt *n* : sal *f* gema
rocky ['rɑki] *adj* **rockier; -est 1** : rocoso, pedregoso **2** UNSTEADY : inestable
rod ['rɑd] *n* **1** BAR : barra *f*, varilla *f*, vara *f* (de madera) ⟨a fishing rod : una caña (de pescar)⟩ **2** : medida *f* de longitud equivalente a 5.03 metros (5 yardas)
rode → **ride**[1]
rodent ['ro:dənt] *n* : roedor *m*
rodeo ['ro:di,o:, ro'deɪ,o:] *n, pl* **-deos** : rodeo *m*
roe ['ro:] *n* : hueva *f*
rogue ['ro:g] *n* SCOUNDREL : pícaro *m*, -ra *f*; pillo *m*, -lla *f*
roguish ['ro:gɪʃ] *adj* : pícaro, travieso
role ['ro:l] *n* : papel *m*, función *f*, rol *m*
roll[1] ['ro:l] *vt* **1** : hacer rodar ⟨to roll the ball : hacer rodar la pelota⟩ ⟨to roll one's eyes : poner los ojos en blanco⟩ **2** : liar (un cigarrillo) **3** *or* **to roll up** : enrollar ⟨to roll (oneself) up into a ball : hacerse una bola⟩ **4** FLATTEN : estirar (masa), laminar (metales), pasar el rodillo por (el césped) **5 to roll up one's sleeves** : arremangarse — *vi* **1** : rodar ⟨the ball kept on rolling : la pelota siguió rodando⟩ **2** SWAY : balancearse ⟨the ship rolled in the waves : el barco se balanceó en las olas⟩ **3** REVERBERATE, SOUND : tronar (dícese del trueno), redoblar (dícese de un tambor) **4 to roll along** PROCEED : ponerse en marcha **5 to roll around** : revolcarse **6 to roll by** : pasar **7 to roll over** : dar una vuelta
roll[2] *n* **1** LIST : lista *f* ⟨to call the roll : pasar lista⟩ ⟨to have on the roll : tener inscrito⟩ **2** *or* **bread roll** : panecito *m*, bolillo *m Mex* **3** : rollo *m* (de papel, de tela, etc.) ⟨a roll of film : un carrete⟩ ⟨a roll of bills : un fajo⟩ **4** : redoble *m* (de tambores), retumbo *m* (del trueno, etc.) **5** ROLLING, SWAYING : balanceo *m*
roller ['ro:lər] *n* **1** : rodillo *m* **2** CURLER : rulo *m*
roller coaster ['ro:lər,ko:stər] *n* : montaña *f* rusa
roller–skate ['ro:lər,skeɪt] *vi* **-skated; -skating** : patinar (sobre ruedas)
roller skate *n* : patín *m* (de ruedas)
rollicking ['rɑlɪkɪŋ] *adj* : animado, alegre
rolling pin *n* : rodillo *m*
Roman[1] ['ro:mən] *adj* : romano
Roman[2] *n* : romano *m*, -na *f*
Roman Catholic *n* : católico *m*, -ca *f* — **Roman Catholic** *adj*
Roman Catholicism *n* : catolicismo *m*
romance[1] [ro'mænts, 'ro:,mænts] *vi* **-manced; -mancing** FANTASIZE : fantasear
romance[2] *n* **1** : romance *m*, novela *f* de caballerías **2** : novela *f* de amor, novela *f* romántica **3** AFFAIR : romance *m*, amorío *m*
Romanian [rʊ'meɪniən, ro-] *n* **1** : rumano *m*, -na *f* **2** : rumano *m* (idioma) — **Romanian** *adj*
Roman numeral *n* : número *m* romano
romantic [ro'mæntɪk] *adj* : romántico — **romantically** [-tɪkli] *adv*
romp[1] ['rɑmp] *vi* FROLIC : retozar, juguetear
romp[2] *n* : retozo *m*
roof[1] ['ru:f, 'rʊf] *vt* : techar
roof[2] *n, pl* **roofs** ['ru:fs, 'rʊfs; 'ru:vz, 'rʊvz] **1** : techo *m*, tejado *m*, techado *m* **2 roof of the mouth** : paladar *m*
roofing ['ru:fɪŋ, 'rʊfɪŋ] *n* : techumbre *f*
rooftop ['ru:f,tɑp, 'rʊf-] *n* ROOF : tejado *m*
rook[1] ['rʊk] *vt* CHEAT : defraudar, estafar, timar
rook[2] *n* **1** : grajo *m* (ave) **2** : torre *f* (en ajedrez)
rookie ['rʊki] *n* : novato *m*, -ta *f*
room[1] ['ru:m, 'rʊm] *vi* LODGE : alojarse, hospedarse
room[2] *n* **1** SPACE : espacio *m*, sitio *m*, lugar *m* ⟨to make room for : hacer lugar para⟩ **2** : cuarto *m*, habitación *f* (en una casa), sala *f* (para reuniones, etc.) **3** BEDROOM : dormitorio *m*, habitación *f*, pieza *f* **4** (*indicating possibility or opportunity*) ⟨room for improvement : posibilidad de mejorar⟩ ⟨there's no room for error : no hay lugar para errores⟩
roomer ['ru:mər, 'rʊmər] *n* : inquilino *m*, -na *f*
rooming house *n* : pensión *f*
roommate ['ru:m,meɪt, 'rʊm-] *n* : compañero *m*, -ra *f* de cuarto
roomy ['ru:mi, 'rʊmi] *adj* **roomier; -est 1** SPACIOUS : espacioso, amplio **2** LOOSE : suelto, holgado ⟨a roomy blouse : una blusa holgada⟩
roost[1] ['ru:st] *vi* : posarse, dormir (en una percha)
roost[2] *n* : percha *f*
rooster ['ru:stər, 'rʊs-] *n* : gallo *m*
root[1] ['ru:t, 'rʊt] *vi* **1** : arraigar ⟨the plant rooted easily : la planta arraigó con facilidad⟩ ⟨deeply rooted traditions : tradiciones profundamente arraigadas⟩ **2** : hozar (dícese de los cerdos) ⟨to root around in : hurgar en⟩ **3 to root for** : apoyar a, alentar — *vt* **to root out** *or* **to root up** : desarraigar (plantas), extirpar (problemas, etc.)
root[2] *n* **1** : raíz *f* (de una planta) **2** ORIGIN : origen *m*, raíz *f* **3** CORE : centro *m*, núcleo *m* ⟨to get to the root of the matter : ir al centro del asunto⟩
rootless ['ru:tləs, 'rʊt-] *adj* : desarraigado
rope[1] ['ro:p] *vt* **roped; roping 1** TIE : amarrar, atar **2** LASSO : lazar **3 to rope off** : acordonar
rope[2] *n* : soga *f*, cuerda *f*
rosary ['ro:zəri] *n, pl* **-ries** : rosario *m*
rose[1] → **rise**[1]
rose[2] ['ro:z] *adj* : rosa, color de rosa

rose[3] *n* **1** : rosal *m* (planta), rosa *f* (flor) **2** : rosa *m* (color)

rosebush [ˈroːzˌbʊʃ] *n* : rosal *m*

rosemary [ˈroːzˌmɛri] *n, pl* **-maries** : romero *m*

rosette [roˈzɛt] *n* : escarapela *f* (hecho de cintas), roseta *f* (en arquitectura)

Rosh Hashanah [ˌrɑʃhɑˈʃɑnə, ˌroːʃ-] *n* : el Año Nuevo judío

rosin [ˈrɑzən] *n* : colofonia *f*

roster [ˈrɑstər] *n* : lista *f*

rostrum [ˈrɑstrəm] *n, pl* **-trums** *or* **-tra** [-trə] : tribuna *f*, estrado *m*

rosy [ˈroːzi] *adj* **rosier; -est** **1** : sonrosado, de color rosa **2** PROMISING : prometedor, halagüeño

rot[1] [ˈrɑt] *v* **rotted; rotting** *vi* : pudrirse, descomponerse — *vt* : pudrir, descomponer

rot[2] *n* : putrefacción *f*, descomposición *f*, podredumbre *f*

rotary[1] [ˈroːt̬əri] *adj* : rotativo, rotatorio

rotary[2] *n, pl* **-ries** **1** : máquina *f* rotativa **2** TRAFFIC CIRCLE : rotonda *f*, glorieta *f*

rotate [ˈroːˌteɪt] *v* **-tated; -tating** *vi* REVOLVE : girar, rotar — *vt* **1** TURN : hacer girar, darle vueltas a **2** ALTERNATE : alternar

rotation [roˈteɪʃən] *n* : rotación *f*

rote [ˈroːt] *n* **to learn by rote** : aprender de memoria

rotor [ˈroːt̬ər] *n* : rotor *m*

rotten [ˈrɑtən] *adj* **1** PUTRID : podrido, putrefacto **2** CORRUPT : corrompido **3** BAD : malo ⟨a rotten day : un día malísimo⟩

rottenness [ˈrɑtənnəs] *n* : podredumbre *f*

rotund [roˈtʌnd] *adj* **1** ROUNDED : redondeado **2** PLUMP : regordete *fam*, llenito *fam*

rouge [ˈruːʒ, ˈruːdʒ] *n* : colorete *m*

rough[1] [ˈrʌf] *vt* **1** ROUGHEN : poner áspero **2 to rough out** SKETCH : esbozar, bosquejar **3 to rough up** BEAT : darle una paliza (a alguien) **4 to rough it** : vivir sin comodidades

rough[2] *adj* **1** COARSE : áspero, basto **2** UNEVEN : desigual, escabroso, accidentado (dícese del terreno) **3** : agitado (dícese del mar), tempestuoso (dícese del tiempo), violento (dícese del viento) **4** VIOLENT : violento, brutal ⟨a rough neighborhood : un barrio peligroso⟩ **5** DIFFICULT : duro, difícil **6** CRUDE : rudo, tosco, burdo ⟨a rough cottage : una casita tosca⟩ ⟨a rough draft : un borrador⟩ ⟨a rough sketch : un bosquejo⟩ **7** APPROXIMATE : aproximado ⟨a rough idea : una idea aproximada⟩

rough[3] *n* **1 the rough** : el rough (en golf) **2 in the rough** : en borrador

roughage [ˈrʌfɪdʒ] *n* : fibra *f*

roughen [ˈrʌfən] *vt* : poner áspero — *vi* : ponerse áspero

roughly [ˈrʌfli] *adv* **1** : bruscamente ⟨to treat roughly : maltratar⟩ **2** CRUDELY : burdamente **3** APPROXIMATELY : aproximadamente, más o menos

roughneck [ˈrʌfˌnɛk] *n* : matón *m*

roughness [ˈrʌfnəs] *n* : rudeza *f*, aspereza *f*

roulette [ruːˈlɛt] *n* : ruleta *f*

round[1] [ˈraʊnd] *vt* **1** : redondear ⟨she rounded the edges : redondeó los bordes⟩ **2** TURN : doblar ⟨to round the corner : dar la vuelta a la esquina⟩ **3 to round off** : redondear (un número) **4 to round off** *or* **to round out** COMPLETE : rematar, terminar **5 to round up** GATHER : reunir

round[2] *adv* → **around**[1]

round[3] *adj* **1** : redondo ⟨a round table : una mesa redonda⟩ ⟨in round numbers : en números redondos⟩ ⟨round shoulders : espaldas cargadas⟩ **2 round trip** : viaje *m* de ida y vuelta

round[4] *n* **1** CIRCLE : círculo *m* **2** SERIES : serie *f*, sucesión *f* ⟨a round of talks : una ronda de negociaciones⟩ ⟨the daily round : la rutina cotidiana⟩ **3** : asalto *m* (en boxeo), recorrido *m* (en golf), vuelta *f* (en varios juegos) **4** : salva *f* (de aplausos) **5 round of drinks** : ronda *f* **6 round of ammunition** : disparo *m*, cartucho *m* **7 rounds** *npl* : recorridos *mpl* (de un cartero), rondas *fpl* (de un vigilante), visitas *fpl* (de un médico) ⟨to make the rounds : hacer visitas⟩

round[5] *prep* → **around**[2]

roundabout [ˈraʊndəˌbaʊt] *adj* : indirecto ⟨to speak in a roundabout way : hablar con rodeos⟩

roundly [ˈraʊndli] *adv* **1** THOROUGHLY : completamente **2** BLUNTLY : francamente, rotundamente **3** VIGOROUSLY : con vigor

roundness [ˈraʊndnəs] *n* : redondez *f*

roundup [ˈraʊndˌʌp] *n* **1** : rodeo *m* (de animales), redada *f* (de delincuentes, etc.) **2** SUMMARY : resumen *m*

round up *vt* **1** : rodear (ganado), reunir (personas) **2** SUMMARIZE : hacer un resumen de

roundworm [ˈraʊndˌwərm] *n* : lombriz *f* intestinal

rouse [ˈraʊz] *vt* **roused; rousing** **1** AWAKE : despertar **2** EXCITE : excitar ⟨it roused him to fury : lo enfureció⟩

rout[1] [ˈraʊt] *vt* **1** DEFEAT : derrotar, aplastar **2 to rout out** : hacer salir

rout[2] *n* **1** DISPERSAL : desbandada *f*, dispersión *f* **2** DEFEAT : derrota *f* aplastante

route[1] [ˈruːt, ˈraʊt] *vt* **routed; routing** : dirigir, enviar, encaminar

route[2] *n* : camino *m*, ruta *f*, recorrido *m*

routine[1] [ruːˈtiːn] *adj* : rutinario — **routinely** *adv*

routine[2] *n* : rutina *f*

rove [ˈroːv] *v* **roved; roving** *vi* : vagar, errar — *vt* : errar por

rover [ˈroːvər] *n* : vagabundo *m*, -da *f*

row¹ ['ro:] *vt* **1** : avanzar a remo ⟨to row a boat : remar⟩ **2** : llevar a remo ⟨he rowed me to shore : me llevó hasta la orilla⟩ — *vi* : remar

row² ['raʊ] *n* **1** : paseo *m* en barca ⟨to go for a row : salir a remar⟩ **2** LINE, RANK : fila *f*, hilera *f* **3** SERIES : serie *f* ⟨three days in a row : tres días seguidos⟩ **4** RACKET : estruendo *m*, bulla *f* **5** QUARREL : pelea *f*, riña *f*

rowboat ['ro:ˌbo:t] *n* : bote *m* de remos

rowdiness ['raʊdinəs] *n* : bulla *f*

rowdy¹ ['raʊdi] *adj* **-dier; -est** : escandaloso, alborotador

rowdy² *n, pl* **-dies** : alborotador *m*, -dora *f*

rower ['ro:ər] *n* : remero *m*, -ra *f*

royal¹ ['rɔɪəl] *adj* : real — **royally** *adv*

royal² *n* : persona de linaje real, miembro de la familia real

royalty ['rɔɪəlti] *n, pl* **-ties** **1** : realeza *f* (posición) **2** : miembros *mpl* de la familia real **3** **royalties** *npl* : derechos *mpl* de autor

rub¹ ['rʌb] *v* **rubbed; rubbing** *vt* **1** : frotar, restregar ⟨to rub one's hands together : frotarse las manos⟩ **2** MASSAGE : friccionar, masajear **3** CHAFE : rozar **4** POLISH : frotar, pulir **5** SCRUB : fregar **6** **to rub elbows with** : codearse con **7** **to rub someone the wrong way** : sacar de quicio a alguien, caerle mal a alguien — *vi* **to rub against** : rozar

rub² *n* **1** RUBBING : frotamiento *m*, fricción *f* **2** DIFFICULTY : problema *m*

rubber ['rʌbər] *n* **1** : goma *f*, caucho *m*, hule *m Mex* **2** **rubbers** *npl* OVERSHOES : chanclos *mpl*

rubber band *n* : goma *f* (elástica), gomita *f*

rubber–stamp ['rʌbər'stæmp] *vt* **1** APPROVE : aprobar, autorizar **2** STAMP : sellar

rubber stamp *n* : sello *m* (de goma)

rubbery ['rʌbəri] *adj* : gomoso

rubbish ['rʌbɪʃ] *n* : basura *f*, desechos *mpl*, desperdicios *mpl*

rubble ['rʌbəl] *n* : escombros *mpl*, ripio *m*

ruble ['ru:bəl] *n* : rublo *m*

ruby ['ru:bi] *n, pl* **-bies** **1** : rubí *m* (gema) **2** : color *m* de rubí

rudder ['rʌdər] *n* : timón *m*

ruddy ['rʌdi] *adj* **-dier; -est** : rubicundo (dícese de la cara, etc.), rojizo (dícese del cielo)

rude ['ru:d] *adj* **ruder; rudest** **1** CRUDE : tosco, rústico **2** IMPOLITE : grosero, descortés, maleducado **3** ABRUPT : brusco ⟨a rude awakening : una sorpresa desagradable⟩

rudely ['ru:dli] *adv* : groseramente

rudeness ['ru:dnəs] *n* **1** IMPOLITENESS : grosería *f*, descortesía *f*, falta *f* de educación **2** ROUGHNESS : tosquedad *f* **3** SUDDENNESS : brusquedad *f*

rudiment ['ru:dəmənt] *n* : rudimento *m*, noción *f* básica ⟨the rudiments of Spanish : los rudimentos del español⟩

rudimentary [ˌru:də'mɛntəri] *adj* : rudimentario, básico

rue ['ru:] *vt* **rued; ruing** : lamentar, arrepentirse de

rueful ['ru:fəl] *adj* **1** PITIFUL : lastimoso **2** REGRETFUL : arrepentido, pesaroso

ruffian ['rʌfiən] *n* : matón *m*

ruffle¹ ['rʌfəl] *vt* **-fled; -fling** **1** AGITATE : agitar, rizar (agua) **2** RUMPLE : arrugar (ropa), despeinar (pelo) **3** ERECT : erizar (plumas) **4** VEX : alterar, irritar, perturbar **5** : fruncir volantes en (tela)

ruffle² *n* FLOUNCE : volante *m*

ruffly ['rʌfəli] *adj* : con volantes

rug ['rʌg] *n* : alfombra *f*, tapete *m*

rugged ['rʌgəd] *adj* **1** ROUGH, UNEVEN : accidentado, escabroso ⟨rugged mountains : montañas accidentadas⟩ **2** HARSH : duro, severo **3** ROBUST, STURDY : robusto, fuerte

ruin¹ ['ru:ən] *vt* **1** DESTROY : destruir, arruinar **2** BANKRUPT : arruinar, hacer quebrar

ruin² *n* **1** : ruina *f* ⟨to fall into ruin : caer en ruinas⟩ **2** : ruina *f*, perdición *f* ⟨to be the ruin of : ser la perdición de⟩ **3** **ruins** *npl* : ruinas *fpl*, restos *mpl* ⟨the ruins of the ancient temple : las ruinas del templo antiguo⟩

ruinous ['ru:ənəs] *adj* : ruinoso

rule¹ ['ru:l] *v* **ruled; ruling** *vt* **1** CONTROL, GOVERN : gobernar (un país), controlar (las emociones) **2** DECIDE : decidir, fallar ⟨the judge ruled that . . . : el juez falló que . . . ⟩ **3** DRAW : trazar con una regla — *vi* **1** GOVERN : gobernar, reinar **2** PREVAIL : prevalecer, imperar **3** **to rule against** : fallar en contra de

rule² *n* **1** REGULATION : regla *f*, norma *f* **2** CUSTOM, HABIT : regla *f* general ⟨as a rule : por lo general⟩ **3** GOVERNMENT : gobierno *m*, dominio *m* **4** RULER : regla *f* (para medir)

ruler ['ru:lər] *n* **1** LEADER, SOVEREIGN : gobernante *mf*; soberano *m*, -na *f* **2** : regla *f* (para medir)

ruling ['ru:lɪŋ] *n* : resolución *f*, fallo *m*

rum ['rʌm] *n* : ron *m*

Rumanian [rʊ'meɪniən] → **Romanian**

rumble¹ ['rʌmbəl] *vi* **-bled; -bling** : retumbar, hacer ruidos (dícese del estómago)

rumble² *n* : estruendo *m*, ruido *m* sordo, retumbo *m*

ruminant¹ ['ru:mənənt] *adj* : rumiante

ruminant² *n* : rumiante *m*

ruminate ['ru:məˌneɪt] *vi* **-nated; -nating** **1** : rumiar (en zoología) **2** REFLECT : reflexionar, rumiar

rummage ['rʌmɪʤ] *v* **-maged; -maging** *vi* : hurgar — *vt* RANSACK : revolver ⟨they rummaged the attic : revolvieron el ático⟩

rummy [ˈrʌmi] *n* : rummy *m* (juego de naipes)

rumor[1] [ˈruːmər] *vt* : rumorear ⟨it is rumored that . . . : se rumorea que . . ., se dice que . . .⟩

rumor[2] *n* : rumor *m*

rump [ˈrʌmp] *n* **1** : ancas *fpl*, grupa *f* (de un animal) **2** : cadera *f* ⟨rump steak : filete de cadera⟩

rumple [ˈrʌmpəl] *vt* **-pled; -pling** : arrugar (ropa, etc.), despeinar (pelo)

rumpus [ˈrʌmpəs] *n* : lío *m*, jaleo *m fam*

run[1] [ˈrʌn] *v* **ran** [ˈræn]; **run; running** *vi* **1** : correr ⟨she ran to catch the bus : corrió para alcanzar el autobús⟩ ⟨run and fetch the doctor : corre a buscar al médico⟩ **2** : circular, correr ⟨the train runs between Detroit and Chicago : el tren circula entre Detroit y Chicago⟩ ⟨to run on time : ser puntual⟩ **3** FUNCTION : funcionar, ir ⟨the engine runs on gasoline : el motor funciona con gasolina⟩ ⟨to run smoothly : ir bien⟩ **4** FLOW : correr, ir **5** LAST : durar ⟨the movie runs for two hours : la película dura dos horas⟩ ⟨the contract runs for three years : el contrato es válido por tres años⟩ **6** : desteñir, despintar (dícese de los colores) **7** EXTEND : correr, extenderse **8 to run for office** : postularse, presentarse — *vt* **1** : correr ⟨to run 10 miles : correr 10 millas⟩ ⟨to run errands : hacer los mandados⟩ ⟨to run out of town : hacer salir del pueblo⟩ **2** PASS : pasar **3** DRIVE : llevar en coche **4** OPERATE : hacer funcionar (un motor, etc.) **5** : echar ⟨to run water : echar agua⟩ **6** MANAGE : dirigir, llevar (un negocio, etc.) **7** EXTEND : tender (un cable, etc.) **8 to run a risk** : correr un riesgo

run[2] *n* **1** : carrera *f* ⟨at a run : a la carrera, corriendo⟩ ⟨to go for a run : ir a correr⟩ **2** TRIP : vuelta *f*, paseo *m* (en coche), viaje *m* (en avión) **3** SERIES : serie *f* ⟨a run of disappointments : una serie de desilusiones⟩ ⟨in the long run : a la larga⟩ ⟨in the short run : a corto plazo⟩ **4** DEMAND : gran demanda *f* ⟨a run on the banks : una corrida bancaria⟩ **5** (*used for theatrical productions and films*) ⟨to have a long run : mantenerse mucho tiempo en la cartelera⟩ **6** TYPE : tipo *m* ⟨the average run of students : el tipo más común de estudiante⟩ **7** : carrera *f* (en béisbol) **8** : carrera *f* (en una media) **9 to have the run of** : tener libre acceso de (una casa, etc.) **10 ski run** : pista *f* (de esquí)

runaway[1] [ˈrʌnəˌweɪ] *adj* **1** FUGITIVE : fugitivo **2** UNCONTROLLABLE : incontrolable, fuera de control ⟨runaway inflation : inflación desenfrenada⟩ ⟨a runaway success : un éxito aplastante⟩

runaway[2] *n* : fugitivo *m*, -va *f*

rundown [ˈrʌnˌdaʊn] *n* SUMMARY : resumen *m*

run–down [ˈrʌnˈdaʊn] *adj* **1** DILAPIDATED : ruinoso, destartalado **2** SICKLY, TIRED : cansado, débil

rung[1] *pp* → **ring**[1]

rung[2] [ˈrʌŋ] *n* : peldaño *m*, escalón *m*

run–in [ˈrʌnˌɪn] *n* : disputa *f*, altercado *m*

runner [ˈrʌnər] *n* **1** RACER : corredor *m*, -dora *f* **2** MESSENGER : mensajero *m*, -ra *f* **3** TRACK : riel *m* (de un cajón, etc.) **4** : patín *m* (de un trineo), cuchilla *f* (de un patín) **5** : estolón *m* (planta)

runner–up [ˌrʌnərˈʌp] *n, pl* **runners–up** : subcampeón *m*, -peona *f*

running [ˈrʌnɪŋ] *adj* **1** FLOWING : corriente ⟨running water : agua corriente⟩ **2** CONTINUOUS : continuo ⟨a running battle : una lucha continua⟩ **3** CONSECUTIVE : seguido ⟨six days running : por seis días seguidos⟩

runny [ˈrʌni] *adj* **-nier; -est** **1** WATERY : caldoso **2 to have a runny nose** : moquear

run over *vt* : atropellar — *vi* OVERFLOW : rebosar

runt [ˈrʌnt] *n* : animal *m* pequeño ⟨the runt of the litter : el más pequeño de la camada⟩

runway [ˈrʌnˌweɪ] *n* : pista *f* de aterrizaje

rupee [ruːˈpiː, ˈruːˌ-] *n* : rupia *f*

rupture[1] [ˈrʌptʃər] *v* **-tured; -turing** *vt* **1** BREAK, BURST : romper, reventar **2** : causar una hernia en — *vi* : reventarse

rupture[2] *n* **1** BREAK : ruptura *f* **2** HERNIA : hernia *f*

rural [ˈrʊrəl] *adj* : rural, campestre

ruse [ˈruːs, ˈruːz] *n* : treta *f*, ardid *m*, estratagema *f*

rush[1] [ˈrʌʃ] *vi* : correr, ir de prisa ⟨to rush around : correr de un lado a otro⟩ ⟨to rush off : irse corriendo⟩ — *vt* **1** HURRY : apresurar, apurar **2** ATTACK : abalanzarse sobre, asaltar

rush[2] *adj* : urgente

rush[3] *n* **1** HASTE : prisa *f*, apuro *m* **2** SURGE : ráfaga *f* (de aire), torrente *m* (de aguas), avalancha *f* (de gente) **3** DEMAND : demanda *f* ⟨a rush on sugar : una gran demanda para el azúcar⟩ **4** : carga *f* (en futbol americano) **5** : junco *m* (planta)

russet [ˈrʌsət] *n* : color *m* rojizo

Russian [ˈrʌʃən] *n* **1** : ruso *m*, -sa *f* **2** : ruso *m* (idioma) — **Russian** *adj*

rust[1] [ˈrʌst] *vi* : oxidarse — *vt* : oxidar

rust[2] *n* **1** : herrumbre *f*, orín *m*, óxido *m* (en los metales) **2** : roya *f* (en las plantas)

rustic[1] [ˈrʌstɪk] *adj* : rústico, campestre — **rustically** [-tɪkli] *adv*

rustic[2] *n* : rústico *m*, -ca *f*; campesino *m*, -na *f*

rustle[1] [ˈrʌsəl] *v* **-tled; -tling** *vt* **1** : hacer susurrar, hacer crujir ⟨to rustle a newspaper : hacer crujir un periódico⟩ **2** STEAL : robar (ganado) — *vi* : susurrar, crujir

rustle[2] *n* : murmullo *m*, susurro *m*, crujido *m*
rustler [ˈrʌsələr] *n* : ladrón *m*, -drona *f* de ganado
rusty [ˈrʌsti] *adj* **rustier; -est** : oxidado, herrumbroso
rut [ˈrʌt] *n* **1** GROOVE, TRACK : rodada *f*, surco *m* **2 to be in a rut** : ser esclavo de la rutina
ruthless [ˈru:θləs] *adj* : despiadado, cruel — **ruthlessly** *adv*
ruthlessness [ˈru:θləsnəs] *n* : crueldad *f*, falta *f* de piedad
Rwandan [rʊˈandən] *n* : ruandés *m*, -desa *f* — **Rwandan** *adj*
rye [ˈraɪ] *n* **1** : centeno *m* **2** *or* **rye whiskey** : whisky *m* de centeno

S

s [ˈɛs] *n, pl* **s's** *or* **ss** [ˈɛsəz] : decimonovena letra del alfabeto inglés
Sabbath [ˈsæbəθ] *n* **1** : sábado *m* (en el judaísmo) **2** : domingo *m* (en el cristianismo)
saber [ˈseɪbər] *n* : sable *m*
sable [ˈseɪbəl] *n* **1** BLACK : negro *m* **2** : marta *f* cebellina (animal)
sabotage[1] [ˈsæbəˌtaʒ] *vt* **-taged; -taging** : sabotear
sabotage[2] *n* : sabotaje *m*
sac [ˈsæk] *n* : saco *m* (anatómico)
saccharin [ˈsækərən] *n* : sacarina *f*
saccharine [ˈsækərən, -ˌri:n, -ˌraɪn] *adj* : meloso, empalagoso
sachet [sæˈʃeɪ] *n* : bolsita *f* (perfumada)
sack[1] [ˈsæk] *vt* **1** FIRE : echar (del trabajo), despedir **2** PLUNDER : saquear
sack[2] *n* BAG : saco *m*
sacrament [ˈsækrəmənt] *n* : sacramento *m*
sacramental [ˌsækrəˈmɛntəl] *adj* : sacramental
sacred [ˈseɪkrəd] *adj* **1** RELIGIOUS : sagrado, sacro ⟨sacred texts : textos sagrados⟩ **2** HOLY : sagrado **3 sacred to** : consagrado a
sacrifice[1] [ˈsækrəˌfaɪs] *vt* **-ficed; -ficing** **1** : sacrificar **2 to sacrifice oneself** : sacrificarse
sacrifice[2] *n* : sacrificio *m*
sacrilege [ˈsækrəlɪʤ] *n* : sacrilegio *m*
sacrilegious [ˌsækrəˈlɪʤəs, -ˈli:-] *adj* : sacrílego
sacrosanct [ˈsækroˌsæŋkt] *adj* : sacrosanto
sad [ˈsæd] *adj* **sadder; saddest** : triste — **sadly** *adv*
sadden [ˈsædən] *vt* : entristecer
saddle[1] [ˈsædəl] *vt* **-dled; -dling** : ensillar
saddle[2] *n* : silla *f* (de montar)
sadism [ˈseɪˌdɪzəm, ˈsæ-] *n* : sadismo *m*
sadist [ˈseɪdɪst, ˈsæ-] *n* : sádico *m*, -ca *f*
sadistic [səˈdɪstɪk] *adj* : sádico — **sadistically** [-tɪkli] *adv*
sadness [ˈsædnəs] *n* : tristeza *f*
safari [səˈfari, -ˈfær-] *n* : safari *m*
safe[1] [ˈseɪf] *adj* **safer; safest** **1** UNHARMED : ileso ⟨safe and sound : sano y salvo⟩ **2** SECURE : seguro **3 to be on the safe side** : para mayor seguridad **4 to play it safe** : ir a la segura
safe[2] *n* : caja *f* fuerte
safeguard[1] [ˈseɪfˌgard] *vt* : salvaguardar, proteger
safeguard[2] *n* : salvaguarda *f*, protección *f*
safekeeping [ˈseɪfˈki:pɪŋ] *n* : custodia *f*, protección *f* ⟨to put into safekeeping : poner en buen recaudo⟩
safely [ˈseɪfli] *adv* **1** UNHARMED : sin incidentes, sin novedades ⟨they landed safely : aterrizaron sin novedades⟩ **2** SECURELY : con toda seguridad, sin peligro
safety [ˈseɪfti] *n, pl* **-ties** : seguridad *f*
safety belt *n* : cinturón *m* de seguridad
safety pin *n* : alfiler *m* de gancho, alfiler *m* de seguridad, imperdible *m Spain*
saffron [ˈsæfrən] *n* : azafrán *m*
sag[1] [ˈsæg] *vi* **sagged; sagging** **1** DROOP, SINK : combarse, hundirse, inclinarse **2** : colgar, caer ⟨his jowls sagged : le colgaban las mejillas⟩ **3** FLAG : flaquear, decaer ⟨his spirits sagged : se le flaqueó el ánimo⟩
sag[2] *n* : combadura *f*
saga [ˈsagə, ˈsæ-] *n* : saga *f*
sagacious [səˈgeɪʃəs] *adj* : sagaz
sage[1] [ˈseɪʤ] *adj* **sager; -est** : sabio — **sagely** *adv*
sage[2] *n* **1** : sabio *m*, -bia *f* **2** : salvia *f* (planta)
sagebrush [ˈseɪʤˌbrʌʃ] *n* : artemisa *f*
Sagittarius [ˌsæʤəˈtɛriəs] *n* : Sagitario *mf*
said → **say**
sail[1] [ˈseɪl] *vi* **1** : navegar (en un barco) **2** : ir fácilmente ⟨we sailed right in : entramos sin ningún problema⟩ — *vt* **1** : gobernar (un barco) **2 to sail the seas** : cruzar los mares
sail[2] *n* **1** : vela *f* (de un barco) **2** : viaje *m* en velero ⟨to go for a sail : salir a navegar⟩
sailboat [ˈseɪlˌbo:t] *n* : velero *m*, barco *m* de vela
sailfish [ˈseɪlˌfɪʃ] *n* : pez *m* vela
sailor [ˈseɪlər] *n* : marinero *m*
saint [ˈseɪnt, *before a name* ˌseɪnt *or* sənt] *n* : santo *m*, -ta *f* ⟨Saint Francis : San Francisco⟩ ⟨Saint Rose : Santa Rosa⟩
saintliness [ˈseɪntlinəs] *n* : santidad *f*
saintly [ˈseɪntli] *adj* **saintlier; -est** : santo
sake [ˈseɪk] *n* **1** BENEFIT : bien *m* ⟨for the children's sake : por el bien de los

niños⟩ **2** (*indicating an end or a purpose*) ⟨art for art's sake : el arte por el arte⟩ ⟨let's say, for argument's sake, that he's wrong : pongamos que está equivocado⟩ **3 for goodness' sake!** : ¡por (el amor de) Dios!

salable *or* **saleable** [ˈseɪləbəl] *adj* : vendible

salacious [səˈleɪʃəs] *adj* : salaz — **salaciously** *adv*

salad [ˈsæləd] *n* : ensalada *f*

salamander [ˈsæləˌmændər] *n* : salamandra *f*

salami [səˈlɑmi] *n* : salami *m*

salary [ˈsæləri] *n, pl* **-ries** : sueldo *m*

sale [ˈseɪl] *n* **1** SELLING : venta *f* **2** : liquidación *f*, rebajas *fpl* ⟨on sale : de rebaja⟩ **3 sales** *npl* : ventas *fpl* ⟨to work in sales : trabajar en ventas⟩

salesman [ˈseɪlzmən] *n, pl* **-men** [-mən, -ˌmɛn] **1** : vendedor *m*, dependiente *m* (en una tienda) **2 traveling salesman** : viajante *m*, representante *m*

salesperson [ˈseɪlzˌpɚsən] *n* : vendedor *m*, -dora *f*; dependiente *m*, -ta *f* (en una tienda)

saleswoman [ˈseɪlzˌwʊmən] *n, pl* **-women** [-ˌwɪmən] **1** : vendedora *f*, dependienta *f* (en una tienda) **2 traveling saleswoman** : viajante *f*, representante *f*

salient [ˈseɪljənt] *adj* : saliente, sobresaliente

saline [ˈseɪˌliːn, -ˌlaɪn] *adj* : salino

saliva [səˈlaɪvə] *n* : saliva *f*

salivary [ˈsæləˌvɛri] *adj* : salival ⟨salivary gland : glándula salival⟩

salivate [ˈsæləˌveɪt] *vi* **-vated; -vating** : salivar

sallow [ˈsæloː] *adj* : amarillento, cetrino

sally[1] [ˈsæli] *vi* **-lied; -lying** SET OUT : salir, hacer una salida

sally[2] *n, pl* **-lies** **1** : salida *f* (militar), misión *f* **2** QUIP : salida *f*, ocurrencia *f*

salmon [ˈsæmən] *ns & pl* **1** : salmón *m* (pez) **2** : color *m* salmón

salon [səˈlɑn, ˈsæˌlɑn, sæˈlɔ̃] *n* : salón *m* ⟨beauty salon : salón de belleza⟩

saloon [səˈluːn] *n* **1** HALL : salón *m* (en un barco) **2** BARROOM : bar *m*

salsa [ˈsɔlsə, ˈsɑl-] *n* : salsa *f* mexicana, salsa *f* picante

salt[1] [ˈsɔlt] *vt* : salar, echarle sal a

salt[2] *adj* : salado

salt[3] *n* : sal *f*

saltwater [ˈsɔltˌwɔt̬ər, -ˌwɑ-] *adj* : de agua salada

salty [ˈsɔlt̬i] *adj* **saltier; -est** : salado

salubrious [səˈluːbriəs] *adj* : salubre

salutary [ˈsæljəˌtɛri] *adj* : saludable, salubre

salutation [ˌsæljəˈteɪʃən] *n* : saludo *m*, salutación *f*

salute[1] [səˈluːt] *v* **-luted; -luting** *vt* **1** : saludar (con gestos o ceremonias) **2** ACCLAIM : reconocer, aclamar — *vi* : hacer un saludo

salute[2] *n* **1** : saludo *m* (gesto), salva *f* (de cañonazos) **2** TRIBUTE : reconocimiento *m*, homenaje *m*

Salvadoran [ˌsælvəˈdorən] → **El Salvadoran**

salvage[1] [ˈsælvɪʤ] *vt* **-vaged; -vaging** : salvar, rescatar

salvage[2] *n* **1** SALVAGING : salvamento *m*, rescate *m* **2** : objetos *mpl* salvados

salvation [sælˈveɪʃən] *n* : salvación *f*

salve[1] [ˈsæv, ˈsav] *vt* **salved; salving** : calmar, apaciguar ⟨to salve one's conscience : aliviarse la conciencia⟩

salve[2] *n* : ungüento *m*

salvo [ˈsælˌvoː] *n, pl* **-vos** *or* **-voes** : salva *f*

same[1] [ˈseɪm] *adj* : mismo, igual ⟨the results are the same : los resultados son iguales⟩ ⟨he said the same thing as you : dijo lo mismo que tú⟩

same[2] *pron* : mismo ⟨it's all the same to me : me da lo mismo⟩ ⟨the same to you! : ¡igualmente!⟩

sameness [ˈseɪmnəs] *n* **1** SIMILARITY : identidad *f*, semejanza *f* **2** MONOTONY : monotonía *f*

sample[1] [ˈsæmpəl] *vt* **-pled; -pling** : probar

sample[2] *n* : muestra *f*, prueba *f*

sampler [ˈsæmplər] *n* **1** : dechado *m* (de bordado) **2** COLLECTION : colección *f* **3** ASSORTMENT : surtido *m*

sanatorium [ˌsænəˈtoriəm] *n, pl* **-riums** *or* **-ria** [-iə] : sanatorio *m*

sanctify [ˈsæŋktəˌfaɪ] *vt* **-fied; -fying** : santificar

sanctimonious [ˌsæŋktəˈmoːniəs] *adj* : beato, santurrón

sanction[1] [ˈsæŋkʃən] *vt* : sancionar, aprobar

sanction[2] *n* **1** AUTHORIZATION : sanción *f*, autorización *f* **2 sanctions** *npl* : sanciones *fpl* ⟨to impose sanctions on : imponer sanciones a⟩

sanctity [ˈsæŋktət̬i] *n, pl* **-ties** : santidad *f*

sanctuary [ˈsæŋkʧʊˌɛri] *n, pl* **-aries** **1** : presbiterio *m* (en una iglesia) **2** REFUGE : refugio *m*, asilo *m*

sand[1] [ˈsænd] *vt* : lijar (madera)

sand[2] *n* : arena *f*

sandal [ˈsændəl] *n* : sandalia *f*

sandbank [ˈsændˌbæŋk] *n* : banco *m* de arena

sandpaper *n* : papel *m* de lija

sandpiper [ˈsændˌpaɪpər] *n* : andarríos *m*

sandstone [ˈsændˌstoːn] *n* : arenisca *f*

sandstorm [ˈsændˌstɔrm] *n* : tormenta *f* de arena

sandwich[1] [ˈsændˌwɪʧ] *vt* : intercalar, encajonar, meter (entre dos cosas)

sandwich[2] *n* : sandwich *m*, emparedado *m*, bocadillo *m Spain*

sandy [ˈsændi] *adj* **sandier; -est** : arenoso

sane [ˈseɪn] *adj* **saner; sanest** **1** : cuerdo **2** SENSIBLE : sensato, razonable

sang → **sing**
sanguine [ˈsæŋgwən] *adj* **1** RUDDY : sanguíneo, rubicundo **2** HOPEFUL : optimista
sanitarium [ˌsænəˈtɛriəm] *n, pl* **-iums** *or* **-ia** [-iə] → **sanatorium**
sanitary [ˈsænətɛri] *adj* **1** : sanitario ⟨sanitary measures : medidas sanitarias⟩ **2** HYGIENIC : higiénico **3 sanitary napkin** : compresa *f*, paño *m* higiénico
sanitation [ˌsænəˈteɪʃən] *n* : sanidad *f*
sanitize [ˈsænəˌtaɪz] *vt* **-tized; -tizing 1** : desinfectar **2** EXPURGATE : expurgar
sanity [ˈsænət̬i] *n* : cordura *f*, razón *f* ⟨to lose one's sanity : perder el juicio⟩
sank → **sink**
Santa Claus [ˈsæntəˌklɔz] *n* : Papá Noel, San Nicolás
sap[1] [ˈsæp] *vt* **sapped; sapping 1** UNDERMINE : socavar **2** WEAKEN : minar, debilitar
sap[2] *n* **1** : savia *f* (de una planta) **2** SUCKER : inocentón *m*, -tona *f*
sapling [ˈsæplɪŋ] *n* : árbol *m* joven
sapphire [ˈsæˌfaɪr] *n* : zafiro *m*
sarcasm [ˈsɑrˌkæzəm] *n* : sarcasmo *m*
sarcastic [sɑrˈkæstɪk] *adj* : sarcástico — **sarcastically** [-t̬ɪkli] *adv*
sarcophagus [sɑrˈkɑfəgəs] *n, pl* **-gi** [-ˌgaɪ, -ˌʤaɪ] : sarcófago *m*
sardine [sɑrˈdiːn] *n* : sardina *f*
sardonic [sɑrˈdɑnɪk] *adj* : sardónico — **sardonically** [-nɪkli] *adv*
sarsaparilla [ˌsæspəˈrɪlə, ˌsɑrs-] *n* : zarzaparrilla *f*
sash [ˈsæʃ] *n* **1** : faja *f* (de un vestido), fajín *m* (de un uniforme) **2** *pl* **sash** : marco *m* (de una ventana)
sassafras [ˈsæsəˌfræs] *n* : sasafrás *m*
sassy [ˈsæsi] *adj* **sassier; -est** → **saucy**
sat → **sit**
Satan [ˈseɪtən] *n* : Satanás *m*, Satán *m*
satanic [səˈtænɪk, seɪ-] *adj* : satánico — **satanically** [-nɪkli] *adv*
satchel [ˈsæʧəl] *n* : cartera *f*, saco *m*
sate [ˈseɪt] *vt* **sated; sating** : saciar
satellite [ˈsæt̬əˌlaɪt] *n* : satélite *m* ⟨spy satellite : satélite espía⟩
satiate [ˈseɪʃiˌeɪt] *vt* **-ated; -ating** : saciar, hartar
satin [ˈsætən] *n* : raso *m*, satín *m*, satén *m*
satire [ˈsæˌtaɪr] *n* : sátira *f*
satiric [səˈtɪrɪk] *or* **satirical** [-ɪkəl] *adj* : satírico
satirize [ˈsæt̬əˌraɪz] *vt* **-rized; -rizing** : satirizar
satisfaction [ˌsæt̬əsˈfækʃən] *n* : satisfacción *f*
satisfactory [ˌsæt̬əsˈfæktəri] *adj* : satisfactorio, bueno — **satisfactorily** [-rəli] *adv*
satisfy [ˈsæt̬əsˌfaɪ] *v* **-fied; -fying** *vt* **1** PLEASE : satisfacer, contentar **2** CONVINCE : convencer **3** FULFILL : satisfacer, cumplir con, llenar **4** SETTLE : pagar, saldar (una cuenta) — *vi* SUFFICE : bastar
saturate [ˈsæʧəˌreɪt] *vt* **-rated; -rating 1** SOAK : empapar **2** FILL : saturar
saturation [ˌsæʧəˈreɪʃən] *n* : saturación *f*
Saturday [ˈsæt̬ərˌdeɪ, -di] *n* : sábado *m*
Saturn [ˈsæt̬ərn] *n* : Saturno *m*
satyr [ˈseɪt̬ər, ˈsæ-] *n* : sátiro *m*
sauce [ˈsɔs] *n* : salsa *f*
saucepan [ˈsɔsˌpæn] *n* : cacerola *f*, cazo *m*, cazuela *f*
saucer [ˈsɔsər] *n* : platillo *m*
sauciness [ˈsɔsinəs] *n* : descaro *m*, frescura *f*
saucy [ˈsɔsi] *adj* **saucier; -est** IMPUDENT : descarado, fresco *fam* — **saucily** *adv*
Saudi [ˈsaʊdi, ˈsɔ-] → **Saudi Arabian**
Saudi Arabian *n* : saudita *mf*, saudí *mf* — **Saudi Arabian** *adj*
sauna [ˈsɔnə, ˈsaʊnə] *n* : sauna *mf*
saunter [ˈsɔntər, ˈsɑn-] *vi* : pasear, parsearse
sausage [ˈsɔsɪʤ] *n* : salchicha *f*, embutido *m*
sauté [sɔˈteɪ, soː-] *vt* **-téed** *or* **-téd; -téing** : saltear, sofreír
savage[1] [ˈsævɪʤ] *adj* : salvaje, feroz — **savagely** *adv*
savage[2] *n* : salvaje *mf*
savagery [ˈsævɪʤri, -ʤəri] *n, pl* **-ries 1** FEROCITY : ferocidad *f* **2** WILDNESS : salvajismo *m*
savanna [səˈvænə] *n* : sabana *f*
save[1] [ˈseɪv] *vt* **saved; saving 1** RESCUE : salvar, rescatar **2** PRESERVE : preservar, conservar **3** KEEP : guardar, ahorrar (dinero), almacenar (alimentos) **4** : guardar (en informática)
save[2] *prep* EXCEPT : salvo, excepto, menos
savior [ˈseɪvjər] *n* **1** : salvador *m*, -dora *f* **2 the Savior** : el Salvador *m*
savor[1] [ˈseɪvər] *vt* : saborear
savor[2] *n* : sabor *m*
savory [ˈseɪvəri] *adj* : sabroso
saw[1] → **see**
saw[2] [ˈsɔ] *vt* **sawed; sawed** *or* **sawn** [ˈsɔn]; **sawing** : serrar, cortar (con sierra)
saw[3] *n* : sierra *f*
sawdust [ˈsɔˌdʌst] *n* : aserrín *m*, serrín *m*
sawhorse [ˈsɔˌhɔrs] *n* : caballete *m*, burro *m* (en carpintería)
sawmill [ˈsɔˌmɪl] *n* : aserradero *m*
saxophone [ˈsæksəˌfoːn] *n* : saxofón *m*
say[1] [ˈseɪ] *v* **said** [ˈsɛd]; **saying; says** [ˈsɛz] *vt* **1** EXPRESS, UTTER : decir, expresar ⟨to say no : decir que no⟩ ⟨that goes without saying : ni que decir tiene⟩ ⟨no sooner said than done : dicho y hecho⟩ ⟨to say again : repetir⟩ ⟨to say one's prayers : rezar⟩ **2** INDICATE : marcar, poner ⟨my watch says three o'clock : mi reloj marca las tres⟩ ⟨what does the sign say? : ¿qué pone el letrero?⟩ **3** ALLEGE : decir ⟨it's said that she's pretty : se dice que es bonita⟩ — *vi* : decir

say[2] *n, pl* **says** ['seɪz] : voz *f*, opinión *f* ⟨to have no say : no tener ni voz ni voto⟩ ⟨to have one's say : dar uno su opinión⟩

saying ['seɪɪŋ] *n* : dicho *m*, refrán *m*

scab ['skæb] *n* **1** : costra *f*, postilla *f* (en una herida) **2** STRIKEBREAKER : rompehuelgas *mf*, esquirol *mf*

scabbard ['skæbərd] *n* : vaina *f* (de una espada), funda *f* (de un puñal, etc.)

scabby ['skæbi] *adj* **scabbier; -est** : lleno de costras

scaffold ['skæfəld, -ˌfo:ld] *n* **1** *or* **scaffolding** : andamio *m* (para obreros, etc.) **2** : patíbulo *m*, cadalso *m* (para ejecuciones)

scald ['skɔld] *vt* **1** BURN : escaldar **2** HEAT : calentar (hasta el punto de ebullición)

scale[1] ['skeɪl] *v* **scaled; scaling** *vt* **1** : escamar (un pescado) **2** CLIMB : escalar (un muro, etc.) **3 to scale down** : reducir — *vi* WEIGH : pesar ⟨he scaled in at 200 pounds : pesó 200 libras⟩

scale[2] *n* **1** *or* **scales** : balanza *f*, báscula *f* (para pesar) **2** : escama *f* (de un pez, etc.) **3** EXTENT : escala *f*, proporción *f* ⟨wage scale : escala salarial⟩ **4** : escala *f* (en música, en cartografía, etc.) ⟨to draw to scale : dibujar a escala⟩

scallion ['skæljən] *n* : cebollino *m*, cebolleta *f*

scallop ['skɑləp, 'skæ-] *n* **1** : vieira *f* (molusco) **2** : festón *m* (decoración)

scalp[1] ['skælp] *vt* : arrancar la cabellera a

scalp[2] *n* : cuero *m* cabelludo

scalpel ['skælpəl] *n* : bisturí *m*, escalpelo *m*

scaly ['skeɪli] *adj* **scalier; -est** : escamoso

scam ['skæm] *n* : estafa *f*, timo *m fam*, chanchullo *m fam*

scamp ['skæmp] *n* : bribón *m*, -bona *f*; granuja *mf*; travieso *m*, -sa *f*

scamper ['skæmpər] *vi* : corretear

scan[1] ['skæn] *vt* **scanned; scanning 1** : escandir (versos) **2** SCRUTINIZE : escudriñar, escrutar ⟨to scan the horizon : escudriñar el horizonte⟩ **3** PERUSE : echarle un vistazo a (un periódico, etc.) **4** EXPLORE : explorar (con radar), hacer un escáner de (en ecografía) **5** : escanear (una imagen)

scan[2] *n* **1** : ecografía *f*, examen *m* ultrasónico (en medicina) **2** : imagen *f* escaneada (en una computadora)

scandal ['skændəl] *n* **1** DISGRACE, OUTRAGE : escándalo *m* **2** GOSSIP : habladurías *fpl*, chismes *mpl*

scandalize ['skændəlˌaɪz] *vt* **-ized; -izing** : escandalizar

scandalous ['skændələs] *adj* : de escándalo

Scandinavian[1] [ˌskændə'neɪviən] *adj* : escandinavo

Scandinavian[2] *n* : escandinavo *m*, -va *f*

scanner ['skænər] *n* : escáner *m*, scanner *m*

scant ['skænt] *adj* : escaso

scanty ['skænti] *adj* **scantier; -est** : exiguo, escaso ⟨a scanty meal : una comida insuficiente⟩ — **scantily** [-təli] *adv*

scapegoat ['skeɪpˌgo:t] *n* : chivo *m* expiatorio, cabeza *f* de turco

scapula ['skæpjələ] *n, pl* **-lae** [-ˌli:, -ˌlaɪ] *or* **-las** → **shoulder blade**

scar[1] ['skɑr] *v* **scarred; scarring** *vt* : dejar una cicatriz en — *vi* : cicatrizar

scar[2] *n* : cicatriz *f*, marca *f*

scarab ['skærəb] *n* : escarabajo *m*

scarce ['skɛrs] *adj* **scarcer; -est** : escaso

scarcely ['skɛrsli] *adv* **1** BARELY : apenas **2** : ni mucho menos, ni nada que se le parezca ⟨he's scarcely an expert : ciertamente no es experto⟩

scarcity ['skɛrsəṭi] *n, pl* **-ties** : escasez *f*

scare[1] ['skɛr] *vt* **scared; scaring** : asustar, espantar

scare[2] *n* **1** FRIGHT : susto *m*, sobresalto *m* **2** ALARM : pánico *m*

scarecrow ['skɛrˌkro:] *n* : espantapájaros *m*, espantajo *m*

scarf ['skɑrf] *n, pl* **scarves** ['skɑrvz] *or* **scarfs 1** MUFFLER : bufanda *f* **2** KERCHIEF : pañuelo *m*

scarlet ['skɑrlət] *n* : escarlata *f* — **scarlet** *adj*

scarlet fever *n* : escarlatina *f*

scary ['skɛri] *adj* **scarier; -est** : espantoso, pavoroso

scathing ['skeɪðɪŋ] *adj* : mordaz, cáustico

scatter ['skæṭər] *vt* : esparcir, desparramar — *vi* DISPERSE : dispersarse

scavenge ['skævəndʒ] *v* **-venged; -venging** *vt* : rescatar (de la basura), pepenar *CA, Mex* — *vi* : rebuscar, hurgar en la basura ⟨to scavenge for food : andar buscando comida⟩

scavenger ['skævəndʒər] *n* **1** : persona *f* que rebusca en las basuras; pepenador *m*, -dora *f CA, Mex* **2** : carroñero *m*, -ra *f* (animal)

scenario [sə'næriˌo:, -'nɑr-] *n, pl* **-ios 1** PLOT : argumento *m* (en teatro), guión *m* (en cine) **2** SITUATION : situación *f* hipotética ⟨in the worst-case scenario : en el peor de los casos⟩

scene ['si:n] *n* **1** : escena *f* (en una obra de teatro) **2** SCENERY : decorado *m* (en el teatro) **3** VIEW : escena *f* **4** LOCALE : escenario *m* **5** COMMOTION, FUSS : escándalo *m*, escena *f* ⟨to make a scene : armar un escándalo⟩

scenery ['si:nəri] *n, pl* **-eries 1** : decorado *m* (en el teatro) **2** LANDSCAPE : paisaje *m*

scenic ['si:nɪk] *adj* : pintoresco

scent[1] ['sɛnt] *vt* **1** SMELL : oler, olfatear **2** PERFUME : perfumar **3** SENSE : sentir, percibir

scent[2] *n* **1** ODOR : olor *m*, aroma *m* **2** : olfato *m* ⟨a dog with a keen scent : un perro con un buen olfato⟩ **3** PERFUME : perfume *m*

scented [ˈsɛntəd] *adj* : perfumado

scepter [ˈsɛptər] *n* : cetro *m*

sceptic [ˈskɛptɪk] → **skeptic**

schedule[1] [ˈskɛˌʤu:l, -ʤəl, *esp Brit* ˈʃɛdˌju:l] *vt* **-uled; -uling** : planear, programar

schedule[2] *n* **1** PLAN : programa *m*, plan *m* ⟨on schedule : según lo previsto⟩ ⟨behind schedule : atrasado, con retraso⟩ **2** TIMETABLE : horario *m*

scheme[1] [ˈski:m] *vi* **schemed; scheming** : intrigar, conspirar

scheme[2] *n* **1** PLAN : plan *m*, proyecto *m* **2** PLOT, TRICK : intriga *f*, ardid *m* **3** FRAMEWORK : esquema *f* ⟨a color scheme : una combinación de colores⟩

schemer [ˈski:mər] *n* : intrigante *mf*

schism [ˈsɪzəm, ˈskɪ-] *n* : cisma *m*

schizophrenia [ˌskɪtsəˈfri:niə, ˌskɪzə-, -ˈfrɛ-] *n* : esquizofrenia *f*

schizophrenic [ˌskɪtsəˈfrɛnɪk, ˌskɪzə-] *n* : esquizofrénico *m*, -ca *f* — **schizophrenic** *adj*

scholar [ˈskɑlər] *n* **1** STUDENT : escolar *mf*; alumno *m*, -na *f* **2** EXPERT : especialista *mf*

scholarly [ˈskɑlərli] *adj* : erudito

scholarship [ˈskɑlərˌʃɪp] *n* **1** LEARNING : erudición *f* **2** GRANT : beca *f*

scholastic [skəˈlæstɪk] *adj* : académico

school[1] [ˈsku:l] *vt* : instruir, enseñar

school[2] *n* **1** : escuela *f*, colegio *m* (institución) **2** : estudiantes *mfpl* y profesores *mpl* (de una escuela) **3** : escuela *f* (en pintura, etc.) ⟨the Flemish school : la escuela flamenca⟩ **4 school of fish** : banco *m*, cardumen *m*

schoolboy [ˈsku:lˌbɔɪ] *n* : escolar *m*, colegial *m*

schoolgirl [ˈsku:lˌgərl] *n* : escolar *f*, colegiala *f*

schoolhouse [ˈsku:lˌhaʊs] *n* : escuela *f*

schoolmate [ˈsku:lˌmeɪt] *n* : compañero *m*, -ra *f* de escuela

schoolroom [ˈsku:lˌru:m, -ˌrʊm] → **classroom**

schoolteacher [ˈsku:lˌti:ʧər] *n* : maestro *m*, -tra *f*; profesor *m*, -sora *f*

schoolwork [ˈsku:lˌwərk] *n* : trabajo *m* escolar

schooner [ˈsku:nər] *n* : goleta *f*

science [ˈsaɪən*t*s] *n* : ciencia *f*

science fiction *n* : ciencia ficción *f*

scientific [ˌsaɪənˈtɪfɪk] *adj* : científico — **scientifically** [-fɪkli] *adv*

scientist [ˈsaɪəntɪst] *n* : científico *m*, -ca *f*

scintillating [ˈsɪntəˌleɪt̬ɪŋ] *adj* : chispeante, brillante

scissors [ˈsɪzərz] *npl* : tijeras *fpl*

sclerosis [skləˈro:səs] *n, pl* **-roses** : esclerosis *f*

scoff [ˈskɑf] *vi* **to scoff at** : burlarse de, mofarse de

scold [ˈsko:ld] *vt* : regañar, reprender, reñir

scoop[1] [ˈsku:p] *vt* **1** : sacar (con pala o cucharón) **2 to scoop out** HOLLOW : vaciar, ahuecar

scoop[2] *n* : pala *f* (para harina, etc.), cucharón *m* (para helado, etc.)

scoot [ˈsku:t] *vi* : ir rápidamente ⟨she scooted around the corner : volvió la esquina a toda prisa⟩

scooter [ˈsku:t̬ər] *n* : patineta *f*, monopatín *m*, patinete *m*

scope [ˈsko:p] *n* **1** RANGE : alcance *m*, ámbito *m*, extensión *f* **2** OPPORTUNITY : posibilidades *fpl*, libertad *f*

scorch [ˈskɔrʧ] *vt* : chamuscar, quemar

score[1] [ˈskor] *v* **scored; scoring** *vt* **1** RECORD : anotar **2** MARK, SCRATCH : marcar, rayar **3** : marcar, meter (en deportes) **4** GAIN : ganar, apuntarse **5** GRADE : calificar (exámenes, etc.) **6** : instrumentar, orquestar (música) — *vi* **1** : marcar (en deportes) **2** : obtener una puntuación (en un examen)

score[2] *n, pl* **scores 1** *or pl* **score** TWENTY : veintena *f* **2** LINE, SCRATCH : línea *f*, marca *f* **3** : resultado *m* (en deportes) ⟨what's the score? : ¿cómo va el marcador?⟩ **4** GRADE, POINTS : calificación *f* (en un examen), puntuación *f* (en un concurso) **5** ACCOUNT : cuenta *f* ⟨to settle a score : ajustar una cuenta⟩ ⟨on that score : a ese respecto⟩ **6** : partitura *f* (musical)

scorn[1] [ˈskɔrn] *vt* : despreciar, menospreciar, desdeñar

scorn[2] *n* : desprecio *m*, menosprecio *m*, desdén *m*

scornful [ˈskɔrnfəl] *adj* : desdeñoso, despreciativo — **scornfully** *adv*

Scorpio [ˈskɔrpiˌo:] *n* : Escorpio *mf*, Escorpión *mf*

scorpion [ˈskɔrpiən] *n* : alacrán *m*, escorpión *m*

Scot [ˈskɑt] *n* : escocés *m*, -cesa *f*

Scotch[1] [ˈskɑʧ] *adj* → **Scottish**[1]

Scotch[2] *npl* **the Scotch** : los escoceses

scot–free [ˈskɑtˈfri:] *adj* **to get off scot–free** : salir impune, quedar sin castigo

Scots [ˈskɑts] *n* : escocés *m* (idioma)

Scottish[1] [ˈskɑt̬ɪʃ] *adj* : escocés

Scottish[2] *n* → **Scots**

scoundrel [ˈskaʊndrəl] *n* : sinvergüenza *mf*; bellaco *m*, -ca *f*

scour [ˈskaʊər] *vt* **1** EXAMINE, SEARCH : registrar (un área), revisar (documentos, etc.) **2** SCRUB : fregar, restregar

scourge[1] [ˈskərʤ] *vt* **scourged; scourging** : azotar

scourge[2] *n* : azote *m*

scout[1] [ˈskaʊt] *vi* **1** RECONNOITER : reconocer **2 to scout around for** : explorar en busca de

scout[2] *n* **1** : explorador *m*, -dora *f* **2** *or* **talent scout** : cazatalentos *mf*

scow [ˈskaʊ] *n* : barcaza *f*, gabarra *f*

scowl[1] [ˈskaʊl] *vi* : fruncir el ceño

scowl[2] *n* : ceño *m* fruncido

scram [ˈskræm] *vi* **scrammed; scramming** : largarse
scramble[1] [ˈskræmbəl] *v* **-bled; -bling** *vi* **1** : trepar, gatear (con torpeza) ⟨he scrambled over the fence : se trepó a la cerca con dificultad⟩ **2** STRUGGLE : pelearse (por) ⟨they scrambled for seats : se pelearon por los asientos⟩ — *vt* **1** JUMBLE : mezclar **2 to scramble eggs** : hacer huevos revueltos
scramble[2] *n* : rebatiña *f*, pelea *f*
scrap[1] [ˈskræp] *v* **scrapped; scrapping** *vt* DISCARD : desechar — *vi* FIGHT : pelearse
scrap[2] *n* **1** FRAGMENT : pedazo *m*, trozo *m* **2** FIGHT : pelea *f* **3** *or* **scrap metal** : chatarra *f* **4 scraps** *npl* LEFTOVERS : restos *mpl*, sobras *fpl*
scrapbook [ˈskræpˌbʊk] *n* : álbum *m* de recortes
scrape[1] [ˈskreɪp] *v* **scraped; scraping** *vt* **1** GRAZE, SCRATCH : rozar, rascar ⟨to scrape one's knee : rasparse la rodilla⟩ **2** CLEAN : raspar ⟨to scrape carrots : raspar zanahorias⟩ **3 to scrape off** : raspar (pintura, etc.) **4 to scrape up** *or* **to scrape together** : juntar, reunir poco a poco — *vi* **1** RUB : rozar **2 to scrape by** : arreglárselas, ir tirando
scrape[2] *n* **1** SCRAPING : raspadura *f* **2** SCRATCH : rasguño *m* **3** PREDICAMENT : apuro *m*, aprieto *m*
scratch[1] [ˈskrætʃ] *vt* **1** : arañar, rasguñar ⟨to scratch an itch : rascarse⟩ **2** MARK : rayar, marcar **3 to scratch out** : tachar
scratch[2] *n* **1** : rasguño *m*, arañazo *m* (en la piel), rayón *m* (en un mueble, etc.) **2** : sonido *m* rasposo ⟨I heard a scratch at the door : oí como que raspaban a la puerta⟩
scratchy [ˈskrætʃi] *adj* **scratchier; -est** : áspero, que pica ⟨a scratchy sweater : un suéter que pica⟩
scrawl[1] [ˈskrɔl] *v* : garabatear
scrawl[2] *n* : garabato *m*
scrawny [ˈskrɔni] *adj* **scrawnier; -est** : flaco, escuálido
scream[1] [ˈskri:m] *vi* : chillar, gritar
scream[2] *n* : chillido *m*, grito *m*
screech[1] [ˈskri:tʃ] *vi* : chillar (dícese de las personas o de los animales), chirriar (dícese de los frenos, etc.)
screech[2] *n* **1** : chillido *m*, grito *m* (de una persona o un animal) **2** : chirrido *m* (de frenos, etc.)
screen[1] [ˈskri:n] *vt* **1** SHIELD : proteger **2** CONCEAL : tapar, ocultar **3** EXAMINE : someter a una revisión, hacerle un chequeo (a un paciente) **4** SIEVE : cribar
screen[2] *n* **1** PARTITION : biombo *m*, pantalla *f* **2** SIEVE : criba *f* **3** : pantalla *f* (de un televisor, una computadora, etc.) **4** MOVIES : cine *m* **5** *or* **window screen** : ventana *f* de tela metálica
screenplay [ˈskri:nˌpleɪ] *n* SCRIPT : guión *m*
screw[1] [ˈskru:] *vt* : atornillar — *vi* **1 to screw in** : atornillarse **2 to screw up** *fam* : meter la pata
screw[2] *n* **1** : tornillo *m* (para fijar algo) **2** TWIST : vuelta *f* **3** PROPELLER : hélice *f*
screwdriver [ˈskru:ˌdraɪvər] *n* : destornillador *m*, desarmador *m Mex*
scribble[1] [ˈskrɪbəl] *v* **-bled; -bling** : garabatear
scribble[2] *n* : garabato *m*
scribe [ˈskraɪb] *n* : escriba *m*
scrimmage [ˈskrɪmɪdʒ] *n* : escaramuza *f*
scrimp [ˈskrɪmp] *vi* **1 to scrimp on** : escatimar **2 to scrimp and save** : hacer economías
script [ˈskrɪpt] *n* **1** HANDWRITING : letra *f*, escritura *f* **2** : guión *m* (de una película, etc.)
scriptural [ˈskrɪptʃərəl] *adj* : bíblico
scripture [ˈskrɪptʃər] *n* **1** : escritos *mpl* sagrados (de una religión) **2 the Scriptures** *npl* : las Sagradas Escrituras
scriptwriter [ˈskrɪptˌraɪt̬ər] *n* : guionista *mf*, libretista *mf*
scroll [ˈskro:l] *n* **1** : rollo *m* (de pergamino, etc.) **2** : voluta *f* (adorno en arquitectura)
scrotum [ˈskro:t̬əm] *n, pl* **scrota** [-t̬ə] *or* **scrotums** : escroto *m*
scrounge [ˈskraʊndʒ] *v* **scrounged; scrounging** *vt* **1** BUM : gorrear *fam*, sablear *fam* (dinero) **2 to scrounge around for** : buscar, andar a la busca de — *vi* **to scrounge off someone** : vivir a costa de alguien
scrub[1] [ˈskrʌb] *vt* **scrubbed; scrubbing** : restregar, fregar
scrub[2] *n* **1** THICKET, UNDERBRUSH : maleza *f*, matorral *m*, matorrales *mpl* **2** SCRUBBING : fregado *m*, restregadura *f*
scrubby [ˈskrʌbi] *adj* **-bier; -est 1** STUNTED : achaparrado **2** : cubierto de maleza
scruff [ˈskrʌf] *n* **by the scruff of the neck** : por el cogote, por el pescuezo
scrumptious [ˈskrʌmpʃəs] *adj* : delicioso, muy rico
scruple [ˈskru:pəl] *n* : escrúpulo *m*
scrupulous [ˈskru:pjələs] *adj* : escrupuloso — **scrupulously** *adv*
scrutinize [ˈskru:tənˌaɪz] *vt* **-nized; -nizing** : escrutar, escudriñar
scrutiny [ˈskru:təni] *n, pl* **-nies** : escrutinio *m*, inspección *f*
scuba [ˈsku:bə] *n* **1** *or* **scuba gear** : equipo *m* de submarinismo **2 scuba diver** : submarinista *mf* **3 scuba diving** : submarinismo *m*
scuff [ˈskʌf] *vt* : rayar, raspar ⟨to scuff one's feet : arrastrar los pies⟩
scuffle[1] [ˈskʌfəl] *vi* **-fled; -fling 1** TUSSLE : pelearse **2** SHUFFLE : caminar arrastrando los pies
scuffle[2] *n* **1** TUSSLE : refriega *f*, pelea *f* **2** SHUFFLE : arrastre *m* de los pies
scull[1] [ˈskʌl] *vi* : remar (con espadilla)

scull[2] *n* OAR : espadilla *f*
sculpt [ˈskʌlpt] *v* : esculpir
sculptor [ˈskʌlptər] *n* : escultor *m*, -tora *f*
scuptural [ˈskʌlptʃərəl] *adj* : escultórico
sculpture[1] [ˈskʌlptʃər] *vt* **-tured; -turing** : esculpir
sculpture[2] *n* : escultura *f*
scum [ˈskʌm] *n* **1** FROTH : espuma *f*, nata *f* **2** : verdín *m* (encima de un líquido)
scurrilous [ˈskərələs] *adj* : difamatorio, calumnioso, injurioso
scurry [ˈskəri] *vi* **-ried; -rying** : corretear
scurvy [ˈskərvi] *n* : escorbuto *m*
scuttle[1] [ˈskʌtəl] *v* **-tled; -tling** *vt* : hundir (un barco) — *vi* SCAMPER : corretear
scuttle[2] *n* : cubo *m* (para carbón)
scythe [ˈsaɪð] *n* : guadaña *f*
sea[1] [ˈsi:] *adj* : del mar
sea[2] *n* **1** : mar *mf* ⟨the Black Sea : el Mar Negro⟩ ⟨on the high seas : en alta mar⟩ ⟨heavy seas : mar gruesa, mar agitada⟩ **2** MASS : mar *m*, multitud *f* ⟨a sea of faces : un mar de rostros⟩
seabird [ˈsi:ˌbərd] *n* : ave *f* marina
seaboard [ˈsi:ˌbord] *n* : litoral *m*
seacoast [ˈsi:ˌko:st] *n* : costa *f*, litoral *m*
seafarer [ˈsi:ˌfærər] *n* : marinero *m*
seafaring[1] [ˈsi:ˌfærɪŋ] *adj* : marinero
seafaring[2] *n* : navegación *f*
seafood [ˈsi:ˌfu:d] *n* : mariscos *mpl*
seagull [ˈsi:ˌgʌl] *n* : gaviota *f*
sea horse [ˈsi:ˌhɔrs] *n* : hipocampo *m*, caballito *m* de mar
seal[1] [ˈsi:l] *vt* **1** CLOSE : sellar, cerrar ⟨to seal a letter : cerrar una carta⟩ ⟨to seal an agreement : sellar un acuerdo⟩ **2 to seal up** : tapar, rellenar (una grieta, etc.)
seal[2] *n* **1** : foca *f* (animal) **2** : sello *m* ⟨seal of approval : sello de aprobación⟩ **3** CLOSURE : cierre *m*, precinto *m*
sea level *n* : nivel *m* del mar
sea lion *n* : león *m* marino
sealskin [ˈsi:lˌskɪn] *n* : piel *f* de foca
seam[1] [ˈsi:m] *vt* **1** STITCH : unir con costuras **2** MARK : marcar
seam[2] *n* **1** STITCHING : costura *f* **2** LODE, VEIN : veta *f*, filón *m*
seaman [ˈsi:mən] *n*, *pl* **-men** [-mən, -ˌmɛn] **1** SAILOR : marinero *m* **2** : marino *m* (en la armada)
seamless [ˈsi:mləs] *adj* **1** : sin costuras, de una pieza **2** : perfecto ⟨a seamless transition : una transición fluida⟩
seamstress [ˈsi:mpstrəs] *n* : costurera *f*
seamy [ˈsi:mi] *adj* **seamier; -est** : sórdido
séance [ˈseɪˌɑnts] *n* : sesión *f* de espiritismo
seaplane [ˈsi:ˌpleɪn] *n* : hidroavión *m*
seaport [ˈsi:ˌport] *n* : puerto *m* marítimo
sear [ˈsɪr] *vt* **1** PARCH, WITHER : secar, resecar **2** SCORCH : chamuscar, quemar
search[1] [ˈsərtʃ] *vt* : registrar (un edificio, un área), cachear (a una persona), buscar en — *vi* **to search for** : buscar
search[2] *n* : búsqueda *f*, registro *m* (de un edificio, etc.), cacheo *m* (de una persona)
searchlight [ˈsərtʃˌlaɪt] *n* : reflector *m*
seashell [ˈsi:ˌʃɛl] *n* : concha *f* (marina)
seashore [ˈsi:ˌʃor] *n* : orilla *f* del mar
seasick [ˈsi:ˌsɪk] *adj* : mareado ⟨to get seasick : marearse⟩
seasickness [ˈsi:ˌsɪknəs] *n* : mareo *m*
seaside → **seacoast**
season[1] [ˈsi:zən] *vt* **1** FLAVOR, SPICE : sazonar, condimentar **2** CURE : curar, secar ⟨seasoned wood : madera seca⟩ ⟨a seasoned veteran : un veterano avezado⟩
season[2] *n* **1** : estación *f* (del año) **2** : temporada *f* (en deportes, etc.) ⟨baseball season : temporada de beisbol⟩
seasonable [ˈsi:zənəbəl] *adj* **1** : propio de la estación (dícese del tiempo, de las temperaturas, etc.) **2** TIMELY : oportuno
seasonal [ˈsi:zənəl] *adj* : estacional — **seasonally** *adv*
seasoning [ˈsi:zənɪŋ] *n* : condimento *m*, sazón *f*
seat[1] [ˈsi:t] *vt* **1** SIT : sentar ⟨please be seated : siéntense, por favor⟩ **2** HOLD : tener cabida para ⟨the stadium seats 40,000 : el estadio tiene 40,000 asientos⟩
seat[2] *n* **1** : asiento *m*, plaza *f* (en un vehículo) ⟨take a seat : tome asiento⟩ **2** BOTTOM : fondillos *mpl* (de la ropa), trasero *m* (del cuerpo) **3** : sede *f* (de un gobierno, etc.)
seat belt *n* : cinturón *m* de seguridad
sea urchin *n* : erizo *m* de mar
seawall [ˈsi:ˌwɑl] *n* : rompeolas *m*, dique *m* marítimo
seawater [ˈsi:ˌwɔtər, -ˌwɑ-] *n* : agua *f* de mar
seaweed [ˈsi:ˌwi:d] *n* : alga *f* marina
seaworthy [ˈsi:ˌwərði] *adj* : en condiciones de navegar
secede [sɪˈsi:d] *vi* **-ceded; -ceding** : separarse (de una nación, etc.)
seclude [sɪˈklu:d] *vt* **-cluded; -cluding** : aislar
seclusion [sɪˈklu:ʒən] *n* : aislamiento *m*
second[1] [ˈsɛkənd] *vt* : secundar, apoyar (una moción)
second[2] *or* **secondly** [ˈsɛkəndli] *adv* : en segundo lugar
second[3] *adj* : segundo
second[4] *n* **1** : segundo *m*, -da *f* (en una serie) **2** : segundo *m*, ayudante *m* (en deportes) **3** MOMENT : segundo *m*, momento *m*
secondary [ˈsɛkənˌdri] *adj* : secundario
secondhand [ˈsɛkəndˈhænd] *adj* : de segunda mano
second lieutenant *n* : alférez *mf*, subteniente *mf*
second–rate [ˈsɛkəndˈreɪt] *adj* : mediocre, de segunda categoría

secrecy [ˈsiːkrəsi] *n, pl* **-cies** : secreto *m*

secret[1] [ˈsiːkrət] *adj* : secreto — **secretly** *adv*

secret[2] *n* : secreto *m*

secretarial [ˌsɛkrəˈtriəl] *adj* : de secretario, de oficina

secretariat [ˌsɛkrəˈtriət] *n* : secretaría *f*, secretariado *m*

secretary [ˈsɛkrəˌtri] *n, pl* **-taries** **1** : secretario *m*, -ria *f* (en una oficina, etc.) **2** : ministro *m*, -tra *f*; secretario *m*, -ria *f* ⟨Secretary of State : Secretario de Estado⟩

secrete [sɪˈkriːt] *vt* **-creted; -creting** **1** : secretar, segregar (en fisiología) **2** HIDE : ocultar

secretion [sɪˈkriːʃən] *n* : secreción *f*

secretive [ˈsiːkrət̬ɪv, sɪˈkriːt̬ɪv] *adj* : reservado, callado, secreto

sect [ˈsɛkt] *n* : secta *f*

sectarian [sɛkˈtriən] *adj* : sectario

section [ˈsɛkʃən] *n* : sección *f*, parte *f* (de un mueble, etc.), sector *m* (de la población), barrio *m* (de una ciudad)

sectional [ˈsɛkʃənəl] *adj* **1** : en sección, en corte ⟨a sectional diagram : un gráfico en corte⟩ **2** FACTIONAL : de grupo, entre facciones **3** : modular ⟨sectional furniture : muebles modulares⟩

sector [ˈsɛktər] *n* : sector *m*

secular [ˈsɛkjələr] *adj* **1** : secular, laico ⟨secular life : la vida secular⟩ **2** : seglar (dícese de los sacerdotes, etc.)

secure[1] [sɪˈkjʊr] *vt* **-cured; -curing** **1** FASTEN : asegurar (una puerta, etc.), sujetar **2** GET : conseguir

secure[2] *adj* **-curer; -est** : seguro — **securely** *adv*

security [sɪˈkjʊrət̬i] *n, pl* **-ties** **1** SAFETY : seguridad *f* **2** GUARANTEE : garantía *f* **3** **securities** *npl* : valores *mpl*

sedan [sɪˈdæn] *n* **1** *or* **sedan chair** : silla *f* de manos **2** : sedán *m* (automóvil)

sedate[1] [sɪˈdeɪt] *vt* **-dated; -dating** : sedar

sedate[2] *adj* : sosegado — **sedately** *adv*

sedation [sɪˈdeɪʃən] *n* : sedación *f*

sedative[1] [ˈsɛdət̬ɪv] *adj* : sedante

sedative[2] *n* : sedante *m*, calmante *m*

sedentary [ˈsɛdənˌtɛri] *adj* : sedentario

sedge [ˈsɛʤ] *n* : juncia *f*

sediment [ˈsɛdəmənt] *n* : sedimento *m* (geológico), poso *m* (en un líquido)

sedimentary [ˌsɛdəˈmɛntəri] *adj* : sedimentario

sedition [sɪˈdɪʃən] *n* : sedición *f*

seditious [sɪˈdɪʃəs] *adj* : sedicioso

seduce [sɪˈduːs, -ˈdjuːs] *vt* **-duced; -ducing** : seducir

seduction [sɪˈdʌkʃən] *n* : seducción *f*

seductive [sɪˈdʌktɪv] *adj* : seductor, seductivo

see[1] [ˈsiː] *v* **saw** [ˈsɔ]; **seen** [ˈsiːn]; **seeing** *vt* **1** : ver ⟨I saw a dog : vi un perro⟩ ⟨see you later! : ¡hasta luego!⟩ **2** EXPERIENCE : ver, conocer **3** UNDERSTAND : ver, entender **4** ENSURE : asegurarse ⟨see that it's correct : asegúrese de que sea correcto⟩ **5** ACCOMPANY : acompañar **6** **to see off** : despedir, despedirse de — *vi* **1** : ver ⟨seeing is believing : ver para creer⟩ **2** UNDERSTAND : entender, ver ⟨now I see! : ¡ya entiendo!⟩ **3** CONSIDER : ver ⟨let's see : vamos a ver⟩ **4** **to see to** : ocuparse de

see[2] *n* : sede *f* ⟨the Holy See : la Santa Sede⟩

seed[1] [ˈsiːd] *vt* **1** SOW : sembrar **2** : despepitar, quitarle las semillas a

seed[2] *n, pl* **seed** *or* **seeds** **1** : semilla *f*, pepita *f* (de una fruta) **2** SOURCE : germen *m*, semilla *f*

seedless [ˈsiːdləs] *adj* : sin semillas

seedling [ˈsiːdlɪŋ] *n* : plantón *m*

seedpod [ˈsiːdˌpɑd] → **pod**

seedy [ˈsiːdi] *adj* **seedier; -est** **1** : lleno de semillas **2** SHABBY : raído (dícese de la ropa) **3** RUN-DOWN : ruinoso (dícese de los edificios, etc.), sórdido

seek [ˈsiːk] *v* **sought** [ˈsɔt]; **seeking** *vt* **1** : buscar ⟨to seek an answer : buscar una solución⟩ **2** REQUEST : solicitar, pedir **3** **to seek to** : tratar de, intentar de — *vi* SEARCH : buscar

seem [ˈsiːm] *vi* : parecer

seeming [ˈsiːmɪŋ] *adj* : aparente, ostensible

seemingly [ˈsiːmɪŋli] *adv* : aparentemente, según parece

seemly [ˈsiːmli] *adj* **seemlier; -est** : apropiado, decoroso

seep [ˈsiːp] *vi* : filtrarse

seer [ˈsiːər] *n* : vidente *mf*, clarividente *mf*

seesaw[1] [ˈsiːˌsɔ] *vi* **1** : jugar en un subibaja **2** VACILLATE : vacilar, oscilar

seesaw[2] *n* : balancín *m*, subibaja *m*

seethe [ˈsiːð] *vi* **seethed; seething** **1** : bullir, hervir **2** **to seethe with anger** : rabiar, estar furioso

segment [ˈsɛgmənt] *n* : segmento *m*

segmented [ˈsɛgˌmɛntəd, sɛgˈmɛn-] *adj* : segmentado

segregate [ˈsɛgrɪˌgeɪt] *vt* **-gated; -gating** : segregar

segregation [ˌsɛgrɪˈgeɪʃən] *n* : segregación *f*

seismic [ˈsaɪzmɪk, ˈsaɪs-] *adj* : sísmico

seize [ˈsiːz] *v* **seized; seizing** *vt* **1** CAPTURE : capturar, tomar, apoderarse de **2** ARREST : detener **3** CLUTCH, GRAB : agarrar, coger, aprovechar (una oportunidad) **4** **to be seized with** : estar sobrecogido por — *vi or* **to seize up** : agarrotarse

seizure [ˈsiːʒər] *n* **1** CAPTURE : toma *f*, captura *f* **2** ARREST : detención *f* **3** : ataque *m* ⟨an epileptic seizure : un ataque epiléptico⟩

seldom [ˈsɛldəm] *adv* : pocas veces, rara vez, casi nunca

select[1] [səˈlɛkt] *vt* : escoger, elegir, seleccionar (a un candidato, etc.)

select[2] *adj* : selecto

selection [səˈlɛkʃən] *n* : selección *f*, elección *f*

selective [səˈlɛktɪv] *adj* : selectivo
selenium [səˈliːniəm] *n* : selenio *m*
self [ˈsɛlf] *n, pl* **selves** [ˈsɛlvz] **1** : ser *m*, persona *f* ⟨the self : el yo⟩ ⟨with his whole self : con todo su ser⟩ ⟨her own self : su propia persona⟩ **2** SIDE : lado (de la personalidad) ⟨his better self : su lado bueno⟩
self-addressed [ˌsɛlfəˈdrst] *adj* : con la dirección del remitente ⟨include a self-addressed envelope : incluya un sobre con su nombre y dirección⟩
self-appointed [ˌsɛlfəˈpɔɪntəd] *adj* : autoproclamado, autonombrado
self-assurance [ˌsɛlfəˈʃʊrənts] *n* : seguridad *f* en sí mismo
self-assured [ˌsɛlfəˈʃʊrd] *adj* : seguro de sí mismo
self-centered [ˌsɛlfˈsɛntərd] *adj* : egocéntrico
self-confidence [ˌsɛlfˈkɑnfədənts] *n* : confianza *f* en sí mismo
self-confident [ˌsɛlfˈkɑnfədənt] *adj* : seguro de sí mismo
self-conscious [ˌsɛlfˈkɑntʃəs] *adj* : cohibido, tímido
self-consciously [ˌsɛlfˈkɑntʃəsli] *adv* : de manera cohibida
self-consciousness [ˌsɛlfˈkɑntʃəsnəs] *n* : vergüenza *f*, timidez *f*
self-contained [ˌsɛlfkənˈteɪnd] *adj* **1** INDEPENDENT : independiente **2** RESERVED : reservado
self-control [ˌsɛlfkənˈtroːl] *n* : autocontrol *m*, control *m* de sí mismo
self-defense [ˌsɛlfdɪˈfɛnts] *n* : defensa *f* propia, defensa *f* personal ⟨to act in self-defense : actuar en defensa propia⟩ ⟨self-defense class : clase de defensa personal⟩
self-denial [ˌsɛlfdɪˈnaɪəl] *n* : abnegación *f*
self-destructive [ˌsɛlfdɪˈstrʌktɪv] *adj* : autodestructivo
self-determination [ˌsɛlfdɪˌtərməˈneɪʃən] *n* : autodeterminación *f*
self-discipline [ˌsɛlfˈdɪsəplən] *n* : autodisciplina *f*
self-employed [ˌsɛlfɪmˈplɔɪd] *adj* : que trabaja por cuenta propia, autónomo
self-esteem [ˌsɛlfɪˈstiːm] *n* : autoestima *f*, amor *m* propio
self-evident [ˌsɛlfˈɛvədənt] *adj* : evidente, manifiesto
self-explanatory [ˌsɛlfɪkˈsplænəˌtori] *adj* : fácil de entender, evidente
self-expression [ˌsɛlfɪkˈsprʃən] *n* : expresión *f* personal
self-government [ˌsɛlfˈgʌvərmənt, -vərn-] *n* : autogobierno *m*
self-help [ˌsɛlfˈhɛlp] *n* : autoayuda *f*
self-important [ˌsɛlfɪmˈpɔrtənt] *adj* **1** VAIN : vanidoso, presumido **2** ARROGANT : arrogante
self-indulgent [ˌsɛlfɪnˈdʌldʒənt] *adj* : que se permite excesos
self-inflicted [ˌsɛlfɪnˈflɪktəd] *adj* : autoinfligido
self-interest [ˌsɛlfˈɪntrəst, -təˌrst] *n* : interés *m* personal
selfish [ˈsɛlfɪʃ] *adj* : egoísta
selfishly [ˈsɛlfɪʃli] *adv* : de manera egoísta
selfishness [ˈsɛlfɪʃnəs] *n* : egoísmo *m*
selfless [ˈsɛlfləs] *adj* UNSELFISH : desinteresado
self-made [ˌsɛlfˈmeɪd] *adj* : próspero gracias a sus propios esfuerzos
self-pity [ˌsɛlfˈpɪṭi] *n, pl* **-ties** : autocompasión *f*
self-portrait [ˌsɛlfˈpɔrtrət] *n* : autorretrato *m*
self-propelled [ˌsɛlfproˈpɛld] *adj* : autopropulsado
self-reliance [ˌsɛlfriˈlaɪənts] *n* : independencia *f*, autosuficiencia *f*
self-respect [ˌsɛlfriˈspɛkt] *n* : autoestima *f*, amor *m* propio
self-restraint [ˌsɛlfriˈstreɪnt] *n* : autocontrol *m*, moderación *f*
self-righteous [ˌsɛlfˈraɪtʃəs] *adj* : santurrón, moralista
self-sacrifice [ˌsɛlfˈsækrəˌfaɪs] *n* : abnegación *f*
selfsame [ˈsɛlfˌseɪm] *adj* : mismo
self-service [ˌsɛlfˈsərvɪs] *adj* **1** : de autoservicio **2 self-service restaurant** : autoservicio *m*
self-sufficiency [ˌsɛlfsəˈfɪʃəntsi] *n* : autosuficiencia *f*
self-sufficient [ˌsɛlfsəˈfɪʃənt] *adj* : autosuficiente
self-taught [ˌsɛlfˈtɔt] *adj* : autodidacta
sell [ˈsɛl] *v* **sold** [ˈsoːld]; **selling** *vt* : vender — *vi* : venderse
seller [ˈsɛlər] *n* : vendedor *m*, -dora *f*
selves → **self**
semantic [sɪˈmæntɪk] *adj* : semántico
semantics [sɪˈmæntɪks] *ns & pl* : semántica *f*
semaphore [ˈsɛməˌfor] *n* : semáforo *m*
semblance [ˈsɛmbləntss] *n* : apariencia *f*
semen [ˈsiːmən] *n* : semen *m*
semester [səˈmɛstər] *n* : semestre *m*
semicolon [ˈsɛmiˌkoːlən, ˈsɛˌmaɪ-] *n* : punto y coma *m*
semiconductor [ˈsɛmikənˌdʌktər, ˈsɛˌmaɪ-] *n* : semiconductor *m*
semifinal [ˈsɛmiˌfaɪnəl, ˈsɛˌmaɪ-] *n* : semifinal *f*
seminar [ˈsɛməˌnɑr] *n* : seminario *m*
seminary [ˈsɛməˌnɛri] *n, pl* **-naries** : seminario *m*
Semitic [səˈmɪṭɪk] *adj* : semita
senate [ˈsɛnət] *n* : senado *m*
senator [ˈsɛnəṭər] *n* : senador *m*, -dora *f*
send [ˈsɛnd] *vt* **sent** [ˈsɛnt]; **sending** **1** : mandar, enviar ⟨to send a letter : mandar una carta⟩ ⟨to send word : avisar, mandar decir⟩ **2** PROPEL : mandar, lanzar ⟨he sent it into left field : lo mandó al jardín izquierdo⟩ ⟨to send up dust : alzar polvo⟩ **3 to send into a rage** : poner furioso
sender [ˈsɛndər] *n* : remitente *mf* (de una carta, etc.)

Senegalese [ˌsɛnəgəˈliːz, -ˈliːs] *n* : senegalés *m*, -lesa *f* — **Senegalese** *adj*
senile [ˈsiːˌnaɪl] *adj* : senil
senility [sɪˈnɪləṭi] *n* : senilidad *f*
senior[1] [ˈsiːnjər] *adj* **1** ELDER : mayor ⟨John Doe, Senior : John Doe, padre⟩ **2** : superior (en rango), más antiguo (en años de servicio) ⟨a senior official : un alto oficial⟩
senior[2] *n* **1** : superior *m* (en rango) **2** **to be someone's senior** : ser mayor que alguien ⟨she's two years my senior : me lleva dos años⟩
senior citizen *n* : persona *f* de la tercera edad
seniority [ˌsiːˈnjɔrəṭi] *n* : antigüedad *f* (en años de servicio)
sensation [sɛnˈseɪʃən] *n* : sensación *f*
sensational [sɛnˈseɪʃənəl] *adj* : que causa sensación ⟨sensational stories : historias sensacionalistas⟩
sense[1] [ˈsɛnts] *vt* **sensed; sensing** : sentir ⟨he sensed danger : se dio cuenta del peligro⟩
sense[2] *n* **1** MEANING : sentido *m*, significado *m* **2** : sentido *m* ⟨the sense of smell : el sentido del olfato⟩ **3 to make sense** : tener sentido
senseless [ˈsɛntsləs] *adj* **1** MEANINGLESS : sin sentido, sin razón **2** UNCONSCIOUS : inconsciente
senselessly [ˈsɛntsləsli] *adv* : sin sentido
sensibility [ˌsɛntsəˈbɪləṭi] *n, pl* **-ties** : sensibilidad *f*
sensible [ˈsɛntsəbəl] *adj* **1** PERCEPTIBLE : sensible, perceptible **2** AWARE : consciente **3** REASONABLE : sensato ⟨a sensible man : un hombre sensato⟩ ⟨sensible shoes : zapatos prácticos⟩ — **sensibly** [-bli] *adv*
sensibleness [ˈsɛntsəbəlnəs] *n* : sensatez *f*, solidez *f*
sensitive [ˈsɛntsəṭɪv] *adj* **1** : sensible, delicado ⟨sensitive skin : piel sensible⟩ **2** IMPRESSIONABLE : sensible, impresionable **3** TOUCHY : susceptible
sensitiveness [ˈsɛntsəṭɪvnəs] → **sensitivity**
sensitivity [ˌsɛntsəˈtɪvəṭi] *n, pl* **-ties** : sensibilidad *f*
sensitize [ˈsɛntsəˌtaɪz] *vt* **-tized; -tizing** : sensibilizar
sensor [ˈsɛnˌsɔr, ˈsɛntsər] *n* : sensor *m*
sensory [ˈsɛntsəri] *adj* : sensorial
sensual [ˈsɛntʃuəl] *adj* : sensual — **sensually** *adv*
sensuality [ˌsɛntʃəˈwæləṭi] *n, pl* **-ties** : sensualidad *f*
sensuous [ˈsɛntʃuəs] *adj* : sensual
sent → **send**
sentence[1] [ˈsɛntənts, -ənz] *vt* **-tenced; -tencing** : sentenciar
sentence[2] *n* **1** JUDGMENT : sentencia *f* **2** : oración *f*, frase *f* (en gramática)
sentiment [ˈsɛntəmənt] *n* **1** BELIEF : opinión *f* **2** FEELING : sentimiento *m* **3** → **sentimentality**
sentimental [ˌsɛntəˈmɛntəl] *adj* : sentimental
sentimentality [ˌsɛntəˌmɛnˈtæləṭi] *n, pl* **-ties** : sentimentalismo *m*, sensiblería *f*
sentinel [ˈsɛntənəl] *n* : centinela *mf*, guardia *mf*
sentry [ˈsɛntri] *n, pl* **-tries** : centinela *mf*
sepal [ˈsiːpəl, ˈsɛ-] *n* : sépalo *m*
separable [ˈsɛpərəbəl] *adj* : separable
separate[1] [ˈsɛpəˌreɪt] *v* **-rated; -rating** *vt* **1** DETACH, SEVER : separar **2** DISTINGUISH : diferenciar, distinguir — *vi* PART : separarse
separate[2] [ˈsɛprət, ˈsɛpə-] *adj* **1** INDIVIDUAL : separado, aparte ⟨a separate state : un estado separado⟩ ⟨in a separate envelope : en un sobre aparte⟩ **2** DISTINCT : distinto
separately [ˈsɛprətli, ˈsɛpə-] *adv* : por separado, separadamente, aparte
separation [ˌsɛpəˈreɪʃən] *n* : separación *f*
sepia [ˈsiːpiə] *n* : color *m* sepia
September [sɛpˈtɛmbər] *n* : septiembre *m*, setiembre *m*
septic [ˈsɛptɪk] *adj* : séptico ⟨septic tank : fosa séptica⟩
sepulchre [ˈsɛpəlkər] *n* : sepulcro *m*
sequel [ˈsiːkwəl] *n* **1** CONSEQUENCE : secuela *f*, consecuencia *f* **2** : continuación *f* (de una película, etc.)
sequence [ˈsiːkwənts] *n* **1** SERIES : serie *f*, sucesión *f*, secuencia *f* (matemática o musical) **2** ORDER : orden *m*
sequester [sɪˈkwɛstər] *vt* : aislar
sequin [ˈsiːkwən] *n* : lentejuela *f*
sequoia [sɪˈkwɔɪə] *n* : secoya *f*, secuoya *f*
sera → **serum**
Serb [ˈsərb] *or* **Serbian** [ˈsərbiən] *n* **1** : serbio *m*, -bia *f* **2** : serbio *m* (idioma) — **Serb** *or* **Serbian** *adj*
Serbo–Croatian [ˌsərbokroˈeɪʃən] *n* : serbocroata *m* (idioma) — **Serbo–Croatian** *adj*
serenade[1] [ˌsɛrəˈneɪd] *vt* **-naded; -nading** : darle una serenata (a alguien)
serenade[2] *n* : serenata *f*
serene [səˈriːn] *adj* : sereno — **serenely** *adv*
serenity [səˈrɛnəṭi] *n* : serenidad *f*
serf [ˈsərf] *n* : siervo *m*, -va *f*
serge [ˈsərʤ] *n* : sarga *f*
sergeant [ˈsɑrʤənt] *n* : sargento *mf*
serial[1] [ˈsɪriəl] *adj* : seriado
serial[2] *n* : serie *f*, serial *m* (de radio o televisión), publicación *f* por entregas
serially [ˈsɪriəli] *adv* : en serie
series [ˈsɪrˌiːz] *n, pl* **series** : serie *f*, sucesión *f*
serious [ˈsɪriəs] *adj* **1** SOBER : serio **2** DEDICATED, EARNEST : serio, dedicado ⟨to be serious about something : tomar algo en serio⟩ **3** GRAVE : serio, grave ⟨serious problems : problemas graves⟩
seriously [ˈsɪriəsli] *adv* **1** EARNESTLY : seriamente, con seriedad, en serio **2** SEVERELY : gravemente

seriousness [ˈsɪriəsnəs] *n* : seriedad *f*, gravedad *f*

sermon [ˈsərmən] *n* : sermón *m*

serpent [ˈsərpənt] *n* : serpiente *f*

serrated [səˈreɪt̬əd, ˈsɛrˌeɪt̬əd] *adj* : dentado, serrado

serum [ˈsɪrəm] *n, pl* **serums** *or* **sera** [ˈsɪrə] : suero *m*

servant [ˈsərvənt] *n* : criado *m*, -da *f*; sirviente *m*, -ta *f*

serve [ˈsərv] *v* **served; serving** *vi* **1** : servir ⟨to serve in the navy : servir en la armada⟩ ⟨to serve on a jury : ser miembro de un jurado⟩ **2** DO, FUNCTION : servir ⟨to serve as : servir de, servir como⟩ **3** : sacar (en deportes) — *vt* **1** : servir ⟨to serve God : servir a Dios⟩ **2** HELP : servir ⟨it serves no purpose : no sirve para nada⟩ **3** : servir (comida o bebida) ⟨dinner is served : la cena está servida⟩ **4** SUPPLY : abastecer **5** CARRY OUT : cumplir, hacer ⟨to serve time : servir una pena⟩ **6 to serve a summons** : entregar una citación

server [ˈsərvər] *n* **1** : camarero *m*, -ra *f*; mesero *m*, -ra *f* (en un restaurante) **2** *or* **serving dish** : fuente *f* (para servir comida) **3** : servidor *m* (en informática)

service[1] [ˈsərvəs] *vt* **-viced; -vicing 1** MAINTAIN : darle mantenimiento a (una máquina), revisar **2** REPAIR : arreglar, reparar

service[2] *n* **1** HELP, USE : servicio *m* ⟨to do someone a service : hacerle un servicio a alguien⟩ ⟨at your service : a sus órdenes⟩ ⟨to be out of service : no funcionar⟩ **2** CEREMONY : oficio *m* (religioso) **3** DEPARTMENT, SYSTEM : servicio *m* ⟨social services : servicios sociales⟩ ⟨train service : servicio de trenes⟩ **4** SET : juego *m*, servicio *m* ⟨tea service : juego de té⟩ **5** MAINTENANCE : mantenimiento *m*, revisión *f*, servicio *m* **6** : saque *m* (en deportes) **7 armed services** : fuerzas *fpl* armadas

serviceable [ˈsərvəsəbəl] *adj* **1** USEFUL : útil **2** DURABLE : duradero

serviceman [ˈsərvəsˌmæn, -mən] *n, pl* **-men** [-mən, -ˌmɛn] : militar *m*

service station → **gas station**

servicewoman [ˈsərvəsˌwʊmən] *n, pl* **-women** [-ˌwɪmən] : militar *f*

servile [ˈsərvəl, -ˌvaɪl] *adj* : servil

serving [ˈsərvɪŋ] *n* HELPING : porción *f*, ración *f*

servitude [ˈsərvəˌtuːd, -ˌtjuːd] *n* : servidumbre *f*

sesame [ˈsɛsəmi] *n* : ajonjolí *m*, sésamo *m*

session [ˈsɛʃən] *n* : sesión *f*

set[1] [ˈsɛt] *v* **set; setting** *vt* **1** SEAT : sentar **2** *or* **set down** PLACE : poner, colocar **3** ARRANGE : fijar, establecer ⟨to set the date : poner la fecha⟩ ⟨he set the agenda : estableció la agenda⟩ **4** ADJUST : poner (un reloj, etc.) **5** (*indicating the causing of a certain condition*) ⟨to set fire to : prenderle fuego a⟩ ⟨she set it free : lo soltó⟩ **6** MAKE, START : poner, hacer ⟨I set them working : los puse a trabajar⟩ — *vi* **1** SOLIDIFY : fraguar (dícese del cemento, etc.), cuajar (dícese de la gelatina, etc.) **2** : ponerse (dícese del sol o de la luna)

set[2] *adj* **1** ESTABLISHED, FIXED : fijo, establecido **2** RIGID : inflexible ⟨to be set in one's ways : tener costumbres muy arraigadas⟩ **3** READY : listo, preparado

set[3] *n* **1** COLLECTION : juego *m* ⟨a set of dishes : un juego de platos, una vajilla⟩ ⟨a tool set : una caja de herramientas⟩ **2** *or* **stage set** : decorado *m* (en el teatro), plató *m* (en el cine) **3** APPARATUS : aparato *m* ⟨a television set : un televisor⟩ **4** : conjunto *m* (en matemáticas)

setback [ˈsɛtˌbæk] *n* : revés *m*, contratiempo *m*

set in *vi* BEGIN : comenzar, empezar

set off *vt* **1** PROVOKE : provocar **2** EXPLODE : hacer estallar (una bomba, etc.) — *vi or* **to set forth** : salir

set out *vi* : salir (de viaje) — *vt* INTEND : proponerse

settee [sɛˈtiː] *n* : sofá *m*

setter [ˈsɛt̬ər] *n* : setter *mf* ⟨Irish setter : setter irlandés⟩

setting [ˈsɛt̬ɪŋ] *n* **1** : posición *f*, ajuste *m* (de un control) **2** : engaste *m*, montura *f* (de una gema) **3** SCENE : escenario *m* (de una novela, etc.) **4** SURROUNDINGS : ambiente *m*, entorno *m*, marco *m*

settle [ˈsɛt̬əl] *v* **settled; settling** *vi* **1** ALIGHT, LAND : posarse (dícese de las aves), depositarse (dícese del polvo) **2** SINK : asentarse (dícese de los edificios) ⟨he settled into the chair : se arrellanó en la silla⟩ **3** : instalarse (en una casa), establecerse (en una ciudad o región) **4 to settle down** : calmarse, tranquilizarse ⟨settle down! : ¡tranquilízate!, ¡cálmate!⟩ **5 to settle down** : sentar cabeza, hacerse sensato ⟨to marry and settle down : casarse y sentar cabeza⟩ — *vt* **1** ARRANGE, DECIDE : fijar, decidir, acordar (planes, etc.) **2** RESOLVE : resolver, solucionar ⟨to settle an argument : resolver una discusión⟩ **3** PAY : pagar ⟨to settle an account : saldar una cuenta⟩ **4** CALM : calmar (los nervios), asentar (el estómago) **5** COLONIZE : colonizar **6 to settle oneself** : acomodarse, hacerse cómodo

settlement [ˈsɛt̬əlmənt] *n* **1** PAYMENT : pago *m*, liquidación *f* **2** COLONY : asentamiento *m* **3** RESOLUTION : acuerdo *m*

settler [ˈsɛt̬ələr] *n* : poblador *m*, -dora *f*; colono *m*, -na *f*

setup [ˈsɛtˌʌp] *n* **1** ASSEMBLY : montaje *m*, ensamblaje *m* **2** ARRANGEMENT : disposición *f* **3** PREPARATION : preparación *f* **4** TRAP, TRICK : encerrona *f*

set up *vt* **1** ASSEMBLE : montar, armar **2** ERECT : levantar, erigir **3** ESTABLISH : establecer, fundar, montar (un negocio) **4** CAUSE : armar ⟨they set up a clamor : armaron un alboroto⟩
seven[1] [ˈsɛvən] *adj* : siete
seven[2] *n* : siete *m*
seven hundred[1] *adj* : setecientos
seven hundred[2] *n* : setecientos *m*
seventeen[1] [ˌsɛvənˈtiːn] *adj* : diecisiete
seventeen[2] *n* : diecisiete *m*
seventeenth[1] [ˌsɛvənˈtiːnθ] *adj* : decimoséptimo
seventeenth[2] *n* **1** : decimoséptimo *m*, -ma *f* (en una serie) **2** : diecisieteavo *m*, diecisieteava parte *f*
seventh[1] [ˈsɛvənθ] *adj* : séptimo
seventh[2] *n* **1** : séptimo *m*, -ma *f* (en una serie) **2** : séptimo *m*, séptima parte *f*
seventieth[1] [ˈsɛvəntiəθ] *adj* : septuagésimo
seventieth[2] *n* **1** : septuagésimo *m*, -ma *f* (en una serie) **2** : setentavo *m*, setentava parte *f*, septuagésima parte *f*
seventy[1] [ˈsɛvənti] *adj* : setenta
seventy[2] *n, pl* **-ties** : setenta *m*
sever [ˈsɛvər] *vt* **-ered; -ering** : cortar, romper
several[1] [ˈsɛvrəl, ˈsɛvə-] *adj* **1** DISTINCT : distinto **2** SOME : varios ⟨several weeks : varias semanas⟩
several[2] *pron* : varios, varias
severance [ˈsɛvrənts, sɛvə-] *n* **1** : ruptura *f* (de relaciones, etc.) **2 severance pay** : indemnización *f* (por despido)
severe [səˈvɪr] *adj* **severer; -est 1** STRICT : severo **2** AUSTERE : sobrio, austero **3** SERIOUS : grave ⟨a severe wound : una herida grave⟩ ⟨severe aches : dolores fuertes⟩ **4** DIFFICULT : duro, difícil — **severely** *adv*
severity [səˈvrəti] *n* **1** HARSHNESS : severidad *f* **2** AUSTERITY : sobriedad *f*, austeridad *f* **3** SERIOUSNESS : gravedad *f* (de una herida, etc.)
sew [ˈsoː] *v* **sewed; sewn** [ˈsoːn] *or* **sewed; sewing** : coser
sewage [ˈsuːɪʤ] *n* : aguas *fpl* negras, aguas *fpl* residuales
sewer[1] [ˈsoːər] *n* : uno que cose
sewer[2] [ˈsuːər] *n* : alcantarilla *f*, cloaca *f*
sewing [ˈsoːɪŋ] *n* : costura *f*
sex [ˈsɛks] *n* **1** : sexo *m* ⟨the opposite sex : el sexo opuesto⟩ **2** COPULATION : relaciones *fpl* sexuales
sexism [ˈsɛkˌsɪzəm] *n* : sexismo *m*
sexist[1] [ˈsɛksɪst] *adj* : sexista
sexist[2] *n* : sexista *mf*
sextant [ˈsɛkstənt] *n* : sextante *m*
sextet [sɛkˈstɛt] *n* : sexteto *m*
sexton [ˈsɛkstən] *n* : sacristán *m*
sexual [ˈsɛkʃʊəl] *adj* : sexual — **sexually** *adv*
sexuality [ˌsɛkʃʊˈæləti] *n* : sexualidad *f*
sexy [ˈsɛksi] *adj* **sexier; -est** : sexy
shabbily [ˈʃæbəli] *adv* **1** : pobremente ⟨shabbily dressed : pobremente vestido⟩ **2** UNFAIRLY : mal, injustamente
shabbiness [ˈʃæbinəs] *n* **1** : lo gastado (de ropa, etc.) **2** : lo mal vestido (de personas) **3** UNFAIRNESS : injusticia *f*
shabby [ˈʃæbi] *adj* **shabbier; -est 1** : gastado (dícese de la ropa, etc.) **2** : mal vestido (dícese de las personas) **3** UNFAIR : malo, injusto ⟨shabby treatment : mal trato⟩
shack [ˈʃæk] *n* : choza *f*, rancho *m*
shackle[1] [ˈʃækəl] *vt* **-led; -ling** : ponerle grilletes (a alguien)
shackle[2] *n* : grillete *m*
shad [ˈʃæd] *n* : sábalo *m*
shade[1] [ˈʃeɪd] *v* **shaded; shading** *vt* **1** SHELTER : proteger (del sol o de la luz) **2** *or* **to shade in** : matizar los colores de — *vi* : convertirse gradualmente ⟨his irritation shaded into rage : su irritación iba convirtiéndose en furia⟩
shade[2] *n* **1** : sombra *f* ⟨to give shade : dar sombra⟩ **2** : tono *m* (de un color) **3** NUANCE : matiz *m* **4** : pantalla *f* (de una lámpara), persiana *f* (de una ventana)
shadow[1] [ˈʃædoː] *vt* **1** DARKEN : ensombrecer **2** TRAIL : seguir de cerca, seguirle la pista (a alguien)
shadow[2] *n* **1** : sombra *f* **2** DARKNESS : oscuridad *f* **3** TRACE : sombra *f*, atisbo *m*, indicio *m* ⟨without a shadow of a doubt : sin sombra de duda, sin lugar a dudas⟩ **4 to cast a shadow over** : ensombrecer
shadowy [ˈʃædowi] *adj* **1** INDISTINCT : vago, indistinto **2** DARK : oscuro
shady [ˈʃeɪdi] *adj* **shadier; -est 1** : sombreado (dícese de un lugar), que da sombra (dícese de un árbol) **2** DISREPUTABLE : sospechoso (dícese de una persona), turbio (dícese de un negocio, etc.)
shaft [ˈʃæft] *n* **1** : asta *f* (de una lanza), astil *m* (de una flecha), mango *m* (de una herramienta) **2** *or* **mine shaft** : pozo *m*
shaggy [ˈʃægi] *adj* **shaggier; -est 1** HAIRY : peludo ⟨a shaggy dog : un perro peludo⟩ **2** UNKEMPT : enmarañado, despeinado (dícese del pelo, de las barbas, etc.)
shake[1] [ˈʃeɪk] *v* **shook** [ˈʃʊk]; **shaken** [ˈʃeɪkən]; **shaking** *vt* **1** : sacudir, agitar, hacer temblar ⟨he shook his head : negó con la cabeza⟩ **2** WEAKEN : debilitar, hacer flaquear ⟨it shook her faith : debilitó su confianza⟩ **3** UPSET : afectar, alterar **4 to shake hands with someone** : darle la mano a alguien, estrecharle la mano a alguien — *vi* : temblar, sacudirse
shake[2] *n* : sacudida *f*, apretón *m* (de manos)
shaker [ˈʃeɪkər] *n* **1 salt shaker** : salero *m* **2 pepper shaker** : pimentero *m* **3 cocktail shaker** : coctelera *f*
shake–up [ˈʃeɪkˌʌp] *n* : reorganización *f*
shakily [ˈʃeɪkəli] *adv* : temblorosamente

shaky [ˈʃeɪki] *adj* **shakier; -est 1** SHAKING : tembloroso **2** UNSTABLE : poco firme, inestable **3** PRECARIOUS : precario, incierto **4** QUESTIONABLE : dudoso, cuestionable ⟨shaky arguments : argumentos discutibles⟩

shale [ˈʃeɪl] *n* : esquisto *m*

shall [ˈʃæl] *v aux, past* **should** [ˈʃʊd] *present s & pl* **shall 1** (*used to express a command*) ⟨you shall do as I say : harás lo que te digo⟩ **2** (*used to express futurity*) ⟨we shall see : ya veremos⟩ ⟨when shall we expect you? : ¿cuándo te podemos esperar?⟩ **3** (*used to express determination*) ⟨you shall have the money : tendrás el dinero⟩ **4** (*used to express a condition*) ⟨if he should die : si muriera⟩ ⟨if they should call, tell me : si llaman, dímelo⟩ **5** (*used to express obligation*) ⟨he should have said it : debería haberlo dicho⟩ **6** (*used to express probability*) ⟨they should arrive soon : deben (de) llegar pronto⟩ ⟨why should he lie? : ¿porqué ha de mentir?⟩

shallow [ˈʃælo:] *adj* **1** : poco profundo (dícese del agua, etc.) **2** SUPERFICIAL : superficial

shallows [ˈʃælo:z] *npl* : bajío *m*, bajos *mpl*

sham[1] [ˈʃæm] *v* **shammed; shamming** : fingir

sham[2] *adj* : falso, fingido

sham[3] *n* **1** FAKE, PRETENSE : farsa *f*, simulación *f*, imitación *f* **2** FAKER : impostor *m*, -tora *f*; farsante *mf*

shamble [ˈʃæmbəl] *vi* **-bled; -bling** : caminar arrastrando los pies

shambles [ˈʃæmbəlz] *ns & pl* : caos *m*, desorden *m*, confusión *f*

shame[1] [ˈʃeɪm] *vt* **shamed; shaming 1** : avergonzar ⟨he was shamed by their words : sus palabras le dieron vergüenza⟩ **2** DISGRACE : deshonrar

shame[2] *n* **1** : vergüenza *f* ⟨to have no shame : no tener vergüenza⟩ **2** DISGRACE : vergüenza *f*, deshonra *f* **3** PITY : lástima *f*, pena *f* ⟨what a shame! : ¡qué pena!⟩

shamefaced [ˈʃeɪm,feɪst] *adj* : avergonzado

shameful [ˈʃeɪmfəl] *adj* : vergonzoso — **shamefully** *adv*

shameless [ˈʃeɪmləs] *adj* : descarado, desvergonzado — **shamelessly** *adv*

shampoo[1] [ʃæmˈpu:] *vt* : lavar (el pelo)

shampoo[2] *n, pl* **-poos** : champú *m*

shamrock [ˈʃæm,rɑk] *n* : trébol *m*

shank [ˈʃæŋk] *n* : parte *f* baja de la pierna

shan't [ˈʃænt] (*contraction of* **shall not**) → **shall**

shanty [ˈʃænti] *n, pl* **-ties** : choza *f*, rancho *m*

shape[1] [ˈʃeɪp] *v* **shaped; shaping** *vt* **1** : dar forma a, modelar (arcilla, etc.), tallar (madera, piedra), formar (carácter) ⟨to be shaped like : tener forma de⟩ **2** DETERMINE : decidir, determinar — *vi or* **to shape up** : tomar forma

shape[2] *n* **1** : forma *f*, figura *f* ⟨in the shape of a circle : en forma de círculo⟩ **2** CONDITION : estado *m*, condiciones *fpl*, forma *f* (física) ⟨to get in shape : ponerse en forma⟩

shapeless [ˈʃeɪpləs] *adj* : informe

shapely [ˈʃeɪpli] *adj* **shapelier; -est** : curvilíneo, bien proporcionado

shard [ˈʃɑrd] *n* : fragmento *m*, casco *m* (de cerámica, etc.)

share[1] [ˈʃɛr] *v* **shared; sharing** *vt* **1** APPORTION : dividir, repartir **2** : compartir ⟨they share a room : comparten una habitación⟩ — *vi* : compartir

share[2] *n* **1** PORTION : parte *f*, porción *f* ⟨one's fair share : lo que le corresponde a uno⟩ **2** : acción *f* (en una compañía) ⟨to hold shares : tener acciones⟩

sharecropper [ˈʃɛr,krɑpər] *n* : aparcero *m*, -ra *f*

shareholder [ˈʃɛr,ho:ldər] *n* : accionista *mf*

shark [ˈʃɑrk] *n* : tiburón *m*

sharp[1] [ˈʃɑrp] *adv* : en punto ⟨at two o'clock sharp : a las dos en punto⟩

sharp[2] *adj* **1** : afilado, filoso ⟨a sharp knife : un cuchillo afilado⟩ **2** PENETRATING : cortante, fuerte **3** CLEVER : agudo, listo, perspicaz **4** ACUTE : agudo ⟨sharp eyesight : vista aguda⟩ **5** HARSH, SEVERE : duro, severo, agudo ⟨a sharp rebuke : una reprimenda mordaz⟩ **6** STRONG : fuerte ⟨sharp cheese : queso fuerte⟩ **7** ABRUPT : brusco, repentino **8** DISTINCT : nítido, definido ⟨a sharp image : una imagen bien definida⟩ **9** ANGULAR : anguloso (dícese de la cara) **10** : sostenido (en música)

sharp[3] *n* : sostenido *m* (en música)

sharpen [ˈʃɑrpən] *vt* : afilar, aguzar ⟨to sharpen a pencil : sacarle punta a un lápiz⟩ ⟨to sharpen one's wits : aguzar el ingenio⟩

sharpener [ˈʃɑrpənər] *n* : afilador *m* (para cuchillos, etc.), sacapuntas *m* (para lápices)

sharply [ˈʃɑrpli] *adv* **1** ABRUPTLY : bruscamente **2** DISTINCTLY : claramente, marcadamente

sharpness [ˈʃɑrpnəs] *n* **1** : lo afilado (de un cuchillo, etc.) **2** ACUTENESS : agudeza *f* (de los sentidos o de la mente) **3** INTENSITY : intensidad *f*, agudeza *f* (de dolores, etc.) **4** HARSHNESS : dureza *f*, severidad *f* **5** ABRUPTNESS : brusquedad *f* **6** CLARITY : nitidez *f*

sharpshooter [ˈʃɑrp,ʃu:t̬ər] *n* : tirador *m*, -dora *f* de primera

shatter [ˈʃæt̬ər] *vt* **1** : hacer añicos ⟨to shatter the silence : romper el silencio⟩ **2 to be shattered by** : quedar destrozado por — *vi* : hacerse añicos, romperse en pedazos

shave[1] [ˈʃeɪv] *v* **shaved; shaved** *or* **shaven** [ˈʃeɪvən]; **shaving** *vt* **1** : afeitar, rasurar ⟨she shaved her legs : se rasuró las piernas⟩ ⟨they shaved (off) his beard : le afeitaron la barba⟩ **2** SLICE : cortar (en pedazos finos) — *vi* : afeitarse, rasurarse

shave[2] *n* : afeitada *f*, rasurada *f*

shaver [ˈʃeɪvər] *n* : afeitadora *f*, máquina *f* de afeitar, rasuradora *f*

shawl [ˈʃɔl] *n* : chal *m*, mantón *m*, rebozo *m*

she [ˈʃiː] *pron* : ella

sheaf [ˈʃiːf] *n, pl* **sheaves** [ˈʃiːvz] : gavilla *f* (de cereales), haz *m* (de flechas), fajo *m* (de papeles)

shear [ˈʃɪr] *vt* **sheared; sheared** *or* **shorn** [ˈʃorn]; **shearing 1** : esquilar, trasquilar ⟨to shear sheep : trasquilar ovejas⟩ **2** CUT : cortar (el pelo, etc.)

shears [ˈʃɪrz] *npl* : tijeras *fpl* (grandes)

sheath [ˈʃiːθ] *n, pl* **sheaths** [ˈʃiːðz, ˈʃiːθs] : funda *f*, vaina *f*

sheathe [ˈʃiːð] *vt* **sheathed; sheathing** : envainar, enfundar

shed[1] [ˈʃd] *vt* **shed; shedding 1** : derramar (sangre o lágrimas) **2** EMIT : emitir (luz) ⟨to shed light on : aclarar⟩ **3** DISCARD : mudar (la piel, etc.) ⟨to shed one's clothes : quitarse uno la ropa⟩

shed[2] *n* : cobertizo *m*

she'd [ˈʃiːd] (*contraction of* **she had** *or* **she would**) → **have, would**

sheen [ˈʃiːn] *n* : brillo *m*, lustre *m*

sheep [ˈʃiːp] *ns & pl* : oveja *f*

sheepfold [ˈʃiːpˌfoːld] *n* : redil *m*

sheepish [ˈʃiːpɪʃ] *adj* : avergonzado

sheepskin [ˈʃiːpˌskɪn] *n* : piel *f* de oveja, piel *f* de borrego

sheer[1] [ˈʃɪr] *adv* **1** COMPLETELY : completamente, totalmente **2** VERTICALLY : verticalmente

sheer[2] *adj* **1** TRANSPARENT : vaporoso, transparente **2** ABSOLUTE, UTTER : puro ⟨by sheer luck : por pura suerte⟩ **3** STEEP : escarpado, vertical

sheet [ˈʃiːt] *n* **1** *or* **bedsheet** [ˈbɛd-ˌʃiːt] : sábana *f* **2** : hoja *f* (de papel) **3** : capa *f* (de hielo, etc.) **4** : lámina *f*, placa *f* (de vidrio, metal, etc.), plancha *f* (de metal, madera, etc.) ⟨baking sheet : placa de horno⟩

sheikh *or* **sheik** [ˈʃiːk, ˈʃeɪk] *n* : jeque *m*

shelf [ˈʃɛlf] *n, pl* **shelves** [ˈʃɛlvz] **1** : estante *m*, anaquel *m* (en una pared) **2** : banco *m*, arrecife *m* (en geología) ⟨continental shelf : plataforma continental⟩

shell[1] [ˈʃɛl] *vt* **1** : desvainar (chícharos), pelar (nueces, etc.) **2** BOMBARD : bombardear

shell[2] *n* **1** SEASHELL : concha *f* **2** : cáscara *f* (de huevos, nueces, etc.), vaina *f* (de chícharos, etc.), caparazón *m* (de crustáceos, tortugas, etc.) **3** : cartucho *m*, casquillo *m* ⟨a .45 caliber shell : un cartucho calibre .45⟩ **4** *or* **racing shell** : bote *m* (para hacer regatas de remos)

she'll [ˈʃiːl, ˈʃɪl] (*contraction of* **she shall** *or* **she will**) → **shall, will**

shellac[1] [ʃəˈlæk] *vt* **-lacked; -lacking 1** : laquear (madera, etc.) **2** DEFEAT : darle una paliza (a alguien), derrotar

shellac[2] *n* : laca *f*

shellfish [ˈʃɛlˌfɪʃ] *n* : marisco *m*

shelter[1] [ˈʃɛltər] *vt* **1** PROTECT : proteger, abrigar **2** HARBOR : dar refugio a, albergar

shelter[2] *n* : refugio *m*, abrigo *m* ⟨to take shelter : refugiarse⟩

shelve [ˈʃɛlv] *vt* **shelved; shelving 1** : poner en estantes **2** DEFER : dar carpetazo a

shenanigans [ʃəˈnænɪgənz] *npl* **1** TRICKERY : artimañas *fpl* **2** MISCHIEF : travesuras *fpl*

shepherd[1] [ˈʃɛpərd] *vt* **1** : cuidar (ovejas, etc.) **2** GUIDE : conducir, guiar

shepherd[2] *n* : pastor *m*

shepherdess [ˈʃɛpərdəs] *n* : pastora *f*

sherbet [ˈʃərbət] *or* **sherbert** [-bərt] *n* : sorbete *m*, nieve *f Cuba, Mex, PRi*

sheriff [ˈʃɛrɪf] *n* : sheriff *mf*

sherry [ˈʃɛri] *n, pl* **-ries** : jerez *m*

she's [ˈʃiːz] (*contraction of* **she is** *or* **she has**) → **be, have**

shield[1] [ˈʃiːld] *vt* **1** PROTECT : proteger **2** CONCEAL : ocultar ⟨to shield one's eyes : taparse los ojos⟩

shield[2] *n* **1** : escudo *m* (armadura) **2** PROTECTION : protección *f*, blindaje *m* (de un cable)

shier, shiest → **shy**

shift[1] [ˈʃɪft] *vt* **1** CHANGE : cambiar ⟨to shift gears : cambiar de velocidad⟩ **2** MOVE : mover **3** TRANSFER : transferir ⟨to shift the blame : echarle la culpa (a otro)⟩ — *vi* **1** CHANGE : cambiar **2** MOVE : moverse **3 to shift for oneself** : arreglárselas solo

shift[2] *n* **1** CHANGE, TRANSFER : cambio *m* ⟨a shift in priorities : un cambio de prioridades⟩ **2** : turno *m* ⟨night shift : turno de noche⟩ **3** DRESS : vestido *m* (suelto) **4** → **gearshift**

shiftless [ˈʃɪftləs] *adj* : perezoso, vago, holgazán

shifty [ˈʃɪfti] *adj* **shiftier; -est** : taimado, artero ⟨a shifty look : una mirada huidiza⟩

shilling [ˈʃɪlɪŋ] *n* : chelín *m*

shimmer [ˈʃɪmər] *vi* GLIMMER : brillar con luz trémula

shin[1] [ˈʃɪn] *vi* **shinned; shinning** : trepar, subir ⟨she shinned up the pole : subió al poste⟩

shin[2] *n* : espinilla *f*, canilla *f*

shine[1] [ˈʃaɪn] *v* **shone** [ˈʃoːn] *or* **shined; shining** *vi* **1** : brillar, relucir ⟨the stars were shining : las estrellas brillaban⟩ **2** EXCEL : brillar, lucirse — *vt* **1** : alumbrar ⟨he shined the flashlight at it : lo alumbró con la linterna⟩ **2** POLISH : sacarle brillo a, lustrar

shine[2] *n* : brillo *m*, lustre *m*

shingle[1] [ˈʃɪŋgəl] *vt* **-gled; -gling** : techar

shingle[2] *n* : tablilla *f* (para techar)

shingles [ˈʃɪŋgəlz] *npl* : herpes *m*

shinny [ˈʃɪni] *vi* **-nied; -nying** → **shin**[1]

shiny [ˈʃaɪni] *adj* **shinier; -est** : brillante

ship[1] [ˈʃɪp] *vt* **shipped; shipping 1** LOAD : embarcar (en un barco) **2** SEND : transportar (en barco), enviar ⟨to ship by air : enviar por avión⟩

ship[2] *n* **1** : barco *m*, buque *m* **2** → **spaceship**

shipboard [ˈʃɪpˌbord] *n* **on ~** : a bordo

shipbuilder [ˈʃɪpˌbɪldər] *n* : constructor *m*, -tora *f* naval

shipment [ˈʃɪpmənt] *n* **1** SHIPPING : transporte *m*, embarque *m* **2** : envío *m*, remesa *f* ⟨a shipment of medicine : un envío de medicina⟩

shipping [ˈʃɪpɪŋ] *n* **1** SHIPS : barcos *mpl*, embarcaciones *fpl* **2** TRANSPORTATION : transporte *m* (de mercancías)

shipshape [ˈʃɪpˈʃeɪp] *adj* : ordenado

shipwreck[1] [ˈʃɪpˌrɛk] *vt* **to be shipwrecked** : naufragar

shipwreck[2] *n* : naufragio *m*

shipyard [ˈʃɪpˌjɑrd] *n* : astillero *m*

shirk [ˈʃərk] *vt* : eludir, rehuir ⟨to shirk one's responsibilities : esquivar uno sus responsabilidades⟩

shirt [ˈʃərt] *n* : camisa *f*

shiver[1] [ˈʃɪvər] *vi* **1** : tiritar (de frío) **2** TREMBLE : estremecerse, temblar

shiver[2] *n* : escalofrío *m*, estremecimiento *m*

shoal [ˈʃoːl] *n* : banco *m*, bajío *m*

shock[1] [ˈʃɑk] *vt* **1** UPSET : conmover, conmocionar **2** STARTLE : asustar, sobresaltar **3** SCANDALIZE : escandalizar **4** : darle una descarga eléctrica a

shock[2] *n* **1** COLLISION, JOLT : choque *m*, sacudida *f* **2** UPSET : conmoción *f*, golpe *m* emocional **3** : shock *m* (en medicina) **4** *or* **electric shock** : descarga *f* eléctrica **5** SHEAVES : gavillas *fpl* **6 shock of hair** : mata *f* de pelo

shock absorber *n* : amortiguador *m*

shocking [ˈʃɑkɪŋ] *adj* **1** : chocante **2 shocking pink** : rosa *m* estridente

shoddy [ˈʃɑdi] *adj* **shoddier; -est** : de mala calidad ⟨a shoddy piece of work : un trabajo chapucero⟩

shoe[1] [ˈʃuː] *vt* **shod** [ˈʃɑd]; **shoeing** : herrar (un caballo)

shoe[2] *n* **1** : zapato *m* ⟨the shoe industry : la industria del calzado⟩ **2** HORSESHOE : herradura *f* **3 brake shoe** : zapata *f*

shoelace [ˈʃuːˌleɪs] *n* : cordón *m* (de zapatos)

shoemaker [ˈʃuːˌmeɪkər] *n* : zapatero *m*, -ra *f*

shone → **shine**

shook → **shake**

shoot[1] [ˈʃuːt] *v* **shot** [ˈʃɑt]; **shooting** *vt* **1** : disparar, tirar ⟨to shoot a bullet : tirar una bala⟩ **2** : pegarle un tiro a, darle un balazo a ⟨he shot her : le pegó un tiro⟩ ⟨they shot and killed him : lo mataron a balazos⟩ **3** THROW : lanzar (una pelota, etc.), echar (una mirada) **4** PHOTOGRAPH : fotografiar **5** FILM : filmar — *vi* **1** : disparar (con un arma de fuego) **2** DART : ir rápidamente ⟨it shot past : pasó como una bala⟩

shoot[2] *n* : brote *m*, retoño *m*, vástago *m*

shooting star *n* : estrella *f* fugaz

shop[1] [ˈʃɑp] *vi* **shopped; shopping** : hacer compras ⟨to go shopping : ir de compras⟩

shop[2] *n* **1** WORKSHOP : taller *m* **2** STORE : tienda *f*

shopkeeper [ˈʃɑpˌkiːpər] *n* : tendero *m*, -ra *f*

shoplift [ˈʃɑpˌlɪft] *vi* : hurtar mercancía (de una tienda) — *vt* : hurtar (de una tienda)

shoplifter [ˈʃɑpˌlɪftər] *n* : ladrón *m*, -drona *f* (que roba en una tienda)

shopper [ˈʃɑpər] *n* : comprador *m*, -dora *f*

shore[1] [ˈʃor] *vt* **shored; shoring** : apuntalar ⟨they shored up the wall : apuntalaron la pared⟩

shore[2] *n* **1** : orilla *f* (del mar, etc.) **2** PROP : puntal *m*

shoreline [ˈʃorˌlaɪn] *n* : orilla *f*

shorn → **shear**

short[1] [ˈʃɔrt] *adv* **1** ABRUPTLY : repentinamente, súbitamente ⟨the car stopped short : el carro se paró en seco⟩ **2 to fall short** : no alcanzar, quedarse corto

short[2] *adj* **1** : corto (de medida), bajo (de estatura) **2** BRIEF : corto ⟨short and sweet : corto y bueno⟩ ⟨a short time ago : hace poco⟩ **3** CURT : brusco, cortante, seco **4** : corto (de tiempo, de dinero) ⟨I'm one dollar short : me falta un dólar⟩

short[3] *n* **1 shorts** *npl* : shorts *mpl*, pantalones *mpl* cortos **2** → **short circuit**

shortage [ˈʃɔrtɪʤ] *n* : falta *f*, escasez *f*, carencia *f*

shortcake [ˈʃɔrtˌkeɪk] *n* : tarta *f* de fruta

shortchange [ˈʃɔrtˈʧeɪnʤ] *vt* **-changed; -changing** : darle mal el cambio (a alguien)

short circuit *n* : cortocircuito *m*, corto *m* (eléctrico)

shortcoming [ˈʃɔrtˌkʌmɪŋ] *n* : defecto *m*

shortcut [ˈʃɔrtˌkʌt] *n* **1** : atajo *m* ⟨to take a shortcut : cortar camino⟩ **2** : alternativa *f* fácil, método *m* rápido

shorten [ˈʃɔrtən] *vt* : acortar — *vi* : acortarse

shorthand [ˈʃɔrtˌhænd] *n* : taquigrafía *f*

short–lived [ˈʃɔrtˈlɪvd, -ˈlaɪvd] *adj* : efímero

shortly [ˈʃɔrtli] *adv* **1** BRIEFLY : brevemente ⟨to put it shortly : para decirlo en pocas palabras⟩ **2** SOON : dentro de poco

shortness [ˈʃɔrtnəs] *n* **1** : lo corto ⟨shortness of stature : estatura baja⟩ **2** BREVITY : brevedad *f* **3** CURTNESS : brusquedad *f* **4** SHORTAGE : falta *f*, escasez *f*, carencia *f*

shortsighted [ˈʃɔrtˌsaɪt̬əd] → **nearsighted**
shot [ˈʃɑt] *n* **1** : disparo *m*, tiro *m* ⟨to fire a shot : disparar⟩ **2** PELLETS : perdigones *mpl* **3** : tiro *m* (en deportes) **4** ATTEMPT : intento *m*, tentativa *f* ⟨to have a shot at : hacer un intento por⟩ **5** RANGE : alcance *m* ⟨a long shot : una posibilidad remota⟩ **6** PHOTOGRAPH : foto *f* **7** INJECTION : inyección *f* **8** : trago *m* (de licor)
shotgun [ˈʃɑtˌgʌn] *n* : escopeta *f*
should → **shall**
shoulder[1] [ˈʃoːldər] *vt* **1** JOSTLE : empujar (con el hombro) **2** : ponerse al hombro (una mochila, etc.) **3** : cargar con (la responsabilidad, etc.)
shoulder[2] *n* **1** : hombro *m* ⟨to shrug one's shoulders : encogerse los hombros⟩ **2** : arcén *m* (de una carretera)
shoulder blade *n* : omóplato *m*, omoplato *m*, escápula *f*
shouldn't [ˈʃʊdənt] (*contraction of* **should not**) → **shall**
shout[1] [ˈʃaʊt] *v* : gritar, vocear
shout[2] *n* : grito *m*
shove[1] [ˈʃʌv] *v* **shoved; shoving** : empujar bruscamente
shove[2] *n* : empujón *m*, empellón *m*
shovel[1] [ˈʃʌvəl] *vt* **-veled** *or* **-velled; -veling** *or* **-velling 1** : mover con (una) pala ⟨they shoveled the dirt out : sacaron la tierra con palas⟩ **2** DIG : cavar (con una pala)
shovel[2] *n* : pala *f*
show[1] [ˈʃoː] *v* **showed; shown** [ˈʃoːn] *or* **showed; showing** *vt* **1** DISPLAY : mostrar, enseñar **2** REVEAL : demostrar, manifestar, revelar ⟨he showed himself to be a coward : se reveló como cobarde⟩ **3** TEACH : enseñar **4** PROVE : demostrar, probar **5** CONDUCT, DIRECT : llevar, acompañar ⟨to show someone the way : indicarle el camino a alguien⟩ **6** : proyectar (una película), dar (un programa de televisión) — *vi* **1** : notarse, verse ⟨the stain doesn't show : la mancha no se ve⟩ **2** APPEAR : aparecer, dejarse ver
show[2] *n* **1** : demostración *f* ⟨a show of force : una demostración de fuerza⟩ **2** EXHIBITION : exposición *f*, exhibición *f* ⟨flower show : exposición de flores⟩ ⟨to be on show : estar expuesto⟩ **3** : espectáculo *m* (teatral), programa *m* (de televisión, etc.) ⟨to go to a show : ir al teatro⟩
showcase [ˈʃoːˌkeɪs] *n* : vitrina *f*
showdown [ˈʃoːˌdaʊn] *n* : confrontación *f* (decisiva)
shower[1] [ˈʃaʊər] *vt* **1** SPRAY : regar, mojar **2** HEAP : colmar ⟨they showered him with gifts : lo colmaron de regalos, le llovieron los regalos⟩ — *vi* **1** BATHE : ducharse, darse una ducha **2** RAIN : llover
shower[2] *n* **1** : chaparrón *m*, chubasco *m* ⟨a chance of showers : una posibilidad de chaparrones⟩ **2** : ducha *f* ⟨to take a shower : ducharse⟩ **3** PARTY : fiesta *f* ⟨a bridal shower : una despedida de soltera⟩
show off *vt* : hacer alarde de, ostentar — *vi* : lucirse
show up *vi* APPEAR : aparecer — *vt* EXPOSE : revelar
showy [ˈʃoːi] *adj* **showier; -est** : llamativo, ostentoso — **showily** *adv*
shrank → **shrink**
shrapnel [ˈʃræpnəl] *ns & pl* : metralla *f*
shred[1] [ˈʃrɛd] *vt* **shredded; shredding** : hacer trizas, desmenuzar (con las manos), triturar (con una máquina) ⟨to shred vegetables : cortar verduras en tiras⟩
shred[2] *n* **1** STRIP : tira *f*, jirón *m* (de tela) **2** BIT : pizca *f* ⟨not a shred of evidence : ni la mínima prueba⟩
shrew [ˈʃruː] *n* **1** : musaraña *f* (animal) **2** : mujer *f* regañona, arpía *f*
shrewd [ˈʃruːd] *adj* : astuto, inteligente, sagaz — **shrewdly** *adv*
shrewdness [ˈʃruːdnəs] *n* : astucia *f*
shriek[1] [ˈʃriːk] *vi* : chillar, gritar
shriek[2] *n* : chillido *m*, alarido *m*, grito *m*
shrill [ˈʃrɪl] *adj* : agudo, estridente
shrilly [ˈʃrɪli] *adv* : agudamente
shrimp [ˈʃrɪmp] *n* : camarón *m*, langostino *m*
shrine [ˈʃraɪn] *n* **1** TOMB : sepulcro *m* (de un santo) **2** SANCTUARY : lugar *m* sagrado, santuario *m*
shrink [ˈʃrɪŋk] *vi* **shrank** [ˈʃræŋk] *or* **shrunk** [ˈʃrʌŋk]; **shrunk** *or* **shrunken** [ˈʃrʌŋkən]; **shrinking 1** RECOIL : retroceder ⟨he shrank back : se echó para atrás⟩ **2** : encogerse (dícese de la ropa)
shrinkage [ˈʃrɪŋkɪʤ] *n* : encogimiento *m* (de ropa, etc.), contracción *f*, reducción *f*
shrivel [ˈʃrɪvəl] *vi* **-veled** *or* **-velled; -veling** *or* **-velling** : arrugarse, marchitarse
shroud[1] [ˈʃraʊd] *vt* : envolver
shroud[2] *n* **1** : sudario *m*, mortaja *f* **2** VEIL : velo *m* ⟨wrapped in a shroud of mystery : envuelto en un aura de misterio⟩
shrub [ˈʃrʌb] *n* : arbusto *m*, mata *f*
shrubbery [ˈʃrʌbəri] *n, pl* **-beries** : arbustos *mpl*, matas *fpl*
shrug [ˈʃrʌg] *vi* **shrugged; shrugging** : encogerse de hombros
shrunk → **shrink**
shuck[1] [ˈʃʌk] *vt* : pelar (mazorcas, etc.), abrir (almejas, etc.)
shuck[2] *n* **1** HUSK : cascarilla *f*, cáscara *f* (de una nuez, etc.), hojas *fpl* (de una mazorca) **2** SHELL : concha *f* (de una almeja, etc.)
shudder[1] [ˈʃʌdər] *vi* : estremecerse
shudder[2] *n* : estremecimiento *m*, escalofrío *m*
shuffle[1] [ˈʃʌfəl] *v* **-fled; -fling** *vt* MIX : mezclar, revolver, barajar (naipes) — *vi* : caminar arrastrando los pies

shuffle² *n* **1** : acto *m* de revolver ⟨each player gets a shuffle : a cada jugador le toca barajar⟩ **2** JUMBLE : revoltijo *m* **3** : arrastramiento *m* de los pies

shun [ˈʃʌn] *vi* **shunned; shunning** : evitar, esquivar, eludir

shunt [ˈʃʌnt] *vt* : desviar, cambiar de vía (un tren)

shut [ˈʃʌt] *v* **shut; shutting** *vt* **1** CLOSE : cerrar ⟨shut the lid : tápalo⟩ **2 to shut out** EXCLUDE : excluir, dejar fuera a (personas), no dejar que entre (luz, ruido, etc.) **3 to shut up** CONFINE : encerrar — *vi* : cerrarse ⟨the factory shut down : la fábrica cerró suspuertas⟩

shut–in [ˈʃʌtˌɪn] *n* : inválido *m*, -da *f* (que no puede salir de casa)

shutter [ˈʃʌt̬ər] *n* **1** : contraventana *f*, postigo *m* (de una ventana o puerta) **2** : obturador *m* (de una cámara)

shuttle¹ [ˈʃʌt̬əl] *v* **-tled; -tling** *vt* : transportar ⟨she shuttled him back and forth : lo llevaba de acá para allá⟩ — *vi* : ir y venir

shuttle² *n* **1** : lanzadera *f* (para tejer) **2** : vehículo *m* que hace recorridos cortos **3** → **space shuttle**

shuttlecock [ˈʃʌt̬əlˌkɑk] *n* : volante *m*

shut up *vi* : callarse ⟨shut up! : ¡cállate (la boca)!⟩

shy¹ [ˈʃaɪ] *vi* **shied; shying** : retroceder, asustarse

shy² *adj* **shier** *or* **shyer** [ˈʃaɪər]; **shiest** *or* **shyest** [ˈʃaɪəst] **1** TIMID : tímido **2** WARY : cauteloso ⟨he's not shy about asking : no vacila en preguntar⟩ **3** SHORT : corto (de dinero, etc.) ⟨I'm two dollars shy : me faltan dos dólares⟩

shyly [ˈʃaɪli] *adv* : tímidamente

shyness [ˈʃaɪnəs] *n* : timidez *f*

Siamese¹ [ˌsaɪəˈmiːz, -ˈmiːs-] *adj* : siamés ⟨Siamese twins : hermanos siameses⟩

Siamese² *n* **1** : siamés *m*, -mesa *f* **2** : siamés *m* (idioma) **3** *or* **Siamese cat** : gato *m* siamés

sibling [ˈsɪblɪŋ] *n* : hermano *m*, hermana *f*

Sicilian [səˈsɪljən] *n* : siciliano *m*, -na *f* — **Sicilian** *adj*

sick [ˈsɪk] *adj* **1** : enfermo **2** NAUSEOUS : mareado, con náuseas ⟨to get sick : vomitar⟩ **3** : para uso de enfermos ⟨sick day : día de permiso (por enfermedad)⟩

sickbed [ˈsɪkˌbɛd] *n* : lecho *m* de enfermo

sicken [ˈsɪkən] *vt* **1** : poner enfermo **2** REVOLT : darle asco (a alguien) — *vi* : enfermar(se), caer enfermo

sickening [ˈsɪkənɪŋ] *adj* : asqueroso, repugnante, nauseabundo

sickle [ˈsɪkəl] *n* : hoz *f*

sickly [ˈsɪkli] *adj* **sicklier; -est** **1** : enfermizo **2** → **sickening**

sickness [ˈsɪknəs] *n* **1** : enfermedad *f* **2** NAUSEA : náuseas *fpl*

side [ˈsaɪd] *n* **1** : lado *m*, costado *m* (de una persona), ijada *f* (de un animal) **2** : lado *m*, cara *f* (de una moneda, etc.) **3** : lado *m*, parte *f* ⟨he's on my side : está de mi parte⟩ ⟨to take sides : tomar partido⟩

sideboard [ˈsaɪdˌbord] *n* : aparador *m*

sideburns [ˈsaɪdˌbərnz] *npl* : patillas *fpl*

sided [ˈsaɪdəd] *adj* : que tiene lados ⟨one-sided : de un lado⟩

side effect *n* : efecto *m* secundario

sideline [ˈsaɪdˌlaɪn] *n* **1** : línea *f* de banda (en deportes) **2** : actividad *f* suplementaria (en negocios) **3 to be on the sidelines** : estar al margen

sidelong [ˈsaɪdˌlɔŋ] *adj* : de reojo, de soslayo

sideshow [ˈsaɪdˌʃoː] *n* : espectáculo *m* secundario, atracción *f* secundaria

sidestep [ˈsaɪdˌstɛp] *v* **-stepped; -stepping** *vi* : dar un paso hacia un lado — *vt* AVOID : esquivar, eludir

sidetrack [ˈsaɪdˌtræk] *vt* : desviar (una conversación, etc.), distraer (a una persona)

sidewalk [ˈsaɪdˌwɔk] *n* : acera *f*, vereda *f*, andén *m CA*, *Col*, banqueta *f Mex*

sideways¹ [ˈsaɪdˌweɪz] *adv* **1** : hacia un lado ⟨it leaned sideways : se inclinaba hacia un lado⟩ **2** : de lado, de costado ⟨lie sideways : acuéstese de costado⟩

sideways² *adj* : hacia un lado ⟨a sideways glance : una mirada de reojo⟩

siding [ˈsaɪdɪŋ] *n* **1** : apartadero *m* (para trenes) **2** : revestimiento *m* exterior (de un edificio)

sidle [ˈsaɪdəl] *vi* **-dled; -dling** : moverse furtivamente

siege [ˈsiːʤ, ˈsiːʒ] *n* : sitio *m* ⟨to be under siege : estar sitiado⟩

siesta [siːˈɛstə] *n* : siesta *f*

sieve [ˈsɪv] *n* : tamiz *m*, cedazo *m*, criba *f* (en mineralogía)

sift [ˈsɪft] *vt* **1** : tamizar, cerner ⟨sift the flour : tamice la harina⟩ **2** *or* **to sift through** : examinar cuidadosamente, pasar por el tamiz

sifter [ˈsɪftər] *n* : tamiz *m*, cedazo *m*

sigh¹ [ˈsaɪ] *vi* : suspirar

sigh² *n* : suspiro *m*

sight¹ [ˈsaɪt] *vt* : ver (a una persona), divisar (la tierra, un barco)

sight² *n* **1** : vista *f* (facultad) ⟨out of sight : fuera de vista⟩ **2** : algo visto ⟨it's a familiar sight : se ve con frecuencia⟩ ⟨she's a sight for sore eyes : da gusto verla⟩ **3** : lugar *m* de interés (para turistas, etc.) **4** : mira *f* (de un rifle, etc.) **5** GLIMPSE : mirada *f* breve ⟨I caught sight of her : la divisé, alcancé a verla⟩

sighting [ˈsaɪt̬ɪŋ] *n* : avistamiento *m*

sightless [ˈsaɪtləs] *adj* : invidente, ciego

sightseer [ˈsaɪtˌsiːər] *n* : turista *mf*

sign¹ [ˈsaɪn] *vt* **1** : firmar ⟨to sign a check : firmar un cheque⟩ **2** *or* **to sign on** HIRE : contratar (a un empleado), fichar (a un jugador) — *vi* **1** : hacer una seña ⟨she signed for him to stop : le hizo una seña para que se parara⟩ **2** : comunicarse por señas

sign[2] *n* **1** SYMBOL : símbolo *m*, signo *m* ⟨minus sign : signo de menos⟩ **2** GESTURE : seña *f*, señal *f*, gesto *m* **3** : letrero *m*, cartel *m* ⟨neon sign : letrero de neón⟩ **4** TRACE : señal *f*, indicio *m*

signal[1] [ˈsɪgnəl] *vt* **-naled** *or* **-nalled; -naling** *or* **-nalling** **1** : hacerle señas (a alguien) ⟨she signaled me to leave : me hizo señas para que saliera⟩ **2** INDICATE : señalar, indicar — *vi* : hacer señas, comunicar por señas

signal[2] *adj* NOTABLE : señalado, notable

signal[3] *n* : señal *f*

signature [ˈsɪgnəˌʧʊr] *n* : firma *f*

signet [ˈsɪgnət] *n* : sello *m*

significance [sɪgˈnɪfɪkən*t*s] *n* **1** MEANING : significado *m* **2** IMPORTANCE : importancia *f*

significant [sɪgˈnɪfɪkənt] *adj* **1** IMPORTANT : importante **2** MEANINGFUL : significativo — **significantly** *adv*

signify [ˈsɪgnəˌfaɪ] *vt* **-fied; -fying** **1** : indicar ⟨he signified his desire for more : haciendo señas indicó que quería más⟩ **2** MEAN : significar

sign language *n* : lenguaje *m* por señas

signpost [ˈsaɪnˌpoːst] *n* : poste *m* indicador

silence[1] [ˈsaɪlən*t*s] *vt* **-lenced; -lencing** : silenciar, acallar

silence[2] *n* : silencio *m*

silent [ˈsaɪlənt] *adj* **1** : callado ⟨to remain silent : quedarse callado, guardar silencio⟩ **2** QUIET, STILL : silencioso **3** MUTE : mudo ⟨a silent letter : una letra muda⟩

silently [ˈsaɪləntli] *adv* : silenciosamente, calladamente

silhouette[1] [ˌsɪləˈwɛt] *vt* **-etted; -etting** : destacar la silueta de ⟨it was silhouetted against the sky : se perfilaba contra el cielo⟩

silhouette[2] *n* : silueta *f*

silica [ˈsɪlɪkə] *n* : sílice *f*

silicon [ˈsɪlɪkən, -ˌkɑn] *n* : silicio *m*

silk [ˈsɪlk] *n* : seda *f*

silken [ˈsɪlkən] *adj* **1** : de seda ⟨a silken veil : un velo de seda⟩ **2** SILKY : sedoso ⟨silken hair : cabellos sedosos⟩

silkworm [ˈsɪlkˌwərm] *n* : gusano *m* de seda

silky [ˈsɪlki] *adj* **silkier; -est** : sedoso

sill [ˈsɪl] *n* : alféizar *m* (de una ventana), umbral *m* (de una puerta)

silliness [ˈsɪlinəs] *n* : tontería *f*, estupidez *f*

silly [ˈsɪli] *adj* **sillier; -est** : tonto, estúpido, ridículo

silo [ˈsaɪˌloː] *n, pl* **silos** : silo *m*

silt [ˈsɪlt] *n* : cieno *m*

silver[1] [ˈsɪlvər] *adj* **1** : de plata ⟨a silver spoon : una cuchara de plata⟩ **2** → **silvery**

silver[2] *n* **1** : plata *f* **2** COINS : monedas *fpl* **3** → **silverware** **4** : color *m* plata

silverware [ˈsɪlvərˌwær] *n* **1** : artículos *mpl* de plata, platería *f* **2** FLATWARE : cubertería *f*

silvery [ˈsɪlvəri] *adj* : plateado

similar [ˈsɪmələr] *adj* : similar, parecido, semejante

similarity [ˌsɪməˈlærət̬i] *n, pl* **-ties** : semejanza *f*, parecido *m*

similarly [ˈsɪmələrli] *adv* : de manera similar

simile [ˈsɪməˌliː] *n* : símil *m*

simmer [ˈsɪmər] *v* : hervir a fuego lento

simper[1] [ˈsɪmpər] *vi* : sonreír como un tonto

simper[2] *n* : sonrisa *f* tonta

simple [ˈsɪmpəl] *adj* **simpler; -plest** **1** INNOCENT : inocente **2** PLAIN : sencillo, simple **3** EASY : simple, sencillo, fácil **4** STRAIGHTFORWARD : puro, simple ⟨the simple truth : la pura verdad⟩ **5** NAIVE : ingenuo, simple

simpleton [ˈsɪmpəltən] *n* : bobo *m*, -ba *f*; tonto *m*, -ta *f*

simplicity [sɪmˈplɪsət̬i] *n* : simplicidad *f*, sencillez *f*

simplification [ˌsɪmpləfəˈkeɪʃən] *n* : simplificación *f*

simplify [ˈsɪmpləˌfaɪ] *vt* **-fied; -fying** : simplificar

simply [ˈsɪmpli] *adv* **1** PLAINLY : sencillamente **2** SOLELY : simplemente, sólo **3** REALLY : absolutamente

simulate [ˈsɪmjəˌleɪt] *vt* **-lated; -lating** : simular

simulation [ˌsɪmjəˈleɪʃən] *n* : simulación *f*

simultaneous [ˌsaɪməlˈteɪniəs] *adj* : simultáneo — **simultaneously** *adv*

sin[1] [ˈsɪn] *vi* **sinned; sinning** : pecar

sin[2] *n* : pecado *m*

since[1] [ˈsɪn*t*s] *adv* **1** : desde entonces ⟨they've been friends ever since : desde entonces han sido amigos⟩ ⟨she's since become mayor : más tarde se hizo alcalde⟩ **2** AGO : hace ⟨he's long since dead : murió hace mucho⟩

since[2] *conj* **1** : desde que ⟨since he was born : desde que nació⟩ **2** INASMUCH AS : ya que, puesto que, dado que

since[3] *prep* : desde

sincere [sɪnˈsɪr] *adj* **-cerer; -est** : sincero — **sincerely** *adv*

sincerity [sɪnˈsɛrət̬i] *n* : sinceridad *f*

sinew [ˈsɪnˌjuː, ˈsɪˌnuː] *n* **1** TENDON : tendón *m*, nervio *m* (en la carne) **2** POWER : fuerza *f*

sinewy [ˈsɪnjʊi, ˈsɪnʊi] *adj* **1** STRINGY : fibroso **2** STRONG, WIRY : fuerte, nervudo

sinful [ˈsɪnfəl] *adj* : pecador (dícese de las personas), pecaminoso

sing [ˈsɪŋ] *v* **sang** [ˈsæŋ] *or* **sung** [ˈsʌŋ]; **sung; singing** : cantar

singe [ˈsɪnʤ] *vt* **singed; singeing** : chamuscar, quemar

singer [ˈsɪŋər] *n* : cantante *mf*

single[1] [ˈsɪŋgəl] *vt* **-gled; -gling** *or* **to single out** **1** SELECT : escoger **2** DISTINGUISH : señalar

single[2] *adj* **1** UNMARRIED : soltero **2** SOLE : solo ⟨a single survivor : un solo

sobreviviente⟩ ⟨every single one : cada uno, todos⟩
single[3] *n* **1** : soltero *m*, -ra *f* ⟨for married couples and singles : para los matrimonios y los solteros⟩ **2** *or* **single room** : habitación *f* individual **3** DOLLAR : billete *m* de un dólar
single–handed [ˈsɪŋgəlˈhændəd] *adj* : sin ayuda, solo
singly [ˈsɪŋgli] *adv* : individualmente, uno por uno
singular[1] [ˈsɪŋgjələr] *adj* **1** : singular (en gramática) **2** OUTSTANDING : singular, sobresaliente **3** STRANGE : singular, extraño
singular[2] *n* : singular *m*
singularity [ˌsɪŋgjəˈlærət̬i] *n, pl* **-ties** : singularidad *f*
singularly [ˈsɪŋgjələrli] *adv* : singularmente
sinister [ˈsɪnəstər] *adj* : siniestro
sink[1] [ˈsɪŋk] *v* **sank** [ˈsæŋk] *or* **sunk** [ˈsʌŋk]; **sunk; sinking** *vi* **1** : hundirse (dícese de un barco) **2** DROP, FALL : descender, caer ⟨to sink into a chair : dejarse caer en una silla⟩ ⟨her heart sank : se le cayó el alma a los pies⟩ **3** DECREASE : bajar — *vt* **1** : hundir (un barco, etc.) **2** EXCAVATE : excavar (un pozo para minar), perforar (un pozo de agua) **3** PLUNGE, STICK : clavar, hincar **4** INVEST : invertir (fondos)
sink[2] *n* **1 kitchen sink** : fregadero *m*, lavaplatos *m Chile, Col, Mex* **2 bathroom sink** : lavabo *m*, lavamanos *m*
sinner [ˈsɪnər] *n* : pecador *m*, -dora *f*
sinuous [ˈsɪnjʊəs] *adj* : sinuoso — **sinuously** *adv*
sinus [ˈsaɪnəs] *n* : seno *m*
sip[1] [ˈsɪp] *v* **sipped; sipping** *vt* : sorber — *vi* : beber a sorbos
sip[2] *n* : sorbo *m*
siphon[1] [ˈsaɪfən] *vt* : sacar con sifón
siphon[2] *n* : sifón *m*
sir [ˈsər] *n* **1** (*in titles*) : sir *m* **2** (*as a form of address*) : señor *m* ⟨Dear Sir : Muy señor mío⟩ ⟨yes sir! : ¡sí, señor!⟩
sire[1] [ˈsaɪr] *vt* **sired; siring** : engendrar, ser el padre de
sire[2] *n* : padre *m*
siren [ˈsaɪrən] *n* : sirena *f*
sirloin [ˈsərˌlɔɪn] *n* : solomillo *m*
sirup → **syrup**
sisal [ˈsaɪsəl, -zəl] *n* : sisal *m*
sissy [ˈsɪsi] *n, pl* **-sies** : mariquita *f fam*
sister [ˈsɪstər] *n* **1** : hermana *f* **2 Sister** : hermana *f*, Sor *f* ⟨Sister Mary : Sor María⟩
sisterhood [ˈsɪstərˌhʊd] *n* **1** : condición *f* de ser hermana **2** : sociedad *f* de mujeres
sister–in–law [ˈsɪstərɪnˌlɔ] *n, pl* **sisters–in–law** : cuñada *f*
sisterly [ˈsɪstərli] *adj* : de hermana
sit [ˈsɪt] *v* **sat** [ˈsæt]; **sitting** *vi* **1** : sentarse, estar sentado ⟨he sat down : se sentó⟩ **2** ROOST : posarse **3** : sesionar ⟨the legislature is sitting : la legislatura está en sesión⟩ **4** POSE : posar (para un retrato) **5** LIE, REST : estar (ubicado) ⟨the house sits on a hill : la casa está en una colina⟩ — *vt* SEAT : sentar, colocar ⟨I sat him on the sofa : lo senté en el sofá⟩
sitcom [ˈsɪtˌkɑm] → **situation comedy**
site [ˈsaɪt] *n* **1** PLACE : sitio *m*, lugar *m* **2** LOCATION : emplazamiento *m*, ubicación *f*
sitter [ˈsɪt̬ər] → **baby–sitter**
sitting room → **living room**
situated [ˈsɪʧʊˌeɪt̬əd] *adj* LOCATED : ubicado, situado
situation [ˌsɪʧʊˈeɪʃən] *n* **1** LOCATION : situación *f*, ubicación *f*, emplazamiento *m* **2** CIRCUMSTANCES : situación *f* **3** JOB : empleo *m*
situation comedy *n* : comedia *f* de situación
six[1] [ˈsɪks] *adj* : seis
six[2] *n* : seis *m*
six–gun [ˈsɪksˌgʌn] *n* : revólver *m* (con seis cámaras)
six hundred[1] *adj* : seiscientos
six hundred[2] *n* : seiscientos *m*
six–shooter [ˈsɪksˌʃuːt̬ər] → **six–gun**
sixteen[1] [sɪksˈtiːn] *adj* : dieciséis
sixteen[2] *n* : dieciséis *m*
sixteenth[1] [sɪksˈtiːnθ] *adj* : decimosexto
sixteenth[2] *n* **1** : decimosexto *m*, -ta *f* (en una serie) **2** : dieciseisavo *m*, dieciseisava parte *f*
sixth[1] [ˈsɪksθ, ˈsɪkst] *adj* : sexto
sixth[2] *n* **1** : sexto *m*, -ta *f* (en una serie) **2** : sexto *m*, sexta parte *f*
sixtieth[1] [ˈsɪkst̬iəθ] *adj* : sexagésimo
sixtieth[2] *n* **1** : sexagésimo *m*, -ma *f* (en una serie) **2** : sesentavo *m*, sesentava parte *f*
sixty[1] [ˈsɪkst̬i] *adj* : sesenta
sixty[2] *n, pl* **-ties** : sesenta *m*
sizable *or* **sizeable** [ˈsaɪzəbəl] *adj* : considerable
size[1] [ˈsaɪz] *vt* **sized; sizing** **1** : clasificar según el tamaño **2 to size up** : evaluar, apreciar
size[2] *n* **1** DIMENSIONS : tamaño *m*, talla *f* (de ropa), número *m* (de zapatos) **2** MAGNITUDE : magnitud *f*
sizzle [ˈsɪzəl] *vi* **-zled; -zling** : chisporrotear
skate[1] [ˈskeɪt] *vi* **skated; skating** : patinar
skate[2] *n* **1** : patín *m* ⟨roller skate : patín de ruedas⟩ **2** : raya *f* (pez)
skateboard [ˈskeɪtˌbord] *n* : monopatín *m*
skater [ˈskeɪt̬ər] *n* : patinador *m*, -dora *f*
skein [ˈskeɪn] *n* : madeja *f*
skeletal [ˈskələt̬əl] *adj* **1** : óseo (en anatomía) **2** EMACIATED : esquelético
skeleton [ˈskɛlətən] *n* **1** : esqueleto *m* (anatómico) **2** FRAMEWORK : armazón *mf*
skeptic [ˈskɛptɪk] *n* : escéptico *m*, -ca *f*
skeptical [ˈskɛptɪkəl] *adj* : escéptico
skepticism [ˈskɛptəˌsɪzəm] *n* : escepticismo *m*

sketch[1] [ˈskɛtʃ] *vt* : bosquejar — *vi* : hacer bosquejos
sketch[2] *n* **1** DRAWING, OUTLINE : esbozo *m*, bosquejo *m* **2** ESSAY : ensayo *m*
sketchy [ˈskɛtʃi] *adj* **sketchier; -est** : incompleto, poco detallado
skewer[1] [ˈskju:ər] *vt* : ensartar (carne, etc.)
skewer[2] *n* : brocheta *f*, broqueta *f*
ski[1] [ˈski:] *vi* **skied; skiing** : esquiar
ski[2] *n, pl* **skis** : esquí *m*
skid[1] [ˈskɪd] *vi* **skidded; skidding** : derrapar, patinar
skid[2] *n* : derrape *m*, patinazo *m*
skier [ˈski:ər] *n* : esquiador *m*, -dora *f*
skiff [ˈskɪf] *n* : esquife *m*
skill [ˈskɪl] *n* **1** DEXTERITY : habilidad *f*, destreza *f* **2** CAPABILITY : capacidad *f*, arte *m*, técnica *f* ⟨organizational skills : la capacidad para organizar⟩
skilled [ˈskɪld] *adj* : hábil, experto
skillet [ˈskɪlət] *n* : sartén *mf*
skillful [ˈskɪlfəl] *adj* : hábil, diestro
skillfully [ˈskɪlfəli] *adv* : con habilidad, con destreza
skim[1] [ˈskɪm] *vt* **skimmed; skimming 1** *or* **to skim off** : espumar, descremar (leche) **2** : echarle un vistazo a (un libro, etc.), pasar rozando (una superficie)
skim[2] *adj* : descremado ⟨skim milk : leche descremada⟩
skimp [ˈskɪmp] *vi* **to skimp on** : escatimar
skimpy [ˈskɪmpi] *adj* **skimpier; -est** : exiguo, escaso, raquítico
skin[1] [ˈskɪn] *vt* **skinned; skinning** : despellejar, desollar
skin[2] *n* **1** : piel *f*, cutis *m* (de la cara) ⟨dark skin : piel morena⟩ **2** RIND : piel *f*
skin diving *n* : buceo *m*, submarinismo *m*
skinflint [ˈskɪn,flɪnt] *n* : tacaño *m*, -ña *f*
skinned [ˈskɪnd] *adj* : de piel ⟨tough-skinned : de piel dura⟩
skinny [ˈskɪni] *adj* **skinnier; -est** : flaco
skip[1] [ˈskɪp] *v* **skipped; skipping** *vi* : ir dando brincos — *vt* : saltarse
skip[2] *n* : brinco *m*, salto *m*
skipper [ˈskɪpər] *n* : capitán *m*, -tana *f*
skirmish[1] [ˈskərmɪʃ] *vi* : escaramuzar
skirmish[2] *n* : escaramuza *f*, refriega *f*
skirt[1] [ˈskərt] *vt* **1** BORDER : bordear **2** EVADE : evadir, esquivar
skirt[2] *n* : falda *f*, pollera *f*
skit [ˈskɪt] *n* : sketch *m* (teatral)
skittish [ˈskɪt̬ɪʃ] *adj* : asustadizo, nervioso
skulk [ˈskʌlk] *vi* : merodear
skull [ˈskʌl] *n* **1** : cráneo *m*, calavera *f* **2 skull and crossbones** : calavera *f* (bandera pirata)
skunk [ˈskʌŋk] *n* : zorrillo *m*, mofeta *f*
sky [ˈskaɪ] *n, pl* **skies** : cielo *m*
skylark [ˈskaɪ,lɑrk] *n* : alondra *f*
skylight [ˈskaɪ,laɪt] *n* : claraboya *f*, tragaluz *m*
skyline [ˈskaɪ,laɪn] *n* : horizonte *m*
skyrocket [ˈskaɪ,rɑkət] *vi* : dispararse
skyscraper [ˈskaɪ,skreɪpər] *n* : rascacielos *m*
slab [ˈslæb] *n* : losa *f* (de piedra), tabla *f* (de madera), pedazo *m* grueso (de pan, etc.)
slack[1] [ˈslæk] *adj* **1** CARELESS : descuidado, negligente **2** LOOSE : flojo **3** SLOW : de poco movimiento
slack[2] *n* **1** : parte *f* floja ⟨to take up the slack : tensar (una cuerda, etc.)⟩ **2 slacks** *npl* : pantalones *mpl*
slacken [ˈslækən] *vt* : aflojar — *vi* : aflojarse
slacker [ˈslækər] *n* : vago *m*, -ga *f*; holgazán *m*, -zana *f*
slag [ˈslæg] *n* : escoria *f*
slain → **slay**
slake [ˈsleɪk] *vt* **slaked; slaking** : saciar (la sed), satisfacer (la curiosidad)
slam[1] [ˈslæm] *v* **slammed; slamming** *vt* **1** : cerrar de golpe ⟨he slammed the door : dio un portazo⟩ **2** : tirar o dejar caer de golpe ⟨he slammed down the book : dejó caer el libro de un golpe⟩ — *vi* **1** : cerrarse de golpe **2 to slam into** : chocar contra
slam[2] *n* : golpe *m*, portazo *m* (de una puerta)
slander[1] [ˈslændər] *vt* : calumniar, difamar
slander[2] *n* : calumnia *f*, difamación *f*
slanderous [ˈslændərəs] *adj* : difamatorio, calumnioso
slang [ˈslæŋ] *n* : argot *m*, jerga *f*
slant[1] [ˈslænt] *vi* : inclinarse, ladearse — *vt* **1** SLOPE : inclinar **2** ANGLE : sesgar, orientar, dirigir ⟨a story slanted towards youth : un artículo dirigido a los jóvenes⟩
slant[2] *n* **1** INCLINE : inclinación *f* **2** PERSPECTIVE : perspectiva *f*, enfoque *m*
slap[1] [ˈslæp] *vt* **slapped; slapping** : bofetear, cachetear, dar una palmada (en la espalda, etc.)
slap[2] *n* : bofetada *f*, cachetada *f*, palmada *f*
slash[1] [ˈslæʃ] *vt* **1** GASH : cortar, hacer un tajo en **2** REDUCE : reducir, rebajar (precios)
slash[2] *n* : tajo *m*, corte *m*
slat [ˈslæt] *n* : tablilla *f*, listón *m*
slate [ˈsleɪt] *n* **1** : pizarra *f* ⟨a slate roof : un techo de pizarra⟩ **2** : lista *f* de candidatos (políticos)
slaughter[1] [ˈslɔt̬ər] *vt* **1** BUTCHER : matar (animales) **2** MASSACRE : masacrar (personas)
slaughter[2] *n* **1** : matanza *f* (de animales) **2** MASSACRE : masacre *f*, carnicería *f*
slaughterhouse [ˈslɔt̬ər,haʊs] *n* : matadero *m*
Slav [ˈslɑv, ˈslæv] *n* : eslavo *m*, -va *f*
slave[1] [ˈsleɪv] *vi* **slaved; slaving** : trabajar como un burro
slave[2] *n* : esclavo *m*, -va *f*
slaver [ˈslævər, ˈsleɪ-] *vi* : babear

slavery [ˈsleɪvəri] *n* : esclavitud *f*

Slavic [ˈslɑvɪk, ˈslæ-] *adj* : eslavo

slavish [ˈsleɪvɪʃ] *adj* **1** SERVILE : servil **2** IMITATIVE : poco original

slay [ˈsleɪ] *vt* **slew** [ˈsluː]; **slain** [ˈsleɪn]; **slaying** : asesinar, matar

slayer [ˈsleɪər] *n* : asesino *m*, -na *f*

sleazy [ˈsliːzi] *adj* **sleazier; -est 1** SHODDY : chapucero, de mala calidad **2** DILAPIDATED : ruinoso **3** DISREPUTABLE : de mala fama

sled[1] [ˈslɛd] *v* **sledded; sledding** *vi* : ir en trineo — *vt* : transportar en trineo

sled[2] *n* : trineo *m*

sledge [ˈslɛʤ] *n* **1** : trineo *m* (grande) **2** → **sledgehammer**

sledgehammer [ˈslɛʤˌhæmər] *n* : almádena *f*, combo *m Chile, Peru*

sleek[1] [ˈsliːk] *vt* SLICK : alisar

sleek[2] *adj* : liso y brillante

sleep[1] [ˈsliːp] *vi* **slept** [ˈslɛpt]; **sleeping** : dormir

sleep[2] *n* **1** : sueño *m* **2 to go to sleep** : dormirse

sleeper [ˈsliːpər] *n* **1** : durmiente *mf* ⟨to be a light sleeper : tener el sueño ligero⟩ **2** *or* **sleeping car** : coche *m* cama, coche *m* dormitorio

sleepily [ˈsliːpəli] *adv* : de manera somnolienta

sleepiness [ˈsliːpinəs] *n* : somnolencia *f*

sleepless [ˈsliːpləs] *adj* : sin dormir, desvelado ⟨to have a sleepless night : pasar la noche en blanco⟩

sleepwalker [ˈsliːpˌwɔkər] *n* : sonámbulo *m*, -la *f*

sleepy [ˈsliːpi] *adj* **sleepier; -est 1** DROWSY : somnoliento, soñoliento ⟨to be sleepy : tener sueño⟩ **2** LETHARGIC : aletargado, letárgico

sleet[1] [ˈsliːt] *vi* **to be sleeting** : caer aguanieve

sleet[2] *n* : aguanieve *f*

sleeve [ˈsliːv] *n* : manga *f* (de una camisa, etc.)

sleeveless [ˈsliːvləs] *adj* : sin mangas

sleigh[1] [ˈsleɪ] *vi* : ir en trineo

sleigh[2] *n* : trineo *m* (tirado por caballos)

sleight of hand [ˌslaɪṭəvˈhænd] : prestidigitación *f*, juegos *mpl* de manos

slender [ˈslɛndər] *adj* **1** SLIM : esbelto, delgado **2** SCANTY : exiguo, escaso ⟨a slender hope : una esperanza lejana⟩

sleuth [ˈsluːθ] *n* : detective *mf*; sabueso *m*, -sa *f*

slew → **slay**

slice[1] [ˈslaɪs] *vt* **sliced; slicing** : cortar

slice[2] *n* : rebanada *f*, tajada *f*, lonja *f* (de carne, etc.), rodaja *f* (de una verdura, fruta, etc.), trozo *m* (de pastel, etc.)

slick[1] [ˈslɪk] *vt* : alisar

slick[2] *adj* **1** SLIPPERY : resbaladizo, resbaloso **2** CRAFTY : astuto, taimado

slicker [ˈslɪkər] *n* : impermeable *m*

slide[1] [ˈslaɪd] *v* **slid** [ˈslɪd]; **sliding** [ˈslaɪdɪŋ] *vi* **1** SLIP : resbalar **2** GLIDE : deslizarse **3** DECLINE : bajar ⟨to let things slide : dejar pasar las cosas⟩ — *vt* : correr, deslizar

slide[2] *n* **1** SLIDING : deslizamiento *m* **2** SLIP : resbalón *m* **3** : tobogán *m* (para niños) **4** TRANSPARENCY : diapositiva *f* (fotográfica) **5** DECLINE : descenso *m*

slier, sliest → **sly**

slight[1] [ˈslaɪt] *vt* : desairar, despreciar

slight[2] *adj* **1** SLENDER : esbelto, delgado **2** FLIMSY : endeble **3** TRIFLING : leve, insignificante ⟨a slight pain : un leve dolor⟩ **4** SMALL : pequeño, ligero ⟨not in the slightest : en absoluto⟩

slight[3] *n* SNUB : desaire *m*

slightly [ˈslaɪtli] *adv* : ligeramente, un poco

slim[1] [ˈslɪm] *v* **slimmed; slimming** : adelgazar

slim[2] *adj* **slimmer; slimmest 1** SLENDER : esbelto, delgado **2** SCANTY : exiguo, escaso

slime [ˈslaɪm] *n* **1** : baba *f* (secretada por un animal) **2** MUD, SILT : fango *m*, cieno *m*

slimy [ˈslaɪmi] *adj* **slimier; -est** : viscoso

sling[1] [ˈslɪŋ] *vt* **slung** [ˈslʌŋ]; **slinging 1** THROW : lanzar, tirar **2** HANG : colgar

sling[2] *n* **1** : honda *f* (arma) **2** : cabestrillo *m* ⟨my arm is in a sling : llevo el brazo en cabestrillo⟩

slingshot [ˈslɪŋˌʃɑt] *n* : tiragomas *m*, resortera *f Mex*

slink [ˈslɪŋk] *vi* **slunk** [ˈslʌŋk]; **slinking** : caminar furtivamente

slip[1] [ˈslɪp] *v* **slipped; slipping** *vi* **1** STEAL : ir sigilosamente ⟨to slip away : escabullirse⟩ ⟨to slip out the door : escaparse por la puerta⟩ **2** SLIDE : resbalarse, deslizarse **3** LAPSE : caer ⟨to slip into error : equivocarse⟩ **4 to let slip** : dejar escapar **5 to slip into** PUT ON : ponerse — *vt* **1** PUT : meter, poner **2** PASS : pasar ⟨she slipped me a note : me pasó una nota⟩ **3 to slip one's mind** : olvidársele a uno

slip[2] *n* **1** PIER : atracadero *m* **2** MISHAP : percance *m*, contratiempo *m* **3** MISTAKE : error *m*, desliz *m* ⟨a slip of the tongue : un lapsus⟩ **4** PETTICOAT : enagua *f* **5** : injerto *m*, esqueje *m* (de una planta) **6 slip of paper** : papelito *m*

slipper [ˈslɪpər] *n* : zapatilla *f*, pantufla *f*

slipperiness [ˈslɪpərinəs] *n* **1** : lo resbaloso, lo resbaladizo **2** TRICKINESS : astucia *f*

slippery [ˈslɪpəri] *adj* **slipperier; -est 1** : resbaloso, resbaladizo ⟨a slippery road : un camino resbaloso⟩ **2** TRICKY : artero, astuto, taimado **3** ELUSIVE : huidizo, escurridizo

slipshod [ˈslɪpˌʃɑd] *adj* : descuidado, chapucero

slip up *vi* : equivocarse

slit[1] [ˈslɪt] *vt* **slit; slitting** : cortar, abrir por lo largo

slit[2] *n* **1** OPENING : abertura *f*, rendija *f* **2** CUT : corte *m*, raja *f*, tajo *m*
slither ['slɪðər] *vi* : deslizarse
sliver ['slɪvər] *n* : astilla *f*
slob ['slɑb] *n* : persona *f* desaliñada ⟨what a slob! : ¡qué cerdo!⟩
slobber[1] ['slɑbər] *vi* : babear
slobber[2] *n* : baba *f*
slogan ['slo:gən] *n* : lema *m*, eslogan *m*
sloop ['slu:p] *n* : balandra *f*
slop[1] ['slɑp] *v* **slopped; slopping** *vt* : derramar — *vi* : derramarse
slop[2] *n* : bazofia *f*
slope[1] ['slo:p] *vi* **sloped; sloping** : inclinarse ⟨the road slopes upward : el camino sube (en pendiente)⟩
slope[2] *n* : inclinación *f*, pendiente *f*, declive *m*
sloppy ['slɑpi] *adj* **sloppier; -est** **1** MUDDY, SLUSHY : lodoso, fangoso **2** UNTIDY : descuidado (en el trabajo, etc.), desaliñado (de aspecto)
slot ['slɑt] *n* : ranura *f*
sloth ['slɔθ, 'slo:θ] *n* **1** LAZINESS : pereza *f* **2** : perezoso *m* (animal)
slouch[1] ['slaʊʧ] *vi* : andar con los hombros caídos, repantigarse (en un sillón)
slouch[2] *n* **1** SLUMPING : mala postura *f* **2** BUNGLER, IDLER : haragán *m*, -gana *f*; inepto *m*, -ta *f* ⟨to be no slouch : no quedarse atrás⟩
slough[1] ['slʌf] *vt* : mudar de (piel)
slough[2] ['slu:, 'slaʊ] *n* SWAMP : ciénaga *f*
Slovak ['slo:ˌvɑk, -ˌvæk] *or* **Slovakian** [slo:'vɑkiən, -'væ-] *n* : eslovaco *m*, -ca *f* — **Slovak** *or* **Slovakian** *adj*
Slovene ['slo:ˌvi:n] *or* **Slovenian** [slo:'vi:niən] *n* : esloveno *m*, -na *f* — **Slovene** *or* **Slovenian** *adj*
slovenly ['slʌvənli, 'slɑv-] *adj* : descuidado (en el trabajo, etc.), desaliñado (de aspecto)
slow[1] [slo:] *vt* : retrasar, reducir la marcha de — *vi* : ir más despacio
slow[2] *adv* : despacio, lentamente
slow[3] *adj* **1** : lento ⟨a slow process : un proceso lento⟩ **2** : atrasado ⟨my watch is slow : mi reloj está atrasado, mi reloj se atrasa⟩ **3** SLUGGISH : lento, poco activo **4** STUPID : lento, torpe, corto de alcances
slowly [slo:li] *adv* : lentamente, despacio
slowness [slo:nəs] *n* : lentitud *f*, torpeza *f*
sludge ['slʌʤ] *n* : aguas *fpl* negras, aguas *fpl* residuales
slug[1] ['slʌg] *vt* **slugged; slugging** : pegarle un porrazo (a alguien)
slug[2] *n* **1** : babosa *f* (molusco) **2** BULLET : bala *f* **3** TOKEN : ficha *f* **4** BLOW : porrazo *m*, puñetazo *m*
sluggish ['slʌgɪʃ] *adj* : aletargado, lento
sluice[1] ['slu:s] *vt* **sluiced; sluicing** : lavar en agua corriente
sluice[2] *n* : canal *m*
slum ['slʌm] *n* : barriada *f*, barrio *m* bajo
slumber[1] ['slʌmbər] *vi* : dormir
slumber[2] *n* : sueño *m*
slump[1] ['slʌmp] *vi* **1** DECLINE, DROP : disminuir, bajar **2** SLOUCH : encorvarse, dejarse caer (en una silla, etc.)
slump[2] *n* : bajón *m*, declive *m* (económico)
slung → **sling**
slunk → **slink**
slur[1] ['slər] *vt* **slurred; slurring** : ligar (notas musicales), tragarse (las palabras)
slur[2] *n* **1** : ligado *m* (en música), mala pronunciación *f* (de las palabras) **2** ASPERSION : calumnia *f*, difamación *f*
slurp[1] ['slərp] *vi* : beber o comer haciendo ruido — *vt* : sorber ruidosamente
slurp[2] *n* : sorbo *m* (ruidoso)
slush ['slʌʃ] *n* : nieve *f* medio derretida
slut ['slʌt] *n* PROSTITUTE : ramera *f*, fulana *f*
sly ['slaɪ] *adj* **slier** ['slaɪər]; **sliest** ['slaɪəst] **1** CUNNING : astuto, taimado **2** UNDERHANDED : soplado — **slyly** *adv*
slyness ['slaɪnəs] *n* : astucia *f*
smack[1] ['smæk] *vi* **to smack of** : oler a, saber a — *vt* **1** KISS : besar, plantarle un beso (a alguien) **2** SLAP : pegarle una bofetada (a alguien) **3 to smack one's lips** : relamerse
smack[2] *adv* : justo, exactamente ⟨smack in the face : en plena cara⟩
smack[3] *n* **1** TASTE, TRACE : sabor *m*, indicio *m* **2** : chasquido *m* (de los labios) **3** SLAP : bofetada *f* **4** KISS : beso *m*
small ['smɔl] *adj* **1** : pequeño, chico ⟨a small house : una casa pequeña⟩ ⟨small change : monedas de poco valor⟩ **2** TRIVIAL : pequeño, insignificante
smallness ['smɔlnəs] *n* : pequeñez *f*
smallpox ['smɔlˌpɑks] *n* : viruela *f*
smart[1] ['smɑrt] *vi* **1** STING : escocer, picar, arder **2** HURT : dolerse, resentirse ⟨to smart under a rejection : dolerse ante un rechazo⟩
smart[2] *adj* **1** BRIGHT : listo, vivo, inteligente **2** STYLISH : elegante — **smartly** *adv*
smart[3] *n* **1** PAIN : escozor *m*, dolor *m* **2** **smarts** *npl* : inteligencia *f*
smartness ['smɑrtnəs] *n* **1** INTELLIGENCE : inteligencia *f* **2** ELEGANCE : elegancia *f*
smash[1] ['smæʃ] *vt* **1** BREAK : romper, quebrar, hacer pedazos **2** WRECK : destrozar, arruinar **3** CRASH : estrellar, chocar — *vi* **1** SHATTER : hacerse pedazos, hacerse añicos **2** COLLIDE, CRASH : estrellarse, chocar
smash[2] *n* **1** BLOW : golpe *m* **2** COLLISION : choque *m* **3** BANG, CRASH : estrépito *m*
smattering ['smæt̬ərɪŋ] *n* **1** : nociones *fpl* ⟨she has a smattering of programming : tiene nociones de programación⟩ **2** : un poco, unos cuantos ⟨a

smattering of spectators : unos cuantos espectadores⟩

smear[1] ['smɪr] *vt* **1** DAUB : embadurnar, untar (mantequilla, etc.) **2** SMUDGE : emborronar **3** SLANDER : calumniar, difamar

smear[2] *n* **1** SMUDGE : mancha *f* **2** SLANDER : calumnia *f*

smell[1] ['smɛl] *v* **smelled** *or* **smelt** ['smɛlt]; **smelling** *vt* : oler, olfatear ⟨to smell danger : olfatear el peligro⟩ — *vi* : oler ⟨to smell good : oler bien⟩

smell[2] *n* **1** : olfato *m*, sentido *m* del olfato **2** ODOR : olor *m*

smelly ['smɛli] *adj* **smellier; -est** : maloliente

smelt[1] ['smɛlt] *vt* : fundir

smelt[2] *n, pl* **smelts** *or* **smelt** : eperlano *m* (pez)

smile[1] ['smaɪl] *vi* **smiled; smiling** : sonreír

smile[2] *n* : sonrisa *f*

smirk[1] ['smərk] *vi* : sonreír con suficiencia

smirk[2] *n* : sonrisa *f* satisfecha

smite ['smaɪt] *vt* **smote** ['smo:t]; **smitten** ['smɪtən] *or* **smote; smiting 1** STRIKE : golpear **2** AFFLICT : afligir

smith ['smɪθ] *n* : herrero *m*, -ra *f*

smithy ['smɪθi] *n, pl* **smithies** : herrería *f*

smock ['smɑk] *n* : bata *f*, blusón *m*

smog ['smɑg, 'smɔg] *n* : smog *m*

smoke[1] ['smo:k] *v* **smoked; smoking** *vi* **1** : echar humo, humear ⟨a smoking chimney : una chimenea que echa humo⟩ **2** : fumar ⟨I don't smoke : no fumo⟩ — *vt* : ahumar (carne, etc.)

smoke[2] *n* : humo *m*

smoke detector [dɪ'tɛktər] *n* : detector *m* de humo

smoker ['smo:kər] *n* : fumador *m*, -dora *f*

smokestack ['smo:kˌstæk] *n* : chimenea *f*

smoky ['smo:ki] *adj* **smokier; -est 1** SMOKING : humeante **2** : a humo ⟨a smoky flavor : un sabor a humo⟩ **3** : lleno de humo ⟨a smoky room : un cuarto lleno de humo⟩

smolder ['smo:ldər] *vi* **1** : arder sin llama **2** : arder (en el corazón) ⟨his anger smoldered : su rabia ardía⟩

smooth[1] ['smu:ð] *vt* : alisar

smooth[2] *adj* **1** : liso (dícese de una superficie) ⟨smooth skin : piel lisa⟩ **2** : suave (dícese de un movimiento) ⟨a smooth landing : un aterrizaje suave⟩ **3** : sin grumos ⟨a smooth sauce : una salsa sin grumos⟩ **4** : fluido ⟨smooth writing : escritura fluida⟩

smoothly ['smu:ðli] *adv* **1** GENTLY, SOFTLY : suavemente **2** EASILY : con facilidad, sin problemas

smoothness ['smu:ðnəs] *n* : suavidad *f*

smother ['smʌðər] *vt* **1** SUFFOCATE : ahogar, sofocar **2** COVER : cubrir **3** SUPPRESS : contener — *vi* : asfixiarse

smudge[1] ['smʌʤ] *v* **smudged; smudging** *vt* : emborronar — *vi* : correrse

smudge[2] *n* : mancha *f*, borrón *m*

smug ['smʌg] *adj* **smugger; smuggest** : suficiente, pagado de sí mismo

smuggle ['smʌgəl] *vt* **-gled; -gling** : contrabandear, pasar de contrabando

smuggler ['smʌgələr] *n* : contrabandista *mf*

smugly ['smʌgli] *adv* : con suficiencia

smut ['smʌt] *n* **1** SOOT : tizne *m*, hollín *m* **2** FUNGUS : tizón *m* **3** OBSCENITY : obscenidad *f*, inmundicia *f*

smutty ['smʌt̬i] *adj* **smuttier; -est 1** SOOTY : tiznado **2** OBSCENE : obsceno, indecente

snack ['snæk] *n* : refrigerio *m*, bocado *m*, tentempié *m fam* ⟨an afternoon snack : una merienda⟩

snag[1] ['snæg] *v* **snagged; snagging** *vt* : enganchar — *vi* : engancharse

snag[2] *n* : problema *m*, inconveniente *m*

snail ['sneɪl] *n* : caracol *m*

snake ['sneɪk] *n* : culebra *f*, serpiente *f*

snakebite ['sneɪkˌbaɪt] *n* : mordedura *f* de serpiente

snap[1] ['snæp] *v* **snapped; snapping** *vi* **1** : intentar morder (dícese de un perro, etc.), picar (dícese de un pez) **2** : hablar con severidad ⟨he snapped at me! : ¡me gritó!⟩ **3** BREAK : romperse, quebrarse (haciendo un chasquido) — *vt* **1** BREAK : partir (en dos), quebrar **2** : hacer (algo) de un golpe ⟨to snap open : abrir de golpe⟩ **3** RETORT : decir bruscamente **4** CLICK : chasquear ⟨to snap one's fingers : chasquear los dedos⟩

snap[2] *n* **1** CLICK, CRACK : chasquido *m* **2** FASTENER : broche *m* **3** CINCH : cosa *f* fácil ⟨it's a snap : es facilísimo⟩

snapdragon ['snæpˌdrægən] *n* : dragón *m* (flor)

snapper ['snæpər] → **red snapper**

snappy ['snæpi] *adj* **snappier; -est 1** FAST : rápido ⟨make it snappy! : ¡date prisa!⟩ **2** LIVELY : vivaz **3** CHILLY : frío **4** STYLISH : elegante

snapshot ['snæpˌʃɑt] *n* : instantánea *f*

snare[1] ['snær] *vt* **snared; snaring** : atrapar

snare[2] *n* : trampa *f*, red *f*

snare drum *n* : tambor *m* con bordón

snarl[1] ['snɑrl] *vi* **1** TANGLE : enmarañar, enredar **2** GROWL : gruñir

snarl[2] *n* **1** TANGLE : enredo *m*, maraña *f* **2** GROWL : gruñido *m*

snatch[1] ['snæʧ] *vt* : arrebatar

snatch[2] *n* : fragmento *m*

sneak[1] ['sni:k] *vi* : ir a hurtadillas — *vt* : hacer furtivamente ⟨to sneak a look : mirar con disimulo⟩ ⟨he sneaked a smoke : fumó un cigarrillo a escondidas⟩

sneak[2] *n* : soplón *m*, -plona *f*

sneakers ['sni:kərz] *npl* : tenis *mpl*, zapatillas *fpl*

sneaky ['sni:ki] *adj* **sneakier; -est** : solapado

sneer[1] ['snɪr] *vi* : sonreír con desprecio
sneer[2] *n* : sonrisa *f* de desprecio
sneeze[1] ['sni:z] *vi* **sneezed; sneezing** : estornudar
sneeze[2] *n* : estornudo *m*
snicker[1] ['snɪkər] *vi* : reírse disimuladamente
snicker[2] *n* : risita *f*
snide ['snaɪd] *adj* : sarcástico
sniff[1] ['snɪf] *vi* **1** SMELL : oler, husmear (dícese de los animales) **2 to sniff at** : despreciar, desdeñar — *vt* **1** SMELL : oler **2 to sniff out** : olerse, husmear
sniff[2] *n* **1** SNIFFING : aspiración *f* por la nariz **2** SMELL : olor *m*
sniffle ['snɪfəl] *vi* **-fled; -fling** : respirar con la nariz congestionada
sniffles ['snɪfəlz] *npl* : resfriado *m*
snip[1] ['snɪp] *vt* **snipped; snipping** : cortar (con tijeras)
snip[2] *n* : tijeretada *f*, recorte *m*
snipe[1] ['snaɪp] *vi* **sniped; sniping** : disparar
snipe[2] *n, pl* **snipes** *or* **snipe** : agachadiza *f*
sniper ['snaɪpər] *n* : francotirador *m*, -dora *f*
snippet ['snɪpət] *n* : fragmento *m* (de un texto, etc.)
snivel ['snɪvəl] *vi* **-veled** *or* **-velled; -veling** *or* **-velling 1** → **snuffle 2** WHINE : lloriquear
snob ['snɑb] *n* : esnob *mf*, snob *mf*
snobbery ['snɑbəri] *n, pl* **-beries** : esnobismo *m*
snobbish ['snɑbɪʃ] *adj* : esnob, snob
snobbishness ['snɑbɪʃnəs] *n* : esnobismo *m*
snoop[1] ['snu:p] *vi* : husmear, curiosear
snoop[2] *n* : fisgón *m*, -gona *f*
snooze[1] ['snu:z] *vi* **snoozed; snoozing** : dormitar
snooze[2] *n* : siestecita *f*, siestita *f*
snore[1] ['snor] *vi* **snored; snoring** : roncar
snore[2] *n* : ronquido *m*
snort[1] ['snɔrt] *vi* : bufar, resoplar
snort[2] *n* : bufido *m*, resoplo *m*
snout ['snaʊt] *n* : hocico *m*, morro *m*
snow[1] ['sno:] *vi* **1** : nevar ⟨I'm snowed in : estoy aislado por la nieve⟩ **2 to be snowed under** : estar inundado
snow[2] *n* : nieve *f*
snowball ['sno:ˌbɔl] *n* : bola *f* de nieve
snowdrift ['sno:ˌdrɪft] *n* : ventisquero *m*
snowfall ['sno:ˌfɔl] *n* : nevada *f*
snowplow ['sno:ˌplaʊ] *n* : quitanieves *m*
snowshoe ['sno:ˌʃu:] *n* : raqueta *f* (para nieve)
snowstorm ['sno:ˌstɔrm] *n* : tormenta *f* de nieve, ventisca *f*
snowy ['sno:i] *adj* **snowier; -est** : nevoso ⟨a snowy road : un camino nevado⟩
snub[1] ['snʌb] *vt* **snubbed; snubbing** : desairar
snub[2] *n* : desaire *m*
snub–nosed ['snʌbˌno:zd] *adj* : de nariz respingada
snuff[1] ['snʌf] *vt* **1** : apagar (una vela) **2** : sorber (algo) por la nariz
snuff[2] *n* : rapé *m*
snuffle ['snʌfəl] *vi* **-fled; -fling** : respirar con la nariz congestionada
snug ['snʌg] *adj* **snugger; snuggest 1** COMFORTABLE : cómodo **2** TIGHT : ajustado, ceñido ⟨snug pants : pantalones ajustados⟩
snuggle ['snʌgəl] *vi* **-gled; -gling** : acurrucarse ⟨to snuggle up to someone : arrimársele a alguien⟩
snugly ['snʌgli] *adv* **1** COMFORTABLY : cómodamente **2** : de manera ajustada ⟨the shirt fits snugly : la camisa queda ajustada⟩
so[1] ['so:] *adv* **1** (*referring to something indicated or suggested*) ⟨do you think so? : ¿tú crees?⟩ ⟨so it would seem : eso parece⟩ ⟨I told her so : se lo dije⟩ ⟨he's ready, or so he says : según dice, está listo⟩ ⟨it so happened that . . . : resultó que . . . ⟩ ⟨do it like so : hazlo así⟩ ⟨so be it : así sea⟩ **2** ALSO : también ⟨so do I : yo también⟩ **3** THUS : así, de esta manera **4** : tan ⟨he'd never been so happy : nunca había estado tan contento⟩ **5** CONSEQUENTLY : por lo tanto
so[2] *conj* **1** THEREFORE : así que **2** *or* **so that** : para que, así que, de manera que **3 so what?** : ¿y qué?
soak[1] ['so:k] *vi* : estar en remojo — *vt* **1** : poner en remojo **2 to soak up** ABSORB : absorber
soak[2] *n* : remojo *m*
soap[1] ['so:p] *vt* : enjabonar
soap[2] *n* : jabón *m*
soapsuds ['so:pˌsʌdz] → **suds**
soapy ['so:pi] *adj* **soapier; -est** : jabonoso ⟨a soapy taste : un gusto a jabón⟩ ⟨a soapy texture : una textura de jabón⟩
soar ['sor] *vi* **1** FLY : volar **2** RISE : remontar el vuelo (dícese de las aves) ⟨her hopes soared : su esperanza renació⟩ ⟨prices are soaring : los precios están subiendo vertiginosamente⟩
sob[1] ['sɑb] *vi* **sobbed; sobbing** : sollozar
sob[2] *n* : sollozo *m*
sober ['so:bər] *adj* **1** : sobrio ⟨he's not sober enough to drive : está demasiado borracho para manejar⟩ **2** SERIOUS : serio
soberly ['so:bərli] *adv* **1** : sobriamente **2** SERIOUSLY : seriamente
sobriety [sə'braɪət̬i, so-] *n* **1** : sobriedad *f* ⟨sobriety test : prueba de alcoholemia⟩ **2** SERIOUSNESS : seriedad *f*
so–called ['so:'kɔld] *adj* : supuesto, presunto ⟨the so-called experts : los expertos, así llamados⟩
soccer ['sɑkər] *n* : futbol *m*, fútbol *m*
sociable ['so:ʃəbəl] *adj* : sociable
social[1] ['so:ʃəl] *adj* : social — **socially** *adv*
social[2] *n* : reunión *f* social

socialism [ˈsoːʃəˌlɪzəm] *n* : socialismo *m*
socialist[1] [ˈsoːʃəlɪst] *adj* : socialista
socialist[2] *n* : socialista *mf*
socialize [ˈsoːʃəˌlaɪz] *v* **-ized; -izing** *vt* **1** NATIONALIZE : nacionalizar **2** : socializar (en psicología) — *vi* : alternar, circular ⟨to socialize with friends : alternar con amigos⟩
social work *n* : asistencia *f* social
society [səˈsaɪəṭi] *n, pl* **-eties** **1** COMPANIONSHIP : compañía *f* **2** : sociedad *f* ⟨a democratic society : una sociedad democrática⟩ ⟨high society : alta sociedad⟩ **3** ASSOCIATION : sociedad *f*, asociación *f*
socioeconomic [ˌsoːsioˌiːkəˈnɑmɪk, -ˌɛkə-] *adj* : socioeconómico
sociology [ˌsoːsiˈɑləʤi] *n* : sociología *f*
sociological [ˌsoːsiəˈlɑʤɪkəl] *adj* : sociológico
sociologist [ˌsoːsiˈɑləʤɪst] *n* : sociólogo *m*, -ga *f*
sock[1] [ˈsɑk] *vt* : pegar, golpear, darle un puñetazo a
sock[2] *n* **1** *pl* **socks** *or* **sox** [ˈsɑks] : calcetín *m*, media *f* ⟨shoes and socks : zapatos y calcetines⟩ **2** *pl* **socks** [ˈsɑks] PUNCH : puñetazo *m*
socket [ˈsɑkət] *n* **1** *or* **electric socket** : enchufe *m*, toma *f* de corriente **2** : glena *f* (de una articulación) ⟨shoulder socket : glena del hombro⟩ **3 eye socket** : órbita *f*, cuenca *f*
sod[1] [ˈsɑd] *vt* **sodded; sodding** : cubrir de césped
sod[2] *n* TURF : césped *m*, tepe *m*
soda [ˈsoːdə] *n* **1** *or* **soda water** : soda *f* **2** *or* **soda pop** : gaseosa *f*, refresco *m* **3** *or* **ice–cream soda** : refresco *m* con helado
sodden [ˈsɑdən] *adj* SOGGY : empapado
sodium [ˈsoːdiəm] *n* : sodio *m*
sodium bicarbonate *n* : bicarbonato *m* de soda
sodium chloride → **salt**
sofa [ˈsoːfə] *n* : sofá *m*
soft [ˈsɔft] *adj* **1** : blando ⟨a soft pillow : una almohada blanda⟩ **2** SMOOTH : suave (dícese de las texturas, de los sonidos, etc.) **3** NONALCOHOLIC : no alcohólico ⟨a soft drink : un refresco⟩
softball [ˈsɔftˌbɔl] *n* : softbol *m*
soften [ˈsɔfən] *vt* : ablandar (algo sólido), suavizar (la piel, un golpe, etc.), amortiguar (un impacto) — *vi* : ablandarse, suavizarse
softly [ˈsɔftli] *adv* : suavemente ⟨she spoke softly : habló en voz baja⟩
softness [ˈsɔftnəs] *n* **1** : blandura *f*, lo blando (de una almohada, de la mantequilla, etc.) **2** SMOOTHNESS : suavidad *f*
software [ˈsɔftˌwær] *n* : software *m*
soggy [ˈsɑgi] *adj* **soggier; -est** : empapado
soil[1] [ˈsɔɪl] *vt* : ensuciar — *vi* : ensuciarse
soil[2] *n* **1** DIRTINESS : suciedad *f* **2** DIRT, EARTH : suelo *m*, tierra *f* **3** COUNTRY : patria *f* ⟨her native soil : su tierra natal⟩
sojourn[1] [ˈsoːˌʤərn, soːˈʤərn] *vi* : pasar una temporada
sojourn[2] *n* : estadía *f*, estancia *f*, permanencia *f*
solace [ˈsɑləs] *n* : consuelo *m*
solar [ˈsoːlər] *adj* : solar ⟨the solar system : el sistema solar⟩
sold → **sell**
solder[1] [ˈsɑdər, ˈsɔ-] *vt* : soldar
solder[2] *n* : soldadura *f*
soldier[1] [ˈsoːlʤər] *vi* : servir como soldado
soldier[2] *n* : soldado *mf*
sole[1] [ˈsoːl] *adj* : único
sole[2] *n* **1** : suela *f* (de un zapato) **2** : lenguado *m* (pez)
solely [ˈsoːli] *adv* : únicamente, sólo
solemn [ˈsɑləm] *adj* : solemne, serio — **solemnly** *adv*
solemnity [səˈlɛmnəṭi] *n, pl* **-ties** : solemnidad *f*
solicit [səˈlɪsət] *vt* : solicitar
solicitous [səˈlɪsəṭəs] *adj* : solícito
solicitude [səˈlɪsəˌtuːd, -ˌtjuːd] *n* : solicitud *f*
solid[1] [ˈsɑləd] *adj* **1** : macizo ⟨a solid rubber ball : una bola maciza de caucho⟩ **2** CUBIC : tridimensional **3** COMPACT : compacto, denso **4** STURDY : sólido **5** CONTINUOUS : seguido, continuo ⟨two solid hours : dos horas seguidas⟩ ⟨a solid line : una línea continua⟩ **6** UNANIMOUS : unánime **7** DEPENDABLE : serio, fiable **8** PURE : macizo, puro ⟨solid gold : oro macizo⟩
solid[2] *n* : sólido *m*
solidarity [ˌsɑləˈdærəṭi] *n* : solidaridad *f*
solidify [səˈlɪdəˌfaɪ] *v* **-fied; -fying** *vt* : solidificar — *vi* : solidificarse
solidity [səˈlɪdəṭi] *n, pl* **-ties** : solidez *f*
solidly [ˈsɑlədli] *adv* **1** : sólidamente **2** UNANIMOUSLY : unánimemente
soliloquy [səˈlɪləkwi] *n, pl* **-quies** : soliloquio *m*
solitaire [ˈsɑləˌtɛr] *n* : solitario *m*
solitary [ˈsɑləˌtɛri] *adj* **1** ALONE : solitario **2** SECLUDED : apartado, retirado **3** SINGLE : solo
solitude [ˈsɑləˌtuːd, -ˌtjuːd] *n* : soledad *f*
solo[1] [ˈsoːˌloː] *vi* : volar en solitario (dícese de un piloto)
solo[2] *adv & adj* : en solitario, a solas
solo[3] *n, pl* **solos** : solo *m*
soloist [ˈsoːloɪst] *n* : solista *mf*
solstice [ˈsɑlstɪs] *n* : solsticio *m*
soluble [ˈsɑljəbəl] *adj* : soluble
solution [səˈluːʃən] *n* : solución *f*
solve [ˈsɑlv] *vt* **solved; solving** : resolver, solucionar
solvency [ˈsɑlvəntsi] *n* : solvencia *f*
solvent [ˈsɑlvənt] *n* : solvente *m*
Somali [soˈmɑli, sə-] *n* : somalí *mf* — **Somali** *adj*
somber [ˈsɑmbər] *adj* **1** DARK : sombrío, oscuro ⟨somber colors : colores

oscuros〉 **2** GRAVE : sombrío, serio **3** MELANCHOLY : sombrío, lúgubre

sombrero [səm'brɛr,o:] *n, pl* **-ros** : sombrero *m* (mexicano)

some[1] ['sʌm] *adj* **1** : un, algún 〈some lady stopped me : una mujer me detuvo〉 〈some distant galaxy : alguna galaxia lejana〉 **2** : algo de, un poco de 〈he drank some water : tomó (un poco de) agua〉 **3** : unos 〈do you want some apples? : ¿quieres unas manzanas?〉 〈some years ago : hace varios años〉

some[2] *pron* **1** : algunos 〈some went, others stayed : algunos se fueron, otros se quedaron〉 **2** : un poco, algo 〈there's some left : queda un poco〉 〈I have gum; do you want some? : tengo chicle, ¿quieres?〉

somebody ['sʌmbədi, -,bɑdi] *pron* : alguien

someday ['sʌm,deɪ] *adv* : algún día

somehow ['sʌm,haʊ] *adv* **1** : de alguna manera, de algún modo 〈I'll do it somehow : lo haré de alguna manera〉 **2** : por alguna razón 〈somehow I don't trust her : por alguna razón no me fío de ella〉

someone ['sʌm,wʌn] *pron* : alguien

someplace ['sʌm,pleɪs] → **somewhere**

somersault[1] ['sʌmər,sɔlt] *vi* : dar volteretas, dar un salto mortal

somersault[2] *n* : voltereta *f*, salto *m* mortal

something ['sʌmθɪŋ] *pron* : algo 〈I want something else : quiero otra cosa〉 〈she's writing a novel or something : está escribiendo una novela o no sé qué〉

sometime ['sʌm,taɪm] *adv* : algún día, en algún momento 〈sometime next month : durante el mes que viene〉

sometimes ['sʌm,taɪmz] *adv* : a veces, algunas veces, de vez en cuando

somewhat ['sʌm,hwʌt, -,hwɑt] *adv* : algo, un tanto

somewhere ['sʌm,*h*wɛr] *adv* **1** (*indicating location*) : en algún lugar 〈it must be somewhere else : estará en otra parte〉 **2** (*indicating destination*) : a algún lugar

son ['sʌn] *n* : hijo *m*

sonar ['so:,nɑr] *n* : sonar *m*

sonata [sə'nɑṯə] *n* : sonata *f*

song ['sɔŋ] *n* : canción *f*, canto *m* (de un pájaro)

songbird ['sɔŋ,bərd] *n* : pájaro *m* cantor

songwriter ['sɔŋ,raɪṯər] *n* : compositor *m*, -tora *f*

sonic ['sɑnɪk] *adj* **1** : sónico **2 sonic boom** : estampido *m* sónico

son–in–law ['sʌnɪn,lɔ] *n, pl* **sons–in–law** : yerno *m*, hijo *m* político

sonnet ['sɑnət] *n* : soneto *m*

sonorous ['sɑnərəs, sə'norəs] *adj* : sonoro

soon ['su:n] *adv* **1** : pronto, dentro de poco 〈he'll arrive soon : llegará pronto〉 **2** QUICKLY : pronto 〈as soon as possible : lo más pronto posible〉 〈the sooner the better : cuanto antes mejor〉 **3** : de buena gana 〈I'd sooner walk : prefiero caminar〉

soot ['sʊt, 'su:t, 'sʌt] *n* : hollín *m*, tizne *m*

soothe ['su:ð] *vt* **soothed; soothing 1** CALM : calmar, tranquilizar **2** RELIEVE : aliviar

soothsayer ['su:θ,seɪər] *n* : adivino *m*, -na *f*

sooty ['sʊṯi, 'su:-, 'sʌ-] *adj* **sootier; -est** : cubierto de hollín, tiznado

sop[1] ['sɑp] *vt* **sopped; sopping 1** DIP : mojar **2** SOAK : empapar **3 to sop up** : rebañar, absorber

sop[2] *n* **1** CONCESSION : concesión *f* **2** BRIBE : soborno *m*

sophisticated [sə'fɪstə,keɪṯəd] *adj* **1** COMPLEX : complejo **2** WORLDLY-WISE : sofisticado

sophistication [sə,fɪstə'keɪʃən] *n* **1** COMPLEXITY : complejidad *f* **2** URBANITY : sofisticación *f*

sophomore ['sɑf,mor, 'sɑfə,mor] *n* : estudiante *mf* de segundo año

soporific [,sɑpə'rɪfɪk, ,so:-] *adj* : soporífero

soprano [sə'præ,no:] *n, pl* **-nos** : soprano *mf*

sorcerer ['sɔrsərər] *n* : hechicero *m*, brujo *m*, mago *m*

sorceress ['sɔrsərəs] *n* : hechicera *f*, bruja *f*, maga *f*

sorcery ['sɔrsəri] *n* : hechicería *f*, brujería *f*

sordid ['sɔrdɪd] *adj* : sórdido

sore[1] ['sor] *adj* **sorer; sorest 1** PAINFUL : dolorido, doloroso 〈I have a sore throat : me duele la garganta〉 **2** ACUTE, SEVERE : extremo, grande 〈in sore straits : en grandes apuros〉 **3** ANGRY : enojado, enfadado

sore[2] *n* : llaga *f*

sorely ['sorli] *adv* : muchísimo 〈it was sorely needed : se necesitaba urgentemente〉 〈she was sorely missed : la echaban mucho de menos〉

soreness ['sornəs] *n* : dolor *m*

sorghum ['sɔrgəm] *n* : sorgo *m*

sorority [sə'rɔrəṯi] *n, pl* **-ties** : hermandad *f* (de estudiantes femeninas)

sorrel ['sɔrəl] *n* **1** : alazán *m* (color o animal) **2** : acedera *f* (hierba)

sorrow ['sɑr,o:] *n* : pesar *m*, dolor *m*, pena *f*

sorrowful ['sɑrofəl] *adj* : triste, afligido, apenado

sorrowfully ['sɑrofəli] *adv* : con tristeza

sorry ['sɑri] *adj* **sorrier; -est 1** PITIFUL : lastimero, lastimoso **2 to be sorry** : sentir, lamentar 〈I'm sorry : lo siento〉 **3 to feel sorry for** : compadecer 〈I feel sorry for him : me da pena〉

sort[1] ['sɔrt] *vt* **1** : dividir en grupos **2** CLASSIFY : clasificar **3 to sort out** ORGANIZE : poner en orden **4 to sort out** RESOLVE : resolver

sort[2] *n* **1** KIND : tipo *m*, clase *f* ⟨a sort of writer : una especie de escritor⟩ **2** NATURE : índole *f* **3 out of sorts** : de mal humor
sortie [ˈsɔrṭi, sɔrˈti:] *n* : salida *f*
SOS [ˌɛsˌo:ˈɛs] *n* : SOS *m*
so–so [ˈso:ˈso:] *adj & adv* : así así, de modo regular
soufflé [su:ˈfleɪ] *n* : suflé *m*
sought → **seek**
soul [ˈso:l] *n* **1** SPIRIT : alma *f* **2** ESSENCE : esencia *f* **3** PERSON : persona *f*, alma *f*
soulful [ˈso:lfəl] *adj* : conmovedor, lleno de emoción
sound[1] [ˈsaʊnd] *vt* **1** : sondar (en navegación) **2** *or* **to sound out** PROBE : sondear **3** : hacer sonar, tocar (una trompeta, etc.) — *vi* **1** : sonar ⟨the alarm sounded : la alarma sonó⟩ **2** SEEM : parecer
sound[2] *adj* **1** HEALTHY : sano ⟨safe and sound : sano y salvo⟩ ⟨of sound mind and body : en pleno uso de sus facultades⟩ **2** FIRM, SOLID : sólido **3** SENSIBLE : lógico, sensato **4** DEEP : profundo ⟨a sound sleep : un sueño profundo⟩
sound[3] *n* **1** : sonido *m* ⟨the speed of sound : la velocidad del sonido⟩ **2** NOISE : sonido *m*, ruido *m* ⟨I heard a sound : oí un sonido⟩ **3** CHANNEL : brazo *m* de mar, canal *m* (ancho)
soundless [ˈsaʊndləs] *adj* : sordo
soundlessly [ˈsaʊndləsli] *adv* : silenciosamente
soundly [ˈsaʊndli] *adv* **1** SOLIDLY : sólidamente **2** SENSIBLY : lógicamente, sensatamente **3** DEEPLY : profundamente ⟨sleeping soundly : durmiendo profundamente⟩
soundness [ˈsaʊndnəs] *n* **1** SOLIDITY : solidez *f* **2** SENSIBLENESS : sensatez *f*, solidez *f*
soundproof [ˈsaʊndˌpru:f] *adj* : insonorizado
soundtrack [ˈsaʊn*d*ˌtræk] *n* : banda *f* sonora
sound wave *n* : onda *f* sonora
soup [ˈsu:p] *n* : sopa *f*
sour[1] [ˈsaʊər] *vi* : agriarse, cortarse (dícese de la leche) — *vt* : agriar, cortar (leche)
sour[2] *adj* **1** ACID : agrio, ácido (dícese de la fruta, etc.), cortado (dícese de la leche) **2** DISAGREEABLE : desagradable, agrio
source [ˈsors] *n* : fuente *f*, origen *m*, nacimiento *m* (de un río)
sourness [ˈsaʊərnəs] *n* : acidez *f*
south[1] [ˈsaʊθ] *adv* : al sur, hacia el sur ⟨the window looks south : la ventana mira al sur⟩ ⟨she continued south : continuó hacia el sur⟩
south[2] *adj* : sur, del sur ⟨the south entrance : la entrada sur⟩ ⟨South America : Sudamérica, América del Sur⟩
south[3] *n* : sur *m*
South African *n* : sudafricano *m*, -na *f* — **South African** *adj*
South American[1] *adj* : sudamericano, suramericano
South American[2] *n* : sudamericano *m*, -na *f*; suramericano *m*, -na *f*
southbound [ˈsaʊθˌbaʊnd] *adj* : con rumbo al sur
southeast[1] [saʊˈθi:st] *adj* : sureste, sudeste, del sureste
southeast[2] *n* : sureste *m*, sudeste *m*
southeasterly [saʊˈθi:stərli] *adv & adj* **1** : del sureste (dícese del viento) **2** : hacia el sureste
southeastern [saʊˈθi:stərn] *adj* → **southeast**[1]
southerly [ˈsʌðərli] *adv & adj* : del sur
southern [ˈsʌðərn] *adj* : sur, sureño, meridional, austral ⟨a southern city : una ciudad del sur del país, una ciudad meridional⟩ ⟨the southern side : el lado sur⟩
Southerner [ˈsʌðərnər] *n* : sureño *m*, -ña *f*
South Pole : Polo *m* Sur
southward [ˈsaʊθwərd] *or* **southwards** [-wərdz] *adv & adj* : hacia el sur
southwest[1] [saʊθˈwɛst, *as a nautical term often* saʊˈwɛst] *adj* : suroeste, sudoeste, del suroeste
southwest[2] *n* : suroeste *m*, sudoeste *m*
southwesterly [saʊθˈwɛstərli] *adv & adj* **1** : del suroeste (dícese del viento) **2** : hacia el suroeste
southwestern [saʊθˈwɛstərn] *adj* → **southwest**[1]
souvenir [ˌsu:vəˈnɪr, ˈsu:vəˌ-] *n* : recuerdo *m*, souvenir *m*
sovereign[1] [ˈsɑvərən] *adj* : soberano
sovereign[2] *n* **1** : soberano *m*, -na *f* (monarca) **2** : soberano *m* (moneda)
sovereignty [ˈsɑvərənti] *n, pl* **-ties** : soberanía *f*
Soviet [ˈso:viˌɛt, ˈsɑ-, -viət] *adj* : soviético
sow[1] [ˈso:] *vt* **sowed; sown** [ˈso:n] *or* **sowed; sowing 1** PLANT : sembrar **2** SCATTER : esparcir
sow[2] [ˈsaʊ] *n* : cerda *f*
sox → **sock**
soy [ˈsɔɪ] *n* : soya *f*, soja *f*
soybean [ˈsɔɪˌbi:n] *n* : soya *f*, soja *f*
spa [ˈspɑ] *n* : balneario *m*
space[1] [ˈspeɪs] *vt* **spaced; spacing** : espaciar
space[2] *n* **1** PERIOD : espacio *m*, lapso *m*, período *m* **2** ROOM : espacio *m*, sitio *m*, lugar *m* ⟨is there space for me? : ¿hay sitio para mí?⟩ **3** : espacio *m* ⟨blank space : espacio en blanco⟩ **4** : espacio *m* (en física) **5** PLACE : plaza *f*, sitio *m* ⟨to reserve space : reservar plazas⟩ ⟨parking space : sitio para estacionarse⟩
spacecraft [ˈspeɪsˌkræft] *n* : nave *f* espacial
spaceflight [ˈspeɪsˌflaɪt] *n* : vuelo *m* espacial

spaceman ['speɪsmən, -ˌmæn] *n, pl* **-men** [-mən, -ˌmɛn] : astronauta *m*, cosmonauta *m*
spaceship ['speɪsˌʃɪp] *n* : nave *f* espacial
space shuttle *n* : transbordador *m* espacial
space suit *n* : traje *m* espacial
spacious ['speɪʃəs] *adj* : espacioso, amplio
spade[1] ['speɪd] *v* **spaded; spading** *vt* : palear — *vi* : usar una pala
spade[2] *n* **1** SHOVEL : pala *f* **2** : pica *f* (naipe)
spaghetti [spə'gɛt̮i] *n* : espagueti *m*, espaguetis *mpl*, spaghetti *mpl*
spam ['spæm] *n* : spam *m*, correo *m* electrónico no solicitado
span[1] ['spæn] *vt* **spanned; spanning** : abarcar (un período de tiempo), extenderse sobre (un espacio)
span[2] *n* **1** : lapso *m*, espacio *m* (de tiempo) ⟨life span : duración de la vida⟩ **2** : luz *f* (entre dos soportes)
spangle ['spæŋgəl] *n* : lentejuela *f*
Spaniard ['spænjərd] *n* : español *m*, -ñola *f*
spaniel ['spænjəl] *n* : spaniel *m*
Spanish[1] ['spænɪʃ] *adj* : español
Spanish[2] *n* **1** : español *m* (idioma) **2 the Spanish** *npl* : los españoles
spank ['spæŋk] *vt* : darle nalgadas (a alguien)
spar[1] ['spɑr] *vi* **sparred; sparring** : entrenarse (en boxeo)
spar[2] *n* : palo *m*, verga *f* (de un barco)
spare[1] ['spær] *vt* **spared; sparing 1** : perdonar ⟨to spare someone's life : perdonarle la vida a alguien⟩ **2** SAVE : ahorrar, evitar ⟨I'll spare you the trouble : le evitaré la molestia⟩ **3** : prescindir de ⟨I can't spare her : no puedo prescindir de ella⟩ ⟨can you spare a dollar? : ¿me das un dólar?⟩ **4** STINT : escatimar ⟨they spared no expense : no repararon en gastos⟩ **5 to spare** : de sobra
spare[2] *adj* **1** : de repuesto, de recambio ⟨spare tire : llanta de repuesto⟩ **2** EXCESS : de más, de sobra ⟨spare time : tiempo libre⟩ **3** LEAN : delgado
spare[3] *n or* **spare part** : repuesto *m*, recambio *m*
sparing ['spærɪŋ] *adj* : parco, económico — **sparingly** *adv*
spark[1] ['spɑrk] *vi* : chispear, echar chispas — *vt* PROVOKE : despertar, provocar ⟨to spark interest : despertar interés⟩
spark[2] *n* **1** : chispa *f* ⟨to throw off sparks : echar chispas⟩ **2** GLIMMER, TRACE : destello *m*, pizca *f*
sparkle[1] ['spɑrkəl] *vi* **-kled; -kling 1** FLASH, SHINE : destellar, centellear, brillar **2** : estar muy animado (dícese de una conversación, etc.)
sparkle[2] *n* : destello *m*, centelleo *m*
sparkler ['spɑrklər] *n* : luz *f* de bengala
spark plug *n* : bujía *f*
sparrow ['spæro:] *n* : gorrión *m*
sparse ['spɑrs] *adj* **sparser; -est** : escaso — **sparsely** *adv*
spasm ['spæzəm] *n* **1** : espasmo *m* (muscular) **2** BURST, FIT : arrebato *m*
spasmodic [spæz'mɑdɪk] *adj* **1** : espasmódico **2** SPORADIC : irregular, esporádico — **spasmodically** [-dɪkli] *adv*
spastic ['spæstɪk] *adj* : espástico
spat[1] → **spit[1]**
spat[2] ['spæt] *n* : discusión *f*, disputa *f*, pelea *f*
spatial ['speɪʃəl] *adj* : espacial
spatter[1] ['spæt̮ər] *v* : salpicar
spatter[2] *n* : salpicadura *f*
spatula ['spætʃələ] *n* : espátula *f*, paleta *f* (para servir)
spawn[1] ['spɔn] *vi* : desovar, frezar — *vt* GENERATE : generar, producir
spawn[2] *n* : hueva *f*, freza *f*
spay ['speɪ] *vt* : esterilizar (una perra, etc.)
speak ['spi:k] *v* **spoke** ['spo:k]; **spoken** ['spo:kən]; **speaking** *vi* **1** TALK : hablar ⟨to speak to someone : hablar con alguien⟩ ⟨who's speaking? : ¿de parte de quien?⟩ ⟨so to speak : por así decirlo⟩ **2 to speak out** : hablar claramente **3 to speak out against** : denunciar **4 to speak up** : hablar en voz alta **5 to speak up for** : defender — *vt* **1** SAY : decir ⟨she spoke her mind : habló con franqueza⟩ **2** : hablar (un idioma)
speaker ['spi:kər] *n* **1** : hablante *mf* ⟨a native speaker : un hablante nativo⟩ **2** : orador *m*, -dora *f* ⟨the keynote speaker : el orador principal⟩ **3** LOUDSPEAKER : altavoz *m*, altoparlante *m*
spear[1] ['spɪr] *vt* : atravesar con una lanza
spear[2] *n* : lanza *f*
spearhead[1] ['spɪrˌhɛd] *vt* : encabezar
spearhead[2] *n* : punta *f* de lanza
spearmint ['spɪrmɪnt] *n* : menta *f* verde
special ['spɛʃəl] *adj* : especial ⟨nothing special : nada en especial, nada en particular⟩ — **specially** *adv*
specialist ['spɛʃəlɪst] *n* : especialista *mf*
specialization [ˌspɛʃələ'zeɪʃən] *n* : especialización *f*
specialize ['spɛʃəˌlaɪz] *vi* **-ized; -izing** : especializarse
specialty ['spɛʃəlt̮i] *n, pl* **-ties** : especialidad *f*
species ['spi:ˌʃi:z, -ˌsi:z] *ns & pl* : especie *f*
specific [spɪ'sɪfɪk] *adj* : específico, determinado — **specifically** [-fɪkli] *adv*
specification [ˌspɛsəfə'keɪʃən] *n* : especificación *f*
specify ['spɛsəˌfaɪ] *vt* **-fied; -fying** : especificar
specimen ['spɛsəmən] *n* **1** SAMPLE : espécimen *m*, muestra *f* **2** EXAMPLE : espécimen *m*, ejemplar *m*
speck ['spɛk] *n* **1** SPOT : manchita *f* **2** BIT, TRACE : mota *f*, pizca *f*, ápice *m*
speckled ['spɛkəld] *adj* : moteado

spectacle ['spɛktɪkəl] *n* **1** : espectáculo *m* **2 spectacles** *npl* GLASSES : lentes *fpl*, gafas *fpl*, anteojos *mpl*, espejuelos *mpl*

spectacular [spɛk'tækjələr] *adj* : espectacular

spectator ['spɛk,teɪṭər] *n* : espectador *m*, -dora *f*

specter *or* **spectre** ['spɛktər] *n* : espectro *m*, fantasma *m*

spectrum ['spɛktrəm] *n, pl* **spectra** [-trə] *or* **spectrums 1** : espectro *m* (de colores, etc.) **2** RANGE : gama *f*, abanico *m*

speculate ['spɛkjə,leɪt] *vi* **-lated; -lating 1** : especular (en finanzas) **2** WONDER : preguntarse, hacer conjeturas

speculation [,spɛkjə'leɪʃən] *n* : especulación *f*

speculative ['spɛkjə,leɪṭɪv] *adj* : especulativo

speculator ['spɛkjə,leɪṭər] *n* : especulador *m*, -dora *f*

speech ['spi:ʧ] *n* **1** : habla *f*, modo *m* de hablar, expresión *f* **2** ADDRESS : discurso *m*

speechless ['spi:ʧləs] *adj* : enmudecido, estupefacto

speed[1] ['spi:d] *v* **sped** ['spɛd] *or* **speeded; speeding** *vi* **1** : ir a toda velocidad, correr a toda prisa ⟨he sped off : se fue a toda velocidad⟩ **2** : conducir a exceso de velocidad ⟨a ticket for speeding : una multa por exceso de velocidad⟩ — *vt* **to speed up** : acelerar

speed[2] *n* **1** SWIFTNESS : rapidez *f* **2** VELOCITY : velocidad *f*

speedboat ['spi:d,bo:t] *n* : lancha *f* motora

speed bump *n* : badén *m*

speed limit *n* : velocidad *f* máxima, límite *m* de velocidad

speedometer [spɪ'dɑməṭər] *n* : velocímetro *m*

speedup ['spi:d,ʌp] *n* : aceleración *f*

speedy ['spi:di] *adj* **speedier; -est** : rápido — **speedily** [-dəli] *adv*

spell[1] ['spɛl] *vt* **1** : escribir, deletrear (verbalmente) ⟨how do you spell it? : ¿cómo se escribe?, ¿cómo se deletrea?⟩ **2** MEAN : significar ⟨that could spell trouble : eso puede significar problemas⟩ **3** RELIEVE : relevar

spell[2] *n* **1** TURN : turno *m* **2** PERIOD, TIME : período *m* (de tiempo) **3** ENCHANTMENT : encanto *m*, hechizo *m*, maleficio *m*

spellbound ['spɛl,baʊnd] *adj* : embelesado

speller ['spɛlər] *n* : persona *f* que escribe ⟨she's a good speller : tiene buena ortografía⟩

spelling ['spɛlɪŋ] *n* : ortografía *f*

spend ['spɛnd] *vt* **spent** ['spɛnt]; **spending 1** : gastar (dinero, etc.) **2** PASS : pasar (el tiempo) ⟨to spend time on : dedicar tiempo a⟩

spendthrift ['spɛnd,θrɪft] *n* : derrochador *m*, -dora *f*; despilfarrador *m*, -dora *f*

sperm ['spərm] *n, pl* **sperm** *or* **sperms** : esperma *mf*

spew ['spju:] *vi* : salir a chorros — *vt* : vomitar, arrojar (lava, etc.)

sphere ['sfɪr] *n* : esfera *f*

spherical ['sfɪrɪkəl, 'sfɛr-] *adj* : esférico

spice[1] ['spaɪs] *vt* **spiced; spicing 1** SEASON : condimentar, sazonar **2** *or* **to spice up** : salpimentar, hacer más interesante

spice[2] *n* **1** : especia *f* **2** FLAVOR, INTEREST : sabor *m* ⟨the spice of life : la sal de la vida⟩

spick–and–span ['spɪkənd'spæn] *adj* : limpio y ordenado

spicy ['spaɪsi] *adj* **spicier; -est 1** SPICED : condimentado, sazonado **2** HOT : picante **3** RACY : picante

spider ['spaɪdər] *n* : araña *f*

spigot ['spɪgət, -kət] *n* : llave *f*, grifo *m*, canilla *Arg, Uru*

spike[1] ['spaɪk] *vt* **spiked; spiking 1** FASTEN : clavar (con clavos grandes) **2** PIERCE : atravesar **3** : añadir alcohol a ⟨he spiked her drink with rum : le puso ron a la bebida⟩

spike[2] *n* **1** : clavo *m* grande **2** CLEAT : clavo *m* **3** : remache *m* (en voleibol) **4** PEAK : pico *m*

spill[1] ['spɪl] *vt* **1** SHED : derramar, verter ⟨to spill blood : derrame sangre⟩ **2** DIVULGE : revelar, divulgar — *vi* : derramarse

spill[2] *n* **1** SPILLING : derrame *m*, vertido *m* ⟨oil spill : derrame de petróleo⟩ **2** FALL : caída *f*

spin[1] ['spɪn] *v* **spun** ['spʌn]; **spinning** *vi* **1** : hilar **2** TURN : girar **3** REEL : dar vueltas ⟨my head is spinning : la cabeza me está dando vueltas⟩ — *vt* **1** : hilar (hilo, etc.) **2** : tejer ⟨to spin a web : tejer una telaraña⟩ **3** TWIRL : hacer girar

spin[2] *n* : vuelta *f*, giro *m* ⟨to go for a spin : dar una vuelta (en coche)⟩

spinach ['spɪnɪʧ] *n* : espinacas *fpl*, espinaca *f*

spinal column ['spaɪnəl] *n* BACKBONE : columna *f* vertebral

spinal cord *n* : médula *f* espinal

spindle ['spɪndəl] *n* **1** : huso *m* (para hilar) **2** : eje *m* (de un mecanismo)

spindly ['spɪndli] *adj* : larguirucho *fam*, largo y débil (dícese de una planta)

spine ['spaɪn] *n* **1** BACKBONE : columna *f* vertebral, espina *f* dorsal **2** QUILL : púa *f* (de un animal) **3** THORN : espina *f* **4** : lomo *m* (de un libro)

spineless ['spaɪnləs] *adj* **1** : sin púas, sin espinas **2** INVERTEBRATE : invertebrado **3** WEAK : débil (de carácter)

spinet ['spɪnət] *n* : espineta *f*

spinster ['spɪntstər] *n* : soltera *f*

spiny ['spaɪni] *adj* **spinier; -est** : con púas (dícese de los animales), espinoso (dícese de las plantas)

spiral[1] [ˈspaɪrəl] *vi* **-raled** *or* **-ralled; -raling** *or* **-ralling** : ir en espiral
spiral[2] *adj* : espiral, en espiral ⟨a spiral staircase : una escalera de caracol⟩
spiral[3] *n* : espiral *f*
spire [ˈspaɪr] *n* : aguja *f*
spirit[1] [ˈspɪrət] *vt* **to spirit away** : hacer desaparecer
spirit[2] *n* **1** : espíritu *m* ⟨body and spirit : cuerpo y espíritu⟩ **2** GHOST : espíritu *m*, fantasma *m* **3** MOOD : espíritu *m*, humor *m* ⟨in the spirit of friendship : en el espíritu de amistad⟩ ⟨to be in good spirits : estar de buen humor⟩ **4** ENTHUSIASM, VIVACITY : espíritu *m*, ánimo *m*, brío *m* **5 spirits** *npl* : licores *mpl*
spirited [ˈspɪrət̬əd] *adj* : animado, energético
spiritless [ˈspɪrətləs] *adj* : desanimado
spiritual[1] [ˈspɪrɪʧʊəl, -ʧəl] *adj* : espiritual — **spiritually** *adv*
spiritual[2] *n* : espiritual *m* (canción)
spiritualism [ˈspɪrɪʧʊəˌlɪzəm, -ʧə-] *n* : espiritismo *m*
spirituality [ˌspɪrɪʧʊˈæləṭi] *n, pl* **-ties** : espiritualidad *f*
spit[1] [ˈspɪt] *v* **spit** *or* **spat** [ˈspæt]; **spitting** : escupir
spit[2] *n* **1** SALIVA : saliva *f* **2** ROTISSERIE : asador *m* **3** POINT : lengua *f* (de tierra)
spite[1] [ˈspaɪt] *vt* **spited; spiting** : fastidiar, molestar
spite[2] *n* **1** : despecho *m*, rencor *m* **2 in spite of** : a pesar de (que), pese a (que)
spiteful [ˈspaɪtfəl] *adj* : malicioso, rencoroso
spitting image *n* **to be the spitting image of** : ser el vivo retrato de
spittle [ˈspɪṭəl] *n* : saliva *f*
splash[1] [ˈsplæʃ] *vt* : salpicar — *vi* **1** : salpicar **2 to splash around** : chapotear
splash[2] *n* **1** SPLASHING : salpicadura *f* **2** SQUIRT : chorrito *m* **3** SPOT : mancha *f*
splatter [ˈsplæṭər] → **spatter**
splay [ˈspleɪ] *vt* : extender (hacia afuera) ⟨to splay one's fingers : abrir los dedos⟩ — *vi* : extenderse (hacia afuera)
spleen [ˈspliːn] *n* **1** : bazo *m* (órgano) **2** ANGER, SPITE : ira *f*, rencor *m*
splendid [ˈsplɛndəd] *adj* : espléndido — **splendidly** *adv*
splendor [ˈsplɛndər] *n* : esplendor *m*
splice[1] [ˈsplaɪs] *vt* **spliced; splicing** : empalmar, unir
splice[2] *n* : empalme *m*, unión *f*
splint [ˈsplɪnt] *n* : tablilla *f*
splinter[1] [ˈsplɪntər] *vt* : astillar — *vi* : astillarse
splinter[2] *n* : astilla *f*
split[1] [ˈsplɪt] *v* **split; splitting** *vt* **1** CLEAVE : partir, hender ⟨to split wood : partir madera⟩ **2** BURST : romper, rajar ⟨to split open : abrir⟩ **3** DIVIDE, SHARE : dividir, repartir — *vi* **1** : partirse (dícese de la madera, etc.) **2** BURST, CRACK : romperse, rajarse **3** *or* **to split up** : dividirse
split[2] *n* **1** CRACK : rajadura *f* **2** TEAR : rotura *f* **3** DIVISION : división *f*, escisión *f*
splurge[1] [ˈsplərʤ] *v* **splurged; splurging** *vt* : derrochar — *vi* : derrochar dinero
splurge[2] *n* : derroche *m*
spoil[1] [ˈspɔɪl] *vt* **1** PILLAGE : saquear **2** RUIN : estropear, arruinar **3** PAMPER : consentir, mimar — *vi* : estropearse, echarse a perder
spoil[2] *n* PLUNDER : botín *m*
spoke[1] → **speak**
spoke[2] [ˈspoːk] *n* : rayo *m* (de una rueda)
spoken → **speak**
spokesman [ˈspoːksmən] *n, pl* **-men** [-mən, -ˌmɛn] : portavoz *mf*; vocero *m*, -ra *f*
spokeswoman [ˈspoːksˌwʊmən] *n, pl* **-women** [-ˌwɪmən] : portavoz *f*, vocera *f*
sponge[1] [ˈspʌnʤ] *vt* **sponged; sponging** : limpiar con una esponja
sponge[2] *n* : esponja *f*
spongy [ˈspʌnʤi] *adj* **spongier; -est** : esponjoso
sponsor[1] [ˈspɑntsər] *vt* : patrocinar, auspiciar, apadrinar (a una persona)
sponsor[2] *n* : patrocinador *m*, -dora *f*; padrino *m*, madrina *f*
sponsorship [ˈspɑntsərˌʃɪp] *n* : patrocinio *m*, apadrinamiento *m*
spontaneity [ˌspɑntəˈniːəṭi, -ˈneɪ-] *n* : espontaneidad *f*
spontaneous [spɑnˈteɪniəs] *adj* : espontáneo — **spontaneously** *adv*
spoof [ˈspuːf] *n* : burla *f*, parodia *f*
spook[1] [ˈspuːk] *vt* : asustar
spook[2] *n* : fantasma *m*, espíritu *m*, espectro *m*
spooky [ˈspuːki] *adj* **spookier; -est** : que da miedo, espeluzante
spool [ˈspuːl] *n* : carrete *m*
spoon[1] [ˈspuːn] *vt* : comer, servir, o echar con cuchara
spoon[2] *n* : cuchara *f*
spoonful [ˈspuːnˌfʊl] *n* : cucharada *f* ⟨by the spoonful : a cucharadas⟩
spoor [ˈspʊr, ˈspor] *n* : rastro *m*, pista *f*
sporadic [spəˈrædɪk] *adj* : esporádico — **sporadically** [-dɪkli] *adv*
spore [ˈspor] *n* : espora *f*
sport[1] [ˈsport] *vi* FROLIC : retozar, juguetear — *vt* SHOW OFF : lucir, ostentar
sport[2] *n* **1** : deporte *m* ⟨outdoor sports : deportes al aire libre⟩ **2** JEST : broma *f* **3 to be a good sport** : tener espíritu deportivo
sporting [ˈsporṭɪŋ] *adj* : deportivo ⟨a sporting chance : buenas posibilidades⟩
sportsman [ˈsportsmən] *n, pl* **-men** [-mən, -ˌmɛn] : deportista *m*

sportsmanship [ˈsportsmən,ʃɪp] *n* : espíritu *m* deportivo, deportividad *f Spain*
sportswoman [ˈsports,wʊmən] *n, pl* **-women** [-,wɪmən] : deportista *f*
sporty [ˈsporṭi] *adj* **sportier; -est** : deportivo
spot[1] [ˈspɑt] *v* **spotted; spotting** *vt* **1** STAIN : manchar **2** RECOGNIZE, SEE : ver, reconocer ⟨to spot an error : descubrir un error⟩ — *vi* : mancharse
spot[2] *adj* : hecho al azar ⟨a spot check : un vistazo, un control aleatorio⟩
spot[3] *n* **1** STAIN : mancha *f* **2** DOT : punto *m* **3** PIMPLE : grano *m* ⟨to break out in spots : salirle granos a alguien⟩ **4** PREDICAMENT : apuro *m*, aprieto *m*, lío *m* ⟨in a tight spot : en apuros⟩ **5** PLACE : lugar *m*, sitio *m* ⟨to be on the spot : estar en el lugar⟩
spotless [ˈspɑtləs] *adj* : impecable, inmaculado — **spotlessly** *adv*
spotlight[1] [ˈspɑt,laɪt] *vt* **-lighted** *or* **-lit** [-,lɪt]; **-lighting 1** LIGHT : iluminar (con un reflector) **2** HIGHLIGHT : destacar, poner en relieve
spotlight[2] *n* **1** : reflector *m*, foco *m* **2 to be in the spotlight** : ser el centro de atención
spotty [ˈspɑṭi] *adj* **spottier; -est** : irregular, desigual
spouse [ˈspaʊs] *n* : cónyuge *mf*
spout[1] [ˈspaʊt] *vt* **1** : lanzar chorros de **2** DECLAIM : declamar — *vi* : salir a chorros
spout[2] *n* **1** : pico *m* (de una jarra, etc.) **2** STREAM : chorro *m*
sprain[1] [ˈspreɪn] *vt* : sufrir un esguince en
sprain[2] *n* : esguince *m*, torcedura *f*
sprawl[1] [ˈsprɔl] *vi* **1** LIE : tumbarse, echarse, despatarrarse **2** EXTEND : extenderse
sprawl[2] *n* **1** : postura *f* despatarrada **2** SPREAD : extensión *f*, expansión *f*
spray[1] [ˈspreɪ] *vt* : rociar (una superficie), pulverizar (un líquido)
spray[2] *n* **1** BOUQUET : ramillete *m* **2** MIST : rocío *m* **3** ATOMIZER : atomizador *m*, pulverizador *m*
spray gun *n* : pistola *f*
spread[1] [ˈsprɛd] *v* **spread; spreading** *vt* **1** *or* **to spread out** : desplegar, extender **2** SCATTER, STREW : esparcir **3** SMEAR : untar (mantequilla, etc.) **4** DISSEMINATE : difundir, sembrar, propagar — *vi* **1** : difundirse, correr, propagarse **2** EXTEND : extenderse
spread[2] *n* **1** EXTENSION : extensión *f*, difusión *f* (de noticias, etc.), propagación *f* (de enfermedades, etc.) **2** : colcha *f* (para una cama), mantel *m* (para una mesa) **3** PASTE : pasta *f* ⟨cheese spread : pasta de queso⟩
spreadsheet [ˈsprɛd,ʃiːt] *n* : hoja *f* de cálculo
spree [ˈspri] *n* **1** : acción *f* desenfrenada ⟨to go on a shopping spree : comprar como loco⟩ **2** BINGE : parranda *f*, juerga *f* ⟨on a spree : de parranda, de juerga⟩
sprig [ˈsprɪg] *n* : ramita *f*, ramito *m*
sprightly [ˈspraɪtli] *adj* **sprightlier; -est** : vivo, animado ⟨with a sprightly step : con paso ligero⟩
spring[1] [ˈsprɪŋ] *v* **sprang** [ˈspræŋ] *or* **sprung** [ˈsprʌŋ]; **sprung; springing** *vi* **1** LEAP : saltar **2** : mover rápidamente ⟨the lid sprang shut : la tapa se cerró de un golpe⟩ ⟨he sprang to his feet : se paró de un salto⟩ **3 to spring up** : brotar (dícese de las plantas), surgir **4 to spring from** : surgir de — *vt* **1** RELEASE : soltar (de repente) ⟨to spring the news on someone : sorprender a alguien con las noticias⟩ ⟨to spring a trap : hacer saltar una trampa⟩ **2** ACTIVATE : accionar (un mecanismo) **3 to spring a leak** : hacer agua
spring[2] *n* **1** SOURCE : fuente *f*, origen *m* **2** : manantial *m*, fuente *f* ⟨hot spring : fuente termal⟩ **3** : primavera *f* ⟨spring and summer : la primavera y el verano⟩ **4** : resorte *m*, muelle *m* (de metal, etc.) **5** LEAP : salto *m*, brinco *m* **6** RESILIENCE : elasticidad *f*
springboard [ˈsprɪŋ,bord] *n* : trampolín *m*
springtime [ˈsprɪŋ,taɪm] *n* : primavera *f*
springy [ˈsprɪŋi] *adj* **springier; -est 1** RESILIENT : elástico **2** LIVELY : enérgico
sprinkle[1] [ˈsprɪŋkəl] *vt* **-kled; -kling** : rociar (con agua), espolvorear (con azúcar, etc.), salpicar
sprinkle[2] *n* : llovizna *f*
sprinkler [ˈsprɪŋkələr] *n* : rociador *m*, aspersor *m*
sprint[1] [ˈsprɪnt] *vi* : echar la carrera, esprintar (en deportes)
sprint[2] *n* : esprint *m* (en deportes)
sprinter [ˈsprɪntər] *n* : esprínter *mf*
sprite [ˈspraɪt] *n* : hada *f*, elfo *m*
sprocket [ˈsprɑkət] *n* : diente *m* (de una rueda dentada)
sprout[1] [ˈspraʊt] *vi* : brotar
sprout[2] *n* : brote *m*, retoño *m*, vástago *m*
spruce[1] [ˈspruːs] *v* **spruced; sprucing** *vt* : arreglar — *vi or* **to spruce up** : arreglarse, acicalarse
spruce[2] *adj* **sprucer; sprucest** : pulcro, arreglado
spruce[3] *n* : picea *f* (árbol)
spry [ˈspraɪ] *adj* **sprier** *or* **spryer** [ˈspraɪər]; **spriest** *or* **spryest** [ˈspraɪəst] : ágil, activo
spun → **spin**
spunk [ˈspʌŋk] *n* : valor *m*, coraje *m*, agallas *fpl fam*
spunky [ˈspʌŋki] *adj* **spunkier; -est** : animoso, corajudo
spur[1] [ˈspər] *vt* **spurred; spurring** *or* **to spur on** : espolear (un caballo), motivar (a una persona, etc.)

spur[2] *n* **1** : espuela *f*, acicate *m* **2** STIMULUS : acicate *m* **3** : espolón *m* (de aves gallináceas)

spurious ['spjʊriəs] *adj* : espurio

spurn ['spərn] *vt* : desdeñar, rechazar

spurt[1] ['spərt] *vt* SQUIRT : lanzar un chorro de — *vi* SPOUT : salir a chorros

spurt[2] *n* **1** : actividad *f* repentina ⟨a spurt of energy : una explosión de energía⟩ ⟨to do in spurts : hacer por rachas⟩ **2** JET : chorro *m* (de agua, etc.)

sputter[1] ['spʌtər] *vi* **1** JABBER : farfullar **2** : chisporrotear (dícese de la grasa, etc.), petardear (dícese de un motor)

sputter[2] *n* **1** JABBER : farfulla *f* **2** : chisporroteo *m* (de grasa, etc.), petardeo *m* (de un motor)

spy[1] ['spaɪ] *v* **spied; spying** *vt* SEE : ver, divisar — *vi* : espiar ⟨to spy on someone : espiar a alguien⟩

spy[2] *n* : espía *mf*

squab ['skwɑb] *n, pl* **squabs** *or* **squab** : pichón *m*

squabble[1] ['skwɑbəl] *vi* **-bled; -bling** : reñir, pelearse, discutir

squabble[2] *n* : riña *f*, pelea *f*, discusión *f*

squad ['skwɑd] *n* : pelotón *m* (militar), brigada *f* (de policías), cuadrilla *f* (de obreros, etc.)

squadron ['skwɑdrən] *n* : escuadrón *m* (de militares), escuadrilla *f* (de aviones), escuadra *f* (de naves)

squalid ['skwɑlɪd] *adj* : miserable

squall ['skwɔl] *n* **1** : aguacero *m* tormentoso, chubasco *m* tormentoso **2** **snow squall** : tormenta *f* de nieve

squalor ['skwɑlər] *n* : miseria *f*

squander ['skwɑndər] *vt* : derrochar (dinero, etc.), desaprovechar (una oportunidad, etc.), desperdiciar (talentos, energías, etc.)

square[1] ['skwær] *vt* **squared; squaring** **1** : cuadrar **2** : elevar al cuadrado (en matemáticas) **3** CONFORM : conciliar (con), ajustar (con) **4** SETTLE : saldar (una cuenta) ⟨I squared it with him : lo arreglé con él⟩

square[2] *adj* **squarer; -est** **1** : cuadrado ⟨a square house : una casa cuadrada⟩ **2** RIGHT-ANGLED : a escuadra, en ángulo recto **3** : cuadrado (en matemáticas) ⟨a square mile : una milla cuadrada⟩ **4** HONEST : justo ⟨a square deal : un buen acuerdo⟩ ⟨fair and square : en buena lid⟩

square[3] *n* **1** : escuadra *f* (instrumento) **2** : cuadrado *m*, cuadro *m* ⟨to fold into squares : plegar en cuadrados⟩ **3** : plaza *f* (de una ciudad) **4** : cuadrado *m* (en matemáticas)

squarely ['skwærli] *adv* **1** EXACTLY : exactamente, directamente, justo **2** HONESTLY : honradamente, justamente

square root *n* : raíz *f* cuadrada

squash[1] ['skwɑʃ, 'skwɔʃ] *vt* **1** CRUSH : aplastar **2** SUPPRESS : acallar (protestas), sofocar (una rebelión)

squash[2] *n* **1** *pl* **squashes** *or* **squash** : calabaza *f* (vegetal) **2** *or* **squash racquets** : squash *m* (deporte)

squat[1] ['skwɑt] *vi* **squatted; squatting** **1** CROUCH : agacharse, ponerse en cuclillas **2** : ocupar un lugar sin derecho

squat[2] *adj* **squatter; squattest** : bajo y ancho, rechoncho *fam* (dícese de una persona)

squat[3] *n* **1** : posición *f* en cuclillas **2** : ocupación *f* ilegal (de un lugar)

squaw ['skwɔ] *n* : india *f* (norteamericana)

squawk[1] ['skwɔk] *vi* : graznar (dícese de las aves), chillar

squawk[2] *n* : graznido *m* (de un ave), chillido *m*

squeak[1] ['skwi:k] *vi* : chillar (dícese de un animal), chirriar (dícese de un objeto)

squeak[2] *n* : chillido *m*, chirrido *m*

squeaky ['skwi:ki] *adj* **squeakier; -est** : chirriante ⟨a squeaky voice : una voz chillona⟩

squeal[1] ['skwi:l] *vi* **1** : chillar (dícese de las personas o los animales), chirriar (dícese de los frenos, etc.) **2** PROTEST : quejarse

squeal[2] *n* **1** : chillido *m* (de una persona o un animal) **2** SCREECH : chirrido *m* (de frenos, etc.)

squeamish ['skwi:mɪʃ] *adj* : impresionable, sensible ⟨he's squeamish about cockroaches : las cucarachas le dan asco⟩

squeeze[1] ['skwi:z] *vt* **squeezed; squeezing** **1** PRESS : apretar, exprimir (naranjas, etc.) **2** EXTRACT : extraer (jugo, etc.)

squeeze[2] *n* : apretón *m*

squelch ['skwɛltʃ] *vt* : aplastar (una rebelión, etc.)

squid ['skwɪd] *n, pl* **squid** *or* **squids** : calamar *m*

squint[1] ['skwɪnt] *vi* : mirar con los ojos entornados

squint[2] *adj or* **squint–eyed** ['skwɪnt,aɪd] : bizco

squint[3] *n* : ojos *mpl* bizcos, bizquera *f*

squire ['skwaɪr] *n* : hacendado *m*, -da *f*; terrateniente *mf*

squirm ['skwərm] *vi* : retorcerse

squirrel ['skwərəl] *n* : ardilla *f*

squirt[1] ['skwərt] *vt* : lanzar un chorro de — *vi* SPURT : salir a chorros

squirt[2] *n* : chorrito *m*

stab[1] [stæb] *vt* **stabbed; stabbing** **1** KNIFE : acuchillar, apuñalar **2** STICK : clavar (con una aguja, etc.), golpear (con el dedo, etc.)

stab[2] *n* **1** : puñalada *f*, cuchillada *f* **2** JAB : pinchazo *m* (con una aguja, etc.), golpe *m* (con un dedo, etc.) **3** **to take a stab at** : intentar

stability [stə'bɪləti] *n, pl* **-ties** : estabilidad *f*

stabilize ['steɪbə,laɪz] *v* **-lized; -lizing** *vt* : estabilizar — *vi* : estabilizarse

stable[1] [ˈsteɪbəl] *vt* **-bled; -bling** : poner (ganado) en un establo, poner (caballos) en una caballeriza
stable[2] *adj* **-bler; -blest** **1** FIXED, STEADY : fijo, sólido, estable **2** LASTING : estable, perdurable ⟨a stable government : un gobierno estable⟩ **3** : estacionario (en medicina), equilibrado (en psicología)
stable[3] *n* : establo *m* (para ganado), caballeriza *f* o cuadra *f* (para caballos)
staccato [stəˈkɑt̬oː] *adj* : staccato
stack[1] [ˈstæk] *vt* **1** PILE : amontonar, apilar **2** COVER : cubrir, llenar ⟨he stacked the table with books : cubrió la mesa de libros⟩
stack[2] *n* **1** PILE : montón *m*, pila *f* **2** SMOKESTACK : chimenea *f*
stadium [ˈsteɪdiəm] *n, pl* **-dia** [-diə] *or* **-diums** : estadio *m*
staff[1] [ˈstæf] *vt* : proveer de personal
staff[2] *n, pl* **staffs** [ˈstæfs, stævz] *or* **staves** [ˈstævz, ˈsteɪvz] **1** : bastón *m* (de mando), báculo *m* (de obispo) **2** *pl* **staffs** PERSONNEL : personal *m* **3** *or* **stave** : pentagrama *m* (en música)
stag[1] [ˈstæg] *adv* : solo, sin pareja ⟨to go stag : ir solo⟩
stag[2] *adj* : sólo para hombres
stag[3] *n, pl* **stags** *or* **stag** : ciervo *m*, venado *m*
stage[1] [ˈsteɪʤ] *vt* **staged; staging** : poner en escena (una obra de teatro)
stage[2] *n* **1** PLATFORM : estrado *m*, tablado *m*, escenario *m* (de un teatro) **2** PHASE, STEP : fase *f*, etapa *f* ⟨stage of development : fase de desarrollo⟩ ⟨in stages : por etapas⟩ **3 the stage** : el teatro *m*
stagecoach [ˈsteɪʤˌkoːʧ] *n* : diligencia *f*
stagger[1] [ˈstægər] *vi* TOTTER : tambalearse — *vt* **1** ALTERNATE : alternar, escalonar (turnos de trabajo) **2** : hacer tambalear ⟨to be staggered by : quedarse estupefacto por⟩
stagger[2] *n* : tambaleo *m*
staggering [ˈstægərɪŋ] *adj* : asombroso
stagnant [ˈstægnənt] *adj* : estancado
stagnate [ˈstægˌneɪt] *vi* **-nated; -nating** : estancarse
staid [ˈsteɪd] *adj* : serio, sobrio
stain[1] [ˈsteɪn] *vt* **1** DISCOLOR : manchar **2** DYE : teñir (madera, etc.) **3** SULLY : manchar, empañar
stain[2] *n* **1** SPOT : mancha *f* **2** DYE : tinte *m*, tintura *f* **3** BLEMISH : mancha *f*, mácula *f*
stainless [ˈsteɪnləs] *adj* : sin mancha ⟨stainless steel : acero inoxidable⟩
stair [ˈstær] *n* **1** STEP : escalón *m*, peldaño *m* **2 stairs** *npl* : escalera *f*, escaleras *fpl*
staircase [ˈstærˌkeɪs] *n* : escalera *f*, escaleras *fpl*
stairway [ˈstærˌweɪ] *n* : escalera *f*, escaleras *fpl*
stake[1] [ˈsteɪk] *vt* **staked; staking** **1** : estacar, marcar con estacas (una propiedad) **2** BET : jugarse, apostar **3 to stake a claim to** : reclamar, reivindicar
stake[2] *n* **1** POST : estaca *f* **2** BET : apuesta *f* ⟨to be at stake : estar en juego⟩ **3** INTEREST, SHARE : interés *m*, participación *f*
stalactite [stəˈlækˌtaɪt] *n* : estalactita *f*
stalagmite [stəˈlægˌmaɪt] *n* : estalagmita *f*
stale [ˈsteɪl] *adj* **staler; stalest** : viejo ⟨stale bread : pan duro⟩ ⟨stale news : viejas noticias⟩
stalemate [ˈsteɪlˌmeɪt] *n* : punto *m* muerto, impasse *m*
stalk[1] [ˈstɔk] *vt* : acechar — *vi* : caminar rígidamente (por orgullo, ira, etc.)
stalk[2] *n* : tallo *m* (de una planta)
stall[1] [ˈstɔl] *vt* **1** : parar (un motor) **2** DELAY : entretener (a una persona), demorar — *vi* **1** : pararse (dícese de un motor) **2** DELAY : demorar, andar con rodeos
stall[2] *n* **1** : compartimiento *m* (de un establo) **2** : puesto *m* (en un mercado, etc.)
stallion [ˈstæljən] *n* : caballo *m* semental
stalwart [ˈstɔlwərt] *adj* **1** STRONG : fuerte ⟨a stalwart supporter : un firme partidario⟩ **2** BRAVE : valiente, valeroso
stamen [ˈsteɪmən] *n* : estambre *m*
stamina [ˈstæmənə] *n* : resistencia *f*
stammer[1] [ˈstæmər] *vi* : tartamudear, titubear
stammer[2] *n* : tartamudeo *m*, titubeo *m*
stamp[1] [ˈstæmp] *vt* **1** : pisotear (con los pies) ⟨to stamp one's feet : patear, dar una patada⟩ **2** IMPRESS, IMPRINT : sellar (una factura, etc.), acuñar (monedas) **3** : franquear, ponerle estampillas a (correo)
stamp[2] *n* **1** : sello *m* (para documentos, etc.) **2** DIE : cuño *m* (para monedas) **3** *or* **postage stamp** : sello *m*, estampilla *f*, timbre *m CA, Mex*
stampede[1] [stæmˈpiːd] *vi* **-peded; -peding** : salir en estampida
stampede[2] *n* : estampida *f*
stance [ˈstænts] *n* : postura *f*
stanch [ˈstɔnʧ, ˈstɑnʧ] *vt* : detener, estancar (un líquido)
stand[1] [ˈstænd] *v* **stood** [ˈstʊd]; **standing** *vi* **1** : estar de pie, estar parado ⟨I was standing on the corner : estaba parada en la esquina⟩ **2** *or* **to stand up** : levantarse, pararse, ponerse de pie **3** (*indicating a specified position or location*) ⟨they stand third in the country : ocupan el tercer lugar en el país⟩ ⟨the machines are standing idle : las máquinas están paradas⟩ **4** (*referring to an opinion*) ⟨how does he stand on the matter? : ¿cuál es su postura respecto al asunto?⟩ **5** BE : estar ⟨the house stands on a hill : la casa está en una colina⟩ **6** CONTINUE : seguir ⟨the order still stands : el mandato sigue vi-

gente⟩ — *vt* 1 PLACE, SET : poner, colocar ⟨he stood them in a row : los colocó en hilera⟩ 2 TOLERATE : aguantar, soportar ⟨he can't stand her : no la puede tragar⟩ 3 **to stand firm** : mantenerse firme 4 **to stand guard** : hacer la guardia

stand[2] *n* 1 RESISTANCE : resistencia *f* ⟨to make a stand against : resistir a⟩ 2 BOOTH, STALL : stand *m*, puesto *m*, kiosko *m* (para vender periódicos, etc) 3 BASE : pie *m*, base *f* 4 : grupo *m* (de árboles, etc.) 5 POSITION : posición *f*, postura *f* 6 **stands** *npl* GRANDSTAND : tribuna *f*

standard[1] [ˈstændərd] *adj* 1 ESTABLISHED : estándar, oficial ⟨standard measures : medidas oficiales⟩ ⟨standard English : el inglés estándar⟩ 2 NORMAL : normal, estándar, común 3 CLASSIC : estándar, clásico ⟨a standard work : una obra clásica⟩

standard[2] *n* 1 BANNER : estandarte *m* 2 CRITERION : criterio *m* 3 RULE : estándar *m*, norma *f*, regla *f* 4 LEVEL : nivel *m* ⟨standard of living : nivel de vida⟩ 5 SUPPORT : poste *m*, soporte *m*

standardization [ˌstændərdəˈzeɪʃən] *n* : estandarización *f*

standardize [ˈstændərˌdaɪz] *vt* **-ized; -izing** : estandarizar

standard time *n* : hora *f* oficial

stand by *vt* : atenerse a, cumplir con (una promesa, etc.) — *vi* 1 : mantenerse aparte ⟨to stand by and do nothing : mirar sin hacer nada⟩ 2 : estar preparado, estar listo (para un anuncio, un ataque, etc.)

stand for *vt* 1 REPRESENT : significar 2 PERMIT, TOLERATE : permitir, tolerar

standing [ˈstændɪŋ] *n* 1 POSITION, RANK : posición *f* 2 DURATION : duración *f*

stand out *vi* 1 : destacar(se) ⟨she stands out from the rest : se destaca entre los otros⟩ 2 **to stand out against** RESIST : oponerse a

standpoint [ˈstændˌpɔint] *n* : punto *m* de vista

standstill [ˈstændˌstɪl] *n* 1 STOP : detención *f*, paro *m* ⟨to come to a standstill : pararse⟩ 2 DEADLOCK : punto *m* muerto, impasse *m*

stand up *vt* : dejar plantado ⟨he stood me up again : otra vez me dejó plantado⟩ — *vi* 1 ENDURE : durar, resistir 2 **to stand up for** : defender 3 **to stand up to** : hacerle frente (a alguien)

stank → **stink**

stanza [ˈstænzə] *n* : estrofa *f*

staple[1] [ˈsteɪpəl] *vt* **-pled; -pling** : engrapar, grapar

staple[2] *adj* : principal, básico ⟨a staple food : un alimento básico⟩

staple[3] *n* 1 : producto *m* principal 2 : grapa *f* (para engrapar papeles)

stapler [ˈsteɪplər] *n* : engrapadora *f*, grapadora *f*

star[1] [ˈstɑr] *v* **starred; starring** *vt* 1 : marcar con una estrella o un asterisco 2 FEATURE : estar protagonizado por — *vi* : tener el papel principal ⟨to star in : protagonizar⟩

star[2] *n* : estrella *f*

starboard [ˈstɑrbərd] *n* : estribor *m*

starch[1] [ˈstɑrtʃ] *vt* : almidonar

starch[2] *n* : almidón *m*, fécula *f* (comida)

starchy [ˈstɑrtʃi] *adj* **starchier; -est** : lleno de almidón ⟨a starchy diet : una dieta feculenta⟩

stardom [ˈstɑrdəm] *n* : estrellato *m*

stare[1] [ˈstær] *vi* **stared; staring** : mirar fijamente

stare[2] *n* : mirada *f* fija

starfish [ˈstɑrˌfɪʃ] *n* : estrella *f* de mar

stark[1] [ˈstɑrk] *adv* : completamente ⟨stark raving mad : loco de remate⟩ ⟨stark naked : completamente desnudo⟩

stark[2] *adj* 1 ABSOLUTE : absoluto 2 BARREN, DESOLATE : desolado, desierto 3 BARE : desnudo 4 HARSH : severo, duro

starlight [ˈstɑrˌlaɪt] *n* : luz *f* de las estrellas

starling [ˈstɑrlɪŋ] *n* : estornino *m*

starry [ˈstɑri] *adj* **starrier; -est** : estrellado

start[1] [ˈstɑrt] *vi* 1 JUMP : levantarse de un salto, sobresaltarse, dar un respingo 2 BEGIN : empezar, comenzar 3 SET OUT : salir (de viaje, etc.) 4 : arrancar (dícese de un motor) — *vt* 1 BEGIN : empezar, comenzar, iniciar 2 CAUSE : provocar, causar 3 ESTABLISH : fundar, montar, establecer ⟨to start a business : montar un negocio⟩ 4 : arrancar, poner en marcha, encender ⟨to start the car : arrancar el motor⟩

start[2] *n* 1 JUMP : sobresalto *m*, respingo *m* 2 BEGINNING : principio *m*, comienzo *m* ⟨to get an early start : salir temprano⟩

starter [ˈstɑrt̬ər] *n* 1 : participante *mf* (en una carrera, etc.); jugador *m* titular, jugadora *f* titular (en beisbol, etc.) 2 APPETIZER : entremés *m*, aperitivo *m* 3 *or* **starter motor** : motor *m* de arranque

startle [ˈstɑrt̬əl] *vt* **-tled; -tling** : asustar, sobresaltar

start–up [ˈstɑrtˈʌp] *adj* : de puesta en marcha

starvation [stɑrˈveɪʃən] *n* : inanición *f*, hambre *f*

starve [ˈstɑrv] *v* **starved; starving** *vi* : morirse de hambre — *vt* : privar de comida

stash [ˈstæʃ] *vt* : esconder, guardar (en un lugar secreto)

stat [ˈstæt] → **statistic**

state[1] [ˈsteɪt] *vt* **stated; stating** 1 REPORT : puntualizar, exponer (los hechos, etc.) ⟨state your name : diga su nombre⟩ 2 ESTABLISH, FIX : establecer, fijar

state[2] *n* 1 CONDITION : estado *m*, condición *f* ⟨a liquid state : un estado líquido⟩ ⟨state of mind : estado de ánimo⟩

⟨in a bad state : en malas condiciones⟩ **2** NATION : estado *m*, nación *f* **3** : estado *m* (dentro de un país) ⟨the States : los Estados Unidos⟩
stateliness ['steɪtlinəs] *n* : majestuosidad *f*
stately ['steɪtli] *adj* **statelier; -est** : majestuoso
statement ['steɪtmənt] *n* **1** DECLARATION : declaración *f*, afirmación *f* **2** *or* **bank statement** : estado *m* de cuenta
stateroom ['steɪt,ru:m, -,rʊm] *n* : camarote *m*
statesman ['steɪtsmən] *n, pl* **-men** [-mən, -,mɛn] : estadista *mf*
static[1] ['stæṭɪk] *adj* : estático
static[2] *n* : estática *f*, interferencia *f*
station[1] ['steɪʃən] *vt* : apostar, estacionar
station[2] *n* **1** : estación *f* (de trenes, etc.) **2** RANK, STANDING : condición *f* (social) **3** : canal *m* (de televisión), estación *f* o emisora *f* (de radio) **4 police station** : comisaría *f* **5 fire station** : estación *f* de bomberos, cuartel *m* de bomberos
stationary ['steɪʃə,nɛri] *adj* **1** IMMOBILE : estacionario, inmovible **2** UNCHANGING : inmutable, inalterable
stationery ['steɪʃə,nɛri] *n* : papel *m* y sobres *mpl* (para correspondencia)
station wagon *n* : camioneta *f* ranchera, camioneta *f* guayín *Mex*
statistic [stə'tɪstɪk] *n* : estadística *f* ⟨according to statistics : según las estadísticas⟩
statistical [stə'tɪstɪkəl] *adj* : estadístico
statistician [,stætə'stɪʃən] *n* : estadístico *m*, -ca *f*
statue ['stæ,ʧu:] *n* : estatua *f*
statuesque [,stæʧʊ'ɛsk] *adj* : escultural
statuette [,stæʧʊ'ɛt] *n* : estatuilla *f*
stature ['stæʧər] *n* **1** HEIGHT : estatura *f*, talla *f* **2** PRESTIGE : talla *f*, prestigio *m*
status ['steɪṭəs, 'stæ-] *n* : condición *f*, situación *f*, estatus *m* (social) ⟨marital status : estado civil⟩
statute ['stæ,ʧu:t] *n* : ley *f*, estatuto *m*
staunch ['stɔnʧ] *adj* : acérrimo, incondicional, leal ⟨a staunch supporter : un partidario incondicional⟩ — **staunchly** *adv*
stave[1] ['steɪv] *vt* **staved** *or* **stove** ['sto:v]; **staving 1 to stave in** : romper **2 to stave off** : evitar (un ataque), prevenir (un problema)
stave[2] *n* : duela *f* (de un barril)
staves → **staff**
stay[1] ['steɪ] *vi* **1** REMAIN : quedarse, permanecer ⟨to stay in : quedarse en casa⟩ ⟨he stayed in the city : permaneció en la ciudad⟩ **2** CONTINUE : seguir, quedarse ⟨it stayed cloudy : siguió nublado⟩ ⟨to stay awake : mantenerse despierto⟩ **3** LODGE : hospedarse, alojarse (en un hotel, etc.) — *vt* **1** HALT : detener, suspender (una ejecución, etc.) **2 to stay the course** : aguantar hasta el final
stay[2] *n* **1** SOJOURN : estadía *f*, estancia *f*, permanencia *f* **2** SUSPENSION : suspensión *f* (de una sentencia) **3** SUPPORT : soporte *m*
stead ['stɛd] *n* **1** : lugar *m* ⟨she went in his stead : fue en su lugar⟩ **2 to stand (someone) in good stead** : ser muy útil a, servir de mucho a
steadfast ['stɛd,fæst] *adj* : firme, resuelto ⟨a steadfast friend : un fiel amigo⟩ ⟨a steadfast refusal : una negativa categórica⟩
steadily ['stɛdəli] *adv* **1** CONSTANTLY : continuamente, sin parar **2** FIRMLY : con firmeza **3** FIXEDLY : fijamente
steady[1] ['stɛdi] *v* **steadied; steadying** *vt* : sujetar ⟨she steadied herself : recobró el equilibrio⟩ — *vi* : estabilizarse
steady[2] *adj* **steadier; -est 1** FIRM, SURE : seguro, firme ⟨to have a steady hand : tener buen pulso⟩ **2** FIXED, REGULAR : fijo ⟨a steady income : ingresos fijos⟩ **3** CALM : tranquilo, ecuánime ⟨she has steady nerves : es imperturbable⟩ **4** DEPENDABLE : responsable, fiable **5** CONSTANT : constante
steak ['steɪk] *n* : bistec *m*, filete *m*, churrasco *m*, bife *m Arg, Chile, Uru*
steal ['sti:l] *v* **stole** ['sto:l]; **stolen** ['sto:lən]; **stealing** *vt* : robar, hurtar — *vi* **1** : robar, hurtar **2** : ir sigilosamente ⟨to steal away : escabullirse⟩
stealth ['stɛlθ] *n* : sigilo *m*
stealthily ['stɛlθəli] *adv* : furtivamente
stealthy ['stɛlθi] *adj* **stealthier; -est** : furtivo, sigiloso
steam[1] ['sti:m] *vi* : echar vapor ⟨to steam away : moverse echando vapor⟩ — *vt* **1** : cocer al vapor (en cocina) **2 to steam open** : abrir con vapor
steam[2] *n* **1** : vapor *m* **2 to let off steam** : desahogarse
steamboat ['sti:m,bo:t] → **steamship**
steam engine *n* : motor *m* de vapor
steamroller ['sti:m,ro:lər] *n* : apisonadora *f*
steamship ['sti:m,ʃɪp] *n* : vapor *m*, barco *m* de vapor
steamy ['sti:mi] *adj* **steamier; -est 1** : lleno de vapor **2** EROTIC : erótico ⟨a steamy romance : un tórrido romance⟩
steed ['sti:d] *n* : corcel *m*
steel[1] ['sti:l] *vt* **to steel oneself** : armarse de valor
steel[2] *adj* : de acero
steel[3] *n* : acero *m*
steely ['sti:li] *adj* **steelier; -est** : como acero ⟨a steely gaze : una mirada fría⟩ ⟨steely determination : determinación férrea⟩
steep[1] ['sti:p] *vt* : remojar, dejar (té, etc.) en infusión
steep[2] *adj* **1** : empinado, escarpado ⟨a steep cliff : un precipicio escarpado⟩ **2** CONSIDERABLE : considerable, marcado **3** EXCESSIVE : excesivo ⟨steep prices : precios muy altos⟩
steeple ['sti:pəl] *n* : aguja *f*, campanario *m*

steeplechase ['sti:pəl,ʧeɪs] *n* : carrera *f* de obstáculos

steeply ['sti:pli] *adv* : abruptamente

steer[1] ['stɪr] *vt* **1** : conducir (un coche), gobernar (un barco) **2** GUIDE : dirigir, guiar

steer[2] *n* : buey *m*

steering wheel *n* : volante *m*

stein ['staɪn] *n* : jarra *f* (para cerveza)

stellar ['stɛlər] *adj* : estelar

stem[1] ['stɛm] *v* **stemmed; stemming** *vt* : detener, contener, parar ⟨to stem the tide : detener el curso⟩ — *vi* **to stem from** : provenir de, ser el resultado de

stem[2] *n* : tallo *m* (de una planta)

stench ['stɛnʧ] *n* : hedor *m*, mal olor *m*

stencil[1] ['stɛntsəl] *vt* **-ciled** *or* **-cilled; -ciling** *or* **-cilling** : marcar utilizando una plantilla

stencil[2] *n* : plantilla *f* (para marcar)

stenographer [stə'nɑgrəfər] *n* : taquígrafo *m*, -fa *f*

stenographic [,stɛnə'græfɪk] *adj* : taquigráfico

stenography [stə'nɑgrəfi] *n* : taquigrafía *f*

step[1] ['stɛp] *vi* **stepped; stepping 1** : dar un paso ⟨step this way, please : pase por aquí, por favor⟩ ⟨he stepped outside : salió⟩ **2 to step on** : pisar

step[2] *n* **1** : paso *m* ⟨step by step : paso por paso⟩ **2** STAIR : escalón *m*, peldaño *m* **3** RUNG : escalón *m*, travesaño *m* **4** MEASURE, MOVE : medida *f*, paso *m* ⟨to take steps : tomar medidas⟩ **5** STRIDE : paso *m* ⟨with a quick step : con paso rápido⟩

stepbrother ['stɛp,brʌðər] *n* : hermanastro *m*

stepdaughter ['stɛp,dɔt̬ər] *n* : hijastra *f*

stepfather ['stɛp,fɑðər, -,fa-] *n* : padrastro *m*

stepladder ['stɛp,lædər] *n* : escalera *f* de tijera

stepmother ['stɛp,mʌðər] *n* : madrastra *f*

steppe ['stɛp] *n* : estepa *f*

stepping–stone ['stɛpɪŋ,sto:n] *n* : pasadera *f* (en un río, etc.), trampolín *m* (al éxito)

stepsister ['stɛp,sɪstər] *n* : hermanastra *f*

stepson ['stɛp,sʌn] *n* : hijastro *m*

step up *vt* INCREASE : aumentar

stereo[1] ['stɛri,o:, 'stɪr-] *adj* : estéreo

stereo[2] *n, pl* **stereos** : estéreo *m*

stereophonic [,stɛrio'fɑnɪk, ,stɪr-] *adj* : estereofónico

stereotype[1] ['stɛrio,taɪp, 'stɪr-] *vt* **-typed; -typing** : estereotipar

stereotype[2] *n* : estereotipo *m*

sterile ['stɛrəl] *adj* : estéril

sterility [stə'rɪlət̬i] *n* : esterilidad *f*

sterilization [,stɛrələ'zeɪʃən] *n* : esterilización *f*

sterilize ['stɛrə,laɪz] *vt* **-ized; -izing** : esterilizar

sterling ['stərlɪŋ] *adj* **1** : de ley ⟨sterling silver : plata de ley⟩ **2** EXCELLENT : excelente

stern[1] ['stərn] *adj* : severo, adusto — **sternly** *adv*

stern[2] *n* : popa *f*

sternness ['stərnnəs] *n* : severidad *f*

sternum ['stərnəm] *n, pl* **sternums** *or* **sterna** [-nə] : esternón *m*

stethoscope ['stɛθə,sko:p] *n* : estetoscopio *m*

stevedore ['sti:və,dor] *n* : estibador *m*, -dora *f*

stew[1] ['stu:, 'stju:] *vt* : estofar, guisar — *vi* **1** : cocer (dícese de la carne, etc.) **2** FRET : preocuparse

stew[2] *n* **1** : estofado *m*, guiso *m* **2 to be in a stew** : estar agitado

steward ['stu:ərd, 'stju:-] *n* **1** MANAGER : administrador *m* **2** : auxiliar *m* de vuelo (en un avión), camarero *m* (en un barco)

stewardess ['stu:ərdəs, 'stju:-] *n* **1** MANAGER : administradora *f* **2** : camarera *f* (en un barco) **3** : auxiliar *f* de vuelo, azafata *f*, aeromoza *f* (en un avión)

stick[1] ['stɪk] *v* **stuck** ['stʌk]; **sticking** *vt* **1** STAB : clavar **2** ATTACH : pegar **3** PUT : poner **4 to stick out** : sacar (la lengua, etc.), extender (la mano) — *vi* **1** ADHERE : pegarse, adherirse **2** JAM : atascarse **3 to stick around** : quedarse **4 to stick out** PROJECT : sobresalir (de una superficie), asomar (por detrás o debajo de algo) **5 to stick to** : no abandonar ⟨stick to your guns : manténgase firme⟩ **6 to stick up** : estar parado (dícese del pelo, etc.), sobresalir (de una superficie) **7 to stick with** : serle fiel a (una persona), seguir con (una cosa) ⟨I'll stick with what I know : prefiero lo conocido⟩

stick[2] *n* **1** BRANCH, TWIG : ramita *f* **2** : palo *m*, vara *f* ⟨a walking stick : un bastón⟩

sticker ['stɪkər] *n* : etiqueta *f* adhesiva

stickler ['stɪklər] *n* : persona *f* exigente ⟨to be a stickler for : insistir mucho en⟩

sticky ['stɪki] *adj* **stickier; -est 1** ADHESIVE : pegajoso, adhesivo **2** MUGGY : bochornoso **3** DIFFICULT : difícil

stiff ['stɪf] *adj* **1** RIGID : rígido, tieso ⟨a stiff dough : una masa firme⟩ **2** : agarrotado, entumecido ⟨stiff muscles : músculos entumecidos⟩ **3** STILTED : acartonado, poco natural **4** STRONG : fuerte (dícese del viento, etc.) **5** DIFFICULT, SEVERE : severo, difícil, duro

stiffen ['stɪfən] *vt* **1** STRENGTHEN : fortalecer, reforzar (tela, etc.) **2** : hacer más duro (un castigo, etc.) — *vi* **1** HARDEN : endurecerse **2** : entumecerse (dícese de los músculos)

stiffly ['stɪfli] *adv* **1** RIGIDLY : rígidamente **2** COLDLY : con frialdad

stiffness ['stɪfnəs] *n* **1** RIGIDITY : rigidez *f* **2** COLDNESS : frialdad *f* **3** SEVERITY : severidad *f*

stifle ['staɪfəl] *vt* **-fled; -fling** SMOTHER, SUPPRESS : sofocar, reprimir, contener ‹to stifle a yawn : reprimir un bostezo›

stigma ['stɪgmə] *n, pl* **stigmata** [stɪg'mɑt̬ə, 'stɪgmət̬ə] *or* **stigmas** : estigma *m*

stigmatize ['stɪgməˌtaɪz] *vt* **-tized; -tizing** : estigmatizar

stile ['staɪl] *n* : escalones *mpl* para cruzar un cerco

stiletto [stə'lɛˌt̬oː] *n, pl* **-tos** *or* **-toes** : estilete *m*

still[1] ['stɪl] *vt* CALM : pacificar, apaciguar — *vi* : pacificarse, apaciguarse

still[2] *adv* **1** QUIETLY : quieto ‹sit still! : ¡quédate quieto!› **2** : de todos modos, aún, todavía ‹she still lives there : aún vive allí› ‹it's still the same : sigue siendo lo mismo› **3** IN ANY CASE : de todos modos, aún así ‹he still has doubts : aún así le quedan dudas› ‹I still prefer that you stay : de todos modos prefiero que te quedes›

still[3] *adj* **1** MOTIONLESS : quieto, inmóvil **2** SILENT : callado

still[4] *n* **1** SILENCE : quietud *f*, calma *f* **2** : alambique *m* (para destilar alcohol)

stillborn ['stɪlˌbɔrn] *adj* : nacido muerto

stillness ['stɪlnəs] *n* : calma *f*, silencio *m*

stilt ['stɪlt] *n* : zanco *m*

stilted ['stɪltəd] *adj* : afectado, poco natural

stimulant ['stɪmjələnt] *n* : estimulante *m* — **stimulant** *adj*

stimulate ['stɪmjəˌleɪt] *vt* **-lated; -lating** : estimular

stimulation [ˌstɪmjə'leɪʃən] *n* **1** STIMULATING : estimulación *f* **2** STIMULUS : estímulo *m*

stimulus ['stɪmjələs] *n, pl* **-li** [-ˌlaɪ] **1** : estímulo *m* **2** INCENTIVE : acicate *m*

sting[1] ['stɪŋ] *v* **stung** ['stʌŋ]; **stinging** *vt* **1** : picar ‹a bee stung him : le picó una abeja› **2** HURT : hacer escocer (físicamente), herir (emocionalmente) — *vi* **1** : picar (dícese de las abejas, etc.) **2** SMART : escocer, arder

sting[2] *n* : picadura *f* (herida), escozor *m* (sensación)

stinger ['stɪŋər] *n* : aguijón *m* (de una abeja, etc.)

stinginess ['stɪndʒinəs] *n* : tacañería *f*

stingy ['stɪndʒi] *adj* **stingier; -est** **1** MISERLY : tacaño, avaro **2** PALTRY : mezquino, mísero

stink[1] ['stɪŋk] *vi* **stank** ['stæŋk] *or* **stunk** ['stʌŋk]; **stunk; stinking** : apestar, oler mal

stink[2] *n* : hedor *m*, mal olor *m*, peste *f*

stint[1] ['stɪnt] *vt* : escatimar ‹to stint oneself of : privarse de› — *vi* **to stint on** : escatimar

stint[2] *n* : período *m*

stipend ['staɪˌpɛnd, -pənd] *n* : estipendio *m*

stipulate ['stɪpjəˌleɪt] *vt* **-lated; -lating** : estipular

stipulation [ˌstɪpjə'leɪʃən] *n* : estipulación *f*

stir[1] ['stər] *v* **stirred; stirring** *vt* **1** AGITATE : mover, agitar **2** MIX : revolver, remover **3** INCITE : incitar, impulsar, motivar **4** *or* **to stir up** AROUSE : despertar (memorias, etc.), provocar (ira, etc.) — *vi* : moverse, agitarse

stir[2] *n* **1** MOTION : movimiento *m* **2** COMMOTION : revuelo *m*

stirrup ['stərəp, 'stɪr-] *n* : estribo *m*

stitch[1] ['stɪtʃ] *vt* : coser, bordar (para decorar) — *vi* : coser

stitch[2] *n* **1** : puntada *f* **2** TWINGE : punzada *f*, puntada *f*

stock[1] ['stɑk] *vt* : surtir, abastecer, vender — *vi* **to stock up** : abastecerse

stock[2] *n* **1** SUPPLY : reserva *f*, existencias *fpl* (en comercio) ‹to be out of stock : estar agotadas las existencias› **2** SECURITIES : acciones *fpl*, valores *mpl* **3** LIVESTOCK : ganado *m* **4** ANCESTRY : linaje *m*, estirpe *f* **5** BROTH : caldo *m* **6 to take stock** : evaluar

stockade [stɑ'keɪd] *n* : estacada *f*

stockbroker ['stɑkˌbroːkər] *n* : corredor *m*, -dora *f* de bolsa

stockholder ['stɑkˌhoːldər] *n* : accionista *mf*

stocking ['stɑkɪŋ] *n* : media *f* ‹a pair of stockings : unas medias›

stock market *n* : bolsa *f*

stockpile[1] ['stɑkˌpaɪl] *vt* **-piled; -piling** : acumular, almacenar

stockpile[2] *n* : reservas *fpl*

stocky ['stɑki] *adj* **stockier; -est** : robusto, fornido

stockyard ['stɑkˌjɑrd] *n* : corral *m*

stodgy ['stɑdʒi] *adj* **stodgier; -est** **1** DULL : aburrido, pesado **2** OLD-FASHIONED : anticuado

stoic[1] ['stoːɪk] *or* **stoical** [-ɪkəl] *adj* : estoico — **stoically** [-ɪkli] *adv*

stoic[2] *n* : estoico *m*, -ca *f*

stoicism ['stoːəˌsɪzəm] *n* : estoicismo *m*

stoke ['stoːk] *vt* **stoked; stoking** : atizar (un fuego), echarle carbón a (un horno)

stole[1] → **steal**

stole[2] ['stoːl] *n* : estola *f*

stolen → **steal**

stolid ['stɑlɪd] *adj* : impasible, imperturbable — **stolidly** *adv*

stomach[1] ['stʌmɪk] *vt* : aguantar, soportar

stomach[2] *n* **1** : estómago *m* **2** BELLY : vientre *m*, barriga *f*, panza *f* **3** DESIRE : ganas *fpl* ‹he had no stomach for a fight : no quería pelea›

stomachache ['stʌmɪkˌeɪk] *n* : dolor *m* de estómago

stomp ['stɑmp, 'stɔmp] *vt* : pisotear — *vi* : pisar fuerte

stone[1] ['stoːn] *vt* **stoned; stoning** : apedrear, lapidar

stone[2] *n* **1** : piedra *f* **2** PIT : hueso *m*, pepa *f* (de una fruta)

Stone Age *n* : Edad *f* de Piedra

stony [ˈsto:ni] *adj* **stonier; -est 1** ROCKY : pedregoso **2** UNFEELING : insensible, frío ⟨a stony stare : una mirada glacial⟩

stood → **stand**

stool [ˈstu:l] *n* **1** SEAT : taburete *m*, banco *m* **2** FOOTSTOOL : escabel *m* **3** FECES : deposición *f* de heces

stoop[1] [ˈstu:p] *vi* **1** CROUCH : agacharse **2 to stoop to** : rebajarse a

stoop[2] *n* **1** : espaldas *fpl* encorvadas ⟨to have a stoop : ser encorvado⟩ **2** : entrada *f* (de una casa)

stop[1] [ˈstɑp] *v* **stopped; stopping** *vt* **1** PLUG : tapar **2** PREVENT : impedir, evitar ⟨she stopped me from leaving : me impidió que saliera⟩ **3** HALT : parar, detener **4** CEASE : dejar de ⟨he stopped talking : dejó de hablar⟩ — *vi* **1** HALT : detenerse, parar **2** CEASE : cesar, terminar ⟨the rain won't stop : no deja de llover⟩ **3** STAY : quedarse ⟨she stopped with friends : se quedó en casa de unos amigos⟩ **4 to stop by** : visitar

stop[2] *n* **1** STOPPER : tapón *m* **2** HALT : parada *f*, alto *m* ⟨to come to a stop : pararse, detenerse⟩ ⟨to put a stop to : poner fin a⟩ **3** : parada *f* ⟨bus stop : parada de autobús⟩

stopgap [ˈstɑp,gæp] *n* : arreglo *m* provisorio

stoplight [ˈstɑp,laɪt] *n* : semáforo *m*

stoppage [ˈstɑpɪʤ] *n* : acto *m* de parar ⟨a work stoppage : un paro⟩

stopper [ˈstɑpər] *n* : tapón *m*

storage [ˈstorɪʤ] *n* : almacenamiento *m*, almacenaje *m*

storage battery *n* : acumulador *m*

store[1] [ˈstor] *vt* **stored; storing** : guardar, almacenar

store[2] *n* **1** RESERVE, SUPPLY : reserva *f* **2** SHOP : tienda *f* ⟨grocery store : tienda de comestibles⟩

storehouse [ˈstor,haʊs] *n* : almacén *m*, depósito *m*

storekeeper [ˈstor,ki:pər] *n* : tendero *m*, -ra *f*

storeroom [ˈstor,ru:m, -,rʊm] *n* : almacén *m*, depósito *m*

stork [ˈstɔrk] *n* : cigüeña *f*

storm[1] [ˈstɔrm] *vi* **1** : llover o nevar tormentosamente **2** RAGE : ponerse furioso, vociferar **3 to storm out** : salir echando pestes — *vt* ATTACK : asaltar

storm[2] *n* **1** : tormenta *f*, tempestad *f* **2** UPROAR : alboroto *m*, revuelo *m*, escándalo *m* ⟨a storm of abuse : un torrente de abusos⟩

stormy [ˈstɔrmi] *adj* **stormier; -est** : tormentoso

story [ˈstori] *n, pl* **stories 1** NARRATIVE : cuento *m*, relato *m* **2** ACCOUNT : historia *f*, relato *m* **3** : piso *m*, planta *f* (de un edificio) ⟨first story : planta baja⟩

stout [ˈstaʊt] *adj* **1** FIRM, RESOLUTE : firme, resuelto **2** STURDY : fuerte, robusto, sólido **3** FAT : corpulento, gordo

stove[1] [ˈsto:v] *n* : cocina *f* (para cocinar), estufa *f* (para calentar)

stove[2] → **stave[1]**

stow [ˈsto:] *vt* **1** STORE : poner, meter, guardar **2** LOAD : cargar — *vi* **to stow away** : viajar de polizón

stowaway [ˈsto:ə,weɪ] *n* : polizón *m*

straddle [ˈstrædəl] *vt* **-dled; -dling** : sentarse a horcajadas sobre

straggle [ˈstrægəl] *vi* **-gled; -gling** : rezagarse, quedarse atrás

straggler [ˈstrægələr] *n* : rezagado *m*, -da *f*

straight[1] [ˈstreɪt] *adv* **1** : derecho, directamente ⟨go straight, then turn right : sigue derecho, luego gira a la derecha⟩ **2** HONESTLY : honestamente ⟨to go straight : enmendarse⟩ **3** CLEARLY : con claridad **4** FRANKLY : francamente, con franqueza

straight[2] *adj* **1** : recto (dícese de las líneas, etc.), derecho (dícese de algo vertical), lacio (dícese del pelo) **2** HONEST, JUST : honesto, justo **3** NEAT, ORDERLY : arreglado, ordenado

straighten [ˈstreɪtən] *vt* **1** : enderezar, poner derecho **2 to straighten up** : arreglar, ordenar ⟨he straightened up the house : arregló la casa⟩

straightforward [streɪtˈfɔrwərd] *adj* **1** FRANK : franco, sincero **2** CLEAR, PRECISE : puro, simple, claro

straightway [ˈstreɪtˈweɪ, -,weɪ] *adv* : inmediatamente

strain[1] [ˈstreɪn] *vt* **1** EXERT : forzar (la vista, la voz) ⟨to strain oneself : hacer un gran esfuerzo⟩ **2** FILTER : colar, filtrar **3** INJURE : lastimarse, hacerse daño en ⟨to strain a muscle : sufrir un esguince⟩

strain[2] *n* **1** LINEAGE : linaje *m*, abolengo *m* **2** STREAK, TRACE : veta *f* **3** VARIETY : tipo *m*, variedad *f* **4** STRESS : tensión *f*, presión *f* **5** SPRAIN : esguince *m*, torcedura *f* (del tobillo, etc.) **6 strains** *npl* TUNE : melodía *f*, acordes *mpl*, compases *fpl*

strainer [ˈstreɪnər] *n* : colador *m*

strait [ˈstreɪt] *n* **1** : estrecho *m* **2 straits** *npl* DISTRESS : aprietos *mpl*, apuros *mpl* ⟨in dire straits : en serios aprietos⟩

straitened [ˈstreɪtənd] *adj* **in straitened circumstances** : en apuros económicos

strand[1] [ˈstrænd] *vt* **1** : varar **2 to be left stranded** : quedar(se) varado, quedar colgado ⟨they left me stranded : me dejaron abandonado⟩

strand[2] *n* **1** : hebra *f* (de hilo, etc.) ⟨a strand of hair : un pelo⟩ **2** BEACH : playa *f*

strange [ˈstreɪnʤ] *adj* **stranger; -est 1** QUEER, UNUSUAL : extraño, raro **2** UNFAMILIAR : desconocido, nuevo

strangely [ˈstreɪnʤli] *adv* ODDLY : de manera extraña ⟨to behave strangely : portarse de una manera rara⟩ ⟨strangely, he didn't call : curiosamente, no llamó⟩

strangeness ['streɪndʒnəs] *n* **1** ODDNESS : rareza *f* **2** UNFAMILIARITY : lo desconocido

stranger ['streɪndʒər] *n* : desconocido *m*, -da *f*; extraño *m*, -ña *f*

strangle ['stræŋgəl] *vt* **-gled; -gling** : estrangular

strangler ['stræŋglər] *n* : estrangulador *m*, -dora *f*

strap[1] ['stræp] *vt* **strapped; strapping 1** FASTEN : sujetar con una correa **2** FLOG : azotar (con una correa)

strap[2] *n* **1** : correa *f* **2 shoulder strap** : tirante *m*

strapless ['stræpləs] *n* : sin tirantes

strapping ['stræpɪŋ] *adj* : robusto, fornido

stratagem ['strætədʒəm, -ˌdʒɛm] *n* : estratagema *f*, artimaña *f*

strategic [strə'ti:dʒɪk] *adj* : estratégico

strategist ['strætədʒɪst] *n* : estratega *mf*

strategy ['strætədʒi] *n, pl* **-gies** : estrategia *f*

stratified ['strætəˌfaɪd] *adj* : estratificado

stratosphere ['strætəˌsfɪr] *n* : estratosfera *f*

stratospheric [ˌstrætə'sfɪrɪk, -'sfɛr-] *adj* : estratosférico

stratum ['streɪtəm, 'stræ-] *n, pl* **strata** [-tə] : estrato *m*, capa *f*

straw *n* **1** : paja *f* ⟨the last straw : el colmo⟩ **2** *or* **drinking straw** : pajita *f*, popote *m Mex*

strawberry ['strɔˌbɛri] *n, pl* **-ries** : fresa *f*

stray[1] ['streɪ] *vi* **1** WANDER : alejarse, extraviarse ⟨the cattle strayed away : el ganado se descarrió⟩ **2** DIGRESS : desviarse, divagar

stray[2] *adj* : perdido, callejero (dícese de un perro o un gato), descarriado (dícese del ganado)

stray[3] *n* : animal *m* perdido, animal *m* callejero

streak[1] ['stri:k] *vt* : hacer rayas en ⟨blue streaked with grey : azul veteado con gris⟩ — *vi* : ir como una flecha

streak[2] *n* **1** : raya *f*, veta *f* (en mármol, queso, etc.), mechón *m* (en el pelo) **2** : rayo *m* (de luz) **3** TRACE : veta *f* **4** : racha *f* ⟨a streak of luck : una racha de suerte⟩

stream[1] ['stri:m] *vi* : correr, salir a chorros ⟨tears streamed from his eyes : las lágrimas brotaban de sus ojos⟩ — *vt* : derramar, dejar correr ⟨to stream blood : derramar sangre⟩

stream[2] *n* **1** BROOK : arroyo *m*, riachuelo *m* **2** RIVER : río *m* **3** FLOW : corriente *f*, chorro *m*

streamer ['stri:mər] *n* **1** PENNANT : banderín *m* **2** RIBBON : serpentina *f* (de papel), cinta *f* (de tela)

streamlined ['stri:mˌlaɪnd] *adj* **1** : aerodinámico (dícese de los automóviles, etc.) **2** EFFICIENT : eficiente, racionalizado

street ['stri:t] *n* : calle *f*

streetcar ['stri:tˌkɑr] *n* : tranvía *m*

strength ['strɛŋkθ] *n* **1** POWER : fuerza *f* **2** SOLIDITY, TOUGHNESS : solidez *f*, resistencia *f*, dureza *f* **3** INTENSITY : intensidad *f* (de emociones, etc.), lo fuerte (de un sabor, etc.) **4** : punto *m* fuerte ⟨strengths and weaknesses : virtudes y defectos⟩ **5** NUMBER : número *m*, complemento *m* ⟨in full strength : en gran número⟩

strengthen ['strɛŋkθən] *vt* **1** : fortalecer (los músculos, el espíritu, etc.) **2** REINFORCE : reforzar **3** INTENSIFY : intensificar, redoblar (esfuerzos, etc.) — *vi* **1** : fortalecerse, hacerse más fuerte **2** INTENSIFY : intensificarse

strenuous ['strɛnjʊəs] *adj* **1** VIGOROUS : vigoroso, enérgico **2** ARDUOUS : duro, riguroso

strenuously ['strɛnjʊəsli] *adv* : vigorosamente, duro

stress[1] ['strɛs] *vt* **1** : someter a tensión (física) **2** EMPHASIZE : enfatizar, recalcar **3 to stress out** : estresar

stress[2] *n* **1** : tensión *f* (en un material) **2** EMPHASIS : énfasis *m*, acento *m* (en lingüística) **3** TENSION : tensión *f* (nerviosa), estrés *m*

stressful ['strɛsfəl] *adj* : estresante

stretch[1] ['strɛtʃ] *vt* **1** EXTEND : estirar, extender, desplegar (alas) **2 to stretch the truth** : forzar la verdad, exagerar — *vi* : estirarse

stretch[2] *n* **1** STRETCHING : extensión *f*, estiramiento *m* (de músculos) **2** ELASTICITY : elasticidad *f* **3** EXPANSE : tramo *m*, trecho *m* ⟨the home stretch : la recta final⟩ **4** PERIOD : período *m* (de tiempo)

stretcher ['strɛtʃər] *n* : camilla *f*

strew ['stru:] *vt* **strewed; strewed** *or* **strewn** ['stru:n]; **strewing 1** SCATTER : esparcir (semillas, etc.), desparramar (papeles, etc.) **2 to strew with** : cubrir de

stricken ['strɪkən] *adj* **stricken with** : aquejado de (una enfermedad), afligido por (tristeza, etc.)

strict ['strɪkt] *adj* : estricto — **strictly** *adv*

strictness ['strɪktnəs] *n* : severidad *f*, lo estricto

stricture ['strɪktʃər] *n* : crítica *f*, censura *f*

stride[1] ['straɪd] *vi* **strode** ['stro:d]; **stridden** ['strɪdən]; **striding** : ir dando trancos, ir dando zancadas

stride[2] *n* : tranco *m*, zancada *f*

strident ['straɪdənt] *adj* : estridente

strife ['straɪf] *n* : conflictos *mpl*, disensión *f*

strike[1] ['straɪk] *v* **struck** ['strʌk]; **striking** *vt* **1** HIT : golpear (a una persona) ⟨to strike a blow : pegar un golpe⟩ **2** DELETE : suprimir, tachar **3** COIN, MINT : acuñar (monedas) **4** : dar (la hora) **5** AFFLICT : sobrevenir ⟨he was stricken with a fever : le sobrevino una fiebre⟩ **6** IMPRESS : impresionar, parecer ⟨her voice struck me : su voz me impresionó⟩ ⟨it struck him as funny : le pareció chistoso⟩ **7** : encender (un fósforo) **8** FIND : descubrir (oro, petróleo) **9** ADOPT : adoptar (una pose, etc.) — *vi* **1** HIT : golpear ⟨to strike against : chocar contra⟩ **2** ATTACK : atacar **3** : declararse en huelga

strike[2] *n* **1** BLOW : golpe *m* **2** : huelga *f*, paro *m* ⟨to be on strike : estar en huelga⟩ **3** ATTACK : ataque *m*

strikebreaker [ˈstraɪkˌbreɪkər] *n* : rompehuelgas *mf*, esquirol *mf*

strike out *vi* **1** HEAD : salir (para) **2** : ser ponchado (en béisbol) ⟨the batter struck out : poncharon al bateador⟩

striker [ˈstraɪkər] *n* : huelguista *mf*

strike up *vt* START : entablar, empezar

striking [ˈstraɪkɪŋ] *adj* : notable, sorprendente, llamativo ⟨a striking beauty : una belleza imponente⟩ — **strikingly** *adv*

string[1] [ˈstrɪŋ] *vt* **strung** [ˈstrʌŋ]; **stringing** **1** THREAD : ensartar ⟨to string beads : ensartar cuentas⟩ **2** HANG : colgar (con un cordel)

string[2] *n* **1** : cordel *m*, cuerda *f* **2** SERIES : serie *f*, sarta *f* (de insultos, etc.) **3 strings** *npl* : cuerdas *fpl* (en música)

string bean *n* : judía *f*, ejote *m Mex*

stringent [ˈstrɪndʒənt] *adj* : estricto, severo

stringy [ˈstrɪŋi] *adj* **stringier; -est** : fibroso

strip[1] [ˈstrɪp] *v* **stripped; stripping** *vt* : quitar (ropa, pintura, etc.), desnudar, despojar — *vi* UNDRESS : desnudarse

strip[2] *n* : tira *f* ⟨a strip of land : una faja⟩

stripe[1] [ˈstraɪp] *vt* **striped** [ˈstraɪpt]; **striping** : marcar con rayas o listas

stripe[2] *n* **1** : raya *f*, lista *f* **2** BAND : franja *f*

striped [ˈstraɪpt, ˈstraɪpəd] *adj* : a rayas, de rayas, rayado, listado

strive [ˈstraɪv] *vi* **strove** [ˈstroːv]; **striven** [ˈstrɪvən] *or* **strived; striving** **1 to strive for** : luchar por lograr **2 to strive to** : esforzarse por

strobe [ˈstroːb] *or* **strobe light** *n* : luz *f* estroboscópica

strode → **stride**

stroke[1] [ˈstroːk] *vt* **stroked; stroking** : acariciar

stroke[2] *n* : golpe *m* ⟨a stroke of luck : un golpe de suerte⟩

stroll[1] [ˈstroːl] *vi* : pasear, pasearse, dar un paseo

stroll[2] *n* : paseo *m*

stroller [ˈstroːlər] *n* : cochecito *m* (para niños)

strong [ˈstrɔŋ] *adj* **1** : fuerte **2** HEALTHY : sano **3** ZEALOUS : ferviente

stronghold [ˈstrɔŋˌhoːld] *n* : fortaleza *f*, fuerte *m*, bastión *m* ⟨a cultural stronghold : un baluarte de la cultura⟩

strongly [ˈstrɔŋli] *adv* **1** POWERFULLY : fuerte, con fuerza **2** STURDILY : fuertemente, sólidamente **3** INTENSELY : intensamente, profundamente **4** WHOLEHEARTEDLY : totalmente

struck → **strike**[1]

structural [ˈstrʌktʃərəl] *adj* : estructural

structure[1] [ˈstrʌktʃər] *vt* **-tured; -turing** : estructurar

structure[2] *n* **1** BUILDING : construcción *f* **2** ARRANGEMENT, FRAMEWORK : estructura *f*

struggle[1] [ˈstrʌgəl] *vi* **-gled; -gling** **1** CONTEND : forcejear (físicamente), luchar, contender **2** : hacer con dificultad ⟨she struggled forward : avanzó con dificultad⟩

struggle[2] *n* : lucha *f*, pelea *f* (física)

strum [ˈstrʌm] *vt* **strummed; strumming** : rasguear

strung → **string**[1]

strut[1] [ˈstrʌt] *vi* **strutted; strutting** : pavonearse

strut[2] *n* **1** : pavoneo *m* ⟨he walked with a strut : se pavoneaba⟩ **2** : puntal *m* (en construcción, etc.)

strychnine [ˈstrɪkˌnaɪn, -nən, -ˌniːn] *n* : estricnina *f*

stub[1] [ˈstʌb] *vt* **stubbed; stubbing** **1 to stub one's toe** : darse en el dedo (del pie) **2 to stub out** : apagarse

stub[2] *n* : colilla *f* (de un cigarrillo), cabo *m* (de un lápiz, etc.), talón *m* (de un cheque)

stubble [ˈstʌbəl] *n* **1** : rastrojo *m* (de plantas) **2** BEARD : barba *f*

stubborn [ˈstʌbərn] *adj* **1** OBSTINATE : terco, obstinado, empecinado **2** PERSISTENT : pertinaz, persistente — **stubbornly** *adv*

stubbornness [ˈstʌbərnnəs] *n* **1** OBSTINACY : terquedad *f*, obstinación *f* **2** PERSISTENCE : persistencia *f*

stubby [ˈstʌbi] *adj* **stubbier; -est** : corto y grueso ⟨stubby fingers : dedos regordetes⟩

stucco [ˈstʌkoː] *n, pl* **stuccos** *or* **stuccoes** : estuco *m*

stuck → **stick**[1]

stuck–up [ˈstʌkˈʌp] *adj* : engreído, creído *fam*

stud[1] [ˈstʌd] *vt* **studded; studding** : tachonar, salpicar

stud[2] *n* **1** *or* **stud horse** : semental *m* **2** : montante *m* (en construcción) **3** HOBNAIL : tachuela *f*, tachón *m*

student [ˈstuːdənt, ˈstjuː-] *n* : estudiante *mf*; alumno *m*, -na *f* (de un colegio)

studied [ˈstʌdid] *adj* : intencionado, premeditado

studio [ˈstuːdiˌoː, ˈstjuː-] *n, pl* **studios** : estudio *m*

studious [ˈstuːdiəs, ˈstjuː-] *adj* : estudioso — **studiously** *adv*

study[1] [ˈstʌdi] *v* **studied; studying** **1** : estudiar **2** EXAMINE : examinar, estudiar

study[2] *n, pl* **studies** **1** STUDYING : estudio *m* **2** OFFICE : estudio *m*, gabinete *m* (en una casa) 3 RESEARCH : investigación *f*, estudio *m*

stuff[1] ['stʌf] *vt* : rellenar, llenar, atiborrar ⟨a stuffed toy : un juguete de peluche⟩

stuff[2] *n* 1 POSSESSIONS : cosas *fpl* 2 ESSENCE : esencia *f* 3 SUBSTANCE : cosa *f*, cosas *fpl* ⟨some sticky stuff : una cosa pegajosa⟩ ⟨she knows her stuff : es experta⟩

stuffing ['stʌfɪŋ] *n* : relleno *m*

stuffy ['stʌfi] *adj* **stuffier; -est** 1 CLOSE : viciado, cargado ⟨a stuffy room : una sala mal ventilada⟩ ⟨stuffy weather : tiempo bochornoso⟩ 2 : tapado (dícese de la nariz) 3 STODGY : pesado, aburrido

stumble[1] ['stʌmbəl] *vi* **-bled; -bling** 1 TRIP : tropezar, dar un traspié 2 FLOUNDER : quedarse sin saber qué hacer o decir 3 **to stumble across** *or* **to stumble upon** : dar con, tropezar con

stumble[2] *n* : tropezón *m*, traspié *m*

stump[1] ['stʌmp] *vt* : dejar perplejo ⟨to be stumped : no tener respuesta⟩

stump[2] *n* 1 : muñón *m* (de un brazo o una pierna) 2 *or* **tree stump** : cepa *f*, tocón *m* 3 STUB : cabo *m*

stun ['stʌn] *vt* **stunned; stunning** 1 : aturdir (con un golpe) 2 ASTONISH, SHOCK : dejar estupefacto, dejar atónito, aturdir

stung → **sting**[1]

stunk → **stink**[1]

stunning ['stʌnɪŋ] *adj* 1 ASTONISHING : asombroso, pasmoso, increíble 2 STRIKING : imponente, impresionante (dícese de la belleza)

stunt[1] ['stʌnt] *vt* : atrofiar

stunt[2] *n* : proeza *f* (acrobática)

stupefy ['stu:pəˌfaɪ, 'stju:-] *vt* **-fied; -fying** 1 : aturdir, atontar (con drogas, etc.) 2 AMAZE : dejar estupefacto, dejar atónito

stupendous [stʊ'pɛndəs, stjʊ-] *adj* 1 MARVELOUS : estupendo, maravilloso 2 TREMENDOUS : tremendo — **stupendously** *adv*

stupid ['stu:pəd, 'stju:-] *adj* 1 IDIOTIC, SILLY : tonto, bobo, estúpido 2 DULL, OBTUSE : lento, torpe, lerdo

stupidity [stʊ'pɪdəṭi, stjʊ-] *n* : tontería *f*, estupidez *f*

stupidly ['stu:pədli, 'stju:-] *adv* 1 IDIOTICALLY : estúpidamente, tontamente 2 DENSELY : torpemente

stupor ['stu:pər, 'stju:-] *n* : estupor *m*

sturdily ['stərdəli] *adv* : sólidamente

sturdiness ['stərdinəs] *n* : solidez *f* (de muebles, etc.), robustez *f* (de una persona)

sturdy ['stərdi] *adj* **sturdier; -est** : fuerte, robusto, sólido

sturgeon ['stərdʒən] *n* : esturión *m*

stutter[1] ['stʌṭər] *vi* : tartamudear

stutter[2] *n* STAMMER : tartamudeo *m*

sty ['staɪ] *n* 1 *pl* **sties** PIGPEN : chiquero *m*, pocilga *f* 2 *pl* **sties** *or* **styes** : orzuelo *m* (en el ojo)

style[1] ['staɪl] *vt* **styled; styling** 1 NAME : llamar 2 : peinar (pelo), diseñar (vestidos, etc.) ⟨carefully styled prose : prosa escrita con gran esmero⟩

style[2] *n* 1 : estilo *m* ⟨that's just his style : él es así⟩ ⟨to live in style : vivir a lo grande⟩ 2 FASHION : moda *f*

stylish ['staɪlɪʃ] *adj* : de moda, elegante, chic

stylishly ['staɪlɪʃli] *adv* : con estilo

stylishness ['staɪlɪʃnəs] *n* : estilo *m*

stylist ['staɪlɪst] *n* : estilista *mf*

stylize ['staɪˌlaɪz, 'staɪə-] *vt* : estilizar

stylus ['staɪləs] *n, pl* **styli** ['staɪˌlaɪ] 1 PEN : estilo *m* 2 NEEDLE : aguja *f* (de un tocadiscos)

stymie ['staɪmi] *vt* **-mied; -mieing** : obstaculizar

suave ['swɑv] *adj* : fino, urbano

sub[1] ['sʌb] *vi* **subbed; subbing** → **substitute**[1]

sub[2] *n* 1 → **substitute**[2] 2 → **submarine**

subcommittee ['sʌbkəˌmɪṭi] *n* : subcomité *m*

subconscious[1] [səb'kɑntʃəs] *adj* : subconsciente — **subconsciously** *adv*

subconscious[2] *n* : subconsciente *m*

subcontract [ˌsʌb'kɑnˌtrækt] *vt* : subcontratar

subculture ['sʌbˌkʌltʃər] *n* : subcultura *f*

subdivide [ˌsʌbdə'vaɪd, 'sʌbdəˌvaɪd] *vt* **-vided; -viding** : subdividir

subdivision ['sʌbdəˌvɪʒən] *n* : subdivisión *f*

subdue [səb'du:, -'dju:] *vt* **-dued; -duing** 1 OVERCOME : sojuzgar (a un enemigo), vencer, superar 2 CONTROL : dominar 3 SOFTEN : suavizar, atenuar (luz, etc.), moderar (lenguaje)

subgroup ['sʌbˌgru:p] *n* : subgrupo *m*

subhead ['sʌbˌhɛd] *or* **subheading** [-ˌhɛdɪŋ] *n* : subtítulo *m*

subject[1] [səb'dʒɛkt] *vt* 1 CONTROL, DOMINATE : controlar, dominar 2 : someter ⟨they subjected him to pressure : lo sometieron a presiones⟩

subject[2] ['sʌbdʒɪkt] *adj* 1 : subyugado, sometido ⟨a subject nation : una nación subyugada⟩ 2 PRONE : sujeto, propenso ⟨subject to colds : sujeto a resfriarse⟩ 3 **subject to** : sujeto a ⟨subject to congressional approval : sujeto a la aprobación del congreso⟩

subject[3] ['sʌbdʒɪkt] *n* 1 : súbdito *m*, -ta *f* (de un gobierno) 2 TOPIC : tema *m* 3 : sujeto *m* (en gramática)

subjection [səb'dʒɛkʃən] *n* : sometimiento *m*

subjective [səb'dʒɛktɪv] *adj* : subjetivo — **subjectively** *adv*

subjectivity [ˌsʌbˌdʒɛk'tɪvəṭi] *n* : subjetividad *f*

subjugate ['sʌbdʒɪˌgeɪt] *vt* **-gated; -gating** : subyugar, someter, sojuzgar

subjunctive [səb'ʤʌŋktɪv] *n* : subjuntivo *m* — **subjunctive** *adj*
sublet ['sʌb,lɛt] *vt* **-let; -letting** : subarrendar
sublime [sə'blaɪm] *adj* : sublime
sublimely [sə'blaɪmli] *adv* **1** : de manera sublime **2** UTTERLY : absolutamente, completamente
submarine[1] ['sʌbmə,ri:n, ,sʌbmə'-] *adj* : submarino
submarine[2] *n* : submarino *m*
submerge [səb'mərʤ] *v* **-merged; -merging** *vt* : sumergir — *vi* : sumergirse
submission [səb'mɪʃən] *n* **1** YIELDING : sumisión *f* **2** PRESENTATION : presentación *f*
submissive [səb'mɪsɪv] *adj* : sumiso, dócil
submit [səb'mɪt] *v* **-mitted; -mitting** *vi* YIELD : rendirse ⟨to submit to : someterse a⟩ — *vt* PRESENT : presentar
subnormal [,sʌb'nɔrməl] *adj* : por debajo de lo normal
subordinate[1] [sə'bɔrdən,eɪt] *vt* **-nated; -nating** : subordinar
subordinate[2] [sə'bɔrdənət] *adj* : subordinado ⟨a subordinate clause : una oración subordinada⟩
subordinate[3] *n* : subordinado *m*, -da *f*; subalterno *m*, -na *f*
subordination [sə,bɔrdən'eɪʃən] *n* : subordinación *f*
subpoena[1] [sə'pi:nə] *vt* **-naed; -naing** : citar
subpoena[2] *n* : citación *f*, citatorio *m*
subscribe [səb'skraɪb] *vi* **-scribed; -scribing** **1** : suscribirse (a una revista, etc.) **2 to subscribe to** : suscribir (una opinión, etc.), estar de acuerdo con
subscriber [səb'skraɪbər] *n* : suscriptor *m*, -tora *f* (de una revista, etc.); abonado *m*, -da *f* (de un servicio)
subscription [səb'skrɪpʃən] *n* : suscripción *f*
subsequent ['sʌbsɪkwənt, -sə,kwɛnt] *adj* : subsiguiente ⟨subsequent to : posterior a⟩
subsequently ['sʌb,sɪkwɛntli, -kwənt-] *adv* : posteriormente
subservient [səb'sərviənt] *adj* : servil
subside [səb'saɪd] *vi* **-sided; -siding** **1** SINK : hundirse, descender **2** ABATE : calmarse (dícese de las emociones), amainar (dícese del viento, etc.)
subsidiary[1] [səb'sɪdi,ɛri] *adj* : secundario
subsidiary[2] *n, pl* **-ries** : filial *f*, subsidiaria *f*
subsidize ['sʌbsə,daɪz] *vt* **-dized; -dizing** : subvencionar, subsidiar
subsidy ['sʌbsədi] *n, pl* **-dies** : subvención *f*, subsidio *m*
subsist [səb'sɪst] *vi* : subsistir, mantenerse, vivir
subsistence [səb'sɪstənts] *n* : subsistencia *f*
substance ['sʌbstənts] *n* **1** ESSENCE : sustancia *f*, esencia *f* **2** : sustancia *f* ⟨a toxic substance : una sustancia tóxica⟩ **3** WEALTH : riqueza *f* ⟨a woman of substance : una mujer acaudalada⟩
substandard [,sʌb'stændərd] *adj* : inferior, deficiente
substantial [səb'stænʧəl] *adj* **1** ABUNDANT : sustancioso ⟨a substantial meal : una comida sustanciosa⟩ **2** CONSIDERABLE : considerable, apreciable **3** SOLID, STURDY : sólido
substantially [səb'stænʧəli] *adv* : considerablemente
substantiate [səb'stænʧi,eɪt] *vt* **-ated; -ating** : confirmar, probar, justificar
substitute[1] ['sʌbstə,tu:t, -,tju:t] *v* **-tuted; -tuting** *vt* : sustituir — *vi* **to substitute for** : sustituir
substitute[2] *n* **1** : sustituto *m*, -ta *f*; suplente *mf* (persona) **2** : sucedáneo *m* ⟨sugar substitute : sucedáneo de azúcar⟩
substitute teacher *n* : profesor *m*, -sora *f* suplente
substitution [,sʌbstə'tu:ʃən, -'tju:-] *n* : sustitución *f*
subterfuge ['sʌbtər,fju:ʤ] *n* : subterfugio *m*
subterranean [,sʌbtə'reɪniən] *adj* : subterráneo
subtitle ['sʌb,taɪṭəl] *n* : subtítulo *m*
subtle ['sʌṭəl] *adj* **-tler; -tlest** **1** DELICATE, ELUSIVE : sutil, delicado **2** CLEVER : sutil, ingenioso
subtlety ['sʌṭəlti] *n, pl* **-ties** : sutileza *f*
subtly ['sʌṭəli] *adv* : sutilmente
subtotal ['sʌb,to:ṭəl] *n* : subtotal *m*
subtract [səb'trækt] *vt* : restar, sustraer
subtraction [səb'trækʃən] *n* : resta *f*, sustracción *f*
suburb ['sʌ,bərb] *n* : municipio *m* periférico, suburbio *m*
suburban [sə'bərbən] *adj* : de las afueras (de una ciudad), suburbano
subversion [səb'vərʒən] *n* : subversión *f*
subversive [səb'vərsɪv] *adj* : subversivo
subway ['sʌb,weɪ] *n* : metro *m*, subterráneo *m Arg, Uru*
succeed [sək'si:d] *vt* FOLLOW : suceder a — *vi* : tener éxito (dícese de las personas), dar resultado (dícese de los planes, etc.) ⟨she succeeded in finishing : logró terminar⟩
success [sək'sɛs] *n* : éxito *m*
successful [sək'sɛsfəl] *adj* : exitoso, logrado — **successfully** *adv*
succession [sək'sɛʃən] *n* : sucesión *f* ⟨in succesion : sucesivamente⟩
successive [sək'sɛsɪv] *adj* : sucesivo, consecutivo — **successively** *adv*
successor [sək'sɛsər] *n* : sucesor *m*, -sora *f*
succinct [sək'sɪŋkt, sə'sɪŋkt] *adj* : sucinto — **succinctly** *adv*
succor[1] ['sʌkər] *vt* : socorrer
succor[2] *n* : socorro *m*

succotash [ˈsʌkəˌtæʃ] *n* : guiso *m* de maíz y frijoles
succulent[1] [ˈsʌkjələnt] *adj* : suculento, jugoso
succulent[2] *n* : suculenta *f* (planta)
succumb [səˈkʌm] *vi* : sucumbir
such[1] [ˈsʌtʃ] *adv* **1** SO : tan ⟨such tall buildings : edificios tan grandes⟩ **2** VERY : muy ⟨he's not in such good shape : anda un poco mal⟩ **3 such that** : de tal manera que
such[2] *adj* : tal ⟨there's no such thing : no existe tal cosa⟩ ⟨in such cases : en tales casos⟩ ⟨animals such as cows and sheep : animales como vacas y ovejas⟩
such[3] *pron* **1** : tal ⟨such was the result : tal fue el resultado⟩ ⟨he's a child, and acts as such : es un niño, y se porta como tal⟩ **2** : algo o alguien semejante ⟨books, papers and such : libros, papeles y cosas por el estilo⟩
suck [ˈsʌk] *vi* **1** : chupar (por la boca), aspirar (dícese de las máquinas) **2** SUCKLE : mamar — *vt* : sorber (bebidas), chupar (dulces, etc.)
sucker [ˈsʌkər] *n* **1** : ventosa *f* (de un insecto, etc.) **2** : chupón *m* (de una planta) **3** → **lollipop** **4** FOOL : tonto *m*, -ta *f*; idiota *mf*
suckle [ˈsʌkəl] *v* **-led; -ling** *vt* : amamantar — *vi* : mamar
suckling [ˈsʌklɪŋ] *n* : lactante *mf*
sucrose [ˈsuːˌkroːs, -ˌkroːz] *n* : sacarosa *f*
suction [ˈsʌkʃən] *n* : succión *f*
Sudanese [ˌsuːdənˈiːz, -ˈiːs] *n* : sudanés *m*, -nesa *f* — **Sudanese** *adj*
sudden [ˈsʌdən] *adj* **1** : repentino, súbito ⟨all of a sudden : de pronto, de repente⟩ **2** UNEXPECTED : inesperado, improviso **3** ABRUPT, HASTY : precipitado, brusco
suddenly [ˈsʌdənli] *adv* **1** : de repente, de pronto **2** ABRUPTLY : bruscamente
suddenness [ˈsʌdənnəs] *n* **1** : lo repentino **2** ABRUPTNESS : brusquedad *f* **3** HASTINESS : lo precipitado
suds [ˈsʌdz] *npl* : espuma *f* (de jabón)
sue [ˈsuː] *v* **sued; suing** *vt* : demandar — *vi* **to sue for** : demandar por (daños, etc.)
suede [ˈsweɪd] *n* : ante *m*, gamuza *f*
suet [ˈsuːət] *n* : sebo *m*
suffer [ˈsʌfər] *vi* : sufrir — *vt* **1** : sufrir, padecer (dolores, etc.) **2** PERMIT : permitir, dejar
sufferer [ˈsʌfərər] *n* : persona que padece (una enfermedad, etc.)
suffering [ˈsʌfərɪŋ] *n* : sufrimiento *m*
suffice [səˈfaɪs] *vi* **-ficed; -ficing** : ser suficiente, bastar
sufficient [səˈfɪʃənt] *adj* : suficiente
sufficiently [səˈfɪʃəntli] *adv* : (lo) suficientemente, bastante
suffix [ˈsʌˌfɪks] *n* : sufijo *m*
suffocate [ˈsʌfəˌkeɪt] *v* **-cated; -cating** *vt* : asfixiar, ahogar — *vi* : asfixiarse, ahogarse
suffocation [ˌsʌfəˈkeɪʃən] *n* : asfixia *f*, ahogo *m*
suffrage [ˈsʌfrɪdʒ] *n* : sufragio *m*, derecho *m* al voto
suffuse [səˈfjuːz] *vt* **-fused; -fusing** : impregnar (de olores, etc.), bañar (de luz), teñir (de colores), llenar (de emociones)
sugar[1] [ˈʃʊgər] *vt* : azucarar
sugar[2] *n* : azúcar *mf*
sugarcane [ˈʃʊgərˌkeɪn] *n* : caña *f* de azúcar
sugary [ˈʃʊgəri] *adj* **1** : azucarado ⟨sugary desserts : postres azucarados⟩ **2** SACCHARINE : empalagoso
suggest [səgˈdʒɛst, sə-] *vt* **1** PROPOSE : sugerir **2** IMPLY : indicar, dar a entender
suggestible [səgˈdʒɛstəbəl, sə-] *adj* : influenciable
suggestion [səgˈdʒɛstʃən, sə-] *n* **1** PROPOSAL : sugerencia *f* **2** INDICATION : indicio *m* **3** INSINUATION : insinuación *f*
suggestive [səgˈdʒɛstɪv, sə-] *adj* : insinuante — **suggestively** *adv*
suicidal [ˌsuːəˈsaɪdəl] *adj* : suicida
suicide [ˈsuːəˌsaɪd] *n* **1** : suicidio *m* (acto) **2** : suicida *mf* (persona)
suit[1] [ˈsuːt] *vt* **1** ADAPT : adaptar **2** BEFIT : convenir a, ser apropiado a **3** BECOME : favorecer, quedarle bien (a alguien) ⟨the dress suits you : el vestido te queda bien⟩ **4** PLEASE : agradecer, satisfacer, convenirle bien (a alguien) ⟨does Friday suit you? : ¿le conviene el viernes?⟩ ⟨suit yourself! : ¡como quieras!⟩
suit[2] *n* **1** LAWSUIT : pleito *m*, litigio *m* **2** : traje *m* (ropa) **3** : palo *m* (de naipes)
suitability [ˌsuːṭəˈbɪləṭi] *n* : idoneidad *f*, lo apropiado
suitable [ˈsuːṭəbəl] *adj* : apropiado, idóneo — **suitably** [-bli] *adv*
suitcase [ˈsuːtˌkeɪs] *n* : maleta *f*, valija *f*, petaca *f Mex*
suite [ˈswiːt, *for 2 also* ˈsuːt] *n* **1** : suite *f* (de habitaciones) **2** SET : juego *m* (de muebles)
suitor [ˈsuːṭər] *n* : pretendiente *m*
sulfur [ˈsʌlfər] *n* : azufre *m*
sulfuric acid [ˌsʌlˈfjʊrɪk] *adj* : ácido *m* sulfúrico
sulfurous [ˌsʌlˈfjʊrəs, ˈsʌlfərəs, ˈsʌlfjə-] *adj* : sulfuroso
sulk[1] [ˈsʌlk] *vi* : estar de mal humor, enfurruñarse *fam*
sulk[2] *n* : mal humor *m*
sulky [ˈsʌlki] *adj* **sulkier; -est** : malhumorado, taimado *Chile*
sullen [ˈsʌlən] *adj* **1** MOROSE : hosco, taciturno **2** DREARY : sombrío, deprimente
sullenly [ˈsʌlənli] *adv* **1** MOROSELY : hoscamente **2** GLOOMILY : sombríamente
sully [ˈsʌli] *vt* **sullied; sullying** : manchar, empañar

sultan [ˈsʌltən] *n* : sultán *m*
sultry [ˈsʌltri] *adj* **sultrier; -est** **1** : bochornoso ⟨sultry weather : tiempo sofocante, tiempo bochornoso⟩ **2** SENSUAL : sensual, seductor
sum[1] [ˈsʌm] *vt* **summed; summing** **1** : sumar (números) **2** → **sum up**
sum[2] *n* **1** AMOUNT : suma *f*, cantidad *f* **2** TOTAL : suma *f*, total *f* **3** : suma *f*, adición *f* (en matemáticas)
sumac [ˈʃuːˌmæk, ˈsuː-] *n* : zumaque *m*
summarize [ˈsʌməˌraɪz] *v* **-rized; -rizing** : resumir, compendiar
summary[1] [ˈsʌməri] *adj* **1** CONCISE : breve, conciso **2** IMMEDIATE : inmediato ⟨a summary dismissal : un despido inmediato⟩
summary[2] *n, pl* **-ries** : resumen *m*, compendio *m*
summer [ˈsʌmər] *n* : verano *m*
summery [ˈsʌməri] *adj* : veraniego
summit [ˈsʌmət] *n* **1** : cumbre *f*, cima *f* (de una montaña) **2** *or* **summit conference** : cumbre *f*
summon [ˈsʌmən] *vt* **1** CALL : convocar (una reunión, etc.), llamar (a una persona) **2** : citar (en derecho) **3 to summon up** : armarse de (valor, etc.) ⟨to summon up one's strength : reunir fuerzas⟩
summons [ˈsʌmənz] *n, pl* **summonses** **1** SUBPOENA : citación *f*, citatorio *m Mex* **2** CALL : llamada *f*, llamamiento *m*
sumptuous [ˈsʌmptʃʊəs] *adj* : suntuoso
sum up *vt* **1** SUMMARIZE : resumir **2** EVALUATE : evaluar — *vi* : recapitular
sun[1] [ˈsʌn] *vt* **sunned; sunning** **1** : poner al sol **2 to sun oneself** : asolearse, tomar el sol
sun[2] *n* **1** : sol *m* **2** SUNSHINE : luz *f* del sol
sunbeam [ˈsʌnˌbiːm] *n* : rayo *m* de sol
sunblock [ˈsʌnˌblɑk] *n* : filtro *m* solar
sunburn[1] [ˈsʌnˌbərn] *vi* **-burned** [-ˌbərnd] *or* **-burnt** [-ˌbərnt]; **-burning** : quemarse por el sol
sunburn[2] [ˈsʌnˌbərn] *n* : quemadura *f* de sol
sundae [ˈsʌndi] *n* : sundae *m*
Sunday [ˈsʌnˌdeɪ, -di] *n* : domingo *m*
sundial [ˈsʌnˌdaɪl] *n* : reloj *m* de sol
sundown [ˈsʌnˌdaʊn] → **sunset**
sundries [ˈsʌndriz] *npl* : artículos *mpl* diversos
sundry [ˈsʌndri] *adj* : varios, diversos
sunflower [ˈsʌnˌflaʊər] *n* : girasol *m*, mirasol *m*
sung → **sing**
sunglasses [ˈsʌnˌglæsəz] *npl* : gafas *fpl* de sol, lentes *mpl* de sol
sunk → **sink[1]**
sunken [ˈsʌŋkən] *adj* : hundido
sunlight [ˈsʌnˌlaɪt] *n* : sol *m*, luz *f* del sol
sunny [ˈsʌni] *adj* **sunnier; -est** : soleado
sunrise [ˈsʌnˌraɪz] *n* : salida *f* del sol
sunscreen [ˈsʌnˌskriːn] *n* : filtro *m* solar
sunset [ˈsʌnˌsɛt] *n* : puesta *f* del sol
sunshine [ˈsʌnˌʃaɪn] *n* : sol *m*, luz *f* del sol
sunspot [ˈsʌnˌspɑt] *n* : mancha *f* solar
sunstroke [ˈsʌnˌstroːk] *n* : insolación *f*
suntan [ˈsʌnˌtæn] *n* : bronceado *m*
sup [ˈsʌp] *vi* **supped; supping** : cenar
super [ˈsuːpər] *adj* : súper ⟨super! : ¡fantástico!⟩
superabundance [ˌsuːpərəˈbʌndənts] *n* : superabundancia *f*
superb [sʊˈpərb] *adj* : magnífico, espléndido — **superbly** *adv*
supercilious [ˌsuːpərˈsɪliəs] *adj* : altivo, altanero, desdeñoso
supercomputer [ˈsuːpərkəmˌpjuːt̬ər] *n* : supercomputadora *f*
superficial [ˌsuːpərˈfɪʃəl] *adj* : superficial — **superficially** *adv*
superfluous [sʊˈpərflʊəs] *adj* : superfluo
superhighway [ˈsuːpərˌhaɪˌweɪ, ˌsuːpərˈ-] *n* : autopista *f*
superhuman [ˌsuːpərˈ*h*juːmən] *adj* **1** SUPERNATURAL : sobrenatural **2** HERCULEAN : sobrehumano
superimpose [ˌsuːpərɪmˈpoːz] *vt* **-posed; -posing** : superponer, sobreponer
superintend [ˌsuːpərɪnˈtɛnd] *vt* : supervisar
superintendent [ˌsuːpərɪnˈtɛndənt] *n* : portero *m*, -ra *f* (de un edificio); director *m*, -tora *f* (de una escuela, etc.); superintendente *mf* (de policía)
superior[1] [sʊˈpɪriər] *adj* **1** BETTER : superior **2** HAUGHTY : altivo, altanero
superior[2] *n* : superior *m*
superiority [sʊˌpɪriˈɔrət̬i] *n, pl* **-ties** : superioridad *f*
superlative[1] [sʊˈpərlət̬ɪv] *adj* **1** : superlativo (en gramática) **2** SUPREME : supremo **3** EXCELLENT : excelente, excepcional
superlative[2] *n* : superlativo *m*
supermarket [ˈsuːpərˌmɑrkət] *n* : supermercado *m*
supernatural [ˌsuːpərˈnætʃərəl] *adj* : sobrenatural
supernaturally [ˌsuːpərˈnætʃərəli] *adv* : de manera sobrenatural
superpower [ˈsuːpərˌpaʊər] *n* : superpotencia *f*
supersede [ˌsuːpərˈsiːd] *vt* **-seded; -seding** : suplantar, reemplazar, sustituir
supersonic [ˌsuːpərˈsɑnɪk] *adj* : supersónico
superstar [ˈsuːpərˌstɑr] *n* : superestrella *f*
superstition [ˌsuːpərˈstɪʃən] *n* : superstición *f*
superstitious [ˌsuːpərˈstɪʃəs] *adj* : supersticioso
superstructure [ˈsuːpərˌstrʌktʃər] *n* : superestructura *f*
supervise [ˈsuːpərˌvaɪz] *vt* **-vised; -vising** : supervisar, dirigir
supervision [ˌsuːpərˈvɪʒən] *n* : supervisión *f*, dirección *f*

supervisor [ˈsuːpərˌvaɪzər] *n* : supervisor *m*, -sora *f*
supervisory [ˌsuːpərˈvaɪzəri] *adj* : de supervisor
supine [sʊˈpaɪn] *adj* **1** : en decúbito supino, en decúbito dorsal **2** ABJECT, INDIFFERENT : indiferente, apático
supper [ˈsʌpər] *n* : cena *f*, comida *f*
supplant [səˈplænt] *vt* : suplantar
supple [ˈsʌpəl] *adj* **-pler; -plest** : flexible
supplement¹ [ˈsʌpləˌmɛnt] *vt* : complementar, completar
supplement² [ˈsʌpləmənt] *n* **1** : complemento *m* ⟨dietary supplement : complemento alimenticio⟩ **2** : suplemento *m* (de un libro o periódico)
supplementary [ˌsʌpləˈmɛntəri] *adj* : suplementario
supplicate [ˈsʌpləˌkeɪt] *v* **-cated; -cating** *vi* : rezar — *vt* : suplicar
supplier [səˈplaɪər] *n* : proveedor *m*, -dora *f*; abastecedor *m*, -dora *f*
supply¹ [səˈplaɪ] *vt* **-plied; -plying** : suministrar, proveer de, proporcionar
supply² *n, pl* **-plies** **1** PROVISION : provisión *f*, suministro *m* ⟨supply and demand : la oferta y la demanda⟩ **2** STOCK : reserva *f*, existencias *fpl* (de un negocio) **3 supplies** *npl* PROVISIONS : provisiones *fpl*, víveres *mpl*, despensa *f*
support¹ [səˈport] *vt* **1** BACK : apoyar, respaldar **2** MAINTAIN : mantener, sostener, sustentar **3** PROP UP : sostener, apoyar, apuntalar, soportar
support² *n* **1** : apoyo *m* (moral), ayuda *f* (económica) **2** PROP : soporte *m*, apoyo *m*
supporter [səˈportər] *n* : partidario *m*, -ria *f*
supportive [səˈportɪv] *adj* : que apoya ⟨his family is very supportive : su familia lo apoya mucho⟩
suppose [səˈpoːz] *vt* **-posed; -posing** **1** ASSUME : suponer, imaginarse **2** BELIEVE : suponer, creer **3 to be supposed to** : tener que, deber
supposed [səˈpoːzd, -ˈpoːzəd] *adj* : supuesto — **supposedly** [səˈpoːzədli] *adv*
supposition [ˌsʌpəˈzɪʃən] *n* : suposición *f*
suppository [səˈpɑzəˌtori] *n, pl* **-ries** : supositorio *m*
suppress [səˈprɛs] *vt* **1** SUBDUE : sofocar, suprimir, reprimir (una rebelión, etc.) **2** : suprimir, ocultar (información) **3** REPRESS : reprimir, contener ⟨to suppress a yawn : reprimir un bostezo⟩
suppression [səˈprɛʃən] *n* **1** SUBDUING : represión *f* **2** : supresión *f* (de información) **3** REPRESSION : represión *f*, inhibición *f*
supremacy [sʊˈprɛməsi] *n, pl* **-cies** : supremacía *f*
supreme [sʊˈpriːm] *adj* : supremo
Supreme Being *n* : Ser *m* Supremo
supremely [sʊˈpriːmli] *adv* : totalmente, sumamente
surcharge [ˈsərˌtʃɑrdʒ] *n* : recargo *m*
sure¹ [ˈʃʊr] *adv* **1** ALL RIGHT : por supuesto, claro **2** (*used as an intensifier*) ⟨it sure is hot! : ¡hace tanto calor!⟩ ⟨she sure is pretty! : ¡qué linda es!⟩
sure² *adj* **surer; -est** : seguro ⟨to be sure about something : estar seguro de algo⟩ ⟨a sure sign : una clara señal⟩ ⟨for sure : seguro, con seguridad⟩
surely [ˈʃʊrli] *adv* **1** CERTAINLY : seguramente **2** (*used as an intensifier*) ⟨you surely don't mean that! : ¡no me digas que estás hablando en serio!⟩
sureness [ˈʃʊrnəs] *n* : certeza *f*, seguridad *f*
surety [ˈʃʊrət̬i] *n, pl* **-ties** : fianza *f*, garantía *f*
surf [ˈsərf] *n* **1** WAVES : oleaje *m* **2** FOAM : espuma *f*
surface¹ [ˈsərfəs] *v* **-faced; -facing** *vi* : salir a la superficie — *vt* : revestir (una carretera)
surface² *n* **1** : superficie *f* **2 on the surface** : en apariencia
surfboard [ˈsərfˌbord] *n* : tabla *f* de surf, tabla *f* de surfing
surfeit [ˈsərfət] *n* : exceso *m*
surfer [ˈsərfər] *n* : surfista *mf*
surfing [ˈsərfɪŋ] *n* : surf *m*, surfing *m*
surge¹ [ˈsərdʒ] *vi* **surged; surging** **1** : hincharse (dícese del mar), levantarse (dícese de las olas) **2** SWARM : salir en tropel (dícese de la gente, etc.)
surge² *n* **1** : oleaje *m* (del mar), oleada *f* (de gente) **2** FLUSH : arranque *m*, arrebato *m* (de ira, etc.) **3** INCREASE : aumento *m* (súbito)
surgeon [ˈsərdʒən] *n* : cirujano *m*, -na *f*
surgery [ˈsərdʒəri] *n, pl* **-geries** : cirugía *f*
surgical [ˈsərdʒɪkəl] *adj* : quirúrgico — **surgically** [-kli] *adv*
surly [ˈsərli] *adj* **surlier; -est** : hosco, arisco
surmise¹ [sərˈmaɪz] *vt* **-mised; -mising** : conjeturar, suponer, concluir
surmise² *n* : conjetura *f*
surmount [sərˈmaʊnt] *vt* **1** OVERCOME : superar, vencer, salvar **2** CLIMB : escalar **3** CAP, TOP : coronar
surname [ˈsərˌneɪm] *n* : apellido *m*
surpass [sərˈpæs] *vt* : superar, exceder, rebasar, sobrepasar
surplus [ˈsərˌplʌs] *n* : excedente *m*, sobrante *m*, superávit *m* (de dinero)
surprise¹ [səˈpraɪz, sər-] *vt* **-prised; -prising** : sorprender
surprise² *n* : sorpresa *f* ⟨to take by surprise : sorprender⟩
surprising [səˈpraɪzɪŋ, sər-] *adj* : sorprendente — **surprisingly** *adv*
surrender¹ [səˈrɛndər] *vt* **1** : entregar, rendir **2 to surrender oneself** : entregarse — *vi* : rendirse
surrender² *n* : rendición *m* (de una ciudad, etc.), entrega *f* (de posesiones)

surreptitious [ˌsərəpˈtɪʃəs] *adj* : subrepticio — **surreptitiously** *adv*
surrogate [ˈsərəgət, -ˌgeɪt] *n* : sustituto *m*
surround [səˈraʊnd] *vt* : rodear
surroundings [səˈraʊndɪŋz] *npl* : ambiente *m*, entorno *m*
surveillance [sərˈveɪlənts, -ˈveɪljənts, -ˈveɪənts] *n* : vigilancia *f*
survey¹ [sərˈveɪ] *vt* **-veyed; -veying 1** : medir (un terreno) **2** EXAMINE : inspeccionar, examinar, revisar **3** POLL : hacer una encuesta de, sondear
survey² [ˈsərˌveɪ] *n, pl* **-veys 1** INSPECTION : inspección *f*, revisión *f* **2** : medición *f* (de un terreno) **3** POLL : encuesta *f*, sondeo *m*
surveyor [sərˈveɪər] *n* : agrimensor *m*, -sora *f*
survival [sərˈvaɪvəl] *n* : supervivencia *f*, sobrevivencia *f*
survive [sərˈvaɪv] *v* **-vived; -viving** *vi* : sobrevivir — *vt* OUTLIVE : sobrevivir a
survivor [sərˈvaɪvər] *n* : superviviente *mf*, sobreviviente *mf*
susceptibility [səˌsɛptəˈbɪləṭi] *n, pl* **-ties** : vulnerabilidad *f*, propensión *f* (a enfermedades, etc.)
susceptible [səˈsɛptəbəl] *adj* **1** VULNERABLE : vulnerabie, sensible ⟨susceptible to flattery : sensible a halagos⟩ **2** PRONE : propenso ⟨susceptible to colds : propenso a resfriarse⟩
suspect¹ [səˈspɛkt] *vt* **1** DISTRUST : dudar de **2** : sospechar (algo), sospechar de (una persona) **3** IMAGINE, THINK : imaginarse, creer
suspect² [ˈsʌsˌpɛkt, səˈspɛkt] *adj* : sospechoso, dudoso, cuestionable
suspect³ [ˈsʌsˌpɛkt] *n* : sospechoso *m*, -sa *f*
suspend [səˈspɛnd] *vt* : suspender
suspenders [səˈspɛndərz] *npl* : tirantes *mpl*
suspense [səˈspɛnts] *n* : incertidumbre *f*, suspenso *m* (en una película, etc.)
suspenseful [səˈspɛntsfəl] *adj* : de suspenso
suspension [səˈspɛntʃən] *n* : suspensión *f*
suspicion [səˈspɪʃən] *n* **1** : sospecha *f* **2** TRACE : pizca *f*, atisbo *m*
suspicious [səˈspɪʃəs] *adj* **1** QUESTIONABLE : sospechoso, dudoso **2** DISTRUSTFUL : suspicaz, desconfiado
suspiciously [səˈspɪʃəsli] *adv* : de modo sospechoso, con recelo
sustain [səˈsteɪn] *vt* **1** NOURISH : sustentar **2** PROLONG : sostener **3** SUFFER : sufrir **4** SUPPORT, UPHOLD : apoyar, respaldar, sostener
sustainable [səˈsteɪnəbəl] *adj* : sostenible
sustenance [ˈsʌstənənts] *n* **1** NOURISHMENT : sustento *m* **2** SUPPORT : sostén *m*
svelte [ˈsfɛlt] *adj* : esbelto
swab¹ [ˈswɑb] *vt* **swabbed; swabbing 1** CLEAN : lavar, limpiar **2** : aplicar a (con hisopo)
swab² *n or* **cotton swab** : hisopo *m* (para aplicar medicinas, etc.)
swaddle [ˈswɑdəl] *vt* **-dled; -dling** [ˈswɑdəlɪŋ] : envolver (en pañales)
swagger¹ [ˈswægər] *vi* : pavonearse
swagger² *n* : pavoneo *m*
swallow¹ [ˈswɑloː] *vt* **1** : tragar (comida, etc.) **2** ENGULF : tragarse, envolver **3** REPRESS : tragarse (insultos, etc.) — *vi* : tragar
swallow² *n* **1** : golondrina *f* (pájaro) **2** GULP : trago *m*
swam → **swim¹**
swamp¹ [ˈswɑmp] *vt* : inundar
swamp² *n* : pantano *m*, ciénaga *f*
swampy [ˈswɑmpi] *adj* **swampier; -est** : pantanoso, cenagoso
swan [ˈswɑn] *n* : cisne *f*
swap¹ [ˈswɑp] *vt* **swapped; swapping** : cambiar, intercambiar ⟨to swap places : cambiarse de sitio⟩
swap² *n* : cambio *m*, intercambio *m*
swarm¹ [ˈswɔrm] *vi* : enjambrar
swarm² *n* : enjambre *m*
swarthy [ˈswɔrði, -θi] *adj* **swarthier; -est** : moreno
swashbuckling [ˈswɑʃˌbʌklɪŋ] *adj* : de aventurero
swat¹ [ˈswɑt] *vt* **swatted; swatting** : aplastar (un insecto), darle una palmada (a alguien)
swat² *n* : palmada *f* (con la mano), golpe *m* (con un objeto)
swatch [ˈswɑtʃ] *n* : muestra *f*
swath [ˈswɑθ, ˈswɔθ] *or* **swathe** [ˈswɑð, ˈswɔð, ˈsweɪð] *n* : franja *f* (de grano segado)
swathe [ˈswɑð, ˈswɔð, ˈsweɪð] *vt* **swathed; swathing** : envolver
swatter [ˈswɑṭər] → **flyswatter**
sway¹ [ˈsweɪ] *vi* : balancearse, mecerse — *vt* INFLUENCE : influir en, convencer
sway² *n* **1** SWINGING : balanceo *m* **2** INFLUENCE : influjo *m*
swear [ˈswær] *v* **swore** [ˈswor]; **sworn** [ˈsworn]; **swearing** *vi* **1** VOW : jurar **2** CURSE : decir palabrotas — *vt* : jurar
swearword [ˈswærˌwərd] *n* : mala palabra *f*, palabrota *f*
sweat¹ [ˈswɛt] *vi* **sweat** *or* **sweated; sweating 1** PERSPIRE : sudar, transpirar **2** OOZE : rezumar **3 to sweat over** : sudar la gota gorda por
sweat² *n* : sudor *m*, transpiración *f*
sweater [ˈswɛṭər] *n* : suéter *m*
sweatshirt [ˈswɛtˌʃərt] *n* : sudadera *f*
sweaty [ˈswɛṭi] *adj* **sweatier; -est** : sudoroso, sudado, transpirado
Swede [ˈswiːd] *n* : sueco *m*, -ca *f*
Swedish¹ [ˈswiːdɪʃ] *adj* : sueco
Swedish² *n* **1** : sueco *m* (idioma) **2 the Swedish** *npl* : los suecos
sweep¹ [ˈswiːp] *v* **swept** [ˈswɛpt]; **sweeping** *vt* **1** : barrer (el suelo, etc.), limpiar (suciedad, etc.) ⟨he swept the books

aside : apartó los libros de un manotazo⟩ **2** *or* **to sweep through** : extenderse por (dícese del fuego, etc.), azotar (dícese de una tormenta) — *vi* **1** : barrer, limpiar **2** : extenderse (en una curva), describir una curva ⟨the sun swept across the sky : el sol describía una curva en el cielo⟩

sweep[2] *n* **1** : barrido *m*, barrida *f* (con una escoba) **2** : movimiento *m* circular **3** SCOPE : alcance *m*

sweeper [ˈswi:pər] *n* : barrendero *m*, -ra *f*

sweeping [ˈswi:pɪŋ] *adj* **1** WIDE : amplio (dícese de un movimiento) **2** EXTENSIVE : extenso, radical **3** INDISCRIMINATE : indiscriminado, demasiado general **4** OVERWHELMING : arrollador, aplastante

sweepstakes [ˈswi:pˌsteɪks] *ns & pl* **1** : carrera *f* (en que el ganador se lleva el premio entero) **2** LOTTERY : lotería *f*

sweet[1] [ˈswi:t] *adj* **1** : dulce ⟨sweet desserts : postres dulces⟩ **2** FRESH : fresco **3** : sin sal (dícese de la mantequilla, etc.) **4** PLEASANT : dulce, agradable **5** DEAR : querido

sweet[2] *n* : dulce *m*

sweeten [ˈswi:tən] *vt* : endulzar

sweetener [ˈswi:tənər] *n* : endulzante *m*

sweetheart [ˈswi:tˌhɑrt] *n* : novio *m*, -via *f* ⟨thanks, sweetheart : gracias, cariño⟩

sweetly [ˈswi:tli] *adv* : dulcemente

sweetness [ˈswi:tnəs] *n* : dulzura *f*

sweet potato *n* : batata *f*, boniato *m*

swell[1] [ˈswɛl] *vi* **swelled; swelled** *or* **swollen** [ˈswo:lən, ˈswʌl-]; **swelling 1** *or* **to swell up** : hincharse ⟨her ankle swelled : se le hinchó el tobillo⟩ **2** *or* **to swell out** : inflarse, hincharse (dícese de las velas, etc.) **3** INCREASE : aumentar, crecer

swell[2] *n* **1** : oleaje *m* (del mar) **2** → **swelling**

swelling [ˈswɛlɪŋ] *n* : hinchazón *f*

swelter [ˈswɛltər] *vi* : sofocarse de calor

swept → **sweep**[1]

swerve[1] [ˈswərv] *vi* **swerved; swerving** : virar bruscamente

swerve[2] *n* : viraje *m* brusco

swift[1] [ˈswɪft] *adj* **1** FAST : rápido, veloz **2** SUDDEN : repentino, súbito — **swiftly** *adv*

swift[2] *n* : vencejo *m* (pájaro)

swiftness [ˈswɪftnəs] *n* : rapidez *f*, velocidad *f*

swig[1] [ˈswɪg] *vi* **swigged; swigging** : tomar a tragos, beber a tragos

swig[2] *n* : trago *m*

swill[1] [ˈswɪl] *vt* : chupar, beber a tragos grandes

swill[2] *n* **1** SLOP : bazofia *f* **2** GARBAGE : basura *f*

swim[1] [ˈswɪm] *vi* **swam** [ˈswæm]; **swum** [ˈswʌm]; **swimming 1** : nadar **2** FLOAT : flotar **3** REEL : dar vueltas ⟨his head was swimming : la cabeza le daba vueltas⟩

swim[2] *n* : baño *m*, chapuzón *m* ⟨to go for a swim : ir a nadar⟩

swimmer [ˈswɪmər] *n* : nadador *m*, -dora *f*

swindle[1] [ˈswɪndəl] *vt* **-dled; -dling** : estafar, timar

swindle[2] *n* : estafa *f*, timo *m fam*

swindler [ˈswɪndələr] *n* : estafador *m*, -dora *f*; timador *m*, -dora *f*

swine [ˈswaɪn] *ns & pl* : cerdo *m*, -da *f*

swing[1] [ˈswɪŋ] *v* **swung** [ˈswʌŋ]; **swinging** *vt* **1** : describir una curva con ⟨he swung the ax at the tree : le dio al árbol con el hacha⟩ **2** : balancear (los brazos, etc.), hacer oscilar **3** SUSPEND : colgar — *vi* **1** SWAY : balancearse (dícese de los brazos, etc.), oscilar (dícese de un objeto), columpiarse, mecerse (en un columpio) **2** SWIVEL : girar (en un pivote) ⟨the door swung shut : la puerta se cerró⟩ **3** CHANGE : virar, cambiar (dícese de las opiniones, etc.)

swing[2] *n* **1** SWINGING : vaivén *m*, balanceo *m* **2** CHANGE, SHIFT : viraje *m*, movimiento *m* **3** : columpio *m* (para niños) **4 to take a swing at someone** : intentar pegarle a alguien

swipe[1] [ˈswaɪp] *vt* **swiped; swiping 1** STRIKE : dar, pegar (con un movimiento amplio) **2** WIPE : limpiar **3** STEAL : birlar *fam*, robar

swipe[2] *n* BLOW : golpe *m*

swirl[1] [ˈswərl] *vi* : arremolinarse

swirl[2] *n* **1** EDDY : remolino *m* **2** SPIRAL : espiral *f*

swish[1] [ˈswɪʃ] *vt* : mover (produciendo un sonido) ⟨she swished her skirt : movía la falda⟩ — *vi* : moverse (produciendo un sonido) ⟨the cars swished by : se oían pasar los coches⟩

swish[2] *n* : silbido *m* (de un látigo, etc.), susurro *m* (de agua), crujido *m* (de ropa, etc.)

Swiss [ˈswɪs] *n* : suizo *m*, -za *f* — **Swiss** *adj*

swiss chard *n* : acelga *f*

switch[1] [ˈswɪʧ] *vt* **1** LASH, WHIP : azotar **2** CHANGE : cambiar de **3** EXCHANGE : intercambiar **4 to switch on** : encender, prender **5 to switch off** : apagar — *vi* **1** : moverse de un lado al otro **2** CHANGE : cambiar **3** SWAP : intercambiarse

switch[2] *n* **1** WHIP : vara *f* **2** CHANGE, SHIFT : cambio *m* **3** : interruptor *m*, llave *f* (de la luz, etc.)

switchboard [ˈswɪʧˌbord] *n* : conmutador *m*, centralita *f*

swivel[1] [ˈswɪvəl] *vi* **-veled** *or* **-velled; -veling** *or* **-velling** : girar (sobre un pivote)

swivel[2] *n* : base *f* giratoria

swollen *pp* → **swell**[1]

swoon[1] [ˈswu:n] *vi* : desvanecerse, desmayarse

swoon[2] *n* : desvanecimiento *m*, desmayo *m*

swoop[1] [ˈswuːp] *vi* : abatirse (dícese de las aves), descender en picada (dícese de un avión)
swoop[2] *n* : descenso *m* en picada
sword [ˈsɔrd] *n* : espada *f*
swordfish [ˈsɔrdˌfɪʃ] *n* : pez *m* espada
swore, sworn → **swear**
swum *pp* → **swim**[1]
swung → **swing**[1]
sycamore [ˈsɪkəˌmor] *n* : sicomoro *m*
sycophant [ˈsɪkəfənt, -ˌfænt] *n* : adulador *m*, -dora *f*
syllabic [səˈlæbɪk] *adj* : silábico
syllable [ˈsɪləbəl] *n* : sílaba *f*
syllabus [ˈsɪləbəs] *n, pl* **-bi** [-ˌbaɪ] *or* **-buses** : programa *m* (de estudios)
symbol [ˈsɪmbəl] *n* : símbolo *m*
symbolic [sɪmˈbɑlɪk] *adj* : simbólico — **symbolically** [-kli] *adv*
symbolism [ˈsɪmbəˌlɪzəm] *n* : simbolismo *m*
symbolize [ˈsɪmbəˌlaɪz] *vt* **-ized; -izing** : simbolizar
symmetrical [səˈmɛtrɪkəl] *or* **symmetric** [-trɪk] *adj* : simétrico — **symmetrically** [-trɪkli] *adv*
symmetry [ˈsɪmətri] *n, pl* **-tries** : simetría *f*
sympathetic [ˌsɪmpəˈθɛt̬ɪk] *adj* **1** PLEASING : agradable **2** RECEPTIVE : receptivo, favorable **3** COMPASSIONATE, UNDERSTANDING : comprensivo, compasivo
sympathetically [ˌsɪmpəˈθɛt̬ɪkli] *adv* : con compasión, con comprensión
sympathize [ˈsɪmpəˌθaɪz] *vi* **-thized; -thizing** : compadecer ⟨I sympathize with you : te compadezco⟩
sympathy [ˈsɪmpəθi] *n, pl* **-thies** **1** COMPASSION : compasión *f* **2** UNDERSTANDING : comprensión *f* **3** AGREEMENT : solidaridad *f* ⟨in sympathy with : de acuerdo con⟩ **4** CONDOLENCES : pésame *m*, condolencias *fpl*
symphonic [sɪmˈfɑnɪk] *adj* : sinfónico
symphony [ˈsɪmpfəni] *n, pl* **-nies** : sinfonía *f*
symposium [sɪmˈpoːziəm] *n, pl* **-sia** [-ziə] *or* **-siums** : simposio *m*
symptom [ˈsɪmptəm] *n* : síntoma *m*
symptomatic [ˌsɪmptəˈmæt̬ɪk] *adj* : sintomático
synagogue [ˈsɪnəˌgɑg, -ˌgɔg] *n* : sinagoga *f*
sync [ˈsɪŋk] *n* : sincronización *f* ⟨in sync : sincronizado⟩
synchronize [ˈsɪŋkrəˌnaɪz, ˈsɪn-] *v* **-nized; -nizing** *vi* : estar sincronizado — *vt* : sincronizar
syncopate [ˈsɪŋkəˌpeɪt, ˈsɪn-] *vt* **-pated; -pating** : sincopar
syncopation [ˌsɪŋkəˈpeɪʃən, ˌsɪn-] *n* : síncopa *f*
syndicate[1] [ˈsɪndəˌkeɪt] *vi* **-cated; -cating** : formar una asociación
syndicate[2] [ˈsɪndɪkət] *n* : asociación *f*, agrupación *f*
syndrome [ˈsɪnˌdroːm] *n* : síndrome *m*
synonym [ˈsɪnəˌnɪm] *n* : sinónimo *m*
synonymous [səˈnɑnəməs] *adj* : sinónimo
synopsis [səˈnɑpsɪs] *n, pl* **-opses** [-ˌsiːz] : sinopsis *f*
syntactic [sɪnˈtæktɪk] *adj* : sintáctico
syntax [ˈsɪnˌtæks] *n* : sintaxis *f*
synthesis [ˈsɪnθəsɪs] *n, pl* **-theses** [-ˌsiːz] : síntesis *f*
synthesize [ˈsɪnθəˌsaɪz] *vt* **-sized; -sizing** : sintetizar
synthetic[1] [sɪnˈθt̬ɪk] *adj* : sintético, artificial — **synthetically** [-t̬ɪkli] *adv*
synthetic[2] *n* : producto *m* sintético
syphilis [ˈsɪfələs] *n* : sífilis *f*
Syrian [ˈsɪriən] *n* : sirio *m*, -ria *f* — **Syrian** *adj*
syringe [səˈrɪnʤ, ˈsɪrɪnʤ] *n* : jeringa *f*, jeringuilla *f*
syrup [ˈsərəp, ˈsɪrəp] *n* : jarabe *m*, almíbar *m* (de azúcar y agua)
system [ˈsɪstəm] *n* **1** METHOD : sistema *m*, método *m* **2** APPARATUS : sistema *m*, instalación *f*, aparato *m* ⟨electrical system : instalación eléctrica⟩ ⟨digestive system : aparato digestivo⟩ **3** BODY : organismo *m*, cuerpo *m* ⟨diseases that affect the whole system : enfermedades que afectan el organismo entero⟩ **4** NETWORK : red *f*
systematic [ˌsɪstəˈmæt̬ɪk] *adj* : sistemático — **systematically** [-t̬ɪkli] *adv*
systematize [ˈsɪstəməˌtaɪz] *vt* **-tized; -tizing** : sistematizar
systemic [sɪsˈtɛmɪk] *adj* : sistémico

T

t [ˈtiː] *n, pl* **t's** *or* **ts** [ˈtiːz] : vigésima letra del alfabeto inglés
tab [ˈtæb] *n* **1** FLAP, TAG : lengüeta *f* (de un sobre, una caja, etc.), etiqueta *f* (de ropa) **2** → **tabulator** **3** BILL, CHECK : cuenta *f* **4 to keep tabs on** : tener bajo vigilancia
tabby [ˈtæbi] *n, pl* **-bies** **1** *or* **tabby cat** : gato *m* atigrado **2** : gata *f*
tabernacle [ˈtæbərˌnækəl] *n* : tabernáculo *m*
table [ˈteɪbəl] *n* **1** : mesa *f* ⟨a table for two : una mesa para dos⟩ **2** LIST : tabla *f* ⟨multiplication table : tabla de multiplicar⟩ **3 table of contents** : índice *m* de materias
tableau [tæˈbloː, ˈtæˌ-] *n, pl* **-leaux** [-ˈbloːz, -ˌbloːz] : retablo *m*, cuadro *m* vivo (en teatro)
tablecloth [ˈteɪbəlˌklɔθ] *n* : mantel *m*
tablespoon [ˈteɪbəlˌspuːn] *n* **1** : cuchara *f* (de mesa) **2** → **tablespoonful**

tablespoonful [ˈteɪbəlˌspuːnˌfʊl] *n* : cucharada *f*
tablet [ˈtæblət] *n* **1** PLAQUE : placa *f* **2** PAD : bloc *m* (de papel) **3** PILL : tableta *f*, pastilla *f*, píldora *f* ⟨an aspirin tablet : una tableta de aspirina⟩
table tennis *n* : tenis *m* de mesa
tableware [ˈteɪbəlˌwær] *n* : vajillas *fpl*, cubiertos *mpl* (de mesa)
tabloid [ˈtæˌblɔɪd] *n* : tabloide *m*
taboo[1] [təˈbuː, tæ-] *adj* : tabú
taboo[2] *n* : tabú *m*
tabular [ˈtæbjələr] *adj* : tabular
tabulate [ˈtæbjəˌleɪt] *vt* **-lated; -lating** : tabular
tabulator [ˈtæbjəˌleɪt̬ər] *n* : tabulador *m*
tacit [ˈtæsɪt] *adj* : tácito, implícito — **tacitly** *adv*
taciturn [ˈtæsɪˌtərn] *adj* : taciturno
tack[1] [ˈtæk] *vt* **1** : sujetar con tachuelas **2 to tack on** ADD : añadir, agregar
tack[2] *n* **1** : tachuela *f* **2** COURSE : rumbo *m* ⟨to change tack : cambiar de rumbo⟩
tackle[1] [ˈtækəl] *vt* **-led; -ling 1** : taclear (en futbol americano) **2** CONFRONT : abordar, enfrentar, emprender (un problema, un trabajo, etc.)
tackle[2] *n* **1** EQUIPMENT, GEAR : equipo *m*, aparejo *m* **2** : aparejo *m* (de un buque) **3** : tacleada *f* (en futbol americano)
tacky [ˈtæki] *adj* **tackier; -est 1** STICKY : pegajoso **2** CHEAP, GAUDY : de mal gusto, naco *Mex*
tact [ˈtækt] *n* : tacto *m*, delicadeza *f*, discreción *f*
tactful [ˈtæktfəl] *adj* : discreto, diplomático, de mucho tacto
tactfully [ˈtæktfəli] *adv* : discretamente, con mucho tacto
tactic [ˈtæktɪk] *n* : táctica *f*
tactical [ˈtæktɪkəl] *adj* : táctico, estratégico
tactics [ˈtæktɪks] *ns & pl* : táctica *f*, estrategia *f*
tactile [ˈtæktəl, -ˌtaɪl] *adj* : táctil
tactless [ˈtæktləs] *adj* : indiscreto, poco delicado
tactlessly [ˈtæktləsli] *adv* : rudamente, sin tacto
tadpole [ˈtædˌpoːl] *n* : renacuajo *m*
taffeta [ˈtæfət̬ə] *n* : tafetán *m*, tafeta *f Arg, Mex, Uru*
taffy [ˈtæfi] *n, pl* **-fies** : caramelo *m* de melaza, chicloso *m Mex*
tag[1] [ˈtæg] *v* **tagged; tagging** *vt* **1** LABEL : etiquetar **2** TAIL : seguir de cerca **3** TOUCH : tocar (en varios juegos) — *vi* **to tag along** : pegarse, acompañar
tag[2] *n* **1** LABEL : etiqueta *f* **2** SAYING : dicho *m*, refrán *m*
tail[1] [ˈteɪl] *vt* FOLLOW : seguir de cerca, pegarse
tail[2] *n* **1** : cola *f*, rabo *m* (de un animal) **2** : cola *f*, parte *f* posterior ⟨a comet's tail : la cola de un cometa⟩ **3 tails** *npl* : cruz *f* (de una moneda) ⟨heads or tails : cara o cruz⟩
tailed [ˈteɪld] *adj* : que tiene cola
tailgate[1] [ˈteɪlˌgeɪt] *vi* **-gated; -gating** : seguir a un vehículo demasiado de cerca
tailgate[2] *n* : puerta *f* trasera (de un vehículo)
taillight [ˈteɪlˌlaɪt] *n* : luz *f* trasera (de un vehículo), calavera *f Mex*
tailor[1] [ˈteɪlər] *vt* **1** : confeccionar o alterar (ropa) **2** ADAPT : adaptar, ajustar
tailor[2] *n* : sastre *m*, -tra *f*
tailpipe [ˈteɪlˌpaɪp] *n* : tubo *m* de escape
tailspin [ˈteɪlˌspɪn] *n* : barrena *f*
taint[1] [ˈteɪnt] *vt* : contaminar, corromper
taint[2] *n* : corrupción *f*, impureza *f*
take[1] [ˈteɪk] *v* **took** [ˈtʊk]; **taken** [ˈteɪkən]; **taking** *vt* **1** CAPTURE : capturar, apresar **2** GRASP : tomar, agarrar ⟨to take the bull by the horns : tomar al toro por los cuernos⟩ **3** CATCH : tomar, agarrar ⟨taken by surprise : tomado por sorpresa⟩ **4** CAPTIVATE : encantar, fascinar **5** INGEST : tomar, ingerir ⟨take two pills : tome dos píldoras⟩ **6** REMOVE : sacar, extraer ⟨take an orange : saca una naranja⟩ **7** : tomar, coger (un tren, un autobús, etc.) **8** NEED, REQUIRE : tomar, requerir ⟨these things take time : estas cosas toman tiempo⟩ **9** BRING, CARRY : llevar, sacar, cargar ⟨take them with you : llévalos contigo⟩ ⟨take the trash out : saca la basura⟩ **10** BEAR, ENDURE : soportar, aguantar (dolores, etc.) **11** ACCEPT : aceptar (un cheque, etc.), seguir (consejos), asumir (la responsabilidad) **12** SUPPOSE : suponer ⟨I take it that . . . : supongo que . . . ⟩ **13** (*indicating an action or an undertaking*) ⟨to take a walk : dar un paseo⟩ ⟨to take a class : tomar una clase⟩ **14 to take place** HAPPEN : tener lugar, suceder, ocurrir — *vi* : agarrar (dícese de un tinte), prender (dícese de una vacuna)
take[2] *n* **1** PROCEEDS : recaudación *f*, ingresos *mpl*, ganancias *fpl* **2** : toma *f* (de un rodaje o una grabación)
take back *vt* : retirar (palabras, etc.)
take in *vt* **1** : tomarle a, achicar (un vestido, etc.) **2** INCLUDE : incluir, abarcar **3** ATTEND : ir a ⟨to take in a movie : ir al cine⟩ **4** GRASP, UNDERSTAND : captar, entender **5** DECEIVE : engañar
takeoff [ˈteɪkˌɔf] *n* **1** PARODY : parodia *f* **2** : despegue *m* (de un avión o cohete)
take off *vt* REMOVE : quitar ⟨take off your hat : quítate el sombrero⟩ — *vi* **1** : despegar (dícese de un avión o un cohete) **2** LEAVE : irse, partir
take on *vt* **1** TACKLE : abordar, emprender (problemas, etc.) **2** ACCEPT : aceptar, encargarse de, asumir (una responsabilidad) **3** CONTRACT : contratar (trabajadores) **4** ASSUME : adoptar, asumir, adquirir ⟨the neighborhood took on a dingy look : el barrio asumió una apariencia deprimente⟩

takeover [ˈteɪkˌoːvər] *n* : toma *f* (de poder o de control), adquisición *f* (de una empresa por otra)

take over *vt* : tomar el poder de, tomar las riendas de — *vi* : asumir el mando

taker [ˈteɪkər] *n* : persona *f* interesada ⟨available to all takers : disponible a cuantos estén interesados⟩

take up *vt* **1** LIFT : levantar **2** SHORTEN : acortar (una falda, etc.) **3** BEGIN : empezar, dedicarse a (un pasatiempo, etc.) **4** OCCUPY : ocupar, llevar (tiempo, espacio) **5** PURSUE : volver a (una cuestión, un asunto) **6** CONTINUE : seguir con

talc [ˈtælk] *n* : talco *m*

talcum powder [ˈtælkəm] *n* : talco *m*, polvos *mpl* de talco

tale [ˈteɪl] *n* **1** ANECDOTE, STORY : cuento *m*, relato *m*, anécdota *f* **2** FALSEHOOD : cuento *m*, mentira *f*

talent [ˈtælənt] *n* : talento *m*, don *m*

talented [ˈtæləntəd] *adj* : talentoso

talisman [ˈtælɪsmən, -lɪz-] *n, pl* **-mans** : talismán *m*

talk[1] [ˈtɔk] *vi* **1** : hablar ⟨he talks for hours : se pasa horas hablando⟩ **2** CHAT : charlar, platicar — *vt* **1** SPEAK : hablar ⟨to talk French : hablar francés⟩ ⟨to talk business : hablar de negocios⟩ **2** PERSUADE : influenciar, convencer ⟨she talked me out of it : me convenció que no lo hiciera⟩ **3 to talk over** DISCUSS : hablar de, discutir

talk[2] *n* **1** CONVERSATION : charla *f*, plática *f*, conversación *f* **2** GOSSIP, RUMOR : chisme *m*, rumores *mpl*

talkative [ˈtɔkət̬ɪv] *adj* : locuaz, parlanchín, charlatán

talker [ˈtɔkər] *n* : conversador *m*, -dora *f*; hablador *m*, -dora *f*

talk show *n* : programa *m* de entrevistas

tall [ˈtɔl] *adj* : alto ⟨how tall is he? : ¿cuánto mide?⟩

tallness [ˈtɔlnəs] *n* HEIGHT : estatura *f* (de una persona), altura *f* (de un objeto)

tallow [ˈtæloː] *n* : sebo *m*

tally[1] [ˈtæli] *v* **-lied; -lying** *vt* RECKON : contar, hacer una cuenta de — *vi* MATCH : concordar, corresponder, cuadrar

tally[2] *n, pl* **-lies** : cuenta *f* ⟨to keep a tally : llevar la cuenta⟩

talon [ˈtælən] *n* : garra *f* (de un ave de rapiña)

tambourine [ˌtæmbəˈriːn] *n* : pandero *m*, pandereta *f*

tame[1] [ˈteɪm] *vt* **tamed; taming** : domar, amansar, domesticar

tame[2] *adj* **tamer; -est 1** DOMESTICATED : domesticado, manso **2** DOCILE : manso, dócil **3** DULL : aburrido, soso

tamely [ˈteɪmli] *adv* : mansamente, dócilmente

tamer [ˈteɪmər] *n* : domador *m*, -dora *f*

tamp [ˈtæmp] *vt* : apisonar

tamper [ˈtæmpər] *vi* **to tamper with** : adulterar (una sustancia), forzar (un sello, una cerradura), falsear (documentos), manipular (una máquina)

tampon [ˈtæmˌpɑn] *n* : tampón *m*

tan[1] [ˈtæn] *v* **tanned; tanning** *vt* **1** : curtir (pieles) **2** : broncear — *vi* : broncearse

tan[2] *n* **1** SUNTAN : bronceado *m* ⟨to get a tan : broncearse⟩ **2** : color *m* canela, color *m* café con leche

tandem[1] [ˈtændəm] *adv or* **in tandem** : en tándem

tandem[2] *n* : tándem *m* (bicicleta)

tang [ˈtæŋ] *n* : sabor *m* fuerte

tangent [ˈtændʒənt] *n* : tangente *f* ⟨to go off on a tangent : irse por la tangente⟩

tangerine [ˈtændʒəˌriːn, ˌtændʒəˈ-] *n* : mandarina *f*

tangible [ˈtændʒəbəl] *adj* : tangible, palpable — **tangibly** [-bli] *adv*

tangle[1] [ˈtæŋgəl] *v* **-gled; -gling** *vt* : enredar, enmarañar — *vi* : enredarse

tangle[2] *n* : enredo *m*, maraña *f*

tango[1] [ˈtæŋˌgoː] *vi* : bailar el tango

tango[2] *n, pl* **-gos** : tango *m*

tangy [ˈtæŋi] *adj* **tangier; -est** : que tiene un sabor fuerte

tank [ˈtæŋk] *n* : tanque *m*, depósito *m* ⟨fuel tank : depósito de combustibles⟩

tankard [ˈtæŋkərd] *n* : jarra *f*

tanker [ˈtæŋkər] *n* : buque *m* cisterna, camión *m* cisterna, avión *m* cisterna ⟨an oil tanker : un petrolero⟩

tanner [ˈtænər] *n* : curtidor *m*, -dora *f*

tannery [ˈtænəri] *n, pl* **-neries** : curtiduría *f*, tenería *f*

tannin [ˈtænən] *n* : tanino *m*

tantalize [ˈtæntəˌlaɪz] *vt* **-lized; -lizing** : tentar, atormentar (con algo inasequible)

tantalizing [ˈtæntəˌlaɪzɪŋ] *adj* : tentador, seductor

tantamount [ˈtæntəˌmaʊnt] *adj* : equivalente

tantrum [ˈtæntrəm] *n* : rabieta *f*, berrinche *m* ⟨to throw a tantrum : hacer un berrinche⟩

tap[1] [ˈtæp] *vt* **tapped; tapping 1** : ponerle una espita a, sacar líquido de (un barril, un tanque, etc.) **2** : intervenir (una línea telefónica) **3** PAT, TOUCH : tocar, golpear ligeramente ⟨he tapped me on the shoulder : me tocó en el hombro⟩

tap[2] *n* **1** FAUCET : llave *f*, grifo *m* ⟨beer on tap : cerveza de barril⟩ **2** : extracción *f* (de líquido) ⟨a spinal tap : una punción lumbar⟩ **3** PAT, TOUCH : golpecito *m*, toque *m*

tape[1] [ˈteɪp] *vt* **taped; taping 1** : sujetar o arreglar con cinta adhesiva **2** RECORD : grabar

tape[2] *n* **1** : cinta *f* (adhesiva, magnética, etc.) **2** → **tape measure**

tape measure *n* : cinta *f* métrica

taper[1] [ˈteɪpər] *vi* **1** : estrecharse gradualmente ⟨its tail tapers towards the tip : su cola va estrechándose hacia la punta⟩ **2** *or* **to taper off** : disminuir gradualmente

taper[2] *n* **1** CANDLE : vela *f* larga y delgada **2** TAPERING : estrechamiento *m* gradual

tapestry [ˈtæpəstri] *n, pl* **-tries** : tapiz *m*

tapeworm [ˈteɪpˌwərm] *n* : solitaria *f*, tenia *f*

tapioca [ˌtæpiˈoːkə] *n* : tapioca *f*

tar[1] [ˈtɑr] *vt* **tarred; tarring** : alquitranar

tar[2] *n* : alquitrán *m*, brea *f*, chapopote *m Mex*

tarantula [təˈræntʃələ, -ˈræntələ] *n* : tarántula *f*

tardiness [ˈtɑrdinəs] *n* : tardanza *f*, retraso *m*

tardy [ˈtɑrdi] *adj* **-dier; -est** LATE : tardío, de retraso

target[1] [ˈtɑrgət] *vt* : fijar como objetivo, dirigir, destinar

target[2] *n* **1** : blanco *m* ⟨target practice : tiro al blanco⟩ **2** GOAL, OBJECTIVE : meta *f*, objetivo *m*

tariff [ˈtærɪf] *n* DUTY : tarifa *f*, arancel *m*

tarnish[1] [ˈtɑrnɪʃ] *vt* **1** DULL : deslustrar **2** SULLY : empañar, manchar (una reputación, etc.) — *vi* : deslustrarse

tarnish[2] *n* : deslustre *m*

tarpaulin [tɑrˈpɔlən, ˈtɑrpə-] *n* : lona *f* (impermeable)

tarragon [ˈtærəˌgɑn, -gən] *n* : estragón *m*

tarry[1] [ˈtæri] *vi* **-ried; -rying** : demorarse, entretenerse

tarry[2] [ˈtɑri] *adj* **1** : parecido al alquitrán **2** : cubierto de alquitrán

tart[1] [ˈtɑrt] *adj* **1** SOUR : ácido, agrio **2** CAUSTIC : mordaz, acrimonioso — **tartly** *adv*

tart[2] *n* : tartaleta *f*

tartan [ˈtɑrtən] *n* : tartán *m*

tartar [ˈtɑrt̬ər] *n* **1** : tártaro *m* ⟨tartar sauce : salsa tártara⟩ **2** : sarro *m* (dental)

tartness [ˈtɑrtnəs] *n* **1** SOURNESS : acidez *f* **2** ACRIMONY, SHARPNESS : mordacidad *f*, acrimonia *f*, acritud *f*

task [ˈtæsk] *n* : tarea *f*, trabajo *m*

taskmaster [ˈtæskˌmæstər] *n* **to be a hard taskmaster** : ser exigente, ser muy estricto

tassel [ˈtæsəl] *n* : borla *f*

taste[1] [ˈteɪst] *v* **tasted; tasting** *vt* : probar (alimentos), degustar, catar (vinos) ⟨taste this soup : prueba esta sopa⟩ — *vi* : saber ⟨this tastes good : esto sabe bueno⟩

taste[2] *n* **1** SAMPLE : prueba *f*, bocado *m* (de comida), trago *m* (de bebidas) **2** FLAVOR : gusto *m*, sabor *m* **3** : gusto *m* ⟨she has good taste : tiene buen gusto⟩ ⟨in bad taste : de mal gusto⟩

taste bud *n* : papila *f* gustativa

tasteful [ˈteɪstfəl] *adj* : de buen gusto

tastefully [ˈteɪstfəli] *adv* : con buen gusto

tasteless [ˈteɪstləs] *adj* **1** FLAVORLESS : sin sabor, soso, insípido **2** : de mal gusto ⟨a tasteless joke : un chiste de mal gusto⟩

taster [ˈteɪstər] *n* : degustador *m*, -dora *f*; catador *m*, -dora *f* (de vinos)

tastiness [ˈteɪstinəs] *n* : lo sabroso

tasty [ˈteɪsti] *adj* **tastier; -est** : sabroso, gustoso

tatter [ˈtæt̬ər] *n* **1** SHRED : tira *f*, jirón *m* (de tela) **2 tatters** *npl* : andrajos *mpl*, harapos *mpl* ⟨to be in tatters : estar por los suelos⟩

tattered [ˈtæt̬ərd] *adj* : andrajoso, en jirones

tattle [ˈtæt̬əl] *vi* **-tled; -tling** **1** CHATTER : parlotear *fam*, cotorrear *fam* **2 to tattle on someone** : acusar a alguien

tattletale [ˈtæt̬əlˌteɪl] *n* : soplón *m*, -plona *f fam*

tattoo[1] [tæˈtuː] *vt* : tatuar

tattoo[2] *n* : tatuaje *m* ⟨to get a tattoo : tatuarse⟩

taught → **teach**

taunt[1] [ˈtɔnt] *vt* MOCK : mofarse de, burlarse de

taunt[2] *n* : mofa *f*, burla *f*

Taurus [ˈtɔrəs] *n* : Tauro *mf*

taut [ˈtɔt] *adj* : tirante, tenso — **tautly** *adv*

tautness [ˈtɔtnəs] *n* : tirantez *f*, tensión *f*

tavern [ˈtævərn] *n* : taberna *f*

tawdry [ˈtɔdri] *adj* **-drier; -est** : chabacano, vulgar

tawny [ˈtɔni] *adj* **-nier; -est** : leonado

tax[1] [ˈtæks] *vt* **1** : gravar, cobrar un impuesto sobre **2** CHARGE : acusar ⟨they taxed him with neglect : fue acusado de incumplimiento⟩ **3 to tax someone's strength** : ponerle a prueba las fuerzas (a alguien)

tax[2] *n* **1** : impuesto *m*, tributo *m* **2** BURDEN : carga *f*

taxable [ˈtæksəbəl] *adj* : sujeto a un impuesto

taxation [tækˈseɪʃən] *n* : impuestos *mpl*

tax–exempt [ˈtæksɪgˈzɛmpt, -ɛg-] *adj* : libre de impuestos

taxi[1] [ˈtæksi] *vi* **taxied; taxiing** *or* **taxying; taxis** *or* **taxies** **1** : ir en taxi **2** : rodar sobre la pista de aterrizaje (dícese de un avión)

taxi[2] *n, pl* **taxis** : taxi *m*, libre *m Mex*

taxicab [ˈtæksiˌkæb] *n* → **taxi**[2]

taxidermist [ˈtæksəˌdərmɪst] *n* : taxidermista *mf*

taxidermy [ˈtæksəˌdərmi] *n* : taxidermia *f*

taxpayer [ˈtæksˌpeɪər] *n* : contribuyente *mf*, causante *mf Mex*

TB [ˌtiːˈbiː] → **tuberculosis**

tea [ˈtiː] *n* **1** : té *m* (planta y bebida) **2** : merienda *f*, té *m* (comida)

teach [ˈtiːtʃ] *v* **taught** [ˈtɔt]; **teaching** *vt* : enseñar, dar clases de ⟨she teaches math : da clases de matemáticas⟩ ⟨she taught me everything I know : me enseñó todo lo que sé⟩ — *vi* : enseñar, dar clases

teacher [ˈtiːʧər] *n* : maestro *m*, -tra *f* (de enseñanza primaria); profesor *m*, -sora *f* (de enseñanza secundaria)
teaching [ˈtiːʧɪŋ] *n* : enseñanza *f*
teacup [ˈtiːˌkʌp] *n* : taza *f* para té
teak [ˈtiːk] *n* : teca *f*
teakettle [ˈtiːˌktəl] *n* : tetera *f*
teal [ˈtiːl] *n, pl* **teal** *or* **teals** : cerceta *f* (pato)
team[1] [ˈtiːm] *vi or* **to team up 1** : formar un equipo (en deportes) **2** COLLABORATE : asociarse, juntarse, unirse
team[2] *adj* : de equipo
team[3] *n* **1** : tiro *m* (de caballos), yunta *f* (de bueyes o mulas) **2** : equipo *m* (en deportes, etc.)
teammate [ˈtiːmˌmeɪt] *n* : compañero *m*, -ra *f* de equipo
teamster [ˈtiːmstər] *n* : camionero *m*, -ra *f*
teamwork [ˈtiːmˌwərk] *n* : trabajo *m* en equipo, cooperación *f*
teapot [ˈtiːˌpɑt] *n* : tetera *f*
tear[1] [ˈtær] *v* **tore** [ˈtor]; **torn** [ˈtorn]; **tearing** *vt* **1** RIP : desgarrar, romper, rasgar (tela) ⟨to tear to pieces : hacer pedazos⟩ **2** *or* **to tear apart** DIVIDE : dividir **3** REMOVE : arrancar ⟨torn from his family : arrancado de su familia⟩ **4** **to tear down** : derribar — *vi* **1** RIP : desgarrarse, romperse **2** RUSH : ir a gran velocidad ⟨she went tearing down the street : se fue como rayo por la calle⟩
tear[2] *n* : desgarradura *f*, rotura *f*, desgarro *m* (muscular)
tear[3] [ˈtɪr] *n* : lágrima *f*
teardrop [ˈtɪrˌdrɑp] *n* → **tear**[3]
tearful [ˈtɪrfəl] *adj* : lloroso, triste — **tearfully** *adv*
tease[1] [ˈtiːz] *vt* **teased; teasing 1** MOCK : burlarse de, mofarse de **2** ANNOY : irritar, fastidiar
tease[2] *n* **1** TEASING : burla *f*, mofa *f* **2** : bromista *mf*; guasón *m*, -sona *f*
teaspoon [ˈtiːˌspuːn] *n* **1** : cucharita *f* **2** → **teaspoonful**
teaspoonful [ˈtiːˌspuːnˌfʊl] *n, pl* **-spoonfuls** [-ˌfʊlz] *or* **-spoonsful** [-ˌspuːnzˌfʊl] : cucharadita *f*
teat [ˈtiːt] *n* : tetilla *f*
technical [ˈtɛknɪkəl] *adj* : técnico — **technically** [-kli] *adv*
technicality [ˌtɛknəˈkæləṭi] *n, pl* **-ties** : detalle *m* técnico
technician [tɛkˈnɪʃən] *n* : técnico *m*, -ca *f*
technique [tɛkˈniːk] *n* : técnica *f*
technological [ˌtɛknəˈlɑʤɪkəl] *adj* : tecnológico
technology [tɛkˈnɑləʤi] *n, pl* **-gies** : tecnología *f*
teddy bear [ˈtɛdi] *n* : oso *m* de peluche
tedious [ˈtiːdiəs] *adj* : aburrido, pesado, monótono — **tediously** *adv*
tediousness [ˈtiːdiəsnəs] *n* : lo aburrido, lo pesado
tedium [ˈtiːdiəm] *n* : tedio *m*, pesadez *f*
tee [ˈtiː] *n* : tee *mf*
teem [ˈtiːm] *vi* **to teem with** : estar repleto de, estar lleno de
teenage [ˈtiːnˌeɪʤ] *or* **teenaged** [-eɪʤd] *adj* : adolescente, de adolescencia
teenager [ˈtiːnˌeɪʤər] *n* : adolescente *mf*
teens [ˈtiːnz] *npl* : adolescencia *f*
teepee → **tepee**
teeter[1] [ˈtiːṭər] *vi* : balancearse, tambalearse
teeter[2] *n or* **teeter–totter** [ˈtiːṭər-ˌtɑṭər] → **seesaw**
teeth → **tooth**
teethe [ˈtiːð] *vi* **teethed; teething** : formársele a uno los dientes ⟨the baby's teething : le están saliendo los dientes al niño⟩
telecast[1] [ˈtɛləˌkæst] *vt* **-cast; -casting** : televisar, transmitir por televisión
telecast[2] *n* : transmisión *f* por televisión
telecommunication [ˈtɛləkəˌmjuːnəˈkeɪʃən] *n* : telecomunicación *f*
telegram [ˈtɛləˌgræm] *n* : telegrama *m*
telegraph[1] [ˈtɛləˌgræf] *v* : telegrafiar
telegraph[2] *n* : telégrafo *m*
telepathic [ˌtɛləˈpæθɪk] *adj* : telepático — **telepathically** [-θɪkli] *adv*
telepathy [təˈlɛpəθi] *n* : telepatía *f*
telephone[1] [ˈtɛləˌfoːn] *v* **-phoned; -phoning** *vt* : llamar por teléfono a, telefonear — *vi* : telefonear
telephone[2] *n* : teléfono *m*
telescope[1] [ˈtɛləˌskoːp] *vi* **-scoped; -scoping** : plegarse (como un telescopio)
telescope[2] *n* : telescopio *m*
telescopic [ˌtɛləˈskɑpɪk] *adj* : telescópico
televise [ˈtɛləˌvaɪz] *vt* **-vised; -vising** : televisar
television [ˈtɛləˌvɪʒən] *n* : televisión *f*
tell [ˈtɛl] *v* **told** [ˈtoːld]; **telling** *vt* **1** COUNT : contar, enumerar ⟨all told : en total⟩ **2** INSTRUCT : decir ⟨he told me how to fix it : me dijo cómo arreglarlo⟩ ⟨they told her to wait : le dijeron que esperara⟩ **3** RELATE : contar, relatar, narrar ⟨to tell a story : contar una historia⟩ **4** DIVULGE, REVEAL : revelar, divulgar ⟨he told me everything about her : me contó todo acerca de ella⟩ **5** DISCERN : discernir, notar ⟨I can't tell the difference : no noto la diferencia⟩ — *vi* **1** SAY : decir ⟨I won't tell : no voy a decírselo a nadie⟩ **2** KNOW : saber ⟨you never can tell : nunca se sabe⟩ **3** SHOW : notarse, hacerse sentir ⟨the strain is beginning to tell : la tensión se empieza a notar⟩
teller [ˈtɛlər] *n* **1** NARRATOR : narrador *m*, -dora *f* **2** *or* **bank teller** : cajero *m*, -ra *f*
temerity [təˈmɛrəṭi] *n, pl* **-ties** : temeridad *f*
temp [ˈtɛmp] *n* : empleado *m*, -da *f* temporal
temper[1] [ˈtɛmpər] *vt* **1** MODERATE : moderar, temperar **2** ANNEAL : templar (acero, etc.)

temper[2] *n* **1** DISPOSITION : carácter *m*, genio *m* **2** HARDNESS : temple *m*, dureza *f* (de un metal) **3** COMPOSURE : calma *f*, serenidad *f* ⟨to lose one's temper : perder los estribos⟩ **4** RAGE : furia *f* ⟨to fly into a temper : ponerse furioso⟩

temperament [ˈtɛmpərmənt, -prə-, -pərə-] *n* : temperamento *m*

temperamental [ˌtɛmpərˈmɛntəl, -prə-, -pərə-] *adj* : temperamental

temperance [ˈtɛmprən*t*s] *n* : templanza *f*, temperancia *f*

temperate [ˈtɛmpərət] *adj* : templado (dícese del clima, etc.), moderado

temperature [ˈtɛmpərˌʧʊr, -prə-, -pərə-, -ʧər] *n* **1** : temperatura *f* **2** FEVER : calentura *f*, fiebre *f*

tempest [ˈtɛmpəst] *n* : tempestad *f*

tempestuous [tɛmˈpɛsʧʊəs] *adj* : tempestuoso

temple [ˈtɛmpəl] *n* **1** : templo *m* (en religión) **2** : sien *f* (en anatomía)

tempo [ˈtɛmˌpo:] *n, pl* **-pi** [-ˌpi:] *or* **-pos** : ritmo *m*, tempo *m* (en música)

temporal [ˈtɛmpərəl] *adj* : temporal

temporarily [ˌtɛmpəˈrɛrəli] *adv* : temporalmente, provisionalmente

temporary [ˈtɛmpəˌrɛri] *adj* : temporal, provisional, provisorio

tempt [ˈtɛmpt] *vt* : tentar

temptation [tɛmpˈteɪʃən] *n* : tentación *f*

tempter [ˈtɛmptər] *n* : tentador *m*

temptress [ˈtɛmptrəs] *n* : tentadora *f*

ten[1] [ˈtɛn] *adj* : diez

ten[2] *n* **1** : diez *m* (número) **2** : decena *f* ⟨tens of thousands : decenas de millares⟩

tenable [ˈtɛnəbəl] *adj* : sostenible, defendible

tenacious [təˈneɪʃəs] *adj* : tenaz

tenacity [təˈnæsət̬i] *n* : tenacidad *f*

tenancy [ˈtɛnən*t*si] *n, pl* **-cies** : tenencia *f*, inquilinato *m* (de un inmueble)

tenant [ˈtɛnənt] *n* : inquilino *m*, -na *f*; arrendatario *m*, -ria *f*

tend [ˈtɛnd] *vt* : atender, cuidar (de), ocuparse de — *vi* : tender ⟨it tends to benefit the consumer : tiende a beneficiar al consumidor⟩

tendency [ˈtɛndən*t*si] *n, pl* **-cies** : tendencia *f*, proclividad *f*, inclinación *f*

tender[1] [ˈtɛndər] *vt* : entregar, presentar ⟨I tendered my resignation : presenté mi renuncia⟩

tender[2] *adj* **1** : tierno, blando ⟨tender steak : bistec tierno⟩ **2** AFFECTIONATE, LOVING : tierno, cariñoso, afectuoso **3** DELICATE : tierno, sensible, delicado

tender[3] *n* **1** OFFER : propuesta *f*, oferta *f* (en negocios) **2 legal tender** : moneda *f* de curso legal

tenderize [ˈtɛndəˌraɪz] *vt* **-ized; -izing** : ablandar (carnes)

tenderloin [ˈtɛndrˌlɔɪn] *n* : lomo *f* (de res o de puerco)

tenderly [ˈtɛndərli] *adv* : tiernamente, con ternura

tenderness [ˈtɛndərnəs] *n* : ternura *f*

tendon [ˈtɛndən] *n* : tendón *m*

tendril [ˈtɛndrɪl] *n* : zarcillo *m*

tenement [ˈtɛnəmənt] *n* : casa *f* de vecindad

tenet [ˈtɛnət] *n* : principio *m*

tennis [ˈtɛnəs] *n* : tenis *m*

tenor [ˈtɛnər] *n* **1** PURPORT : tenor *m*, significado *m* **2** : tenor *m* (en música)

tenpins [ˈtɛnˌpɪnz] *npl* : bolos *mpl*, boliche *m*

tense[1] [ˈtɛn*t*s] *v* **tensed; tensing** *vt* : tensar — *vi* : tensarse, ponerse tenso

tense[2] *adj* **tenser; tensest** **1** TAUT : tenso, tirante **2** NERVOUS : tenso, nervioso

tense[3] *n* : tiempo *m* (de un verbo)

tensely [ˈtɛn*t*sli] *adv* : tensamente

tenseness [ˈtɛn*t*snəs] → **tension**

tension [ˈtɛnʧən] *n* **1** TAUTNESS : tensión *f*, tirantez *f* **2** STRESS : tensión *f*, nerviosismo *m*, estrés *m*

tent [ˈtɛnt] *n* : tienda *f* de campaña

tentacle [ˈtɛntɪkəl] *n* : tentáculo *m*

tentative [ˈtɛntət̬ɪv] *adj* **1** HESITANT : indeciso, vacilante **2** PROVISIONAL : sujeto a cambios, provisional

tentatively [ˈtɛntət̬ɪvli] *adv* : provisionalmente

tenth[1] [ˈtɛnθ] *adj* : décimo

tenth[2] *n* **1** : décimo *m*, -ma *f* (en una serie) **2** : décimo *m*, décima parte *f*

tenuous [ˈtɛnjʊəs] *adj* : tenue, débil ⟨tenuous reasons : razones poco convincentes⟩

tenuously [ˈtɛnjʊəsli] *adv* : tenuemente, ligeramente

tenure [ˈtɛnjər] *n* : tenencia *f* (de un cargo o una propiedad), titularidad *f* (de un puesto académico)

tepee [ˈti:ˌpi:] *n* : tipi *m*

tepid [ˈtɛpɪd] *adj* : tibio

tequila [təˈki:lə] *n* : tequila *m*

term[1] [ˈtərm] *vt* : calificar de, llamar, nombrar

term[2] *n* **1** PERIOD : término *m*, plazo *m*, período *m* **2** : término *m* (en matemáticas) **3** WORD : término *m*, vocablo *m* ⟨legal terms : términos legales⟩ **4** **terms** *npl* CONDITIONS : términos *mpl*, condiciones *fpl* **5** **terms** *npl* RELATIONS : relaciones *fpl* ⟨to be on good terms with : tener buenas relaciones con⟩ **6 in terms of** : con respecto a, en cuanto a

terminal[1] [ˈtərmənəl] *adj* : terminal

terminal[2] *n* **1** : terminal *m*, polo *m* (en electricidad) **2** : terminal *m* (de una computadora) **3** STATION : terminal *f*, estación *f* (de transporte público)

terminate [ˈtərməˌneɪt] *v* **-nated; -nating** *vi* : terminar(se), concluirse — *vt* : terminar, poner fin a

termination [ˌtərməˈneɪʃən] *n* : cese *m*, terminación *f*

terminology [ˌtərməˈnɑləʤi] *n, pl* **-gies** : terminología *f*

terminus [ˈtərmənəs] *n, pl* **-ni** [-ˌnaɪ] *or* **-nuses** **1** END : término *m*, fin *m* **2** : terminal *f* (de transporte público)

termite [ˈtərˌmaɪt] *n* : termita *f*
tern [ˈtərn] *n* : golondrina *f* de mar
terrace[1] [ˈtɛrəs] *vt* **-raced; -racing** : formar en terrazas, disponer en bancales
terrace[2] *n* **1** PATIO : terraza *f*, patio *m* **2** : terraplén *m*, terraza *f*, bancal *m* (en agricultura)
terra–cotta [ˌtɛrəˈkɑt̬ə] *n* : terracota *f*
terrain [təˈreɪn] *n* : terreno *m*
terrapin [ˈtɛrəpɪn] *n* : galápago *m* norteamericano
terrarium [təˈræriəm] *n, pl* **-ia** [-iə] *or* **-iums** : terrario *m*
terrestrial [təˈrɛstriəl] *adj* : terrestre
terrible [ˈtɛrəbəl] *adj* : atroz, horrible, terrible
terribly [ˈtɛrəbli] *adv* **1** BADLY : muy mal **2** EXTREMELY : terriblemente, extremadamente
terrier [ˈtɛriər] *n* : terrier *mf*
terrific [təˈrɪfɪk] *adj* **1** FRIGHTFUL : aterrador **2** EXTRAORDINARY : extraordinario, excepcional **3** EXCELLENT : excelente, estupendo
terrify [ˈtɛrəˌfaɪ] *vt* **-fied; -fying** : aterrorizar, aterrar, espantar
terrifying [ˈtɛrəˌfaɪɪŋ] *adj* : espantoso, aterrador
territory [ˈtɛrəˌtori] *n, pl* **-ries** : territorio *m* — **territorial** [ˌtɛrəˈtoriəl] *adj*
terror [ˈtɛrər] *n* : terror *m*
terrorism [ˈtɛrərˌɪzəm] *n* : terrorismo *m*
terrorist[1] [ˈtɛrərɪst] *adj* : terrorista
terrorist[2] *n* : terrorista *mf*
terrorize [ˈtɛrərˌaɪz] *vt* **-ized; -izing** : aterrorizar
terry [ˈtɛri] *n, pl* **-ries** *or* **terry cloth** : (tela de) toalla *f*
terse [ˈtərs] *adj* **terser; tersest** : lacónico, conciso, seco — **tersely** *adv*
tertiary [ˈtərʃiˌɛri] *adj* : terciario
test[1] [ˈtɛst] *vt* : examinar, evaluar — *vi* : hacer pruebas
test[2] *n* : prueba *f*, examen *m*, test *m* ⟨to put to the test : poner a prueba⟩
testament [ˈtɛstəmənt] *n* **1** WILL : testamento *m* **2** : Testamento *m* (en la Biblia) ⟨the Old Testament : el Antiguo Testamento⟩
testicle [ˈtɛstɪkəl] *n* : testículo *m*
testify [ˈtɛstəˌfaɪ] *v* **-fied; -fying** *vi* : testificar, atestar, testimoniar — *vt* : testificar
testimonial [ˌtɛstəˈmoːniəl] *n* **1** REFERENCE : recomendación *f* **2** TRIBUTE : homenaje *m*, tributo *m*
testimony [ˈtɛstəˌmoːni] *n, pl* **-nies** : testimonio *m*, declaración *f*
test tube *n* : probeta *f*, tubo *m* de ensayo
testy [ˈtɛsti] *adj* **-tier; -est** : irritable
tetanus [ˈtɛtənəs] *n* : tétano *m*, tétanos *m*
tête–à–tête [ˌtɛt̬əˈtɛt, ˌteɪt̬əˈteɪt] *n* : conversación *f* en privado
tether[1] [ˈtɛðər] *vt* : atar (con una cuerda), amarrar
tether[2] *n* : atadura *f*, cadena *f*, correa *f*
text [ˈtɛkst] *n* **1** : texto *m* **2** TOPIC : tema *m* **3** → **textbook**
textbook [ˈtɛkstˌbʊk] *n* : libro *m* de texto
textile [ˈtɛkˌstaɪl, ˈtɛkstəl] *n* : textil *m*, tela *f* ⟨the textile industry : la industria textil⟩
textual [ˈtɛkstʃʊəl] *adj* : textual
texture [ˈtɛkstʃər] *n* : textura *f*
Thai [ˈtaɪ] *n* **1** : tailandés *m*, -desa *f* **2** : tailandés *m* (idioma) — **Thai** *adj*
than[1] [ˈðæn] *conj* : que, de ⟨it's worth more than that : vale más que eso⟩ ⟨more than you think : más de lo que piensas⟩
than[2] *prep* : que, de ⟨you're better than he is : eres mejor que él⟩ ⟨more than once : más de una vez⟩
thank [ˈθæŋk] *vt* : agradecer, darle (las) gracias (a alguien) ⟨thank you! : ¡gracias!⟩ ⟨I thanked her for the present : le di las gracias por el regalo⟩ ⟨I thank you for your help : le agradezco su ayuda⟩
thankful [ˈθæŋkfəl] *adj* : agradecido
thankfully [ˈθæŋkfəli] *adv* **1** GRATEFULLY : con agradecimiento **2** FORTUNATELY : afortunadamente, por suerte ⟨thankfully, it's over : se acabó, gracias a Dios⟩
thankfulness [ˈθæŋkfəlnəs] *n* : agradecimiento *m*, gratitud *f*
thankless [ˈθæŋkləs] *adj* : ingrato ⟨a thankless task : un trabajo ingrato⟩
thanks [ˈθæŋks] *npl* **1** : agradecimiento *m* **2 thanks!** : ¡gracias!
Thanksgiving [θæŋksˈgɪvɪŋ, ˈθæŋksˌ-] *n* : el día de Acción de Gracias (fiesta estadounidense)
that[1] [ˈðæt] *adv* (*in negative constructions*) : tan ⟨it's not that expensive : no es tan caro⟩ ⟨not that much : no tanto⟩
that[2] *adj, pl* **those** : ese, esa, aquel, aquella ⟨do you see those children? : ¿ves a aquellos niños?⟩
that[3] *conj & pron* : que ⟨he said that he was afraid : dijo que tenía miedo⟩ ⟨the book that he wrote : el libro que escribió⟩
that[4] *pron, pl* **those** [ˈðoːz] **1** : ése, ésa, eso ⟨that's my father : ése es mi padre⟩ ⟨those are the ones he likes : ésos son los que le gustan⟩ ⟨what's that? : ¿qué es eso?⟩ **2** (*referring to more distant objects or time*) : aquél, aquélla, aquello ⟨those are maples and these are elms : aquéllos son arces y éstos son olmos⟩ ⟨that came to an end : aquello se acabó⟩
thatch[1] [ˈθætʃ] *vt* : cubrir o techar con paja
thatch[2] *n* : paja *f* (usada para techos)
thaw[1] [ˈθɔ] *vt* : descongelar — *vi* : derretirse (dícese de la nieve), descongelarse (dícese de los alimentos)
thaw[2] *n* : deshielo *m*

the[1] [ðə, *before vowel sounds usu* ðiː] *adv* **1** (*used to indicate comparison*) ⟨the sooner the better : cuanto más pronto, mejor⟩ ⟨she likes this one the best : éste es el que más le gusta⟩ **2** (*used as a conjunction*) : cuanto ⟨the more I learn, the less I understand : cuanto más aprendo, menos entiendo⟩

the[2] *art* : el, la, los, las ⟨the gloves : los guantes⟩ ⟨the suitcase : la maleta⟩ ⟨forty cookies to the box : cuarenta galletas por caja⟩

theater *or* **theatre** [ˈθiːət̬ər] *n* **1** : teatro *m* (edificio) **2** DRAMA : teatro *m*, drama *m*

theatrical [θiˈætrɪkəl] *adj* : teatral, dramático

thee [ˈðiː] *pron* : te, ti

theft [ˈθɛft] *n* : robo *m*, hurto *m*

their [ˈðɛr] *adj* : su ⟨their friends : sus amigos⟩

theirs [ˈðɛrz] *pron* : (el) suyo, (la) suya, (los) suyos, (las) suyas ⟨they came for theirs : vinieron por el suyo⟩ ⟨theirs is bigger : la suya es más grande, la de ellos es más grande⟩ ⟨a brother of theirs : un hermano suyo, un hermano de ellos⟩

them [ˈðɛm] *pron* **1** (*as a direct object*) : los (*Spain sometimes* les), las ⟨I know them : los conozco⟩ **2** (*as indirect object*) : les, se ⟨I sent them a letter : les mandé una carta⟩ ⟨give it to them : dáselo (a ellos)⟩ **3** (*as object of a preposition*) : ellos, ellas ⟨go with them : ve con ellos⟩ **4** (*for emphasis*) : ellos, ellas ⟨I wasn't expecting them : no los esperaba a ellos⟩

thematic [θiˈmæt̬ɪk] *adj* : temático

theme [ˈθiːm] *n* **1** SUBJECT, TOPIC : tema *m* **2** COMPOSITION : composición *f*, trabajo *m* (escrito) **3** : tema *m* (en música)

themselves [ðəmˈsɛlvz, ðɛm-] *pron* **1** (*as a reflexive*) : se, sí ⟨they enjoyed themselves : se divirtieron⟩ ⟨they divided it among themselves : lo repartieron entre sí, se lo repartieron⟩ **2** (*for emphasis*) : ellos mismos, ellas mismas ⟨they built it themselves : ellas mismas lo construyeron⟩

then[1] [ˈðɛn] *adv* **1** : entonces, en ese tiempo ⟨I was sixteen then : tenía entonces dieciséis años⟩ ⟨since then : desde entonces⟩ **2** NEXT : después, luego ⟨we'll go to Toronto, then to Winnipeg : iremos a Toronto, y luego a Winnipeg⟩ **3** BESIDES : además, aparte ⟨then there's the tax : y aparte está el impuesto⟩ **4** : entonces, en ese caso ⟨if you like music, then you should attend : si te gusta la música, entonces deberías asistir⟩

then[2] *adj* : entonces ⟨the then governor of Georgia : el entonces gobernador de Georgia⟩

thence [ˈðɛnts, ˈθɛnts] *adv* : de ahí, de ahí en adelante

theologian [ˌθiːəˈloːdʒən] *n* : teólogo *m*, -ga *f*

theological [ˌθiːəˈlɑdʒɪkəl] *adj* : teológico

theology [θiˈɑlədʒi] *n, pl* **-gies** : teología *f*

theorem [ˈθiːərəm, ˈθɪrəm] *n* : teorema *m*

theoretical [ˌθiːəˈrɛt̬ɪkəl] *adj* : teórico — **theoretically** *adv*

theorist [ˈθiːərɪst] *n* : teórico *m*, -ca *f*

theorize [ˈθiːəˌraɪz] *vi* **-rized; -rizing** : teorizar

theory [ˈθiːəri, ˈθɪri] *n, pl* **-ries** : teoría *f*

therapeutic [ˌθɛrəˈpjuːt̬ɪk] *adj* : terapéutico — **therapeutically** *adv*

therapist [ˈθɛrəpɪst] *n* : terapeuta *mf*

therapy [ˈθɛrəpi] *n, pl* **-pies** : terapia *f*

there[1] [ˈðær] *adv* **1** : ahí, allí, allá ⟨stand over there : párate ahí⟩ ⟨over there : por allí, por allá⟩ ⟨who's there? : ¿quién es?⟩ **2** : ahí, en esto, en eso ⟨there is where we disagree : en eso es donde no estamos de acuerdo⟩

there[2] *pron* **1** (*introducing a sentence or clause*) ⟨there comes a time to decide : llega un momento en que tiene uno que decidir⟩ **2 there is, there are** : hay ⟨there are many children here : aquí hay muchos niños⟩ ⟨there's a good hotel downtown : hay un buen hotel en el centro⟩

thereabouts [ðærəˈbaʊts, ˈðærəˌ-] *or* **thereabout** [-ˈbaʊt, -ˌbaʊt] *adv* **or thereabouts** : por ahí, más o menos ⟨at five o'clock or thereabouts : por ahí de las cinco⟩

thereafter [ðærˈæftər] *adv* : después ⟨shortly thereafter : poco después⟩

thereby [ðærˈbaɪ, ˈðærˌbaɪ] *adv* : de tal modo, de ese manera, así

therefore [ˈðærˌfor] *adv* : por lo tanto, por consiguiente

therein [ðærˈɪn] *adv* **1** : allí adentro, ahí adentro ⟨the contents therein : lo que allí se contiene⟩ **2** : allí, en ese aspecto ⟨therein lies the problem : allí está el problema⟩

thereof [ðærˈʌv, -ˈɑv] *adv* : de eso, de esto

thereupon [ˈðærəˌpɑn, -ˌpɔn; ˌðærəˈpɑn, -ˈpɔn] *adv* : acto seguido, inmediatamente (después)

therewith [ðærˈwɪð, -ˈwɪθ] *adv* : con eso, con ello

thermal [ˈθərməl] *adj* **1** : térmico (en física) **2** HOT : termal

thermodynamics [ˌθərmodaɪˈnæmɪks] *ns & pl* : termodinámica *f*

thermometer [θərˈmɑmət̬ər] *n* : termómetro *m*

thermos [ˈθərməs] *n* : termo *m*

thermostat [ˈθərməˌstæt] *n* : termostato *m*

thesaurus [θɪˈsɔrəs] *n, pl* **-sauri** [-ˈsɔrˌaɪ] *or* **-sauruses** [-ˈsɔrəsəz] : diccionario *m* de sinónimos

these → **this**

thesis ['θi:sɪs] *n, pl* **theses** ['θi:ˌsi:z] : tesis *f*

they ['ðeɪ] *pron* : ellos, ellas ⟨they are here : están aquí⟩ ⟨they don't know : ellos no saben⟩

they'd ['ðeɪd] (*contraction of* **they had** *or* **they would**) → **have, would**

they'll ['ðeɪl, 'ðɛl] (*contraction of* **they shall** *or* **they will**) → **shall, will**

they're ['ðɛr] (*contraction of* **they are**) → **be**

they've ['ðeɪv] (*contraction of* **they have**) → **have**

thiamine ['θaɪəmɪn, -ˌmi:n] *n* : tiamina *f*

thick[1] ['θɪk] *adj* **1** : grueso ⟨a thick plank : una tabla gruesa⟩ **2** : espeso, denso ⟨thick syrup : jarabe espeso⟩ — **thickly** *adv*

thick[2] *n* **1 in the thick of** : en medio de ⟨in the thick of the battle : en lo más reñido de la batalla⟩ **2 through thick and thin** : a las duras y a las maduras

thicken ['θɪkən] *vt* : espesar (un líquido) — *vi* : espesarse

thickener ['θɪkənər] *n* : espesante *m*

thicket ['θɪkət] *n* : matorral *m*, maleza *f*, espesura *f*

thickness ['θɪknəs] *n* : grosor *m*, grueso *m*, espesor *m*

thickset ['θɪk'sɛt] *adj* STOCKY : robusto, fornido

thick–skinned ['θɪk'skɪnd] *adj* : poco sensible, que no se ofende fácilmente

thief ['θi:f] *n, pl* **thieves** ['θi:vz] : ladrón *m*, -drona *f*

thieve ['θi:v] *v* **thieved; thieving** : hurtar, robar

thievery ['θi:vəri] *n* : hurto *m*, robo *m*, latrocinio *m*

thigh ['θaɪ] *n* : muslo *m*

thighbone ['θaɪˌbo:n] *n* : fémur *m*

thimble ['θɪmbəl] *n* : dedal *m*

thin[1] ['θɪn] *v* **thinned; thinning** *vt* : hacer menos denso, diluir, aguar (un líquido), enrarecer (un gas) — *vi* : diluirse, aguarse (dícese de un líquido), enrarecerse (dícese de un gas)

thin[2] *adj* **thinner; -est 1** LEAN, SLIM : delgado, esbelto, flaco **2** SPARSE : ralo, escaso ⟨a thin beard : una barba rala⟩ **3** WATERY : claro, aguado, diluido **4** FINE : delgado, fino ⟨thin slices : rebanadas finas⟩

thing ['θɪŋ] *n* **1** AFFAIR, MATTER : cosa *f*, asunto *m* ⟨don't talk about those things : no hables de esas cosas⟩ ⟨how are things? : ¿cómo van las cosas?⟩ **2** ACT, EVENT : cosa *f*, suceso *m*, evento *m* ⟨the flood was a terrible thing : la inundación fue una cosa terrible⟩ **3** OBJECT : cosa *f*, objeto *m* ⟨don't forget your things : no olvides tus cosas⟩

think ['θɪŋk] *v* **thought** ['θɔt]; **thinking** *vt* **1** : pensar ⟨I thought to return early : pensaba regresar temprano⟩ **2** BELIEVE : pensar, creer, opinar **3** PONDER : pensar, reflexionar **4** CONCEIVE : ocurrirse, concebir ⟨we've thought up a plan : se nos ha ocurrido un plan⟩ — *vi* **1** REASON : pensar, razonar **2** CONSIDER : pensar, considerar ⟨think of your family first : primero piensa en tu familia⟩

thinker ['θɪŋkər] *n* : pensador *m*, -dora *f*

thinly ['θɪnli] *adv* **1** LIGHTLY : ligeramente **2** SPARSELY : escasamente ⟨thinly populated : poco populado⟩ **3** BARELY : apenas

thinness ['θɪnnəs] *n* : delgadez *f*

thin–skinned ['θɪn'skɪnd] *adj* : susceptible, muy sensible

third[1] ['θərd] *or* **thirdly** [-li] *adv* : en tercer lugar ⟨she came in third : llegó en tercer lugar⟩

third[2] *adj* : tercero ⟨the third day : el tercer día⟩

third[3] *n* **1** : tercero *m*, -ra *f* (en una serie) **2** : tercero *m*, tercera parte *f*

third world *n* **the Third World** : el Tercer Mundo *m*

thirst[1] ['θərst] *vi* **1** : tener sed **2 to thirst for** DESIRE : tener sed de, estar sediento de

thirst[2] *n* : sed *f*

thirsty ['θərsti] *adj* **thirstier; -est** : sediento, que tiene sed ⟨I'm thirsty : tengo sed⟩

thirteen[1] [ˌθər'ti:n] *adj* : trece

thirteen[2] *n* : trece *m*

thirteenth[1] [ˌθər'ti:nθ] *adj* : décimo tercero

thirteenth[2] *n* **1** : decimotercero *m*, -ra *f* (en una serie) **2** : treceavo *m*, treceava parte *f*

thirtieth[1] ['θərt̬iəθ] *adj* : trigésimo

thirtieth[2] *n* **1** : trigésimo *m*, -ma *f* (en una serie) **2** : treintavo *m*, treintava parte *f*

thirty[1] ['θərt̬i] *adj* : treinta

thirty[2] *n, pl* **thirties** : treinta *m*

this[1] ['ðɪs] *adv* : así, a tal punto ⟨this big : así de grande⟩

this[2] *adj, pl* **these** ['ði:z] : este ⟨these things : estas cosas⟩ ⟨read this book : lee este libro⟩

this[3] *pron, pl* **these** : esto ⟨what's this? : ¿qué es esto?⟩ ⟨this wasn't here yesterday : esto no estaba aquí ayer⟩

thistle ['θɪsəl] *n* : cardo *m*

thong ['θɔŋ] *n* **1** STRAP : correa *f*, tira *f* **2** FLIP-FLOP : chancla *f*, chancleta *f*

thorax ['θorˌæks] *n, pl* **-raxes** *or* **-races** ['θorəˌsi:z] : tórax *m*

thorn ['θɔrn] *n* : espina *f*

thorny ['θɔrni] *adj* **thornier; -est** : espinoso

thorough ['θəro:] *adj* **1** CONSCIENTIOUS : concienzudo, meticuloso **2** COMPLETE : absoluto, completo — **thoroughly** *adv*

thoroughbred ['θəroˌbrɛd] *adj* : de pura sangre (dícese de un caballo)

Thoroughbred *n or* **Thoroughbred horse** : pura sangre *mf*

thoroughfare ['θəroˌfær] *n* : vía *f* pública, carretera *f*

thoroughness ['θəronəs] *n* : esmero *m*, meticulosidad *f*

those → **that**
thou [ˈðaʊ] *pron* : tú
though[1] [ˈðoː] *adv* **1** HOWEVER, NEVERTHELESS : sin embargo, no obstante **2 as ~** : como si ⟨as though nothing had happened : como si nada hubiera pasado⟩
though[2] *conj* : aunque, a pesar de ⟨though it was raining, we went out : salimos a pesar de la lluvia⟩
thought[1] → **think**
thought[2] [ˈθɔt] *n* **1** THINKING : pensamiento *m*, ideas *fpl* ⟨Western thought : el pensamiento occidental⟩ **2** COGITATION : pensamiento *m*, reflexión *f*, raciocinio *m* **3** IDEA : idea *f*, ocurrencia *f* ⟨it was just a thought : fue sólo una idea⟩
thoughtful [ˈθɔtfəl] *adj* **1** PENSIVE : pensativo, meditabundo **2** CONSIDERATE : considerado, atento, cortés — **thoughtfully** *adv*
thoughtfulness [ˈθɔtfəlnəs] *n* : consideración *f*, atención *f*, cortesía *f*
thoughtless [ˈθɔtləs] *adj* **1** CARELESS : descuidado, negligente **2** INCONSIDERATE : desconsiderado — **thoughtlessly** *adv*
thousand[1] [ˈθaʊzənd] *adj* : mil
thousand[2] *n, pl* **-sands** *or* **-sand** : mil *m*
thousandth[1] [ˈθaʊzəntθ] *adj* : milésimo
thousandth[2] *n* **1** : milésimo *m*, -ma *f* (en una serie) **2** : milésimo *m*, milésima parte *f*
thrash [ˈθræʃ] *vt* **1** → **thresh 2** BEAT : golpear, azotar, darle una paliza (a alguien) **3** FLAIL : sacudir, agitar bruscamente
thread[1] [ˈθrɛd] *vt* **1** : enhilar, enhebrar (una aguja) **2** STRING : ensartar (cuentas en un hilo) **3 to thread one's way** : abrirse paso
thread[2] *n* **1** : hilo *m*, hebra *f* ⟨needle and thread : aguja e hilo⟩ ⟨the thread of an argument : el hilo de un debate⟩ **2** : rosca *f*, filete *m* (de un tornillo)
threadbare [ˈθrɛdˈbær] *adj* **1** SHABBY, WORN : raído, gastado **2** TRITE : trillado, tópico, manido
threat [ˈθrɛt] *n* : amenaza *f*
threaten [ˈθrɛtən] *v* : amenazar
threatening [ˈθrɛtənɪŋ] *adj* : amenazador — **threateningly** *adv*
three[1] [ˈθriː] *adj* : tres
three[2] *n* : tres *m*
3–D [ˈθriːˈdiː] *adj* → **three–dimensional**
three–dimensional [ˈθriːdəˈmɛntʃənəl] *adj* : tridimensional
threefold [ˈθriːˌfoːld] *adj* TRIPLE : triple
three hundred[1] *adj* : trescientos
three hundred[2] *n* : trescientos *m*
threescore [ˈθriːˈskor] *adj* SIXTY : sesenta
thresh [ˈθrɛʃ] *vt* : trillar (grano)
thresher [ˈθrɛʃər] *n* : trilladora *f*
threshold [ˈθrɛʃˌhoːld, -ˌoːld] *n* : umbral *m*
threw → **throw**[1]
thrice [ˈθraɪs] *adv* : tres veces
thrift [ˈθrɪft] *n* : economía *f*, frugalidad *f*
thriftless [ˈθrɪftləs] *adj* : despilfarrador, manirroto
thrifty [ˈθrɪfti] *adj* **thriftier; -est** : económico, frugal — **thriftily** [ˈθrɪftəli] *adv*
thrill[1] [ˈθrɪl] *vt* : emocionar — *vi* **to thrill to** : dejarse conmover por, estremecerse con
thrill[2] *n* : emoción *f*
thriller [ˈθrɪlər] *n* **1** : evento *m* emocionante **2** : obra *f* de suspenso
thrilling [ˈθrɪlɪŋ] *adj* : emocionante, excitante
thrive [ˈθraɪv] *vi* **throve** [ˈθroːv] *or* **thrived; thriven** [ˈθrɪvən] **1** FLOURISH : florecer, crecer abundantemente **2** PROSPER : prosperar
throat [ˈθroːt] *n* : garganta *f*
throaty [ˈθroːt̬i] *adj* **throatier; -est** : ronco (dícese de la voz)
throb[1] [ˈθrɑb] *vi* **throbbed; throbbing** : palpitar, latir (dícese del corazón), vibrar (dícese de un motor, etc.)
throb[2] *n* : palpitación *f*, latido *m*, vibración *f*
throe [ˈθroː] *n* **1** PAIN, SPASM : espasmo *m*, dolor *m* ⟨the throes of childbirth : los dolores de parto⟩ **2 throes** *npl* : lucha *f* larga y ardua ⟨in the throes of : en el medio de⟩
throne [ˈθroːn] *n* : trono *m*
throng[1] [ˈθrɔŋ] *vt* CROWD : atestar, atiborrar, llenar — *vi* : aglomerarse, amontonarse
throng[2] *n* : muchedumbre *f*, gentío *m*, multitud *f*
throttle[1] [ˈθrɑtəl] *vt* **-tled; -tling 1** STRANGLE : estrangular, ahogar **2 to throttle down** : desacelerar (un motor)
throttle[2] *n* **1** : válvula *f* reguladora **2 at full throttle** : a toda máquina
through[1] [ˈθruː] *adv* **1** : a través, de un lado a otro ⟨let them through : déjenlos pasar⟩ **2** : de principio a fin ⟨she read the book through : leyó el libro de principio a fin⟩ **3** COMPLETELY : completamente ⟨soaked through : completamente empapado⟩
through[2] *adj* **1** DIRECT : directo ⟨a through train : un tren directo⟩ **2** FINISHED : terminado, acabado ⟨we're through : hemos terminado⟩
through[3] *prep* **1** : a través de, por ⟨through the door : por la puerta⟩ ⟨a road through the woods : un camino que atraviesa el bosque⟩ **2** BETWEEN : entre ⟨a path through the trees : un sendero entre los árboles⟩ **3** BECAUSE OF : a causa de, como consecuencia de **4** (*in expressions of time*) ⟨through the night : durante la noche⟩ ⟨to go through an experience : pasar por una experiencia⟩ **5** : a, hasta ⟨from Monday through Friday : de lunes a viernes⟩

throughout[1] [θru:ˈaʊt] *adv* **1** EVERYWHERE : por todas partes **2** THROUGH : desde el principio hasta el fin de (algo)

throughout[2] *prep* **1** : en todas partes de, a través de ⟨throughout the United States : en todo Estados Unidos⟩ **2** : de principio a fin de, durante ⟨throughout the winter : durante todo el invierno⟩

throve → **thrive**

throw[1] [ˈθro:] *vt* **threw** [ˈθru:]; **thrown** [ˈθro:n]; **throwing** **1** TOSS : tirar, lanzar, echar, arrojar, aventar *Col, Mex* ⟨to throw a ball : tirar una pelota⟩ **2** UNSEAT : desmontar (a un jinete) **3** CAST : proyectar ⟨it threw a long shadow : proyectó una sombra larga⟩ **4 to throw a party** : dar una fiesta **5 to throw into confusion** : desconcertar **6 to throw out** DISCARD : botar, tirar (en la basura)

throw[2] *n* TOSS : tiro *m*, tirada *f*, lanzamiento *m*, lance *m* (de dados)

thrower [ˈθro:ər] *n* : lanzador *m*, -dora *f*

throw up *v* VOMIT : vomitar, devolver

thrush [ˈθrʌʃ] *n* : tordo *m*, zorzal *m*

thrust[1] [ˈθrʌst] *vt* **thrust; thrusting** **1** SHOVE : empujar bruscamente **2** PLUNGE, STAB : apuñalar, clavar ⟨he thrust a dagger into her heart : la apuñaló en el corazón⟩ **3 to thrust one's way** : abrirse paso **4 to thrust upon** : imponer a

thrust[2] *n* **1** PUSH, SHOVE : empujón *m*, empellón *m* **2** LUNGE : estocada *f* (en esgrima) **3** IMPETUS : ímpetu *m*, impulso *m*, propulsión *f* (de un motor)

thud[1] [ˈθʌd] *vi* **thudded; thudding** : producir un ruido sordo

thud[2] *n* : ruido *m* sordo (que produce un objeto al caer)

thug [ˈθʌg] *n* : matón *m*

thumb[1] [ˈθʌm] *vt* : hojear (con el pulgar)

thumb[2] *n* : pulgar *m*, dedo *m* pulgar

thumbnail [ˈθʌm,neɪl] *n* : uña *f* del pulgar

thumbtack [ˈθʌm,tæk] *n* : tachuela *f*, chinche *f*

thump[1] [ˈθʌmp] *vt* POUND : golpear, aporrear — *vi* : latir con vehemencia (dícese del corazón)

thump[2] *n* THUD : ruido *m* sordo

thunder[1] [ˈθʌndər] *vi* **1** : tronar ⟨it rained and thundered all night : llovió y tronó durante la noche⟩ **2** BOOM : retumbar, bramar, resonar — *vt* ROAR, SHOUT : decir a gritos, vociferar

thunder[2] *n* : truenos *mpl*

thunderbolt [ˈθʌndər,bo:lt] *n* : rayo *m*

thunderclap [ˈθʌndər,klæp] *n* : trueno *m*

thunderous [ˈθʌndərəs] *adj* : atronador, ensordecedor, estruendoso

thundershower [ˈθʌndər,ʃaʊər] *n* : lluvia *f* con truenos y relámpagos

thunderstorm [ˈθʌndər,stɔrm] *n* : tormenta *f* con truenos y relámpagos

thunderstruck [ˈθʌndər,strʌk] *adj* : atónito

Thursday [ˈθərz,deɪ, -di] *n* : jueves *m*

thus [ˈðʌs] *adv* **1** : así, de esta manera **2** SO : hasta (cierto punto) ⟨the weather's been nice thus far : hasta ahora ha hecho buen tiempo⟩ **3** HENCE : por consiguiente, por lo tanto

thwart [ˈθwɔrt] *vt* : frustrar

thy [ˈðaɪ] *adj* : tu

thyme [ˈtaɪm, ˈθaɪm] *n* : tomillo *m*

thyroid [ˈθaɪ,rɔɪd] *n or* **thyroid gland** : tiroides *mf*, glándula *f* tiroidea

thyself [ðaɪˈsɛlf] *pron* : ti, ti mismo

tiara [tiˈærə, -ˈɑr-] *n* : diadema *f*

Tibetan [təˈbɛtən] *n* **1** : tibetano *m*, -na *f* **2** : tibetano *m* (idioma) — **Tibetan** *adj*

tibia [ˈtɪbiə] *n, pl* **-iae** [-bi,i:] : tibia *f*

tic [ˈtɪk] *n* : tic *m*

tick[1] [ˈtɪk] *vi* **1** : hacer tictac **2** OPERATE, RUN : operar, andar (dícese de un mecanismo) ⟨what makes him tick? : ¿qué es lo que lo mueve?⟩ — *vt or* **to tick off** CHECK : marcar

tick[2] *n* **1** : tictac *m* (de un reloj) **2** CHECK : marca *f* **3** : garrapata *f* (insecto)

ticket[1] [ˈtɪkət] *vt* LABEL : etiquetar

ticket[2] *n* **1** : boleto *m*, entrada *f* (de un espectáculo), pasaje *m* (de avión, tren, etc.) **2** SLATE : lista *f* de candidatos

tickle[1] [ˈtɪkəl] *v* **-led; -ling** *vt* **1** AMUSE : divertir, hacerle gracia (a alguien) **2** : hacerle cosquillas (a alguien) ⟨don't tickle me! : ¡no me hagas cosquillas!⟩ — *vi* : picar

tickle[2] *n* : cosquilleo *m*, cosquillas *fpl*, picor *m* (en la garganta)

ticklish [ˈtɪkəlɪʃ] *adj* **1** : cosquilloso (dícese de una persona) **2** DELICATE, TRICKY : delicado, peliagudo

tidal [ˈtaɪdəl] *adj* : de marea, relativo a la marea

tidal wave *n* : maremoto *m*

tidbit [ˈtɪd,bɪt] *n* **1** BITE, SNACK : bocado *m*, golosina *f* **2** : dato *m* o noticia *f* interesante ⟨useful tidbits of information : informaciones útiles⟩

tide[1] [ˈtaɪd] *vt* **tided; tiding** *or* **to tide over** : proveer lo necesario para aguantar una dificultad ⟨this money will tide you over until you find work : este dinero te mantendrá hasta que encuentres empleo⟩

tide[2] *n* **1** : marea *f* **2** CURRENT : corriente *f* (de eventos, opiniones, etc.)

tidily [ˈtaɪdəli] *adv* : ordenadamente

tidiness [ˈtaɪdinəs] *n* : aseo *m*, limpieza *f*, orden *m*

tidings [ˈtaɪdɪŋz] *npl* : nuevas *fpl*

tidy[1] [ˈtaɪdi] *vt* **-died; -dying** : asear, limpiar, poner en orden

tidy[2] *adj* **-dier; -est** **1** CLEAN, NEAT : limpio, aseado, en orden **2** SUBSTANTIAL : grande, considerable ⟨a tidy sum : una suma considerable⟩

tie[1] [ˈtaɪ] *v* **tied; tying** *or* **tieing** *vt* **1** : atar, amarrar ⟨to tie a knot : atar un nudo⟩ ⟨to tie one's shoelaces : atarse los cordones⟩ **2** BIND, UNITE : ligar, atar **3** : empatar ⟨they tied the score : empataron el marcador⟩ — *vi* : empatar ⟨the two teams were tied : los dos equipos empataron⟩

tie[2] *n* **1** : ligadura *f*, cuerda *f*, cordón *m* (para atar algo) **2** BOND, LINK : atadura *f*, ligadura *f*, vínculo *m*, lazo *m* ⟨family ties : lazos familiares⟩ **3** *or* **railroad tie** : traviesa *f* **4** DRAW : empate *m* (en deportes) **5** NECKTIE : corbata *f*

tier [ˈtɪr] *n* : hilera *f*, escalón *m*

tiff [ˈtɪf] *n* : disgusto *m*, disputa *f*

tiger [ˈtaɪgər] *n* : tigre *m*

tight[1] [ˈtaɪt] *adv* TIGHTLY : bien, fuerte ⟨shut it tight : ciérralo bien⟩

tight[2] *adj* **1** : bien cerrado, hermético ⟨a tight seal : un cierre hermético⟩ **2** STRICT : estricto, severo **3** TAUT : tirante, tenso **4** SNUG : apretado, ajustado, ceñido ⟨a tight dress : un vestido ceñido⟩ **5** DIFFICULT : difícil ⟨to be in a tight spot : estar en un aprieto⟩ **6** STINGY : apretado, avaro, agarrado *fam* **7** CLOSE : reñido ⟨a tight game : un juego reñido⟩ **8** SCARCE : escaso ⟨money is tight : escasea el dinero⟩

tighten [ˈtaɪtən] *vt* : tensar (una cuerda, etc.), apretar (un nudo, un tornillo, etc.), apretarse (el cinturón), reforzar (las reglas)

tightly [ˈtaɪtli] *adv* : bien, fuerte

tightness [ˈtaɪtnəs] *n* : lo apretado, lo tenso, tensión *f*

tightrope [ˈtaɪtˌroːp] *n* : cuerda *f* floja

tights [ˈtaɪts] *npl* : leotardo *m*, malla *f*

tightwad [ˈtaɪtˌwɑd] *n* : avaro *m*, -ra *f*; tacaño *m*, -ña *f*

tigress [ˈtaɪgrəs] *n* : tigresa *f*

tile[1] [ˈtaɪl] *vt* **tiled; tiling** : embaldosar (un piso), revestir de azulejos (una pared), tejar (un techo)

tile[2] *n* **1** *or* **floor tile** : losa *f*, baldosa *f*, mosaico *m Mex* (de un piso) **2** : azulejo *m* (de una pared) **3** : teja *f* (de un techo)

till[1] [ˈtɪl] *vt* : cultivar, labrar

till[2] *n* : caja *f*, caja *f* registradora

till[3] *prep & conj* → **until**

tiller [ˈtɪlər] *n* **1** : cultivador *m*, -dora *f* (de la tierra) **2** : caña *f* del timón (de un barco)

tilt[1] [ˈtɪlt] *vt* : ladear, inclinar — *vi* : ladearse, inclinarse

tilt[2] *n* **1** SLANT : inclinación *f* **2** **at full tilt** : a toda velocidad

timber [ˈtɪmbər] *n* **1** : madera *f* (para construcción) **2** BEAM : viga *f*

timberland [ˈtɪmbərˌlænd] *n* : bosque *m* maderero

timbre [ˈtæmbər, ˈtɪm-] *n* : timbre *m*

time[1] [ˈtaɪm] *vt* **timed; timing** **1** SCHEDULE : fijar la hora de, calcular el momento oportuno para **2** CLOCK : cronometrar, medir el tiempo de (una competencia, etc.)

time[2] *n* **1** : tiempo *m* ⟨the passing of time : el paso del tiempo⟩ ⟨she doesn't have time : no tiene tiempo⟩ **2** MOMENT : tiempo *m*, momento *m* ⟨this is not the time to bring it up : no es el momento de sacar el tema⟩ **3** : vez *f* ⟨she called you three times : te llamó tres veces⟩ ⟨three times greater : tres veces mayor⟩ **4** AGE : tiempo *m*, era *f* ⟨in your grandparents' time : en el tiempo de tus abuelos⟩ **5** TEMPO : tiempo *m*, ritmo *m* (en música) **6** : hora *f* ⟨what time is it? : ¿qué hora es?⟩ ⟨it's time for dinner : es hora de comer⟩ ⟨at the usual time : a la hora acostumbrada⟩ ⟨to keep time : ir a la hora⟩ ⟨to lose time : atrasar⟩ **7** EXPERIENCE : rato *m*, experiencia *f* ⟨we had a nice time together : pasamos juntos un rato agradable⟩ ⟨to have a rough time : pasarlo mal⟩ ⟨have a good time! : ¡que se diviertan!⟩ **8** **at times** SOMETIMES : a veces **9** **for the time being** : por el momento, de momento **10** **from time to time** OCCASIONALLY : de vez en cuando **11** **in time** PUNCTUALLY : a tiempo **12** **in time** EVENTUALLY : con el tiempo **13** **time after time** : una y otra vez

timekeeper [ˈtaɪmˌkiːpər] *n* : cronometrador *m*, -dora *f*

timeless [ˈtaɪmləs] *adj* : eterno

timely [ˈtaɪmli] *adj* **-lier; -est** : oportuno

timepiece [ˈtaɪmˌpiːs] *n* : reloj *m*

timer [ˈtaɪmər] *n* : temporizador *m*, cronómetro *m*

times [ˈtaɪmz] *prep* : por ⟨3 times 4 is 12 : 3 por 4 son 12⟩

timetable [ˈtaɪmˌteɪbəl] *n* : horario *m*

timid [ˈtɪmɪd] *adj* : tímido — **timidly** *adv*

timidity [təˈmɪdəṯi] *n* : timidez *f*

timorous [ˈtɪmərəs] *adj* : timorato, miedoso

timpani [ˈtɪmpəni] *npl* : timbales *mpl*

tin [ˈtɪn] *n* **1** : estaño *m*, hojalata *f* (metal) **2** CAN : lata *f*, bote *m*, envase *m*

tincture [ˈtɪŋktʃər] *n* : tintura *f*

tinder [ˈtɪndər] *n* : yesca *f*

tine [ˈtaɪn] *n* : diente *m* (de un tenedor, etc.)

tinfoil [ˈtɪnˌfɔɪl] *n* : papel *m* (de) aluminio

tinge[1] [ˈtɪnʤ] *vt* **tinged; tingeing** *or* **tinging** [ˈtɪnʤɪŋ] TINT : matizar, teñir ligeramente

tinge[2] *n* **1** TINT : matiz *m*, tinte *m* sutil **2** TOUCH : dejo *m*, sensación *f* ligera

tingle[1] [ˈtɪŋgəl] *vi* **-gled; -gling** : sentir (un) hormigueo, sentir (un) cosquilleo

tingle[2] *n* : hormigueo *m*, cosquilleo *m*

tinker [ˈtɪŋkər] *vi* **to tinker with** : arreglar con pequeños ajustes, toquetear (con intento de arreglar)

tinkle[1] [ˈtɪŋkəl] *vi* **-kled; -kling** : tintinear

tinkle[2] *n* : tintineo *m*

tinsel [ˈtɪntsəl] *n* : oropel *m*

tint[1] [ˈtɪnt] *vt* : teñir, colorear

tint[2] *n* : tinte *m*

tiny [ˈtaɪni] *adj* **-nier; -est** : diminuto, minúsculo

tip[1] [ˈtɪp] *v* **tipped; tipping** *vt* **1** *or* **to tip over** : volcar, voltear, hacer caer **2** TILT : ladear, inclinar ⟨to tip one's hat : saludar con el sombrero⟩ **3** TAP : tocar, golpear ligeramente **4** : darle una propina (a un mesero, etc.) ⟨I tipped him $5 : le di $5 de propina⟩ **5** : adornar o cubrir la punta de ⟨wings tipped in red : alas que tienen las puntas rojas⟩ **6 to tip off** : dar información a — *vi* TILT : ladearse, inclinarse

tip[2] *n* **1** END, POINT : punta *f*, extremo *m* ⟨on the tip of one's tongue : en la punta de la lengua⟩ **2** GRATUITY : propina *f* **3** ADVICE, INFORMATION : consejo *m*, información *f* (confidencial)

tip–off [ˈtɪpˌɔf] *n* **1** SIGN : indicación *f*, señal *f* **2** TIP : información *f* (confidencial)

tipple [ˈtɪpəl] *vi* **-pled; -pling** : tomarse unas copas

tipsy [ˈtɪpsi] *adj* **-sier; -est** : achispado

tiptoe[1] [ˈtɪpˌto:] *vi* **-toed; -toeing** : caminar de puntillas

tiptoe[2] *adv* : de puntillas

tiptoe[3] *n* : punta *f* del pie

tip–top[1] [ˈtɪpˈtɑp, -ˌtɑp] *adj* EXCELLENT : excelente

tip–top[2] *n* SUMMIT : cumbre *f*, cima *f*

tirade [ˈtaɪˌreɪd] *n* : diatriba *f*

tire[1] [ˈtaɪr] *v* **tired; tiring** *vt* : cansar, agotar, fatigar — *vi* : cansarse

tire[2] *n* : llanta *f*, neumático *m*, goma *f*

tired [ˈtaɪrd] *adj* : cansado, agotado, fatigado ⟨to get tired : cansarse⟩

tireless [ˈtaɪrləs] *adj* : incansable, infatigable — **tirelessly** *adv*

tiresome [ˈtaɪrsəm] *adj* : fastidioso, pesado, tedioso — **tiresomely** *adv*

tissue [ˈtɪˌʃu:] *n* **1** : pañuelo *m* de papel **2** : tejido *m* ⟨lung tissue : tejido pulmonar⟩

titanic [taɪˈtænɪk, tə-] *adj* GIGANTIC : titánico, gigantesco

titanium [taɪˈteɪniəm, tə-] *n* : titanio *m*

titillate [ˈtɪtəlˌeɪt] *vt* **-lated; -lating** : excitar, estimular placenteramente

title[1] [ˈtaɪṭəl] *vt* **-tled; -tling** : titular, intitular

title[2] *n* : título *m*

titter[1] [ˈtɪṭər] *vi* GIGGLE : reírse tontamente

titter[2] *n* : risita *f*, risa *f* tonta

tizzy [ˈtɪzi] *n, pl* **tizzies** : estado *m* agitado o nervioso ⟨I'm all in a tizzy : estoy todo alterado⟩

TNT [ˌti:ˌɛnˈti:] *n* : TNT *m*

to[1] [ˈtu:] *adv* **1** : a un estado consciente ⟨to come to : volver en sí⟩ **2 to and fro** : de aquí para allá, de un lado para otro

to[2] *prep* **1** (*indicating a place*) : a ⟨to go to the doctor : ir al médico⟩ ⟨I'm going to John's : voy a la casa de John⟩ **2** TOWARD : a, hacia ⟨two miles to the south : dos millas hacia el sur⟩ **3** ON : en, sobre ⟨apply salve to the wound : póngale ungüento a la herida⟩ **4** UP TO : hasta, a ⟨to a degree : hasta cierto grado⟩ ⟨from head to toe : de pies a cabeza⟩ **5** (*in expressions of time*) ⟨it's quarter to seven : son las siete menos cuarto⟩ **6** UNTIL : a, hasta ⟨from May to December : de mayo a diciembre⟩ **7** (*indicating belonging or possession*) : de, a ⟨the key to the lock : la llave del candado⟩ **8** (*indicating response*) : a ⟨dancing to the rhythm : bailando al compás⟩ **9** (*indicating comparison or proportion*) : a ⟨it's similar to mine : es parecido al mío⟩ ⟨they won 4 to 2 : ganaron 4 a 2⟩ **10** (*indicating agreement or conformity*) : a, de acuerdo con ⟨made to order : hecho a la orden⟩ ⟨to my knowledge : a mi saber⟩ **11** (*indicating inclusion*) : en cada, por ⟨twenty to the box : veinte por caja⟩ **12** (*used to form the infinitive*) ⟨to understand : entender⟩ ⟨to go away : irse⟩

toad [ˈto:d] *n* : sapo *m*

toadstool [ˈto:dˌstu:l] *n* : hongo *m* (no comestible)

toady [ˈto:di] *n, pl* **toadies** : adulador *m*, -dora *f*

toast[1] [ˈto:st] *vt* **1** : tostar (pan) **2** : brindar por ⟨to toast the victors : brindar por los vencedores⟩ **3** WARM : calentar ⟨to toast oneself : calentarse⟩

toast[2] *n* **1** : pan *m* tostado, tostadas *fpl* **2** : brindis *m* ⟨to propose a toast : proponer un brindis⟩

toaster [ˈto:stər] *n* : tostador *m*

tobacco [təˈbæko:] *n, pl* **-cos** : tabaco *m*

toboggan[1] [təˈbɑgən] *vi* : deslizarse en tobogán

toboggan[2] *n* : tobogán *m*

today[1] [təˈdeɪ] *adv* **1** : hoy ⟨she arrives today : hoy llega⟩ **2** NOWADAYS : hoy en día

today[2] *n* : hoy *m* ⟨today is a holiday : hoy es día de fiesta⟩

toddle [ˈtɑdəl] *vi* **-dled; -dling** : hacer pininos, hacer pinitos

toddler [ˈtɑdələr] *n* : niño *m* pequeño, niña *f* pequeña (que comienza a caminar)

to–do [təˈdu:] *n, pl* **to–dos** [-ˈdu:z] FUSS : lío *m*, alboroto *m*

toe [ˈto:] *n* : dedo *m* del pie

toenail [ˈto:ˌneɪl] *n* : uña *f* del pie

toffee *or* **toffy** [ˈtɔfi, ˈtɑ-] *n, pl* **toffees** *or* **toffies** : caramelo *m* elaborado con azúcar y mantequilla

toga [ˈto:gə] *n* : toga *f*

together [təˈgɛðər] *adv* **1** : juntamente, juntos (el uno con el otro) ⟨Susan and Sarah work together : Susan y Sarah trabajan juntas⟩ **2 ~ with** : junto con

togetherness [təˈgɛðərnəs] *n* : unión *f*, compañerismo *m*

togs [ˈtɑgz, ˈtɔgz] *npl* : ropa *f*

toil[1] [ˈtɔɪl] *vi* : trabajar arduamente

toil[2] *n* : trabajo *m* arduo

toilet [ˈtɔɪlət] *n* **1** : arreglo *m* personal **2** BATHROOM : (cuarto de) baño *m*, servicios *mpl* (públicos), sanitario *m Col, Mex, Ven* **3** : inodoro *m* ⟨to flush the toilet : jalar la cadena⟩

toilet paper *n* : papel *m* higiénico

toiletries [ˈtɔɪlətriz] *npl* : artículos *mpl* de tocador

token [ˈtoːkən] *n* **1** PROOF, SIGN : prueba*f*, muestra*f*, señal*m* **2** SYMBOL : símbolo *m* **3** SOUVENIR : recuerdo *m* **4** : ficha *f* (para transporte público, etc.)

told → **tell**

tolerable [ˈtɑlərəbəl] *adj* : tolerable — **tolerably** [-bli] *adv*

tolerance [ˈtɑlərən*t*s] *n* : tolerancia *f*

tolerant [ˈtɑlərənt] *adj* : tolerante — **tolerantly** *adv*

tolerate [ˈtɑləˌreɪt] *vt* **-ated; -ating** **1** ACCEPT : tolerar, aceptar **2** BEAR, ENDURE : tolerar, aguantar, soportar

toleration [ˌtɑləˈreɪʃən] *n* : tolerancia *f*

toll[1] [ˈtoːl] *vt* : tañer, sonar (una campana) — *vi* : sonar, doblar (dícese de las campanas)

toll[2] *n* **1** : peaje *m* (de una carretera, un puente, etc.) **2** CASUALTIES : pérdida *f*, número *m* de víctimas **3** TOLLING : tañido *m* (de campanas)

tollbooth [ˈtoːlˌbuːθ] *n* : caseta *f* de peaje

tollgate [ˈtoːlˌgeɪt] *n* : barrera *f* de peaje

tomahawk [ˈtɑməˌhɔk] *n* : hacha *f* de guerra (de los indígenas norteamericanos)

tomato [təˈmeɪt̬o, -ˈmɑ-] *n, pl* **-toes** : tomate *m*

tomb [ˈtuːm] *n* : sepulcro *m*, tumba *f*

tomboy [ˈtɑmˌbɔɪ] *n* : marimacho *mf*; niña *f* que se porta como muchacho

tombstone [ˈtuːmˌstoːn] *n* : lápida *f*

tomcat [ˈtɑmˌkæt] *n* : gato *m* (macho)

tome [ˈtoːm] *n* : tomo *m*

tomorrow[1] [təˈmɑro] *adv* : mañana

tomorrow[2] *n* : mañana *m*

tom–tom [ˈtɑmˌtɑm] *n* : tam-tam *m*

ton [ˈtən] *n* : tonelada *f*

tone[1] [ˈtoːn] *vt* **toned; toning** **1** *or* **to tone down** : atenuar, suavizar, moderar **2** *or* **to tone up** STRENGTHEN : tonificar, vigorizar

tone[2] *n* : tono *m* ⟨in a friendly tone : en tono amistoso⟩ ⟨a greyish tone : un tono grisáceo⟩

tongs [ˈtɑŋz, ˈtɔŋz] *npl* : tenazas *fpl*

tongue [ˈtʌŋ] *n* **1** : lengua *f* **2** LANGUAGE : lengua *f*, idioma *m*

tongue–tied [ˈtʌŋˌtaɪd] *adj* **to get tongue–tied** : trabársele la lengua a uno

tonic[1] [ˈtɑnɪk] *adj* : tónico

tonic[2] *n* **1** : tónico *m* **2** *or* **tonic water** : tónica *f*

tonight[1] [təˈnaɪt] *adv* : esta noche

tonight[2] *n* : esta noche *f*

tonsil [ˈtɑn*t*səl] *n* : amígdala *f*, angina *f Mex*

tonsillitis [ˌtɑn*t*səˈlaɪt̬əs] *n* : amigdalitis *f*, anginas *fpl Mex*

too [ˈtuː] *adv* **1** ALSO : también **2** EXCESSIVELY : demasiado ⟨it's too hot in here : aquí hace demasiado calor⟩

took → **take**[1]

tool[1] [ˈtuːl] *vt* **1** : fabricar, confeccionar (con herramientas) **2** EQUIP : instalar maquinaria en (una fábrica)

tool[2] *n* : herramienta *f*

toolbox [ˈtuːlˌbɑks] *n* : caja *f* de herramientas

toot[1] [ˈtuːt] *vt* : sonar (un claxon o un pito)

toot[2] *n* : pitido *m*, bocinazo *m* (de un claxon)

tooth [ˈtuːθ] *n, pl* **teeth** [ˈtiːθ] : diente *m*

toothache [ˈtuːθˌeɪk] *n* : dolor *m* de muelas

toothbrush [ˈtuːθˌbrʌʃ] *n* : cepillo *m* de dientes

toothless [ˈtuːθləs] *adj* : desdentado

toothpaste [ˈtuːθˌpeɪst] *n* : pasta *f* de dientes, crema *f* dental, dentífrico *m*

toothpick [ˈtuːθˌpɪk] *n* : palillo *m* (de dientes), mondadientes *m*

top[1] [ˈtɑp] *vt* **topped; topping** **1** COVER : cubrir, coronar **2** SURPASS : sobrepasar, superar **3** CLEAR : pasar por encima de

top[2] *adj* : superior ⟨the top shelf : la repisa superior⟩ ⟨one of the top lawyers : uno de los mejores abogados⟩

top[3] *n* **1** : parte *f* superior, cumbre *f*, cima *f* (de un monte, etc.) ⟨to climb to the top : subir a la cumbre⟩ **2** COVER : tapa *f*, cubierta *f* **3** : trompo *m* (juguete) **4 on top of** : encima de

topaz [ˈtoːˌpæz] *n* : topacio *m*

topcoat [ˈtɑpˌkoːt] *n* : sobretodo *m*, abrigo *m*

topic [ˈtɑpɪk] *n* : tema *m*, tópico *m*

topical [ˈtɑpɪkəl] *adj* : de interés actual

topmost [ˈtɑpˌmoːst] *adj* : más alto

top–notch [ˈtɑpˈnɑtʃ] *adj* : de lo mejor, de primera categoría

topographic [ˌtɑpəˈgræfɪk] *or* **topographical** [-fɪkəl] *adj* : topográfico

topography [təˈpɑgrəfi] *n, pl* **-phies** : topografía *f*

topple [ˈtɑpəl] *v* **-pled; -pling** *vi* : caerse, venirse abajo — *vt* : volcar, derrocar (un gobierno, etc.)

topsoil [ˈtɑpˌsɔɪl] *n* : capa *f* superior del suelo

topsy–turvy [ˌtɑpsiˈtərvi] *adv & adj* : patas arriba, al revés

torch [ˈtɔrtʃ] *n* : antorcha *f*

tore → **tear**[1]

torment[1] [tɔrˈmɛnt, ˈtɔrˌ-] *vt* : atormentar, torturar, martirizar

torment[2] [ˈtɔrˌmɛnt] *n* : tormento *m*, suplicio *m*, martirio *m*

tormentor [tɔrˈmɛntər] *n* : atormentador *m*, -dora *f*

torn *pp* → **tear**[1]

tornado [tɔrˈneɪdo] *n, pl* **-does** *or* **-dos** : tornado *m*

torpedo[1] [tɔrˈpiːdo] *vt* : torpedear

torpedo[2] *n, pl* **-does** : torpedo *m*

torpid [ˈtɔrpɪd] *adj* **1** SLUGGISH : aletargado **2** APATHETIC : apático

torpor [ˈtɔrpər] *n* : letargo *m*, apatía *f*

torrent [ˈtɔrənt] *n* : torrente *m*

torrential [təˈrɛntʃəl, tə-] *adj* : torrencial

torrid [ˈtɔrɪd] *adj* : tórrido

torso [ˈtɔrˌsoː] *n, pl* **-sos** *or* **-si** [-ˌsiː] : torso *m*

tortilla [tɔrˈtiːjə] *n* : tortilla *f* (de maíz)
tortoise [ˈtɔrt̬əs] *n* : tortuga *f* (terrestre)
tortoiseshell [ˈtɔrt̬əsˌʃɛl] *n* : carey *m*, concha *f*
tortuous [ˈtɔrtʃʊəs] *adj* : tortuoso
torture[1] [ˈtɔrtʃər] *vt* **-tured; -turing** : torturar, atormentar
torture[2] *n* : tortura *f*, tormento *m* ⟨it was sheer torture! : ¡fue un verdadero suplicio!⟩
torturer [ˈtɔrtʃərər] *n* : torturador *m*, -dora *f*
toss[1] [ˈtɔs, ˈtɑs] *vt* **1** AGITATE, SHAKE : sacudir, agitar, mezclar (una ensalada) **2** THROW : tirar, echar, lanzar — *vi* : sacudirse, moverse agitadamente ⟨to toss and turn : dar vueltas⟩
toss[2] *n* THROW : lanzamiento *m*, tiro *m*, tirada *f*, lance *m* (de dados, etc.)
toss–up [ˈtɔsˌʌp] *n* : posibilidad *f* igual ⟨it's a toss-up : quizá sí, quizá no⟩
tot [ˈtɑt] *n* : pequeño *m*, -ña *f*
total[1] [ˈtoːtəl] *vt* **-taled** *or* **-talled; -taling** *or* **-talling 1** *or* **to total up** ADD : sumar, totalizar **2** AMOUNT TO : ascender a, llegar a
total[2] *adj* : total, completo, absoluto — **totally** *adv*
total[3] *n* : total *m*
totalitarian [toːˌtæləˈtɛriən] *adj* : totalitario
totalitarianism [toːˌtæləˈtɛriəˌnɪzəm] *n* : totalitarismo *m*
totality [toːˈtælət̬i] *n, pl* **-ties** : totalidad *f*
tote [ˈtoːt] *vt* **toted; toting** : cargar, llevar
totem [ˈtoːtəm] *n* : tótem *m*
totter [ˈtɑtər] *vi* : tambalearse
touch[1] [ˈtʌtʃ] *vt* **1** FEEL, HANDLE : tocar, tentar **2** AFFECT, MOVE : conmover, afectar, tocar ⟨his gesture touched our hearts : su gesto nos tocó el corazón⟩ — *vi* : tocarse
touch[2] *n* **1** : tacto *m* (sentido) **2** DETAIL : toque *m*, detalle *m* ⟨a touch of color : un toque de color⟩ **3** BIT : pizca *f*, gota *f*, poco *m* **4** ABILITY : habilidad *f* ⟨to lose one's touch : perder la habilidad⟩ **5** CONTACT : contacto *m*, comunicación *f* ⟨to keep in touch : mantenerse en contacto⟩
touchdown [ˈtʌtʃˌdaʊn] *n* : touchdown *m* (en futbol americano)
touching [ˈtʌtʃɪŋ] *adj* MOVING : conmovedor
touchstone [ˈtʌtʃˌstoːn] *n* : piedra *f* de toque
touch up *vt* : retocar
touchy [ˈtʌtʃi] *adj* **touchier; -est 1** : sensible, susceptible (dícese de una persona) **2** : delicado ⟨a touchy subject : un tema delicado⟩
tough[1] [ˈtʌf] *adj* **1** STRONG : fuerte, resistente (dícese de materiales) **2** LEATHERY : correoso ⟨a tough steak : un bistec duro⟩ **3** HARDY : fuerte, robusto (dícese de una persona) **4** STRICT : severo, exigente **5** DIFFICULT : difícil **6** STUBBORN : terco, obstinado
tough[2] *n* : matón *m*, persona *f* ruda y brusca
toughen [ˈtʌfən] *vt* : fortalecer, endurecer — *vi* : endurecerse, hacerse más fuerte
toughness [ˈtʌfnəs] *n* : dureza *f*
toupee [tuːˈpeɪ] *n* : peluquín *m*, bisoñé *m*
tour[1] [ˈtʊr] *vi* : tomar una excursión, viajar — *vt* : recorrer, hacer una gira por
tour[2] *n* **1** : gira *f*, tour *m*, excursión *f* **2 tour of duty** : período *m* de servicio
tourism [ˈtʊrˌɪzəm] *n* : turismo *m*
tourist [ˈtʊrɪst, ˈtər-] *n* : turista *mf*
tournament [ˈtərnəmənt, ˈtʊr-] *n* : torneo *m*
tourniquet [ˈtərnɪkət, ˈtʊr-] *n* : torniquete *m*
tousle [ˈtaʊzəl] *vt* **-sled; -sling** : desarreglar, despeinar (el cabello)
tout [ˈtaʊt] *vt* : promocionar, elogiar (con exageración)
tow[1] [ˈtoː] *vt* : remolcar
tow[2] *n* : remolque *m*
toward [ˈtord, təˈwɔrd] *or* **towards** [ˈtordz, təˈwɔrdz] *prep* **1** (*indicating direction*) : hacia, rumbo a ⟨heading toward town : dirigiéndose rumbo al pueblo⟩ ⟨efforts towards peace : esfuerzos hacia la paz⟩ **2** (*indicating time*) : alrededor de ⟨toward midnight : alrededor de la medianoche⟩ **3** REGARDING : hacia, con respecto a ⟨his attitude toward life : su actitud hacia la vida⟩ **4** FOR : para, como pago parcial de (una compra o deuda)
towel [ˈtaʊəl] *n* : toalla *f*
tower[1] [ˈtaʊər] *vi* **to tower over** : descollar sobre, elevarse sobre, dominar
tower[2] *n* : torre *f*
towering [ˈtaʊərɪŋ] *adj* : altísimo, imponente
town [ˈtaʊn] *n* : pueblo *m*, ciudad *f* (pequeña)
township [ˈtaʊnˌʃɪp] *n* : municipio *m*
tow truck [ˈtoːˌtrʌk] *n* : grúa *f*
toxic [ˈtɑksɪk] *adj* : tóxico
toxicity [tɑkˈsɪsət̬i] *n, pl* **-ties** : toxicidad *f*
toxin [ˈtɑksɪn] *n* : toxina *f*
toy[1] [ˈtɔɪ] *vi* : juguetear, jugar
toy[2] *adj* : de juguete ⟨a toy rifle : un rifle de juguete⟩
toy[3] *n* : juguete *m*
trace[1] [ˈtreɪs] *vt* **traced; tracing 1** : calcar (un dibujo, etc.) **2** OUTLINE : delinear, trazar (planes, etc.) **3** TRACK : describir (un curso, una historia) **4** FIND : localizar, ubicar
trace[2] *n* **1** SIGN, TRACK : huella *f*, rastro *m*, indicio *m*, vestigio *m* ⟨he disappeared without a trace : desapareció sin dejar rastro⟩ **2** BIT, HINT : pizca *f*, ápice *m*, dejo *m*
trachea [ˈtreɪkiə] *n, pl* **-cheae** [-kiˌiː] : tráquea *f*

tracing paper *n* : papel *m* de calcar
track[1] ['træk] *vt* **1** TRAIL : seguir la pista de, rastrear **2** : dejar huellas de ⟨he tracked mud all over : dejó huellas de lodo por todas partes⟩
track[2] *n* **1** : rastro *m*, huella *f* (de animales), pista *f* (de personas) **2** PATH : pista *f*, sendero *m*, camino *m* **3** *or* **railroad track** : vía *f* (férrea) **4** → **racetrack 5** : oruga *f* (de un tanque, etc.) **6** : pista *f* (deporte) **7 to keep track of** : llevar la cuenta de
track–and–field ['trækənd'fi:ld] *adj* : de pista y campo
tract ['trækt] *n* **1** AREA : terreno *m*, extensión *f*, área *f* **2** : tracto *m* ⟨digestive tract : tracto digestivo⟩ **3** PAMPHLET : panfleto *m*, folleto *m*
traction ['trækʃən] *n* : tracción *f*
tractor ['træktər] *n* **1** : tractor *m* (vehículo agrícola) **2** TRUCK : camión *m* (con remolque)
trade[1] ['treɪd] *v* **traded; trading** *vi* : comerciar, negociar — *vt* EXCHANGE : intercambiar, canjear
trade[2] *n* **1** OCCUPATION : oficio *m*, profesión *f*, ocupación *f* ⟨a carpenter by trade : carpintero de oficio⟩ **2** COMMERCE : comercio *m*, industria *f* ⟨free trade : libre comercio⟩ ⟨the book trade : la industria del libro⟩ **3** EXCHANGE : intercambio *m*, canje *m*
trade–in ['treɪd,ɪn] *n* : artículo *m* que se canjea por otro
trademark ['treɪd,mɑrk] *n* **1** : marca *f* registrada **2** CHARACTERISTIC : sello *m* característico (de un grupo, una persona, etc.)
trader ['treɪdər] *n* : negociante *mf*, tratante *mf*, comerciante *mf*
tradesman ['treɪdzmən] *n, pl* **-men** [-mən, -,mɛn] **1** CRAFTSMAN : artesano *m*, -na *f* **2** SHOPKEEPER : tendero *m*, -ra *f*; comerciante *mf*
trade wind *n* : viento *m* alisio
tradition [trə'dɪʃən] *n* : tradición *f*
traditional [trə'dɪʃənəl] *adj* : tradicional — **traditionally** *adv*
traffic[1] ['træfɪk] *vi* **trafficked; trafficking** : traficar (con)
traffic[2] *n* **1** COMMERCE : tráfico *m*, comercio *m* ⟨the drug traffic : el narcotráfico⟩ **2** : tráfico *m*, tránsito *m*, circulación *f* (de vehículos, etc.)
traffic circle *n* : rotonda *f*, glorieta *f*
trafficker ['træfɪkər] *n* : traficante *mf*
traffic light *n* : semáforo *m*, luz *f* (de tránsito)
tragedy ['trædʒədi] *n, pl* **-dies** : tragedia *f*
tragic ['trædʒɪk] *adj* : trágico — **tragically** *adv*
trail[1] ['treɪl] *vi* **1** DRAG : arrastrarse **2** LAG : quedarse atrás, retrasarse **3 to trail away** *or* **to trail off** : disminuir, menguar, desvanecerse — *vt* **1** DRAG : arrastrar **2** PURSUE : perseguir, seguir la pista de
trail[2] *n* **1** TRACK : rastro *m*, huella *f*, pista *f* ⟨a trail of blood : un rastro de sangre⟩ **2** : cola *f*, estela *f* (de un meteoro) **3** PATH : sendero *m*, camino *m*, vereda *f*
trailer ['treɪlər] *n* **1** : remolque *m*, tráiler *m* (de un camión) **2** : caravana *f* (vivienda ambulante)
train[1] ['treɪn] *vt* **1** : adiestrar, entrenar (atletas), capacitar (trabajadores), amaestrar (animales) **2** POINT : apuntar (un arma, etc.) — *vi* : entrenar(se) (físicamente), prepararse (profesionalmente) ⟨she's training at the gym : se está entrenando en el gimnasio⟩
train[2] *n* **1** : cola *f* (de un vestido) **2** RETINUE : cortejo *m*, séquito *m* **3** SERIES : serie *f* (de eventos) **4** : tren *m* ⟨passenger train : tren de pasajeros⟩
trainee [treɪ'ni:] *n* : aprendiz *m*, -diza *f*
trainer ['treɪnər] *n* : entrenador *m*, -dora *f*
training ['treɪnɪŋ] *n* : adiestramiento *m*, entrenamiento *m* (físico), capacitación *f* (de trabajadores)
traipse ['treɪps] *vi* **traipsed; traipsing** : andar de un lado para otro, vagar
trait ['treɪt] *n* : rasgo *m*, característica *f*
traitor ['treɪţər] *n* : traidor *m*, -dora *f*
traitorous ['treɪţərəs] *adj* : traidor
trajectory [trə'dʒɛktəri] *n, pl* **-ries** : trayectoria *f*
tramp[1] ['træmp] *vi* : caminar (a paso pesado) — *vt* : deambular por, vagar por ⟨to tramp the streets : vagar por las calles⟩
tramp[2] *n* **1** VAGRANT : vagabundo *m*, -da *f* **2** HIKE : caminata *f*
trample ['træmpəl] *vt* **-pled; -pling** : pisotear, hollar
trampoline [,træmpə'li:n, 'træmpə,-] *n* : trampolín *m*, cama *f* elástica
trance ['trænts] *n* : trance *m*
tranquil ['træŋkwəl] *adj* : calmo, tranquilo, sereno — **tranquilly** *adv*
tranquilize ['træŋkwə,laɪz] *vt* **-ized; -izing** : tranquilizar
tranquilizer ['træŋkwə,laɪzər] *n* : tranquilizante *m*
tranquillity *or* **tranquility** [træŋ'kwɪləţi] *n* : sosiego *m*, tranquilidad *f*
transact [træn'zækt] *vt* : negociar, gestionar, hacer (negocios)
transaction [træn'zækʃən] *n* **1** : transacción *f*, negocio *m*, operación *f* **2 transactions** *npl* RECORDS : actas *fpl*
transatlantic [,træntsət'læntɪk, ,trænz-] *adj* : transatlántico
transcend [træn'sɛnd] *vt* : trascender, sobrepasar
transcendent [træn*t*'sɛndənt] *adj* : trascendente — **transcendence** [træn*t*'sɛndən*t*s] *n*
transcendental [,træn*t*,sɛn'dɛntəl, -sən-] *adj* : trascendental ⟨transcendental meditation : meditación trascendental⟩

transcribe [træn'skraɪb] *vt* **-scribed; -scribing** : transcribir
transcript ['træn,skrɪpt] *n* : copia *f* oficial
transcription [træn'skrɪpʃən] *n* : transcripción *f*
transfer[1] [trænts'fər, 'trænts,fər] *v* **-ferred; -ferring** *vt* **1** : trasladar (a una persona), transferir (fondos) **2** : transferir, traspasar, ceder (propiedad) **3** PRINT : imprimir (un diseño) — *vi* **1** MOVE : trasladarse, cambiarse **2** CHANGE : transbordar, cambiar (de un transporte a otro) ⟨he transfers at E Street : hace un transborde a la calle E⟩
transfer[2] ['trænts,fər] *n* **1** TRANSFERRING : transferencia *f* (de fondos, de propiedad, etc.), traslado *m* (de una persona) **2** DECAL : calcomanía *f* **3** : boleto *m* (para cambiar de un avión, etc., a otro)
transferable [trænts'fərəbəl] *adj* : transferible
transference [trænts'fərənts] *n* : transferencia *f*
transfigure [trænts'fɪgjər] *vt* **-ured; -uring** : transfigurar, transformar
transfix [trænts'fɪks] *vt* **1** PIERCE : traspasar, atravesar **2** IMMOBILIZE : paralizar
transform [trænts'fɔrm] *vt* : transformar
transformation [,træntsfər'meɪʃən] *n* : transformación *f*
transformer [trænts'fɔrmər] *n* : transformador *m*
transfusion [trænts'fju:ʒən] *n* : transfusión *f*
transgress [trænts'grɛs, trænz-] *vt* : transgredir, infringir
transgression [trænts'grɛʃən, trænz-] *n* : transgresión *f*
transient[1] ['træntʃənt, 'trænsiənt] *adj* : pasajero, transitorio — **transiently** *adv*
transient[2] *n* : transeúnte *mf*
transistor [træn'zɪstər, -'sɪs-] *n* : transistor *m*
transit ['træntsɪt, 'trænzɪt] *n* **1** PASSAGE : pasaje *m*, tránsito *m* ⟨in transit : en tránsito⟩ **2** TRANSPORTATION : transporte *m* (público) **3** : teodolito *m* (instrumento topográfico)
transition [træn'sɪʃən, -'zɪʃ-] *n* : transición *f*
transitional [træn'sɪʃənəl, -'zɪʃ-] *adj* : de transición
transitive ['træntsəṭɪv, 'trænzə-] *adj* : transitivo
transitory ['træntsə,tori, 'trænzə-] *adj* : transitorio
translate [trænts'leɪt, trænz-; 'trænts,-, 'træns,-] *vt* **-lated; -lating** : traducir
translation [trænts'leɪʃən, trænz-] *n* : traducción *f*
translator [trænts'leɪṭər, trænz-; 'trænts,-, 'træns,-] *n* : traductor *m*, -tora *f*
translucent [trænts'lu:sənt, trænz-] *adj* : translúcido
transmission [trænts'mɪʃən, trænz-] *n* : transmisión *f*
transmit [trænts'mɪt, trænz-] *vt* **-mitted; -mitting** : transmitir
transmitter [trænts'mɪṭər, trænz-; 'trænts,-, 'træns,-] *n* : transmisor *m*, emisor *m*
transom ['træntsəm] *n* : montante *m* (de una puerta), travesaño *m* (de una ventana)
transparency [trænts'pærəntsi] *n, pl* **-cies** : transparencia *f*
transparent [trænts'pærənt] *adj* **1** : transparente, traslúcido ⟨a transparent fabric : una tela transparente⟩ **2** OBVIOUS : transparente, obvio, claro — **transparently** *adv*
transpiration [,træntspə'reɪʃən] *n* : transpiración *f*
transpire [trænts'paɪr] *vi* **-spired; -spiring** **1** : transpirar (en biología y botánica) **2** TURN OUT : resultar **3** HAPPEN : suceder, ocurrir, tener lugar
transplant[1] [trænts'plænt] *vt* : trasplantar
transplant[2] ['trænts,plænt] *n* : trasplante *m*
transport[1] [trænts'port, 'trænts,-] *vt* **1** CARRY : transportar, acarrear **2** ENRAPTURE : transportar, extasiar
transport[2] ['trænts,port] *n* **1** TRANSPORTATION : transporte *m*, transportación *f* **2** RAPTURE : éxtasis *m* **3** *or* **transport ship** : buque *m* de transporte (de personal militar)
transportation [,træntspər'teɪʃən] *n* : transporte *m*, transportación *f*
transpose [trænts'po:z] *vt* **-posed; -posing** : trasponer, trasladar, transportar (una composición musical)
transverse [trænts'vərs, trænz-] *adj* : transversal, transverso, oblicuo — **transversely** *adv*
trap[1] ['træp] *vt* **trapped; trapping** : atrapar, apresar (en una trampa)
trap[2] *n* : trampa *f* ⟨to set a trap : tender una trampa⟩
trapdoor ['træp'dor] *n* : trampilla *f*, escotillón *m*
trapeze [træ'pi:z] *n* : trapecio *m*
trapezoid ['træpə,zɔɪd] *n* : trapezoide *m*, trapecio *m*
trapper ['træpər] *n* : trampero *m*, -ra *f*; cazador *m*, -dora *f* (que usa trampas)
trappings ['træpɪŋz] *npl* **1** : arreos *mpl*, jaeces *mpl* (de un caballo) **2** ADORNMENTS : adornos *mpl*, pompa *f*
trash ['træʃ] *n* : basura *f*
trashy ['træʃi] *adj* : de pacotilla
trauma ['trɔmə, 'traʊ-] *n* : trauma *m*
traumatic [trə'mæṭɪk, trɔ-, traʊ-] *adj* : traumático
travel[1] ['trævəl] *vi* **-eled** *or* **-elled; -eling** *or* **-elling** **1** JOURNEY : viajar **2** GO, MOVE : desplazarse, moverse, ir ⟨the waves travel at uniform speed : las ondas se desplazan a una velocidad uniforme⟩

travel[2] *n or* **travels** *npl* : viajes *mpl*
traveler *or* **traveller** [ˈtrævələr] *n* : viajero *m*, -ra *f*
traverse [trəˈvərs, træˈvərs, ˈtrævərs] *vt* **-versed; -versing** CROSS : atravesar, extenderse a través de, cruzar
travesty [ˈtrævəsti] *n, pl* **-ties** : parodia *f*
trawl[1] [ˈtrɔl] *vi* : pescar con red de arrastre, rastrear
trawl[2] *n or* **trawl net** : red *f* de arrastre
trawler [ˈtrɔlər] *n* : barco *m* de pesca (utilizado para rastrear)
tray [ˈtreɪ] *n* : bandeja *f*, charola *f Bol, Mex, Peru*
treacherous [ˈtrɛʧərəs] *adj* **1** TRAITOROUS : traicionero, traidor **2** DANGEROUS : peligroso
treacherously [ˈtrɛʧərəsli] *adv* : a traición
treachery [ˈtrɛʧəri] *n, pl* **-eries** : traición *f*
tread[1] [ˈtrɛd] *v* **trod** [ˈtrɑd]; **trodden** [ˈtrɑdən] *or* **trod; treading** *vt* TRAMPLE : pisotear, hollar — *vi* **1** WALK : caminar, andar **2 to tread on** : pisar
tread[2] *n* **1** STEP : paso *m*, andar *m* **2** : banda *f* de rodadura (de un neumático, etc.) **3** : escalón *m* (de una escalera)
treadle [ˈtrɛdəl] *n* : pedal *m* (de una máquina)
treadmill [ˈtrɛdˌmɪl] *n* **1** : rueda *f* de andar **2** ROUTINE : rutina *f*
treason [ˈtriːzən] *n* : traición *f* (a la patria, etc.)
treasure[1] [ˈtrɛʒər, ˈtreɪ-] *vt* **-sured; -suring** : apreciar, valorar
treasure[2] *n* : tesoro *m*
treasurer [ˈtrɛʒərər, ˈtreɪ-] *n* : tesorero *m*, -ra *f*
treasury [ˈtrɛʒəri, ˈtreɪ-] *n, pl* **-suries** : tesorería *f*, tesoro *m*
treat[1] [ˈtriːt] *vt* **1** DEAL WITH : tratar (un asunto) ⟨the article treats of poverty : el artículo trata de la pobreza⟩ **2** HANDLE : tratar (a una persona), manejar (un objeto) ⟨to treat something as a joke : tomar(se) algo a broma⟩ **3** INVITE : invitar, convidar ⟨he treated me to a meal : me invitó a comer⟩ **4** : tratar, atender (en medicina) **5** PROCESS : tratar ⟨to treat sewage : tratar las aguas negras⟩
treat[2] *n* : gusto *m*, placer *m* ⟨it was a treat to see you : fue un placer verte⟩ ⟨it's my treat : yo invito⟩
treatise [ˈtriːt̬ɪs] *n* : tratado *m*, estudio *m*
treatment [ˈtriːtmənt] *n* : trato *m*, tratamiento *m* (médico)
treaty [ˈtriːt̬i] *n, pl* **-ties** : tratado *m*, convenio *m*
treble[1] [ˈtrɛbəl] *vt* **-bled; -bling** : triplicar
treble[2] *adj* **1** → **triple 2** : de tiple, soprano (en música) **3 treble clef** : clave *f* de sol
treble[3] *n* : tiple *m*, parte *f* de soprano
tree [ˈtriː] *n* : árbol *m*
treeless [ˈtriːləs] *adj* : carente de árboles
trek[1] [ˈtrɛk] *vi* **trekked; trekking** : hacer un viaje largo y difícil
trek[2] *n* : viaje *m* largo y difícil
trellis [ˈtrɛlɪs] *n* : enrejado *m*, espaldera *f*, celosía *f*
tremble [ˈtrɛmbəl] *vi* **-bled; -bling** : temblar
tremendous [trɪˈmɛndəs] *adj* : tremendo — **tremendously** *adv*
tremor [ˈtrɛmər] *n* : temblor *m*
tremulous [ˈtrɛmjələs] *adj* : trémulo, tembloroso
trench [ˈtrɛnʧ] *n* **1** DITCH : zanja *f* **2** : trinchera *f* (militar)
trenchant [ˈtrɛnʧənt] *adj* : cortante, mordaz
trend[1] [ˈtrɛnd] *vi* : tender, inclinarse
trend[2] *n* **1** TENDENCY : tendencia *f* **2** FASHION : moda *f*
trendy [ˈtrɛndi] *adj* **trendier; -est** : de moda
trepidation [ˌtrɛpəˈdeɪʃən] *n* : inquietud *f*, ansiedad *f*
trespass[1] [ˈtrɛspəs, -ˌpæs] *vi* **1** SIN : pecar, transgredir **2** : entrar ilegalmente (en propiedad ajena)
trespass[2] *n* **1** SIN : pecado *m*, transgresión *f* ⟨forgive us our trespasses : perdónanos nuestras deudas⟩ **2** : entrada *f* ilegal (en propiedad ajena)
tress [ˈtrɛs] *n* : mechón *m*
trestle [ˈtrɛsəl] *n* **1** : caballete *m* (armazón) **2** *or* **trestle bridge** : puente *m* de caballete
triad [ˈtraɪˌæd] *n* : tríada *f*
trial[1] [ˈtraɪəl] *adj* : de prueba ⟨trial period : período de prueba⟩
trial[2] *n* **1** : juicio *m*, proceso *m* ⟨to stand trial : ser sometido a juicio⟩ **2** AFFLICTION : aflicción *f*, tribulación *f* **3** TEST : prueba *f*, ensayo *m*
triangle [ˈtraɪˌæŋgəl] *n* : triángulo *m*
triangular [traɪˈæŋgjələr] *adj* : triangular
tribal [ˈtraɪbəl] *adj* : tribal
tribe [ˈtraɪb] *n* : tribu *f*
tribesman [ˈtraɪbzmən] *n, pl* **-men** [-mən, -ˌmɛn] : miembro *m* de una tribu
tribulation [ˌtrɪbjəˈleɪʃən] *n* : tribulación *f*
tribunal [traɪˈbjuːnəl, trɪ-] *n* : tribunal *m*, corte *f*
tributary [ˈtrɪbjəˌtɛri] *n, pl* **-taries** : afluente *m*
tribute [ˈtrɪbˌjuːt] *n* : tributo *m*
trick[1] [ˈtrɪk] *vt* : engañar, embaucar
trick[2] *n* **1** RUSE : trampa *f*, treta *f*, artimaña *f* **2** PRANK : broma *f* ⟨we played a trick on her : le gastamos una broma⟩ **3** : truco *m* ⟨magic tricks : trucos de magia⟩ ⟨the trick is to wait five minutes : el truco está en esperar cinco minutos⟩ **4** MANNERISM : peculiaridad *f*, manía *f* **5** : baza *f* (en juegos de naipes)
trickery [ˈtrɪkəri] *n* : engaños *mpl*, trampas *fpl*
trickle[1] [ˈtrɪkəl] *vi* **-led; -ling** : gotear, chorrear

trickle[2] *n* : goteo *m*, hilo *m*

trickster ['trɪkstər] *n* : estafador *m*, -dora *f*; embaucador *m*, -dora *f*

tricky ['trɪki] *adj* **trickier; -est 1** SLY : astuto, taimado **2** DIFFICULT : delicado, peliagudo, difícil

tricycle ['traɪsəkəl, -ˌsɪkəl] *n* : triciclo *m*

trident ['traɪdənt] *n* : tridente *m*

triennial ['traɪ'ɛniəl] *adj* : trienal

trifle[1] ['traɪfəl] *vi* **-fled; -fling** : jugar, juguetear

trifle[2] *n* : nimiedad *f*, insignificancia *f*

trifling ['traɪflɪŋ] *adj* : trivial, insignificante

trigger[1] ['trɪgər] *vt* : causar, provocar

trigger[2] *n* : gatillo *m*

trigonometry [ˌtrɪgə'nɑmətri] *n* : trigonometría *f*

trill[1] ['trɪl] *vi* QUAVER : trinar, gorjear — *vt* : vibrar ⟨to trill the *r* : vibrar la *r*⟩

trill[2] *n* **1** QUAVER : trino *m*, gorjeo *m* **2** : vibración *f* (en fonética)

trillion ['trɪljən] *n* : billón *m*

trilogy ['trɪləʤi] *n, pl* **-gies** : trilogía *f*

trim[1] ['trɪm] *vt* **trimmed; trimming 1** DECORATE : adornar, decorar **2** CUT : recortar **3** REDUCE : recortar, reducir ⟨to trim the excess : recortar el exceso⟩

trim[2] *adj* **trimmer; trimmest 1** SLIM : esbelto **2** NEAT : limpio y arreglado, bien cuidado

trim[3] *n* **1** CONDITION : condición *f*, estado *m* ⟨to keep in trim : mantenerse en buena forma⟩ **2** CUT : recorte *m* **3** TRIMMING : adornos *mpl*

trimming ['trɪmɪŋ] *n* : adornos *mpl*, accesorios *mpl*

Trinity ['trɪnəṭi] *n* : Trinidad *f*

trinket ['trɪŋkət] *n* : chuchería *f*, baratija *f*

trio ['tri:ˌo:] *n, pl* **trios** : trío *m*

trip[1] ['trɪp] *v* **tripped; tripping** *vi* **1** : caminar (a paso ligero) **2** STUMBLE : tropezar **3 to trip up** ERR : equivocarse, cometer un error — *vt* **1** : hacerle una zancadilla (a alguien) ⟨you tripped me on purpose! : ¡me hiciste la zancadilla a propósito!⟩ **2** ACTIVATE : activar (un mecanismo) **3 to trip up** : hacer equivocar (a alguien)

trip[2] *n* **1** JOURNEY : viaje *m* ⟨to take a trip : hacer un viaje⟩ **2** STUMBLE : tropiezo *m*, traspié *m*

tripartite [traɪ'pɑrˌtaɪt] *adj* : tripartito

tripe ['traɪp] *n* **1** : mondongo *m*, callos *mpl*, pancita *f Mex* **2** TRASH : porquería *f*

triple[1] ['trɪpəl] *vt* **-pled; -pling** : triplicar

triple[2] *adj* : triple

triple[3] *n* : triple *m*

triplet ['trɪplət] *n* **1** : terceto *m* (en poesía, música, etc.) **2** : trillizo *m*, -za *f* (persona)

triplicate ['trɪplɪkət] *n* : triplicado *m*

tripod ['traɪˌpɑd] *n* : trípode *m*

trite ['traɪt] *adj* **triter; tritest** : trillado, tópico, manido

triumph[1] ['traɪəmpf] *vi* : triunfar

triumph[2] *n* : triunfo *m*

triumphal [traɪ'ʌmpfəl] *adj* : triunfal

triumphant [traɪ'ʌmpfənt] *adj* : triunfante, triunfal — **triumphantly** *adv*

trivia ['trɪviə] *ns & pl* : trivialidades *fpl*, nimiedades *fpl*

trivial ['trɪviəl] *adj* : trivial, intrascendente, insignificante

triviality [ˌtrɪvi'æləṭi] *n, pl* **-ties** : trivialidad *f*

trod, trodden → **tread**[1]

troll ['tro:l] *n* : duende *m* o gigante *m* de cuentos folklóricos

trolley ['trɑli] *n, pl* **-leys** : tranvía *m*

trombone [trɑm'bo:n] *n* : trombón *m*

trombonist [trɑm'bo:nɪst] *n* : trombón *m*

troop[1] ['tru:p] *vi* : desfilar, ir en tropel

troop[2] *n* **1** : escuadrón *m* (de caballería) **2** GROUP : grupo *m*, banda *f* (de personas) **3 troops** *npl* SOLDIERS : tropas *fpl*, soldados *mpl*

trooper ['tru:pər] *n* **1** : soldado *m* (de caballería) **2** : policía *m* montado **3** : policía *m* (estatal)

trophy ['tro:fi] *n, pl* **-phies** : trofeo *m*

tropic[1] ['trɑpɪk] *or* **tropical** [-pɪkəl] *adj* : tropical

tropic[2] *n* **1** : trópico *m* ⟨tropic of Cancer : trópico de Cáncer⟩ **2 the tropics** : el trópico

trot[1] ['trɑt] *vi* **trotted; trotting** : trotar

trot[2] *n* : trote *m*

trouble[1] ['trʌbəl] *v* **-bled; -bling** *vt* **1** DISTURB, WORRY : molestar, perturbar, inquietar **2** AFFLICT : afligir, afectar — *vi* : molestarse, hacer un esfuerzo ⟨they didn't trouble to come : no se molestaron en venir⟩

trouble[2] *n* **1** PROBLEMS : problemas *mpl*, dificultades *fpl* ⟨to be in trouble : estar en un aprieto⟩ ⟨heart trouble : problemas de corazón⟩ **2** EFFORT : molestia *f*, esfuerzo *m* ⟨to take the trouble : tomarse la molestia⟩ ⟨it's not worth the trouble : no vale la pena⟩

troublemaker ['trʌbəlˌmeɪkər] *n* : agitador *m*, -dora *f*; alborotador *m*, -dora *f*

troublesome ['trʌbəlsəm] *adj* : problemático, dificultoso — **troublesomely** *adv*

trough ['trɔf] *n, pl* **troughs** ['trɔfs, 'trɔvz] **1** : comedero *m*, bebedero *m* (de animales) **2** CHANNEL, HOLLOW : depresión *f* (en el suelo), seno *m* (de olas)

trounce ['traʊnts] *vt* **trounced; trouncing 1** THRASH : apalear, darle una paliza (a alguien) **2** DEFEAT : derrotar contundentemente

troupe ['tru:p] *n* : troupe *f*

trousers ['traʊzərz] *npl* : pantalón *m*, pantalones *mpl*

trout ['traʊt] *n, pl* **trout** : trucha *f*

trowel ['traʊəl] *n* **1** : llana *f*, paleta *f* (de albañil) **2** : desplantador *m* (de jardinero)

truant ['tru:ənt] *n* : alumno *m*, -na *f* que falta a clase sin permiso

truce [ˈtru:s] *n* : tregua *f*, armisticio *m*
truck¹ [ˈtrʌk] *vt* : transportar en camión
truck² *n* **1** : camión *m* (vehículo automóvil), carro *m* (manual) **2** DEALINGS : tratos *mpl* ⟨to have no truck with : no tener nada que ver con⟩
trucker [ˈtrʌkər] *n* : camionero *m*, -ra *f*
truculent [ˈtrʌkjələnt] *adj* : agresivo, beligerante
trudge [ˈtrʌʤ] *vi* **trudged; trudging** : caminar a paso pesado
true¹ [ˈtru:] *vt* **trued; trueing** : aplomar (algo vertical), nivelar (algo horizontal), centrar (una rueda)
true² *adv* **1** TRUTHFULLY : lealmente, sinceramente **2** ACCURATELY : exactamente, certeramente
true³ *adj* **truer; truest 1** LOYAL : fiel, leal **2** : cierto, verdadero, verídico ⟨it's true : es cierto, es la verdad⟩ ⟨a true story : una historia verídica⟩ **3** GENUINE : auténtico, genuino — **truly** *adv*
true–blue [ˈtru:ˈblu:] *adj* LOYAL : leal, fiel
truffle [ˈtrʌfəl] *n* : trufa *f*
truism [ˈtru:ˌɪzəm] *n* : perogrullada *f*, verdad *f* obvia
trump¹ [ˈtrʌmp] *vt* : matar (en juegos de naipes)
trump² *n* : triunfo *m* (en juegos de naipes)
trumped–up [ˈtrʌmptˈʌp] *adj* : inventado, fabricado ⟨trumped-up charges : falsas acusaciones⟩
trumpet¹ [ˈtrʌmpət] *vi* **1** : sonar una trompeta **2** : berrear, bramar (dícese de un animal) — *vt* : proclamar a los cuatro vientos
trumpet² *n* : trompeta *f*
trumpeter [ˈtrʌmpət̬ər] *n* : trompetista *mf*
truncate [ˈtrʌŋˌkeɪt, ˈtrʌn-] *vt* **-cated; -cating** : truncar
trundle [ˈtrʌndəl] *v* **-dled; -dling** *vi* : rodar lentamente — *vt* : hacer rodar, empujar lentamente
trunk [ˈtrʌŋk] *n* **1** : tronco *m* (de un árbol o del cuerpo) **2** : trompa *f* (de un elefante) **3** CHEST : baúl *m* **4** : maletero *m*, cajuela *f Mex* (de un auto) **5 trunks** *npl* : traje *m* de baño (de caballero)
truss¹ [ˈtrʌs] *vt* : atar (con fuerza)
truss² *n* **1** FRAMEWORK : armazón *m* (de una estructura) **2** : braguero *m* (en medicina)
trust¹ [ˈtrʌst] *vi* : confiar, esperar ⟨to trust in God : confiar en Dios⟩ — *vt* **1** ENTRUST : confiar, encomendar **2** : confiar en, tenerle confianza a ⟨I trust you : te tengo confianza⟩
trust² *n* **1** CONFIDENCE : confianza *f* **2** HOPE : esperanza *f*, fe *f* **3** CREDIT : crédito *m* ⟨to sell on trust : fiar⟩ **4** : fideicomiso *m* ⟨to hold in trust : guardar en fideicomiso⟩ **5** : trust *m* (consorcio empresarial) **6** CUSTODY : responsabilidad *f*, custodia *f*
trustee [ˌtrʌsˈti:] *n* : fideicomisario *m*, -ria *f*; fiduciario *m*, -ria *f*
trustful [ˈtrʌstfəl] *adj* : confiado — **trustfully** *adv*
trustworthiness [ˈtrəstˌwərðinəs] *n* : integridad *f*, honradez *f*
trustworthy [ˈtrəstˌwərði] *adj* : digno de confianza, confiable
trusty [ˈtrəsti] *adj* **trustier; -est** : fiel, confiable
truth [ˈtru:θ] *n, pl* **truths** [ˈtru:ðz, ˈtru:θs] : verdad *f*
truthful [ˈtru:θfəl] *adj* : sincero, veraz — **truthfully** *adv*
truthfulness [ˈtru:θfəlnəs] *n* : sinceridad *f*, veracidad *f*
try¹ [ˈtraɪ] *v* **tried; trying** *vt* **1** : enjuiciar, juzgar, procesar ⟨he was tried for murder : fue procesado por homicidio⟩ **2** : probar ⟨did you try the salad? : ¿probaste la ensalada?⟩ **3** TEST : tentar, poner a prueba ⟨to try one's patience : tentarle la paciencia a uno⟩ **4** ATTEMPT : tratar (de), intentar **5** *or* **to try on** : probarse (ropa) — *vi* : tratar, intentar
try² *n, pl* **tries** : intento *m*, tentativa *f*
tryout [ˈtraɪˌaʊt] *n* : prueba *f*
tsar [ˈzɑr, ˈtsɑr, ˈsɑr] → **czar**
T–shirt [ˈti:ˌʃərt] *n* : camiseta *f*
tub [ˈtʌb] *n* **1** CASK : cuba *f*, barril *m*, tonel *m* **2** CONTAINER : envase *m* (de plástico, etc.) ⟨a tub of margarine : un envase de margarina⟩ **3** BATHTUB : tina *f* (de baño), bañera *f*
tuba [ˈtu:bə, ˈtju:-] *n* : tuba *f*
tube [ˈtu:b, ˈtju:b] *n* **1** PIPE : tubo *m* **2** : tubo *m* (de dentífrico, etc.) **3** *or* **inner tube** : cámara *f* **4** : tubo *m* (de un aparato electrónico) **5** : trompa *f* (en anatomía)
tubeless [ˈtu:bləs, ˈtju:b-] *adj* : sin cámara (dícese de una llanta)
tuber [ˈtu:bər, ˈtju:-] *n* : tubérculo *m*
tubercular [tʊˈbərkjələr, tjʊ-] → **tuberculous**
tuberculosis [tʊˌbərkjəˈlo:sɪs, tjʊ-] *n, pl* **-loses** [-ˌsi:z] : tuberculosis *f*
tuberculous [tʊˈbərkjələs, tjʊ-] *adj* : tuberculoso
tuberous [ˈtu:bərəs, ˈtju:-] *adj* : tuberoso
tubing [ˈtu:bɪŋ, ˈtju:-] *n* : tubería *f*
tubular [ˈtu:bjələr, ˈtju:-] *adj* : tubular
tuck¹ [ˈtʌk] *vt* **1** PLACE, PUT : meter, colocar ⟨tuck in your shirt : métete la camisa⟩ **2** : guardar, esconder ⟨to tuck away one's money : guardar uno bien su dinero⟩ **3** COVER : arropar (a un niño en la cama)
tuck² *n* : pliegue *m*, alforza *f*
Tuesday [ˈtu:zˌdeɪ, ˈtju:z-, -di] *n* : martes *m*
tuft [ˈtʌft] *n* : penacho *m* (de plumas), copete *m* (de pelo)
tug¹ [ˈtʌg] *v* **tugged; tugging** *vi* : tirar, jalar, dar un tirón — *vt* : jalar, arrastrar, remolcar (con un barco)
tug² *n* **1** : tirón *m*, jalón *m* **2** → **tugboat**
tugboat [ˈtʌgˌbo:t] *n* : remolcador *m*

tug–of–war [ˌtʌgəˈwɔr] *n, pl* **tugs–of–war** : tira y afloja *m*
tuition [tuˈɪʃən] *n or* **tuition fees** : tasas *fpl* de matrícula, colegiatura *f Mex*
tulip [ˈtu:lɪp, ˈtju:-] *n* : tulipán *m*
tumble[1] [ˈtʌmbəl] *v* **-bled; -bling** *vi* **1** : dar volteretas (en acrobacia) **2** FALL : caerse, venirse abajo — *vt* **1** TOPPLE : volcar **2** TOSS : hacer girar
tumble[2] *n* : voltereta *f*, caída *f*
tumbler [ˈtʌmblər] *n* **1** ACROBAT : acróbata *mf*, saltimbanqui *mf* **2** GLASS : vaso *m* (de mesa) **3** : clavija *f* (de una cerradura)
tummy [ˈtʌmi] *n, pl* **-mies** BELLY : panza *f*, vientre *m*
tumor [ˈtu:mər, ˈtju:-] *n* : tumor *m*
tumult [ˈtu:ˌmʌlt, ˈtju:-] *n* : tumulto *m*, alboroto *m*
tumultuous [tʊˈmʌlʧʊəs, tju:-] *adj* : tumultuoso
tuna [ˈtu:nə, ˈtju:-] *n, pl* **-na** *or* **-nas** : atún *m*
tundra [ˈtʌndrə] *n* : tundra *f*
tune[1] [ˈtu:n, ˈtju:n] *v* **tuned; tuning** *vt* **1** ADJUST : ajustar, hacer más preciso, afinar (un motor) **2** : afinar (un instrumento musical) **3** : sintonizar (un radio o televisor) — *vi* **to tune in** : sintonizar (con una emisora)
tune[2] *n* **1** MELODY : tonada *f*, canción *f*, melodía *f* **2 in tune** : afinado (dícese de un instrumento o de la voz), sintonizado, en sintonía
tuneful [ˈtu:nfəl, ˈtju:n-] *adj* : armonioso, melódico
tuner [ˈtu:nər, ˈtju:-] *n* : afinador *m*, -dora *f* (de instrumentos); sintonizador *m* (de un radio o un televisor)
tungsten [ˈtʌŋkstən] *n* : tungsteno *m*
tunic [ˈtu:nɪk, ˈtju:-] *n* : túnica *f*
tuning fork *n* : diapasón *m*
Tunisian [tu:ˈni:ʒən, tju:ˈnɪziən] *n* : tunecino *m*, -na *f* — **Tunisian** *adj*
tunnel[1] [ˈtʌnəl] *vi* **-neled** *or* **-nelled; -neling** *or* **-nelling** : hacer un túnel
tunnel[2] *n* : túnel *m*
turban [ˈtərbən] *n* : turbante *m*
turbid [ˈtərbɪd] *adj* : turbio
turbine [ˈtərbən, -ˌbaɪn] *n* : turbina *f*
turboprop [ˈtərbo:ˌprɑp] *n* : turbopropulsor *m* (motor), avión *m* turbopropulsado
turbulence [ˈtərbjələnts] *n* : turbulencia *f*
turbulent [ˈtərbjələnt] *adj* : turbulento — **turbulently** *adv*
tureen [təˈri:n, tjʊ-] *n* : sopera *f*
turf [ˈtərf] *n* SOD : tepe *m*
turgid [ˈtərʤɪd] *adj* **1** SWOLLEN : turgente **2** : ampuloso, hinchado ⟨turgid style : estilo ampuloso⟩
Turk [ˈtərk] *n* : turco *m*, -ca *f*
turkey [ˈtərki] *n, pl* **-keys** : pavo *m*
Turkish[1] [ˈtərkɪʃ] *adj* : turco
Turkish[2] *n* : turco *m* (idioma)
turmoil [ˈtərˌmɔɪl] *n* : agitación *f*, desorden *m*, confusión *f*
turn[1] [ˈtərn] *vt* **1** : girar, voltear, volver ⟨to turn one's head : voltear la cabeza⟩ ⟨she turned her chair toward the fire : giró su asiento hacia la hoguera⟩ **2** ROTATE : darle vuelta a, hacer girar ⟨turn the handle : dale vuelta a la manivela⟩ **3** SPRAIN, WRENCH : dislocar, torcer **4** UPSET : revolver (el estómago) **5** TRANSFORM : convertir ⟨to turn water into wine : convertir el agua en vino⟩ **6** SHAPE : tornear (en carpintería) — *vi* **1** ROTATE : girar, dar vueltas **2** : girar, doblar, dar una vuelta ⟨turn left : doble a la izquierda⟩ ⟨to turn around : dar la media vuelta⟩ **3** BECOME : hacerse, volverse, ponerse **4** SOUR : agriarse, cortarse (dícese de la leche) **5 to turn to** : recurrir a ⟨they have no one to turn to : no tienen quien les ayude⟩
turn[2] *n* **1** : vuelta *f*, giro *m* ⟨a sudden turn : una vuelta repentina⟩ **2** CHANGE : cambio *m* **3** CURVE : curva *f* (en un camino) **4** : turno *m* ⟨they're awaiting their turn : están esperando su turno⟩ ⟨whose turn is it? : ¿a quién le toca?⟩
turnaround [ˈtərnəˌraʊnd] *n* PROCESSING : procesamiento *m*
turncoat [ˈtərnˌko:t] *n* : traidor *m*, -dora *f*
turn down *vt* **1** REFUSE : rehusar, rechazar ⟨they turned down our invitation : rehusaron nuestra invitación⟩ **2** LOWER : bajar (el volumen)
turn in *vt* : entregar ⟨to turn in one's work : entregar uno su trabajo⟩ ⟨they turned in the suspect : entregaron al sospechoso⟩ — *vi* : acostarse, irse a la cama
turnip [ˈtərnəp] *n* : nabo *m*
turn off *vt* : apagar (la luz, la radio, etc.)
turn on *vt* : prender (la luz, etc.), encender (un motor, etc.)
turnout [ˈtərnˌaʊt] *n* : concurrencia *f*
turn out *vt* **1** EVICT, EXPEL : expulsar, echar, desalojar **2** PRODUCE : producir **3** → **turn off** — *vi* **1** : concurrir, presentarse ⟨many turned out to vote : muchos concurrieron a votar⟩ **2** PROVE, RESULT : resultar
turnover [ˈtərnˌo:vər] *n* **1** : empanada *f* (salada o dulce) **2** : volumen *m* (de ventas) **3** : rotación *f* (de personal) ⟨a high turnover : un alto nivel de rotación⟩
turn over *vt* **1** TRANSFER : entregar, transferir (un cargo o una responsabilidad) **2** : voltear, darle la vuelta a ⟨turn the cassette over : voltea el cassette⟩
turnpike [ˈtərnˌpaɪk] *n* : carretera *f* de peaje
turnstile [ˈtərnˌstaɪl] *n* : torniquete *m* (de acceso)
turntable [ˈtərnˌteɪbəl] *n* : tornamesa *mf*
turn up *vi* **1** APPEAR : aparecer, presentarse **2** HAPPEN : ocurrir, suceder (inesperadamente) — *vt* : subir (el volumen)
turpentine [ˈtərpənˌtaɪn] *n* : aguarrás *m*, trementina *f*

turquoise [ˈtər͵kɔɪz, -͵kwɔɪz] *n* : turquesa *f*
turret [ˈtərət] *n* **1** TOWER : torre *f* pequeña **2** : torreta *f* (de un tanque, un avión, etc.)
turtle [ˈtərt̬əl] *n* : tortuga *f* (marina)
turtledove [ˈtərt̬əl͵dʌv] *n* : tórtola *f*
turtleneck [ˈtərt̬əl͵nɛk] *n* : cuello *m* de tortuga, cuello *m* alto
tusk [ˈtʌsk] *n* : colmillo *m*
tussle[1] [ˈtʌsəl] *vi* **-sled; -sling** SCUFFLE : pelearse, reñir
tussle[2] *n* : riña *f*, pelea *f*
tutor[1] [ˈtu:t̬ər, ˈtju:-] *vt* : darle clases particulares (a alguien)
tutor[2] *n* : tutor *m*, -tora *f*; maestro *m*, -tra *f* (particular)
tuxedo [͵tək'si:͵do:] *n, pl* **-dos** *or* **-does** : esmoquin *m*, smoking *m*
TV [͵ti:ˈvi:, ˈti:͵vi:] → **television**
twain [ˈtweɪn] *n* : dos *m*
twang[1] [ˈtwæŋ] *vt* : pulsar la cuerda de (una guitarra) — *vi* : hablar en tono nasal
twang[2] *n* **1** : tañido *m* (de una cuerda de guitarra) **2** : tono *m* nasal (de voz)
tweak[1] [ˈtwi:k] *vt* : pellizcar
tweak[2] *n* : pellizco *m*
tweed [ˈtwi:d] *n* : tweed *m*
tweet[1] [ˈtwi:t] *vi* : piar
tweet[2] *n* : gorjeo *m*, pío *m*
tweezers [ˈtwi:zərz] *npl* : pinzas *fpl*
twelfth[1] [ˈtwɛlfθ] *adj* : duodécimo
twelfth[2] *n* **1** : duodécimo *m*, -ma *f* (en una serie) **2** : doceavo *m*, doceava parte *f*
twelve[1] [ˈtwɛlv] *adj* : doce
twelve[2] *n* : doce *m*
twentieth[1] [ˈtwʌntiəθ, ˈtwɛn-] *adj* : vigésimo
twentieth[2] *n* **1** : vigésimo *m*, -ma *f* (en una serie) **2** : veinteavo *m*, veinteava parte *f*
twenty[1] [ˈtwʌnti, ˈtwɛn-] *adj* : veinte
twenty[2] *n, pl* **-ties** : veinte *m*
twice [ˈtwaɪs] *adv* : dos veces 〈twice a day : dos veces al día〉 〈it costs twice as much : cuesta el doble〉
twig [ˈtwɪg] *n* : ramita *f*
twilight [ˈtwaɪ͵laɪt] *n* : crepúsculo *m*
twill [ˈtwɪl] *n* : sarga *f*, tela *f* cruzada
twin[1] [ˈtwɪn] *adj* : gemelo, mellizo
twin[2] *n* : gemelo *m*, -la *f*; mellizo *m*, -za *f*
twine[1] [ˈtwaɪn] *v* **twined; twining** *vt* : entrelazar, entrecruzar — *vi* : enroscarse (alrededor de algo)
twine[2] *n* : cordel *m*, cuerda *f*, mecate *m CA, Mex, Ven*
twinge[1] [ˈtwɪnʤ] *vi* **twinged; twinging** *or* **twingeing** : sentir punzadas
twinge[2] *n* : punzada *f*, dolor *m* agudo
twinkle[1] [ˈtwɪŋkəl] *vi* **-kled; -kling 1** : centellear, titilar (dícese de las estrellas o de la luz) **2** : chispear, brillar (dícese de los ojos)
twinkle[2] *n* : centelleo *m* (de las estrellas), brillo *m* (de los ojos)
twirl[1] [ˈtwərl] *vt* : girar, darle vueltas a — *vi* : girar, dar vueltas (rápidamente)
twirl[2] *n* : giro *m*, vuelta *f*
twist[1] [ˈtwɪst] *vt* : torcer, retorcer 〈he twisted my arm : me torció el brazo〉 — *vi* : retorcerse, enroscarse, serpentear (dícese de un río, un camino, etc.)
twist[2] *n* **1** BEND : vuelta *f*, recodo *m* (en el camino, el río, etc.) **2** TURN : giro *m* 〈give it a twist : hazlo girar〉 **3** SPIRAL : espiral *f* 〈a twist of lemon : una rodajita de limón〉 **4** : giro *m* inesperado (de eventos, etc.)
twisted [ˈtwɪstəd] *adj* : retorcido 〈a twisted mind : una mente retorcida〉
twister [ˈtwɪstər] **1** → **tornado 2** → **waterspout**
twitch[1] [ˈtwɪʧ] *vi* : moverse nerviosamente, contraerse espasmódicamente (dícese de un músculo)
twitch[2] *n* : espasmo *m*, sacudida *f* 〈a nervous twitch : un tic nervioso〉
twitter[1] [ˈtwɪt̬ər] *vi* CHIRP : gorjear, cantar (dícese de los pájaros)
twitter[2] *n* : gorjeo *m*
two[1] [ˈtu:] *adj* : dos
two[2] *n, pl* **twos** : dos *m*
twofold[1] [ˈtu:ˈfo:ld] *adv* : al doble
twofold[2] [ˈtu:͵fo:ld] *adj* : doble
two hundred[1] *adj* : doscientos
two hundred[2] *n* : doscientos *m*
twosome [ˈtu:səm] *n* COUPLE : pareja *f*
tycoon [taɪˈku:n] *n* : magnate *mf*
tying → **tie**[1]
type[1] [ˈtaɪp] *v* **typed; typing** *vt* **1** TYPEWRITE : escribir a máquina, pasar (un texto) a máquina **2** CATEGORIZE : categorizar, identificar — *vi* : escribir a máquina
type[2] *n* **1** KIND : tipo *m*, clase *f*, categoría *f* **2** *or* **printing type** : tipo *m*
typeface [ˈtaɪp͵feɪs] *n* : tipo *m* de imprenta
typewrite [ˈtaɪp͵raɪt] *v* **-wrote; -written** : escribir a máquina
typewriter [ˈtaɪp͵raɪt̬ər] *n* : máquina *f* de escribir
typhoid[1] [ˈtaɪ͵fɔɪd, taɪˈ-] *adj* : relativo al tifus o a la tifoidea
typhoid[2] *n or* **typhoid fever** : tifoidea *f*
typhoon [taɪˈfu:n] *n* : tifón *m*
typhus [ˈtaɪfəs] *n* : tifus *m*, tifo *m*
typical [ˈtɪpɪkəl] *adj* : típico, característico — **typically** *adv*
typify [ˈtɪpə͵faɪ] *vt* **-fied; -fying** : ser típico o representativo de (un grupo, una clase, etc.)
typist [ˈtaɪpɪst] *n* : mecanógrafo *m*, -fa *f*
typographic [͵taɪpəˈgræfɪk] *or* **typographical** [-fɪkəl] *adj* : tipográfico — **typographically** [-fɪkli] *adv*
typography [taɪˈpɑgrəfi] *n* : tipografía *f*
tyrannical [təˈrænɪkəl, taɪ-] *adj* : tiránico — **tyrannically** [-nɪkli] *adv*
tyrannize [ˈtɪrə͵naɪz] *vt* **-nized; -nizing** : tiranizar
tyranny [ˈtɪrəni] *n, pl* **-nies** : tiranía *f*
tyrant [ˈtaɪrənt] *n* : tirano *m*, -na *f*
tzar [ˈzɑr, ˈtsɑr, ˈsɑr] → **czar**

U

u [ˈjuː] *n, pl* **u's** *or* **us** [ˈjuːz] : vigésima primera letra del alfabeto inglés
ubiquitous [juːˈbɪkwət̬əs] *adj* : ubicuo, omnipresente
udder [ˈʌdər] *n* : ubre *f*
UFO [ˌjuːˌɛfˈoː, ˈjuːˌfoː] *n, pl* **UFO's** *or* **UFOs** (*u*nidentified *f*lying *o*bject) : ovni *m*, OVNI *m*
Ugandan [juːˈgændən, -ˈgɑn-; uːˈgɑn-] *n* : ugandés *m*, -desa *f* — **Ugandan** *adj*
ugliness [ˈʌglinəs] *n* : fealdad *f*
ugly [ˈʌgli] *adj* **uglier; -est** **1** UNATTRACTIVE : feo **2** DISAGREEABLE : desagradable, feo ⟨ugly weather : tiempo feo⟩ ⟨to have an ugly temper : tener mal genio⟩
Ukrainian [juːˈkreɪniən, -ˈkraɪ-] *n* **1** : ucraniano *m*, -na *f* **2** : ucraniano *m* (idioma) — **Ukrainian** *adj*
ukulele [ˌjuːkəˈleɪli] *n* : ukelele *m*
ulcer [ˈʌlsər] *n* : úlcera *f* (interna), llaga *f* (externa)
ulcerate [ˈʌlsəˌreɪt] *vi* **-ated; -ating** : ulcerarse
ulceration [ˌʌlsəˈreɪʃən] *n* **1** : ulceración *f* **2** ULCER : úlcera *f*, llaga *f*
ulcerous [ˈʌlsərəs] *adj* : ulceroso
ulna [ˈʌlnə] *n* : cúbito *m*
ulterior [ˌʌlˈtɪriər] *adj* : oculto ⟨ulterior motive : motivo oculto, segunda intención⟩
ultimate [ˈʌltəmət] *adj* **1** FINAL : último, final **2** SUPREME : supremo, máximo **3** FUNDAMENTAL : fundamental, esencial
ultimately [ˈʌltəmətli] *adv* **1** FINALLY : por último, finalmente **2** EVENTUALLY : a la larga, con el tiempo
ultimatum [ˌʌltəˈmeɪt̬əm, -ˈmɑ-] *n, pl* **-tums** *or* **-ta** [-t̬ə] : ultimátum *m*
ultrasound [ˈʌltrəˌsaʊnd] *n* **1** : ultrasonido *m* **2** : ecografía *f* (técnica o imagen)
ultraviolet [ˌʌltrəˈvaɪələt] *adj* : ultravioleta
umbilical cord [ˌʌmˈbɪlɪkəl] *n* : cordón *m* umbilical
umbrage [ˈʌmbrɪʤ] *n* **to take umbrage at** : ofenderse por
umbrella [ˌʌmˈbrɛlə] *n* **1** : paraguas *m* **2 beach umbrella** : sombrilla *f*
umpire[1] [ˈʌmˌpaɪr] *v* **-pired; -piring** : arbitrar
umpire[2] *n* : árbitro *m*, -tra *f*
umpteenth [ˌʌmpˈtiːnθ] *adj* : enésimo
unable [ˌʌnˈeɪbəl] *adj* : incapaz ⟨to be unable to : no poder⟩
unabridged [ˌʌnəˈbrɪʤd] *adj* : íntegro
unacceptable [ˌʌnɪkˈsɛptəbəl] *adj* : inaceptable
unaccompanied [ˌʌnəˈkʌmpənid] *adj* : solo, sin acompañamiento (en música)
unaccountable [ˌʌnəˈkaʊntəbəl] *adj* : inexplicable, incomprensible — **unaccountably** [-bli] *adv*
unaccustomed [ˌʌnəˈkʌstəmd] *adj* **1** UNUSUAL : desacostumbrado, inusual **2** UNUSED : inhabituado ⟨unaccustomed to noise : inhabituado al ruido⟩
unacquainted [ˌʌnəˈkweɪnt̬əd] *adj* **to be unacquainted with** : desconocer, ignorar
unadorned [ˌʌnəˈdɔrnd] *adj* : sin adornos, puro y simple
unadulterated [ˌʌnəˈdʌltəˌreɪt̬əd] *adj* **1** PURE : puro ⟨unadulterated food : comida pura⟩ **2** ABSOLUTE : completo, absoluto
unaffected [ˌʌnəˈfɛktəd] *adj* **1** : no afectado, indiferente **2** NATURAL : sin afectación, natural
unaffectedly [ˌʌnəˈfɛktədli] *adv* : de manera natural
unafraid [ˌʌnəˈfreɪd] *adj* : sin miedo
unaided [ˌʌnˈeɪdəd] *adj* : sin ayuda, solo
unambiguous [ˌʌnæmˈbɪgjʊəs] *adj* : inequívoco
unanimity [ˌjuːnəˈnɪmət̬i] *n* : unanimidad *f*
unanimous [jʊˈnænəməs] *adj* : unánime — **unanimously** *adv*
unannounced [ˌʌnəˈnaʊnst] *adj* : sin dar aviso
unanswered [ˌʌnˈæntsərd] *adj* : sin contestar
unappealing [ˌʌnəˈpiːlɪŋ] *adj* : desagradable
unappetizing [ˌʌnˈæpəˌtaɪzɪŋ] *adj* : poco apetitoso, poco apetecible
unarmed [ˌʌnˈɑrmd] *adj* : sin armas, desarmado
unassisted [ˌʌnəˈsɪstəd] *adj* : sin ayuda
unassuming [ˌʌnəˈsuːmɪŋ] *adj* : modesto, sin pretensiones
unattached [ˌʌnəˈtæʧt] *adj* **1** LOOSE : suelto **2** INDEPENDENT : independiente **3** : solo (ni casado ni prometido)
unattractive [ˌʌnəˈtræktɪv] *adj* : poco atractivo
unauthorized [ˌʌnˈɔθəˌraɪzd] *adj* : sin autorización, no autorizado
unavailable [ˌʌnəˈveɪləbəl] *adj* : no disponible
unavoidable [ˌʌnəˈvɔɪdəbəl] *adj* : inevitable, ineludible
unaware[1] [ˌʌnəˈwær] *adv* → **unawares**
unaware[2] *adj* : inconsciente
unawares [ˌʌnəˈwærz] *adv* **1** : por sorpresa ⟨to catch someone unawares : agarrar a alguien desprevenido⟩ **2** UNINTENTIONALLY : inconscientemente, inadvertidamente
unbalanced [ˌʌnˈbæləntst] *adj* : desequilibrado
unbearable [ˌʌnˈbærəbəl] *adj* : insoportable, inaguantable — **unbearably** [-bli] *adv*
unbecoming [ˌʌnbɪˈkʌmɪŋ] *adj* **1** UNSEEMLY : impropio, indecoroso **2** UNFLATTERING : poco favorecedor

unbelievable [ˌʌnbəˈliːvəbəl] *adj* : increíble — **unbelievably** [-bli] *adv*

unbend [ˌʌnˈbɛnd] *vi* **-bent** [-ˈbɛnt]; **-bending** RELAX : relajarse

unbending [ˌʌnˈbɛndɪŋ] *adj* : inflexible

unbiased [ˌʌnˈbaɪəst] *adj* : imparcial, objetivo

unbind [ˌʌnˈbaɪnd] *vt* **-bound** [-ˈbaʊnd]; **-binding** **1** UNFASTEN, UNTIE : desatar, desamarrar **2** RELEASE : liberar

unbolt [ˌʌnˈboːlt] *vt* : abrir el cerrojo de, descorrer el pestillo de

unborn [ˌʌnˈbɔrn] *adj* : aún no nacido, que va a nacer

unbosom [ˌʌnˈbʊzəm, -ˈbuː-] *vt* : revelar, divulgar

unbreakable [ˌʌnˈbreɪkəbəl] *adj* : irrompible

unbridled [ˌʌnˈbraɪdəld] *adj* : desenfrenado

unbroken [ˌʌnˈbroːkən] *adj* **1** INTACT : intacto, sano **2** CONTINUOUS : continuo, ininterrumpido

unbuckle [ˌʌnˈbʌkəl] *vt* **-led; -ling** : desabrochar

unburden [ˌʌnˈbərdən] *vt* **1** UNLOAD : descargar **2 to unburden oneself** : desahogarse

unbutton [ˌʌnˈbʌtən] *vt* : desabrochar, desabotonar

uncalled–for [ˌʌnˈkɔldˌfɔr] *adj* : inapropiado, innecesario

uncanny [ənˈkæni] *adj* **-nier; -est** **1** STRANGE : extraño **2** EXTRAORDINARY : raro, extraordinario — **uncannily** [-ˈkænəli] *adv*

unceasing [ˌʌnˈsiːsɪŋ] *adj* : incesante, continuo — **unceasingly** *adv*

unceremonious [ˌʌnˌsɛrəˈmoːniəs] *adj* **1** INFORMAL : sin ceremonia, sin pompa **2** ABRUPT : abrupto, brusco — **unceremoniously** *adv*

uncertain [ˌʌnˈsərtən] *adj* **1** INDEFINITE : indeterminado **2** UNSURE : incierto, dudoso **3** CHANGEABLE : inestable, variable ⟨uncertain weather : tiempo inestable⟩ **4** HESITANT : indeciso **5** VAGUE : poco claro

uncertainly [ˌʌnˈsərtənli] *adv* : dudosamente, con desconfianza

uncertainty [ˌʌnˈsərtənti] *n, pl* **-ties** : duda *f*, incertidumbre *f*

unchangeable [ˌʌnˈʧeɪnʤəbəl] *adj* : inalterable, inmutable

unchanged [ˌʌnˈʧeɪnʤd] *adj* : sin cambiar

unchanging [ˌʌnˈʧeɪnʤɪŋ] *adj* : inalterable, inmutable, firme

uncharacteristic [ˌʌnˌkærɪktəˈrɪstɪk] *adj* : inusual, desacostumbrado

uncharged [ˌʌnˈʧɑrʤd] *adj* : sin carga (eléctrica)

uncivilized [ˌʌnˈsɪvəˌlaɪzd] *adj* **1** BARBAROUS : incivilizado, bárbaro **2** WILD : salvaje

uncle [ˈʌŋkəl] *n* : tío *m*

unclean [ˌʌnˈkliːn] *adj* **1** IMPURE : impuro **2** DIRTY : sucio

unclear [ˌʌnˈklɪr] *adj* : confuso, borroso, poco claro

Uncle Sam [ˈsæm] *n* : el Tío Sam

unclog [ˌʌnˈklɑg] *vt* **-clogged; -clogging** : desatascar, destapar

unclothed [ˌʌnˈkloːðd] *adj* : desnudo

uncomfortable [ˌʌnˈkʌmpfərt̬əbəl] *adj* **1** : incómodo (dícese de una silla, etc.) **2** UNEASY : inquieto, incómodo

uncommitted [ˌʌnkəˈmɪt̬əd] *adj* : sin compromisos

uncommon [ˌʌnˈkɑmən] *adj* **1** UNUSUAL : raro, poco común **2** REMARKABLE : excepcional, extraordinario

uncommonly [ˌʌnˈkɑmənli] *adv* : extraordinariamente

uncompromising [ˌʌnˈkɑmprəˌmaɪzɪŋ] *adj* : inflexible, intransigente

unconcerned [ˌʌnkənˈsərnd] *adj* : indiferente — **unconcernedly** [-ˈsərnədli] *adv*

unconditional [ˌʌnkənˈdɪʃənəl] *adj* : incondicional — **unconditionally** *adv*

unconscious[1] [ˌʌnˈkɑnʧəs] *adj* : inconsciente — **unconsciously** *adv*

unconscious[2] *n* : inconsciente *m*

unconsciousness [ˌʌnˈkɑnʧəsnəs] *n* : inconsciencia *f*

unconstitutional [ˌʌnˌkɑntstəˈtuːʃənəl, -ˈtjuː-] *adj* : inconstitucional

uncontrollable [ˌʌnkənˈtroːləbəl] *adj* : incontrolable, incontenible — **uncontrollably** [-bli] *adv*

uncontrolled [ˌʌnkənˈtroːld] *adj* : incontrolado

unconventional [ˌʌnkənˈvɛnʧənəl] *adj* : poco convencional

unconvincing [ˌʌnkənˈvɪntsɪŋ] *adj* : poco convincente

uncouth [ˌʌnˈkuːθ] *adj* CRUDE, ROUGH : grosero, rudo

uncover [ˌʌnˈkʌvər] *vt* **1** : destapar (un objeto), dejar al descubierto **2** EXPOSE, REVEAL : descubrir, revelar, exponer

uncultivated [ˌʌnˈkʌltəˌveɪt̬əd] *adj* : inculto

uncurl [ˌʌnˈkərl] *vt* UNROLL : desenrollar — *vi* : desenrollarse, desrizarse (dícese del pelo)

uncut [ˌʌnˈkʌt] *adj* **1** : sin cortar ⟨uncut grass : hierba sin cortar⟩ **2** : sin tallar, en bruto ⟨an uncut diamond : un diamante en bruto⟩ **3** UNABRIDGED : completo, íntegro

undaunted [ˌʌnˈdɔntəd] *adj* : impávido

undecided [ˌʌndiˈsaɪdəd] *adj* **1** IRRESOLUTE : indeciso, irresoluto **2** UNRESOLVED : pendiente, no resuelto

undefeated [ˌʌndiˈfiːt̬əd] *adj* : invicto

undeniable [ˌʌndiˈnaɪəbəl] *adj* : innegable — **undeniably** [-bli] *adv*

under[1] [ˈʌndər] *adv* **1** LESS : menos ⟨$10 or under : $10 o menos⟩ **2** UNDERWATER : debajo del agua **3** : bajo los efectos de la anestesia

under[2] *adj* **1** LOWER : (más) bajo, inferior **2** SUBORDINATE : inferior **3** : insuficiente ⟨an under dose of medicine : una dosis insuficiente de medicina⟩

under[3] *prep* **1** BELOW, BENEATH : debajo de, abajo de ⟨under the table : abajo de la mesa⟩ ⟨we walked under the arch : pasamos por debajo del arco⟩ ⟨under the sun : bajo el sol⟩ **2** : menos de ⟨in under 20 minutes : en menos de 20 minutos⟩ **3** (*indicating rank or authority*) : bajo ⟨under the command of : bajo las órdenes de⟩ **4** SUBJECT TO : bajo ⟨under suspicion : bajo sospecha⟩ ⟨under the circumstances : dadas las circunstancias⟩ **5** ACCORDING TO : según, de acuerdo con, conforme a ⟨under the present laws : según las leyes actuales⟩

underage [ˌʌndərˈeɪʤ] *adj* : menor de edad

underbrush [ˈʌndərˌbrəʃ] *n* : maleza *f*

underclothes [ˈʌndərˌklo:z, -ˌklo:ðz] → **underwear**

underclothing [ˈʌndərˌklo:ðɪŋ] → **underwear**

undercover [ˌʌndərˈkʌvər] *adj* : secreto, clandestino

undercurrent [ˈʌndərˌkərənt] *n* **1** : corriente *f* submarina **2** UNDERTONE : corriente *f* oculta, trasfondo *m*

undercut [ˌʌndərˈkʌt] *vt* **-cut; -cutting** : vender más barato que

underdeveloped [ˌʌndərdɪˈvɛləpt] *adj* : subdesarrollado, atrasado

underdog [ˈʌndərˌdɔg] *n* : persona *f* que tiene menos posibilidades

underdone [ˌʌndərˈdʌn] *adj* RARE : poco cocido

underestimate [ˌʌndərˈɛstəˌmeɪt] *vt* **-mated; -mating** : subestimar, menospreciar

underexposed [ˌʌndərɪkˈspo:zd] *adj* : subexpuesto (en fotografía)

underfoot [ˌʌndərˈfʊt] *adv* **1** : bajo los pies ⟨to trample underfoot : pisotear⟩ **2 to be underfoot** : estorbar ⟨they're always underfoot : están siempre estorbando⟩

undergarment [ˈʌndərˌgɑrmənt] *n* : prenda *f* íntima

undergo [ˌʌndərˈgo:] *vt* **-went** [-ˈwɛnt]; **-gone** [-ˈgɔn]; **-going** : sufrir, experimentar ⟨to undergo an operation : someterse a una intervención quirúrgica⟩

undergraduate [ˌʌndərˈgræʤʊət] *n* : estudiante *m* universitario, estudiante *f* universitaria

underground[1] [ˌʌndərˈgraʊnd] *adv* **1** : bajo tierra **2** SECRETLY : clandestinamente, en secreto ⟨to go underground : pasar a la clandestinidad⟩

underground[2] [ˈʌndərˌgraʊnd] *adj* **1** SUBTERRANEAN : subterráneo **2** SECRET : secreto, clandestino

underground[3] [ˈʌndərˌgraʊnd] *n* : movimiento *m* o grupo *m* clandestino

undergrowth [ˈʌndərˈgro:θ] *n* : maleza *f*, broza *f*

underhand[1] [ˈʌndərˌhænd] *adv* **1** SECRETLY : de manera clandestina **2** *or* **underhanded** : sin levantar el brazo por encima del hombro (en deportes)

underhand[2] *adj* **1** SLY : solapado **2** : por debajo del hombro (en deportes)

underhanded [ˌʌndərˈhændəd] *adj* **1** SLY : solapado **2** SHADY : turbio, poco limpio

underline [ˈʌndərˌlaɪn] *vt* **-lined; -lining** **1** : subrayar **2** EMPHASIZE : subrayar, acentuar, hacer hincapié en

underlying [ˌʌndərˈlaɪɪŋ] *adj* **1** : subyacente ⟨the underlying rock : la roca subyacente⟩ **2** FUNDAMENTAL : fundamental, esencial

undermine [ˌʌndərˈmaɪn] *vt* **-mined; -mining** **1** : socavar (una estructura, etc.) **2** SAP, WEAKEN : minar, debilitar

underneath[1] [ˌʌndərˈni:θ] *adv* : debajo, abajo ⟨the part underneath : la parte de abajo⟩

underneath[2] *prep* : debajo de, abajo de

undernourished [ˌʌndərˈnərɪʃt] *adj* : desnutrido

underpants [ˈʌndərˌpænts] *npl* : calzoncillos *mpl*, calzones *mpl*

underpass [ˈʌndərˌpæs] *n* : paso *m* a desnivel

underprivileged [ˌʌndərˈprɪvlɪʤd] *adj* : desfavorecido

underrate [ˌʌndərˈreɪt] *vt* **-rated; -rating** : subestimar, menospreciar

underscore [ˈʌndərˌskor] *vt* **-scored; -scoring** → **underline**

undersea[1] [ˌʌndərˈsi:] *or* **underseas** [-ˈsi:z] *adv* : bajo la superficie del mar

undersea[2] *adj* : submarino

undersecretary [ˌʌndərˈsɛkrəˌtɛri] *n, pl* **-ries** : subsecretario *m*, -ria *f*

undersell [ˌʌndərˈsɛl] *vt* **-sold; -selling** : vender más barato que

undershirt [ˈʌndərˌʃərt] *n* : camiseta *f*

undershorts [ˈʌndərˌʃɔrts] *npl* : calzoncillos *mpl*

underside [ˈʌndərˌsaɪd, ˌʌndərˈsaɪd] *n* : parte *f* de abajo

undersized [ˌʌndərˈsaɪzd] *adj* : más pequeño de lo normal

understand [ˌʌndərˈstænd] *v* **-stood** [-ˈstʊd]; **-standing** *vt* **1** COMPREHEND : comprender, entender ⟨I don't understand it : no lo entiendo⟩ ⟨that's understood : eso se comprende⟩ ⟨to make oneself understood : hacerse entender⟩ **2** BELIEVE : entender ⟨to give someone to understand : dar a alguien a entender⟩ **3** INFER : tener entendido ⟨I understand that she's leaving : tengo entendido que se va⟩ — *vi* : comprender, entender

understandable [ˌʌndərˈstændəbəl] *adj* : comprensible

understanding[1] [ˌʌndərˈstændɪŋ] *adj* : comprensivo, compasivo

understanding[2] *n* **1** GRASP : comprensión *f*, entendimiento *m* **2** SYMPATHY : comprensión *f* (mutua) **3** INTERPRETATION : interpretación *f* ⟨it's my understanding that . . . : tengo la impresión de que . . ., tengo entendido que . . .〉 4 AGREEMENT : acuerdo *m*, arreglo *m*

understate [ˌʌndərˈsteɪt] *vt* **-stated; -stating** : minimizar, subestimar

understatement [ˌʌndərˈsteɪtmənt] *n* : atenuación *f* 〈that's an understatement : decir sólo eso es quedarse corto〉

understudy [ˈʌndərˌstʌdi] *n, pl* **-dies** : sobresaliente *mf*, suplente *mf* (en el teatro)

undertake [ˌʌndərˈteɪk] *vt* **-took** [-ˈtʊk]; **-taken** [-ˈteɪkən]; **-taking 1** : emprender (una tarea), asumir (una responsabilidad) **2** PROMISE : comprometerse (a hacer algo)

undertaker [ˈʌndərˌteɪkər] *n* : director *m*, -tora *f* de funeraria

undertaking [ˈʌndərˌteɪkɪŋ, ˌʌndərˈ-] *n* **1** ENTERPRISE, TASK : empresa *f*, tarea *f* **2** PLEDGE : promesa *f*, garantía *f*

undertone [ˈʌndərˌto:n] *n* **1** : voz *f* baja 〈to speak in an undertone : hablar en voz baja〉 **2** HINT, UNDERCURRENT : trasfondo *m*, matiz *m*

undertow [ˈʌndərˌto:] *n* : resaca *f*

undervalue [ˌʌndərˈvælˌju:] *vt* **-ued; -uing** : menospreciar, subestimar

underwater[1] [ˌʌndərˈwɔt̬ər, -ˈwɑ-] *adv* : debajo (del agua)

underwater[2] *adj* : submarino

under way [ˌʌndərˈweɪ] *adv* : en marcha, en camino 〈to get under way : ponerse en marcha〉

underwear [ˈʌndərˌwær] *n* : ropa *f* interior, ropa *f* íntima

underworld [ˈʌndərˌwərld] *n* **1** HELL : infierno *m* **2 the underworld** CRIMINALS : la hampa, los bajos fondos

underwrite [ˈʌndərˌraɪt, ˌʌndərˈ-] *vt* **-wrote** [-ˌro:t, -ˈro:t]; **-written** [-ˌrɪtən, -ˈrɪtən]; **-writing 1** INSURE : asegurar **2** FINANCE : financiar **3** BACK, ENDORSE : suscribir, respaldar

underwriter [ˈʌndərˌraɪt̬ər, ˌʌndərˈ-] *n* INSURER : asegurador *m*, -dora *f*

undeserving [ˌʌndiˈzərvɪŋ] *adj* : indigno

undesirable[1] [ˌʌndiˈzaɪrəbəl] *adj* : indeseable

undesirable[2] *n* : indeseable *mf*

undeveloped [ˌʌndiˈvɛləpt] *adj* : sin desarrollar, sin revelar (dícese de una película)

undies [ˈʌndi:z] → **underwear**

undignified [ˌʌnˈdɪgnəfaɪd] *adj* : indecoroso

undiluted [ˌʌndaɪˈlu:t̬əd, -də-] *adj* : sin diluir, concentrado

undiscovered [ˌʌndɪˈskʌvərd] *adj* : no descubierto

undisputed [ˌʌndɪˈspju:t̬əd] *adj* : indiscutible

undisturbed [ˌʌndɪˈstərbd] *adj* : tranquilo (dícese de una persona), sin tocar (dícese de un objeto)

undivided [ˌʌndɪˈvaɪdəd] *adj* : íntegro, completo

undo [ˌʌnˈdu:] *vt* **-did** [-ˈdɪd]; **-done** [-ˈdʌn]; **-doing 1** UNFASTEN : desabrochar, desatar, abrir **2** ANNUL : anular **3** REVERSE : deshacer, reparar (daños, etc.) **4** RUIN : arruinar, destruir

undoing [ˌʌnˈdu:ɪŋ] *n* : ruina *f*, perdición *f*

undoubted [ˌʌnˈdaʊt̬əd] *adj* : cierto, indudable — **undoubtedly** *adv*

undress [ˌʌnˈdrɛs] *vt* : desvestir, desabrigar, desnudar — *vi* : desvestirse, desnudarse

undrinkable [ˌʌnˈdrɪŋkəbəl] *adj* : no potable

undue [ˌʌnˈdu:, -ˈdju:] *adj* : excesivo, indebido — **unduly** *adv*

undulate [ˈʌnʤəˌleɪt] *vi* **-lated; -lating** : ondular

undulation [ˌʌnʤəˈleɪʃən] *n* : ondulación *f*

undying [ˌʌnˈdaɪɪŋ] *adj* : perpetuo, imperecedero

unearth [ˌʌnˈərθ] *vt* **1** EXHUME : desenterrar, exhumar **2** DISCOVER : descubrir

unearthly [ˌʌnˈərθli] *adj* **-lier; -est** : sobrenatural, de otro mundo

uneasily [ˌʌnˈi:zəli] *adv* : inquietamente, con inquietud

uneasiness [ˌʌnˈi:zinəs] *n* : inquietud *f*

uneasy [ˌʌnˈi:zi] *adj* **-easier; -est 1** AWKWARD : incómodo **2** WORRIED : preocupado, inquieto **3** RESTLESS : inquieto, agitado

uneducated [ˌʌnˈɛʤəˌkeɪt̬əd] *adj* : inculto, sin educación

unemployed [ˌʌnɪmˈplɔɪd] *adj* : desempleado

unemployment [ˌʌnɪmˈplɔɪmənt] *n* : desempleo *m*

unending [ˌʌnˈɛndɪŋ] *adj* : sin fin, interminable

unendurable [ˌʌnɪnˈdʊrəbəl, -ɛn-, -ˈdjʊr-] *adj* : insoportable, intolerable

unequal [ˌʌnˈi:kwəl] *adj* **1** : desigual **2** INADEQUATE : incapaz, incompetente 〈to be unequal to a task : no estar a la altura de una tarea〉

unequaled *or* **unequalled** [ˌʌnˈi:kwəld] *adj* : sin igual

unequivocal [ˌʌnɪˈkwɪvəkəl] *adj* : inequívoco, claro — **unequivocally** *adv*

unerring [ˌʌnˈɛrɪŋ, -ˈər-] *adj* : infalible

unethical [ˌʌnˈɛθɪkəl] *adj* : poco ético

uneven [ˌʌnˈi:vən] *adj* **1** ODD : impar (dícese de un número) **2** : desigual, desnivelado (dícese de una superficie) 〈uneven terrain : terreno accidentado〉 **3** IRREGULAR : irregular, poco uniforme **4** UNEQUAL : desigual

unevenly [ˌʌnˈi:vənli] *adv* : desigualmente, irregularmente

uneventful [ˌʌnɪˈvɛntfəl] *adj* : sin incidentes, tranquilo

unexpected [ˌʌnɪkˈspɛktəd] *adj* : imprevisto, inesperado — **unexpectedly** *adv*

unfailing [ˌʌnˈfeɪlɪŋ] *adj* **1** CONSTANT : constante **2** INEXHAUSTIBLE : in-

agotable **3** SURE : a toda prueba, indefectible
unfair [ˌʌnˈfær] *adj* : injusto — **unfairly** *adv*
unfairness [ˌʌnˈfærnəs] *n* : injusticia *f*
unfaithful [ˌʌnˈfeɪθfəl] *adj* : desleal, infiel — **unfaithfully** *adv*
unfaithfulness [ˌʌnˈfeɪθfəlnəs] *n* : infidelidad *f*, deslealtad *f*
unfamiliar [ˌʌnfəˈmɪljər] *adj* **1** STRANGE : desconocido, extraño ⟨an unfamiliar place : un lugar nuevo⟩ **2 to be unfamiliar with** : no estar familiarizado con, desconocer
unfamiliarity [ˌʌnfəˌmɪliˈærət̬i] *n* : falta *f* de familiaridad
unfashionable [ˌʌnˈfæʃənəbəl] *adj* : fuera de moda
unfasten [ˌʌnˈfæsən] *vt* : desabrochar, desatar (una cuerda, etc.), abrir (una puerta)
unfavorable [ˌʌnˈfeɪvərəbəl] *adj* : desfavorable, mal — **unfavorably** [-bli] *adv*
unfeeling [ˌʌnˈfiːlɪŋ] *adj* : insensible — **unfeelingly** *adv*
unfinished [ˌʌnˈfɪnɪʃd] *adj* : inacabado, incompleto
unfit [ˌʌnˈfɪt] *adj* **1** UNSUITABLE : inadecuado, impropio **2** UNSUITED : no apto, incapaz **3** : incapacitado (físicamente) ⟨to be unfit : no estar en forma⟩
unflappable [ˌʌnˈflæpəbəl] *adj* : imperturbable
unflattering [ˌʌnˈflæt̬ərɪŋ] *adj* : poco favorecedor
unfold [ˌʌnˈfoːld] *vt* **1** EXPAND : desplegar, desdoblar, extender ⟨to unfold a map : desplegar un mapa⟩ **2** DISCLOSE, REVEAL : revelar, exponer (un plan, etc.) — *vi* **1** DEVELOP : desarrollarse, desenvolverse ⟨the story unfolded : el cuento se desarrollaba⟩ **2** EXPAND : extenderse, desplegarse
unforeseeable [ˌʌnforˈsiːəbəl] *adj* : imprevisible
unforeseen [ˌʌnforˈsiːn] *adj* : imprevisto
unforgettable [ˌʌnfərˈgɛt̬əbəl] *adj* : inolvidable, memorable — **unforgettably** [-bli] *adv*
unforgivable [ˌʌnfərˈgɪvəbəl] *adj* : imperdonable
unfortunate¹ [ˌʌnˈfɔrʧənət] *adj* **1** UNLUCKY : desgraciado, infortunado, desafortunado ⟨how unfortunate! : ¡qué mala suerte!⟩ **2** INAPPROPRIATE : inoportuno ⟨an unfortunate comment : un comentario poco feliz⟩
unfortunate² *n* : desgraciado *m*, -da *f*
unfortunately [ˌʌnˈfɔrʧənətli] *adv* : desafortunadamente
unfounded [ˌʌnˈfaʊndəd] *adj* : infundado
unfreeze [ˌʌnˈfriːz] *v* **-froze** [-ˈfroːz]; **-frozen** [-ˈfroːzən]; **-freezing** *vt* : descongelar — *vi* : descongelarse
unfriendliness [ˌʌnˈfrɛndlinəs] *n* : hostilidad *f*, antipatía *f*
unfriendly [ˌʌnˈfrɛndli] *adj* **-lier; -est** : poco amistoso, hostil
unfurl [ˌʌnˈfərl] *vt* : desplegar, desdoblar — *vi* : desplegarse
unfurnished [ˌʌnˈfərnɪʃt] *adj* : desamueblado
ungainly [ˌʌnˈgeɪnli] *adj* : desgarbado
ungodly [ˌʌnˈgɔdli, -ˈgɑd-] *adj* **1** IMPIOUS : impío **2** OUTRAGEOUS : atroz, terrible ⟨at an ungodly hour : a una hora intempestiva⟩
ungrateful [ˌʌnˈgreɪtfəl] *adj* : desagradecido, ingrato — **ungratefully** *adv*
ungratefulness [ˌʌnˈgreɪtfəlnəs] *n* : ingratitud *f*
unhappily [ˌʌnˈhæpəli] *adv* **1** SADLY : tristemente **2** UNFORTUNATELY : desafortunadamente, lamentablemente
unhappiness [ˌʌnˈhæpinəs] *n* : infelicidad *f*, tristeza *f*, desdicha *f*
unhappy [ˌʌnˈhæpi] *adj* **-pier; -est 1** UNFORTUNATE : desafortunado, desventurado **2** MISERABLE, SAD : infeliz, triste, desdichado **3** INOPPORTUNE : inoportuno, poco feliz
unharmed [ˌʌnˈhɑrmd] *adj* : salvo, ileso
unhealthy [ˌʌnˈhɛlθi] *adj* **-thier; -est 1** UNWHOLESOME : insalubre, malsano, nocivo a la salud ⟨an unhealthy climate : un clima insalubre⟩ **2** SICKLY : de mala salud, enfermizo
unheard–of [ˌʌnˈhərdəv] *adj* : sin precedente, inaudito, insólito
unhinge [ˌʌnˈhɪnʤ] *vt* **-hinged; -hinging 1** : desquiciar (una puerta, etc.) **2** DISRUPT, UNSETTLE : trastornar, perturbar
unholy [ˌʌnˈhoːli] *adj* **-lier; -est 1** : profano, impío **2** UNGODLY : atroz, terrible
unhook [ˌʌnˈhʊk] *vt* **1** : desenganchar, descolgar (de algo) **2** UNDO : desabrochar
unhurt [ˌʌnˈhərt] *adj* : ileso
unicorn [ˈjuːnəˌkɔrn] *n* : unicornio *m*
unidentified [ˌʌnaɪˈdɛntəˌfaɪd] *adj* : no identificado ⟨unidentified flying object : objeto volador no identificado⟩
unification [ˌjuːnəfəˈkeɪʃən] *n* : unificación *f*
uniform¹ [ˈjuːnəˌfɔrm] *adj* : uniforme, homogéneo, constante
uniform² *n* : uniforme *m*
uniformed [ˈjuːnəˌfɔrmd] *adj* : uniformado
uniformity [ˌjuːnəˈfɔrmət̬i] *n, pl* **-ties** : uniformidad *f*
unify [ˈjuːnəˌfaɪ] *vt* **-fied; -fying** : unificar, unir
unilateral [ˌjuːnəˈlæt̬ərəl] *adj* : unilateral — **unilaterally** *adv*
unimaginable [ˌʌnɪˈmæʤənəbəl] *adj* : inimaginable, inconcebible
unimportant [ˌʌnɪmˈpɔrtənt] *adj* : intrascendente, insignificante, sin importancia
uninhabited [ˌʌnɪnˈhæbət̬əd] *adj* : deshabitado, desierto, despoblado

uninhibited [ˌʌnɪnˈhɪbət̬əd] *adj* : desenfadado, desinhibido, sin reservas
uninjured [ˌʌnˈindʒərd] *adj* : ileso
unintelligent [ˌʌnɪnˈtɛlədʒənt] *adj* : poco inteligente
unintelligible [ˌʌnɪnˈtɛlədʒəbəl] *adj* : ininteligible, incomprensible
unintentional [ˌʌnɪnˈtɛntʃənəl] *adj* : no deliberado, involuntario
unintentionally [ˌʌnɪnˈtɛntʃənəli] *adv* : involuntariamente, sin querer
uninterested [ˌʌnˈɪntəˌrɛstəd, -trəstəd] *adj* : indiferente
uninteresting [ˌʌnˈɪntəˌrɛstɪŋ, -trəstɪŋ] *adj* : poco interesante, sin interés
uninterrupted [ˌʌnˌɪntəˈrʌptəd] *adj* : ininterrumpido, continuo
union [ˈju:njən] *n* **1** : unión *f* **2** *or* **labor union** : sindicato *m*, gremio *m*
unionize [ˈju:njəˌnaɪz] *v* **-ized; -izing** *vt* : sindicalizar, sindicar — *vi* : sindicalizarse
unique [jʊˈni:k] *adj* **1** SOLE : único, solo **2** UNUSUAL : extraordinario
uniquely [jʊˈni:kli] *adv* **1** EXCLUSIVELY : exclusivamente **2** EXCEPTIONALLY : excepcionalmente
unison [ˈju:nəsən, -zən] *n* **1** : unísono *m* (en música) **2** CONCORD : acuerdo *m*, armonía *f*, concordia *f* **3 in ~** SIMULTANEOUSLY : simultáneamente, al unísono
unit [ˈju:nɪt] *n* **1** : unidad *f* **2** : módulo *m* (de un mobiliario)
unitary [ˈju:nəˌtɛri] *adj* : unitario
unite [jʊˈnaɪt] *v* **united; uniting** *vt* : unir, juntar, combinar — *vi* : unirse, juntarse
unity [ˈju:nət̬i] *n, pl* **-ties** **1** UNION : unidad *f*, unión *f* **2** HARMONY : armonía *f*, acuerdo *m*
universal [ˌju:nəˈvərsəl] *adj* **1** GENERAL : general, universal ⟨a universal rule : una regla universal⟩ **2** WORLDWIDE : universal, mundial — **universally** *adv*
universe [ˈju:nəˌvərs] *n* : universo *m*
university [ˌju:nəˈvərsət̬i] *n, pl* **-ties** : universidad *f*
unjust [ˌʌnˈdʒʌst] *adj* : injusto — **unjustly** *adv*
unjustifiable [ˌʌnˌdʒʌstəˈfaɪəbəl] *adj* : injustificable
unjustified [ˌʌnˈdʒʌstəˌfaɪd] *adj* : injustificado
unkempt [ˌʌnˈkɛmpt] *adj* : descuidado, desaliñado, despeinado (dícese del pelo)
unkind [ˌʌnˈkaɪnd] *adj* : poco amable, cruel — **unkindly** *adv*
unkindness [ˌʌnˈkaɪndnəs] *n* : crueldad *f*, falta *f* de amabilidad
unknowing [ˌʌnˈno:ɪŋ] *adj* : inconsciente, ignorante — **unknowingly** *adv*
unknown [ˌʌnˈno:n] *adj* : desconocido
unlawful [ˌʌnˈlɔfəl] *adj* : ilícito, ilegal — **unlawfully** *adv*
unleash [ˌʌnˈli:ʃ] *vt* : soltar, desatar
unless [ənˈlɛs] *conj* : a menos que, salvo que, a no ser que
unlike[1] [ˌʌnˈlaɪk] *adj* **1** DIFFERENT : diferente, distinto **2** UNEQUAL : desigual
unlike[2] *prep* **1** : diferente de, distinto de ⟨unlike the others : distinto a los demás⟩ **2** : a diferencia de ⟨unlike her sister, she is shy : a diferencia de su hermana, es tímida⟩
unlikelihood [ˌʌnˈlaɪkliˌhʊd] *n* : improbabilidad *f*
unlikely [ˌʌnˈlaɪkli] *adj* **-lier; -est** **1** IMPROBABLE : improbable, poco probable **2** UNPROMISING : poco prometedor
unlimited [ˌʌnˈlɪmət̬əd] *adj* : ilimitado
unload [ˌʌnˈlo:d] *vt* **1** REMOVE : descargar, desembarcar (mercancías o pasajeros) **2** : descargar (un avión, un camión, etc.) **3** DUMP : deshacerse de — *vi* : descargar (dícese de un avión, un camión, etc.)
unlock [ˌʌnˈlɑk] *vt* **1** : abrir (con llave) **2** DISCLOSE, REVEAL : revelar
unluckily [ˌʌnˈlʌkəli] *adv* : desgraciadamente
unlucky [ˌʌnˈlʌki] *adj* **-luckier; -est** **1** : de mala suerte, desgraciado, desafortunado ⟨an unlucky year : un año de mala suerte⟩ **2** INAUSPICIOUS : desfavorable, poco propicio **3** REGRETTABLE : lamentable
unmanageable [ˌʌnˈmænɪdʒəbəl] *adj* : difícil de controlar, poco manejable, ingobernable
unmarried [ˌʌnˈmærid] *adj* : soltero
unmask [ˌʌnˈmæsk] *vt* EXPOSE : desenmascarar
unmerciful [ˌʌnˈmərsɪfəl] *adj* MERCILESS : despiadado — **unmercifully** *adv*
unmistakable [ˌʌnmɪˈsteɪkəbəl] *adj* : evidente, inconfundible, obvio — **unmistakably** [-bli] *adv*
unmoved [ˌʌnˈmu:vd] *adj* : impasible ⟨to be unmoved by : permanecer impasible ante⟩
unnatural [ˌʌnˈnætʃərəl] *adj* **1** ABNORMAL, UNUSUAL : anormal, poco natural, poco normal **2** AFFECTED : afectado, forzado ⟨an unnatural smile : una sonrisa forzada⟩ **3** PERVERSE : perverso, antinatural
unnecessary [ˌʌnˈnɛsəˌsɛri] *adj* : innecesario — **unnecessarily** [-ˌnɛsəˈsɛrəli] *adv*
unnerve [ˌʌnˈnərv] *vt* **-nerved; -nerving** : turbar, desconcertar, poner nervioso
unnoticed [ˌʌnˈno:t̬əst] *adj* : inadvertido ⟨to go unnoticed : pasar inadvertido⟩
unobstructed [ˌʌnəbˈstrʌktəd] *adj* : libre, despejado
unobtainable [ˌʌnəbˈteɪnəbəl] *adj* : inasequible
unobtrusive [ˌʌnəbˈstru:sɪv] *adj* : discreto
unoccupied [ˌʌnˈɑkjəˌpaɪd] *adj* **1** IDLE : desempleado, desocupado **2** EMPTY : desocupado, libre, deshabitado
unofficial [ˌʌnəˈfɪʃəl] *adj* : extraoficial, oficioso, no oficial

unorganized [ˌʌnˈɔrgəˌnaɪzd] *adj* : desorganizado
unorthodox [ˌʌnˈɔrθəˌdɑks] *adj* : poco ortodoxo, poco convencional
unpack [ˌʌnˈpæk] *vt* : desempacar — *vi* : desempacar, deshacer las maletas
unpaid [ˌʌnˈpeɪd] *adj* : no remunerado, no retribuido ⟨an unpaid bill : una cuenta pendiente⟩
unparalleled [ˌʌnˈpærəˌlɛld] *adj* : sin igual
unpatriotic [ˌʌnˌpeɪtriˈɑṭɪk] *adj* : antipatriótico
unpleasant [ˌʌnˈplɛzənt] *adj* : desagradable — **unpleasantly** *adv*
unplug [ˌʌnˈplʌg] *vt* **-plugged; -plugging** **1** UNCLOG : destapar, desatascar **2** DISCONNECT : desconectar, desenchufar
unpopular [ˌʌnˈpɑpjələr] *adj* : impopular, poco popular
unpopularity [ˌʌnˌpɑpjəˈlærəṭi] *n* : impopularidad *f*
unprecedented [ˌʌnˈprɛsəˌdɛntəd] *adj* : sin precedentes, inaudito, nuevo
unpredictable [ˌʌnpriˈdɪktəbəl] *adj* : impredecible
unprejudiced [ˌʌnˈprɛʤədəst] *adj* : imparcial, objetivo
unprepared [ˌʌnpriˈpærd] *adj* : no preparado ⟨an unprepared speech : un discurso improvisado⟩
unpretentious [ˌʌnpriˈtɛnʧəs] *adj* : modesto, sin pretensiones
unprincipled [ˌʌnˈprɪntsəpəld] *adj* : sin principios, carente de escrúpulos
unproductive [ˌʌnprəˈdʌktɪv] *adj* : improductivo
unprofitable [ˌʌnˈprɑfəṭəbəl] *adj* : no rentable, poco provechoso
unpromising [ˌʌnˈprɑməsɪŋ] *adj* : poco prometedor
unprotected [ˌʌnprəˈtɛktəd] *adj* : sin protección, desprotegido
unprovoked [ˌʌnprəˈvoːkt] *adj* : no provocado
unpublished [ˌʌnˈpʌblɪʃt] *adj* : inédito
unpunished [ˌʌnˈpʌnɪʃt] *adj* : impune ⟨to go unpunished : escapar sin castigo⟩
unqualified [ˌʌnˈkwɑləˌfaɪd] *adj* **1** : no calificado, sin título **2** COMPLETE : completo, absoluto ⟨an unqualified denial : una negación incondicional⟩
unquestionable [ˌʌnˈkwɛsʧənəbəl] *adj* : incuestionable, indudable, indiscutible — **unquestionably** [-bli] *adv*
unquestioning [ˌʌnˈkwɛsʧənɪŋ] *adj* : incondicional, absoluto, ciego
unravel [ˌʌnˈrævəl] *v* **-eled** *or* **-elled; -eling** *or* **-elling** *vt* **1** DISENTANGLE : desenmarañar, desenredar **2** SOLVE : aclarar, desenmarañar, desentrañar — *vi* : deshacerse
unreal [ˌʌnˈriːl] *adj* : irreal
unrealistic [ˌʌnˌriːəˈlɪstɪk] *adj* : poco realista
unreasonable [ˌʌnˈriːzənəbəl] *adj* **1** IRRATIONAL : poco razonable, irrazonable, irracional **2** EXCESSIVE : excesivo ⟨unreasonable prices : precios excesivos⟩
unreasonably [ˌʌnˈriːzənəbli] *adv* **1** IRRATIONALLY : irracionalmente, de manera irrazonable **2** EXCESSIVELY : excesivamente
unrefined [ˌʌnriˈfaɪnd] *adj* **1** : no refinado, sin refinar (dícese del azúcar, de la harina, etc.) **2** : poco refinado, inculto (dícese de una persona)
unrelated [ˌʌnriˈleɪṭəd] *adj* : no relacionado, inconexo
unrelenting [ˌʌnriˈlɛntɪŋ] *adj* **1** STERN : severo, inexorable **2** CONSTANT, RELENTLESS : constante, implacable
unreliable [ˌʌnriˈlaɪəbəl] *adj* : que no es de fiar, de poca confianza, inestable (dícese del tiempo)
unrepentant [ˌʌnriˈpɛntənt] *adj* : impenitente
unresolved [ˌʌnriˈzɑlvd] *adj* : pendiente, no resuelto
unrest [ˌʌnˈrɛst] *n* : inquietud *f*, malestar *m* ⟨political unrest : disturbios políticos⟩
unrestrained [ˌʌnriˈstreɪnd] *adj* : desenfrenado, incontrolado
unrestricted [ˌʌnriˈstrɪktəd] *adj* : sin restricción ⟨unrestricted access : libre acceso⟩
unrewarding [ˌʌnriˈwɔrdɪŋ] *adj* THANKLESS : ingrato
unripe [ˌʌnˈraɪp] *adj* : inmaduro, verde
unrivaled *or* **unrivalled** [ˌʌnˈraɪvəld] *adj* : incomparable
unroll [ˌʌnˈroːl] *vt* : desenrollar — *vi* : desenrollarse
unruffled [ˌʌnˈrʌfəld] *adj* **1** SERENE : sereno, tranquilo **2** SMOOTH : tranquilo, liso ⟨unruffled waters : aguas tranquilas⟩
unruliness [ˌʌnˈruːlinəs] *n* : indisciplina *f*
unruly [ˌʌnˈruːli] *adj* : indisciplinado, díscolo, rebelde
unsafe [ˌʌnˈseɪf] *adj* : inseguro
unsaid [ˌʌnˈsɛd] *adj* : sin decir ⟨to leave unsaid : quedar por decir⟩
unsanitary [ˌʌnˈsænəˌtɛri] *adj* : antihigiénico
unsatisfactory [ˌʌnˌsæṭəsˈfæktəri] *adj* : insatisfactorio
unsatisfied [ˌʌnˈsæṭəsˌfaɪd] *adj* : insatisfecho
unscathed [ˌʌnˈskeɪðd] *adj* UNHARMED : ileso
unscheduled [ˌʌnˈskɛˌʤuːld] *adj* : no programado, imprevisto
unscientific [ˌʌnˌsaɪənˈtɪfɪk] *adj* : poco científico
unscrupulous [ˌʌnˈskruːpjələs] *adj* : inescrupuloso, sin escrúpulos — **unscrupulously** *adv*
unseal [ˌʌnˈsiːl] *vt* : abrir, quitarle el sello a
unseasonable [ˌʌnˈsiːzənəbəl] *adj* **1** : extemporáneo ⟨unseasonable rain

: lluvia extemporánea⟩ **2** UNTIMELY : extemporáneo, inoportuno
unseemly [ˌʌnˈsi:mli] *adj* **-lier; -est 1** INDECOROUS : indecoroso **2** INAPPROPRIATE : impropio, inapropiado
unseen [ˌʌnˈsi:n] *adj* **1** UNNOTICED : inadvertido **2** INVISIBLE : oculto, invisible
unselfish [ˌʌnˈsɛlfɪʃ] *adj* : generoso, desinteresado — **unselfishly** *adv*
unselfishness [ˌʌnˈsɛlfɪʃnəs] *n* : generosidad *f*, desinterés *m*
unsettle [ˌʌnˈsɛtəl] *vt* **-tled; -tling** DISTURB : trastornar, alterar, perturbar
unsettled [ˌʌnˈsɛtəld] *adj* **1** CHANGEABLE : inestable, variable ⟨unsettled weather : tiempo inestable⟩ **2** DISTURBED : agitado, inquieto ⟨unsettled waters : aguas agitadas⟩ **3** UNDECIDED : pendiente (dícese de un asunto), indeciso (dícese de una persona) **4** UNPAID : sin saldar, pendiente **5** UNINHABITED : despoblado, no colonizado
unshaped [ˌʌnˈʃeɪpt] *adj* : sin forma, informe
unsightly [ˌʌnˈsaɪtli] *adj* UGLY : feo, de aspecto malo
unskilled [ˌʌnˈskɪld] *adj* : no calificado
unskillful [ˌʌnˈskɪlfəl] *adj* : inexperto, poco hábil
unsnap [ˌʌnˈsnæp] *vt* **-snapped; -snapping** : desabrochar
unsociable *adj* : poco sociable
unsolved [ˌʌnˈsɔlvd] *adj* : no resuelto, sin resolver
unsophisticated [ˌʌnsəˈfɪstəˌkeɪt̬əd] *adj* **1** NAIVE, UNWORLDLY : ingenuo, de poco mundo **2** SIMPLE : simple, poco sofisticado, rudimentario
unsound [ˌʌnˈsaʊnd] *adj* **1** UNHEALTHY : enfermizo, de mala salud **2** : poco sólido, defectuoso (dícese de una estructura, etc.) **3** INVALID : inválido, erróneo **4 of unsound mind** : mentalmente incapacitado
unspeakable [ˌʌnˈspi:kəbəl] *adj* **1** INDESCRIBABLE : indecible, inexpresable, incalificable **2** HEINOUS : atroz, nefando, abominable — **unspeakably** [-bli] *adv*
unspecified [ˌʌnˈspɛsəˌfaɪd] *adj* : indeterminado, sin especificar
unspoiled [ˌʌnˈspɔɪld] *adj* **1** : conservado, sin estropear (dícese de un lugar) **2** : que no está mimado (dícese de un niño)
unstable [ˌʌnˈsteɪbəl] *adj* **1** CHANGEABLE : variable, inestable, cambiable ⟨an unstable pulse : un pulso irregular⟩ **2** UNSTEADY : inestable, poco sólido (dícese de una estructura)
unsteadily [ˌʌnˈstɛdəli] *adv* : de modo inestable
unsteadiness [ˌʌnˈstɛdinəs] *n* : inestabilidad *f*, inseguridad *f*
unsteady [ˌʌnˈstɛdi] *adj* **1** UNSTABLE : inestable, variable **2** SHAKY : tembloroso
unstoppable [ˌʌnˈstɑpəbəl] *adj* : irrefrenable, incontenible
unsubstantiated [ˌʌnsəbˈstæntʃiˌeɪt̬əd] *adj* : no corroborado, no demostrado
unsuccessful [ˌʌnsəkˈsɛsfəl] *adj* : fracasado, infructuoso
unsuitable [ˌʌnˈsu:t̬əbəl] *adj* : inadecuado, impropio, inapropiado ⟨an unsuitable time : una hora inconveniente⟩
unsuited [ˌʌnˈsu:t̬əd] *adj* : inadecuado, inepto
unsung [ˌʌnˈsʌŋ] *adj* : olvidado
unsure [ˌʌnˈʃʊr] *adj* : incierto, dudoso
unsurpassed [ˌʌnsərˈpæst] *adj* : sin par, sin igual
unsuspecting [ˌʌnsəˈspɛktɪŋ] *adj* : desprevenido, desapercibido, confiado
unsympathetic [ˌʌnˌsɪmpəˈθɛt̬ɪk] *adj* : poco comprensivo, indiferente
untangle [ˌʌnˈteɪŋgəl] *vt* **-gled; -gling** : desenmarañar, desenredar
unthinkable [ˌʌnˈθɪŋkəbəl] *adj* : inconcebible, impensable
unthinking [ˌʌnˈθɪŋkɪŋ] *adj* : irreflexivo, inconsciente — **unthinkingly** *adv*
untidy [ˌʌnˈtaɪdi] *adj* **1** SLOVENLY : desaliñado **2** DISORDERLY : desordenado, desarreglado
untie [ˌʌnˈtaɪ] *vt* **-tied; -tying** *or* **-tieing** : desatar, deshacer
until[1] [ˌʌnˈtɪl] *prep* : hasta ⟨until now : hasta ahora⟩
until[2] *conj* : hasta que ⟨until they left : hasta que salieron⟩ ⟨don't answer until you're sure : no contestes hasta que (no) estés seguro⟩
untimely [ˌʌnˈtaɪmli] *adj* **1** PREMATURE : prematuro ⟨an untimely death : una muerte prematura⟩ **2** INOPPORTUNE : inoportuno, intempestivo
untold [ˌʌnˈto:ld] *adj* **1** : nunca dicho ⟨the untold secret : el secreto sin contar⟩ **2** INCALCULABLE : incalculable, indecible
untouched [ˌʌnˈtʌtʃt] *adj* **1** INTACT : intacto, sin tocar, sin probar (dícese de la comida) **2** UNAFFECTED : insensible, indiferente
untoward [ˌʌnˈtɔrd, -ˈto:ərd, -təˈwɔrd] *adj* **1** : indecoroso, impropio (dícese del comportamiento) **2** ADVERSE, UNFORTUNATE : desafortunado, adverso ⟨untoward effects : efectos perjudiciales⟩ **3** UNSEEMLY : indecoroso
untrained [ˌʌnˈtreɪnd] *adj* : inexperto, no capacitado
untreated [ˌʌnˈtri:t̬əd] *adj* : no tratado (dícese de una enfermedad, etc.), sin tratar (dícese de un material)
untroubled [ˌʌnˈtrʌbəld] *adj* : tranquilo ⟨to be untroubled by : no estar afectado por⟩
untrue [ˌʌnˈtru:] *adj* **1** UNFAITHFUL : infiel **2** FALSE : falso
untrustworthy [ˌʌnˈtrʌstˌwərði] *adj* : de poca confianza (dícese de una persona), no fidedigno (dícese de la información)

untruth [ˌʌn'tru:θ, 'ʌnˌ-] *n* : mentira *f*, falsedad *f*

untruthful [ˌʌn'tru:θfəl] *adj* : mentiroso, falso

unusable [ˌʌn'ju:zəbəl] *adj* : inútil, inservible

unused [ˌʌn'ju:zd, *in sense 1 usually* -'ju:st] *adj* **1** UNACCUSTOMED : inhabituado **2** NEW : nuevo **3** IDLE : no utilizado (dícese de la tierra) **4** REMAINING : restante ⟨the unused portion : la porción restante⟩

unusual [ˌʌn'ju:ʒʊəl] *adj* : inusual, poco común, raro

unusually [ˌʌn'ju:ʒʊəli, -'ju:ʒəli] *adv* : excepcionalmente, extraordinariamente, fuera de lo común

unwanted [ˌʌn'wɑntəd] *adj* : superfluo, de sobre

unwarranted [ˌʌn'wɔrəntəd] *adj* : injustificado

unwary [ˌʌn'wæri] *adj* : incauto

unwavering [ˌʌn'weɪvərɪŋ] *adj* : firme, inquebrantable ⟨an unwavering gaze : una mirada fija⟩

unwelcome [ˌʌn'wɛlkəm] *adj* : importuno, molesto

unwell [ˌʌn'wɛl] *adj* : enfermo, mal

unwholesome [ˌʌn'ho:lsəm] *adj* **1** UNHEALTHY : malsano, insalubre **2** PERNICIOUS : pernicioso **3** LOATHSOME : repugnante, muy desagradable

unwieldy [ˌʌn'wi:ldi] *adj* CUMBERSOME : difícil de manejar, torpe y pesado

unwilling [ˌʌn'wɪlɪŋ] *adj* : poco dispuesto ⟨to be unwilling to : no estar dispuesto a⟩

unwillingly [ˌʌn'wɪlɪŋli] *adv* : a regañadientes, de mala gana

unwind [ˌʌn'waɪnd] *v* **-wound** [-'waʊnd]; **-winding** *vt* UNROLL : desenrollar — *vi* **1** : desenrollarse **2** RELAX : relajar

unwise [ˌʌn'waɪz] *adj* : imprudente, desacertado, poco aconsejable

unwisely [ˌʌn'waɪzli] *adv* : imprudentemente

unwitting [ˌʌn'wɪt̬ɪŋ] *adj* **1** UNAWARE : inconsciente **2** INADVERTENT : involuntario, inadvertido ⟨an unwitting mistake : un error inadvertido⟩ — **unwittingly** *adv*

unworthiness [ˌʌn'wərðinəs] *n* : falta *f* de valía

unworthy [ˌʌn'wərði] *adj* **1** UNDESERVING : indigno ⟨to be unworthy of : no ser digno de⟩ **2** UNMERITED : inmerecido

unwrap [ˌʌn'ræp] *vt* **-wrapped; -wrapping** : desenvolver, deshacer

unwritten [ˌʌn'rɪtən] *adj* : no escrito

unyielding [ˌʌn'ji:ldɪŋ] *adj* : firme, inflexible, rígido

unzip [ˌʌn'zɪp] *vt* **-zipped; -zipping** : abrir el cierre de

up[1] ['ʌp] *v* **upped** ['ʌpt]; **upping; ups** *vt* INCREASE : aumentar, subir ⟨they upped the prices : aumentaron los precios⟩ — *vi* **to up and** : agarrar y *fam* ⟨she up and left : agarró y se fue⟩

up[2] *adv* **1** ABOVE : arriba, en lo alto ⟨up in the mountains : arriba en las montañas⟩ **2** UPWARDS : hacia arriba ⟨push it up : empújalo hacia arriba⟩ ⟨the sun came up : el sol salió⟩ ⟨prices went up : los precios subieron⟩ **3** (*indicating an upright position or waking state*) ⟨to sit up : ponerse derecho⟩ ⟨they got up late : se levantaron tarde⟩ ⟨I stayed up all night : pasé toda la noche sin dormir⟩ **4** (*indicating volume or intensity*) ⟨to speak up : hablar más fuerte⟩ **5** (*indicating a northerly direction*) ⟨the climate up north : el clima del norte⟩ ⟨I'm going up to Canada : voy para Canadá⟩ **6** (*indicating the appearance or existence of something*) ⟨the book turned up : el libro apareció⟩ **7** (*indicating consideration*) ⟨she brought the matter up : mencionó el asunto⟩ **8** COMPLETELY : completamente ⟨eat it up : cómetelo todo⟩ **9** : en pedazos ⟨he tore it up : lo rompió en pedazos⟩ **10** (*indicating a stopping*) ⟨the car pulled up to the curb : el carro paró al borde de la acera⟩ **11** (*indicating an even score*) ⟨the game was 10 up : empataron a 10⟩

up[3] *adj* **1** (*risen above the horizon*) ⟨the sun is up : ha salido el sol⟩ **2** (*being above a normal or former level*) ⟨prices are up : los precios han aumentado⟩ ⟨the river is up : las aguas están altas⟩ **3** : despierto, levantado ⟨up all night : despierto toda la noche⟩ **4** BUILT : construido ⟨the house is up : la casa está construida⟩ **5** OPEN : abierto ⟨the windows are up : las ventanas están abiertas⟩ **6** (*moving or going upward*) ⟨the up staircase : la escalera para subir⟩ **7** ABREAST : enterado, al día, al corriente ⟨to be up on the news : estar al corriente de las noticias⟩ **8** PREPARED : preparado ⟨we were up for the test : estuvimos preparados para el examen⟩ **9** FINISHED : terminado, acabado ⟨time is up : se ha terminado el tiempo permitido⟩ **10 to be up** : pasar ⟨what's up? : ¿qué pasa?⟩

up[4] *prep* **1** (*to, toward, or at a higher point of*) ⟨he went up the stairs : subió la escalera⟩ **2** (*to or toward the source of*) ⟨to go up the river : ir río arriba⟩ **3** ALONG : a lo largo, por ⟨up the coast : a lo largo de la costa⟩ ⟨just up the way : un poco más adelante⟩ ⟨up and down the city : por toda la ciudad⟩

upbraid [ˌʌp'breɪd] *vt* : reprender, regañar

upbringing ['ʌpˌbrɪŋɪŋ] *n* : crianza *f*, educación *f*

upcoming [ˌʌp'kʌmɪŋ] *adj* : próximo

update[1] [ˌʌp'deɪt] *vt* **-dated; -dating** : poner al día, poner al corriente, actualizar

update[2] ['ʌpˌdeɪt] *n* : actualización *f*, puesta *f* al día

upend [ˌʌp'ɛnd] *vt* **1** : poner vertical **2** OVERTURN : volcar

upgrade[1] [ˈʌpˌɡreɪd, ˌʌpˈ-] *vt* **-graded; -grading 1** PROMOTE : ascender **2** IMPROVE : mejorar

upgrade[2] [ˈʌpˌɡreɪd] *n* **1** SLOPE : cuesta *f*, pendiente *f* **2** RISE : aumento *m* de categoría (de un puesto), ascenso *m* (de un empleado) **3** IMPROVEMENT : mejoramiento *m*

upheaval [ˌʌpˈhiːvəl] *n* **1** : levantamiento *m* (en geología) **2** DISTURBANCE, UPSET : trastorno *m*, agitación *f*, conmoción *f*

uphill[1] [ˌʌpˈhɪl] *adv* : cuesta arriba

uphill[2] [ˈʌpˌhɪl] *adj* **1** ASCENDING : en subida **2** DIFFICULT : difícil, arduo

uphold [ˌʌpˈhoːld] *vt* **-held; -holding 1** SUPPORT : sostener, apoyar, mantener **2** RAISE : levantar **3** CONFIRM : confirmar (una decisión judicial)

upholster [ˌʌpˈhoːlstər] *vt* : tapizar

upholsterer [ˌʌpˈhoːlstərər] *n* : tapicero *m*, -ra *f*

upholstery [ˌʌpˈhoːlstəri] *n, pl* **-steries** : tapicería *f*

upkeep [ˈʌpˌkiːp] *n* : mantenimiento *m*

upland [ˈʌplənd, -ˌlænd] *n* : altiplanicie *f*, altiplano *m*

uplift[1] [ˌʌpˈlɪft] *vt* **1** RAISE : elevar, levantar **2** ELEVATE : elevar, animar (el espíritu, la mente, etc.)

uplift[2] [ˈʌpˌlɪft] *n* : elevación *f*

upon [əˈpɔn, əˈpɑn] *prep* : en, sobre ⟨upon the desk : sobre el escritorio⟩ ⟨upon leaving : al salir⟩ ⟨questions upon questions : pregunta tras pregunta⟩

upper[1] [ˈʌpər] *adj* **1** HIGHER : superior ⟨the upper classes : las clases altas⟩ **2** : alto (en geografía) ⟨the upper Mississippi : el alto Mississippi⟩

upper[2] *n* : parte *f* superior (del calzado, etc.)

uppercase [ˌʌpərˈkeɪs] *adj* : mayúsculo

upper hand *n* : ventaja *f*, dominio *m*

uppermost [ˈʌpərˌmoːst] *adj* : más alto ⟨it was uppermost in his mind : era lo que más le preocupaba⟩

upright[1] [ˈʌpˌraɪt] *adj* **1** VERTICAL : vertical **2** ERECT : erguido, derecho **3** JUST : recto, honesto, justo

upright[2] *n* : montante *m*, poste *m*, soporte *m*

uprising [ˈʌpˌraɪzɪŋ] *n* : insurrección *f*, revuelta *f*, alzamiento *m*

uproar [ˈʌpˌror] *n* COMMOTION : alboroto *m*, jaleo *m*, escándalo *m*

uproarious [ˌʌpˈroriəs] *adj* **1** CLAMOROUS : estrepitoso, clamoroso **2** HILARIOUS : muy divertido, hilarante — **uproariously** *adv*

uproot [ˌʌpˈruːt, -ˈrʊt] *vt* : desarraigar

upset[1] [ˌʌpˈsɛt] *vt* **-set; -setting 1** OVERTURN : volcar **2** SPILL : derramar **3** DISTURB : perturbar, disgustar, inquietar, alterar **4** SICKEN : sentar mal a ⟨it upsets my stomach : me sienta mal al estómago⟩ **5** DISRUPT : trastornar, desbaratar (planes, etc.) **6** DEFEAT : derrotar (en deportes)

upset[2] *adj* **1** DISPLEASED, DISTRESSED : disgustado, alterado **2 to have an upset stomach** : estar mal del estómago, estar descompuesto (de estómago)

upset[3] [ˈʌpˌsɛt] *n* **1** OVERTURNING : vuelco *m* **2** DISRUPTION : trastorno *m* (de planes, etc.) **3** DEFEAT : derrota *f* (en deportes)

upshot [ˈʌpˌʃɑt] *n* : resultado *m* final

upside–down [ˌʌpˌsaɪdˈdaʊn] *adj* : al revés

upside down [ˌʌpˌsaɪdˈdaʊn] *adv* **1** : al revés **2** : en confusión, en desorden

upstairs[1] [ˌʌpˈstærz] *adv* : arriba, en el piso superior

upstairs[2] [ˈʌpˌstærz, ˌʌpˈ-] *adj* : de arriba

upstairs[3] [ˈʌpˌstærz, ˌʌpˈ-] *ns & pl* : piso *m* de arriba, planta *f* de arriba

upstanding [ˌʌpˈstændɪŋ, ˈʌpˌ-] *adj* HONEST, UPRIGHT : honesto, íntegro, recto

upstart [ˈʌpˌstɑrt] *n* : advenedizo *m*, -za *f*

upswing [ˈʌpˌswɪŋ] *n* : alza *f*, mejora *f* notable ⟨to be on the upswing : estar mejorándose⟩

uptight [ˌʌpˈtaɪt] *adj* : tenso, nervioso

up to *prep* **1** : hasta ⟨up to a year : hasta un año⟩ ⟨in mud up to my ankles : en barro hasta los tobillos⟩ **2 to be up to** : estar a la altura de ⟨I'm not up to going : no estoy en condiciones de ir⟩ **3 to be up to** : depender de ⟨it's up to the director : depende del director⟩

up–to–date [ˌʌptəˈdeɪt] *adj* **1** CURRENT : corriente, al día ⟨to keep up-to-date : mantenerse al corriente⟩ **2** MODERN : moderno

uptown [ˈʌpˈtaʊn] *adv* : hacia la parte alta de la ciudad, hacia el distrito residencial

upturn [ˈʌpˌtərn] *n* : mejora *f*, auge *m* (económico)

upward[1] [ˈʌpwərd] *or* **upwards** [-wərdz] *adv* **1** : hacia arriba **2 ~ of** : más de

upward[2] *adj* : ascendente, hacia arriba

upwind [ˌʌpˈwɪnd] *adv & adj* : contra el viento

uranium [jʊˈreɪniəm] *n* : uranio *m*

Uranus [jʊˈreɪnəs, ˈjʊrənəs] *n* : Urano *m*

urban [ˈərbən] *adj* : urbano

urbane [ˌərˈbeɪn] *adj* : urbano, cortés

urchin [ˈərʧən] *n* **1** SCAMP : granuja *mf*; pillo *m*, -lla *f* **2 sea urchin** : erizo *m* de mar

Urdu [ˈʊrduː, ˈər-] *n* : urdu *m*

urethra [jʊˈriːθrə] *n, pl* **-thras** *or* **-thrae** [-ˌθriː] : uretra *f*

urge[1] [ˈərʤ] *vt* **urged; urging 1** PRESS : instar, apremiar, insistir ⟨we urged him to come : insistimos en que viniera⟩ **2** ADVOCATE : recomendar, abogar por **3 to urge on** : animar, alentar

urge[2] *n* : impulso *m*, ganas *fpl*, compulsión *f*

urgency [ˈərʤən*t*si] *n, pl* **-cies** : urgencia *f*

urgent [ˈərʤənt] *adj* **1** PRESSING : urgente, apremiante **2** INSISTENT : insistente **3 to be urgent** : urgir
urgently [ˈərʤəntli] *adv* : urgentemente
urinal [ˈjʊrənəl, *esp Brit* jʊˈraɪnəl] *n* : orinal *m* (recipiente), urinario *m* (lugar)
urinary [ˈjʊrəˌnɛri] *adj* : urinario
urinate [ˈjʊrəˌneɪt] *vi* **-nated; -nating** : orinar
urination [ˌjʊrəˈneɪʃən] *n* : orinación *f*
urine [ˈjʊrən] *n* : orina *f*
urn [ˈərn] *n* **1** VASE : urna *f* **2** : recipiente *m* (para servir café, etc.)
Uruguayan [ˌʊrəˈgwaɪən, ˌjʊr-, -ˈgweɪ-] *n* : uruguayo *m*, -ya *f* — **Uruguayan** *adj*
us [ˈʌs] *pron* **1** (*as direct object*) : nos ⟨they were visiting us : nos visitaban⟩ **2** (*as indirect object*) : nos ⟨he gave us a present : nos dio un regalo⟩ **3** (*as object of preposition*) : nosotros, nosotras ⟨stay with us : quédese con nosotros⟩ ⟨both of us : nosotros dos⟩ **4** (*for emphasis*) : nosotros ⟨it's us! : ¡somos nosotros!⟩
usable [ˈju:zəbəl] *adj* : utilizable
usage [ˈju:sɪʤ, -zɪʤ] *n* **1** HABIT : costumbre *f*, hábito *m* **2** USE : uso *m*
use[1] [ˈju:z] *v* **used** [ˈju:zd, *in phrase "used to" usually* ˈju:stu:]; **using** *vt* **1** EMPLOY : emplear, usar **2** CONSUME : consumir, tomar (drogas, etc.) **3** UTILIZE : usar, utilizar ⟨to use tact : usar tacto⟩ ⟨he used his friends to get ahead : usó a sus amigos para mejorar su posición⟩ **4** TREAT : tratar ⟨they used the horse cruelly : maltrataron al caballo⟩ **5 to use up** : agotar, consumir, gastar — *vi* (*used in the past with* **to** *to indicate a former fact or state*) : soler, acostumbrar ⟨winters used to be colder : los inviernos solían ser más fríos, los inviernos eran más fríos⟩ ⟨she used to dance : acostumbraba bailar⟩
use[2] [ˈju:s] *n* **1** APPLICATION, EMPLOYMENT : uso *m*, empleo *m*, utilización *f* ⟨out of use : en desuso⟩ ⟨ready for use : listo para usar⟩ ⟨to be in use : usarse, estar funcionando⟩ ⟨to make use of : servirse de, aprovechar⟩ **2** USEFULNESS : utilidad *f* ⟨to be of no use : no servir (para nada)⟩ ⟨it's no use! : ¡es inútil!⟩ **3 to have the use of** : poder usar, tener acceso a **4 to have no use for** : no necesitar ⟨she has no use for poetry : a ella no le gusta la poesía⟩
used [ˈju:zd] *adj* **1** SECONDHAND : usado, de segunda mano ⟨used cars : coches usados⟩ **2** ACCUSTOMED : acostumbrado ⟨used to the heat : acostumbrado al calor⟩
useful [ˈju:sfəl] *adj* : útil, práctico — **usefully** *adv*
usefulness [ˈju:sfəlnəs] *n* : utilidad *f*
useless [ˈju:sləs] *adj* : inútil — **uselessly** *adv*
uselessness [ˈju:sləsnəs] *n* : inutilidad *f*
user [ˈju:zər] *n* : usuario *m*, -ria *f*
usher[1] [ˈʌʃər] *vt* **1** ESCORT : acompañar, conducir **2 to usher in** : hacer pasar (a alguien) ⟨to usher in a new era : anunciar una nueva época⟩
usher[2] *n* : acomodador *m*, -dora *f*
usherette [ˌʌʃəˈrɛt] *n* : acomodadora *f*
usual [ˈju:ʒuəl] *adj* **1** NORMAL : usual, normal **2** CUSTOMARY : acostumbrado, habitual, de costumbre **3** ORDINARY : ordinario, típico
usually [ˈju:ʒuəli, ˈju:ʒəli] *adv* : usualmente, normalmente
usurp [jʊˈsərp, -ˈzərp] *vt* : usurpar
usurper [jʊˈsərpər, -ˈzər-] *n* : usurpador *m*, -dora *f*
utensil [jʊˈtɛntsəl] *n* **1** : utensilio *m* (de cocina) **2** IMPLEMENT : implemento *m*, útil *m* (de labranza, etc.)
uterine [ˈju:t̬əˌraɪn, -rən] *adj* : uterino
uterus [ˈju:t̬ərəs] *n, pl* **uteri** [-ˌraɪ] : útero *m*, matriz *f*
utilitarian [ju:ˌtɪləˈtɛriən] *adj* : utilitario
utility [ju:ˈtɪlət̬i] *n, pl* **-ties 1** USEFULNESS : utilidad *f* **2 public utility** : empresa *f* de servicio público
utilization [ˌju:t̬ələˈzeɪʃən] *n* : utilización *f*
utilize [ˈju:t̬əlˌaɪz] *vt* **-lized; -lizing** : utilizar, hacer uso de
utmost[1] [ˈʌtˌmo:st] *adj* **1** FARTHEST : extremo, más lejano **2** GREATEST : sumo, mayor ⟨of the utmost importance : de suma importancia⟩
utmost[2] *n* : lo más posible ⟨to the utmost : al máximo⟩
utopia [jʊˈto:piə] *n* : utopía *f*
utopian [jʊˈto:piən] *adj* : utópico
utter[1] [ˈʌt̬ər] *vt* : decir, articular, pronunciar (palabras)
utter[2] *adj* : absoluto — **utterly** *adv*
utterance [ˈʌt̬ərənts] *n* : declaración *f*, articulación *f*

V

v [ˈvi:] *n, pl* **v's** *or* **vs** [ˈvi:z] : vigésima segunda letra del alfabeto inglés
vacancy [ˈveɪkəntsi] *n, pl* **-cies 1** EMPTINESS : vacío *m*, vacuidad *f* **2** : vacante *f*, puesto *m* vacante ⟨to fill a vacancy : ocupar un puesto⟩ **3** : habitación *f* libre (en un hotel) ⟨no vacancies : completo⟩
vacant [ˈveɪkənt] *adj* **1** EMPTY : libre, desocupado (dícese de los edificios,

etc.) **2** : vacante (dícese de los puestos) **3** BLANK : vacío, ausente ⟨a vacant stare : una mirada ausente⟩
vacate [ˈveɪˌkeɪt] *vt* **-cated; -cating** : desalojar, desocupar
vacation[1] [veɪˈkeɪʃən, və-] *vi* : pasar las vacaciones, vacacionar *Mex*
vacation[2] *n* : vacaciones *fpl* ⟨to be on vacation : estar de vacaciones⟩
vacationer [veɪˈkeɪʃənər, və-] *n* : turista *mf*, veraneante *mf*, vacacionista *mf CA, Mex*
vaccinate [ˈvæksəˌneɪt] *vt* **-nated; -nating** : vacunar
vaccination [ˌvæksəˈneɪʃən] *n* : vacunación *f*
vaccine [vækˈsiːn, ˈvækˌ-] *n* : vacuna *f*
vacillate [ˈvæsəˌleɪt] *vi* **-lated; -lating** **1** HESITATE : vacilar **2** SWAY : oscilar
vacillation [ˌvæsəˈleɪʃən] *n* : indecisión *f*, vacilación *f*
vacuous [ˈvækjʊəs] *adj* **1** EMPTY : vacío **2** INANE : vacuo, necio, estúpido
vacuum[1] [ˈvæˌkjuːm, -kjəm] *vt* : limpiar con aspiradora, pasar la aspiradora por
vacuum[2] *n, pl* **vacuums** *or* **vacua** [ˈvækjʊə] : vacío *m*
vacuum cleaner *n* : aspiradora *f*
vagabond[1] [ˈvægəˌbɑnd] *adj* : vagabundo
vagabond[2] *n* : vagabundo *m*, -da *f*
vagary [ˈveɪgəri, vəˈgɛri] *n, pl* **-ries** : capricho *m*
vagina [vəˈʤaɪnə] *n, pl* **-nae** [-ˌniː, -ˌnaɪ] *or* **-nas** : vagina *f*
vagrancy [ˈveɪgrəntsi] *n, pl* **-cies** : vagancia *f*
vagrant[1] [ˈveɪgrənt] *adj* : vagabundo
vagrant[2] *n* : vagabundo *m*, -da *f*
vague [ˈveɪg] *adj* **vaguer; -est** **1** IMPRECISE : vago, impreciso ⟨a vague feeling : una sensación indefinida⟩ ⟨I haven't the vaguest idea : no tengo la más remota idea⟩ **2** UNCLEAR : borroso, poco claro ⟨a vague outline : un perfil indistinto⟩ **3** ABSENTMINDED : distraído
vaguely [ˈveɪgli] *adv* : vagamente, de manera imprecisa
vagueness [ˈveɪgnəs] *n* : vaguedad *f*, imprecisión *f*
vain [ˈveɪn] *adj* **1** WORTHLESS : vano **2** FUTILE : vano, inútil ⟨in vain : en vano⟩ **3** CONCEITED : vanidoso, presumido
vainly [ˈveɪnli] *adv* : en vano, vanamente, inútilmente
valance [ˈvælənts, ˈveɪ-] *n* **1** FLOUNCE : volante *m* (de una cama, etc.) **2** : galería *f* de cortina (sobre una ventana)
vale [ˈveɪl] *n* : valle *m*
valedictorian [ˌvæləˌdɪkˈtoriən] *n* : estudiante *mf* que pronuncia el discurso de despedida en ceremonia de graduación
valedictory [ˌvæləˈdɪktəri] *adj* : de despedida
valentine [ˈvælənˌtaɪn] *n* : tarjeta *f* que se manda el Día de los Enamorados (el 14 de febrero)
Valentine's Day *n* : Día *m* de los Enamorados
valet [ˈvæˌleɪ, væˈleɪ, ˈvælət] *n* : ayuda *m* de cámara
valiant [ˈvæljənt] *adj* : valiente, valeroso
valiantly [ˈvæljəntli] *adv* : con valor, valientemente
valid [ˈvæləd] *adj* : válido
validate [ˈvæləˌdeɪt] *vt* **-dated; -dating** : validar, dar validez a
validity [vəˈlɪdəti, væ-] *n* : validez *f*
valise [vəˈliːs] *n* : maleta *f* (de mano)
valley [ˈvæli] *n, pl* **-leys** : valle *m*
valor [ˈvælər] *n* : valor *m*, valentía *f*
valorous [ˈvælərəs] *adj* : valeroso, valiente
valuable[1] [ˈvæljʊəbəl, ˈvæljəbəl] *adj* **1** EXPENSIVE : valioso, de valor **2** WORTHWHILE : valioso, apreciable
valuable[2] *n* : objeto *m* de valor
valuation [ˌvæljʊˈeɪʃən] *n* **1** APPRAISAL : valoración *f*, tasación *f* **2** VALUE : valuación *f*
value[1] [ˈvælˌjuː] *vt* **-ued; -uing** **1** APPRAISE : valorar, avaluar, tasar **2** APPRECIATE : valorar, apreciar
value[2] *n* **1** : valor *m* ⟨of little value : de poco valor⟩ ⟨to be a good value : estar bien de precio, tener buen precio⟩ ⟨at face value : en su sentido literal⟩ **2 values** *npl* : valores *mpl* (morales), principios *mpl*
valueless [ˈvæljuːləs] *adj* : sin valor
valve [ˈvælv] *n* : válvula *f*
vampire [ˈvæmˌpaɪr] *n* **1** : vampiro *m* **2** *or* **vampire bat** : vampiro *m*
van[1] [ˈvæn] → **vanguard**
van[2] *n* : furgoneta *f*, camioneta *f*
vanadium [vəˈneɪdiəm] *n* : vanadio *m*
vandal [ˈvændəl] *n* : vándalo *m*
vandalism [ˈvændəlˌɪzəm] *n* : vandalismo *m*
vandalize [ˈvændəlˌaɪz] *vt* : destrozar, destruir, estropear
vane [ˈveɪn] *n or* **weather vane** : veleta *f*
vanguard [ˈvænˌgɑrd] *n* : vanguardia *f*
vanilla [vəˈnɪlə, -ˈnɛ-] *n* : vainilla *f*
vanish [ˈvænɪʃ] *vi* : desaparecer, disiparse, desvanecerse
vanity [ˈvænəti] *n, pl* **-ties** **1** : vanidad *f* **2** *or* **vanity table** : tocador *m*
vanquish [ˈvæŋkwɪʃ, ˈvæn-] *vt* : vencer, conquistar
vantage point [ˈvæntɪʤ] *n* : posición *f* ventajosa
vapid [ˈvæpəd, ˈveɪ-] *adj* : insípido, insulso
vapor [ˈveɪpər] *n* : vapor *m*
vaporize [ˈveɪpəˌraɪz] *v* **-rized; -rizing** *vt* : vaporizar — *vi* : vaporizarse, evaporarse
vaporizer [ˈveɪpəˌraɪzər] *n* : vaporizador *m*
variability [ˌvɛriəˈbɪləti] *n, pl* **-ties** : variabilidad *f*
variable[1] [ˈvɛriəbəl] *adj* : variable ⟨variable cloudiness : nubosidad variable⟩

variable[2] *n* : variable *f*, factor *m*
variance [ˈvɛriənts] *n* **1** DISCREPANCY : varianza *f*, discrepancia *f* **2** DISAGREEMENT : desacuerdo *m* ⟨at variance with : en desacuerdo con⟩
variant[1] [ˈvɛriənt] *adj* : variante, divergente
variant[2] *n* : variante *f*
variation [ˌvɛriˈeɪʃən] *n* : variación *f*, diferencias *fpl*
varicose [ˈværəˌkoːs] *adj* : varicoso
varicose veins *npl* : varices *fpl*, várices *fpl*
varied [ˈvɛrid] *adj* : variado, dispar, diferente
variegated [ˈvɛriəˌgeɪt̬d] *adj* : abigarrado, multicolor
variety [vəˈraɪət̬i] *n, pl* **-ties** **1** DIVERSITY : diversidad *f*, variedad *f* **2** ASSORTMENT : surtido *m* ⟨for a variety of reasons : por diversas razones⟩ **3** SORT : clase *f* **4** BREED : variedad *f* (de plantas)
various [ˈvɛriəs] *adj* : varios, diversos
varnish[1] [ˈvɑrnɪʃ] *vt* : barnizar
varnish[2] *n* : barniz *f*
varsity [ˈvɑrsət̬i] *n, pl* **-ties** : equipo *m* universitario
vary [ˈvɛri] *v* **varied; varying** *vt* : variar, diversificar — *vi* **1** CHANGE : variar, cambiar **2** DEVIATE : desviarse
vascular [ˈvæskjələr] *adj* : vascular
vase [ˈveɪs, ˈveɪz, ˈvɑz] *n* : jarrón *m*, florero *m*
vassal [ˈvæsəl] *n* : vasallo *m*, -lla *f*
vast [ˈvæst] *adj* : inmenso, enorme, vasto
vastly [ˈvæstli] *adv* : enormemente
vastness [ˈvæstnəs] *n* : vastedad *f*, inmensidad *f*
vat [ˈvæt] *n* : cuba *f*, tina *f*
vaudeville [ˈvɔdvəl, -ˌvɪl; ˈvɔdəˌvɪl] *n* : vodevil *m*
vault[1] [ˈvɔlt] *vi* LEAP : saltar
vault[2] *n* **1** JUMP : salto *m* ⟨pole vault : salto de pértiga, salto con garrocha⟩ **2** DOME : bóveda *f* **3** : bodega *f* (para vino), bóveda *f* de seguridad (de un banco) **4** CRYPT : cripta *f*
vaulted [ˈvɔltəd] *adj* : abovedado
vaunted [ˈvɔntəd] *adj* : cacareado, alardeado ⟨a much vaunted wine : un vino muy alardeado⟩
VCR [ˌviːˌsiːˈɑr] *n* : video *m*, videocasetera *f*
veal [ˈviːl] *n* : ternera *f*, carne *f* de ternera
veer [ˈvɪr] *vi* : virar (dícese de un barco), girar (dícese de un coche), torcer (dícese de un camino)
vegetable[1] [ˈvɛʤtəbəl, ˈvɛʤət̬ə-] *adj* : vegetal
vegetable[2] *n* **1** : vegetal *m* ⟨the vegetable kingdom : el reino vegetal⟩ **2** : verdura *f*, hortaliza *f* (para comer)
vegetarian [ˌvɛʤəˈtɛriən] *n* : vegetariano *mf*
vegetarianism [ˌvɛʤəˈtɛriəˌnɪzəm] *n* : vegetarianismo *m*
vegetate [ˈvɛʤəˌteɪt] *vi* **-tated; -tating** : vegetar
vegetation [ˌvɛʤəˈteɪʃən] *n* : vegetación *f*
vegetative [ˈvɛʤəˌteɪt̬ɪv] *adj* : vegetativo
vehemence [ˈviːəmənts] *n* : intensidad *f*, vehemencia *f*
vehement [ˈviːəmənt] *adj* : intenso, vehemente
vehemently [ˈviːəməntli] *adv* : vehementemente, con vehemencia
vehicle [ˈviːəkəl, ˈviːˌhɪkəl] *n* **1** *or* **motor vehicle** : vehículo *m* **2** MEDIUM : vehículo *m*, medio *m*
vehicular [viˈhɪkjələr, və-] *adj* : vehicular ⟨vehicular homicide : muerte por atropello⟩
veil[1] [ˈveɪl] *vt* **1** CONCEAL : velar, disimular **2** : cubrir con un velo ⟨to veil one's face : cubrirse con un velo⟩
veil[2] *n* : velo *m* ⟨bridal veil : velo de novia⟩
vein [ˈveɪn] *n* **1** : vena *f* (en anatomía, botánica, etc.) **2** LODE : veta *f*, vena *f*, filón *m* **3** STYLE : vena *f* ⟨in a humorous vein : en vena humorística⟩
veined [ˈveɪnd] *adj* : veteado (dícese del queso, de los minerales, etc.)
velocity [vəˈlɑsət̬i] *n, pl* **-ties** : velocidad *f*
velour [vəˈlʊr] *or* **velours** [-ˈlʊrz] *n* : velour *m*
velvet[1] [ˈvɛlvət] *adj* **1** : de terciopelo **2** → **velvety**
velvet[2] *n* : terciopelo *m*
velvety [ˈvɛlvət̬i] *adj* : aterciopelado
venal [ˈviːnəl] *adj* : venal, sobornable
vend [ˈvɛnd] *vt* : vender
vendetta [vɛnˈdɛt̬ə] *n* : vendetta *f*
vendor [ˈvɛndər] *n* : vendedor *m*, -dora *f*; puestero *m*, -ra *f*
veneer[1] [vəˈnɪr] *vt* : enchapar, chapar
veneer[2] *n* **1** : enchapado *m*, chapa *f* **2** APPEARANCE : apariencia *f*, barniz *m* ⟨a veneer of culture : un barniz de cultura⟩
venerable [ˈvɛnərəbəl] *adj* : venerable
venerate [ˈvɛnəˌreɪt] *vt* **-ated; -ating** : venerar
veneration [ˌvɛnəˈreɪʃən] *n* : veneración *f*
venereal disease [vəˈnɪriəl] *n* : enfermedad *f* venérea
venetian blind [vəˈniːʃən] *n* : persiana *f* veneciana
Venezuelan [ˌvɛnəˈzweɪlən, -zʊˈeɪ-] *n* : venezolano *m*, -na *f* — **Venezuelan** *adj*
vengeance [ˈvɛnʤənts] *n* : venganza *f* ⟨to take vengeance on : vengarse de⟩
vengeful [ˈvɛnʤfəl] *adj* : vengativo
venial [ˈviːniəl] *adj* : venial ⟨a venial sin : un pecado venial⟩
venison [ˈvɛnəsən, -zən] *n* : venado *m*, carne *f* de venado
venom [ˈvɛnəm] *n* **1** : veneno *m* **2** MALICE : veneno *m*, malevolencia *f*

venomous [ˈvɛnəməs] *adj* : venenoso
vent[1] [ˈvɛnt] *vt* : desahogar, dar salida a ⟨to vent one's feelings : desahogarse⟩
vent[2] *n* **1** OPENING : abertura *f* (de escape), orificio *m* **2** *or* **air vent** : respiradero *m*, rejilla *f* de ventilación **3** OUTLET : desahogo *m* ⟨to give vent to one's anger : desahogar la ira⟩
ventilate [ˈvɛntəlˌeɪt] *vt* **-lated; -lating** : ventilar
ventilation [ˌvɛntəlˈeɪʃən] *n* : ventilación *f*
ventilator [ˈvɛntəlˌeɪt̬ər] *n* : ventilador *m*
ventricle [ˈvɛntrɪkəl] *n* : ventrículo *m*
ventriloquism [vɛnˈtrɪləˌkwɪzəm] *n* : ventriloquia *f*
ventriloquist [vɛnˈtrɪləˌkwɪst] *n* : ventrílocuo *m*, -cua *f*
venture[1] [ˈvɛntʃər] *v* **-tured; -turing** *vt* **1** RISK : arriesgar **2** OFFER : aventurar ⟨to venture an opinion : aventurar una opinión⟩ — *vi* : arriesgarse, atreverse, aventurarse
venture[2] *n* **1** UNDERTAKING : empresa *f* **2** GAMBLE, RISK : aventura *f*, riesgo *m*
venturesome [ˈvɛntʃərsəm] *adj* **1** ADVENTUROUS : audaz, atrevido **2** RISKY : arriesgado
venue [ˈvɛnˌjuː] *n* **1** PLACE : lugar *m* **2** : jurisdicción *f* (en derecho)
Venus [ˈviːnəs] *n* : Venus *m*
veracity [vəˈræsət̬i] *n, pl* **-ties** : veracidad *f*
veranda *or* **verandah** [vəˈrændə] *n* : terraza *f*, veranda *f*
verb [ˈvərb] *n* : verbo *m*
verbal [ˈvərbəl] *adj* : verbal
verbalize [ˈvərbəˌlaɪz] *vt* **-ized; -izing** : expresar con palabras, verbalizar
verbally [ˈvərbəli] *adv* : verbalmente, de palabra
verbatim[1] [vərˈbeɪt̬əm] *adv* : palabra por palabra, textualmente
verbatim[2] *adj* : literal, textual
verbose [vərˈboːs] *adj* : verboso, prolijo
verdant [ˈvərdənt] *adj* : verde, verdeante
verdict [ˈvərdɪkt] *n* **1** : veredicto *m* (de un jurado) **2** JUDGMENT, OPINION : juicio *m*, opinión *f*
verge[1] [ˈvərʤ] *vi* **verged; verging** : estar al borde, rayar ⟨it verges on madness : raya en la locura⟩
verge[2] *n* **1** EDGE : borde *m* **2 to be on the verge of** : estar a pique de, estar al borde de, estar a punto de
verification [ˌvɛrəfəˈkeɪʃən] *n* : verificación *f*
verify [ˈvɛrəˌfaɪ] *vt* **-fied; -fying** : verificar, comprobar, confirmar
veritable [ˈvɛrət̬əbəl] *adj* : verdadero — **veritably** *adv*
vermicelli [ˌvərməˈtʃɛli, -ˈsɛli] *n* : fideos *mpl* finos
vermin [ˈvərmən] *ns & pl* : alimañas *fpl*, bichos *mpl*, sabandijas *fpl*
vermouth [vərˈmuːth] *n* : vermut *m*
vernacular[1] [vərˈnækjələr] *adj* : vernáculo
vernacular[2] *n* : lengua *f* vernácula
versatile [ˈvərsət̬əl] *adj* : versátil
versatility [ˌvərsəˈtɪlət̬i] *n* : versatilidad *f*
verse [ˈvərs] *n* **1** LINE, STANZA : verso *m*, estrofa *f* **2** POETRY : poesía *f* **3** : versículo *m* (en la Biblia)
versed [ˈvərst] *adj* : versado ⟨to be well versed in : ser muy versado en⟩
version [ˈvərʒən] *n* : versión *f*
versus [ˈvərsəs] *prep* : versus
vertebra [ˈvərtəbrə] *n, pl* **-brae** [-ˌbreɪ, -ˌbriː] *or* **-bras** : vértebra *f*
vertebrate[1] [ˈvərtəbrət, -ˌbreɪt] *adj* : vertebrado
vertebrate[2] *n* : vertebrado *m*
vertex [ˈvərˌtɛks] *n, pl* **vertices** [ˈvərtəˌsiːz] **1** : vértice *m* (en matemáticas y anatomía) **2** SUMMIT, TOP : ápice *m*, cumbre *f*, cima *f*
vertical[1] [ˈvərtɪkəl] *adj* : vertical — **vertically** *adv*
vertical[2] *n* : vertical *f*
vertigo [ˈvərtɪˌgoː] *n, pl* **-goes** *or* **-gos** : vértigo *m*
verve [ˈvərv] *n* : brío *m*
very[1] [ˈvɛri] *adv* **1** EXTREMELY : muy, sumamente ⟨very few : muy pocos⟩ ⟨I am very sorry : lo siento mucho⟩ **2** (*used for emphasis*) ⟨at the very least : por lo menos, como mínimo⟩ ⟨the very same dress : el mismo vestido⟩
very[2] *adj* **verier; -est** **1** EXACT, PRECISE : mismo, exacto ⟨at that very moment : en ese mismo momento⟩ ⟨it's the very thing : es justo lo que hacía falta⟩ **2** BARE, MERE : solo, mero ⟨the very thought of it : sólo pensarlo⟩ **3** EXTREME : extremo, de todo ⟨at the very top : arriba de todo⟩
vesicle [ˈvɛsikəl] *n* : vesícula *f*
vespers [ˈvɛspərz] *npl* : vísperas *fpl*
vessel [ˈvɛsəl] *n* **1** CONTAINER : vasija *f*, recipiente *m* **2** BOAT, CRAFT : nave *f*, barco *m*, buque *m* **3** : vaso *m* ⟨blood vessel : vaso sanguíneo⟩
vest[1] [ˈvɛst] *vt* **1** CONFER : conferir ⟨to vest authority in : conferirle la autoridad a⟩ **2** CLOTHE : vestir
vest[2] *n* **1** : chaleco *m* **2** UNDERSHIRT : camiseta *f*
vestibule [ˈvɛstəˌbjuːl] *n* : vestíbulo *m*
vestige [ˈvɛstɪʤ] *n* : vestigio *m*, rastro *m*
vestment [ˈvɛstmənt] *n* : vestidura *f*
vestry [ˈvɛstri] *n, pl* **-tries** : sacristía *f*
vet [ˈvɛt] *n* **1** → **veterinarian** **2** → **veteran**[2]
veteran[1] [ˈvɛt̬ərən, ˈvɛtrən] *adj* : veterano
veteran[2] *n* : veterano *m*, -na *f*
Veterans Day *n* : día *m* del Armisticio (celebrado el 11 de noviembre en los Estados Unidos)
veterinarian [ˌvɛt̬ərəˈnɛriən, ˌvɛt̬əˈnɛr-] *n* : veterinario *m*, -ria *f*
veterinary [ˈvɛt̬ərəˌnɛri] *adj* : veterinario
veto[1] [ˈviːt̬o] *vt* **1** FORBID : prohibir **2** : vetar ⟨to veto a bill : vetar un proyecto de ley⟩

veto² *n, pl* **-toes** **1** : veto *m* ⟨the power of veto : el derecho de veto⟩ **2** BAN : veto *m*, prohibición *f*
vex ['vɛks] *vt* : contrariar, molestar, irritar
vexation [vɛk'seɪʃən] *n* : contrariedad *f*, irritación *f*
via ['vaɪə, 'vi:ə] *prep* : por, vía
viability [ˌvaɪə'bɪləṯi] *n* : viabilidad *f*
viable ['vaɪəbəl] *adj* : viable
viaduct ['vaɪəˌdʌkt] *n* : viaducto *m*
vial ['vaɪəl] *n* : frasco *m*
vibrant ['vaɪbrənt] *adj* **1** LIVELY : vibrante, animado, dinámico **2** BRIGHT : fuerte, vivo (dícese de los colores)
vibrate ['vaɪˌbreɪt] *vi* **-brated; -brating** **1** OSCILLATE : vibrar, oscilar **2** THRILL : bullir ⟨to vibrate with excitement : bullir de emoción⟩
vibration [vaɪ'breɪʃən] *n* : vibración *f*
vicar ['vɪkər] *n* : vicario *m*, -ria *f*
vicarious [vaɪ'kæri:əs, vɪ-] *adj* : indirecto — **vicariously** *adv*
vice ['vaɪs] *n* : vicio *m*
vice admiral *n* : vicealmirante *mf*
vice president *n* : vicepresidente *m*, -ta *f*
viceroy ['vaɪsˌrɔɪ] *n* : virrey *m*, -rreina *f*
vice versa [ˌvaɪsɪ'vərsə, ˌvaɪs'vər-] *adv* : viceversa
vicinity [və'sɪnəṯi] *n, pl* **-ties** **1** NEIGHBORHOOD : vecindad *f*, inmediaciones *fpl* **2** NEARNESS : proximidad *f*
vicious ['vɪʃəs] *adj* **1** DEPRAVED : depravado, malo **2** SAVAGE : malo, fiero, salvaje ⟨a vicious dog : un perro feroz⟩ **3** MALICIOUS : malicioso
viciously ['vɪʃəsli] *adv* : con saña, brutalmente
viciousness ['vɪʃəsnəs] *n* : brutalidad *f*, ferocidad *f* (de un animal), malevolencia *f* (de un comentario, etc.)
vicissitudes [və'sɪsəˌtu:dz, vaɪ-, -ˌtju:dz] *npl* : vicisitudes *fpl*
victim ['vɪktəm] *n* : víctima *f*
victimize ['vɪktəˌmaɪz] *vt* **-mized; -mizing** : tomar como víctima, perseguir, victimizar *Arg, Mex*
victor ['vɪktər] *n* : vencedor *m*, -dora *f*
Victorian [vɪk'to:riən] *adj* : victoriano
victorious [vɪk'to:riəs] *adj* : victorioso — **victoriously** *adv*
victory ['vɪktəri] *n, pl* **-ries** : victoria *f*, triunfo *m*
victuals ['vɪṯəlz] *npl* : víveres *mpl*, provisiones *fpl*
video¹ ['vɪdiˌo:] *adj* : de video ⟨video recording : grabación de video⟩
video² *n* **1** : video *m* (medio o grabación) **2** → **videotape²**
video camera *n* : videocámara *f*
videocassette [ˌvɪdiokə'sɛt] *n* : videocasete *m*, videocassette *m*
videocassette recorder → **VCR**
video game *n* : videojuego *m*, juego *m* de video
videotape¹ ['vɪdioˌteɪp] *vt* **-taped; -taping** : grabar en video, videograbar
videotape² *n* : videocinta *f*
vie ['vaɪ] *vi* **vied; vying** ['vaɪɪŋ] : competir, rivalizar
Vietnamese [viˌɛtnə'mi:z, -'mi:s] *n* **1** : vietnamita *mf* **2** : vietnamita *m* (idioma) — **Vietnamese** *adj*
view¹ ['vju:] *vt* **1** OBSERVE : mirar, ver, observar **2** CONSIDER : considerar, contemplar
view² *n* **1** SIGHT : vista *f* ⟨to come into view : aparecer⟩ **2** ATTITUDE, OPINION : opinión *f*, parecer *m*, actitud *f* ⟨in my view : en mi opinión⟩ **3** SCENE : vista *f*, panorama *f* **4** INTENTION : idea *f*, vista *f* ⟨with a view to : con vistas a, con la idea de⟩ **5 in view of** : dado que, en vista de (que)
viewer ['vju:ər] *n or* **television viewer** : telespectador *m*, -dora *f*; televidente *mf*
viewpoint ['vju:ˌpɔɪnt] *n* : punto *m* de vista
vigil ['vɪʤəl] *n* **1** : vigilia *f*, vela *f* **2 to keep vigil** : velar
vigilance ['vɪʤələnts] *n* : vigilancia *f*
vigilant ['vɪʤələnt] *adj* : vigilante
vigilante [ˌvɪʤə'lænˌti:] *n* : integrante *mf* de un comité de vigilancia (que actúa como policía)
vigilantly ['vɪʤələntli] *adv* : con vigilancia
vigor ['vɪgər] *n* : vigor *m*, energía *f*, fuerza *f*
vigorous ['vɪgərəs] *adj* : vigoroso, enérgico — **vigorously** *adv*
Viking ['vaɪkɪŋ] *n* : vikingo *m*, -ga *f*
vile ['vaɪl] *adj* **viler; vilest** **1** WICKED : vil, infame **2** REVOLTING : asqueroso, repugnante **3** TERRIBLE : horrible, atroz ⟨vile weather : tiempo horrible⟩ ⟨to be in a vile mood : estar de un humor de perros⟩
vilify ['vɪləˌfaɪ] *vt* **-fied; -fying** : vilipendiar, denigrar, difamar
villa ['vɪlə] *n* : casa *f* de campo, quinta *f*
village ['vɪlɪʤ] *n* : pueblo *m* (grande), aldea *f* (pequeña)
villager ['vɪlɪʤər] *n* : vecino *m*, -na *f* (de un pueblo); aldeano *m*, -na *f* (de una aldea)
villain ['vɪlən] *n* : villano *m*, -na *f*; malo *m*, -la *f* (en ficción, películas, etc.)
villainess ['vɪlənɪs, -nəs] *n* : villana *f*
villainous ['vɪlənəs] *adj* : infame, malvado
villainy ['vɪləni] *n, pl* **-lainies** : vileza *f*, maldad *f*
vim ['vɪm] *n* : brío *m*, vigor *m*, energía *f*
vindicate ['vɪndəˌkeɪt] *vt* **-cated; -cating** **1** EXONERATE : vindicar, disculpar **2** JUSTIFY : justificar
vindication [ˌvɪndə'keɪʃən] *n* : vindicación *f*, justificación *f*
vindictive [vɪn'dɪktɪv] *adj* : vengativo
vine ['vaɪn] *n* **1** GRAPEVINE : vid *f*, parra *f* **2** : planta *f* trepadora, enredadera *f*
vinegar ['vɪnɪgər] *n* : vinagre *m*

vinegary [ˈvɪnɪgəri] *adj* : avinagrado
vineyard [ˈvɪnjərd] *n* : viña *f*, viñedo *m*
vintage[1] [ˈvɪntɪʤ] *adj* **1** : añejo (dícese de un vino) **2** CLASSIC : clásico, de época
vintage[2] *n* **1** : cosecha *f* ⟨the 1947 vintage : la cosecha de 1947⟩ **2** ERA : época *f*, era *f* ⟨slang of recent vintage : argot de la época reciente⟩
vinyl [ˈvaɪnəl] *n* : vinilo
viola [viːˈoːlə] *n* : viola *f*
violate [ˈvaɪəˌleɪt] *vt* **-lated; -lating 1** BREAK : infringir, violar, quebrantar ⟨to violate the rules : violar las reglas⟩ **2** RAPE : violar **3** DESECRATE : profanar
violation [ˌvaɪəˈleɪʃən] *n* **1** : violación *f*, infracción *f* (de una ley) **2** DESECRATION : profanación *f*
violence [ˈvaɪlən*t*s, ˈvaɪə-] *n* : violencia *f*
violent [ˈvaɪlənt, ˈvaɪə-] *adj* : violento
violently [ˈvaɪləntli, ˈvaɪə-] *adv* : violentamente, con violencia
violet [ˈvaɪlət, ˈvaɪə-] *n* : violeta *f*
violin [ˌvaɪəˈlɪn] *n* : violín *m*
violinist [ˌvaɪəˈlɪnɪst] *n* : violinista *mf*
violoncello [ˌvaɪələnˈʧɛloː, ˌviː-] → **cello**
VIP [ˌviːˌaɪˈpiː] *n, pl* **VIPs** [-ˈpiːz] : VIP *mf*, persona *f* de categoría
viper [ˈvaɪpər] *n* : víbora *f*
viral [ˈvaɪrəl] *adj* : viral, vírico ⟨viral pneumonia : pulmonía viral⟩
virgin[1] [ˈvərʤən] *adj* **1** CHASTE : virginal ⟨the virgin birth : el alumbramiento virginal⟩ **2** : virgen, intacto ⟨a virgin forest : una selva virgen⟩ ⟨virgin wool : lana virgen⟩
virgin[2] *n* : virgen *mf*
virginity [vərˈʤɪnəṭi] *n* : virginidad *f*
Virgo [ˈvərˌgoː, ˈvɪr-] *n* : Virgo *mf*
virile [ˈvɪrəl, -ˌaɪl] *adj* : viril, varonil
virility [vəˈrɪləṭi] *n* : virilidad *f*
virtual [ˈvərʧuəl] *adj* : virtual ⟨a virtual dictator : un virtual dictador⟩ ⟨virtual reality : realidad virtual⟩
virtually [ˈvərʧuəli, ˈvərʧəli] *adv* : en realidad, de hecho, casi
virtue [ˈvərˌʧuː] *n* **1** : virtud *f* **2 by virtue of** : en virtud de, debido a
virtuosity [ˌvərʧuˈɑsəṭi] *n, pl* **-ties** : virtuosismo *m*
virtuoso [ˌvərʧuˈoːsoː, -zoː] *n, pl* **-sos** *or* **-si** [-ˌsiː, -ˌziː] : virtuoso *m*, -sa *f*
virtuous [ˈvərʧuəs] *adj* : virtuoso, bueno — **virtuously** *adv*
virulence [ˈvɪrələn*t*s, ˈvɪrjə-] *n* : virulencia *f*
virulent [ˈvɪrələnt, ˈvɪrjə-] *adj* : virulento
virus [ˈvaɪrəs] *n* : virus *m*
visa [ˈviːzə, -sə] *n* : visa *f*
vis–à–vis [ˌviːzəˈviː, -sə-] *prep* : con relación a, con respecto a
viscera [ˈvɪsərə] *npl* : vísceras *fpl*
visceral [ˈvɪsərəl] *adj* : visceral
viscosity [vɪsˈkɑsəṭi] *n, pl* **-ties** : viscosidad *f*
viscount [ˈvaɪˌkæʊnt] *n* : vizconde *m*
viscountess [ˈvaɪˌkæʊntɪs] *n* : vizcondesa *f*
viscous [ˈvɪskəs] *adj* : viscoso
vise [ˈvaɪs] *n* : torno *m* de banco, tornillo *m* de banco
visibility [ˌvɪzəˈbɪləṭi] *n, pl* **-ties** : visibilidad *f*
visible [ˈvɪzəbəl] *adj* **1** : visible ⟨the visible stars : las estrellas visibles⟩ **2** OBVIOUS : evidente, patente
visibly [ˈvɪzəbli] *adv* : visiblemente
vision [ˈvɪʒən] *n* **1** EYESIGHT : vista *f*, visión *f* **2** APPARITION : visión *f*, aparición *f* **3** FORESIGHT : visión *f* (del futuro), previsión *f* **4** IMAGE : imagen *f* ⟨she had visions of a disaster : se imaginaba un desastre⟩
visionary[1] [ˈvɪʒəˌnɛri] *adj* **1** FARSIGHTED : visionario, con visión de futuro **2** UTOPIAN : utópico, poco realista
visionary[2] *n, pl* **-ries** : visionario *m*, -ria *f*
visit[1] [ˈvɪzət] *vt* **1** : visitar, ir a ver **2** AFFLICT : azotar, afligir ⟨visited by troubles : afligido con problemas⟩ — *vi* : hacer (una) visita
visit[2] *n* : visita *f*
visitor [ˈvɪzəṭər] *n* : visitante *mf* (a una ciudad, etc.), visita *f* (a una casa)
visor [ˈvaɪzər] *n* : visera *f*
vista [ˈvɪstə] *n* : vista *f*
visual [ˈvɪʒuəl] *adj* : visual ⟨the visual arts : las artes visuales⟩ — **visually** *adv*
visualize [ˈvɪʒuəˌlaɪz] *vt* **-ized; -izing** : visualizar, imaginarse, hacerse una idea de — **visualization** [ˌvɪʒəwələˈzeɪʃən] *n*
vital [ˈvaɪṭəl] *adj* **1** : vital ⟨vital organs : órganos vitales⟩ **2** CRUCIAL : esencial, crucial, decisivo ⟨of vital importance : de suma importancia⟩ **3** LIVELY : enérgico, lleno de vida, vital
vitality [vaɪˈtæləṭi] *n, pl* **-ties** : vitalidad *f*, energía *f*
vitally [ˈvaɪṭəli] *adv* : sumamente
vital statistics *npl* : estadísticas *fpl* demográficas
vitamin [ˈvaɪṭəmən] *n* : vitamina *f* ⟨vitamin deficiency : carencia vitamínica⟩
vitreous [ˈvɪtriəs] *adj* : vítreo
vitriolic [ˌvɪtriˈɑlɪk] *adj* : mordaz, virulento
vituperation [vaɪˌtuːpəˈreɪʃən, -ˌtjuː-] *n* : vituperio *m*
vivacious [vəˈveɪʃəs, vaɪ-] *adj* : vivaz, animado, lleno de vida
vivaciously [vəˈveɪʃəsli, vaɪ-] *adv* : con vivacidad, animadamente
vivacity [vəˈvæsəṭi, vaɪ-] *n* : vivacidad *f*
vivid [ˈvɪvəd] *adj* **1** LIVELY : lleno de vitalidad **2** BRILLIANT : vivo, intenso ⟨vivid colors : colores vivos⟩ **3** INTENSE, SHARP : vívido, gráfico ⟨a vivid dream : un sueño vívido⟩
vividly [ˈvɪvədli] *adv* **1** BRIGHTLY : con colores vivos **2** SHARPLY : vívidamente
vividness [ˈvɪvədnəs] *n* **1** BRIGHTNESS : intensidad *f*, viveza *f* **2** SHARPNESS : lo gráfico, nitidez *f*

vivisection [ˌvɪvəˈsɛkʃən, ˈvɪvəˌ-] *n* : vivisección *f*
vixen [ˈvɪksən] *n* : zorra *f*, raposa *f*
vocabulary [voːˈkæbjəˌlɛri] *n, pl* **-laries** 1 : vocabulario *m* 2 LEXICON : léxico *m*
vocal [ˈvoːkəl] *adj* 1 : vocal 2 LOUD, OUTSPOKEN : ruidoso, muy franco
vocal cords *npl* : cuerdas *fpl* vocales
vocalist [ˈvoːkəlɪst] *n* : cantante *mf*, vocalista *mf*
vocalize [ˈvoːkəlˌaɪz] *vt* **-ized; -izing** : vocalizar
vocation [voˈkeɪʃən] *n* : vocación *f* ⟨to have a vocation for : tener vocación de⟩
vocational [voˈkeɪʃənəl] *adj* : profesional ⟨vocational guidance : orientación profesional⟩
vociferous [voˈsɪfərəs] *adj* : ruidoso, vociferante
vodka [ˈvɑdkə] *n* : vodka *m*
vogue [ˈvoːg] *n* : moda *f*, boga *f* ⟨to be in vogue : estar de moda, estar en boga⟩
voice[1] [ˈvɔɪs] *vt* **voiced; voicing** : expresar
voice[2] *n* 1 : voz *f* ⟨in a low voice : en voz baja⟩ ⟨to lose one's voice : quedarse sin voz⟩ ⟨the voice of the people : la voz del pueblo⟩ **2 to make one's voice heard** : hacerse oír
voice box → **larynx**
voiced [ˈvɔɪst] *adj* : sonoro
voice mail *n* : correo *m* de voz
void[1] [ˈvɔɪd] *vt* : anular, invalidar ⟨to void a contract : anular un contrato⟩
void[2] *adj* 1 EMPTY : vacío, desprovisto ⟨void of content : desprovisto de contenido⟩ 2 INVALID : inválido, nulo
void[3] *n* : vacío *m*
volatile [ˈvɑlət̬əl] *adj* : volátil, inestable
volatility [ˌvɑləˈtɪlət̬i] *n* : volatilidad *f*, inestabilidad *f*
volcanic [vɑlˈkænɪk] *adj* : volcánico
volcano [vɑlˈkeɪˌnoː] *n, pl* **-noes** *or* **-nos** : volcán *m*
vole [ˈvoːl] *n* : campañol *m*
volition [voˈlɪʃən] *n* : volición *f*, voluntad *f* ⟨of one's own volition : por voluntad propia⟩
volley [ˈvɑli] *n, pl* **-leys** 1 : descarga *f* (de tiros) 2 : torrente *m*, lluvia *f* (de insultos, etc.) 3 : salva *f* (de aplausos) 4 : volea *f* (en deportes)
volleyball [ˈvɑliˌbɔl] *n* : voleibol *m*
volt [ˈvoːlt] *n* : voltio *m*
voltage [ˈvoːltɪʤ] *n* : voltaje *m*
volubility [ˌvɑljəˈbɪlət̬i] *n* : locuacidad *f*
voluble [ˈvɑljəbəl] *adj* : locuaz
volume [ˈvɑljəm, -ˌjuːm] *n* 1 BOOK : volumen *m*, tomo *m* 2 SPACE : capacidad *f*, volumen *m* (en física) 3 AMOUNT : cantidad *f*, volumen *m* 4 LOUDNESS : volumen *m*
voluminous [vəˈluːmənəs] *adj* : voluminoso
voluntary [ˈvɑlənˌtɛri] *adj* : voluntario — **voluntarily** [ˌvɑlənˈtɛrəli] *adv*
volunteer[1] [ˌvɑlənˈtɪr] *vt* : ofrecer, dar ⟨to volunteer one's assistance : ofrecer la ayuda⟩ — *vi* : ofrecerse, alistarse como voluntario
volunteer[2] *n* : voluntario *m*, -ria *f*
voluptuous [vəˈlʌpʧuəs] *adj* : voluptuoso
vomit[1] [ˈvɑmət] *v* : vomitar
vomit[2] *n* : vómito *m*
voodoo [ˈvuːˌduː] *n, pl* **voodoos** : vudú *m*
voracious [vɔˈreɪʃəs, və-] *adj* : voraz
voraciously [vɔˈreɪʃəsli, və-] *adv* : vorazmente, con voracidad
vortex [ˈvɔrˌtɛks] *n, pl* **vortices** [ˈvɔrtəˌsiːz] : vórtice *m*
vote[1] [ˈvoːt] *vi* **voted; voting** : votar ⟨to vote Democratic : votar por los demócratas⟩
vote[2] *n* 1 : voto *m* 2 SUFFRAGE : sufragio *m*, derecho *m* al voto
voter [ˈvoːt̬ər] *n* : votante *mf*
voting [ˈvoːt̬ɪŋ] *n* : votación *f*
vouch [ˈvæʊʧ] *vi* **to vouch for** : garantizar (algo), responder de (algo), responder por (alguien)
voucher [ˈvæʊʧər] *n* 1 RECEIPT : comprobante *m* 2 : vale *m* ⟨travel voucher : vale de viajar⟩
vow[1] [væʊ] *vt* : jurar, prometer, hacer voto de
vow[2] *n* : promesa *f*, voto *m* (en la religión) ⟨a vow of poverty : un voto de pobreza⟩
vowel [ˈvæʊəl] *n* : vocal *m*
voyage[1] [ˈvɔɪɪʤ] *vi* **-aged; -aging** : viajar
voyage[2] *n* : viaje *m*
voyager [ˈvɔɪɪʤər] *n* : viajero *m*, -ra *f*
vulcanize [ˈvʌlkəˌnaɪz] *vt* **-nized; -nizing** : vulcanizar
vulgar [ˈvʌlgər] *adj* 1 COMMON, PLEBIAN : ordinario, populachero, del vulgo 2 COARSE, CRUDE : grosero, de mal gusto, majadero *Mex* 3 INDECENT : indecente, colorado (dícese de un chiste, etc.)
vulgarity [ˌvʌlˈgærət̬i] *n, pl* **-ties** : grosería *f*, vulgaridad *f*
vulgarly [ˈvʌlgərli] *adv* : vulgarmente, groseramente
vulnerability [ˌvʌlnərəˈbɪlət̬i] *n, pl* **-ties** : vulnerabilidad *f*
vulnerable [ˈvʌlnərəbəl] *adj* : vulnerable
vulture [ˈvʌlʧər] *n* : buitre *m*, zopilote *m CA, Mex*
vying → **vie**

W

w [ˈdʌbəlˌjuː] *n, pl* **w's** *or* **ws** [-ˌjuːz] : vigésima tercera letra del alfabeto inglés

wad[1] [ˈwɑd] *vt* **wadded; wadding 1** : hacer un taco con, formar en una masa **2** STUFF : rellenar

wad[2] *n* : taco *m* (de papel), bola *f* (de algodón, etc.), fajo *m* (de billetes)

waddle[1] [ˈwɑdəl] *vi* **-dled; -dling** : andar como un pato

waddle[2] *n* : andar *m* de pato

wade [ˈweɪd] *v* **waded; wading** *vi* **1** : caminar por el agua **2 to wade through** : leer (algo) con dificultad — *vt or* **to wade across** : vadear

wading bird *n* : zancuda *f*, ave *f* zancuda

wafer [ˈweɪfər] *n* : barquillo *m*, galleta *f* de barquillo

waffle [ˈwɑfəl] *n* **1** : wafle *m* **2 waffle iron** : waflera *f*

waft [ˈwɑft, ˈwæft] *vt* : llevar por el aire — *vi* : flotar

wag[1] [ˈwæg] *v* **wagged; wagging** *vt* : menear — *vi* : menearse, moverse

wag[2] *n* **1** : meneo *m* (de la cola) **2** JOKER, WIT : bromista *mf*

wage[1] [ˈweɪʤ] *vt* **waged; waging** : hacer, librar ⟨to wage war : hacer la guerra⟩

wage[2] *n or* **wages** *npl* : sueldo *m*, salario *m* ⟨minimum wage : salario mínimo⟩

wager[1] [ˈweɪʤər] *v* : apostar

wager[2] *n* : apuesta *f*

waggish [ˈwægɪʃ] *adj* : burlón, bromista (dícese de una persona), chistoso (dícese de un comentario)

waggle [ˈwægəl] *vt* **-gled; -gling** : menear, mover (de un lado a otro)

wagon [ˈwægən] *n* **1** : carro *m* (tirado por caballos) **2** CART : carrito *m* **3** → **station wagon**

waif [ˈweɪf] *n* : niño *m* abandonado, animal *m* sin hogar

wail[1] [ˈweɪl] *vi* : gemir, lamentarse

wail[2] *n* : gemido *m*, lamento *m*

wainscot [ˈweɪnskət, -ˌskɑt, -ˌskoːt] *or* **wainscoting** [-skət̬ɪŋ, -ˌskɑ-, -ˌskoː-] *n* : boiserie *f*, revestimiento *m* de paneles de madera

waist [ˈweɪst] *n* : cintura *f* (del cuerpo humano), talle *m* (de ropa)

waistline [ˈweɪstˌlaɪn] → **waist**

wait[1] [ˈweɪt] *vi* : esperar ⟨to wait for something : esperar algo⟩ ⟨wait and see! : ¡espera y verás!⟩ ⟨I can't wait : me muero de ganas⟩ — *vt* **1** AWAIT : esperar **2** DELAY : retrasar ⟨don't wait lunch : no retrase el almuerzo⟩ **3** SERVE : servir, atender ⟨to wait tables : servir (a la mesa)⟩

wait[2] *n* **1** : espera *f* **2 to lie in wait** : estar al acecho

waiter [ˈweɪt̬ər] *n* : mesero *m*, camarero *m*, mozo *m Arg, Chile, Col, Peru*

waiting room *n* : sala *f* de espera

waitress [ˈweɪtrəs] *n* : mesera *f*, camarera *f*, moza *f Arg, Chile, Col, Peru*

waive [ˈweɪv] *vt* **waived; waiving** : renunciar a ⟨to waive one's rights : renunciar a sus derechos⟩ ⟨to waive the rules : no aplicar las reglas⟩

waiver [ˈweɪvər] *n* : renuncia *f*

wake[1] [ˈweɪk] *v* **woke** [ˈwoːk]; **woken** [ˈwoːkən] *or* **waked; waking** *vi or* **to wake up** : despertar(se) ⟨he woke at noon : se despertó al mediodía⟩ ⟨wake up! : ¡despiértate!⟩ — *vt* : despertar

wake[2] *n* **1** VIGIL : velatorio *m*, velorio *m* (de un difunto) **2** TRAIL : estela *f* (de un barco, un huracán, etc.) **3** AFTERMATH : consecuencias *fpl* ⟨in the wake of : tras, como consecuencia de⟩

wakeful [ˈweɪkfəl] *adj* **1** SLEEPLESS : desvelado **2** VIGILANT : alerta, vigilante

waken [ˈweɪkən] → **awake**

walk[1] [ˈwɔk] *vi* **1** : caminar, andar, pasear ⟨you're walking too fast : estás caminando demasiado rápido⟩ ⟨to walk around the city : pasearse por la ciudad⟩ **2** : ir andando, ir a pie ⟨we had to walk home : tuvimos que ir a casa a pie⟩ **3** : darle base por bolas (a un bateador) — *vt* **1** : recorrer, caminar ⟨she walked two miles : caminó dos millas⟩ **2** ACCOMPANY : acompañar **3** : sacar a pasear (a un perro)

walk[2] *n* **1** : paseo *m*, caminata *f* ⟨to go for a walk : ir a caminar, dar un paseo⟩ **2** PATH : camino *m* **3** GAIT : andar *m* **4** : marcha *f* (en beisbol) **5 walk of life** : esfera *f*, condición *f*

walker [ˈwɔkər] *n* **1** : paseante *mf* **2** HIKER : excursionista *mf* **3** : andador *m* (aparato)

walking stick *n* : bastón *m*

walkout [ˈwɔkˌaʊt] *n* STRIKE : huelga *f*

walk out *vi* **1** STRIKE : declararse en huelga **2** LEAVE : salir, irse **3 to walk out on** : abandonar, dejar

walkway [ˈwɔkˌweɪ] *n* **1** SIDEWALK : acera *f* **2** PATH : sendero *m* **3** PASSAGEWAY : pasadizo *m*

wall[1] [ˈwɔl] *vt* **1 to wall in** : cercar con una pared o un muro, tapiar, amurallar **2 to wall off** : separar con una pared o un muro **3 to wall up** : tapiar, condenar (una ventana, etc.)

wall[2] *n* **1** : muro *m* (exterior) ⟨the walls of the city : las murallas de la ciudad⟩ **2** : pared *f* (interior) **3** BARRIER : barrera *f* ⟨a wall of mountains : una barrera de montañas⟩ **4** : pared *f* (en anatomía)

wallaby [ˈwɑləbi] *n, pl* **-bies** : ualabí *m*

walled [ˈwɔld] *adj* : amurallado

wallet [ˈwɑlət] *n* : billetera *f*, cartera *f*

wallflower [ˈwɔlˌflaʊər] *n* **1** : alhelí *m* (flor) **2 to be a wallflower** : comer pavo

wallop[1] [ˈwɑləp] *vt* **1** TROUNCE : darle una paliza (a alguien) **2** SOCK : pegar fuerte

wallop² *n* : golpe *m* fuerte, golpazo *m*
wallow¹ [ˈwɑˌloː] *vi* **1** : revolcarse ⟨to wallow in the mud : revolcarse en el lodo⟩ **2** DELIGHT : deleitarse ⟨to wallow in luxury : nadar en lujos⟩
wallow² *n* : revolcadero *m* (para animales)
wallpaper¹ [ˈwɔlˌpeɪpər] *vt* : empapelar
wallpaper² *n* : papel *m* pintado
walnut [ˈwɔlˌnʌt] *n* **1** : nuez *f* (fruta) **2** : nogal *m* (árbol y madera)
walrus [ˈwɔlrəs, ˈwɑl-] *n, pl* **-rus** *or* **-ruses** : morsa *f*
waltz¹ [ˈwɔlts] *vi* **1** : valsar, bailar el vals **2** BREEZE : pasar con ligereza ⟨to waltz in : entrar tan campante⟩
waltz² *n* : vals *m*
wan [ˈwɑn] *adj* **wanner; -est** **1** PALLID : pálido **2** DIM : tenue ⟨wan light : luz tenue⟩ **3** LANGUID : lánguido ⟨a wan smile : una sonrisa lánguida⟩ — **wanly** *adv*
wand [ˈwɑnd] *n* : varita *f* (mágica)
wander [ˈwɑndər] *vi* **1** RAMBLE : deambular, vagar, vagabundear **2** STRAY : alejarse, desviarse, divagar ⟨she let her mind wander : dejó vagar la imaginación⟩ — *vt* : recorrer ⟨to wander the streets : vagar por las calles⟩
wanderer [ˈwɑndərər] *n* : vagabundo *m*, -da *f*; viajero *m*, -ra *f*
wanderlust [ˈwɑndərˌlʌst] *n* : pasión *f* por viajar
wane¹ [ˈweɪn] *vi* **waned; waning** **1** : menguar (dícese de la luna) **2** DECLINE : disminuir, decaer, menguar
wane² *n* **on the wane** : decayendo, en decadencia
wangle [ˈwæŋgəl] *vt* **-gled; -gling** FINAGLE : arreglárselas para conseguir
wannabe [ˈwɑnəˌbiː] *n* : aspirante *mf* (a algo); imitador *m*, -dora *f* (de alguien)
want¹ [ˈwɑnt, ˈwɔnt] *vt* **1** LACK : faltar **2** REQUIRE : requerir, necesitar **3** DESIRE : querer, desear
want² *n* **1** LACK : falta *f* **2** DESTITUTION : indigencia *f*, miseria *f* **3** DESIRE, NEED : deseo *m*, necesidad *f*
wanting [ˈwɑntɪŋ, ˈwɔn-] *adj* **1** ABSENT : ausente **2** DEFICIENT : deficiente ⟨he's wanting in common sense : le falta sentido común⟩
wanton [ˈwɑntən, ˈwɔn-] *adj* **1** LEWD, LUSTFUL : lascivo, lujurioso, licencioso **2** INHUMANE, MERCILESS : despiadado ⟨wanton cruelty : crueldad despiadada⟩
wapiti [ˈwɑpəṭi] *n, pl* **-ti** *or* **-tis** : uapití *m*
war¹ [ˈwɔr] *vi* **warred; warring** : combatir, batallar, hacer la guerra
war² *n* : guerra *f* ⟨to go to war : entrar en guerra⟩
warble¹ [ˈwɔrbəl] *vi* **-bled; -bling** : gorjear, trinar
warble² *n* : trino *m*, gorjeo *m*
warbler [ˈwɔrblər] *n* : pájaro *m* gorjeador, curruca *f*
ward¹ [ˈwɔrd] *vt* **to ward off** : desviar, protegerse contra
ward² *n* **1** : sala *f* (de un hospital, etc.) ⟨maternity ward : sala de maternidad⟩ **2** : distrito *m* electoral o administrativo (de una ciudad) **3** : pupilo *m*, -la *f* (de un tutor, etc.)
warden [ˈwɔrdən] *n* **1** KEEPER : guarda *mf*; guardián *m*, -diana *f* ⟨game warden : guardabosque⟩ **2** *or* **prison warden** : alcaide *m*
wardrobe [ˈwɔrdˌroːb] *n* **1** CLOSET : armario *m* **2** CLOTHES : vestuario *m*, guardarropa *f*
ware [ˈwær] *n* **1** POTTERY : cerámica *f* **2 wares** *npl* GOODS : mercancía *f*, mercadería *f*
warehouse [ˈwærˌhaʊs] *n* : depósito *m*, almacén *m*, bodega *f Chile, Col, Mex*
warfare [ˈwɔrˌfær] *n* **1** WAR : guerra *f* **2** STRUGGLE : lucha *f* ⟨the warfare against drugs : la lucha contra las drogas⟩
warhead [ˈwɔrˌhɛd] *n* : ojiva *f*, cabeza *f* (de un misil)
warily [ˈwærəli] *adv* : cautelosamente, con cautela
wariness [ˈwærinəs] *n* : cautela *f*
warlike [ˈwærˌlaɪk] *adj* : belicoso, guerrero
warm¹ [ˈwɔrm] *vt* **1** HEAT : calentar, recalentar **2 to warm one's heart** : reconfortar a uno, alegrar el corazón **3 to warm up** : calentar (los músculos, un automóvil, etc.) — *vi* **1** : calentarse **2 to warm to** : tomarle simpatía (a alguien), entusiasmarse con (algo)
warm² *adj* **1** LUKEWARM : tibio, templado **2** : caliente, cálido, caluroso ⟨a warm wind : un viento cálido⟩ ⟨a warm day : un día caluroso, un día de calor⟩ ⟨warm hands : manos calientes⟩ **3** : caliente, que abriga ⟨warm clothes : ropa de abrigo⟩ ⟨I feel warm : tengo calor⟩ **4** CARING, CORDIAL : cariñoso, cordial **5** : cálido (dícese de colores) **6** FRESH : fresco, reciente ⟨a warm trail : un rastro reciente⟩ **7** (*used for riddles*) : caliente
warm–blooded [ˈwɔrmˈblʌdəd] *adj* : de sangre caliente
warmhearted [ˈwɔrmˈhɑrṭəd] *adj* : cariñoso
warmly [ˈwɔrmli] *adv* **1** AFFECTIONATELY : calurosamente, afectuosamente **2 to dress warmly** : abrigarse
warmonger [ˈwɔrˌmɑŋgər, -ˌmʌŋ-] *n* : belicista *mf*
warmth [ˈwɔrmpθ] *n* **1** : calor *m* **2** AFFECTION : cariño *m*, afecto *m* **3** ENTHUSIASM : ardor *m*, entusiasmo *m*
warm–up [ˈwɔrmˌʌp] *n* : calentamiento *m*
warn [ˈwɔrn] *vt* **1** CAUTION : advertir, alertar **2** INFORM : avisar, informar
warning [ˈwɔrnɪŋ] *n* **1** ADVICE : advertencia *f*, aviso *m* **2** ALERT : alerta *f*, alarma *f*
warp¹ [ˈwɔrp] *vt* **1** : alabear, combar **2** PERVERT : pervertir, deformar — *vi* : pandearse, alabearse, combarse

warp[2] *n* **1** : urdimbre *f* ⟨the warp and the weft : la urdimbre y la trama⟩ **2** : alabeo *m* (en la madera, etc.)

warrant[1] [ˈwɔrənt] *vt* **1** ASSURE : asegurar, garantizar **2** GUARANTEE : garantizar **3** JUSTIFY, MERIT : justificar, merecer

warrant[2] *n* **1** AUTHORIZATION : autorización *f*, permiso *m* ⟨an arrest warrant : una orden de detención⟩ **2** JUSTIFICATION : justificación *f*

warranty [ˈwɔrənti, ˌwɔrənˈtiː] *n, pl* **-ties** : garantía *f*

warren [ˈwɔrən] *n* : madriguera *f* (de conejos)

warrior [ˈwɔriər] *n* : guerrero *m*, -ra *f*

warship [ˈwɔrˌʃɪp] *n* : buque *m* de guerra

wart [ˈwɔrt] *n* : verruga *f*

wartime [ˈwɔrˌtaɪm] *n* : tiempo *m* de guerra

wary [ˈwæri] *adj* **warier; -est** : cauteloso, receloso ⟨to be wary of : desconfiar de⟩

was → **be**

wash[1] [ˈwɔʃ, ˈwɑʃ] *vt* **1** CLEAN : lavar(se), limpiar, fregar ⟨to wash the dishes : lavar los platos⟩ ⟨to wash one's hands : lavarse las manos⟩ **2** DRENCH : mojar **3** LAP : bañar ⟨waves were washing the shore : las olas bañaban la orilla⟩ **4** CARRY, DRAG : arrastrar **5 to wash away** : llevarse (un puente, etc.) — *vi* **1** : lavarse (dícese de una persona o la ropa) ⟨the dress washes well : el vestido se lava bien⟩ **2 to wash against** *or* **to wash over** : bañar

wash[2] *n* **1** : lavado *m* ⟨to give something a wash : lavar algo⟩ **2** LAUNDRY : artículos *mpl* para lavar, ropa *f* sucia **3** : estela *f* (de un barco)

washable [ˈwɔʃəbəl, ˈwɑ-] *adj* : lavable

washboard [ˈwɔʃˌbord, ˈwɑʃ-] *n* : tabla *f* de lavar

washbowl [ˈwɔʃˌboːl, ˈwɑʃ-] *n* : lavabo *m*, lavamanos *m*

washcloth [ˈwɔʃˌklɔθ, ˈwɑʃ-] *n* : toallita *f* (para lavarse)

washed–out [ˈwɔʃtˈaʊt, ˈwɑʃt-] *adj* **1** : desvaído (dícese de colores) **2** EXHAUSTED : agotado, desanimado

washed–up [ˈwɔʃtˈʌp, ˈwɑʃt-] *adj* : acabado (dícese de una persona), fracasado (dícese de un negocio, etc.)

washer [ˈwɔʃər, ˈwɑ-] *n* **1** → **washing machine** **2** : arandela *f* (de una llave, etc.)

washing [ˈwɔʃɪŋ, ˈwɑ-] *n* WASH : ropa *f* para lavar

washing machine *n* : máquina *f* de lavar, lavadora *f*

washout [ˈwɔʃˌaʊt, ˈwɑʃ-] *n* **1** : erosión *f* (de la tierra) **2** FAILURE : fracaso *m* ⟨she's a washout : es un desastre⟩

washroom [ˈwɔʃˌruːm, ˈwɑʃ-, -ˌrʊm] *n* : servicios *mpl* (públicos), baño *m*, sanitario *m Col, Mex, Ven*

wasn't [ˈwʌzənt] (*contraction of* **was not**) → **be**

wasp [ˈwɑsp] *n* : avispa *f*

waspish [ˈwɑspɪʃ] *adj* **1** IRRITABLE : irritable, irascible **2** CAUSTIC : cáustico, mordaz

waste[1] [ˈweɪst] *v* **wasted; wasting** *vt* **1** DEVASTATE : arrasar, arruinar, devastar **2** SQUANDER : desperdiciar, despilfarrar, malgastar ⟨to waste time : perder tiempo⟩ — *vi or* **to waste away** : consumirse, chuparse

waste[2] *adj* **1** BARREN : yermo, baldío **2** DISCARDED : de desecho **3** EXCESS : sobrante

waste[3] *n* **1** → **wasteland** **2** MISUSE : derroche *m*, desperdicio *m*, despilfarro *m* ⟨a waste of time : una pérdida de tiempo⟩ **3** RUBBISH : basura *f*, desechos *mpl*, desperdicios *mpl* **4** EXCREMENT : excremento *m*

wastebasket [ˈweɪstˌbæskət] *n* : cesto *m* (de basura), papelera *f*, zafacón *m Car*

wasteful [ˈweɪstfəl] *adj* : despilfarrador, derrochador, pródigo

wastefulness [ˈweɪstfəlnəs] *n* : derroche *m*, despilfarro *m*

wasteland [ˈweɪstˌlænd, -lənd] *n* : baldío *m*, yermo *m*, desierto *m*

watch[1] [ˈwɑʧ] *vi* **1** *or* **to keep watch** : velar **2** OBSERVE : mirar, ver, observar **3 to watch for** AWAIT : esperar, quedar a la espera de **4 to watch out** : tener cuidado ⟨watch out! : ¡ten cuidado!, ¡ojo!⟩ — *vt* **1** OBSERVE : mirar, observar **2** *or* **to watch over** : vigilar, cuidar **3** : tener cuidado de ⟨watch what you do : ten cuidado con lo que haces⟩

watch[2] *n* **1** : guardia *f* ⟨to be on watch : estar de guardia⟩ **2** SURVEILLANCE : vigilancia *f* **3** LOOKOUT : guardia *mf*, centinela *f*, vigía *mf* **4** TIMEPIECE : reloj *m*

watchdog [ˈwɑʧˌdɔg] *n* : perro *m* guardián

watcher [ˈwɑʧər] *n* : observador *m*, -dora *f*

watchful [ˈwɑʧfəl] *adj* : alerta, vigilante, atento

watchfulness [ˈwɑʧfəlnəs] *n* : vigilancia *f*

watchman [ˈwɑʧmən] *n, pl* **-men** [-mən, -ˌmɛn] : vigilante *m*, guarda *m*

watchword [ˈwɑʧˌwərd] *n* **1** PASSWORD : contraseña *f* **2** SLOGAN : lema *m*, eslogan *m*

water[1] [ˈwɔţər, ˈwɑ-] *vt* **1** : regar (el jardín, etc.) **2 to water down** DILUTE : diluir, aguar — *vi* : lagrimear (dícese de los ojos), hacérsele agua la boca a uno ⟨my mouth is watering : se me hace agua la boca⟩

water[2] *n* : agua *f*

water buffalo *n* : búfalo *m* de agua

watercolor [ˈwɔţərˌkʌlər, ˈwɑ-] *n* : acuarela *f*

watercourse [ˈwɔţərˌkors, ˈwɑ-] *n* : curso *m* de agua

watercress [ˈwɔţərˌkrɛs, ˈwɑ-] *n* : berro *m*

waterfall [ˈwɔt̬ərˌfɔl, ˈwɑ-] *n* : cascada *f*, salto *m* de agua, catarata *f*

waterfowl [ˈwɔt̬ərˌfaʊl, ˈwɑ-] *n* : ave *f* acuática

waterfront [ˈwɔt̬ərˌfrʌnt, ˈwɑ-] *n* **1** : tierra *f* que bordea un río, un lago, o un mar **2** WHARF : muelle *m*

water lily *n* : nenúfar *m*

waterlogged [ˈwɔt̬ərˌlɔgd, ˈwɑt̬ər-ˌlɑgd] *adj* : lleno de agua, empapado, inundado (dícese del suelo)

watermark [ˈwɔt̬ərˌmɑrk, ˈwɑ-] *n* **1** : marca *f* del nivel de agua **2** : filigrana *f* (en el papel)

watermelon [ˈwɔt̬ərˌmɛlən, ˈwɑ-] *n* : sandía *f*

water moccasin → moccasin

waterpower [ˈwɔt̬ərˌpaʊər, ˈwɑ-] *n* : energía *f* hidráulica

waterproof[1] [ˈwɔt̬ərˌpruːf, ˈwɑ-] *vt* : hacer impermeable, impermeabilizar

waterproof[2] *adj* : impermeable, a prueba de agua

watershed [ˈwɔt̬ərˌʃɛd, ˈwɑ-] *n* **1** : línea *f* divisoria de aguas **2** BASIN : cuenca *f* (de un río)

waterskiing [ˈwɔt̬ərˌskiːɪŋ, ˈwɑ-] *n* : esquí *m* acuático

waterspout [ˈwɔt̬ərˌspaʊt, ˈwɑ-] *n* WHIRLWIND : tromba *f* marina

watertight [ˈwɔt̬ərˌtaɪt, ˈwɑ-] *adj* **1** : hermético **2** IRREFUTABLE : irrebatible, irrefutable ⟨a watertight contract : un contrato sin lagunas⟩

waterway [ˈwɔt̬ərˌweɪ, ˈwɑ-] *n* : vía *f* navegable

waterworks [ˈwɔt̬ərˌwərks, ˈwɑ-] *npl* : central *f* de abastecimiento de agua

watery [ˈwɔt̬əri, ˈwɑ-] *adj* **1** : acuoso, como agua **2** : aguado, diluido ⟨watery soup : sopa aguada⟩ **3** : lloroso ⟨watery eyes : ojos llorosos⟩ **4** WASHED-OUT : desvaído (dícese de colores)

watt [ˈwɑt] *n* : vatio *m*

wattage [ˈwɑt̬ɪʤ] *n* : vataje *m*

wattle [ˈwɑt̬əl] *n* : carúncula *f* (de un ave, etc.)

wave[1] [ˈweɪv] *v* **waved; waving** *vi* **1** : saludar con la mano, hacer señas con la mano ⟨she waved at him : lo saludó con la mano⟩ **2** FLUTTER, SHAKE : ondear, agitarse **3** UNDULATE : ondular — *vt* **1** SHAKE : agitar **2** BRANDISH : blandir **3** CURL : ondular, marcar (el pelo) **4** SIGNAL : hacerle señas a (con la mano) ⟨he waved farewell : se despidió con la mano⟩

wave[2] *n* **1** : ola *f* (de agua) **2** CURL : onda *f* (en el pelo) **3** : onda *f* (en física) **4** SURGE : oleada *f* ⟨a wave of enthusiasm : una oleada de entusiasmo⟩ **5** GESTURE : señal *f* con la mano, saludo *m* con la mano

wavelength [ˈweɪvˌlɛŋkθ] *n* : longitud *f* de onda

waver [ˈweɪvər] *vi* **1** VACILLATE : vacilar, fluctuar **2** FLICKER : parpadear, titilar, oscilar **3** FALTER : flaquear, tambalearse

wavy [ˈweɪvi] *adj* **wavier; -est** : ondulado

wax[1] [ˈwæks] *vi* **1** : crecer (dícese de la luna) **2** BECOME : volverse, ponerse ⟨to wax indignant : indignarse⟩ — *vt* : encerar

wax[2] *n* **1** BEESWAX : cera *f* de abejas **2** : cera *f* ⟨floor wax : cera para el piso⟩ **3** *or* **earwax** [ˈɪrˌwæks] : cerilla *f*, cerumen *m*

waxen [ˈwæksən] *adj* : de cera

waxy [ˈwæksi] *adj* **waxier; -est** : ceroso

way [ˈweɪ] *n* **1** PATH, ROAD : camino *m*, vía *f* **2** ROUTE : camino *m*, ruta *f* ⟨to go the wrong way : equivocarse de camino⟩ ⟨I'm on my way : estoy de camino⟩ **3** : línea *f* de conducta, camino *m* ⟨he chose the easy way : optó por el camino fácil⟩ **4** MANNER, MEANS : manera *f*, modo *m*, forma *f* ⟨in the same way : del mismo modo, igualmente⟩ ⟨there are no two ways about it : no cabe la menor duda⟩ ⟨no way! : ¡de ninguna manera!⟩ **5** (*indicating a wish*) ⟨have it your way : como tú quieras⟩ ⟨to get one's own way : salirse uno con la suya⟩ **6** STATE : estado *m* ⟨things are in a bad way : las cosas marchan mal⟩ **7** RESPECT : aspecto *m*, sentido *m* **8** CUSTOM : costumbre *f* ⟨to mend one's ways : dejar las malas costumbres⟩ **9** PASSAGE : camino *m* ⟨to get in the way : meterse en el camino⟩ **10** DISTANCE : distancia *f* ⟨to come a long way : hacer grandes progresos⟩ **11** DIRECTION : dirección *f* ⟨come this way : venga por aquí⟩ ⟨which way did he go? : ¿por dónde fue?⟩ **12 by the way** : a propósito, por cierto **13 by way of** VIA : vía, pasando por **14 out of the way** REMOTE : remoto, recóndito **15 → under way**

wayfarer [ˈweɪˌfærər] *n* : caminante *mf*

waylay [ˈweɪˌleɪ] *vt* **-laid** [-ˌleɪd]; **-laying** ACCOST : abordar

wayside [ˈweɪˌsaɪd] *n* : borde *m* del camino

wayward [ˈweɪwərd] *adj* **1** UNRULY : díscolo, rebelde **2** UNTOWARD : adverso

we [ˈwiː] *pron* : nosotros, nosotras

weak [ˈwiːk] *adj* **1** FEEBLE : débil, endeble **2** : flojo, pobre ⟨a weak excuse : una excusa poco convincente⟩ **3** DILUTED : aguado, diluido ⟨weak tea : té poco cargado⟩ **4** FAINT : tenue (dícese de los colores, las luces, los sonidos, etc.)

weaken [ˈwiːkən] *vt* : debilitar — *vi* : debilitarse, flaquear

weakling [ˈwiːklɪŋ] *n* : alfeñique *m fam*; debilucho *m*, -cha *f*

weakly[1] [ˈwiːkli] *adv* : débilmente

weakly[2] *adj* **weaklier; -est** : débil, enclenque

weakness [ˈwiːknəs] *n* **1** FEEBLENESS : debilidad *f* **2** FAULT, FLAW : flaqueza *f*, punto *m* débil

wealth [ˈwɛlθ] *n* **1** RICHES : riqueza *f* **2** PROFUSION : abundancia *f*, profusión *f*

wealthy [ˈwɛlθi] *adj* **wealthier; -est** : rico, acaudalado, adinerado

wean [ˈwi:n] *vt* **1** : destetar (a los niños o las crías) **2 to wean someone away from** : quitarle a alguien la costumbre de

weapon [ˈwɛpən] *n* : arma *f*

weaponless [ˈwɛpənləs] *adj* : desarmado

weaponry [ˈwɛpənri] *n* : armamento *m*

wear[1] [ˈwær] *v* **wore** [ˈwor]; **worn** [ˈworn]; **wearing** *vt* **1** : llevar (ropa, un reloj, etc.), calzar (zapatos) ⟨to wear a happy smile : sonreír alegremente⟩ **2** *or* **to wear away** : desgastar, erosionar (rocas, etc.) **3 to wear out** : gastar ⟨he wore out his shoes : gastó sus zapatos⟩ **4 to wear out** EXHAUST : agotar, fatigar ⟨to wear oneself out : agotarse⟩ — *vi* **1** LAST : durar **2 to wear off** DIMINISH : disminuir **3 to wear out** : gastarse

wear[2] *n* **1** USE : uso *m* ⟨for everyday wear : para todos los días⟩ **2** CLOTHING : ropa *f* ⟨children's wear : ropa de niños⟩ **3** DETERIORATION : desgaste *m* ⟨to be the worse for wear : estar deteriorado⟩

wearable [ˈwærəbəl] *adj* : que puede ponerse (dícese de una prenda)

wear and tear *n* : desgaste *m*

weariness [ˈwɪrinəs] *n* : fatiga *f*, cansancio *m*

wearisome [ˈwɪrisəm] *adj* : aburrido, pesado, cansado

weary[1] [ˈwɪri] *v* **-ried; -rying** *vt* **1** TIRE : cansar, fatigar **2** BORE : hastiar, aburrir — *vi* : cansarse

weary[2] *adj* **-rier; -est 1** TIRED : cansado **2** FED UP : harto **3** BORED : aburrido

weasel [ˈwi:zəl] *n* : comadreja *f*

weather[1] [ˈwɛðər] *vt* **1** WEAR : erosionar, desgastar **2** ENDURE : aguantar, sobrellevar, capear ⟨to weather the storm : capear el temporal⟩

weather[2] *n* : tiempo *m*

weather–beaten [ˈwɛðərˌbi:tən] *adj* : curtido

weatherman [ˈwɛðərˌmæn] *n, pl* **-men** [-mən, -ˌmɛn] METEOROLOGIST : meteorólogo *m*, -ga *f*

weatherproof [ˈwɛðərˌpru:f] *adj* : que resiste a la intemperie, impermeable

weather vane → **vane**

weave[1] [ˈwi:v] *v* **wove** [ˈwo:v] *or* **weaved; woven** [ˈwo:vən] *or* **weaved; weaving** *vt* **1** : tejer (tela) **2** INTERLACE : entretejer, entrelazar **3 to weave one's way through** : abrirse camino por — *vi* **1** : tejer **2** WIND : serpentear, zigzaguear

weave[2] *n* : tejido *m*, trama *f*

weaver [ˈwi:vər] *n* : tejedor *m*, -dora *f*

web[1] [ˈwɛb] *vt* **webbed; webbing** : cubrir o proveer con una red

web[2] *n* **1** COBWEB, SPIDERWEB : telaraña *f*, tela *f* de araña **2** ENTANGLEMENT, SNARE : red *f*, enredo *m* ⟨a web of intrigue : una red de intriga⟩ **3** : membrana *f* interdigital (de aves) **4** NETWORK : red *f* ⟨a web of highways : una red de carreteras⟩ **5 the Web** : la web

webbed [ˈwɛbd] *adj* : palmeado ⟨webbed feet : patas palmeadas⟩

Web site *n* : sitio *m* web

wed [ˈwɛd] *vt* **wedded; wedding 1** MARRY : casarse con **2** UNITE : ligar, unir

we'd [ˈwi:d] (*contraction of* **we had, we should,** *or* **we would**) → **have, should, would**

wedding [ˈwɛdɪŋ] *n* : boda *f*, casamiento *m*

wedge[1] [ˈwɛʤ] *vt* **wedged; wedging 1** : apretar (con una cuña) ⟨to wedge open : mantener abierto con una cuña⟩ **2** CRAM : meter, embutir

wedge[2] *n* **1** : cuña *f* **2** PIECE : porción *f*, trozo *m*

wedlock [ˈwɛdˌlɑk] → **marriage**

Wednesday [ˈwɛnzˌdeɪ, -di] *n* : miércoles *m*

wee [ˈwi:] *adj* : pequeño, minúsculo ⟨in the wee hours : a las altas horas⟩

weed[1] [ˈwi:d] *vt* **1** : desherbar, desyerbar **2 to weed out** : eliminar, quitar

weed[2] *n* : mala hierba *f*

weedy [ˈwi:di] *adj* **weedier; -est 1** : cubierto de malas hierbas **2** LANKY, SKINNY : flaco, larguirucho *fam*

week [ˈwi:k] *n* : semana *f*

weekday [ˈwi:kˌdeɪ] *n* : día *m* laborable

weekend [ˈwi:kˌɛnd] *n* : fin *m* de semana

weekly[1] [ˈwi:kli] *adv* : semanalmente

weekly[2] *adj* : semanal

weekly[3] *n, pl* **-lies** : semanario *m*

weep [ˈwi:p] *v* **wept** [ˈwɛpt]; **weeping** : llorar

weeping willow *n* : sauce *m* llorón

weepy [ˈwi:pi] *adj* **weepier; -est** : lloroso, triste

weevil [ˈwi:vəl] *n* : gorgojo *m*

weft [ˈwɛft] *n* : trama *f*

weigh [ˈweɪ] *vt* **1** : pesar **2** CONSIDER : considerar, sopesar **3 to weigh anchor** : levar anclas **4 to weigh down** : sobrecargar (con una carga), abrumar (con preocupaciones, etc.) — *vi* **1** : pesar ⟨it weighs 10 pounds : pesa 10 libras⟩ **2** COUNT : tener importancia, contar **3 to weigh on one's mind** : preocuparle a uno

weight[1] [ˈweɪt] *vt* **1** : poner peso en, sujetar con un peso **2** BURDEN : cargar, oprimir

weight[2] *n* **1** HEAVINESS : peso *m* ⟨to lose weight : bajar de peso, adelgazar⟩ **2** : peso *m* ⟨weights and measures : pesos y medidas⟩ **3** : pesa *f* ⟨to lift weights : levantar pesas⟩ **4** BURDEN : peso *m*, carga *f* ⟨to take a weight off one's mind : quitarle un peso de encima a uno⟩ **5**

IMPORTANCE : peso *m* **6** INFLUENCE : influencia *f*, autoridad *f* ⟨to throw one's weight around : hacer sentir su influencia⟩

weighty ['weɪṭi] *adj* **weightier; -est 1** HEAVY : pesado **2** IMPORTANT : importante, de peso

weird ['wɪrd] *adj* **1** MYSTERIOUS : misterioso **2** STRANGE : extraño, raro — **weirdly** *adv*

welcome[1] ['wɛlkəm] *vt* **-comed; -coming** : darle la bienvenida a, recibir

welcome[2] *adj* : bienvenido ⟨to make someone welcome : acoger bien a alguien⟩ ⟨you're welcome! : ¡de nada!, ¡no hay de qué!⟩

welcome[3] *n* : bienvenida *f*, recibimiento *m*, acogida *f*

weld[1] ['wɛld] *v* : soldar

weld[2] *n* : soldadura *f*

welder ['wɛldər] *n* : soldador *m*, -dora *f*

welfare ['wɛl,fær] *n* **1** WELL-BEING : bienestar *m* **2** : asistencia *f* social

well[1] ['wɛl] *vi or* **to well up** : brotar, manar

well[2] *adv* **better** ['bɛṭər]; **best** ['bɛst] **1** RIGHTLY : bien, correctamente **2** SATISFACTORILY : bien ⟨to turn out well : resultar bien, salir bien⟩ **3** COMPLETELY : completamente ⟨well-hidden : completamente escondido⟩ **4** INTIMATELY : bien ⟨I knew him well : lo conocía bien⟩ **5** CONSIDERABLY, FAR : muy, bastante ⟨well ahead : muy adelante⟩ ⟨well before the deadline : bastante antes de la fecha⟩ **6 as well** ALSO : también **7 → as well as**

well[3] *adj* **1** SATISFACTORY : bien ⟨all is well : todo está bien⟩ **2** DESIRABLE : conveniente ⟨it would be well if you left : sería conveniente que te fueras⟩ **3** HEALTHY : bien, sano

well[4] *n* **1** : pozo *m* (de agua, petróleo, gas, etc.), aljibe *m* (de agua) **2** SOURCE : fuente *f* ⟨a well of information : una fuente de información⟩ **3** *or* **stairwell** : caja *f*, hueco *m* (de la escalera)

well[5] *interj* **1** (*used to introduce a remark*) : bueno **2** (*used to express surprise*) : ¡vaya!

we'll ['wi:l, wɪl] (*contraction of* **we shall** *or* **we will**) **→ shall, will**

well–balanced ['wɛl'bælənst] *adj* : equilibrado

well–being ['wɛl'bi:ɪŋ] *n* : bienestar *m*

well–bred ['wɛl'brɛd] *adj* : fino, bien educado

well–defined [,wɛldi'faɪnd] *adj* : bien definido

well–done ['wɛl'dʌn] *adj* **1** : bien hecho ⟨well-done! : ¡bravo!⟩ **2** : bien cocido

well–known ['wɛl'no:n] *adj* : famoso, bien conocido

well–meaning ['wɛl'mi:nɪŋ] *adj* : bienintencionado, que tiene buenas intenciones

well–nigh ['wɛl'naɪ] *adv* : casi ⟨well-nigh impossible : casi imposible⟩

well–off ['wɛl'ɔf] **→ well–to–do**

well–rounded ['wɛl'raʊndəd] *adj* : completo, equilibrado

well–to–do [,wɛltə'du:] *adj* : próspero, adinerado, rico

Welsh ['wɛlʃ] *n* **1** : galés *m*, galesa *f* **2** : galés *m* (idioma) — **Welsh** *adj*

welt ['wɛlt] *n* **1** : vira *f* (de un zapato) **2** WHEAL : verdugón *m*

welter ['wɛltər] *n* : fárrago *m*, revoltijo *m* ⟨a welter of data : un fárrago de datos⟩

wend ['wɛnd] *vi* **to wend one's way** : ponerse en camino, encaminar sus pasos

went → go[1]

wept → weep

were → be

we're ['wɪr, 'wər, 'wi:ər] (*contraction of* **we are**) **→ be**

werewolf ['wɪr,wʊlf, 'wɛr-, 'wər-, -,wʌlf] *n, pl* **-wolves** [-,wʊlvz, -,wʌlvz] : hombre *m* lobo

west[1] ['wɛst] *adv* : al oeste

west[2] *adj* : oeste, del oeste, occidental ⟨west winds : vientos del oeste⟩

west[3] *n* **1** : oeste *m* **2 the West** : el Oeste, el Occidente

westerly ['wɛstərli] *adv & adj* : del oeste

western ['wɛstərn] *adj* **1** : Occidental, del Oeste **2** : occidental, oeste

Westerner ['wɛstərnər] *n* : habitante *mf* del oeste

West Indian *n* : antillano *m*, -na *f* — **West Indian** *adj*

westward ['wɛstwərd] *adv & adj* : hacia el oeste

wet[1] ['wɛt] *vt* **wet** *or* **wetted; wetting** : mojar, humedecer

wet[2] *adj* **wetter; wettest 1** : mojado, húmedo ⟨wet clothes : ropa mojada⟩ **2** RAINY : lluvioso **3 wet paint** : pintura *f* fresca

wet[3] *n* **1** MOISTURE : humedad *f* **2** RAIN : lluvia *f*

we've ['wi:v] (*contraction of* **we have**) **→ have**

whack[1] ['*h*wæk] *vt* : golpear (fuertemente), aporrear

whack[2] *n* **1** : golpe *m* fuerte, porrazo *m* **2** ATTEMPT : intento *m*, tentativa *f*

whale[1] ['*h*weɪl] *vi* **whaled; whaling** : cazar ballenas

whale[2] *n, pl* **whales** *or* **whale** : ballena *f*

whaleboat ['*h*weɪl,bo:t] *n* : ballenero *m*

whalebone ['*h*weɪl,bo:n] *n* : barba *f* de ballena

whaler ['*h*weɪlər] *n* **1** : ballenero *m*, -ra *f* **2 → whaleboat**

wharf ['*h*wɔrf] *n, pl* **wharves** ['*h*wɔrvz] : muelle *m*, embarcadero *m*

what[1] ['*h*wɑt, '*h*wʌt] *adv* **1** HOW : cómo, cúanto ⟨what he suffered! : ¡cómo sufría!⟩ **2 what with** : entre ⟨what with one thing and another : entre una cosa y otra⟩

what[2] *adj* **1** (*used in questions*) : qué ⟨what more do you want? : ¿qué más quieres?⟩ ⟨what color is it? : ¿de qué color es?⟩ **2** (*used in exclamations*) : qué ⟨what an idea! : ¡qué idea!⟩ **3** ANY, WHATEVER : cualquier ⟨give what help you can : da cualquier contribución que puedas⟩

what³ *pron* **1** (*used in direct questions*) : qué ⟨what happened? : ¿qué pasó?⟩ ⟨what does it cost? : ¿cuánto cuesta?⟩ **2** (*used in indirect statements*) : lo que, que ⟨I don't know what to do : no sé que hacer⟩ ⟨do what I tell you : haz lo que te digo⟩ **3 what for** WHY : porqué **4 what if** : y si ⟨what if he knows? : ¿y si lo sabe?⟩

whatever¹ [*h*wɑṭ'ɛvər, ˌ*h*wʌṭ-] *adj* **1** ANY : cualquier, cualquier . . . que ⟨whatever way you prefer : de cualquier manera que prefiera, como prefiera⟩ **2** (*in negative constructions*) ⟨there's no chance whatever : no hay ninguna posibilidad⟩ ⟨nothing whatever : nada en absoluto⟩

whatever² *pron* **1** ANYTHING : (todo) lo que ⟨I'll do whatever I want : haré lo que quiera⟩ **2** (*no matter what*) ⟨whatever it may be : sea lo que sea⟩ **3** WHAT : qué ⟨whatever do you mean? : ¿qué quieres decir?⟩

whatsoever¹ [ˌ*h*wɑtso'ɛvər, ˌ*h*wʌṭ-] *adj* → **whatever¹**

whatsoever² *pron* → **whatever²**

wheal ['*h*wi:l] *n* : verdugón *m*

wheat ['*h*wi:t] *n* : trigo *m*

wheaten ['*h*wi:tən] *adj* : de trigo

wheedle ['*h*wi:dəl] *vt* **-dled; -dling** CAJOLE : engatusar ⟨to wheedle something out of someone : sonsacarle algo a alguien⟩

wheel¹ ['*h*wi:l] *vt* : empujar (una bicicleta, etc.), mover (algo sobre ruedas) — *vi* **1** ROTATE : girar, rotar **2 to wheel around** TURN : darse la vuelta

wheel² *n* **1** : rueda *f* **2** *or* **steering wheel** : volante *m* (de automóviles, etc.), timón *m* (de barcos o aviones) **3 wheels** *npl* : maquinaria *f*, fuerza *f* impulsora ⟨the wheels of government : la maquinaria del gobierno⟩

wheelbarrow ['*h*wi:lˌbærˌo:] *n* : carretilla *f*

wheelchair ['*h*wi:lˌʧær] *n* : silla *f* de ruedas

wheeze¹ ['*h*wi:z] *vi* **wheezed; wheezing** : resollar, respirar con dificultad

wheeze² *n* : resuello *m*

whelk ['*h*wɛlk] *n* : buccino *m*

whelp¹ ['*h*wɛlp] *vi* : parir

whelp² *n* : cachorro *m*, -rra *f*

when¹ ['*h*wɛn] *adv* : cuándo ⟨when will you return? : ¿cuándo volverás?⟩ ⟨he asked me when I would be home : me preguntó cuándo estaría en casa⟩

when² *conj* **1** (*referring to a particular time*) : cuando, en que ⟨when you are ready : cuando estés listo⟩ ⟨the days when I clean the house : los días en que limpio la casa⟩ **2** IF : cuando, si ⟨how can I go when I have no money? : ¿cómo voy a ir si no tengo dinero?⟩ **3** ALTHOUGH : cuando ⟨you said it was big when actually it's small : dijiste que era grande cuando en realidad es pequeño⟩

when³ *pron* : cuándo ⟨since when are you the boss? : ¿desde cuándo eres el jefe?⟩

whence ['*h*wɛnts] *adv* : de donde

whenever¹ [*h*wɛn'ɛvər] *adv* **1** : cuando sea ⟨tomorrow or whenever : mañana o cuando sea⟩ **2** (*in questions*) : cuándo

whenever² *conj* **1** : siempre que, cada vez que ⟨whenever I go, I'm disappointed : siempre que voy, quedo desilusionado⟩ **2** WHEN : cuando ⟨whenever you like : cuando quieras⟩

where¹ ['*h*wɛr] *adv* : dónde, adónde ⟨where is he? : ¿dónde está?⟩ ⟨where did they go? : ¿adónde fueron?⟩

where² *conj* : donde, adonde ⟨she knows where the house is : sabe donde está la casa⟩ ⟨she goes where she likes : va adonde quiera⟩

where³ *pron* : donde ⟨Chicago is where I live : Chicago es donde vivo⟩

whereabouts¹ ['*h*wɛrəˌbaʊts] *adv* : dónde, por dónde ⟨whereabouts is the house? : ¿dónde está la casa?⟩

whereabouts² *ns & pl* : paradero *m*

whereas [*h*wɛr'æz] *conj* **1** : considerando que (usado en documentos legales) **2** : mientras que ⟨I like the white one whereas she prefers the black : me gusta el blanco mientras que ella prefiere el negro⟩

whereby [*h*wɛr'baɪ] *adv* : por lo cual

wherefore ['*h*wɛrˌfor] *adv* : por qué

wherein [*h*wɛr'ɪn] *adv* : en el cual, en el que

whereof [*h*wɛr'ʌv, -ɑv] *conj* : de lo cual

whereupon ['*h*wɛrəˌpɑn, -ˌpɔn] *conj* : con lo cual, después de lo cual

wherever¹ [*h*wɛr'ɛvər] *adv* **1** WHERE : dónde, adónde **2** : en cualquier parte ⟨or wherever : o donde sea⟩

wherever² *conj* : dondequiera que, donde sea ⟨wherever you go : dondequiera que vayas⟩

wherewithal ['*h*wɛrwɪˌðɔl, -ˌθɔl] *n* : medios *mpl*, recursos *mpl*

whet ['*h*wɛt] *vt* **whetted; whetting 1** SHARPEN : afilar **2** STIMULATE : estimular ⟨to whet the appetite : estimular el apetito⟩

whether ['*h*wɛðər] *conj* **1** : si ⟨I don't know whether it is finished : no sé si está acabado⟩ ⟨we doubt whether he'll show up : dudamos que aparezca⟩ **2** (*used in comparisons*) ⟨whether I like it or not : tanto si quiero como si no⟩ ⟨whether he comes or he doesn't : venga o no⟩

whetstone ['*h*wɛtˌsto:n] *n* : piedra *f* de afilar

whey ['*h*weɪ] *n* : suero *m* (de la leche)

which¹ ['*h*wɪʧ] *adj* : qué, cuál ⟨which tie do you prefer? : ¿cuál corbata prefieres?⟩ ⟨which ones? : ¿cuáles?⟩ ⟨tell me which house is yours : dime qué casa es la tuya⟩

which[2] *pron* **1** : cuál ⟨which is the right answer? : ¿cuál es la respuesta correcta?⟩ **2** : que, el (la) cual ⟨the cup which broke : la taza que se quebró⟩ ⟨the house, which is made of brick : la casa, la cual es de ladrillo⟩

whichever[1] [*h*wɪʧˈɛvər] *adj* : el (la) que, cualquiera que ⟨whichever book you like : cualquier libro que te guste⟩

whichever[2] *pron* : el (la) que, cualquiera que ⟨take whichever you want : toma el que quieras⟩ ⟨whichever I choose : cualquiera que elija⟩

whiff[1] [ˈ*h*wɪf] *v* PUFF : soplar

whiff[2] *n* **1** PUFF : soplo *m*, ráfaga *f* **2** SNIFF : olor *m* **3** HINT : dejo *m*, pizca *f*

while[1] [ˈ*h*waɪl] *vt* **whiled; whiling** : pasar ⟨to while away the time : matar el tiempo⟩

while[2] *n* **1** TIME : rato *m*, tiempo *m* ⟨after a while : después de un rato⟩ ⟨in a while : dentro de poco⟩ **2 to be worth one's while** : valer la pena

while[3] *conj* **1** : mientras ⟨whistle while you work : silba mientras trabajas⟩ **2** WHEREAS : mientras que **3** ALTHOUGH : aunque ⟨while it's very good, it's not perfect : aunque es muy bueno, no es perfecto⟩

whim [ˈ*h*wɪm] *n* : capricho *m*, antojo *m*

whimper[1] [ˈ*h*wɪmpər] *vi* : lloriquear, gimotear

whimper[2] *n* : quejido *m*

whimsical [ˈ*h*wɪmzɪkəl] *adj* **1** CAPRICIOUS : caprichoso, fantasioso **2** ERRATIC : errático — **whimsically** *adv*

whine[1] [ˈ*h*waɪn] *vi* **whined; whining 1** : lloriquear, gimotear, gemir **2** COMPLAIN : quejarse

whine[2] *n* : quejido *m*, gemido *m*

whinny[1] [ˈ*h*wɪni] *vi* **-nied; -nying** : relinchar

whinny[2] *n, pl* **-nies** : relincho *m*

whip[1] [ˈ*h*wɪp] *v* **whipped; whipping** *vt* **1** SNATCH : sacar (rápidamente), arrebatar ⟨she whipped the cloth off the table : arrebató el mantel de la mesa⟩ **2** LASH : azotar **3** DEFEAT : vencer, derrotar **4** INCITE : incitar, despertar ⟨to whip up enthusiasm : despertar el entusiasmo⟩ **5** BEAT : batir (huevos, crema, etc.) — *vi* FLAP : agitarse

whip[2] *n* **1** : látigo *m*, azote *m*, fusta *f* (de jinete) **2** : miembro *m* de un cuerpo legislativo encargado de disciplina

whiplash [ˈ*h*wɪpˌlæʃ] *n or* **whiplash injury** : traumatismo *m* cervical

whippet [ˈ*h*wɪpət] *n* : galgo *m* pequeño, galgo *m* inglés

whir[1] [ˈ*h*wər] *vi* **whirred; whirring** : zumbar

whir[2] *n* : zumbido *m*

whirl[1] [ˈ*h*wərl] *vi* **1** SPIN : dar vueltas, girar ⟨my head is whirling : la cabeza me está dando vueltas⟩ **2 to whirl about** : arremolinarse, moverse rápidamente

whirl[2] *n* **1** SPIN : giro *m*, vuelta *f*, remolino *m* (dícese del polvo, etc.) **2** BUSTLE : bullicio *m*, torbellino *m* (de actividad, etc.) **3 to give it a whirl** : intentar hacer, probar

whirlpool [ˈ*h*wərlˌpu:l] *n* : vorágine *f*, remolino *m*

whirlwind [ˈ*h*wərlˌwɪnd] *n* : remolino *m*, torbellino *m*, tromba *f*

whisk[1] [ˈ*h*wɪsk] *vt* **1** : llevar ⟨she whisked the children off to bed : llevó a los niños a la cama⟩ **2** : batir ⟨to whisk eggs : batir huevos⟩ **3 to whisk away** *or* **to whisk off** : sacudir

whisk[2] *n* **1** WHISKING : sacudida *f* (movimiento) **2** : batidor *m* (para batir huevos, etc.)

whisk broom *n* : escobilla *f*

whisker [ˈ*h*wɪskər] *n* **1** : pelo *m* (de la barba o el bigote) **2 whiskers** *npl* : bigotes *mpl* (de animales)

whiskey *or* **whisky** [ˈ*h*wɪski] *n, pl* **-keys** *or* **-kies** : whisky *m*

whisper[1] [ˈ*h*wɪspər] *vi* : cuchichear, susurrar — *vt* : decir en voz baja, susurrar

whisper[2] *n* **1** WHISPERING : susurro *m*, cuchicheo *m* **2** RUMOR : rumor *m* **3** TRACE : dejo *m*, pizca *f*

whistle[1] [ˈ*h*wɪsəl] *v* **-tled; -tling** *vi* : silbar, chiflar, pitar (dícese de un tren, etc.) — *vt* : silbar ⟨to whistle a tune : silbar una melodía⟩

whistle[2] *n* **1** WHISTLING : chiflido *m*, silbido *m* **2** : silbato *m*, pito *m* (instrumento)

whit [ˈ*h*wɪt] *n* BIT : ápice *m*, pizca *f*

white[1] [ˈ*h*waɪt] *adj* **whiter; -est** : blanco

white[2] *n* **1** : blanco *m* (color) **2** : clara *f* (de huevos) **3** *or* **white person** : blanco *m*, -ca *f*

white blood cell *n* : glóbulo *m* blanco

whitecaps [ˈ*h*waɪtˌkæps] *npl* : cabrillas *fpl*

white–collar [ˈ*h*waɪtˈkɑlər] *adj* **1** : de oficina **2 white–collar worker** : oficinista *mf*

whitefish [ˈ*h*waɪtˌfɪʃ] *n* : pescado *m* blanco

whiten [ˈ*h*waɪtən] *vt* : blanquear — *vi* : ponerse blanco

whiteness [ˈ*h*waɪtnəs] *n* : blancura *f*

white–tailed deer [ˈ*h*waɪtˈteɪld] *n* : ciervo *f* de Virginia

whitewash[1] [ˈ*h*waɪtˌwɔʃ] *vt* **1** : enjalbegar, blanquear ⟨to whitewash a fence : enjalbegar una valla⟩ **2** CONCEAL : encubrir (un escándalo, etc.)

whitewash[2] *n* **1** : jalbegue *m*, lechada *f* **2** COVER-UP : encubrimiento *m*

whither [ˈ*h*wɪðər] *adv* : adónde

whiting [ˈ*h*waɪt̬ɪŋ] *n* : merluza *f*, pescadilla *f* (pez)

whitish [ˈ*h*waɪt̬ɪʃ] *adj* : blancuzco

whittle [ˈ*h*wɪt̬əl] *vt* **-tled; -tling 1** : tallar (madera) **2 to whittle down** : reducir,

recortar ⟨to whittle down expenses : reducir los gastos⟩
whiz[1] *or* **whizz** [ˈ*h*wɪz] *vi* **whizzed; whizzing 1** BUZZ : zumbar **2 to whiz by** : pasar muy rápido, pasar volando
whiz[2] *or* **whizz** *n, pl* **whizzes 1** BUZZ : zumbido *m* **2 to be a whiz** : ser un prodigio, ser muy hábil
who [ˈhuː] *pron* **1** (*used in direct and indirect questions*) : quién ⟨who is that? : ¿quién es ése?⟩ ⟨who did it? : ¿quién lo hizo?⟩ ⟨we know who they are : sabemos quiénes son⟩ **2** (*used in relative clauses*) : que, quien ⟨the lady who lives there : la señora que vive allí⟩ ⟨for those who wait : para los que esperan, para quienes esperan⟩
whodunit [huːˈdʌnɪt] *n* : novela *f* policíaca
whoever [huːˈɛvər] *pron* **1** : quienquiera que, quien ⟨whoever did it : quienquiera que lo hizo⟩ ⟨give it to whoever you want : dalo a quien quieras⟩ **2** (*used in questions*) : quién ⟨whoever could that be? : ¿quién podría ser?⟩
whole[1] [ˈhoːl] *adj* **1** UNHURT : ileso **2** INTACT : intacto, sano **3** ENTIRE : entero, íntegro ⟨the whole island : toda la isla⟩ ⟨whole milk : leche entera⟩ **4 a whole lot** : muchísimo
whole[2] *n* **1** : todo *m* **2 as a whole** : en conjunto **3 on the whole** : en general
wholehearted [ˈhoːlˈhɑrt̬əd] *adj* : sin reservas, incondicional
whole number *n* : entero *m*
wholesale[1] [ˈhoːlˌseɪl] *v* **-saled; -saling** *vt* : vender al por mayor — *vi* : venderse al por mayor
wholesale[2] *adv* : al por mayor
wholesale[3] *adj* **1** : al por mayor ⟨wholesale grocer : tendero al por mayor⟩ **2** TOTAL : total, absoluto ⟨wholesale slaughter : matanza sistemática⟩
wholesale[4] *n* : mayoreo *m*
wholesaler [ˈhoːlˌseɪlər] *n* : mayorista *mf*
wholesome [ˈhoːlsəm] *adj* **1** : sano ⟨wholesome advice : consejo sano⟩ **2** HEALTHY : sano, saludable
whole wheat *adj* : de trigo integral
wholly [ˈhoːli] *adv* **1** COMPLETELY : completamente **2** SOLELY : exclusivamente, únicamente
whom [ˈhuːm] *pron* **1** (*used in direct questions*) : a quién ⟨whom did you choose? : ¿a quién elegiste?⟩ **2** (*used in indirect questions*) : de quién, con quién, en quién ⟨I don't know whom to consult : no sé con quién consultar⟩ **3** (*used in relative clauses*) : que, a quien ⟨the lawyer whom I recommended to you : el abogado que te recomendé⟩
whomever [huːmˈɛvər] *pron* WHOEVER : quienquiera, quien ⟨marry whomever you please : cásate con quien quieras⟩
whoop[1] [ˈ*h*wuːp, ˈ*h*wʊp] *vi* : gritar, chillar
whoop[2] *n* : grito *m*
whooping cough *n* : tos *f* ferina
whopper [ˈ*h*wɑpər] *n* **1** : cosa *f* enorme **2** LIE : mentira *f* colosal
whopping [ˈ*h*wɑpɪŋ] *adj* : enorme
whore [ˈhor] *n* : puta *f*, ramera *f*
whorl [ˈ*h*wɔrl, ˈ*h*wərl] *n* : espiral *f*, espira *f* (de una concha), línea *f* (de una huella digital)
whose[1] [ˈhuːz] *adj* **1** (*used in questions*) : de quién ⟨whose truck is that? : ¿de quién es ese camión?⟩ **2** (*used in relative clauses*) : cuyo ⟨the person whose work is finished : la persona cuyo trabajo está terminado⟩
whose[2] *pron* : de quién ⟨tell me whose it was : dime de quién era⟩
why[1] [ˈ*h*waɪ] *adv* : por qué ⟨why did you do it? : ¿por qué lo hizo?⟩
why[2] *n, pl* **whys** REASON : porqué *m*, razón *f*
why[3] *conj* : por qué ⟨I know why he left : yo sé por qué salió⟩ ⟨there's no reason why it should exist : no hay razón para que exista⟩
why[4] *interj* (*used to express surprise*) : ¡vaya!, ¡mira!
wick [ˈwɪk] *n* : mecha *f*
wicked [ˈwɪkəd] *adj* **1** EVIL : malo, malvado **2** MISCHIEVOUS : travieso, pícaro ⟨a wicked grin : una sonrisa traviesa⟩ **3** TERRIBLE : terrible, horrible ⟨a wicked storm : una tormenta horrible⟩
wickedly [ˈwɪkədli] *adv* : con maldad
wickedness [ˈwɪkədnəs] *n* : maldad *f*
wicker[1] [ˈwɪkər] *adj* : de mimbre
wicker[2] *n* **1** : mimbre *m* **2** → **wickerwork**
wickerwork [ˈwɪkərˌwərk] *n* : artículos *mpl* de mimbre
wicket [ˈwɪkət] *n* **1** WINDOW : ventanilla *f* **2** *or* **wicket gate** : postigo *m* **3** : aro *m* (en croquet), palos *mpl* (en críquet)
wide[1] [ˈwaɪd] *adv* **wider; widest 1** WIDELY : por todas partes ⟨to travel far and wide : viajar por todas partes⟩ **2** COMPLETELY : completamente, totalmente ⟨wide open : abierto de par en par⟩ **3 wide apart** : muy separados
wide[2] *adj* **wider; widest 1** VAST : vasto, extensivo ⟨a wide area : una área extensiva⟩ **2** : ancho ⟨three meters wide : tres metros de ancho⟩ **3** BROAD : ancho, amplio **4** *or* **wide–open** : muy abierto **5 wide of the mark** : desviado, lejos del blanco
wide–awake [ˈwaɪdəˈweɪk] *adj* : (completamente) despierto
wide–eyed [ˈwaɪdˈaɪd] *adj* **1** : con los ojos muy abiertos **2** NAIVE : inocente, ingenuo
widely [ˈwaɪdli] *adv* : extensivamente, por todas partes
widen [ˈwaɪdən] *vt* : ampliar, ensanchar — *vi* : ampliarse, ensancharse
widespread [ˈwaɪdˈsprɛd] *adj* : extendido, extenso, difuso
widow[1] [ˈwɪˌdoː] *vt* : dejar viuda ⟨to be widowed : enviudar⟩
widow[2] *n* : viuda *f*

widower [ˈwɪdowər] *n* : viudo *m*
width [ˈwɪdθ] *n* : ancho *m*, anchura *f*
wield [ˈwiːld] *vt* **1** USE : usar, manejar ⟨to wield a broom : usar una escoba⟩ **2** EXERCISE : ejercer ⟨to wield influence : influir⟩
wiener [ˈwiːnər] → **frankfurter**
wife [ˈwaɪf] *n, pl* **wives** [ˈwaɪvz] : esposa *f*, mujer *f*
wifely [ˈwaɪfli] *adj* : de esposa, conyugal
wig [ˈwɪg] *n* : peluca *f*
wiggle[1] [ˈwɪgəl] *v* **-gled; -gling** *vt* : menear, contonear ⟨to wiggle one's hips : contonearse⟩ — *vi* : menearse
wiggle[2] *n* : meneo *m*, contoneo *m*
wiggly [ˈwɪgəli] *adj* **-glier; -est** **1** : que se menea **2** WAVY : ondulado
wigwag [ˈwɪg͵wæg] *vi* **-wagged; -wagging** : comunicar por señales
wigwam [ˈwɪg͵wɑm] *n* : wigwam *m*
wild[1] [ˈwaɪld] *adv* **1** → **wildly** **2 to run wild** : descontrolarse
wild[2] *adj* **1** : salvaje, silvestre, cimarrón ⟨wild horses : caballos salvajes⟩ ⟨wild rice : arroz silvestre⟩ **2** DESOLATE : yermo, agreste **3** UNRULY : desenfrenado **4** CRAZY : loco, fantástico ⟨wild ideas : ideas locas⟩ **5** BARBAROUS : salvaje, bárbaro **6** ERRATIC : errático ⟨a wild throw : un tiro errático⟩
wild[3] *n* → **wilderness**
wild card *n* **1** : factor *m* desconocido **2** : comodín *m* (carta o símbolo)
wildcat [ˈwaɪld͵kæt] *n* **1** : gato *m* montés **2** BOBCAT : lince *m* rojo
wilderness [ˈwɪldərnəs] *n* : yermo *m*, desierto *m*
wildfire [ˈwaɪld͵faɪr] *n* **1** : fuego *m* descontrolado **2 to spread like wildfire** : propagarse como un reguero de pólvora
wildflower [ˈwaɪld͵flaʊər] *n* : flor *f* silvestre
wildfowl [ˈwaɪld͵faʊl] *n* : ave *f* de caza
wildlife [ˈwaɪld͵laɪf] *n* : fauna *f*
wildly [ˈwaɪldli] *adv* **1** FRANTICALLY : frenéticamente, como un loco **2** EXTREMELY : extremadamente ⟨wildly happy : loco de felicidad⟩
wile[1] [ˈwaɪl] *vt* **wiled; wiling** LURE : atraer
wile[2] *n* : ardid *m*, artimaña *f*
will[1] [ˈwɪl] *v, past* **would** [ˈwʊd]; *pres sing & pl* **will** *vt* WISH : querer ⟨do what you will : haz lo que quieras⟩ — *v aux* **1** (*expressing willingness*) ⟨no one would take the job : nadie aceptaría el trabajo⟩ ⟨I won't do it : no lo haré⟩ **2** (*expressing habitual action*) ⟨he will get angry over nothing : se pone furioso por cualquier cosa⟩ **3** (*forming the future tense*) ⟨tomorrow we will go shopping : mañana iremos de compras⟩ **4** (*expressing capacity*) ⟨the couch will hold three people : en el sofá cabrán tres personas⟩ **5** (*expressing determination*) ⟨I will go despite them : iré a pesar de ellos⟩ **6** (*expressing probability*) ⟨that will be the mailman : eso ha de ser el cartero⟩ **7** (*expressing inevitability*) ⟨accidents will happen : los accidentes ocurrirán⟩ **8** (*expressing a command*) ⟨you will do as I say : harás lo que digo⟩
will[2] *vt* **1** ORDAIN : disponer, decretar ⟨if God wills it : si Dios lo dispone, si Dios quiere⟩ **2** : lograr a fuerza de voluntad ⟨they were willing him to succeed : estaban deseando que tuviera éxito⟩ **3** BEQUEATH : legar
will[3] *n* **1** DESIRE : deseo *m*, voluntad *f* **2** VOLITION : voluntad *f* ⟨free will : libre albedrío⟩ **3** WILLPOWER : voluntad *f*, fuerza *f* de voluntad ⟨a will of iron : una voluntad férrea⟩ **4** : testamento *m* ⟨to make a will : hacer testamento⟩
willful *or* **wilful** [ˈwɪlfəl] *adj* **1** OBSTINATE : obstinado, terco **2** INTENTIONAL : intencionado, deliberado — **willfully** *adv*
willing [ˈwɪlɪŋ] *adj* **1** INCLINED, READY : listo, dispuesto **2** OBLIGING : servicial, complaciente
willingly [ˈwɪlɪŋli] *adv* : con gusto
willingness [ˈwɪlɪŋnəs] *n* : buena voluntad *f*
willow [ˈwɪ͵loː] *n* : sauce *m*
willowy [ˈwɪlowi] *adj* : esbelto
willpower [ˈwɪl͵paʊər] *n* : voluntad *f*, fuerza *f* de voluntad
wilt [ˈwɪlt] *vi* **1** : marchitarse (dícese de las flores) **2** LANGUISH : debilitarse, languidecer
wily [ˈwaɪli] *adj* **wilier; -est** : artero, astuto
wimp [ˈwɪmp] *n* **1** COWARD : gallina *f*, cobarde *mf* **2** WEAKLING : debilucho *m*, -cha *f*, alfeñique *m*
win[1] [ˈwɪn] *v* **won** [ˈwʌn]; **winning** *vi* : ganar — *vt* **1** : ganar, conseguir **2 to win over** : ganarse a **3 to win someone's heart** : conquistar a alguien
win[2] *n* : triunfo *m*, victoria *f*
wince[1] [ˈwɪnts] *vi* **winced; wincing** : estremecerse, hacer una mueca de dolor
wince[2] *n* : mueca *f* de dolor
winch [ˈwɪntʃ] *n* : torno *m*
wind[1] [ˈwɪnd] *vt* : dejar sin aliento ⟨to be winded : quedarse sin aliento⟩
wind[2] [ˈwaɪnd] *v* **wound** [ˈwaʊnd]; **winding** *vi* MEANDER : serpentear — *vt* **1** COIL, ROLL : envolver, enrollar **2** TURN : hacer girar ⟨to wind a clock : darle cuerda a un reloj⟩
wind[3] [ˈwɪnd] *n* **1** : viento *m* ⟨against the wind : contra el viento⟩ **2** BREATH : aliento *m* **3** FLATULENCE : flatulencia *f*, ventosidad *f* **4 to get wind of** : enterarse de
wind[4] [ˈwaɪnd] *n* **1** TURN : vuelta *f* **2** BEND : recodo *m*, curva *f*
windbreak [ˈwɪnd͵breɪk] *n* : barrera *f* contra el viento, abrigadero *m*
windfall [ˈwɪnd͵fɔl] *n* **1** : fruta *f* caída **2** : beneficio *m* imprevisto
wind instrument *n* : instrumento *m* de viento

windlass [ˈwɪndləs] *n* : cabrestante *m*

windmill [ˈwɪnd,mɪl] *n* : molino *m* de viento

window [ˈwɪn,doː] *n* **1** : ventana *f* (de un edificio o una computadora), ventanilla *f* (de un vehículo o avión), vitrina *f* (de una tienda) **2** → **windowpane**

windowpane [ˈwɪn,doː,peɪn] *n* : vidrio *m*

window–shop [ˈwɪndo,ʃɑp] *vi* **-shopped; -shopping** : mirar las vitrinas

windpipe [ˈwɪnd,paɪp] *n* : tráquea *f*

windshield [ˈwɪnd,ʃiːld] *n* **1** : parabrisas *m* **2 windshield wiper** : limpiaparabrisas *m*

windup [ˈwaɪnd,ʌp] *n* : conclusión *f*

wind up *vt* END : terminar, concluir — *vi* : terminar, acabar

windward[1] [ˈwɪndwərd] *adj* : de barlovento

windward[2] *n* : barlovento *m*

windy [ˈwɪndi] *adj* **windier; -est 1** : ventoso ⟨it's windy : hace viento⟩ **2** VERBOSE : verboso, prolijo

wine[1] [ˈwaɪn] *v* **wined; wining** *vi* : beber vino — *vt* **to wine and dine** : agasajar

wine[2] *n* : vino *m*

wing[1] [ˈwɪŋ] *vi* FLY : volar

wing[2] *n* **1** : ala *f* (de un ave, un avión, o un edificio) **2** FACTION : ala *f* ⟨the right wing of the party : el ala derecha del partido⟩ **3 wings** *npl* : bastidores *mpl* (de un teatro) **4 on the wing** : al vuelo, volando **5 under one's wing** : bajo el cargo de uno

winged [ˈwɪŋd, ˈwɪŋəd] *adj* : alado

wink[1] [ˈwɪŋk] *vi* **1** : guiñar el ojo **2** BLINK : pestañear, parpadear **3** FLICKER : parpadear, titilar

wink[2] *n* **1** : guiño *m* (del ojo) **2** NAP : siesta *f* ⟨not to sleep a wink : no pegar el ojo⟩

winner [ˈwɪnər] *n* : ganador *m*, -dora *f*

winning [ˈwɪnɪŋ] *adj* **1** VICTORIOUS : ganador **2** CHARMING : encantador

winnings [ˈwɪnɪŋz] *npl* : ganancias *fpl*

winnow [ˈwɪ,noː] *vt* : aventar (el grano, etc.)

winsome [ˈwɪnsəm] *adj* CHARMING : encantador

winter[1] [ˈwɪntər] *adj* : invernal, de invierno

winter[2] *n* : invierno *m*

wintergreen [ˈwɪntər,griːn] *n* : gaulteria *f*

wintertime [ˈwɪntər,taɪm] *n* : invierno *m*

wintry [ˈwɪntri] *adj* **wintrier; -est 1** WINTER : invernal, de invierno **2** COLD : frío ⟨she gave us a wintry greeting : nos saludó fríamente⟩

wipe[1] [ˈwaɪp] *vt* **wiped; wiping 1** : limpiar, pasarle un trapo a ⟨to wipe one's feet : limpiarse los pies⟩ **2 to wipe away** : enjugar (lágrimas), borrar (una memoria) **3 to wipe out** ANNIHILATE : aniquilar, destruir

wipe[2] *n* : pasada *f* (con un trapo, etc.)

wire[1] [ˈwaɪr] *vt* **wired; wiring 1** : instalar el cableado en (una casa, etc.) **2** BIND : atar con alambre **3** TELEGRAPH : telegrafiar, mandarle un telegrama (a alguien)

wire[2] *n* **1** : alambre *m* ⟨barbed wire : alambre de púas⟩ **2** : cable *m* (eléctrico o telefónico) **3** CABLEGRAM, TELEGRAM : telegrama *m*, cable *m*

wireless [ˈwaɪrləs] *adj* : inalámbrico

wiretapping [ˈwaɪr,tæpɪŋ] *n* : intervención *f* electrónica

wiring [ˈwaɪrɪŋ] *n* : cableado *m*

wiry [ˈwaɪri] *adj* **wirier; -est 1** : hirsuto, tieso (dícese del pelo) **2** : esbelto y musculoso (dícese del cuerpo)

wisdom [ˈwɪzdəm] *n* **1** KNOWLEDGE : sabiduría *f* **2** JUDGMENT, SENSE : sensatez *f*

wisdom tooth *n* : muela *f* de juicio

wise[1] [ˈwaɪz] *adj* **wiser; wisest 1** LEARNED : sabio **2** SENSIBLE : sabio, sensato, prudente **3** KNOWLEDGEABLE : entendido, enterado ⟨they're wise to his tricks : conocen muy bien sus mañas⟩

wise[2] *n* : manera *f*, modo *m* ⟨in no wise : de ninguna manera⟩

wisecrack [ˈwaɪz,kræk] *n* : broma *f*, chiste *m*

wisely [ˈwaɪzli] *adv* : sabiamente, sensatamente

wish[1] [ˈwɪʃ] *vt* **1** WANT : desear, querer **2 to wish (something) for** : desear ⟨they wished me well : me desearon lo mejor⟩ — *vi* **1** : pedir (como deseo) **2** : querer ⟨as you wish : como quieras⟩

wish[2] *n* **1** : deseo *m* ⟨to grant a wish : conceder un deseo⟩ **2 wishes** *npl* : saludos *mpl*, recuerdos *mpl* ⟨to send best wishes : mandar muchos recuerdos⟩

wishbone [ˈwɪʃ,boːn] *n* : espoleta *f*

wishful [ˈwɪʃfəl] *adj* **1** HOPEFUL : deseoso, lleno de esperanza **2 wishful thinking** : ilusiones *fpl*

wishy–washy [ˈwɪʃi,wɔʃi, -,wɑʃi] *adj* : insípido, soso

wisp [ˈwɪsp] *n* **1** BUNCH : manojo *m* (de paja) **2** STRAND : mechón *m* (de pelo) **3** : voluta *f* (de humo)

wispy [ˈwɪspi] *adj* **wispier; -est** : tenue, ralo (dícese del pelo)

wisteria [wɪsˈtɪriə] *n* : glicinia *f*

wistful [ˈwɪstfəl] *adj* : añorante, anhelante, melancólico — **wistfully** *adv*

wistfulness [ˈwɪstfəlnəs] *n* : añoranza *f*, melancolía *f*

wit [ˈwɪt] *n* **1** INTELLIGENCE : inteligencia *f* **2** CLEVERNESS : ingenio *m*, gracia *f*, agudeza *f* **3** HUMOR : humorismo *m* **4** JOKER : chistoso *m*, -sa *f* **5 wits** *npl* : razón *f*, buen juicio *m* ⟨scared out of one's wits : muerto de miedo⟩ ⟨to be at one's wits' end : estar desesperado⟩

witch [ˈwɪʧ] *n* : bruja *f*

witchcraft [ˈwɪʧ,kræft] *n* : brujería *f*, hechicería *f*

witch doctor *n* : hechicero *m*, -ra *f*

witchery [ˈwɪʧəri] *n, pl* **-eries** **1** → **witchcraft** **2** CHARM : encanto *m*

witch–hunt [ˈwɪʧˌhʌnt] *n* : caza *f* de brujas

with [ˈwɪð, ˈwɪθ] *prep* **1** : con ⟨I'm going with you : voy contigo⟩ ⟨coffee with milk : café con leche⟩ **2** AGAINST : con ⟨to argue with someone : discutir con alguien⟩ **3** (*used in descriptions*) : con, de ⟨the girl with red hair : la muchacha de pelo rojo⟩ **4** (*indicating manner, means, or cause*) : con ⟨to cut with a knife : cortar con un cuchillo⟩ ⟨fix it with tape : arréglalo con cinta⟩ ⟨with luck : consuerte⟩ **5** DESPITE : a pesar de, aún con ⟨with all his work, the business failed : a pesar de su trabajo, el negocio fracasó⟩ **6** REGARDING : con respecto a, con ⟨the trouble with your plan : el problema con su plan⟩ **7** ACCORDING TO : según ⟨it varies with the season : varía según la estación⟩ **8** (*indicating support or understanding*) : con ⟨I'm with you all the way : estoy contigo hasta el fin⟩

withdraw [wɪðˈdrɔ, wɪθ-] *v* **-drew** [-ˈdru:]; **-drawn** [-ˈdrɔn]; **-drawing** *vt* **1** REMOVE : retirar, apartar, sacar (dinero) **2** RETRACT : retractarse de — *vi* : retirarse, recluirse (de la sociedad)

withdrawal [wɪðˈdrɔəl, wɪθ-] *n* **1** : retirada *f*, retiro *m* (de fondos, etc.), retraimiento *m* (social) **2** RETRACTION : retractación *f* **3** **withdrawal symptoms** : síndrome *m* de abstinencia

withdrawn [wɪðˈdrɔn, wɪθ-] *adj* : retraído, reservado, introvertido

wither [ˈwɪðər] *vt* : marchitar, agostar — *vi* **1** WILT : marchitarse **2** WEAKEN : decaer, debilitarse

withhold [wɪθˈho:ld, wɪð-] *vt* **-held** [-ˈhld]; **-holding** : retener (fondos), aplazar (una decisión), negar (permiso, etc.)

within[1] [wɪðˈɪn, wɪθ-] *adv* : dentro

within[2] *prep* **1** : dentro de ⟨within the limits : dentro de los límites⟩ **2** (*in expressions of distance*) : a menos de ⟨within 10 miles of the ocean : a menos de 10 millas del mar⟩ **3** (*in expressions of time*) : dentro de ⟨within an hour : dentro de una hora⟩ ⟨within a month of her birthday : a poco menos de un mes de su cumpleaños⟩

without[1] [wɪðˈaʊt, wɪθ-] *adv* **1** OUTSIDE : fuera **2** **to do without** : pasar sin algo

without[2] *prep* **1** OUTSIDE : fuera de **2** : sin ⟨without fear : sin temor⟩ ⟨he left without his briefcase : se fue sin su portafolios⟩

withstand [wɪθˈstænd, wɪð-] *vt* **-stood** [-ˈstʊd]; **-standing** **1** BEAR : aguantar, soportar **2** RESIST : resistir, resistirse a

witless [ˈwɪtləs] *adj* : estúpido, tonto

witness[1] [ˈwɪtnəs] *vt* **1** SEE : presenciar, ver, ser testigo de **2** : atestiguar (una firma, etc.) — *vi* TESTIFY : atestiguar, testimoniar

witness[2] *n* **1** TESTIMONY : testimonio *m* ⟨to bear witness : atestiguar, testimoniar⟩ **2** : testigo *mf* ⟨witness for the prosecution : testigo de cargo⟩

witticism [ˈwɪt̬əˌsɪzəm] *n* : agudeza *f*, ocurrencia *f*

witty [ˈwɪt̬i] *adj* **-tier; -est** : ingenioso, ocurrente, gracioso

wives → **wife**

wizard [ˈwɪzərd] *n* **1** SORCERER : mago *m*, brujo *m*, hechicero *m* **2** : genio *m* ⟨a math wizard : un genio en matemáticas⟩

wizened [ˈwɪzənd, ˈwi:-] *adj* : arrugado, marchito

wobble[1] [ˈwɑbəl] *vi* **-bled; -bling** : bambolearse, tambalearse, temblar (dícese de la voz)

wobble[2] *n* : tambaleo *m*, bamboleo *m*

wobbly [ˈwɑbəli] *adj* : bamboleante, tambaleante, inestable

woe [ˈwo:] *n* **1** GRIEF, MISFORTUNE : desgracia *f*, infortunio *m*, aflicción *f* **2** **woes** *npl* TROUBLES : penas *fpl*, males *mpl*

woeful [ˈwo:fəl] *adj* **1** SORROWFUL : afligido, apenado, triste **2** UNFORTUNATE : desgraciado, infortunado **3** DEPLORABLE : lamentable

woke, woken → **wake[1]**

wolf[1] [ˈwʊlf] *vt or* **to wolf down** : engullir

wolf[2] *n, pl* **wolves** [ˈwʊlvz] : lobo *m*, -ba *f*

wolfram [ˈwʊlfrəm] → **tungsten**

wolverine [ˌwʊlvəˈri:n] *n* : glotón *m* (animal)

woman [ˈwʊmən] *n, pl* **women** [ˈwɪmən] : mujer *f*

womanhood [ˈwʊmənˌhʊd] *n* **1** : condición *f* de mujer **2** WOMEN : mujeres *fpl*

womanly [ˈwʊmənli] *adj* : femenino

womb [ˈwu:m] *n* : útero *m*, matriz *f*

won → **win**

wonder[1] [ˈwʌndər] *vi* **1** SPECULATE : preguntarse, pensar ⟨to wonder about : preguntarse por⟩ **2** MARVEL : asombrarse, maravillarse — *vt* : preguntarse ⟨I wonder if they're coming : me pregunto si vendrán⟩

wonder[2] *n* **1** MARVEL : maravilla *f*, milagro *m* ⟨to work wonders : hacer maravillas⟩ **2** AMAZEMENT : asombro *m*

wonderful [ˈwʌndərfəl] *adj* : maravilloso, estupendo

wonderfully [ˈwʌndərfəli] *adv* : maravillosamente, de maravilla

wonderland [ˈwʌndərˌlænd, -lənd] *n* : país *m* de las maravillas

wonderment [ˈwʌndərmənt] *n* : asombro *m*

wondrous [ˈwʌndrəs] → **wonderful**

wont[1] [ˈwɔnt, ˈwo:nt, ˈwɑnt] *adj* : acostumbrado, habituado

wont[2] *n* : hábito *m*, costumbre *f*

won't [ˈwo:nt] (*contraction of* **will not**) → **will[1]**

woo [ˈwu:] *vt* **1** COURT : cortejar **2** : buscar el apoyo de (clientes, votantes, etc.)

wood[1] [ˈwʊd] *adj* : de madera
wood[2] *n* **1** *or* **woods** *npl* FOREST : bosque *m* **2** : madera *f* (materia) **3** FIREWOOD : leña *f*
woodchuck [ˈwʊd,ʧʌk] *n* : marmota *f* de América
woodcut [ˈwʊd,kʌt] *n* **1** : plancha *f* de madera (para imprimir imágenes) **2** : grabado *m* en madera
woodcutter [ˈwʊd,kʌt̬ər] *n* : leñador *m*, -dora *f*
wooded [ˈwʊdəd] *adj* : arbolado, boscoso
wooden [ˈwʊdən] *adj* **1** : de madera ⟨a wooden cross : una cruz de madera⟩ **2** STIFF : rígido, inexpresivo (dícese del estilo, de la cara, etc.)
woodland [ˈwʊdlənd, -,lænd] *n* : bosque *m*
woodpecker [ˈwʊd,pɛkər] *n* : pájaro *m* carpintero
woodshed [ˈwʊd,ʃɛd] *n* : leñera *f*
woodsman [ˈwʊdzmən] → **woodcutter**
woodwind [ˈwʊd,wɪnd] *n* : instrumento *m* de viento de madera
woodworking [ˈwʊd,wərkɪŋ] *n* : carpintería *f*
woody [ˈwʊdi] *adj* **woodier; -est 1** → **wooded 2** : leñoso ⟨woody plants : plantas leñosas⟩ **3** : leñoso (dícese de la textura), a madera (dícese del aroma, etc.)
woof [ˈwʊf] → **weft**
wool [ˈwʊl] *n* : lana *f*
woolen[1] *or* **woollen** [ˈwʊlən] *adj* : de lana
woolen[2] *or* **woollen** *n* **1** : lana *f* (tela) **2 woolens** *npl* : prendas *fpl* de lana
woolly [ˈwʊli] *adj* **-lier; -est 1** : lanudo **2** CONFUSED : confuso, vago
woozy [ˈwuːzi] *adj* **-zier; -est** : mareado
word[1] [ˈwərd] *vt* : expresar, formular, redactar
word[2] *n* **1** : palabra *f*, vocablo *m*, voz *f* ⟨word for word : palabra por palabra⟩ ⟨in one's own words : en sus propias palabras⟩ ⟨words fail me : me quedo sin habla⟩ **2** REMARK : palabra *f* ⟨by word of mouth : de palabra⟩ ⟨to have a word with : hablar (dos palabras) con⟩ **3** COMMAND : orden *f* ⟨to give the word : dar la orden⟩ ⟨just say the word : no tienes que decirlo⟩ **4** MESSAGE, NEWS : noticias *fpl* ⟨is there any word from her? : ¿hay noticias de ella?⟩ ⟨to send word : mandar un recado⟩ **5** PROMISE : palabra *f* ⟨to keep one's word : cumplir uno su palabra⟩ **6 words** *npl* QUARREL : palabra *f*, riña *f* ⟨to have words with : tener unas palabras con, reñir con⟩ **7 words** *npl* TEXT : letra *f* (de una canción, etc.)
wordiness [ˈwərdinəs] *n* : verbosidad *f*
wording [ˈwərdɪŋ] *n* : redacción *f*, lenguaje *m* (de un documento)
word processing *n* : procesamiento *m* de textos
word processor *n* : procesador *m* de textos
wordy [ˈwərdi] *adj* **wordier; -est** : verboso, prolijo
wore → **wear**[1]
work[1] [ˈwərk] *v* **worked** [ˈwərkt] *or* **wrought** [ˈrɔt]; **working** *vt* **1** OPERATE : trabajar, operar ⟨to work a machine : operar una máquina⟩ **2** : lograr, conseguir (algo) con esfuerzo ⟨to work one's way up : lograr subir por sus propios esfuerzos⟩ **3** EFFECT : efectuar, llevar a cabo, obrar (milagros) **4** MAKE, SHAPE : elaborar, fabricar, formar ⟨a beautifully wrought vase : un florero bellamente elaborado⟩ **5 to work up** : estimular, excitar ⟨don't get worked up : no te agites⟩ — *vi* **1** LABOR : trabajar ⟨to work full-time : trabajar a tiempo completo⟩ **2** FUNCTION : funcionar, servir
work[2] *adj* : laboral
work[3] *n* **1** LABOR : trabajo *m*, labor *f* **2** EMPLOYMENT : trabajo *m*, empleo *m* **3** TASK : tarea *f*, faena *f* **4** DEED : obra *f*, labor *f* ⟨works of charity : obras de caridad⟩ **5** : obra *f* (de arte o literatura) **6** → **workmanship 7 works** *npl* FACTORY : fábrica *f* **8 works** *npl* MECHANISM : mecanismo *m*
workable [ˈwərkəbəl] *adj* **1** : explotable (dícese de una mina, etc.) **2** FEASIBLE : factible, realizable
workaday [ˈwərkə,deɪ] *adj* : ordinario, banal
workbench [ˈwərk,bɛnʧ] *n* : mesa *f* de trabajo
workday [ˈwərk,deɪ] *n* **1** : jornada *f* laboral **2** WEEKDAY : día *m* hábil, día *m* laborable
worker [ˈwərkər] *n* : trabajador *m*, -dora *f*; obrero *m*, -ra *f*
working [ˈwərkɪŋ] *adj* **1** : que trabaja ⟨working mothers : madres que trabajan⟩ ⟨the working class : la clase obrera⟩ **2** : de trabajo ⟨working hours : horas de trabajo⟩ **3** FUNCTIONING : que funciona, operativo **4** SUFFICIENT : suficiente ⟨a working majority : una mayoría suficiente⟩ ⟨working knowledge : conocimientos básicos⟩
workingman [ˈwərkɪŋ,mæn] *n, pl* **-men** [-mən, -,mɛn] : obrero *m*
workman [ˈwərkmən] *n, pl* **-men** [-mən, -,mɛn] **1** → **workingman 2** ARTISAN : artesano *m*
workmanlike [ˈwərkmən,laɪk] *adj* : bien hecho, competente
workmanship [ˈwərkmən,ʃɪp] *n* **1** WORK : ejecución *f*, trabajo *m* **2** CRAFTSMANSHIP : artesanía *f*, destreza *f*
workout [ˈwərk,aʊt] *n* : ejercicios *mpl* físicos, entrenamiento *m*
work out *vt* **1** DEVELOP, PLAN : idear, planear, desarrollar **2** RESOLVE : solucionar, resolver ⟨to work out the answer : calcular la solución⟩ — *vi* **1** TURN OUT : resultar **2** SUCCEED : lograr, dar resultado, salir bien **3** EXERCISE : hacer ejercicio

workroom [ˈwərkˌruːm, -ˌrʊm] *n* : taller *m*
workshop [ˈwərkˌʃɑp] *n* : taller *m* ⟨ceramics workshop : taller de cerámica⟩
workstation [ˈwərkˌsteɪʃən] *n* : estación *f* de trabajo (en informática)
world[1] [ˈwərld] *adj* : mundial, del mundo ⟨world championship : campeonato mundial⟩
world[2] *n* : mundo *m* ⟨around the world : alrededor del mundo⟩ ⟨a world of possibilities : un mundo de posibilidades⟩ ⟨to think the world of someone : tener a alguien en alta estima⟩ ⟨to be worlds apart : no tener nada que ver (uno con otro)⟩
worldly [ˈwərldli] *adj* **1** : mundano ⟨wordly goods : bienes materiales⟩ **2** SOPHISTICATED : sofisticado, de mundo
worldwide[1] [ˈwərldˈwaɪd] *adv* : mundialmente, en todo el mundo
worldwide[2] *adj* : global, mundial
World Wide Web *n* : World Wide Web *f*
worm[1] [ˈwərm] *vi* CRAWL : arrastrarse, deslizarse (como gusano) — *vt* **1** : desparasitar (un animal) **2 to worm one's way into** : introducirse en ⟨he wormed his way into her confidence : se ganó su confianza⟩ **3 to worm something out of someone** : sonsacarle algo a alguien
worm[2] *n* **1** : gusano *m*, lombriz *f* **2 worms** *npl* : lombrices *fpl* (parásitos)
wormy [ˈwərmi] *adj* **wormier; -est** : infestado de gusanos
worn *pp* → **wear**[1]
worn–out [ˈwornˈaʊt] *adj* **1** USED : gastado, desgastado **2** TIRED : agotado
worried [ˈwərid] *adj* : inquieto, preocupado
worrier [ˈwəriər] *n* : persona *f* que se preocupa mucho
worrisome [ˈwərisəm] *adj* **1** DISTURBING : preocupante, inquietante **2** : que se preocupa mucho (dícese de una persona)
worry[1] [ˈwəri] *v* **-ried; -rying** *vt* : preocupar, inquietar — *vi* : preocuparse, inquietarse, angustiarse
worry[2] *n, pl* **-ries** : preocupación *f*, inquietud *f*, angustia *f*
worse[1] [ˈwərs] *adv* (*comparative of* **bad** *or of* **ill**) : peor
worse[2] *adj* (*comparative of* **bad** *or of* **ill**) : peor ⟨from bad to worse : de mal en peor⟩ ⟨to get worse : empeorar⟩ ⟨to feel worse : sentirse peor⟩
worse[3] *n* : estado *m* peor ⟨to take a turn for the worse : ponerse peor⟩ ⟨so much the worse : tanto peor⟩
worsen [ˈwərsən] *vt* : empeorar — *vi* : empeorar(se)
worship[1] [ˈwərʃəp] *v* **-shiped** *or* **-shipped; -shiping** *or* **-shipping** *vt* : adorar, venerar ⟨to worship God : adorar a Dios⟩ — *vi* : practicar una religión
worship[2] *n* : adoración *f*, culto *m*
worshiper *or* **worshipper** [ˈwərʃəpər] *n* : devoto *m*, -ta *f*; adorador *m*, -dora *f*
worst[1] [ˈwərst] *vt* DEFEAT : derrotar
worst[2] *adv* (*superlative of* **ill** *or of* **bad** *or* **badly**) : peor ⟨the worst dressed of all : el peor vestido de todos⟩
worst[3] *adj* (*superlative of* **bad** *or of* **ill**) : peor ⟨the worst movie : la peor película⟩
worst[4] *n* **the worst** : lo peor, el (la) peor ⟨the worst is over : ya ha pasado lo peor⟩
worsted [ˈwʊstəd, ˈwərstəd] *n* : estambre *m*
worth[1] [ˈwərθ] *n* **1** : valor *m* (monetario) ⟨ten dollars' worth of gas : diez dólares de gasolina⟩ **2** MERIT : valor *m*, mérito *m*, valía *f* ⟨an employee of great worth : un empleado de gran valía⟩
worth[2] *prep* **to be worth** : valer ⟨her holdings are worth a fortune : sus propiedades valen una fortuna⟩ ⟨it's not worth it : no vale la pena⟩
worthiness [ˈwərðinəs] *n* : mérito *m*
worthless [ˈwərθləs] *adj* **1** : sin valor ⟨worthless trinkets : chucherías sin valor⟩ **2** USELESS : inútil
worthwhile [wərθˈhwaɪl] *adj* : que vale la pena
worthy [ˈwərði] *adj* **-thier; -est 1** : digno ⟨worthy of promotion : digno de un ascenso⟩ **2** COMMENDABLE : meritorio, encomiable
would [ˈwʊd] *past of* **will 1** (*expressing preference*) ⟨I would rather go alone than with her : preferiría ir sola que con ella⟩ **2** (*expressing intent*) ⟨those who would ban certain books : aquellos que prohibirían ciertos libros⟩ **3** (*expressing habitual action*) ⟨he would often take his kids to the park : solía llevar a sus hijos al parque⟩ **4** (*expressing contingency*) ⟨I would go if I had the money : iría yo si tuviera el dinero⟩ **5** (*expressing probability*) ⟨she would have won if she hadn't tripped : habría ganado si no hubiera tropezado⟩ **6** (*expressing a request*) ⟨would you kindly help me with this? : ¿tendría la bondad de ayudarme con esto?⟩
would–be [ˈwʊdˈbiː] *adj* : potencial ⟨a would-be celebrity : un aspirante a celebridad⟩
wouldn't [ˈwʊdˀnt] (*contraction of* **would not**) → **would**
wound[1] [ˈwuːnd] *vt* : herir
wound[2] *n* : herida *f*
wound[3] [ˈwaʊnd] → **wind**[2]
wove, woven → **weave**[1]
wow [ˈwaʊ] *interj* : ¡guau!, ¡híjole! *Mex*, ¡hala! *Spain*
wrangle[1] [ˈræŋgəl] *vi* **-gled; -gling** : discutir, reñir ⟨to wrangle over : discutir por⟩
wrangle[2] *n* : riña *f*, disputa *f*
wrap[1] [ˈræp] *v* **wrapped; wrapping** *vt* **1** COVER : envolver, cubrir ⟨to wrap a package : envolver un paquete⟩

⟨wrapped in mystery : envuelto en misterio⟩ **2** ENCIRCLE : rodear, ceñir ⟨to wrap one's arms around someone : estrechar a alguien⟩ **3 to wrap up** FINISH : darle fin a (algo) — *vi* **1** COIL : envolverse, enroscarse **2 to wrap up** DRESS : abrigarse ⟨wrap up warmly : abrígate bien⟩

wrap[2] *n* **1** WRAPPER : envoltura *f* **2** : prenda *f* que envuelve (como un chal, una bata, etc.)

wrapper [ˈræpər] *n* : envoltura *f*, envoltorio *m*

wrapping [ˈræpɪŋ] *n* : envoltura *f*, envoltorio *m*

wrath [ˈræθ] *n* : ira *f*, cólera *f*

wrathful [ˈræθfəl] *adj* : iracundo

wreak [ˈriːk] *vt* : infligir, causar ⟨to wreak havoc : crear caos, causar estragos⟩

wreath [ˈriːθ] *n, pl* **wreaths** [ˈriːðz, ˈriːθs] : corona *f* (de flores, etc.)

wreathe [ˈriːð] *vt* **wreathed; wreathing 1** ADORN : coronar (de flores, etc.) **2** ENVELOP : envolver ⟨wreathed in mist : envuelto en niebla⟩

wreck[1] [ˈrɛk] *vt* : destruir, arruinar, estrellar (un automóvil), naufragar (un barco)

wreck[2] *n* **1** WRECKAGE : restos *mpl* (de un buque naufragado, un avión siniestrado, etc.) **2** RUIN : ruina *f*, desastre *m* ⟨this place is a wreck! : ¡este lugar está hecho un desastre!⟩ ⟨to be a nervous wreck : tener los nervios destrozados⟩

wreckage [ˈrɛkɪʤ] *n* : restos *mpl* (de un buque naufragado, un avión siniestrado, etc.), ruinas *fpl* (de un edificio)

wrecker [ˈrɛkər] *n* **1** TOW TRUCK : grúa *f* **2** : desguazador *m* (de autos, barcos, etc.), demoledor *m* (de edificios)

wren [ˈrɛn] *n* : chochín *m*

wrench[1] [ˈrɛnʧ] *vt* **1** PULL : arrancar (de un tirón) **2** SPRAIN, TWIST : torcerse (un tobillo, un músculo, etc.)

wrench[2] *n* **1** TUG : tirón *m*, jalón *m* **2** SPRAIN : torcedura *f* **3** *or* **monkey wrench** : llave *f* inglesa

wrest [ˈrɛst] *vt* : arrancar

wrestle[1] [ˈrɛsəl] *v* **-tled; -tling** *vi* **1** : luchar, practicar la lucha (en deportes) **2** STRUGGLE : luchar ⟨to wrestle with a dilemma : lidiar con un dilema⟩ — *vt* : luchar contra

wrestle[2] *n* STRUGGLE : lucha *f*

wrestler [ˈrɛsələr] *n* : luchador *m*, -dora *f*

wrestling [ˈrɛsəlɪŋ] *n* : lucha *f*

wretch [ˈrɛʧ] *n* : infeliz *mf*; desgraciado *m*, -da *f*

wretched [ˈrɛʧəd] *adj* **1** MISERABLE, UNHAPPY : desdichado, afligido ⟨I feel wretched : me siento muy mal⟩ **2** UNFORTUNATE : miserable, desgraciado, lastimoso ⟨wretched weather : tiempo espantoso⟩ **3** INFERIOR : inferior, malo

wretchedly [ˈrɛʧədli] *adv* : miserablemente, lamentablemente

wriggle [ˈrɪgəl] *vi* **-gled; -gling** : retorcerse, menearse

wring [ˈrɪŋ] *vt* **wrung** [ˈrʌŋ]; **wringing 1** *or* **to wring out** : escurrir, exprimir (el lavado) **2** EXTRACT : arrancar, sacar (por la fuerza) **3** TWIST : torcer, retorcer **4 to wring someone's heart** : partirle el corazón a alguien

wringer [ˈrɪŋər] *n* : escurridor *m*

wrinkle[1] [ˈrɪŋkəl] *v* **-kled; -kling** *vt* : arrugar — *vi* : arrugarse

wrinkle[2] *n* : arruga *f*

wrinkly [ˈrɪŋkəli] *adj* **wrinklier; -est** : arrugado

wrist [ˈrɪst] *n* **1** : muñeca *f* (en anatomía) **2** *or* **wristband** [ˈrɪst-ˌbænd] CUFF : puño *m*

writ [ˈrɪt] *n* : orden *f* (judicial)

write [ˈraɪt] *v* **wrote** [ˈroːt]; **written** [ˈrɪtən]; **writing** : escribir

write down *vt* : apuntar, anotar

write off *vt* CANCEL : cancelar

writer [ˈraɪt̬ər] *n* : escritor *m*, -tora *f*

writhe [ˈraɪð] *vi* **writhed; writhing** : retorcerse

writing [ˈraɪt̬ɪŋ] *n* **1** : escritura *f* **2** HANDWRITING : letra *f* **3 writings** *npl* WORKS : escritos *mpl*, obra *f*

wrong[1] [ˈrɔŋ] *vt* **wronged; wronging** : ofender, ser injusto con

wrong[2] *adv* : mal, incorrectamente

wrong[3] *adj* **wronger** [ˈrɔŋər]; **wrongest** [ˈrɔŋəst] **1** EVIL, SINFUL : malo, injusto, inmoral **2** IMPROPER, UNSUITABLE : inadecuado, inapropiado, malo **3** INCORRECT : incorrecto, erróneo, malo ⟨a wrong answer : una mala respuesta⟩ **4 to be wrong** : equivocarse, estar equivocado

wrong[4] *n* **1** INJUSTICE : injusticia *f*, mal *m* **2** OFFENSE : ofensa *f*, agravio *m* (en derecho) **3 to be in the wrong** : haber hecho mal, estar equivocado

wrongdoer [ˈrɔŋˌduːər] *n* : malhechor *m*, -chora *f*

wrongdoing [ˈrɔŋˌduːɪŋ] *n* : fechoría *f*, maldad *f*

wrongful [ˈrɔŋfəl] *adj* **1** UNJUST : injusto **2** UNLAWFUL : ilegal

wrongly [ˈrɔŋli] *adv* **1** : injustamente **2** INCORRECTLY : erróneamente, incorrectamente

wrote → **write**

wrought [ˈrɔt] *adj* **1** SHAPED : formado, forjado ⟨wrought iron : hierro forjado⟩ **2** *or* **wrought up** : agitado, excitado

wrung → **wring**

wry [ˈraɪ] *adj* **wrier** [ˈraɪər]; **wriest** [ˈraɪəst] **1** TWISTED : torcido ⟨a wry neck : un cuello torcido⟩ **2** : irónico, sardónico (dícese del humor)

X

x¹ *n, pl* **x's** *or* **xs** ['ɛksəz] **1** : vigésima cuarta letra del alfabeto inglés **2** : incógnita *f* (en matemáticas)
x² ['ks] *vt* **x–ed** ['ɛkst]; **x–ing** *or* **x'ing** ['ɛksiŋ] DELETE : tachar
xenon ['zi:ˌnɑn, 'zɛ-] *n* : xenón *m*
xenophobia [ˌzɛnə'fo:biə, ˌzi:-] *n* : xenofobia *f*
Xmas ['krɪsməs] *n* : Navidad *f*
x–ray ['ɛksˌreɪ] *vt* : radiografiar
X ray ['ɛksˌreɪ] *n* **1** : rayo *m* X **2** *or* **X–ray photograph** : radiografía *f*
xylophone ['zaɪləˌfo:n] *n* : xilófono *m*

Y

y ['waɪ] *n, pl* **y's** *or* **ys** ['waɪz] : vigésima quinta letra del alfabeto inglés
yacht¹ ['jɑt] *vi* : navegar (a vela), ir en yate ⟨to go yachting : irse a navegar⟩
yacht² *n* : yate *m*
yak ['jæk] *n* : yac *m*
yam ['jæm] *n* **1** : ñame *m* **2** SWEET POTATO : batata *f*, boniato *m*
yank¹ ['jæŋk] *vt* : tirar de, jalar, darle un tirón a
yank² *n* : tirón *m*
Yankee ['jæŋki] *n* : yanqui *mf*
yap¹ ['jæp] *vi* **yapped; yapping** **1** BARK, YELP : ladrar, gañir **2** CHATTER : cotorrear *fam*, parlotear *fam*
yap² *n* : ladrido *m*, gañido *m*
yard ['jɑrd] *n* **1** : yarda *f* (medida) **2** SPAR : verga *f* (de un barco) **3** COURTYARD : patio *m* **4** : jardín *m* (de una casa) **5** : depósito *m* (de mercancías, etc.)
yardage ['jɑrdɪʤ] *n* : medida *f* en yardas
yardarm ['jɑrdˌɑrm] *n* : penol *m*
yardstick ['jɑrdˌstɪk] *n* **1** : vara *f* **2** CRITERION : criterio *m*, norma *f*
yarn ['jɑrn] *n* **1** : hilado *m* **2** TALE : historia *f*, cuento *m* ⟨to spin a yarn : inventar una historia⟩
yawl ['jɔl] *n* : yola *f*
yawn¹ ['jɔn] *vi* **1** : bostezar **2** OPEN : abrirse
yawn² *n* : bostezo *m*
ye ['ji:] *pron* : vosotros, vosotras
yea¹ ['jeɪ] *adv* YES : sí
yea² *n* : voto *m* a favor
year ['jɪr] *n* **1** : año *m* ⟨last year : el año pasado⟩ ⟨he's ten years old : tiene diez años⟩ **2** : curso *m*, año *m* (escolar) **3** **years** *npl* AGES : siglos *mpl*, años *mpl* ⟨I haven't seen them in years : hace siglos que no los veo⟩
yearbook ['jɪrˌbʊk] *n* : anuario *m*
yearling ['jɪrlɪŋ, 'jərlən] *n* : animal *m* menor de dos año
yearly¹ ['jɪrli] *adv* : cada año, anualmente
yearly² *adj* : anual
yearn ['jərn] *vi* : anhelar, ansiar
yearning ['jərnɪŋ] *n* : anhelo *m*
yeast ['ji:st] *n* : levadura *f*
yell¹ ['jɛl] *vi* : gritar, chillar — *vt* : gritar
yell² *n* : grito *m*, alarido *m* ⟨to let out a yell : dar un grito⟩
yellow¹ ['jɛlo] *vi* : ponerse amarillo, volverse amarillo
yellow² *adj* **1** : amarillo **2** COWARDLY : cobarde
yellow³ *n* : amarillo *m*
yellow fever *n* : fiebre *f* amarilla
yellowish ['jɛloɪʃ] *adj* : amarillento
yellow jacket *n* : avispa *f* (con rayas amarillas)
yelp¹ ['jɛlp] *vi* : dar un gañido (dícese de un animal), dar un grito (dícese de una persona)
yelp² *n* : gañido *m* (de un animal), grito *m* (de una persona)
yen ['jɛn] *n* **1** DESIRE : deseo *m*, ganas *fpl* **2** : yen *m* (moneda japonesa)
yeoman ['jo:mən] *n, pl* **-men** [-mən, -mɛn] : suboficial *mf* de marina
yes¹ ['jɛs] *adv* : sí ⟨to say yes : decir que sí⟩
yes² *n* : sí *m*
yesterday¹ ['jɛstərˌdeɪ, -di] *adv* : ayer
yesterday² *n* **1** : ayer *m* **2 the day before yesterday** : anteayer
yet¹ ['jɛt] *adv* **1** BESIDES, EVEN : aún ⟨yet more problems : más problemas aún⟩ ⟨yet again : otra vez⟩ **2** SO FAR : aún, todavía ⟨not yet : todavía no⟩ ⟨as yet : hasta ahora, todavía⟩ **3** : ya ⟨has he come yet? : ¿ya ha venido?⟩ **4** EVENTUALLY : todavía, algún día **5** NEVERTHELESS : sin embargo
yet² *conj* : pero
yew ['ju:] *n* : tejo *m*
yield¹ ['ji:ld] *vt* **1** SURRENDER : ceder ⟨to yield the right of way : ceder el paso⟩ **2** PRODUCE : producir, dar, rendir (en finanzas) — *vi* **1** GIVE : ceder ⟨to yield under pressure : ceder por la presión⟩ **2** GIVE IN, SURRENDER : ceder, rendirse, entregarse
yield² *n* : rendimiento *m*, rédito *m* (en finanzas)
yin and yang ['jɪnænd'jæŋ, -'jɑŋ] *n* : yin *m* y yang *f*
yodel¹ ['jo:dəl] *vi* **-deled** *or* **-delled; -deling** *or* **-delling** : cantar al estilo tirolés
yodel² *n* : canción *f* al estilo tirolés
yoga ['jo:gə] *n* : yoga *m*
yogurt ['jo:gərt] *n* : yogur *m*, yogurt *m*
yoke¹ ['jo:k] *vt* **yoked; yoking** : uncir (animales)
yoke² *n* **1** : yugo *m* (para uncir animales)

⟨the yoke of oppression : el yugo de la opresión⟩ **2** TEAM : yunta *f* (de bueyes) **3** : canesú *m* (de ropa)

yokel [ˈjoːkəl] *n* : palurdo *m*, -da *f*

yolk [ˈjoːk] *n* : yema *f* (de un huevo)

Yom Kippur [ˌjoːmkɪˈpʊr, ˌjɑm-, -ˈkɪpər] *n* : el Día *m* del Perdón, Yom Kippur

yon [ˈjɑn] → **yonder**

yonder[1] [ˈjɑndər] *adv* : allá ⟨over yonder : allá lejos⟩

yonder[2] *adj* : aquel ⟨yonder hill : aquella colina⟩

yore [ˈjoːr] *n* **in days of yore** : antaño

you [ˈjuː] *pron* **1** (*used as subject — familiar*) : tú; vos (*in some Latin American countries*); ustedes *pl*; vosotros, vosotras *pl Spain* **2** (*used as subject — formal*) : usted, ustedes *pl* **3** (*used as indirect object — familiar*) : te, les *pl* (se *before lo, la, los, las*), os *pl Spain* ⟨he told it to you : te lo contó⟩ ⟨I gave them to (all of, both of) you : se los di⟩ **4** (*used as indirect object — formal*) : lo (*Spain sometimes* le), la; los (*Spain sometimes* les), las *pl* **5** (*used after a preposition — familiar*) : ti; vos (*in some Latin American countries*); ustedes *pl*; vosotros, vosotras *pl Spain* **6** (*used after a preposition — formal*) : usted, ustedes *pl* **7** (*used as an impersonal subject*) ⟨you never know : nunca se sabe⟩ ⟨you have to be aware : hay que ser consciente⟩ ⟨you mustn't do that : eso no se hace⟩ **8 with you** (*familiar*) : contigo; con ustedes *pl*; con vosotros, con vosotras *pl Spain* **9 with you** (*formal*) : con usted, con ustedes *pl*

you'd [ˈjuːd, ˈjʊd] (*contraction of* **you had** *or* **you would**) → **have, would**

you'll [ˈjuːl, ˈjʊl] (*contraction of* **you shall** *or* **you will**) → **shall, will**

young[1] [ˈjʌŋ] *adj* **younger** [ˈjʌŋgər]; **youngest** [-gəst] **1** : joven, pequeño, menor ⟨young people : los jóvenes⟩ ⟨my younger brother : mi hermano menor⟩ ⟨she is the youngest : es la más pequeña⟩ **2** FRESH, NEW : tierno (dícese de las verduras), joven (dícese del vino) **3** YOUTHFUL : joven, juvenil

young[2] *npl* : jóvenes *mfpl* (de los humanos), crías *fpl* (de los animales)

youngster [ˈjʌŋkstər] *n* **1** YOUTH : joven *mf* **2** CHILD : chico *m*, -ca *f*; niño *m*, -ña *f*

your [ˈjʊr, ˈjoːr, jər] *adj* **1** (*familiar singular*) : tu ⟨your cat : tu gato⟩ ⟨your books : tus libros⟩ ⟨wash your hands : lávate las manos⟩ **2** (*familiar plural*) : su, vuestro *Spain* ⟨your car : su coche, el coche de ustedes⟩ **3** (*formal*) : su ⟨your houses : sus casas⟩ **4** (*impersonal*) : el, la, los, las ⟨on your left : a la izquierda⟩

you're [ˈjʊr, ˈjoːr, ˈjər, ˈjuːər] (*contraction of* **you are**) → **be**

yours [ˈjʊrz, ˈjoːrz] *pron* **1** (*belonging to one person — familiar*) : (el) tuyo, (la) tuya, (los) tuyos, (las) tuyas ⟨those are mine; yours are there : ésas son mías; las tuyas están allí⟩ ⟨is this one yours? : ¿éste es tuyo?⟩ **2** (*belonging to more than one person — familiar*) : (el) suyo, (la) suya, (los) suyos, (las) suyas; (el) vuestro, (la) vuestra, (los) vuestros, (las) vuestras *Spain* ⟨our house and yours : nuestra casa y la suya⟩ **3** (*formal*) : (el) suyo, (la) suya, (los) suyos, (las) suyas

yourself [jərˈsɛlf] *pron, pl* **yourselves** [-ˈslvz] **1** (*used reflexively — familiar*) : te, se *pl*, os *pl Spain* ⟨wash yourself : lávate⟩ ⟨you dressed yourselves : se vistieron, os vestisteis⟩ **2** (*used reflexively — formal*) : se ⟨did you hurt yourself? : ¿se hizo daño?⟩ ⟨you've gotten yourselves dirty : se ensuciaron⟩ **3** (*used for emphasis*) : tú mismo, tú misma; usted mismo, usted misma; ustedes mismos, ustedes mismas *pl*; vosotros mismos, vosotras mismas *pl Spain* ⟨you did it yourselves? : ¿lo hicieron ustedes mismos?, ¿lo hicieron por sí solos?⟩

youth [ˈjuːθ] *n, pl* **youths** [ˈjuːðz, ˈjuːθs] **1** : juventud *f* ⟨in her youth : en su juventud⟩ **2** BOY : joven *m* **3** : jóvenes *mfpl*, juventud *f* ⟨the youth of our city : los jóvenes de nuestra ciudad⟩

youthful [ˈjuːθfəl] *adj* **1** : de juventud **2** YOUNG : joven **3** JUVENILE : juvenil

youthfulness [ˈjuːθfəlnəs] *n* : juventud *f*

you've [ˈjuːv] (*contraction of* **you have**) → **have**

yowl[1] [ˈjæʊl] *vi* : aullar

yowl[2] *n* : aullido *m*

yo–yo [ˈjoːˌjoː] *n, pl* **-yos** : yoyo *m*, yoyó *m*

yucca [ˈjʌkə] *n* : yuca *f*

Yugoslavian [ˌjuːgoˈslɑviən] *n* : yugoslavo *m*, -va *f* — **Yugoslavian** *adj*

yule [ˈjuːl] *n* CHRISTMAS : Navidad *f*

yuletide [ˈjuːlˌtaɪd] *n* : Navidades *fpl*

yuppie [ˈjʌpi] *n* : yuppy *mf*

Z

z [ˈziː] *n, pl* **z's** *or* **zs** : vigésima sexta letra del alfabeto inglés
Zambian [ˈzæmbiən] *n* : zambiano *m*, -na *f* — **Zambian** *adj*
zany¹ [ˈzeɪni] *adj* **-nier; -est** : alocado, disparatado
zany² *n, pl* **-nies** : bufón *m*, -fona *f*
zap¹ [ˈzæp] *vt* **zapped; zapping 1** ELIMINATE : eliminar **2** : enviar o transportar rápidamente — *vi* : ir rápidamente
zap² *n* **1** ZEST : sabor *m*, sazón *f* **2** BLAST : golpe *m* fuerte
zap³ *interj* : ¡zas!
zeal [ˈziːl] *n* : fervor *m*, celo *m*, entusiasmo *m*
zealot [ˈzɛlət] *n* : fanático *m*, -ca *f*
zealous [ˈzɛləs] *adj* : celoso — **zealously** *adv*
zebra [ˈziːbrə] *n* : cebra *f*
zenith [ˈziːnəθ] *n* **1** : cenit *m* (en astronomía) **2** PEAK : apogeo *m*, cenit *m* ⟨at the zenith of his career : en el apogeo de su carrera⟩
zephyr [ˈzɛfər] *n* : céfiro *m*
zeppelin [ˈzɛplən, -pəlɪn] *n* : zepelín *m*
zero¹ [ˈziːro, ˈzɪro] *vi* **to zero in on** : apuntar hacia, centrarse en (un problema, etc.)
zero² *adj* : cero, nulo ⟨zero degrees : cero grados⟩ ⟨zero opportunities : oportunidades nulas⟩
zero³ *n, pl* **-ros** : cero *m* ⟨below zero : bajo cero⟩
zest [ˈzɛst] *n* **1** GUSTO : entusiasmo *m*, brío *m* **2** FLAVOR : sabor *m*, sazón *f*
zestful [ˈzɛstfəl] *adj* : brioso
zigzag¹ [ˈzɪgˌzæg] *vi* **-zagged; -zagging** : zigzaguear
zigzag² *adv & adj* : en zigzag
zigzag³ *n* : zigzag *m*
Zimbabwean [zɪmˈbɑbwiən, -bweɪ-] *n* : zimbabuense *mf* — **Zimbabwean** *adj*
zinc [ˈzɪŋk] *n* : cinc *m*, zinc *m*
zing [ˈzɪŋ] *n* **1** HISS, HUM : zumbido *m*, silbido *m* **2** ENERGY : brío *m*
zinnia [ˈzɪniə, ˈziː-, -njə] *n* : zinnia *f*
Zionism [ˈzaɪəˌnɪzəm] *n* : sionismo *m*
Zionist [ˈzaɪənɪst] *n* : sionista *mf*
zip¹ [ˈzɪp] *v* **zipped; zipping** *vt or* **to zip up** : cerrar el cierre de — *vi* **1** SPEED : pasarse volando ⟨the day zipped by : el día se pasó volando⟩ **2** HISS, HUM : silbar, zumbar
zip² *n* **1** ZING : zumbido *m*, silbido *m* **2** ENERGY : brío *m*
zip code *n* : código *m* postal
zipper [ˈzɪpər] *n* : cierre *m*, cremallera *f*, zíper *m CA, Mex*
zippy [ˈzɪpi] *adj* **-pier; -est** : brioso
zircon [ˈzərˌkɑn] *n* : circón *m*, zircón *m*
zirconium [ˌzərˈkoːniəm] *n* : circonio *m*
zither [ˈzɪðər, -θər] *n* : cítara *f*
zodiac [ˈzoːdiˌæk] *n* : zodíaco *m*
zombie [ˈzɑmbi] *n* : zombi *mf*, zombie *mf*
zone¹ [ˈzoːn] *vt* **zoned; zoning 1** : dividir en zonas **2** DESIGNATE : declarar ⟨to zone for business : declarar como zona comercial⟩
zone² *n* : zona *f*
zoo [ˈzuː] *n, pl* **zoos** : zoológico *m*, zoo *m*
zoological [ˌzoːəˈlɑʤɪkəl, ˌzuːə-] *adj* : zoológico
zoologist [zoˈɑləʤɪst, zuː-] *n* : zoólogo *m*, -ga *f*
zoology [zoˈɑləʤi, zuː-] *n* : zoología *f*
zoom¹ [ˈzuːm] *vi* **1** : zumbar, ir volando ⟨to zoom past : pasar volando⟩ **2** CLIMB : elevarse ⟨the plane zoomed up : el avión se elevó⟩
zoom² *n* **1** : zumbido *m* ⟨the zoom of an engine : el zumbido de un motor⟩ **2** : subida *f* vertical (de un avión, etc.) **3** *or* **zoom lens** : zoom *m*
zucchini [zʊˈkiːni] *n, pl* **-ni** *or* **-nis** : calabacín *m*, calabacita *f Mex*
Zulu [ˈzuːluː] *n* **1** : zulú *mf* **2** : zulú *m* (idioma) — **Zulu** *adj*
zygote [ˈzaɪˌgoːt] *n* : zigoto *m*, cigoto *m*

100 Important English Idioms
100 Frases idiomáticas importantes en inglés

ace

(to have) an ace in the hole → ***(tener) un as bajo la manga***
: a powerful and often secret advantage or strategy that can be used if needed ⟨*his popularity among elderly voters gives him an ace in the hole for the coming election*⟩

(to come/be) within an ace of → ***(estar) a un paso de (lograr o sufrir algo)***
: (to be) very close to experiencing something either positive or negative ⟨*they came within an ace of winning the championship*⟩

alley

to be right up one's alley → ***ser lo mío/tuyo (etc.)***
: to fit one's interest or strengths ⟨*I love books, so volunteering at the library is right up my alley*⟩

ant

(to have/get) ants in one's pants → ***(estar) impaciente/inquieto***
: (to experience) a strong feeling of excitement and impatience ⟨*the children got ants in their pants waiting for the show to begin*⟩

apart

to come apart at the seams → ***venirse abajo***
: to fail, break apart, or be in very bad condition ⟨*this house is coming apart at the seams*⟩

apple

the apple of one's eye → ***la niña de los ojos de alguien***
: a person or thing that one cherishes ⟨*his daughter is the apple of his eye*⟩

arm

(to cost) an arm and a leg → ***(costar) un ojo de la cara***
: (to be) a very large amount of money ⟨*it's a reliable car, and it doesn't cost an arm and a leg*⟩

ax

(to have) an ax to grind → ***(tener) intereses personales (en algo)***
: (to have) a hidden and often selfish purpose for doing something ⟨*she claims she has no ax to grind in criticizing the proposal*⟩

ball

to drop the ball → ***fallar***
: to make a mistake especially by not doing something important ⟨*I think the mayor dropped the ball by not hiring more police officers*⟩

to start the ball rolling → ***poner (algo) en marcha***
: to begin an activity or process ⟨*she tried to get the ball rolling by asking him a few questions*⟩

ball game

a whole new ball game → ***se viró la tortilla***
: a situation or activity that has changed ⟨*dealing with the economy is a whole new ball game now*⟩

bar

to raise/lower the bar → ***subir/bajar el nivel de lo exigido***
: to change a standard used to judge success ⟨*the police department raised the bar for hiring future officers*⟩

bark

to bark up the wrong tree → ***errar, equivocarse***
: to try to do something in a way that will not be successful ⟨*she claims researchers are barking up the wrong tree by focusing on conventional treatments*⟩

beans

to spill the beans → ***descubrir el pastel***

: to reveal secret information ⟨*the party is a surprise, so don't spill the beans*⟩

belt

to tighten one's belt → ***apretarse el cinturón/la correa, ahorrar***

: to make changes in order to save money ⟨*companies are tightening their belts during the recession*⟩

birds

to be birds of a feather → ***ser tal para cual***

: to be of the same kind or nature ⟨*those two guys are birds of a feather*⟩

bite

to bite off more than one can chew → ***tratar de abarcar demasiado***

: to take on more responsibility than one can handle ⟨*I really bit off more than I could chew when I took on this project*⟩

boat

to miss the boat → ***perder el tren***

: to fail to make use of an opportunity ⟨*if I don't act now I could miss the boat on this investment*⟩

to rock the boat → ***hacer olas***

: to cause trouble by changing or trying to change a situation that others are comfortable with ⟨*the system isn't perfect, but nobody wants to rock the boat*⟩

bone

to have a bone to pick (with someone) → ***tener que ajustar cuentas (con alguien)***

: to have something to argue or complain about (with someone) ⟨*I have a bone to pick with you about your barking dog*⟩

burn

to burn a hole in one's pocket → ***darle ganas (a alguien) de gastar dinero***

: to cause an eagerness to spend money one has ⟨*he just got his tax refund, and it's burning a hole in his pocket*⟩

to burn the midnight oil → ***quemarse las pestañas/cejas***

: to work or study until very late at night ⟨*the students have been burning the midnight oil preparing for exams*⟩

bush

to beat around the bush → ***andarse con rodeos***

: to avoid saying something by talking about other things ⟨*stop beating around the bush and tell me why you're here*⟩

candle

to not hold a candle to (someone or something) → ***no llegar ni a la suela del zapato (a alguien), no poder comparar con (algo)***

: to not be on the same level as or as good as (something or someone) ⟨*this new movie doesn't hold a candle to the original*⟩

castles

to build castles in the air → ***construir castillos en el aire***

: to focus on a dream, plan, or idea that has little chance of success ⟨*he's just building castles in the air if he thinks he can open a restaurant without any money*⟩

chew

to chew the fat → ***charlar, platicar***

: to talk together in a friendly or casual way ⟨*they would sit for hours and chew the fat*⟩

chicken

to count one's chickens before they hatch → ***vender la piel del oso antes de cazarlo***

: to plan for something desired before knowing it will definitely happen ⟨*don't count your chickens before they hatch—we don't know yet if she will accept our offer*⟩

chop

to bust one's chops → ***molestar a alguien a modo de chiste***

: to tease or criticize in a playful way ⟨*my boss likes to bust my chops when I don't look sharp*⟩

class

to be in a class by oneself → ***ser único/raro***

: to be very different from others in a good or bad way ⟨*there have been a lot of corporate scandals, but this one is in a class by itself*⟩

cleaner

to take (someone) to the cleaner's → ***dejar limpio/pelado (a alguien), dejar sin dinero (a alguien)***

: to get all or most of someone's money or possessions often in an unfair way ⟨*his former business partner took him to the cleaners, leaving him with all the bills*⟩

color

to show one's true colors → ***revelarse como (cierto tipo de persona)***

: to reveal one's real nature or character ⟨*he seemed nice at first, but he showed his true colors during the crisis*⟩

contention

(to be a) bone of contention → ***(ser la) nota discordante, (ser la) manzana de la discordia***

: (to be) something that causes anger and disagreement ⟨*the tariffs have been a bone of contention between the two nations*⟩

corner

to back/paint oneself into a corner → ***meterse en camisa de once varas, meterse en un lìo***

: to put oneself into a difficult position ⟨*the candidate backed/painted himself into a corner by proposing a tax increase*⟩

cry

to cry wolf → ***dar la voz de alarma (sin causa)***

: make people think there is danger when there is really none ⟨*news organizations have been warned not to cry wolf*⟩

dark

to keep (someone) in the dark → ***ocultarle algo (a alguien)***

: to keep (someone) in a state of not knowing about something ⟨*the public was kept in the dark about the agreement*⟩

drummer

to march to the beat of a different drummer → ***ser poco convencional***

: to think, live, or behave in an unusual way ⟨*his strange behavior was no surprise—he had always marched to the beat of a different drummer*⟩

duck

to take to something like a duck (takes) to water → ***tener un talento innato para algo***

: to learn something very quickly or easily ⟨*she took to dancing like a duck (takes) to water*⟩

ear

to play it by ear → ***improvisar, hacer algo sobre la marcha***

: to do something without special preparation; improvise ⟨*I don't know how they'll react to our proposal, so we'll just have to play it by ear*⟩

eight ball

to be behind the eight ball → ***estar en un apuro***

: to be in a bad position ⟨*the loss of this contract puts the company behind the eight ball*⟩

envelope

to push the envelope → ***trascender los límites***

: to go beyond the usual or normal limits by doing something especially new or risky ⟨*the director was pushing the envelope with his experimental new films*⟩

eye

to see eye to eye → ***estar de acuerdo (con alguien)***

: to have the same opinion; agree ⟨*they don't see eye to eye on the issue of taxes*⟩

fence

to sit on the fence → ***nadar entre dos aguas***
: to be unable to decide about something ⟨*he tried to persuade those still sitting on the fence to vote in his favor*⟩

fiddle

to play second fiddle → ***ser plato de segunda mesa***
: to be relegated to a less important position or status than someone or something else ⟨*the new player had to play second fiddle to the star of the team*⟩

fish

to feel like/be a fish out of water → ***sentirse/estar como gallina en corral ajeno***
: to be a person who is in a place or situation that seems unnatural or uncomfortable ⟨*he's a small-town boy who feels like a fish out of water here in the big city*⟩

foot

to put one's foot in one's mouth → ***meter la pata***
: to say something that causes unintended embarrassment or hurt feelings ⟨*I really put my foot in my mouth when I asked her about her job. I didn't know she'd just been fired*⟩

gold

to go for the gold → ***picar alto, aspirar a mucho***
: to put forth maximum effort to seek top success, prize, or honors ⟨*no holding back! I'm going for the gold*⟩

grease

to grease the palm of (someone) → ***untarle la mano (a alguien), sobornar (a alguien)***
: to give (someone) money for doing something illegal or dishonest for you ⟨*they had to grease the palms of a few officials to get the building permits they needed*⟩

heaven

to be a match made in heaven → ***hacer buena pareja***
: to be a match/marriage that is very good and successful ⟨*their happy marriage was a match made in heaven*⟩

high note

on a high note → ***con una nota positiva***
: in a pleasant or enjoyable way ⟨*our vacation ended on a high note when we got to meet the ambassador*⟩

horn

to blow one's own horn → ***darse bombo***
: to talk about oneself or one's achievements especially proudly ⟨*we've had a very successful year, and I think we have a right to blow our own horn*⟩

to get on the horn → ***llamar por teléfono***
: to contact someone by telephone ⟨*he got on the horn to the police*⟩

ice

to break the ice → ***romper el hielo***
: to say or do something that helps people relax and begin talking ⟨*he opened the meeting with a joke to break the ice*⟩

insult

to add insult to injury → ***por si fuera poco***
: to do or say something that makes a bad situation worse ⟨*most people were forced to work longer hours each week, and to add insult to injury, the company decided not to give pay raises*⟩

jury

the jury is still out on (something) → ***(algo) todavía no es seguro***
: something has not yet been decided or has not yet become clear ⟨*the jury is still out on whether the new restaurant will succeed*⟩

kill

to kill two birds with one stone → ***matar dos pájaros de un tiro***
: to achieve two things by doing a single action ⟨*we can kill two birds with one stone by dropping off the mail when we go the grocery store*⟩

knife

to (go) under the knife → ***operarse***

: to have a medical operation ⟨*I'm going under the knife to have my appendix removed tomorrow*⟩

knot

to tie the knot → ***casarse***

: to get married ⟨*when are you two going to tie the knot?*⟩

lead balloon

to go over like a lead balloon → ***caerle/sentarle muy mal (a alguien)***

: to fail completely ⟨*he told a joke about his mother-in-law and it went over like a lead balloon*⟩

leg

to pull someone's leg → ***tomarle el pelo (a alguien)***

: to playfully make someone believe something that is not true ⟨*I panicked when he said the test was tomorrow, but then I realized he was just pulling my leg*⟩

lid

to keep a lid on (something) → ***mantener (algo) oculto/tapado***

: to prevent (something) from being widely known ⟨*she tried to keep a lid on news of the company's financial situation*⟩

limelight

to be in the limelight → ***estar en el candelero***

: to be experiencing public attention or notice ⟨*when his new book caused an unexpected controversy, he was in the limelight once again*⟩

line

to line one's pockets → ***embolsarse dinero, meter la mano en la caja/lata***

: to take or get a lot of money by doing something illegal or dishonest ⟨*corrupt officials have been lining their pockets at the public's expense*⟩

luck

to be down on one's luck → ***estar pasando (por) una mala racha***

: to be suffering through a difficult time ⟨*she asked for a handout because she's been down on her luck lately*⟩

lunch

to be out to lunch → ***estar desconectado de la realidad, no estar en sus cabales***

: to be unaware of what is really happening because of confusion or mental instability ⟨*I could not understand his rambling; I think that guy's out to lunch*⟩

marble

to lose one's marbles → ***perder la chaveta***

: to become insane ⟨*when he started ranting about how the government was out to get him, I thought he'd lost his marbles*⟩

memory

to take a stroll/trip/walk (etc.) down memory lane → ***rememorar viejos tiempos***

: to think or talk about pleasant things from the past ⟨*we took a stroll down memory lane, talking about our time at school together*⟩

move

to move heaven and earth → ***mover cielo y tierra***

: to do everything possible to accomplish something ⟨*he vowed that he would move heaven and earth to finish the project on schedule*⟩

music

to be music to one's ears → ***sonarle a música celestial (a alguien), ser música celestial (para alguien)***

: to be something that one is happy to hear ⟨*when she said she'd marry me, that was music to my ears*⟩

nose

to pay through the nose → ***pagar un dineral***

: to pay a very high price ⟨*I found the perfect dress, but I paid through the nose for it*⟩

nowhere

in the middle of nowhere → ***quién sabe dónde***

: very far from other people or houses ⟨*I had to walk three miles after my car broke down in the middle of nowhere*⟩

p's and q's
to mind your p's and q's → ***tener cuidado con lo que se hace***
: to be careful about behaving in a polite or proper way ⟨*we knew to mind our p's and q's around our aunt*⟩

page
to borrow/take a page from someone's book → ***seguir el ejemplo de alguien***
: to do the same thing that someone else has done ⟨*you may want to borrow/take a page from his book and study harder for your finals*⟩

pop
to pop the question → ***proponerle matrimonio a alguien***
: to propose marriage to someone ⟨*she got tired of waiting for him to pop the question*⟩

preach
to preach to the choir → ***tratar de convencer a los que ya están convencidos***
: to speak for or against something to people who already agree with your opinions ⟨*his speeches to supporters won't win him any more votes, for he's just preaching to the choir*⟩

pull
to pull a fast one (on someone) → ***jugarle una mala pasada (a alguien)***
: to deceive or trick (someone) ⟨*someone might try to pull a fast one on you, so be careful*⟩

raise
to raise the dead → ***resuscitar a los muertos***
: to cause a dead person to rise from the grave ⟨*that noise is loud enough to raise the dead*⟩

river
to send someone up the river → ***encarcelar a alguien***
: to send someone to prison ⟨*they sent him up the river for 10 years*⟩
to sell someone down the river → ***traicionar a alguien***
: to betray someone ⟨*I can't believe my best friend would sell me down the river*⟩

rope
to learn/know the ropes → ***aprender/saber como se hacen las cosas***
: to become/be familiar with the special way things are done in a particular place or activity ⟨*it will take a few weeks for new employees to learn the ropes*⟩

rub
to rub elbows (with someone) → ***codearse (con alguien)***
: to meet and talk (with someone) in a friendly, informal way ⟨*the awards dinner gave me the opportunity to rub elbows with some of today's greatest American poets*⟩

ruffle
to ruffle a few feathers → ***hacer enojar a la gente***
: to upset or offend one or more persons ⟨*his critical remarks ruffled a few feathers of board members*⟩

sack
to hit the sack → ***irse a la cama***
: to go to bed for the night ⟨*I'm tired, so I'm going to hit the sack*⟩

saddle
to be back in the saddle → ***recuperar el control***
: to be once again in control ⟨*after a few setbacks, he's back in the saddle*⟩

screw
to have a screw loose → ***faltarle un tornillo (a alguien), tener un tornillo suelto***
: to be crazy ⟨*you've got to have a screw loose to think that's a good idea*⟩

seventh heaven
to be in seventh heaven → ***estar en el séptimo cielo***
: to be in a state of extreme happiness and joy ⟨*when I told her she was about to become a grandma, she was in seventh heaven*⟩

shoes
to fill someone's shoes → ***ocupar el puesto de alguien***
: to do what someone else does with the same level of quality or success ⟨*I don't think anyone will be able to fill her shoes after she retires*⟩

to put oneself in someone's shoes → ***ponerse en el pellejo de alguien***
: to imagine oneself in another person's situation ⟨*when considering how much to donate to the homeless, try to put yourself in their shoes*⟩

shoot

to shoot from the hip → ***hablar sin detenerse a pensar***
: to act or speak quickly without thinking about the possible results ⟨*I haven't thought up a formal plan, so I'm shooting from the hip with this suggestion*⟩

socks

to knock/blow someone's socks off → ***impresionar/deslumbrar a alguien***
: to affect or impress one in a very strong and favorable way ⟨*here's a song that will knock your socks off*⟩

stab

to stab (someone) in the back → ***darle una puñalada por la espalda (a alguien)***
: to betray someone's trust ⟨*he's the kind of person who gets you to trust him then stabs you in the back*⟩

stop

to pull out all the stops → ***dar el do de pecho, tirar/echar la casa por la ventana***
: to do everything possible to achieve success ⟨*when he throws a party, he really pulls out all the stops*⟩

straw

to clutch/grasp at straws → ***agarrarse a/de cualquier esperanza***
: to try to solve a problem by doing things that probably will not help ⟨*economists were grasping at straws to end the global financial crisis*⟩

think

to have another think coming → ***estar muy equivocado***
: to be wrong or mistaken ⟨*if he thinks he can fool me, he has another think coming*⟩

thunder

to steal someone's thunder → ***adelantársele a alguien (al anunciar o revelar algo)***
: to prevent someone from enjoying rightful success or attention by doing or saying whatever that person was planning to do or say ⟨*I didn't mean to steal your thunder, but I just had to tell your mom about your promotion*⟩

torch

to carry a torch → ***seguir enamorado de alguien (sin ser correspondido)***
: to continue to have romantic feelings for someone who does not return the feelings ⟨*is she still carrying a torch for him after all this time?*⟩

wart

warts and all → ***con todos sus defectos***
: despite someone's or something's flaws ⟨*he was often selfish and thoughtless, but she loved him, warts and all*⟩

wash

to wash one's hands of (someone or something) → ***lavarse las manos de (alguien o algo)***
: to refuse to be involved with (something or someone) anymore ⟨*I've tried to help them, but they won't listen to me, so I'm washing my hands of the whole mess*⟩

wear

to wear the pants → ***llevar los pantalones, mandar***
: to be the one to make the important decisions for a group ⟨*you'd better ask her permission because she wears the pants in the family*⟩

wet

to get one's feet wet → ***iniciarse en algo, dar sus primeros pasos en algo***
: to begin a new job or activity with relatively simple tasks to become more familiar with it ⟨*the new office assistant got her feet wet by doing some simple filing tasks*⟩

wringer

to put (someone) through the wringer → ***hacerle sudar la gota gorda a alguien, agotar a alguien***
: to put someone through a series of very difficult or unpleasant experiences ⟨*they were put through the wringer by the insurance investigator*⟩

Números/Numbers

Números cardinales/Cardinal Numbers

Español/Spanish		Inglés/English
uno	1	one
dos	2	two
tres	3	three
cuatro	4	four
cinco	5	five
seis	6	six
siete	7	seven
ocho	8	eight
nueve	9	nine
diez	10	ten
once	11	eleven
doce	12	twelve
trece	13	thirteen
catorce	14	fourteen
quince	15	fifteen
dieciséis	16	sixteen
diecisiete	17	seventeen
dieciocho	18	eighteen
diecinueve	19	nineteen
veinte	20	twenty
veintiuno	21	twenty-one
veintidós	22	twenty-two
veintitrés	23	twenty-three
veinticuatro	24	twenty-four
veinticinco	25	twenty-five
veintiséis	26	twenty-six
veintisiete	27	twenty-seven
veintiocho	28	twenty-eight
veintinueve	29	twenty-nine
treinta	30	thirty
treinta y uno	31	thirty-one
treinta y dos	32	thirty-two
treinta y tres	33	thirty-three
treinta y cuatro	34	thirty-four
treinta y cinco	35	thirty-five
treinta y seis	36	thirty-six
treinta y siete	37	thirty-seven
treinta y ocho	38	thirty-eight
treinta y nueve	39	thirty-nine
cuarenta	40	forty
cuarenta y uno	41	forty-one
cincuenta	50	fifty
sesenta	60	sixty
setenta	70	seventy
ochenta	80	eighty
noventa	90	ninety
cien	100	hundred
ciento uno	101	hundred one
ciento dos	102	hundred two
doscientos	200	two hundred
trescientos	300	three hundred
cuatrocientos	400	four hundred
quinientos	500	five hundred
seiscientos	600	six hundred
setecientos	700	seven hundred
ochocientos	800	eight hundred
novecientos	900	nine hundred
mil	1,000	thousand

Números ordinales/Ordinal Numbers

Español/Spanish		Inglés/English
primero, -ra	1st	first
segundo, -da	2nd	second
tercero, -ra	3rd	third
cuarto, -ta	4th	fourth
quinto, -ta	5th	fifth
sexto, -ta	6th	sixth
séptimo, -ma	7th	seventh
octavo, -va	8th	eighth
noveno, -na	9th	ninth
décimo, -ma	10th	tenth
undécimo, -ma	11th	eleventh
duodécimo, -ma	12th	twelfth
decimotercero, -ra	13th	thirteenth
decimocuarto, -ta	14th	fourteenth
decimoquinto, -ta	15th	fifteenth
decimosexto, -ta	16th	sixteenth
decimoséptimo, -ma	17th	sevententh
decimoctavo, -va	18th	eighteenth
decimonoveno, -na *or* decimonono, -na	19th	nineteenth
vigésimo, -ma	20th	twentieth
vigésimoprimero, vigésimaprimera	21st	twenty-first
vigésimosegundo, vigésimasegunda	22nd	twenty-second
trigésimo, -ma	30th	thirtieth
cuadragésimo, -ma	40th	fortieth
quincuagésimo, -ma	50th	fiftieth
sexagésimo, -ma	60th	sixtieth
septuagésimo, -ma	70th	seventieth
octogésimo, -ma	80th	eightieth
nonagésimo, -ma	90th	ninetieth
centésimo, -ma	100th	hundredth
ducentésimo	200th	two hundredth
tricentésimo	300th	three hundredth
cuadringentésimo	400th	four hundredth
quingentésimo	500th	five hundredth
sexcentésimo	600th	six hundredth
septingentésimo	700th	seven hundredth
octingésimo	800th	eight hundredth
noningentésimo	900th	nine hundredth
milésimo	1,000th	one thousandth

Abreviaturas comunes en español
Common Spanish Abbreviations

SPANISH ABBREVIATION AND EXPANSION		ENGLISH EQUIVALENT	
abr.	abril	**Apr.**	April
a/c	a cargo de	**c/o**	care of
A.C., a.C.	antes de Cristo	**BC**	before Christ
a. de J.C.	antes de Jesucristo	**BC**	before Christ
ago.	agosto	**Aug.**	August
a.m.	ante meridiem (de la mañana)	**a.m., AM**	ante meridiem (before noon)
Apdo., Aptdo.	apartado (de correos)	—	P.O. box
A.T.	Antiguo Testamento	**O.T.**	Old Testament
av., avda.	avenida	**ave.**	avenue
ayte.	ayudante	**asst.**	assistant
blvar., br.	bulevar	**blvd.**	boulevard
c/, C/	calle	**st.**	street
C	centígrado, Celsius	**C**	centigrade, Celsius
C.	compañía	**Co.**	company
CA	corriente alterna	**AC**	alternating current
cap.	capítulo	**ch., chap.**	chapter
c.c.	centímetros cúbicos	**cc, cu. cm.**	cubic centimeters
CC	corriente continua	**DC**	direct current
cg.	centígramo	**cg**	centigram
CI	coeficiente intelectual *o* de inteligencia	**IQ**	intelligence quotient
Cía.	compañía	**Co.**	company
cm.	centímetro	**cm**	centimeter
col.	columna	**col.**	column
C.P.	código postal	—	zip code
c/u	cada uno, cada una	**ea.**	each
d.C.	después de Cristo	**AD**	anno Domini (in the year of our Lord)
dcha.	derecha	—	right
d. de J.C.	después de Jesucristo	**AD**	anno Domini (in the year of our lord)
dep., dpto.	departamento	**dept.**	department
DF, D.F.	Distrito Federal	—	Federal District
dic.	diciembre	**Dec.**	December
do.	domingo	**Sun.**	Sunday
Dr.; Dra.	doctor; doctora	**Dr.**	doctor
E, E.	Este, este	**E**	East, east
edif.	edificio	**bldg.**	building
EEUU, EE.UU.	Estados Unidos	**US, U.S.**	United States
ej.	por ejemplo	**e.g.**	for example
ene.	enero	**Jan.**	January
etc.	etcétera	**etc.**	et cetera
f	femenino	**f**	female
F	Fahrenheit	**F**	Fahrenheit
feb.	febrero	**Feb.**	February
g., gr.	gramo	**g., gm, gr.**	gram
gob.	gobierno	**govt.**	government
h.	hora	**hr.**	hour
Hnos.	hermanos	**Bros.**	brothers
izq.	izquierda	**l.**	left

juev.	jueves	**Thurs.**	Thursday
jul.	julio	**Jul.**	July
jun.	junio	**Jun.**	June
kg.	kilogramo	**kg**	kilogram
km.	kilómetro	**km**	kilometer
l.	litro	**l, lit.**	liter
lun.	lunes	**Mon.**	Monday
m	masculino	**m**	male, masculine
m	metro	**m**	meter
mar.	marzo	**Mar.**	March
mart.	martes	**Tues.**	Tuesday
Méx.	mexicano, México	**Mex.**	Mexican, Mexico
mg.	miligramo	**mg**	milligram
miérc.	miércoles	**Wednes.**	Wednesday
min	minuto	**min.**	minute
ml.	mililitro	**ml**	mililiter
mm.	milímetro	**mm**	millimeter
N, N.	Norte, norte	**N, no.**	North, north
n.º	número	**no.**	number
NE	nordeste	**NE**	northeast
NN.UU.	Naciones Unidas	**UN**	United Nations
NO	noroeste	**NW**	northwest
nov.	noviembre	**Nov.**	November
N.T.	Nuevo Testamento	**N.T.**	New Testament
NU	Naciones Unidas	**UN**	United Nations
núm.	número	**num.**	number
NY	Nueva York, New York	**NY**	New York
O, O.	Oeste, oeste	**W**	West, west
oct.	octubre	**Oct.**	October
p., pág.	página	**p., pg.**	page
P	(talla) pequeña	**S**	small
págs.	páginas	**pp.**	pages
RCP	reanimación cardiopulmonar, resucitación cardiopulmonar	**CPR**	cardiopulmonary resuscitation
P.D.	postdata	**P.S.**	postscript
p. ej.	por ejemplo	**e.g.**	for example
p.m.	post meridiem (de la tarde)	**p.m., PM**	post meridiem (afternoon)
pº	paseo	**Ave.**	avenue
PR	Puerto Rico	**PR**	Puerto Rico
ptas., pts.	pesetas	—	—
pto.	punto	**pt.**	point
r.p.m.	revoluciones por minuto	**rpm.**	revolutions per minute
s.	siglo	**c., cent.**	century
S, S.	Sur, sur	**S, so.**	South, south
S., Sto., Sta.	san, santo, santa	**St.**	saint
S.A.	sociedad anónima	**Inc.**	incorporated (company)
sáb.	sábado	**Sat.**	Saturday
SE	sudeste, sureste	**SE**	southeast
seg.	segundo, segundos	**sec.**	second, seconds
sep., sept.	septiembre	**Sept.**	September
S.L.	sociedad limitada	**Ltd.**	limited (corporation)
SO	sudoeste, suroeste	**SW**	southwest
Sr.	Sénior	**Sr.**	Senior
tb.	también	—	also
tel., Tel.	teléfono	**tel.**	telephone
v	versus	**v., vs.**	versus
v.g., v.gr.	verbigracia	**e.g.**	for example
vier., viern.	viernes	**Fri.**	Friday
vol.	volumen	**vol.**	volume

Common English Abbreviations
Abreviaturas comunes en inglés

LA ABREVIATURA INGLÉS Y LA AMPLIACIÓN		EL EQUIVALENTE ESPAÑOL	
AAA	American Automobile Association	—	—
AC	alternating current	**CA**	corriente alterna
AD	anno Domini (in the year of our Lord)	**d.C., d. de J.C.**	después de Cristo, después de Jesucristo
AK, Alas.	Alaska	—	Alaska
AL, Ala.	Alabama	—	Alabama
a.m., AM	ante meridiem (before noon)	**a.m.**	ante meridiem (de la mañana)
Am., Amer.	America, American	—	América, americano
amt.	amount	—	cantidad
ans.	answer	—	respuesta
Apr.	April	**abr.**	abril
AR, Ark.	Arkansas	—	Arkansas
asst.	assistant	**ayte.**	ayudante
atty.	attorney	—	abogado, -da
Aug.	August	**ago.**	agosto
ave.	avenue	**av., avda.; pº**	avenida; paseo
AZ, Ariz.	Arizona	—	Arizona
BC	before Christ	**a.C., A.C., a. de J.C.**	antes de Cristo, antes de Jesucristo
BCE	before the Christian Era, before the Common Era	—	antes de la era cristiana, antes de la era común
bet.	between	—	entre
bldg.	building	**edif.**	edificio
blvd.	boulevard	**blvar., br.**	bulevar
Br., Brit.	Britain, British	—	Gran Bretaña, británico
Bro(s).	brother(s)	**Hno(s).**	hermano(s)
c, cm	centimeter	**cm.**	centímetro
c., cent.	century	**s.**	siglo
C	Celsius, centigrade	**C**	Celsius, centígrado
CA, Cal., Calif.	California	—	California
Can., Canad.	Canada, Canadian	—	Canadá, canadiense
cap.	capital (place)	—	capital
cap.	capital (letter)	—	mayúscula
cc, cu. cm	cubic centimeters	**c.c.**	centímetros cúbicos
CEO	chief executive officer	—	presidente, -ta (de una corporación)
ch., chap.	chapter	**cap.**	capítulo
Co.	company	**C., Cía.**	compañía
CO, Colo.	Colorado	—	Colorado
c/o	care of	**a/c**	a cargo de
COD	cash on delivery, collect on delivery	—	(pago) contra reembolso
col.	column	**col.**	columna
corp.	corporation	—	corporación
CPR	cardiopulmonary resuscitation	**RCP**	reanimación cardiopulmonar, resucitación cardiopulmonar
CT, Conn.	Connecticut	—	Connecticut

D.A.	district attorney	—	fiscal (del distrito)
DC	direct current	**CC**	corriente continua
DC	District of Columbia	—	—
DE, Del.	Delaware	—	Delaware
Dec.	December	**dic.**	diciembre
dept.	department	**dep., dpto.**	departamento
doz.	dozen	—	docena
Dr.	doctor	**Dr., Dra.**	doctor, doctora
E	East, east	**E, E.**	Este, este
ea.	each	**c/u**	cada uno, cada una
e.g.	for example	**v.g., v.gr.**	verbigracia
EMT	emergency medical technician	—	técnico, -ca en urgencias médicas
Eng.	England, English	—	Inglaterra, inglés
esp.	especially	—	especialmente
etc.	et cetera	**etc.**	etcétera
f	female	**f**	femenino
F	Fahrenheit	**F**	Fahrenheit
Feb.	February	**feb.**	febrero
fem.	feminine	—	femenino
FL, Fla.	Florida	—	Florida
Fri.	Friday	**vier., viern.**	viernes
ft.	feet, foot	—	pie(s)
g, gm	gram	**g., gr.**	gramo
Ga., GA	Georgia	—	Georgia
gal.	gallon	—	galón
govt.	government	gob.	gobierno
gr.	gram	**g., gr.**	gramo
HI	Hawaii	—	Hawai, Hawaii
hr.	hour	**h.**	hora
ht.	height	—	altura
IA, Ia.	Iowa	—	Iowa
ID	Idaho	—	Idaho
IL, Ill.	Illinois	—	Illinois
in.	inch	—	pulgada
IN, Ind.	Indiana	—	Indiana
Inc.	incorporated (company)	**S.A.**	sociedad anónima
Jan.	January	**ene.**	enero
Jul.	July	**jul.**	julio
Jun.	June	**jun.**	junio
Jr.	Junior	**Jr.**	Júnior
kg	kilogram	**kg.**	kilogramo
km	kilometer	**km.**	kilómetro
KS, Kan., Kans.	Kansas	—	Kansas
KY, Ky.	Kentucky	—	Kentucky
l	liter	**l.**	litro
l.	left	**izq.**	izquierda
L	large	**G**	(talla) grande
LA, La.	Louisiana	—	Luisiana, Louisiana
lb.	pound	—	libra
Ltd.	limited (corporation)	**S.L.**	sociedad limitada
m	male, masculine	**m**	masculino
m	meter	**m**	metro
M	medium	**M**	(talla) mediana
MA, Mass.	Massachusetts	—	Massachusetts
Mar.	March	**mar.**	marzo
masc.	masculine	—	masculino
MD, Md.	Maryland	—	Maryland
M.D.	Doctor of Medicine	—	doctor de medicina
ME, Me.	Maine	—	Maine
Mex.	Mexican, Mexico	**Méx.**	mexicano, México
mg	milligram	**mg.**	miligramo
mi.	mile	—	milla
MI, Mich.	Michigan	—	Michigan
min.	minute	**min**	minuto

ml	mililiter	**ml.**	mililitro
mm	millimeter	**mm.**	milímetro
MN, Minn.	Minnesota	—	Minnesota
mo.	month	—	mes
MO, Mo.	Missouri	—	Missouri
Mon.	Monday	**lun.**	lunes
mpg	miles per gallon	—	millas por galón
mph	miles per hour	—	millas por hora
MS, Miss.	Mississippi	—	Mississippi, Misisipí
mt., mtn.	mount, mountain	—	monte, montaña
MT, Mont.	Montana	—	Montana
N	North, north	**N**	Norte, norte
NC	North Carolina	—	Carolina del Norte, North Carolina
ND, N. Dak.	North Dakota	—	Dakota del Norte, North Dakota
NE	northeast	**NE**	nordeste
NE, Neb., Nebr.	Nebraska	—	Nebraska
NH	New Hampshire	—	New Hampshire
NJ	New Jersey	—	Nueva Jersey, New Jersey
NM., N. Mex.	New Mexico	—	Nuevo México, New Mexico
no.	north	**N**	norte
no.	number	**n.º**	número
Nov.	November	**nov.**	noviembre
N.T.	New Testament	**N.T.**	Nuevo Testamento
NV, Nev.	Nevada	—	Nevada
NW	northwest	**NO**	noroeste
NY	New York	**NY**	Nueva York, New York
Oct.	October	**oct.**	octubre
OH, O	Ohio	—	Ohio
OK, Okla.	Oklahoma	—	Oklahoma
OR, Ore., Oreg.	Oregon	—	Oregon
O.T.	Old Testament	**A.T.**	Antiguo Testamento
oz.	ounce, ounces	—	onza, onzas
p.	page	**p.**	página
PA, Pa., Penn.	Pennsylvania	—	Pennsylvania, Pensilvania
PD	police department	—	departamento de policía
pg.	page	**pág.**	página
pkg.	package	—	paquete
p.m., PM	post meridiem (afternoon)	**p.m.**	post meridiem (de la tarde)
P.O.	post office	—	oficina de correos, correo
pp.	pages	**págs.**	páginas
PR	Puerto Rico	**PR**	Puerto Rico
pres.	president	—	presidente, -ta
P.S.	postscript	**P.D.**	postdata
P.S.	public school	—	escuela pública
pt.	point	**pto.**	punto
PTA	Parent-Teacher Association	—	—
PTO	Parent-Teacher Organization	—	—
q, qt.	quart	—	cuarto de galón
r., rt.	right	**dcha.**	derecha
rd.	road	**c/, C/**	calle
recd.	received	—	recibido
RI	Rhode Island	—	Rhode Island
rpm	revolutions per minute	**r.p.m.**	revoluciones por minuto

rte.	route	—	ruta
S	small	**P**	(talla) pequeña
S	South, south	**S**	Sur, sur
Sat.	Saturday	**sáb.**	sábado
SC	South Carolina	—	Carolina del Sur, South Carolina
SD, S. Dak.	South Dakota	—	Dakota del Sur, South Dakota
SE	southeast	**SE**	sudeste, sureste
sec.	second, seconds	**seg.**	segundo, segundos
Sept.	September	**sep., sept.**	septiembre
so.	south	**S**	sur
sq.	square	—	cuadrado
Sr.	Senior	**Sr.**	Sénior
st.	street	**c/, C/**	calle
St.	saint	**S., Sto., Sta.**	santo, santa
Sun.	Sunday	**dom.**	domingo
SW	southwest	**SO**	sudoeste, suroeste
t., tsp.	teaspoon	—	cucharadita
T, tb., tbsp.	tablespoon	—	cucharada (grande)
tel.	telephone	**tel., Tel.**	teléfono
Thu., Thur., Thurs.	Thursday	**juev.**	jueves
TM	trademark	—	marca (de un producto)
TN, Tenn.	Tennessee	—	Tennessee
Tue., Tues.	Tuesday	**mart.**	martes
TX, Tex.	Texas	—	Texas
UN	United Nations	**NU, NN.UU.**	Naciones Unidas
US	United States	**EEUU, EE.UU.**	Estados Unidos
USA	United States of America	**EEUU, EE.UU.**	Estados Unidos de América
usu.	usually	—	usualmente
UT	Utah	—	Utah
v., vs.	versus	**v**	versus
VA, Va.	Virginia	—	Virginia
vol.	volume	**vol.**	volumen
VP	vice president	—	vicepresidente, -ta
VT, Vt.	Vermont	—	Vermont
W	West, west	**O**	Oeste, oeste
WA, Wash.	Washington (state)	—	Washington
Wed.	Wednesday	**miérc.**	miércoles
WI, Wis., Wisc.	Wisconsin	—	Wisconsin
wt.	weight	—	peso
WV, W. Va.	West Virginia	—	Virginia del Oeste, West Virginia
WY, Wyo.	Wyoming	—	Wyoming
yd.	yard	—	yarda
yr.	year	—	año

Nations of the World
Naciones del mundo

ENGLISH/INGLÉS	SPANISH/ESPAÑOL
Africa/África	
Algeria	Argelia
Angola	Angola
Benin	Benin
Botswana	Botswana, Botsuana
Burkina Faso	Burkina Faso
Burundi	Burundi
Cameroon	Camerún
Cape Verde	Cabo Verde
Central African Republic	República Centroafricana
Chad	Chad
Comoros	Comores, Comoras
Congo, Democratic Republic of	Congo, República Democrática del
Congo, Republic of the	Congo, República del
Djibouti	Yibuti, Djibouti
Egypt	Egipto
Equatorial Guinea	Guinea Ecuatorial
Eritrea	Eritrea
Ethiopia	Etiopía
Gabon	Gabón
Gambia	Gambia
Ghana	Ghana
Guinea	Guinea
Guinea-Bissau	Guinea-Bissau
Ivory Coast	Costa de Marfil
Kenya	Kenya, Kenia
Lesotho	Lesotho, Lesoto
Liberia	Liberia
Libya	Libia
Madagascar	Madagascar
Malawi	Malawi, Malaui
Mali	Malí
Mauritania	Mauritania
Mauritius	Mauricio
Morocco	Marruecos
Mozambique	Mozambique
Namibia	Namibia
Niger	Níger
Nigeria	Nigeria
Rwanda	Ruanda, Rwanda
São Tomé and Príncipe	Santo Tomé y Príncipe
Senegal	Senegal
Seychelles	Seychelles
Sierra Leone	Sierra Leona
Somalia	Somalia
South Africa, Republic of	Sudáfrica, República de
Sudan	Sudán
Swaziland	Suazilandia, Swazilandia
Tanzania	Tanzanía, Tanzania
Togo	Togo
Tunisia	Túnez
Uganda	Uganda
Zambia	Zambia
Zimbabwe	Zimbabwe, Zimbabue

ENGLISH/INGLÉS	SPANISH/ESPAÑOL

Antarctica/Antártida

No independent countries
No tiene países independientes

Asia/Asia

Afghanistan	Afganistán
Armenia	Armenia
Azerbaijan	Azerbaiyán, Azerbaiján
Bahrain	Bahrein
Bangladesh	Bangladesh
Bhutan	Bután, Bhután
Brunei	Brunei
Cambodia	Camboya
China	China
Cyprus	Chipre
East Timor	Timor Oriental
Georgia	Georgia
India	India
Indonesia	Indonesia
Iran	Irán
Iraq	Iraq, Irak
Israel	Israel
Japan	Japón
Jordan	Jordania
Kazakhstan	Kazajistán, Kazajstán
Korea, North	Corea del Norte
Korea, South	Corea del Sur
Kuwait	Kuwait
Kyrgyzstan	Kirguizistán, Kirguistán
Laos	Laos
Lebanon	Líbano
Malaysia	Malasia
Maldives	Maldivas
Mongolia	Mongolia
Myanmar	Myanmar
Nepal	Nepal
Oman	Omán
Pakistan	Pakistán, Paquistán
Philippines	Filipinas
Qatar	Qatar
Saudi Arabia	Arabia Saudita, Arabia Saudí
Singapore	Singapur
Sri Lanka	Sri Lanka
Syria	Siria
Taiwan	Taiwán, Taiwan
Tajikistan	Tayikistán
Thailand	Tailandia
Turkey	Turquía
Turkmenistan	Turkmenistán
United Arab Emirates	Emiratos Árabes Unidos
Uzbekistan	Uzbekistán
Vietnam	Vietnam
Yemen	Yemen

Europe/Europa

Albania	Albania
Andorra	Andorra
Austria	Austria
Belarus	Bielorrusia, Belarús
Belgium	Bélgica
Bosnia and Herzegovina	Bosnia-Herzegovina

ENGLISH/INGLÉS	SPANISH/ESPAÑOL
Bulgaria	Bulgaria
Croatia	Croacia
Czech Republic	República Checa
Denmark	Dinamarca
Estonia	Estonia
Finland	Finlandia
France	Francia
Germany	Alemania
Greece	Grecia
Hungary	Hungría
Iceland	Islandia
Ireland	Irlanda
Italy	Italia
Kosovo	Kosovo
Latvia	Letonia
Liechtenstein	Liechtenstein
Lithuania	Lituania
Luxembourg	Luxemburgo
Macedonia	Macedonia
Malta	Malta
Moldova	Moldova
Monaco	Mónaco
Montenegro	Montenegro
Netherlands	Países Bajos
Norway	Noruega
Poland	Polonia
Portugal	Portugal
Romania	Rumania, Rumanía
Russia	Rusia
San Marino	San Marino
Serbia	Serbia
Slovakia	Eslovaquia
Slovenia	Eslovenia
Spain	España
Sweden	Suecia
Switzerland	Suiza
Ukraine	Ucrania
United Kingdom	Reino Unido
Vatican City	Ciudad del Vaticano

North America/Norteamérica

Antigua and Barbuda	Antigua y Barbuda
Bahamas	Bahamas
Barbados	Barbados
Belize	Belice
Canada	Canadá
Costa Rica	Costa Rica
Cuba	Cuba
Dominica	Dominica
Dominican Republic	República Dominicana
El Salvador	El Salvador
Grenada	Granada
Guatemala	Guatemala
Haiti	Haití
Honduras	Honduras
Jamaica	Jamaica
Mexico	México, Méjico
Nicaragua	Nicaragua
Panama	Panamá
Saint Kitts and Nevis	Saint Kitts y Nevis, San Cristóbal y Nieves
Saint Lucia	Santa Lucía
Saint Vincent and the Grenadines	San Vicente y las Granadinas

ENGLISH/INGLÉS	SPANISH/ESPAÑOL
Trinidad and Tobago	Trinidad y Tobago
United States of America	Estados Unidos de América

Oceania/Oceanía

Australia	Australia
Fiji	Fiji, Fiyi
Kiribati	Kiribati
Marshall Islands	Islas Marshall
Micronesia, Federated States of	Micronesia, Estados Federados de
Nauru	Nauru
New Zealand	Nueva Zelanda, Nueva Zelandia
Palau	Palaos
Papua New Guinea	Papúa Nueva Guinea, Papua Nueva Guinea
Samoa	Samoa
Solomon Islands	Islas Salomón
Tonga	Tonga
Tuvalu	Tuvalu
Vanuatu	Vanuatu

South America/Sudamérica

Argentina	Argentina
Bolivia	Bolivia
Brazil	Brasil
Chile	Chile
Colombia	Colombia
Ecuador	Ecuador
Guyana	Guyana
Paraguay	Paraguay
Peru	Perú
Suriname	Surinam
Uruguay	Uruguay
Venezuela	Venezuela

Metric System: Conversions
Sistema métrico: conversiones

Length

unit	number of meters	approximate U.S. equivalents
millimeter	0.001	0.039 inch
centimeter	0.01	0.39 inch
meter	1	39.37 inches
kilometer	1,000	0.62 mile

Longitud

unidad	número de metros	equivalentes aproximados de los EE.UU.
milímetro	0.001	0.039 pulgada
centímetro	0.01	0.39 pulgada
metro	1	39.37 pulgadas
kilómetro	1,000	0.62 milla

Area

unit	number of square meters	approximate U.S. equivalents
square centimeter	0.0001	0.16 square inch
square meter	1	10.76 square feet
hectare	10,000	2.47 acres
square kilometer	1,000,000	0.39 square mile

Superficie

unidad	número de metros cuadrados	equivalentes aproximados de los EE.UU.
centímetro cuadrado	0.0001	0.16 pulgada cuadrada
metro cuadrado	1	10.76 pies cuadrados
hectárea	10,000	2.47 acres
kilómetro cuadrado	1,000,000	0.39 milla cuadrada

Volume

unit	number of cubic meters	approximate U.S. equivalents
cubic centimeter	0.000001	0.061 cubic inch
cubic meter	1	1.31 cubic yards

Volumen

unidad	número de metros cúbicos	equivalentes aproximados de los EE.UU
centímetro cúbico	0.000001	0.061 pulgada cúbica
metro cúbico	1	1.31 yardas cúbicas

Capacity

unidad	number of liters	approximate U.S. equivalents		
		CUBIC	DRY	LIQUID
liter	1	61.02 cubic inches	0.91 quart	1.06 quarts

Capacidad

unidad	número de litros	equivalentes aproximados de los EE.UU.		
		CÚBICO	SECO	LÍQUIDO
litro	1	61.02 pulgadas cúbicas	0.91 cuarto	1.06 cuartos

Mass and Weight

unit	number of grams	approximate U.S. equivalents
milligram	0.001	0.015 grain
centigram	0.01	0.15 grain
gram	1	0.035 ounce
kilogram	1,000	2.20 pounds
metric ton	1,000,000	1.10 short tons

Masa y peso

unidad	número de gramos	equivalentes aproximados de los EE.UU.
miligramo	0.001	0.015 grano
centigramo	0.01	0.15 grano
gramo	1	0.035 onza
kilogramo	1.000	2.20 libras
tonelada métrica	1,000,000	1.10 toneladas cortas